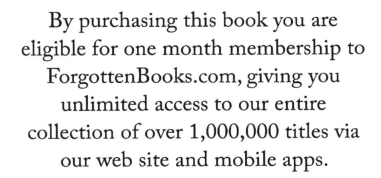

ISBN 978-0-428-68956-8
PIBN 11300602

BROOKLYN
DAILY EAGLE
ALMANAC.

1921

A Book of Information, General of the World, and Special of New York City and Long Island.

Vol. XXXVI., Jan., 1921. Yearly Subscription to EAGLE LIBRARY Two Dollars and Fifty Cents.
Almanac Number, One Dollar and Fifty Cents.

Office of Publication
EAGLE BUILDING, BROOKLYN-NEW YORK CITY.

INDEX

IMPORTANT NOTICE—The following index to the 1921 Brooklyn Eagle Almanac has been entirely revised and rearranged according to the most up-to-date library and encyclopedic indexing methods. A straight alphabetical arrangement has been followed in order to facilitate quick and easy reference to any subject.

CAUTION—In using this index, disregard such geographical titles as, for example, "Kings County Sheriff" and look only for "Sheriffs," where will be found the page numbers for each of the local county sheriffs offices. Similarly, the "Metropolitan Museum of Art" will be found under "Museums"; the "New York State Canal Board" will be found under "Canal." Likewise, the "United States Department of Agriculture" at Washington will be found under "Agriculture," etc., etc.

SPECIAL NOTICE Regarding Societies and Associations—Owing to the thousands of organizations about which detailed information is contained in the Eagle Almanac, it is obviously impossible to index each under its individual title. For quick reference all these organizations have been grouped or classified under chapter headings according to the general purpose or function of the society. Consult the following list of these chapters for the KIND of organization you are looking for. For example: The "American Seamen's Friend Society" is classified under "Hospitals, Homes and Societies for Relief," and is found with the Manhattan list of those devoted to "Special Relief." Similarly, the "Froebel Society of Brooklyn" is classified in the "Literary Societies" chapter under the Brooklyn list.

INDEX TO SECTIONS UNDER HOSPITALS, HOMES AND SOCIETIES FOR RELIEF.

INDEX TO CHAPTERS UNDER SOCIETIES AND ASSOCIATIONS.

DETAILED INDEX.

First consult "Additions and Changes During Printing," on page xxvi, and make corrections in main body of Almanac on the pages indicated. Do this immediately. Otherwise you might overlook important changes and be misinformed.

A

See Additions and Corrections of Almanac Text on page xxviii.

DETAILED INDEX—*Continued.*

B

See Additions and Corrections of Almanac Text on page xxviii.

DETAILED INDEX—*Continued.*

See Additions and Corrections of Almanac Text on page xxviii.

DETAILED INDEX—*Continued.*

See Additions and Corrections of Almanac Text on page xxviii.

THE

PEOPLES NATIONAL BANK

OF BROOKLYN

Ralph Ave. and Quincy St. at Broadway

Total Resources, $6,000,000

OFFICERS

George W. Spence, President
Charles Wissman, Vice President
Walter F. Cawthorne, Cashier
Arthur W. Spolander, Assistant Cashier

DIRECTORS

Wm. H. Agricola
George W. Baker
Arthur R. Koch
Henry C. Bohack
Clinton P. Case
George F. Trommer
Frederick W. Luecke
Marshall McLean
Frederick L. Mills
Henry L. Schelling
George W. Spence
Charles Wissman

MODERN SAFE DEPOSIT AND STORAGE VAULTS

Boxes to rent, $5.00 per year.

Our Foreign Department is prepared to send money to all parts of the World. Let us handle your Foreign business for you.

Depository of the City and State of New York and United States Postal Savings

DETAILED INDEX—*Continued.*

D

See Additions and Corrections of Almanac Text on page xxviii.

DETAILED INDEX—*Continued.*

See Additions and Corrections of Almanac Text on page xxviii.

DETAILED INDEX—*Continued.*

See Additions and Corrections of Almanac Text on page xxviii.

DETAILED INDEX—*Continued.*

See Additions and Corrections of Almanac Text on page xxviii.

DETAILED INDEX—*Continued.*

M

N

See Additions and Corrections of Almanac Text on page xxviii.

DETAILED INDEX—*Continued.*

O

P

See Additions and Corrections of Almanac Text on page xxviii.

DETAILED INDEX—*Continued.*

Q

See Additions and Corrections of Almanac Text on page xxviii.

DETAILED INDEX—*Continued.*

R

S

See Additions and Corrections of Almanac Text on page xxviii.

DETAILED INDEX—*Continued.*

T

See Additions and Corrections of Almanac Text on page xxviii.

DETAILED INDEX—*Continued.*

U

V

See Additions and Corrections of Almanac Text on page xxviii.

DETAILED INDEX—*Continued.*

W

Y

Z

See Additions and Corrections of Almanac Text on page xxviii.

INDEX TO PREVIOUS VOLUMES.

(Some of the important items in former Eagle Almanacs.)

(The number following the year is the page number of that volume.)

ADVERTISERS' INDEX.

(Roman numeral pages in front of Almanac; Arabic numerals in back of book.)

IMPORTANT!

ADDITIONS AND CHANGES DURING PRINTING OF ALMANAC.

It is suggested that you make note of the following additions and changes which occurred while The Eagle Almanac was at press, putting the changes in the proper place in the body of the book on the pages noted below. Do this at once and you will run no risk of being misinformed or having overlooked important last-minute changes up to the date of this list, Jan. 14, 1921.

Libraries of L. I.

Pt. Washington Free—W. M. Mitchell, Lib.; 8,000 vols.

Museums.

Dyckman House—Hours. Sun. and Mon., 1-5 P.M. Other days, 10 A.M. to 5 P.M.

Long Island Societies and Associations.

Nassau Co. Soc. for the Prevention of Cruelty to Children—1920. Mineola, L. I. Dirs.: E. C. Brower, Roslyn; Robt. Gair, Jr., Glen Cove; Molly M. Davis, Brookville; Benj. Stern, Roslyn.

Port Jefferson Business Men's Assn —Pt. Jefferson, L. I. J. D. Meeker, Pres.; G. H. Loper, Sec.

Riverhead Chapter, Eastern Star—Mrs. J. T. Young, Matron, Laurel; Miss R. P. Terry, Sec.; Mrs. M. M. Burr, Treas.

Savings Banks, N. Y. C.

Dime Savings Bank, Bkln.—Russell S. Walker, Pres., deceased.

Hospitals, Homes and Socs. for Relief.

Queens—Mary Immaculata Hosp., Jamaica. Med. and Surg. Staff: Dr. E. W. Shipman, Ch., Richmond Hill; Dr. E. J. Buxbaum, Sec.-Treas., Jamaica.

Societies and Associations.

Art Clubs—Bkln. Soc. of Artists—Benjamin Eggleston elected President.

Bds. of Trade, etc.—National-Amer. Chamber of Commerce of Mexico—530 mem. Wm. F. Saunders, Sec., Apartado 82 bis, Mexico City.

Bds. of Trade—Queens—Lawrence-Cedarhurst Bd. of Trade. Edward M. Raeder, Pres.; P. C. Vandewater, Sec.; P. W. Skidmore, Treas.

Business, Commercial and Agricultural Socs., National—Assn. of National Advertisers—M. H. Wright, Pres., Philadelphia, Pa.; C. D. Ellsworth, N. Y. City; H. U. Winston, Cleveland, O., and R. N. Fellows, Chicago, V.-Prests.

Educational and Scientific Socs.—Bkln. Music School Settlement, 122-6 St. Felix. Mrs. Benj. Prince, Pres.; Mrs. Walter Hannett, Cor. Sec.; Miss Rosamond Roberts, Exec. Sec.; G. Foster Smith, Treas.

Irish Socs., Bkln.—Amer. Assn. for the Recognition of the Irish Republic, Prospect Council. J. McSweeny, Pres.; Jos. Hickey, Sec.; Mrs. H. Kelly, Treas., 824 President

Literary Socs—Fenelon Reading Circle; Mrs. J. Campbell Keough elected Pres.

Patriotic and Commemorative Socs.—Army and Navy Union, U. S. of Amer. Naval Branch No. 1., Borough Hall, Bkln. Fredk. E. Haskins, Commdr., 767 Washington av., Bkln.; E. Allcock, Adj., 360 B'way, Mhtn.—Custer Garrison No. 2, Borough Hall, Bkln.; C. Herst, Commdr.—Virginia Dare Chapter, D. A. R. Mrs. G. C. Taft, Regent; Miss Eliz. Bedford, Sec.

Religious Socs.—Worlds Y. W. C. A. Miss M. Dingman appointed Industrial Sec.

Secret and Benefit Socs.—National Assn. of Naval Veterans, 1861-1865. Monitor Assn., Borough Hall, Bkln.; Fredk. E. Haskins, Sec., 767 Washington av., Bkln.

Sporting Clubs, Country Clubs—Neponsit Club, Rockaway Beach. Dr. Lewis Morris, Pres

Sporting Clubs, Golf Clubs—Brentwood Golf Club, Brentwood, L. I. Emerson McWhorter, Pres.

War Veterans' Assn.—Veterans of Foreign Wars of the U. S., Dept. of N. Y., Room 12, Borough Hall, Bkln. Dept. Commdr., James F. Rorke; Dept. Adj., Alvah R. Stetson; Dept. Commdr., Wm. J. S. Dineen.—Bkln. Posts (No., name of post. adj., address): 10. Lt. Quentin Roosevelt, P. J. Robinson, 520 6th av.; 44. V. H. Bridgeman, L. Hutzel, 272 St. Nicholas av.; 107. Argonne, A. R. Stetson, 240 61st; Lt. Col. M. N. Lieberman, G. F. Silvia, 68 Hicks; 124. Semper Fidelis, J. F. Rorke, 431 56th; Ridgewood, E. H. Meyerhoefer, 336 Knickerbocker av.; Sultana Naval, P. S. Rowan; Maj. J. McKenna, H. R. La Tourette, 297 Grove; 213. Caduccus, A. F. Dorbecker, 1721 Woodbine; 244. Williamsburg, L. F. Pike, 44 Sumner av.; 260. Jos. A. Wynn, J. A. Brunner, 80 Sunnyside av.; 292. Pvt. J. R. McClue, J. A. Mageska, 1032 N. Y. av.; 301. Raymond A. McIver, J. J. McIver, 1307 St. Johns pl.; 309. Philip P. Grey, F. Weller, 655 Lexington av.; 310. Jos. S. Beatty, Earl Fulton, 747 McDonough; 412. Sgt. F. J. Vermilyn, Geo. R. Tracy, 113 Ellery; 452. Corp. T R. Nulty, Jos. Nulty, 642A Leonard; 463. Kendenberg-Callahan, Wm. J. Grecia, 48 Eaton pl.; 487. Lt. Saml. Solovei, S. Grossman, 45 Christopher av.; 500. Johnson-Fireman, H. C. Feurbach, 103 Bleecker; 510. Harry H. Schneider, S. Goldberg, 221 Lewis av.; 515. Bartel Pritchard, F W. Rox, 8731 111th; 569. Sylvester Loughlin, Edw. Smith, 720 5th av.; 570. Arthur C. Mayer, J. F. Connolly, 3296 Fulton; 571. Chas. P. Prince, J. W. McCarthy, 271 Etna.

Unclassified Socs.—National. Fire Marshals' Assn. of North America. J. A. Macy, Pres., Des Moines, Ia.; L. T. Hussey, Sec.-Treas., Topeka, Kan.

International — International Federation of American Homing Pigeon Fanciers; an important object of the soc. is to locate the owner of strayed homing pigeons; the data contained in the band on the leg of the pigeon will enable the secretary to locate the owner. F. P. Lueke, Pres., 1353 Park pl., Bkln.; John Fisher, Sec.-Treas., 203 Montgomery, Bloomfield, N. J.—Bkln. Concourse of Homing Pigeon Fanciers, 15 Garden. Wm. T. Walsh, Pres., 1121 St Marks av.; D. Gibson, Sec., 105 Lynch. Homing Pigeon Clubs—Manhattan Club, W Cordua, Sec., 644 Bedford av, Bkln; South Bkln Club, H. A. Immig, Sec., 603 6th av.; Queensboro Club, Wm. Draycott, Sec., 150 Snediker av., Union Course; Maspeth Club, Wm. Graneman, Sec., 1 Sophie, Maspeth: East N. Y. Club, H. Jacobs, Sec., 534 Jerome; Metropolitan Club, H. Becker, Sec., 1026 Metropolitan av., Bkln; Long Is. Club, J. Bermel Pres., 153 Wayne, Glendale, Greenpoint Club, Carl Hultz, Sec., 11 Van Dam, Bkln.

New York City Churches.

Bkln.—Jewish—Synagogue of Congregation Sons of Israel, 21st and Benson av., dedicated.

Bkln.—Presbyterian—Syrian Protestant, Pacific and Clinton. Org. 1904. Contrib. mem., 90. Total amt. raised, $12,000. Value church property, $27,500.

Bkln.—Roman Catholic—Church of St. Ephren, 7th av. and 75th. Rector, Rev. Richard Kennedy.

Queens—Disciples of Christ — Ridgewood Christian, Forest av. Pastors, K. Page and W. A. R. McPherson. Org. 1908. Contrib. mem., 175. S. S. mem., 240. Total amt. raised, $3,000. Value church property, $75,000.

Political Organizations.

Anawanda Dem. Club, Woodward av. and Linden, Boro of Queens. 1,100 mem. Jos. T. Quinn, Pres.; Louis C. Himmelsbach, Sec.

Anthony Bucalos Rep. League, 128 Central av., Bkln. G. Vascellaro, Pres.

Non-Partisan League of Kings Co., 1935 Park pl., Bkln. Frank S. Flannigan, Pres.

Washington Dem. Club (10th A. D.), J. J. Barnum elected Pres.; J. F. McNeeley elected Cor. Sec.

Statistics of Principal Countries.

Albania—Italian Mandatory.

Austria—Michael Hainisch elected Pres.

Bavaria—Minister President, Dr. von Kahr.

British Empire—Pacific Islands, High Commr., Sir. C. H. Redwell.

Danzig—Administrator, Sir Reginald Tower.

Mesopotamia—Commr, Sir P. Z. Cox.

Nepal—Sovereign, Maharaja Shamsher Jang.

Prussia—President, Herr Braun.

A Navy balloon, which left Rockaway Point, N. Y., Dec. 13, 1920, and had been missing ever since, reported on Jan. 2, 1921, having landed safely ten miles north of Moose Factory, Ontario, after a flight of 800 miles. This breaks the world's record for distance in a balloon.

NEW YORK STATE LEGISLATURE, 1921.

SENATE COMMITTEES, 1921-22.
(Announced Jan. 12, 1921.)

Finance—Hewitt, Thompson, Lockwood, Walton, Towner, Davenport, Knight, Gibbs, Carson, Baumes, Robinson, Lusk, Boylan, Twomey, Walker.

Judiciary—Burlingame, Walton, Knight, Gibbs, Pitcher, Whitley, Baumes, Swift, Karle, Duell, Meyer, Tolbert, Lusk, Cotillo, Schackno, Walker.

Cities—Mullan, Gibbs, Lockwood, Burlingame, Lowman, Swift, Fearon, Campbell, Smith, Lusk, Farrell, McGarry, Schackno, Walker.

Public Service—Knight, Ferris, Baumes, Whitley, Carson, Robinson, Thayer, Wiswall, Kavanaugh, Duggan, Lusk, Downing, McCue, Walker.

Internal Affairs—Lowman, Knight, Carson, Ferris, Robinson, Bloomfield, Thayer, Ames, Draper, Campbell, Lusk, McGarry, Strauss, Walker.

Codes—Walton, Knight, Whitley, Baumes, Pitcher, Lowman, Simpson, Draper, Harris, Cotillo, Schackno, Walker.

Taxation and Retrenchment—Davenport, Mullan, Burlingame, Whitley, Towner, Burling, Kavanaugh, Tolbert, Kaplan, Boylan, McCue.

Insurance—Towner, Gibbs, Karle, Fearon, Ames, Wiswall, Duggan, Seidel, Downing, McCue, Twomey.

Agriculture—Ferris, Towner, Carson, Knight, Burling, Ames, Bloomfield, Downing, Strauss.

Public Education—Lockwood, Carson, Davenport, Pitcher, Swift, Draper, Reischmann, Lusk, Cotillo, Downing, Walker.

Conservation—Thompson, Ferris, Tolbert, Smith, Draper, Harris, Martin, Farrell, Strauss.

Banks—Pitcher, Burling, Whitley, Swift, Kaplan, Martin, Taylor, Cotillo, McCue.

Civil Service—Robinson, Lockwood, Smith, Taylor, Harris, Reischmann, Seidel, McGarry, Farrell.

Commerce and Navigation—Karle, Thompson, Whitley, Campbell, Kavanaugh, Kaplan, Seidel, Twomey, McCue.

Canals—Whitley, Gibbs, Pitcher, Ames, Wiswall, Duggan, McGarry, McCue.

Public Health—Gibbs, Lowman, Karle, Bloomfield, Taylor, Seidel, Twomey, Strauss.

Military Affairs—Swift, Duell, Thayer, Meyer, Martin, Downing, Schackno.

Labor and Industry—Duell, Knight, Mullan, Burling, Baumes, Boylan, McGarry.

Privileges and Elections—Meyer, Walton, Robinson, Wiswall, Kavanaugh, Cotillo, Schackno.

Penal Institutions—Simpson, Towner, Harris, Farrell, McGarry.

Printed and Engrossed Bills—Baumes, Davenport, Simpson, Schackno, Strauss.

Public Printing—Fearon, Taylor, Reischmann, Boylan, Farrell.

Revision—Burling, Martin, Reischmann, Schackno, Cotillo.

STANDING COMMITTEES, 1921 ASSEMBLY.
(Announced Jan. 12, 1921.)

Ways and Means—McGinnies, Chautauqua; Seaker, St. Lawrence; Lord, Chenango; Fenner, Tompkins; Yale, Putnam; Mead, Orange; Hutchinson, Fulton-Hamilton; Steinberg, New York; Moore, Westchester; Harrington, Clinton; Roosevelt, Nassau; Mullen, Kings; Hamill, New York; Leininger, Queens; Beasley, Erie.

Judiciary—Martin, Oneida; Rowe, Erie; Lown, Yates; Jenks, Broome; Everett, St. Lawrence; Stitt, Kings; Ullman, New York; Smith, Onondaga; Westall, Westchester; Moran, Lewis; Barnes, Oswego; Bloch, New York; McKee, Bronx.

General Laws—Richford, Chemung; Booth, Oneida; Brady, Erie; Neary, Queens; Halpern, Queens; Blodgett, Schenectady; Druss, Kings; Warren, New York; Aronson, New York; Borkowski, Erie; O'Connor, New York; Walsh, Bronx; Galgano, New York.

Affairs of Cities—Blakely, Westchester; Wells, Kings; Whitcomb, Broome; Slacer, Erie; Booth, Oneida; Crowley, Monroe; Chamberlin, Onondaga; Gaffers, Albany; Jesse, New York; Blodgett, Schenectady; Pette, Queens; McArdle, Kings; Kiernan, New York.

Agriculture—Witter, Tioga; Lord, Chenango; Cowee, Rensselaer; Gage, Wyoming; Soule, Onondaga; Long, Delaware; Rice, Cortland; Webb, Dutchess; Betts, Wayne; Greenwald, Schoharie; Porter, Essex; Gray, Sullivan; Brooks, Madison.

Internal Affairs—Wheelock, Livingston; Cheney, Erie; Hager, Cayuga; Harris, Monroe; Miller, Genesee; Smith, Saratoga; Dobson, Seneca; Van Wagenen, Ulster; Yale, Putnam; Finch, Columbia; Kirkland, Cattaraugus; Bartholomew, Washington; Ellsworth, Franklin.

Railroads—Seaker, St. Lawrence; Yale, Putnam; Caulfield, Kings; Trahan, Westchester; Baum, Queens; Wallace, New York; Kirkland, Cattaraugus; Finch, Columbia; Frerichs, Richmond; Nichols, New York; Reilly, Kings; Hamill, New York; Taylor, Kings.

Electricity, Gas and Water Supply—Fenner, Tompkins; Slacer, Erie; Whitcomb, Broome; Campbell, Albany; Gempler, Kings; Halpern, Queens; Lewis, Monroe; Sackett, Ontario; Reiss, New York; Porter, Essex; Crowe, Kings; McLoughlin, Kings; Leininger, Queens.

Insurance—Gardner, Dutchess; Crowley, Monroe; Caulfield, Kings; Morrissey, Rensselaer; MacFarland, Warren; Seelbach, Erie; Doherty, Kings; Franchot, Niagara; Gaffers, Albany; Trahan, Westchester; Rayher, New York; McDonald, Bronx; Cosgrove, Richmond.

Banks—Cheney, Erie; Mead, Orange; Gardner, Dutchess; Hunter, Steuben; Wheelock, Livingston; Hawkins, New York; Dobson, Seneca; McCleary, Montgomery; Warren, Kings; Moran, Lewis; Druss, Kings; Merrigan, Albany; Wackerman, Kings.

Taxation and Retrenchment—Judson, Monroe; Chamberlin, Onondaga; Downs, Suffolk; Moore, Westchester; Van Wagenen, Ulster; Morrissey, Rensselaer; Bly, Kings; Franchot, Niagara; Rayher, New York; Frerichs, Richmond; Lieberman, New York; Reiburn, New York; Lyman, Bronx.

Public Education—Harris, Monroe; Soule, Onondaga; Gage, Wyoming; Peck, Rockland; Miss M. L. Smith, New York; Jacobs, Greene; Greenwald, Schoharie; Wright, Chatauqua; Bailey, Suffolk; Moses, Kings; McKee, Bronx; McArdle, Kings; O'Connor, New York.

Public Health—Lattin, Orleans; Smith, Saratoga; Rowe, Erie; Miss M. L. Smith, New York; Jesse, New York; Hausner, Schuyler; Smith, Otsego; Sackett, Ontario; Wright, Chautauqua; Lewis, Monroe; Clayton, Kings; Bloch, New York; Henderson, Bronx.

Canals—Zimmerman, Erie; Judson, Monroe; Booth, Oneida; Hawkins, New York; Jeffery, Niagara; Blodgett, Schenectady; Dobson, Seneca; Smith, Onondaga; Giaconne, Kings; Bartholomew, Washington; Barnes, Oswego; Beasley, Erie; Merrigan, Albany.

Excise—Gage, Wyoming; Richford, Chemung; Long, Delaware; Hager, Cayuga; Betts, Wayne; Williams, Oneida; Seelbach, Erie; Witter, Tioga; Moore, Kings; Di Pirro, New York; Schwab, Queens; Burchill, New York; Orr, Bronx.

Labor and Industries—Brady, Erie; Downs, Suffolk; Lattin, Orleans; Miller, Genesee; Lown, Yates; Roosevelt, Nassau; Jacobs, Greene; Jeffery, Niagara; McCleary, Montgomery; Mastick, Westchester; Kelly, Kings; Hackenberg, New York; Antin, Bronx.

Commerce and Navigation—Caulfield, Kings; Cowee, Rensselaer; Ullman, New York; Seelbach, Erie; Hausner, Schuyler; Aronson, New York; Campbell, Schenectady; McArdle, Kings; Schwab, Queens; Reilly, Kings; Orr, Bronx.

Charitable and Religious Societies—Peck, Rockland; Smith, Saratoga; Webb, Dutchess; Williams, Oneida; MacFarland, Warren; Pette, Queens; Trahan, Westchester; Clayton, Kings; Borkowski, Erie; McDonald, Bronx; Burchill, New York; McLoughlin, Kings; Solomon, Kings.

Military Affairs—Wells, Kings; Webb, Dutchess; Steinberg, New York; Wallace, New York; Brundage, Orange; Neary, Queens; Fox, New York; Wheelock, Livingston; Roosevelt, Nassau; Carroll, Kings; Barnes, Oswego; McLoughlin, Kings; Walsh, Bronx.

Public Printing—Betts, Wayne; Chamberlin, Onondaga; Long, Delaware; Duke, Allegany; Campbell, Albany; Baum, Queens; Stitt, Kings; Moses, Kings; Kiernan, New York; McDonald, Bronx; Solomon, Kings.

Claims—Steinberg, New York; McWhinney, Nassau; Mullen, Kings; Pette, Queens; Gempler, Kings; Reiss, New York, Moore, Kings; Di Pirro, New York; Giaconne, Kings; Dickstein, New York; Wackerman, Kings.

Public Institutions—Mead, Orange; Everett, St. Lawrence; Cheney, Erie; Campbell, Albany; Bly, Kings; Harris, Monroe; Baum, Queens; Brooks, Madison; Cosgrove, Richmond; Antin, Bronx; Jager, Kings.

Printed and Engrossed Bills—Miller, Genesee; Fenner, Tompkins; Cole, Steuben; Westall, Westchester; Reilly, Kings.

Social Welfare—Miss M. L. Smith, New York; Duke, Allegany; Brady, Erie; Bly, Kings; Doherty, Kings; Neary, Queens; Lieberman, New York; Schwab, Queens; Reiburn, New York; Lyman, Bronx; Jager, Kings.

COUNTY OFFICIALS, NEW YORK STATE.

County.	County Seat.	Representatives in Congress.	County Judge.	Surrogate.	District Attorney.	Sheriff.	County Clerk.	County Treasurer.	Supt. of Poor.
Albany	Albany	P.G.Ten Eyck	G.Addington	E.J.Staley	T.C.Roland	Frank Coss	L. C. Warner	Wm.B.Leroy	A.C.Quentel
Allegany	Belmont	D.A.Reed	*E.Reynolds	E.Reynolds	Lee Fassett	A.Bluestone	D.P.Snyder	D.S.Burdick	W.H.Hall
Bronx	New York	(See U.S.Govt.)	L.D.Gibbs	G.M.S.Schulz	E.J.Glennon	T.H.O'Neil	R.L.Moran	Chamberlain	Charities Dpt
Broome	Binghamton	J.D.Clarke	*Benj.Baker	Benj.Baker	U.C.Lyons	B.M.Holcomb	F.P.Ockerman	W.F.Sherwood	G.F.Briggs
Cattaraugus	Little Valley	D.A.Reed	G.A.Larkin	A.A.Bird	A.M.Laidlaw	R.T.Mallory	F.M.Merrill	B.L.Andrews	W.P.Kysor
Cayuga	Auburn	N.J.Gould	E.S.Mosher	W.E.Woodin	B.Kenyon	F.W.Hendrick	C.J.Warne	F.A.Eldredge	A.L.Smith
Chautauqua	Mayville	D.A.Reed	A.B.Ottaway	H.N.Crosby	W.S.Stearns	J.S.McCallum	Ellen P. Yates	W.J.Doty	G.W.Colgrove
Chemung	Elmira	A.B.Houghton	*C.B.Swartw'd	C.B.Swartw'd	R.F.Nichols	H.E.Chapman	H.E.Copley	R.M.Dennis	A.R.Hoke
Chenango	Norwich	J.D.Clarke	*J.P.Hill	J.P.Hill	W.N.Truesdell	H.F.Hovey	I.J.Tillman	E.W.Camp	F.J.Quinn
Clinton	Plattsburg	B.H.Snell	J.K.Collins	V. F. Boire	H.A.Jerry	W.H.Coffe	J.N.Landry	S.D.Healey	C.D.Rea
Columbia	Hudson	C.B.Ward	J.L.Crandell	J.V.W'tb'k,Jr.	J.C.Tracy	F.Carter,Jr	C.H.DeWitt	E.Westover	W.N.Goold
Cortland	Cortland	W.W.Magee	G.M.Champlin	J.E.Eggleston	J.F.Tobin	R.E.Wright	G.M.Hoagland	F.J.Bentley	F.T.Newcomb
Delaware	Delhi	J.D.Clarke	*A.J.McNaught	A.J.McNaught	A.L.O'Connor	W.L.V'D'rm'k	E.J.Turnbull	H.S.Graham	J.F.Foreman
Dutchess	Poughkeepsie	H'm'n Fish,Jr.	C.W.H.Arnold	D.J.Gleason	R.E.Aldrich	C.F.Morehouse	H.N.Winch's'r	A.P.Russell	F.W.Hallock
Erie	Buffalo	J.M.Mead C.MacGregor	T.H.Noonan	L.B.Hart	G.B.Moore	W.F.Waldron	J.H.Meahl	S.A.Anderson	Charities Dept.
Essex	Eliz'bethtown	B.H.Snell	*B. A. Pyrke	B. A. Pyrke	O.B.Brewster	F.Dashnaw	N.D.Barnard	W.G.Wallace	H.H.Nye
Franklin	Malone	B.H.Snell	*F.G.Paddock	F.G.Paddock	E.C.Lawrence	A.A.Edwards	F.R.Kirk	J. A. Latour	J.Q.King
Fulton	Johnstown	F.Crowther	F.Talbot	T.C.Calderw'd	J.W.Titcomb	F. H. Vickery	E.D.Gordon	J.R.Robertson	M.Dutcher
Genesee	Batavia	A.D.Sanders	*N.K.Cone	N.K.Cone	J.L.Kelly	D.L.Elliott	C.B.Pixley	J.W.Mullen	G.H.Craft
Greene	Catskill	C.B.Ward	*J.C.Tallmadge	J.C.Tallmadge	H.McK.Curtis	G.W.Osborn	W.B.Donahue	W.S.Sherman	I.T.Tolley
Hamilton	LakePleasant	F.Crowther	*T.D.Sullivan	T.D.Sullivan	H.E.Gill	H.D.Kellogg	John Ostrander	C. L. Fry	S.W.Morrison
Herkimer	Herkimer	H.P.Snyder	*Chas. Bell	Chas. Bell	W.E.Ward	W.H.Cress	W.Qu'k'nbush	S.C.Burch	M.J.Casler
Jefferson	Watertown	L.W.Mott	C.B.Alverson	Jos.Atwell	J.B.Cooper	E.S.Gillette	F.H.Moore	B.S.Hayes	F. S. Dunaway
Kings	Brooklyn	(SeeU.S.Govt.)	See Co. Officials in G.N.Y.	G. A. Wingate	H.E.Lewis	J.Drescher	Wm.E.Kelly	Chamberlain N. Y. City	Charities Dept
Lewis	Lowville	L.W.Mott	*Milton Carter	Milton Carter	F.L.Smith	N.J Peck	P.J.Ulrich	E.H.Barnes	L.T.Strong
Livingston	Geneseo	A.D.Sanders	*L.R.Doty	L.R.Doty	W.A.Wheeler	Wm.Mann	J.H.Black	E.B.Wilhelm	J.Green
Madison	Wampsville	L.W.Mott	*J.D.Senn	J.D.Senn	E.A.Kiley	E.E.Cummings	L.L.Saunders	F.M.Elliott	L.Close
Monroe	Rochester	T.B.Dunn A.D.Sanders	W.K.Gillette	S.S.Brown	W.F.Love	F.S.Couchman	J.L.Hotchkiss	A.D.Chapman	W.E.Porter
Montgomery	Fonda	F.Crowther	C.E.Hardies	F.Sponable	N. J. Herrick	S.Hodge	H. D. Loder	T.F.Brown	R.E.Keesler
Nassau	Mineola	F.C.Hicks	L.J.Smith	L.D.Howell	C.R.Weeks	C.W.Smith	T.S.Cheshire	W.E.Luyster	C. Van Deusen
New York	New York	(SeeU.S.Govt.)	See Co. Officials in G.N.Y.	J.P.Cohalan Jas.A.Foley	E.Swann	D.H.Knott	W.F.Schneider	Chamberlain	Charities Dept
Niagara	Lockport	S.W.Dempsey	C.Hickey	C.Hickey	B.A.Duquette	C.A.Smith	F.H.Fogal	L.E.Huston	J.Shimer
Oneida	Utica	H.P.Snyder	F.H.Hazard	E.W.Jones	W.R.Lee	A.W.Pickard	(Vacant)	W.A.Foster	J.T.Howe
Onondaga	Syracuse	W.W.Magee	D.R.Cobb	J.W.Sadler	F.P.Malpass	E.G.Ten Eyck	A.C.Mead	H.C.Ranson	H.D.Nott'ham
Ontario	Canandaigua	N.J.Gould	H.W.Fitch	H.I.Dunton	N.D.Lapham	R.H.Gulvin	H.D.Aldrich	H.E.Snyder	F.W.Hollis
Orange	Goshen	H'm'n Fish,Jr.	R.Wiggins	E.C.Smith	J.D.Wilson,Jr.	W.M.Leonard	G.F.Gregg	J.L.Sloan	W.F.Durland
Orleans	Albion	J.S.Parker	*G.B.Fluhrer	G. B. Fluhrer	W.H.Munson	J.S.Porter	H.D.Bartlett	H.E.Coleburn	L. S. Hill
Oswego	Oswego	L.W.Mott	H. D. Coville	C.I.Miller	F.D.Culkin	L.J.Parsons	E.L.Vincent	G.H.Fuller	C.A.Stone
Otsego	Cooperstown	J.D.Clarke	U.G.Welch	S.L.H'tingt'n	A.A.Pierson	B.F.Van Zandt	W.I.Smith	B.G.Johnson	M.J.Esmay
Putnam	Carmel	H'm'n Fish,Jr.	*J.B.Southard	J.B.Southard	P.A.Anderson	H.B.Stephens	E.S.Agor	E.D.Stannard	J.Brooks
Queens	Jamaica	J.J.Kindred	B.J.Humphrey	Daniel Noble	Dana Wallace	John Wagner	E.W.Cox	Chamberlain	Charities Dept.
Rensselaer	Troy	P.G.Ten Eyck	P.H.Russell	C.S.McChesney	J. P. Taylor	B.Sharpe	H.Dahl	D. Runkle	H.A.Sheldon
Richmond	Richmond	D.J.Riordan	*J.H.Tiernan	J.H.Tiernan	J.P.Maloy	W. K. Walsh	C.L.Bostwick	Chamberlain	Charities Dept.
Rockland	New City	J.W.Husted	*M.B.Patterson	M.B.Patterson	M.Lexow	A.H.Merritt	J.W.Sherwood	W.G.Hamilton	E.D.Ten Eyck
St.Lawrence	Canton	B.H.Snell	J. C. Crapser	A.R.Herriman	J. C. Dolan	L.A.Fishbeck	N.W.Halle	R.P.Johnston	H.A.Olmstead
Saratoga	Ballston Spa.	Jas.S.Parker	L.B.McKelvey	W.S.Ostrander	C.B.Andrus	A.L.Reynolds	J.F.Hennessy	W.W.Bl'ckmer	F.J.Dunn
Schenectady	Schenectady	F.Crowther	J.J.McMullen	A.M.Vedder	J.R.Parker	D.Manning	G.T.Bradt	W.E.Walker	J. H. Chisholm
Schoharie	Schoharie	C.B.Ward	*D.Beekman	D. Beekman	C.B.Mayham	Geo.Oliver	H.W.Wright	T.Colby	H.J.Rose
Schuyler	Watkins	A.B.Houghton	*G.M.Velie	G.M.Velie	E.C.Barkman	L.E.Kenyon	C.E.Titus	B.E.Birge	C.M.Bronson
Seneca	Waterloo	N.J.Gould	*G.F.Bodine	G.F.Bodine	L.S.Church	C.P.Seeley	G.T.Purcell	O.C.Cone	C.W.Slaughter
Steuben	Bath	A.B.Houghton	W.J.Cheney	E.C.Smith	E.S.Brown	F.L.Nolton	L.H.Brown	W.P Dean	J.S.Brundage

Suffolk	Riverhead	F.C.Hicks	G.H.Furman	R.S.Pelletrau	L.M.Young	J.F.Kelly	J.F.Richards'n	S.M.Scudder	J.Baker
Sullivan	Monticello	C.B.Ward	*G.H.Smith	G.H.Smith	H.F.Gardner	G.N.Hembdt	G.D.Pelton	C.A.Shaw	F.E.Rhodes
Tioga	Owego	A.B.Houghton	*G.F.Andrews	G.F.Andrews	N.Turk	G.S.Bixby	A. L. Decker	T.H.Reddish	A.Lainhart
Tompkins	Ithaca	A.B.Houghton	*W.M.Kent	W.M.Kent	A.G.Adams	Chas.Green	C.D.Tarbell	R.L.Post	W.D.Baldwin
Ulster	Kingston	C.B.Ward	J.M.Fowler	W.N.Gill	F.G.Traver	W.J.Smith	C.K.Loughran	J.Lounsbery	W.S.Hartshorn
Warren	Lake George	Jas.S.Parker	*G. S. Raley	G.S.Raley	J.S.Kiley	R.J.Bolton	E.C.Sisson	B.W.Sprague	E.W.Griggs
Washington	Hudson Falls	Jas.S.Parker	E.C.Rogers	Fred'k Fraser	W.S.Bascom	F.A.Brown	G.W.Curry	H. J. Stevens	M.S.Graham
Wayne	Lyons	N.J.Gould	*C.W.Knapp	C.W.Knapp	W.T.Purchase	J.Newman	C.A.Noble	G.S.Reeves	C.A.Stalker
Westchester	White Plains	J.W.Husted	F.L.Young	G.A.Slater	L.P.Davis	C.E.Nossiter	D.J.Cashin	Wm. Archer	Charities Bd
Wyoming	Warsaw	A.D.Sanders	*J.E.Norton	J.E.Norton	L. A. Walker	Jno.Simons,Jr.	B.F.Williams	C.B.Smallwood	C.F.Wing
Yates	Penn Yan	N.J.Gould	*G.H.Baker	G.H.Baker	C.W.Kimball	C.W.Blodgett	F. R. Durry	H.O.Bennett	J.W.Ball

*County Judge and Surrogate. Corrected according to returns filed with Sec. of State up to Jan. 17, 1921.

SUBURBAN NEW JERSEY COUNTY OFFICIALS.

County.	County Seat.	Representatives in Congress.	County Judge.	Surrogate.	District Attorney.	Sheriff.	County Clerk.	County Collector.	Chairman Board of Freeholders.
Bergen	Hackensack	R.Perkins	J.B.Zahiskie	J.B.Hopper	A.C.Hart	J.Kingsley,Jr.	G.VanBuskirk	J.C.Mercer	Jos.Kingly.
Essex	Newark	F.R.Lehlbach. R.W.Parker	W.P.Martin H.V.Osborne F.G.Stickel,Jr.	H.Isherwood	J.H.Harrison	J.R.Flavell	J.H.Scott	R.W.Booth	A.W.Harrison.
Hudson	Jersey City	C.F.X.O'Brien A.E.Olpp H.W.Taylor	J.W.McCarthy R.Doherty J.A.Blair	J.F.Norton	*P.P.Garven	J.Magner	J.J.McGovern.	J.F.S.Fitzp'k.	O.L.AufderH'd
Passaic	Paterson	A.H.Radcliffe	W.W.Watson	FredericBeggs	*Michael Dunn	J.McCutcheon.	J.J.Slater	Geo.W.Batbyl.	R.Sinclair
Union	Elizabeth	E.R.Ackerman	C.B.Pierce	C.N.Codding	*W.L.Hetfield.	J.E.Warner	Wm.B.Martin.	N.R.Leavitt	G.J.Teller.

*Prosecuting.

LOSS OF LIFE IN PANICS AND DISASTROUS FIRES.

Date and structure.	Deaths.
Dec. 5, 1876, Bkln. Theater	289
June 28, 1880, Seawanhaka off Wards Isl.	24
Dec. 8, 1881, Ring-Theater, Vienna, Austria.	850
June 16, 1883, school, Sunderland, England.	200
Apr. 30, 1884, poorhouse, Van Buren Co., Mich.	30
Dec. 18, 1884, St. John's Home, Bkln	22
Feb. 12, 1885, Blockley Almshouse, Phila.	50
May 25, 1887, Opera Comique, Paris	200
Sept. 4, 1887, theater, Exeter, England	200
Mar. 21, 1888, Banquet Theater, Portugal	200
Mar. 26, 1889, factory, Kent av., Bkln	22
July 21, 1889, building at Lu-Chow, China	400
Jan. 9, 1890 Shantung Theater, China	250
Aug. 22, 1891, Taylor Bldg., N. Y. City	61
Feb. 6, 1892, Hotel Royal, N. Y. City	28
Apr. 27, 1892, Central Theater, Phila	28
Apr. 1, 1896, 36 Union, Bkln. (tenement)	10
Aug. 12, 1896, Ching Un Dist. Theater, China.	200
May 4, 1897, Charity Bazaar, Paris	150
Mar. 17, 1899, Windsor Hotel, N. Y. City	45
June 30, 1900, Hoboken piers and ships	145
Feb. 2, 1902, Park Av. Hotel, N. Y. City	21
Sept. 20, 1902, Shiloh Baptist Church, Birmingham, Ala	115
Jan. 27, 1903, Colney-Hatch Asylum, London, England	52
Nov. 22, 1903, lodging house, Johnstown, Pa.	28
Dec. 30, 1903, Iroquois Theater, Chicago	602
June 15, 1904, the Gen. Slocum disaster	1,021
Nov. 22, 1904, 184 Troutman, Bkln	12
Mar. 20, 1905, shoe factory, Brockton, Mass.	100
Apr. 18, 1906, San Francisco fire	500
July 29, 1907, tenement, 222 Chrystie, Mhtn.	20
Dec. 7, 1907, coal mine, Fairmont, Va.	400
Jan. 4, 1908, Rhodes Theater, Boyertown, Pa.	169
Mar. 4, 1908, school, Collingwood, Ohio	174
Feb. 2, 1909, theater in Acapulco, Mexico	300
Nov. 26, 1910, factory, Newark, N. J.	23
Mar. 5, 1911, theater, Bologole, Russia	90
Mar. 25, 1911, 23 Washington pl., Mhtn., Triangle Shirtwaist Co.	145
Apr. 9, 1911, bldg., Bombay, British India.	200
Aug. 26, 1911, Canonsburg, Pa.	26
Jan. 9, 1912, Equitable Life Bldg., 120 B'way, N. Y. City	6
May 27, 1912, film explosion and theater fire, Villereal, Spain	80
July 8, 1912, factory fire nr. Lipesh, Russia	60
Nov. 23, 1912, Starch factory, Waukegan, Ill.	25
Apr. 23, 1913, mine explosion, Pittsburgh, Pa.	96
Aug. 3, 1913, mine expl'n, Glasgow, Scotland	22
Oct. 14, 1913, mine explosion, Cardiff, Wales	400
Dec. 3, 1913, lodging house, Boston, Mass.	30
Dec. 25, 1913, theater panic, Calumet, Mich.	72
Apr. 17, 1914, West Side tenement, N. Y. C.	12
Mar. 13, 1915, Crew-Levick explosion, Bkln.	5
Nov. 2, 1915, 66 No. 6th, Williamsburgh	13
Nov. 6, 1915, 285-287 No. 6th, Wmsb'rg	12
Jan. 8, 1916, explosion, str. Aztec, Erie Basin, Bkln.	7
Jan. 24, 1916, explosion, Buffalo	15
Mar. 6, 1916, explosion in jail, El Paso, Texas	18
May 10, 1916, theatre, Wallaceton, Va.	26
May 15, 1916, explosion, powder plant, Repauno, N. J.	8
July 24, 1916, explosion, tunnel under Lake Erie	22
July 30, 1916, explosion, Black Tom Island, N. J.	2
Oct. 5, 1916, Christian Brothers' College, St. Louis, Mo.	9
Oct. 17, 1916, dye concern, Astoria, L. I. C.	9
Oct. 26, 1916, St. Elizabeth's Hospital, Farnham, Quebec	19
Dec. 6, 1917, sections of Halifax and Dartmouth, N. S.	1,800
Apr. 13, 1918, State Hospital, Norman, Okla.	40
May 28, 1918, 2900 W. 3d, Coney Island	2
Sept. 7, 1918, Amer. Button Co., Newark, N. J.	12
Oct. 4-5, 1918, Explosions, T. A. Gillespie Loading Co.	50
March 17, 1919, United Electric Light Co.	2
March 27, 1919, Richmond Hill Circle, L. I.	3
May 24, 1919, S. S. Virginia	15
June 20, 1919, Mayaguez Theatre, San Juan, Porto Rico	150
Oct. 25, 1919—Franowitz, Silesia	40
Nov. 18, 1919, Howell, Mich.	4
Nov. 23, 1919, Villa Platte, La.	28
Nov. 14, 1920, moving picture theatre, Mhtn.	6
Nov. 20, 1920, tenement house, Mhtn.	9
Dec. 2, 1920, studio apartment, Mhtn.	5

NEW YORK STATE FUNDS, JUNE 30, 1920.

GENERAL BALANCE SHEET OF THE STATE

Resources.

General Fund:	
Total cash for general purposes	$32,986,346.17
Revenue Required for General Fund:	
Budget appropriations in force	139,856,463.46
Canal Fund (other than maintenance, etc.):	
Construction	152,190,583.99
Investments (J. R. Shanley Est. Co.)	469,600.00
Cash	3,626,253.82
Canal Debt Sinking Fund:	
Investments at par	42,907,087.63
Cash (statement I)	1,661,351.40
Highway Improvement Fund:	
Construction	78,461,847.68
Cash	3,257,633.81
Highway Debt Sinking Fund:	
Investments at par	23,225,153.43
Cash	407,032.66
Saratoga Springs State Reservation Fund:	
Purchase of land, etc.	523,991.59
Cash	8.41
Palisades Interstate Park Fund:	
Extensions and improvements	4,756,320.58
Cash	243,679.42
Sinking Fund:	
Investments at par	820,360.00
Cash	31,157.42
State Forest Preserve Fund:	
Land, etc.	1,272,906.49
Cash	1,227,093.51
Sinking Fund:	
Investments at par	331,100.00
Cash	116,242.68
Federal Rural Post Road Fund	100,000,00
Principal investments at par	8,753,230.88
Principal cash	1,997,545.24
Revenue cash	9,762.20
Total resources	$498,232,242.47

Appropriations, Liabilities and Surplus.

General Fund:	
Appropriations in force	$141,249,400.00
Surplus, July 1, 1920	31,593,409.63
Canal fund (other than maintenance, etc.):	
Funded debt	148,000,000.00
Compt. temporary certif.	2,600,000.00
Sinking Fund Reserves	44,568,439.03
Construction appropriation fund	2,914,500.00
Miscellaneous receipts on account of construction appropriated	2,156,003.64
Miscellaneous receipts on account of construction unappropriated	615,934.17
Highway Improvement Fund:	
Funded debt	30,000,000.00
Compt. temporary certf.	200,000.00
Sinking Fund Reserves	23,632,176.09
Miscellaneous receipts on account of construction unappropriated	339,274.41
Miscellaneous receipts on account of construction appropriated	279,707.03
Saratoga Springs State Reservation Fund:	
Funded debt	524,000.00
Palisades Interstate Park Fund:	
Funded debt	5,000,000,00
Sinking Fund Reserves	851,517.43
State Forest Preserve Fund:	
Funded debt	2,500,000.00
Sinking Fund Reserves	447,342.68
Federal Rural Post Road Fund.	100,000.00
Trust Fund Reserves	10,760,538.82
Total appropriations, liabilities and surplus	$498,232,242.47

COMPARATIVE STATISTICS, STATE OF NEW YORK, OCTOBER, 1, 1880, TO JUNE 30, 1920

Year.	Assessed value of real and personal property.	Direct State tax rate (mills).	Direct State taxes levied.	Funded State debt (gross).	Treasury transactions for general purposes of government. Receipts.	Expenditures.	Excess receipts over expenditures or dec. (—).
1881	$2,681,257,606	2.25	$6,032,825.61	$9,109,054.87	$12,468,522.33	$10,682,396.01	$1,786,126.32
1882	2,783,682,567	2.45	6,820,022.29	9,109,054.87	9,503,255.57	10,198,222.16	—694,966.59
1883	2,872,257,325	3.25	9,334,836.31	8,473,854.87	10,064,675.22	10,254,333.73	—189,658.51
1884	3,014,591,372	2.575	7,762,572.78	8,461,854.87	11,974,624.28	11,168,954.79	805,669.49
1885	3,094,731,457	2.96	9,160,405.11	9,461,854.87	11,416,472.68	12,196,939.79	—780,467.11
1886	3,224,682,343	2.95	9,512,812.91	9,327,204.87	12,912,109.21	11,509,585.94	1,402,523.27
1887	3,361,128,177	2.70	9,075,046.08	7,567,004.87	13,261,660.07	11,988,408.07	1,273,252.00
1888	3,469,199,945	2.62	9,089,303.86	6,965,354.87	13,585,113.40	13,533,366.40	51,747.00
1889	3,567,429,757	3.52	12,557,352.74	6,774,854.87	12,687,410.54	13,327,862.99	—640,452.45
1890	3,683,653,062	2.34	8,619,748.17	4,964,304.87	14,460,586.37	13,152,610.26	1,307,976.11
1891	3,779,393,746	1.375	5,196,666.40	2,927,654.87	14,836,028.02	13,837,616.33	998,411.69
1892	3,931,741,499	1.98	7,784,848.16	763,160.00	10,364,427.56	14,018,830.67	—3,654,403.11
1893	4,038,058,949	2.58	10,418,192.08	660.00	13,842,181.27	15,115,836.39	—1,273,655.12
1894	4,199,882,058	2.18	9,155,742.88	660.00	15,131,290.37	16,192,049.13	—1,060,758.76
1895	4,292,082,167	3.24	13,906,346.23	660.00	17,211,858.20	17,550,012.81	—338,154.61
1896	4,368,712,903	2.69	11,751,837.71	2,320,660.00	24,786,181.54	21,422,352.33	3,363,829.21
1897	4,506,985,694	2.67	12,023,651.80	5,765,660.00	22,387,587.29	21,384,294.58	1,003,292.71
1898	4,898,611,019	2.08	10,189,110.93	9,340,660.00	23,183,541.32	24,839,031.79	—1,655,490.47
1899	5,076,396,824	2.49	12,640,228.09	10,185,660.00	22,717,694.96	22,061,592.93	656,102.03
1900	5,461,302,752	1.96	10,704,153.39	10,130,660.00	28,072,441.06	25,152,296.65	2,920,144.41
1901	5,686,921,678	1.20	6,824,306.01	10,075,660.00	26,455,869.72	23,395,030.08	3,060,839.64
1902	5,754,400,382	.13	748,072.05	9,920,660.00	23,149,609.26	23,260,249.19	—110,639.93
1903	5,854,500,121	.13	761,085.02	9,665,660.00	23,516,080.02	23,240,381.04	275,698.98
1904	7,446,476,127	.13	968,041.90	9,410,660.00	24,981,651.16	25,938,464.87	—956,813.71
1905	7,738,165,640	.154	1,191,677.51	11,155,660.00	25,286,916.86	27,359,485.90	—2,072,569.04
1906	8,015,090,722	None	....	10,630,660.00	34,059,518.54	27,424,363.08	6,635,155.46
1907	8,565,379,394	None	....	17,290,660.00	35,032,053.87	32,619,734.94	2,412,318.93
1908	9,173,568,245	None	....	26,230,660.00	33,996,769.90	34,318,052.13	—321,282.23
1909	9,666,118,681	None	....	41,230,660.00	31,567,185.51	39,237,426.69	—7,670,241.18
1910	9,821,620,552	None	....	57,230,660.00	37,905,876.73	38,332,015.66	—426,138.93
1911	10,121,277,458	.60	6,072,766.48	79,730,660.00	36,138,376.06	38,119,377.16	—1,981,001.10
1912	11,022,985,914	1.00	11,022,985.91	109,702,660.00	50,492,863.56	44,858,059.07	5,634,804.49
1913	11,128,498,055	.5805	6,460,093.12	135,355,660.00	55,521,777.76	50,011,422.53	5,510,355.23
1914	11,385,137,127	None	....	159,260,660.00	50,907,945.40	53,828,583.62	—2,920,638.22
1915	12,070,420,887	1.70	20,519,715.51	186,400,660.00	42,141,009.68	57,342,600.39	—15,201,590.71
1916	11,790,628,803	None	....	211,404,660.00	61,437,404.35	52,725,240.14	8,712,1[illegible].21
1917	12,091,437,643	1.08	13,058,752.65	236,309,660.00	61,593,111.04	60,881,297.84	711,813.20
1918	12,520,819,811	1.06	13,272,069.00	236,214,660.00	76,034,631.50	73,392,123.34	2,642,508.16
1919	12,758,021,964	1.06	13,523,503.27	236,119,660.00	80,458,633.85	78,941,313.01	1,517,320.84
1920	12,989,432,733	2.695	3[illegible],006,323.91	236,024,000.00	115,678,480.46	94,100,071.61	21,578,408.85
Totals	....	....	....	....	$1,241,223,426.49	1,208,911,876.04	$32,311,550.45

NEW YORK STATE LAWS.

Of the 952 new laws passed by the 1920 Legislature, some of the most important are indicated below. They are divided according to bject, numbers on the left side referring to apter. Dates at end of paragraph indicate te of Brooklyn Eagle in which full text of law is printed.

Agriculture.

1—Dog license fees; distributing money; appropriation. June 15.
406—Exhibit, agriculture; dairying. July 31.
288—Farm machinery, rental by State. July 31.
90—Sale of agricultural seeds. July 10.

Appropriations.

165—Annual appropriation bill, $74,163,173.63. ly 17.
582—Supplemental annual appropriation bill, 98,682.98. Aug. 28.
50—Canals, Erie, Oswego, Cham., unexpended lance, $1,425,361.37, reappropriation. July 3.
49—Hudson River Canal Terminals, unexpended balance, $82,274.74, reappropriation. July 3.
435—Charitable, Reformatory institutions, nployees, $153,000. July 31.
669—Highway improvement, $261,359.79. ug. 12.
670—Highway improvement, $10,000,000. ug. 12.
697—Hospital officers and employees, $1,120,-0. Aug. 14.
9—Industrial Commission, new building, $545,-0. June 15.
8—Administering Income Tax Law, $500,000. une 15.
519—Palisades Interstate Park, lands, $500,-0. Aug. 7.
903—Purchase of radium, $225,000. Aug. 28.
154—Rural post roads, $3,750,000. July 10.
680—School teachers' salaries, $20,550,000. ug. 14.
80—State, county highways, maintenance, ,500,000. July 3.
892—Tunnel, New York-New Jersey, construction of, $1,000,000. Aug. 28.

Banking Law.

167—Restrictions on savings bank deposits. ly 10.
546—Examination of banks and trust companies. Aug. 7.
703—Personal loan companies, brokers. Aug. 14.
67—Residence of savings banks trustees. ly 3.

Banks.

379—Deposit of State moneys. July 31.
454—Safe deposit boxes, surrogates examine. ly 31.

Boxing.

912—Provides for Boxing Commission. Aug. 28.

Business Law—General.

939—Contracts, advances on, personal property. Aug. 28.
940—Contracts, advances, personal property, aiver. Aug. 28.

Canals.

(See also Appropriations.)

698—Grain terminals, New York City and Oswego, appropriation. Aug. 14.
541—Railroads within canal terminals. Aug. 7.
402—Terminals, construction, appropriation. July 31.

Charities Law.

308—Temporary detention of females. July 31.
774—Mental defective delinquent women. Aug. 21.

Civil Practice.

925—Civil Practice Act. Aug. 28.
926—Civil Practice Act. depositions. Aug. 28.

Code—Civil.

471—New York City Court, jurisdiction. July 28.
133—Summary proceedings, tenant, objectionable, proof. July 10.
139—Summary proceedings, excessive rent, defense. July 10.
134—Summary proceedings, stay of, deposit rent. July 10.
132—Summary proceedings, defense, counterclaim. July 10.
135—Tenants, holding over, defense, counterclaim. July 10.

Education Law.

680—Increase of salaries of teachers and employees. Aug. 14.
73—Salaries of teachers in New York City schools. July 3.

Election Law.

875—Providing for absentee voting. Aug. 28.

Highway Law.

96—Registration fees, motor vehicles. July 10.
684—Lights, motor vehicles. Aug. 14.

Labor.

601—Children in factories and mercantile establishments, examination. Aug. 9.
603—Employees, physical examination. Aug. 14.
275—Enacting Arbitration Law. July 26.

Liquor Tax Law.

911—Liquors, intoxicating, defined to mean liquors containing more than 2.75 percent of alcohol by weight. Aug. 28.

Motor Vehicles.

119—Misdemeanor to wilfully remove or alter number or identification mark. (See also Highway Law.) July 10.

New York Charter.

79—Change name of Public Charities Dept. July 3.
427—City officers, employees, retirement. July 31.
800—Firemen, policemen, dependent relatives. July 24.
509—Appointing patrolmen. Aug. 14.

Penal Law.

569—Makes it a misdemeanor to knowingly transmit to any newspaper false statements. Aug. 7.

Rent Laws.

Chapters 942, 943, 944, 945, 946, 947, 949, 950, 951, 952; published in pamphlet form by Brooklyn Daily Eagle.

WAR BONUSES IN TWELVE STATES.

A soldier bonus of $10 for each month's serv- in the World War was carried at the New ork election by popular referendum. It is esnated that 400,000 ex-service men and women ill share in this grant. In Washington and ew Jersey similar results were obtained, ashington voting $15 per month for every onth of service up to Armistice Day and New ersey granting her returned soldiers $10 per onth, with a maximum of $100. New York's aximum is $250. With the three States just entioned, the list of States which has voted ch bonuses to their returned soldiers numrs twelve, namely: Massachusetts, Vermont, ew Hampshire, Minnesota, Wisconsin, Rhode land, North Dakota, South Dakota and Maine. these, North Dakota, which pays her fightg sons and daughters $25 for each month of rvice, without setting a limit, is the most liberal.

Twenty-two nations on Dec. 20, 1920, signed e protocol giving executive approval to the ague plan for an International Court of Juste. Portugal, Switzerland, Denmark and Saldor also agree to compulsory arbitration.

WORLD'S LARGEST WOODEN DRY DOCK.

The largest wooden sectional dry dock in the world has been constructed by the Morse Dry Dock and Repair Company of Brooklyn. It is built in sections, each complete with separate pumping plant, and in such a manner that a 15,000-ton vessel, 475 ft. long, can be raised by three sections, the whole of the six sections being able to accommodate vessels of 725 ft. in length and 30,000 tons burden. Its first great task was to raise the 630-ft. steamer Minnesota clear of the water, which it did in twenty-five minutes.

The 1920 annual report of the Commissioner-General of Immigration shows that in the past year 90,025 aliens were admitted to the United States from Canada and 52,361 from Mexico, which breaks all records for immigration from those countries.

Cambridge University, England, by a vote of 904 to 712, on Dec. 8, 1920, refused women full membership in the university on equal terms with men. Most of the other English universities, including Oxford, have granted full membership to women.

FAILURES IN THE UNITED STATES.

Reported by R. G. Dun & Co.	Number *1919	Number *1920	Liabilities *1919	Liabilities *1920
MANUFACTURERS:				
Iron foundries and nails	26	31	$1,639,841	$4,033,984
Machinery and tools	180	228	13,539,291	24,517,036
Woolens, carpets and knit goods	7	14	98,991	1,000,218
Cottons, lace and hosiery	21	23	1,441,701	1,230,707
Lumber, carpenters and coopers	251	185	4,923,592	11,784,940
Clothing and millinery	178	368	2,075,369	8,826,023
Hats, gloves and furs	25	84	243,548	2,617,086
Chemicals and drugs	39	34	1,203,960	758,799
Paints and oils	9	11	165,973	290,416
Printing and engraving	61	48	836,330	1,471,869
Milling and bakers	151	284	2,195,128	3,210,116
Leather, shoes and harness	53	80	944,739	3,016,956
Liquors and tobacco	50	61	925,490	1,284,397
Glass, earthenware and bricks	48	25	3,003,920	811,309
All others	802	907	22,884,692	37,359,697
Total manufacturing	1,901	2,383	$56,122,075	$102,146,953
TRADERS:				
General stores	449	477	$4,555,629	$6,397,481
Groceries, meats and fish	1,376	1,550	8,300,548	11,064,521
Hotels and restaurants	324	351	3,439,526	3,787,041
Liquors and tobacco	218	156	1,418,346	1,728,118
Clothing and furnishing	322	468	2,878,591	5,944,057
Dry goods and carpets	191	320	2,066,265	7,142,672
Shoes, rubbers and trunks	133	132	1,272,263	1,656,510
Furniture and crockery	76	73	812,973	704,209
Hardware, stoves and tools	87	73	1,476,866	1,292,495
Chemicals and drugs	136	100	808,234	810,323
Paints and oils	26	15	827,106	310,963
Jewelry and clocks	73	101	596,448	1,581,273
Books and papers	24	20	280,661	175,038
Hats, furs and gloves	21	118	294,149	6,655,005
All others	605	939	8,024,966	25,857,638
Total trading	4,061	4,894	$37,152,571	$75,107,340
Agents, brokers, etc	591	660	$23,965,732	$67,296,309
Total commercial	6,553	7,937	$117,240,378	$244,550,602

*Report covers 12 months from Dec. 1 to Nov. 30; all other figures for calendar year.

Commercial Failures.

Year.	No.	Liabilities.
1878	10,478	$234,383,132
1879	6,658	98,149,053
1880	4,735	65,752,000
1881	5,583	81,155,932
1882	6,738	101,547,564
1883	9,184	172,874,172
1884	10,968	226,343,427
1885	10,637	124,220,321
1886	9,834	114,644,119
1887	9,634	167,560,944
1888	10,679	123,829,973
1889	10,882	148,784,337
1890	10,907	189,856,964
1891	12,273	189,868,638
1892	10,344	114,044,167
1893	15,242	346,779,889
1894	13,885	172,992,856
1895	13,197	173,196,060
1896	15,088	226,096,834
1897	13,351	154,332,071
1898	12,186	130,662,899
1899	9,337	90,879,889
1900	10,774	138,495,673
1901	11,002	113,092,379
1902	11,615	117,476,769
1903	12,069	145,444,185
1904	12,199	144,202,311
1905	11,520	102,676,172
1906	10,682	119,201,515
1907	11,725	197,385,225
1908	15,690	222,315,684
1909	12,924	154,603,465
1910	12,652	201,757,097
1911	13,441	191,061,665
1912	15,399	202,319,352
1913	16,037	272,672,288
1914	18,280	357,908,859
1915	22,156	302,286,148
1916	16,993	196,212,256
1917	13,855	182,441,371
1918	9,982	163,019,979
1919	6,451	113,291,237
*1920	7,937	244,550,602

DISASTERS AT SEA.

Marine Disasters.	Lives Lost.
1880. Jan. 31—Atlanta, British training ship, left Bermuda; never heard from	290
1881. Aug. 30—Teuton, Cape of Good Hope	200
1884. April 19—State of Florida and bark Ponema sunk in midocean after collision	145
1887. Jan. 29—Kapunda, collided with bark Ada Melore off coast of Brazil	300
1887. Nov. 15—Wah Young, caught fire between Canton and Hongkong	
1890. Jan. 2—Persia, wrecked off Corsica	
1890. Feb. 17—Duburg, wrecked in China Sea	400
1890. March 1—Quetia, in Torres Straits	[illegible]
1890. Sept. 19—Turkish frigate Ertogrul foundered off Japan	540
1890. Dec. 27—Shanghai, burned in China Sea	101
1891. March 17—Utopia, Anchor Line, collision with the Anson off Gibraltar	574
1892. Jan. 13—Namehow, in China Sea	414
1892. Oct. 28—Romania, wrecked off Corsica	113
1893. Feb. 8—Trinairia, wrecked off Spain	115
1893. June 22—British battleship Victoria sunk in collision with the Camperdown off Syria	357
1894. June 25—Norge, wrecked on Rockall Reef, in North Atlantic	600
1895. Jan. 30—Elbe, German steamer, sunk in collision with the Crathie, in North Sea	335
1895. March 11—Spanish cruiser Reina Regenta foundered in Mediterranean	400
1898. July 2—Bourgogne, French Line, sunk in collision with Cromartyshire	571
1904. June 15—General Slocum, excursion steamboat, burned going through Hell Gate, New York	1,000
1905. Sept. 12—Japanese warship Mikasa sunk after explosion in Sasepo Harbor	599
1907. Feb. 12—Larchmont, in collision with the Harry Hamilton in Long Island Sound	183
1908. July 28—Chinese warship Jing King foundered off Hongkong	300
1908. Nov. 6—Taish, sunk off Etoro Isl	150
1909. Nov. 25—Sardinia, burned at entrance to Port of Valletta, Malta	100
1910. April 26—Aurora, sunk by iceberg in North Atlantic	187
1912. April 14—Titanic, White Star Line, sunk in Atlantic Ocean after hitting iceberg	1,503
1912. Sept. 28—Kickermaru, off coast Japan	1,000
1913. March 1—Calvados, lost in blizzard in Sea of Marmora	200
1913. May 24—Nevada, sunk after striking mine in Gulf of Smyrna	[illegible]
1913. Oct. 9—Volturno, fire mid-Atlantic	[illegible]
1914. Apr. 1—Sealing steamer Southern Cross lost after severe storm off Cape Race	[illegible]
1914. May 30—Empress of Ireland, of Canadian Pacific fleet, sunk by collier Storstadt in fog on St. Lawrence River	[illegible]
1915. May 7—Lusitania of Cunard Line, torpedoed and sunk off south coast of Ireland by German submarine	[illegible]
1915. July 24—Eastland, excursion steamer, turned over at pier in Chicago River	[illegible]
1916. Mar. 5—Spanish S.S. Principe de Asturias sunk off Santos, Brazil	[illegible]
1916. Oct. 20—Str. Merida sunk in Lake Erie	[illegible]
1916. Oct. 21—Barge D. L. Filer in Lake Erie	[illegible]
1916. Oct. 21—Str. J. B. Colgate in Lake Erie	[illegible]
1916. Nov. 3—Strs. Connemara and Retriever, collision in North Sea	[illegible]
1916. Nov. 6—Str. Pio IX, off Canary Isls	[illegible]
1917. Dec. 8—Eugene F. Moran, tug, foundered and sunk off Atlantic City	[illegible]
1918. Feb. 24—Red Cross liner Florizel foundered in storm off Cape Race	[illegible]
1918. Feb. 6—British S. S. Miguel De Larrinaga foundered in mid-ocean	[illegible]
1918. Oct. 25—Steamer Princess Sophia sunk during storm off Alaska	[illegible]
1919. Sept. 9—Spanish passenger liner Valbanera sunk in hurricane off Rebecca Shoal Lighthouse, 40 miles from Key West, Fla.	[illegible]
1919. Dec. 19—British S. S. Lien Shing lost at sea, off Saigon	[illegible]
1919. Dec. 19—British S. S. Manxman sunk in midocean	[illegible]
1919. Dec. 20—Oil Tanker J. A. Chanslor wrecked off Cape Blanco	[illegible]
1919. Dec. 29—Belgian S. S. Anton Von Driel wrecked off St. Shott's, N. F.	[illegible]
1920. Jan. 10—British S. S. Troveal sunk in English Channel	[illegible]
1920. Jan. 12—French S. S. L'Affrique sunk in Bay of Biscay	[illegible]
1920. Jan. 19—Str. Macona foundered off coast of Norway	[illegible]
1920. Apr. 18—Str. William O'Brien sunk in Atlantic	[illegible]

THE BROOKLYN EAGLE ALMANAC.

VOLUME XXXVI. JANUARY, 1921.

THE 1921 EAGLE ALMANAC AND ITS FEATURES

THE current year marks the thirty-sixth anniversary of THE EAGLE ALMANAC, and the eightieth anniversary of THE BROOKLYN DAILY EAGLE. Four score years ago, when the United States was still a fledgling among the nations and Brooklyn little more than a country town the first EAGLE was issued. Its beginnings were humble, but the sturdy character and good business judgment of its founder, Isaac Van Anden, and the manner in which his nephew, Colonel William Hester, and his associates, have carried forward the splendid Van Anden traditions for the past sixty years, have developed THE EAGLE into one of the great newspapers of America and of the world.

THE EAGLE ALMANAC expresses THE EAGLE's desire to record in more compact and permanent form than that of a daily newspaper the chronicle of the year's events. These are times of change and transition. The World War has been over for more than two years, but real peace has not yet come. Men and parties, governments and policies, are shifting and changing rapidly and constantly. It is difficult to follow the day's events. In such a time the complete records provided in the pages of this ALMANAC are of particular value.

During the past year the United States has experienced one of her quadrennial national political campaigns. This issue of THE EAGLE ALMANAC records the facts of that campaign and of the biennial election of Governor and other officials of the State. The tabulation of the election results is complete and of itself gives this issue permanent historic value. The tables are as accurate as careful checking and rechecking can make them. THE EAGLE ALMANAC is proud of its record for accuracy, a record which it has developed with the help of its readers. As always the ALMANAC Editor will appreciate your calling his attention to any errors you may discover in the issue, even though they relate to minor matters. The fourteenth census of the United States was taken in 1920. Some remarkable growths have been shown during the last ten years and the figures published in THE ALMANAC show many changes in the rank of the larger cities.

Striking examples of THE EAGLE spirit and enterprise were exemplified in several instances in 1920. On the invitation of Franklin K. Lane, then Secretary of the Interior, THE BROOKLYN DAILY EAGLE Grand Canyon National Park Dedication Tour was organized. With the Canyon dedication as the central feature the month's tour, from April 8 to May 8, included practically all the beauties and wonders and historic points of interest in the Southwest and California. In 1919, an EAGLE Excursion party inaugurated a 1,600 miles motor tour through National Parks, and this followed the 1915 EAGLE Excursion to the San Francisco Fair.

THE EAGLE raised a fund for the decoration of Brooklyn graves in France on Memorial Day under the supervision of the Paris Bureau. The extensive plans of the American Legion along this same line caused the bureau to include the photography as well as the laying of flowers upon the graves, the photographs being sent to the relations of the soldiers through the Index department. Cemeteries in Flanders and from Calais to Verdun in the north of France were visited during a period from May 29 to August 30, 1920.

THE EAGLE's fifth annual Current Events Bee, held in the auditorium of the Manual Training High School on March 19, 1920, was one of the most spirited and closely contested of any so far held.

Popular features of EAGLE work are THE EAGLE Current Events Talks, held each Tuesday during the winter months in the Auditorium of the EAGLE Building.

THE EAGLE INFORMATION BUREAU continued during the year with work of rendering valuable aid to the public. It also published a Summer Resort Guide, a Winter Resort Guide and an Educational Directory.

During the past year THE ALMANAC AND LIBRARY DEPARTMENT has issued the following important publications: Code of Ordinances of the City of New York; The Rent Relief Bills; Long Island Auto Guide; The Code of Criminal Procedure; The Penal Law; National Parties and Platforms; The Charter of the City of New York; and The Code of Civil Procedure. The issue of these documents in convenient and inexpensive form is of great help to many people. At the present high price of composition and paper not all of these publications pay their way, but their publications has frequently been characterized as a public service.

BOROUGH OF BROOKLYN STREET AND AVENUE DIRECTORY

The letters and numbers following names indicate position of the thoroughfare on the map in pocket of the Almanac

Note that in case of long thoroughfares, important cross streets with corner numbers are given. A * placed in the right or left column of figures denotes that the thoroughfare does not extend to that side. For railroad connections, etc., consult the map.

A (E 4), Washington av., n. Flushing av., E. to E. av.
A, 31st ward (H 10), Knapp n. av. V, S E. to creek
Aberdeen (J 5), 1861 B'way N. E. to Evergreen Cem.
Adams (D 3), E. R., bet. Wash'n and Pearl, S.E. to Fulton.
133 128 Sands.
281 290 Johnson.
Adelphi (E 4), 108 Flushing av., S. to Atlantic av.
149 146 Myrtle av.
265 272 DeKalb av.
423 430 Fulton.
Adelphi pl. (L 4), from Crescent bet. Ridgewood av. and Fulton, E. to Hemlock.
Agate ct. (G 5), 1483 Atlantic av., N.—one block.
Ainslie (F 2), 15 Marcy av., S.E. and E to Bush'k av.
Aitken pl. (G 6), Empire blvd. n. B'klyn av., S. to Lefferts av.
Alabama av. (K 5), Jamaica av., junc. Fulton, S. E. to Vandalia av.
Albany av. (G 5), 1558 Fulton, S. to Av. K.
149 148 Bergen.
277 274 St. Johns pl.
519 516 E. N. Y. av.
911 910 Church av.
Albemarle rd. (E 7), West av. bet. Caton av. and Church av. E. to Nostrand av.
Albemarle ter. (F 7), from E. 21st bet. Church av. * and Albemarle rd.
Alice ct. (G 5), 1463 Atlantic av.—one block.
Alton pl. (G 8), Flatbush av. bet. Hubbard pl. & Overbaugh pl. N.E. to E. 40th.
Amber (M 5), Dumont av., S. to Borough line.
Amboy (J 5), 1464 East New York av., S. to E. 98th.
Amersfort pl. (F 7), Flatbush av. at E. 26th, S. E. to Germania pl.
Ames la. (J 7), E. 92d, bet. Av. D and Nolan's la., N. E. to Av B at Rockaway P'kway.
Amherst (F 11), Shore Boulevard, E. of West End av., S. to Oriental Boulevard.
Amity (C 4) E.R., bet. Pacific & Congress, E. to Court.
Anchorage pl. (D 3), bet. Plymouth and Water.
Anna ct. (K 6), from Will pl., S to Stanley av.
Anthony (G 2), 544 Morgan av., E to Newtown creek.
Apollo (G 2), 235 Meeker av., N. to Newtown creek.
Apple (E 4), Lemon, bet. Fleeman & Clinton avs., S to Flushing av.
Appoline ct. (J 8), from E. 66th S. of Av. L., N. E. to E. 68th.
Argyle rd. (E 7), Caton av. bet. Rugby and Westminster rds., S. to Av. H.
Arion pl. (G 4), Broadway E. to Bushwick av.
Arlington av. (K 5), 148 Jamaica av., E. to Fulton.
Arlington pl. (F 5), 56 Halsey, S. to Fulton.
Arthur (K 9), from E. 74th, bet. Av. Y and Av. Z, N. and N. W. to Av. V.
Ash (F 1), 1162 Manhattan av., E. to Oakland.
Ashford (K 5), 416 Jamaica av., S. E. to Borden av
Ashland pl. (E 4), 104 DeKalb av., S. to Fl'b'sh av.
Atkins av. (L 5), 3116 Atlantic av., S.E. to Borden av.
Atlantic av. (C 4), E. R., bet. State & Pacific, S. E. to Schroeders av.
581 594 Flatbush av.
1167 1222 Bedford av.
1517 1588 Albany av.
2465 2466 VanSinderen av.
2791 2792 Van Sicklen av.
3037 3026 Essex.
3317 3316 Euclid av.
Atlantic av., 30th wd. (B 9), Parrott pl., bet. 90th & 92d, E. to Delaplaine.
Atlantic av., 31st ward (C 11), Gravesend bay, bet. Mermaid av. & Beach 50th, S. & E to W. 5th.
Atlantic Basin (C 4), bounded by Conover (Com. wf.), Clinton wf., Buttermilk Channel and India wharf.
Auburn pl. (E 4), 97 St. Edwards, S. E. to N. Portland av.
Autumn av. (L 4), 898 Jamaica av., S. to Jamaica bay.
Av. A (H 7), Ralph av. at E. 87th, N. E. to E. 98th.
Av. B, 29th ward, now Beverly rd.
Av. B (H 7), E. 56th opp. Beverly rd., E. & N. E. to E. 98th.
Av. C (E 7), West av., opp. 36th, E. to Coney Isl'd av.
Av. D (F 7), Flatbush av., opp. Ditmas av., E. to Fresh creek
Av. F (E 8), West av., opp. 42d, E. to E. 8th.
Av. G (F 8), West av., opp. 44th, E. & N. E. to Flatbush av.
Av. H (E 8), Ocean P'kway, S. of Foster av., E. to Paerdegat av.
Av. I (E 8), West av., opp. 49th, E. to Ralph av.
Av. J (E 8), West av., opp. 52d, E. to Bergen av., and (J 7), from E. 80th, N.E. to E. 108th.
Av. K. (E 8), Ocean Parkway, E. to Bergen av., and (J 7), from E. 80th, N. E. to E. 108th.
Av. L (E 8), Gravesend av., bet. Avs. K & M, E. to Bergen av., and (J 8), fr. E. 80th, N.E. to E. 108th.
Av. M (E 9), West av., opp. 23d av., E. to Bergen av., and (J 8), from E. 80th, N. E. to E. 108th.
Av. N (E 9), West av., opp. 61st, E. to Bergen av., and (J 8), from E. 80th, N E. to E. 108th.
Av. O (D 9), Bay Parkway opp. 72d, E. to Ralph av.
Av. P (D 9), Bay Parkway opp. 77th, E. & N. E. to Flatbush av.
Av. Q (D 9), Stillwell av., opp. 23d av., E. & N.E. to Flatbush av.
Av. R (D 9), Stillwell av., bet. 80th & 81st, E. & N. E. to Flatbush av.
Av. S (D 10), Stillwell av., opp. 83d, E. & N. E. & E. to Av. T.
Av. T (D 10), Stillwell av., opp. 85th, E. & N. E. to Bergen av.
Av. U (D 10), Stillwell av., bet. 26th av. & Bay 43d, E. & N. E. to Bergen Av.
Av. V (D 10), Stillwell av., opp. 27th av., E. & N. E. to Paerdegat av. S.
Av. W (D 10), Stillwell av., bet. Bay 47th & 28th av., E. & N. E. to Paerdegat av., S.
Av. X (D 10), Stillwell av., bet. Bay 49th & Bay 50th. E. & N. E. to Paerdegat av. S.
Av. Y (D 10). Harway Basin. S. of Bay 50th, E. & N. E. to E. 74th.
Av. Z (D 11), Gravesend Bay at Warehouse av., E. & N.E to Jamaica bay, and (K 9), from E. of E. 69th, N. E. to E. 74th.
B (E 4), Washington av., n. of Lemon, E. to E. av.
B, 31st ward (H 10), Knapp, n. Av. V, S. E. to creek.
Bainbridge (G 5), 491 Sumner av., E to B'way.
209 200 Reid av.
419 422 Howard av.
Baisleys la. (J 7), n. Av. J, N. E. to E. 100th.
Baltic (C 4), E. R., bet. Warren & Harrison, S. E to 5th av.
Bancroft pl. (H 5) 1008 Herkimer, S. to Atlantic av.
Banker (F 2), Nassau av., n. N. 14th, N. to Calyer.
Barbey (K 5), 332 Highland b'lvd, S.E. to Borden av.
Barbey pl. (K 4), fr. Robert bet. Heath pl. & Robert pl., S. to Highland blvd.
Barrett (H 5), East New York av., opp. Lincoln pl., S to E. 98th.
Bartlett (G 4), 648 Flushing av., N. E. to B'way.
Bassett av. (J 9), from National av., S. W. to Mill Basin Channel.
Batchelder (G 9), Gerritsen av., bet. Fillmore av. & Av. S, S. to Sheepshead bay.
Bath av. (B 9), Battery av., S. of 92d, S. E. to Stillwell av.
Battery av. (B 8), 86th, bet. Dahlgren pl. & 7th av., S. W. to Warehouse av.
Bay (C 5), 59 Otsego. S. E. to Gowanus canal.
Bay av. (F 8), Locust av. bet. E. 16th and Ocean av., to Kings Highway.
Bay Court (F 11), E. 16th E. to E 18th.
Bay parkway, (E 8), Ocean Parkway S. of av. I, S. to Gravesend bay.
Bay Ridge av. (A 7), 69th, New York bay, S. E. to Bay P'kway: also see (B 8), bet. 74th and 76th.
Bay Ridge Parkway (C 8), 8th av. bet. 66th & 68th, N. W. to 3d av.
Bay View av. (C 11), Holland av., E. to W. 37th.
Bay 1st (C 9), 86th, n. 12th av., S.W to DykerHeig'ts Park.
Bay 2d (C 9), 86th, n. 13th av., S. W. to Dyker Heights Park.
Bay 3d (C 9), now 13th av.
Bay 5th (C 9), 86th, n. 14th av. S. W to Benson av.
Bay 6th (C 9), now 14th av.
Bay 7th (C 9), 86th, n. 14th av., S. W. to Cropsey av
Bay 8th (C 9), 85th, n. 15th av., S. W. to Gravesend bay.
Bay 9th (C 9), now 15th av.
Bay 10th & 11th (C 9), 86th, S.W. to Cropsey av.
Bay 12th (C 9), now 16th av.
Bay 13th & 14th (C 9), 86th, S. W. to Cropsey av.
Bay 15th (C 9) now 17th av.
Bay 16th (C 9), from New Utrecht av. at 81st., S. W. to Cropsey av.
Bay 17th (C 9), 86th S. W to Gravesend bay.
Bay 18th (C 9), now 18th av.
Bay 19th (C 9), 86th, S. W. to Gravesend bay.
Bay 20th (C 9), 86th, S. W. to Cropsey av.
Bay 21st (C 9) now 19th av.
Bay 22d (C 9), 86th, S. W. to Gravesend bay.
Bay 23d (D 9), 86th, S. W. to Cropsey av.
Bay 24th (D 9), now 20th av.
Bay 25th & 26th (D 9), 86th, S.W. to Cropsey av.
Bay 27th (D 9), now 21st av.
Bay 28th (D 9), Gravesend bay to 86th.
Bay 29th (D 9), Gravesend bay to 86th.
Bay 30th (D 10), now Bay P'kway.
Bay 31st (D 10), 86th S. W. to Cropsey av.
Bay 32d (D 10), 86th, S. W. to Gravesend bay.
Bay 33d (D 10), now 23d av.
Bay 34th & 35th (D 10), 86th, S. W. to Gravesend bay.
Bay 36th (D 10). now 24th av.
Bay 37th (D 10), 86th, S. W. to Gravesend bay.
Bay 38th (D 10), 86th, S. W. to Cropsey av
Bay 39th (D 10), now 25th av.
Bay 40th & 41st (D 10), 86th, S. W. to Gravesend bay.
Bay 42d (D 10). now 26th av.
Bay 43d & 44th (D 10), Stillwell av, S. W. to Gravesend bay.
Bay 45th (D 10). now 27th av.
Bay 46th & 47th (D 10), Stillwell av., S. W. to Gravesend bay.
Bay 48th (D 10). now 28th av.
Bay 49th & 50th (D 10), Stillwell av., S. W. to Gravesend bay.
Bayard (F 2), 318 Union av., E. to Humboldt.

BOROUGH OF BROOKLYN STREET AND AVENUE DIRECTORY—*Continued.*

Beach la. (E 10), Van Sicklen, n. Av. V, W to Gravesend bay.

Beach pl. (C 4), 22 Degraw, S.W. to Sackett—1 block.

Beach 37th (C 11), Atlantic av. (Sea Gate), S. to Atlantic ocean.

Beach 38th, 40th and 42d (C11), Surf av. (Sea Gate), S. W. to Atlantic ocean.

Beach 43d & 44th (C 11), Atlantic av. (31st Ward). S. W. to Atlantic ocean.

Beach 45th to 48th (C 11), Surf av. (Sea Gate), S. W. to Atlantic ocean.

Beach 49th to 51st (C 11), Surf av. (Sea Gate), N. W. to Gravesend bay.

Beadel (G 2), 124 Kingsland av., E. to Newtown cr.

Beard (C 5), 102 Otsego, N. W. to New York bay.

Beaumont (G 11) Shore blvd., bet. Amherst and Coleridge, S. to Oriental blvd.

Beaver (G4), 816 Flushing av. S. E to Bushwick av.

Bedford av. (F 2), 631 Manhattan av., S. & S. E. & S. W. to Emmons av.
278 288 Grand.
387 402 Broadway.
855 882 Myrtle av.
124_ 1262 Fulton.
1498 1504 St. Johns pl.
1749 1750 Empire blvd.
2189 2190 Church av.
2681 2616 Flatbush av.
3415 3416 Av. M.
4188 4184 Av. U.
4848 4842 Emmons av.

Bedford pl. (G 5), 24 Brevoort pl.. S. to Atlantic av.

Bell (F1), Commercial, opp. Clay, N W. to Newtown cr.

Belmont av. (J5), 469 Rockaway av., E. to Boro. line.

Belvidere (G 4), 879 Broadway, E. to Beaver.

Bennett ct. (B 8), 72d, bet. Ridge ct. & 4th av. runs N.

Bennett's la. (C 9), Kings Highway at 84th, S. to Gravesend bay.

Benson av. (B 9), 7th av., opp. 90th, S. E. to Stillwell av.

Bergen (D 4), 185 Court, E. to East New York av.
248 252 Nevins.
467 484 Flatbush av.
1017 1010 Bedford av.
1787 1780 Buffalo av.

Bergen av. (J 8), fr. Ralph av. at Av. J, S. E. and S. to E. 74th at Av. Y.

Bergen 1st to Bergen 20th (J 8), inclusive, from Bergen av.. N.E. to Paerdegat av. S.

Bergen Beach rd. (H 8), E 51st. at Av. M, E. to Bergen Beach.

Bergen pl. (B 7), Wakeman pl., W. of 2d av., S. to 67th.

Berkeley pl. (E 5), 185 5th av., E. to Plaza.

Berriman (L5), 3092 Atlantic av., S. E. to Borden av.

Berry (F 2), 72 N. 14th, S. W. to Division av.

Beverly rd. (E 7), E 2d, opp. 14th av. E. to E. 56th.

Blake av. (H 6), E. 98th, at Ralph av., to Boro. line.

Bleecker (H 4), 943 Bushwick av., N. E. to Boro. line.

Blue (F 1), Commercial, bet. Dupont & Franklin, N.W. to Newtown creek.

Boerum (G 3), 519 B'way, E. to Bogart.

Boerum pl. (D4), 114 Livingston, S. to Bergen.

Bogart (H 3), 993 Flushing av., N. to Ten Eyck.

Boliver (E4), 3 Fleet, E. to St. Edwards.

Bond (D 4), 496 Fulton, S. to Gowanus canal.

Borden av. (L7), fr. Fresh Creek Basin, N. E. to Borough line.

Boulevard ct. (F 10), E. 4th, N. of Av. X, E. to Ocean Parkway.

Bowery (E 11), W. 16th, E. to W. 11th.

Bowne (C 5), 18 Richards, N. W. to Conover.

Box (F 1), 76 Commercial, E. to Oakland.

Bradford (K5), 158 Jamaica av., S. & S. E. to Borden av.

Bragg (G 9), Gerritsen av., S. of Av. T, S. to Sheepshead bay.

Brant (G 1), 89 Paidge av., N. E. to Newtown creek.

Bremen (G4), name changed to Stanwix av.

Brenda ct. (J 8), from E. 66th bet. av. L and av. M, N. E. to E. 68th.

Brevoort pl. (F5), 545 Franklin av., E. to Bedford av.

Bridge (A 4), East river, bet. Gold & Jay, S. to Fulton.

Bridge rd. (D 8), fm. 226 Sands, S. E. to Navy, 1 blk.

Bridgewater (G 2), 329 Meeker av., N. W. to Norman av.

Brigham (G 10), Gerritsen av., at Av. U, S. to Sheepshead bay.

Brighton Beach av. (F11), from Ocean Parkway at Surf av., N. E. to Coney Island av.

Brighton ct. (E 10), E. 2d, N. of Av. Z, E. to Ocean Parkway.

Bristol (J5), E. New York av. bet. Hopkinson av. and Chester, S. to E. 98th.

Broadway (E3), E.R., bet. S. 8th & S. 6th, S. E. to Fulton.
299 302 Marcy av.
* 620 Wallabout
755 752 Flushing av.
949 944 Myrtle av.
1115 1118 DeKalb av.
1369 1364 Gates av.
* 1886 Sumpter.
2119 * Jamaica av.

Brooklyn av. (G 5), 1420 Fulton, S. to Flatbush av.
289 286 Eastern Parkway.
1207 1208 Av. C.

Broome (G 2), 558 Graham av., E. to Humboldt.

Brown (G 9), Gerritsen av., bet. Av. R and Fillmore to Sheepshead bay.

Bryant (C 5), Henry st. sl., S of Halleck, S. E. to Gowanus bay.

Buckingham rd. (F 7), now E. 16th, Church av. opp. Guilford pl., S. to Foster av.

Buffalo av. (H 5), 1872 Fulton, S. to E. N. Y. av.
297 294 E. Parkway.

Bulwer Pl. (K 4), from Vermont av. at Evergreen cemetery, S. E. to Highland blvd.

Burnett (G 9), Nostrand av., bet. Av. P & Av. Q, S. E. to Av. X.

Burr pl. (G 4), 18 Noll, S. —one-half block.

Bush (C 5), 105 Dwight, S. E. to Gowanus canal.

Bushwick av. (G 3), 802 Metropolitan av., S. & S. E. to Jamaica av.
99 96 Grand.
219 216 Meserole.
455 454 Flushing av.
677 662 Myrtle av.
1049 1050 Gates av.
1267 1266 Halsey
1579 1580 E. Parkway.
1787 —— Jamaica av.

Bushwick pl. (G 3), 244 Meserole to Boerum.

Butler (D 4), 261 Court, S. E. & E. to 5th av.

Butler pl. (E 5), Sterling pl., E. of Vanderbilt av. W. to Prospect pk Plaza.

Byrne pl. (K 8), from Denton av., W. of E. 91st, W. to Jamaica Bay.

C (E 4), Wash'n av.. N. of Lemon, E. to East av.

Cactus pl. (J5), 2025 B'way, N. E. to Bushwick av.

Calhoun (G 3), 328 Morgan av., E. to Stewart av.

Calyer (F 2), E.R. bet. Oak & Quay E. to Kingsland av.

Cambridge pl. (F 4), 200 Greene av., S. to Fulton.

Cameron ct. (D 8), from 66th, bet. 17th and Ovington ct., S. to 67th.

Campus pl. (L 4), from Crescent, bet. Ridgewood av. and Fulton, E. to Hemlock.

Canal av. (C 11), W. 37th. opp. Cypress av., E. to Sheepshead bay.

Canarsie av. (G 6), Montgomery E. of Nostrand av., S. E. to Canarsie la.

Canarsie la. (H 7), from Schenectady av. at Holy Cross Cem., S. E. and N. E to E. 92d (that part from Flatbush av. to Schenectady av. being now part of Cortelyou rd.)

Carlton av. (E 4), 86 Flushing av., S. to Flatbush av.
149 148 Myrtle av.
421 408 Fulton
659 636 Flatbush av.

Carroll (C 5), 59 Hamilton av., S E. to E. N. Y. av.
223 232 Court.
615 628 Fifth av.
875 900 Washington av.
1161 1186 Nostrand av.
1649 1676 Utica av.

Catharine (G 3), 925 Grand, N. to Metropolitan av.

Cathedral pl. (D 4), from Jay, bet. Chapel and Tillary, E. to Bridge.

Caton av. (E 7), Gravesend av. at Fort Hamilton p'kway, E to Ocean p'kway and from Ocean p'kway, S. of Henry N.E. to Flatbush av.

Caton pl. (E 7), Ocean p'way, S. of Fort Hamilton p'kway, N. E. to Coney Island av.

Cedar (H 4), 751 Bushwick av., N. E. to Central av.

Cedar (F 9), E. 16th, n. Av. M, N. E. to Ocean av.

Cedar pl. (F 6), Montgomery, bet. Franklin av. & Pine pl., S. to Empire blvd.

Celestial ct. (J 8), from E. 66th, bet. av. M and av. N, N. E. to E. 68th.

Central av. (H 3), 944 Flushing av., S. E to Evergreen cemetery.
189 208 Myrtle av.
445 470 Putnam av.

Centre (C5), 479 Columbia, S. E. to Gowanus canal.

Centre pl. (D10), 26th av., n. Harway av., S. to Bay 43d.

Chapel (D 4), 228 Jay, E. to Bridge.

Charles (D 4), 186 York, S. to Sands.

Charles pl. (H 4), 1215 Myrtle av., N. W.

Chauncey (G 5), 1629 Fulton, E. to Borough line.

Cheever pl. (D 4), 182 Harrison, S. W. to Degraw.

Cherry (G 2), 510 Vandervoort av., E. to Newtown creek.

Chester (J 5), East New York av., E. of Bristol. S. to E. 98th.

Chester av. (D 7), 3415 Ft. Hamilton p'kway, E. S. to Church av.

Chester ct. (F 6), from Flatbush av., S. of Lincoln rd., W. to E. 21st.

Chestnut (L 4). Jamaica av., bet. Richmond & Euclid av., S. to Atlantic av., & from Liberty av., S. to Sutter av.

Chestnut av. (F 9), 1809 Coney Island av., N. E. to Bay av.

Christopher av. (J 5), East New York av., bet. Stone & Sackman, S. to Av. D.

Church av. (E 7), 36th, bet. 13th & 14th avs., E. & N. E. to E. 98th.
101 102 Gravesend av.
601 602 Eastern P'kway.
901 902 Coney Island av.
2201 2202 Flatbush av.
5001 5002 Utica av.

Clara (E 7), 126 West av., S. W. to 36th av.

Clarendon rd. (F 7) 1129 Flatbush av., E. to Ralph av.

Clark (D 4), 135 Columbia hts., S. E. to Fulton.

Clarkson av. (F 6), 789 Flatbush av., E. & N. E. to E. 98th.

Classon av. (F 4), 700 Kent av., S. & S. W. to Washington av. at President.
201 188 Myrtle av.
555 538 Fulton.

Clay (F 1), from 36 Commercial, E. to Paidge av.

Clermont av. (E 4), 128 Flushing av., S. to Atlantic av.

Cleveland (K5), 442 Jamaica av., S. E. to Borden av.

Cleveland pl. (D5), 536 Baltic, S. to Butler—1 block.

Clifford pl. (F 2), 120 Calyer, S. E. to Meserole av.

Clifton pl. (F 4), 65 St. James pl., E. to Marcy av.

Clinton (D 4), 262 Fulton, S. W. to Gowanus creek.
138 148 Livingston.
445 458 First pl.
577 582 Hamilton av.

Clinton av. (E3), Wallabout Channel, S. to Atlantic av.
495 490 Fulton.

Clinton pl. (L4), fr W. side of Crescent, N. of Etna.

BOROUGH OF BROOKLYN STREET AND AVENUE DIRECTORY—*Continued.*

Clinton wharf (C 5), Atlantic dock, from Commercial wharf to S. pier.

Clymer (E 3), Wallabout canal, bet. Wash'n av., Cross, N. E. to Division av.

Coffey (C 5), 60 Otsego, N. W. to New York bay.

Coleman (G 8), Av. P, bet. Kimball & Hendrickson, S. E. to Jamaica bay.

Coleman la. (H 9), Fillmore av., n. E. 38th, S. E. to Av. X.

Coleridge (F 11), Shore boulevard, bet. Beaumont and Dover, S. to Oriental boulevard.

Coles (C 5), 359 Columbia, S E. to Henry.

College pl. (D 4), 42 Love la., N. E. half block.

Collins av. (L7), fr. Louisiana av., at Fresh Creek basin N. E. to Fountain av.

Colonial rd. (B 7), 66th, opp. 1st av., S. to 92d.

Columbia (C4), 18 Atlantic av., S. W. to Gowanus bay.
828 814 Hamilton av.
499 476 Bush.

Columbia Heights (D 3), 18 Fulton, S. to Pierrepont.

Columbia pl. (D 4), 34 Joralemon, S. to Atlantic av.

Columbus pl. (H 5), 926 Herkimer, S. to Atlantic av.

Commerce (C5), 380 Columbia, N. W. to Conover.

Commercial (A 1), 18 Dupont, N. E. to Manhattan av.

Commercial wf. (F 1), Atlantic dock, from India wharf, S. W. to William.

Concord (D 4), 215 Fulton, E. to Navy.

Concourse Drive (E 11), continuation of Surf av. from W. 5th to Sea Breeze av.

Condit pl. (L 4), 27 Autumn av., E. to Nichols av.

Conduit av. (L 5), Atlantic av. n. Fountain av., S. E. to Borough line.

Coney Island av. (E 6), junc. Windsor pl. & Terrace pl., S. E. to Atlantic ocean.
478 474 Church av.
1043 1044 Foster av.
2047 2050 Kings Highway.

Congress (C 4), E. R., bet. Amity & Warren, S. E. to Court.

Conklin av. (J 7), Remsen av. S. of Glenwood rd., N. E. to E. 100th.

Conover (C 5), 60 Hamilton av., S. W. to N. Y. bay.

Conselyea (F 3), 218 Union av., E. to Humboldt.

Conway (J 5), Norman pl., n. Truxton, N. E. to Evergreens cemetery.

Cook (G 3), 671 B'way, E. to Bogart.

Cooper (J 5), 1711 B'way, N. E. to Borough line.

Cornelia (H 4), 1479 B way, N. E to Borough line.

Cornells al. (E 4), 137 Gold, E. to Green la.

Cortelyou rd. (E 7), West, opp. 38th, N. E. to Flatbush av.

Cortland (E 11), Neptune av., bet. Richard & Henry, S. to Sheepshead bay rd.—one block.

Cottage pl. (D 11), now part of Warehouse av.

Court (D 4), 340 Fulton, S. to Gowanus bay.
79 78 Livingston.
803 804 Degraw.
551 582 Hamilton av.

Court sq. (D 4), 342 Fulton, S. to Livingston.

Covert (J 4), 1639 Broadway, N. E. to Borough line.

Cowenhoven la. (B 7), 5th av., opp. Senator, E. to 18th at 53d.

Coyle (G 7), Gerritsen av., junction Av. T, S. to Sheepshead bay.

Cozine av. (K6), Louisiana av., bet. Wortman av. & Fairfield av., E. to Borough line.

Cranberry (D 4), 77 Columbia heig'ts, S. E. to Fulton

Crawford av. (F10), Ocean p'kway, opp. Boulevard ct. E. to E. 12th.

Creamer (C 5), 89 Otsego, S. E. to Gowanus canal.

Crescent (L 4) Jamaica av., n. Euclid av., S. to Jamaica bay.

Crescent pl. (L 4), from Crescent, N. of Ridgewood av., E. to Hemlock.

Crooke av. (F6), Parade pl., bet. Woodruff and Caton avs., N. E. to Ocean av.

Cropsey av. (B 9), Battery av., S. of 103d, S. E. to Stillwell av.

Cropsey la. (D 10), Cropsey av., S. Bay 34th, S. W. to Warehouse av.

Crosby av. (K 4), fr. Vermont av. at Evergreen Cemetery, N. E. to Bulwer pl.

Cross (E 3), East River, S. Division av., E. to Kent av.

Crown (F 6), 909 Washington av., E. to East New York av.

Crystal (L5), Magenta, bet. Fountain av. and Conduit av., S. to Sutter av.

Crystal pl. (L 5), fr. Fountain av., bet. Hegeman and Vienna avs., E. to Holly.

Cumberland (E 4), 66 Flushing av., S. to Atlantic av.

Cypress av. (H3), 1324 Flushing av., S. E. to Bor. line.

Cypress av. (Sea Gate) (C 11), Manhattan av., E. to W. 37th.

D (E 4), Washington av., bet. C & E, E. to West av.

Dahill rd. (E 7), from Ft. Hamilton Parkway at Caton av., S. to Kings Highway.

Dahlia pl. (J 5), 2055 B'way, N. E. to Bushwick av.

Dahlgren pl. (B 8), 86th, bet. Gatling pl. & Battery av., S. W. to U. S Gov't Reservation.

Damask ct. (J 8), from E. 66th, bet. av. M. and av. N, N. E. to E 68th.

Danforth (L 4), from Crescent, S. of Etna, E. to Autumn av.

Dean (D 4), 167 Court, E. to East New York av.
141 136 Hoyt.
451 454 Flatbush av.
845 846 Grand av.
1345 1344 Brooklyn av.
2227 2228 Hopkinson av.

Debevoise (G 3), 701 B'way, E. to Bushwick av.

Debevoise av. (G 3), 125 Maspeth av., N. W. to Beadel.

Debevoise pl. (E 4), 21 Fleet, S. to DeKalb av.

De Bruyns la. (D 9), 86th, bet. 19th & 20th avs., S. to Gravesend bay.

Decatur (G 5), 498 Tompkins av., E. & N. E. to Borough line.

Degraw (C 4), East River, bet. Sedgwick & Sackett, S. E. to 5th av.
115 118 Columbia.
283 302 Court.

DeKalb av. (D 4), 469 Gold, E. to Borough line.
498 484 Franklin av.
1125 1116 Broadway.
1758 1748 Borough line

DeKoven ct. (F 8), Rugby rd., n. Foster av., E. to E. 17th.

Delamere pl. (F 7), 2302 Foster av., S. to Emmons av.

Delaplaine (B 9), 86th, n. 12th av., S. to Dyker Heights Park.

Delevan (C 5), 384 Columbia, N. W. to Van Brunt.

Delmonico pl. (G 4), 652 Flushing av., S. E. to Park av.

Dennett pl. (D 5), 198 Luquer, S. to Nelson.

Denton av. (K 7), from Jamaica Bay at Canarsie Beach Pk., N. E. to Rockaway P'kway.

Denton pl. (D 5), 528 Carroll, S. W. to First.

Denyse la. (D 11), 2401 Cropsey av., S. W. to Gravesend bay.

Derussy (B 9), 86th, bet. 10th & 11th avs., S. to Dyker Beach Park.

De Sales pl. (J 5), 1885 B'way, N. E. to Evergreens cemetery.

Desmond ct. (F 10), E. 7th S. of Av. X, E. to E. 12th.

Devoe (F 3), 184 Union av., E. to Morgan av.

Dewey pl. (H 5), 1060 Herkimer, S. to Atlantic av.

Diamond (G 2), 168 Driggs av., N. to Greenpoint av.

Dickinson (G 3), 308 Morgan av., N. E. to Newtown creek.

Dikeman (C 5), 38 Otsego, N. W. to N. Y. bay.

Dinsmore pl. (L5), 283 Norwood av., E. to Logan.

Ditmars (G 4), 995 Broadway, N. E. to Bushwick av.

Ditmas av., 29th ward, (E 7), 501 West, E. to Flatbush av.

Ditmas av., 32d ward (H7), fr. Farragut rd. at Schenectady av., N. E. to E. 98th.

Division av. (E 3), E. R., S. of S. 11th, E. to B'way.
335 296 Broadway.

Division pl. (G2), 108 Kingsland av., E. to Newtown cr.

Dixon pl. (E 4), 246 York, S. to Sands.

Dobbin (F 2), 29 Nassau av., N. to Meserole av.

Dock (D 3), E. R., bet. Fulton & Main, S. to Front.

Dodworth (H 4), 1095 B'way, N. E. to Bushwick av.

Dooley (G 11), 2251 Emmons av., N. W.

Dorchester rd. (E 7), Coney Island av., N. of 18th av., N. E. to Flatbush av.

Doscher (L 5), 980 Liberty av., S. to Belmont av.

Doughty (D 3), 13 Furman, E. to Hicks.

Douglass (D 5), 283 Court, S. E. to 5th av., & from 1378 East New York av., S. to E. 98th.
283 278 Third av.
1953 1954 Sutter av.

Dover (G 11), Shore Boulevard, bet. Coleridge & Exeter, S to Oriental Boulevard.

Downing (F 4), 2 Quincy, S. to Fulton.

Dresden (L4), name changed to Highland pl.

Drew av. (M 5), Borough line at McKinley av., S. to Jamaica Bay.

Driggs av. (G 2), 201 Meeker av., W., S. W. & S. to Division av.
307 308 Manhattan av.
693 694 Grand.

Duck (G 1), 109 Paidge av., N. E. to Newtown creek.

Duffield (D 4), Nassau, S. to Fulton.

Dumont av. (H 6), E. 98th, n. Tapscott, E. to Borough line.

Dunham pl. (E 3), 29 B'way, N. E. to S. 6th—one block.

Dunne ct. (F10), E. 7th, N. of Av. Y, E. to E. 12th.

Dupont (F 1), E. R. at West, E. to Paidge av.

Durland pl. (J 7), Glenwood rd. bet. E. 92d & E. 93d, S. to Conklin av.

Duryea ct. (D 8), 66th, E. of 16th av., S. to 67th.

Duryea pl. (F 7), Flatbush av. bet. Vernon av. & Beverly rd., E. to E. 22d.

Dwight (C 5), 382 Columbia, S. W. to Beard.

E (E 3), Washington av., bet. D & F, E. to West av.

Eagle (F1), East River, bet. Dupont & Freeman, E. to Paidge av.

Earl (H 6), East New York av., at E. 49th, E. to Remsen av.

East av. (F 4), Flushing av. opp. Ryerson, N. to R.

E. 1st (E 10), from Av. T, E. of Stryker, S. to Canal av.

E. 2d (E 7), from Vanderbilt E. of Gravesend av., S. to Canal av. and (F 11), fr. Neptune av., E. of Ocean P'kway, S. W. to Brighton Beach av.

E. 3d (E 7), from Vanderbilt, opp. 20th, S. to av. Y and (F 11), from Canal av., E. of Ocean P'kway, S. W. to Neptune av., thence S. E. to Brighton Beach av.

E. 4th (E 6), from Vanderbilt, opp. 19th, S. to av. X and (F 11), from Canal av., S. E. to Neptune av., thence S. E. to Brighton Beach av.

E. 5th (E 6), 426 Vanderbilt, S. to Boulevard ct. and (F 11), fr. Neptune av., S. E. to Brighton Beach av.

E. 6th (F 10), 602 Av. Y, S. to Brighton Beach av.

BOROUGH OF BROOKLYN STREET AND AVENUE DIRECTORY—*Continued.*

E. 7th (E 6), fr. Reeve pl., E. of Ocean P'kway, S. to Canal av. and (F 11), fr. Neptune av., S. E. to Brighton Beach av.
E. 8th (E 7), 11 Ocean p'kway, S. to Av. V.
E. 9th (E 7), Beverly rd., W. of Coney Island av., S. to Av. V.
E. 10th (E 7), Caton Av. E of Coney Island av., S. to Av. Q.
E. 11th (F 10), 1102 Av. W, S. to Sea Breeze av.
E. 12th (F 8), 1202 Av. H, S. to Surf av.
E. 13th (F 8), 1302 Av. H, S. to Surf av.
E. 14th (F 8), 1402 Av. H, S. to Emmons av.
E. 15th (F 8), 1502 Av. H, S. to Emmons av.
E. 16th to E. 18th inclusive (F 7) Caton av., S. to Emmons av.
E. 19th (F 7), Tennis ct., W. of Ocean av., S. to Emmons av.
E. 21st (F6), Caton av., E. of Ocean av., S. to Foster av.
E. 22d (F7), Albemarle rd., E of Flatbush av., S. to Foster av.
E. 23d (F 7), 2226 Tilden av., S. to Foster av.
E. 24th (F 7), Flatbush av. at Newkirk av., S. to Foster av.
E. 25th (F 7), Beverly rd. bet. Lott & Prospect (29th ward), S. to Foster av.
E. 26th (F 7), Beverly rd. opp. Prospect (29th ward), S. to Emmons av.
E. 27th (F 8), Av. G. at Amersfort pl., S. to Emmons av.
E. 28th & E. 29th (F 7), Albemarle rd., bet. Rogers & Nostrand avs., S. to Emmons av.
E. 30th (G 9), Nostrand av., n. Flatlands av., S.E. to Av. X.
E. 31st (G 7), Church av. E. of Nostrand av., S. & S. E. to Av. S.
E. 32d (G 7), Church av. W. of New York av., S. & S. E. to Av. W.
E. 33d (G 9), Av. N, near Kings Highway, S. E. to Jamaica bay.
E. 34th (G6), 418 Winthrop, S. & S. E to Jamaica bay.
E. 35th (G 6), 430 Clarkson av., S. & S.E. to Jamaica bay.
E. 36th (G 8), Flatbush av., opp. B'klyn av., S. to Jamaica bay.
E. 37th (G 6), Winthrop, E. of B'klyn av., S. & S. E. to Jamaica bay.
E. 38th (G6), Clarkson av., E. of B'klyn av., S. & S. E. to Jamaica bay.
E. 39th (G6), Clarkson av., E. of E. 38th, S. & S. E. to Lott pl.
E. 40th (G6), Clarkson av., W. of Albany av., S. & S. E. to Flatlands av.
E. 41st (F 8), Av. K, opp. Albany av., S. E. to Flatlands av.
E. 42d (G6), Clarkson av., E. of Albany av., S. to Av. K.
E. 43d (G 6) Clarkson av., W. of Troy av., S. to Flatbush av.
E. 45th & E. 46th (G 6), East New York av., bet. Troy & Schenectady avs., S. to Flatbush av.
E. 48th & E. 49th (H 6), East New York av., bet. Schenectady & Utica avs., S. to Flatbush av.
E. 51st (H 6), Remsen av., E. of Utica av., S. to Flatbush av.
E. 52d to E. 59th (H 6), Remsen av., S. & S. E. to av. U.
E. 61st (J 9), Ralph av., opp. Av. O, S.E. to av. U.
E. 62d (J 8), now Mill av.
E. 63d (J 8), Av. N, E. of Ralph av., S. E. to av. X.
E. 64th (J 8), Ralph av., n. Av. N, S. E. to av. U.
E. 65th (H 8), Ralph av., at Av. M, S. E. to av. U.
E. 66th (H 8), Ralph av., bet. Avs. L & M, S.E. to av. U.
E. 67th (J 8), from av. T, S. E. to av. U.
E. 68th (J 8), from Ralph av., bet. av. K and av. L, S. E. to av. Z.
E. 69th (J 8), from Ralph av., S. E. to Av. Z.
E. 70th (J8), from Av. K at Bergen av., S.E. to Av. Z.
E. 71st (J8), from Av. L at Bergen av., S.E. to Av. Z.
E. 72d (J8), from Av. M at Bergen av., S.E. to Av. Z.
E. 73d (J 8), from Av. N nr. Bergen av., S. E. to Av. Z.
E. 74th (J 8), from Bergen av. at Av. T, S. E. to av. Z.
E. 75th (H8), Ralph av., at Glenwood rd. S.E. to Flatlands av.
E. 76th (H7), Ralph av., n. Glenwood rd., S. E. to Paerdegat 1st.
E. 77th (H 7), Ralph av., at Farragut rd. S.E. to Paerdegat 1st.
E. 78th (H 7), from Ralph av., N. of Farragut rd. S. E. to Paerdegat 1st.
E. 79th (H 7), Ralph av., at Foster av., S. E. to Paerdegat 1st.
E. 80th (H 7), Ralph av., at Foster av., S. E. to Seaview av.
E. 81st (H 7), Ralph av., S. E. to Av. L.
E. 82d (H 7), from Ralph av., S. E. to Av. M.
E. 83d (H 7), from Ralph av., S. E. to Av. N.
E. 84th (H 7), from Ralph av., S. E. to Seaview av.
E. 85th (H 7), from Ralph av., S. E. to Seaview av.
E. 86th (H 7), from Ralph av., S. E. to Seaview av.
E. 87th (H 7), from Ralph av., S. E. to Seaview av.
E. 88th (H 7), Ralph av., S. E. to Seaview av.
E. 89th (H 6), Ralph av., S. E. to Seaview av.
E. 91st (H 6), from East New York av., S. E. to Seaview av. and fr. Denton av., S. E. to Jamaica Bay.
E. 92d (H 6), from East New York av., S. E. to Av. M. and from Av. N S. E. to Seaview av. and from Denton av., S. E. to Jamaica Bay.
E. 93d & E. 94th (H 6), E. N. Y. av., S. E. to Jamaica bay.
E. 95th (H6), East New York av., S E. to Rockaway av.
E. 96th (H 6), East New York av., S.E. to Denton av.
E. 98th (H 6), East New York av., S. E. to Jamaica bay.
E. 99th (J 7), Av. D, S. E. to Skidmore av.
E. 100th to E. 105th (J 6), inclusive, from Av. D, S. E. to Skidmore av.
E. 106th (J 6), from Av. D, S. E. to Av. J.
E. 107th (K 6), Av. D, S. E to Av. J.
E. 108th (K6), Fresh creek, S. E. to Skidmore av.
East New York av. (G 6), New York av. op. Lincoln rd., N. E. to Fulton.

943 944 Utica av.
1879 — St. Johns pl.
— 1508 Chester

Eastern Parkway (E 5), Plaza, E. to Highland Park.

185 188 Washington av.
399 402 Bedford av.
701 704 Brooklyn av.
1291 1292 Buffalo av.

Eckford (G 2), 101 Newton, N. W. to Greenpoint av.
Edward pl. (D 11), W. 30th bet. Surf av. & Atlantic ocean—runs W.
Egan av. (L 7), from Louisiana av., at Fresh Creek Basin, N. E. to Borough line.
Eldert (J 4), 1613 B'way, N. E. to Borough line.
Elderts lane (formerly Enfield st.) (L 4), Jamaica av., bet. Grant av. and Borough line, S to Jamaica bay.
Elizabeth pl. (D3), 26 Fulton, S. W. to Doughty—one block.
Ellery (F 4), 55 Nostrand av., E. & N.E. to Beaver.
Elliott pl. (See S. Elliott & N. Elliott pls.)
Elm av. (F 9), 1339 Coney Island av., N.E to Bay av.
Elm pl. (D 4), 472 Fulton S. W. to Livingston.
Elmore pl. (F 7), 2202 Foster av., S. to Emmons av.
Elmwood av. (E 8), Gravesend av., bet. Foster av. and Av. I, E. to Ocean p'kway.
Elton (K 5), Jamaica av., bet. Cleveland & Linwood, S. E. to Borden av.
Emerald (M 5), Dumont av., at Borough line, S. to Borough line.
Emerson pl. (F 4), 308 Flushing av., S. to Lafayette av.
Emmers la. (F 10), Shore rd. at Av. Y, N. E. to Ocean av.
Emmett (D 4), 48 Atlantic av., S. to Amity.
Emmons av. (F 11), E. 14th, opp. Canal av., E. to Knapp.
Empire blvd. (F6), 463 Flatbush av., E. to East New York av.
Enfield (see Elderts lane).
Engert av. (G 2), 518 Manhattan av., E. to Meeker av.
Erasmus (F 7), Bedford av., bet. Church av. & Grant, E. to Nostrand av.
Erie Basin (C 5), ft. of Otsego, Dwight, Richards & Van Brunt.
Essex (L 5), Jamaica av., bet. Linwood & Shepherd av., S. E. to Borden av.
Estate rd. (E 9), E. 4th, bet. Avs. P and Q, E. to Ocean parkway.
Etna (L 4), 21 Dresden, E. to Borough line.
Euclid av. (L4) Jamaica av., bet. Chestnut & Crescent, S. to Wortman av.
Evans (E 3), 59 Hudson av., E. to Navy Yard.
Evergreen av. (G 3), 216 Cook, S. E. to Evergreens cemetery.

423 478 Gates av.
605 660 Halsey st.
789 844 Evergreens cem.

Evergreen pl. (K5), 82 New Jersey av. W.
Exeter (G 11), Shore Boulevard, W. of Ocean av., to Oriental Boulevard.
F (E 3), Washington av., S. of Wallabout pl., E. to West av.
Fair (E 4), 145 Prince, E. to Fleet pl.
Fairfield av. (K6) Fresh ck., bet. Cozine & Vandalia avs., E. to Borough line.
Fairview pl. (G 6), 312 Martense av. to Church av.
Falmouth (G 11), Shore B'lev'd, E. of Ocean av., S. to Oriental Boulev'd.
Fanchon pl. (K 5), Highland Boulevard, bet. Gillen pl. & Pellington pl. S. to Jamaica av.
Farragut rd. (F 7), fr. 1109 Ocean av., E. to Schenectady av. & fr. Glenwood rd. N. E. to Fresh Creek.
Fayette (G 4), 791 B'way, N E. to Beaver.
Fenimore (F 6), Ocean av., bet. Rutland rd. & Hawthorne, E. to Troy av.
Ferris (C 5), 201 William, S. W. to Beard.
Ferry pl. (C 5), 1 Hamilton av., N. E. to Sackett.
Fillmore av. (G 9), Gerritsen av., bet. Avs. R & S, N. E. to Av. T.
Fillmore pl. (F 3), 667 Driggs, S. E. to Roebling.
Fiske pl. (E 5), 804 Carroll, S. W. to Garfield pl.
Flatbush av. (D 4), from Nassau bet. Jay & Bridge S. to Jamaica bay.

149 128 Atlantic av.
381 384 Sterling pl.
739 740 Clarkson.
881 882 Church av.
1267 1268 Bedford av.
1555 1560 Nostrand av.
2105 2106 Av. N.

Flatlands 1st to Flatlands 11th (K 7), inclusive, from E. 105th, N.E. to E. 108th.
Flatlands av. (F9), Av. P, at Delamere pl., N. E. to Fresh creek.
Fleeman av. (E 4), Flushing av., W. of Washington av., N.
Fleet (B 4), 374 Hudson av., S. W. to DeKalb av.
Fleet pl. (E 4), 208 Tillary, S. to Fleet.
Fleets al. (D3), 49 York, N.

BOROUGH OF BROOKLYN STREET AND AVENUE DIRECTORY—*Continued.*

Flint (D 3), 64 Front, S. E. to Prospect.
Floods al. (D 4), 22 Johnson, S. to Myrtle av.
Florence (G 3), 846 Grand, S. to Maujer.
Floyd (C 3), 97 Nostrand av., E. to B'way.
Flushing av. (E4), Navy, opp. Nassau, E. to Boro. line.
887 828 Classon av.
* 520 Nostrand.
765 764 B'way.
1875 1414 Borough line.
Folsom pl. (L 5), 265 Linwood, E. to Essex.
Forbell av. (M 5), Glen at Borough line, S. to Jamaica bay.
Force Tube av. (L4), Highland Boulevard, E. of Linwood, S. E. to Richmond.
Ford (G 9), Gerritsen av. at Av. S, S. to Sheepshead bay.
Forest pl. (B 8), 414 88th, S. W. to 90th.
Forrest (G 4), 501 Bushwick av., E. & N. E. to Flushing av.
Ft. Greene pl. (E 4), 125 De Kalb av., S. to Atlantic av.
Ft. Hamilton p'kway (E 7), Ocean parkway at Prospect av., S. W. to Fort Hamilton.
2731 —— E. 5th.
3923 —— 40th.
5728 —— 58th.
6923 6924 70th.
* 9540 97th.
Ft. Hill pl. (B 9), Dahlgren pl., E. to Battery av.
Foster av. (E 8), Gravesend av., opp. 47th, E. to E. 53d and fr. Glenwood rd. at Utica av., N. E. to Fresh creek.
587 588 Ocean parkway
1983 1984 Ocean av.
2923 2924 Nostrand av.
4023 4024 Albany av.
Fountain av. (L 5), 3218 Atlantic av., S. E. to Borden av.
Fountain 1st to Fountain 8th (M6), inclusive, from Montauk av., N. E. to Fountain av.
Fountain pl. (L 5), from Fountain av. bet. Dumont and Hegeman avs. E. to Holly.
Franklin (F2), N.14th, opp. Kent av., N. to Commercial.
Franklin av. (F4), 106 Wallabout, S. & S. W. to Washington av.
511 512 Fulton.
711 712 Park pl.
943 926 Montgomery.
Franklin av., 29th ward (E 7), now 18th av.
Freedom sq. (H 4), at junction of Myrtle av., Bushwick av. and Willoughby av.
Freeman (F 1), E. R., bet. Eagle & Greene, E. to Paidge av.
Front (D 3), 27 Fulton, E. to Hudson av.
Frost (F 2), 284 Union av., E. to Newtown creek.
Fuller pl. (E 6), 160 Windsor pl. S W.
Fulton (D 3), E. R. at Fulton Ferry, S. E. & E. to Borough line.
135 * Sands.
351 * Myrtle av.
* 544 Flatbush av.
725 642 Lafayette av.
965 908 Washington av.
1149 1182 Franklin av.
1293 1278 Nostrand av.
* 1558 Albany av.
* 1752 Utica av.
2057 2152 Rockaway av.
2641 2642 Pennsylvania av
2787 2788 Van Sicklen av.
3095 * Arlington av.
4393 4394 Elderts lane.
Fulton pl. (D 4), closed.
Furman (D 3), 6 Fulton, S. W. to Atlantic av.
Furman av. (J 5), 1881 B'way, N. E. to Evergreens cemetery.
G (E 3), Wallabout pl. E. of West av. S. W.
Gallatin pl. (D 4), 406 Fulton, S. to Livingston.
Garden (G 3), 840 Flushing av., S.E. to Bushwick av.
Garden, 29th ward (H 6), E. 48th bet. Clarkson & Lenox rd., E. to Utica av.
Garden pl. (D 4), 90 Joralemon, S. W. to State.
Gardner av. (H 3), 1225 Flushing av., N. to Meeker av.
Garfield pl. (D5), 261 4th av., S. E. to Prospect pk. W.
Garnet (C5), 311 Hamilton av., S.E. to Go'nus canal.
Garrison (D 3), 44 Front, S. E. to York.
Gates av. (E 5), 873 Fulton, E. to Borough line.
321 310 Bedford av.
893 850 Reid av.
1071 1086 Broadway.
Gatling pl. (B 8), 86th, bet. Ft. Hamilton av. & Dahlgren pl., S. W. to 92d.
Gelston av. (B 8), 86th, bet. 5th av. & Ft. Hamilton av., S. W. to 94th.
Gem (F 2), 37 N. 15th, N. to Meserole av.
George (H 4), 87 Evergreen av., N. E. to Knickerbocker av.
Georgia av. (K5), 24 Jamaica av., S. to Vandalia av.
259 260 Belmont av.
547 548 Riverdale av.
Gerald ct. (F 10), E. 7th S. of Av. Y, E. to Coney Island av.
Germania pl. (G 8), Amersfort pl. at E. 29th, N. E. to Flatbush av.
Gerritsen av. (G 9), Nostrand av., at Av. Q, S. E. to Jamaica bay.
Gerry (F 4), 459 Marcy av., N. E. to Broadway.
Gillen pl. (K 5), Jamaica av., junc. Broadway, N. to Bushwick av.
Gilmore ct. (F 10), from E. 11th to E.12th, N. of Voorhies av.
Girard (G11), Shore blvd., bet. Falmouth & Hastings, S. to Oriental blvd.
Glen (L 5), Atlantic av., junc. Conduit av., E. to Borough line.
Glenada pl. (G 5), 142 Decatur, S. to Fulton.
Glenmore av. (J 5), 367 Rockaway av., E. to Borough line.
815 816 Alabama av.
1023 1024 Euclid av.
Glenwood rd. (G8), fr. 1491 Flatbush av., E. to E. 56th and from Paerdegat av., N. E. to Fresh creek.
Gold (D3), East River, bet. Bridge & Hudson av., S. to Fulton.
351 344 Myrtle av.
Goodwin pl. (H 4), 1086 Greene av., S. E. to Grove.
Gothic al. (D 4), 185 Adams, E. to Pearl.
Grace ct. (D 4), 248 Hicks, runs N. W. & N.
Grafton (H 5), East New York av., at Pitkin av., S. to E. 98th.
Graham av. (G4), 747 Broadway, N. to Driggs av.
335 342 Metropolitan av.
467 476 Meeker av.
Grand (E 3), East River, bet. S. 1st and N. 1st, S. E. & E. to Newtown cr'k.
499 500 Union av.
815 818 Bushwick av.
Grand st. Extension (F 3), Havemeyer, at S 4th, E. to Grand.
Grand av. (F4), 276 Flushing av., S. & S W. to Park pl.
367 388 Gates av.
657 670 Washington av.
Granite (J 5), 1813 B'way, N. E. to Borough line.
Grant av. (L 4), Jamaica av., bet. Nichols av. and Elderts lane, S. to Jamaica bay.
Grant sq. (F 5), Bergen to Pacific at Bedford av.
Grattan (H 3), 54 Bogart, E. to Flushing av.
Gravesend av. (E9), 10th av., opp. 20th, S. to Canal av.
Gravesend Neck rd. (E 10), 351 Van Sicklen av. E. to Ocean av.
Green la. (E 3), 256 Front, S. to Sands.
Green (F 2), East River, bet. Freeman & Huron, E. to Kingsland av.
Greene av. (E 4), 123 S. Oxford, E. to Borough line.
353 348 Franklin av.
725 726 Sumner av.
1087 1108 Bushwick av.
Greenpoint av. (F 2), East River, bet. Kent & Milton, E. to Newtown creek.
137 158 Manhattan av.
403 414 Kingsland av.
Greenwood av. (E 7), 205 Gravesend av., N. E. to Coney Island av.
Grove (H 4), 1315 B'way, N. E. to Borough line.
Grove av. (B 9), Derussey, at Atlantic av. (30th wd.), N. E. to 11th av.
Grove pl. (E 4), 13 Hanover pl., S. E.
Gubner (B9), 86th n. 10th av., S. W. to 7th av.
Guernsey (F 2), 49 Nassau av., N. to Oak.
Guilford pl. (F 7), Caton av., W. of Parade pl., S. to Church av.
Gunther pl. (J 5), 1258 Herkimer, S. to Atlantic av
H (E 3), Wallabout pl. to Washington av.
Hale av. (L 4), Jamaica av. bet. Force Tube av. & Norwood, S. to Atlantic av.
Hall (E 4), 232 Flushing av., S. to DeKalb av.
Halleck (C 5), 99 Otsego, E. to Gowanus canal.
Halsey (F 5), 1228 Bedf av., E. to Borough li
513 554 Stuyvesant a
969 968 Broadway.
Hamburg av. (H 3), no changed to Wilson a
275 260 Greene av.
487 472 Jefferson av.
Hamilton av. (C 4), E. R er, at Sackett, S. to 3d
353 362 Court.
543 590 Third av.
Hampton av. (F 11), End av., bet. Manhat & Oriental Bouleva E. to Manhattan Blvd
Hampton pl. (G 5), 1 Park pl., S. to St. Johns
Hancock (F 5), 491 Frank av., E. to Borough lin
643 654 Reid áv.
1081 1084 Bushwick av.
Hanover pl. (E 4), 516 F ton, S. W. to Livingst
Hanson pl. (E 4), 123 Fl bush av., E. to Fulton
Harbor View ter. (A8), fr 80th, bet. Shore rd. a Narrows av., S. to 82d
Haring (G 9), Gerrits av. at Av. R, S. to E mons av.
Harmon (H 4), 891 Bushwick av., N. E. to Borough line.
Harper ct. (D 4), 255 Ja E. to Lawrence.
Harrison (C 4) E. R., b Baltic & Irving, E. Court.
Harrison al. (E 3), Eva Hudson av., to Navy Y
Harrison av. (F 3), 1 Division av., S. E. Flushing av
Harrison pl. (H3), 72 Boga E. to Flushing av.
Hart (F 4), 185 Nostra av. E. to Borough line
469 470 Broadway.
809 810 Knick'bocker a
Harway av. (D 10), Cropsey av. at Bay 37th, E. to Av. Z.
Hastings (G11), Shore bl bet. Girard & Irwin, S. Oriental blvd.
Hausman (G 2), 211 Meek av., N. to Norman av.
Havemeyer (E 3), 270 9th, S. W. to Division a
Havens pl. (J 5), 1494 Herk mer, S. W. to Atlantic a
Hawthorne (F 6), 659 Fla bush av., E. to Troy a
Heath pl. (K4), fr. Robe S. to Highland blvd.
Hegeman av. (J 6), E. 98 at Ames, E. to Boro. lin
Heisser sq. (H 4), juncti of Knickerbocker a Myrtle av. and Bleeck
Hemlock (L 4), Jama av. bet. Crescent & Ra road av., S. to Atlant av., & from Liberty a S. to Jamaica bay.
Hendrickson (G 8), Fla lands av. at Av. M, E. to Mill creek.
Hendrix (K5), 236 Highla b'lvd. S. E. to Borden a
Henry (D 4), 106 Fulton, W. to Gowanus bay.
193 190 Montague.
317 306 Atlantic av.
531 518 Union.
683 676 Hamilton av.
Henry, 29th ward (E 7 E. 8th, S. of Caton pl. Ocean p'kway.

BOROUGH OF BROOKLYN STREET AND AVENUE DIRECTORY—*Continued.*

Henry, 31st ward (E 11), Canal av., bet. Richard & W. 5th, S. to Neptune av.
Henry pl. (G 1), 171 Paidge av., N.E. to Newtown crk.
Herbert (G 2), 151 Richardson, N.E. to Kingsland av.
Herkimer (F 5), 1263 Bedford av., E. to Williams pl.
195 196 N. Y. av.
447 448 Albany av.
1119 1120 Saratoga av.
1433 1434 Sackman.
Herkimer pl. (F 5), Perry pl. n. Atlantic av., S. E. to Nostrand av.
Herzl (J 5), 1432 East New York ave., S. to E. 98th.
Hewes (F 4), Wallabout pl. n. Classon av., N. E. to Union av.
Heyward (F 4), 61 Wallabout, N. E. to B'way.
Hicks (D 3), 64 Fulton, S. W. to Gowanus bay.
337 332 Atlantic av.
— 546 Union.
695 674 Hamilton av.
919 908 Halleck.
High (D 4), 161 Fulton, E. to Navy.
Highland av. (Sea Gate) (C 11), Gravesend bay, S. to Mermaid av.
Highland Boulevard (K 5) Bushwick av., at Dahlia pl., N. E. to Highland park.
Highland pl. (L 4) from Jamaica av. at Fo ce Tube av., S. to Atlantic av.
Highland View av. (D 11), Warehouse av.. n. Surf av.. W. to W. 23d.
Hill (L 5), Conduit av., bet. Magenta & Liberty av., E. to Autumn av.
Himrod (H 4), 867 Bushwick av., N.E to Borough line.
Hinckley pl. (E 7), E. 8th. bet. Turner pl. & Beverly rd., E. to E. 11th.
Hinsdale (J 5), 2510 Atlantic av.. S. to Fresh creek.
508 504 Riverdale av.
Hobson av. (H 9), Flatbush av., n. Fillmore av., W. to E. 36th.
Holland (G 1), 149 Paidge av., N.E. to Newtown crk.
Holly (L 5), Sutter av., bet. Chestnut & Euclid avs., S. to Stanley av.
Holmes la. (J 7), E. 92d, n. Av. K, E. to E. 100th.
Homecrest av. (F 9), Av. U, bet. E. 12th & E. 13th, S. to Emmons av.
Hooper (F 3), 667 Kent av., N. E. to Grand.
Hope (F 3), 155 Roebling, S. E. to Union av.
Hopkins (F 4), 37 Nostrand av., E. to B'way.
Hopkinson av. (J 4), 1596 B'way, S. to E. 98th.
175 176 Fulton.
383 384 E. N. Y. av.
Howard av. (H 4), 1392 B'way. S. to E. 98th.
261 264 Fulton.
Howard ct. (D 3), Main, bet. Water & Front. S. W.
Howard pl. (E 6), 130 Windsor pl., S. W.
Hoyt (D 4), 448 Fulton, S. W. to 5th.
145 146 Bergen.
305 306 Union.
Hubbard (D 10), Mill rd., n. Bay 41st, S.W. to Gravesend bay.
Hubbard, (F 10), Av. X, n. Ocean pkway, S. to Neptune av.
Hubbard pl. (G 8), Flatbush av., bet. Av. K & Alton pl., N. E. to E. 40th.
Hudson av. (E 4), East River, bet. Gold & Navy Yard, S. to Fulton.
351 354 Myrtle av.
Hudson pl. (E 4), 210 Sands.
Hull (J 5), 1945 Fulton, E. to Broadway.
Humboldt (G 2), 808 Flushing av., N. to Meserole av.
365 370 Metropolitan av.
557 576 Engert av.
Hunts al. (D 4), 227 Henry, S. E.
Hunterfly pl. (H 5), 752 Herkimer, S. to Atlantic av.
Hunterfly rd. (H 6), Sutter av., at Tapscott, S. E. to Hegeman.
Huntington (C 5), 419 Columbia, S. E. to Smith.
Huron (F 2), East River, bet. Greene & India, E. to Kingsland av.
I (E 3), Wallabout Market.
Imlay (C 5), 80 Hamilton av., S. W. to William.
India (F 2), East River, bet. Huron & Java, E. to Kingsland av.
India wf. (C 5), Commercial wf. at Summit, N. to N. Pier, Atlantic Dock.
Ingraham (G 3), 92 Bogart, E. to Flushing av.
Institute Park. East Side Lands (E 5), bounded by Eastern pkway, Washington & Flatbush avs.
Irving (C 4), East River, bet. Harrison & Sedgwick, S. E. to Columbia.
Irving av. (H 3), Flushing av., at Thames, S. E. to Borough line.
155 144 DeKalb av.
299 290 Myrtle av.
411 420 Putnam av.
Irving pl. (F 5), 180 Gates av., S. to Fulton.
Irvington pl. (F 8), E. 16th n. of Foster av. & E. to E. 17th.
Irwin (G 11), Shore Boulevard, bet Hastings & Jaffrey, S. to Oriental Boulevard.
Island av. (J 8), Av. N, at Ralph av., E. to Paerdegat av. S.
J (F 4), Wallabout Market.
Jackson (F 3), 252 Union av., E. to Newtown creek.
Jackson ct. (E 3), 248 Front, runs S.
Jackson pl. (D 6), 284 16th, S.W. to Prospect av.
Jaffrey (G 11), Shore Boulevard, bet. Irwin & Kensington, S. to Oriental Boulevard.
Jamaica av. (K 5), Fulton junc., East New York av., E. to Borough line.
207 184 Miller av.
— 388 Ridgewood av.
— 644 Norwood av.
— 834 Crescent.
Jardine pl. (J 5), 1458 Herkimer, S.W. to Atlantic av.
Jardine pl. (L 4), now Washington pl.
Java (F 2), East River, bet. India & Kent, E. to Greenpoint av.
Jay (D 3), East River, bet. Pearl & Bridge, S. to Fulton.
405 420 Fulton.
Jefferson (G 4), 917 B'way, N. E. to Cypress av.
Jefferson av. (F 5), 19 Ormond pl., E. to Boro. line.
181 185 Nostrand av.
417 448 Throop av.
711 696 Reid av.
1021 966 Broadway.
Jerome (K 5), 352 Jamaica av., S. E. to Borden av.
Jerome av. (G 10), Ocean av., S. of Av. Z, E. to Av. Z at E. 24th.
Jewel (G 2), 648 Humboldt, N.W. to Greenpoint av.
John (D 3), 1 Adams, E. to Little.
Johnson (D 4), 311 Fulton, E. to Leo pl.
Johnson, 29th ward (E 7), now part of Caton av.
Johnson av. (F 3), 498 B'way, E. to Flushing av.
421 404 Morgan av.
Johnson av., 29th ward (E 8), now part of Parkville av.
Johnson la. (E 10), Village rd., n. Av. U, N.E. to E. 15th.
Johnson pl. (F 7), Church av., n. Bedford av., S. to Snyder av.
Joralemon (C 4), bet. Montague & State, East River to Fulton.
Judge (G 3), 245 Powers, N. W. to Devoe.
Junius (J 5), East New York av., opp. Pacific, S. to Fresh creek.
K (F 4), Wallabout pl., W.
Kane pl. (H 5), 894 Herkimer, S. to Atlantic av.
Kathleen pl. (F 10), E. 7th bet. Gerald ct. & Av. Z, E. to Coney Island av.
Keap (F 3), Wallabout canal, bet. Rodney & Hooper, N.E. to Union av.
119 126 Bedford av.
297 302 Broadway.
Kemble av. (J 9), from Av. V at Mill av., S. W. and S. to National av.
Kenilworth pl. (F 7), Farragut rd., bet. Amersfort pl. & Flatbush av., S. E. to Germania pl.
Kenmore pl. (F 6), Woodruff av., S. to Caton av.
Kenmore ter. (F 7), from E. 21st, bet. Church av. and Albemarle rd.
Kensington (G 11), Shore Boulevard, E of Jaffrey, S. to Oriental Boulevard.
Kent (F 2), East River, bet. Java and Greenpoint av., E. to Whale creek canal.
Kent av. (F 2), N. 14th, opp. Franklin, S. & S. E. to Lafayette av.
101 110 N. 8th.
203 218 Metropolitan av.
401 402 Broadway.
759 768 Flushing av.
1021 1034 Lafayette av.
Kermit pl. (E 7), Coney Island av., at Parade Grounds, W. to East 8th.
Kills Path (L 4), Jamaica av., opp. Euclid av., N. to Borough line.
Kimball (G 8), Flatlands av. opp. E. 38th, S.E. to Jamaica bay.
King (C 5), 474 Columbia, N. W. to Buttermilk ch.
Kings Highway (D 9), Bay Pkway. E. & N. E. to Flatbush av.
Kings pl. (E 9), Kings Highway, bet. W. 1st & W 2d, S. E.
Kingsland av. (G 3), 71 Maspeth av., N. and N. W. to Newtown Creek
165 164 Meeker av.
471 466 Greenpoint av.
Kingston av. (G 5), 1490 Fulton, S. to Winthrop.
125 120 Bergen.
251 246 St. Johns pl.
Knapp (G 10), Gerritsen av., bet. Av. U & Av. V, S. to Emmons av.
Knickerbocker av. (H 3), Johnson av., at Morgan av., S.E. to Borough line.
— 136 Flushing av.
313 314 Hart.
— 458 Myrtle av.
783 784 Halsey.
Kosciusko (F 4), 989 Bedford av., E. to Bushwick av.
378 360 Sumner av.
Kosciusko pl. (F 4), 999 Kent av., E.—half block.
Kossuth pl. (H 4), 1169 Broadway., N. E. to Bushwick av.
Lafayette (E 4), 41 Fleet, E. to Raymond.
Lafayette, 31st ward (F 9), Elm av., at E. 16th, S. to Cedar av.
Lafayette av. (E 4), 73 Flatbush av., E. to Bushwick av.
149 138 Carlton av.
273 262 Washington av.
487 498 Bedford av.
823 824 Sumner av.
1103 1108 Broadway.
Lafayette av., 30th ward (B 9), 7th av., at Parrott pl., E. to Bay 1st.
Lafayette ct. (E 8), E. 4th. bet. Avs L & M, E. to Ocean p'kway.
La France ct. (J 8), from E. 66th. bet. Av. N and Island av. N.E. to E. 68th.
LaGrange (G 3), 868 Grand, S. to Maujer.
Lake (G 2), 6 Bridgewater, N. E. to Newtown creek.
Lake, 31st ward (E 9), Kings Highway at Av. R, S. to 86th.
Lakeland pl. (F 11), from Ocean View av., E. of E. 2d. S. E. to Brighton Beach av.
Lancaster av. (F 10), Ocean pkway, S. of Av. W. E. to E. 12th.
Langham (G 11), Shore blvd, E. of Kensington, S. to Oriental blvd.
Laurel av. (Sea Gate) (C 11). Manhattan av., E. to W. 37th.
Lawrence (D 4), Tillary, bet. Jay & Bridge, S. to Fulton.
Lawrence av. (E 8), 47th, bet. Webster & Washington avs, N. E. to Ocean Parkway.
Lawton (H 4), 1067 B'way, N. E. to Bushwick av.
Lee av. (F 3), 146 Division av., S. E. to Lorimer.
Lefferts av. (F 6), 511 Flatbush av., E. to Utica av.
Lefferts pl. (F 5), 249 St. James pl., S. E. to Franklin av.
Lemon (E 4), Clinton av., N. of Peach, E. to Washington av.

BOROUGH OF BROOKLYN STREET AND AVENUE DIRECTORY—*Continued.*

Lenox rd. (F 6), 781 Flatbush av., E. to 98th.
Leo pl. (E 4), 78 St. Edwards, S.W. to Myrtle av.
Leonard (G 3), 619 B'way, N. W. to Greenpoint av.
217 210 Grand.
509 512 Driggs av.
Lewis av. (G 4), 352 Floyd, S. to Fulton.
293 298 Putnam av.
449 448 Fulton.
Lewis pl. (E 7), Coney Island av., bet. Beverly rd. & Matthews pl., E. to E. 11th.
Lexington av. (F 4), 317 Grand av.. E. to B'way.
191 174 Bedford av.
557 528 Sumner av.
Lexington av., 30th ward (B 9), 7th av. at Parrott pl., E. to 12th av
Liberty (D 4), 6 High, S. to Fulton, at Tillary.
Liberty (L 4), Eldert la., bet. Etna and Ridgewood av., W. to Richards la.
Liberty, 31st ward (F 9), Locust av. at E. 14th, S. to Elm av.
Liberty av. (J5), East New York av. bet. Rockaway av. & Thatford av., E. to Borough line.
219 220 Snediker av.
509 510 Van Sicklen av.
741 742 Essex.
985 986 Crystal.
1043 1044 Crescent.
Lincoln av. (L 4), Etna, bet. Autumn & Nichols avs., S. to Jamaica bay.
Lincoln pl. (E 5), 161 5th av., E. to E. New York av.
167 168 7th av.
409 414 Washington av.
655 656 Bedford av.
957 958 Brooklyn av.
1543 1544 Buffalo av.
Lincoln rd. (F 6), 99 Ocean av., E. to E. New York av.
Linden (H 4), 1349 B'way, N. E. to Borough line.
Linden av. (F 6), 581 Flatbush av., E. to 98th.
Linwood (K 5), 502 Jamaica av., S. E. to Borden av.
Little (D 3), East River, bet. Hudson av. & Navy Yard, S. W. to Evans.
Little's la. (E 7), Cortelyou rd. at Coney Island av., S. W. to 16th av.
Little Nassau (F 4), 37 Taaffe, E.
Livingston (D 4), 17 Sidney pl., E. to Flatbush av.
Livonia av. (H 6), E. 98th, at Howard av., E. to New Lots rd.
Lloyd (F 7), 2728 Church av. S. to Erasmus.
Lloyd ct. (E 9), W. 3d, bet. Avs. R & S, E. to Van Sicklen.
Locust av. (F 8), 1623 Coney Isl. av.. N. E. to Ocean av.
Locust (G 4), 857 B'way E. to Beaver.
Locke av. (L 6), from Louisiana av. at Fresh Creek Basin, N. E. to Fountain av.
Logan (L 4), Jamaica av., bet. Norwood av. & Richmond. S. and S. E. to Vandalia av.
Lombardy (G 2), 144 Kingsland av., E. to Newtown creek.
Lorimer (G 2), 157 Wallabout, N. E. and N. to Noble.
245 240 Broadway.
475 476 Grand.
787 788 Bayard.
1049 1050 Meserole av.
Lorraine (C 5), 19 Otsego, S. E. to Hamilton av.
Lorraine av. (J 6), E. 98th at Amboy, E. to Boro line.
193 194 Stone av.
861 862 Hinsdale.
685 686 Bradford.
893 900 Linwood.
Lott (F 7), 50 Erasmus, S. to Canarsie la.
Lott av. (J 6), E. 98th opp. Church av., E. to New Lots av.
Lott pl. (G 8), Flatbush av., n. Kings Highway, E. to E. 40th.
Lotts or Littles la. (E 7), Cortelyou rd., at Coney Island av., S.W. to 16th av.
Louis pl. (H 5), 1090 Herkimer, S.W. to Atlantic av.
Louisa (E 7), Gravesend av., bet. Albemarle rd. & Church av., S.W. to 36th.
Louisiana av. (K 6), Williams av., n. New Lots av., S. E. to Borden av.
Lourdes pl. (J 5), Furman av., bet. B'way & Bushwick av.. E. to Aberdeen.
Love la. (D 4), E. of 159 Henry, W. to Hicks.
Ludlam pl. (F 6), Montgomery, W. of Rogers av., S. to Sullivan.
Luquer (C 5), 377 Columbia, S. E. to Smith.
Lyme av. (Sea Gate) (C 11), Manhattan av.. E. to W. 37th.
Lynch (F 4), 95 Wallabout, N. E. to B'way.
Mack pl. (D 4), 171 Bridge, E. to Gold.
Mackay pl. (A 7), Shore rd. n. 70th, E. to 1st av.
Mackenzie (G 11), Shore Boulev'd, E. of Langham, to Oriental Boulevard.
Macon (F 4), 19 Arlington pl., E. to Hopkinson av.
339 320 Sumner av.
847 830 Saratoga av.
Madison (F 5), 493 Classon av., E. to Borough line.
473 484 Sumner av.
893 940 Broadway.
Magenta (L 5), now part of McKinley av.
Main (D 3), E. R., at Catharine Ferry. S. to Fulton.
Main rd. (H 6), now E. 92d.
Malbone (F6), name changed to Empire blvd.
Malta (K 6), New Lots av., bet. Williams av. & Alabama av., S. E. to Fairfield av.
Manhasset pl. (C 5), 106 Rapelye, S. to Coles.
Manhattan av. (G 3), 677 B'way, N. to Newtown creek.
231 238 Grand.
549 558 Driggs av.
897 898 Greenpoint av.
1205 1206 Newtown creek.
Manhattan av. (Sea Gate) (C11), Gravesend bay at Highland av., S. to Mermaid av.
Manhattan Boulevard (G 10), now Shore Boulev'd.
Manhattan ct. (F 11), E. 2d, S. of Av. Y, E. to Ocean Parkway.
Manor ct. (F 10), E. 7th, S. of Av. Z, E. to Coney Island av.
Mansfield pl. (F7), 2402 Foster av., S. to Emmons av.
Maple (F 6), 557 Flatbush av. E. to Troy av.
Maple av. (Sea Gate) (C11), Highland av., S. of Gravesend bay, E. to W. 37th.
Maple ct. (E7), E. 17th from Caton av., S. to Church av.
Marcy av. (F 3), 490 Metropolitan av., S. W. & S. E. & S. to Fulton.
171 178 Broadway.
273 286 Hewes.
461 454 Flushing av.
575 566 Myrtle av.
665 664 DeKalb av.
847 850 Putnam av.
Marine av. (A 8), 92d, at 1st av., S. E. to Ft. Hamilton pkway.
Marion (H 5), 1707 Fulton. E. to B'way.
Market av. (E 4), Flushing av, opp. Hall, N. to F.
Marlborough ct. (F 8), Foster av., bet. Brighton Beach R. R. and Rugby rd.
Marlborough rd. (F 7), Caton av., bet. Buckingham & Rugby rds, S. to Foster av.
Marsh (G 9), Nostrand av.. at Av. P, S. E. to Av. X.
Marshall (D3), East River, ft. of Adams, E. to Little.
Marshall's la. (K 7), E. 92d at Av. K., S. E. to Rockaway pkway.
Martense (F7), 859 Flatbush av., E. to New York av.
Martense ct. (F7), from N. side of Martense, E. of Flatbush av.
Maspeth av. (G 3), Humboldt, n. Metropolitan av., N. E. to Newtown creek.
Matthews pl. (E 7), Coney Island av., bet. Lewis pl. and Slocum pl., E. to E. 11th.
Maujer (F 3), 393 S. 1st, E. to Newtown creek.
879 360 Morgan av.
501 468 Metropolitan av
McDonough (G 5), 945 Marcy av., E. to B'way.
361 372 Stuyvesant av.
813 822 Broadway.
McDougal (H 5), 1875 Fulton, E. to B'way.
McKenney (D 3), 50 Doughty, S.W. to Poplar.
McKibbin (G 3), 557 B'way, E. to Bogart.
201 200 Bushwick av.
McKinley av. (L 5), from N. end of Fountain av., E. to Eldert la.
Meadow (G2), 86 Waterbury, E. to Metropolitan av.
Meadow la. (K 7), E. 83d, n. Av. J, N. E. to E. 92d.
Meeker av. (G 2), 115 Richardson, N. E. to Newtown creek.
128 108 N. Henry.
— 318 Varick av.
Melrose (G 4), 923 B'way, N. E. to Irving av.
Menehan (H 4), 969 Bushwick av., N. E. to Borough line.
Mercein (D3), B'klyn bridge n. York. N E. to Garrison.
Mermaid av. (C 11), from Surf av. at Sea Gate av., E. to Stillwell av. and from Coney Island av., E. to E. of Homecrest av.
Meserole (F 3), 44 Union av., E. to Borough line.
149 154 Graham av.
369 382 Morgan av.
Meserole av. (F2), 12 Franklin, E. to Kingsland av.
118 104 Manhattan av.
318 306 Kingsland av.
Metropolitan av. (F2), E. R.. bet. N. 1st & N. 3d, S. E. & E. to Newtown ck.
201 204 Bedford av.
— 802 Bushwick av.
1027 1026 Morgan av.
1207 — Maujer.
— 1280 Ten Eyck.
Metz av. (E 4), Fleeman av. West to Clinton av.
Middagh (D 4), 59 Columbia hts., S. E. to Fulton.
Middleton (F 4), 121 Wallabout, N.E. to Throop av.
Midwood (F6), 581 Flatbush av., E. to Troy av.
Milford (L5), 3166 Atlantic av., S. E. to Vandalia av.
Mill (C 5), 457 Columbia, E. to Hamilton av.
Mill, 18th Ward (H 3), Stewart av., at English Kills, E. to Newt'n creek.
Mill av. (J 8), from Ralph av., S. of Island av., S.E. and S. to National av.
Mill la. (J 8), from Ralph av.. S. of Island av., E. to E. 64th.
Mill rd., 31st ward (D 10), from Cropsey av., at 25th av., S. E. to Bay 47th.
Mill rd., 32d ward (J 6), Hopkinson av., at Vienna av., E. to Fresh creek.
Miller av. (K 5), 176 Highland b'lvd, S. E. to Borden av.
141 142 Fulton.
339 340 Pitkin av.
Miller pl. (G 6), Empire blvd., n. B'klyn av., S. to Lefferts av.
Milton (F 2), East River, bet. Noble & Greenpoint av., E. to Manhattan av.
Milton pl. (K4), fr. Crosby av., bet. Vermont av. and Bulwer pl., S. to Highland blvd.
Minna (E 7), 26 West av., S. W. to 36th.
Moffat (J 5), 1735 B'way, N. E. to Borough line.
Monitor (G 2), 225 Richardson, N. to Greenpoint av.
Monroe (F 4) 471 Classon av., E. to B'way.
113 122 Bedford av.
887 — Broadway.
Monroe pl. (D 4), 100 Clark, S. W. to Pierrepont.
Monsell (G 6), Montgomery, n. Schenectady av., S. to Malbone.
Montague (D 4), E. R., bet. Pierrepont and Remsen, E. to Court.
Montague ter. (D 4), 46 Montague, S. to Remsen.
Montauk av. (L 5), 3146 Atlantic av., S. E. to Borden av.
Montauk ct. (F 10), E. 7th bet. Manor ct. & Voorhies av., E. to Coney Island av

BOROUGH OF BROOKLYN STREET AND AVENUE DIRECTORY—*Continued.*

Monteith (G 3), 475 Bushwick av., E. to Evergreen av.
Montgomery (F 6), Washington av., n. Crown, E. to East New York av.
Montgomery, 29th ward (E 7), 416 Coney Island av., S. W. to E. 7th.
Montgomery pl. (E 5), 185 8th av., S. E. to Prospect Park.
Montrose av. (F 3), B'way, opp. Penn, E. to Boro. line.
389 392 Morgan av.
Moore (G 3), 607 B'way, E. to Bogart.
Morgan av. (H 3), 1029 Flushing av., N. to Norman av.
229 228 Ten Eyck.
368 368 Maspeth av.
568 560 Driggs av.
Morrell (G3), 848 Flushing av., N. to Bushwick av.
Morrisd (B 9), 86th, n. Delaplaine, S. to Dyker Heights Park.
Morse (G 2), 22 Bridgewater, N. E. to Newtown creek.
Morton (E 3), 589 Kent av., N. E. to Bedford av.
Morton av. (H 9), Fillmore av. at E. 52d, W. to Coleman la.
Moultrie (G 2), 747 Humboldt, N. to G'point av.
Myrtle av. (D 4), 351 Fulton, E. to Borough line.
115 106 Bridge.
237 220 Navy.
401 400 Vanderbilt av.
679 686 Bedford av.
751 754 Nostrand av.
975 952 Throop av.
1147 1132 Broadway.
1437 1410 Greene av.
Narrows av. (A 7), 53 Bay Ridge av., S. to Bay Ridge Parkway.
Nassau (D 4), 187 Fulton, E. to Navy.
Nassau av. (F 2), 87 N. 14th, N. E. to Varick.
243 244 Kingsland av.
Nassau pl. (E 4), 252 Nassau, S. to Concord.
National av. (J 9), fr. ft. of Mill av., W. to Bassett av.
Nautilus av. (Sea Gate) (C 11), Manhattan av., E. to W. 37th.
Navy (E 4), 243 York, S. to DeKalb av.
Naylors al. (D 4), Liberty, n. Nassau, E., half block.
Nelson (C 5), 399 Columbia, S. E. to Smith.
Neptune av. (F 11), 2 E. 14th, W. to Surf av., at Beach 45th, E. to Emmons av.
Nevins (E 4), 8 Flatbush av., S. W. to Carroll.
New (F 3), 193 B'way, E. to S. 4th.
New (E 11), Cortland bet. Neptune av. & Sheepshead bay rd., S.E. to W. 5th.
New Atlantic av. (J 5), Havens pl., S. E. to East New York av.
New Jersey av. (K 5) Highland Boulevard, bet. Pellington pl. & Vermont av., S. and S. E. to Locke av.
211 212 Liberty av.
305 306 Pitkin av.
857 858 Stanley av.
New Lots av. (J 6), Watkins, at Hegeman av., N. E. to Fountain av.
New Utrecht (B9), Bay 1st, n. 86th, S. W. to Benson av.
New Utrecht av. (D7), from 9th av. at 38th, S. to 86th.
New York av. (G 5), 1350 Fulton, S. to Av. N.
121 120 Bergen.
291 300 E. P'kway.
425 442 Empire blvd.
919 9:0 Church av.
1213 1214 Av. C.
Newell (G2), 196 Driggs av., N. W. to Greenpoint av.
Newkirk av. (E8), 639 Ocean pkway, E. to E. 35th.
Newport (J 6), E. 98th at Barrett, E. to New Lots av.
Newton (G 2), 426 Leonard, N. E. to Engert av.
Nichols av. (L 4), 946 Jamaica av., S. to Atlantic av.
Noble (F2), East River, bet. Oak & Milton, E. to Manhattan av.
Nolan's la. (J 7), E. 92d, n. Av. D, N. E. to E. 98th.
Noll (G 4), 525 Bushwick av., E. to Flushing av.
Norfolk (G11), Shore Boulevard, E. of Mackenzie, S. to Oriental Boulevard.
Norman av. (F 2), Banker, opp. Wythe av., N. E. to Bridgewater.
205 202 Moultrie.
301 298 Morgan av.
Norman pl. (J 5), 76 Truxton, S. E. to Fulton.
N. Elliott pl. (E 4), 16 Flushing av., S. to Myrtle av.
N. Henry (G 2), 209 Richardson, N. to Paidge av.
N. Oxford (E 4), 48 Flushing av., S. to Myrtle av.
N. Portland av. (E4) 30 Flushing av., S. to Myrtle av.
N. 1st (F 3), E. R., bet. Grand & Metropolitan av., S. E. to Driggs.
N. 3d (F 2), E. R., bet. Metropolitan av. & N. 4th, S. E. to Metropolitan av.
N. 4th (F 2), E. R., bet. N. 3d & N. 5th, S. E. to Metropolitan av.
N. 5th (F 2), E. R., bet. N. 4th & N. 6th, S. E. to Metropolitan av.
N. 6th (F 2), E. R., bet. N. 5th & N. 7th, S. E. to Metropolitan av.
N. 7th (F 2), E. R., bet. N. 6th & N. 8th, S. E. to Union av.
N. 8th (F 2), E. R., bet. N. 7th & N. 9th, S. E. to Union av.
N. 9th (F 2), E. R., bet. N. 8th & N. 10th, S. E. to Havemeyer, at Withers.
N. 10th (F 2), E. R., bet. N. 9th & N. 11th, S.E. to Union av.
N. 11th (F 2), E. R., bet. N. 10th & N. 12th, S. E. to Union av.
N. 12th (F 2), E. R., bet. N. 11th & N. 13th, S. E. to Union av.
N. 13th (F 2), E. R., bet. N. 12th & N. 14th, S. E. to Union av
N. 14th (F 2), E. R., bet. N. 13th & N. 15th, S. E. to Driggs av.
N. 15th (F 2), 2 Franklin, S. E. to Driggs av.
Norwood av. (L4), Jamaica av., bet. Logan & Hale, S. to Atlantic av.
Nostrand av. (F 4), 520 Flushing av., S. to Sheepshead bay.
185 152 Myrtle av.
268 290 Lafayette av.
349 388 Gates av.
495 534 Fulton.
641 680 St. Marks av.
791 832 Eastern P'kway
1151 1152 Rutland road.
1451 1452 Church av.
1837 1838 Av. D.
2375 2376 Av. J.
2799 2810 Kings Highway.
3429 3440 Av. U.
3857 3858 Av. Z.
Noyes pl. (M 6), from Egan av. nr. Spring Creek Basin, S. E. to Borden av.
Nutria al. (D 4), 207 Adams, E. to Pearl.
Oak (F 2), E. R., bet. Noble & Calyer, E. to Guernsey.
Oakland (G 2), 228 Driggs av., N. W. to Newtown cr.
263 264 Kent.
319 316 Huron.
403 402 Clay.
Oakland pl. (F 7), Albemarle rd., bet. Bedford av. & Lott, S. to Vernon av.
Ocean av. (F 6), Flatbush av., opp. Malbone, S. to Oriental Boulevard.
205 — Fenimore.
519 520 Church av.
1009 1010 Newkirk av.
1683 1684 Av. L.
2811 2812 Av. X.
Ocean av., 30th ward (B9), 11th av., n. 86th, S. E. to New Utrecht.
Ocean ct. (E 10), E. 3d, S. of Av. X, E. to Hubbard.
Ocean Parkway (E7), Coney Island av., opp. Parkside av., W. & S. to Concourse.
417 418 Cortelyou rd.
1195 1196 Av. L.
2089 2090 Av. U.
2589 2590 Av. Z.
Ocean pl. (J 5), 1228 Herkimer, S. W. to Atlantic av.
Ocean View av. (F 11), from Ocean P'kway, S. of Neptune av., N. E. to Coney Island av.
Oceanic av. (Sea Gate) (C 11), Mermaid av., E. to W. 37th.
Old Bridge rd. (E 4), 226 Sands, S. E. to Navy.
Old Wood Point rd. (G 3), 1 Maspeth av., N. E. to Withers, to Metropolitan av.
Olive (G 3), 889 Grand, N. to Maspeth av.
Olive pl. (J 5), 1342 Herkimer, S.W. to Atlantic av.
Oliver (A 8), Shore blvd., n. 93d, N.E. to Marine av.
Onderdonk av., part of (H 3), Meadow, S. E. to Meserole.
Orange (D 4), 99 Columbia hts., E. to Fulton.
Orient av. (G 3), 823 Metropolitan av., E. to Newtown creek.
Orient ct. (F 11), E. 7th, bet. Voorhies & Canal avs., E. to Coney Island av.
Oriental Boulevard (F11), West End av., S. of Hampton av. E. to Irwin.
Ormond pl. (F 5), 92 Putnam av., S. to Fulton.
Osborn (J 5), East New York av., at Liberty av., S. to Av. D.
Otis pl. (F 11), from Neptune av., W. of Coney Island av., S. to Ocean View av.
Otsego (C 5), Dwight at Bush, S. W. to Beard.
Overbaugh (G 8), Flatbush av., n. Av. L, N. E. to E. 46th.
Overton pl. (E11), W. 11th, n. Neptune av., W. to W. 12th.
Ovington av. (B 7), Ridge Boulev'd, bet. Bay Ridge av. & 71st E. to 7th av. & 10th av. S of Bay Ridge av., E. to New Utrecht av.
Ovington ct (D8) 66th, bet. Duryea ct. & Cameron ct., S. to 67th.
Oxford (See N. Oxford & S. Oxford.)
Oxford (G 11), Shore Boulevard, E. of Norfolk, S. to Oriental Boulevard.
Pacific (C 4), East River, bet. Atlantic av. & Amity, E. to East New York av.
197 198 Court.
389 390 Bond.
617 608 Flatbush av.
843 818 Vanderbilt av.
1287 1256 Nostrand av.
2003 1958 Ralph av.
Paerdegat av. N. (J8), from Ralph av. at Av. H, S.E. to Flatlands av., and from ft. of E. 76th, S. E. to Seaview av.
Paerdegat av. S. (J8), from Glenwood rd. at E. 56th, S. E. to Flatlands av., & from Ralph av. at Av. I, S. E. and S. to Av. Z.
Paerdegat 1st to Paerdegat 15th (J 8), inclusive, fr. Paerdegat av. North, N. E. to E. 80th
Paidge av. (F 1), 418 Oakland, S. E. to Whale creek canal.
Palmer pl. (M 6), fr. Egan av. nr. Spring Creek Basin, S. E. to Borden av.
Palmetto (H 4), 1387 B'way, N. E. to Borough line.
Parade pl. (F 6), Parkside av., S. to Caton av.
Park (G 4), 837 B'way, E. to Beaver.
Park av. (E 4), 261 Hudson av., E. to B'way.
275 266 Washington av.
463 452 Franklin av.
569 560 Nostrand av.
Park pl. (E 5), 97 5th av., E. to East New York av.
— 166 Flatbush av.
441 442 Grand av.
829 830 Nostrand av.
1239 1240 Troy av.
Parkside av. (E6), Coney Isl. av., opp. Ocean p'kway, N. E. and E. to New York av.
Parkville av. (E 8), from 47th, bet. Lawrence and Foster avs., N. E. to Coney Island av.
Parkway ct. (E 10), E. 3d, bet. Ocean ct. & Av. Y, E. to Hubbard.
Parrott pl. (B 9), 88th, at 7th av., S. W. to 92d.
Patchen av. (H 4), 1166 B'way, S. to Fulton.
Peach (E 4), Clinton av., bet. Pear & Lemon, E. to Apple.

BOROUGH OF BROOKLYN STREET AND AVENUE DIRECTORY—*Continued.*

Pear (E 4), Clinton av., bet. Flushing av. & Peach, E. to Apple.

Pearl (D 3), E.R., bet. Adams & Jay, S. to Fulton

Pellington pl. (K 5), Highland B'l'vard, bet. Fanchon pl. and New Jersey av., S. to Jamaica av.

Pembroke (G 11), Shore Boulev'd, E. of Norfolk, S to Oriental Boulevard.

Penn (F 4), 707 Kent av., N. E. to B'way

Pennsylvania av. (K 5), 72 Jamaica av., S.E. to Borden av.

235 236 Pitkin av.

625 630 New Lots av.

Pequot (F 1), 29 Paidge av. N. E. to Newtown creek.

Percival (C 5), 787 Clinton, S. E. to Gowanus bay.

Perry pl. (F 5), 1167 Atlantic av., N. to Herkimer pl.

Phillip's al. (D 3), York, nr. Adams, S. to Prospect.

Pierrepont (D 4), 208 Columbia Heights, E. to Fulton.

Pierrepont pl. (D 4), 2 Pierrepont, S. to Montague.

Pilling (J 5), 1783 B'way, N. E. to Borough line.

Pine (L4), Etna, bet. Euclid & Crescent & Conduit av., S. to Cozine av.

Pine pl. (F 6), Montgomery, bet. Cedar pl. & Bedford av., S. to Sullivan.

Pineapple (D 4), 115 Columbia Heights, E. to Fulton.

Pink (F 1), Commercial, opp. Franklin, N. W. to Newtown creek.

Pioneer (C 5), 450 Columbia, N. W. to Atlantic dock.

Pitkin av. (H 5), Ralph, at Eastern p'kway, E. to Borough line.

* 1444 East New York av.

1621 1622 Hopkinson av.

1837 1838 Sackman.

2127 2128 Vermont.

2433 2434 Linwood.

2741 2742 Pine.

Plaza (E 5), boundary of the entrance of Prospect Park, at Flatbush av. & Vanderbilt av.

Plaza st. (E 5), Plaza at Eastern p'way, N. & W. & S. to the Plaza at Berkeley pl.

Pleasant pl. (J 5), 1312 Herkimer, S. to Atlantic av.

Plymouth (D3), East River n. Water, N. E. to Little.

Polhemus pl. (E5), 784 Carroll, S. W. to Garfield pl.

Poplar (D 3), 37 Columbia hts. S. E. to Henry.

Poplar av. (Sea Gate (C) 11), Highland av., opp. Manhattan av., E. to W. 37th.

Poplar pl. (D 3), closed.

Portal (H 5), from Eastern p'kway at Lincoln Terrace park, S. to East New York av.

Porter av. (H3), 1005 Flushing av., N. to Meeker av.

131 132 Meserole.

321 336 Maspeth av.

Portland av. (See N. Portland & S. Portland avs.)

Powell (J 5), East New York av., bet. Sackman & Junius, S. to Av. D.

Powers (F 3), 148 Union av., E to Catharine.

Prescott pl. (H 5), 980 Herkimer, S. to Atlantic av.

President (C 4), 31 Hamilton av., S.E. to East New York av.

269 270 Court.

657 658 Fifth av.

991 1002 Franklin av.

1333 1340 Brooklyn av.

Prince (E 4), 220 Concord, S. to Fleet.

Prince ct. (E 3), Front, n. Gold, S. to York.

Prospect (D 4), 107 Main, N. E. to Navy.

Prospect, 29th ward (F 7), 2056 Church av., S. to Beverly rd.

Prospect av. (D 6), Gowanus Bay, bet. Hamilton & 17th, S. E. to Ocean pkway.

Prospect Park West (E 5), that part of 9th av. from Union at park entrance, S.W. to Greenwood cemetery.

Prospect pl. (E 5), 77 Fifth av., E. to E. New York av.

109 120 Flatbush av.

403 406 Grand av.

795 800 Nostrand av.

1379 1384 Utica av.

Prospect ter. (D 4), 132 Prospect, S.

Provost (F 2), 255 Greenpoint av., N. to Paidge av.

Pulaski (F 4), 208 Nostrand av., E. to B'way.

Purdy pl. (H 3), 2 Seneca av., S. E. to Borough line

Putnam av. (F5), 1005 Fulton, E. to Borough line.

287 268 Nostrand av.

421 428 Tompkins av.

789 798 Reid av.

1047 1082 Broadway.

1327 1328 Wilson av.

Quay (F 2), East River, S. of Calyer, E. to Franklin.

Quentin (G 11), Shore blvd., E. of Pembroke, S. to Oriental blvd.

Quincy (F 4), 2 Downing, E. to B'way.

449 474 Throop av.

Radde pl. (J 5), 1174 Herkimer, S. to Atlantic av.

Railroad av. (L4) now Autumn av.

Raleigh pl. (G 7), 344 Martense, S. to Church av.

Ralph av. (H4), 1304 B'way, S. to East New York av., & fr. Remsen av. n. Church av., S. to Av. T

187 188 McDonough.

303 302 Fulton.

427 428 Bergen.

601 600 Eastern pkway.

Randolph (H 3), 88 Varick, E. to Purdy pl.

Ranton (F1), 49 Paidge av., N. E. to Newtown creek.

Rapelye (C 5), 169 Van Brunt, E. to Henry.

Raymond (E 4), 32 Park av., S. to DeKalb av

Red Hook la. (D 4), 354 Fulton, S. W. to Livingston.

Reeve pl. (E 6), 148 Coney Island av., S. W. to Prospect av.

Regent pl. (F 7), Flatbush av. opp. Tilden av., S. W. to E. 19th.

Regent sq. (D 4), the open space at junction of Fulton & Liberty.

Reid (B 5), 456 Van Brunt N. W. to Conover.

Reid av. (H 4), 1064 B'way, S. to Fulton.

195 204 Putnam av.

Remsen (D 4), 271 Furman, S. to Court.

Remsen av. (H6), East New York av. at Utica av., S. E. to Canarsie Beach park.

Repose pl. (K 6), Schenck av., n. New Lots av., E. to Jerome.

Revere pl. (G 5), Dean bet. Kingston av. & Albany av., S. to Bergen.

Richard (E 11), Canal av. bet. W. 6th & Henry, S. to Neptune av.

Richards (C 5), 42 Rapelye, S. W. to Erie Basin.

Richards la. (L 4), Union pl., bet. Nichols & Grant avs., N. to Liberty.

Richardson (F 2), 300 Union av., E. to Kingsland av.

Richmond (L 4), Jamaica av., bet. Logan & Chestnut, S. to Force Tube av.

Ridge ct. (B 8), 72d, E. of 3d av.; runs N.

Ridge Boulevard (B 7), 66th, opp. 2d av., S. to Marine av.

Ridgewood (F 6), Flatbush av., opp. Caton av., E. to New York av.

Ridgewood av. (K 5), Jamaica av. jct. Jerome, E. to Borough line.

Ridgewood av., 28th ward (J 4), Palmetto, nr. Irving av., E. to Putnam av.

Ripley (G 11), Shore blvd., E of Quentin, S. to Oriental blvd.

River (E 3), 290 Kent av., N. to N. 3d.

Riverdale av. (J 6), E. 98th at Grafton, N. E. to New Lots av

Roberge pl. (E 11), W. 5th, E. to W. 3d.

Robert (K 4), from Bulwer pl., N. E. to Highland blvd.

Robert pl. (K 4), from Robert, S. to Highland blvd.

Robinson (F 6), now part of Parkside av.

Rochester av. (H 5), 1814 Fulton, S. to East New York av.

167 178 Prospect pl.

Rock (H 3), 22 Bogart, E. to Morgan av.

Rockaway av. (J 5), 1712 B'way, S. W. to E. 98th.

131 144 Fulton.

327 326 Prospect pl.

Rockaway av., 32d ward (K8), Rockaway p'kway at Sea View av., S. to E. 93d.

Rockaway Parkway (H 6), East New York av., opp. Buffalo av., S. E. to Jamaica bay.

Rockwell pl. (B 4), 82 De-Kalb av., S. to Flatbush av.

Rodney (F 3), Wallabout canal, bet. Ross & Keap, N. E. to Metropolitan av.

397 412 Grand.

Roebling (F 2), 303 Union av., S. to Division av.

297 306 Broadway.

347 354 Division av.

Rogers av. (F 5), Dean, at Bedford av., S. to Av. F.

199 180 E. P'kway.

317 300 Montgomery.

525 526 Rutland rd.

819 320 Church av.

Romaine ter. (E 4), the small Plaza at N. W. corner Ft. Greene pk & steps leading to Prison Ship Martyrs' Monument.

Rose pl. (J 5), 1995 Broadway, N. E. to Bushwick av.

Ross (F 3), Wallabout canal bet. Wilson & Rodney, N. E. to Division av.

Royce (J 8), from Bergen av. at Av. V, S.E. to Av. X

Ruby (M 5), Borough line bet. Blake & Dumont avs., S. to Borough line.

Rugby rd. (E 7), Caton av., bet. Marlborough and Argyle rds., S. to Av. H.

Rush (E 3), 521 Kent av., E. to Division av.

Russell (G 2), 99 Meeker av., N. to Greenpoint av.

Russell pl. (J 5), 1144 Herkimer, S. to Atlantic av.

Russell sq. (H 5), junction Pitkin & East New York avs.

Rutherford pl. (C 9), from 17th av., S. of Benson av. S E. to 18th av.

Rutland rd. (F 6), 597 Flatbush av., E. to E. 98th.

Rutledge (F 4), 27 Wallabout, N. E. to B'way.

Ryder (G 8), Kings Highway bet. E. 38th & Flatbush av., S. E. to Jamaica bay.

Ryder av. (E 9), Gravesend av., bet. Avs. N & O N.E. to Coney Island av.

Ryder's la. (G 9), Kings Highway at E. 25th, S. E. to Av. U.

Ryerson (F 4), 254 Flushing av., S. to Lafayette av.

Sackett (C 4), East River, bet. Degraw & Union, S. E. to 5th av.

297 308 Court.

585 600 Third av.

Sackman (J 5) 1986 Eastern P'kway, S. to Av. D.

St. Andrews pl. (G 5), 304 Herkimer, S. to Atlantic av.

St. Charles pl. (F 5), St. Johns pl., bet. St. Francis pl. & Bedford av, S. to Lincoln pl.

St. Edwards (E 4), 2 Flushing av., S. to Willoughby.

St. Felix (E 4), 117 DeKalb av., S. to Hanson pl.

St. Francis pl. (F 5), St. Johns pl., bet. Franklin av. & St. Charles pl., S. to Lincoln pl.

St. James pl. (F 4), 330 De Kalb av., S. to Atlantic av.

St. Johns pl. (E 5), 137 5th av., E. to East New York av.

165 170 7th av.

325 326 Underhill av.

541 542 Franklin av.

884 854 Bedford av.

1075 1096 Brooklyn av.

1355 1378 Schenectady av.

St. Marks av. (E5), 61 5th av., E. to East New York av.

367 380 Grand av.

833 850 Brooklyn av.

1391 1398 Ralph av.

St. Marks pl. (E 5), 3d av., opp. Wyckoff E. to 4th av.

BOROUGH OF BROOKLYN STREET AND AVENUE DIRECTORY—*Continued.*

St. Nicholas av. (H 2), 1272 Flushing av, S. E. to Borough line.

St. Pauls ct. (F 6), St. Pauls pl., S. of Caton av., E. to Ocean av.

St. Pauls pl. (F6), Parkside av. bet. Parade pl. & Ocean av., S. E. to Church av.

Sandford (F 4), 500 Flushing av., S. to DeKalb av.

Sands (D 4), 185 Fulton, E. to Navy.

97 94 Jay.

223 220 Hudson av.

Sapphire (M 5), from Dumont av., at Borough line, S. to Borough line.

Saratoga av. (H 4), 1486 B'way, S. to E. 98th.

219 214 Fulton.

361 356 St. Marks av.

Schaeffer (J 4), 1663 Broadway, N. E. to Boro line.

Schenck av. (K 5), 290 Jamaica av., S.E. to Borden av.

179 180 Atlantic av.

321 322 Pitkin av.

773 774 Vienna av.

Schenck av. 32d ward (K 8), E. 92d, n. Jamaica bay, E. to E. 94th st.

Schenectady av. (H 5), 1692 Fulton, S. to Flatbush av.

161 170 Prospect pl.

331 344 Carroll

415 416 Empire blvd.

535 536 Winthrop.

879 880 Church av.

Schermerhorn (D 4), 135 Clinton, S. E. to Flatbush av.

365 370 Third av.

Scholes (F 3), 62 Union av., E. to Newtown creek.

221 218 Bushwick av.

513 516 Stewart av.

Schroeders av. (L 7), from Louisiana av. at Fresh Creek Basin, N. E. to Borough line.

Scott av. (H3), Troutman, at St. Nicholas av., N. to Newtown creek.

Sea pl. (D 11), W. 32d, bet. Surf av. & the Atlantic ocean; runs W.

Sea Breeze av. (E 11), W. 5th, bet. Sheepshead Bay rd. & Surf av., E. to Coney Island av.

Sea Gate av. (C 11), Bay View av., S. to Mermaid av.

Sea View av. (K 8), from Paerdegat av. North, N. E. to Fresh creek basin.

Seabring (C 5), 356 Columbia, N. W. to VanBrunt.

Sedgwick (C4), East River, bet. Irving & Degraw, S. E. to Columbia.

Sedgwick pl. (B 7), Wakeman pl., E. of 1st av., S. to 67th.

Seeley (E 6), 85 Gravesend av., N.E. to Coney Island av.

Seigel (G 3), 579 B'way, E. to Bogart.

Senator (B 7), from Colonial rd. at Bay Ridge Pk., E. to 6th av.

Seneca av. (H 3), 281 Randolph, N. to Newtown creek.

Sentinel pl. (L 5), 281 Euclid av., E.

Setauket (F 1), 69 Paidge av., N. E. to Newtown creek.

Sharon (G3), 40 Orient av., E. to Morgan av.

Shawnett (F 1), 9 Paidge av., N. E. to Newtown creek.

Sheepshead Bay rd. (E 11), W. 8th, S. of Neptune av., S. E. & E. to Coney Island av.

Sheepshead Bay rd. (F 10), Av. W. at E. 12th, S. E. to Emmons av. and E. 18th.

Sheepshead ct. (F 11), E. 16th to Sheepshead Bay rd.

Sheffield av. (K 5), 48 Jamaica av., S. E. to Vandalia av.

Shell rd. (E 10), Gravesend av. & Av. X, S. W. to Canal av.

Shepherd av. (L 4), Jamaica av., bet. Essex and Dresden, S. E. to Borden av.

Sheridan av. (L 5), 3488 Atlantic av., S. to Jamaica bay.

Sherlock pl. (J 5), 1398 Herkimer, S. to Atlantic av.

Sherman (E 6), 53 10th av., S.E. & S. to Ocean parkway.

Shore Boulevard (F 11), Neptune av., at Coney Island av., E. to end of Coney Island.

Shore rd. (B 7), 66th at 1st av., S. W., S. & S. E. to 4th av., at 101st.

Shore rd., 31st ward (F 10), Voorhies la., E. 16th, S. to Emmons av.

Sidney pl. (D 4), 128 Joralemon, S. to State.

Sigourney (C 5), 79 Otsego, S. E. to Gowanus bay.

Silliman pl. (B 7), now Ovington av.

Skidmore av. (K 8), from E 95th, nr. Canarsie pk., N. E. to 108th.

Skidmore la. (J 7), E. 92d, bet. Flatlands av. & Av. J, N. E. to E. 101st.

Skillman (F4), 414 Flushing av., S. to Lafayette av.

Skillman av. (F3), 236 Union av., E. to Kingsland av.

Slocum pl. (E 7), Coney Isl. av., bet. Matthews pl. and Cortelyou rd., E. to 12th.

Smith (D 4), 382 Fulton, S. W. to Gowanus bay.

301 300 Union.

577 544 Hamilton av.

Smiths al. (E 4), 240 High, S. to Nassau.

Smiths la., (E 4), E. 87th. n. Farragut rd., N. E. to Rockway pkway.

Snediker av. (J 5), 2486 Atlantic av, S. to Fresh creek.

Snyder av. (F 7), 945 Flatbush av., E. to Ralph av.

Somers (J 5), 2017 Fulton, E. to Broadway.

Somerset (G11), Shore blvd., E of Ripley, S. to Oriental blvd.

S. Elliott pl. (E 4), 185 DeKalb av., S. to Atlantic av.

S. Oxford (E 4), 156 DeKalb av., S to Atlantic av.

S. Portland av. (E 4), 144 De Kalb, S. to Atlantic av.

S. 1st (E 3), E R., bet. Grand & S. 2d, S. E. to Union av.

147 140 Bedford av.

— 402 Union av.

S. 2d (E 3), E.R., bet. S. 1st & S. 3d, S. E. to Union av.

139 140 Bedford av.

415 — Union av.

S. 3d (E 3), E. R. bet. S. 2d & S. 4th, S.E. to Union av.

127 130 Bedford av.

415 402 Union av.

S. 4th (E3), E.R., bet. S. 3d & S. 5th, S.E. to Union av.

129 126 Bedford av.

427 432 Union av

S. 5th (E3), E.R., bet. S. 4th & S. 6th, S.E. to Union av.

127 138 Bedford av.

445 464 Union av.

S. 6th (E 3), E. R., bet. S. 5th & B'way, S. E. to B'way.

119 — Bedford av.

S. 8th (E 3), E.R., bet. B'way & S. 9th, E. to B'way.

121 130 Bedford av.

S. 9th (E 3), E. R., bet. S. 8th & S. 10th, E. to Broadway.

125 116 Bedford av.

299 294 Broadway.

S. 10th (E 3), E. R., bet. S. 9th and S. 11th, E. to Bedford av.

S. 11th (E 3), E. R., bet. S. 10th & Division av., E. to Berry.

Southgate ct. (E 10), Stryker bet. Stryker ct. & Av. X, E. to W. 1st.

Spencer (F 4), 464 Flushing av., S. to DeKalb av.

Spencer ct. (F 4), 552 De Kalb av., S. to Kosciusko.

Spencer pl. (F 5), 28 Hancock, S. to Fulton.

Spoffard av. (J 6), now Stanley av.

Sprague's al. (D4), 225 Fulton, E. to Liberty.

Spring 1st (M 6), from Sheridan av., N. E. to Forbell av.

Spring 2d (M 6), from Sheridan av., N. E. to Forbell av.

Stagg (F 3), 80 Union av., E. to Newtown creek.

167 154 Graham av.

381 378 Morgan av.

Stanhope (H 4), 843 Bushwick av., N.E. to Cypress av.

Stanley av. (J 6), E. 98th at Hopkinson av, E. to Borough line.

Stanwix (G 4), 621 Bushwick av., N. to Flushing av.

Starr (H4), 125 Central av., N. E. to Borough line.

State (D 4), 363 Furman, S. E. to Flatbush av.

181 202 Court.

513 566 Flatbush av.

Stephens ct. (F 7), Flatbush av., bet. Newkirk & Foster avs., S. W.

Sterling (F 6), Washington av., bet. Lefferts av. & Empire blvd., E. to Brooklyn av.

Sterling pl. (E 5), 117 5th av., E. to East New York av.

177 184 Flatbush av.

458 458 Washington av.

939 940 New York av.

1441 1442 Utica av.

1927 1916 E. New York av.

Steuben (F 4), 292 Flushing av., S. to Lafayette av.

Stewart (J 3), 1941 B'way, N. E. to Evergreens cem.

Stewart av. (H 3) 1183 Flushing av., N. to Meeker av.

Stewart av. 30th ward (C 8), 7th av. at 66th, S. to 5th av.

Stilwell (D 10), Mill rd. at Bay 43d, S. W. to Gravesend bay.

Stillwell av. (D 9), Bay p'kway, n. Av. P, to Surf.

Stilwell la. (K 7), E. 92d, n. Av. K, S. W. to E. 88th.

Stockholm (H 4), 819 Bushwick av., N. E. to Borough line.

Stockton (F 4), 115 Nostrand av., E. to B'way.

Stoddard pl. (F 6), Montgomery, E. of Bedford av., S. W. to Sullivan.

Stone av. (J 5), 1806 B'way, S. to Av. D.

201 202 Dean.

365 366 Pitkin av.

641 642 Livonia av.

Story (E 7), West av. bet. Louisa & Church av., S. W. to 36th.

Stratford rd. (E 7), Caton av., bet Westminster rd. & E. 10th, S to Foster av.

Strong pl. (D 4), 174 Harrison, S. to Degraw

Stryker (D 10), Mill rd. at Bay 40th, S. W. to Gravesend bay.

Stryker (E 10), E. 2d, n. Av. R, S. to Av. X.

Stryker ct. (E 10), from Stryker S. of Av. W, E. to W. 1st.

Stuart (G 9), Nostrand av., at Av. Q. S. E. to Av. X.

Stuyvesant av. (G 4), 958 B'way, S. to Fulton.

157 168 Lexington av.

429 440 Fulton.

Sullivan (C 5), 90 Dwight, N. W. to N. Y. bay.

Sullivan, 29th ward (F 6), 1189 Washington av., E. to Nostrand av.

Summit (C 5), 15 Conover, S. E. to Henry.

Sumner av. (G 4), 270 Hopkins, S. to Fulton.

289 286 Gates av.

505 500 Fulton.

Sumner pl. (G4), 771 B'way, N. E. to Flushing av.

Sumpter (H 5), 1808 Fulton, E. to B'way.

Sunnyside av. (K 5), Vermont, n. Highland boulevard, E. to Highland pk.

Sunnyside ct. (K5), Sunnyside av., opp. Barbey, to Highland park.

Surf av. (H 4), W. 5th, opp Concourse drive, W. & N. W. to Gravesend bay.

Sutter av. (H 6), E. 98th, bet. E. N. Y. av., & Blake av. to Borough line.

87 88 Saratoga av.

663 664 New Jersey av.

1267 1268 Euclid av

Sutton (G 2), 177 Meeker av., N to Norman av.

Suydam (H 4), 1033 Broadway, N.E. to Boro. line.

Suydam la. (H 6), Church av., n. Utica av., S. to Canarsie la.

Suydam pl. (H5), 808 Herkimer, S.W. to Atlantic av.

Sycamore (E 4), 39 Raymond, S. E. to St. Edwards.

Taaffe pl. (F4), 348 Flushing av., S. to Lafayette av.

BOROUGH OF BROOKLYN STREET AND AVENUE DIRECTORY—*Continued.*

Talman (D 4), 119 Pearl, E. to Charles.
Tapscott (H 6), E. N. Y. av. bet. Union & Howard av., S. E. to 98th.
Taylor (E 3), 29 Washington av., N. E. to Lee av.
Tehama (E 7), 94 West av., S. W. to 36th.
Temple ct. (E6), Seeley, bet. Coney Island av. & 17th, N. W.
Temple sq. (E 4), Flatbush av. at Schermerhorn.
Ten Eyck (F 3), 98 Union av., E. to Metropolitan av.
377 392 Morgan av.
528 576 Metropolitan av.
Tennis ct. (F 7), 111 E. 18th, E. to Ocean av.
Terrace pl. (E 6), 61 Gravesend av., N. E. to Prospect av.
Thames (H 3), 38 Bogart E. to Flushing av.
Thatford av. (J 5), East New York av., at Liberty av., S. to Av. D.
Thomas (G 2), 554 Varick av., N.E. to Newt'n creek.
Thompson pl. (E 11), W. 5th bet. Sheepshead Bay rd. & Sea Breeze av., W.
Thornhill (G 11), Shore blvd, E. of Somerset S. to Oriental blvd.
Thornton (G 4), 125 Throop av., N. E. to B'way.
Throop av. (G4), 584 B'way, S. to Fulton.
288 246 Myrtle av.
449 480 Gates av.
639 660 Fulton.
Tiffany pl. (C4), 100 Harrison, S. to Degraw.
Tilden av. (F 7), 1011 Flatbush av., E. to Ralph av.
Tillary (D 4), 279 Fulton, to St. Edwards.
Times Plaza (E 4), at Junction of Flatbush av., Atlantic av. and 4th av.
Tompkins av. (G 4), 650 Flushing av., S. to Fulton.
118 106 Myrtle av.
321 316 Gates av.
497 494 Fulton.
Tompkins pl. (D 4), 224 Harrison, S. to Degraw.
Townsend (G 2), 558 Stewart av., N. E. to Newtown creek.
Tremont (C 5), now Visitation pl.
Troutman (G4), 1171 Myrtle av., N.E. to Borough line.
Troy av. (G 5), 1628 Fulton, S. to Flatbush av.
117 126 Bergen.
285 292 Eastern p'kway.
401 408 Montgomery.
Truxton (J 5), 2091 Fulton, E. to B'way.
Turner pl. (E 7), E. 8th. bet. Church av. and Hinkley pl., E. to E. 11th.
Underhill av. (F 5), 908 Atlantic av., S. to Eastern p'kway.
Underhill pl. (E5), Eastern p'kway, opp. Underhill av., S.W. to Flatbush av.
Union, 26th ward (L 4), Autumn av., bet. Etna & Ridgewood av., S. & E. to Eldert la.
Union (C 4), from 5 Hamilton av., S.E. to Rochester av., and from Portal at Lincoln Terrace pk., S. E. and S. to E. 98th.
299 284 Court.
599 560 Third av.
917 870 Eighth av.
1405 1366 Brooklyn av.
Union av. (F 3), 511 B'way, N. to N. 12th.
121 130 Grand.
* 236 Skillman av.
315 — N. 12th.
Union la. (D 4), 34 Myrtle av., S.
Union pl. (L 4), from Autumn av. to Grant av.
United States (E 3), 17 Little, E. to Navy Yard.
Utica av. (H 5), 1752 Fulton, S. to Flatbush av.
109 110 Bergen.
319 320 President.
865 866 Church av.
1341 1342 Foster av.
Van Brunt (C4), 22 Harrison S. W. to New York bay.
309 336 King.
Van Buren (G4), 254 Tompkins av. E. & N. E. to Bushwick av.
Vandalia av. (K 7), from Louisiana av., N. E. to Spring creek, thence E. to Borough line.
Vandalia 1st to Vandalia 10th (K 7) inclusive, fr. Louisiana av., N. E. to Pennsylvania av.
Vandam (G 2), 257 Meeker av., N.E. to Newtown cr'k.
Vanderbilt (E 6), 123 Gravesend av., N. E. to Coney Island av.
Vanderbilt av. (E 4), 144 Flushing av., S. to Flatbush av.
159 148 Myrtle av,
545 512 Atlantic av.
711 680 Plaza.
Vanderveer (J 5), 1915 B'way, N. E. to Evergreens cemetery.
Vanderveer pl. (F 7), Flatbush av., opp. E. 23d, E. to E. 23d.
'**Vandervoort av.** (G 3), 1077 Grand, N. to Meeker av.
Vandervoort pl. (H 3), 56 Thames, S. to Flushing av.
Vandyke (C 5), 80 Otsego. N. W., to New York bay.
Van Houten's la. (J 7), E. 91st, n. Av. J, E. to E. 96th.
Van Sicklen (E 9), Kings Highway, bet. Kings pl. & Lake pl., S. to 86th.
Van Sicklen av. (K 5), 206 Jamaica av., S.E. to Borden av.
293 294 Pitkin av.
Van Sinderen av. (J 5), Fulton, bet. Sackman & Williams pl., S. to Fresh crk.
Varet (G 3), 639 B'way, E. to Bogart.
Varick (G 2), 295 Meeker av., N. to Newtown creek.
Varick av. (H 3), 1145 Flushing av., N. to Meeker av.
249 248 Grand.
463 464 Division pl.
Varkens Hook rd. (J 7), E. 88th, at Canarsie la., S. to Meadow la.
Verandah pl. (D 4), 375 Henry, E. to Clinton.
Vermont (K5), 2366 Eastern pkway, S. and S. E. to Collins av.
105 106 Fulton.
305 306 Pitkin av.
Vermont av. (K 4), from Highland blvd., N. E. to Boro line (thence in Boro of Queens.)
Vernon av. (F 4), 158 Nostrand av., E. to B'way.
271 272 Sumner av.
408 412 B'way.
Verona (C 5), 404 Columbia, N. W. to Conover.
Verona pl. (G 5), 86 Macon, S. to Fulton.
Vienna av. (J 6), name changed to Lorraine av.
Village rd. (E 10), Van Sicklen, S. of Av. V, E. & N. to Johnson's la.
Vine (D 3), 27 Columbia hgts., E. to McKinney.
Virginia pl. (H 5), 1182 Park pl., S. to Sterling pl.
Visitation pl. (C 5), 426 Columbia, N. W. to Van Brunt
Voorhies av. (F 10), Hubbard, bet. Av. Z & Canal av., E. to Knapp.
Voorhies la. (F10), Sheepshead Bay rd, bet. Av. Z & Voorhies av., N. E. to Ocean av.
Waalbocht pl. (E3), Washington av., S. of Taylor, S. E. to Hewes.
Wakeman pl. (B7), Colonial rd., N. of 67th, E. to 3d av.
Walsh ct. (E8), from E. 3d, S of Foster av. E. to E. 5th.
Waldorf ct. (F 8), 735 Rugby rd., E. to E. 17th.
Waldron pl. (D 3), 129 York, N
Wallabout (F 4), Williamsburgh road, bet. Flushing av. & Wallabout canal, E. to B'way.
— 238 Nostrand av.
341 426 Broadway.
Walton (F 4), 198 Wallabout, N. E. to B'way.
Walworth (F 4), 484 Flushing av., S. to DeKalb av.
Warehouse (K 6), now Will pl.
Warehouse av. (B 9), Battery av., at 106th, S. E. & S. to Atlantic ocean.
Warren (C 4), E. R., bet. Congress & Baltic, S. E. to 5th av.
239 264 Court.
667 696 Fifth av.
Warren pl.' (D 4), 148 Warren, S. to Baltic.
Warwick (K 5), Highland Boulevard, E. of Barbey, S. E. to Borden av.
201 202 Fulton.
417 418 Pitkin av.
Washington (D 3), E. R., bet. Main & Adams, S. to Fulton.
Washington av. (E 3), 556 Kent av., S. to Flatbush av.
179 176 Myrtle av.
307 306 DeKalb av.
507 530 Fulton.
659 684 St. Marks av.
Washington av., 29th ward (E 8), now part of Parkville av.
Washington pl. (F6), Washington av., N. of Sullivan, N.E. to Franklin av.
Washington pl. (L4), from W. side of Crescent, S. of Jamaica av.
Washington Plaza (F 3), at Brooklyn end of Williamsburg Bridge.
Water (D 3), 1 Fulton, E. to Hudson av.
Water, 17th ward (F 1), 428 Oakland, S. E. to Shawnett.
Waterbury (G 3), 303 Johnson av., N. to Grand.
Waters av. (C 9), Kings Highway, bet. 13th & 14th avs., S. W. to Benson av.
Watkins (J 5), E. N. Y. av., bet. Osborn & Stone av., S. to Av. D.
Waverly av. (E 4), 188 Flushing av., S. to Atlantic av.
155 152 Myrtle av.
495 492 Fulton.
Way-home (E 4), 219 Gold, runs E.—half block.
Webster av. (E 8), 47th, bet. 18th & Lawrence avs., N. E. to Coney Island av.
Webster pl. (D 6), 264 16th, S. W. to Prospect av.
Weirfield (J 4), 1551 B'way, N. E. to Borough line.
Weldon (L 5), Conduit av., bet. Glen & Magenta, E. to Autumn av.
Wellington ct. (F 8), 769 Rugby rd., E. to E. 17th.
West (F 2), Bushwick creek, bet. Franklin & E. R., N. to Newtown creek.
West, 29th ward (E 7), that part from Ft. Hamilton Parkway to Kings Highway, now known as Dahill rd.
West (E 10), from Av. U, E. of Gravesend av., S. to Canal av.
West av. 19th ward (E 4), Flushing av., bet. Washington & Market avs., N. to Waalbocht pl.
West av. 31st ward (E 11), bet. Canal & Neptune avs., E. to Ocean p'kway.
West End av. (F11), Shore blvd., W. of Amherst, S. to Oriental boulevard.
W. 1st (E9), 65th, bet. West & W. 2d, to Sea Breeze av.
W. 2d (E 9), 65th E. of 24th av., S. to Sea Breeze av.
W. 3d (E9), Av. O at 65th, S to Av. S, & fm. Av. X, S. to Sea Breeze av.
W. 4th (E 9), 65th, S. to Av. T.
W. 5th (E9), 65th, opp. 23d av., S. to Atlantic ocean.
W. 6th (E 9), 65th, bet. 22d av. & Bay p'kway, S. to Sheepshead Bay rd.
W. 7th (E 9), Bay p'kway, opp. 66th, S. to Av. X.
W. 8th (E 9), Bay p'kway, opp. 67th, S. to Av. X, & fm. Canal av. to Atlantic ocean.
W. 9th, 31st ward (E 9), Bay p'kway, S. to Av. X.
W. 9th (C 5), 489 Columbia. S. E. to Smith.
W. 10th (D9), Bay p'kway, opp. 70th, S. to Canal av., & fm. Surf av., S. to Atlantic ocean.
W. 11th (D9), Bay p'kway, opp. 71st, S. to Canal av.
W. 12th (D9), Bay p'kway, bet. 71st and 72d, S. to Surf av.
W. 13th (D9), Bay p'kway, opp. 74th. S. to Canal av.
W. 15th (D 10), Av. Y, S. to Surf av.
W. 16th (D 10), Av. Y, S. to Atlantic ocean.
W. 17th (D 10), Av. Y, S. to Surf av.
W. 18th (D 11), Av. Z, to Canal av.

BOROUGH OF BROOKLYN STREET AND AVENUE DIRECTORY—*Continued.*

W. 19th to W. 21st inclusive (D 11) from Av. Z the streets run alternately to Surf av. & to Atlantic ocean. There is no W. 22d st.

W. 23d (D 11), from Canal av., S. to Atlantic ocean.

W. 24th (D 11), from Canal av., S. to Surf av.

W. 25th to W. 30th, inclusive (D 11). from Canal av., S. to Atlantic ocean. There is no W. 26th st.

W. 31st (D 11), from Canal av., S. to Surf av.

W. 32d (D 11), from Canal av., S. to Atlantic ocean.

W. 33rd (D11), from Canal av., S. to Surf av.

W. 35th (C 11), fr. Gravesend Bay, S. to Atlantic ocean.

W. 36th (C 11), fr. Gravesend Bay. S. to Surf av.

W. 37th (C 11), Bay View av., S. to Atlantic ocean.

Westminster rd. (E 7), Caton av., bet. Argyle & Stratford rds., S. to Av. H.

Whipple (G4), 669 Flushing av., N E. to Broadway.

White (G 3), 209 Cook, N. to Johnson av.

Whitwell pl. (D 5), 504 Carroll, S. W. to 1st.

Will pl. (K 6). from Williams av., S. of Vienna av., E. to Louisiana av.

Williams ct. (F 10), from E. 11th to E. 12th, S. of av. Z.

Williams av. (J 5), East New York av. bet. Hinsdale & Alabama av., S. to Fresh creek.

Williams pl. (J 5), 2486 Fulton. S.W. to East New York av.

Williamsburgh rd. (F 4), 307 Flushing av., N. to Wallabout.

Willinck (F6), Washington av., S. of Montgomery E. to Franklin av.

Willoughby (D 4), 405 Fulton. E. to St. Edwards.

Willoughby av. (E 4), 177 Washington Park, E. to Borough line.

203 202 Grand av.
371 372 Bedford av.
511 512 Marcy av.
867 878 Broadway.
1099 1100 Wilson av.
1419 1420 Cypress av.

Willow (D 3), 20 Poplar, S.W. to Pierrepont.

Willow pl (D 4) 52 Joralemon, S. W. to State.

Wilson (E 3), Wallabout canal, bet. Taylor & Ross, N. E. to Division av.

Wilson av. (H3), 1002 Flushing av., S. E. to Evergreens cemetery.

275 260 Greene av.
487 472 Jefferson av.

Windsor pl. (D 6) 477 7th av., S.E. to Coney Isl'd av.

Winthrop (F 6), 675 Flatbush av. E. to E. 98th.

Withers (F 3), 269 N. 9th, E. to Newtown creek.

Wolcott (C 5), 110 Dwight, N. W. to New York bay.

Wood pl. (J 4), 61 Autumn av., E. to Nichols av.

Woodbine (H4), 1407 Broadway, N.E. to Borough line.

Woodhull (C 5), 111 Hamilton av., S. E. to Henry.

Woodruff av. (F 6), Parade pl., bet. Parkside av. & Crooke av., N. E. to Flatbush av.

Woodside av. (F9), Gravesend av., S. of Av. Q, E to E. 2d.

Wortman av. (K 6), Louisiana av., bet. Stanley & Cozine av., N. E. to Borough line.

Wyckoff (D 4), 208 Court, E. to Third av.

Wyckoff av. (H 3), 1224 Flushing av., S. E. to Borough line.

Wyona (K 5), 146 Jamaica av., S. & S.E. to Borden av.

119 100 DeKalb av.
261 290 Ralph av.

Wythe av. (F 2), 146 Banker, S. E. & S. W. to Wallabout.

271 306 Grand.
505 542 Division av.
745 780 Rutledge.

York (D 3), 71 Fulton, E. to Navy.

1st (D 5), 361 Hoyt, S. E. to Prospect Park West.

1st, 29th ward (E 8), 18th av. at E. 8th, S.E. to Foster av.

1st av. (C6), E. 40th, at Gowanus bay, S. W. to 66th.

1st pl. (C 5). 587 Henry, S. E. to Smith.

1st pl. 31st ward (E 10), Lake S. of Village rd., E. to Gravesend av.

2d (D 5), 363 Smith, S. E. to Prospect Park W.

2d av. (D 5), Gowanus canal, at 5th, S.W. to Bay Ridge parkway.

2d pl. (C 5), 607 Henry, S. E. to Smith.

2d pl., 31st ward (E 10), Van Sicklen, S. of Village rd., E. to Gravesend av.

3d (D 5), 383 Smith, S. E. to Prospect Park W.

227 230 Third av.
571 574 Eighth av.

3d, 29th ward (E 8), 18th av., E. of Gravesend av., S. E. to Foster av.

3d av. (E 4), 70 Flatbush av., S. W. to N. Y. bay.

249 250 Union.
455 460 Ninth.
755 754 Twenty-fifth.
3901 3902 Thirty-ninth.
6001 6002 Sixtieth.
7123 7184 Seventy-second.
9923 — One hundredth.

3d pl. (D 5), 627 Henry, S. E. to Smith.

3d pl., 31st ward (E 10), Van Sicklen at Av. W, E. to Lake pl.

4th (D 5), 403 Smith, S. E. to Prospect Park W.

4th av. (E 5), 122 Flatbush av., S. to Bay Ridge parkway.

211 222 Union.
485 444 Ninth.
747 758 Twenty-fifth.
3901 3902 Thirty-ninth.
6001 6002 Sixtieth.
9923 9924 One-hundredth.

4th pl. (D 5), 647 Henry, S. E. to Smith.

5th (D 5), 423 Smith, S. E. to Prospect Park W.

333 338 Fifth av.

5th av. (E 5), 620 Atlantic av., S. W. to 4th av. at 95th.

205 208 Union.
441 444 Ninth.
* 748 Twenty-fifth.
3901 3902 Thirty-ninth.
6001 6002 Sixtieth.
7101 7102 Seventy-first.
9501 9502 Ninety-fifth.

6th (D 5), 443 Smith, S.E. to Prospect Park W.

331 340 Fifth av.

6th av. (E 5), 674 Atlantic av., S. W. to Fort Hamilton Parkway.

207 202 Union.
441 432 Ninth.
689 670 Twentieth.
3901 3902 Thirty-ninth.
6001 6002 Sixtieth.
7101 7102 Seventy-first.
8401 8402 Eighty-fourth.

7th (D 5), 451 Smith, S. E. to Prospect Park W.

331 324 Fifth av.

7th av. (E 5), 300 Flatbush av., S W. to 107th.

207 212 Third.
327 328 Ninth.
569 572 Twentieth.
3901 3902 Thirty-ninth.
6001 6002 Sixtieth.
7101 7102 Seventy-first.

8th (D5), 2d, bet. 7th & 9th, S.E. to Prospect Park W.

281 280 Fifth av.

8th av. (E 5), 364 Flatbush av., S. W. to 7th av. at 73d.

901 902 Ninth.
1901 1902 Nineteenth.
3901 3902 Thirty-ninth.
6001 6002 Sixtieth.

9th (D 5), 501 Smith, S. E. to Prospect Park W.

183 190 Third av.
571 584 Prospect P'k W.

9th av. (C 7), 37th, S. W. to Fort Hamilton pkway.

3701 3702 Thirty-seventh.
5701 5702 Fifty-seventh.
— 6901 Ovington av.

10th (D 5), Gowanus canal, bet. 9th & 11th, S. E. to Prospect Park W.

371 372 Fifth av.

10th av. (E 6), 517 15th, S. W. to 7th av.

11th (D 5), Gowanus canal, bet. 10th & 12th, S. E. to Prospect Park W.

327 328 Fifth av.

11th av. (E 6), 547 15th, S. W. to Dyker Heights Park.

12th (D5). Gowanus canal. bet. 11th & 13th, S. E. to Prospect Park W.

281 280 Fifth av.

12th av. (E 7). West av., bet. Minna & Tehama, S. W. to Dyker Heights Pk.

13th (D 5), Gowanus canal, bet. 12th & Hamilton av., S. E. to Prospect Pk. W.

267 270 Fifth av.

13th av. (D7), 36th opp. Louisa, S. W. to Benson av.

14th (D 5), from 435 Hamilton av., S. E to Prospect Park W.

249 258 Fifth av.

14th av. (E 7), 206 West, S. W. to Benson av.

15th (D 5). 473 Hamilton av., S.E. to Coney Isl. av.

211 214 Fifth av.
479 484 Prospect Pk. W.

15th av. (E 7), West av., at 36th, S. W. to Gravesend bay.

16th (D 6), 501 Hamilton av., S. E. to Coney Is. av.

205 174 Fifth av.
463 434 Prospect P'k W.

16th av. (E 7), West av., at 39th, S. W. to Gravesend bay.

17th (D 6), Gowanus bay, bet. Prospect av. & 18th, S. E. to Terrace pl.

247 240 Fifth av.
491 498 Prospect P'k W.

17th av. (E8). West av., at 42d, S. W. to Gravesend bay.

18th (D 6), Gowanus bay, bet. 17th & 19th, S. E. to Vanderbilt.

233 238 Fifth av.
501 494 Prospect Pk. W.

18th av. (E 8), Coney Island av., opp. Ditmas av., S. E. to Cropsey av.

19th (D 6), Gowanus bay, bet. 18th & 20th, S. E. to Vanderbilt.

239 238 Fifth av.
485 478 Prospect P'k W.

19th av. (E 8), West av., at 47th, S. W. to Gravesend bay.

20th (D 6), Gowanus bay, bet. 19th & 21st, S. E. to Vanderbilt.

241 238 Fifth av.
491 486 Prospect P'k W.

20th av. (E 8), West av., at 50th, S. W. to Gravesend bay.

21st (D 6), Gowanus bay, bet. 20th & 22d, S. E. to Gravesend av.

21st av. (E 8), West av., at 53d, S. W. to Graves'd bay.

22d (H 6). Gowanus bay, bet. 21st & 23d, S. E. to West av.

22d av., Bay parkway (E 8), Ocean parkway, bet. Avs. I & J, S. W. to Gravesend bay.

23d (D6). Gowanus bay, bet. 22d & 24th. S. E. to 7th av.

23d av. (E 9). West av., at 59th, S. W. to Gravesend bay.

24th (C 6), Gowanus bay, bet. 23d & 25th, S. E. to 6th av.

24th av. (E 9), West av., bet. 61st and 62d, S. W. to Cropsey av.

25th (C 6), Gowanus bay, bet. 24th & 26th. S. E. to 5th av.

25th av. (D 10). Stillwell av., at 84th, S. W. to Gravesend bay.

26th (C 6), Gowanus bay, bet. 25th & 27th, S. E. to 5th av.

26th av. (D 10), Stillwell av., nr. 86th, S. W. to Gravesend bay.

27th (C 6), Gowanus bay, bet. 26th & 28th, S. E. to 5th av.

27th av. (D 10). Stillwell av., at Bath av., S. W. to Gravesend bay.

28th (C 6), Gowanus bay, bet. 27th & 29th, S. E. to 5th av.

28th av. (D 10), Bath av. nr. Stillwell av., S. W. to Gravesend bay.

29th to 34th, inclusive (C 6), Gowanus bay, S. E. to 5th av.

35th (C 6), Gowanus bay, S. E. to 4th av., and 14th av. to West.

36th (C6), Gowanus bay bet. 35th & 37th. S.E. to West.

37th (C 6), Gowanus bay, bet. 36th & 38th, S. E. to West.

38th (C6), Gowanus bay, at 2d av., S.E. to West.

BOROUGH OF BROOKLYN STREET AND AVENUE DIRECTORY—*Continued.*

39th (C 6), Gowanus bay, bet. 38th & 40th, S. E. to West.

40th (C 6), 1st av., bet. 39th and 41st. S. E. to West.

41st (C 6), 1st av., bet. 40th & 42d, S. E. to West.

42d (C 6), 1st av., bet. 41st & 43d, S. E. to West.

43d (C 6), 1st av., bet. 42d & 44th, S. E. to West.

44th (C 6), 1st av., bet. 43d & 45th, S. E. to West.

45th (C6), 1st av., bet. 44th and 46th, S.E. to 18th av.

46th (B 6), 1st av., bet. 45th and 47th, S. E. to 18th av.

47th (B6), 1st av., bet. 46th & 48th, S. E. to Gravesend av.

48th (B7), 1st av., bet. 47th & 49th, S. E. to West.

49th (B 7), 1st av., bet. 48th & 50th, S. E. to West.

50th (B 6). New York bay, bet. 49th & 51st, S. E. to West.

51st (B 6), New York bay, bet. 50th & 52d, S. E. to West.

52d (B 6), New York bay, bet. 51st & 53d, S. E. to West.

53d(B7), NewYork bay, bet. 52d & 54th, S. E. to West.

54th (B 8), New York bay, bet. 53d & 55th. S. E. to West.

55th (B 8), New York bay. bet. 54th & 56th, S. E. to 19th av.

56th (B 8), New York bay, bet. 55th & 57th, S. E. to 19th av.

57th (B 8), New York bay. bet. 56th & 58th, S. E. to West.

58th (B 8), New York bay, bet. 57th & 59th, S. E. to West.

59th (B 8), New York bay, bet. 58th & 60th, S. E. to West.

60th (B 8), New York bay, S. E. to Gravesend av.

61st to 64th inclusive (B 8), New York bay, S. E to West.

65th (B 8), New York bay, S. E. to Gravesend av.

66th to 68th inclusive (B 9), New York bay, S. E. to 22d av., Bay parkway.

69th (A 7), now Bay R'ge av.

70th (A 7), New York bay, n. Mackay pl., E. to 2d av., and from 7th av., opp. Ovington av., S. E. to 22d av., Bay parkway.

71st to 75th inclusive (A 7 & 8), New York bay, E. to 22d av., Bay parkway.

76th (A 8), 1725 Narrows av., S. W. to Bay parkway

77th (A 8), New York bay, S. E. to Bay parkway.

78th (A 8), 7725 Narrows av., S. E. to Stillwell av.

79th to 83d, inclusive (A 8), New York bay, S. E. to Stillwell av.

84th (A 8), Colonial rd., bet. 83d and 85th, S. E. to Stillwell av.

85th (A 8), 8428 Narrows av., S. E. to Stillwell av.

86th (A 8), Shore rd., E. to Gravesend av.
499 500 5th av.
1099 1100 11th av.
— 1672 17th av.

87th (A8), New York bay, S. E. to 5th Av.

88th (A8), New York bay S. E. to 7th av.

89th (A 8), 8823 Narrows av., S. E. to 5th av.

90th (A 8), Ridge blvd., S. E. to 7th av.

91st (A 8), New York bay, S. E. to 5th av.

92d (A 8), New York bay, S. E. to 7th av.

93d (A 8), New York bay, E. & S. E. to 4th av.

94th & 95th (A 9), New York bay, E. & S. E. to Ft. Hamilton parkway.

96th (A 9), New York bay, E. & S. E. to 4th av.

97th & 99th (A9), N. Y. bay. E. to Ft. Hamilton pkway

100th (A9) 9928 3d av., S. E. to Ft. Hamilton pkway.

101st (A 9), from 3d av., S. E. to Ft. Hamilton av.

102d (B 9), Battery av., S. E. to 7th av.

103d (B 9), Battery av., S. E. to 7th av.

105th (B9), Battery av., S. E. to 7th av.

BOROUGH OF MANHATTAN STREET AND AVENUE DIRECTORY

Note that in case of long thoroughfares, important cross streets with corner numbers are given. With these numbers and by referring to the maps, the location of any point in the city can readily be ascertained.

The letters and numbers following names indicate position of the thoroughfare on the map in pocket of the Almanac.

Abingdon sq. (B13), Bleecker, from Bank to 8th av., from 2 to 20, 8th av., and from 585 to 609 Hudson.

Academy (B 5), fr. Harlem River, N. of Dyckman, N. W. to Seaman av.

Adrian av. (B 4), fr Terrace View av. n. W. 225th, N. to W. 228th.

Albany (C 15), from 122 Greenwich. W. to N. R.

Alexander Hamilton sq. (B 7), at junction of Amsterdam av. & Hamilton pl., W. 143d to W. 144th.

Allen (D 14), from 104 Division, N. to E. Houston.

Amsterdam av. (B 11), continuation of 10th av., fr. W. 59th. N. to Ft. George av.
585 W. 86th. 986 W. 106th.
1815 W. 125th. 1917 W. 155th.

Ann (C 15), fr. 222 Broadway, E. to Gold.

Arden (B5), fr. Naegle av., bet. Sickles and Thayer, N. W. to Broadway.

Astor ct. (C12), from 21 W. 33d, N. to W. 34th.

Astor pl. (C 13), from 744 Broadway, E. to 3d av.

Attorney (D 14), 236 Division, N. to E. Houston.

Audubon av. (B 6), from St. Nicholas av. at W. 165th, bet. Amsterdam av. and Broadway, N. to Fort George av.

Audubon pl. (B7), fr B'way at W. 157th, N. to W. 158th.

Av. A (D 14), from 230 E. Houston, N. to E. 93d.
224 E. 14th. 372 E. 23d.

Av. B (D 14), from 294 E. Houston, N. to E. R.
282 281 E. 14th.

Av. C (D 14), from 358 E. Houston, N. to E. R.

Av. D (E 14), from 426 E. Houston, N. to E. R.

B st. (A 5), 284 Dyckman, S

Bank (C 13). fr. 85 Greenwich av., W. to N. R.

Barclay (C 15), from 227 B'way, W. to N. R.

Barrow (C 14), from 134 Washington pl., W. to N. R.

Batavia (D 15), from 78 Roosevelt, E. to James.

Battery pl. (C 15), from 1 B'way, W. to N. R.

Baxter (D 15), from 166 Park row, N. to Grand.

Bayard (D 14), from 70 Division, W. to Baxter.

Beach (C 14), from 250 W. B'way, W. to N. R.

Beaver (C 15), from 8 Broadway, E. to Pearl.

Bedford (C 14), fr. 180 W. Houston, N. to Ch'topher.

Beekman (C 15), from 34 Park row, S. E. to E. R.

Beekman pl. (D12), from 429 E. 49th, N. to E. 51st.

Bennett av. (B 6), W. 181st, W. of B'way, N. & E. to B'way.

Benson (C 14), from 107 Leonard, N.

Bethune (B 13), from 591 Hudson, W. to N. R.

Birmingham (D 14), from 84 Henry, S. to Madison.

Bishop's la. (C 15), 174 Chambers, S. to Warren.

Bleecker (D14), 318 Bowery W. and N. to 8th av.
138-139 W Broadway.

Bloomfield (B 13), from 7 10th av., W. to N. R.

Bolton av. (B5), fr. B'wy & Dyckman, N. W. to Spuyten Duyvil creek.

Bond (C 14), from 658 B'way, E. to Bowery.

Bowery (D 14), from 13 Chatham sq., N. to E. 4th.
284 279 E. Houston.

Bowling gr. (C 15), from Whitehall, W. to State.

Bradhurst av. (B 7), junction of Edgecombe av. & W. 142d., N. to W. 155th

Bridge (C 15), from 15 State. E. to Broad.

Broad (C 15), from 21 Wall, S. to E. R.

Broadway (C 15), from 1 Battery pl., N. to Spuyten Duyvil creek (cont. in the Borough of the Bronx).
207 210 Fulton.
271 — Chambers.
417 416 Canal.
461 458 Grand.
641 640 Bleecker.
853 858 E. 14th.
957 958 E. 23d.
1311 1300 W. 34th.
1467 1470 W. 42d.
1805 1810 W. 59th.
2079 — W. 72d.
2315 2318 W. 84th.
— 2556 W. 96th.
2755 2756 W. 106th.
3137 3134 W. 125th.
3329 — W. 135th.
3741 3740 W. 155th.
4341 — W. 185th
— 5100 W. 219th.
5147 — Indian road.
— 5228 W. 226th.
5241 — W. 228th.

Broadway al. (D 13), fr. 158 E. 26th, N. to E. 27th.

Broadway ter. (B 6), from Fairview av. E. to W. 193d, E. of Broadway.

Broome (E 14), from 15 East, W. to Hudson.
337 336 Bowery.
441 442 Broadway.
499 500 W. Broadway.

Bryant park (C 12), bet. 5th & 6th avs., W. 40th and W. 42d.

Buena Vista av. (B 6), now Haven av.

Burling sl. (D15), from 234 Pearl, S. E. to E. R.

C st. (A 5), from Dyckman, W. of B st., S.

Canal (D 14), from 182 East Broadway, W. to N. R.
283 B'way. 375 W. B'way.

Cannon (E 14), from 538 Grand, N. to E. Houston.

Carlisle (C 15), from 112 Greenwich, W. to N. R.

Carmine (C 14), from No. 1 6th av., W. to Varick.

Caroline (C 15), from 211 Duane, N. to Jay.

Catharine (D 14), from 1 Division, S. to Cherry.

Catharine la. (C 14), fr. 344 B'way, E. to Lafayette.

Catharine sl. (D15), fr. 115 Cherry, S. to East River.

Cathedral p'kway (C 9), W. 110th from 5th av. to Riverside Drive.

Cedar (C 15), from 181 Pearl, W. to N. R.

Central pk. S. (C 11), W. 59th, 5th av. to 8th av.

Central park W. (B11), 8th av., W. 59th to W. 110th.

Centre (C 15), from City Hall Park, N. to Broome.

Centre mkt. pl. (C 14), 172 Grand, N. to Broome.

Chambers (C 15), from 96 Park row, W. to North River.

Charles (C 13), fr. 87 Greenwich av., W. to North R.

Charles la. (B 13), from 692 Washington, W. to West.

Charlton (C 14), from 29 Macdougal, W. to North River.

Chatham sq. (D 14). from 2 Mott, E. & S. to Oliver.

Chelsea sq. (B13), bet. 9th & 10th avs. and W 20th and 21st.

Cherry (D 15), from 340 Pearl, E. to East River.

Chestnut (D 15), from 8 Oak, N. to Madison.

Chittenden av. (A 6), from Northern av., N. of W. 181st, W. & N. to Riverside Drive.

BOROUGH OF MANHATTAN STREET AND AVENUE DIRECTORY—*Continued.*

Chittenden pl. (A 5), from Chittenden av., N. to Northern av.

Christopher(C13),3 Greenwich av., W. to North River.

Chrystie (D 14), 44 Division, N. to E. Houston.

Church (C 15), from 99 Liberty, N. to Canal.

City Hall pl.(C 15), from 15 Chambers,N.E. to Pearl.

Claremont av. (B 9), W. 116th, bet. Broadway and Riverside Drive, N. to W. 127th.

Claremont pl. (B 8), from Claremont av., N. of W. 122d, W. to Riverside Dr.

Clarke (C 14), from 538 Broome, N. to Spring.

Clarkson st. (C 14), from 225 Varick, W. to North River.

Cleveland pl. (C 14), from 404 Broome, N. to Spring. Formerly called Marion.

Clevelandsq.(D14), Public place to front the Manhattan Bridge terminal.

Cliff(D 15), from 101 John, N. E. to Hague.

Clinton(D 14), from 298 E. Houston,S. to East River.

Clinton ct. (C 13), r. 52 W. 8th.

Coenties' al. (C 15), from 73 Pearl to 40 Stone

Coenties' sl. (C15), from 66 Pearl, S. to East River.

Cold Spring rd. (B4), fr.W. 218th, W. to Indian rd.

Collister (C 14), from 51 Beach, N. to Laight.

Colonial parkway (B 7), fr. W. 155th and St. Nicholas pl., N. to Amsterdam av.

Columbia (E 14), from 520 Grand, N to E. Houston.

Columbia pl. (D 13), E. 8th, bet. Av. C and Av. D.

Columbus av. (B 11), continuation of 9th av., from W. 59th, N. to W. 110th.
254 257 W. 72d.
534 — W. 86th.
934 935 W. 106th.

Columbus Circle (B 11), B'way & 8th av., W. 58th to W. 60th.

Columbus pk. (D 14), bet. Mulberry and Baxter and Park and Bayard.

Commerce (C 14), from 286 Bleecker, W. to Barrow.

Congress (C 14), from 177 W.Houston, S. to King.

Convent av. (B 8), from Morningside av. and W. 127th, N. to W. 152d and St. Nicholas av.

Convent Hill (B 8), W. 130th, bet. St. Nicholas and Convent avs.

Cooper (B 5), Academy, bet. Broadway and Seaman av., N. to Indian rd.

Cooper sq. E. (D 13), 43 E. 4th, N. to Astor pl.

Cooper sq. W. (D 13), 41 E. 4th, N. to Astor pl.

Corbin pl. (A 5), from Ft. Washington av., at Ft. Tryon pl., E. to Ft. Washington av.

Corlears (E 14), from 587 Grand, S. to East River.

Corlears Hook pk. (E 14), bet. Corlears & Jackson & Cherry & South.

Cornelia (C 14), from 158 W. 4th, W. to Bleecker.

Cortlandt (C 15), from 171 Broadway, W. to North River.

Cortlandt al. (C 14), from 270 Canal, S. to Franklin.

Cottage pl.(C14),Hancock.

Crosby (C 14), from 28 Howard, N. to Bleecker.

Crosby pl. (B 4), fr. Prescott av. n. Nichols pl.,N. E., W.& S. to Prescott av.

Croton (B 7), from Amsterdam av. c. W. 165th N. W. to Audubon av.

Cuyler's al. (D 15), from 28 South, W. to Water.

D st. (A 5), from Dyckman, W. of C st. S.

Delancey (D 14), from 178 Bowery, E. to East River.

Depeyster (D 15), from 187 Water, S to East River.

Desbrosses (C 14), from 195 Hudson, W. to North R.

DeWitt Clinton pk. (B11), bet. 11th av. and Hudson River & W. 52d & W. 54th.

Dey(C 15), from 191 Broadway, W. to North River.

Division (D 14), from 1 Bowery, E. to Grand.

Dominick (C 14), from 18 Clarke, W. to Hudson.

Dover (D 15), from 340 Pearl, S. to East River.

Downing (C 14), from 216 Bleecker, W. to Varick.

Doyers (D 14), from 18 Chatham sq., N. to Pell.

Dry Dock (D 13), from 423 E. 10th, N. to E. 12th.

Duane(D15), from 40 Rose W. to North River.

Dunscomb pl. (D 12), E. 50th, bet. 1st av. and Beekman pl.

Dutch(C15),from 49 John, N. to Fulton.

Dyckman (B 5), N. end of Harlem Driveway N. W. to North River.

East (E 14), from 750 Water, N. to Rivington.

E. Broadway(D14),19 Chatham sq., E. to Grand.

East End av. (D 10), fr. E. 79th, E. of Av. A, N. to E. 89th.

E. Houston(C 14), from 608 B'way, E. to East River.

E. 4th (D 14), from 694 Broadway, E. to East R.

NOTE.—The numerical streets from E. 8th st. to E. 89th st., run E. fr 5th ave. to East River; fr. E. 90th to E. 142d run E from 5th av. to Harlem River, with the exception of E. 10th st., and are numbered on their N. E. and S. E. corners according to the following system:

N.E.C.S.E.C.
1 2 5th av.
101 100 4th av and Park av.
201 200 3d av.
301 300 2d av.
401 400 1st av.
501 500 Av. A & Pleasant av.
601 600 Av. B and E. End av.
701 700 Av. C.
801 800 Av. D.

Edgar(C15),from 59 Greenwich, E. to Trinity pl.

Edgecombe av. (B 7), St. Nicholas av & W. 136th, N. to W. 155th.

Eldridge (D 14), from 86 Division,N.to E.Houston.

Elizabeth (D 14), from 52 Bayard, N. to Bleecker.

Elm (C 15), 14 Reade, N. to Worth.

Elwood (B 5), fr. Hillside av., W. to Broadway.

Emerson (B 4), from Seaman av. to Prescott av.

Essex (D 14), from 160 Division, N. to E. Houston.

Essex mkt. pl. (D14), from 68 Ludlow, E. to Essex.

Exchange al.(C15), from 55 B'way, W. to Trinity pl.

Exchange ct.(C15), 74 Exchange pl.

Exchange pl. (C 15), from 6 Hanover, W. to B'way.

Exterior(D 11), fr E. 64th, E. of Av. A, N.E. to E. 81st.

Extra pl.(D 14), rear 101 st.

Fairview av. (B 5), St. Nicholas av., N. of W 193d, W. to Broadway.

Farmer's mkt. (B 13), Washington, c. Gansevoort.

Ferry (D 15), from 86 Gold S. E. to Pearl.

Finn sq. (C 14), West Broadway, Leonard and Franklin.

Fletcher (D 15), from 208 Pearl, S. to E. R.

Forsyth (D 14), fr. 68 Division, N. to E Houston.

Fort Charles pl. (B 4), Jacobus pl. N. E. to Marble Hill av.

Fort Charles pl. W. (B 4), now Van Corlear pl.

Fort George av. (B5), Amsterdam av., N. of W. 190th W. to St. Nicholas av.

Fort Tryon pl. (A 5), from Fort Washington av. at Corbin pl., S. W. to Riverside Drive.

Fort Washington av.(B 7), Broadway at W. 159th, N. to B'way at Elwood.

Frankfort (C15), from 170 Nassau, E. to Pearl.

Franklin (D 14), from 64 Baxter, W. to N. R.

Franklin pl. (C 14), from 68 Franklin, N. to White.

Franklin sq. (D 15), from 10 Cherry to Pearl.

Franklin ter. (B 13), r 364 W. 26th.

Front (C 15), from 49 Whitehall, E. to Roosevelt, and from South. c. Montgomery, E. to E. R.
113 Wall. 199 Fulton.

Fulton (D 15), from 93 South, W. to N. R.
158 165 Broadway.

Fulton fish mkt. (D 15), bet. Piers 17 and 18, East River.

Fulton mkt. (D 15), Fulton, cor. South.

Gansevoort (B 13), from 356 W. 4th, W. to N. R.

Gay (C 13), 141 Waverley pl., N. to Christopher.

Goerck (E 14), from 574 Grand, N. to 3d.

Gold (C 15), fr. 87 Maiden la., N. to Frankfort.

Gouverneur (D 14), from 75 Division, S. to Water.

Gouverneur la. (D 16), fr. 48 South, W. to 93 Water.

Gouverneur sl. (E 14), fr. 371 South, N. to 613 Water.

Gramercy pk. (C 13), bet. E. 20th and E. 21st.

Grand (C 14), from 78 Varick, E. to E. R.
52 49 W. Broadway.
114 119 Broadway.
234 235 Bowery.

Great Jones (C 14), from 682 B'way, E. to Bowery.

Greeley sq. (C12), junction of Broadway and 6th av. from W. 32d to W. 34th.

Greene (C 14), from 331 Canal, N. to E. 8th.
33 36 Grand.
183 182 Bleecker.
263 260 E. 8th.

Greenwich (C 15), from 4 Battery pl., N. to Gansevoort.
190 197 Fulton.
480 477 Canal.
586 583 W. Houston.

Greenwich av.(C 13), from 105 6th av., N. to 8th av.

Grove (C 14), fr. 488 Hudson, E. to Waverley pl.

Hague (D 15), from 367 Pearl, W. to Cliff.

Hall pl. (D 14), from 211 6th, N. to 7th.

Hamilton (D 15), from 73 Catharine, E to Market.

Hamilton Fish pk (D 14), bet. Stanton and E. Houston, Pitt and Sheriff

Hamilton pl. (B 8), from Broadway at W. 136th, N. E to Amsterdam av.

Hamilton ter. (B 7), from W. 141st W. of St Nicholas av., N. to W. 144th.

Hancock (C 14), fr. 176 W. Houston, N. to Bleecker.

Hancock pl. (B 8), Manhattan from St. Nicholas av. to Morningside av.

Hancock sq. (B 8), bet. St. Nicholas & Manhattan avs. & W. 123d.

Hanover (C 15), from 57 Wall, S. to Pearl.

Hanover sq. (D 15), on Pearl, from 106 S E. to East River.

Harlem mkt. (D 9), 1st av. c. E. 102d.

Harlem River Driveway (B7), from W. 155th & St Nicholas pl., N. to Dyckman.

Harrison (C 14), from 81 Hudson, W. to N. R.

Harry Howard sq. (C 14), bounded by Canal, Walker, Baxter and Mulberry.

Haven av. (B 6), W. 169th, bet. Ft. Washington av. and Riverside Drive, N. to W. 181st.

Henderson pl. (D10), from 541 E. 86th, N.

Henry (D 14), from 14 Oliver, E. to Grand.

Herald sq. (C12), bounded by Broadway, 6th av., W. 34th and W. 36th sts.

Hester (D 14), from 216 Division, W. to Centre.

High Bridge pk. (C7), bet. W. 155th & Washington Bridge & Harlem River Driveway & Colonial pk.

Hillside av. (B 5), Broadway, at Naegle av., E. to St. Nicholas av.

Horatio (B 13), 129 Greenwich av., W. to N. River.

Howard (C 14), from 201 Centre, W. to Mercer.

Hubert (C 14), fr. 149 Hudson, W. to North River.

Hudson (C 15), from 139 Chambers, N. to 9th av.
213 206 Canal.
385 384 W. Houston.
583 586 Bank.

BOROUGH OF MANHATTAN STREET AND AVENUE DIRECTORY—*Continued.*

Indian rd. (B 4), fr. B'way opp. Isham, N. to Broadway.
Irving pl. (C 13), from 117 E. 14th, N. to E. 20th.
Isham (B 4), from 10th av. and W. 209th, N. W. to Broadway.
Jackson (E 14), from 338 Henry, S. to E. R.
Jacob (D 15), fr. 19 Ferry, N. to Frankfort.
Jacobus pl. (B 5), from Terrace View av., n. Leyden, N. to Ft. Charles pl.
James (D 15), fr. 215 Park Row, S. to James sl.
James sl. (D 15), from 77 Cherry, S. to E. R.
Jane (C 13), fr. 118 Greenwich av., W. to N. R.
Jay (C 15), fr. 61 Hudson, W. to N. R.
Jefferson (D 14), from 179 Division, S. to E. R.
Jefferson mkt. (C 13), 6th av., cor. Greenwich av.
Jersey (C 14), from 127 Crosby, E. to Mulberry,
John (C 15), fr. 184 Broadway, E. to Pearl.
Jones (C 14), from 174 W. 4th, W. to Bleecker.
Jones al. (C 14), Shinbone al., W. of Lafayette, N.E. to W. of Great Jones.
Jones la. (D 15), from 101 Front, S. to E. R.
Judson pl. (C 14), Thompson fr. W. 3d to W. 4th.
Jumel pl. (B 6), from W. 167th, nr. Amsterdam av., N. to Edgecombe rd.
Jumel ter. (B 7), from W. 160th, nr. St. Nicholas av., N. to W. 162d.
Kenmare (C 14), from 205 Lafayette, E. to Bowery.
King (C 14), from 41 Macdougal, W. to N. R.
Lafayette (C 15), fr. Centre at Reade, N. to E. 8th.
Laight (C 14), from 398 Canal, W. to N. R.
La Salle (B 8), from Roosevelt sq., W. to Claremont av. (formerly part of W. 125th).
Lawrence (B 8), fr. 405 W. 126th, N. W. to W. 129th.
Lenox av. (C 9), from W. 110th, N. to Harlem R.
299 298 W. 125th.
Leonard (C 14), from 92 Hudson, E. to Baxter.
86 W. B'way. 98 B'way.
Leroy (C 14), from 248 Bleecker, W. to N. R.
Lewis (E 14), from 556 Grand, N. to E. 8th.
Lexington av. (C 13), 121 E. 21st, N. to Harlem R.
17 E. 23d. 1275 E. 86th.
237 E. 34th. 1487 E. 96th.
389 E. 42d. 1689 E 106th.
695 E. 57th. 1869 E. 116th.
995 E. 72d. 2068 E. 125th.
Leyden (B 4), from Terrace View av., n. Jacobus pl., W. to Tunissen pl.
Liberty (C 15), from 76 Maiden la., W. to N. R.
Liberty pl. (C 15), from 57 Liberty, N. to Maiden la.
Lincoln pl. (D 9), from 167 E. 118th, N.
Lispenard (C 14), from 277 W. Broadway, E. to Broadway.
Little W. 12th (B 13), from 89 Gansevoort, W. to N. R.
Livingston pl. (D 13), fr. 325 E. 15th N. to E. 17th.
London ter. (B 13), N. Side W. 23d, bet. 9th and 10th avs.
Long Acre sq. now Times sq.
Ludlow (D 14), f'm 144 Division, N. to E. Houston.
Macdougal (C 14), from 219 Spring, N. to W. 8th.
Macdougal al. (C 13), from Macdougal, n. W. 8th, E.
Macomb's pl. (C 7), from 2830 8th av., N. E. to Harlem River.
Madison (D 15), from 426 Pearl, E. to Grand.
Madison av. (C 13), from 29 E. 23d, N. to Harlem R.
183 E. 34th. 1350 E. 95th.
315 E. 42d. 1569 E. 106th.
629 E. 59th. 1767 E. 116th.
875 E. 73d. 1943 E. 125th.
1171 E. 86th.
Madison sq. (C 13), bet. 5th and Madison avs. and E. 23d and E. 26th.
Madison sq. N. (C 13), E. 26th, bet. 5th & Madison avs.
Magraw pl. (B 6), W. 181st W. of Bennett av., N. to W. 183d.
Maiden la. (C 15), from 172 Broadway, S. E. to East River.
Mall (C 15), B'way, opp. Park pl., E. to Park row.
Mangin (E 14), from 590 Grand, N. to E. Houston.
Manhattan, 11th ward (E 14), from 444 E. Houston, N. to 3d.
Manhattan, 12th ward (B 8), now part of W. 125th.
Manhattan av. (B 9), from 25 W. 100th, N. to St. Nicholas av.
Manhattan mkt. (B 12), 11th av. cor. W. 34th.
Manhattan pl. (C 15), from 10 Elm, W. & S. to Reade.
Marble Hill av. (B 4), W. 225th W. of Broadway N. W to Spuyten Duyvil creek.
Marginal (B 13), from 401 W. 12th, N. to W. 22d.
Market (D 14), from 61 Division, S. to E. R.
Marketfield (C 15), from 72 Broad, W.
Mercer (C 14), from 311 Canal, N. to E. 8th.
Milligan pl. (C 19), 139 6th av.
Minetta (C 14), 209 Bleecker, N. to Minetta la.
Minetta la. (C 14), from 113 Macdougal, W. to 6th av.
Minetta pl. (C 14), rear 2 Minetta.
Mission pl. (D 14), from 58 Park, N. to Worth.
Mitchel sq. (B 6), Br'dway and St. Nicholas av., W. 166th to W. 170th.
Mitchell pl. (D 12), E. 49th, bet. 1st av. and Beekman pl.
Monroe (D 15), from 59 Catharine, E. to Grand,
Montgomery (D 14), from 247 Division, S. to E. R.
Moore (C 15), from 30 Pearl, S. to E. R.
Morningside av. (B 9), W. 110th, opp. Manhattan av., N. to W. 127th.
Morningside Drive (B 9), W. 110th, opp. Columbus av., N. to W. 122d.
Morningside pk. (B 9), bet. Morningside av. and Morningside dr. and W. 110th and W. 123d.
Morris (C 15), from 27 Broadway, W. to N. R.
Morton (C 14), from 270 Bleecker, W. to N. R.
Mott (D 14), from 200 Park row, N. to Bleecker.
Mt. Morris pk. (C 8), bet Madison av. and Mt. Morris pk. W. and E. and W. 120th and E. and W. 124th.
Mt. Morris pk. W. (C 8), W. 120th bet. 5th & Lenox avs., N. to W. 124th.
Mt. Morris pl. (C 8), W. 124th, bet. 5th & Lenox avs.
Moylan pl. (B 8), from Amsterdam av. at W. 125th, W. to B'dway (formerly part of 126th.)
Mulberry (D 14), from 186 P'k Row, N. to Bleecker.
Mulry sq. (C 13), formed by Greenwich av., 7th av., Perry and W. 11th.
Murray (C 15), from 247 Broadway, W. to North River.
Naegle av. (B 5), Broadway and Hillside av., N. E. to Amsterdam av.
Nassau (C 15), from 20 Wall, N. to Park row.
69 70 John.
135 136 Beekman.
—— 170 Frankfort.
New (C 15), from 7 Wall, S to Beaver.
New Bowery (D 15), from 396 Pearl, N. to Park row.
New Chambers (D 15), 107 Park row, E. to Cherry.
Nichols pl. (A 4), from Prescott av., bet. Crosby pl. and Emerson, W.
Norfolk (D 14), from 180 Division, N. to E. Houston.
North Moore (C 14), fr. 234 W. B'way, W. to N. R.
North William (C 15), fr. 16 Frankfort, N. to Park row.
Northern av. (A 6), from W. 177th, W. of Haven av., N. to Fort Wash. av.
Oak (D 15), from 392 Pearl, E. to Catharine.
Old Broadway (B 8), 117 Manhattan N. to W. 133d.
Old sl. (D 15), from 106 Pearl, S. to East River.
Oliver (D 15), from 68 New Bowery, S. to East River.
Orchard (D 14), from 124 Division, N. to E. Houston
Ottendorfer sq. (C 15), Centre, bet. Chambers and Reade.
Overlook ter. (B 6), W. 184th W. of Bennett av., N. to Ft Washington av.
Park (C 15), from 36 Centre, E. to Mott.
Park av. (C 12), continuation of 4th av., from E. 34th, N. to E. Fordham rd., Borough of Bronx.
136 E. 42d. 1038 E. 86th.
500 E. 59th. 1636 E 116th.
756 E. 72d. 1816 E. 125th.
Park pl. (C 15), from 237 Broadway, W. to North River.
Park row (C 15), from 1 Ann, E. to Chatham sq.
Park ter E. (B 4), from P'k, W. of B'way, N. to W. 218th.
Park ter. W. (B 4), from Indian rd at Isham Park, N. E. to W. 218th.
Patchin pl. (C 13) 111 W. 10th
Pearl (C 15), from 14 State, E. and N. W. to B'way.
149 152 Wall.
263 266 Fulton.
463 464 Park row.
Peck sl. (D 15), from 312 Pearl, E. to South.
Pelham (D 14), from 96 Monroe, S. to Cherry.
Pell (D 14), from 18 Bowery, W. to Mott.
Pentz pl. (B 8), W. 140th and St. Nicholas ter., S.
Perry (C 13), from 55 G'wich av., W. to North R.
Pershing sq (C 12), Park av. from S. of E. 41st to N. of E. 42nd.
Pike (D 14), from 107 Division, S. to E. R.
Pine (C 15), from 106 Broadway, E. to East R.
Pinehurst av. (B 6), from W. 177th, W. of Ft. Washington av., N. to W. 181st
Pitt (D 14), from 276 Division, N. to E. Houston.
Platt (D 15), from 221 Pearl, W. to William.
Pleasant av. (D 9), from E. 100th E. of 1st av., N. to Harlem River.
Post av. (B 5), from 123 Dyckman, N. to 10th av.
Prescott av. (A 5), fr. 261 Dyckman, N to Spuyten Duyvil creek.
Prince (D 14), from 230 Bowery W. to Macdougal.
79 B'way. 145 W. B'way.
Prospect pl. (D 12), from E. 40th, bet. 2d and 1st avs., N. to E. 43d.
Rachel la. (E 14), from 4 Goerck, E. to Mangin.
Reade (D 15), from 22 Duane, W. to North R.
Rector (C 15), fr. 78 Broadway, W. to North River.
Renwick (C 14), from 508 Canal, N. to Spring.
Ridge (D 14), from 254 Division, N. to E. Houston.
River View ter. (D 11), from E 58th E. of Av. A, N. to E. 59th.
Riverside Drive (B 11), W. 72d bet. West End & 12th avs., N to Dyckman.
Riverside park, bet. Riverside drive & Hudson River, from W. 72d to W. 129th.
Riverside ter. (A 6), E. side of Riverside Drive from W. 177th to W. 181st.
Rivington (D 14), from 213 Bowery, E. to East River
Robert Morris pk. (B 7), bet. W. 160th and W. 162d and Colonial parkway and Jumel ter.
Roosevelt (D 15), from 187 Park row, S. to East R.
Roosevelt sq. (B 8), Morningside av., W. 124th and W. 125th.
Rose (D 15), from 34 Frankfort, N. E. to Pearl.
Rutgers (D 14), from 26 Canal, S to East River.
Rutgers pk. (D 14), foot of Rutgers.
Rutgers pl. (D 14), Monroe, Jefferson to Clinton.
Rutherfurd pl. (D 13), from 224 E. 17th, S. to E. 15th.

BOROUGH OF MANHATTAN STREET AND AVENUE DIRECTORY—*Continued.*

St. Clair pl. (B 8), from Broadway, W. to N. R. formerly part of W. 129th).

St. Johns la. (C 14), from 9 Beach, N. to Laight.

St. Lukes pl. (C 14), Leroy st., from 68 to 99.

St. Marks pl. (D 13) 8th st. from 77 Cooper sq. E., E. to Av. A.

St Nicholas av. (C 9), fr. Lenox av. and W. 110th, N. W. to Dyckman.

St. Nicholas pk. (B 8), bet. W. 128th and W. 141st. and St. Nicholas av. and St. Nicholas ter.

St. Nicholas pl. (B 7), from St. Nicholas av. & W. 149th, N. to W. 155th.

St. Nicholas ter. (B 8), W. 127th & St. Nicholas av., N. to W. 140th.

Scammel (D 14), from 299 East Broadway, S. to Water.

Seaman av. (B 4), from Bolton rd., bet. Broadway and Prescott av. N to Isham.

Sheridan sq. (C 14), at junction of W. 4th, Christopher and Grove.

Sheriff (E 14), from 502 Grand, N. to 2d.

Sherman av. (B 5), from Broadway and Elwood, N. to 10th av.

Sherman sq. (B 11), at junction of Broadway and Amsterdam av. at W. 73d.

Shinbone al. (C 14), fr 11 Bleecker, N. and N. W. to Jones al.

Sickles (B 5), from Naegle av., bet. Elwood and Arden, W. to B'way.

South (C 15), fr. 66 Whitehall, E. to East River.

South William (C 15), from 7 William, W. to Broad.

Spencer pl. (C 13), W. 4th, bet. Christopher and W. 10th.

Spring (D 14), from 188 Bowery, W. to North River.

Spruce (C 15), from 41 Park row, S. E. to Gold.

Stable ct. (C 13), from 14 Cooper sq. W., W. and N.

Stanton (D 14), from 245 Bowery, E. to East River.

Staple (C 15), from 169 Duane, N. to Harrison.

State (C 15), from 48 Whitehall, N. to Bowling Green.

Stone (C 15), from 18 Whitehall, E. to William.

Straus sq. (B 9), junction B'way and West End av., from W. 106th to W. 107th.

Stuyvesant (D 12), from 29 3d av., E. to 2d av.

Stuyvesant al. (D 13), fr. 208 E. 11th, N. to E. 12th.

Stuyvesant sq. (D 13), bet. Rutherfurd pl. and Livingston pl. and E. 15th and E. 17th.

Suffolk (D 14), from 202 Division, N. to E Houston.

Sullivan (C 14), from 415 Canal, N. to W. 4th.

Sutton pl. (D 11), Av. A from E. 58th to E. 60th.

Sylvan ct. (D 8), from 168 E. 121st, N.

Sylvan pl. (D 8), from 158 E. 120th, N. to E. 121st.

Sylvan ter. (B 7), Jumel ter., nr. W. 160th, W. to St. Nicholas av.

Temple (C 15), from 88 Liberty, S. to Cedar.

Terrace View av. (B 4), W. 225th, opp. Leyden, N. to W. 228th.

Thames (C 15), 113 Broadway, W. to Greenwich.

Thayer (B 5), from Naegle av., bet. Arden & Dyckman, W. to Broadway.

Theatre al. (C 15), from 19 Ann, N. to Beekman.

Thomas (C 15), 317 Broadway, W. to Hudson.
74 73 W. Broadway.

Thompson (C 14), from 395 Canal, N. to W. 4th.

Tiemann pl. (B 8) (formerly part of W. 127th), from W. 125th (formerly Manhattan st.), W. to Riverside Drive.

Times sq. (C 12), the open space at the junction of Broadway, 7th av. and W. 43d.

Tompkins (E 14), fr. 606 Grand, N. to East River.

Tompkins sq. (D 13), bet. Avs. A and B and E. 7th and E. 10th.

Trimble pl. (C 15), 115 Duane, N. to Thomas.

Trinity pl. (C 15), from 6 Morris, N. to Liberty.

Tunissen pl. (B 4), from Harlem River, N. to Terrace View av.

Union pl. (C 13), 4th av., fr. E. 17th to E. 19th.

Union sq., E. (C 13), 4th av., from E. 14th to E. 17th.

Union sq., W. (C 13), Broadway, from E. 14th to E. 17th.

University pl. (C 13), from 29 Waverley pl., N. to E. 14th.

Van Corlear pl. (B 4), fr. Jacobus pl., N. W. to W. 227th.

Vandam (C 14), fr. 13 Macdougal, W. to Greenwich.

Vanderbilt av. (C 12), from 27 E. 42d to E. 45th.

Vandewater (D 15), from 54 Frankfort, E to Pearl.

Vannest pl. (C 13), Charles from W. 4th to Bleecker.

Varick (C 14), from 130 Franklin, N. to Carmine.
70 Canal
205 204 W. Houston.

Vermilye av. (B 5), from Dyckman, N. of Sherman av., N. E. to W. 211th.

Vesey (C 15), from B'way (opp. 222), W. to N. River.
66 W. Broadway.

Vestry (C 14), from 428 Canal, W. to North River.

Wadsworth av. (B 6), fr. W. 173d and Broadway, N. to St. Nicholas av.

Wadsworth ter. (B 5), W. of Wadsworth av., from W. 188th to Fairview av.

Walker (C 14), from 258 W. B'way, E. to Canal.
68 69 Broadway.

Wall (C 15), fr. 86 Broadway, E. to E. R.

Warren (C 15), from 259 B'way, W. to N. R.
61 62 W. Broadway.

Washington (C 15), from 6 Battery pl., N. to W. 14th.
194 191 Fulton.
286 285 Chambers.
476 475 Canal.
566 565 W. Houston.
732 731 Bank.

Washington mkt. (C 15), Fulton, cor. West.

Washington mews (C 13), from 1 5th av., E. to University pl.

Washington pl. (C 13), 718 B'way, W. to Grove.

Washington sq. (C 13), bet. Wooster and Macdougal and W. 4th and Waverley pl.

Washington sq. E. (C 14), from 48 W. 4th, N. to Waverley pl.

Washington sq. N. (C 13), Waverley pl., 29 to 89.

Washington sq. S. (C 14), W. 4th from 54 to 126.

Washington sq. W. (C 14), Macdougal st., from 143 to 165.

Washington ter. (B 5), W. 186th, bet. Amsterdam & Audubon avs., runs S.

Water (C 15), from 41 Whitehall, E. to E. R.
113 Wall. 199 Fulton.

Watts (C 14), from 366 W. Broadway W. to North River.

Waverley pl. (C 13), from 727 Broadway, W. and N. to Bank.

Weehawken (B 14), from 304 W. 10th, S. to Christopher.

West (C 15), from 12 Battery pl., N. to 10th av.
130 Fulton.
185 Chambers.
298 Canal.
441 Bank.

West Broadway (C 15), fr. 66 Vesey, N. to W. 4th.
296 Canal. 518 Bleecker.

West End av. (B 11), fr. 601 W. 59th to W. 107th.
259 254 W. 72d.
539 536 W. 86th.
739 738 W. 96th.

W. Houston (C 14), from 609 B'way, W. to N. R.

West Washington mkt. (B 13), West, bet. Gansevoort and Bloomfield.

W. 3d, (C 14), from 681 Broadway, W. to 6th av.

W. 4th (C 14), from 697 Broadway, W. & N. W. to W. 13th.
30 31 Greene.
154 151 6th av.
298 299 Bank.

NOTE.—The numerical streets running west from 5th av. up to W. 59th are numbered on the northwest and southwest corners according to the following system:

N.W.C.	S.W.C.	
1	2	5th av.
101	100	6th av.
201	200	7th av.
301	300	8th av.
401	400	9th av.
501	500	10th av.
601	600	11th av.

W. 8th (C 13), from 8 5th av., W. to 6th av.

W. 9th (C 13), from 22 5th av., W. to 6th av.

West 10th to W. 109th.

NOTE.—The numerical streets from W. 10th to W. 58th, run west fr. 5th av. to N. R.; from W. 61st st. to W. 72d, from Cent. Pk. West to N. R.; fr. W. 73d to W. 109th, except W. 78-79-80th from Central Park West to Riverside Drive, and are numbered on their northwest and southwest corners as follows:

N. W. C.	S. W. C.	
1	2	Central pk. W.
101	100	Columbus av.
201	200	Amsterdam av.
301	300	W. End av.

W. 78th (B 10), Columbus av., W. to Riverside Dr.

W. 79th (B 10), Columbus av., W. to Riverside Dr.

W. 80th (B 10), Columbus av., W. to Riverside Dr

NOTE.—The numerical streets north of W. 110th, which run west from 5th av., are numbered on their northwest and southwest corners according to the following system:

N. W. C.	S. W. C.	
1	2	5th av.
101	100	Lenox av.
201	200	7th av.
301	300	8th av.
401	400	Columbus av.
501	500	Amsterdam av.

W. 110th. Cathedral parkway (C 9), from 5th av., W. to Riverside Drive.

W. 111th to W. 120th (C 9 & 8), from 5th av., W. to Riverside Drive.

W. 121st (C 8), from 10 Mt. Morris pk. W., W. to Riverside Drive.

W. 122d (C 8), from 18 Mt. Morris pk. W., W. to Riverside Drive.

W. 123d (C 8), from 30 Mt. Morris pk. W., W. to Riverside Drive.

W. 124th (C 8), from 2002 5th av., W. to Riverside Drive.

W. 125th (C 8), fr. 2020 5th av., W. and N. W. to N. R. (former section W of Roosevelt sq. now La Salle st. and Manhattan st. changed to part of W. 125th).
86 88 Lenox av.
278 279 8th av.
388 383 Morn'gside av.

W. 126th (C 8), from 2040 5th av., W. to Lawrence (section W. of Amsterdam av. now Moylan pl.).

W. 127th (C 8), fr. 2056 5th av., W. to Lawrence (section W. thereof now Tiemann pl.).

W. 128th (C 8), fr. 2076 5th av., W. to Amsterdam av.

W. 129th (C 8), from 2098 5th av., W. to Broadway (section W. thereof now St. Claire pl.).

W. 130th (C 8), from 2118 5th av., W. to N. R.

W. 131st (C 8), from 2138 5th av., W. to N. R.

W. 132d (C 8), from 2158 5th av., W. to N. R.

W. 133d (C 8), 2174 5th av., W. to N. R.

W. 134th (C 8), from 2192 5th av., W. to N R.

W. 135th (C 8), 2218 5th av., W. to Riverside Dr.

BOROUGH OF MANHATTAN STREET AND AVENUE DIRECTORY—*Continued.*

W. 136th (C 8), from 2234 5th av., W. to St. Nicholas av., and from Amsterdam av. W. to N. R.
W. 137th (C 8), from 2260 5th av., W. to St. Nicholas av., and from Amsterdam av. W. to N. R.
W. 138th (C 8), from 2280 5th av., W. to N. R.
W. 139th (C 8), from 2300 5th av., W. to N. R.
W. 140th to W. 142d (C 8 & 7), from 5th av., W. to N. R.
W. 143d to W. 148th (C 7), from Harlem R., W. to N. R.
W. 149th (C 7), from 779 Lenox av., W. to N. R.
W. 150th to W. 153d (C 7), from Harlem R., W. to N. R.
W. 154th (C 7), from 7th av., W. to Amsterdam av.
W. 155th (C 7), from 7th av., W. to N. R.
W. 156th (B 7), from 921 St. Nicholas av., W. to Broadway.
W. 157th (B 7), from Colonial parkway, W. to Audubon pl.
W. 158th (B 7), from 957 St. Nicholas av., W. to N. R.
W. 159th (B 7), from Colonial parkway, W. to Broadway.
W. 160th (B7), from Colonial parkway, W. to Riverside drive.
W. 161st (B 7), from 2036 Amsterdam av., W. to Riverside Drive.
W. 162d to W. 164th (B 7 & 6), from Edgecombe Road to Riverside Drive.
W. 165th (B 6), Colonial parkway, W. to N. R.
W. 166th (B6), fr. Colonial parkway, W. to Ft. Was ington av.
W. 167th (B 6), from Colonial parkway, W. to Ft. Washington av.
W. 168th (B 6), fr. 2378 Amsterdam av., W. to Fort Washington av.
W. 169th (B 6), from Amsterdam av., W. to Riverside Drive.
W. 170th (B 6), from Colonial parkway, W. to Buena Vista av.
W. 171st (B6), fr. Amsterdam av., W. to Haven av.
W. 172d (B 6), fr. Amsterdam av., W. to Broadway.
W. 173d (B 6), fr. Amsterdam av., W. to Broadway.
W. 174th to W. 178th (B8), fr. Amsterdam av., W. to Broadway.
W. 179th & W. 180th (B6), fr. Amsterdam av., W. to Northern av.
W. 181st (B 6), from 2440 Amsterdam av., W. to Riverside Drive.
W. 182d (B 6), from 2460 Amsterdam av., W. to Broadway.
W. 183d (B 6), from 2480 Amsterdam av., to a private av. not yet named W. of Magraw pl.
W. 184th (B 6), from 2494 Amsterdam av., W. to Overlook ter.
W. 185th (B 6), from Colonial pkway, New av. W. to Broadway.
W. 186th (B 5), from 2540 Amsterdam av., W. to Overlook ter.
W. 187th (B 5), from Amsterdam av., W. to Ft. Washington av.
W. 188th (B 5), from Amsterdam av., W. to Wadsworth av.
W. 189th (B 5), from Amsterdam av., W. to Bennett av.
W. 190th & W. 191st (B 5), from Audubon av., W. to Wadsworth av.
W. 192d (B5), fr. Audubon av., W. to Bennett av.
W. 193d (B5), fr. Audubon av., W. to Wadsworth av.
W. 201st (B5), fr. Harlem River, W. to Academy.
W. 202d & W. 203d (B 5), from Harlem River, W. to 10th av.
W. 204th (B5), from Harlem River to Seaman av.
W. 205th to W. 210th (B5 & 4); (except **W. 207th**) from Harlem River to 10th av.
W. 207th (B 5), fr. Harlem River, N. W. to Isham.
W. 211th and W. 212th (B 4), Harlem R. W. to Broadway.
W. 213th to W. 215th (B 4), Harlem River W. to Indian Road.
W. 216th (B 4), from Harlem River W. to Broadway.
W. 217th (B 4), from Park Ter. E., W. to Park Ter. W.
W. 218th (B4), from Harlem River, W. to Harlem River.
W. 219th (B 4), from Harlem Riv., W. to Indian rd.
W. 220th (B 4), Harlem River, W. to Seaman av.
W. 225th (B 4), Harlem River, W. to Leyden.
W. 227th (B 4), Harlem River, W. to Adrian pl.
W. 228th (B 4), Broadway, W. to Adrian pl.
White (C 14), from 229 W. B'way, E. to Baxter.
White's pl. (C 13), r. 214 W. 18th.
Whitehall (C 15), from 2 Broadway, S. to East River.
Willett (D 14), from 482 Grand, N. to E. Houston.
William (C 15), from 105 Pearl, N.E. to 447 Pearl.
44 Wall. 140 Fulton.
Winthrop pl. (C14), Greene bet. Waverley pl. & E. 8th.
Wooster (C 14), from 85 Canal, N. to W. 4th.
Worth (C14), from 72 Hudson, E. to Park row.
York (C14), 9 St. Johns la., E. to W. Broadway.
1st (D 14), from 308 Bowery, E. to Av. A.
1st av. (D 14), from 166 E. Houston N. to Harlem River.
237 232 E. 14th.
391 392 E. 23d.
593 — E. 34th.
739 788 E. 42d.
1037 1044 E. 57th.
1615 1616 E. 84th.
1855 — E. 96th.
2049 2050 E. 106th.
2437 2434 E. 125th.
2d (D 14), from 238 Bowery, E. to Av. D.
2d av. (D 14), from 118 E. Houston, N. to Harlem River.
225 228 E. 14th.
397 398 E. 23d.
621 620 E. 34th.
781 782 E. 42d.
1077 1082 E. 57th.
1385 1392 E. 72d.
1657 1656 E. 86th.
2061 2062 E. 106th.
2259 2258 E. 116th.
2433 2438 E. 125th.
3d (D 14), from 345 Bowery, E. to East River.
3d av. (D13), fr. St. Marks pl., N. to Harlem River.
124 123 E. 14th.
296 299 E. 23d.
504 505 E. 34th.
658 657 E. 42d.
948 951 E. 57th.
1248 1245 E. 72d.
1922 1923 E. 106th.
2298 2297 E. 125th.
— Continued in the Borough of the Bronx.
4th av. (C13), fr. Astor pl., at E. 8th, N. to E. 34th.
158 157 E. 14th.
312 289 E. 23d.
5th (D14), from 19 Cooper sq. E., E to East River.
5th av. (C 13), fr. 13 Washington sq. N. (57 Waverley pl.), N. to Harlem River.
82 67 W. & E. 14th.
186 185 W. & E. 23d.
350 353 W. & E. 34th.
500 499 W. & E. 42d.
— 775 E. 59th.
— 908 E. 72d.
— 1029 E. 84th.
— 1149 E. 96th.
— 1249 E. 106th.
1416 1415 W. & E. 116th.
2020 2021 W. & E. 125th.
2218 2217 W. & E. 135th.
6th (D14), from 39 Cooper sq. E., E. to East River.
6th av. (C 14), from Carmine, N. to Central p'k S.
207 208 W. 14th.
373 374 W. 23d.
785 sq. W. 42d.
7th (D 13), from opp. 62 Cooper sq. W., E. to East River.
7th av. (C13), fr. Carmine at Varick, N. to Central pk. S., and fr. W. 110th, N. to Harlem River.
60 53 W. 14th.
220 219 W. 23d.
440 439 W. 34th.
596 599 W. 42d.
2094 2039 W. 125th.
8th av. (D 13), from 598 Hudson, N. to Harlem R.
79 78 W. 14th.
259 254 W. 23d.
479 474 W. 34th.
657 658 W. 42d.
969 968 W. 57th.
2151 2144 W. 116th.
— 2330 W. 125th.
2525 2534 W. 135th.
2725 2728 W. 145th.
9th av. (B 13), from Gansevoort, N. to W. 59th and from W. 201st, W. of Academy, N. to Broadway.
43 — W. 14th.
— 206 W. 23d.
429 — W. 34th.
581 580 W. 42d.
10th av. (B 13), from 542 West, N. to W. 59th, and from Academy at W. 202d, N. to Broadway.
57 56 W. 14th.
219 220 W. 23d.
427 424 W. 34th.
578 574 W. 42d.
11th av. (B 13), from Little W. 12th, N. to W. 59th.
179 180 W. 23d.
393 394 W. 34th.
551 552 W. 42d.
851 852 W. 59th.
12th av. (B 12), from foot W. 30th, N. to W. 72d.
13th av. (B 13), fr. W. 22d, W. of 11th av., N. to W. 30th.

HEIGHT OF NOTABLE BUILDINGS.

Structure.	Feet.	Structure.	Feet	Structure.	Feet
Amiens cathedral	383	Florence cathedral	387	St. Peter's, Rome	433
Bunker Hill monument	221	Fribourg cathedral	386	Strassburg cathedral	465
Capitol, Washington	288	Milan cathedral	360	St. Stephen's, Vienna	470
City hall, Philadelphia	535	Pyramid, Great	451	Washington monument	556
Cologne cathedral	512	Rouen cathedral	464	Woolworth Bldg., N. Y	750
Eiffel tower	984	St. Paul's, London	404		

LONGEST RIVERS IN THE WORLD.

River.	Miles.	River.	Miles.	River.	Miles.	River.	Miles.
Mississippi-Mo.	4,194	Yangtze	3,000	Amur	2,700	Volga	2,325
Nile	3,670	La Plata	2,950	Mekong	2,600	Hwangho	2,300
Amazon	3,300	Lena	2,860	Niger	2,600	Yukon	2,050
Ob	3,235	Kongo	2,800	Yenesei	2,500	Colorado	2,000

BOROUGH OF BRONX STREET AND AVENUE DIRECTORY

The following resolution, adopted by the Board of Aldermen March 21, 1882, and approved by the Mayor March 28, 1882, will explain the plan of numbering the streets north of Harlem River: That Willis Avenue be numbered, commencing at the Harlem River, and that said numbering run continuously through Willis, Melrose and Webster avenues. That all other avenues in the Twenty-third and Twenty-fourth Wards, having a generally northerly and southerly direction, be given the same number at the cross street nearest their southern terminus as that on Willis, Melrose, and Webster avenues at the intersection of said cross street, and then numbered accordingly.

The prefix West is given to all cross streets in the Twenty-third and Twenty-fourth Wards lying west of Jerome av., which runs from Harlem River at Macomb's Dam Bridge to City line, and that the prefix East is given to all cross streets lying east of said avenue and the Harlem River.

The letters and numbers following names indicate position of the thoroughfare on the map in pocket of Almanac.

Abbatt pl. (G 3), fr. Seymour av., E. to Eastchester road.

Abbot (D 1), fr. Aldrich. N. of Bronx River, E. to Baldwin.

Adams (F 5), fr. Walker av., at E. 180th, N. W. to Morris pk. av.

Adams pl. (D 5), from E. 182d E. of Arthur av., N. to Crescent av.

Adee av. (E 3), from 3000 Bronx pk. E., E. to Hutchinson river.

Albany crescent (B 3), fr. Kingsbridge ter. N. to Bailey av.

Alden pl. (D 5), from Park av., bet. E. 178th & E. 179th, W. to Webster av.

Aldrich (D 1), from Bronx River, N. of E. 242d, N. to Bronx River.

Aldus (E 6), 1000 S. Boulevard, E. to Whitlock av.

Alexander av. (B 8), from 331 E. 132d, N. to E. 143d.

Allaire av. (H 5), fr. Zerega av. bet. Lacombe & Farrington avs., N. to Lafayette av.

Allerton av. (E 3), fr. 2700 Bronx pk. E., E. to Hutchinson av.

Amethyst (F 4), from Sagamore, N. W. to Unionport rd.

Amundson av. (F 1), fr. 1425 E. 233d, N. W. to City line.

Anderson av. (C 7), from 885 Jerome av., N. to Shakespeare av.

Andrews av. (C 5), from 1641 Aqueduct av., N. to W. Fordham rd.

Anna pl. (D 6), now Kinderman pl.

Anthony av. (D 5), fr. Clay av. E. 173d, N. to Grand Boulevard & Concourse.

Appleton av. (G 4), from Vreeland av. near Westchester creek, N. to Wilkinson av.

Aqueduct av. (C 6), now University av.

Aqueduct av. E. (C 5), from 81 W. 180th, N. to W. 184th.

Aqueduct av. W. (C 4), fr. W. 188th, E of University av., N. to W. Kingsbridge rd.

Archer (F 5), fr. 1500 Beach av., E. to Storrow.

Arden sq. (E 2), bet. Curtis and Tillotson avs., and Eastchester rd. and Fenton av.

Arlington av. (B 4), from 601 Kappock, N. to Independence av.

Army av. (C 4), from W. 197th, W. of Jerome av., N. to W. 206th.

Arnow av. (E 3), from 2900 Bronx pk. E., E. to Hutchinson av.

Arnow pl. (H 3), fr. Westchester av., N. of Morris pk. av., E. to Eastern blvd.

Arthur av. (D 5), from 631 Crotona pk. N., N. to Pelham av.

Astor av. (E 4), fr. Olinville av., bet. Thwaite's pl. and Waring av., E. to Stillwell av.

Austin pl. (E 7), from E. 144th, bet. Timpson pl. & Whitlock av., N. E. to Whitlock av.

Avenue St. John (E 7), fr. Prospect av., at Dawson, S. to Timpson pl.

Bacon (G 7), from East River, N. to Edgewater rd.

Bagley av. (J 6), from Yznaga av., bet. Evans and Seamans avs., N. W. to Causeway.

Bailey av. (C 4), from 2500 Sedgwick av., N. to W. 234th.

Bailey pl. (C 4), from 3410 Bailey av., N. to Fort Independence.

Bainbridge av. (D 4), fr. E. Fordham rd., opp. Elm pl., N. E. to Jerome av.

Baisley av. (H 4), fr. 1225 Bradford av., N. E. to Shore drive.

Baker av. (F 4), from 1680 Garfield, E. to Matthews av.

Balcom av. (J 5), fr. East River, bet. Buttrick and Swinton avs., N. W. to Appleton av.

Baldwin (D 1), from E. 242d, Bronx River, N. to City line.

Barbour (G 4), fr. Barnard, bet. Haswell and Barlow, N. E. to Bates.

Barker av. (E 4), from 651 Pelham parkway, N. to Duncomb av.

Barkley av. (H 5), from E. 177th, bet. Lafayette av. and Eastern blvd., N. E. to Shore drive.

Barlow, now called Poplar.

Barnard (G 4), fr. Haswell, bet. Eastchester rd. and McAlpin av., N. W. to Eastchester rd.

Barnes av. (F 4), fr. Baker av bet. Wallace & Matthews avs., N. to Bissel av. and from Baychester av. N. to City line.

Barnett pl. (F 4), from Barnes av., S. of Rhinelander av., E. to Matthews av.

Barrett av. (H 6), from Castle Hill av., opposite Zerega av., N. W. and N. to Lafayette av.

Barretto (F 7), fr. Edgewater rd., bet. Casanova and Ryawa av., N. to Fox.

Barry (F 7), fr. Oak Point av., bet. Cabot and Dupont, N. E. to Tiffany.

Bartholdi (E 3), fr. 3300 White Plains rd, E. to Bronxwood av.

Bartow av. (F 3), from E. Gun Hill rd., at Tiemann av., N. E. to Hutchinson river.

Bassett av. (G 3), fr. Eastchester rd., opp. Sacket, N. E. to Hutchinson av.

Bassford av. (D 4), from E. 182d, bet. Washington & Bathgate avs., N. to 3d av.

Bates (G 4), fr. Barbour N. of Barnard, W. to Barlow.

Bathgate av. (D 5), from Wendover av., W. of 3d av., N. to E. 191st.

Bay (City I.) (K 8^1 & J 7^2), from Eastchester bay, bet. Tier & Fordham, E. to City Island av., and from King av., E. to L. I. Sound.

Baychester av. (G 3), from Pelham Bay pk. E. of Edson av., N. W. to Bissell av.

Beach (City Island) (K^1 2 & J^2 7), from Eastchst'r bay, E. to L. I. Sound.

Beach av. (24th ward) (G 6), from Bronx River, bet. Taylor and St. Lawrence avs., N. to Walker av.

Beacon av., now part of E. 174th.

Bear Swamp Road, now called Bronxdale av.

Beaumont av. (D 4), from 701 Grote, N. to E. 189th.

Beck (E 7), 622 Prospect av., E. to Intervale av.

Becker (H 3), Eastern boulevard at Buhre av., N. W. to Morris Park av.

Bedford pk. Boulevard, see East and West Bedford Pk. Boulevard.

Beebe av., now called Orloff av.

Beech ter. (E 7), from 360 Crimmins av., E. to Beekman av.

Beekman av. (E 7), from E. 141st, bet. Crimmins and Cypress avs. N. to St. Mary's.

Belden (City Island) (K 8), fr. City Island av., S. of Rochelle, E. to L. I. Sound.

Bell av. (F 1), fr. 4001 Pratt av., N. W. to City line.

Belmont, now Mt. Eden av.

Belmont av. (D 5), from 701 E. 175th, N. to Fordham University grounds.

Belmont pl. (D 4), now that part of E. 184th bet. Lorillard pl. & Arthur av.

Benedict av. (G 5), from 1330 Pugsley av., E. to Unionport rd.

Benson av. (G 4), fr. Lane av., N. of Westchester av., N. W. to Walker av.

Bergen av. (D 7), from 494 Willis av., N. E. to Brook av.

Betts av. (H 6), from Clason's pt. rd., at Bronx River, N. to Compton av.

Bissel av. (E 1), from 4500 Barnes av., N. E. to City line.

Black (H 5), fr. 750 Zerega av., E. to Westchester creek.

Blackrock av. (G 5), from 1060 Virginia av., E. to Westchester creek.

Blackstone av. (B 3), Spuyten Duyvil pkway, at W. 237th, N. to W. 256th.

Blair av. (K 5^1 & J 10^2), fr. Shore Drive, bet. Reynolds & Longstreet avs., N. to Shore Drive

Blondell av. (G 4), from Walker av., at Westchester sq., N. W. to Barlow.

Bogart av. (G 4), from N. Y., N. H. & H. R R., at Bear Swamp rd., N. W. to Bronx & Pelham p'kway.

Boller av. (G 3), from Bassett av. N., bet. Palmer and Hunter avs., N. W. to Eden ter.

Bolton av. (H 6), from Bronx R. av., bet. White Plains rd. and Underhill av., N. to Ludlow av.

Bonner pl. (D 6), from Morris av, bet. E. 163d and E. 164th, runs E.

Boone av. (E 6), from Freeman, bet. West Farms rd. and Westchester av., N. to E. 176th.

Boscobel av. (C 6), from Jerome av., opp. Cromwell av., N. W. to Aqueduct av.

Boscobel pl. (C 6), from Boscobel av., bet. Plimpton and Aqueduct avs., W. to Undercliff av.

Boston av. (C 3), now called Boston ter.

Boston rd. (D 7), fr. 3302 3d av., N. E. to City line.

Boston ter., now part of Albany Crescent.

Bouck av. (F 3), fr. 1275 Pelham pkway N., N. to Boston rd.

Bowne (City Island) (K^1 2 & J^2 7), fr. Eastchester bay, bet. Beach and Ditmas, E. to L. I. Sound.

Boyd av. (E 2), from 1751 Edenwald av., N. W. to Barnes av.

Boynton av. (F 6), from Bronx River av., bet. Ward and Elder avs., N. to Bronx River av.

BOROUGH OF BRONX STREET AND AVENUE DIRECTORY—*Continued.*

Bradford av. (H 4), from 1200 Ft. Schuyler rd., N. to La Salle.

Bradley (D 1), fr. Aldrich, N. of Abbot, E. to Baldwin.

Brady av. (E4), from 2100 Bear Swamp rd., E. to Neil av.

Bridge (City Island) (J^1 2 & H^2 7), fr. City Island av., N. of the Bridge, E. to Minnieford av.

Briggs av. (D 4), from E. Kingsbridge rd., bet. Valentine av. and Coles pl., N. E. to Mosholu Parkway.

Brinsmade av. (J 5), from Shore drive, bet. Huntington and Swinton avs., N. W. to Eastern blvd.

Bristow (E 6), from 1319 Stebbins av., N. to Boston rd.

Britton (E 8), from 2800 Bronx pk.E., E.to White Plains rd.

Broadway, 24th wd. (B 4), fr. Spuyten Duyvil cr.; N. and N.E. to City line.

Brockett av., now called St. Raymond av.

Bronx (E 5), fr. E. Tremont av., E. of Boston rd., N. to E. 181st.

Bronx arcade (D 8), from 365 E.138th, N. to E.142d.

Bronx Boulevard (D 8), Burke av., opp. Bronx pk. E.. N. to City line.

Bronx Park av. (E 5), fr. Van Nest av., S. of E. 177th, N. & E. to Morris pk av.

Bronx Park East (F 4), fr. 601 Bronx & Pelham pkway. N. to Burke av.

Bronx River av. (H 6), fr. Clason's pt., W.. N. W. and N.E. to Rosedale av.

Bronx River P'kway (D8), from N. end of Bronx Pk., N. to City Line.

Bronx and Pelham Parkway (E 5), fr. Southern blvd., opp. Pelham av., E. to Pelham bay park.

Bronxdale av. (F 4), from West Farms rd., W. to Bronx park E.

Bronxwood av. (F4), from Rhinelander av., at Bear Swamp rd., N. W. to Barnes av.

Brook av. (D 8), fr. 511 E. 132d, N. to Wendover av.

Brown pl (D8), from 491 E. 132d, N. to E. 138th.

Bruner av. (G 3), fr. Bassett av. N., W. of Mayor, N. W. to Barnes av.

Brush av. (J 6), from Yznaga av., W. of Taber av., N. and N. E. to Waterbury av.

Bryant av. (G 10), from Edgewater rd., bet. Faile and Drake, N.to E. 182d.

Buchanan pl. (C 5), from Jerome av., bet. W. 182d and W. 183d, W. to Aqueduct av.

Buck (G 4), from Zerega av., bet. Maclay av. and Fuller, N. to Seddon.

Buhre av. (G 4), fr. 3000 McAlpin av., E. to E. blvd.

Bullard av. (D 1), from 581 E. 236th, N. to E. 242d.

Burke av. (E 3), fr. Bronx River at N side of Bronx pk. E. to Hutchinson R.

Burnet pl. (E 7), from 820 Garrison av., S. E. to Tiffany.

Burnside av. (C 5), see East Burnside av., see West Burnside av.

Burr av. (G 3), fr. Eastern blvd at Westchester av., N. to Bronx and Pelham pkway.

Bush (C 5), fr. 2024 Creston av., E. to Anthony av.

Bushnell av. (G 3), fr. E. Gun Hill road at Bruner av., N. E. to Hutchinson av.

Bussing av. (E 2), from Barnes av. at E. 232d, N. E. to City line.

Butler pl. (G 4), from 1360 Zerega av., N. E. to Herschel.

Buttrick av. (J 5), from East River, bet. Robinson and Balcom avs., N. W. to Mendell.

Byron av. (D 2), fr. 751 E. 233d N. to Bissel av.

Cabot (F 7). from East River, N. to Leggett av.

Cale (C 3), from Van Cortlandt av. W., at Orloff av., N. to Van Cortlandt park S.

Calhoun av. (K 5^1 & J 10^2) from Shore drive, bet. Quincy and Revere avs., N. W. to Eastern blvd.

Cambrelleng av. (D 4), fr. 681 Grote. N. to Pelham av.

Cambridge av. (B 3), from W. 232d, at Oxford av., N. to Riverdale av.

Cameron pl. (C 5), from 2170 Jerome av., E. to Morris av.

Camp (E 1), fr. Baychester av., bet. Hoyt and Bissell av., N. E. to Wilder.

Canal pl. (D 8), from E. 138th, E. of Park av., N. to W. 144th.

Canal st. W. (D 8), from E. 135th, bet. Park av. and Mott Haven Canal, N. to E. 138th.

Cannon pl. (C 3), from Giles pl., N. of Heath av.. W. & N. to W. 238th.

Carlisle pl. (E3), from E. 211th, bet. Holland and Barnes avs., N. to E. 218th.

Caroll (City Island) (K 8^1 & J 7^2), from Eastchester bay; bet. Schofield and Orchard, E. to L. I. Sound.

Carpenter av. (D 2), fr. E. 219th, at Bronx blvd., N. to City line.

Carr (D 7), fr. 708 German pl., E. to St. Anns av.

Carrigan pl. (C 3), from W. 208th, E. of Goulden av., N. E. to Mosholu Parkway South.

Carroll pl. (C 6), from 181 E. 165th, N. to McClellan.

Carter av. (D 5), fr. E. 173d, bet. Anthony & Webster avs., N. to E. Tremont av.

Cary av. (H 5), from Hale av., at Stark pl., N. to Foote av.

Casanova (F 7), from 1221 Viele av., N. to Spofford av.

Castle Hill av. (H 6), from Castle Hill pk., at mouth of Westchester crk., N. to Walker av.

Caswell av. (G 7), fr. 100 Drake, E. to East River.

Cauldwell av. (E 7), from 621 Westchester av., N. to Boston rd.

Causeway (H5), from Ferris av. to Evans av., S. of Randall av.

Cayuga av. (B 3), from W. 244th, E. of Malcolm pl., N. to W. 246th.

Cedar av., 23d wd. (C 5), fr. 1800 Sedgwick av. N. to W. Fordham rd.

Cedar la. (C 7), fr. 140 E. 150th, runs N.

Centre (City Island) (K 8^1 & J 8^2), fr. Eastchester bay, S. of Schofield, E. to Long Island Sound.

Chaffee av. (K 5^1 & J 10^2), fr. Shore dr. at Throg's Neck blvd., E. to L. I. Sound.

Chanute av. (F 6), now called Manor av., from Bronx River, bet. Craighill & Ward avs., N. to Bronx River av.

Chapin av. (D2), fr. Bronx blvd., opp. E. 219th, N. to E. 228th.

Charlotte (E 6), from Jennings, bet. Wilkins pl. and Minford pl., N. to Crotona pk. E.

Chatterton av. (G 5), fr. 1031 Virginia av.. E. to Westchester creek.

Chesbrough av. (G 4), fr. 1474 Williamsbridge rd., E. & N. to Westchester creek.

Chester (E2), fr. 3524 Eastchester rd., N. E. to E. 222d.

Chestnut (E 3), from 3300 Barnes av., E. to Bronxwood av.

Chisholm (E 6), 1289 Intervale av., N. to Jennings.

City Island av. (City I'ld) (K 8^1 & J 8^2), fr. L. I Sound, at Belden Pt. pk. N. to Eastchester bay.

City Island rd. (H 3), Bartow station, E. and S. to City Island.

Claflin av (C 4), fr. Eames pl., bet. Webb av. and University av., N. to Reservoir av.

Claremont parkway (D 6), from 1570 Webster av., E. to Fulton av.

Clarence av. (J4), fr. Shore Drive at Schley av., N. to Baisley av.

Clarke pl. W. (C 6), see E. Clarke pl., see W. Clarke pl.

Clason's Point rd. (H 6), from Clason's pt., N. W. to Westchester av

Clay av. (D 6), from 3291 Park av., N. to E. 176th.

Clifford pl. (C 5), fr. 1700 Jerome av., E. to Walton av.

Clinton av. (D 6), from E. 169th, bet. Franklin av. and Boston rd., N. to E. 182d.

Clinton pl. (C 5), from Jerome av., bet. W. 181st & W. 182d, W. to Aqueduct av.

Close av. (F 6), fr. Bronx River av., bet. Lafayette and Story avs., N. to Bronx River av.

Coddington av. (H 4), fr. 1400 Ft. Schuyler rd.. N. E. to Eastern blvd.

Colden av. (F4), from Sackett av., E. of Radcliffe av., N.W. to Bogart av. and from Astor av., N. W. to E. Gun Hill rd.

Colgate av. (F 6), fr. Bronx River av. at Lafayette av., N. to Bronx River av.

College av. (D 7), from Morris av. at E. 141st, N. to Teller av.

Colonial av. (G 3), from Westchester av., bet. St. Paul and Burr avs., N. to Bronx & Pelham pkway.

Commerce av. (B 6), from W. 170th, W. of Sedgwick av., N. to W. 176th.

Commerce av. (G 5), from 1100 Zerega av., N. E. and N. to Walker av.

Commonwealth av. (G 6), fr. Bronx River av., bet. St. Lawrence and Rosedale, N. to Walker av.

Compton av. (H 6), from Clason's pt., N. & N. W. to Patterson av.

Concord av. (E 7), from E. 141st, bet. Robbins and Wales avs., N. to E. 152d.

Concourse (C 6), see Grand Boulevard & Concourse.

Conner (F 2), fr. 3700 Pratt av., E. & S. E. to Hutchinson River.

Continental av. (G 3), fr. Westchester av., bet. Wilkinson and St. Paul avs., N. to Bronx and Pelham parkway.

Cooper av., now Putnam pl.

Copeland (H 5), fr. Brush av. N. of E. 177th, N.E. to Graff av.

Coppee (H5), fr. 650 Zerega av. E. to Westchester cr.

Corlear av. (B 3), from Spuyten Duyvil creek, bet. Kingsbridge & Tibbett avs., N. to W. 240th.

Cornell av. (H 6), fr. nr. mouth of Bronx River E. to Pugsley's creek.

Corsa av. (F2), fr. 1475 Burke av., N.W. to Oakley.

Corsa la. (E2), from Eastchester rd. at Needham av., N. W. to Bronxwood av.

Coster (F 7), fr. 51 Edgewater rd., N. to Hunt's Point av.

Cottage la. (B 4), from W. 230th, bet. Bailey av. & B'way N. to Albany rd.

Cottage pl. (D 6), from E. 170th, bet. Fulton and Franklin avs., N. to Crotona pk. S.

Courtlandt av. (D 7), from 2773 3d av, N. to E. 163d.

Craighill av., now called Stratford av.

Cranford av. (D 1), from Baychester av., at White Plains rd., N. E. to City line.

Crawford av. (E 2), from 3900 Laconia av., N.E. to Eden ter.

Crescent av. (D 4), from 2306 Arthur av., N. E. to E. 187th.

BOROUGH OF BRONX STREET AND AVENUE DIRECTORY—*Continued.*

Creston av. (C 5), from E. Tremont av., bet. Morris av. and Echo pl., N. to Minerva pl.

Crimmins av. (E 7), from E. 141st, E. of St. Anns av., N. to St. Marys.

Croes av. (G 6), fr. Bronx R. av., bet. Noble and Patterson avs, N. to Bronx River av.

Cromwell av. (C 7), from Exterior at E. 150th, N. to Macomb's rd.

Crosby av. (H 4), from Eastern Boulevard, bet. Edison & Layton avs, N. to Westchester av. at Edison av.

Cross (City Island) (J 2^1 & H 7^2) from Eastchester Bay, bet. Elizabeth and Beach, E. to L. I. Sound.

Crotona av. (D 6), from 1375 Boston rd., N. to S. Boulevard.

Crotona pk. E. (E 6), Prospect av., N. of Boston rd., N. E to S. Boulevard.

Crotona pk. N. (D 5), from 1780 Arthur av., E. to E. 175th.

Crotona pk. S. (D 6), from Fulton av. opp. St. Pauls pl., E. to Prospect av.

Crotona pk. W. (D 6), that part of Fulton av. bet. Crotona pk S. & E. 175th.

Crotona p'kway (E 5), S. Boulev'd fr. E. 175th N. to Bronx pk.

Crotona pl. (D 6), fr. St. Pauls pl., bet. 3d & Fulton avs., N. to E. 171st.

Cruger av. (F4), fr. Bronxdale av., E. of White Plains rd. N. W. to E. Gun Hill rd., that part S. of Bronxdale av. being now part of Hunt av.

Cullinden av., now called Wissman av.

Curtis (E 2), from 3524 Fenton av., N.E. to Eastchester rd.

Cypress av. (E 8), fr. 671 E. 132d, N. to St. Marys.

Cyrus pl. (D 4), from 4700 Park av., E. to 3d av.

Dahlgren (G 7), from 1581 Ryawa av., N. to Edgewater rd.

Daly av. (E 5), from E. 176th, W. of Boston rd., N. to E. 182d.

Damis av., now called Colgate av.

Daniel (H 4), fr. 1650 Plymouth av., E. to Crosby av.

Dark (F 1), fr. 4000 Pratt av., E. to Dyre.

Dash's la. (B 3), from W. 242d. W. of Tibbett's av., N.W. & S. W. to Fieldston rd.

Davidson av. (C 5), fr. 21 W. 177th, N. to W. 194th.

Davis av. (J 5), fr. Shore drive, bet. Robinson and Buttrick avs., N. W. to Lafayette avs.

Dawson (E 7), from 718 Prospect av., N. E. to Intervale av.

Dean av. (J 4), fr. Shore Drive, N. of Philip av., N. to Baisley av.

Decatur av. (D 4), from E. Fordham rd., W. of Webster av., N.E. to E. 211th.

DeKalb av. (C 3), from 51 E. 208th, N. to E. 213th.

Delafield av. (A 3), fr. 450 W. 247th, N. to W. 263d.

Delanoy av. (G 3), from Pelham parkway N., at Stillwell av., N. to E. Gun Hill rd.

Delavall (G 2), from Hutchinson av. N. of Adee av., N. W. to Boston rd.

Demeyer (G 3), from 1851 Bassett av. N., N. to E. Gun Hill rd.

Depot pl. (B 6), from Harlem River, N. of W. 167th, E. to Sedgwick av.

Depot sq. E. (D4), fr. Depot sq. S., N. to Depot sq. N.

Depot sq. N. (D 4), from Webster av., S. of E. 201st, E. to Depot sq. E.

Depot sq. S. (D 4), from Webster av., N. of E. 200th, E. to Depot sq. E.

De Reimer av. (G 3), fr. 2025 Bassett av. N., N.W. to Nereid av.

Devoe av. (E 5), from E. 174th, E. of Bronx River, N. to E. 180th.

Devoe ter. (C 4), fm. 2420 Webb av., E. & N. to W. 190th.

Dewey av. (H 6), fr. Westchester creek, N. of Yznaga av., N. E. to Throg's Neck Boulevard.

Deyo (F 3), fm. 3150 Fenton av., N. E. to Eastchester rd.

Dickinson av. (C 3), from Sedgwick av., E. of Saxon av., N. to Van Cortland Park S.

Digney av. (E 2), from E. 233d at Edenwald av., N. W. to E. 237th.

Ditmars (City Island) (K2^1 & J7^2), from Eastchester Bay, S. of Bowne, E. to L. I. Sound.

Dock, now that part of W. 177th, bet. Harlem River and Sedgwick av.

Dongan (E 6), now part of E. 163d, fr. Westchester av. to S. Boulevard.

Doris (G 5), Westchester av., opp. Havemeyer av., N. W. to Glebe av.

Dorsey (G 4), fr. 1650 Zerega av., N.E. to Seddon.

Doughty (C 7), from E. 158th, W. of Cromwell av., N. to E. 161st.

Douglas av. (A3), from 670 W. 240th, N. to W. 247th.

Douglas pl. (J 4), now Scott pl.

Drake (G 7), from E. River, N. to Seneca av.

Dudley av. (H 4), from 1450 Ft. Schuyler rd., N. E. to Crosby av.

Duncan (E 3), from 3300 Bronxwood av., E. to Laconia av.

Duncomb av. (E 3), from Bronx Boulevard, N. of Magenta, N. E. to Olinville av.

Dupont (F 7), from 1101 Oak Point av., N. to Leggett av.

Duryea (F 1), from 1451 E 233d, N.W to City line.

Dyre av. (G 2), fr. Hutchinson av. at Arnow av., N.W. and N. to City line.

Dyre pl. (F2), now part of Dyre av.

Eads (H 5), from E. 177th bet. Copeland & Holley, N.E. to Graff av.

Eagle av. (D 7), from E. 149th, E. of St. Anns av., N. to E. 163d.

Eames pl. (C 4), from University av., N. of West Kingsbridge rd, W. to Webb av.

Earl (F4), now that part of Sackett av., bet. Bear Swamp rd & Radcliffe av.

Earley (City Island) (K 3^1 & J 8^2), fr. Eastchester Bay, bet. Pell and Winter, E. to City Island av.

East Bay av. (F 7), from 400 Cabot, E. to Bronx R.

East Bedford Pk. Boulevard (C 3), from 2950 Jerome av., E. to Bronx Pk.

East Belmont (C 6), now part of Mount Eden av.

East Burnside av. (C 5), from 2040 Jerome av. E. to Valentine av.

East Clarke pl. (C6), fr. 1820 Jerome av., E. to Grand Boulevard & Concourse.

East Fordham rd. (C 4), from 2442 Jerome av., E. to Webster av.

East Gun Hill rd. (D3), fr. 3500 Jerome av. E. to Baychester av.

East Kingsbridge rd. (C 4), fr. 2670 Jerome av., E. & S.E. to E. Fordham rd.

East Mosholu pkway N. (C 3), the N. side of Mosholu p'kway, E. of Jerome av.

East Mosholu pkway S. (C 3), the S. side of Mosholu p'kway, E. of Jerome av.

East Tremont av. (C 5), fr. 1966 Jerome av. E. to Bronx River.

East Van Cortlandt av. (C 3), fr. 3200 Jerome av., E. to Woodlawn rd.

E. 129th (continued from Manhattan Borough) (D 8), from Willow av., nr. Bronx Kills, E. to Walnut av.

E. 130th (continued from Manhattan Borough) (D 8), from 2 St. Anns av. E. to Locust av.

E. 131st (continued from Manhattan Borough) (D 8), from 62 St. Anns av. E. to Locust av.

E. 132d, 23d ward (D 8), from 82 Lincoln av., E. to East River.

E. 133d, 23d ward (D 8), from 2412 3d av., E. to East River.

E. 134th, 23d ward (D 8), from W. of 3d av., E. to East River.

E. 135th, 23d ward (D 8), from 2468 Park av., E. to East River.

E. 136th, 23d ward (D 8), from 190 Rider av., E. to East River.

E. 137th, 23d ward (D 8), from 220 Rider av., E. to East River.

E. 138th, 23d ward (C 8), from Harlem River, E. to East River.

E. 139th, 23d ward (D 8), from 276 Rider av., E. to Locust av.

E. 140th, 23d ward (D 8), from Exterior, E. to East River.

E. 141st, 23d ward (D 8), from 2680 Park av., E. to Locust av.

E. 142d, 23d ward (D 7), from 390 Rider av., E. to S. blvd.

E. 143d (D 7), fr. E. 144th bet. Rider & Morris avs. E. to St. Anns av.

E. 144th (D 7), from 414 River av., E. to Whitlock av.

E. 145th (D 7), from 290 E. 146th, E. to Timpson pl.

E. 146th (D 7), from Exterior; S. of E. 149th E. to Mott av., and fr. 466 River av., E. to St. Anns av.

E. 147th (D 7), from 2792 3d av., E. to Austin pl.

E. 148th (D 7), 2818 from Park av., E. to St. Anns av.

E. 149th (C 7), from Harlem R., E. and S. to East River

E. 150th (C 7), fr. Harlem River, E. to Prospect av.

E. 151st (C 7), from Exterior, S. of E. 157th, S. E. and E. to Prospect av.

E. 152d (D 7), fr. 2938 Park av., E. to Prospect av.

E. 153d (C7), from E. 157th, W. of Cromwell av., S. E. and E. to Brook av.

E. 154th (D 7), from 2996 Park av., E. to 3d av.

E. 155th (D 7), from 3016 Park av., E. to 3d av., and fr. 780 Westchester av., E. to Prospect av.

E. 156th (C 7), from 750 Mott av., E. and S to Worthen.

E. 157th (C 7), from 800 Exterior, E. to St. Anns av.

E. 158th (C 7), from N. Y. C. & H. R. R. R., E. to Westchester av.

E. 159th (C 7), 850 Walton av., E. to Eagle av.

E. 160th (D7), fr. 860 Morris av. E. to Westchester av.

E. 161st (C7), from 848 Jerome av., E. to Hewitt pl.

E. 162d (C 7), from 940 Jerome av., E. to Sheridan av. and fr. Sherman av., E. to Westchester av.

E. 163d (C7), fr. 940 Grand Boulevard & Concourse, E. to S. blvd.

E. 164th (C 6), 1000 Jerome av., E. to Trinity av., and fr. 980 Prospect av., E. to Stebbins av.

E. 165th (C 6), fr. 1050 Jerome av., E. to Whitlock av.

E. 166th (C6), from 1050 Walton av., E. to Prospect av.

E. 167th (C 6), from 1210 Jerome av., E. to Westchester av.

E. 168th (C6), from River av., at Jerome av., E. to Prospect av.

E. 169th (C 6), fr. Jerome av., at Gerard av., E. to E. 167th.

E. 170th (C6), fr. 1400 Jerome av., E. to Charlotte.

E. 171st (C 6), fr. 1450 Jerome av., E. to Fulton av.

E. 172d (C 6), fr. 1500 Jerome av., E. to Bronx River av.

BOROUGH OF BRONX STREET AND AVENUE DIRECTORY—*Continued.*

E. 173d (C 5), from 1680 Grand Boulevard & Concourse, E. to Manor av.

E. 174th (C5), fr. 1650 Jerome av., E. to Devoe av. and from 1760 Boston rd., E. to E. 177th and St. Lawrence av.

E. 175th (C 5), from 1750 Jerome av., E. to Boston rd.

E. 176th (C5), fr. 1850 Jerome av., E. to Bronx River.

E. 177th (C 5), fr. 1900 Jerome av., E. to Grand Boulevard & Concourse, & fr. Bronx River, E. to Locust Pt.

E. 178th (C 5), from 1980 Creston av., E. to Boston rd. and from 860 Bronx pk. av., E. to Van Nest av

E. 179th (C 5), fr. 2000 Jerome av., E. to Bronx pk. av.

E. 180th (C5), fr. 2080 Creston av., E. to Walker av.

E. 181st (C 5), from 2150 Jerome av., E. to Bronx.

E. 182d (C 5), fr. 2230 Jerome av., E. to Southern blvd.

E. 183d (C 4), fr. 2294 Jerome av., E. to Southern blvd.

E. 184th (C4), fr. 2374 Jerome av., E. to Arthur av.

E. 185th (D 4), from 4596 Park av., E. to Southern blvd.

E. 186th (D4), fr. 4640 Park av., E. to Belmont av.

E. 187th (C 4), from 2426 Grand Boulevard and Concourse, E. to Southern blvd.

E. 188th (C 4), from E. Fordham rd., bet. Morris & Creston avs., E. to Beaumont av.

E. 189th (C 4), fr. 2488 Webster av., E. to Southern blvd.

E. 190th (C 4), fr. 2500 Jerome av., E. to E. Fordham rd.

E. 191st (C 4), fr. Morris av., at St James pk., E. to Creston av., and from 2540 Bathgate av., E. to Hughes av.

E. 192d (C4), 2580 Creston av., E. to Valentine av.

E. 193d (C 4), fr. 2640 Jerome av., E. to Webster av.

E. 194th (C 4), from E. Kingsbridge rd., at Valentine av. E. to Continental av.

E. 195th (D 4), from 2688 Marion av., E. to Hobart av.

E. 196th (C 4), fr. 2750 Jerome av., E. to Burr av.

E. 197th (C4), fr. 2820 Creston av., E. to Hobart av.

E. 198th (C 4), fr. 2850 Jerome av., E. to Webster av.

E. 199th (C 3), fr. 2922 Jerome av., S. E. to Webster av.

E. 200th (C 3), now called Bedford pk. blvd.

E. 201st (D 3), from 3020 Grand Boulevard & Concourse, E. to Webster av.

E. 202d (D 3), from 3040 Grand Boulevard & Concourse, E. to Briggs av., and from 3066 Webster av., E. to Bronx Park.

E. 203d (D 3), from 3120 Grand Boulevard & Concourse, E. to Mosholu Parkway and from 3090 Webster av. E. to Bronx park.

E. 204th (C 3), from 3116 Jerome av., E. to Bronx park.

E. 205th (C 3), fr. 3150 Jerome av., E. to Mosholu pkway and from 3100 Woodlawn rd., E. to Webster av.

E. 206th (C 3), from 3170 Grand Boulevard & Concourse, E. to Perry av.

E. 207th (D 3), from 3200 Woodlawn rd. E. to Webster av.

E. 208th (C 3), from 3400 Jerome av., S. E. and E. to Bainbridge av.

E. 209th (D 3), from 3300 Perry av., E. to Parkside pl.

E. 210th (C 3), from E. 208th, at DeKalb av., E. to Reservoir Oval W., & fr. Webster av. S. of E. Gun Hill rd., E. to Duncomb av.

E. 211th (D 3), fr. Woodlawn rd., N. of E. Gun Hill rd. E. to Boston rd.

E. 212th (C 3), from 3560 Jerome av., E. to Woodlawn rd., fr. 3560 White Plains rd. E. to Holland av., and fr. 3560 Bronxwood av., E. to Boston rd.

E. 213th (C 3), from 3600 Jerome av., E. to Woodlawn rd., and fr. Bronx river E. to Boston rd.

E. 214th (D2), from 3630 White Plains rd., E. to Wilson av.

E. 215th (D 2), fr. 3660 White Plains rd., E. and N. E. to Wilson av.

E. 216th (D 2), fr. Bronx River P'kway, N. of E. Gun Hill rd., E to Wilson av.

E. 217th (D 2), fr. 3724 White Plains rd., E. to Laconia av.

E. 218th (D 2), from 3750 White Plains rd., E. to Oakley.

E. 219th (D 2), from Bronx River P'kway at Carpenter av., E. to Oakley.

E. 220th (D2), from Bronx River P'kway, E. to Oakley.

E. 221st (D2) 3850 Carpenter av., E. to Eastchester rd.

E. 222d (D2), Bronx River P'kway, Wakefield, E. to Hutchinson av.

E. 223d (D 2), from 3924 Carpenter av., E. to Laconia av.

E. 224th (D 2), from Bronx River Parkway, Wakefield, E. to Laconia av.

E. 225th (D 2), from 3974 Carpenter av., E. to Mickle av.

E. 226th (D2), from Bronx River Parkway, Wakefield, E. to Laconia av.

E. 227th (D 2), from 4024 Carpenter av. E. to Laconia av.

E. 228th (D 2), fr. Bronx River Parkway, Wakefield, E. to Laconia av.

E. 229th (D2), from Bronx River Parkway, E. to Laconia av.

E. 230th (D 2), from 4124 Carpenter av., E. to Wickham av.

E. 231st (D2), from 4150 Carpenter av., E. to Bruner av.

E. 232d (D 2), from 4174 Bronx Blvd., E. to Ely av.

E. 233d (C 2), Jerome av., S. of Mt. Vernon av., E. to Hutchinson river.

E. 234th (D2), from E. 233d, bet. Kepler & Katonah avs., E. to Bussing av.

E. 235th (C 2 & D 2), from 4270 Mt. Vernon av., E. to Bronx river, and from 4250 Carpenter av., E. to Bronxwood av.

E. 236th (C 2 & D 1), from 4290 Mt. Vernon av., E. to Bronx river, and from 4350 Bullard av., E. to Barnes av.

E. 237th (C 2), from Napier av., at Mt. Vernon av., E. to Vireo av., and fr. 4356 Bullard av., E. to Barnes av.

E. 238th (C 2), from Mt. Vernon av. at Oneida av., E. to Vireo av.

E. 239th (C 2 & D 1), from 4350 Mt. Vernon av., E. to Vireo av., and from 4500 Bullard av., E. to Barnes av.

E. 240th (C 1 & D 1), from 4370 Mt. Vernon av., E. to McLean av., & from 4600 Bullard av., E. to Furman av.

E. 241st (C 1), from 4390 Mt. Vernon av., E. to White Plains rd.

E. 242d (C 1), from 4440 Mt. Vernon av., E. to City line and fr. Bronx R., E to Penfield.

E. 243d (D1), from Robertson, S. of City line, E. to Barnes av.

Eastburn av. (D 5), 231 E. Belmont, N. to Grand Boulevard & Concourse.

Eastchester Landing rd. (F 1), now Connor.

Eastchester pl. (G1), from Tillotson av., N. of Hutchinson River, N.W. to Hollers av.

Eastchester rd. (G4), from Walker av., opp. Benson av. N. & N. W. to Laconia av.

Eastern Boulevard, 23d ward (F 7), now Oak Point av.

Eastern Boulevard, 24th ward (H 5), E. 177th at Seabury av., E. and N. and E. to Hutchinson R.

Echo pl. (C 5), E. Tremont av., bet. Creston av. and the Grand Boulevard and Concourse, E. to Echo pk.

Eden av. (C 6), now Selwyn av.

Eden ter. (F 2), fr. Boston rd., at Needham av., N. W. to E. 233d.

Edenwald av. (E 2), from Bronxwood av., at E. 233d, N. E. to City line.

Edgehill av. (B 4), from W. 227th, bet. Netherland and Johnson avs., N. to W. 230th.

Edgewater rd. (F 7), from Manida at East R., N. & N. W. to West Farms rd.

Edison av. (J 5), fr. Dewey av., at E. 177th, N. W. and N. to Wilkinson av.

Edson av. (G 2), fr. 1951 Bassett av. N., N. W. to Bissel av.

Edwards av. (H 4), from Waterbury av., W. of Fort Schuyler rd., N. to Balcom av.

Effingham av. (H 6), from Zerega av. bet. Norton and Lacombe avs., N. to Lafayette av.

Elberon av. (G 4), from 1831 Eastchester rd., N. W. to Pelham pkway S.

Elder av. (F 6), from Bronx River av. at Seward av., N. to Bronx River av.

Elizabeth (City Island) (J 2[1] & H 7[2]), from Eastchester bay, bet Sutherland and Cross, E. to L. I. Sound.

Elliott pl. (C 6), fr. 1374 Jerome av., E. to Grand Boulevard & Concourse.

Ellis av. (G 5), from 1230 Virginia av., E. to Commerce av.

Ellison av. (H 4), from Whittemore av., bet. Balcom av. & Ft. Schuyler rd. N. to Edwards av.

Ellsworth av. (J 4), from Shore Dr., bet. Throg's Neck Boulevard & Vincent av., N. to Waterbury av.

Elm pl. (D 4), fr. E. 187th, E. of Tiebout av., N. to E. Fordham rd.

Elsmere pl. (E 5), from 1932 Prospect av., E. to S. Boulevard.

Elton av. (D 7), from 3d av., at E. 158d, N. to Brook av.

Elwood pl. (E 2), from E. 212th, bet. Laconia av. & Boston rd., N to E. 214th.

Ely av. (G 2), from 1901 Bassett av., N. W. to Bissel av.

Emerson av. (J 5), fr. East River, S. of Robinson av., N. W. to Lafayette av.

Emmet (D 4), from Pelham av., E. of Washington av., N.

Ericson pl. (G 4), fr. 1470 Ft. Schuyler rd., N. W. to Appleton av.

Evadna av., now Roberts av.

Evans av. (J 6), from Old Ferry Pt., N. W. to Randall av.

Evelyn pl. (C 4), from Jerome av., bet. W. 183d & North, W. to Aqueduct av., E.

Evergreen av. (F 6), from Bronx River av., bet. Wheeler & Lafayette avs., N. to Bronx River av.

BOROUGH OF BRONX STREET AND AVENUE DIRECTORY—*Continued.*

Exterior (C 8 & B 5), E. 185th, W. of Park av., N. to Jerome av., and fr. W. 179th, N. to W. 230th.

Faile (F 7), from East River N. to 1200 Westchester av.

Fairfax av. (H 4), from Layton av., E. of Kearney av., N. to Waterbury av.

Fairfield av. (B 4), fr. 630 Kappock, N. to Spuyten Duyvil pkway.

Fairmount av. (H 4), from Eastern Boulevard, bet. Layton and Baisley avs., N. E. to Ruth pl.

Fairmount pl. (D 5), from 1900 Crotona av., E. to S. Boulevard.

Falconer (G 7), fr. Hunt's Point av., at Edgewater rd., N. to Edgewater rd.

Faraday av., now Iselin av.

Farragut (G 7), from E. R., N. to Edgewater rd.

Farrington av. (H 5), Zerega av. bet. Allaire and Randall avs., N. to Lafayette av.

Featherbed la. (C8), from 1651 Jerome av., W. to Aqueduct av.

Fenfell av. (F 6), now called Evergreen av.

Fenton av. (F 3), 1451 Pelham pkway N., N. W. to Hicks.

Ferncliff pl. (C 7), from E 151st st., at Cromwell av., runs S. W.

Ferris av. (G 3), Baychester, now that part of Mace av. bet. E. Gun Hill rd. and Hutchinson av.

Ferris av. (J 6), from Yznaga av., E. of Seaman av., N. to E. 177th.

Ferris pl. (G 4), fr. Westchester sq., S. of Walker av., E. to Commerce.

Field pl. (C 4), from 2354 Morris av., E. to Ryer av.

Fieldston rd. (B 3), from Riverdale av., at W. 236th, N. to City line.

Fillmore (F 4), Van Nest av., bet. Garfield and Unionport rd., N. W. to Bronx Park E.

Findlay av. (D 6), from E. 164th, bet. College and Teller avs., N. to 170th.

Fink av. (G 4), fr. Walker av., at Westchester sq., E. to Lang av.

Fish av. (F 3), fr. 1851 Pelham pkway N., N. W. to Oakley.

Fletcher (D 4), from 2196 Washington av., E. to Bassford av.

Folin (D 5), fr. E. 181st, at Tiebout av. N.E. to E. 182d.

Foote av. (H5), from Randall av., at Ferris av., S. E. to Emerson av.

Ford (D 5), fr. 2270 Tiebout av., E. to Webster av.

Fordham (City Island) (K 3^1 & J 7^2), fr. Eastchester bay, bet. Bay & Orchard, E. to L. I. Sound.

Fordham rd. (C 4), see East Fordham rd. and see West Fordham rd.

Forest (G4) now Lurting av.

Forest av. (E 7), Westchester av., bet. E. 155th and E. 156th, N. to E. 168th.

Fort Independence (C 3), from Heath av., W. of Kingsbridge ter., N. to W. 238th.

Fort Schuyler rd. (K 5^1 & J 10^2), fr. Shore drive, bet. Revere and Logan avs., N. to Westchester cr.

Fowler av. (G4), from Bear Swamp rd. at Pierce av., N. to Neil av.

Fox (E 7), fr. 580 Prospect av., N.E. to Intervale av.

Fox sq. (E 6), at junction of Westchester av. and West Farms rd.

Franklin av., (D 6), 3368 3d av., N. to Crotona pk. South.

Freeman (E 6), from 1268 Union av., E. to Westchester av.

Frisby av. (G 4), fr. 1500 Zerega av., N. E. to Walker av.

Fteley av. (G6), fr. Bronx River av., at Lacombe av., N. to Bronx River av.

Fuller (G 4), fr. 1750 Zerega av., N. E. to Seddon.

Fulton (E 3) (Olinville), fr Bronx Pk. E. bet Mace & Allerton avs., E. to White Plains road.

Fulton av. (D6), fr. E. 166th, bet. 3d & Franklin avs., N. to E. 175th.

Furman av. (D 1), from 725 E. 236th, N. to E. 241st.

Gainsboro av. (H 4), Middletown rd., W. of Eastern blvd., N. W. to Morris pk. av.

Gale pl. (C 3), from Orloff av., N. of Van Cortlandt av., W. and N. to Van Cortlandt park S.

Garden (D 5), fr. Grote, W. of Crotona av., S. E. to Southern blvd.

Garden pl. (D 1), from E. 240th, bet. White Plains rd. & Furman av., N. to E. 241st.

Garfield (F 5), fr. Walker av., opp. Thieriot, N. W. to Morris Park av.

Garrison av. (E 7), from Leggett av., bet. Whitlock av. and Barry, N. E. to Bronx River.

Garrison sq., now called Truxton sq.

Gates pl. (C 3), fr. 41 W. Mosholu pkway N., N.E. to W. Gun Hill rd.

Gaynor av. (C3), from W. 206th, E. of Goulden av., N. E to Mosholu Parkway South.

Genner av. (F 6), fr. Bronx River av., bet. Ward and Elder avs., N. to Bronx River av.; now called Boynton av.

Gerard av. (C 7), from 340 Exterior, North to Jerome av.

German pl. (D 7), name changed to Hegney pl.

Gilbert pl. (F 6), from 850 Hunt's Point av., E. to Faile.

Gildersleeve av. (H 6), from Bronx River, bet. O'Brien and Cornell avs., E. to Pugsley's creek.

Giles pl. (C 3), from Heath av., at Sedgwick av., N. and E. to Sedgwick av.

Gillespie av. (H 4), from Waterbury av., bet. Edison and Crosby avs., N. to Middletown rd.

Gilroy pl. (C 3), from W. 208th. E. of Carrigan pl., N. E. to Mosholu Parkway South.

Givan av. (E 3), fr. E. Gun Hill rd., at Pearsall av., N. E. to Hutchinson av.

Givan sq. (F3), bet. E. Gun Hill rd. & Arnow av., and Eastchester rd. and Fenton av.

Gleason av. (F 5), fr. 1200 Metcalf av., E. to Seabury av.

Glebe av. (G 5), fr. Westchester av., bet. Castle Hill & Havemeyer avs., N. and N. E. to Overing.

Glover (G 5), from 2301 Westchester av., N. W. to Castle Hill av.

Goble pl. (C6), fr. Inwood av., bet. W. 172d and Belmont, W. to Macomb's rd.

Goodridge av. (B 3), fr. W. 247th, at Highland av., N. & W. to Riverdale av., form'ly called Alamo av.

Goulden av. (C 4), from Reservoir av. at W. 197th, N. on East side of Reservoir to Mosholu P'kway.

Gouverneur av. (C 3), fr. 3901 Sedgwick av. N. to Van Cortlandt pk. S.

Gouverneur pl. (D 6), 3420 Park av., E. to Washington av.

Grace av. (G3), fr. Pelham pkway N., W. of Baychester av., N. W. to Bissel av.

Graff av. (J 5), fr. Shore drive, bet. Buttrick and Balcom avs., N. W. to Westchester creek.

Graham sq. (D 8), at junction of 3d av., Morris av. and E. 188th.

Graham sq. (C 6), fr. 1140 Lawrence av., N. & N.W. to Lawrence av.

Grand av. (C 5), from 1620 Macomb's rd., N. E. & N. to Kingsbridge rd.

Grand Boulevard and Concourse, fr. E. 161st opp. Mott av. N. to Mosholu pkway.

1099	1098 E. 166th.
1901	1900 E. Tremont av.
2501	2500 E. Fordham rd.
3001	3000 Bedford pk blvd

Grand View pl. (C 6), fr. E. 167th bet. the Grand blvd & Concourse & Walton avs., N. to E. 168th.

Grant av. (D 7), from E. 161st, bet. Sherman and Morris avs., N. to E. 170th.

Grant Circle, see Hugh J Grant Circle.

Gray (F 5), from E. 177th at Westchester av., N. to Guerlain.

Greene pl. (H 4), fr. Ft. Schuyler rd., bet. Otis & Berkley avs. E. to Edison av.

Grenada pl. (E 2), from Bruner av., at E 231st, N. E. to E. 233d.

Greystone av. (B 3), from 3300 Riverdale av., N. to W. 246th.

Gridley av., now part of Lafayette av.

Grinnell pl. (E 7), fr. 1161 Oak Point av., N. and W. to Garrison av.

Grosvenor av. (B 3), from W. 246th. at Douglas av., N. and W to Iselin av.

Grote (D 5), from E. 182d bet. Belmont and Crotona avs., E. to Southern blvd.

Grover pl. (K 5^1 & J 10^2), from Shore drive, S. of Chaffee av., E. to Pennyfield av.

Guerlain (F5), 1560 Beach av., E. to Unionport rd.

Gun Hill rd. (C 3), see East Gun Hill rd.; see West Gun Hill rd.

Gunther av. (G 3), Stillwell av., bet. Delanoy & Wickham avs., N. W. to Barnes av.

Haight av. (G4), Walker av bet. Lurting av. & Eastchester rd., N. to Bronx and Pelham Parkway.

Hale av. (J 6), from Ferris av. nr. Seaman av., E. to Dewey av.

Half Moon pl. (A 3), from W. 240th, bet. Delafield av. and Seward pl., N. and E. to Independence av.

Hall of Fame ter. (C 5), from University av & W. 181st, W. to Sedgwick av.

Hall pl. (E 6), from E. 165th, bet. Stebbins av. and Rogers pl., N. to Intervale av.

Halleck (G 7), from 81 Edgewater road, N. to Edgewater road.

Halperin av. (G 4), from 1424 Williamsbridge rd., E. to Ponton av.

Halsey (G 4), Wellington av., at Zerega av., N. E. & E. to Commerce av.

Hammersley av. (F 3), fr. E. Gun Hill rd., at Seymour av., N.E. to Hutchinson av.

Hampden pl. (C 5), from W. 183d, bet. Cedar and Sedgwick avs., N. E. to W. Fordham rd.

Hanson av. (K 5^1 & J 9^2), from Shore Drive, E. of Hooker av., N. to E. 177th.

Harlem River ter. (C 5), from Cedar av., S. of W. 181st, N. to Bailey av.

Harper av. (G 3), fr. 2175 Hassett av. N., N. W. & N. to City line.

Harriet pl. (H 4), now part of Revere av.

Harrington av. (H 4), fr. 1424 Ft. Schuyler rd., N. E. to Gillespie av.

Harrison av. (C 5), from Featherbed la., opp. Inwood av., N. to W. 181st.

Harrod av. (G 6), Bronx River av., at Randall av., N. to Bronx River av.

Harts, now part of Barrett av.

Haskin (H 4), from 1160 Ft. Schuyler Road, N. E. to Edison av.

Haswell (G4), Eastchester rd., N. of Blondel av., E. to McAlpin av.

Havemeyer av. (H 5), 2301 Lacombe av. N. to Westchester av.

BOROUGH OF BRONX STREET AND AVENUE DIRECTORY—*Continued.*

Haviland av. (G5), fr. 1130 Virginia av., E. to Commerce av.

Hawkstone (C6), 1560 Walton av., E. to the Grand blvd. and Concourse.

Haynes av. (H 5), fr. Foote av., at Schley av., N. W. and N. to Parsons av.

Heath av. (C 4), from 2600 Bailey av. N. to Sedgwick av.

Heathcote av. (G 1), fr. Givan av., W. of Hutchinson av., N. to Boston rd.

Hegney pl. (D 7), from Westchester av., bet. Brook & St. Anns avs., N. to Brook av.

Hendrick ter., now part of Spuyten Duyvil rd.

Hering av. (G 4), fr. N.Y., N. H. & H. R. R., opp. Blondell av., N. W. & N. to Boston rd.

Herkimer pl. (C 2), fr. E. 238d. W. of Napier av., N. to E. 235th.

Hermany av. (G 5), from 860 White Plains rd., E. to Zerega av.

Herschel (G 4), Wellington av., at Seabury av., N. W. to Westchester av.

Hewitt pl. (E 7), E. 156th, E. of Prospect av., N. to Westchester av.

Hickory (E 3), N. Oak drive, E. of Holland av., N. to E. Gun Hill rd.

Hicks (E 2), fr. 3574 Wilson av., N. E. to Eastchester rd.

Highland av. (B 3), now Grosvenor av.

Hill av. (F 1), 1851 E. 233d, N. W. to City line.

Hobart av. (H 4), from Baisley av., bet. Crosby and Wilkinson avs., N. W. and N. to E. 196th.

Hoe av. (E 6), Whitlock av., bet Hunt's Pt. av. & Faile, N. to Boston rd.

Hoffman (D 4), fr. 571 E. 184th, N. to E 191st.

Hoguet av. (G5), fr. m Unionport rd., at Protectory av., N. to Walker av.

Holland av. (F 4), Baker av., bet. Cruger & Wallace avs., N. to E. 215th.

Hollers av. (F2), fr. Boller av., nr. Boston rd., N.E. to Pelham Bay park W.

Holley (H 5), fr. E. 177th, bet. Hutton and Eads, N. E. to Graff av

Hollywood av. (K 5^1 & J 10^2), fr. Shore Drive, W. of Throg's Neck blvd., N. to Middletown rd.

Holt pl. (D 3), Reservoir Oval E., bet. E. 207th & E. 209th, E. to Perry av.

Home (D 6), 1158 Boston rd., E. to Westchester av.

Hone av. (G 4), Walker av., bet. Paulding & Lurting avs., N.W. and N. to E. Gun Hill rd.

Honeywell av. (E 5), from 901 E. Tremont av., N. E. to Bronx park S.

Hooker av. (K5^1 & J9^2), fr. Shore Drive, bet. Longstreet and Hanson avs., N. to E. 177th.

Hornaday pl. (E 5), from 2140 Crotona pkway, E. to Honeywell av.

Horton (City Island) (K 8), from Eastchester bay, N. of Rochelle, E. to L. I. Sound.

Hosmer av. (J 5), fr. Shore Drive, bet. Emerson and Robinson avs., N. W. to Lafayette av.

Houghton av. (G 5), from Bolton av., bet. Ludlow and Story avs., E. to Westchester creek.

Howe av. (H 6), Castle Hill pk. at mouth of Pugsleys creek, N. to Lafayette av.

Hoxie (E 1), E. 241st, bet. Bissell & Barnes avs., N. W. to Cranford.

Hoyt (E1), 4424 Baychester av., N. E. to Wilder av.

Hubbell (G 4), fr. Dorsey, bet. Zerega av. and Seddon, W. to Maclay av.

Hugh J. Grant Circle (F 5), at intersection of E. 177th & Westchester av.

Hughes av. (D5), fr. 641 E. Tremont av., N. to E. 191st.

Huguenot av. (G 1), from Pelham Bay pk. W., N. W. to Boston rd.

Hull av. (D 3), 351 E. Mosholu pkway N. E. and N. to E. 211th.

Hunt av. (F 4), from Baker av., bet. White Plains rd. and Holland av., N. W. and N. to Bronxdale av.

Hunt's Point av. (G 7), from East River, N. W. to Southern blvd.

Hunter av. (G 3), fr. 2101 Bassett av. N., N. W. to Pratt av.

Hunter av. (City Island) (K 8^1 & J 7^2), Tier, bet. City Island and William avs., N. to Bowne.

Huntington av. (J5), from Shore Drive, bet. Balcom and Brinsmade avs., N. W. to Eastern blvd.

Husson av. (H 6), Bronx River av., at Clason's pt. rd., N. to Compton av.

Hutchinson av. (G 2), fr. Bassett av. N. E. of Harper av., N. to Boston rd.

Hutton (H 5), fr. E. 177th, bet. Mendell and Holley, N. E. to Graff av.

Huxley av. (B 2), Mosholu av., bet. Spencer and Newton avs., N. to W. 262d.

Independence av. (A 4), from 2500 Palisade av., N. to W. 261st.

Intervale av. (E 7), from Southern blvd., bet. Longwood av. & Tiffany, N. to Wilkins av.

Inwood av. (C 6), from 1290 Cromwell av., N. to Featherbed la.

Irvine (F6), Seneca av., E. of Hunt's Pt. av., N. to Garrison av.

Iselin av. (B 3), fr. Spuyten Duyvil pkway, bet. Fieldston rd. and Von Humboldt av. N. W. & N. E. to Newton av.

Ittner pl. (D 5), 1754 Webster av., E. to Park av.

Ives (G4), 1830 Eastchester rd., E. to Bassett av.

Jackson av. (E 8), from South'n Blvd. at E. 138th N. to Boston rd.

Jarrett pl. (G 4), fr Eastchester rd. bet. Williamsbridge rd. & Blondell av., N. to Poplar.

Jarvis av. (H4), from Eastern Blvd., bet. Coddington av. and Middletown rd., N. W. to Buhre av.

Jefferson pl. (D6), fr. 1880 Franklin av., E. to B'ton rd.

Jennings (E 6), fr. Union av., at Boston rd., E. to West Farms road.

Jerome av. (C 7), Harlem R., W. of Macomb's Dam bridge, N. to City line.
— 1000 E. 164th.
1401 1400 W. & E. 170th.
1901 1900 W. & E. 177th.
2501 2500 W. & E 190th.
3501 3500 W. & E. Gun Hill rd.

Jesup av. (C6), fr. Boscobel av., at W. 170th, N. to Featherbed la.

Jessup pl. (C 6), Jesup av., N. of Boscobel av., W. to Shakespeare av.

Johnson av. (B 4), from Spuyten Duyvil rd., at Palisade av., S. E. and N. E. and N. to Spuyten Duyvil parkway.

Kane (G 7), from Caswell av., at Edgewater rd., N. to Randall av.

Kappock (A 4), 2501 Johnson av., N. & N. W. to Spuyten Duyvil rd.

Katonah (D2), from 301 E. 233d. N. to Mt. Vernon av.

Kearney av. (K5^1 & J10^2), from Shore Drive, bet. Throg's Neck blvd. and Meagher av., N. to Shore Drive and fr. Layton av. E. of Throg's Neck blvd., N. to Waterbury av.

Kelly (E 7), from 660 Prospect av., N. E. and N. to Intervale av.

Kepler av. (C 2), from 201 E. 233d, N. to Mt. Vernon av.

Kinderman pl. (D 6), fr. Webster av., bet. E. 169th and E. 170th, E. to Brook av.

King av. (City Isl'd) (K 8^1 and J 7^2), fr. Carroll, E. of Minnieford av., N. to Beach, and from Elizabeth, E. of Minnieford av., N. to Terrace.

King's College pl. (D 3), fr. E. Gun Hill rd., bet. Tryon and Cooper avs., N. to E. 211th.

Kingsbridge av. (B 4), fr. Terrace View av., bet. Broadway and Corlear pl., N. to W. 238th.

Kingsbridge rd. (C 4), see East Kingsbridge rd.; see West Kingsbridge rd.

Kingsbridge ter. (C 4), fr. Heath av., S. of W. Kingsbridge rd., N. to Heath av.

Kingsland av. (G 3), fr. 1625 Pelham pkway N., N. to Laconia av.

Kinsella (F 4), Matthews av., bet. Van Nest and Morris Park avs., E. to Bronxdale avs.

Kirk (G 4), from 1430 Seabury av, N. E. to Commerce av.

Knapp (F3), fr. E. Gun Hill rd., opp. Fenton av., N.E. to Eastchester rd.

Knox pl. (C 3), 12 W. Mosholu pkway. N., N.E. to W. Gun Hill rd.

Kossuth av. (D 3), from 75 E. Mosholu pkway N., N. to DeKalb av.

Lacombe av. (G 6), from Bronx River av., at Fteley av., E. to Westchester creek.

Laconia av. (F 3), from Williamsbridge rd., at Bronx & Pelham pkway, N. to Ely av.

Lafayette av. (E 7), from Longwood av. bet. S. Boulevard and Whitlock avs., E. to Shore Drive.

Lafayette pl. (E 6), from Prospect av., W. of Boston rd. runs S.

Lafontaine av. (D 5), fr. 581 E. Tremont av., N. to Quarry rd.

Lakewood (F 4), fr. Hering av., bet. Morris pk. and Rhinelander avs., N. E. to Narragansett av.

Lamport pl. (J 5), from Revere av., bet. Randall and Schley avs., E. to Ft. Schuyler rd.

Landing rd. (C 4), from Harlem River, N. of W. Fordham rd., E. to near Sedgwick av.

Lane av. (G 4), from Westchester av. at Overing, N. to Walker av.

Lang av. (G4), Westchester av. at Middletown rd., N. W. to McAlpin av.

La Salle av. (H 4), fr. 1850 Ft. Schuyler rd., N E to Eastern blvd.

Latting (H4), Westchester ck., N. of Waterbury av., N. E. to Ft. Schuyler rd.

Laurie av. (G4), 3050 McAlpin av., E. to Mulford av.

Lawrence av. (C 6), from Lind av., S. of W. 166th, N. to W. 167th.

Lawton av. (H6), fr. Brush av., N. of Yznaga av., N. E. to Ferris av. and from Shore Drive at Balcom av., N.E. to Shore Drive, N. of E. 177th.

Layton av. (H 4), from 3000 Eastern blvd., E. to Long Island Sound.

Lebanon (E 5), from 440 Devoe av., E. to Morris pk. av.

Lee (G 4), from 1650 Appleton av., E. to Westchester av.

Leggett av. (E 7), fr. 742 Prospect av., S. E. to Truxton.

Leland av. (H 6), fr. Bronx River av., at Gildersleeve av., N. to Walker av.

Lester (E 3), 2050 Barker av., E. to White Plains rd.

Liebig av. (A 2), Mosholu av., bet. W. 256th and Tyndall av., N. to City line.

Light (F1), 3800 Pratt av., E. to Provost av.

Lincoln, now Hone av.

Lincoln av. (D 8), from Harlem R., E. of 3d av. Bridge, N. to E. 138th.

Lind av. (C 7), now part of University av.

Lisbon pl. (D 3), from E. 205th, E. of Grand Boulevard and Concourse, E. to E. Mosholu pkway S.

BOROUGH OF BRONX STREET AND AVENUE DIRECTORY—*Continued.*

Livingston av. (B8), from Spuyten Duyvil pkway, bet. Fieldston rd. and Waldo av., N. to W. 252d.

Locust av. (E 8), from 921 E. 132d, N. to E. 141st.

Lodovick av. (G 3), 1701 Pelham pkway N., N.W. to E. Gun Hill rd.

Logan av. (K 5^1 & J 10^2), from Shore Drive, E. of Fort Schuyler rd., N. to Berkley av.

Longfellow av. (F 7), from 1341 Viele av., N. to Boston rd.

Longstreet av. (K 5^1 and J 9^2), Shore Drive, bet. Blair and Hooker avs., N. to Shore Drive.

Longwood av. (E 7), from 840 Westchester av., S.E. to Tiffany.

Loomis (G 4), 1860 Eastchester rd., E. to Bassett av.

Lorillard pl. (D 4), fr. 4500 3d av., N. to E. Fordham rd.

Loring pl. (C 5), from W. Tremont av., bet. Osborne pl. and Andrews av., N. to W. Fordham rd.

Low av. (C 4), from Jerome av., near W. 198th, N. to W. 206th.

Lowell (E 6), fr. Longfellow av., bet. E. 165th & Westchester av. E. to Whitlock av.

Lowerre pl. (D2), E. 226th, bet. White Plains rd. and Carpenter av., N. to E. 230th.

Lowmede pl. (E8), now that part of Bronx Blvd. bet. E.210th & Gun Hill rd. E.

Ludlow av. (F 6), Whitlock av., at Longfellow av., E. to Westchester creek.

Ludlow sq. (F 6), at junction of Clason's pt. rd. & Ludlow av.

Lurting av. (G 4), Walker av., bet. Hone av. and Haight av. N.W. to Bronx & Pelham pkway & from Mace av., bet. Hone and Laconia avs., N. to E. Gun Hill rd.

Lydig av. (E 4), fr. Boston rd., W. of Bear Swamp rd., E. to Neil av.

Lyman pl. (E 6), Stebbins av., bet. E. 169th & Chisholm, N. to Freeman.

Lyon av. (G 5), 1400 Castle Hill av., E. & N. E. to Zerega av.

Lyvere (F4), from Hoguet av., S. of Walker, E. & N. to Walker av.

Mace av. (E 8), from 2500 Bronx pk. E., E. to Hutchinson av.

Maclay av. (G 4), 1700 Parker, N. E. to Walker av.

Macomb's rd. (C 6), from Jerome av., opp. Marcy pl., N. to Aqueduct av.

Macy pl. (E 7), from 772 Prospect av., S. E. to Hewitt pl.

Magenta (D 3), fr. Bronx River P'kway, at Newell, E. to Colden av.

Mahan av. (H 4), Middletown rd., bet. Jarvis and Gainboro avs., N.W. and N. to Morris pk. av.

Main (E5), now Walker av.

Maitland av. (G 4), Pelham rd., opp. the Bridge, E. to Mayflower av.

Manida (F 7), from 41 Edgewater road, N. to Garrison av.

Manor av. (F6), fr. Bronx R. bet. Craighill and Ward avs., N. to Bronx R. av.

Mansion (F 5), Noble av., at Bronx River av., E. to Beach av.

Mapes av. (E 5), 801 E. Tremont av., N.E. to E. 182d.

Marcy pl. (C6), 1350 Jerome av., E. to Sheridan av.

Marine (City Island), (K 8^1), fr. City Isl'd av., N. of Horton, E. to L. I. Sound.

Marion av. (D 4), from E. 184th, bet. Tiebout av. and Granite pl., N. E. to Mosholu pkway.

Marmion av. (E 5), from 851 Crotona pk. N., N. to S. Boulevard.

Marshall av. (K5^1 & J10^2), from Shore Drive, at Meagher av. E. to E. 177th.

Martha av. (D 2), fr. 401 E. 235th, N. to City line

Matilda av. (D 1), 651 E. 236th, N. to E. 242d.

Matthews av. (F 4), Baker av., E. of Barnes av., N. to Burke av.

Mayflower av. (H 4), from Ft. Schuyler rd., bet. Puritan and Bradford avs., N. W. & N. to Bronx and Pelham parkways.

Mayor (G 3), 1825 Pelham parkway, N., N. W. to Bruner av.

McAlpin av. (G 4), Eastchester rd., at Blondell av., E. to N.Y., N.H. & H. R. R.

McClellan (C 6), from 1150 Jerome av., E. to Findlay av.

McDonald (F 3), fr. Seymour av., bet. Saratoga & Rhinelander avs., N.E. to Bassett av.

McGraw av. (F 5), from 1380 Beach av., E. to Unionport rd.

McKinley sq. (D 6), the triangular space at Boston rd. & E. 169th.

McLean av. (D 1), from Vireo av., N. of E. 239th, S. E. to Webster av.

McOwen av. (G 1), fr. Pelham Bay park W., N. W. to Boston rd.

Mead (F 5), 1660 Garfield, E. to Unionport rd.

Meagher av. (K5^1 & J10^2) from Shore Drive, bet. Kearney & Pennyfield avs., N. to Shore Drive.

Melrose av. (D 7), fr. 3d av. opp. Willis av., N. to E. 165th.

Melville (F 5), Walker av., bet. Van Buren & Taylor, W. to Morris park av.

Mendell (H 5), E. 177th, at Eastern Boulevard, N. E. to Graff av.

Merriam av. (C 6), fr. Ogden av., bet. W. 168th and W. 169th, N. to University av.

Merrill (F 5), 1460 Rosedale av., E. to Beach av.

Merritt av. (G 2), Hutchinson av., bet. Delavall and Hammersley av., N. W. to City line.

Merry av. (H 4), from La Salle av., bet. Hobart & Hollywood avs., N. to Middletown rd.

Metcalf av. (G 6), Bronx River av., bet. Lacombe and Randall avs., N. to Bronx River av.

Meyers (H 4), 1130 Fort Schuyler road, N. E. to Edison av.

Mickle av. (G3), fr. 1571 Bronx and Pelham parkway, N. to Laconia av.

Middletown rd. (G 4), fr. Westchester av. at Appleton av., N. E. to Eastern blvd.

Mildred pl. (G 3), Pilgrim av., bet. Morris pk. and Wilkinson avs., E. to Edison av.

Miles av. (J 5), fr. Baxter Creek, Inlet, N. E. to Westchester Bay.

Minerva pl. (C 4), fr. 2880 Jerome av., S. E. to the Grand Boulevard and Concourse.

Minford pl. (E 6), fr. 901 Jennings, N. to Boston rd.

Minnieford av. (City Isl'd) (K 8^1 & J 7^2), fr. Schofield, E. of City Island av., N. to Pelham Bay.

Mohegan av. (E 5), from E. 175th, W. of S. Boulevard, N. to Bronx pk. S.

Monroe av. (D 5), fr. 331 E. Belmont av., N. to E. Tremont av.

Monterey av. (D 5), from 551 E. Tremont av., N. to Quarry rd.

Montgomery av. (C6), from W. 174th, bet. Aqueduct and Popham avs., N. to W. Tremont av.

Monticello av. (F1), 1375 E. 233d, N. W. to City line.

Morgan av. (F 3), 1425 Pelham pkway N. to E. Gun Hill rd.

Morris av. (D 8), from 2557 3d av., N. to Jerome av.

Morris Park av. (F 5), fr. Van Nest av., at E. 177th, N.E. & E. to E. Boulev'd.

Morrison av. (G 6), Bronx River av., bet. Harrod and Craighill avs., N. to Bronx River av.

Morton pl. (C 5), Harrison av., N. of W. Tremont av., W. to University av.

Mosholu av. (A2), fr. Delafield av. at W. 245th, N. E. and S.E. to Jerome av.

Mosholu pkwy (D3), Bronx pk., at E. 201st, N. W., to Van Cortlandt pk.

Mosholu pkway, N. (D 3)-See East Mosholu parkway N. See West Mosholu parkway N.

Mosholu parkway S. See E. Mosholu pkway S. See W. Mosholu parkway S.

Mott av. (D8), fr. Park av., S. of E. 138th, N. to E. 161st.

Mott Haven Canal (D8), fr. Harlem River, bet. Park and 3d avs., N. to E. 138th.

Mt. Eden av. (C 6), fr. 1630 Clay av., W. to Macombs rd.

Mt. Hope av., now called Monroe av.

Mt. Hope pl. (C 5), from 1876 Jerome av., E. to Anthony av.

Mt. Vernon av. (C3), 1 E. 233d, N. E. to City line.

Mulford av. (G 4), Middletown rd., bet. Appleton and Mayflower avs., N. to Wilkinson av.

Muliner av. (F 4), from Morris pk. av., bet. Matthews and Bronxdale avs., N. to Pelham parkway, S.

Mulvey (F 1), fr. E. 233d, bet. Merritt and Provoost avs. N. to City line.

Munn av. (G 5), from 2274 Westchester av., E. to Commerce av.

Munroe av., now Tomlinson av.

Murdock av. (F 1), fr 1825 E. 233d, N. W. to City line.

Napier av. (C 2), from 51 E. 233d, N. to Mt. Vernon av.

Narragansett av. (G 4), fr. Seymour av., bet. Morris pk. and Saratoga avs., N.W. to Bronx and Pelham pkway.

Navy av (C 4), from Jerome av., N. of W. 197th, N. to W. 206th.

Needham av. (E 2), fr. E. 216th, at Wilson av., N E. to Boston rd.

Neill av. (F 4), fr. Bronxdale av., at Hunt av., E. to Bronx and Pelham parkway.

Nelson av., 23d ward (C 6), from 120 W. 164th, N. to Macomb's rd.

Nelson pl., now Grenada pl.

Nereid av. (D1), fr. Bronx River Parkway, N. E. to City line.

Netherland av. (B 4), from 550 Kappock, N. to W. 261st.

Newbold av. (G 5), from 1260 Virginia av., E. to Commerce av.

Newell av. (D 3), Burke av., E. of Bronx River, N. to E. Gun Hill rd.

Newman av. (H 6), fr. 60 Bronx River av., N. to Lafayette av.

Newport av. (G 4), Sackett av., at Eastchester rd., N. W. to Neill av.

Newton av., now part of Post rd.

Nindham pl. (C 4), from W. Kingsbridge rd., bet. Heath av. & Kingsbridge ter. E. to Kingsbridge ter.

Noble av. (G 6), fr. Bronx River av., bet. Rosedale and Croes avs., N. to Bronx River av.

Noell av. (G 2), fr. Hutchinson av., bet. Hammersley and Burke avs., N. W. to Boston rd.

Norman av. (C 3), from 3930 Sedgwick av., N. to Van Cortlandt Park S.

North (C 4), 2347 Jerome av., W. to Aqueduct av. E.

North Oak Drive (E 3), Cruger av., S. of Bartholdi, E to South Oak dr.

Norton av. (H 6), from 400 Olmstead av., E. to Westchester creek.

Oak Point av. (F 7), 500 Cabot, E. to Bronx River.

Oak ter. (E 7), from 340 Crimmins av., E. to Beekman av.

BOROUGH OF BRONX STREET AND AVENUE DIRECTORY—*Continued.*

Oak Tree pl. (D 5), from 2144 Lafontaine av., E. to Hughes av.

Oakland pl. (D 5), from 2062 Belmont av., E. to Prospect av.

Oakley (E 2), from 3724 Laconia av., N. E. to Eastchester av.

O'Brien av. (H 9), Bronx River, bet. Rosedale and Gildersleeve avs., E. to Pugsley's creek.

Odell (G 5), 1400 Unionport rd., N. to Purdy.

Ogden av. (C 7), from 805 Jerome av., N. to University av.

Olinville av. (E 5), from Bronx & Pelham pkway, between Barker av. and White Plains rd., N. to E. 219th.

Oliver pl. (D 4), from 2838 Marion av. S. E. to Webster av.

Olmstead av. (H 6), Barrett av., at Norton av., N. to Walker av.

Oneida av. (C 2), fr. 101 E. 233d, N. to Mt Vernon av.

Orchard (City Island) (K 8^3 & J 7^2), fr. Eastchester bay, bet. Carroll & Fordham, E. to Minnieford av.

Orloff av. (C 3), from W. 238th and Cannon pl., S. E. to VanCortlandt pk. S.

Osborne pl. (C 5), fr. W. Tremont av., E. of Sedgwick, N. to W. 180th.

Osgood (D 1), fr. E. 242d, bet. Matilda & Richardson avs., N. to E. 243d.

Otis av. (H4), Ft. Schuyler rd., E. of Eastern blvd., E. to Layton av

Overing (G 4), fr. Westchester av., opp. Seabury av., N. W. to Walker av.

Oxford av. (B 3), W. 232d, bet. Cambridge & Johnson avs, N. to W. 237th.

Paine (H 4), Bradford av., bet. Baisley & Waterbury av., N. E. to Crosby av.

Palisade av. (B4), Johnson av. at Spuyten Duyvil rd., W. & N. to W. 261st.

Palisade pl. (C 5), from 1781 Popham av., N. W. to Sedgwick av.

Palmer av. (G 3), fr. 2051 Bassett av. N., N. W. to Eden terrace.

Park, now part of Cauldwell av.

Park av. (continued from Mhtn. Borough) (D 8), fr. Harlem River, W. of 3d av., N. to 3d av.

2469	2468	E. 135th.
—	3084	E. 156th.
3455	3454	E. 167th.
4569	4568	E. 184th.

Park View pl. (B2), now part of Valles av.

Park View ter. (C 4), now part of Jerome av.

Parker (G 4), Wellington av., bet. Westchester & Zerega avs., N. W. to Castle Hill av.

Parkside pl. (D 8), from Webster av., N. of E. 205th, N. to Webster av.

Parsons av. (H 5), from Dewey av. at Foote av., N. W. to Philip av.

Pascal pl., now part of Waldo av.

Patterson av. (G 6), Bronx River, S. of Lacombe av., E. to Pugsley's creek.

Paulding av. (G 4), from N. Y., N. H. & H. R. R., E. of Colden av., N. W. to Bronx and Pelham P'kway, and from Astor av., N. W. and N. to E. 233d.

Payne (G 7), fr. 91 Edgewater road, N. to Edgewater rd.

Pearsall av. (F 3), from 1225 Pelham pkway N., to Boston rd.

Peartree av. (G 2), Hutchinson av., at Burke av., N. W. to Boston rd.

Pelham av., now part of E. Fordham rd., bet. Webster av. and Southern blvd.

Pelham Bay Park W. (G 1), fr. 3300 Huguenot av., N. W. and N. to City line.

Pelham Bridge rd. (H 2), from Pelham Bridge in Pelham Bay pk. N.E. to City line.

Pelham pkway N. (E 4), the N. side of Bronx and Pelham pkway.

Pelham pkway S. (E 4), the south side of Bronx and Pelham pkway.

Pelham rd., now called Appleton av.

Pell (City Island), (K 8^1 and J 8^2), fr. Eastchester Bay, bet. Earley and Reynolds, E. to City Isl'd av.

Penfield (D 1), from 4770 White Plains rd., E. to City line.

Pennyfield av. (K 5^1 and J 10^2), from Public pk., Throg's Neck, N. to Shore Drive.

Perot (C3), fr. Kingsbridge ter., N. of Albany Crescent, E. to Sedgwick av.

Perry av. (D 3), from 321 Bedford Park Boulev'rd, N. E. to E. 211th.

Philip av. (H 5), from 800 Ferris av., N. E. to Shore Drive.

Pierce av. (F4), from 1600 Bronxdale av., N. E. to Sackett av.

Pilgrim av. (H 4), from Middletown rd., bet. Mayflower and Edison avs., N. to Wilkinson av.

Pillow pl. (K 5^1 & J10^2), from Shore Drive, S. of Marshall av., E. to Pennyfield av.

Pilot av. (City Isl'd) (K 8^1 and J8^2), from Eastchester Bay, S. of Reynolds, E. towards L. I. Sound.

Pinkney av. (G 1), from Hutchinson av., N. of Givan av., N. to Boston rd.

Pitman av. (E1), from 4300 Barnes av., N.E. to City line.

Plimpton av. (C 6), 149 W. 169th, N. to Featherbed la.

Plymouth av. (H 4), from 2930 Zulette av., N. to Roberts av.

Point (City Island) (K 8^1 and J 8^2), now Rochelle.

Pond pl. (D 4), fr. E. 197th. bet. Bainbridge & Marion avs., N. to E. 198th.

Pontiac pl. (E 7), from 600 Trinity av., E. to Jackson av.

Ponton av. (G 4), Walker av., E. of Roberts av., N. E. & N. to Wilkinson av.

Pope pl. (K 4^1 and J 9^2), Sampson av., bet. Longstreet av. & Shore Drive, N. to Shore Drive.

Popham av. (C 6), fr. W. 174th, bet. Montgomery & Undercliff avs., N. & E to Montgomery av.

Poplar, (F 4), from 1500 Bronxdale av., N. E. to Bates.

Porter (G 7), from E.R., N. to Edgewater rd.

Post rd. (B 3), fr. Broadway at Spuyten Duyvil pkway. N. to W. 260th.

Powell av. (G 5), fr. 1160 Virginia av., E. to Commerce av.

Powers av. (E 8), E. 141st, bet. Cypress and Robbins av., N. to St. Marys.

Pratt av. (F2), Hunter av, N. of Needham av., N.E. to City line.

Preble (G 7), from E. R., N. to Edgewater rd.

Prentiss av. (K5^1 & J 10^2), Shore Drive, bet. Pennyfield and Reynolds avs. N. to Shore Drive.

President av. (C 4), from W. 197th, E. of Reservoir av., N. to W. 206th.

Prospect av., 23d Wd. (E 7), from S. Boulevard, at E. 149th N. to E. 189th.

Prospect pl. (D 5), from 1758 Clay av., E. to Anthony av.

Protectory av. (G 5), McGraw av., at Unionport rd., N. E. and N. W. to Walker av.

Provost av. (F1), fr. Hutchinson av., at Hammersley av., N. W. and N. E. to City line.

Pugsley av. (H 6), East River, W. of Clason's pt. rd., N. to McGraw av.

Purdy (G 5), Westchester av., bet. Unionport rd. and Castle Hill av., N. to Walker av.

Puritan av. (H4), from 1240 Fort Schuyler rd., N to La Salle.

Putnam av. E. (B 3), W. 238th, W. of Albany rd. N to Vancortlandt pk. S.

Putnam av. W. (B 3), from 171 W. 238d, N. to Vancortlandt pk. S.

Putnam pl. (D F), from Reservoir Oval E., W. of Reservoir pl., E. to 211th.

Quarry rd. (D 5), 4878 3d av., N. E. to Arthur av.

Quimby av. (G5), 930 White Plains rd., E. to Westchester creek.

Quincy av. (J5^1& J10^2), fr. Shore Drive, bet. Swinton and Calhoun avs., N. W. to Eastern blvd.

Radcliffe av. (F 4), from 975 Sackett av., N. W. to Colden av., nr. Brady av., and from Astor av., N. W. to Magenta.

Rae (D 7), 658 Hegney pl., E. to St. Anns av.

Randall av. 23d Wd (F 7), Truxton, at Leggett av., E. to Shore Drive.

Randolph av. (F 6), now that part of E. 172d, E. of Bronx River av.

Reed pl. (B 4), from 2850 Heath av. W. to Bailey av.

Reiss pl. (E 4), fr. Bronx pk. E., N. of Bronx and Pelham pkway, E. to Barker av.

Reservoir av. (C 4), from 50 W. Kingsbridge rd., N. W. to Sedgwick av.

Reservoir Oval E. (D 3), from Bainbridge av. at Vancortlandt av., E. and N. E. & N. to Putnam pl.

Reservoir Oval W. (D 3), from Bainbridge av. opp. E. 208th, N E. & E. to Putnam pl.

Reservoir pl. (D 3), from Reservoir Oval E., N. E. to E. Gun Hill rd.

Revere av. (K 5^1 & J 10^2), from East River, E. of Swinton av., N. W. to St. Raymond's Cemetery.

Review pl. (B 2), from W. 238th, bet. Broadway and Putnam av. W., N. to Vancortlandt pk. S.

Reynold (City Island) (K8^1 & J 8^2), fr. Eastchester bay, N. of Pilot, E. to City Island av.

Reynolds av. (K5^1 & J10^2), Shore Drive, bet. Prentiss and Blair av., N. to Shore Drive.

Rhinelander av. (F 4), fr. 1900 Unionport rd., E. to Stillwell av.

Richardson av. (D 1), fr. E. 236th, N. to E. 242d.

Rider av. (D 8), 201 E. 135th, N. to E. 144th.

Ridge pl. (D 7), from 336 Mott av. E.

Ritter pl. (E 6), 1286 Union av., E. to Prospect av.

River av. (C 7), from 101 E. 144th, N. to Jerome av.

Riverdale av. (B 3), from Spuyten Duyvil rd., bet. W. 231st and W. 232d, N. to City line.

Robbins av. (E 8), now called Jackson av.

Roberts av. (G 4), Walker av., at Williamsbridge rd., N. E. and E. to Eastern blvd.

Robertson (D 1), E. 242d, bet. Carpenter & Matilda avs., N. to E. 243d.

Robinson av. (J 5), from East River, bet. Emerson and Buttrick avs., N W. to Lafayette av.

Rochambeau av. (D 3), from Bainbridge av. bet. Mosholu pkway and Woodlawn rd., N. W. and N. to E. 212th.

Rochelle (City Island) (K8), fr. Eastchester bay, S. of Horton, E. to L. I. Sound.

Rockwood (C 6), fr. 1530 Walton av., E. to Grand Boulevard & Concourse.

Rodman pl. (E 5), from 1914 Longfellow av., E. to West Farms rd.

Roebling av. (G 4), fr. 1574 Appleton av., E. to Edison av.

Rogers pl. (E 6), Dawson, bet. Stebbins and Intervale avs., N. to Hall pl.

BOROUGH OF BRONX STREET AND AVENUE DIRECTORY—*Continued.*

Rombouts av. (G 2), Adee av., W. of Hutchinson av., N. W. and N. E. to City line.

Ropes av. (G 1), from Pelham Bay pk. W., N. W. to Boston rd.

Rosedale av. (G 6), from East river, bet. Commonwealth and Noble avs., N. to Walker av.

Roselle (G 4), Silver, bet. Walker av. & Williamsbridge rd., N. W. to Poplar.

Rosewood (D 3), Bronx River P'kway, S. of Magenta, E. to Cruger av.

Rowe (G 4), 1360 Seabury av., E. to Commerce av.

Rowland (G 4), 2431 Westchester av., N.W. to St. Raymond's av.

Ruth pl. (J 4), from Shore Drive at Layton av., N. W. to Dean av.

Ryawa av. (F 7), from East River, at Barretto, E. to East River.

Ryer av. (D 5), from E. 178th, at Echo pk, N. to E. 187th.

Sackett av. (F 4), from 1550 Bronxdale av, N. E. to Eastchester rd.

Sacrahong (G 7), from 111 Edgewater rd. N. to Edgewater rd.

Sagamore (F 4), from W. of Unionport rd. at White Plains rd., E. to Hunt av.

St. Anns av. (D 8), from 571 E. 132d. N. to 3d av.

St. George Crescent (D 3), from E. 206th, E. of the Grand Boulevard & Concourse, N. to Vancortlandt av.

St. John av. (E7), see Avenue St. John.

St. Lawrence av. (G 6), 880 Bronx River av., N. to Walker av.

St. Marys (D 7), from St. Anns av. opp. E. 143d, E. to S. Boulevard.

St. Ouen (D 1), from 4730 White Plains rd., E. to Wilder av.

St. Paul av. (G 3), Westchester av., bet. Mahan av. & Eastern Blvd., N.W. to Bronx & Pelham parkway.

St. Pauls pl. (D 8), from 1418 Webster av. E. to Fulton av.

St. Peters av. (G 4), fr. 2465 Westchester av., N. W. to Walker av.

St. Raymond av. (G 5), fr. 1600 Protectory av., E. and N. E. to Wilkinson av.

Sampson av. (J 5), from Emerson av., bet. Dewey and Miles avs., E. to Shore Drive.

Sand (G5), fr. 1450 Unionport rd., N. to Protectory av.

Sands pl. (G3), from Westchester av., N. of Arnow av., E. to E. Blvd.

Saratoga av., now called Wilkinson av.

Saxon av. (C 3), 3961 Sedgwick av., N. to Vancortlandt park, S.

Schieffelin av. (E2), from Tiemann av., at E. 226th N. E. to Eden ter.

Schieffelin's la. (F 2), fr. Boston rd., bet. Bruner & Ely avs., N. and N. E. to Palmer av.

Schley av. (H 5), from Hale av., bet. Seaman av. and Stark av., N. E. to Shore Drive.

Schofield (City Isl.) (K 3[1] & J 7[2]), from Eastchester bay, bet. Carroll and Centre, E. to L. I. Sound.

Schurz av. (K 5[1] & J 10[2]), from Ft. Schuyler rd., at Shore Drive, E. to E. 177th.

Schuyler (G 4) fr. Seabury av., at Kirk, E. to Commerce av.

Schuyler pl. (H 3), from Arnow av., bet. Westchester av. and E. Boulevard, N. to Sands pl.

Scott pl. (J 4), from Ft. Schuyler rd., bet. Sullivan pl. and Philip av., E. to Edison av.

Screvin av. (H 6), fr. 300 Barrett av., W. & N. to Lafayette av.

Scribner av. (H 5), from 1126 Balcom av., E. to Eastern blvd.

Seabury av. (H5), Eastern Boulevard, at E. 177th, N. to Westchester av.

Seabury pl. (H 6), fr. Charlotte, opp. E. 170th, N. to Boston rd.

Seaman av. (J 6), from Brush av., S. of Randall av., E. and N. E. to Foote av.

Secor av. (F 1), from Hollers av. to City line.

Seddon (G 4), from 2475 St. Raymond av., W. to Walker av.

Sedgwick av. (C 7), from 795 Jerome av., N. E. to Mosholu pkway.

Selwyn av. (C 6), from 1451 Morris av., N. to E. 174th.

Seminole (Westches'r hts) (F3), fr. Elberon av., bet. Morris Park & Rhinelander avs., N. W. to Neil av.

Seminole av., now called Livingston av.

Seminole pl. (G 3), from Seymour av, bet. Abbatt pl. and McDonald, E. to Stillwell av.

Seneca av. (F 6), from 870 Hunt's Point av., E. to Bronx River.

Seton av. (F 1), fr. 1401 E. 233d, N. W. to City line.

Seward av. (F6), fr. Bronx River av., at Elder av., E. to Westchester creek.

Seward pl. (A3), now part of Sycamore av.

Seymour av. (G 4), Morris pk. av., at Eastchester rd., N. W. to Hicks.

Shakespeare av. (C 6), from 1171 Jerome av., N. to Featherbed la.

Sheridan av. (C 7), E. 158d, bet Mott and Park avs., N. to E. Belmont.

Sherman av. (D 7), 221 E. 161st, N. to E. 168th.

Shore Drive (J 5), fr. Baxter creek Inlet, E. and N. to Baisley av.

Shrady pl. (C3), fr. Heath av., N. of Summit pl., E. to Kingsbridge terrace.

Sigma pl. (A 2), from 5905 Independence av., S. & N to Palisade av.

Silver (G4), fr. 2560 Walker av., N.E. to Williamsbridge rd.

Simpson (E 6), from 940 Fox, N. to Freeman.

Sommer pl. (H 4), Fort Schuyler rd., bet. Berkley and Gridley av., E. to Edison av.

South Oak Drive (E3), Cruger av., N. of Burke, E. to Bronxwood av.

Southern Boulevard (D 8), fr. 124 St. Anns av., N. and N.W. to Webster av.

Spencer av. (B 2), from 5781 Mosholu av., N. to City line.

Spencer pl. (D 7), 181 E. 144th, N. to E. 150th.

Spencer sq. (F3), between Arnow & Allerton avs., and Colden and Bronxwood avs.

Spofford av. (F 7), from Tiffany opp. Longwood av., E. to Bronx River.

Spruce, Pelham Bay View Park (F3), from Palmer Boulevard, bet. Hemlock & Poplar, N. to Leroy.

Spuyten Duyvil p'kway (B 4), 660 Kappock, N. E. & E. to Broadway.

Spuyten Duyvil rd. (A 4), runs fr. Spuyten Duyvil parkway to Palisade av.

Stark av. (H6), from Brush av., N. of Dewey av. E. and N. E. to Foote av.

Starling av. (G 5), Unionport rd., at Protectory av., E. to Glebe av.

Stearns (G4), fr. Glover bet. St. Raymond and Castle Hill avs., N.E. to Parker.

Stebbins av. (E7), Dawson, bet. Longwood av. & Rogers pl. N. to Boston rd.

Steenwick av. (G2), Hutchinson av., at E. 222d, N. W. and N. to City line.

Stephens av. (H 6), from 63 Bronx River av., N. to Compton av.

Steuben av. (D 3), from 121 E. Mosholu p'kway, N., N. to E. Gun Hill rd.

Stevens pl. (D 4), E. 187th, bet. Tiebout and Marion avs., N. to E. 189th.

Stevenson pl. (C 3), from Sedgwick av., N. of W. 238th, S. E. to Sedgwick av.

Stillwell av. (G 3), from 2000 Eastchester rd, N.E. to Varian av.

Storrow (F 5), fr. E. 177th, at Westchester av., N. to Unionport rd.

Story av. (F 6), fr. Bronx River, bet. Ludlow and Lafayette avs., E. to Zerega av.

Strang av. (E2), 4174 Laconia av., N.E. to Pratt av.

Stratford av. (F 6), from Bronx River av., bet. Morrison & Manor avs., N. to Bronx River av.

Strong (C 4), from Jerome av., N. of W. 196th, W. to University av.

Suburban pl. (E 5), from Boston rd., E. of E. 172d, N. to Crotona pk. E.

Sullivan pl. (J 4), fr. Ft. Schuyler rd., bet. Gridley av. and Douglas pl., E. to Edison av.

Summit av. (C 7), W. 161st, bet. Ogden & Sedgwick av., N. to W. 166th.

Summit pl. (C 3), from Kingsbridge ter., N. of Perot, W. to Bailey av.

Sutherland (City Island) (J2[1] & H7[2]), City Island av., N. of Elizabeth, E. to L. I. Sound.

Swinton av. (J 5), from East River, bet. Balcom and Revere avs., N. W. to Eastern blvd.

Sycamore av. (A 3), from W. 240th, at Palisade av., N. to W. 254th.

Sylvan av. (B2), from W. 253d, W. of Newton av., N. to Iselin av.

Taber av. (J6), fr. Yznaga av., bet. Brush & Evans av, N. W. to Stark av.

Taylor av. (G 6), from 800 Bronx River av., N. to Morris pk av.

Teasdale pl. (D 6), 960 Boston rd., E. to Trinity av.

Teller av. (D 7), Park av., at E. 162d, N. to Morris av.

Tenbroeck av. (G 4), fr. 1201 Pierce av., N. W. and N. to E. Gun Hill rd.

Terrace pl. (D 7), 600 Eagle av. E. to Park av.

Terrace (City Island) (J2[1] & H7[2]), Minnieford av., N. of Bridge E. towards L. I. Sound.

Thieriot av. (H 6), Bronx River av., bet. Gildersleeve and O'Brien avs., N. to Walker av.

Third av. (D 8) (continued fr. Manhattan Borough), from Harlem River N. to E Fordham rd.

2655	2654	E. 142d.
2923	2922	E. 152d.
3251	3250	E. 163d
4215	4214	E. Tremont av.
4653	4652	E. 187th.

Throg's Neck Boulevard (K 5[1] & J 10[2]), fr. Shore Drive bet. Hollywood & Kearney avs., N. to Eastern blvd.

Throgmorton av. (J 4), fr. Ellsworth av. at Lafayette av., N. to Baisley av.

Throop av. (F3), from 1251 Pelham pkway N., N. to E. Gun Hill rd.

Thwaites pl. (E 4), from 2250 Bronx pk. E., E. to White Plains rd.

Tibbett av. (B 4), from 300 West 230th, N. to Cayuga av.

Tiebout av. (D 5), E. 180th, bet. Webster and Valentine avs., N. to E. Fordham rd.

Tiemann av. (G 3), fr. 1651 Pelham pkway, N. W. to Laconia av.

Tier (City Island) (K 3[1] & J 7[2]), S. of Ditmars, E. to King av.

Tiffany (F 6), from East River, at Viele av., N. to E. 169th.

Tilden (E 3), fr. E. Gun Hill rd. at Holland av., E. to Paulding av.

BOROUGH OF BRONX STREET AND AVENUE DIRECTORY—*Continued.*

Tillotson av. (F 2), 3400 Fenton av. E. to Pelham Bay park W.

Timpson pl. (E 7), E. 144th, E. of Southern blvd., N. E. to Whitlock av.

Tinton av. (E 7), Southern blvd, at E. 145th, N. to E. 169th.

Tomlinson av. (G 4), from Sacket av. W. of Williamsbridge rd., N. W. to Pelham parkway S.

Topping av. (D 5), E. Belmont, bet. Mt. Hope and Clay avs., N. to E. 176th.

Torry av. (H 6), from 880 Barrett av., N. to Lafayette av.

Townsend av. (C 6), from 51 E. 170th, N. to E. 176th.

Trafalgar pl. (E 5), E. 175th, bet. Waterloo pl. and Southern blvd., N. to E. 176th.

Trask av. (H 6), from 420 Barrett av., N. to Lafayette av.

Tratman av. (G 4), from 1450 Zerega av., N. E. to Benson av.

Tremont av. (C 5), see East Tremont av.; see West Tremont av.

Trinity av. (E 7), from 691 E. 147th, N. to E. 166th.

Truxton (F 7), East River, E. of Dupont, N. to Longwood av.

Truxton sq. (F 7), at junction of Longwood and Spofford avs. and Tiffany and Truxton.

Tryon av. (D 3), Reservoir Oval W., E. of Wayne av., N. to E. 211th.

Tudor pl. (C 6), Walton av., bet. McClellan & E. 167th, E. to Grand Boulevard and Concourse.

Turnbull av. (G 5), from 880 White Plains rd., E. to Zerega av.

Turneur av. (H 6), Zerega av., S. of Norton av., N. to Lafayette av.

Twiggs pl. (K 4' & J 9"), fr. Longstreet av., bet. Sampson and Miles avs., E. to Shore Drive.

Tyndall av. (A 2), from 5661 Mosholu av., N. to City line.

Undercliff av. (C 6), from 1370 Sedgwick av., N. to Sedgwick av.

Undercliff pl., (C 6), fr. Undercliff av., S. of Washington Bridge, E. to University av.

Underhill av. (H 6), from Bronx River av., bet. Bolton and Cornell avs., N. to Gleason av.

Union av. 23d ward (E 7), 500 Southern blvd., N. to Boston rd.

Union pl. (C 6), Lind av., N. of W. 166th, E. to W. 167th.

Unionport rd. (G 5), Westchester av., bet. Olmstead av. and Purdy, N.W. to White Plains rd.

University av. (C 5), from 950 Sedgwick av., N. to W. Kingsbridge rd.

Valentine av. (D 5), fr. E. Tremont av., at Webster av. N. to E. 204th.

Valentine av. (J 4), now Throgmorton av.

Valles av. (B 2), W. 254th, between Sylvan av. and Fieldston rd., N. to W. 256th.

Van Buren (F 5), from 1760 Walker av., N. W. to Morris park av.

Vance (G 3), from 1875 Bassett av., N. W. to Demeyer.

Vancortlandt av. (C 3), See East Vancortlandt av. See West Vancortlandt av.

Vancortlandt park S. (C 3), W. Mosholu parkway S., at Dickinson pl., W. to Broadway.

Van Hoesen (F 4), from Eastchester rd. at junction with Stillwell av., S. W. to Seminole av., and from Seminole av., N. W. to Bronx and Pelham p'kway.

Van Nest av. (E 5), from 120 E. 177th, E. to Eastchester rd.

Van Wyck av. E. (C 4), from Jerome av., E. of Van Wyck av. W., N.E. to Jerome av.

Van Wick av. W. (C 4), from Jerome av. at Low av., N. E. to Jerome av.

Varian av. (G 3), fr. 2400 Hutchinson av., N. W. to Conner.

Victor (F 4), Unionport rd. at Van Nest av., N. to Rhinelander av.

Viele av. (F 7), from 800 Tiffany, E. to Bronx River.

Villa av. (C 3), from 101 Bedford pk. blvd., N. to E. Vancortlandt av.

Vincent av. (J 4), from Shore Drive, bet. Ellsworth & Wilcox avs., N. to Waterbury av.

Vireo av. (D 2), from 501 E. 233d, N. to City line.

Virginia av. (G 5), from 1921 Ludlow av., N. to Westchester av.

Von Humboldt av. (now called Delafield av.), (B 3), from Spuyten Duyvil pkway., bet. Faraday and Riverdale avs., N. to City line.

Vreeland av. (H 4), 2675 Waterbury av., N. to Appleton av.

Vyse av. (E 6), 1121 W. Farms rd., N. to Bronx pk S.

Wakefield sq. (E 2), on Bronxwood av., bet. E. 221st and E. 223d.

Waldo av. (B 4), from W. 236th, at Greystone av., N. to W. 252d.

Wales av. (E 7), fr. Southern blvd., at E. 141st, N. to Westchester av.

Walker av. (E 5), from Bronx River, at E. 177th, E. to Westchester creek.

Wallace av. (F 4), 755 Baker av., N. W. & N. to South Oak drive.

Walnut av. 23d ward (E 8), from 881 E. 132d, N. to E. 141st.

Walton av. (C 8), from E. 138th, bet. Mott av. and Exterior, N. to E. Fordham rd.

Ward av. (F 6), from 680 Bronx River av., N. to Bronx River av.

Waring av. (E 4), fr. 2400 Bronx pk. E., E. to Givins Basin.

Washington av. (D 7), from 3d av. at E. 159th, N. to E. Fordham rd.

Waterbury av. (G 5), fr. Westchester av., bet. Havemeyer and Glebe avs., N.E. to Eastchester blvd., & from Wilcox av. N. E. to Eastchester bay.

Waterloo pl. (E 5), E. 175th bet. Vineyard pl. and Trafalgar pl., N. to E. 176th.

Waters av. (G 4), fr. 1500 Appleton av., N. W. to McAlpin av.

Watson av. (F 6), Bronx River av., bet. Westchester and Ludlow avs., E. to Westchester creek.

Watson's la. (F 6), fr. Watson av., at Elder av., N. & N. E. to Walker av.

Wayne av. (D 3), E. 210th, E. of Woodlawn rd., N. W. and N. to E. 211th.

Webb av. (C 4), W. 188th, E. of Sedgwick av., N. to Reservoir av.

Webster av. (D 6), E. 165th, at Brook av., N. to City line.

— 1900 E. Tremont av.
2535 — E. Fordham rd.
2875 2872 Bedford pk. bvd.
3501 3500 E. Gun Hill rd.

Weeks av. (D 5) from 261 E. Belmont, N. to E. 176th.

Weiher ct. (D 6), fr. 1010 Wash'n av. E. to 3d av.

Wellington av., now called Munn av.

Wellman av. (G 4), 1524 Ericson pl., E. to Dudley av.

West, now called Hornaday pl.

West Bedford Pk. Boulevard (C 3), from 2951 Jerome av., W. to Goulden av.

W. Belmont (C 6), now part of Mt. Eden av.

W. Burnside av. (C 5), 2041 Jerome av., W. to Sedgwick av.

W. Clarke pl. (C 6), from 1321 Jerome av., W. to Inwood av.

W. Farms rd. (E 6), from Westchester av. at Hoe av., N. E. to Boston rd.

1301 1300 Freeman.
1761 1760 E. 174th.

W. Fordham rd. (C 4), fr. 2641 Jerome av., W. to Harlem River.

W. Gun Hill rd. (C 3), 3501 Jerome av., W. to Mosholu pkway.

W. Kingsbridge rd. (C 4), 2671 Jerome av., W. and N. to Harlem River.

W. Mosholu pkway. N. (C 3), the north side of Mosholu parkway, W. of Jerome av.

W. Mosholu pkway. S. (C 3), the south side of Mosholu parkway W. of Jerome av.

W. Tremont av. (C 5), 1967 Jerome av., W. to Sedgwick av.

W. Vancortlandt av. (C 3), Sedgwick av., at Gouverneur av., N. W. to Vancortlandt park S.

W. 161st (C 7), fr. 901 Ogden av., W. to Sedgwick av.

W. 162d (C 7), fr. 951 Anderson av., W. to Summit av.

W. 163d (C 7), 985 Woodycrest av., W. to Ogden av.

W. 164th (C 6), 995 Anderson av., W. to Harlem River.

W. 165th (C 6), 1061 Jerome av., W. to Sedgwick av.

W. 166th (C 6), from 1111 Jerome av., W. to Lind av.

W. 167th (C 6), fr. Washington av., W. to Harlem River.

W. 168th (C 6), Boscobel av., N. of Jerome av., W. to W. 167th.

W. 169th (C 6), Jerome av., N. of Cromwell av., W. to Sedgwick av.

W. 170th (C 6), fr. 1401 Jerome av., W. to Commerce av.

W. 171st (C 6), Ogden av., S. of University av., W. to Harlem River.

W. 172d (C 6), from 1501 Jerome av., W. to University av.

W. 174th (C 5), fr. 1701 Jerome av., W. to Undercliff av.

W. 175th (C 5), fr. Grand av., at W. 174th, W. to Undercliff av.

W. 176th (C 5), fr. 1851 Jerome av., W. to Harlem River.

W. 177th (C 5), fr. 1901 Jerome av., W. to Harlem River.

W. 178th (C 5), Sedgwick av., S. of W. Burnside av., W. to Harlem River.

W. 179th (C 5), from University av. at W. Burnside av., W. to Harlem River.

W. 180th (C 5), fr. 2001 Davidson av., W. to Osborne pl.

W. 181st (C 5), fr. 2151 Jerome av., W. to University av.

W. 182d (C 5), Jerome av., S. of Buchanan pl., W. to Cedar av.

W. 183d (C 5), Jerome av., N. of Buchanan pl., W. to Sedgwick av.

W. 184th (C 4), fr. 2375 Jerome av., W. to Harlem River.

W. 185th (C 4), fr. Jerome av., N. of W. 184th, N. to Davidson av.

W. 188th (C 4), Grand av., N. of W. Fordham rd., W. to Sedgwick av.

W. 189th (C 4), Exterior, W. to Harlem River.

W. 190th (C 4), fr. 2501 Jerome av., W. to Webb av.

W. 191st (B 2), Exterior, W. to Harlem River.

W. 192d (C 4), from Jerome av., S. of W. Fordham rd., W. to Harlem River.

W. 193d (C 4), Heath av., N. of Kingsbridge ter., W. to Bailey av.

BOROUGH OF BRONX STREET AND AVENUE DIRECTORY—*Continued.*

W. 195th (C 4), from Jerome av., W. to Sedgwick av.

W. 196th (C 4), from 2749 Jerome av., W. to Reservoir av.

W. 197th (C 4), from Jerome av., W. to Sedgwick av.

W. 198th (C 4), from 2849 Jerome av., W. to Goulden av.

W. 199th (C 3), from Low av., W. to Goulden av.

W. 204th (C 3), from Jerome av., W. to Goulden av.

W. 205th (C 3), from Jerome av., W. to Goulden av.

W. 206th (C 3), from junction of Jerome av. and Low av., N. W. to Goulden av.

W. 207th (C 3), from Gaynor av. S of W. 208th, N. W. to Goulden av.

W. 208th (C 3), from Gaynor av., S. of Mosholu Parkway South, N. W. to Goulden av.

W. 209th (C 3), from Jerome av., S. of Mosholu Parkway South, N. W. to Gaynor av.

W. 227th (B 4). Spuyten Duyvil rd.. at Johnson av., W. to Independence av.

W. 229th (C 4), Sedgwick av., N. of W. Kingsbridge rd. W. to Bailey av.

W. 230th (C 4), Kingsbridge ter., S. of Albany Crescent, W. to Independence av.

W. 231st (B 3), from Bailey av., N. of Albany Crescent, W. to Palisade av.

W. 232d (B 3), from 3201 Broadway, W. to Spuyten Duyvil rd.

W. 233d (B 3), Bailey av., at Albany Crescent, W. to Broadway.

W. 234th (B 3), fr. 3401 Bailey av., W. to Riverdale av.

W. 235th (B 3), fr. 3501 Riverdale av., W. to Palisade av.

W. 236th (B 3), fr. 3601 Bailey av., W. and S. and W. to Hudson River.

W. 237th (B 3), fr. 3701 Putnam av. W., W. to Yonkers av.

W. 238th (C 3), from 3801 Sedgwick av., W. & N. W. to Yonkers av.

W. 239th (B 3), fr. 3901 Putnam av. W., W. to Yonkers av.

W. 240th (B 3), from 5871 Broadway, W. to Hendrick ter.

W. 242d (B 3), fr. 4200 Waldo av., W. and S. W. to Fieldston rd.

W. 244th (B 3), fr. 6000 Broadway, S. W to Spuyten Duyvil pkway.

W. 245th (B 3), from 4501 Waldo av., S. W. to Fieldston rd.

W. 246th (B 3), from 6001 Broadway, N. and W. to Seward pl.

W. 247th (B 3), from 4700 Riverdale av., W. to Hudson River.

W. 248th (A 3), fr. 4801 Independence av., W. to Hudson River.

W. 249th (B 2), fr. 4901 Riverdale av., W. to Sycamore av.

W. 250th (B 2), fr. Post rd., S. of W. 251st, W. to Independence av.

W. 251st (B 2), from 6201 Broadway, W. to Post rd.

W. 252d (B 2), fr. 6251 Broadway, W. to Sycamore av.

W. 253d (B 2), fr. 6321 Broadway, W. to Hudson River.

W. 254th (B 2), from 6351 Broadway, W. Fieldston rd., 5401 Von Humboldt av., W. to N. R.

W. 255th (B 2), from 5421 Fieldston rd., W. to Riverdale av.

W. 256th (B 2), from 6421 Broadway, W. to Independence av.

W. 259th (B 2), fr. 6531 Broadway, W. to Netherland av.

W. 260th (B 2), fr. 6571 Broadway, W. to Riverdale av.

W. 261st (B 2), from 6641 Broadway, W. to Hudson River.

W. 262d (B 2), fr. 6771 Broadway, W. to Tyndall av.

W. 263d (A 2), from Spencer av. at City line, W. to Riverdale av.

Westchester Arcade (E 7), from Westchester av., opp. Wales av., W. to Jackson av.

Westchester av. (D 7), from 2870 3d av., N. E to Eastern Boulevard.

641	640	Trinity av.
801	800	Union av.
—	1040	S. Boulevard.
1501	1500	Wheeler av.
1801	1800	Beach av.
—	2300	Wellington av.
—	2500	Seabury av.

Westchester sq. (G 4), at junction of Walker av. and Westchester av.

Westervelt av. (G 3). fr. 1601 Bronx and Pelham parkway, N. W. to E. Gun Hill rd.

Wheeler av. (F6), 700 Bronx R. av., N. to Bronx R. av.

White Plains rd. (H 6), East river, W. of Pugsley av., N. to City line.

501	500	Lacombe av.
1301	1300	Westchester av.
1601	1600	Walker av.
2201	2200	Bronx and Pelham pkway.
3501	3500	E. Gun Hill rd.
4201	4200	E. 233d.

Whitlock av. (E 7), from S. Boulevard, bet. E. 141st and E. 142d, N. E. & N. to Westchester av.

Whittemore av. (H 4), fr. Balcom av., S. of Waterbury av., E. to Fort Schuyler rd.

Whittier (F 7), from 1361 Viele av. N. to Ludlow av.

Wickham av. (G 3), from Stillwell av., bet. Gunther and Bruner avs., N. W. to Barnes av.

Wiegand pl. (C 5), from W. 180th, bet. University and Andrews avs., N. to W. 181st.

Wilcox av. (J 4), Shore Drive, bet. Vincent and Clarence avs., N. to Waterbury av.

Wilder av. (E1), from 1801 E. 233d, N. W. to City line.

Wilgus (E 3), from 2950 Bronx Park, E., E. to White Plains rd.

Wilkins av. (E 6), Southern blvd., at Freeman, N. to Crotona Park E.

Wilkinson av. (G 3), from Westchester Cr. at Ponton av., E. to Eastern blvd.

Willett av. (D3), fr. E. Gun Hill rd., bet. Olinville av. and White Plains rd., N. to E. 219th.

William av. (City Island) (K 3[1] & J 3[2]), from Pilot N. to Ditmars.

William pl. (H 4), fr. Dudley av., bet. Ft. Schuyler rd. and Mayflower av., N. to Maitland av.

Williamsbridge rd. (G 4), from Walker av., opp. Frisby av., N. E. to Bronxwood av.

Willis av. (D 8), from 401 E. 132d, N. to 3d av.

Willow av. (E8), fr. Bronx Kills, N. to E. 138th.

Wilson av. (F 3), 1301 Neill av., N., N. W. to Needham av.

Winters (City Island (K3[1]) & J 3[2]), fr. Eastchester bay, N. of Earley, E. to L. I. Sound.

Wissman av (K 5[1] & J 9[2]) from E. 177th at Pennyfield av., E. to Shore Dr.

Wood av. (F 5) E. 177th at Beach av., E. to Storrow.

Woodhull av. (F 3), 1551 Bronx and Pelham parkway N., N. to Arnow av.

Woodlawn rd. (D 3), now that part of E. 204th bet. Bainbridge av. & Bronx pk. and that part of Bainbridge av. bet. E. 204th and Jerome av.

Woodycrest av. (C 7), 847 Jerome av. N. to W. 168th.

Worthen (F 7), from 1181 Oak Point av., N. and W. to Garrison av.

Wright av. (G 3), fr. 2125 Bushnell av., N., N. W. to Boston road.

Wyatt (E5), fr. 860 Devoe av., E. to Van Nest av.

Wythe pl. (C 6), from 151 E. 170th, N. to E. 172d.

Yates av. (G4), 1160 Sackett av., N. W. and N. to E. Gun Hill rd.

Yonkers av. (A 3), from W. 236th, bet. Independence and Palisade avs., N. to W. 239th.

Young av. (F 3), 1325 Pelham pkway, N., N. to E. Gun Hill rd.

Yznaga av. (J 6), fr. Westchester creek, S. of Lawton av., E. to Baxter creek Inlet.

Zerega av. (H 6), from Castle Hill av., opp. Barrett av., N. E. and N. W. to Castle Hill av.

Zulette av. (G 4), from Ft. Schuyler av. at Westchester creek, E. to Jarvis av.

BOROUGH OF QUEENS STREET AND AVENUE DIRECTORY

To locate any thoroughfare in the Borough of Queens, look for it in alphabetical order by name of street, regardless of the village or sectional name. Then the letters and numbers following names will indicate position of the thoroughfare on map in pocket of Almanac.

In case of duplicate names, in different sections of the Borough, consult each on map, which will show the one sought.

Aberdeen rd. (L 6) from Grand Central parkway, W. of Midland parkway, N. E. to 190th.

Abingdon rd. (H 7) (Richmond Hill), from Union Turnpike, S. and E. to Cuthbert pl.

Abner (N 14) (Edgemere), from Beach 40th, E. to Beach 38th.

Academy (B 4) (L. I. C.), from Q'nsborough Pl'za, N. E. to Newtown av.

Acorn pl. (F 5), from Van Dine. E. to Junction av.

Ada (E 6), from Juniper av., N. E to Firth av.

Adair (N 9) (Springfield), from Pineville Lane, E. to Springfield blvd.

Adams (E 5) (Winfield), from Queens Boulevard, S. and E to Queens Boulevard.

Addison pl. (C 5) (Laurel Hill), from Laurel Hill Boulevard, N. to Anable av.

Adel rd. (L 7), from Home Lawn av., S. of Aspen pl., S. E. to Hillside av.

Adirondack Blvd. (G 16) (R'way Beach), from Ocean Promenade, N. W. to Beach Channel dr.

Admiral (E 7), fr. Metropolitan, S E to Sigsbee.

Adolph (L 8) (Jamaica), now part of 171st pl.

Adrian rd. (M 6), fr. 195th, S. of Midland pkway, E. to 197th.

BOROUGH OF QUEENS STREET AND AVENUE DIRECTORY—*Continued.*

Adriatic (D 7), from Andrews E. to Fresh Pond rd.

Agate pl. (J 7), from Austin, N.E. to Queens blvd.

Agnes pl. (G 7), from Myrtle av., N. to Edsall av.

Aguilar av. (K 6), from Kissena rd. at 72d av., S. E to Parsons av

Ainsworth av. (P 4), from Langston av., E. of Grand Central pkway, N. E. & N. to 61st av.

Albert (C 4) (L. I. C.), from Jackson av., N. E. to Jam. av. and (D 8) (L. I. C.), from Astoria av., N. E. to Wolcott av.

Albion (E 5), from Queens blvd., N. E. to S. Railroad av.

Albertis (G 5), from Corona av., N. W. to Fillmore av

Alcott pl. (N 18) (Far Rockaway), from Norton dr., N. E. to Mott Basin.

Alden av. (E 8), from Wyckoff av., N.E. to Pansey.

Alderton (F 6), from Woodhaven av., S. E. to Holyoke.

Aldrich (D 6) (Winfield), from Hawthorne, N. to Laurel Hill blvd.

Alexander av. (M 4) (Bayside), from Jackson av., N. W. to Park av.

Allegheney av. (H 7), from Burns, N. E. to Queens blvd

Allen (H 4), from Jackson av., E. to Jackson av.

Allendale (K 8) (Jamaica), from 95th av., S. E. to Liberty av.

Alley Pond rd. (O 4), a semicircular road running from Easthampton rd. to Hanford pkway, through proposed park, between Alley creek and Alley pond.

Alma (F 7), from Graeme av., N. to Central av.

Almeda av. (L 14) (R'way Beach), from Barbadoes Drive, E. to Beach 63d.

Almont rd. (O 18) (Far R'way), from Annapolis av., N. E. to Virginia.

Alonzo rd. (O 18) (Far R'way), from City line, W. to Beach 9th.

Alp pl. (O 18), (Far Rockaway), fr. McNeil blvd., N. to City line.

Alpha pl. (E 8) (Glendale), from Suburban, N. to Myrtle av.

Alpine (N 4), from Cloverdale blvd., S. of Birmingham rd., N. E. and S. E. to Hoxie.

Alsop (K 8) (Jamaica), now part of Kissena rd. and 150th.

Alstyne av. (G 5) (Newtown), from Hanover av., E. to Radcliff.

Alto pl. (L 3) (Whitestone), from Beechhurst, E. to Toronto.

Alton av. (F 6) from Burford, N. E. to Woodhaven av.

Alwick rd. (L 9), from Van Wyck blvd., S. of Rockaway bvld., E. to 140th.

Alwin rd. (M 6), fr. 198th S. of Midland parkway, E. to Rosedale blvd.

Amador rd. (N 4), from Northern pkway, at border of proposed park, S. E. to Easthampton rd.

Amber (G 9) (Woodhav'n), from Sutter av., S. to Dumont av., and from Cozine av., S. to Jamaica.

Amboy lane (O 7) (Queens), from 218th E. to Springfield blvd.

Ambrose (J 7), from Hillside av., N. to Kew Gardens rd.

Amelia rd. (M 9), from 179 N. E. to Merrill.

Ames pl. (F 6) from Florence av., N. E. to Woodhaven av.

Amory av. (D 7), from Metropolitan av., S. E. to Bleecker.

Amory ct. (D 7), from Grandview av., N. E. to Zeliler.

Amos (N 10), from 147th, W. of Springfield blvd., S. to 149th av.

Amstel blvd. (K 14) (Rockaway Beach), from St. Cloud rd., S. E. & E & N. E & E. to Rockaway Beach blvd.

Anable (B 5) (L. I. C.), from L. I. R. R., N. W. to Jackson av.,

Anable av. (B 5) (L.I.C.) from Meadows, S. E. to Calvary Cemetery.

Anaconda av. (M 6), from 73d av. at 193d, S. E. to Union Turnpike.

Anchor (F 8) (North Beach), from 35th, E. to Flushing Bay.

Anderson rd. (N 9) (Jamaica), from Merrick blvd., N. E. to 180th.

Anderson av. (D 4) (Woodside), from Newtown rd. S. E. to Rowan av.

Andes (M 7), from Liberty av., N. to Westwood.

Andrews (D 7), from Zeiller, N. E. and N. to Mt. Olivet av.

Ankener (E 5), from Calamus av., S. and S. E. to Metropolitan av.

Anna (O 10) (Rosedale), fr. Hoff. N. to Conselyea.

Anna pl. (E 8), fr. Pansey, N. E. to Fresh Pond rd.

Annandale la. (P 3), from Little Neck rd., E. of Browvale drive, S. & S. E. to 60th av.

Annapolis (O 18) (Far R'way), from Empire av., S.E. to McNeil blvd.

Anniston av. (P 4), from Winchester boulev'd at Bradshaw av., N. E. to Marathon av.

Anthon (D 7), from Myrtle av., N. E. to Putnam av.

Anthony (H 5) (Flushing), from Wateredge av., N. E. to Lawrence.

Appleton (M 10), fr. Rockaway blvd., opp. 160th, N. E. to S. Conduit av.

Arcade av. (M 7), from Dunkirk, N.E. to Liberty av.

Arch (B 5) (L. I. C.), from L. I. R.R., N. W. to Jackson av.

Archer av. (K 8) (Jamaica), from Van Wyck blvd., E. to 160th.

Arctic (D 7), from Flushing av., S. E. to Fresh Pond rd.

Arda pl. (D 6) (Laurel Hill), from Waters, N. to Borden av.

Argo (L 5), from 164th at Kissena pk., E to 166th.

Arkansas (H 9), from Peconic av., N. E. to Suwanee av.

Arlington ter. (K 8) (Jamaica), from Inwood, N. E. to Sutphin blvd.

Armand pl. (D 8), from Cypress av., N. E. to Walter.

Armour (N 10), fr. Springfield blvd., opp. Springfield la., S. W. to 147th av.

Arnold (D 7), fr. Metropolitan av., N. E. to Arctic.

Arona pl. (L 8) (Jamaica), now 165th pl.

Arrow (G 7), from Yellowstone av., S. E. to Roman av.

Arrow av. (M 10), from S. Conduit av., W. of New York av., S.E. to Farmers blvd.

Arthur (N 10), from S. Conduit av., S. W. to Sheffield av.

Arundel pl. (N 4), fr. 56th av., bet. Penshurst pl. & Chatsworth pl., S. and S. W. to Penshurst pl.

Arverne bld. (L 14), from Amstel blvd. at Beach 62d, S. E. to Rockaway Beach blvd.

Ascan av. (H 7), fr. Metropolitan av., N. E. to Burns.

Ash av. (J 4) (Flushing), from Kissena blvd., N. E. to Murray.

Ashburton av. (M 4) (Bayside), from Consdale, N. E. to Bayside blvd.

Ashby av. (L 4), fr. Cemetery la., S. of Rocky Hill rd., E. to Utopia pkway.

Ashford (O 6), from 88th av., W. of Winchester blvd., S. to Braddock av.

Ashland (G 8) (Woodhaven), from Boro line to Myrtle av., now part of Park lane S., thence part of 85th av.

Aske (F 5) (Elmhurst), fr. Roosevelt av., S. E. to Van Dine.

Aspen pl. (L 7), fr. Home Lawn av., S. of Kendrick rd., S. E. to Mayfield rd.

Astoria av. (C 8) (L. I.C.), from Van Alst av., E. to Jackson av.

Astoria pl. (C 8) (L. I.C.), from Barclay, S. E. to Hallett.

Atfield av. (K 9), fr. Rockaway blvd., N. W. to Liberty av., thence now part of 132d.

Atglen pl. (K 8) (Jamaica), now part of 107th av.

Athalia pl. (J 2) (College Pt.), from Fletcher av., N. to Draper av.

Atkinson av. (P 6), from Winchester blvd., S. of 91st av., N. E. to Braddock av.

Atlantic av. (F 8) (Woodhaven), continued from Boro line, E. to Van Wyck av. (Richmond Hill.)

Atom (H 6), from Queens blvd., N. E. to 120th.

Auburndale la. (L 4), fr. Station rd., bet. 171st and 172d, S. to Fresh Meadow rd.

Audley (H 7) (Richmond Hill), from Babbage, N. W. to Forest Park, now part of 116th.

Audley (H 7) (Richmond Hill), from Forest Park, E. to Grenfeld.

Augustina av. (O 18), (Far R'way), fr. Beach 12th, S. W. to Bayport pl.

Austin (F 6), fr. Eliot av., S.E. to Metropolitan av.

Ava pl. (L 7), from Devonshire rd., between Adel rd. and Dalny rd., S. to Gilman av.

Avery (H 4) (Flushing), from Wateredge av., N. E. to Lawrence.

Avery av. (H 4) (Flushing), from Lawrence, N. E. to Saull.

Avis rd. (P 14) (Far R'way), from McNeil blvd. E. to City line.

Avon rd. (M 7) (Jamaica), from Radnor rd., N. to Kent rd.

Ayr av. (D 6) (Winfield), from Hawthorne, N. to Betts av.

Azalea, (E 7), from Metropolitan av., N. W. to Eliot av.

Aztec pl. (N 14) (Far Rockaway), from Grasmere ter., N. W. to Far Rockaway blvd.

Babbage (H 7) (Richmond Hill), from Forest Park, S. E. to Jamaica av, at Richmond Hill sta.

Babbitt (A 4) (L. I. C.), from Bulkhead line. S. E. to Vernon av.

Babylon av. (M 7), from Dunkirk, N.E. to Liberty av.

Backus (H 7), from Austin, N.E. to Queens blvd.

Badger av. (M 10), from S. Conduit av., W. of Arrow av., S. E. to Farmers blvd.

Bagley av. (L 4), fr. Cemetery la., S. of Ashby av., E. to Utopia parkway.

Baisley blvd. (L 11), from 163d av., E. of Cornell Basin, N. E. to Farmers blvd.

Bajen pl. (G 9) (Woodhaven), from Perkins, E. to Ferry.

Baker av. (K 9), fr. Rockaway blvd., N. W. to Liberty av., other parts now 134th.

Baldwin (D 4) (L. I. C.), from Vandeventer av., N. E. to Astoria av., and (E 3) (L. I. C.), from Wolcott av., N. E. to bulkhead line.

Baldwin (E 7), from Laura, N. to Metropolitan av.

Baldwin av. (G 7), from Selfridge av., N. E. to Burns.

BOROUGH OF QUEENS STREET AND AVENUE DIRECTORY—*Continued.*

Balfour (H 6), fr. Queens blvd., N. E. to 120th.

Ballard la. (N 7) (Hollis), from 198th. E. to 204th.

Balsam av. (N 10), from Farmers blvd., S. of S. Conduit av., S. E. to Arthur.

Baltic (D 6), from Andrews, E. to Mt. Olivet av.

Bancroft (D 6) (Winfield), from Hawthorne, N. to Tyler.

Bandera (L 10), from S. Conduit av., W. of Oka, S. E. to Byron.

Bandman av. (K 8) (Jamaica), now part of 105th av.

Banks av. (G 4), from Astoria av., E. to Flushing bay.

Banta pl. (F 5), from Van Dine, E. to Junction av.

Barbadoes dr. (L 14) (R'way Beach), from Beach 72d at Failing av., N. W. & N. & N. E. & E. to Beach 63d.

Barbara (F 7), from Graeme av., N. to Central av.

Barclay (C 8) (L. I. C.), from Hoyt av., N E. to Winthrop av.

Barclay av. (J 4) (Flushing), from Kissena blvd. N. E. to 156th.

Bard (E 6), from Burford, N E. to Woodhaven av.

Bardwell av. (O 7), from 207th, E. to 212th.

Bark (F 8) (North Beach), from 38th, E. to Flushing bay.

Barkins (G 5) (Corona Hgts.), from Alstyne av., S. E. to Rodman.

Barlow pl. (K 2) (Whitestone), from Ridgeway av, N. E. to Arndt pl.

Barn (B 5) (L. I. C.), from L. I. R. R., N. W. to Jackson av.

Barnett av. (C 5) (L.I.C.), from Laurel Hill av., N. E. and E. to Woodside av.

Barnwell (E 5), from Queens Blvd., N. E. to South Railroad av.

Barr (M 10), from Rockaway blvd., opp. 159th, N. E. to Grayland av.

Barron (L 9) (Jamaica), from 116th av., S. E. to Foch blvd.

Barry rd. (K 14) (R'way Beach), fr. Beach 84th.

Barrymore (G 6) (Newtown), fr. Queens blvd., N. W. to Corona av.

Barthold pl. (J 5) (Flushing), from 187th, E. to Jaggar av.

Bartlett (M 10), from Rockaway blvd., S. of Appleton, N. E. to Duncan av.

Barton av. (K 4), from 149th pl., E. to 150th.

Bartow (C 4) (L. I. C.), from Jackson av., N. E. to Jamaica av., and (C 8) (L I. C.) from Astoria av., N. E. to Ditmas av.

Bascom av. (M 9), from 140th, S. of Rockaway blvd., E. to 143d.

Bassett rd. (M 10), from Cogswell, S. of Geraldine av., S. E. to Judith.

Battery rd. (N 13) (Far R'way), from McBride E. to Pinson.

Baxter (F 5) (Elmhurst), from B'way, N. E. to Roosevelt av.

Bay (N 11) (Springfield), from Boulevard E.

Bay Park pl. (N 13) (Far Rockaway), from Healy av., N. W. to Bayswater av.

Bayard (H 4), from Peartree av., E to Flushing River.

Bayfield av. (L 14) (R'way Beach), from Barbadoes dr. to Beach 63d.

Baylies (G 4), from Polk av., N. to Jackson av.

Bayport pl. (O 13) (Far R'way), from Dinsmore av., N. W. to Augustina av.

Bayshore rd. (N 3), from McKnight dr at Little Neck Bay N. along Shore of Little Neck Bay and thence S. to L. I. R. R., W. of Little Neck Sta.

Bayside av. (J 3) (College Pt), from Union, S. of 30th av., N E. to 154th.

Bayside la. (K 3), fr. 29th av., W. of 163d, N. E. to Cross Island blvd.

Bayswater av. (N 13) (Far R'way), from Dickens W. to Norton dr.

Bayview (O 3) (LittleNeck), from Morgan pl., S. E. to Broadway.

Beach 2nd (P 14) (Far Rockaway), from Ocean Promenade, N. to Sea Girt av.

Beach 3rd (P 14) (Far Rockway), from Ocean Promenade, N. to Sea Girt av.

Beach 4th (P 14) (Far R'way), fr. Ocean Promenade, N. to Reads Lane.

Beach 5th (O 14) (Far R'way), fr. Ocean Promenade, N. to Sea Girt av.

Beach 6th (O 14) (Far R'way), fr. Ocean Promenade, N. to Sea Girt av.

Beach 7th (O 14) (Far R'way), from Ocean Promenade, N. to Frisco av.

Beach 8th (O 14) (Far R'way), fr. Ocean Promenade, N. to Sea Girt av., and from Frisco av. N. to Cornaga av.

Beach 9th (O 14) (Far R'way), fr. Ocean Promenade, N. to Far Rockaway blvd.

Beach 11th (O 14) (Far R'way). fr. Ocean Promenade, N. to Sea Girt av. and from Heyson rd., N. to Plainview av.

Beach 12th (O 14) (Far R'way), from Ocean Promenade, N. to City line.

Beach 13th (O 14) (Far R'way), fr. Ocean Promenade, N. to Mott av.

Beach 14th (O 14) (Far R'way), fr. Ocean Promenade, N. to Frisco av.

Beach 15th (O 14) (Far R'way) from Heyson rd., N. to New Haven av.

Beach 16th (O 14) (Far R'way), fr. Ocean Promenade, N. to Sea Girt av.

Beach 17th (O 14) (Far R'way), fr. Ocean Promenade, N. E. to Brookhaven av.

Beach 19th (O 14) (Far R'way), fr. Ocean Promenade, N. to Mott av.

Beach 20th (O 14) (Far R'way), from Ocean Promenade, N. to Mott av.

Beach 21st (O 14) (Far R'way), fr. Ocean Promenade, N. and N. E. to Mott av.

Beach 22d (N 14) (Far R'way), from Camp rd., N. to Far Rockaway blvd.

Beach 24th (N 14) (Far R'way) fr. Ocean Promenade, N. to Sea Girt av., and from Cornaga av., N. to Dickens.

Beach 25th (N 14) (Far R'way), from Ocean Promenade, N. to Sea Girt av., and from Camp rd., N. W. to Mott Basin.

Beach 26th (N 14) (Far R'way) fr. Ocean Promenade, N. to Edgemere av.

Beach 27th (N 14) (Far R'way), from Ocean Promenade, N. to Collier av., and from Healy av., N. to Bayswater av.

Beach 28th (N 14) (Far R'way), from Ocean Promenade, N. to Brookhaven av., and from Bayswater av., N. E. to Mott Basin.

Beach 29th (N 14) (Far R'way), from Ocean Promenade, N. to Brookhaven av., and fr. Far Rockaway blvd., N. W. to Healy av.

Beach 30th (N 14) (Far R'way), from Ocean Promenade, N. to Lewmay rd., and from Sea Girt av., N. to Brookhaven av.

Beach 31st (N 14) (Far R'way), from Ocean Promenade, N. to Lewmay rd., and from Sea Girt av., N. to Brookhaven av.

Beach 32d (N 14) (Edgemere), fr. Ocean Promenade, N. and N. W. to Norton dr.

Beach 33d (N 14) (Edgemere), fr. Ocean Promenade, N. to Brookhaven av.

Beach 34th (N 14) (Edgemere), fr. Ocean Promenade, N. to Brookhaven av.

Beach 35th (N 14) (Edgemere, fr. Ocean Promenade, N. to Norton av.

Beach 36th (N 14) (Edgemere). fr. Ocean Promenade. N. to Norton av.

Beach 37th (N 14) (Edgemere), fr. Ocean Promenade. N. to Norton av.

Beach 38th (N 14) (Edgemere), fr. Ocean Promenade. N. to Norton av.

Beach 39th (N 14) (Edgemere), fr. Ocean Promenade, N. to Norton av.

Beach 40th (N 14) (R'way, Beach), fr. Ocean Promenade, N. to Beach 41st.

Beach 41st (M 14) R'way, Beach), fr. Ocean Promenade, N. to Norton av.

Beach 41st pl. (M 14) (Rockaway Beach), fr. Beach 42d, N. E. to Beach 41st.

Beach 42d (M 14) (R'way Beach), fr. Ocean Promenade, N. to Norton av.

Beach 43d (M 14) (R'way Beach), fr. Ocean Promenade, N. to Norton av.

Beach 44th (M 14) (R'way Beach), fr. Ocean Promenade, N. to Conch rd.

Beach 45th (M 14) (R'way Beach), fr. Ocean Promenade, N. to Conch rd.

Beach 46th (M 14) (R'way Beach), fr. Ocean Promenade, N. to Norton av.

Beach 46th pl. (M 14), fr. Ocean Promenade, N. to Edgemere av.

Beach 47th (M 14) (R'way Beach), fr. Ocean Promenade, N. to Norton av.

Beach 48th (M 14) (R'way Beach), fr. Ocean Promenade, N. to Norton av.

Beach 49th (M 14) (R'way Beach), fr. Ocean Promenade, N. to Norton av.

Beach 50th (M 14) (R'way Beach), fr. Ocean Promenade, N. to Norton av.

Beach 51st (M 14) (R'way Beach), fr. Ocean Promenade, N. to Amstel blvd.

Beach 52d (M 14) (R'way Beach), fr. Ocean Promenade, N. to Amstel blvd.

Beach 53d (M 14) (R'way Beach), fr. Ocean Promenade, N. to Amstel blvd.

Beach 54th (M 14) (R'way Beach), fr. Ocean Promenade, N. to Amstel blvd.

Beach 55th (M 14) (R'way Beach), fr. Ocean Promenade, N. to Amstel blvd.

Beach 56th (M 14) (R'way Beach), fr. Ocean Promenade, N. to Amstel blvd.

Beach 57th (M 14) (R'way Beach), fr. Ocean Promenade, N. to Amstel blvd.

Beach 58th (M 14) (R'way Beach), fr. Ocean Promenade, N. to Amstel blvd.

Beach 59th (M 14) (R'way Beach), fr. Ocean Promenade, N. to Amstel blvd.

Beach 60th (M 14) (R'way Beach), fr. Ocean Promenade, N. to Rockaway Beach blvd.

Beach 61st (L 14) (R'way Beach), fr. Ocean Promenade, N. to Rockaway Beach blvd.

Beach 62d (L 14) (R'way Beach), fr. Ocean Promenade, N. to Amstel blvd.

Beach 63d (L 14) (R'way Beach), fr. Ocean Promenade, N. to Barbadoes dr.

Beach 64th (L 14) (R'way Beach), fr. Ocean Promenade, N. to Decosta av.

Beach 65th (L 14) (R'way Beach), fr. Ocean Promenade, N. to Barbadoes dr.

Beach 66th (L 14) (R'way Beach), fr. Ocean Promenade, N. to Decosta av.

BOROUGH OF QUEENS STREET AND AVENUE DIRECTORY—*Continued.*

Beach 67th (L 14) (R'way Beach), fr. Ocean Promenade, N. to Barbadoes dr.

Beach 68th (L 14) (R'way Beach). fr. Ocean Promenade, N. to Barbadoes dr.

Beach 69th (L 14) (R'way Beach), from Ocean Promenade, N. to Barbadoes dr.

Beach 70th (L 14) (R'way Beach), fr. Ocean Promenade. N. to Amstel blvd.

Beach 71st (L 14) (Rockaway Beach), fr. Ocean Promenade, N. to Amstel blvd.

Beach 72d (L 14) (Rockaway Beach), fr. Ocean Promenade. N. to Barbadoes dr.

Beach 73d (L 14) (R'way Beach), fr. Ocean Promenade, N. to Amstel blvd.

Beach 74th (L 14) (R'way Beach). fr. Ocean Promenade, N. to Amstel blvd.

Beach 75th (L14) (R'way Beach), fr. Ocean Promenade, N. to Amstel blvd.

Beach 76th (L 14) (R'way Beach). fr. Ocean Promenade, N. to Brookside av.

Beach 77th (L14) (R'way Beach), fr. Ocean Promenade, N. to Bulkhead line.

Beach 78th (L14) (R'way Beach), fr. Ocean Promenade, N. to R'way Beach blvd.

Beach 79th (K14) (R'way Beach), fr. Ocean Promenade, N. to Brookside av.

Beach 80th (K14) (R'way Beach, fr Ocean Promenade N. to Bulkhead line.

Beach 81st (K 14) (R'way Beach). fr. Ocean Promenade, N. to Finnard av.

Beach 82d (K 14) (R'way Beach), fr. Ocean Promenade, N. to Hammels Sta.

Beach 83d (K 14) (R'way Beach), fr Ocean Promenade, N to Hammels Sta.

Beach 84th (K14) (R'way Beach), fr. Ocean Promenade, N. to Java.

Beach 85th (K14) (R'way Beach), fr. Ocean Promenade, N. to Beach Channel dr.

Beach 86th (K14) (R'way Beach), fr. Ocean Promenade, N. to Beach Channel dr.

Beach 87th (K14) (R'way Beach), fr. Ocean Promenade, N. to Beach Channel dr.

Beach 88th (K14) (R'way Beach). fr. Ocean Promenade, N. to Holland av, and from R'way Beach blvd., N. W. to Beach Channel dr.

Beach 89th (K14) (R'way Beach), from Gull ct., N. W. to Beach Channel dr.

Beach 90th (K14) (R'way Beach), fr. Holland av., N. W. to Beach Channel dr.

Beach 91st (K 15) (R'way Beach), fr. Ocean Promenade, N. W. to Beach Channel dr.

Beach 92d (K 15) (R'way Beach), fr. Ocean Promenade, N. W. to Beach Channel dr.

Beach 93d (K 15) (R'way Beach), fr. Ocean Promenade, N. W. to Holland av.

Beach 94th to Beach 102d, both inclusive, (K and J 15) (R'way Beach), fr. Ocean Promenade, N. W. to Beach Channel dr.

Beach 103d (J 15), (R'way Beach), now Seaside av.

Beach 104th to Beach 106th, both inclusive, (J 15)(R'way Beach). fr. Ocean Promenade, N. W. to Beach Channel dr.

Beach 107th (J15) (Rockway Beach), fr. Ocean Promenade, N. W. to St. Marks av.

Beach 108th (J15) (R'way Beach), fr. Ocean Promenade, N. W. to Beach Channel dr.

Beach 109th (J15) (R'way Beach), fr. Ocean Promenade, N. W. to Wainwright ct.

Beach 110th (J15) (R'way Beach), fr. Ocean Promenade. N. W. to R'way Beach blvd.

Beach 111th (J15) (R'way Beach), fr Ocean Promenade, N. W. to R'way Beach blvd.

Beach 112th (J15) (R'way Beach), fr. Ocean Promenade, N. W. to R'way Beach blvd.

Beach 113th (J15) (R'way Beach), fr. Ocean Promenade, N. W. to R'way Beach blvd.

Beach 114th (J15) (R'way Beach), fr. Ocean Promenade. N. W. to R'way Beach blvd.

Beach 115th (J15) (R'way Beach), fr. Ocean Promenade. N. W. to R'way Beach blvd.

Beach 116th to Beach 141st, both inclusive. (H and G 15) (Rockaway Beach), fr. Ocean Promenade, N. W. to Beach Channel dr.

Beach 143d (G 16) (Rockaway Beach), fr. Ocean Promenade, N. W. to Cronston av.

Beach 144th (G16) (Rockaway Beach), fr. Ocean Promenade, N. W. to Cronston av.

Beach 145th (G16) (Rockaway Beach), fr. Ocean Promenade, N. W. to Beach Channel dr.

Beach 146th (G16) (Rockaway Beach), fr. Ocean Promenade, N. W. to Beach Channel dr.

Beach 147th (G16) (Rockaway Beach), fr. Ocean Promenade, N. W. to Beach Channel dr.

Beach 148th (G16) (Rockaway Beach), fr. Ocean Promenade, N. W. to Beach Channel dr.

Beach 149th (G16) (Rockaway Beach), fr. Ocean Promenade, N. W. to Beach Channel dr.

Beach Channel dr. (G 15) (R'way Beach), from Seaside Pk., N. E. and E. and N. E. to Brookside av.

Beach pl. (N 8), from Bayshore rd., bet. 233d and McKnight dr., S. to 28th rd.

Beacon pl. (M 13) (Far Rockaway), from Mott av., N. E. to Mott Basin.

Beattie av. (H 10), from Vanderveer av., N. E. to Thedford.

Beaumont rd. (O 14) (Far R'way), from Beach 11th, E. to Beach 9th.

Beaver (B 5) (L.I.C.), from Review av., N.E. to Borden av.

Beaver rd. (K 8), from 150th, N. E. to 160th.

Beck rd. (O 13) (Far Rockaway), from Annapolis av., N. E. to Virginia.

Bedell (L 8), from 159th, S. E. to 137th av.

Beebe (B 4) (L. I. C.), from Van Alst av., S. E. to Jackson av.

Beech (B 5) (L. I. C.), from L. I. R. R., N. W. to Jackson av.

Beech av. (J4) (Flushing), from Kissena blvd., N. E. to 156th.

Beechhurst av. (K 2) (Whitestone), fr. Beeckman, S. E. to Jackson av.

Beechy rd. (H 7), from Burns, S. and S. E. to Overhill.

Belknap (N 9), from 139th av., N. and N. W. to Merrick rd.

Bell blvd. (M 2), from Little Bay av, at Little Bay, S.E. Grand Central parkway.

Bella pl. (D 6) (Maspeth), from Flushing av., east of Willow, S. one block.

Bellwood av. (P 6), from Winchester blvd., S. of Atkinson av., N. E. to Braddock av.

Belmont (E 8), from Cabot pl., S E. two blocks.

Belmont av. (G 9) (Woodhaven), from Boro. line, E. to Emerald.

Benham (F 5) (Elmhurst), from Roosevelt av., S.E. to Van Dine.

Bent pl. (J 5), from Webb av., opp. 187th, S., E. and N. to Webb av. opp. 188th.

Bentley rd. (O 10), from 218th, S. of Cascade av., S. E. to Brookville blvd.

Benton (N 9) (Springfield), from 121st av., S. E. to Williamson.

Berkeley (N 10) fr. Langdon, at proposed New Park, S. to 149th av.

Berlin av. (C 6) (Laurel Hill), from Creek, N. to Borden av.

Berme pl. (C 8) (L. I. C.), from Barclay, S. E. to Van Alst av.

Berrian av. (D8) (L.I.C.), from Bulkhead line at Berrian Creek, S. E. and E. and S. E. and E. and S. E. to Jackson av.

Bertha pl. (G 7), from Myrtle av., N. to Edsall av.

Berwick rd. (M 7) (Jamaica), from Henley rd., S. to Dalny.

Bessemer (H 8) (Richmond Hill), from Forest Park, S. E. to Jamaica av. at Richmond Hill sta.

Bessemund av. (N 13), (Far R'way), from Beach 25th S. W. to Norton dr.

Beta (E 8) (Glendale), fr. Suburban. N. to Myrtle av.

Bethune pl. (E 7), (Middle Village), from Penelope, S. E. to Lowell av.

Betts av. (D 6) (Maspeth), from Maspeth av., N. to Queens blvd.

Benson av. (D 5) (Winfield), from Betts av., E. to Trimble av.

Beverley rd. (J 7) (Richmond Hill), from Union Turnpike, S. and E. to Bravoort.

Bielby (D 6) (Maspeth), from Rust, E. to Van Cott av.

Bigelow av. (H 11), fr. Jamaica Bay, N. to Sutter av.

Billings (O 6), from 88th av., W. of Ashford, S. to Braddock av.

Birch (J 11), fr. Jamaica Bay. N. and N. W. to Liberty av., thence now part of 120th.

Birdsall av. (O 13) (Far Rockaway), from Pinson, E. to Redfern av.

Birmingham rd. (N 4), fr. Cloverdale blvd., S. of Amador rd., E. and S.E. to Easthampton rd.

Bittman (E 6), fr. Grand S. E. to Metropolitan av.

Blackwell (C 4) (L. I. C.), from Jackson av., N. E. to Jamaica av., and (C3) (L. I. C), from Astoria av., N. E to Ditmars av.

Blaine (F 6), from Bowne. S. E. to Phelps av.

Blake av. (G 9) (Woodhaven). from Boro line, E. and S.E to 128th.

Blakely (L 8) (Jamaica), from Beaver rd., S.E to Liberty av.

Bleecker (D 7), continued from Boro. line. N. E. & E. to Fresh Pond rd.

Bliss (C 5) (L. I. C.), from Borden av., N. to Barnett av.

Bloomer (D 6), from Borden av., N. to Maurice av.

Bloomfield (F 6), from Calamus av., S. E. to Jupiter av.

Bloomfield pl. (F 6), from Penelope, S. E. to Satterlee av.

Blossom av. (J 4) (Flushing), from Wateredge av., E. and N. E. to Saull.

Blossom av. (H 5) (Flushing), from Wateredge av., N. E. to Lawrence.

Bodine (A 4) (L. I. C), from bulkhead line, S. E. to Sherman pl.

Bolton rd. (O 13) (Far R'way), from Beach 9th, E. to Virginia.

Bolzes (N 9), from Salem av., N. to Baisley av.

Boody pl. (D 4) (Woodside), from Jackson av., N. to Grand av.

BOROUGH OF QUEENS STREET AND AVENUE DIRECTORY—*Continued.*

Boone (N 9) (Springfield), from Merrick rd., S. E. to Ridgedale.

Booth (F 6), fr. Woodhaven av., S. E. to Queens blvd.

Borden av. (A 5) (L. I. C.), from Front, S. E. to Grand at Brown pl.

Borkel pl. (O 6), from 90th av., S. of Braddock av., S. E. to Winchester blvd.

Boston (G 2) (College Pt.) from Tallman av., E. to Mamaroneck.

Boulevard (B 4) (L. I. C.), fr. Queensboro bridge, N. E. to Winthrop av.

Bourton (F6), from Woodhaven av., S. E. to Orville.

Bow (H7), fr. Continental av., E. and S. to Groton.

Bowne, (F 6), from Corinth av., N. E. to Calamus av.

Bowne (J 4) (Flushing), from Northern blvd., S. E. to Rose av.

Boyce av. (M 4) (Bayside), from 206th, E. to 208th.

Boynton (M 10), fr. Rockaway blvd., E. of S. Conduit av., S. to junction of 149th av. and 158th.

Brackenridge av. (G 2), (College Pt.), now Poppenhusen av. and part of 5th av.

Braddock av. (O 6), from Springfield boulev'd, at Whitehall ter., E. to Jackson av.

Bradley av. (B 6), from Newtown creek, N. and N. W. to Borden av.

Bradshaw av. (P 4), from Rushford, S. of 62d av., E. and N. E. to 251st.

Brady (G4), from Carvall, N. to Polk av.

Bragaw (C 5) (L. I. C.), from Hunters Pt. av., N. to Skillman av.

Brattle rd. (P 3) (Little Neck), fr. 245th at York av., N. E. to Little Neck rd.

Breck pl. (F 6), fr Bowne, S. E. to Eliot av.

Briar pl. (N 13) (Far R'way), from Camp pl., N. to Brookhaven av.

Bridgewater av. (P 4), fr. Golf rd., at Roff, N.E. to Grand Central pkway.

Briell (C 4) (L.I.C.), from Jackson av., N. E. to Jamaica av.

Briggs av. (J 9), from R'way blvd., N. W. to Liberty av., thence now part of 117th.

Brinkerhoff av. (K 8), from 111th av., N.E. to Farmers blvd.

Brisban (K 8), from 95th av., S. to Liberty av.

Bristol (H 9), from Peconic av., N. E. to Sutter av.

Britton av. (F 5) (Elmhurst), from B'way, N. E. to Roosevelt av.

Broad (D 6) (Maspeth), from L. I. R. R., N. to Newtown av.

Broad (O 11), from Hook creek, E. to Rockaway Turnpike.

Broadway (B 4) (L. I. C.), from bulkhead line, S. E. and S. to Queens blvd.

Broadway (J 4) (Flushing), from Flushing River, E. to Cemetery la.; E. of that point known as Jackson av.

Brocher rd. (M 9), from 172, N. E. to Merrill.

Brokaw (N 10), from S. Conduit av., W. of Arthur, S. to Sheffield av.

Brousus (G 5) (Corona Hghts.), fr. South Railroad av., S. to Martense av.

Brookhaven av. (N14) (Far R'way), fr. Beach 35th, N. E. and E. to Beach 17th.

Brookside (O 3), from Old House Landing rd., S.W. & S. to 38th av.

Brookside av. (L14) (Rockaway Beach), fr. Beach 72d, N. W. to Beach Channel dr.

Brookville blvd. (O 9), from City line at Covington, S. W. to 147th av., thence S.E. to Rockaway blvd. at Hook Creek Basin.

Brower pl. (F6), from Woo N. E. to Queens blvd.

Brown av. (O 3), fr. 247th, N.W. to Old House Landing rd.

Brown pl. (E 6), fr. Grand, S. E. to Juniper.

Browvale dr. (O 3), from Jackson av., E. to Little Neck rd.

Browvale la. (P 3), from Browvale dr., S. to Annandale la.

Bruce rd. (K 15) (R'way Beach), fr. Beach 90th, E. to Beach 87th.

Brunswick av. (O13) (Far R'way), from McNeil blvd., S. W. to Nameoke av.

Brush (F 7) (Glendale), from Myrtle av., N. W. to Edsall av.

Bryant av. (D 5) (Winfield), from Laurel Hill blvd., N. to Benson av.

Bryce rd. (F 4) (Corona), from Junction av., N. to 39th.

Buchman av. (D 7), from Myrtle av., N.W. to Putnam av.

Buck (P 5), from Cullman av., E. of Winchester blvd., S. E. and S. to Grand Central pkway.

Buckley (C 5) (L. I. C.), from Hunters Pt. av., N. to Meadow.

Buckner pl. (J 7), from Queens blvd., N. E. to 190th.

Bud pl. (J 4) (Flushing), from 36th av. to 36th rd.

Buell (G 4), from 51st, N. W. to Banks av.

Bulger pl. (H 4) (Flushing), from Wateredge av., N. E. to Meadow.

Bullet av. (P 6) (Creedmoor), from Douglaston av., E. to Pistol.

Bullock (D 6), from Borden av., N. to Maurice av.

Bulwer pl. (E 9), from Boro. line, N. W. to Vermont av.

Burchell av. (L 14) (R'way Beach), from Barbadoes dr., E. to Beach 69th.

Burchell pl. (L 14) (R'way Beach), fr. Beach 65th, E. to Beach 60th.

Burford (F 6), from Ames pl., S. E. to Satterlee av.

Burgoyne av. (N 10), from Springfield blvd., S. of Sheffield av., S. E. to 211th.

Burling (K 4) (Flushing), from Cherry av., S. E. to Oak av.

Burns (F 6), from Woodhaven av., S.E. to Union Turnpike.

Burnside av. (D4) (Woodside), from Charlotte, E to Astoria av.

Burrough av. (E 6), from Jay av., N. to Woodside av.

Burrough pl. (D 5), from Woodside av., N. to Roosevelt av.

Burton (L2) (Whitestone), from Shore Acres blvd., E. of 166th, S. to Willets Pt. blvd.

Busby av. (M 6), from 73d av. at 194th, S. E. and N. E. to Peck av.

Bush (E 8), from Cypress av., E. 1 block.

Buskirk pl. (F 6), from Woo, N. E. to Queens blvd.

Butler (G 4), from Banks av., N. W. to Schurz av.

Butte pl. (O 4), fr. 230th, S. of 56th av., E. to Easthampton rd.

Byrd (J 5) (Flushing), fr. Cherry av., S. to Peck av.

Byron (M 10), from S. Conduit av., W. of 158th, S. W. to Baisley blvd., and from 150th av., S. W. to 152d av.

Cabinet (D 4) (L. I. C.), from Vandeventer av., N. E. to Astoria av., and (E 3) (L. I. C.), from Wolcott av., N. E. to bulkhead line.

Cabot pl. (E 8), fr. Cypress av., S. W. 1 block.

Cadmus pl. (N 13) (Far R'way), from Plunkett av., N. E. to Mott Basin.

Caffrey av. (O 14) (Far Rockaway), from City line, S. W. to Brookhaven av.

Calamus (E 5), fr. Maurice av., E. & S. E. to Woodhaven av.

Caldwell av. (E 6), from Harriett av., N. E. to Queens blvd.

California av. (H 5), from Wateredge av., N. E. to Saull.

Cambria av. (O 4), fr. Overbrook dr., S. of Deepdale av., N. E. to Morenci la.

Camden av. (M 7), from Dunkirk, N.E. to Liberty av.

Camelia (B 3) (L. I. C.), from Boulevard, S. E. to Crescent.

Cameron (D5), from Grout av., N. to Woodside av.

Camp rd. (N14) (Far Rockaway), from Beach 21st, S. W. to Edgemere av.

Caney la. (P 10) (Rosedale), from Brookville blvd., S. E. and N. E. to City line.

Capron (E 7), from Admiral, N. to Metropolitan.

Carll la. (K 3), from Willets Pt. blvd., E. of 160th, S. E. to Cross Isl. blvd.

Carlton (F6), fr. Woodhaven av., S. E. to Orville.

Carmen (E 5), from Maurice av., E. to Lauronson.

Carol (K 8) (Jamaica), from Van Wyck av., E. to Sutphin rd.

Carolin (C 5) (L. I. C.), from Borden av., N. to Jackson av.

Carolina rd. (O 4), from Hanford pkway, S. of Wessington av., E. to Douglaston av.

Carroll pl. (D 6) (Maspeth), from Jay av., N. to Garfield.

Carter (M 10), now parts of Masterson av. and 156th.

Carter pl. (F 6), from Grand, S. E. to Caldwell av.

Carver (C 3) (L. I. C.), from Newtown, N. E. to Astori av.

Cary pl. (O 3), fr. 36th av., opp. 243d, S. E. to 244th.

Cascade av. (O 10), from 218th, S. of 147th av., E. to Edgewood.

Case (F 5) (Elmhurst), fr. Roosevelt av., S. E. to VanDine.

Case pl. (F 5), from Van Dine, E. to Junction av.

Caspian (D7), from Flushing av., S. E. & E. to Eliot av.

Cassel av. (C 6) (Laurel Hill), from Hobson av., E. to Willow av.

Castlewood (P 4), fr. Little Neck rd., S. of Gurley la., E. and S. E. and S. to City line.

Catalpa av. (D 7), from Myrtle av., N. E. and E. to Shaler.

Cedar (J 10), fr. Peconic av., N. E. to Rockaway blvd.

Cedar (N 3) (Douglaston), from Regatta pl., N. E. to Douglaston av.

Cedar av. (J 9), fr. R'way Blvd., N. W. to Liberty av., thence now 113th.

Cedar pl. (C 3) (L. I. C.), from Edwards, S. E. to Hallett.

Cedarcroft pl. (L 7), from Home Lawn av., N. of Hillside av., N. E. to Adel rd.

Cedric rd. (K 9), fr. 128th, N. of Sutter av., E. to 130th.

Central av. (E 7) (Glendale), from Otto, N. E. to Selfridge.

Centre (D 8), fr. Wyckoff av., N. E. to Myrtle av.

Chadwick (L 10), from S. Conduit av., W. of Bandera, S. E. to Byron.

Chaffee (E 7), from Kossuth pl., N. W. to Cornelia.

BOROUGH OF QUEENS STREET AND AVENUE DIRECTORY—*Continued.*

Chancellor (P4), fr. Langford, S. of 62d av., S. E. and N. E. to Commonwealth av.

Chandler (O 13) (Far R'way), from Dix, N. to Battery pl.

Channel av. (J 10), from Fairfield av., S. to Jamaica Bay.

Channing rd. (O 18) (Far R'way), from Beach 9th W. to Neilson.

Chapin pl. (O 18) (Far Rockaway), from Beck rd., F. W. to Almont rd.

Charlecote Ridge (L 7), fr. Grand Central parkway at Home Lawn av., S.E. and S. to Henley rd.

Charles (D 6) (Maspeth), from Rust, E. to Flushing av.

Charles (O10) (Rosedale), from Hoff, N. to Conselyea av.

Charlotte (D 4) (Woodside), from 20th, E. to Burnside av.

Charlotte pl. (E 8), from Alden av., N. to Otto.

Chatsworth pl. (N4), from 56th av., bet. Arundel pl. and 226th, S. E. to 61st av.

Chauncey (C 3) (L. I. C.), from Hoyt av., N. E. to Winthrop av.

Cheney (N 9), from Farmers av., E. to Bennet.

Cherry av. (J 4) (Flushing), from Peck av., N. E. to 156th.

Chestnut (J 10), from Peconic av., N. & N. W. to Liberty av., thence now 112th.

Chestnut av. (C 3) (L. I. C.), from Vandeventer av., N. E. to Astoria av.

Chevy Chase rd. (M 6), fr. Union Turnpike, W. of Holliswood av., S. to Hillside av.

Chicago (F 5) (Newtown), from Queens blvd., N.W. to Corona av.

Chippewa (H 9), from Peconic av., N. E. to Rockaway blvd.

Chittenden (H 6), from Queens blvd., N. E. to 120th.

Christie (G 5), from Marlowe av., N. E. to Waldron.

Chrystina av. (M9), fr. Salem av., N. to Thorpe pl.

Church (J 9) (Richmond Hill), from R'way blvd., N. W. to Liberty av., thence now 118th.

Clara (F 7), from Graeme av., N. to Central av.

Clark (C 3) (L. I. C.), from Main, E. to Crescent.

Clark av. (D 6) (Laurel Hill), from Rust, N. to Borden av.

Claude av. (L 8), from 160th N. E. to 111th av.

Claymore av. (M 10), from S. Conduit av., W. of Badger av., S. E. to Farmers blvd.

Clayton rd. (L 7) (Jamaica), from 164th, S. of Tilly av., E. to 165th.

Clermont av. (D 7), from Hibberd av., N. to Maurice av.

Cleveland av. (D5) (Wo'dside), from Queens blvd. N. to Skillman av.

Cliff pl. (M 2) (Bayside), from Rumford, E. to Bell av.

Clifford av. (N10) (Springfield), from Springfield blvd., S. of S. Conduit av., S. E. to 216th.

Clifton av. (C 6) (Laurel Hill), fr. Newtown creek, N. to Borden av.

Clinton av. (C 6), from Debevoise av., E. and N. E. to Fisk av.

Clio av. (M 6) (Hollis), fr. Keno av., S. to Dunton av., W.

Clover pl. (E 8), from Cypress av., S. W. two blocks.

Cloverdale blvd. (N 4), fr. junction of Northern parkway and Amador rd., S. E. to Union Turnpike.

Club Court (N 4), on elevation to the South of Kenilworth pl. and S. to 56th av.

Clyde (G 6), from Thornton, S. E. to Stafford av.

Coast (F3) (North Beach), from 89th, E. to Flushing Bay.

Codwise pl. (F 5), from Grand, N. to Queens blvd.

Coe pl. (F 5), from Vorhees pl., E. to Junction av.

Cogswell (M 10), fr. 152d av., E. of 160th, N. E. to Farmers blvd.

Cold Spring rd. (N18) (Far R'way), from Waterloo rd., E. to Beach 25th, N.

Colden (J 4) (Flushing), from Franklin av., S. E. to Kissena blvd.

Coler av. (E 5), from Queens blvd., E. to Fitch av.

Coleridge av. (Q4), fr. Golf rd., W. of Langston av., N. E. to Grand Central parkway.

Colfax (O7), from Bardwell av., S.E. to 214th.

Colgan av. (F 6), from Van Horn, N. E. to Woodhaven av.

College pl. (H 2) (College Pt.), from Powells Cove blvd., E. of 120th, S. E. to 122d.

College Point Causeway (H 3) (College Pt.), fr. 122d, S. of 26th av., S. E. to Willets Pt. blvd.

Collier av. (N 14) (Far Rockaway), fr. Beach 22d, W. to Brookhaven av.

Collins av. (D 7), from Metropolitan av., N. to Grand.

Collins pl. (H 4), fr. 34th av., E. of Lawrence, S. to Northern blvd.

Colloway (G 5) (Corona Hghts.), from Lewis av., S. to Martense av.

Cologne av. (C 6), from Hull av., N. to Columbine.

Colonial av. (H 6), from Queens blvd., N. W. to Rodman.

Columbia av. (D 6) (Maspeth), fr. Flushing av., N. to Adams.

Columbine av. (C 6) (Laurel Hill), from Laurel Hill blvd., E. to Borden av.

Coman (H4), from Riverside av., E. to Flushing river.

Comfort av. (N 10), from Kirkland, near Farmers blvd., E. to Berkeley.

Commercial av. (N 10), fr. N. Y. blvd., near Farmers blvd., E. to Berkeley.

Commonwealth blvd. (P 4), from Marathon av., bet. Anniston and Bradshaw avs., S. and S. E. to City line.

Como (M 6) (Hollis), from Keno av., E. to Pinto av.

Compton ter. (L 7) (Jamaica), now part of 88th av.

Conch pl. (M 14) (R'way Beach), from Beach 44th to Beach 45th.

Conch rd. (M 14) (R'way Beach), fr. Norton av., at Beach 45th, N. W. at side of Norton Basin.

Concord (P 8), from Lakeville rd., near City line, S.E. & S. to Little Neck rd.

Concord av. (P 8), continued from Nassau County, from City line, N. of Glenwood av., S. E. to Lakeville rd.

Conduit av. (G 9) (Woodhaven), from Boro. line, S. E. to Peconic av.

Congress av. (C 5) (Laurel Hill), from Laurel Hill blvd., E. to Borden av.

Conover (M 10), fr. Rockaway blvd., near S. Conduit av., N. E. to S. Conduit av.

Conroy (N 10), from S. Conduit av., W. of Brokaw, S. to Langdon av.

Constantia pl. (G 7), from Myrtle av., N. to Edsall av.

Continental av. (G 7), from Union Turnpike, N. E. to Burns.

Cook (F 7) (Glendale), fr. Proctor, E. to Central av.

Coombs (M 9) (Springfield), from 202d, S. E. to Lakeview av.

Cooper (C 3) (L. I. C.), fr. Grand av., N. E. to Newtown av.

Cooper (D 8), cont'd from Boro. line, N. E. to Cypress av.

Copeland av. (F 7) (Glendale), from Myrtle av., N. E. and E. to Woodhaven av.

Corbett (F 6), fr. Jupiter av., S. E. to Satterlee av.

Corey (E6), from Berford, N. E. to Woodhaven av.

Corinth (F 6), from Ankener, S. E. to Satterlee av.

Cornaga av. (N 14) (Far R'way), from Beach 20th, N. E. to City line.

Cornbury pl. (F 6), from Bowne, S.E. to Eliot av.

Cornelia (D 8), continued from Boro. line, N. E. and E. to Shaler.

Cornell (G 7), from Woodhaven av., N.E. to Orville.

Cornish (F5), from Queens blvd., N. E. to South Railroad av.

Corona av. (F 5) (Newtown), from Maurice, N. E. and E. and N. E. and S. E. to Rodman.

Corporal Stone (M 3), from 35th av. at 214th, S. to 40th av.

Couch (G 4), from Astoria av., N. W. to Banks av.

Court (B 5) (L.I.C.), from L. I. R. R., N. W. to Thompson av.

Courtney av. (L 4), from Cemetery la., S. of Bagley av., E. to Utopia parkway.

Covert av. (D 7), from Borough line, S. E. to Myrtle av.

Covington (O 8), fr. Spr'gfield blvd., S. E. to City line.

Cowen rd. (M 10), from Cogswell, N. of 150th av., S. E. to 150th av.

Cox pl. (D 6) (Maspeth), from Grand, E. to Flushing av.

Cozine av. (G 10) (Woodhaven), from Borough line, E. and S.E. to 128th.

Craft av. (P 11), fr. 151st av., near City line, N. E. to Rosedale blvd.

Crandall la. (M 9), from Cheney, N. and N. E. to Caxton av.

Crane (B 5) (L. I. C.), from L. I. R. R., N. W. to Jackson av.

Cranston (L 9), from Baisley blvd. at 132d av., S. E. to N. Conduit av.

Craven rd. (N 10), from Brokaw, S. of S. Conduit av., E. to Arthur.

Creek (B5) (L. I. C.) from Borden av., N. E. to Meadow.

Creek (C 6), from Hobson av., S. E. to Rust at Clark av.

Creek (D 7), from Flushing av., N. to Rust at Lawall av.

Crescent (B 5) (L. I. C.), from Nott av., N. E. to Winthrop av.

Cresskill (K 8), from 95th av., S. to 101st av.

Crocheron av. (K4) (Flushing), fr. Northern blvd. at 161st, N. E. to Cross Isl. blvd. E. thereof being now part of 35th av.

Croft rd. (J 15) (R'way Beach), fr. Beach 107th, N. E. to Beach 105th.

Crommelin av. (J 4) (Flushing), from Lawrence, S. E. to Byrd.

Cronston av. (G15) (R'way Beach), fr. Beach Channel dr., at Beach 143d, N. E. to Beach Channel dr. at Beach 124th.

Crosby av. (E 9), from Vermont av., at Boro. line, N. E. to Bulwer pl.

Cross Island blvd. (K 2), from 6th av., S. of Merritt rd., S. E. to Union Turnpike

Crossover rd. (M10), from Cogswell, S. of Rockaway blvd., S.E. to Farmers blvd.

Croydon rd. (L 7) (Jamaica), from Homelawn av., E. and N. E. to Midland Parkway.

BOROUGH OF QUEENS STREET AND AVENUE DIRECTORY—*Continued.*

Crager's rd. (K 14) (R'way Beach), from Scheer to Amstel blvd.

Cryder's la. (K 2) (Whitestone), from Cross Isl. blvd., S. of 15th av., N. E. to Little Bay av.

Crystal av. (O 5), from Springfield blvd., S. of Union Turnpike, S. to Hartland av.

Cullman av. (O 5), from Cloverdale blvd.. at 73d av., N. E. to Little Neck rd.

Curtis (G 4), from Banks av., N. W. to Sigel av.

Curzon rd. (H 7), fr. Park Lane South, S. of Mayfair rd.. S., E. to 116th.

Cushman pl. (G 5) (Newtown), from Martense, N.W. to Gfrry av.

Cuthbert pl. (J 7) (Richmond Hill), fr. Lefferts av., S. E. and S. to Metropolitan av.

Cutler (F 6), from Van Horn, N. E. to Queens blvd.

Cypress av. (D7), cont'd from Borough line, S. E. and E. to Fresh Pond rd.

Cyrus (O 6), fr. 88th av., W. of Billings, S. to Braddock av

Dabney av. (O 13) (Far Rockaway), from City line, S. W. to Leland.

Dahlia av. (J4) (Flushing), from Saull, E. to Jagger.

Dakota av. (K 9), from Rockaway blvd., N. W. to Liberty av.; other parts being now 135th.

Dale rd. (L 7) (Jamaica), from 160th, S. of Archer av., E. to Union Hall.

Dalny rd. (L 7) (Jamaica), from Wexford ter. N. and E. to Holliswood av.

Dana (E 6), from Berford, N. E. to Woodhaven av

Dartmouth (F 6), from Woodhaven av., S. E. to E. to Continental av.

Darvall (G 4), from Alburtus av., E. to Flushing river.

Davenport av. (O 6), from Springfield blvd., S. of 92d av., N. E. to Braddock av.

Davidson pl. (C3) (L. I.C.) from Emily ter., S. E. to Hallett.

Davis (B 5) (L. I. C.), from L. I. R. R., N. W. to Jackson av.

Davit (F3) (North Beach), from 42d, E. to Flushing Bay.

Dayton pl. (M2) (Bayside) from Little Bay av.. at Bell blvd., S. E. to 26th av.

Deal la. (N 9), from Merrick rd., E. to Caxton av.

Dearborn av. (O 8), from 117th av., S.E. to City line.

Debevoise (B 4) (L. I. C.), from Jackson av., N. E. to Jamaica av.

Debevoise av. (C 3) (L. I. C.), from Astoria av., N. E. to Ditmars av.

Debevoise av. (C 6), (Laurel Hill), from Creek, N. to Borden av.

DeBoe (E8) (Glendale), fr. Suburban, N, W. to Myrtle av.

Decatur (D 8), continued from Boro. line, N. E. to Myrtle av.

Decker (E 6) (Maspeth), fr. Grand, N to Henry.

Decosta av. (L 14) (R'way Beach), from Barbadoes dr., E. to Beach 69th and from Beach 67th, E. to Beach 63d.

Deepdale av. (O 4), from Overlook dr., S. of Wessington av., N. E. to Browvale la.

Deepdene (H 7), from Underwood, E. to Rockrose.

Deer (J 10), from Fairfield av., S. to Jamaica bay.

Deerfield rd. (N14) (Edgemere), from Beach 82d, W. to Beach 80th.

Deesen (M10), from Crossover rd., S. of Cogswell, N. E. to Duncan av.

Defoe (N 9) (Springfield), Pineville la., E. to Ridgeville.

Degen av. (N9) (Jamaica), now part of 130th av.

DeKalb av. (C 7), cont'd from Boro. line, N. E. to Woodward av.

DeKoven (H6), fr. Queens blvd., N. E. to 120th.

Delavall av. (H 4)' from Bayard, N. to Flushing river.

Delaware av. (K 4) (Flushing), from Burling, N.E. to 156th.

Delia (G 7), from Myrtle av., N. to Central av.

Dell pl. (P 4), from Chancellor, W. of Maynard, S. to Cullman av.

Delmar av. (L 5), fr. Cemetery la., at Wheaton la., E. and N.E. to Hollis Court blvd.

DeLong (H 4) (Flushing), from Wateredge av., S. to Sanford av.

Delta pl. (E8) (Glendale), from Suburban, N. to Myrtle av.

Denman (F5) (Elmhurst), from Roosevelt, S. E. to Van Dine.

Dennington av. (H 11), fr. Jamaica bay, N. to Sutter av., thence now 88th.

Dennis (N9), from Farmers av., E. to Bennet.

Denton (L 7) (Jamaica), from Archer av., S.E. to South rd.

Depew av. (M 7), from Dunkirk, N.E. to Liberty av.

Depeyster (G 4), from Roosevelt av., N. W. to Jackson av.

Depot rd. (K 4), fr. 156th. N. E. to 160th, the eastern section being now part of 39th av.

Deppe (O 3), fr. 240th, S. of L. I. R. R., N. E. and E. to Northern blvd.

Dermott av. (P 5), from Winchester blvd., S. of Hollins av., N. E. to Grand Central blvd.

DesMoines (H 9), from Peconic av., N. to Rockaway blvd.

DeSota rd. (K 15) (R'way Beach), fr. Beach 94th, N. E. to Beach 92d.

DeVine (G 5), from Marlowe av., N. E. to Waldron.

Devonshire rd. (L 7), from Home Lawn av., N. of Gilman av., N. E. to Dalny rd.

Dewey pl. (K 7), from Admiral, N. to Metropolitan av.

Dewitt av. (Q 4), fr. Langston av., at Golf rd., N. E. to Grand Central parkway.

Dey (B 4) (L. I. C.), from Hopkins av., S. E. to Crescent.

Diamond (H 8) from Park av., N. to Union Turnpike. (N 13) (Far R'way), fr. Cornaga av., N. to Mott Basin.

Dickens av. (N 14) (Far R'way), fr. Cornaga av., S. W. to Norton dr.

Dickson (D 5) (L. I. C.), from Greenpoint av., N. to Jackson av.

Diener (K 15), name changed to Holland av.

Dill pl. (E 8), from Alden av., N. to Otto.

Dillon (L 8) (Jamaica), from Claude av., S.E. to 114th av.

Dinsmore av. (O 13) (Far R'way), from Beach 9th S. W. to Mott av.

Ditmars av. (C3) (L.I.C.), from Boulevard, S. E. and E. and S. E. to Astoria av.

Division (F5), fr. Calamus av., S. E. to Caldwell.

Dix av. (O 13) (Far Rockaway), from McBride, E. to Redfern av.

Dock (A 5) (L.I. C.), from Bulkhead line, E. to Front.

Dock (H 4) (Flushing), fr. Grove, N. to Water.

Dodge (O 6), from 88th av., W. of Cyrus, S. to Braddock av.

Doncaster pl. (L 6), from Grand Central parkway, E. of Utopia parkway, N. to Edgerton pl.

Doncaster rd. (L6) (Jamaica), now part of Grand Central parkway.

Dormans rd. (N 8) (Jamaica), from Murdock av., E. to Farmers blvd.

Dorothy (E 6), fr. Brown, N. E. to Firth av.

Doubleday (E 7), from Madison, N.W. to Traffic.

Douglas av. (L 7) (Jamaica), fr. 166th, E to 175th.

Douglaston av. (O 3), from Northern blvd., S. to Hanford parkway.

Douglaston blvd. (O 3), fr. Bayshore rd., S. to Northern blvd.

Douglaston parkway (O4), from 61st av., near Alley Pond, S. E. to Southern parkway.

Dow pl. (O 4), from Hanford pkway, S. of 62d av., N. E. to Redfield.

Downing (H 3), from 30th av., E. of Higgins, S. E. to 34th av.

Drake (D6) (Winfield), fr Hawthorne, N. to Tyler.

Drew av. (G 10), from Vandalia av., S. to Jamaica bay.

Dreyer av. (C 4) (L. I. C.), from Laurel Hill av., N. E. to Newtown rd.

Drummond (N 10), fr. N. Conduit av., W. of 183d, S. and S. E. to Springfield la.

Duane (D 4) (Woodside), from Jackson av., N. E. to 31st av.

Duer rd. (O 3), from proposed Basin at Old House Landing rd., S.E. to Peru drive.

Dulon (G 4), from Sigel av., N. to Ditmars.

Dumfries pl. (L 6), from 80th, E. of Tryon rd., S. to Kildare av.

Dumont av. (G 9) (Woodhaven), from Boro. line, E. to Hawtree av.

Dunbar (N 13) (Far Rockaway), from Norton dr., N. E. to Mott Basin.

Duncan av. (M 10), from S. Conduit av., W. of Claymore av., S. E. to Farmers blvd.

Dune (O 14) (Far R'way), from Sea Girt av., N.W. to Edgemere av.

Dunham av. (G 10), from Boro. line, E. to L. I. R.R.

Dunkirk (N 8), fr. Farmers blvd., N.W. to Liberty av.

Dunn pl. (J 4) (Flushing), from Franklin av., S. E. to Cherry av.

Dunton av. (N 6) (Hollis), from Dunton av. West, E. to Rosedale blvd.

Dunton av. West (M 6) (Hollis), from Salerno av. S. E. to Dunton av.

Durand av. (P 11) (Rosedale), at City line, E. of Craft av., runs N. E. to Rosedale blvd. at City line.

Duryea (B 6), fr. Review av., N. E. to Bradley av.

Dutch Kills (B 5) (L.I.C.), from Thompson, N. W. to Jackson av.

Dwight av. (N 14) (Far R'way), fr. Norton dr., N. E to Beach 29th.

Dyer (D4) (Woodside), fr. Jackson av., E. to Charlotte.

Dyer (G 4), from 51st, to Lent.

Eads la. (N9), from Farmers av., E. to Caxton av.

East av. (A 5) (L. I. C.), from Newtown creek, N. & N.E. to South Jane.

East Williston av. (Q 5), from Little Neck rd., S. of 85th av., N. E. to City line.

Easthampton rd. (N 3), from Bayshore rd., W. of proposed Basin, S. E. to Southern blvd.

Eberly (N 10), from S. Conduit av., W. of Drummond, S. to Mayer av.

Echo pl. (M 6), from 85th av., E. of Holliswood av., S. to Grand Central parkway.

Eddy pl. (P 4), from York av., at Langford, E. to Rushford.

Edgar pl. (E 8), from Tappen ter., E. to Vermont av.

Edgemere av. (N14) (Edgemere), from Rockaway Beach blvd., E. to Fernside pl.

BOROUGH OF QUEENS STREET AND AVENUE DIRECTORY—*Continued.*

Edgerton blvd. (L7), from Grand Central parkway, W. of Midland parkway, S. E. to Hillside av.

Edgerton pl. (L 6), from foot of Utopia parkway, N. E. to Tudor rd.

Edgewater la. (N 3), from 85th av., at 216th, E. to 222d.

Edgewood (N 9) (Springfield), from Farmers av., S. E. to City line.

Edison pl. (F7) (Glendale), from Indiana pl., N. W. to Edsall av.

Edisto (J 9), from R'way blvd., N. W. to Liberty av.

Edith pl. (E 6), from Eliot av., S. E. to Lutheran Cemetery.

Edmonson (N 9) (Springfield), from Farmers av., S. E. to Springfield blvd.

Edmore av. (P 6), fr. Winchester blvd., S. of Davenport av., N. E. to 240th.

Edna (O 13) (Far Rockaway), from Dabney av. N. E. to City line.

Edsall av. (E7) (Glendale), from Otto, E. to Delta.

Edson (G4), from Alburtis av., E. to Flushing river

Edward (C 3) (L. I. C.), from Astoria pl., N. E. to Potter av.

Effington av. (L 5), from Cemetery la., S. of Delmar av., S. E. and E. to Utopia parkway.

Egan av. (G 10), from Boro. line, E. and S. E. to 128th.

Egerton blvd. (L 7) (Jamaica), Wexford ter., N. and W. to Home Lawn av.

Eggert pl. (N 13) (Far R'way), from Mott av., N. to Mott Basin.

Egmont (N 13) (Far Rockaway), from Mott av., N. E. to Mott Basin.

Eighteenth (E 5), from Woodside av., N. to Hazen.

Eighteenth av. (D 4) (L.I. C.), from Jackson av., N. E. to Vandeventer av., and (D 3) (L. I. C.), from Astoria av., N. E. to Walcott av.

Eighteenth av. (G 2) (College Pt.), from 110th, at Flushing bay, E. to 112th and from 114th, E. to 127th, and from 128th, E. to 142d, and (K 2), from Parsons blvd., E. to Cross Isl. blvd., and from 157th, E. to Utopia parkway.

Eighth (A5) (L.I.C.), from Bulkhead line, S. E. to Jackson av.

Eighth (D 5) (Woodside), from Woodside av., N. to Patterson av.

Eighth av. (C 4) (L. I. C.), from Jamaica av., N. E. to Astoria av., and (D3) (L. I. C.), from Ditmas av., N. E. to Riker av.

Eighth av. (H 2) (College Pt.), from 117th, S. of 7th av., E. to 122d, and from 141st, E. to Cross Isl. blvd.

Eighth rd. (K 2), fr. 149th, S. of 8th av., E. to 150th.

Eightieth (G 8) (Woodhaven), from Park la. So., S. E. to Sutter av.

Eightieth av. (Q 5), from Union Turnpike, at 252d, N. E. to City line.

Eightieth dr. (L 6), from 171st, S. of Union Turnpike, N. E. to Chevy Chase rd.

Eightieth rd. (L 6), from 173d, S. of Union Turnpike, N.E. to Holliswood av., and (P 5), from Commonwealth blvd., S. of Union Turnpike, N.E. to 246th.

Eighty-first (G 8) (Woodhaven), from 92d av., S. E. to Liberty av., & from Pitkin av., S. to Sutter av.

Eighty-first av. (J7), from 126th, S. of Grand Central parkway, N. E. to 134th, and from 135th E. to 138th, and from 141st, N. E. to Parsons av., and (K 6), from 164th, N. E. to 171st, and from 173d N. E. to Utopia pkway, and (M 6), from Holliswood av., N.E. to Union Turnpike, and (P 5), fr. Gettysburg, S. of Union Turnpike, N. E. to City line.

Eighty-first dr. (L6), from 173d, S. of 81st rd., N. E. to Utopia parkway.

Eighty-first rd. (L6), from 170th, S. of 81st av., N.E. to Utopia parkway.

Eighty-second (G8) (Woodhaven), from 92d av., S. E. to 101st.

Eighty-second av. (J 7), from Kew Gardens rd., N. E. to 139th, and from Goethals av. at eastern boundary of proposed park, N. E. to Utopia pkway, and (P 5), from Gettysburg, S. of 81st av., N. E. to City line.

Eighty-second dr. (K 7), from 135th, S. of 82d rd., N. E. to Grand Central pkway, and from Kissena rd., N. E. to 153d, and from Parsons av. E. to 161st, and (Q 5), from 252d, S. of 82d rd., N. E. to 255th.

Eighty-second rd. (J 7), from Kew Gardens rd., S. of 82d av., N. E. to 130th, and from 135th N. E. to 138th, and from 147th N. E. to Parsons av., and (L 6), from Goethals av., N. of Grand Central pkway, N. E. to 175th, and (Q 5), from 252d, S. of 82d av., N. E. to 255th.

Eighty-third (G8) (Woodhaven), from Atlantic av., E. of 82nd, S. E. to 101st av.

Eighty-thirdav. (J7) (Black Stump), from Kew Gardens rd., N. of Maple Grove Cem., N. E. to Grand Central parkway, and from 170th, N. E. to Home Lawn av., and (P 5), fr. Gettysburg, N. of Hillside av., N.E. to City line.

Eighty-thirddr. (J7) (Black Stump), fr 137th at Maple Grove Cemetery, N. E. and E. to 164th.

Eighty-third road (J 7) (Black Stump), from 137th at Maple Grove Cemetery, N.E. to Grand Central parkway.

Eighty-fourth (G8) (Woodhaven), from 86th av., S. E. to 86th rd., and from 89th av., S. E. to Liberty av.

Eighty-fourth av. (H 7) (Richmond Hill), from Myrtle av., E. of Park la. South, N. E. to 122d, and (J7) (Black Stump) from 137th at Maple Grove Cem., N. E. and E. to 164th, and from 164th, E. and S. E. to 84th dr., and (L7), from 168th, N. E. to Home Lawn av, and (M 6), from Rosedale blvd., N. E. to Hollis Court blvd.

Eighty-fourth dr. (J 7), from Queens blvd., S. of 84th rd., N.E. to 84th av., and (Q 5), from 253d, S. of Hillside av., N. E. to 256th.

Eighty-fourth rd. (J 7), from Queens blvd. at 137th, N. E. to Parsons av., and (L 7), from 170th, N. E. to 172d, and (P 5), from Hillside av., opp. 243d, E. to 244th, and fr. Little Neck rd., S. of Hillside av., N.E. to 256th.

Eighty-fifth (G 8) (Woodhaven), from Park la. So., S. E. to 101st av., and from Liberty av., S. E. to Sutter av.

Eighty-fifth av. (G8) (Richmond Hill), from 83d, S. of Park la. South, E. to 85th, and from 91st E. to 96th, and from 102d N. E. to 110th, and fr. Myrtle av., N. E. to Metropolitan av., and (J 7) (Black Stump), fr. 137th at Maple Grove Cem., N. E. to 165th, and (M6), fr. Chevy Chase rd., N.E. & E. to Grand Central parkway, and (P 6), from Hillside av., at 240th, E. and N. E. to City line.

Eighty-fifth dr. (G 8) (Woodhaven), from 74th S. of 85th rd., E. to 79th, and fr. 80th, E. to 85th, and from 102d, N. E. to 104th, and (K 7) (Black Stump), from 139th, S. of 85th av., N. E. and E. to 144th, and from 148th E. and N. E. to Parsons av., and (P 6), from Commonwealth dr., S. of 85th av., N. E. to 247th.

Eighty-fifth rd. (G 8), (Woodhaven), from 74th S. of Park la. South, E. to 79th, and from 80th E. to property line and from 83d, E. to 98th, and fr. 101st, N. E. to 104th, and (K7) (Black Stump), from 85th av. at 141st, E. to 143d, and from 148th, E. to Kissena rd., and (M6), from Chevy Chase rd., N. E. to 194th, and (P 6), from 241st, S. of 85th av., E. to Commonwealth blvd., & fr. 253d, N.E. to Little Neck rd.

Eighty-sixth (G8) (Woodhaven), from Park la. So., S. E. to Sutter av.

Eighty-sixth av. (G 8) (Woodhaven), from 74th S. of 85th dr., E. to 80th, and from 83d, E. to 86th, and from 91st, E. to 96th, and from 101st, N. E. to 115th, and (J 7) (Black Stump), from 137th at Maple Grove Cem., N.E. and E. to 143d, and from 148th, N. E. to Parsons av., and (M 6), from Lonsdale av., N. E. to Grand Central parkway, and (P 6), from Gettysburg, at Hillside av., E. and N. E. to City line.

Eighty-sixth dr. (G 8) (Woodhaven), from 91st S. of 86th rd., E. to 94th, and (P 6), fr. Commonwealth blvd., S. of 86th av., E. to 248th.

Eighty-sixth rd. (G 8) (Woodhaven), fr. 74th, S. of 86th av., E. to 79th and from 80th, E. to property line, and from 83d, E. to 84th, and from 89th, E. to 93th, and from 102d, N. E. to 104th, and (K 7) (Black Stump), from Queens blvd. S. of 86th av., E to 143d, and (P 6), fr. Sargent, S. of Hillside av., E. to Gettysburg and from 241st, E. to Commonwealth blvd.

Eighty-seventh (G 8) (Woodhaven), fr. Park la. So., S. E. to 101st av., and from Liberty av., S. E. to Sutter av.

Eighty-seventh av. (G 8) (Woodhaven), from Elderts la., S. of Jamaica av., E. to 75th, and from 78th, E. to 85th, and from 100th, N. E. to 104th, and (J 7) (Black Stump), from Kew Gardens rd., S. of Maple Grove Cem., N. E, E. and N. E. to Parsons av., and (O 6), fr. Grand Central parkway, at Springfield blvd., N. E. to City line.

Eighty-seventh dr. (K 7), from Queens blvd., N. of Hillside av., E. to 143d, and (Q 6), from Commonwealth blvd., S. of 87th av., E. to Little Neck rd.

Eighty-seventh rd. (G 8) (Woodhaven), from Elderts la., S. of 87th av., E. to 75th, and from 78th, E. to 85th, and (K 7) (Black Stump), from Queens blvd., S. of 87th av., E. to 143d, and from 144th, N. E. to Parsons av., and from Gilman av., N. E. to 164th, and (Q 6), from 252d, S. of 87th av., E. and N. E. to City line.

Eighty-eighth (G 8) (Woodhaven), from Park la. So., S. E. to Sutter av.

Eighty-eighth av. (G 8) (Woodhaven), from Elderts la., S. of 87th rd., N. E. to Woodhaven av.,

BOROUGH OF QUEENS STREET AND AVENUE DIRECTORY—*Continued.*

and from 100th, N. E. to 104th, and from 181st, N. E. to 182d, and from 189th, N. E. to 160th, and from 165th, N. E. to 171st, and from 175th, N.E. to 178th, and (O 6), from Hillside av., N. of Braddock av., E. to 247th.

Eighty-eighth dr. (G 8) (Woodhaven), from 78th, S. of 88th rd., E. to 89th, and (P 6), from 242d, S. of 88th rd., E. and N. E. to 88th rd.

Eighty-eighth rd. (G 8) (Woodhaven), from Eldert la., S. of 88th av., E. to 75th, and fr. 78th, E. to 85th, and from 139th, E. to 144th, and (P 6), from 242d, S. of 88th av., E. to Jamaica av.

Eighty-ninth (G8) (Woodhaven), from Park la. So., S. E. to Sutter av.

Eighty-ninth av. (G 8) (Woodhaven), fr. Brooklyn Boro line, N. of Rockaway blvd., N.E. to 188th, and from 189th, N. E. to 178th, and from 181st, N. E. to 191st, and from 196th, E. and N. E. to Braddock av., and (P 6), from Ransom, S. of 88th av., E. and N.E. to 249th.

Eighty-ninth rd. (N 7), (Hollis) from 196th E. to 198th, and from 211th to 212th.

Elbertson F5 (Elmhurst), from Roosevelt av., S. E. to Kingsland av.

Elbow pl. (J 3) (Flushing), now Miller and part of 33d av.

Elder av. (J 4) (Flushing), from Peck av., N. E. to Kissena blvd.

Elderts la. (F 8) (Woodhaven), fr. Jamaica av., S. to Atlantic av., and from Vandalia av., S. to Jamaica Bay.

Eleventh (A 5) (L. I. C.), from Vernon av., S. E. to Jackson av.

Eleventh (D4) (Woodside), from Jackson av., N. to Grand av.

Eleventh av. (C4) (L.I.C.), from Jamaica av., N. E. to Astoria av., and (D3), (L. I. C), from Walcott av., N. E. to Riker av.

Eleventh av. (G2) (College Pt.), from Powells Cove blvd., S. of 9th av., E. to 115th, and (K 2), from 147th, E. to 153d, and from 154th, E. to 166th.

Elinor (E6), from Harriett av., N. E. to Firth av.

Eliot av. (D 7), from Metropolitan av., N. E. to Queens blvd.

Elizabeth av. (L14) (R'way Beach), from Barbadoes dr. E. to Beach 68th.

Elk et. (O18) (Far R'way) from Beach 20th, N. W. to Beach 22d.

Elkhorn (J16)' from Fairfield, S. to Jamaica Bay.

Elkmont av. (P 5), from Commonwealth blvd. S. of Underhill av., N. E. to Little Neck rd.

Ella (G 7), fr. Myrtle av., N. to Central av.

Ellis pl. (N 10), from N. Y. blvd., W. of Farmers blvd., N. E. to Farmers blvd.

Elm (B 3) (L. I. C.), from Boulevard, S. E. to 2d av.

Elm av. (K 4) (Flushing), from Burling av., N. E. to 156th.

Elmhurst av. (F 5) (Elmhurst), from Broadway, N. E. to Roosevelt av.

Elmira av. (M 7), from Brinkerhoff av., N. E. to Liberty av.

Elroy av. (O 18) (Far R'way), from Frisbie, N. E. to City line.

Elsie pl. (C5), fr. Packard, E. to Calvary Cemetery.

Elvira av. (O 14) (Far R'way), from City line, S. W. to Beach 9th.

Ely av. (B 5) (L. I. C.), from Jackson av., N. & N. E. to Newtown av.

Emerald (G9), from Sutter av., S. to Dumont av., and from Wortman av., S. to Jamaica Bay.

Emily (G 7), from Woodhaven av., E. to Baldwin.

Emily ter. (C 3) (L. I. C.), from Astoria pl., N. E. to Potter av.

Emma (D 7), from Flushing av., S. E. to Metropolitan av.

Empire av. (O 18) (Far R'way), from City line, S. W. to Cornaga av.

Enfield pl. (N 4), r. Garland, S. of Oakland Lake, S. to 56th av.

Engine (F3) (North Beach), from Ditmars av., E. to Flushing bay.

English (A 4) (L. I. C.), from Bulkhead line, S. E. to Vernon av.

Eno pl. (N 18) (Far Rockaway), from Norton dr., to Westbourne av.

Enright rd. (N 18) (Far R'way), fr. Gipson, W. to Dickens.

Epsilon pl. (E 8), fr. Anna pl., N. to Myrtle av.

Epsom Course (N6) (Hollis), fr. Grand Central Parkway, S. and E. and N. to Grand Central Parkway.

Ericsson (G 4), fr. Banks av., N. W. to Sigel av.

Escalente (H9), fr. Peconic av., N. E. to Rockaway blvd.

Esser (D 6), from Rust, E. to Maspeth av.

Ethan av. (Q 4), fr. Castlewood, between Dewitt and Langston avs., N. E. to Grand Central pkwy.

Etna (G 5) (Newtown), fr. Gfrry av., N.W. to Parcell.

Euclid (H 6), fr. Queens blvd., N. E. to 120th.

Eva (D 6), from Hemlock pl. N. to Flushing av.

Evans rd. (L 8), fr. Liberty av., N. E. to 159th.

Eveleth rd. (N 9) (Jamaica), from Merrick blvd., N. E. to 180th.

Evelin (D 7), from Fresh Pond rd., E. to Mount Olivet av.

Everdell av. (O 18) (Far Rockaway), from Beach 20th, E. to Greenport rd.

Everitt pl. (N8) fr. Westchester av., S.E. to Baisley blvd.

Everton (F 6), fr. Woodhaven av., S. E. to Orville.

Excelsior (M10), fr. Crossover rd., S. of Deeson, N. E. to N. Y. blvd.

Exeter (G6), fr. Thornton, S. E. to Continental av.

Exter (L 4) (Flushing), from Linn, N. to Beechhurst av.

Faber ter. (N 18) (Far R'way), from Granada pl., N. W. and N. E. to Mott Basin.

Failing av. (L 14) (R'way Beach), from Beach 72d. E. to Beach 69th.

Fairbanks av. (E 5), from Woodside av., E. to Baxter av.

Fairbury av. (P 6), from Winchester blvd., S. of Edmore av., N. E. to 240th.

Fairchild av. (L 5), from Wheaton la., S. of Effington av., E. to Utopia parkway.

Fairfax av. (P 4), fr. Marathon av., S. of Overbrook dr., N. E. to Annandale la.

Fairfield av. (G10), from Boro. line, E. and S. E. to 128th.

Fairmont (E 8), fr. Alden av., S. E. to Ozone ter.

Fairview av. (D 7), from Stanhope, S. E. to Forest av.

Falcon av. (N 14) (Far R'way), from Bay 29th, S. W. to Norton dr.

Fanning (G 5) (Newtown), from Sothern av., E. to Marlowe av.

Far Rockaway blvd. (N14), from Beach 35th, N. E. to City line.

Fargo (N 10), from Comfort av., W. of Drummond, S. to 147th av.

Farmers blvd. (M 7) (Hollis), from Jamaica av. at Colton av., S. E. and S. and S. W. to 163d av.

Farmington (J 10), from Flynn, S. to Jamaica Bay.

Farrington (H 3) (Flushing), from 130th, at 20th av., S. E. to Northern blvd.

Fennard (K 14) (R'way Beach), from Beach 82d to Beach 80th.

Fennimore av. (P 4), from 60th av., at 251st, N. E. and E. to City line.

Ferguson (G 4) (Corona), from Sackett, N. E. to Flushing river.

Fern pl. (M 8) (Jamaica), from 107th av., S. E. to 108th rd.

Ferndale av. (K 8) (Jamaica), from 143d, N. E. to Sutphin bvld.

Fernside pl. (N 14) (Far R'way), from Sea Girt av., N.E. to Edgemere av.

Fernwood rd. (L2) (Whitestone), from 162d, S. of 13th av., N. E. to 166th.

Ferrara av. (N 6) (Hollis), from Rosedale blvd., N. E. and N. to Grand Central Parkway.

Fidde (G 5), from Calloway, N. E. to Waldron.

Field pl. (G5) (Newtown), from Martense, N. W. to Gfrry av.

Fife (H 6), from Queens blvd., N. E. to 120th.

Fifteenth av. (D 4) (L. I. C.), from Jamaica av., N. E. to Astoria av., and (D 3) (L. I. C.), from Wolcott av., N. E. to Bulkhead line.

Fifteenth av. (G 2) (College Pt.), from Flushing Bay, E. to 150th, and (K 2), from Cross Isld. blvd., E. to Willets Pt. blvd., and (M 2), from Willets Pt. blvd., N. E. to 215th pl.

Fifteenth dr. (K 2), from 147th, S. of 15th rd., E. and N. E. to Cross Isld. blvd., and from Locke av., E. to Utopia pkway.

Fifteenth rd. (K 2), from 147th, at 15th av., E. to 150th, and from 200th, E. to 204th.

Fifth (A 5) (L. I. C.), from Front, E. to East.

Fifth (D 5) (Woodside), from Queens blvd., N. to Patterson av.

Fifth av. (C 4) (L. I. C.), from Jamaica av., N. E. to Astoria av.

Fifth av. (H 2) (College Point), from College pl., S. of Powells Cove blvd. E. to Powells Cove blvd., and (J 2) (Whitestone), from 144th, E. to Powells Cove blvd.

Fiftieth (G 4), from Polk av., N. to Astoria av.

Fiftieth av. (L 5), from Utopia parkway, at Underhill av., N. E. to Bell av., and from 215th, E. to 216th, and from 217th, N. E. to Springfield blvd.

Fifty-first (G7), fr. Queens blvd., N. to Flushing bay.

Fifty-first av. (N 4), from Bell av., S. of Rocky Hill rd., N. E. to Springfield blvd., and (O 4), fr. Redfield, N. E. to 244th.

Fifty-second (G 4), from Jackson av., N. to Astoria av.

Fifty-second av. (O 4), fr. Redfield, N. of Sanborn av., N. E. to 244th.

Fifty-third (G 4), fr. Jackson av., N. to Flushing bay.

Fifty-third av. (L 5), from Utopia parkway, S. of Peck av., N. E. to Bell av., and from 217th, N. E. to Springfield blvd.

Fifty-fourth (G 4), from Jackson av., N. to Flushing bay.

Fifty-fourth av. (N 4), fr. 217th, S. of 53d av., N. E. to Springfield blvd.

Fifty-fifth (G 4), fr. Jackson av., N. to Flushing bay.

Fifty-sixth av. (J5), from 142d, S. of Peck av., S.E. to 150th and from 161st E. and N. E. to Easthampton rd.

Fifty-sixth dr. (J5), from Jagger av., S.E. to 140th.

Fifty-sixth rd. (J 5), from Lawrence, S. of Peck av., S. E. to 150th.

BOROUGH OF QUEENS STREET AND AVENUE DIRECTORY—*Continued.*

Fifty-seventh av. (J 5), from Wateredge av., S. of Hammell av., E. to 186th.

Fifty-seventh rd. (J 5), from Wateredge av., S. of 57th av., E. to North Hempstead Turnpike.

Fifty-eighth av. (J 5), fr. Rodman, S. of 57th rd., E. and S.E. to 155th, and from Fresh Meadow rd., E. to 174th, and from Utopia parkway, N. E. to Springfield blvd., and from Arundel pl., N. E. to Easthampton rd.

Fifty-eighth rd. (J 5), fr. Wateredge av., S. of 57th rd., E. and S. E. to 155th.

Fifty-ninth av. (J5), from Rodman, S. of 58th rd., E. and S. E. and E. to 164th at St. Mary's Cemetery, and from 166th, E. to 170th, and from Fresh Meadow rd., S. E. to Utopia parkway; and (N 5), from 220th, N. E. to Springfield blvd., and from 230th N.E. to Easthampton rd., and (P 4), from Annandale la., E. to 262d.

Fillmore av. (D 4) (Woodside), from Broadway, E. to 48th.

Finlay (N 10), from S. Conduit av., W. of Eberly, S. to Commercial av.

Finnard av. (K 14) (R'way Beach), from Beach 80th to Beach 88d.

First (D 5) (Woodside), from Queens blvd., N. to 21st av.

First av. (C 4) (L. I. C.), from Jamaica av., N. E. to Grand av.

First av. (J 2) (Whitestone), from Parsons blvd., at Powells Cove blvd., N. E. to 150th.

First pl. (N 3) (Bayside), from Bayside blvd., E. to Bay.

Firth av. (E 6), fr. Grand, S. E. to Metropolitan.

Firwood pl. (M 7), from Brinkerhoff av., S. E. to Hilburn av.

Fisher av. (L 9), from Yardley, N.E. to Altmar.

Fisk (E6) (Maspeth), from Grand, N. to Fillmore.

Fitch av. (E 5), fr. Queens blvd., E. to Kingsland av.

Fitting (C 5) (L. I. C.), from Nott av., N. to Jackson av.

Fleet (G 6), fr. Woodhaven av., S. E. and E. to Continental av.

Flemming pl. (F6), from Florence av., N. E. to Woodhaven av.

Flint (J 9), from Peconic av., N. E. to Rockaway blvd.

Flora (E 6), from Harriett av., N. E. to Firth av.

Florence av. (F 6), from Eliot av., S.E. to Jupiter av.

Florence av. (P 10) (Rosedale), now that part of 240th, S. of 147th av.

Flossie (H 7), from Union Turnpike, N. to Metropolitan av.

Floyd (K2) (Bayside), now part of Shore Acres blvd.

Flushing (A 5) (L. I. C.), from Bulkhead line, E. to Vernon av.

Flushing av. (C 7), cont'd from Boro. line, N. E. to Grand.

Flynn av. (G 10), from Boro. line, S. E. to 128th.

Foam pl. (O13) (Far Rockaway), from Dinsmore pl., N. W. to Far Rockaway blvd.

Foch blvd. (K 9), from Rockaway blvd., N.E. to Hook Creek blvd.

Folsom av. (E 7) (Glendale), from Luther pl., N. W. to Otto.

Fonda av. (M7), from Dunkirk, N.E. to Liberty av.

Foote (G4), from Sigel av., N. to Ditmars.

Foothill ter. (M 7) (Jamaica), from Kent rd., N. E. to Rosedale blvd.

Forbell av. (G 10), from Vandalia av., S. to Jamaica bay.

Ford (F 7) (Glendale), fr. Myrtle av., N. W. & N. to Graeme.

Forest av. (D8), from Walter, N. W. to Metropolitan av.

Forest av. (J5) (Flushing), now part of Franconia av.

Forest Parkway (G 8) (Woodhaven), fr. Park Lane, E. of 80th, S. to Jamaica av.

Forley (F 5) (Elmhurst), from Roosevelt av., S. E. to Kingsland av.

Fortieth (G5), from Lake, N. W. to Flushing bay.

Fortieth av. (H 4), from Wateredge av., S. of 37th av., N. E. to 154th and (M8) fr. Bell blvd., E. to 221st and (N 4) fr. 224th, N.E. to Easthampton rd. and fr. 230th, N. E. to McKnight dr. and (O3) fr. Douglaston blvd. E. and N.E. to 240th and fr. 247th N.E. to Morgan.

Fortieth rd. (H 4), from Wateredge av., S. of 40th av., N. E. to Main.

Forty-first (G 5), fr. Lake, N. W. to Flushing bay.

Forty-first av. (H 4), from DeLong, N. E. to 156th, and from 168th, S. of Station rd., N. E. to Auburndale la. and (N 4) from 214 E. to 224th and (O 4) from 224th, E. to Douglaston blvd. and from Westmoreland rd., N. E. to Boro line.

Forty-first dr. (O 3), from Old House Landing rd., N. E. to Boro line.

Forty-first rd. (J 4), from Lawrence, S. of 41st av., N. E. to Jagger and (O 3) from Old House Landing rd., N. E. to Westmoreland.

Forty-second (G 5), from Lake, N. W. to Flushing bay.

Forty-second av. (L 4), fr. Auburndale la., S. of Station rd., N. E. to Cross Isld. blvd. and (M 4) from Cross Isld. blvd., E. to 43rd av. and (O 3) from Douglaston blvd. E. to 243rd and fr. Old House Landing rd., E. to Westmoreland.

Forty-second rd. (L 4), fr. 196th, S. of 42d av., N. E. to Cross Isld. blvd.

Forty-third (F 5), from Lake, N.W. to Ditmars av.

Forty-third av. (K 4), fr. 156th, S. of Sanford av., E. to Northern blvd. and (M 4) from Cross Isld. blvd., E. to Easthampton rd. and (O 4) from 230th E. to Boro line.

Forty-fourth (G 4), from Sackett, N. to Astoria av.

Forty-fourth av. (M 4), fr. 196th, S. of Northern blvd. N. E. to Northern blvd. and (O 4) fr. Douglaston blvd., E. to Cary pl. and from Old House Landing rd., E. to Westmoreland.

Forty-fifth (G 5), fr. Sackett, N. to Astoria av.

Forty-fifth av. (K 4), from 156th, S. of 43d av., E. and N. E. to Northern blvd.

Forty-fifth dr. (M 4), from Rosedale blvd., S. of 45th rd., N. E. to 215th.

Forty-fifth rd. (M 4), from 196th, S. of 45th av., N.E. to 215th, and from 220th pl., E. to Northern parkway.

Forty-sixth (G5), fr. Sackett, N. to Astoria av.

Forty-sixth av. (K4), from Parsons blvd., E. and N. E. to Northern blvd.

Forty-sixth rd. (M4), from 198th, S. of 46th av., N.E. to 215th.

Forty-seventh (G 4), from Hayes av., N. to Astoria av.

Forty-seventh av. (M 4), from Rosedale blvd., at Rocky Hill rd., N. E. to Springfield blvd.

Forty-seventh rd. (M 4), from Rocky Hill rd., at 203d, N. E. to 206th.

Forty-eighth (G 4), from Polk av., N. to Astoria av.

Forty-eighth av. (L 5), fr. Utopia parkway, opp. Gladwin av., N. E. to Rocky Hill rd.

Forty-ninth (G 4), from Polk av., N. to Astoria av.

Forty-ninth av. (N4), from 213th, S. of Rocky Hill rd., N.E. to Bell blvd., and from 215th, E. to 216th, and from 217th, N. E. to Springfield blvd.

Fosdick av. (E 7) (Glendale), fr. Indiana pl., N. W. to L.I.R.R.

Foster av. (C 5) (L. I. C.) from Skillman av., E. to Greenpoint av.

Foster pl. (N 10) (Springfield), now Ellis pl.

Fosters Meadow rd. (O 10) now part of Brookville blvd.

Fourteenth (A 4) (L.I.C.), from Bulkhead line, S.E. to Ely av.

Fourteenth (E 5) (Woodside), from Broadway, N. to 12th.

Fourteenth av. (D 4) (L. I.C.), from Jamaica av., N. E. to Astoria av.

Fourteenth av. (G 2) (College Pt.), from Flushing Bay, E. to 162d, and (M2) from Bell blvd., E. to 216th.

Fourteenth rd. (G 2) (College Pt), from Powells Cove blvd., S. of 14th av., E. to 123d, and from 132d, E. to 133d pl., and (K 2), from 14th av., S. E. and N. E. to 152d, and from 164th, E. to Utopia parkway.

Fourth (A 5) (L. I. C.), from Front, E. to Canal.

Fourth (D 5) (Woodside), from Queens blvd., N. to Patterson av.

Fourth av. (C 4) (L. I. C.), from Jamaica av., N. E. to Astoria av., and (D3) (L. I. C.), from Ditmars av., N.E. to Winthrop av.

Fourth av. (H 2) (College Pt.), from 123th, S of 3d av., E. to Powells Cove blvd., and (J 2) (Whitestone), from Powells Cove blvd., E. to 144th, and from 145th pl. E. to 149th, and from 150th, E. to Powells Cove blvd.

Fowler (H 4) (Flushing), from Wateredge av., N. E. to Lawrence.

Fox (B 5) (L. I. C.), from Review av., N.E. to Borden av.

Foxall (D 7), from Onderdonk av., N. E. to Fresh Pond rd.

Frame pl. (J 4) (Flushing) from 41st av., S. to Maple av.

Frances (G 7), from Myrtle av., N. to Central av.

Franconia av. (J 4) (Flushing), from Byrd, N. E. to Murray.

Franklin (B 3) (L. I. C.), from Bulkhead line, E. to Van Alst av.

Franklin av. (J 4) (Flushing), from Saull, N. E. to Parsons blvd.

Frankton (P 10) (Rosedale), from City line, S W. to 147th av.

Frederick (C 7), from Gilbert, N. E. to Creek.

Freeborn (N 10), from 147th av., E. of Farmers blvd., S. E. to Springfield blvd.

Freedom av. (H 9) (Woodhaven), from Suwanee, av., N. W. to Liberty av., thence now 102d.

Freman av. (B 4) (L. I. C.), from Bulkhead line, S. E. to Jackson av.

Fremont (E 8), from Central av., N. to Cornelia.

French (G 4), from 51st, to Lent.

Fresh Meadow rd. (L 4) from Auburndale la., E. to Utopia parkway.

Fresh Pond rd. (D6) (Maspeth), fr. Flushing av., S.& S.E. to Borough line.

Frigate (F3) (N'th Beach), from Ditmars av., E. to Flushing bay.

Frisbie (O13) (FarR'way), from City line, S. to Redfern av.

Frisco av. (O 14) (Far Rockaway), fr. City line, S.W. to New Haven av.

BOROUGH OF QUEENS STREET AND AVENUE DIRECTORY—*Continued.*

Front (A 5) (L. I. C.), fr. Newtown creek, N. E. to 5th.

Frost av. (K 9), fr. R'way blvd., N. W. to Liberty av., thence now part of 131st.

Fuller pl. (H 4) (Flushing), from 41st av., S. to Maple av.

Fullerton (P 4), fr. Rushford, bet. Chancellor and Redfield, S. E. and S.W. to Winchester blvd.

Fulton (D6), from Maurice av., E. to Connecting Railroad.

Fulton av. (B 8) (L. I C.), from Bulkhead line, E. to Main.

Funston (E7), fr. Admiral, N. to Metropolitan av.

Furman av. (D 7), from Flushing av., N. W. to Maspeth av.

Galley (E 3), from Riker av., N. to Bowery bay.

Galway av (M 8), from Dunkirk, N.E. to Rye pl.

Gamma (E 8) (Glendale), from Suburban, N. to Myrtle av.

Garden (J 4) (Flushing), from Lincoln, N. to Washington.

Gardner (M 2), from Little Bay av., E. of 209th, S. and S. E to Hollis ct. blvd.

Garfield (D 5) (Winfield), from Laurel Hill blvd., E. to Railroad av.

Garland (N 4), from Cloverdale blvd., S. of Oakland Lake, W. and S. to 56th av.

Garonne (J 9), from Peconic av., N. E. to Rockaway blvd.

Garrett (N 9), from 132d av., S. E. to Farmers blvd.

Garrick (H 7), fr. Queens blvd., N. E. to 120th.

Garrison av. (C 7), from Flushing av., N. W. to Maspeth av.

Garrison rd. (L 6), now that part of 82d av. between Goethals av. and Utopia parkway.

Gates av. (D 8), continued from Boro. line, N. E. and E. to Traffic.

Gay (F5) (Newtown), from Gfrry av., N.W. to South Railroad av.

Gaylord av. (K 7), now that part of 84th rd. between Queens blvd. and Parsons av.

Gaylord rd. (P 14) (Far R'way), from Reads la., N. E. to Annapolis av.

Gem pl. (K14) (Rockaway Beach), from Beach 87th, E. to Beach 86th.

Genesee (G 9) (Woodhaven), from Sutter av., S. to Jamaica bay.

George (D 8), fr. Wyckoff av., N. E. to Myrtle av.

Geranium av. (J4) (Flushing), from Colden, N. E. to Kissena blvd.

Gerard pl. (G 6), from Occident, S. E. to Yellowstone av.

Gertrude (G 7), from Myrtle av., N. to Central av.

Gettysburg (P 5), fr. Union Turnpike, at Old Creedmoor Rifle Range, S. & S. E. to Jamaica av.

Gfrry av. (F 5) (Newtown) fr. Pike, E. to Marlowe av.

Gibbon (L 5) (Bayside), fr. Peck av., bet. Cemetery la. and Utopia parkway, S. to 61st.

Gilbert (B 5) (L. I. C.), from Review av., N. E. to Borden av.

Gilbert (C 7), from Metropolitan av., N W. to Maspeth av.

Gillmore (G4), from Banks av., N. W. to Sigel av.

Gilman av. (K 7), from Parsons av., N. of Hillside av., N. E. to Dainy rd.

Gilroy av. (H5), fr. Hewitt av., N. W. to Flushing bay.

Gipson (N 13) (Far Rockaway), from Far Rockaway blvd., N. to Mott Basin.

Girard av. (N 10), from N. Y. blvd., N. of 147th av., E. to Berkeley.

Gladstone av. (N 10), from S. Conduit av. at 205th, S. E. to Edgewood.

Gladwin av. (L5), fr. Cemetery la., S. of Effington av., S. E. and E. to Utopia parkway.

Gladys (E 6), from Harriett av., N.E. to Firth av.

Glassboro av. (K 8) (Jamaica), from 189th, N.E. to Sutphin blvd.

Gleane (F 5) (Elmhurst), from Baxter av., S. E. to Kingsland av.

Gleason pl. (D 4) (L.I.C.), from Vandeventer av., N. E. to Wilson av.

Glenmore av. (G9) (Woodhaven), from Boro. line, E. to Bayside Cemetery.

Glenwood (O 3) (Little Neck), fr. 39th rd., near City line, S. E. to Lakeville rd.

Goethals av. (K 7), from Grand Central parkway at 141st, N. E. and S. to Grand Central parkway at 170th.

Goldfield (L 10), fr. 150th, S. of S. Conduit av., S. E. and S. W. to 152d av.

Goldington (G 6), from Woodhaven av., S. E. to Orville.

Goldsmith (F5), fr. Grand, N. to Maurice av.

Golf rd. (P 4), from Little Neck rd., N. of Langston av., N.E. to Langston av.

Gomer av. (G 2) (College Pt.), from Bulkhead line, E. and N. E. to Canfield av. (Whitestone).

Goodrich (C 3) (L. I. C.), from Astoria av., N. E. to Winthrop av.

Goodwin pl. (H 7), from Queens blvd., N. E. to 120th.

Gordon av. (M 8) (Jamaica), now part of 178th.

Gorsline pl. (E 5), from Grand, N. to Queens blvd.

Gosman av. (C5) (L. I. C.), from Borden av., N. to Jackson av.

Gotham rd. (K 9), from 128th, S. of Rockaway blvd., E. to 180th.

Gothic dr. (L 7), from Gilman av., E. of proposed park, N. and N. E. to Home Lawn av.

Gould av. (C 5) (L. I. C.), from Greenpoint av., E. to Calvary Cemetery.

Govan pl. (L 3) (Whitestone), fr. Utopia Parkway, E. to Barrington.

Gown (H 6) from Queens blvd., N. E. to 120th.

Grace (C 4) (L.I.C.), from Jackson av., N. E. to Jamaica av.

Grace (N 10), from S. Conduit av., W. of Finley, S. to Comfort av.

Graeme av. (F 7) (Glendale), from Proctor, E. to Baldwin.

Graham av. (B 4) (L.I.C.), from Bulkhead line, S. E. to Jackson av.

Granada pl. (N 13) (Far R'way), from Mott av., N. E. to Mott Basin.

Grand (C 7), from Boro. line cont'd, N. E. to Queens blvd.

Grand av. (B 3) (L. I. C.), from Main, S. E. & E. to Flushing bay.

Grand Central parkway (J 7), from Queens blvd. at 120th, N. E., E. and N. E. to City line.

Grandview av. (D 7), from Flushing av., S. E. to Fresh Pond rd.

Granger (G 5) (Corona Hghts.), from Martense av., S. E. to Rodman.

Grannatt pl. (L 9), from Rockaway blvd. at Baisley blvd., S.E. to 133d av.

Grape av. (K 4) (Flushing), from Burling av., N. E. to Kissena blvd.

Grapnel (F 3) (North Beach), from Ditmars av., E. to Flushing bay.

Grasmere ter. (N 13) (Far R'way), fr. Beach 25th, N. E. and N. to Mott av.

Grau pl. (J 7), fr. Queens blvd., N. E. to 120th.

Graves pl. (F8) (Woodhaven), now part of 85th rd.

Gravett pl. (J 5), from Larch av., at Cedar Grove Cemetery, E. and S. to Melbourne av.

Graylands av. (M 10), fr. S. Conduit av., E. of Rockaway blvd., S.E. to Appleton.

Grayson (N 8) (Sp'gfield), from 121st av., S. E. to Pineville la.

Greelyville (L 2) (Bayside), now part of 205th.

Green (M 10), now parts of Masterson av. and 157th.

Greenbridge av. (M 10), from 150th av., E. of Cogswell, N. E. to Duncan av.

Greene av. (D 7), cont'd from Boro. line, N. E. to Forest av.

Greenoak (B3) (L I.C.), fr. Temple, N. W. to Main.

Greenpoint av. (B6) (L. I. C.), from Boro. line continued, N.E. to Skillman av.

Greenport rd. (O 14) (Far R'way), from Beach 19th, N. E. to Cornaga av.

Greenwood av. (J 10), fr. Peconic av., N. & N. W. to Liberty av., thence now 111th.

Gregory (O 4), fr. 69d av., E. of Hanford parkway, S. E. to Langford.

Greiffenberg (F 6), from Grand, S. E. to Metropolitan av.

Grenfell (J 7) (Richmond Hill), from Union Turnpike, S. to Lefferts av.

Griffin av. (M 4) (Bayside), from 208th, E. to 214th.

Griffith av. (F 7) (Glendale), from Myrtle av., N. W. and N. to Metropolitan av.

Grimm av. (G 10), from Borough line, E. & S. E. to 128th.

Grosvenor rd. (H7) (Richmond Hill), from Park Lane South, S. of Metropolitan av., S.E. to 116th.

Groton (G 6), from Selfridge, S. E. to Roman av.

Grout av. (D 5), from Greenpoint av., E. to Broadway.

Grove (D 8), cont'd from Boro. line, N. E. and E. to Traffic.

Guilford (H 7), from Metropolitan av., N. E. to Kessel.

Gainsburg rd. (K 8) (Jamaica), from 150th, E. and N. to Liberty av.

Guion av. (J 9), fr. R'way blvd., N. W. to Liberty av., thence now 108th.

Gulick (M 8), from New York av., N. E. to Van Allen.

Gull ct. (K 14) (Rockaway Beach), bet. Beach 88th and Beach 89th.

Gunther (G 5) (Corona), from Alburtis av., N. E. to Flushing river.

Gurley la. (P 4), fr. 255th, S. of 61st av., E. and S. E. to Ainsworth av.

Gwydir (F 6), fr. Caldwell av., S. E. to Satterlee av.

Hackensack (J 10), from Lambertson av., S. to Jamaica bay.

Hackett pl. (H 6), from Austin, N. E. to Queens blvd.

Hague pl. (L 9), fr. Baisley av., S. of Cranston, S. E. to 133d av.

Haight (H 4), (Flushing), from 41st av., S. to Maple av.

Halle av. (C 6) (Laurel Hill), from Laurel Hill blvd., E. to Willow av.

Halleck av. (D 8), from Ouderdonk av., N. E. to Shaler.

Hallett (C 3) (L. I. C.), from Astoria av., N. E. to Winthrop av.

Halsey (B 3) (L. I. C.), from Bulkhead line, N. to Bulkhead line.

Hamilton av. (A 5) (L. I. C.), from Vernon av., N. E. to Vernon av.

Hamilton av. (J 9), from R'way blvd., N. W. to Liberty av., thence now part of 115th.

BOROUGH OF QUEENS STREET AND AVENUE DIRECTORY—*Continued.*

Hamilton pl. (D 6) (Maspeth), fr. Whitlock av., N. W. to Jay av.

Hamlin la. (O 5), fr. 234th, N. of Underhill av., N.E. to 236th.

Hammell av. (H 5) (Flushing), from Wateredge av., N. E. to Jagger av.

Hammel's blvd. (L 14), fr. Amstel blvd. at Beach 75th, S. W. and N. W. to Beach Channel dr.

Hammond (F 5) (Newtown), from Gay, E. to Hanover av.

Hampton (F5) (Elmhurst) from Baxter av., S. E. to Kingsland av.

Hancock (A 5) (L. I. C.), from Vernon av., N. E. to Vernon av.

Hancock (D 8), continued from Boro line, N. E. to Myrtle av.

Hancock pl. (D5) (L.I.C.), from Queens blvd., N. to Greenpoint av.

Hand rd. (O 3), fr. 251st, E. of Jackson av., N. E. to Browvale dr.

Hanford parkway (O 4), from 46th av., nr. Jackson av., S. E. to Southern parkway.

Hanford pl. (O 4), fr. Hanford pkway, opp. York av., S. to 61st av.

Hanlon (O 7), from 100th av., S. E. to City line.

Hannah (G 7), from Myrtle av., N. to Central av.

Hannibal (M 7), from Camden av., S. E. to Farmers blvd.

Hanover av. (G 6) (Newtown), fr. Queens blvd., N. W. to South Railroad av.

Hantz rd. (M 14) (R'way Beach), bet. Beach 44th and Beach 45th, N. of Amstel blvd.

Harbor (F4) (NorthBeach) from Dulon, E. to Flushing bay.

Harding (N 10), from S. Conduit av., E. of Farmers blvd., S. to Commercial av.

Hardy (P 4), from Kay, E. of Winchester blvd., E. to Dell pl.

Harlem pl. (L 8) (Flushing), now part of 80th av.

Harman (D7), cont'd from Boro. line, N. E. to Metropolitan av.

Harms (M 9) (Jamaica), from Baisley blvd., S. E. to 133d av.

Harnay la. (N 4), fr 215th, at 32d av., E. and S. to 43d av.

Harold av. (C 5) (L. I. C.), from Borden av., N. to Jackson av.

Harper av. (H 4), from L. I. R. R. N. W. to Flushing river.

Harriett av. (E 6), from Caldwell av., S. E. to Eliot.

Harris av. (B 4) (L. I. C.), from Bulkhead line, S. E. to Crescent.

Harsell (A 4) (L. I. C.), from Bulkhead line, S. E. to Vernon av.

Hart (C 7), cont'd from Boro. line, N.E. to Woodward av.

Hart (F 5) (Newtown), fr. South Railroad av., S.E. to Corona av.

Hartland av. (N 5), from Kingsbury av., E. of Bell av., S. E. to Grand Central pkway.

Harvard rd. (O 3) (Little Neck), from Virginia rd., N. to Broadway.

Harvest (H 6), fr. Queens blvd., N. E. to 120th.

Harway pl. (M 2) (Bayside), from Willets Pt. blvd. at Bell blvd., S. E. to 23d av.

Hassock (O 13) (Far Rockaway), from Nameoke av., N. W. to City line.

Hastings av. (O 10), from 211th, S. of Clifford av., S. E. to 216th.

Haswell (G 6), fr. Woodhouse av., S.E. to Orville.

Hatch av. (H 10), from Jamaica bay, N. to Sutter av.

Hatton la. (O 5), from Springfield blvd., S. of Union Turnpike, E. to Grand Central pkway.

Havemeyer (G5) (Corona), from Alburtis av, N. E. to Flushing river.

Haven rd. (O 10), from 219th, S. of Cascade av., S. E. to Brookville blvd.

Hawkins pl. (M 2) (Whitestone), from Little Bay av., S. E. to Willets pt. rd.

Hawthorn (N 10) (Springfield), from Farmers av. S. E. to Springfield rd.

Hawthorn av. (K4) (Flushing), from Burling av., N. E. to 156th.

Hawthorne (D 5), from Betts, E. to Drake.

Hawtree av. (H 9), from Sutter av., S. to Vienna av., and from Dunham av., S. to Jamaica bay.

Hawtree Creek rd. (J10), from Peconic av., N. E. to Van Wyck av.

Hayes av. (D 4) (Woodside), from Broadway, E. to Astoria av.

Hayward (B 5) (L. I. C.), from Borden av., N. to Meadow.

Hayward pl. (M7) (Jamaica), from Palermo av., N. E. to Palo Alto av.

Hazen (D 3) (L. I. C.), fr. Astoria av., N. E. to Bulkhead line.

Head of the Vleigh (J 7), formerly from Union Turnpike at 188th, N. E. and N to Kissena rd.

Healy av. (N 13) (Far Rockaway), from Gipson. S. W. to Waterloo rd.

Hebberd (D6), from Creek E. to Rust.

Hebberd av. (D 6), from Flushing av., E. to Fresh Pond rd.

Hedwig (D 6), from Mt. Olivet av., N. to Flushing av.

Hegeman av. (G9) (Woodhaven), from Boro. line, E. and S. E. to 128th.

Heiser (C 5) (L. I. C.), from Anable av., N. to Jackson av.

Helen (E 7), from Edith pl., N. E. to Firth av.

Hemlock pl. (D 6), from Collins av., E. to Mt. Olivet Cemetery.

Hemstead av. (O 7), fr. L. I. R. R., S. E. to City line.

Henderson av. (M 7) (Jamaica), from 185th, E. to Farmers blvd.

Hendricks (F 6), from Juniper av., S. E. to Satterlee av.

Henley rd. (L 7) (Jamaica), from Devonshire rd. at Kendrick rd, N. E. and E. to Holliswood av.

Henning la. (P 5), from 79th av., W. of Winchester blvd., N. E. to Winchester blvd.

Henrietta (G7), from Central av., E. to Baldwin.

Henry (B (L. I. C.), fr. Ely av., 4). E. to Hunter av. 8

Henry (E 5) (Winfield), from Borough av., E. and S.E. to Queens blvd.

Henry (H 4) (Flushing), from Sanford av., N. to Water.

Henry (L 9) (Idlewild), fr. Van Wyck blvd., S. to Rockaway blvd.

Henry (H 4) (Flushing), from 41st av., N. to Wateredge av.

Herald av. (H 9) (Woodhaven), from Rockaway blvd., N. W. to Liberty av., thence now 107th.

Herald av. (H 10) (Aqueduct), fr. Dunham av., N. to L. I. R. R.

Herbert (D 6) (Maspeth), from Rust, E. to Clermont av.

Herrick av. (G 9), from Metropolitan av., N. E. to Dartmouth.

Herriman av. (L 7) (Jamaica), now part of 161st.

Hessler av. (L 14) (R'way Beach), from Barbadoes dr, E. to Beach 69th.

Hewitt av. (H 5), fr. 120th at Varick, N. E., W. and N. W. to Flushing bay.

Hewlett av. (P 4), from Thornhill av.. W. of City line, S. E. to 77th av.

Heyson rd. (O 14) (Far R'way), from Beach 9th, W. and S. to Sea Girt av.

Hiawatha av. (N 7) (Hollis), fr. 98th, E. & N. E. to 198th.

Hicks av. (D 5), from Tyler, N. to L. I. R. R.

Hicks pl. (D 5), fr. Queens blvd.. N. to Broadway.

Hicksville rd. (O 14) (Far R'way), from Beach 9th, E. and N. E. to Beach 9th.

Higbie av. (M 9), now part of 140th av.; (L 10), now part of 147th av., (N 10), now Burgoyne av.

Higgins (H 3) (College Point), from 25th rd. at 129th, S. E. to 32d av.

High (D 6), from Rust, N. to Maspeth av.

High (N 11) (Springfield), from Boulevard E.

Hilburn av. (M 8) from Dunkirk, N. E. to Liberty av.

Hill (C 5) (L. I. C.), from Gale, N. to Meadow.

Hill (D 6) (Maspeth), from Rust, E. to Clermont av.

Hillmeyer av. (L14) (R'way Beach), from Barbadoes dr.. E. to Beach 63d.

Hillside av. (G 5) (Corona Hghts.), from Lewis av., S. E. to Rodman.

Hillside av. (H 8) (Richmond Hill), from Myrtle av., N. E. to City line.

Hillyer pl. (E5), from L. I. R. R., N. to Queens blvd.

Hilton (E 5), from Nagy, E. to Lauronson.

Himrod (D 7) continued, from Boro. line, N. E. to Metropolitan av.

Hinman (F 7) (Glendale), from Cook, N. W. to Metropolitan av.

Hinsdale av. (Q 6) (Floral Park), continued from N. of Whittier av.

Hobart (D 4) (L. I. C.), fr. Vandeventer av., N. E. to Rex pl.

Hobart av. (N 10), from Fargo, N. of 147th av., E. to Berkeley.

Hobson av. (C 6) (Laurel Hill), fr. Newtown Creek, N. E. to Borden av.

Holland av. (H 4), from Roosevelt av., N. W. to Flushing bay.

Holland av. (Q 6) (Floral Park), continued N. fr. City line.

Holland av. (K 15) (R'way Beach), fr. Beach 87th, W. to Beach 94th.

Hollins av. (P 5), fr. Winchester blvd.. S. of Cullman av., N. E. to Grand Central pkway.

Hollis av. (M 7), from Jamaica av., S. E. and E. to Springfield blvd.

Hollis Court blvd. (L 4) from Rocky Hill rd., at 191st, S. E. & E. & S. W. & S. E. & S. to Jamaica av.

Holliswood av. (L 5) (Bayside), from Utopia parkway, N. of Delmar av., S. E. to Hillside av.

Holly (J 5) (Flushing), fr. Peck av., N. E. to Jamaica av. (Flushing).

Holly av. (J 5) (Flushing), from Byrd, N. E. to Parsons blvd.

Hollywood av. (K4) (Flushing), from 149th, N. E. to 156th.

Holmes (D 5) (Winfield), from Laurel Hill blvd., N. to Queens blvd.

Homans av. (F 6), from Woo, N. E. to Justice.

Home (F 4), from Roosevelt av., N. to Polk av.

Home Lawn av. (L 7) (Jamaica), from southern end of Utopia parkway, S. W. to Hillside av.

Home pl. (N 8), from Dunkirk, S. E. to Quencer.

Homer Lee av. (M 7) (Jamaica), now part of 178th.

Honeywell (C 5) (L. I. C.), from Hunters Pt. av., N. & N. W. to Jackson av.

Hook Creek blvd. (P 6) (Queens), from Jamaica av., S. to Cowan av.

Hooker (E 7) (Glendale), from Myrtle av., N. W. to Otto.

BOROUGH OF QUEENS STREET AND AVENUE DIRECTORY—*Continued.*

Hope av. (L 5), from 168th, S. of Peck av., E. to Utopia parkway.

Hopkins av. (B 4) (L.I.C.), from Van Alst av., N.E. to Clark.

Horatio (N 4), fr. Amador rd., bet. Northern parkway and Easthampton rd., S. to Hoxie.

Horstman av. (G10), from Boro. line, E. & S. E. to 128th.

Horton (F 5) (Newtown), from Justice, E. to Marlowe av.

Hosack (F7) (Glendale), fr. Proctor, E. to Weisse av.

Housatonic (J 10), from Peconic av., N. E. to Rockaway blvd.

House Ldg. (O3) (Douglaston), from L. I. R. R., N.W. to Little Neck Bay.

Howard (B 6) (L. I. C.), from Review av., N. E. to Bradley av.

Howe pl. (F 6), fr. Corinth av., N. E. to Calamus av.

Howell av. (D 5) (Woodside) fr. 5th, S. E. to 8th.

Howland (C 3) (L. I. C.), from Hoyt av., N. E. to Winthrop av.

Hoxie (N 4), from Cloverdale blvd., S. of Alpine, S. E., N. E. and E. to Birmingham rd.

Hoyt av. (C 3) (L. I. C.), from Boulevard, S. E. to Astoria av.

Hude (O 13) (Far R'way), from Brunswick av., S. E. to Far R'way blvd.

Hudson (G 9) (Woodhaven), from Sutter av., S. to Jamaica Bay.

Hughes (D 7) from Forest av., E. to Shaler.

Hull av. (C6), from Laurel Hill blvd., E. & N. E. to Schenk av.

Hulst (C 5) (L. I. C.), from Greenpoint av., N. to Skillman av.

Humphreys (G 4), from Astoria, N. W. to Forty-third.

Hungry Harbor rd. (P 10) (Rosedale) from Rosedale blvd., opp. 148th rd. E. to City line.

Hunt (F 5) (Corona), fr. Van Dine, N. E. to Louona av.

Hunt pl. (G 5) (Corona), from Louona av., N. E. to Alburtis av.

Hunter av. (B 5) (L. I. C.), from Nott av., N. E. to Plaza.

Hunter's Point av. (A 5) (L.I.C.), fr. Jackson av., E. & S. E. to Borden av.

Huntley (M 10), fr. Crossover rd., S. of Excelsior, N. E. to Duncan av.

Hurley la. (O 6), fr. Grand Central parkway, N. of 87th av., N. E. to Strongburst av.

Huxley (O 10) (Rosedale), from Brookville blvd. at Newhall av., S. E. to City line.

Hyatt av. (E6), fr. Borden av., N. to Woodside av.

Ibis (H 6), from Queens blvd., N. E. to 120th.

Ickelston rd. (P 14) (Far R'way), from Annapolis S. W. to Reads la.

Idgeon (A 5), from Bulkhead line, E. to West av.

Illinois (J 10), from Peconic av., N. E. to Rockaway blvd.

Illion av. (M 8), fr. Dunkirk, N. E. to Farmers blvd.

Imlay rd. (N13) (Far Rockaway), from Beach 28th, E. to Beach 25th, North.

Ina court (N 4), from Enfield pl., N. of 56th av., E. to Cloverdale blvd.

Indiana pl. (F 8), from Fosdick av., N. E. to Ridgewood pl.

Ingold pl. (H 3) (College Point), from Kinney av., N. to Inman av.

Ingram (G 7), from Selfridge, S. E. to Puritan.

Inlet (F 4), from Curtis, E. to Ditmars av.

Inman av. (H 2) (College Point), from Eldorado, E. to Rockville.

Inman pl. (G 2) (College Point), from Tallman av., E. to Chelsea.

Inwood (K 8) (Jamaica), from Liberty av., S. E. to 111th av., and from Rockaway blvd., S. to 135th av.

Iola rd. (N 13) (Far Rockaway), from Sunnyside, E. to Beach 24th.

Iowa rd. (P 3), from Little Neck rd., E. of West End dr., N. E. to City line.

Ireland pl. (E 5), from L. I. R. R., N. to Queens blvd.

Irene (E 7), from Juniper, N. E. to Firth av.

Iroquois (G 9) (Woodhaven), from Sutter av., S. to Jamaica Bay.

Irving av. (D5) (Winfield), from Tyler, N. to Queens blvd.

Irving av. (D 8), cont'd from Boro. line, S. E. to Moffat.

Irvona (L 8), from Lambertville av., N. W. to Cumberland.

Irwin pl. (N 9), from Baisley blvd., S.W. to Leslie rd.

Isabella (C 3) (L. I. C.), from Grand av., N. E. to Astoria av.

Isabella (G7), from Myrtle av., N. to Metropolitan av.

Ithaca (F 5) (Elmhurst), from Baxter av., S. E. to Kingsland av.

Ivanhoe av. (H 2) (College Pt.), from Schlesinger, E. to Greenville.

Ives pl. (P 5), from Cullman av., bet. Maynard and Dell pl., S. to Hollins av.

Ivy (F5) (Newtown), from Justice, E. to Sothern av.

Jackson av. (A 5) (L.I.C.), from Vernon av., near Borden av., N. E. and E. to Flushing river; that part E. of Flushing river being now Northern blvd.

Jacksons Mill rd. (E 5), from Broadway, N. E. and E. to 40th.

Jacobus pl. (E 5), fr. Calamus av., N. to Queens blvd.

Jagger (J 4) (Flushing), from 41st av., S. E. to Peck av.

Jamaica av. (B3) (L.I.C.), from Blvd., S. E. to Patterson av.

Jamaica av. (F 8) (Woodhaven), cont'd fr. Boro. line, E. and N. E. to City line.

James (D 6), from Rust, E. to Flushing av.

James (H 4) (Flushing), from 41st av., N. to 37th av.

Janet pl. (H 4) (Flushing), from Wateredge av., S. to 40th av.

Jansen av. (E 6), from Harriett av., N. E. to Corinth av.

Jardine rd. (P 14) (Far R'way), from Reads la., N. E. to McNeil av.

Jassamine av. (K4) (Flushing), from Burling av., N. E. to 156th.

Java pl. (K 14) (R'way Beach), fr. Beach 85th, N. E to Beach Channel dr.

Javington (M4) (Bayside), from Jackson av., N. W. to Little Bay av.

Jay av. (C 6), from Willow av., N. E. to Mueller.

Jefferson av. (D 8), cont'd from Boro. line, N. E. to Myrtle av.

Jenkins (J 4) (Flushing), from Franklin av., S. E. to Elder av.

Jennico (J 7) (Richmond Hill), from Austin, N. E. to Kew Gardens rd.

Jennings (F5) (Newtown), from Justice E. to Sothern av.

Jessie pl. (D 5) (L. I. C.), from Nott av., N. to Queens blvd.

Jewel (H 6), from Queens blvd., N. E. to 120th.

Jewel av. (J6), from 120th S. of 69th rd., N. E. and E. to 73d.

Joe pl. (H 4) (Flushing), from 40th av. to 40th rd.

Johanna (H 7), fr. Union T'npike, N. to Metropolitan av.

John (D 7), fr. Bleecker, N. to Metropolitan av.

John (H 4) (Flushing), fr. Water, E. to Railroad.

Johnson (E 6), fr Grand, S. E. to Metropolitan av.

Jones av. (C 6) (Laurel Hill), from Laurel Hill blvd., E. to Clark av.

Joost (F 6), from Van Horn, N. E. to Woodhaven av.

Jordan (L 3), from 28th av., E. of Utopia parkway, S. E. to 35th av.

Jordan av. (M 8), from Dunkirk, N. E. to Farmers blvd.

Joy av. (C6) (Laurel Hill), from Laurel Hill blvd., E. to Borden av.

Judge (F 5) (Elmhurst), from Baxter av., S. E. to Kingsland av.

Judith (M 10), from 150th av., opp. 162d, N. E. to Farmers blvd.

Judson (A 4) (L. I. C.), from Bulkhead line, S. E. to Vernon av.

Julia (G 7), from Forest Park, N. to Copeland av.

Junction av. (G 6), from Queens blvd., N. W. to Burnside av.

Juniper av. (J 5) (Flushing), from Colden, N. E. to Kissena blvd.

Juniper av. (E 6), from Grand, S. E. to Metropolitan.

Juno (G 7), from Yellowstone av., S.E. to Roman av.

Jupiter av. (E 7), from Juniper av., N.E. and N. to Queens blvd.

Justice (F 5) (Newtown), from Broadway, S. E. and E. to Junction av.

Kalmia av. (K 4) (Flushing), from Colden, N. E. to Kissena blvd., and from Burling, N. E. and E. to 156th.

Katharine (E 7), from Juniper, N. E. to Firth av.

Katie (G 7), from Woodhaven av., E. to Baldwin.

Kay (P 4), from Winchester blvd., S. of Chancellor, S. E. to Cullman av.

Kay pl. (P 5), from Fullerton, E. of Winchester blvd., E. to Cullman av.

Kearney (G 4), from Astoria av., N. W. to Grand av.

Keeseville av. (N 7), from Murdock av., N. E. to Farmers blvd.

Kellogg av. (P 5), fr. Upland la., S. of Underhill av., E. to Winchester blvd.

Kelp rd. (L 14) (R'way Beach), from Beach 67th to Beach 62th.

Kelvin (H6), from Queens blvd., N. E. to 120th.

Kendrick rd. (L 7), from Home Lawn av., S. of Croydon av., S.E. to Henley rd.

Kenilworth av. (O 8), fr. Rosedale blvd., N. E. to Murdock av.

Kenilworth pl. (N4), from Garland, near Oakland Lake, E. to Cloverdale blvd.

Kennebec (G 9) (Woodhaven), from Sutter av., S. to Jamaica bay.

Kennedy av. (P 4), from Grand Central parkway, bet. Little Neck rd. and Castlewood, N. E. and E. to Grand Central pkway.

Keno av. (M 6) (Hollis), from Palermo av., E. to Messina av.

Kensington pl. (H7), from Austin, N. E. to Queens blvd.

Kent rd. (M 6), fr. Union Turnpike, W. of Chevy Chase rd. S., S. E. and S. to Hillside av.

Kenton av. (P 14) (Far R'way), from McNeil blvd., W. to Beach 9th.

Kenyon av. (P 4), fr. Marathon av., S. of Fairfax av., N. E. to Annandale la.

Kessel (G 6), from Woodhaven av., S.E. to Union Turnpike.

Ketcham (F5) (Elmhurst) from Baxter av., S. E. to Kingsland av.

BOROUGH OF QUEENS STREET AND AVENUE DIRECTORY—*Continued.*

Kew Gardens rd. (J7), fr. Queens blvd. at Grand Central parkway, S. E. to Metropolitan av.

Keystone rd. (J 7) (Richmond Hill), fr. Kew Gardens rd., S. of Maple Grove Cemetery, N. E. to 135th.

Kiever (G5) (Corona Hts.) from Lewis av., S. E. to Martense av.

Kildare av. (L 6), from Utopia parkway, opp. 82d av., N. E. to 80th dr.

Kindred (C 3) (L. I. C.), from Hoyt av., N. E. to Winthrop av.

Kingsbury av. (N 5), from Bell av., S. of Underhill av., N. E. to Grand Central pkway.

Kingsland av. (F 5) (Elmhurst), from Warner av., N. E. to Havemeyer av.

Kingsley (J 7) (Richmond Hill), from Austin, N. E. to Kew Gardens rd.

Kingston ter. (G 5) (Newtown), from Martense, N. W. to Gfrry av.

Kip pl. (E 5), from Calamus av., N. to Henry.

Kirkland (N10), fr. Farmers blvd., S. of N. Y. blvd., S. E. to 148th av.

Kirkwall rd. (M 6), from 85th rd., E. of Chevy Chase rd., S. to Dalny.

Kissena blvd. (J 4) from Main, S. E. to Peck av.

Kissena rd. (K 5), from Peck av. at S. W. cor. of Kissena pk., S. and S. E. to Hillside av.

Kite (L 5), from 166th, E. to Lithonia av.

Kittredge (N 10), fr. 149th av., E. of Lombard, S. E. to 152d av.

Klondike (J 10), from Jamaica bay, N. E. to Rockaway blvd.

Kneeland pl. (E 5), from L. I R. R., N. to Queens blvd.

Koerner (F 5), from L. I. R. R., N. E. to VanHorn.

Kolyer (E 6) (Maspeth), from Grand, N. to Stoutenburgh.

Kossuth pl. (E 7), from Fresh Pond rd., S. E. to Myrtle av.

Kouwenhoven (C 4) (L. I. C.), from Jackson av., N. E. to Jamaica av., and (D 3) (L.I.C.), from Astoria av., N. E. to Winthrop av.

Kress pl. (O 4), fr. Birmingham rd., bet. Horatio and Hoxie, N.E. to Easthampton rd.

Laburnum av. (K 5) (Flushing), from Peck av., N. E. to Fresh Meadow rd.

Laconia (F 6), from Woo, N. E. to Justice.

Lafayette (E8) (Glendale), from Indiana pl., N. W. to L. I. R. R.

LaForge (F 7) (Middle Village), from Metropolitan av., N. W. and N. to Queens blvd.

Lake (F 5) (Corona), from Junction av., N.E. to Alburtis av.

Lake View blvd. East (L 9) (Jamaica), from 116th av., S. to Baisley blvd.

Lake View blvd. West (L9) (Jamaica), from Foch blvd., S. to Sutphin blvd.

Lakeville rd. (P 3), from Little Neck rd., E. of Iowa rd., E. to City line.

Lakewood av. (K 8) (Jamaica), from 109th av., N. E. to Sutphin blvd.

Lambert (F 7) (Glendale), from Myrtle av., N. W. to Edsall av.

Lambertson av. (G 10), fr. Boro. line, E. to Hackensack.

Lamont av. (E 5) (Elmhurst), from Kingsland av., N. E. to VanDine.

Langdale av. (P 4), from Union Turnpike, at City line, S. to City line.

Langdon av. (N 10), from Finley, S. of Mayer, E. to Berkeley.

Langford (P4), from York av., at Eddy pl., S. and S. W. to Hanford pkway.

Langston av. (P 4), from Grand Central pkway, at Commonwealth blvd., N. E. to City line.

Lansing (O10) (Rosedale), from S. Conduit av., E. of Cedarhurst branch of L. I. R. R., S. E. to 216th.

Larby pl. (L 8), from New York av., E. to Belleville.

Larch av. (J 5), from Peck av., E. of 142d, S. E. and S. to 69th av.

Larkin av. (L 14) (R'way Beach), from Rockaway Beach blvd., at Beach 67th, E. to Rockaway Beach blvd. at Beach 64th.

Latham la. (M 9), from 169th, N. of 144th, W. and S. to N. Conduit av.

Lathrop (B 4) (L. I. C.), from Jackson av., N. E. to Jamaica av.

Laura (G 7), from Woodhaven av., E. to Baldwin.

Laurel Hill av. (C 5) (L. I. C.), from Borden av., N. to Jackson av.

Laurel Hill blvd. (B 6), from Newtown creek, N. E. and E. to Broadway.

Laurelton parkway (O 9), from North Conduit av., N. E. to Merrick rd.

Lauronson (E 6), fr. Calamus av., N.W. to Queens blvd.

Law (E 6), from Grand, S. E. to Metropolitan av.

Lawall av. (C 7), from Newtown creek, N. E. to Rust.

Lawn av. (H 8) (Woodhaven), from Liberty av., S. to Suwanee av.

Lawrence (C 3) (L. I. C.), from Astoria av., N. E. to Winthrop av.

Lawrence (H 3), fr. junction of 132d and 32d av., S. E. to North Hempstead turnpike.

Lawrence blvd. (M4) (Bayside), from Demorest, N. E. to 12th.

Lawrence pl. (J 5), from North Hempstead turnpike at Lawrence, S. to 61st av.

Lax av. (H 2) (College Pt.), from 122d, S. of 5th av., N. E. to 3d av.

Layton (F 5) (Elmhurst), from Baxter av., S.E. to Britton av.

Leavitt (J 3) (Flushing), from 32d av., at 141st, S.W. and S. to Northern blvd.

Lee av. (E 5), from Queens blvd., N. to Rowan av.

Leeds (P 4), from Brattle rd., E. of Annandale la., N. E. to Little Neck rd.

Lefferts (J 7) (Richmond Hill), from Metropolitan av., S. E. to Liberty av.

Lefferts av. (J 11), from Jamaica bay, N. and N. W. to Liberty av. (that part from Liberty av. to Metropolitan av. being now known as Lefferts street); and fr. Metropolitan av. to Kew Gardens being now known as Lefferts blvd.

Lefferts blvd. (H 7), from Metropolitan av., N. E. to Kew Gardens rd.

Leggett pl. (K 2), from 7th av., E. of Cross Isld. blvd., S. to 9th av.

Lehigh (G 9), from Sutter av., S. to Jamaica bay.

Leith pl. (O 3), fr. Brattle rd., W. of Little Neck rd., S. E. to Leeds.

Leith rd. (P 4), fr. Annandale la., opp. Morenci la., N. E. to Brattle rd.

Leland (O 13) (Far Rockaway), from Redfern av. N. W. to City line.

Lenett av. (P 14) (Far R'way), from McNeil blvd., W. to Beach 9th.

Lenox (K 5), from Woodside av., N. to Broadway.

Lent (G 4), from Polk av., N. to Jackson av.

Leslie rd. (N 9) (Jamaica), from Merrick blvd., N. E. to 180th.

Lessing av. (H 3) (College Pt.), from Tallman av., E. to Whitestone av.

Leverich av. (F 5), from Roosevelt av., N. to Fillmore av.

Lewis (K 10), from Conduit, N. to Old South rd.

Lewis av. (F6), from Division, N. E. to Corona av.

Lewiston av. (N 7), from Murdock av., N. E. to Farmers blvd.

Lewmay rd. (N 14) (Far R'way), fr. Beach 29th, W. to Beach 32d.

Liberty av. (G 9) (Woodhaven), from Boro. line, E. and N. E. and S. E. to Farmers blvd.

Lilac (D 7), fr Metropolitan av., N.W. to Eliot av.

Lily (H 7), from Union Turnpike, N. to Metropolitan av.

Lincoln (B 8) (L. I. C.), from Hopkins av., S. E. to Crescent.

Lincoln av. (D 5) (L.I.C.), from Queens blvd., N. to Middleburg av.

Linden (D 8), cont'd from Boro. line, N. E. and E. to Traffic.

Linden (H 3), from 20th av., at 131st, S. E. to Northern blvd.

Lisbet pl. (E 6), from Eliot av., S. E. to Lutheran Cemetery.

Lithonia av. (L 5), from 164th, at Kissena park, E. to Cemetery la.

Little Bay av. (L2) (Whitestone), from Utopia Parkway, at Little Bay E. and N. E. to boundary line of Ft. Totten.

Little Neck blvd. (N 2), from Willets Pt. blvd., at Little Neck Bay, S.E. to McKnight dr.

Little Neck rd. (P 3), from Jackson av., W. of City line, S. E. to Jamaica av.

Liverpool (K 8) (Jamaica), from 94th av., S. E. to 111th av., that part S. thereof being now part of 147th.

Livingston (H 6), from Queens blvd., N. E. to 120th.

Livorno pl. (N 6) (Hollis), from Revenna pl., N. E. to Messina.

Lizzard (J 10), from Jamaica bay, N.E. to Rockaway blvd.

Lloyd rd. (K 8) (Jamaica), from Van Wyck blvd., N E. to Liberty av.

Locke av. (K 2), fr. Cross Isld. blvd., N. of 17th av., N. E. to 15th av.

Lockwood (B 4) (L. I. C.), from Jackson av., N. E. to Jamaica av.

Locust (C 5) (L. I. C.), from Borden av., N. to Jackson av.

Lombard (N 10), fr. Farmers blvd., N. of 147th av., S. E. to 181st.

Long (M 9), from Foch blvd., S. E. to Baisley blvd.

Longfellow av. (D5) (Winfield), from Tyler, N. to Queens blvd.

Longview av. (H 5) (Corona Heights), from Corona av., E. to Riverside av.

Loretta rd. (O 14) (Far R'way), fr. Beach 22d, S. W. to Far R'kaway blvd.

Lott av. (G 8) (Woodhaven), from Atlantic av., N. to Ashland.

Lotta pl. (G 6), from Austin, N.E. to Queens blvd.

Lotus av. (E8), from Anna pl., N. to Myrtle av.

Loubet (G 7), fr. Selfridge, S. E. to Ascan av.

Loubet pl. (G 7), fr. Woodhaven av., S. E. to Orville.

Louisa (G 7), from Forest Park, N. to Woodhaven av.

Louona av. (G 5), from North Railroad, N. to Roosevelt av.

Lovingham pl. (N 8), from Westchester av., S. E. to Baisley blvd.

Lowell av. (F 7) (Middle Village), fr. Metropolitan av., N. E. to Woodhaven av.

Lowell av (Q 6) (Floral Park), from Little Neck rd., N. E. to City line.

Lowery (C 5) (L. I. C.), fr. Hunters Point av., N. to Skillman av.

Lucas (N 8), fr. 120th av., S. E. to Williamson av.

BOROUGH OF QUEENS STREET AND AVENUE DIRECTORY—*Continued.*

Lucern pl. (K 4) (Flushing), from 18th, E. to 22d.

Lucy (E 7), from Juniper, N. E. to Firth av.

Lucy (H 7) from Union Turnpike, N. to Metropolitan av.

Ludlum (M 8), from Dawson, N. E. to Oakfield.

Ludlum av. (N 7) (Jamaica), from 187th, E. to Farmers blvd.

Lugger (G4), from Ditmars av., E. to Flushing Bay.

Luke pl. (N 4), from Bell av., S. of 53d av., S. E. to 56th av.

Lurting (F 5) (Newtown), from Corona av., N. E. to Flushing River.

Luther pl. (E 8), from De Boe pl., E. to Fosdick av.

Lux rd. (K 8) (Jamaica), from Remington, N. E. to Inwood.

Laydig (G 5), from North Railroad av., N. W. to Lake bet. 40th and 41st.

Layster (C 4) (L. I. C.), from Jackson av. N. E. to Jamaica av., and (D3) (L. I. C.), fr. Astoria av., N. E. to Wolcott av.

Lydia (G 7) from Union Turnpike, N. to Metropolitan av.

Lyman (P 6), fr. 88th av., W. of Gettysburg, S. to Braddock av.

Lynch av. (J 4) (Flushing), from Lawrence, N. E. to Saull.

Lynxville (O 4), from McKnight dr., S. of 36th av., S. E. to Jackson av.

Lyon av. (G 4), fr. Astoria av., E. to Flushing Bay.

Macdonald (J 4) (Flushing), from Franklin av., S. E. to Elder av.

Macnish (F 5), fr. Vietor pl., S. to Kingsland av.

Macon Lane (N 9) from Merrick rd., E. to Caxton av.

Madden (C5) (L. I. C.), fr. Borden av., N. to Skillman av., & L. I. freight yard, N. to Jackson.

Madison (D 8) continued from Boro. line, N.E. & E. to Traffic.

Madison av. (P7) (Queens), from 222d, N. E. & N. to Rocky Hill rd.

Maetrich (N9), from 150th av., N. to 127th av.

Magnolia pl. (J 4) (Flushing), from Ash av. to Beach av.

Main (C 3) (L. I. C.), from Bulkhead line, E. to Astoria av.

Main (J 4) (Flushing), from Northern blvd., S. to 41st av.

Makarower (G 5) (Corona Heights), from Lewis av., S.E. to Martense av.

Malcolm (D 6), from Hebberd, N. W. to Grand.

Mangin av. (N 8) (Jamaica), from Murdock av., N. E. to Farmers blvd.

Manheim (F 5) from L. I. R. R., N. E. to Seabury.

Manley (B5) (L. I. C.), from Borden av., N. to Meadow.

Manor av. (H11), from Jamaica Bay, N.W. to Sutter av.

Manse (G 7), fr. Selfridge, S. E. to Ascan av.

Manse pl. (G 7), fr. Woodhaven av., S. E. to Yellowstone av.

Mansfield av. (E 4) (L. I. C.), from Astoria av., E. to Flushing Bay.

Mansion (D 5), from 5th, E. to Schroeder.

Mansley (K 8) (Jamaica), from Remington, N. E. to Merrick rd.

Manson (F 7) (Glendale), from Myrtle av., N. to Copeland av.

Maple av. (H 4) (Flushing), from Sanford av., N. E. to Kissena blvd.

Marabel (D 6), from Maspeth N. to Borden av.

Marathon av. (O 3), from Morgan av., E. of Old House Landing rd., S.E. to Little Neck rd.

Marc (C 3) (L. I. C), from Grand av., N. E. to Newtown av.

Marengo av. (M 6) (Hollis), fr. Grand Central Parkway, S. & E. to Rosedale blvd.

Margaret (G 7), fr. Union Turnpike, S.E. to Nannie.

Marianna (L 5), from 65th av., E. of Utopia parkway, S. to 73d av.

Marinette (O 3), fr. Bayshore rd., at Douglaston av., S.E. to Bayshore rd.

Marion (B 4) (L. I. C.), fr. North Jane, N. E. to Ridge.

Marion av. (E 7), from Juniper av., N.E. and N. to Queens blvd.

Marion pl. (B5) (L. I. C.), from Fourteenth, N. E. to South Jane.

Markwood (H 7), fr. North Greenway terrrace, E. to Union Turnpike.

Marlowe av. (G 6) from Queens blvd., N. W. to South Railroad av.

Marne pl. (M 8) (Jamaica), from Sayres av., S. E. to Westchester av.

Mars pl. (N 9), from Eveleth, S.E. to Farmers av.

Marsden (M 8) (Jamaica), from 114th av., S. E. to Foch blvd., and from Smith, S. E. to 129th av.

Marshall pl. (E 8), from connecting line near Alden av., N. E. Walter.

Martell pl. (H7), from Austin, N.E. to Queens blvd.

Martense (F5), fr. Queens blvd., N. E. & N. to Corona av.

Martha (G 7), from Forest Park, N. to Woodhaven av.

Martin (D 7), from Flushing av., S. E. to Arnold.

Martin av. (J 7) (Richmond Hill), now that part of 81st av., between 126th and 134th.

Mary (D 7) from Metropolitan av., N. to Flushing av.

Maryland rd. (O 4) (Little Neck), from Hanford pkway, S. of Carolina rd., E. to Douglaston av.

Maspeth av. (C 6), cont'd from Boro. line, N. E. & E. to Flushing av.

Massina av. (N 6) (Hollis), from Romeo, S. E. to Lonsdale av.

Masterson av. (M 10), fr. S. Conduit av., W. of Emery av., S. E. to Farmers blvd.

Mastic pl. (M 2) (Bayside), from Pinehurst, E. to Bell av.

Matthewson lane (N9), fr. Farmers, E. to Merrick rd.

Matthias av. (L 8), from Dillon, N. E. to 166th.

Maure av. (K 9), from Rockaway blvd., N. W. to Liberty av.

Maurice av. (D 6), from Maspeth av., N. E. & E. to Sothern av.

Maxine (J 7), from Queens blvd., N. E. to 120th.

Mayda rd. (O 10) (Rosedale), from Brookville blvd., S. E. to 147th av.

Mayer av. (N 10) (Springfield), from Farmers blvd., S. of Sheffield av., E. to Drummond.

Mayfair rd. (H 7), from Park Lane South, S. of Grosvenor rd., S. E. to 116th.

Mayfield rd. (L 7), from Croydon rd., bet. Home Lawn av. and Charlecote Ridge, S. W. to Adel rd.

Maynard (P 4), from 61st av., E. of Winchester blvd., S. to Cullman av.

Mayville (M 7), from Brinkerhoff av., S.E. to Murdock av.

Mazeau (E 6), from Whitney, S. E. to Metropolitan av.

McArthur (E 7), from Admiral, N. to Metropolitan av.

McBride (N 13) (Far Rockaway), from Cornaga av., N. to Mott Basin.

McClellan pl. (C 3) (L. I. C.), from Barclay, S. E. to Van Alst av.

McComb pl. (F 7) (Glendale), from Myrtle av., N.W. to Edsall av.

McCook (E 4) (L. I. C.), from Astoria av., N. to Hazen.

McCormick av. (H 9) (Richmond Hill), from Suwanee av., N. W. to Liberty, thence now part of 103d.

McIntosh (G 4) from Astoria av., N.W. to Forty-third.

McKinley av. (E 7) (Glendale), from Myrtle av., N. W. to Otto.

McKinley pl. (G 5), from Way av., N. E. to Barkins.

McKnight dr. (O 3), from Bayshore rd., at 27th av., S. E. and S. W. to Jackson av.

McNeil blvd. (P 14) (Far R'way), fr. Ocean Promenade, N. W. to City line.

McPherson (E 7), from Shaler, N.W. to Cornelia.

Meade (E 7) (Glendale), from Myrtle av., N. W. to Otto.

Meadow (B 5) (L. I. C.), from Hunters Pt. av., N. E. to Thompson av.

Meadow (H4) (Flushing), from California av., E. of Flushing River, N.W. to Water.

Meagher (E 4) (L. I. C.), from Astoria av., N. to Hazen.

Medina pl. (F 5) (Newtown), from Gfrry av., N. W. to Corona av.

Meehan av. (P 14) (Far Rockaway), fr. McNeil blvd., W. to Beach 19th.

Mekin av. (M 4) (Bayside), from 204th to 207th.

Melbourne av. (J 5), from Larch av. at Cedar Grove Cemetery, E. to Kissena rd.

Memorial (F7) (Glendale), from Proctor, E. to Weisse av.

Memphis av. (O10) (Rosedale), from 226th, S. E. to 239th.

Mentone (O9) (Laurelton), from 208th, S. E. to N. Conduit av.

Merchant (C 3) (L. I. C.), now Kindred.

Mermaid av. (M14) (R'way Beach), fr. Amstel av., E. to Far R'way blvd.

Merrick blvd. (L 7) (Jamaica), from South rd., S. E. and E. to City line.

Merrill (M 8), from Victoria rd., S. E. to 125th av.

Merrimac (G 9), from Sutter av., S. to Jamaica bay.

Merritt (G 5), from Lurting, E. to Fanning, and from Fanning, N. E. to Flushing river.

Merritt rd. (K 2), from 150th, S. of Powells Cove blvd., S. E. to 151st.

Meta pl. (D 6) (Maspeth), from Flushing av., opp. Willow, S. 1 block.

Metcalf av. (L 5), from 164th at Kissena park, E. and N. E. to Fresh Meadow rd.

Meteor (H6), from Queens blvd., N. E. to 120th.

Metropolitan av. (C 7), from Boro. line, cont'd S. E. to Jamaica av., at Jamaica.

Metz av. (E5), from Fisk av., E. to 19th.

Metz pl. (E5), from 22d, E. to Broadway.

Mexico (N 8), from Murdock av., S. to Westchester av.

Meyers av. (E 5), from Queens blvd., N. to Broadway.

Mickle (G4), from Alburtis av., E. to Brady.

Middagh (E 5), fr. Queens blvd., N. to Roosevelt av.

Middleburg av. (C5) (L. I. C.), from Laurel Hill av., E. to Stryker av.

Middleway Circle (H 7), bet. Burns and Continental av., and Slocum Crescent.

Midland parkway (M 7) (Jamaica), from Hillside av., N. and N. E. and E. to Peck av.

Milburn (N9) (Springfield) from 121st av., S. E. to Williamson.

Miles pl. (E 7), from Admiral, N. to Metropolitan av.

BOROUGH OF QUEENS STREET AND AVENUE DIRECTORY—*Continued.*

Milford (L 9), from Yukon av., N. W. to Tuckahoe av.
Mill (F 3) (North Beach), from Wolcott av., S. E. to 42d.
Mill (L 9), from Floridaway, N.W. to Baisley av.
Miller (H 8), fr. 83d av., E. of L. I. R.R., S. to 88d av.
Mills (B 3) (L. I. C.), from Bulkhead line, N. to Bulkhead line.
Milton (D 7), from Flushing av., N. W. to Maspeth av.
Milville (F 8) (Woodhahaven), from Boro. line, E. to Eads av.
Milwood av. (E 8), from Walter, E. to Epsilon pl.
Minna (D 6), from Mt. Olivet av., E. to Mt. Olivet Cemetery.
Mississippi (J 10), from Jamaica bay, N. E. to Rockaway blvd.
Missouri (J 10), from Peconic av., N. E. to Rockaway blvd.
Mobile rd. (O 18) (Far R'way), from Cornaga av., N. E. to Reads la.
Modjeska (G 6), fr. Woodhaven av., N.E. to Queens blvd.
Moffat (D 8), cont'd from Boro. line, N. E. to Irving av.
Mohavia (M 9), from Pittsford av., N. W. to Baisley av.
Moline (P 6), from 88th av., W. of Lyman, S. to Braddock av.
Monitor (G 4), from Ditmars av., E. to Flushing bay.
Monson (B 3) (L. I. C.), from Bulkhead line, N. to Bulkhead line.
Montague av. (F 7) (Glendale), from Myrtle av., N. W. to Central av.
Montauk av. (M 4) (Bayside), from Bell av., E. to Bayside blvd.
Montauk (N 8), from Westchester av., S. E. to Farmers blvd.
Monterey (O 7) (Queens), from Springfield blvd., W. and S.W. to 217th.
Monteverde av. (E6) (Maspeth), from Grand, N. to Railroad av.
Montgomery av. (C 6), (Laurel Hill), from Newtown creek, N. to Borden av.
Moore (C5) (L. I. C.), from Hunters Pt. av., N. to Meadow.
Morehead (P 10) (Rosedale), from City line, W. to Rosedale blvd.
Morenci la. (P 4), fr. Marathon av., N. of Thebes la., E. and S. E. to Annandale la.
Morgan (O 3), fr. 40th av., S. E to Northern blvd.
• **Moritz** (L 6) (Jamaica), S. E. from Union av.
Morrell av. (H 10), from Boro. line, E. to Lefferts av.
Morris av. (H 5), from Hewitt av., N. W. to Flushing bay.
Morton av. (F 7) (Glendale), from St. Germans N. to Metropolitan av.
Moss rd. (G 7) (Richmond Hill), from Woodhaven av., E. to 91th on Southern border of Forest Pk.
Mott av. (N18) (Far Rockaway), from Bulkhead line, S. E. to Beach 9th.
Mount (B5) (L. I. C.), from Borden av., N. to Thompson av.
Mount Holyoke (G6), from Woodhaven av., N. E. to Queens blvd.
Mount Olivet av. (D 7), from Flushing av., E. and S. to Metropolitan av.
Mowbray (J 7) (Richmond Hill), from Kew Gardens rd., N. E. 2 blocks.
Mowbray pl. (J 7) (Richmond Hill), from Austin, N.E. to Kew Gardens rd.
Mueller (E 6) (Maspeth), from Flushing av., N. to Jay av.
Muhlenberg av. (H 4) (Flushing), from Sanford av., S. E. and E. to Lawrence.
Mulberry av. (K5) (Flushing), from Golden av., N. E. to Kissena blvd.
Muller av. (J 7), now that part of 82d rd. between Kew Gardens rd. and 130th.
Murdock av. (N 8), from Mangins av. and Dormans rd., N. E. and E. to City line.
Murison pl. (C 3) (L.I.C.), from Edward, S. E. to Hallett.
Murray (K 2) (Flushing), from 14th rd., at 150th, S. E., S. and S. E. to 156th.
Murray la. (K 3) (Flushing), from Bayside av., E. of 150th, S. E. to Murray.
Musk Fort (P 6) (Creedmoor), from Bullet av., N. to Powder.
Musket (P 6), fr. Hillside av., S. of the Creedmoor Rifle Range, S. to 87th av.
Mymand pl. (D 7), from Fresh Pond rd., E. to Mt. Olivet av.
Myrtle av. (D 8), continued from Boro. line, E. to Jamaica av. (Richmond Hill).
Nagy (F 7) (Middle Village), from Metropolitan av., N.W. & N. to Henry.
Nameoke (O 18) (Far R'way), from Cornaga av., N. W. to Far Rockaway blvd.
Nameoke av. (O 18) (Far R'way), from Far Rockaway blvd., N. W. to Gipson.
Nannie (G 7), from Woodhaven av., E. to Diamond.
Nansen (G 7), from Selfridge, S. E. to Metropolitan av.
Nansen pl. (G 7), from Woodhaven av., S. E. to Yellowstone av.
Napier av. (J 9) fr. Rockaway blvd., N. W. to Liberty av., thence now 109th.
Nasby pl. (N14) (Far Rockaway), fr. Ocean Crest blvd., N. to Far Rockaway blvd.
Nashville av. (N9) (Springfield), from Edmonson, N. E. to Rosedale blvd.
Navy (G 4), from Ditmars av., N. E. to Flushing bay.
Nebraska av. (K 9), from Rockaway blvd., N. W. to Liberty av., thence now part of 133d.
Negundo av. (K 5) (Flushing), from Golden, N. E. to Parsons av.
Neilson (O 18) (Far Rockaway), from Greenport rd., N. W. to Far Rockaway blvd.
Nellis (N 8) (Springfield), from 133d av., S. E. to Springfield blvd.
Nenagh ter. (N 14) (Far R'way), fr. Beach 25th, S. W. to Bay 29th.
Neosho (J 9), from R'way blvd., N. W. to Liberty av.
Neponsit av. (G15) (Rockaway Beach), fr. Beach 149th, N. E. to Adirondack blvd.
Nepton (N9) (Springfield), from Ridgedale, E. to Springfield blvd.
Nero av. (M 6) (Jamaica), from Santiago, E. to Sancho.
New Haven av. (J 7) (Jamaica), from Hillside av., S. to Jamaica av.
New Haven av. (N 14) (Far R'way), from Grasmere ter., E. and S. E. to Plainview av.
New York blvd. (L 7), from Jamaica av., S E. to Springfield blvd.
Newbold (J 7) (Richmond Hill), from Kew Gardens rd., N. E. 2 blocks.
Newbold pl. (J 7) (Richmond Hill), from Austin, N.E. to Kew Gardens rd.
Newburg (N 8), from Murdock av., S. to Westchester av.
Newcomb av. (M 9) (Jamaica), now part of 132d av.
Newhall av. (O 10), from Brookville blvd., nr. L.I. R.R., S. E. to 147th av.
Newport av. (G 15) (Rockaway Beach), fr. Beach 149th, N. E. to Beach Channel dr.
Newtown av. (C 3) (L.I.C.), fr. Grand av. at 4th av., N. W. to Astoria av.
Newtown av. (D 6), from Borden av., at Betts av., E. to Borden av.
Newtown rd. (D 4), from Woodside av., N. W. to Grand av.
Niagara av. (G 9), from Sutter av., S. to Jamaica bay.
Nicolls (G 5) (Newtown), from Way av., N. E. to Flushing river.
Nineteenth (E 5), from Queens blvd., N. to Hazen.
Nineteenth av. (D 4) (L.I. C.), fr. Jackson av., N. E. to Vandeventer, and (D 3) (L. I. C.), from Astoria av., N. E. to Wolcott av.
Nineteenth av. (K 2) (Whitestone), from Parsons blvd., at proposed park, E and N. E. to Little Neck blvd.
Ninetieth (G 8) (Woodhaven), from Park la. So., S.E. to Atlantic av., and from 95th av., S. E. to Sutter av.
Ninetieth av. (G8) (Woodhaven), from 78th at 89th av., E. to 84th, and from 100th, N. E. to 107th, and from Van Wyck blvd., N.E. to 143d, and from Sutphin blvd., N. E. to 150th, and from 153d, N. E. to 161st, and from 166th, N. E. to Braddock av., and (P6), from 242d, E. to Commonwealth av.
Ninetieth rd. (G8) (Woodhaven), from 78th, S. of 90th av., E. to 84th and from 148th, E to 150th, and from 153d, E. to 155th, and (M 7) (Hollis), from 192d, N. E. to 198d.
Ninety-first (G 8) (Woodhaven), from Park la. So., S.E. to Jamaica av., and from 88th av., S. E. to Atlantic av., and from 95th av., S. E. to Sutter av.
Ninety-first av. (G 8) (Woodhaven), from Boro line, S. of Rockaway blvd., N. E. to Sutphin blvd., and from 166th, N. E. to 169th, and from 172d, N. E. to 175th, and from 179th pl., N. E. to 184th, and from 186th, N.E. to 189th, and (M 7), from 196th, E. to 197th, and from 93d av., at 209th, N. E. to Braddock av., and (P6), from 242d, E. to Jackson av.
Ninety-first rd. (M 7), from 183d, E. to 184th, and (O 6), from 212th, E. to 213th, and from Springfield blvd., S. of 91st av., N. E. to Braddock av.
Ninety-second (G8) (Woodhaven), from Jamaica av., S. E. to Sutter av.
Ninety-second av. (G 8) (Woodhaven), fr. 100th, S of 91st av., N. E. to 110th, and from 127th, N. E. to 132d, and (O 6), from 212th, at 93d av., N. E. to Braddock av.
Ninety-second rd. (L 7), from 168th, E. to 170th, and (P 6), from Winchester blvd., E. to Gettysburg.
Ninety-third (H8) (Woodhaven), from Atlantic av., S E. to Sutter av.
Ninety-third av. (G 8) (Woodhaven), from Elderts la., S. of 93d av., E. to 76th, and from 100th, N. E. to 107th, and from 112th, N. E. to 114th, and (L 8) (Jamaica), from New York blvd., E. to 165th, and from 168th, E. to 183d, and (M 7), from Jamaica av., at 198th, N. E. to Braddock av.
Ninety-third rd. (N 6), from 211th, N. E. to Hollis Court blvd., and (O 6), from 211th, E. to

BOROUGH OF QUEENS STREET AND AVENUE DIRECTORY—*Continued.*

Hollis blvd., and from 217th, N. E. to 219th, and from Springfield blvd., N. E. to 240th.

Ninety-fourth (G8) (Woodhaven), from Park la. So., S.E. to 89th av., and from Woodhaven blvd., S. E. to 103d av.

Ninety-fourth av. (H 8) (Richmond Hill), from 97th, S. of Atlantic av., N. E. to 106th, and from 124th. N.E. to Beaver rd., and (N 7), from Jamaica av., at 202d, N. E. to 224th.

Ninety-fourth dr. (O 6), from 216th, N. E. to Springfield blvd., and from 220th, N.E. to 221st.

Ninety-fourth rd. (O 7), from 210th, E. to 211th, and from 216th, N. E. to Springfield blvd., and from 220th, N.E. to 221st.

Ninety-fifth (H 8) (Woodhaven), from Jamaica av., S.E. to 103d av., and from Liberty av., S. E. to 108th av.

Ninety-fifth av. (G 9) (Woodhaven), fr. Brooklyn Boro. line, S. of Atlantic av., N.E. to Beaver rd., and (P6), from 222d, S. of Jamaica av., N. E. to City line.

Ninety-sixth (H 8) (Woodhaven), from Park la. So., S.E. to 97th av., and from 103d av., S. E. to Sutter av.

Ninety-sixth av. (P 6), from Jamaica av., near Springfield blvd., S. and E. to 224th.

Ninety-sixth rd. (O 6) (Queens), from 220th, E. to 224th.

Ninety-seventh (H 8) (Woodhaven), from Jamaica av., S. E. to Sutter av.

Ninety-seventh av. (G 9) (Woodhaven), fr. Brooklyn Boro. line, S. of 95th av., N. E. to 150th, and (O 6), from Springfield blvd., E. to 224th.

Ninety-eighth (H8) (Woodhaven), from Park la. So., S.E. to Atlantic av., and from 95th av., S. E. to Sutter av.

Ninety-eighth av. (M 7) (Hollis), from Farmers av., E. and N. to Jamaica av., and from Hempstead av., E. to Springfield blvd., and from 222d E. to City line.

Ninety-ninth (H8) (Woodhaven), from 99th av., S. E. to Sutter av.

Ninety-ninth av. (H 8) (Woodhaven), fr. 95th, S. of 97th av., N. E. to 99th, and (N 7), from Hollis av., E. to Hempstead av., and from Sigourney av., E. to Raywick, and from 218th E. to City line.

Ninth (A5) (L. I. C.), from Bulkhead line, S. E. to Jackson av.

Ninth (D 4) (Woodside), from Broadway, N. to Charlotte.

Ninth av. (C 4) (L. I. C.), from Jamaica av., N. E. to Astoria av., and (D 3) (L.I.C.), from Winthrop av., N. E. to Bulkhead line.

Ninth av. (H 2) (College Pt.), from Powells Cove blvd.. S. of 7th av., E. to 151st pl., and from 154th, E. to 166th.

Noble (A4) (L. I. C.), from Bulkhead line, S. E. to Vernon av.

Noell (H 4), from Jackson av., N. to Flushing river.

Nolins av. (H 11), from Niagara av., E. to Leffert av.

Nome (H 6), from Queens blvd. N. E. to 120th.

Nora (E 7) (Middle Village), from Juniper av., N. E. to Firth av.

Norfolk (F5), from Queens blvd., N. E. to Xenia.

Normal rd. (K 7), from Parsons av. at 86th av., N. E. to 164th

Norman (D 8), fr. Wykoff av., N. E. to Myrtle av.

North Conduit av. (N 9), from 128th, N. of W. Conduit, E. to City line.

North Greenway terraces (H 7), from Middleway Circle. S. E. to Union Turnpike.

North Hempstead Turnpike (J5), from junction of Lawrence and Rodman, E. and S. E. to Hollis Court blvd.

North Henry (C3) (L.I.C.), from Newtown av., N. E. to Astoria av.

North Jane (B 4) (L.I.C.), from Vernon av., S.E. to Plaza.

North Railroad av. (F 5), (Elmhurst), fr. VanNest, N. E. to Tiemann av.

North Villa pl. (J 8), from Jamaica av., N to Kew Gardens rd.

North Washington pl. (C3) (L. I. C.), from Willow, E. to Hallett.

North William (C 3) (L. I. C.), from Willow, E. to Van Alst av.

Northern blvd. (J 4). from Flushing River eastward to Nassau County line.

Northern parkway (N 4), from Jackson av., bet. 220th pl. and Harnay la., S. E. to Cloverdale blvd.

Norton av. (M 14) (R'way Beach). fr. Beach 49th, N. E. and S. E. to Far Rockaway blvd.

Norton drive (N 14) (Far Rockaway), from Far Rockaway blvd., N. W. along shore of Norton Basin to Mott Basin.

Nott (B 5) (L. I. C.), from Thompson av., N. W. to Jackson av.

Nott av. (A 5) (L. I. C.), from Bulkhead line, S.E. to Jackson av., and from Creek, E. to Jessie pl.

Nurge (D 7), fr. Metropolitan av., N. E. to Arctic.

Nutley pl. (N 9), fr. Eveleth rd., E. to Farmers blvd.

Oak av. (K 5) (Flushing), from Peck av., N.E. and E. to 164th

Oakley (D 4) (L. I. C.), from Vandeventer av., N. E. to Astoria av., and (E 3) (L. I. C.), from Wolcott av., N. E. to Bulkhead line.

Oakman av. (O 14) (Far Rockaway). from Beach 9th, E. to McNeil blvd.

Occident (G 6), from Austin, N. E. to 120th.

Ocean av. (H 8) (Woodhaven), now 99th and 100th.

Ocean ct. (L 14) (R'way Beach), from Beach 59th to Beach 58th.

Ocean Crest blvd. (N 14) (Far R'way), from Grasmere ter., S. W. to Norton dr.

Ocean Promenade (G 15) (R'way Beach), fr. Seaside Pk., N. E. and E. to City line.

Ocean View av. (H 11), fr. Jamaica Bay, N. to Sutter av., thence now 89th.

Odonnell rd. (L 8) (Jamaica). from 114th av., N.E. to 166th.

Ohio (K 9) (Richmond Hill). from Warburton av., N. W. to Liberty av.

Oka (L 10), from S. Conduit av., W. of Byron, S. to Byron.

Ola pl. (N13) (Far R'way), from Sunnyside, E. to Beach 24th, N.

Olcott (G7), from Selfridge S. E. to Metropolitan av.

Old (O 3) (Little Neck), from Willow, N. W. to Morgan pl.

Old House Landing rd. (O 3), from 38th av., W. of Boro line, S.E. to Deppe.

Old South rd. (G 9), from Pitkin av., S. E. and E. to 128th, thence now part of 135th av.

Olga (E 7) (Middle Village), from Juniper av., N. to Firth av.

Olgate (N 9), from Freeport. N.W. to VanAlien.

Olive pl. (H 7), from Continental av., S. E. to South Greenway terraces.

Oliver (B 5) (L. I. C.), from Borden av., N. to Hunters Pt. av.

Olivia (G7), from Martha, E. to Diamond.

Olmsted pl. (F 8) (Glendale), from Indiana pl., N. W. to Edsall av.

Omega (G6), from Austin, N. E. to 120th.

Onderdonk (C7), fr. Boro. line, N. E. to Myrtle av.

One Hundredth (H 8) (Richmond Hill), from 87th av., S. E. to 88th av., and from 90th av., S. E. to 91st av., and from 92d av., S.E. to 93d av., and from Atlantic av., S. E. to Liberty av.

One Hundredth av. (N 7), from Hollis av., N. E. to 210th, and from 218th. E. to City line.

One Hundredth rd. (P 7), from 222d, E. to City line.

One Hundred and First (H 8) (Richmond Hill). from Park la. So., S. E. to Jamaica av., and from 95th av., S. E. to Liberty av.

One Hundred and First av. (G9) (Woodhaven), from Brooklyn Boro. line, S. of 97th av., N. E. to Liberty av., and (O 7), from 218th, E. to Springfield blvd.

One Hundred and Second (H 8) (Richmond Hill), from Park la. So., S. E. to Liberty av.

One Hundred and Second av. (G 8) (Woodhaven), from 81st, S of 101st av., N. E. to 89th, and (J 8), from 127th. N. E. to 129th, and from 134th, N. E. to Allendale and (N7), from Farmers av., E. to Hollis av., and from 210th, E. to 217th pl., and from Springfield blvd., S. E. to 221st, and from 224th, S E. to Stewart la.

One Hundred and Second rd. (G 9) (Woodhaven), from 81st, S. of 102d av., N.E. to Rockaway blvd.; and (J 8), from 127th, N. E. to 129th.

One Hundred and Third (H 8) (Richmond Hill), from 95th av., S. E. to Liberty av.

One Hundred and Third av. (H 9) (Woodhaven), from Liberty av., at 84th, N.E. to VanWyck blvd., and (N7), from Farmers blvd.. E. to Hollis av., and from 217th, S. E. to 217th pl., and from Raywick, S. E. to 218th pl., and from 220th, S.E. to Hook Creek blvd.

One Hundred and Third rd. (L7) (Jamaica), from 171st E. to 172nd.

One Hundred and Fourth (H 8) (Richmond Hill), from Park la. So., S. E. to Liberty av.

One Hundred and Fourth av. (J8) (Richmond Hill), from 127th, S. of 103d av., N. E. to 129th, and (K 8) (Jamaica), from Van Wyck blvd.. N.E. to Remington, and from Merrick blvd, N. E. to 172d, and from Liberty av., N. E. to Farmers blvd., and (N 7), from 208th, E. to 218th pl., and from Springfield blvd., S E to Hook Creek blvd.

One Hundred and Fourth rd. (L7) (Jamaica), from 164th, E to 164th pl., and from 166th. E to Merrick blvd.. and from 172d, E. to 180th.

One Hundred and Fifth (H 8) (Richmond Hill), fr. Park la. So., S. E. to Jamaica av., and fr. 95th av., S. E. to Liberty av.

One Hundred and Fifth av. (K8) (Jamaica), from Remington, N.E. to 150th, and from Merrick blvd., N. E. to 172d. and from 178th, N.E. to 180th, and (N 7), fr. Farmers blvd., E. to 193d, and (O 7), from Raywick, S. E. to Hollis av., and fr. 220th, S. E. to City line

One Hundred and Fifth rd. (K 8) (Jamaica), from VanWyck blvd., N.E. to 142d.

BOROUGH OF QUEENS STREET AND AVENUE DIRECTORY—*Continued.*

One Hundred and Sixth (H 8) (Richmond Hill), fr. Park la. S., S.E. to Jamaica av., & fr. Atlantic av., S. E. to Liberty av.

One Hundred and Sixth av. (G 9) (Woodhaven), from 85th, S. of Liberty av., E. to 86th, and (K 8) (Jamaica), fr. Van Wyck blvd., N. E to 142d, and from Pinegrove, N.E. to 150th, and from Merrick blvd., E to 169th, and (O 7), from 215th, E. to Raywick, and fr. 220th, S. E. to City line.

One Hundred and Seventh (H 8) (Richmond Hill), from Park la. So., S. E. to Liberty av.

One Hundred and Seventh av. (G 9) (Woodhaven). from 85th, S. of 106th av., E. to Rockaway blvd., and (K 8) (Jamaica), from Van Wyck blvd., N.E. to 180th, and (O 7), from Springfield blvd., S. E. to City line.

One Hundred and Seventh rd. (K8) (Jamaica), from 139th, E. to 142d.

One Hundred and Eighth (H 8) (Richmond Hill). from Myrtle av., S. E. to Liberty av.

One Hundred and Eighth av. (G 9) (Woodhaven), from 85th, S. of 107th av., E. to 86th, and from Woodhaven blvd., E. to 96th, and (K8) (Jamaica), from Spa pl., N E. to Fern pl., and from 177th, S.E. and E. to 180th, and (O 7), from Springfield blvd., S. E. to City line.

One Hundred and Eighth rd. (L8) (Jamaica), from 167th, N. E. to Merrick blvd., and from 176th, E. to 177th.

One Hundred and Eighth dr. (L8) (Jamaica), from 164th, N. E. to Merrick blvd.

One Hundred and Ninth (H 8) (Richmond Hill), from Myrtle av., S. E. to Liberty av.

One Hundred and Ninth av. (G 9) (Woodhaven), from 85th, S. of 108th av., E. to 86th, and from Woodhaven blvd., N. E. to 99th, and (K 9) (Jamaica), from Van Wyck blvd., N.E. to 180th, and (N 7), from 208th. E. to 211th, and fr m 217th pl., S. E. to City line.

One Hundred and Ninth rd. (L8) (Jamaica), from 139th, N.E to 141st, and from Sutphin blvd., N.E. to 155th, and from 155th, E. to Merrick blvd., and (N 7), from Farmers av., N. E. to Hollis av.

One Hundred and Ninth dr. (L 8) (Jamaica), from Sutphin blvd., N. E. to 155th, and from 164th, E. to 167th.

One Hundred and Tenth (G 2) (College Pt.), from Powells Cove blvd., S. to Powells Cove blvd., and (H 8) (Richmond Hill), from Myrtle av., S. E. to Liberty av.

One Hundred and Tenth av. (N 7), from 194th, N. E. to 198th, and from 205th, N. E. to Rosedale blvd., and from Colfax, N. E. and S. E. to 225th.

One Hundred and Tenth rd. (L8) (Jamaica), from Liverpool, N.E. to 155th, and from New York blvd., N. E. to 164th pl., and from 167th, N. E. to 169th, and (N 7), fr Farmers blvd., N. E. to 195th.

One Hundred and Eleventh (G 2) (College Pt.), from 14th av., E. of 110th, S. to 14th rd., and (H 8) (R'mond Hill), fr. Myrtle av., S. E. to Liberty av.

One Hundred and Eleventh av. (K8) (Jamaica), from Van Wyck blvd., N. E. to Sayres av., and (N 7), from Farmers blvd., N. E. to 212th. and from 221st, E. to City line.

One Hundred and Eleventh rd. (L8) (Jamaica), from Sutphin blvd., N. E. to 155th, and from Merrick blvd., N. E to 172d, and (N 8), from Farmers blvd., N.E. to 196th, and from 205th, N.E. to Rosedale blvd., and fr. Colfax, E. to Springfield blvd.

One Hundred and Twelfth (G 2) (College Pt.), from Powells Cove blvd., S. to Powells Cove blvd., and (H 8) (R'mond Hill), fr. 84th av., S E. to Lib'ty av.

One Hundred and Twelfth av. (L8)) Jamaica), from Sutphin blvd., N. E. to 155th, and from 176th, N. E. to 180th, and (N 9), from Farmers blvd., N. E. to 212th, and from Springfield blvd., E. to City line.

One Hundred and Twelfth rd. (L8) (Jamaica), from 157th, N.E. to 159th, and from Dillon, E. to New York blvd., and (N 8), from Farmers blvd., N. E. to 196th, and from 205th, to Rosedale blvd., and fr. Colfax, E. to 212th.

One Hundred and Thirteenth (G 2) (College Pt.), from 14th av., E. of 112th, S. to 14th rd., and (H 7) (Richmond Hill), from 84th av., S. E. to Liberty av.

One Hundred and Thirteenth av. (L 8) (Jamaica), from Sutphin blvd. N. E. to 157th, and from 169th, E. to Merrick blvd., and from Marne pl., E. to 175th, and (N 8), from Murdock av., N. E. and E. to City line.

One Hundred and Thirteenth rd. (N 8), from Murdock av., N. E. to 196th, and from 205th, to Rosedale blvd., and from Springfield blvd., E. to City line.

One Hundred and Fourteenth (G 2) (College Pt.), from 12th av., E. of Powells Cove blvd., S. to Powells Cove blvd., and (H 7) (Richmond Hill), from Bessemer, S. E. to Liberty av.

One Hundred and Fourteenth av. (K 8) (Jamaica), from Van Wyck blvd., N. E. to Mangin av., and Dormans rd.

One Hundred and Fourteenth drive (N 8), from Murdock av., S. E. and N.E. to 196th, and fr. 205th N.E. to Rosedale blvd.

One Hundred and Fourteenth rd. (L 8) (Jamaica), from Sutphin blvd., N. E. to 157th, and from Westchester av., N. E. to 180th, and (N 8), from Murdock av., S. E. and N.E. to 196th, and fr. 205th N. E. to Rosedale blvd.

One Hundred and Fifteenth (G 2) (College Pt.), from Poppenhusen av., E. of Powells Cove blvd., S. to 14th rd., and (H 7) (Richmond Hill), from Park la. So., S. E. to Liberty av.

One Hundred and Fifteenth av. (K 8) (Jamaica), from Van Wyck blvd., N. E. to 157th, and from New York blvd., N.E. to Westchester av., and (M 8), from Murdock av., E. and N. E. to Murdock av.

One Hundred and Fifteenth dr. (L 9) (Jamaica), from Sutphin blvd., N.E. to 157th, and (N 8), from Farmers blvd., N. E. to 196th, and fr. 205th, N. E. to Rosedale blvd.

One Hundred and Fifteenth rd. (L 9) (Jamaica), from Sutphin blvd., N.E. to Bedell, and (N 8), from Farmers blvd., N.E. to 196th, and from 205th, N. E. to Rosedale blvd.

One Hundred and Sixteenth (G 2) (College Pt.), from 10th av., E. of 115th, S. to 14th rd., and (H 7) (Richmond Hill), from Metropolitan av., S E. to Liberty av.

One Hundred and Sixteenth av. (K 9) (Jamaica), from Van Wyck blvd., N. E. to New York blvd., and from Marsden. N.E. to Westchester av., and (N 8), from Farmers blvd., N. E. to City line.

One Hundred and Sixteenth dr. (L 9) (Jamaica), from Sutphin blvd., N. E. to 116th rd.

One Hundred and Sixteenth rd. (L 9) (Jamaica), from 142d, N. E. to 148d, and from Sutphin blvd., N. E. to 157th, and (N 8), from Farmers blvd., N. E. to 196th, and from 205th, N.E. to Rosedale blvd.

One Hundred and Seventeenth (H 2) (College Pt.), from Powells Cove blvd., at College Pt., S. E. and S. to Powells Cove blvd., and (H 7) (Richmond Hill), from 84th av., S. E. to Babbage and from Myrtle av., S. E. to Liberty av.

One Hundred and Seventeenth av. (N 8), now part of Foch blvd.

One Hundred and Seventeenth rd. (N 8), from Farmers blvd., N. E. to 196th.

One Hundred and Eighteenth (H 2) (College Pt.), from 9th av., E. of 117th, S. to 15th av., and (H 7) (Richmond Hill), from Metropolitan av., S. E. to Hillside av., and from Jamaica av, S. E. to Liberty av.

One Hundred and Eighteenth av. (L 9) (Jamaica), from Van Wyck blvd., E. to 139th, and from Sutphin blvd., N. E. to Lake View blvd. West, and fr m Lake View blvd. East, N. E. to New York blvd., and (N 8), from Farmers blvd., N. E. to 209th.

One Hundred and Eighteenth rd. (M 9) (Jamaica), from Lake View blvd. East, N. E. to New York blvd., and from Montauk, N. E. to 196th.

One Hundred and Nineteenth av. (L 9) (Jamaica), from 143d, N. E. to Lake View blvd West, and from Lake View blvd. East to Bedell, and from Marsden, N. E. to Baisley blvd., and (N 8), from Farmers blvd., N. E. to City line.

One Hundred and Nineteenth pl. (H 2) (College Pt.), from Powells Cove blvd., S. E. to Poppenhusen av.

One Hundred and Nineteenth rd. (L 9) (Jamaica), from 142d pl., E. to 148d, and from Sutphin blvd., E. to Lake View blvd. West, and from Lake View blvd. East, N. E. to New York blvd., and from Baisley blvd., E. to 180th, and from Montauk, N. E. to 189th.

One Hundred and Nineteenth dr. (N 8) (Jamaica), from Montauk, N. E. to Farmers blvd.

One Hundred and Twentieth (H 2) (College Pt.), from Powells Cove blvd. E. of 119th pl., S. E. to Poppenhusen av., and from 9th av. S. to 20th av., and (H 5), from Radcliff, S. to Riverside av., thence S. E. to Queens blvd., and (J 7) (Richmond Hill), from 84th, S. E. to Liberty av.

One Hundred and Twentieth av. (L 9) (Jamaica), from Van Wyck blvd., N. E. to Lake View blvd. West, and from Lake View blvd. East, N.E. to City line.

One Hundred and Twentieth rd (L 9) (Jamaica), from Lake View blvd. East, N. E. to New York blvd., and (N 8), from Farmers blvd., N. E. to 192d.

One Hundred and Twenty-first (H 2) (College Pt.), from Powells Cove blvd. E. of College pl., S. to Poppenhusen av., and from 10th av., S. to 28th

BOROUGH OF QUEENS STREET AND AVENUE DIRECTORY—*Continued.*

av., and from 80th av., S. to Tallman blvd., and (J 7) (Richmond Hill), from 84th av., S. E. to Liberty av.

One Hundred and Twenty-first av. (L 9) (Jamaica), from Sutphin blvd., N. E. to Lake View blvd. West, and from Lake View blvd. East, N.E. to New York blvd., and from Montauk, N. E. to City line.

One Hundred and Twenty-first rd. (N 8), fr. Farmers blvd., N. E. to 192d.

One Hundred and Twenty-second (H 2) (College Pt.), from 3d, S. of Powells Cove blvd., S. to Tallman blvd., and (J 7) (Richmond Hill), from Metropolitan av., S. E. to Jamaica av.

One Hundred and Twenty-second av. (L 9) (Jamaica), from 142d, E. to 148d, and from Sutphin blvd., N. E. to Lake View blvd. West, and from Lake View blvd. East, N.E. to Smith, and (N 8), from Farmers blvd., N. E. to Nashville av., and from Covington, N. E. to City line.

One Hundred and Twenty-third (H 2) (College Pt.) from 5th av., E. of Lax av., S. to Tallman blvd., and (J 7) (Richmond Hill), from Metropolitan av., S. E. to 89th av., and from Atlantic av., S. E. to Liberty av.

One Hundred and Twenty-third av. (L 9) (Jamaica), from Van Wyck blvd., E. to Lake View blvd. West, and (O 8), from Covington, N. E. to City line.

One Hundred and Twenty-fourth (H 2) (College Pt.), from 5th av., E. of 123d, S. to Tallman blvd. and (J 7), from Grand Central pkway., S. E. to Queens blvd., and (Richmond Hill), from Metropolitan av., S. E. to 89th av., and from Atlantic av., S. E. to Liberty av.

One Hundred and Twenty-fourth av. (L 9) (Jamaica), from 153d, E. to Lake View blvd. West, and (O 8), from Covington, N. E. to City line.

One Hundred and Twenty-fifth (H 2) (College Pt.), from Powells Cove blvd. S. to Tallman blvd., and (J 7), from Grand Central parkway, S. E. to Queens blvd., and (Richmond Hill), from Metropolitan av., S. and S. E. to 89th av., and fr. Atlantic av., S. E. to Liberty av.

One Hundred and Twenty-fifth av. (M 9) (Jamaica), from 172d, N. E. to Merrick blvd., and (O 8), from Covington, N.E. to City line.

One Hundred and Twenty-sixth (H 2) (College Pt.), from 3d av., E. of 125th, S. to Tallman blvd., and (J 7), from Grand Central parkway, S. E. to 92d, and (Richmond Hill), from Metropolitan av., S. and S. E. to 91st av., and from Atlantic av., S. E. to Liberty av.

One Hundred and Twenty-sixth av. (M 9) (Jamaica), from Marsden, N.E. to Merrick blvd., and (O 8), from Covington, N. E. to City line.

One Hundred and Twenty-seventh (H 2) (College Pt.), from Powells Cove blvd., E. of 125th, S. E. and S. to Tallman blvd., and (H 5), from Wateredge av., E. of the Flushing river, S. E. to Webb av., and (J 7) (Richmond Hill), from Hillside av., S. to Jamaica av., and from 89th av., S. E. to 92d av., and from Atlantic av., S. E. to Jamaica av.

One Hundred and Twenty-seventh av. (M 9) (Jamaica), from 172d, N. E. to Merrick blvd.

One Hundred and Twenty-seventh dr. (D 8), from 218th, S. E. to 219th.

One Hundred and Twenty-seventh rd. (P 8), from 218th, S. E. to 219th, and 221st, S. E. to City line.

One Hundred and Twenty-eighth (H 2) (College Pt.), from 3d av., E. of 127th, S. to 18th av., and from 14th av., S. to Tallman blvd., and (H 5), from Wateredge av., S. of 61st av., S. E. to 61st rd., and (K 9), fr. Rockaway blvd., S. to N. Conduit av., and from S. Conduit av., S. to 163d av.

One Hundred and Twenty-eighth av. (M 9) (Jamaica), from 157th, N. E. to New York blvd., and from 172d, N. E. to Maetrich, and (P 8), from 214th, S. E. to City line.

One Hundred and Twenty-eighth dr. (O 8), from 214th, S. E. to 217th, and from 221st, S. E. to City line.

One Hundred and Twenty-eighth pl. (H 8) (College Pt.), from 23d rd., W. of L.I.R.R., S. to 25th av.

One Hundred and Twenty-eighth rd. (P 8), from 221st, E. to City line.

One Hundred and Twenty-ninth (H8) (College Pt.), from E. R. at W. point of Powells Cove, S. to 3d av., and from 4th av. S. to 13th av., and from 13th rd., S. to 25th av., and from 25th rd., S. to Tallman blvd., and (H 5), from Wateredge av., at 61st, S. E. to 61st rd., and (J8) (Richmond Hill), from Jamaica av., S. E. to 91st av., and from Atlantic av., S. E. to Liberty av., and (K 9), from Cedric rd., W. of 130th, S. to N. Conduit av., and from S. Conduit av., S. to 163d av.

One Hundred and Twenty-ninth av. (L 9), from 142d, S. of Sutter av., E. to 143d, and from 144th, E. to 145th, and (M 9) (Jamaica), from Baisley blvd., N. E. to Merrick blvd., and (O 8), from 209th, S. E. to City line.

One Hundred and Thirtieth (H 2), from 6th av., E. of 129th, S. to 13th av., and from 18th rd., S. to 25th av., and from 28th av., S. to College Pt. Causeway, and (H5), from 61st av., W. of Rodman, S. E. to 83d av., and (J 7) (Richmond Hill), from Metropolitan av., S. E. to Liberty av., and (K 9), from Rockaway blvd., S. to 163d av.

One Hundred and Thirtieth av. (L 9), from 135th pl., S. of Sutter av., E. to 150th, and from 156th, N. E. to New York blvd. and from 176th, E. to Merrick blvd., and (O 8), from Springfield, S. E. to City line.

One Hundred and Thirtieth pl. (K 10), from 133d av., W. of 131st, S. to N. Conduit av., and from S. Conduit av., S. to 156th av.

One Hundred and Thirtieth rd. (N 9) (Jamaica), from 178th, E. to Merrick blvd., and (O 8), from 202d, S. E. to 203d, and from Brookville blvd., S. E. to City line.

One Hundred and Thirty-first (H 2) (College Pt.), from Powells Cove blvd., at Powells Cove, S. to 20th av., and from 30th av., S. to 31st rd., and (H 5), from Avery, E. of Meadow, S. E. to Rodman, and (J7) (Richmond Hill), from Metropolitan av., S E to 88th av., and from Atlantic av., S. E. to Liberty av., and (K 9), from Rockaway blvd., S. to N. Conduit av., and from S. Conduit av., S. to 156th av.

One Hundred and Thirty-first av. (K 9), fr. 130th, S. of Sutter av., E. to 134th, and from 137th, E. to 140th, and from 142d, E. to 143d, and (M 9) (Jamaica), from 158th, N. E. to New York blvd., and from 176th, E. to Merrick blvd., and (N 9), from Springfield blvd., S. E. to City line.

One Hundred and Thirty-first dr. (P9), from 225th S. E. to 227th.

One Hundred and Thirty-first rd. (N9), from 202d, S. E. to 203d, and from 219th, E. to City line.

One Hundred and Thirty-second (H 2) (College Pt.), from Powells Cove blvd., E. of 131st, S. to 12th av., and from 13th rd., S. to Linden, and from 31st rd., S. to 32d av., and (J7) (Richmond Hill), from Metropolitan av., S.E. to 89th av., and from 90th av., S. E. to 92d av., and from Atlantic av., S. E. to Liberty av., and (K 9), from Rockaway blvd., S. to 156th av.

One Hundred and Thirty-second av. (L 9), from 137th, S. of 131st av., E. to 140th, and from Baisley blvd., S. of Rockaway blvd., N.E. to Bedell, and from Garrett, N. E. to 178th, and (N 9) (Springfield), fr. Springfield blvd., S. E. to City line.

One Hundred and Thirty-second rd. (N 9) (Springfield), from Williamson av., S. E. to 203d, and from Brookville blvd., S. E. to 238th.

One Hundred and Thirty-third (H 2) (College Pt.), from 7th av., E. of 132d, S. to 12th av., and from 15th av., S. to 25th av., and (J 5), from 56th rd., E. of Lawrence, S. to North Hempstead Turnpike, and (J 7) (Richmond Hill), from Jamaica av., S. E. to 91st av., and from Atlantic av., S. E. to Liberty av., and (K 9), from Rockaway blvd., S. to 135th av., and from 150th av., S. to 163d av.

One Hundred and Thirty-third av. (K 9), from 128th, S of Sutter av., E. to 150th, and from Baisley blvd., N. E. to Rockaway blvd., and (M 9) (Jamaica) from 159th, N. E. to New York blvd., and from Garrett, N. E. to 178th, and (N 9) (Springfield), fr. Springfield blvd., S. E. to Merrick rd.

One Hundred and Thirty-third dr. (P 9) (Rosedale), from 228th, S. E. to City line.

One Hundred and Thirty-third pl. (H2), from 18th av., W. of 135th, S. W. to 15th av.

One Hundred and Thirty-third rd. (N 9) from Garrett, N. E. to Farmers blvd., and (Springfield), from Williamson av., S. E. to 203d, and fr 218th, S.E. to 219th, and from 228th, S. E. to City line.

One Hundred and Thirty-fourth (H 2) from 15th av., E. of 133d, S. to 26th av., and (J 5), from Peck av., E. of Lawrence, S. to 61st av, and (J 7), from 78th rd., E. of 130th, S. E. to 83d av., and from Keystone rd., E. of Kew Gardens rd., S. E. to 87th av., and (Richmond Hill), from Jamaica av., S.E. to 91st av., and from Atlantic av., S. E. to Liberty av., and (K 9), from Rockaway blvd., S. to 163d av.

One Hundred and Thirty-fourth av. (K 9), from 134th, S. of 133d av., E. to 135th, and from 137th

BOROUGH OF QUEENS STREET AND AVENUE DIRECTORY—*Continued.*

E. to 140th, and from Baisley blvd., N. E. to Bedell, and from Garrett, N. E. to Farmers blvd., and (P 9), from 225th, S. E. to City line.

One Hundred and Thirty-fourth pl. (K 10), from Rockaway blvd., W. of 135th, S. to N. Conduit av.

One Hundred and Thirty-fourth rd. (N 9) (Sp'ngfield), from Springfield blvd., S. E. to 207th, and from 218th, S. E. to Laurelton Parkway.

One Hundred and Thirty-fifth (H 2), from Powells Cove blvd., at Powells Cove, S. to Willets Pt. blvd., and (J 5), from Hammell av., S. to North Hempstead Turnpike. & from 61st av., S. to 63d rd., and from 68th rd., S. E. to 83d av, and (J 7), from Keystone rd., S. E. to Hillside av., and (Richmond Hill), from Jamaica av., S. E. to 91st av., and from 101st av., S. E to Liberty av., and (K9), from Rockaway blvd., S. to 163d av.

One Hundred and Thirty-fifth av. (K 9), from 128th, S. of 133d av., E. to 150th, and from Baisley blvd., N. E. to Rockaway blvd., and (N 9), from Bennett, N. E. to Caxton av., and from Springfield blvd., S. E. to City line.

One Hundred and Thirty-fifth pl. (K 9), from Rockaway blvd., W. of Van Wyck blvd., S. to 135th av., and from S. Conduit av., S. to 163d av.

One Hundred and Thirty-fifth rd. (O 9) (Rosedale), from 229th, S. E. to City line.

One Hundred and Thirty-sixth (J 2), from 7th av., E. of 135th, S. to 12th av., and from 13th av., S. to 31st av., and (J 5), from 56th rd., at Hammell av., S. to Webb av., and (J 7), from 87th av., S. E. to Jamaica av.

One Hundred and Thirty-sixth av. (M 9), from N. Conduit av., E. of Baisley blvd., N. E. to Rockaway blvd., and (N9), fr. Farmers blvd., N. E. to Caxton av., and from Springfield blvd., S. E. to 206th, and from Laurelton Parkway, S. E. to City line.

One Hundred and Thirty-sixth pl. (N 9), from Farmers blvd., E. to Thurston.

One Hundred and Thirty-sixth rd. (N 9) (Springfield), from Springfield blvd., S. E. to 201st, and fr. 227th, S. E. to City line.

One Hundred and Thirty-seventh (J 2), from 7th av., E. of 136th, S. to 12th av., and from 13th av., S. to Leavitt, and (J 5), from 56th rd., E. of 136th, S. to North Hempstead Turnpike, and from 63d av., S. to Webb av., and (J 7), from 78th rd., S. E. to Grand Central parkway, and from 83d av., S. E., S. and S. E. to Jamaica av., and (L 9), from Sutter av., S. to 135th av., and from S. Conduit av., S. to 163d av.

One Hundred and Thirty-seventh av. (M 9), from Rockaway blvd., S. of 134th av., N. E. to Caxton av., and from Springfield blvd., S. E. to City line.

One Hundred and Thirty-seventh dr. (O 9) (Rosedale), fr. Rosedale blvd., S. E. to Brookville blvd.

One Hundred and Thirty-seventh rd. (N 9), from 174th, E. to Farmers blvd. and fr. Springfield blvd., S. E. to 206th, and from 227th, S. E. to City line.

One Hundred and Thirty-eighth (J 2), from Powells Cove blvd., at Powells Cove, S. to 32d av., and (J 5), from Peck av., W. of Jaggar av., S. to Webb av., and from 68th rd., S. E. to 82d dr., and (J 7), from 85th av. S. E. to Archer av., and from 106th av., S. E. to Foch blvd., and (L 10), from 135th av., S. to N. Conduit av., and from S. Conduit av., S. to 163d av.

One Hundred and Thirty-eighth av. (M 9), from N. Conduit av., W. of Rockaway blvd., N. E. to Rockaway blvd., and (N 9) (Springfield), from L. I. R. R., S. E. to North Conduit av.

One Hundred and Thirty-eighth dr. (O 10) (Rosedale), from Laurelton Parkway, S. E. to Rosedale blvd.

One Hundred and Thirty-eighth pl. (K 7) (Jamaica), from Jamaica av., S. E. to Archer av., and from 94th av., S. E. to 95th av.

One Hundred and Thirty-eighth rd. (M 9) (Sp'ngfield), from Springfield blvd., S. E. to 205th.

One Hundred and Thirty-ninth (J 2), from 13th av., E. of 138th, S. to 30th av., and (J 5), from 63d av., E. of 138th, S. to Webb av., and (J 7), fr. Grand Central pkway, S. E. to Archer av., and from 107th av., S. E. to 120th av., and (L 10), from 135th, S. to N. Conduit av., and fr. S. Conduit av., S. to 163d av.

One Hundred and Thirty-ninth av. (N 9) (Springfield), from Southgate, S. E. to Hook Creek blvd.

One Hundred and Thirty-ninth rd. (N 9), from 177th, E. to Farmers blvd.

One Hundred and Fortieth (J 2), from 13th av., E. of 139th, S. to 32d av., and (J 5), from Peck av., E. of Jagger av., S. to 58th rd., and (J7), from Grand Central pkway, S. E. to 82d dr., and (K 8), from 111th av., S. E. and S. to 163d av.

One Hundred and Fortieth av. (M 9), from Rockaway blvd., N. of N. Conduit av., N. E. and E. to Lakeview av., and (O 10), from S. Conduit av., S. E. to 226th.

One Hundred and Forty-first (J 2), from Powells Cove blvd., at Powells Cove, S. to 12th av., and from 13th av., S. to 32d av., and (J 5), from 56th rd. E. of 140th, S. W. to North Hempstead Turnpike, and from 69th av., S. E. to Grand Central pkway, and from Grand Central pkway, S. E. to 85th dr, and (K 8), from 109th av., S. E. and S. to Rockaway blvd.

One Hundred and Forty-first av. (N 9), fr. Farmers blvd., E. to Edgewood, and fr. Springfield blvd., S. E. to 226th.

One Hundred and Forty-second (J 2), from 12th av., E. of 141st, S. to Willets Pt. blvd., and (J 5), from Peck av., W. of Larch av., S. E. and S. to Webb av., and (J 7), from Grand Central pkway, S. E. to 82d dr., and (K 8), from Liberty av., S. E. to N. Conduit av., and from S. Conduit av., S. to 163d av.

One Hundred and Forty-second av. (N 9), from 174th, S. of 140th av., E. to 180th, and from 182d, E. to Springfield blvd., and fr. Brookville blvd., S. E. to 226th.

One Hundred and Forty-second pl. (L 9) (Jamaica), from Foch blvd., S. to Rockaway blvd.

One Hundred and Forty-third (J 2), from 13th av., E. of 142d, S. to 15th av., and from 20th av., S. to Willets Pt. blvd., and (K 7), from Grand Central parkway, E of 142d, S. E. to 82d dr., and from 85th av., S to Hillside av., and (K 7), from Jamaica av., S. E. to 95th av., and from 109th av., S. E. and S. to 163d av.

One Hundred and Forty-third av. (N 9) (Springfield), fr. Farmers blvd, S. E. to North Conduit av., and from Brookville blvd., S. E. to 231st.

One Hundred and Forty-third rd. (N 10), from 172d, S. of 140th av., E. to 179th, and fr. Springfield blvd., S. E. to 205th.

One Hundred and Forty-fourth (J 2), from Parsons blvd., near Powells Cove, S. W. and S. to 15th av., and from 20th av., S. to 21st av., and from 23d av., S. to 25th av., and (J 6), from Larch av., at Melbourne av., S. E. and S. to Jamaica av., and (L 9), from 111th av., S. E. and S. to N. Conduit av., and from S. Conduit av., S. to 163d av.

One Hundred and Forty-fourth av. (N 10) (Rosedale), from N. Y. blvd., N. of N. Conduit av., E. to Springfield blvd., and from Brookville blvd., S. E. to 236th.

One Hundred and Forty-fourth pl. (J 2), from 14th av., E. of 144th, S. to 15th av., and (K 7), from Jamaica av., S. E. to Archer av.

One Hundred and Forty-fifth (J 3), from 29th av., E. of Parsons blvd., S. to Bayside av., and from 33d av., S. to 34th av., and (K 7), from 88th av., S. to Jamaica av., and (L 8), from 11th av., S. E. and S. to 133d av., and from S. Conduit av., S. to 161st av.

One Hundred and Forty-fifth av. (L 10), from 150th, S. of S. Conduit av., E. to Baisley blvd., and from Byron, S. E. to Boynton, and (O 10), fr. Brookville blvd., S. E. to 236th.

One Hundred and Forty-fifth dr. (M 10), from Byron, S. of 145th rd., S. E. to 155th.

One Hundred and Forty-fifth pl. (J 2), from Powells Cove blvd., E. of Parsons blvd., S. E. to 7th av., and from 10th av., S. E. to 12th av., and from 13th av., S. E. to 14th av., and from 29th av., S. to Bayside av., and from 33d av., S. to 34th av.

One Hundred and Forty-fifth rd. (M 10), from Byron, S. of 145th av., S. E. to 155th, and from Boynton, S. E. to Cogswell.

One Hundred and Forty-sixth (J 2), from 10th av., E. of 145th pl., S. E. to 12th av., and from 13th av., S. E. to 15th av., and from 20th av., S. to Northern blvd., and (K 7), from Hillside av., S. to Archer av., and from Sutphin blvd., S. to Liberty av., and from 111th av., S. E. and S. to 160th av.

One Hundred and Forty-sixth av. (L 10), from Goldfield, S. of 145th av., E. and S. E. to Cogswell.

One Hundred and Forty-sixth pl. (J 2), from 10th av., E. of 146th, S. E. to 12th av., and from 13th av., S. to 17th av.

One Hundred and Forty-sixth rd. (L 10), from Goldfield, S. of 146th av. E. to 153d, and from Byron, S. E. to 155th.

One Hundred and Forty-seventh (J2), from Powells Cove blvd., E. of 145th pl., S. E. and S. to Bayside av., and from 33d av., S. to 34th av., and from 35th av., S. to

BOROUGH OF QUEENS STREET AND AVENUE DIRECTORY—*Continued.*

Parsons blvd., and (J 6), from Gravett pl., S. E. to Grand Central parkway, and (L 8), from 111th av., S. E. and S. to N. Conduit av., and fr. S. Conduit av., S. to 159th av.

One Hundred and Forty-seventh av. (L 10), from Van Wyck blvd., S. of S. Conduit av., S. E. to Cogswell, and fr. Farmers blvd., E. to City line.

One Hundred and Forty-seventh dr. (O 10), from 219th, S. of 147th rd., E. to Edgewood, and from Huxley, E. to Rosedale blvd.

One Hundred and Forty-seventh pl. (K 7) (Jamaica), from Jamaica av., S. to Archer av., and from 95th av., S. E. to Liberty av.

One Hundred and Forty-seventh rd. (O 10), from 219th, S. of 147th av., E. to Edgewood, and from Huxley, E. to City line.

One Hundred and Forty-eighth (J 2), from 10th av, E. of 147th S. E to 15th av., and from Willets Pt. blvd., S. to 25th av.. and from 29th av., S. to 35th av., and (J 5), from 56th rd.. E. to Larch av., S. W. to Reeves av., and (K 7), from Grand Central parkway, S. E. and S. to Archer av., and from 94th av., S. E. to 150th, and from 111th av., S. E. to Foch blvd., and (L 9), from Rockaway blvd., S. to N. Conduit av., and fr. S. Conduit av. S. to 157th av.

One Hundred and Forty-eighth av. (M 10), from Baisley blvd., at Byron, S. E. to Boynton, and from Lombard, E. to Drummond, and from Berkeley, E. to Amos, and from 208th, S. E. to 216th, and from Huxley, E. to City line.

One Hundred and Forty-eighth dr. (O 10), from Brookville blvd.. S. of 148th rd., E. to Edgewood, and from Huxley, E. to City line.

One Hundred and Forty-eighth rd. (N 10), from Lombard, S. of 148th av., E. to N. Y. blvd., and (O 10), from Brookville blvd., E. to Edgewood, and from Huxley, E. to City line.

One Hundred and Forty-ninth (K 2), from Powells Cove blvd., E. of 147th, S. E. and E. to 46th av., and (K 6), from 79th av., E. of 147th, S.E. to Union Turnpike, and from 85th rd., S. E. to 85th dr.. and (K 7), from Jamaica av., S. to Archer av., and from 95th av., S. to 97th av.. and from 114th av., S. E. to 116th av., and (L 9), from Rockaway blvd., S. to N. Conduit av., and from S. Conduit av., S. to 155th av.

One Hundred and Forty-ninth av. (M 10), from Baisley blvd., S. of 148th av., E. to 158th, and from Lombard, E. S. E. and E. to City line.

One Hundred and Forty-ninth dr. (O 11), from 220th, S. of 149th rd., E. to 223d, and from Huxley. E. to Weller la.

One Hundred and Forty-ninth pl. (J 2), from 2d av., E. of 149th, S. E. to 5th av.. and from 33d av., S. to Beach av.

One Hundred and Forty-ninth rd. (N 10), from Lombard. S. of 149th av., E. and S.E. to Sp'gfield blvd., and from 205th, S. E. to 208th. and from 220th, E to Brookville blvd., and from 223d E. to 225th, and from Huxley. E. to City line.

One Hundred and Fiftieth (K 2), from Powells Cove blvd., S E. and S. to Sanford av., and (J 5), from Peck av., S. W., S. and S. E. to 75th av., and (K 7), from Hillside av., S.E. to Sutphin blvd., and (L 9), from Rockaway blvd., S. and S. W. to 163d av

One Hundred and Fiftieth av. (K 10), from 128th, S. of S. Conduit av., E to Springfield blvd.. and from 205th, S.E. to 208th. and from 220th, E. and S. E. to Craft av., near City line.

One Hundred and Fiftieth dr. (N 10), from Lombard, S. of 150th rd., E. to Drummond, and from Brookville blvd., E. to 226th.

One Hundred and Fiftieth pl. (K 2), from 6th av., E. of 150th, S. E. to 7th av, and from 14th rd., S. E. to 17th av., and from Bayside av., S E. to 40th av.

One Hundred and Fiftieth rd. (N 10), from Lombard. S. of 150th av, E to Springfield blvd., and from Brookville blvd., E. to 226th.

One Hundred and Fifty-first (K 2), from Powells Cove blvd., E. of 5th av., S. to Cross Isld. blvd., and (K 5), from Peck av., S. W. to North Hempstead turnpike, & (K 7), from 84th rd., S. E. to 85th dr, and (K 7), from Jamaica av., S. to Twombly rd., and from 94th av., S. to Beaver rd., and (L 10) fr. Goldfield, S. and S. W. to 155th av.

One Hundred and Fifty-first av. (L 10), from 151st, S. of 150th av., E. to Goldfield, and from Baisley blvd., E. to 158th, and from Cogswell, E. to 162d. and from Lombard, E to N. Y. blvd., and from Springfield blvd., S. E. to City line.

One Hundred and Fifty-first dr. (N 10), from N. Y. blvd., S. of 151st rd., E. to Springfield blvd.

One Hundred and Fifty-first pl. (K 2). from Powells Cove blvd, E. of 151st, S. to 10th av.

One Hundred and Fifty-first rd. (M 10), from Byron, S. of 150th av., E. to 158th, and from Lombard, E. to Drummond.

One Hundred and Fifty-second (K 2), from Powells Cove blvd.. E. of 151st pl., S. to 14th rd., and from Bayside av., S. to 33d av., and (K 5), from Peck av., S. W. to North Hempstead turnpike, and from 79th av., S. E. to Union turnpike, and from Grand Central parkway. S E. to 85th dr., and (K 7), from 88th av.. S. E. to 89th av., and from Jamaica av., S. E. to Archer av.. and from 118th av., S. E. to 119th av.. and from 123d av., S. E. to Lake View blvd. West, and (L 10), from 147th av., at Goldfield, S. to 150th av.

One Hundred and Fifty-second av. (K 10), from 128th, S. of 150th av., E. to Rockaway blvd., and fr. Lombard, E and S.E. to 232d, at Hook Creek Basin.

One Hundred and Fifty-second pl. (K 2), from eastern end of Powells Cove blvd., S. to 10th av.

One Hundred and Fifty-second rd. (N 10), from Lombard, S. of 152d av., E. to Springfield blvd., and from 229th, S. E. to 232d.

One Hundred and Fifty-third (K 2), from 10th av., at Whitestone Landing Sta., S. to 14th av., and from Bayside av., S. to Northern blvd., and (K 5), from Peck av., S. W. to Reeves av., and from Melbourne av., S. E. to Grand Central parkway, and (K 7), from Hillside av., S. E. to Jamaica av.. and from South rd., S. E. to 107th av., and from 108th av., S. E. to 112th av., and from Foch blvd., S.E. to Lake View blvd. West, and from Baisley blvd, S. E. to 182d av., and (L 10), from S. Conduit av., S. E. and S. W. to 152d av.

One Hundred and Fifty-third av. (M 10), from Baisley blvd., S. of 152d av, E. to 161st, and from 171st, S. E. to 173d, and from Lombard. S. E. to Hook Creek Basin, near City line.

One Hundred and Fifty-third pl. (K 2), from 14th av., E. of 153d, S. to Cross Isld. blvd.

One Hundred and Fifty-third rd. (M 10), from 171st. S. of 153d av., S.E. to 173d, and from Lombard, S. of Rockaway blvd., S. E. to 181st, and from 217th, S. E. to 232d.

One Hundred and Fifty-fourth (K 2), from 7th av., E. of 152d pl., S. to 41st av., and from Barclay av., S. to Sanford av., and (L 8), from South rd., S. E. to 109th av., and from 118th av., S. E. to 119th av., and (M 9), from Baisley blvd., S. E. to 140th av.

One Hundred and Fifty-fourth av. (M 10), from Baisley blvd., S. of 153d av., S. E. to Springfield blvd.

One Hundred and Fifty-fourth dr. (M 10), from 156th, S. of 154th av., S. E. to 161st, and from 171st, S. E. to 173d, and from 177th, S.E. to Sp'gfield blvd., and from 220th, S. E. to Head of Bay blvd.

One Hundred and Fifty-fourth pl. (K 5), from 59th av., E. of Kissena rd., S. to 61st av.

One Hundred and Fifty-fourth rd. (M 10), from 158th, S. of 154th av., S. E. to 161st, and from 171st, S. E. to 173d, and from 177th, S.E. to Head of Bay blvd.

One Hundred and Fifty-fifth (K 2), from 14th av., E. of 154th, S. to Locke av., and from 29th av., S. to 41st av., and from Sanford av., S. to Beech av., and (K 5), from North Hempstead turnpike, S. to 73d av., and (K 7), from 90th av., S. to 90th rd.. and from South rd., S. E. to Lake View blvd. West, and from Baisley blvd., S. E. and S. to N. Conduit av., and from S. Conduit av., S. E. to 147th av., and from 154th av., S. W. to 163d av.

One Hundred and Fifty-fifth av. (K 10), from 128th, S. of 152d av., S. E. to 150th, and from Baisley blvd., S. E. to Head of Bay blvd.

One Hundred and Fifty-sixth (K 2), from 14th av., E. of 155th. S. to 16th av., and from 29th av., S. to Depot rd., and (K 4), from Station rd., S. to Oak av., and from North Hempstead turnpike, S. to 73d av., and (L 8), from Guinzburg rd., S. E. to 114th av., and from Baisley blvd., S. E. and S. to N. Conduit av., and from S. Conduit av., S. W. to 163d av.

One Hundred and Fifty-sixth av. (K 10), from 128th. S. of 155th av., S. E. to west side of Cornell basin, and from east side of Cornell basin, S. E. to Head of Bay blvd.

One Hundred and Fifty-seventh (K 2), from 7th av., E. of 154th, S. to Depot rd., and (K 4), from Station rd., S to Oak av., and from North Hempstead turnpike, S. to 73d av., and (L 8),

BOROUGH OF QUEENS STREET AND AVENUE DIRECTORY—*Continued.*

from South rd. to Foch blvd, and from Baisley blvd., S. E. and S. to N. Conduit av., and (M 10), from 155th av., S. W. to 163d av.

One Hundred and Fifty-seventh av. (L 10), from 147th, S. of 156th av., S. E. to 150th.

One Hundred and Fifty-eighth (K 2), from East River, E. of Whitestone Landing, S. to 7th av., and from 14th av., S. to Locke av., and from 29th av., S. to Depot rd., and from Station rd., S. to Oak av, and (L 8), from South rd., S. E. to New York blvd., and from 129th av., S. E. and S. to N. Conduit av., and from Rockaway blvd., S. W. to 156th av.

One Hundred and Fifty-ninth (K 2), from Shore Acres blvd., E. of 158th, S. to 7th av., and from 14th av., S. to 15th av., and from 29th av., S. to Depot rd., and (K 4), fr. Station rd., S. to Oak av., and from North Hempstead turnpike, S. to 73d av., and fr. Union turnpike, S. E. to Goethals av., and from 82d dr., S.W. to Grand Central parkway, and from 84th av., S. to Parsons av., & (L 7). from Archer av., S. E. to New York blvd., and from 133d av., S. E. and S. to N. Conduit av., and from Rockaway blvd., S. to 152d av., and from 156th av., S. W. to 163d av.

One Hundred and Fifty-ninth av. (K 10), from 128th, S. of 156th av., S. E. to 130th, at Bergen Basin, and from 133d, S. E. to 150th at Cornell Basin, and from Baisley blvd., S. E. to Head of Bay blvd.

One Hundred and Fifty-ninth dr. (L 10), from 146th, S. of 159th rd., S. E. to 150th.

One Hundred and Fifty-ninth rd. (L 10), from 146th, S. of 159th av., S. E. to 150th.

One Hundred and Sixtieth (K 2), from Shore Acres blvd., E. of 159th, S. to Depot rd., and (K 4), from Station rd., S. to Oak av., and from North Hempstead turnpike, S. E. to Goethals av., and from 82d dr. S. to Normal rd., and (L 7), from Hillside av., S. E. to Claude av., and from 133d av., S. E. and S. to N.Conduit av., and from Rockaway blvd., S. to 153d av., and from 155th rd., S. to 163d av.

One Hundred and Sixtieth av. (K 10), from 128th, S. of 159th av., S. E. to Bergen basin, and from Bergen basin, S E. to Cornell basin, and from Cornell basin, S. E. to Head of Bay blvd.

One Hundred and Sixtieth dr. (L 11), from 145th, S. of 160th rd., S.E. to 150th.

One Hundred and Sixtieth rd. (L 11), from 145th, S. of 160th av., S.E. to 150th.

One Hundred and Sixty-first (K 2), from Shore Acres blvd., E. of 160th, S. to 7th av., and from 14th av., S. to 15th av., and from 29th av., S. to Northern blvd., and (K 4), from Station rd., S. to Oaks av., and from Kissena park, S. to 72d, and from Union turnpike, S. to Goethals av., and from 82d dr., S. to Grand Central parkway, and from 84th av., S. to Normal rd., and (L 7), from Hillside av., S. E. to Jamaica av., and from 133d av., S. E. and S. to N. Conduit av., and from 152d av., S.W. to 163d av.

One Hundred and Sixty-first av. (K 10), from 128th, S. of 160th av., S. E. to 130th, and from 133d, S. E. to 150th, and from Baisley blvd., S. E. to Head of Bay blvd.

One Hundred and Sixty-first pl. (M 9) (Jamaica), from 122d av., S. to Baisley blvd.

One Hundred and Sixty-first rd. (L 11), from 144th, S. of 161st av., S. E. to 150th.

One Hundred and Sixty-second (L 2), from Shore Acres blvd., E. of 161st, S. to 15th av., and from 29th av., S. to Oak av., and (K 5), from Peck av., E. of 161st, S. and S. E. to Goethals av., and (K 7), from 84th dr., S. E. to Normal rd., and (L 7), from Hillside av., S.E. to Jamaica av, and (M 10), from 150th av., S. W. to 163d av.

One Hundred and Sixty-second av. (L 11), from 144th, S. of 161st rd., S E. to 150th.

One Hundred and Sixty-third (L 2), from Cryders la., E. of 162d, S. to Depot rd., and from Northern blvd., S to 46th av., and (K 5), fr. Fresh Meadow rd., W. of Flushing Cemetery, S. to Oak av., and from Peck av., E. of 162d, S. to 72d av., and (L 7), from Hillside av., S.E. to Jamaica av., and (M 10), from Judith, S. W. to 163d av.

One Hundred and Sixty-third av. (K 11), from 128th, S. of 161st av., S. E. to Bergen basin, and from Bergen basin, S. E. to Cornell basin, and from Cornell basin, S.E. to Head of Bay blvd.

One Hundred and Sixty-third pl. (K 5), from Fresh Meadow rd., E. of 163d, S. to Oak av.

One Hundred and Sixty-fourth (L 2), from Cryders la., E. of 163d, S. to 15th av., and from 25th av., S. to Depot rd., and from Station rd., S. to 46th av., and (K 5), from Fresh Meadow rd., E. of 163d pl., S.E. to Jamaica av, and from Tilly av., S. E. to 110th rd., and from Foch blvd., S.E. to 122d av., and (M 10), from Judith, S. W. to 163d av.

One Hundred and Sixty-fourth pl. (K 6), from Union Turnpike, E. of 164th, S. E. to Goethals av., and (L 8), from 104th rd., S. E. to 111th av.

One Hundred and Sixty-fifth (L 2), from Cryders la., E. of 164th, S. to 15th av., and from Bayside la., S. to Depot rd., and from Station rd., S. to 46th av., and (K 5), from Peck av., E. of 164th, S. to North Hempstead Turnpike, and from 61st av., S. to 72d av., and fr. 78th av., S. to Union Turnpike, and fr. Union Turnpike, S. E. to Goethals av., and from 84th dr., S. E. to 108th av., and from 114th av., S.E. to 116th av., and from Foch blvd., S. E to Smith, and from Baisley blvd., S. E. to 132d av., and (M 10), from Cross-over rd., S. W. to 163d av.

One Hundred and Sixty-fifth pl. (L 8) (Jamaica), from 108th av., S E. to 108th dr.

One Hundred and Sixty-sixth (L 2), from Shore Acres blvd., E. of 162d, S. to Depot rd., and from Station rd., S. to 46th av., and (L 5), fr. Fresh Meadow rd., S. of Flushing Cem., S. W. to Kite, and from Peck av., S to 59th av., and from 61st av., S. to Goethals av., and (L 7), from Gilman av., S. E. to Liberty av., and from South rd., S. E. to 104th rd., and from 107th av., S. E. to 108th av., and from Brinkerhoff av., S. E. to Foch blvd., and from Bedell, S. E to 137th av.

One Hundred and Sixty-seventh (L 3), from 27th av., E. of 166th, S. to 46th av., and (L 5), fr. Fresh Meadow rd., S. of Flushing Cem., S. W. and S. to Underhill av., and fr. Peck av., S. to 59th av., and from 61st av., S. to 73d av., and from 75th av., S. E. to Goethals av., and from Gothic dr., S. E. to Hillside av., and (L 8), from 108th av., S. E. to Foch blvd., and from Bedell, S. E and S. to 140th av., and (M 10), from Rockaway blvd., S. W. to 163d av.

One Hundred and Sixty-eighth (L 3), from Cross Isld. blvd., E. of Bayside la., S. to Depot rd., and fr. Station rd., S. to 46th av., and (L 5), fr. Fresh Meadow rd, S. of Flushing Cem., S. W. to Lithonia av., and from Peck av., S. to 59th av., and from 61st av., S. and S. E. to Liberty av., and from Brinkerhoff av., S. E. to 119th av., and from Bedell, S. E. to 144th av., and (M 10), from Rockaway blvd., S. W. to 163d av.

One Hundred and Sixty-eighth pl. (L 5), from Grand Central pkway, E. of 168th, S. E. to 90th av., and from Liberty av., S. E. to 104th av.

One Hundred and Sixty-ninth (L 3), from Utopia parkway, at 17th rd., S. to Depot rd., and from Station rd., S. to 46th av., and (L 5), fr. Fresh Meadow rd., S. of Flushing Cemetery, S. W. to Lithonia av., and from Peck av, S. to 59th av., and from 60th av., S. and S. E. to Goethals av., and (L 7), from Grand Central pkway, S. E. to Jamaica av., and from Liberty av., S.E. to 107th av., and from Brinkerhoff av., S. E. to Marsden, and from Bedell, S. E. to N.Conduit av., and (M 10), from Rockaway blvd., S. W. to 163d av.

One Hundred and Sixty-ninth pl. (M 8) (Jamaica), from Merrick blvd., S E. to Brinkerhoff av.

One Hundred and Seventieth (L 3), from Cross Isld. blvd., at 27th av., S to Depot rd., and from Station rd., S. to 46th av., and (L 5), from Peck av., E. of 169th, S. to 59th av., and from 60th av., S. and S. E. to Goethals av., and (L 7), from Grand Central parkway, S.E. to Gothic dr., and (L 7), from Hillside av., S. E. to 108th av., and from 111th av., S. E. to Sayres av., and from 114th av., S. E. to Marsden, and from Bedell, S. E. to 144th av., and (M 10), from Rockaway blvd., S. W. to 163d av.

One Hundred and Seventy-first (L 3), from Cross Isld. blvd., S. of 170th, S. to Depot rd., and from Station rd., S. to 46th av., and (L 5), fr. Fresh Meadow rd., W of Wheaton la., S. W. to Underhill av, and from Peck av, S. to North Hempstead Turnpike, & from 60th av., S. and S. E. to 82d av., and (L 7), from Hillside av., S.E. to Jamaica av., and from Liberty av., S. E. to Merrick blvd., and from 116th av., S. E. to Baisley blvd., and from 129th av., S. E. to 144th av., and (M 11), from Rockaway blvd., S. W. to 163d av.

One Hundred and Seventy-first pl. (L 7) (Jamaica), from 105th av., S. E. to Brinkerhoff av.

One Hundred and Seventy-second (L 3), from 26th av., W. of Utopia parkway, S. to Depot rd.,

BOROUGH OF QUEENS STREET AND AVENUE DIRECTORY—*Continued.*

and from Station rd., S. to Hollis ct. blvd., and (L 5), from Peck av., E. of 171st, S. to North Hempstead Turnpike, and from 60th av., S. & S.E. to Home Lawn av., and (L 7), from Hillside av., S. E. to 93d av., and from Liberty av., S. E. to Sayres av., and from Westchester av., S.E. to 115th av., and from Foch blvd., S. E. to Marsden, and from Bedell, S. E. to N. Conduit av., and (M 11), from 155th av., S. W. to 163d av.

One Hundred and Seventy-second pl. (L 6), from 81st rd., E. of 172d, S. E. to 82d av.

One Hundred and Seventy-third (L 5), from Peck av., W. of Fresh Meadow rd , S. to Fresh Meadow rd., and from 61st av., S. and S. E. to Grand Central pkway, and (L 7), from Hillside av., S. E. to 89th av., and from 91st av., S. E. to 93d av., and from Liberty av., S. E. to Sayres av., and from Westchester av., S.E. to Foch blvd., and from Bedell, S. E. and S. to 143d rd , and (M 11), from Rockaway blvd., S. W. to 155th av.

One Hundred and Seventy-fourth (L5), from Fresh Meadow rd., at 56th av., S. to 59th av., and from 59th av., S. E. and S. to 65th av., and from 65th av., W. of Fresh Meadow rd., S and S.E. to Union Turnpike, and (M 8), from 108th av., S. E. to Sayres av., and from 114th av., S. E. to 119th av., and from Bedell, S. E. and S. to 143d rd., and (M 11), from 155th av., S. W. to 163d av.

One Hundred and Seventy-fourth pl. (M 9) (Jamaica), from 125th av., S.E. to 129th av.

One Hundred and Seventy-fifth (L 5), from Hope av., at Fresh Meadow rd., S., S. E. and S. to 67th av., and from 69th av.. S. and S.E. to Home Lawn av., and (L 7), from Hillside av., S. E. to 93d av., and from Douglas av., S. E. to 107th av., and from 108th av. to Merrick blvd., and from Bedell S. E. to 137th av., and from 137th rd., S. to 140th av., and (M 11), from Rockaway blvd., S. W. to 155th.

One Hundred and Seventy-fifth pl. (M 8) (Jamaica), from Sayres av., S. E. to 120th av.

One Hundred and Seventy-sixth (L 6), from 75th av., W. of Utopia parkway, S. to Union Turnpike, and (L 7), from 90th av., S. E. to 93d av., and from Liberty av., S. E. to 107th av., and from 108th rd., S. E. to Baisley blvd., and from 125th av., S. E. to 127th av., and from 130th av., S. E. to 131st av., and from Bedell, S.E. and S. to 140th av., and (M 11), from 155th av., S. W. to 163d av.

One Hundred and Seventy-sixth pl. (N 9) (Jamaica), from 130th av., S. to 131st av.

One Hundred and Seventy-seventh (L 6), from 73d av., E. of Utopia parkway, S. E. to Union Turnpike, and (M 7), fr. Jamaica av., S. E. to 120th av., and from 127th av., S. E. to 131st av., and from 137th rd., S. to 140th av., and (M 11), from Rockaway blvd., S. W. to 155th av.

One Hundred and Seventy-seventh pl. (M 8) (Jamaica), from Westchester av., S. E. to 119th av., and from Baisley blvd., S. E. to 120th av.

One Hundred and Seventy-eighth (L 6), from 73d av., E. of 177th, S. E. to Union Turnpike, and (M 7), from Hillside av., S.E. to 93d av., and from Liberty av., S. E. to Leslie rd., and from 130th av., S. E. to Farmers blvd., and from 137th rd., S. to 140th av., and (M 11), from 155th av., S. W. to 163d av.

One Hundred and Seventy-eighth pl. (M 7) (Jamaica), from Jamaica av., S.E. to 93d av., and from Sayres av., S. E. to Belover rd., and from 130th av., S. E. to Farmers blvd.

One Hundred and Seventy-ninth (L 6), from 69th av., at Marianna, S. E. to Union Turnpike, and (M 7), from Hillside av., S.E. to Jamaica av., and from 107th av., S. E. to Leslie rd., and (N 10), from 143d av., E. of Farmers blvd., S. to 144th av., and from 155th av., at Lombard, S. W. to 163d av.

One Hundred and Seventy-ninth pl. (M 7) (Jamaica), from Hillside av., S.E. to 93d av., and from 108th av., S. E. to 180th.

One Hundred and Eightieth (L 6), from 67th av., at Marianna, S. E. to Union Turnpike, and (M 7), from Wexford ter., S. to Jamaica av., and from Liberty av., S. E. to Farmers blvd., and (N 10), from 140th av., S. to N. Conduit av., and from Lombard, S. W. to 163d.

One Hundred and Eightieth pl. (M 7) (Jamaica), from Jamaica av., S. E. to 93d av.

One Hundred and Eighty-first (L5), from 64th av., E. of Utopia parkway, S.E. to Union Turnpike, and (M 7), from Wexford ter., S. to Jamaica av., and (N 10), fr. 140th S. to N. Conduit av., and from R'way blvd., W. of Springfield blvd., S. W. to 154th av., and from 155th av., S. W. to 163d av.

One Hundred and Eighty-first pl. (M 7) (Jamaica), from Jamaica av., S. E. to 93d av.

One Hundred and Eighty-second (L 5), from Utopia parkway, S. of North Hempstead Turnpike, S. E. to Union Turnpike, and (M 7), from Wexford ter., S. to Jamaica av., and (N 9), fr. Farmers blvd., S. E. and S. to North Conduit av

One Hundred and Eighty-second pl. (M 7) (Jamaica), from Hillside av., S E. to 93d av.

One Hundred and Eighty-third (L 5), from North Hempstead Turnpike, E. of Utopia parkway, S.E. to Union Turnpike, and (M 7), from Hillside av., S. E. to Liberty av., and (N 9), from 140th av., S. to 144th av.

One Hundred and Eighty-fourth (L 5) (Bayside), from Utopia pkway, S. of 58d av., S. E. to Union Turnpike, and (M 7), from Hillside av., S. E. to Jamaica av., and from 104th av., S. E. to Liberty av., and (N 9), from 140th av., S. to N. Conduit av.

One Hundred and Eighty-fourth pl. (M 7) (Jamaica), from Hillside av., S. E. to Jamaica av.

One Hundred and Eighty-fifth (L 5) (Bayside), fr. 58d av., E. of Utopia pkway, S. E. to Union Turnpike, and (M 7), from Hillside av., S. E. to Jamaica av., and from Henderson av., S. E. to Liberty av., and (N 9), from 141st av., S. to N. Conduit av.

One Hundred and Eighty-sixth (L 5) (Bayside), fr. 58d av., at Peck av., S. E. to Union Turnpike, and (M 7), from Hillside av , S.E. to Jamaica av., and from Henderson av., S. E. to Liberty av., and (N 9), from North Conduit av., S. E. to 141st av.

One Hundred and Eighty-seventh (L 4), from Hollis ct. blvd., S. to Rocky Hill rd., and from Utopia parkway, S. E. to Underhill av., and from Peck av., S. E. to Union Turnpike, and (M 7), from Hillside av., S. E. to Jamaica av., and from Henderson av., S. E. to Liberty av.

One Hundred and Eighty-seventh pl. (M7) (Hollis), from Hillside av., S. E. to Jamaica av., and from Henderson av., S. E. to Liberty av.

One Hundred and Eighty-eighth (M7) (Hollis), fr. Hillside av., S. E. to Jamaica av., and from Henderson av., S. E. to Liberty av.

One Hundred and Eighty-ninth (L 4) (Bayside), from Station rd., E. of Utopia pkway, S. and S. E. to Underhill av., and from 56th av., S. E. to Aberdeen rd and (M 7), from Hillside av., S. E. to Jamaica av., and from Henderson av., S. E. to Liberty av., and from Farmers blvd., S E. to 120th av.

One Hundred and Ninetieth (L 3) (Bayside), fr. Cross Isld. blvd., E. of Utopia parkway, S. to Depot rd., and from Station rd., S. and S. E. to 56th av., and from Peck av., S.E. to Radnor rd., and (M 7), from Hillside av., S. to Hollis av., and from 109th rd., S. E. to Zuider av.

One Hundred and Ninetieth pl. (M6), fr. Radnor rd., at 85th av., S. E. to 85th rd., and (N 7), fr. 109th rd., E. of Farmers blvd., S. E. to 110th rd.

One Hundred and Ninety-first (L 4) (Bayside), fr. Cross Isld. blvd., E. of 19th, S. to Depot rd., and from Station rd., S. and S. E. to Underhill av., and from Peck av., S. E. to 85th av., and (M 7), fr. Hillside av., S. E. to 110th rd., and fr. 115th dr , S. E. to Nashville av.

One Hundred and Ninety-second (L 4) (Bayside), from Cross Isld. blvd., E. of 191st, S. and S. E. to 85th av., and (M 7), fr. Hillside av., S. E. to Jamaica av., and fr. Portville av., S. to 110th rd., and from 116th rd., S. E. to Nashville av.

One Hundred and Ninety-third (L 4) (Bayside), fr. Cross Isld. blvd., E. of 192d, S. to 85th av., and from Crocheron av., S. to Depot rd., and from Station rd., S. and S. E. to Underhill av., and fr. Peck av., S.E. to 73d av., and (M6), from Anaconda av., S. E. to 85th av., and (M 7), from Hillside av., S. E. to 109th rd., and from 117th rd., S. E. to Williamson av.

One Hundred and Ninety-fourth (L 4) (Bayside), from Crocheron av., E. of 193d, S to Depot rd., and from Station rd., S. and S. E. to Underhill av., and from Peck av., S. E. to 73d av., and (M 6), from Anaconda av., S. E. to Grand Central parkway, and (M 7), from Hillside av., S. E. to Nashville av.

One Hundred and Ninety-fifth (L 4) (Bayside), fr. Cross Isld. blvd., at 86th av., S. to Depot rd., and from Station rd., S. and S. E. to 73d av., and (M 6), Anaconda av., S E. to Grand Central pkway, and (M 7), from Hillside av., S.E. to 111th av., and from 116th rd., S. E. to 12?d av.

BOROUGH OF QUEENS STREET AND AVENUE DIRECTORY—*Continued.*

One Hundred and Ninety-sixth (L 4) (Bayside), from Station rd., W. of Crosslsld.blvd., S. and S. E. to Underhill av., and from Peck av., S. E. to Busby av., and (M 6), from Union Turnpike, S. E. to Midland parkway, and (M 7), from Hillside av., S. E. to 122d av.

One Hundred and Ninety-seventh (M 4) (Bayside), fr. 45th rd., W. of 198th, S. and S. E. to Underhill av., and from Peck av., S. E. to Busby av., and (M 6), from Union Turnpike, S.E. to Grand Central pkway, and (N 7), from Hillside av., S. E. to Springfield blvd.

One Hundred and Ninety-eighth (M 4) (Bayside), from 45th rd., W. of Rosedale blvd., S. and S. E. to Underhill av., and from Peck av., S. E. to Busby av., and (M 6), from Union Turnpike, S. E. to 85th av., and (N 7), from Hillside av., S. E. to 122d av.

One Hundred and Ninety-ninth (M 4) (Bayside), from Rocky Hill rd., W. of Rosedale blvd., S. E. to Underhill av., & from Peck av., S. E. to Busby av., and (M 6), from Union Turnpike, S. E. to Alwin rd., and (N 6), fr. Hillside av., S. E. to Springfield blvd.

Oneida pl. (L 9), from Liverpool, E. to Sutphin rd.

Onslow (J 7) (Richmond Hill), from Kew Gardens rd., to E. of Queens blvd.

Onslow pl. (J7) (Richmond Hill), from Austin, N. E. to Kew Gardens rd.

Opdyke (G 5) (Corona Heights), fr. Corona av., N. E. to Flushing river.

Opitz av. (H 8) (College Pt.), from Tallman av., E. and S. E to Bayside av.

Orange (B 4) (L. I. C.), from Hopkins av., S. E. to Crescent.

Orchard (B 8) (L. I. C.), from Bulkhead, E. to blvd.

Orchard (B 5) (L. I. C.), from L. I. R. R., N. W. to Hunter av.

Ord rd. (O 8), from 250th, N. of Marathon av., N. E. to 251st.

Oregon (L 10), from S. Conduit av., E. of Baisley blvd., S. E. to Byron.

Oregon pl. (L 10), fr. 134th av., nr. Baisley blvd., S. E. & S. to N. Conduit av.

Orlop (G 4), from Jackson av., N. to Flushing Bay.

Orontes (F 5), fr. Queens blvd., N. E. & N. to Corona av.

Orr pl. (G 7), from Metropolitan av., N. E. to Olcott.

Orton (B 5) (L.I.C.), from Borden av., N. to Meadow.

Orville (G6), from Burns, S. to Metropolitan av.

Oswego av. (G 9), from Sutter av., S. to Jamaica Bay.

Otis av. (G 6), from Quality, N. W. to Norfolk.

Otto (E 8), from Charlotte pl., S. E. & S. to L. I. R. R.

Outville (K 9) (Jamaica), fr. Irwin, N.E. to Espen.

Overbrook dr. (O 4), from Snell av., at Thebes la., S. E. and N. E. to City line.

Overhill (H 7), fr. North Greenway ter., N. E. to Burns.

Ovid pl. (N8), from Quencer, N. to Murdock av.

Owens (C 7), from Metropolitan av., N. W. to Maspeth av.

Oxford (H 4) (Flushing), now Anthony.

Ozone ter. (E 8), from Cypress av., E. 1 block.

Pacific (D 6), fr. L.I.R.R., E. to Mount Olivet Cemetery.

Pacific (O 11), from Old Mill Creek, E. to Fosters Meadow rd.

Packard (C 5) (L. I. C.), from Borden av., N. to Jackson av.

Padua pl. (M 6) (Hollis), from Keno av., S. E. to Ferrara av.

Palace av. (M4) (Bayside), from Alexander av., E. to Bell av.

Palermo av. (M6) (Hollis), fr. Grand Central Parkway, S. & W. to Holliswood av.

Palmer (G 5), fr. Queens blvd., E. to Xenia.

Palmetto (D 8), continued from Boro line, N. E. & E. to Traffic.

Palo Alto av. (M 6) (Hollis), from Nero av., S. to Hillside av.

Panama (J 10), from Jamaica Bay, N. E., to Rockaway blvd.

Pansy (E 8), from Anna pl., N. to Myrtle av.

Parcell (F 5) (Newtown), fr. Corona av., E. to Gay.

Park av. (M 4) (Bayside), from Barrington, N. E. to 2d.

Park Lane South (G 8) (Woodhaven), from 74th at Brooklyn Boro line, N. E. along Southern boundary of Forest Park to Metropolitan av.

Park pl. (B 4) (L. I. C.), from Freeman, N. to Webster.

Park pl. (C 8) (L. I. C.), from Hoyt av., N. E. to Potter av.

Park ter. (C 8) (L. I. C.), from Barclay, S. E. to Van Alst av.

Parsons av. (K 5), from Kissena park, S. and S. E. to Hillside av.

Parsons blvd. (J 2), from east point of Powells Cove, S. to Rose av., and (K 7), from Hillside av., S. E. to Jamaica av.

Passaic (K 9) (Richmond Hill), from R'way blvd., N. W. to Liberty av.

Patterson (D 4) (Woodside), from Duane, E. to Astoria av.

Paulina (G 7), from Martha, E. to Diamond.

Pavo rd. (K7), from Union Hall, N. between Gilman av. and Yuma la., E. to 166th.

Pawnee (J 10) fr. Peconic av., N. E. to Rockaway blvd.

Payne pl. (H7), fr. Austin, N. E. to Queens blvd.

Payntar av. (B4) (L.I.C.), from Vernon av., S. E. to Jackson av.

Payton pl. (H 4) (Flushing), from Wateredge av., S. to 40th av.

Pearsall (B 5) (L. I. C.), from Review av., N. E. to Hunters Pt. av.

Pearson (B 5) (L. I. C.), from L.I.R.R., N. W. to Jackson av.

Peartree av. (H 7) from Queens blvd., N. W. to Jackson av.

Peck av. (J 4), from Lawrence, S. E., E. and S.E. to Grand Central pkway.

Peconic av. (J 10), from Lefferts av. at Morrell, N. W. to Sutter av.

Peel (D 4) (Woodside), from Fillmore av., N. to Hayes av.

Pell (H 4), from Darvall, N. E. to Jackson av.

Pembroke av. (P 8), from Little Neck rd., E. of Jackson av., N. E. to Glenwood av.

Pembroke pl. (J 7) (Richmond Hill), fr. Austin, N. E. to Kew Gardens rd.

Pendleton (H 8) (College Pt.), now part of 125th.

Penelope (E7) (Middle Village), from Juniper av., N. E. to Queens blvd.

Penn rd. (K 14) (R'way Beach), from Beach 83d E. to Beach 81st.

Penshurst pl. (N 4), from 56th av., E. of Springfield blvd., S. and S. E. to 61st av.

Perego pl. (G6), from Austin, N.E. to Queens blvd.

Perry av. (D 6), fr. Clark av., E. & N.E. to Borden av.

Peru dr. (O 8), from 250th, E. of L. I. R. R., N. E. to City line.

Peters Round (M 7), from 91st av. to 184th.

Petit pl. (F 5) (Elmhurst), fr. Broadway, N. E. to Ithaca.

Petry pl. (D 4) (L. I. C.), from Vandeventer av., N. and N. E. to Wilson av.

Phelps av. (F 6), from Corinth av., N. E. to Calamus av.

Phillips pl. (C 8) (L.I. C.), from Edward, S. E. to Hallett.

Phlox pl. (K4) (Flushing), from Beech av., S. to Cherry av.

Phroane av. (L 8) (Jamaica), from New York blvd., N. E. to 160th.

Pidgeon Meadow rd. (L4), Western and Southern boundary of Flushing Cemetery, from 46th av. to Auburndale la.

Pierce av. (B 4) (L. I. C.), from Bulkhead line, S. E. to Jackson av.

Pike (F 5) (Newtown), from Maurice av., N. W. to Corona av.

Pilgrim (H 6), from Austin, N. E. to 120th.

Pinckney (N 6) (Hollis), f . Grand Central Parkway, N. E. to 212th.

Pine (B 6), from Review av., N. E. to Bradley av.

Pinegrove (K 8) from Liberty av., S. E. to Ferndale av.

Pineville lane (N 9) (S'pgfield), from Merrick rd., N. E to Williamson av.

Pinson (O 13) (Far Rockaway), from Dix, N. to Hassock.

Pinto av. (M 6) (Hollis), fr. Keno av., N. to Grand Central Parkway.

Pistol (P 6) (Creedmoor), from Hillside av., S. to 87th av.

Pitkin av. (G 9) (Woodhaven), from Boro. line, E. & S. E. to Bayside Cemetery.

Plainfield (L7) (Jamaica), from Bergen av., E. to Warwick av.

Plainview av. (O 14) (Far R'way), from Beach 21st, E. to McNeil blvd.

Platt av. (H 11), from Owego av., E. to Gherardi av

Plaza (B 4) (L. I. C.), at entrance to Queens Borough bridge.

Pleasant pl. (L 8) (Jamaica), from Merrick rd., N. W. to Hartford av.

Pleasure av. (D8) (L.I.C.), from Lawrence, S. E. to Rapelje av.

Plover (E 6), from Kolyer, E. to connecting R.R.

Plunkett av. (N 13) (Far R'way), from Faber ter., W. to Point Breeze pl.

Poe pl. (D 5), from Grout av., N. to Broadway.

Point Breeze pl. (M 13) (Far R'way), fr. Norton dr., N. E. to Mott Basin.

Point cres. (J 2), from 7th av., E. of 138th, S. E. to 141st.

Polk (E 5) (Woodside), fr. Meyers av., E. to Darvall.

Polo pl. (G7), from Woodhaven av., E. to Orville.

Pomeroy (C 4) (L. I. C.), from Jackson av., N. E. to Jamaica av., and (D3) (L. I. C.), from Astoria av., N. E. to Ditmars av.

Pompeii (M 6) (Hollis), fr. Dunton av. West, N. E. to Marengo av.

Pontiac (P 6), from 88th av., W. of Moline, S. to Braddock av.

Pope (E 4) (L. I. C.), fr. Astoria av., N. to Hazen.

Poplar (K 5) (Flushing), from Colden, N. E. to Parsons blvd.

Poppenhusen av. (G 2) (College Pt.), from Powells Cove blvd., S. of College Pt., N.E. to College pl.

Port (G 4), from Jackson av., N. to Flushing bay.

Portia pl. (P 5), fr. Hanford pkway, bet. Langford and Rushford, S. E. and N. E. to Winchester blvd.

BOROUGH OF QUEENS STREET AND AVENUE DIRECTORY—*Continued.*

Portland av. (H 10), from Hatch av., N. E. to Conduit av., and (H9), from Rockaway blvd., N. W. to Liberty av., thence now part of 106th.

Portsmouth (H 7), from Austin, N. E. to Queens blvd.

Potomac (G 9), from Sutter av., S. to Jamaica Bay.

Potter av. (C 3) (L. I. C.), from Boulevard, S. E. to Astoria av.

Powell (E 6), from Grand, S. E. to Satterlee av.

Powells Cove blvd. (H 3), from 22d rd., at Flushing Bay northward along east shore of Flush'g Bay to College Pt., thence eastward along shore to 152d pl. at Whitestone Landing.

Poyer (F 5) (Newtown), fr. South Railroad av., S.E. to Maurice av.

Poyston (M 3) (Bayside), from Kirkwood, N. E. to Highwood.

Preston (B 6), fr. Review av., N. E. to Bradley av.

Preston la. (O 10), from 149th av., E. of 218th, N. and E. to Brookville blvd.

Price (D 4), (Woodside), from Patterson av., N. to Grand av.

Prince (J 4) (Flushing), from 38d av., W. of Farrington. S. to 40th av.

Princeton (K 8), from Liberty av., S. E. to Lakewood av.

Proctor (F 7) (Glendale), from Myrtle av., N. W. to Metropolitan av.

Prospect (B 5) (L. I. C.), from Hunter av., N. E. to Webster av.

Prospect av. (D 7), from Putnam av., N. W. to L. I. R. R.

Prospect Circle (M 6), fr. Aberdeen rd., W. of Holliswood av., in a northerly direction continuing in circular formation between Holliswood av. & Chevy Chase rd.

Provoost (G 5) (Corona Heights), from Corona Heights, N. E. to Flushing River.

Pulaski (F 7), from Proctor, E. to Weisse av.

Purdy (D 3) (L I. C.), fr. Astoria av., N. E. to Wolcott av.

Puritan (H 7), fr. Puritan av., N.E. to Queens blvd.

Puritan av. (H 7), from Metropolitan av., N. E. to Queens blvd.

Purves (B 5) (L. I. C.), from Thompson av., N. W. to Crescent.

Putnam av. (D 8) cont. from Boro. line, N.E. & E. to Fresh Pond rd.

Quality (G 6), from Austin, N. E. to 120th.

Quality pl. (N 9) fr. Garrett, E. to Farmers av.

Quay (G 4), from Jackson av., N. to Flushing bay.

Quebec (J11), from Jamaica Bay, N. E. & N. W. to Liberty av.

Queens (B5) (L. I. C), fr. L. I. R. R., N. W. to Jackson av.

Queens boulevard (B 5), (L. I. C.), from Thompson av., S. E. to Jamaica av. (Jamaica.)

Quencer rd. (N 8), from Dunkirk, S. E. to Farmers blvd.

Quince (K 5) (Flushing), from Kissena blvd., N.E. to Oak av.

Quinn (D 4) (L. I. C.), fr. Grand av., N.E. to Rex pl.

Radcliff (G5) fr. Waldron, N. E. to Flushing River.

Radde (B 5) (L. I. C.), from Hunter av., N. E. to Ridge.

Radnor rd. (M 7), fr. Hillside av., E. of Midland parkway, N. and N.E. to Rosedale blvd.

Railroad av. (D 5), from Tyler av., E. to N. E. to L. I. R. R.

Rainier pl. (M 2) (Bayside), from Quitman, E. to Bell av.

Ralph (D 7), continued from Boro line, N. E. & E. to Traffic.

Ramsey (E6), fr. Grand, S. E. to Metropolitan av.

Range (P 6) (Creedmoor), from Hillside av., S. to 87th av.

Rankin av. (L 9), from Bedford, to S. of Bank.

Ransom (P 6), from 88th av., W. of Pontiac, S. to Braddock av.

Rapelje (B 4) (L. I. C.), from Jackson av., N. E. to Jamaica av.

Rapelje av. (C3) (L. I. C.), from Astoria av., N. E. to Ditmars av.

Rariton (J 11), from Jamaica Bay, N. E. & N. W. to Liberty av.

Ravenna pl. (N6) (Hollis), from Romeo, S. E. to Ferrara av.

Rawson (C 5) (L. I. C.), fr. Hunters Pt. av., N. to Meadow.

Raywick (O 7) (Queens), from 98th av., S. W. to Hollis av.

Reads la. (O18) (Far Rockaway), from Beach 9th, S. E. to McNeil av.

Redfern av. (O 18) (Far R'way), from Mott av., N. E. to McNeil av.

Redfield (O 4), from Hanford pkway, bet. Maryland rd. and Alley Pond rd., E. and S. E. to Winchester blvd.

Reeder (F 5) (Newtown), from Queens blvd., N to Maurice av.

Reel (E 5) (Woodside), fr. Fillmore, N. to Hayes.

Reeves av. (J 5), fr. Larch av., E. on north'n boundary of City of N. Y. Parental Home, to 61st av.

Regina av. (O 18) (Far R'way), from Regina blvd., W. to McBride.

Regina blvd. (O 18) (Far R'way), from Regina av., N. to City line.

Rehan pl. (G 6), fr. Webb, N. W. to Rodman.

Reinhart rd. (M 14) (R'way Beach), bet. Beach 44th and Beach 45th, S. of Amstel blvd.

Reliance pl. (H 7), fr. Austin, N.E. to Queens blvd.

Remington (K 8), from 96th av., S. E. to 109th av.

Remsen (C 3) (L. I. C.), from Grand av., N. to Boulevard.

Remsen (D 6) (Maspeth), from Mt. Olivet Cemetery, N. W. to Hull av.

Remsen av. (F 6), fr. Corinth av., N. E. to Calamus.

Rene pl. (D 7), fr. Grandview av., N. E. to Metropolitan av.

Review av. (B 6), from Bradley av., N. W. to Borden av.

Rex rd. (M 7) (Jamaica), from 175th, N. E. to Fern pl.

Reynolds (E 7), from Myrtle av., N. to Edsall av.

Rhine (P 4), from Commonwealth blvd., at Bradshaw av., S. to Grand Central pkway.

Rice (C 7), from Metropolitan av., N. W. to Maspeth av.

Richard av. (E 7) (Glendale), from Myrtle av., N. W. to Otto.

Richey (C 7), from Flushing av., N. W. to Maspeth av.

Richland av. (M 6), from Union Turnpike at Rosedale blvd., N. E. to Peck av.

Richmond Hill av. (H 7) (Richmond Hill), from Metropolitan av., N. and E. to Lefferts av.

Ridge (B 6) (L. I. C.), fr. Boulevard, S. E. to Crescent.

Ridgedale (N 9) (Springfield), from L. I. R. R., N. E. to 182d rd.

Ridgewood pl. (F7) (Glendale), from Indiana pl., N. W. to Edsall av.

Riker av. (D 3) (L. I. C.), from 7th av., S. E. and E. to Berrian av.

Rio pl. (M 6) (Jamaica), from Holliswood av., E. to Santiago.

Rio Grande (J 10), from Peconic av., N. E. to Rockaway blvd.

River (A5) (L. I. C.), from Newtown creek, N. to Dock.

Riverside av. (H 5), from 120th, near Rodman, N. W. to Flushing bay.

Riverton (N 8), from 119th rd., N. to Baisley blvd.

Roach (F 5), (Newtown), from South Railroad av., S.E. to Corona av.

Robard lane (O 7) (Queens), from Hollis av., S. to Monterey.

Robert (E9), from Bulwer pl., N. E. to Highland park.

Robin (E 6), from Kalyer, E. to Connecting R. R.

Robinson (J 4) (Flushing), from Cherry av., S.E. to Rose av.

Robinswood (L 2) (Whitestone), from Cryders la., E. of Fernwood rd., N. E. to 166th.

Rock (P 4), from 61st av., W. of Marathon av., S. to 62d av.

Rockaway Beach blvd. (G 15) (R'way Beach), fr. Beach 149th, N. E. and E. and N. E. to Beach 35th (Edgemere).

Rockaway blvd. (F 8), (Woodhaven), fr. Elderts la., at Brooklyn Boro. line, S. E. to City line.

Rockaway turnpike (M10), from Rockaway blvd., at Conduit, S.E. to City line.

Rockrose (H 7), from South Greenway terrace, E. to Burns.

Rocky Hill rd. (L 4), (Flushing), from Cemetery la., at 46th av., S.E. and N. E. to Springfield blvd.

Rodman (G 5), fr. Queens blvd., N. E. to junction of Lawrence and North Hempstead Turnpike.

Roe rd. (N 8) (Jamaica), from Irwin pl., N. E. to 120th av.

Roe pl. (L 2), from Little Bay av., at 206th, S. W. to Willets Pt. blvd.

Roff (P 4), fr. Grand Central pkway, E. to Golf rd.

Rogers (A 4) (L. I. C.), fr. Bulkhead line, S. E. to Vernon av.

Rogers (C 7), from Grand, N. W. to Maspeth av.

Roman av. (H 7), from Metropolitan av., N. E. to South Greenway ter.

Rombouts pl. (E 5), from Woodside av., N. to Broadway.

Rome dr. (N 8) (Jamaica), from Dunkirk, N. E. to Quencer rd.

Romeo (N 6) (Hollis), from Epsom Course, S. and E. and N. to Grand Central Parkway.

Rookingham (M 3) (Bayside), fr. Crocheron av., N. W. to Poppenhusen av.

Roosevelt av. (D 5), from L. I. R.R., E. to Holland av.

Rose av. (K5) (Flushing), from Peck av., N. E. to Oak av.

Rosecrans (E 3) (L. I. C.), from Astoria av., N. to Hazen.

Rosedale blvd. (N 6), from Union Turnpike at Motor Parkway, S. E. to City line at Hook Creek.

Rowan (D6), from Borden av., N. to Broadway.

Roxton (G6), from Thornton, N. E. to Queens blvd.

Ruby (G 9), from Sutter av., S. to Dumont av., and from Fairfield av., S. to Jamaica bay.

Rudder (H 4), from Jackson av., N. to Flushing bay.

Rugby av. (P4), fr. Thornhill av., E. of 248th, S.E. and N. E. to Thebes la.

Rural av. (N 9) (Springfield), from Williamson av., N. E. to Sears.

Rushford (P 4), from Winchester blvd., opp. Sidney, S. W. and S. to Southern parkway.

Rushville rd. (M 6) (Jamaica), from Grand Central Parkway, N. W. to Black Stump rd.

BOROUGH OF QUEENS STREET AND AVENUE DIRECTORY—*Continued.*

Ruskin (G 6), from Queens blvd., N. E. to 120th.

Rust (D 6), from Clinton av., S. E. to Flushing av.

Ruth (G 7), fr. Woodhaven av., N. to Union Turnpike.

Rutledge (B 4) (L. I. C.), from Freeman av., N. E. to Graham av.

Ryder av. (J 11), from Lefferts av., S. E. to 128th.

Rye pl. (M 7), from Brinkerhoff av., S. E. to Hilburn av.

Ryerson av. (E 6) (Maspeth), from Fulton, N. to Railroad av.

Sabre (P 6) (Creedmoor), from 88th av., S. to Braddock av.

Sackett (G 5) (Corona), from Roosevelt av., N. E. to Ferguson.

Sage (O 18) (Far R'way), from Empire av., N. W. to Brunswick av.

St. Claud rd. (K 14) (R'way Beach), from Scheer to Amstel blvd.

St. Felix av. (D 8), from connecting line nr. Cooper, E. to Epsilon pl.

St. Germans (F 7) (Glendale), from Proctor, E. to Weisse av.

St. James (F5), fr. Queens blvd., N.E. to South Railroad av.

St Mark's av. (J15) (R'way Beach), from Beach 102d, W. to Beach 110th.

St. Nicholas av. (D7), cont. from Boro. line, S. E. to Myrtle av.

Salerno av. (M 6) (Hollis), from Palermo av., E. to Clio av.

Salvini (H 6), fr. Queens blvd., N. E to 120th.

Sample (G6), from Austin, N. E. to 120th.

Samuelson (F 7), from Ankener, N. E. to Division.

Sanborn av. (O 4), fr. Hanford pkway, N. E. to Annandale la.

Sancho av. (M 6) (Hollis), fr. Keno av., N. & N. E. to Grand Central pkway.

Sanders pl. (K 8), from 95th av. S. E. to 101st av.

Sandol (E 8), from Alden av., N. to Myrtle av.

Sanford (B 4) (L. I. C.), from Bulkhead line, S.E. to Sherman.

Sanford av. (H 4) (Flushing), from Flushing river, N.E. and E. to Northern blvd.

Santiago (M6), from Grand Central Parkway, S. E. to Palermo av.

Sapphire (G 9), fr. Sutter av., S. to Dumont av., and from Stanley av., S. to Jamaica bay.

Sarah (H 7), from Union Turnpike, N. to Metropolitan av.

Sargent (P 6), fr. Hillside av., S. to 87th av.

Satterlee av. (F7) (Middle Village), from Metropolitan av., N. E. to Woodhaven.

Saull (J 4) (Flushing), fr. Maple av., S. to Peck av.

Saultell (H 5), from Rodman, N. to Corona av.

Saunders pl. (F 6), from Woodhaven av., S. E. to Jupiter av.

Savannah (J 10), fr. Peconic av., N. E. to R'way blvd.

Sawyer la. (O 6), fr. Grand Central pkway, N. E. to Springfield blvd.

Sawyer pl. (O 6), fr. Whitehall ter., N. E. to Sawyer la.

Sayres av. (M 8) (Jamaica) from New York blvd. N. E. to Brinkerhoff av.

Scheer (K 14) (Rockaway Beach), from St. Cloud rd., S. E. to Crugers rd.

Schenck av. (E 6) (Maspeth), from Grand, N. to Queens blvd.

Schieren (D4) (Woodside), from Patterson av., N. E. to Wilson av.

Schley (E 7), from Myrtle av., N. to Edsall av.

School (B 5) (L. I. C), fr. Borden av., N. to Thompson av.

Schroeder (D 5) (Woodside), from Queens blvd., N. to Mansion.

Schurz av. (E4) (L. I. C.), from 12th, E. to Flushing bay.

Scudder (G 6), fr. Queens blvd., N. E. to 120th.

Sea Girt (N 14) (Edgemere), from Rockaway Beach blvd., E. to Beach 32d.

Sea Girt av. (P 14) (Far R'way), from McNeil blvd., W. to Beach 32d.

Seabury (F 5), fr. Grand, S. E. to Woodhaven av.

Seafoam ct. (L 14) (R'way Beach), from Beach 63d to Beach 62d.

Seaford pl. (M 3) (Bayside), from Newlands, E. to Bayshore rd.

Sears (N 9) (Springfield), from Springfield blvd., N. W. to 122d av.

Seaside av. (J 15) (R'way Beach), from Ocean Promenade, N. W. to Beach Channel dr.

Seattle (H 8) (Woodhaven), from Suwanee av., N. W. to Liberty av., thence now part of 105th.

Second (D 5) (Woodside), from Woodside av., N. to 21st av.

Second av. (C 4) (L. I. C.), from Jamaica av., N. E. to Astoria av., and (D3) (L.I.C.), fr. Ditmars av., N. E. to Winthrop av.

Second av. (M 2) (College Pt.), from Tallman cres., E. to Powells Cove blvd., and (J 2) (Whitestone), from 145th pl., N. E. to 150th.

Second pl. (N3) (Bayside), from Bayside blvd., E. to Little Neck bay.

Second rd. (J 2) (Whitestone), from 147th, S. of 2d av., E. to 149th.

Sedgwick (E 7), from Halleck av., N. to Cornelia.

See rd. (P 5), from Southern pkway, bet. Cullman and 73d avs., S. E. to 73d av.

Selfridge (G 6), fr. Fleet, S. to Metropolitan av.

Selover rd. (N9) (Jamaica), fr. Merrick blvd. N, E. to 180th.

Seminole av. (J 6), from Queens blvd., N. W. to Rodman.

Seneca av. (D 8), from Myrtle av., S. E. to St. Felix av.

Seventeenth (E 5), from Queens blvd., N. to 12th.

Seventeenth av. (D 4) (L. I. C.), from Jackson av., N.E. to Vandeventer av., and (D 3) (L. I. C.), fr. Astoria av., N.E. to Wolcott av.

Seventeenth av. (K 2) (Whitestone), from Parsons blvd., at proposed park, E. and N. E. to Little Neck blvd.

Seventeenth rd. (K 2), fr. Parsons blvd., at proposed park, E. to Utopia parkway.

Seventh (A 5) (L. I. C.), from Bulkhead line, S. E. to Jackson av.

Seventh (D4) (Woodside), from Jackson av., N. to Grand av.

Seventh av. (C4), (L.I.C.), from Jamaica av., N. E. to Astoria av., and (D3) (L.I.C.), fr. Ditmars av., N. E. to Bulkhead line.

Seventh av. (M 2) (College Pt.), from Powells Cove blvd., S. of College Pt., E. to Utopia parkway.

Seventh rd. (J 2), from Powells Cove blvd., at Powells Cove, S. E. to 144th.

Seventieth av. (J 6), from 120th, S. of Jewel av., N. E. to Kissena rd.

Seventieth rd. (J 6), from 120th, S. of 70th av., N. E. to Kissena rd.

Seventy-first av. (J6), from 120th, S of 70th rd., N. E. and E. to 172d, and (N 5), from 220th, S. of 69th av., N.E. to Springfield blvd., and from 234th, E. to Southern parkway.

Seventy-first rd. (J6), from 120th, S. of 71st av., N. E. to Kissena rd.

Seventy-second av. (J 6), from 120th, S. of 71st rd. N.E to Kissena rd., and from Aguilar av., at 157th, E. to 166th. and (O 5), from 234th, S. of Cullman av., E. to Southern pkway, and (P 5), from 247th, E. to 249th.

Seventy-second dr. (J 6), from 120th, S. of 72d rd., N. E. to 153d.

Seventy-second rd. (J 6), from 120th, S. of 72d av., N. E. to Kissena rd.

Seventy-third av. (J 6), from 120th, S. of 72d dr., S.E. to Winchester blvd., and (P4), from 247th, N. E. to Little Neck rd.

Seventy-fourth (G 8) (Woodhaven), fr. Park la. So., S. to Jamaica av.

Seventy-fourth av. (L 6), from 175th, S. of 73d av., N. E. to Utopia pkway, and (O 5), from Springfield blvd., S. of 73d av., N. E. to 223d, and from 234th, E. to Southern pkway, and (P 5), from 247th, N. of Underhill av., N.E. to Langston av.

Seventy-fourth rd. (O 5), from Springfield blvd., S. of 74th av., N. E. to 223d.

Seventy-fifth (G 8) (Woodhaven), from Jamaica av., S. E. to 101st av., and from Liberty av., S. to Sutter av.

Seventy-fifth av. (J 6), fr. 120th, S. of 73d av., N.E. to Grand Central pkway.

Seventy-fifth rd. (J 6), fr. 120th, S. of 75th av., N. E. to 166th.

Seventy-sixth (G8) (Woodhaven), from Park la. So., S. E. to Sutter av.

Seventy-sixth av. (J 6), from 120th, S. of 75th rd., N. E. to 182d, and (O 5), from Springfield blvd., S. of 75th av., E. to 225th, and from 229th, E. to 231st, and (Q 4), from Union Turnpike, N. E. to City line.

Seventy-sixth rd. (J 6), from 120th, S. of 76th av., N. E. to 166th.

Seventy-seventh (G 8) (Woodhaven), from Jamaica av., S. E. to Sutter av.

Seventy-seventh av. (J 6), from 120th, S. of 76th rd., N. E. to 166th, and (O 5), from Springfield blvd., S. of 76th av., E. to 225th, and from 231st, N. E. to 232d, and (Q 5), from Union Turnpike, N. E. to City line.

Seventy-seventh rd. (J 6), from 120th, S. of 77th av., N. E. to 173d.

Seventy-eighth (G 8) (Woodhaven), from Jamaica av., S. E. to Sutter av.

Seventy-eighth av. (J 7), from 120th, S. of 77th rd., N. E. to 166th, and (P 5), fr. Commonwealth blvd., S. Elkmont av., N. E. to 246th, and (Q 5), from Union Turnpike, N.E. to City line.

Seventy-eighth rd. (J 7), from 120th, S. of 78th av., N. E to 164th.

Seventy-ninth (G8) (Woodhaven), from Park la. So., S. E. to Jamaica av., and from 92d av., S. to Rockaway blvd., and from Glenmore av., S. to Sutter av.

Seventy-ninth av. (J 6), from 138th, N. of Union Turnpike, N.E. to Union Turnpike at 164th, and (O 5), from Springfield blvd., S. of Kingsbury av., N. E. to Tomah, and from Stronghurst av., N. E. to Winchester blvd., and fr. Commonwealth blvd., N. E. to 246th, and (Q 5), from Union Turnpike, N. E. to City line.

Seward av. (O 6), fr. 87th av., E. of Stronghurst av., N. E. and E. to Winchester blvd.

Shaler (E 7), from Chaffee), N. E. and N. to Traffic.

BOROUGH OF QUEENS STREET AND AVENUE DIRECTORY—*Continued.*

Shapon pl. (L 8), now part of 109th rd.

Sheer (K 14) (Rockaway Beach), fr. Crugers rd., N.W. to St. Cloud rd.

Sheffield (J 15) (R'way Beach), name changed to St. Marks av.

Sheffield av. (N10) (Springfield), fr. Farmers blvd., S. of Balsam av., S.E. to 211th.

Shelbourne (H 7), from Austin, N. E. to Queens blvd.

Sherman (B 4) (L I. C.), from North Jane, N. E. to Grand av.

Sherman pl. (B 4) (L I. C.), from 14th, N. E. to South Jane.

Shiloh av. (P5), fr. Union Turnpike, at Commonwealth blvd., N. E. to City line.

Shore av. (K8) (Jamaica), from Remington, N. E. to 154th.

Shore Acres blvd. (K 2), from 7th av., E. of 154th N. and E. and S. to 7th av., at Little Neck Bay.

Shorthill (H 7), fr. South Greenway terrace, N. to Puritan av.

Shoshone (J11), fr. Jamaica bay, N. E. and N. W. to Liberty av.

Siboutsen (F 4), fr. Junction av., N. E. to 43d.

Sidney (P 4), from Winchester blvd., W. of Marathon av., S. to 61st av.

Sidway pl. (N 9), from Selover, S. E. to Farmers blvd.

Sigel av. (E 4) (L. I. C.), from 12th, E. to Flushing bay.

Sigourney av. (O 7) (Bellair), fr. 98th av., S. E. to 218th.

Sigsbee pl. (E 7), fr. Shaler, N. E. and N. to Metropolitan av.

Silver (D 7), from Forest av., E. to Fresh Pond rd.

Simonson (E 5), fr. Grand, N. to Queens blvd.

Simpson (C 7), from Metropolitan av., N. W. to Maspeth av.

Singer (M 8) (Jamaica), from Haldimand, N. W. to Burtis.

Sixteenth (E 5), fr. Woodside av., N. to 12th.

Sixteenth av. (D 4) (L. I. C.), from Jamaica av., N. E. to Astoria av., (D 3) (L. I. C.), from Wolcott av., N. E. to Bulkhead line.

Sixteenth av. (K 2) (Whitestone), from Locke av., E. of 154th, N. E. to Little Neck blvd.

Sixteenth rd. (K 2), from 147th, S. of 15th dr., E. to 150th pl., and from 154th, E. to Utopia parkway.

Sixth (A5) (L. I. C.), from Bulkhead line, S. E. to Jackson av.

Sixth av. (C 4) (L. I. C.), from Jamaica av., N. E. to Astoria av., (D 3) (L. I.C.), from Ditmars av., N. E. to Winthrop av.

Sixth av. (H 2) (College Pt.), from Poppenhusen av., at 119th, E. to 131st, and (J 2), from 145th pl., E. to Merritt rd., and from 151st, E. to 151st pl.

Sixth rd. (K 2) (Whitestone), from 151st, S. of 6th av., E. to Powells Cove blvd.

Sixtieth av. (J 5), from Wateredge av., S. of 59th rd., E. and S. E. to Kissena rd., and (L 5), from 169th to 170th, and from 171st to 172d, and (P 4), from Winchester blvd., N. E. and E. to City line.

Sixtieth rd. (P 4), from Little Neck rd., S. of 60th av., E. to 262d.

Sixty-first av. (H 5), from Hewitt av., W. of Flushing river, S. E, E. and N. E. to City line.

Sixty-first rd. (H 5), from Wateredge av., N of Rodman, N. E. to Rodman, and from 185th, at Cedar Grove Cem., E. and S. E. to Reeves av.

Sixty-second av. (H 5), fr. Wateredge av., S. of Rodman, N. E. to 180th, and from 185th, at Cedar Grove Cem., E and S E. to Reeves av., and (N 5), fr. 220th, S. of 61st av., N. E. to Springfield blvd., and (O4), from Hanford pkway, N.E. to Redfield, and from 244th, S. E. and N. E. and E. to 251st.

Sixty-second dr. (H 5), fr. Wateredge av., S. of 62d rd., N. E. to 180th.

Sixty-second rd. (H 5), fr. Wateredge av., S. of 62d av., N. E. to 180th, and from 185th, at Cedar Grove Cem., E. to 142d.

Sixty-third av. (H5), from Wateredge av., S. of 62d dr., N. E. to 180th, and from 185th, at Cedar Grove Cem., E. to 142d, and (P 4), from Marathon av., S. of 62d av., E. to 255th.

Sixty-third dr. (H 5), from Wateredge av., S. of 63d rd., N. E. to 180th.

Sixty-third rd. (H5), from Wateredge av., S. of 63d av., N. E. to 180th, and from 185th, at Cedar Grove Cem., E. to 186th.

Sixty-fourth av. (H 5), fr. Wateredge av., N. of Webb av., N.E. to 180th, and (K 5), from Kissena rd., E. to 155th, and (L 5), from Fresh Meadow pkway, at 61st av., N.E. to Easthampton rd.

Sixty-fourth rd. (H 5), fr. Wateredge av., S. of Webb av., N.E. to 180th, at Cedar Grove Cem.

Sixty-fifth av. (H 6), from Wateredge av., S. of 64th rd., N. E. to 180th, at Cedar Grove Cem., and (K 5), from Kissena rd., E. to 183d, and (N5), fr. 220th, S. of 64th av., N. E. to Springfield blvd., and from 233d, N. E. to Easthampton rd.

Sixty-fifth rd. (H 6), from Wateredge av., S. of 64th av., N. E. to 180th, at Cedar Grove Cem.

Sixty-sixth av. (H6), from Wateredge av., S. of 65th rd., N. E. to 180th, at Cedar Grove Cem., and (N5), from 220th, S. of 65th av., N.E. to Springfield blvd., and fr. 233d, N.E. to Easthampton rd.

Sixty-sixth rd. (H6), from Wateredge av., S. of 66th av., N. E. to 180th, at Cedar Grove Cem.

Sixty-seventh av. (H 6), from Wateredge av., S. of 66th rd., N.E. to 180th at Cedar Grove Cem., and (K 5), from Kissena rd., E. and N.E. to Easthampton rd.

Sixty-seventh rd. (H 6), from Wateredge av., S. of 67th av., N.E. to 180th at Cedar Grove Cem.

Sixty-eighth av. (J 6), from Wateredge av., S. of 67th rd., N.E. to 180th at Cedar Grove Cem., and from 144th, N.E to Melbourne av., and (N5), from 220th, S. of 67th av., N. E. to Springfield blvd., and from 233d, N. E. to 234th.

Sixty-eighth dr. (J 6), fr. Wateredge av., S. of 68th rd., N. E. to Melbourne av.

Sixty-eighth rd. (J 6), fr. Wateredge av., S. of 68th, N. E. to 188th, and from Larch av., N. E to Melbourne av.

Sixty-ninth av. (H 6), fr. 120th, S. of Meteor, N.E., E. and N. E. to Easthampton rd.

Sixty-ninth rd. (H6), from 120th, S. of 69th av., N. E. to Kissena rd.

Skillman (B 5) (L. I. C.), from Academy, S. and E. to Jackson av.

Skillman av. (C 5) (L. I. C.), fr. Thompson av., N. E. & E. to Woodside av.

Sloan (N9), from 139th av., N. to 137th av.

Slocum (E 8), from Anna pl., N. to Myrtle av.

Slocum Crescent (H 7), fr. Continental av., S. E. and N. E. to Burns.

Sloop (H 4), from Jackson av., N. to Flushing bay.

Smart (J 4) (Flushing), from Cherry av., S.E. to Negundo av.

Smith (M 8), (Jamaica), from Foch blvd. S. to Baisley blvd.

Snell av. (O 4), from Jackson av., at 46th av., S. E. and E. and N. E. to Jackson av.

Soho pl. (M 6) (Jamaica), from Holliswood av., E. to Santiago.

Sophie (C 7), fr. Flushing av., N.W. to Maspeth av.

Sothern av. (G 6) (Newtown), fr. Queens blvd., N. W. to South Railroad av.

South (G 5), fr. Martense av., S. E. to Rodman.

South rd. (K 8) (Jamaica), from Remington, N. E. to Merrick blvd.

South Conduit av. (K 10), from 128th, S. of the Conduit, E. to City line.

South Greenway Terrace (H 7), from Middleway Circle, S. E. to Union Turnpike.

South Jane (B4) (L. I. C.), from Vernon av., S. E. to Plaza.

South Railroad av. (F 5) (Elmhurst), fr. Queens blvd., N. E. to Tiemann av.

South Washington (B 4) (L. I. C.), from Academy, S. E. to Jackson av.

Southern parkway (P 5), from junction of Hanford and Douglaston pkways, S. to Grand Central pkway.

Southgate (N 9), fr. 137th av., S. to Edgewood.

Spa pl. (K8), from Lakewood av., S. E. to Arlington ter.

Spencer av. (O 6), from Grand Central parkway, E. to Hillside av.

Sprague (F 7) (Glendale), from Myrtle av., N. W. to Edsall av.

Spray View av. (M 14) (Edgemere), fr. Beach 86th, E. to Beach 82d.

Spring (B 6), from Review av., N. E. to Bradley av.

Springfield blvd. (N 4), fr. Harnay la., bet. 218th & 220th, S. E. and S. W. to 168d av.

Springfield la. (N 10), fr. Springfield blvd., N. of 147th av., S. E. to 152d av.

Spruce (J 4), from Liberty av., N. W. to St. Anns av. (Richmond Hill.)

Spruce (O 6) (Queens), from Springfield rd., E. to Jefferson av.

Stafford av. (G 7), from Metropolitan av., N. E. to Yellowstone av.

Standard pl. (K 7), (Jamaica), from Jamaica av. S. to Archer av.

Stanhope (D 7) continued fr. Boro. line, N. E. to Metropolitan av.

Stanley av. (G 9) (Woodhaven), from Boro. line, E. & S. E. to 128th.

Starling (E 6), from Kolyer, E. to Grand.

Starr (C 7), continued fr. Boro. line, N. E. to Metropolitan av.

Starr av. (B 6) from Pine, N. W. to Borden av.

Statham (M 2) (Bayside), from Neander av., N. to Gellert av.

Statham pl. (M 3) (Bayside) from Poppenhusen av., N. to Mulford av.

Station rd. (K 4), from 156th, E. to 162d, and (L 4), from Northern blvd., S. of L.I.R.R., N. E. to Cross Isld. blvd.

Stead (J 7), fr. Keystone, S. to Degraw.

Stedman (D5), from Betts. av., E. to Drake.

Steenwyck (G 4), fr. Polk av., N. to Jackson av.

Steinway (C 4) (L. I. C.), from Jackson av., N. E. to Jamaica av.

BOROUGH OF QUEENS STREET AND AVENUE DIRECTORY—*Continued.*

Steinway av. (D 8) (L. I. C.), from Astoria av., N. E. to Winthrop av.

Stemler (C 4) (L. I. C.), from Jackson av., N. E. to Jamaica av.

Stephen (D 8), from Wyckoff av., N. E. to Myrtle av.

Steuben (F 7) (Glendale), fr. Proctor, E. to Weisse av.

Stevens (B 8) (L. I. C.), from Fulton av., N. to Bulkhead line.

Stewart lane (P 7), from 100th av., E. and S. E. to Hempstead av.

Stockholm (C 7) cont'd fr. Boro line, N.E. to Woodward av.

Stockton (N9) (Jamaica), from Farmers blvd., N. W. to Zuider av.

Stone (D 5) (L. I. C.), from Queens blvd., N. to Barnett av.

Stoothoff av. (J 9), from Rockaway blvd., N. W. to Liberty av., thence now 114th.

Story (G 5) (Corona Heights), from Corona av., N. E. to Hewitt av.

Story rd. (L 14) (R'way Beach), fr. Beach 69th, E. to 68th.

Stoutenburg av. (D 5), from Maurice av., E. to Decker.

Stowe pl. (K 2) (Whitestone), from Barlow, N. W. to Arndt.

Stratford (H 7), from Metropolitan av., N. E. to Kessel.

Stratton (H 8) (College Pt.). from 130th, at 23d av., S. E. to 31st av.

Strong (G 5), fr. Barkins, N. E. to Hewitt av.

Stronghurst av. (O 6), fr. 87th av., E. of Grand Central pkway, N. E. to Underhill av.

Stryker av. (D 5) (Woodside), fr. Woodside av., S. E. to Roosevelt av.

Styler rd. (K 8), fr. Tuckerton, N. E. to 156th.

Suburban (E 8), fr. Epsilon pl., E. to Folsom av.

Suffolk dr. (N 8), from Newburg, E. to Farmers blvd.

Sullivan rd. (N 8), from Dunkirk, N. E. to Quencer rd.

Summer (H7), from South Greenway ter., North 2 blocks.

Summerfield (D 8), from Wyckoff av., N. E. to Myrtle av.

Summit (E 7), from Metropolitan av., N. W. to Eliot av.

Sunbury rd. (N 9) (Jamaica), fr. Merrick blvd. N.E. to 120th av.

Sunfield av. (Q4), fr. Ethan av., N. E. to City line.

Sunnyside (N 18) (Far Rockaway), fr. Mott av., N. E. to Beach 28th N.

Sunswick (B 4) (L. I. C.), from North Jane, N. E. to Graham av.

Surrey rd. (L 6), fr. Union Turnpike, E. of Utopia parkway. S. E. to Midland pkway.

Sutphin blvd. (K 7), (Jamaica), fr. Hillside av., S. E. to Rockaway blvd.

Sutter av. (G 9) (Woodhaven), fr. Boro. line, E. & S. E. to 150th.

Suwanee av. (H 9), from Rockaway blvd., N.E. to Van Wyck blvd., that part E. thereof being now part of 109th av.

Suydam (C 7), continued from Boro. line, N. E. to Woodward av.

Suydam (O 7), (Hollis), fr. 99th av., S. E. to Hollis av.

Swan rd. (L 14) (R'way Beach), fr. Beach 69th, E. to Beach 68th.

Sybilla (G 7), from Metropolitan av., S. & S. E. to Union Turnpike.

Sylvan (E. 8), from Alden av., N. to Millwood av.

Syringa pl. (J 4) (Flushing), from Ash av. to Beech av.

Talbot (J 7), from Metropolitan av., N. to Iris.

Tallman blvd. (H 8), from 29th av., at Flushing Bay, S. and E. along shore of Flushing Bay to Willets Pt. blvd.

Tallman cres. (H2) (College Pt.), from 129th, S. of Powells Cove blvd., S.W. and S. to 3d av.

Tappen ter. (E 8), from Vermont av., N. to Cypress av.

Taylor (C 8) (L. I. C.), fr. Remsen, E. to Crescent.

Teal dr. (M 14) (Rockaway Beach), bet Beach 41st and Beach 41st pl., S. of Norton av.

Temple (B 8) (L. I. C.), fr. Boulevard, S.E. to Crescent av.

Tennessee (J 10), fr. Peconic av., N. E. to Rockaway blvd.

Tennis pl. (H7) fr. Exeter, N. E. to Queens blvd.

Tenth (A 5) (L. I. C.), fr. Bulkhead line, S. E. to Jackson av.

Tenth (D 5) (Woodside), from Broadway, N. to Jackson av.

Tenth (L 10), from Cornell Basin, E. to Garfield av.

Tenth av. (C 4) (L. I. C.), from Jamaica av., N. E. to Astoria av., (D 8) (L. I. C.), fr. Winthrop av., N. E. to Bulkhead line.

Tenth av. (G 2) (College Pt.), from 115th, S. of 9th av., E. to 117th, and fr. 120th E. to College pl., and (J 2), from 141st, E. to Parsons blvd., and from Parsons blvd., E. to Utopia parkway.

Terry (M 9), (Jamaica), from Baisley blvd., S. E. to 133d av.

Tesla pl. (F 7) (Glendale), from Myrtle av., N.W. to Edsall pl.

Thames (J 11), fr. Jamaica Bay, N. E. & N. W. to Liberty av.

Thebes la. (O 4), fr. Overbrook dr., at Snell av., N. E. and S. E. to Overbrook dr.

Thedford av. (H 9) (Woodhaven), from Sutter av., S. to Conduit av., and from Dunham av., S. to Jamaica Bay.

Theodore (D 8) (L. I. C.), from Astoria av., N. E. to Wolcott av.

Theresa (G 7), fr. Sybilla, N. to Metropolitan av.

Thew av. (F 6), from Corinth av., S. E. to Satterlee av.

Third (A 5) (L. I. C.), fr. Front, E. to Canal.

Third (D 5) (Woodside), fr. Queens blvd., N. to Jackson av.

Third av. (C 4) (L. I. C.), from Jamaica av., N. E. to Newtown av.

Third av. (H 2) (College Pt.), from Powells Cove blvd., E. to Powells Cove blvd., and (J 2) (Whitestone), fr. Parsons blvd. E. to Powells Cove blvd.

Third rd. (H 2) (College Pt.), from Powells Cove blvd., E. of 121st, E. to 3d av.

Thirteenth (A5) (L.I. C.), from Bulkhead line, S. E. to Hunter av.

Thirteenth (E 5) (Woodside), from Broadway, N. E. to 12th.

Thirteenth av. (D4) (L. I. C)., from Jamaica av., N. E. to Astoria av., (D 8) (L. I. C.), from Wolcott av., N. E. to Bulkhead line.

Thirteenth av. (G 2) (College Pt.), from Powells Cove blvd. at Flushing Bay, E. to 114th, and from 122d, E to 126th and from 128th, E. to 131st. and from 133d pl., E. to 147th, and from 154th E. to Fernwood rd., and from 166th, E. to Utopia pkway. and from Bell blvd., N. E. to 215th pl.

Thirteenth dr. (J 2), from 144th, S. of 13th rd., E. to Parsons blvd.

Thirteenth rd. (H2), from 129th, S. of L.I. R.R., E. to 133d pl., and from 144th, E. to Parsons blvd.

Thirtieth (F5), fr. Roosevelt av., N. to Bowery bay.

Thirtieth av. (H 8), from Tallman blvd., at Flushing Bay. E. to Bayside av.. and from Utopia parkway, N. E. to Jordan, and (O 8), from Bayshore rd., E. of Little Neck Bay, E. to Bayshore rd.

Thirty-first (F 5), from Roosevelt av., N. to Bowery bay.

Thirty-first av. (H 8). from Tallman blvd., at Flushing Bay, E. to Willets Pt. blvd., and (O 8), fr. Bayshore rd., E. of Little Neck Bay, E. to Bayshore rd.

Thirty-first dr. (J8), from Ulmer, S of 31st rd., N. E. to Farrington, and from 138th, N. E. to 140th.

Thirty-first rd. (H 8); fr. Tallman blvd. at Flushing Bay, E. & N.E. to 30th av., nr. Union and (M 8), from 216th E. to 218th.

Thirty-second (F 5), from Roosevelt av., N. to Bowery bay.

Thirty-second (L4) (Flushing), from Queens av., N. to Franconia av.

Thirty-second av. (J 8), fr. Lawrence, at 132d, N. E. and E. and N. E. to Bell blvd., and (M 8), from Bell blvd., E. to Little Neck blvd., and (O 8), from Bayshore rd., E. of Little Neck Bay, E. to Bayshore rd.

Thirty-second rd. (L 8), from Cross Isld. blvd., S. of 32d av., N. E. to Jordan and (M 8), from Bell blvd., E. to Little Neck blvd., and (O 8), from Bayshore rd., E. of Little Neck Bay, E. to Douglaston blvd.

Thirty-third (F 5), from Roosevelt av., N. to Bowery bay.

Thirty-third av. (H 4), fr. Lawrence, S. of 32d av., E. to Downing, and from Miller, E. to Farrington, and from Leavitt, S. E. to Union, and fr. Union E. and N.E. to 219th and (O8) from Bayshore rd., E. of Little Neck Bay, E. to Bayshore rd.

Thirty-third rd. (K 8), fr. Murray, S. of 33d av., E. to 153d, and from 209th, N. E. to 215th.

Thirty-fourth (F 5), from Roosevelt av., N. to Bowery bay.

Thirty-fourth av. (H 4), fr. Lawrence, at Flushing Bay, E. to Downing, and from Linden, E. to 137th, and from Leavitt, S. E. to Union, and from Union, E. to 153d, and from 192d, at Cross Isld. Blvd., N.E. to Little Neck blvd., and (O8), from Bayshore rd., E. of Little Neck Bay, E. to Bayshore rd.

Thirty-fourth rd. (M 8), from 209th, S. of 34th av., N. E. to 218th.

Thirty-fifth (F 5), from Roosevelt av., N. to Bowery bay.

Thirty-fifth av. (J4), from L.I.R.R., N. of Northern blvd., N.E. to Little Neck blvd., and (O 8), from Bayshore rd., E. of Little Neck Bay, E. to Bay shore rd.

Thirty-sixth (F 5), from Roosevelt av., N. to Bowery bay.

Thirty-sixth av. (K 4), fr. Lawrence, S. of Northern blvd., E. to Prince, and from Cross Isld. blvd., N. E. to 221st, and (O4) fr. Bayshore rd., E. of Little Neck Bay, E. to Bayshore rd.

Thirty-sixth rd. (J 4), fr. Lawrence, S. of 36th av., E. to Prince.

Thirty-seventh (G 5), fr. Hunt, N. W. to Flushing bay.

BOROUGH OF QUEENS STREET AND AVENUE DIRECTORY—*Continued.*

Thirty-seventh av. (H 4), from Wateredge av., at Flushing River, N. E. to 147th, and (L 4), from Utopia parkway, E. to Cross Isld. blvd., and (N 3), from 221st, E. to Easthampton rd., and (O 3), from Bayshore rd., E. of Little Neck Bay, E. to Bayshore rd., and from Old House Landing rd., N. E. to Duer.

Thirty-seventh rd. (O 3), from Bayshore rd., E. of Little Neck Bay, E. to Douglaston blvd., and from Will pl., N. E. to 37th av.

Thirty-eighth (F 4), from Jackson av., N. to Flushing bay.

Thirty-eighth av. (J 4), from Prince, S. of 37th av., N. E. to 150th and (L 4), from Cross Isld. blvd., N. E. to 224th, and (N 3), from 230th, E. to 233rd, and (O 3), from McKnight dr., to Will pl., and from Bayshore rd., N. E. to Duer.

Thirty-eighth dr. (N 3), from 224th, E. to Easthampton rd., and from 230th, E. to Douglaston blvd., and (O 3), from 240th, E. to Will pl.

Thirty-eighth rd. (N 3), from 230th, E. to Will pl.

Thirty-ninth (F 4), from Fillmore av., N. to Riker av.

Thirty-ninth av. (J 4), from Lawrence, N. E. to Union, and (L 4), from 170th, E. to Easthampton rd., and (N 3), from 230th, E. to Wainscott av., and (O3), from Bayshore rd., N. E. to Duer.

Thirty-ninth rd. (N 4), fr. 224th, E. to Easthampton rd., and from 230th, E. to McKnight dr., and (O3), from Westmoreland, N. E. to Boro line.

Thomas (B 6), fr. Review av., N E. to Bradley av.

Thompson av. (B 5) (L. I. C.), from Jackson av., E. to Queens blvd

Thornhill av. (P 4), from Overbrook dr., N. E. to City line.

Thornton (G 6), fr. Fleet, N.W. and N.E. to Queens blvd.

Thorpe rd. (M 9), fr 125th av., N. E. to Merrill.

Thrall av. (H 9), fr. Sutter av., S. to Jamaica bay.

Thrush (E 6), fr Kolyer, E. to Connecting R. R.

Thurman (G 6), from Queens blvd., N. E. to 120th.

Thursby av. (L 14) (R'way Beach), from Barbadoes dr., E. to Beach 63d.

Thurston (N 9), fr. Farmers rd., S. E. to 140th av.

Tiemann av. (G 5), from Corona av., N. W. to Polk av.

Tilly av. (L 7) (Jamaica), from New York blvd., E. to 165th.

Tioga dr. (N8), fr. Dunkirk, N. E. and S. E. to Farmers blvd.

Tisdale (B 3) (L. I. C.), from Stevens, E. to Remsen.

Titus (C4) (L. I. C.), from Jackson av., N. E. to Jamaica av. (D 3) (L. I. C.), from Astoria av., N. E. to Wolcott av.

Todd pl. (O 5), fr. Union T'npike, S to Hatton la.

Toledo (F 5) (Newtown), from Queens blvd., S. to South Railroad av.

Tomah (O 5), from Cloverdale blvd., S. to Union Turnpike.

Tompkins pl. (F 8) (Glendale). from Indiana pl., N. W. to Edsall av.

Totten (L 2) (Whitestone), from 7th av., E. of Burton, S. to Utopia parkway.

Towaly av. (O 13) (Far R'way), from Farragut, S. E. and S. to Cornaga av.

Townsend av. (C 5) (Laurel Hill), from Laurel Hill blvd., E. to Borden av.

Towns pl. (C5), from Laurel Hill av., E. to Bliss.

Traffic (D 7), from Fresh Pond rd., S. E. to Sigsbee pl.

Trains Meadow rd. (F 3), from Ditmars av., S. E. to Astoria av.

Trappe pl. (L7) (Jamaica), from Puntine, E. to Cliffside.

Traverse rd. (P 3), from 251st, N.E. to Browvale la.

Tredell (K 2) (Whitestone), from Roxboro av., E. to Botanic.

Tredwell (G 6), fr. Queens blvd., N.E. to 120th.

Trimble av. (D 5), from Queens blvd., N. to Woodside av.

Trimble pl. (D 5), from Woodside av., N. to Broadway.

Trist pl. (N13) (Far Rockaway), from Bayswater, N. to Westbourne av.

Trotter (F 7) (Glendale), fr. Ford, N. E. to Weisse av.

Troutman (C7), continued from Boro. line, N. E. to Metropolitan av.

Troutville rd. (N 9), (Jamaica), from Irwin pl. N. E. to 178th.

Trowbridge (C8) (L.I C), fr. Boulevard, E. to Van Alst av.

Tryon rd. (L6) (Jamaica), from 80th dr., E. to Utopia pkway, S. and S. E. to Aberdeen rd.

Tuckahoe av. (J 9), from R'way blvd., N. E. to Van Wyck blvd., that part E. thereof being now part of 111th av.

Tuckerton (K 8), from Blakely S. to South rd.

Tudor pl. (E 8), from Vermont av., N. to Cypress av.

Tudor rd. (L6) (Jamaica), fr. Grand Central parkway, E. of Doncaster pl., N. E. to Chevy Chase rd.

Turin dr. (N 8), from Newburg, E. to Farmers blvd.

Twelfth (A 5) (L. I. C.), from Vernon av., S. E. to Jackson.

Twelfth (E 5) (Woodside), from Fillmore av., N. and N. E. to 22d.

Twelfth av. (D4) (L. I. C.), from Jamaica av., N. E. to Astoria av., and (D3), (L. I. C.), from Wolcott av., N. E. to Bulkhead line.

Twelfth av. (G 2) (College Pt.), from Powells Cove blvd., S. of 111th av., E. to 153d, and from 154th, E. to Utopia parkway.

Twelfth rd. (K 2), from 147th, at 12th av., S. E. and E. to Fernwood rd.

Twentieth (E 5), fr. Laurel Hill blvd., N. to Hazen.

Twentieth av. (D 4) (L. I. C.), from Jackson av., N. E. to Vandeventer av.

Twentieth av. (H 3) (College Pt.), from Powells Cove blvd. at Flushing Bay, E. to Utopia parkway, and (M 3), from Hanway pl., N.E. to Bell blvd.

Twentieth rd. (K 3), from 146th, S. of 20th av., E. to 169th.

Twenty-first (E 5), from Laurel Hill blvd., N. to Riker av.

Twenty-first av. (D 4) (L. I.C.), fr. Jackson av., N. E. to Vandeventer av.

Twenty-first av. (H3) (College Pt.), from 122d, S. of 20th av., E. to 124th, and from 143d, E. to Willets Pt. blvd., and from 160th, E. and N. E. to Bell blvd.

Twenty-first rd. (L 3), fr. Carll la., at 163d, E. to Utopia parkway, and (M 3), from 216th, N. of 22d av., E. to 218th.

Twenty-second (E 5), from Fitch av., N. to Bowery bay.

Twenty-second av. (H 3), from Powells Cove blvd., S. of 21th av., E. and N. E. to 203d av.

Twenty-second rd. (J 3), from 142d, S. E. to 23d av., and (M 3), fr. 214th, S. of 22d av., E. to 215th.

Twenty-third (E 5), from Broadway, N. to Riker av.

Twenty-third av. (H 3), from Flushing Bay, S. of 22d av., E. and N. E. to Bell blvd.

Twenty-fourth (E5), from Baxter av., N. to Riker av.

Twenty-fourth av. (J 3), from Parsons blvd., S. of 23d av., E. and N. E. to 203d.

Twenty-fourth rd. (K 3), from 149th, at Willets Pt. blvd., E. and N. E. to 203d.

Twenty fifth (E 5), from Baxter av., N. to Bowery bay.

Twenty-fifth av. (H 3), fr. 119th, at Flushing Bay, E. to Parsons blvd., and from 149th, E. to Utopia parkway.

Twenty-fifth dr. (J 3), fr. Union, S. of 25th av., E. to Cross Isld. blvd.

Twenty-fifth rd. (H 3), fr. 119th, at Flushing Bay, E. to Higgins av., and from Parsons blvd., E. to 147th.

Twenty-sixth (F 5), from Baxter av., N. to Bowery bay.

Twenty-sixth av. (H 3), from 119th, at Flushing Bay, E. and N. E. to Gardner, and (O 3), fr. Bayshore rd., E. of Little Neck Bay, E. to Marinette.

Twenty-seventh (F 5), fr. Roosevelt av., N. to Bowery bay.

Twenty-seventh av. (J 3), from Parsons blvd., S. of 26th av., E. to 168th, and from Cross Isld. blvd., N. E. to 172d, and from Utopia parkway, N. E. to 200th, and from 209th pl., N. E. to 210th, and (O 3), from Bayshore rd., E. of Little Neck Bay, E. to Bayshore rd.

Twenty-eighth (F5), from Roosevelt av., N. to Bowery bay.

Twenty-eighth av. (H 3), from 119th, at Flushing Bay, E. to Higgins, and from Ulmer, E. to Bayside la., and from Cross Isld. blvd., N. E. to Little Neck Bay, and (O 3), from Bayshore rd., E. of Little Neck Bay, E. to Bayshore rd.

Twenty-ninth (F 5), from Roosevelt av., N. to Bowery bay.

Twenty-ninth av. (H 3), from Flushing Bay, E. to 122d, and from Union E. and N. E. to Little Neck blvd., and (O 3), from Bayshore rd., E. of Little Neck Bay, E. to Bayshore rd.

Twenty-ninth rd. (J 3), from Union, S. of 29th av., E. to 147th.

Two Hundredth (L2), from Utopia parkway, at 14th rd., S. to 22d av., and from 26th av., S. E. to Cross Isld. blvd., and (N 7) (Hollis), from 99th av., S. E. to Nashville av., and from 130th av., S. W. to 136th av.

Two Hundred and First (L 2), from Utopia parkway, at Little Bay, S. and S.E. to 38th av., and from Station rd., S. E. to Northern blvd., and from Rocky Hill rd., S. E. to Underhill av., and from Peck av., S. E. to Busby av., and (N 6), fr. Union Turnpike, S. E. to Grand Central Parkway, and fr. Hillside av., S. E. to Nashville av., and from 130th av., S. W. to 138th av.

Two Hundred and Second (L 2), from Little Bay av., at Cryders la., S. to 22d av., and from 26th av., S.E. to 38th av., and from Station rd., S. E. to North Hempstead Turnpike, and (M 5), fr. Peck

BOROUGH OF QUEENS STREET AND AVENUE DIRECTORY—*Continued.*

av., S. E. to Busby av., and (N 6) from Union Turnpike, S. E. to Grand Central pkway, and from Hillside av., S. E. to Nashville av., and from 130th av., S. W. to Coombs.

Two Hundred and Third (L 2), from Little Bay av., E. of 202d, S. and S. E. to Linn, and from Station rd., S. E. to Northern blvd., and fr. Rocky Hill rd., S. E. to Hollis Court blvd., and from Peck av., S. E. to Busby av., and (N 6), from Richland av., S. E. to Grand Central Parkway, and from 99th av., S. E. to Springfield blvd., and fr. 130th av., S. W. to 138th av., and (N 10), from S. Conduit av., S. W. to Springfield la.

Two Hundred and Fourth (L 2), from Little Bay, S. and S. E. to Underhill av., and from Peck av., S. E. to Busby av., and (N 6), from Union Turnpike, S. E. to Grand Central Parkway, and fr. Hillside av., S. E. to Covington, and from 130th av., S. W. to North Conduit av., and (N 10), fr. S. Conduit av., S. W. to Springfield la.

Two Hundred and Fifth (L 2), from Little Bay av., E. of 204th, S. and S. E. to Linn, and from Station rd., S. E. to Northern blvd., and fr. Rocky Hill rd., S. E. to Underhill av., and (N 5), from 73d av., S. E. to Busby av., and from Richland av., S. E. to Grand Central parkway, and from Hillside av., S. E. to Springfield blvd., and (O 9), from 130th av., S. W. to 147th av., and (N 10), from 149th av., S. W. to 168d av.

Two Hundred and Sixth (L 2), from Little Bay av., E. of 205th, S. and S. E. to Linn, and from Station rd., S. E. to Underhill av.; and from Peck av., S. E. to Hollis Court blvd., and (N 6), from Union Turnpike, S. E. to 86th av., and from 99th av., S. E. to Hollis av., and from 130th av., S. W. to Lakeview av., and (N 10), from S. Conduit av., S. W. to 149th av., and from 151st av., S. W. to 168d av.

Two Hundred and Seventh (L 2), from Little Bay av., E. of 206th, S. E. to Linn, and fr. Station rd., S. E. to Northern blvd., and from 47th av., S. E. to Underhill av., and fr. Peck av., S. E. to Busby av., and from 81st av., S. E. to 86th av., and from Hillside av., S. E. to Covington, and (O 9), from 130th av., S. W. to N. Conduit av., and (N 10), from S. Conduit av., S. W. to 149th av., and from 151st av., S. W. to 168d av.

Two Hundred and Eighth (L 2), fr. Little Bay av., E. of 207th, S. and S. E. to Northern blvd., and from 47th av., S. E. to Underhill av., and from Peck av., S. E. to Busby av., and from Richland av., S. E. to 86th av., and from Hillside av., S. E. to Jamaica av., and from 99th av., S. E. to Covington, and (O 9), fr. 130th av., S. W. to 168d av.

Two Hundred and Ninth (L 2), fr. Little Bay av., E. of 208th, S. and S. E. to Northern blvd., and from Hillside av., S. E. to Jamaica av., and from 99th av. to 100th av., and from 104th av., S. E. to Hollis av., and from Colfax S. E. to Covington, and from 129th av., S. W. to L. I. R. R., and (N 10), from S. Conduit av., S. W. to 168d av.

Two Hundred and Ninth pl. (M 2), from Little Neck av., E. of Gardiner, S. and S. E. to 33d av., and (O 7) (Hollis), from Hollis av., S. E. to Colfax av.

Two Hundred and Tenth (M 2), from Dayton pl., near Little Bay av., S. and S. E. to Northern blvd., and from 47th av., S. E. to Underhill av., and from Peck av., S. E. to Busby av., and from Richland av., S. E. and S. W. to Lonsdale av., and from Whitehall Terrace, S. E. to Hollis av., and from Colfax S. E. to Covington, and fr. 130th av., S. W. to 141st av., and (N 10), from S. Conduit av., S. W. to junction of 168d av., and Head of Bay blvd.

Two Hundred and Tenth pl. (M 2), from Dayton pl., E. of 210th, S. to 32d av., and (N 6) (Hollis), from 89th av., S. E. to 94th av., and from 210th, S. E. to Hollis av.

Two Hundred and Eleventh (M 3), from Dayton pl., E. of 210th pl., S. and S. E. to Underhill av., and (N 6), from Richland av., S. E. to 86th, and from Hillside av., S. E. to Hollis av., and from Colfax S. E. to Covington, and from 130th av., S. W. to Mentone, and from South Conduit av., S. E. to Head of Bay blvd.

Two Hundred and Eleventh pl. (N 6) (Hollis), from 90th av., S. E. to 93d av., and from 99th av., S. E. to 212th.

Two Hundred and Twelfth (M 3), from Dayton pl., E. of 211th, S. to 33d rd., and from 47th av., S. E. to Underhill av., and (N 6) from Richland av., S. E. to Covington, and from 129th av., S. W. to 145th av., and (O 10), from Edgewood, S. W. to Head of Bay blvd.

Two Hundred and Twelfth pl. (N 6) (Hollis), from Hillside av., S. E. to Jamaica av.

Two Hundred and Thirteenth (M 3), from 23d av., E. of 212th, S. to Northern blvd., and fr. 47th av., W. of Bell av., S. E. to 75th av., and (N 6), from Richland av., S. E. to 86th av., and fr. Hillside av., S. E. to Jamaica av., and from 99th av., S. E. to 104th av., and from Hollis av., S. E. to Murdock av., and fr. 130th av., S. W. to 145th av., and (O 10), from Edgewood, S. W. to Head of Bay blvd.

Two Hundred and Thirteenth pl. (O 6) (Hollis), from 93d av., S. E. to Jamaica av.

Two Hundred and Fourteenth (M 3), from 26th av., E. of Bell blvd., S. to 35th av., and from 50th av., S. E. to Underhill av., and from Richland av., S. E. to Hollis Court blvd., and from Hillside av., S E. to Jamaica av., and (O 7), from Hollis av., S. E. to Covington, thence S. W. to Head of Bay blvd.

Two Hundred and Fourteenth pl. (M 3), from 23d av., E. of 214th, S. to Northern blvd., and (O 6) from Whitehall terrace, S. E. to Jamaica av.

Two Hundred and Fifteenth (M 2), from Willets Pt. blvd., E. of Bell blvd., S. E. to 51st av., and from 53d av., S. E. to Underhill av., and from Peck av., S. E. to 86th av., and (O 6), from Hillside av., S. E. to Jamaica av., and from 99th av., S. E. to 128th av., and from 130th av., S. W. to Lansing, and (O 10), from Edgewood, S. W. to Head of Bay blvd.

Two Hundred and Fifteenth pl. (M 2), from Little Bay av., N. of Bell blvd., S. E. to 31st av., and fr. Harnay la., S. to Rocky Hill rd., and (O 6), from Hillside av., S. E. to Jamaica av.

Two Hundred and Sixteenth (M 2), from Willets Pt. blvd., E. of 215th, S. E. to Bell blvd., and (O 6), from Hillside av., S. E. to Jamaica av., and from Hempstead av., S. E. to Springfield blvd., and from 130th av., S. W. to Head of Bay blvd.

Two Hundred and Seventeenth (M 2), from Little Neck blvd., E. of 216th, S. E. to 29th av., and fr. Edgewater la., S. to 31st av., and from Harnay la., S. to Underhill av., and from Union Turnpike, S. E. to Grand Central pkway, and (O 6), from Hillside av., S. E. to Jamaica av., and from Hempstead av., S. E. to Springfield blvd., and from Covington, S. W. to North Conduit av., and (O 10), from 149th av., S. W. to Head of Bay blvd.

Two Hundred and Seventeenth pl. (O 6), from Peck av., W. of 218th, S. E. to 86th av., and (O 7) (Hollis), fr. Hempstead av., S. E. to 104th av., and from Hollis av., S. E. to 110th av.

Two Hundred and Eighteenth (N 3), from 28th av., W. of Little Neck blvd., S. to 31st av., and from Harnay la., S. to Rocky Hill rd., and from 56th av., S. E. to Underhill av., and from Peck av., S. E. to 85th av., and (O 6) (Queens), from Hillside av., S. E. and S. to Hempstead av., and from Murdock av., S. E. and S. W. to North Conduit av., and (O 10), from 147th av., S. W. to Head of Bay blvd.

Two Hundred and Eighteenth pl. (O 6), from Whitehall terrace, S. of Springfield blvd., S. E. to 93d av., and fr. Hempstead av., S. to Hollis av.

Two Hundred and Nineteenth (N 3), from Bayshore rd., at 22d av., S. to 24th av., and from 26th av., S. to 31st av., and from 56th av., S. E. to Underhill av., and fr. Hillside av., S. E. to 94th av., and from 97th av., S. to 108th av., and from 112th av., S. E. and S. W. to Laurelton pkway, and (O 10), from 147th av., S. W. to Head of Bay blvd.

Two Hundred and Twentieth (N 3), from Wainscott av., W. of 221st, S. to 31st av., and from Harnay la., S. to 46th av., and from 56th av., S. E. to Hartland av., and (O 6), from 89th av., S. E. to 91st av., and from 91st rd., S. E. to Jamaica av., and from 96th rd., S. E. to 108th av., and from Murdock av., S. E. & S. W. to 131st av., and (O 10), from Bentley rd., S. W. to Preston la., and from 149th av., S. W. to Head of Bay blvd.

Two Hundred and Twentieth pl. (N 4), from Harnay la., W. of 221st, S. to 46th av., and from 73d av., S. E. to Underhill av.

Two Hundred and Twenty-first (N 3), from Edgewater la., S. to Jackson av., and from Sp'gfield blvd., S. E. to Underhill av., and from Kingsbury av., S. E. to Hartland av., and (O 6), fr. Braddock av., S. E. to 91st av., and from 91st rd., S. E. to Winchester blvd., and from 94th av., S. to 96th av., and from 96th rd., S. E. to 99th av., and from 100th av., S. W. and S. to 129th av., and (O 11), from 151st av., S. W. to Rockaway blvd.

BOROUGH OF QUEENS STREET AND AVENUE DIRECTORY—*Continued.*

Two Hundred and Twenty-first pl. (O 6), fr. Braddock av., W. of 90th av., S.E. to Winchester blvd.

Two Hundred and Twenty-second (N 4), from 33d av., S. to Northern blvd., and from 61st av., S.E. to 73d av., and fr. Springfield blvd., S. to Underhill av., and from Kingsbury av., S. E. to Hartland av., and (O 6), fr. Braddock av., S. to Hempstead av., and from 109th av., S. W. to 110th av., and from Murdock av., S. E. to Covington, and (O11) from 149th av., E. of Brookville blvd., S. to 149th dr., and from 150th av., W. of Brookville blvd., S. W. to Rockaway blvd.

Two Hundred and Twenty-third (N 3), from Crocheron av., W. of Bayshore rd., S. to 31st av., and from 43d av., S. to Northern Parkway, and from 61st av., S. E. to Springfield blvd., and (O 5), from Kingsbury av., W. of Springfield blvd., S. E. to Crystal av., and (P 7), from Hanlon av., S. W. and S. E. to Hook Creek blvd., and (O 11), from 149th av., S. to 150th av., and fr. Brookville blvd., S.W. to Rockaway blvd.

Two Hundred and Twenty-fourth (N 3), from Bayshore rd., nr. 35th av., S. to 41st av. and from 43d av., S. to Northern blvd., and from 58th av., S.E. to 75th av., and (P6), from Braddock av, S. to 96th av., and from 96th rd., S. to Hempstead av., and from Murdock av., S. E. to Hook Creek blvd., and (P 9), from Merrick rd., S. W. to N. Conduit av., and from S. Conduit av., S. W. to Huxley, and (O10), from 147th av., S. to 149th av., and (O 11), from 151st av., at Brookville blvd., S.W. to Rockaway blvd.

Two Hundred and Twenty-fifth (N3), from 27th av., W. of Easthampton rd., S. E. to 28th dr., and fr. 33d av., S. to 46th av., and (O 5), from 61st av., S. E. to Underhill av, and (P 7), from Hempstead av., S.W. and S.E. to Hook Creek blvd., and (O 11), from 149th av., S. W. to 150th av., and from 151st av., S. W. to Rockaway blvd.

Two Hundred and Twenty-sixth (N 4), from 33d av., W. of 227th, S. to 46th av., and from Cloverdale av., S. E. to Underhill av., and (P 7), from Murdock av., S. to Hook Creek blvd., and (P 9), from 130th rd., S. W. to N. Conduit av., and from S. Conduit av., S. W. to 147th av., and (O 11), from 149th av., S.W. to Rockaway blvd.

Two Hundred and Twenty-seventh (N 4), from 33d av., W. of Easthampton rd., S.E to 46th av., and (O 6), from Stronghurst av., S.E. to 87th av., and (P 7) (Queens), from Hook blvd., S. W. and S. to Hook Creek blvd, and from 130th av., S. W. to North Conduit av., and (O 11), from 149th av., S.W. to Rockaway blvd.

Two Hundred and Twenty-eighth (N 4), fr. Jackson av., W. of Easthampton rd., S. to 46th av., and from Hoxie, S.E. to Underhill av., and (O 5), fr. Grand Central parkway, S. to Stronghurst av., and from Seward av., S.E. to 87th av., and (P 7) (Queens), from 112th av., S. to Hook Creek blvd., and from 130th rd., S. W. to Memphis av, and (O 10), fr. Newhall av., S. to 147th av., and from Edgewood S.W. to Rockaway blvd.

Two Hundred and Twenty-ninth (O 4), from Hoxie, W. of Birmingham rd., S. E. to Underhill av., and (O 5), from Kingsbury av., S. E. to Grand Central pkway, and from Stronghurst av., S. E. to 87th av., and (P 7) (Queens), from 112th av., S. to Hook Creek blvd., and from 134th av., S. W. to Memphis av., and (O 11), from Edgewood, W. of Craft av., S.W. to Rockaway blvd.

Two Hundred and Thirtieth (N 3), from Bayshore rd., E. of proposed Basin, S. E. to 46th av., and from 46th av., S. E. to 75th av., and from Stronghurst av., S. E. to 87th av., and (P 10), fr. Hook Creek blvd., S. W. to 143d av., and (O 11), from Brookville blvd., S. to Rockaway blvd.

Two Hundred and Thirty-first (O 4), from 36th av., W. of 232d, S. E. to 46th av., and from 61st av., S. E. to Underhill av., and fr. Union Turnpike, S. E. to 87th av., and (P 10), from Hook Creek blvd., S. W. to Weller av., and (O 11), from 153d rd., W. of Brookville blvd., S. to Rockaway blvd.

Two Hundred and Thirty-second (O 4), from 36th av., W. of 233d, S. E. to 46th av., and from Easthampton rd., at 61st av., S. E. to Underhill av., and from Union Turnpike, S. E. to 87th av., and (P 10), from City line, S.W. and S. to 148th rd., and (O 11), from junction of Craft av. and 151st av., S. to Brookville blvd.

Two Hundred and Thirty-third (N 3), from Bayshore rd., bet. 230th and Beach pl., S. E. to Wainscott av, and from 36th av., S. E. to 46th av., and (O 5), from Easthampton rd., S. E. to Underhill av., and from Stronghurst av., S. E. to Winchester blvd., and (P 10), from City line, S. W. to Weller av.

Two Hundred and Thirty-fourth (O 5), from Easthampton rd. at 61st av., S. E. to Underhill av., and fr. Union Turnpike, S.E. to Winchester blvd.

Two Hundred and Thirty-fifth (O 3), from 27th av., E. of Douglaston av., S. to 28th av., and (O 5), from Easthampton rd., S. to 69th av., and from Union Turnpike, S. to Hillside av.

Two Hundred and Thirty-sixth (O 3), from 28th av., W. of 237th, S. to 28th rd., and (O 5), from Easthampton rd., S. to Grand Central pkway, and from Union T'npike S. to Winchester blvd., and (P 10), from City line, S.W. and S. to City line at Huxley.

Two Hundred and Thirty-seventh (O 3), from 19th av., E. of Douglaston av., S. to 28th rd., and (P 5), from Easthampton rd., S. to 73d av., and from Union Turnpike, S. to Winchester blvd., and (P 6), from Gettysburg, S. to 87th av., and from 88th av., S. to Braddock av., and (P 10), from City line, S. W. to Mayda rd., and (P 11), from 149th dr., S. to Craft av., near City line.

Two Hundred and Thirty-eighth (O 3), from 28th rd., W. of 239th, S. to 29th av., and (P 6), from Gettysburg, S. to 87th av., and from 88th av., S. to Braddock av., and (P 10), from City line, S. W. to 147th av., and (P 11), fr. 149th dr., S. to Craft av., near City line.

Two Hundred and Thirty-ninth (O 3), from 28th rd., W. of 240th, S. to 29th av., and from Lynxville, S. to 46th av., and (P 5), from Gettysburg, S. to 87th av., and from 88th av., S. to Braddock av., and (P 10), fr. City line, S. W. to 147th av., and (P11), fr. 149th rd., S. to Craft av., nr. City line.

Two Hundred and Fortieth (O 3), from Douglaston av., bet. 17th & 18th avs., S. to Northern blvd., and (P 5), from 82d av., S. to 87th av., and from 88th av., S. to Jamaica av., and (P 10), fr. City line, N. of Frankton, S. W. and S. to Hook Creek.

Two Hundred and Forty-first (O 4), from Snell av., W. of Douglaston av., S. to Wessington av., and (P 5), from Gettysburg, S. E. and S. to 87th av., and from 88th av., S. and S. E. to Jamaica av., and (P 11), from 149th rd., S. to Craft av. at City line.

Two Hundred and Forty-second (O 3), from 36th av., W. of Cary pl., S. to 37th av., and (P 5), from Union Turnpike at Gettysburg, S. E. to Hillside av., and from 88th av., S. and S. E. to Jamaica av., and (P 10), from 240th, S. to City line at Hook Creek.

Two Hundred and Forty-third (O 3) from Morgan av., at L. I. R. R., S. to 36th av., and from Northern blvd., S. to Van Zandt av., and (P 5), fr. Union Turnpike, S. E. to Hillside av., and fr. Braddock av., S. E. to Jamaica av., and (P11) from 149th dr., S. to Hook Creek.

Two Hundred and Forty-fourth (O 3), from 36th av., E. of Cary pl., S. E. to Redfield, and (P 5), from Union Turnpike, S. E. and S. to Braddock av., and (P 11), fr. 149th rd., S. to Hook Creek.

Two Hundred and Forty-fifth (O 4), fr. Northern blvd., W. of Snell av., S.E. and S. to Redfield, and (P 6), from 91st av., S. to Braddock av., and (P11), from Hook Creek to City line.

Two Hundred and Forty-sixth (O 3), from Morgan av., at L. I. R.R., S. E. to Jackson av., and (P5), from Elkmont av., S. E. to 85th av., and from 85th av. at Commonwealth blvd., S. to 87th av., and from 91st av., S. to Jamaica av.

Two Hundred and Forty-seventh (O 3), from L. I. R. R., at Morgan av., S. E. to Jackson av., and from Van Zandt av., S. E. to Sanborn av., and (P 5), from Langston av., S. and S. E. to Underhill av., and from Elkmont av., S. E. to 86th av., and from 88th av., S. to Jamaica av.

Two Hundred and Forty-eighth (O 3), from Morgan av., W. of Marathon av., S. E. to Overbrook dr., and (P 5), from 73d av., S. E. to Underhill av., and from Elkmont av., S. E. to 87th dr.

Two Hundred and Forty-ninth (P 5), from Langston av., W. of 250th, S. E. to Jackson av.

Two Hundred and Fiftieth (O 3), from Deppe S. E. to Marathon av., and (P4), from 60th av., E. of Marathon av., S. to 61st av., and from Langston av., S. E. to Underhill av., and from Elkmont av., S. E. to 87th dr., and from 88th rd., S. to Jamaica av.

Two Hundred and Fifty-first (O 3), from Jackson av., W. of Browvale dr., S. E. and E. to Deepdale av., and (P 4), fr. Overbrook dr., S. to Cullman av., and from Langston av., S. E. to Underhill

BOROUGH OF QUEENS STREET AND AVENUE DIRECTORY—*Continued.*

av., and from Elkmont av., S.E. to 87th dr., and from 88th rd., S. E. to Northern blvd.

Two Hundred and Fifty-second (P 4), from 60th av., W. of 253d, S. E. to Grand Central parkway, and from Langston av., S. E. to Underhill av., and from Elkmont av., S. E. to 87th dr.

Two Hundred and Fifty-third (P 4), from 60th av., opp. Annandale la., S. E. to Grand Central parkway, and (Q 5), fr. 83d av., S. to 87th dr.

Two Hundred and Fifty-fourth (P 4), fr. Thornhill av., E. of Annandale la., S. E. to Fennimore av., and from 60th av., S. E. to Cullman av., and (Q 5), from Little Neck rd., S. E. and S. to 82d av., and from 86th av., S. to 87th dr.

Two Hundred and Fifty-fifth (P 3), from Little Neck rd., opp. Concord, S. E. to Little Neck rd., and (Q 5), from Shiloh av., S. E. & S. to Hillside av., and from Little Neck rd., S. to Jamaica av.

Two Hundred and Fifty-sixth (P 3), from City line, bet. Lakeville rd. and Thornhill av., and from 59th av., S. E. to Fennimore av., and from 59th av., S. E. to 61st av., and (Q 5), from Shiloh av., S. E. and S. to Little Neck rd.

Two Hundred and Fifty-seventh (Q 5), fr Little Neck rd., S. of 258th, S. E. to Underhill av., and from Shiloh av., S. E. and S. to City line.

Two Hundred and Fifty-eighth (P 5), from Little Neck rd., S. of Langston av., S. E. and S. to City line.

Two Hundred and Fifty-ninth (P 4), from Langston av., S. E. to Underhill av., and from Shiloh av., S. E. and S. to City line.

Two Hundred and Sixtieth (P 4), from Hewlett av., E. of Little Neck rd., S. E. to Fennimore av., and from Langston av., S.E. to Underhill av., and fr. Shiloh av., S. E. and S. to City line.

Two Hundred and Sixty-first (P 4), from Hewlett av., bet. 216th and Overbrook dr., S. E. to 59th av., and from Langston av., S. E. to Underhill av., and from Shiloh av., S. E. and S. to City line.

Two Hundred and Sixty-second (P 4), from Hewlett av. at Overbrook dr., S. E. and S. to Kennedy av., and (Q 4), fr. Langston av., S. E. to Underhill av., and from Shiloh av., S. E. and S. to City line.

Two Hundred and Sixty-third (Q 4), from Langston av, opp. Golf rd., S. E. and S. to City line.

Two Hundred and Sixty-fourth (P 3), from Fennimore av., W. of Hewlett av., S. E. to 61st av., and (Q 4), from Langston av., S. E. to Underhill av., and from Shiloh av., S. E. and S. to City line.

Two Hundred and Sixty-fifth (Q 4), from Hewlett av., S. of Fennimore av., S. and S. E. to Grand Central pkway, and from Langston av., S. E. to Underhill av., and from Shiloh av., S. E. and S. to City line.

Two Hundred and Sixty-sixth (Q 4), from Hewlett av., at 60th av., S. to 61st av., and from Langston av., S. E. to Underhill av., and from Shiloh av., S. E. and S. to City line.

Two Hundred and Sixty-seventh (Q 4), fr. Hewlett av., S. of 60th av., S. and S. E. to Grand Central parkway.

Two Hundred and Sixty-eighth (Q 4), fr. Langston av., at 74th av., S. E. to Underhill av., and from Shiloh av., S. E. and S. to Hillside av.

Two Hundred and Sixty-ninth (Q 4), fr. Langston av., W. of 268th, S. E. to Underhill av., and from Shiloh av., S. E. and S. to Langdale av.

Two Hundred and Seventieth (Q 4), from Langston av. at Hewlett av., S. E. to Underhill av., and from Shiloh av., S. E. and S. to Langdale av.

Two Hundred and Seventy-first (Q 4), from Hewlett av. at Langston av., S. E. to Underhill av., and from Shiloh av., S. E. and S. to Langdale av.

Twombly (K7) (Jamaica), now part of Archer av. and Twombly rd.

Twombly pl. (K 7) (Jamaica), from Jamaica av., S. to Archer av.

Twombly rd. (K 7) (Jamaica), from 151st, E. to 152d.

Tyler (D 5), from Laurel Hill av., S. E. to Railroad av.

Ulmer (H 8) (College Pt.), from 25th av., E. of L. I. R. R., S. E. to 81st dr.

Ulster av. (J 9), fr. Rockaway blvd., N. E. to Van Wyck blvd., that part E. thereof being now parts of 114th av. and Mangin av.

Underhill av. (L 5) (Bayside), fr. 164th at Kissena park, E., S. E. and N. E. to City line.

Underwood (H 7), fr. North Greenway terrace, N. E. to Burns.

Union (J 8), from Willets Pt. blvd., W. of Parsons blvd., S. W. to Franklin av., and from Cherry av., S.E. to Negundo av.

Union ct. (F 6), from Division, N.E, to Calamus av.

Union Hall North (K 7), from Yuma la., W. of 164th, S.E. to Hillside av.

Union Turnpike (G 7), from Myrtle av., at Forest park, N.E. to Queens blvd., and (J 7), from Grand Central pkway. at 188th, N. E. to City line.

Unionhall (L 7), from Jamaica av., S. E. to 111th av.

Unity (G 5) (Corona Hgts), from Corona av., N. E. to Gilroy av.

University av. (J 8) (Whitestone), from Parsons av., E. to Pinford.

Upland la. (P 5), fr. Grand Central pkway, S. W. to 79th av.

Uppervillepl. (K2) (Whitestone), from Oakridge av., N. E. to Atwater.

Upton pl. (D 4) (Woodside), fr. Charlotte, N. to Jamaica av.

Uris (G 6), from Austin, N. E. to 120th.

Ursina rd. (N9) (Jamaica), from Irwin pl., N. E. to 178th.

Ursula (G7), from L.I.R.R. N. to Metropolitan av.

Urquhart (G 6), fr. Queens blvd., N. E to 120th.

Utopia Parkway (L 2), from 7th av., at Little Bay, S. and S E. to Grand Central pkway.

Valentine (E7) (Glendale), from Myrtle av., N. W. to Otto.

Van Alst av. (B5) (L. I. C.), from Jackson av., N. and N. E. to Winthrop av.

Van Buren (C 5) (L. I. C.), from Borden av., N. to Skillman av., and L. I. freight yard, N. to Jackson av.

Van Cleef (G 5) (Corona Heights), from Orontes, S. E. to Rodman.

Van Cortlandt av. (D8), fr. Myrtle av., N. E. to Kossuth pl.

Van Cott av. (D6), fr. Grand, N. to Maurice av.

Vandalia av. (G 10), from Boro. line, E. and S.E. to 128th.

Van Dam (B 5) (L. I. C.), from Borden av., N. to Meadow.

Vandeveer av. (H 11), fr. Jamaica bay, N. to Sutter av.

Vandeventer av. (C 3) (L. I. C.), from 2d av., S. E. to Grand av.

Van Dine (F 5), fr. Kingsland av., N. to Roosevelt av.

Van Dusen (E6), from Whitlock av., S. E. to Satterlee av.

Van Horn (F 5), fr. Grand, S. E. to Woodhaven av.

Van Kleeck (F5), fr. Grand, N. to Queens blvd.

Van Loon (F5) (Newtown) from Grand, N. to Maurice av.

Van Mater (B6), from Review av., N. E. to Bradley av.

Van Pelt (C 5) (L. I. C.), from Greenpoint av., N. to Skillman av.

Van Sicklen av. (J 10), fr. Lefferts av., S. E. to Raritan.

Van Twiller (G 6), from Queens blvd., N. E. to 120th.

Van Wyck blvd. (K 8), from Jamaica av., S. E. and S. to 163d av.

Van Zandt av. (O 4), from Douglaston av., S. of Wessington av., N. E. to Annandale la.

Varian (F7) (Glendale), fr. Ford, N. E. to Edsall av.

Varick (H 5) (Corona Heights), from Corona av., N. E. to 120th.

Vassar (G 7), from Woodhaven av., N. E. to Orville.

Vaux (D 5) (Woodside), from Queens blvd., N. to Jackson av.

Vermont av. (K9), fr. Boro. line, N. E. and N. to Cypress av.

Vernon av. (A 5) (L. I. C.), fr. Jackson av., N. E. to Broadway.

Verona (G 6), fr. Queens blvd., N. E. to 120th.

Viaduct (B 5) (L. I. C.), from Plaza, S. E. to Queens blvd.

Victoria dr. (M 9) (Jamaica), from 172d N. E. to Merrill.

Victoria rd. (M 9) (Jamaica), from Merrill E. to Merrick blvd.

Vienna av. (G 9) (Woodhaven), from Boro. line, E. and S. E to 128th.

Victor pl. (F 5) (Elmhurst), from Broadway, N. E. to Judge.

Vincent (D7), from Ralph, N. to Elliot av.

Viola (G 7), from L. I. R. R., N. to Metropolitan av.

Virginia (O 18) (Far Rockaway), from Cornaga av., N. W. to Brunswick av.

Vistula av. (J 9), from Rockaway blvd., N. E. to Van Wyck blvd., that part E. thereof being now part of 115th av.

Vogt pl. (J2) (Whitestone), from Fletcher av., N. to Jonathan.

Vorhees pl. (F5), fr. Hunt, N. to Roosevelt av.

Wabash (J 10), from Peconic av., N. E. to Rockaway blvd.

Wainwright ct. (J 15) (Rockaway Beach), fr. Beach 109th, N. E. to Beach 106th.

Walker av. (H 9), from Sutter av., S. to Jamaica bay.

Wallace (D 4) (L. I. C.), from Vandeventer av., N. E. to Rex pl.

Wallace pl. (J7), fr. Queens blvd., N. E. to 120th.

Wallach (A 4) (L. I. C), fr. Bulkhead line, S. E. to Vernon av.

Walnut (J 9), from R'way blvd., N. W. to Liberty av., thence now part of 116th.

Walter (E 8), from Alden av., N. to Millwood av.

Waltham (K 8), from 95th av., S. E. to Lakewood av.

BOROUGH OF QUEENS STREET AND AVENUE DIRECTORY—*Continued.*

Wanda (G 7), from L. I. R. R., N. to Metropolitan av.
Warburton av. (K 9), from Rockaway blvd., N. E. to Van Wyck blvd., that part E. thereof being now part of 116th av.
Ward (E 6), from Grand, S. E. to Metropolitan av.
Wardell (B 3) (L. I. C.), from Fulton av., N. to Boulevard.
Wareham rd. (L 7), from Croydon rd., W. of Midland pkway, S.E. to Dalny rd.
Warner av. (F 5) (Elmhurst), from Kingsland av., N. E. to Roosevelt av.
Warren (K 9), from Rockaway blvd., N.W to Liberty av.
Warwick cres. (L 7) (Jamaica), from Hillside av., S. E. to 175th.
Washington av. (B 4) (L. I. C.), from Bulkhead line, S. E. to Jackson av.
Washington Circle (H 15) (R'way Beach), Rockaway Beach blvd., bet. Beach 120th and Beach 121st.
Water (H 4) (Flushing), from Flushing river, at Willow, N. to Washington.
Wateredge av. (J 7), from Grand Central parkway, E. of Queens blvd., N. W., N. and N.W. to Lawrence.
Waterloo pl. (N 13) (Far R'way), fr Waterloo rd., N. E. to Mott av.
Waterloo rd. (N 13) (Far R'way), from Nortons dr., W. and N. and N.W. to Norton dr.
Waters av. (C 6) (Laurel Hill), from Laurel Hill blvd., E. to Borden av.
Waterview (N 13) (Far R'way), from Healey av., N. W. to Bayswater av.
Watjean ct. (N 14) (Far R'way), from Fernside pl., N. W. to Edgemere av.
Watson pl. (M 8) (Jamaica), from 107th av., S.E. to 177th.
Way av. (G 5), from Martense av., N.W. to Roosevelt av.
Wayland av. (E 7), from Mt. Olivet av., N. E. to Juniper av.
Wayne (F 7) (Glendale), from Proctor, E. to Weisse av.
Webb (G 6), from Queens blvd., N. E. to 120th.
Webb av. (H 5), from Riverside av., N.E. through Cedar Grove Cem. to junction of 63d & Larch avs.
Webb pl. (K 2), from 153d pl., S. of 14th av., S. W. to 15th av.
Webster av. (B 4) (L. I. C.), from Bulkhead line, S.E. to Jackson av.
Weeks la. (M 4), fr. Rosedale av., S. of Rocky Hill rd., N. E. to Rocky Hill rd.
Well pl. (C 3) (L. I. C.), from Astoria av., N. to Washington.
Weimar (F 5), from L. I. R. R., N. E. to Queens blvd.
Weirfield (D 8), cont'd from Boro. line, N. E. to Myrtle av.
Weisse av. (E 6), fr. Grand, S. E. to Myrtle av.
Weller av. (O 10) (Rosedale), from Brookville blvd., S. E. & S. to 147th rd.
Weller la. (P 10), from 147th av., E. of 236th, S. to Craft av. at City line.
Welling (B 3) (L. I. C.), from Greenoak, E. to Main.
Welton av. (E 8) fr. Anna pl., N. to Myrtle av.
Wessington av. (O 4), fr. Hanford parkway, S. of Snell av., N. E. to Marathon av.
West av. (A 5) (L. I. C.) from Borden av., N. W. to Nott av.
West av. (J 4) (Flushing), from Forest av., S. E. to Peck av.
West Brook (H 2) (College Point), fr. Fletcher av., N. to Tallman av.
West End dr. (P 3), from Little Neck rd., E. of Pembroke av., N. E. and E. to Glenwood av.
Westbourne av. (N 13) (Far R way), fr. Beach 25th, W. to Dunbar.
Westchester av. (M 8), fr. Merrick blvd., E. to Farmers blvd.
Westervelt (H 5) (Corona Heights), fr. Corona av., E. to Flushing River.
Westgate lane (N 9) from 137th av., S. E. to 140th av.
Westmoreland (O 3), from 39th rd., at Old House Landing rd., S. E. to Northern blvd.
Westside (G 5), from Rodman, N. to Corona av.
Westwood (M 7), fr. Liberty av., N. E. to Farmers blvd.
Wetherole pl. (F 6), from Woodhaven av., S. E. to Jupiter av.
Wexford ter. (L 7) (Jamaica), fr. Hillside av., N. E. to Holliswood av.
Wharf (H 4), from Jackson av., N. to Flushing Bay.
Wheatley (O 13) (Far Rockaway), fr. Brunswick, S.E. to Far R'way blvd.
Wheeler (E 7), from Admiral, N. to Metropolitan av.
Whitehall terrace (N 6) (Hollis), from Rosedale blvd., N. E. to Springfield blvd.
Whitlock av. (E 6), from Hamilton pl., N. E. to Queens blvd.
Whitney (C 3) (L. I. C.), fr. Crescent av., S. E. to Academy.
Whitney (D 6), fr. Maurice av., E. to Grand.
Whitson (H 7) fr. Roman av., S. E. to Union Turnpike.
Whittier av. (D 5) (Winfield), from Tyler, N. to Queens blvd.
Wickham (H 5) (Corona Heights), from Corona av., N. E to 120th.
Wilbur av. (B 4) (L. I. C.), from Vernon av., S. E. to Academy.
Wilcox (G 4), from Polk av. N. W. to Jackson av.
Will pl. (O 3), from Bayshore rd., at 27th rd., S. to 28th rd.
Willets Pt. blvd. (H 3), from Flushing River, N. E. to boundary line of Fort Totten.
William (B 5) (L. I. C.), from Thirteenth, N.E. to Graham av.
Williamson av. (N 9) (Sp'gfield), Edmondson, N. E. and E. to Springfield blvd.
Willoughby av. (7 C) continued from Boro. line, N. E. to Woodward av.
Willow (C 3) (L. I. C.), fr. Main, N. to Hoyt av.
Willow av. (D 6), from Grand, N. to Borden av.
Willshire (H 3) (Flushing), now Downing.
Wilson av. (D 3) (L. I. C.), from 10th av., S. E to Grand av.
Winans (C 4) (L.I.C.), from Jackson av., N. E. to Jamaica av.
Winchester blvd. (P 4), from Marathon av., at Overbrook dr., S.W. and S. to 93d av.
Windsor (H 7), fr. Austin, N. E. to Queens blvd.
Winifred (D 7), fr. Fresh Pond rd., E. to Azalea.
Winter (H 7) from Ascan av., E. to Summer.
Winthrop av. (D 3) (L.I.C.), from Bulkhead line, S. E. to Wolcott av.
Wolcott av. (C 3) (L.I.C.), from Blvd., S. E. & E. to Berrian.
Woo (F 5), from Grand, S. E. to Buskirk pl.
Wood (E 4) (L. I. C.), from Astoria av., N. to Hazen.
Wood (M 7), fr. Dunkirk, S. E. to Murdock av.
Woodbine (D 8) continued, from Boro line, N. E. & E. to Traffic.
Woodhaven av. (F 6), from Queens blvd., S. E. to Park la. So., and from Sutter av., S. to Jamaica Bay.
Woodhaven blvd. (G 8), fr. Park la. So., S.E. to Sutter av.
Woodhull (H 5), now Longview av.
Woodhull av. (M 7) (Hollis), from Jamaica av., near Hollis av., to Jamaica av.
Woodland av. (G 9), from Jamaica bay, N. E. to Sutter av.
Woodlawn av. (G 8) (Woodhaven) fr. Atlantic av., N. to Ashland.
Woodmere (H 8) (Richmond Hill), fr. Woodmere pl., E. to Herald av.
Woodside av. (D 5) (Woodside), from Jackson av., S. to Middleburg av. and E. to Broadway.
Woodward av. (C 7), from Metropolitan av., S. E. to Forest av.
Woolley (F 6), from Cornbury pl., N. E. to Calamus av.
Woolsey (C 3) (L. I. C.), fr. Main, N. to Hoyt av.
Woolsey av. (C 3) (L. I. C.), from Blvd., S. E. to Astoria av.
Worth (A 4) (L. I. C.), from Bulkhead line, S. E. to Vernon av.
Worth (H 5) (Flushing), from Flushing river, N. to Jefferson.
Worthington av. (E 5), fr. Woodside av., N. to Middagh.
Wortman av. (G 10) (Woodhaven), from Boro. line, E. to Aqueduct sta.
Wren pl. (M 8) (Jamaica), from 107th av., S. E. to 108th av.
Wright av. (D 5) (Woodside), fr. Queens blvd., N. E. to Seventh.
Wurster (H 5) (Corona Heights), fr. Corona av., N. E. to 120th.
Wyckoff av. (D 8) cont'd from Boro. line, S. E. to Alden av.
Xenia pl. (G 5) (Corona Hgts.), from Martense av., S. E. to Rodman.
Xenophon (H 3) (College Pt.), now part of 133d.
Yacht (H 4), from Jackson N. to Flushing Bay.
Yale (M 7) (Jamaica), now part of 179th.
Yalu (G 6), from Queens blvd., N. E to 120th.
Yardley (L 9), from Yukon av., N. W. to Warburton av.
Yates rd. (L 8) (Jamaica), from Sutphin blvd., N. E. to 154th.
Yellowstone av. (G 7), from Woodhaven av., N. & E. & N. to Yalu.
York av. (O 4), from Hanford parkway, S. of Sanborn av., N. E. to Overbrook dr.
Young (B 5) (L. I. C.), from Review av., N. E. to Hunters Point av.
Yukon av. (K 9), now part of Foch blvd.
Yuma la. (K 7), fr. Union Hall North, between Gilman av. and Pavo rd., W., N. and N. E. to 164th.
Zeiller (D 7), from Flushing av., S. E. to Metropolitan av.
Zion (P 3), from Jackson av., bet. Marathon av. and 248th, S. E. to Thebes la.
Zoller rd. (N 9) (Jamaica), from Merrick blvd., N. E. to 180th.
Zulder (K 9), from Rockaway blvd., N. E. to Van Wyck blvd., that part E. thereof being now part of 120th av.
Zuni (G 6), from Queens blvd., N. E. to 120th.

First Month **JANUARY** 31 Days

Moon's Phases	D.	H.	M.
New Moon.	9	0	27
First Quar.	17	1	31
Full Moon	23	6	08
Last Quar.	30	3	02

CALENDAR FOR GREATER NEW YORK (Standard Time)

Day of Month	Day of Week	Day of Year	Sun at Noon Mark Mean time H. M. S.	Sun Rises H. M.	Sun Sets H. M.	Moon Rises H. M.	Moon Sets H. M.
1	Sat	1	12 3 40	7 20	4 39	0 12	11 44
2	S	2	12 4 08	7 20	4 40	1 15	12 18
3	Mo	3	12 4 36	7 20	4 41	2 15	12 54
4	Tu	4	12 5 03	7 20	4 42	3 14	1 31
5	W	5	12 5 30	7 20	4 43	4 09	2 13
6	Th	6	12 5 57	7 20	4 44	5 01	2 59
7	Fri	7	12 6 23	7 20	4 44	5 49	3 48
8	Sat	8	12 6 49	7 20	4 45	6 33	4 40
9	S	9	12 7 14	7 20	4 46	7 14	5 35
10	Mo	10	12 7 39	7 20	4 48	7 50	6 31
11	Tu	11	12 8 03	7 20	4 49	8 22	7 28
12	W	12	12 8 27	7 20	4 50	8 53	8 24
13	Th	13	12 8 50	7 19	4 51	9 22	9 23
14	Fri	14	12 9 12	7 19	4 52	9 52	10 21
15	Sat	15	12 9 33	7 18	4 53	10 21	11 22
16	S	16	12 9 54	7 18	4 54	10 52	.. ..
17	Mo	17	12 10 14	7 18	4 55	11 26	0 24
18	Tu	18	12 10 34	7 17	4 56	12 07	1 28
19	W	19	12 10 52	7 17	4 57	12 53	2 33
20	Th	20	12 11 10	7 16	4 58	1 47	3 38
21	Fri	21	12 11 27	7 16	5 00	2 49	4 41
22	Sat	22	12 11 44	7 15	5 01	3 57	5 39
23	S	23	12 11 59	7 14	5 02	5 09	6 31
24	Mo	24	12 12 14	7 14	5 03	6 24	7 17
25	Tu	25	12 12 28	7 13	5 04	7 37	7 59
26	W	26	12 12 41	7 12	5 06	8 48	8 35
27	Th	27	12 12 54	7 12	5 07	9 57	9 11
28	Fri	28	12 13 05	7 11	5 08	11 02	9 44
29	Sat	29	12 13 16	7 10	5 09	.. ..	10 18
30	S	30	12 13 26	7 09	5 10	0 05	10 54
31	Mo	31	12 13 30	7 08	5 11	1 06	11 31

Second Month **FEBRUARY** 28 Days

Moon's Phases	D.	H.	M.
New Moon.	7	7	37
First Quar.	15	1	53
Full Moon.	23	4	32

CALENDAR FOR GREATER NEW YORK (Standard Time)

Day of Month	Day of Week	Day of Year	Sun at Noon Mark. Mean time H. M. S.	Sun Rises H. M.	Sun Sets H. M.	Moon Rises H. M.	Moon Sets H. M.
1	Tu	32	12 13 44	7 07	5 13	2 03	12 13
2	W	33	12 13 52	7 06	5 14	2 56	12 58
3	Th	34	12 13 58	7 05	5 15	3 46	1 45
4	Fri	35	12 14 04	7 04	5 17	4 32	2 36
5	Sat	36	12 14 10	7 03	5 18	5 13	3 29
6	S	37	12 14 14	7 02	5 19	5 51	4 25
7	Mo	38	12 14 18	7 00	5 21	6 25	5 22
8	Tu	39	12 14 21	6 59	5 22	6 56	6 19
9	W	40	12 14 23	6 58	5 23	7 27	7 17
10	Th	41	12 14 24	6 57	5 24	7 56	8 15
11	Fri	42	12 14 24	6 56	5 26	8 25	9 15
12	Sat	43	12 14 24	6 55	5 27	8 56	10 16
13	S	44	12 14 23	6 53	5 28	9 29	11 18
14	Mo	45	12 14 21	6 52	5 29	10 06	.. ..
15	Tu	46	12 14 18	6 51	5 30	10 48	0 21
16	W	47	12 14 15	6 50	5 31	11 37	1 25
17	Th	48	12 14 11	6 48	5 33	12 33	2 25
18	Fri	49	12 14 06	6 47	5 34	1 36	3 23
19	Sat	50	12 14 00	6 46	5 35	2 44	4 17
20	S	51	12 13 54	6 44	5 36	3 56	5 05
21	Mo	52	12 13 47	6 43	5 37	5 09	5 48
22	Tu	53	12 13 40	6 41	5 38	6 22	6 28
23	W	54	12 13 32	6 40	5 40	7 33	7 04
24	Th	55	12 13 23	6 39	5 41	8 42	7 40
25	Fri	56	12 13 13	6 37	5 42	9 48	8 15
26	Sat	57	12 13 03	6 36	5 43	10 52	8 52
27	S	58	12 12 53	6 34	5 44	11 53	9 29
28	Mo	59	12 12 42	6 33	5 45	.. ..	10 10

NOTE. Heavy-faced type indicates afternoon or p. m. time.

Third Month **MARCH** 31 Days

Moon's Phases	D.	H.	M.
Last Quar.	1	9	08
New Moon.	9	1	09
First Quar.	16	10	49
Full Moon.	23	3	19
Last Quar.	31	4	13

CALENDAR FOR GREATER NEW YORK (Standard Time)

Day of Month	Day of Week	Day of Year	Sun at Noon Mark Mean time H. M. S.	Sun Rises H. M.	Sun Sets H. M.	Moon Rises H. M.	Moon Sets H. M.
1	Tu	60	12 12 31	6 31	5 46	0 48	10 54
2	W	61	12 12 19	6 30	5 47	1 40	11 41
3	Th	62	12 12 06	6 29	5 48	2 27	12 31
4	Fri	63	12 11 53	6 27	5 50	3 10	1 23
5	Sat	64	12 11 40	6 25	5 51	3 49	2 18
6	S	65	12 11 26	6 23	5 52	4 24	3 14
7	Mo	66	12 11 12	6 21	5 54	4 58	4 11
8	Tu	67	12 10 57	6 20	5 55	5 29	5 08
9	W	68	12 10 42	6 18	5 56	5 58	6 08
10	Th	69	12 10 27	6 17	5 57	6 28	7 08
11	Fri	70	12 10 11	6 15	5 58	7 00	8 10
12	Sat	71	12 9 55	6 14	5 59	7 33	9 11
13	S	72	12 9 39	6 12	6 00	8 09	10 14
14	Mo	73	12 9 22	6 10	6 01	8 48	11 18
15	Tu	74	12 9 05	6 09	6 02	9 34	.. ..
16	W	75	12 8 48	6 07	6 03	10 27	0 18
17	Th	76	12 8 31	6 06	6 04	11 25	1 15
18	Fri	77	12 8 13	6 04	6 05	12 28	2 09
19	Sat	78	12 7 56	6 02	6 06	1 37	2 58
20	S	79	12 7 38	6 01	6 07	2 48	3 41
21	Mo	80	12 7 20	5 59	6 08	3 59	4 21
22	Tu	81	12 7 02	5 57	6 09	5 09	4 57
23	W	82	12 6 43	5 56	6 10	6 18	5 33
24	Th	83	12 6 25	5 54	6 12	7 27	6 09
25	Fri	84	12 6 07	5 53	6 12	8 32	6 46
26	Sat	85	12 5 48	5 51	6 14	9 36	7 23
27	S	86	12 5 30	5 49	6 14	10 36	8 04
28	Mo	87	12 5 11	5 48	6 16	11 30	8 47
29	Tu	88	12 4 53	5 46	6 16	.. ..	9 34
30	W	89	12 4 35	5 44	6 18	0 20	10 23
31	Th	90	12 4 16	5 43	6 19	1 06	11 15

Fourth Month **APRIL** 30 Days

Moon's Phases	D.	H.	M.
New Moon.	8	4	05
First Quar.	15	5	12
Full Moon.	22	2	49
Last Quar.	29	11	09

CALENDAR FOR GREATER NEW YORK (Standard Time)

Day of Month	Day of Week	Day of Year	Sun at Noon Mark Mean time H. M. S.	Sun Rises H. M.	Sun Sets H. M.	Moon Rises H. M.	Moon Sets H. M.
1	Fri	91	12 3 58	5 41	6 20	1 47	12 09
2	Sat	92	12 3 40	5 39	6 21	2 23	1 05
3	S	93	12 3 22	5 37	6 22	2 57	2 01
4	Mo	94	12 3 05	5 35	6 23	3 28	2 58
5	Tu	95	12 2 47	5 34	6 25	3 58	3 57
6	W	96	12 2 30	5 32	6 26	4 28	4 57
7	Th	97	12 2 13	5 31	6 27	5 00	5 58
8	Fri	98	12 1 56	5 29	6 28	5 32	7 01
9	Sat	99	12 1 39	5 27	6 29	6 08	8 05
10	S	100	12 1 23	5 26	6 30	6 48	9 10
11	Mo	101	12 1 07	5 24	6 31	7 32	10 12
12	Tu	102	12 0 51	5 23	6 32	8 24	11 12
13	W	103	12 0 35	5 21	6 33	9 21	.. ..
14	Th	104	12 0 20	5 20	6 34	10 22	0 06
15	Fri	105	Fast	5 18	6 35	11 28	0 55
16	Sat	106	11 59 50	5 17	6 36	12 36	1 39
17	S	107	11 59 36	5 15	6 37	1 44	2 20
18	Mo	108	11 59 22	5 14	6 38	2 53	2 56
19	Tu	109	11 59 09	5 12	6 39	4 01	3 31
20	W	110	11 58 55	5 11	6 40	5 08	4 06
21	Th	111	11 58 43	5 09	6 41	6 14	4 41
22	Fri	112	11 58 30	5 08	6 42	7 19	5 18
23	Sat	113	11 58 19	5 07	6 43	8 20	5 56
24	S	114	11 58 07	5 05	6 44	9 18	6 38
25	Mo	115	11 57 56	5 04	6 45	10 11	7 25
26	Tu	116	11 57 46	5 02	6 46	10 59	8 13
27	W	117	11 57 36	5 01	6 47	11 42	9 05
28	Th	118	11 57 27	5 00	6 48	.. ..	9 58
29	Fri	119	11 57 18	4 58	6 49	0 21	10 54
30	Sat	120	11 57 09	4 57	6 50	0 55	11 50

Fifth Month **MAY.** 31 Days

Moon's Phases.	D.	H.	M.
New Moon.	7	4	02
First Quar.	14	10	25
Full Moon.	21	3	15
Last Quar.	29	4	45

CALENDAR FOR GREATER NEW YORK (Standard Time)

Day of Month	Day of Week	Day of Year	Sun at Noon Mark Mean time H. M. S.	Sun Rises H. M.	Sun Sets H. M.	Moon Rises H. M.	Moon Sets H. M.
1	S	121	11 57 03	4 55	6 52	1 27	12 46
2	Mo	122	11 56 54	4 54	6 53	1 58	1 44
3	Tu	123	11 56 48	4 52	6 54	2 28	2 42
4	W	124	11 56 42	4 51	6 55	2 58	3 43
5	Th	125	11 56 36	4 50	6 56	3 30	4 46
6	Fri	126	11 56 31	4 49	6 57	4 04	5 50
7	Sat	127	11 56 27	4 48	6 58	4 43	6 56
8	S	128	11 56 23	4 46	6 59	5 26	8 01
9	Mo	129	11 56 20	4 45	7 00	6 16	9 03
10	Tu	130	11 56 17	4 44	7 01	7 12	10 01
11	W	131	11 56 15	4 43	7 02	8 14	10 53
12	Th	132	11 56 13	4 42	7 03	9 20	11 40
13	Fri	133	11 56 12	4 41	7 04	10 28	.. ..
14	Sat	134	11 56 12	4 40	7 05	11 36	0 21
15	S	135	11 56 12	4 39	7 06	12 44	0 58
16	Mo	136	11 56 13	4 38	7 07	1 51	1 33
17	Tu	137	11 56 14	4 38	7 08	2 57	2 07
18	W	138	11 56 15	4 36	7 08	4 02	2 40
19	Th	139	11 56 18	4 36	7 09	5 06	3 16
20	Fri	140	11 56 21	4 35	7 10	6 08	3 53
21	Sat	141	11 56 24	4 34	7 11	7 07	4 33
22	S	142	11 56 28	4 33	7 12	8 02	5 17
23	Mo	143	11 56 32	4 32	7 13	8 52	6 04
24	Tu	144	11 56 37	4 32	7 14	9 38	6 56
25	W	145	11 56 43	4 31	7 15	10 18	7 48
26	Th	146	11 56 49	4 31	7 15	10 54	8 48
27	Fri	147	11 56 55	4 30	7 16	11 28	9 39
28	Sat	148	11 57 02	4 29	7 17	11 59	10 35
29	S	149	11 57 09	4 29	7 18	.. ..	11 31
30	Mo	150	11 57 17	4 28	7 19	0 28	12 29
31	Tu	151	11 57 26	4 28	7 19	0 57	1 28

Sixth Month **JUNE.** 30 Days

Moon's Phases.	D.	H.	M.
New Moon.	6	1	15
First Quar.	13	4	00
Full Moon.	20	4	41
Last Quar.	28	8	17

CALENDAR FOR GREATER NEW YORK (Standard Time)

Day of Month	Day of Week	Day of Year	Sun at Noon Mark Mean time H. M. S.	Sun Rises H. M.	Sun Sets H. M.	Moon Rises H. M.	Moon Sets H. M.
1	W	152	11 57 35	4 27	7 20	1 28	2 29
2	Th	153	11 57 44	4 27	7 21	2 00	3 31
3	Fri	154	11 57 53	4 26	7 22	2 36	4 36
4	Sat	155	11 58 03	4 26	7 22	3 17	5 42
5	S	156	11 58 14	4 26	7 23	4 04	6 47
6	Mo	157	11 58 24	4 25	7 24	4 58	7 49
7	Tu	158	11 58 35	4 25	7 24	5 59	8 46
8	W	159	11 58 47	4 25	7 25	7 05	9 38
9	Th	160	11 58 58	4 24	7 26	8 16	10 20
10	Fri	161	11 59 10	4 24	7 26	9 26	11 00
11	Sat	162	11 59 22	4 24	7 27	10 35	11 36
12	S	163	11 59 34	4 24	7 27	11 44	.. ..
13	Mo	164	11 59 47	4 23	7 28	12 50	0 10
14	Tu	165	Slow	4 23	7 29	1 55	0 44
15	W	166	12 0 12	4 23	7 29	2 58	1 17
16	Th	167	12 0 24	4 23	7 29	4 00	1 54
17	Fri	168	12 0 37	4 23	7 30	5 00	2 32
18	Sat	169	12 0 50	4 23	7 30	5 55	3 14
19	S	170	12 1 03	4 23	7 31	6 47	4 00
20	Mo	171	12 1 16	4 24	7 31	7 34	4 49
21	Tu	172	12 1 29	4 24	7 31	8 16	5 41
22	W	173	12 1 42	4 24	7 31	8 55	6 35
23	Th	174	12 1 55	4 24	7 31	9 29	7 31
24	Fri	175	12 2 07	4 25	7 31	10 00	8 26
25	Sat	176	12 2 20	4 25	7 32	10 31	9 22
26	S	177	12 2 33	4 25	7 32	10 59	10 19
27	Mo	178	12 2 45	4 26	7 32	11 28	11 16
28	Tu	179	12 2 58	4 26	7 32	11 59	12 15
29	W	180	12 3 10	4 27	7 31	.. ..	1 16
30	Th	181	12 3 22	4 27	7 31	0 39	2 17

Seventh Month **JULY.** 31 Days

Moon's Phases.	D.	H.	M.
New Moon.	5	8	36
First Quar.	11	11	16
Full Moon.	19	7	08
Last Quar.	27	9	20

CALENDAR FOR GREATER NEW YORK (Standard Time)

Day of Month	Day of Week	Day of Year	Sun at Noon Mark Mean time H. M. S.	Sun Rises H. M.	Sun Sets H. M.	Moon Rises H. M.	Moon Sets H. M.
1	Fri	182	12 3 34	4 27	7 31	1 09	3 21
2	Sat	183	12 3 45	4 28	7 31	1 52	4 26
3	S	184	12 3 57	4 29	7 31	2 43	5 30
4	Mo	185	12 4 08	4 29	7 31	3 40	6 30
5	Tu	186	12 4 18	4 30	7 30	4 44	7 24
6	W	187	12 4 29	4 31	7 30	5 54	8 13
7	Th	188	12 4 39	4 31	7 30	7 07	8 56
8	Fri	189	12 4 48	4 32	7 29	8 20	9 35
9	Sat	190	12 4 58	4 33	7 29	9 31	10 11
10	S	191	12 5 06	4 33	7 28	10 40	10 46
11	Mo	192	12 5 15	4 34	7 28	11 46	11 20
12	Tu	193	12 5 23	4 35	7 28	12 51	11 57
13	W	194	12 5 30	4 36	7 27	1 54	.. ..
14	Th	195	12 5 37	4 36	7 27	2 54	0 34
15	Fri	196	12 5 44	4 37	7 26	3 50	1 14
16	Sat	197	12 5 49	4 38	7 26	4 43	1 58
17	S	198	12 5 55	4 38	7 25	5 31	2 45
18	Mo	199	12 6 00	4 39	7 24	6 15	3 36
19	Tu	200	12 6 04	4 40	7 24	6 55	4 29
20	W	201	12 6 08	4 41	7 23	7 30	5 24
21	Th	202	12 6 11	4 42	7 22	8 03	6 20
22	Fri	203	12 6 14	4 43	7 21	8 34	7 16
23	Sat	204	12 6 16	4 43	7 21	9 03	8 12
24	S	205	12 6 17	4 44	7 20	9 32	9 09
25	Mo	206	12 6 18	4 45	7 19	10 01	10 06
26	Tu	207	12 6 19	4 46	7 18	10 33	11 04
27	W	208	12 6 19	4 47	7 17	11 07	12 05
28	Th	209	12 6 18	4 48	7 16	11 46	1 06
29	Fri	210	12 6 17	4 49	7 15	.. ..	2 09
30	Sat	211	12 6 15	4 50	7 14	0 30	3 12
31	S	212	12 6 12	4 50	7 13	1 23	4 12

Eighth Month **AUGUST.** 31 Days

Moon's Phases.	D.	H.	M.
New Moon.	3	3	18
First Quar.	10	9	14
Full Moon.	18	10	28
Last Quar.	26	7	51

CALENDAR FOR GREATER NEW YORK (Standard Time)

Day of Month	Day of Week	Day of Year	Sun at Noon Mark Mean time H. M. S.	Sun Rises H. M.	Sun Sets H. M.	Moon Rises H. M.	Moon Sets H. M.
1	Mo	213	12 6 09	4 51	7 12	2 28	5 09
2	Tu	214	12 6 05	4 52	7 11	3 30	6 01
3	W	215	12 6 01	4 53	7 10	4 41	6 47
4	Th	216	12 5 56	4 54	7 09	5 55	7 29
5	Fri	217	12 5 51	4 55	7 08	7 09	8 08
6	Sat	218	12 5 45	4 56	7 07	8 21	8 44
7	S	219	12 5 38	4 57	7 06	9 31	9 20
8	Mo	220	12 5 31	4 58	7 04	10 39	9 57
9	Tu	221	12 5 23	4 59	7 03	11 44	10 34
10	W	222	12 5 14	5 00	7 02	12 45	11 14
11	Th	223	12 5 05	5 01	7 01	1 44	11 57
12	Fri	224	12 4 55	5 02	6 59	2 38	.. ..
13	Sat	225	12 4 45	5 03	6 57	3 28	0 43
14	S	226	12 4 34	5 05	6 56	4 14	1 32
15	Mo	227	12 4 22	5 06	6 55	4 55	2 24
16	Tu	228	12 4 10	5 07	6 53	5 32	3 19
17	W	229	12 3 59	5 07	6 52	6 06	4 14
18	Th	230	12 3 46	5 08	6 50	6 37	5 10
19	Fri	231	12 3 32	5 09	6 49	7 07	6 06
20	Sat	232	12 3 18	5 10	6 48	7 35	7 03
21	S	233	12 3 04	5 11	6 46	8 05	8 00
22	Mo	234	12 2 49	5 12	6 45	8 36	8 57
23	Tu	235	12 2 34	5 13	6 43	9 08	9 57
24	W	236	12 2 18	5 14	6 42	9 45	10 57
25	Th	237	12 2 02	5 15	6 40	10 26	11 58
26	Fri	238	12 1 45	5 16	6 39	11 14	12 58
27	Sat	239	12 1 28	5 17	6 37	.. ..	1 [illegible]
28	S	240	12 1 11	5 18	6 36	0 08	2 [illegible]
29	Mo	241	12 0 54	5 19	6 34	1 10	3 [illegible]
30	Tu	242	12 0 36	5 20	6 33	2 17	4 [illegible]
31	W	243	12 0 17	5 21	6 31	3 29	5 20

Ninth Month SEPTEMBER. 30 Days

CALENDAR FOR GREATER NEW YORK (Standard Time)

Moon's Phases.	D.	H.	M.
New Moon.	1	10	33
First Quar.	8	10	30
Full Moon.	17	2	20
Last Quar.	24	4	18

Day of Month	Day of Week	Day of Year	Sun at Noon Mark Mean time	Sun Rises	Sun Sets	Moon Rises	Moon Sets
			H. M. S.	H. M.	H. M.	H. M.	H. M.
1	Th	244	11 59 59	5 22	6 30	4 42	6 01
2	Fri	245	11 59 40	5 23	6 28	5 56	6 38
3	Sat	246	11 59 21	5 24	6 26	7 09	7 16
4	S	247	11 59 01	5 25	6 25	8 19	7 53
5	Mo	248	11 58 42	5 26	6 23	9 27	8 31
6	Tu	249	11 58 22	5 27	6 21	10 32	9 11
7	W	250	11 58 02	5 27	6 20	11 34	9 53
8	Th	251	11 57 41	5 29	6 18	12 31	10 40
9	Fri	252	11 57 21	5 29	6 17	1 24	11 28
10	Sat	253	11 57 00	5 31	6 15	2 11	.. ..
11	S	254	11 56 39	5 32	6 13	2 54	0 20
12	Mo	255	11 56 18	5 33	6 11	3 32	1 18
13	Tu	256	11 55 57	5 34	6 09	4 07	2 08
14	W	257	11 55 36	5 35	6 08	4 39	3 04
15	Th	258	11 55 15	5 36	6 06	5 10	4 00
16	Fri	259	11 54 53	5 37	6 04	5 39	4 57
17	Sat	260	11 54 32	5 38	6 03	6 08	5 54
18	S	261	11 54 11	5 39	6 01	6 39	6 51
19	Mo	262	11 53 50	5 40	5 59	7 11	7 51
20	Tu	263	11 53 28	5 41	5 58	7 47	8 50
21	W	264	11 53 07	5 42	5 56	8 27	9 51
22	Th	265	11 52 46	5 43	5 55	9 11	10 51
23	Fri	266	11 52 25	5 44	5 53	10 02	11 51
24	Sat	267	11 52 04	5 45	5 51	10 59	12 47
25	S	268	11 51 44	5 46	5 49	.. ..	1 39
26	Mo	269	11 51 23	5 47	5 48	0 02	2 28
27	Tu	270	11 51 03	5 48	5 46	1 09	3 12
28	W	271	11 50 43	5 49	5 44	2 20	3 53
29	Th	272	11 50 23	5 50	5 43	3 31	4 31
30	Fri	273	11 50 04	5 51	5 41	4 43	5 09

Tenth Month OCTOBER. 31 Days

CALENDAR FOR GREATER NEW YORK (Standard Time)

Moon's Phases.	D.	H.	M.
New Moon.	1	7	26
First Quar.	8	3	12
Full Moon.	16	6	0
Last Quar.	23	11	32
New Moon.	30	6	39

Day of Month	Day of Week	Day of Year	Sun at Noon Mark Mean time	Sun Rises	Sun Sets	Moon Rises	Moon Sets
			H. M. S.	H. M.	H. M.	H. M.	H. M.
1	Sat	274	11 49 44	5 52	5 40	5 55	5 46
2	S	275	11 49 25	5 53	5 38	7 05	6 23
3	Mo	276	11 49 07	5 54	5 36	8 13	7 04
4	Tu	277	11 48 48	5 54	5 35	9 18	7 46
5	W	278	11 48 30	5 56	5 33	10 19	8 32
6	Th	279	11 48 13	5 56	5 31	11 14	9 20
7	Fri	280	11 47 55	5 58	5 30	12 04	10 12
8	Sat	281	11 47 38	5 59	5 28	12 49	11 05
9	S	282	11 47 22	6 00	5 26	1 29	.. ..
10	Mo	283	11 47 06	6 01	5 24	2 05	0 00
11	Tu	284	11 46 50	6 03	5 23	2 39	0 55
12	W	285	11 46 35	6 04	5 21	3 10	1 51
13	Th	286	11 46 20	6 05	5 19	3 40	2 47
14	Fri	287	11 46 06	6 06	5 18	4 10	3 45
15	Sat	288	11 45 53	6 07	5 17	4 40	4 42
16	S	289	11 45 40	6 08	5 15	5 12	5 42
17	Mo	290	11 45 27	6 09	5 13	5 47	6 43
18	Tu	291	11 45 15	6 10	5 12	6 26	7 44
19	W	292	11 45 04	6 11	5 11	7 09	8 45
20	Th	293	11 44 53	6 12	5 09	7 59	9 45
21	Fri	294	11 44 43	6 13	5 08	8 54	10 43
22	Sat	295	11 44 34	6 14	5 06	9 54	11 36
23	S	296	11 44 25	6 15	5 05	10 59	12 25
24	Mo	297	11 44 17	6 16	5 04	.. ..	1 09
25	Tu	298	11 44 10	6 18	5 02	0 06	1 50
26	W	299	11 44 04	6 19	5 01	1 15	2 28
27	Th	300	11 43 58	6 20	5 00	2 25	3 04
28	Fri	301	11 43 53	6 21	4 58	3 34	3 40
29	Sat	302	11 43 49	6 22	4 57	4 43	4 17
30	S	303	11 43 46	6 23	4 56	5 52	4 55
31	Mo	304	11 43 43	6 24	4 55	6 58	5 37

Eleventh Month NOVEMBER. 30 Days

CALENDAR FOR GREATER NEW YORK (Standard Time)

Moon's Phases.	D.	H.	M.
First Quar.	7	10	54
Full Moon.	15	8	39
Last Quar.	22	6	41
New Moon.	29	8	26

Day of Month	Day of Week	Day of Year	Sun at Noon Mark Mean time	Sun Rises	Sun Sets	Moon Rises	Moon Sets
			H. M. S.	H. M.	H. M.	H. M.	H. M.
1	Tu	305	11 43 41	6 25	4 53	8 02	6 22
2	W	306	11 43 40	6 27	4 52	9 01	7 09
3	Th	307	11 43 40	6 28	4 51	9 55	8 01
4	Fri	308	11 43 40	6 29	4 50	10 43	8 54
5	Sat	309	11 43 42	6 30	4 49	11 26	9 49
6	S	310	11 43 44	6 31	4 47	12 04	10 45
7	Mo	311	11 43 47	6 33	4 46	12 39	11 40
8	Tu	312	11 43 51	6 34	4 45	1 10	.. ..
9	W	313	11 43 55	6 36	4 44	1 41	0 36
10	Th	314	11 44 01	6 37	4 43	2 10	1 33
11	Fri	315	11 44 07	6 38	4 42	2 40	2 30
12	Sat	316	11 44 14	6 39	4 41	3 11	3 29
13	S	317	11 44 22	6 40	4 40	3 45	4 30
14	Mo	318	11 44 31	6 41	4 39	4 22	5 31
15	Tu	319	11 44 41	6 42	4 38	5 04	6 34
16	W	320	11 44 52	6 44	4 38	5 52	7 36
17	Th	321	11 45 02	6 45	4 37	6 47	8 36
18	Fri	322	11 45 15	6 46	4 36	7 47	9 32
19	Sat	323	11 45 28	6 47	4 35	8 51	10 24
20	S	324	11 45 41	6 48	4 35	9 59	11 10
21	Mo	325	11 45 56	6 49	4 34	11 06	11 51
22	Tu	326	11 46 12	6 50	4 33	.. ..	12 30
23	W	327	11 46 28	6 52	4 33	0 14	1 05
24	Th	328	11 46 45	6 53	4 32	1 23	1 40
25	Fri	329	11 47 03	6 54	4 32	2 30	2 15
26	Sat	330	11 47 22	6 55	4 31	3 37	2 52
27	S	331	11 47 41	6 56	4 31	4 42	3 31
28	Mo	332	11 48 01	6 57	4 31	5 47	4 13
29	Tu	333	11 48 22	6 58	4 30	6 47	4 59
30	W	334	11 48 44	6 59	4 30	7 44	5 49

Twelfth Month DECEMBER. 31 Days

CALENDAR FOR GREATER NEW YORK (Standard Time)

Moon's Phases.	D.	H.	M.
First Quar.	7	8	20
Full Moon.	14	9	51
Last Quar.	21	2	54
New Moon.	29	0	39

Day of Month	Day of Week	Day of Year	Sun at Noon Mark Mean time	Sun Rises	Sun Sets	Moon Rises	Moon Sets
			H. M. S.	H. M.	H. M.	H. M.	H. M.
1	Th	335	11 49 06	7 00	4 30	8 35	6 42
2	Fri	336	11 49 29	7 01	4 29	9 21	7 37
3	Sat	337	11 49 52	7 02	4 29	10 01	8 33
4	S	338	11 50 16	7 03	4 29	10 37	9 29
5	Mo	339	11 50 41	7 04	4 29	11 10	10 25
6	Tu	340	11 51 06	7 05	4 29	11 41	11 21
7	W	341	11 51 32	7 06	4 29	12 10	.. ..
8	Th	342	11 51 58	7 07	4 29	12 39	0 17
9	Fri	343	11 52 25	7 08	4 29	1 09	1 14
10	Sat	344	11 52 52	7 08	4 29	1 41	2 13
11	S	345	11 53 19	7 09	4 29	2 17	3 14
12	Mo	346	11 53 47	7 10	4 29	2 56	4 15
13	Tu	347	11 54 15	7 11	4 29	3 41	5 19
14	W	348	11 54 43	7 12	4 29	4 34	6 21
15	Th	349	11 55 12	7 12	4 30	5 33	7 21
16	Fri	350	11 55 41	7 13	4 30	6 38	8 16
17	Sat	351	11 56 10	7 14	4 30	7 46	9 06
18	S	352	11 56 40	7 14	4 31	8 56	9 51
19	Mo	353	11 57 09	7 15	4 31	10 05	10 33
20	Tu	354	11 57 39	7 16	4 31	11 15	11 08
21	W	355	11 58 09	7 16	4 32	.. ..	11 43
22	Th	356	11 58 39	7 17	4 32	0 22	12 19
23	Fri	357	11 59 09	7 17	4 33	1 28	12 54
24	Sat	358	11 59 39	7 18	4 34	2 33	1 31
25	S	359	Slow	7 18	4 34	3 36	2 11
26	Mo	360	12 00 39	7 18	4 35	4 38	2 55
27	Tu	361	12 01 08	7 19	4 35	5 35	3 42
28	W	362	12 01 38	7 19	4 36	6 28	4 33
29	Th	363	12 02 07	7 19	4 37	7 15	5 26
30	Fri	364	12 02 37	7 20	4 37	7 59	6 22
31	Sat	365	12 03 06	7 20	4 38	8 36	7 19

HIGH WATER AT NEW YORK (GOVERNOR'S ISLAND).

Following high water tables were prepared and furnished by the United States Coast and Geodetic Survey at New York City. The time given is Eastern Standard Time. ●, new moon; ☽, 1st quar.; ○, full moon; ☾, 3d quar.; E, moon on equator; N, S, moon farthest north or south of equator; A, P, moon in apogee or perigee; ⊙1 sun at vernal equinox; ⊙2 sun at summer solstice; ⊙3 sun at autumnal equinox; ⊙4 sun at winter solstice.

Moon.	Date of Mo.	JANUARY.				Moon.	FEBRUARY.				Moon.	MARCH.				Moon.	APRIL.			
		A. M.		P. M.			A. M.		P. M.			A. M.		P. M.			A. M.		P. M.	
		High Water	Low Water	High Water	Low Water		High Water	Low Water	High Water	Low Water		High Water	Low Water	High Water	Low Water		High Water	Low Water	High Water	Low Water
		h. m.	h. m.	h. m.	h. m.		h. m.	h. m.	h. m.	h. m.		h. m.	h. m.	h. m.	h. m.		h. m.	h. m.	h. m.	h. m.
	1	1 54	8 12	12	8 33		3 21	9 41	3 46	9 54	☾	1 40	8 09	2 08	8 24	A	2 58	9 27	3 33	9 45
	2	2 54	9 14	14	9 29		4 17	10 38	4 41	10 47	S	2 42	9 09	13	9 23		3 52	10 20	4 29	10 38
	3	3 53	10 12	13	10 21	S	5 07	11 29	5 31	11 36		3 41	10 07	11	10 19		4 44	11 08	5 15	11 28
	4	4 44	11 05	06	11 12		5 53	.. ..	6 16	12 15	A	4 35	10 59	04	11 10		5 29	11 52	5 57	.. ..
	5	5 32	11 54	54	11 58	A	6 33	0 21	6 57	12 57		5 23	11 46	49	1 56		6 10	0 12	6 34	12 32
S	6	6 16	.. ..	39	12 39		7 10	1 03	7 34	1 36		6 05	.. ..	30	2 29	E	6 47	0 53	7 07	1 08
	7	6 55	0 42	18	1 21	●	7 44	1 42	8 07	2 13		6 48	0 40	08	1 07		7 21	1 32	7 39	1 44
	8	7 33	1 23	56	2 01		8 14	2 18	8 38	2 49		7 18	1 20	33	1 48	●	7 54	2 09	8 11	2 17
A●	9	8 07	2 03	32	2 41		8 42	2 53	9 05	3 22	●	7 50	1 59	09	2 18		8 28	2 46	8 43	2 50
	10	8 38	2 41	06	3 16	E	9 09	3 27	9 31	3 51	E	8 19	2 31	37	2 49		9 03	3 24	9 20	3 24
	11	9 05	3 17	35	3 54		9 37	3 58	10 03	4 19		8 46	3 06	05	3 18		9 43	4 06	10 00	4 02
	12	9 34	3 52	1 04	4 28		10 13	4 33	10 42	4 48		9 17	3 39	39	3 47	N	10 25	4 50	10 47	4 47
	13	10 04	4 26	1 38	5 00		10 54	5 14	11 27	5 25		9 52	4 15	1 16	4 19		11 18	5 44	11 42	5 42
E	14	10 40	5 04	1 18	5 35		11 42	6 07	.. ..	6 14		10 34	4 56	1 02	4 58		.. ..	6 49	12 22	6 57
	15	11 24	5 50	.. ..	6 12	☽	0 21	7 19	12 40	7 21		11 28	5 49	1 55	5 49	☽	0 49	7 59	1 44	8 21
	16	0 05	6 48	1 14	7 02		1 28	8 40	1 54	8 44	N☽	.. ..	6 57	1 23	6 59	P	13	9 09	3 09	9 33
☽	17	1 01	8 00	15	8 05	N	2 47	9 52	3 25	9 59		1 03	8 17	41	8 28		35	10 11	4 20	10 38
	18	2 07	9 12	25	9 18		4 07	10 55	4 44	11 05		2 25	9 30	16	9 46		42	11 08	5 18	11 37
	19	3 19	10 17	48	10 18		5 14	11 49	5 44	.. ..		3 51	10 24	33	10 58	E	42	.. ..	6 12	12 01
	20	4 27	11 16	56	11 20	P	6 13	0 05	6 44	12 45	⊙1	4 59	11 32	35	11 58		36	0 31	7 01	12 50
N	21	5 29	.. ..	00	12 13		7 07	0 59	7 37	1 36		5 59	.. ..	29	2 24		25	22	7 48	37
	22	6 26	16	56	1 04	○	7 58	1 52	8 28	2 23	E	6 52	0 46	20	1 18	○	10	10	8 33	2 21
P○	23	7 19	11	51	1 55	E	8 47	2 43	9 17	3 12	○	7 42	1 34	08	2 01		56	56	9 18	3 06
	24	8 11	04	44	2 44		9 35	3 33	10 05	3 59		8 30	2 27	54	2 46		39	42	9 55	3 49
	25	9 02	57	36	3 31		10 24	4 24	10 53	4 45		16	3 15	39	3 32		1 23	26	10 36	4 33
	26	9 53	51	1 28	4 24		11 13	5 16	11 45	5 35		1 01	4 02	1 23	4 17	S	1 06	13	11 17	5 19
E	27	10 45	45	1 23	5 14		.. ..	6 11	12 05	6 28		1 47	4 50	1 10	5 08		1 58	00	..	6 11
	28	11 40	41	.. ..	6 08		0 42	7 08	1 04	7 25		35	5 41	1 57	5 52		00	51	12 45	7 04
	29	0 20	41	12 38	7 03		.. ..	.. ..	.. ..	.. ..	S	.. ..	6 33	1 27	6 47	A☾	51	45	1 42	8 04
☾	30	1 20	43	1 41	8 00		.. ..	.. ..	.. ..	.. ..		0 50	7 31	27	7 46		48	41	2 42	9 04
	31	2 21	45	2 44	8 58		.. ..	.. ..	.. ..	.. ..	☾	1 50	8 29	32	8 47		.. ..	.. ..	.. ..	.. ..

Moon.	Date of Mo.	MAY.				Moon.	JUNE.				Moon.	JULY.				Moon.	AUGUST.			
		A. M.		P. M.			A. M.		P. M.			A. M.		P. M.			A. M.		P. M.	
		High Water	Low Water	High Water	Low Water		High Water	Low Water	High Water	Low Water		High Water	Low Water	High Water	Low Water		High Water	Low Water	High Water	Low Water
		h. m.	h. m.	h. m.	h. m.		h. m.	h. m.	h. m.	h. m.		h. m.	h. m.	h. m.	h. m.		h. m.	h. m.	h. m.	h. m.
	1	2 49	9 33	33	10 00		3 32	10 16	4 19	10 58		3 31	10 14	4 19	11 14		5 22	11 45	57	.. ..
	2	3 49	10 23	29	10 50		4 31	11 03	5 07	11 49		4 40	11 11	5 16	.. ..		6 26	0 37	51	12 44
E	3	4 39	11 09	13	11 38		5 25	11 50	5 51	.. ..		5 45	0 09	6 15	12 06	P●	7 24	1 29	46	39
	4	5 27	11 51	58	.. ..		6 16	0 37	6 42	37	N	6 45	1 01	7 08	1 01		8 19	2 20	38	34
	5	6 10	0 22	32	12 31		7 07	1 24	7 27	22	●	7 41	1 52	8 01	1 55		9 12	3 11	31	28
	6	6 50	1 05	09	1 09	N●	7 56	2 11	8 14	10	P	8 35	2 42	8 52	2 48	E	10 05	4 01	1 24	22
●	7	7 30	1 47	47	1 48		8 46	2 59	9 01	00		9 28	3 32	9 44	3 42		10 58	4 52	18	17
	8	8 11	2 30	26	2 27	P	9 36	3 48	9 52	51		10 22	4 22	10 37	4 37		11 53	5 42	.. ..	14
	9	8 53	3 12	09	3 11		10 30	4 37	10 42	45		11 17	5 13	11 32	5 34		0 12	6 35	12 49	14
N	10	9 38	3 58	53	3 55		11 28	5 29	11 38	44	E	.. ..	6 05	12 14	6 33	☽	1 10	7 30	47	13
P	11	10 27	4 46	1 43	4 48		.. ..	6 25	12 29	47	☽	0 28	7 00	1 13	7 34		2 10	8 28	46	12
	12	11 25	5 40	1 40	5 48	E☽	0 42	7 21	1 32	54		1 29	7 56	2 13	8 36		3 12	9 25	44	1 10
	13	.. ..	6 39	31	6 56		1 46	8 21	2 36	58	•	2 32	8 53	3 13	9 37	S	4 11	10 20	39	1 03
☽	14	0 50	7 42	43	8 08		2 58	9 19	3 37	1 00		3 35	9 49	4 11	10 36		5 06	11 13	29	1 53
	15	2 00	8 45	55	9 13		3 58	10 16	4 36	1 59		4 35	10 45	5 05	11 30		5 56	.. ..	15	1 01
E	16	3 14	9 45	01	10 21		4 59	11 09	5 29	1 54		5 31	11 36	5 55	.. ..		6 40	0 38	56	1 47
	17	4 22	10 42	59	11 20		5 54	.. ..	6 19	1 01	S	6 21	0 21	6 41	12 25	A	7 21	1 20	34	30
	18	5 22	11 35	51	.. ..		6 44	0 44	7 04	1 48		7 07	1 07	7 23	1 11	○	7 59	2 00	08	2 10
	19	6 15	0 14	40	12 25	S	7 31	1 31	7 47	34	○	7 49	1 50	8 03	1 54		8 32	2 38	40	2 48
	20	7 05	1 04	26	1 12	○	8 14	2 15	8 27	19		8 29	2 31	8 38	2 36	E	9 04	3 14	09	25
○	21	7 51	1 51	10	1 57	⊙2	8 55	2 57	9 04	01	A	9 06	3 11	9 10	3 16		9 31	3 47	37	00
	22	8 36	2 36	50	2 42		9 34	3 39	9 39	41		9 40	3 49	9 40	3 54		10 00	4 18	1 07	35
S	23	9 18	3 20	29	3 20	A	10 11	4 19	10 10	22		10 11	4 25	10 08	4 30		10 34	4 46	1 44	12
	24	9 59	4 08	1 06	4 07		10 47	4 58	10 41	02	E	10 40	4 57	10 39	5 07		11 13	5 18	27	56
	25	10 39	4 46	1 42	4 50		11 22	5 35	11 18	42		11 12	5 30	1 14	5 45		11 59	5 58	.. ..	51
	26	11 21	5 29	17	5 35		11 57	6 14	11 50	27		11 49	6 01	1 56	6 30	☾	0 17	6 49	12 55	59
A	27	.. ..	6 13	[illegible]	6 23	E	.. ..	6 53	12 37	18	☾	.. ..	6 39	2 36	7 26	N	1 18	7 58	00	10
	28	.. ..	7 00	50	7 16	☾	0 34	7 36	1 24	15		0 45	7 26	1 29	8 31		2 31	9 14	15	1 16
☾	29	0 35	7 48	39	8 13		1 24	8 24	2 18	17		1 42	8 27	2 31	9 38		3 52	10 25	28	16
E	30	1 27	8 38	32	9 10		2 23	9 18	3 18	1 16		2 51	9 35	3 41	10 42		5 05	11 29	34	.. ..
	31	2 30	9 27	27	10 06		.. ..	.. ..	.. ..	.. ..	N	4 07	10 42	4 49	11 42		6 08	0 12	33	12 28

The full moon nearest to Sept. 21 is popularly known as the "harvest moon." This is because the moon then rises for several consecutive evenings at nearly the same hour, giving an unusual number of moonlight evenings. This is the most noticeable in the higher latitudes and quite disappears at the equator. The "hunter's moon" is the first full moon following the harvest moon.

HIGH WATER AT NEW YORK (GOVERNOR'S ISLAND)—*Continued.*

Moon.	Date of Mo.	September A.M. High Water	September A.M. Low Water	September P.M. High Water	September P.M. Low Water	Moon.	October A.M. High Water	October A.M. Low Water	October P.M. High Water	October P.M. Low Water
		h. m.	h. m.	h. m.	h. m.		h. m.	h. m.	h. m.	h. m.
P ●	1	7 05	1 05	7 28	1 24	●	7 36	1 30	8 01	2 00
	2	7 58	1 56	8 22	2 18		8 26	2 19	8 52	2 51
E	3	8 50	2 46	9 13	3 10	S	9 16	3 08	9 42	3 42
	4	9 41	3 36	10 05	4 04		10 05	3 57	10 34	4 33
	5	10 33	4 25	10 57	4 56		10 55	4 46	11 27	5 26
	6	11 26	5 16	11 51	5 51		11 48	5 39	.. ..	6 20
	7	.. ..	6 09	12 20	6 48	S	0 23	6 35	12 43	7 16
☽	8	0 43	7 04	1 18	7 46	☽	1 21	7 33	1 40	8 12
S	9	1 48	8 02	2 16	8 44		2 20	8 30	2 38	9 06
	10	2 48	9 00	3 14	9 39		3 16	9 26	3 31	9 57
	11	3 46	9 54	4 09	10 32	A	4 07	10 18	4 22	10 45
	12	4 39	10 47	4 58	11 21		4 58	11 06	5 07	11 28
A	13	5 26	11 36	5 48	.. ..		5 34	11 52	5 48	.. ..
	14	6 10	0 06	6 24	12 21	E	6 12	0 10	6 26	12 33
	15	6 48	0 47	7 02	1 03		6 47	0 48	7 01	1 18
	16	7 24	1 25	7 36	1 42	○	7 19	1 24	7 34	1 52
E ○	17	7 56	2 02	8 08	2 20		7 50	1 57	8 07	2 30
	18	8 26	2 36	8 37	2 56		8 21	2 30	8 41	3 08
	19	8 55	3 08	9 06	3 32		8 57	3 04	9 19	3 48
	20	9 24	3 38	9 40	4 09		9 37	3 40	10 03	4 33
	21	10 00	4 09	10 20	4 48	N	10 22	4 24	10 54	5 24
	22	10 43	4 45	11 06	5 35		11 15	5 18	11 55	6 23
⊙ 3	23	11 33	5 31	.. ..	6 33	☾	.. ..	6 27	12 17	7 28
N ☾	24	0 01	6 30	12 32	7 41		1 09	7 44	1 31	8 38
	25	1 08	7 47	1 41	8 50		2 28	8 57	2 49	9 34
	26	2 27	9 03	3 00	9 55		3 37	10 08	4 00	10 31
	27	3 46	10 13	4 13	10 53	E P	4 39	11 03	5 01	11 25
	28	4 52	11 16	5 17	11 49		5 34	11 58	5 57	.. ..
P	29	5 51	.. ..	6 15	12 13		6 26	0 16	6 50	12 51
E	30	6 45	0 40	7 09	1 07	●	7 15	1 05	7 40	1 41
	31	.. ..	.. ..	.. ..	.. ..		8 03	1 52	8 30	2 31

Date of Mo.	Moon.	November A.M. High Water	November A.M. Low Water	November P.M. High Water	November P.M. Low Water	Moon.	December A.M. High Water	December A.M. Low Water	December P.M. High Water	December P.M. Low Water
		h. m.	h. m.	h. m.	h. m.		h. m.	h. m.	h. m.	h. m.
1		8 50	2 41	9 19	3 20		9 09	3 02	9 41	3 43
2		9 36	3 29	10 08	4 09		9 51	3 48	10 27	4 29
3	S	10 23	4 18	10 58	4 59		10 33	4 35	11 14	5 16
4		11 11	5 08	11 51	5 49		11 16	5 25	.. ..	6 03
5		.. ..	6 02	12 02	6 42	A	0 08	6 17	12 01	6 52
6		0 46	6 58	12 56	7 34		0 54	7 12	12 48	7 41
7	☽	1 43	7 55	1 51	8 28	☽	1 47	8 08	1 40	8 31
8	A	2 37	8 51	2 45	9 17	E	2 38	9 04	2 36	9 19
9		3 28	9 44	3 37	10 04		3 27	9 56	3 31	10 05
10	E	4 15	10 34	4 23	10 49		4 12	10 45	4 22	10 48
11		4 57	11 19	5 07	11 29		4 55	11 31	5 10	11 31
12		5 35	.. ..	5 48	12 08		5 36	.. ..	5 55	12 17
13		6 10	0 09	6 27	12 44		6 17	0 13	6 40	1 01
14		6 46	0 46	7 05	1 25	○	6 59	0 56	7 25	1 45
15	○	7 21	1 23	7 43	2 01	N	7 42	1 39	8 12	2 30
16		7 58	2 00	8 23	2 48		8 28	2 26	9 00	3 17
17	N	8 38	2 40	9 08	3 33	P	9 14	3 16	9 52	4 06
18		9 22	3 24	9 56	4 20		10 04	4 10	10 49	4 57
19		10 11	4 16	10 53	5 18		11 00	5 09	11 51	5 52
20		11 06	5 15	11 58	6 10		.. ..	6 14	12 02	6 50
21	P	.. ..	6 24	12 10	7 11	E ☾	0 57	7 21	1 10	7 51
22	☾	1 09	7 36	1 23	8 14	⊙ 4	2 04	8 29	2 21	8 50
23		2 20	8 45	2 36	9 13		3 08	9 33	3 29	9 48
24	E	3 26	9 49	3 44	10 09		4 08	10 32	4 30	10 44
25		4 25	10 48	4 45	11 03		5 03	11 28	5 26	11 35
26		5 18	11 43	5 40	11 54		5 53	.. ..	6 18	12 19
27		6 09	.. ..	6 33	12 35		6 40	0 25	7 06	1 06
28		6 56	0 42	7 22	1 24	S	7 24	1 11	7 50	1 52
29	●	7 42	1 30	8 10	2 11	●	8 06	1 55	8 33	2 35
30	S	8 26	2 16	8 56	2 58		8 45	2 39	9 14	3 17
31		.. ..	.. ..	.. ..	.. ..		9 22	3 21	9 53	3 58

SIGNS OF THE PLANETS, ETC.

⊙ The Sun.	☿ Mercury.	⊕ The Earth.	♃ Jupiter.	♅ Uranus.
☾ The Moon.	♀ Venus.	♂ Mars.	♄ Saturn.	♆ Neptune.

SIGNS OF THE ZODIAC.

Spring Signs. 1. ♈ Aries. 2. ♉ Taurus. 3. ♊ Gemini.	Summer Signs. 4. ♋ Cancer. 5. ♌ Leo. 6. ♍ Virgo.	Autumn Signs. 7. ♎ Libra. 8. ♏ Scorpius. 9. ♐ Sagittarius.	Winter Signs. 10. ♑ Capricornus. 11. ♒ Aquarius. 12. ♓ Pisces.

TIDE TABLES—ATLANTIC COAST.*

NEW YORK, LONG ISLAND, THE SOUND, CUBA AND PORTO RICO.

Compiled from data in Tide Tables published by U. S. Coast and Geodetic Survey. To obtain approximate time and height of high water at following stations, add to or subtract from time and height at New York (Governor's Island), viz.:

Stations.	Time. H. M.	Height. Feet.	Stations.	Time. H. M.	Height. Feet.
Albany, N. Y.	+10 30	−2.0	Matanzas, Cuba	+ 1 35	−2.7
Amagansett Coast Guard Sta., L. I.	− 0 10	−2.2	Mayaguez, Porto Rico	+ 1 00	−3.3
Asbury Park, N. J.	− 0 50	−0.3	Montauk Point, L. I., N. Y.	− 0 05	−2.4
Atlantic City (Million Dollar Pier)	− 1 00	−0.3	New Haven, Conn.	+ 2 50	+1.6
Barnegat Inlet, N. J. (Entrance)	− 0 20	−2.2	New London, Conn.	+ 1 15	−1.9
Block Island, R. I. (Basin Harbor)	− 0 45	−1.4	Newport, R. I.	− 1 00	−0.9
Bridgeport, Conn.	+ 3 00	+2.8	North Brother Lt., N. Y.	+ 3 30	+2.5
Brooklyn Bridge, N. Y.	+ 0 20	−0.2	Orient Point, L. I., N. Y.	+ 1 40	−1.7
Brooklyn Navy Yard	+ 0 40	−0.4	Oyster Bay, L. I., N. Y.	+ 3 00	+2.9
Cardenas, Cuba	+ 2 20	−3.0	Point Judith Lt., R. I.	− 0 50	−1.3
Cienfuegos, Cuba (Entrance)	+ 1 55	−3.6	Port Gibara, Cuba	− 0 15	−2.5
Coney Island, N. Y.	− 0 40	+0.3	Pt. Jefferson Entrance, L. I., N. Y.	+ 2 55	+1.8
Dobbs Ferry, N. Y.	+ 1 20	−0.7	Port Nuevitas, Cuba (Entrance)	+ 0 30	−3.1
East Rockaway Inlet, L. I., N. Y.	− 0 35	−0.3	Princess Bay Lt., S. I.	− 0 30	+0.9
Execution Rocks Lt., N. Y.	+ 3 05	+2.9	Providence, R. I.	− 0 40	+0.2
Falkner Island Lt., Conn.	+ 2 40	+1.0	Rockaway Inlet, L. I., N. Y.	− 0 35	+0.2
Fall River, Mass.	− 0 45	+0.5	San Juan, Porto Rico	+ 1 16	−3.3
Fire Island Inlet, N. Y.	− 0 50	−2.4	Santiago de Cuba, Cuba (Entrance)	+14 05	−3.3
Great Captain's Island Lt., Conn.	+ 3 00	+2.9	Saybrook Breakwater Lt.	+ 2 10	−0.8
Greenport, L. I., N. Y.	+ 2 05	−2.0	Shinnecock Coast Guard Sta., L. I.	− 0 30	−1.9
Guantanamo, Cuba	+13 40	−3.4	South Amboy, N. J.	− 0 25	+0.9
Havana, Cuba	+ 1 30	−3.5	Southold Landing, L. I., N. Y.	+ 2 55	−1.9
Hell Gate, Astoria Ferry	+ 1 55	+0.7	Spuyten Duyvil, N. Y.	+ 0 45	−0.4
Hell Gate, Hallets Point Lt.	+ 2 35	+1.1	Stamford, Conn.	+ 3 00	+2.9
Horton Point Lt., L. I., N. Y.	+ 2 35	−0.4	Stonington, Conn.	+ 0 45	−1.7
Jamesport, L. I., N. Y.	+ 4 00	−2.0	The Battery, Manhattan	+ 0 00	+0.0
Kingsbridge, Harlem River	+ 1 00	−0.1	The Narrows, N. Y.	− 0 35	+0.2
Little Gull Island Lt., N. Y.	+ 1 00	−1.9	Throggs Neck Lt., N. Y.	+ 3 10	+2.8
Long Branch, N. J.	− 0 50	−0.1	West 72d St., Manhattan	+ 0 20	−0.2
Manzanillo, Cuba	− 8 50	−1.3	West Point, N. Y.	+ 3 15	−1.6

*For more accurate differences see "Tide Tables," published annually by the U. S. Coast and Geodetic Survey.

ASTRONOMICAL CALCULATIONS FOR 1921.

By B. Hart Wright, DeLand, Fla.

The year 1921 corresponds to the following eras: The 145-6th year of Independence of the U. S. of America; the year 5681-82 of the Jewish era; the year 5682 begins at sunset, Oct. 2; the year 8030 of the Greek Church, beginning Jan. 14, which is the new style reckoning for Jan. 1. This difference of 13 days will continue until Feb. 29, 2100; the Mohammedan era, 1339-40, the year 1340, beginning Sept. 3. Jan. 1 is the 2,422,691st day since the beginning of the Julian Period.

CHRONOLOGICAL CYCLES—Dominical or Sunday Letter, B. Epact, Moon's Age, Jan. 1, 21. Lunar Cycle, or Golden Number, 3. Solar Cycle, 26. Roman Indiction, 4. Dionysian Period, 250. Jewish Lunar Cycle, 19. Julian Period, 6634.

THE SEASONS—Eastern Standard Time.

	Begins		D.	H.	M.		Lasts D.	H.	M.		Begins		D.	H.	M.		Lasts D.	H.	M.
Winter	1920	Dec.	21	10	17	P.M.	89	0	26	Autumn	1921	Sept.	23	9	20	A.M.	89	18	40
Spring	1921	Mch.	20	10	51	P.M.	92	19	37	Winter	1921	Dec.	22	4	8	A.M.	—	—	—
Summer	1921	June	21	6	36	P.M.	93	14	36			Tropical year					365	5	19

To obtain correct time by the Sun, Moon, planets or stars, see page 66, 1918 Eagle Almanac.

ECLIPSES, 1921.

There will be four eclipses this year, as follows:

I.—Annular of the Sun, Apr. 8, invisible in the U. S., visible in Arctic region, Eastern Atlantic, Europe, Asia and Africa.

II.—Total of the Moon on the morning of Apr. 22, visible throughout the Western continent and in the U. S. as follows in Eastern Standard time:

Partial begins at 1:03 a.m.
Total begins at 2:23 a.m.
Middle greatest eclipse at 2:44 a.m.
Total ends at 3:05 a.m.
Partial ends at 4:26 a.m.

III.—Total of the Sun Oct. 1, invisible in the U. S., visible in S. America, etc.

IV.—Partial of the Moon, Oct. 16, visible in the U. S. as follows in E. Standard Time:

Begins at 4:14 p.m.*
Middle or greatest eclipse at 5:54 p.m.
Ends at 7:34 p.m.

*The moon will rise about 5:10 p.m., therefore in eclipse at rising.

THE PLANETS.

MORNING STARS.

MERCURY, April 1 to 10 and Nov. 15 to 20.
VENUS, after April 22.
MARS, after June 29.
JUPITER, after Sept. 22.
SATURN, from Sept. 21 to Dec. 29.

EVENING STARS.

MERCURY, Feb. 10 to 15 and Sept. 25 to Oct. 5.
VENUS, until April 22.
MARS, until June 29.
JUPITER, until Sept. 22.
SATURN, until Sept. 21 and after Dec. 29.

BRIGHTEST OR BEST SEEN.

MERCURY, within the time limits given above, when visible as a Morning or Evening Star. VENUS, March 17 to 24 and May 24 to 31. MARS, at the beginning and end of the year, but not when at his best. JUPITER, in March. SATURN, in March. URANUS, in August-September, and NEPTUNE, in January and February.

INVISIBLE OR VERY DIM.

MERCURY, always, except as noted above. VENUS, April 20 to 25. MARS, June and July. JUPITER, in September. SATURN, in September. URANUS and NEPTUNE, always.

NOTE—VENUS, MARS, JUPITER AND SATURN will be very near together in October, and VENUS will leave the group in November.

ALL NIGHT STARS.

Only JUPITER and SATURN will shine all night, and that in March.

STORY OF OUR WORLD FAMILY FOR 1921.

THE SUN—During the solar eclipse of May 29, 1919, it was discovered that such stars as were rendered photographically visible by the eclipse were not in their proper place, as shown by night photographs, taken when far from solar influences. This supports the theory of Dr. Einstein, of the materiality and rigidity of the so-called interstellar ether, proving light is subject to gravitational laws, contrary to all previous concepts, and necessitating the remaking of the laws of the universe. Twice within the year the light of the Sun will be intercepted by the intervention of the Moon. See eclipses. Very unusual and astounding activities in the luminous solar envelope were witnessed in 1918-19. The very unusually great and marvelously beautiful auroral displays have proven a relationship, which, conjointly with distinct terrestrial disturbing factors, makes the soliterraneous storm period conditions. The larger of the great Sun spots may be easily seen through a smoked glass or by throwing the Sun's image on a screen in a darkened room. Note their change in form as they draw near or recede from the Sun's center, due to the Sun's convexity.

MERCURY, being so near the Sun, can only be seen when near certain of the points of greatest angular distance from the Sun and, like him, must be uninhabitable to any and all forms of life. These conditions may not be widely different from those upon the Earth during and prior to the igneous period of the Earth's geologic history, while yet the waters were unformed, existing in gaseous or elemental stage. The primeval rain, which washed our heavy laden atmosphere and prepared it for ministering to human comfort, has not yet come to those bodies, within the orbit of the Earth and younger than we are by countless ages. (See under "The Planets" for times of visibility of Mercury.)

VENUS, our interior and younger neighbor, may be in that stage of evolution corresponding to the time when our fossiliferous rocks were being formed, and her atmosphere, being still dense with impurities, reflects a large portion of the light received from the Sun. This causes her dazzling brilliancy. It is not improbable that such forms of life as characterized our similar stage of Earth evolution may exist there. Inasmuch as she receives about twice the amount of light and heat that we do, this evolutionary process may be much further advanced than was the case with the Earth at her age. She will be at her brightest possible phase in March, as an Evening Star, and in May as a Morning Star, being invisible in April, when between us and the Sun, after which she will remain a Morning Star to the end of the year, when she will be close to the Sun and, therefore, dim. Venus is a rapid traveler and her itinerary for the year will be as follows. At the beginning of the year Venus will be in Capricornus, a few degrees west of the Y of Aquarius; on the 9th she will be in Aquarius, east of the Y and 41' S. of Uranus and 5° S. of the Moon on the 13th; crosses the prime meridian of the heavens on the 2d-3d of February and in line with the east side of the Square of Pegasus, a few degrees N. of her. Her greatest distance east of the Sun, 47°, will be reached Feb. 10, and she will be occulted by the Moon Feb. 11, but she will have set here at that time, being at setting almost merged into the Moon. March 10 she will be just S. of the principal bright stars in Aries, Hamel and Sheratan; becomes stationary March 21, when west of the Pleiades and then retrogrades or goes back westward until May 11 to where she was March 1, near the stars in the horn of the Ram, having passed her point of greatest brilliancy March 17 and 7° to the north of Mars April 4 and 8° N. of Moon April 8, becoming dim April 10; invisible April 19-25, during which time she passes to the west of the Sun, becoming a Morning Star, rapidly increasing in brightness until the latter part of May; reaches the Pleiades and greatest distance west of the Sun July 1, having passed her stationary point on May 11, after which she again goes forward to her point of greatest brilliancy as a Morning Star when just south of the bright stars in the horn of the Ram again. She reaches the Hyades the middle of July and passes 3° N. of Aldebaran July 17. She will be 2° N. of the Moon July 31, when about midway between Sirius and Capella, and about Aug. 24-30 between Procyon on the S. and Castor and Pollux on the N., being 4° N. of the Moon on the 30th. On Sept. 13 she will be 5° N. of Neptune, just below the point of the Sickle, and on the 24th passes less than one-half of 1 degree N. of the brilliant Regulus (see Chart of the Heavens) in the end of the handle of the Sickle, and 5° N. of the Moon on the 28th. On Oct. 3 11′ S. of Mars, so close as to almost merge their light as they brighten the glorious morning light of autumn close to the E. horizon, and on the 22d of Oct. she will pass about one-half of 1 degree N. of Jupiter with the brilliant Denebola about 5° N. and W. of her; 2° N. of Moon on Oct. 29 and 1° S. of Moon Nov. 28. She will pass about 4° N. of Spica Virginis Nov. 6 and 4° S. of the Moon Dec. 28, when close to the Sun and dim, being close to her most distant point from us attainable.

MARS will not be a conspicuous object at all during the year, being a fairly bright Evening Star at the first; dim in May, invisible in June-July, dim in Aug. as a Morning Star and slightly brighter at the end of the year than at its beginning. The big telescopes tell us when snow, frost and freezing take place with the Martians, and doubtless their bold airmen, if able to reach the Earth, would consider us pigmies of stature and attainments. At the beginning of the year Mars will be in almost the same position as Venus and they will be less than one-half of a degree apart on the 9th, Mars being the most northern, and also only 15′ S. of Uranus (see under Uranus); passes 5° S. of the Moon Jan. 13, becoming quite dim in April, when he will be passing the Pleiades. About the middle of Sept., when fairly bright in the eastern morning sky, he will be seen only about 1° N. of Regulus, making a glorious pair; 53′ S. of Saturn Nov. 14 and only 10′ N. of Jupiter Nov. 26, all splendid combinations, especially the last, when they will almost appear as one; 3° N. of Spica Dec. 11.

JUPITER and SATURN will share with Venus a large part of the glories of the evening western sky for the first three months and, in fact, Jupiter and Saturn are so close throughout the year that all we need to do is to state that the former is the brightest and farther west by about 5 or 6 degrees at the first and gradually approaching until they are in conjunction on Sept. 14, when both will be too near the Sun to be seen. Towards the end of the year, when they are again bright as Morning Stars, Jupiter will be the most eastern by a little greater lead than Saturn had at the beginning of the year. This conjunction of the two major members of our family is an unusual event and will attract much attention, more especially as Mars is in the bunch also (see under Mars), and also Venus and the Moon from Oct. 22 to 29 in the edge of the morning twilight as follows: Venus, 35′ S. of Saturn Oct. 22 and 31′ N. of Jupiter Oct. 25, Saturn 3¾°, Jupiter 2° and Mars 3° N. of Moon Oct. 28, and Venus 2° N. on the 29th. Then again Nov. 25-28 all will be bunched and lastly Dec. 22-28 all will be within the last half of Leo and the first half of Virgo. Note how the respective distances of the planets from the Sun for even dates compare. Both planets will be invisible in Sept. and dim in Aug. and Oct. The rings of Saturn will be invisible this year because edgewise to the Earth.

URANUS will be most favorably situated for observation in August and September, but unless one has an instrument and knowledge of adjustments, it will be useless to look for him, and the same is true of Neptune, whose most favorable position will be in January and February.

METEORS—The great meteorite or aerolite which dropped into Lake Michigan with such great disturbance of all electro-magnetic conditions over a very great area, was probably one of the greatest foreign bodies ever come to Earth. It is unfortunate it can never be studied by man, but it is from the same source as all others, and probably did not differ from the Corn. Peary specimen from Greenland at the door of the American Museum of Natural History, on Central Park West, New York City. All come from an orbit which lies between Mars and Jupiter, but so very eccentric that it extends far out beyond the outermost members of our system.

CHURCH DAYS, FIXED AND MOVABLE FEASTS AND ANNIVERSARIES.

New Year's Day (Circumcision)	Jan.	1
Epiphany (Twelfth Day)	"	6
Alex. Hamilton's Birthday	"	11
Greek Church New Year's Day	"	14
Lee's Birthday	"	19
Septuagesima Sunday	"	23
Conversion of St. Paul	"	25
Sexagesima Sunday	"	30
Purification B. V. M.	Feb.	2
Candlemas or "Ground Hog Day	"	2
Quinquagesima Sunday	"	6
Shrove Tuesday (Mardi Gras)	"	8
Ash Wednesday, Lent begins	"	9
Roosevelt Nat'l Memorial Day	"	9
Lincoln's Birthday	"	12
Quadragesima Sunday	"	13
St. Valentine's Day	"	14
Ember Days		16, 18, 19
Washington's Birthday	"	22
St. Matthias	"	24
Longfellow's Birthday	"	27
St. David's Day	Mch.	1
Mid-Lent Sunday	"	6
Andrew Jackson's Birthday	"	15
St. Patrick's Day	"	17
Palm Sunday	"	20
Good Friday	"	25
Annunciation (Lady Day)	"	25
Easter Sunday	Mch.	27
Low Sunday	Apr.	3
Thos. Jefferson's Birthday	"	13
St. George	"	23
St. Mark	"	25
Memorial Day (Southern)	"	26
Gen. Grant's Birthday	"	27
Rogation Sunday	May	1
Philip and James	"	1
Dewey Day	"	1
Ascension Day	"	5
Arbor Day	"	6
Mothers' Day (2d Sun.)	"	8
Pentecost (Whit Sunday)	"	15
Peace Day	"	18
Ember Days		18, 20, 21
Trinity Sunday	"	22
Corpus Christi	"	26
Memorial Day (Northern)	"	30
Jeff Davis' Birthday	June	3
St. Barnabas	"	11
Flag Day	"	14
Bunker Hill Day (Mass.)	"	17
Nativity of John the Baptist	"	24
Peter and Paul	"	29
Independence Day	July	4
St. Swithin's Day; Stony Point Day	"	15
Mary Magdalen	"	22
St. James	"	25
Transfiguration	Aug.	6
Name of Jesus	"	7
Feast of Assumption B. V. M.	"	15
St. Bartholomew	Aug.	24
Battle of L. I., 1776	"	24
St. John the Baptist Beheaded	"	29
Labor Day	Sept.	5
Lafayette Day (N.Y.C.)	"	6
Nativity of Mary	"	8
Exaltation of Holy Cross	"	14
Antietam Day	"	17
Saint Matthew	"	21
Ember Days		21, 23, 24
St. Michael and All Angels	"	29
Hebrew New Year*	Oct.	3
Nat'l Fire Prevention Day	"	9
Columbus Day	"	12
Day of Atonement (Yom-Kippur)	"	12
First Day of Tabernacles (Sucoth)	"	17
St. Luke	"	18
Sts. Simon and Jude	"	28
Hallowe'en	"	31
All Saints' Day	Nov.	1
All Souls' Day	"	2
Martinmas. Armistice Day	"	11
Thanksgiving Day	"	24
St. Catherine	"	25
First Sunday in Advent	"	27
St. Andrew	"	30
Conception B. V. M.	Dec.	8
Ember Days		14, 16, 17
St. Thomas	"	21
Christmas Day	"	25
St. John the Evangelist	"	27
Holy Innocents	"	28

*Begins at sunset of the 2d, but the 3d is the New Year's Day, which ends at sunset.

There are 17 public schools in the Canal Zone, with 1,764 pupils in the white schools and 1,010 in the colored schools. School property is valued at $550,000 and the annual expenditure is $140,000.

The distinction is claimed for Wesleyan Female College of Macon, Ga, that it was the first woman's college in the world. It was established by the Methodist Episcopal Church, in 1836.

GREEK CHURCH OR RUSSIAN CALENDAR—A.D. 1921, A.M. 8030.

New Style.	Old Style.	Holy Days.	New Style.	Old Style.	Holy Days.
Jan. 7.....	Dec. 25, '20.	Christmas.	June 12....	May 30....	Holy Ghost.
Jan. 14.....	Jan. 1, '21.	Circumcision.	July 12....	June 29....	Peter & Paul Chief Apos.
Jan. 19.....	Jan. 6.....	Epiphany.	Aug. 19....	Aug. 6....	Transfiguration.
Jan. 30.....	Jan. 17.. ..	Carnival Sunday.	Aug. 28....	Aug. 15....	Repose of Theotokos.
Feb. 9.....	Jan. 27.....	Ash Wednesday.	Sept. 21...	Sept. 8....	Nativity of Theotokos.
Feb. 13.....	Jan. 31.....	1st Sunday in Lent.	Sept. 27....	Sept. 14....	Exaltation of Theotokos.
Feb. 15.....	Feb. 2.....	Hypopante (Purification).	Oct. 14....	Oct. 1....	Patronage of Theotokos.
Mch. 20.....	Mch. 7.....	Palm Sunday.	Nov. 28....	Nov. 15. ..	1st day of Nativity.
Mch. 25.....	Mch. 12.....	Great (Good) Friday.	Dec. 4....	Nov. 21....	Entrance of Theotokos.
Mch. 27.....	Mch. 14.....	Holy Pasche (Easter).	Dec. 22....	Dec. 9....	Conception of Theotokos.
May 5....	Apr. 22.....	Ascension (Holy) Thr.	Jan. 7. '22	Dec. 25....	Christmas.
May 6....	Apr. 23.....	St. George.	Jan. 14....	Jan. 1, '22	Circumcision.
May 15....	May 2.....	Pentecost.			

The difference between old and new style will continue to be 13 days until Feb. 29, 2100.

MOHAMMEDAN CALENDAR—YEAR 1339-40.

The year 1339 is the 19th year of the 45th Cycle of 30 years and is a common year of 354 days.

Year.	Month No.	Name.	Begins.	Lasts Days.	Year.	Month No.	Name.	Begins.	Lasts Days.
1339..	5....	Jomhadi I....................	Jan. 10	30	1339..	12....	Dulheggia	Aug. 5	29
" ..	6....	Jomhadi II....................	Feb. 9	29	1340..	1....	Muharrem	Sept. 3	30
" ..	7....	Rajeb	Mch. 10	30	" ..	2....	Saphar	Oct. 3	29
" ..	8....	Sheban	Apr. 9	29	" ..	3....	Rabia I....................	Nov. 1	30
" ..	9....	Ramadan (Fast)....................	May 8	30	" ..	4....	Rabia II	Dec. 1	29
" ..	10....	Schawall	June 7	29	" ..	5....	Jomhadi I	Dec. 30	30
" ..	11....	Dulkaeda	July 6	30					

JEWISH OR HEBREW CALENDAR—YEAR 5681-82, A.M.

The year 5681 is the 19th and last of the 299th cycle of 19 years—a leap year, 2d Adar or VeAdar, being added, making 384 days.

Month. No.	Name.	Day	Feast or Festival.	Gregorian Date	Month. No.	Name.	Day.	Feast or Festival.	Gregorian Date
5	Sh'vat (5681)	1	Rosh-Chodesh..........	Jan. 10.	12	Av..........	1	Rosh-Chodesh..........	Aug. 5.
6	Adar........	1	Rosh-Chodesh..........	Feb. 8-9.	12	Av..........	9	Fast of Av..........	Aug. 13*.
7	2d Adar.....	1	Rosh-Chodesh..........	Mch. 10-11.	13	Ellul.......	1	Rosh-Chodesh..........	Sept. 3-4.
7	2d Adar.....	13	Fast of Esther..........	Mch. 23.	1	Tishri (5682)	1	1st Day of New Year..	Oct. 3†.
7	2d Adar.....	14-15	Purim..........	Mch. 24-25.	1	Tishri.......	3	Fast of Gedaliah.......	Oct. 5.
8	Nissan......	1	Rosh-Chodesh..........	Apr. 9.	1	Tishri.......	10	Yom-Kippur..........	Oct. 12.
8	Nissan......	15	1st Day of Passover....	Apr. 23.	1	Tishri.......	15	1st Day of Tabernacles	Oct. 17.
9	Iyar.........	1	Rosh-Chodesh..........	May 8-9.	1	Tishri.......	21	Hoshannah-Rabbah...	Oct. 23.
9	Iyar.........	18	Lag B'Omer..........	May 26.	1	Tishri.......	22	Sh'mini Atseres........	Oct. 24.
9	Iyar.........	18	33d Day of Omer.......	May 26.	1	Tishri.......	23	S'mchas-Torah.........	Oct. 25.
10	Sivan........	1	Rosh-Chodesh..........	June 7.	2	Chesvan....	1	Rosh-Chodesh..........	Nov. 1-2.
10	Sivan........	6	1st Day of Pentecost...	June 12.	3	Kislev......	1	Rosh-Chodesh..........	Dec. 1-2.
11	Tammuz....	1	Rosh-Chodesh..........	July 6-7.	3	Kislev......	25	1st Day of Chanukah..	Dec. 26.
11	Tammuz....	17	Fast of Tammuz..........	July 23*.	4	Tebet.......	1	Rosh-Chodesh..........	Dec. 31

*Observed the following day. †Begins at sunset Oct. 2.

DATES OF COMING EASTERS.

Easter will occur this year on March 27. It is determined by the date of first full moon after the vernal equinox. Following are the dates of this festival for the balance of this century:

1922..Apr. 16	1935..Apr. 21	1948..Mar. 28	1961..Apr. 2	1974..Apr. 14	1987..Apr. 19
1923..Apr. 1	1936..Apr. 12	1949..Apr. 17	1962..Apr. 22	1975..Mar. 30	1988..Apr. 3
1924..Apr. 20	1937..Mar. 28	1950..Apr. 9	1963..Apr. 14	1976..Apr. 18	1989..Mar. 26
1925..Apr. 12	1938..Apr. 17	1951..Mar. 25	1964..Mar. 29	1977..Apr. 10	1990..Apr. 15
1926..Apr. 4	1939..Apr. 9	1952..Apr. 13	1965..Apr. 18	1978..Mar. 26	1991..Mar. 31
1927..Apr. 17	1940..Mar. 24	1953..Apr. 5	1966..Apr. 10	1979..Apr. 15	1992..Apr. 11
1928..Apr. 8	1941..Apr. 13	1954..Apr. 18	1967..Mar. 26	1980..Apr. 6	1993..Apr. 11
1929..Mar. 31	1942..Apr. 5	1955..Apr. 10	1968..Apr. 14	1981..Apr. 19	1994..Apr. 3
1930..Apr. 20	1943..Apr. 25	1956..Apr. 1	1969..Apr. 6	1982..Apr. 11	1995..Apr. 16
1931..Apr. 5	1944..Apr. 9	1957..Apr. 21	1970..Mar. 29	1983..Apr. 3	1996..Apr. 7
1932..Mar. 27	1945..Apr. 1	1958..Apr. 6	1971..Apr. 11	1984..Apr. 22	1997..Mar. 30
1933..Apr. 16	1946..Apr. 21	1959..Mar. 29	1972..Apr. 20	1985..Apr. 7	1998..Apr. 12
1934..Apr. 1	1947..Apr. 6	1960..Apr. 17	1973..Apr. 22	1986..Mar. 30	1999..Apr. 4
					2000..Apr. 23

DIFFERENCE IN TIME.

Daylight saving-time law, which was in force in 1918, was repealed by Congress in 1919. It is in effect, however, in N. Y. C. through Bd. of Aldermen ordinance.

At 12 o'clock noon in N. Y. City the time is as follows in other cities:

Amsterdam, 5:20 P.M.; Antwerp, 5:17 P.M.; Athens, 6:35 P.M.; Berlin, 5:54 P.M.; Bombay, 9:51 P.M.; Bremen, 5:33 P.M.; Brussels, 5:17 P.M.; Buenos Ayres, 1:02 P.M.; Calcutta, 10:49 P.M.; Constantinople, 6:56 P.M.; Geneva, 5:25 P.M.; Hamburg, 5:40 P.M.; Havana, 11:24 A.M.; Havre, 5:00 P.M. Hong Kong, 12:37 A.M.;* Liverpool, 4:48 P.M.; London, 5:00 P.M.; Madrid, 4:46 P.M.; Melbourne, 2:40 A.M.;* Mexico City, 10:19 A.M.; Panama, 11:38 A.M.; Paris, 5:09 P.M.; Rio de Janeiro, 2:08 P.M.; Rome, 5:50 P.M.; St. Petersburg, 7:01 P.M.; Stockholm, 6:12 P.M.; Valparaiso, 12:09 P.M.; Vienna, 6:06 P.M.; Yokohama, 2:19 A.M.

*Morning of the following day.

EAGLE CURRENT EVENTS BEE.

Samuel Levine, Jr., a 19-year-old student of the Bushwick H. S., who came to this country from Russia only six years ago, won The Eagle's fifth annual Current Events Bee, held in the auditorium of the Manual Training H. S., on March 19, 1920. Second honors were captured by Irving Cyrull of the Brooklyn Evening H. S., which competed for the first time this year. The Bee, one of the most spirited and closely contested of any so far held, began with a concert by the Musical Art Society of Manual Training H. S., and, after the singing of "America" by the audience and contestants, Herbert F. Gunnison, publisher of The Eagle, presented $5 gold pieces to the students of the 17 different schools who were winners in the contests for the best lists of questions on current topics, and the bronze medals to the school champions. H. V. Kaltenborn, assistant managing editor of The Eagle, was interrogator, and the judges were Judge Frederick E. Crane, the Rev. Joseph V. S. McClancy, superintendent of Catholic schools in Brooklyn, and Meier Steinbrink, attorney

WEIGHTS AND MEASURES.

LINEAR MEASURE.

12 in.=1 foot. 3 ft.=1 yd. 5½ yds.=1 rod. 40 rods=1 furlong. 320 rods=1 mile. 5,280 ft.=1 mile. 3 miles=1 league.

The hand (4 in.) is to measure horses' heights. The nautical mile is 6,085 ft. 1 knot to 1.1528 statute miles. 1 degree is 67.168 statute miles.

3 barleycorns=1 inch, used by shoemakers. 6 feet=1 fathom, used to measure depths at sea. 3 feet=1 pace, and 5 paces—1 rod, used in pacing distances. 8 furlongs=1 mile. 9 inches=1 span. 18 inches=1 cubit.

SURVEYORS' LINEAR MEASURE.

7.92 inches=1 link. 25 links=1 rod. 4 rods, or 100 links=1 chain. 80 chains=1 mile.

SQUARE MEASURE.

144 sq. in.=1 sq. ft. 9 sq. ft.=1 sq. yd. 30¼ sq. yds.=1 sq. rod. 160 sq. rods=1 acre. 640 acres=1 sq. mile.

The side of a square having an area of an acre is approximately 208¾ feet.

SURVEYORS' SQUARE MEASURE.

625 sq. links=1 sq. rod. 16 sq. rods=1 sq. chain. 10 sq. chains=1 acre.

A square mile of land is called a section. In some parts of the country a township contains 36 square miles.

MARINERS' MEASURE.

6 ft.=1 fathom. 120 fathoms=1 cable lgh. 7½ cable lghs.=1 mile. 5,280 ft.=1 statute mile. 6,085 ft.=1 nautical mile. 3 marine miles=1 marine league.

CUBIC MEASURE.

1,728 cu. in.=1 cu. ft. 27 cu. ft.=1 cu. yd.
67.2 cu. in.=1 qt. dry measure.
1 cu. ft.=7.48 gals., liquid measure.

DRY MEASURE.

2 pints=1 quart. 4 pecks=1 bushel.
8 quarts=1 peck.

LIQUID MEASURE.

4 gills=1 pt. 2 pts.=1 qt. 4 qts.=1 gal. 31½ gal.=1 bbl. 2 bbls.=1 hogshead.

PAPER MEASURE.

24 sheets=1 quire. 2 reams=1 bundle.
20 quires=1 ream. 5 bundles=1 bale.

CIRCULAR MEASURE.

60 sec.= 1 min. 60 min.=1 degree. 360 degrees=1 circle. 1 degree=60 geographical miles. 1 geographical mile=1.1527 statute miles. 1 degree of equator=69.124 statute miles.

TIME MEASURE.

60 sec.=1 min. 60 min.=1 hour. 24 hours=1 day. 365 days=1 year. 100 years=1 century.

CLOTH MEASURE.

2¼ in.=1 nail. 4 nails=1 quarter. 4 quarters =1 yd.

COUNTING.

12 things=1 doz. 12 doz.=1 gross. 12 gross= 1 great gross. 20 things=1 score.

MISCELLANEOUS.

3 in.=1 palm. 4 in.=1 hand. 6 in.=1 span. 18 in.=1 cubit. 21.8 in.=bible cubit. 2½ ft.=1 military pace.

SIZES OF BOOKS.

(First figure pages, 2d, leaves; 3d, sheet.)

Folio, 4, 2, 1; quarto (4to.), 8, 4, 1; octavo (8vo.), 16, 8, 1; duodecimo (12mo.), 24, 12, 1; octodecimo (18mo.), 36, 18, 1.

APOTHECARIES' WEIGHT.

20 grains=1 scruple. 8 drams=1 ounce.
3 scruples=1 dram. 12 ounces=1 pound.

AVOIRDUPOIS WEIGHT.

16 drams=1 oz. 16 oz.=1 lb. 100 lbs.=1 cwt. 20 cwt.=1 ton.

Long ton—2,240 lbs., used most in G. Britain.

TROY WEIGHT.

24 grains=1 pennyweight. 20 pennyweights= 1 oz. 12 oz.=1 lb.

1 caret in diamond measure=3.2 troy grains.

Metric System.

Metric system is in general use in all principal nations with exception of Gt. Britain, Russia and the U. S., where it is authorized but not compulsory. For scientific purposes its use is common throughout world.

LINEAR MEASURE.

10 millimetres=1 centimetre (6.394 in.). 10 centim.=1 decim. (3.937 in.). 10 decim.=1 metre (39.37 in.). 10 metres=1 dekam. (393.7 in.). 10 dekam.=1 hectom. (328 ft. 1 in.). 10 hectom.=1 kilom. (3,280 ft. 10 in.). 10 kilom.=1 myriam. (6.2137 mi.).

SQUARE MEASURE.

1 sq. metre=1 centare (1,550 sq. in.). 100 sq. metres=1 are (119.6 sq. yds.). 10,000 sq. metres=1 hectare (2.471 acres).

CUBIC MEASURE.

1 cu. centimetre=1 millitre (.061 cu. in., dry measure; .27 fluid dram, liquid measure). 10 milli.=1 centil. (.6102 cu. in., dry; .338 fl. oz., liquid). 10 centil.=1 decil. (6.1022 cu. in., dry; .845 gill). 10 decil.=1 litre (.908 qts., dry; 1.0567 qts., liquid). 10 litres=1 dekal. (9.08 qts., dry; 2.6417 gal., liquid). 10 dekal.=1 hectol. (2 bu. 3.35 pecks, dry; 26.417 gal., liquid). 10 hectols.=1 kilol, or stere. (1.308 cu. in., dry; 264.17 gals., liquid).

METRIC EQUIVALENTS.

1 grain=0.06480 gram. 1 oz.=28.3495 grams. 1 lb.=0.45359 kilogram. 1 dram (apoth.)= 3.6967 grams. 1 scruple (apoth.)=1,2322 grams. 1 qt. (dry)=1.1012 liters. 1 peck (dry)=8.8098 liters. 1 bushel=0.35239 hectoliter. 1 qt. (liq.) =0.95636 liter. 1 gallon=3.78543 liters. 1 in.= 25.4001 millimeters. 1 in.=2.54001 centimeters. 1 in.=0.0254 meter. 1 ft.=0.3048 meter. 1 yd.= 0.9144 meter. 1 mile=1.6093 kilometers. 1 sq. in.=645.16 sq. millimeters. 1 sq. ft.=0.0829 sq. meter. 1 sq. yd.=0.8361 sq. meter. 1 sq. mile= 2.5900 sq. kilometers. 1 acre=0.4017 hectare. 1 cubic in.=16.387 cubic millimeters. 1 cubic ft.= 0.02832 cubic meter. 1 cubic yd.=0.7645 cubic meter.

Cubic Inches in U.S. Standard Capacity Measures

LIQUID MEASURE.

1 gal. contains 231 cu. in.; ½ gal., 115.5; 1 qt., 57.75; 1 pt., 28.875; ½ pt., 14.437; 1 gill contains 7.218; 1 fluid oz., 1.804; 1 dram, .225.

DRY MEASURE.

1 bushel contains 2150.42 cu. in.; ½ bushel, 1075.21; 1 peck, 537.60; ½ peck, 268.80; ¼ peck, 134.40; 1 qt., 67.20; 1 pint, 33.60; ½ pint, 16.80.

Biblical Weights Reduced to Troy Weight.

The gerah, 1-20th of a shekel, 12 gr.; the bekah, ½ a shekel, 5 pwt.; the shekel, 10 pwt.; the maneh, 60 shekels, 2 lbs., 6 oz.; the talent, 50 manehs, or 3,000 shekels, 125 lbs.

Electrical Units Defined.

Ohm—Unit of resistance; represents resistance offered to an unvarying electric current by a column of mercury at the temperature of ice, 14.5421 grams in mass, of a cross-sectional area of 1.00003 sq. millimeters and of the length of 106.3 centimeters.

Ampere—Unit of current; decomposes .0009324 of a gram of water in 1 second or deposits silver at the rate of .001118 of a gram per sec. when passed through a solution of nitrate of silver in water.

Volt—Unit of electro motive force; 1 volt equals 1 ampere of current passing through a substance having 1 ohm of resistance.

Coulomb—Unit of quantity; amount of electricity transferred by a current of 1 ampere in 1 sec.

Farad—Unit of capacity; capacity of a condenser charged to a potential of 1 volt by 1 coulomb. A microfarad is one millionth of a farad.

Joule—Unit of work; equivalent to energy expended in 1 sec. by 1 ampere current in 1 ohm resistance.

Watt—Unit of power; equivalent to work done at the rate of 1 joule per sec. A kilowatt is 1,000 watts.

TABLE OF SPECIFIC GRAVITY.

Compared with water.

Water, distilled	100	Iron, cast	721
Water, sea	103	Ivory	183
Alcohol	84	Lead	1,135
Aluminum	256	Mahogany	106
Ash	84	Maple	75
Brass	84	Marble	270
Butter	94	Milk, cow's	103
Cedar	61	Milk, goat's	104
Chalk	279	Oak	117
Coal	130	Platina	2,150
Copper	895	Porcelain	226
Cork	24	Silver	1,047
Ebony	133	Steel	783
Fir	55	Sulphur	203
Glass	289	Tin	729
Gold	1,926	Walnut	67
Ice	92	Zinc	691

THE 1920 CENSUS.

The Director of the Census submitted to the Speaker of the House of Representatives on Dec. 17, 1920, a statement, for apportionment purposes, of the official population of continental United States, as shown by the returns of the Fourteenth Decennial Census, taken as of Jan. 1, 1920.

The population of continental United States, as finally determined, is 105,708,771, a gain of 25,663 over the preliminary figures given out, subject to correction, on Oct. 7, namely, 105,683,108. In 1910 continental United States had a population of 91,972,266 and in 1900 a population of 75,994,575, thus showing an increase since 1910 of 13,736,505, or 14.9 per cent., as compared with an increase from 1900 to 1910 of 15,977,691, or 21 per cent. As stated by Director Rogers on Oct. 7, when the preliminary figures (105,683,108) were announced, the large falling off in the rate of growth for the country as a whole, as shown by these figures, is due mainly to an almost complete cessation of immigration for more than five years preceding the taking of the census in Jan., 1920, and in some degree also to an epidemic of influenza and to the casualties resulting from the World War.

The results of the census of population in 1920 at first glance may seem somewhat disappointing and open to question possibly, but the substantial accuracy of the enumeration in January is fully borne out by comparison with estimates based upon the probable excess of births over deaths throughout the decade and the excess of immigration over emigration. From all available data, it may be roughly estimated that the annual excess of births over deaths throughout the United States is approximately 1 per cent. This rate compounded would indicate an increase of approximately 10.5 per cent. during the decade. Thus the nearly 92,000,000 persons present in the United States in 1910 might be expected to increase to about 101,700,000 in 1920. In addition, the excess of immigration over emigration during the decade was approximately 3,733,000. Since the bulk of these foreign-born persons came to the country during the first 4 years of the decade, it may be roughly estimated that the increase due to excess of births over deaths in their families was about 10 per cent. Thus the population of the country may be assumed to have been augmented by about 4,100,000 during the decade through excess of immigration over emigration. The two estimates taken together would indicate, therefore, probable population of 105,800,000, or only a small fraction of 1 per cent. more than the total shown by the returns of the Fourteenth Census.

The figures of the present census also show that the trend of population from the country to the city has become greatly accentuated since 1910, and that, for the first time in the country's history, more than half the entire population is now living in urban territory, as defined by the Census Bureau. That is to say, of the 105,708,771 persons enumerated in the Fourteenth Census, preliminary tabulations show that 54,816,209, or 51.9 per cent., are living in incorporated places of 2,500 inhabitants or more, and 50,866,899, or 48.1 per cent., in rural territory. At the census of 1910 the corresponding percentages were 46.3 and 53.7, respectively, showing a loss of 5.6 per cent. in the proportion for the population living in rural territory. To show more clearly the change in the proportion of the population living in rural territory now as compared with ten years ago, the rural population can be divided into two classes, namely, 9,864,196, or 9.3 per cent. of the total population living in incorporated places of less than 2,500 inhabitants and 41,002,703, or 38.8 per cent. of the total population living in what may be called purely country districts. At the census of 1910 the population living in incorporated places of less than 2,500 inhabitants formed 8.8 per cent., while the population living in purely country districts formed 44.8 per cent. of the total population.

The increase since 1910 in the population as a whole, as before stated, was 14.9 per cent., but during the decade there has been an increase in that portion of the population living in urban territory of 12,192,826, or 28.6 per cent., and in that portion living in rural territory of 1,518,016, or only 3.1 per cent.; and if the comparison is extended to cover the two classes of rural territory, it appears that that portion living in incorporated places of less than 2,500 inhabitants shows an increase of 1,745,371, or 21.5 per cent., whereas that portion living in purely country districts shows an actual decrease of 227,355, or six-tenths of 1 per cent.

The percentages of increase shown for the several States vary greatly, due in part to the causes which have been noted as affecting the increase in the population of the country as a whole, but also in part to the abnormal internal movement of population required to meet the excessive demands of the war work in certain sections. For three States, Mississippi, Nevada and Vermont, there have been small decreases in population, the largest decrease being for Nevada, 5.5 per cent.

POPULATION AND RANK OF LARGEST CITIES

CITIES.	*	1920.	*	1910.	*	1900.
New York, N. Y..	1	5,620,048	1	4,766,883	1	3,437,202
Chicago, Ill.	2	2,701,705	2	2,185,283	2	1,698,575
Philadelphia, Pa...	3	1,823,158	3	1,549,008	3	1,293,697
Detroit, Mich.	4	993,739	9	465,766	13	285,704
Cleveland, O.	5	796,836	6	560,663	7	381,768
St. Louis, Mo.	6	772,897	4	687,029	4	575,238
Boston, Mass.	7	748,060	5	670,585	5	560,892
Baltimore, Md. ...	8	733,826	7	558,485	6	508,957
Pittsburgh, Pa. ..	9	588,103	8	533,905	11	321,616
Los Angeles, Cal..	10	576,673	17	319,198	36	102,479
San Francisco, Cal.	11	508,410	11	416,912	9	342,782
Buffalo, N. Y......	12	506,775	10	423,715	8	352,387
Milwaukee, Wis. ..	13	457,147	12	373,857	14	285,315
Washington, D. C..	14	437,571	16	331,069	15	278,718
Newark, N. J.......	15	414,216	14	347,469	16	246,070
Cincinnati, O.	16	401,247	13	363,591	10	325,902
New Orleans, La..	17	387,219	15	339,075	12	287,104
Minneapolis, Minn.	18	380,582	18	301,408	19	202,718
Kansas City, Mo...	19	324,410	20	248,381	22	163,752
Seattle, Wash.	20	315,652	21	237,194	48	80,671
Indianapolis, Ind..	21	314,194	22	233,650	21	169,164
Jersey City, N. J..	22	297,864	19	267,779	17	206,433
Rochester, N. Y...	23	295,750	25	218,149	24	162,608
Portland, Ore.	24	258,288	28	207,214	42	90,426
Denver, Col.	25	256,369	27	213,381	25	133,859
Toledo, O.	26	243,109	30	168,497	26	131,822
Providence, R. I..	27	237,595	23	224,326	20	175,597
Columbus, O.	28	237,031	29	181,511	28	125,560
Louisville, Ky.	29	234,891	24	223,928	18	204,731
St. Paul, Minn. ...	30	234,595	26	214,744	23	163,065
Oakland, Cal.	31	216,361	32	150,174	56	66,960
Akron, O.	32	208,435	81	69,067	87	42,728
Atlanta, Ga.	33	200,616	31	154,839	43	89,872
Omaha, Neb.	34	191,601	41	124,096	35	102,555
Worcester, Mass...	35	179,754	33	145,986	29	118,421
Birmingham, Ala..	36	178,270	36	132,685	99	38,415
Syracuse, N. Y.....	37	171,717	34	137,249	30	108,374
Richmond, Va. ...	38	171,667	39	127,628	46	85,050
New Haven, Conn.	39	162,519	35	133,605	31	108,027
Memphis, Tenn. ..	40	162,351	37	131,105	37	102,320
San Antonio, Tex.	41	161,379	54	96,614	71	53,321
Dallas, Tex.	42	158,976	58	92,104	88	42,638
Dayton, O.	43	152,559	43	116,577	45	85,333
Bridgeport, Conn...	44	143,538	49	102,054	54	70,996
Houston, Tex.	45	138,076	65	78,800	85	44,633
Hartford, Conn. ..	46	138,036	51	98,915	49	79,850
Scranton, Pa.	47	137,783	38	129,867	38	102,026
Gd. Rapids, Mich..	48	137,634	44	112,571	44	87,565
Paterson, N. J. ..	49	135,860	40	125,600	32	105,171
Youngstown, O. ..	50	132,358	64	79,066	84	44,885
Springfield, Mass..	51	129,563	59	88,926	60	62,059
Des Moines, Ia. ..	52	126,468	61	86,368	59	62,139
N. Bedford, Mass...	53	121,217	53	96,652	58	62,442
Fall River, Mass...	54	120,485	42	119,295	33	104,863
Trenton, N. J.	55	119,289	52	96,815	53	73,307
Nashville, Tenn. ..	56	118,342	45	110,364	47	80,865
Salt L. City, Utah.	57	118,110	57	92,777	70	53,531
Camden, N. J. ...	58	116,309	56	94,538	52	75,935
Norfolk, Va.	59	115,777	82	67,452	80	46,624
Albany, N. Y.	60	113,344	50	100,253	40	94,151
Lowell, Mass.	61	112,759	46	106,294	39	94,969
Wilmington, Del...	62	110,168	60	87,411	51	76,508
Cambridge, Mass...	63	109,694	47	101,839	41	91,886
Reading, Pa.	64	107,784	55	96,071	50	78,961
Fort Worth, Tex...	65	106,482	75	73,312	151	26,688
Spokane, Wash. ...	66	104,437	48	104,402	100	36,848
Kansas City, Kan.	67	101,177	62	82,331	76	51,418
Yonkers, N. Y.....	68	100,176	63	79,803	79	47,931

*Rank.

POPULATION OF CITIES UNDER 100,000.

Following is a table of cities of 25,000 to 100,000 inhabitants in the 1920 census in the order of their rank, with comparative figures for 1900 and 1910. The figures for 1920 census are subject to correction:

Rk.	City.	1920	1910	1900
69	Lynn, Mass.	99,148	89,336	68,513
70	Duluth, Minn.	98,917	78,466	52,969
71	Tacoma, Wash.	96,965	83,743	37,714
72	Elizabeth, N. J.	95,682	73,409	52,130
73	Lawrence, Mass.	94,270	85,892	62,559
74	Utica, N. Y.	94,156	74,419	56,383
75	Erie, Pa.	93,372	66,525	52,733
76	Somerville, Mass.	93,091	77,236	61,643
77	Flint, Mich.	91,599	38,550	13,103
78	Jacksonville, Fla.	91,558	57,699	28,429
79	Waterbury, Conn.	91,410	73,141	51,139
80	Oklahoma City, Okla.	91,258	64,205	10,037
81	Schenectady, N. Y.	88,723	72,826	31,682
82	Canton, O.	87,091	50,217	30,667
83	Fort Wayne, Ind.	86,549	63,933	45,115
84	Evansville, Ind.	85,264	69,647	59,007
85	Savannah, Ga.	83,252	65,064	54,244
86	Manchester, N. H.	78,384	70,063	56,987
87	St. Joseph, Mo.	77,939	77,403	102,979
88	Knoxville, Tenn.	77,818	36,346	32,637
89	El Paso, Tex.	77,543	39,279	15,906
90	Bayonne, N. J.	76,754	55,545	32,722
91	Peoria, Ill.	76,121	66,950	56,100
92	Harrisburg, Pa.	75,917	64,186	50,167
93	San Diego, Cal.	74,683	39,578	17,700
94	Wilkes-Barre, Pa.	73,833	67,105	51,721
95	Allentown, Pa.	73,502	51,913	35,416
96	Wichita, Kan.	72,128	52,450	24,671
97	Tulsa, Okla.	72,075	18,182	1,390
98	Troy, N. Y.	72,013	76,813	60,651
99	Sioux City, Iowa	71,227	47,828	33,111
100	South Bend, Ind.	70,983	53,684	35,999
101	Portland, Me.	69,272	58,571	50,145
102	Hoboken, N. J.	68,166	70,324	59,364
103	Charleston, S. C.	67,957	58,833	55,807
104	Johnstown, Pa.	67,327	55,482	35,936
105	Binghamton, N. Y.	66,800	48,443	39,647
106	East St. Louis, Ill.	66,740	58,547	29,655
107	Brockton, Mass.	66,138	56,878	40,063
108	Terre Haute, Ind.	66,083	58,157	36,673
109	Sacramento, Cal.	65,857	44,696	29,282
110	Rockford, Ill.	65,651	45,401	31,051
111	Little Rock, Ark.	64,997	45,941	38,307
112	Pawtucket, R. I.	64,248	51,622	39,231
113	Passaic, N. J.	63,824	54,773	27,777
114	Saginaw, Mich.	61,903	50,510	42,345
115	Springfield, O.	60,840	46,921	38,253
116	Altoona, Pa.	60,331	52,127	38,973
117	Holyoke, Mass.	60,203	57,730	45,712
118	Mobile, Ala.	60,151	51,521	38,469
119	New Britain, Conn.	59,316	43,916	25,998
120	Springfield, Ill.	59,183	51,678	34,159
121	Racine, Wis.	58,593	38,002	29,102
122	Chester, Pa.	58,030	38,537	33,988
123	Chattanooga, Tenn.	57,896	44,604	30,154
124	Lansing, Mich.	57,327	31,229	16,485
125	Covington, Ky.	57,121	53,270	42,938
126	Davenport, Ia.	56,727	43,028	35,254
127	Berkeley, Cal.	55,886	40,434	13,214
128	Long Beach, Cal.	55,593	17,809	2,252
129	Gary, Ind.	55,378	16,802	......
130	Lincoln, Neb.	54,934	43,973	40,169
131	Portsmouth, Va.	54,387	33,190	17,427
132	Wheeling, W. Va.	54,322	41,641	38,878
133	Haverhill, Mass.	53,884	44,115	37,175
134	Lancaster, Pa.	53,150	47,227	41,459
135	Macon, Ga.	52,995	40,665	23,272
136	Augusta, Ga.	52,548	41,040	39,441
137	Tampa, Fla.	51,252	37,782	15,839
138	Roanoke, Va.	50,842	34,874	21,495
139	Niagara Falls, N. Y.	50,760	30,445	19,457
140	East Orange, N. J.	50,710	34,371	21,506
141	Atlantic City, N. J.	50,682	46,150	27,838
142	Bethlehem, Pa.	50,358	12,837	10,758
143	Huntington, W. Va.	50,177	31,161	11,923
144	Topeka, Kan.	50,022	43,684	33,608
145	Malden, Mass.	49,103	44,404	33,664
146	Kalamazoo, Mich.	48,858	39,437	24,404
147	Hamtramck, Mich.	48,615	3,559	......
148	Winston-Salem, N. C.	48,395	22,700	13,650
149	Jackson, Mich.	48,374	31,433	25,180
150	Quincy, Mass.	47,876	32,642	23,899
151	Pay City, Mich.	47,554	45,166	27,628
152	York, Pa.	47,512	44,750	33,708
153	Highland Park, Mich.	46,499	4,120	427
154	Charlotte, N. C.	46,338	34,014	18,091
155	Newton, Mass.	46,054	39,806	33,587
156	McKeesport, Pa.	45,975	42,694	34,227
157	Cedar Rapids, Ia.	45,566	32,811	25,656
158	Pasadena, Cal.	45,354	30,291	9,117
159	Elmira, N. Y.	45,305	37,176	35,672
160	Cicero Town, Ill.	44,995	14,557	16,310
161	New Castle, Pa.	44,938	36,280	28,339
162	Fresno, Cal.	44,616	24,892	12,470
163	Galveston, Tex.	44,255	36,981	37,789
164	Shreveport, La.	43,874	28,015	16,013
165	Decatur, Ill.	43,818	31,140	20,754
166	Woonsocket, R. I.	43,496	38,125	28,204
167	Montgomery, Ala.	43,464	38,136	30,346
168	Chelsea, Mass.	43,184	32,452	34,072
169	Pueblo, Col.	42,908	44,395	28,157
170	Mount Vernon, N. Y.	42,726	30,919	21,228
171	Salem, Mass.	42,529	43,697	35,956
172	Pittsfield, Mass.	41,751	32,121	21,766
173	Lakewood, O.	41,732	15,181	3,355
174	Perth Amboy, N. J.	41,707	32,121	17,699
175	Butte, Mont.	41,611	39,165	30,470
176	Lexington, Ky.	41,534	35,099	26,369
177	Lima, O.	41,306	30,508	21,723
178	Fitchburg, Mass.	41,013	37,826	31,531
179	Kenosha, Wis.	40,472	21,371	11,606
180	Beaumont, Tex.	40,422	20,640	9,427
181	Stockton, Cal.	40,296	23,253	17,506
182	Everett, Mass.	40,120	33,484	24,336
183	Wichita Falls, Tex.	40,079	8,200	2,480
184	West Hoboken, N. J.	40,068	35,403	23,094
185	Stamford, Conn.	40,067	28,836	18,839
186	Oak Park, Ill.	39,830	19,444	......
187	Hamilton, O.	39,675	35,279	23,914
188	Springfield, Mo.	39,631	35,201	23,267
189	Superior, Wis.	39,624	40,384	31,091
190	Charleston, W. Va.	39,608	22,996	11,099
191	San Jose, Cal.	39,604	28,946	21,500
192	Dubuque, Ia.	39,141	38,494	36,297
193	Medford, Mass.	39,038	23,150	18,244
194	Jamestown, N. Y.	38,917	31,297	22,892
195	Waco, Tex.	38,500	26,425	20,686
196	Joliet, Ill.	38,406	34,670	29,353
197	Madison, Wis.	38,378	25,531	19,164
198	Brookline, Mass.	37,748	27,792	19,935
199	Columbia, S. C.	37,524	26,319	21,108
200	Lorain, O.	37,295	28,883	16,028
201	Evanston, Ill.	37,215	24,978	19,259
202	Taunton, Mass.	37,137	34,259	31,036
203	Muskegon, Mich.	36,570	24,062	20,818
204	Muncie, Ind.	36,524	24,005	20,942
205	Aurora, Ill.	36,397	29,807	24,147
206	Waterloo, Ia.	36,230	26,693	12,580
207	Chicopee, Mass.	36,214	25,401	19,167
208	New Rochelle, N. Y.	36,213	28,867	14,720
209	Williamsport, Pa.	36,198	31,860	28,757
210	Auburn, N. Y.	36,192	34,668	30,345
211	Battle Creek, Mich.	36,164	25,267	18,563
212	Council Bluffs, Ia.	36,162	29,292	25,802
213	Hammond, Ind.	36,004	20,925	12,376
214	Quincy, Ill.	65,978	36,587	36,252
215	East Chicago, Ind.	35,967	19,098	3,411
216	Newport News, Pa.	35,596	20,205	19,635
217	Rock Island, Ill.	35,177	24,335	19,493
218	Poughkeepsie, N. Y.	35,000	27,936	24,029
219	Austin, Tex.	34,876	29,860	22,258
220	Meriden, Conn.	34,739	32,066	28,695
221	Pontiac, Mich.	34,273	14,432	9,769
222	Easton, Pa.	33,813	28,523	25,238
223	Danville, Ill.	33,756	27,871	16,354
224	Amsterdam, N. Y.	33,524	31,267	20,929
225	Wilmington, N. C.	33,372	25,748	20,976
226	Orange, N. J.	33,268	29,630	24,141
227	Oshkosh, Wis.	33,162	33,062	28,284
228	Portsmouth, O.	33,011	23,481	17,870
229	Ogden, Utah	32,804	25,580	18,313
230	New Brunswick, N. J.	32,779	23,388	20,006
231	Norristown, Pa.	32,319	27,875	22,265
232	Hazleton, Pa.	32,277	25,452	14,230
233	Lewiston, Me.	31,791	26,247	23,761
234	Watertown, N. Y.	31,285	26,730	21,696
235	Columbus, Ga.	31,125	20,554	17,614
236	Pensacola, Fla.	31,035	22,982	17,747
237	Green Bay, Wis.	31,017	25,236	18,684
238	Petersburg, Va.	31,002	24,127	21,810
239	Sheboygan, Wis.	30,955	26,398	22,962
240	Waltham, Mass.	30,915	27,834	23,481
241	Moline, Ill.	30,709	24,199	17,248
242	Newburgh, N. Y.	30,366	27,805	24,943
243	La Crosse, Wis.	30,363	30,417	28,895
244	Muskogee, Okla.	30,277	25,278	4,254
245	Newport, R. I.	30,255	27,149	22,441
246	Colorado Springs, Col.	30,105	29,078	21,085
247	Kokomo, Ind.	30,067	17,010	10,609
248	Lynchburg, Va.	29,956	29,494	18,891
249	West New York, N. J.	29,926	13,560	5,267
250	Joplin, Mo.	29,855	32,073	26,023
251	Cumberland, Md.	29,837	21,839	17,128
252	Anderson, Ind.	29,767	22,476	20,178
253	Norwich, Conn.	29,685	28,219	24,637
254	Zanesville, O.	29,569	28,026	23,538
255	Miami, Fla.	29,549	5,471	1,681
256	Cranston, R. I.	29,407	21,107	13,343
257	Newport, Ky.	29,317	30,300	28,301
258	Phoenix, Ariz.	29,053	11,134	5,544

POPULATION OF CITIES UNDER 100,000—*Continued.*

Rk.	City.	1920	1910	1900
259	Revere, Mass.	28,823	18,219	10,395
260	Fort Smith, Ark.	28,811	23,975	11,587
261	Montclair, N. J.	28,810	21,550	13,962
262	Alameda, Cal.	28,806	23,383	16,464
263	Bloomington, Ill.	28,725	25,768	23,286
264	Steubenville, O.	28,508	22,391	14,349
265	Asheville, N. C.	28,504	18,762	14,694
266	Nashua, N. H.	28,379	26,005	23,898
267	Hagerstown, Md.	28,066	16,507	13,591
268	Marion, O.	27,891	18,232	11,862
269	Clarksburg, W. Va.	27,869	9,201	4,050
270	Mansfield, O.	27,824	20,768	17,640
271	Norwalk, Conn.	27,700	24,211	19,932
272	Plainfield, N. J.	27,700	20,550	15,369
273	Everett, Wash.	27,644	24,814	7,838
274	Elgin, Ill.	27,454	25,976	22,433
275	East Cleveland, O.	27,292	9,179	2,757
276	Warren, O.	27,050	11,081	8,529
277	Richmond, Ind.	26,765	22,324	18,226
278	Kearney, N. J.	26,724	18,659	10,896
279	Newark, O.	26,718	25,404	18,157
280	Kingston, N. Y.	26,688	25,908	24,535
281	Clifton, N. J.	26,470	11,869	5,351
282	Rome, N. Y.	26,341	20,497	15,343
283	Bangor, Me.	25,978	24,803	21,850
284	Port Huron, Mich.	25,944	18,863	19,158
285	New London, Conn.	25,688	19,659	17,548
286	Bellingham, Wash.	25,570	24,298	11,062
287	Irvington, N. J.	25,480	11,877	5,255
288	Sioux Falls, S. D.	25,176	14,094	10,266

CENTER OF POPULATION FOR U. S.

Position of Center of Population.

Yr.	North Lat.	West Long.	Approximate Location by Important Towns.	‡
1790..	39 16.5	76 11.2	23 m. E. of Baltimore, Md.	...
1800..	39 16.1	76 56.5	18 m. W. of Baltimore, Md.	41
1810..	39 11.5	77 37.2	40 m. NWW. Wash'gton, D.C.	36
1820..	39 5.7	78 33.0	16 m. N. of Woodstock, Va.	50
1830..	38 57.9	79 16.9	19 m. WSW. Moorefield, W. Va.	39
1840..	39 2.0	80 18.0	16 m. S. Clarksburg, W. Va.	55
1850..	38 59.0	81 19.0	23 m. S. E. Parkersb'g, W. Va.	55
1860..	39 0.4	82 48.8	20 m. S. of Chillicothe, O...	81
1870..	39 12.0	83 35.7	48 m. E. by N. Cincinnati, O.	44
1880..	39 4.1	84 39.7	8 m. W. by S. Cincinnati, O.	58
1890..	39 11.9	85 32.9	20 m. E. of Columbus, Ind...	49
1900..	39 9.5	85 48.9	6 m. S. E. of Columbus, Ind.	15
1910..	39 12.0	86 30.0	W. part Bloomington, Ind..	39
1920*.				

*Not yet determined by the Census Bureau.
‡Miles; preceding decade's westward movement.

CENTER OF AREA FOR U. S.

The center of area of the United States, excluding Alaska and Hawaii and other recent accessions, is in Northern Kansas, 10 miles north of Smith Center, county seat of Smith County, in approximate latitude 39 deg. 55 min., and approximate longitude 98 deg. 50 min. The center of population, according to 1910 census, was, therefore, about three-fourths of a degree, 51 miles south, and 12¼ deg., about 657 miles, east of the center of area. The center of population, according to 1920 census, is not yet determined.

POPULATION OF LONG ISLAND.

NASSAU COUNTY.

Towns and Villages.	1920.	1915.	1910.
Total	125,727	116,825	83,930
Glen Cove City	8,664	8,875	......
Hempstead town	70,397	63,271	44,297
East Rockaway village..	2,005	1,607	1,200
Freeport village	8,599	7,463	4,836
Hempstead village	6,382	6,073	4,964
Lawrence village	2 861	1,870	1,189
Rockville Centre village.	6,262	5,223	3,667
North Hempstead town	26,370	23,687	17 881
Mineola village	3,016	2,318	1,981
Oyster Bay township	20,296	29,867	21,802
Sea Cliff village	2,108	1,981	1,694
Farmingdale village	2,091	1,856	1,567

SUFFOLK COUNTY.

Total	110,241	104,342	96,138
Babylon town	11,315	11,190	9,030
Amityville village	3,265	2,780	2 517
Babylon village	2,523	3,100	2,600
Brookhaven town	21,847	19,591	16,737
Patchogue village	4,031	4,506	3,824
Bellport village	614	499	419
Easthampton town	4,852	5,164	4,722
Sag Harbor village	2,993	3,245	3 408
Huntington town	13,893	15,244	12,004
Northport village	1,977	2,527	2,096
Islip town	20,704	17,658	18,346
Riverhead town	5,753	5,730	5,345
Shelter Island town	890	1,153	1,064
Smithtown town	9,114	4,988	7 073
Southampton town	11,726	13,453	11,240
Southampton village	2,635	3,092	2,509
Southold town	10,147	10,008	10,577
Greenport village	3,122	3,735	3,089

TOTAL POPULATION OF LONG ISLAND BY COUNTIES.

	1920.	1915.	1910.	1900.
Kings	2,018,356	1,798,513	1,634,351	1,166,582
Queens	469,042	396,727	284,041	152,999
Nassau	125,727	116,825	83,930	55,448
Suffolk	110,241	104,342	96,138	77,582
Totals	2,723,366	2,416,407	2,098,460	1,452,611

AREA AND POPULATION CONTINENTAL U. S. EACH CENSUS, 1790-1920.

Census.	Year.	Sq.m.	Pop.	Inc.	%
1	1790	867,980	3,929,214	....	...
2	1800	867,980	5,308,483	1,378,969	35.1
3	1810	1,685,865	7,239,881	1,931,398	36.4
4	1820	1,753,588	9,638,453	2,398,572	33.1
5	1830	1,753,588	12,866,020	3,227,567	33.5
6	1840	1,753,588	17,069,453	4,203,433	32.7
7	1850	2,944,337	23,191,876	6,122,423	35.9
8	1860	2,973,965	31,443,321	8,251,445	35.6
9	1870	2,973,965	38,558,371	7,115,050	22.6
10	1880	2,973,965	50,155,783	11,630,838	30.2
11	1890	2,973,965	62,947,714	12,790,557	25.5
12	1900	2,974,159	75,994,575	13,046,861	20.7
13	1910	2,973,890	91,972,266	15,977,691	21.0
14	1920	....	105,683,108	13,710,842	14.9

POPULATION NEW YORK STATE, 1790-1920.

Yrs	Pop.	Inc.	Pc.	Yrs	Pop.	Inc.	Pc.
1790	340,120	....	....	1870	4,382,759	502,024	12.9
1800	589,051	248,931	73.2	1880	5,082,871	700,112	16.0
1810	959,049	369,998	62.8	1890	6,003,174	914,962	18.0
1820	1,372,812	413,763	43.1	1900	7,268,894	1,265,720	21.1
1830	1,918,608	546,796	39.8	1910	9,113,614	1,844,720	25.4
1840	2,428,921	510,313	26.6	*1915	9,687,744	574,130	6.2
1850	3,097,394	668,473	27.5	1920	10,384,144	1,270,530	13.9
1860	3,880,735	783,341	25.3				

*State Census.

DENSITY OF NEW YORK STATE.

N. Y. State has 60 cities. Their aggregate population, 1920 census, is 8,091,975, or 77.9% of the total population ofthe State. There are 62 counties, their population ranging from 3,970 in Hamilton County to 2,284,103 in New York County. The latest available record gives the State a total land area of 47,654 sq. miles. The average number of persons to each sq. mile is 217.9. In 1910 it was 191.2.

LARGEST CITIES OF THE WORLD.

Cities.	Miles to N. Y.	Year.	Population.
London, Metropolitan*	3,233	1918	7,432,929
New York	.....	1920	5,620,048
Paris	3,518	1911	2,888,110
Chicago	900	1920	2,701,705
Tokio	7,727	1917	2,349,803
Petrograd	5,007	1915	2,318,645
Vienna	4,740	1914	2,149,800
Berlin	3,830	1910	2,071,257
Philadelphia	90	1920	1,823,158
Moscow	5,012	1915	1,817,100
Buenos Ayres	5,871	1918	1,637,155
Osaka	7,977	1916	1,460,218
Hankow	9,500	1917	†1,321,000
Rio Janeiro	4,770	1911	1,128,637
Constantinople	5,810	1912	†1,203,000
Calcutta	9,830	1911	1,122,313
Glasgow	3,370	1918	1,111,428
Pekin	10,500	1917	†1,000,000
Shanghai	9,920	1917	†1,000,000
Detroit	743	1920	993,739
Bombay	8,120	1911	979,445
Hamburg	3,652	1910	931,035
Warsaw	4,150	1913	909,491
Canton	9,085	1910	†900,000
Budapest	4,303	1910	880,371
Birmingham, Eng.	3,100	1917	870,211
Cleveland	568	1920	796,836
St. Louis	1,048	1920	772,897
Sydney, N. S. W.	9,691	1917	770,300
Montreal	404	1918	750,000
Boston	217	1920	748,060
Liverpool	3,052	1911	746,421
Baltimore	188	1920	733,826
Melbourne	9,945	1917	708,240

*Registrar General's report. †Estimated.

AREA AND POPULATION OF STATES AND TERRITORIES.

States & Ter.	Admitted to Union.	Capital.	*Area Sq. M.	§	1880. Census.	§	1890. Census.	§	1900. Census.	§	1910. Census.	§	1920. Census.
Alabama	Dec. 14, 1819	Montgomery	51,279	17	1,262,505	17	1,513,017	18	1,828,697	18	2,138,093	18	2,348,174
Arizona	Feb 14, 1912	Phoenix	113,810	44	40,440	48	59,620	49	122,931	46	204,354	46	333,903
Arkansas	June 15, 1836	Little Rock	52,525	25	802,525	24	1,128,179	25	1,311,564	25	1,574,449	25	1,752,204
California	Sept. 9, 1850	Sacramento	155,652	24	864,694	22	1,208,130	21	1,485,053	12	2,377,549	8	3,426,861
Colorado	Aug. 1, 1876	Denver	103,658	35	194,327	31	412,198	31	539,700	32	799,024	33	939,629
Connecticut	**Jan. 9, 1788	Hartford	4,820	28	622,700	29	746,258	29	908,420	31	1,114,756	29	1,380,631
Delaware	**Dec. 7, 1787	Dover	1,965	38	146,608	42	168,493	46	184,735	47	202,322	47	223,003
Dist. Columbia	†July 16, 1790	....	60	36	177,624	39	230,392	42	278,718	43	331,069	42	437,571
Florida	March 3, 1845	Tallahassee	54,861	34	269,493	32	391,422	32	528,542	33	752,619	32	968,470
Georgia	**Jan. 2, 1788	Atlanta	58,725	13	1,542,180	12	1,837,353	11	2,216,331	10	2,609,121	12	2,895,832
Idaho	July 3, 1890	Boise	83,354	46	32,610	45	84,385	47	161,772	45	325,594	43	431,866
Illinois	Dec. 3, 1818	Springfield	56,043	4	3,077,871	3	3,826,351	3	4,821,550	3	5,638,591	3	6,485,280
Indiana	Dec. 11, 1816	Indianapolis	36,045	6	1,978,301	8	2,192,404	8	2,516,462	9	2,700,876	11	2,930,390
Iowa	March 3, 1845	Des Moines	55,586	10	1,624,615	10	1,911,896	10	2,231,853	15	2,224,771	16	2,404,021
Kansas	Jan. 29, 1861	Topeka	81,774	20	996,096	19	1,427,096	22	1,470,495	22	1,690,949	24	1,769,257
Kentucky	Feb. 4, 1791	Frankfort	40,181	8	1,648,690	11	1,858,635	12	2,147,174	14	2,289,905	15	2,416,630
Louisiana	April 8, 1812	Baton Rouge	45,409	22	939,946	25	1,118,587	23	1,381,625	24	1,656,388	22	1,798,509
Maine	March 3, 1820	Augusta	29,895	27	648,936	30	661,086	30	694,466	34	742,371	35	768,014
Maryland	**April 28, 1788	Annapolis	9,941	23	934,943	27	1,042,390	26	1,188,044	27	1,295,346	28	1,449,661
Massachusetts	**Feb. 6, 1788	Boston	8,039	7	1,783,085	6	2,238,943	7	2,805,346	6	3,366,416	6	3,852,356
Michigan	Jan. 26, 1837	Lansing	57,480	9	1,636,937	9	2,093,889	9	2,420,982	8	2,810,173	7	3,668,412
Minnesota	May 11, 1858	St. Paul	80,858	26	780,773	20	1,301,826	19	1,751,394	19	2,075,708	17	2,387,125
Mississippi	Dec. 10, 1817	Jackson	46,362	18	1,131,597	21	1,289,600	20	1,551,270	21	1,797,114	23	1,790,618
Missouri	March 2, 1821	Jefferson City	68,727	5	2,168,380	5	2,679,184	5	3,106,665	7	3,293,335	9	3,404,055
Montana	Feb. 22, 1889	Helena	146,201	45	39,159	44	132,159	44	243,329	40	376,053	39	548,889
Nebraska	March 1, 1867	Lincoln	76,808	30	452,402	26	1,058,910	27	1,066,300	29	1,192,214	31	1,296,372
Nevada	Oct. 13, 1864	Carson City	109,821	43	62,266	49	45,761	49	42,335	49	81,875	49	77,407
N. Hampshire	**June 21, 1788	Concord	9,031	31	346,991	33	376,530	36	411,588	39	430,572	41	443,083
New Jersey	**Dec. 18, 1787	Trenton	7,514	19	1,131,116	18	1,144,933	16	1,883,669	11	2,537,167	41	3,155,900
New Mexico	Jan. 6, 1912	Santa Fe	122,503	41	119,565	43	153,593	45	195,310	44	327,301	44	360,350
New York	**July 26, 1788	Albany	47,654	1	5,082,871	1	5,997,853	1	7,268,894	1	9,113,614	1	10,384,829
N. Carolina	Nov. 21, 1789	Raleigh	48,740	15	1,399,750	16	1,617,947	15	1,893,810	16	2,206,287	14	2,559,123
N. Dakota	Feb. 22, 1889	Bismarck	70,183	40	c135,177	41	182,719	41	319,146	37	577,056	36	645,680
Ohio	Nov. 30, 1802	Columbus	40,740	3	3,198,062	4	3,672,316	4	4,157,545	4	4,767,121	4	5,759,394
Oklahoma	Nov. 16, 1907	Oklahoma City	69,414	..	....	46	61,834	38	398,331	23	1,657,155	21	2,028,283
Oregon	Feb. 14, 1859	Salem	95,607	37	174,768	38	313,767	35	413,536	35	672,765	34	783,389
Pennsylvania	**Dec. 12, 1787	Harrisburg	44,832	2	4,282,891	2	5,258,014	2	6,302,115	2	7,665,111	2	8,720,017
Rhode Island	**May 29, 1790	Providence	1,067	33	276,531	35	345,506	34	428,556	38	542,610	38	604,397
S. Carolina	**May 23, 1788	Columbia	30,495	21	995,577	23	1,151,149	24	1,340,316	26	1,515,400	26	1,683,724
S. Dakota	Feb. 22, 1889	Pierre	76,868	..	d	37	328,808	37	401,570	36	583,888	37	636,547
Tennessee	June 1, 1796	Nashville	41,687	12	1,542,359	13	1,767,518	14	2,020,616	17	2,184,789	19	2,337,885
Texas	Dec. 29, 1845	Austin	262,398	11	1,591,749	7	2,235,523	6	3,048,710	5	3,896,542	5	4,663,228
Utah	Jan. 4, 1896	Salt Lake City	82,184	39	143,963	40	207,905	43	276,749	41	373,351	40	449,396
Vermont	Feb. 18, 1791	Montpelier	9,124	32	332,286	36	332,422	40	343,641	42	355,956	45	352,428
Virginia	**June 26, 1788	Richmond	40,262	14	1,512,565	15	1,655,980	17	1,854,184	20	2,061,612	20	2,309,187
Washington	Feb. 22, 1889	Olympia	66,836	42	75,116	34	349,390	33	518,103	30	1,141,990	30	1,356,621
W. Virginia	Dec. 31, 1862	Charleston	24,022	29	618,457	28	762,794	28	958,800	28	1,221,119	27	1,463,701
Wisconsin	March 3, 1847	Madison	55,256	16	1,315,497	14	1,686,880	13	2,069,042	13	2,333,860	13	2,632,067
Wyoming	July 10, 1890	Cheyenne	97,594	47	20,789	47	60,705	50	92,531	49	145,965	48	194,402
Alaska	†July 27, 1868	Juneau	590,884	..	....	..	32,052	..	63,592	..	64,356	..	54,899
Guam	††Dec. 10, 1898	Agana	225	..	....	..	....	..	9,676	..	11,806	..	13,275
Hawaii	‡July 7, 1898	Honolulu	6,449	..	....	..	89,990	..	154,001	..	191,909	..	255,912
Porto Rico	††Dec. 10, 1898	San Juan	3,435	..	....	..	....	..	953,243	..	1,118,012	..	1,299,809
Samoa (Amer.)	‡‡Nov. 14, 1899	Pago Pago	102	..	....	..	....	..	5,679	..	7,251	..	8,056
Virgin Islands	rDec. 14, 1916	....	....	..	....	..	....	..	....	..	....	..	‡26,051

Grand total population for 1900, 77,256,630; 1910, 92,402,151; per cent. increase, 20.89; 1920 census, Continental U. S., 105,708,771; outlying possessions, 12,148,738. Total, 117,857,509. Philippine population, census of 1903, 7,635,426, est.; 1918, 10,350,640. Panama Canal Zone, 22,858. Tutuila Group, 7,550, report of 1916. ‡Statistisk Aarbog of Denmark, 1916. **Ratified the constitution. †Organized as Territories. ††Ceded by Treaty of Paris. ‡Date of approval of Act of Congress annexing Hawaii. ‡‡Treaty with Great Britain and Germany. cDakota Territory. dSee North Dakota. §Rank. *Land area as of July, 1913, compiled by the Bureau of the Census from data furnished by officials. rSale ratified by Danish people.

COMPARATIVE POPULATION OF NEW YORK STATE.

With a population of 10,384,144, N. Y. State has more people than any one of these European countries. Belgium, Roumania, Greece, Netherlands, Portugal, Sweden, Bulgaria, Switzerland, Finland, Denmark or Norway. It has more than Scotland and Ireland combined at the last census (1911): it has almost twice as many as Australia and it exceeds all Canada by one-third.

N. Y. State is more populous than any country in South America, except Brazil, and it exceeds any country in North America, except Mexico.

Its increase of 1,270,530 from 1910 to 1920 was at the rate of 13.9 per cent.

More than half the population of the State is contained in New York City.

State population, 1920 10,384,144
N. Y. City, 1920 (55% of State population). 5,620,048
Remainder of State 4,764,097

POPULATION OF NEW YORK CITY AND SUBURBS.

In the following table population has been computed for New York City and cities and towns located in territory adjacent to the central city:

	Area, acres.	1920, pop'n.	1910, pop'n.	PC. inc.
Metropolitan Dist.	616,927.6	7,377,186	6,218,651	18.6
In city proper.	183,555.0	5,620,048	4,766,883	17.9
Outside urban portions......	433,372.6	1,757,138	1,451,768	21.0

With the adjacent territory of New York are the following municipalities of 5,000 or over, 1920 figures. New York: Yonkers city, 100,176; Mount Vernon city, 42,726; New Rochelle city, 36,213; Mamaroneck village, 6,276. New Jersey: Newark city, 414,216; Jersey City, 297,864; Paterson city, 135,866; Elizabeth city, 95,682; Hoboken city, 68,166; Bayonne city, 76,754; Passaic city, 63,824; West Hoboken town, 40,068; East Orange city, 50,710; Perth Amboy city, 41,707; Orange city, 33,260; Montclair town, 28,810; Union town, 20,651; Kearney town, 26,724; Bloomfield town, 22,019; Harrison town, 15,721; Hackensack town, 17,667; West New York town, 29,926; Irvington town, 25,480; Englewood city, 11,617; Rahway city, 11,042; Rutherford borough, 9,497; South Orange village, 7,274; Nutley town, 9,421; Roosevelt borough, 11,047; Guttenberg town, 6,726.

POPULATION AND AREA OF NEW YORK STATE BY COUNTIES.

County.	County Seat.	†Area Sq.M.	Census. 1900.	‡Census. 1905.	Census. 1910.	‡1915. Total.	‡1915. Aliens.	Census. 1920.
Albany	Albany	527	165,571	171,497	173,666	183,330	14,240	186,106
Allegany	Belmont	1,047	41,501	43,257	41,412	40,216	762	36,842
Bronx*	Bronx	41½	200,507	271,630	430,980	615,600	122,466	732,016
Broome	Binghamton	705	69,149	72,282	78,809	90,641	7,425	69,149
Cattaraugus	Little Valley	1,342	65,643	66,196	65,919	72,756	5,419	71,323
Cayuga	Auburn	703	66,234	65,309	67,106	65,751	4,065	65,221
Chautauqua	Mayville	1,069	88,314	96,880	105,126	116,818	9,957	115,348
Chemung	Elmira	407	54,063	51,600	54,662	59,017	2,103	65,872
Chenango	Norwich	894	36,568	36,783	35,575	36,648	915	34,969
Clinton	Plattsburg	1,049	47,430	47,282	48,230	47,561	2,318	43,898
Columbia	Hudson	644	43,211	42,868	43,658	44,111	3,418	38,930
Cortland	Cortland	503	27,576	29,508	29,249	30,074	1,223	29,625
Delaware	Delhi	1,449	46,413	56,788	45,575	45,995	1,573	42,774
Dutchess	Poughkeepsie	806	81,670	81,632	87,661	91,044	7,022	91,747
Erie	Buffalo	1,034	433,686	473,700	528,985	571,897	64,914	634,588
Essex	Elizabethtown	1,836	30,707	32,452	33,458	32,461	1,544	31,871
Franklin	Malone	1,678	42,853	47,012	45,717	46,181	3,463	43,541
Fulton	Johnstown	516	42,842	42,330	44,534	45,625	3,459	44,927
Genesee	Batavia	496	34,561	35,878	37,615	40,707	3,881	37,976
Greene	Catskill	643	31,478	31,130	30,214	30,091	1,131	25,796
Hamilton	Lake Pleasant	1,700	4,947	4,912	4,373	4,491	196	3,970
Herkimer	Herkimer	1,459	51,049	53,856	56,356	64,109	7,777	64,962
Jefferson	Watertown	1,274	76,748	80,459	80,382	81,009	6,196	82,250
Kings	Brooklyn	§81	1,166,582	1,358,686	1,634,351	1,798,513	357,292	2,018,356
Lewis	Lowville	1,270	27,427	26,642	24,849	25,947	1,196	23,704
Livingston	Geneseo	631	37,059	36,450	38,037	38,427	2,710	36,830
Madison	Wampsville	650	40,545	39,690	39,289	41,742	1,788	39,535
Monroe	Rochester	663	217,854	239,434	283,212	319,310	38,435	352,034
Montgomery	Fonda	398	47,488	49,928	57,567	61,030	8,993	57,928
Nassau	Mineola	274	55,448	69,477	83,930	116,825	17,305	125,727
New York	New York	63	2,050,600	2,384,010	2,762,522	2,137,747	665,463	2,284,103
Niagara	Lockport	522	74,961	84,744	92,036	108,550	16,767	118,705
Oneida	Utica	1,250	132,800	139,341	154,157	167,331	22,555	182,485
Onondaga	Syracuse	781	168,735	178,441	200,298	213,992	19,522	241,465
Ontario	Canandaigua	649	49,605	52,689	52,286	54,628	2,758	52,652
Orange	Goshen	834	103,859	108,267	116,001	118,118	9,892	119,844
Orleans	Albion	396	30,164	31,323	32,000	33,919	2,566	28,619
Oswego	Oswego	966	70,881	70,110	71,664	75,929	4,734	71,045
Otsego	Cooperstown	1,009	48,939	48,209	47,216	48,534	1,293	46,200
Putnam	Carmel	233	13,787	14,169	14,665	12,767	1,028	10,802
Queens	Jamaica	105	152,999	198,240	284,041	396,727	45,634	469,042
Rensselaer	Troy	663	121,697	122,637	122,276	121,330	5,755	113,129
Richmond	Richmond	48	67,021	72,845	85,969	98,634	13,847	116,531
Rockland	New City	183	38,298	45,032	46,873	46,903	4,543	45,548
St. Lawrence	Canton	2,701	89,083	90,045	89,005	90,291	7,138	88,121
Saratoga	Ballston Spa	823	61,089	62,658	61,917	62,982	4,212	60,029
Schenectady	Schenectady	206	46,852	71,334	88,235	98,625	12,310	109,363
Schoharie	Schoharie	642	26,854	25,294	23,855	23,005	565	21,303
Schuyler	Watkins	336	15,811	15,122	14,004	13,954	421	13,098
Seneca	Waterloo	336	28,114	25,815	26,972	25,249	1,355	24,735
Steuben	Bath	1,401	82,822	81,814	83,362	83,630	2,304	80,627
Suffolk	Riverhead	924	77,582	81,653	96,138	104,342	12,134	110,241
Sullivan	Monticello	1,002	32,306	34,795	33,808	38,189	3,134	33,163
Tioga	Owego	520	27,951	26,907	25,624	25,549	458	24,212
Tompkins	Ithaca	476	33,830	34,151	33,647	36,535	1,651	35,285
Ulster	Kingston	1,140	88,422	86,660	91,769	85,367	5,410	74 979
Warren	Lake George	879	29,943	31,935	32,223	32,977	1,301	31,673
Washington	Hudson Falls	837	45,624	47,376	47,778	46,955	2,211	44,888
Wayne	Lyons	599	48,660	48,564	50,179	53,476	3,371	48,827
Westchester	White Plains	448	184,257	228,950	283,055	321,713	48,644	344,086
Wyoming	Warsaw	601	30,413	31,355	31,880	33,028	1,482	30,077
Yates	Penn Yan	343	20,318	19,408	18,642	18,841	585	16,641

Total area State, 47,654 sq. m. *Decrease. †U. S. 1910 Census figures. §To Jamaica Bay Bulkhead, not Borough lines. ‡N. Y. State Census. 1915 Census includes institution inmates, difference between number of aliens and total shows number of citizens in each county. *New County, Laws of 1912. See previous volumes of Eagle Almanac for 1880 and 1890 Census figures.

POPULATION OF N. Y. CITY BY BOROUGHS.

Year.	N.Y.C.	Boroughs: Mhtn.	Br'nx	Bkln.	Qu'ns	Rich.
1790 ...	49,401	33,131	1,781	4,495	6,159	3,825
1800 ...	79,216	60,515	1,755	5,740	6,642	4,564
1810 ...	119,734	96,373	2,267	8,303	7,444	5,347
1820 ...	152,056	123,706	2,782	11,187	8,246	6,135
1830 ...	242,278	202,589	3,023	20,535	9,049	7,082
1840 ...	391,114	312,710	5,346	47,613	14,480	10,965
1850 ...	696,115	515,547	8,032	138 882	18,593	15,061
1860 ...	1,174,779	813,660	23,593	279,122	32,903	25 492
1870 ...	1,478,103	942,292	37,393	419,921	45 468	33,029
1880 ...	1,911,698	1,164,673	51,980	599,495	56,559	38,991
1890 ...	2,507,414	1,441,216	88,908	838,547	87,050	51,693
1900 ...	3,437,202	1,850,093	200,507	1,166,582	152,999	67,021
1910 ...	4,766,883	2,331,542	430 980	1,634,351	284,041	85,969
1915 ...	5,047,221	2,137,747	615,600	1,798,513	396,727	98,634
1920 ...	5,620,048	2,284,103	732,016	2,018,356	469,042	116,531

The population of the present City of New York has grown to 5,620,048 in 1920, or an increase since 1910 of 17.9 per cent. The population per acre in each of the five boroughs is: Manhattan, 162; Bronx, 33; Brooklyn, 38; Queens, 7; Richmond, 3.

Per Cent. Increase by Boroughs.

Boroughs.	1910 to 1920. Number.	1910 to 1920. Per Cent.	1900 to 1910. Number.	1900 to 1910. Per Cent
Manhattan	*47,439	*2.0	481,449	26.0
Bronx	301,036	69.8	230,473	114.4
Brooklyn	384,005	23.5	467,769	40.0
Queens	185,001	63.1	131,042	85.6
Richmond	30,562	35.6	18,948	28.2
Total inc.	853,165	17.9	1,329,681	38.7

*Decrease.

COINAGE MINTS AND ASSAY OFFICES.

Coinage mints of the United States are located in Philadelphia, Pa.; San Francisco, Cal., and Denver, Col. The Government Mint Assay Offices are in Carson City, Nev., and New Orleans, La. The U. S. Assay Offices are in New York, N. Y.; Boise, Idaho; Helena, Mont.; Deadwood, S. D.; Seattle, Wash., and Salt Lake City, Utah. The mint in Philadelphia was established in 1792 and the others as follows: San Francisco, 1852, and Denver, 1904.

POPULATION INCORPORATED CITIES AND VILLAGES, N. Y. STATE.

Cities of over 100,000.	1920.	*1915.	1910.
New York City	5,620,048	5,047,221	4,766,883
Manhattan	2,284,103	2,137,747	2,331,542
Bronx	732,016	615,600	430,980
Brooklyn	2,018,356	1,798,513	1,634,351
Queens	469,042	396,727	284,041
Richmond	116,531	98,634	85,969

Cities of over 100,000.	1920.	*1915.	1910.
Buffalo	506,775	454,630	423,715
Rochester	295,750	248,465	218,149
Syracuse	171,717	145,293	137,249
Albany	113,344	107,979	100,253
Yonkers	100,176	90,948	79,803

*N. Y. State Census. In the following table letter c indicates city. See 1915 Eagle Almanac for 1890 and 1900 Census figures.

City or Village.	1920.	1915.	1910.
Adams	1,557	1,671	1,458
Addison	1,699	1,754	2,004
Afton	782	754	729
Akron	1,960	1,856	1,677
Albion	4,683	5,988	5,016
Alden	755	777	828
Alexander	194	259	212
Alexandria Bay	1,649	2,062	1,899
Alfred	698	677	739
Allegany	1,350	1,327	1,293
Altamont	797	805	674
Altmar	315	390	363
Amityville	3,265	2,780	2,517
Amsterdam c	33,524	34,319	31,267
Andes	394	405	414
Andover	1,132	1,154	1,136
Angelica	972	1,138	1,056
Angola	1,367	1,194	898
Antwerp	1,029	1,057	974
Arcade	1,372	1,568	1,294
Ardsley	730	442	537
Argyle	198	223	231
Arkport	463	538	562
Athens	1,844	1,925	1,956
Attica	2,015	2,013	1,869
Auburn c	36,142	32,468	34,668
Aurora	717	396	493
Avoca	1,019	1,083	1,057
Avon	2,585	2,430	2,053
Babylon	2,523	3,100	2,600
Bainbridge	1,259	1,201	1,159
Baldwinville	3,685	3,220	3,009
Ballston Spa	4,103	4,344	4,138
Barker	431	550	441
Batavia c	13,541	13,278	11,613
Bath	4,795	4,1‑3	3,884
Beacon c	10,996	10,165	10,629
Belleville	306	280	344
Bellport	614	499	419
Belmont	1,021	1,031	1,094
Bemus Point	227	270	38
Bergen	576	639	637
Binghamton c	66,800	53,668	48,443
Black River	937	857	916
Blasdell	1,401	940	849
Bloomingdale	490	394	382
Bolivar	1,146	1,260	1,318
Boonville	1,914	1,909	1,794
Brewster	859	1,402	1,296
Briar Cliff M'n'r	1,027	1,221	950
Bridgewater	232	258	245
Brightwaters	250	1,000	...
Brockport	2,930	3,368	3,579
Brocton	1,383	1,292	1,781
Bronxville	3,055	2,240	1,863
Brookfield	317	400	395
Brownville	976	885	854
Burdett	380	375	382
Caledonia	1,170	1,241	1,290
Cambridge	1,559	1,727	1,528
Camden	1,941	2,181	2,170
Camillus	808	840	763
Canajoharie	2,415	2,474	2,273
Canandaigua c	7,356	7,501	7,217
Canaseraga	651	668	754
Canastota	3,995	3,849	3,247
Candor	699	749	737
Canisteo	2,201	2,314	2,259
Canton	2,631	2,624	2,701
Cape Vincent	913	1,102	1,155
Carthage	4,320	3,871	3,563
Castile	1,013	962	1,040
Castleton	1,595	1,583	1,396
Cato	404	388	374
Catskill	4,728	5,371	5,296
Cattaraugus	1,347	1,276	1,165
Cayuga	300	373	348
Cayuga Hts.	179	...	...
Cazenovia	1,683	1,928	1,861
Cedarhurst	2,838	2,657	1,747
Celoron	757	720	619
Central Square	448	481	429
Champlain	1,140	1,279	1,280
Chateaugay	1,291	1,196	1,045
Chatham	2,710	2,389	2,251
Chaumont	595	682	708
Cherry Creek	527	720	606
Cherry Valley	728	762	792

City or Village.	1920.	1915.	1910.
Chester	1,049	1,280	1,210
Chittenango	650	1,074	678
Churchville	613	583	565
Clayton	1,849	1,879	1,941
Clayville	999	972	649
Cleveland	541	660	687
Clifton Springs	1,628	1,664	1,600
Clinton	1,270	1,264	1,236
Clyde	2,528	2,699	2,695
Cobleskill	2,410	2,362	2,088
Cohocton	843	938	838
Cohoes c	22,987	23,433	24,709
Cold Brook	261	274	338
Cold Springs	1,422	935	2,549
Constableville	380	391	407
Cooperstown	2,725	2,634	2,484
Copenhagen	554	695	585
Corfu	458	515	413
Corinth	2,576	2,415	2,166
Corning c	15,820	13,459	13,730
Cornwall	1,755	2,240	2,638
Cortland c	13,294	12,367	11,504
Coxsackie	2,121	2,309	2,494
Croghan	646	659	621
Croton-on-H'd'n.	2,286	2,243	1,806
Cuba	1,611	1,645	1,556
Dannemora	1,606	869	1,146
Dansville	4,681	4,018	3,938
Delhi	1,969	1,743	1,760
Delevan	547	567	...
Depew	5,850	4,932	3,921
Deposit	1,943	1,779	1,864
De Ruyter	519	604	538
Dexter	1,164	1,145	1,005
Dobbs Ferry	4,401	4,030	3,455
Dolgeville	3,448	3,326	2,685
Dresden	621	826	345
Dryden	707	722	709
Dundee	1,143	1,236	1,228
Dunkirk c	19,336	17,870	17,221
Earlville	792	845	874
East Aurora	3,703	3,445	2,781
East Bloomfield.	356	...	...
East Randolph	544	582	593
East Rochester	3,901	3,471	2,398
East Rockaway.	2,005	1,607	1,200
East Syracuse	4,106	3,839	3,274
Eastwood	2,194	777	810
Edwards	577	504	476
Elba	386	439	351
Elbridge	382	475	462
Elizabethtown	518	630	505
Ellenville	3,116	3,073	3,114
Ellicottville	950	881	985
Ellisburg	275	316	702
Elmira c	45,393	40,093	37,176
Elmira Heights.	4,188	3,154	2,732
Elmsford	1,635	1,380	411
Endicott	9,500	5,581	2,408
Esperance	269	241	263
Fabius	240	340	344
Fairhaven	552	624	571
Fairport	4,626	3,556	3,112
Falconer	2,742	2,342	2,141
Farmingdale	2,091	1,856	1,567
Farnham	516	636	540
Fayetteville	1,584	1,779	1,481
Fishkill	479	531	516
Fleischmann's	525	767	568
Fonda	747	1,120	1,100
Forestport	383	505	507
Forestville	620	740	721
Fort Ann	338	436	436
Fort Covington	836	828	877
Fort Edward	3,871	3,662	3,762
Fort Plain	2,747	2,923	2,762
Frankfort	4,198	4,213	3,303
Franklin	476	441	473
Franklinville	2,015	2,065	1,568
Fredonia	6,051	5,828	5,285
Freeport	8,599	7,463	4,836
Freeville	303	337	318
Friendship	1,026	1,199	1,218
Fulton c	13,043	11,138	10,480
Fultonville	869	955	812
Gainesville	341	340	327
Galway	94	104	112
Geneseo	2,157	2,253	2,087

City or Village.	1920.	1915.	1910.
Geneva c	14,648	13,232	12,446
Gilbertsville	419	451	455
Glen Cove	8,664	8,875	...
Glen Park	661	650	522
Glens Falls c	16,638	16,323	15,243
Gloversville c	22,075	21,178	20,642
Goshen	2,843	3,511	3,081
Gouverneur	4,143	4,164	4,128
Gowanda	2,673	2,524	2,012
Grand-View-on-Hudson	175	355	368
Granville	3,024	3,890	3,920
Great Neck Estates	339	175	...
Green Island	4,411	4,533	4,737
Greene	1,297	1,272	1,275
Greenport	3,122	3,735	3,089
Greenwich	2,384	2,315	2,314
Groton	2,235	1,445	1,260
Hagaman	855	952	875
Hamburg	3,185	2,744	2,134
Hamilton	1,505	1,588	1,689
Hammond	409	418	404
Hammondsport	417	1,560	1,254
Hancock	1,326	1,356	1,329
Hannibal	400	432	330
Harriman	690	854	...
Harrisville	900	991	921
Hastg's-on-H'n.	5,526	5,461	4,652
Haverstraw	5,226	5,418	5,669
Hempstead	6,382	6,073	4,964
Henderson	299	380	340
Herkimer	10,453	9,577	7,520
Hermon	457	607	587
Heuvelton	5,459	556	529
Highland Falls	2,588	2,518	2,470
Hillburn	1,112	1,017	1,090
Hilton	827	817	627
Hobart	587	596	544
Holland Patent.	328	339	337
Holley	1,625	1,780	1,679
Homer	2,356	2,871	2,696
Honeoye Falls	1,107	1,258	1,169
Holcomb	488	...	...
Hoosick Falls	4,896	5,406	5,532
Hornell c	15,025	14,352	13,617
Horseheads	2,078	1,949	1,778
Hudson c	11,745	11,544	11,417
Hudson Falls	5,761	5,585	5,189
Hunter	683	405	406
Ilion	10,169	8,900	6,588
Interlaken	73	663	693
Irvington	2,701	2,379	2,319
Ithaca c	17,004	16,750	14,802
Jamestown c	38,917	37,780	31,297
Johnson	8,587	5,400	3,775
Johnstown c	10,906	10,687	10,447
Jordan	1,012	1,063	978
Keeseville	813	1,795	1,835
Kenmore	3,160	1,700	1,020
Kinderhook	732	827	698
Kingston c	26,688	26,354	25,908
Lackawanna c	17,918	15,737	14,549
Lacona	461	476	443
Lake George	630	750	632
Lake Placid	2,099	1,977	1,682
Lakewood	714	702	564
Lancaster	6,059	5,094	4,364
Larchmont	2,468	2,060	1,958
La Salle	3,813	2,402	1,299
Laurens	228	364	242
Lawrence	2,861	1,870	1,189
Leroy	4,203	4,084	3,771
Leicester	279	305	304
Lewiston	723	741	713
Liberty	2,459	2,395	2,072
Lima	843	922	866
Limestone	454	463	684
Lisle	294	347	329
Little Falls c	13,029	13,022	12,273
Little Valley	1,253	1,307	1,368
Liverpool	1,831	1,691	1,388
Livonia Station.	743	857	823
Lockport c	21,308	18,693	17,970
Long Beach	....	662	230
Lowville	3,127	3,244	2,940
Lynbrook	4,275	3,055	2,206
Lyndonville	738	832	647

POPULATION OF INCORPORATED CITIES AND VILLAGES, NEW YORK STATE—*Con.*

City or Village.	1920	1915	1910
Lyons	318	4,742	4,460
Lyons Falls	818	863	759
McGrawville	1,032	887	931
Macedon	526	1,147	536
Madison	265	317	309
Malone	7,556	7,404	6,477
Mamaroneck	6,276	7,290	5,699
Manchester	1,467	1,115	881
Manlius	1,296	1,304	1,314
Mannsville	265	627	330
Marathon	665	1,006	1,079
Marcellus	989	991	917
Margaretville	650	648	669
Marlborough	807	795	920
Massena	5,993	4,614	2,951
Mayfield	592	595	590
Mayville	442	1,201	1,122
Mechanicville c	8,166	8,208	6,634
Medina	6,011	6,079	5,683
Meridian	274	313	313
Mexico	1,336	1,474	1,233
Middleburg	986	1,059	1,114
Middleport	1,416	1,427	1,530
Middletown c	18,420	16,381	15,313
Middleville	790	710	625
Milford	505	560	511
Millbrook	1,096	1,252	1,136
Millerton	829	890	858
Mineola	3,016	2,318	1,981
Minoa	867	668	...
Mohawk	2,919	2,577	2,079
Monroe	1,527	1,519	1,195
Montgomery	906	957	941
Monticello	2,330	2,132	1,941
Montour Falls	1,560	1,281	1,208
Mooers	512	522	560
Moravia	1,331	1,393	1,324
Morris	420	466	535
Morristown	489	479	540
Morrisville	497	682	500
Mount Kisco	3,901	2,902	2,802
Mount Morris	3,312	3,884	2,782
Mount Vernon c	42,726	37,049	30,919
Munnsville	377	...	...
Naples	1,148	1,138	1,093
Nassau	655	697	529
Nelliston	664	716	737
Nelsonville	423	979	765
Newark	6,964	6,468	6,227
Newark Valley	821	808	925
New Berlin	1,070	1,131	1,114
Newburgh c	30,366	27,876	27,805
Newfield	302	341	354
New Hartford	1,621	1,459	1,195
New London	90	213	108
New Paltz	1,056	1,261	1,230
Newport	708	697	583
New Rochelle c	36,213	31,758	28,867
Niagara Falls c	50,760	42,257	30,445
Nichols	554	586	533
North Bangor	362	334	...
North Collins	1,158	1,068	964
North Pelham	....	1,874	1,311
Northport	1,977	2,327	2,096
N'th Tarrytown	5,927	4,877	5,421
N. Tonawanda c	15,482	13,498	11,955
Northville	1,190	1,635	1,130
Norwich c	8,268	8,342	7,422
Norwood	1,808	1,579	1,993
Nunda	1,152	1,140	1,043
Nyack	4,444	4,291	4,619
Oakfield	1,422	1,307	1,231
Odessa	366	335	330
Ogdensburg c	14,609	14,338	15,933
Old Forge	565	515	465
Olean c	20,506	17,981	14,743
Oneida c	10,541	9,472	8,317
Oneida Castle	446	399	393
Oneonta c	11,582	10,474	9,491
Oramel	123	126	131
Oriskany Falls	1,014	973	892
Ossining	10,739	10,326	11,480
Oswego c	23,626	25,426	23,368
Otego	540	579	676
Ovid	438	591	548
Owego	4,147	4,570	4,633
Oxford	1,590	1,594	1,654

City or Village.	1920	1915	1910
Painted Post	2,170	1,329	1,224
Palatine Bridge	443	408	392
Palmyra	2,480	2,465	2,268
Panama	298	352	337
Parish	476	521	490
Patchogue	4,031	4,506	[illegible]
Pawling	1,032	1,070	848
Peekskill	15,868	15,502	15,245
Pelham	5,195	793	681
Pelham Manor	1,754	1,115	832
Penn Yan	5,215	4,725	4,597
Perry	4,717	5,009	4,388
Perrysburg	271	...	...
Phelps	2,200	1,375	1,354
Philadelphia	794	847	842
Philmont	1,919	2,060	1,813
Phoenix	1,747	1,655	1,642
Piermont	1,600	1,481	1,380
Pike	304	344	422
Pine Hill	248	646	417
Pittsford	1,328	1,376	1,205
Plandome	319	255	117
Plattsburg c	10,909	10,134	11,138
Pleasant Valley	384	429	427
Pleasantville	3,590	2,464	2,207
Poland	349	315	332
Port Byron	1,035	1,115	1,085
Port Chester	16,573	15,129	12,809
Port Dickinson	883	583	437
Port Henry	2,183	2,584	2,266
Port Jervis c	10,171	9,413	9,564
Port Leyden	735	753	764
Portville	704	765	758
Potsdam	4,039	4,157	4,036
Poughkeepsie c	35,000	32,714	27,936
Prattsburg	654	696	684
Prospect	282	339	278
Pulaski	1,895	1,860	1,788
Randolph	1,310	1,341	1,298
Ravena	2,093	1,700	...
Red Creek	499	525	457
Red Hook	827	923	960
Remsen	448	417	421
Rensselaer c	10,823	11,210	10,711
Rensselaer Falls	328	374	367
Rhinebeck	1,397	1,587	1,548
Richburg	351	380	451
Richfield Sp'ngs	1,388	1,623	1,503
Richmondville	581	567	599
Richville	302	316	307
Rifton	....	346	745
Rockville Centre	6,262	5,223	3,667
Rome c	26,341	21,926	20,497
Rosendale	655	804	1,125
Rouse Point	1,700	1,783	1,638
Rushville	656	459	463
Rye	5,308	5,339	3,964
Sacketts Harbor	1,094	829	868
Saddle Rock	71	71	77
Sag Harbor	2,993	3,245	3,408
St. Johnsville	2,469	2,705	2,536
Salamanca c	9,276	8,370	5,792
Salem	1,083	1,096	1,250
Saltaire	12	...	...
Sands Point	284	535	152
Sandy Creek	566	669	617
Saranac Lake	1,119	4,918	4,983
Saratoga S'gs c	13,181	12,864	12,693
Saugerties	4,013	4,490	3,929
Savannah	516	531	521
Savona	554	571	587
Scarsdale	3,506	2,717	...
Schaghticoke	568	794	765
Schenectady c	88,723	80,381	72,826
Schenevus	499	537	576
Schoharie	851	1,124	996
Schuylerville	1,625	1,711	1,614
Scotia	4,358	3,790	2,957
Scottsville	784	900	...
Sea Cliff	2,108	1,981	1,694
Seneca Falls	6,389	7,018	6,588
Sharon Springs	400	531	459
Sherburne	1,104	1,016	960
Sherman	847	919	836
Shoreham	11	151	...
Sherrill	1,761	...	...
Shortsville	1,300	1,228	1,112

City or Village.	1920	1915	1910
Sidney	2,670	2,641	2,507
Silver Creek	2,262	3,220	2,512
Silver Springs	1,155	893	974
Sinclairville	514	582	542
Skaneateles	1,835	1,768	1,615
Sloan	1,791	2,202	1,259
Smyrna	261	247	257
Sodus	1,329	...	...
Solvay	7,352	5,886	5,139
Southampton	2,635	3,092	2,509
South Dayton	655	...	...
S'th Glens Falls	2,158	2,106	2,247
South Nyack	1,799	1,950	2,068
Spencer	661	653	669
Spencerport	926	848	1,000
Spring Valley	4,428	2,804	2,353
Springville	2,331	2,688	2,246
Stamford	947	1,060	972
Stillwater	932	1,041	1,004
Suffern	3,154	2,781	2,663
Sylvan Beach	105	196	169
Tannersville	597	758	660
Tarrytown	5,807	5,752	5,600
Theresa	857	1,053	932
Ticonderoga	2,102	2,754	2,475
Tivoli	876	1,080	1,034
Tonawanda c	10,068	9,147	8,290
Trenton	269	316	289
Troy c	72,013	75,488	76,813
Trumansburg	1,011	1,181	1,186
Tuckahoe	3,509	2,753	2,722
Tully	477	559	551
Tupper Lake	2,508	3,910	3,067
Turin	327	339	349
Unadilla	1,157	1,125	1,009
Union	3,303	1,922	1,544
Union Springs	642	784	798
Unionville	402	387	351
Upper Nyack	535	642	691
Utica c	94,156	80,589	74,419
Palatie	1,301	1,410	1,229
Valley Falls	633	795	835
Van Etten	350	407	476
Vernon	541	532	451
Victor	945	1,031	891
Victory Mills	725	657	748
Voorheesville	614	550	633
Waddington	702	726	731
Walden	5,493	5,196	4,004
Walton	3,598	3,606	3,103
Wampsville	276	222	212
Wappinger's F'ls	3,235	3,742	3,196
Warsaw	3,622	3,424	3,206
Warwick	2,420	2,505	2,318
Washingtonville	631	635	631
Waterford	2,637	3,047	3,245
Waterloo	3,809	4,343	3,931
Watertown c	31,263	26,895	26,730
Watervliet c	16,073	14,990	15,074
Waterville	1,255	1,564	1,410
Watkins	2,785	2,760	2,817
Waverly	5,270	5,119	4,855
Wayland	1,790	1,699	1,392
Webster	1,247	1,439	1,032
Weedsport	1,379	1,448	1,344
Wellsburg	465	478	432
Wellsville	5,046	4,695	4,382
West Carthage	1,666	1,587	1,393
Westfield	3,413	3,319	2,985
W. Haverstraw	2,018	2,330	2,369
Westport	669	716	692
West Winfield	725	788	726
Whitehall	5,258	4,666	4,917
White Plains c	21,031	18,681	15,949
Whiteboro	3,038	2,493	2,375
Wh'tney Point	665	760	744
Williamsville	1,733	1,272	1,105
Wilson	631	741	656
Windsor	598	665	637
Wolcott	1,186	1,346	1,216
Woodhull	300	352	316
Woodridge	941		...
Woodsburgh	220	169	261
Wurtsboro	362	408	478
Wyoming	396	...	...
Yorkville	1,512	1,098	691
Youngstown	539	571	556

JAPANESE POPULATION OF HAWAII.

The Japanese population of Hawaii is announced by the Census Bureau as 109,269 out of a total population of 255,512. The Japanese constitute 42.7 per cent. of the 1920 population of the islands. The actual increase of Japanese on the island during the last decade was 29,594, or 37.1 per cent., as against a percentage gain of 30.4 per cent. made during the ten years, 1900-10. Figures on the sex of the Japanese population in 1920, as compared with 1910 and 1900, show a much larger increase in the number of women and girls than in the number of men and boys. The female portion of the population amounted to 23.3 per cent. in 1900, as compared with 42.7 per cent. in 1920.

AREA, POPULATION AND DENSITY OF BOROUGHS.

The determination of an exact area of New York City and its boroughs is a debatable matter. This is due to the irregular waterfront lines and the existence of considerable areas under water, marsh lands, or meadow lands, which different surveyors compute differently. Some base their figures within pierhead lines, others within bulkhead lines and still others within borough lines. No official figures exist for the exact areas of the boroughs. With regard to Mhtn. Boro., the total acreage figures given below is approximately correct. There has been considerable filling in on the smaller islands, the area of which has not been computed. The Eagle Almanac gives below the areas of the Assembly Districts, as apportioned by the 1917 Legislature (see index for boundaries), computed by the topographical bureaus of each borough; also the areas computed by wards by the Health Department. The discrepancies are explained above. The Eagle Almanac gives the preference to the Topographical Bureau figures, as same are computed for the official use of each Borough President's office.

BY ASSEMBLY DISTRICTS.

Brooklyn. 1920—2,018,356.

A.D...	Census	Ac'ge	Density
1......	86,912	888	97.8
2......	109,104	18,894	5.7
3......	90,760	1,749	51.8
4......	82,336	805	102.2
5......	67,808	612	110.7
6......	85,895	494	190.0
7......	77,455	1,195	64.8
8......	79,658	676	117.8
9......	92,734	3,318	27.9
10......	75,835	826	91.8
11......	78,062	960	81.3
12......	77,872	1,398	55.7
13......	83,437	1,088	76.6
14......	97,344	572	170.1
15......	73,027	873	75.0
16......	97,110	5,168	18.7
17......	75 487	701	107.6
18......	95,245	2,864	33.2
19......	86,719	545	159.1
20......	99,357	920	107.9
21......	84,484	1,856	45.5
22......	122,637	4,720	25.9
23......	99,058	585	171.0
Total..	2,018,356	51,807	38.9

Manhattan. 1920—2,284,103.

A.D...	Census	Ac'ge	Density
1......	137,522	1,204	114.2
2......	147,115	438	335.8
3......	113,098	760	148.8
4......	94,980	245	420.3
5......	103,166	486	212.2
6......	99,165	572	173.3
7......	85,486	542	157.7
8......	109,522	267	410.1
9......	82,994	369	224.9
10......	79,801	1,102	72.4
11......	79,314	364	217.8
12......	121,539	686	177.1
13......	76,008	485	156.7
14......	120,879	437	276.6
15......	96,072	1,316	73.0
16......	108,117	364	297.0
17......	85,663	411	208.4
18......	141,790	633	223.9
19......	78,052	344	226.8
20......	83 156	500	166.3
21......	76,982	366	210.3
22......	74,895	503	148.8
23......	88,787	1,624	546.1
Total..	2,284,103	14,056	162.5

Bronx. 1920—732,016.

A.D...	Census	Ac'ge	Density
1......	110,315	822	134.2
2......	117,611	1,921	61.2
3......	83,042	1,763	47.1
4......	84,195	523	160.9
5......	88,428	554	159.6
6......	70,482	14,405	4.8
7......	89,123	556	160.2
8......	88,820	6,136	14.4
Total..	732,016	21,680	27.9

Queens. A.D.	Census	Richmond. A.D.	Census
1.....	78,806	1.....	55,681
2.....	73,273	2.....	60,850
3.....	76,593		
4.....	83,175		
5.....	83,228		
6.....	73,968		
Total	469,042	Total.	116,531

Total acreage, New York City, 201,059 acres, or 315.11 sq. miles.

ACREAGE, POPULATION AND DENSITY BY WARDS.

(Prepared by Bureau of Records, Dept. of Health, N. Y. C. Population figures, 1910 U. S. Census. 1915 N. Y. State Census figures not used by Health Dept. 1920 U. S. Census figures not yet computed.)

Brooklyn.

Ward.	Acre'ge	Census	Density
1	233.0	21,851	93.8
2	97.7	6,894	70.6
3	161.4	15,910	98.6
4	111.3	10,477	94.1
5	119.4	19,401	162.5
6	302.9	46,437	153.3
7	458.5	44,037	96.0
8	1,843.2	82,687	44.9
9	623.6	50,501	81.0
10	318.7	41,238	129.4
11	252.6	21,659	85.7
12	663.1	29,262	44.1
13	230.3	30,091	130.7
14	282.6	33,329	117.9
15	244.8	35,887	146.6
16	244.8	68,244	278.7
17	823.3	70,346	85.5
18	873.0	35,708	40.9
19	413.8	44,860	108.4
20	461.4	27,463	59.5
21	483.2	78,741	163.0
22	1,361.6	81,283	59.7
23	736.0	65,561	89.1
24	1,198.5	80,466	67.2
25	567.8	63,597	112.0
26	3,590.2	177,963	49.5
27	400.7	76,000	189.6
28	884.4	77,451	87.6
29	3,800.0	72,351	19.0
30	5,401.1	76,406	14.1
31	6,312.3	30,988	4.9
32	5,479.5	17,419	3.2
Total..	38,977.8	1,634,508	41.9

Manhattan.

Ward.	Acre'ge	Census	Density
1	154.0	9,750	63.0
2	81.0	933	11.5
3	95.0	1,915	20.2
4	83.0	21,336	257.1
5	168.0	5,666	33.7
6	86.0	19,670	228.7
7	198.0	102,101	515.6
8	183.0	33,182	181.4
9	322.0	64,099	201.6
10	110.0	66,439	604.0
11	196.0	136,548	696.7
12	6,154.0	806,648	131.1
13	107.0	64,651	604.3
14	96.0	38,321	399.3
15	198.0	30,584	154.5
16	349.0	55,926	160.2
17	331.0	172,334	520.6
18	450.0	62,821	139.6
19	1,481.0	292,950	197.7
20	444.0	73,308	165.1
21	411.0	62,345	151.7
22	1,529.0	209,154	136.8
Total..	13,226.0	2,331,491	176.3

Bronx.

Ward.	Acre'ge	Census	Density
23	4,267.0	268,880	63.0
24	22,255.8	162,062	7.3
Total..	26,522.8	430,942	16.2

Queens.

Ward.	Acre'ge	Census	Density
1	4,741	61,763	13.3
2	14,085	105,219	7.2
3	19,358	37,171	1.7
4	33,432	67,412	1.8
5	5,900	12,476	2.2
Total..	77,516	284,041	3.5

Richmond.

Ward.	Acre'ge	Census	Density
1	3,340.0	27,201	8.1
2	4,130.0	16,871	4.1
3	10,050.0	19,312	1.9
4	8,180.0	10,062	1.2
5	10,900.0	11,428	1.0
Total..	36,600.0	85,969	2.3

Total population of N. Y. City, U. S. Census, 1920, 5,620,048. Total acreage, 201,059. Total density per acre, 27.9. U. S. Census, 1910, 4,766,883. Total acreage, 192,842.6. Total density per acre, 24.3. State Census, 1915, 5,047,221. The Federal Bureau of the Census reports the total land area in acres in N. Y. City for July 1, 1915, as 183,555; Bkln., 44,911; Mhtn., 14,038; Bronx, 26,889; Queens, 67,142; Richmond, 30,575.

FEDERAL RAILROAD CONTROL.

Government control of the railroads began on Dec. 28, 1917, and continued until March 1, 1920, when the railroads were returned to owners.

The Government's gross loss in operation of the railroads during Federal control was $900,478,000, according to the final report of the Railroad Administration Director of Finance.

OIL CONSUMING COUNTRIES.

The position of the United States among the oil-consuming countries of the world is shown below, which indicates that this country uses over four-sevenths of the world's consumption. World's consumption by barrels, estimated: United States, 280,000,000; British Empire, 70,000,000; Russia, 63,000,000; France, Italy, Roumania, etc., 23,100,000; rest of world, 56,000,000.

FOREIGN-BORN POPULATION OF NEW YORK CITY.

Totals by nationalities, prepared by Bureau of the Census of Dept. of Commerce and Labor.

Countries	Brooklyn 1910.	Brooklyn 1900.	Manhattan 1910.	Manhattan 1900.	Bronx 1910.	Bronx 1900.	Queens 1910.	Queens 1900.	Richmond 1910.	Richmond 1900.	N. Y. City 1910	N. Y. City 1900.
Australia	222	152	456	257	60	34	33	21	20	13	791	477
Austria	36,421	9,119	139,367	77,061	10,647	1,997	5,638	1,954	1,130	345	193,203	90,476
Belgium	508	338	1,390	709	175	96	141	65	60	32	2,249	1,221
Canada—French	709	762	1,609	1,441	301	153	184	125	29	30	2,844	2,511
Canada—Other	8,086	7,814	11,383	9,153	2,097	1,173	1,039	674	576	534	23,181	19,248
Cuba & W. Indies	2,179	1,356	3,328	2,093	211	132	91	65	57	37	5,966	3,682
Denmark	3,623	2,932	2,754	1,777	769	397	634	284	209	214	7,989	5,604
England	28,312	27,543	36,466	32,298	6,861	3,893	4,576	3,100	1,904	1,787	78,119	68,721
Finland	2,617	1,515	3,598	1,883	534	138	222	123	120	74	7,400	3,733
France	2,846	2,601	13,055	10,259	1,029	615	1,139	950	322	310	18,261	14,735
Germany	87,897	107,679	119,174	165,879	36,586	24,381	30,223	20,547	5,362	5,692	279,242	324,198
Greece	1,017	172	6,615	1,100	249	14	70	19	53	4	8,004	1,309
Holland	1,443	852	2,112	1,508	384	109	177	96	63	48	4,180	2,607
Hungary	8,369	2,449	56,713	28,007	5,928	550	1,577	241	749	269	73,336	31,516
Ireland	70,543	83,296	151,046	166,041	18,264	12,820	8,658	7,958	4,017	4,858	252,528	275,073
Italy	100,390	37,119	199,619	95,930	25,169	7,862	11,107	3,003	4,239	1,435	340,524	145,429
Newfoundland	525	......	256	......	39	......	21	......	18	......	859	......
Norway	15,129	7,969	4,019	1,099	1,199	444	539	240	1,375	735	22,251	11,387
Portugal	389	146	678	95	120	17	38	7	22	6	1,247	271
Roumania	7,809	935	22,092	9,453	2,124	97	147	5	38	9	32,210	10,499
Russia	160,433	31,458	248,855	143,581	27,691	2,221	8,389	2,513	2,212	656	483,580	180,423
Scotland	7,913	7,784	10,631	9,133	2,403	1,338	1,588	1,079	563	493	23,098	19,827
South America	569	314	1,081	531	115	46	61	29	28	14	1,854	934
Spain	1,075	559	2,043	852	103	30	49	16	53	18	3,323	1,475
Sweden	16,489	14,595	13,216	10,933	3,177	1,458	1,444	759	622	471	34,948	25,316
Switzerland	2,163	1,849	5,802	4,912	1,355	822	854	548	211	228	10,415	8,369
Turkey in Asia	1,772	......	4,109	......	174	......	198	......	50	......	6,303	......
Turkey in Europe	407	248	3,064	1,069	156	26	35	45	17	12	3,679	1,400
Wales	544	561	902	865	191	113	76	103	62	44	1,775	1,686
Other Nationalities	1,162	1,354	2,606	3,904	354	282	145	142	88	204	4,354	5,786
Total foreign-born white	571,356	353,769	1,104,029	782,714	148,935	61,258	79,115	44,615	24,278	18,581	1,927,713	1,260,918

DISTRIBUTION OF IMMIGRATION.

The following table shows the distribution of immigrants by groups of States for 1920. This is based upon the immigrant's own statement of his intended future residence. Island possessions of the U. S. are omitted. A comparison in percentages with 1914 is added:

Group of States.	No. immigrants entering 1920.	Per cent. 1920.	Per cent. 1914.
New England	75,000	17.0	12.8
Middle Atlantic	151,000	37.0	48.0
East North Central	67,000	15.0	21.0
West North Central	15,000	3.6	4.8
South Atlantic	14,000	3.2	2.8
East South Central	1,500	0.3	0.3
West South Central	41,000	9.6	1.4
Mountain	13,000	3.1	1.9
Pacific	47,000	11.0	4.7

WORLD'S JEWISH POPULATION.

David Trietsch, the Jewish statistician, has estimated the present number of Jews in the world to be 15,430,000. According to figures presented by the *American Israelite* the Hebrew population of the world is distributed as follows:

Poland	3,300,000	France	150,000
Ukraine	3,300,000	Algeria and Tunis	150,000
United States	3,100,000	Arabia	130,000
Russia (including Serbia)	900,000	Greece	120,000
		Holland	110,000
Roumania	650,000	Morocco	110,000
Germany	540,000	Argentina	100,000
Hungary	450,000	Canada	100,000
Czecho-Slovakia	450,000	Turkey	100,000
British Isles	300,000	Palestine	100,000
Austria	300,000	Australasia	20,000
Lithuania	250,000	*European countries	200,000
Jugo-Slavia	200,000		
Africa (excluding Morocco, Tunis and Algeria)	170,000	*Asiatic countries	100,000
		*American countries	30,000

*Not separately enumerated.

550,000 BROOKLYN HOMES.

The Brooklyn Bureau of Charities has compiled figures showing that Brooklyn, with an area of over 80 square miles, has 67,590 one-family houses, 52,938 two-family houses and 48,980 apartment houses. The total population, 2,018,356, which is greater than the combined population of St. Louis, Cincinnati, San Francisco and New Orleans, lives in 550,000 homes. There are 189 public schools, with a registration of 347,313. This is more than in any other borough and 36 per cent. of the entire registration for the city.

PRINCIPAL PUBLICATIONS IN FOREIGN LANGUAGES IN NEW YORK CITY.

Represented by Amer. Assn. of Foreign Language Newspapers, Inc., 30 East 23d, Mhtn.

Arabic—Al Hoda, 81 West.

Armenian—Gotchnag, 265 Lexington av.

Bohemian—Hlas Lidu, 432 E. 71st; Listy, 1390 2d av.

Chinese—Chinese Reform News, 176 Park Row; Republic News, 108 Park Row.

Croatian—Narodni List, 61 Park Row; Jugoslovenski Svijet, 357 W. 52d.

Danish—Norlyset, 132 Nassau.

Finnish—New Yorkin Uutiset, 740 40th, Bkln.; Finska Amerikanaren, 1116 Ocean av., Bkln.

French—Courrier des Etats-Unis, 195 Fulton.

Greek—Atlantis, 117 W. 31st; National Herald, 140 W. 26th.

Hebrew—Jewish Morning Journal, 77 Bowery; Jewish Daily News, 187 E. B'way; Forward, 175 E. B'way; Day Warheit, 183 E. B'way; Die Zeit, 153 E. B'way.

Hungarian—Amerikai Magyar Nepszava, 178 2d av.

Italian—Bolletino della Sera, 178 Worth; Araldo Italiano, 434 Lafayette; Progresso Italo-Americano, 42 Elm; Giornale Italiano, 434 Lafayette; La Follia di New York, 226 Lafayette.

Japanese—Jap. Amer. Commercial Wkly., 411 8th av.; Japanese Times, 35 6th av.

Lithuanian—Vienybe Lietuvniku, 124 Grand, Bkln; Tevyne, 307 W. 30th.

Norwegian—Nordisk Tidende, 4423 3d av., Bkln.

Polish—Telegram Codzienny, 90 E. 10th; Nowy Swiat, 424 E. 9th, Kurger Narodowy, 61 Park Row.

Russian—Novoyit Russkoye Slovo, 19 E. 7th.

Servian—Srpski Dnevnik, 417 Lafayette.

Slovak—Slovak v. Amerike, 1482 B'way; New Yorske Dennik, 502 E. 73d.

Slovenic—Glas Naroda, 82 Cortlandt.

Spanish—La Prensa, 245 Canal.

Swedish—Nordstjernan, 108 Park Row; Arbetaren, 45 Rose.

German papers, not in the above association, are: Staats Zeitung, Ev'g Herold, 182 William.

JAPANESE POPULATION OF PACIFIC COAST STATES.

The Japanese population of California, announced by the Census Bureau, is 70,196, an increase of 23,840, or 69.7 per cent. compared with 1910. The Japanese population of Washington is 17,114, an increase of 4,195, or 32.4 per cent. The Japanese population of Oregon is given as 4,022, an increase of 604 or 17.7 per cent.

RACES OF THE WORLD.

The six great races of mankind are divided as follows: Mongolian, 655,000,000; Caucasian, 645,000,000; Negro, 100,000,000; Semitic, 81,000,000; Malayan, 52,000,000; Red Indian, 23,000,000. Total, 1,646,000,000.

GAZETTEER OF LONG ISLAND.

Population figures from 1910 U. S. Census, 1915 N. Y. State Census, 1920 U. S. Census (marked *) and estimated by postmasters. Routes and air-line distances are reckoned from Bkln. Boro Hall. L. I. R. R. stations are designated by letters following name of place: H—Hempstead Br.; F R—Far Rockaway Br.; L B—Long Beach Br.; W—Wading River Br.; P W—Port Washington Br.; M—Main Line; O—Oyster Bay Br.; Mo—Montauk Div. A number following name of a place means that nearest R. R. line to it is in that village opposite same number in first column.

	PLACES.	Pop'l	Miles Ro-ute	Miles Air line	Town where located.
1	Acabouack, 3	458	108	99	Easthamp.
2	Albertson, O	250	20	18	No. Hemp.
3	Amagansett, Mo. ..	869	104	96	Easthamp.
4	Amityville Mo	*3,265	31½	23	Babylon
5	Apaquogue, 62	10	103	95	Easthamp.
6	Aquebogue, M	545	76½	70	Riverhead
7	Artist's Lake, 348..	35	63	54	Brookhaven
8	Atlanticville, 261 ...	626	79	72	Southhamp.
9	Babylon, Mo	*2,523	37	34	Babylon
10	Baiting Hollow, 38.	428	72	65	Riverhead
11	Baldwin, Mo.	3,000	21½	19	Hempstead
12	Barnes' Hole, 3.....	15	106	97	Easthamp.
13	Barnes' Landing, 3.	.....	106	97	Easthamp.
14	Barnum Island, 148.	75	21½	15	Hempst'd
15	Bartlett, 25	.....	57	52	Brookhvn.
16	Bayport, Mo.	750	57	53	Islip
17	Bay Shore, Mo......	3,025	41	36	Islip
18	Bayville, 171	625	30	27	Oyster Bay
19	Bedelltown, 137	167	26	23	Oyster Bay
20	Beechwood, M	.....	30	28	Hempst'd.
21	Bellerose, M	325	14	12	Hempst'd.
22	Belle Terre, 252.....	60	58½	53	Brookhvn.
23	Belmont Park, M ..	.....	14	12	Hempst'd.
24	Bellmore, Mo.	500	26	23	Hempst'd.
25	Bellport, Mo	*614	58	53	Brookhvn.
26	Bethpage, 27........	150	30	27½	Oyster Bay
27	Bethpage Junc., M.	25	29½	27½	Oyster Bay
28	Blue Point, Mo.	373	53	48	Brookhvn.
29	Bohamia, 267	550	50	42	Islip.
30	Brentwood, M	500	41	37½	Islip
31	Breslau, 165	500	(Now Lindenhurst.)		
32	Bridgehampton, Mo	1,394	95	87	Southhmp.
33	Bridgeport, 322	375	17	13½	Hempst'd.
3a	Brightwaters, 17 ..	*250	40	35	Islip
34	Broad Hollow, 182..	100	33	30	Babylon
35	Brookhaven, Mo. ..	150	60	55	Brookhvn.
36	Brooklyn, 263	244	74	68	Southamp.
37	Brookville, 312	150	30	26	Oyster Bay
38	Calverton, M	425	69	64	Riverhead
39	Canoe Place, 111....	162	83	75	Southamp.
40	Cedarhurst, F R...	*2,838	20	13	Hempst'd.
41	Cedar Island, 165...	.....	37	32	Babylon
41a	Centreville, 263.	.....	(Now Roanoke)		
42	Central Islip, M....	400	43	39½	Islip
43	Central Park, M....	350	28	27	Oyster Bay
44	Centre Island, 288...	75	34	30	Oyster Bay
45	Centre M'rhes, Mo.	1,100	66½	61½	Brookhvn.
46	Centerport, 117	470	38	33	Huntingt'n
47	Christian Hook, 230	.....	(Now Oceanside.)		
47a	†Clinton road, H..	.....	19½	17	Hempst'd
48	Cockle's Harbor, 118	50	100	90	Shelter Isl'd
49	Cold Spring, W	50	32	30	Huntington
50	Cold Sp'g Har., 49..	650	35	31	Huntington
51	Commack, 215	153	42	33	Huntington
52	Copiague, Mo.	350	32½	30	Babylon
53	Coram, 186	*100	56	52	Brookhvn.
54	Crane Neck, 306.....	50	56	50	Brookhvn.
55	Cutchogue, M.......	931	85½	79	Southold
56	Darlington, 291	35	49	45	Smithtown
57	Deer Park, M.......	50	36½	33	Babylon
58	Dering Harbor 118.	*3	96	90	Shelter Isl'd
59	Dix Hills, 117.......	125	39	33	Huntington
60	Dosoris, 107..........	193	28	25	Oyster Bay
61	E. Beach, 215........	.....	42	36	Huntington
62	Easthampton, Mo..	*4,832	101	91½	Easthamp.
63	East Islip, 146......	200	44	40	Islip
64	East Meadow, 118..	360	97	90	Southold
65	East Meadow, 131..	350	24	21	Hempst'd.
66	East Moriches, Mo.	525	68	63	Brookhvn.
67	East Neck, 142	625	36	31	Huntington
68	East Northport, 142	325	41	34	Huntington
69	East Norwich, 238..	400	33	30	Oyster Bay
70	East Patchogue, Mo	80	56	51	Brookhvn.
71	Eastport, Mo.	425	70½	65	Brookhvn.
72	East Quogue, 261...	300	78	70	Southamp.
73	East Rocka'y, L B	*2,005	19½	15	Hempst'd.
74	East Setauket, 285..	91	57	51	Brookhvn.
75	East Williston, O..	359	20	17	No. Hemp.
76	Eaton's Neck, 117..	160	40	34	Huntingt'n
77	Eaton's Point, 117..	150	41	34	Huntingt'n
78	Echo, 252	346	57½	52	Brookhvn.
79	Edgewood, M	90	38½	35	Islip
80	Elmont, 23	150	15	13	Hempst'd.
81	Elm Point, 115......	45	17	12	No. Hemp
82	Elwood, 215	200	40	35	Huntingt'n
83	Fairground, 142	500	35	31	Huntingt'n
84	Fanny Bartlett, 62.	.....	107	97	Easthamp.
85	Farmingdale, M ...	*2,091	30	28	Oyster Bay
86	Farmingville, 140...	135	53	48	Brookhvn.
87	Fenhurst, 134	.....	(now Hewlett).		
88	Fireplace, 3	5	110	90	Easthamp.
89	Fire Island, 17......	25	47	39	Islip
90	Flanders, 263	263	76	70	Southamp.
91	Floral Park, M	1,771	15	13	Hempst'd
92	Flower Hill, 246.....	75	17½	15	N. Hemp.
93	Flowerfield, W	50	51	47	Smithtown
94	Fort Salonga, 154...	68	46	40	Smithtown
96	Foster Meadows, 269	600	16	13	Hempst'd
97	Franklin Square, 23	800	16½	14	Hempst'd.
99	Freeport, Mo	*8,599	23	20	Hempstead
100	Freetown, 62	200	103	94	Easthamp.
101	Fresh Pond, 38......	50	72	65	Riverhead
102	Fresh Pond, 107.....	200	29	24	Smithtown
103	Friar's Head, 263...	.....	78	70	Riverhead
104	Garden City, H ...	*2,420	18½	16	Hempst'd.
105	Gardiner's Island, 3	25	115	104	Easthamp.
106	Georgica, 325	20	100	91	Easthamp.
107	Glen Cove, O	*8,664	27	25	Glen Cove
108	Glen Head, O......	200	25	23	Oyster Bay
109	Glenwood L'd'g, 108	500	25½	23	Oyster Bay
110	Golf Grounds, Mo. .	.....	87	80	Southamp.
111	Good Ground, Mo..	825	82½	75	Southamp.
112	Grassy Hollow, 62..	28	105	96	Easthamp.
113	Great Hog Neck, 300	138	93	85	Southold
114	Great Neck, P W..	*339	38	33	Huntingt'n
115	Great Neck, 117....	.....	14	12	No. Hemp
116	Great River, Mo....	350	45½	40½	Islip
117	Greenlawn, W	500	37	33	Huntingt'n
118	Greenport, M	*3,122	94½	87	Southold
119	Greenvale, O	.....	(Part of Glen Head		
120	Greenville, 277	638	51	45	Islip
121	Greenwich Pt., 131.	.....	(Now Roosevelt)		
122	Hagermann, Mo...	250	56	51	Brookhvn.
123	Halesite, 142	500	37	32	Huntingt'n
124	Half Hollow, 57.....	125	37	32	Huntingt'n
125	Hampton B'ch, 261.	.....	80	71	Southamp.
126	Hampton Park, 294	.....	91	84	Southamp.
127	Harbor Hill, 216...	.....	24	20	No. Hemp
128	Hardscrabble, 325...	10	100	91	Easthamp.
130	Hauppage, 291	95	50	44	Smithtown
131	Hempstead, H	*6,382	20	17	Hempstead
132	Hempst'd Cr's'g, H	.....	19	16½	Hempstead
133	Hempst'd Gdns., H	214	23½	19	Hempstead
134	Hewlett, F. R......	1,500	17½	14	Hempstead
135	Hewlett Pt., 114....	.....	17	12	No. Hemp
136	Hicks' Beach, 164...	.....	23	18	Hempstead
137	Hicksville, M	1,650	25	23	Oyster Bay
138	Hog Neck, 273.......	193	102	92	Southamp.
139	Holbrook, 232	210	50	44	Islip
140	Holtsville, M	142	52	48	Brookhvn.
141	Horton's Pt., 300....	.....	92	84	Southold
142	Huntington, W ...	*13897	35	31	Huntington
144	Hyde Park, M	1,800	16½	14	Hempstead
145	Inwood, F R	2,000	20½	20	Hempstead
146	Islip, Mo	*20704	43½	38½	Islip
147	Jacob's Hill, 263....	.....	78	70	Riverhead
148	Jekyll Island, L B.	.....	21½	15	Hempstead
149	Jamesport, M	353	78½	72	Riverhead
150	Jericho, 137	489	26	23	Oyster Bay
151	Jerusalem, 326.......	300	29	26	Hempstead
152	Jerusalem, 43	87	28	27	Oyster Bay
153	Jones' Beach, 179...	.....	30	26	Oyster Bay
154	Kings Park, W	375	43½	40	Smithtown
155	Kingstown	40	105	97	Easthamp.
156	Lake Grove, 267.....	401	53½	47	Brookhvn.
157	Lake Ronk'nk'a, 267	200	51	42	Islip
158	Lake View, H	300	15	12	No. Hemp.
159	Lakeville, 114	200	22	18½	Hempstead
160	Larkfield, 215........	575	40	35	Huntington
161	Lattingtown, 171 ...	195	30	27	Oyster Bay
162	Laurel, M	100	80	73½	Riverhead
163	Laurelton, 238	100	34	31	Oyster Bay
164	Lawrence, F R	*2,861	20	13	Hempstead
165	Lindenhurst, Mo....	1,890	34	31	Babylon
166	Little Hog Neck, 55	.....	88	80	Southold
167	Little Neck, 117.....	245	39	34	Huntingt'n
168	Lloyd Harbor, 142..	.....	37	32	Huntingt'n
169	Lloyd Neck, 142.....	325	37	32	Huntingt'n
170	Locust Grove, 137...	50	27	24	Oyster Bay

†Shuttle trolley is operated between Garden City sta. and Clinton rd. sta.

GAZETTEER OF LONG ISLAND—*Continued.*

	PLACES.	Pop'l	Miles Ro-ute	Miles Air line	Town where located
171	Locust Valley, O...	530	29	27	Oyster Bay
172	Long Beach, L B..	662	23¾	15	Hempstead
173	Lower Melville, 242.	225	34	29	Huntingt'n
174	Lynbrook, Mo	*4,275	18	13	Hempstead
174a	Malberne, H.......	800	23	20	Hempstead
175	Manhansett, 118....	.....	98	89	Shelter Isl'd
176	Manhasset, P W...	700	15½	13	No. Hemp.
177	Mannetto Hill, 137..	65	26	24	Oyster Bay
178	Manorville, M......	322	65	60	Brookhvn.
179	Massapequa, Mo. ..	300	29	26	Oyster Bay
180	Mastic, Mo.	100	44	59	Brookhvn
181	Matinecock, O......	175	30	27	Oyster Bay
182	Mattituck, M........	1,268	84	75	Southold
183	Meadowbrook, 131 ..	250	22	19	Hempst'd.
184	Meadow Glen, 154..	265	45	41	Smithtown
185	Mecox, 32	262	98	88	Southamp.
186	Medford, M.........	100	54¼	50	Brookhvn
187	Melville, 242	231	35	29	Huntingt'n
187a	Merillon, M	.....	24¼	22	Hempstead
188	Merrick, Mo.	275	17¼	15	N. Hemp.
189	Miamogue Pt., 149..	.....	79	70	Riverhead
190	Midd'e Island, 186..	290	59	55	Brookhvn.
191	Middleville, 154	710	45	40	Smithtown
192	Milburn, 11	2,596	23	20	Hempstead
193	Miller's Place, W..	159	60¼	55	Brookhvn.
194	Mill Neck, O	800	31	28	Oyster Bay
195	Mill Side, 307.......	.....	73	66	Southamp.
196	Mineola, M..........	*3,016	18¼	16	No. Hemp
197	Montauk, Mo	50	116	106	Easthamp.
198	Montauk Pt., 197....	10	121	111	Easthamp
199	Moriches, Mo.	225	64	59	Brookhvn.
200	Mt. Pleasant, 267...	.....	49	42	Islip
201	Mt. Sinai, 143	210	63	57	Brookhvn
202	Munson, 305	125	17	13	Hempstead
203	Napeague B'ch, Mo	20	108	99	Easthamp
205	N's'u-by-the-Sea,172	.....	23¾	15	Hempstead
206	Nassau Boulev'd, H	300	19¼	17	Hempstead
206a	Nesconset, 274	700	53	49	Smithtown
207	New Cassell, 331....	200	22	19	No. Hemp.
208	New Hyde Park, M	1,000	16¼	14	No. Hemp
209	New Suffolk, 55.....	275	87	78	Southold
210	Newtown, 111.......	.....	83	75	Southamp.
211	New Village, 267...	150	54	48	Brookhvn.
212	Nissequogue, 274 ...	125	52	46	Smithtown
213	N. Babylon, 347....	150	36	32	Babylon
214	No. Islip, 42.......	.....	45	38	Islip
215	Northport, W	*1,977	39½	35	Huntingt'n
216	North Roslyn, O...	300	23	19	No. Hemp.
217	No. Sea, 110	75	90	83	Southamp.
218	Northville, 6 (Now Sound Av.)				Riverhead
219	N. Wad'g River,324	.....	69	62	Riverhead
220	Northwest, 273......	10	100	90	Easthamp.
221	North Side, 294.....	.....	96	87	Southamp.
223	Norwood (Now Malverne)				Hempstead
224	Noyack, 327	70	100	90	Southamp.
225	Oak Beach, 9	20	42	36	Babylon.
226	Oakdale, Mo.	190	47¼	43	Islip
227	Oak Island, 9	.....	42	36	Babylon.
228	Oak Neck, 171.......	.....	31	28	Oyster Bay
229	Oakville, 261	50	79	71	Southamp.
230	Oceanside, L B	300	19¼	15	Hempstead
231	Old Fields, 117	520	37	33	Huntingt'n
232	Old Holbrook, M...	.....	50	46	Islip
233	Old Westbury, 331..	500	23	19	No. Hemp.
234	Oneck, 332	60	75	78	Southamp.
235	Oregon Hills, 182...	.....	85	78	Southold
236	Orient, 118	756	100	92	Southold
237	Orient Point, 118....	148	104	96	Southold
238	Oyster Bay O	*20296	33	30	Oyster Bay
240	Patchogue, Mo	*4,031	54	49	Brookhvn.
241	Peconic, M..........	921	88	81	Southold
242	Pinelawn, M	36	32¼	28¼	Babylon
243	Pine View, 242	450	35	30	Huntingt'n
244	Piping Rock, 171 ...	.....	29	27	Oyster Bay
245	Plainedge, 27	150	30	28	Oyster Bay
246	Plandome, P W...	*319	16½	13	N. Hemp.
247	Plainview, 137	150	26	24	Oyster Bay
248	Plattsdale, 75	143	21	17	No. Hemp.
249	Plum Island, 118...	250	106	98	Southold
250	Point o' Woods, 17.	.....	46	40	Brookhvn.
251	Ponquogue, 111	240	84	76	Southamp.
252	Port Jefferson, W..	2,200	57½	52	Brookhvn.
253	Port Wash'gt'n.PW	2,000	18¼	16	No. Hemp.
254	Potunk, 332	55	75	68	Southamp.
256	Powder Hill, 325....	.....	100	90	Easthamp.
257	Promised Land, Mo.	75	106	97	Easthamp.
258	Quantuck Bay, 332..	.....	78	76	Southamp.
259	Queenswater, L B..	115	23	15	Hempstead
260	Quiogue, 332	271	77	75	Southamp.
261	Quogue, Mo.	600	77½	70	Southamp.
262	Remsenburg, 301 ...	300	73	66	Southamp.
263	Riverhead, M	*5,753	73½	67	Riverhead
263a	Roanoke, M........	.....	76	69	Riverhead.
265	Rocky Point, W....	210	64½	59	Brookhvn.
266	Rockv'le C'tre, Mo.	*6,262	19½	17	Hempstead
267	Ronkonkoma, M ...	370	48	36	Islip
268	Roosevelt, 131	2,000	22	19	Hempstead
269	Rosedale, Mo.	720	14½	12½	Hempstead
270	Roslyn, O	2,000	22	18	No. Hemp.
271	Sagaponack, 32	385	97	89	Southamp.
272	Sagg, 32.......... ...	(Now Sagaponack)			
273	Sag Harbor, Mo ..	*2,993	99½	92	S.&Easthptn
274	St. James, W.......	215	50	48	Smithtown
275	St. Johnland, 154...	275	44	40	Smithtown
276	Sands Point, 253,...	*284	21	16	No. Hemp.
277	Sayville, Mo.	2,200	50¼	45½	Islip
278	Scuttle Hole, 32....	165	96	87	Southamp.
279	Sea Cliff, O	*2,108	28¼	26	Oyster Bay
280	Seaford, Mo.	508	28	25	Hempstead
281	Searington, 2	75	21½	18	No. Hemp.
283	Sebonac, 110	6	88	81	Southamp.
284	Selden, 140	90	54	50	Brookhvn.
285	Setauket, W	615	55	50	Brookhvn.
285a	Shelter Island 118	*890	98	87	Shelter Isl'd
286	Shelter Is'd Hts..118	557	96	87	Shelter Isl'd
287	Shinnec'k Hills, Mo	.....	85¾	78	Southamp.
288	Shoreham, W	*11	65½	60	Brookhvn.
289	Short Beach, 179...	.....	35	27	Oyster Bay
291	Smithtown, W	*9 114	47	43	Smithtown
292	Smitht'n Br'ch, 291	700	48	43	Smithtown
294	Southampton, Mo..	*2,637	89½	82	Southamp.
295	South Haven, 35....	59	62	57	Brookhvn.
296	S'th Jamesport, 149.	290	79	72	Riverhead
297	So. Lynbrook, L B.	268	18¾	15	Hempstead
298	Sound Avenue, 6. ..	1,633	79	22	Riverhead
299	So. Northport, 215..	120	40	35	Huntingt'n
300	Southold, M	*10147	90	93	Southold
301	Speonk, Mo.	198	73	66½	Southamp.
302	Springs (The), 62..	450	105	97	Easthamp.
303	Springville, 111	190	83	76½	Southamp.
304	Squiretown, 111	25	83	76	Southamp.
305	Stewart Manor, H..	25	16½	14	Hempstead
306	Stony Brook, W....	506	53	48	Brookhvn.
308	Strong's Neck, 306.	25	56	50	Brookhvn.
309	Suffolk Downs, Mo.	.....	84	77	Southamp.
310	Sunken Meadow, 154	210	45	40	Smithtown
311	Sweet's Hollow, 242	450	35	30	Huntingt'n
312	Syosset, W	200	29	27	Oyster Bay
314	Terryville, 252	100	59	54	Brookhvn.
315	Thomaston, P W..	1,000	14	12	No. Hemp.
316	Tiana, 111	50	83	76	Southamp.
318	Tuckahoe, 110	50	87½	80	Southamp.
319	Tuthill's Mi'ls, 38..	.....	70	64	Brookhvn.
320	Uniondale, 131	500	29	19	Hempstead
322	Valley Stream, Mo.	1,100	16½	14	Hempstead
323	Vernon Valley, 215.	375	41	36	Huntingt'n
324	Wading River, W..	399	68¾	63	Riverhead
325	Wainscott, Mo......	100	97½	90	Easthamp.
326	Wantagh, Mo.	275	27	26	Hempstead
327	Water Mill, Mo.....	173	92	84½	Southamp.
330	Waverly, 140	100	53	46	Brookhvn.
331	Westbury Sta., M..	1,000	21½	19	No. Hemp.
332	Westhampton, Mo..	441	74½	67	Southamp.
333	Westhptn B'ch, 332.	170	75	67	Southamp.
334	West Hempstead, H	300	20½	17	Hempstead
335	West Hills, 49	320	34	29	Huntingt'n
336	West Islip, 9	520	39	35	Islip
337	West Neck, 142	425	39	32	Huntingt'n
339	West Sayville, 277..	550	51	45	Islip
341	Wheatley, 216	215	27	21	Oyster Bay
343	Wickapogue, 294....	100	91	83	Southamp.
344	Woodbury, 49	207	32	30	Oyster Bay
345	Woodmere, F R....	577	18	14	Hempstead
346	Wreck Lead, L B..	50	23	15	Hempstead
347	Wyandanch, M	73	34½	30	Babylon
348	Yaphank, M	300	58½	54	Brookhvn.

PANAMA CANAL TRAFFIC.

The number of commercial vessels which had traversed the Panama Canal since its opening in 1914 had reached 10,212 at the close of the fiscal year ended last June 30. The average monthly number of vessels making the passage has risen steadily until it reached 144.9 in the first half of the year 1920.

RESULTS OF THE DRAFT.

Of the total registrants in the selective draft in this country, 36.22 were held for military service; 2.89 were given agricultural deferment, 39.57 were given dependency deferments, 1.81 industrial deferment, 8.33 were aliens, 5.27 were physically disqualified and .72 of 1 were deserters.

PARKS AND DRIVES IN NEW YORK CITY.

Total Park Area of New York City.

Including all lands laid out as parks. Manhattan, 1,487 acres; Bronx, 3,929.19; Brooklyn, 1,165; Queens, 1,186; Richmond, 63. Total, 7,830.19.

Total Length Parkways, etc.

Manhattan, 40,100 feet; Bronx, 48,892; Brooklyn, 153,120; Queens, 1,320; Richmond, ——. Total, 243,432.

See previous vols. of Eagle Almanac for history of parks in N. Y. City and monuments.

BROOKLYN.

Park System of Bkln. comprises 51 parks, playgrounds and open spaces, with an area of 1,165 acres, and 15 parkways and streets, with total length of 30 miles. The total assessed valuation of Bkln.'s park property amounts to approximately 80 millions of dollars. Park Dept. Offices, Litchfield Mansion, Prospect Park, Bkln. (For Officers and Employees see City Government Chapter.)

Frederic B. Pratt and Alfred T. White gave to N. Y. C. in Oct., 1917, 123 acres of land about Gerritsen's Basin, Jamaica Bay, worth $280,755.48, for use as a park. They also agreed to reimburse the city for the cost of an additional 24.5 acres to be acquired through condemnation proceedings to complete the park around the basin.

Name and Location of Parks.

[Name, location and acquisition, acreage, appraised valuation.]

Amersfort—Av. J, E. 38th, Av. I and E. 39th—Acq. Nov. 11, 1901, improved 1905—3.56—$64,500.

Bedford—Kingston and Bkln. avs., Prospect and Park pls.—Purchased 1892 for $149,000—4.10—$325,000.

Bensonhurst—Bay P'kway and Gravesend Bay, 21st and Cropsey av.—Acq. 1896—12—$240,000.

Borough Hall—Joralemon, Court and Fulton—Part of old Remsen est., purchased 1837—1.70—†$3,314,000.

Bkln. Botanic Garden and Arboretum (incl. 12.69 acres of Bk. Inst. A. A. Lands)—Eastern P'kway, Washington and Flatbush avs. and Empire blvd.—Part of original purchase of Prospect Park—In 1909 City of N. Y. entered into an agreement with Bkln. Inst. for estbt. and maintenance by Inst. of the Botanic Garden—61.39—†$9,885,000.

Bkln. Heights Parks—Columbia Heights, fronting on Furman—Authorized by act of Legislature in 1866—.86—$131,500.

Bushwick—Knickerbocker and Irving avs., Starr and Suydam—Purchased 1890 for $104,000—6.86—$305,000.

Canarsie—Skidmore, Sea View and Denton avs., E. 88th and E. 93d, Byrne pl. and Jamaica Bay—Acq. 1896—30.50—$115,000.

.Carroll—President, Court, Carroll and Smith—Authorized by act of Legislature in 1850. Acq. 1852. Opened as a public sq. in 1853. Improved in 1856. Remodeled in 1892—1.90—$165,000.

City—St. Edwards and Navy, Park and Flushing avs.—Authorized by Common Council 1835. Purchased 1837—7.50—$491,000.

C. I. Concourse Lands (excl. of Seaside Park)—W. 5th and Sea Breeze av. and Atlantic Ocean—Authorized by Common Council 1874—59.70—$1,132,000.

Cooper Gore—Junc. Metropolitan and Orient avs. —Purchased 1896 for $2,655—.15—$7,000.

Cooper—Maspeth and Morgan avs., Sharon and Olive—Presented by Peter Cooper—6.10—$140,000.

Cuyler Gore—Cumberland and Fulton and Greene av.—Acq. 1845—.08—$25,000.

Dreamland—W. 5th and W. 8th, Surf av. and Atlantic Ocean—Acq. 1904—14.70—$839,500.

Dyker Beach—7th av. and Bay 8th, Cropsey av., 14th av. and Gravesend Bay—Acq. 1895—139.80—$778,000.

Ft. Greene—DeKalb av., Washington Pk., Willoughby and St. Edwards and Myrtle av.—Authorized by act of Legislature 1847. Placed under control of Park Commnrs. 1868—28.90—$3,098,500.

Ft. Hamilton—4th av., 101st, Ft. amilton av. and Shore rd.—Acq. 1895—4.60—$539,000H

Fulton—Chauncey and Fulton and Stuyvesant av.—Acq. 1906—2—$143,500.

Grant Square Gore Park—Bedford and Rogers avs. and Bergen—00.013—$1,000.

Gravesend—18th and 19th avs., 55th and 58th—Acq. 1917—6.92—$55,700.

Highland—Jamaica av. and U. S. Natl. Cemetery, Boro. Line, Reservoir and Warwick Extension—Purchased 1891 for $181,640.60—40.86—$491,500.

Highland Park Addition—Heath pl., Highland Park, Vermont av., Private Property and Highland blvd.—5.19—$200,000.

†Incl. value of bldgs. on land.

Irving Square—Wilson and Knickerbocker avs. and Weirfield and Halsey—Acq. 1895—2.96—$281,000.

Lincoln Ter.—Estn. P'kway, Buffalo and Rochester avs. and President—Acq. 1895—7.60—$151,200.

Lincoln Ter. Pk. Addition—President, Rochester av., Carroll, Buffalo av., Eastern Parkway, Portal and East N. Y. av.—7.40—$150,000.

Linton—Bradford, Blake, Dumont and Miller avs. —Acq. 1896—2.29—$81,000.

McKinley—Ft. Hamilton and 7th avs. and 73d—Authorized by Bd. of Est. 1902, acq. 1903—8.50—$201,210.

Milestone—18th av., north of 82d—Acq. 1917—.007 —$400.

Prospect—Prospect Park W. and Flatbush, Ocean, Parkside avs. and Prospect Pk. S. W.—Acq. 1859. Completed 1867—526—$30,766,000.

Red Hook—Richards, Verona, Dwight and Pioneer—Purchased 1892 for $131,250—5.28—$182,000.

Saratoga Sq.—Saratoga and Howard avs., Halsey and Macon—Acq. 1895—3.20—$223,600.

Seaside—Ocean P'kway, Concourse, W. 5th and Sea Breeze av.—Authorized by Legislature 1874—16.30—$625,000.

Stuyvesant Gore—Stuyvesant and Vernon avs. and B'way—Acq. 1884—.08—$6,000.

Sunset—41st and 44th, 5th and 7th avs.—Purchased 1891 for $162,000—24.50—$844,500.

Tompkins—Tompkins, Greene, Marcy and Lafayette avs.—Acq. 1839. Placed under control of Bkln. Park Commsnrs. 1869. Improved in 1870—7.80—$460,000.

Underhill Gore—Underhill and Washington avs. and Pacific.—Acq. 1877—.10—$6,500.

Vanderveer—E. N. Y. and Pitkin avs., Barrett and Grafton—Presented in 1896 by P. L. Vanderveer—.21—$15,000.

Winthrop—Nassau and Driggs avs., Russell and Monitor—Purchased 1899 for $132,825—9.10—$505,000.

Woodpoint Gore—Bushwick, Metropolitan and Maspeth avs. Constructed 1895, land being acq. at time No. 2d was improved by widening street 14 ft. —.05—$1,000.

Unnamed Parks.

A—Etrn. P'kway, Washington and Classon avs. —0.155—$7,000.

B—Roebling, Division and Lee avs.—.14—$14,500.

C—4th av. and 5th av. and 94th—.018—$1,000.

D—Myrtle, Willoughby and Bushwick avs.—.0033—$400.

E—Chauncey and Fulton and Lewis av.—Acq. 1906 —.01—$1,500.

F—Monitor, Engert and Meeker avs.—Acq. 1917—.005—$500.

Combined Parks and Playgrounds.

[Name, location and acquisition, acreage, appraised valuation.]

McCarren—Berry, Lorimer, Leonard, Bayard and No. 12th, Nassau, Driggs, Mhtn. and Union avs.—Acq. in sections at various dates from 1899 to 1912 —38.42—$1,321,000.

McLaughlin—Bridge, Tillary and Jay.—Acq. 1904—3.30—$367,500.

Williamsburg Bridge—Bedford and Kent avs., So. 5th and So. 6th.—Acq. 1900 at time of construction of Wmsburg. Br. and was transferred to Dept. of Parks from Dept. of Bridges in 1903—4.30 —$275,000.

Gerritsen Basin, Jamaica Bay—Acq. 1917—123—$280,755.48.

Williamsburg Pk—Boerum, Johnson av., Lorimer and Leonard—(Board of Est. approved purchase Oct., 1917. Acq. in 1918)—1.83—$119,550.

Playgrounds.

Betsy Head Memorial—Livonia, Dumont, Hopkinson avs. and Douglass and Dumont, Blake, Hopkinson avs. and Bristol.—Acq. 1912. Opened 1915—10.50—$370,000.

Bushwick—Putnam av., bet. Knickerbocker and Irving avs.—Acq. 1907—2.80—$68,000.

Fort Greene Park Playground—Plaza at n. w. cor. of Park—3 (included in park).

McKibbin—Seigel, White and McKibbin.—Acq. 1903—1.37—$70,000.

New Lots—Sackman, Riverdale, Newport and Christopher avs.—Purchased 1895—2.29—$73,000.

Parade Ground—Coney Isl., Parkside and Caton avs.—Opened 1866—39.16—$1,500,000.

Red Hook—Richards, King, Dwight and Pioneer. —Acq. 1906—2.29—$52,000.

Parkways and Streets.

[Name, location, acreage, appraised valuation.]

Bay P'kway—Ocean P'kway, bet. Avs. I and J, Bensonhurst Beach—30.99—$1,000,000.

PARKS AND DRIVES—BROOKLYN—*Continued.*

Bay Ridge P'kway—Ft. Hamilton av., bet. 66th and 67th, to 1st av., bet. 66th and Wakeman pl.—40.89—$717,700.

Buffalo Av.—Etrn. P'kway, bet. Rochester and Ralph avs., to E. N. Y. av., bet. E. 96th and E. 98th—1.98—$31,000.

Bushwick Av.—Myrtle av., bet. Ditmars and Charles pl., to Jamaica av., bet. Sheffield and New Jersey avs.—31.41—$500,000.

Etrn. P'kway—Prospect Pk. Plaza to Ralph av., bet. Union and Lincoln pl.—61.12—$3,000,000.

.Etrn. P'kway Extn.—Ralph av., bet. Union and Lincoln pl., to Bushwick av., bet. De Sales pl. and Stewart—18.55—$1,300,000.

Ft. Hamilton Av.—Ocean P'kway and Prospect av., to Ft. Hamilton—48.15—$1,000,000.

Highland Blvd.—Bushwick av., bet. Dahlia and Gillen pls., to Highland Park—9—$150,000.

Lincoln Rd.—Ocean av. to Bedford av., bet. Lefferts av. and Maple—2.61—$138,900.

Ocean P'kway—Prospect Pk. Circle to Coney Isl. Concourse—140—$4,000,000.

Parkside Av.—Prospect Pk. Circle to Flatbush av. at Robinson—3.15—$433,800.

Plaza St.—Prospect Pk. Plaza—4.31—$229,400.

Pennsylvania Av.—Jamaica av., bet. Sheffield and New Jersey avs., to Jamaica Bay—19.24—$630,100.

Rockaway P'kway—Buffalo av. at E. N. Y. av., to Canarsie Beach, bet. E. 96th and E. 98th—40.90—$773,000.

Shore Rd.—1st av., bet. 66th and Wakeman pl., to Ft. Hamilton—119.3—$5,000,000.

BROOKLYN BOTANIC GARDEN.

The Bkln. Botanic Garden, located bet. Eastern P'kway and Empire Blvd. and Flatbush and Washington avs., was opened to the public on Linnaeus's birthday, May 13, 1911. The garden comprises about 50 acres of land, on which are located the various plantations, the conservatories and the laboratory building. The object of the garden is the advancement and diffusion of a knowledge and love of plants, and its special aim is to be of service to the local community.

The grounds are open free to the public daily at 8 A.M., except Sundays and holidays, when they open at 10 A.M. There is a graded membership, the dues of annual members being $10 a year. Special privileges are offered to members.

A Bureau of Information is maintained concerning all matters of plant life and gardening, the determination of specimens, care of lawns and gardens, trees and shrubs, insect pests and plant diseases. This service is free to the public. The Native Wild Flower Garden contains about 900 species that grow without cultivation within 100 miles of New York City; the Rock Garden contains over 600 species of Alpine and other rock-loving plants; the Japanese Garden has been pronounced the most perfect specimen of that kind of garden in any public park in America; the general Systematic Garden, chiefly of European herbs and shrubs, occupies the central portion of the grounds; the Ecological Garden illustrates the relation of plants to various factors of environment, such as water, light, gravity, insects, etc. The Iris Garden extends along the brook and the Children's Gardens, containing over 250 individual plots, are at the south end of the grounds. A library of over 10,000 books and pamphlets on plant life and gardening is open free to the public, and also the herbarium of over 150,000 specimens. Illustrated lectures and occasional exhibits are also open free. The conservatories contain a collection of tropical and sub-tropical plants, including those used for food, fiber and other economic purposes, including banana, sugar-cane, tea, coffee, rubber, hemp, papyrus, figs, citrous fruits, etc.

The buildings, costing over $280,000, were erected at the joint expense of the city and the Board of Trustees of the Brooklyn Institute of Arts and Sciences, of which the Botanic Garden is a department. The Japanese Garden was constructed and is maintained wholly at private expense, and the library, herbarium and all plants on the grounds and in the conservatories are obtained by private funds.

Reached by Flatbush av. trolley from Park Row by B. R. T. subway (Brighton Beach Line) to Prospect Pk. Sta., where transfer for Botanic Garden El. Sta., by Interborough subway to Brooklyn Museum Sta. (Eastern P'kway Line), and by most surface lines in Brooklyn. Prospectus of courses and booklet of information free by addressing the secretary. The director of the garden is Dr. C. Stuart Gager.

MANHATTAN.

Names and Location of Parks.

[Name first and in order, acreage and location.]

Abingdon Sq.—0.202—8th av. and Hudson.

Alex. Hamilton Sq.—0.001—143d and Hamilton pl.

Battery—21.199—Ft. of B'way.

Beach St.—0.028—Beach and W. B'way.

Bowling Green—0.517—B'way and Whitehall.

Bryant—4.775—6th av. and 42d.

Canal St.—0.318—Canal and West.

Carl Schurz—12.546—84th to 89th, E. R.

Central—843.019—5th to 8th avs., 59th to 110th.

Chelsea—3.117—27th to 28th, 9th to 10th avs.

Christopher St.—0.139—Christopher and W. 4th.

City Hall—8.289—B'way and Chambers.

Colonial—12.79—Edgecombe to Bradhurst avs. 145th to 155th.

Columbus—2.75—Mulberry and Bayard.

Cooper—0.229—3d av. and 7th.

Corlear's Hook—8.3—Corlear's and South.

DeWitt Clinton—7.377—52d to 54th, N. R.

Duane St.—0.108—Duane and Hudson.

Empire Park—0.344—B'way and 63d.

Grand St.—0.096—Grand and E. B'way.

Greeley Sq.—0.144—6th av. and 32d.

Hamilton Fish—3.673—Houston and Willett

Hancock Sq.—0.072—St. Nicholas av., 123d.

Harlem Lane—1.27—7th av. and 153d.

Herald Sq.—0.042—6th av. and 35th.

Hudson—1.7—Hudson and Leroy.

Jackson Sq.—0.227—8th av. and Horatio.

Jeanette—0.728—Coenties Slip and South.

John Jay—3.004—E. 76th to E. 78th, East River.

Kuyter—0.298—South approach to 3d av. Bridge.

Lincoln Sq.—0.069—B'way and 66th.

Madison Sq.—6.84—B'way and 23d.

Mhtn. Sq.—17.582—Central Park West, 77th to 81st.

Mitchel Sq.—0.286—166th, B'way and St. Nicholas av.

Morningside—31.238—110th to 123d, Columbus to Amsterdam avs.

Mt. Morris—20.174—Mt. Morris to Madison av., 120th to 124th.

Paradise—0.114—Mission pl. and Worth.

Park Av. Parks—3.118—Park av., 34th to 40th, 50th to 96th.

Riverside—140.037—N. R., 72d to 129th.

Riverside Dr. Extension—24.000—N. R., 135th to 158th.

Roger Morris—1.546—Jumel Terrace, Edgecombe rd., 160th to 162d.

Rutgers—0.478—Rutgers slip and South.

Ryan—0.18—2d av. and 42d.

St. Gabriel's—2.947—35th to 36th, 1st and 2d avs.

St. Nicholas—19.728—St. Nicholas av., to St. Nicholas Terrace, 130th to 141st.

Sherman Sq.—0.001—B'way and 70th.

Straus—0.072—B'way and 108th.

Stuyvesant—4.229—Rutherford pl., 16th.

Thomas Jefferson—15.529—111th, 1st av., 114th, Harlem River.

Tompkins Sq.—10.508—Av. A and 7th.

Union Sq.—3.483—B'way and 14th.

Washington Sq.—8.115—5th av., Waverley pl.

Wm. H. Seward—3.315—Canal and Jefferson.

Unimproved Parks.

Ft. Washington—40.81—Ft. Wash. Point, Hudson River.

High Bridge—75.766—155th to a line 150 ft. north of Washington Bridge, west side of H. R. Driveway and 155th to 159th, east side of H. R. Driveway.

Isham—10.593—213 and B'way, to Harlem Ship Canal.

St. Nicholas Park—7.507—West of St. Nicholas Terrace and extensions at 130th and 141st.

Improved and Unnamed Parks.

Park—0.340—B'way and 138th.

Park—1.037—17th and 18th, Av. C and E. R.

Triangle—0.038—St. Nicholas av. and 137th.

Triangle—0.024—St. Nicholas av. and 150th.

Triangle—0.095—B'way and 73d.

Triangle—0.018—Mhtn. av. and 114th.

Triangle—0.074—7th av. and 117th.

Triangle—0.048—Lafayette, Kenmare and Cleveland pl.

Parks—7.543—Center of B'way, 60th to 123d.

Parks—3.621—Center of B'way, 137th to 168th.

Parks—1.904—Center of 7th av., 110th to Harlem River.

PARKS AND DRIVES—MANHATTAN—*Continued*

Parks—0.716—Center of Delancey, Bowery to Clinton.

Addition to Riverside Pk.—2.064—122d, Riverside Drive to Claremont av.

Park—1.849—W. 23d and 11th av.

Unimproved and Unnamed Parks.

Extension of Riverside Pk.—48.215—N. Y. C. & H. R. R. to bulkhead line of Hudson River, 72d to 129th.

West of Harlem River Driveway and n. of High Bridge Park—23.013.

Extension to Corlear's Hook Pk.—South to pierhead line—2.343.

Park—3,567—E. of Riverside Drive about 190th.

Playgrounds.‡

Abingdon Sq.—8th av. and Hudson.
Astor Field—149th and 8th av.
Battery Park†—State and Battery pl.
Bennett Field*—184th and B'way.
Carl Schurz Park—86th and E. R.
Carmensville—151st, 152d and Amsterdam av.
Central Park*—Sheep Meadow and 99th.
Chelsea Park*†—27th and 10th av.
Cherry and Market*†—Cherry and Market.
Clark—174th and Ft. Washington av.
Corlear's Hook Park*†—Corlear's Hook and Jackson.
Colonial Park—150th and Bradhurst av.
Columbus Park*†—Baxter and Worth.
DeWitt Clinton Park*†—53d and 11th av.
Esplanade (Wmsburg. Br.)—Delancey.
E. 12th, nr. Av. A.
E. 17th St. Park—17th and E. R.
E. 19th, bet. 1st av. and Av. A.
E. 67th, bet. 1st and 2d avs.
Grace—W. 104th, nr. Columbus av.
Hamilton Fish Park*†—Houston and Pitt.
Highbridge Park—170th and Amsterdam av
Hudson Park—Clarkson and Hudson.
Jackson Sq. Park—Horatio and 8th av.
Jasper Oval*—137th and Convent av.
John Jay—77th and E. R.
Mt. Morris—120th and Madison av.
Reservoir Oval*—174th and Amsterdam av.
Riverside Park*—96th and Riverside Drive.
Riverside Oval*—77th and Riverside Drive and Riverside, 83d.
Ryan Park—42d and Pleasant pl.
St. Gabriel's Park*†—35th and 2d av.
St. Nicholas Park—133d and St. Nicholas av.
Seward Park*†—Canal and Jefferson.
Thos. Jefferson Pk.*†—114th and Pleasant av.
Tompkins Sq. Park†—10th and Av. A.
W. 59th St.*†—59th, bet. 10th and 11th avs.
W. 59th St. Gymnasium—(Boys and girls), 59th, bet. 10th and 11th avs.
Yorkville†—101st, bet. 2d and 3d avs.
"Five Points"—0.187—Baxter and Worth.
Queensboro*†—Ft. of E. 59th.
Water Gate—134th and Convent av.
Ft. Washington—177th and Ft. Washington Point.
Hamilton Fish Indoor Gymnasium—(Boys and girls), Houston and Pitt.
Washington Sq.—W. 4th and Waverley pl.
18th and 10th av.
44th and 12th av.

*Has ball grounds. †Has athletic fields. ‡See Index for recreation piers.

Gymnasiums.

Cherry and Olive; 5 Rutgers pl.; 348 E. 54th; 407 W. 28th; Carmine, cor. Varick.

Lands Acquired for Playgrounds.

59th to 60th, w. of Amsterdam av.—0.519.
Nos. 180 to 184 Cherry—0.392.
South side 101st, bet. 2d and 3d avs.—0.846.
Corner Worth and Baxter—0.187.
W. of Sutton pl., bet. 59th and 60th—1,239.
151st and 152d, E. of Amsterdam av.—0.142.
W. of 1st av., bet. 67th and 68th—1.383.
Additional land at Carmansville Playground, 152d and Amsterdam av.—0.432.

Parkways.

Location.	L'gth, ft.	W'dth, ft
Harlem River Driveway......	11,562	100 to 150
Morningside Drive	8,538	90
122d, w. of 10th av	1,450	80
123d, w. of Morningside Park.....	819	60
Riverside Drive...............	17,000	90 to 168
Riv'side Dr. Ext., 135th to 158th	6,560	....

The Aquarium.

Battery Park Aquarium opened Dec., 1896. Free. Open every day in the year. Summer, 9 a.m. until 5 p.m.; winter, 10 a.m. to 4 p.m.

Exhibits—Fish, 200 kinds, making with Mammals, Crustaceans, Mollusks and Reptiles, a total of many thousand specimens. Average yearly attendance for 15 years, 2,400,000. Hatchery, 6,000,000 food fish distributed.

THE BRONX.

Office: Zbrowski Mansion, Claremont Park.

Names and Location of Parks.

[Name first, then acreage and location.]

Bronx—719.12—E. 180th, Boston rd., E. 182d, Southern blvd., St. John's College property, N. Y. C. & H. R. R. R., Burke av., Morris Park av. and White Plains dr.

Claremont—38—Teller av., Belmont, Clay av. and 170th.

Crotona—154.60—Tremont av., 3d av. and Fulton av., Crotona Pk., s., e., and n., and Arthur av.

DeVoe—5.87—188th, Fordham rd., Aqueduct av. and Sedgwick av.

Echo—4—Webster and Burnside avs.

Franz Sigel—17.47—Mott av., Walton av., 152d and 158th.

Joseph Rodman Drake Park—2.80—Hunt's Point rd. and Longfellow av.

Macomb's Dam—27—Jerome av., 162d, Cromwell's av. and Harlem River.

Melrose—0.83—161st and 162d, Courtlandt and Vanderbilt avs.

Pelham Bay—1,756—N. E. end of city.

Poe—2.33—E. 192d, Kingsbridge rd., Gd. blvd. and Concourse.

Rose Hill Park—0.72—Pelham av., Park av., Webster av.

St. James—11.83—Jerome av., Creston av. and E. 191st.

St. Mary's—34.2—St. Anns av., St. Marys, 149th and Robbins av.

University—2.75—Cedar and Sedgwick avs., 181st.

Van Cortlandt—1,132.35—City line, B'way, Van Cortlandt and Mt. Vernon avs.

Washington Bridge—8.45—Sedgwick av., Harlem River, Washington Bridge.

Parkways.

	Length, ft.
Crotona—100 ft. wide	3,315
Spuyten Duyvil—60 to 180 ft. wide.......	12,500
Mosholu—600 ft. wide	12,070
Bronx and Pelham—400 ft. wide	20,500

Zoological Park.

The N. Y. Zoological Park is located at the geographical center of Bronx Borough, in the southern section of Bronx Park. It occupies a site of 264 acres. Is reached by Interborough subway to 180th (Bronx Pk.) Sta., 3d av. L to Pelham av., Harlem R. R. to Fordham and all surface cars to West Farms.

The park is the joint production of the N. Y. Zoological Soc. and the City of N. Y., but it is managed solely by the society. In several respects it stands at the head of the zoological parks and gardens of the world, notably in area of grounds occupied by animals, in the total number of living animals, birds and reptiles exhibited. The total number of living creatures on exhibition on Jan. 1, 1918, was 4,054 specimens, representing 1,130 species. There are 14 large animal buildings, 10 animal buildings of the second class and 14 large groups of outdoor dens, aviaries and corrals. The attendance of visitors in 1918 was 1,770,437. Open 10 A.M., closes half hour before sunset.

Admission is free on five days of each week, including all holidays and Sun., but on Mon. and Thurs. an admission fee of 25c. is charged. The City of N. Y. provides the annual maintenance fund and the Zoological Soc. furnishes all the living collections. The park was opened to the public on Nov. 9, 1899. The names of the officers are as follows: Prof. Henry Fairfield Osborn, Pres. of the Zoological Soc.; Madison Grant, Sec.; Wm. T. Hornaday, Director and General Curator of the Zoological Park.

Botanical Garden.

The Botanical Garden, area 380.12 acres, is located at the northerly end of Bronx Park; is open all times, its buildings from 10 a.m. to 4:30 p.m. summer; 10 a.m. to 4 p.m. winter. Reached by 3d av. L and Harlem Div., N. Y. Central. Contains extensive plantations, greenhouses and a large museum collection, library and laboratories, also free public lectures every Sat. afternoon from April to Nov.

PARKS AND DRIVES—THE BRONX—*Continued.*

Grand Boulevard and Concourse.

The Concourse, under the jurisdiction of the Borough of The Bronx, is designed to provide connection bet. Mhtn. and the park system in the northern and eastern portions of The Bronx. The estimated cost of the work of construction was $1,052,158, and the actual cost at contract price, $1,139,748.79. The contract was let Aug. 20, 1902, the lowest bid being $1,011,822. The ground was broken for the work by President Haffen on Oct. 2, 1902, at the junction of Morris av. and 175th. The time estimated for its construction was 1,000 working days. The contract for this work was formally accepted Nov. 2, 1909.

The entrance to the Concourse, including Cedar (Franz Sigel) Park, is a stretch of land 2,300 ft. long from 400 to 500 ft. wide and extends from N. Y. Central and Hudson River R. R. to E. 164th; the route of the Concourse is along the ridge bet. Jerome and Webster avs. It is about 4 miles long and 182 ft. wide, crossing a deep valley at E. 175th, with a beautiful masonry arch. It has a central driveway for fast driving, 56 ft. in width; a macadamized driveway on each side, 24 ft. in width, for general traffic, and access to abutting property. There is a 20-ft. sidewalk on each side; trucking is prohibited and there are no bicycle paths.

Spaces bet. the driveways and the paths were planted with the trees and sodded; over 2,000 trees were planted.

The Concourse is connected with Mhtn. by means of the Madison Av. Bridge and 149th St. Bridge at Lenox av., through Mott av., and also by means of E. 161st and Central Macomb's Dam Bridge with 7th Av. Blvd. and Washington Hgts.

Bronx River Parkway Reservation.

The Bronx River P'kway Reservation extends along both sides of Bronx River from northerly line of Botanical Gardens, or Bronx Park, to lands of Bd. of Water Supply at the Kensico Reservoir and dam, total length of 15½ miles.

QUEENS.

Office: "The Overlook," Forest Park.

The area of parks and parkway of Queens consists of 1,180.58 acres. Forest Park, the largest of the system, contains public golf links, golf house, baseball grounds, tennis courts, administration and service buildings and extensive greenhouse.

Names and Location of Parks.

[Name, acreage and location.]

Ashmead—0.27, Canal, Park pl. and South, Jamaica. Astoria—56.25, Barclay, Hoyt av., Ditmars av. and East River, Astoria. Baisley's Pond—75.00, Baisley av., Sutphin rd. and New York av., Jamaica. College Point—1.14, 5th av. and 15th, College Point. Flushing—1.02, B'way and Main, Flushing. Forest—536, Myrtle av., Union turnpike, Park lane, Ashland and Cypress Hills Cemetery. Highland—49.50, Bulwer pl., Vermont av., Cypress av. and Borough Line. Jacob Riis—262.58, Neponsit, Rockaway. Kings—11.60, Fulton, Alsop, Ray and Shelton av., Jamaica. Kissena—86.12, Rose and Oak, Flushing. Leavitt—7.61, Myrtle av., Leavitt and Congress, Flushing. Linden—3, Lake, Alburtis av., Hunt pl. and Culver pl., Corona. Old Newtown Cemetery—0.87, Toledo and Court, Corona. One-Mile Pond—16, Merrick rd. and Central av., Jamaica. Pauper's Cemetery—3, Queens av., bet. 24th and 26th, Flushing. Police Training Farm—28.12, Hempstead turnpike and Jamaica av., adjacent to Kissena Park, Flushing. Rainey—8.00. Vernon and Graham avs., Astoria. Rockaway—17.87, 110th to 126th, Triton av. and Atlantic Ocean. Rockaway Park. Upland—5.67, Highland av., nr. Hillcrest av., Jamaica. Wayanda—2, Hollis av., nr. Springfield rd., Queens.

Triangles and Parking Spaces.

Triangles—0.5—Jackson av. and 6th (unofficial); 0.1—Jackson av. and 11th; 0.1—Jackson av. and 12th. 0.8—Vernon and Nott avs., L. I. C.; 0.2—Hoyt and Flushing av., Astoria; 0.5—College av. 13th, College Point—0.01—Myrtle and Cypress, Ridgewood.

Parking Spaces—0.3—Jamaica av., bet. Crescent and 3d av., Astoria; 0.65—Hayes av., from Junction av. to 43d, Corona; 0.91—Nott av., from Vernon to Jackson avs., L. I. C.; 0.9—4th av., bet. 17th and 18th, College Point; 26.5 (Conduit Lands) —along Bkln. Conduit, from Highland Park to City Line.

Parkway.

Forest—2.5—Jamaica av. to Forest Park.

Public Golf Links.

Located in Forest Park, on Myrtle, Woodhaven and Jamaica avs., consists of 118 acres and an 18-hole course. Golf house at Forest P'kway.

RICHMOND.

Names and Location of Parks.

[Names first, then acreage and location.]

Public Park at Port Richmond—1.28—B'way, Bennett, Heberton av. and Vreeland.

Washington Sq.—1.46—Bay, Water and Canal, Stapleton.

Unimproved Parks.

Park at Westerleigh—2.92—Maine and Willard avs.

Silver Lake—57.9—Richmond turnpike and Silver Lake, Brighton Hgts.

Playgrounds.

St. Peters—Richmond Terrace, New Brighton.
Westerleigh—Westerleigh.

PLAYGROUNDS UNDER PRIVATE JURISDICTION, NEW YORK CITY.

PARKS AND PLAYGROUNDS ASSOCIATION OF THE CITY OF NEW YORK.*

1123 Broadway, Mhtn.

Brooklyn Committee, 50 Court, Bkln.

Playgrounds.

BROOKLYN—Greenpoint, Kent and West. P. S. 29—Front and Jay.—Newkirk av. and E. 31st.—N. Y. av.—†Monteith, bet. Bremen and Evergreen av.—York, nr. Fulton and Willoughby; Provost and Eagle.—Parkside av., P. S. 99 Annex.—Ballground connected with all playgrounds.

The following are equipped and maintained by the association during the summer:

Playgrounds.

Henry, bet. E. B'way and Gouverneur.—Bowling Green, Washington.—15th, bet. 5th and 6th avs. (opp. N. Y. Hospital)—244 Spring.—B'way, bet. W. 225th and W. 226th.—103d and 5th av.—Villa av., bet. 204th and 205th.

Roofs.

Greenwich House, 27 Barrow.—West Side School, 417 W. 38th.—Music School, 55 E. 3d.—Educational Alliance, 197 E. B'way.—Jacob A. Riis House, 48 Henry.—Univ. Settlement, 184 Eldridge.

Yards.

Gerry Society Annex, 442 W. 23d.—312 E. 31st. —304 E. 34th.—339 E. 37th.

Hospitals and Institutions.

Metropolitan Hospital and City Home on Blackwell's Island.

Street Centers.

67th, bet. West End and Amsterdam avs.; W. 63d, bet. West End av. and Amsterdam av.; E. 101st, bet. Park and Lex. avs.; W. 131st, bet. Lenox and 5th avs.; W. 140th, bet. Lenox and 7th avs.; Henry, bet. Catherine and Market.

Excursions to Bronx and Van Cortlandt Parks.

Baseball League is played on the "round robin" principle so that teams are kept together through the summer. 105 teams registered in Manhattan and the Bronx. 2,000 boys registered. In addition to its summer activities, the assn. maintains flag centers as funds will allow.

NATIONAL HIGHWAYS PROTECTIVE SOCIETY.*

1 W. 34th, Mhtn.

Playgrounds.

Little Children's Recreation Park, 69th and 2d av., Mhtn.

NATIONAL PLANT, FLOWER AND FRUIT GUILD.*

70 5th av., Mhtn.

Recreation Centers.

MANHATTAN—66th and Av. A. and Bowling Green.

*Private association; for officers see "Societies, Civic Assns." See also Parks and Drives chapter, Public School chapter and Settlements. Additional playgrounds are maintained by Parks and Playgrounds Assn. during summer. †All year playground.

The two highest mountains on the American Continent are Aconcagua, 23,290 feet, and Tupungato, 23,000 feet. They are both in the Andes in South America.

NATIONAL AND STATE PARKS.

NATIONAL PARKS.

Name.	Acres.	Est'd.	State.
*Yellowstone	2,142,720	1872	Mont., Wyo. & Ida.
*Hot Springs Reserv'n.	911.63	1832	Ark.
*†Nat. Zoological Pk.	170	1889	D. C.
§Chickamauga and Chattanooga (Mil.)	6,543	1890	Ga. & Tenn.
§Antietam Battlefield	50	1890	Md.
*Sequoia	161,597	1890	Cal.
*General Grant	2,536	1890	Cal.
*Yosemite	719,622	1890	Cal.
§Shiloh	3,546	1894	Tenn.
§Gettysburg	2,451	1895	Pa.
§Vicksburg	1,323	1899	Miss.
*Mt. Rainier	207,360	1899	Wash.
*Crater Lake	159,360	1902	Ore.
*Platt	848	1902-'04	Okla.
*Wind Cave	10,899	1903	S. Dak.
*Sully's Hill Park	780	1904	N. Dak.
*Mesa Verde	48,966	1905-'13	Colo.
*Glacier	981,681	1910	Mont.
*Rocky Mountain	254,327	1915-'17	Colo.
*Hawaii	75,295	1916	Hawaii
§Lincoln's Birthplace	......	1916	Kentucky.
*Lassen Volcanic	79,561.58	1916	Cal.
§Guilford Courthouse	125	1917	N. Car.
*Mt. McKinley	1,408,000	1917	Alaska
*Grand Canyon	613,120	1919	Ariz.
*Lafayette	5,000	1919	Me.
*Zion	5,000	1919	Utah.

*Administered by the Natl. Park Service, Dept. of Interior.
†Under Smithsonian Inst.
§Administered by the War Dept.
*†Part of park system of Dist. of Col., but under supervision of the U. S.

NATIONAL MONUMENTS.
ADMINISTERED BY NATL. PARK SERVICE, INTERIOR DEPT.

1st, name; 2d, State; 3d, date; 4th, area (acres):

Devil's Tower, Wyo., 1906, 1,152; Montezuma Castle, Ariz., 1906, 160; El Morro, N. Mex., 1906, 1917, 240; Chaco Canyon, N. Mex., 1907, *20,629; †Muir Woods, Cal., 1908, 295; Pinnacles, Cal., 1908, 2,080; Tumacacori, Ariz., 1908, 10; Shoshone Cavern, Wyo., 1909, 210; ‡Natural Bridges, Utah, 1909, 1916, *2,740; Gran Quivira, N. Mex., 1909, 160; Sitka, Alaska, 1910, 57; ‖Rainbow Bridge, Utah, 1910, 160; Lewis and Clark Cavern, Mont., 1908, 1911, 160; Colorado, Col., 1911, 13,883; Petrified Forest, Ariz., 1906, 1911, 25,625; ‖Navajo, Ariz., 1909, 1912, 360; Papago Saguaro, Ariz., 1914, 2,050; Dinosaur, Utah, 1915, 80; Capulin Mountain, N. Mex., 1916, 681; Verendrye, N. D., 1917, 253; §Casa Grande, Ariz., 1918, 480; Katmai, Alaska, 1918, *1,088,000; Scotts Bluff, Neb., 1919, 2,053; †Yucca House, Col., 1919, 9.6.

*Estimated area. †Donated to U. S. ‡Originally set aside by proclamation of Apr. 16, 1908, and contained only 120 acres. ‖Within an Indian reservation. §Originally set aside Mar. 2, 1889, as a Natl. Park.

*NATIONAL GAME PRESERVES.
(Wholly or Part in Natl. Forests.)

Name.	Natl. forest & State.	Area.
Grand Canyon	Tusayan and Kaibab, Ariz.	1,492,928
Wichita	Wichita, Okla	61,480
Elk Refuge	Jackson, Wyo.	2,600
Montana Natl. Bison Range	Moiese, Mont	18,521
Niobrara	Valentine, Neb	14,000
Pisgah	Pisgah Natl. Forest, N. C.	79,461
Sully Hill	Sully Hill Natl. Pk., N. D.	780
Wind Cave	Wind Cave Natl. Pk., S. D.	4,000

*All national parks are natl. game preserves.

STATE PARKS.
(Name, area and year established.)

California—Capitol Park, 33; 1860-74—California Redwood Park, 7,750, 1901—University Farm, Davis, 799; 1905—Santa Monica (sta.), 20; 1887—State Capital, 33; 1887—Chico (sta), 29; 1898—Sutters Fort, 8; 1870—University of California, 531; 1868—Whitaker Forest, 320; 1910.

Connecticut—Cornwall Forest, 1,200; 1912—Israel Putnam Camp Ground, 100; 1903—Portland Forest, 1,500; 1903—Simsbury Forest, 300; 1908—Union Forest, 500; 1905.

Massachusetts—*Blue Hills (res.), 4,906; 1893-1898—*Beaver Brook, 58; 1893—*Middlesex Falls (res.), 1,845; 1894—*Stony Brook (res.), 463; 1894—*Hemlock Gorge (res.), 23; 1895—*Hart's Hill (res.), 22; 1900—*Charles River (res.), 711; 1896—*Mystic River (res.), 54; 1899—Neponset River (res.), 922; 1899—*King's Beach and Lynn Shore (res.), 22; 1895—*Revere Beach (res.), 65; 1895—*Winthrop Shore (res.), 16; 1899—*Quincy Shore (res.), 32; 1900—*Nantasket Beach (res.), 25; 1899—Bunker Hill (res.), 6; 1919—Wachusett Mt. (res.), 1,500; 1900—Greylock (res.), 8,458; 1900—Mt. Tom (res.), 1,000—Mt. Everett, 1,106.

Michigan—Mackinac Island State Park, 1,015; 1895—Michigan Forest Res., 235,061.38; 1901—Interlocker State Park, 200; 1917—Total amount land for forestry purposes, 600,000.

Minnesota—Itasca Park, 20,000; 1891—St. Croix Park, 150; 1895—Alexander Ramsey, 86; 1911—Minneopa State Park, 60; 1905—Ft. Ridgley, 80; 1913—Horace Austin, 1913.

New York—Niagara Falls Park, 197; 1883-1884—Niagara Falls Park in Canada, 730—Watkins Glen (res.), 104; 1906—Adirondack Preserve, 1,767,778; 1885—Catskill Preserve, 118,772; 1885—International Park, 180; 1895—†Fire Island Park, 118; 1908—Palisades Interstate Park, 24,000; 1910—Saratoga Springs Park, 304; 1911—Indian Ladder, 350; 1914.

Pennsylvania—In 26 counties there are 1,048,682 acres of forest land established and maintained by the State for commercial purposes.

Wisconsin—Interstate Park, Dalles of St. Croix, 550; 1835-1901—Peninsula, 3,700; 1909—Brule River, 6,000; 1905—Nelson Dewey Park, 1,671; 1911-1915—Devil's Lake, 1,040; 1909—Cushing Mem. Park, 8; 1911—Pattison Park, Douglas Co., 660; 920—Perrot Park, Trempealeau Co., 910; 1920.

Wyoming—Big Horn Hot Springs, State Reserve (res.), 640; 1897.

*Metropolitan Park. †For history of Fire Island Park see page 447, 1909 Almanac.

RAILROAD PASSENGER STATIONS IN MANHATTAN.

B. & O., ft. W. 23d and Liberty, 7th av. and 32d, Hudson Terminal.

Central of N. J., ft. W. 23d and Liberty; Sandy Hook Route (in summer), ft. W. 42d and Cedar, also.

D., L. & W., ft. Barclay, Christopher and W. 23d.

Erie, ft. Chambers and W. 23d, Hudson Terminal.

Hudson Terminal, Cortlandt, Dey, Church and Fulton. Hudson and Manhattan R. R., Newark and Jersey City to Morton, Mhtn., to Christopher, to 6th av., along 6th av. to 33d.

Lehigh Valley, ft. W. 23d and Liberty, 7th av. and 32d, Hudson Terminal.

Long Island, 7th av. and 33d, ft. E. 34th, Atlantic av. Br., junction Flatbush and Atlantic avs., Bkln.

N. J. & N. Y., ft. Chambers and W. 23d.

N. Y. & Long Branch, ft. Liberty, W. 23d, 7th av. and 32d, Hudson Terminal. In summer, ft. W. 42d and Cedar, also.

N. Y. C. & H. R., Grand Central, 42d and 4th av.; 125th; Harlem Div., 4th av. and 42d; 125th; Putnam Div., Sedgwick av. (Bronx), High Bridge.

N. Y., N. H. & H., Grand Central, 4th av. and 42d; 125th.

N. Y., O. & W., ft. of Cortlandt and W. 42d.

N. Y., Susquehanna & Western, ft. Chambers and W. 23d.

Northern of New Jersey, ft. of Chambers and W. 23d.

Pennsylvania, ft. Cortlandt and Desbrosses, 7th av., 31st to 33d and Hudson Terminal.

Philadelphia & Reading, ft. W. 23d and Liberty.

Staten Island, ft. Whitehall.

West Shore, ft. Cortlandt and W. 42d. Grand Central.

VEHICULAR N. Y.-N. J. TUNNEL.

Ground was broken in October, 1920, for the great twin-tube vehicular tunnel designed by a Brooklyn engineer, Clifford M. Holland, and which is to join the States of New York and New Jersey. Its estimated cost of construction will be $57,000,000. This will be equally borne by the two States.

FOREST, FISH AND GAME LAWS OF NEW YORK STATE.

Based on Chap. 647, Laws of 1911, and subsequent amendments and additions. Revised to Jan. 1, 1921.

SEASONS.

Open seasons for game and fish in N. Y. State includes first and last dates given.

Quadrupeds and birds protected by law shall not be taken except after sunrise and before sunset. Fish protected by law shall not be taken except by angling unless otherwise specifically permitted.

GAME.

Beaver—No open season.

Deer—No open season. Wild deer of either sex, other than fawn, having horns not less than three inches in length, may be taken in the counties of Clinton, Essex, Franklin, Fulton, Hamilton, Herkimer, Jefferson, Lewis, Oneida, Oswego, Saratoga, St. Lawrence, Warren and Washington (Oct. 15-Nov. 15). In Ulster, Sullivan, Rensselaer, Delaware and Orange Counties (Nov 1-15, inclusive). In Dutchess County (Nov. 1-15, inclusive).

Under a license issued by Conservation Comm., venison may be possessed from Nov. 21-Feb. 1 by the owner for consumption only. Application not honored after Nov. 20.

No person shall take more than one such deer in an open season, nor transport more than one carcass or part thereof at any one time.

Deer shall not be hunted with dogs; no jacklight or other artificial light, trap, saltlick or other device to entrap or entice deer shall be used, made or set, nor shall any deer be taken by aid or use thereof. No deer shall be taken while in the water.

No dog of either sex shall be taken into the Adirondack or Catskill Park or into forests inhabited by deer or harbored or possessed therein unless the owner shall first obtain a license from the Conservation Commission for such dog.

Venison legally taken may be possessed from Oct. 15 to Nov. 20.

Land Turtle—No open season.

Sable or Marten—Nov. 10-March 15, any manner, day or night.

Mink—Nov. 10-March 15; any manner, day or night.

Muskrat—Dec. 1-March 31, with exceptions.

Muskrat houses must not be injured or disturbed. The shooting of muskrat is prohibited, as well as taking them with box, wire or cage trap.

Rabbits, Varying Hares and Cottontail Rabbits—Oct. 1-March 1.

No person shall take more than 6 either all of one kind or partly of each in 1 day.

Hares and rabbits not to be hunted with ferrets except in counties where permitted by resolution of Commission.

The owner or occupant of enclosed or occupied farms and lands or a person duly authorized in writing by such owner or occupant may take except by use of ferrets, on such owner's or occupant's premises at any time in any manner hares or rabbits which are injuring their property.

There is no close season for Belgian hares, jack rabbits or rabbits bred in captivity.

Varying hares and cottontail rabbits may be bought and sold during the open season. (See Additional Protective Orders.)

Varying hares and cottontail rabbits when bred in captivity may be bought and sold for food purposes during the close season provided a license so to do shall have first been obtained from the Conservation Comn. Additional protection has been granted to varying hares and cottontail rabbits.

Raccoon—In any manner, day or night, Nov. 10-Feb. 10.

Skunk—Nov. 10-Feb. 10, in any manner, day or night, except by smoking or use of chemicals, and must not be hunted, pursued or killed by dogs.

Squirrels, Black, Gray and Fox—Oct. 1-Nov. 15. EXCEPTION: Long Island, Nov. 1-Dec. 31. 5 squirrels limit. No such squirrels shall be taken within the corporate limits of any city or village.

BIRDS.

Duck, Goose, Brant—Sept. 16-Dec. 31, and may be possessed Sept. 16-Jan. 10. EXCEPTION: Long Island, Oct. 16-Jan. 31. May be possessed from Oct. 16-Feb. 10.

Wood Duck, Eider Duck and Swan—No open season. Ducks, geese and brant shall not be taken except from the land, from a blind or floating device used to conceal the hunter (other than a sail or powerboat) from a rowboat when the same shall be within 50 ft. of shore or of a natural growth of flags or in pursuit of wounded birds.

EXCEPTION: Ducks, geese and brant may be taken during the open season therefor by aid of any floating device other than sail or powerboats at any distance from shore on Long Island Sound, Shinnecock, Gardiner, Reeves, Flanders and Peconic bays, Lake Erie, Niagara River and Oneida Lake, and in Great South Bay west of Smith's Point and east of the Nassau-Suffolk county line

No more than 25 ducks in aggregate of all kinds in 1 day shall be taken by one person nor more than 8 geese in the aggregate of all kinds, nor more than 8 brant, during the open season, occupying the same boat, blind or battery.

Grouse or Partridge—Oct. 15-Nov. 15. EXCEPTION: Long Island, Nov. 1-Dec. 31. No more than 2 grouse or partridge in 1 day nor 10 in open season, and on L. I. not more than 2 in 1 day and 15 in an open season, and may be possessed for an additional period of 5 days next succeeding the open season.

Partridge, Hungarian or European Gray Legged—No open season.

Wild Pheasants (Hungarian, Dark-Necked, Ring-Necked, commonly called English Mongolian or Chinese)—Last 2 Thurs. in Oct., and first 2 Saturdays in Nov. EXCEPTION: Long Island, Nov. 1-Dec. 31.

Only the cock or male bird may be taken and no more than 3 male pheasants in the open season, except on L. I., where limit is 4 male pheasants in 1 day and 30 in open season.

Quail—No open season until 1925. EXCEPTION: Long Island, Nov. 1-Dec. 31. Limit, 6 quail in 1 day, not more than 40 in an open season on L. I. Special provisions for rails, Amer. coots, etc.

Shore Birds, Black-bellied and Golden Plovers and Greater and Lesser Yellowlegs—Aug. 16-Nov. 30. A person may take not to exceed 15 black-bellied and golden plovers and greater and lesser yellowlegs in the aggregate of all kinds in one day.

Wilson Snipe or Jack Snipe—Sept. 16-Dec. 31. EXCEPTION: Long Island, Oct. 16-Jan. 31. A person may take not to exceed 25 Wilson snipe or jack snipe in 1 day.

Woodcock—Oct. 1-Nov. 30. Limit, 6 woodcock in 1 day, not more than 24 in open season.

FISH.

Bass, Black and Oswego—June 16-Nov. 30. Minimum length 10 in. Limit per day to 1 person 15; to a boat, 2 or more persons, 25. Shall not be sold or offered for sale.

Striped Bass—No close season. Minimum length, 12 in.

Bullheads—(See Lake George.)

Frogs, Green, Spring and Bull—June 1-Mar. 31.

Icefish or Smelt (taken from Lake Champlain or from inland waters)—No close season. Minimum length, 6 in. No size limit in marine district.

Lake Trout—Not less than 15 in. April 1-Sept. 30. EXCEPTION: Lakes Erie and Ontario. No close season. Limit, 10 lake trout in 1 day, but whenever 2 or more persons are angling from same boat, not to exceed 15, except in Lakes Erie and Ontario they may be taken in any number. (See Lake George.)

Maskallonge—June 16-Dec. 31. Minimum length 24 in. Taking through the ice prohibited.

Pickerel and Pike—May 1-Mar. 1. In St. Lawrence River; minimum length, 20 in.; day limit to a person, 12. (See Lake George.)

Pikeperch (Wall-eyed Pike, commonly called Pike and Yellow Pike)—May 10-Mar. 1. Minimum length 12 in. (See Lake George.)

Yellow Perch—Yellow Perch from Cazenovia Lake, Otisco Lake, Skaneateles Lake, Cross Lake, Onondaga Lake and Jamesville reservoir. May 1-March 1. No close season in other waters.

Sturgeon—Shortnosed—July 1-April 30. 20 in. **Lake and Sea**—No close season. 42 in.

Trout (Brook, Speckled, Brown, Rainbow, Steelhead and Red-Throat)—First Sat. in April-Aug. 31. 6 in.; day limit, 10 lbs. to person. Shall not be sold or offered for sale, whether taken within or without the State.

Whitefish—Not less than 1¾ lbs. in the round—April 1-Sept. 30.

HOTELS AND APARTMENT HOTELS.

Ap., apartment hotel.

Brooklyn.

Bossert—Montague and Hicks.
Brevoort—47 Brevoort pl. Ap.
Brighton Beach (Sum.)—B. B.
Bristol Family Hotel—1284 Pacific.
Buena Vista—Ft. 24th.
Chatlaine—Bedford and Dean.
Clarendon—Washington & Johnson.
Colonna—173 8th av. Ap.
Franklin Arms—66 Orange. Ap.
Harbor View—62 Montague. Ap.
Hollywood Inn—Cropsey av.
Maewyl—1152 Pacific. Ap.
Mansion House—187 Hicks. Ap.
Margaret—97 Columbia H'gts. Ap.
Markham—637 St. Marks av. Ap.
Marquise—126 Herkimer. Ap.
Mohawk—379 Washington av. Ap.
Montague—103 Montague. Ap.
Osmund—1140 Pacific. Ap.
Shelburne—Brighton Beach.
St. George—51 Clark.
Standish Arms — 169 Columbia Hts. Ap.
Touraine—23 Clinton. Ap.

Manhattan and Bronx.

Abbey Inn—Ft. Washington av., nr. W. 198th.
The Aberdeen—540 W. 146th. Ap.
Aberdeen—17 W. 32d.
Abingdon—7 Abingdon sq.
Alabama—13 E. 11th.
Alcazar—43 W. 32d.
Alexandria—250 W. 103d. Ap.
America—104 E. 15th.
Amsterdam—57 Lexington av.
Anderson—102 W. 80th. Ap.
Annex—See McAlpin.
Ansonia—B'way and 73d.
Arlington—18 W. 25th.
Ashton—1312 Madison av.
Astor—44th and B'way.
Athens—56 E. 42d.
Bartholdi Inn—171 W. 45th.
Belleclaire—2173 B'way.
Belmont Hotel—Park av. & 42d.
Beresford—Central Pk. W., 81st-82d
Bergin—225 7th av.
Berkeley—20 5th av. Ap.
Biltmore—Madison av., 43d & 44th.
Bonta—B'way and 94th.
Bradford—65 E. 11th.
Breslin—1194 B'way.
Bretton Hall—2350 B'way.
Brevoort—11 5th av.
Bristol—129 W. 48th.
Broadway Central—673 B'way.
Broztell—3 E. 27th.
Brunswick—1236 Madison av. Ap.
Bryant Park Studio—80 W. 40th.
Buckingham—5th av. and 50th.
Burlington—505 W. 134th. Ap.
Caledonia—28 W. 26th.
Calumet—340 W. 57th.
Cecilia—515 W. 147th. Ap.
Chatham—Vanderbilt av. & 48th
Chelsea Hotel—222 W. 23d.
Claremont—126th & Riverside P'k
Claridge—B'way. cor. 44th.
Clendening—202 W. 103d.
Collingwood—45 W. 35th.
Colonial—8th av. and 125th.
Commodore—42d & Lexington av.
Continental—1448 Broadway.
Cumberland—B'way and 54th.
Dakota—1 W. 72d. Ap.
De France—142 W. 49th.
Devon—70 W. 55th.
Empire—1895 B'way.
Endicott—Columbus av. & 81st.
Essex—Madison av., cor. 56th.
Evelyn—101 W. 78th.
Felix-Portland—132 W. 47th.
Flanders—133-137 W. 47th.
Fifty-first St.—33 W. 51st. Ap.
Garden—63 Madison av.
Gotham—5th av. and 55th.
Grampion—182 St. Nicholas av. Ap.
Great Northern—118 W. 57th.
Greeley Sq.—B'way and 34th.
Gregorian—42 W. 35th.
Grenoble—56th and 7th av.
Grosvenor—37 5th av.
Hargrave—112 W. 72d.
Hawthorne—70-72 W. 49th.
Herald Square—116 W. 34th.
Hermitage—592 7th av.
Hoffman Arms—640 Madison av.
Holley—36 Washington sq. W.
Hotel Algonquin—59-65 W. 44th.
Hotel Calvert—145 W. 41st.
Hotel Churchill—856 Broadway.
Hotel Hamilton—73d and B'way.
Hotel Irving—26 Gramercy Pk
Hotel Lafayette—31 University pl.
Hotel Latham—4 E. 28th.
Hotel Plaza—5th av. and 59th.
Imperial—B'way, 31st & 32d.
Iroquois—49 W. 44th.
Judson—53 Washington sq. S.
La Salle—30 E. 60th.
Le Marquis—12 E. 31st.
Leonori—701 Madison av.
Long Acre—157-163 W. 47th.
Lorraine—2 E. 45th.
Lucerne—201 W. 79th.
McAlpin—B'way and 34th.
Madison Sq.—37 Madison av.
Majestic—71st, 72d & Ct. Pk. W.
Manhattan Sq.—54 W. 77th.
Marie A'toin'te—B'way, 66th-67th.
Markwell—220 W. 49th.
Marlborough—B'way and 36th.
Marlton—3 W. 8th.
Marseilles—B'way & 103d.
Martha Washington—29 E. 29th.
Martinique—See McAlpin.
Maryland—104 W. 49th.
Mills' Hotels—No. 1, 160 Bleecker; No. 2, 16 Rivington; No. 3, 161 W. 36th.
Monticello—35 W. 64th.
Murray Hill—112 Park av.
Narragansett—B'way and 93d.
Netherland—5th av. and 59th.
New Weston—31 E. 49th.
Newton—2528 B'way.
Nobleton—126 W. 73d.
Normandie—B'way and 38th.
Orleans—100 W. 80th.
Park Av.—32d & 33d, on Park av.
Patterson—58 W. 46th.
Pennsylvania—7th av. & 32d.
Preston—363 4th av.
Prince George—14 E. 28th.
Richmond—70 W. 46th.
Ritz-Carlton—Mad. av., 46th.
Robert Fulton—228 W. 71st.
Royalton—44 W. 44th.
St. Andrew—B'way and 72d.
St. George—49 E. 12th.
St. Hubert—120 W. 57th.
St. James—109-113 W. 45th.
St. Margaret—129 W. 47th.
St. Paul—46 W. 60th.
St. Regis (The)—55th and 5th av.
San Jacinto—18 E. 60th.
San Remo—Central Pk. W. & 74th
Savoy—767 5th av. Ap.
Schuyler—59 W. 45th.
Schuyler Arms—307 W. 98th.
Selkirk—308 W. 82d.
Seville—Madison av., cor. 29th.
Sevillia—117 W. 58th.
Seymour—44 W. 45th.
Shanley's—B'way and 43d, 1204 B'way, 383 6th av.
Sherman Sq.—2039 B'way.
Sherry's—5th av. and 44th.
Somerset—150 W. 47th.
Strand—502 W. 14th.
Stratford—11 E. 32d.
Theresa—7th av. and 125th.
Times Sq.—206 W. 43d.
Touraine—9 E. 39th.
Twelve Fifth Av.—12 5th av.
Union Square—18 Union sq. E.
Vanderbilt—34th and Park av.
Van Rensselaer—17-19 E. 11th.
Waldorf-Astoria—5th av. & 34th.
Wallick—43d and B'way.
Walton—104 W. 70th.
Warrington—161-163 Madison av.
Webster—40 W. 45th.
Wellington—7th av. and 55th.
Willard—256 W. 76th.
Wolcott—4 W. 31st.
Woodstock—127 W. 43d.
Woodward—Broadway and 55th.
Y. M. C. A., West Side Branch (for members)—318 W. 57th.
York—7th av. and 36th.

Queens.

Ann Jeannette (Sum.) — Rockaway Pk.
Arms (Sum.)—Far Rockaway.
Arverne (Summer)—Arverne.
Belle Harbor House—Belle Harbor.
Belvidere (Summer)—Edgemere.
Chelsea—Far Rockaway.
Colonial (Summer)—Arverne.
Commercial—Queens.
Edgemere Club (Summer)—Edgemere.
Flushing—Flushing.
Forest Hills—Forest Hills.
Holliswood Hall — Hillside av., Hollis.
Hotel Far Rockaway—Far Rockaway.
Imperial—Arverne.
Kew Gardens—Kew Gardens.
Narragansett House (Summer)—Seaside.
N. Y. Hotel—Seaside.
Ostend (Sum.)—Far Rockaway.
Prince—Arverne, L. I.
Tak-a-Fou-Sha (Summer) — Far Rockaway.
Waldorf—Rockaway Beach.

Richmond.

Castleton—Castleton Corners.
Cliff House—Tompkinsville.
Hugot's—St. George.
Knickerbocker—New Brighton.
Manhattan—Huguenot Pk.
Terra Marine—Huguenot Pk.
Washington—New Dorp.

GREAT SHIP CANALS OF THE WORLD.

Canal.	Yr. op'd.	Length, miles.	D'th, ft.	W'th, ft.*	Cost.
‡Cape Cod (U. S.)	1914	8	25	150	$12,000,000
Corinth (Greece)	1893	4	26.25	72	5,000,000
Elbe and Trave (Germany)	1900	41	10	72	5,831,000
Kiel (Germany)	†1895	61	45	150	94,000,000
Kronstadt-St. Petersburg (Russia)	1890	16	20.50	220	10,000,000
Lake Venern—Gotenburg (Sweden)	1917	52	13.2	100	....
Manchester ship (England)	1894	35.5	26	120	75,000,000
Marseilles—Rhone	‡1916	60	9.8	82	20,000,000
Panama (U. S.)	1914	50.5	45	300	375,000,000
Sault Ste. Marie (Canada)	1895	1.11	20.25	142	2,791,873
Sault Ste. Marie (U. S.)	1855	1.6	22	100	10,000,000
Suez (Egypt)	1869	90	31	108	100,000,000
Welland (Canada)	1887	26.75	14	100	25,000,000

*At the bottom. †Reconstruction began in 1907 and completed June, 1914. ‡Barges and vessels up to 600 tons can navigate the canal.

PUBLIC HALLS.

Brooklyn.

Following list does not include all assembly and dance halls.

Academy of Music—Lafayette av. and Ashland pl.
Acme—330 7th av.
Arcadia Hall—918 Halsey.
Association—55 Hanson pl.
Aurora Grata Cathedral—Bedford av., nr. Madison.
Bedford Y. M. C. A.—Bedford av., cor. Monroe.
Boys Welcome Hall—185 Chauncey.
Broadway Casino—792 B'way.
Central Y.M.C.A.—55 Hanson pl.
Clermont Rink—189 Clermont av.
Eastern District Y. M. C. A., Marcy av. and So. 9th.
Eckford—206 and 269 Calyer.
Galen—184 Joralemon.
Grand Bushwick—428 Bushwick av.
Hart's Hall—1030 Gates av.
Historical—Pierrepont and Clinton
Imperial—15 Red Hook lane.
Independence—89 Osborn.
Jefferson—5 Court sq.
Johnston Building—12 Nevins.
Kismet Temple Mosque — Herkimer, nr. Nostrand av.
Labor Lyceum—949 Wil'by av.
Masonic Temple—Lafayette av., cor. Clermont.
McCaddin—Berry, nr. So. 3d.
Memorial—376 Schermerhorn.
Palm Garden—275 Hamburg av.
Pouch Mnsn.—345 Clinton av.
Prospect Hall—261 Prospect av.
Regina Mansion, 601 Willoughby av.
Saengerbund—61 Smith.
Schwaben—472 Knickerbocker av.
St. Malachy's—Atlantic av., cor. Hendrix.
Somer's Hall—126 Rockaway av.
Trommer's Hall—1632 Bush'k av.
Waverly Hall—165 Waverly av.
Wil'by Mansion—663 Wil'by av.

Manhattan and Bronx.

Aeolian—34 W. 43d.
Am. Museum Nat. Hist. Lecture Hall—Central Pk. W. and 77th.
Amsterdam Opera House — 340 W. 44th.
Apollo—126 Clinton, 975 1st av.
Association—215 W. 23d; 318 W. 57th; 153 E. 86th; 5 W. 125th.
Berkeley Lyceum—19 W. 44th.
Bronx Casino—2994 3d av.
Bronx Lyceum—705 Courtlandt av.
Carnegie Hall—883 7th av.
Cooper Union—E. 8th and 4th av.
Gaelic Ath. Assn. of Am.—211 E. 45th.
Gr. Cent. Pal.—488 Lexington av.
Madison Sq. Concert—31 E. 26th.
Madison Sq. Garden—51 Mad. av.
Masonic—46 W. 24th, 1475 Williamsbridge rd., Westchester; 1931 Washington av.
Masonic Temple—310 Lenox av.
Mozart—328 E. 86th.
Murray Hill Lyceum—160 E. 34th.
Niblo's Garden—3690 3d av.
Tammany—145 E. 14th.
Union Square—8 Union Sq. E.
Y. M. C. A.—215 W. 23d.
Y. M. H. A.—148 E. 92d.

Queens.

Arverne Casino—Arverne, L. I.
Astoria Assembly Rooms — 22 Flushing av., L. I. City.
Bohemian—Woolsey av., Astoria.
Broadway—458 B'way, L. I. City.
Colonial—Arverne.
Columbia—Willow, Rich. Hill.
Good Templar—Springfield.
Hollis Assn.—Fulton, Hollis.
Jamaica Town Hall—Fulton.
Knights of Columbus—40 Madison av., Flushing; 76 Main, L. I. City.
Lyceum—Queens.
Masonic—161 Broadway, Flushing; 165 Fulton av., L. I. City; 246 Jackson av., L. I. City; 60 Mott av., Far Rockaway; 114 Grand av., Astoria.
Masonic Temple—46 Union av., Jamaica.
Odd Fellows—University, cor. Clinton, Woodhaven 71 B'way, Flushing; 96 2d av., L. I. City; 39 W. 18th, Whitestone; 106 Locust, Flushing.
St. Mary's Lyceum—117 5th, L. I. City; 80 Flushing av., Jamaica.

Richmond.

Labor Lcm.—22 Roff, Stapleton.
Masonic—Bennett, cor. Richmond av., Port Richmond.
Masonic Temple—234 Main.
Odd Fellows—14 Brook.

BROOKLYN INSTITUTE OF ARTS AND SCIENCES.

Bkln. Institute of Arts and Sciences has the following 4 general divisions: Dept. of Education, Academy of Music Bldg.; Dept. of Museums, Museum Bldg., Eastern P'kway and Washington av.; Children's Museum, Bedford Park, Bkln. av., and Dept. of Botanic Garden, Washington and Flatbush avs.; Dept. of Biological Laboratory at Cold Spring Harbor, L. I.

Central office, Academy of Music Bldg., Lafayette av., bet. Fulton and Flatbush av.

Officers, Board of Trustees—A. A. Healy, Hon. Pres.; Frank L. Babbott Pres.; W. H. Crittenden, Edward C. Bum, W. A. Putnam, Vice-Presidents; G. Foster Smith, Treas.; Herman Stutzer, Sec.

Council of Assoc. Members—Rev. Chas. C. Albertson, Pres.; J. Herbert Low, Sec.

Trustees—C. C. Albertson, S. P. Avery, F. L. Babbott, H. L. Batterman, E. L. Beers, H. H. Benedict, E. C. Blum, G. M. Boardman, D. A. Boody, R. R. Bowker, G. W. Brush, S. P. Cadman, W. J. Coombs, W. C. Courtney, W. H. Crittenden, A. DeSilver, J. G. Dettmer, G. D. Fahnestock, J. D. Fairchild, J. W. Frothingham, A. M. Hatch, A. A. Healy, H. W. Healy, F. S. Jones, Martin Joost, E. R. Kennedy, L. V. Lockwood, E. P. Maynard, W. J. Matheson, E. W. McCarty, J. H. Morgan, H. J. Morse, C. J. Peabody, A. D. Pell, J. H. Post, G. D. Pratt, W. A. Putnam, D. S. Ramsay, H. F. Noyes, Francis H. Sloan, G. Foster Smith, Herman Stutzer, J. T. Underwood, E. G. Warner, A. T. White, Alex. M. White.

Dept. of Education, C. D. Atkins, Dir., has 9,500 members.

School of Pedagogy—L. H. White, Ch.; 22 teachers, 783 students.

DEPARTMENTS AND THEIR PRESIDENTS.

Agriculture, C. A. Peters; Architecture, Arne Dehli; Astronomy, A. J. Brooks; Botany, G. C. Wood; Domestic Science, Mrs. F. K. Perkins; Dramatic Art, M. Tucker; Electricity, S. Sheldon; Engineering, A. S. Tuttle, Sec.; Ethnology, S. Hagar; Fine Arts, W. H. Goodyear; Geography, H. L. Bridgman; Geology, J. Mickleborough; Microscopy, S. C. Wheat; Mineralogy, F. T. Bather, Sec.; Music, R. H. Woodman; Pedagogy, W. L. Felter; Philately, T. P. Hyatt; Philology, W. Boughton; Philosophy, E. H. Griggs; Photography, W. E. Macnaughtan; Physics, E. R. von Nardroff; Political Science, J. H. Low; Psychology, J. J. Schonhoven; Chess Club, E. Behr.

Evening Art Classes—Four courses of instruction, J. H. Boston, Inst.

BRANCHES OF THE DEPT. OF EDUCATION OF THE INSTITUTE.

Huntington—C. E. Shepard, Ch.; Mrs. J. S. Sammis, Sec.

Jamaica—B. J. Humphrey, Ch.; Dr. O. D. Humphrey, Sec.

BROOKLYN MUSEUM OF FINE ARTS, ETHNOLOGY AND NATURAL HISTORY.

Open week days, 9 A.M. to 5 P.M.; Sat., 9 A.M. to 6 P.M.; Sun., 2 to 6 P.M. On Mon. and Tues. a fee of 25c. for adults and 10c. for children is charged. On other days admission is free, including holidays.

A tract of land at Eastern P'kway and Washington av., containing 11 9-10 acres and valued at $900,000, was leased by former City of Bkln. to the Institute for a term of 100 yrs. On this site the 1st section of the Museum bldg. was completed in May, 1897, and opened to public June 2, 1897; 2d section was completed in 1905, and 3d section in 1909; 5th section was started in 1911. Entire structure, when completed, will cover an area of 560 ft. square, with 4 interior courts. W. H. Fox, Dir.

Children's Museum, Bedford Park, Brooklyn av. and Prospect pl., is open daily from 9 A.M. to 5:30 P.M.; Sun., 2 to 5:30 P.M. Free. Miss Anna B. Gallup. (See Index.)

Botanic Garden, C. S. Gage. (See Index.)

Biological Laboratory, Cold Spring Harbor, L. I. C. B. Davenport, Dir. Dormitory for students.

Carnegie Institution Branch, Cold Spring Harbor, L. I.—C. B. Davenport, Dir. Work in conjunction with Bkln. Institute biological laboratory.

CAPITAL PUNISHMENT IN THE UNITED STATES.

Capital punishment prevails in all of the States of the Union, except Arizona, Kansas, Maine, Minnesota, North Dakota, Oregon, Rhode Island, Washington and Wisconsin. In Michigan the only crime punishable by death is treason. The death penalty was abolished in the State of Washington in 1913. It was abolished in Iowa in 1872 and restored in 1878. It was also abolished in Colorado in 1897, but was restored in 1901. Hanging is the ordinary mode of execution, but in Arkansas, Indiana, Massachusetts, New York, Nebraska, Ohio, Pennsylvania, Vermont, Virginia and Oklahoma electrocution is the legal method. In Nevada hanging or shooting is optional with the condemned.

CIVIL SERVICE INFORMATION.

FEDERAL.

Officers—Three commissioners are appointed by the President to assist him in preparing suitable rules for carrying the civil service act into effect and in enforcing the law and the rules.

General Rules—The fundamental principles governing appointments to Federal civil positions are found in the civil service act itself. The present rules were approved March 20, 1903, and went into effect April 15, 1903. They have since been revised in part from time to time. The classified service includes all officers and employees in the executive civil service of the United States except mere unskilled laborers, persons whose appointments are subject to confirmation by the Senate and certain persons whose positions are exempted from the operation of the civil service act under the terms of the laws creating the positions.

Examinations—These are conducted by boards of examiners chosen from among persons in Government employ and are held as frequently as the needs of the service require in all the States and Territories, at convenient places.

Qualifications of Applicants—The Commission is authorized to exclude from any examination a person who is not a citizen of or who does not owe allegiance to the United States; who does not come within the age limitations prescribed; who is physically disqualified for the service which he seeks; who is addicted to the habitual use of alcoholic beverages to excess or to the use of opium, morphine or other narcotic drugs; who has been dismissed from the public service for delinquency or misconduct; who has made a false statement in his application or has been guilty of fraud or deceit in any manner connected with his application or examination, or has been guilty of crime or infamous or notoriously disgraceful conduct; who has been dishonorably discharged from the United States Army, Navy or Marine Corps, or who is otherwise unfit, in the opinion of the Commission, for the position sought.

STATE.

Detailed information by addressing "State Civil Service Commission, Albany, N. Y."

The State Civil Service Rules provide for:

(a) Exempt Class—Includes deputies of principal officers; secretaries of boards or commissions; clerks and deputy clerks of courts; all other positions for filling of which examinations are found not to be practicable.

(b) Non-Competitive Class—Includes minor positions in institutions where competition is impracticable; also a few subordinate positions in the State Departments.

(c) Labor Class—Includes unskilled laborers, skilled laborers and positions of similar character not included in competitive or non-competitive classes.

Examiners—Appointed by State Civil Service Commission. Work under direction of Chief Examiner.

Applications—Applications for positions in competitive class must be executed in applicant's handwriting on blank form supplied by and forwarded to "State Civil Service Commission, Albany, N. Y.," but not until examination has been ordered.

Examinations—Held as the needs of the service require, usually in series at intervals of five or six weeks during the year. Examinations usually in writing, each subject rated on basis of 100. Every candidate who receives a rating of at least 60 per cent. on each subject of the examination and general average of not less than 75 per cent. is eligible.

State Civil Service Commission.

The State Civil Service Commission consists of 3 members, appointed by the Gov. and with the advice and consent of the State Senate, not more than 2 of them to be adherents of the same political party. The salary is $5,000 a year for pres. and $5,000 per year for associate commr., beginning July 1, 1920, with necessary traveling expenses; term of office 6 years. The commission has power to appoint a secretary, a chief examiner and such other officers, clerks and examiners as may be deemed necessary. The commission has supervision of the administration of the civil service law and rules in the 59 cities of the State. It has charge and control of examinations and appointments in the service of the State, the counties of Albany, Bronx, Chautauqua, Erie, Kings, Monroe, Nassau, New York, Niagara, Oneida, Onondaga, Orange, Queens, Rensselaer, Richmond, Suffolk, Ulster and Westchester and the villages of Ilion, Ossining, Peekskill and Port Chester. During the year 1919, 19,000 persons filed application forms for examinations. Of these 15,663 were actually examined and upward of 3,000 appointments were made to competitive places. On Jan. 1, 1920, there were 20,664 positions, not including laborers, subject to the jurisdiction of the commission. These positions were classified as follows: Unclassified service, 1,516; classified service, A, exempt, 1,496; B, competitive, 11,114; C, non-competitive, 6,538. In addition there were on Jan. 1, 1920, 315 persons on military duty as follows: Unclassified service, 5; exempt class, 6; competitive class, 98; non-competitive class, 206.

MUNICIPAL.

Detailed information at the Municipal Civil Service Commission, Municipal Bldg., Mhtn.

Applications — Applications for positions in competitive class must be filed in applicant's handwriting, addressed to the secretary of the Municipal Civil Service Commission of New York City. Application forms not issued or received until examination has been ordered and advertised. All candidates must be citizens of the U. S. Applications for Labor Class positions may be filed at any time.

NEW YORK STATE REGENTS' EXAMINATIONS, 1921.

Regents' examinations, under the control of the Education Department (Examinations Division) will be held in 1921 as follows:

ACADEMIC—Jan. 17-21, inc., at New York, Albany, Syracuse and Buffalo, and about 900 academies and high schools.

June 13-17, inc., at New York, Albany, Syracuse and Buffalo, and about 900 academies and high schools.

Sept. 12-14, inc., at New York, Albany, Syracuse and Buffalo only. The Sept. examinations are for professional and technical students exclusively.

Morning session, 9:15. Afternoon, 1:15.

For State life certificates, Aug. 15-19, inc., at Albany, Binghamton, Buffalo, Chautauqua, Cortland, Elmira, Hornell, Hudson Falls, Ithaca, Malone, Kingston, Liberty, New York, Norwich, Oneonta, Ogdensburg, Plattsburg, Rochester, Syracuse, Utica and Watertown.

For college graduate certificates, May 26-27, at N. Y., Albany, Syracuse, Buffalo, Elmira and Canton.

Aug. 18-19, at New York, Albany, Syracuse, Rochester, Ithaca, Chautauqua, Canton.

PUBLIC ACCOUNTANT—Examinations for certificates for certified public accountant will be held Jan. 25-27 and June 28-30, at New York, Albany, Syracuse and Buffalo. Candidates will be notified as to exact place.

MEDICAL—Examinations for license to practice medicine will be held Jan. 25-28, May 24-27, June 28-July 1, Sept. 27-30, at New York, Albany, Syracuse and Buffalo. Same places for optometry examinations, Jan., June and Sept.

Application should be made 10 days in advance and candidates will be notified as to exact place. Admission to the medical licensing examinations requires a fee of $25 and sworn evidence that the candidate is more than 21 years of age, of good moral character and has the general education required preliminary to receiving the M.D. degree in this State.

Examinations for license to practice dentistry and veterinary medicine will be held at the same places and on the same dates as the examinations for medical license, except that no dental examinations will be held in May.

Examinations for certificates as registered nurse will be held Jan. 25-27 and June 28-30, at New York, Albany, Syracuse and Buffalo. Candidates will be notified as to exact place.

PHARMACY—Examinations will be held on Jan. 25-27, May 24-26, June 28-30 and Sept. 27-29, at Albany, Buffalo and New York for both pharmacists and druggists.

FERRY COMPANIES IN NEW YORK.

ARCHIE'S FERRY—Daily trips (summer), bet. Sheepshead Bay and Roxbury. In winter 4 trips a day. Capt. Archie. Emmons and Ocean avs.

BERGEN BEACH AND CANARSIE FERRY CO.—Sunday trips bet. Bergen Beach and Canarsie during summer.

BKLN. AND RICHMOND FERRY—Between Bay Ridge av. (69th st.) to St. George, S. I. Leaves each side, week days, half hourly from 6 a.m. to 7:30 p.m.; Sundays, half hourly from 7 a.m. to 9:30 p.m.

McAVOY EXC. LINE—Canarsie to Rockaway Point, landing at Barren Island and Roxbury. All year service. Arthur McAvoy, Pres., 1457 E. 95th, Canarsie.

ROCKAWAY BEACH EXC. LINE (INC.)—P. H. Reid, Jr., Pres. Sheepshead Bay to Rockaway Pt., Breezy Pt., Roxbury and Bitz's, half hourly, 5.30 a.m. to 11 p.m., summer schedule.

10TH AND 23D ST. FERRY CO. (INC.)—W. E. Holmes, Supt. Ft. Greenpoint av. to E. 23, Mhtn. 6 a.m. to 10 p.m. every 15 min., 10 p.m. to 6 a.m. every 30 min. Su. and holidays, 8 a.m. to 10 p.m. every 15 min., 10 p.m. to 6 a.m. every 30 min.

UNION FERRY CO. OF N. Y. AND BKLN.—Thos. Read, Pres.; Geo. P. Hotaling, Vice Pres.; J. O'Brien, Asst. Sec. and Treas.; G. M. Bedell, Supt. Office, ft. Atlantic av., Bkln. Fulton Ferry—Fulton to Fulton, Mhtn. Hamilton Ferry—Hamilton av. to Whitehall, Mhtn. South Ferry—Atlantic av. to Whitehall, Mhtn.

Manhattan and Bronx.

ASTORIA CITY FERRY—From E. 92d.

BLACKWELL'S ISLAND—Ferry at ft. of E. 86th leaves at a quarter of and a quarter after the hour. Visiting days, Metropolitan Hosp., Thur. and Sun., 11 a.m. to 4 p.m.

COMMUNIPAW FERRIES—Operated by Central R. R. of N. J. From Liberty st. to Communipaw, Jersey City. Connects with C. R. R. of N. J., P. & R. R. R. From W. 23d to Communipaw.

DYCKMAN ST. AND ENGLEWOOD—From ft. Dyckman every 15 min. from 6 a.m. to 11 p.m. On Sat., Sun. and holidays every 10 min. from 6 a.m. to midnight.

ELLIS ISLAND—From Battery Park Barge Office, ft. Whitehall.

ENGLEWOOD CLIFFS (PALISADES INTERSTATE PARK)—See Dyckman St. and Englewood.

GOVERNOR'S ISL.—Govt. boat under direction of Quartermaster, Governor's Island. From Barge Office, Battery, 7:15, then every 30 min. to 11.45 p.m., then 1:00 a.m. Pass: Also from Middle Slip No. 6, South St. Terminal, from 6:45 a.m. to 6 p.m. daily, except Sun., on 30 min. schedule.

HART'S ISLAND—From E. 26th, 10 a.m., except Sun. and holidays. Visitors must obtain passes from Dept. of Correction, Room 2532, Municipal Bldg.

HOBOKEN FERRIES, D. L. & W.—Barclay, Christopher and W. 23d to Hoboken; W. 23d to 14th, Hoboken.

LONG ISLAND R. R.—E. 34th to L. I. City—Leave New York (E. 34th) week days, 5 a.m., then every 20 min. to 7:24 a.m., then every 12 m'n. to 6:48 p.m., then every 20 minutes to 10:30 p.m. Sun., 7:10 a.m. and every 20 min. to 9:50 p.m. Leave Long Island City week days, 4:50 a.m., then every 20 min. to 7:12 a.m., then every 12 min. to 6:30 p.m., then every 20 min. to 10.20 p.m. Sun., 7 a.m., then every 20 minutes to 9:40 p.m.

MHTN. STATE HOSPITAL—See Ward's Is.

MUNICIPAL FERRY CO.—Owned by city. From Whitehall, Mhtn., to St. George, Rich.; from 39th, Bkln., to Whitehall, Mhtn.

N. Y. CENTRAL—From ft. W. 42d and Cortlandt to West Shore R. R. station, Weehawken, N. J. Office, Weehawken, N. J.

N. Y. CITY CHILDREN'S HOSP., RANDALL'S IS.—Ferry from E. 26th and 125th St. Piers, 8 a.m. Pass from Dept. Public Welfare, Municipal Bldg.

NORTH BROTHER ISLAND—From E. 132d. By boat about every hour from 7:15 a.m. to 1:00 a.m. Jurisdiction Bd. of Health.

PAVONIA FERRY CO.—Chambers and W. 23d to Pavonia av., Jersey City, connecting with Erie R. R. F. D. Underwood, Pres.; G. Mihard, Sec.; W. J. Moody, Treas.; P. M. Coyne, Supt. Office, Jersey City.

PENN. R. R. FERRIES—From Cortlandt and Desbrosses to Montgomery, Jersey City. Connects with Penn. R. R.

RIKER'S ISLAND—Ft. 26th, at 10 a.m., except Sun. and holidays. Pass from Dept. of Correction, Municipal Bldg.

RIVERSIDE AND FT. LEE FERRY CO.—W. 130th to Edgewater, N. J.

STATUE OF LIBERTY—From Battery Pier to Bedloe's Island. Every day hourly from 8 a.m. to 7 p.m. Time from statue, 20 min. later.

WARD'S ISLAND, MANHATTAN STATE HOSPITAL—Visiting days, Sat., Sun. and Mon. Steamer leaves ft. E. 116th., 1 p.m., and half hourly after until 3 p.m. All other days steam ferry leaves same pier on half hourly trips on the hour and half hour from 6:30 a.m. to 12 midnight. Fare, 5c. Passes may be obtained from Dr. M. B. Heyman, Supt.

W. 23D ST. FERRY, MHTN., TO JERSEY CITY—Connects with C. R. R. of N. J., P. and R. Erie R. R. and D., L. and W. R. R. at Hoboken.

L. I. STEAMBOATS AND FERRIES.

Astoria and New York. Babylon, Oak Island and Oak Island Beach. Bay Shore and Ocean Beach. Bay Shore and Point o' Woods. Bay Shore and Saltaire. Canarsie and Bergen Beach. Canarsie and Rockaway Beach. Clason Pt. and College Pt. Clason Pt. and Whitestone. College Pt. and New York. Coney Island and New York. Freeport, Point Comfort and Point Lookout. Flushing and New York (fr. only). Fort Totten (U. S. Govt. boat). New London Route—Sag Harbor, Shelter Island Hgts., Greenport. Patchogue to Cherry Grove, Point o' Woods, Ocean Beach, Fire Island and Long Cove. Oyster Bay and Greenwich. Oyster Bay, New Rochelle and Rye. Port Jefferson and Bridgeport, Conn. Rockaway Beach and New York. Sea Gate and New York (see Eagle L. I. Motorcar Guide, issued each spring, for time schedules. Price 35 cts.).

STATE INSTITUTE OF APPLIED AGRICULTURE ON L. I., FARMINGDALE, N. Y.

The object of the State Inst. of Applied Agriculture is to open the road to successful farming to the boys and girls and men and women of N. Y. C., L. I., and the neighboring sections of the State.

The courses are designed with particular reference to the needs of people who have had little or no farm experience. Carefully planned practical work is combined with the study of the underlying principles of scientific agriculture. Classes continue throughout the 12 months of the year, and the students follow the complete cycle of agricultural production from the preparation of the ground to the harvesting of the crop. The course of study, while progressive, leading from one subject to another in logical order, is so arranged as to fit the student in a minimum amount of time to do actual farm work. The Institute Farm of 308 acres is the students' main laboratory.

The admission requirement for the regular 3-years' course is a year of high school training or its equivalent. Persons who have the equivalent of a grammar school education may be admitted to a preparatory course of one year, on completion of which they are eligible for the regular course. Tuition is free to residents of N. Y. State, and there are no laboratory fees.

Short courses especially adapted for school teachers are given during July and Aug. Special courses for farmers are given during Dec., Jan. and Feb. Special courses made up of subjects selected from the regular courses may be arranged to meet the needs and qualifications of mature people.

Director, A. A. Johnson. Trustees: W. M. Baldwin, Pres.; Garden City, L. I.; F. P. Nohowel, V.-Pres., Bay Shore, L. I.; W. W. Niles, Sec., 120 Mosholu P'kway, N. Y. C.; I. J. Long, Treas., Bay Shore, L. I.; J. W. Heineman, Hollis, L. I.; H. D. Nessler, 1 W. 85th, N. Y. C.; Mrs. Robert Low Pierrepont, 140 Columbia hgts., Bkln.; Miss Hilda Ward, Roslyn, L. I.; J. Angleman, New Brighton, S. I.

FEDERAL EMPLOYEES.

The number of Federal employees at the various years named has been as follows: 1816, 6,327; 1863, 49,212; 1881, 107,095; 1909, 208,215; 1920, 740,000.

LOCATION OF PIERS.

Manhattan.

NORTH RIVER.

No. Street.

- A—Battery pl.
- 1 (new) Battery pl.
- 1 (old) Battery pl.
- 1, 3 Battery pl.
- 1 Morris.
- 6, 7 Morris & Rector.
- 8 Rector.
- 9 Rector & Carlisle.
- 10 Albany.
- 11 Cedar.
- 13 Cortlandt & Dey.
- 14 Fulton.
- 15 Vesey & Barclay.
- 16 Barclay & Park pl.
- 17 Park pl.
- 18 Murray.
- 19 Warren.
- 20 Chambers.
- 21 Duane.
- 22 Jay.
- 23 Harrison.
- 24 Franklin.
- 25 No. Moore.
- 26 Beach.
- 27 Hubert.
- 28 Laight.
- 29 Vestry.
- 31 Watts.
- 32, 33, 34 Canal.
- 35 Spring.
- 36 Spring & Charlton.
- 37 Charlton.
- 38 King.
- 39 W. Houston.
- 40 Clarkson.
- 41 Leroy.
- 42 Morton.

No. Street.

- 43 Barrow (recreation).
- 44 Christopher.
- 45 W. 10th.
- 46 Charles.
- 47 Perry.
- 48 W. 11th.
- 49 Bank.
- 50 Bethune & W. 12th.
- 51 Jane.
- 52 Gansevoort.
- Gansevoort Market South.
- Gansevoort Market Middle.
- Gansevoort Market North.
- 53 Bloomfield.
- 54 W. 13th.
- 56 W. 14th.
- 57 W. 15th.
- 58 W. 16th.
- 59 W. 18th.
- 60 W. 19th.
- 61 W. 21st.
- 62 W. 22d.
- 63 W. 23d.
- 64 W. 24th.
- 65 W. 25th.
- 66 W. 26th.
- 67 W. 27th.
- 68 W. 28th.
- 69 W. 29th.
- 70 W. 30th.
- 71 W. 31st.
- 72 W. 32d.
- 73 W. 33d.
- 74 W. 34th.
- 75 W. 35th.
- 76 W. 36th.
- 77 W. 37th.
- 78 W. 38th.
- 79 W. 39th.
- 80 W. 40th.

No. Street.

- 81 W. 41st.
- 83 W. 43d.
- 84 W. 44th.
- 86 W. 46th.
- 87 W. 47th.
- 88 W. 48th.
- 89 W. 49th.
- 90 W. 50th. (recreation)
- 91 W. 51st.
- 92 W. 52d.
- 93 W. 53d.
- 94 W. 54th.
- 95 W. 55th.
- 96 W. 56th.
- 97 W. 57th.
- 98 W. 58th.
- 99 W. 59th.
- B W. 63d.
- D W. 64th.
- E W. 65th.
- F W. 67th.
- G W. 68th.
- I W. 70th.
- 79th St.
- 80th St.
- 95th St.
- 96th St.
- 97th St.
- 97th North (Naval Reserve).
- 129th St. (recreation).
- 131st St.
- 132d St.
- 133d St.
- 134th St.
- 135th St.
- 155th St.
- 156th St.
- 157th St.
- 158th St.

EAST RIVER.

No. Street.

- 4 Broad.
- 5, 6, 7, 8 Coenties Slip.
- 9 Coenties & Old Slip.
- 10 Old Slip.
- 11 Gouverneur la.
- 12, 13 Wall.
- 14 Maiden la.
- 15 Fletcher & Burling slip.
- 16 Burling slip.
- 17 Fulton.
- 18 Beekman.
- 19, 20 Peck slip.
- 21 Dover.
- 22 James slip.
- 25 Oliver.
- 26, 27 Catharine.
- 28 Catharine & Market.
- 29 Market.
- 30 Pike & Market (recreation).
- 31, 32 Pike.
- 33 Pike & Rutgers.
- 34 Rutgers.
- 35 Rutgers & Jefferson.
- 36 Jefferson.

No. Street.

- 37 Clinton.
- 38 Clinton & Montgomery.
- 39, 40 Montgomery.
- 41, 42 Gouverneur.
- 43 Gouverneur & Jackson.
- 44, 45 Jackson.
- 47 Delancey.
- 50 Rivington.
- 51 Rivington & Stanton.
- 52 Stanton.
- 53 Houston., So.
- 54 Houston, No.
- E. 3d St. (recreation).
- E. 4th St.
- E. 5th St.
- E. 6th St.
- E. 7th St.
- E. 8th St.
- E. 9th St.
- E. 10th St.
- E. 11th St.
- E. 12th St.
- E. 13th St.
- E. 18th St.
- E. 19th St.
- E. 20th St.
- E. 21st St.

No. Street.

- E. 22d St.
- E. 24th St. (recreation)
- E. 25th St.
- E. 26th St.
- E. 28th St.
- E. 29th St.
- E. 30th St.
- E. 31st St.
- E. 32d St.
- E. 33d St.
- E. 34th St.
- E. 35th St.
- E. 36th St.
- E. 37th St.
- E. 38th St.
- E. 39th St.
- E. 45th St.
- E. 46th St.
- E. 47th St.
- E. 49th St.
- E. 53d St.
- E. 60th St.
- E. 61st St.
- E. 62d St.
- E. 86th St.
- E. 90th St.
- E. 91st St.
- E. 94th St.
- E. 95th St.
- E. 96th St.
- E. 99th St.
- E. 100th St.

HARLEM RIVER.

Location.

- E. 102d St.
- E. 103d St.
- E. 104th St.
- E. 107th St.
- E. 108th St.
- E. 109th St.
- E. 110th St.

Location.

- E. 112th St. (recreation).
- E. 116th St.
- Bet. E. 116th & 117th St.
- E. 117th St.
- E. 118th St.

Location.

- E. 119th St.
- E. 120th St.
- Bet. E. 126th & 127th St.
- E. 128th St.
- E. 209th St.

Brooklyn.

Location.

- Bay Ridge av.
- 64th St.
- Army 4 59th.
- Army 3 60th.
- Army 2 61st.
- Army 1 62d.
- 57th St.
- Bush 1.
- Bush 2.
- Bush 3.
- Bush 4.
- Bush 5.
- Bush 6.
- Bush 7.
- Bush 8.
- 35th St.
- 33d St.
- 31st St.
- 30th St.
- 29th St.
- Erie Basin 1.
- Erie Basin 2.
- Pier 48.
- Pier 47.
- Pier 46.
- Pier 45.
- Pier 41.
- Pier 40.
- Pier 39.
- Pier 38.
- Pier 37.
- Pier 36.
- Pier 35.
- Pier 34.
- Pier 33.
- Pier 32.
- Pier 30.
- Pier 29.
- Pier 27.

Location.

- Pier 26.
- Pier 24.
- Pier 22.
- Pier 18.
- Pier 17.
- Pier 16.
- State Barge Canal Pier, Gowanus.
- Pier 15.
- Pier 12.
- Pier 11.
- Pier 10.
- Pier 9.
- Pier 8.
- Pier 7.
- Pier 6.
- Pier 5.
- Pier 4.
- Fulton St.
- Pier 3.
- Pier 2.
- Pier 1.
- Adams St.
- Jay St., So.
- Jay St., No.
- Jay St., Terminal.
- Bridge St.
- Gold St.
- Hudson Av.
- Wallabout 1
- Wallabout 2
- Wallabout 3
- Wallabout 4
- Wallabout 5
- S. 5th St.
- S. 3d St.
- S. 2d St.

Location.

- S. 1st St.
- N. 1st St.
- N. 2d St. (recreation)
- N. 3d St.
- N. 4th St.
- N. 5th St.
- Bet. N. 5th & 6th.
- N. 6th St.
- N. 7th St.
- N. 8th St.
- N. 9th St.
- Bet. N. 9th & 10th.
- N. 10th St.
- N. 11th St.
- Bet. N. 11th & 12th.
- Quay St.
- Oak St.
- Bet. Oak & Noble.
- Noble St.
- Milton St.
- Kent St.
- Java St.
- India St.
- Huron St.
- Green St.
- Freeman St.
- Eagle St.
- Bet. Eagle & Dupont.
- Bet. Dupont & Clay.
- Whale Creek.
- Flatbush av.

Queens.

- Pidgeon St.
- Flushing St.
- 6th St., L. I. C.
- 7th St., So. L. I. C.
- 7th St., No. L. I. C.
- 8th St., L. I. C.
- Mott av.
- Jamaica av.
- Whitestone Ldg.
- 3d St., L. I. C.
- 4th St., L. I. C.
- 5th St., L. I. C.
- 5th St., L. I. C., North

Bronx.

- Fordham rd., Harlem River.
- E. 132d, E. R.
- E. 136th, E. R.
- E. 138th, E. R.
- Tiffany, E. R.
- Main, City Isl.
- 4 Cabot.
- 3, 2 Cabot & Truxton.
- 1 Truxton.

Staten Island.

- Clifton.
- South St.
- Coal 3, 2, 1, St. George.
- B. & O. 8, 7, 6, 5, 4, 3, 2, 1, St. George.
- 1, 2, 3, 4, Tompkinsville.
- Canal St.
- 19, 20, 21, Stapleton.
- Rosebank.

Hoboken, Jersey City, &c.

Location and New York Ferry.

Am. Docks, adjoining Ferry, Tompkinsville, S.I.
Brooklyn E. D., Terminal, ft. Warren. Cort.
Campbell Stores, ft. 6th, Hoboken. Hoboken.
Clyde S. S. Co., ft. 11th, Hoboken. Hoboken.
Erie Long Docks, ft. Pavonia av., Jersey City; Chambers, W. 23d.
Holland-American Line, ft. 5th. Hoboken.
Lloyd-Sabaudo, ft. Grand, Jersey City.
National Docks, ft. Phillips. Communipaw and West 23d.
Scandinavian-American Line, 17th. Hoboken.
U. S. Army, 1st and Newark, Hoboken.
U. S. Army, ft. 2d, 3d, 4th. Hoboken.
Wilson Line, ft. 7th. Hoboken.

DOCKMASTERS' OFFICES.

Dist. 1, Ft. Watts, N. R.; 2, Ft. 46th, N. R.; 3, Ft. 52d, N. R.; 4, Ft. 129th, N. R.; 5, Ft. 157th, N. R.; 6, Pier 11, E. R.; 7, Pier 33, E. R.; 8, Ft. E. 22d, E. R.; 9, Ft. E. 62d, E. R.; 10, Ft. E. 100th, H. R.; 11, Ft. E. 125th, H. R.; 12, Ft. 184th, H. R. (Bronx side); 13, Mn'cp'l Ferry Term'l, Ft. 39th, Bkln.; 14, Ft. Bay Ridge av., Bkln.; 15, Pier 1, Wallabout Canal; 16, Ft. Jamaica av., Astoria; 8A, Ft. E. 22d, E. R.; 15A, Pier 1, Wallabout Canal; 16A, Rockaway Beach.

Alaska gets its name from "Al-ay-es-ka," a native Eskimo or Innuit word meaning "great country."

STEAMSHIP AND STEAMBOAT LINES, PRINCIPAL OFFICES AND SAILINGS.

The "*" denotes that the passenger service is discontinued during the winter season. ‡Panama Canal Routes. §Funnel colors.

[For special information about any line communicate with Eagle Information Bureau.]

Note—Unless otherwise stated, addresses of piers and offices are in Manhattan. Foreign sailing schedules are subject to change.

Albany Day Line—See Hudson River Line.

Albertina—See Merchants S. S. Co.

‡**Am. and Australian S. S. Line**—Office, Norton, Lilly & Co., 26 Beaver. Weekly for all ports in Australia. New Zealand via Panama Canal or Cape of Good Hope. **Fr. British flag.** §**Blue sq.**, white and red.

Am.-African Line—Office, Norton, Lilly & Co., 26 Beaver. Sailings for So. and E. Africa monthly. **Pass. and Fr. British flag.** §**Blue sq.**, red diamond.

‡**Am.-Asiatic S. S. Co.**—See Prince Line.

Am.-Indian S. S. Line—Office, Norton, Lilly & Co., 26 Beaver. **Sailings** monthly for Mediterranean, Gulf of Aden, India and Red Sea ports. Pass. and Fr. British flag. §Blue with white diamonds E. & B.

American Line—Pier 62, N. R. Office, 9 B'way. Sat., Plymouth, Cherbourg, Southampton, Hamburg. Pass. and Fr.; 6 steamers. Amer. flag. §Black, white band, black top.

Am.-Manchurian S. S. Line—Office, Norton, Lilly & Co., 26 Beaver. Sailings every 3 weeks to Aden, Straits Settlements, Philippines, China and Japan. **Fr. British flag.** §**Blue and white A. & M.**

Am.-Mediterranean-Levant Line—Office, Norton, Lilly & Co., 26 Beaver. To and from New York, Phila., **Levant. Calling en route at ports in the Mediterranean, Levant and Black Sea, as inducements offer. Pass. and Fr. British flag.** §Red and white, A. L. in sq.

Anchor Line—Pier 64, N. R., ft. W. 24th. Office, 24 State. **For Glasgow and Mediterranean. Fr. and Pass.**

Atlantic Transport Line—Pier 58, N. R., ft. W. 16th. Office, 9 B'way. Sat. for London direct. Pass. and fr.; 13 steamers. British and American flag. §**Red, with black top.**

‡**Barber Lines**—Piers 36, 37 and 38, Atlantic Basin, Bkln. Barber Steamship Lines, Inc., 17 Battery pl. To China and Japan, via Red Sea ports and Panama Canal, sailing monthly, calling at Aden, Singapore, Manila, Hong Kong, Shanghai, Kobe and Yokohama; to Havre and Dunkirk fortnightly; to Argentine, Uruguay, every 10 days, calling at Montevideo, Buenos Ayres, Rosario and Bahia Blanca. Agents for Union Clan Line to South and East Africa to Australia sailing monthly for Brisbane, Sydney, Melbourne, Adelaide and New Zealand.

Bay State Line—Pier 19, E. R., Peck Slip. For Providence, daily and Sun., Nov. 1-Mar. 31, 5 p.m.; Apr. 1-Oct. 31, 5:30 p.m. Fr. and Pass.

Bayonne Trans. Co.—Pier 50, N. R., ft. Bethune st. Office, 100 William. Daily except Sun., for Bayonne, N. J. Fr. §Red B. T. Co., on white.

*Bear Mt. Line—Leaves from Battery for Bear Mountain on Hudson, daily and Sun. Battery, 8 a.m.; W. 132d, 9.30 a.m. Office, 17 State.

Belgian Line (Lloyd Royal Belge)—141 Broadway. Pier 13, N. R. Antwerp, Havre, Rouen. Semi-monthly. §White and red band.

Ben Franklin Trans. Co.—Ft. Franklin. Office, at pier. Daily N. Y. for Yonkers, except Sun., 2 and 5 p.m. From Yonkers to Pier 24 N. R., 8 a.m. and 6 p.m. Fr. only.

Booth S. S. Co., Ltd.—17 Battery pl. Loading berth, Pier 4, Martin's Stores, Bkln.; 1 and 2 sailings in alternate months, to Para and to Manaos, and one monthly to Maranham and Ceara and Parnahyba, Brazil, and Iquitos, Peru, Maccio, Pernambuco, Cabedello and Natal.

Bridgeport Line—Pier 28, E. R., ft. of Catharine. Weekdays only, 3 p.m.; 22d st, 3:15 p.m., for Bridgeport, Conn. Fare, 95c. Fr. and Pass.

Bristol City Line—Ft. W. 29th. Office, 25 Whitehall. Weekly sailings for Bristol, Eng.; 10 steamers. British flag. §Black, white band, blue star in center.

*Catskill Evening Lines—Ft. Christopher, N. R., Pier 43. Office at pier. Mon., Wed., Fri. at 5:30 p.m. for Athens, Catskill, Hudson, Stockport, Coxsackie. Fr. only. Also for stations on Albany Southern R. R., Boston-Albany R. R., N. Y. C. R. R., Rutland R. R.

***Central-Hudson Steamboat Co.—Pier 24, N. R., ft. Franklin. Office, at pier. Leave daily except Sunday for Hudson River landings as far as Kingston. Sunday landings to Newburgh only.**

***Central R. R. of N. J. Boats—Pier 10, N. R., ft. Cedar, and Pier 81, N. R., ft. W. 42d. Office, 143 Liberty. Daily for Atlantic Highlands,** making connections for points south. During spring and fall 3 trips are made each way weekdays and 2 trips on Sunday. During summer 6 trips are made each way weekdays and 5 trips on Sun. **Pass.; 3 boats. §Red disk.**

Central Vermont Ry. Co. Steamers leave New Pier 29, E. R., daily. Receiving stations at Bkln., Jay st., Bush Termls. Offices at piers and 82 Wall. Daily for New England, Canadian and Western States Points. Fr.

Clyde Line—Pier 36, N. R., ft. Spring. Offices, Pier 36, N. R., and 489 5th av. **Sails Tues., Thurs. and Sat. at 12.00 for Charleston, S. C., and Jacksonville, Fla. Semi-monthly, Santo Domingo.**

Colonial Line—Pier 39, N. R., ft. W. Houston. Daily, 5:30 P.M. (summer), 5 P.M. (winter) for Providence.

Commonwealth Dominion, Ltd., Cunard Australasian Service—Pier 10, Robert Stores, Bkln. Fremantle, Adelaide, Melbourne, Sydney, Brisbane, Auckland, Wellington, Lyttleton and Dunedin. §Red, black top.

Compagnie Generale Transatlantique Line—See French Line.

Compania Trasatlantica (Spanish Royal Mail Line) Pier 8, E. R. For Havana, Vera Cruz, Cadiz and Barcelona, and northern Spanish ports once a month. Pass. and fr. Spanish flag.

Cosulich Line (Societa Triestina di Navy)—17 Battery pl. Pier 7. Bush Term., Bklyn. Naples, Palermo. Patras, Dubrovnik, Fiume, Trieste and Venice. Wed. and St. §Black, red, white and red.

Cunard Line—Piers 53, 54, 56 and 71, W. 14th. Office, 21-24 State. **Services from N. Y., Boston, Philadelphia, Baltimore, Portland and Canadian ports to Liverpool, London, Bristol, Southampton, Plymouth, Cherbourg, Havre, Antwerp, Rotterdam, Hamburg and Danzig.** Service to Mediterraean and Levant ports. Fr. and pass. British flag. §Red, black bands, black top.

C. W. Davis Line—New Pier 30, E. R., ft. Market and Pike. Office, on pier. For New Rochelle, Mamaroneck. Fr. only. Daily, 11 a.m., Sundays and Mondays excepted. §Buff.

Eastern S. S. Corporation—See Metropolitan S. S. Line and Maine S. S. Line.

Fabre Lines—Pier ft. 31st, Bkln. Office, 17 State. **Sails weekly for Azores, Lisbon, Barcelona and Algiers, Palermo, Naples, Nice and Marseilles. Pass. and fr. French flag. §Blue,** white and red.

Fall River Line—Pier 14, N. R., ft. Fulton. Oct. 1 to May, daily 5 p.m., then daily 5:30 p.m. **for Newport and Fall River. Fr. Office on pier.**

France and Canada S. S. Corp.—120 B'way.

French Line (Compagnie Generale Transatlantique)—Pier 57, ft. 15th, N. R., pass. steamers. and Pier 84, ft. W. 44th, for cargo steamers. Office, 19 State. Weekly sailings for Havre and Bordeaux. Fr. and pass. Also from France to West Indies, Mexico, Central Amer., Intercolonial, Mediterranean and Coastwise lines. §Red with black top band.

Funch, Edye Co.—Various loading termls. Office, 8-10 Bridge. For So. African ports. Fr. only, steamers monthly.

Furness Bermuda Line—34 Whitehall. Pier 95, N. R. Sailings Wednesdays and Saturdays. §Black, red, black.

Gans Steamship Line—Erie Basin, Bkln. Office, 12 B'way. For Spanish and Portuguese ports. §Blue band, white G.

Grace Line—From Pier 33, Atlantic Terml., Bkln, bi-weekly for west coast of So. America. W. R. Grace & Co., 104 Pearl. §Green, with black top and white band.

Greek Line—Office 20 Pearl. N. Y. and Piraeus.

***Hartford Line—Pier 20, E. R., Peck Slip. Office on pier, and Pier 19, E. R.; daily except Sun., at 5 p.m., for Hartford and Connecticut river landings. Fr. and pass.; 2 boats.**

Holland-Amer. Line—Ft. 5th, Hoboken, N. J. Office, 24 State st. Sailings upon application for Rotterdam, via Plymouth and Boulogne. Fr. and pass. Dutch flag. §Buff with green, white and green bands.

Houston Line—R. P. Houston & Co. Office, Room 1124, 17 Battery pl. **Sails from Pier 3, Erie** Basin, Bkln., every 2 weeks for **Montevideo,**

STEAMSHIP AND STEAMBOAT LINES—*Continued.*

Buenos Ayres, La Plata, Rosario and upriver ports. Regular sailings to So. and E. African ports. Mail and fr. British flag. §Red, black top.

*Hudson Nav. Co.—Pier 32, N. R., ft. Canal. Office on pier. Daily at 6 p.m.; W. 132d, 6:30 p.m. For Albany and Troy. Fr. and pass.; 7 boats.

*Hudson River Day Line—Ft. Desbrosses, W. 42d and W. 129th, N. R. Office, Desbrosses st. pier. Daily for Albany and intermediate landings; 4 boats. §Buff.

*Iron S. B. Co.—Pier 1 (new), N. R., and W. 129th. Office, 17 Battery pl. Daily for Coney Island and Rockaway Beach, during period May 30 to Labor Day.

Isthmian S. S. Lines—39 Cortlandt. Regular sailings, via Panama Canal, to San Francisco, Seattle, Vancouver (B. C.), etc. Loading berth, Pier ft. 29th, Bkln.

Kerr S. S. Co.—Pier ft. 57th, Bkln. Office 17 Battery pl., Mhtn. Fr. to Danzig and Hamburg.

Joy Line—Now Bay State Line.

Kingston Line—See Central Hudson S. B. Co.

Lamport & Holt Line—Piers 7 & 8, Bkln., and 14 & 15, Hoboken. Office, 42 B'way, N. Y. Sails for Brazil, Uruguay and Argentina. Fr. and pass. Fr. to Manchester, England, every 2 weeks. British flag. §Blue, with white band and black top.

La Veloce Italian Line—Pier 97, ft. W. 57th. Office, 1 State. Sailings from New York to Naples and Genoa. Pass. and fr. Italian flag.

Lloyd Brazileiro—Pier 5, Bush Docks, Bkln. Office, 44 Whitehall. Regular service bet. N. Y. and Brazilian ports. Pass. and fr. §White, buff and white.

Lloyd Italiano Societa Di Navigazione.—Merged with Navigazione Generale Italiano.

Lloyd Royal Belge—See Belgian Line.

Lloyd-Sabaudo—Pier 95, N. R., ft. W. 55th. Office, 34 Whitehall. To Naples, Genoa, Palermo.

*Lower Hudson Steamboat Co.—Freight only. Ft. Franklin. Daily for Ossining, Tarrytown, Irvington, Croton. Leave Franklin, Pier 24, N. R., 1 p.m.

Mallory Line—Pier 38, N. R. Offices, Pier 36, N. R., and 489 Fifth ave., N. Y. For Galveston. Fr. and pass.

Metropolitan S. S. Line, owned by Eastern S. S. Lines, Inc.—Operates line bet. N. Y. and Boston. Pier 18, N. R., ft. of Murray. Offices at pier and Boston. Daily at 5 p.m. Pass. and exp. Fr. Tues., Thurs. and Sat.

Middlesex Trans. Co.—Pier 45, E. R. Daily at 3 p.m., except Sun. New Brunswick, N. J. Fr. §Buff, with black top.

*Montauk S. B. Co.—Pier E. 34th.

Morgan Line—See Southern Pacific Co.

*Morton Line—Ft. Bloomfield, at 11:30 a.m., for Verplank and Peekskill. Fr.

Munson S. S. Line—Pier 9 and 10, E. R. Office 82 Beaver. For Cuban ports. Sailings every week for fr. Pass. service fortnightly. S. American passenger service, Brazil, Uruguay, Argentine, frequent sailings. §Blue, with white strip and black top.

*Murray's Line—New Pier 5, E. R. Office, 33 Coenties Slip. Albany and Troy. Fr. only. 5 boats.

Navigazione Generale Italiana. Office, 1 State. Pier 97, ft. W. 57th. New York to Naples and Genoa. Pass. and Fr. Italian flag.

Nelson Lines—Sanderson & Son, Gen. Agts., 26 Broadway, phone Broad 2360.

*New Bedford Line—Ft. Houston, Pier 40, N. R. Pass. service during summer only. Fr. service throughout year.

Newburgh Line—See Central Hudson S. B. Co.

New Haven Line—Pier 28, E. R., ft. Catharine. Fr. only. Special Sun. excursions during summer months.

New London Line—Pier 40, N. R., ft. Houston. Office, on pier. Week days, 5:30 p.m.; ft. E. 22d, 6 p.m., for New London. Fr. and pass.

N. Y. and Cuba Mail S. S. Co.—Piers 13 and 14, E. R. Genl. office, ft. of Wall. Sat. to Havana, Cuba; Progreso, Vera Cruz and Tampico, Mexico. Fr. and pass. Amer. flag. §Two white bands.

N. Y. and L. B. S. Co.—See Patten Line.

N. Y. and N. J. Steamboat Co.—Pier 32, E. R. Daily, except Sun. and holidays, 10 a.m., for Perth Amboy and landings on Staten Island Sound and Kill von Kull. Fr. only. Daily except Sun. and holidays, 2 p.m., for Perth Amboy, Keyport. Fr. only. Keyport stops discontinued during winter.

N. Y. and Porto Rico S. S. Co.—Pier 35, Atlantic Basin, Bkln. Office, 11 B'way. Sat., 12 noon for Porto Rican ports. U. S. mails. Fr. and pass.; 9 boats. Amer. flag. §Yellow band with white strip.

‡N. Y. and So. Amer. Line—From ft. 29th, Bkln. Office, 11 B'way. Direct fr. service thru Panama Canal to Chile, Peru and west coast So. American countries. §Yellow, blue and red band with white diamonds.

N. Y. and W. India Line—See Quebec S. S. Co.

No. and E. River S. B. Co.—See Stamford Line.

North River S. B. Co.—See Raleigh.

Norton Line—Office, Norton, Lilly & Co., 26 Beaver. Sailings every three weeks for Montevideo, Uruguay, Buenos Ayres, Argentina and Rosario. So. Amer. ports. Pass. and fr. Amer. flag.

Norwegian-Amer. Line — Ft. of 30th, Bkln. Office, 8-10 Bridge, N. Y. Sailings Bergen, Stavanger, Kristiansand and Kristiania. Pass. and fr.

Norwich Line—See New London Line.

Ocean Steamship Co., Ltd.; The China Mutual Steam Navigation Co., Ltd.—Pier 3, Bush Terml., ft. 47th, Bkln. Office, 8-10 Bridge, Mhtn. Two services, 1 via Suez Canal to Aden, Singapore, Manila and Hong Kong, sailing twice each month; and 1 via Panama Canal to Kobe, Yokohama and Shanghai, sailings twice each month. Fr. §Blue.

Ocean S. S. Co. of Savannah (Savannah Line) —Pier 35, N. R., ft. Spring. Office at pier. Call Spring 3595 for sailings for Savannah, Ga. Pass. and fr.

Pacific Steam Navigation Co., Sanderson & Son, Gen. Agts., 26 B'way, phone Broad 2360.

‡Panama R. R. S. S. Line—Pier 67, ft. W. 27th, N. R. Office, 24 State. For Cristobal, Canal Zone. Pass. and fr. 16 boats. Amer. flag. §White band.

*Patten Line—Gansevoort Market Pier, 2 p.m.; Battery, 2:35 p.m. Daily (except Sunday) for Long Branch, N. J., and intermediate points. Sundays and holidays, Battery, 8:30 and 9:30 a.m.

Phelps Line—Pier 7, ft. 41st, Bkln. Office, 17 Battery pl., Mhtn. To Naples, Patras, Dubrovnik, Trieste.

*Peoples Line — Pier 32, N. R., ft. Canal, 6 p.m. and 132d, 6:30 p.m. Office, on piers. Daily for Albany. Pass. and fr. 4 steamers.

Phoenix Line—(Ellerman's) British flag. Freight service, New York-Antwerp, Pier 7th st., Hoboken, N. J. Agents, Sanderson & Son, 26 B'way.

Port Chester Trans. Co.—Pier 30, E. R., ft. of Market. Mon., Wed., Fri., 12 noon. Port Chester, N. Y. Fr. only.

Portland Line—See Maine S. S. Co.

Poughkeepsie Line—See Central Hudson S. B. Co.

Prince Line—Pier 4, Bush Docks, ft. 45th, Bkln. Furness, Withy Co., Ltd., Gen. Agts., Furness House, Whitehall, N. Y. Regular sailings for Brazil, the River Plate, So. African ports, China, Japan and Philippines. Also regular sailings between N. Y. and Straits Settlements, Manila, China and Japan, via Panama and otherwise.

*Providence Line—Pier 14 (new), N. R., ft. Fulton. Office on pier. Fr. only. Service operated all year.

Quebec S. S. Co.—Pier 47, N. R. Office, 34 Whitehall. Sails every 2 weeks for W. Indies. Fr. and pass. British flag. §Red top.

*Raleigh—Pier 24, ft. Franklin. Daily except Sun., 2 p.m.; Sat., 1 p.m., for Hastings, Dobbs Ferry, Nyack and Haverstraw. Fr. only.

Red Cross Line—Pier ft. Java, Greenpoint, Bkln. Office, 17 Battery pl., Mhtn. Weekly sailings for Halifax, N. S., and St. John's, N. F., during summer; every 18 days during winter. Fr. and pass.; 1 boat. §White field, red cross.

Red "D" Line—Pier 11, Bkln. Office, 82 Wall. Every other Wed. for Mayaguez, La Guayra, Curacao and Maracaibo; every other Wed. for San Juan, Curacao, La Guayra and Porto Cabello. Pass. and fr. Amer. flag. §Buff, with black top.

Red Star Line—Pier 61, N. R. Office, 9 B'way. For Southampton and Antwerp. Pass. and fr. Amer. and British flags. §Black, with white bands.

Royal Dutch West India Mail—Pier 8, ft. 39th, Bkln. Fr. and pass. Office, 10 Bridge. For Hayti, Curacao, Venezuela, Trinidad, Paramaribo and Amsterdam. Dutch flag.

Royal Mail Steam Packet Co., Sanderson & Son, Gen. Agts., 26 B'way, phone 2360.

Russian-Amer. Line—Office, 55 B'way.

Sandy Hook Route—See Central R. R. of N. J.

STEAMSHIP AND STEAMBOAT LINES—*Continued.*

*Saugerties and N. Y. S. B. Co.—Outer end Pier 43, N. R., ft. Christopher. Office, Saugerties, N. Y. Daily, except Sun., at 6 p.m.; (Sats., July and Aug., 1 p.m.) for Saugerties, Tivoli, Rhinecliff, Barrytown, Ulster Landing and Hyde Park. Lv. Saugerties daily, except Sat., at 6 p.m.

Savannah S. S. Line—See Ocean S. S. Co.

Scandinavian-Amer. Line—Ft. 17th, Hoboken. Pass. office, 1 B'way. Fr. office, 8 Bridge. Christiansand, Christiana and Copenhagen. Pass. and fr. Danish flag. §Black, red, black.

Sea Bird—See Merchants S. B. Co.

Seaboard and Gulf S. S. Co.—Pier 32 E. R. Office, on pier. Steamer service between Atlantic Coast ports, Gulf of Mexico, West Indies (as cargo offers.) Tramp steamers everywhere. Proposed service between U. S., Gulf, Central and South Amer. Fr. only.

*Sea Gate Boat, Battery to Sea Gate (private).

*Sightseeing Yachts, Tourist, H. C. Caswell and Halcyon—From Battery around Manhattan Island, 10:30 a.m., 2:30 p.m. Down Bay to Sandy Hook and Ocean, 1:30 p.m. from Battery Park Pier.

Southern Pacific S. S. Line—Pier 48, N. R., ft. W. 11th. Office, Pier 49, N. R., and 165 B'way. Weekly sailings for New Orleans. Pass. and fr. Three sailings weekly for Galveston, fr. only.

Spanish Royal Mail Line—See Campania Transatlantica.

Stamford Line—Pier 30, E. R., ft. Market. Daily, 10:30 a.m., except Sun. and holidays for Stamford. Fr.

Starin New Haven Line—Pier 18, N. R. Sailings week days at 7 p.m., for N. H. Fr. only.

Steamer Squantum—Battery. Daily hourly from 9 a.m. to 7 p.m. for Liberty Island.

Steele S. S. Line—50 Broad, N. Y. C. Sailings from New Orleans to Manchester, Bremen, Havre, Dunkirk, Bordeaux and St. Nazaire. From Galveston to Liverpool. From Texas City to Bremen, Hamburg, Havre, Dunkirk, Bordeaux, St. Nazaire.

Swedish-American Line—Pier ft. W. 55th. To Gothanburg direct. Office, 24 State.

Thingvalla Line—See Scandinavian-Amer.

Transatlantica Italiana—5 State and Pier 25, N. R. To Naples and Genoa every ten days.

Transoceanica S. S. Co.—Piers 96 and 97, N. R. Office, 17 Battery pl. Regular service to Genoa, Naples, Palermo and Messina. Pass. and. fr Italian flag. §Yellow, with two black bands.

Trinidad Line—Pier 24, Bkln. Office, 29 B'way. Every fortnight, Grenada, Trinidad and Demerara, making connections for Tobago, Ciudad, Bolivar and upper Orinoco River points. Fr. and pass.; 3 steamers. British flag. §Red, with black top.

Troy Line—See Hudson Nav. Co. Line.

The Union-Castle Mail Steamship Co., Ltd.—Sanderson & Son, Passenger Agts., 26 B'way.

Union Clan Line—See Barber Lines.

‡United Fruit Co. Steamship Service. Office, 17 Battery pl. Between N. Y. and Havana, Cuba; Kingston, Jamaica, Cristobal, C. Z.; Bocas del Toro, Panama; Cartagena, Pto. Colombia and Santa Marta, Colombia; Pto. Limon, Costa Rica. Between New Orleans, Havana, Cuba; Cristobal, C. Z.; Bocas del Toro, Panama; Pto. Barrios, Guatemala; Tela, Honduras; Belize, British Honduras. Connections can be made at Cristobal for all West coasts, ports of Central and South America. Frequent service maintained from N. Y. and New Orleans to above ports.

U. S. and A. Lines, Inc., Pier 26, Bkln. Office. 8-10 Bridge, Mhtn. Steamer service for Australian and New Zealand ports, also So. Africa, So. America, Asiatic ports. Fr. only. §Red, white and blue bands.

U. S. and Pacific Line—See Grace Line.

U. S. Govt. Boat—Ft. Whitehall. Frequent trips daily to Governor's Island. Ft. Slocum boat leaves Pier 12, E. R., 1:00 p.m. Tu., Th. and Sat. Boats to Ft. Hancock leave daily. Two trips weekly to Ft. Hamilton, Ft. Wadsworth and Sandy Hook.

U. S. Mail S. S. Co.—Pass. office, 45 B'way; fr. office, 120 B'way.

Ward Line—See New York and Cuba Mail S.S. Co.

West Coast Line—Pier 45, ft. Conover, Bkln. Agents, Wessel, Duval & Co., 25 Broad. Sails monthly for Chile and Peru. Fr. 10 to 12 boats. American and Norwegian flags. §White H in red band.

West India Steamship Co.—Office, 26 Beaver. Mexico, Cuba and West Indies, So. America.

White Star Line—Piers 59 and 60, N. R. Office. 9 B'way. Liverpool, Cherbourg, Southampton, Mediterranean ports, Egypt. Pass. and fr.; 11 boats. British flag. §Buff, with black top.

TRANSATLANTIC PASSENGER STEAMERS FROM NEW YORK.

Steamships.	First Trip.	Gross Ton'ge.	Indic. H. P.	Lgth.	†Speed.
AMERICAN LINE.					
New York	1888	10,080	16,000	576	19
Philadelphia	1889	10,233	16,800	576	19
St. Louis	1895	10,231	17,500	554	19
St. Paul	1895	10,231	17,000	554	19
Leviathan§	1914	54,300	80,000	950	24
CUNARD LINE (a).					
Caronia	1905	19,687	20,000	650	19
Pannonia	1904	9,851	......	486	14
Saxonia	1900	14,270	10,400	580	15
Carmania	1905	19,524	20,000	650	19
Mauretania (b)	1907	31,937	70,000	790	26
Aquitania (c)	1914	47,000	60,000	868	24
Royal George	1907	11,146	14,500	526	19½
Imperator	1913	52,000	62,000	919	22⅝
Scythia	1920	21,000	13,000	600	16
K. A. Victoria	1905	25,000	......	700	..
FABRE LINE.					
Roma	1902	5,291	6,000	426	16
Britannia	1903	9,500	6,000	426	16
Madonna	1905	5,533	6,200	450	16½
Venezia	1907	6,827	7,200	460	16½
Canada	1912	9,654	10,000	500	17½
Patria	1914	11,885	12,000	530	18½
Providence (Bldg.)	....	17,000	18,000	540	19
FRENCH LINE (e).					
La Savoie	1901	13,410	22,000	580	20
La Touraine	1890	8,429	12,000	536	18
La Lorraine	1899	11,372	12,000	580	20
Lafayette	1915	12,000	14,800	690	20
Niagara	1907	9,614	7,300	484	16
Chicago	1908	14,150	9,600	520	16
France	1912	24,839	47,000	732	23½
Rochambeau	1911	17,417	13,000	580	18
Paris (launched)	1916	......	45,000	639	23
HOLLAND-AMERICA LINE. (Netherlands-American Steam Navigation Co.)					
Ryndam	1902	12,527	7,500	560	15½
Noordam	1902	12,531	7,500	560	15½
New Amsterdam	1906	17,250	10,500	615	16½
Rotterdam	1908	24,149	15,000	668	17
RED STAR LINE.					
Finland	1902	12,241	11,300	580	15
Lapland	1908	18,694	16,000	620	17
Belgic	1914	26,500	.....	670	..
Kroonland	1902	12,241	11,300	580	15
Zeeland	1901	12,100	11,300	580	15
ATLANTIC TRANSPORT LINE.					
Minnekahda	1918	17,221	......	646	15
NORWEGIAN-AMERICAN LINE.					
Bergensfjord	1913	10,709	9,400	530	17½
Stavangerfjord	1918	12,978	10,400	552	17½
SCANDINAVIAN-AMERICAN LINE.					
Oscar II	1901	10,000	8,000	515	16
Hellig Olav	1902	10,000	8,000	515	16
United States	1903	10,000	8,000	515	16
Frederik VIII	1914	12,000	10,000	542	17
WHITE STAR LINE (d).					
Celtic	1901	20,904	15,000	697	15
Canopic	1900	12,096	8,000	578	13
Cretic	1902	13,518	7,300	601	13
Cedric	1903	21,035	15,000	697	15
Baltic	1904	23,876	13,300	726	15
Adriatic	1907	24,541	17,000	726	17
Megantic	1909	14,878	11,000	565	18
Olympic	1911	46,359	46,000	882	22

†Average speed per hour in knots or nautical miles (6,085 ft.). (a) Lusitania of Cunard Line, which was torpedoed off Irish coast on May 7, 1915, held record from Queenstown to N. Y. (1909), 4d., 11h., 42m.; N. Y. to Queenstown (1911), 4d., 15h., 50m. (b) N. Y. to Queenstown (1909), 4d., 13h., 41m.; Queenstown to N. Y. (1910), 4d., 10h., 41m. (c) On maiden trip from Liverpool to N. Y., 5d., 17h., 43m., best day's run, 602 knots. (d) Arabic of White Star Line torpedoed off Irish coast on Aug. 19, 1915, and sunk. Celtic torpedoed in March, 1918, off Irish coast. (e) La Provence of this line sunk on Feb. 26, '16, in Mediterranean. (a) Transylvania of this line torpedoed May 4, 1917, in Mediterranean. Tuscania torpedoed, Feb. 6, 1918. §Awarded to this line by Allied Peace Council.

ELECTRIC ROADS IN NEW YORK CITY.

BROOKLYN.

The surface and elevated lines in Brooklyn are controlled by the following companies:

BROOKLYN RAPID TRANSIT SYSTEM—In Dec., 1918, went into the hands of a receiver. L. M. Garrison, receiver. Controls Bkln. Heights R. R. Co.; controls New York Consolidated R. R. Co. (formed by merger of Bkln. Union Elevated R. R. Co., Sea Beach Ry. Co. and Canarsie R. R. Co.), John H. Hallock, Pres.; South Bkln. Ry Co., A. R. Piper, Pres. (lessee of Prospect Park & Coney Island R. R., Ralph Peters, Pres.); Nassau Electric R. R. Co., T. S. Williams, Pres.; Bklyn., Queens Co. & Suburban R. R. Co., C. D. Meneely, V.-Pres.; Coney Island & Gravesend Ry. Co., H. C. Duval, Pres., and Coney Island & Bkln. R. R. Co., T. S. Williams, Pres., which are operated independently.

Executive Officers of Bkln. Rapid Transit Co.—Col. Timothy S. Williams, Pres.; C. D. Meneely, V.-Pres., M. O. B. & Treas.; J. H. Bennington, Sec.; Geo. D. Yeomans, Gen. Counsel. Offices, 85 Clinton.

Operating Staff of Constituent Companies—W. S. Menden, Gen. Mgr. for the Receiver; A. R. Piper, Asst. Gen. Mgr.; W. Seibert, Supt. of Surface Trans.; J. E. Eagan, Supt. of Trans.; C. L. Crobbs, Chief Eng. Way and Structure; W. G. Gove, Supt. of Equipment; A. R. Piper, Gen. Fr. Agent; C. E. Roehl, Elec. Eng.; I. Isaacsen, Gen. Claim Agent; L. Van Cott, Purch. Agent.

Accounting Dept.—Howard Abel, Comp.

BROOKLYN CITY R. R. CO.—On Oct. 19, 1919, this co. took over for operation its lines formerly leased to Bkln. Heights R. R. Co.—Frank Lyman Pres.; H. F. Noyes, V.-Pres.; H. H. Porter, V.-Pres. and Gen. Mgr.; S. B. Olney, Sec.; C. E. Morgan, Asst. to Gen. Mgr.; G. W. Jones, Treas.; E. H. Reed, Auditor; Wm. Siebert, Supt. of Trans. Office, 168 Montague.

*BUSH TERMINAL R. R.—Office, ft. 48th, I. T. Bush, Pres.; R. G. Simonds, Vice-Pres.; P. L. Gerhardt, Traffic Mgr.; R. S. Williams, Sec.; J. A. Heinrich, Treas.; G. F. Kivilin, Purch. Agent.

CONEY ISLAND AND BROOKLYN R. R. CO.—Office, 85 Clinton. T. S. Williams, Pres.; C. D. Meneely, Vice Pres. and Treas.; J. H. Bennington, Sec.

*MANHATTAN BRIDGE 3-CENT LINE—Office, 333 Gold. Frederick W. Rowe, Pres.; E. T. Horwill, Treas.; Walter Hammitt, Sec.; Arthur Porter, Supt.

NEW YORK MUNICIPAL RAILWAY CORPORATION, organized to construct and operate the B. R. T.'s share of the enlarged rapid transit system of the city, including the new B'way subway in Mhtn., with the other new routes and extensions allotted to the company, and to operate the 4th av. subway in Bkln. Office, 85 Clinton. N. F. Brady, Ch. of Bd.; Col. T. S. Williams, Pres.; C. D. Meneely, V.-Pres. and Treas.; J. H. Harding, Vice-Pres.; H. R. Potts, Asst. Sec.

*VAN BRUNT ST. AND ERIE BASIN R. R. CO.—Office, 264 Van Brunt. John F. Murphy, Pres.; D. W. Sullivan, V.-Pres.; Wyllys Terry, Sec. and Treas.

Surface Lines.

AVENUE C—From Flatbush and Ave. C to Coney Island av., via Ave. C.

BERGEN ST.—From Woodhaven, via Liberty av., E. New York av., St. Johns pl., Buffalo av., Bergen, Boerum pl., Adams, Sands, to Park Row and to Flatbush-Atlantic subway.

BERGEN BEACH SHUTTLE — From Bergen Beach, via E. 76th, Ave. U, Island av., Ave. N., E. 49th.

BROADWAY—From Delancey, via Williamsburg Bridge, via B'way, Fulton, Crescent, to Cypress Hills.

BROADWAY FERRY SHUTTLE—From Bridge Plaza to B'way Ferry only, via B'way.

BROOKLYN BRIDGE LOCAL—From Park Row to Sands, via Bkln. Bridge.

*BUSH TERMINAL LINE—From 39th St. Ferry to 1st av., through private property to Pier 1, ft. 51st. From 28th on 2d av. to 41st, through to 1st av., then on 1st av. to 63d.

BUSHWICK AV. — From Myrtle and Wyckoff, via Myrtle av., Bushwick av., Meserole, S. 4th, Havemeyer, Bridge Plaza, Williamsburg Bridge, to Delancey.

CALVARY CEMETERY—From Greenpoint Ferry, via Greenpoint av., to Calvary Cemetery.

CHURCH AV.—Rockaway av. and New Lots rd., via New Lots rd., E. B'way, Church av., 37th, 13th av., 39th, 2d av. and private property to ferry.

CONEY ISLAND, NORTON'S POINT—From West End Term. (C. I.), to Norton's Point, via N. Y. and C. I. branch of So. B. Ry. Co.

COURT ST.—Bush st. depot to Park Row, via Hamilton av., Court, Fulton, to Park Row.

CROSSTOWN—From Erie Basin, via Richards, Woodhull, Columbia, Atlantic av., Court, Joralemon, Willoughby, Raymond, Park av., Washington av., Kent av., B'way, Bedford av., Manhattan av. and 4th, L. I. City. Return same route, except Driggs av. instead of Bedford av., and Navy instead of Raymond.

CYPRESS HILLS—From Wyckoff and Myrtle avs., via Myrtle, Cypress avs., Cypress Hills.

DEKALB AV.—From Park Row to Sands, to Washington, to Fulton, to DeKalb av., to Seneca av., with branch to Fulton Ferry and extensions to Grandview av. and Ridgewood, to Myrtle av., via Seneca av.

FIFTEENTH ST.—Hamilton Ferry, via Hamilton av., 15th, Prospect Pk. W. and 20th.

FIFTH AV.—From Ft. Hamilton, via 4th, 5th and Atlantic avs., to South Ferry; Atlantic av., to Fulton Ferry, via Boerum pl., and Adams, also Flatbush-Atlantic subway loop.

FLATBUSH AV.—From Park Row, via Fulton, Flatbush av., Ave. N., to E. 49th.

FLATBUSH AV. SHUTTLE—Flatbush av. and Av. U, via Flatbush av. to Av. N.

FLATBUSH-SEVENTH AV. LINE—From Prospect Pk. W. and 20th, via 20th, 7th av., Flatbush av., Livingston, Borough Hall, Court, Joralemon and Boerum pl. to Livingston.

FLUSHING AV.—From Park Row, via Sands, Navy, Flushing av., Grand, to Maspeth and Jackson av. depot; to Park Row, runs via Grand, Flushing av., to Hudson av. and Nassau, Sands, to Bridge.

FLUSHING-RIDGEWOOD — From Ridgewood, via Lutheran Line, Fresh Pond rd., to Flushing av., to Grand, to Union av., to Corona av., to Lawrence av., to Prospect, Jaeger av., to Bradford av., Flushing.

FRANKLIN AV.—From Delancey, Mhtn., via Wmsbg. Bridge, S. 8th, Wythe av., Franklin av., Empire blvd. (Willink entrance to Prospect Park). Circle to Boulevard, to Coney Island during summer months.

FULTON ST.-Park Row, via Fulton, to E. N. Y.

GATES-PROSPECT PARK (during the summer season only)—From Ridgewood to Prospect Park Loop, via Myrtle av., Gates av., Nostrand av., Malbone, Flatbush av.

GRAHAM AV.—From Park Row to Sands, Navy, Flushing av., Graham av., Driggs av., Manhattan av., Greenpoint av., to Greenpoint Ferry and L. I. City.

GRAND ST.—North Beach, to Bowery Bay rd., Junction av., Union av., Grand, Marcy av., S. 4th, Havemeyer, S. 5th, Wmsbg. Bridge, to Delancey, Mhtn.

GRAND ST. SHUTTLE—From Grand and Marcy av., via Grand, Kent av., to B'way Ferry.

GREENE AND GATES AV.—From Park Row, via Fulton, to Greene av., Franklin av., Gates av., Myrtle av., to Myrtle and Wyckoff avs., Ridgewood.

GREENPOINT—From Mhtn. av., to Boro. Hall, Commercial, Franklin, Kent av., Classon av., Myrtle av., to Boro. Hall.

HAMILTON AV.—From Hamilton Ferry, via Hamilton av., to 3d av., to 65th.

HAMILTON FERRY LINE—From Hamilton Ferry, on Hamilton av., to 9th, Prospect Park, W. 15th, to Boulevard.

HICKS ST.—From Hamilton av., to Atlantic av., via Hicks.

HOLY CROSS—From Nostrand av., via Sheldon av., to Holy Cross Cemetery.

HOYT AND SACKETT STS.—From Bergen St. Depot, to Hamilton Ferry, via Bergen, Hoyt and Sackett.

JAMAICA AV.—From Jamaica, via Fulton, Jamaica av. to E. N. Y.

LORIMER ST.—From Box, via Mhtn. av., Nassau av., Lorimer, to Nostrand av., to Empire blvd., to Prospect Park Loop. Cars are operated to Greenpoint Ferry after midnight to 5 A.M. only.

MANHATTAN BRIDGE 3-CENT LINE—From Flatbush av. and Fulton, through Flatbush av. extension to and across Mhtn. Bridge. Returns same route. Franchise permits of extensions.

*Independent lines.

ELECTRIC ROADS IN NEW YORK CITY—BROOKLYN—*Continued.*

MEEKER AV.—From Newtown Creek (Calvary Cemetery), to Graham av., via Meeker av.

METROPOLITAN—From Delancey, via Wmsbg. Bridge, Bridge Plaza, S. 4th, Marcy av. to Grand, to Metropolitan av., to Jamaica av.

MONTAGUE ST.—From Hicks, via Montague, to Court.

MYRTLE AV.—From Park Row, via Fulton, Myrtle av., to Ridgewood.

NASSAU AV.—From Manhattan and Nassau avs., through Nassau, Varick and Meeker avs., to Newtown Creek (Calvary Cemetery).

NEW LOTS AV.—Rockaway and Hegeman avs. to Berriman, via New Lots av.

NOSTRAND AV. — Delancey, via Wmsbg. Bridge, to Roebling, Lee, Nostrand avs., to Flatbush and Nostrand avs.

NOSTRAND AV. SHUTTLE—From Flatbush and Nostrand avs., to Kings Highway, via Nostrand av.

NOSTRAND-PROSPECT PARK (during the summer only) — From Delancey, via Wmsbg Bridge, Roebling, Lee av., Nostrand av., Malbone, Flatbush av., to Prospect Park Loop.

OCEAN AV.—From B'way Ferry, B'way, Marcy av., Fulton, Nostrand av., Bergen, Rogers av., Av. F, Ocean av., to Emmons.

PARK AV.—From Central av. and Cooper to Park Row, via Central av., Jefferson, Beaver, Park, Park av., Navy, Concord and Washington.

PUTNAM AV. AND HALSEY ST.—From Park Row, via Fulton, to Putnam av., Nostrand av., Halsey, to Wyckoff av.

RALPH-ROCKAWAY AV.—From Rockaway and Church avs., via Rockaway av., E. N. Y. av., St. Johns pl., Ralph av. and B'way, to Delancey, via Wmsbg. Bridge; also shuttle from Rockaway and Church avs. to Ralph av. and St. Johns pl., via E. 98th and Ralph av.

REID AV.—From Delancey, via Wmsbg. Bridge, via B'way, to Reid av., Fulton, Utica av., to Church and Utica avs.

RICHMOND HILL—From Ridgewood, via Myrtle av., to Richmond Hill.

ROGERS AV.—From Ocean av. and Av. I, via Ocean av., Farragut rd., Rogers av., to Sterling pl., to Washington av., to Atlantic av., to Flatbush av., to Livingston, to Boro. Hall. Return via Boerum pl., to Livingston, to Flatbush av. and return.

SEA GATE—From Sea Gate, to Sheepshead Bay, via Surf av., W. 8th, Neptune av., W. 6th, Neptune av. and Emmons av. CULVER SHUTTLE—From Sea Gate to Culver Depot via Surf av.

SEVENTH AV.—Greenwood Cemetery, 20th, via 7th av., Flatbush av., Atlantic av., Boerum pl., Adams, Sands, Bridge, to Park Row. Additional service during A.M. and P.M. rush hours operated to South Ferry.

SIXTEENTH AV.—From 16th av. and 63d, to 16th and Gravesend avs., via 16th.

†SIXTY-FIFTH ST.—BAY RIDGE—From Bay 19th and Bath av., via Bath av., 14th av., 86th, to 5th av.

SIXTY-FIFTH ST.-FT. HAMILTON—From Ft. Hamilton to 65th and 3d av., via 4th av., 99th, 3d av. Some trips operated to 39th and 2d av., A.M. and P.M. rush hours, via 2d av. ton Ferry.

SMITH AND NINTH ST.—From Park Row, Mhtn., via Bridge, to Washington, through High to Jay, to Smith, to 9th, to Prospect Park West, to 15th, to Coney Island av., to Neptune av. and Coney Island, with branch connecting with Fulton Ferry.

ST. JOHNS PL. LINE—From Buffalo and St. Johns pl., via St. Johns pl., Rogers av., Sterling pl., Washington av., Atlantic av., Flatbush av., Livingston, Court, Joralemon, Fulton, Borough Hall, returning via Boerum pl., Livingston.

SUMNER AV.—From Delancey, via Wmsbg. Bridge, B'way, Sumner av., Fulton, Troy av., Bergen.

THIRD AV.—From Borough Hall, via Fulton, Flatbush av., 3d av., to 65th.

THIRTY-NINTH ST. FERRY-CONEY ISLAND—Coney Island to 39th St. Ferry, via Stillwell av., Bath av., 14th av., 86th, 5th av., to 39th St. Ferry. Tr. to Church av. line at 39th and 5th av.

TOMPKINS AV.—From Delancey, via Wmsbg. Bridge, Roebling, Division av., Harrison av., Tompkins av., Fulton, Empire blvd., Prospect Pk.

UNION AV.—From Greenpoint Ferry, via Greenpoint av., to Mhtn., Driggs, Union avs., B'way, Throop, Flushing, Knickerbocker, Myrtle avs., to Ridgewood.

UNION ST.—From Hamilton Ferry, to Court, Union, Prospect Park West and 20th. Summer to Coney Island, via 20th and P. P. & C. I. R. R.

UTICA AV.—From Church and Utica avs. to Av. N, via Utica av.

VAN BRUNT ST. AND ERIE BASIN LINE—Hamilton Ferry to Erie Basin. Route: From Hamilton Ferry, through Hamilton av., Van Brunt, Beard, Hallock to Columbia, Erie Basin.

VANDERBILT AV.—Prospect Pk. W. and 20th to Park Row, via Prospect Pk. W., Vanderbilt and Park avs., Navy, Concord, Washington and Bridge. Runs during summer to Coney Island, via 20th and P. P. & C. I. R. R.

WILLIAMSBURG BRIDGE LOCAL—From Bridge Plaza to Delancey, via Wmsbg. Bridge.

WILSON AV.—From Canarsie, via Rockaway P'kway, Rockaway av., Cooper, Wilson, Morgan, Johnson avs., Union av., S. 5th, Marcy av., B'way, Wmsbg. Bridge, to Delancey.

WYCKOFF AV.—Ridgewood to Delancey and Bridge Plaza, via Wyckoff av., Flushing av., Morgan av., Harrison pl., Bogart, McKibbin, B'way.

EIGHTH AV.—From Bay Ridge av., via 8th av., 39th, to 39th St. Ferry.

GRAVESEND AV.—From Coney Island av., via Gravesend av. and 20th, to Prospect Pk. W.

PARK SLOPE—From Av. C and Coney Island av., via Coney Island av., Prospect Pk. S., Prospect Pk. W., Flatbush av., Fulton, to Borough Hall. Return via Court and Livingston.

Elevated Lines.

All Brooklyn elevated lines operated by The N. Y. Consolidated R. R. Co.

BROADWAY LINE—Trains run through from Canarsie to Chambers (Mhtn.), via B'way and Centre St. Loop. Transfer to trolley at Marcy av. for B'way Ferry. Transfer at Canal for West End, Sea Beach and Broadway Subways.

CULVER LINE (Coney Island), via Gravesend av. and 38th, to 36th; thence via 5th av. line to Park Row. Change at 9th av. to West End Subway.

FULTON ST.—From Park Row to Lefferts av., Morris Park, via Fulton, Williams pl., Snediker av., Pitkin av., Euclid av. and Liberty av.

LEXINGTON AV.—Park Row to 168th, Jamaica; †53 min. Also Chambers to Jamaica during rush hours, via Centre St. Loop; †45 min.

MYRTLE AV.—Park Row to Metropolitan av. (Lutheran Cemetery); time, 32 min. Transfer at Vanderbilt av. for East N. Y. Connects at Wyckoff av. for Richmond Hill, Glendale and Cypress Hills surface cars. Connect at Fresh Pond rd. for Flushing cars. Also Chambers (Mhtn.), to Metropolitan av., during rush hours, via Centre St. Loop, B'way and Myrtle av.; †29 min.

Long Island Railroad Company.

LONG ISLAND R. R. CO.—Controlled by the Penn. R. R. Co., operates 394.54 miles of road. Brooklyn line, from Flatbush av. to Jamaica, 9.39 miles, leased from the Nassau Electric R. R. Co., successor to the Atlantic Av. R. R. Co. At Jamaica connects with trains for all parts of Long Island. Officers: Ralph Peters, Pres.; Henry Tatnall, A. J. County, Vice-Prests.; F. E. Haff, Sec.; C. L. Addison, Asst. Secs.; J. R. Sarage, Gen. Supt.; Donall Wilson, Gen. Freight Agt.; P. H. Woodward, Gen. Passgr. Agt.; T. J. Ludlum, Auditor. Principal offices and address, Pennsylvania Station, N. Y. Brooklyn station and offices at Flatbush and Atlantic avs. Engineering and operating officials' offices in Jamaica.

MANHATTAN AND THE BRONX.

Surface Line Companies.

The surface lines in Manhattan and The Bronx are controlled by the following lines:

NEW YORK RAILWAYS CO.—Job E. Hedges, Receiver; Frank Hedley, Gen. Mgr.; W. A. Anderson, Sec.; J. H. Campbell, Treas. Office, 165 B'way.

THIRD AV. RAILWAY CO.—S. W. Huff, Pres., 130th and 3d av. (Controls Drydock, E. B'way and Battery R. R. Co.; 42d St., Manhattanville and St. Nicholas Av. Ry. Co.; Union Ry. Co.; Southern Blvd. R. R. Co.; Yonkers R. R. Co.; Westchester Elec. R. R. Co.; N. Y. City Interborough Ry. Co.; Mid-Crosstown Ry. Co.; Belt Line Ry. Corp.; Kingsbridge R. R. and Bronx Traction Co.)

Elevated Line Companies.

INTERBOROUGH RAPID TRANSIT CO.—Offices, 165 B'way. Lessee of all lines of the Manhattan Ry. Co. Frank Hedley, Pres.; A. Belmont, Ch. Board; Edw. J. Berwind, Ch. Ex. Com.; J. H. Campbell, Treas.; H. M. Fisher, Sec.; E. F. J. Gaynor, Auditor.

ELECTRIC ROADS IN NEW YORK CITY—MANHATTAN AND BRONX—*Continued.*

MANHATTAN RAILWAY CO.—165 B'way. Alfred Skitt, Pres.; P. V. Trainque, Asst. Sec.-Treas. Lines: 2d av., 3d av., 6th av., 9th av. and suburban line.

Elevated Lines.

NINTH AV.—So. Ferry to 135th. Transfer to 6th av. line at 135th. †36 min. During rush hours, to Woodlawn, connecting with N. Y. and Putnam Ry. at Sedgwick av.

SECOND AV.—So. Ferry to 129th. †35 min., and from 129th to Bronx Park over the 3d av. line. Transfers to 3d av. line at Chatham sq. and 129th. To Bronx Park. †21 min.

SIXTH AV. LINE—So. Ferry to Woodlawn (connecting with N. Y. and Putnam Ry. at Sedgwick av.). †64 min.

THIRD AV.—So. Ferry to 129th, and from 129th to E. 238th. Transfers to 2d av. line at Chatham sq. City Hall to 129th, †30 min., and to Bronx Park, †51 min.; from So. Ferry to 129th, †34 min., and to E. 238th. †65½ min.

Hudson Tubes.

HUDSON & MANHATTAN R. R. CO.—General offices, 30 Church. Oren Root, Pres.; J. V. Davies, Ch. Eng.; J. S. O'Neale, Treas.; F. H. Sillick, Compt.; R. B. Kay, Sec.-Treas. Routes: Hudson Terminal to Summit av., Jersey City; Mhtn. Transfer, Harrison and Park pl., Newark; Hudson Terminal to Hoboken; B'way and 33d to Hoboken; B'way and 33d to Summit av., Jersey City. Connection is made from Hudson Terminal with the Pennsylvania R. R. at Mhtn Transfer, and Exchange pl., J. C. Stations in Mhtn.: Hudson Terminal, entrances on Cortlandt, Dey and Fulton, near Church; Christopher, bet. Hudson and Greenwich; 6th av., at 9th, 14th, 19th, 23d, 28th, 32d and 33d. Stations in N. J.: Penn. R. R. station at Exchange pl., J. C.; Erie R. R. station, Pavonia av., J. C.; D., L. & W. station, Hoboken; Grove and Henderson, J. C.; Summit av., J. C.; Mhtn. Transfer; Harrison, Park pl, Newark. Connection from uptown stations to Newark trains made at Grove-Henderson station. From 33d to Newark, †35 min.; from Hudson Terminal to Mhtn. Transfer, †16 min.; from Hudson Terminal to Park pl., Newark, †20 min.

†Running time.

QUEENS.

Surface Lines and Companies.

LONG ISLAND ELECTRIC RAILWAY CO.—Inc. 1894. Capital stock, $600,000. Officers: C. L. Addison, Pres., Penn. Station, Mhtn.; W. O. Wood, Vice Pres. and Gen. Mgr., L. I. City; W. F. Brown, Sec. and Treas., Penn. Station, Mhtn. Operates 16.30 miles of track. Jamaica to Queens, Jamaica to City Line, Bkln.; Jamaica to Far Rockaway.

NEW YORK AND QUEENS COUNTY—Offices, 7 and 9 Borden av., L. I. City. W. O. Wood, Pres. and Gen. Mgr.

OCEAN ELECTRIC RAILWAY—Office, Penn. R. R. Station, 33d, Mhtn. Operating old Rockaway Village R. R. A. J. County, Pres.; W. F. Brown, Sec. Routes: From passenger station, L. I. R. R., at Far Rockaway, to Far Rockaway Beach, and from railroad station to Arverne, Rockaway Beach, Rockaway Park, Belle Harbor and Neponsit.

RICHMOND.

RICHMOND LIGHT AND RAILROAD CO.—C. W. Huntington, Pres.. R. L. Rand, V.-Pres.; J. E. Phillips, Sec.-Treas.

SOUTHFIELD BEACH RY CO.—Same officers as above. Summer only, Midland Beach to So. Beach.

STATEN ISLAND MIDLAND RY. CO.—C. W. Huntington, Pres.; R. L. Rand, V.-Pres.; A. M. Stillwell, Sec.-Asst. Treas.; A. Watson, Treas. and Asst. Sec. Gen. offices, New Brighton. Lines: From St. George, through Tompkinsville, Stapleton, Grant City, Egbertville to Richmond. From Grant City to Midland Beach. From Concord, through Westerleigh, Port Richmond to Bergen Point Ferry. From Eckstein's Brewery and Manor rd. to Richmond Terrace, W. N. B. Silver Lake Line from St. George Ferry to Port Richmond via Richmond turnpike.

STATEN ISLAND RAPID TRANSIT RAILWAY CO.—H. B. Voorhees, Gen. Mgr. Lines: St. George to Arlington, St. George to So. Beach.

STATEN ISLAND RAILWAY CO. (Steam)—Same officers as above. Clifton to Tottenville.

N. Y. CITY SUBWAY SYSTEM.

B. R. T. Routes and Stations.

BROOKLYN-MANHATTAN-QUEENS SUBWAY.

BROADWAY-4TH AV. SUBWAY.

86th, Bay Ridge; 77th, Bay Ridge av. (trolley connection for Bath Beach), 59th (junction with Sea Beach Line; see table following); 53d, 45th, 36th (junction with West End Line; see table following); 25th, Prospect av., 9th, Union, Pacific (transfer to West End and Sea Beach Lines); DeKalb av. (transfer to Brighton Beach Line); Court (Montague St. Tunnel), Whitehall, Rector and Trinity pl., Cortlandt and Church, City Hall and B'way, Canal and B'way (free transfer with West End Line, Sea Beach Line and Centre St. Loop; also connection with Lexington Av. Line of Interborough), Prince and B'way, 8th and B'way, Union sq.-14th (connection with Lexington Av. Line, I. R. T.), 23d and B'way, 28th, 34th, Times sq. (connection with 7th Av. West Side Subway and Shuttle Service to Grand Central Station), 49th, 57th, 5th av. and 60th, Lexington av. and 60th, Queensboro Plaza (connects with I. R. T. to Astoria and Corona).

WEST END LINE, B. R. T.

From Times sq. to Bath Beach, Bensonhurst and Coney Island.

Runs over Broadway Subway from Times sq. to Canal, thence over Manhattan Bridge to Myrtle av., DeKalb av., thence over 4th Av. Subway to 36th; 36th; 9th av., near 39th: free transfer with Culver El., via Gravesend av. to Coney Island; Fort Hamilton P'kway, 50th-Borough Pk., 55th and New Utrecht av., 62d and New Utrecht av. (free transfer with Sea Beach Line), 71st, Homewood; 79th and New Utrecht av., 18th av.-Van Pelt Manor for Bath Beach, 20th av. and 86th, Bay P'kway-Bensonhurst, 25th av. and 86th, Bay 50th, Coney Island-Stillwell av. Short Line Service during rush hours between 62d and City Hall (Mhtn.), via Montague St. Tunnel.

SEA BEACH LINE, B. R. T.

From Times sq. to Coney Island.

Runs over Broadway Subway from Times sq. to Canal, thence over Manhattan Bridge to DeKalb av., thence over 4th Av. Subway to 59th: 59th, 8th av., Fort Hamilton av., New Utrecht av. (free transfer with West End Line), 18th av., 20th av., 22d av., Kings Highway, Av. U, 86th, Coney Island-Stillwell av.

BRIGHTON BEACH LINE, B. R. T.

Operates from Queensboro Plaza over the Broadway Subway to Whitehall, thence via Montague St. Tunnel to Court (connection with I. R. T. subways), DeKalb av. (free transfer with 4th Av., West End and Sea Beach Lines), Atlantic av. (L. I. Depot), 7th av., Prospect Park (shuttle service to Franklin av., Fulton St. El.), Parkside av., Church av., Beverley rd., Cortelyou rd., Newkirk av., Av. H, Av. J, Elm av., Kings Highway, Av. U, Neck rd., Sheepshead Bay, Brighton Beach, Ocean P'kway, W. 8th, Coney Island-Stillwell av.

On Sundays and holidays and from 7 P.M. to 12 midnight daily, operates via Manhattan Bridge to Times sq. Short Line Service during rush hours from Prospect Park Station, via Manhattan Bridge to Times sq.

CENTRE ST. LOOP, B. R. T.

Broadway, Brooklyn, elevated trains over Williamsburgh Bridge, then as subway to Essex, Bowery, Canal, Chambers.

I. R. T. Routes and Stations.

EASTERN PARKWAY LINE.

New Lots av., Van Siclen av., Pennsylvania av., Junius, Rockaway av., Saratoga av., Sutter av., Utica av., Kingston av., Nostrand av., Franklin av., Brooklyn Museum, Prospect Pk. Plaza, Bergen, Atlantic av.

NOSTRAND AV. BRANCH.

Flatbush av., Newkirk av., Beverley rd., Church av., Winthrop, Sterling, President, Franklin av., Brooklyn Museum, Prospect Pk. Plaza, Bergen, Atlantic av.

WEST SIDE SUBWAY—7TH AV. LINE, I. R. T.

VAN CORTLANDT PK. BRANCH.

Through trains from New Lots av. (Eastern P'kway Line) and Flatbush av. (Nostrand Av. Branch) to Van Cortlandt Pk.

Atlantic av., Nevins, Hoyt, Borough Hall, Clark and Henry, Wall (William), Fulton, Park pl., Chambers (junction with train from South Ferry, Rector, Cortlandt), Franklin, Canal, Houston.

ELECTRIC ROADS IN NEW YORK CITY—MANHATTAN AND BRONX—*Continued.*

Christopher, 14th, 18th, 23d, 28th, Pennsylvania Sta., Times sq. (shuttle service to Grand Central, also connection with B. R. T. Subway), 50th, 59th, 66th, 72d, 79th, 86th, 91st, 96th (junction of Bronx Pk. Br., via Lenox av.), 103d, 110th, 116th, Manhattan (125th), 137th, 145th, 157th, 168th, 181st, 191st, Dyckman, 207th, 215th, 225th, 231st, 238th, Van Cortlandt Pk. (connects with trolley for Yonkers).

BRONX PARK BRANCH.

Through trains from President (Nostrand Av. Br.) to 180th, Bronx Pk. As Van Cortlandt Pk. Br. from Atlantic av. to 96th.

96th, 110th, 116th, 125th, 135th (junction with 145th, Lenox av. trains), Mott av. (transfer to Lexington Av. Line), 149th and 3d av. (free transfer with 3d Av. El), Jackson av., Prospect Av., Intervale av., Simpson, Freeman, 174th, 177th (transfer to Lexington Av. Line for E. 180th—Morris Pk. Av. Sta.), 180th, Bronx Pk.

EAST SIDE SUBWAY.

(For Eastern P'kway and Nostrand Av. Lines, see preceding tables.)

LEXINGTON AV. LINE, I. R. T.—JEROME AV. AND WOODLAWN BRANCH.

Atlantic av., Nevins (transfer point for Eastern P'kway Line and Nostrand Av. Br.), Hoyt, Borough Hall—2 blocks from Myrtle Av. and Lexington Av. El. (Joralemon St. Tunnel), Bowling Green (transfer to So. Ferry), Wall (B'way), Fulton, Brooklyn Bridge (local trains around City Hall Loop), Worth, Canal (connection with B. R. T. Subways), Spring, Bleecker, Astor pl., 14th (connection with B. R. T. Subways), 18th, 23d, 28th, 33d, Grand Central Sta. (transfer to Queensboro Line, also to West Side Subway, via Shuttle Service), 51st, 59th, 68th, 77th, 86th, 96th, 103d, 110th, 116th, 125th (transfer to Pelham Bay Pk. Br.), 138th, Mott Haven; 149th and Mott av. (transfer to E. 180th—Morris Park av. Branch and West Side Subway), 161st and Jerome av., 167th and Jerome av. (connection with 6th Av. and 9th Av. El.), 170th and Jerome av., Belmont, 176th, N. Y. University, 183d, Fordham rd., Kingsbridge rd., Bedford Pk. blvd., Moshulu P'kway, Woodlawn.

E. 180TH ST. (MORRIS PARK AV.) BRANCH.

As Jerome Av. Br. from Atlantic av. to Mott av. (149th).

Mott av. (transfer to West Side Subway), 149th, 3d av. (free transfer with 3d Av. El.), Jackson av., Prospect av., Intervale av., Simpson, Freeman, 174th, 177th (transfer for 180th—Bronx Park—West Side Subway Terminal), E. 180th (Morris Pk. av.—transfer to White Plains Rd. Br.).

White Plains Connection.

(Note—Connection at E. 180th (Morris Pk. av.) Station for Mt. Vernon, New Rochelle and White Plains via New York, Westchester and Boston Ry. Time: Mt. Vernon, 9 minutes; White Plains, 30 minutes.

PELHAM BAY PARK BRANCH, FROM 125TH ST., I. R. T. (EAST SIDE SUBWAY).

125th, 3d av., Brook av., Cypress av., E. 143d, E. 149th, South blvd.: Longwood av., Huntspoint av., Whitlock av., Elder av., Sound View av., St. Lawrence av., E. 177th, Castle Hill av., Zerega av., Westchester sq., Middletown rd., Buhre av., Pelham Bay Pk.

WHITE PLAINS ROAD BRANCH, I. R. T.

E. 180th (Morris Pk. av.), Bronx Pk. E., Pelham P'kway, Allerton av., Burke av., Gun Hill rd., 219th, 225th, 233d, 238th, 241st.

QUEENSBOROUGH LINE, I. R. T.—CORONA BRANCH.

Grand Central, Jackson av. and 4th, Hunters Pt. av., 11th and Jackson av., Queensboro Plaza (free transfer with 2d Av. El. from 57th), Rawson, Lowery, Bliss, Lincoln av., Woodside (connection with L. I. R. R.), Fisk av., B'way, 25th, Elmhurst av., Junction av., Alburt's av.

ASTORIA BRANCH.

Runs as above from Grand Central to Queensboro Plaza.

Queensboro Plaza, Beebe av., Washington av., B'way, Grand av., Hoyt av., Ditmars av.

NEW YORK CITY MOTOR BUS SERVICE.

Manhattan.

The operation of the following bus lines is in control of the Dept. of Plant and Structures:

1—MADISON AND CHAMBERS ST. LINE—Terminals: Delancey and E. R.; Chambers St. Ferry, N. R. Route, East, Grand, Madison, New Chambers. Return: Madison, Grand, Tompkins to Delancey. Length: About 2 miles.

2—DELANCEY AND SPRING ST. LINE—Terminals: Delancey and E. R.; Desbrosses Ferry, N. R. Route: Delancey, Bowery, Spring, W. B'way, Watts, to Desbrosses Ferry. Return: Same route. Length: About 2 miles.

3—AVENUE C LINE—Terminals: 10th and Av. C; Desbrosses Ferry, N. R. Route, westbound: 10th and Av. C, 4th, 1st av., Houston, Washington, Watts, to Desbrosses Ferry. Return: Eastbound: Desbrosses Ferry, Watts, Greenwich, Charlton, Prince, Bowery, Stanton, Pitts, Av. C, to 10th. Length: About 3⅛ miles.

4—EIGHTH ST. LINE—Terminals. Brooklyn Plaza, Williamsburg Bridge; 7th av. and 23d, Mhtn. Route, south and eastbound: 23d and 7th av., Greenwich av., 8th, Av. A, Essex, Delancey, Williamsbug Bridge, Brooklyn Plaza. Return: North and westbound: Brooklyn Plaza, Williamsburg Bridge, Clinton, Av. B, 2d, Av. A, 9th, Stuyvesant, 8th, Greenwich av., 7th av. and 23d. Length: About 4 miles.

5—14TH ST. LINE—Terminals: Brooklyn Plaza, Williamsburg Bridge, W. 23d St. Ferries. Route, south and eastbound: 23d St. Ferries, Marginal, 14th, Av. A, E. Houston, Essex, Delancey, Williamsburg Bridge, Brooklyn Plaza. Return, north and westbound: Brooklyn Plaza, Williamsburg Bridge, Clinton, Av. B, 2d, Av. A, 14th, Marginal, 23d St. Ferries. Length: About 4½ miles.

6—YORKVILLE-86TH ST. LINE—Terminals: 86th and B'way; 92d and Av. A. Route: 92d, Av. A, 86th, through 86th to 5th av., to 85th, through Central Pk. to 86th, to B'way, to 87th, to West End av., to 86th, to B'way. Return: Starting from 86th and B'way, over same route. Length: 2 miles.

Queens Bus Lines.

12—FLUSHING-BAYSIDE LINE — Terminals: Flushing Bridge; Bayside. Route: Jackson av., to B'way, to Bell av., to Bayside Railroad Depot. Return: Over same route.

13—CORONA LINE—Terminals: Flushing (Main St. Depot); Corona. Route: Main St. Depot (Flushing), to Jackson av., to Shell rd., to Albertus av., to Long Island R. R. Depot at Corona. Return: Over same route.

FIFTH AVENUE COACH CO. MOTOR BUS ROUTES.

Fare 10 cents on all lines, with free transfers at certain points.

A large number is attached to the busses operating the different routes, corresponding to the numbers given in the following list, also a sign with white letters on black shows principal streets traversed, and in white letters on red shows the terminal.

1—FIFTH AVENUE—Bet. Washington sq. and 110th, as traffic demands. Running time, 35, 39 and 46 min.

2—FIFTH AND SEVENTH AVENUES—5th av., from Washington sq. to 110th, to 7th av., to 153d, to McComb's pl., to 155th St. Viaduct, to St. Nicholas pl. (Polo Grounds) Leave 155th and St. Nicholas pl. from 7:17 A.M. to 9:07 A.M. every 10 min. Leave 125th and 7th av. from 6:42 A.M. to 11:47 P.M. every 2 to 10 min. Running time, 41, 45 and 53 min.

Sundays—Leave 155th and St. Nicholas pl. from 7:30 A.M. to 8:19 P.M. every 5 to 10 min. After above time, busses leave 145th and 7th av. from 8.29 P.M. to 12:13 A.M. every 5 to 10 min. Running time, 46 and 51 min.

3—FIFTH AND ST. NICHOLAS AVENUES—5th av., from 22d and 5th av. to 110th, to Manhattan av., to St. Nicholas av., to 181st, connecting at 181st with No. 7 service for 193d and St. Nicholas av. (Fort George). Leave 181st and St. Nicholas av. 7 A.M. to 11:43 P.M. every 3½ to 10 min. Running time, 54, 57 and 64 min.

Sundays—Leave from 193d and St. Nicholas av. (Fort George) to Washington sq. from 7:29 A.M. to 11:59 P.M. every 5 to 10 min. Running time, 64 min.

4—FIFTH AVENUE, CATHEDRAL P'KWAY, RIVERSIDE DRIVE AND BROADWAY—32d, from Pennsylvania Sta. (7th av. entrance) to 5th av., to 110th, Cathedral P'kway, to Riverside dr., to 135th, to B'way, to 168th. Leave 168th and B'way from 7 A.M. to 11:49 P.M. every 6 to 10 min. Running time 55, 59 and 66 min. Leave 157th and B'way from 7:22 A.M. to 6 P.M. every 8 to 10 min. Running time, 51, 55 and 62 min. Shoppers' Service (week days only)—Fifth Avenue, Cathedral Parkway and Riverside Drive—5th av., from Washington sq. and 22d to 110th, Cathedral P'kway, to Riverside dr. and 113th. Leave Riverside dr. and 113th from 9:01 A.M. to 4:26 P.M. every 5 min. Running time, 43, 47 and 54 min.

ELECTRIC ROADS IN NEW YORK CITY—MANHATTAN AND BRONX—*Continued*

5—FIFTH AVENUE, 57TH STREET, RIVERSIDE DRIVE AND BROADWAY TO 168TH STREET—5th av., from Washington sq. to 57th, to B'way, to 72d, to Riverside dr., to 135th, to B'way, to 168th. Leave 168th and B'way from Nov. 11 from 6:39 A.M. to 11:44 P.M. every 3½ to 10 min. Fifth Avenue, 57th Street, Riverside Drive and Broadway to 168th Street, to 181st Street — 5th av., from 22d to 57th, to B'way, to 72d, to Riverside dr., to 135th, to B'way, to 168th, to St. Nicholas av., to 181st, connecting at 181st with No. 7 serv.ce for 193d and St. Nicholas av. (Fort George). Leave 181st and St. Nicholas av. from 7:25 A.M. to 8:35 A.M. and from 12:23 P.M. to 4:57 P.M. every 10 min. Running time, 60, 64, 73 and 81 min.

Sundays—Leave 168th and B'way from 7.49 A.M. to 3:30 P.M. every 5 to 10 min. Bet. 3:30 P.M. and 11:41 P.M. buses operated from 193d and St. Nicholas av. (Fort George) every 5 to 10 min. Running time, 60 and 69 min. Shoppers' Serv'ce (week days only)—Fifth Avenue, 57th Street, Broadway and Riverside Drive to 113th Street—5th av., from Washington sq. to 57th, to B'way, to 72d, to Riverside dr., to 113th. Leave 113th and Riverside dr. from 9:01 A.M. to 5:01 P.M. every 5 min. Running time, 42, 46 and 54 min.

6—72D STREET CROSSTOWN—E. 72d, from 1st av. to 5th av., to 57th, to B'way, to W. 72d to Central Pk. W. Leave 1st av. every 15 min. from 8 A.M. to 6 P.M. Leave Central Pk. W. every 15 min. from 8:20 A.M. to 6:30 P.M. Running time, 21 and 22 min.

7—WASHINGTON HEIGHTS AND HARLEM LINE (week days only)—St. Nicholas av., 193d (Fort George), to 168th, to Edgecomb rd., to 155th St. Viaduct, to Macomb's pl., to 153d, to 7th av., to 125th. Leave 125th and 7th av. from 8:35 A.M. to 12 midnight every 10 to 20 min. Running time, 44, 43 and 54 min.

8—FIFTH AVENUE, 57TH STREET, RIVERSIDE DRIVE AND BROADWAY—32d, from Pennsylvania Sta. (8th av. entrance) to 5th av., to 57th, to B'way, to 72d, to Riverside dr., to 135th, to B'way and to 157th. Leave 157th and B'way from 7:08 A.M. to 6:01 P.M. every 5 to 10 min. Running time, 51, 55 and 63 min. Leave 135th and B'way from 7:31 A.M. to 5 P.M. every 5 to 10 min. Running time, 44, 48 and 56 min.

9—CENTRAL PARK WEST, WASHINGTON SQUARE—Shoppers' Service (week days only)—5th av., from Washington sq. to 57th, to B'way, to 72d to Central Pk. W.

LONG ISLAND ELECTRIC RAILROADS.

For Electric Railroads in New York City, see index.

Name.	Terminal Points.	Miles.	Min. Time.	Fare.
Glen Cove Railroad	Sea Cliff Station to Glen Cove Landing	3.25	20	.05
Huntington R. R. Co	Huntington to Melville	9	40	...
Northport Traction Co	Northport Station to Northport Harbor	2.75	15	.05
L. I. Electric Railway	Jamaica to Far Rockaway	9	45	.10
L. I. Electric Railway	Belmont Park to Grant av (old City Line, Bkln.)	6.25	36	.05
N. Y. & L. I. Traction Co	Mineola to Jamaica	9.50	45	.15
N. Y. & L. I. Traction Co	Hempstead to Jamaica	9.50	48	.15
N. Y. & L. I. Traction Co	Mineola to Rockaway Blvd. sta. (Bkln.)	24.50	120	.30
Ocean Electric Railway	Far Rockaway to Neponsit	7.50	38	.08
Nassau Co. R. R	Sea Cliff to Sea Cliff Station	1.50	10	.05

LEGAL HOLIDAYS IN THE UNITED STATES.

(See index for church days, feasts and anniversaries.)

Jan. 1—New Year's Day: Dist. of Col., territories and all States, except Ark. and Mass. (in Maine a bank holiday only legally.)

Jan. 8—Anniversary Battle New Orleans: La.

Jan. 19—Lee's Birthday: Fla., Ga., N. C., S. C., Va., Ala., Miss. and Ark.

Feb. 8—Mardi Gras: Ala., Fla., La.

Feb. 12—Lincoln's Birthday: Ill., Minn., N. Y., Conn., Wash., N. D., Pa., S. D., Wyo., Nev., Del., Kans., Mont., Mich., W. Va., Utah, Iowa, Col., N. M., Cal., Ore., Ind.

Feb. 22—Washington's Birthday: Dist. of Col., territories and all States.

Mar. 2—Anniversary Texas Independence: Tex.

Mar. 25—Good Friday: Ala., Conn., La., Minn., N. J., Pa., Tenn., Md., Del., Fla., Porto Rico.

April 12—Anniversary of the adoption of the Halifax Resolution: N. C.

April 13—Thomas Jefferson's Birthday: Ala.

April 19—Patriots' Day: Mass., Me.

April 21—Anniversary Battle San Jacinto: Tex.

April 26—Confederate Memorial Day: Ala., Fla., Ga., Miss.

May 10—Confederate Day: N. C., S. C.

May 20—Anniversary of signing of Mecklenburg Declaration of Independence: N. C.

May 30—Confederate Memorial Day: Va.

May 30—Memorial Day: In Dist. of Col., all States, except Ark., Fla., Ga., La., Miss., N. C., S. C., Tex.

June 3—Jefferson Davis' Birthday: Fla., Ga., S. C., Ala., Tenn., Tex., Miss. Confederate Decoration Day in La., Confederate Day, Tenn.

June 9—Bkln.: Sunday Schls. Anniversary Day—1st Thursday. If Decoration Day falls within same week, 2d Thursday. For public schls. in Borough of Bkln.

June 11—Kamehameha Day: In Ter. Hawaii.

June 15—Pioneer Day: Idaho.

July 4—Independence Day: All States and territories and Dist. of Columbia.

July 10—Admission Day: Wyo.

July 24—Pioneer Day: Utah.

July 25—Landing of Am. Troops: Porto Rico.

Aug. 1—Colorado Day: Col.

Aug. 16—Bennington Battle Day: Vt.

Sept. 5—Labor Day: Parish of Orleans, La.; Dist. of Col. and all States, except Wyo.

Sept. 9—Admission Day: Cal.

Sept. 12—Old Defenders' Day: Md.

Oct. 12—Columbus Day: Ala., Ark., Del., Ind., Kans., W. Va., Vt., Idaho, Ore., Tex., Wash., Me., Col., N. Y., N. J., R. I., Conn., Mich., Mo., Ohio, Md., Mass., Pa., Ill., Mont., Cal., Ky., Ariz., N. H., N. M., Nev., Neb., Okla.

Oct. 18—Alaska Day: Alaska.

Oct. 31—Admission Day: Nev.

Nov. 1—All Saints' Day: La.

Nov. 5—Pioneer Day: Mont. (observed in public schools).

Nov. 8—General Election Day: All States, except Ala., Ark., Conn., Del., Ga., Me., Mass., Miss., Neb., N. C., Utah, Vt., Ohio, Kans.

Nov. 11—Armistice Day: Oregon, Minn., Mich., Texas, Mass., Ala., Md., N. C. and Cal.

Nov. 24—Thanksgiving Day: All States and territories and Dist. of Col.; not statutory in some States.

Dec. 25—Christmas Day: All States, Dist. of Col. and all territories.

Arbor Day is a legal holiday in N. D., Ill., Minn., Me. and Wyo., day being set by Gov. in Neb., Apr. 21; Mont., 3d Tues. in Apr.; Ariz., 1st Mon. in Feb.; Utah. Apr. 14; R. I., 2d Fri. in May; Idaho, 1st Fri. after May 1; Fla., 1st Fri. in Feb.; Ga., 1st Fri. in Dec.

Fast Day whenever appointed in Apr., N. H. Thurs. of Fair Week, S. C. Every Sat. after 12 o'clock, noon, is a legal holiday in N. Y., N. J., Penn., Md., N. C., Ind., Mich., Ohio, Cal., Tenn., Va. and Dist. of Col.; in La. and Mo. in cities over 100,000; in Ill., in cities over 200,000 in New Castle Co., Del., and in Charleston and Richmond Cos., S. C. New Year's Day, Feb. 22, May 30, July 4, Labor Day, Thanksgiving Day and Christmas Day are legal holidays by act of Congress applying to all governmental executive depts. only, but are not necessarily executive by Congress itself. There is no natl. holiday, not even July 4th. There is no general statute on the subject.

U. S. BIRTH AND DEATH RATES.

In the birth registration area of the U. S. 1,373,438 infants were born alive in 1919, representing a birth rate of 22.3 per 1,000 of population. The total number of deaths in the same area was 798,104, or 13.0 per 1,000. The births exceeded the deaths by 72.1 per cent.

LIBRARIES AND READING ROOMS.

Brooklyn.

PUBLIC LIBRARY.

Brooklyn Public Library (free)—Central office, 26 Brevoort pl. Circulation from Jan. 1, 1919, to Dec. 31, 1919, 5,333,671. Volumes in library, 962,522. Open 9 A.M. to 9 P.M. Board of Trustees: David A. Boody, Pres.; Frank L. Babbott, Vice-Pres.; John Hill Morgan, Sec.; R. R. Appleton, Treas.; Frank Lyman, Roscoe C. E. Brown, Paul Grout, William A. White, Nathaniel H. Levi, Francis L. Noble, William H. Good, Richard R. Bowker, Eugene Charles Alder, Darwin R. James, Jr., Horace J. Morse, Theodore L. Frothingham, William H. English, Simeon B. Chittenden, C. A. Webber, J. J. Cashman, John Dowd, F. J. Sullivan. Ex-officio members, The Mayor, Comptroller and Borough President.

Administration Dept.—Frank P. Hill, Chief Librarian; J. A. Lowe, Asst. Lib'n.; C. W. Foss, Ref. Lib.; Theresa Hitchler, Supt. of Cataloguing Dept.; Pauline Goler, Librarian's Sec.; W. E. Lanchantin, Fin. Clerk; L. N. Martin, Supt. of Supplies; C. E. Farrington, Chief Clk. Book Order Dept.; Clara W. Hunt, Supt. of Children's Dept.; Julia A. Hopkins, Supt. of Staff Instruction; L. N. Feipel, Editor of Publications.

Branches and Branch Librarians—Astral, Franklin and India, J. Grace Merry. Bay Ridge, 73d and Ridge blvd., Laura Taylor. Bedford, Franklin av., opp. Hancock. Mary Casamajor. Borough Park, 1325 56th, Helen R. Bull. Brownsville, Glenmore av. and Watkins, Hedwig Roghé. Brownsville Children's, Stone and Dumont avs., Mrs. Flora De Gogorza. Bushwick, Bushwick av. and Seigel, Hilda W. Green, Carroll Park, Clinton and Union, Nellie B. Fatout. City Park, St. Edwards and Auburn pl., Stella H. Foote. Concord, Concord and Jay, Maude B. Adams. DeKalb, Bushwick and DeKalb avs., Jane Conard. East, Arlington av. and Warwick, Ella C. Selden. Eastern Parkway, Eastern P'kway and Schenectady av., Grace E. McDowell. Flatbush, Linden av., nr. Flatbush av., Grace L. Donaghy. Fort Hamilton, 4th av. and 95th, Mrs. Helen M. Smith. Greenpoint, Norman av. and Leonard, Eliza Witham. Kensington, 771 Gravesend av., Ellen C. McIlroy. Kings Highway, 1608 Kings Highway, Elsie M. Reed. Leonard, Devoe and Leonard, Fannie C. Boles. Macon, Lewis av. and Macon, Mary E. Mathews (Act.). Montague, 197 Montague, Miss A. M. Colby, New Utrecht, 86th and 20th av., Julia R. Gwyn. Pacific, 4th av. and Pacific, Mrs. Ella M. B. Perry. Prospect, 6th av. and 9th, Emma McE. Olcott. Public School 89, Newkirk av. and E. 31st, Lila G. Hart. Red Hook, Richards and Visitation pl., Helen R. Burdett. Ridgewood, 496 Knickerbocker av., Fanny A. Sheldon. Saratoga, Hopkinson av. and Macon, Edna H. Bancroft. Schermerhorn, 198 Livingston, Lillian J. McMahon. Sheepshead Bay, 1667 Sheepshead Bay rd., Alice H. Meigs. South 4th av. and 51st, Bertha G. Crozier. Tompkins Park, in Tompkins Park, Elizabeth S. Williams. Williamsburg, Division and Marcy avs., Gwendolen Brown. Winthrop, North Henry and Engert av., Edith E. Schwegler.

Work on the Flatbush av. wing of the central Library Bldg. (Flatbush av. and Eastern Parkway), the foundation of which was laid some time ago, was continued during 1919, and the first story of the wing is nearing completion. The entire building which will be one of the handsomest structures of its kind, will cost approximately $8,000,000. It will occupy a site extending 486 ft. on Flatbush av., and 332 ft. on Eastern Parkway, and a frontage of 70 ft. on the Prospect Park Plaza, opposite to the Memorial Arch and extending 486 ft. along the Mt. Prospect Reservoir in the rear. The site covers 5,900 sq. ft., or 2¼ acres. The building will be five stories high and will have a book capacity of 2,500,000 volumes. Ground was broken on June 5, 1912. The Flatbush av. wing is under construction. The Public Library system of the borough, which embraces 31 branches, 3 stations (small branches open afternoons), a department of traveling libraries, and a library for the blind, with about 963,000 volumes, has an annual circulation of over 5,000,000. By gift from the Carnegie Foundation the city now owns in Brooklyn 20 library buildings, the average cost of which has been $80,000.

Dept. Traveling Libraries—Bedford av., opp. Hancock. Mary J. Thackray.

Information regarding librarians' courses should be addressed to Miss Julia A. Hopkins, Bedford Branch, Franklin av. and Hancock.

Library for the Blind—Mrs. Beryl H. Goodshaw.

31 Branch librarians, salaries from $1,320 to $1,980; 23 assistant branch librarians, $1,260 to $1,320; 74 library assistants, $1,020 to $1,200; 68 junior library assistants, $840 to $960; 20 children's librarians, $1,260 to $1,320; 12 assistant children's librarians, $1,020 to $1,080; 16 cataloguers, $960 to $1,500; 20 head caretakers, $1,020 to $1,200; 16 caretakers, $390 to $960; 32 cleaners, $510 to $660; 54 junior clerks, $420 to $600.

OTHER BROOKLYN LIBRARIES.

Brooklyn Botanic Garden Library—Eastern P'kway and Washington av. 15,000 vols. 400 periodicals. Devoted to botany, horticulture, gardening and like subjects. Open daily, 9 A.M. to 5 P.M., except Su. and holidays.

Brooklyn Daily Eagle—Free circulating library for employes. Eagle Bldg. 8,000 vols.

Brooklyn Institute of Arts and Sciences—Central Museum Library, Eastern P'kway and Washington av., 724,293 vols. Reference only. Special library of books on art, natural history and ethnology. Miss S. A. Hutchinson, Lib.

Children's Museum Library (Bkln. Inst. Arts and Sciences)—185 Brooklyn av. 8,275 vols. Reference only. Library of nature books, natural sciences, travel and history. For use of teachers and students as well as children. Open 10 A.M. to 5 P.M. daily; 2 P.M. to 5 P.M. Sunday. Miss M. S. Draper, Lib.

Christian Science Reading Rooms—216A Livingston, 1272 Bedford av., 67th, bet. 3d and 4th avs., 251 E. 21st and 85 7th av.

Friends' Library—110 Schermerhorn. 600 vols. (Quakerania.) Open for reference. Hours: Tues. and Thurs. mornings. Arrangements made with persons wishing to consult old records. Librarian in attendance at close of meeting on Sun. morning. Anna L. Curtis, Lib.

Law—Room 201, Court House. E. T. Horwill, Ch.; Otto Wetzel, Lib. 45,804 vols. Open 8:45 A.M. to 11 P.M.; June 15 to July 31 to 5:30 P.M.; Aug., 1 P.M.

Long Island Historical Soc.—Clinton, cor. Pierrepont. 89,762 vols. Reference only for members or those introduced by members. Emma Toedteberg, Lib. Open 8:30 A.M. to 6 P.M.

Medical Soc. of the County of Kings (free)—1313-1317 Bedford av. 75,000 vols., 20,000 pamphlets and 700 current journals. Open 10 A.M. to 6 P.M. Chas. Frankenberger, Lib.

New Church Library (free)—108 Clark, cor. Monroe pl. 9:30 A.M. to 5 P.M., Sat. 9:30 to 1 P.M. Swedenborg's Works and collateral literature.

Pratt Institute Free Library—Ryerson, bet. DeKalb and Willoughby avs. 120,000 vols. Circulation, 220,000. Edward F. Stevens, Lib. Circulating Dept. Reference Dept., Reading Room, Applied Science Reference Room, Art Reference Room, Art Gallery, open week days, 9 A.M. to 9:30 P.M. Children's room closes at 6 P.M. Story hour, Fri. evenings.

Pratt Inst. School of Library Science—E. F. Stevens, Dir.; Josephine A. Rathbone, Vice-Dir., 220 Ryerson.

Spicer Memorial—Polytechnic Inst. Free to students. 10,000 vols. Edith C. Squires, Lib.

Underhill Soc. Library—248 Maple. 1,700 vols. 5,225 magazines and pamphlets. 1,635 photos and pictures. Miss L. H. Underhill, Lib.

Y. M. C. A. Central—55 Hanson pl. Ethel S. Brown, Lib.; Edna M. Collins, Asst. Lib.

Young Women's Christian Assn.—Schermerhorn and Flatbush av. Free to members; reading room free to women. Open 9 A.M. to 9:30 P.M. 12,857 vols. Georgia W. Rathbone, Lib.

Manhattan and Bronx.

PUBLIC LIBRARY.

New York Public Library—Astor, Lenox and Tilden Foundations. Est. by consolidation of the Astor Library, Lenox Library and the Tilden Trust, May 23, 1895. The Astor Library was founded 1849 by John Jacob Astor. The Lenox Library in 1870 by James Lenox.

The permanent site of the consolidated library is 5th av., bet. 40th and 42d, known as Bryant Park. The cornerstone of the building was laid Nov. 10, 1902. The building was dedicated May 23, 1911, and opened to the public the following day.

LIBRARIES AND READING ROOMS—MANHATTAN AND BRONX—*Continued.*

The trustees of the library are: W. W. Appleton, C. H. Dodge, S. Greenbaum, E. S. Harkness, Archbishop Hayes, A. C. James, L. C. Ledyard, J. G. Milburn, J. P. Morgan, M. J. O'Brien, S. H. Olin, W. B. Parsons, Elihu Root, C. H. Russell, E. W. Sheldon, William Sloane, G. W. Smith, I. N. Phelps Stokes, Henry Walters, Payne Whitney and The Mayor, Comptroller and Pres. of the Bd. of Aldermen, ex-officio. E. H. Anderson, Dir., 476 5th av.

Headquarters, 476 5th av., bet. 40th and 42d. Circulating branches: 33 E. B'way (Chatham sq.), 192 E. B'way (Seward Park), 61 Rivington, 388 E. Houston (Hamilton Fish Park), 66 Leroy (Hudson Park), 331 E. 10th (Tompkins sq.), 135 2d av. (Ottendorfer), 251 W. 13th (Jackson sq.), 228 E. 23d (Epiphany), 209 W. 23d (Muhlenberg), 303 E. 36th (St. Gabriel's Park), 457 W. 40th, 42d and 5th av. (Central), 123 E. 50th (Cathedral), 742 10th av. (Columbus), 121 E. 58th, 328 E. 67th, 190 Amsterdam av. (Riverside), 1465 Av. A (Webster), 222 E. 79th (Yorkville), 444 Amsterdam av. (St. Agnes), 112 E. 96th, 206 W. 100th (Blomingdale), 174 E. 110th (Aguilar), 203 W. 115th, 9 W. 124th (Harlem Library), 224 E. 125th, 73 Mhtn. (Bruce), 103 W. 135th, 503 W. 145th (Hamilton Grange), 1000 St. Nicholas av. (Washington Heights), 535 W. 179th (Ft. Washington), 321 E. 140th (Mott Haven), 759 E. 160th (Woodstock), 910 Morris av. (Melrose), 78 W. 168th (High Bridge), 610 E. 169th (Morrisania), 1866 Washington av. (Tremont), 3041 Kingsbridge av. (Kingsbridge), 5 Central av., St. George; 75 Bennett, Pt. Richmond. 132 Canal, Stapleton; 7430 Amboy rd., Tottenville. Statistics for year ending Dec. 30, 1919. In the reference dept., 892,298 desk applicants consulted 2,244,452 volumes; 1,437,178 volumes and pamphlets were in the reference dept.; in the circulating dept., 9,892,648 volumes were taken for home use; 139,510 new borrowers were registered during the year; the number of volumes in the department was 1,177,896.

The Carnegie gift announced Mar. 15, 1901, provided for 42 branch library buildings; an amendatory agreement was made Mar. 26, 1902, increasing the number to 50 for the boroughs of Manhattan, the Bronx and Richmond, which will cost over $3,006,000. The first of these branches was opened Dec. 13, 1902, at 222 E. 79th. 37 have been erected and 6 others housed in buildings otherwise provided.

Municipal Reference Br.—Municipal Bldg., Room 512.

Library School—Information regarding library courses may be had by addressing the Principal, 476 5th av.

OTHER MHTN. AND BRONX LIBRARIES.

Aeronautic Library—299 Madison av. Est. 1915. 1,500 vols. Open 9 A.M. to 5 P.M. H. C. Wirth, Mng. Dir.

Amer. Geographical Soc.—B'way and 156th. Est. 1852. 55,700 vols., 48,171 sheet maps and 938 Atlases. Open to the public the whole year. Week days from 9:30 A.M. to 5 P.M. Su. (exhibitions only), 2 to 5 P.M.

Amer. Inst.—322-324 W. 23d. Est. 1828. Open 9 to 4. 15,000 vols. for ref. W. A. Eagleston, Lib.

Amer. Museum of Natural History—77th and Central Park West. Est. 1869. Open free every day in the year: Week days and holidays, 9 A.M. to 5 P.M.; Sundays, 1 P.M. to 5 P.M. 100,000 vols. R. W. Tower, Curator of Library and Publications. Free for reference. Natural sciences and anthropology.

Amer. Numismatic Soc.—B'way at 156th. Est. 1858. 4,000 vols. 550 mem. For public consultation. S. P. Noe, Sec.; H. Wood, Curator.

Amer. Soc. Mech. Engineers—(See Engineering Soc. Library.)

Assn. of the Bar Library—42 W. 44th. 129,152 vols. Franklin O. Poole, Lib.

Astor—(See New York Public Library.)

Benjamin & Townsend—Bellevue Hospital, ft. E. 26th. Est. 1889. Open 9 to 5. 3,500 vols. Alex. Kennedy, Lib.

Bethany Memorial Free Reading Room—67th and 1st av. Open afternoon and evening daily, except Su. A. B. Churchman.

Bryson Lib. of the Teachers' College—W. 120th, nr. B'way. Est. 1888. 68,882 vols. Free for lending, etc., to students of Teachers' and Barnard colleges, Columbia Univ. Elizabeth G. Baldwin, Lib.

Cathedral—Consolidated with N. Y. Public.

Catholic Club—120 Central Park S. Est. 1871. Free to members and families and persons introduced by members. Also to students in schools and colleges. Open to mems. 30,000 vols. Thos. B. Lee, Lib.

Catholic Reading Room for Seamen—422 West. 2,500 vols. Rev. P. J. Magrath, Dir.

Century Library—7 W. 43d. 12,000 vols. For members of Century Assn. C. W. Gordon, Lib.

Christian Science Reading Rooms—159 W. 72d, 154 Nassau, 680 Madison av., 33 W. 42d, 606 W. 110th, 600 W. 181st, 225 5th av., 149 E. 86th, Mhtn.; 505 Tremont av., Bronx.

Columbia University—B'way and 116th. Est. 1754. Open 8:30 A.M. to 10 P.M. 725,000 vols. Free to adults for consultation on introduction. W. H. Carpenter, Act. Lib.

Cooper Union—8th and 4th av. Open 8 A.M. to 10 P.M.; on Sun., from Sept. to June, 12 M. to 9 P.M. 58,000 vols. F. A. Curtis, Lib.

Corporation Counsel Library—Municipal bldg. Exclusively for use of Corporation Counsel and assistants. 13,100 vols. J. M. Valles, Lib.

DeWitt Memorial—286 Rivington. Est. 1882. Open 3 to 7 P.M. 3,000 vols. 6,300 mem. M. R. Birnie, Lib. Free circulating.

Directory Library—R. L. Polk & Co., Inc. Publishers of 'Trow's Directories, 125-135 Church. State, city and local directories of United States and Canada, over 3,000 vols. Open 8:30 A.M. to 5 P.M.

Engineering Societies Library—29 W. 39th. Open daily, except Sun. and holidays, 9 A.M. to 10 P.M. 155,000 vols. Free to the public for reference. H. W. Craver, Dir.

Foreign Missions Library (free)—156 5th av. Est. 1840. 11,747 vols. Open 9 A.M. to 5 P.M. except Sun. and holidays. Miss S. A. Pinder, Lib.

Friends' Library—221 E. 15th. 3,050 vols. Open for reference. Hours: Mon., Wed., 9 to 12 A.M.; Fri., 1:30 to 5 P.M. Librarian in attendance at close of meeting on Sun. morning. Arrangements made with persons wishing to consult old records. (Quakerania.) Anna L. Curtis, Lib.

General Soc. Mechanics and Tradesmen—Free Library and Reference Room, 16-24 W. 44th. Est. 1820. Open 9 A.M. to 8 P.M., except Sun. and holidays. 97,900 vols. H. W. Parker, Lib. Connected with the library is the Slade (architectural), 1,137 vols.; DeMilt (reference), 16,879 vols., and the Kendall Collection (architectural), 92 vols. R. T. Davies, Treas.-Sec.

Hispanic Soc. of Amer.—156th, W. of B'way. Est. 1904. A. M. Huntington, Pres.; H. F. Osborn, Vice-Pres.; G. B. Grinnell, Sec. Museum and public reference lib. 100,000 vols. Spain, Portugal, Latin America. Museum open to the public from 9 A.M. to 5 P.M. week days, ex. Sun. and Mon.

Hudson Guild Library—436 W. 27th. 5,000 vols.

Huntington Free Library—Westchester sq. Est. 1891. Open 9 A.M. to 10 P.M. Sun., 2 to 9 P.M. 5,000 vols. Miss Emma K. Volz.

Lenox—See N. Y. Public Library.

Library—City Clerk—Board of Aldermen—Municipal Bldg. Est. 1847. Open 9 A.M. to 5 P.M. 2,500 vols. Philip Baer, Lib. Free for reference.

Library of the N. Y. Homeopathic Med. College and Flower Hospital—1886. 63d and Av. A. 13,000 vols. Frances Holly, Lib.

Libreria Economica Italiana—215 Spring. 200,000 vols. E. Filomarino & Co.

Loan Libraries for Ships—76 Wall. Supported by American Seamen's Friend Soc. Sends out on ships cases of 43 books each. Total vols., 660,321. W. Elling, Lib.

Masonic—50 W. 24th. Est. 1868. Open 2 to 10:30 P.M. 12,600 vols. E. B. Silver, Grand Lib.

Mercantile Library Assn. of N. Y.—Astor pl. Est. 1820. Open 9 A.M. to 5 P.M. 250,368 vols. Chas. H. Cox, Lib.

Methodist—150 5th av. Open 9 A.M. to 5 P.M. 7,000 vols. M. Young, Act. Lib.

Metropolitan Museum of Art—Central Park, 82d and 5th av. Open 10 to 5 weekdays; holidays and Saturdays, 10 to 6. 37,400 vols., 48,600 photographs. Wm. Clifford, Lib.

N. Y. Academy of Medicine—17-21 W. 43d. Est. 1847. Open 9 A.M. to 2 P.M. 116,130 vols. J. S. Brownne, Res. Lib.

N. Y. Anti-Vivisection Soc.—456 4th av. Books, magazines and other anti-vivisection literature free. Diana Belais, Pres.

LIBRARIES AND READING ROOMS—*Manhattan and Bronx—Continued.*

N. Y. Genealogical and Biographical Soc.—226 W. 58th. Est. 1869. 18,000 vols. Free to members. Open week days, 10 to 6, and Mon. eve., 8 to 10 P.M. Visitors welcomed.

N. Y. Historical Soc.—170 Central Park West. Est. 1804. Open daily, 9 A.M. to 5 P.M. Closed Sun., Christmas, New Year's Day, July 4 and month of Aug.; open other holidays 1 to 5 P.M. Amer. history. For reference. R. H. Kelby, Lib.

N. Y. Law Institute—Room 932, Equitable Bldg. Est. 1828. 91,508 vols. 820 mem. J. F. Couilliou, Act. Lib.

N. Y. Port Soc.—Free reading room for seamen. 166 11th av. Open week days 10 A.M. to 10 P.M.; Sundays, 2 to 9 P.M. Rev. K. Palmer Miller, Gen. Sec.

N. Y. Produce Exchange—B'way and Beaver. Est. 1862. Open 9 A.M. to 3:30 P.M. Free to members.

N. Y. Society—109 University pl. Est. 1754. 9 A.M. to 5:30 P.M. 100,000 vols. F. B. Bigelow, Lib. Free for reference.

N. Y. Univ. Gen. Library—Univ. Heights. Org. 1831. 86,800 vols. Open daily. Law—Washington sq. 28,060 vols. Open daily. Pedagogy—Univ. Bldg., Washington sq. Open daily. 10,665 vols. Belle Corwin, M.D., Lib.

Railroad Br. Y. M. C. A.—309 Park av. 24,467 vols. Theo. F. Judd, Act. Lib.

Reform Club—9 So. William. Sidney Newborg, Sec.

Riverdale—Riverdale, N. Y. Open Mon., Wed. and Sat. evenings, 7:30 to 9:30; Wed. and Sat. afternoons, 3 to 5. Martha Faison, Lib.

Russell Sage Foundation Library—130 E. 22d. 19,000 sociological books and 51,000 pamphlets. Free to the public. Open 8:45 A.M. to 6 P.M.; June, July, Aug., Sept., 9 A.M. to 5 P.M. week days; Sat., 12 noon. F. W. Jenkins, Lib.

Union Settlement Library—241 E. 104th. 1,516 vols. Isabel Molumphy, Lib., 237 E. 104th.

Union Theological Seminary—B'way and 120th. 141,602 vols, 70,411 pamphlets, 240 manuscripts, Rev. H. P. Smith, Lib.

Vedanta Soc. Library—50 W. 67th. 600 vols.

Womrath's New Fiction (pay)—2191, 2544, 2792, 3489 B'way, 21 W. 45th, 15 E. 28th. Grand Centl. Sta., 642 and 976 Madison av.

Y. M. C. A.—2 W. 45th. Free to public for reference. Est. 1852. 100,000 total number of vols. distributed among 14 branches. 23d St. Branch—215 W. 23d. 12,400 vols., A. A. Clarke, Lib. West Side Branch—318 W. 57th, 45,200 vols., F. R. Petrie, Lib.

Y. M. H. A. Library—Lexington av. and 92d. 14,500 vols. Miss M. B. Adler, Lib.

Y. W. C. A., Central Branch—610 Lexington av. Open 9 A.M. to 9:30 P.M. Circulation dept. open to association members only. Membership, $1 per year. Reading and reference rooms free. 9,000 vols. M. F. Blair, Lib.

Queens.

PUBLIC LIBRARY.

The Queens Borough Public Library—Office, 402 Fulton, Jamaica, L. I. Public circulating. Incorp. 1896 as the L. I. City Public Library Incorp. as the Queens Borough Public Library April 17, 1907. Officers: Prest., J. H. Leich; Vice-Pres., J. W. Dolan; Sec., Owen J. Dever; Treas., W. A. Duncan; Asst. Treas., Edward L. Hein. Trustees: J. A. Dayton, N. Y.; J. W. Dolan, Kew Gardens; O. J. Dever, Middle Village; W. A. Duncan, Far Rockaway; F. L. Feuerbach, Richmond Hill; E. L. Hein, Woodhaven; J. H. Leich, Woodhaven; T. J. O'Brien, Brooklyn; F. O'Keefe, Brooklyn; G. W. Pople, Flushing; J. T. Quinn, Ridgewood; M. J. Shugrue, Corona; H. F. Strebel, Brooklyn; H. Stoesser, M.D., Union Course; G. A. Vandenhoff, Astoria.

Director, John C. Atwater. Branches, Astoria, Main and Woolsey, L. I. City; Bayside, Elsie pl., Bayside; Broadway, 298 Steinway av., L. I. City; Corona, 57 Kingsland av., Corona; Elmhurst, B'way and Maurice av., Elmhurst; Far Rockaway, Central and Mott avs., Far Rockaway; Flushing, Jamaica and Jagger avs., Flushing; Grandview, Grandview and Forest avs., Ridgewood; Hollis, Fulton and Iroquois av., Hollis; Jamaica, 402 Fulton, Jamaica; Nelson, 244 Jackson av., L. I. City; Ozone Park, 4138 Jerome av., Ozone Park, L. I.; Poppenhusen, 13th and 1st av., College Point; Queens, Whittier and Wertland av., Queens; Richmond Hill, Hillside av., Richmond Hill; Ridgewood, 754 Seneca av., Ridgewood; Seaside, Boulevard and Oceanus av., Rockaway Beach; Steinway, 441 Potter av., L. I. City; Whitestone, 30 8th av., Whitestone; Woodhaven, 1229 Jamaica av., Woodhaven; Woodside, Greenpoint and Betts avs., Woodside. Traveling Libraries—Arverne, Blvd. and Park av.; Cedar Manor, 292 N. Y. av., Jamaica; Douglaston, Main av.; Dunton, 31 Jerome av.; Evergreen, 1020 Fresh Pond rd.; Forest Hills, Greenway Terrace, Glendale, 2896 Myrtle av.; Jackson Hgts., 25th and Baxter av., Elmhurst; Laurel Hill, Montgomery and Cypress av.; Little Neck, Old House Landing rd.; Louona Park, 80 43d, Corona; Maspeth, 80 Grand; Middle Village, 2177 Metropolitan av.; Morris Park, Atlantic av.; Ravenswood, Vernon av., L. I. City; Rockaway Park, 5th av., nr. L. I. R. R.; So. Ozone Park, Rockaway rd. and Pressberger av.; Springfield, Higbie av., nr. Elec. R. R.; Winfield, Queens blvd. and Ramsey; St. Albans. Numerous other distributing agencies of Traveling Library, such as Community Stations, Village Collections and Institutional Stations.

All Branch Libraries are open daily, except Sunday, from 9 A.M. to 9 P.M. Bayside and Whitestone are open Monday, Wednesday and Friday from 10 A.M. to 6 P.M., and Tuesday, Thursday and Saturday from 1 to 9 P.M., and Steinway, Monday, Wednesday and Friday, 12 M. to 9 P.M., and Tuesday, Thursday and Saturday from 10 A.M. to 6 P.M. Hollis and Queens on Tuesday, Thursday and Saturday from 12 M. to 9 P.M., and Monday, Wednesday and Friday from 9 A.M. to 5:30 P.M.

All Branch Libraries are open from 9 A.M. to 12 M. on all holidays, except New Year's Day, Fourth of July, Labor Day, Thanksgiving and Christmas, on which days they are closed all day.

OTHER QUEENS LIBRARIES.

Christian Science Reading Rooms—Greenwood av., Richmond Hill; 95 Grove, Flushing; Central av. at Neilson av., Far Rockaway; 178 Continental av., Forest Hills; 10 Union av., Jamaica, L. I.

Supreme Court Library in the County of Queens—Court House, L. I. City. 8,101 vols. Harry A. Horton, Lib.

Richmond.

Christian Science Reading Rooms—61 Richmond Turnpike, Tompkinsville; Castleton and Oakland avs., W. New Brighton.

See New York Public Library under Mhtn.

LIBRARIES OF LONG ISLAND.

Location.	Name.	Librarian.	No. Vols.
Amityville	Free	Helen Badger	2,200
Babylon	Babylon	Gladys Conklin	5,223
Bay Shore	Free	E. S. Smith	4,985
Bellport	Public	Mrs. W. W. Hulse	4,000
Bridgeham'ton	Hampton	M. T. van Scoy	13,131
Cold Spring H.	Free	E. J. Wright	5,111
Cutchogue	Free	D. E. Morrell	1,781
Easthampton	Free	E. C. Hedges	12,200
East Quogue	Free	E. Van Hise	1,110
E. Rockaway	B'seley Free	A. Davison	4,500
Freeport	Public	A. B. Rogan	5,000
Garden City	Cathedral Sc.	B. G. Wood	5,300
Garden City	St. Paul's Sc.	F. A. Suter	2,000
Glen Cove	Public	E. C. Thorne	10,500
Great Neck	Great Neck	Mrs. H. W. Craver	6,568
Greenport	Floyd Mem	Miss E. Deale	3,325
Hempstead	Hempstead	Miss C. Webb	6,104
Huntington	Association	Mrs. M. F. Gains	10,000
Islip	St. Mark's	Miss F. B. Smith	6,000
Locust Valley	Friends' Aca	LaVerne Baldwin	3,221
Lynbrook	Free	Mrs. W. J. Raeb'rn	2,006
Massapequa	D. F. Jones	Hy. F. Fallot	3,648
Mattituck	Free	C. Jackson	4,632
Merrick	Free Circu'g	Miss L. Miller	3,893
Northport	Public	Miss E. Partridge	5,991
Oyster Bay	Free	Lule P. Sammis	7,690
Patchogue	Free	Alma Custead	7,500
Pt. Washingt'n	Free	W. M. Mitchell	7,034
Riverhead	Free	Mrs. C. M. C. Terry	3,254
Riverhead	Roanoke	Mrs. C. J. Young	1,227
Riverhead	Sound Ave	C. P. Smith	1,050
Rockville C'tre	Public	A. H. Decker	9,592
Roslyn	Bryant	W. Witte	2,100
Sag Harbor	Pierson H. S.	G. R. Lyon	2,100
Sag Harbor	J. Jerm'm Me.	O. P. Young	13,081
Sea Cliff	Public	May Dibbell	4,773
Setauket	Emma Clark	Jos'ine Elbertson	5,091
Shelter Island	Public	D. B. Payne	7,079
Smithtown Br.	Smithtown	C. H. Peek	6,314
Southampton	Rogers Mem	J. W. Foster	12,8[illegible]
Southold	Free	A. A. Spooner	5,800
Westbury	Public	Martha Tompkins	1,459
W'thampton	Free	A. S. Meeker	3,963

UNIVERSITIES, COLLEGES, ACADEMIES AND PRIVATE SCHOOLS.

Leading Institutions Outside of N. Y. City.

Name, location and name of President or Dean. *Girls. †Boys. §Co-educational. (For special school information consult Bkln. Eagle Information Bureau and Educational Directory.)

Amherst College†—Amherst, Mass. Alex. Meiklejohn.

Berea College§—Berea, Ky. Wm. G. Frost.

Boston Univ.§—Boston, Mass. L. H. Murlin.

Bowdoin College†—Brunswick, Me. K. C. M. Sills.

Brown Univ.§—Providence, R. I. W. H. P. Faunce.

Bryn Mawr College*—Bryn Mawr, Pa. Helen H. Taft.

Bucknell Univ.§—Lewisburg, Pa. E. W. Hunt.

Clark Univ. (Colored)§—So. Atlanta, Ga. H. A. King.

Colgate Univ.†—Hamilton, N. Y. E. B. Bryan.

Cornell Univ.§—Ithaca, N. Y. J. G. Schurman.

Dartmouth College†—Hanover, N. H. E. M. Hopkins.

De Pauw Univ.§—Greencastle, Ind. G. R. Grose.

Drake Univ.§—Des Moines, Ia. A. Holmes.

Florida State College*—Tallahassee, Fla. E. Conradi.

George Washington Univ.—§—Washington, D. C. W. C. Collier.

Georgetown Univ.†—Washington, D. C. J. B. Creeden.

Grinnell College§—Grinnell, Ia. J. H. T. Main.

Harvard Univ.†—Cambridge, Mass. A. L. Lowell.

Illinois College§—Jacksonville, Ill. C. H. Rammelkamp.

Indiana Univ.§—Bloomington, Ind. Wm. L. Bryan.

Iowa State Coll. of Agriculture—Ames, Ia. R. A. Pearson.

Johns Hopkins Univ.§—Baltimore, Md. F. J. Goodnow.

Knox College§—Galesburg, Ill. J. L. McConaughy.

Lehigh Univ.†—South Bethlehem, Pa. H. S. Drinker.

Leland Stanford, Jr., Univ.§—Stanford U. P. O., Cal. R. L. Wilbur.

Louisiana State Univ.§—Baton Rouge, La. T. A. Boyd.

Marquette Univ.§—Milwaukee, Wis. H. C. Noonan.

Mass. Inst. of Technology§—Boston, Mass. R. C. Maclaurin.

Mt. Holyoke College*—South Hadley, Mass. Mary E. Woolley.

Northwestern Univ.§—Evanston and Chicago, Ill. L. H. Hough.

Oberlin College§—Oberlin, Ohio. H. C. King.

Ohio State Univ.§—Columbus, Ohio. W. O. Thompson.

Ohio Univ.§—Athens, Ohio. A. Ellis.

Pennsylvania State College§—State College, P. O. Edwin E. Sparks.

Princeton Univ.†—Princeton, N. J. J. G. Hibben.

Purdue Univ.§—Lafayette, Ind. W. E. Stone.

Radcliffe College*—Cambridge, Mass. L. B. R. Briggs.

Rutgers College†—New Brunswick, N. J. W. H. Demarest.

St. Lawrence Univ.§—Canton, N. Y. R. E. Sykes.

St. Louis Univ.§—St. Louis, Mo. W. F. Robinson.

Simmons College*—Boston, Mass. H. Lefavour.

Smith College*—Northampton, Mass. Wm. A. Neilson.

State College of Washington§—Pullman, Wash. E. O. Holland.

State Univ. of Iowa§—Iowa City, Iowa. W A. Jessup.

State Univ. of Montana§—Missoula, Mont. E. O. Sisson.

Stevens Inst. of Technology†—Hoboken, N. J. A. C. Humphreys.

Syracuse Univ.§—Syracuse, N. Y. J. R. Day.

Temple Univ.§—Philadelphia, Pa. R. H. Conwell.

Tufts College†—Medford, Mass. J. E. Cousens.

Univ. of Alabama§—Tuscaloosa, Ala. G. H. Denny.

Univ. of Arizona§—Tucson, Ariz. R. B. Von Kleinsmid.

Univ. of Arkansas§—Fayetteville, Ark. J. C. Futrall.

Univ. of Buffalo§—Buffalo, N. Y. C. P. Norton.

Univ. of California§—Berkeley, Cal. B. I. Wheeler.

Univ. of Chicago§—Chicago, Ill. H. P. Judson.

Univ. of Colorado§—Boulder, Col. Geo. Norlin.

Univ. of Denver§—Denver, Col. H. A. Buchtel.

Univ. of Detroit†—Detroit, Mich. W. T. Doran.

Univ. of Florida†—Gainesville, Fla. A. A. Murphree.

Univ. of Georgia†—Athens, Ga. D. C. Barrow.

Univ. of Idaho§—Moscow, Idaho. E. H. Lindly.

Univ. of Illinois§—Urbana, Ill. E. J. James.

Univ. of Kansas§—Lawrence, Kan. F. Strong.

Univ. of Kentucky§—Lexington, Ky. F. L. McVey.

Univ. of Maine§—Orono, Me. R. J. Aley.

Univ. of Maryland—Baltimore, Md. Thos. Fell.

Univ. of Michigan§—Ann Arbor, Mich. M. L. Burton.

Univ. of Minnesota§—Minneapolis, Minn. M. L. Burton.

Univ. of Mississippi§—University, Miss. J. N. Powers.

Univ. of Missouri§—Columbia, Mo. A. R. Hill.

Univ. of Montana§—Missoula, Mont. E. O. Sisson.

Univ. of Nebraska§—Lincoln, Neb. S. Avery.

Univ. of Nevada§—Reno, Nev. W. E. Clark.

Univ. of New Mexico§—Albuquerque, N. M. D. R. Boyd.

Univ. of North Carolina†—Chapel Hill, N. C. H. W. Chase.

Univ. of North Dakota§—Grand Forks, N. D. T. F. Kane.

Univ. of Notre Dame†—Notre Dame, Ind. Rev. J. Cavanaugh, D.D.

Univ. of Oklahoma§—Norman, Okla. S. D. Brooks.

Univ. of Oregon§—Eugene, Ore. P. L. Campbell.

Univ. of Pennsylvania§—Philadelphia, Pa. J. H. Penniman, Act. Provost.

Univ. of Pittsburgh§—Pittsburgh, Pa. S. B. McCormick.

Univ. of Rochester§—Rochester, N. Y. R. Rhees.

Univ. of South California§—Los Angeles, Cal. G. F. Bovard.

Univ. of South Carolina§—Columbia, S. C. Wm. S. Currell.

Univ. of South Dakota§—Vermilion, S. D. R. L. Slagle.

Univ. of Tennessee§—Knoxville, Tenn. A. H. Morgan.

Univ. of Texas§—Austin, Tex. R. E. Vinson.

Univ. of Utah§— Salt Lake City, Utah. J. A Widtsoe.

Univ. of Vermont—Burlington, Vt. G. H. Perkins.

Univ. of Virginia†—Charlottesville, Va. E. A. Alderman.

Univ. of Washington§—Seattle, Wash. H. Suzzallo.

Univ. of Wisconsin§—Madison, Wis. E. A. Birge.

Univ. of Wyoming§—Laramie, Wyo. A. Nelson.

Valparaiso Univ.§—Valparaiso, Ind. H. K. Brown.

Vanderbilt Univ.§—Nashville, Tenn. J. H. Kirkland.

Vassar College*—Poughkeepsie, N. Y. H. N. MacCracken.

Washington and Jefferson College†—Washington, Pa. S. C. Black.

Washington and Lee Univ.†—Lexington, Va. H. L. Smith.

Washington Univ.§—St. Louis, Mo. F. A. Hall (Chanc'r).

Wellesley College*—Wellesley, Mass. Miss E. F. Pendleton.

Wesleyan Univ.†—Middletown, Conn. Wm. A. Shanklin.

Western Reserve Univ.§—Cleveland, O. C. F. Thwing.

West Virginia Univ.§—Morgantown, W. Pa. F. B. Trotter.

William and Mary College†—Williamsburg, Va. J. A. C. Chandler.

Williams College†—Williamstown, Mass. H. A. Garfield.

Yale Univ.†—New Haven, Conn. A. T. Hadley.

Brooklyn.

COLLEGES.

Adelphi College*—Clifton and St. James pl. F. D. Blodgett, Pres.

Brooklyn College—265 Nostrand av. Rev. J. A. Farrell.

Brooklyn Law School of St. Lawrence University§—Eagle bldg.; W. P. Richardson, Dean.

St. Francis College and Academy†—41 Butler. Brother Jariath, Pres.

St. John's College†—Willoughby av., cor. Lewis. Rev. J. W. Moore, Pres

St. Joseph's Day College*—245 Clinton av.

PREPARATORY SCHOOLS.

Acad. of the Visitation*—Ridge blvd. and 89th. Sis. F. Agnes.

Adelphi Academy§—Lafayette av. and St. James pl. E. C. Alder. Prin.

Bedford Institute*—221 McDonough.

Berkeley Institute*—183 Lincoln pl. Ina C. Atwood, Pres.

Brooklyn Heights Sem.*—18 Pierrepont.

UNIVERSITIES, COLLEGES, ACADEMIES AND PRIVATE SCHOOLS—BROOKLYN—*Continued.*

Chase's, Mrs. J. A., Sch.§—976-978 St. Marks av.
Eastern Dist. Business Sch.§—775 DeKalb av.
Flatbush School§—1603 Newkirk av.
Friends' School§—112 Schermerhorn.
Froebel Acad.§—176 Bkln. av. L. J. Forbes.
Heffley Collegiate Prep. *Sch.§—243 Ryerson.
Miss Kennedy's Private Schl.—211 Carroll.
Lincoln School§—284 South 9th.
Lockwood Acad.§—138 So. Oxford.
Misses McCreary's School§—657 Ocean av.
Marquand Prep. Sch.†—55 Hanson pl. C. O. Warren.
Mrs. Perkins' School§—112 Woodruff av.
Moeller's Boarding Schl.§—5000 15th av.
N. Y. Preparatory School§—Franklin and Jefferson av.
Packer Collegiate Inst.*—170 Joralemon. J. H. Denbigh.
Poly Prep. Country Day Sch.†—Dyker Hts. J. D. Allen.
Pratt Inst.§—215 Ryerson. F. B. Pratt.
Prospect Heights School†—217 Lincoln pl.
St. Agnes' Seminary*—283-287 Union. Sis. of St. Joseph.
St. Angela's Hall*—286 Washington av. Sis. St. Celestine.
St. Francis Academy—41 Butler.
St. John's Coll. High Sch.†—75 Lewis av.
Y. M. C. A., Bed. Br.†—1121 Bedford av.
Y. M. C. A., Central Br.†—55 Hanson pl.
Y. M. C. A., East. Dist.†—179 Marcy av.
Y. M. H. A.†—345 9th.
Y. W. C. A., Central Br.*—Schermerhorn and Flatbush av.

TECHNICAL SCHOOLS.

Heffley School of Engineering†—243 Ryerson. N. P. Heffley, Pres.
Marquand School†—55 Hanson pl.
Polytechnic Inst. of Bkln.†—85 Livingston. F. W. Atkinson, Pres.
Pratt Inst.§—215 Ryerson. F. B. Pratt, Pres.
Y. M. C. A., Central Br.†—55 Hanson pl. M. S. Tuttle, Pres. Eastern Dist. Br.—179 Marcy av.

BUSINESS.

Accountancy Inst. of Bklyn.—55 Hanson pl.
Alpha School—2 Sumner av.
Avon School—1317 B'way.
Browne's Bus. Coll.—Flatbush & Lafayette avs.
Columbia Bus. Inst.—23 Flatbush av.
Curtis Bus. Schl.—140 Ft. Greene pl.
Drake's Business Schl.—Bedford av. and Fulton.
Eastern Dist. Bus. Inst.—775 DeKalb av.
Ellsworth Schl.—912 Flatbush av.
Euclid Schl.—1309 Fulton.
Excelsior Bus. Schl.—2582 Atlantic av.
Flatbush Com. Schl.—824 Flatbush av.
Flatbush-Kensington Bus. Schl.—1509 37th.
Heffley-Greenpoint Schl.—894 Manhattan av.
Heffley Inst.—243-245 Ryerson.
Kissick's Bus. Inst.—37 Ft. Greene pl.
Lambs Bus. Training Schl.—327 9th.
L. I. Bus. Schl.—143-149 South 8th.
Marquand School—55 Hanson pl.
Middleton's Bus. Schl.—9th and 6th av.
Miner's Bus. Acad.—720 Hancock.
People's School—1781 Pitkin av.
Plymouth Inst.—Orange and Hicks.
Queensboro Bus. Inst.—Cypress and Myrtle avs.
St. Joseph's Com'l High Schl.—342 Bridge.
The C. F. Young Schl. of Sten.—148 Montague.
Wood's Bus. Schl.—287 B'way.
Y. M. C. A., Bed. Br.—1125 Bedford av.; Cent. Br., 55 Hanson pl.; E. D. Br., 179 Marcy av.
Y. M. H. A.—345 9th.
Y. W. C. A.—376 Schermerhorn.

LAW.

Bkln. Law School of St. Lawrence Univ.—Eagle Bldg.

MEDICAL.

Bkln. Coll. of Pharmacy§—265 Nostrand av.
Long Island Coll. Hospital†—Medical Coll. in Polhemus Mem. Clinic, Henry, cor. Amity.

MUSIC.

Bkln. Acad. of Mus. Art—547-49 Greene av.
Bkln. Con. of Music—Franklin and Lefferts pl.
Bkln. Music Schl. Settlement—122-126 St. Felix.
Bushwick Cons. of Music—36 Palmetto.
Central Mus. Schl. (Y. M. C. A.)—55 Hanson pl.
Fique Musical Inst.—128 DeKalb av.
Grand Ital. Cons. Music—542 State.
Hager's Studio of Music—51 Harman.
Hassell Cons. of Music—853 Marcy av.
Henry Mollenhauer's Cons. of Music—73 Livingston.
King Music Studios—6 Spencer pl.
Lenox Schl. of Pop. Music—757 Halsey.
Leschetizsky Conserv. of Music—964 St. Marks av.
Louis Mollenhauer's Con. of Music—71 Marlborough rd.
Master Schl. of Music—110 Remsen.
Munson Inst. of Music—357 Ovington av.
People's Mus. Inst. of Bkln.—126 Macon.
Roth Studio—405 9th.
Slack's Schl. of Music—6 Alice ct.
St. John's Coll. Cons. Music—82 Lewis av.
Stagg Studio of Music—107 Miller av.
Tollefsen Studio—946 President.
Venth Cons. of Music—115 McDonough.
Victoria Music Studio. Inc.—435 Bergen.
Winn Schl. of Pop. Mus.—691 DeKalb av.
Woelber Schl. of Music—784A Quincy.

MISCELLANEOUS.

Amer. Concentration Schl.—283 St. John's pl.
Automobile Schl. (Bedford Y. M. C. A.)—1104 Bedford av.
Berlitz Schl. of Languages—218 Livingston.
B'way Dancing Acad.—1050 B'way.
Brooklyn Auto Schl.—1029 Bedford av.
Brooklyn Inst. Art and Sciences§—Lafayette av., cor. Ashland pl. (See index for details.)
Chateau du Parc Acad. of Dram. and Operatic Arts—Chauteau du Parc.
De Severinus Art Schl.—1076 Bergen.
Equitable Gymnasium—120 B'way.
Koch's Acad. of Dancing—1252 Bedford av.
Koch's Dancing Schl.—158 Park pl.
McEvoy Schl. of Pedagogy—6 3d av.
Montague Physical Training Inst.—185 Montague.
New Way Auto Schl.—B'way and Willoughby.
North Amer. Auto Schl.—586 Atlantic av. and 219 Havemeyer.
St. John's Theo. Sem.—Lewis av. and Hart.
Stelle Riding Academy—Caton pl. & Pk. Circle.
Stern School of Dancing—952 B'way.
Westerley's Riding Schl.—Cortelyou rd. and Rogers av.
Yoerger's Boxing Sch.—952 B'way.

Manhattan and Bronx.

COLLEGES.

Barnard College*—B'way and 119th. Miss V. C. Gildersleeve, Dean.
Coll. City of N. Y.†—St. Nicholas av. and 139th S. E. Mezes.
Coll. of Mt. St. Vincent*—261st. Sr. M. Ambrose.
Columbia Univ.§—116th, Morningside Heights. N. M. Butler, Pres.
Columbia Unv. Law Schl.—Riverside Heights.
Fordham Univ.†—191st and 3d av. E. P. Tivnan.
Hunter*—68th and Park av. G. S. Davis, Pres.
Manhattan Coll.†—131st and B'way. Christian Brothers. Rev. Brother Jasper.
N. Y. Univ.§—Schools. (1) College of Arts and Pure Science, University Heights. (2) College of Engineering. (3) Washington Square College, Washington sq. (4) School of Commerce, Accounts and Finance; Wall St. Division, 90 Trinity pl. (5) School of Law. (6) Graduate School. (7) School of Pedagogy. (8) Graduate School of Business Administration, 90 Trinity pl. (9) Training School for Teachers of Retail Selling. (10) Medical College, 1st av. and E. 26th. (11) Veterinary College. (12) Summer School. (13) Women's Law Class, 32 Waverly pl.. E. E. Brown, Chancellor; LeRoy E. Kimball, Bursar; M. E. Loom's, Registrar.

PREPARATORY SCHOOLS.

Acad. of Mt. St. Vincent.*—West 261st.
Academy of Sacred Heart*—533 Madison av.
Ballard Schl. (Y. W. C. A.)*—610 Lexington av.
Barnard Schl.†—W. 244th.
Barnard Schl.*—423 W. 148th.
Berkeley-Irving Schl.†—309 W. 83d.
Brown Schl. of Tutoring§—241 W. 75th.
Buckley Schl.†—120 E. 74th.
Clark Schl.†—301 W. 72d.
Clason Pt. Military Acad.†—Clason Pt.
Collegiate Schl.†—241 W. 77th.
Columbia Gram. Sch.†—5 W. 93d.
Cooper Union§—8th and 4th av.
De La Salle Inst.†—108 Central Pk. South.
Dwight Schl.†—72 Park av.
Ethical Culture Schl.§—Central Park West and 63d.
Franklin Schl.†—18 W. 89th.
Friends' Seminary§—226 E. 16th.
Gardner Schl. for Girls—11 E. 51st.
Hamilton Inst. for Girls—90th and Riverside Drive.
Hamilton Inst.†—599 West End av.
Holy Cross Acad.*—343 W. 42d.

UNIVERSITIES, COLLEGES, ACADEMIES AND PRIVATE SCHOOLS—MHTN. AND BRONX—*Con.*

Horace Mann Schl.§—551 W. 120th.
Horace Mann Schl.†—W. 246th.
Kelvin Schl.†—331 W. 70th.
Kohut Schl.†—Riverdale.
Lawrence Smith Schl.—111 E. 60th.
L'Ecole Francaise—12 E. 95th.
Loyola Schl.†—Park av. and 83d.
Massee Summer Tutoring Schl.§—507 5th av.
McBurney Schl.†—318 W. 57th.
Miss Fawcett's Schl.*—57 E. 73d.
Mrs. Scoville's Schl.*—2042 5th av.
New York Prep. Schl.§—72 Park av.
Rayson Schl.*—164 W. 75th.
Riverdale Country Schl.†—W. 252d.
Riverside Schl.*—879 West End av.
Scudder Schl.*—316 W. 72d.
St. Agatha Schl.*—553 W. End av.
St. Ann's Acad.†—Lex. av. and 76th.
St. George's Schl.†—59 E. 64th.
Trinity Schl.†—139 W. 91st.
Xavier High Schl.†—30 W. 16th.
Y. M. C. A. 23d St. Prep. Schl.—215 W. 23d.
Y. M. C. A. West Side†—318 W. 57th.

TECHNICAL.

Baron de Hirsh Trade Schl.†—222 E. 64th.
Cooper Union§—4th av. and 8th.
Hebrew Tech. Inst.†—36 Stuyvesant.
Hebrew Tech. Schl. for Girls—240 2d av.
N. Y. Electrical Schl.†—30 W. 17th.
N. Y. Nautical College—318 W. 57th.
N. Y. Trade Schl.†—1st av. and 67th.
U. S. Aero Schl.—38 Park Row.
Webb Institute of Naval Architecture—188th and Sedgwick av.
Y. M. C. A. West Side†—318 W. 57th.

BUSINESS.

Chelsea Schl.—215 W. 23d.
Chief Schl.—207 W. 35th.
Drake's Business Schl.—154 Nassau.
Eastman Gaines Schl.—123d and Lenox av.
Elliott-Fisher Billing—88 Park pl.
Fifth Av. Schl. of Secs.—503 5th av.
Fritz's Business Schl.—334 5th av.
Gaffey's Shorthand Schl.—25 W. 34th.
Haskins Business Inst.—150 W. 55th.
Interboro Inst.—63 Park Row.
Kimball Bus. Schl.—116 W. 14th.
Miller Business Schl.—E. 23d and Lex. av.
Mull's Schl.—144 Columbus av.
Natl. Training Schl. for Filing—125 W. 42d.
N. Y. Inst. of Accountancy—215 W. 23d.
N. Y. Schl. of Filing—1170 B'way.
New York Schl. of Secretaries—33 W. 42d.
N. Y. Univ. Schl. of Com'ce, Accounts & Finance—32 Waverly pl.
Pace Inst. of Accountancy—30 Church.
Packard Com. Schl.—Lexington av. and 35th.
Paine's Uptown Bus. Schl.—1931 B'way.
Pernin Shorthand Schl.—628 World bldg.
Reed Business Schl.—150 Nassau.
Titus Civil Service Schl.—121 E. 11th.
U. S. Secretarial Schl.—542 5th av.
Y. M. C. A. West Side—318 W. 57th.

LAW.

Columbia Univ. Law Schl.—Riverside Heights.
Fordham Univ. Law Schl.—233 B'way.
N. N. Univ. Law Schl.—32 Waverly Pl.

MEDICAL.

Bodce Dental Trade Schl.—136 W. 52d.
Coll. of Dental & Oral Surg.—302 E. 35th.
Coll. of Pharmacy, N. Y. C.—115 W. 68th.
Cornell Univ. Med. Coll.—1st av. and E. 28th.
Eclectic Osteopathic Inst.—110 W. 90th.
N. Y. Homeo. Med. Coll.—460 E. 64th.
New York Polyclinic Med. Schl. and Hospital—345 W. 50th.
New York Post-Graduate Med. Schl. and Hospital§—301 E. 20th.
Univ. and Bellevue Hosp. Med. Coll.†—E. 26th.

MUSIC.

Dudley Buck—50 W. 67th.
Elinor Comstock Mus. Schl.—41 E. 80th.
Granberry Piano Schl.—Carnegie Hall.
Guilmant Organ Schl.—44 W. 12th.
Institute of Musical Art—120 Claremont av.
Lachmund Cons. of Piano Playing—Steinway Hall.
National Cons. of Music—126 W. 79th.
N. Y. Amer. Cons. of Music—163 W. 72d.
New York College of Music—128-130 E. 58th.
N. Y. Schl. of Musical Arts—Central Park West.
Nichols Vocal and Piano Schl.—504 Carnegie Hall.
Virgil Piano Conserv.—11 W. 68th.
Woelber Schl. of Music—810 Carnegie Hall.

MISCELLANEOUS.

American Inst. of Phrenology§—1358 B'way.
Art Students' League of N. Y.—215 W. 57th.
Berlitz Schl. of Languages—28-30 W. 34th.
Cortina Acad. of Languages—12 E. 46th.
Dancing Carnival—69 W. 66th.
Fisk Finger Print Schl.—95 Liberty.
Gen. Theo. Sem.—175 9th av.
Henderson Schl. (Elocution)—Aeolian Hall.
Jewish Theo. Sem. of Amer.—531 W. 123d.
Lemcke's Cooking Schl.—26 W. 94th.
McDowell Dressmaking and Millinery Schl.—25 W. 35th.
Meffert's Swimming Schl.—Woolworth Bldg.
N. Y. Mergenthaler Linotype Schl.—244 W. 23d.
Montessori Children's House—673 West End av.
Natl. Acad. of Design—175 W. 109th.
Navigation and Marine Engineering Schl.—25 South.
N. Y. Coll. of Chiropractics—1416 B'way.
New York Inst. for the Instruction of the Deaf and Dumb—99 Ft. Washington av.
N. Y. Inst. for the Education of the Blind—412 9th av.
N. Y. Inst. of Photography—141 W. 36th.
New York Schl. of Applied Design for Women—160 Lexington av.
N. Y. Schl. of Engraving—15 John.
New York Schl. of Expression—318 W. 57th.
New York Schl. of Fine and Applied Arts—2239 B'way.
New York Schl. of Journalism§—32 Waverly pl.
New York Schl. of Social Work—105 E. 22d.
N. Y. State Veterinary Coll.—333 E. 26th.
Rand Schl. of Social Science—7 E. 15th.
Reeves' Conserv. of Dancing—2642 B'way.
Remey's Dancing Schl.—127 Columbus av.
Renouard Training Schl. for Embalmers—162 E. 23d.
Savage Schl. for Phys. Educ.—308 W. 59th.
Topel Swimming Schl.—2561 B'way.
Union Theological Seminary§—B'way and 120th.
Uttmark's Nautical Coll.—8 State.
Y. M. C. A.—318 W. 57th, 215 W. 23d.

Queens.

Broadway Riding Academy—Far Rockaway.
Browne's Jamaica Bus. Schl.—Jamaica.
Gomez Schl. of Elocution—14 S. 27th, Flushing.
Kew Forest Schl.—Forest Hills.
Loder Commercial Schl.—Jamaica.
Plaza Business Schl.—L. I. City.
Queensboro Commercial Schl.—L. I. City.
Richmond Hill Business Schl.—Rich. Hill.
St. Agnes Acad.§—College Point.

Richmond.

Acad. Lady Blessed Sacrament*—Gryme's Hill.
Staten Island Acad.§—New Brighton.
Staten Island Aviation Schl.—Graham Beach.

Long Island.

Acad. of St. Joseph*—Brentwood.
Acad. of Sacred Heart of Mary*—Sag Harbor.
Burroughs Schl.†—Great Neck.
Craven School†—Mattituck.
Friends' Acad.§—Locust Valley.
St. Mary's Cathedral Schl.*—Garden City.
St. Paul's Cathedral Schl.†—Garden City.
Winnwood§—Lake Grove.
State Inst. of Applied Agri.—Farmingdale. W. M. Baldwin.

N. Y. STATE HIGHWAY IMPROVEMENT

There are about 80,000 miles of public highways, of which by statute about 3,772 miles are designated as State routes, to be improved at sole expense of State; about 8,516 miles of county highways, which are to be improved at joint expense of State and counties, leaving about 68,000 miles of town highways, which are to be improved and maintained by local town authorities, assisted by county supts. and under supervision and direction of dept., at the joint expense of towns and State.

Up to Jan. 1, 1920, 7,230 miles of State and county highways have been completed; 6,300 miles of town roads macadamized; 6,900 miles of town roads improved as gravel highways; 24 miles of concrete, and approximately 56,000 miles of town roads widened, shaped and crowned and made safe for travel.

The Dept. of Highways was established in 1908.

New York City has an average of one fire every 21 minutes, day and night.

COPYRIGHTS, PATENTS AND TRADE-MARKS.

COPYRIGHTS.

UNDER LAW OF JULY 1, 1909.

Periodicals—1. Publish the issue upon which copyright protection is desired, printing therein the required copyright notice, before making any application to the Copyright Office for registration.

2. Promptly after the publication of each issue, send 2 copies thereof to the Copyright Office, Washington, D. C., with an application for registration (upon Form B1) and a remittance for the statutory fee of $1, which sum includes the cost of a certificate under seal. Such certificate "shall be admitted in any court as prima facie evidence of the facts stated therein."

Books—Print and publish with a notice of copyright, then register, using Form A1. Manuscript of a book cannot be registered.

Notice of Copyright—The law prescribes that the copyright notice shall consist either of the word "Copyright" or the abbreviation "Copr.," accompanied by the name of the copyright proprietor, and the year in the case of a literary, musical or dramatic work.

Type-setting in the U. S.—Section 15 of the law provides "That of the printed book or periodical * * * the text of all copies accorded protection under this Act, * * * shall be printed from type set within the limits of the U. S. either by hand or by the aid of any kind of type-setting machine, or from plates made within the limits of the U. S. from type set therein, or, if the text be produced by lithographic process, or photo-engraving process, then by a process wholly performed within U. S." An affidavit of such American manufacture must be filed.

Franking Privilege—The Postmaster, if requested, shall give a receipt for articles and mail them without cost to copyright claimant.

Fees—The statutory fee for the registration of any one issue of a periodical is $1, including a certificate under seal as explained above. Non-certificate, 50c., entries are not permissible under the new law, except in the case of photographs. Each issue of a copyright periodical requires its own registration fee of $1.

Contributions to Periodicals—Section 3 of the law provides "That the copyright provided by this Act shall protect all the copyrightable component parts of the work copyrighted, and all matter therein in which copyright is already subsisting, but without extending the duration or scope of such copyright. The copyright upon composite works or periodicals shall give to the proprietor thereof all the rights in respect thereto which he would have if each part were individually copyrighted under this Act."

Titles—The general title of a newspaper, magazine, or other periodical cannot be protected under the copyright law. There must be deposited 2 complete copies of each issue, promptly after publication.

Remittances should be made by money order, payable to the Register of Copyrights.

Application Forms—Form for affidavit of Amer. printing is on reverse of Form A1. A1—Book by citizen or resident of the U. S. A2—Book reprinted in U. S. with new copyright matter. A3—Book by foreign author in foreign language. A4—Ad interim—Book published abroad in the Eng. language. A5—Contribution to a newspaper or periodical. B1—Periodical; registration of single issue, accompanied by cash. B2—Periodical; fee to be charged against credit. C—Lecture, sermon or address. D1—Published dramatic composition. D2—Dramatic composition not reproduced for sale. D3—Dramatico-musical composition (published). D4—Dramatico-musical composition (unpublished). E—Musical composition published for 1st time. E1—Musical composition republished with new copyright matter. E2—Musical composition not reproduced for sale. F—Published map. G—Work of art (painting, drawing or sculpture); or model or design for a work of art. I1—Drawing or plastic work of a scientific or technical character (published). I2—Same (unpublished). J1—Photograph published for sale. J2—Photograph not reproduced for sale. K—Print or pictorial illustration. L1—Motion picture photo-play (published). L2—Same (unpublished). [illegible] M2—Same (unpublished). Motion picture scenarios are not entitled to registration unless they have been printed and published. Like other unpublished works, they are protected by common law.

For works not reproduced in copies for sale—Copyright may also be had of certain classes of works (see a, b, c below) of which copies are not reproduced for sale, by filing in this office an application for registration, with the statutory fee of $1, sending therewith.

(a) Lectures, addresses, dramatic or musical compositions, complete Mss. or typewritten copy.

(b) Photographs, 1 print.

(c) Works of art (paintings, drawings, sculpture); drawings or plastic works of a scientific or technical character, 1 photograph or other identifying reproduction.

Application for the renewal of subsisting copyrights—Application for renewal may be filed within 1 year prior to expiration of term by:

(1)—The author of the work if still living; (2) the widow, widower or children of the author if the author is not living; (3) the author's executor, if such author, widow, widower, or children be not living; (4) if the author, widow, widower, and children are all dead and the author left no will, then the next of kin.

Fee for recording of renewal claim is 50c.

For the new renewal term of 28 years, use Renewal Form R1.

For the extension of an existing renewal term from 14 years to 28 years, use Extension Form R2.

PATENTS.

Applications for letters patent must be made to the Com. of Patents, and signed by inventors.

A complete application comprises a petition, specification, affidavit, drawing and fee.

A reissue is granted to original patentee when original patent is inoperative on account of defective or insufficient specification.

Fees: Filing original application, $15; issuing of patent, $20; designs (3½ yrs.), $10; designs (7 yrs.), $15; designs (14 yrs.), $30; reissue, $30; filing disclaimer, $10. Certified copies of printed patents, designs, trademarks, 85c. Uncertified printed copies of specifications and drawings, 10c. each; for manuscript copies, for every 100 words or fraction thereof, 10c.; for certificate of search, $1; for each brief from digest of assignments, 20c.; for assistance to attorneys and others in the examination of publications in the Scientific Library, an hour or less, $1; each additional hour or fraction thereof, $1. Recording every assignment, agreement, power of attorney or other paper, of 300 words or under, $1. For over 300 and under 1,000 words, $2. For over 1,000 words, $1 for each additional 1,000 or fraction thereof.

There must be a drawing made with India ink alone, on pure white paper, the thickness of three sheets of Bristol board, and containing a calendered and smooth surface. All drawings must be made with pen only and every line and letter, signature and shading must be absolutely black. The size of the sheet must be exactly 10x15 inches, and there must be an inch margin on each side, leaving the "sight" exactly 8x13 inches. When the view is longer than the width of the sheet, it may be turned on its side, while the signature of the inventor must be placed at the lower right hand corner, but, in no instance, shall they encroach upon the drawing.

Caveats—Law repealed in 1910.

TRADE MARKS.

A trade mark may be registered by any person, firm or corporation in the U. S. or located in any foreign country which, by treaty, convention or law, affords similar privileges to citizens of the U. S., and who is entitled to the exclusive use of any trade mark and uses the same in commerce with foreign nations or among the several States, or with Indian tribes.

On filing an application for registration of a trade mark, $10 must be paid. If the applicant be a corporation, it must be specified under the laws of what State or nation incorporated.

One hundred and forty-nine persons are killed by accident in the United States each day, according to statistics compiled by the National Safety Council.

VOLCANOES AND EARTHQUAKES

Prepared by the National Geographic Society of Washington, D. C. Gilbert Grosvenor, President.

Studies of the volcanic phenomena in the Mt. Katmai region, Alaska, made by the expedition under Robert F. Griggs for the National Geographic Society, have shown that where the lava rose in the throat of Katmai in the great eruption of 1912, it had a temperature of less than 1,000 degrees Centigrade. The lava stood in this position until it had melted about a cubic mile of the rock of the old mountain, and then exploded with terrific violence. The source of these vast accessions of energy has not yet been accounted for.

Salton Sink, in the Imperial Valley, California, which has for many years been an area of mud volcanoes emitting steam and sulphurous gases, the roar of whose vents can be heard for miles, is gradually drying up. The lake, which is about eighteen miles long, nine miles wide and 169 feet below sea level, is said to be retreating at the rate of a mile a year. The salt-encrusted land thus left is being rapidly seized by homesteaders. Geologists estimate that the area has changed from sea to desert and back again to sea fifty times or more during its history.

The United States Weather Bureau records show that there were 101 earthquake shocks strong enough to be felt by persons during 1919. More than 4,500 correspondents in various parts of the country are recording such quakes and sending in full accounts to the Bureau.

One of the heaviest quakes felt in years in Juneau, Alaska, shook buildings badly on December 14, 1919. Katmai volcano, near Kodiak, Alaska, is believed to have been the place about which the shocks centered.

A series of severe earthquake shocks beginning on January 3, was felt in the entire region around Vera Cruz, Mexico, many people having been killed and much property destroyed. The village of San Juan Coscomatepec showed a toll of 30 dead and many buildings demolished; Huatusco an equal number, and Jalapa, fifty victims. In Vera Cruz several people were killed and much property was destroyed, and the villages of Teocelo and Couztlan were virtually destroyed. The course of the San Francisco River was changed, watermains in the city of Vera Cruz were broken and thousands of trees in a forest twenty-five miles from the city were uprooted. Though clearly tectonic, and not characteristic of volcanic earthquakes, the center of this one seemed to be in the neighborhood of Mt. Orizaba. The small and apparently extinct volcano Cero de San Miguel, near Cordoba, also erupted, bursting in twain. The new crater threw out smoke, ashes and flame, and a lava stream 200 yards wide which resulted in about 200 deaths.

On January 31 and February 1, 1920, an earthquake in the State of Minas Geraes, Brazil, of an intensity without precedent in that region shook down a number of houses and created a panic among the inhabitants, who say the rumblings sounded as if they were produced by the explosion of tons of dynamite or the breaking of enormous quantities of rocks far within the interior of the earth. Since this disturbance the National Observatory of Rio de Janeiro has decided to install a seismograph in the State of Minas Geraes, another in the State of Rio Grande do Sul at Porto Alegroe and a third in the State of Matto Grosso at Cuyaba.

Widespread disaster was caused in the Province of Emilia and the Apennine Mountains to the west by a violent earthquake coming at 7:55 on September 7, followed by minor earth tremors for several days. In Fivizzano, nearly all the houses were shaken down and 432 persons were killed. As a result of the 300 subterranean concussions on that date, more than a hundred towns and villages, particularly those in the vicinity of the marble quarries at Carrara, were badly damaged and some were completely demolished, rendering ten thousand people homeless. Pizzo d'Ucello, a mountain near Spezia, burst into active volcanic eruption and avalanches were started in the Swiss Alps as results of the violence of the quake. This volcano threw out enormous columns of thick dark smoke in an umbrella-shaped cloud from its crater, and all the wells and streams near the mountain were impregnated with sulphur.

A severe earthquake, with the town of Yunlin as its center, which damaged buildings and caused some deaths, occurred throughout Formosa on June 5.

Grakali and other villages within a radius of sixty miles west of Tiflis were shaken by an earthquake which killed several hundred persons and made thousands of others homeless.

A new volcanic field in the Bayuda Desert, half-way between Merowe and Berber, was discovered by Dr. Chalmers Mitchell on his Trans-African airplane flight. He concludes from his observations that the eruptions were not later than the Kainozoic Age.

Among his important discoveries in the Sahara, Col. J. Tilho recently announced that Emi Kussi in the Tibesti highlands is the largest of a series of extinct volcanoes. Its crater is well formed and there is now a thick deposit of sodium carbonate on the floor.

In December, 1919, the abnormally high lava column of Kilauea collapsed 400 feet, completely changing the appearance of the crater. The fire lakes became molten maelstroms and the floor of the great crater was covered with outpourings of molten lava, as the crags and pinnacles which have for the last two years been prominent on the landscape sank into the depths.

On February 16, French Oceanica was swept over by a tidal wave, the greatest losses being on Makalea Island.

Professor Emelio Oddone, noted seismologist of Naples, has been in Mexico studying the causes and effects of the earthquakes there. With his new invention, the inerviameter, he he has taken measurements of energy and motion of the quakes.

Violent earthquake shocks were reported from Ferrara, Italy, on June 4; from Tuscany in Italy, on June 10; a slight quake from Cannes, in France, on November 29, 1919; from Florence on October 26, 1919, and a severe shock from Rome on September 12, 1919. In the latter quake, houses are reported to have collapsed or to have been badly damaged at Bagni, Asciana, Montorio, Radicofani, Pian Castagnajo, Badia, San Salvatore and Cello.

Two pronounced shocks were reported from Anchorage, Alaska, on June 25, 1920. Though they did no great damage, their efforts extended for one hundred miles north of the city.

Three distinct earthquake shocks were felt throughout the State of Washington and northward through British Columbia on January 24, 1920.

Los Angeles reports a sharp quake on July 16, 1920, the earth tremors being recorded on the seismographs at Georgetown University, Washington, D. C., approximately 2,300 miles from the center of greatest disturbance.

Earthquake shocks of considerable intensity were recorded by the Weather Bureau seismographs in Chicago on March 29, though the center of the quake was probably 1,200 miles from the city.

Mount Lassen, the only active volcano in the United States, burst into sputtering eruption on April 3, casting forth great clouds of smoke and ashes in an unusually violent manner.

A slight earthquake, accompanied by a dull rumbling sound, was experienced at Comrie, Scotland, on September 13, 1920.

Giarre, at the base of Mount Etna, on the Island of Sicily, was shaken by a violent earthquake on September 27, 1920. Property was destroyed and many persons were injured in Giarre, where the shock was greatest. The nearby village of Codadivolpe was practically demolished.

Crihuela, in Spain, suffered a sharp quake on September 26, 1920.

DIRECT DIPLOMACY WITH CANADA.

A statement read in the Canadian Parliament in Ottawa and formally made public by the British Embassy in Washington, declares the purpose of the British Government to have the King of England appoint a "Canadian Minister to the United States," who shall have office room in the Embassy Building in Washington, shall have direct charge of all negotiations on Canadian affairs, and at times, in the absence of the Empire's Ambassador, shall exercise his powers with reference to all questions.

POLAR EXPLORATIONS

Prepared by the National Geographic Society of Washington, D. C. Gilbert Grosvenor, President.

After having drifted across the waters north of Asia and Europe from Norway since June, 1918, Capt. Roald Amundsen reached Nome, Alaska, during the past summer. Here he secured extra provisions and set sail on August 8 in his ship, the "Maude," especially designed to withstand the pressure of Polar ice, for Wrangel Island. From this point he planned to lock his boat in the ice and drift across the Polar basin. He hopes that the drift will at least take him near enough the North Pole for him to make a dash for it, but he has declared that the chief object of his expedition is to compile scientific data on the Arctic region.

The United States Army Air Service Alaskan Flying Expedition, which made the trip to Nome from Long Island in 112 hours of flying time, secured much data on hitherto uncharted areas among the Canadian glaciers.

The well-known Danish explorer, Knud Rasmussen, returned late in 1919, from Angmagssalik, the largest settlement on the east coast of Greenland. This was the last village visited by him in making his study of the differences between the culture, language and traditions of every tribe and clan in the country. No one has ever before come into such direct personal contact with a whole people as Rasmussen has with the people of Greenland.

Baffin Land, a very rich and alluring field for explorers and scientists, will be the object of an expedition which will set out in the summer of 1921 under Donald B. MacMillan, one of Peary's lieutenants on the expedition that reached the North Pole. During the following winter the coast of Baffin Land will be explored and the next summer the party will attempt to penetrate the interior. Very little is now known about the territory whose whole western shore of perhaps 1,000 miles in length, is but vaguely defined on charts. Its vast lakes and towering mountains are mythical to us, and its flora and fauna have practically never been studied.

The steamer Thor I, of the British Imperial Antarctic Expedition, under the leadership of John L. Cope, bound for the unknown regions around the South Pole, put into Norfolk (Virginia) Harbor on October 25, 1920, for coal. The party will proceed to Deception Island, in the Falkland group, where they will take a smaller steamer and head for Graham Land, the southernmost land known, to explore during the next eighteen months 1,200 miles of absolutely unknown and unexplored territory. The expedition is equipped with airplanes and a wireless apparatus with which they expect to communicate with headquarters in London. It is reported that this two-year survey is preliminary to a five-year expedition which will be inaugurated upon the return of Mr. Cope.

Lange Koch, the young Danish scientist and explorer, set out this summer on a two-year expedition to the region around North Point, Greenland, in order thus to proclaim Danish sovereignty over all of Greenland.

A natural science and geological expedition is being organized by Dr. Olaf Holtedahl, of Christiania University, Norway, to explore the Nova Zembla region, Arctic Russia, and establish a temporary meteorologic station there.

Germany is said to be making extensive preparations for Arctic explorations by airplane, with a principal base on the west coast of Spitzbergen.

A systematic survey of Spitzbergen carried out annually by the Norwegian Government was continued during the past year under Adolf Hoel, extending hydrographic surveys from the northern entrance of Bell Sound to the mouth of Horn Sound, the charts recently published as a result of these expeditions being vast improvements on those heretofore issued.

TRANSACTIONS OF THE NEW YORK CLEARING HOUSE.

77 to 83 Cedar st., Manhattan. (Compiled by Wm. J. Gilpin, Manager.)

The largest daily transactions on record were on Dec. 16, 1919, when the exchanges amounted to $1,384,614,055.95. Balances, $135,234,927.90, or total of $1,519,848,983.85. The largest exchanges were on Jan. 2, 1920, $1,385,807,180.86. The largest balances were on June 17, 1920, $157,020,486.37. The following shows transactions of Clearing House for sixty-seven years:

Years Ending Sept. 30.	No. Members	Capital.	Clearings for Year.	Average Daily Clearings.	Balances for Year.	Average Daily Balances.	Bal. to Cl'r'gs
							Per Ct
1854-1899.......	......	....	$1,231,423,418,499.23	$87,415,590.26	$58,640,345,106.12	$4,162,727.60	4.76
1900............	64	$74,222,700	51,964,588,564.51	170,936,146.61	2,730,411,810.27	8,981,716.48	5.26
1901............	62	81,722,700	77,020,672,493.65	254,193,638.59	3,515,037,741.05	11,600,784.62	4.56
1902............	60	100,672,700	74,753,189,435.56	245,898,649.46	3,377,504,072.11	11,110,210.76	4.51
1903............	56	113,072,700	70,833,655,940.29	233,005,447.17	3,315,516,487.48	10,906,304.23	4.68
1904............	54	115,972,700	59,672,796,804.41	195,648,514.11	3,105,858,575.60	10,183,142.87	5.20
1905............	54	115,972,700	91,879,318,369.00	302,234,599.89	3,953,875,974.80	13,006,170.97	4.33
1906............	55	118,150,000	103,754,100,091.25	342,422,772.57	3,832,621,023.87	12,648,914.27	3.69
1907............	54	129,100,000	95,315,421,237.96	313,537,569.86	3,813,926,108.35	12,545,809.56	4.00
1908............	50	126,350,000	73,630,971,913.18	241,413,022.66	3,469,632,271.41	11,179,122.30	4.63
1909............	51	127,350,000	99,257,662,411.03	326,565,468.45	4,194,484,028.37	13,797,644.83	4.22
1910............	50	132,350,000	102,553,959,069.28	338,461,911.11	4,195,293,966.90	13,845,854.67	4.09
1911............	67	170,275,000	92,420,120,091.67	305,016,597.99	4,388,563,113.06	14,483,706.64	4.74
1912............	65	174,275,000	96,672,300,863.67	319,050,497.89	5,051,262,291.57	16,670,832.64	5.22
1913............	64	179,900,000	98,121,520,297.15	323,833,400.32	5,144,130,384.69	16,977,328.00	5.24
1914............	62	175,300,000	89,760,344,971.31	296,238,762.28	5,128,647,302.16	16,926,228.72	5.71
1915............	62	178,550,000	90,842,707,723.90	299,810,916.58	5,340,846,740.16	17,626,556.89	5.87
1916............	63	185,550,000	147,180,700,461.18	484,147,070.60	8,561,624,447.46	28,163,238.31	5.82
1917............	63	200,750,000	181,534,031,387.84	601,106,064.20	12,147,791,432.60	40,224,474.94	6.69
1918............	59	205,650,000	174,524,179,028.72	575,987,389.53	17,255,062,671.17	56,947,401.55	9.88
1919............	60	220,350,000	214,703,444,468.43	708,592,225.96	20,950,477,482.92	69,143,490.04	9.75
1920............	55	261,650,000	252,338,249,466.28	830,060,031.13	25,216,212,385.55	82,498,067.05	9.99
Totals, avgs.	..	....	$3,570,157,362,589.60	$171,520,084.20	$207,269,155,417.66	$10,131,942.87	5.80

MOTOR VEHICLE REGISTRATIONS.

The following table gives the motor vehicle and motorcycle registrations for 1919 automobile year in Greater New York and New York State:

COUNTIES.	Pleasure.	Omnibus.	Commercial.	Trailers.	Dealers.	Total cars including exempts.	No. of motorcycles.
Bronx	9,418	945	2,598	26	55	13,042	912
Kings	43,126	1,415	11,810	162	183	56,696	2,868
New York	54,070	5,839	21,893	391	467	82,660	3,114
Queens	16,030	652	3,785	89	95	20,651	1,231
Richmond	4,106	285	971	10	20	5,392	152
Totals, New York City	126,750	9,136	41,057	678	820	178,441	8,277
Totals, New York State	446,593	22,572	97,346	2,470	2,681	571,662	28,561

NATURALIZATION AND QUALIFICATION OF VOTERS.

Under the Federal Statutes, the Bureau of Naturalization, U. S. Dept. of Labor, Washington, D. C., has charge of all matters concerning the naturalization of aliens. The offices of the Chief Naturalization Examiner of that Bureau for the N. Y. Dist. are 3d Floor, No. 1 Beekman, Mhtn.

WHERE TO MAKE APPLICATION — Top floor Brooklyn Post Office Bldg. for residents of Brooklyn, Long Island and Staten Island.

Room 7, Hall of Records, Brooklyn, for residents of Brooklyn.

Room 304, Hall of Records, Mhtn., for residents of Mhtn.

Bronx Co. Court House, 161st and 3d av., for the Bronx.

P. O. Bldg., Mhtn., for Mhtn., Bronx, Columbia and Rockland, Putnam, Orange, Dutchess, Sullivan, Greene, Ulster and Westchester counties, or in Co. Clerk's office in the county in which applicant resides.

CITIZENSHIP—The Federal statutes declare the following persons to be citizens:

All persons born in United States and subject to the jurisdiction thereof, excluding Indians not taxed.

All persons legally naturalized.

All children born out of jurisdiction of United States, whose fathers are at time of their birth citizens thereof, but the right of citizenship shall not descend to children whose fathers have never resided in the United States.

A child born without the U. S. of alien parents shall be deemed a citizen of the U. S. by virtue of the naturalization of or resumption of Amer. citizenship by the parent, provided that such naturalization or resumption takes place during the minority of such child and that the citizenship of such minor child shall begin at the time such minor child begins to reside permanently in the U. S.

An American woman who marries a foreigner takes the nationality of her husband. At the termination of the marital relation she may resume her American citizenship, if abroad by registering as an American citizen within 1 year with a consul of the U. S., or by returning to reside in the U. S., or if residing in the U. S. by continuing to reside therein.

All persons who were citizens of Hawaii on Aug. 12, 1898, are citizens of the U. S. All citizens of Porto Rico, as defined by Sec. 7 of the Act of April 12, 1900, are declared by the Act of Mar. 2, 1917, to be citizens of the U. S. Filipinos who serve not less than 3 years in the U. S. Navy, and who have declared their intention to become citizens, may be naturalized.

NATURALIZATION—The applicant for citizenship must have resided in the United States for the continued term of at least 5 years next preceding his application, and 1 year within State or Territory where the court is held that admits him. Not less than 2 nor more than 7 years before he files his petition for naturalization he must declare, on oath, before the clerk of any court authorized to naturalize, his intention to become a citizen. Any person over 18 years of age may declare intention. There is a fee of $1 for receiving and filing declaration of intention; of $2 for filing petition, and of $2 for making final order and issuing citizenship certificates, if granted, the whole fee being payable when petition is filed. Blanks for statement of the facts material for first or final papers may be obtained from court clerk or from public evening schools for foreigners or from chief examiner.

The petitioner must be accompanied by at least two witnesses who are citizens of the United States who have known the applicant for at least five years and have known him to be a resident of the United States for five years and of the State or Territory for one year.

Children under the age of 21 at the time of the naturalization of their parents who become residents of the United States during their minority, are considered citizens.

When any naturalized citizen shall have resided 2 years in the foreign state from which he came, or for 5 years in any other foreign state it shall be presumed that he has ceased to be an American citizen and the place of his general abode shall be deemed his place of residence during said years. This presumption may be overcome by registering with an American consul.

NATURALIZATION OF PERSONS WHO HAVE SERVED IN THE ARMY OR NAVY DURING THE WORLD WAR—The Act of Congress, approved May 9, 1918, provides that: "Any alien serving in the military or naval service of the U. S. during the war (World War) may file his petition for naturalization without making the preliminary declaration of intention and without proof of the required five years' residence within the U. S., provided he appears with his two witnesses before the appropriate representative of the Bureau of Naturalization and passes the preliminary examination hereby required before filing his petition for naturalization in the office of the clerk of the court, and any petition for naturalization filed under the provisions of this subdivision may be heard immediately."

Persons of foreign birth who served in the military or naval forces of the United States during the European War, after final examination and acceptance by the military or naval authorities, and who have been honorably discharged, may be naturalized in the same manner as those who applied for citizenship while in the service.

NATURALIZATION FORBIDDEN—Only free white persons and persons of African birth or African descent can be naturalized.

QUALIFICATIONS OF VOTERS—Every person N. Y. State, 21 yrs. old, is entitled to vote if he or she shall be on or before the day of election a citizen of the United States 90 days, a resident of the State 1 year, a resident of the county 4 months, a resident of the election district 30 days. A person otherwise qualified whose birthday is on the day following election is entitled to vote. A minor who has been convicted of felony and has served out his or her term during his or her minority is not entitled to vote when of age.

SOLDIERS' AND SAILORS' INSURANCE.

Dir. R. G. Cholmeley-Jones of the Bur. of War Risk Insurance, in the Treas. Dept., made public on Mar. 31, 1920, schedules of terms and rates under Amendment of Dec. 24, 1919, of the War Risk Insurance Act. Converted insurance will be issued for $1,000 or any larger amount in multiples of $500 up to $10,000, but not to exceed the amount of term insurance carried, on any of the following forms: Ordinary Life, 20-Payment Life, 30-Payment Life, 20-Year Endowment, 30-Year Endowment and Endowment at age 62. Premiums may be paid monthly, quarterly, semi-annually or annually. Death benefits on converted insurance are payable in one sum, in limited installments or in continuous installments, at the option of the insured. total permanent disability benefits payable to insured, regardless of age, when total permanent disability occurs.

For not more than 5 years after the war, or until the earlier conversion of the term insurance, as provided, the monthly term premium shall be in accordance with following table of rates, increasing at each anniversary of the policy to the rate for his or her then attained age (1st, attained age; 2d, monthly rate):

TABLE OF PREMIUMS FOR $5,000.
(Ages 15 to 65.)

15, $3.15; 16, $3.15; 17, $3.15; 18, $3.20; 19, $3.20; 20, $3.20; 21, $3.25; 22, $3.25; 23, $3.25; 24, $3.30; 25, $3.30; 26, $3.35; 27, $3.35; 28, $3.40; 29, $3.45; 30, $3.45; 31, $3.50; 32, $3.55; 33, $3.60; 34, $3.65; 35, $3.70; 36, $3.75; 37, $3.80; 38, $3.85; 39, $3.95; 40, $4.05; 41, $4.10; 42, $4.20; 43, $4.35; 44, $4.45; 45, $4.60; 46, $4.75; 47, $4.95; 48, $5.15; 49, $5.40; 50, $5.70; 51, $6; 52, $6.35; 53, 6.75; 54, $7.20; 55, $7.65; 56, $8.20; 57, $8.80; 58, $9.50; 59, $10.25; 60, $11.05; 61, $12; 62, $13; 63, $14.10; 64, $15.35; 65, $16.75.

The first ship flying the German flag to arrive in the Port of New York since July, 1914, docked Nov. 4, 1920, at one of the Army base piers in South Brooklyn. It was the "Sophie Rickmers," a 4,863 gross ton freighter, which had just been completed at the Rickmers yard at Bremerhaven.

LONG ISLAND SOCIETIES AND ASSOCIATIONS.

NASSAU AND SUFFOLK COUNTIES.

(See index for L. I. Country Clubs, Golf, etc.).

Alumnae and Alumni.

Friends' Academy Alumni Assn., Locust Valley—H. H. Tredwell, Pres.; Hilda Waldron, Sec., East Norwich.

Glen Cove High School Alumni Assn.—1911. J. Dunn, Treas.; Miss E. Hyde, Sec., Glen Cove.

Boards of Trade and Civic Improvement.

Babylon Taxpayers Assn.—1914. 100 mem. Alfred Harris, Pres.; H. C. Hepburn, Sec.

Bayport Bd. of Trade—1915. 45 mem. F. D. Smith, Pres.; M. C. L'Hommedieu, Sec.

Bay Shore Board of Trade and Impt. Assn.—W. W. Hulse. Pres.; F. T. Hulse, Treas.

Belle Terre Assn.—1916. Chas. W. Riecks, Pres.; C. L. Woody, Sec.

Bellmore Bd. of Trade—1916. 195 mem. C. M. Vanderoef, Pres.; W. de Minn, Sec.

Bridgehampton Bd. of Trade—1908. 50 mem. A. G. Halsey, Pres.; E. H. Dickerson, Sec.

Brook Haven Village Impt. Assn.—Clyde Furst, Pres.; J. E. Johnson, Sec.; F. P. Reeve, Treas.

City Club of Glen Cove—1916. 200 mem. Mrs. W. H. Seaman, Pres.; Mrs. G. E. Raynor, Rec. Sec.; Mrs. S. Fyfe, Cor. Sec.

Cold Spring Harbor Village Impt. Society—1899. 100 mem. J. H. J. Stewart, Pres.; Fredk. C. Thomas, Sec.

Community Service of Patchogue—A. Bosch, Pres.; Frank Guttridge, Ch.; J. R. Drue, Sec.

Commuters Club—Centre Moriches. Jos. Haag, Pres.; George Pfaff, Sec., 109 Lafayette, Mhtn.

East End Chamber of Commerce of Greenport—1920. 75 mem. Ansel V. Young, Pres.; Chas. G. Bailey, Sec., Greenport.

Easthampton Board of Trade—1907. 12 mem. A. H. Culver, Pres., Easthampton; Welby Boughton, Sec.

Easthampton Neighborhood Assn.—1914. 214 mem. C. R. Sleight, Pres.; Mrs. N. N. Tiffany, Sec.

East Moriches Improvement Assn.—1911. J. H. Miller, Pres.; J. D. Howell, V. Pres.; W. J. Howell, Sec.

Farmingdale Bd. of Trade, Inc.—Dr. J. F. Michel, Pres.; Edwin H. Bailey, Sec.

Farmingdale Tax Payers Assn.—1920. 92 mem. G. Carl, Pres.; L. Garity, Sec.

Floral Park Board of Trade—118 mem. A. H. Goldsmith, Pres.; Ray Stokely, Sec.

Glen Cove City Chamber of Commerce—1920. J. W. Townsend, Pres.; D. J. Fogarty, Sec., 146 Glen, Glen Cove.

Glen Cove Neighborhood Assn.—1914. 769 mem. F. B. Cowan, Pres.; C. P. Valentine, Exec.-Sec.

Glen Morris Civic Club—1915. 239 mem. P. S. MacDwyer, Pres.; E. L. Helmig, Sec.

Glenwood Landing Impt. Assn.—1914. I. N. Sievwright, Pres.; A. H. Larsen, Sec.

Great Neck Business Men's Assn.—E. E. Le Cluse, Pres.; G. V. Bullen, Sec., Great Neck.

Greenport Board of Trade, amalgamated with East End Chamber of Commerce of Greenport.

Hempstead Chamber of Commerce—1919. 300 mem. E. C. Hinkle, Pres.; J. L. Kornicker, Sec.

Hunters Garden Assn.—F. B. Howell, Pres.; Jno. Hagen, Sec., Riverhead.

Huntington Assn.—F. E. Farnsworth, Pres.; C. E. Shepard, Sec.

Huntington Business Men's Protective Assn.—1920. H. A. Murphy, Ch.; C. N. Sammis, Jr., Sec.

Inwood Impt. Soc.—1905. 75 mem. C. H. Parks, Pres.; Wm. Adams, Sec.

Islip Business Men's Assn.—1919. W. Haff, Pres.; Roscoe Clock, Sec.

Jamaica Village Soc.—E. L. Maeder, Pres.; Arvine Baylis, Sec.

Jamesport Camp Ground Impt. Soc.—1916. Rev. W. I. Bowman, Pres.; Miss Alice Ludlam, Sec.

Lawrence-Cedarhurst Board of Trade—1919. 75 mem. S. E. Newton, Pres.; P. C. Vandewater, Sec., Cedarhurst.

Lindenhurst Board of Trade—1909. August Voldenauer, Pres.; Robt. W. Wild, Cor. Sec.

Long Island Waterways Assn.—1912. N. B. Kilmer, Pres.; E. N. Edwards, Sec., 1 Railroad av., Freeport.

Lynbrook Civic Assn.—1910. 71 mem. E. G. Hedden, Pres.; A. Schwartz, Sec.

Malverne Club—1918. 75 mem. A. Roy Camp, Pres.; A. H. Wagg, Sec.

Massapequa Board of Trade—M. H. Ormsbee, Pres.; R. D. Sylvester, Sec., Massapequa.

Matinecock Neighborhood Assn.—Locust Valley. 1909. A. J. Hans, Pres.; J. H. Mould, Sec., Locust Valley.

Merrick Civic League—1915. Curtis H. Bowne, Pres.; Harry Leich, Sec.

Mineola Board of Trade—G. Schmidt, Pres.; A. F. Buhler, Sec.

Nassau Co. Assn.—1920. A. T. Davison, Pres.; J. A. Albertson, Sec., Westbury.

Patchogue Baymen's Protective Assn.—E. C. Sweezy, Pres.; E. S. Furman, Sec.

Port Jefferson Village Impt. Soc.—Miss Myra Platt, Pres.; Mrs. L. M. Tookee, Sec.

Real Estate Exchange of L. I.—See Boards of Trade, Queens.

Rockville Centre Business Men's Assn.—1918. 40 mem. Frank Goodwin, Pres.; S. Ellis, Sec.

Roslyn Neighborhood Assn.—1915. 800 mem. N. S. Jones, Pres.; W. Eastman, Sec.; R. E. Haas, Exec. Sec.

St. Albans Impt. Assn.—F. J. Frantzen, Pres.; W. Rylance, Sec.

Sag Harbor Ladies Village Improvement Soc.—Miss I. R. Miles, Pres.; Miss M. E. Stanton, Sec.

Setauket Neighborhood Assn.—300 mem. E. M. Wells, Pres.; Mrs. H. Helbig, Sec., Setauket.

Smithtown Society—1915. 91 mem. Alonzo Potter, Pres.; Miss Caroline Thompson, Sec.

Southampton Bd. of Trade—D. J. Gilmartin, Pres.; O. C. Gardner, Sec.

Suffolk Co. Taxpayers—1914. H. L. Kenyon, Pres.; M. Shiebler, Sec., Shelter Isl. Hts.

Valley Stream Civic Assn.—G. W. Ruppel, Pres.; G. A. Herrmann, Rec. Sec.

Westbury Protective Assn.—H. W. Underhill, Pres.; H. E. Hawxhurst, Sec.

Women's Vil. Impt. Assn. of Sayville—1916. 45 mem. Mrs. A. V. Green, Pres.; Miss C. Edwards, Sec.

Business, Commercial and Agricultural.

Agricultural Soc. of Queens and Nassau—See Bus. and Com. Soc., Queens.

Associated Physicians of L. I.—See Bus. and Com., Bkln.

Board of Fire Underwriters of Suffolk Co.—1908. 164 mem. A. Edwards, Pres., Huntington; J. Bagshaw, Sec.-Treas., Riverhead.

Bridgehampton Evergreen Cemetery Assn.—Stephen Hedges, Pres.; E. O. Hedges, Sec.

Chevrolet Associated Dealers of L. I.—1920. 14 mem. F. L. Cooley, Pres.; S. E. Newton, Sec.

Cold Spring Harbor Biological Laboratory—See Educational and Scientific Socs.

Cold Spring Harbor Station for Experimental Evolution. See Educational and Scientific Socs.

Greenport Club—1916. 50 mem. D. W. Tuthill, Pres.; A. M. Tasker, Sec.

Greenport Oyster Growers Protective Assn.—G. E. Griffing, Pres.; G. N. Flack, Sec.

Greenport Sterling Cemetery Assn.—L. F. Terry, Pres.; A. Tasker, Sec.; J. W. Beebee, Supt.

Huntington Poultry and Pet Stock Assn.—1910. 175 mem. A. V. Sammis, Pres.; W. H. Payne, Sec., Huntington Sta.

Huntington Rural Cemetery Assn.—J. F. Wood, Pres.; Miss N. E. Pearsall, Sec. and Supt.

Inland Waterway League of L. I.—1908. W. W. Hulse, Pres.; I. J. Long, Sec., Bay Shore.

L. I. Cauliflower Assn.—Riverhead. C. H. Aldrich, Pres.; C. J. McNulty, Sec., Laurel.

L. I. Commercial Teachers' Assn.—1915. 39 mem. Miss A. Mattson, Pres.; Miss Louise Lewis, Sec., Sea Cliff.

L. I. Farmers' Club—1880. 52 mem. E. V. Titus, Pres.; J. E. Willets, Sec., Glen Cove.

L. I. Poultry Assn.—Farmingdale. 1920. 25 mem. Robert Seaman, Pres.; E. T. Banner, Sec., Farmingdale.

Lynbrook Real Estate Exch.—P. A. Blake, Pres.; W. H. O'Brien, Sec.

Nassau Co. Bar Assn.—C. I. Wood, Pres.; W. C. Roe, Sec., Jamaica.

Nassau Co. Farm and Home Bureau Assn.—Court House, Mineola. Farm Dept., 650 mem.; Home Dept., 500 mem. E. V. Titus, Pres., Glen Cove; L. Van de Water Jr., Sec., Hempstead.

LONG ISLAND SOCIETIES AND ASSOCIATIONS—BUSINESS, ETC.—*Continued.*

Nassau Co. Horticultural Soc., Glen Cove— T. Twigg, Pres.; E. Harris, Sec., Glen Cove.

Northport Farmers Club—E. A. Crowe, Pres.; F. B. Smith, Sec., Ft. Salonga.

Oyster Bay Horticultural Soc.—1912. Geo. Hale, Pres.; J. R. McCulloch, Sec., Oyster Bay.

Patchogue Cedar Grove Cem. Assn.—G. L. Chichester, Pres.; J. C. Mills, Treas.; J. B. Swezey, Sec.

Pinelawn Cem.—John R. Weeks, Pres.; W. H. Locke, Jr., Sec., 188 Montague, Bkln.

Port Jefferson Cedar Hill Cem. Assn.—H. P. Hawkins, Pres.; A. K. Woodhull, Sec.

Real Estate Exch. of L. I.—See Business Socs., Mhtn.

Riverhead Cem. Assn.—G. M. Vail, Pres.; U. B. Howell, Sec. and Treas.

Ronkonkoma Business Men's Assn.—C. W. Hawkins, Sec.

Sag Harbor Oakland Cem. Assn.—W. R. Reimann, Pres.; F. S. Pulver, Sec.

Southampton Horticultural Soc.—S. R. Candler, Pres.; J. Dickson, Sec.

Suffolk Co. Agricultural Soc.—1858. 350 mem. H. S. Brush, Pres.; Harry Lee, Sec., Riverhead.

Suffolk Co. Bar Assn.—Hon. G. H. Furman, Pres.; R. J. Hawkins, Sec., Patchogue.

Suffolk Co. Farm and Home Bureau Assn.—E. R. Lupton, Pres., Mattituck; J. C. Corwith, Sec., Water Mill.

Suffolk Co. Press Assn.—L. B. Green, Pres.; I. J. Long, Sec., Bay Shore.

Charitable.

Amer. Red Cross (South Suffolk Co. Chap.)—1917. Mrs. W. B. Cutting, Ch.; W. Kingsland Macy, Sec., Islip.

Bkln. Home for Blind, Crippled and Defective Children—Port Jefferson, L. I. Est. 1907. Office, 4 Court sq., Bkln. For support, care, education, medical and surgical treatment of blind, crippled and defective children. 325 inmates. Rt. Rev. Chas. McDonnell, Pres.; Sister Teresa, Supt.; G. F. Shiebler, Gen. Agt.

Central Islip State Hosp.—See N. Y. State Govt.

Children's Home—Mineola, L. I. Care of destitute children 4 to 14 yrs. Children received from Nassau Co. and Greater N. Y. 65 inmates. Mrs. A. M. Cordier, Pres.; G. H. Leavitt, Treas., Bayside.

Country Home for Convalescent Babies—Sea Cliff, L. I. Mrs. W. D. Guthrie, Pres.; Mrs. William T. Sheehan, Sec.; Loretto F. G. Ames, Supt.

Eastern L. I. Hospital—Greenport. Est. 1905. J. H. Marshall, M.D., Pres.; J. L. Kahler, Sec.

Hempstead Town Poor Farm—Uniondale. Est. 1866. 50 inmates. D. Morrison, Pres.-Treas.; A. H. Goldsmith, Sec.

House of St. Giles the Cripple—Garden City, L. I. Inc. 1891. Church home and hospital for destitute crippled children under 16 yrs. 64 inmates. Rt. Rev. F. Burgess, D.D., Pres.; F. L. Sniffin, Treas.; B. B. Mosher, Exec. Officer; Miss A. F. Hasbrouck, Supt.

Tiny Tim Assn.—See Bkln. Charities.

Howard Orphanage and Industrial School, Indian Head Farm—Kings Park, L. I. Est. 1868. L. H. Wood, 20 Nassau, Mhtn.

International Sunshine Soc., Sapphire Branch of Sea Cliff—1911. Mrs. C. S. Chelborg, Pres.; Mrs. E. M. Sedden, Sec.-Treas.

Jones' Inst.—Hicksville L. I. Est. 1834. For the poor of Oyster Bay and North Hempstead Towns. 41 inmates. J. A. Albertson, Pres.; Chas. Van Nostrand, Supt.

Kings Park State Hosp., Kings Park—See Hospitals for Insane, under N. Y. State Govt.

Manhattan State Hosp.—See Central Islip, under Hospitals for Insane, N. Y. State Govt.

Mercy Hospital—Hempstead. Nursing Sisters of Sick Poor. Rt. Rev. Mgr. Edw. McCarty, Pres.

Nassau Hosp. Assn.—Mineola. 1896. Care of sick, injured and wounded. 1,682 inmates cared for. W. M. Baldwin, Pres.; Ada F. Adams, Supt.

Nazareth Trade School—Farmingdale. 1900. Mother M. Celestine, Supt. Training of boys from 5 to 16 yrs. of age. 387 inmates.

Orchard House Settlement—Glen Cove. 1920. Mrs. H. P. Davison, Hon. Ch.; Mrs. E. A. Frank, Exec. Ch.; Mrs. P. Dana, Treas.; Mrs. D. N. Gay, Sec. Highland av., Glen Cove.

Patchogue Public Health Clinic. 1914. River av. School. Meets every 4 wks. Dr. W. E. Gordon, Pres.; F. A. Potter, Treas.; Dr. W. A. Reeve, Sec.

St. Charles' Hospital—Port Jefferson. 1907. Care of blind, crippled and defective children. Under charge of Daughters of Wisdom. Mgr. McDonnell, Pres.

Soc. of St. Johnland—Kings Park, L. I. Inc. 1870. R. L. Harrison, Pres., 49 West 20th, Mhtn.; Alice P. Thomson, Supt. Maintains homes for aged men, women and aged couples and cares for friendless children. Work is conducted on cottage system. Has two cottages for boys and two for girls; a kindergarten and graded school; an infirmary and resident nurse; cottage homes for working families. Requirements for admission are worthiness of character, good health, the need of a home and partial payment of cost of maintenance. Suitable homes and employment found for children who have reached the age limit and are not taken away by relatives or friends. Non-sec. Contributions should be sent to Robt. W. B. Elliott, Treas., 49 W. 20th, Mhtn.

Southampton Hospital—Southampton. 1909. To establish, support and manage an institution for the purpose of affording medical and surgical aid to sick and disabled persons. G. W. Curtis, Pres.; Alice M. Large, Supt.

Southside Hospital—Babylon. Est. 1911. 18 beds. Miss M. Manning, Supt.

Suffolk Co. Almshouse—Yaphank. 140 inmates. A. W. Young, Keeper; Mrs. Young Matron; Jonathan Baker, Supt., Easthampton. Children's Home under same general supervision. 14 inmates. Mrs. Ruth Overton, Matron.

Wayside Home—Valley Stream. Est. 1880. Rescue wayward girls, 16 yrs. and over, committed by courts of four L. I. counties for 1st offenses. Avg. 35 inmates. Mrs. H. Hobart Porter, Pres.; Miss E. A. Hafford, Supt.

Woodcleft Fresh Air Home—1906. Freeport. Affords summer outings for poor children. Affiliated with the Soc. of St. Vincent de Paul. W. D. S. Kelly, Ch.

Community Service.

Community Assn.—Bay Shore and Brightwaters. J. A. Mollenhauer, Pres.; Roy B. Davis, Sec.; Chas. Kuhn, Treas., Brightwaters.

Community Club of Westbury—1920. 45 mem. Mrs. P. H. Quinan, Pres.; Miss Edith Johnson, Sec.

Community League—Cedarhurst. 1919. 300 mem. W. S. Pettit, Pres.; R. B. Brownlee, Sec., Woodmere.

Community League of Hewlett, Woodmere, Cedarhurst, Lawrence and Inwood—Cedarhurst. 1920. 1,000 mem. T. H. Harris, Pres.; R. B. Brownlee, Sec., Woodmere.

Community Service Club—Floral Park. 1919. 33 mem. Miss M. A. Walters, Pres.; Miss M. Indzonka, Sec.

Freeport Community Council—1920. Benj. Asch, Pres.; Mrs. R. H. Earon, Sec.

Girls' Community Service Club of Hempstead—13 Main, Hempstead. 1920. 100 mem. May E. Barth, Pres.; Mary Rhodes, Sec.

Hollis Court Community Club—1920. E. S. Harrison, Sec., Queens.

Medford Community Social Club—1920. T. J. Quinn, Pres.; F. J. Brown, Sec.

Rockville Centre Community House—1920. 500 mem. R. H. Boggs, Pres.; W. R. Burdick and D. A. Fraser, Secs.

Educational and Scientific.

Biological Laboratory of the Bklyn. Inst. of Arts and Sciences—Board of Managers, W. J. Matheson, 21 Burling Slip, Mhtn., Pres.; C. B. Davenport, Dir.

Cold Spring Harbor Station for Experimental Evolution—Carnegie Inst. of Washington. C. B. Davenport, Dir.; G. H. Clafin, Supt.

Eugenics Record Office, Carnegie Inst. of Washington. Cold Spring Harbor—Est. 1910. C. B. Davenport, Dir.; H. H. Laughlin, Supt.

L. I. Harvard Club—Univ. Club, Bkln. 1903. 60 mem. B. Meredith Langstaff, Pres.; Warren J. Kibby, Sec.

Nassau Co. School Men's Council—1919. 40 mem. J. T. P. Calkins, Pres.; F. B. Watson, Sec., Rockville Centre.

Nassau Co. Schoolmasters Club—T. P. Calkins, Pres., Hempstead.

Nassau Co. Teachers' Assn.—H. J. Ackerson, Pres.; Alma M. Glendenny, Sec., Mineola.

Teachers' Assn., First Dist., Suffolk Co.—1919. 250 mem. J. Hughes, Pres.; E. E. Flanagan, Sec., Riverhead.

LONG ISLAND SOCIETIES AND ASSOCIATIONS—*Continued.*

Literary.

Amityville Literary Soc.—60 mem. Mrs. M. P. Myton, Pres.; Mrs. L. W. Baylis, Sec.

Babylon Literary Soc.—100 mem. Dr. W. H. Deale, Pres.; Mrs. J. R. Higbie, V.-Pres.; Mrs. E. B. Howell, Sec.

Bay Shore Free Library—Mrs. V. B. Hulse, Pres.; Mrs. J. J. Gibson, Sec.; Eliz. S. Smith, Libr.

Bellport Literary Assn.—Miss M. H. Garrard, Pres.; C. M. Walsh, Sec.

Culture Club of Huntington—Mrs. Fred B. Sammis, Pres.; Miss Ina Van Sise, Sec.

East Quogue Library Assn.—D. A. Vail, Sec.

Floyd Memorial Library—F. W. Corey, Pres.; J. L. Kahler, Sec.

Fortnightly Club of Rockville Centre—Mrs. L. H. Rockwell, Pres.; Mrs. H. W. Reeve, 104 Windsor av.

Hempstead Library—Miss Fanny Mulford, Pres.; Miss H. Mulford, Sec.; Mrs. F. Y. Harlow, Treas.

Huntington Br. of the Bkln. Inst.—1908. C. E. Shepard, Pres.; D. Conklin, Treas.; Mrs. I. S. Sammis, Sec.

Huntington Historical Soc.—Mrs. I. S. Sammis, Pres.; Mrs. Alfred B. Sammis, Sec.

Huntington Library Assn.—A. W. Sammis, Pres.; Hiram Paulding, Sec.

Mattituck Literary Soc.—Chas. Gildersleeve, Pres.; Miss Lizzie M. Tuthill, Sec.

Nassau Co. Historical and Genealogical Soc.—J. S. Cooley, M.D., Pres.; J. D. Fish, Sec., Hempstead.

Orient Lyceum Assn.—P. Weller, Pres.; P. K. Edwards, Sec.

Oyster Bay Woman's Club—Miss A. Steinsieck, Pres.; Mrs G. Hutchinson, Sec.

Riverhead Lecture Assn.—G. M. Vail, Pres.; Geo. Burns, Sec.; E. W. Tooker, Treas.

Sag Harbor Historical and Antiquarian Soc.—J. H. Hunt, Pres.

St. Nicholas Soc. of Nassau Island—1848. 250 mem. Dr. A. DeW. Mason, Pres.; W. R. Lott, Sec., Hollis av., Hollis.

Sea Cliff Public Library Board—Mrs. C. S. Chellborg, Pres.; Mrs. C. M. Sedden, Sec.; May Dibbell, Libr.

Southampton Literary Soc.—Wm. K. Dunwell, Pres.; Mrs. A. R. Corwith, Sec.

Southold Browning Soc. 1905. Mrs. E. B. Hallock, Pres.; Mrs. Agnes Cochran, Sec.-Treas.

Southold Free Library Assn.—Dr. J. W. Stokes, Pres.; R. G. Terry, Sec.; Annie A. Spooner, Libr.

Suffolk Co. Historical Soc.—Dr. Charles E. Craven, Pres.; Miss Ruth Ackerly, Sec., Riverhead.

Westhampton Free Library Assn.—E. H. Bishop, Pres.; Miss A. S. Meeker, Sec., Westhampton Beach.

Winter Night Study Club—Islip. 103 mem. E. Greenwood, Pres.; G. Hall, Sec., East Islip.

Women's Study Club of Patchogue—Mrs. J. A. Canfield, Pres.; Mrs. F. W. Shaw, Sec.

Medical.

Medical Soc. of Glen Cove and the Townships of Oyster Bay and North Hempstead—1920. 35 mem. Dr. J. B. Connolly, Pres.; Dr. E. R. Schilling, Sec., Glen Cove.

North Shore Medical Soc.—Huntington. 1916. 34 mem. Dr. I. F. Barnes, Pres.; Dr. James H. Shawe, Sec., Huntington.

South Side Clinical Soc.—Dr. J. L. Halsey, Pres.; Dr. E. S. Moore, Sec.-Treas., Bay Shore.

Suffolk Co. Medical Soc.—David Edwards, Pres., Easthampton; Dr. Frank Overton, Sec., Patchogue.

Musical.

Music Lovers' Soc.—Baldwin. 1914. Fred. Kirby, Pres. and Dir.; G. M. Bode, Sec.

Setauket Community Chorus—50 mem. Mrs. W. H. Steward Jr., Ch.; B. C. Peters, Dir., Northport.

Smithtown Community Chorus—76 mem. Mrs. Alonzo Potter, Ch.; B. C. Peters, Dir., Northport.

Patriotic and Commemorative.

Huntington D. A. R. (Ketewamoke Chap.), Inc.—Mrs. Gilbert Scudder, Regent; Miss Nettie E. Pearsall, Sec.

Huntington Sons of Am. Revolution—1909. 44 mem. I. Swezey, Pres.; E. Samuels, Sec.

Orient Monument Assn.—1906. J. H. Young, Pres.; E. E. Luce, Sec.

Southampton Town Colonial Soc.—L. E. Terry, Pres.; Mrs. E. P. White, Sec.

Theodore Roosevelt Italian-American Club—Bay Shore. 1919. A. Albonese, Pres.; G. Guinta, Sec.

Political.

For Political County Committees of L. I., see Index, Political Committees.

Religious.

Archdeaconry of Queens and Nassau—See Religious Soc., Queens.

Brotherhood, First Congregational Ch., Bay Shore—60 mem. F. Sherry, Pres.; C. H. Moore, Cor. Sec.

Christian Brotherhood—1915. Baldwin. 35 mem. G. M. Bode, Pres.; Chas. P. Buckley, Sec.

Christian Soldiers—50 mem. G. W. Hildreth, Comm.; E. M. Robinson, Sec., Riverhead.

Diocese of Long Island (P. E.)—Rt. Rev. Frederick Burgess, Bishop, Garden City; Rev. R. Rogers, Sec., 306 McDonough, Bkln.

Holy Name Soc., Our Lady of Good Counsel, R. C. Ch., Lawrence—1911. 80 mem. T. D. Mulcahy, Pres.; Geo. King, Sec.

Jamesport Camp Meeting Assn.—Rev. W. A. Layton, Pres.; G. M. Vail, Sec., Riverhead.

Ladies' Catholic Benevolent Legion, Holy Redeemer Branch 1336—1914. 60 mem. Rev. J. L. O'Toole, Dir., Freeport.

Lake Grove Bible Soc.—S. T. Smith, Pres.; H. L. Gould, Sec.

Lake Grove Women's Missionary Soc.—Mrs. Jas. B. Gould, Pres.; Mrs. W. W. Buland, Sec.

L. I. Baptist Assn.—See Religious Soc., Bkln.

L. I. Bible Soc.—Rev. Arthur Newman, Pres.; Rev. Jas. M. Denton and Rev. J. Rippere, V.-Prests.; Rev. A. F. Johnson, Rec. Sec.; Erastus Post, Cor. Sec., Westhampton.

L. I. District of the Inter. Order of the King's Daughters and Sons—Mrs. Cleon R. Clark, Dist. Pres., 771 Lincoln pl., Bklyn.

Men's Bible Class, First Presbyt. Ch., Sag Harbor—1909. 20 mem. J. F. Davis, Pres.; Edward Hill, Sec.-Treas.

Men's Club, First M. E. Ch., Pt. Jefferson—1916. 90 mem. R. G. Swenk, Pres.; R. B. Wheeler, Sec.

Men's Club, First M. E. Ch., Southampton—1913. 80 mem. D. C. Palmer, Pres.; R. Whitman, Sec.

Men's Club, First Presbyt. Ch., Babylon—1906. 50 mem. J. S. Ames, Pres.; G. H. Walbridge, Sec.

Men's Club, First Presbyt. Ch., Oyster Bay—1913. 50 mem. W. J. Smith, Jr., Pres.; Geo. Hastings, Sec.

Men's Club, M. E. Ch., Freeport—G. F. DuBois, Pres.; F. Lee, Sec.

Men's Club, Redeemer P. E. Ch., Merrick—1908. 70 mem. W. S. Christy, Sec.

Men's Club of St. John's P. E. Ch., Huntington—W. H. Sammons, Pres.; W. J. Smith, Sec.

Men's Club of St. Paul's P. E. Ch., Patchogue—1913. 9 mem. Jos. Banner, Pres.; E. R. Chambers, Sec.

Mens Holy Name Soc. Our Lady of Good Counsel, R. C. Ch., Lawrence, 1911. 80 mem.

Montauk District Sunday School Assn.—Amagansett.

North Classis of L. I. (Ref.)—Rev. Chas. K. Clearwater, Sec., Elmhurst.

North Side Sunday School Assn.—J. S. Ryder, Supt., Miller pl.; Miss F. N. Tyler, Sec.-Treas., Smithtown Branch.

Orient Bible Soc.—L. H. Hallock, Pres.; S. H. Tuthill, Sec.

Orient District Sunday School Assn.—G. M. Vail, Pres.; Mrs. E. W. Tooker, Sec., Riverhead.

Port Jefferson Bible Soc.—H. M. Randhall, Pres.; G. H. Soper, Sec.

Presbytery of L. I.—Comprises churches of Brookhaven town and all towns eastward; Rev. C. E. Craven, D.D., Stated Clk., Mattituck.

Riverhead Town Union of C. E. Officers—I. S. Warner, Pres.; Miss Mary L. Aldrich, Sec., Aquebogue.

South Classis of L. I. (Ref.)—Rev R. A. Watson, Pres.; J. S. Gardner, Stated Clerk, Somerville, N. J.

Suffolk Assn. of Cong. Churches and Ministers—Rev. W. H. Fitch, Registrar, Riverhead.

Suffolk Co. Camp Meeting Assn.—1834. Jamesport. Rev. W. A. Layton, Pres.; G. M. Vail, Sec., Riverhead.

Suffolk Co. C. E. Union—H. B. Vail, Cor. Sec., Riverhead.

LONG ISLAND SOCIETIES AND ASSOCIATIONS—Religious—*Continued.*

Suffolk Co. Sunday School Assn.—Patchogue. 1859. 139 schools. Jos. Perrottet, Pres.; C. G. Sands, Sec.; H. T. Weeks, Supt.

Western District Sunday School Assn.—D. D. Overton, Pres.; C. G. Sands, Sec., Islip.

Whosoever Will Soc.—Mrs. Louis C. Burling, Pres., Southampton; Mrs. Belle Payne, Sec.

Willing Workers Soc.—Freeport. 1920. Mrs. B. F. Post, Pres.; Mrs. E. B. Washburn, Sec., Freeport.

Winthrop Club, Westbury—1917. 150 mem. H. T. Paterson, Pres.; W. H. Bennem, Jr., Sec.

Woman's Christian Temperance Union—See Temperance Soc.

Woman's H. and F. Miss. Soc. of Presbytery of L. I.—Mrs. C. E. Craven, Pres.; Mrs. W. J. Post, L. I. Sec., Southampton; Mrs. E. J. Thomson, Treas., Bridgehampton.

Yaphank Bible Soc.—R. F. Hawkins, Pres.; F. W. Edwards, Sec.

Missions.

Halesite at Halesite—Mission of Cent. Pres. Ch. at Huntington. Prayer meeting services every Mon. evening. Attendance, 35.

Chapel of First Ch. of Huntington—S. S. weekly. 80 mem. Evangelistic services weekly.

Springs Chapel (Pres.)—The Springs Chapel of Easthampton Pres. Ch. 40 mem. Sunday school attendance about 50. G. E. Miller, Supt.

Stony Brook at Stony Brook—1886. Mission of Setauket Pres. Ch. Self-supporting. 54 mem. Attendance, 55. Sunday school, 80. Chas. E. Cole, Supt. Preaching services Sun., 4 P.M., summer; 3:30 P.M., winter.

Social.

Amityville Club—R. J. Ireland, Pres.; E. J. Heartt, Sec.

Cutchogue Pequash Recreation Club—W. M. Beebe, Pres.; S. W. Horton, Sec., Peconic.

Floral Park Field Club, Inc.—1919. 152 mem. W. A. Wright, Pres.; Theo. Hawkinson, Sec.

Flanders Club—Wm. B. Boulton, Pres.; O. D. Munn, Sec., 233 Broadway, Mhtn.

Friday Club—Lynbrook. 1903. C. Schweitzer, Pres.; Mrs. G. B. Phillips, Sec.

Hollis Court Community Club—E. S. Harrison, Sec., Queens.

Hollis Woman's Club—1915. 120 mem. Mrs. J. S. Shevlin, Pres.; Mrs. H. Barroll, Jr., Sec.

Huntington Bay Club—1920. Huntington. 300 mem. Geo. B. Cortelyou, Pres.; M. A. Warren, Sec., 52 Wall, Mhtn.

Huntington Union Club—G. Hendrickson, Pres.; J. C. Conklin, Sec.

Ladies' Whist Club—Southold. 1909. Mrs. L. N. Sanford, Pres.; Mrs. A. T. Dickerson, Sec.

Merrick Social Club—1919. R. Keil, Pres.; A. H. Otto, Sec.

Mineola Club, Mineola—75 mem. Geo. H. Hansen, Jr., Pres.; E. A. Tubbs, Sec.

Riverhead Pot and Kettle Club—24 mem., limited. B. Rogers, Pres.; Adam Hill, Sec.-Treas.

Rocklyn Club—Lynbrook. Inc. 1920. 84 mem. W. A. Strong, Pres.; E. F. Peckham, Sec., Lynbrook.

Sea Cliff Good of the Village Assn.—Mrs. C. A. Carpenter, Pres.; Mrs. C. S. Chellborg, Sec.

Sodality of St. Patrick's—Bay Shore. 50 mem. Miss MacDonald, Pres.; Miss Irene G. Cahill, Sec.

South Shore College Club—1919. Mrs. E. B. Howell, Pres., Babylon; Miss Marian Smith, Sec., Islip.

Miscellaneous.

Allied Citizens of America (Riverhead Chap.)—F. H. Tuthill, Pres.; Hallock Luce, Sec., Riverhead.

Freeport Mutual Benev. Assn.—Jacob Williams, Pres.; A. J. Post, Sec.

Greta-Theo Holding House—Roslyn. 1920. Under supervision of Co-Operative Girls' Club. See Working Girls' Clubs, Mhtn.

Hempstead Mutual Benefit Assn.—Wm. Stoffel, Pres.; H. E. Velsor, Sec.

L. I. Council of Women's Clubs—20,000 mem. Mrs. Clinton B. Smith, Pres., 137 Maple av., Flushing; Mrs. R. Chapman, Rec. Sec.

L. I. Motor P'kway, Inc., Garden City—W. K. Vanderbilt, Jr., Pres.; R. C. Gasser, Sec. Owns Petit Trianon restaurant at Lake Ronkonkoma.

L. I. R. R. Employees Mutual Relief Assn.—Jamaica. 1886. 8,400 mem. P. H. Woodward, Ch.; T. F. Hogan, Sec., Jamaica.

Mask and Wig Club—1916. 51 mem. A. N. Johnson, Pres.; F. S. Joerissen, Sec., Freeport.

Nassau Co. Assn.—1916. Alfred T. Davison, Pres., Freeport; J. A. Albertson, Sec., Westbury.

Nassau Co. Firemen's Assn.—1903. Mineola. 2,000 mem. A. Campbell, Pres., Glen Cove; J. J. Kramer, Sec., Glen Cove.

Orient Washington Temperance Soc.—H. Terry, Pres.; H. C. King, Sec., Orient.

Patchogue Assn. of Exempt Firemen—C. F. Chapman, Pres.; J. B. Swezey, Sec.

Patchogue Mfgs. Co. Employees Assn.—150 mem. W. Miller, Pres.; E. R. Chambers, Sec. Patchogue, L. I.

Patchogue Sorosis—Miss L. A. Davis, Pres.; Mrs. E. Woolford, Sec.

Piping Rock Horse Show Assn.—Locust Valley. Paul D. Cravath, Pres.; G. E. Fahys, Ch. Exec. Com.

Point o' Woods Assn.—A. M. Ryon, Flushing, Pres.; H. L. Street, Sec., 170 B'way, Mhtn.

Royal Arcanum Hosp. Assn. of L. I.—F. A. Miller, Pres.; H. Sessler, Sec., Baldwin, L. I.

Southampton Kennel Club—1913. 100 mem. H. P. Robbins, Pres.; Henry D. Whitfield, Sec., 597 5th av., Mhtn.

Southern N. Y. Vol. Firemen's Assn.—See Veteran Firemen's Assn., Bkln.

Suffolk Co. Mutual Benefit Assn.—F. S. Hill, Pres.; J. Bagshaw, Sec., Riverhead.

Suffolk Co. Vol. Firemen's Assn.—W. K. Post, Pres.; J. F. Flugrath, Sec., Babylon.

Veteran Assn., Co. H, 119th Regt.—J. H. Smith, Pres.; M. R. Smith, Sec., Hempstead.

Welfare Soc.—1915. Port Washington. Mrs. Chas. Ross, Pres.; Mrs. H. Smith, Cor. Sec.

PUBLICATIONS IN NASSAU AND SUFFOLK COUNTIES.

AMITYVILLE—Record, Fri.; Sun., Fri.
BABYLON—Leader, Fri.; S. Side Signal, Fri.
BAYSHORE—Journal, Sat.
BRIDGEHAMPTON—News, Fri.
CENTRE MORICHES—Record, Fri.
EASTHAMPTON—Star, Fri.
EAST NORWICH—Enterprise, Sat.
FARMINGDALE—Times, Fri.; Furrow, mo.
FLORAL PARK—Nassau Event, Tues.; Record, Fri.
FREEPORT—Nassau Co. Review, Fri.
GARDEN CITY—New Country Life, mo.; Garden Magazine, mo.; Short Stories, mo.; World's Work, mo.; Inter-America, mo.; Red Cross Magazine, mo.; Revista del Mundo, quart.
GLEN COVE—Echo, Sat.; Examiner, Sat.; City Record and News, Sat.
GREAT NECK—North Hempstead Record, Sat.
GREAT NECK STATION—N. Side Tribune, Fri.
GREENPORT—Rep. Watchman, Sat.; Suffolk Times, Fri.
HEMPSTEAD—Inquirer, Fri.; Sentinel, Thur.
HICKSVILLE—News, Fri.; Courier, Wed.
HUNTINGTON—Long Islander, Fri.; Suffolk Bulletin, Fri.
HUNTINGTON STATION—L. I. Herald, Fri.
ISLIP—Herald, Tu.
LONG BEACH—Press and Oceanside News, Sat.
LYNBROOK—New Era and Malverne News, Wed.
MINEOLA—Nassau County Gazette, Fri.; Nassau County, Sun, Sat.
NORTHPORT—Journal, Fri.; Law Notes, mo.
OYSTER BAY—Guardian, Fri.; Pilot, Fri.
PATCHOGUE—Advance, Fri.; Argus, Fri.
PORT JEFFERSON—Echo, Sat.; Times, Sat.
PORT WASHINGTON—News, Fri.; Nassau Guide, Fri.
RIVERHEAD—County Review, Fri.; News, Sat.; L. I. Agriculturist, mo.
ROCKVILLE CENTRE—S. Side Observer, Fri.; Owl, Thur.
ROSLYN—News, Fri.
SAG HARBOR—Express, Thur.; News, Fri.
SAYVILLE—Suffolk County News, Fri.
SEA CLILFF—News, Sat.; Recorder, Fri.
SMITHTOWN BRANCH—Messenger, Fri.
SOUTHAMPTON—Press, Thur.; Sea Side Times, Thur.
SOUTHOLD—L. I. Traveler, Fri.
WESTBURY—Times, Fri.
WESTHAMPTON BEACH—Hampton Chronicle, Fri.
WHITESTONE—Herald, Sat.

LONG ISLAND CHURCHES—NASSAU COUNTY.

Name of Church and Location.	Name of Pastor and Address.	Organized	Contrib'g Mem.	S. S. Members.	Total Amt. Raised	Value Church Prop'ty.
Baptist.						
First, Grove st., Freeport	E. Dennett, Freeport	1895	185	119	$2,377	$20,000
First, Hempstead	S. W. Stackhouse, Hempstead	1884	85	60	2,200	20,000
First, Lynbrook	G. W. Holmes, Lynbrook	1914	26	49	....	15,000
First, Carlton av., Port Washington	W. J. Rutherford, Port Washington	1873	31	45	2,500	12,000
First, Rockville Centre	A. F. Johnson, 76 So. Village av	1870	137	150	5,000	50,000
Oyster Bay, Oyster Bay	C. S. Wightman, Oyster Bay	1724	68	50	1,780	24,000
Shiloh, Rockville Centre	I. P. Harrell, 15 Banks av	1909	70	40	2,000	2,500
Christian Science.						
Christian Science, Hempstead	Mrs. Annie O'Hara	....	.....	....	....	....
Christian Science, Patchogue	Mrs. Emma B. Carter, Patchogue	....	.....	....	....	....
Christian Science, Rockville Centre	H. E. Jahnke, Clerk	1912	.....	....	....	....
Christian Science, Sea Cliff	C. E. Church—First Reader	1908	.....	....	....	1,500
Congregational.						
Bethany, East Rockaway	E. L. Shaver	1885	88	98	2,000	15,000
Memorial Cong., Wantagh av	Wm. B. Allis, 15 W. 38th, N. Y	1889	71	100	2,000	15,000
Friends.						
Bethpage Meeting, Farmingdale	John C. Merritt, Farmingdale	1727	5	....	30	2,000
Jericho, Hicksville	Amy Willets, Jericho	1787	45	....	300	2,500
Jerusalem, near Wantagh	C. S. Garner, Clerk, Wantagh	1827	5	....	2,280	2,000
Manhasset Preparative, Manhasset	A. W. Lapham, Clk., Pt. Wash'ton	....	29	....	....	....
Matinecock, Preparative, Locust Valley	James Willits, Clerk, Glen Cove	1725	105	....	300	8,000
Westbury Hicksite, Post av	Grace Hicks, Clerk, Westbury	1700	65	....	495	12,000
Westbury Orthodox, Friends	Stephen W. Post, Clerk, Westbury	1828	20	40	1,000	6,000
Jewish.						
Tiferth, Israel, Glen Cove	S. Karasick	1899	60	40	....	15,000
Lutheran.						
Christ, Floral Park	Ralph M. Durr, 2 Holland av	1912	120	141	3,363	10,000
Christ, Freeport	C. H. Miller, Freeport	1909	100	100	3,256	6,000
Epiphany (German & English), Hempd.	W. R. Meyer, Hempstead	1897	150	125	2,400	12,000
Grace, Smithville South	Supply	1916	35	40	500	3,000
Holy Trinity, Park av., Rockville Centre	B. Mohrtens, Rockville Centre	1899	84	115	3,008	12,156
St. John's, Lynbrook	F. E. Reissig, Lynbrook	1912	75	100	....	6,000
St. John's, Merrick	C. Zinssmeister, Bkln	1917	44	37	1,871	3,500
St. Luke's, Farmingdale	W. H. Steinbicker	1911	79	87	2,300	9,500
St. Paul's, Valley Stream	W. M. Ruccius, Lynbrook	1912	30	100	....	3,000
St. Peter's, Baldwin	Wm. Steinbicker, Rock'le Centre	1916	42	39	2,000	1,300
St. Stephen's, Hicksville	R. E. Peterman, Hicksville	1910	180	190	3,000	20,000
St. Trinity Evang., Hicksville	Wm. D. Rusch, Hicksville	1863	200	140	2,200	20,000
Methodist Episcopal.						
Baldwin, Merrick rd., Baldwin	D. M. Lewis, Baldwin	1840	251	379	4,000	14,000
Bellmore, Newbridge	J. L. Robinson, Bellmore	1839	59	88	1,050	11,500
Carpenter Memorial, Glen Cove	W. D. Carnes, Glen Cove	1785	176	217	6,624	56,000
East Meadow, Church st., East Meadow	J. V. Williams, East Meadow	1867	73	30	600	6,000
Farmingdale, Farmingdale	H. H. Mower	1840	105	178	2,100	12,300
First, Port Washington	H. D. Jones, Port Washington	1852	289	465	7,602	30,000
First, Roosevelt	R. R. Roberts, Roosevelt	1911	105	200	1,500	4,000
First Church, Valley Stream	United with Grace, Valley Stream.					
Floral Park, Verbena av., Floral Park	E. S. Jackson, Floral Park	1890	250	469	4,864	16,000
Freeport, Pine st., Freeport	W. E. Thompson	1833	748	695	11,379	60,000
Grace, Valley Stream	Roy M. Terry, Valley Stream	1904	153	231	1,400	12,000
Great Neck, Great Neck	Wm. Redheffee, Great Neck	1872	132	130	2,600	26,000
Hempstead, Hempstead	S. O. Curtice, Hempstead	1812	496	368	11,752	54,000
Hicksville, Hicksville, Inc., Plain Edge	W. Pickering	1901	120	227	2,200	14,500
Lawrence, Lawrence	M. O. Lepley, Lawrence	1831	135	359	6,484	46,000
Oceanside	Gustave Laass	1895	125	166	1,600	20,000
Roslyn, Roslyn	A. P. Corliss, Roslyn	1814	100	100	1,200	6,500
St. James', Lynbrook	A. A. Bouton, Lynbrook	1785	350	371	5,000	26,000
St. John's, Elmont	Roy M. Terry, Valley Stream	1850	53	50	600	9,000
St. Mark's, Rockville Centre	Richard Hegarty, Rockville Centre	1871	480	600	10.000	60,000
St. Paul's, Bayville	G. W. Keeling	1867	60	70	1,000	7,000
St. Paul's, South st., Oyster Bay	J. J. Blythe, Oyster Bay	1872	201	209	5,000	30,000
Sea Cliff, Sea Cliff	L. K. Moore, Sea Cliff	1874	200	275	7,000	60,000
Seaford, Seaford	Theo. Bennett, 324 E. 32d, Bkln	1859	75	100	1,300	5,500
Searingtown, Searingtown	A. P. Corliss, Roslyn	1778	40	45	400	5,000
Wesley, East Norwich	Elbert C. Hoag, East Norwich	1834	46	98	4,422	12,000
Westbury, Westbury	D. Dorchester, Westbury	1901	125	105	1,435	7,000
Woodbury, Woodbury	Eugene W. Shrigley	1857	120	96	2,107	14,000
Woodmere, B'way, Woodmere	G. A. Bronson, Woodmere	1878	144	220	6,000	40,000
Methodist Episcopal—African.						
Bethel, Freeport	W. O. Huff, Passaic, N. J	1902	75	65	1,400	9,000
Bethel, Westbury	G. A. Lonzo, Westbury	1887	80	50	2,500	8,000
Calvary, Glen Cove	T. H. Lawrence, Glen Cove	1843	100	86	3,000	16,000
Mount Olive, Port Washington	James Stirling, 1208 Fulton, Bkln	1870	65	34	700	5,000
St. Peter, Douglaston	L. W. DeShields, 256 W. 35th, Mhtn	1870	100	25	900	4,000
Salem, Mineola av., Roslyn	Rev. R. E. DuVall, Roslyn Hts	1862	42	40	1,100	3,000
Meth. Epis.—African, Zion.						
Jackson Memorial, Cross st., Hempstead	M. L. Harvey, Hempstead	1830	41	50	1,500	5,000
Lakeville	A. Johnson, 1957 Dean, Bkln	1835	25	25	800	3,000
St. Hood A. M. E. Zion Church, Oyster Bay.	J. S. Cooper, Oyster Bay	1857	55	62	1,275	15,000
Methodist Episcopal—German.						
St. Paul's, Willis av., Mineola	Otto Mann, Mineola	1901	50	30	1,025	12,000
Wesley Hall, Sea Cliff	A. F. Waible, Sea Cliff	1891	54	40	3,200	4,000
Methodist Protestant.						
First, Church st., Baldwin	J. H. Tuthill, Baldwin	1875	140	300	3,500	25,000
First, Denton av., Lynbrook	W. S. Dunn, Lynbrook	1785	198	225	5,005	35,000
St. Paul's, Inwood	R. F. Day, Inwood	1879	230	400	5,600	36,000

LONG ISLAND CHURCHES—NASSAU COUNTY—*Continued.*

Name of Church and Location.	Name of Pastor and Address.	Organised	Contrib'g Mem.	S. S. Members.	Total Amt. Raised	Value Church Prop'ty.
Presbyterian.						
Bellmore, Bellmore	G. J. Becker, Bible House, Mhtn.	1877	50	75	$1,000	$5,000
Christ's First, Fulton av., Hempstead.	F.M.Kerr, 353 Fulton av., Hmpstd.	1644	360	290	11,000	50,000
First, Church st., Freeport	J. S. Gould, Freeport	1849	373	285	4,457	25,000
First, School st., Glen Cove	F. B. Cowan, Glen Cove	1869	243	130	9,500	60,000
First, Oceanside	J. H. Bigelow, 5000 B'way, Mhtn.	1871	115	160	3,400	10,000
First, East Main, Oyster Bay	H. R. Fancher, Oyster Bay	1845	160	140	4,500	50,000
Glenwood, Glenwood Landing	James Newell Grace, Roslyn	1889	66	60	750	3,000
Mineola Presby. Church, Mineola	G. G. Dunshee, Mineola	1902	150	200	3,250	15,000
New Hyde Park	Gottlieb Ruesch, New Hyde Park.	1902	105	70	1,749	25,000
Rockville Centre	A. H. Rennie, Rockville Centre	1909	140	140	2,800	12,000
Roosevelt, Roosevelt	H. E. Moyer	....	.....	....	......	......
Roslyn, Roslyn	James Newell Grace Roslyn	1852	115	65	2,200	12,000
St. Paul's, Elmont	Augustus C. Espach, Hempstead	1864	118	70	1,443	22,000
Protestant Episcopal.						
All Saints, Middle Neck rd., Great Neck	Kirkland Huske, Great Neck	1887	360	165	9,922	150,000
Cathedral of Incarnation, Garden City.	B'p Burgess. Dean O. F. R. Treder.	1885	450	181	16,351	1,250,000
Christ, Merrick rd., Lynbrook	J. V. Cooper, Lynbrook	1903	200	174	3,747	20,000
Christ, Manhasset	Chas. H. Ricker, Manhasset	1803	185	98	5,300	80,000
Christ, Oyster Bay	G. E. Talmage, Oyster Bay	1705	536	115	18,000	67,000
Church of Ascension, Rockville Centre.	F. H. Handsfield, Rockville Cen.	1885	208	136	3,915	38,000
Church of Nativity, Willis av., Mineola	G. W. McMullin, Mineola	1899	100	60	1,340	24,000
Church of the Advent, Westbury	R. D. Pope, Westbury	1910	145	100	10,702	60,000
Grace, Massapequa	William Wiley, Massapequa	1846	144	62	1,999	50,000
Holy Trinity, Hicksville	G. W. McMullin, Mineola	1900	23	25	200	10,000
Redeemer, Merrick	W. H. Littebrandt, Merrick	1881	50	95	4,600	30,000
St. Elizabeth, Floral Park	G W. McMullin, Mineola	1910	100	100	1,002	3,000
St. George's, Hempstead	Chas. H. Snedeker, 120 Prospect st	1704	380	220	6,500	10,000
St. James, Franklin Square	G. V. Gilreath, Garden City	....	45	50	......	2,500
St. John's, Hempstead (colored)	W. S. McKinney. 41 Grand, Jam'a.	1902	40	42	......	3,000
St. John's, Cold Spring Harbor	H. A. Barrett	1835	200	58	7,000	20,000
St. Luke, Sea Cliff	J. R. Alten	1890	165	117	5,200	42,000
St. Matthias" (col'd), Smithville, South.	W. S. McKinney, 41 Grand, Jam'a.	1902	20	12	......	2,500
St. Mary's, Amityville	Vedder Van Dyck, Amityville	1889	.....	....	......	......
St. Michael and All Angels, Seaford	A. Smith, Roosevelt	1889	51	45	......	17,000
St. Paul's, Glen Cove	Jas. S. Holland	1834	.....	....	......	......
St. Paul's, Roosevelt	....	1901	40	65	247	6,000
St. Stephen's, Port Washington	Rev.Dr.W.E.Bentley, Pt. Wash'n.	1892	208	96	3,796	42,000
St. Thomas', Farmingdale	G. W. MacMullin, Farmingdale	1874	80	90	1,500	14,200
Transfiguration, Freeport	R. H. Scott, Freeport	1894	330	190	5,000	30,000
Trinity, Hewlett	A. L. Bumpus, Hewlett	1844	329	155	15,927	47,600
Trinity, Roslyn	G. S. Mullen, Roslyn	1869	238	143	4,473	100,000
Trinity Chapel, Valley Stream	A. L. Bumpus, Hewlett	1920	26	42	2,500	......
Reformed Church in America.						
First, Hicksville	Vacant	1883	50	50	2,000	20,000
First Reformed, New Hyde Park	B. Milton Smith, New H. P.	1892	60	75	1,500	15,000
North Hempstead, Manhasset	Oscar Maddaus, Manhasset	1732	177	150	5,272	50,000
Oyster Bay Reformed, Brookville	W. H. Jackson, Glen Head	1732	120	75	3,500	40,000
Reformed Church, Locust Valley	Ed. W. Miller, D.D., Locust Val.	1869	100	125	5,150	15,000
Miscellaneous.						
The Community Church, Great Neck	Edward P. Farnham	1914	100	100	5,000	......

Roman Catholic Churches of Nassau Co.†

Name of Church and Location.	Name of Pastor.	Organized	No. of P'r'hioners	S. S. Members.	Value Ch'ch Prop.
Church of Our Holy Redeemer, Freeport	John L. O'Toole	1900	900	175	$126,000
Corpus Christi, Mineola	James M. Burke	1895	430	110	30,000
*Holy Ghost, New Hyde Park	Francis Videnz, 1 assistant	1898	400	....	20,000
Holy Name of Mary, Valley Stream	Peter P. McGovern	1902	600	130	40,000
Our Lady of Good Counsel, Inwood	John J. Mahan	1910	700	150	30,000
Our Lady of Loretto, Hempstead	Robt. E. Boyle, 1 assistant	1870	700	190	25,000
*St. Agnes,' Rockville Centre	Peter Quealy	1887	400	170	30,000
St. Aloysius, Great Neck	Patrick Rogers	....	800	180	100,000
St. Barnabas, Bellmore	John J. Galvin	1912	....	175	27,000
*St. Boniface (German), Elmont	Ignatius Zeller, 1 assistant	1850	700	150	22,000
St. Boniface Martyr, Sea Cliff	Louis J. Sloane	1897	600	130	40,000
St. Brigid's, Westbury	William F. McGinnis, 1 assistan	1853	740	236	5,600
St. Christopher, Baldwin	John A. McGoldrick	1915	400	....	65,000
St. Catherine of Sienna, Franklin Square	Conrad Lutz	1906	200	100	20,000
St. Dominic's, Oyster Bay	Charles J. Canivan	1870	375	93	40,000
St. Gertrude's, Bayville	Charles J. Canivan	1910	260	75	6,000
*St. Hedwig's, Floral Park	Francis Wilamowski	1902	5,000	75	50,000
St. Hyacinth's, Glen Cove (Polish)	Charles Sarnecki	1909	750	200	12,000
*St. Ignatius, Hicksville	Lawrence Fuchs, 1 assistant	1859	480	90	35,000
*St. Joachim, Cedarhurst	Henry Jordan, 1 assistant	1893	350	80	50,000
St. Joseph, Garden City	E. A. Holran	1901	375	50	50,000
St. Joseph's, Hewlett	John Farrell	1872	250	40	7,000
St. Kilian, Farmingdale	Benedictine Fathers	1895	400	74	50,000
St. Martha's, Uniondale	Wm. Manka	1906	200	50	3,000
St. Mary's, Manhasset	Thos. F. Quinn	1855	200	40	100,000
St. Mary's, Roslyn	Louis N. Martel	1871	1,100	125	58,000
St. Mary's of the Isle, Long Beach	Edward Hoar	1912	....	....	......
*St. Patrick's, Glen Cove	Bernard O'Reilly, 1 assistant	1854	900	150	75,000
St. Peter of Alcantara, Port Washington	Joseph A. Carroll, 1 assistant	1901	900	100	110,000
St. Raymond's, Lynbrook	Wm. J. McKenna	1909	450	150	45,000
St. William the Abbot, Seaford	Attended from Bellmore	....	....	....	......

Has a parochial school. †Compiled through aid and courtesy of Secretary, Diocese of Brooklyn.

Totals Nassau County.

From figures reported by individual churches. Catholic totals from Diocese Hdqtrs., Bkln.

Denominations.	Con-trib'g Mem.	S.S. Mem-bers.	Total Amount Raised.	Value Church Pr'p'rty	Denominations.	Con-trib'g Mem.	S.S. Mem-bers.	Total Amount Raised.	Value Church Pr'p'rty
Baptist	602	513	$15,857	$143,500	Methodist Protest't.	568	925	$14,105	$96,000
Christian Science	...	...	......	1,500	Presbyterian	1,995	1,685	46,049	289,000
Congregational	159	198	4,000	30,000	Protestant Epis'pal	4,627	2,594	136,721	2,113,800
Friends	274	40	8,405	62,500	Reformed	507	475	17,422	140,000
Jewish	60	40	......	15,000	Roman Catholic	*18,635	3,051	......	1,172,000
Lutheran	1,129	1,177	20,535	106,450	Miscellaneous	100	100	5,000	......
Methodist Episcopal	5,221	6,541	111,199	664,300					
Meth. Epis.—African	462	300	9,600	45,000	Grand total	34,564	33,462	$386,693	$4,918,050
M. E.—African Zion	121	187	3,575	23,000					
Meth. Epis. German	104	70	4,225	16,000					

*Number of parishioners.

SUFFOLK COUNTY.

Name of Church and Location.	Name of Pastor and Address.	Or gan-ised	Con-trib'g Mem.	S. S. Mem-bers.	Total Amt. Raised	Value Church Prop'ty.
Baptist.						
Blue Point, Blue Point	R. H. Kundle, Blue Point	1865	40	50	$1,300	$4,000
Ebenezer, Babylon	J. Blackston, 18 Evergreen, Jam'a.	1883	16	16	150	1,500
Evergreen, Huntington	Wm. R. Roper, Huntington	1913	15	18	250	4,000
First, Main st. and Carl av., Babylon	A. S. Lowrie, Babylon	1871	137	60	1,700	18,000
First, East Marion	Vacant	1845	150	125	3,402	16,800
First, Main st., Greenport	Vacant	1831	175	160	2,392	15,000
First, Patchogue	W.A.Kloeppel, 39 Jayne av., Patc'e	1889	100	125	2,600	12,000
First, Main st., Port Jefferson	John Bauer, Pt. Jefferson	1861	95	75	1,900	18,000
Huntington, Huntington	N. R. Smith, Huntington	1868	60	60	1,737	15,000
Peoples, Madison st., Sag Harbor	F. Nightingale, Sag Harbor	1844	50	62	3,472	10,000
Union, Main st., Cold Spring Harbor	Supply	1848	60	30	....	4,000
Congregational.						
Baiting Hollow, Baiting Hollow	C. Fersch, Calverton	1791	95	70	2,441	7,000
Calverton Chapel, Calverton	Vacant	1880	.....	....	....	1,000
First, First av., Bay Shore	C. S. MacDowell	1860	240	225	5,000	75,000
First, Main st., Patchogue	L. H. Johnston, Patchogue	1793	479	250	690	75,000
First, Orient	——, Orient	1735	175	135	2,400	20,000
First, Main st., Riverhead	C. C. Cornwell, Riverhead	1834	296	180	7,500	40,000
First, Wading River	Geo. H. Smith	1785	65	60	1,158	15,000
Jamesport, Main st., Jamesport	E. N. Kirby, Jamesport	1725	103	60	1,100	8,000
Mount Sinai, Mount Sinai	F. Voorhees, Millers Place	1789	122	60	1,750	9,500
Old Steeple Church, Aquebogue	Wm. S. Woodworth	1750	123	108	1,776	11,500
Sayville, Main st., Sayville	Wm. T. Edds, Sayville	1858	65	136	2,188	20,000
Sound Avenue, Sound av., Riverhead	W. H. Fitch, Riverhead	1829	186	208	5,330	27,000
Jewish.						
Hebrew Congregation, Huntington Sta.	Benj. Levine	1906	48	....	500	5,000
Temple Mishkan Israel, Sag Harbor	(Holidays only)	1899	47	....	....	....
Lutheran.						
Christ's, Islip Terrace	H. Zoller, Patchogue	1915	40	25	500	1,500
Emanuel, Patchogue	H. Zoller, Patchogue	1912	70	70	1,500	10,400
Holbrook, Holbrook	A. H. Meili, Sayville	1896	9	28	300	1,000
St. John's, Lindenhurst	A. H. Schaefer, Lindenhurst	1876	170	225	2,512	13,500
St. John's, Greene av., Sayville	A. H. Meili, Sayville	1894	50	40	2,000	7,000
St. Peter's Evang. Luth., Greenport	Otto Posselt, Greenport	1868	70	25	1,000	7,000
St. Peter's Luth., Huntington Sta	P. H. Pallmeyer, Huntington Sta.	1907	90	110	2,000	10,000
Methodist Episcopal.						
Bayport, Main st., Bayport	V. W. Mitchell, Bayport	1873	42	60	1,696	7,500
Bellport, Bellport	Wm. Dalziel, Bellport	1857	58	78	600	4,400
Brookhaven, Brookhaven	W. H. Barton, Patchogue	1857	51	37	800	3,500
Calverton, Calverton	E. W. Shrigley, Jr., Southold	1888	40	33	500	2,300
Centerport, Centerport	W. C. Blakeman, Centerport	1901	65	50	900	7,500
Central Islip, Central Islip	J. V. Williams, Central Islip	1879	25	35	444	6,000
Centre Moriches, Centre Moriches	A. L. Hubbard, Centre Moriches	1839	120	114	2,297	15,000
Cold Spring Harbor, Cold Spring Hbor.	....	1842	50	52	800	5,000
Commack, Commack	Chas. E. Williams, Commack	1782	84	150	800	7,000
Coram, Middle Island	L. F. Worley, Coram	1857	60	30	750	7,500
East Moriches, N. Main, East Moriches	H. C. Crosier, East Moriches	1874	83	80	2,000	10,000
East Quogue, East Quogue	J. T. Langlois, East Quogue	1853	100	90	1,600	12,000
First, Broadway, Amityville	W. H. Burgwin, Amityville	1792	300	388	11,222	35,500
First, Deer Park av., Babylon	W. S. Jackson, Babylon	1831	375	250	500	40,000
First, Main st., Bay Shore	C. E. Benedict, Bay Shore	1828	342	....	....	34,000
First M. E. Church, Bridgehampton	J. F. Dunkerke, Bridgehampton	1816	200	185	3,385	25,000
First, Cutchogue	C. A. Knesal	1827	150	139	2,700	13,000
First, Easthampton	J. W. Griffith, Easthampton	1894	100	80	2,000	15,000
First Church, Main st., Huntington	H. M. Hancock, Huntington	1828	301	258	4,000	24,000
First, Main st., Port Jefferson	R. C. Carlson, Port Jefferson	1818	289	240	3,000	32,000
First, Southampton	Henry Trinkaus, Southampton	1843	418	289	5,638	42,500
Flanders, Flanders	H. S. Trueman, Flanders	1895	25	20	750	4,000
Good Ground, Good Ground	W. M. Warden	1828	150	190	1,850	17,000
Greenport, Main st., Greenport	C. A. Quigley, Greenport	1828	248	175	3,200	25,000
Hauppage	A. A. Ball, Hauppage	1806	40	56	1,500	6,000
Islip	Wm. M. Carr, Islip	1809	250	150	3,000	40,000
Jamesport, South Jamesport	H. S. Trueman, Flanders	1860	10	9	400	4,000
Lake Grove	Hy. Still, Lake Grove	1795	100	50	1,139	15,000
Lucien Memorial, Kings Park	J. W. Dodson, Kings Park	1896	65	85	2,120	7,250
Melville, Melville	H. H. Mower, Farmingdale	1840	50	60	636	3,000
M. E. Church, Orient	T. C. Bobilin, Orient	1829	130	150	3,228	10,000
Patchogue, Ocean av., Patchogue	W. E. Schoonhoven, Patchogue	1791	605	532	10,500	50,000
Riverhead, Riverhead	H. M. Richard, Riverhead	1830	305	150	8,000	25,000
Sag Harbor, Sag Harbor	J. A. Macmillan, Sag Harbor	1810	260	215	5,013	25,000
St. James', St. James	A. Rosenberg, Stony Brook	1873	30	50	600	5,000
St. Paul's, Northport	W. B. Maskiell, Northport	1805	400	275	6,500	30,000
Sayville, Sayville	A. J. Pennell, Sayville	1833	200	175	2,500	23,000
Setauket, East Setauket	H. R. Coleman, East Setauket	1843	75	110	1,150	6,000

LONG ISLAND CHURCHES—SUFFOLK COUNTY—*Continued.*

Name of Church and Location.	Name of Pastor and Address.	Organised	Contrib'g Mem.	S. S. Members.	Total Amt. Raised	Value Church Prop'ty.
Methodist Episcopal—Continued.						
Simpson, Amityville	C. M. Wilson, Amityville	1871	120	124	$3,500	$12,000
Smithtown, Smithtown Landing	L. A. Ginlet, Smithtown Branch	1834	47	53	800	5,500
Smithtown, Smithtown Branch	L. A. Ginlet, Smithtown Branch	1846	46	58	800	5,500
Southold, Southold	I. T. Stafford, Southold	1794	152	150	2,300	15,500
Stony Brook, Stony Brook	A. Rosenberg, Stony Brook	1809	72	75	1,600	6,000
Union, East Northport	C. A. Williams, Commack	1903	28	42	700	4,500
Westhampton, Westhampton	Chas. A. Quigley	1832	120	75	2,000	21,000
Westhampton Beach, West'mpton B'ch.	T. B. Miller, Westhampton B'ch.	1891	60	75	2,100	14,500
West Hills, West Hills	....	1843	15	12	300	1,500
Methodist Episcopal—African.						
Allen, Northport	Jos. Stewart, Northport	1886	12	....	450	3,000
Arnett, Port Jefferson	Z. T. Frederick, Port Jefferson	1909	7	32	567	2,100
Bethel, Albany av., Amityville	C. P. Cole, Amityville	1840	70	62	2,350	4,530
Bethel, Babylon	....	1890	30	30	637	2,000
Bethel, Huntington	J. M. Proctor, Huntington	1846	60	35	1,586	5,000
Bethel, Setauket	D. Eato, Setauket, Box 52	1848	60	40	1,548	6,000
Second, Brooks st., Bay Shore	H. H. Harris, Bay Shore	1880	50	42	1,864	7,000
Meth. Epis.—African, Zion.						
African M. E., Riverhead	E. O. Clark, Riverhead	1878	80	42	1,000	5,000
Bellport	J. H. Brockett, Bellport	1880	35	30	400	5,500
Centre Moriches	A. L. Hubbard	1873	127	....	......	17,500
St. David's A. M. E. Zion, Sag Harbor	J. H. Brockett, P. O. Box 785, S.H'r	1840	40	30	1,500	10,000
St. Luke's A. M. E. Zion, Riverhead	R. W. Boyd, Riverhead	1873	36	66	800	12,000
Methodist Protestant.						
First, Eastport	W. L. Angelo, Eastport	1852	121	205	1,600	12,000
Manorville, Manorville	Wm. Bowen, Moriches	1830	20	25	300	2,000
Moriches, Moriches	W. H. Bowen	1900	40	90	1,000	5,000
Pentecostal.						
People's, Sag Harbor	....	1896	12	20	526	3,500
Presbyterian.						
Bellport, Bellport	Supply	1852	30	....	600	15,000
Bethel (colored), Southampton	Thos. C. Ogburn	1917	37	28	530	6,000
Brentwood, Brentwood	Vacant	1891	20	....	1,050	10,000
Brookfield, Manorville	F. J. Pohl, Manorville	1796	38	27	527	5,000
Central, Huntington	Samuel H. Seem, Huntington	1864	332	175	6,150	25,000
Commack, Commack	Vacant	1720	12	....	375	1,500
Cutchogue, Cutchogue	F. Griswold Beebe, Cutchogue	1732	144	143	2,945	12,000
First, Amagansett	C. B. Scoville, Box 36, Amagansett	1860	201	144	2,625	13,000
First, Bridgehampton	Arthur Newman, Bridgehampton	1670	387	199	5,092	40,000
First, Easthampton	N. W. Harkness, Easthampton	1649	520	261	7,200	100,000
First, East Mor'ches	O. R. W. Klose	1902	95	45	1,947	6,200
First, Greenlawn	S. H. Seem, Huntington	1874	50	60	800	2,000
First, Huntington	E. J. Humeston, Huntington	1658	324	240	8,000	50,000
First, Islip	Vacant	1857	227	220	5,000	30,000
First, Main st., Babylon	John M. Brockle, Babylon	1798	260	156	6,000	35,000
First, Main st., Greenport	Wm. Striker, Greenport	1832	232	180	2,300	20,000
First, Main st., Southampton	Geo. W. Rexford	1640	650	250	10,000	100,000
First, Main st., Southold	Wm. H. Lloyd, Southold	1640	156	150	3,000	30,000
First, Northport	U. A. Guss	1795	190	110	4,700	30,000
First, Port Jefferson	Vacant	1870	256	154	4,968	40,000
First, Sag Harbor	Vacant	1766	300	180	3,300	50,000
First, Setauket	T. J. Elms, Setauket	1660	157	164	5,997	19,500
First, Shelter Island	A. L. Shear, Shelter Island	1808	270	280	4,500	24,000
First, Smithtown	E. W. Abbey, Smithtown Branch	1751	180	120	2,500	30,000
First, Stonybrook	T. J. Elms, Setauket	1886	123	87	600	6,000
Mattituck, Mattituck	D. H. Overton, Jr., Mattituck	1715	288	250	4,600	20,000
Melville, Melville	A. Morgan	1829	16	20	417	5,000
Middletown, Middle Island	Jacob Norris, Middle Island	1767	75	25	1,200	2,500
Moriches, Centre Moriches	Vacant	1831	88	55	1,250	10,000
Remsenburg, Remsenburg	Wm. S. C. Webster, Remsenburg	1887	52	25	1,200	1,000
Shinnecock Presby. Ch., South'm't'n	T. C. Ogburn, Southampton	1875	42	60	580	2,800
Southhaven, Southhaven	F. E. Allen, Brookhaven	1747	27	12	1,000	8,500
Westhampton	Thomas Coyle, Westhampton B'ch.	1748	300	250	4,500	18,000
Westhampton Mission, Quogue	Thomas Coyle, Quogue	1890	60	30	450	1,200
Yaphank, Yaphank	James M. Denton, Yaphank	1871	32	16	828	2,500
Protestant Episcopal.						
Atonement, Quogue (4 months)	Summer Church	1884	.....	....	......	....
Caroline, Setauket	Chas. A. Livingston, Setauket	1729	75	40	1,800	10,000
Christ, Main, Bellport	J. P. Smyth, Bellport	1886	50	22	2,490	18,000
Christ, Brentwood	J. Tilley, Central Islip	1872	18	12	783	3,500
Christ, Port Jefferson	Chas. A. Livingston, Setauket	1888	20	20	500	10,000
Christ Church, Sag Harbor	J. C. Welwood, Sag Harbor	1845	155	70	4,700	75,000
Christ, West Islip	E. J. Burlingham, Babylon	1870	110	142	2,619	40,000
Emmanuel, Great River	Wm. N. Webbe, Great River	1862	8	20	3,600	30,000
Grace, Riverhead	Joseph Ryerson, Riverhead	1873	138	100	1,558	17,000
Grace Chapel, Huntington Sta	C. E. Cragg, Huntington	1912	30	37	150	10,000
Holy Trin'ty, Greenport	John H. Heady, Greenport	1865	70	75	2,000	20,000
Messiah, Central Islip	J. Tilley, Central Islip	1869	58	46	2,978	10,500
Redeemer, Mattituck	Joseph Ryerson, Riverhead	1878	20	....	50	3,000
St. Andrew's, Halesite	C. E. Cragg, Huntington	1888	.....	....	......	1,500
St. Andrew's, Yaphank	H. Wilson, Patchogue	1853	25	12	418	....
St. Andrew's Dune, Southampton	Summer Church	1879	.....	....	2,000	10,000
St. Ann's, Bridgehampton	S. C. Fish, Bridgehampton	1906	55	28	4,853	30,000
St. Ann's, Sayville	John H. Prescott, Sayville	1874	100	175	3,000	60,000
St. Ann's Chapel, Babylon	E. J. Burlingham, Babylon	1914	.....	....	......	....
St. Elizabeth's Chapel North Babylon	E. J. Burlingham (Christ Ch. Par.)	1898	.....	....	......	....
St. James', St. James	Wm. Holden, St. James	1853	500	60	6,599	23,500
St. James' Chapel, Stony Brook	Wm. Holden, St. James	1873	35	20	200	3,000
St. John's-on-the-Plains, Bohemiaville	J. H. Prescott, Sayville	1880	.....	75	50	1,200
St. John's, Railroad av., C'tre Moriches	J. P. Smyth	1898	10	9	104	3,000
St. John's, Fisher's Island	Arthur B. Kinsolving	1881	200	....	1,100	5,000

LONG ISLAND CHURCHES—SUFFOLK COUNTY—*Continued.*

Name of Church and Location.	Name of Pastor and Address.	Organised	Contrib'g Mem.	S. S. Members.	Total Amt. Raised	Value Church Prop'ty.
Protestant Episcopal—Continued.						
St. Johns, Main st., Huntington	Chas. E. Cragg, Huntington	1748	430	162	$6,286	$75,000
St. Johns, Southampton	S. C. Fish, Bridgehampton	1908	104	46	3,725	29,500
St. Luke's, Easthampton	E. R. Bourne, Easthampton	1859	500	200	17,600	120,000
St. Mark's, Islip	William Garth, Islip	1847	260	250	10,000	75,000
St. Mary's, Amityville	V. Van Dyck, Amityville	1886	180	85	3,000	15,000
St. Mary's, Shelter Island	J. H. Heady, Greenport	1871	50	25	395	20,000
St. Mary's, Good Ground	S. C. Fish, Bridgehampton	1912	21	23	5,309	12,000
St. Paul's, Rider av., Patchogue	E. A. W. H. Wilson, Patchogue	1843	175	112	2,476	30,000
St. Peter's, Bay Shore	Wm. R. Watson, Bay Shore	1888	190	100	6,395	35,000
Trinity, Main st., Northport	Geo. S. Mullen, Northport	1888	132	50	2,850	40,000
Reformed.						
Sayville, West Sayville	C. Muller, W. Sayville	1866	175	250	3,050	13,000
Universalist.						
First, Main st., Southold	Abram Conklin	1836	50	40	1,850	8,000

Roman Catholic Churches, Suffolk Co., L. I.†

Name of Church and Location.	Name of Pastor.	Organised	No. of P'r'hioners	S. S. Members.	Value Ch'ch Prop.
Church of Our Lady of Poland	Alex. Cizmowski	1918	800	....	....
Immaculate Conception, Westhampton Beach	Joseph Cizmowski	1874	200	30	$12,000
Our Lady of Grace, Fisher's Island	Henry Churchill	1890	700	....	20,000
Our Lady of Ostra Brama, Peconic (Polish)	Joseph Cizmowski	1908	300	75	1,000
*Our Lady of Perpetual Help, Lindenhurst	Tobias E. Farrenkopf	1869	500	100	2,500
Our Lady of the Isle, Shelter Island	Passionist Fathers	1906	450	50	12,000
Our Lady of the Snows, Blue Point	Charles A. Craig	1916	200	...	4,000
Queen of the Most Holy Rosary, Bridgehampton	Attended from Southampton	1912	400	60	30,000
Queen of the Rosary	John J. Gorman	....	.....	....	......
Sacred Heart, Cutchogue	John McCoy	1872	400	80	20,000
Sacred Hearts of Jesus and Mary, South'mpton	Edw. F. Brophy, 1 assistant	1892	600	150	150,000
St. Agnes, Greenport	Francis Connelly	1855	600	125	30,000
*St. Andrew's, Sag Harbor	Peter L. Riekard	1785	1,400	303	75,000
St. Ann's, Brentwood	Thomas Murray	1895	150	20	12,000
St. Francis de Sales, Patchogue	James J. Cronin, 1 assistant	1888	700	100	40,000
St. Hugh's, Huntington Sta	Christian W. Herchenroder	1910	300	60	12,000
St. Isidore's (Polish), Riverhead	Charles Schimmel	1906	700	100	70,000
St. James', St. James	William J. Duhigg	1903	100	15	30,000
St. James', Setauket	Attended from Port Jefferson	1893	200	35	9,000
St. John of God, Central Islip	James J. Kennedy, 1 assistant	1903	500	85	30,000
St. John the Baptist, Wading River	Attended from Manorville	1912	.....	....	......
St. John's, Bohemia	Attended from Sayville	1889	100	20	5,000
St. John's, Centre Moriches	John J. Donlan	1896	330	45	30,000
St. John's, Riverhead	J. F. Curran	1865	400	100	25,000
*St. Joseph's, Babylon	James H. Casey	1876	700	150	130,000
St. Joseph's, Kings Park	J. I. J. Smith	1892	400	200	14,000
St. Joseph's, Ronkonkoma	Thomas K. Fenarty	1886	150	30	8,000
St. Lawrence, Sayville	George A. Gardiner	1897	200	125	75,000
St. Martin's, Amityville	James F. Irwin	1897	350	100	35,000
St Mary's, Bellport	Martin Biggane	1907	300	60	10,000
*St. Mary's, East Islip	Thos. W. Connolly	1898	550	190	45,000
St. Mary's, East Moriches	Attended from Centre Moriches	1888	120	10	4,500
St. Mary's, Port Jefferson	John Genders, 3 assistants	1902	150	60	10,000
St. Patrick's, Bay Shore	Edward Donovan	1850	600	200	30,000
St. Patrick's, Huntington	J. J. F. Robinson, 1 assistant	1849	1,000	200	6,500
St. Patrick's, Southold	Edward McGrath	1854	300	40	24,000
St. Patrick's, Smithtown	Attended from St. James	1835	100	....	10,000
St. Peter and Paul, Manorville	Henry A. Spengler	1912	.....	....	......
St. Philomena, Easthampton	John J. Moran	1894	200	30	25,000
St. Philip Neri's, Northport	James Kehoe	1894	300	50	20,000
St. Rosalie's, Good Ground	Jos. C. Curren	1899	40	22	18,000

*Has a parochial school.

Totals Suffolk County.

From figures reported by individual churches. Catholic totals from Diocese Hdqtrs., Bkln.

Denominations.	Contrib'g Mem.	S.S. Members.	Total Amount Raised.	Value Church Pr'p'rty
Baptist	898	781	$18,903	$118,300
Congregational	1,949	1,492	31,333	30,900
Jewish	95	...	500	5,000
Lutheran	579	523	9,812	50,400
Methodist Episcopal	6,567	5,804	108,818	702,950
Meth. Epis.—African	277	253	8,552	26,680
M. E.—African Zion	318	168	3,700	50,500
Methodist Protest't.	181	320	2,900	19,000
Pentecostal	12	20	526	3,500
Presbyterian	6,171	4,116	$37,731	$776,700
Protestant Epis'pal.	3,719	2,016	96,998	835,700
Reformed	175	250	3,050	13,000
Roman Catholic	*15,120	2,960	......	1,094,500
Universalist	50	40	1,850	8,000
Grand total	36,111	18,743	$324,673	$3,735,130

*Number of parishioners.

LANGUAGES OF THE WORLD.

The principal European languages are divided as follows: English, 160,000,000; German, 110,000,000; Russian, 100,000,000; French, 70,000,000; Spanish, 50,000,000; Italian, 50,000,000; Portuguese, 25,000,000. Swedish is spoken by 5,500,000 persons; Norwegian and Danish by 6,000,000; Serbo-Croatian by 8,000,000; Bohemian or Czech by 7,000,000; Bulgarian by 5,600,000; Dutch by 3,500,000; Polish by 16,000,000; Greek by 9,000,000, and Flemish by 3,500,000. Chinese is spoken by some 400,000,000 people, if all the various dialects are included; Japanese by 53,000,000 and Hindustani by about 100,000,000. There are about 5,000 different languages spoken in the world.

LONG ISLAND OFFICIALS.

OFFICERS OF LONG ISLAND INCORPORATED VILLAGES.

Village.	President.	Village Clerk.	Tax Collector.	Treasurer.
Amityville	F. B. Powell	Wm. Lauder	F. W. Udall	N. V. W. Colyer.
Babylon	C. E. Puttfarcken	James B. Cooper	Frank E. Davis	J. H. Baldwin.
Bayville	W. S. Pierce	Ida F. Perry	Rozina West	C. H. Wright.
Bellport	C. E. Hulse	L. B. Raymond	J. N. Hawkins	J. R. Watkins.
Brightwaters	R. T. Snodgrass	Chas. Kuhn	Ella A. Mandell	W. S. Haviland.
Cedarhurst	J. G. McNicoll	L. M. Raisig	A. T. Moon	G. W. Craft.
Dering Harbor	C. Lane Poor	G. A. Barr	A. T. Towl	W. T. Barr.
Easthampton	J. Baker	R. A. Smith		K. E. Davis.
East Rockaway	W. E. Johnson	Chas. E. Curtis	H. W. Beery	D. S. Denton, Jr.
Farmingdale	N. D. Ketcham	P. W. Evarts	Chas. Post	Jesse Jones.
Floral Park	Geo. H. Downing	E. D. Purcell	B. James	E. C. Ullmann.
Freeport	C. A. Edwards	Sylvester P. Shea	D. F. Seaman	S. Dimon Smith.
Garden City	G. L. Hubbell	T. P. Klopper	E. A. Pratt	F. A. Kimball.
Great Neck Estates	F. Stadelman	F. B. Church	H. Keller	P. W. Thistle.
Greenport	Geo. B. Preston	Ella L. Phillips	F. B. Thornhill	I. L. Price.
Hempstead	J. S. Nichols	E. P. Parsons	C. E. Akley, Jr.	F. Marthing.
Lawrence	C. C. Adams	James Loucheim	H'y Worthington	Peter B. Olney, Jr.
Long Beach	Wm. H. Reynolds	Agnes Bracken	Jas. Abel	H. M. Susswein.
Lynbrook	G. W. Wright	Wm. H. O'Brien	W. Karn	J. S. Simonson.
Mineola	Geo. Schmidt	Albert F. Buhler	D. Harrington	H. Von Oehsen.
Northport	W. E. Call	Israel Carll	F. Gardiner	John K. Sammis.
Patchogue	Dr. E. A. Foster	Edw. B. Woodruff	R. H. Valentine	E. Johanknecht, Jr.
Plandome	A. G. Elvin	L. W. Armstrong	W. Barnwell	O. W. Anthony.
Rockville Centre	M. K. Dunn	G. S. Utter	A. J. Flanagan	Chas. J. Dooley.
Sag Harbor	M. B. Lewis	J. B. Wright	Margaret King	E. F. Jones.
Saltaire	J. T. Mason	Raymond Martin	W. B. Stanton	Harry Bartling.
Sands Point	T. Kingsbury	H. R. Tibbits	H. J. Tibbets	A. V. Fraser.
Sea Cliff	Peter Rohrbach, Jr.	Walter F. Forster	J. E. Jones	G. F. Butler.
Shoreham	F. W. Gridley	J. R. Melville	R. L. Stone	E. F. Stevens.
Southampton	B. H. Bishop	Ethel R. Whitman		F. N. Dunwell.
Woodsburgh	F. H. Hatch	W. Rosenbaum	A. N. Peck	A. N. Peck.

TOWN OFFICERS OF NASSAU AND SUFFOLK COUNTIES.

Town.	Supervisor.	Town Clerk and Address.	Collector and Address.
Babylon	W. T. Louden	E. A. Taylor, Babylon	James B. Kent, Babylon.
Brookhaven	Riley P. Howell	R. B. Ackerly, Patchogue	R. P. Wheeler, Pt. Jefferson.
Easthampton	N. N. Tiffany	J. Y. Strong, Easthampton	Ulysses Lee, Easthampton.
Hempstead	H. R. Smith	F. C. Gilbert, Hempstead	J. H. Foster, Hempstead.
Huntington	A. L. Field	Wm. B. Trainer, Huntington	C. Sammis.
Islip	John Westerbeke	W. C. Haff	M. J. Anderson, Bay Shore
N. Hempstead	C. E. Remsen	W. N. Mullon, Manhasset	Chas. Snedeker, Manhasset
Oyster Bay	C. Chester Painter.	Ed. J. Conlin	F. McQueen, Oyster Bay
Riverhead	B. F. Howell	J. W. Kratoville, Riverhead	F. Downs, Riverhead.
Shelter Island	Chas. H. Smith	E. P. Baldwin, Shelter Isl'd	R. Schweinsberg, Sh. Is. Hts.
Smithtown	C. D. Miller	F. E. Brush, Smitht'n Br.	H. A. Smith, Smithtown Br.
Southampton	B. G. Halsey	Jas. A. Early, Southampton	A. C. Dalzell.
Southold	David W. Tuthill	Joseph N. Hallock, Southold	E. L. Bennett, E. Marion.

NASSAU COUNTY OFFICIAL LIST.

Office.	Name.	Residence.	Office.	Name.	Residence.
Rep. in Cong.	F. C. Hicks	Pt. Washington	County Compt.	E. J. Bennet	R'kville Centre.
State Senator	G. L. Thompson	Kings Park	County Treas.	W. E. Luyster	Glen Cove.
Assembly, 1 D.	T. A. M'Whinney	Lawrence.	Dist. Att'y	C. R. Weeks	Pt. Washington
Assembly, 2 D.	Theo. Roosevelt	Oyster Bay	Supt. of Poor	C. C. VanDeusen	R'kville Centre.
County Judge	L. J. Smith	Hempstead.	Sch. Supt., 1st D	J. S. Cooley, M.I	Mineola.
Surrogate	LeoneD. Howell	Mineola.	Sch. Supt., 2d D	W. C. Mepham	Merrick.
Sheriff	Chas. W. Smith	Lawrance.	Com'r of El'ct's	L. E. Kerwin	Hempstead.
County Clerk	T. S. Cheshire	Woodmere.	Com'r of El'ct's	Chas. U. Stowe.	Hempstead.
Dep. Co. Clerk	O. E. Payne	Glen Cove.	Com'r of Jurors	J. N. Brown	Valley Stream.
Superv'r's Cl'k.					

(For Glen Cove city officials see index.)

SUFFOLK COUNTY OFFICIAL LIST.

Office.	Name.	Residence.	Office.	Name.	Residence.
Rep. in Cong.	F. C. Hicks	Pt. Washington	Sch. Supt., 2d D	J. H. Young	Central Islip.
State Senator	G. L. Thompson.	Kings Park.	Sch. Supt., 3d D	L. J. Smith	Huntington.
Assembly, 1 D.	J. G. Downs	Cutchogue.	Coroner	W. B. Gibson	Huntington.
Assembly, 2 D.	W. G. Carroll	Bayport.	Coroner	M. B. Lewis	Sag Harbor.
County Judge	Geo. H. Furman	Patchogue.	Coroner	C. C. Miles	Greenport.
Surrogate	S. B. Strong 3d.	Setauket.	Coroner	E. S. Moore	Bay Shore.
Dist. Att'y	LeR. M. Young	Babylon.	Coroner	C. W. Hedge	Fisher's Island.
Sheriff	J. F. Kelly	Kings Park.	Superv'r's Cl'k.	J. F. Kelly	Kings Park.
County Clerk	J. F. Richardson	Riverhead.	Sh. Fish Com.	W. R. Cartwright	Shelter Island.
County Treas.	H. P. Tuthill	Mattituck.	Sh. Fish Com.	D. W. Tuthill	Greenport.
Co. Auditor	D. T. Corwin	Riverhead.	Sh. Fish Com.	R. A. Leek	Southampton.
Supt. of Poor	Jonathan Baker	Easthampton.	Com'r of El'ct's	F. S. Pulver	Sag Harbor.
County Sealer	C. P. Smith	Riverhead.	Com'r of El'ct's	A. J. Adams	Riverhead.
Sch. Supt., 1st D	P. B. Matthews	Bridgehampton.			

JUSTICES OF THE PEACE OF LONG ISLAND

Babylon—H. A. Edwards, Paul Bailey, J. B. Cooper, F. J. Wood.

Brookhaven—F. P. Johnson, J. S. Dreyer, E. F. Howell, Robt. Macintosh, Fred'k Marchant, C. C. Neville, C. F. West, W. Court, H. Smith.

Easthampton—Hiram Sherrill, E. F. Jones, M. H. Edwards, D. S. Miller.

Hempstead—W. R. Jones, L. M. Raisig, E. T. Neu, W. F. Southard.

Huntington—A. E. Lowndes, W. E. J. Collins, G. C. Hendrickson, F. H. Koster.

Islip—J. A. Moore, D. D. White, F. R. Nohowel, F. T. Hulse.

North Hempstead—Thos. B. Roeber, Arthur E. Jones, E. E. Le Cluse, A. P. Kohler.

Oyster Bay—Ed. J. Deasy, W. I. Harrold, A. Morey, C. H. Stoll.

Riverhead—W. S. Downs, Wm. F. Flanagan, W. L. Miller, R. Burnside.

Shelter Island—Irving Clark, W. R. Cartwright, J. B. Morrison, P. E. Nostrand.

Smithtown—Benj. D. Blackman, M. B. Blydenburgh, G. S. Hodgkinson, W. F. Flynn, G. B. Purick.

Southampton—Clifford Jackson, C. B. Raynor, C. Humblet, W. C. Greene, R. R. Kendrick.

Southold—W. W. Griffin, C. G. Corey, H. H. Terry, F. E. Hine, J. H. Rambo.

LONG ISLAND SCHOOL BOARDS AND DISTRICTS, 1919-1920.

(First name following town is president, or trustee if followed by T.; 2d name, clerk.)

Nassau County.

FIRST DISTRICT.

James S. Cooley, M.D., Supt., Mineola.

Union School Districts.

TOWN OF NORTH HEMPSTEAD.

1. Westbury—Rev. Wm. F. McGinnis, Pres.; G. L. Eastman, Clerk.
3. Roslyn—Ralph Tubby; W. Charlick.
4. *Port Washington—J. H. Decker; Miss M. Mitchell.
5. New Hyde Park—J. N. Krug; Albert Rohrer.
6. Manhasset—W. Barnwell; E. L'Hommedieu.
7. Great Neck—Frank Dickerson; Wm. G. Genner.
10. Mineola—Wm. McCarthy; A. F. Buhler.
11. Carle Place—G. S. Dorwin; Alex. Wickey.

TOWN OF OYSTER BAY.

1. Glenwood—H. Van Cott; Mrs. C. Weber.
4. Locust Valley—B. W. Downing; G. A. Davis.
5. †Glen Cove—G. Wood; F. Ludlam.
6. Bayville—A. W. Flower; O. J. West.
9. Oyster Bay—J. F. Bermingham; Geo. D. Clarke.
16. Wheatley—D. K. Jay; A. F. Simonson.
17. Hicksville—W. Duffy; Wm. Stolz.
21. Central Park—Geo. Benkert; E. S. Stymus.
22. Farmingdale—Wm. H. Kingston; Mrs. R. Franke.
24. Sea Cliff—E. M. Ledden; Fred Jenkins.

*Jurisdiction of P. D. Schrieber, Supt. Dist. has 4 schools. †Jurisdiction of Glen Cove City administration. H. H. Chapman, Supt.

Common School Districts.

TOWN OF NORTH HEMPSTEAD.

2. East Williston—Wm. M. Tompkins, T.; B. A. Griffin.
8. Lakeville—H. J. Fry, T.; Arthur Fogel.
9. Herricks—M. C. Perkins, T.; Miss R. Wicks.

TOWN OF OYSTER BAY.‡

2. Greenvale—G. D. Hegeman, T.; G. T. Powell.
3. Brookville—Chas. Luyster, T.; Chas. Mernin.
8. East Norwich—J. H. Vernon, T.; J. E. E. Remsen.
11. Cold Spring Harbor—C. H. Walters, T.; Miss C Wheeler.
12. Syosset—G. D. Carnes, T.; S. J. Titus.
13. Woodbury—J. L. Baylis, T.; D. S. Whitney.
14. Locust Grove—J. S. Burke, T.; E. W. Underhill.
15. Jericho—R. Seaman, T.; D. Underhill.
18. Plain Edge—C. E. Schwarting, T.; J. P. Thompson.
19. Plain View—J. A. Jantzen, T.; Chas. Fleischer.
20. Bethpage—Miss C. M. Smith, T.; Mrs. C. Baker.
23. Massapequa—E. H. Floyd-Jones, T.; Mrs. T. Killian.

‡Oyster Bay No. 7 (Central Park) and Oyster Bay No. 10 (Oyster Bay Cove) are consolidated with No. 9, Oyster Bay.

SECOND DISTRICT.

W. C. Mepham, Superintendent, Merrick.

Union School Districts.

TOWN OF HEMPSTEAD.

1. Hempstead Village—C. H. Ludlum, M.D.; G. H. Baukney.
2. Uniondale—A. G. Patterson.
4. Smithville South—T. J. Thornton; C. A. Wood.
6. Seaford—Harry Livingston; Mary E. Southard.
7. Bellmore—Charles Russell, Sr.; G. J. Baldwin.
9. Freeport—C. D. Baker; R. E. Donaghy.
10. Baldwin—W. J. Steele, M.D.; Chas. Wheeler.
11. Oceanside—C. A. McGuirl; Gilbert Smith.
12. Norwood—P. W. F. Lindner; F. B. Wheldon.
14. Woodmere—J. A. Carson; R. L. Kane.
15. Lawrence—L. J. Beach; N. J. Pettitt.
16. Elmont—Philip Hoeffner; J. Herman.
17. F'klin Sq.—Herman Utz; P. J. Herman.
19. East Rockaway—C. B. Phipps; C. E. Curtiss.
20. Lynbrook—C. E. Schweitzer; A. O. Albin.
21. Rockville Centre—A. E. Ives, Jr.; Mrs. E. R. Spellman.
22. Floral Park—J. L. Childs; Wallace Thurston.
23. Wantagh—F. E. Bradley; Mrs. B. Jackson.
24. Valley Stream—W. L. Buck; H. Bayer.
27. West Hempstead—F. B. Taylor; James Bacon.
28. Long Beach—Henry Suswein; A. Bracken.

Common School Districts.

TOWN OF HEMPSTEAD.

3. East Meadow—I. Nohearn; Del Smith.
5. Jerusalem—Sidney Seaman; H. L. Stehl.
13. Valley Stream North—Arthur Hendrickson; G. H. Combs.
18. Garden City—G. H. Hubbell; H. A. Frey.
25. Merrick—G. Hewlett; Jas. Emery.
26. Island Trees—J. E. Walsh; O. Stressman.

Suffolk County.

Union School Districts.

FIRST SUPERVISORY DISTRICT.

P. B. Matthews, Dist. Supt., Bridgehampton, L. I.

Easthampton, Dist. No. 1—T. R. Barns, Pres.; D. C. Talmage, Clk., Easthampton, L. I. Easthampton, Dist. No. 5, W. R. Reimann; C. A. Kiernan, Sag Harbor. Southampton, Dist No. 5, G. D. Squires; J. H. Corwin, Good Ground. Southampton, Dist. No. 6, W. D. Van Brunt; W. P. Bishop, Southampton. Southampton, Dist. No. 9, E. Sayre; C. W. Hildreth, Bridgehampton. Southampton, Dist. No. 2, J. B. Cook; J. F. Stevens, Westhampton. Southampton, Dist. No. 11, E. W. Tuthill, D. F. Brown, Eastport.

Riverhead, Dist. No. 5, R. P. Griffing; E. M. Robinson, Riverhead. Southold, Dist. No. 2, J. B. Adams; E. F. Dewey, Orient. Southold, Dist. No. 5, J. N. Hallock; W. H. Terry, Southold. Southold, Dist. No. 9, F. C. Barker; R. A. Hughes, Mattituck. Southold, Dist. No. 10, F. D. Schaumberg; L. F. Terry, Greenport. Shelter Island, Dist. No. 1, F. N. Dickerson; D. H. Young, Shelter Island.

SECOND SUPERVISORY DISTRICT.

J. Henry Young, Supt., Central Islip, L. I.

Brookhaven, Dist. No. 1, R. F. Wells, Pres.; F. H. Wells, Clk., Stony Brook. Brookhaven, Dist. No. 2, Jacob Satterlee; J. B. Gurney, Setauket. Brookhaven, Dist. No. 5, Mrs. G. Raynor, T. J. Morrissey, Lake Ronkonkoma. Brookhaven, Dist. No. 6, Charles Dare; A. O. Smith, Port Jefferson. Brookhaven, Dist. No. 23, Fremont Abrams; Mrs. A. E. Davis, Blue Point. Brookhaven, Dist. No. 27, J. Stephani; W. Rodgers, East Patchogue. Brookhaven, Dist. No. 28, George Kraemer; L. Raymond, Bellport. Brookhaven, Dist. No. 32, C H. Wilcox; H. A. T. Hadges, Center Moriches. Brookhaven, Dist. No. 24, Frank Guttridge; H. J. Bishop, Patchogue. Islip, Dist. No. 1, J. J. Gibson; F. C. Hendrickson, Bay Shore. Islip, Dist. No. 2, C. G. Sands; Wilmarth Haff, Islip. Islip, Dist. No. 3, H. B. Hollins; C. H. Smisek, East Islip. Islip, Dist. No. 4, Dow Clock; H. O. Newton, Sayville. Islip, Dist. No. 5, C. F. Pratt; M. H. L'Hommedieu, Bayport. Islip, Dist. No. 7, W. Lederer; Anton Bartik, Bohemia. Islip, Dist. No. 12, Dr. W. H. Ross; Dr. H. E. Chauvin, Brentwood. Islip, Dist. No. 13, R. H. Story; R. E. O'Donohue, Central Islip.

THIRD SUPERVISORY DISTRICT.

Leonard J. Smith, Supt., Northport, L. I.

Babylon, Dist. No. 1, B. B. Wood, Pres.; Jesse Smith, Clk., Babylon. Babylon, Dist. No. 4, William Rall; E. J. McGraw, Lindenhurst. Babylon, Dist. No. 6, G. V. Greey; R. S. Colt, Amityville. Huntington, Dist. No. 3, T. H. Sammis; W. E. Bryant, Huntington. Huntington, Dist. No. 4, Dr. Frank Quackenbush; Charles Mott, Northport. Smithtown, Dist. No. 1, George Purick; F. E. Brush, Smithtown Branch.

DAYLIGHT SAVING ORDINANCE.

Be it ordained by the Board of Aldermen of The City of New York, as follows:

That the standard time throughout The City of New York is that of the 75th meridian of longitude west from Greenwich, except that at 2 o'clock ante-meridian of the last Sunday in March of each year such standard time throughout The City of New York shall be advanced one hour, and at 2 o'clock ante-meridian of the last Sunday in October of each year such standard time shall, by the retarding of one hour, be returned to the mean astronomical time of the 75th meridian of longitude west from Greenwich, and all courts, public offices and legal and official proceedings shall be regulated thereby. (Adopted by the Board of Aldermen, Oct. 14, 1919; approved by the Mayor, Oct. 24, 1919.)

State figures as of July 1, 1920. **BANKS OF LONG ISLAND—Nassau and Suffolk Counties** National Bank figures as of September 8, 1920.

Institutions.	Location.	President.	Cashier.	Loans and Disc'nts.	Bonds and Invsts.	Due from TrustCos & Banks.	Total Res'rces	Capital.	Circulation.	Surplus & Profits	Total Deposits
National.											
First	Amityville	C. A. Luce	Percy L. Hall	$533,501	$286,183	$404,793	$1,307,969	$25,000	$25,000	$32,355	$1,220,504
Babylon	Babylon	W. F. Norton	W. W. Wood	96,470	440,423	122,856	719,349	50,000	.....	50,882	618,366
First	Bayshore	W. H. Robbins	O. S. Brewster	233,054	419,984	137,493	818,110	50,000	25,000	34,338	704,371
Bridgehampton	Bridgehampton	E. J. Hildrith	E. J. Thomson	257,798	116,285	41,455	432,242	25,000	18,000	20,561	367,198
Peninsula	Cedarhurst	C. C. Adams	A. I. Davidson	....	....	....	....	100,000	.....	.....	....
East Hampton	Easthampton	Hiram Sherrell	G. A. Miller	365,527	328,873	115,039	876,580	25,900	16,000	40,124	809,965
First	East Islip	Chas. L. Wolpert	Harry L. Wolpert	132,045	124,600	32,179	312,067	25,000	25,000	7,047	252,320
First	Farmingdale	J. F. Michel	W. H. Trou	388,522	406,765	76,851	904,934	25,000	25,000	40,404	780,430
First	Freeport	Roswell Davis	Wm. F. Kraft, Jr.	758,356	636,891	155,553	1,624,007	25,000	12,500	58,327	1,524,950
First	Greenport	G. C. Adams	F. B. Corey	416,661	236,984	146,341	844,742	50,000	50,000	70,546	673,207
Peoples	Greenport	Thos. F. Price	I. L. Price	233,812	148,315	78,272	507,008	....	12,500	34,439	405,922
First	Hempstead	Fred Ingraham	C. F. Norton	1,144,007	1,116,407	297,800	2,729,090	....	100,000	110,171	2,412,419
Second	Hempstead	G. H. Bankey	C. H. Ludlum	532,518	20,957	100,865	792,321	100,000	.....	32,235	625,027
First	Huntington	J. F. Wood	W. S. Funnell	274,262	619,239	77,026	1,022,971	50,000	50,000	27,041	905,516
First	Islip	E. R. Smith	Roscoe C. Clock	191,275	259,324	47,749	525,151	25,000	6,250	31,599	459,221
First	Lindenhurst	W. C. Abbott	Geo. Pebler	347,026	107,161	40,825	558,069	25,000	6,500	26,044	482,068
Lynbrook	Lynbrook	J. F. Felton	J. L. Stanley	1,186,005	432,259	270,429	2,025,601	25,000	7,000	83,243	1,886,602
Peoples	Lynbrook	S. J. Broadbury	W. F. Flock	213,223	71,771	48,055	360,971	50,000	25,000	12,500	273,771
First	Mineola	H. W. Andrews	G. Smith	436,248	586,416	153,961	1,255,801	50,000	50,000	37,977	1,115,478
First	Northport	R. Miles	H. K. Soper	364,060	426,106	84,263	934,817	50,000	20,000	21,686	831,111
First	Port Jefferson	O. T. Fanning	F. A. Kline	349,737	544,587	62,394	1,001,256	50,000	50,000	58,054	812,800
Port Washington	Port Washington	H. R. Tibbits	D. M. Croucher	301,235	63,298	63,160	446,550	25,000	.....	9,570	410,979
Suffolk County	Riverhead	T. M. Griffing	B. F. Howell	820,964	404,151	164,804	1,419,481	50,000	50,000	89,148	1,228,233
First	Rockville Centre	J. H. Carl	C. J. Dooley	1,131,580	171,175	551,365	1,907,618	25,000	25,000	79,979	1,767,988
Nassau County	Rockville Centre	D. N. Bulson	B. T. Raynor	343,501	500,985	73,362	959,927	50,000	.....	36,510	871,416
Oystermen's	Sayville	I. H. Green	Dow Clock	194,310	314,926	174,211	757,365	50,000	50,000	109,288	545,960
Nat'l Bk. of Smithtown Br.	Smithtown Branch	J. S. Huntting	J. A. Overton	196,697	305,162	86,062	610,272	25,000	25,000	27,586	531,628
First	Southampton	John Nugent	W. K. Dunwell	789,041	691,853	146,495	1,783,071	100,000	70,000	111,021	1,453,280
Valley Stream	Valley Stream	F. W. Muller	F. C. Haskell	....	....	....	....	25,000	....	....	....
State.											
Amityville	Amityville	Solomon Ketcham	E. J. Heartt	$325,866	$195,577	$24,403	$707,703	$25,000	$597,411	$69,827	$607,260
Babylon	Babylon	J. C. Robbins	G. C. Abbott	154,396	150,024	28,959	377,926	50,000	309,667	17,842	309,734
Centre Moriches	Centre Moriches	J. L. Havens	C. E. Liscum	337,264	195,546	61,750	660,494	25,000	583,496	43,574	583,496
Farmingdale	Farmingdale	Martin Meyer	J. S. Baylis	165,409	166,097	13,558	469,094	25,000	396,443	26,720	413,973
Floral Park	Floral Park	E. L. Frost	C.H.VanNostrand	297,882	381,993	8,944	929,185	25,000	830,509	41,455	830,509
Freeport	Freeport	J. J. Randall	W. S. Hall	795,200	477,215	62,320	1,626,980	100,000	1,058,141	105,061	1,725,406
Glen Cove	Glen Cove	D. N. Gay	J. C. Small	1,211,615	1,166,070	274,042	3,063,814	100,000	2,794,754	113,085	2,826,142
Great Neck	Great Neck	Roswell Eldridge	Austin Hicks	415,717	468,576	49,338	1,140,157	50,000	1,012,867	76,329	1,012,867
Hempstead	Hempstead	....	C. E. Patterson	514,830	935,580	173,512	2,226,735	30,000	1,987,337	199,148	1,987,337
Hempstead Harbor	Roslyn	Jos. H. Bogart	H. C. Hegeman	371,410	444,162	179,037	1,112,408	30,000	936,921	92,398	986,399
Hicksville	Hicksville	H. W. Underhill	J. J. Ulmer	854,417	389,651	21,106	1,468,160	25,000	1,303,021	122,900	1,308,160
Huntington	Huntington	Douglass Conklin	R. W. Downs	1,235,294	923,845	192,119	2,736,981	100,000	2,418,655	189,426	2,445,555
Lawrence	Lawrence	J. C. Schmuck	J. A. Ruth	1,206,088	220,050	223,049	1,874,518	100,000	1,694,868	49,375	1,717,968
Mattituck	Mattituck	J. M. Lupton	E. D. Corwin	237,902	168,816	39,354	480,915	25,000	402,884	36,073	417,884
Nassau County	Great Neck Station	J. L. Schaefer	B. D. Willets	259,572	244,874	72,126	641,178	50,000	554,951	36,217	554,951
Nassau Union	Glen Cove	Richard Downing	H. G. Hayward	396,080	677,598	156,231	1,321,459	100,000	1,097,079	88,685	1,130,079
North Hempstead	Port Washington	H. R. Smith	B. H. Monfort	398,229	445,381	86,799	1,138,141	25,000	1,031,846	56,767	1,059,449
North Shore	Oyster Bay	W. F. Johnson	C. A. Clewer	677,692	256,845	85,713	1,144,088	25,000	1,077,364	38,765	1,077,598
Osborne	Easthampton	C. W. Osborne	N. N. Tiffany	195,502	268,062	37,002	694,516	100,000	526,187	43,295	549,877
Oyster Bay	Oyster Bay	E. M. Griffin	E. F. Cheshire	439,481	618,917	60,393	1,410,381	50,000	1,292,148	64,289	1,292,633
Patchogue	Patchogue	J. A. Potter	F. A. Potter	629,039	160,842	100,752	1,044,549	75,000	823,356	85,182	879,062
Peconic	Sag Harbor	W. E. Denison	F. W. Corwin	256,922	33,211	26,129	343,859	25,000	258,235	29,450	288,467
Port Jefferson	Port Jefferson	H. M. Randall	R. B. Dayton	529,646	255,208	57,064	967,239	25,000	829,686	82,852	846,686
Rockville Centre	Rockville Centre	F. T. DeLano	J. F. Simonson	1,170,338	855,208	100,299	2,555,285	100,000	2,122,439	109,567	2,185,718
Sea Side	W. Hampton Beach	E. F. Post	H. D. Bishop	180,008	85,366	32,171	317,420	25,000	265,247	25,640	266,108
Southold	Southold	Albert A. Folk	A. T. Dickerson	113,917	123,304	19,160	281,673	25,000	197,539	15,733	210,539
Southampton	Southampton	E. A. Hildreth	L. E. Terry	360,079	257,580	57,603	784,982	100,000	547,368	94,386	588,761

South Side	Bay Shore	P. S. Wicks	L. K. Redington	319,029	321,844	45,924	765,154	25,000	644,110	31,809	649,33[illegible]
Suffolk County	Stony Brook	W. P. Youngs	Geo. Hellen	239,576	135,476	25,687	448,676	25,000	394,943	22,549	390,943
Westbury	Westbury	Frank Powers	R. W. McCord	237,440	223,739	16 [illegible]31	621,960	25,000	547,680	33,021	559,065
Savings.											
Riverhead	Riverhead	U. B. Howell.	O. G. Pike	......	......	......	$8,879,990	......	$7,364,643	$1,506,847	-
Roslyn	Roslyn	Thos. Mott	F. E. Willits, Treas.	......	......	.	3,419,949	......	3,139,456	279,896	......
Sag Harbor	Sag Harbor	Wm. D. Halsey	E. L. Tindall	......	......	......	2,681,789	......	2,410,241	270,348	......
Southold	Southold	H. W. Prince	H. H. Huntting	......	......	......	6,925,034	......	5,881,968	1,043,065	......
Union	Patchogue	E. G. Terrell	W. S. Rose	......	......	......	4,554,377	......	4,129,111	424,011	......
Trust Companies.											
Citizens	Patchogue	S. N. Gerard	H. L. Reith	......	......	......	$2,640,380	$100,000	$2,106,986	$159,952	......
Nassau County	Mineola	G. S. Emory	J. O. Bergen	......	......	......	2,640,380	100,000	2,106,986	159,952	......
Northport	Northport	H. S. Mott	Chas. S. Mott, Treas.	......	......	......	941,447	100,000	739,806	52,892	......
Suffolk County	Riverhead	G. M. Vail	John S. Howe	......	......	. -	2,858,088	100,000	2,349,455	147,090	......

NEW YORK CITY SAFE DEPOSIT COMPANIES, JANUARY 1, 1920*

Brooklyn and Queens	President.	Secretary or Treasurer.	Stock Invest-ments.	Vaults and Safes.	Cash Deposited in Banks.	Total Resources	Capital.	Excess of As'ts Over Liabilities
Bank of Long Island, Jamaica	P. A. Rowley	O. G. Alexander, Treas.	$95,190	$16,516	$3,516	$115,222	$100,000	$15,222
Brooklyn City, 177 Montague st	D. H. Lanman	F. O. Edgerton	126,149	......	4,482	136,171	100,000	22,042
Franklin, 166 Montague st	E. C. Delafield	T. Gerrish	28,321	**94,625	2,774	125,721	100,000	25,721
Long Island, 136 Montague st	F. L. Sniffen	H. V. Wing, Sec.	51,000	**2,000	2,794	132,852	100,000	20,581
Security, DeKalb av. and Fulton st	Geo. Cox	A. J. Mauger	23,300	81,034	4,417	130,350	100,000	20,892
Manhattan and Bronx.								
Astor, 57th st. and Madison av	S. Prosser	W. P. Belknap, Treas.	125,796	32,118	2,621	169,179	100,000	56,535
Atlantic, 49 Wall st	G. S. Floyd-Jones	J. M. Hogan	143,060	......	9,086	170,641	100,000	55,428
Bankers, 4 Wall st	Chas. Van Orden	F. Rysavy, Treas.	162,750	16,428	13	179,392	100,000	79,392
Broadway, 23d st. and 4th av	M. J. O'Brien, Jr.	Chas. Strauss	31,989	70,000	......	104,368	100,000	4,368
Bronx, [illegible]t and Park avs	T. T. Fischer	W. M. Stevens, Treas.	......	37,908	9,878	139,847	110,000	5,788
Central Mercantile, 3 East 14th st	G. W. Craft	F. L. Fisher, Cashier	96,980	7,900	3,760	110,756	100,000	10,756
Central Union, [illegible]th av. and 60th st	......	......	8,250	105,560	13,117	130,202	100,000	9,353
Colonial [illegible]ch of [illegible]e, but makes separate	report)	......	......	74,000	32,671	106,571	100,000	8,571
Commercial, Broadway and 41st st	R. R. Moore	Geo. J. Baumann, Treas.	75,915	23,900	52	132,867	100,000	32,867
[illegible]n Exchange, 13 William	W. A. Nash	W. C. Pitkin, Treas.	......	405,208	8,575	413,934	300,000	8,838
Empire, 120 [illegible]way and 580 Fifth av	L. W. Baldwin	P. H. Hudson	15 000	94,870	40,285	150,353	100,000	14,930
Empire City, 5th av. and 21st st	B. J. Greenhut	Edw. Searle	36,655	65,000	2,928	107,123	100,000	7,108
*Equi[illegible]ble, 43 Exchange pl	A. W. Krech	Frank E. Ryon	15,136	**188,628	8,557	213,971	200,000	13,971
Farmers, 475 5th av	E. S. Marston	A. V. Heely	24,562	......	5,130	130,829	100,000	23,284
Fidelity	S. S. Conover	A. H. Mars, Sec.	97,565	22,000	1,344	122,053	100,000	22,053
Fifth Avenue, 250 Fifth av	E. H. Peaslee	W. J. Sturzenegger	128,490	10,000	6,797	145,287	100,000	39,093
Garf[illegible]d, 7 W. 23d	R. W. Poor	G. D. Weeks, Sec.-Treas.	39,157	88,000	6,831	164,738	150,000	9,248
Greenwich, 135 [illegible]m	H. W. Ford	Frank Hammond, Treas.	49,200	52,000	1,127	103,897	100,000	3,897
Guaranty, 524 Fifth av	Chas. H. Sabin	E. G. McWilliam, V.-Pres.	[illegible]0	201,018	51,808	266,918	200,000	30,342
Hanover, 5 Nassau st	W. Woodward	E. A. Van Nest	5,273	190,000	7,117	202,874	200,000	2,495
Hudson, 1411 Broadway	Frank V. Baldwin	R. A. Purdy	104,262	6,000	2,875	115,399	100,000	15,399
Irving, 233 Broadway	H. E. Ward	E. F. Bouker, V.-Pres.	33,156	93,153	......	133,252	100,000	32,981
*Knickerbocker, 358 Fifth av	C. H. Keep	Chas. S. Adams, Treas.	84,317	60,663	2,266	166,384	100,000	66,384
Lincoln, 60-72 East 42d st	F. E. Webb	J. P. Carter Treas	[illegible]0	......	135,701	3,142,977	1,000,000	1,633,730
[illegible]n, 204 Fifth av	A. S. Webb	A. F. Smith, Sec.	29,376	86,925	5,210	124,041	100,000	22,861
Mercan[illegible], 115 Broadway	Wm. Giblin	F. J. Mooney, Sec. Treas.	34,843	235,472	8,276	309,359	200,000	49,756
New Malden [illegible], 170 Broadway	A. Oppenheimer	J. Heynen, Treas.	29,590	75,550	2,955	111,667	100,000	10,967
N. Y. Produce Exchange, Produce Exchange	W. A. Nash	E. G. See	61,375	**173,[illegible]38	20,260	259,828	150,000	105,992
N. Y. Stock Exchange, 10 Broad st	Jas. B. Mabon	M. J. Verdery, Sec.	110 554	24.900	174	135,828	100,000	35,828
Safe [illegible]t Co. of N. Y., 149 Broadway	F. A. Park	W. J. Ramsey	113,184	80,000	12,986	206,370	100,000	106,305
Standard, 25 Broad st	W.J.Barrows, V.-P., Gen. Mgr.	J. M. Cunningham, Sec.	85,705	150,355	1,916	238,461	200,000	33,461
State, 378 Grand st	H. C. Richard	W. L. Burckett	......	160,042	5,103	165,433	100,000	433
Thirty-fourth Street, 41 West 34th st	W. F. H. Koelsch	C. J. Beard, Treas.	......	45,873	4,033	385,062	225,000	52,979
Tiffany & Co.	......	......	94,940	......	15,011	124,098	100,000	16,563
[illegible]d States, 32 [illegible]ty st	J. L. Pendergast	Joseph Adams	290,125	65,203	11,602	379,204	200,000	175,267

Branches: [a]60 B'way, Lenox av. and 125th, 3d av. and 148th. [b]2079 B'way. [c]73d B'way, 125th and 8th av., Madison av. and 75th. [e]220 B'way, Madison av. and 45th.
*Semi-[illegible]al reports not filed. **Includes furniture and fixtures.

NEW YORK CITY SAVINGS BANKS, JULY 1, 1920

Institution.	Location.	President.	Cashier or Secretary.	Total Resources.	Due Depositors	*Surplus.	No. Open Accounts.	Deposits for Year.	†Expenses.
Brooklyn.									
Bay Ridge	5323 Fifth av	M. T. Lewis	R. S. Darbee, Cashier	$5,781,118	$5,565,952	5[illegible]66	17,901	$[illegible],170,190	$15,589
Brevoort	Nostrand av. and Macon	Howard M. Smith	R. Lounsbery, Sec	9,916,112	9,410,859	503,745	22,993	5,891,265	19,312
Brooklyn	Pierrepont, cor. Clinton st	C. Hadden	L. E. Sutton, Compt	71,344,522	64,917,558	6,387,293	76,162	20,041,110	108,112
Bushwick	725 Grand st.	Jare E. Brown	Geo. J. Merked, Cashier	10,598,878	9,888,003	704,874	19,931	4,988,494	19,890
City Savings	Flatbush & Lafayette avs	Remsen Rushmore	H. V. Raymond, Sec	8,719,425	8,329,538	376,544	16,655	5,227,806	25,222
[illegible]e Savings	DeKalb av., cor. Fleet st	R. S. Walker	F. W. Jackson, Treas	76,763,412	70,944,209	5,740,645	128,146	32,265,145	118,025
Dime Sav. of W'msburgh	209 Havemeyer	[illegible]. P. Sturgis	C. M. Lowes, Treas	15,383,408	14,435,851	879,124	18,802	5,889,649	39,305
East Brooklyn	643 Myrtle av	E. F. Barnes	D. Morehouse, Treas	13,685,159	12,795,525	886,307	21,459	6,111,942	28,683
East [illegible] York	2644 Atlantic av	E. A. Richards	J. K. [illegible], Treas	[illegible]1	8,355,988	570,863	15,713	5,267,908	31,517
Flatbush	910 Flatbush av	H. B. Hawkins	D. A Bentien, Sec	4,382,952	4,293,505	89,447	15,835	4,471,846	13,498
Fulton	375 Fulton	Adolph [illegible]	J. C. M. [illegible], Treas	15,978,817	14,936,123	1,042,694	22,002	5,786,639	46,794
Greater [illegible] York	449 Fifth av	C. J. Obermayer	W [illegible]	12,123,916	11,676,153	442,593	30,892	8,416,138	31,480
Greenpoint	Manhattan av. and Calyer	G. W. Felter	F. S. Harlow, Sec	17,797,580	16,327,238	1,458,013	26,316	8,150,042	43,106
Hamburg	1451 Myrtle av	David Engel	G. Unbescheiden, Sec	5,142,982	4,959,682	183,300	12,704	[illegible]457,695	8,235
Home	804 Manhattan av	M. W. Gleason	Vernon M. Powell	1,095,049	1,052,461	42,587	3,141	603,456	4,021
Kings [illegible]	Broadway, cor. Bedford av	H. G. Taylor	M. Muller, Cashier	15,876,036	14,915,299	960,237	14,756	4,168,761	34,251
Lincoln	531 Broadway	Charles Froeb	Henry St[illegible], [illegible]	38,099,344	35,421,542	2,667,802	53,896	18,667,187	49,954
Prudential	B'way and Vernon av	D. W. Kaatze	L. P. Buck	6,463,718	6,218,512	243,983	13,463	4,297,167	14,731
Roosevelt	1024 Gates av	J. W. Fraser	A. M. Shevill, Cashier	18,058,647	17,354,589	695,142	39,248	11,010,636	40,268
South Brooklyn	160-162 Atlantic av	[illegible]. J. Coombs	Bernard A. Burger, Sec.	32,950,[illegible]61	29,576,966	3,313,732	39,077	10,288,639	73,303
Sumner	12 Graham av	A. S. Somers	W. I. Conner, Sec	2,346,708	2,271,087	75,423	5,876	1,698,890	8,110
Williamsburgh	Broadway and Driggs av	Andrew D. Baird	Chas. J. Pasfield	111,330,064	97,658,584	13,611,479	120,858	33,909,563	184,921
Mhtn. and the Bronx.									
[illegible]an Savings	115 West 42d	W. M. Campbell	J. L. Haste, [illegible]	5,805,983	5,586,867	205,182	15,107	4,194,411	22,065
Bank for Sav. City of N. Y.	280 Fourth av	Walter Trimble	L. B. [illegible]ry, Sec	111,179,123	103,878,351	7,300,771	143,643	28,167,613	160,902
Bowery Savings	128-130 Bowery	H. A. Schenck	Jos. G. [illegible]le, Sec	153,795,608	138,985,230	14,810,378	154,301	51,888,545	150,641
Broadway Savings Inst	5 Park place	H. F. Hutchinson	L. F. Ferris, Sec	13,972,884	13,346,239	626,077	15,482	3,450,088	39,459
Bronx	429 Tremont av	T. T. Fischer	W. B. [illegible]tevens, Comp	5,291,520	5,170,351	121,169	14,158	4,117,408	15,072
Central	157 4th av	H. Cillis	Adolph Reppert	117,760,404	109,094,722	8,641,681	136,473	35,411,733	157,974
Citizens	58 Bowery	Henry Sayler	Ed. A. [illegible], Sec	26,144,899	23,636,361	2,508,537	29,064	9,518,667	43,232
Commonwealth	2007 Amsterdam av	J. H. Boschen	C. S. Gaubert, Sec	2,975,358	2,937,598	37,760	10,986	2,254,809	8,216
Dollar	2792 3d av	B. G. Hughes	W. M. Kern, Com	29,377,109	27,714,232	1,657,377	63,581	17,064,621	54,072
Dry Dock	341-343 Bowery	Andrew [illegible]	S. Webster, Sec	80,150,079	73,531,852	6,595,127	95,464	32,500,379	89,081
East River	291 Broadway	N. T. Nichols	L. Van Brunt, Sec	38,674,320	34,312,442	4,361,878	31,489	7,864,787	133,212
Emigrant Industrial	51 Chambers st	J. J. Pulleyn	L. V. O'Donohue, Sec	199,018,113	190,846,792	8,171,321	195,207	53,268,906	438,496
Empire City	231 West 125th st	A. S. Van Winkle	H. C. Murphy, Sec	11,810,648	11,264,169	544,479	27,507	7,774,060	30,274
Excelsior	W. 23d st and 6th av	Wm. J. Roome	J.C. Griswold, Sec	23,844,960	22,607,289	1,237,250	36,149	9,600,627	77,613
Franklin	656-658 8th av.	E. K. Satterlee	H. P. Aichele, Sec	39,396,685	35,782,007	3,602,568	72,761	17,757,150	75,111
Greenwich	246-248 Sixth av	Jas. Quinlan	C. M. Dutcher, Treas	84,903,206	77,926,883	6,935,747	99,559	19,281,585	120,446
Harlem	125th and [illegible]ington av	Wm. E. Trotter	Thos. R. Ebert, Sec	41,458,375	38,668,449	2,790,426	65,135	16,670,795	51,172
Irving	115 Chambers st	H. E. Tener	G. B. Dunning, Sec	21,385,[illegible]68	20,027,917	1,357,770	21,832	4,150,686	38,327
Italian	64 Spring st	J. N. Francolini	P. I. Simonelli, Sec	11,853,807	11,189,972	658,396	23,848	8,918,711	32,656
Maiden Lane	170 Broadway	F. A. Ringler	J. Heynen, Sec	3,272,547	3,199,315	73,231	10,101	2,710,125	10,710
Manhattan	644 Broadway	W. C. Stokes	A. Stiles, Sec	13,820,043	12,806,558	1,003,777	24,013	6,343,706	72,449
Metropolitan	59-61 Cooper sq.	R. D. Andrews	F. H. Moffet, Sec	17,305,662	16,453,989	851,723	20,845	4,815,577	35,717
New York	Eighth av., cor. 14th	Wm Felsinger	C. L. Blakelock, Treas	52,230,362	48,067,636	4,162,725	54,059	12,907,905	64,832
North River	31 W. 34th st	C. Rohe	Geo. T. Connett, Treas	14,555,096	13,754,603	795,569	27,433	7,674,162	37,714
North Side	230 Third av	J. G. Borgstede	A. A. Ekirch, Sec	5,200,451	5,057,046	143,404	13,882	3,843,864	16,117
Seamen's	76 Wall st	Dan'l Barnes	Geo. M. Halsey	83,687,153	78,113,453	5,573,699	93,052	16,403,269	100,221
Union Dime	701 Sixth av	A. P. W. Kinnan	F. M. Leake, Treas	66,303,031	61,423,516	4,830,453	148,295	33,011,870	121,401
Union Square	20 Union square	W. H. Rockwood	H. R. Br'ck'hoff, Sec	20,383,237	19,421,098	972,139	24,172	8,253,168	48,354
United [illegible]tates	606 Madison av	Wm. C. Adams	A. F. Le Gost, Treas	9,939,182	9,547,349	[illegible]82	19,451	5,436,041	24,682
Universal††	87 Liberty st	Wilbur F. Brown	R. K. Meixsell, Sec	1,598,829	1,573,617	22,814	17,357	2,[illegible]99	12,553
West Side	110-112 Sixth av.	C. O. [illegible]w	F. V. Hudson, Sec	7,110,274	6,738,403	371,870	14,756	3,378,410	20,599

Queens and Richmond.									
College Point	313 13th, College Point	W. W. Weitling	G. W. Gillette, S.	2,986,274	2,799,307	186,066	4,937	1,321,359	6,409
Jamaica	360 Fulton st., Jamaica	M. S. Rapelye	C. R. Doughty, Sec	9,557,407	8,938,253	619,154	15,534	4,270,191	19,487
Long Island City	Bridge Plaza, cor. Acad. st.	W. J. Burnett	Jarvis S. Hicks, Sec	17,024,191	15,589,255	1,434,935	30,193	8,677,286	43,447
Queens County	80 Main st., Flushing	Wm. T. James	A. C. Hageman	7,003,096	6,460,065	543,031	12,145	2,999,545	13,862
Richmond County	1619 Richmond Ter., W. N. B.	J. F. Smith	G. H. Fredwell	3,156,660	2,978,825	171,329	7,892	1,699,781	8,780
Staten Island	Stapleton	E. C. Bridgman	H. C. Hagedorn, Cash.	9,494,892	9,004,496	484,753	20,640	4,765,498	36,619

*On estimated market value. †For six months. ††Merged with Bowery Savings Bk.

STATE BANKS OF NEW YORK CITY, JUNE 30, 1920.

Institution.	Location.	President.	Cashier.	Loans and Discounts.	Cash Items.	Due from Trust C's Banks & Bankers.	Res'rces and Liabilities.	Capital.	Due Depositors.	‡Surplus and Undivided Profits.	Total Deposits.
Brooklyn.											
*Coney Island	Surf av., Coney Is.	Wm. J. Ward	G. H. Malley	$1,254,502	$6,504	$85,003	$4,306,635	$200,000	$3,538,443	$132,589	$3,740,389
Homestead	141 Pennsylvania av.	E. L. Rockefeller	G. L. Porter	1,515,183	23,198	193,378	3,483,316	200,000	3,053,751	116,676	3,160,338
*Mechanics	Court & Montague sts.	H. M. De Mott	W. C. Donn	23,980,678	2,977,633	0 4408	42,064,240	1,600,000	32,841,465	1,206,133	39,082,939
Montauk	5th av. & Union st.	J. W. Nash	J. R. Valentine	2,099,324	....	2017	2,703,100	100,000	2,507,074	58,628	2,542,074
Municipal	1783 Pitkin av.	S. J Goldberg	F. A. Gallagher	1,304,919	89,543	40611	2,008,792	02000	1,657,952	105,037	1,698,593
*North Side	225 Havemeyer st.	Paul E. Bonner	Henry r Bl.	6,180,087	472,257	47,251	8,735,042	02000	7,268,504	294,728	8,026,187
West End	20th av at 8th st.	S. Fromm	W. S. Germain	....	....	50,324	388	200,000	.	102,368	.
Queens.											
Hillside	Richmond Hill	Joel Fowler	Fredk. Boschen	514,551	2,946	821,311	1,796,498	100,000	1,617,347	54,350	1,637,347
#Long Is., Bank of	Jamaica (Merged with	the Bank of the Man	hattan Co., 40 Wall.)	....	....	....	....	....	....	....	....
Mhtn. & Bronx.											
*Bank of America	44 Wall st.	Wm. H. Perkins	Chas. E. Curtis	45,602,770	56, 54683	2,326,449	147,841,632	5,500,000	98,381,506	6,108,043	115,904,743
Bank of Gba in N. Y.	34 Wall st.	W. A. M.	C. F. Plarre	1,216,760	..	418,115	2,047,672	00,000	1,725,405	105,051	1,725,405
Bank of Europe	1429 First av.	Thomas Capek	V. W. Woytisek	2,461,519	....	297,331	6,024,614	150,000	55,969	283,642	5,572,799
(f)Bank of U. S	320 5th av.	J. S. Marcus	L. K. Hyde	24, 2401	285 724	4,843,017	32,190,177	1,500,000	26,904,744	606,372	27,267,516
Bk. of Wash'n H'ghts.	1915 Amsterdam av.	John Whalen	J. J. O'Shaughnessy	1,308,820	136,433	366,589	4,485,671	00,000	3,756,025	444,819	3,915,857
Bowery	124-126 Bowery	John S. Sr.	Charles Esaig	2,450,066	242,458	491,845	6,960,932	2000	5,714,969	842,006	880
Broadway Central	2574 Broadway	F. Williams	A. Zieoat	1,859,164	..	301,069	3,224,296	100,000	2,996,477	66,687	3,049,183
Bronx Borough	440 E. Tremont av.	C. A. Becker	T. B. Hanson	1,630,888	5,835	391,234	3,997,017	01600	3,472,645	65,668	3,705,753
Bryant Park	220 W. 42d st.	W. W. Warner	E. F. Giese	1,746,915	33,416	204,227	2,835,789	200,000	2,424,827	147,395	2,481,610
Ctral Mercantile	1 E. 14th st.	G. W. Craft	F. L. Fisher	1,855,712	....	220,224	2,438,975	200,000	2,133,584	90,084	2,133,584
†Chelsea Exchange	266 W. 34th st.	A. E. Stilger	W. W. Tappan	5,486,331	63,693	1,611,106	10,759,941	850	7,864,720	343,218	8,168,246
*Colonial	441 Chus av.	Alexander Walker	G. S. Carr	13,510,930	909,808	1,210,078	18,668,128	600,000	16,341,969	1,400,642	16,513,554
*Columbia	507 5th av.	E. H. Bernheim	G. R. Jewett	21,814,816	1,121,664	497,637	31,883,536	2,000,000	24,448,734	1,374,018	24,685,577
(bb) Commercial Exch.	330 Bowery	L. A. Fahs	G. Kern	5,055,251	414,844	321,414	9,796,390	02000	8,105,892	980,724	8,106,412
*Commonwealth	9094 Bowery	Chas. A. King	Geo F. A. Olt	4,729,262	735,927	152,372	11,299,474	400,000	8,667,685	801,342	9,768,684
Continental	23 Broad st	J. F. Fredericks	F. H. Hornley	6 8859	4 4846	220,331	15,151,774	1, 0000	10,257,968	788,778	10,876,861
*Corn Exchange	13 William st.	W. E. Frew	E. S. Malmar	71,751,351	19,918,949	2,590,855	209,542,894	4,620,000	177,571,681	8,582,001	191,533,047
Cosmopolitan	803 Prospect av.	L. G. Robinson	W. H. Devlin	2,221,864	102,211	516,338	3,353,920	02000	2,873,817	83,029	2,958,817
Fifth Avenue	530 Fifth av.	A. S. Frissell	W. G. Gaston	16,704,869	1,428,518	1,037,543	26,496,692	500,000	22,211,972	2,253,646	22,428,998
*Greenwich	102 Hudson st.	H. W. Ford	Frank Hammond	17,646,238	1,320,019	1,943,738	24,727,271	1,000,000	19,730,531	1,716,919	46808
Henry J. Schnitzer	141 Washington	J. Charmatz	Alex. Silum	0,600	47,883	209,770	416,731	( )800	71,837	88,223	72,983
Industrial	323 4th av.	S. B. Lynd	J. B. Close	6,324,678	....	421,438	7,762,552	1,000,000	493,328	549,519	5,389,496
International	17 Battery pl.	J. C. Colgate	A. J. McGrath	6,825,174	222,630	488,085	10,074,831	500,000	8154,849	388,897	8,177,535
John Nemeth	395 B'way	....	....	1,754,292	8,753	354,075	2,461,352	02000	1,491,283	04,771	08851
*Manhattan Co.	40 Wall st.	Stephen Baker	O. E. Paynter	122,682,338	53,232,107	4,658,316	246,002,904	5,000,000	150,228,987	15,974,509	189,027,477
M. Berardini Bank	34 Mulberry st.	M. Berardini	P. Berardini	53,923	....	509,671	1,372,455	01000	293,218	677,270	542,473
*Metropolitan	4th av. and 23d st.	H. Ollesheimer	A. C. Corby	29,562,146	3,265,273	1,746,238	44,985,426	2,000,000	38,815,079	2,988,206	39,632,060
Mutual	49 W. 33d st.	C. A. Sackett	H. N. Kirkland	10,234,347	80829	257,404	14,428,086	2000	13,138,260	697,356	13,403,544
New Netherland	41 W. 34th st.	W. F. H. Koelsch	C. J. Beard	9,160,085	335,719	486,093	13,609,936	600,000	058,092	682,761	8,169,092
*Pacific	470 Broadway	O. H. Cheney	F. E. Mann	23,887,161	2,375,296	203,013	36, 7 592	1,000,000	27,479,855	1,765,096	28,465,658

(Continued on next page.)

STATE BANKS OF NEW YORK CITY—MANHATTAN AND THE BRONX—*Continued.*

Institution.	Location.	President.	Cashier.	Loans and Discounts.	Cash Items.	Due from Trust C's Banks & Bankers.	Res'rces and Liabilities.	Capital.	Due Depositors.	§Surplus and Undivided Profits.	Total Deposits.
:Slavonic	136 W. 23d st	M. I. Pupin	P. H. [illegible]ovitch	34,411	1,485	91,346	395,550	100,000	245,924	48,724	245,924
Standard	55 Av. B	R. M. [illegible]er	M. Lederer	1,046,346	....	206,465	1,507,691	100,000	[illegible]9,465	145,778	1,114,465
††State	378 Grand st	H. C. Richard	J. Kneisel	51,294,314	3,033,548	3,916,727	78,541,450	2,500,000	72,320,918	2,007,085	73,008,389
Twenty-third Ward	3d av. and 137th st	Chas. P. [illegible]rt	H. J. [illegible]n Cook	4,758,560	298,060	283,719	6,473,654	200,000	54[illegible],661	205,486	6,025,768
Union Liberty	163 E. 23d	R. L Modra	J. J. Bonk	104,150	....	74,010	22[illegible]44	125,000	40,385	2159	75,412
W. R. Grace & Co.	7 Hanover sq	J. L. [illegible]er	Robert F. [illegible]kiser	2,705,488	....	1,685,208	9,127,911	500,000	[illegible]50,777	0 [illegible]26	5,373,205
Yorkville	1511 3d av	A. Zinsser	[illegible]d. Roth	11,338,408	295,370	345,752	16,275,376	200,000	14,579,011	755,903	16,025,824

Branches of above banks: ᵃSurf av. & W. 25th. [illegible]e [illegible]s av. [illegible]h. ᵇ317 9th; Schermerhorn, nr. Flatbush [illegible]; 3d av. [illegible]t, 356 Fulton, 2590 [illegible]av., 136, 1365 B'way. ᵉ33 & 710 [illegible]d. ᶠFlushing, Corona, Far Rockaway, Rockaway Beach, [illegible]de, [illegible]dhaven, Ridgewood, Richmond Hill, Elmhurst, College Point, Long Island [illegible]y. 804 [illegible]h Pond rd., ᵏB'way, cor. 68th; B'way, [illegible]; B'way, cor. 102d; 666 Columbus [illegible], 921 [illegible]s av.; St. Nicholas av. and [illegible]h. ᵐ415 B'way, [illegible]60 So. Blvd. ᵉ[illegible] pl. and [illegible] Ite, [illegible]way and Spring, 253 B'way, Norfolk and Grand, Av. D and [illegible], 5th av. and 20th, 4th av. and 29th, 303 W. [illegible], 7 E. 42d, 101 W. 125th, 85 E. 125th, 72d and Columbus [illegible], B'way and 28th, 2902 B'way, 375 E. 149th, 50 Church, 34 Union sq., Amsterdam av. and [illegible], 7th av. and 33d, St. Nicholas av. and 181st, 13[illegible] E. [illegible], Lex. av. and [illegible], B'way and [illegible]h, 196 Park [illegible], B'way and 55th, Fulton and Pearl, Park av. and 52d, Lexington av. and 72d, Mhtn.; Tremont and Arthur avs., 385 E. Fordham rd., 207th and Post av., Bronx; 894 Man[illegible] [illegible], 44 Court, 19 Flatbush av., 949 B'way, 79 Hamilton av., Bkln.; 41 Jackson av., Bridge Plaza, L. I. City; Flushing, [illegible], L. I., and St. George, S. I. ᵍ77th and 1st av., [illegible]h and 3d av. ʳ135 William, 260 W. [illegible]y, 596 6th av., 874 B'way, 1531 B'way. ˢ100 William, 271 B'way, 565 B'way. ᵗ31 [illegible]n sq. and branches in Queens, [illegible]. ˣ122 Hudson. Madison av. and 28th, 49th and 7th av., [illegible]n av. and 57th. ᶻ960 Boston rd., [illegible]3 3d av. 2301 7th av. ††1400 5th av., 276 5th [illegible], 109 Essex, Mhtn.; Westchester av. and 158th, Bronx; 363 [illegible]ne av., 60 Graham av., Bkln. (bb) B'way and [illegible]. (f) 77 Delan[illegible], Madison av. and [illegible]th. §On market [illegible]. ᵉWith which is [illegible]d the Franklin Trust, 164 Montague, Bkln.; Branches, 569 Fulton, 3d av. and 35th, 1001 Wallabout Mkt., Bkln., and 21 E. [illegible], Mhtn.

NEW YORK CITY TRUST COMPANIES, JUNE 30, 1920.

Institution and Location.	President.	Secretary.	Loans on Collateral.	Stk&Bond Public Securities	[illegible] Private Securities	Resources and [illegible]	Capital.	§Surplus.	Deposits on which int. is paid	ᵃDue Depositors
Brooklyn.										
ᵉBrooklyn, 177 Montague st	E. P. Maynard	W. P. Schenck	$9,898,149	$12,476,840	$11, [illegible]876	$49,242,654	$1,500,000	$2,596,521	$34,620,000	$29,024,825
Hamilton, 189 Montague st	W. E. Edmister	[illegible] Hadden	5,003,204	1,312,896	1,298,965	10,492,723	500,000	[illegible]6	8,389,700	6,678,201
Kings County, 342-346 [illegible]on st	J. D. Fairchild	[illegible] Blake	11,795,573	[illegible]10858	6,274,200	28,393,085	500,000	2,775,749	23,862,500	19,231,874
‡Manufacturers Tr. Co., 774 B'way	N. S. Jonas	[illegible] L. [illegible]er	5,008,262	6,418,802	1,517,397	40,419,074	2,000,000	20[illegible]38	23,398,000	28,202,583
ᵏPeoples, 181 Montague st	[illegible] A. Boody	W. A. Fischer	18,681,490	4,252,220	6,794,393	43,887,758	5[illegible]	1,900,240	31,728,650	34,474,648
Manhattan and The Bronx.										
American, 135 Broadway	H. A. Jahler	[illegible]rd [illegible]ne	5,031,990	[illegible]2	447,572	12,649,246	1,000,000	3[illegible]564	9,591,472	9,447,212
ᵉᵉᵉBankers, 16 [illegible]all st	Seward [illegible]er	R.H.Giles, [illegible]V.Pr.	160,657,746	23,316,111	27,162,475	[illegible]848,720	20,000,000	17, [illegible]0	306,671,493	21[illegible] 196,830
ᵉCentral Union, 80 B'way	[illegible]ge W. Davison	Milton Ferguson	85,174,100	31,343,930	20,724,771	253,969,885	12,500,000	17 15936	187,294,047	[illegible]95
[illegible]a, 60 Broadway	W. V. King	A. W. [illegible]s	35,451,116	4,536,991	13,456,637	134,742,608	5,000,000	7,206,876	84,233,899	190,648,089
Commercial, 41st st. and Broadway	R. R. Moore	J. G. Hemerich	2,952,429	1,316,205	695,225	10,659,279	[illegible]0	422,810	4,221,244	8,028,286
ᵉEmpire, 120 Broadway	L. W. Baldwin	M. J. Brown	19,275 [illegible]4	5,361,142	8,165,666	57,432,799	2,000,000	1,898,502	43,097,389	40,103,377
Corporation, 37 Wall	K. K. McLaren	H. S. Gould	1,976	650,456	....	802,139	500,000	246,793	....	....
ᵖEquitable, 37 Wall st	Alvin W. Krech	W. J. Eck	81,637,100	16,889,305	29,444,677	325,241,217	12,000,000	16,919,693	210 000,000	177,139,151
ᵍFarmers Loan, 16-22 William st	Edwin S. [illegible]on	A. V. [illegible]ly	34,762,759	36,584,513	12,790,131	187,590,349	5,000,000	10,713,349	[illegible]8	[illegible]377
Fidelity, Chambers & Hudson	S. S Conover	A. H. Mars	2,686,956	2,452,494	1,895,650	17,672,190	1,000,000	1,251,696	10,708,000	11 695,522
Fulton, 149 Broadway	H. C. Swords	A. J. Morris	4,898,012	1,086,760	1 2[illegible]06	[illegible],728,977	500,000	[illegible]61	8,200,000	[illegible]0
ᵉGuaranty, 140 Broadway	[illegible] H. Sabin	M. T. Murray, Jr.	304,847,805	66,578,843	38, [illegible]455	907,169,457	25,000,000	33,260,509	453,112,197	556,025,093
Hudson, 1411 Broadway	Frank V. Baldwin	Richard A. Purdy	3,218,712	1,666,555	645,908	9,078,407	500,000	[illegible]4	5,000,400	7,286,844
Italian Discount and Trust	G. P. Kennedy	Hugh Connolly	3,643,815	650,701	10,499	14,569,602	500,000	500,000	11,712,036	9,600,475
††Lawyers Title & Trust Co., 160 B'way	L. V. Bright	W. N. Vail	6,579,732	1,241,450	3,554,285	31,367,603	4,000,000	6,167,439	16,512,000	15,933,323
‡Lincoln, 204 5th av	A. S. Webb	[illegible]s. E. Calhoun	13,530,007	2,582,296	804,979	31 738,532	2,000,000	1,060,590	19,000,000	25,650,811
Mercantile, 115 B'way	C. A. Austin	H. D. Campbell	7,0[illegible],963	1,885,060	1,961,764	[illegible],987	1,000,000	[illegible]21	16,691,400	15,907,573
Metropolitan, 60 Wall st	H. I. Pratt	Geo. N. Hartmann	16, [illegible]22	6,705,791	4,012,308	49,509,595	2,000,000	3 [illegible]14	28,016,700	[illegible]65
N. Y. L. Ins. & T. Co., 52 Wall st	Walter Kerr	Irving L. Roe	597,875	2,719,420	[illegible]3	26,381,909	1,000,000	2,175,690	20,404,109	15 457,098
New York, 26 Broad st	M. N. Buckner	H. Forsyth	40,765,757	3,291,035	7, [illegible]15	107,025,362	3,000,000	11,292,742	63,793,063	[illegible]

rTitle Guar. & T. Co., 176 Broadway	C. H. Kelsey	J. W. Cleveland	12,598,972	2,249,466	5,780,829	56,392,598	5,000,000	13,138,017	30,721,908	30,480,094
**U. S. Mtge. & T. Co., 55 Cedar st	J. W. Platten	H. L. Servoss	34,082,780	4,007,677	4,014,272	84,733,296	2,000,000	4,650,151	64,085,848	55,797,646
United States, 45-47 Wall st	E. W. Sheldon	W. J. Worcester	30,130,939	2,431,925	8,304,956	62,893,174	2,000,000	14,161,928	42,178,900	25,283,809

Branches of above trust companies: *Fulton and Bedford av., Bkln.; 90 B'way, Mhtn. $84 B'way, Bkln.; 8th av. and 34th, Mhtn. kNostrand av., cor. Herkimer; Flatbush and Church avs., 418 and 1455 Myrtle av.; 5th av., cor. 54th; 230 Flatbush av. n858 5th av., 100 W. 125th, Mhtn.; 3d av. and 148th, Bronx. *580 5th av. pMadison av. and 45th, 222 B'way. q475 5th av. r137 W. 125th, Mhtn.; 370 E. 149th, Bronx; 175 Remsen, Bkln.; 350 Fulton, Jamaica; 67 Jackson av., L. I. C. *42d and Madison av.; 5th av. and 60th; 425 5th av. *522 5th av., 266 Grand, Madison av. and 60th. ††381 E. 149th, Bronx; 188 Montague, 44 Court, 1354 B'way, Bkln.; 367 Fulton, Jamaica, Queens. ‡346 B'way, B'way and 72d, 7 Wall. **B'way and 73d, 125th and 8th av., 950 Madison av. *Subject to check. §(Including all undivided profits) on market value. ***Astor merged with; 5th av. and 42d.

TITLE AND MORTGAGE GUARANTEE COMPANIES.

Financial condition of New York City's Real Estate Title and Mortgage Guarantee Cos. for year ending January 1, 1920.

Company.	Address.	President.	Secretary.	Assets.	*Liabilities.	Capital.	Surplus.	Income.	Disb'em'ts
Brooklyn.									
Bond & Mtge. Guarantee	175 Remsen st	C. H. Kelsey	W. B. Clarke	$13,385,458	$1,266,989	$5,000,000	$7,011,468	$2,082,558	$1,623,671
Home Title Ins.	51 Willoughby st	H. B. Davenport	D. S. Coe	1,965,497	837,506	500,000	627,992	490,706	390,179
U. S. Title Guaranty	32 Court st.	C. E. Covert	G.W.Cummings,Jr.	1,474,150	567,952	625,000	281,198	641,339	571,664
Manhattan.									
Lawyers' Mtge.§	59 Liberty st.	R. M. Hurd	O. S. Isbell	9,951,848	594,030	6,000,000	3,357,817	1,397,970	1,112,029
Lawyers' Title & Trust**	160 Broadway	L. V. Bright	W. N. Vail	32,151,638	22,410,515	4,000,000	5,741,123	2,889,474	2,311,270
N. Y. Title & Mtge.†	135 Broadway	H. A. Kahler	Gerhard Kuehne	6,318,594	1,955,150	3,000,000	1,363,444	1,090,196	1,014,922
Title Guarantee & Trust‡	176 Broadway	C. H. Kelsey	J. W. Cleveland	56,642,016	38,848,710	5,000,000	12,793,366	6,489,449	5,849,134

*Except capital. **Branches: 381 E. 149th, Bronx; 188 Montague, 44 Court, 1354 B'way, Bkln.; 367 Fulton, Jamaica. †203 Montague, Bkln.; Bridge Plaza, L. I. City; 375 Fulton, Jamaica, L. I.; 24 Bay, St. George, S. I. §184 Montague, Bkln.; ‡137 W. 125th, Mhtn.; 370 E. 149th, Bronx; 175 Remsen, Bkln.; L. I. City; Jamaica, Queens.

SUMMARY OF NEW YORK STATE TRUST COMPANIES.

The condition of the 97 trust cos. of N. Y. State, June 30, 1920, as compared with 101 companies, June 30, 1919:

RESOURCES.

	June 30, 1919.	June 30, 1920.
Mortgages	$94,344,039	$96,670,010
Public securities	447,272,698	312,517,846
Other securities	354,933,201	334,297,669
Loans on collateral	1,257,558,758	1,098,734,736
Other loans	515,838,315	783,101,972
Overdrafts	392,854	481,106
Real estate	54,393,798	56,442,141
Due from trust companies and banks	160,717,386	201,295,831
Specie	17,109,454	13,018,562
Legal tenders and national bank bills	29,576,114	28,317,136
Bills and checks for next day's clearings	136,796,761	147,592,550
Federal Reserve notes	247,025,773	223,831,836
Other assets	338,967,939	266,024,149
Totals	$3,654,927,090	$3,563,320,535

LIABILITIES.

	June 30, 1919.	June 30, 1920.
Capital	$136,043,000	$145,593,600
Surplus on market value	206,489,635	208,355,236
Due savings banks	57,922,270	52,789,970
Due savings and loan associations, etc.	957,734	721,733
Due as executor and administrator	113,938,314	180,641,372
Deposits preferred because secured by State bonds	11,098,480	20,289,487
Deposits preferred because of pledge of assets	194,333,477	74,588,795
Deposits otherwise preferred	16,719,290	6,796,353
Deposits subject to check	2,241,471,155	2,285,974,065
Due trust companies and banks	274,947,488	266,331,136
Bills payable	133,240,317	66,473,171
Rediscounts	71,708,804	90,248,699
Other liabilities	196,057,126	214,516,968
Totals	$3,654,927,090	$3,567 320,535

SUMMARY OF NEW YORK STATE BANKS.

RESOURCES.

	June 30, 1919.	June 30, 1920.
Public Securities	$167,082,431	$146,827,936
Other securities	93,704,408	98,233,558
Real estate	20,809,089	21,281,453
Mortgages owned	13,195,386	17,320,576
Loans and discounts	570,208,025	751,853,141
Overdrafts	314,099	358,858
Due from trust companies and banks	63,933,433	63,540,062
Specie	17,251,547	14,874,399
Legal tenders and national bank notes	24,376,113	30,274,442
Cash items	172,639,680	163,698,781
Federal Reserve notes	74,636,063	95,075,178
Other assets	52,147,810	57,718,613
Totals	$1,270,298,084	$1,460,567,017

LIABILITIES.

	June 30, 1919.	June 30, 1920.
Capital	$39,603,000	$53,792,910
Surplus on market value	61,911,027	76,303,388
Deposits by Supt. Banks	606,228	619,096
Due savings banks	30,850,998	33,763,640
Due savings and loan associations	1,251,476	1,200,347
Deposits secured by State bonds	4,914,193	7,713,802
Deposits preferred because secured by pledge of part of bank assets	24,233,359	8,204,753
Deposits otherwise preferred	1,679,207	1,774,511
Due depositors	929,324,259	1,111,288,966
Due to trust companies and banks	58,132,081	53,806,450
Rediscounts	6,533,954	10,356,636
Bills payable	58,120,790	42,830,356
Other liabilities	53,137,513	58,903,162
Totals	$1,270,298,084	$1,460,557,017
Total deposits	$1,050,901,901	$1,218,371,565

NATIONAL BANKS IN NEW YORK CITY.

(Figures as of Sept. 8, 1920.)

Bank and Location.	President.	Cashier.	Loans,* Disc'nts.	Capital.	Surplus & Profits.	Total Deposits†	Res'c's& Liab't's.
Brooklyn.							
First, B'way, Havemeyer	Joseph Huber..	A. P. Verity..	$8,639,563	$500,000	$817,530	$11,202,938	$13,215,460
Greenp't, 142 Gr'n't av...	D.E.Frend'ger	W. Wilmurt...	2,845,740	200,000	331,665	3,714,832	4,296,906
Nassau, Court & Jorl'n..	G. F. Smith....	H.Schoenber'r.	14,990,680	1,000,000	1,394,728	16,210,603	18,853,356
Peoples Nat., 882 Quincy..	G. W. Spence..	W.F.Cawth'e.	2,632,700	200,000	262,756	5,372,134	5,917,122
Mhtn. & Bronx.							
Am. Exch., 128 B'way..	L. L. Clarke...	A.P.Lee........	101,066,658	5,000,000	7,438,747	128,727,916	163,354,556
Atlantic, 257 B'way......	H. D. Kountze	F. E. Andruss.	17,765,393	1,000,000	1,137,198	19,828,989	26,506,969
Bk. of N. Y., 48 Wall....	H. L. Griggs...	F.C.Metz.Jr...	37,370,380	2,000,000	7,167,649	55,891,575	77,175,094
Battery Pk., 2 B'way..	E. A. de Lima.	A.H.Merry....	15,021,455	1,500,000	1,614,104	17,022,863	21,859,276
Bronx, 369 E. 149th......	T. J. Quinn....	H.J.B.Willis..	3,248,878	200,000	260,379	3,336,199	3,889,572
Chase, 57 B'way.........	E.V.R.Thayer	Wm.P.Holly...	359,328,953	15,000,000	24,189,497	327,387,426	508,459,736
Chat'm&Ph'ix, 192 Bwy..	L. G. Kaufman	B.L.Haskins...	114,442,229	7,000,000	7,929,781	134,629,695	165,645,982
Chemical, 270 B'way.....	P.H.Johnston..	A.K.Chapman	148,341,285	4,500,000	14,816,756	119,830,298	185,373,369
Coal & Iron, 143 Lib'rty.	J. T. Sproull..	A. H. Day.....	16,254,590	1,500,000	1,590,770	17,892,703	23,361,830
East River, 680 B'way...	A.H.Giannini.	A. H. Gibson..	10,523,153	1,000,000	810,616	13,902,282	16,296,908
Fifth, Lex. & 23d......	E. E. Watts...	W.S.Beckley...	13,964,870	1,000,000	717,360	13,350,775	15,988,807
First, 2 Wall............	F. L. Hine.....	S. A. Welldon	131,462,998	10,000,000	36,127,970	207,009,261	364,587,225
Garfield, 5th av. & 23d...	R. W. Poor....	A.W.Snow.....	11,998,011	1,000,000	1,588,665	16,036,526	19,315,442
Gotham, 1819 B'way.....	H.H.Bizallion.	Horace Howe.	10,036,758	500,000	612,448	11,617,549	15,745,040
Hanover, 11 Nassau.....	W.Woodward..	W.E.Cable,Jr..	99,179,022	3,000,000	20,331,578	161,966,117	187,677,974
Harriman, 5th av.&44th.	J.W.Harriman	H. B. Fonda..	22,193,639	1,000,000	1,767,421	27,831,666	35,679,951
Imp.& Trdrs., 247 B'way.	H. H. Powell..	C.F.Regan.....	42,051,709	1,500,000	8,636,324	34,805,001	52,568,535
Irving, B'way&Park Pl..	H. E. Ward...	P.F.Gray......	210,237,704	12,500,000	10,651,329	243,975,168	318,282,945
Liberty, 120 B'way.......	H. D. Gibson..	Fred. W. Walz.	86,587,842	5,000,000	7,617,870	94,885,276	121,903,518
Mech'cs&Metals, 50 Wall.	G.W.M'Garrah	J.S.House......	182,651,608	10,000,000	16,512,784	198,703,247	262,351,099
Natl. Amer., 8 W. 40th..	J.M.Gerard....	H.I.Stevens...	2,169,060	1,000,000	500,000	1,428,643	2,943,817
N.Bk.of Com., 31 Nassau.	J.S.Alexander.	R.H.Passmore	312,825,413	25,000,000	33,446,173	324,861,019	434,285,900
N'l But.& D'v's. 683 B'wa	W.W.Vale'tine	W.J.Duane....	4,206,858	300,000	164,863	4,365,206	5,908,936
National City, 55 Wall...	J. A. Stillman.	F.N.C.Lenf'y..	495,859,689	25,000,000	61,363,196	528,960,200	716,128,806
Nat'l Park, 214 B'way...	R.Delafield....	E.V.Connolly.	170,267,118	7,500,000	22,737,066	177,142,975	245,599,397
N.Y.Co., 8th av. & 14th...	Oscar Cooper...	A.S.Hurst.....	12,735,862	1,000,000	617,142	14,077,058	16,498,430
Progress, 7th & 28th.....	J.Silberzweig..	A.Silberzweig.	†.........	....	....	....	....
Public, B'way & 25th....	E.S Rothchild	C.H.Baldwin..	46,982,802	2,000,000	2,065,103	67,431,926	75,956,960
Seaboard, 18 B'way......	S.G.Bayne.....	C. H. Marfield	41,277,835	1,000,000	4,599,923	58,491,212	70,318,908
Second, 250 5th av........	W.A.Simonson	Chas.W.Case..	22,277,819	1,000,000	4,552,442	21,321,014	31,809,006
Union Exch., 21st&5th av	S.H.Herman...	Geo.B.Connley.	17,834,378	1,000,000	1,100,908	18,247,834	23,847,261
Queens.							
Bay Side, Bay Side......	Elmer G. Story.	M. Vaughan....	391,886	50,000	39,647	1,216,238	1,360,885
First Nat. of Jamaica..	S.Brinc'hoff...	W.Peterson....	2,003,356	100,000	118,080	4,241,317	4,512,557
First Nat. of Ozone Pk.	J. B. Reimer..	W.L.Hopkins..	1,422,986	50,000	93,216	2,343,009	2,544,595
First Nat., Whitestone.	E. P. Roe......	J.W.Stanley...	426,776	50,000	55,575	611,686	761,966
Flushing National......	C. M. Lowes..	C.E.Meyer.....	500,550	100,000	43,307	1,124,724	1,463,042
Nat. of Far Rockaway	H. G. Heyson.	S. R. Weston..	1,397,861	50,000	62,436	2,735,083	2,882,437
Richmond Hill..........	G.Solms.......	C.B.Mah'er....	335,484	160,080	21,121	315,752	506,898
Ridgewood, Ridgewood..	Louis Berger...	C. V. Gunther.	6,522,755	100,000	245,728	7,471,577	7,978,658
Richmond.							
Mariner's Harbor........	G. T. Egbert..	S. Bedell	498,795	50,000	29,110	606,157	704,829
Pt. Richm'd, 2062 R'd. Te	W.J.Davidson..	E. R. Moody...	939,860	100,000	178,907	2,342,343	2,736,914
Richm'd Bor., Stapleton	J. W. Place...	G.S.Holbert....	980,709	100,000	57,271	1,251,019	1,454,875
Stapleton, Bay & Canal	C. A. Bruns...	M. H. Scott....	730,842	100,000	137,523	1,499,751	1,850,453
Tottenville, 179 Main....	A.B.Potterton.	I. J. Horton...	923,998	25,000	62,288	1,104,498	1,215,123

*And overdrafts. †Individual. ‡On Sept. 8, 1920, was a State Bank.

SUMMARY OF NEW YORK STATE PRIVATE BANKS.

RESOURCES.

	June 30, 1919.	June 30, 1920.
Public securities	$6,322,633	$7,350,036
Private securities	2,910,390	3,339,883
Real estate owned	2,250,032	2,129,087
Mortgages owned	616,515	714,030
Loans and discounts	3,508,783	6,368,542
Accounts receivable	1,147,701	495,527
Due from customers	254,123	278,489
Overdrafts	8,218	18,197
Due from trust companies, banks and bankers	5,792,749	5,645,159
Deposits with express and steamship companies	34,437	30,149
Specie	55,445	257,830
Legal tenders and national bank notes	586,185	681,661
Federal Reserve notes	10,550	...
Foreign money	208,921	293,183
Foreign postage	7,345	4,498
Cash items	320,624	213,821
Other assets	323,046	439,302
Totals	$24,357,697	$28,159,294

LIABILITIES.

	June 30, 1919.	June 30, 1920.
Permanent capital	$1,521,000	$1,974,000
Surplus on market value..	2,867,953	5,032,394
Deposits	16,603,888	18,659,819
Due trust companies banks and bankers	1,551,279	681,594
Bills payable	346,150	485,948
Rediscounts	146,634	154,892
Other liabilities	1,320,793	1,270,647
Totals	$24,357,697	$28,159,294
Total deposits	$18,155,167	$19,241,421

Note—89 private bankers reported in 1919; 98 in 1920.

LIFE INSURANCE COMPANIES' SURPLUS.

The following comparative figures show sources and amounts of increases and decreases, in unassigned funds (surplus) of life insurance cos. authorized in N. Y. State for years ending Jan. 1, 1919 and 1920.

	1919.	1920.
Loss from loading	*$289,476	$22,072,287
Gain from mortality	†12,493,222	85,325,521
Gain from surrendered and lapsed policies	12,931,548	13,042,436
Gain from interest and rents, less amount required to maintain reserve	89,518,400	89,633,040
Loss from annuities	711,604	873,226
Loss from investments	4,526,477	4,687,958
Loss from dividends to policyholders, incl. net incr. or dec. in dividend funds apportioned and unapportioned	127,303,443	1,445,708
Loss from miscellaneous sources	*6,581,048	19,630,594
Total gain	†26,634,410	22,631,483

*Gain. †Loss.

The longest average of life is to be found in Norway.

NEW YORK CITY LIFE INSURANCE COMPANIES.

The following table gives a summary of the business transacted in the State of New York for the year ended January 1, 1920 (including industrial business), by New York City companies:

Institution and Location.	President.	Secretary.	*Pol. in Force.	Prem's rec'd.	Claims incur'd.	Claims paid.
Equitable, 120 Broadway.....	W. A. Day.....	Wm. Alexander	$459,675,612	$20,975,174	$5,708,738	$6,008,045
Guardian Life of Amer., 50 Union Sq....................	Hubert Cillis....	Carl Heye.......	25,077,010	866,421	222,764	254,442
Home, 256 Broadway	W. A. Marshall	W. S. Gaylord..	30,095,126	1,201,768	401,135	443,136
Manhattan, 66 Broadway....	T. E. Lovejoy...	M. De Mott......	8,950,880	279,746	174,291	162,393
Metropolitan, 1 Madison av..	H. Fiske........	J. S. Roberts....	526,745,288	36,714,869	5,545,560	5,785,400
Morris Plan, 680 5th av.......	A. J. Morris....	J. B. Gilder.....	1,234,200	33,957	5,900	5,850
Mutual, 34 Nassau st.........	C. A. Peabody..	Easton & Dix...	350,203,658	14,280,124	6,248,529	6,210,170
New York, 346 Broadway.....	D. P. Kingsley.	S. M. Ballard..	542,323,941	23,928,318	10,155,573	10,668,079
Postal, 511 5th av..............	Wm. R. Malone	Wesley Sisson...	5,240,570	170,766	128,959	122,063
Teachers, 522 5th av..........	H. S. Pritchett.	C. Furst........	197,070	2,395	....	....
United States, 273 Broadway	J. P. Munn.....	A. Wheelwright..	5,481,289	165,106	202,369	189,219

*Amount.

NEW JERSEY AND CONNECTICUT LIFE INSURANCE COMPANIES.

Summary of life insurance business transacted in the States of New Jersey and Connecticut for the year ending January 1, 1920, by the companies of those States.

Companies.	President.	Secretary.	Policies in Force Jan. 1, '19. No.	Policies in Force Jan. 1, '19. Amount.	Prem's Received	Claims Incurred.	Claims Paid.
New Jersey							
Colonial, Jersey City.....	E.J.Heppenheimer	D.Johnston..	123,028	$19,436,135	$728,769	$238,797	$244,721
Mut. Benefit, Newark....	F.Frelinghuysen..	J.W.Johnson	19,931	69,060,378	1,897,937	739,249	707,136
Prudential, Newark......	F.F.Dryden........	W.I.Ham'ton	1,935,587	421,981,778	14,201,214	4,462,139	4,747,358
Connecticut.							
Aetna, Hartford..........	M.G.Bulkeley......	C.E.Gilbert & W.H.Newell.	7,049	25,115,497	775,652	408,538	401,000
Conn. General, Hartford	R.W.Huntington..	R.H.Cole.....	75,711	265,643,470	6,602,656	1,424,909	1,616,495
Conn. Mutual, Hartford.	H S Robinson....	J.H.Greene..	3,962	11,350,788	474,575	328,796	356,076
Phoenix, Mutual, Hart'd..	J.M.Holcombe.....	H.F.Johnson	114,495	253,349,443	8,881,880	2,233,828	2,486,538
The Travelers, Hartford.	L.F.Butler.........	J.L.Howard..	9,369	45,292,783	925,892	345,831	348,486

FIRE AND FIRE-MARINE INSURANCE COMPANIES.

The following table gives the business in the State of New York, by joint-stock Fire and Fire-Marine Insurance Companies of New York City, for the year ended January 1, 1920:

Institution and location.	President.	Secretary.	Prem's rec'd.	Losses paid.	Losses incur'd	Excess pre's.*	Risks written.
Am. Alliance, 1 Liberty.....	C.G.Smith.......	E.M.Cragin......	$247,865	$51,095	$59,145	$188,720	$38,573,444
Am. Eagle, 80 Maiden lane..	Henry Evans....	J. E. Lopez.......	343,843	67,262	85,933	257,909	48,380,904
Am. Equit. Assur., 68 Wil'm	R.A.Corroon.....	T. A. Duffey....	390,970	71,089	90,603	300,366	61,027,971
Am. (Fire), 84 William......	C. F. Sturhahn.	T. B. Boss.......	54,725	447	2,377	52,347	7,329,950
Am. Mer. Marine, 56 Beaver.	C. P. Stewart...	C. H. Gardner..	42,824	5,999	9,216	33,608	11,194,994
Assur of Am., 80 Maiden la	R.B.Rathbone...	C.S.Conklin......	165,693	30,402	30,000	135,693	13,187,635
Bankers & Shippers, 35 Wm..	W. G. Wilcox...	R. Van Iderstine	32,984	732	1,412	31,571	7,225,431
Caledonian-Am., 50 Pine....	C.H.Post........	Milward Prain..	8,699	2,152	2,361	6,338	1,398,565
City of New York, Maiden lane and William st......	M.A.White......	J.C.French......	336,781	126,716	119,328	217,452	44,203,459
Colonial Assur., 80 Maiden la.	L.H.Wise........	E. S. Powell, Jr.	139,200	22,492	13,447	125,753	19,547,413
Commercial Union, 55 John.	A.H.Wray.......	W. M. Ballard..	110,209	42,085	42,618	67,591	13,878,310
Commonwealth, 76 William	C. F. Shallcross.	R.P.Barbour....	271,387	88,522	93,545	177,842	25,862,454
Continental, 80 Maiden lane	Henry Evans....	J.E.Lopez.......	2,232,376	693,559	765,654	1,466,722	336,570,369
Fidelity-Phenix, 80 M'den la.	H.Evans.........	J.E.Lopez.......	1,697,726	607,271	590,130	1,107,595	232,685,755
Globe & Rutgers, 111 William	E.C.Jameson....	J. H. Mulvehill..	1,444,174	767,216	797,077	647,097	151,592,354
Great American, 1 Liberty..	C. G. Smith.....	E.M.Cragin.....	2,018,278	499,360	455,305	1,562,973	301,303,297
Guaranty, 80 Maiden la......	J. S. Sutphen...	E. S. Powell, Jr	Began business 1920.				
Hamilton, 111 William.......	E. C.Jameson...	A.Lenssen, Jr....	93,033	33,430	37,157	55,875	13,319,889
Hanover, 34 Pine............	R.E.Warfield....	E. S. Jarvis......	487,580	199,948	194,455	293,125	65 073,740
Home, 56 Cedar	E.G.Snow........	W. Kurth........	4,001,220	1,698,085	1,676,721	2,324,505	549,130,221
Hudson, 100 William.........	J.M.Wennstrom.	H. N. Morgan...	86,779	6,908	36,801	49,977	22,030,963
ImperialAssur., 100 William.	P.Beresford......	Howard Terhune	143,988	37,736	39,508	104,479	23,153,872
Importers and Exporters, 17 S. William..................	L. Schinasi......	H. Knox.........	82,349	3,516	7,879	74,470	14,004,084
International, 80 Maiden la.	Sumner Ballard.	F.Kortenbeutel..	391,218	204,939	208,767	182,451	41,084,251
†Knickerbocker, 63 Wm.	R. A. Carroon...	T. A. Duffey.....	140,470	36,920	42,839	97,630	12,083,755
Mercantile, 76 William.....	C. F. Shallcross.	R.P.Barbour....	253,896	87,964	92,360	161,536	38,694,240
Merchants, 45 John..........	E.L.Ballard.....	G. L. McIntire..	304,074	94,027	118,246	185,828	28,463,700
National Liberty, 709 6th av..	G. B. Edwards..	G.H.Kehr.......	841,175	256,209	292,721	548,453	106,503,655
N. Y. Equitable, 68 William	R. A. Conroon...	T. A. Duffey.....	172,357	25,587	24,413	147,944	13,114,237
‡N. Y. Natl., 62 William....	G. B. Edwards..	G.H.Kehr.......	......	......	......	......	......
Niagara, 123 William........	O. E. Lane.......	C. A. Lung......	1,169,240	342,139	374,060	795,180	142,365,068
Northern, 1 Liberty	W. Brewster....	Jas. Marshall....	175,005	67,598	71,373	103,632	24,785,663
North River, 95 William.....	J. A. Forster....	D. G. Wakeman.	675,373	235,685	271,247	404,125	81,662,365
Pacific Fire, 59 John.........	C.V.Meserole....	H. B. Lange, Jr.	458,430	196,980	293,772	164,657	25,407,642
Queen Ins.Co.Am., 84 Wil'm	N. S. Bartow....	F. E. Jenkins...	629,820	186,357	196,134	433,685	86,025,379
Safeguard, 57 William......	A.G.McIlw'ne, Jr	H. W. Gray, Jr..	61,734	11,545	11,203	50,530	11,541,850
Star, 80 William............	H. R. Loudon...	R. H. Williams..	104,181	16,387	19,423	84,757	17,746,759
Stuyvesant, 111 William.....	J.S.Frel'gh'sen..	G. S.Hutchings.	216,363	207,782	178,153	38,209	20,410,065
United States, 95 William.	G. R. Branson...	D.G.Wakeman..	982,728	324,548	368,378	614,349	121,601,152
Vulcan, 94 Fulton...........	Isidor Kahn.....	I.Koenigsberger	47,379	20,655	23,495	23,883	4,952,803
Washington Mar., 51 Beaver.	E. Kehaya.......	E. W. Murray...	27,804	696	3,589	24,215	2,958,847
Westchester, 100 William...	O.E.Schaefer....	C. B. G. Gaillard	770,198	270,177	283,827	495,895	113,542,153

*Excess of premiums over losses incurred. †Absorbed by merger the N. Y. Equitable Assurance Co., March 11, 1920. ‡In liquidation.

Brooklyn leads the country in postal savings gains. The borough gained $330,773 and Manhattan $263,353 during the year ending June 30, 1920.

Seattle is building the largest pier in the world. It is 2,566 feet long and 360 feet wide, and will be large enough to dock eleven ocean-going vessels at one time.

CEMETERIES OF N. Y. CITY AND VICINITY.

Name, location and entrance, area acres and office:

Acacia, Woodhaven, L. I., 11¾, Grand, nr. Allen, Mhtn.
‡Ahawath Chesed, Metropolitan av., Queens, 13, 1424 Metropolitan av.
‡Baron Hirsch, Old Stone rd., Pt. Richmond, 100, 131 Essex, Mhtn.
‡Bay Side, Woodhaven, Queens, 45, at cemetery.
Bay View, Ocean av., Jersey City, 18, 15 Exchange pl., Jersey City.
Beechwoods, New Rochelle, N. Y., 35, Beechwood av., New Rochelle.
Bethel, Amboy rd., Tottenville, 7, Tottenville, S. I.
‡Beth-Olom Field, Kills Path and Fresh Pond rd., 7¾, at cemetery.
‡Bnai-Israel, Waverly, N. J., 1, 140 1st, Elizabeth, N. J.
*Calvary, Borden and Greenpoint av.; Queens, 400, 24 E. 52d, Mhtn.
Canarsie Av. K and Remsen av., 12, E. 92d and Av. K, Canarsie.
Cedar Grove, Flushing, L. I., 200, 1 Madison av., Mhtn.
Cedar Lawn, Paterson, N. J., 125, 129 Market, Paterson, N. J.
City Cemetery, Harts Island, 20, at cemetery.
Cypress Hills, Jamaica av. and Crescent, Bkln., 400, at cemetery.
Evergreen (The), Elizabeth, N. J., 90, 1137 N. Broad, Elizabeth, N. J.
Evergreen, Morristown, N. J., 200, 5 South, Morristown, N. J.
Evergreens (The), Bushwick av. and Conway, 300, Bushwick av. and Conway, Bkln.
Fairview, Castleton Corners, 10, 1781 Richmond Terminal, W. N. Brighton.
Ferncliff, Woodlands, N. Y., 100, 3230 3d av., Mhtn.
Flatlands Ref. Church, Flatbush av., Bkln., 3, 1120 Flatbush av., Bkln.
Flushing, Flushing, L. I., 75, at cemetery.
Fountain, Van, W. New Brighton, 3, 216 Taylor, W. New Brighton.
Fresh Pond Crematory, 71 Mt. Olivet av., Boro. of Queens, N. Y. C., 1, Middle Village, L. I.
**Friends, Prospect Park, Bkln., 18, 1662 10th av., Bkln.
Gravesend Village, Neck rd., Bkln., 2, 2 Lake pl., Bkln.
Greenwood (The), 5th av. and 25th, Bkln., 478, 170 B'way, Mhtn.
Greenwood Union, Rye, N. Y., 100, Rye, N. Y.
Hoboken, New Durham, N. J., 17, 225 Washington, Hoboken, N. J.
*Holy Cross, Bkln. and Snyder avs., Bkln., 84, Jay, cor. Chapel.
Kensico, Westchester Co., N. Y., 461, 103 Park av., Mhtn.
Laurel Grove, Totowa, N. J., 200, Colt Bldg., Paterson, N. J.
Linden Hill, Woodward av., Grandview av. and Stanhope, 23, at cemetery.
Lutheran, Metropolitan av., Middle Village, 250, 1837 Metropolitan av., Middle Village.
‡Machpelah, Cypress av., Queens, 13, Fresh Pond rd. and Cypress.
‡Maimonides, Jamaica av., Bkln., 8, at cemetery.
Maple Grove, Kew Gardens, 74, at cemetery.
Middle Village M. E. Church, Middle Village, L. I., ½, 1892 DeKalb av.
Mokon Sholen, Woodhaven, Queens, 9, at cemetery.
Montefiore, Springfield, L. I., 113, 14 Delancey, Mhtn.
Moravian, New Dorp, S. I., 90, at cemetery.
*Most Holy Trinity, 675 Central av., Bkln., 23¾, 675 Central av.
‡Mt. Carmel, Cypress av., Fresh Pond rd., Queens, 45, at cemetery.
Mt. Hebron, Flushing, L. I., 150, 1 Madison av., Mhtn.
‡Mt. Hope, Jamaica av., Bkln., 10, Jamaica and Nichols avs.
Mt. Hope, Westchester Co., N. Y., 200, 290 Lenox av., Mhtn.
Mt. Lebanon, Myrtle av. and Brush, Queens, 85, 8 Rutgers, Mhtn.
‡Mt. Neboh, Fresh Pond rd., Queens, 16, at cemetery.
Mt. Olivet, Maspeth, L. I., 71½, Grand, Maspeth.
Mt. Pleasant, Hawthorne, N. Y., 104, 2 W. 64th, Mhtn.
Mt. Richmond, Richmond, S. I., 28, 245 Grand, Mhtn.
*Mt. St. Mary, Fresh Meadow rd., Boro. of Queens, L. I., 30, 62 Madison av., Flushing.
‡Mt. Zion, Borden and Maurice avs., Queens, 75, 41 Park Row, Mhtn.
New York Bay, Jersey City, N. J., 22, Chapel and Garfield avs.
N. Y. City Marble, 3d st., nr. 1st av., Mhtn., 3, 59 2d, Mhtn.
Oak Hill, Nyack, N. Y., 80, N. Highland av., Nyack, N. Y.
Oakland, Yonkers, N. Y., 70, 51 Warburton av., Yonkers.
Ocean View, Oakwood, S. I., 100, at cemetery.
Pelham, City Island, N. Y., 3, 171 Fordham, City Island.
Pinelawn, Pinelawn, L. I., 1819, 188 Montague.
Prospect, Jamaica, Queens, 4, 7 Union Hall, Jamaica, L. I.
Rosehill, Linden, N. J., 125, 71 W. 23d, Mhtn.
*St. John's, Metropolitan and Weisse avs., Queens, 189, Jay and Chapel, Bkln.
*St. Joseph, Yonkers, N. Y., 22, 141 Ashburton av.
St. Michael's, Astoria, Queens, 73, at cemetery.
St. Monica's, Jamaica, L. I., 1½, 42 Washington, Jamaica.
St. Paul's, B'way, nr. Fulton, Mhtn., 137 Fulton, Mhtn.
*St. Peter's, West New Brighton, 18, 53 St. Marks pl., New Brighton.
*St. Raymond's, Westchester, N. Y., 84, at cemetery
‡Salem Field, Jamaica and Norwood avs., Queens, 80, Jamaica and Euclid avs.
‡Silver Lake, Stapleton, S. I., 4½, 245 Grand, Mhtn.
Silver Mount, Tompkinsville, S. I., 25, 282 Tompkins av., Tompkinsville.
†Shearith Israel, Fresh Pond rd., Bkln., 20¾, at cemetery.
Springfield, Springfield, L. I., 30, at cemetery.
Staten Island, W. New Brighton, S. I., 1½, 63 New, Port Richmond.
Trinity Church, 153d to 155th, Mhtn., 35, 501 W. 153d, Mhtn.
Trinity Churchyard, B'way and Wall, Mhtn., 187 Fulton, Mhtn.
‡Union Fields, Cypress av., Bkln., 32, at cemetery.
U. S. National, Jamaica av. and Hale, Bkln., 18.14, Jamaica av. and Hale.
‡Washington, 22d and Gravesend, Bkln., 100, 2 Rector, Mhtn.
Woodland, Richmond Turnpike, 15, at cemetery.
Woodlawn, 233d and Webster av., Bronx, 400, 20 E. 23d, Mhtn.
Woodrow M. E., Woodrow, S. I., 2, at cemetery.

*Roman Catholic. †Portuguese cemetery. ‡Jewish. **Quaker.

ALTITUDE IN N. Y. CITY.

(Height in ft. above tide water.)

Brooklyn: Atlantic av. and Furman, 7. Clymer and Kent av., 9. Franklin and Flushing avs., 12. Union and Gowanus Canal, 14. Bridge and Myrtle av., 37. Franklin and Myrtle avs., 43. Atlantic and Flatbush avs., 45. Grand and Bushwick av., 47. Atlantic av. and Court, 49. 4th av. and 15th, 50. Myrtle av. and Adams, 61. Bedford av. and Fulton, 63. B'way and Myrtle av., 67. Atlantic and Vanderbilt avs., 71. Fulton and Cumberland, 77. Atlantic and Saratoga avs., 97. Fulton and Hopkinson av., 103. Flatbush and Vanderbilt avs., 125. Eastern P'kway and Franklin av., 134. 9th av. and Union, 142. 9th av. and 15th, 151. 7th av. and 22d, 153. 9th av. and 9th, 156. 9th av. and 20th, 175 (highest point in street system).

Highest point in Bkln. is in Greenwood Cemetery, near 9th av. entrance.

The highest natural elevation in Manhattan is located a short distance west of Ft. Washington av., about 900 ft. north of W. 181st st., near the site of Old Fort Washington. This point is 267 ft. 9 in. above mean sea level at Sandy Hook. Another natural elevation, which is located on Inwood Hill, to the north of Dyckman st., is 232 ft. 9 in. above mean sea level.

The highest point in The Bronx is located in the block bounded by Iselin av., Highland av. and W. 250th st. It is 284 ft. 6 in. above mean high water.

The Savannah, the first steamship to cross the Atlantic, was built in New York and launched Aug. 22, 1818.

HOSPITALS, HOMES AND SOCIETIES FOR RELIEF.

(See also L. I. Societies and Jewish Organizations.)

NATIONAL AND INTERNATIONAL.

Amer. Humane Assn.—Albany, N. Y. Wm. O. Stillman, Pres., 287 State, Albany, N. Y.; N. J. Walker, Sec., Watervliet, N. Y.; L. L. Wilder, Albany, N. Y., Field Sec.; H. P. Schoenberner, Treas., Bkln., N. Y.

Amer. Natl. Red Cross—Washington, D. C. 1881. Reinc. 1905. Chapters in all states and territories, incl. Dist. of Col., Philippines, Porto Rico, Hawaii and Canal Zone. Woodrow Wilson, Pres.; Mabel T. Boardman, Sec., Red Cross Bldg., Washington, D. C.

Amer. Red Star Animal Relief—Albany, N. Y. Under auspices of Amer. Humane Assn.; provides veterinary aid to sick and injured U. S. Army animals, also furnishes aid for animals in cases of great civil disasters. W. O. Stillman, Dir. Gen.; L. L. Wilder, Albany, Gen. Mgr.; H. P. Schoenberner, Bkln., Treas.

Church Pension Fund—14 Wall, N. Y. C. Inst. 1917. Natl. and official Soc. of P. E. Church for pensions for clergy and their widows and orphans. Capital, $8,712,000. Supported by assessments on churches equal to 7½% of salaries paid to rector and curates. Bishop William Lawrence, Pres.; J. P. Morgan, Treas.; Monell Sayre, Sec.

Natl. Child Labor Committee—105 E. 22d, Mhtn. 1904. 17,000 mem. Dr. Felix Adler, Ch.; O. R. Lovejoy, Gen. Sec.

Natl. Child Welfare Assn.—Inc. 70 5th av., Mhtn. Deals with all questions of child welfare and assists in organizing and directing Child Welfare Exhibits. W. H. Wadhams, Pres.; C. F. Powlison, Gen. Sec.

Natl. Conference of Social Work—1874. A. T. Burns, Pres.; Wm. H. Parker, Sec., 315 Plymouth ct., Chicago, Ill. Next meeting, Milwaukee, Wis., June 22-29, 1921.

Natl. Homes for Disabled Volunteer Soldiers—Hdqrs., Natl. Military Home, Ohio. Branches in 9 States. G. H. Wood, Pres.; C. W. Wadsworth, Gen. Treas.

Natl. Plant, Flower and Fruit Guild—70 5th av. Founded 1893. Object, to give to poor in hospitals and tenements sympathy and cheer through distribution of plants, flowers, fruit and jelly and by placing window boxes in tenement and congested dists. To establish home, county and community gardens. Mrs. J. W. Stewart, Pres.; Miss E. E. Shaw, Sec.; Mrs. G. E. Paul, Exec. Sec.; Miss V. D. H. Furman, Treas.

Needlework Guild of Amer.—Est. 1885. Inc. 1896. Natl. office, 505 Franklin Bldg., Phila. Mrs. T. H. Newberry, Pres.; Miss R. K. Bender, Sec., 525 branches. Furnishes garments and household linen annually to hospitals, homes and other charities. Special collections in times of disaster.

Soc. of Inner Mission and Rescue Work—Office, 564 2d, Bkln. Est. 1909. Missionary and social work for general betterment and uplift. Gives help and advice to strangers and immigrants, helping them to find employment, and fights white slavery. Maintains a Mission Hall at 268 Hamilton av., Bkln., and home for children too old for orphan asylum, 564 2d, Bkln. Rev. V. A. M. Mortensen, Pres.; Rev. J. F. W. Kitzmeyer, Sec.

Travelers' Aid Soc.—See Unclassified Soc., Nat.

Vassar Students' Aid Soc.—Inc. 1889. 1,225 mem. Mrs. K. B. Miller, Pres.; Mrs. W. G. Van Loon, Sec., 249 Lark, Albany, N. Y.

STATE.

For other State Relief see L. I. Socs., N. Y. State Govt. and end of this chapter.

Convention of Socs. for Prevention of Cruelty in N. Y. State—A. Elwood Corning, Newburg, N. Y., Pres.; C. H. Warner, Sec., 111 Warburton av., Yonkers.

BROOKLYN.

Hospitals, Dispensaries and Asylums.

For amount of money appropriated to charitable institutions for 1918 see the City Budget.

Ambulance Service—Ambulances are kept in readiness at many of the hospitals, and may be called to any part of the city at any hour, by telephoning Police Hdqts., 7000 Main.

Babies Hosp.—See Seaside Hosp., under Bkln. Children's Aid Soc.; Relief of Children.

Bay Ridge Hosp., Dispensary and Training Sch. for Nurses—See Victory Memorial Hosp.

Bedford Dispensary and Hosp.—Name changed to Ocean Hill Memorial Dispensary and Hosp.

Beth Moses Hosp.—1920. Stuyvesant av. and Hart. I. Levin, Pres.; D. Werbelowsky, Sec.; I. Rokeach, Treas.; J. Carlinger, Supt.

Bethany Deaconesses' and Hosp. Soc.—Est. 1894. 237 St. Nicholas av. Meth. Epis. 731 patients cared for. Nursing sick and missionary work. Rev. G. Bobilin, Supt.; Rev. H. H. Heck, Treas.; Myrtha Binder, Head Deaconess. Visiting days, Tues., Fri. and Sun., 2 to 4 P.M.

Bradford St. Hosp.—109 Bradford. (Branch of Kings Co. Hosp.) For emergency cases and general dispensary. Non-sec. Property has been purchased at Penn. and Livonia avs., as the site for new hosp. Under charge of Dept. of Charities. Miss Margaret Lacey, Nurse in Charge.

Bkln. Central Dispensary—Leased to city for purposes of carrying on tuberculosis work.

Bkln. City Dispensary—11 Tillary. Est. 1846. Dental Clinic; Food Clinic; Maternity Center. Chas. F. Neergaard, Pres.; Miss Bird, Reg.

Bkln. E. D. Dispensary and Hosp.—Consolidated with the Williamsburg Hosp.

Bkln. E. D. Homeopathic Dispensary—194 S. 3d. Est. 1872. Number of treatments, 4,547; prescriptions, 6,514; new patients, 1,903; operations, 1,430. Dr. G. W. Schaedel, Pres.; R. L. Woods, Sec.

Bkln. Eye and Ear Hosp.—94 Livingston and 79 Schermerhorn Est. 1868. Treats poor suffering from diseases of eye, ear, nose, throat. 5,319 house patients; 105,586 persons assisted; 348 average daily attendance. S. B. Chittenden, Pres.; H. R. Baker, Supt.

Bkln. Home for Consumptives—240 Kingston av. Est. 1881. 100 inmates. Mrs. T. W. Wardell, Pres.; Mrs. Charles Adams, Sec.

Bkln. Hosp. (The)—DeKalb av. and Raymond. Est. 1845. Non-sec. Care and treatment of sick or injured, excepting contagious and chronic cases. H. I. Pratt, Pres.; W. G. Nealley, M.D., Supt. Includes the following depts.: General Hosp. 306 beds; 6,499 patients; 33,138 prescriptions. Visiting days, 1:30 to 2:30 P.M. daily; 6 to 6:30 P.M., Tues. and Fri. Dispensary est. 1912. Ambulance service—2 ambulances, 2,927 calls answered. Training Sch. for Nurses. Est. 1880. 120 pupils. Miss Kate Madden, R. N., Dir. of Nurses.

Bkln. Maternity—See Prospect Heights Hosp.

Bkln. Nursery and Infants' Hosp.—396 Herkimer. Org. 1871. Children under 6 yrs. 150 cared for. Visiting days, 1st Su. each month, 10-12; 2d Th., 2-5 p.m. Mrs. Emma Dale Webb, Supt.

Bkln. State Hosp. for Insane (formerly L. I. State Hosp.)—Clarkson, nr. Albany av. Census, 1,333. Treated during year, 2,016. Farm colony located at Creedmoor, L. I. I. G. Harris, Med. Supt.

Bkln. Throat Hosp.—See Wmsbg. Hosp.

Brownsville and E. N. Y. Hosp., Inc. (The)—Rockaway P'kway and Av. A. Completed 1920. Hospital for Brownsville and E. N. Y. office, 1855 Pitkin av.; Jacob Falk, Sec.

Bushwick and East Bkln. Dispensary—Myrtle and Lewis avs. Est. 1878. 7,674 persons treated; 7,203 prescriptions. Open daily, Sun. and holidays excepted, 2-4 P.M.; Sat. 10:30-12 noon. E. F. Barnes, Pres.; F. H. Wagner, Supt.

Bushwick Hosp.—Howard and Putnam avs. Inc. 1891. 90 beds. Visiting hours daily, 2-4, 7-8. Margaret L. Fisher, Supt. Jewett Training Sch. for Nurses.

Caledonian Hosp. of City of N. Y.—53 Woodruff av. D. G. C. Sinclair, Pres.; C. F. Garlich, Sec., 600 Jefferson av.

Women's Soc. of the Caledonian Hosp.—1909. 130 mem. Mrs. C. F. Garlichs, Pres., 600 Jefferson av.

Carson C. Peck Memorial Hospital. Albany av. and Crown. Est. 1919. C. P. Case, Pres.; C. F. Neergaard, Sec.; H. H. Warfield, Supt.

Coney Island Hosp.—Ocean P'kway, nr. Av. Z. 120 beds. Under charge of Dept. of Public Welfare. Adam Eberle, M.D., Dep. Med. Supt.

Cumberland St. Hosp. and Training Sch. for Nurses—105-111 Cumberland. Est. 1902. Under direction Dept. Public Welfare. For sick poor. 3,291 patients. 1,837 ambulance cases. Dispensary treatments, 21,221; bed capacity, 200.

Day Camp Rutherford—See Bkln. Bureau of Charities, Special Relief.

East N. Y. Dispensary, 131 Watkins—1895. For treatment of sick poor. 35,000 persons treated. 20,000 prescriptions. M. Ginsburg, Pres.; Matilda J. Weithorn, Reg.

HOSPITALS, HOMES AND SOCIETIES FOR RELIEF—BROOKLYN—*Continued.*

Faith Home for Incurables—546 Park pl. Est. 1875. For incurable women, supported by voluntary contributions. 75 patients. Visiting days, daily, 2-5 P.M. Mrs. C. F. Young, Sec.

German Hosp.—(See Wyckoff Heights Hosp.).

Greenpoint Hosp.—Dept. of Public Welfare—Kingsland av. and Bullion. 1915. Capacity of 210 beds. Serves Greenpoint and north side sections. R. G. Laub, M.D., Med. Supt.

Harbor Hosp.—Cropsey and 23d avs. 1914. To give medical and surgical treatment to those of moderate means at moderate prices. J. M. Sullivan, R. N., Supt.

Hospital of the Holy Family—155 Dean. Est 1909. (R.C.) Sister M. Ursulina, Supt.

Ladies' Auxiliary—1909. Mrs. J. G. Cavanagh, Pres., 904 Ocean P'kway.

Hospital of the House of St. Giles the Cripple—Bkln. av. and President. Capacity, 45. Out-patient Dept., 50 daily. Miss A. F. Hasbrouck, in charge.

Israel Hosp. of Bkln. and Dispensary—Now United Israel-Zion Hosp.

Jewish Hosp.—Classon and St. Marks avs. 1901. Non-sec., under Jewish auspices. Affords medical and surgical aid and nursing to sick and disabled persons. 6,158 persons admitted. E. C. Blum, Pres.; I. Isaacson, Hon. Sec.

Training Sch. for Nurses—P. H. Lustig, Pres.; Miss A. M. Sabol, Supt. of Nurses.

Jewish Hosp. Dispensary—1901. Classon and St. Marks avs. Open 2-4 P.M. 40,000 persons treated. Operated as part of the Jewish Hosp. E. C. Blum, Pres.; I. Isaacsen, Hon. Sec.

Kings Co. Hosp.—Clarkson, bet. Albany av. and Clove rd. Est. 1849. Non-sec. Under charge of Comm. of Public Welfare. 16,849 patients. Daily number of patients, 885. Dr. M. D. Jones, Supt. Training Sch. for Nurses—Isabelle Burrows, Supt.

Kings Co. Hosp. for Chronic Diseases—Clarkson, nr. N. Y. av. 600 beds. Dr. Mortimer D. Jones, Med. Supt.

Kingston Av. Hosp.—Kingston av. and Fenimore. Est. 1889. Under charge of Dept. of Health. For contagious diseases. Patients mostly children. Capacity, 650 beds. Dr. W. T. Cannon, Res. Phys.

L. I. Coll. Hosp.—Henry, Pacific and Amity. Est. 1857. Care and treatment of sick, promotion medical science and instruction. 9,143 patients; daily number of patients, 413; Dr. P. S. Dudley, Pres.; A. L. Mason, Sec.; Dr. R. E. Shaw, Supt. Training Sch. for Nurses—Est. 1883. 130 pupils. 26 graduates. Miss M. E. Robinson, R.N., Supt.

Guild of the L. I. College Hosp.—Meets in Guild Room of Hospital. Org. 1897. 90 mem. To provide linen and garments and for comfort of sick poor of the hospital. Miss M. T. Seaman, Pres.; Mrs. A. L. Mason, Sec.

L. I. College Hosp. Dispensary—Amity, cor Henry. Est. 1858. 16,113 persons assisted. 68,544 treatments. R. E. Shaw, Registrar.

Lutheran Hosp. Assn.—E. N. Y. av. and Junius. Est. 1881. 1,050 inmates. Visiting days, every day, 2-4 P.M. D. Tietjen, Pres.; A. H. Legenhausen, Fin. Sec.; Augusta E. Abel. Supt.

Luth. Hosp. Assn. Clinic for Ear, Nose and Throat—E. N. Y. av. and Junius. Same officers as Luth. Hosp. 18,306 treatments.

Maternity Hosp. of Brownsville and E. N. Y. —1395 Eastern P'kway. Mrs. Anna Heater, Ch.

Memorial Dispensary—827 Sterling pl. Est. 1881. Medical aid to women and children. 1,311 prescriptions given. Dr. L. A. Cort, Pres.; Dr. M. E. Ellis, Res. Phys.

Memorial Hosp. for Women and Children—827 Sterling pl. Est. 1883. Dr. L. A. Cort, Pres.; Dr. M. F. Fleckles, Sec.

Methodist Episcopal Dispensary—7th av. and 7th. Est. 1895. 2,825 patients.

Methodist Episcopal Hosp.—6th st., 7th and 8th avs. Est. 1881. 12,072 patients. A. P. Sloan, Pres.; Rev. J. E. Holmes, Supt.

Norwegian Lutheran Deaconesses' Home and Hosp.—4th av. and 46th. Est. 1883. All cases, except contagious ones, without regard to creed or nationality. Free to poor. 180 beds. Patients treated in wards and private rooms, 3,289; ambulance calls, 4,261. Does outside relief work for the poor. Visiting days: Mon., Wed., Fri. and Su., 2-3 P.M.; Tu. and Thur., 6-7 P.M. Lauritz Larsen, Pres.; A. N. Rygg, Sec.

Ladies' Auxiliary—Mrs. B. Gunsten, Pres.; Mrs. Ahlstrom, Cor. Sec.; Marie Johnsen, Rec. Sec.

Ocean Hill Memorial Dispensary and Hosp.—343 Ralph av. Non-sec. Open week days. F. G. Seymour, Pres.; C. Rippier, Sec., 736 Jefferson av.

Polhemus Memorial Clinic—Henry, cor. Amity. Est. 1897. Free. W. B. Davenport, Pres., 189 Montague; H. H. Burley, Supt.

Prospect Heights Hosp. and Bkln. Maternity—Washington av., cor. St. Johns pl. Est. 1871. General hospital for the treatment of surgical, medical and maternity cases. 68 inmates. Mrs. R. Shaw, Pres.; Mrs. G. M. Gibson, Supt.

St. Catharine's Hosp. and Dispensary—Bushwick av., nr. Ten Eyck Est. 1875, under charge of Sisters of St. Dominic. 260 inmates. Rt. Rev. C. E. McDonnell, D.D., Pres.; Mother M. Cornelia, O.S.D., Supt.

St. Catherine's Hosp. Men's Aid Soc.—138 Montrose av. Org. 1877. To aid the sick in hospital. Geo. Schuettinger, Pres.; J. Roethlem, Sec., 230 Graham av. Ladies' Aid Soc. of St. Catherine's Hosp.—Org. 1899. Mrs. J. J. Haggerty, Pres.; Miss M. E. Morris, Sec.

St. Christopher's Hosp. for Babies and Training Sch. for Nursery Maids—277-283 Hicks. Est. 1896. 100 patients (under 4 yrs.). Mrs. W. D. Sargent, Pres.; Isabel Gordon, Supt.; Hy. B. MacKown, Bus. Mgr.

St. John's Hosp. (Church Charity Foundation of L. I.)—Atlantic and Albany avs. Est. 1851. Under Prot. Epis. denomination. 2,070 patients. Rev. P. F. Swett, Supt.

St. Mary's Hosp. (The)—St. Marks and Buffalo avs. Est. 1879. (R. C.) 4,202 patients. Rt. Rev. C. E. McDonnell, Pres. Visiting days, Su., Tu., Thur., 3-5 P.M.

St. Mary's Hosp. Ladies' Aid Soc.—St. Marks and Rochester avs. Org. 1886. Mrs. A. P. Conklin, Pres.; Mrs. A. L. Harriman, R.N., Sec.

Training School for Nurses—J. B. La Marsh, Dir. St. Mary's Junior Aux., Miss Teresa M. Smith, Pres.

St. Peter's Hosp.—Henry, bet. Congress and Warren. Est. 1864. (R. C.). Under charge of Sisters of the Poor of St. Francis. 3,551 patients. Visiting days, Thur. and Su., 2-4 P.M. Sister Siegfrieda, Supt.

Samaritan Hosp.—4th av. cor. 17th. Est. 1906. Free dispensary. A. H. Smith, Pres.; E. Kirby, R.N., Supt.

Seaside Hosp.—See Bkln. Children's Aid Soc., under Relief of Children, Bkln.

Seney Hosp.—See Meth. Epis. Hosp.

Swedish Hosp.—Sterling pl. and Rogers av. Est. 1906. Non-sec. 80 patients. Chas. Edling, Pres.; Dorothea Gothson, Supt.

Trinity Hosp.—1835. E. N. Y. av. Est. 1912. 30 inmates. Dr. W. F. Campbell, Surg.-in-Chief; Miss G. V. McMahon, Supt.

United Israel-Zion Hosp.—1246 42d. For treatment of all diseases, incl. dentistry. Patients treated, 5,533; prescriptions, 3,993. Newman Dube, Pres.; Boris Fingerhood, Exec. Dir. Med. Staff.

United States Naval Hosp.—Flushing av., opp. Ryerson. Est. 1824. For officers and enlisted personnel of the U. S. Navy and Marine Corps. Commanding officer, C. H. T. Lowndes, Capt. M. C., U. S. N.

Victory Memorial Hosp. (formerly Bay Ridge Hosp., Dispensary and Training Sch. for Nurses) —92d and 7th av. Org. 1899. Inc. 1904. Non-sec. 7,269 treatments, 9,824 prescriptions. L. H. Smith, Pres.; L. F. Moynahan, Sec.; L. Merklein, Treas.

Williamsburgh Hosp. and Dispensary —106-112 S. 3d. Est. 851. 1,535 inmates; 6,390 dispensary treatments; 4,093 prescriptions; 2,282 ambulance calls. Visiting days, Tues., Thur., Su., 2-4, and Mon., Wed. and Fri., 7-8 P.M. J. H. Post, Pres.; Margaret T. Herlihy, R. N., Supt. In 1917 the Eastern Dist. Hosp. was merged with this.

Williamsburg Mission to the Jews—Throop av. and Walton. Sar Shalom Dispensary. Free medical treatment daily, 1-4 P.M. Rev. Leopold Cohn, Supt., 27 Throop av. Chief of Staff. Dr. F. H. Richardson.

Wyckoff Heights Hospital—St. Nicholas av., Stanhope and Stockholm. (Formerly German Hosp.) Est. 1889. Opened 1899. 3,170 treated Hospital, 4,615 treated Dispensary, 1,650 ambulance cases. Visiting days, Su. and Wed., 2-4 P.M.; 7:30-8:30 P.M. F. A. Schurman, Pres.; Charles Arras, Supt.

Zion Hosp.—United with Israel Hosp. under name United Israel-Zion Hosp.

HOSPITALS, HOMES AND SOCIETIES FOR RELIEF—BROOKLYN—*Continued.*

Relief of the Aged.

Baptist Home of Bkln.—Greene av., cor. Throop. Est. 1869. To care for indigent Baptists. 70 inmates. Wm. B. Fox, Pres., 296 Jefferson av.; Miss A. I. McGuire, Cor. Sec., 484 Willoughby av.; Mrs. H. T. Alden, Rec. Sec., 185 Quincy; H. R. Ferguson, Treas.; Mrs. Van Winkle, Matron.

Bkln. Hebrew Home and Hosp. for the Aged—Dumont and Howard avs. Est. 1913. 184 inmates. Mrs. Chas. Rosenthal, Pres.

Auxiliary to the Bkln. Hebrew Home and Hosp. for the Aged—Jonathan Schneider, Pres.; C. Augustus Kestin, Treas.

Bkln. Home for Aged Colored People (over 65 yrs.)—St. Johns pl., cor. Kingston av. Est. 1891. 36 inmates. Mrs. P. Bogert, Pres.; Mrs. D. M. Staebler, Sec., 690 Macon; Mrs. C. E. Dame, Supt.

Bkln. Home for Aged Men and Aged Couples (over 70 yrs.)—745 Classon av. Est. 1878. 120 inmates. Mrs. W. D. Spalding, Pres.; Mrs. Jas. H. Hollingshead, 1st V.-Pres.; Mrs. Wm. V. Hester, Cor. Sec.; Mrs. O. E. Reimer, Sec.; Mrs. E. M. Lang, Supt.

Bkln. Meth. Epis. Church Home for Aged and Infirm (over 65 yrs.)—Park pl., cor. New York av. Est. 1883. 100 inmates. Mrs. A. I. Preston, Pres.; Emma S. Rushmore, Supt.

Congregational Home for the Aged—1910. Linden av., bet. Rogers and Bedford avs. 46 inmates. A. G. Cooper, Pres.; Mrs. F. J. Clark, Sec.; Miss M. Stryker, Supt.

Danish Home for the Aged—1051 41st. 1906. To provide home for worthy Danes over 65 yrs. Admission $300 for life if able to pay. Cap. 23. Jas. Rasmussen, Pres.; V. Bancke, Sec., 1105 Halsey.

German Evangelical Home for the Aged—Chauncey, nr. Bushwick av. Est. 1879. To provide food, shelter, clothing to persons 60 yrs. and over. 263 inmates. Mrs. C. Kaupp, Pres.; Mrs. A. Heins, Sec.; Mrs. D. Streubel, Treas.; Mrs. M. E. L. Werner, Supt.

Graham Home for Old Ladies (over 60 yrs.)—320 Washington av. Non-sec. Est. 1851. 80 inmates. Miss F. E. White, Pres.; Miss J. C. Dunham, Supt.

Greenpoint Home for the Aged (Ladies' Benevolent Assn.)—Oak and Guernsey. Est. 1882. Age limit, 65 yrs.; Mrs. G. M. Owen, Pres., 218 Guernsey; Mrs. J. H. Stobbe, Sec., 654 E. 23d.

Home for Aged, Church Charity Foundation—Herkimer, nr. Albany av. (See also Miscellaneous.) For communicants of P. E. Church, 65 yrs. and upward. 72 inmates.

Home for Aged of Little Sisters of Poor—DeKalb and Bushwick avs. Also 8th av. and 16th. Est. 1868. Men and women over 60 yrs. 255 inmates. Sister Pascaline, Supt.

Jewish Home for Aged and Infirm—871 Bushwick av. 1912. 100 inmates. Non-sec. From 60 years up. Dr. P. A. Siegelstein, Pres.; Dora Sonnenblick, Matron.

Marein-Heim (Home) for Aged—18th av. and 64th. Est. 1895. Founded by the German Ladies' Assn. to provide a home for worthy poor German men and women of Bkln. over 60 yrs. of age. 50 inmates. Miss M. Behr, Pres.; Mrs. J. Heubech, Treas., 184 8th av.; Mrs. E. Zerboni, Matron.

N. Y. City Home for Aged and Infirm, Bkln. Division—Now known as Kings Co. Hosp. for Chronic Diseases. See Hospitals.

Norwegian Christian Home for Aged—1250 67th. Inc. 1911. P. Rasmussen, Pres.; Miss Alma Beij, Sec.; Miss A. Fuhr, Matron.

N. Y. City Home for Aged and Infirm, Bkln. Division—Clarkson, near New York av. Est. 1831. Treated 1,906. Dr. M. D. Jones, Supt.

Norwegian Christian Home for Aged—1250 67th. Inc. 1911. P. Rasmussen, Pres.; Miss Alma Beij, Sec.; Miss H. Gunvalsen, Matron.

Presbyterian Home for Aged—390 Ocean Parkway. Est. 1917. Rev. N. W. Wells, Pres.; A. G. Van Cleve, Sec.; R. M. Hart, Treas., 32 Court.

Swedish Augustana Home for the Aged—1680 60th. 1908. (65 yrs.). 42 inmates. Rev. J. D. Danielson, Pres.; V. Berger, Sec., 1675 60th; John H. Benson, Mgr.

Wartburg Home for Aged and Infirm (over 65 yrs.)—2598 Fulton. Est. 1875. (Lutheran). 84 inmates. A. Dihlmann, Pres.; Otto Graesser, Sec., 602 E. 9th, Mhtn.

Relief of Children.

Babies' Pure Milk and Health stations are located throughout Bkln. Information and addresses of same may be obtained from the Dept. of Health or from the Bkln. Children's Aid Soc.

Bedford Day Nursery—See Bkln. Bureau of Charities, Special Relief.

Beecher Home. (See Orphan Asylum Soc. of Bkln.)

Boys Welcome Hall—185 Chauncey. Est. 1892. Free evening resort for boys from 9 to 18 yrs. Maintains gymnasium, library, billiard table, bowling alleys. Boy Scout Troop and summer camp, educational classes and religious work. Attendance, 30,000 yearly. W. S. Twiddy, Pres.; G. C. May, Treas.; W. R. Shaw, Exec. Sec.

Bkln. Baptist Orphanage—Ocean av. and Ave. S. Est. 1901. To care for orphans. 4-18 yrs. Wm. H. MacMurray, Pres.; Max Schimpf, Sec., 245 Carroll.

Ladies' Aux.—Mrs. R. B. Hull, Pres.; Mrs. J. F. Hoag, Sec.

Bkln. Benev. Soc.—84 Amity. Est. 1845. Care of orphans and poor. Rt. Rev. C. E. McDonnell, Pres.; J. M. Sheridan, Agt.

Bkln. Boys' Club—Inc. (Auspices of Boys' Club Org. and Aid Soc.). 123 5th av. Org. 1901. For repression of juvenile crime, promotion of good citizenship and morality. D. E. Jayne, Supt.; F. H. Stevenson, Treas.

Bkln. Children's Aid Soc.—72 Schermerhorn. Est. 1866. Protetction, care and shelter of friendless youth. H. O. Wood, Pres.; A. E. Wakeman, Gen. Sec. Maintains following branches: (1) Bureau of Counsel, Investigation and Relief—Gives relief and advice. Over 6,000 persons aided. (2) Placing Out Dept. finds homes for children; work for boys and girls and places for mothers with children; 500 such homes and situations secured. (3) The Working Boys Home—14-18 yrs., and temporary shelter for homeless children of all ages. Lodgings, 2,600. Mrs. Margaret Walters, Matron. (4) Summer Relief Work—(a) Seaside Home, Far Rockaway. 1876. Mothers and sick children 1 day to 2 weeks. Resident phys. and corps of trained nurses. 8,700 cared for. Mrs. M. H. Dyckman, Mgr. (b) Seaside Hosp., every modern hospital equipment for the care of infants. 300 cared for. Mrs. S. B. Lott, Supt. (c) Herriman Farm, Monsey, N. Y. Farm School and Industrial Training, F. N. Patterson, Supt. (d) Free milk for babies in co-operation with Dept. of Health, 25 stations. (e) Country fortnight outings, co-operating with Tribune Fresh Air Fund. 1,400 Bkln. boys and girls given two weeks' stay. Applications for each dept., 72 Schermerhorn.

Bkln. Hebrew Orphan Asy.—See Jewish Org.

Bkln. Home for Blind, Crippled and Defective Children—See Charitable Inst., L. I.

Bkln. Industrial School Assn. and Home for Destitute Children—217 Sterling pl. 1854. Miss L. G. Zabriskie, Pres.; Miss N. T. Lazell, Sec.; Mrs. B. A. Connolly, Supt.

Bkln. Juvenile Probation Assn.—102 Court. To assist and extend juvenile probation work by co-operating with the Children's Court and correctional institutions. It co-ordinates and supervises all volunteer effort done in connection with the court and is the clearing house for Big Brother and Big Sister work. R. J. Wilkin, Pres.; David H. Lanman, Treas., 177 Montague; Miss Gertrude Grasse, Sec.

Bkln. Nursery and Infants' Hosp.—See Hospitals.

Bkln. Soc. for Prevention of Cruelty to Children (The)—105 Schermerhorn. Inc. 1880. Has jurisdiction over Bkln. and Nassau County.

Main lines of work: (1) Investigates complaints of parental negligence, cruelty and other injustice to children under 16 yrs. of age; (2) Rescues children from squalid and depraved surroundings and affords them a fresh start in asylums or foster homes; (3) Instructs and compels ignorant, careless parents to deal with their children properly, to improve home conditions and to allow needed medical or surgical treatment; (4) Befriends and studies the needs of neglected and exceptional children, and secures the co-operation of medical, charitable, reformative and other agencies; (5) Cares for homeless, maltreated and arrested children in the society's shelter; (6) Prosecutes adults who commit crimes against children; (7) Secures law enforcement and decency in moving picture theaters, saloons, shore resorts and similar places; (8) Investigates applications for the release of children from institutions; (9) Takes charge of the temporary detention quarters in the Bkln. and Queens Children's Courts, and otherwise assists these and other courts; (10) Inquires into local child welfare needs, promotes legislation, and serves as a bureau of information and advice.

Statistics for 1919. Families involved in complaints, 6,491; children involved in complaints, 20,000; children received in shelter, 4,118. James A. Smith, Pres.; John J. Williams, Treas.; Arthur W. Towne, Supt.

Central Day Nursery. See Bkln. Bureau of Charities. Special Relief.

Children's Christmas for Children—1909. (Christmas Red Stocking Com.) 150 mem. To provide Christmas gifts for destitute children. Mrs. J. S. Waterman, Pres.

Convent of Sisters of Mercy—273 Willoughby av. Girls bet. 2 and 16 years and infants. Est. 1855. 1,327 inmates. Mother M. Ursula, Mother Superior. Branches, 12th av. and 64th, Bkln., and Syosset, L. I. Also home for infants. Syosset branch is for boys.

Dominican Home—See Orphan Home of the Nuns of the Order of St. Dominic.

Dyker Heights Home—See Internatl. Sunshine Branch for the Blind.

First Hebrew Day Nursery and Kindergarten —See Jewish Org.

Flatbush Boys' Club and Community Center—Org. 1903. Inc. 1909. 2523 Snyder av. Resort for boys and girls up to 18 yrs. Maintains gymnasium, library, swimming pool and educational classes. Open all day and evening. 600 mem.

Friend-in-Need Day Nursery—95 Bradford. Est. 1908. Age limit, 12 yrs. 30 children (average) cared for daily. Mrs. J. C. Creveling, Pres.; Mrs. J. H. Wells, Sec.; Mrs. Hardiman, Matron.

Gardner Sunshine Day Nursery—562 Herkimer. Est. 1902. Care for little children of working mothers. 7,000 children cared for. Mrs. N. L. Mead, Pres., 139 Rutledge; Mrs. T. Findlay, Mat.; Elsie G. Hartcorn, Sec.

Gillespie Memorial Day Nursery—See Industrial School Assn., Bkln., E. D.

Hebrew Day Nursery of Brownsville—See Jewish Org.

Hebrew Educational Soc.—(See Jewish Org.).

Home of the House of St. Giles the Cripple—See Charitable Soc., L. I.

Howard Orphanage and Industrial Schl.—See Charitable Inst., L. I.

Immaculate Conception Day Nursery—117 Sands. 38 Front. Est. 1893. 44,951 children cared for. Mrs. William C. Courtney, Pres.; Miss M. Harkins, Matron. Ladies' Assn.—117 Sands. Org. 1893. 60 mem. Miss E. G. McLaughlin, Sec., 129 St. Johns pl.

Industrial School Assn. of Bkln., E. D.—141-153 S. 3d. Est. 1854. Children 2-16 yrs. Instructs in elementary branches, domestic duties and manual training, provides food and clothing. Main Home, 141 S. 3d. 400 inmates. Kindergarten; 482 Humboldt; 50 inmates. Gillespie Memorial; 210 Richardson. Summer Home, Hauppage, L. I. Col. A. D. Baird, Pres.; D. T. Wilson, Sec.; A. J Fernandez Supt.

Internatl. Sunshine Branch for the Blind—Nursery and home at 84th and 13th av. Kindergarten at 83d and 13th av. Est. 1904. Care, maintenance and education of blind children. Daily average, 30. Mrs. C. W. Alden, Pres.; Mrs. N. E. C. Furman, Sec., 8432 107th, Richmond Hill; Dr. Grace P. Masmillen, Supt.

Kallman Orphanage—18th av. and 67th. Est. 1898. Age limit, 4-15 years. Non-sec. 80 inmates. C A. Ogren, Pres.; John Lindblom, Mgr.

King's Daughters' Day Nursery—87 Java. Est. 1901. Inc. Non-sec. Infants and young children cared for during working hours for mothers who are widowed or deserted. Mrs. C. Treber, Pres., 2721 Bedford av.; Mrs. Wm. Tyler, 146 Kent, Sec.

Milk Stations—See Babies Pure Milk and Health Stations.

Norwegian Children's Home Assn.—43 Gubner. Non-sec. A. N. Rygg, Pres.; O. Hertzwig, Sec., 544 81st.

Orphan Asylum Soc. of City of Bkln.—1435 Atlantic av. Est. 1833. Children 3-14 yrs. Orphans and half-orphans. 200 inmates. Mrs. A. Dreyer, Pres.; Mrs. W. H. Meserole, Cor. Sec.; Mrs. F. A. Henschien, Supt.

Orphan Home of the Nuns of the Order of St. Dominic—Est. 1861. Headquarters where children are received, 153 Graham av. Branches maintained: Sorrowful Mother, Harrison pl.; St. Dominic's, New Hyde Park, L. I.; Nazareth Trade School, Farmingdale, L. I.; St. Rose's Industrial School for Girls, Melville, L. I. M. Augustine Fleck, O.S.D., Pres.; Sister M. Perpetua, O.S.D., Mgr.

Otilie Orphan Asylum—See Relief Institutions of Queens Borough.

Prospect Day Nursery—176 14th. 1920. Non-sec. Has room for 40 children, where mothers are employed during the day. Under auspices of Runsdorf Maternity Soc., Mrs. S. Harris, Pres.

Ridgewood Day Nursery Assn.—227 Knickerbocker av. Est. 1905. To provide protection for children while mothers earn their livelihood. Mrs. A. B. Moriarty, Pres., Prin. P. S. No. 162; Miss E. Reich. Matron.

Roman Catholic Orphan Asylum Soc.—Room 14, 4 Court sq. Genl. Agt., G. F. Shiebler. Est. 1826. 3 to 14 yrs. Inmates in all asylums. 2,000. Rt. Rev. C. E. McDonnell, Pres.; J. F. Keany, V.-Pres.; J. J. Walsh, Treas.; J. J. Gartland, Sec. Object of soc. is to protect and educate orphans and half-orphans bet. ages 3 and 14 yrs. Institutions maintained by the society: St. John's Home for Boys, Albany and St. Marks avs., in charge of Sisters of St. Joseph. Sister Jane Frances, Supt.—Branch of St. John's Protectory, Hicksville, L. I. Country Home, Sister M. Adelaide, Supt.—St. John's Summer Home, Coney Island. Open during summer only.—St. Joseph's Female Orphan Asylum, Willoughby and Sumner avs., in charge of Sisters of Charity. Sister M. Antonina, Supt.—St. Paul's Industrial School—Clinton and Congress. Girls from St. Joseph's are transferred to St. Paul's, where they receive a training fitting them to be self-supporting when discharged from the institution.—Emerald Assn. Est. 1839. To provide funds for the Roman Catholic Orphan Asylums through medium of the Emerald Ball. C. J. Druhan, Pres.; J. F. Casey, Sec.

Runsdorf Maternity Soc.—176 14th. Mrs. L. J. Runsdorf, Hon. Pres.; Mrs. S. Harris, Pres. Conducts day nursery.

St. Agnes' Day Nursery (R. C.)—415 Degraw. Est. 1895. 12,520 children assisted. Mrs. Edward Feeney, Pres.; Mrs. H. J. McCann, Treas.; Mrs. M. J. Shea, Sec., 13 2d.

St. Joseph's Day Nursery—873 Pacific. Est. 1896. Care of children of working women during working hours. Age limit—girls, 14 years; boys, 9. Non-sec. 7,191 children cared for. Clothing and food given to 9,274 persons. Mrs. D. B. Griffin, Pres.; Mrs. Jos. McMahon, V.-Pres.; Miss Ann E. O'Rourke, Sec.; Miss Anne G. Keany, Treas.; Miss E. A. Leddy, Matron.

St. Malachy's Home—Atlantic and Van Sicklen avs. Est. 1876 (R. C.) For destitute children, 2-16 yrs. 122 inmates. Mother M. Louis Pres.; Sister M. Edmund, Supt. Branch, Rockaway Park—Est. 1895. For destitute children, 2-16 yrs. 340 inmates. Mother M. Louis, Pres.; Sister M. Angeline, Supt. St. Joseph's Home—Flushing, 1903. For destitute children, 2-16 yrs. 341 inmates. Mother M. Louis, Pres.; Sister M. Agnes Marie, Supt.

St. Vincent's Home for Boys—Boerum pl. and State. Est. 1869 (R. C.). 200 inmates. Supported by voluntary contributions. Rt. Rev. C. E. McDonnell, Pres.; Rev. P. F. Kelly, Rector and Treas.; St. Vincent's Guild—Mrs. N. G. Wall, Pres.; Mrs. J. F. Whalen, Sec. Junior Aid Soc.—Miss Anna R. Rush, Pres:; Miss Mary Rush, Sec.

Seaside Home, Coney Island—See Bkln. Children's Aid Soc.

Sheltering Arms Nursery (P. E.)—Work continued by Bkln. Children's Aid Soc.

Tiny Tim Soc.—To help raise funds for the Hospital of the House of St. Giles the Cripple. Mrs. J. A. Mollenhauer, Pres.; Miss Annie Olney, Sec., 163 Herkimer.

Upanin Club—See Soc., miscellaneous.

Williamsburg Day Nursery—(See Bkln. Bureau of Charities. Special Relief).

Special Relief.

Amer. Natl. Red Cross—Bkln. Chapter. Org. 1905. 163 Remsen. Adrian Van Sinderen, Ch.; A. E. Vaughan, Exec. Sec.; Mrs. Marian Sargent, Sec

Barbados Soc. in N. Y.—Org. 1906. Garfield pl. and 6th av. To relieve needy Barbadians and for social intercourse among members. 65 mem. A. Smith, Pres.; G. S. Reed, Sec., 455 Prospect pl.

HOSPITALS, HOMES AND SOCIETIES FOR RELIEF—BKLN.—SPECIAL RELIEF—*Continued.*

Boarding Homes for Working Girls—See King's Daughters House, Y. W. C. A. and St. Peter's Home.

Bkln. Assn. for Improving the Condition of the Poor—104 Livingston. Org. 1843. Inc. 1864. E. H. Pilsbury, Pres.; F. L. Sniffen, Treas.; Miss J. M. Hixon, Gen. Agt. Supported by voluntary contributions. Relieves promptly all cases in need of assistance. Non-sec. Exchange and Training Schl. for blind; conducts salesroom where articles made by the blind are sold. Also educational classes for the adult blind, helping them to become self-supporting. Housekeeping centers, model apartment, classes in cooking and clubs for girls in home-making. Visits made in the homes, giving instructions in cooking and housekeeping that better homes can be maintained on a more economical basis. Orthopaedic Clinic; contributes to support of clinic for children at L. I. Coll. Hosp. Conducts a Dental Clinic, also a Malnutrition Clinic. Women and children are given days and weeks outings during the summer at the A. I. C. P. Rest, Coney Is., and in co-operation with other organizations.

Brooklyn Bureau of Charities—1878. Inc. 1887. Consolidated with the Union for Christian Work. 1901. Central office, 69 Schermerhorn. Open 8 A.M. to 6:30 P.M., except Sun. and holidays, 10-12 A.M. only. Dist. offices, 9 A.M. to 5 P.M., except Sun. and holidays. A. T. White, Pres. Emeritus; Darwin R. James, Jr., Pres.; F. B. Pratt, J. H. Post, A. M. White, Vice-Pres.; E. P. Maynard, Treas.; G. H. Thirkield, Asst. Treas.; S. B. Chittenden, Counselor; G. H. Hall, Med. Advisor; Thos. J. Riley, Gen. Sec. Bd. of Directors: W. F. Atkinson, A. V. Barnes, Mrs. W. S. Brewster, W. H. Childs, I. H. Cary, W. I. Frothingham, H. F. Gunnison, W. Hammitt, T. W. Hynes, D. R. James, Jr., J. Liebman, Miss E. C. Low, J. G. Low, Mrs. E. P. Maynard, E. P. Maynard, Rev. E. W. McCarty, F. C. Munson, F. C. B. Page, J. H. Post, C. M. Pratt, F. B. Pratt, D. D. Roberts, G. F. Smith, G. W. Smith, H. K. Twitchell, A. Van Sinderen, A. M. White, A. T. White. Object: The Brooklyn Bureau of Charities aims to relieve distress and suffering of all kinds; to rescue the poor from hunger and want and to restore them to self-support; to teach the blind; to aid the crippled; to stamp out tuberculosis; to improve housing conditions; to protect the interests of the poor in the lower courts, and to eradicate street begging by imposters. The Bureau maintains offices and workers in every section of Brooklyn. It is absolutely non-sectarian, recognizing no distinction of race or creed, and derives its entire support from voluntary contributions.

Administration and Finance—69 Schermerhorn. Thos. J. Riley, Ph.D., Gen. Sec.; Aaron M. Lopez, Asst. to Gen. Sec.; T. W. Hanigan, Fin. Sec.; Edwin Madvig, Auditor.

Service and Relief—69 Schermerhorn. Mrs. May Harding, Supt.; Homeless Dept., Mrs. Mary Hammell. District offices—Bedford, 1660 Fulton; Bushwick, 723 Hart; East New York, 141 Pennsylvania av.; East Williamsburgh, 255 Division av.; Flatbush, 876a; Flatbush av.; Fort Greene, 506 Grand av.; Gowanus, 321 9th; Greenpoint, 182 Franklin; Navy Yard, 322 Jay; Red Hook, 419 Clinton; Southern, 5704 4th av.; St. Mark's, 1660 Fulton; Williamsburgh, 255 Division av.

Day Nursery Committee—69 Schermerhorn. Aaron M. Lopez, Sec.; Central Day Nursery, 69 Schermerhorn; Williamsburgh Day Nursery, 255 Division av.

Wood Yard and Laundries—1660 Fulton. Geo. M. Galloway, Supt.; Bedford Laundry, 1660 Fulton; Williamsburgh Laundry, 255 Division av.; Wood Yard, 1660 Fulton.

Committee on the Prevention of Tuberculosis—69 Schermerhorn. Nels Nelson, Sec. This committee aims by educational literature and public talks to reduce the spread of tuberculosis; conducts open air classes and assists in maintaining tuberculosis sanatorium.

Housing Committee — 69 Schermerhorn. Robt. Stuart, Sec. This committee aims to improve housing conditions in Brooklyn.

Committee on Criminal Courts—69 Schermerhorn. Mendicancy Officer, J. D. Godfrey. This committee aims to secure from the lower courts the best results for social betterment and to prevent street begging by imposters.

Committee on the Blind—Aaron M. Lopez, Sec.; Miss H. B. Griswold, Dir. of Work. Headquarters for the Blind—287 Schermerhorn. This committee aims to make the blind self-supporting through education and training. The committee maintains a Crafts Shop at 306 Livingston, where the work of the blind is for sale.

Committee on Crippled Children—69 Schermerhorn. Miss Ethel Evans, Sec. This committee aims to provide proper medical care, education and recreation for every crippled child in Brooklyn.

Confidential Social Service Exchange—69 Schermerhorn. Aaron M. Lopez, Sec.; Miss Dorcas Campbell, Asst. Sec. A clearing house for the convenience of all societies in Brooklyn and Queens.

School Lunch Commitee—69 Schermerhorn. Aaron M. Lopez, Sec.; Mrs. Addie C. Cox, Supervisor. This committee formerly provided nourishing food in the public schools at nominal cost at its lunch counters and in special classes. The Bd. of Education is now doing this work and the committee is engaged in special work.

Bkln. City Mission and Tract Soc.—See Missions.

Bkln. Deaconesses' Home (M. E.)—238 President. 1892. Accom. 22. Rev. Frank Upham, Pres.; Mrs. H. W. Byrnes, Supt.

Bkln. Federation of Jewish Charities—See Jewish Organizations.

Bkln. Female Employment Soc.—93 Court. Est. 1854. All kinds of sewing. Sewing School. Mrs. W. A. Putman, Pres.; Mrs. A. S. C. Montgomery, Sec., 39 Remsen.

Bkln. Guild for Deaf Mutes—Org. 1892. Assist destitute, hold debates, lectures. Meets first Thurs. each month in parish building of St. Mark's Church, Adelphi, nr. DeKalb av. Service is also conducted in St. Mark's Church; Rev. J. Chamberlain, pastor among deaf mutes, Sun. at 3 P.M. A. J. McLaren, Pres.; Mrs. H. Leibsohn, Sec., 8645 17th.

Bkln. Lodging Houses—Majority open all night. Lodgings, 10-50 cts. per night. 302 Bedford av.; 339 and 658 B'way; 29, 35, 50, 66, 76, 109, 178, 223, 289 and 296 Fulton, 134 Grand; 32, 80 Hamilton av; 6 Henry; 17 Myrtle av; 355 Pearl; 70 Summit; 10, 14, 16 Tillary; 109 S. 6th; 4306 3d av.; 236 Market av.; 6 Washington av.; 344 East av.; 124 West av.; 370 40th.

Bkln. Training Sch. and Home for Young Girls (9-16 yrs.)—1483 Pacific. Est. 1887. Mrs. J. J. Roberts, Pres., 841 President; Miss C. Murton Walker, Treas.; Mrs. H. L. Gray, Supt.

Catholic Women's Assn.—See Religious Soc.

Christmas and Easter Letter Mission—Org. 1881. Distributes Christmas and Easter letters and greetings among inmates of prisons, hospitals, institutions, homes, factories, railroad employees, life-saving stations, etc., in U. S. and Alaska. Also to our soldiers abroad and at home. Miss M. M. Pendleton, Sec.-Treas., 215 Monroe.

Church Home for the Blind—452 Herkimer. Est. 1896. (Church Charity Foundation. See Miscl.) To care for homeless blind women. 24 inmates. Deaconess Hodgkiss, in charge.

Congregation of the Holy Name of Jesus—Mother House, Holy Name Convent, Mt. Kisco, N. Y.; St. Clare's private school for girls at Mt. Kisco, N. Y., summer outings to country for children; Rev. Mother Superior, Holy Name Convent, Mt. Kisco, N. Y.

District Nursing Committee—67 Schermerhorn. —(See Bkln. Bur. of Charities).

Florence Nightingale Federation of the M. E. Hosp.—1916. 6th, 7th avs. to 8th av. Mrs. Wm. Kennedy, Pres.; Miss Julia Ring, Rec. Sec.; Mrs. W. L. Davison, Cor. Sec., 29 7th av.

Hosp. Saturday and Sunday Assn.—62 Joralemon. Est. 1881. To interest public in hospital charity. W. G. Low, Pres.; A. F. Hewlett, Sec., 68 Remsen.

Industrial Home for the Blind—514-524 Gates av. Est. 1893. Age limit, 18 yrs. and upward. 38 inmates. W. C. Humstone, Pres.; E. P. Morford, Supt.

King's Daughters House (boarding house for working girls)—18 Sidney pl. 35 boarders. Miss Sophie L. Meserole, Pres.; Miss Isabel W. White, Supt.

Legal Aid Soc.—Room 204, Eagle Bldg. Renders legal aid to those unable to procure assistance elsewhere and promotes measures for their

HOSPITALS, HOMES AND SOCIETIES FOR RELIEF—BKLN.—SPECIAL RELIEF—*Continued.*

protection. **Chas. E. Hughes, Pres.; C. P. Kitchel, Sec., 43 Cedar, Mhtn.; L. McGee, Atty., Eagle Bldg.**

Needlework Guild in America—Bkln. Br. Org. 1891. 75 institutions helped. Meets once a year. **Mrs. J. E. Langstaff, Pres., 19 7th av.; Miss M. L. Wintringham, Treas., 168 Hicks; Mrs. E. F. Howell, Sec., 9 Arlington pl. Flatbush Br.—Org. 1897. 81 mem. Mrs. H. L. Bartlett, Pres.; Mrs. P. Browne, Sec., 543 Ocean av. Flatlands Br.—Org. 1897. 53 directors. Mrs. M. Becker, Pres.; Mrs. A. L. Fuller, Sec., 543 E. 24th. So. Midwood. New Utrecht Br.—Org. 1897. 70 directors. Mrs. John F. Berry, Pres.; Mrs. J. Lott, Sec., 237 82d.**

Nursing Sisters of the Sick Poor (R. C.) 439 Henry. Est. 1906. Care of the sick poor. 252 cases cared for. **Rev. Mother M. Emma, Superior; Mrs. John B. Fraser, Pres.**

Old South Bkln. Dental Dispensary, Inc.—1917. 139 Harrison. Conducted by Old South Bkln. Civic League. Hours, 9-5 A.M. daily, except Sat. 9-12., Tu. and Thur. 7:30 to 9:30 P.M Mrs. Natalie Holden Lander, Sec.

Ozanam Home—40-48 Concord. Org. 1901. (R. C.) Temporary relief for women. 750 assisted. **Very Rev. Mons. Francis J. O'Hara, Pres.;** Wm. D. S. Kelly, Sec.; **Miss S. Gough, Supt.**

Provident Loan—Smith and Livingston, 24 Graham av. and Pitkin and Rockaway avs. See Provident Loan Soc. of N. Y., Special Relief, Mhtn.

Recreation Home for Women and Children—Harway av., Gravesend Beach. Inc. 1898. Temporary home for recuperation. Mrs. G. W. Rasch, Pres.; Miss K. S. Dreier, Cor. Sec., 135 Central Pk. W., Mhtn.; Mrs. Oley, Matron.

St. Peter's Home for Working Girls (R. C.)—395 Hicks. Est. 1890. Home for working girls of moderate means. 6 sisters, 65 inmates. Sisters of St. Joseph.

Salvation Army Industrial Home—Bkln. Hdqtrs., 430 Keap. Care of homeless men. 7,500 cared for. J. Kingsepp, Mgr.

Scandinavian Young Women's Home (Fridhem)—149 So. Portland av. Est. 1901. Under charge of Swedish Ev. Pilgrim (Cong.) Church. Home for immigrant and servant girls. Rev. H. A. Benson, Pres.

Social Service Com. of Kings Co. Hosp.—Org. 1910. 21 mem. To aid sick poor. Mrs. Bruce R. Duncan, Ch.; Miss Daisy Gaus, Sec., 497 Halsey.

Soc. for Aid of Friendless Women and Children—20 Concord. Temporary shelter for women. Permanent home for girls, from 2 to 18, and boys, from 2 to 6. Est. 1868. 110 inmates. Have a summer home. Mrs. F. W. Hopkins, Pres.; Mrs. C. Boyer, Supt.

Soc. of Inner Mission and Rescue Work—See National Socs.

Soc. of St. Vincent de Paul—General office, Room 38, 4 and 5 Court sq. Org. 1855. An organization connected with the Catholic churches. Dispenses general charity without regard to denomination. Work is done by a conference in each church. Governed by a council of the president and vice president of each conference. Officers of the council are: T. W. Hynes, Pres., 1332 Pacific; Jos. Kunkel, Sec., 492 Throop av. Council meets 2d Thur. each month at the Pro-Cathedral school hall, Jay.

Conferences and Presidents.

Assumption—F. McPartland, 48 Columbia hgts.
Blessed Sacrament—L. J. Mulligan, 75 Ashford.
Epiphany—T. M. James, 132 Clymer.
Gate of Heaven—Thos. O'Hare, Ozone Pk., L. I.
Holy Family—J. J. Gallagher, 415 10th.
Holy Innocents—J. F. Ackerman, 360 E. 19th.
Holy Name—Thos. Hogan, 29 Fuller pl.
Holy Rosary—J. F. Mallon, 724 Herkimer.
Immaculate Conception—F. Kelly, 240 Rutland rd.
Immaculate Heart of Mary—J. F. Decker, 2721 Ft. Hamilton av.
Most Holy Trinity—G. J. Peters, 191 Graham av.
Nativity—J. A. Creighton, 163 Putnam av.
Our Holy Redeemer—S. D. O'Mara, Freeport, L. I.
Our Lady of Angels—Ludwig Merklein, 428 Ovington av.
Our Lady of Good Counsel—H. D. McGrane, 533 Madison.
Our Lady of Mercy—T. Coffey, 464 Pacific.
Our Lady of Perpetual Help—W. S. Bartley, 450 59th.
Our Lady of Victory—C. Partridge, 228 McDonough.
Queen of All Saints—R. H. Farley, 284 DeKalb av.
Sacred Heart—J. Long, 116 Clermont av.
St. Agnes—T. J. Kavanagh, 361 Degraw.
St. Ambrose—W Dooling, 17 Van Buren.
St. Ann—T. Tully, 164 High.
St. Anthony—M. H. Kavanagh, 141 Kent.
St. Augustine—W. H. Bennett, 156 St. Johns pl.
St. Barbara—W. Drennan, 965 Bushwick av.
St. Benedict—S. Haas, 966 Herkimer.
St. Brigid—E. J. Collins, 1721 Gates av.
St. Catharine of Alexandria—C. D. Sanderson, 4619 Ft. Hamilton P'kway.
St. Charles Borromeo—G. Rausch, 67 Atlantic av.
St. Edward—J. Bailey, 32 Auburn pl.
St. Finbar—E. J. Huott, 46 Bay 17th.
St. Francis Xavier—W. F. O'Brien, 439 6th.
St. Gabriel—E. O'Rourke, 299 Arlington av.
St. Gregory—J. J. Cunningham, 225 Brooklyn av.
St. Ignatius—F. Kerr, 698 Sterling pl.
St. James—J. Larmour, 226 Clermont av.
St. John the Baptist—L. W. Malone, 929C 18th.
St. John the Evangelist—M. J. Rush, 163 23d.
St. Joseph—W. Tormey, 1010 Fulton.
St. Lucy—Andrea Basile, 812 Kent av.
St. Mary Star-of-the-Sea, Far Rockaway—E. J. Healy, Bay View av., Far Rockaway.
St. Mary Star-of-the-Sea—J. Medlar, 71 2d.
St. Matthew—W. T. Matthews, 1286 Prospect pl.
St. Michael (E. N. Y.)—C. Rudershavarn, 2747 Fulton.
St. Michael's, Flushing—D. Barry, 57 Madison av., Flushing.
St. Michael—Jas. Cain, 530 44th.
St. Patrick—L. I. City. R. Flood, 171 Beebe av., L. I. C.
St. Parick—Ft. Hamilton. H. A. Napier, 259 93d.
St. Patrick—J. A. McCarthy, 239 Emerson pl.
St. Paul—D. J. Printy, 296 Warren.
St. Peter—J. Armstrong, 179 Baltic.
Sts. Peter and Paul—J. Gallagher, 112 Clymer.
St. Rita—Ravenswood, L. I. C. J. McConnell, 67 Sherman, L. I. C.
St. Stephen's—P. D. Bradshaw, 426 Clinton.
St. Teresa—T. Monahan, Mhtn. Beach.
St. Thomas Aquinas—W. H. Pettes, 301 7th.
St. Vincent de Paul—Martin Devaney, 238 N. 7th.
Transfiguration—J. O'Rourke, 271 Division av.

Visiting Nurse Association of Brooklyn, Inc.—80 Schermerhorn. Object: To give skilled nursing care to the sick in their homes; to teach personal hygiene, cleanliness and the prevention of diseases. The association maintains a staff of trained nurses to give nursing care under the physician's direction to the sick in their homes. The nursing service covers the Borough of Brooklyn. A separate staff is maintained for home treatment and follow-up work of cases of infantile paralysis in Kings County. Fees charged according to the circumstances of the individual patient and at the discretion of the nurse. The same service is given, however, to those who are not able to pay. Branch Offices: 136 B'way, 732 Flushing av., 1022 Gates av., 105 Fleet pl., 1696 Myrtle av., 6005 14th av., 861 Manhattan av., 887 Flatbush av., 2523 Snyder av., Bond and Wyckoff, 131 Baltic. Mrs. J. Morton Halstead, Act. Pres.; Mrs. F. L. Pomeroy, Rec. Sec.; Miss Marion Libby, Cor. Sec.; Miss Mary W. Chapman, Treas.; Miss Eliz. Stringer, R. N., Supt.

Women's Aux. of St. Vincent de Paul Soc.—1903. 439 Henry. Promotes welfare of the poor, sick and friendless, besides taking an active interest in the affairs of the Nursing Sisters and Ozanam Home. Visit public hospitals, jail and penitentiary and maintains 4 settlements for Italian children. Mrs. J. Byrne, V.-Pres.; Miss N. O'Reilly, Sec.

White Cross Hosp. and Relief Assn.—1562 Fulton. Est. 1908. 300 mem. Relief sick and needy, first aid to injured. **Maintains hospital tents at Rockaway Beach, Canarsie, Coney Island, South Beach, Roxbury, Rockaway Pt., P'kway Baths and Dreamland Pk. Wm. W. Butcher, Pres.; W. H. Marquand, Treas.; Alex. MacNaughton, Sec., 253 61st.**

HOSPITALS, HOMES AND SOCIETIES FOR RELIEF—BKLN.—SPECIAL RELIEF—*Continued.*

Women's Work Exchange and Decorative Art Soc.—130 Montague. To assist gentlewomen to dispose of their handiwork. Mrs. F. W. Moss, Pres.

Young Ladies' Aid and Literary Soc. Inc. 1908. 143 McKibbin. S. Wolf, 502 Willoughby av.

Reformatories.

Disciplinary Training Sch. for Boys—Abolished. Reformation work of juvenile delinquents. Emma M. Finn, Mncpl. Bldg., N. Y.

House of the Good Shepherd—Hopkinson av. and Pacific. Est. 1868. Reformation of erring women (R. C.). 500 inmates. Sister M. Joachim, Sec.; Sister M. St. Anselm, Supt.

Truant Schools—Org. 1870. Under charge of Bd. of Education.—(See Public Schools.)

Wayside Home—Removed to Valley Stream, L. I.

Women's Branch House—(See Bkln. City Mission and Tract Soc. under Missions.)

Settlements.

Bkln. Neighborhoods Assn.—1908. 50 mem. Social and Civic Betterment. For closer union of individual, social and settlement workers. S. Barnard, Pres., 176 Nassau.

Catholic Settlement Assn.—Org. 1910. 180 Gold. Maintains Dr. White Memorial, 180 Gold; Visitation Branch, Visitation pl.; St. Anne's Branch. Purposes: To provide a centre for wholesome recreation and to meet the needs, both physical and spiritual, of the poor of the neighborhood. Trained nurse in attendance at the Dr. White Memorial. Mrs. Mathias Figueira, Pres.; Mrs. W. H. Sefton, Cor. Sec., 444 79th.

Columbia House Settlement (formerly Willow Pl. Chapel House)—25-27 Columbia pl. Est. 1906. Maintains a kindergarten, sewing schl., dressmaking, cooking, carpentry, athletic teams, gymnasium, library, penny bank, music sch., indoor playground; also clubs for men and women, boys and girls. Country fortnight outing for children. Mrs. D. MacLean, Head Worker.

Emmanuel House—131 Steuben. Maintained by Emmanuel Bapt. Ch. Reading and game rooms, gymnasium, free sewing sch., kindergarten, Sun. sch., athletic assn.

Greenpoint Neighborhood House—85 Java. Org. 1895. Supported by the Pratt Inst. Neighborship Assn. Maintains a kindergarten and various clubs for young men, women, boys and girls. Gives instruction in sewing, dressmaking, millinery, cooking, gymnastics, dancing, manual training and music. Eve. classes in English to foreigners. Has a trained nurse in residence, who does district nursing in the neighborhood. Florence E. Clendenning, Head Worker.

Hall Memorial House—157 Montague. Org. 1895. Center for social work for boys and men, under auspices of Holy Trinity Ch. A corps of young men residents, assisted by other volunteers. Conducts athletics, social, industrial and civic clubs for boys of all ages. Men's club and billiard and poolroom, library, gymnasium and baths. Sections for civic, social, musical purpose. 400 mem. Rev. J. H. Melish, Pres.

Holy Trinity Guild House—122 Pierrepont. Org. 1905. Center for social work for women, girls and children in connection with Holy Trinity P. E. Church. A corps of volunteers conducts the work. Maintains Dorcas Soc., Mothers' Meeting and Employment Soc. for women, Girls' Friendly Soc. for young working women. Candidates' clubs and sewing sch. Florence L. Drinker, Head Worker.

Italian Settlement—90 Adams. G. W. Thompson, Pres.; W. E. Davenport, Head Worker.

Lincoln Settlement—105 Fleet pl. Est. 1908. Center for physical, educational and social betterment. Work largely among the colored. Day Nursery, a nurse of the District Nursing Assn. in attendance. The settlement conducts classes and clubs among children and adults. W. H. Baldwin, Pres.; Miss H. Jackson, Sec.; Dr. V. Morton Jones, Head Worker.

Little Italy Neighborhood Assn.—146 Union. Neighborhood House for Italians. Est. 1904. There are 4 residents and the work is directed by the head worker, and a board of 30 mem. There are the usual clubs, classes, kindergarten, gymnasium, a trained nurse and first aid room. O. T. Carroll, Pres.; Mrs. T. W. Reynolds, Treas.; Miss M. Knox, Head Worker.

Maxwell Kindergarten House—245 Concord. A kindergarten settlement for mothers and little children. Is headquarters for kindergarten mothers' clubs of public schools. Miss F. Curtis, Pres.; Miss M. E. Bittner, Head Worker.

Music Sch. Settlement (Bkln. Branch)—See Educational Socs.

People's Institute United Neighborhood Guild, Inc.—176 Nassau. Purpose: To maintain neighborhood clubhouses and social centers to promote education, social and civic welfare of the community and to co-operate with others in movements for public good. Maintains its building as a meeting place for social and civic clubs, gymnasium and athletics, festivals, music and dancing. Mrs. H. E. Dreier, Pres.; Seymour Barnard, Dir.

Pratt Inst. Neighborhood Assn.—215 Ryerson. C. Pratt, Pres.; Margaret Middleditch, Sec.

School Settlement Assn.—120 Jackson. Est. 1901. Settlement conducted by Alumnae Associations of Adelphi, Berkeley, Bkln. Training Schl. for Teachers, Girls High, Packer Inst. and Miss Rounds. Classes for children in sewing, cooking, music, dramatics, story-telling, folk dancing, games, etc. Basketball and baseball teams. Social and athletic clubs for young men and women. Summer playground. Americanization classes. Helen L. Moss, Head Worker.

Social Guild—1913. 800 mem. (Temporarily inactive). Lillian Wolf Chamow, Sec., 502 Willoughby av.

Upanin Club—(See Miscellaneous Socs., Bkln.)

Willoughby House Settlement—97 Lawrence. Org. 1900. Inc. 1905. Maintains boys', girls and young women's clubs and classes, mothers' club, men's club, gymnasium, pool room, fresh air camp. Miss May Belle Williams, Pres., 284 Gates av; Miss Mina A. Clement, Treas.; Miss A. B. Van Nort, Head Worker; Ida M. Ryerson, Asst.; H. S. Williamson, Dir. of Men's and Boys' Work.

Humane Societies.

Amer. Soc. for Prevention of Cruelty to Animals—Bkln. office, 114 Lawrence. Est. 1866. Alfred Wagstaff, Pres.

Soc. for Prevention of Abuse in Animal Experimentation—204 Montague. Branch, Rochester, N. Y. Org. 1907. J. B. Y. Warner, Pres.; F. P. Bellamy, Treas.

South Bkln. Veterinary Hosp.—Est. 1904. 1-3 16th. Dr. H. J. Brotheridge.

Miscellaneous.

Church Charity Foundation of L. I. (P. E.)—Albany, cor. Atlantic av. Est. 1851. Bd. of Mgrs.: Rt. Rev. F. Burgess, Pres.; M. W. Byers, Sec., 188 McDonough; Rev. P. F. Swett, Supt. Maintains following depts.: Orphan House, St. John's Hospital, Church Home for the Blind, Home for the Aged, Sisters' House and Training Schl. for Nurses.

City Prison, Borough of Bkln., under Dept. of Correction—149 Raymond. 10,688 prisoners received during the year. Visiting days, every day bet. 10 and 11:30 A.M., Su. and holidays excepted. Warden Robert Barr.

Morgue—On Kings Co. Hosp. Grounds. Est. 1863. Under charge of Dept. of Public Charities.

MANHATTAN.

Hospitals, Dispensaries and Asylums.

Ambulances are kept in readiness at many of the hospitals and may be called to any part of the city at any hour by telephone from police stations or by telephoning Police Hdqts., 3100 Spring, for the transfer to hospitals of accident cases and diseases not contagious. Bd. of Ambulance Service, City of N. Y.—(See Municipal Government Chapter.)

Babies' Hosp.—135 E. 55th. Est. 1887. Country branch, Oceanic, N. J., open during summer months. For care of poor sick children under 3 yrs. 75 beds. 1,920 children assisted. J. S. Hoyt, Pres.; Miss M. A. Smith, Supt. Hosp.; Miss M. Wood, Supt. Nurses.

Bellevue Hosp.—Ft. E. 26th. Est. 1816. 546,329 day treatments. Geo. O'Hanlon, M.D., Gen. Med. Supt.; M. L. Fleming, M.D., Asst. Med. Supt. Maintains an Out Patient Dept., ft. E. 26th.

Bellevue Training Sch. for Nurses—440 E. 26th. Inc. 1873. 469 pupils in training at Bellevue and Allied Hospitals, Harlem, Fordham and Gouverneur. Pres. Bd. of Women Mgrs., Mrs. W. C. Osborn; Miss C. J. Buink, Gen. Supt. Training Schools.

HOSPITALS, HOMES AND SOCIETIES FOR RELIEF—MHTN.—HOSPS., DISPS. & ASYLS.—*Con.*

Beth Israel Hosp.—Monroe, Jefferson and Cherry. Inc. 1890. Medical and surgical care of sick poor. 2,489 patients; 68,541 persons assisted in dispensary; 64,743 prescriptions issued. J. H. Cohen, Pres.; L. J. Frank, Supt.

Ladies' Aux. Soc.—900 mem. Mrs. A. F. Hess, Pres.

Bloomingdale Clinic of St. Michael's (P. E.) Ch.—225 W. 99th. 4,739 treatments given. The Rector, Pres.; Mrs. G. R. Lewis, Treas.; Clara G. Granger, Reg.; Physicians in Charge: Dr. J. C. Fisk, Dr. A. G. Biddle, Dr. J. M. McTierman, Dr. A. H. Appel, H. R. Cronk.

Broad St. Hospital—129 Broad. E. Walker, Pres., 25 Broad.; Dr. A. J. Barker Savage, Sec.

Burke Relief Foundation (Winifred Masterson)—Inc. 170 B'way. Org. 1902. To maintain and conduct a convalescent home and similar charities at White Plains and elsewhere. Commenced operations in Apr., 1915, at White Plains. Admission House, 325 E. 57th. F. K Sturgis, Pres.; F. H. Denman, Sec.; Dr. F. Brush, Supt.

Children's Hosp.—(See N. Y. City Children's Hospitals and Schools.)

City Hosp.—Blackwell's Island. Est. 1849. In charge Dept. Public Welfare. General Hospital, including Maternity, Neurological and Children's Pavilions. For destitute sick suffering from non-contagious diseases. Admission through office of admitting physician, Reception Hospital, Queensboro Bridge, Blackwell's Island. 4,305 patients; 1,060 beds. Visiting days, Th., Su., 11 A.M. to 4 P.M. Bird S. Coler, Comm.; Dr. C. B. Bacon, Med. Supt.

Columbus Hosp. and Columbus Hosp. Dispensary—226 E. 20th. Inc. 1895. 125 beds. In charge of the Missionary Sisters of Sacred Heart of Jesus. 1,498 inmates cared for. Mother M. Josephine, Supt. Visiting days, Tu., Th., 2:30-4 P.M.; Su., 2:30-4:30 P.M.

Training School for Nurses—Opened 1911. Capacity 35 pupils.

Community Hospital—17-21 W. 101st. Est. 1863. Non-sec. 2,812 patients. 5,301 dispensary patients; 4,984 prescriptions given. Wm. H. Dieffenbach, M.D., Pres.; Howard Van Note, Sec.; J. H. Storer, M.D., Treas.; E. A. Laurence, R. N., Supt.

Custodial Asylum—See N. Y. City Children's Hospitals and Asylums.

DeMilt Dispensary—245 E. 23d. Inc. 1851. Free medicines and a charge of 10c. for medicines to those able to pay. Open 10 A.M. to 4 P.M. R. G. Mead, Pres.; E. M. Townsend, Treas., 345 B'way; T. J. Kearns, M.D., House Phy.

DuBois Fund for Assisting Respectable Poor to Obtain Services of Trained Nurse—Org. 1887. 911 Park av. Mrs. T. Olyphant, Treas.

Emergency Receiving Hosp. — Storehouse, Blackwell's Island. Est. 1911. Under direction Dept. of Public Welfare. Temporary treatment pending their removal to Blackwell's Island hospitals. Ambulance service. 13,072 patients cared for. Dr. W. H. Conley, Med. Supt.

Epileptic Hospital—See City Hosp.

Floating Hosp. of St. John's Guild—See Relief of Children.

Flower Hosp.—E. 64th and Av. A. Est. 1860. H. C. Smith, V.-Pres.; E. R. Tinkler, Treas.; L. Johnson, Sec.; H. D. Thomason, Supt. Capacity, 200 beds. Dispensary open daily, 10-12 A.M. and 2-4 P.M. Hosp. visiting hours: Private rooms, governed by physician, 10 A.M. to 9 P.M. daily; rooms of more than one bed and wards, 2-4 and 7-8 P.M. daily; clinical wards, Tu., Th., Su., 2-4 P.M.; Mon., Fri., 7-9 P.M.

French Benev. Soc. Hosp. and Dispensary—450-458 W. 34th. 2,501 inmates. 25,222 prescriptions. L. Jouvaud, Pres. Visiting days, Tu., Fri. and Su., 2-4 P.M.

German Hosp. and Dispensary—Name changed to Lenox Hill Hosp.

German Poliklinik (Dispensary) — Name changed to Stuyvesant Polyclinic.

Good Samaritan Dispensary—Broome, cor. Essex. Inc. 1848. Free treatment; medicine, 10 cents each prescription to those who can pay. Open daily. 134,854 patients; 109,076 prescriptions given. Dr. L. F. Bishop, Pres.; Dr. E. Schultze, Phy. in Chief.

Gouverneur Hosp.—Ft. Gouverneur. Est. 1885. A reception hosp. for accidents and medical indoor and outdoor treatment. Patients cared for, 5,353; out patients dept., 137,979. Visiting days, Tu., Fri., 6-8 P.M.; Su., 2-4 P.M.; Dr. J. W. Brannan, Pres.; Dr. G. O'Hanlon, Genl. Med. Supt.; J. A. Stowers, Asst. Supt.

Hahnemann Hosp.—Park av., bet. 67th and 68th. Inc. 1869. Maintains Training School for Nurses. Accommodation for poor requiring treatment and private rooms for pay patients. Capacity, 138 beds. Visiting days, Su., Wed. and Fri., 2-4 P.M. T. Frank Manville, Pres.; W. E. Woodbury, M.D., Dir.

Harlem Dispensary—108 E. 128th. Inc. 1868. Open daily except Su., holidays, 1:30-3:30 P.M. Free to poor. No. of visitors, 4,489; 3,306 prescriptions given. E. F. Corey, Pres.; G. H. Corey, Treas.; G. S. Walker, Sec.

Harlem Eye and Ear Hospital—Lexington av. and 127th. Inc. 1881. Hospital of 25 beds and clinic for free treatment of poor. 10,000 persons treated. E. E. Hinkle, Pres.; Dr. C. B. Meding, Sec. and Exec. Surgeon, 113 E. 54th.

Harlem Hosp. and Out Patient Dept.—Lenox av. and 136th. Est. 1887. Branch of Bellevue and Allied Hosps. Visiting days: Tu., Fri., 6-8 P.M.; Su., 1-4 P.M. Children's visiting days, 2-3 P.M. on Tu., Fri. and Su. Clinic days, every day except Su. and holidays: Surgical, 10-12 A.M.; medical, 2-4 P.M. Cardiac Clinic, Th., 7:30 to 9:30 P.M.; Mental Clinic, Wed., 4 to 6 and 8 to 9 P.M. C. D. O'Neil, Res. Supt. (See also Tuberculosis Clinic.)

Har Moriah Hosp.—138 E. 2d. Est. 1909. For treatment of all acute medical and surgical cases. 1,283 inmates. F. Baron, Supt.

Herman Knapp Mem. Eye Hosp.—500 W. 57th. Inc. 1869. A dispensary and hosp. for treatment of diseases of eye and school of ophthalmology. Receives patients free when necessary. Others admitted at reasonable rates. 50 beds. Maintains a dispensary or out-patient dept. 10th av., cor. 57th, for free treatment of the poor. 13,044 patients cared for during past year. School of ophthalmology, 500 W. 57th; for instruction in eye surgery to graduates of medicine. F. V. S. Crossby, Pres.; R. L. Morris, Treas., 16 Wall; Dr. A. Knapp, Exec. Surg., 10 E. 54th.

Hospital and House of Rest for Consumptives —Bolton rd., nr. Dyckman. Org. 1869. Care of consumptives in all stages of disease. 175 under treatment in yr. M. F. Griggs, Pres.; I. A. Porter, Act. Supt.

Hosp. for Joint Diseases—1919 Madison av. Est. 1907. Non-sec. Disp. buildings at 41 E. 123d. To treat acute and chronic joint diseases and prevent and correct deformities. Treatments, 92,875. Lewis Straus, Pres.; Dr. H. W. Frauenthal, Sug.-in-Chief.

House of Annunciation for Crippled and Incurable Children, 3740 B'way. Inc. 1893. Free for destitute girls, 4 to 16 yrs. Maintains St. Elizabeth's House, a summer home at Wilton, Conn. 50 patients. Rev. L. T. Cole, D.D., Pres.; T. H. Myers, Orthopedic Surg.; W. S. McMurdy, House Phy.

House of Calvary—Macomb's rd. and Featherbed la. Est. 1899. (Cath.) Care of destitute men and women suffering from incurable cancer and allied diseases. Free. Capacity, 100 beds. Catherine C. McParlan, Sec.

House of the Holy Comforter, Free Church Home for Incurables (P. E.)—196th and Grand Concourse. Inc. 1880. Free home for incurable women and children. 60 inmates. Beverly Chew, Pres.; J. S. Barnes, Treas., 52 Vanderbilt av.; Miss M. R. Swarr, Supt.

Hudson Street Hosp.—See N. Y. Hosp.

Infirmary of College of Dental and Oral Surgery of N. Y.—302 W. 35th. Est. 1893. Dr. Wm. Carr, Dean.

Jewish Maternity Hosp.—270-272 E. B'way. Est. 1906. To attend women during their lying-in period. Non-sec. 50 beds. 50 cribs. S. Finkelstein, Pres.; B. B. Rhein, Supt.

J. Hood Wright Mem. Hosp.—See Knickerbocker Hosp.

Knickerbocker Hosp.—503 W. 131st. Inc. 1862. Free to poor; maintains an ambulance service. Visiting days, Su., Tu. and Fri., 2-4 P.M. Visiting hours also bet. 7-8 Tu. and Fri. evenings. M. G. Foster, Pres.; Lucy M. Moore, Supt.

Laura Franklin Free Hosp. for Children—19 E. 111th. Org. 1885. 2-12 yrs. Non-sec. 1,140 patients. Visiting days, Su., 2-3 P.M. W. Delano, Jr., Pres., 50 E. 42d; F. L. Lurkins, R.N., Supt. Has a registered training school.

Lenox Hill Hosp.—77th, bet. Lex. and Park avs. Est. 1857. Free to sick poor. Inmates cared for, 5,113. Fritz Achelis, Pres.; Geo. F. Sauer, Supt. Visiting days, Wed., Su., 2-4 P.M. Maintains Training Schl. for Nurses.

Louisa Minturn Hosp. for Scarlet Fever and Diphtheria—Ft. of E. 16th. Private rooms; each patient may be attended by own physician. Dr. E. L. Dow, Ch. Exec. Com.

Lutheran Hosp. of Mhtn. Inc. 1911—Convent av. and 144th. Complete new hospital and nurses' home opened 1916. G. N. Wenner, Pres.; F. N. Bunger, Sec., 140 W. 123d.

Mhtn. Eye, Ear and Throat Hosp.—210 E. 64th. Inc. 1869. Free to indigent persons. Dispensary open week days, 2-3 P.M. 13,558 indoor patients; 63,720 outdoor patients; 173,947 visits; 60,009 prescriptions. J. A. Haskell, Pres., 764 B'way; R. O'Brien, Supt.

Mhtn. Maternity and Dispensary—Inc. 1901. 327 E. 60th. Free and pay wards. Private rooms. Charity cases attended in homes in hosp. dist. Affiliated course for student nurses. Courses for physicians and students. M. Taylor, Pres.; Nancy E. Cadmus, Supt.

Mhtn. State Hosp.—See State Government.

Memorial Hosp.—Central Park W. and W. 106th. Inc. 1887. Treatment of cancer and allied diseases. Free wards, pay wards and private rooms. Medical dept. under the supervision of Cornell Univ. Herbert Parsons, Pres.; Archibald Douglas, Sec.; F. R. Appleton, Ch. Exec. Com.; G. F. Holmes, Supt.

Metropolitan Hosp.—Blackwell's Island. Under Dept. of Public Welfare. Est. 1875. Dr. W. H. Conley, Med. Supt. Visiting days, Th. and Su., 11 A.M. to 4 P.M.

Metropolitan Throat Hosp.—351 W. 34th. Inc. 1874. Free to poor. Non-sec. 1,716 new cases registered. 5,014 in attendance. Dispensary open daily, 2-4 P.M. E. Floyd-Jones, Pres.; G. B. Hope, Med. Supt.

Misericordia Hosp.—531 E. 86th. Org. 1887. Maternity, General Hosp. 447 inmates. Sister of the Holy Heart of Mary, Pres.; Sister St. Emily, Supt. of Nurses.

Mt. Moriah Hosp. (See Har Moriah.)

Mount Sinai Hosp.—5th av. and 100th. Inc. 1852. Non-sec. Free to poor. Accident cases admitted free. 521 beds. 9,913 cases treated. Dispensary, Madison av. and 100th, for free treatment. 214,059 consultations and treatments. Outdoor Relief and District Corps care for cases outside of hospital and furnish nurses at homes of poor. Geo. Blumenthal, Pres.; Dr. S. S. Goldwater, Dir. Visiting days, medical wards, Mon. and Th., 2-3; surgical wards, Tu. and Sat., 2-3.

Training Sch. for Nurses—Madison av. and 100th. Inc. 1881. Hugo Blumenthal, Pres.; Miss E. A. Greener, R.N., Supt.

N. Y. City Children's Hospital, Randall's Island, Dept. Public Welfare. Est. 1868. For care and treatment of feebleminded and epileptic. Transfers cases of these types to State Institutions. Maintains hospital and a laboratory for study of feebleminded and epileptic and also training school and industrial dept. Receives patients from Gr. New York over 2 years. 2,000 beds. The Mental Clinic, formerly Clinic for Atypical Children and Outdoor Patient Dept., now located at Post Graduate Hospital. This clinic opens every morning ex. Wed., 9 A.M. to 11 A.M. On Tu. and Wed. clinic held at Cumberland St. Hospital, Bkln. Dr. J. F. Vavasour, Med. Dir.

N. Y. Dispensary—34-36 Spring. Est. 1790. Free medical and surgical aid to sick poor. 134,697 persons assisted during yr. T. W. Cleaveland, Phys.-in-Chief.

N. Y. Eye and Ear Infirmary—2d av., cor. 13th. Org. 1820. Limited number of free beds. Total number of beds, 175; number of indoor patients, 6,348; visits to dispensary, 167,700; prescriptions, 73,400. Dispensary open daily. Free to poor. J. J. Riker, Pres.; L. Iselin, Treas.; T. K. Robertson, Supt. Maintains a school of instruction for graduate physicians and a training school for nurses.

N. Y. Foundling Hosp.—175 E. 68th. Est. 1869. (Cath.) To care for needy and homeless mothers, foundlings and deserted children, from infants to 2 yrs. 4,960 cared for. Needy and homeless mothers, 582. Children adopted, 480. Controlled by the Sisters of Charity. Mother M. Josepha, Pres.; Sister Anna Michella, Dir.

Ladies' Aux.—Mrs. J. V. Bouvier, Hon. Pres.; Mrs. Jos. H. Sammis, Pres.; Miss Cath. Brady, Sec.

N. Y. Homeopathic Medical College and Flower Hospital—See Flower Hosp.

N. Y. Hosp. (Soc. of)—6 to 16 W. 16th and 7 to 21 W. 15th. Inc. 1771. E. W. Sheldon, Pres.; P. Tuckerman, Treas. Hosp. for pay and free patients. 12,478 patients during year. Thos. Howell, M.D., Supt. Out-Patients Dept. at 8 W. 16th. Open except Su. and holidays, 10:30-12, 2-3 P.M. Number treated, 12,536; prescriptions, 37,934. Training School for Nurses, 8 W. 16th. Bloomingdale Hospital for Insane, White Plains, N. Y. Treated 622 at Convalescent Homes, White Plains, 941. Wm. L. Russell, M.D., Med. Supt.

N. Y. Infant Asylum—Inc. 1865. See N. Y. Nursery and Child's Hospital.

N. Y. Infirmary for Women and Children—321 E. 15th. Est. 1853. 23,966 assisted in dispensary; 19,629 prescriptions given. E. C. Henderson, Pres.; Lucy F. Ryder, R.N., Supt.

N. Y. Medical College and Hosp. for Women Homeopathic)—Non-Community Hospital.

N. Y. Nursery and Child's Hosp. (founded 1910 by consolidation of the Nursery and Child's Hospital and N. Y. Infant Asylum). Supported by public funds, voluntary contributions and board of paying patients. Dr. E. L. Partridge, Pres.; Miss Rye Morley, Supt. Application for admission to be made for private patients in the Reservation Office and for ward patients at the Registration Desk in the clinic. Receives foundlings and sick children and has power, through State Charities Aid Assn., to procure the adoption of suitable foster parents. A number of private rooms and wards are provided for patients who are able to pay, where patients may, if they so desire, be attended by their own physicians subject to regulations of Medical Board. Includes the Old Marion St. Maternity Hosp. (Inc. 1827), which gives without charge medical attendance during confinement. Also operates Boarding Out Dept., where children are boarded out in homes in N. Y. City and vicinity.

N. Y. Ophthalmic and Aural Inst.—See Herman Knapp Mem. Eye Hosp.

N. Y. Ophthalmic Hosp.—201 E. 23d. Inc. 1852. Free to needy afflicted with disease of eye, ear, nose and throat. Affords facilities for instruction of medical students. (Homeopathic.) 1,142 indoor patients; 9,352 outdoor cases; 32,320 prescriptions. F. Moss, Pres.; Dr. G. I. Hall, Res. Surg.; Mrs. V. L. Dicks, Supt.

N. Y. Orthopedic Dispensary and Hosp.—420 E. 59th. Est. 1866. Free to poor, with special reference to diseases and deformities of bones and joints. Gives instruction in same. Receives for treatment children and adults. 1,003 patients, 78,463 hospital days care given; 14,486 patients in dispensary; Miss Theodora S. Root, Supt.; R. A. Hibbs, Surg.-in-Chief. Country Branch at White Plains, N. Y. Mrs. S. M. Bridgman, Supt.

N. Y. Polyclinic Med. School and Hosp.—341-351 W. 50th. Inc. 1882. Rev. C. H. Parkhurst, Pres.; David Webster, V.-Pres.; J. A. Wyeth, Sec.; A. A. Jaller, Supt. Maintains free dispensary to the poor. Visiting days, Tu., Fri. and Su., 2-4 P.M.

Free Dispensary of the N. Y. Polyclinic Med. Sch. and Hosp.—341-351 W. 50th. Inc. 1882. Gives medical advice and medicines to poor. Non-sec. Open daily, except Su. and holidays, from 9 A.M. to 5 P.M.

N. Y. Post-Graduate Med. School and Hosp.—2d av., cor. 20th. Org. 1882. Dr. F. E. Sondern, Pres.; Dr. A. F. Chace, Sec.; A. H. Candlish, Supt. Maintains hospital of 416 beds, for treatment of patients suffering from general diseases. Consists of wards for women, children and men, and babies' ward. School for graduate physicians also. Margaret Fahenstock Training Schl. for Nurses, 304 E. 20th.

N. Y. Skin and Cancer Hosp.—2d av. and 19th. Inc. 1882. 100 beds. Visiting days, Tu., Th., Sa., Su., 2-4 P.M. Dispensary gives free advice and treatment to poor every day except Su. and holidays, 9-10 A.M. 10,050 new patients. 33,849 visits made to dispensary. E. D. Murphy, Pres.; Dr. F. Haas, Sec.; Miss S. Burns, Supt.

N. Y. Soc. for Relief of Ruptured and Crippled—321 E. 42d. Inc. 1863. For curable children from 4 to 14 yrs. and adults. 225 beds. Dispensary for outdoor patients. Wm. C. Osborn, Pres., 170 B'way; V. P. Gibney, Surg.-in-Chief; J. D. Flick, Supt.

N. Y. Throat, Nose and Lung Hosp.—229 E. 57th. Inc. 1893. H. D. Brewster, Pres.; E. J. Bermingham, Exec. Surg.

N. Y. Univ. and Bellevue Hosp. Med. College, 1st av. and 26th. Est. 1898. E. E. Brown, Ph.D., LL.D., Chancellor; S. A. Brown, M.D., Dean of Faculty. Dispensary in Medical College Bldg. Aid and medicine free to sick poor.

Northeastern Dispensary—222 E. 59th. Inc. 1862. Free to poor. 10,237 patients treated; 25,747 prescriptions dispensed. S. F. Hallock, Pres.; E. G. Foster, Sec.; Dr. A. F. Taylor, Supt. and House Phy.

Northern Dispensary—165 Waverly pl. Inc. 1828. 12,319 cases; 8,876 prescriptions dispensed. R. L. Harrison, Pres.; W. D. Luks, Supt.

Northwestern Dispensary—9th av. and 36th. Inc. 1852. No charge for medicine and surgical dressings to the worthy poor of the district bounded by 23d to 59th and 5th av. to Hudson River. S. W. Fairchild, Pres.; Dr. H. C. Hanscom, Phy.-in-Charge.

Nursery and Child's Hosp.—Inc. 1854.—(See N. Y. Nursery and Child's Hosp.)

Old Marion St. Maternity Hosp.—Inc. 1827. —(See N. Y. Nursery and Child's Hosp.).

Oppenheimer Inst.—60 E. 67th. Medical treatment of persons addicted to alcohol or drugs. F. H. Miesse, Sec.; W. P. Youngs, Mgr. Dir.

Paralytic Hosp.—See City Hosp.

Park Hosp. (formerly N. Y. Red Cross Hosp and Training School)—395 Central Park W. Inc. 1902. Non-sec. Allen Wardwell, Pres.; Marjorie V. Thompson, Supt.

Pasteur Inst.—(See N. Y. Bacteriological Inst.

People's Hosp.—203 2d av. Est. 1907. 2,000 inmates. 10,000 prescriptions. J. Goldman, Pres.; W. I. Sirovich, M.D., Supt.

Post-Graduate Hosp.—See N. Y. Post-Graduate Hosp.

Presbyterian Hosp.—41 E. 70th. Inc. 1868. 4,734 patients; 18,156 out patients. Out Patients Dept. cares for outdoor patients who are residents of N. Y. C. School of Nursing and Registry for Nurses. Wm. Sloane, Pres.; C. H. Young, M.D., Supt.

Riverside Hosp. (Dept. of Health), North Brother Island—Est. 1885. 600 inmates. For infectious diseases, including tuberculosis, city. Dr. Thos. F. Joyce, Hosp. Phy.

Rockefeller Inst.—E. 66th and Av. A. Est. 1901. Research for prevention and treatment of disease. Dr. Simon Flexner, Dir. Inst.; R. Cole, M.D., Dir. Hosp.; Nancy P. Ellicott, Supt; E. B. Smith, Bus. Mgr.

Roosevelt Hosp.—58th and 59th, 9th and 10th avs. Inc. 1864. A notable feature is the Syms operating building for aseptic treatment of operative cases and large open air wards for the fresh air treatment of medical cases. Patients cared for in hosp., 5,472; 34,614 persons assisted. W. E. Roosevelt, Pres.; C. B. Grimshaw, Supt. Maintains an Outdoor Dept. Visiting days, Su., Wed., Fri., 1 to 2 P.M.

St. Andrew's Convalescent Hosp.—237 E. 17th. Est. 1886. For women and girls recovering from illness, etc. In charge of Sisterhood of St. John the Baptist (P. E.). W. M. Barnum, Pres.; C. L. Kingsley, Treas., 55 Liberty.

St. Ann's Maternity—130 E. 69th. Est. 1869. 359 patients. Connected with N. Y. Foundling Hosp.; receives both pay and free patients. Sister Anna Michella, Dir.

St. Bartholomew's Clinic—215 E. 42d. Est. 1890. Medical and surgical treatment to poor. 51,129 persons treated; 20,173 prescriptions. Rev. L. Parks, Pres.; J. W. Fiske, Gen. Mgr.

St. Elizabeth's Home for Convalescent Women—Office, 375 Lafayette. Founded and maintained by Soc. of St. Vincent de Paul. Home situated at Spring Valley, N. Y. J. F. Boyle, Pres. Sisters of Mercy in charge of home.

St. Elizabeth's Hosp.—415 W. 51st. Inc. 1870. 65 beds. In charge of Sisters of St. Francis. Visiting days, every afternoon, 2:30-3:30, and evening, 6:30-7:30. Mother M. Celso, Supt.

St. Francis' Home of Sisters of Poor of St. Francis—609 5th. Org. 1865. Home for aged, suffering from chronic diseases. Cap., 305. Sister Gonzaga, Supt.

St. Gregory Hospital—See Volunteer Hosp.

St. Joseph's Asyl. Blind Girls under 14.—See Charitable Institutions, Richmond Borough.

St. Luke's Hosp. (Prot. Epis.)—Cathedral Hgts., 113th and Amsterdam av. Inc. 1850. 380 beds. 8,109 inmates; 29,737 persons aided; number of days of treatment accorded patients, 122,759. Prescriptions given, 77,079. C. H. Russell, Pres.; G. F. Clover, Supt.; G. Blagden, Sec.; W. P. Bliss, Treas., 71 B'way.

St. Mark's Hosp.—175 2d av. Inc. 1890. Non-sec. No contagious diseases admitted. Visiting days Wed. and Su. Dr. B. T. Tilton, Pres.; E. F. Lohr, Supt.

St. Mary's Free Hosp. for Children—405-411 W. 34th. Org. 1870. For treatment of sick, maimed and crippled children, from 2 to 14 yrs. 2,331 patients during year. Conducted by Episcopal Sisterhood of St. Mary. Sister Catharine, Sister Supt. Children's Dispensary, 435 9th av. 13,543 treatments given. Noyes Memorial Home, Peekskill, for convalescent patients. Summer Branch, Norwalk, Conn., for convalescents. Visiting days, Th., 11-12 A.M.; Su., 3-4 P.M.

St. Rose's Home for Cancer—71 Jackson, Mhtn., and Rosary Hill Home, Hawthorne, N. Y. Est. 1899. For destitute men and women. Under charge of Dominican Sisters, but is non-sec. Visiting days, in city, Th. and Su.; in country, any day. Mother M. Alphonsa Lathrop, O.S.D., and Mother M. Rose Huber, O.S.D., Supt.

St. Vincent's Hosp.—11th and 12th and 7th av. Org. 1849—For poor of both sexes. 365 beds. Patients, 6,000. Out patient dept. open daily, 2-4 P.M. Ambulance service. In charge of Sisters of Charity of St. Vincent de Paul. Visiting days, Tu., Fri. and Su., 3-5 P.M. Training Sch. for Nurses. Sister Clement Maria, Supt.

Seaside Hosp. for Children of St. John's Guild—See Relief of Children.

Sloane Hosp. for Women—Est. 1888. 447 W. 59th. An obstetrical and gynecological hospital, with 107 obstetrical ward beds, 17 obstetrical private beds, 100 cribs, 24 gynecological ward beds and 21 gynecological private beds. Dr. W. Ward, Pres.; Dr. S. Swift, Res. Phys.

Soc. of the Lying-in Hosp.—17th and 18th and 2d av. Org. 1798. Sub-station, 314 Broome. Capacity of Hosp., including Private Patients' Pavilion, 155 beds. Admitted to Hosp., 3,161. Outdoor Dept., 1,997 patients cared for. L. C. Ledyard, Pres.; Dr. W. H. Spiller, Supt.

Stuyvesant Polyclinic (Dispensary)—137 2d av. Inc. 1883. Free treatment of sick poor. 41,426 persons assisted; 40,304 prescriptions. Dr. H. J. Boldt, Pres.; Dr. C. Pfister, Sec.

Sydenham Hosp.—Est. 1892. 343 E. 116th. Medical care for all needy sick. 1,782 patients cared for; 18,883 persons assisted in dispensary; 51,844 prescriptions given. A. W. Kempner, Pres.; Lucas Toch, Supt.

Trinity Dispensary—209 Fulton. Medical and surgical aid to poor. Dr. J. A. Wilson, Phys.-in-Charge.

Tuberculosis Hosp. Admission Bureau—See Miscellaneous.

U. S. Immigrant Hosps.—Ellis Island, N. Y. Harbor. Erected 1900. (a) General Hosp. (b) Contagious Disease Hosp. Care and treatment temporarily of diseased or defective arriving aliens. J. W. Kerr, Chief Med. Officer.

U. S. Public Health Service—Dispensary. 245 Barge Office, So. Ferry. 10,500 admissions to treatment. 7,500 physical examinations for the A. B. Seamen, Masters and Pilots, etc.

Vanderbilt Clinic (Allied with the College of Physicians and Surgeons)—60th, cor. Amsterdam av. Est. 1888. A dispensary for sick poor. Open daily, except Su. and holidays. 32,192 cared for; 161,031 visits of patients to clinic. Dr. W. Darrach, Pres.; F. Miller, Supt.

Volunteer Hosp.—Water and Beekman. 1,105 inmates cared for; 36,006 dispensary patients. Gen. B. Booth, Pres.; E. S. Allen, Supt.

Ward's Island—See Manhattan State Hosp.

West Side Dispensary and Hosp.—328 W. 42d. Inc. 1872. Treatment of poor. Open week days 9 A.M. to 9 P.M. Jas. P. Cahan, Pres.; A. V. Mentz, Supt.

Wilkes Dispensary for Children—435 9th av. Est. 1881. Age limit, 14 yrs. Treatment of sick and crippled children. 17,144 treatments given; 7,379 prescriptions filed. Under charge of Sisters of St. Mary. E. Sutton, Supt.

Willard Parker Hosp.—Est. 1884. Ft. E. 16th. For diphtheria, measles, scarlet fever, whooping cough, mumps. 1,000 beds. E. Giddings, M.D., Res. Phys.

Winifred Masterson Burke Relief Foundation—See Burke Relief Foundation.

Woman's Hosp. in the State of N. Y.—141 W. 109th. Est. 1857. 242 beds. Out Patient Dept. Open daily, except Su. and holidays, 9-10 A.M. and 2-3 P.M. G. L. Winthrop, Pres.; F. J. Shepard, Sec.; F. L. Hine, Treas.; J. V. Norris, Supt.

Women's Rescue and Industrial Home—See Special Relief.

HOSPITALS, HOMES AND SOCIETIES FOR RELIEF—MHTN.—RELIEF OF AGED—*Continued*.

Relief of Aged.

Assn. for Relief of Respectable Aged, Indigent Females in City of N. Y.—104th, cor. Amsterdam av. Inc. 1815. Age over 65. $300 entrance fee. None received who have lived as servants. Acc. 120. Must be residents of Mhtn. or Bronx. Mrs. W. E. Roosevelt, Pres.; Miss B. Potter, Sec., 140 E. 56th.

Baptist Home for Aged—For persons over 65 yrs. 116 E. 68th. Est. 1869. 87 inmates. Mrs. A. M. Hyatt, Pres.; Mrs. F. M. Burr, Sec., Englewood, N. J.; S. B. Detterding, Supt.

Chapin Home for the Aged and Infirm—(See Queens.)

Home for Aged and Infirm Hebrews—(See Jewish Org.)

Home for Old Men and Aged Couples (Prot. Epis.)—112th and Amsterdam av. Inc. 1872. 63 inmates. E. B. Sexton, Pres.; R. P. Kent, Sec., 184 Montague, Bkln.

Home of Daughters of Jacob—(See Jewish Org.)

Homes for the Aged of the Little Sisters of the Poor (both sexes)—Inc. 1871. 213 E. 70th. Sister Marie Josephine de la Croix, Pres.; Sister Agathe de St. Ambroise, Superior, 135 W. 106th. Sister Jeremiah de St. Ann, Superior, E. 183d and Belmont av. Visiting days, Su., Th.

Isabella Home—Amsterdam av., cor. 190th. Est. 1875. Inc. 1889. For men over 65, women 60. Home for aged and sick without regard to creed, sex or nationality. 172 beds. Mrs. A. Woerishoffer, Pres.; Adolf Kuttroff, V.-Pres.; August Zinsser, Jr., Treas.; Mr. and Mrs. C. von Boetticher, Supt. and Matron.

Meth. Epis. Ch. Home—Amsterdam av. and 92d. Est. 1850. For aged members of M. E. churches in N. Y. City. 115 inmates. Mrs. M. K. Robinson, Pres. Emeritus; Mrs. G. Waldo Smith, Pres.; Mrs. J. Pennington, Matron.

N. Y. City Home for Aged and Infirm, Mhtn. Div., including City Home and Neurological Hospitals—Blackwell's Island. Est. 1846. For infirm, destitute adult persons, incurables and diseases of nervous system. Capacity, 2,996. C. B. Cosgrove, Supt.

Presbyterian Home for Aged Women—49 E. 73d. Inc. 1866. Applicants must be residents of N. Y. City, over 65 yrs. of age, members of a Presbyterian or Reformed Dutch Ch. for 3 yrs. Colored persons not received. Acc. 45. Mrs. Jas. E. Ware, 1st Dir.; Miss E. M. Olcott, Sec., 111 W. 13th; Miss Davis, Matron.

Relief for Veteran Soldiers and Sailors—Applications made to Bur. of Investigations, Centre and White, Mhtn.; Arthur and Tremont av., Bronx; 327 Schermerhorn, Bkln.; Town Hall, Flushing; Borough Hall, St. George, S. I. V. S. Dodworth, Dir.; Agnes M. Mulry, Asst. Dir., Municipal Bldg.

St. Joseph's Home for the Aged—209 W. 15th. Org. 1868. Women over 60 yrs. of age. Inmates pay according to accommodations. 240 inmates. In charge of Sisters of Charity of St. Vincent de Paul.

St. Luke's Home for Aged Women (60 yrs. old)—2914 B'way. Est. 1852. Must be communicants P. E. churches of city and Diocese of N. Y. contributing to Home, and residents of city 5 yrs. 84 inmates. Rev. E. M. Stires, D.D., Pres. Bd. of Trustees; W. T. Innes, Treas., 32 E. 20th; Mrs. J. H. Copeland, Matron; Mrs. C. De W. Bridgman, Sec. Bd. of Mgrs.

Samaritan Home for the Aged—414 W. 22d. Inc. 1867. Prot.; both sexes over 65. 32 inmates. Admission fee, $300. Mrs. G. E. Kissel, Pres.; L. F. Fallan, Treas., 49 Wall; Mrs. T. Henscheim, Matron.

Swiss Benevolent Soc.—Org. 1851. Maintains home for aged Swiss of both sexes at 35 W. 67th. 42 permanents. 25 transients. H. Escher, Jr., Pres.; C. A. Challendes, Supt.

Trinity Chapel Home—1666 Bussing av. Org. 1865. For poor aged women, communicants of any P. E. parish in Mhtn. or Bronx, over 60 yrs. Rev. J. Wilson Sutton, Pres.

Trustees of the Home for Aged Women of the Church of the Holy Communion—See "Soc. of St. Johnland," under L. I. Charitable Soc.

Relief of Children.

Abigail Free Sch. and Kindergarten—15 Charles. Org. 1889. Non-sec. Receives free poor children under 7 yrs. of age; gives secular, industrial, religious training, free lunch and evening meal daily. Patriotic meetings for older boys and girls, 4-5:30 P.M. Expended $4,265. Supported by voluntary contributions. 41 average daily kindergarten attendance. Capt. J. H. Barker, Pres., New Rochelle, N. Y.; E. P. Devare Gen. Mgr.

Assn. for Befriending Children and Young Girls—See House of the Holy Family. Special Relief.

Assn. of Day Nurseries of N. Y. City—289 4th av. Org. 1895. For conference and mutual benefit in day nursery work. Mrs. C. Furst Pres.; Miss H. M. Sears, Exec. Sec., 10 A.M. to 4 P.M.; Sat., 10 A.M. to 1 P.M.

Babies' Dairy—416 E. 65th, 523 E. 78th, 511 W. 41st and 342 E. 116th. Org. 1908. Inc. 1911 To supply modified milk to sick infants. R. A Benson, M.D., Phy.-in-Charge; Mrs. J. Clemens, Sec., 10 E. 71st.

Babies' Pure Milk and Health Stations are located throughout Mhtn. and the Bronx. Mncpl. Milk Stas. The baby health stations, formerly conducted by Nathan Straus, are now under supervision of the Bureau of Child Hygiene of the Dept. of Health. For information apply to the Dept. of Health.

Baptist Fresh Air Home Soc.—100 W. 162d Inc. 1892. Conducts Fresh Air Home for Sunday Schl. children and does general fresh air work. R. L. Haring, Pres.

Bethany Day Nursery and Kindergarten—67th and 1st av. Org. 1887. Cares for children under 6 yrs. and provides refuge after school hours for children from 6 to 12 years, whose parents work during day. Average atttendance, 100 Supported by donations. Mrs. J. C. Kerr, Cor. Sec.; Miss E. Clash, Supt.

Beth-El Sisterhood—See Jewish Org.

Bethlehem Day Nursery of Church of Incarnation—249 E. 30th. Inc. 1885. For infants and children from 1 week to 7 yrs. of age, of working women who pay 10c. a day for each child. 15,000 children cared for. Miss F. A. Smith, Pres.; Mrs. J. J. Riker, Treas., 110 E. 37th.

Big Brother Movement—200 5th av. 1904. 492 mem. F. C. Hoyt, Pres.; C. A. Taussig, Sec.; R. C. Sheldon, Gen. Sec.

Bloomingdale Day Nursery—62 W. 97th. Org. 1894. Care of children, from 2 months to 7 yrs. of working mothers, who pay 15c. daily for widows, 25c. daily when father and mother are both working, for each child. 75 children cared for daily. Mrs. W. H. Browning, Pres.; Mrs. C. E. Lilley, Matron.

Boys' Club (The)—161 Av. A. Org. 1876. Training for citizenship through athletics, debating, music, movies and literary work. Mem. 7,000. Non-sec. Open all day and evenings. H. S. Brooks, Sec., 195 B'way; C. Wheeler, Dir.

Boys' Club Org. and Aid Soc.—489 5th av. Inc. 1910. For industrial, moral and physical betterment of boys and girls. Boys and girls helped, about 6,000 annually. Rev. W. E. Steckel, Pres.; J. L. Dudley, Sec.; A. C. Kenyon, Supt.

Brightside Day Nursery and Kindergarten—See Jewish Org.

Bryson Day Nursery—149 Av. B. Inc. 1898. For care of children 1 month to 7 yrs. old; 10c. per day charged for each child. Classes daily, 9-12 A.M., 1-4 P.M. Mrs. W. B. James, Pres.; Mrs. H. P. Robbins, Sec., 19 E. 80th; Florence D. Solliday, Supt.

Catharine Mission Day Nursery and Kindergarten—22 Catharine sl. Org. 1888. About 100 children cared for daily. Gospel service every evening. Mothers' meeting Wednesday afternoon. Bible classes and Sunday School. 2:30 P.M. Free med. treatment for women and children. Free reading room. Industrial classes. Miss M. A. Delaney, Supt.; Dr. L. Delaney-Barbour, Res. Phys.

Catholic Guardian Soc.—139 E. 17th. Inc. 1913. Looks after children discharged from the Catholic Institutions and maintains a free Employment Bureau and a temporary shelter for these children. Archbishop Hayes, Pres.; Rev. S. Ludlow, Exec. Sec.

Catholic Home Bureau for Dependent Children—289 4th av. Inc. 1899. Places annually about 200 Catholic dependent children in free foster family homes. J. J. Deery, Pres.; Wm. C. Daly, Sec.; E. J. Butler, Exec. Sec.

Cheering Circle of King's Daughters—Bronx, N. Y. City. Org. 1888. For fresh air work among children. Mrs. S. A. Carman, Pres.; Mrs. F. M. Squires, Sec., 311 E. 201st.

Children's Aid Soc.—United Charities Bldg., 105 E. 22d. Org. 1853. W. C. Osborn, Pres.; E. G. Merrill, Treas.; C. L. Brace, Sec. For education

HOSPITALS, HOMES AND SOCIETIES FOR RELIEF—MHTN.—RELIEF OF CHILDREN—*Continued.*

of poor children, caring for boys and girls in lodging houses, and procuring homes in rural districts and in the West. Has provided with homes and places of employment since its organization some 75,000 boys and girls. At industrial schools upward of 8,000 poor children have received aid and instruction. Dental clinics have been established in 5 industrial schools. 1,100 children were treated during the year. The work of the society includes the lodging houses for boys and girls located as follows: Brace Memorial, or Newsboys, for Boys, 14 New Chambers, W. L. Butcher, Supt.; Elizabeth Home for Girls, 307 E. 12th, Mrs. J. G. Colby, Matron; 44th St., for Boys, 247 E. 44th, A. Huck, Supt.; Shelter for Women and Children, 311 E. 12th. Mrs. J. G. Colby, Matron. Also 10 day and 8 eve. industrial schools for which see Kindergarten. Maintains the following:

Emergency Shelter for Women and Children—311 E. 12th. Affords evicted and homeless women and children temporary shelter for a night or two, or longer if warranted by circumstances, until another place of abode can be established. Mrs. J. G. Colby, Matron.

Summer Charities: Children's Summer Home and Haxtum Cottage for Crippled Girls at Bath Beach; Health Home, at West Coney Island, for mothers and sick children. Home for convalescent children, Chappaqua, N. Y. Boys' Camps at Valhalla, N. Y., and at the Goodhue Home, West New Brighton, S. I. Martha Summer Home, Ossining, N. Y. Goodhue Home, S. I., for under-developed and convalescent boys.

Sick Children's Mission—7 branch stations, with physicians and nurses who visit sick poor at their homes with supplies and free medical attendance. Hdqtrs., 136 E. 127th. C. R. Conklin, Dir.

Emigration and Placing Out Office, for providing homeless children with homes in the West—105 E. 22d. Open 9 A.M. to 5 P.M. Poor families having friends or prospect of work in any part of the country assisted with transportation. R. N. Brace, Supt., 105 E. 22d. Maintains supplementary to its industrial schools the following: Brace Farm Training School, Valhalla, N. Y. For giving street boys instruction in agricultural pursuits preparatory to placing them in country homes. Wm. Wood, Supt.

Children's Clinic, Dental Dept. of Health—343 Pleasant av. Dr. S. Streim and Anna Moore, R.N.

Crippled Children's East Side Free Sch.—155 Henry, and Oakhurst, N. J. Non-sec. Est. 1901. To improve physical condition of and educate crippled children so as to render them self-supporting. 200 pupils. Mrs. A. Lehman, Pres.; Mrs. Harry Goldsmith, Cor. Sec., 333 W. 76th; Mrs. S. Landman, Supt.

Darrach Home for Crippled Children—118 W. 104th. Est. 1889. Home for friendless crippled children. 16 inmates. Mrs. N. M. Pond, Pres.; Mrs. W. L. Baner, Sec., 40 W. 68th; Miss J. K. O'Leary, Matron.

Day Nursery for Babies of Office Cleaners—120 Cedar. Miss S. E. Miler, Matron.

Dobbs House—512 E. 87th. Maintain all-year-round Polly Platt Library for juniors and small children. Neighborhood playground for school children. Child welfare station. Miss F. G. Benjamin, Pres.; Mrs. A. W. Francis, Vice-Pres.

Dominican Convent of Our Lady of the Rosary—329 E. 63d. Est. 1876. Under care Cath. Ch. Cares for and trains destitute children from 2-16 yrs., committed by magistrates. 1,000 inmates. Superioress, Mother M. Thomas, Pres.; Sr. M. Benvenuta, Sec.

Down Town Day Nursery—120 Cedar. Org. 1903. 50 children cared for daily. Mrs. H. Harriman, Pres.; Miss S. E. Miles, Supt.

East Side Day Nursery—See Jewish Org.

Five Points House of Industry—Office, 454 W. 23d. Cottage colony, Pomona, N. Y. Est. 1850. Cares for destitute children from 2-16 yrs. T. T. Wells, Pres.; C. B. Boorom, Supt.

Free Home for Young Girls—318 Mosholu Parkway. Est. 1867. Inc. 1879. Home and Training Sch. for young girls for self-support, bet. ages of 12 and 18. 27 inmates. Mrs. E. R. Adee, Pres.; Mrs. Geo. Cole, Supt.

Free Industrial Sch. for Crippled Children—471 W. 57th. Supported by annual dues of members and voluntary contributions. 60 children average daily attendance. They are conveyed to and from their homes in an auto bus. All crippled children admitted. Public school educational advantages. Manual training is a special feature. Nurses and physicians in attendance. Braces and all orthopedic appliances are supplied without charge. These are children debarred from public schools because of a physical disability. W. Scott, Pres.; Mrs. E. D. Jones, Treas. Summer Home of this Soc. is called the Lulu Thorley Lyons Home for Crippled and Delicate Children, at Claverack, N. Y. Open during months of June, July and Aug. for reception of crippled children of city school.

God's Providence House—330 Broome. Est. 1895. Under care P. E. Church. Kindergarten, day nursery, settlement work. 17,430 children cared for. Rev. L. E. Sunderland, Supt.; Miss E. R. Hopkins, Head Worker.

Grace Church Day Nursery—94 4th av. (Prot. Epis.) Est. 1878. For children 1 mo. to 12 yrs. of working women. Kindergarten instruction. Daily average, 85. Open 7 A.M. to 6:30 P.M. Mrs. Thos. Folsom, Pres.; Deaconess, J. L. Gardner, House Mother.

Guild of the Infant Saviour—Room 418, 105 E. 22d. Org. 1900. Inc. 1901. Co-operates with maternity and foundling hospitals, obtains temporary shelter for destitute mothers with infants, upon discharge from these institutions, secures employment for them, preferably in the country. Mrs. R. McGinnis, Pres.; Mrs. T. S. O'Brien, Sec.

Halsey Day Nursery of St. Thomas' P. E. Ch.—227 E. 59th. 1897. Cares for children 4 weeks to 9 yrs. of age. Kindergarten instruction and care of school children. Annual attendance, 21,102. Mrs. Ira Barrons, Pres., 521 Park av.; Miss M. W. Ferris, Supt.

Hebrew Day Nursery—See Jewish Org.

Hebrew Infant Asylum—See Jewish Org.

Hebrew Orphan Asylum of the City of N. Y.—See Jewish Org.

Holy Family's Day Nursery—252 E. 112th. In charge of Sisters of Pious Soc. of Missions. To care for children whose parents go out to work. 150 cared for. Sister Mary Matilde, Superior.

Home Garden of N. Y. City—See Settlements.

Howard Mission and Home for Little Wanderers—225 E. 11th. Inc. 1864. To aid poor neglected children and to provide permanent homes. J. F. Havemeyer, Pres.; H. L. McGee, Sec. and Treas.; Miss Jennie Hudson, Supt.

Inst. for Improved Instruction of Deaf Mutes—904-922 Lex. av. Org. 1867. Education of deaf by oral method. Pupils able to pay are charged $450 per annum; others free. 250 pupils. F. H. Levy, Pres.; H. Taylor, Supt. and Prin.

Internatl. Sunshine Soc., Blind Babies' Dept.—96 5th av. Org. 1896. Mrs. John Alden, Pres. Gen.; Mrs. Nellie E. C. Furman, Sec.; Mrs. A. O. Buck, Treas. Nursery and Kindergarten, 84th and 13th av., Bkln. Arthur Home, Hosp. and Kindergarten, Pine Grove av., Summit, N. J. Mrs. Minnie J. Force, Sec.

Jewell Day Nursery—20 Macdougal. For children 6 wks. to 7 yrs. of women who must support themselves. Mrs. A. M. Dodge, Pres., 563 Park av.; Miss E. V. Miles, Supt.

Kip's Bay Day Nursery—402 E. 50th. Org. 1902. For care of children under 6, whose mothers are the breadwinners of family. Mrs. W. G. Borland, Pres.; Miss E. Billings, Sec., 279 Madison av.; Miss A. L. Gifford, Supt.

Lisa Day Nursery (1894)—458 W. 20th. Care and instruction of children under 7 yrs. Miss S. A. Moller, Pres.; Miss O. Elliott, Matron.

Little Missionaries Day Nursery—93 St. Marks pl. Org. 1896. For children under 15 yrs. Voluntary contributions. 150 daily. L. H. Rolston, Pres.; D. M. Torrey, Sec. and Treas.; Miss S. Curry, Mgr.

"Little Mothers'" Aid Assn. (The)—236 2d av. Est. 1890. Has no salaried officers. Supported by voluntary contributions. Gives summer outings, practical instruction in domestic hygiene (including care of infants), cooking, sewing, cleanliness and kindness to children who have care of younger ones while their mothers are at work. The Homemaking Circles are at 236 2d av., 66 Greenwich; Loving Arms Nursery, 746 11th av., Mhtn.; also supported by Brooklyn Auxiliary at 41 Rush, Bkln. Mrs. C. Burns, Pres.; Mrs. G. Henry Roesl, Bkln., Aux. Ch.; M. L. Hawkins, Sec. Has 4 day nurseries.

HOSPITALS, HOMES AND SOCIETIES FOR RELIEF—MHTN.—RELIEF OF CHILDREN—*Continued.*

Madonna Day Nursery—178 Cherry. Est. 1910. 2 mo. to 12 yrs. Provides a day home for children of working mothers (R. C.). Inmates cared for, 100. Sister Marianne, Supt.

Mary F. Walton Assn.—Lincoln House (Branch of Henry St. Settlement). Est. 1895. For free education of colored children from 3-6 yrs. Miss K. W. Sewall, Treas., 29 E. 77th.

Masters Sch. Day Nursery—519 E. 86th. Accommodates 100 children. School children's lunch supplied. Supports Neighborhood House, 512 E. 87th. Library for juniors, daily clubs and classes, mothers' club and a health station twice weekly for babies and pre-school age children. Doctor and trained nurse in attendance. Miss F. G. Benjamin, Pres.; Mrs. A. W. Francis, V.-Pres.; Miss M. J. MacKay, Dir.

Milk Stations—See Babies' Pure Milk and Health Stations.

Mission of the Immaculate Virgin for the Protection of Homeless and Destitute Children—381 Lafayette. Branches: Mt. Loretto, S. I., home for 2,000 orphan boys and girls, 4-14 yrs.; St. Benedict's Home, Rye, N. Y.; Home for Colored Orphan Boys and Girls. Most Rev. P. J. Hayes, Pres.; Rev. M. J. Fitzpatrick, Rector. Res., 381 Lafayette, Mhtn.

Nazareth Nursery—214 W. 15th. Bet. 40 and 50 children are received daily while their mothers work. Sisters of St. Francis in charge. Sister M. Liguori, Superior.

N. Y. Child Welfare Com.—70 5th av. Investigates conditions affecting child life in city and works to improve them. R. Van Iderstine, Pres.; F. C. Myers, Exec. Sec.

N. Y. Foundling Hosp.—See Hospitals, Mhtn.

N. Y. Inst. for Instruction of Deaf and Dumb (Free)—See Colleges and Academies.

N. Y. Milk Com.—1906. 30 Broad, Rm. 1505. Object: Impt. of milk supply and reduction of infant mortality. S. G. Williams, Ch.; M. F. Ray, Sec.

N. Y. Nursery and Child's Hosp.—See Hospitals.

N. Y. Soc. for Prevention of Cruelty to Children—51 Irving pl. Inc. 1875. In 1919, 18.169 complaints received and investigated. J. D. Lindsay, Pres.; E. K. Coulter, Gen. Mgr.

Orphans Home and Asylum of P. E. Church in N. Y.—Convent av. and 135th. Inc. 1859. Cares for orphans and half-orphans; boys from 3-8 yrs. and girls from 3-8 yrs. Summer home, Beacon, N. Y. 110 inmates. Mrs. B. K. Stevens, Pres.; Mrs. R. E. Jones, Sec., 611 W. 112th; Rev. James Sheerin, Supt.

People's Univ. Extension Soc. of N. Y.—1425 B'way. Est. 1898. Teaching self-help to poor mothers and children, including cripples, blind and mental defectives, by means of free classes in manual training, domestic economy, corrective physical tr., hygiene, sanitation, etc. R. Johnson, Pres.; J. E. Whitney, Sec.

Presentation Day Nursery—228-230 E. 32d. 1905. Children 2 wks. to 14 yrs., of poor working mothers. Employment bureau for the mothers. Has night shelter and settlement for children of poor mothers in hospitals. Fresh air outings and day excursions. Rt. Rev. Bishop Hayes, Pres.; Miss H. N. Murphy, Directress.

Riverside Day Nursery—149 W. 63d. Org. 1887. Children 3 mos. to 8 yrs. of age of working women. Mrs. A. L. Gardiner, Pres.; B. A. Jackson, Treas., 254 W. 73d.

Roman Catholic Orphan Asylum—Office, 24 E. 52d. Org. 1817. Inc. 1852. Boys' and Girls' Asylum, Sedgwick av. and Kingsbridge rd., Bronx, in which orphan children bet. 4 and 10 yrs. of age are received. 1,000 inmates. Most Rev. Patrick J. Hayes, Pres.; Francis O'Neill, Sec.; E. J. Quin, Gen. Agt.

St. Agnes' Nursery—7 Charles. Inc. 1890. Care of children by the day of working mothers. Mrs. R. R. Livingston, Pres.; Mrs. J. Stovesend, Supt.

St. Ann's Day Nursery, Parish of Our Lady of Good Counsel—240 E. 90th. Care of children of working mothers. Average 30 daily. Rt. Rev. J. N. Connolly, Rector; Miss N. Hennessy, in charge.

St. Barnabas' House of the N. Y. P. E. City Mission Soc.—See Special Relief.

St. George's Evening Trade Sch.—Now operated by the N. Y. Assn. for Improving the Condition of the Poor.

St. John's Guild—Office, 103 Park av. Org. 1866. Free relief to sick poor children. Maintains a floating hospital, seaside hospital. 39,000 cared for during year. D. G. Maynard, Pres.; J. L. Seligman, Sec.; D. Olcott, 2d, Treas.; L. F. Hayden, Gen. Agt.

Floating Hospital of St. John's Guild—Daily in summer carries 1,200 persons—mothers with **sick children—on week days for 26 miles of sailing; provides medical treatment with hospital care. Hot and cold salt water bathing. Provides the midday meal and sterilized milk morning and afternoon for young children.** Number of beneficiaries received during the summer of 1919, 33,000. L. F. Hayden, Gen. Agt.

The Floating Hospital makes trips to the Lower Bay for the benefit of sick poor children July and Aug., and to Seaside Hospital for Children, Cedar Grove, New Dorp, S. I., which is open for medical and surgical care for sick babies, from June 1-Oct. 1.

Seaside Hosp. of St. John's Guild—New **Dorp, S. I. Receives dangerously sick babies** with their mothers, from June 1-Oct. 1. 375 **beds. No contagious diseases admitted. D. G. Maynard, Pres.**

St. Joseph's Day Nursery—469 W. 57th. 1890. Children from 2 mos. to 12 yrs. Attendance, 80 daily. Has free employment bureau for domestic help. J. J. Cunningham, Pres.; W. H. Carr, Sec.

St. Michael's Home for Destitute Children—See Charitable Institutions, Richmond.

St. Vincent de Paul, Asylum of—215 W. 39th. Inc. 1868. Under auspices of Church of St. Vincent de Paul. Age 4 yrs. and up. 180 inmates. Has Fresh Air Fund for sending children to seaside in summer. Under charge of Sisters Marianites of Holy Cross. Very Rev. T. Wucher, S.P.M., Pres.; L. H. de Milhau, Treas., 2 Rector; Mother Mary of St. Timothy, Supt.

St. Vincent de Paul Day Nursery and Sch.—69 S. Washington sq. 10 mo. to 16 yrs. 300 inmates. St. Vincent de Paul's Villa, Sea Cliff, L. I. Summer Home for children of day nursery. School, 200 children; Kindergarten, 75; Nursery, 18. Mrs. Alfred Chapin, Pres.; Sr. Mary of St. Irene, in charge.

St. Vincent de Paul Summer Home Office, 216 W. 15th. Founded and maintained by Soc. of **St. Vincent de Paul. Home situated at Spring** Valley, N. Y. Cap. 350. Offers to poor Roman **Catholic children, from 5-12 yrs. of City of N. Y., a 2-weeks' vacation during summer months. Sisters of Mercy charge of home.**

Salvation Army Slum Day Nurseries—94 Cherry. 24.058 children cared for during year. Jennie R. Ward, Staff-Capt.

Sanitarium for Hebrew Children—See Jewish Org.

Santa Claus Assn.—387 4th av. Inc. 1913. **Purveyors of Christmas spirit. Letters gathered from post office written to Santa Claus by poor children. Letters turned over to volunteers who will attend to one case personally. 36,000 children reached Dec., 1915. Supported** by public subscription. J. D. Gluck, Pres.

Sheltering Arms—504 W. 129th. Inc. 1864. Temporary home for children 6-12 yrs. Acc. 180 children. W. R. Peters, Pres.; Mrs. A. S. Page, Supt.

Silver Cross Day Nursery—249 E. 117th. Est. 1890. 25,000 children cared for under 12 yrs. Mrs. S. E. Clendenning, Pres.; Mrs. E. M. Baxter, Supt.

Soc. for Ethical Culture, Children's Canteen Federation for Child Study—33 Central Pk. W. 1918. 1,131 children cared for. Mrs. H. S. Gans, Pres.; Winifred S. Gibbs, Dietician.

Soc. for the Relief of Half-Orphans and Destitute Children—110 Manhattan av. Relief of half-orphans and destitute children, 4-10 yrs. Est. 1835. Present number, 165. Cap. 165. Miss E. O. Butler, Pres.; Mrs. J. R. Wheeler, Sec., 433 W. 117th; Miss A. De Yoe, Supt.

Sunbeam Day Nursery of Fifth Av. Pres. Ch—1147 1st av. Org. 1896. Children 2 wks. to 6 yrs. Average attendance, 59. Mrs. Marshall, Pres.; Miss M. A. Powell, Matron.

Sunnyside Day Nursery—221 E. 104th. Org. 1882. Care of children from 2 mos. to 6 yrs. of poor working mothers. 24,315 children cared for. Mrs. G. E. Kissel, Pres.; Miss B. Pratt, Sec.; Miss L. Lawrence, Supt.

Tribune Fresh Air Fund—154 **Nassau. Org. 1877. Inc. 1888. Provides free country outings** for poor children 5-16 yrs., for a fortnight during summer. An average of 9,500 children are sent into country for 2 wks. each yr., including a large number from Bkln. Bor. O. M. Reid, Pres.; L. M. Conly, Mgr.

Tuberculosis Preventorium for Children—105 E. 22d. Org. 1909. To prevent the development and spread of tuberculosis, primarily among children. A. F. Hess, M.D., Pres.; M. M. Mann, Sec.

United Relief Work of the Soc. for Ethical Culture—See Special Relief.

Virginia Day Nursery of the Woman's Branch of the N. Y. City Mission Soc.—Open 7 A.M. to 6:30 P.M. 632 E. 5th. Average attendance, 89. Mrs. S. Sloan, Pres.; Mrs. G. R. Getman, Supt. and Matron.

Washington Heights Day Nursery—See St. Vincent de Paul Day Nursery.

Wayside Day Nursery—216 E. 20th. Org. 1883. Average 56 children daily. Cares for children while mothers work. Mrs. W. H. Geishenen, Pres., 375 Park av.; Miss A. Chawner, Matron.

West Side Day Nursery, Industrial Sch. and Kindergarten—264-266 W. 40th. Org. 1883. Children under 14 yrs.; cares for young children of working mothers, and teaches the older girls industrial work. Inmates of nursery, 13,126; industrial schl., 3,005. Mrs. C. S. Smith, Pres.; Miss M. C. Phelps, Sec.; Mrs. E. A. Pratt, Supt.

Winifred Wheeler Day Nursery and Kindergarten of the East Side Settlement House—540 E. 76th. Est. 1891. For the day care of children from 2 wks. to 7 yrs., while their mothers work. 100 children. Mr. R. S. Pierrepont, Pres.; Gertrude Ferguson, R. N.

Special Relief.

Actors' Fund of Amer.—701 7th av. Org. 1882. Provides assistance for disabled and needy members of theatrical profession and burial for such as leave no means therefor. Actors' Fund Home, W. New Brighton, S. I.; opened 1902. Daniel Frohman, Pres.; Sam A. Scribner, Treas.; Gus Hill, Sec.; W. C. Austin, Asst. Sec.

Agency for Assisting and Providing Situations for Destitute Mothers with Infants—Est. 1893. 745 situations provided last yr. Arrangements made for expectant mothers. Convalescent care arranged for young mothers leaving maternity hosps. Expenses about $22,000 annually. Homer Folks, Sec.; Miss H. C. Butler, Treas.; Miss M. R. Mason, Supt., 105 E. 22d.

Amelia Relief Soc.—See Settlements.

Amer. Red Cross—N. Y. Co. Chapter, 119 W. 40th. Mr. J. H. Perkins, Ch.; W. K. Draper, Vice-Ch.; J. B. Moore, Sec.; M. N. Buckner, Treas.

Amer. Seamen's Friend Soc.—Inc. 1833. 76 Wall. Natl. Soc. for Seamen. Object: To improve the social and religious condition of seamen. Chaplains and Institutes in leading seaports of this and foreign countries. Provides libraries for out-going vessels. Publishes Sailor's Magazine. Maintains Sailors Home and Institute, with accommodations for officers and seamen, games and reading rooms, 507 West. Rev. J. B. Calvert, D.D., Pres.; Rev. G. S. Webster, D.D., Sec.; Clarence C. Pinneo, Treas.

Amer. Committee for Devastated France—(See War Relief Socs.)

Armenian Colonial Assn.—265 Lexington av. Org. 1910. To help Armenians to become good citizens of the U. S. Rev. H. G. Benneyan, Dir.

Army and Navy Dept. of Internatl. Committee Y. M. C. A., 347 Madison av. To provide soldiers and sailors as many social, educational, physical and religious privileges as possible. W. Sloane, Ch.; J. S. Tichenor, F. A. McCarl and Bert C. Pond, Secs.; B. H. Fancher, Treas.

Army Relief Soc.—275 Lexington av. Org. 1900. Relief of orphans and widows of officers and enlisted men of Regular Army. Mrs. Henry L. Stimson, Pres.; Miss E. Lamont, Cor. Sec.; C. R. Agnew, Treas., 16 William.

Assn. of Catholic Charities (Ladies of Charity)—667 Lexington av. For promotion of Cath. activities and social welfare work. Twenty-one standing committees. Miss G. Iselin, Pres.; Miss T. R. O'Donohue, Sec.

Baron de Hirsch Fund—See Jewish Org.

Belgian Bureau—429-431 W. 47th, Mhtn. Relief of Belgian Immigrants and gen. welfare of Belgians. Rt. Rev. J. F. Stillemans, Dir.

Belgian Soc. of Benevolence—431 W. 47th. Est. 1869. Relieves indigent Belgians. Supported by subscriptions. L. Hagenaers, Pres.; Rev. O. A. Nys, Sec.; O. G. Schovaers, Treas.

Beth-El Sisterhood—See United Hebrew Charities.

Bible and Fruit Mission to Public Hosps. of N. Y. City (Inc.) Org. 1878. To minister spiritually and physically to patients in our public hospitals. Rev. J. F. Talcott, Treas., 16 E. 66th.

Blind Babies—International Sunshine Home for Blind Babies. Maintained by Intl. Sunshine Br. for the Blind, 84th st. and 13th av., Dyker Heights, Bkln. Mrs. Grace Macmillan, Supt.

Blind Men's Imp. Club of N. Y.—1906. 111 E. 59th. W. I. Scandlin, Pres.; L. J. Furman, Sec.

Blodgett Memorial Country Home Assn.—Conducted by Bd. of Trustees from Grace Emmanuel Church and Vestry of Holy Trinity Church jointly. For temporary care and culture of children and persons who may be in need of the country and rest. Rev. Wm. K. McGown, Pres.; Rev. H. P. Nichols, D.D., Ch. of Bd. of Trustees. Office, 213 E. 115th.

Blue Anchor Soc.—105 E. 22d. Org. 1880. Relief to rescued from shipwrecks; supplies coast guard or lifesaving stations throughout U. S. under Govt. requisition with clothing. Mrs. F. T. Hume, Pres.; Mrs. E. L. Young, Treas.

Brace Memorial Newsboys' House—244 William. Est. 1854. Number boys cared for, 1,936; lodgings furnished, 32,747; meals furnished, 65,343; 1,854 boys provided employment; 1,027 boys sent to Army and Navy; boys in U. S. Service, 5,460; runaways returned to parents, 325; taken from court, 104; 469 boys registered in Neighborhood and House clubs. Aggregate attendance, 102,233. Wm. C. Osborne, Pres.; C. L. Brace, Sec.; Wm. L. Butcher, Supt.

Charity Fund of the Chamber of Commerce—65 Liberty. Org. 1883. Consists of $60,000, bequeathed by J. C. Green and $150,000 bequeathed by Amos R. Eno, the income of which is applied to relief of distressed merchant members of the Chamber. C. T. Gwynne, Sec.

Charity Organization Soc.—Org. 1882. Central office, 105 E. 22d. Objects: To be a center of inter-communication bet. various churches and charitable agencies; foster harmonious co-operation and check evils of overlapping of relief; investigate cases referred for inquiry; provide visitors to attend cases; obtain relief for suitable cases; procure work for poor; promote social and sanitary reforms.

Officers of Central Council—R. W. deForest, Pres.; O. T. Bannard, V.-Pres.; H. T. White, Treas.; Lawson Purdy, Sec. and Gen. Dir.

Ex-officio members: The Mayor, Comm. of Police, Comm. of Health, Comm. of Public Welfare, Comm. of Correction, U. S. Comm. of Immigration, Comm. Tenement House Dept., Pres. of N. Y. Assn. Improving Condition of Poor; J. A. McKim, representing State Charities Aid Assn.; Prof. Samuel McCune Lindsay, representing Columbia University. Supported by voluntary contributions and legacies. Under the auspices of the society are maintained the following:

Social Service Exch.—A central bureau enabling each of various agencies interested in same family to share in knowledge, experience and plans of the others, with a view to establishing wise co-operation which shall be most helpful to the family.

Registration Bureau, in which the society's records are filed and from which reports are sent to co-operating agencies.

Joint Application Bureau, maintained jointly with the Assn. for Improving the Condition of the Poor, open every day in the year from 9 A.M. to midnight.

Fourteen district offices in charge of the treatment of families under care residing within their respective boundaries.

Laundry—516 W. 28th. Temporary employment and training for women.

Industrial Bldg. and Wood Yard—516 W. 28th. Labor, lodgings and meals provided.

The Society publishes "The Charities Directory," has a Committee on the Prevention of Tuberculosis, a Tenement House Committee, a Committee on Criminal Courts, a Committee on District Work, a Committee on Home Economics, a Bureau of Advice and Information, a Schl. of Social Work.

Christian Aid Assn.—7 Bible House, 4th av. and 9th. Supported by voluntary contributions. Mrs. A. Stanwood, founder, in charge.

Clara de Hirsch Home for Working Girls—225 E. 63d. Est. 1897. 160 residents. To benefit working girls, 14-21 yrs. Clara de Hirsch, Foundation, $400,000. Mrs. O. S. Straus, Pres.; Mrs. Walter Liebman, Sec., 55 E. 82d; Miss R. Sommerfeld, Supt.

HOSPITALS, HOMES AND SOCIETIES FOR RELIEF—MANHATTAN—SPECIAL RELIEF—*Continued.*

Hannah Lavanbury Home—319 E. 17th. Mrs. Oscar Straus, Pres.; Miss Julia Rosenberg, Supt.

Committee on Prevention of Tuberculosis of Charity Org. Soc. of N. Y. City—1902. 105 E. 22d. L. Veiller, Ch.

Consumers' League of City of N. Y.—289 4th av. To ameliorate the conditions of employment of working women and children, and to secure wholesome conditions in production and distribution of goods consumed by public. Miss Amey Aldrich, Pres.

Corporation for Relief of Widows and Children of Clergymen of P. E. Church in State of N. Y.—Inc. 1769. 98 annuities. Rev. E. C. Chorley, D.D., Garrison, N. Y., Sec.; W. Harison, Treas., 43 Cedar.

Council of Jewish Women—See Jewish Org.

Deborah Benevolent Sewing Soc.—See United Hebrew Charities.

East Side Settlement and Neighborhood House—441 E. 123d. For destitute children. Soup kitchen (free) for unemployed. Open all yr. L. B. Elliman, Pres.; H. C. Eva, Supt.; W. R. K. Taylor, Treas., 49 Wall; O. DeL. Coster, Sec.

Emanu-El Sisterhood of Personal Service—See United Hebrew Charities.

Emigrant Mission Committee of the German Evang. Luth. Synod of Mo., Ohio and other States, at N. Y. City—See Lutheran Immigrant Soc.

French Benev. Soc. of N. Y.—450 W. 34th. Org. 1889. Assist needy. Supported by contributions and patients' fees. L. Jouvaud, Pres.; V. Fulchiron, Sec. Maintains relief bureau; general relief. Night refuge; temporary shelter and food. Dispensary; free advice to sick, 5,449 treated; 18,474 consultations. Free medical attendance to indigent French in their homes. Hosp. for sick poor. French indigent patients admitted free.

Friends' Employment Soc.—226 E. 16th. Org. 1862. Inc. 1902. Gives employment in sewing to worthy women. Supported by contributions. E. S. Clarke, Treas., 557 W. 174th; Emily W. Lawton, Sec.

Friends' Home Assn.—To provide home for Friends at moderate cost. G. A. McDowell, Pres., 103 Morningside av.; H. A. Hawkins, Sec., Rutherford, N. J.

German Ladies' Soc. for Relief of Destitute Widows, Orphans and Sick Persons—Org. 1844. Inc. 1860. Supported by donations and permanent fund. 3,400 cases relieved. Miss M. Schurz, Pres., 565 Park av.

German Soc. of City of N. Y.—147 4th av. Org. 1784. Inc. 1804. Gives medical advice and general relief to needy German immigrants and their descendants. Families assisted, 2,328; individuals, 608; patients treated by phys., 810. H. C. Kudlich, Pres.; A. Bossert, Mgr.

Girls' Friendly Soc. Lodge—155 E. 54th. Est. 1908. To provide a home for working girls at moderate cost. Mrs. H. M. Beers, House Mother.

Golden Rule Alliance of Amer.—75 5th av Engaged in general charitable work and helping blind and working girls. M. F. Holman, Sec.

Grace House in the Fields. Summer Home of Grace P. E. Ch., Mhtn.—New Canaan, Conn. Vacation to mothers, children and working girls. C. L. Slattery, Rector.

Grace Institute—149 W. 60th. Inc. 1897. Endowed by W. R. Grace. To furnish women and girls. Free instruction in cooking, sewing, millinery, laundry, stenography and typewriting. Non-sec. Personal application is required. 1,706 pupils. J. P. Grace, Pres.; W. R. Grace, Sec. In charge of the Sisters of Charity of Mt. St. Vincent, N. Y. City.

Harlem Relief Soc.—Inc. 1893. Supported by voluntary contributions. Mrs. C. F. MacLean, Pres.; Mrs. A. L. Barrett, Sec., 2162 University av.

Havens Relief Fund Soc.—Org. 1870. Administers an endowment received from the late C. G. Havens; gives temporary relief, through almoners. A. N. Hand, Pres.; C. M. Bleecker, Sec., 49 Wall.

Heartsease Home for Women and Babies—413 E. 51st. Org. 1899. A home for friendless women, mothers and infants; adoption of babies and a boarding-out dept. for babies. Instruction given. Supported by voluntary contributions. Annie L. Richardson, Pres.; Louise B. Schofield, Sec.

Hebrew Free Loan—See Jewish Organizations.

Helping Hand Assn. of the City of N. Y.—416-418 W. 54th. Inc. 1865. Provides employment for destitute women and instruction in sewing. Supported by voluntary contributions. Mrs. E. J. Herrick, 1st Dir.; Miss L. Ziesse, visitor.

Holy Cross House—300 E. 4th. Boarding house for working girls. Sisters St. John Baptist, in charge.

Home Bureau Medical House (Inc.)—36 W. 39th. Est. 1890. Physicians', nurses' and mothers' headquarters for all necessities of the sick room and nursery. Nurse's registry, sterilized surgical obstetrical supplies, food for invalids, children and diabetics, invalid furniture, for sale or to rent, etc. Mrs. Mary Hatch Willard, Pres.

Home for Homeless Boys—441-447 E. 123d; office, 340 Madison av. Est. 1899. To care for destitute, homeless boys and help them to obtain work. Non-sec. and free. Accommodating 100 boys at one time. L. B. Elliman, Pres.; H. C. Eva, Supt.; W. R. K. Taylor, Treas., 49 Wall; O. DeL. Coster, Sec.

Hosp. Book and Newspaper Soc.—105 E. 22d. Branch of State Charities Aid Assn. Est. 1874. Receives donations of reading matter for distribution among hospitals, other public institutions and wherever needed. Miss A. D. Weeks, Sec.

House of the Holy Family—136 2d av. Est. 1870. To receive and give mental, religious and industrial education to wayward girls, 10 to 20 yrs. of age. 70 girls cared for. Under charge of Sisters of Divine Compassion (R. D. C.) Rev. Mother M. Aloysia, R. D. C., Superior. Gen. Assn. for Befriending Children and Young Girls; co-operates with Sisters of Divine Compassion in support of House of the Holy Family.

Hungarian Relief Soc.—32 Pearl. Est. 1897. To aid Hungarian immigrants.

Immigrant Girls' Home of Women's Home Missionary Soc. of M. E. Church—273 W. 11th. A temporary resting place. Mrs. A. R. Alberti, Supt.

Immigrant Mission of the Methodist Episcopal Church.—25 Pearl. Rev. C. Samuelson, Missionary.

Industrial Building and Wood Yard—See Charity Org. Soc.

Industrial Christian Alliance—243 W. 11th. Est. 1891. Shelter, 35 Perry. Helps the homeless and unemployed man, who is able and willing to work, by giving him temporary employment, which provides food and lodging while he is seeking work. Maintains a free employment bureau. Families also assisted. Geo. T. Brokaw, Pres.; Lucy L. Smedley, Head Worker; C. W. Knight, Mgr. (No paid officers.)

Industrial Removal Soc.—174 2d av. Philanthropic agency to distribute Jewish immigrants in interior sections of U. S. and designed to relieve congestion in N. Y. Isidore Frank, Acting Mgr.

Internatl. Medical Missionary Soc.—156 5th av. and Goshen, Mass. Students assisted and summer home for Missionaries maintained at Goshen, Mass. Org. 1881. Rev. G. H. Dowkontt, M.D., Sec., 421 56th, Bkln.; J. E. Giles, M.D., Treas., 156 5th av.

Internatl. Sunshine Soc. (Blind Babies)—Headquarters, 96 5th av., Mhtn. Org. 1896. Mrs. Cynthia Westover Alden, Pres.-Gen.; Mrs. Nellie E. C. Furman, Sec.; Mrs. A. O. Buck, Treas, 55 Cherry, Elizabeth, N. J. Internatl. Sunshine Nursery and Kindergarten for Blind Babies—83d and 12th av., Bkln. Mrs. G. MacMillen, Supt. Internatl. Sunshine Arthur Home, Hospital and Kindergarten for Blind Babies and Backward Blind Children—Pine Grove, Summit, N. J. Mrs. Minnie J. Force, Sec., 96 5th av., Mhtn.

Irish Emigrant Soc.—51 Chambers and 29 Reade. Inc. 1841. Aid and protection to immigrants. M. F. McDermott, Pres.; Thos. V. Brady, Treas.; J. J. Foley, Sec.

I. T. Hopper Home—See Women's Prison Assn.

Island Mission for Cheering the Poor and Sick in Public Charitable Institutions—Mrs. C. Jones, Pres.; Miss A. Marks, Sec.

Italian Benev. Inst. and Hosp.—Ft. E. 83d. For relief of sick and needy Italians. Maintains a dispensary and hospital of 100 beds. Dr J. W. Perilli, Pres.

Jeanne d'Arc Home for French Immigrant Girls—251 W. 24th. Protection of French girls while seeking employment. 2,210 girls cared for.

Rev. T. Wucher, Pres.; Mother Marie Clotilde, Matron.

Jewish Girls Welfare Soc.—See Jewish Soc.

Ladies' Christian Union of C. of N. Y.—Maintains Young Women's Home, 49 W. 9th; Branch Home, 308 2d av.; The Eva, 153 E. 62d; The Rosemary, 24 W. 12th; The Katharine, 118 W. 13th; The Milbank Memorial, 11 W. 10th. Promotes temporal, moral and religious welfare of self-supporting young women. 600 transients and residents. Mrs. L. H. Burr, Pres.; Mrs. W. W. Clark, Sec., 532 Clinton av., Bkln.

Ladies' Hebrew Lying-in Relief Soc.—Meets at Sydenham Hosp., 337 E. 116th. Inc. 1877. 1,129 persons aided. Mrs. F. Cohen, Pres.

Ladies of St. Vincent de Paul—120 W. 24th. Org. 1845. For French widows, old and infirm women and orphans under charge of Soeurs Marianites de St. Croix. 47 orphans cared for. Day nursery, 69 S. Washington sq. Money, clothing and work distributed 1st Th. of each month. Mme. C. de Vivier, Pres.; Miss A. Delmonico, Sec., 40 E. 83d.

Leake and Watts Assn.—Org. 1884. Takes care of its needy members in case of sickness and provides free burial for same in case of death. J. R. Gait, Pres.; Wm. Tresselt, Cor. Sec., 151 Bloomfield av., Passaic, N. J.; Geo. J. Hunt, Sec., 383 E. 157th.

Leake Dole of Bread—Founded 1792. Open from 9 A.M. to 1 P.M., Sa. mornings. Bequest of John Leake (interest on $2,500). 67 loaves distributed to poor parishioners at St. Luke's Chapel, Trinity Parish, 481 Hudson, weekly.

Legal Aid Soc. (The)—Est. 1876. Main office, 239 B'way; Seaman's Branch, 1 B'way; West Side Branch, 253 W. 58th; Harlem Branch, 51 E. 125th; Bkln. Branch, Eagle Bldg. Renders legal aid to those unable to procure assistance elsewhere and promotes measures for their protection. Chas. E. Hughes, Pres.; Carl L. Schurz, Vice-Pres.; C. P. Kitchel, Sec., 43 Cedar; Allen Wardwell, Treas., 15 Broad; J. G. Milburn, Act. Treas.; L. McGee, Attorney.

Life Saving Benev. Assn. of N. Y.—1849. 51 Wall. C. Eldert, Pres.; C. M. Bleecker, Sec., Mhtn.

Little Sisters of the Assumption (R. C.) (French Sisterhood)—Branch est. in America 1891. Nurse sick poor in their own homes free. Sister Marie Louise, Supt. of house, 246 E. 15th; Sister Marie Elizabeth, Supt., of 340 Convent av.

Lutheran Immigrant Soc.—Synod of Mo., Ohio and other States, at N. Y. City, 234 E. 62d. Org. 1885. Inc. 1889. To do mission work among immigrants and to be helpful in general. H. F. Ressmeyer, Pres.; Rev. O. H. Restin, Supt.

Madison av. Exchange for Women's Work—577 Madison av. Inc. 1886. 15 per cent. charged on sales. Mrs. Ira Barrows, Pres.; Mrs. Chauncey Kerr, Sec.; Mrs. H. Hudson, Supt.

Maedchenheim (Girls Home) Soc.—217 E. 62d. Supported by German Baptists. Permanent or temporary home for servant girls and place for social intercourse. Mrs. L. Maeder, Pres.; Mrs. R. E. Hoefflin, Sec., 1127 Fulton av., Bronx; H. E. Altherr, Matron.

Manhattan Ladies' Relief Assn.—Inc. 1896. Aids the needy by donations of money. Mrs. M. Schleneth, Pres., 417 Main, New Rochelle; Mrs. Chas. Schuler, Sec., 2250 Hughes av.

Marine Soc. of the City of N. Y.—1770. 80 Broad. 200 mem. For improvement of maritime knowledge and relief of indigent and distressed members. A. B. Conner, Pres.; W. A. Pendleton, Treas.; W. E. Crockett, Sec.

Mission of Our Lady of the Rosary—7 State. Temporary home for Irish immigrant girls. Girls discharged to the Mission by the immigration authorities are received, no charge being made for board and lodging or for placing in employment. Rev. M. J. Henry, Dir.

Municipal Lodging House—432 E. 25th. Est. 1896. Normal accommodations for 847 transient lodgers. House has 6 light, airy sleeping rooms, double deck white enamel beds, shower baths, formaldehyde fumigating plant, dining room and laundry. Provides medical clinic and free employment bur. Dispossessed families, mothers with babies, sick and aged given special care. In 1917 the lodging house provided a total of 92,405 accommodations to homeless persons. E. E. McMahon, Supt.; L. J. Miller, Steward.

Natl. Plant, Flower and Fruit Guild, N. Y. Branch—70 5th av. Mrs. James Roosevelt, Hon. Pres.; Mrs. G. E. Paul, Sec. See Natl. Guild, under Charities.

Natl. Urban League (for Social Service among Negroes)—1911. Conducts Big Brother and Big Sister work, maintains convalescent and detention homes, conducts boys' and girls' clubs, acts as clearing house for social welfare work among colored people, finds new openings of employment, trains Negro social workers, improves housing conditions, makes investigations. E. K. Jones, Nat. Sec., 127 E. 23d; J. H. Hubert, N. Y. Sec., 2303 7th av.; R. J. Elzy, Bkln. Sec., 102 Court, Bkln.

Needlework Guild of Amer. N. Y. City Branch—Org. 1891. Miss G. Bigelow, Pres.; Miss H. Eliz. Howson, Sec., 489 West End av. See Natl. Soc. under Charities.

N. Y. Assn. for Improving the Condition of the Poor—105 E. 22d. Org. 1843. Inc. 1848. C. N. Bliss, Jr., Pres.; Geo. Blagden, Treas.; A. Nichols, Sec.; B. B. Burritt, Gen. Dir. Under direction of board of 40 managers; supported by voluntary contributions. (1) Dept. of Family Welfare, Bureau of Relief, 5,000 families cared for in their homes; Bureau of Fresh Air operates Sea Breeze, West Coney Island, for mothers and children; also Boys Camp, Girls Farm and Old Folks Summer Outing Home. 81,366 days entertainment in 1919. Home Hosp. for treatment of combined tuberculosis and poverty; Caroline Rest School for Mothers at Hartsdale, N. Y. Old Men's Toy Shop where 81 old men were given daily work. Sewing Rooms at which 75 women were helped daily toward self-support. Home instruction and relief given by 25 district visitors, 35 visiting nurses, 8 dietitians and 6 visiting housekeepers. (2) Dept. of Social Welfare, Bureau of Welfare of School Children, Bureau of Public Health and Hygiene, Bureau of Food Supply. N. Y. State Comm. on Ventilation. Special activities: Milbank Memorial Laundry, 325 E. 38th; Mulberry Community House, 256 Mott, housing medical and dental clinics; People's Kitchen, 10th av., cor. 29th; Men's Coffee House, cor. Hudson and Leroy.

N. Y. Assn. for the Blind—111 E. 59th. Est. 1906. To prevent unnecessary blindness and to help the blind to help themselves. Supported by voluntary contributions. Dr. J. H. Finley, Pres.; Miss W. Holt, Sec.; F. L. Eldridge, Treas.

N. Y. City Indian Assn.—Org. 1882. To strengthen Christian public sentiment in favor of Indians of our country and aid in mission work among them. Mrs. B. E. Rabell, Pres.; Miss H. M. Thompson, Treas., 76 W. 86th.

N. Y. City Mission Soc.—See Missions.

N. Y. Colored Mission—8 W. 131st. Maintains an apartment house for women and day nursery. Employment office, classes in sewing and singing and Sabbath School. A visitor. Dr. J. L. Barton, Pres.; Mrs. Lloyd Cofer, Supt.

N. Y. Deaconess Assn.—1175 Madison av. Org. 1889. Inc. 1893. Deaconesses nurse and relieve sick and poor in tenement districts and work elsewhere under the direction of pastors. Supported by voluntary contributions. Bishop Luther B. Wilson, Pres.; C. R. Saul, Treas.; Miss M. J. Kistler, Supt.

N. Y. Diet Kitchen Assn. (The)—Inc. 1873. Central office: 33 W. 42d. Mrs. H. Villard, Pres.; Mrs. Jos. W. Tilton, Treas., 33 W. 42d; Miss M. L. Daniels, Dir. Assn. supports 8 milk stas. and maintains a corps of 15 nurses for health and general welfare work among families connected with the assn.'s stations. Activities of assn. incl. dispensing of pure milk, carrying on of health conferences for babies and older children, registration and oversight of prospective mothers, home visiting and instruction of mothers in baby and general hygiene, talks, cooking classes at stas., and active co-operation with other health and social service agencies of the dists. and with Dept. of Health. Location of stations: Wickham, 169 Mott; Anne Barbara, 1254 2d av.; Gibbons, 453 E. 121st; Tuck, 35 W. 139th; Riverside, 126 W. 100th; Raymond, 437 W. 41st; Demorest, 583 Courtlandt av., Bronx; Villard, 500 W. 126th.

N. Y. Exchange for Woman's Work—541 Madison av. Inc. 1878. Accepts for sale womens' and childrens' apparel, also domestic and fancy articles. Commission of 15 per cent. charged. Vocational Bur. secures positions for professional women, governesses, business managers and clerical workers. Mrs. J. S. Ward, Pres.; Mrs. S. H. Ordway, Sec.; Miss V. D. H. Furman, Treas.; Ida J. Dutton, Bus. Mgr.

HOSPITALS, HOMES AND SOCIETIES FOR RELIEF—MANHATTAN—SPECIAL RELIEF—*Continued.*

N. Y. Home for Homeless Boys—441-447 E. 123d. Office, 340 Madison av. H. C. Eva, Supt. L. B. Elliman, Pres.; O. DeL. Coster, Sec.; W. R. K. Taylor, Treas., 49 Wall. Soldiers and Sailors Service House at 447 E. 123d free to all enlisted men from camp.

N. Y. House and School of Industry—120 W. 16th. Org. 1850. Assists infirm and destitute women by giving them employment in needlework. Orders taken for fine sewing. Store for sale of undergarments, house and hotel articles. Voluntary contributions. Mrs. Nathan W. Green, Pres.; Miss H. L. Knox, Treas.; Miss G. W. Sargent, Sec., 28 E. 35th.

N. Y. League for the Hard of Hearing—126 E. 59th. 1910. 650 mem. Harold Hays, M.D., Pres.; Annetta W. Peck, Exec. Sec.

N. Y. Lodging House—Est. and supervised by different charity orgs.—Majority remain open all night. Salvation Army Hotels, 225 Bowery, 243 Bowery; Mills Hotels, No. 1, 160 Bleecker; No. 2, 2 Rivington; No. 3, 161 W. 36th; Salvation Army Industrial Homes, 508 W. 48th, 229 E. 120th; Industrial Christian Alliance, 35 Perry; Bowery Y. M. C. A., 153 Bowery; Bowery Mission Hotel, 242 E. B'way; Municipal Lodging House, 432 E. 25th; Volunteers of America, 176th and Webster av.; Charity Organization Soc. Woodyard, 516 W. 28th.

N. Y. Practical Aid Soc.—347 W. 56th. Inc. 1891. To render immediate aid in food, medical attendance and other relief to worthy women and children. 2,000 persons assisted. W. W. Urquhart, Pres.; Mrs. M. S. Trimmer, Supt.

N. Y. Press Club—21 Spruce. Org. 1872. Has fund for charity and free burial of deceased journalists. E. P. Howard, Pres.; C. H. Redfern, Sec.

Newsboys' Lodging House—Name changed to Brace Memorial Newsboys' House.

Night Refuge, see St. Mary's Home for the protection of Young Women.

Olive Tree Inn Lodging House for Men—338-342 E. 23d.

Poor Adult Blind Bu. of Investigations—Municipal Bldg. Branches: 124 E. 59th, Mhtn.; Bergen Bldg., Tremont and Arthur avs., Bronx; 327 Schermerhorn, Bkln.; Town Hall, Flushing; Borough Hall, S. I. An annual appropriation is distributed by Dept. of Public Welfare among adult blind citizens not inmates of any institution and over 21 yrs. and who have resided continuously in N. Y. C. for 2 yrs. immediately preceding date of application. V. S. Dodworth, Dir.

Prison Assn. of N. Y.—135 E. 15th. Inc. 1846. Aims to improve penal and reformatory systems. Furnishes legal aid for those unjustly accused. Aids discharged prisoners with employment, food, clothing, tools and shelter. Cares for prisoners' families. Receives persons on probation and on parole. E. Smith, Pres.; O. F. Lewis, Gen. Sec.; D. M. Sawyer, Sec.

Prisoners Aid Dept. of Salvation Army—124 W. 14th. Est. 1906. Aids prisoners and their families. Miss E. Booth, Pres.; Col. E. J. Parker, Prison Sec.; Brigadier T. Cowan, Chaplain men's dept.; Capt. S. Sheppard, Probation and Parole Officer; Lieut. E. Becker, Sec., Brighter Day League.

Provident Loan Soc. of N. Y.—Exec. Office, 346 4th av.; Loan Offices, 346 4th av., 186 Eldridge, 736 7th av., 124th and Lex. av., 148th and Courtlandt av., 409 Grand, Essex, cor. Houston, 180 E. 72d, 2365 8th av., 55 Chambers; Bkln., cor. Smith and Livingston, 24 Graham av., and Pitkin av., cor. Rockaway. Inc. 1894. Org. to do general pawnbroking business. Loans on pledges of personal property at rate of 1% per month. On all pledges redeemed within 2 weeks ½% interest charged. Certificates of contribution issued. $8,200,000; bonds outstanding, $1,363,000. Otto T. Bannard, Pres.; M. L. Schiff, Treas.

Regina Angelorum Home for Working Girls.—112-118 E. 106th. Conducted by the Sisters of Mercy. Sr. M. Vincent, Superior.

Rodeph Sholom Sisterhood—See United Hebrew Charities.

Sailors' Home—See Amer. Seamen's Friends Soc.

Sailors' Snug Harbor—See Richmond.

St. Andrew's Soc.—See Scottish Soc., Mhtn.

St. Barnabas' House of N. Y. (P. E.) City Mission Soc.—304-306 Mulberry. Org. 1865. Temporary place for homeless women and children, women discharged from prison and convalescent women discharged from hospitals. 50 beds for adults, 35 for children. Fresh Air Fund Excursions made during summer. Rev. L. E. Sunderland, Supt.; L. Cromwell, Treas., 38 Bleecker; Miss E. R. Hopkins, Head Worker.

St. David's Soc. of the State of N. Y.—289 4th av. Org. 1835. Inc. 1841. To afford pecuniary relief to worthy Welsh people. 92 aided. J. C. Williams, Pres.; G. M. Lewis, Sec.; A. H. Williams, Treas.

St. George's Soc.—361 W. B'way. Founded 1770. Assists needy English residents. Recent arrivals not eligible. Dr. W. E. Lambert, Pres.; F. H. Trimble, Sec.; L. D. Langley, Almoner.

St. Mary's Home for the Protection of Young Women—143 W. 14th. Est. 1877. Night Refuge for Homeless Women—144 W. 15th. Women sheltered and fed. Articles of clothing given. Miss S. M. Osborne, Pres., 143 W. 14th.

St. Peter's Union for Catholic Seamen—422 West. Maintains reading rooms. Rev. P. J. Magrath, Dir.

St. Phillips Villa—Est. 1902. 417 Broome and 218th and B'way. To provide home and positions for Catholic friendless boys, 14-16 yrs. of age. House at 218th used as summer home. Bro. Bonitus, Supt.

St. Raphael Italian Ben. Soc.—Org. 1891. To assist Italian immigrants. Maintains immigrant home at 8-10 Charlton. Dr. G. Ferrante, Sec., Rev. G. Moretto, Rep.

St. Raphael's Soc. for Protection of German Catholic Immigrants—6 State. Org. 1883. Sisters of St. Agnes in charge.

St. Thomas' Summer Home—East Marion, L. I. N. Y. office, 229 E. 59th. Est. 1892. To give two-weeks' outing to those connected with parish of St. Thomas' P. E. Ch., Mhtn. Rev. E. M. Stires, D.D., Rec. All work sustained by the church. Rev. J. S. Haight, Vicar in Charge.

Salvation Army—Internatl. hdqrs., 101 Queen Victoria, London, England. The following are internatl. statistics for year ended Dec., 1918: Countries and colonies occupied, 66; corps and outposts, 10,591; under direction of 26,838 officers, cadets and employees, with 68,676 local officers, and 31,389 bandsmen. Hdqtrs. in Amer., 122 W. 14th, Mhtn. Inc. in U. S., 1899. A religious body founded on military principles by the late Wm. Booth at Mile End, Eng., July 5, 1865. Is incorporated in the States of N. Y., Pa., Ill., Mass., Cal. and Mich. The U. S. is divided into three depts., with hdqtrs. in New York, Chicago and San Francisco. Miss Evangeline Booth is in charge. Commr. Thos. Estill in command of the Eastern territory; Commr. Wm. Peart in charge of the Midwest and Lieut. Commr. Adam Gifford in charge of the West.

The following statistics refer to the U. S. and are for the year ended Sept., 1919: Corps and outposts numbered 963; 5,949,454 persons attended the indoor meetings and 117,599 open air meetings were held; local officers and bandsmen who gave their services gratuitously numbered 9,422; at the 63,968 meetings, held for young people, there was an attendance of 1,869,994; War Crys published, 6,171,940. Relief Insts. for the poor included 84 industrial homes, with a sleeping accommodation of 2,171; 6,655 men were admitted; 1,485,209 meals and 518,142 beds were supplied; 57 workingmen's hotels, with sleeping accommodations for 5,323; beds supplied, 1,498,887. Slum Posts and Nurseries—Posts and nurseries, 11; hours spent in active service, 116,577; families visited, 10,375; children sheltered, 47,982. Rescue and Maternity Homes—Homes and hosps., 26; accommodations, 1,425; girls admitted, 2,314; girls passed out, 2,151; meals supplied, 1,307,328; beds supplied, 436,117; children admitted, 1,991; children passed out, 1,941; women in homes end of year, 648; children in homes end of year, 693. Missing and Inquiry—Inquiries, 1,917; found, 522. Children's Homes—Homes, 3; accommodation, 440; beds supplied, 130,029; meals supplied, 394,548. Prison Work—Hours spent visiting, 9,903; prisoners prayed with and advised, 68,211; prisoners assisted on discharges, 2,843; situations found, 69. General Statistics—Christmas dinners (1918), 201,760; Thanksgiving dinners (1918), 16,466; persons afforded temp. relief outside Industrial Homes and Hotels, 709,351; mothers given summer outings, 4,977; children given summer outings, 33,366; men found employment outside own Insts., 46,590; meals given outside own Insts., 294,456; beds given outside own Insts., 97,268; pounds of ice distributed, 315,913; pounds of coal distributed, 1,632,627.

HOSPITALS, HOMES AND SOCIETIES FOR RELIEF—MANHATTAN—SPECIAL RELIEF—*Continued.*

Sands Fund of P. E. Ch.—220 E. 23d. The interest of which is used at the discretion of Bishop of N. Y. for clergymen of the Diocese of N. Y. The Bishop of N. Y., R. M. Pott, Rev. C. K. Gilbert. Dexter Blagden, Trustee.

Seamen's Christian Assn.—Est. 1888. 399 West. To assist seafaring men. Attendance, 85,192; 11,303 men shipped; 313 lodgings. H. P. Beach, Pres.; S. Wright, Supt.

Shaaray Tefila Sisterhood—See United Hebrew Charities.

Shelter for Respectable Girls (P. E.)—Org. 1871. Inc. 1880. 212 E. 46th. Gives to girls and young women a temporary home if strangers in the city or seeking employment. 371 inmates; 1,168 women aided. Rev. H. M. Barbour, D.D., Pres.; Katherine Gillmore, House Deaconess.

Shut-in Soc.—Inc. 1885. For encouragement and comfort of invalids, printing and distribution of publications adapted to such work. Publishes monthly periodical, "The Open Window." Ed., Miss A. Breath. Has library and loans wheel chairs to members. Numbers 3,000 invalids and 1,000 associates. Mrs. C. E. Merrill, Pres.; Miss M. H. Hadley, Sec. and Treas., 129 E. 34th.

Sisters of Bon Secours—1195 Lex. av. Inc. 1883. Who nurse the sick in their homes, irrespective of creed or nationality. Sister Winifred, Pres. and Superioress.

Slavonic Immigrant Soc.—1907. 436 W. 23d. Provides temporary shelter in home for Slavonic immigrants, and maintains free employment bureau. Prof. M. I. Pupin, Pres.; A. B. Koukol, Sec.

Soc. for Italian Immigrants—6 Water. Est. 1901. To protect and aid arriving and outgoing Italian immigrants; maintains an immigrant lodging house and free labor bureau. Non-sec. 168,439 persons assisted, fed and lodged since 1908. E. G. Fabbri, Pres.; A. V. Tozzi, Mgr.

Soc. for Relief of Widows and Orphans of Med. Men of N. Y.—1842. 17 W. 43d. W. T. Alexander, Pres.; A. F. Currier, Sec.

Soc. for the Employment and Relief of Poor Women—104 E. 20th. Org. 1844. Unitarian. Supplies sewing to women in their homes Subscribers pay $8 for each applicant for season. 85 to 100 women given sewing. Miss H. C. Butler, Pres.; Mrs. Ernst Wehncke, Sec., 822 President, Bkln.; Mrs. G. R. Bishop, Treas Maintains a repository, 146 E. 16th, for sale of garments.

Soc. for Relief of Poor Widows with Small Children—Inc. 1802. Aids those of good character with 2 children under 14 not assisted by authorities. Miss S. Grace Fraser, 1st Dir.; Margaret A. Jackson, Sec., 556 Madison av. Apply only by letter.

Soc. of Inner Mission and Rescue Work—See National Charitable Soc.

Soc. of Lutheran Hosp.—See Lutheran Hosp., Mhtn.

Soc. of the Helpers of the Holy Souls of City of N. Y. (The)—114 E. 86th. Inc. 1894. Catholic community devoted to care of sick poor in their own homes and other works of mercy. Mother Mary of St. Catherine, Superior.

Soc. of Justice—1919. 1482 B'way. To aid meritorious and indigent persons charged or convicted of criminal offenses, who, through poverty, are unable to supply counsel. Rev. P. S. Grant, Pres; Loretta Caruthers, Sec.

Soc. of St. Vincent de Paul—Org. 1865. Inc. 1872. Object: 1st, a practice of a Christian life; 2d, to visit and aid poor; 3d, to promote the elementary and religious instruction of poor children; 4th, to distribute moral and religious books; 5th, to undertake other charitable work. Internat'l hdqrs., Paris, France.

Metropolitan Central Council of N. Y.—1860. 216 W. 15th. Superior Council of the U. S. has circumspection of all conferences in the U. S. Meets at office W. after 1st M. each month. J. F. Boyle, Pres.; M. J. Scanlan, Treas.

Particular Council of N. Y.—Has circumspection of conferences in N. Y. C. S. of 100th. Meets 216 W. 15th, 2d M. each month. J. F. Boyle, Pres.; P. H. Bird, Sec., 216 W. 15th. 653 mem. Relieved 5,489 families.

Conferences and Presidents.

Carmelite—Rev. D. O'Connor, 338 E. 29th.
Corpus Christi—Hugh Reilly, 521 W. 123d.
Epiphany—J. O'Connell, 335 Av. A.
Guardian Angel—P. H. Bird, 452 W. 22d.
Holy Cross—Jas. O'Connell, 424 W. 43d.
Holy Innocents—M. Connelly, 309 W. 55th.
Holy Name—J. J. Lynch, 175 W. 95th.
Holy Trinity—M. A. O'Connell, 115 W. 84th.
Immaculate Conception—Thos. J. Walsh, 225 W. 15th.
Most Holy Redeemer—C. Werckle, 237 E. 12th.
Nativity—E. M. Kelly, 331 E. 9th.
Our Lady of Good Counsel—230 E. 90th. Very Rev. Mgr. J. N. Connolly, Sp. Dir.
Our Lady of Guadaloupe—G. B. Puga, 466 W. 146th.
Our Lady of Perpetual Help—Edw. Colligan, 321 E. 65th.
Our Lady of Sorrows—Jos. Spergal, 247 E. 3d.
Sacred Heart—T. I. Traub, 447 W. 51st.
Sacred Heart of Jesus and Mary—D. Patrone, 158 E. 26th.
St. Agnes—Leo Kearney, 253 Mosholu Pkway.
St. Alphonsus—P. J. O'Connell, 285 W. Houston.
St. Ambrose—Wm. Moran, 498 W. 55th.
St. Ann—J. Donat, 214 E. 12th.
St. Anthony—John O'Connor, 560 W. 180th.
St. Anthony's Chapel—N. Picciano, 307 E. 48th.
St. Benedict, the Moor—York Russell, M.D., 244 W. 131st.
St. Bernard—P. J. Ward, 225 W. 15th.
St. Boniface—V. Stockman, 353 E. 83d.
St. Bridget—W. F. Quirk, Sr., 298 E. 7th.
St. Columbia—T. E. Anderson, 66 W. 88th.
St. Frances de Sales—P. Kane, 174 E. 96th.
St. Francis Xavier—R. J. Doherty, 30 W. 16th.
St. Gabriel—J. J. Killian, 316 E. 37th.
St. Gregory the Great—Chas. F. McKenna, 155 W. 91st.
St. Ignatius—V. Maickel, 540 E. 87th.
St. Jean Baptist—J. Maher, 185 E. 76th.
St. Joachim—E. De Stefano, 4 Mulberry.
St. John the Baptist—B. Lawrence, 352 W. 45th.
St. John the Evangelist—Jas. J. Doherty, 410 E. 58th.
St. Joseph (6th av.)—J. J. Doris, 288 W. 12th.
St. Lawrence—J. H. Fargis, 37 Liberty.
St. Malachy—W. J. Kelly, 446 W. 51st.
St. Matthew—H. P. Falls, 170 W. End av.
St. Monica—W. Slattery, 57 E. 86th.
St. Nicholas—J. Schaff, 151 Av. A.
St. Patrick (Cathedral)—J. C. Rooney, 155 E. 49th.
St. Patrick (Mott st.)—W. McNamara, 120 34th, Woodcliff, N. J.
St. Paul the Apostle—T. F. Farrell, 147 W. 93d.
St. Peter—T. J. Gallagher, 31 Barclay.
St. Raphael—R. J. Fitzgerald, 434 W. 47th.
St. Rose—L. Rconey, 1 Cannon.
St. Stephen—J. McDonald, 515 2d av.
St. Veronica—T. A. Wolfe, 275 W. 11th.
St. Vincent Ferrer—Jas. P. Scully, 588 Park av.
St. Wenceslaus—J. A. Komarek, 432 E. 66th.
Transfiguration—M. Barroni, 208 9th, Bkln.

State Charities Aid Assn. Visiting Committee—Office, Room 710, 105 E. 22d. Object: To visit systematically all wards and buildings of Bellevue and Allied Hospitals of Dept. of Health and of Dept. of Public Welfare; to secure such improvements as will contribute to mental, moral and physical well-being of inmates. Submits frequent letters to Com. of Health and to Com. Pub. Welfare; also special reports to Trustees of Bellevue upon necessary improvements and to Board of Estimate and Apportionment upon appropriations needed for hospitals, etc. Organizes employment for sick and infirm in above institutions. Has subcommittees for Boroughs of Mhtn., The Bronx, Bkln., Queens and Richmond. Homer Folks, Pres.; M. N. Buckner, Treas.; Miss M. R. Taber, Sec.; Miss M. L. Putnam and Mr. F. Kierman, Asst. Secs. Supported by voluntary contributions.

Sunshine Soc.—See Internatl. Sunshine Soc. Also Universal Sunshine Soc.

Swedish Luth. Immigrant Home—5 Water. Est. 1895. 3,305 cared for. Rev. S. G. Ohman, Pres.; Rev. Axel C. H. Helander, Supt.

Swiss Benev. Soc.—See Relief for Aged, Mhtn.

Syrian Soc. of City of N. Y.—Est. 1892. Educational and industrial institution for Syrian and Arabic speaking immigrants; teach tnem English. A. F. Haddad, 89 Broad.

Temple Israel Sisterhood—See United Hebrew Charities.

Trained Attendants on Sick (Ballard School of Y. W. C. A.)—53d and Lexington av. Org. 1872. Gives instruction to women to become attendants on invalids, companions and practical nurses. 3 mo. course, beginning Oct. Dr. Jeannette Hamill, Dir.; Miss G. B. Ballard, Ch.

United Hebrew Charities of the City of N. Y.—356-358 2d av. Inc. 1877. Grants relief to the deserving Jewish poor throughout the City of N. Y. Leopold Plaut, Pres.; Miss F. Taussig, Exec. Dir.

United Hospital Fund of N. Y. (formerly the Hosp. Sat. and Sun. Assn. of N. Y. City)—Org. 1879. 105 E. 22d. Helps to maintain the free work of the hospitals by raising money, which is distributed on the basis of the actual amount of free services rendered by each of the United Hospitals, regardless of race or creed. This is ascertained from carefully audited reports of the work, income and expenses of the hospitals. Distribution in 1920 was $850,000. Robert Olyphant, Pres.; Albert H. Wiggin, Treas., 57 B'way; F. D. Greene, Gen. Sec.

United Relief Work of Soc. for Ethical Culture—33 Central Park W. Inc. 1879. Furnishes free scholarships in Ethical Culture School. Dist. Nursing Dept. sends trained nurses into homes of poor. L. G. Rose, Pres.; M. Beckhard, Treas.; Mrs. F. Alder, Ch., 152 W. 77th.

U. S. Dept. of Labor, U. S. Employment Service—H. D. Sayer, Federal Dir., 120 E. 28th.

Universal Sunshine Soc.—80 Lafayette. Object: To send flowers and fruit to sick people and work principally among invalids. Mrs. C. Burns, Pres.; Mrs. J. Pierce, Sec., 80 Lafayette.

Vassar Students Aid Soc.—Org. 1890. To lend pecuniary aid without interest to students of Vassar College. Mrs. D. Bissell, Pres., 219 W. 79th; Miss Adelina Kuhn, Sec., 3100 B'way.

Virginia Hotel for Women—228 E. 12th. Org. 1910. Young women charged $6-$9 per wk., including 3 meals a day and use of laundry. About 90 guests. Mrs. W. Herbert, Pres.; Miss M. Blagden, Sec.

Volunteers of America.—1896. 34 W. 28th. Gen. and Mrs. Ballington Booth, Co-Commanders-in-Chief; W. J. Crafts, Treas. The organization is religious and philanthropic, with branches throughout the United States. During the year 339,732 free lodgings have been given the poor, while 919,220 have been furnished at nominal charge or in exchange for work. Homes for women are maintained. Children are cared for, and many hundreds taken to fresh-air camps; upward of 30,000 children have been helped with clothing, etc.; 720,460 free meals have been given, and 311,574 meals paid for by work or other means; 926,036 persons attended services inside; 2,654,558 attended the open-air services during the year. Thousands of copies of Christian literature were circulated in State's prisons, jails, hospitals, soldiers' homes and children's homes.

Washington Sq. Home for Friendless Girls—9 W. 8th. Dr. Edwd. L. Partridge, Pres.; Wm. A. Greer, Sec.

West Side Aid for Friendless Men.—243 W. 11th. Est. 1909. Helping men to help themselves. C. W. Knight, Gen. Mgr.; L. L. Smedley, Sec.; Mrs. B. Smedley, Matron. (No paid officers.)

White Rose Home for Colored Working Girls—262 W. 136th. 2,220 cared for, travelers protected, conducts industrial classes. Miss M. L. Stone, Pres., 435 Central Park W.; Mrs. S. E. Wilkerson, Treas.; Mrs. G. Blick, Sec.; H. L. Ferrell, Supt.

Women's Prison Assn. and Isaac T. Hopper Home—110 2d av. Inc. 1845. Improvement of condition of prisoners, support and encouragement of reformed convicts. Dr. A. S. Daniel, Pres.; Miss M. V. Clark, Exec. Sec., 110 2d av.; Mrs. H. W. Smith, Supt.

Women's Rescue Home and Hospital of the Salvation Army—316-318 E. 15th. Helpful advice given to any woman in trouble and needing a friend. Lt.-Col. Emma J. Brown, Supt.

Working Girls' Vacation Soc.—105 E. 22d. Org. 1883. For unmarried working girls. Provides 2 weeks' vacation in country. Maintains 2 homes at Santa Clara, N. Y., for outings to girls of consumptive tendencies. Other homes at Farmington, Conn.; Greens Farms, Conn.; Cobalt, Conn.; Chester, N. Y.; Hadlyme, Conn., and at North Long Branch, N. J. Mrs. W. Herbert, Pres.; Mrs. J. Rogers, V.-Pres.

Working Women's Protective Union—289 4th av. Org. 1863. To promote interests of working women other than domestics, to provide them with legal protection from impositions of employers. Dr. H. D. Chapin, Pres.; A. M. Hudnut, Treas.; Miss E. R. Ogilby, Supt.

Young Friends' Aid Assn.—Org. 1873. Inc. 1890. 226 E. 16th. Gives temporary aid. J. C. Kitchin, Pres.; J. Hibberd Taylor, Treas.; Anna L. Curtis, Cor. Sec.

Y. M. C. A.—Has employment bureaus at 23d St. Branch (fee charged). 215 W. 23d. West Side Branch (fee charged), 318 W. 57th. Bronx Union Branch (fee charged), 470 E. 161st. French Branch (free), 109 W. 54th. Bowery Branch (fee charged), 8 E. 3d. Harlem Branch (fee charged), 5 W. 125th. W. M. Kingsley, Pres.

Young Women's Home Soc. of French Evangelical Church—341 W. 30th. Org. 1888. Maintains French Evang. Home for Young Women. Provides for respectable unemployed teachers, governesses and French-speaking women and procures employment for them. Miss E. Bolliet, Supt.

Reformatories.

Florence Crittenton League—427 W. 21st. Est. 1883. Inc. 1914. Helping wayward girls and unfortunate women; 532 assisted in 1918. Also takes girls pending trial from the courts. Peter T. Barlow, Pres.; Mrs. J. N. Borland, V.-Pres.; Miss E. H. Davison, Sec. It is entirely supported by voluntary contributions.

House of the Good Shepherd (R. C.)—Ft. 90th and E. R. Inc. 1858. Reformation of inebriates and fallen women committed by city magistrates or those who present themselves voluntarily. Capacity, 500. Sister M. Alexis, Sup'r.

House of the Holy Family—See Special Relief.

Inwood House—Org. 1833. Dyckman and River rd. Gives home to women desirous of reforming. Has a nursery dept., laundry and sewing room. 97 inmates. Mrs. L. Watjen, Pres.; Mrs. Irvin Cornell, Sec.; Mrs. S. C. Douglass, Supt.

Margaret Strachan Home for Young Women—Taken over by Salvation Army.

Midnight Mission—United Charities Bldg. For training of wayward girls, 14 to 20 yrs. Country branch, St. Michael's Home at Mamaroneck, in charge of Sisters of St. John the Baptist. Dr. S. F. Morris, Pres.; F. Parkman, Sec.-Treas., 24 Nassau.

N. Y. City Reformatory of Misdemeanants—New Hampton Farms, Orange Co., N. Y. Under jurisdiction of Dept. of Correction. The Legislature of 1905 passed an act, known as Chap. 305 of Laws of 1905, amending Chap. 627 of Laws of 1904, establishing the "N. Y. City Reformatory of Misdemeanants," to which institution the magistrates of any court of N. Y. City may, after conviction, commit for first offense only on any charge, offense, misdemeanor or crime, other than a felony, all male persons whom they shall deem in their discretion to be a proper subject for reformatory treatment, bet. ages of 16 and 30, to an indeterminate sentence not exceeding 3 yrs. The first inmate was received Dec. 22, 1905. Number cared for, 7,927. S. W. Brewster, Supt. Branch Reformatory Honor Camp, City Farms, Warwick, N. Y. Est. 1920.

St. Zita's Home for Friendless Women—143 W. 14th. Inc. May, 1893. To shelter and provide employment for friendless women. Sister Mary Magdalen, Supt.

Soc. for Reformation of Juvenile Delinquents, City of N. Y.—House of Refuge, Randall's Island ferry ft. of E. 125th. Est. 1824. A reformatory; receives male children under 16 convicted of juvenile delinquency, from 1st, 2d, 3d and 9th Judicial Dists of the State; over 16 and under 18, convicted of a misdemeanor from all Judicial Dists of State. They are given a common school education, industrial instruction and military training. Capacity, 1,000 inmates. Supported by State. Isaac Townsend, Pres.; Ed. C. Barber, Supt.

Washington Square Home—9 W. 8th. Org. 1873. Temporary home for mothers with babies. E. L. Partridge, M.D., Pres.; W. Foulke, Treas.; Miss F. L. Giddings, Supt.

Settlements.

Alfred Corning Clark Neighborhood House—283 Rivington. Opened 1899. To educate and train children of the neighborhood by kindergartens, clubs, etc.; also gymnasium, clubs, and classes for boys and young men. Edward Clark Club House for men opened in 1905.

HOSPITALS, HOMES AND SOCIETIES FOR RELIEF—MANHATTAN—SETTLEMENTS—*Continued.*

Amelia Relief Soc.—115 E. 101st. Org. 1896. Care for worthy needy in their homes, settlement work in own building. Financial, medical aid, supply clothing, etc. Mem. 350. Mrs. K. Solomon, Pres., 226 W. 70th.

Amer. Sunshine Assn. Settlement—352 W. 40th. Day Centre. Visiting and relief. Office, 147 W. 23d. Miss M. A. Gorham, Pres.

Christodora House—147 Av. B and Northover Camp, Bound Brook, N. J. Org. 1897. For physical, social, intellectual and spiritual development of people in crowded portions of city and co-operation with civic, religious and philanthropic work carried on in neighborhood. Mrs. A. C. James, Pres.; Miss C. I. MacColl, Head Worker.

Chrystie St. House—75 Horatio. Temporary home for otherwise homeless and destitute young men, 16 to 30 years old, until able to support themselves. M. W. Maclay, Ch.; Stephen G. Williams, Treas., 30 Broad.

College Settlement (The)—84 and 86 1st. Org. 1889. A home in neighborhood of working people in which educated men and women live in order to furnish a common meeting ground for all classes for their mutual benefit and education. It forms a social center for its neighborhood and further carries on its work through various clubs and classes, to which about 2,000 people belong. It is supported by an association formed for that purpose. Mrs. A. N. Noble, Head Worker.

Doe Ye Nexte Thynge Soc.—Settlement House, 18 Leroy. Inc. 1886. Org. to bring its members into closer relationship with the people of the lower West Side. Maintains a Settlement house where clubs and classes for men and women, boys and girls are held. Also a visiting branch and coal club. Mrs. Ansel Phelps, Pres., 125 E. 61st; Miss M. R. Blair, Head Worker.

East Side House—East River and 76th. Inc. 1891. Org. for promoting a better social order. Maintains following activities: Day nursery, kindergarten, afternoon clubs and classes for boys and girls of school age, evening clubs for adult men and women, a music school, gymnasium, summer camps for men, boys and girls; various school extension classes. Average attendance, 1,500. R. S. Pierrepont, Pres.; M. de G. Trenholm, Head Worker.

Frank Bottome Memorial—See Margaret Bottome Memorial.

Grace Church Neighborhood House—98 4th av. (P. E.). Lunch room for working girls, clubs for boys and girls. Roof garden, men's lunch, reading room, etc. Mrs. T. Folsom, Pres.; Deaconess Gardner, House Mother.

Grace Church Settlement—415 E. 13th. To elevate condition of the neighborhood. Weekday prayer four days a week in chapel. Service in main chapel each Sunday, 8 A.M., 11 A.M. and 8 P.M.—4 P.M. in Italian. Maintains Grace Hospital, 414 E. 14th, including House of Simeon, a home for old men; House of Anna, home for old women, and House of the Holy Child, an asylum for children; the Parish House, 413-415 E. 13th. Branch of the N. Y. Kindergarten Assn.; a cooking school, sewing and manual, gymnasium, swimming, baths and a variety of associations and classes; the clubhouse, which has rooms for men's and boys' clubs and classes for manual training. St. Luke's Assn., which helps the sick, buries dead, employs a physician, has a dispensary, open 2-4 P.M., Mon., Wed. and Fri., and also a trained nurse to care for sick poor at their homes. There are Friendly Societies, King's Daughters, St. Andrew's Brotherhood, Young Men's Clubs, Battalion, Boys Scouts, etc. Rev. F. G. Urbano and Rev. E. White in charge.

Greenwich House—27 Barrow. Settlement House maintained by Co-op. Social Settlement Soc. Org. 1902. Center for social, educational and civic improvement, carried on in conjunction and association with people residing in neighborhood. Herbert Parsons, Pres.; Mary K. Simkhovitch, Dir.; B. E. Pollak, Treas., 27 Barrow.

Haarlem House (formerly Home Garden of N. Y. City, founded 1898, inc. 1901)—311 E. 116th. A community house. Social clubs, athletics, lectures, Americanization work; a summer camp, Camp Dixon, Ridgefield, Conn. Supported by voluntary contributions. Miss I. M. Cammann, Sec.; B. M. Gage, Dir.

Hamilton House—72 Market. Inc. 1902. Branch of Henry St. Settlement. Maintains Kindergarten, Maternity Clinic. Office of Henry St. nurses. Club and classes for children and adults of the neighborhood. Italian Needle Work Guild. Home work given out. Henrietta Gersdansky, Head Worker.

Hartley House—413 W. 46th. Org. 1897. Social settlement, clubs and classes for children and adults. Cooking school, circulating library, gymnasium, playground. Vacation farm at Towaco, N. J. Miss M. Mathews, Head Worker.

Henry Street Settlement (Nurses)—Org. 1892. Central office, 265 Henry. Branches, 232 E. 79th, 72 Market and 202 W. 63d. Br. offices for nursing service at 27 Barrow, 441 W. 28th, 1836 Amsterdam av, 311 E. 116th, 237 E. 104th, 232 E. 79th, 505 E. Tremont av., 525 W. 47th, 916 Brook av., 435 E. 17th, 5222 B'way, 72 Market, 2303 7th av., 677 Morris av., Staten Islander Bldg., Tompkinsville, S. I. Maintains district nursing service covering Mhtn., Bronx and Richmond; first aid rooms, convalescent and fresh air homes in country, classes in art, festival dancing, dramatics, manual training, sewing, social and literary clubs, kindergartens, study rooms and gymnasium. Also Neighborhood Playhouse, 466 Grand. Vocational scholarships. Information Center for Council of Women's Organizations. Miss L. D. Wald, Head Resident.

Hudson Guild—Org. 1896. 436 W. 27th. Object: To organize neighborhood for social betterment, to teach ethics of organization among wage earners and to improve moral, mental and physical condition of its members. Class instruction free. Clubs and classes for people of all ages. Free kindergarten, playground, baths and free employment bureau. Health league, dental clinic, summer play school, co-operative store, co-operative vacation farm, printing apprentices' school, supported by Employing Printers' Section, Typographical Union and the Guild. Public meetings for the discussion of labor questions. A. M. Bing, Pres., 119 W. 40th; J. L. Elliott, Head Worker.

Kennedy House—Org. 1906. 423 W. 43d. To be a good neighbor in all which that word implies. Mrs. S. W. Child, Pres.; Jessie Powell-Arnold, Head Worker.

Lenox Hill Settlement—511 E. 69th. Est. 1894. Object: To be a good neighbor in organized and unorganized ways. T. S. McLane, Pres.; Rosalie Manning, Head Worker.

Lighthouse No. 1—111 E. 59th. Headquarters of N. Y. Assn. for Blind. Settlement for the blind. Dr. J. H. Finley, Pres.; Miss W. Holt, Sec.

Madison House—Org. 1898. 216 Madison. General Settlement purposes. M. Kirchberger, Pres.; Miss Ruth Larned, Head Worker.

Margaret Bottome Memorial—King's Daughters Settlement. 344 E. 124th. To better conditions of children and women of East Side Harlem. Mrs. J. S. Conabeer, Pres.; Mrs. W. R. Clark, Sec., 523 W. 158th.

Music School Settlement—51-55 E. 3d. Inc. 1903. For the extension of good musical education. 1,000 pupils. Mrs. Frank B. Rowell, Pres.; M. Chaffee, Dir.

Normal College Alumnae House—See Lenox Hill House.

Nurses Settlement—See Henry St. Settlement.

People's Home Settlement of the People's Home Church—543 E. 11th. Est. 1901. Miss G. E. Resseguie, Deaconess-in-Charge.

Recreation Rooms and Settlement—Org. 1898. 186 Chrystie. Educational and social improvement of neighborhood, scholarships, maternity clinic. Mrs. Cyrus Sulzberger, Pres.; Miss Josephine Schain, Head Worker.

Richmond Hill House—28 Macdougal. Social settlement with 6 resident workers and board of managers, composed jointly of resident and non-resident members. The settlement was originally the West Side Branch of University Settlement, became an independent settlement 1903. The work is among Italians. There are the usual clubs and classes and special effort is made along industrial and art lines. Donald Scott, Pres.; E. T. Tefft, Treas.; H. Ward, Sec.; C. Hook, Head Worker.

Riis (Jacob A.) Neighborhood Settlement—48 Henry. Conducts kindergarten, sewing, cooking and gymnasium classes; clubs for men, women and children; dances. Has roof garden and baths. Summer camp for boys and one for girls in the Inter-State Park Reservation. Mrs. Jacob A. Riis, Pres.; Miss H. H. Jessup, Head Worker.

HOSPITALS, HOMES AND SOCIETIES FOR RELIEF—MANHATTAN—SETTLEMENTS—*Continued.*

St. Rose's Settlement of Catholic Social Union—257 E. 71st. Org. 1898. To enlist Catholics of leisure in personal service of poor, to give religious instruction to neglected and ignorant, whether children or adults. Maintains free circulating library, sewing and cooking classes, gymnasium, classes in Christian doctrine, social clubs for young people of both sexes. Friendly visiting. Rev. C. M. Thuente, O. P. Founder; Spr. Dir., Rev. H. Heffernan, O. P.; Pres., Mrs. Wm. Arnold, Babylon, L. I.

Speyer School—94-96 Lawrence (127th and Amsterdam av.) Building donated by James Speyer; dedicated 1902. Experimental Junior High School and annex to P. S. School 43, Mhtn., under joint supervision of Bd. of Education and Columbia Univ. Rapid advancement classes for pupils from all upper West Side public schools; pupil self-govt. Training for citizenship, aft. classes, orchestra. J. K. Van Denburg, Ph.D., Prin.

Sunshine Settlement—Est. 1900. Inc. 1917. 122 White. Has social center for working girls, young boys and mothers of neighborhood and has various industrial classes; maintains clubs, vacation funds, library, kindergarten, practical lectures, health classes, medical and otherwise. C. Irving Hall, Pres.; S. E. Furry, Sec. Has given legal aid and medical aid and sent hundreds of the poor to the country and seashore during the summer and has supplied a number of volunteers to the Army from its clubs who were trained in first aid work. Office, 53 Bible House.

Union Settlement Assn.—237 E. 104th. Est. 1895. To co-operate with neighbors and citizens generally for social and civic betterment. Non-sec. Kindergartens, study room, sewing school, gymnasium, nurses, clubs and classes for men, women and children, 2 summer homes for girls and boys. A. C. McGiffert, Pres.; J. Sloane, Treas.; G. S. White, Sec. and Head Worker.

University Settlement—184 Eldridge. Est. 1886. Maintains about 145 clubs, public baths, gymnasium, boys' camp at Beacon, N. Y.; school girls' camp at Montclair, N. J., and vacation camps for older girls and boys. Holds lectures, debates, concerts, etc. Systematic investigations of local and municipal social problems, also branch of Provident Loan Soc. J. Speyer, Pres.; Hugo Kohlman, Sec.; J. S. Eisinger, Head Worker.

Warren Goddard House (Inc. 1901 as Friendly Aid Settlement, name changed in 1902)—246 E. 34th. Object: To be of service to the neighborhood. It maintains a kindergarten, lunch room for school children and working mothers, gymnasium, young men's, women's, boys' and girls' clubs and classes in dressmaking, embroidery, basketry, cooking, carpentry, housekeeping, singing, piano, literature; the Hayden housekeeping center, 325 E. 31st, model flat where all branches of homemaking are taught. The Soc. maintains four summer homes. The settlement is maintained by the Friendly Aid Soc. Recently opened club for men in uniform, for soldiers and sailors of U. S. and of her Allies. Club rooms open 9 A.M. to 10:30 P.M. Baths, gymnasium, pool, piano, reading and writing rooms. Geo. McAneny, Pres.; Miss E. Kendall, Sec., 14 Central Park W.; H. D. Plant, Treas., 361 B'way; Miss E. B. Bowles, Head Worker.

West Side Branch Y. W. C. A. Boarding home—460 W. 44th. Est. 1892. Is a center for religious, educational, social and physical improvement, a boarding home, etc. Accommodates 32 girls. Harriet Wright, Matron.

West Side Juvenile Club—326 Greenwich. Inc. 1902, 300 boys, 300 girls. Has library, gymnasium, carpentry, sewing classes, etc. H. S. Davis, Pres.; J. H. Stewart, 43 Exch. pl., Treas.; T. A. Renkel, Supt.

White Door Gospel Settlement—Org. 1897. 211 Clinton. For home-making, good citizenship, upbuilding of character. 1,100 mem. Prentice Sanger, Pres.; Harriet Irwin, Head Worker.

Humane Societies.

Amer. Soc. for Prevention of Cruelty to Animals—50 Madison av. Inc. 1866. During yr. it prosecuted 1,900, investigated 6,782 cases of cruelty and removed and cared for 76,625 homeless, sick and injured cats and dogs. Maintains dispensary and hosp. for animals and shelter for dogs and cats and an ambulance house at Av. A and 24th, Mhtn. Office and ambulance house at 114 Lawrence, and shelter at 233 Butler, Bkln., and shelter on Wave, Richmond; has ambulances and life saving apparatus for sick and injured animals. Special agents authorized to enforce laws of State located in principal cities and towns. Supported by voluntary contributions and bequests. A. Wagstaff, Pres.; R. Welling, Sec.

Bide-a-Wee Home Assn., Inc., for Friendless Animals—410 E. 38th. Rescues about 10,000 animals annually. Supported by voluntary contributions. Operates city home and country home at Wantagh, L. I., for friendless animals and has placed from 6,000 to 7,000 dogs and cats in good homes during 1917. Free emergency hospital. Mrs. H. U. Kibbe, Pres.; Miss E. R. B. Champion, Sec.

Horse Aid Soc. of N. Y., Inc.—Hdqtrs. 149 W. 38th. Bronx Branch, 2707 Walker av.; Bkln. Branch, 270 Reid av. Inc. 1910. Free clinic for horses and domestic animals. Instruction in proper care and treatment of animals. Free employment bureau for drivers. Horse Aid Drivers' Club, Horse Aid Helpers' Club, instructing children to be kind to every living thing. Entirely supported by voluntary contributions. Mrs. J. M. Ehrlich, Pres.; Mrs. J. Bloom, Sec.

Humane Soc. of N. Y.—102 Fulton. Inc. 1904. Prevention of cruelty to animals. D. Belais, Pres.

N. Y. State Vet. Col. at N. Y. Univ.—26th and 1st av. Inc. 1857. Maintains hosp. for animals and dispensary at which free veterinary advice is given to poor persons and treatment to their animals. Dr. W. H. Hoskins, Dean.

N. Y. Women's League for Animals, Inc.—Free hospital and dispensary. 350 Lafayette. Est. 1910. 1,500 mem. Mrs. James Speyer, Pres.; Mrs. Mary E. Dunn, Sec., 350 Lafayette.

Miscellaneous.

Bur. of Investigation, Boarding Out and Transportation—Municipal Bldg. Branches: Dept. Public Welfare, 124 E. 59th, Mhtn.; Bergen Bldg., Tremont and Arthur avs., Bronx; 327 Schermerhorn, Bkln.; Town Hall, Flushing; Borough Hall, St. George, S. I. Tuberculosis Hosp. Admission Bureau, 124 E. 59th, Mhtn. Provides hospital treatment for sick poor, distributes pension to poor adult blind semi-annually; provides relief for veterans of Civil and Spanish wars and members of their families, pays transportation of non-residents to their homes, provides home care for aged persons, investigates cases proposed by private hospitals as public charges, adjusts claims for non-support or present such claims to the appropriate court, commits dependent children to institutions. Visits and supervises in family homes children who have been accepted as public charges and boarded out. V. S. Wodworth, Dir.

City Hosp. Schl. of Nursing, Blackwell's Island. Est. 1875. T. H. Le Febvre, R. N., Principal.

Clearing House for Mental Defectives. Post-Graduate Med. Sch. and Hospital, 20th and 2d av. Examines persons suspected of being mentally deficient and arranges for their admission to institutions or prescribes the proper course of treatment at home. Max G. Schlapp, M.D., Dir.

Dept. of Correction—1898. Municipal Bldg. Charge of city and district prisons, reformatories, etc.

N. Y. Co. Penitentiary—Blackwell's Island. Est. 1832. Reception and Classification Division, persons sentenced under Chap. 579, Laws 1915. 1 day to 3 years. Average number of inmates for yr., 4,217. Visiting days, daily. Sat., Su. and holidays excepted. J. A. McCann, Act. Warden.

N. Y. Morgue—Bellevue Hosp. grounds, E. 29th. Est. 1866. Temporary receiving institution for the city's dead. Forty per cent. of the total received are buried by the city, sixty per cent. by friends. Distributes unclaimed bodies to medical colleges and postgraduate schools. M. J. Rickard, Supt.

Rockefeller Foundation—1913. 61 B'way. To promote well being of mankind throughout the world. Geo. E. Vincent, Pres.; E. R. Embree, Sec.

Russell Sage Foundation—130 E. 22d. Inc. 1907. For the improvement of social and living conditions in U. S. R. W. de Forest, Pres.; J. M. Glenn, Sec. and Gen. Dir.

Tuberculosis Hosp. Admission Bureau, Dept. of Public Welfare—124 E. 59th. Receives applications for admission to tuberculosis hospitals and sanatoria, and preventoria for children. S. Potter, Supt.

HOSPITALS. HOMES AND SOCIETIES FOR RELIEF—MANHATTAN—MISCELLANEOUS—*Continued.*

Workhouse—Blackwell's Island. For prisoners convicted of intoxication, disorderly conduct, vagrancy and minor offenses. Average number of prisoners, 1,480. Visiting days, any day except Sat., Su. and holidays. 1 visit allowed every 30 days for 1st month and 2 visits a month thereafter. Passes issued at the Pass Bureau, Rm. 2532, 25th floor, Municipal Bldg., Mhtn. M. M. Lilly, Supt.

BRONX.

Hospitals, Dispensaries and Asylums.

Bronx Eye and Ear Infirmary—459 E. 141st. Est. 1903. For poor only. Treatment of eye, ear, nose and throat diseases, 2:30-4 P.M., daily except Su. and holidays. Dr. C. H. Smith, Sec.; Miss M. Rau, Supt.

Fordham Hosp.—Southern Blvd. and Crotona av. One of Bellevue and Allied Hosp. Has dispensary and ambulance service. Visiting hours: Su., Wed., 2-4 P.M.; Fri., 6-8 P.M., to adults only. Dr. J. W. Brannan, Pres. Bd. of Trustees; Miss H. Malmgren, Supt.

Home for Destitute Blind—Grand Concourse and E. 193d. 93 inmates. L. S. Morris, Pres.; C. C. Bull, Sec.; Fred'k. F. de Rham, Treas., 44 Wall; Miss K. E. Bower, Matron.

Home for Incurables—3d av., bet. 182d and 184th. Non-sec. Inc. 1866. 300 inmates. One-third of beds are free. Visiting days, daily, 11 A.M. to 5 P.M. Ogden Mills, Pres.; J. L. Thomas, Sec.; J. V. Smith, M.D., Med. Supt.

Lebanon Hosp. Assn.—Westchester and Cauldwell avs. Inc. 1893. General Hospital. Dispensary open, daily, 2-4 P.M. Non-sec. Samuel Arnstein, Pres., 2 W. 72d; G. E. Halpern, Supt. Visiting days for ward patients, Su., Wed., 2-4 P.M.; Thur., 7-8 P.M. Training school for nurses.

Lincoln Hosp. and Home—E. 141st and Southern Blvd. Est. 1839. Reception in Hosp. and Dispensary of patients regardless of race, creed or color, and in home of aged, infirm colored persons, both sexes. 6,734 patients; 21,244 treatments in dispensary, 8,522 prescriptions given; emergency treatments, 1,821; 7,358 ambulance calls. Visiting days, Tu., Fri., Su., 2-4 P.M. Miss M. W. Booth, Pres.; F. Gwyer, M.D., Supt.

Montefiore Home & Hosp. for Chronic Diseases—Gunhill rd., nr. Jerome av. Inc. 1884. Non-sec. Charity hosp. for patients in chronic stages of disease. 500 patients cared for. Families of those in the home, if necessary, assisted from Julius Hallgarten fund. S. G. Rosenbaum, Pres.; H. M. Lehman, Treas.; Dr. S. Wachsmann, Med. Dir.; M. D. Goodman, Supt. Maintains the Montefiore Home Country Sanitarium at Bedford Hills, N. Y., for treatment of patients in the incipient stage of tuberculosis. Dr. B. Silverman, Med. Supt. Cap., 225; 1,978 patients.

St. Francis Hosp., in charge of Sisters of Poor of St. Francis—E. 142d, bet. Brook and St Anns avs. Opened 1906. Cap. 450. Sister Antoniana, Sup.

St. Joseph's Hosp. for Consumptives. Under care of Sisters of Poor of St. Francis—E. 143d, nr. Brook av. Opened 1882. Care of consumptives. Free to poor. 525 beds. Visiting days, Su., Thur., 2-4 P.M.

Relief of Aged.

Peabody Home for Aged and Indigent Women. 2064 Boston rd. Inc. 1874. Free and non-sec. Age 65 yrs. and over. 32 inmates. R. Y. Hebden, Sec.-Treas., 64 Wall. Ladies Aux. Assn.—Reorg. 1910. 16 mem. Assist in management of home. Mrs. E. W. Warren, Pres.

Relief of Children.

Am. Female Guardian Soc. and Home for the Friendless, 936 Woodycrest av. Org. 1834. Inc. 1849. Selena M. Campbell, Pres.; Mrs. L. P. Mendenhall, Treas. To care for destitute children, boys under 12, girls under 16, and when surrendered place them in homes. 5 industrial schools located at: Home School, 936 Woodycrest av.; Industrial School, No. 1, 303 E. 109th; No. 8, 218 E. 148th; No. 7, 243 E. 103d; No. 12, 2247 2d av.; Summer Home (Wright Memorial), Oceanport, N. J., where home children are cared for from July to Sept.

Colored Orphan Asylum—W. 261st, Riverdale. N. Y. Est. 1836. Institution for care and training of colored children bet ages of 2 and 16 yrs. Cap., 290. Mrs. Willard Parker, Head Dir.; Dr. Mason Pitman, Supt.

Messiah Home for Children—Spring Valley, N. Y. Org. 1885. Supported by private contributions. Lydia C. French, Sec., 929 Park av., Mhtn.

St. Elizabeth Industrial School—Bathgate av. and E. 188th. Org. 1885. Teaches industries to poor children from 6-16 yrs. (R. C.) Miss M. A. Kennedy, Pres.; B. Smyth, Sec.

Sevilla Home for Children—Inc. 1889. Lafayette av., and Manida. Home receives destitute girls bet. 5 and 10 yrs. Non-sec. S. Sloan, Pres.; Miss J. F. M. Cobban, Supt.

Special Relief.

Ch. of God Missionary Home—2132 Grand av. C. J. Blewitt, Pres.; M. A. Blewitt, Sec.-Treas.

Oliver Tilden's Woman's Relief Corps—1931 Washington av. Inc. 1887. To assist dependent veterans, their wives and orphans. M. A. Nolan, Pres.; Mrs. E. W. Pulis, Sec., 297 E. 146th.

Soc. of St. Vincent de Paul, Particular Council of the Bronx—509 Willis av. Has circumspection of conferences in the Bronx. 450 mem. 645 families relieved during 1919. James J. Reid, Pres.; J. E. Dougherty, Sec.

Reformatories.

N. Y. Catholic Protectory—Inc. 1863. Westchester, N. Y. City. Office, 415 Broome, Mhtn. Branches: Lincoln Agricultural Sch., Lincolndale (formerly Somers Center), N. Y.; St. Philip's Home for Industrious Boys, 417 Broome, Mhtn. Office, 415 Broome. For destitute and delinquent Catholic children from 3-16 yrs., as follows: 1st, Children under 16 intrusted for protection and reformation. 2d, bet. 7 and 16, committed by magistrates. 3d, those committed or transferred by Dept. of Public Welfare. Boys taught trades in male dept. at Westchester. Boys taught agriculture, dairy work, etc., at Lincoln Agri. Sch. Girls taught industrial employments and domestic work at female dept. Positions found for boys at St. Philip's Home. Number cared for, 4,337. Myles Tierney, Pres.; John J. Falahee, Treas.; Jos. P. Grace, Sec.; John O'Toole, Actuary; Rev. Bro. Cleophas, Dir. Male Dept.; Rev. Sister P. M. Charita, Sup. Girls' Dept.; Rev. Bro. Clementian, Dir. Lincoln Agri. Sch.; Rev. Bro. Bonitus, Dir. St. Philip's Home.

QUEENS.

American Red Cross, Queens Co. Chapter—Bridge Plaza, L. I. City. J. J. Conway, Ch.; Edmund J. Clarry, Sec., Elmhurst; J. G. Embree, Treas.

Associated Charities—64 Main, Flushing. H. G. Murray, Pres.; R. B. Howard, Gen. Sec.

Belknap Summer Home for Day Nursery Children—Far Rockaway. Est. 1901. 225 children cared for. Miss E. DeG. Cuyler, Pres., 903 Park av., Mhtn.

Big Sisters of Queens Borough—207 Borough Hall, L. I. City. Mrs. Smith Alford, Pres.; Mrs. H. E. Hendrickson, Ch. Court Committee.

Chapin Home for Aged and Infirm—Jamaica. Inc. 1869. Non-Sec. (Age 65). To provide a home for the aged and infirm. 100 inmates. Under care Universalist Church. Mrs. H. E. Fox, Pres.; Mrs. C. L. Stickney, Rec. Sec., 560 W. 149th, Mhtn.; R. Brenton, Supt.

Flushing Female Assn.—Lincoln, Flushing. Est. 1814. Education and assistance of poor of colored race. Miss L. R. Peck, Pres.; Miss A. Breath, Sec., 146 Franklin pl., Flushing.

Flushing Hosp. and Disp.—Forest and Parsons avs., Flushing. Est. 1883. W. H. Walker, Pres.; A. D. Nash, Sec.; Thos. B. Lowerre, Supt.; Miss Helen Lyman, Supt. Nurses.

Flushing Hosp. Aid Soc.—Flushing. Est. 1907. To aid Flushing Hosp. and Dispensary. F. S. Yale, Pres., Flushing; A. P. Laighton, Sec. Woman's Aux., Flushing Br., Mrs. W. M. Simmons, Pres.; Mrs. B. C. Eldridge, Sec. Bayside Br., Mrs. J. E. McKee, Pres.; Mrs. A. G. Maury, Sec. Douglaston Br., Mrs. J. Billings, Pres.; Mrs. G. L. Lewis, Sec. "Green Twigs," Mrs. C. B. Martin, Pres.; Miss A. Clark, Sec. Forest Hills Br., Mrs. N. Rae, Pres.; Mrs. J. Gétz, Sec.

Free Dental Clinic for Poor Children—374 Fulton, Jamaica. Operated by Dept. of Health. To care for teeth of poor schl. children. Esther Kirchenbaum, D.D.S., B. Kutyn, D.D.S.

Jamaica Hosp.—Jamaica. Est. 1891. Giving medical and surgical aid. 1,500 patients treated. Visiting days, Tu., Th. and Su., 2-4, 7-9 P.M. Mrs. Frank Denton, Pres.; Mrs. H. Carman, Sec.; Mrs. G. Yeaton, Treas.; Miss Rosa A. Saffeir, R. N., Supt.

HOSPITALS, HOMES AND SOCIETIES FOR RELIEF—*QUEENS—Continued.*

Jamaica Hosp. League—Mrs. Starr Brinckerhoff, Pres.; Mrs. Geo. Polhemus, Sec.; Mrs. A. Lee, Treas.

Morris Park Aux.—Mrs. S. Pettitt, Jr., Pres.; Mrs. A. C. Estabrooke, Treas.

Woodhaven Aux.—Mrs. H. M. De Ronde, Pres.; Mrs. C. Tillinghast, Sec.

Springfield Aux.—Mrs. E. Thomson, Pres.; Mrs. Parker, Sec.

Grace Ch. Hosp. League—Mrs. G. Morris, Pres.; Mrs. C. Hicks, Sec.

Hollis Hosp. League—Mrs. P. Fleury, Pres.; Mrs. A. S. Hanna, Sec.

Forest Park Aux.—Mrs. B. George, Pres.; Miss C. Brockman, Sec.

Council of Jewish Women Aux.—Mrs. W. Gold, Pres.; Mrs. S. J. Gutter, Sec.

Liberty Aux.—Mrs. H. I. Huber, Pres.; Mrs. R. M. Von Gassbeck, Sec.

Roosevelt Aux.—Mrs. Pusch, Ch.

Kew Gardens Aux.—Mrs. E. R. Rich, Pres.; Mrs. G. Floyd, Sec.

Ladies' Employment Society of Flushing—Lincoln, Flushing. Org. 1867. To supply needy women with sewing during Jan., Feb., Mar. Mrs. T. S. Willets, Pres.; Mrs. J. S. Eadie, Sec., Flushing.

Mary Immaculata Hosp.—Ray and Shelton av., Jamaica. Est. 1902. 100 bed Hosp. Tr. Schl. for Nurses. 1,561 Hosp. patients during past year. 1,414 ambulance calls. Mother Augustine Fleck, O.S.D., Pres.; Sister M. Thos. Straub, O.S.D., Treas. and Superior; Sister M. Eugenia, O.S.D., Supt.; Sister M. Josephanna, Supt. of Tr. Schl.

Woman's Aux.—Mrs. J. Schnellein, Pres.; Mrs. L. A. Shaughness, Sec.; Mrs. Thos. Corrigan, V.-Pres.

Daughters of Charity—Miss J. Schuellin, Pres.; Miss E. Glennan, Sec.

Otillie Orphan Asylum—Kaplan av., cor. Degraw av., Jamaica. Est. 1892. Under charge of members of German Ref. and Pres. Churches of Bkln. and Mhtn. in connection with Otillie Orphan Asylum Soc. of N. Y. Inc. 1892. Accommodates orphans and half-orphans from 4-11 yrs. 127 inmates. Rev. Wenzl Walenta, Pres.; M. Braun, Sec., 233 Grove, Bkln.; Rev. G. A. Godduhn, Supt.

Parental School, Flushing, L. I.—See Public Schools of City of New York.

Philanthropic Committee of 20th Century Club—Richmond Hill. Est. 1899. Investigating all applications for assistance; securing work and giving aid in sickness. Mrs. W. De Groot, Pres.; Mrs. C. Brace, Ch.

Public School Relief Assn.—P. S. No. 89, Elmhurst—Est. 1905. Supplies poor school children with shoes, stockings, underwear, etc., during winter months. Mrs. E. P. Johnson, Pres.; Mrs. S. S. Wagner, Ch., Hampton, Elmhurst.

Queensboro Soc. for the Prevention of Cruelty to Children—Butler Bldg., Jamaica. 1920. H. Pushae Williams, Pres.; Alex. Dienst, Sec., Front, L. I. City.

Rockaway Beach Hosp. and Dispensary—Hammels av., Rockaway Beach. Est. 1908. Free medical and surgical aid. G. Bennett, Pres.; E. H. Frost, Supt.

St. Anthony's Hosp.—Woodhaven av., nr. Elm, Woodhaven. Est. 1914. To aid tuberculosis patients. Acc. about 420 patients. In charge of Sisters of the Poor of St. Francis.

St. George's Seaside Cottages—Rockaway Park. Est. 1884. To give week's stay to the members of St. George's Parish. 800 are provided for during season in this way. Bungalows are provided for families, each of whom remains 2 weeks. A group of thirty young women is accommodated for week ends. Day trips are conducted for mothers and children and on Sun. for men and girls of parish. On Sun. a religious service is conducted on the beach by a clergyman of St. George's P. E. Church, by whom the work is supported. E. W. Chappell, Deaconess in Charge., N. Y. office, 207 E. 16th.

St. John's L. I. City Hosp.—Jackson av., cor. 12th, L. I. City. Est. 1891. To give relief to the sick. 4,301 patients treated. Has ambulance service. Rt. Rev. C. E. McDonnell, Pres.; Sister M. Philomene, Supt.

St. Joseph's Home—Flushing. See St. Malachy Home, Relief of Children, Bkln.

St. Joseph's Hosp.—Broadway, Far Rockaway. Est. 1905. Non-sec. 1,439 inmates. Cap. 100 beds. Training sch., 18 nurses and Supt. Rev. J. McNamee, Pres.; Sister M. Febronia, Supt.

St. Mary's Hosp. (See Mary Immaculata Hosp.)

Sanitarium for Hebrew Children of the City of N. Y.—See Jewish Org.

United Workers—30 Monroe, Flushing. Org. 1892. Has a day nursery, clothing bureau, friendly and visiting committee. Mrs. J. Macdonald, Pres.; Mrs. H. P. Williams, 390 Sanford av., Flushing.

RICHMOND.

Actors' Fund Home—1910. West New Brighton. Age limit, men, 60 yrs.; women, 55. Daniel Frohman, Pres.; Jas. Halfpenny, Supt.

Bethlehem Orphan's and Half Orphan's Asylum—Fingerboard rd., Ft. Wadsworth. Inc. 1886. Children 3-12 yrs. of Luth. Church. 140 inmates. Theo. Lamprecht, Pres.; Wm. Essig, Sec., 130 Ridgewood av., Bkln.; Rev. M. T. Holls, Supt.

Charity Org. Soc.—W. New Brighton. Org. 1885. To help poor to help themselves. 70 families assisted. Mrs. G. W. Curtis, Pres.; Miss L. H. Irving, Sec., 103 Henderson av., New Brighton.

Female Infants' Home and Grotto of Our Lady of Lourdes—Mt. Loretto, Pleasant Plains. Accommodates 100. Sister M. Scholastica, Superior.

Lakeview Home—See Jewish Org.

Mariners' Family Asylum—Org. 1843. Stapleton, S. I. To provide an asylum for aged and destitute widows, wives, mothers, sisters and daughters of seamen of the port of N. Y., often known as "The Old Ladies Home." Admission fee, $200. Cap. 60. Mrs. Hy. Cattermole, Cor. Sec. Visiting day, Th.

Needlework Guild of Amer.—New Brighton Br. Est. 1892. New garments collected for institutions. Mrs. R. Monell, Pres.; Miss M. W. Alexander, Sec.

New Brighton Day Nursery—5th, New Brighton. Under auspices of Woman's Club of Staten Isl. Est. 1901. To care for children while mothers are out at work. 4,000 children cared for. Mrs. W. B. Wilkinson, Ch.

The N. Y. C. Farm Colony—W. New Brighton, S. I. Maintained by City of N. Y. for care of the relatively able-bodied men unable to maintain themselves. Inmates are expected to work on farm and industrial shops operated in connection with the institution. Farm Colony Cottages built for aged couples, citizens who are unable to maintain themselves. Administration combined with Sea View Hospital. G. Kremer, M.D., Med. Supt.

Port Richmond Day Nursery—93 Park av., Port Richmond. Org. 1895. To care for children of working women and furnish temporary relief in emergencies. Mrs. Wm. Wheeler, Pres.; Mrs. E. L. Benjamin, Treas., 239 Heberton av., Port Richmond; Mrs. H. J. Murray, Sec.; Mrs. Edith Fountain, Matron.

Richmond Co. Soc. for Prevention of Cruelty to Children—Castleton av., Tompkinsville. Inc. 1880. Judge T. C. Brown, Pres.; Mrs. L. W. Clark, Sec.; Mrs. M. R. Smith, Supt., 111 Farview av., New Brighton.

Sailors' Snug Harbor—New Brighton, S. I. Est. 1801. Home for aged, decrepit and worn-out sailors. 714 inmates. Capt. G. E. Beckwith, Gov.; Jas. Henry, Comp., 262 Greene, Mhtn.

St. Joseph's Asylum for Blind Girls Under 14—Mt. Loretto, Prince Bay, S. I. Branch of Mission of Immaculate Virgin. Rev. M. J. Fitzpatrick, Superior, 381 Lafayette, Mhtn.

St. Michael's Home for Destitute Children—Green Ridge. Est. 1884. House of reception and branch home, 424 W. 34th, Mhtn. 400 inmates. Rev. W. A. Dougherty, Pres.

St. Vincent's Hosp. of the Borough of Richmond—Bard and Castleton avs., West New Brighton. Org. 1903. 1,689 inmates. Non-sec. Dr. E. Callahan, Pres. of the Med. Board; conducted by Sisters of Charity.

Sea View Hosp., West New Brighton, S. I. 1913. Cap. 1,777. Includes the following divisions: Hospital, sanatorium for tuberculosis, preventorium for the predisposed, colony for dependent men, cottages for aged couples and women; psychopathic service for the alleged insane. Dr. G. Kremer, Med. Supt.

Soc. for Relief of Destitute Children of Seamen—New Brighton. Est. 1846. Home for children

HOSPITALS, HOMES AND SOCIETIES FOR RELIEF—RICHMOND—*Continued.*

2-10 yrs., receiving public school education. Supported by contributions and income from gifts and legacies. Miss M. T. Marsh, Dir.; M. A. Irving, Treas.

State Charities Aid Assn.—Visiting committee for Boro. of Richmond, City Visiting committee. Org. 1873. Visits systematically the Sea View Farms, and recommends such reforms as may be practicable for improvement of mental, moral and physical conditions of inmates. Mrs. T. M. Rianhard, Ch.; Miss M. R. Taber, Sec., 105 E. 22d, Mhtn.

Staten Island Diet Kitchen Assn.—Grant and Van Duzer, Tompkinsville. Est. 1882. Object, relief of destitute sick and distribution of nourishing food. 217 persons assisted in 1917. Mrs. T. Livingston Kennedy, Pres., 314 Westervelt av., New Brighton; Mrs. F. DeRevere, Sec., Stapleton; Miss Warnecke, Matron.

Staten Island Hospital—Tompkinsville. Est. 1863. Care of medical, surgical, obstetrical, children and contagious cases. 3,780 inmates cared for. W. L. DeBost, Pres.; Dr. Chas. W. Goodwin, Supt. Has a training school for nurses. 40 pupils; a dispensary and ambulance service.

Surgical Appliance Fund Assn.—Org. 1891. Provides for needy cripples, artificial limbs and surgical braces. Miss A. F. Hicks, Ch., New Brighton, S. I.

Swedish Home for Aged People—20 Bristol av., West New Brighton. 1912. 27 inmates. E. F. Johnson, Pres.; C. K. Johansen, Sec., 108 Park Row, Mhtn.; O. Kallstrand, Mgr.

U. S. Marine Hosp.—Stapleton. Est. 1883. For care and treatment of sick and disabled seamen of merchant marine, U. S. Coast Guard, Engineer Corps of Army, or Mississippi River Commission, and officers and crews of lighthouse establishment and Coast Survey of U. S., officers and men of the Army and Navy, injured civilian employees of U. S., patients referred by Bureau War Risk Ins. and U. S. employees. Hosp. last yr.: Admissions, 3,200 out patients, office and Barge Office. 10,500 admissions to treatment, 7,500 physical examinations for the A. B. seamen, masters and pilots.

Victoria Home for Aged British Men and Women—1915. West New Brighton, S. I. Mrs. H. H. Pike, Pres.; Mrs. J. F. Mackenzie, Sec.; Mrs. T. E. Hurdus, Treas.

MISCELLANEOUS RELIEF SOCIETIES—NEW YORK STATE AND VICINITY.

For Long Island Charities see Index.

Hospitals.

Bloomingdale Hosp. for Mental Disorders—White Plains, N. Y. Est. 1771 by Soc. of N. Y. Hosp. E. W. Sheldon, Pres.; Dr. Wm. L. Russell, Med. Supt. Office hrs., 8 W. 16th, Mhtn., at noon all business days.

Daisy Fields Home and Hosp. for Crippled Children—Englewood, N. J. Est. 1893. Treatment free. 18 patients. Supported by voluntary contributions. Mrs. L. D. Mowry, Pres.; Mrs. R. Prosser, Ch. House Comm.; Mrs. G. L. Miller, Sec., Brayton, Englewood, N. J.; Miss M. E. Bennett, Supt.

Loomis Sanatorium for Treatment of Tuberculosis. Loomis, Sull. Co., N. Y. Rates in main division, $30-$50 per wk.; Intermediate Div., $20 per wk.; Annex Div., $15 per wk. Applicants for admission must submit on special form report of examination by their physician. B. H. Waters, Phys.-in-Chief.

St. Andrew's Rest—Woodcliff Lake, N. J. Est. 1887. Summer Br. of St. Andrew's Convalescent Hosp. 350 cared for. Sisters of St. John Baptist in charge.

St. Eleanor's Home for Convalescents—Tuckahoe, N. Y. Free accommodation of convalescents. Supported by private individual and under direction of Sisters of Charity. Sister M. Isidore, Supt.

Sanatorium Gabriels—See Tuberculosis Hosp.

Seton Hosp. for Men—Spuyten Duyvil. Inc. 1892. Treats all stages of consumption regardless of creed or color. Cap. 200-250, nearly all beds being subsidized by Dept. of Public Welfare, but there is a limited number of pay beds. Visiting days, Th. and Su., 2-4 P.M. Under direction of Sisters of Charity. Sister Frances Ignatius, Supt. Nazareth Branch for women and children.

Stony Wold Sanatorium—Lake Kushaqua, N. Y. Inc. 1901. Cares for incipient cases of tuberculosis. Receives women and girls, from 6 yrs. up. Mrs. J. E. Newcomb, Pres., R. 40, 1974 B'way.

Bkln. Hgts. Aux. of Stony Wold Sanatorium—150 Joralemon. 30 mem. To raise funds to pay for care of Bkln. working girls, young married women and children suffering from tuberculosis, at Stony Wold Sanatorium. Mrs. T. R. French, Ch.; Mrs. E. A. Freshman, Sec., 200 Hicks, Bkln.

Relief of Aged.

Baptist Ministers' Home Soc. of N. Y.—1023 E. 2d, Bkln. Est. 1882. For aged and disabled ministers, their wives, widows and minor children. G. W. Nicholson, Pres.; A. T. Brooks, D.D., Sec.-Treas.

Colored Home for Aged and Orphans—Essex Co., Montclair, N. J. Cares for adults over 65 yrs. Non-sec. Inmates, 21. Geo. Brown, Pres.; Mrs. A. M. Lynch, Sec., 7 Arch, Newark, N. J.

Firemen's Home of the State of N. Y.—Inc. 1890. Hudson, N. Y. Care for indigent volunteer firemen. 150 inmates. F. Baldwin, Pres.; W. H. Swartwout, Sec.; 276 Rutland rd., Bkln.; J. W. Eaton, Treas., Babylon, L. I.; E. H. Seehusen, Supt., Hudson, N. Y.

Fritz Reuter Altenheim—4361 Blvd., North Bergen, N. J. Est. 1897. Home for men over 60 and women over 55. W. J. Ruesch, Pres.; H. C. Eibs, Sec., 77 Bowers, Jersey City, N. J.; W. J. Solms, Supt.

Gallaudet Home for Aged and Infirm Deaf Mutes—Org. 1885. Near Poughkeepsie. 60 yrs. Office, address Mrs. D. C. Foster, 132 So. Hamilton, Poughkeepsie. 28 inmates. H. R. Jewett, Sec.; Miss V. B. Gallaudet, Asst. Gen. Mgr.

German Masonic Home—Tappan, N. Y. Est. 1888. Owned and conducted by German Masonic Temple Assn., N. Y., for Masons over 65 yrs., their wives or widows over 60 yrs. 34 inmates. L. Burger, Pres.; Louis Kleinbohl, Sec., 623 Linden av.; G. Leyendecker, Supt.

Home for the Aged and Infirm of the Independent Order of B'nai B'rith. See Jewish Org.

Mary Louise Heins Memorial—Mt. Vernon, N. Y. Ages, 65-86. Dr. G. C. Berkemeier, Pres., Mt. Vernon, N. Y.

Masonic Home and Asylum—Utica, N. Y. Est. 1893. For indigent Masons, their wives, widows and orphans of deceased members. 461 inmates. W. A. Rowan, Pres.; Wm. J. Wiley, Supt.

Miriam Osborn Memorial Home Assn.—Harrison, N. Y. Est. 1892. To provide home for respectable aged gentlewomen in needy circumstances, over 65 yrs., who have been residents of N. Y., Bronx or Westchester counties for previous 10 yrs. Admission fee, $500. H. C. Adams, Sec.

Pringle Memorial Home—Poughkeepsie, N. Y. Est. 1900. For aged and indigent gentlemen, preferably literary men (65 yrs.). 12 inmates. C. M. Fenton, Pres.; F. Hasbrouck, Ch. House Comm.; Mrs. I. T. Haight, Matron; Geo. C. Riley, Sec., Ellicott sq., Buffalo, N. Y.

Seabury Memorial Home—325 Highland av., Mt. Vernon, N. Y. Inc. 1888. Home for aged who have earned their living in literature, art, music, education or any of various professions. Non-sec. Applications must be made to Bd. of Trustees at Home. Alex. Wilson, Pres.; A. H. Seabury, Sec.; A. T. Sweet, Treas.; J. E. Osgood, Supt.

United Odd Fellows' Home and Orphanage Assn.—Unionport, N. Y. Inc. 1886. Home for aged and asylum for orphans of Odd Fellows. 94 inmates and 75 children. M. Berliner, Pres.; A. Menge, Supt.

Relief of Children.

Assn. of Little Mothers' League—1915. Dr. J. E. Baker, Ch.; Mrs. C. S. Whitman, Dir.

Asylum of Sisters of St. Dominick—Blauvelt, N. Y. Est. 1878. Inc. 1890. Home and Industrial Sch. for Children. Age limit, 16. 760 inmates. Mgr. Edwards, Pres.; Mother M. Marcella, Provincial.

Baptist Fresh Air Home Soc.—Somers, N. Y. Inc. 1892. Conducts Fresh Air Home for children of the Baptist Sunday Schl. and does general fresh air work. G. Leask, Pres., 54 William, N. Y. C.; C. H. Sears, Sec., 276 5th av., N. Y. C.

Christian Herald Children's Home—Est. 1894. Inc. 1898. Nyack-on-Hudson. Children of tenements from 6-11 yrs. for 10 days' vacation. Supported by voluntary contributions through Christian Herald. G. H. Patterson, Pres., Bible House, Mhtn.; Miss E. Goering, Supt.

HOSPS., HOMES AND SOCIETIES FOR RELIEF—N. Y. STATE & VIC.—RELIEF OF CHILDREN—*Con.*

Edgewater Creche—Englewood, N. J. 1884. Conducts fresh air work for mothers and children under 6. Also all-year convalescence home for babies of 2 years old and under. Mrs. I. H. Cornell, Pres.; L. C. Kellogg, Sec., 105 E. 22d, Mhtn.

Hebrew Sheltering Guardian Soc., Pleasantville, N. Y.—See Jewish Org.

Jennie Clarkson Home for Children (The)—Valhalla, N. Y. Inc. 1892. Age limit, for reception under 10 yrs. Care of orphans, half-orphans, destitute children. Has farm of 50 acres. 54 inmates. E. McK. Whiting, Pres.; J. M. Lesser, Sec., 126 Liberty. M. K. Sherwin, Supt.

Lulu Thorley Lyons Home for Crippled and Delicate Children—Claverack, N. Y. See Free Industrial Sch. for Crippled Children, under Relief of Children, Mhtn.

Missionary Sisters, Third Order of St. Francis—St. Joseph's Home for Destitute Children, Peekskill, N. Y. House of Reception, 12 W. 129th, Mhtn. Both sexes under 16 yrs.

Morristown Summer Shelter—Morristown, N. J. Org. 1890. Fresh Air Home for young girls, 4-14 yrs. Open from June to Sept. Cap., 60. Mrs. J. A. H. Hopkins, Pres.; M. F. Pierson, Sec., Colles av., Morristown, N. J. Mrs. W. W. Cutler, Treas.

Orphan Asylum Soc.—Hastings-on-Hudson, N. Y. Office, Room 521, United Charities Bldg. Inc. 1806. Maintains free Prot. orphanage on cottage plan for destitute orphans, both sexes, from 2-10 yrs. Ten cottages, cap. 240 children. Mrs. B. Perkins, 1st Dir.; Mrs. J. S. Sheppard, Treas.; R. R. Reeder, Supt.

Recreation Home—1905. Rockland Lake, N. Y. 2 houses. 3-12 yrs. of age. Charges $7 per wk., and $1 for auto trip fare to the home. Rev. W. H. Lawall, Nyack, N. Y., in charge.

Rethmore Home—Tenafly, N. J. Inc. 1892. fresh air home for children of N. Y. in summer. Age limit, 12 yrs. Mrs. J. H. Browning, Mgr.

Robins' Nest—Tarrytown-on-Hudson, N. Y. Inc. 1901. Summer home for convalescent children from Hospital for Ruptured and Crippled, 3-12 yrs.; 35 children cared for. Mrs. Howard Carroll, Pres.; Miss M. V. Lewis, Sec.; Miss Abbatt, Matron.

Sacred Heart Orphan Asylum—West Park on the Hudson, N. Y. Reception house, ft. Washington av. and 190th. In charge of Missionary Sisters of the Sacred Heart of Jesus.

St. Agatha's Home for Children—Nanuet, N. Y. Inc. 1885. 700 inmates. Reception House, 175 E. 68th. In charge of Sisters of Charity. Sister Mary Albert, Supt.

St. Benedict's Home for Destitute Colored Children of Both Sexes—Rye, N. Y. Est. 1886. 4-14 yrs. 160 inmates. Rev. M. J. Fitzpatrick, Mgr., 375 Lafayette, Mhtn.; Sister Modesta, Supt.

St. Christopher's Home for Destitute Children—Dobbs Ferry, N. Y. Founded 1881. Inc. 1885. Adopted cottage system in 1890. Maintains school for training of destitute children. Under patronage of Meth. Epis. Ch. 130 resident children. 25 children in a cottage. 40 placed out under supervision. Supported by voluntary contributions. Mrs. R. S. Ransom, Pres., Hartsdale, N. Y; Miss Ida G. Thompson, Supt.

Soc. of St. Martha—Bronxville, N. Y. Org. 1881. Epis. Training in household economy in all its branches to young girls over 6 yrs. 10 inmates. Rev. Mother Elizabeth, founder.

Speedwell Soc.—Morristown, N. J. Est. 1902. Provides temporary homes in country for convalescent and abandoned children. Non-sec. Mrs. H. A. Alexander, Pres.; Mrs. A. F. Mabon, Treas.; Miss M. I. Warne, Supt., 32½ Sussex av., Morristown.

Trustees of Leake and Watts' Orphan House in City of N. Y.—Inc. 1831. City Line. P. O. Yonkers, N. Y. (Ludlow or Lowerre sta. and Van Cortlandt Pk. subway). Free, private pay and city charges. 6-16 yrs. Non-sec. Cap. 300. Rev. Howard Duffield, Pres., 20 5th av. A. S. McClain, Supt.

Tuberculosis Preventorium for Children—Farmingdale, N. J. Est. 1909. To prevent the development and spread of tuberculosis primarily among children. 4,412 admitted. 200 beds. 12 beds for infants of tubercular families. Dr. A. F. Hess, Pres.; Miss J. P. Quinby, Supt.

Wartburg Orphans Farm Sch. of Evang. Luth. Ch.—Mt. Vernon. Est. 1864. Half and full orphans of both sexes bet. 2-10 yrs. given educational and industrial training. Maintains farm, printing house and kindergarten. 340 inmates. Rev. G. C. Berkemeier, Dir.

Watts de Peyster Industrial Home and Sch. for Girls—Tivoli-on-Hudson. Madalin P. O., N. Y. Inc. 1894. 60 capacity. Entrance age, 4-12, remaining until 17 yrs. To educate and train orphans and half-orphans to become self-supporting. Mrs. M. F. Park, Ch., 27 E. 62d, N. Y. C.; Miss I. M. Wharton, Supt.

Special Relief.

Burke Relief Foundation for Convalescents—1915. White Plains. 300 beds. Admission Dept., 325 E. 57th, Mhtn. Dr. F. Brush, Med. Dir., White Plains.

Gilbert A. Robertson Home—Scarsdale, N. Y. Inc. 1890. Summer home for poor families. Supported by endowment and contributions. W. N. Blakeman, Jr., Pres.; Candler Cobb, Sec., 46 Front.

Meadow Brook (Hope Hall)—Orangeburg. N. Y. Under auspices of Volunteers of Amer. Home for discharged prisoners. 40 inmates. W. Zabel, Supt., Orangeburg, N. Y.

Rest for Convalescents—B'way, White Plains. Inc. 1893. Temporary care for Protestant women over 16 yrs. Mrs. J. P. Duncan, Pres.; Mrs. H. Duffield, Sec., 20 5th av.; A. M. Rockwell, Supt.

St. Joseph's Inst. for Improved Instruction of Deaf Mutes—Org. 1869. Inc. 1875. Schl. for boys, Eastern Blvd. and Ferry Pt. rd., Westchester; Miss A. M. Larkin, Supt. Sch. for girls, same location as boys' sch.; Miss J. J. O'Hara, Supt. Girls' br., 113 Buffalo av., Bkln., Miss R. A. Fagan, Supt. Cap. of both schs. and br., 500. Children over 12 appointed by State Supt. of Public Instruction, bet. 5 and 12 admitted by Comm. of Public Welfare.

Solomon and Betty Loeb Memorial Home for Convalescents—East View, N. Y. Est. 1906. Admitting office, 356 2d av., N. Y. C. Admission days, Mon. and Th., 10-11 A.M. Women and children, 5 to 14 years of age. J. J. Hanauer, Pres.; Mrs. R. M. Israel, Supt.

Reformatories.

Berkshire Industrial Farm—Canaan, N. Y. Inc. 1886. Non-sec. Natl. training sch. for unruly and delinquent boys, conducted under religious influence. Boys taken by deed of surrender by parent for 4 yrs., with earlier discharge for good behavior, by commitment by magistrate with consent of supt., or by transfer from institutions. 140 inmates. S. T. Carter, Jr., Pres., Plainfield, N. J.; E. B. Hilliard, Supt.

Charlton Industrial Farm School—Ballston Lake, N. Y. Est. 1895. Home for wayward and homeless boys from 8-12 yrs. 30 inmates. Frank L. Smith, Pres.; W. I. Cavert, Sec.; L. H. Sears, Supt.

"Chester Crest," N. Y. Christian Home for Intemperate Men—Mt. Vernon, N. Y. Accommodations for all classes. Under management of bd. of directors. Booklet free. Rev. G. S. Avery, Res. Mgr.

Door of Hope—Tappan, N. Y. Mhtn. office, 122 W. 14th. Inc. 1892. Under supervision of Salvation Army and in conjunction with Door of Hope Bd. of Mgrs. For reclaiming fallen girls under 30 yrs. Staff Capts., Mrs. E. M. Whittemore, Pres.; M. Evans, Matron.

George Junior Republic of N. J.—Transferred to mother Republic at Freeville, N. Y.

George Junior Republic Assn.—Freeville, N. Y. Org. 1895. To care for neglected delinquent and other children bet. 14 and 21. W. R. George, Founder, in active charge of work.

House of Mercy (P. E.)—213th, Inwood-on-Hudson. Inc. 1855. For reception and reformation of destitute and fallen women. 110 inmates. Sister Gertrude, Superior; M. P. Parks, Sec., 104 E. 64th, Mhtn.

Jewish Protectory and Aid Soc., Hawthorne, N. Y.—See Jewish Org.

N. Y. Juvenile Asylum—Dobbs Ferry. N. Y. office, 103 Park av. Est. 1851. For children 7-16. Care, education and training of neglected, truant and delinquent boys. Places children in homes. 600 inmates. E. Dwight, Pres.; Guy Morgan, Supt.

St. Germain's Home of the House of the Good Shepherd—Mt. Florence, Peekskill, N. Y. Reception house, 504 E. 90th, Mhtn. Cap. 300.

HOSPS., HOMES AND SOCIETIES FOR RELIEF—N. Y. STATE AND VIC.—REFORMATORIES—*Con.*

Controlled by Roman Catholic Nuns of Good Shepherd. Sister M. Divine Heart, Supt.; Sister M. St. Austin, Sec.

St. Michael's Home—Mamaroneck, N. Y. Home Training Schl. Br. of Midnight Mission. Home for wayward girls. In charge of Sisterhood of St. John the Baptist. 50 inmates. S. F. Morris, Pres.; F. Parkman, Treas., 24 Nassau. Officers of St. Michael's Ladies' Assn.; Mrs. S. F. Morris, Pres.; Mrs. C. S. Brown, Sec., 247 Lexington av. Office of Midnight Mission, 105 E. 22d.

PRIVATE SANITARIUMS—NEW YORK CITY AND LONG ISLAND.

Brooklyn.

Muncie Sanit.—117 Macon. Surgical, chronic and all cases except contagious. Est. 1883. 156 inmates during yr. Florence J. Kennedy, Supt.

Midwood Sanit.—19 Winthrop. Est. 1907. Acute surgical cases. Acc. for 32 patients. Dr. Burt D. Harrington.

Skene Sanit.—759 President. Inc. 1902. L. G. Baldwin, M.D., Pres.; M. Louisa McMahon, Supt.

Willis Sanit.—54 St. Pauls pl. Aged and incurables, except insanity. H. Willis, M.D., Mgr.

Manhattan and Bronx.

Bronx Sanit.—1259 Washington av. G. E. Huether, Pres., 163 W. 85th; Dr. A. F. Brugman, Sec.; Miss G. V. Boggs, Supt.

Brown's Sanit.—220 E. 53d. Est. 1893. Female patients only. Dr. Schaub, Pres.; Mrs. Brown, Supt.

Hill Sanit., Inc.—317 W. 136th. Est. 1906. Acc. 40. Medical, surgical and maternity cases. Geo. W. Hill, Pres.

Minzesheimer Sanit.—138-140 E. 61st. Est. 1907. Medical, surgical and obstetrical cases. Camilla L. Minzesheimer, Pres.

Sprague Inst.—141 W. 36th. Est. 1898. For rheumatism, lumbago, gout, sciatica, neuritis, neurasthenia, stiff joints, etc. 50 rooms. No medicine administered. S. B. Whitington, Supt.

Long Island.

Breezehurst Terrace Sanit. for Nervous and Mental Diseases, Drug Addiction and Invalidism—Whitestone. Mhtn. office, 58 Central Park W. Est. 1890. 35 inmates. Dr. D. A. Harrison, Cons. Phy.; Dr. D. R. Lewis in charge.

Brunswick Home—Amityville. Inc. 1887. Epileptics, aged and feeble-minded persons, alcoholism and drug habitues. 250 inmates. Dr. C. Markham, Supt. in charge.

Dr. Combes' Sanit.—Jackson and Flushing avs., Corona. Mental and nervous diseases. Dr. E. T. Murray, Phys. in charge.

Long Island Home—Amityville. Est. 1882. Mental and nervous cases. 138 inmates. F. L. Bailey, Pres. Dr. O. J. Wilsey, Phys. in charge.

Louden Hall Cottage Home Sanit.—Amityville. Care and treatment of aged, decrepit and mentally enfeebled persons; opium and alcoholic cases. John Louden, Supt.

River Crest Sanit.—Astoria. Office, 616 Madison av., N. Y. C. Org. 1897. Daily average, 120. Mild mental and nervous diseases, alcoholic and drug addictions. Dr. J. J. Kindred, Consultant; Dr. Wm. E. Dold, Phys. in charge.

Ross Health Resort—Brentwood. Rest cure, nervous cases, convalescents. W. H. Ross, Phys.

Sanford Hall Hosp.—Jamaica av., nr. Franklin pl., Flushing. Est. 1841. Mental and nervous diseases. Dr. W. S. Brown, Phys. in charge.

Suffolk Co. Sanit. (Suffolk Co. Tuberculosis Hosp.)—Holtsville, L. I. 1917. Capacity, 48. Dr. E. P. Kolb, Supt.

TUBERCULOSIS CLINICS IN N. Y. CITY.

A prospective patient is supposed to go to the nearest clinic.

Brooklyn.

Dept. of Health, Bay Ridge Clinic, 60th and 2d av., Mon., Wed. and Fri., 2 to 4 P.M.

Dept. of Health Boat Camp, ft. N. 2d, 9 A.M. to 5 P.M. Day patients do not remain at night.

Dept. of Health, Brownsville, 64 Pennsylvania av., daily, 2 to 4 P.M.; Children's Clinic, Sat., 10 A.M. to 12 M.

Dept. of Health, Bedford, 420 Herkimer, daily, 2 to 4 P.M.; Children's Clinic, Sat., 10 A.M. to 12 M.

Dept. of Health, Prospect, Fleet and Willoughby, daily, 2 to 4 P.M.; Tu. and Th., 8 to 9 P.M.; Children's Clinic, Sat., 10 A.M. to 12 M.

Dept. of Health, E. D. Clinic, 306 South 5th, daily, 2 to 4 P.M.; Children's Clinic, Sat., 10 A.M. to 12 M.

Dept. of Health, Parkville, 974 West, Mon., Wed. and Fri., 2 to 4 P.M.; Children's Clinic, Sat., 10 A.M. to 12 M.

Manhattan.

A tuberculosis hospital admission bureau is maintained by the Dept. of Health, 128 Prince, for admissions to Otisville Sanatorium and Riverside Hosp. The Dept. of Public Welfare conducts a Hospital Admission Bureau for all hospitals and sanatoria at 124 E. 59th. Also children of tubecular parents to preventoria. Hours, 9 A.M. to 5 P.M.

Boat Camp "Manhattan," ft. E. 91st, 9 A.M. to 5 P.M. For Preventorium children.

Jefferson Clinic, 341 Pleasant av., daily, 10 A.M. to 12 M.; Tu., Th. and Sat., 2 to 4 P.M.; Tu., 8 to 9 P.M.

Stuyvesant Clinic, 111 E. 10th, Tu., Th., Sat., 10 A.M. to 12 M.; every aft., 2 to 4 P.M.; Children's Clinic, Sat., 10 A.M. to 12 M.

Yorkville Clinic, 439 E. 57th, every aft., 2 to 4 P.M.; Wed., 8 to 9 P.M.; Children's Clinic, Sat., 10 to 12 A.M.

Washington Clinic, Prince and Wooster, daily, 2 to 4 P.M.; Th., 8 to 9 P.M.; Children's Clinic, Sat., 10 A.M. to 12 M.

Chelsea Clinic, 307 W. 33d, daily, 2 to 4 P.M.; Th., 8 to 9 P.M.; Children's Clinic, Sat., 10 A.M. to 12 M.

Corlears Clinic, 331 Broome, daily, 2 to 4 P.M.; Th., 8 to 9 P.M.; Children, Sat., 10 A.M. to 12 M.

Riverside, 481 W. 145th, daily, 2 to 4 P.M.; Th., 8 to 9 P.M.; Children, Sat., 10 A.M. to 12 M.

Associate Clinics: Bellevue Dispensary, ft. E. 26th, daily, 2 to 4 P.M.

Gouverneur Hosp. Dispensary, ft. Gouverneur, Mon., Wed. and Fri., 2 to 4 P.M.; Tu., Th. and Sat., 4 to 6 P.M.

Harlem Hosp. and Out Patient Dept., 136th and Lenox av., daily, 2 to 4 P.M., and Th., 7:30 to 9:30 P.M.; Children, Tu. and Sat., 10 to 12 A.M.

Mt. Sinai Hosp. Dispensary, Madison av. and 100th, daily, 10 to 11 A.M.; 1 to 3 P.M.

N. Y. Dispensary, 34 Spring, daily, 11 A.M. to 1 P.M., except Tu. and Th.

N. Y. Hosp. Dispensary, 8 W. 16th, Mon., Fri., 2 to 3 P.M.; Tu., 7:30 to 9 P.M.; Children, Wed., 3 to 5 P.M.

Presbyterian Hosp. Dispensary, 70th and Madison av., daily, 1:30 to 2:30 P.M.

St. Luke's Hosp. Dispensary, Amsterdam av. and 113th, adults, Tu. and Thur., 1:30 to 2:30 P.M.; Fri., 7 to 8 P.M.; Children, Sat., 9 to 10 A.M.

Ladies' Auxiliary, Tuberculosis Com.—Mrs. J. Sheppard, Ch.

Tuberculosis Hospital Admission Bureau, 124 E. 59th, 9 A.M. to 5 P.M.

Vanderbilt Clinic, Amsterdam av. and 60th, daily, 9:30 to 2:30 P.M., except Su. and holidays.

Bronx.

Dept. of Health, Mott Haven, 493 E. 139th, daily, 10 A.M. to 12 M.; Tu., 8 to 9 P.M.; Children's Clinic, Sat., 10 to 12 A.M.

Dept. of Health, Tremont, 3d av. and St. Pauls pl., daily, 2 to 4 P.M.; Th., 8 to 9 P.M.; Children's Clinic, Sat., 9 to 11 A.M.

Queens.

Dept. of Health Clinic, 374 Fulton, Jamaica, M., W., Fri., 2 to 4 P.M.; Th., 8 to 9 P.M.

Dept. of Health Clinic, 127 46th, Corona, Mon., Wed. and Fri., 2 to 4 P.M.; Thur., 8 to 9 P.M.

Dept. of Health Clinic, 138 Hunter av., L. I. City. Mon., Wed. and Fri., 2 to 4 P.M.; Thur., 8 to 9 P.M.

Dept. of Health Clinic, 753 Onderdonk av., Ridgewood. Tu., Th., Sat., 2 to 4 P.M.; Wed., 8 to 9 P.M.

Richmond.

Dept. of Health, Bay and Baltic, Stapleton, S. I., Mon., Wed., Fri., 2-4 P.M.

HOSPITALS, HOMES AND SOCIETIES FOR RELIEF—*Continued.*

TUBERCULOSIS HOSPITALS IN N. Y. STATE.

Tuberculosis Hospitals and Sanatoriums located outside of Greater New York maintained by cities, counties and hospital associations. For requirements for admission, etc., address Committee on Prevention of Tuberculosis of State Charities Aid Assn., 105 E. 22d, Mhtn.

Albany Hosp., Albany. All stages. Public cases only. No private cases. Dr. H. C. Goodwin, Supt.

Chemung Co. Tuberculosis Sanatorium, Elmira. Dr. E. T. Bush, Supt.

Edward Meany Sanatorium, Taughannock Falls, N. Y. Tompkins Co. Sanatorium. $11.50 per week to Tompkins Co. patients. Non-residents of Co., $15 per week. Keith Sears, M.D., Supt.

Erie Co. Hosp., Buffalo, N. Y. Building destroyed by fire, June, 1918. Patients cared for by contract by City Hosp.

Estelle and Walter C. Odell Mem. Sanatorium for Tuberculosis, Newburgh, N. Y. All stages. Up to $14 per week. Dr. R. A. Miller, Supt.

Hill Crest and Uplands, Santa Clara. Summer vacation houses, for working girls and women threatened with tuberculosis.

Iola Sanatorium. (See Monroe Co. Tuberculosis Hosp.)

J. N. Adam Memorial Hosp., Perrysburg. Favorable cases from Buffalo, N. Y. Pulmonary, bone and joint. Dr. C. L. Hyde, Supt.

Loomis Sanatorium, Loomis. Incipient and moderately advanced. $15-$40 per wk. Dr. B. H. Waters, Phys. in charge.

Monroe Co. Tuberculosis Sanatorium, Rochester, N. Y. Dr. J. J. Lloyd, Supt.

Montefiore Home, Bedford Hills. Incipient cases. Cap., 225. Free beds. B. Stivelman, M.D., Med. Supt.

Montgomery Co. Tuberculosis Hosp., Amsterdam, N. Y. Dr. V. M. Parkinson, Supt.

The Broome County Tuberculosis Hosp. All stages. 78 beds. Dr. Blinn A. Buell, Supt.

N. Y. City Municipal Sanatorium for Tuberculosis, Otisville. Free institution maintained by the Dept. of Health. Admission through the Hospital Diagnostic Sta. of the Dept. of Health, 130 Prince, Mhtn. R. J. Wilson, M.D., Dir.

Oak Mount Sanatorium, East Bloomfield. Care and treatment of pulmonary tuberculosis. Dr. W. A. Bing, Supt.

Oneida Co. Hosp., Rome, N. Y. All stages. Dr. R. L. Bartlett, Supt.

Oswego Co. Sanatorium, Richland, N. Y. All stages. Dr. L. F. Hollis, Supt.

Pawling Sanatorium, Wynantokill, N. Y.—A new 200-bed tuberculosis hospital. Dr. F. L. S. Reynolds, Supt.

Rainbow Sanatorium, Rainbow Lake. Free to all stages. Ind. Order of Foresters. Rates to others, $2.50 per day. Dr. J. S. Emans, Supt.

Ray Brook (State Hosp.), Ray Brook. Incipient and early cases only. Free. Dr. H. A. Bray, Supt. Apply local boards of health.

Samuel W. Bowne Memorial Hosp., Poughkeepsie. All stages. Also children. $10-$15 per wk. G. N. Kimball, Pres.; H. St. J. Williams, M.D., Supt.

Sanatorium Gabriels, Gabriels. Conducted by Sisters of Mercy, $18-$25 per wk. Dr. H. J. Blankmyer, Res. Phys.

Sprain Ridge Hospital, Yonkers. Incipient cases only. $2-$7 per wk. Mrs. H. Smith, Supt.

Stony Wold Sanatorium, Lake Kushaqua, N. Y. Incipient and sometimes moderately advanced. $9 per wk. Also a few free beds. M. F. Lent, Supt.

Summit View Sanatorium, Gloversville, N. Y. All stages. Fulton Co. patients pay according to their ability up to $10 per wk. Other patients, $12 per wk. Dr. W. Shaw, Supt.

Sunnycrest Sanatorium, Auburn. All stages. $12 to $14 per wk. K. Bohrman, Supt.; A. F. Hodgman, Med. Attend.

Trudeau Sanatorium—Trudeau, N. Y. Est. 1885. To offer hygienic, dietetic and climatic treatment to consumptives who otherwise could not obtain it. 150 patients. $10 to $17.50 per wk. Dr. W. B. James, Pres.; Dr. F. H. Heise, Res. Phys.; C. R. Armstrong, Supt.

Ulster Co. Tuberculosis Hosp., Kingston. All stages. Free to county patients; non-residents, $12 per wk. Dr. A. C. Gates, Supt.

Westchester Co. Tuberculosis Hosp., East Plew. All stages. $10 per wk. Only Westchester Co. residents accepted. Admitted upon application to Commr. of Charities and Corrections. Dr. F. E. Russell, Phys. in Charge.

Workmen's Circle Sanatorium, Liberty. Incipient cases. Dr. J. B. Fish, Supt.

Yonkers Municipal Hosp. for Advanced Cases, Yonkers. Louise Landers, Supt.

MILITARY TRAINING IN N. Y. STATE.

The Military Training Commsn. consists of the Maj. Gen. commanding the Natl. Guard ex-officio, who is ch., and two other members, one appointed by the Board of Regents of the Univ. of the State and one by the Governor. The terms of the appointed members are 4 years.

Under the terms of Article 1-A of the military law, which is the act creating the Military Training Commsn., every boy in the State above the age of 16 years and not over the age of 19 years, except boys exempted by the commsn., must receive such military training as the commsn. may prescribe for periods aggregating not more than three hours in each week during the school or college year in the case of school boys and for 41 weeks in each year in the case of boys who are not pupils. The training is to be conducted under the supervision of the commsn. by male teachers and physical instructors of schools and colleges when assigned by governing bodies and accepted by the commsn., by officers and enlisted men of the Natl. Guard and Naval Militia or such officers and enlisted men of the U. S. Army as may be available. In the discretion of the commsn. the military training requirement may be met in part by "such vocational training or vocational experience as will, in the opinion of the commsn., specifically prepare boys of the ages named for service useful to the State, in the maintenance of defense, in the promotion of public safety, in the conservation and development of the State's resources, or in the construction and maintenance of public improvements."

Within the limits of appropriation the commsn. may conduct summer camps for boys subject to military training, attendance at the camps to be voluntary.

The commsn. issues to every boy who complies with the requirements of the law a certificate to that effect, which a boy of the ages specified must possess in order to attend school or be employed.

The commsn. is also directed to advise and confer with the Board of Regents of the Univ. of the State as to courses of instruction in physical training to be prescribed for elementary and secondary schools as provided in the amendment to the education law, passed at the same session of the Legislature, calling for not less than 20 minutes a day of physical training for all school children over 8 years of age. The commsn. is to provide for the observation and inspection of physical training work in the schools.

Armories of the Natl. Guard and Naval Militia when not required for the use of the regular organization, and arms and other equipment of the Natl. Guard and Naval Militia not required at the time, are to be made available to the Military Training Commsn. for conducting its work. School authorities are authorized to permit the use of school buildings and grounds for this same purpose.

CONTRIBUTORS TO CHARITIES.

The New York Association for Improving the Condition of the Poor, with 11,642 contributors, heads the list of all the charitable organizations in the United States in the number of individual contributors. With more than 11,000, the Brooklyn Bureau of Charities now has the second largest popular support, the United Charities of Chicago coming third and the New York Charity Organization Society, fourth.

WAR RELIEF.

(New York City Headquarters.)

Allied.

Amer. Artists' Comm. of One Hundred Relief Fund for Families of French Soldier-Artists—W. A. Coffin, Ch.; W. B. Faxon, Treas., 215 W. 57th.

Amer. Authors Fund for Relief of Wounded Soldiers of Allied Nations—Care State St. Trust Co., 33 State St., Boston, Mass.

Amer. Committee for Devastated France—1918. 16 E. 39th, Mhtn., and 15 Blvd. Lannes, Paris. 3000 mem. M. T. Herrick, Pres.; Miss Eliz. Scarborough, Sec., 104 E. 40th.

Amer. Fund for French Wounded—Rm. 1106, 71 B'way. Mrs. Walter P. Bliss, Treas.

Amer. Girls' Aid—165 B'way. Gladys Hollingsworth Attwood, Ch.

Amer. Memorial Hospital, Inc.—61 B'way. Miss Edith Bangs, Ch., Central Union Trust Co., Depository, Mhtn.

Amer. Zionist Medical Unit—Zionist Organization of Amer., 55 5th av. Miss Henrietta Szold.

Belgian Relief Fund—431 W. 47th. J. P. Morgan & Co., Depository.

British War Relief Assn., Inc.—247 5th av. Major Louis L. Seaman, M.D., Pres.; Henry Clews, Treas.

Cardinal Mercier Fund for Special Belgian Relief—431 W. 47th. J. P. Morgan & Co., Depository.

Colonie de Franceville of Madame F. Berkeley Smith, 16 Place de la Madeleine, Paris—Mrs. W. D. Hines, 122 E. 70th.

Comm. for Men Blinded in Battle—W. Forbes Morgan, Treas., 111 E. 59th.

Commission for Relief in Belgium—115 B'way. Herbert Hoover, Ch.

Comm. on Relations with France and Belgium—A. R. Kimball, Treas., 105 E. 22d.

Duryea War Relief, Inc. (Secours Duryea)—202 Madison av. Mrs. N. L. Duryea, Pres.

Fatherless Children of France, Inc.—1918. 665 5th av. Depository, J. P. Morgan & Co.; S. L. Cromwell, Pres.; Alex. J. Hemphill, Treas.; Chas. MacVeagh, Sec.

Franco-Amer. Comm. for Protection of Children of Frontier of France—F. R. Coudert, Ch. and Treas., 2 Rector.

Lafayette Fund—Francis Roche, Treas., Vanderbilt Hotel.

Le Paquet de L'Orphelin, 299 B'way, Rm. 1612.

L'Union des Arts, 653 5th av. Moreta Maynard, Sec.

Lithuanian Central War Relief Comm., Inc.—294 8th av.

Natl. Allied Relief Comm., Inc.—2 W. 45th. John Moffat, C. B. E., Ch.; Miss I. E. Morton, Sec.; J. A. Blair, Jr., Treas.; Metropolitan Trust Co., Depository.

Noel du Soldat Belge Fund—P. Dumont, 10 Bridge.

Permanent Blind Relief War Fund for Soldiers and Sailors of the Allies, Inc.—A. W. Kerch, Gen. Treas., 590 5th av.

Roumanian Relief Comm. of Amer.—43 Cedar. W. Nelson Cromwell, Ch.; T. Tileston Wells, Ch. Exec. Comm.; H. Clews, Treas.

Russian Amer. Relief Assn.—Care Natl. City Bank, 55 Wall. V. Demianof, Treas.

Serbian Aid Fund—1 Madison av. O. T. Bannard, Treas.; Mabel R. Greene, Sec.; Madame S. Gronitch, Dir.

Serbian Child Welfare of Amer.—7 W. 8th. Wm. Jay Schieffelin, Ch.; A. B. Hepburn, Treas.

Armenian, Jewish, Polish.

Amer. Jewish Relief Comm. For War Sufferers from the War—A. Lehman, Treas., 20 Exch. pl.

Central Comm. for the Relief of Jews Suffering Through the War—51 Chambers. H. Fischel, Treas.; S. Bero, Gen. Mgr.

Joint Distribution Comm. of Amer. Funds for Jewish War Sufferers—F. M. Warburg, Ch., 52 William; P. Baerwald, Treas.; A. Lucas, Sec., 20 Exchange pl.

Jewish People's Relief Comm.—175 E. B'way. S. J. Goldberg, Treas.; Isadore Garelick, Sec.

Near East Relief—1 Madison av. James L. Barton, Ch.; C. H. Dodge, Treas.; Chas. V. Vickrey, Sec.

Paderewski Fund for Poland (formerly Polish Victims' Relief Fund)—Aeolian Bldg., 33 W. 42d. W. H. Taft, Pres.; F. A. Vanderlip, Hon. Treas.; W. O. Gorski, Ex. Sec.

THE HALL OF FAME.

In March, 1900, the late Chancellor MacCracken of New York University, announced that $250,000 had been given that institution for a Hall of Fame of great Americans. The conditions were that 50 names might be chosen in 1900 and 5 more each succeeding 5 years through the 20th century. 100 electors from all of the 45 States were asked to make nominations and to indicate each one his choice of 50 names. Upon Oct. 1, 1900, it appeared that 97 electors had voted and that 29 names had received a majority of 51 votes. The number of votes for each was as follows: George Washington, 97; Abraham Lincoln, 96; Daniel Webster, 96; Benjamin Franklin, 94; Ulysses S. Grant, 93; John Marshall, 91; Thomas Jefferson, 91; Ralph Waldo Emerson, 87; Robert Fulton, 86; Henry W. Longfellow, 85; Washington Irving, 83; Jonathan Edwards, 82; Samuel F. B. Morse, 82; David G. Farragut, 79; Henry Clay, 74; Nathaniel Hawthorne, 73; George Peabody, 74; Peter Cooper, 69; Robert E. Lee, 68; Eli Whitney, 69; John J. Audubon, 67; Horace Mann, 67; Henry Ward Beecher, 64; James Kent, 65; Joseph Story, 64; John Adams, 62; Wm. E. Channing, 58; Gilbert Stuart, 62; Asa Gray, 51.

In 1904 the constitution of the Hall was amended to provide for choosing separately 10 names of famous American women in 1905, and 2 in each succeeding quinquennium.

In Oct., 1905, the Senate received the ballots of 95 electors, of whom only 85 undertook to consider the names of women. A majority of 51 was demanded, but in the case of the names of women a majority of only 47. The following 8 persons were found to be duly chosen: John Quincy Adams, 60; James Russell Lowell, 59; William T. Sherman, 58; James Madison, 56; John G. Whittier, 53; Mary Lyon, 59; Emma Willard, 50; Maria Mitchell, 48.

In Oct., 1910, the Senate received the votes of 97 electors; 51 votes were required for choice; 10 names were added, as follows: Harriet Beecher Stowe, 74; Oliver Wendell Holmes, 69; Edgar Allan Poe, 69; James Fenimore Cooper, 62; Phillips Brooks, 60; William Cullen Bryant, 59; Frances E. Willard, 56; Andrew Jackson, 53; George Bancroft, 53, and John Lothrop Motley, 51.

For the election in 1915, the 100 electors were called to choose not more than 23 American men and not more than 11 famous American women. 97 electors sent ballots, 3 having died during year; 9 names were chosen by a majority of 49 or more electors, as follows: Alexander Hamilton, 70; Mark Hopkins, 69; Francis Parkman, 68; Louis Agassiz, 64; Elias Howe, 61; Joseph Henry, 56; Rufus Choate, 52; Daniel Boone, 52; with one woman, Charlotte Cushman, 53.

The Constitution was amended in 1914, by striking out the separable election of foreign-born Americans, so that the 4 foreign names which had been chosen in 1905 and 1910 were resubmitted in 1915 for election in competition with native-born Americans. Two names, Alexander Hamilton and Louis Agassiz, were approved. The others, John Paul Jones and Roger Williams, lacked a majority, but remain in nomination for 1920. Thus 50 famous men in all have been admitted, and 6 famous women. Total, 56. For the election in 1920 the 102 electors were called to choose not more than twenty men and not more than ten women. 101 electors sent ballots; six men were elected and one woman: Samuel Langhorne Clemens, James Buchanan Eads, Patrick Henry, Thomas William Greene Morton, Augustus Saint Gaudens, Roger Williams and Alice Freeman Palmer.

Communications should be addressed to Executive Office, Hall of Fame, 347 Madison av., New York City.

The new House of Assembly of New Jersey consists of 60 members. Harry Runyon of Warren County, was the sole Democrat chosen on Election Day. The remaining 59 Assemblymen, who include 2 women, 2 ministers and a negro, are Republican.

SOCIETIES AND ASSOCIATIONS.

These Organizations are arranged alphabetically under headings as shown on first page of Index.

ALUMNI AND ALUMNAE ASSOCIATIONS.

International.

Internatl. Federation of Catholic Alumnae—1914. 83,000 mem. Vy. Rev. Jas. Cardinal Gibbons, Hon. Pres.; Mrs. J. J. Sheeran, Pres., 219 76th, Bkln.; Miss H. R. O'Neil, Sec., 259 84th, Bkln.

National.

Alumnae Assn. of Smith College—College Hall, Northampton, Mass. 1881. 7,850 mem. Mrs. Dwight W. Morrow, Pres. Gen.; Florence H. Snow, Sec.

Alumni Assn. of Amer. Rhodes Scholars—1907. Mass. Inst. of Technology, Cambridge, Mass. 500 mem. L. W. Cronkhite, Pres.; Frank Aydelotte, Sec., Mass. Inst. of Tech., Cambridge, Mass.

Amer. Nurses Assn.—35,000 mem. Miss C. D. Noyes, Pres.; Miss Katherine DeWitt, Sec., 19 West Main, Rochester, N. Y. Next convention, 1922, at Seattle, Wash.

Assn. of Collegiate Alumnae—1881. 10,000 mem. Mrs. L. K. M. Rosenberry, Pres.; Mrs. G. S. Martin, Exec. Sec., 934 Stewart av., Ithaca, N. Y.

Assn. of Graduates of U. S. Military Academy—1870. West Point, N. Y. 1,500 mem. Gen. S. E. Tillman, Pres.; Capt. W. A. Ganoe, Sec.

Vanderbilt Med. Alumni—Org. 1908. 520 mem. Dr. F. M. Williams, Pres.; Dr. Wm. Litterer, Sec.-Treas., Nashville, Tenn.

Women's Univ. Club—1891. 1,200 mem. 106 E. 52d, Mhtn. Mrs. T. Jex Preston, Jr., Pres.; Mrs. T. J. Goddard, Cor. Sec.

Brooklyn.

Adelphi Academy Alumni Assn.—1908. 300 mem. T. L. Leeming, Pres.; Luman Wing, Sec., Dongan Hills, S. I.

Adelphi College Alumnae Assn.—1900. 250 mem. Mrs. J. L. Robinson, Pres.; Miss E. M. McKechnie, Sec., 1164 Pacific.

Alumnae Assn. Bkln. Law Schl. (Women)—1910. 21 mem. Miss Amy Wren, Pres.; Miss Rose Gottlieb, Sec., 44 Court.

Alumnae Assn. of College of Mt. St. Vincent on Hudson—1896. 360 mem. Mrs. N. C. Brosnan, Pres.; Miss O. Carroll, Sec., 135 E. 92d, Mhtn.

Alumnae Assn. of M. E. Hosp. Training Schl. for Nurses—1896. Miss M. Bellamy, Pres.; Mrs. C. B. Hoag, Sec.

Alumnae Assn. of St. Agnes' Academy—1897. 300 mem. 285 Union. Miss M. Hansbery, Pres.; Miss M. Moore, Sec., 208 Warren.

Alumnae Assn. of Williamsburgh Hosp. Training Schl. for Nurses—1915. 45 mem. Mrs. A. Fallberg, Pres.

Alumni Assn. of Boys' High Schl.—1907. 175 mem. A. A. Tausk, Cor. Sec.; R. I. Raiman, Rec. Sec.

Alumni Assn. of Bkln. Eve. High Schl. for men—1917. 350 mem. W. L. Schweikert, Pres., 620 E. 32d; H. J. Dybinski, Sec., 378 State.

Alumni Assn. Cumberland St. and Bkln. Homeopathic Hosp.—1900. 132 mem. Dr. W. T. Hopper, Pres.; Dr. W. R. Izard, Sec., 141 St. Marks av.; W. H. Price, Treas.

Alumni Assn. P. S. No. 3—Hancock, nr. Bedford av. 1,000 mem. F. P. Taylor, Pres.; J. H. Evans, Sec.

Alumni Assn., P. S. No. 10—1906. 7th av., 17th. 1,000 mem. J. Rice, Pres.; F. Clark, Sec., 445 14th.

Alumni Assn. of St. Catherine's Hosp.—60 mem. J. A. Driscoll, M.D., 171 Washington Pk.

Alumni Assn. of St. John's College—1881. 75 Lewis av. 350 mem. Alfred J. Jollon, Pres.; Jos. V. Boland, Sec., 282 Arlington av.

Alumni Assn. of Sch. of Fine and Applied Arts of Pratt Inst.—1909. 296 Lafayette av. Mrs. Berthoud, Pres.; Miss M. T. Jones, Sec.

Alumni Soc. of the Bkln. Hebrew Orphan Asylum—1902. 200 mem. Dr. I. H. Rogow, Pres.; L. Katzoff, Sec.

Associate Alumnae Adelphi Acad.—1910. 325 mem. Miss Jessie H. Righter, Pres., 1357 Dean; Mrs. C. W. Middleton, Cor. Sec.

Associate Alumnae, Packer Collegiate Inst.—1882. 1,099 mem. Mrs. L. C. Caruana, Pres.; Miss Mildred J. Baxter, Sec., 173 Columbia hts.

Association P. S. No. 17—1914. No. 5th and Driggs av. 138 mem.

Berkeley Alumnae Assn.—Berkeley Inst. —1887. 191 Lincoln pl. 195 mem. Mrs. R. E. Merwin, Pres., 796 Carroll; Mrs. E. R. McPherson, Cor. Sec., 202 8th av.

Bkln. Alumni Assn. of Amherst College—350 mem. G. P. Hitchcock, Pres.; H. L. Warner, Sec., 85 Clinton.

Bkln. Chautauqua Alumni—1888. 60 mem. J. A. Lant, Pres.; Miss Laurence, Sec., 610 Delamere pl.

Bkln. College Club—1125 Carroll. 1919. 624 mem. J. A. Reilly, Pres.; L. J. Mannion, Jr., Sec., 900A Greene av.

Bkln. Hosp. Training Schl. Alumnae—1903. 187 mem. Mrs. H. F. McChesney, Pres.; M. E. Holt, Treas., 66 Montague.

Cornell Alumni Assn.—1905. 1,200 mem. J. L. Moffatt, Pres.; E. I. Thompson, Sec., 44 Court.

Erasmus Hall Alumni Assn.—5,000 mem. G. E. Boynton, 304 E. 18th. Mem. of Faculty in charge.

Graduates Assn. of the Pratt Inst. Schl. of Library Science—411 mem. Mrs. F. De Gogorza, Pres.; Mrs. C. H. Tapping, Sec., 161 Emerson pl.

Hamilton College Alumni Assn.—1901. •50 mem. Bayard L. Peck, Pres.; W. C. Du Bois, Sec., 165 B'way, Mhtn.

Harvard Club of L. I.—60 mem. B. M. Langstaff, Pres.; W. J. Kibby, Sec., Univ. Club of Bkln.

Henry D. Woodworth Assn. (P. S. No. 17)—1914. 450 mem. Moses B. Schmidt, Pres.; J. P. Hogan, Sec.; Wm. O. West, Treas., 1227 Fulton.

Manual League—1919. 1,817 mem. Bert W. Hendrickson, Pres.; Mardette Frost, Sec., 397 Park pl.

Norwegian Hosp. Alumni—27 mem. H. T. Spelman, Pres.; H. Fisher, Sec., 312 Lewis av.

Old South Fourth St. Alumni Assn.—1906. Ed. J. Clarry, Pres.; M. D. Barnes, Sec., Woolworth Bldg., Mhtn.

Polytechnic Alumni Assn.—85 Livingston. 1904. 400 mem. W. H. Oulson, Pres.; M. G. Woolfson, Sec., 619 Eastern P'kway.

Polytechnic Preparatory Alumni Assn.—4,000 mem. Lawrence C. Hull, Pres.; Dr. M. W. Henry, Treas., 2589 Bedford av.; H. Holt, Sec.

Pratt Inst. Chemical Alumni Assn.—1901. E. J. Murphy, Pres.; C. W. Schmitz, Sec.

Pratt Inst. Kindergarten Alumnae Assn.—1892. 500 mem. Miss M. A. Gardner, Pres., 371 Gates av.; Miss Ora M. Nutt, Sec., 6 St. James pl.

Rounds Alumnae Assn.—1896. 204 mem. Mrs. L. R. Bewden, Pres.; Mrs. J. N. Carpenter, Sec., 90 Greene av.

St. Anthony's Alumnae—729 Leonard. 1913. Margaret Baatenburger, Pres.; Mary McAllister, Sec.

St. Anthony's Parochial Alumni Assn.—1913. Leonard, nr. Greenpoint av. J. A. McClellan, Pres.; Patrick A. Finn, Sec.

St. John's Graduate Nurses' Alumni Assn., Atlantic and Albany avs.—1919. 80 mem. Mrs. F. Dyott, Pres.; Miss L. Cowan, Sec.

St. Joseph's College Alumnae—1920. St. Joseph's Coll. Marjorie Nolan, Pres.; Adaline Canning, Sec.

St. Mary's Hosp. Alumni—1903. 90 mem. Dr. C. G. O'Connor, Pres.; Dr. O. A. Gordon, Jr., Sec., 71 Halsey.

Visitation Alumnae—1904. Ridge blvd. and 89th. M. A. Hook, Pres., 1001 Ocean av.; Mrs. Orville Peters, Sec., 570 Pacific.

Yale Alumni Assn. of L. I.—1904. Hamilton Club. 650 mem. A. F. Jenks, Pres.; H. C. Martin, Sec., 25 Madison av., Mhtn.

Manhattan and The Bronx.

Alfred Club (Alumni Assn. of Alfred Univ.)—1908. 55 mem. F. C. White, Pres.; A. C. Prentice, M.D., Sec., 226 W. 78th.

Alumnae Assn. of Bellevue Train. Schl. for Nurses—1889. 426 E. 26th. 515 mem. C. B. Bristol, Pres.; M. E. Allen, Sec.

Alumnae Assn. of Rutgers Female Inst. and Col.—1867. 40 mem. Mrs. C. C. Kennedy, Pres.; Miss E. F. Merritt, Cor. Sec., 155 W. 93d.

Alumnae Assn. of Women's Law Class of N. Y. Univ.—1891. 300 mem. Miss I. M. Pettus, Pres.; Miss M. E. A. MaGuire, Sec., 27 2d pl., Bkln.

Alumni Assn. of Amity Theological Schl.—1905. 242 mem. Chas. Bolte, Pres.; C. F. Weindell, Sec., 138 E. 31st.

SOCIETIES AND ASSOCIATIONS—ALUMNI AND ALUMNAE—MHTN. AND BRONX—*Continued.*

Alumni Assn. of Clason Pt. Military Academy —Clason Pt. J. Rorke, Pres.; J. Hoctor, Treas.; Chas. Rebholz, Sec.

Alumni Assn. of the Col. of St. Francis Xavier—1879. 850 mem. C. M. O'Keefe, Pres.; J. A. McNamara, Sec., 165 B'way.

Alumni Assn. of Eclectic Med. College—1870. 239 E. 14th. 894 mem. Dr. A. M. Ralston, Sec., 121 Henry, Bkln.

Alumni Assn. of Grammar Schl. No. 40—1908. 350 mem. Gen. G. W. Wingate, Pres.; J. W. McDonald, Sec., 425 W. 120th.

Alumni Assn. of the Law Schl. of Columbia Univ.—1860. Columbia Univ. 850 mem. G. W. Morray, Pres.; J. P. Carter, Sec., 32 Liberty.

Alumni Assn. of Manhattan College—B'way, at 131st. 1869. 1,500 mem. J. E. Kiffin, Pres.; J. T. Stack, Sec., 312 Union, Bkln.

Alumni Assn. of Mt. Washington Collegiate Inst. N. Y.—1884. 125 mem. W. H. Sage, Pres.; J. N. Henriques, Sec., 468 W. 144th.

Alumni Assn. of N. Y. Col. of Dentistry—1880. 118 mem. Dr. R. O. Taylor, Pres.; Dr. L. J. Solow, Sec., 33 W. 42d.

Alumni Assn. of N. Y. Col. of Pharmacy—1870. 119 W. 68th. 1,500 mem. Leo Roon, Pres.; L. N. Brown, Sec.

Alumni Assn. of N. Y. Homeopathic Med. Col. and Hosp.—1883. 850 mem. Dr. N. H. Ives, Pres.; Dr. E. S. Munson, Sec., 8 W. 49th.

Alumni Assn. N. Y. State Veterinary College at N. Y. Univ.—1889. 1,200 mem. Dr. T. E. Smith, Pres.; Dr. A. Eichorn, Sec., Pearl River, N. Y.

Alumni Assn. of N. Y. Univ. Law Schl.—1884. 3,500 mem. Hon. E. L. Garvin, Pres.; H. E. Lippincott, Sec., 1 E. 45th.

Alumni Assn. of P. S. No. 14—1905. 175 mem. J. H. Halsey, Pres.; Miss M. A. Corbett, Sec., 921 Av. O, Bkln.

Alumni Assn. of the School of Architecture of Columbia Univ.—116th, Morningside hgts. 125 mem. R. J. Reilley, Pres.; Arthur Ware, Sec., 1170 B'way

Alumni Assn. of Stevens Inst. of Technology—1876. Stevens Tech., Hoboken, N. J. 1,900 mem. E. E. Hinkle, Pres.; G. G. Freygang, Sec.

Amherst Assn. of N. Y.—700 mem. G. B. Mallon, Pres.; F. S. Bale, Sec., 120 B'way.

Associate Alumni of Col. of the City of N. Y. —Inc. 1853. 138th and St. Nicholas Terrace. 3,600 mem. Lee Kohns, Pres.; J. Holman, Sec., 371 Grand.

Associate Alumni of Gen. Theological Sem.—1832. 950 mem. Rev. John Keller, Sec., 2 Clark, Glen Ridge, N. J.

Associate Alumnae of Hunter Col. of the City of N. Y.—1871. Park av. and 8th. 2,452 mem. Mrs. W. C. Popper, Pres.; Miss J. Seligmann, Sec., 124 E. 80th.

Associated Alumni of Mt. Sinai Hosp.—250 mem. Dr. H. L. Celler, Pres.; Dr. H. E. Lindeman, Sec., 102 W. 75th.

Assn. of Alumni of Col. of Phy. and Surg. of the Medical Dept. Columbia Univ.—1859. 375 mem. W. Mendelson, Pres.; Dr. H. E. Hale, Sec., 64 W. 50th.

Assn. of Alumni of Columbia Col.—1874. 1,700 mem. Maj. A. W. Putnam, Pres.; R. W. Macbeth, Sec., 450 5th av.

Assn. of Alumni of N. Y. Hosp.—1908. 250 mem. Dr. W. Culbert, Pres.; C. E. Farr, Sec., 8 W. 16th.

Assn. of Collegiate Alumnae (N. Y. Branch)—1886. 175 mem. Mrs. Milton L'Ecluse, Pres.; Mrs. Herbert Bowles, Cor. Sec., 1664 Nelson av., Bronx.

Assn. of Johns Hopkins Alumni in N. Y. and N. J.—1893. 80 mem. G. S. Brown, Pres.; John Griffin, V.-Pres.; Arthur Wright, Sec., 111 B'way.

B. D. L. Sutherland Assn. or Grove St. Grammar Schl.—1914. 725 mem. W. W. Cohen, Pres.; E. E. Elkins, Sec., 2892 Bailey av.

Barnard Col. Alumnae Assn. — Mrs. P. Achilles, Pres.; Miss A. C. Reiley, Ex. Sec., Students Hall, B'way and 117th.

Bowdoin Alumni Assn.—1869. 450 mem. H. D. Gibson, Pres., 120 B'way; J. W. Frost, Sec., 14 Wall.

Brown University Club—1875. 250 mem. A. B. Meacham, Pres., 59 Wall; C. B. Fernald, Sec.

Columbia Alumni Federation—1913. Central Bd. of more than 20 alumni assns., with membership of 6,000. Stephen G. Williams, Pres.; C. G. Proffitt, Exec. Sec., 311 East Hall, Columbia Univ.

Columbia Univ. Club—See Social Clubs.

Cornell Univ. Club—See Social Clubs.

Dartmouth Col. Alumni Assn. of N. Y.—1866. 750 mem. C. G. Du Bois, Pres.; M. Whittemore, Sec., 165 B'way.

Dwight Alumni Assn.—1891. 400 mem. C. E Hughes, Pres.; Geo. C. Austin, Sec., 135 B'way.

Eastern Alumni Assn. of Univ. of Chicago—1898. E. H. Ahrens, Sec., 461 4th av.

Elmira Col. Club—Mrs. L. T. Le Wold, Pres.; Mrs. C. Tolley, Sec.

Emerson Alumni Club—1905. 80 mem. Mrs. K. A. Arnidson, Pres.; Miss Helen M. Roarty, Sec., 206 Lexington av., Bkln.

Fordham Univ. Alumni—Fordham. 1859. 1,600 mem. O. S. Tierney, Pres.; E. Gilleran, Sec., Fordham Univ.

Gallaudet Alumni Assn.—1907. 45 mem. Dr. T. F. Fox, Pres.; Dr. E. W. Nies, Sec., 503 W. 149th, Mhtn.

General Alumni Assn., N. Y. Univ.—1919. 22 W. 43d. 15,000 mem. Howard F. Langland, Exec. Sec.

George White Alumni Assn.—1901. Savoy Hotel. 200 mem. P. A. Weinberg, 634 5th av., Pres.; Mrs. J. J. Cody, Treas., 1269 Lexington av.

Hamilton Col. Alumni Assn. of N. Y. City—1912. Dr. L. B. Sherman, Pres.; H. C. Bates, Sec., Metropolitan Life Ins. Co., N. Y.

Harvard Club—See Social Clubs.

Kenyon Col. Alumni Assn. of the East—148 mem. C. E. Milmine, Pres., 29 E. 80th; Rev. F. R. Jones, Sec., Willard Parker Hospital, ft. E. 16th.

Lafayette Alumni Assn.—1883. 1,000 mem. H. N. Hempstead, Pres.; W. D. Bushnell, Sec., 120 B'way.

Lehigh Univ. Club of Greater N. Y.—See Social Clubs.

Mass. Agricultural Col. Club of N. Y.—1886. 200 mem. W. L. Morse, Pres.; A. T. Beals, Sec., 2929 B'way.

Mt. Holyoke Alumnae Assn.—Miss H. B. Prescott, Pres.; Miss Helen S. Watt, Sec., 23 W. 54th.

N. Y. Alumni Assn. Albany State Normal Col. —S. J. Slawson, Pres.: F. A. Duncan, Sec., Custom House, N. Y. City.

N. Y. Alumni Assn. of Colgate Univ.—E. B. Shallow, Pres.; E. H. Whitney, Sec., 241 W. 37th, N. Y. C.

N. Y. Alumni Assn. of Univ. of Vermont—450 mem. Dr. H. E. Lewis, Pres.; H. E. Wood, Sec., 15 Broad.

N. Y. Alumni Club (Univ. of Chicago)—L. J. MacGregor, Sec., care of Halsey, Stuart & Co., 49 Wall.

N. Y. Assn. of the Alumni of Phillips Acad., Andover—1891. 1,600 mem. F. R. Appleton, Pres.; F. H. Simmons, Sec., 110 Centre.

N. Y. Assn. Alumni of the Univ. of Virginia—400 mem. Dr. J. H. Claiborne, Pres.; F. A. Jenkins, Sec., 14 Wall.

N. Y. Graduates Soc. of McGill Univ.—1895. 80 mem. W. W. Colpitts, Pres.; W. H. Donnelly, Sec., 178 Woodruff av., Bkln.

N. Y. Soc. of Queens Univ., Canada—1901. 52 mem. J. R. Losee, Sec., 200 W. 58th.

Oberlin Alumni (N. Y. Assn.)—1884. O. C. Sanborn, Pres., 80 B'way.

Ohio State Univ. Assn. of N. Y.—1900. C. W. Burkett, Pres.; H. A. Carr, Sec.-Treas., 80 Maiden lane.

Potsdam State Normal Schl. Alumni Assn. of N. Y.—1893. 300 mem. C. H. Cherrey, Pres., White Plains; J. Dowsey, Sec., Tarrytown, N. Y.

Princeton Club—See Social Clubs.

Roosevelt Hosp. Alumni Assn.—1896. 59th and 9th av. 176 mem. S. R. Burnap, M.D., Pres.; P. M. Barker, M.D., Sec., 100 W. 59th.

Rutgers College Alumni Assn. of City of N. Y. —1,300 mem. R. H. Neilson, Pres.; T. S. Voorhees, Sec., 111 B'way.

St. Lawrence Univ. Club—200 mem. Cleland R. Austin, Pres.; Edwin B. Wilson, Sec., 409 E. 26th, Bkln.

St. Paul's Schl. (Garden City) Alumni Assn.—1889. 1,165 mem. Chas. S. Butler, Pres., Garden City, L. I.; A. J. Daly, Sec., Garden City, L. I.

Seton Hall Col. Alumni Assn.—1860. 600 mem. E. F. Kinkead, Pres.; G. H. Gleeson, Sec., 738 Broad, Newark, N. J.

Soc. of Alumni of Amer. Academy of Dramatic Arts—1888. Laura Sedgwick Collins, Pres.; Wales Winter, Treas., Longacre Bldg.

SOCIETIES AND ASSOCIATIONS—ALUMNI AND ALUMNAE—MHTN. AND BRONX—*Continued.*

Soc. of Alumni of Bellevue Hosp.—1886. 875 mem. 50 Vanderbilt av. C. B. Slade, Pres.

Soc. of Alumni of the Sloane Hosp. for Women—1888. 203 mem. Dr. E. M. Collie, Jr., Pres.; Dr. S. Swift, Cor. Sec., 55 E. 61st.

Soc. of Alumni of St. Luke's Hosp.—1893. 200 mem. Dr. F. Beekman, Pres.; Dr. M. K. Smith, Sec.

Sun Alumni Assn.—1904. 200 mem. Edward G. Riggs, Pres.; Willis Holly, Sec.-Treas., Municipal Bldg., Rm. 1007.

Technology Club of N. Y.—1895. 1,200 mem. L. D. Gardner, Pres.; T. C. Desmond, Sec., 17 Gramercy Pk.

Thomas Hunter Assn.—1897. 600 mem. A. E. Cressinger, Pres.; F. R. Fortmeyer, Sec., P. O. Box 740. Mhtn.

Trinity Col. Alumni (N. Y. Assn.)—1870. 400 mem. R. Thorne, Pres.; F. C. Hinkel, Jr., Sec., 75 Beekman.

U. S. Naval Acad. Alumni Assn. of N. Y.—1895. 500 mem. R. M. Thompson, Pres., 1607 23d, Washington, D. C.

Union Col. Alumni Assn.—1888. 36 Stuyvesant. 500 mem. Dr. F. H. Giddings, Pres.; Wm. Allen, Sec., 149 B'way.

Univ. of Ill. Alumni Assn.—200 mem. Evans E. A. Stone, Pres.; W. B. Lazew, Sec., 50 Church.

Univ. of Mich. Club—450 mem. H. E. Chickering, Pres.; H. W. Ford, Sec.-Treas., 50 Church.

Univ. of Pa. Club—See Social Clubs.

Univ. of Rochester Alumni Assn.—1884. 875 mem. Burt L. Fenner, Pres.; H. C. Michaels, Sec., 404 4th av.

Virginia Military Inst. Alumni Assn., N. Y. Chapter—J. C. Meem, Pres., 149 Remsen, Bkln.; Earl Rankin, Sec., Produce Exchange, Mhtn.

Wellesley Club of N. Y.—1890. 767 mem. Mrs. F. H. Filley, Pres.; Mrs. H. Sichel, Cor. Sec., 424 W. 20th.

Wesleyan Univ. Club of N. Y.—700 mem. Wm. A. Jones, Pres.

Wilson Col. Club of Greater N. Y.—1907. 159 mem. Mrs. F. Welsh, Pres.; Mrs. F. Chalinor, Sec., 27 Argyle rd., Flatbush.

Yale Club—See Social Clubs.

ART CLUBS.

National.

Amer. Fed. of Arts—1909. 228 chapters. R. W. de Forest, Pres.; Leila Mechlin, Sec., 1741 N. Y. av., Washington, D. C.

Amer. Inst. of Architects—1857. Washington, D. C. 288 fellows; 1,464 mem. Chapters in 38 cities. H. H. Kendall, Pres.; W. S. Parker, Sec.; E. C. Kemper, Exec.-Sec., The Octagon House, Washington, D. C.

Amer. Painters, Sculptors and Grovers—1919. 49 mem. 647 5th av., N. Y. C.

Amer. Soc. of Landscape Architects—1899. F. L. Olmstead, Pres.; A. F. Brinckerhoff, Sec., 527 5th av., Mhtn.

Amer. Students Club—4 Rue Joseph-Bara, Paris, France. Rodman Wanamaker, Pres.; H. W. Methven, Sec.; F. C. Friescke, Ch. Bd. of Gov.

Amer. Water Color Soc.—1867. 215 W. 57th. Mhtn. 130 mem. W. S. Robinson, Pres.; J. W. Dunsmore, Sec.

Natl. Arts Club—1898. 1,800 mem. 15 Gramercy Pk. John G. Agar, Pres.; J. C. Oswald, Sec.

Natl. Institute Arts and Letters—1898. 250 mem. C. Gilbert, Pres.; J. B. Fletcher, Columbia Univ., Sec.

Natl. Sculpture Soc.—1893. 215 W. 57th, Mhtn. 350 mem. F. G. R. Ronti, Pres.; E. W. Keysen, Sec.

Natl. Soc. of Craftsmen—1906. 10 E. 47th. Mhtn. 300 mem. C. E. Pellew, Pres.; Miss Jane Hoagland, Act. Sec.

Natl. Soc. of Mural Painters—1895. 92 mem. Geo. W. Breck, Pres.; A. Covey, Sec., 215 W. 57th, Mhtn.

Soc. of Independent Artists—600 mem. Jno. Sloan, Pres.; A. S. Baylinson, Sec., 1947 B'way, N. Y. C.

Brooklyn.

Allied Arts Assn.—175 Duffield. 1907. 81 mem. E. V. Brewster, Pres.; W. G. Bowdoin, Sec.

Amer. Inst. of Architects (Bkln. Chap.)—T. E. Snook, Pres.; MacDonald Mayer, Sec., Gardens Apt., Forest Hills, L. I.

Bkln. Academy of Photography—1888. 35 mem. Wm. Arnold, Pres.; H. W. Hodges, Sec., 177 Montague.

Bkln. Art Assn.—Academy of Music. H. J. Morse, Pres.; Herman Stutzer, Sec.

Bkln. Art Club—1878. Professional artists only. Benj. Eggleston, Pres.; Wedworth Wadsworth, Sec., Durham, Conn.

Bkln. Art Guild—246 Fulton. 38 mem. Miss Edith Sawyer, Pres.; Miss E. L. Hollis, Sec., 111 Decatur.

Bkln. Inst. of Arts and Sciences—See Index.

de Severinus Art Students League—1912. Mme. L. de Severinus, Pres., 1076 Bergen; Miss E. Schenkbar, Sec.

Bkln. Soc. of Artists—1917. 85 mem. F. J. Boston, Pres.; H. E. Field, Sec., 106 Columbia Hts.

Bkln. Water Color Club—1919. 40 mem. B. Egleston, Pres.; H. B. Tschudy, Sec., H. Field, 106 Columbia Hts.

Pratt Art Alumni Assn.—1906. 296 Lafayette av. Miss Adele Lay, Pres.; Wm. Gotham, Sec.

Rembrandt Club of Bkln.—1880. 100 mem. F. L. Babbott, Pres.; Howard S. Hadden, Sec., 248 Henry.

Manhattan and Bronx.

Amer. Criterion Soc.—Hotel Plaza. 1912. 550 mem. Mrs. Leonard L. Hill, Pres.; Mrs. Sidney B. Whitlock, Sec., Sea Gate.

Amer. Fine Arts Soc.—1889. 215 W. 57th. C. J. Miller, Sec.

Amer. Institute of Architects (N. Y. Chap.)—1867. 215 W. 57th. 275 mem. B. L. Fenner, Pres.; H. R. Shreve, Sec., 215 W. 57th.

Architectural League of N. Y.—1880. 215 W. 57th. 675 mem. J. M. Hewlett, Pres.; L. G. White, Sec.

Art Alliance of America—1914. 10 E. 47th. 816 mem. W. F. Purdy, Pres.

Art Students League of N. Y.—1875. 215 W. 57th. 482 members. 1,551 students. Gifford Beal, Pres.; J. Howell, Sec.

Bronx Soc. of Arts and History (The)—1905. Lorillard Mansion, Bronx Pk. 100 mem. W. Stebbin Smith, Pres., 462 E. 167th; Gunther K. Ackerman, Sec., The Mansion, Bronx Pk.

Fine Arts Federation of N. Y.—215 W. 57th. 1895. Council of all principal art societies of city. 96 member delegates elected from constituent societies. A. D. W. Brunner, Pres.; A. S. Bard, Treas.; W. L. Harris, Sec., 120 Central Park So.

Metropolitan Museum of Art—1870. Central Pk., 82d. 8,694 mem. R. W. DeForest, Pres.; H. W. Kent, Sec.; Ed. Robinson, Dir. Open 10 A.M. to 6 P.M. in summer, 10 A.M. to 5 P.M. in winter; Sun., 1 P.M. to 6 P.M. Admission free, except on Mon. and Fri., when a charge of 25c. is made. Copyists obtain permission to work on all days except Sat. afternoons, Sun. and legal holidays. (See index also for museums.)

Municipal Art Soc. of N. Y.—119 E. 19th. Inc. 1898. 700 mem. Object to encourage municipal art. J. Howland Hunt, Pres.: Mrs. H. B. Keen Sec.

Natl. Acad. of Design—1825. Amsterdam av. and 109th. 262 mem. 130 academicians, 132 associates. E. H. Blashfield, Pres.; C. C. Curran, Sec.

N. Y. School of Applied Design for Women—1892. 160 Lexington av. Miss E. J. Pond, Sup.

N. Y. Soc. of Architects—1906. United Engineering Bldg., Mhtn. 400 mem. J. R. Gordon, Pres.; W. T. Towner, Sec., 100 Morningside Drive, Mhtn.

N. Y. Water Color Club—1890. 220 mem. H. B. Snell, Pres.; Ed. C. Volkert, Sec., 215 W. 57th.

Pen and Brush Club (The)—1898. 134 E. 19th. 245 mem. Miss Ida M. Tarbell, Pres.; Miss Reinette Lovewell, Sec., 128 W. 99th.

Salamagundi—1871. 47 5th av. 900 mem. J. M. Rhind, Pres.; W. Neumuller, Cor. Sec.

School Art League of N. Y. City—1911. Object: To foster art education in public schls. 5 W. 47th. J. P. Haney, Ch.; Florence N. Levy, Sec.

Sketch Club of N. Y.—1898. 150 mem. S. F. Miller, Pres.; W. J. Blackburn, Sec., 1 Madison av.

Soc. of Beaux Arts Architects—1894. 126 E. 75th. 278 mem. B. W. Morris, Pres.; P. A. Cusacks, Sec., 12 E. 46th.

Soc. of Illustrators—1899. 225 mem. C. D. Gibson, Pres.; H. L. Sparks, Treas.; F. De Sales, Casey, Sec.; Ray Greenleaf, Cor. Sec., 50 Union sq.

Queens.

Queensboro Soc. of Allied Arts and Crafts—1910. Dr. C. H. Miller, N. A., Pres., Queenslawn Pk., Queens; Mrs. Geo. Tonner Sec., Hollis.

SOCIETIES AND ASSOCIATIONS—*Continued*

BOARDS OF TRADE AND CIVIC IMPROVEMENT ASSOCIATIONS.

Note—In many instances organizations classifying themselves as Business Associations (pages 164-169) are similar in character to Boards of Trade, but to avoid repetition they are not included in following list.

National and International.

Amer. Chamber of Commerce—1905, Naples, Italy. J. P. Spanier, A. Piccoli, Sec., 14 via Marina Nuova, Naples, Italy.

Amer. Civic Assn.—1904. Washington, D. C. 2,600 mem. J. H. McFarland, Pres.; E. E. Marshall, Sec., 914 Union Trust Bldg., Washington, D. C.

Amer. Soc. for Municipal Improvements—1894. 600 mem. Geo. H. Norton, Buffalo, N. Y., Pres.; C. C. Brown, Sec., Valparaiso, Ind.

British Empire Chamber of Commerce in the U. S. of America—1920. 165 B'way, Mhtn. 250 mem. E. F. Darrell, Ch.; Ryerson Ritchie, Sec.

Far Western Travelers Assn.—St. Francis, San Francisco, Cal., and Hotel Claridge, N. Y. City. 1913. 1,150 mem. Col. J. B. Patton, Pres.; S. L. Mein'nger, Sec., Hotel Claridge, N. Y. City.

Franco-Amer. Bd. of Commerce and Industry—1919. 175 5th av., N. Y. C. 200 mem. Emile Utard, Pres.; Theodore Seltzer, Sec.

Internatl. Chamber of Commerce—1920. 33 rue Jean Goujon, Paris, France. The purpose of the Internatl. Chamber is to ascertain the commercial intercourse of nations, to secure harmony of actions on all internatl. questions affecting commerce and industry, and to promote peace, progress and cordial relations among countries and their citizens by the co-operation of business men and their organizations devoted to the development of commerce and industry. Etienne Clementel, Pres.; Edouard Dolleans, Sec.

Natl. Citizens' Alliance, Inc.—1890. Object: Anti-Monopoly, personal liberty. 1,189 mem. 134 W. 20th, Mhtn. Harding Weston, Pres.; Henry Nichols, Sec., 134 W. 20th, Mhtn.

Natl. Civic Federation—1900. Object: To organize best minds of nation in educational movement for advancement of industrial and social progress. Alton B. Parker, Pres.; R. M. Easley, Ch. Exec. Council, 1 Madison av., Mhtn.

Natl. Florists' Board of Trade—1898. 48 Wall, Mhtn. E. McK. Whiting, Pres.; H. A. Wood, Sec., 48 Wall.

Natl. Highways Protective Soc.—1909. 80 Maiden la., Mhtn. E. S. Cornell, Sec.

Natl. Housing Assn.—1910. R. W. de Forest, Pres.; Lawrence Veiller, Sec., 105 E. 22d, Mhtn.

Natl. Jewelers' Board of Trade—1899. 15 Maiden la. 1,200 mem. A. Lorsch, Pres.; F. C. Backus, Sec.

Natl. Municipal League—1894. 2,500 mem. L. Purdy, Pres.; C. R. Woodruff, Sec., 701 North American Bldg., Phila., Pa.

Woman's Natl. River and Harbor Congress—1908. Washington, D. C. Mrs. J. M. Strout, Pres.; Mrs. E. G. Laurence, Sec., 856 Locust, Cincinnati, O.

State.

N. Y. Civic League—1910. 452 B'way, Albany, N. Y. W. Sheafe Chase, Pres., 451 Bedford av., Bkln.; Rev. O. R. Miller, State Supt.; H. P. Freece, Treas.

Brooklyn.

Allied Boards of Trade and Taxpayers' Assn.—1904. Hart's Hall, Gates av. and B'way. 3,300 mem. M. Adler, Pres.; M. J. McDonough, Sec., 983 Madison.

Allied Civic Assns. of Greater Ridgewood and E. D.—1911. Irving av., cor. Cornelia. 25 orgs. B. A. Ruoff, Pres.; Wm. Hart, Sec., 1434 Myrtle av.

Amer. Assn. for the Planting and Preservation of City Trees—1909. 150 mem. G. V. Brower, Pres.; Miss A. B. Gallup, Sec., Bkln. Children's Museum, Bkln. av, and Park pl. Has a Junior League of 6,000 mem., divided into 11 chapters in P. S. libraries and settlements. Children from kindergarten to high school age. Miss M. W. Carmichael, Dir.

Associated Civic Assns. of Bkln.—1915. 1180 Fulton. 40 organizations in central body. Herbert L. Carpenter, Pres.; Wm. D. O'Donnell, Sec.

Atlantic Av. and Bkln. Impt. Assn.—1908. 846 Fulton. 250 mem. E. J. Megarr, M.D., 586 Washington av., Pres.; L. Arnold, Sec., 846 Fulton.

Atlantic Av. Business Men's and Taxpayers' Assn. of E. N. Y. 1911. 2730 Atlantic av. 200 mem. S. J. Phillips, Pres.; L. Middleman, Sec.

Atlantic Av. Civic Assn.—1909. 90 mem. H. L. O'Brien, Pres. and Sec., 69 Court.

Bath Beach and Bensonhurst Bd. of Trade—1902. 2079 Cropsey av. 75 mem. D. A. Kistler, Pres.; J. F. Duhamel, Sec., 202 Bay 28th.

Bath Beach Taxpayers' Assn.—1910. 102 mem. Phil. Sheridan, Pres.; M. G. Magrath, Sec., 203 Bay 8th.

Bay Ridge Chamber of Commerce—1917. 250 mem. S. H. Duffy, Pres.; Anthony Huber, Sec., 421 51st.

Bedford Av. Crosstown Subway League—1912. 469 Franklin av. F. Clayton, Pres.; C. C. Mollenhauer, Sec., 147 B'way.

Bedford and Park Ave. Bd. of Trade—1908. 507 Park av. 70 mem. E. Bick, Pres.; A. H. Wilson, Sec., 41 Clifton pl.

Bedford Hgts. Bd. of Trade—700 Franklin av. C. Partridge, Pres.; G. P. Losee, Sec.; W. G. Halpin, Cor. Sec., 700 Franklin av.

Boro. Park Hgts. Civic Assn.—1911. 150 mem. M. S. Harris, Pres.; W. W. Tracy, Sec., 4602 Ft. Hamilton P'kway.

Broadway Bd. of Trade—1898. 1028 Gates av. 300 mem. N. H. Levi, Pres.; E. F. Reuter, Sec., 1336 B'way.

Bkln. Business Men's Assn.—1910. 151 Remsen. John Michel, Pres.; S. J. Corsa, Sec.

Bkln. Chamber of Commerce—32 Court. 3,000 mem. J. S. Davis, Pres.; Mayo Fesler, Sec.

Bkln. Com. on City Planning—1912. 807 mem. F. B. Pratt, Pres.; J. W. Tumbridge, Sec., Hotel St. George.

Bkln. Hgts. Assn.—1910. 500 mem. C. J. Peabody, Pres.; J. W. Tumbridge, Sec., 51 Clark.

Canarsie Bd. of Trade—1904. 300 mem. A. Stahle, Pres.; F. H. Campbell, Sec., 1221 Remsen av.

Central Borough Board of Public Improvement—1906. 175 mem. W. H. Benjes, Pres.; F. A. Byrne, Sec., 296 Lenox rd.

Central Comm. Flatbush Civic Organizations—1912. G. Boochever, Ch.; F. C. Wandmacher, Sec., 1290 N. Y. av.

Central Flatbush Taxpayers' Assn.—1906. 125 mem. G. C. Emerich, Pres.; Gregory Weinstein, Sec., 296 Lenox rd.

Citizens' Assn. of Bay Ridge and Fort Hamilton—1885. 271 mem. W. B. Hatfield, Pres.; J. J. Sheeran, Sec., 219 76th.

City Line Bd. of Trade—Grant and Liberty av., G. U. Forbell, Pres.; C. S. Forbell, Sec.

Clinton Av. Assn.—1899. 90 mem. F. T. Aldridge, Pres., 406 Clinton av.; W. B. Greenman, Sec., 256 Clinton av.

Commerce Club—1912. W. S. Miller, Pres.; J. E. MacDermott, Sec., 807 Mhtn. av.

Coney Isl. Carnival Co., Inc.—W. F. Mangels, Pres.; L. A. Squier, Sec., W. 8th, C. I.

Cypress Hills Bd. of Trade—1906. P. S. No. 65. 275 mem. Chas. S. Forbell, Pres.; F. D. Kruse, Sec., 58 Hale av.

Cypress Hills Taxpayers' and Citizens' Protective Union (Inc.)—267 Nichols av. 1911. 40 mem. Morris Adler, Pres.

DeKalb Impt. Assn.—1914. J. Kampner, Pres.; G. F. McCann, Sec., 113 Lewis av.

Dem. County Com. Sub-Com. on Civic Affairs—J. H. McCooey, Ch. Ex. Com., 4 Court sq.

Dimas Pk. Assn.—1908. 125 mem. M. S. Marden, Pres.; C. Addoms, Sec.

Downtown Taxpayers' Assn.—1904. P. S. No. 5. 200 mem. Dr. J. J. Colgan, Pres.; Morris Garlick, Sec., 181 Gold.

E. D. Bd. of Trade—1900. 500 mem. 157 Meeker av. J. Garlinge, Pres.; R. W. Boenig, Sec., 157 Meeker av.

E. D. Club—See Social Clubs.

East Bkln. Citizens' Assn.—1912. 200 mem. E. F. Barnes, Pres.; Van D. Macumber, Sec., 926 Bedford av.

East Flatbush Taxpayers' Assn.—1904. 4917 Church av. 125 mem. F. R. Horton, Pres.; D. C. Taylor, Sec., 426 E. 45th.

Eastern P'kway Civic League—1914. 827 Nostrand av. H. J. Levy, Pres.; J. B. Allen, Sec.

Eastern P'way Subway Assn.—1903. Eastern P'kway and Bkln. av. 8,000 mem. F. W. Rowe, Pres.; A. S. Drescher, Sec., 1613 President.

Erie Basin Bd. of Trade—1910. 195 Richards. 180 mem. W. F. Silleck, Pres.; A. J. Hildebrand, Sec.

Fiske Terrace Assn.—1906. 150 mem. J. A. Derthick, Pres.; Ben. M. Joquish, Sec., 782 E. 18th.

Flatbush Chamber of Commerce, Inc.—1916. 842 Flatbush av. 281 mem. Lewis H. Pounds, Pres.; Carl S. Heidenreich, Sec.

SOCIETIES AND ASSNS.—BOARDS OF TRADE AND CIVIC IMPROVEMENT—BROOKLYN—*Continued.*

Flatbush Community Center—1920. 100 mem. Dr. I. G. Harris, Pres.; F. C. Wandmacher, Sec., 1290 New York av.

Flatbush Playgrounds Assn.—Amalgamated with Bkln. Parks and Playgrounds Com.

Flatbush Taxpayers' Assn.—1896. 750 mem. Flatbush Water Works Co., 2 Lenox rd. Geo. A. Taft, Pres.; F. C. Wandmacher, Sec., 1290 N. Y. av.

Ft. Hamilton Citizens' Assn.—1906. 40 mem. J. P. Taylor, Pres.; Eugene Lucas, Sec., 242 94th.

F'klin Bd. of Trade—1913. E. W. McGuire, Pres.; A. L. Perkiens, Sec., 1161 Fulton.

Fulton St. Bd. of Trade—90. 350 mem. J. L. Baker, M.D., Pres.; A. Hoffman, Sec., 1211 Dorchester rd.

Glenwood Impt. Assn.—1907. 60 mem. J. R. Corbin, Pres.; L. Longuemare, Sec., 2412 Glenwood rd.

Grace Greenwood Civic Club—Buckingham Chateau, Flatbush. 1911. 60 mem. Mrs. Wm. Reed, Pres.; Mrs. Geo. Brandow, Historian; Mrs. Geo. Osgood, Sec., 278 Carroll.

Grand Av. Assn.—1909. J. A. Smith, 424 Grand av.; E. W. Haviland, Sec., 403 Grand av.

Grand St. Impt. Assn.—1898. 100 mem. T. P. Fritz, Pres., 806 Halsey; J. McGrade, Sec.

Gravesend Beach Bd. of Trade—1914. 90 mem. J. F. Duhamel, Pres., 8650 19th av.; C. N. Gates, Sec.

Gravesend Bd. of Trade—1909. 75 mem. F. C. Rudloff, Pres., 263 Webster av.; W. A. Reller, Sec.

Greenpoint Hebrew Civic Club, Inc.—1908. 861 Mhtn. av. 100 mem. Mayer Sachs, Pres.; S. Silverman, Sec.

Greenpoint Taxpayers' and Citizens' Assn.—1914. 250 mem. Edw. Welch, Pres., 205 N. Henry; Chas. F. Hulseman, Sec., 837 Manhattan av.

Greenpoint Women's Civic Club—1918. Mrs. F. Roddatz, Pres.; Mrs. M. McKell, Sec.

Highland Park Civic Assn.—1914. 331 Jamaica av. 300 mem. Judge E. A. Richards, Pres.; Russell F. Thomas, Sec.

Italian-Amer. Civic Union—1910. D. Cuozzo, Pres.; J. Virdone, Sec., 50 Court.

Jamaica Bay Impt. Assn.—1905. 500 mem. A. Wheeler, Pres.; N. B. Killmer, Sec., 396 State.

Kensington and Parkville Impt. League—1907. 300 mem. C. H. Teeter, Pres.; J. H. Ewald, Sec., 783 E. 4th.

Kings and Queens Co. Bakers' Bd. of Trade—1404 Decatur. 1916. 450 mem. Jacob Roeser, Pres.; Jos. E. Mueller, Sec.

Kings County Grand Jurors Assn.—1919. Room 1, Hall of Records. 700 mem. Wm. M. Tomlins, Jr., Pres.; Clarence E. Spayd, Sec., 130 Columbia Hts.

Kings Highway Bd. of Trade—1905. 500 mem. G. A. Marshall, Pres.; L. A. Chapple, Sec., 1620 E. 15th.

Lefferts Park Impt. League—1902. 120 mem. J. R. Pinover, Pres.; J. F. Steppe, Sec., 1551 71st.

Lincoln Pl. Tree Assn.—1912. 798 Lincoln pl. 60 mem. G. C. Wood, Pres.; Arthur Pratt, Sec.

Livingston St. Assn.—1920. L. Kalischer, Pres., 283 Livingston; J. Turner, Treas.

Manufacturers' and Business Men's Assn. (now Chamber of Commerce of Bkln.)

Men's Club of Bay Ridge—80th and Bay Ridge blvd. 1902. 200 mem. E. C. Babcock, Pres.; D. W. Taylor, Sec., 441 78th.

Midwood Manor Assn.—1911. 350 mem. A. Goldwasser, Pres., 953 E. 8th.

Midwood Park Property Owners' Assn.—1909. W. H. Heissenbuttel, Pres.; A. G. Harkness, Sec., 671 E. 19th.

Municipal Club—1897. 100 mem. M. W. Gleason, Pres.; A. B. Roome, Sec., 100 William, Mhtn.

New Lots Bd. of Trade—1908. 996 Blake av. 715 mem. J. Hessel, Pres.; J. Jens, Cor. Sec., 198 Hendrix.

New Utrecht Impt. Assn.—1908. 1765 79th. 75 mem. M. C. Schill, Pres.; F. C. Licari, Sec.

N. Y. Harbor Protective and Development Assn. —150 Nassau. A. Van Wyck, Pres.; J. D. Tucker, Sec., 2679 E. 24th, Bkn.

North Flatbush Bd. of Trade—1914. 1120 Nostrand av. 105 mem. J. J. Ludeke, Pres.; A. J. Snee, Sec., 54 Rutland rd.

Nostrand Ave. Bd. of Trade—1913. 100 mem. 363 Nostrand av. John Herries, Pres.; J. V. Martin, Sec.

Oakland St. Prop. Owners' Impt. Assn.—1912. 97 Oakland. 150 mem. J. J. Holwell, Pres.; Henry Bopp, Sec.

Ocean Hill Bd. of Trade—1902. 160 mem. E. E. Pabst, Pres.; Harry P. Butler, Sec., 394 E. 2d.

Old **South Bkln.** Civic League, Inc.—1913. 139 Harrison. Mrs. N. H. Lander, Exec. Sec. Conducts dental dispensary. Americanization work done under supervision of Miss E. A. Holden, Sec.

Parade Park Assn.—1908. E. N. Whiting, Pres.; J. H. Windels, Sec., 1506 Caton av.

Parks and Playgrounds Comm. (Bkln. Com.)—1911. 50 Court. F. C. Munson, Ch.; L. W. Betts, Sec.

Prospect Heights Citizens' Assn.—1904. 600 mem. A. G. Reeves, Pres.; C. D. McBride, Sec., 135 Berkeley pl.

Prospect Park South Assn.—1905. 186 mem. Arthur M. Howe, Pres., 205 Rugby rd.; E. W. Harter, Sec., 121 Marlborough rd.

Ridgewood Bd. of Trade—1902. 431 Irving av. 360 mem. Edw. Domschke, Pres.; F. Richter, Sec., 431 Irving av.

Sheepshead Bay Bd. of Trade—A. W. Dennen, Pres.; A. W. Houck, Sec.; J. D. Tucker, Sec. Exec. Com., 2679 E. 24th.

So. Bkln. Bd. of Trade—1896. Prospect Library, 6th av. and 9th. 700 mem. A. Link, Pres.; Albertine McIntyre, Sec., 513 5th av.

So. Bkln. Business Men's League—1910. 150 mem. 589 4th av. Gustave Hartung, Pres.; B. J. Becker, Sec., 875 Fulton.

So. Midwood Residents' Assn.—1901. 280 mem. H. C. Wetterau, Pres.; J. E. Byrne, Sec., 648 Delamere pl.

Stuyvesant Hgts. Impt. Soc.—1910. 28 mem. H. R. Ritch, Pres.; E. B. Parsons, Sec., 483 Macon.

Sunset Park Civic Assn.—4117 8th av. 1907. 160 mem. J. O. Seifert, Pres.; G. R. Bennett, Sec.

Taxpayers' Improvement Assn. of Windsor Ter. —1900. 1305 Prospect av. 100 mem. Jas. F. Decker, Pres.; D. Cuozzo, Sec., 619 Greenwood av.

Taxpayers' Protective Assn. of Bkln.—1918. 576 Decatur. 26,000 mem. J. I. Rosenbrock, Pres.; C. F. Harwood, Sec., 576 Decatur.

Thirty-first Ward Taxpayers' Assn.—1904. 1624 E. 10th. 332 mem. R. C. Doggett, Pres.; C. E. Brady, Sec., 1624 E. 10th.

Thirty-second Ward Taxpayers' Assn.—1895. 1514 Flatbush av. 225 mem. A. S. Crumm, Pres. and Sec., 1490 Flatbush av.

Tompkins-Lafayette Bd. of Trade—1913. 450 Throop av. 200 mem. R. T. Brown, Pres.; A. T. King, Sec.

Twenty-eighth Ward Taxpayers' Protective Assn. —1895. 472 Wilson av. 400 mem. J. J. Chambers, Pres.; P. A. Franke, Sec.

Twenty-fourth Ward Bd. of Trade—1904. 294 New York av. 200 mem. John H. Wacker, Pres., 981 Lincoln pl.; J. J. McDonnell, Sec.

United Civic and Commercial Assns.—75 orgs. 10,000 mem. C. H. Fuller, Pres.; J. F. Geis, Sec., 457 Classon av.

Urban Club—1894. 75 mem. Mrs. D. Porter, Pres.; Mrs. John Biddle Clark, Sec., 60 1st pl.

Utica Hgts. Bd. of Trade—69 Utica av. J. I. Gottlieb, Pres., 1775 Pacific; M. S. Shindelman, Sec.

Van Sicklen Taxpayers' Assn. (Inc.)—1911. 200 mem. 545 Neptune av. C. N. Brewster, Pres.; H. Conrad, Sec.

Vanderveer Pk. Taxpayers' Assn.—Av. D and N. Y. av. 175 mem. J. C. Lowe, Pres.; A. J. Brown, Sec., 316 E. 29th.

West End Bd. of Trade—1897. 200 mem. J. J. O'Leary, Pres.; A. Huber, Sec., 421 51st.

West End Impt. League of Coney Island—Surf av. and W. 22d. 200 mem. W. C. Canning, Pres.; C. H. Wilson, Sec., 2420 Surf av.

West Flatbush League—1914. 305 Church av. 200 mem. H. T. Woods, Pres.; Jos. C. O'Dea, Sec., 210 Albemarle rd.

Williamsburg and Greenpoint Bd. of Trade—1906. 277 mem. W. Prentice, Pres., 286 Graham av.; P. C. Traeger, Sec.

Women's Health Protective Assn.—1890. 85 mem. Mrs. A. E. Fraser, Pres., 226 Quincy; Mrs. H. W. Nichols, Sec., 209 Underhill av.

Women's Municipal League, Prospect Heights Branch—1905. 100 mem. Mrs. F. B. Pratt, Pres.; Mrs. W. I. Tuttle, Sec., 130 Willoughby av. Flatbush Branch—1909. Flatbush. Mrs. E. S. Shumway, Pres.; Mrs. R. B. Browne, Sec., 543 Ocean av.

Woodlawn Taxpayers' Assn.—1920. 200 mem. W. K. Van Meter, Pres.; Albert Billington, Sec., 112 av. N.

Wyckoff Heights Taxpayers' Assn.—1910. 98 Wyckoff av. 600 mem. C. Busch, Pres.; R. J. Schneider, Sec., 446 Harman.

Manhattan and Bronx.

Anti-Policy Soc.—1904. M. M. Marks, Pres.; C. P. Blaney, Sec., 140 Nassau.

Assn. for N. Y.—233 B'way. W. H. Black, Pres.; F. D. Gallatin, Sec., 160 B'way.

SOCIETIES AND ASSNS.—BDS. OF TRADE AND CIVIC IMPROVEMENT—MHTN. AND BRONX—*Continued.*

Board of Trade of Fur Industry—C. S. Porter, Ch.; D. C. Mills, Clerk. 303 5th av.

Broadway Assn.—1912. 1270 B'way. 1500 mem. J. D'M. Thompson, Pres.; H. G. Opdycke, Managing Dir.

Bronx Bd. of Trade—1894. 137th and 3d av. 972 mem. J. Brackenridge, Pres.; Chas. E. Reid, Sec.

Bureau of Municipal Research—1906. Inc. 1907. 261 B'way. Chas. A. Beard, Dir.; R. F. Cutting, Ch. Object: Impartial analysis of problems of governmental administration in city and state; constructive publicity.

Training Sch. for Public Service—Dr. C. A. Beard, Dir.

Field work in other cities and state governments; scientific research in preparation of administrative handbooks, service manuals and monographs to aid administrators.

Central Mercantile Assn.—500 mem. 111 5th av. C. Cowl, Pres.; J. E. Kean, Sec.

Chamber of Commerce of State of N. Y.—1768. 65 Liberty, Mhtn. 1,800 resident mem. 100 non-resident. Darwin P. Kingsley, Pres.; G. T. Gwynne, Sec.

Chelsea Neighborhood Assn.—1912. 244 W. 23d. 600 mem. B. Moore, Pres.; J. C. Kempvall, Sec.

Citizens' Union—(See Political Organizations.)

City Club of N. Y. (The)—1892. 55 W. 44th. 2,100 mem. N. S. Spencer, Pres.; R. V. Ingersoll, Sec.

Committee of Fourteen—1905. To suppress commercialized vice. P. S. Straus, Ch.; F. H. Whitin, Gen. Sec., 27 E. 22d.

Crockery Bd. of Trade of N. Y.—1891. 126 5th av. K. L. Wedgwood, Pres.; L. S. Owen, Sec.

Downtown League—1,100 mem. D. Robinson, Pres., 154 Nassau.

Federated Civic Assns. of N. Y.—1912. 542 5th av. R. G. Cooke, Pres.

Fifth Av. Assn.—1907. 542 5th av. 1,300 mem. R. G. Cooke, Pres.; W. J. Pedrick, Jr., Gen. Man.; S. F. Hart, Exec. Sec.

Franco-Amer. Bd. of Commerce and Industry—See National.

Hardware Bd. of Trade—1877. 291 B'way. 400 mem. C. A. Hauck, Sec.

Harlem Bd. of Commerce—1896. 500 mem. 290 Lenox av. J. G. Smith Pres.; T. P. Ward, Sec.

Harlem Property Owners' Assn.—1901. 67 W. 125th. 825 mem. I. Hyman, Pres., 119 Nassau; Fred. Kraus, Sec.

Leaf Tobacco Bd. of Trade of the City of N. Y.—166 Front. 1881. 95 firms. Jos. Mendelsohn, Pres.; Chas. Fox, Sec.

Long Isl. Real Estate Bd.—S. Yates, Pres., 47 W. 34th; Carl B. Elmer, Sec.; G. H. Rome, Treas.

Neighbors' Union—48 Henry. 1919. 200 mem. A. D. Moore, Pres.; Ida Oppenheimer, Sec.

New Club for Men and Women—17 W. 44th (temp.); 113-123 W. 43d (perm.). 1920. S. McC. Lindsay, Pres.; Miss C. S. Baker, Sec.; L. P. B. Gould, Treas.

N. Y. Bd. of Trade and Transportation—1873. 38 Park row. 800 firms. L. Kohns, Pres.; F. S. Gardner, Sec.

N. Y. Harbor Protective and Development Assn.—150 Nassau. A. Van Wyck, Pres.; J. D. Tucker, Sec., 2679 E. 24th, Bkln.

North Side Bd. of Trade—Name changed to Bronx Bd. of Trade.

Parks and Playgrounds Assn. of City of N. Y.—1905. 2,000 mem. 1123 B'way. Geo. G. Battle, Pres.; Miss L. Morton, Sec.

Real Estate Exchange of L. I.—1907. 47 W. 34th. S. Yates, Pres.; Carl B. Elmer, Sec.

Reform Club—1888. 600 mem. 9 So. William. Ed. J. Shriver, Pres.; S. Newborg, Sec.

School Garden Assn. of N. Y. (The)—1908. 600 active. 3,500 associate mem. Dr. G. Straubenmuller, Pres.; Dr. Marguerite T. Lee, Sec., G. H. School, Bkln.

Stationers' and Publishers' Bd. of Trade—1875. 90 Nassau. 120 mem. H. C. Bainbridge, Jr., Pres.; Gordon Cameron, Sec.

Taxpayers' Alliance—177th and 3d av. 1894. 6,000 mem. J. F. Cavanagh, Pres.; E. L. Franz, Sec.

Thirty-fourth St. Bd. of Trade—1918. 47 W. 34th. V. Green, Pres.; W. B. Gibbs, Sec.

Tree Planting Assn.—1897. 100 B'way. 240 mem. C. Thaddeus Terry, Pres.; A. T. Wimonett, Sec.

Washington Sq. Assn.—263 Greene. A. R. Shattuck, Pres.; E. Collyer, Sec.

West End Assn.—1884. 671 mem. A. W. Otis, Pres.; L. Cary, Sec., 685 Madison av.

West Side Taxpayers' Assn.—1874. 267 W. 34th. 600 mem. G. Stege, Pres.; J. J. Tabolt, Sec., 558 8th av.

Woman's Health Prot. Assn.—1884. 125 mem. 424 Central Pk. W. Mrs. R. Trautmann, Pres., Mrs. W. W. Jeffries, Cor. Sec., 474 Central Pk. W.

Women's City Club—22 Park av. 1915. 3,000 mem. Miss Mary Garrett Hay, Pres.; Miss E. Stebbins, Sec.

Women's Municipal League—14 E. 46th. 1,500 mem. Mrs. F. C. Hodgdon, Pres.; Miss H. Duey, Exec. Sec.

Queens.

Astoria Taxpayers and Business Men's Assn.—1902. 158 Franklin, Astoria. 200 mem. J. B. Tisdale, Pres.; Henry Martin, Sec., 1033 2d av., L. I. C.

Belle Harbor Property Owners' Assn.—1908. S. H. Molleson, Sec., 165 B'way, Mhtn.; T. W. Donnelly, Treas.

Bellaire-Hollis Court Community Club—1919. 90 mem. R. H. Burton, Pres.; E. S. Harrison, Sec., Queens rd., Hollis Court.

Business Men's Assn. of Far Rockaway—1912. 85 mem. A. Geib, Pres.; Chas. Lockhart, Sec., National Bank Bldg., Far Rockaway.

Business Men's Assn. of Flushing—1893. 275 mem. G. W. Pople, Pres.; L. S. Case, Sec., 109 Main.

Citizens' Alliance for Good Government of Queens Co.—1915. 380 9th av., L. I. City. 12,000 mem. C. Gerks, Pres.; John Hering, Sec., 532 B'way, L. I. City.

Citizens Assn. of Queens and Bellaire—1916. Queens. 300 mem. E. H. Buhler, Pres.; W. J. Gill, Sec.

Civic Assn. of Corona—1912. 300 mem. L. Loysch, Pres.; T. J. Murphy, Sec., 17 46th.

Civic Federation of the Town of Hempstead—W. S. Pettit, Pres.; A. H. Wagg, Sec, Malverne.

Civic League of Little Neck—1911. 96 mem. W. A. Hunter, Pres.; J. Kimmins, Sec., Little Neck.

College Point Taxpayers' Assn.—1898. 200 mem. F. G. Froehlich, Pres.; C. Yost, Sec., 18 15th st., College Pt.

Douglaston Civic Assn.—1907. 218 mem. W. H. Van Steenbergh, Pres.; G. Howard, Treas.; F. J. Page, Sec.

East Elmhurst Assn.—1909. 91 mem. J. E. Bleekman, Pres., East Elmhurst; H. O. Hanson, Treas.

Elmhurst Taxpayers' Assn.—1909. 200 mem. Leon A. Caswell, Sec., 7 Toledo, Elmhurst.

Evergreen Bd. of Trade—1078 Cypress av. 1905. 100 mem. F. Suesser, Pres.; P. Braun, Sec., 1623 Decatur.

Farmers and Taxpayers' Assn. of 3d Ward—1908. Bayside. 80 mem. Theodore Foulke, Pres.; C. U. Powell, Sec., Sanford av., Flushing.

Flushing Cit. Assn.—1886. 350 mem. G. W. Benton, Pres.; L. S. Case, Sec., 109 Main, Flushing.

Flushing Public Playground Assn.—1910. Mrs. C. B. Smith, Pres.; C. B. Smith, Jr., Sec., 137 Maple av., Flushing.

Flushing United Assn.—1918. 600 mem. J. H. Clark, Jr., Pres.; G. S. Halleran, Sec., 10 Leavitt av.

Forest Pk. Taxpayers' Assn. of Woodhaven—850 mem. T. E. Smith, Pres.; E. L. Hein, Sec., 4 Stanton, Woodhaven.

Glendale Taxpayers' Assn.—1911. 150 mem. E. N. Kassel, Pres.; A. Weber, Sec., Tesla pl.

Homestead Civic Assn.—1909. Jamaica and Woodhaven avs. 900 mem. H. F. Tourte, Pres.; E. P. Axenroth, Sec., 713 87th, Woodhaven.

Jamaica Bd. of Trade—1919. Butler Bldg. H. J. Mullen, Pres.; M. C. Bunyan, Sec.

Jamaica Cit. Assn.—1898. Town Hall. 200 mem. G. E. Polhemus, Pres.; W. E. Stecher, Sec., Jamaica.

Jamaica Creeks One and Two Co-operative League—1916. 140 mem. A. Sauer, Pres.; L. W. Bermas, Sec., 324 Halsey, Bkln.

Jamaica East End Civic Assn.—1910. 125 mem. W. T. Yale, Pres.; D. H. Meldon, Sec., 24 Ackroyd av., Jamaica.

Jamaica Sta. Assn.—1913. Hillcrest office. 100 mem. G. E. Cogswell, Pres.; H. C. McNulty, Sec., Hillcrest office, Jamaica.

Jamaica Village Soc.—E. L. Maeder, Pres.; A. S. Baylis, Sec., 19 Burdette pl., Jamaica.

Ladies' Co-op. Guild, Queens—1887. 40 mem. Mrs. A. E. Hendricskon, Pres.; Mrs. C. G. Stewart, Sec., Queens, L. I.

L. I. League—1908. 13 Herriman av., Jamaica. 264 mem. A. C. Hankins, Pres.; A. J. Eno, Sec.

Maspeth Civic and Improvement Assn.—8 Maspeth av. 1916. 170 mem. A. Frontera, Pres.; J. L. Gorman, Sec., 3 Lex. av., Maspeth.

Men's Christian and Civic League of Elmhurst—160 mem. L. S. Patterson, Pres., 26 Chicago.

SOCIETIES AND ASSOCIATIONS—BDS. OF TRADE AND CIVIC IMPROVEMENT—QUEENS—*Continued.*

Metropolitan Av. Bd. of Trade—Middle Village. 1914. 30 mem. D. W. Peterson, Pres.; Joseph Kreyger, 9 Columbia pl., Maspeth, L. I.

Morris Park Citizens' Assn.—1908. Morris Park. 350 mem. H. A. Schaper, Pres.; W. D. Bowie, Rec. Sec., 1122 S. Vine.

Ozone Park Bd. of Trade, Inc.—1904. 80 mem. O. W. Svenson, Pres.; E. Livett, Sec., 1448 Beaufort, Woodhaven.

Progress Soc. of the Rockaways—1908. 350 mem Masonic Temple, Far Rockaway. B. E. Seigelstein, Pres., 99 Nassau, N. Y. C.; H. A. Wolff, Sec.

Queens Boro. Bd. of Trade—1900. 250 Jackson av., L. I. City. 322 mem. H. C. Schreiter, Pres.; M. L. Lissberger, Ch.; G. W. Luft, Sec.

Quensborough Hill Taxpayers' Assn—1910. 80 mem. G. W. Coter, Pres.; F. Voelker, Sec., Hawthorne, Flushing.

Real Estate Exchange of Long Island—47 W. 34th, Mhtn. S. Yates, Pres.; C. B. Elmer, Sec.

Richmond Hill Civic Assn.—Masonic Temple. 1,600 mem. G. A. De Vestern, Pres.; H. F. J. Ehlert, Sec., 9140 114th.

Richmond Hill South Civic Assn.—Liberty av. and 113th. 1920. 105 mem. J. C. Kemp, Pres.; A. H. Smith, Sec., 10,733 110th.

Ridgewood Chamber of Commerce—Cornelia, nr. Cypress av. F. A. Homann, Pres.

Rockaway Bd. of Trade, Inc.—1912. 500 mem. T. C. McKennee, Pres.; T. C. Warren, Sec.

Rockaway Park Citizens' Assn.—1902. 115 mem. L. I. Sherman, Pres.; J. J. Brennan, Jr., Sec., Rockaway Pk.

Roosevelt Civic Soc.—1920. 200 mem. W. T. Smith, Pres.; H. Markwalter, Sec.

St. Albans Impt. Assn.—1906. The Hall, Locust av., St. Albans. 125 mem. T. Bosshard, Pres.; W. Rylaner, Cor. Sec., St. Albans.

Twentieth Century Club—1896. Richmond Hill. 240 mem. Mrs. D. W. Thompson, Pres.; Mrs. J. C. Atwater, Cor. Sec., 663 114th.

Union Course Civic Assn.—110 Shaw av. 1917. 238 mem. W. Pfeiffer, Pres.; W. R. Thurman, Sec., 77 Rector, Union Course.

United Civic Assns. of Borough of Queens—1902. 140 del. T. G. Ellsworth, Pres.; T. J. Murphy, Sec., 17 46th, Corona.

Upper Flushing Impt. Assn.—150 mem. C. U. Powell, Pres.; W. W. Read, Sec., 4 S. 17th.

Woman's Club of Bayside—1917. 120 mem. Mrs. Robt. P. Magee, Pres.; Mrs. H. Stewart McKnight, Sec., Great Neck.

Woodmere Impt. Soc.—1910. 165 mem. C. G. Galston, Pres.; Wm. Rosenbaum, Treas.

Woodside Impt. Assn.—Louis Lang, Sec., 13 1st, Woodside.

Richmond.

Staten Island Civic League—105 Stuyvesant pl., New Brighton. 1913. 1,200 mem. Dr. L. A. Dreyfus, Pres.; Wm. W. Mills, Ex-Officer, 103 St. Marks pl., New Brighton.

BUSINESS, COMMERCIAL AND AGRICULTURAL ASSOCIATIONS.

International.

American R. R. Assn., Signal Division—1895. F. W. Pflegling, Ch.; H. S. Balliet, Sec., 75 Church, Mhtn.

Associated Advertising Clubs of the World—Chas. A. Otis, Pres., Cleveland, O.; P. S. Florea, Sec.-Treas., 110 W. 40th, N. Y. C.

Grotius Soc. (The)—105 mem. 2 Kings Bench Walk Temple, E. C. London, Eng. Sir John MacDonell, K. C. B., Pres.; H. H. L. Bellot, Sec.

Internatl. Assn. of Casualty and Surety Underwriters, 80 Maiden Lane, Mhtn.—Arthur E. Childs, Pres.; F. Robertson Jones, Sec.

Internatl. Assn. of Display Men—1,000 mem. E. D. Pierce, Pres.; D. B. Brigg, Sec., 1520 Woolworth Bldg., N. Y. C. Next convention, Chicago, July 14 to 17, 1919.

Internatl. Assn. of Rotary Clubs—1910. 910 So. Michigan av., Chicago. 55,000 mem. Estes Snedecor, Pres.; C. R. Perry, Sec.

Internatl. Assn. of Window Trimmers—Name changed to Internatl. Assn. of Display Men.

Internatl. Labor Conference—1919. Provided for in the Treaty of Versailles. Organization pending the creation of a League of Nations. Sec. of Labor Wilson, Ch., Washington, D. C.

Internatl. Water Lines Passenger Assn.—1904. 50 mem. W. F. Wasley, Pres.; G. M. Muskoka Lakes, Gravehurst, Ont.; M. R. Nelson, Sec.-Treas., 911 Hubbell Bldg., Des Moines, Ia.

Women Lawyers' Assn.—1899. 250 mem. E. M. Bullowa, Pres.; E. V. Carlucci, Sec., 150 Nassau, N. Y. C.

National.

Actuarial Soc. of Amer.—1889. 281 mem. 256 B'way, Mhtn. W. A. Hutcheson, Pres.; W. M. Strong, Sec.

Amer. Asiatic Assn.—1898. 627 Lexington av., Mhtn. 300 mem. To promote good relations with Asiatic countries. L. C. Griscom, Pres.; J. Foord, Sec., 627 Lexington av., Mhtn.

Amer. Assn. Dining Car Supts.—1900. 76 mem. E. W. Westlake, Pres.; S. W. Derr, Sec., P. & R. R. R.—C. R. R. of N. J. (Reading Terminal), Phila., Pa.

Amer. Assn. of Foreign Language Newspapers, Inc. 1908. 30 E. 23d, Mhtn. 745 newspapers. Nathan H. Seidman, Pres.

Amer. Assn. of Freight Agents—1888. 1100 mem. C. E. Fish, Pres. B. & O. R. R., Cincinnati, O.; R. O. Wells, Sec. Agt., Ill. Central R. R., Chicago, Ill.

Amer. Assn. of Genl. Baggage Agents—1882. 75 mem. W. D. Carrick, Pres.; E. R. Reynolds. Sec., C. & S. W. R. R., Chicago, Ill.

Amer. Assn. of Nurserymen—1875. Princeton, N. J. 400 mem. L. C. Stack, Pres., Louisiana, Mo.; John Watson, Ex. Sec., Princeton, N. J.

Amer. Assn. of Passenger Traffic Officers—1855. 250 mem. W. J. Black, Pres.; W. C. Hope, Sec., 143 Liberty, Mhtn.

Amer. Assn. of R. R. Supts.—1909. W. S. Williams, Pres.; J. Rothschild, Sec.-Treas., 400 Union Sta., St. Louis, Mo.

Amer. Assn. of the Baking Industry—G. Smith, Mobile, Ala., Pres.; D. P. Chindblom, Sec., 1405 Ashland Block, Chicago, Ill.

Amer. Bankers Assn.—1875. 5 Nassau, Mhtn. 22,400 mem. J. S. Drum, Pres.; G. E. Bowerman, Exec. Sec.

Amer. Bar Assn.—1878. 11,500 mem. H. L. Carson, Pres., Phil., Pa.; W. Thos. Kemp, Sec., Munsey Bldg., Baltimore, Md.

Amer. Booksellers Assn.—1900. 350 mem. E. L. Herr, Pres.; F. G. Melcher, Sec., 62 W. 45th, N. Y. C.

Amer. Bottlers of Carbonated Beverages—1919. 41 Woodward av., Detroit, Mich. 3,000 mem. J. Vernor, Jr., Pres.; J. Owens, Sec.

Amer. Bureau of Shipping—1867. 66 Beaver, Mhtn. S. Taylor, Pres.; J. W. Cantillion, Sec.

Amer. Copyright League—1883. R. U. Johnson, Sec., Room 1412, 347 Madison av., Mhtn.

Amer. Cotton Mfrs. Assn.—1897. Helen F. Johnson, Pres., Greensboro, N. C.; W. D. Adams, Sec.-Treas., Charlotte, N. C.

Amer. Electric Ry. Assn.—1882. 3,500 mem. John H. Pardee, Pres.; E. B. Burritt, Sec., 8 W. 40th, Mhtn.

Amer. Foundrymen's Assn., Inc.—1,200 mem. A. O. Backert, Pres.; C. E. Hoyt, Sec.-Treas., 113 W. Monroe, Chicago, Ill.

Amer. Gas Assn.—1918. 130 E. 15th, Mhtn. G. B. Cortelyou, Pres.; O. H. Fogg, Sec.-Mgr.

Amer. Gladiolus Soc.—1910. 380 mem. H. E. Meader, Pres., Dover, N. H.; A. C. Beal, Sec., 21 Kelvin pl., Ithaca, N. Y.

Amer. Guernsey Cattle Club—1878. 1,000 mem. R. Scoville, Pres.; Wm. H. Caldwell, Sec., Peterboro, N. H.

Amer. Hackney Horse Soc.—Inc. 1891. 350 mem. R. C. Vanderbilt, Pres.; G. C. Gue, Sec., 460 Fulton av., Hempstead, N. Y.

Amer. Hardware Mfrs. Assn.—1901. 4106 Woolworth Bldg., Mhtn. 550 mem. Frederick H. Payne, Pres.; F. D. Mitchell, Sec.

Amer. Inst. of Accountants—1887. 1 Liberty, Mhtn. 1,384 mem. W. H. Rand, Pres.; A. P. Richardson, Sec.

Amer. Inst. of Actuaries—1909. C. H. Beckett, Pres.; Wm. O. Morris, Sec., 1702 N. Am. Bldg., Chicago, Ill.

Amer. Inst. of Banking—1900. 32,500 mem. S. D. Beckley, Pres.; Robt. B. Locke, V.-Pres.; Geo. E. Allen, Educ. Dir.; R. W. Hill, Sec, 5 Nassau, N Y. C.

Amer. Inst. of Marine Underwriters—1898. 15 William. H. Appleton, Pres.; W. H. McGee, Sec.

Amer. Jersey Cattle Club—1868. 324 W. 23d, Mhtn. 900 mem. M. D. Munn, Pres.; R. M. Gow, Sec.

Amer. Mfrs. Export Assn.—1909. 160 B'way, Mhtn. 1,500 mem. W. L. Saunder, Pres.; A. W. Willmann, Sec.; F. Van Leer, Jr., Editor Assn. Publications.

SOCIETIES AND ASSOCIATIONS—BUSINESS, COMMERCIAL AND AGRICULTURAL—NATIONAL—*Con.*

Amer. Meat Packers' Assn.—22 W. Monroe, Chicago, Ill. 1906. 185 mem. Thos. E. Wilson, Pres.; C. B. Heinemann, Sec.

Amer. Natl. Assn. of Masters of Dancing—Fenton T. Bott, Pres., Dayton, O.

Amer. Natl. Retail Jewelers Assn.—1906. 5,000 mem. A. A. Everts, Pres.; A. W. Anderson, Sec., Neenah, Wis.

Amer. Newspaper Publishers Assn.—903-7 World Bldg., Mhtn. 545 newspapers. T. R. Williams, Pres.; L. B. Palmer, Mgr.

Amer. Newspaper Publishers' Assn. Bureau of Advertising, World Bldg., Mhtn. W. A. Thomson, Dir.; T. H. Moore, Associate Dir.

Amer. Paper and Pulp Assn.—1878. 18 E. 41st, Mhtn. Geo. W. Sisson, Jr., Pres.; H. P. Baker, Sec.

Amer. Ry. Assn.—1886. 75 Church, Mhtn. 775 railroads. R. H. Aishton, Pres.; J. E. Fairbanks, Gen. Sec. and Treas.

Amer. Railway Engineering Assn.—1898. Chicago, Ill. 1,700 mem. H. R. Safford, Pres.; E. H. Fritch, Sec., 431 So. Dearborn, Chicago, Ill.

Amer. Ry. Bridge and Bldg. Assn.—1891. 800 mem. F. E. Weise, Pres.; C. A. Lichty, Sec., 319 N. Waller av., Chicago, Ill.

Amer. R. R. Assn., Section III, Mechanical. 1867. W. J. Tollerton, Ch.; V. R. Hawthorne, Sec., 1426 Manhattan Bldg., Chicago, Ill.

Amer. Road Builders' Assn.—1902. 11 Waverly pl., Mhtn. G. P. Coleman, Pres.; E. L. Powers, Sec.

Amer. Saddle Horse Breeders' Assn.—1891. Louisville, Ky. 333 mem. C. M. Thomas, Pres.; R. H. Lillard, Sec., 434 W. Main, Louisville, Ky.

Amer. Seed Trade Assn.—1883. 250 mem. H. G. Hastings, Pres.; C. E. Kendel, Sec., 216 Prospect av., S. E., Cleveland, O.

Amer. Soc. of Agricultural Engrs.—1907. 385 mem. F. N. G. Kranich, Pres.; J. B. Davidson, Sec. and Treas., Iowa State College, Ames, Iowa.

Amer. Soc. of Civil Engineers—1852. 33 W. 39th, Mhtn. 9,200 mem. F. S. Curtiss, Pres.; C. W. Hunt, Sec., 33 W. 39th.

Amer. Soc. of Heating and Ventilating Engineers—1894. Dr. E. V. Hill, Pres.; C. W. Obert, Sec., 29 W. 39th, Mhtn.

Amer. Soc. Mechanical Engineers—1880. 29 W. 39th, Mhtn. 13,000 mem. Fred J. Miller, Pres.; C. W. Rice, Sec.

Amer. Supply and Machinery Mfrs. Assn.—1905. 4106 Woolworth Bldg., Mhtn. 300 mem. Chas. W. Beaver, Pres.; F. D. Mitchell, Sec.

Amer. Sweet Pea Soc.—1909. W. A. Sperling, Pres., 30-32 Barclay; E. C. Vick, Sec.

Amer. Warehousemen's Assn.—300 firms. 60 E. 42d, Mhtn. James F. Keenan, Pres.; C. L. Criss, Sec.; Walter C. Reid, Treas., 60 E. 42d, Mhtn.

Amer. Water Works Assn.—Org. 1881. 1,500 mem. Beekman C. Little, Pres., Rochester, N. Y.; J. M. Diven, Sec., 153 W. 71st, N. Y. C.

Associated Press (The)—1900. 1,260 mem. Frank B. Noyes, Pres.; M. E. Stone, Gen. Mgr., 51 Chambers.

Assn. of North Amer. Directory Publishers—1898. 125 Church, Mhtn. 42 companies. Geo. W. Overton, Pres.; E. J. Loranger, Sec.-Treas.

Assn. of Edison Illuminating Cos.—1885. 29 W. 39th, Mhtn. 73 mem. W. H. Johnson, Pres.; P. S. Millar, Sec.

Assn. of Railway Executives—1913. 320 Munsey Bldg., Washington, D. C., and 61 B'way, Mhtn. 119 R. R. Cos. Thos. DeWitt Cuyler, Ch.; R. S. Binkerd, Asst. to the Ch., 61 B'way, Mhtn.

Audit Bureau of Circulations—1914. 1,460 mem. L. B. Jones, Pres.; S. Clague, Mgr.-Dir., Century Bldg., Chicago, Ill.

Ayrshire Breeders Assn.—1875. Inc. 1886. 1,470 mem. Capt. A. Henry Higginson, Pres., So. Lincoln, Mass.; J. G. Watson, Sec.-Treas., Brandon, Vt.

Carriage Builders' Natl. Assn.—1872. 400 mem. F. H. Delker, Pres.; G. W. Huston, Sec., Cincinnati, O.

Casualty Actuarial and Statistical Soc. of Amer.—1914. 200 mem. B. D. Flynn, Pres.; G. R. Fondiller, Sec., 120 B'way, N. Y. C.

Chamber of Commerce of U. S. of Amer.—1913. Hdqtrs., Mills Bldg., Wash., D. C. Joseph H. DeFrees, Pres.; E. H. Goodwin, V.-Pres.; D. A. Skinner, Sec. N. Y. office, Woolworth Bldg.; San Francisco office, Merchants Exch. Bldg.; Chicago office, Otis Bldg.; St. Louis office, care of Chamber Commerce, St. Louis.

Commercial Law League of America—1895. 108 S. La Salle, Chicago, Ill. 6,500 mem. G. A. Bacon, Pres.; W. C. Sprague, Sec.

Committee of Amer. Shipbuilders—1920. 30 Church, N. Y. C. J. A. Powell, Ch.; H. C. Hunter, Sec.

Common Brick Manufacturers' Assn. of America—1913. 1300 Schofield Bldg., Cleveland, O. 300 mem. W. Schlake, Pres.; R. P. Stoddard, Sec.

Electrical Manufacturers Club—1905. 130 mem. LeRoy Clark, Pres.; F. L. Bishop, Sec., Hartford, Conn.

Farmers' Natl. Congress—1880. 10,000 mem. J. H. Kimble, Pres.; J. H. Patten, Sec., Washington, D. C.

Gen. Agency Assn. of the Equitable Life Assurance Soc.—1905. 100 mem. Courtenay Barber, Pres., 617 People's Gas Bldg., Chicago, Ill.; R. H. Lake, Sec., Bank of Commerce Bldg., Memphis, Tenn.

Inst. for Government Research—1916. Washington, D. C. W. F. Willoughby, Dir. Object: A natl. assn. of citizens with view to promoting efficiency and economy in natl. govt.

Jewelers Security Alliance of U. S.—1883. 15 Maiden la., Mhtn. 7,050 mem. A. K. Sloan, Pres.; J. H. Noyes, Sec.

Laundryowners Natl. Assn.—1883. 2,000 mem. Geo. W. Hooper, Pres.; W. E. Fitch, V.-Pres. and Mgr., La Salle, Ill.

League for Industrial Rights—1902. L. F. Sherman, Ex. Sec., 135 B'way, Mhtn.

Manufacturing Perfumers' Assn. of U. S. (The)—1894. 175 mem. F. W. Jones, Pres.; C. M. Baker, Sec., 309 B'way, N. Y. C.

Master Boiler Makers' Assn.—95 Liberty, Mhtn. 1906 400 mem. Chas. P. Patrick, Pres., Chicago, Ill.; Harry D. Vought, Sec.

Natl. Assn. of Book Publishers—1920. 334 5th av., Mhtn. 80 mem. J. W. Hiltman, Pres.; F. C. Dodd, Sec.

Natl. Assn. of Brass Mfrs.—1886. 65 mem. H. N. Gillette, Pres.; W. M. Webster, Com., 1818 City Hall Sq., Chicago, Ill.

Natl. Assn. of Clothiers—1897. 752 B'way. 250 mem. Eli Strouse, Pres.; Irving Crane, Sec., 13 Astor pl., Mhtn.

Natl. Assn. of Comptrollers and Accounting Officers—1905. 150 mem. C. C. Pashby, Pres., Memphis, Tenn.; M. Foote, Sec., 501 City Hall, Chicago, Ill.

Natl. Assn. of Cotton Mfrs.—1854. 45 Milk, Boston, Mass. 1,200 mem. R. B. Lowe, Pres.; R. R. Wilson, Sec.

Natl. Assn. of Credit Men—1896. 33,098 mem. W. F. H. Koelich, Pres.; J. H. Tregoe, Sec.-Treas., 41 Park Row, N. Y. C.

Natl. Assn. of Electrical Contractors and Dealers—1901. 2,020 mem. W. C. Peet, Pres.; W. H. Morton, Gen. Mgr., 110 W. 40th, Mhtn.

Natl. Assn. of Engine and Boat Mfrs.—1904. Mhtn. H. R. Sutphen, Pres.; Ira Hand, Sec., 29 W. 39th, Mhtn.

Natl. Assn. of Ice Industries—1917. H. D. Norvell, Pres., Cleveland, O.; Leslie C. Smith, Sec., Chicago, Ill.; H. W. Cole, Sec., Eastern Div., 18 E. 41st, Mhtn.

Natl. Assn. of Leather Belting Mfrs.—1887. 50 mem. G. H. Blake, Sec., P. O. Box 859, City Hall Sta., N. Y. C.

Natl. Assn. of Letter Carriers—1889. 35,000 mem. E. J. Gainor, Pres.; E. J. Cantwell, Sec., Kenois Bldg., Washington, D. C.

Natl. Assn. of Life Underwriters—1889. 15,000 mem. J. S. Edwards, Pres.; E. M. Ensign, Cor. Sec., 23 W. 43d, Mhtn.

Natl. Assn. of Mfrs.—1895. 5,000 mem. S. C. Mason, Pres.; Geo. S. Boudinot, Sec., 30 Church, Mhtn.; J. P. Bird, Gen. Mgr.

Natl. Assn. of Master Plumbers of the U. S.—1908. D. E. Duskin, Pres., 1613 Pine, Phila., Pa.; J. R. Hopkin, Sec.

Natl. Assn. of Mercantile Agencies—1907 200 mem. W. S. Rauch, Pres., Newark, N. J.; J. R. Truesdale, Sec.-Treas., 1310 Wick Bldg., Youngstown, O.

Natl. Assn. of Newsdealers and Stationers—1917. 5,000 mem. Wm. H. Pickering, Pres.; L. Joseph, Sec., 391 Fulton, Bkln.

Natl. Assn. of Music Merchants. 1901. 1,200 mem. E. P. Hamilton, Pres.; C. L. Dennis, Sec., 105 W. 40th, N. Y. C.

Natl. Assn. of Postmasters—1898. 7,500 mem. C. M. Selph, Pres.; Frank C. Sites, Sec.-Treas., Harrisburg, Pa.

SOCIETIES AND ASSOCIATIONS—BUSINESS, COMMERCIAL AND AGRICULTURAL—NATIONAL—*Con.*

Natl. Assn. of Railway and Utilities Commissioners—1888. 250 mem. J. B. Walker, Sec., Pelham, N. Y.

Natl. Assn. of Railway Agents—J. E. Van Deusen, Pres.; W. M. Drury, Sec., Coldwater, Mich.

Natl. Assn. of Real Estate Boards, Inc.—1908. 12,500 mem. 206 Boards. F. E. Taylor, Pres., Portland, Ore.; T. S. Ingersoll, Sec., 527 Andrus Bldg., Minneapolis, Minn.

Natl. Assn. of Retail Druggists—1898. 168 N. Michigan Blvd., Chicago, Ill. 15,000 mem. T. F. Hagenow, Pres.; S. C. Henry, Sec.

Natl. Assn. of Retail Grocers—1896. 100,000 mem. J. A. Ulmer, Pres., Toledo, O.; Frank B. Connolly, Act. Sec., 319 Sheldon Bldg., San Francisco, Cal.

Natl. Assn. of Stationers and Mfrs. of the U. S. A.—1904. 1,500 mem. Ralph H. Bauer, Pres.; M. W. Byers, Sec., 41 Park Row, Mhtn.

Natl. Assn. of Theatrical Producing Mgrs.—1907. 200 mem. Wm. A. Brady, Pres.; H. E. Cooley, Sec., 137 W. 48th, Mhtn.

Natl. Assn. of U. S. Civil Service Employees at Navy Yards and Stations—1908. 1,000 mem. F. De W. Armour, Pres.; H. N. Niebling, Sec., 1874 E. 12th, Bkln.

Natl. Assn. of Wool Mfrs.—1864. 50 State, Boston, Mass. F. S. Clark, Pres.; P. T. Cherington, Sec.

Natl. Automobile Chamber of Commerce (Inc.)—1913. 366 Madison av., Mhtn. 123 mem. Chas. Clifton, Pres.; A. J. Brousseau, Sec.; A. Reeves, Gen. Mgr.

Natl. Board of Review of Motion Pictures—1909. 70 5th av., Mhtn. 225 mem. E. D. Martin, Ch.; W. D. McGuire, Jr., O. G. Cocks, W. A. Barrett, W. M. Covill and Alice Evans, Secs.

Natl. Board of Fire Underwriters—76 William, Mhtn. 178 mem. Charles L. Case, Pres.; G. G. Bulkley, Sec.; W. E. Mallalieu, Gen. Mgr., 76 William, Mhtn.

Natl. Board of Marine Underwriters—Farmers Loan and Trust Bldg., 63-65 Beaver, Mhtn. H. Bird, Pres.; E. G. Driver, Asst. Sec.

Natl. Boot and Shoe Mfrs. Assn.—1904. 395 mem. J. F. McElwain, Pres.; Sol. Wile, Sec., Granite Bldg., Rochester, N. Y.

Natl. Canners Assn.—1907. 1739 H, Washington, D. C. W. J. Sears, Pres.; F. C. Gorrell, Sec.

Natl. Conjurers' Assn.—1911. 109 W. 54th, Mhtn. Fredk. M. Schubert, Pres.; Clinton Burgess, Sec., 241 W. 115th, Mhtn.; H. B. Lindaberry, Treas.

Natl. Editorial Assn.—4,000 mem. Wm. Wilke, Pres.; Geo. Schlosser, Sec., Wersington Springs, S. D.

Natl. Electric Light Assn.—1885. 12,000 mem. M. J. Insull, Pres.; M. H. Ayles Worth. Exec. Mgr., 29 W. 39th.

Natl. Erectors' Assn.—1906. 286 5th av., Mhtn. 50 mem. S. P. Mitchell, Ch.; C. E. Cheney, Sec.

Natl. Foreign Trade Council—1914. 1 Hanover sq. India House, Mhtn. 75 mem. J. A. Farrell, Ch.; O. K. Davis, Sec.

Natl. Florists' Bd. of Trade—(See Bds. of Trade.)

Natl. Founders' Assn.—(See Unclassified).

Natl. Grange, Patrons of Husbandry—1867. Assn. of Farmers. S. J. Lowell, Master; C. M. Freeman, Sec., Tippecanoe City, O.

Natl. (Wholesale) Hardware Assn.—1895. 700 mem. R. H. Treman, Treman, King & Co., Pres., Ithaca, N. Y.; T. J. Fernley, Sec., 505 Arch, Phila.

Natl. Harness Mfrs. Assn.—1896. Cincinnati, O. 5,000 mem. E. L. Richards, Pres.; G. M. Scherz, Sec., 1006 Freeman av., Cincinnati, O.

Natl. Home Furnishers' Assn.—A. Leon, Pres.; F. I. Smith, Sec., Knickerbocker Bldg., 116 W. 39th, Mhtn.

Natl. Horse Show Assn.—1883. 500 mem. R. A. Fairbairn, Pres.; Chas. W. Smith, Sec., 16 E. 23d, Mhtn.

Natl. Industrial Conference Bd.—1916. 10 E. 39th, Mhtn. Fredk. P. Fish, Pres.; M. W. Alexander, Managing Dir.

Natl. Inst. of Inventors—1914. 118 Fulton, Mhtn. 3,612 mem. Thos. Howard, Exec. Ch.; Paul Revere Fay, Sec.

Natl. Jewelers' Bd. of Trade—(See Bds. of Trade.)

Natl. League of Postmasters—1904. 15,000 mem. Geo. Busscher, Jr., Pres.; H. H. Collins, Sec., Zanesville, O.

Natl. Leather and Shoe Finders Assn.—1909. 363 mem. H. E. Bragg, Pres.; Geo. A. Knapp, Sec., 812 Pontiac Bldg., St. Louis, Mo.

Natl. Lumber Exporters Assn.—1900. Ed. Barber, Pres., Cincinnati, O.; H. M. Dickson, Sec., 60 Knickerbocker Bldg., Baltimore, Md.

Natl. Negro Business League—1900. 3,000 mem. R. R. Moton, Pres., Tuskegee Inst., Ala.; E. J. Scott, Sec., Howard Univ., Washington, D. C.

Natl. Piano Mfrs. Assn. of Amer.—1897. 125 mem. Otto Schultz, Pres.; H. W. Hill, Asst. Sec., 105 W. 40th, Mhtn.

Natl. Retail Dry Goods Assn.—1911. 2,000 mem. S. P. Halle, Pres.; Lew Hahn, Managing Dir., 200 5th av., Mhtn.

Natl. Retail Hardware Assn. (The)—1901. 18,000 mem. Matthias Ludlow, Pres.; H. P. Sheets, Treas.-Sec., Argos, Ind.

Natl. Retail Liquor Dealers Assn. of Amer.—1892. Geo. J. Carroll, Pres., Elizabeth, N. J.; R. J. Halle, Sec., Garrick Bldg., Chicago.

Natl. Retail Monument Dealers Assn. of Amer., Inc.—1906. C. Price, Pres., Kenton, O.; L. H. Schlesselman, Sec., Lafayette, Ind.

Natl. Safety Council—168 No. Michigan av., Chicago, Ill. 1913. 6,000,000 mem. R. C. Richards, Pres.; S. J. Williams, Sec.; L. Resnick, Dir. of Publicity.

Natl. Shorthand Reporters Assn.—1899. 850 mem. E. L. Allen, Pres., Pittsburgh, Pa.; A. C. Gaw, Sec., 815 Masonic Temple, Chicago, Ill.

Natl. Soc. of Craftsmen—(See Art Clubs.)

Natl. Wholesale Grocers Assn. of the U. S.—1906. 1,300 mem. A. Davies, Pres.; J. B. Newman, Act. Sec., 6 Harrison, Mhtn.

Natl. Wholesale Jewelers Assn.—1908. 180 mem. N. R. Fuller, Pres.; T. A. Fernley, Sec., 505 Arch, Phila., Pa.

Natl. Wholesale Lumber Dealers Assn.—1894. 66 B'way, Mhtn. 460 mem. J. H. McClure, Pres.; E. F. Perry, Sec., Mhtn.

Periodical Publishers Assn. of Amer.—1902. 29 mem. 200 5th av., Mhtn. F. L. Collins, Pres.; C. H. Hathaway, Sec.

Photographers Assn. of Amer.—1880. 421 Claxton Bldg., Cleveland, O. 4,000 mem. C. L. Lewis, Pres.; J. C. Abel, Sec.

Railway Accounting Officers' Assn.—1888. 1116 Woodward Bldg., Washington. D. C. 900 mem. J. G. Drew, Pres.; E. R. Woodson, Sec.

Railway Business Assn.—1908. 466 mem. 30 Church, Mhtn. A. B. Johnson, Pres.; F. W. Noxon, Sec.

Amer. Railway Development Assn.—135 mem. H. O. Hartzell, Pres.; J. B. Lamson, Sec. and Treas., 547 W. Jackson blvd., Chicago, Ill.

Retail Clerks' Int. Prot. Assn.—1890. 60,000 mem. E. E. Baker, Pres.; H. J. Conway, Sec.-Treas., Lock Drawer 248, Lafayette, Ind.

Rubber Assn. of America—1900. 52 Vanderbilt av., Mhtn. 671 mem. H. E. Sawyer, Pres.; A. L. Viles, Sec. and Gen. Mgr.

Silk Assn. of Amer. (The)—1872. 354 4th av., Mhtn. 484 mem. Chas. Cheney, Pres.; Ramsay Peugnet, Sec.

Soc. of Automotive Engineers, Inc.—1909. 5,000 mem. J. G. Vincent, Pres.; C. F. Clarkson, Sec. and Gen. Mgr., 29 W. 39th, Mhtn.

Soc. of Railway Club Secretaries—1872. W. E. Cade, Jr., Boston, Ch.; H. D. Vought, Sec.-Treas., 95 Liberty, Mhtn.

Tobacco Merchants' Assn. of U. S.—1915. 5 Beekman, Mhtn. Jesse A. Bloch, Pres.; Chas. Dushkind, Sec.

Train Dispatchers Assn. of Amer.—1888. 1,200 mem. E. T. Mulquin, Pres.; J. P. Finan, Sec., Box 622, Needles, Cal.

Traveling Engineers Assn.—1,400 mem. G. A. Kell, Pres.; W. O. Thompson, Sec., Cleveland, O.

Treasurers Club of Amer.—301 W. 22d, Mhtn. 1888. 150 mem. J. H. J. Scullion, Pres.; A. J. Schnebbe, Sec.

United Master Butchers Assn. of Amer.—1885. 88,000 mem. C. Grismer, Pres.; J. A. Kotal, Sec., 5328 S. Halsted, Chicago, Ill.

United Press Assn.—W. W. Hawkins, Pres.; R. H. Fancher, Sec., World Bldg., Mhtn.

U. S. Brewers Assn., 50 Union Sq., Mhtn.—1862. 704 mem. C. W. Feigenspan, Pres.; H. F. Fox. Sec.

U. S. Newsprint League—1920. W. J. Pape, Pres., Waterbury, Conn.; J. B. Finan, Sec., Cumberland, Md.

SOCIETIES AND ASSOCIATIONS—BUSINESS, COMMERCIAL AND AGRICULTURAL—*Continued.*

Women Lawyers Assn.—1899. 290 mem. Miss E. M. Bullowa, Pres.; Miss Edviga Carlucci, Sec., 150 Nassau, N. Y. C.

Woman's Natl. Farm and Garden Assn., Inc.—1914. 2,400 mem. Mrs. F. King, Pres.; Miss S. H. Webb, Sec., 414 Madison av., Mhtn.

State.

Central Railway Club—1878. Hotel Statler, Buffalo, N. Y. 800 mem. M. W. Hassett, Pres., Buffalo, N. Y.

Farmers and Market Gardeners Union of N. Y. and N. J.—G. E. Van Sicklen, Pres.; J. M. Bergen, Sec., Woodhaven, L. I.

Legislative Correspondents Assn. of State of N. Y.—1890. Capitol, Albany. 75 mem. Russell Hathaway, Jr., Pres.; H. G. McCoy, Sec., Post Standard, Syracuse, N. Y.

N. Y. Electric Railway Assn.—T. C. Cherry, Pres., Syracuse, N. Y.; W. R. Stanton, Sec., N. Y. State Railways, Rochester, N. Y.

N. Y. State Assn. of Builders—1896. 1,750 mem. E. K. Fenno, Pres.; Ed. A. Keeler, Sec., 425 Orange, Albany.

N. Y. State Assn. of Chiefs of Police—1899. 75 mem. J. A. Wood, Pres.; Jas L. Hyatt, Sec., Chief of Police, Albany.

N. Y. State Assn. of Electrical Contractors and Dealers—1899. 550 mem. M. H. Johnson, Ch.; J. P. Ryan, Sec., 26 Cortlandt, Mhtn.

N. Y. State Assn. of Elocutionists—Prof. H. McTilroe, Pres.; Miss F. M. Schermer, Sec., 328 No. Washington, Herkimer.

N. Y. State Assn. of Postmasters—1907. 250 mem. A. R. Cornwall, Pres., Watertown, N. Y.; F. A. Ray, Sec., Herkimer, N. Y.

N. Y. State Assn. of Real Estate Boards—1905. Utica. 1,200 mem. J. D. White, Pres.; S. Yates, Treas.; M. C. Dobson, Sec.

N. Y. State Assn. of Retail Grocers—1901. Buffalo. 2,500 mem. P. de Puyt, Pres.; Chas. Thorpe, Sec., 164 Bush, Bronx, N. Y.

N. Y. State Bankers Assn.—1894. Composed of 8 groups consisting of 1,109 banks. The local groups are: No. VII., composed of Bkln. and L. I. banks and Group No. VIII., composed of Mhtn., Bronx and Richmond. S. G. H. Turner, Pres., Elmira; E. J. Gallien, Sec., 128 B'way, Mhtn.

N. Y. State Bar Assn.—1876. Albany. 3,226 mem. N. L. Miller, Pres., Syracuse; F. E. Wadhams, Sec., 78 Chapel, Albany; Albert Hessberg, Treas., Albany.

N. Y. State Board of Certified Public Accountant Examiners—F. W. Lafrentz, Pres.; C. S. McCulloh, Sec., 43 Exchange pl., Mhtn.

N. Y. State Breeders Assn.—1841. 500 mem. C. J. Huson, Pres.; Albert E. Brown, Sec., Dept. Farms and Markets, Albany.

N. Y. State Circulation Managers' Assn.—1917. 72 mem. M. J. Burke, Pres., Bkln. Daily Eagle, Bkln.; J. O'Conner, Sec., Knickerbocker Press, Albany.

N. Y. State Embalmers' Assn.—1900. 600 mem. Geo. Schuerman, Pres., Rochester, N. Y.; W. A. Drinkwine, Sec., 528 W. Onondaga, Syracuse.

N. Y. State Hay and Grain Dealers' Assn.—1905. 250 mem. F. Williams, Pres.; D. C. Jones, Sec.-Treas., Weedsport, N. Y.

N. Y. State Horticultural Soc.—1919. 1,600 mem. H. E. Wellman, Pres., Kendall, N. Y.; Ed. C. Gillett, Sec.-Treas., Penn Yan.

N. Y. State Hotel Assn.—1887. 334 5th av., Mhtn. E. C. Green, Pres.; M. A. Cadwell, Sec.

N. Y. State Laundrymen's Assn.—1908. 285 mem. A. W. Cummings, Pres.; W. T. Whitbeck, Sec., 29 Northland av., Buffalo.

N. Y. State League of Savings and Loan Assns.—Geo J. Beyer, Pres.; A. W. McEwan, Sec., 2161 Bathgate av., Bronx.

N. Y. State Oystermen's Protective Assn.—A. F. Merrell, Pres.; H. I. Merrell, Sec., Ft. Pike, Mhtn.

N. Y. State Press Assn.—1853. 200 mem. Walter B. Sanders, Pres., Nunda, N. Y.; Elias Vair, Sec.-Treas., Waterloo, N. Y.

N. Y. State Soc. of Certified Public Accountants—1897. 120 B'way. 450 mem. J. S. M. Goodloe, Pres.; J. F. Farrell, Sec.

N. Y. State Stenographers Assn.—1876. 250 mem. Henry Davis, Pres.; H. M. Kidder, Sec., 5 Beekman, Mhtn.

N. Y. State Undertakers Assn.—1880. 694 mem. Fred. Hulberg, Pres.; G. L. Gilham, Sec.-Treas., 150 W. 13th, Mhtn.

N. Y. State Waterways Assn.—1909. 500 mem. H. W. Hill, Pres., Buffalo; George Clinton, Jr., Sec., Buffalo.

N. Y. Wholesale Grocers Assn.—1888. 136 mem. Ed. Cumpson, Pres.; H. M. Foster, Sec., 6 Harrison, Mhtn.

Professional Photographers Soc. of N. Y.—1907. 235 mem. J. E. Mack, Pres.; B. J. Holcombe, Sec., Rochester, N. Y.

Savings' Bank Assn. of State of N. Y.—1893. John J. Pulleyn, Pres.; Harrison H. Wheaton, Exec. Mgr., 56 W. 45th, Mhtn.

Trust Companies Assn.—1904. 65 companies. Willard V. King, Pres.; F. E. Norton, Sec.; J. C. Powers, Treas., The Fidelity Trust Co., Rochester, N. Y.

Brooklyn.

Amer. Soc. of Swedish Engineers—1888. 271 Hicks. 380 mem. N. V. Hansell, Pres.; R. Strindberg, Sec., 271 Hicks.

Associated Brewery Clerks of N. Y. C.—275 Wilson av. F. A. Clemens, Pres.; F. E. Knell, Sec., 343 Dill pl., Glendale, L. I.

Assn. of Depositors of the Union Bank of Bkln.—1911. 73 Albany av. 400 mem. J. C. F. Baur, Pres.; John Woodenbury, Sec.

Assn. of Union Bakery Proprietors—1919. 1404 Decatur. 350 mem. Walter D. Ebinger, Pres.; Herman Sturm, Sec., 801 Cypress av.

Automobile Service Assn. of Bkln.—1920. 1255 Bedford av. 85 mem. G. T. McFarland, Pres.; Fred. M. Smith, Sec., 254 13th.

Board of Real Estate Brokers—189 Montague. W. R. Burling, Pres.; I. Cortelyou, Sec.

Bkln. Bar Assn.—1889. 675 mem. 123 Remsen. H. S. Rasquin, Sec.

Bkln. Engineers' Club—1896. 400 mem. F. W. Skinner, Pres.; Jos. Strachan, Sec., 117 Remsen.

Bkln. German Boss Bakers' Assn.—See German Socs.

Bkln. Group of the N. Y. Employing Printers' Assn.—1919. Hdqtrs., 23 W. 43d, Mhtn. 71 mem. Einar Schatvet, Pres., 221 77th; J. Andrew Hildebrand, Sec., 64 Sullivan.

Bkln. Insurance Brokers' Assn.—1911. 157 Remsen. 400 mem. John Boylan, Pres.; G. H. Holden, Sec.

Bkln. Labor Lyceum Assn.—1882. 500 mem. 949 Willoughby av. C. A. Heitmann, Pres.; C. R. Jaehngen, Sec.; J. H. Hofmann, Mgr.

Bkln. Master Bakers Purchasing Assn.—1911. 1404 Decatur. 281 mem. Martin Keidel, Pres.; Bruno Bleul, Sec.

Bkln. Retail Hardware Dealers Assn.—1910. 12 Nevins. 117 mem. H. R. L. Rohlfs, Pres.; R. Pearsall, Sec., 151 Macon.

Builders Assn.—1903. 369 Fulton. 115 mem. A. D. Constant, Pres.; W. F. Clayton, Sec., 369 Fulton.

Chamber of Commerce, Bkln.—(See Bds. of Trade.)

Combined Assns. of Engineers of the Boro. of Bkln.—125 So. Elliott pl. Chas. A. Enggren, Ch.; W. F. Brundage, Sec.

Commerce Club of Bkln.—1913. 750 Mhtn. av. W. S. Miller, Pres.; J. E. McDermott, Sec.

Coney Island Mardi Gras Assn., now Coney Isl. Carnival Co., Inc.—See Boards of Trade.

Electrical Contractors Assn. of L. I.—1898. 99 mem. 8 Nevins. H. Tollner, Pres.; H. F. Walcott, Rec. Sec., 714 Monroe.

Hotel Assn. of Bkln. Heights—1917. J. W. Tumbridge, Pres., Hotel St. George.

Kings Co. Lawyers Assn.—1911. 125 mem. J. J. Clancy, Pres.; S. A. Pease, Sec., 186 Remsen.

Kings and Queens Co. Coach Owners' Assn.—259 Lexington av. 275 mem. Lee A. Disbrow, Pres. and Sec.

Lawyers Club of Bkln.—1904. 112 mem. A. E. Goddard, Pres.; F. C. Haven, Sec., 189 Montague.

L. I. Bottlers' Assn. (Inc.)—1895. 367 Park av. 108 mem. J. O'Connell, Pres.; W. B. Hatfield, Sec.

L. I. Undertakers' Assn.—1874. H. T. Pyle, Pres.; J. B. Brophy, Sec., 5708 New Utrecht av.

Mechanics and Traders' Exchange—367-371 Fulton. 200 mem. W. L. Castle, Pres.; D. J. Morrison, Sec.

Motor Vehicle Dealers' Assn.—1920. C. M. Bishop, Pres.; C. J. Maxson, Sec., 1180 Fulton.

N. Y. Employing Printers' Assn., Bkln. group—See Bkln. Group.

Rotary Club of Bkln.—1913. 352 mem. George W. Baker, Pres.; Fred. H. Timpson, Sec., 307 Washington.

Retail Druggists' Protective Assn.—1909. Saengerbund Hall. V. Lind, Sec., 417 Hicks.

Sheepshead Bay Boat Owners' Assn.—Sheepshead Bay. Capt. F. Plage, Pres.; J. D. Tucker, Hon. and Active Pres., 2679 E. 24th; Capt. J. Martin, V.-Pres.; Dave Martin, Jr., Sec.

SOCIETIES AND ASSOCIATIONS—BUSINESS, COMMERCIAL AND AGRICULTURAL—*Continued.*

Travelers' Assn. of the Local Paint and Allied Trades (Inc.)—1907. 8 Nevins. 75 mem. D. C. Anderson, Pres.; B. M. Jordan, Sec., 84 Herkimer.

Underwriters' Soc. of Bkln.—C. H. Bainbridge, Pres.; F. Stussy, Jr., Sec., 172 Montague.

United Master Butchers Assn., Bkln. Br.—1886. 401 Bridge. A. Rosen, Pres.; W. C. Helling, Sec., 3432 Fulton.

United Retail Grocers' Assn.—401 Bridge. 1,000 mem. P. Becker, Pres.; Henry Lohman, Sec., 1702 8th av., Bkln. Fulton Exch.—Meets at 401 Bridge; J. Glawatz, Pres.; Herman Haase, Sec., Lafayette av., cor. Cumberland. Stuyvesant Hgts. Exch.—Fulton, cor. Troy av.; J. G. Ficken, Pres.; Louis Meyer, Sec., Troy av. and Fulton.

Wallabout Market Merchants' Assn.—1894. Geo. Dressler, Pres., 1201 Metz; Arthur Newman, Sec.

West End Bd. of Realty Brokers—1910. E. E. Hart, Pres.; Henry Michaels, Sec., 2222 80th.

Manhattan and Bronx.

Advertising Club of N. Y. (Inc.)—1920. 47 E. 25th. 1,200 mem. D. W. Hopkins, Pres.; S. R. Clarke, Exec. Sec.

Amer. Inst. of Banking, N. Y. Chapter—4,000 mem. G. A. Kinney, Pres., Chase Natl. Bank.

Associated Employees of Dept. of Water Supply, Gas and Electricity (Inc.)—F. A. Byrne, Sec., 1428 E. 10th, Bkln.

Associated Fur Mfrs. (Inc.)—303 5th av. F. Kaufman, Pres.; D. C. Mills, Mgr.

Assn. of Average Adjusters of U. S.—1879. 56 Beaver. 149 mem. J. S. Gilbertson, Ch.; Henry Pegram, Sec.

Assn. of the Bar of the City of N. Y.—1869. 2,333 mem. 42 W. 44th. J. G. Milburn, Pres.; C. H. Strong, Sec., 27 Cedar; F. O. Poole, Lib.

Assn. of the Bar, County of Bronx—1187 Washington av. 1902. 248 mem. H. C. Knoepple, 5 Beekman, Pres.; F. C. Hirleman, Sec., 391 E. 149th.

Assn. of Commercial Travelers, Book and Stationery Trade—C. B. Nourse, Pres.; John Hovendon, Sec., 156 5th av.

Assn. of Dealers in Masons' Building Materials—15-17 W. 46th. F. E. Wise, Pres.; S. J. Treat, Sec.

Assn. of Employing Printers of N. Y. C.—1917. Flatiron Bldg. E. F. Ellert, Pres.; F. E. Wilder, Sec., 416 W. 13th.

Assn. of Master Plumbers of City of N. Y.—155 E. 58th. M. J. Kennedy, Pres.; J. J. Dixon, Sec., 29 Atlantic av., Bkln.; Alex. J. Brown, Exec. Sec., 155 E. 58th. Bkln. Branch—F. L. Steele, Pres., 126 Meserole av., Bkln. Bronx Branch—E. Duklauer, Pres.; V. F. Bernesser, Sec., 1156 Hoe av. Mhtn. Branch—J. L. Knight, Pres.; J. H. Booth, Sec., 155 E. 58th. Richmond Branch—C. A. Schleiminger, Pres.; Jos. F. Elliott, Sec., 1271 N. Y. av., Rosebank. Queens Branch—F. B. Robertson, Pres.; J. F. Rogers, Sec., 131 Main, Flushing.

Assn. of N. Y. Advertising Agencies—F. H. Little, Ch.; W. T. Mullally, Sec.-Treas., 198 B'way.

Automobile Dealers' Assn. (Inc.)—1911. 700 mem. 1845 B'way. W. C. Poertner, Pres.; H. T. Gardner, Sec.

Board of Underwriters of N. Y. (Marine)—1820. 51 Wall. C. Eldert, Pres.; Clayton Platt, Sec., 51 Wall.

Booksellers of the City of N. Y.—1902. 33 mem. C. E. Butler, Pres.; P. Stammer, Sec.

Bottlers Mfrs. Assn.—75 mem. 218 E. 37th. P. F. O'Neill, Pres.; R. E. Schoder, Sec.

Building Trades Employers' Assn. of N. Y.—1903. 34 W. 33d. 1,000 mem. R. Taylor, Pres.; S. B. Donnelly, Sec.

Chamber of Commerce of State of N. Y.—See Bds. of Trade.

Children's Dress Mfrs. Assn.—1913. 75 mem. 200 5th av. D. R. Zackvary, Pres.; C. Rosenbaum, Sec., 24 W. 37th; E. M. Hecker, Mgr.

Clothing Mfrs. Assn. of N. Y., Inc.—752 B'way. 200 mem. W. O. Bandler, Pres.; Irving Crane, Sec.

Consolidated Stock Exchange of N. Y.—1876. 36 Beaver. 500 mem. W. S. Silkworth, Pres.; J. E. Lynch, Sec., Port Washington, L. I.

Correspondents' Club—1894. World Bldg. 25 active, 17 associate mem. A. M. Kemp, Pres.; B. S. Kearns, Sec., 1005 World Bldg.

Cotton Garment Mfrs. of N. Y. City—1913. 80 mem. 1 Madison av. B. Melberg, Pres.; M. H. Rosenberg, Sec.

Customs Brokers and Clerks Assn., Inc.—1897. 17 State. 250 mem. J. T. Rafferty, Pres. G. S. Young, Sec., 132 Pearl.

Dairymen's League—1907. 303 5th av. 81,000 mem. R. D. Cooper, Pres.; A. Manning, Sec.

Dress and Waist Mfrs. Assn.—1909. 235 mem. 200 5th av. H. B. Rosen, Pres.; G. S. Lewy, Gen. Mgr.

Drug and Chemical Club—1894. 100 William. 500 mem. Wm. Jay Schieffelin, Pres.; W. P. Young, Sec.

Electrical Contrs.' Assn.—1892. 42 mem. J. P. Ryan, Sec., 26 Cortlandt.

Employing Plasterers' Assn.—1899. 103 Park av. 24 firms. J. W. Braid, Pres.; T. Smith, Sec.

French Chamber of Commerce—1896. 456 4th av. H. E. Gourd, Pres.; F. Boulin, Sec.

Fulton Market Fishmongers' Assn.—1869. C. G. Miller, Pres.; Wm. H. Cornell, Sec., 10 Fulton, Wholesale Fish Market.

Gen. Soc. of Mechanics and Tradesmen of the City of N. Y.—1785. 16-24 W. 44th. 450 mem. Jas. Hopkins, Pres.; R. T. Davies, Sec.

Hardware Club of N. Y.—1892. 750 mem. 253 B'way. R. G. Thompson, Pres.; J. E. Ogden, Sec.

Harlem Bd. of Commerce—1896. 290 Lenox. 500 mem. J. G. Smith, Pres.; Thos. P. Ward, Sec.

Hide and Leather Assn.—1903. 150 mem. R. E. Binger, Pres.; Ralph E. Hallock, Sec., 176 William.

Hotel Assn. of N. Y. City—1878. 334 5th av. T. D. Green, Pres.; R. D. Blackman, Sec.

Illuminating Engineering Soc.—1906. 29 W. 39th. 1,600 mem. Gen. Geo. H. Harries, Pres.; Clarence L. Law, Sec., 29 W. 39th.

Insurance Soc. of N. Y.—1901. 1,200 mem. Allen E. Clough, Pres.; E. R. Hardy, Sec., 84 William.

Italian Chamber of Commerce—99 Hudson. 1887. 565 mem. L. J. Scaramelli, Pres.; A. C. Bonaschi, Sec., 1966 Valentine av.

Jewelers' 24-Karat Club of N. Y.—1902. 15 Maiden la. 200 mem. Lee Reichman, Pres.; W. J. Ward, Sec., 15 Maiden la.

Life Underwriters' Assn. of N. Y. (The)—1887. 1,000 mem. R. L. Jones, Pres.; L. H. Andrews, Sec., 217 B'way.

Lower Wall St. Business Men's Assn.—1883. Object: To encourage patriotism and philanthropy among business men. Wm. Bayne, Jr., Pres.; A. Wakeman, Sec., 63 Wall.

Machinery Club of N. Y. C.—1907. 1,350 mem. 50 Church. J. R. Vandyck, Pres.; E. A. Stillman, Sec.

Marble Industry Employers' Assn.—1889. 37 mem. John Eisele, Pres.; Wm. K. Fertig, Sec., 137 Madison av.

Maritime Assn. of the Port of N. Y.—78 Broad. Inc. 1874. 1,200 mem. Rafael Rios, Pres.; Walter F. Firth, Sec., 78 Broad.

Mason Builders' Assn.—1884. 130 mem. F. E. Conover, Pres.; John McClurg, Sec., 334 5th av.

Mechanics and Traders' Ex.—1863. 35 W. 32d. F. N. Howland, Pres.; C. E. Cheney, Sec.

Merchant Tailors Soc. of the City of N. Y.—R. Bennett, Pres.; W. A. Richmond, Sec., 241 5th av.

Merchants Protective Assn.—1903. 100 mem. 305 B'way. H. P. McKenney, Pres.; A. C. Brew, Sec.

Merchants' Assn. of N. Y.—1897. 9th floor, Woolworth Bldg. 6,600 mem. Wm. Fellowes Morgan, Pres.; S. C. Mead, Sec.

Metropolitan League Co-operative Savings and Loan Assns.—1893. W. D. Carter, Pres.; A. W. McEwan, Sec., 2161 Bathgate av.

Mining and Metallurgical Soc. of Amer.—1908. 300 mem. 115 B'way. W. Lindgren, Pres.; F. F. Sharpless, Sec.

Municipal Civil Service Commission Employees Soc.—Municipal Bldg. F. A. Byrne, 1428 E. 10th, Bkln., Pres.; J. F. Kavanaugh, Sec.

Municipal Engineers of the City of N. Y.—1903. 600 mem. J. H. Fitch, Pres.; V. S. Moon, Sec., 29 W. 39th.

Natl. Assn. of Clothiers—752 B'way. 300 mem. Eli Strouse, Pres.; Irving Crane, Sec.

Natl. Employment Exch.—1909. 30 Church. Secures employment for office workers. O. T. Bannard, Pres.; G. S. Anthony, Gen. Mgr.

Natl. League of Commission Merchants of the U. S.—N. Y. Branch, 97 Warren. 1893. A. R. Kunz, Pres.; R. C. Jackson, Sec., 335 Washington.

Natl. Workmen's Compensation Service Bureau—13 Park Row. A. W. Whitney, Gen. Mgr.; W. H. Cameron, Sec.-Treas.

SOCIETIES AND ASSOCIATIONS—BUSINESS, COMMERCIAL AND AGRICULTURAL—MHTN. & BRONX—*Con.*

N. Y. Board of Fire Underwriters—1867. 123 William. 158 mem. E. A. Ludlum, Pres.; Bennett Ellison, Sec., 83 William.

N. Y. City Undertakers' Assn.—1884. 175 mem. George W. Freeborn, Pres.; G. L. Gilham, Sec., 150 W. 13th, Mhtn.

N. Y. Civil Service Soc. (Inc.)—1909. 9,000 mem. F. J. Prial, Pres.; W. R. Bradley, Sec., 2129 Cortelyou rd., Bkln.

N. Y. Clearing House Assn.—77 Cedar. Composed of 39 banks and 13 trust cos., Asst. Treas. of U. S. and Federal Reserve Bank of N. Y., 14 banks and trust cos. in city and vicinity make exchanges through banks that are members. A. H. Wiggin, Pres.; H. K. Twitchell, Sec.; W. J. Gilpin, Mgr.; C. E. Bacon, Asst. Mgr.

N. Y. Coffee and Sugar Exchange, Inc.—1885. 323 mem. Hanover sq. C. A. Fairchild, Pres.; E. F. Diercks, Sec., 66 Beaver; C. B. Stroud, Supt.

N. Y. Cotton Exchange—1870. 60-62 Beaver. 450 mem. Leopold S. Bache, Pres.; Leigh M. Pearsall, Sec.

N. Y. County Lawyers' Assn.—1908. 3,700 mem. 165 B'way. C. E. Hughes, Pres.; Geo. C. Austin, Sec.

N. Y. Credit Men's Assn.—1895. 320 B'way. 4,300 mem. E. S. Boteler, Pres.; A. H. Alexander, Sec., 320 B'way.

N. Y. Cut Flower Exchange—1892. 55-57 W. 26th. 150 mem. J. Schneider, Pres.; V. S. Dorval, Sec., Woodside, N. Y.

N. Y. Electrical Soc.—1881. 845 mem. W. N. Dickinson, Pres.; G. H. Guy, Sec., 29 W. 39th.

N. Y. Employing Printers' Assn.—1920. 23-31 W. 43d. 900 mem. E. F. Eilers, Pres.; F. E. Wilder, Sec.; S. C. Gordon, Exec. Sec.

N. Y. Fruit Exchange—1885. 204 Franklin. 225 mem. W. A. Camp, Pres.; A. Zucca, Treas.; J. B. Greason, Sec.; F. W. Geiger, Mgr.

N. Y. Furniture Warehousemen's Assn., Inc.—1897. 300 mem. Grant Mayne, Pres.; C. S. Morris, Sec., 39 W. 66th.

N. Y. Law Inst.—1830. 120 B'way. 850 mem. Elihu Root, Pres.; A. E. Hinrichs, Sec., 52 Wall.

N. Y. Lumber Trade Assn.—1886. Wm. C. Reid, Pres.; H. B. Coho, Sec., 18 B'way.

N. Y. Mercantile Ex.—1872. 6 Harrison. 416 mem. J. D. Mahr, Pres.; H. I. Snyder, Sec.

N. Y. Metal Ex.—111 B'way. 203 mem. Chas. J. Marsh, Pres.; Carl Mayer, Sec.

N. Y. News Bureau Assn.—26 Beaver. 1881 Edward Rascovar, Pres.; F. J. Rascovar, Sec.

N. Y. Piano Mfrs.' Assn.—1899. 75 firms. R. B. Aldcroftts, Pres.; Albert Behning, Sec., 217 W. 125th.

Madison Sq. Garden Poultry Show, Inc.—1888. T. A. Havemeyer, Pres.; D. Lincoln Orr, Sec., Orr's Mills, N. Y.

N. Y. Produce Exchange—1861. B'way, cor. Beaver. 1,900 mem. Walter B. Pollock, Pres.; L. B. Howe, Sec.

N. Y. R. R. Club—1872. 2,200 mem. H. C. Manchester, Pres.; Harry D. Vought, Sec., 95 Liberty.

N. Y. State Bankers' Assn.—Group No. 8, composed of Mhtn., Bronx and Richmond banks, trust cos. and bankers. 128 B'way, N. Y. C. Chas. H. Sabin, Pres.; E. Stauffen, Sec., Liberty Natl. Bank, N. Y. C.

Group No. 7, composed of banks, trust cos. and bankers of L. I. and Bkln. G. S. Emory, Ch.; R B. Dayton, Sec., Cash., Bank of Port Jefferson, N. Y.

N. Y. Stock Exchange—Broad and Wall. W. H. Remick, Pres.; E. V. D. Cox, Sec.

N. Y. Typographical Soc.—1809. Room 805, 25 W. 43d. 265 mem. R. D. Williams, Pres.; John McKinley, Jr., Sec., 7 Glenada pl., Bkln.

Old Colony Club—1916. Hotel Biltmore. Exec. Offices, 1451 B'way. A. J. Norton, Pres.; J. T. Madden, Sec.

Paint, Oil and Varnish Club of N. Y.—1887. 17 Battery pl.—257 mem. H. J. Schnell, Pres.; H. G. Sidebottom, Sec.

Professional Chauffeurs' Club of Amer.—240 W. 55th. Ed. Fagan, Pres.

Publishers Assn. of N. Y. City—903-7 World Bldg. H. L. Bridgman, Ch.; L. B. Palmer, Sec.-Treas.

Railway Car Manufacturers' Assn.—1915. 61 B'way. W. F. M. Goss, Pres.; W. C. Tabbert, Sec.

Real Estate Board of N. Y.—217 B'way. 1908. 1,500 mem. S. H. Tyng, Pres.; D. A. Clarkson, V.-Pres.; J. I. Walsh, Treas.; Wm. M. Benjamin, Sec.

Real Estate Owners Protective Assn.—432 mem. J. S. Schwab, Pres.; W. C. Capleas, Sec., 747 Amsterdam av.

Retail Coal Exch.—1888. 6 Church. 30 mem. Henry Breunich, Pres.; A. F. Keckeisen, Sec.

Retail Dealers' Protective Assn.—1871. 34 W. 33d. G. I. Wichman, Pres.; Walter Grafton, Sec.; conducted as a commercial agency.

Rotary Club of N. Y.—1909. Hotel McAlpin. 510 mem. R. J. Knoeppel, Pres.; W. J. Beamish, Sec., Hotel McAlpin.

Silk Travelers' Assn., Inc.—1916. 1,100 mem. Park Av. Hotel. F. I. Cox, Pres.; H. W. Smith, Sec., 373 4th av.

Sphinx Club—1896. 400 mem. R. F. Huntsman, Pres.; T. A. Barrett, Sec.; R. S. Scarburgh, Treas., 26 Beaver.

Soc. of Naval Architects and Marine Engineers—1893. 29 W. 39th. 1,600 mem. Rear-Admiral Washington L. Capps, Pres.; D. H. Cox, Sec.-Treas.

Soc. of Restaurateurs—1914. 1451 B'way. 350 mem. August Janssen, Pres.; C. J. Kaemmerlen, Sec.

Surety Underwriters' Assn. of N. Y.—Geo. H Hayes, Pres.; M. A. Craig, Sec., 45 William.

Teachers' Co-op. Bldg. and Loan Assn. (N. Y. C.)—170 E. 60th. J. G. Furey, Pres.; C. T. Sesman, Sec.

Traffic Club of N. Y. (The)—1906. 1,600 mem. Waldorf-Astoria. Fred E. Signer, Pres.; C. A. Swope, Sec., 309 B'way.

Transportation—1895. Hotel Manhattan, 725 mem. W. P. Hall, Pres.; J. F. Fairlamb, Sec.

United Real Estate Owners' Assn.—1902. 280 B'way. 10,000 mem. Stewart Browne, Pres.; Isaac Hyman, Sec.

Van Owners' Assn. of Greater N. Y.—1913. 144 Columbus av. 175 mem. C. S. Morris, Pres.; Grant Wayne, Sec., 210 W. 39th.

Wholesale Coal Trade Assn.—1917. 95 mem. C. Andrade, Jr., Pres.; Chas. S. Allen, Sec., 90 West.

Women's Civil Service League—1912. Rm. 526 Municipal Bldg. 160 mem. Mrs. M. F. Merchant, Pres.; Mrs. M. J. Smart, Sec., 464 Eastern P'kway, Bkln.

Working Women's Prot. Union—1863. 289 4th av. H. D. Chapin, M.D., Pres.; E. R. Ogilby, Supt.

Queens.

Agricultural Soc. of Queens-Nassau Counties—1841. 1,000 mem. Robert C. Baird, Pres.; Lott Van de Water, Jr., Sec., 126 Franklin, Hempstead.

Chamber of Commerce of the Borough of Queens—1911. 800 mem. H. Pushae Williams, Pres.; W. I. Willis, Sec., Queensboro Bridge Plaza, L. I. C.

Myrtle Av. Chamber of Commerce—1913. 175 mem. Edward Miethke, Pres.; M. Shaffran, Sec., 2689 Myrtle av.

Newtown Liquor Dealers' Assn.—1896. 48 mem. J. Menn, Pres., Corona.; P. Sperling, Sec.

Queens Co. Bar Assn.—1874. County Court House, L. I. City. 206 mem. Wm. Rasquin, Jr., Pres.; R. Richardson, Sec., Flushing.

Retail Butchers' Assn.—1898. 100 mem. P. Ferris, Sr., Pres.; A. Koch, Sec., 39 13th. College Point.

Springfield Cem. Assn.—G. R. Higbie, Pres.; N. Smith Carpenter, Sec., St. Albans.

Richmond.

Richmond Co. Liberty League—1897. 94 mem. Peter McHugh, Pres.; Chas. Felten, Sec., 653 Van Duzer, Stapleton.

Staten Island Chamber of Commerce—1895. 200 mem. St. George. C. G. Kolff, Pres.; L. W. Kaufmann, Sec.

DRAMATIC SOCIETIES.

International and National.

Internatl. Alliance of Theatrical Stage Employees and Moving Picture Machine Operators of U. S. and Canada—1893. 19,000 mem. James Lemke, Pres.; F. G. Lemaster, Sec., 110 W. 40th, Mhtn.

National Shakespeare Federation—1918. Washington, D. C. Mrs. Johnston, Pres.; Chas. O'H. Craigie, Treas., 1729 Que st., Washington, D. C.; Laura Sedgwick Collins, Sec., Hotel Chelsea, Mhtn.

SOCIETIES AND ASSOCIATIONS—DRAMATIC SOCIETIES—*Continued.*

Brooklyn.

Adelphi Academy Dramatic Assn.—1908. H. J. Nevius, Pres.; Harriet Greason, Sec., 481 Washington av.

Bkln. Drama-Comedy Club—1920. Acad. of Music. 500 mem. Edyth Totten, Pres.; Mrs. R. G. Hargrave, Sec., 8670 Bay 21st; Carl Fique, Mus. Dir., 128 DeKalb av.

Bkln. Royal Vaudeville Club—1911. 50 mem. V. F. Warner, Pres.; H. B. Pratt, Sec., 826 Decatur.

Bkln. Teachers' Assn. Dram. Club—20 mem. A. Ewart, Dir., 90 Downing.

Burky Studio Players—1915. 14 mem. Hy. Burky, Mgr., 1236 Halsey.

Byron Dram. Soc.—1905. 26 mem. G. B. Bradford, Pres.; A. K. Allison, Sec., 8934 Brandon av., Woodhaven.

Catholic Dram. Soc.—1910. 803 97th, Woodhaven, L. I. F. J. Mulligan, Dram. Dir.; Casper Thomas, Bus. Mgr.

Crescent Dram. Soc.—1905. 172 St. Marks av. 20 mem. J. P. Martin, Pres.; W. R. Redmond, Sec. 250 Park pl.

Gregorian Players—1917. 1006 Sterling pl. 100 mem. Geo. Mainardy, Pres.; Adelaid Schmidt, Sec.; Wm. J. McLaughlin, Dir.

Ionian Players—1901. 246 Jamaica av. 21 mem. Frank May, Pres.; N. L. Smith, Sec.

Mercedes Players—1909. 75 mem. F. A. Donohue, Pres.; Miss E. Savage, Rec. Sec., 275A Wyckoff.

Natl. Players—1910. 100 mem. 29 Aberdeen. J. F. Ross, Pres.; F. I. Ross, Sec.

Packer Alumnae Dramatic Assn.—1900. 140 mem. Marguerite Krantz, Pres.; Katherine Burr, Sec., 108 E. 18th.

Park Dram. Soc.—1900. 25 mem. H. R. Beringer, Pres., 1187 E. 19th.

Park Slope Players—1906. 763A Union. 25 mem. Wilbur Lorraine, Pres.; F. W. H. Nelson, Jr., Sec., 329 68th.

Stuyvesant Heights Dram. Co.—1912. 20 mem. 90 Downing. Annette Ewart, Pres.

Thespian Stock Co.—1897. 20 mem. 735 Fulton. H. C. Edwards, Mgr., 754 Halsey.

Ulk Dram. Club—1880. Prospect Hall. 35 mem. E. Bergmann, Pres.; L. Wichers, Sec., 638 4th av.

Xaverians—1905. 97 mem. P. A. Kennedy, Pres.; W. R. Grace, Sec., 133 St. Johns pl.

Manhattan.

Actors' Equity Assn.—1913. 115 W. 47th. 9,000 mem. John Emerson, Pres.; Frank Gillmore, Sec.; Grant Stewart, Rec. Sec.

Actors' Fidelity League—1919. 122 W. 43d. 990 mem. Henry Miller, Pres.; Howard Kyle, Sec.

Actors' Fund of America—1882. 707 7th av. 3,000 mem. Daniel Frohman, Pres.; W. C. Austin, Sec.

Actors' International Assn.—1894. 701 7th av. 600 mem. Harry De Veaux, Pres.; John Welsh, Sec.

Actors' Order of Friendship (Edwin Forrest Lodge No. 2)—1888. 139 W. 47th. 400 mem. R. Galland, Pres.; Wm. H. Young, Sec.

Associated Artists and Actors—1440 B'way. J. W. Fitz Patrick, Pres.; H. Mountford, Sec.-Treas.

Catholic Actors' Guild of America—1914. 220 W. 42d. 1,000 mem. Brandon Tynan, Pres.; E. J. Kelly, Sec.

Dramatic Soc. of Washington Sq. College—1920. 32 Waverley pl. 65 mem. Adolph Meyer, Pres.; H. Axworthy, Sec.

Natl. Assn. of Theatrical Producing Managers—See Business Assns., National.

Natl. Vaudeville Artists' Club—229 W. 46th. Edwards Davis, Pres.; Henry Chesterfield, Sec.

New York Drama League, Inc.—7 E. 42d. S. M. Tucker, Pres.; Miss L. V. Day, Sec.

Players (The)—1888. 16 Gramercy Pk. John Drew, Pres.; John C. Travis, Sec.

Players' Club—1906. Columbia Univ. 175 mem. H. Geiger, Pres.; L. F. Dickinson, Sec., 52 W. 129th.

Professional Woman's League—1893. 144 W. 55th. 250 mem. Helen Whitman Ritchie, Pres.; Mrs. C. A. Schultz, Sec.

Soc. of Amer. Dramatists and Composers—1891. 148 W. 45th. 124 mem. Geo. M. Cohan, Pres.; P. Wilde, Sec.

Theater Club—1910. Hotel Astor. 400 mem. Mrs. J. H. Parker, Pres.; Mrs. Alice Hughes, Sec., 35 W. 32d.

United Theatrical Assn.—Richard A. Purdy, Pres.; Clara Morris, V.-Pres.; Edith F. Ranger, Sec., 418 W. 43d.

Queens.

Cardinal Players—St. Rose Hall, Rockaway Beach. 1905. 28 mem. Albert Ringk, Pres.; Robt. Regan, Sec., Rockaway Beach.

Park Players—1918. 122 Grove, Jamaica. Harold Range, Pres.; Edna McBride, Sec.

EDUCATIONAL AND SCIENTIFIC SOCIETIES

National and International.

Aeronautical Soc. of America—29 W. 39th. F. M. H. Avram, Pres.; A. H. Fisher, Sec.

Am. Acad. in Rome—1905. 101 Park av., Mhtn. W. R. Mead, Pres.; C. G. La Farge, Sec.; W. A. Boring, Treas.

Am. Acad. of Arts and Letters—50 mem. W. M. Sloane, Pres.; R. U. Johnson, Sec., Rm. 1412, 347 Madison av., Mhtn.

Am. Assn. for the Advancement of Science—1847. 15,000 mem. L. O. Howard, Pres.; Burton E. Livingston, Perm. Sec., Smithsonian Inst., Washington, D. C.

Amer. Assn. of Teachers of Journalism—Prof. H. F. Harrington, Pres.; Prof. J. R. Brumm, Sec.-Treas., Univ. of Ill.

Amer. Assn. of University Professors—2,300 mem. E. Capps, Pres., Princeton Univ.; H. W. Tyler, Sec., Mass. Inst. of Technology, Cambridge, Mass.

Am. Assn. to Promote the Teaching of Speech to the Deaf—1890. 1,400 mem. Hdqts., Rochester, N. Y., and Volta Bureau, Washington, D. C. Harris Taylor, Pres., N. Y. C.; A. E. Pope, Sec., Trenton, N. J.

Am. Astronomical Society—1899. 350 mem. F. Schlesinger, Pres.; Joel Stebbins, Sec., Urbana, Ill.

Am. Bird Banding Assn.—1908. Am. Mus. of Nat. Hist., N. Y. C. 400 mem. Howard C. Cleaves, Sec., Albany, N. Y.

Am. Chemical Soc.—1876. 15,693 mem. W. A. Noyes, Pres.; C. L. Parsons, Sec., 1709 G, N. W., Washington, D. C.

Am. Climatological and Clinical Assn.—1884. 150 mem. C. E. Edson, M.D., Pres.; A. K. Stone, M.D., Sec., Framingham Center, Mass.

Am. Council on Education—1918. 818 Connecticut av., Washington, D. C. 140 mem. H. P. Judson, Ch.; Dr. S. P. Capen, Dir.

Am. Dermatological Assn.—1876. Dr. Jay F. Schamberg, Pres.; Dr. Udo J. Wile, Sec., Univ. Hosp., Ann Arbor, Mich.

Am. Dahlia Soc.—Richd. Vincent, Jr., Pres., White Marsh, Md.; Edw. C. Vick, Sec., 205 Elwood av., Newark, N. J.

Am. Dialect Soc.—1889. 330 mem. Prof. J. W. Bright, Pres.; Dr. Percy W. Long, Sec., Harvard Univ., Cambridge, Mass.

Am. Economic Assn.—1885. 2,600 mem. Prof. H. J. Davenport, Pres.; R. B. Westerfield, Sec.-Treas., Yale Univ., New Haven, Conn.

Am. Entomological Soc.—1859. Logan sq., Phila., Pa. 150 mem. Dr. H. Skinner, Pres., Logan sq., Phila., Pa.; R. C. Williams, Jr., Sec.

Am. Ethnological Soc.—1842. Inc. 1916. Am. Museum of Nat. History, Mhtn. 7 monthly meetings. Theresa Mayer, Pres.; R. H. Lowie, Sec., Am. Museum of Nat. History, Mhtn.

Am. Folklore Soc.—1888. 400 mem. E. C. Parsons, Pres.; Chas. Peabody, Sec., Cambridge, Mass.

Am. Genetic Assn.—1903. 3,300 mem. David Fairchild, Pres.; Geo. M. Rommel, Sec., Box 472, 11th St. Sta., Washington, D. C.

Am. Geographical Soc. of N. Y.—1852. B'way and 156th, Mhtn. 3,367 mem. I. Bowman, Dir.

Am. Historical Assn.—1884. Washington, D. C. 2,600 mem. Ed. Channing, Pres., Harvard Univ.; John S. Bassett, Sec., Smith College, Northampton, Mass.

Am. Inst. of Electrical Engineers—1884. 33 W. 39th, Mhtn. 10,655 mem. C. Townley, Pres.; F. L. Hutchinson, Sec.

Am. Inst. of Instruction—1830. 500 mem. W. E. Mason, Pres.; J. J. Mahoney, Sec., Lowell, Mass.

Am. Inst. of Mining and Metallurgical Engineers—1871. 9,000 mem. Herbert Hoover, Pres.; Bradley Stoughton, Sec., 29 W. 39th, Mhtn.

Am. Irish Historical Soc.—1897. 35 W. 39th, Mhtn. 1,400 mem. J. I. C. Clarke, Pres.; S. P. Cahill, Sec.

Am. Jewish Historical Soc.—1892. 38 Park row, Mhtn. 399 mem. Cyrus Adler, Pres.; A. M. Friedenberg, Sec.

SOCIETIES AND ASSOCIATIONS—EDUCATIONAL—NATIONAL AND INTERNATIONAL—*Continued.*

Amer. Library Assn.—1876. To promote and secure public library service for all Americans everywhere. A. S. Tyler, Pres.; Carl H. Milam, Sec., 78 E. Washington, Chicago, Ill.; Assn. Hdqtrs. 4,000 mem. The assn. provided library service for the Army, Navy and Marines during the war. This library service was taken over by the War Dept. in Nov., 1919. The assn. provides library service to the Coast Guard and Lighthouse Service, U. S. Public Health Hospitals and U. S. Shipping Board and other merchant marine vessels. The assn. also publishes books and pamphlets on library work. M. W. Meyer, in charge of publicity. Herbert Putnam, Librarian of Congress, Gen. Dir., Library of Congress, Washington, D. C.

Am. Mathematical Soc.—1894. 750 mem. F. Morley, Pres.; F. N. Cole, Sec., 501 W. 116th, Mhtn.

Am. Microscopical Soc.—1878. 330 mem. Dr. T. W. Galloway, Pres.; Prof. P. S. Welch, Sec., Ann Arbor, Mich.

Am. Nature Study Soc.—1905. Ithaca, N. Y. 1,900 mem. Prof. J. A. Drushel, Pres., St. Louis, Mo.; Prof. Anna B. Comstock, Sec., Ithaca, N. Y.

Am. Oriental Soc.—1842. 499 mem. Prof. Talcott Williams, Pres.; Dr. C. J. Ogden, Cor. Sec., 628 W. 114th, Mhtn. To promote Oriental studies, to encourage research in Eastern languages and literatures, and to publish books and papers dealing with those subjects. Middle West Br. 1917. Prof. A. H. Lybyee, Pres.; A. T. Olmstead, Sec., Urbana, Ill.

Am. Philosophical Soc.—1727 Independence sq., Phila., Pa. W. B. Scott, Pres.; I. Minis Hays, A. W. Goodspeed, V.-Pres.; Geo. E. Hale, A. A. Noyes, H. L. Carson, H. F. Keller, B. M. Davis, Secs.

Am. Physical Soc.—1899. 1,200 mem. Prof. J. S. Ames, Pres.; D. C. Miller, Sec., Case Sch. of Applied Science, Cleveland, O.

Am. Political Science Assn.—1903. 1,500 mem. Paul S. Reinsch, Pres.; F. A. Ogg, Sec., Univ. of Wisconsin, Madison, Wis.

Am. Social Science Assn.—1865. G. G. Battle, Pres.; J. B. Townsend, Sec., 110 W. 40th.

American Soc. of Church History—1888. 200 mem. Object: To promote and stimulate historical study and research, especially in the field of church history. Rev. Prof. Robt. H. Nichols, Pres., Auburn Theological Seminary, Auburn, N. Y.; Rev. Prof. F. W. Loetscher, Sec., Princeton, N. J.

Am. Soc. of Internat. Law—1906. Object: To foster study of internat. law and promote the establishment of international relations on the basis of law and justice. Elihu Root, Pres.; J. B. Scott, Sec., Washington, D. C.

Am. Soc. of Naturalists—1883. 400 mem. Dr. J. Loeb, Pres.; Prof. A. Franklin Shull, Sec., Univ. of Mich., Ann Arbor, Mich.

Am. Soc. for Psychical Research—1906. 44 E. 23d, Mhtn. 1,000 mem. G. Ogden Tubby, Act. Sec.

Am. Soc. of Zoologists—1903. 311 mem. G. A. Drew, Pres.; W. C. Allen, Sec., Lake Forest, Ill.

Am. Sociological Soc.—1906. 1,020 mem. F. W. Blackmar, Pres.; S. E. W. Bedford, Sec., 68th and Ellis av., Chicago, Ill.

Am. Statistical Assn.—1839. 900 mem. Geo. E. Roberts, Pres.; R. E. Chaddock, Sec., Kent Hall, Columbia Univ., N. Y.

Am. University Union in Europe—1917. Journalism Bldg., Columbia Univ., N. Y. C. Prof. H. B. Hutchins, Pres.; Prof. J. W. Cunliffe, Sec.

Archaeological Inst. of Amer.—1879. Washington, D. C. 42 affiliated socs. 3,000 mem. Prof. J. C. Egbert, Pres.; Prof. G. M. Whicher, Gen. Sec., Hunter College, N. Y. C.

Armenian Educational Soc. of Amer.—M. Karagheusian, Pres.; D. A. Dikijian, Sec., 46 Morrison av., W. Somerville, Mass.

Assn. of Amer. Law Schools—1900. 49 Law Schools. E. A. Gilmore, Pres.; H. C. Jones, Sec., Morgantown, W. Va.

Assn. of Amer. Library Schools—1915. Josephine Adams Rathbone, Pres., Library School, Pratt Inst., Bkln.; Florence A. Curtis, Sec., Ill. Univ. Library School, Urbana, Ill.

Assn. of Amer. Universities (The)—1900. 24 mem. Offices filled by universities. Pres., Ohio State Univ., Columbus, O.; V.-Pres., Univ. of Kansas, Lawrence, Kan.; Sec., Univ. of Chicago, Chicago, Ill.

Assn. of Colleges and Preparatory Schools of Middle States and Maryland—1887. 300 colleges and schools. Walter Marsh, Pres.; G. W. McClelland, Sec., Univ. of Pa., Phila., Pa.

Assn. of History Teachers, Middle States and Maryland—1903. 375 mem. D. C. Knowlton, Pres.; R. W. Kelsey, Sec., Haverford College, Haverford, Pa.

Botanical Soc. of America—1906. 775 mem. N. L. Britton, Pres.; J. R. Schramm, Sec., Cornell Univ., Ithaca, N. Y.

Camp Directors Assn. of Amer.—1910. Columbia Univ. 76 mem. H. W. Little, Pres.; E. H. Lehman, Sec., 214 W. 100th.

Carnegie Foundation—Est. by Andrew Carnegie, 1905. Inc. by act of Congress, 1906. Object: Providing retiring allowances for teachers and officers of universities, colleges and technical schools in the U. S., Canada and Newfoundland and the general advancement of higher education. Pres., H. S. Pritchett; Sec., Clyde Furst, 522 5th av., **Mhtn. Has board of 25 trustees who are presidents of universities and colleges and financiers.**

Carnegie Inst. of Washington—Washington, D. C. Founded by Andrew Carnegie, 1902. Inc. by act of Congress, 1904. Object: To encourage investigation, research and discovery and the application of knowledge to the improvement of mankind. Ch. Bd. Trustees, Elihu Root; Sec. Bd. Trustees, C. H. Dodge; Pres., R. S. Woodward.

Catholic Educational Assn.—2,500 mem. 1651 E. Main, Columbus, O. Rev. F. W. Howard, Sec. To promote Christian education and morality.

Catholic Summer School of Amer.—Cliff Haven, N. Y. Very Rev. J. J. Donlan, D.D., Pres.; C. Murray, Sec., 321 W. 43d, Mhtn.

Chautauqua Inst.—1874. Chautauqua, N. Y. 500,000 mem. A. E. Bestor, Pres.; Dr. G. E. Vincent, Hon. Pres.

Chemistry Teachers' Club of N. Y. City—1902. 100 mem. J. H. Branson, Treas., Horace Mann School, Mhtn.

Esperanto Assn. of N. A.—1908. 3,000 mem. E. S. Payson, Pres.; G. W. Lee, Sec., Boston, Mass.

Farmers' Club of the Amer. Inst.—324 W. 23d, Mhtn. Wm. A. Eagleson, Sec.

General Educational Board—1902. 61 B'way, Mhtn. 16 mem. Object: To promote and systematize educational beneficence in the U. S. W. Buttrick, Pres. L. G. Myers, Treas.; A. Flexner and Trevor Arnett, Secs. $10,000,000 cash given to the Board by J. D. Rockefeller, Oct. 2, 1905; $11,000,000, April 1, 1907, and $10,000,000, July 7, 1909. $20,000,000. Sept. 20, 1919, for medical education, and $50,000,000, Dec. 18, 1919, for teachers' salaries.

Geological Soc. of Amer.—1888. 425 mem. I. C. White, Pres.; E. O. Hovey, Sec., Am. Mus. **Nat. Hist., W. 77th and Central Park W., Mhtn.**

Germanic Museum **Assn.—1901. Meets in Cambridge. F. P. Fish, Pres.; C. S. Houghton, Sec. and Treas., 60 State, Boston, Mass.**

Hispanic Soc. of Am.—(See Literary Soc.)

Intercollegiate Socialist Soc.—1905. 70 5th av. 1,500 mem. Arthur Gleason, Act. Pres.; H. W. Laidler, Sec.

Internatl. Acad. of Science, Arts and Letters (Inc.)—1910. 75 mem. Dr. T. G. Lewis, Pres.; C. N. Murray, Sec., 1639 W st., S. E., Washington, D. C.

Internatl. Federation of University Women—Prof. Caroline Spurgeon, Pres., Bedford Coll., London, Eng.; Dean Virginia Gildersleeve, Ch., Barnard Coll., N. Y. C.

Internatl. Kindergarten Union — (See Kindergarten Assns.)

Mathematical Assn. of America—1915. 27 King, Oberlin, O. 1,100 individual mems. and 47 institutional mems. David E. Smith, Pres.; W. D. Cairns, Sec., Oberlin Coll., O.

Modern Language Assn. of Amer.—1883. 1,500 mem. John M. Manly, Pres.; Carleton Brown, Sec., 416 8th av., S. E., Minneapolis, Minn.

Naples Table Assn. for Promoting Lab. Research by women (The)—1898. **Miss B. Boody, Pres.; Dr. F. Sabin, Sec., Johns Hopkins Med. Sch.—Baltimore, Md.**

Natl. Acad. of Sciences—Inc. by Congress 1863. Annual meeting, Washington, 3d Mon. in April. 190 mem. 37 foreign associates. C. D. Walcott, Pres.; G. E. Hale, Foreign Sec.; C. G. Abbot, Home Sec.; F. L. Ransome, Treas., Washington, D. C.

Natl. Assn. for Study and Education of Exceptional Children—1905. "Watchung Crest," Plainfield, N. J. T. Stempfel, Pres.; W. H. Grossmann, Genl. Sec. and Treas.

Natl. Assn. of Corporation Schools—Louis L. Park, Pres., Schenectady, N. Y.; N. S. Sloane, Bkln., and H. S. Dennison, Framingham, Mass., V.-Prests.

Natl. **Assn. of the Deaf—1880. Inc. 1900. 1,700** mem. **Dr. J. H. Cloud, Pres.; A. L. Roberts, Sec., Kendall Green, Washington, D. C.**

Natl. Education Assn.—1857. 50,000 mem. **F. M.** Hunter, Pres., Supt. of Schools, Oakland, Cal.; J. W. Crabtree, Sec., 1201 16th, Washington, D. C.

SOCIETIES AND ASSOCIATIONS—EDUCATIONAL—NATIONAL AND INTERNATIONAL—*Continued.*

Natl. Geographic Soc.—Memorial Hall, Washington, D. C. 750,000 mem. Gilbert Grosvenor, Pres., Washington, D. C.

Natl. Historical Soc.—1915. 37 W. 39th, N. Y. C. F. Allaben, Pres.; Mabel T. R. Washburn, Sec.; Dudley Butler, Treas.

Nat. Inst. of Social Sciences—1,000 mem. E. R. Johnson, Pres.; J. Knight, Sec., 110 W. 40th.

Natl. Kindergarten Assn.—1909. 8 W. 40th, Mhtn. Supported by voluntary gifts. Object. To have kindergartens established in every public school. Major B. Martin, Pres.; Miss Bessie Locke, Cor. Sec.

Natl. Soc. for Vocational Education—1906. 2,500 mem. 140 W. 42d, Mhtn. Wm. J. Bogan, Pres.

Natl. Speech Arts Assn.—1891. Chas. M. Holt, Pres.; Miss J. E. Tharp, Sec., New Orleans, La.

Natl. Tax Assn.—1907. N. P. Haugen, Harvard Univ., Pres., Z. W. Bliss, V. Pres., F. R. Fairchild, Sec., Yale Univ., New Haven, Conn.; A. E. Holcomb, Treas., 195 B'way, Mhtn.

New Piasa Chautauqua Assn.—C. Bernet, Pres.; M. E. Johnson, Gen. Mgr., St. Louis, Mo.

Persian-Armenian Educational Soc. of Amer.—767 Lexington av. M. H. Maroot, Pres.; S. Shahboodaghian, Sec.

Reptile Study Soc. of Amer.—1916. 782 E. 175th. 450 mem. Allen S. Williams, Dir.; Elizabeth Remington, Sec.

Russian Missionary Soc., Inc.—1880. Spring Garden, Phila., Pa. Cortland Myers, Pres.; Wm. Fetler, Gen. Dir.; G. Percy Fox, Treas. Sends out and supports missionaries in Russia and other Slavic countries. Publishes "The Friend of Russia" and also tracts in the Russian language.

Smithsonian Inst., Washington, D. C.—Est. 1846 by act of Congress, under bequest of James Smithson of England. Object: Increase and diffusion of knowledge among men. Accomplished by scientific research and publication. Government branches administered by Inst. U. S. Natl. Museum, Natl. Gallery of Art, Intern. Exchanges, Bureau of Amer. Ethnology, Natl. Zoological Pk., Astrophysical Observatory and Interntl. Catalogue of Scientific Literature.

Society Professional Lecturers and Lyceum Entertainers—1916. H. E. Shelland, Pres., Queens rd., Hollis Court, L. I.

Soc. for Promotion of Agricultural Science—1880. 150 mem. H. Osborn, Pres., Columbus, O.; C. P. Gillette, Sec., Fort Collins, Col.

Soc. for Promotion of Engineering Education—1893. 1,550 mem. M. E. Cooley, Pres.; F. L. Bishop, Sec., Pittsburgh, Pa.

Soc. of Chemical Industry—1881. 52 E. 41st, N. Y. C. 800 Amer. mem. C. E. Sholes, Amer. Ch.; Dr. Allen Rogers, Amer. Sec., Pratt Inst., Bkln., N. Y.

Soc. of Directors of Physical Education in Colleges—62 mem. Dr. Ed. Fauner, Pres.; Dr. D. B. Reed, Sec., Univ. of Chicago, Chicago, Ill.

Southern Education Assn., 1890: Conference for Education in the South, 1898, consolidated, 1915—J. P. McConnell, Pres.; A. P. Bourland, Sec., 1707 Kilbourne pl., Washington, D. C.

U. S. Catholic Historical Soc.—1885. 500 mem. S. Farrelly, Pres.; J. H. Fargis, Cor. Sec., 47 Cedar, Mhtn.

U. S. Geographic Board—1890. Washington, D. C. 16 mem. To this board are referred all questions concerning geographical names arising in the depts., and its decisions are final. C. H. Merriam, Ch.; C. S. Sloane, Sec.

Volta Bureau for the Increase and Diffusion of Knowledge Relating to the Deaf—1887. Volta Bldg., Washington, D. C. Founded and endowed by Alexander Graham Bell. Fred De Land, Supt., Volta Bureau Bldg., Washington, D. C.

University Forum of Amer., 316 W. 88th.—Conducts series of practical lectures by business, professional and political leaders in universities included in membership. Evenings in N. Y. City, every Tues. 100 universities in U. S. Canada and Europe. Alex. Cumming, Pres., office, 550 W. 113th, N. Y. C.; Henry Cleys, Treas.

Women's Educational and Industrial Union—1877. 264 Boylston, Boston, Mass. 4,383 mem. Miss Marion Churchill, Pres.; Miss Eliz. W. Schermerhorn, Sec.

State.

Assn. of Colleges in the State of N. Y.—1906. 39 mem. Frederick C. Ferry, Pres.; A. S. Downing, Sec. 1st Asst. Com. Dir. of Professional Education, Albany.

N. Y. Electric Railway Assn.—1883. T. C. Cherry, Pres.; Wm. F. Stanton, Sec.-Treas., 267 State, Rochester, N. Y.

N. Y. State Assn. of Academic Principals—H. H. Denham, Pres.; E. P. Smith, Sec., Education Dept., Albany, N. Y.

N. Y. State Assn., Elocutionists—1899. Prof. H. M. Tilroe, Pres.; Miss Frances Schermer, Sec., 328 N. Washington, Herkimer, N. Y.

N. Y. State Historical Assn.—1899. 1,000 mem. Geo. A. Blauvelt, Pres.; F. B. Richards, Sec.-Treas., Glens Falls.

N. Y. State Library Assn.—1920. 385 mem. Caroline Webster, Pres.; Lucia Henderson, Jamestown, N. Y., Sec., Prendergast Free Library.

N. Y. State Teachers Assn.—1843. 9,567 mem. J. S. Wright, Pres.; R. A. Searing, Sec., 617 Goodman, Rochester, N. Y.

Brooklyn.

American City Government League (Bureau of Government Research)—Leo Kenneth Mayer, Dir., 8 Adelphi pl.

Associated Schl. Bds. of Bklyn.—1911. 82 mem. James F. Hurley, Pres.; Miss M. M. Dammann, Sec., 412 Stone av.

Assn. of Retired Teachers of City of N. Y., Inc.—Hdqts., 2425 Ocean av. Margaret J. F. Lamson, Pres.; E. A. McAndrew, Rec. Sec.; E. Raymond, Cor. Sec.

Bird Lovers' Club of Bkln.—L. Walsh, Pres.; G. B. Wilmott, Sec., 1138 E. 37th.

Bkln. Aquarium Soc.—1911. 4th av. and Pacific. 185 mem. Dr. F. Schneider, Pres.

Bkln. Botanic Garden—See index.

Bkln. Class Teachers' Org.—1899. 4,276 mem. Isabel A. Ennis, Pres., 250 Washington av.

Bkln. Conchological Club—1904. 17 mem. I. Tuthill, Pres.; H. J. Aitkin, Sec., Central Museum, Bkln. Inst. of Arts and Sciences.

Bkln. Cottage Assn.—1899. 45 mem. To further the interests of Catholic Summer Schl. Assn. Frank McLoughlin, Pres.; Miss Margaret O'Reilly, Sec., 184 Hewes.

Bkln. Engrs. Club—1896. 117 Remsen. W. T. Chevalier, Pres.; J. Strachan, Sec.

Bkln. Heads of Dept. Assn.—190 mem. Miss A. M. Chambers, Pres.; Miss F. L. Reid, Sec., 6 Spencer pl.

Bkln. Inst. of Arts and Sciences—(See index.)

Bkln. Music Schl. Settlement—122-6 St. Felix. Object: To give musical instruction of high standard in all branches at a price within reach of all. Mrs. Chas. J. McDermott, Pres.; K. K. Mussey, Dir.

Bkln. Philosophical Assn.—1878. 40 mem. H. Cooper, Pres.; Wm. A. Winham, Sec., 146 Newton.

Bkln. Principals Council—80 mem. Frank J. Arnold, Pres.; Augustus Ludwig, Sec., P. S. 164.

Bkln. Spelling Reform Soc.—1918. J. Bowden, Pres., 24 Clifton pl.; Miss M. R. Osborne, Sec.

Bkln. Teachers' Assn. — 1874. 5,984 mem. G. M. Davison, Pres.; D. J. Cone, Sec., P. S. 145.

Bkln. Zoological Assn.—1915. M. Arens, Sec., 532 8th. Object: The study and promotion of zoology and kindred subjects, also acquisition and care of animals in Prospect Park.

Brownsville Labor Lyceum—1910. 219 Sackman. S. Hurok, Pres.; M. Shmayonik, Sec.

Contemporary Club—40 mem. Mrs. M. S. Johnson, Pres.; Mrs. T. H. Hardy, Sec., 618 Madison.

Flatbush Garden League—1917. Bkln. Botanic Bldg. Mrs. Eva L. Carson, Pres.; Miss E. Louise Hollis, Sec., 111 Decatur.

Forums—(See Mhtn. and Bronx.)

Friday Afternoon Club—1887. Meets alternate Fridays, Oct. to Apr. 50 mem. Mrs. A. L. Janes, Pres.; Mrs. J. V. Jewell, Cor. Sec., 1371 Dean st.

Friendly Tourists' Club—1895. 25 mem. Mrs. F. Alfred, Pres.; Mrs. J. C. Morton, Sec., 447 Macon.

Hampton Assn. of Bkln.—A. B. Trowbridge, Pres.; H. S. Adams, Sec., 129 Pierrepont, Box 18.

Kings Co. Historical Soc.—41 Amersfort pl. 200 mem. C. A. Ditmas, Pres.; F. M. Raynor, Rec. Sec., 285 Decatur.

Lincoln Soc.—(See Literary.)

L. I. Harvard Club—1903. Univ. Club. 60 mem. B. Meredith Langstaff, Pres.; Warren J. Kibby, Sec.

L. I. Historical Soc.—Pierrepont and Clinton. Willard Bartlett, Pres.; C. H. Burdett, Sec.

SOCIETIES AND ASSOCIATIONS—EDUCATIONAL—BROOKLYN—*Continued.*

Modern Science Club—1898. 125 S. Elliott pl. 350 mem. C. H. Haggerty, Pres.; J. P. Martin, Fin. Sec.; J. Kleiner, Sec.

Navy and Marine Workers Educational Council—Edwd. H. Markolf, Pres., 147 Waverly av.; R. T. Broaddhus, Sec.

People's Inst., United Neighborhood Guild, Inc.—Seymour Barnard, Dir., 176 Nassau.

Priscilla Study Club—Mrs. L. D. Burroughs, Pres., 1609 Dorchester rd.

Progress Club—1905. 407 mem. 180 Remsen. Employees of the Bkln. Union Gas Co. L. G. Tomaselli, Pres.; O. J. Aumuller, Sec., 176 Remsen.

Shakespeare Club of Bkln.—1903. 24 mem. Mrs. B. T. Cook, Pres.; Mrs. R. Tyers, Cor. Sec., 50 Midwood.

Women Principals Assn.—1901. Mrs. M. L. Ledwith, Pres.; Miss S. A. Griffin, Sec., P. S. 84.

Manhattan and Bronx.

Acad. of Political Science in the City of N. Y.—1880. Columbia Univ. 4,100 mem. Prof. S. M. Lindsay, Pres.; Prof. R. C. McCrea, Sec.

Am. Inst. Electrical Engineers—1884. 33 W. 39th. 10,655 mem. 36 "sections" and 63 "branches." A. W. Berresford, Pres.; F. L. Hutchinson, Sec.

Am. Microscopical Soc. of the City of N. Y.—1865. 130 mem. O. G. Mason, Sec., Bellevue Hosp., Mhtn.

Am. Museum of Natural History—1869. Central Park W., cor. 77th. 5,300 mem. H. F. Osborn, Pres.; H. P. Davison, Treas.; Adrian Iselin, Sec.; F. A. Lucas, Dir. (See Index, "Museums.")

Armstrong Assn.—Name changed to Hampton Assn.

Armenian Students' Assn. of Amer.—1910. 300 mem. D. H. Kabakjian, Pres., Lansdowne, Pa.; Ed. Bedrossian, Sec.

Assn. Assistants to Principals—200 mem. Lucille Nicol, Pres.; Jane E. Monahan, Sec.

Assn. of Doctors of Pedagogy of N. Y. Univ. —1896. 102 mem. L. M. Rochester, Pd.D., Pres.; J. J. Savitz, Pd.D., Sec., Trenton, N. J.

Assn. of Men Teachers in Elementary Schools of the City of N. Y.—1911. I. L. Ach, Pres.; R. L. Cottrell, Sec., 209 Greene av., Bkln.

Assn. of Model Teachers in Training Schools for Teachers—A. Grace Gibson, Pres., 260 W. 44th. F. Ursula Payne, V.-Pres., 335 Fenimore, Bkln., Elsie Abrahams, Sec.

Assn. of Primary Principals — (See Women Principals' Assn.)

Assn. of Women High School Teachers—1910. Miss Anna McAuliffe, Pres., 154 E. 91st; Miss C. C. Swenson, Sec., 87 Locust, Flushing, L. I.

Century Theater Club—Hotel Commodore. 1903. 500 mem. Mrs. A. O. Ihlseng, Pres.; Mrs. R. A. Weed, Sec., 815 W. 180th.

City History Club of N. Y.—1896. 105 W. 40th. R. 709. 40 classes. 1,000 children and adults enrolled. Mrs. A. B. Hepburn, Pres.; Mrs. C. Van Anda, Sec.; Mary F. Smart, Cor. Sec.

Civic Forum (The)—1907. 17 W. 44th. Henry Clews, Ch. Exec. Comm.; R. E. Ely, Dir.

Clio Club—1888. Hotel Astor. 130 mem. Mrs. Willis P. Miner, Pres.; Mrs. C. E. Hazeltine, Sec., 106 Morningside Drive.

College Women's Club—(See Special Relief, Relief Soc., Mhtn.)

Congress of States Societies—Hotel Gregorian, N. Y. City. Mrs. T. J. Vivian, Pres.; Mrs. C. D. Hirst, Cor. Sec.

Eastern Palmer Penmanship Teachers' Assn. —1910. 1,500 mem. W. L. Nolan, Pres.; C. J. Newcomb, Sec., 5th floor, 30 Irving pl.

Economic Club of N. Y. (The)—1907. 17 W. 44th. 1,200 mem. Geo. W. Wickersham, Pres.; R. E. Ely, Sec.

Educational Alliance (The)—1889. 197 E. B'way. 3,800 mem. Samuel Greenbaum, Pres.; B. M. L. Ernst, Sec., 31 Liberty; Dr. Henry Fleischman, Admin.

Educational Dramatic League—1913. 105 W. 40th. Mrs. A. Belmont, Pres.; Miss R. Crothers, Sec.

Emile Pedagogical Soc.—1887. Union Sq. Hotel. 150 mem. Dr. J. P. Conroy, Pres.; J. A. Higgins, Sec., 148 E. 63d.

Emma Willard Assn.—1891. To promote higher education among women. 300 mem. Mrs. F. W. Welchman, Pres., 64 Montague, Bkln.

Esperanto Soc.—Information may be obtained from A. S. Arnold, 1476 B'way, or C. C. Coigne, 3633 Creston av., Bronx.

Federation of Parents Assns. of the Public Schls. of the City of N. Y.—1915. W. 215th and B'way. G. S. Griffin, Pres.

First Aid to the Injured Soc.—1882. 105 E. 22d. John A. Wade, Pres.; L. F. Bishop, M.D., Sec.; E. C. S. Graham, Exec. Sec.

Hampton Assn. of N. Y.—1893. 19 W. 44th. 972 mem. Wm. Jay Schieffelin, Pres.; Alfa C. Pearsall, Sec.

High School Teachers' Assn. of N. Y. City—1905. 1,216 mem.• Harold Buttrick, Pres.; Miss M. C. McCarthy, Sec., Erasmus Hall H. S.

Horticultural Soc. of N. Y.—1900. Am. Mus. of Nat. His. and N. Y. Botanical Garden. 850 mem. T. A. Havemeyer, Pres.; G. V. Nash, Sec., N. Y. Botanical Garden, Bronx.

Humanitarian League—1914. 228 W. 75th. Misha Appelbaum, Founder and Pres.

Interborough Assn. of Women Teachers—1906. Mrs. G. C. S. Forsythe, Pres.; Miss Helen A. McKeon, Sec, 564½ Clinton, Bkln.

Intercollegiate Socialist Soc. (N. Y. Chapt.)—70 5th av. 500 mem. L. A. Grout, Sec.

Internl. Forum Assn., Inc.—Hdqts., 12 W. 11th, N. Y. C. An organization for the establishment of new forums. The assn. is also a bureau of information and clearing house for Forum speakers. Dr. P. S. Grant, Pres.; H. A. Lynch, Sec.

Bkln. Civic Forum (P. S. 84. Stone and Glenmore avs., Bkln.)—N. H. Seidman, 876 Eastern P'kway, Bkln.

Bushwick Civic Forum, Bushwick Community Centers, Inc. (DeKalb av. Library, Bkln.) —C. M. Sheeran, Dir.; L. K. Mayer, Sec., 8 Adelphi pl.

Columbia Univ. Inst. of Arts, Columbia Univ. (Horace Mann Aud.) Milton J. Davies, in charge of the Inst.

Community Work Director, Evening Schl. No. 45, Lafayette av., Bkln. M. Cogen, Dir., 1236 Union, Bkln.

Free Synagogue Forum (Free Synagogue, 36 W. 68th)—W. S. Hilborn, Ch., 31 Liberty.

Harlem Forum (Wadleigh H. S., 115th, nr. 7th av.)—Dr. H. Keller, Pres., 143 W. 86th.

The Little Forum—G. L. Cohen, 100 E 101st.

League for Political Education—1894. 17 W. 44th. 4,000 mem. R. E. Ely, Dir.; H. W. Taft, Pres.; Mary B. Cleveland, Exec. Sec.

Community (Community Ch. of N. Y., 34th and Park av.)—Rev. J. H. Holmes, Dir.; Bertha Ruffner, Sec., 29 E. 29th.

New Era Forum (New Era Club)—L. S. Posner, Dir.; J. Klansner, Sec., 274 E. B'way.

People's Forum (Cooper Union)—E. F. Sanderson, Dir., 70 5th av.; E. D. Martin, Asst. Dir.

Public Forum, Inc. (Ch. of the Ascension)—Rev. P. S. Grant, Pres.; Rev. H. A. Lynch, Sec., 12 W. 11th.

St. James Church Forum (St. James' Epis. Church)—Rev. DeW. L. Pelton, Dir.; Chas. F. Reynolds, Sec., 2317 Tiebout av.

St. Mary's Forum—Rev. J. A. McNulty, Dir., 528 Alexander av.

Sunday Morning Forum (Eron Preparatory Sch.)—J. E. Eron, Pres., 187 E. B'way.

Sunday Night Conference (Ch. of the Holy Trinity, Bkln.)—Rev. J. H. Melish, Dir.; R. B. B. Foote, 157 Montague, Bkln.

Sunday Evening Forum of the Labor Temple—Rev. J. C. Day, D.D., 14th and 2d av.

University Forum (University Settlement)—S. B. Kaufman, Dir., 184 Eldridge.

Washington Heights Forum—H. Lichtenberg, Pres.; J. Lyons, Sec., 75 Sherman av.

Women's Forum (Hotel Biltmore)—Miss H. Varick Boswell, Pres.; Mrs. H. A. LeVey, Sec., 609 W. 127th.

Y. M. H. A. Forum—Rabbi Lee J. Levinger, Dir.; J. Nadel, Sec., 148 E. 92d.

League for Political Education—1894. 17 W. 44th. 5,000 mem. H. W. Taft, Ch.; R. E. Ely, Dir.

Life as a Fine Art Club—1909. Hotel Commodore. 175 mem. Mildred M. Easton, Pres.; Helen W. Malone, Sec., 410 Riverside dr.

Linnaean Soc. of N. Y.—1878. Meets at American Mus. of Nat. History, 8:15 P.M. 2, 4 Tu. from Oct. to June. 111 mem. J. Dwight, Pres.; E. R. P. Janvrin, Sec., 515 Park av.

Male High Schl. Teachers' Assn. of N. Y. City —1905. 300 mem. H. B. Penhollow, Pres.; H. M. Hall, Rec. Sec., High Schl. of Commerce.

Modern Historic Records Assn.—1911. 20 Exch. pl. V. J. Dowling, Pres.; J. W. Smith, Sec.

SOCIETIES AND ASSOCIATIONS—EDUCATIONAL—MANHATTAN AND BRONX—*Continued.*

N. Y. Acad. of Sciences—1817. Meets at Amer. Mus. of Nat. His. 700 mem. Edw. L. Thorndike, Pres.; R. W. Tower, Sec. Biology Section meets 2d M.; Geology and Mineralogy Sect., 3d M.; Astronomy, Physics and Chemistry Sect., 1st M.; Sect. of Anthropology and Psychology, 4th M.

N. Y. Assn. for the Blind—111 E. 59th. Dr. John H. Finley, Pres.; Miss Winifred Holt, Sec.

N. Y. Assn. of High Schl. Teachers of German—1900. 350 mem. J. B. E. Jonas, Pres.; Miss M. G. Wendell, Sec., 281 Edgecombe av.

N. Y. Botanical Garden Assn.—1894. Bronx Park. 1,200 mem. E. D. Adams, Pres.; F. L. Stetson, V.-Pres.; N. L. Britton, Sec., Bronx Pk.

N. Y. Browning Soc.—Mrs. J. H. Clark, Pres.; Mrs. Thomas J. Vivian, Sec., 312 Manhattan av.

N. Y. C. Assn. of Men Principals—1917. Wm. Rabenort, Pres.; A. Smith, Cor. Sec., P. S. No. 70, Mhtn.

N. Y. City Assn. of Teachers of English—1903. 248 mem. J. C. Tressler, Pres., Newtown H. S.; M. V. Riblet, Sec., Bryant H. S.

N. Y. City Mothers Club—1899. Waldorf-Astoria. 150 mem. Mrs. Park Matthewson, Pres.; Miss M. Sheitlein, Sec., 48 W. 35th.

N. Y. Classical Club—600 mem. Prof. W. E. Waters, Pres., N. Y. Univ.

N. Y. Entomological Soc.—1892. Amer. Mus. of Natl. Hist. 80 active, 40 cor. mem. L. B. Woodruff, Pres.; C. W. Leng, Sec., Public Museum, S. I.

N. Y. Genealogical and Biographical Soc.—1869. 226 W. 58th. 700 mem. C. W. Bowen, Pres.; H. R. Drowne, Sec., 226 W. 58th.

N. Y. High Schl. Principals Assn.—1903. 45 mem. H. M. Snyder, Sec., Manual Training H. S., Bkln.

N. Y. Hist. Soc.—1804. 170 Central Park W. 839 mem. J. A. Weekes, Pres.; S. Fish, Sec.; R. H. Kelby, Libr.

N. Y. Microscopical Soc.—Inc. 1877. Meets Amer. Mus. of Natl. Hist. 1, 3 F. R. M. Allen, Pres.; G. E. Ashby, Sec., 11 Cliff.

N. Y. Mineralogical Club—1887. Meets at Amer. Mus. of Natl. Hist. 100 mem. G. F. Kunz, Pres.; H. P. Whitlock, Rec. Sec., Amer. Mus. of Natl. Hist., N. Y. C.

N. Y. Schoolmasters' Club—1890. 225 mem. David B. Corson, Pres.; M. D. Quinn, Sec., 101 E. 92d.

N. Y. Soc. of Archaeological Inst. of Amer.—1884. 275 mem. A. P. Ball, Sec., College of City of N. Y.

N. Y. Zoological Soc.—1958. 111 B'way. 2,200 mem. H. F. Osborn, Pres.; Madison Grant, V.-Pres. Has direct control and management of N. Y. Zoological Park and Aquarium.

Oriental Club—1898. 42 Mott. 140 mem. Guy Maine, Pres.; Dr. J. C. Thoms, Sec.

People's Inst.—1897. 70 5th av. E. F. Sanderson, Dir.; E. D. Martin, Asst. Dir.

People's Univ. Extension Soc.—1898. 111 5th av. R. Johnson, Pres.; J. E. Whitney, Sec., Suite 21, 1425 B'way.

Phalo—1880. Membership limited to 50. Mrs. James McCullough, Pres.; Mrs. Margaret E. McGowan, Sec., 104 W. 99th.

Platform Club—1909. A. S. Williams, Pres.; H. W. Merkel, Sec., 185th and Southern Blvd.

Portia Club—1901. 145 mem. Mrs. Ed. A. Albright, Pres.; Mrs. E. Openhym, Cor. Sec., 54 St. Andrews pl., Yonkers, N. Y.

Post Parliament, Inc. (The)—1894. Hotel McAlpin. 125 mem. Mrs. Cora Welles Trow, Pres.; Mrs. Regina Demarest, Sec., 60 W. 76th.

Principals Assn. of the City of N. Y.—1901. 4th Sa. 200 mem. W. Rabenort, Pres.; C. W. Hawkins, Sec., 2667 Heath av., Bronx.

Principals Club—1898. 100 mem. F. H. J. Paul, Pres.; Olive M. Jones, Sec., 38 W. 95th.

Public Education Assn.—1895. 8 W. 40th. C. P. Howland, Pres.; H. W. Nudd, Dir.

Russell Sage Foundation—130 E. 22d. Inc. 1907. For the improvement of social and living conditions in the U. S. R. W. de Forest, Pres.; J. M. Glenn, Sec. and Gen. Dir.

Schoolmasters' Assn.—1887. 250 mem. W. R. Hayward, Pres.; L. W. Johnson, Sec., Adelphi Academy.

Simplified Spelling Board—1 Madison ave. 1906. 47 mem. Advisory Council. 229 mem. C. H. Grandgent, Pres.; H. G. Paine, Sec.

Soc. for Electrical Development, Inc.—522 5th av. 1,300 mem. W. W. Freeman, Pres.

Soc. for Political Study—1886. Hotel Astor. 157 mem. 2, 4 Tu. Mrs. A. N. Palmer, Pres., 53 Winfield av., Mt. Vernon, N. Y.

Soc. of the Music Schl. Settlement—1903. 53 and 55 E. 3d. 1,000 students. Mrs. F. B. Rowell, Pres.; M. Chaffee, Mus. Dir.

Societe des Beaux Arts—1908. Waldorf-Astoria. 100 mem. Mme. Marie Cross Newhans, Pres., 2026 B'way.

Teachers Assn. (The N. Y. City)—1868. Hotel Manhattan. Hugh C. Laughlin, Pres.; J. H. Sherwin, Sec., 78 27th, Elmhurst, N. Y.

Teachers Union of City of N. Y.—1916. 70 5th av. 1,000 mem. H. R. Linville, Pres.; M. Rosenhaus, Rec. Sec., 70 5th av.

Torrey Botanical Club—1871. 250 mem. H. M. Richards, Pres.; F. W. Pennell, Sec., N. Y. Botanical Garden, N. Y. C.

Training Schl. for Public Service—Bureau of Mncpl. Research, 261 B'way. Dr. C. A. Beard.

United Parents' Assn. of Gr. N. Y.—1920. G. E. Pickard, Pres., 230 Decatur, Bkln.; B. Moses, Sec., 1295 Fulton, Bronx.

Webb Inst. of Naval Architecture—1894. Sedgwick av., cor. E. 188th. Education of young men in naval architecture and marine engineering, and home for aged and indigent shipbuilders. 25 guests. S. Taylor, Pres.; G. P. Taylor, Sec.; G. F. Crouch, Rec. Mgr.

Women's Civic Committee of Justice, Inc.—500 mem. 2025 B'way, M. C. Newhaus, Ch.

Woman's Legal Education Soc. (The)—N. Y. Univ. 1890. 20 mem. Miss I. M. Pettus, V.-Pres. and Sec., 106 Central Pk. W.

Women's Press Club—Waldorf Hotel, 5th av. and 34th. Mrs. M. H. Day, Pres.; Mrs. E. L. Carson, Sec.

Women Principals Assn.—1903. Jessie B. Colburn, Pres.; L. M. Rochester, Sec. P. S. 3.

Workingmen's Educational Assn.—1896. 243-47 E. 84th. August Vogt, Pres.; C. Wehrle, Sec.

Queens.

Agricultural Education Assn.—1914. W. G. Elliot, Pres., L. I. City; T. G. Ellsworth, Sec., 243 E. 35th, Mhtn.

Douglaston Mothers' Club—1907. Douglaston, L. I. 100 mem. Mrs. Park Matthewson, Pres., Douglaston; Mrs. E. L. Wertheim, Sec.

Flushing Historical Soc.—1904. 71 B'way. R. E. Parsons, Pres.; H. K. Lines, Sec., 122 Main, Flushing.

Mothers' Club of Forest Hills—Mrs. G. A. Douglas, Pres., Forest Hills, L. I.

Queensboro League of Mothers' Clubs—1918. Mrs. Park Matthewson, Pres., Douglaston, L. I.; Mrs. H. H. Wright, Sec., 86 W. 17th, Flushing.

Teachers' Assn. of the Boro. of Queens—1898. 423 mem. Dr. N. Hewins, Newtown H. S., N. Y. C.

Richmond.

S. I. Inst. of Arts and Sciences—1881. Stuyvesant pl., Wall, St. George. 350 mem. H. R. Bayne, Pres.; C. W. Leng, Sec., St. George.

FRENCH SOCIETIES.

National and International.

Institut Internatl. de Sociologie—1893. For the study of sociological questions. Theophilo Braga, Lisbon, Portugal, Pres.; Rene Worms, Sec., 115 Boulevard St. Germain, Paris.

Natl. Soc. Veterans of the Armies of Land and Sea—(See War Veterans, Natl.)

Brooklyn.

Cercle des Paysans—2863 Atlantic av. 1888. 52 mem. Max Matthias, Pres.; Jules Ballereau, Sec., 112 Berriman.

Franco-Amer. Democratic Club of Kings Co.—2863 Atlantic av. 96 mem. Jos. Colmant, Pres.; Emile Jardinier, Sec., 7 Bedford av, Glendale, L. I.

La Gauloise, Secours Mutuels—2863 Atlantic av. 1885. 56 mem. Emil Marchal, Pres.; Jules Ballereau, Sec., 112 Berriman.

La Fayette, Securs Mutuels—1870. 33 mem. E. Marchal, Pres.; A. Mayer, Sec., 309 Eldert.

La Liberte Lorraine—Palmetto and Seneca avs. 1889. 100 mem. A. Greiner, Pres.; T. A. Thumser, Sec., 1932 Linden.

La Prevoyance, Secours Mutuels—2863 Atlantic av. 1879. 110 mem. Max Matthias, Pres.; Jules Ballereau, Sec., 112 Berriman.

SOCIETIES AND ASSOCIATIONS—FRENCH SOCIETIES—BROOKLYN—*Continued.*

Union des Societes Francaise—2863 Atlantic av. 1884. Jules Frossard, Pres.; J. Ballereau, Sec., 112 Berriman.

Manhattan and Bronx.

BENEFIT.

French Benevolent Soc. of N. Y.—See Special Relief, Mhtn.

L'Amitie—1873. 317 W. 30th. 74 mem. L. Illig, Pres.; Jos. Barthe, Sec., 271 W. 113th.

L'Union Alsacienne—1871. 160 mem. R. Weigel, Pres.; P. Anthon, Sec., 1786 Amsterdam av.

Societe Francaise de Bienfaisance—1809. 450 W. 34th. 450 mem. Lucien Jouvaud, Pres.; Vincent Fulchiron, Sec.

Societe Israelite Francaise—1873. 155 E. 58th. 210 mem. C. Bickard, Pres.; H. I. Rosen, Sec., 575 W. 172d.

Societe Saint Jean Baptiste de Bienfaisance de New York—166 E. 60th. 1850. J. Sausville, Pres.; A. Belanger, Rec. Sec., 212 S. 9th.

Culinary.

Societe Culinaire Philanthropique—1865. 114 W. 48th. 400 mem. O. Gentsch, Pres.; E. Montjean, Sec.

MASONIC.

See Masonic Soc. Index.

MISCELLANEOUS.

Alliance Francaise de N. Y.—200 5th av. 1898. 1,000 mem. F. D. Pavey, Pres.; M. Bergeron, Sec.

Association Generale Des Alsacienes—Lorraine D'Amerique—1917. 2,450 mem. 569 5th av. A. Blum, Pres.; F. Wildenstein, Sec., 647 5th av.

Federation de l'Alliance Francaise aux Etats-Unis et au Canada—1902. 2,500 mem. 200 5th av. J. LeRoy White, Pres.; F. Weill, Sec.

Le Lyceum Societe des Femmes de France in N. Y.—Mme. Carlo Polifeme, O. A., Founder and Pres., 321 W. 92d; M. C. Mertz, Sec.

L'Union Chretienne de Jeunes Gens (French Branch Y. M. C. A.)—109 W. 54th. 1889. 600 mem. E. Twyeffort, Pres.; L. Bichsel, Sec.

Societe Nationale des Professeurs Francais en Amerique—100 St. Nicholas av. 1904. 375 mem. Auguste George, Pres.; Eugene Maloubier, Sec.

GERMAN SOCIETIES.

Brooklyn.

BENEFIT.

*Adler Maennorchor—1872 Fulton. W. Biesel, Pres.; E. Kraus, Sec., 48 Rochester av.; W. Humbach, Cond.

Amt. Dorum Wurster Damen Verein—1117 B'way. Mrs. Katie Thoden, Pres.; Mrs. A. Tyarks, Sec., 20 Cooper.

Amt. Stolzenauer Verein — 253 Atlantic av. E. Strauss, Pres.; H. W. E. Suphan, Sec., 192 E. 32d.

*Ankumer Verein—253 Atlantic av. Wm. Ennebrook, Pres.; H. Weidmann, Sec., 174A 8th.

Arnulf Verein—21 Olive. Fritz Kiesling, Pres.; J. Kunzelmann, Jr., Sec., 292 Powers.

*Badischer K. U. V. No. 1—69 Hamburg av. 135 mem. F. Huber, Pres.; Chas. Diehm, Sec., 299 Jefferson.

*Bremervoerder Verein—401 Bridge. C. H. Hoops, Pres.; H. L. Kuhl, Sec., 212 23d.

*Bkln. E. D. Rifle Corps—2 Ralph av. H. J. Bauer, Capt.; E. J. Tyarks, Sec., 20 Cooper

*Bkln. Hadler Club—Smith and Schermerhorn. A. Flickenschild, Pres.; C. Wibben, Sec., 213 Heyward.

Bkln. Kranken Unterstuetzungs Kasse—Queens County Labor Lyceum, Myrtle and Cypress avs. 60 mem. J. Pieroth, Pres.; H. Frank, Sec., 1389 Madison.

*Bkln. Plattdeutscher Club—Prospect av., cor. 6th av. Hy. Tretisch, Pres.; H. F. Folser, Sec., 121 5th av

*Columbia Bund—J. Buerger, Pres.; Chas. Weich, Sec., 462 Atlantic av. (See page 258, 1917 Eagle Almanac, for sections.)

*Eintracht Sick Benefit Soc. of East N. Y.—1877. 2863 Atlantic av. E. Kuntz, Pres.; George Schwartz, Sec., 701 Glenmore av.

Franklin Bowling Club—1128 Myrtle av. John Boemermann, Pres.; F. H. Lange, Sec. 1819 Stephen.

Frauen Verein Wyckoff Hts. Hospital—1876. Mrs. B. Olbricht, Pres.; Mrs. R. O. Hildebrandt, Sec., Wyckoff Hts. Hospital.

Gruener Zweig K. U. Verein—180 Irving av. 128 mem. A. Hurnisch, Pres.; Chas. Gangloff, Sec., 233 Stockholm.

Hannover Tent T. M.—811 Forest av. Gus Hinrichs, Comm.; H. W. Horeis, Sec., 66 Hart.

*Herzog Karl Theodor Kr. Unt. V., Sect. No. 1—336 Knickerbocker av. A. Krommer, Pres.; G. Otto, Sec., 148 Meserole.

Hessischer K. U. V. Zur Wilhelmhoehe No. 1—221 Wyckoff av. Wm. Hoerschelmann, Pres.; M. Grubert, Sec., 70 S. 8th.

Hildebrandt's Drivers Benefit Soc.—504 Carroll. D. Busch, Pres.; J. Fennell, Sec., 504 Carroll.

Kranken Unt. Verein die Norddeutschen Brueder—251 Atlantic av. F. Thordsen, Pres.; H. Weidmann, Sec., 174A 8th.

Liberty Ben. Soc. No. 1 of Ridgewood—1919 94 mem. 475 Onderdonk av. J. Thomas, Pres.; C. Diehm, Sec., 299 Jefferson.

Marien-Alten-Heim-Gesellschaft—18th av. and 64th. Miss Minna Behr, Pres.; Mrs. J. Oberbeck, Sec.; Mrs. E. Zerboni, Matron.

North Side Tent No. 179, K. O. T. M.—Humboldt and Ten Eyck. H. Gerken, Commander; S. Wise, Sec., 193 Bedford av.

Order of German-Americans—1898. Hdqtrs., 280 So. 5th; Fred'k M. Maurin, Pres.; Frederick Hartmann, Sec., 1297 Greene av.

Otto K. V. Verein—416 Onderdonk av. C. Lang, Pres.; A. Ganzenmuller, Sec., 30 Irving av.

*Plattdeutscher Volksfest Verein of Bkln.—1884. 300 delegates. Smith and Schermerhorn. Wm. Rurck, Pres.; G. A. Kaempffer, Sec., East Elmhurst, L. I.

Rhader Unt.-Verein—253 Atlantic av. D. H. Popper, Pres.; J. H. Grabau, Sec., 1124 Halsey.

*Rheinpfaelzer Volksfest Verein—221 Wyckoff av. C. Kaub, Pres.; A. Gantz, Sec., 1513 Greene av.

*Sachsen Thuringer Sick Benev. Soc. No. 1 of Bkln., Inc.—196 Wilson av. B. Hegner, Pres.; W. Kues, Sec., 242 Linden.

Schleswig-Holsteiner Verein—257 Wilson av. John Lütze, Pres.; G. A. Ohlert, Sec., 293 Irving av.

*Stoteler Club—1025 Lafayette av. A. Krogman, Pres.; C. D. Christoffers, Sec., 818 St. Johns pl.

Vegesacker Club—Smith and Schermerhorn. H. Christoffers, Pres.; F. Grabhorn, Sec., 38 Cranberry.

*Weierbarger Verein—1117 B'way. G. Horn, Pres.; Ernest Thalmann, Sec., 300 6th.

Wyckoff Hts. Hospital Soc. of Bkln. Society—St. Nicholas av. and Stanhope. F. A. Schurmann, Pres.; H. C. A. Wagner, Hon. Sec.; H. Schuessler, Sec., 142-160 St. Nicholas av.

INDEPENDENT PLATTDEUTSCHE AND BENEFIT.

Allemania Lodge, 740, F. and A. M.—Masonic Temple. A. F. Bode, Wor. Master; C. Brau, Sec., 60 Stratford rd.

Deutscher Evangelischer Hilfs Verein—German Evangelical Aid Soc. Home for the Aged. Chauncey, nr. B'way. 1878. Mrs. C. A. Kaupp, Pres.; Miss E. L. Werner, Supt.; Mrs. A. Heins, Sec.

North Side Review, 201 W. B. A. O. F. M.—1117 B'way. Mrs. C. Sclichting, Lady Com.; Mrs. Anna Luhrs, R. K., 593 Evergreen av.

Schwaebischer Kranken Unterstuetzungs Verein, No. 1—936 Seneca av. 1892. 45 mem. T. Albrecht, Pres.; B. Feile, Sec., 333 46th.

Schweizer Bund—353 Covert av. R. Mathis, Pres.; F. Weber, Sec., 148 Montana av., Woodhaven.

Schweizer Club, East N. Y.—118 Jamaica av. G. Hofer, Pres.; A. Cramer, Sec., 40 Bradford.

MUSICAL.

*United Singers of Brooklyn—Bkln. Branch of the Northeastern Saengerbund of America. 1881. Palm Garden, Wilson and Greene avs. A. Greiner, Pres.; A. Bernhardt, Sec., 1742 Myrtle av.; Carl Fique, Cond.

*Adler Maennerchor—1872. 1919 Fulton. W. M. Biesel, Pres.; Wm. Tieman, Sec.; Wm. Humbach, Cond.

*Arion Singing Soc.—See Musical Socs.

SOCIETIES AND ASSOCIATIONS—German—Brooklyn—*Continued.*

Attenhofer Liedertafel—389 Onderdonk av. C. Hausman, Pres.; Geo. Keilbach, Sec., 409 Onderdonk av.; William C. Hollreigel, Cond.

*Bkln. Saengerbund—1862. Smith and Schermerhorn. 420 mem. E. J. Fandrey, Pres.; Max Koeppe, Sec., 653 5th av.; O. Wick, Dir.

*Bkln. Saengerbund Ladies' Chorus—Mrs. C. Goosen, Pres.; Miss F. Storrk, Sec., 217 Montauk av. Mrs. Otto Wick, Dir.

Bkln. Saengerbund Ladies' Soc.—Mrs. C. Segelken, Pres.; Mrs. Leon Doscher, Sec., 501 Atlantic av.

*Gambrinus Maennerchor—1892. 1245 Greene av. 35 mem. J. Piroth, Pres., 2962 Myrtle av.; C. Schekenbach, Sec.; O. Lender, Cond.

Hessischer Saengerbund—Inc. 1876. 817 Onderdonk av. H. Loeffler, Pres.; W. Kues, Sec., 242 Linden; Felix Jaeger, Cond.

*Junger Maennerchor—1913. 221 Wyckoff av. Wm. Mueller, Pres.; Hy. D. D. Kurraner, Sec., 236 Wilson av.; H. Pruemm, Cond.

INDEPENDENT MUSICAL.

*Brooklyn Boys' and Girls' Chorus—1905. Wilson and Greene avs. J. M. Bauer, Pres.; B. K. Maskos, Sec., 855 95th, Woodhaven, L. I.; Ernest Scharpf and B. K. Maskos, Conds.

Katholischer Maennerchor—1911. St. Leonard's Hall, Wilson av. and Jefferson. George Schramm, Pres.; J. J. Giel, Sec., 293 Stagg; Franz Gross, Cond.

Schweizer Damenchor, No. 1—1902. Putnam and Woodward avs. 30 mem. Mrs. A. Freehlich, Pres.; B. Makos, Cond., 855 95th, Woodhaven, L. I.

GYMNASTIC.

*Bkln. E. D. Turn Verein—Bushwick and Gates avs. D. Koos, First Speaker; A. O. Hoercher, Sec.; Wm. Hesse, Instr.

Bkln. Turn Verein—504 Carroll. H. Mattes, Pres.; O. Mattes, Sec., 417 76th.

Columbia Turn Verein—Care of A. Hoch, 13 Newell. Peter Blasius, Ch., 121 Norman av.; A. Hoch, Sec., 13 Newell; Wm. Greve, Instr.

Turnverein Vorwaerts—959 Willoughby av. A. Thielmann, First Speaker; H. R. Ehrhardt, Sec., 71 Truxton; A. Bischoff, Instr.

WAR VETERANS AND SHOOTING.

*Veteranen der Deutschen Armee of Gr. N. Y. —55 Ralph av., cor. Monroe. 37 mem. W. Fritz, Pres.; B. Schirmer, Sec., 158 Sumpter.

*East N. Y. Schuetzenbund—636 Glenmore av. L Grefig, Pres.; P. Fiebig, Sec., 123 Montauk av.

SOCIAL.

Bakers' Progress Club of Bkln.—100 mem. Bkln. Labor Lyceum. Otto Alte, Pres.; M. Kissling, Sec., 300 Palmetto.

Bkln. Labor Lyceum Assn.—See Bus. and Com. Soc.

*Bkln. Scat Club, Inc.—1045 Bushwick av. P. Ollinger, Pres., 1861 Linden; Wm. Breitenback, Sec.

*Dramatischer Club Ulk—Prospect Hall. E. Bergmann, Pres.; L. Wichers, Sec., 638 4th av.; M. Koeppe, Stage Dir., 653 5th av.

*Williamsburg Boss Baecker Verein—Palm Garden. Louis Weber, Pres.; H. Drexsler, Sec., 68 Ashland, Woodhaven.

---

*Formerly affiliated with German Amer. Natl. Alliance, the central organization of Bkln. German societies.

Manhattan and Bronx.

BENEFIT.

Altenbrucher Verein—34-36 9th av. Carl F. Rittel, Pres.; H. Schulze, Sec., 3823 3d av.

Amt. Blumenthaler Club—101 Av. A. L. Kautz, Pres.; Wm. C. Jaeger, Sec., 1238 Madison, Bkln.

Amt. Osterholzer Verein—67 St. Marks pl. G. Havemeyer, Pres.; Rudolph Faust, Sec., 1247 E. 34th, Bkln.

Amt. Ottendorfer Soc.—158 3d av. C. H. Beckmann, Pres.; E. Polack, Sec., 1946 Clinton av.

Arbeiter Kranken und Sterbe-Kasse f. d. Ver Staaten von America (Workmen's Sick and Death Benefit Fund)—Paul Flaeschel, Pres.; P. Sturm, Sec., 1-3 3d av.

Badischer Volkfest Verein—85th and Lexington av. Jos. Peter, Pres.; Fr. G. Holch, Sec., 900 Cauldwell av.

Bavarian Natl. Assn. of No. Amer.—748 B'way, Buffalo, N. Y. P. A. Hoernig, Grand Pres., Bridgeport, O.; C. H. North, Sec., 748 B'way, Buffalo, N. Y.

(See page 261, 1917 Eagle Almanac, for United Sections of Greater New York.)

Bayerischer Volksfest Verein—207 E. 54th. C. Rebhahn, Pres.; G. Pollinger, Sec., 502 W. 139th.

Benevolent Soc. of the U. S. for Propagation of Cremation—Inc. 1911. Every 2d Fri., 7 P.M. Bkln. Labor Lyceum. Geo. Vermaeten, Fin. Sec., 1828 Barnes av., Bronx.

Bremerhavener Club—16 N. William. Chas. Winkelman, Pres.; G. Goerger, Sec., Box 26, R. F. D. No. 2, Huntington, L. I.

Brinkumer Guard—521 6th av. Chris. Wahmann, Capt., 521 6th av.; H. Hainhorst, Sec.

Cannstatter Volksfest Verein—N. Y. Männerchor Halle. Louis Neuffer, Pres.; E. O. Braendle, Sec., 165 E. 89th, Mhtn.

Central Kellner Verein Sterbekasse—1032 1st av. Wm. F. Beseler, Pres.; F. Seligmann, Sec., 1002 Bushwick av., Bkln.

Cuxhavener Club—58 6th av. C. A. Frankenberg, Pres., 58 6th av., N. Y. C.; O. Hagedorn, Sec.

Frauen K. U. V. Schwestern Circle—1877. 507 E. 5th. Mrs. W. Ullrich, Pres.; Mrs. M. Schmidt, Sec., 113 Av. A.

Fuldaer K. U. V. No. 1—492 2d av. E. R. Fortran, Pres.; C. Guckes, Sec., 293 West, W. Hoboken, N. J.

Geestendorfer Club—427 1st av. J. H. Voege, Pres.; F. A. Krupp, Sec., 323 E. 119th.

Lenox Hill Hospital Ladies' Aid Soc.—Krackerwizer's Hall, Lenox Hill Hospital. Mrs. F. Pfeiffer, Pres.; Mrs. Wm. T. Traud, Fin. Sec., Cedar Knolls, Bronxville, N. Y.

United Odd Fellows Home and Orphanage Assn.—Havemeyer and Tremont avs., Unionport, N. Y. C. M. Berliner, Pres.; H. Raeuber, Sec., 211 E. 17th; A. Menge, Supt.

Kellner Kranken U. V. Humanitaet—243 E. 84th. C. Schoenberg, Pres.; B. Korn, Sec., 139 E. 16th.

Knickerbocker Soc.—130 3d av. W. Bogel, Pres.; Carl Grote, Sec., 785 Elton av.

Lamstedter Soc.—H. Fahrenkrug, Pres.; M. Schroeder, Sec., 966 Madison, Bkln.

Langwedeler Verein—130 3d av. Henry Hagermanns, Pres.; C. J. D. Walter, Sec., 180 Frost, Bkln.

Luitpold Ver.—2d av. and 92d. J. Buettner, Pres.; S. G. Kestler, Sec., 216 E. 84th.

Morrisania Plattdeutsche Club—414 E. 158th. Harry Delventhal, Pres.; H. W. Walmann, Sec., 419 E. 144th.

N. Y. Baecker Club—101 Av. A. 285 mem. P. Held, Pres.; C. Hofmann, Sec., 1A Parkside ct., Bkln.

United Odd Fellows Home and Orphanage Assn.—Havemeyer and Tremont avs., Unionport. M. Berliner, Pres.; H. Raeuber, Sec., 211 E. 17th; A Menge, Supt.

Wanna Verein, 158-160 3d av. H. Oest, Pres.; Emil Polack, Sec., 1946 Clinton av.

INDEPENDENT PLATTDEUTSCHE AND BENEFIT.

Home of Daughters of Jacob—1897. 167th, Findlay and Teller avs., Bronx. Mrs. A. J. Dworsky, Pres.; A. Kruger, Supt.; Dr. W. G. Wulfahrt, Sec. 600 inmates.

Knickerbocker Frauen und Jungfrauen Verein No. 1—228 E. 86th. Anna Heins, Pres.; E. Polack, Sec., 1946 Clinton av.

Land Wurster Plattdeutsche Frauen Verein No. 1—228 E. 86th. Mrs. G. Ecken, Pres., 474 E. 144th.

Sachsen-Thueringer K. U. V. No. 1—101 Av. A. M. Hoppe, Pres.; J. B. Becker, Sec., 63 E. 4th.

MUSICAL.

United Singers of New York—1855. Maennerchor Hall. T. W. Henninger, Pres., 205 E. 56th; Jacob Mebus, Sec.; Paul Engelskirchen, Cond. (Following are leading societies affiliated with.)

Allemania Cordialia—228 E. 86th. E. Scharpf, Cond.; J. F. Mueller, Pres.; Geo. Blatz, Sec., 120 Elmwood, Woodhaven, L. I.

N. Y. Maennerchor Eichenkranz — 203-7 E. 56th. A. Braeuer, Pres.; Eugene Harnack, Sec., 335 E. 19th; G. T. Heil, Cond.

Rheinischer Saengerbund—228 E. 86th. J. Mebus, Pres.; P. Hoppe, Sec., 401 E. 77th; I. Jaeger, Cond.

Saengerbund Eurenia—228 E. 86th. 60 mem. T. Keomger, Pres.; John Heusel, Sec., 505 E. 15th; L. Birseck, Cond.

WORKINGMEN'S AND INDEPENDENT MUSICAL.

Arbeiter Maennerchor, N. Y.—243-247 E. 84th. H. Bode, Sec., 504 E. 88th; Alwin Seligmueller, Cond.

Arbeiter Saengerchor—243 E. 84th. August Vogt, Sec., 226 E. 85th.

SOCIETIES AND ASSOCIATIONS—GERMAN—MANHATTAN AND BRONX—*Continued.*

Liederkranz of the City of N. Y.—1847. 111-119 E. 58th. W. O. Kiene, Pres.; C. H. Valentine, Sec.

Staedte Vereinigung New York des Arbeiter Saengerbundes—247 E. 84th. A. Vogt, Sec., 226 E. 85th.

GYMNASTIC.

N. Y. Circuit of North Amer. Gymnastic Union: Vorwaerts T. V.; Bkln., 949 Willoughby av.; Bkln. T. V., 351-353 Atlantic av.; E. D. T. V., Bushwick and Gates avs.; Mt. Vernon T. V., N. 10th and Stevens avs.; Mt. Vernon, N. Y. T. V., 85th and Lexington av.; Central T. V., 213 82d; Bloomingdale T. V., 305 W. 54th; Deutsch-Amer. T. V., 412 E. 158th; T. V. Vorwaerts, N. Y., 525 E. 72d; Columbia T. V., 13 Newell, Bkln.; Woodstock T. V., Forest av. and 158th, Mhtn.; L. I. City T. V., 339 9th av., L. I. C.

Deutsch-Amerikanischer Turn Verein—414 E. 158th. Wm. T. Rehm, 1st Speaker; J. Meissner, Sec., 497 E. 167th.

N. Y. Turn Verein—Lex. av. and 85th.

WAR VETERANS AND SHOOTING.

Deutscher Kriegerbund, N. Y.—1884. 85th and Lexington av., Turnhalle. 500 mem. Christ. Rebhan, Pres.; P. Baumann, Sec., 471 St. Anns av., Bronx. 25 cos. 1, 3 M.

(See pages 264-265, 1917 Eagle Almanac, for companies.)

Mhtn. Schuetzenbund—1865. 222 E. 42d. C. Harth, Pres.; P. H. Kiel, Sec., 665 Oakland pl., Bronx.

New Yorker Schuetzenbund No. 1—620 9th av. Geo. Beck, Pres.; Hugo Weissleder, Sec., 422 W. 37th.

Veteranen, 20 (Turner), N. Y. Volunteers—Lexington av. and 85th. Wm. Hoffensack, Pres., 1007 6th av.; G. Yunginger, Sec., 512 E. 88th.

SOCIAL.

Aschenbroedel Verein—144-146 E. 86th. 1860. 600 mem. Rob. Iver, Pres.; R. Richter, Sec.

Deutscher Fortbildungs-Verein—568 9th av. H. Geiss, Pres.; C. Hummitsch, Sec., 523 W. 47th.

German Press Club—21 Spruce. A. Schoenstadt, Pres.; O. Neuburger, Sec.

Mainzer Carneval Verein—190 3d av. J. Brauneck, Pres.; Fred Mack, Sec., 131 E. 93d.

Stamp Collectors Soc. of N. Y.—Scheffel Hall, 192 3d av. Ed. Ahlborn, Pres.; Chris. Burk, Sec., 1128 Forest av., Bronx.

Social Ladies' Club—N. Y. Turnhalle, 85th and Lexington av. Mrs. L. Speilel, Pres.; Mrs. Ida Fritzing, Sec., 223 1st av., L. I. City.

United Choral Conductors of Amer.—1253 Lexington av. C. Fique, Pres.; L. Vossley, Sec., 1696 Clay av., Bronx.

Vereingte Deutsche Verbande von Gross New York—114 E. 59th. H. F. Haas, N. Y.—Henry Weismann, Bkln.; Hermann Koch, Queens; R. Cronan, Bronx; A. Hoffmeyer, Richmond, Presidents; Henry Pfeiffer, Sec., 349 E. 154th.

Vereinigte Deutsche Gesellschaften der Stadt New York (Central organization of 125 German societies)—1902. 205 E. 56th. H. F. Haas, Pres.; Hy. Pfeiffer, Sec., 635 St. Anns av.

Queens.

*United German Societies of Queens County—Astoria Schuetzenpark. (Societies marked with † are affiliated with.)

BENEFIT.

Arbeiter Kranken-und Sterbe Kasse Astoria—560 mem. 4 Su. F. Marx, Pres.; O. A. Weber, Sec., 727 2d av., L. I. City.

Bayerischer Natl. Verband von North Amerika, Astoria Sec. No. 1, L. I. City—334 10th av. Ad. Bayer, Pres.; C. Zeigler, Sec., 286 Theodore, Steinway, L. I. City.

†Plattdeutscher Verein von L. I. C. und Umgegend—Hettinger's B'way Hall. D. Ehntholdt, Pres.; A. Kroeger, Sec., 370 12th av., L. I. C.

MUSICAL.

†United Singers of Queens County—Astoria Casino, cor. B'way and Steinway av., Astoria. (Central organization of all societies belonging to the Northeastern Federation of German Singers.) O. E. Herrmann, 528 Jamaica av., L. I. C.

†College Point Maennerchor—13th and 3d av. 150 mem. Ed. Kellermann, Pres.; Robert Bauer, Sec.; Chas. Isler, Cond.

†Richmond Hill Quartet—Wimmer's Hall, Lefferts av., Richmond Hill. Fred Ebel, Pres.; Hans Vogt, Sec., 10156 124th, Richmond Hill; Jos. Mengler, Cond.

Richmond.

BENEFIT.

Plattdeutscher Verein von Richmond Co.—Ellmann's Hotel, Stapleton. H. Schwanenberg, Pres.; O. Kruse, Sec., 171 Wright, Stapleton.

DEUTSCHER ORDER DER HARUGARI.

National Officers: O. G. B., W. Holz, Allentown, Pa.; D. G. B., H. A. Seidel, Fitchburg, Mass.; C. G. Kautz, Gr. Sec., Chicago, Ill.; C. Bauer, Gr. Treas., Detroit, Mich.

State Grand Officers: Chas. Kiehle, G. B., Buffalo; A. Koester, Dep. G. B., Rochester; G. Frank, Gr Sec., Buffalo.

(See page 265, 1917 Eagle Almanac, for lodges.)

GREEK LETTER SOCIETIES.

Brooklyn.

Alpha Chi Rho Fraternity, Phi Chi Chap.—73 Court. 1896. 175 mem. E. F. O'Reilly, Chap. Cor.

Alpha Kappa Kappa, Zeta Chapter—128 Amity. 1888. K. MacInnes, Pres.; Wm. H. Genthner, Sec., 96 6th av.

Iota Theta, Bkln. Law Schl., St. Lawrence Univ.—1914. 90 mem. A. Multer, Praetor; L. B. Ginsberg, Scriptor, Room 212, Eagle Bldg.

Phi Delta Phi, Evarts Chap., Bkln. Law Schl., St. Lawrence Univ.—J. D. Barlow, Consul; J. G. von Hofe, Jr., Scriptor, Room 303, Eagle Bldg.

Sigma Omicron—1909. A. C. Watson, Pres.; H. C. Seward, Sec., 623 Av. L.

Theta Phi Law Frat.—Bkln. Law Schl. of St. Lawrence Univ., Eagle Bldg. 1901. 300 mem. F. Lammers, Consul; C. Hoffmann, Scriptor.

Manhattan.

Alpha Delta Phi Club—1890. 136 W. 44th. 1,100 mem. A. C. James, Pres.; G. M. Schurman, Sec.

Alpha Delta Phi Frat.—1832. 136 W. 44th. 13,301 mem. E. M. House, Pres.; R. P. Merritt, Sec.

Beta Theta Pi Club—40 E. 40th. F. H. Sisson, Pres.; W. F. Mozier, Sec.

Chi Psi Fraternity—1841. 5,700 mem. 642 State, Madison, Wis. A. S. Bard, Pres., 25 Broad, Mhtn.; W. B. Champlin, Exec. Sec.

Delta Kappa Epsilon Frat., Yale—1844. 13,500 mem. 43 chaps., 27 Alumni Assns. Ogden Reid, Pres.; Jas. A. Hawes, Gen. Sec., 30 W. 44th.

Delta Kappa Epsilon, N. Y. Chapter—30 W. 44th. 1,800 mem. J. P. Munn, Pres.; Jas. Anderson Hawes, Sec. Publishes DKE magazine quarterly.

Delta Tau Delta Club of N. Y.—1909. 259 Madison av. 275 mem. F. C. Briggs, Pres.; Robt. Bissell, Sec.

Delta Upsilon Club of N. Y.—1887. 500 mem. H. C. Field, Pres.; H. J. Ahlheim, Sec., 165 B'way.

Kappa Alpha (Southern Order), N. Y. City Alumni Chap.—1891. 150 mem. C. E. Whitney, Pres.; B. Smith, V.-Pres.; J. L. Sheppard, Sec., 277 B'way.

Nu Sigma Nu Alumni Assn. of N. Y.—J. C. Fisher, Pres.; L. W. Crossman, Sec. and Treas., 121 W. 11th.

Phi Beta Delta—1903. 131 W. 13th. 600 mem. M. C. Dobrow, Pres.; Dr. L. Schorr, Sec., 238 W. 78th.

Phi Beta Kappa—1858. N. Y. Univ. 384 mem. D. W. Hering, Pres.; W. L. Wright, Jr., Sec., N. Y. Univ., Univ. Hgts.

Phi Beta Kappa (N. Y. Delta Chap.), Columbia Univ.—1869. 790 mem. C. H. Hayes, Pres.; F. W. Scholz, Sec.

Phi Beta Kappa Alumni of N. Y.—1877. 762 mem. Rev. Dr. C. P. Fagnani, Pres.; N. G. McCrea, Sec., Columbia Univ.

Phi Delta Phi Club (Law)—1891. 250 mem. F. N. Van Zandt, Pres.; W. M. Messersmith, Sec., 25 Broad.

Phi Delta Theta—1848. 565 W. 113th. 2,000 mem. Duncan Leys, Pres.

Phi Gamma Delta (Omega Assn.)—1897. 538 W. 114th. 375 mem. Wm. L. Hazen, Pres.; H. H. Frost, Treas.; P. M. Maresi, Sec., 37 Wall.

Phi Gamma Delta Club—34 W. 44th. 850 mem. H. W. Nuckols, Pres.; W. Emery, Sec.

Phi Kappa Psi Frat.—1852. 15,781 mem. W. L. Sheppard, Pres.; H. C. Williams, Sec., 916 Garfield Bldg., Cleveland, O.

SOCIETIES AND ASSOCIATIONS—GREEK LETTER SOCIETIES—*Continued*

Phi Kappa Sigma—1855. 536 W. 114th. 163 mem. L. B. N. Gnaedinger, Pres.; A. S. Kitchen, Sec.

Phi Sigma Delta—1909. 435 W. 117th. 500 mem. J. Barr, Pres.; S. Warshaw, Sec.

Phi Sigma Kappa—1873. 4,000 mem. Dr. W. H. Conley, Pres.; F. P. Rend, Sec., North Amherst, Mass.

Psi Upsilon Club of the City of N. Y.—1886. Madison av. and E. 42d. 800 mem. I. A. Place, Pres.; V. Roberts, Sec.

Sigma Alpha Epsilon Club—1919. 51 W. 48th. 100 mem. Wm. Lilly, Pres.; Don R. Almy, Sec., 46 Cedar.

Sigma Alpha Mu—1909. C. C. N. Y.; 1,100 mem. 25 chaps., 6 Alumbi Clubs. M. E. Reiburn, Pres.; J. Kaplan, Sec., 277 B'way.

Sigma Phi—1827. 1,800 mem. P. J. Ross, Sec., 60 Wall.

Tau Delta Phi—1910. 342 W. 123d. 205 mem. H. Cohen, Pres.; A. Cornhall, Sec.

XI Psi Phi Alumni of N. Y.—1908. 300 mem. W. H. Bourne, Pres.; J. N. Gelson, Sec., 282 Park pl., Bkln.

IRISH SOCIETIES.

National.

Ancient Order of Hibernians in Amer.—See Secret and Benefit Socs.

Gaelic League of Ireland—1898. 624 Madison av. 100,000 mem. Dr. G. B. Kelly, Pres.; Mhtn.

United Irish League of Amer.—1901. Boston, Mass. 306 affiliated branches. M. J. Ryan, Pres.; M. J. Jordan, Sec., Rm. 43, Globe Bldg., Boston, Mass.

Brooklyn.

Emerald Ass'n., 5 Court Sq.—1836. 1,051 mem. C. J. Druhan, Pres.; J. F. Casey, Sec., 470 6th.

Erin's Hope Literary Club (affiliated with Gaelic Leaguo)—1915. Edward Dwyer, The Cedar, Ford, Sheepshead Bay.

Friendly Sons of St. Patrick—1862. C. J. Denham, Pres.; J. J. Gartland, Sec., 1390 Dean.

Friends of Irish Freedom—Geo. Washington Br. E. P. Doyle, Pres., 12 Meserole av.

John McHale, Branch of Gaelic League—1911. J. J. Ruth, Pres., 171 Clarkson av.

St. Patrick Soc.—1850. 4 Court sq. H. T. Woods, Pres., 386 E. 5th; J. J. Lynch, Sec., 56 S. Portland av.

Manhattan.

Amer. Daughters of Ireland—5 E. 35th. Miss Anna Frances Levins, Founder.

Amer.-Irish Historical Soc.—See Educational Socs.

Irish-Amer. Ath. Club—(See Athletic Clubs, Mhtn.).

N. Y. Gaelic Soc.—1876. 342 Amsterdam av. 400 mem. E. Daly, Sec.

Soc. of Friendly Sons of St. Patrick in City of N. Y.—700 mem. D. F. Cohalan, Pres.-Sec.

Queens.

Jamaica Gaelic Soc.—1905. 100 mem. Hillcrest Hall, Bergen av. and Fulton, Jamaica. M. M. Byron, Pres., 348 Maure av., Richmond Hill; J. Fitzgerald, Bergen House, Bergen av., Jamaica.

ITALIAN SOCIETIES.

National.

Soc. of Italian Immigrants—1901. Central office and home, 6 Water, N. Y. C. Ernesto G. Fabbri, Pres.; J. K. Paulding, Sec.; U. M. Coletti, Dir.

Societa San Raffaele—Assistance of women and children immigrants, under control of R. R. Missionary Fathers of St. Charles. Rev. G. Moretto, Dir.; Soc. Home, 8-10 Charlton, Mhtn., conducted by Pallottine Sisters.

Italica Gens.—To assist in finding work and colonization of Italian immigrants. A free federation of the Italian clergy, sustained by Natl. Assn. for Italian Catholic Missionaries. 1910. Central office, 265 B'way, Mhtn.; Rev. G. Grivetti, Dir. and Gen. Mgr.

ORDINE FIGLI D'ITALIA.

Grand Executive Council State of New York—3 St. Marks pl., N. Y. C. Grand officers: Prof. C. Stornello, Venerable; Avo. S. Modica, Sec. Archivista.

ORDINE INDIPENDENTE FIGLI D'ITALIA.

Supreme Lodge of State of N. Y.—E. R. Salerno, Supreme Sec., 5F9 Liberty av.

Loggia Benevento No. 264—1914. 28 Prince, Mhtn. 60 mem. G. Delia, Pres., 32 Leroy, Mhtn.; R. Bucciano Sec.

Brooklyn.

BENEFIT.

Amerigo Vespucci—1908. 250 mem. Louis Principe Pres.; E. D'Angelo, Sec., 2451 Dean.

Antonio Scaloia—238 Columbia. †R. Scotto.

Cittadini St. Angelo dei Lombardi—564 Vanderbilt av. †Raffaele Tarantino.

Circolo Montevago—107 Wilson av. 100 mem. Anthony Saladino, Pres.; M. Maritato, Sec.

Circolo Santa Margeritta Belici—1905. 100 mem. 101 Wilson av.

Congrega Maria S. S. Della Carita di M. S.—73 Troy av.

Congregio Assunta di Pierno, M. S.—F. Fabrizio, Pres., 145 Court; G. Sardo, Sec., 175 Hudson av.

Fior di Menfi—1903. 1010 Willoughby av. 300 mem. P. Catalano, Pres., 34 Irving av. F. Callaci, Sec., 125½ Jefferson.

Fraterno Amore—1883. 225 mem. 40 Union. G. Buffo, Pres.; F. Giri, Cor. Sec., 185 Sackett.

Frigente Pietro—385½ Union. †A. F. Mayo.

Grassanese di M. B.—2340 Pacific. *F. Mattia.

Italian American Assn., East New York—233 Rockaway av. *D. Crachi.

La Bella Sicilia—766 3d av. *J. D'Ambra.

Olimpia di M. S.—73 Troy av.

Progresso e Fratellanza Cittadini di Salaparuta—

Saint Lucy Catholic Club—*A. Mariniello, 1009 40th.

San Bartolo Eoliana di N. Y.—261 Chauncey. *F. Mobilio.

San Giuseppe Vesuviano—719 Liberty av. *V. Gallo.

Santo Cono—32 Withers. †J. B. Casale, 187 Withers.

Societa Citatina di Montevago—1904. 107 Wilson av. 100 mem. S. Bacci, Pres.; F. Lamberta, Sec.

Societa di Mutuo Soccorso Concordia Partanna—102 Montrose av. *S. Ragona.

Societa Menfitana di M. S.—1906. 1010 Willoughby av. 50 mem. S. Cerami, Pres.; G. Mandrachia, Sec.; A. Pisciotta, Treas., 1440 DeKalb av.

United Bootblacks' Protective League—*A. Mariniello, 1009 40th.

SPORTING.

Italian-Amer. Gymnastic Assn.—133 Leonard. John Castorina, Sec.

Manhattan and Bronx.

BENEFIT.

Avellinese—200 Spring. *M. Reppucci.

Circolo Co-operativo Emanuele Gianturco—1900. 524 Broome. F. Solimando, Pres.; F. Mostronardi, Sec., 648 E. 228th.

Cittadini Amanteani—49 Prince. *D. Marano.

Club Avigllanese—1890. 160 mem. 301 W. 25th. V. Pietrafesa, Pres.; A. Verrastro, Sec., 131 Thompson.

Cuochi e Pasticcieri Italo-Svizzeri—108 W. 26th. *O. Monzeglio.

Fraterna Italiana—2410 Lorillard pl. *R. Siconolfi.

Giovanni da Potenza—35 Oak. *Francesco Geraldi.

Italian Barbers Benevolent Soc.—226 E. 80th. G. La Carera, Pres.; S. Nucio, Sec., 226 E. 80th.

Italian Philanthropic Lavoratori della Mensa—144 W. 23d. †C. Scotti.

La Sportiva Italian Aid Soc.—108 W. 46th. F. P. Barbero, Pres.; A. Epis, Sec.

Lecce-Bari-Foggia—1908. 323 E. 112th. 100 mem. R. Cortese, Pres.; V. T. Milano, Sec.

Maria SS. Assunta in Cielo. Church of St. Philip Nevis. Societa del S. Nome. Societa di S. Anna. Societa di S. Antonio di Padova. Rev. Francis Cagnina, 3025 Concourse.

Montalbano d'Elicona—540 E. 187th. †J. Cardillo.

Operaia San Fratello—319 E. 107th. Joseph Savio, Pres.

Societa Italiana Guiseppe Mazzini—1879. 8 Franklin. 350 mem. H. Bonori, Pres.; A. E. Crocco, Sec., 424 3d av., Bkln.

Societa Rimembranza dei Cadutti di Saati—1887. 100 mem. Florence Bldg., 30 2d. B. Rizzo, Pres., 374 Elton, Bkln.; M. Magrini, Sec., 66 Mulberry.

---

†President. *Secretary.

SOCIETIES AND ASSOCIATIONS—ITALIAN—MANHATTAN AND BRONX—*Continued.*

United Bootblacks Protective League—728 9th av. P. Russo, Pres.; E. Tari, Sec., 175 Hudson av., Bkln.

Vincenzo Errante di M. S.—54 Market. F. Erapani, Pres.; J. Cerami, Sec.

EDUCATIONAL.

Italian Educational League—*A. J. Pugliese, Sec., P. S. 21, 223 Mott.

La Giovane Italia—1917. 100 mem. 63 Park Row. T. C. Toledo, Sec., 207 Dyckman.

SPORTING.

Unione Sportiva Italiana—108 W. 45th. F. P. Barbero, Pres.; Angelo De Pol, Sec.

SOCIAL.

Young Men's Progressive Club—320 E. 112th.

†President. *Secretary.

JEWISH ORGANIZATIONS.

Jewish organizations are classified herewith for ease of reference under the following:

CLASSIFICATION.

National organizations (including fraternal orders and Jewish-National societies). Local federations. Charitable organizations (Jewish-sectarian only). Educational organizations. Mutual Benefit societies.

National Organizations.

AMERICAN JEWISH COMMITTEE.

Hdqtrs., 31 Union sq., W., Mhtn.—To prevent infringement of the civil and religious rights of Jews and alleviate the consequences of persecution. L. Marshall, Pres., N. Y.; H. Schneiderman, Act. Sec.

AMERICAN JEWISH CONGRESS.

Hdqtrs., 1 Madison av., Mhtn. Nathan Straus, Hon. Pres.; Julian Mack, Pres.; B. Richards, Sec.

ARBEITER RING.

Headquarters, 175 E. B'way, Mhtn. Org. 1900. 81,000 mem. 635 branches; in Gr. N. Y., 256. Natl. officers: E. H. Jeshurin, Pres.; J. Baskin. Gen. Sec., 175 E. B'way, Mhtn.

(See p. 269-270, 1917 Eagle Almanac, for Bkln., Mhtn. and Bronx branches.)

COUNCIL OF JEWISH WOMEN.

Exec. Office, New Haven, Conn. Immigrant Aid Hqrs., 146 Henry St., Mhtn. Org. 1893. 35,000 mem. Object: To bring about closer relations among Jewish women; to further united efforts in the work of social betterment through religion, philanthropy and education. Mrs. Nathaniel Harris, Pres., Bradford, Pa.; Mrs. Leo Herz, Exec. Sec., New London, Conn. N. Y. Sec.—Mrs. Wm. Sporborg, Hawthorne av., Port Chester, N. Y.

FEDERATION OF JEWISH FARMERS OF AMER.

Hdqtrs., 174 2d av., Mhtn. Org. 1908. To improve the material and social condition of Jewish farmers in Amer. Mem. 2,000. S. Shindler, Pres., Hurleyville, N. Y.; Benj. C. Stone, Sec., 174 2d av., N. Y. C.

INDEPENDENT ORDER B'NAI B'RITH.

Dist. Grand Lodge No. 1, H. Lasker, Pres.; H. Asher, Treas.; M. Levy, Sec., 2307 B'way, Mhtn. Org. 1843. 7,000 mem. 50 lodges.

(See p. 270, 1917 Eagle Almanac for Bkln., Mhtn. and Bronx lodges).

INDEPENDENT ORDER BRITH ABRAHAM.

Org. 1887. 770 lodges and 202,451 mem.; Hon. G. Hartman, Grand Master; M. L. Hollander, Gen. Sec., 37 E. 7th; Alex Goldberg, Treas. (See p. 270-272, 1917 Eagle Almanac, for Bkln., Mhtn., Bronx, Queens, Rich. and Suf. Co. lodges.)

INDEPEND. ORDER FREE SONS OF ISRAEL.

Org. 1849. 8,000 mem.; 81 lodges. Gr. officers, S. J. Liebeskind, Gr. Master; H. J. Hyman, Gr. Rec. Sec., 21 W. 124th, Mhtn.; B. Blumenthal, Gr. Treas.

(See p. 272-273, 1917 Eagle Almanac for Bkln., Mhtn. and Bronx lodges).

INDEPENDENT ORDER SONS OF BENJAMIN.

Org. 1877. 953 3d av., N. Y. City. 4,000 mem. Business being conducted by Supt. of Insurance J. S. Phillips, 298 B'way, N. Y. C..

(See p. 273, 1917 Eagle Almanac for Mhtn. and Bronx lodges).

JEWISH AGRICULTURAL AND INDUSTRIAL AID SOC.

Hdqtrs. 174 2d av. Org. 1900. Assists and encourages agriculture among Jewish immigrants in the United States. Conducts a bureau of information and guidance for intending farmers and grants loans on easy terms and at a low rate of interest to intending farmers as well as to farmers. C. L. Sulzberger, Pres.; E. S. Benjamin, Sec.; G. Davidson, Gen. Mgr.

JEWISH NATIONAL WORKERS ALLIANCE OF AMERICA.

Hdqtrs., 89 Delancey, Mhtn. Org. 1912. 6,100 mem. No. of branches, 112. J. Gordon, Pres.; M. L. Brown, Sec.

(See p. 273-274, 1917 Eagle Almanac for Bkln., Mhtn. and Bronx branches.)

JEWISH SOCIALIST LABOR PARTY POALE ZION OF AMERICA.

Hdqtrs., 153 E. B'way, Mhtn. Org. 1905. 6,270 mem. Affiliated socs., 132. B. Zuckerman, Ch.; H. Ehrenreich, Sec.

(See p. 274, 1917 Eagle Almanac for Mhtn. branches).

ORDER BRITH ABRAHAM.

Hdqtrs., 266 Grand, Mhtn. Org. 1859. 72,000 mem. 460 lodges. Natl. officers, S. Dorf, Gr. Master; G. W. Leisersohn, Gr. Sec.

(See p. 274-275, 1917 Eagle Almanac for Bkln., Mhtn. and Bronx lodges).

ORDER KESHER SHEL BARZEL.

District Grand Lodge No. 1.

Org. 1856. 342 E. 50th, Mhtn. 500 mem. Natl. Officers: J. Ankel, Pres.; M. Greenbaum, Sec., 342 E. 50th, Mhtn.

See p. 275, 1917 Eagle Almanac, for Bklyn., Mhtn. and Bronx lodges).

ORDER SONS OF ZION.

44 E. 23d, Mhtn. Legalized 1910. Mem., 7,000. No. of camps, 108. Officers: Nasi (Gd. Master), Judge J. S. Strahl; Gisbor (Treas.), H. B. Isaacson; Maskir (Sec.), J. Ish-Kishor; Chief Med. Examiner, Dr. S. Neumann.

(See p. 275, 1917 Eagle Almanac for Bkln., Mhtn. and Bronx lodges).

UNITED ORDER TRUE SISTERS.

Hdqtrs., 248 W. 105th, Mhtn. Org. 1846. 6,540 mem. 22 lodges. Gr. officers: L. Schwarzkopf, Gr. Pres.; Rose Baran, Gr. Sec., 248 W. 105th, Mhtn.

(See p. 273, 1917 Eagle Almanac, for Bkln., Mhtn. and Bronx lodges).

UNITED SYNAGOGUE OF AMERICA.

Hdqtrs., 531 W. 123d, Mhtn. Org. 1913. 110 Congregations. 600 mem. Rev. Dr. E. L. Solomon, Pres.; Dr. J. Kohn, Rec. Sec.

YOUNG JUDAEA.

A league of the Zionist Youth. Education Dept. of the Zionist Org. of Amer. 55 5th av. Org. 1909. Mem., 15,000. No. of Circles, 712. D. deSola Pool, Pres.; C. A. Cowen, V.-Pres., S. J. Borowsyk, Sec.; Dr. E. Kohn, Ck. of Leadership. Conducts Leaders Train. Schl. Publishes "Young Judean Leader," J. H. Neuman, Ed.; "Young Judea Magazine."

ZIONIST ORGANIZATION OF AMERICA.

Hdqtrs., 55 5th av. Inc. 1902. To promote the Zionist movement in Amer. L. D. Brandeis, Hon. Pres.; J. W. Mack, Pres.; J. De Haas, Exec. Sec.

Local Federations.

Assn. Reform Rabbis of N. Y. C. and Vicinity—45 E. 75th, Mhtn. Org. 1912. 50 mem. Jos. Silverman, Pres.; Richard Stern, Sec.

Bkln. Jewish Center—Eastern P'kway and Bkln. av. S. Rottenberg, Pres.; S. Horowitz, Treas.; Max N. Koven, Sec.

Federation of Bessarabian Org. Org. 1911. 3,000. Affiliated Societies, 27. Leo Lerner, Pres., 116 Nassau, Mhtn.; Aaron Branower, Treas.; M. Feldman, Sec., 941 Simpson, Bronx.

Federation of Galician and Bucovinian Jews of America—66 2d av. Inc. 1903. A central organization of 417 affiliated societies respectively devoted to charity, mutual aid and educational work. It aims to organize Galician and Bucovinian Jewry throughout America and to relieve sufferings and reconstruct ruins of their brethren in the war-stricken countries of Europe. Federation organized Committee for Reconstruction of Galician Jewry. S. Margoshes, Pres. of Fed.; Jacob Kirschenbaum, Sec.

Federation of Oriental Jews of Amer.—356 2d av. Or. 1912. Affiliated Societies, 24. To Americanize and elevate intellectually and materially the Spanish Greek and Arabic speaking Jewish immigrants from the Levant. J. Gedalecia, Pres.; G. J. Amateau, Sec., 40 W. 115th.

Federation of Roumanian Jews of America—Org. 1906. Maintains home for the aged and infirm convalescent at 4th st., Mount Vernon. Capacity of Home at present, 80; additional buildings under construction. Dr. P. A. Siegelstein, Pres.; Dr. J. E. Braunstein, Sec.

Federation of Russian Polish Hebrews of America—62 W. 113th, Mhtn. No. of branches, 240. Mem. about 50,000. Abr. Rosenberg, Pres.; D. Trautmann, Sec.

Jewish Communal Center of Flatbush—1302-1310 Av. I. Org. 1917. 410 mem. Max Rothstein, Pres.; N. B. Kalis and H. Mehlman, Secs.

Kehillah Jewish Community of N. Y. City—114 5th av., Mhtn. Org. 1909. To further the cause of Judaism in N. Y. City and to represent the Jews of this city with respect to all local matters of Jewish interest. 107 lodges, 19 economic agencies, 60 philan. insts. and 21 Zionist socs. Dr. J. L. Magnes, Ch.; Cyrus L. Sulzberger and B. Semel, V.-Chs.; William Fischman, Treas.; S. Benderly, Ch. Admin. Council.

Zion Center of South Bkln.—327 14th. Org. 1916. 3,000 mem. H. Grayer, Pres.; J. Silverman, Sec.

Charitable Organizations.

(Hosp., dispensaries and other non-sectarian charities see Hosp., Homes and Relief Soc., index.)

Brooklyn.

Bernhard H. Seckels Relief Soc.—Acme Hall, 7th av. and 9th. Org. 1908. 300 mem. To help poor Hebrews. J. Benjamin, Pres.; Mrs. S. J. Horwitz, Sec., 396 8th.

Bkln. Federation of Jewish Charities—12 Graham av. Org. 1909. To provide a permanent, efficient and practical mode of collecting and distributing contributions given for private charitable or philanthropic purposes. Alex. H. Grismar, Pres.; Max Abelman, Exec. Sec.

Bkln. Hebrew Home and Hospital for Aged—1907. Howard and Dumont avs. Mrs. C. Rosenthal, Pres.; Mrs. M. Berger, Sec.

Brooklyn Hebrew Orphan Asylum (Inc. 1878)—Ralph av., Dean and Pacific. For the care and education of Jewish orphans from 4 to 16 yrs. of age. Maintains a boarding-out bureau for its youngest wards. Provides industrial training. Emphasizes after-care work. Present number of wards about 800. Officers: Louis L. Firuski, Pres.; M. B. Schmidt, V.-Pres.; A. N. Bernstein, Treas.; A. L. Jacoby, Supt.

Women's Auxiliary—Ralph av. and Pacific. 1877. 1,000 mem. Mrs. O. Kempner, Pres.; Mrs. G. Coblens, Sec., 351 Jefferson av.

Council of Jewish Women (Bkln. section)—Mrs. A. H. Arons, Pres.; Mrs. E. Celler, Sec., 303 McDonough.

Emanuel Sisterhood of Personal Service—Neighborhood House, 318 E. 82d. Mrs. Alexander Kohut, Pres.

First Hebrew Day Nursery and Kindergarten—174 Leonard st. Cares for children between the ages of 2 and 8 years, whose relatives are unable to otherwise provide for them during the day. When circumstances permit, a charge of 5 or 10 cents is made. Some are free. Temporary night shelter cares for children during the illness or disability of the parents. Mrs. L. Weil, Pres.

Hebrew Free Burial Soc. for the Poor of Bkln.—101 Varet. Inc. 1898. Free burial to deceased poor. Dr. S. A. Gluck, Pres.; L. Meyer, Sec.

Hebrew Gemilath Chasodim (Free Loan) Assn. of Bkln.—31 McKibbin. Org. 1897. 2,800 mem. Lends sums of money from 5 to $300 to the poor without interest. 49,265 applicants. N. Prensky, Pres.; I. Kalina, Sec., 31 McKibbin.

Hebrew Ladies' Aid Soc. of Greenpoint—Est. 1901. Mrs. A. Levy, Pres.; M. Brody, Sec., 108 Noble.

Jewish Home for the Aged and Infirm—871 Bushwick av. Dr. P. A. Siegelstein, Pres.

Tille Memorial Soc., Inc.—Acme Hall, 7th av., cor. 9th. J. Benjamin, Pres.; Mrs. E. A. Tuch, Sec., 872 8th.

United Jewish Aid Socs. of Bkln.—Inc. 1909. 732 Flushing av. Branch offices, 1575 Pitkin av.; Cropsey av. and Bay 24th, Bath Beach. R. Seldner, Pres.; Isaac Meseritz, Sec., 851 Park pl., Bkln. Constituent society of the Bkln. Federation of Jewish Charities. Purpose: To keep intact families deprived of their breadwinners; to rehabilitate impoverished persons and rendering them self-sustaining by means of constructive methods of relief.

Young Men's and Women's Social Service Auxiliary of Bkln., Federation of Jewish Charities—12 Graham av. Org. 1914. About 500 mem. To promote social service and good fellowship. A. D. Schanzer, Pres.; Ira Skutch, Sec.-Treas.

Manhattan and Bronx.

Agudath Achim Chesed Shel Emeth—245 Grand. Org. 1888. Free burial to the deceased of poor or friendless Hebrews. B. Freedman, Pres.; H. E. Adelman, Sec.

Ahavath Chesed Shaar Hashomayim Sisterhood of Personal Service. (See Hosp., etc.—Special Relief.)

Alliance Israelite Universelle—N. Y. Branch, 108 E. 31st. Inc. 1860. Amelioration of the condition of Jews in benighted countries. Julius J. Dukas, Pres.; M. F. Behar, Sec.

Amelia Relief Soc. (See Hosp., etc.—Special Relief.)

Amer. Union of Roumanian Jews—44 7th. Inc. 1906. To relieve the wants of the victims of persecution of our brethren in Roumania. Dr. P. A. Siegelstein, Pres.; A. L. Kalman, Sec.

Hebrew Free Burial and Israel Orphan Asylum Assn.—274-280 2d. Inc. 1903. Judge G. Hartman, Pres.; J. G. Fisher, Supt.

Baron de Hirsch Fund—Room 1715, 80 Maiden Lane. Org. 1891. For the benefit of Russian, Roumanian and Galician immigrants. Trade School, 64th, bet. 2d and 3d avs. Has a farming colony in Woodbine, N. J., together with several factories, Agricultural School, where over 70 boys are taught up-to-date scientific farming, dairying, the manufacture and use of farm tools, etc. There are 2,500 inhabitants, with 4 school houses, 2 synagogues, hotel, public baths and town hall. E. S. Benjamin, Pres.; M. J. Kohler, Hon. Sec.; B. A. Palitz, Gen. Agt.

B'nai Jeshurun Sisterhood of Personal Service. (See Hosp., etc.—Special Relief.)

Brightside Day Nursery and Kindergarten—89 Cannon. Summer Home, Oakhurst, N. J. Org. 1894. Non-sec. Children, 1 week to 6 yrs. old, of working mothers. Attendance, 175 daily. Mrs. S. R. Guggenheim, Pres.; Mrs. F. Sanison, Sec., 417 Park av.

Council of Jewish Communal Inst.—356 2d av. Inc. 1907. To further the cause of charitable and philanthropic endeavor by Jewish community of City of N. Y. L. Arnstein, Pres.; Sol Kohn, Sec., 203 B'way.

Council of Jewish Women—N. Y. Section, 59 W. 92d. Est. 1895. Social betterment through religion, education and Americanization. Mrs. Wm. Sporborg, Pres.; Miss S. X. Schottenfels, Sec.

Employment Dept. of Committee on Outside Activities—356 2d av. Org. 1910. To secure employment for handicapped Jews. Jos. Gedalecia, Mgr.

Harlem Home of the Daughters of Israel—32 E. 119th. Inc. 1914. To provide shelter and a home for poor aged Hebrews. 60 inmates. Mrs. D. Malgood, Pres.; S. Edelstein, Sec.

Hebra Hased Va Amet—2 W. 70th. Relief of sick and burial of dead. S. L. Hyman, Pres.; L. Mankiewicz, Sec., New Rochelle, N. Y.

Hebrew Day Nursery—262 Henry and 61 E. 107th. Care for children of working mothers, 2 to 10 yrs. 250 cared for daily. Dora Silberblatt, Pres.; H. Gottler, Supt.; W. Metchik, Sec.

Hebrew Free Loan Soc. (Inc.)—108 2d av. Branches, 69 E. 116th. 1321 Boston rd., Bronx. 1878 Pitkin av., Bkln. Est. 1892. Loans money to needy on notes without interest guaranteed by responsible endorsers, to be paid in weekly installments. J. Dukas, Pres.; S. Kotcher, Act. Mgr.

Hebrew Kindergarten and Day Nursery—35-37 Montgomery. Inc. 1905. To house during the hours of the day, clothe, feed Jewish children between the ages of 1 month and 6 years whose mothers are obliged to work during the

SOCIETIES AND ASSOCIATIONS—JEWISH—MANHATTAN AND BRONX—*Continued.*

day; to afford free meals to school children between the ages of 6 and 8 years of such mothers. Capacity 350. Dr. P. S. Gardner, Pres.; S. Zuckerman, Sec.

Hebrew Orphan Asylum of the City of N. Y.—Amsterdam av. and 137th. Inc. 1822. Maintains an asylum for Hebrew orphans between 5 and 12 years of age. L. Stern, Pres.; A. Schiff, Sec.; S. Lowenstein, Supt. Ladies' Sewing Soc.—138th and Amsterdam av. Org. 1856. 1,150 mem. Object, to clothe and sew for orphans. Mrs. I. N. Spiegelberg, Pres.; Mrs. G. M. Thurnauer, Sec., 32 W. 91st.

Hebrew Relief Soc.—70th, Central Park W. Est. 1829. Maintains pensioners among Congregation of Shearith Israel Synagogue and dispenses relief through United Hebrew Charities. Supported by members' dues and interest of funds. L. N. Levy, Pres.; L. Mankiewicz, Sec., New Rochelle, N. Y.

Hebrew Sheltering and Immigrant Aid Society of America—229-231 E. B'way. Org. 1890. To shelter, aid, protect and Americanize Jewish immigrants. Non-sec. J. L. Bernstein, Pres.; Leon Moissiff, Hon. Sec.

Hebrew Sheltering Guardian Soc.—Pleasantville, N. Y. Org. 1879. Care of orphans under 16. 250 inmates. A. Lewisohn, Pres.; Dr. Leon W. Goldrich, Ex. Dir.

Home for Aged and Infirm Hebrews of N. Y. (The)—105th and Amsterdam av. Est. 1870. Both sexes over 60 yrs. 340 inmates during year. J. Ballin, Pres.; A. J. Cohn, Sec.

Home for Hebrew Infants—Kingsbridge rd. and University av. Est. 1895. From infancy to 5 yrs. 420 inmates. A. E. Norman, Pres. Has a Young Folks League. S. Wolerstein, Pres.; Clara Haas, V.-Pres.

Home of Daughters of Jacob—167th, Findlay and Teller avs., Bronx. Est. 1897. To shelter poor aged Hebrews over 65 yrs. 600 inmates. Mrs. A. J. Dworsky, Pres.; Wm. G. Wolfert, M.D., Sec.; A. Kruger, Supt.

Home of Sons and Daughters of Israel—230-232 E. 10th. Org. 1909. To maintain a home for aged male and female Hebrews. Cap., 100. Judge A. J. Levy, Pres.; J. Pompan, Sec.

Industrial Removal Office—174 2d av. Est. 1899. Distribution of Jewish immigrants. R. Arkush, Ch.; N. Bijur, Sec.; Isidore Frank, Act. Mgr.

Jewish Consumptives' Relief Soc. of Denver, Col. (Denver Sanatorium)—N. Y. office, 31 Union sq. West. Inc. 1904. To supervise the admission to the sanatorium of applicants from N. Y. and vicinity. N. Y. representative, H. Rosen, Mgr.; G. Miller, Sec.

Jewish Natl. Fund Bureau for Amer.—55 5th av. Inc. 1910. To buy land in Palestine and settle Jewish farmers thereon. S. Abel, Ch.; I. H. Rubin, Sec.

Jewish Protectory and Aid Soc.—M. L. Schiff, Pres., Hawthorne, N. Y.; J. Klein, Supt.

Jewish Up-Lift Soc.—99 Nassau. Inc. 1910. The preservation of morals and suppression of vice. D. Shapiro, Pres.; M. Greenberg, Sec., 99 Nassau.

Ladies' Coal Aid Soc.—203 E. B'way. Org. 1906. To distribute coal free to the Jewish needy of N. Y. City. Mrs. P. Dolinsky, Pres.; I. Taub, Sec.

Ladies' Hebrew Lying-in Relief Soc.—(See Charit. Soc.—Special Relief.)

Montefiore Home and Hospital for Chronic Diseases—Gun Hill rd. and 210th. T. G. Rosenbaum, Pres.; M. D. Goodman, Supt.

Natl. Desertion Bureau—356 2d av. Est. 1911. W. H. Liebmann, Ch.; M. M. Goldstein, Sec. and Counsel.

Natl. Jewish Immigration Council—80 Maiden Lane. Org. 1911. General supervision of all work for Jewish Immigrants at the seaports of the U. S. A. I. Elkus, Pres.

Natl. Union Jewish Sheltering Socs.—229 E. B'way. Org. 1911. L. Sanders, Pres.; I. Hershfield, Sec.

Passover Relief Assn.—Org. 1877. To aid deserving Hebrews in observance of the Passover. M. Silberstein, Pres.; A. Schwarzbaum, Sec., 2677 Creston av., Bronx.

Roumanian Hebrew Aid Assn.—44 7th. Inc. 1899. Charity in every phase. Dr. P. A. Siegelstein, Pres.; A. L. Kalman, Sec.

Sanitarium for Hebrew Children of the City of N. Y.—Rockaway Park. Inc. 1879. N. Y. City Office, 224 W. 34th. 2,500 children cared for; over 13,000 afforded fresh air relief. G. R. Davis, Pres.; Miss M. Drifuss, Supt.

Sisterhood of the Spanish and Portuguese Synagogues in the City of N. Y.—133 Eldridge. Inc. 1910. Mrs. M. M. Menken, Pres.; Mrs. E. O. Belais, Sec., 235 W. 76th.

Soc. for the Welfare of the Jewish Deaf—40-44 W. 115th. To furnish industrial education and secure work for the unemployed Jewish Deaf Mutes of N. Y. A. Erlanger, Pres.; J. Amateau, Sec. and Dir.

Tremont Sisterhood—2064 Grand Boulevard and Concourse. Inc. 1905. Mrs. N. Auerhahn, Pres.; Mrs. E. N. Mayer, Sec., 1674 Nelson av.

Queens.

Council Home for Jewish Girls—Conducted by Brooklyn Section, Council of Jewish Women. Rockaway rd. and Davis av., Jamaica. Mrs. A. H. Arons, Pres., 260 Washington av., Bkln.

State.

Home for the Aged and Infirm of the Independent Order of B'nai B'rith. Dist. No. 1—Yonkers, N. Y. Est. 1882. Hebrews over 65 yrs. M. Goldschmidt, Pres., 49 Wall, Mhtn.; Max Rothschild, Supt.

Ladies' Auxiliary—Yonkers, N. Y. Org. 1882. To clothe female inmates and co-operate with board of governors in contributing to well being of Home. Mrs. E. Loeb, Pres.; E. Marx, Sec.; M. Rothschild, Supt.

Jewish Protectory and Aid Soc.—Hawthorne, N. Y. Est. 1907. To take charge of Jewish children committed to its charge, after conviction, for any delinquency, by a competent authority. 400 inmates. M. L. Schiff, Pres.; J. Klein, Gen. Supt.

Lakeview Home—Arrochar, S. I. Inc. 1909. For wayward girls and unmarried mothers. Gives industrial training, individually adapted to economical independence when discharged from the Home. Cap. of house: Adults, 25; babies, 25. Miss S. American, Hon. Pres.; Mrs. L. G. Kalinpfer, Pres.; Mrs. S. B. Edlin, Supt.

Educational Organizations.

For Schools and Talmud Torahs see index for Colleges, Academies and Private Schools.

Brooklyn.

Glory of Israel Hebrew Inst. of E. N. Y.—1914. 363-371 Pennsylvania av. S. Twersky, Sec.; M. Aronson, Pres.

Hebrew Educational Soc.—Hopkinson and Sutter av. Inc. 1899. Object: The educational and social advancement of the population of Brownsville and East N. Y. O. S. Schlockow, Pres.; N. Friedman, Sec.; H. Brickman, Supt.

Hebrew Free School of Brownsville—400 Stone av.; A. Kaplan, Pres., J. Hendler, Supt.

Hebrew Natl. School—63 Tompkins av., A. Price, Pres., A. J. Eshinskey, Supt.

New Hebrew School of Bkln.—146 Stockton, J. Goldman, Pres., B. Magqin, Supt.

Young Men's Hebrew Assn. of Bath Beach—H. Neaderland, Pres.; E. J. Drachman, Exec. Dir., Cropsey and 20th avs.

Young Men's Hebrew Asso. of Bkln.—345 9th. Inc. 1907. Constituent member of the Bkln. Federation of Jewish Charities. 1,000 mem. G. M. Moscowitz, Pres.; E. H. Paul, Sec., 423 Sterling pl.; Leo A. Harris, Exec. Sec.

Young Men's Hebrew Assn. of Borough Park—1911. 50th and 14th av. Mrs. M. J. Rubin, Pres.; Wm. Cohen, Exec. Dir.

Young Men's and Women's Hebrew Assn. of Williamsburg—B'way, S. 9th and Rodney. Org. 1909. 1,200 mem. D. L. Rubinstein, Pres.; H. Bergoffen, Exec. Dir.

Manhattan and Bronx.

Am. Jewish Historical Soc.—Org. 1892. Office, 38 Park Row, Mhtn. To collect, publish and preserve material bearing on the history of the Jews in Amer. 400 mem. C. Adler, Pres.; A. M. Friedenberg, Sec., 38 Park Row.

Baron de Hirsch Fund—(See Special Relief, Hosp., etc.)

Central Jewish Inst.—1916. 125 E. 85th. To interpret for the Jewish youth and adult Jewish ideals in their American environments.

Eastern Council of Reform Rabbis—1918. 5th av. and 43d. Jos. Silverman, Pres.; B. A. Tinter, Sec.

Educational Alliance—197 E. B'way. Inc. 1893. The Americanization and education of immigrants. S. Greenbaum, Pres.; B. M. L. Ernst, Sec., 31 Liberty. Dr. H. Fleischman, Admin.

SOCIETIES AND ASSOCIATIONS—JEWISH—MANHATTAN AND BRONX—*Continued.*

Emanu-El Brotherhood Social House—309 6th. Inc. 1907. To provide a religious, social and educational center for Hebrews. Rev. J. Silverman, Pres.; Dr. G. A. Kohut, Sec.; T. Roth, Supt.

Esther J. Ruskay Religious Circle—Miss R. Goldstein, Sec., 119 W. 114th.

Federation Settlement, Inc.—236-240 E. 105th. Inc. 1907. A community center for social, cultural and moral benefit. Pauline Markowitz, Head Worker.

Histadruth Achieber—263 Grand. Org. 1909. To support and propagate Hebrew language and literature. S. Goldenberg, Pres., 15 5th av.

Jewish Sabbath Alliance—135 Henry. Inc. 1906. To promote the observance of the Holy Sabbath. Rev. B. Drachman, Pres.; J. H. Luria, Sec.

Madison House—216 Madison. Inc. 1898. A social settlement. I. H. Klein, Pres.; I. B. Scheiber, Sec.; Ruth Larned, Head Worker.

Metropolitan League, Y. M. H. A.—114 5th av. Room 1802. 1911. 7,500 mem. Federation of all Y. M. H. A.'s in Greater N. Y.

N. Y. Board of Jewish Ministers—Inc. 1881. Communal, literary, fraternal. M. Hyamson, Pres., 115 E. 95th.

Sisterhood Spanish and Portuguese Synagogue Neighborhood Home—133 Eldridge. Inc. 1910. Jewish settlement. Mrs. Menken, Pres.; Mrs. E. O. Belais, Sec.

Soc. of Jewish Inst.—Hdqtrs., 1 Madison av. To found and conduct a Jewish Inst. in neighborhood of lower 2d av. S. Suffrin, Pres.; M. Margulies, Sec.; B. G. Richards, Dir.

Soc. of Jewish Social Workers of G. N. Y.—114 5th av. Org. 1905. I. E. Goldwasser, Pres.

Young Men's Educational League—56 St. Marks pl. Org. 1895. To improve its members socially and intellectually. Public lectures held. Chairman elected at every meeting. R. Bernstein, Sec., 1500 Longfellow av.

Young Men's Hebrew Assn.—92d and Lexington av. Inc. 1874. Religious, social, moral, educational improvement of Jewish young men and boys. I. Lehman, Pres.; E. H. Paul, Sec., 52 William. Rabbi Lee J. Levinger, Exec. Dir.

Young Men's Hebrew Assn. of the Bronx—1261 Franklin av. Inc. 1909. Jewish, physical, social and mental advancement. M. M. Fertig, Pres.; L. Weinstein, Sec., 1916 Daly av.; Chas. Nemser, Supt.

Young Women's Hebrew Assn.—31 W. 110th. Inc. 1903. To promote the religious, moral, mental, social and physical welfare of Jewish young women and girls. Mrs. I. Unterberg, Pres.; Mrs. S. I. Hyman, Sec., 981 Park av.; Ray F. Schwartz, Supt.

Mutual Benefit Societies.

Brooklyn.

Daughters and Sons of Jacob—1450 51st. Inc. 1910. J. Greenfield, Pres.; Mrs. Wm. Baily, Sec.

First Umaner Ben. Soc.—581 Glenmore av. Inc. 1898. L. Puchkoff, Pres.

Greenpoint Hebrew Civic Club, Inc.—861 Mhtn. av. Inc. 1908. M. Sachs, Pres.; S. Silverman, Treas.

Jacob S. Strahl Benevolent Soc.—Arcanum Hall, Bedford av. and Fulton. S. D. Johnson, Pres.; I. L. Goldman, Rec. Sec.; M. Gillert, Fin. Sec.; R. Strahl, Treas.

United Brethren Benefit Soc.—Court and State. Org. 1856. 145 mem. M. Hart, Pres.; M. J. Jacobs, Sec., 317 7th st.

United Jewish Aid Soc. of Bkln.—722 Flushing av. I. Meseritz, Sec.

Unity Club of Bkln.—(See Social Clubs.)

Wmsburgh Hebrew Retail Grocers Assn.—143 McKibbin. Org. 1909. L. Alpert, Pres.; D. Yawitz, Sec., 14 Garden.

Young Men's Ben. Soc.—L. Lowenthal, Pres.; Philip Meyrowitz, Sec., 652 Willoughby av.

Manhattan and Bronx.

Bailystoker Y. M. Assn.—J. Halperin, Pres.; H. S. Pinnes, Sec.

David Kantrowitz Family Benev. Assn.—175 E. B'way. L. L. Ratner, Pres.; Harry Tenzer, Sec., 188 S. 2d, Bkln.

First Botoschan American Sick and Benefit Assn.—93 Forsyth. S. M. Feinblatt, Pres.; E. Segall, Sec., 76 E. 7th st.

Habiri—Org. 1908. A Jewish Professional Men's Soc. Ab. J. Goldfarb, Pres.; J. J. Shufro, Sec., 1391 Stebbins av.

Ind. First Odesser K. U. V.—98 Forsyth. Org. 1891. D. Morin, Pres.; S. Carduner, Sec., 73 W. 118th.

Ind. Kalusher K. U. V.—125 Rivington. Inc. 1900. N. Schneider, Pres.; M. Demner, Sec., 214 E. 3d.

Ind. Pedwolosysker K. U. V.—209 E. 2d. N. Pechenick, Pres.; M. Anbinder, Sec., 725 E. 9th.

Ind. Tarnpool, K. U. V.—214 2d. O. W. Lewanhar, Pres.; M. Weishaut, Sec., 88-90 Av. D.

Ind. Warschauer Sick Support Soc.—Org. 1886. C. J. Bernstein, Pres.; I. Bernstock, Sec., 129 Rivington.

Jewish Ministers' Cantors Assn. of America—Jos. Schwartz, Pres.; I. Frank, Cor. Sec., 560 W. 144th.

Judeans, The—Org. 1897. S. Lachman, Pres.; M. J. Kohler, Sec., 52 William.

Progressive Slutzker Y. M. B. A.—264 E. B'way. Org. 1904. Chr. elected at every meeting. N. Cohen, Sec., 280 Christopher av., Bkln.

Relief Soc. of Ekaterinoslaw—98 Forsyth. Inc. 1894. B. Mistroff, Pres.; S. Carduner, Sec., 73 W. 118th.

United Hebrew Community (Adath Israel) of N. Y.—203 E. B'way. Inc. 1901. 9,000 mem. M. H. Phillips, Pres.; S. Mosesson, Sec.

Wolkovisker Y. M. B. A.—235 E. B'way. Inc. 1893. H. Goldenberg, Sec.

Yale Brevda Lodge—747 I. O. B. A. L. B. Hymes, Pres.; N. Brevda, Sec., 84 Delancey.

KINDERGARTEN SOCIETIES.

For other Kindergartens see Pub. Schls. and Relief of Children Chapters.

International and National.

INTERNATIONAL KINDERGARTEN UNION—1892. Next meeting, Detroit, Mich., 1921. 20,000 mem. Miss N. C. Vanderwalker, Pres.; Miss May Murray, Sec., Springfield, Mass.

National.

NATIONAL KINDERGARTEN ASSN.—1909. 8 W. 40th, Mhtn. Object: To have kindergartens, established in every public school. Maj. B. Martin, Pres.; Miss Bessie Locke, Sec.

Brooklyn.

[Name following first address that of Director, unless otherwise given.]

THE BROOKLYN FREE KINDERGARTEN SOC.—1891. 67 Schermerhorn. J. C. Jones, Pres.; Miss Alice H. Dahn, Cor. Sec., 141 Lafayette av.; Miss Gertrude E. Skinner, Supervisor.

1. Brooklyn 1st Free—525 Grand av. Miss Helen Reeve, 516 Nostrand av.

2. Caroline W. Barrett Memorial—Mill and Clinton. Miss C. H. Crane, 474 Washington av.

3. Columbia House—27 Columbia pl. Miss C. Schwalb, 247 Rutledge.

4. Cornelius N. Hoagland—230 Classon av. Miss Louise Porter, 28 Midwood.

5. Hans S. Christian Memorial—Christ Ch., Clinton and Harrison. Miss Caroline Barr, 15 W. 88th, Mhtn.

6. Cuyler Memorial—190 4th av. Miss Jessie Hill, 825 Madison.

7. E. W. Bliss Memorial—191 York. Miss Alice Francis, 178 Summit av., Jersey City.

8. Bethany Memorial—316 Hudson av. Miss A. D. Close, 551 4th.

9. Alice E. Fitts—120 Jackson. Miss E. Garretson, 145 Lefferts pl.

10. Grace Church—Grace ct. and Hicks. Miss Mae J. Shea, 42 Hawthorne.

11. City Park—209 Concord. Miss E. G. Ely, 226 St. James pl.

12. Ellen E. Doty Memorial—1435 Atlantic av. Miss C. B. Eschbach, 83 Kingston av.

13. Little Italy Neighborhood House—146 Union. Mrs. E. G. Marshall, 635 E. 32d.

14. Emmanuel House—131 Steuben. Mrs. G. Brown, 90 Pierrepont.

15. Dietz Memorial—18 Jackson. Miss Pearle Eggleston, 431 W. 146th, Mhtn.

16. Little Friends' Kindergarten—72 Schermerhorn. Miss E. MacNaughton, 589 Pacific.

Manhattan and Bronx.

THE CHILDREN'S AID SOC.—1855. 105 E. 22d. Wm. C. Osborn, Pres.; C. Loring Brace, Sec. Maintains the following free kindergartens, night and industrial schls.:

Av. B—537 E. 16th. Miss E. F. Sinn.

SOCIETIES AND ASSOCIATIONS—KINDERGARTENS—MANHATTAN AND BRONX—*Continued.*

†Fifty-third St.—552 W. 53d. Miss K. Crommelin.

Henrietta—224 W. 63d. Miss M. L. Stewart.

†Italian—Elizabeth and Hester. Mrs. L. E. Weygandt.

†Jones Memorial—407 E. 73d. Miss E. Wells.

*Rhinelander—350 E. 88th. Mrs. E. F. Pettit.

†Sixth St.—630 E. 6th. Miss M. J. Lohn.

†Sullivan St.—219 Sullivan. Miss M. E. Schlegel.

Tompkins Sq.—295 E. 8th, Miss E. F. Sinn.

†West Side—419 W. 38th. Miss D. Kling.

Fifty-third St. Evg.—552 W. 53d. E. M. Barrows.

Henrietta Evg.—224 W. 63d. Miss M. L. Stewart.

Italian Evg.—Elizabeth and Hester. Mrs. L. E. Weygandt.

N. Y. KINDERGARTEN ASSN.—524 W. 42d. 1889. Geo. McAneny, Pres.; Rev. Jas. M. Bruce, Sec.

198 Bleecker. Miss J. B. Ahl.

Alice Carrington Royce—524 W. 42d. Miss J. L. Frame.

Shaw Memorial—61 Henry. Miss L. F. Oswald.

John Winthrop Chanler Memorial—211 Clinton. Miss A. E. Henderson.

Frances Dana Walcott—524 W. 42d. Miss E. I. Cass.

Marion—340 E. 106th. Miss M. A. Kyle.

Geo. Wm. Curtis—299 Henry. Miss Jessie Barnard.

Francis Minturn Memorial—395 Broome. Miss R. Rogers.

Auchmuty—415 E. 13th. Miss L. Wilcox.

East Side—76th and E. R. Miss L. Day.

Anti-Basement Circle—464 E. 64. Miss Henrietta Bergen.

Katherine Stauffer Clark—40 Sutton pl. Miss Whaley.

Ogontz—325 E. 31st. Miss H. Hough.

Anne Browne Alumnae—48 Henry. Miss S. R. Francis.

C. Adolphe Low—407 E. 114th. Miss Bertha Thurston.

People's Home Settlement—543 E. 11th. Miss Eva J. Wallace.

Morning Star—11 Doyers. Miss F. N. Dixon.

Nathan Oppenheim Mem.—94 Cherry. Miss F. L. Dutton.

Union Settlement—237 E. 104th. Miss N. Mawson.

Spring St.—244 Spring. L. R. Carter.

Kenneth—50th, cor. 10th av. Miss J. W. Brush.

Mary F. Walton—202 W. 63d. Miss H. Maesing.

Children's Charitable Union—511 E. 69th. Mrs. A. M. Dashiell.

27 Barrow St.—Miss Helen N. Dodd.

Kindergarten—27 Barron. Miss H. N. Dodd.

Kindergarten—133 W. 4th. Miss E. M. Toggart.

---

*Classes for crippled and defective children.
†Classes for truants.

LITERARY SOCIETIES.

International and National.

Amer. Library Assn.—1876. See Educational Socs.

Amer. Librarians' Home Assn.—150 mem. Maintains a vacation house at Branford, Conn. Mrs. A. S. Donley, Sec., 374 State, Bridgeport, Conn.

Amer. Oriental Soc.—1842. 350 mem. C. R. Lanman, Pres.; C. J. Ogden, 628 W. 114th, N. Y. C.

Authors League of Amer., Inc.—1912. Rex Beach, Pres.; Eric Schuler, Sec., 41 Union Sq. N. Y. C.

Hispanic Soc. of Amer.—156th, west of B'way. 1904. 100 mem. A. M. Huntington, Pres.

Natl. Inst. of Arts and Letters—250 mem. C. Gilbert, Pres.; Prof. J. B. Fletcher, Sec., Columbia Univ., N. Y.

United Amateur Press Assn. of America—1895. 300 mem. R. Erford, Pres., 4337 6th av., Seattle, Wash.; D. N. Florance, Sec., Snohomish, Wash.

State.

N. Y. Library Assn.—1891. Wm. F. Yust, Pres.; N. Louise Ruckteshler, Sec., Norwich.

Brooklyn.

Amateur Writers' Club of Flatbush—1920. 575 E. 29th. Pauline Burstein, Pres.; Anna Burnbaum, Sec., 1072 Rogers av.

Bay Ridge Reading Club—1886. 35 mem. Mrs. O. Heinigke, Pres.; Mrs. J. A. Townsend, Sec., 77 82d.

Bkln. Blue Pencil Club—1908. 30 mem. Mrs. H. P. Adams, Pres., 326 Decatur; A. M. Adams, Sec.

Bkln. Chautauqua Union—See Educational Soc.

Bkln. Heights Seminary Club—1885. 18 Pierrepont, 371 mem. Miss Ellen Y. Stevens, Pres.; Miss Anne Piper, Sec.

Bkln. Woman's Club—114 Pierrepont. 1869. 336 mem. Mrs. Edw. F. Lindridge, Pres.; Mrs. J. M. Wilsom, Sec., 162 Clinton.

Cambridge Club—1890. 50 mem. Mrs. Don C. Seitz, Pres.; Mrs. Stanley Frost, Cor. Sec., 751 Westminster rd.

Central Y. M. C. A. Literary and Debating Soc.—55 Hanson pl. 1884. E. A. King, Pres.; C. W. Morhous, Sec.

Chiropean Club—1896. Pouch Mansion. 305 mem. Miss J. F. Ring, Pres.; Mrs. C. H. Gillespie, Cor. Sec., 1141 Bergen.

Civitas Club of Bkln.—1893. 114 Pierrepont. Mrs. W. P. Earle, Pres.; Mrs. A. C. Leggett, Sec., 231 Park pl.

Collegiate Debating Soc.—1908. 1125 Carroll. 40 mem. R. A. Kearney, Pres.; A. Reheuser, Sec., 348 49th.

Colonia Club (The)—1892. 48 mem. Mrs. T. D. Huntling, Pres.; Miss M. F. Ackerman, Cor. Sec., 776 Argyle rd.

Contemporary Club—40 mem. Mrs. M. F. Johnson, Pres.; Mrs. T. M. Hardy, Sec., 618 Madison.

Diogenes Fellowship—1920. Hdqtrs., Eagle Auditorium, Eagle Bldg. Mrs. Helen Warburton Joy, Founder, 780 Madison av., Mhtn.

Fenelon Reading Circle—1889. Pouch Gallery. 100 mem. Rev. L. A. Oppo, Spir. Dir.; Mrs. G. W. Connell, Pres.; Mrs. A. P. Cooney, 81 Summit, Cor. Sec.

Fortnightly Club of Flatbush (The)—27 mem. Mrs. W. O. Jones, Pres.; Mrs. L. W. Fay, Sec., 578 E. 21st.

Fortnightly Library Club—1895. 38 mem. Mrs. F. J. Swift, Pres.; Mrs. W. B. Nelson, Rec. Sec.; Mrs. C. B. Law, Cor. Sec., 50 Hendrix.

Franklin Literary Soc.—1864. 75 mem. 12 Nevins. A. H. Delano, Ch.; T. E. Crossman, Cor. Sec., 15 Park Row, Mhtn.

Friday Afternoon Club—1887. 50 mem. Mrs. A. L. Janes, Pres.; Mrs. J. V. Jewell, Sec., 1371 Dean.

Froebel Soc.—1884. Masonic Temple. 118 mem. Mrs. C. A. Decker, Pres.; Mrs. C. Fox, Cor. Sec., 698 Greene av.

Hamilton Literary Soc.—1907. Commercial High Sch. Alex. Gross, Pres.; Jules Lehman, Sec., 1018 Park pl.

Illumaniti Club—1908. 100 mem. M. S. MacNutt, Pres.; Mrs. D. V. L. Sheppard, Sec., 66 Fenimore.

Irving League—1904. 15 mem. P. Dilg, Pres.; W. C. Yonge, Sec., 261 Ridgewood av.

Kosmos Club—1894. Mrs. G. J. Corwin, Pres.; Mrs. F. J. Diller, Cor. Sec., 145 Argyle rd.

Leo Lyceum—1889. 2 Carlton av. 110 mem. J. T. Keenan, Pres.; J. A. Wheelin, Sec., 3213 Clarendon rd.

Lincoln Soc.—496 Franklin av. 1913. 100 mem. S. Ross, Pres.; M. Heuvelmans, Sec.

L. I. Library Club, merged with N. Y. Library Club)—(See Literary Socs., Mhtn.)

Monday Club—(See Miscell. Hosp., etc.)

Pensa Literary Club—1898. 25 mem. Mrs. C. A. J. Queck-Berner, Pres.; Mrs. D. E. Hoag, Sec., 633 Greene av.

Photereone Club—1882. 20 mem. Mrs. W. T. Jones, Pres.; Miss M. A. Hawley, Sec., 1815 Dorchester rd.

Prospect Club—1897. 57 mem. Mrs. Eugene W. Sutton, Pres., 379 Washington av.; Mrs. G. A. Preuss, Sec., 496 1st.

Readers' Club (Elocutionists)—1906. 25 mem. Miss I. Spader, Pres.; A. Ewart, Ch. Program Com., 90 Downing.

St. Patrick's Catholic Club—(See Religious Soc.)

SOCIETIES AND ASSOCIATIONS—LITERARY SOCIETIES—BROOKLYN—*Continued.*

St. Peter's Catholic Library Assn.—1878. 114 Warren. 260 mem. C. J. Lockwood, Pres.; Ed. A. Stack, Treas.

Twentieth Century Club—1893. 225 mem. Mrs. M. J. Field, Pres.; Miss M. S. Packard, Sec., 71 Joralemon.

Urban Club—1894. 75 active mem. 10 associates. Mrs. A. J. Perry, Sr., Dir.; Mrs. T. Hanson, Pres.; Mrs. K. C. Bates, Cor. Sec., 376 Clinton.

Utrecht Study Club—1903. 114 Pierrepont. 50 mem. Mrs. G. A. Allen, Pres.; Mrs. F. L. Darrow, Rec. Sec., 364 87th; Mrs. W. E. Shuttleworth, Cor. Sec., Shore rd. and Oliver.

Winter Club—1890. 30 mem. Mrs. Herbert Gardner, Pres.; Mrs. S. Newman, 1855 82d, Sec.

Winter's Night Club—1893. 50 mem. Edward M. Crane, Pres.; Mrs. C. P. Boyle, Sec., 1339 Bedford av.

Writers' Club of Bkln.—1895. 65 mem. Col. F. P. Sellers, Pres.; Rev. A. D. Smith, Sec., 612 Eastern P'kway.

Young Ladies Aid and Literary Soc. Inc.—See Socs. for Relief; Special Relief.

Manhattan and Bronx.

Armenian Colonial Assn.—115 E. 24th. H. G. Benneyem, Dir.

Athene—1914. Waldorf-Astoria. 150 mem. Mrs. Katherine A. Martyn, Pres.; Mrs. Helena L. Rehfuss, Sec. The Lucerne, Amsterdam av. and 79th.

Burns Soc. of the City of N. Y.—1871. 150 mem. Edwd. E. Bartlett, Pres.; H. A. Kenney, Sec., 114 Liberty.

Cathedral Club—(See Social Clubs.)

Century Assn.—1847. 7 W. 43d. 1,300 mem. A. D. Noyes, Sec.

Dickens Fellowship of N. Y.—1904. 15 Gramercy Pk. Dr. Lyman W. Allen, Pres.; Mrs. E. B. Van Deusen, Treas.; Miss Mary B. Sabin, Sec., 2473 Davidson av.

Dixie Club of N. Y.—1905. Hotel Astor, 250 mem. Mrs. E. W. Inslee, Pres.; Mrs. W. A. Downes, Sec., 430 Park av.

Dunlap Soc.—250 mem. Brander Matthews, Pres.; L. E. Shipman, Sec., 16 Gramercy Park.

Eclectic Club—Waldorf-Astoria. 1896. 200 mem. Mrs. A. C. Bage, Pres., 251 W. 92d; Mrs. A. L. Eslanger, Sec., 530 Riverside dr.

Ernest Crosby Club—1901. 267 Henry. 21 mem. J. Krimsky, Pres.; S. Singer, Sec., 1382 5th av.

League of Amer. Pen Women, N. Y. Auxiliary—1920. 150 mem. Mrs. Ruth Rice, Pres., 49 St. Nicholas ter.; Marchese Teodora Marconi, Sec., 3 Washington sq.

Looking Forward Club—1898. Mrs. F. M. Stowell, Pres.; Miss Teresa Sangen, Treas., John Wanamaker's, B'way and 10th.

N. Y. Library Club—1885. E. F. Stevens, Pres., Pratt Inst. Free Library, Bkln.; Miss A. I. Vail, Sec., care of Carter, Ledyard and Milburn, 54 Wall.

Quill Club—1890. 200 mem. R. Taggart, Pres.; C. P. Fagnani, Sec., 606 W. 122d.

Sorosis—1868. Waldorf-Astoria. 200 mem. Mrs. J. L. Childs, Pres.; Mrs. O. D. Brown, Sec., 790 Riverside drive.

Spalding Literary Union—1885. 34 W. 60th. 700 mem. W. A. Davidson, Pres.; Rev. H. F. Riley, C. S. P., Dir.

University Club—1865. 5th av. and 54th. 4,800 mem. A. B. Hepburn, Pres.; S. H. Ordway, Sec.

Queens.

London Literary Assn.—1902. M. E. Leicester, Editor, Jamaica.

Manor Literary Soc.—1910. Bkln. Manor, Woodhaven. 20 mem. E. Trounson, Pres.; Mrs. P. Timmis, Sec., 124 Elmwood, Woodhaven.

Progress Soc. of the Rockaways—(See Bd. of Trade, etc.)

Women's Club—1916. 15 mem. Mrs. H. W. R. Stafford, Sec., Sedgwick, Queens, L. I.

Richmond.

Deems Literary Soc.—1895. Deems Memorial Chapel, Westerleigh. 100 mem. John DeMorgan, Pres.; R. H. Hopkins, Sec.-Treas.

Woman's Club of S. I. (The)—New Brighton. 1893. 175 mem. Mrs. W. A. Boyd, Pres.; Mrs. J. Franklin, Cor. Sec., 461 Oakland av., New Brighton.

MEDICAL SOCIETIES.

International.

Internatl. Alliance of Physicians and Surgeons—1904. 1034 mem. Dr. C. F. Conrad, Organizer. H. Morgenhesser, M.D., Pres.; J. B. Prager, M.D., Sec., 110 W. 90th, Mhtn.

National.

Allied Medical Assns. of America—1911. 1,400 mem. I. Mayer, M.D. Pres.; L. M. Ottofy, M.D., Sec., New Grand Central Theater Bldg., St. Louis, Mo.

Am. Academy of Medicine—1876. 500 mem. Wm. L. Estes, Sr., Pres.; T. W. Grayson, M.D., Sec., 8037 Jenkins Arcade, Pittsburgh, Pa.

Am. Academy of Ophthalmology and Oto-Laryngology—1895. 1,250 mem. Dr. Lee M. Francis, Pres.; Dr. L. G. Peter, Sec., 1529 Spruce, Phila. Pa.

Am. Assn. of Anatomists—400 mem. Prof. C. F. W. McClure, Pres.; Prof. C. R. Stockard, Sec. and Treas., Cornell Medical School, Mhtn.

Am. Assn. of Clinical Research—1909. 419 Boylston. Boston, Mass. R. M. Griswold, M.D., Pres.; Jas. Krauss, M.D., Sec.

Am. Assn. of Obstetricians and Gynecologists—1888. 132 mem. Dr. G. W. Crile, Pres., Cleveland, O.; Dr. E. G. Zinke, Sec., 4 W. 7th, Cincinnati, O. Next meeting Atlantic City, N. J., Sept. 20-22, 1920. Hotel Ambassador.

Am. College of Surgeons—1913. 40 E. Erie Chicago, Ill. 4,180 fellows. Dr. W. J. Mayo, Pres., Rochester, Minn.; Dr. Franklin H. Martin, Sec.; Dr. John G. Bowman, Dir.

Am. Electro Therapeutic Assn.—1891. 17 E. 38th, Mhtn. 250 mem. Dr. B. S. Price, Pres.; Dr. A. B. Hirsh, Sec. Next annual meeting, Washington, D. C., Sept., 1921.

Am. Gynecological Soc.—1876. 96 mem. Dr. W. W. Chipman, Pres.; Dr. G. G. Ward, Jr., Sec., 48 E. 52d, Mhtn.

Am. Homeopathic, Ophthalmological, Otological and Laryngological Sec.—219 mem. Geo. W. McKenzie, Pres.; N. I. Bentley, Sec. 1161 Davis Whitney Bldg., Detroit, Mich.

Am. Inst. of Homeopathy—1844. 3,590 mem. T. A. McCann, Pres.; T. E. Costain, M.D., Sec.-Treas., 829 Marshall Field Bldg., Chicago, Ill.

Am. Laryngological Assn.—1878. 85 mem. Dr. Harris P. Mosher, Pres.; Dr. Geo. M. Coates, Sec., 1736 Pine, Phila., Pa.

Am. Laryngological, Rhinological and Otological Soc., Inc.—Dr. Lee W. Dean, Pres., Iowa City, Ia.; Dr. W. H. Haskin, Sec., 40 E. 41st, Mhtn.

Am. Med. Assn.—1847. 535 N. Dearborn, Chicago, Ill. 48,794 fellows. Surg. Gen. W. C. Broisted, Pres.; Dr. A. R. Craig, Sec.

Am. Medico-Psychological League—1897. Owen Copp, M.D., Pres.: N. W. Mitchell, M.D., Sec.-Treas., Warren, Pa.

Am. Medico-Psychological Assn.—1884. 896 mem. H. C. Eyman, M.D.; H. W. Mitchell, M.D., Sec., Warren, Pa.

Am. Ophthalmological Soc.—1864. 200 mem. Dr. John E. Weeks, Pres.; Dr. T. B. Holloway, Sec.-Treas., 1819 Chestnut, Phila., Pa.

Am. Orthopedic Assn.—1887. Robt. B. Osgood, Pres.; W. W. Plummer, M.D., Sec., 523 Franklin, Buffalo, N. Y. Annual meeting, June, 1921, Boston, Mass.

Am. Osteopathic Assn.—Dr. W. E. Waldo, Pres., Seattle, Wash.; Dr. W. A. Gravatt, Sec., Reibold Bldg., Dayton, O.

Am. Pediatric Soc.—1888. 75 mem. Dr. John Howland, Pres.; Dr. H. C. Carpenter, Sec., 1805 Spruce, Phila., Pa.

Am. Public Health Assn.—1872. 5,708 mem. W. S. Rankin, M.D., Pres., Raleigh, N. C.; A. W. Hedrich, C.P.H., Sec., 169 Mass. av., Boston, Mass. Next meeting at San Francisco, Sept., 1921.

Amer. Soc. for Control of Cancer—25 W. 45th, Mhtn. Dr. Chas. A. Powers, Pres.; T. M. Debevoise, Sec.

Am. Surgical Assn.—160 mem. Next meeting, Toronto, Canada. Dr. John B. Roberts, Pres.; Dr. J. H. Gibbon, Sec., 1608 Spruce, Phila., Pa.

Am. Therapeutic Soc.—1900. 115 mem. Next meeting, Phila., Pa., June, 1920. r. C. E. deM. Sajous, Pres.; r. L. H. Taylor, Sec., The Cecil, Washington, D. C.

Am. Veterinary Med. Assn.—1863. 4,500 mem. C. A. Cary, Pres.; N. S. Mayo, Sec., 4753 Ravenswood av., Chicago.

Assn. of Am. Physicians—1886. 160 active and 25 associate mem. W. S. Thayer, Pres.; T. McCrae, Sec., 1627 Spruce, Phila., Pa.

SOCIETIES AND ASSOCIATIONS—MEDICAL—NATIONAL—*Continued.*

Assn. of Military Surgeons of U. S.—Washington, D. C. Med. Dir., Surg. J. W. Kerr; Col. J. R. Church, M.C., U. S. Army, Sec., Washington, D. C.

Clinical Congress of the Amer. College of Surgeons—Dr. Geo. E. Armstrong, Pres.; Dr. F. H. Martin, Sec.-Gen., 40 E. Erie, Chicago, Ill.

Congress of Amer. Physicians and Surgeons—1888. 1,915 mem. Triennial sessions. Dr. S. Flexner, Pres.; Dr. W. R. Steiner, Sec., 646 Asylum av., Hartford, Conn.

Med. Assn. of Southwest—1905. 975 mem. Dr. E. F. Day, Pres.; Dr. F. H. Clark, Sec., El Reno, Okla.

Natl. Assn. for the Study of Epilepsy—1901. Dr. G. K. Collies, Pres.; Dr. A. L. Shaw, Sec. and Treas., Camden, N. Y.

Natl. Tuberculosis Assn.—1904. 381 4th av. 4,000 mem. Dr. V. C. Vaughn, Pres.; Dr. C. J. Hatfield, Managing Dir.

Natl. Assn. of Progressive Medicine—Dr. J. M. Irving, Pres.; Edw. Carroll, D.O., Sec.; Dr. C. F. Conrad, Organizer and Dir., 110 W. 90th, Mhtn.

Natl. Dental Assn.—1838. 2,000 mem. Dr. H. E. Friesell, Pres.; Dr. Otto U. King, Sec., 127 N. Dearborn, Chicago, Ill.

Natl. Eclectic Med. Assn.—Next meeting, Colorado Springs, Col., June 18-22, 1921. H. W. Felter, M.D., Pres., Cincinnati, O.; W. N. Mundy, M.D., Cor. Sec., Forest, O.

Natl. Med. Assn.—1895. 500 mem. D. W. Byrd, M.D., Pres.; G. W. Cabannis, M.D., Sec., 1744 K., N. W., Washington, D. C.

Natl. First-Aid Assn. of Amer.—Cooper Tavern Bldg., Arlington, Mass. R. G. Wells, Act. Pres. and Treas.; Mrs. M. K. Wells, Sec.

Natl. Soc. of Physical Therapeutics—1893 120 mem. E. P. Mills, M.D., Pres.; F. F. Massey, M.D., Sec., Wernerville, Pa.

Natl. Vol. Emergency Serv.—1900. 6,200 mem. F. E. Davis, Adj.-Gen., 5 Beekman. Mhtn.

Southern Med. Assn.—1907. 6,000 mem. Dr. E. H. Cary, Pres.; Dr. Seale Harris, Sec., Birmingham, Ala.

State.

Assn. of Supts. and Managers of Tuberculosis Hosp. of N. Y. State—Dr. J. H. Marshall, Pres., Southold, L. I.

Eclectic Med. Soc. of the State of N. Y.—1860. 370 mem. L. B. Dawley, M.D., Pres.; T. D. Adlerman, M.D., Sec., 696 St. Marks av., Bkln.

Med. Soc. of the State of N. Y.—17 W. 43d, Mhtn. Next meeting, Bkln., May, 1921. J. R. Kevin, Pres.; Ed. Livingston Hunt, Sec.

N. Y. and New England Assn. of Railway Surgeons—1891. 200 mem. Dr. J. F. Block, Pres.; Dr. Geo. Chaffee, Sec., Bingnamton, N. Y.

N. Y. State Dental Soc.—1868. 2,500 mem. Dr. L. M. Waugh, Pres., 576 5th av., N. Y. C.; A. P. Burkhart, Sec., 52 Genesee, Auburn.

N. Y. State Pharmaceutical Assn.—1879. 1,631 mem. R. S. Lehman, Pres.; E. S. Dawson, Sec., 125 S. Salina, Syracuse.

Pedic Soc. of State of N. Y. (N. Y. Co. Div.)—220 mem. Terrace Garden, E. 58th, Mhtn. M. Redell, Pres.; L. Lewy, Sec., 1624 Av. A, Mhtn.

Brooklyn.

Associated Physicians of L. I.—1898. 900 mem. H. G. Webster, M.D., Pres.; J. C. Hancock, M.D., Sec., 135 Cambridge pl.

Bkln Dental Soc.—1869. 60 mem. Dr. F. C. Walker, Pres.; Dr. W. G. Lewis, Sec., 184 Joralemon.

Bkln. Gynecological Soc.—1890. 1313 Bedford av. 40 mem. Gordon Gibson, Pres.; H. B. Matthews, M.D., Sec., 643 St. Marks av.

Bkln. Med. Assn.—1904. 360 Fulton. 200 mem. T. M. Brennan, Pres.; G. J. Doyle, Sec., 287 Clermont av.

Bkln. Pathological Soc.—1870. 1313 Bedford av. 340 mem. Dr. Thurston Dexter, Pres.; Dr. H. B. Matthews, Sec., 638 St. Mark's av.

Bkln. Soc. of Neurology—1890. Kings Co. Med. Soc. S. Block, M.D., Pres., 502 Washington av.

Bkln. Surgical Soc.—1313 Bedford av. F. D. Jennings, M.D., Pres., 1083 Bushwick av.; R. F. Barker, Sec., 1140 Dean.

East N. Y. Med. Soc.—Dr. B. B. Gerzog, Pres.; Leo Faske, Sec., 1515 Eastern Parkway.

Eclectic Dispensary and Hosp. Soc. of Kings Co.—1902. 309 Hewes. 25 mem. L. Adlerman, M.D., Pres.; M. B. Pearlstien, M.D., Sec., 309 Hewes.

Flatbush Med Soc.—1912. 90 mem. Harold A. Morris, Pres.; Wm. F. C. Steinbugler, Sec.

Greater N. Y. Pharmaceutical Soc.—1909. Wm. T. Creagan, Pres.; T. Lamb, Sec., 84 Livingston.

Homeopathic Med. Soc. of Kings Co.—1857. 150 mem. J. G. Wright, M.D., Pres.; L. D. Broughton, M.D., Sec., 304 Lewis av.

Kings Co. Pharmaceutical Soc.—1877. 265-71 Nostrand av. 500 mem. G. R. Christ, Pres.; C. E. Heimerzheim, Sec., 567 Central av.

Kings Co. Pedic Soc.—Dr. Fred'k Schmitt, Pres.; Dr. H. A. Brown, Sec., 355 Flatbush av.

Medical Soc. of Bay Ridge—1916. 412 73d. 80 mem. Dr. J. W. Malone, Pres.; Dr. Jas. W. Fox, Sec., 418 54th.

Med. Soc. of Kings Co.—1822. 1313 Bedford av. 1,000 mem. Dr. Arthur H. Bogart, Pres.; C. E. Scofield, Sec.

Optometrical Club of Bkln.—1915. 125 S. Elliott pl. 80 mem. Dr. Thos. McBurnie, Pres.; Dr. Harold R. Barnes, Sec., 729 Manhattan av.

Second Dist. Dental Soc.—1868. Library Bldg. of Kings Co. Med. Soc., Bedford av. 440 mem. H. C. Croscup, Pres.; R. D. Harby, Sec., 184 Joralemon.

W'msburgh Med. Soc.—1906. Regina Mansion. 250 mem. Dr. M. J. Levitt, Pres.; Dr. B. B. Berkowitz, Sec., 839 Park pl.

Manhattan and Bronx.

Am. Microscopical Soc. of the City of N. Y.—1865. 130 mem. O. G. Mason, Sec., Bellevue Hosp.

Assn. of Tuberculosis Clinics—1908. 10 E. 39th. 30 free clinics. Jas. A. Miller, M.D., Pres.; John S. Billings, Sec., 10 E. 39th.

Celtic Med. Soc. (N. Y.)—1891. 114 mem. Dr. T. A. Martin, Pres.; Dr. J. J. Rothwell, Sec., 144 W. 76th.

Eastern Med. Soc. (The)—1895. Hotel Brevoort. 630 mem. H. E. Isaacs, Pres.; J. F. Saphir, Sec., 345 W. 88th.

First Dist. Dental Soc.—1868. 17 W. 43d. 1,500 mem. Leland Barrett, Pres.; J. A. Vuilleumier, Sec., 104 E. 40th.

German Med. Soc. of N. Y. City—1860. 286 mem. Dr. R. Denig, Pres.; Dr. W. F. Bopp, Sec., 59 W. 89th.

Harlem Med. Assn. of City of N. Y.—1869. 82 W. 126th. 400 mem. Dr. L. Friedman, Pres.; Dr. M. Schelman, Sec., 119 W. 71st.

Harvard Med. Soc.—58 mem. Dr. B. C. Darling, Pres.; Dr. C. P. Gray, V.-Pres.; Dr. Thos. E. Lavell, Sec., 120 W. 70th.

Homeopathic Med. Soc. of Co. of N. Y.—1857. 17 W. 43d. 416 mem. G. S. Harrington, M.D., Pres.; Reeve Turner, M.D., Sec., 503 W. 149th.

Hospital Graduates' Club—1885. Yale Club. 60 mem. C. A. McWilliams, Pres.; F. S. Matthews, Sec., 62 W. 50th.

Italian Pharmaceutical Assn.—1896. 250 mem. F. Avignone, Pres.; M. de Marsico, Sec., 137 E. 116th.

Lenox Med. and Surgical Soc.—1885. 30 mem. Dr. W. M. Bradshaw, Pres., 130 E. 67th; Dr. I. O. Woodruff, Sec., 152 W. 78th.

Mhtn. Med. Soc.—1906. 75 mem. D. Bissell, Pres.; A. J. Huey, Sec.

Med. Assn. of the Greater City of N. Y.—1899. 600 mem. G. L. Brodhead, M.D., Pres.; E. E. Smith, M.D., Sec., 181 W. 75th.

Med. Soc. of Borough of Bronx—1892. Ebling's Hall. 109 mem. C. A. Clinton, M.D., Pres.; Harry Aranow, Sec., 355 E. 149th.

Med. Soc. of the Co. of N. Y.—1794. 2,756 mem. C. H. Chetwood, M.D., Pres.; D. S. Dougherty, Sec., 11 W. 85th.

Metropolitan Med. Soc. of N. Y. City—80 mem. Dr. B. Sour, Pres.; Dr. M. M. Stark, Sec., 156 W. 86th.

N. Y. Assn. for Med. Education—H. Emerson, Pres.; O. V. Huffman, Sec., 17 W. 43d.

N. Y. Academy of Medicine—1847. 17 W. 43d. 1,700 mem. Dr. Geo. D. Stewart, Pres.; Dr. R. S. Haynes, Sec.

N. Y. Dermatological Soc.—1869. 17 mem. J. M. Winfield, M.D., Pres., 47 Halsey, Bkln.; Fred Wise, M.D., Sec., 24 W. 59th.

N. Y. Medico-Surgical Soc.—1895. Dr. J. R. Bingham, Sec., 575 West End av.

N. Y. Neurological Soc.—1874. 17 W. 43d. 132 mem. W. Timme, Pres.; C. E. Atwood, Sec., 14 E. 60th.

N. Y. Obstetrical Soc.—1863. 70 mem. Dr. W. Ward, Pres.; Dr. Reginald Rawls, Sec., 350 W. 88th.

N. Y. Ophthalmological Soc.—44 mem. H. W. Wooton, Pres.; C. C. McDannold, Sec.-Treas., 100 W. 59th.

N. Y. Osteopathic Clinic—1913. 35 E. 32d. Open 7.30 to 9 p.m., except Wed. and Sat., 1.30 to 9 p.m. W. S. Jones, Pres.; M. Goodbody, Treas.

SOCIETIES AND ASSOCIATIONS—MEDICAL—MANHATTAN AND BRONX—*Continued.*

N. Y. Otological Soc.—1892. 30 mem. J. B. Rae, Pres.; J. R. Page, Sec., 127 E. 62d.

N. Y. Pathological Soc.—1844. 17 W. 43d. 200 mem. Jas. W. Jobling, M.D., Pres.; G. L. Rohdenburg, Sec., 1145 Amsterdam av.

N. Y. Physicians' Mutual Aid Assn.—(See Secret and Benefit Socs., miscellaneous.)

N. Y. Post-Graduate Clinical Soc.—1888. Post-Graduate Medical School & Hosp. 300 mem. G. F. Cahill, Pres.; H. V. Spaulding, Sec., 148 E. 58th; W. G. Vincent, Treas.

N. Y. Surgical Soc.—1879. Academy of Medicine. 60 mem. Dr. Wm. A. Downes, Pres.; Dr. R. S. Hooker, Sec., 175 E. 71st.

N. Y. Tuberculosis Assn.—Inc. 1919. 10 E. 39th. James A. Miller, M.D., Pres.; John S. Billings, M.D., Dir.; Mrs. B. F. Fuller, Exec. Sec.

Northwestern Med. and Surgical Soc. of N. Y. City—1869. 30 mem. Samuel Lloyd, M.D., Pres.; A. E. Biesser, M.D., Sec., 314 W. 58th.

Optometrical Soc. of N. Y.—1897. L. M. Mayer, Pres., 630 Faile; L. Hirschberg, Sec., 2 W. 125th.

Osteopathic Soc. of City of N. Y.—1899. 150 mem. Dr. C. R. Rogers, Pres.; Dr. Wm. D. Fitzwater, Sec., 178 Prospect Park W., Bkln.

Quiz Med. Soc.—1897. 160 mem. Dr. Henry W. Titus, Pres.; Dr. A. C. Burnham, Sec., 111 E. 48th.

Riverside Practitioners' Soc.—1900. 40 mem. Dr. Ed. Cook, Pres.; Dr. J. R. Graham, Sec., 202 W. 86th.

Rockefeller Inst. for Medical Research—66th and Ave. A. S. Flexner, Dir. of Lab.; R. Cole, Dir. of Hosp.; Theobald Smith, Dir. of Dept. of Animal Path.; E. B. Smith, Act. Bus. Mgr.

Soc. of Medical Jurisprudence—1883. N. B. Van Etten, M.D., Pres.; L. H. Moss, M.D., Sec., Richmond Hill, L. I.

Therapeutic Club—1891. 22 mem. W. L. Culbert, Sec., 16 E. 54th.

Woman's Hosp. Soc.—1887. 59 mem. Dr. F. A. Dorman, Pres.; Dr. R. E. Pou, Sec., 20 W. 50th.

Women's Med. Assn. of N. Y. City—1900. 190 mem. Dr. Ethel D. Brown, Pres.; Dr. Isabel MacMillan, Cor. Sec., 251 W. 97th.

Queens.

L. I. City Med. Soc.—1892. 38 mem. Dr. W. J. Burnett, Pres.; Dr. W. G. Frey, Sec., 205 Grand av., L. I. City.

Queens-Nassau Med. Soc.—1899. 210 mem. A. D. Jaques, M.D., Pres.; J. S. Cooley, M.D., Sec., Mineola, L. I.

Richmond.

Richmond Co. Med. Soc.—1896. S. I. Academy. 58 mem. Dr. A. H. Thomas, Pres., New Brighton; Dr. E. W. Presley, Sec., Great Kills.

MEN'S CHURCH CLUBS.

Brooklyn.

Council of Men's Church Clubs of Flatbush—1920. H. F. Gunnison, All Souls Univ. Ch., Pres.; T. P. Peters, St. Marks M. E. Ch., V.-Pres.; W. C. McKee, Flatbush Cong. Ch., Sec., 102 Court; E. W. Mandeville, St. Paul's P. E. Ch., Treas.

BAPTIST.

Berean—37 mem. C. H. Morten, Pres.; E. S. Matthews, Sec., 1672 Dean.

Men's Federation, Hanson pl.—250 mem. G. W. Bovonizer, Pres.; H. W. Weller, Sec., 350 85th.

CONGREGATIONAL.

Church of the Evangel—60 mem. H. H. Kellogg, Pres.; W. Thompson, Sec., 268 Hawthorne.

Flatbush—(Men's League)—250 mem. L. S. Richards, Pres.; R. S. Austin, Sec., 322 E. 19th.

Lewis Av.—100 mem. E. L. Dinsmore, Pres.; S. H. Sweet, Sec., 129 Reid av.

Ocean Av.—130 mem. A. C. H. Andesner, Pres.; L. W. Minchin, Sec., 2813 Av. N.

Park Slope—Geo. R. Warden, Pres., 776 7th.

Parkville—115 mem. S. D. MacDowell, Pres.; A. B. Nichols, Sec., 246 E. 8th.

St. Paul's—130 mem. W. L. Love, M.D., Pres.; A. F. Decker, Jr., Sec., 949 Park pl.

Tompkins Av.—Dr. O. S. Ritch, Pres.; H. H. Romer, Sec., 116 McDonough.

JEWISH.

Bnai Sholaum—150 mem. M. A. Markheim, Pres.; L. Wasserman, Sec., 309 15th.

Cong. B'nai Sholaum (9th St. Temple)—401 9th. M. Friedlander, Rabbi, 10 Pros. Pk. S. W.; M. Talmund, Sexton, 709 8th av.

LUTHERAN.

Bethlehem—30 mem. F. Heuer, Pres.; C. Huber, Sec., 868 E. 47th.

Immanuel—45 mem. F. W. Hinck, Pres.; F. L. Mattfeld, V.-Pres., 418 Tompkins av.; J. Schattauer, Cor. Sec., 263 Rutledge.

Messiah—51 mem. F. E. Frick, Pres.; Carsten H. Ludder, Sec., 161 Meserole av.

Reformation—35 mem. L. Eyring, Pres.; Joseph Frisse, Sec., 186 Warwick.

St. Peter's—175 mem. H. Lohmeyer, Pres.; W. Mahnken, Rec. Sec., 41 Quincy; C. Buhlert, Cor. Sec.

St. Peter's (Hale av.)—50 mem. H. Kramer, Pres.; L. Ritterbusch, Sec., 9524 112th, Richmond Hill.

Trinity (Norweg.)—1911. 70 mem. A. Larsen, Pres., 414 48th.

Zion Norwegian—46 mem. G. Thompson, Pres. K. E. Tobiassen, Sec., 605 57th.

METHODIST EPISCOPAL.

DeKalb Av.—15 mem. J. C. Boyle, Pres.; Wm. Biesecker, Sec., 494B Jefferson av.

First Primitive—19 mem. E. J. Curson, Pres.; C. B. Hague, Sec., 396 Classon av.

Goodsell Memorial—35 mem. H. R. Tucker, Pres.; C. A. Fleming, Sec., 458 Drew av.

Hanson Pl.—53 mem. Wm. Kennedy, Pres.; W. Boylhart, Sec., 13 Fort Greene pl.

Janes—S. W. Daniels, Pres., 658 Monroe; H. Martin, Sec., 569 Halsey.

N. Y. Av.—200 mem. Dr. Geo. C. Wood, Pres.; E. Vanderwater, Sec., 170 Bergen.

Nostrand Av.—Chas. B. Hobart, Sec., 101 Monroe.

St. Mark's—300 mem. Wm. M. Tomlins, Jr., Pres.; F. M. Ellis, Sec., 1231 E. 19th.

Summerfield—C. V. Driggs, Pres.; E. Helme, Sec., 60 Irving pl.; H. W. Mahan, Treas., 55 Hanson pl.

Vanderveer Pk.—60 mem. J. A. Gray, Pres.; J. M. Thompson, V.-Pres., 847 E. 34th.

Warren St.—Harry F. Roper, Sec., 26 Wyckoff.

PRESBYTERIAN.

Arlington Av.—82 mem. W. B. Tiebout, Pres.; A. C. Mitchell, Sec., 69 Highland pl.

Bethany—80 mem. Jas. Cox, Pres.; A. E. Bresee, Sec., 673 Halsey.

Borough Park—42 mem. F. M. Woods, Pres.; J. M. Brunjes, Sec., 457 E. 28th.

Central—W. S. Twiddy, Pres.; W. Hahn, Sec., 191 Jefferson av.

Classon Av.—J. B. McPherson, Pres.; H. B. Ventres, Sec., 366 Monroe.

1st Presbyterian (Bensonhurst)—45 mem. D. Stewart, Pres., 1775 W. 10th; W. Johnson, Sec., 1748 W. 9th.

Flatbush Young Men's—15 mem. H. W. Kleppel, Pres.; E. H. Noll, Sec., 1634 Kenmore pl.

Grace "The Brotherhood"—W. T. Read, Pres.; C. B. Gray, Sec., 612A Jefferson av.

Lafayette Av.—W. W. Owens, Pres.; R. D. Sumner, Sec., 543 4th.

Mount Olivet—100 mem. Chas. Muennich, Pres.; C. Breckle, Sec., 422 Classon av.

Noble St.—34 mem. Rev. R. R. Greenwood, Pres.; J. Morren, Sec., 203 Monitor.

Westminster—21 mem. J. E. Wight, Pres.; G. K. Smith, Sec., 272 Sackett.

PROTESTANT EPISCOPAL.

All Saints—350 mem. W. H. Raab, Pres.; J. A. Hoffman, Sec.

Calvary—A. E. Becker, Pres., 1090 Bushwick av.; S. F. Gerald, Sec.

Christ Church (73d)—W. I. Batty, Pres.; A. Gilmor, Sec.

Church of St. Mark (E. P'kway)—Hon. C. C. Johnson, Pres., 1468 Union; S. P. Bailey, Sec., 243 New York av.

Good Shepherd—H. Ormsbee, Pres., 435 Macon.

Messiah—100 mem. Dr. M. L. de Lorme, Sec., 61 Greene av.

Redeemer—J. Elliott, Sec., 175 Dean.

St. Mark's (Adelphi st.)—30 mem. A. J. Lambertson, Sec., 25 Irving pl.

St. Mary's—H. R. Macdonough, Sec., 230 Classon av.

St. Paul's (Flat.)—100 mem. F. G. Sherrill, Pres.; S. Remlein, Sec., 15 Snyder av.

Trinity (Hgts.)—400 mem. 157 Montague.

SOCIETIES AND ASSOCIATIONS—MEN'S CLUBS—BROOKLYN—*Continued.*

REFORMED.

Dutch Reformed (Flatbush)—E. B. Vanderveer, Pres.; H. A. Jewell, Sec., 185 Lenox rd.
Edgewood—40 mem. C. D. Anderson, Jr., Sec., 4819 11th av.
Emanuel—35 mem. Rev. W. Walenta, Pres.; Jacob Woll, Sec., 1533 Greene av.
First of Wmsburgh.—C. B. Bartram, Act. Pres.; H. Anson, Sec., 818 Vanderveer av., Woodhaven.
New Bkln.—45 mem. Rev. F. C. Erhardt, Pres.; M. Wuttke, Sec., 65 Hull.

UNITARIAN.

Men's Liberal Club—75 mem. R. P. Vidand, Pres., 161 Joralemon; L. M. Symmes, Treas.; J. H. Lathrop, Sec.; 98 Pierrepont.
Second—1907. 25 mem. J. F. Thompson, Pres.; Fred. Brickelmaier, Sec., 1111 Prospect pl.
Unity—25 mem. H. Stewart, Sec., 224 Clermont.

UNIVERSALIST.

All Souls—220 mem. E. B. Wilson, Pres.; W. R. Hill, Sec., 744 Rugby rd.
Church of Good Tidings—Stuyvesant av. and Madison. C. Schober, Pres.; C. Zahn, Sec.
Church of Our Father—75 mem. J. G. Murray, Pres.; E. L. Faris, Sec., 1280 Pacific.

Manhattan and Bronx.

BAPTIST.

First Mariners—F. R. Lombard, Pres., 310 12th, Bkln.
Washington Hgts.—100 mem. R. W. Murray, Pres.

CONGREGATIONAL.

Bethany—35 mem. J. R. Ellerwood, Pres.; Ed. Smith, Sec.-Treas.; J. A. McCagne, 455 10th av.

LUTHERAN.

Advent—30 mem. W. C. Ruth, Pres.; F. P. Freund, Sec., 730 Amsterdam av.
Bethany—40 mem. A. C. Man, Pres.; F. W. Schlatter, Sec., 901 Trinity av.
Christ—20 mem. Fred'k Benzer, Pres.; C. H. Dahmer, Sec., 2151 Morris av., Bronx.
Holy Trinity—25 mem. Geo. Koechig, Pres.; H. L. Gerken, Sec., 26 W. 85th.
St. John's Brotherhood—98 mem. F. Nutzhorn, Pres.; John Nusskern, Sec., 355 Bleecker.
St. Paul's—40 mem. C. Waltemade, Pres.; F. Schellenberg, Sec., 850 E. 156th.
St. Peter's (439 E. 140th)—86 mem. W. Straehler, Pres.; F. Brummer, Sec.; Rev. O. C. Mees, Pastor, 437 E. 140th.

METHODIST EPISCOPAL.

Grace—J. B. Shales, Pres.; R. Breveton, Sec.
St. James—60 mem. Dr. E. R. Birkins, Pres.
Fremont—H. P. Sykes, Pres.; Arthur Geiger, Sec.
Washington Hgts.—100 mem. Dr. H. E. Woolever, Pres., 150 5th av.

PRESBYTERIAN.

Christ—200 mem. A. M. Haas, Sec., 344 W. 36th.
Covenant—40 mem. E. S. Simons, Pres., 13 Maiden la.
Faith—90 mem. F. Harnack, Pres.; E. Shaefer, Sec., 349 W. 48th.
First Presbyterian Ch.—See Religious Socs.
Ft. Washington—135 mem. Thos. I. Crane, Pres., 715 W. 172d. Wm. Van Thoff, Sec., 188 Wadsworth av.
North—L. S. Benton, Pres.; W. J. Mann, Sec., 539 W. 155th.
Second—52 mem. Dr. J. McCabe, Pres.; Jas. Tyrer, Sec., 139 W. 101st.

PROTESTANT EPISCOPAL.

Calvary—120 mem. R. A. Youmans, Pres.; F. L. Swart, Sec.
Grace Chapel (414 E. 14th)—317 mem. Rev. E. White, Pres.
Holy Apostles—60 mem. R. C. Ballard, Sec., 361 W. 25th.
Holy Nativity—40 mem. Chas. Forbach, Pres.; F. Merk, Sec., 3204 Bainbridge av.
Holy Trinity (E. 88th)—75 mem. C. Risiguise, Pres.; F. Rollman, Sec., 316 E. 88th.
Holy Trinity (Lenox av. and 122d)—W. A. Ten Eick, Pres.; E. J. Byrne, Sec., 392 St. Nicholas av.
Intercession—84 mem. W. B. Mussen, Pres.; C. B. Rush, Sec., 617 W. 155th.
St. Albans—20 mem. V. Brewer, Sec., 969 Summit av.
St. Ann's (Morrisania)—50 mem. P. Ruempler, Pres.; J. F. Waring, Sec.
St. Bartholomew's—600 mem. Rev. L. Parks, Pres.; G. McVicker, Supt., 209 E. 42d.
St. John the Evangelist—50 mem. E. Bishop, Pres.; H. Thornquist, Sec., 224 Waverley pl.
St. Luke's (Convent av. and 141st)—75 mem. H. F. Wyckoff, Pres.
St. Margaret's—30 mem. C. H. Boyce, Pres.; T. J. Styles, Sec., 115 B'way.
St. Peter's—35 mem. J. Taffe, Sec., St. Peter's Hall, 340 W. 20th.
St. Philip's—115 mem. R. C. Clark, Pres.; Joseph Madocer, Sec., 626 Lenox av.

REFORMED.

Martha Mem.—16 mem. Rev. E. Burger, Pres.; Wm. Schweizer, Jr., Sec., 665 10th av.; F. Bauer, Treas.
Zion (German)—24 mem. Rev. A. F. Hahn, Pres., 1288 Stebbins av.

Queens.

CONGREGATIONAL.

Christ (Woodhaven)—R. J. Jordan, Sec., 4054 85th rd.
Pilgrim (Bkln. Hills)—84 mem. J. P. Vickery, Pres.; A. H. Griebert, Sec., 9215 107th, Richmond Hill, L. I.

LUTHERAN.

St. Luke's—30 mem. F. E. Tilly, Pres.; L. H. Meyer, Sec., 367 Ferry, Woodhaven.
Zion (Scandinavian)—30 mem. M. Nybo, Pres.; J. Ayre, Sec.

PRESBYTERIAN.

Ridgewood (Forest and Halleck avs.)—C. W. Froessel, Pres., Glendale; C. A. Baecker, Jr., Sec.
First German of E. W'msburg (28 Prospect av., Bkln., Sta. J))—75 mem. M. Linhardt, Pres.; G. Eckert, Sec.
First (Jamaica) (Men's League)—105 mem. R. W. Hunter, Pres., 343 Hillside av.
First (Jamaica) (Ushers' League)—42 mem. W. H. Bergen, Pres., Old So. rd., Jamaica.
French Evangelical (Woodhaven)—24 mem. G. Baechler, Pres.; E. P. Tournu, Sec.

PROTESTANT EPISCOPAL.

All Saints (Bayside)—143 mem. R. P. Magee, Pres.; C. Watson, Sec.
Grace (Jamaica)—115 mem. J. L. Wiltse, Pres., 61 Herriman av., Jamaica; L. Duchate, Sec., 26 Canonbury rd., Jamaica.
Grace (Corona)—34 mem. J. De Jongh, Pres.; J. S. Morrison, Sec., 62 54th.
St. Paul's (Woodside)—45 mem. J. Watson, Pres.; Ch. Story, Sec., 24 5th, Woodside, L. I.

REFORMED.

Flushing—200 mem. R. Martin, Pres.; E. E. Bates, Sec., 393 Amity, Flushing.

Richmond.

Grace M. E. (Pt. Richmond)—40 mem. J. H. Knoebel, Pres.; H. E. Parker, Sec., 85 Albion pl., Pt. Richmond.
Reformed (Pt. Richmond)—160 mem. R. H. Smith, Pres.; W. M. Walsh, Sec., 55 Anderson av.

MUSICAL SOCIETIES.

National.

Amer. Guild of Organists—1896. 29 Vesey, Mhtn. 2,000 mem. Dr. Victor Baier, Warden; Oscar F. Comstock, Gen. Sec.
Juilliard Musical Foundation—1917. Eugene A. Noble, Sec., 136 W. 44th, Mhtn.
Music Publishers Assn. of the U. S. (Inc.)—1895. 8-12 E. 34th, Mhtn. C. A. Woodman, Pres.; E. T. Paull, Sec., 243 W. 42d, Mhtn.
Music Teachers Natl. Assn.—1876. 500 mem. C. N. Boyd, Pres.; Robt. G. McCutchan, Sec., De Pauw Univ., Greencastle, Ind.
Natl. Assn. of Organists—1907. 800 mem. Henry S. Fry, Pres.; W. N. Waters, Sec., 24 W. 60th, Mhtn.
National Opera Club of America—1914. Waldorf-Astoria. 1,000 mem. Katherine Von Klenner, Pres.; Katherine N. Fique, Sec., 128 DeKalb av., Bkln.; Carl Fique, Mus. Dir.

State.

N. Y. State Music Teachers' Assn.—1889. F. H. Haywood, Pres.; S. L. Elmer, Gen. Sec.-Treas., 188 Hawthorne, Bkln.

SOCIETIES AND ASSOCIATIONS—MUSICAL—BROOKLYN—*Continued.*

Brooklyn.

Note—(See also German Socs.)

Aeolian Orchestra—1912. 121 New York av. 40 mem. F. H. Earll, Pres.; Grace Bellows, Conductor 289 Putnam av.

Aeos Soc.—1902. 25 mem. A. F. DePear, Pres.; Wm. J. Hess, Sec., 589 St. Marks av.

Apollo Club—1878. 381 Carlton av. 90 mem. J. A. Smith, Pres.; D. Wescoat, Sec., 69 So. Oxford; J. H. Brown, Cond., 88 So. Oxford.

Argyle Orchestra—1914. 558 81st. 32 mem. W. L. Schweikert, Pres. and Dir.

Arion Singing Soc.—1865. 1002 Bushwick av. 675 mem. Dr. L. Koempel, Pres.; C. W. Gitterman, Sec., 30 Belvidere; E. Scharpf, Mus. Dir.

Arion Ladies' Soc.—Mrs. Louis Brass, Pres.; Miss B. Holsten, Sec.

Arion Dramatic Circle—1906. Dr. G. E. Seyfarth, Dir.; Miss A. Benedict, Sec.

Arion Orchestra—W. J. Peterson, Sr., Pres.; R. Gleissner, Cond.

Arion Ladies' Chorus—Mrs. L. Frese, Pres.; Mrs. O. Gaartner, Sec.

Arion Country Club—Greenwood Lake, N. J. E. H. Hupe, Pres.; M. Werner, Sec.

Assn. for Promoting the Endowment and Development of the Master Schl. of Music—1904. 110 Remsen. Mrs. T. S. Coffin, Pres.; Miss E. M. York, Regr.

Baptist Temple Choir—3d av. and Schermerhorn. 200 mem. W. A. Luyster, Dir., 555 Rugby rd.

Bkln. Choral Soc.—1907. 82 Lewis av. 150 mem. T. B. Glasson, Dir.; Wm. Wise, Pres.

Bkln. Community Chorus (Affiliated with People's Inst. of Bkln.)—176 Nassau. 850 mem. Jas. J. McCabe, Pres.; W. V. Trevoy, Exec. Sec.; Chas. S. Yerbury, Dir.

Bkln. Inst. Sight Singing Class—Academy of Music. 100 mem. C. G. Schmidt, Dir., 246 Hancock.

Bkln. Letter Carriers Band—1909. 1155 Fulton. 40 mem. W. J. Galloway, Pres.; F. J. Fritz, Sec., P. O. Sta. A; H. J. Cochrane, Bandmaster, 296 Halsey.

Bkln. Music School Settlement—See Educational Socs.

Bkln. Oratorio Soc.—1893. Memorial Hall, Schermerhorn. 150 mem. Walter H. Hall, Cond., 39 Claremont av., Mhtn. Under auspices of Columbia Univ. and Bkln Inst.

Bkln. Orchestral Soc.—1889. 60 mem. H. Leipnicker, Pres.; S. H. Lifshey, Sec., 1261 Bedford av.

Bkln. Quartet Club—1871. 75 mem. Prospect Hall. H. Langhorst, Pres.; M. Koeppe, Sec., 653 5th av.

Bkln. Symphony Orchestra—1897. Imperial, Red Hook lane and Fulton. 65 mem. Louis Strauss, Pres.; Geo. F. Flint, Con.

Bkln. Symphony Soc.—Acad. of Music. 1909. 1,220 mem. F. A. M. Burrell, Pres.

Bushwick Community Chorus—50 mem. T. B. Glasson, Dir., 80 Chauncey; C. Sheehan, Pres.

Bushwick Musical Art Soc.—1920. Anton W. Droge, Cond., 1096 B'way.

Chaminade (The) (Ladies Glee Club)—1897. 59 mem. Mrs. Theo. M. Hardy, Pres.; Mrs. E. W. White, Sec., 523 Madison.

Concordia East New York—1859. Fulton and Elton. 230 mem. Chas. H. Veit, Pres.; Emil Martin, Sec.; Carl Hein, Cond.

Conductor Singing Soc., E. N. Y.—2986 Fulton. 250 mem. Chas. H. Veit Sr., Pres.; Emil Martin, Sec.; C. Hein, Cond.

Choral Art Club of Bkln.—1912. 80 mem. A. M. Best, Pres.; H. A. Leggett, Sec., 64 Hancock, Bkln.

Educational Alliance—(See Educational Soc.).

Gillette Glee Club—1910. 582 Flatbush av. 40 mem. Miss H. T. Murphy, Pres.; Miss M. K. Lynch, Sec.

Harmony Glee Club—1894. Palm Garden, 150 mem. Lawrence Derva, Pres.; J. E. Miller, Sec., 1407 Jefferson av.

Juvenile Bkln. Choral Soc.—82 Lewis av. 500 mem. T. B. Glasson, Cond.; Rev. J. W. Moore, Pres.

Indep. Quartet Club—1900. Knickerbocker and DeKalb avs. M. Kaupp, Pres.; H. Bernhardt, Sec.; Ernest Scharpf, Cond.

Laurier Musical Club—1893. 73 mem. L. D. Broughton, Pres.; Miss M. Thoubborn, Sec., 454 5th.

McKinley Orchestra—30 mem. C. O. Morgan, Pres.; C. Weber, Sec. and Mgr., 316 Grant av.

Morning Choral—1919. 40 mem. Mrs. H. B. Tibbetts, Pres.; Mrs. B. W. Colvin, Cor. Sec., 150 Martense.

Mundell Choral Club—1914. 152 Hancock 325 mem. Mrs. C. L. Nichols, Pres.; Miss R. S. Hoogland, Sec., 602 St. Mark's av.; Miss M. L. Mundell, Dir.

Musical and Literary Coterie of E. N. Y.—1873. 64 mem. 113 Arlington av. F. C. Lang, Pres.; C. H. Penny, Sec., 131 Warwick.

Nightingale Club—1894. 100 mem. Mrs. Emma G. Christ, Pres., 990 Madison; Miss Rose O'Brien, Sec., 265 Hooper.

Orchestral Soc. of Bkln. (The)—60 professional musicians. T. B. Glasson, Dir.; J. Lynch, Concert Master, 82 Lewis av.

Peoples' Singing Classes, branches of Peoples' Choral Union—Frank Damrosch, Dir. P. S. No. 15, Thurs., 8 P.M.

Philharmonic Soc. of Bkln.—1857. W. H. Crittenden, Sec., 309 B'way, N. Y. C.

Philomela Ladies' Glee Club—835 Lincoln pl. 1904. 42 mem. Mrs. H. Krey, Pres.; Mrs. L. H. Emerson, Sec., 277 Lefferts av.

Popular (Public) Sight Singing Classes—1893. Beginners and advanced classes, meet Tu. eve., at Memorial Hall, Y. W. C. A. Bldg., Schermerhorn and Flatbush av. 400 mem. W. A. Luyster, Dir., 555 Rugby rd.

Schumann Club—1882. 30 mem. Mrs. J. S. Frothingham, Pres.; Mrs. B. B. Mosher, Sec., 11 Schermerhorn.

Studio Club of Bkln.—1892. "Rusurban," 105 Lefferts pl. 30 mem. G. LeFort Buys, Dir.

Twelfth St. Band and Field Music—60 mem. A. A. Spence, Drum Major; Geo. Wirth, Adjt., 437 3d, Bkln.

University Glee Club—1900. Univ. Club. Clinton H. Heard, Pres.; G. B. Shults, Sec.

Wm. H. Hubbell Camp No. 4 (Spanish War Vets.)—Field Music—1914. 292 Hamburg av. 35 mem. J. Cornell, Major; Geo. Merritt, Sec., 1727 Bleecker.

Woodman Choral Club—1903. Packer Institute. 80 mem. Mrs. H. C. Edwards, 754 Halsey st., Pres.; Mrs. Clark Burnham, Sec., 182 Clinton.

Manhattan and Bronx.

Armenian Students' Assn. of Amer.—1910. 300 mem. Prof. D. Kabakjian, Pres., Univ. of Pa., Phila., Pa.; L. Kazanjian, Sec.

Betrand De Bernyz American Opera Concert and Oratorio Soc. of N. Y.—58 W. 72d. Prof. B. De Bernyz, Pres.; L. C. Harper, Sec.

Choral Soc. of N. Y. Police Dept.—(See Police Glee Club.)

Clef Club—(See Singers and Players of G. N. Y.)

Glee Club of Friendly Sons of St. Patrick—Meets W., 8:15 P M., at Hotel Astor. 45 mem. W. J. Clark, Pres.; W. A. Luyster, Dir., 555 Rugby rd., Bkln.

Mendelssohn Glee Club—1866. 50-52 E. 41st. 60 active, 150 mem. John T. Gillespie, Pres.; W. P. Young, Sec., 76 William.

Met. Life Ins. Glee—Meets Wed., 4:30 P.M., in auditorium of Home Office, 1 Madison av. 36 mem. F. M. Knight, Pres.; Dr. Ion Jackson, Cond., Briarcliff Manor, N. Y.

Music League of America—1 W. 34th. J. I. Adams, Pres.; Marie Keickhofer, Sec.

Musical Art Soc. of N. Y.—1893. Choir of 75. Frank Damrosch, Mus. Dir.; J. S. Sheppard, Sec., 27 Cedar.

N. Y. Bass Drum Club—1878. 100 mem. Ed. Canavann, Pres.; A. Lederhaus, Sec., 210 E. 86th.

N. Y. Community Chorus—1916. 5 Columbus Circle, Mhtn. Mrs. Wm. Shannon, Pres.; H. Barnhart, Dir., 130 E. 22d.

N. Y. Euphony Soc.—1919. Waldorf-Astoria. Mrs. J. J. Gormley, Pres.; Mrs. W. C. Crane, Sec., 500 W. 143d.

N. Y. Federation of Musicians, Inc.—1253 Lex. av. L. A. Steeg, Pres.; J. Marnet, Sec.

N. Y. Mozart Soc.—1909. Hotel Astor. 600 mem. Mrs. Noble McCornell, Pres.; Mrs. Jos. Root, Sec.

Oratorio Soc. of N. Y. (The)—1873. 1 W. 34th. 1,000 mem. C. M. Schwab, Pres.

People's Choral Union of N. Y. C.—1892. 1556 B'way. Joseph Fleming, Pres.; Miss A. Schneider, Sec.; Miss B. M. Palmer, Treas.; Frank Damrosch, Dir.; E. G. Marquard, Cond.

Philharmonic Soc. of N. Y.—1842. 1,000 mem. F. F. Leifels, Sec., Carnegie Hall; Josef Stransky, Cond.

SOCIETIES AND ASSOCIATIONS—MUSICAL—MANHATTAN AND BRONX—*Continued*

Police Glee Club—1916. C. L. Stafford, Dir., 71st Regt. Armory.

Rubinstein Club of N. Y.—1887. Waldorf-Astoria. 550 mem. Mrs. W. R. Chapman, Pres.; Miss Mary J. Baker, Sec., 351 W. 114th.

Schola Cantorum of New York—333 4th av. (Mixed Chorus.) 200 mem. Kurt Schindler, Cond.

Schumann Club of N. Y.—1913. 47 W. 72d. 60 mem. Mrs. Wm. T. Mullally, Pres.; Mrs. Wm. Davidson, Sec.

Singers and Players' Soc. of G. N. Y.—410 mem. Deacon Johnson, Pres. and Dir. Mgr., 134 W. 53d.

Symphony Soc. of N. Y.—1878. 33 W. 42d. H. H. Flagler, Pres.; Richard Welling, Sec., 2 Wall; Carrie Young, Cor. Sec.

University Glee Club of N. Y. C.—1894. 30 E. 42d. 100 active, 200 associate mem. W. S. Haskell, Pres.; D. J. Miller, Sec.

Verdi Club—1917. Waldorf-Astoria. 550 mem. Mrs. F. F. Jenkins, Pres.; Mrs. Leslie Hall, Sec., Haworth, N. J.

Queens.

Musical Soc. of Jamaica—1889. 73 mem. Mrs. J. H. Rumph, Pres.; Mrs. H. G. Doran, Sec., 165 Shelton av., Jamaica.

PATRIOTIC AND COMMEMORATIVE SOCIETIES.

(See Index for War Relief Organizations, The American Legion and War Veterans' Associations.)

International and National.

Amer. Cross of Honor—1898. Washington, D. C. T. H. Herndon, Pres., Washington, D. C.; A. M. Taylor, Sec.

Amer. Flag Assn.—1898. 2,000 mem. C. A. Pugsley, Pres.; C. E. Leonard, Sec., Caryl, Yonkers, N. Y.

Amer. Flag House and Betsy Ross Mem. Assn.—1898. 1,750,000 mem. 239 Arch, Phila. W. A. Carr, Pres.; C. H. Weisgerber, Cor. Sec.

Amer. Irish Historical Soc.—1897. 35 W. 39th, Mhtn. 1,368 mem. J. I. C. Clarke, Pres.; S. C. Cahill, Sec.

Amer. Rights League—1915. 2 W. 45th. For upholding the duty of the Republic in international relations. Major Geo. Haven Putnam, Pres.; L. F. Abbott, Sec.

Amer. Scenic and Historic Preservation Soc.—1895. 500 mem. G. F. Kunz, Pres.; E. H. Hall, Sec., Tribune Bldg., Mhtn.

Amer. School Citizenship League—1908. 405 Marlborough, Boston, Mass. 10,000 mem. R. J. Condon, Pres., Cincinnati, O.; Mrs. Fannie F. Andrews, Sec.

Army and Navy Legion of Valor of U. S. of Amer. G. W. Brush, M.D., Com., 633 E. 16th; J. Brosnan, Adj., 389 3d, Bkln. 230 1st class mem., 77 2d class mem. Composed of men who were awarded medals of honor by Congress and the Distinguished Service Cross for conspicuous gallantry in action.

Army and Navy Union, U. S. A.—1888. 2,228 State, Milwaukee, Wis. 100,000 mem. Lucas A. Van Toor, Natl. Com.; H. W. Lee, Adj.-Gen., 128 E. Price, Phila., Pa.

Army of the Tennessee Assn.—1892. Washington, D. C. H. L. Deam, Pres.; B. W. Bonney, Sec., 1724 Lanier pl., N. W., Washington, D. C.

Assn. for Preservation of Virginia Antiquities—1889. Richmond, Va. 1,500 mem. Mrs. J. T. Ellyson, Pres., 10 E. Franklin, Richmond, Va.; Mrs. J. E. Robinson, Cor. Sec., Richmond, Va.

Aztec Club of 1847—205 mem. Officers of Army, Navy and Marine Corps in Mexican War. Perpetuated by naming as successor son of nearest in blood male relative. H. G. Gibson, Pres.; W. S. Abert, Sec., 1520 H., N. W. Washington, D. C.

Carnation League of Amer. (The)—1901. Members wear carnations, ex-Pres. McKinley's favorite flower, Jan. 29, the anniversary of his birth. L. G. Reynolds, Pres, Dayton, O.

Church Woman's League for Patriotic Service—1919. Mrs. Hamilton Fairfax, Natl. Pres., 8 W. 47th, N. Y. C.

Colonial Dames, Natl. Soc. of—1892. Council meets in Washington every 2 yrs. 9,000 mem. Mrs. J. R. Lamar, Pres.; Mrs. B. Wendell, Sec., Boston, Mass.

Colonial Dames of Amer. (The)—1890. 324 Lexington av., Mhtn. Mrs. T. M. Cheesman, Pres.; Miss E. B. Borrowe, Sec., 507 Madison av.

Colonial Wars, General Soc.—1892. 43 Cedar, Mhtn. 5,600 mem. Wm. Whitehead Ladd, Gov.-Gen.; H. A. Griffin, Sec.-Gen.

Confederate Memorial Literary Soc.—1896. Confederate Museum, Richmond, Va. Miss S. A. Anderson, Pres.

Confederate Southern Memorial Assn.—Mrs. Bryan W. Collier, Cor. Sec.-Gen., College Park, Ga.

Conference Committee on Natl. Preparedness—1915. 1133 B'way, Mhtn. Henry A. Wise Wood, Pres.; Jos. E. Clarke, Sec.

Congress of States Soc.—Hotel Gregorian. Mrs. T. J. Vivian, Pres.; Mrs. C. D. Hirst, Cor. Sec., 137 W. 75th, Mhtn.

Daughters of Amer. Revolution, Natl. Soc.—1890. Memorial Continental Hall, Washington, D. C. 110,350 mem. Mrs. Geo. Maynard Minor, Pres.-Gen.; Mrs. A. Marshall Elliott, Cor. Sec.-Gen.

N. Y. State Society—Mrs. Chas. W. Nash, Regent, Albany, N. Y.; Mrs. Chas. G. Cavanagh, Sec., Bronxville.

Battle Pass Chapter, Bkln.—1905. 59 mem. Mrs. F. H. Baldwin, Regent; Miss J. C. Morton, Sec., 447 Macon.

Ft. Greene Chapter, Bkln.—1896. 226 mem. Mrs. Wm. C. Beecher, Regent, 123 Columbia hgts.; Mrs. L. G. Baldwin, Cor. Sec., 28 Schermerhorn.

Mhtn. Chapter—1898. Mhtn. 125 mem. Mrs. J. B. F. Horreshoff, Regent, 620 West End av.; Mrs. Harvey Seif, Cor. Sec., 203 Park pl., Bkln.

N. Y. City Chapter—1891. 460 mem. Mrs. A. W. Cochran, Regent, 101 W. 85th; Mrs. O. A. Hyde, Rec. Sec.

Knickerbocker Chapter, Mhtn.—1897. 77 mem. Mrs. Simon Baruch, Regent; Miss E. Christie, Sec., Washington sq., Mhtn.

Mary Washington Colonial Chapter, Mhtn.—1896. 160 mem. Miss M. Van B. Vanderpoel, Regent, 30 E. 53d.

Gen. Nathaniel Woodhull Chapter, N. Y. C.—Mrs. T. A. Hay, Regent, 436 Cornelia, Boonton, N. J.; Mrs. Wm. Brough, Cor. Sec., 469 4th, Bkln.; Miss Ruth Woodhull Barnes, Treas., 112 Hempstead av., Hempstead.

Women of '76 Chapter, Bkln.—72 mem. Mrs. F. H. Parcells, Regent; Mrs. R. O. Bothfeld, Cor. Sec., 238 75th, Bkln.

Daughters of Michigan in N. Y.—Mrs. Nellie B. Van Slingerland, Pres.; Mrs. Emma H. McKee, Sec., 160 Congress, Bkln.

Daughters of the Revolution—1891. 33 W. 42d. 3,000 mem. Mrs. Chas. E. Wolbert, Pres.-Gen.; Mrs. W. L. Cunningham, Cor. Sec.-Gen., 2351 Grand Concourse, The Bronx.

Alice Adams Chapter—1909. 45 mem. Mrs. Henry Phillips, Regent; Mrs. A. T. Shorey, Cor. Sec.

Colonial Chapter—Mrs. L. V. Miller, Regent, 276 W. 94th, Mhtn.

Fort Washington Chapter—30 mem. Mrs. J. P. Marshall, Regent, 305 W. 87th, Mhtn.; Mrs. J. Wickham, Sec., 19 W. 106th.

Knickerbocker Chapter—50 mem. Mrs. B. F. Fischer, Regent; Mrs. C. E. Banker, Sec., 307 W. 93d, Mhtn.

L. I. Soc.—1891. 384 mem. Mrs. E. J. Grant, Regent; Mrs. T. Mook, Sec., 72 Hooper, Bkln.

N. Y. State Soc.—1891. Mrs. John F. Hemenway, Regent, 230 W. 76th; Mrs. H. W. Will, Cor. Sec., 138 Prospect ave., Mamaroneck.

New Rochelle Huguenot Chap.—30 mem. Mrs. H. W. Will, Regent.

Mapeckenack Chap., Port Jervis, N. Y.—20 mem. Mrs. C. F. Van Inwegen, Regent.

Daughters of the Union—See National Soc., Daughters of the Union.

Gen. Soc. of Mayflower Descendants—1897. 3,400 mem. Maj.-Gen. Leonard Wood, Gov.-Gen.; A. P. Monroe, Sec.-Gen., 66 Paterson, Providence, R. I. Societies exist in N. Y., Conn., Mass., Pa., Ill., D. C., Ohio, N. J., Wis., R. I., Mich., Me., Col., Cal., Washington, Kan. and Ind. Triennial Congress, Plymouth, Mass., Sept., 1921.

George Washington Memorial Assn.—1898. Washington, D. C. 1,500 mem. Mrs. H. F. Dimock, Pres.; Mrs. N. H. Henry, Sec.; Mrs. F. Northrop, Treas., 21 W. 51st, Mhtn.

Grover Cleveland Birthplace Memorial Assn.—1913. Caldwell, N. J. J. H. Finley, Pres.; W. H. Van Wart, Sec. and Treas., 346 B'way, Mhtn.

SOCIETIES AND ASSOCIATIONS—PATRIOTIC AND COMMEMORATIVE—INT. & NAT'L.—*Continued.*

Guadalupe Club—Mrs. J. J. Nicholson, Pres.; Miss M. L. Hazzard, Cor. Sec., The Farragut, Washington, D. C.

Guardians of Liberty—1304 Masonic Temple, Chicago. Lt. Gen. N. A. Miles, Pres.; H. W. Korsgren, Sec. Exec. Com.

Huguenot Soc. of Amer.—1883. 2 W. 45th, Mhtn. 450 mem. Wm. Mitchell, Esq., Pres.; Miss Margaret A. Jackson, Sec.

Imperial Order. Daughters of the British Empire in the U. S.—Mrs. L. W. Fox, Pres.; Mrs. P. H. Gregory, Sec., 20 W. 83d, Mhtn.

N. Y. City Chapters: King Edward VII, Mrs. Gregory, Regent; King George V, Mrs. C. Y. Sharp, Regent; Victoria, Mrs. Henry Rowley, Regent; Sir George Augustus Elliott, Mrs. Fitzhugh, Regent; Nelson, Mrs. George Quirk, Regent; Niagara, Mrs. Kennard Thomson, Regent; Princess Louise, Mrs. Elkins, Regent; Coronation, Mrs. Webb, Regent; Sir John French, Mrs. Rew, Regent; Beaconsfield, Mrs. Raphael, Regent; Sir Walter Scott, Miss Yvonne Paul, Regent; Lady Borden, Mrs. A. J. Squiers, Regent; Princess Patricia, Mrs. A. O. Tate, Regent; William Shakespeare, Mrs. David Schmitt, Regent; British Isles, Mrs. Arnold, Regent; Lady Wolverton, Mrs. Howell, Regent; Margaret Poulson Murray, Mrs. Walton, Regent; Strathcona, Mrs. Heale, Regent; Waterloo, Mrs. Samuel Jackson, Regent; Baden Powell Chapter for Girls, Miss M. G. Bousfield, Regent.

Inter-Racial Council—233 B'way, Mhtn. Coleman DuPont, Ch.; Wm. H. Barr, Pres.; M. I. Pupin, Sec.

League for Preservation of Amer. Independence—1919. 1133 B'way, Mhtn. Col. Henry Watterson, Pres.; Henry A. Wise Wood, Sec.; Jas. E. Clark, Mgr. Natl. Hdqtrs. Offices also at 418 Union Trust Bldg., Washington, D. C., and 806 Little Bldg., Boston, Mass.

Loyal Coalition—1920. 24 Mt. Vernon, Boston, Mass. Demarest Lloyd, Pres.; Geo. W. Solley, Sec.

Military Order of Foreign Wars—Brig. Gen. S. W. Fountain, Com. Gen., Devon, Pa.; Major David Banks, Sec.-Gen., 23 Park pl., Mhtn.

Military Order of the Loyal Legion of the U. S.—1865. Flanders Bldg., Phila. 6,727 mem. Lieut.-Gen. N. A. Miles, Com.-in-Chief; Brevet Lieut.-Col. J. P. Nicholson, Recorder-in-Chief, 15th and Walnut, Phila., Pa.

Military Order of the Loyal Legion of U. S. Commandery of State of N. Y.—1866. 140 Nassau. 776 mem. Rear Admiral Chas. D. Sigsbee, U. S. N., Com.; Brevet Lieut-Col. W. S. Cogswell, U. S. Vol., Recorder.

Military Order of the World War—1920. 13,500 officers. Gen. Geo. H. Harries, Com.-in-Chief; Capt. C. C. Walton, Jr., Adj.-Gen., 707 Mutual Bldg., Richmond, Va.

Military Soc. of the Frontier—1919. Gordon M. Ash, Pres.; Robt. J. F. McGovern, Sec., 35 N. Pearl, Bridgeton, N. J.

Mount Vernon Ladies' Assn. of the Union—1853. 37 mem. Miss H. C. Comegys, Regent; A. B. Jennings, Rec. Sec., Fairfield, Conn.

Natl. Americanization Comm. — Affiliated with Inter-Racial Council.

Natl. League for Woman's Service—Demobilized Mar. 1, 1920.

Natl. Security League—1914. Hdqtrs., 17 E. 49th, Mhtn. 100,000 mem. Conducting campaign of patriotic education to spread knowledge of constitutional government. Chas. D. Orth, Pres.; E. L. Harvey, Exec. Sec.

Natl. Soc. Children of Amer. Revolution—1895. Washington, D. C. Male and female descendants (minors) of men or women who aided cause of American Independence, as soldiers, sailors, civil officers or recognized patriots. 15,000 mem. Mrs. Chas. W. Brown, Cor. Sec., 1825 Wyoming av., N. W., Washington, D. C.

Natl. Soc. Daughters of the Union—1912. Waldorf-Astoria, Mhtn. 1,000 mem. Mrs. Frank Crowell, Founder. Mrs. Chas. H. Masury, Pres.-Gen.; Mrs. Jas. M. Stewart, Sec., 120 Riverside dr., Mhtn.

Charter Chapter—Dr. F. W. Monell, Regent, 155 W. 75th, Mhtn. Mrs. Wm. R. Stewart, Hon. Regent; Mrs. T. J. Vivian, Sec., 312 Manhattan av., Mhtn.

Natl. Soc. of New England Women.—Mrs. R. F. Cummings, Pres.-Gen.; Mrs. L. A. Welles, Cor. Sec.-Gen., Bronxville, N. Y.

Natl. Soc. of Ohio Women—1904. Mrs. G. M. Clyde, Pres., 229 Lincoln pl., Bkln.

Natl. Soc. of U. S. Daughters of 1812—3,500 mem. Mrs. C. F. R. Jenne, Hartford, Conn., Pres.; Mrs. S. W. Earle, Sec., No. Bank Note Co., Chicago.

State of N. Y. Chap.—1892. 361 mem. Mrs. W. Gerry Slade, Pres., Waldorf-Astoria; Miss M. T. Douglas, Sec.

"Frigate Constitution" Chap. (Bkln.)—Mrs. G. B. Wallis, Regent, 103 Herkimer; Miss L. M. Peck, Sec.

State of Iowa—1906. 54 mem. Mrs. Wood, Regent; Miss M. C. Key, Sec., Council Bluffs, Ia.

Natl. Star-Spangled Banner Assn. of the U. S. A.—1914. Baltimore, Md. J. H. Preston, Pres.; A. S. Goldsborough, Sec., Merchants and Mfrs. Assn., Baltimore, Md.

Naval Order of the U. S.—1890. 356 mem. W. A. Dripps, Gen.-Recorder, 5011 Cedar av., Phila., Pa.

Naval History Soc.—1912. J. Barnes, Pres.; Rear Admiral Bradley A. Fiske, Sec., 35 W. 42d, Mhtn.; R. S. Sloan, Treas.

Navy League of U. S.—1903. 20,000 mem. Lieut.-Col. Henry Breckinridge, Pres.; Wm. M. Galvin, Sec., 528 17th, N. W., Washington, D. C.

Old Time Telegraphers' and Historical Assn. —1880. 1,300 mem. Geo. D. Perry, Pres.; T. E. Fleming, Sec., 195 B'way, Mhtn.

Order of Descendants of Colonial Governors (Hereditary)—1896. Men and women descendants of governors prior to 1750, incl. those who are members of Colonial Dames, Mayflower Descendants and Soc. of Colonial Wars. Miss Gail Treat, Gov.-Gen., East Orange, N. J.

Order of the Founders and Patriots of Amer. —1896. 1,000 mem. H. V. Ames, Univ. of Penn., Gov.-Gen.; W. F. Dix, Sec.-Gen., 34 Nassau, Mhtn.

N. Y. Soc.—1908. 234 mem. H. S. Kissam, Gov.; B. de Beixedon, Sec., 44 Wall, Mhtn.

Order of Pequot and King Phillip—1902. 50 mem. O. L. Frisbee, Ch. for New England States. 200 Cass, Portsmouth, N. H.

Order of Washington—1895. Washington, D. C. 150 mem. Rear Adm. C. H. Stockton, Com.-Gen.; Alfred B. Dent, Sec.-Gen., 900 F, Washington, D. C.

Pan-Amer. Soc. of the U. S.—J. B. Moore, Pres.; H. E. Bard, Sec.

Patriotic Order of Americans—1897. 43,200 mem. Columbus, O. Mrs. Laura L. Beck, Natl. Pres.; G. W. Smith, Natl. Sec., Phillipsburg, N. J.

Patriotic Order Sons of Amer.—1847. 1617 N. Broad, Phila., Pa. G. H. Moyer, Natl. Pres.; H. A. Miller, Sec., 1157 Butler, Easton, Pa.

State Camp of N. Y.—1898. 3,800 mem. I. Britt, Pres.; A. P. Yelvington, Sec., 35 Lewis, Binghamton, N. Y.

Pocahontas Memorial Assn.—1905. Inc. 1906. Washington, D. C. 3,200 mem. Miss E. L. Dorsey, Pres.; Miss L. Reed, Cor. Sec., 6 Iowa Circle, Washington, D. C.

Roosevelt Memorial Assn.—1919. 1 Madison av., N. Y. C. W. B. Thompson, Pres.; H. Hagedorn, Sec.

Soc. of Amer. Officers—See Manhattan Socs.

Soc. of Army and Navy of Confederate States in State of Md.—1871. 409 N. Charles, Baltimore, Md. 510 mem. Lieut. McH. Howard, Pres.; Capt. W. L. Ritter, Sec., Reisterstown, Md.

Society of the Army of Santiago de Cuba—Org. 1898 in Governor's Palace, Santiago de Cuba, "to record history and conserve the memory of the events of the campaign between June 14th and July 17th, 1898." Only those participating in Cuba between those dates are eligible to membership. Pres., Gen. E. D. Dimmick; Sec.-Treas., Col. C. A. Williams, U. S. A.; Historian, Maj. G. Creighton Webb; Reg.-Gen., Gen. P. Reade. Mem., 1,190.

Soc. of the Army of the Potomac—1869. 3,000 mem. Pres., vacant; C. A. Shaw, Treas., 1062 Park pl., Bkln.

Soc. of the Army of Tennessee—1870. Gen. S. Fallows, Pres.; S. Hickendooper, Rec. Sec., Court House, Cincinnati, O.

Soc. of the Cincinnati—1783. 1,020 mem. Hon. Winslow Warren, Pres.-Gen., Dedham, Mass.

Soc. of Descendants of Henry Wolcott—Judson E. Wolcott, Pres., Leader Bldg., Cleveland, O.; Mary Wolcott, Green, Sec., Englewood, Fla.

Soc. of Illinois Women—Mrs. T. S. Slack, Pres.; Mrs. E. H. McKee, Sec., 160 Congress, Bkln.

SOCIETIES AND ASSOCIATIONS—PATRIOTIC AND COMMEMORATIVE—INT. & NAT'L.—*Continued.*

Soc. of Sponsors of U. S. Navy—1909. 918 18th, N. W., Washington, D. C. 350 mem. Mrs. R. T. Hall, Pres.; Miss M. D. Barney, Sec.

Sons of the Amer. Revolution, Natl. Soc.—1889. Washington, D. C. 16,285 mem. J. Harry, Pres.-Gen. 50 State societies, including Hawaii, France and Far Eastern. Philip F. Larner, Sec.-Gen., 918 F., N. W., Washington, D. C.

Empire State Soc. Sons of Amer. Rev.—1890. 1,640 mem. H. F. Remington, Pres.; Capt. C. A. Dubois, Sec., 220 B'way, Mhtn.

Sons of Confederate Veterans, Memphis, Tenn. 50,000 mem. C. Hinton, Adj.-in-Chief, Denver, Col.; Geo. B. Bowling, Qtm.-in-Chief, Memphis, Tenn.; N. B. Forrest, Com.-in-Chief, Biloxi, Miss.

Sons of the Revolution—J. M. Montgomery, Gen.-Pres.; Prof. Wm. Libbey, Gen.-Sec., Princeton, N. J.

State Soc. Sons of Rev.—1876. R. Olyphant, Pres.; J. W. Cleveland, Treas.; H. R. Drowne, Sec., Fraunces Tavern, Mhtn.

Sons and Daughters of Washington—1920. Hdqtrs., 101 S. Manning blvd., Albany, N. Y. Jay W. Forrest, Supreme Grand Master.

Union Soc. of the Civil War—1909. Paul Dana, Pres.-Gen.; W. R. Jones, Sec.-Gen., 30 W. 44th, Mhtn.

United Confederate Veterans—1889. New Orleans, La. 60,000 mem. Gen. K. M. Van Zandt, Pres.; Maj.-Gen. Wm. E. Nickle, Sec., Mobile, Ala.

United Daughters of the Confederacy—1894. 100,000 mem. Mrs. Roy W. McKinney, Pres.-Gen., Paducah, Ky.; Mrs. R. D. Wright, Rec. Sec.-Gen., Newberry, S. C.

U. S. A. Naval and Military Order of the Spanish-Am. War—1899. 78 Broad, Mhtn. 1,300 mem. Capt. Chas. T. Wilt, Com.-in-Chief; Lieut. F. B. Hart, Rec.-in-Chief. Commanderies in N. Y., Mass., Pa., Ill., Conn., Ohio, Cal., Ind., D. C., R. I. Major Thos. R. Fleming, Recorder, N. Y. Com.

U. S. Natl. Honor Guard—Demobolized to reserve of 40,000; standing army of members, 20,000. Miss Theodora Booth, Com., 34 W. 28th, Mhtn.; Miss Agnes Smith, Reserve Com.

U. S. Veteran Navy—(See Secret and Benefit Socs.)

Veteran Corps Artillery—1790. Armory, 33d and Park av., Mhtn. Constituting the Military Soc. of the War of 1812 Veteran Corps. 250 mem. Col. Wm. G. Bates, Com.; Major D. Banks, Adj., 23 Park pl., N. Y. C.

Veterans of Foreign Wars of U. S.—32 Union sq., Mhtn. R. G. Woodside, Com.-in-Chief; Walter I. Joyce, Qrmr.-Gen.

State.

(See also National Societies.)

Colonial Order of the Acorn, N. Y. Chap.—1894. 100 mem. C. S. Van Rensselaer, Chan.; E. Woodward, Rec., 7 W. 44th, Mhtn.

Daughters of Ohio—1901. Waldorf-Astoria. 153 mem. Mrs. E. W. Kingsland, Pres.; Mrs. R. B. Hamilton, Sec., 612 W. 184th, Mhtn.

Native Sons of N. Y.—1912. 473 57th, Bkln. 17,000 mem. R. J. Hurley, Pres. and Founder; R. Granger, Sec., 636 52d, Bkln.

N. Y. State Soc. of the Cincinnati—1783. 25 Broad, Mhtn. 83 mem. T. Olyphant, Pres.; F. B. Hoffman, Sec.

Soc. of Colonial Dames of State of N. Y.—2 W. 47th, Mhtn. 800 mem. Mrs. H. Fairfax, Pres.; Mrs. R. B. Potter, Rec. Sec., Smithtown, L.I.

Soc. of Colonial Wars (in State of N. Y.)—1892. 1,075 mem. H. Duffield, Gov.; T. L. Chrystie, Ses., 43 Cedar, Mhtn.

Soc. of Daughters of Founders and Patriots of Amer. (N. Y. State)—1901. 100 mem. Mrs. C. D. Ward, Pres.; Mrs. J. S. Bradley, Jr., Rec. Sec., 43 Bleecker, Newark, N. J.

Soc. of Mayflower Descendants in the State of N. Y.—1894. 700 mem. H. C. Quinby, Gov.; T. J. Hallowell, Sec., 44 E. 23d, Mhtn.

Soc. of N. Y. State Women—1908. Hotel Astor. 80 mem. Founder, Mrs. Gerard Bancker. Dr. Frances W. Monell, Pres.; Mrs. Regina Demorest, Sec., 60 W. 76th, Mhtn.

Sons of Oriskany—150 mem. Samuel Campbell, Pres.; Peter Flint, Sec.-Treas., 510½ State, Schenectady, N. Y.

Veterans of Foreign Wars of U. S., N. Y. State Commandery—1920. J. F. Rorke, Comm., 431 56th, Bkln.; G. Decker, Sr. Vice Comm., Albany.

Washington Continental Guard—1776. John A. Cutter, Com.; W. W. Ford, Sec., White Plains.

Brooklyn.

(See also National Societies.)

Albany Heights Patriotic League—1918. 239 Albany av. 200 mem. Wm. J. Boers, Pres., 239 Albany av.; Miss Mae Marcus, Sec.

Amer. Anti-Socialistic League—1917. Crescent Hall. 150 mem. V. Hanhart, Pres.; Jos. L. Nowlan, Sec., 458 15th.

Caledonian Club—(See Scottish Soc.)

Colonial Daughters of 17th Century—1896. 300 mem. Members' ancestors must date 1607-1699. Mrs. R. F. Ives, Pres.; Mrs. R. M. Smythe, Cor. Sec., 62 Montague.

Guardians of Liberty (Evergreen Court No. 60). Meets 1, 3 and 5 M. To promote loyalty to ideals of founders of U. S. F. J. Kirchoff, Lock Box 11, Sta. J, Bkln.

Henry Ward Beecher Memorial Assn.—Rev. Dr. N. D. Hillis, Pres.; Chas. J. Schlegel, Treas., 11 St. James pl.

League of the Red, White and Blue, Washington Chapter—1896. 1112 mem. P. S. No. 75. Wm. S. Mills, Pres., 352 Clifton pl.

Little Men and Women of '76. Children of the Amer. Revolution—1894. 103 mem. Mrs. F. W. Hopkins, Pres.; Miss M. Cook, Sec., 47 Sidney pl.

Maine Women's Club of N. Y.—See Manhattan Socs.

Natl. League for Woman's Service, Kings Co. Committee—54 Lafayette av. Mrs. Walter Gibb, Ch.; Mrs. A. F. Cook, Treas.; Miss Minnie B. Geary, Sec.

Natl. Security League, Bkln. Branch—1915. A. R. Latson, Pres.; J. Lounsbery, Sec.; H. J. Davenport, Treas.

Natl. Soc. of New England Women, Bkln. Colony—1905. 345 Clinton av. 300 mem. Mrs. C. H. Sperry, Pres.; Mrs. O. A. Gordon, Vice Pres., 71 Halsey.

New England Soc. in Bkln.—1880. 250 mem. D. A. Boody, Pres.; J. W. Shepard, Rec. Sec., 176 B'way, Mhtn.

New Utrecht Liberty Pole Assn.—1908. 80 mem. J. F. Berry, Pres.; M. S. Hegeman, Sec., 7921 18th av.

Prison Ship Martyrs Monument Assn. of the U. S.—Funds handed over to Red Cross.

St. Nicholas Soc. of Nassau Island—1848. 240 mem. A. DeWitt Mason, Pres.; Wm. R. Lott, Sec., Hollis, L. I.

Soc. of Former Cohoesiers—1914. 140 mem. W. B. Cook, Jr., Sec., 51 Waldorf ct.

Soc. of Old Brooklynites—1880. Kings County Court House. 541 mem. Wm. B. Green, Pres.; C. L. Young, Sec., 311 11th.

Soc. of Patriotic Women of Bkln.—1916. 665 E. 23d. 80 mem. Mrs. Cathrine C. Hynds, Pres.; Mrs. Theresa C. Macoy, Sec., 92 Winthrop.

Sons of North Carolina—1895. 225 mem. 357 Bridge. A. D. Peyton, Pres.; S. L. Taylor, Sec.

Sons and Daughters of New England—1912. 100 mem. Eunice Haskins, Pres.; Mary Witherbee, Rec. Sec.; Mrs. Mark Hatch, Cor. Sec., 381 Jefferson av.

Underhill Soc. of Amer.—1892. 120 mem. Col. J. T. Underhill, Pres.; D. H. Underhill, Cor. Sec., 248 Maple.

U. S. Naval Assn.—1917. 350 mem. J. M. Green, Com; J. L. Stewart, Paymaster, 15 Gamma pl.

Vermont Soc.—1891. 250 mem. A. L. Janes, Pres.; J. L. Barker Sec., 154 Nassau, Mhtn.

Manhattan and Bronx.

(See also National Societies.)

Alabama Soc. of N. Y.—1906. 150 mem. Dr. J. A. Wyeth, Pres., 242 Lexington av.

Albany Soc. of N. Y.—1895. 250 mem. Henry Smith, Pres.; H. B. Skinner, Sec. and Treas., 15 Nassau.

Amer. Defense Soc.—1915. 60,000 mem. 116 E. 24th. C. S. Davison, Pres.; C. S. Thompson, Sec.

California Soc. of N. Y.—1900. 300 mem. John Hays Hammond, Pres.; Henry Varian, Sec.-Treas., Room 103, 66 Park Row.

Canadian Soc. of N. Y.—1897. 300 mem. F. W. Shibley, Pres.; G. D. Bruce, Sec., 120 B'way.

Chautauqua Co. Soc.—1902. 125 mem. H. C. Lake, Pres.; R. D. Adams, Sec., 176 B'way.

Chemung-Tioga Soc.—1904. 500 mem. D. W. Murray, Sec., Rockaway Beach.

Chicago Club, Inc.—1904. Waldorf-Astoria. Mrs. J. M. Gallagher, Pres.; Mrs. W. F. Hissel, Sec., Hotel Hamilton.

SOCIETIES AND ASSOCIATIONS—PATRIOTIC AND COMMEMORATIVE—MHTN. AND BRONX—*Continued.*

Church Woman's League for Patriotic Service—1919. 8 W. 47th. 500 mem. Mrs. H. W. Munroe, Pres.; Miss E. T. Day, Sec.

City History Club—1896. 105 W. 40th. 1,000 mem. Mrs. A. B. Hepburn, Pres.; Mrs. C. Van Anda, Sec.; Mary F. Smart, Cor. Sec.; Dr. F. B. Kelley, Supt. of History Classes.

Columbia Co. Assn.—1901. 382 mem. G. Price, Pres.; C. C. Tough, Sec., 510 E. 73d.

Confederate Veteran Camp of N. Y.—1890. 400 mem. Hotel Astor. C. R. Hatton, Com.; E. Selvage, Adj., 101 Produce Exch.

Conference Committee on Natl. Preparedness. Inc. 1915. Com. publishes booklets, etc., and gratuitously distributes books on natl. defense. The officers are: Ch., Hy. A. Wise Wood; Sec., J. E. Clark, 1133 B'way, N. Y. C.

Cortland Co. Soc. of N. Y. City—1900. 500 mem. Glenn Tisdak, Pres.; Frank Place, Jr., Sec., 17 W. 43d.

Daughters of Indiana in N. Y.—1903. Hotel Astor. 130 mem. Miss M. G. Hay, Pres., 404 Riverside Drive; Mrs. M. Anderson, Cor. Sec.

Daughters of the Union—See National Socs.

Dixie Club of N. Y.—Hotel Commodore. Mrs. E. W. Wright, Pres., 120 W. 70th.

Gen. Slocum Survivors Assn.—1904. 133 mem. Chas. Dersch, Pres.; Edw. Zennegg, Sec., 666 Jamaica av., Bkln.

Georgia Soc. of City of N. Y.—Powell Crichton, Pres.; Harry L. Jones, Sec., 200 5th av.

Grant Monument Assn.—1886. 100 trustees. 165 B'way. Gen. Horace Porter, Hon. Pres.; H. W. Hayden, Pres.; H. C. Quinby, Sec.

Greene Co. Soc. in City of N. Y.—1905. 350 mem. Henry W. Showers, Pres.; J. H. Thomas, Sec. and Treas., 1730 Amsterdam av.

Guardians of Liberty (N. Y. Court No. 1)—Meets 2d and 4th Mondays. 2307 B'way, I. O. B. B. Hall, Mhtn.

Holland Soc. of N. Y. (The)—1885. 1,000 mem. Object: To commemorate Dutch settlement of New Netherlands. A. H. Van Brunt, Pres.; F. R. Keator, Rec. Sec., 90 West.

Indiana Soc.—38 Park Row. 1904. 200 mem. H. Hord, Pres.; F. C. Lucas, Sec.

Iowa New Yorkers—1908. Hotel Astor. 170 mem. Mrs. W. F. Thummel, Pres.; Mrs. G. Boisford, Sec., 3495 B'way.

Iowa Soc. of N. Y.—1907. A. O'Connell, Pres., 51 Chambers; Harry M. Farrell, Sec.

Kansas Soc. of N. Y.—1906. B. F. Woolman, Pres.; Wm. Mitchell, Sec., N. Y. Zoological Park.

League to Enforce Peace—1915. 22 W. 19th. Wm. H. Taft, Pres.; W. H. Short, Sec.

Kentuckians—1904. 225 mem. Evan Shelby, Pres., 63 Wall; J. M. Hartfield, Sec., 14 Wall.

Maiden Lane Historical Soc.—1911. 15 Maiden Lane. 300 mem. A. K. Sloane, Pres.; J. D. Little, Sec., 17 Maiden Lane.

Maine Soc. of N. Y.—1902. 325 mem. Chas. R. Flint, Pres.; W. L. Flye, Sec., 20 High, Glen Ridge, N. J.

Maine Women's Club of N. Y.—1903. 155 mem. Mrs. A. F. Shorey, Pres.; Mrs. A. H. Chadbourne, Sec., 114 Morningside dr.

Marquette Club of the City of N. Y.—Hotel Plaza, 5th av. A. O'Connell, Pres.; K. B. Fox, Sec.; T. Ughetta, Treas.

McGlynn (Dr.) Monument Assn.—1900. 1,500 mem. 220 B'way. S. L. Malone, Pres.; T. J. McMahon, Sec., 2530 Bathgate av., Bronx.

Mexican Soc. of N. Y.—1909. 1,100 mem. F. Juarez, Pres., 27 Warren.

Michigan Soc.—1904. 200 mem. J. C. Weadock, Pres., 14 Wall; T. S. Major, Sec., 2 W. 45th.

Military Order of Foreign Wars of the U. S., N. Y. Commandery—1895. 149 B'way. 450 mem. Col. W. G. Bates, U. S. A., Pres; Major R. A. De Russy, Sec., 52 B'way.

Military Order of the World War, N. Y. Chapter—Hotel Astor. 1920. 900 mem. Col. S. H. Wolfe, Com.; Capt. G. F. Aitken, Adj., 1881 B'way.

Missouri Soc. of City of N. Y.—Bainbridge Colby, Pres., 32 Nassau.

Monticello Club—1897. 66 Morton. 150 mem. T. J. Horgan, Pres.; F. J. Caragher, Treas., 66 Morton.

Natl. California Club—1905. Waldorf-Astoria. 150 mem. Mrs. T. J. Vivian, Pres., 312 Manhattan av; Mrs. L. W. Butler, Cor. Sec., 324 Putnam av, Bkln.

Natl. Soc. of New England Women (N. Y. C. Colony)—350 mem. Mrs. J. F. Yawger, Pres., 448 Riverside dr.; Mrs. J. E. Fox, Sec.

Naval and Military Order, S.-A. War, N. Y. Commandery—1899. 78 Broad. 440 mem. Capt. I. Harris, Com.; Major T. R. Fleming, Rec.

New England Soc.—1805. 1,300 mem. C. W. Bowen, Pres.; H. A. Cushing, Sec., 43 Cedar.

Newfoundland Soc.—1909. 100 mem. E. F. Howell, Pres., 195 B'way; E. Canning, Sec.

N. Y. Caledonian Club—(See Scottish Socs.)

N. Y. League for Americanism—1919. Room 607, 280 Madison av. C. C. Washburn, Pres.; C. D. Babcock, Sec., 471 S. Salina, Syracuse, N. Y.

N. Y. Monuments Commission for Battlefields of Gettysburg, Chattanooga and Antietam—Hall of Records, Mhtn. L. R. Stegman, Ch.; John W. Lynch, Sec.

N. Y. Southern Soc.—1886. 1,000 mem. Wm. A. Barber, Pres.; W. G. Fitzwilson, Sec., 5 Nassau.

Ohio Soc. of N. Y.—1885. Waldorf-Astoria. 1,000 mem. B. B. Avery, Pres.; C. E. Althouse, Sec.

Order of Americans of Armorial Ancestry—1903. 122 mem. Mrs. W. Gerry Slade, Pres., Waldorf-Astoria; Mrs. Jasper Cairns, Registrar, 30 E. 38th.

Pennsylvania Soc.—1899. 1,600 mem. C. M. Schwab, Pres.; Barr Ferree, Sec., 249 W. 13th.

Rensselaer Co. Soc.—1908. 300 mem. T. C. Benson, Pres.; S. M. Bell, Sec., 120 B'way.

St. Lawrence Co. Soc.—1905. Ed. Noble, Pres.; Dr. C. E. Hoag, Sec., 15 E. 48th.

St. Nicholas Club—(See Social Clubs.)

Saratoga Co. Soc.—286 mem. R. M. S. Putnam, Pres.; F. H. Putnam, Sec., 115 W. 104th.

Soc. of American Officers—1909. 18 Gramercy Pk. Maj.-Gn. Robt. Alexander, U. S. A., Pres.; Col. W. C. Brown, U. S. A., Sec.

Soc. of Daughters of Holland Dames, Descendants of the Ancient and Honorable Families of New Netherland—1895. 145 mem. Mrs. J. A. Macdonald, Dir.-Gen.; Mrs. I. De Puy Agnew, Cor. Sec., 987 Madison av.

Soc. of the Genesee—1898. 1,000 mem. J. W. Gerard, Pres., 46 Cedar; Chas. Presbrey, Sec., 456 4th av.

Soc. of Kentucky Women of N. Y.—1907. Euclid Hall. 125 mem. Mrs. Bedell Parker, Pres.; Mrs. C. J. Kiger, Sec., 622 W. 114th.

Soc. of the Sons of Oneida—1897. 250 mem. Chas. H. Wilson, Sec.; C. E. Cady, Treas., 65 Clinton pl.

Soc. of Pennsylvania Women in N. Y.—1913. 275 mem. Mrs. R. Lewis, Pres.; Mrs. E. Brand Beacham, Sec., 249 W. 13th.

Southland Club—1915. Waldorf-Astoria. 140 mem. Mrs. S. Baruch, Pres.; Mrs. H. W. Montague, Sec., 583 Riverside dr.

Steuben Co. Soc.—1894. 400 mem. Thos. Hassett, Pres., Woodmere, L. I.; M. J. Moore, Sec., 141 B'way.

Tennessee Soc. in N. Y.—1905. 350 mem. Dr. Jas. J. King, Pres.; N. P. Cullom, Sec., 165 B'way.

United Historical and Patriotic Socs. and Assns. of N. Y. Comm. of 9—To encourage writing of an accurate history of the State. G. F. Kunz, Ch.; A. Wakeman, Sec., 63 Wall.

Vermont Soc.—(See Bkln.)

Veteran Assn., 2d Battalion Naval Militia, N. Y.—480 mem. J. A. Mollenhauer, Pres.; S. C. Gelston, Treas. 56 Maiden Lane.

Vet. Corps of Artillery. Military Soc. of War of 1812—300 mem. 71st Regt. Armory. Wm. G. Bates, Com.; H. Schieffelin Sayers, Adj., 31 Nassau.

Victory Hall Assn.—1919. 4 E. 43d. Gen. G. W. Wingate, Pres.; C. H. Sabin, Treas.; Arnold Frye, Sec.

Virginians—1889. 242 mem. W. L. McCorkle, Gov.; H. Rogers, Sec., 30 Broad.

Washington Hdqtrs. Assn.—160th and Amsterdam av., Mrs. S. Baruch, Pres., 51 W. 70th; Mrs. J. R. Butler, Sec., 28 Lefferts pl., Bkln.

Woman's Roosevelt Memorial Assn.—1919. 1 E. 57th. 20,000 mem. Mrs. J. H. Hammond, Pres.; Mrs. Chas. A. Bryan, Sec.

Queens.

Good Citizenship League—1891. Flushing. 280 mem. Mrs. Clinton B. Smith, Pres.; Mrs. Wm. K. Waterman, Sec., 12 S. 18th, Flushing.

Jamaica Village Soc.—100 mem. E. L. Maeder, Pres.; A. S. Baylis, Sec., 19 Burdette pl., Jamaica.

King Manor Assn. of L. I.—1900. 265 mem. Mrs. W. W. Gillen, Pres.; Mrs. H. S. Curtis, Sec., 4 Terrace av., Jamaica.

Old New Yorkers Assn.—Ozone Park. O. W. Schiffers, Pres.; C. F. Gottlieb, Sec.

SOCIETIES AND ASSOCIATIONS—*Continued.*

RELIGIOUS SOCIETIES.

(See index for Men's Church Clubs.)

International.

Christian Flag Extension Soc.—1897. To establish universal flag for all Christian denominations. C. C. Overton, Pres., 2750 W. 1st, Coney Island, Bkln., N. Y.

Family Altar League—1907. 380,000 mem. To promote a world-wide observance in Christian homes of the observance of family worship. Rev. W. E. Biederwolf, Pres.; Rev. Wm. Matthew Holderby, 541 Marquette Bldg., Chicago, Ill.

Guild of the Love of God—1904. 9,064 mem. 76 Durham rd., London S. W., England. Rev. A. V. Magee, Pres.; Rev. F. S. DeVona, Sec., St. Clair, Mich.

Interchurch World Movement of North America—1918. 45 W. 18th, Mhtn. Robt. Lansing, Ch.; S. Earl Taylor, Gen. Sec., 111 5th av., Mhtn.

Internatl. Med. Missionary Soc.—1881. 156 5th av., Mhtn. Rev. E. L. Smith, D.D., Pres.; Rev. G. H. Dowkontt, M.D., Sec.

Internatl. Missionary Union—1884. 1,200 mem. Rev. J. S. Stone, M.D., Pres.; Mrs. A. M. Williams, Cor. Sec., 149 W. College, Oberlin, O.; Rev. H. F. Laflamme, Rec. Sec., 105 W. 176th, Mhtn.

Internatl. Order of The King's Daughters and Sons—1886. 280 Madison av., Mhtn. Members in many countries, chiefly in U. S. and Canada. Mrs. R. J. Reed, Pres.; Clara Morehouse, Gen. Sec.

Internatl. S. S. Assn.—1872. 1516 Mallers Bldg., **Chicago, Ill. W. O. Thompson, Pres.; Marion Lawrance, Gen. Sec. Meets in Kansas City, Mo., June, 1922.**

Internatl. Union of Gospel Missions—1914. 205 mem. T. J. Noonan, Pres., 126 Bible House; Mrs. J. H. Wyburn, Sec.

Mth. Brotherhood (The)—58 E. Washington, Chicago, Ill. W. S. Bovard, Gen. Sec.

Russian Bible and Evangelization Soc.—1919. 156 5th av., Mhtn. Geo. E. Howes, Pres.; G. P. Raud, Sec.-Dir.

Spurgeon Memorial Sermon Soc.—1892. Congleton, Cheshire, Eng. Wm. Taverner, Sec. Amer. Hdqtrs., 14 Tillary, Bkln. Rev. E. D. Bailey, Pres.; Rev. T. C. Roberts-Horsfield, Sec.

World's Student Christian Federation—1895. Composed of 25 natl. and internatl. Christian student movements. Dr. J. R. Mott, Ch., 347 Madison av., Mhtn.

World's S. S. Assn.—1889. 216 Metropolitan Tower, Mhtn. John Wanamaker, Pres.; Paul Sturdevant, Treas.; J. W. Kinnear, Ch. Exec. Com.; F. L. Brown, Gen. Sec.

Y. M. C. A.—Internatl. Com. of No. Amer.—1883. 347 Madison av., Mhtn. 200 mem., elected by triennial conventions of delegates from No. Amer. Assns. A. E. Marling, Ch.; J. R. Mott, Gen. Sec. Mem., 868,592; assns., 2,194; paid officers, 5,173; net value of property, $128,019,000. The assns. have striven in a comprehensive and united way to promote the educational, physical and social welfare of the men and boys in America, also to men in the military and naval forces of the U. S., both in America and overseas, and have extended the same helpful ministry to the men of the Allied armies and to prisoners of war in Europe.

National.

BAPTIST.

Amer. Bapt. Foreign Mission Soc.—1814. 276 5th av., Mhtn. Hon. C. E. Milliken, Pres.; W. B. Lipphard, Rec. Sec.

Amer. Bapt. Historical Soc.—1853. 1701 Chestnut, Phila., Pa. Prof. S. B. Meeser, Pres.; Rev. J. W. Lyell, Sec.

Amer. Bapt. Home Mission Soc.—1832. 23 E. 26th, Mhtn. C. L. White, Ex. Sec.; S. Bryant, Treas.

Amer. Bapt. Publication Soc.—1824. 1701-3 Chestnut, Phila., Pa. F. H. Robinson, Pres.; H. V. Meyer, Bus. Mgr. Branches: Boston, Chicago, Los Angeles, New York, St. Louis, Kansas City, Seattle, Toronto.

Bapt. Convention (The Northern)—1907. 1,250,000 mem. E. L. Tustin, Pres., Phila., Pa.; W. C. Bitting, Sec., 5109 Waterman av., St. Louis, Mo.

Bapt. Young People's Union of Amer.—1891. 500,000 mem. W. F. Reynolds, Pres.; Rev. J. A. White, Gen. Sec., 125 N. Wabash av., Chicago, Ill.

Board of Education of the Northern Baptist Convention—1888. 276 5th av., Room 660, Mhtn. C. W. Chamberlain, Pres.; H. R. Chapman, Sec.; F. W. Padelford, Exec. Sec.

Woman's Amer. Bapt. Foreign Mission Soc.—276 5th av., Mhtn. 1913. Mrs. W. A. Montgomery, Pres.; Mrs. T. E. Adams, Rec. Sec., 2033 E. 88th, Cleveland, O.

Woman's Amer. Bapt. Home Mission Soc.—1877. 276 5th av., N. Y. C. Mrs. J. Nuveen, Pres.; Mrs. K. S. Westfall, Exec. Sec.; Mrs. O. R. Judd, Treas.

CATHOLIC.

Catholic Church Extension Soc. of the U. S. A.—1905. 300,000 mem. Missionary work. 180 North Wabash av., Le Moyne Bldg., Chicago, Ill. Rt. Rev. Francis C. Kelley, Pres.; Rt. Rev. E. B. Ledvina, Sec.

Catholic Federation of the U. S. A.—1901. 3,500,000 mem. T. P. Flynn, Pres.; A. Matre, K.S.G., Sec., 175 W. Jackson blvd., Chicago, Ill.

Catholic Missionary Union—1896. Most Rev. P. J. Hayes, D.D., Pres.; Rev. T. A. Daly, C. S. P., Sec.-Treas., 415 W. 59th, Mhtn.

Catholic Young Men's Natl. Union—1875. 204,000 mem. M. J. Slattery, Pres.; T. J. Thornton, Sec.-Treas., 157 N. 15th, Phila., Pa.

U. S. Catholic Historical Soc.—(See Educational Socs.)

CONGREGATIONAL.

Amer. Bd. of Commissioners of Foreign Missions—1810. 14 Beacon, Boston, Mass. 814 mem. N. Y. office, 287 4th av. E. L. Smith, Sec. Conducts foreign missionary work for Cong. churches of U. S. 724 missionaries, 4,836 native workers, 58,620 pupils, 1,244 schools, 75,594 communicants, 710 churches. Auxiliaries: Woman's Bd. of Missions, Boston. Mrs. C. H. Daniels, Pres.; Mrs. F. G. Cook, Treas., Congregational House. Woman's Bd. of Missions of the Interior—Chicago, Mrs. G. M. Clark, Pres.; Mrs. S. E. Hurlbut, Treas., 19 So. La Salle, Chicago, Ill. Woman's Bd. of Missions for the Pacific—Miss H. Brewer, Pres.; Mrs. W. W. Ferrier, Treas., 760 Market, San Francisco, Cal.

Amer. Congregational Assn.—1853. 14 Beacon, Boston. 213 mem. E. M. Noyes, Pres.; Thos. Todd, Jr., **Sec., Boston, Mass.**

Amer. Missionary Assn.—Rev. Dr. Nehemiah Boynton, Pres., Bkln., N. Y.; Rev. Dr. H. P. Dewey, Vice-Pres., Minneapolis, Minn.; Rev. A. Anderson, Rec. Sec., Randolph, Mass.

Cong. Church Bldg. Soc.—1853. 287 4th av., Mhtn. Dr. R. H. Potter, Pres.; G. H. Richards, D.D., and J. R. Smith, D.D., Secs.; C. H. Baker, Treas.

Cong. Education Soc.—1815. 14 Beacon, Boston. Rev. F. M. Sheldon, Gen. Sec.

Woman's Bd. of Missions (Foreign)—503 Cong. House, 14 Beacon, Boston, Mass. Comprises societies in States east of Ohio from Maine to Florida. Mrs. C. H. Daniels, Pres.; Mrs. F. G. Cook, Treas.

EVANGELICAL.

Evangelical Educational Soc.—1862. Rm 19. The **Ch. House, 12th and Walnut, Phila., Pa. 1,000 mem. Rev. S. L. Gilberson, M.A., Gen. Sec.**

LUTHERAN.

Luther League of Amer.—1895. 28,000 mem. in 30 States. Has orgs. in Japan, China, India, Porto Rico, Nova Scotia and Canada. C. T. A. Anderson, Pres.; H. Hodges, Gen. Sec., 846 Drexel Bldg., Phila., Pa.

Lutheran Bd. of Publication—Sheridan Bldg., Phila., Pa. 1918. 21 mem. S. P. Sadtler, Pres.; N. R. Melhorn, Sec.; Grant Hultberg, Mgr., Phila., Pa.

United Luth. Ch. in Amer.—1918. F. H. Kimbel, D.D., Pres.; E. C. Miller, Treas.; M. G. G. Scherer, D.D., Sec., 437 5th av., Mhtn.

METHODIST.

Am. Meth. Historical Soc.—1855. Rev. J. F. Goucher, Pres., Baltimore, Md.: F. G. Porter, Sec., Catonsville, Md.

METHODIST EPISCOPAL.

Board of Sunday Schools of M. E. Church—1827. 58 E. Washington, Chicago, Ill. 29 mem. Bishop Thos. Nicholson, Pres.; W. S. Bovard, Cor. Sec.

Board of Temperance, Prohibition and Public Morals of M. E. Church—204 Pennsylvania av. S. E., Washington, D. C. Bishop Wm. F. McDowell, Pres.; C. T. Wilson, Gen. Sec.

Epworth League of the M. E. Church—1886. Central office, 740 Rush, Chicago, Ill. **Bishop A. W.** Leonard, Pres.; Rev. C. E. Guthrie, Gen. Sec.

SOCIETIES AND ASSOCIATIONS—RELIGIOUS—NATIONAL—*Continued.*

Woman's Home Miss. Soc. of M. E. Church—1880. Natl. hdqtrs., 420 Plum, Cincinnati, O. 270,206 mem. Mrs. W. P. Thirkield, Pres.; Mrs. M. L. Woodruff, Cor. Sec., Allendale, N. J.

METHODIST PROTESTANT.

Woman's Foreign Miss. Soc. of the M. P. Ch.—1879. 9,000 mem. Mrs. H. Hupfield, Pres.; Mrs. G. H. Miller, Cor. Sec., Bellevue, Pa.

PRESBYTERIAN.

Gen. Assem. of Pres. Ch. in U. S. A., Witherspoon Bldg., Phila., Pa.; Rev. S. S. Palmer, Mod.

General Bd. of Education of Pres. Church in U. S. A.—1819. 156 5th av., N. Y. C. Phila. 27 mem. Rev. H. T. Kerr, Pres.; E. P. Hill, Gen. Sec.

Permanent Comm. on Men's Work of Pres. Church in U. S. A.—Rev. J. T. Stone, Ch.; Rev. W. F. Weir, D.D., Gen. Sec., Wooster, O.

Presbyterian Bd. of Ministerial Relief and Sustentation Fund—1855. 12 mem. Witherspoon Bldg., Phila., Pa. Rev. G. F. Greene, D.D., Pres.; Rev. H. B. Master, D.D., Gen. Sec.; Rev. W. W. Heberton, D.D., Treas.

Pres. Historical Soc.—1852. 251 mem. 520 Witherspoon Bldg., Phila., Pa. Henry van Dyke, Pres.; Rev. J. B. Turner, Gen. Sec.

Woman's Bd. of Home Missions of Pres. Ch. in U. S. A.—156 5th av., Mhtn. Mrs. F. S. Bennett, Pres.

PRESBYTERIAN, UNITED.

Board of Home Missions of the United Pres. Ch. of N. Amer.—1858. 209 9th, Pittsburgh, Pa. J. K. McClurkin, Pres.; R. A. Hutchison, Cor. Sec.

PROTESTANT EPISCOPAL.

Brotherhood of St. Andrew—1883. G. F. Shelby, Gen. Sec., Church House, Phila., Pa.

Girls' Friendly Soc. in Amer.—1877. 15 E. 40th. Mhtn. Has 1,004 branches and a membership of 46,290 in U. S. Miss F. W. Sibley, Pres.; Miss M. M. McGuire, Sec.

P. E. Dept. of Missions—1820. J. W. Wood, Exec. Sec., 281 4th av., Mhtn.

P. E. Soc. for Promotion of Evang'l Knowledge—1848. R. H. McKim, D.D., Pres.; A. G. Cummins, Sec., Poughkeepsie, N. Y.

REFORMED.

Particular Synod of Reformed Ch. in Amer., embracing the classes of Hudson, Kingston, North L. I., South L. I., N. Y., Orange, Poughkeepsie and Westchester, Rev. J. M. Martin, Pres., Hudson, N. Y.; Rev. H. Hageman, Stated Clerk, Claverack, N. Y.

UNITARIAN.

Alliance of Unitarian Women—1890. Inc. 1902. 25 Beacon, Boston, Mass. 20,087 mem. Miss L. Lowell, Pres.; Mrs. C. S. Atherton, Sec., 25 Beacon, Boston.

Am. Unitarian Assn.—1825. 25 Beacon, Boston. Rev. S. A. Eliot, D.D., Pres.; Rev. L. C. Cornish, Sec.; H. M. Williams, Treas. N. Y. hdqtrs., 104 E. 20th.

Gen. Con. of Unitarian and Other Christian Churches—1865. Wm. H. Taft, Pres.; Rev. P. Perkins, Sec., 16 Beacon, Boston, Mass.

Unitarian Conference of the Middle States and Canada—1885. M. T. Garvin, Pres., 104 E. 20th, N. Y. C.

Unitarian S. S. Soc.—1827. 25 Beacon, Boston. Rev. W. I. Lawrance, Pres.; G. R. Ferguson, Treas.

UNIVERSALIST.

Gen. Con. of Universalist Ch.—Hon. R. S. Galer, Pres.; Rev. R. F. Etz, Sec., 359 Boylston, Boston, Mass.

Gen. S. S. Assn. of Universalist Ch.—Rev. G. E. Huntley, D.D., Pres., 359 Boylston, Boston, Mass.

Universalist Historical Soc.—1834. Tufts College. 100 mem. H. S. Ballou, Pres.; Rev. W. B. Brigham, Sec., Boston, Mass.

Young People's Christian Union of Universalist Ch.—1889. 359 Boylston, Boston, Mass. 4,200 mem. Rev. C. R. Stetson, Pres.; L. F. Merlin, Sec.-Treas.

OTHER RELIGIOUS SOCIETIES.

Am. Sunday School Union (Inc.)—1824. To establish frontier Sunday Schools. Rev. G. Becker, Sec., Rm. 134, Bible House, Mhtn.

Brotherhood of Andrew and Philip—(Internatl. Council)—1888. An interdenominational soc, for the men of the church, stressing prayer and service. Chapters in 24 denominations throughout the U. S. Rev. R. W. Miller, Hon. Pres., 204 N. 15th, Phila., Pa.

Brotherhood of the Kingdom—1892. Marlborough, N. Y. Rev. L. Williams, Ch. Ex. Com.; Rev. A. S. Cole, Sec.-Treas., Box 843, Kingston, N. Y.

Christian and Missionary Alliance—1897. 690 8th av., Mhtn., Rev. Paul Rader, Pres.; Dr. R. H. Glover, Foreign Sec.; Rev. E. J. Richards, Home Sec., 690 8th av., Mhtn.

Christian Endeavor, United Soc. of—1881. Natl. Hdqtrs., 41 Mt. Vernon, Boston. 79,982 socs., over 4,000,000 mem. Rev. F. E. Clark, Pres.; E. P. Gates, Gen. Sec.

Church Peace Union—1914. 70 5th av., Mhtn. Rev. Wm. P. Merrill, Pres.; Rev. H. A. Atkinson, Sec.

Federal Council of the Churches of Christ in Amer.—1908. 105 E. 22d, Mhtn. Offices also in Washington, D. C., and Chicago. Rev. F. M. North, Pres.; Rev. C. S. Macfarland, Gen. Sec. Represents officially 31 Protestant denominations. Works through commissions, as those upon Evangelism, Social Service, Temperance, Intenational Justice and Good Will, Relations with France and Belgium, Interchurch Federations and Church and Country Life.

Federation of Amer. Zionists—(See Jewish Organizations.)

Free and Open Church Assn.—1875. R. F. Wood, Pres.; Rev. J. A. Goodfellow, Sec., 2353 E. Cumberland, Phila., Pa.; G. Hall, Treas., Franklin Bldg., Phila., Pa.

Gideon's Christian Commercial Travelers' Assn. of Am.—1899. 140 S. Dearborn, Chicago, Ill. A. B. T. Moore, Natl. Sec.

Guild of St. Barnabas for Nurses—1886. 2,300 mem. Religious and social. Rt. Rev. R. Israel, Chaplain-Gen.; Mrs. E. B. Leaf, Sec.-Gen., 2027 Walnut, Phila., Pa.

Lord's Day Alliance of U. S.—1888. 156 5th av., Mhtn. Natl. and Intl. denominational; represents 17 denominations. Jas. Yereance, Pres.; Rev. H. L. Bowlby, D.D., Gen. Sec.; R. G. Davey, Spec. Counsel; G. M. Thomson, Treas.

Missionary Education Movement of the U. S. and Canada—1902. Taken over by Interchurch World Movement of No. Amer., 45 W. 18th.

Natl. Spiritualists' Assn. of the U. S.—1893. 600 Penn. av., S. E., Washington, D. C. 600,000 mem. 600 churches and socs. Dr. G. B. Warne, Pres.; Geo. W. Kates, Sec.

Oriental Esoteric Center and Soc.—1910. 1443 Que, Washington, D. C. Agnes E. Marsland, Pres.; K. M. Hopson, Sec.

Religious Education Assn.—1903. 1440 E. 57th, Chicago, Ill. 3,500 mem. A. E. McGiffert, LL.D., Pres., N. Y.; H. F. Cope, A.M., D.D., Sec.

Seventh Day Adventist Mission Board—Takoma Pk., Washington, D. C. 1861. 173,641 mem. A. G. Daniells, Pres.; W. A. Spicer, Sec., Takoma Pk., Washington, D. C.

Soc. of Inner Mission and Rescue Work—(See Hosp., etc., Natl.)

Student Volunteer Movement for Foreign Missions—1886. 25 Madison av., Mhtn.—J. C. Robbins, Ch. Ex. Com.; R. P. Wilder, Gen. Sec.

Theosophical Soc., Amer. Soc.—1875. 7 048 mem. L. W. Rogers, Natl. Pres., Kimball Bldg., Chicago; B. Jewett, Natl. Sec. Intl. hdqtrs., Adyar, Madras, India. Mrs. A. Besant, Pres.

United Boys' Brigades of Am.—1883. 804 N. Carrolton av., Baltimore, Md. 20,000 mem. Joe H. Cudlipp, Com.-in-Chief.

U. S. Soldiers' Christian Aid Assn.—1861. 5 Beekman, Mhtn. Maj. S. E. Briggs, Pres.; Maj. G. Breck, Sec.-Treas.

Woman's Natl. Sabbath Alliance (The)—1895. 156 5th av., Mhtn. Mrs. S. Y. MacNair, Pres.; Miss C. Murray, Cor. Sec.

Woman's Union Miss. Soc. of Am.—1860. 67 Bible House, Mhtn. Mrs. S. J. Broadwell, Pres.; Mrs. S. T. Dauchy, Sec.

Y. M. C. A. Natl. Board—600 Lexington av., Mhtn. Mrs. R. E. Speer, Pres.; Mrs. L. H. Lapham, Sec.

Young People's Religious Union—1895. 25 Beacon, Boston, Mass. 5,000 mem. Rev. H Page, Pres.; Miss A. B. Pfleghaar, Sec.

State.

Bapt. Miss. Convention of the State of N. Y.—1807. Represents 987 churches, 43 associations, 186,769 church mem. Rev. W. A. Granger, D.D., Pres.; O. R. Judd, Treas.; Rev. E. B. Richmond, Sec., 276 5th av., Mhtn.

Catholic Federation of the State of New York—1905. 50,000 mem. E. F. Cooke, Pres.; J. R. Garvey, Sec., 1207 8th av., Bkln.

Catholic League of the State of N. Y.—Chas. Korz, Pres., Bkln.; J. M. Schifferlin, Rec. Sec., Buffalo, N. Y.

SOCIETIES AND ASSOCIATIONS—RELIGIOUS—STATE—*Continued.*

Colored Baptist Missionary Convention of N. Y. State—1897. 27,880 mem. Rev. G. H. Sims, Pres., 131 W. 131st, Mhtn.; Rev. A. C. Matthews, Cor. Sec., 189A Chauncey, Bkln.

Evangelical Lutheran Synod of N. Y. and New England—1901. 64 congs. 23,244 mem. Rev. F. F. Fry, Pres.; Rev. S. G. Trexler, Sec., 68 Grape, Rochester.

Luther League of N. Y. State—1883. 6,996 Seniors. 1,002 Juniors. Rev. H. D. Shimer, Pres., 1421 State, Schenectady, N. Y.

N. Y. Bapt. Union for Ministerial Education—1850. H. K. Porter, Pres.; G. B. Ewell, Rec. Sec.; Alvah Strong Hall, Rochester.

N. Y. Congregational Conference (Inc.)—1871. Hon. C. H. Hammond, Mod., Buffalo, N. Y.; Rev. W. P. Harmon, Sec., Ticonderoga, N. Y.

N. Y. State Christian Endeavor Union—2,400 socs. 112,400 mem. Rev. F. G. Coffin, Pres., 126 Chestnut, Albany.

N. Y. State Colonization Soc.—1855. 10 mem. Rev. Dr. E. C. Sage, Pres.; L. G. Myers, Treas., 61 B'way, Mhtn.

N. Y. State Convention of Universalists—Carthage. B. A. Field, Pres., Watertown, N. Y.; Rev. G. D. Walker, D.D., Sec., Carthage, N. Y.

N. Y. State Sabbath Assn.—1891. Auxiliary of the Lord's Day Alliance of the U. S. Rev. Dr. D. J. Burrell, Pres.; Rev. H. L. Bowlby, Act. Gen. Sec., 156 5th av., Mhtn.

N. Y. State S. S. Assn.—80 Howard, Albany. 1856 Prof. H. S. Jacoby, Ch. Ex. Com.; Dr. J. Clark, Gen. Supt.

N. Y. Unit. S. S. Union—1892. Unitarian Rooms, 104 E. 20th, Mhtn. 18 Sunday Schools. O. E. Edwards, Jr., Pres.; J. P. Mallett, Sec., 184 Stiles, Elizabeth, N. J.

Synod of N. Y. of the United Luther Ch. in Amer.—Rev. G. Hipsley, D.D., Pres.; Rev. H. Finch, Sec., Johnstown, N. Y.

Universalist Women's Aid Assn. of State of N. Y.—1893. M. D. King, Pres.; Mrs. A. B. Tanner, Sec., 462 Bird av., Buffalo, N. Y.

Woman's Board of Foreign Missions (N. Y. State Branch) (Cong.)—287 4th av., Mhtn. Mrs. N. D. Hillis, Pres.; Miss J. L. Russell, Sec., 353 W. 85th.

Woman's Home Missionary Union, State of N. Y. (Cong.)—Mrs. Wm. Spalding, Pres.; Mrs. J. J. Pearsall, Exec. Sec., 114 Fenimore, Bkln.; Mrs. Wm. A. Kirkwood, Treas.

Women's Missionary Soc. of the Eastern Conference of the Synod of N. Y. and New England. 1912. 1,100 mem. Mrs. R. B. Fenner, Pres.; Mrs J. Wilkens, Roosevelt, N. Y., Sec.

Young Men's Christian Assn.—1866. The State Executive Committee is a corporate body of 36 mem. Hdqtrs., 2 W. 45th, Mhtn. Wm. M. Kingsley, Ch.; S. Woolverton, Treas.; F. W. Pearsall and F. I. Eldridge, State Secs. Total State membership, 88,092, of which 11,637 are railroad men. 3,882 students and 18,461 in boys' depts.

Young People's Christian Union of Universalist Church of N. Y. State, Inc.—419 mem. L. F. Merlin, Pres., 328 Franklin av., Bkln.; Miss Helen Ulrich, Sec., Canton.

Young Women's Christian Assn. (Northeastern Field Committee of)—600 Lexington av., Mhtn. Miss Ruth Colt, Exec. Sec.

Brooklyn.

BAPTIST.

Bapt. Church Extension Soc. of Bkln. and Queens—1886. H. O. Bailey, Pres.; C. S. Cregar, Sec., 175 Remsen.

Baptist Ministers' Home Soc. of N. Y.—1882. 1023 E. 2d. A. T. Brooks, Treas.

Bapt. Ministers' Union—1873. 110 mem. Rev. A. A. Shaw, Pres.; Rev. G. C. McKiernan, Sec., 576 Leonard.

Bapt. Young People's Union—F. H. Grob, Pres.; Miss B. E. Dacker, Sec., 277 76th.

Bapt. Young People's Union of the Second German Ch.—1887. 80 mem. W. Makowsky, Pres., 1151 Greene av., Hilda Becker, Sec., 511 Woodland av., Woodhaven.

L. I. Bapt. Assn.—1867. 74 churches. 23,075 mem. Rev. W. I. Southerton, Mod.; Rev. Geo. C. McKiernan, Clerk, 576 Leonard.

Marcy Av. Forum—1917. Marcy Av. Baptist Ch. Rev. John M. Moore, Pastor, 516 Nostrand av.

Social Union of L. I. Bapt. Assn.—1907. 150 mem. Frank H. Field, Pres., 274 Stirling pl.; Mrs. L. I. Barnes, Sec.

Woman's Amer. Bapt. Home Miss. Soc. (L. I. Branch)—1878. Mrs. R. L. Jones, Pres.; Mrs. E. D. Page, Sec., 274 Gates av.

Women's Bapt. Foreign Miss. Assn. of L. I.—Mrs. R. B. Montgomery, Pres.; Mrs. J. Johnson, Cor. Sec., 414 51st.

Young People's Bapt. Union of Bkln. and L. I.—1877. G. L. Bigger, Pres.; L. A. Duncuff, Sec., 174 Sterling.

CATHOLIC.

Bkln. Catholic Historical Soc.—(See Educational Socs.)

Bkln. Diocesan Union of Catholic Young Men's Socs.—35 socs. in membership. F. McHugh, Pres.; B. J. Buckley, Sec.

Bkln. Federation of German Catholic Socs.—1905. 31 Thornton. 4,360 mem. N. Dietz, Pres.; J. F. Dehler, Sec., 251 Maujer.

Catholic Federation of the Diocese of Bkln.—Branch of the Amer. Federation of Catholic Socs. —1908. 44,525 mem. 216 socs. E. F. Cooke, Pres.; Jos. R. Garvey, Sec., 1207 8th av.

Catholic Women's Civic and Social League—107 Greene av. Miss Josephine M. Bennett, Pres.; Miss Annie Higgins, Rec. Sec., 50 Orange.

Italian Catholic Union of Bkln.—25 Orient av. M. Laura, Pres.

Knights of St. Antony—717 Leonard. 1890. 350 mem. T. C. White, Pres.; W. A. Carley, Sec., 138 Noble.

St. Joseph's Young Men's Union—1889. 701 Dean. 150 mem. T. J. Cuff, Pres.; T. J. Dunnigan, Sec.

Soc. of St. Vincent de Paul—(See Special Relief, Bkln.)

Soc. of the Holy Name. Originated at Council of Lyons, held 1274. Org. of L. I., 1872. 185 socs. Diocesan Union of Holy Name Soc. of Bkln. was formed in 1878. 181 socs. are represented. P. F. Dunn, Pres.; J. R. Garvey, Sec., 1207 8th av.

Vincentian Cath. Club—1919. Driggs av., cor. N. 6th. 150 mem. M. A. Devaney, Pres.; Rev. J. A. Murphy, Spiritual Dir., 167 N. 6th.

CONGREGATIONAL.

Brotherhood of Cong. Ministers—1902. 57 mem. Rev. E. M. Halliday, Pres.; Rev. C. J. Allen, Sec.-Treas., 1776 45th.

Central League—1890. 500 mem. R. M. Gray, Pres.; L. E. Halsey, Sec., 154 Putnam av.

Cong. Church Extension Soc. of N. Y. and Bkln.—1893. 287 4th av., Mhtn. Hon. E. M. Bassett, Pres.; Rev. C. W. Shelton, Sec.

Congregational Club—1888. 125 mem. Rev. E. M. Halliday, Pres.; W. C. McKee, Sec., 102 Court.

Dr. Boynton's Round Table—(Clinton av. Cong. Ch.)—1917. 89 mem. S. C. Fairley, Pres.; D. Bonck, Sec., 394 Grand av.

Men's League of St. Paul's Cong. Ch.—1908. N. Y. av., cor. Sterling pl. 110 mem. W. L. Love, M.D., Pres.; A. F. Decker, Sec., 949 Park pl.

Women's League of Flatbush Cong. Ch.—1901. 300 mem. Mrs. H. A. Higley, Pres.; Mrs. W. J. Dodge, Sec., 1051 E. 10th.

Young Women's Club of Central Cong. Ch.—1916. A. W. Ryall, Pres.; R. Martin, Sec., 75 Hancock.

LUTHERAN.

English Lutheran Missionary Soc. of Bkln., Inc.—1902. 20 churches. Past. S. G. Weiskotten, Pres.; Past. E. R. Jaxheimer, Sec., 165 87th rd., Woodhaven, L. I.

Pastoral Assn. Eastern Conf. N. Y. and N. E. Synod. 30 mem. Past. C. F. Intemann, Pres.; Past. C. G. Toebke, Sec., 12,503 103d av., Richmond Hill.

St. Peter's Luth. Cadet Corps Vet. Assn.—257-263 Skillman. 1895. Religious, athletic, memorial and military training. 90 mem. Capt. Fred Stussy, Jr., Com.; Capt. C. S. Stussy, V.-Com., 642 Monroe.

METHODIST EPISCOPAL.

Allied Men's League of M. E. Churches—(See Bd. of Trade, etc.)

Bkln. and L. I. Church Soc. of M. E. Ch.—1878. 2 managers and pastors from each church in Bkln. and on L. I. and 60 at large. Rev. W. A. Layton, Supt. and Sec., 47 Brevoort pl.

Bkln. and L. I. Preachers Assn. of M. E. Ch.—Fleet, nr. Fulton. 1900. 148 mem. Rev. W. L. Dawson, Pres.; Rev. S. J. Pennell, Sec.

Bkln. South Dist., Epworth League—Central Br. Y. M. C. A. 4,650 mem. H. A. Merlin, Pres.; Miss E. M. Selover, Sec., 1616 Beverly rd.

Florence Nightingale Federation—See Special Relief Socs., Bkln.

Methodist Social Union of Bkln. and L. I.—1894. 225 mem. C. A. Lent, Pres.; E. B. Blatz, Sec., 138 Montague.

SOCIETIES AND ASSOCIATIONS—RELIGIOUS—BROOKLYN—METHODIST EPISCOPAL—*Continued.*

N. Y. East Conference—Rev. W. L. Davidson, Dist. Supt. of Bkln. N. Dist., 62 Montague. Rev. A. S. Kavanagh, Dist. Supt. of Bkln. S. Dist., 352 Clinton.

Woman's Home Miss. Soc. of the N. Y. East Conference of the M. E. Ch.—Mrs. C. A. Soper, Pres., 1523 N. Y. av.; Mrs. K. L. Winter, Sec., 21 Arch, Waterbury, Conn.

PRESBYTERIAN.

Bkln.-Nassau Presbytery — Comprising the Presbyterian churches of Kings and Queens and Nassau cos. 128 ministers and 78 churches. Rev. J. M. Thompson, D.D., Mod.; Rev. J. G. Snyder, Stated Clerk, 9 8th av.

Church Extension Board of the Presbytery of Bkln.-Nassau (Inc.)—1914. R. M. Hart, Pres.; Rev. R. W. Anthony, Exec. Sec., 32 Court.

Federated Aid Soc. of Presbytery of Bkln.—Mrs. I. G. Oldaker, Pres.; Mrs. H. H. Nilsson, Sec., 1717 Grove.

Presbyterian Union of Bkln. and Vicinity—1906. 200 mem. 24 churches. W. F. Atkinson, Pres.; G. P. Moffat, Sec., 148 Monroe.

Women's Home and Foreign Miss. Soc. of the Presbytery of Bkln.—Mrs. W. Carter, Pres.; Mrs. H. C. Palmer, Cor. Sec., 530 1st.

Women's Missionary Soc. of Union Church of Bay Ridge Presby.—1898. 76 mem. Mrs. M. Glen, Pres., 266 83d; Mrs. W. Caye, Sec., 7815 Ridge blvd.

PROTESTANT EPISCOPAL.

Brotherhood of St. Andrew—L. I. Assembly, 170 Remsen. 510 mem. A. Adams, Pres., 421A Lafayette av.; F. J. Murray, Sec., 186 Elton.

Church Club of Diocese of L. I.—1894. 100 mem. 170 Remsen. J. C. Klinck, Pres.; G. M. Allen, Sec.

Daughters of the King (Diocese of L. I.)—8 chaps. 175 mem. Mrs. F. H. Handsfield, Pres., Rockville Centre, L. I.; Miss E. W. Jeffers, Sec., 1068 Hancock.

Diocese of L. I.—(See Religious Socs., L. I.)

Diocesan House of L. I.—170 Remsen. Robert Harrold, Sec.

Girls' Friendly Soc., Diocese of L. I.—1887. Mrs. W. S. Shattuck, Pres.; Miss J. A. H. Schapps, Sec., 753 Bedford av.

St. Thomas' Guild—1887. Rev. D. M. Genns, Pres.; Mrs. S. Beatty, Sec., 1342 Bushwick av.

Trinity Club—157 Montague. 1897. 400 mem. J. H. Melish, Pres.; A. J. Bosthwick, Sec.

Trinity Intermediate Club—157 Montague. 1908. 350 mem. A. J. Bosthwick, Dir.

REFORMED.

Reformed Ch. in Amer.—North Classis of L. I. Rev. C. K. Clearwater, Stated Clerk, 23 Vietor pl., Elmhurst, L. I. South Classis of L. I. Rev. J. F. Berg, Pres.; Rev. J. S. Gardner, Stated Clerk, 266 Altamount pl., Somerville, N. J.

UNITARIAN.

Branch Alliance of Unity Ch.—45 mem. Mrs. M. W. Hughan, Pres.; Mrs. E. F. Hudson, Sec., 556 Greene av.

Natl. Alliance of Unitarian Women (Flatbush Branch), Beverly rd. and E. 19th—1900. 75 mem. Mrs. C. E. Woodbridge, Pres.; Mrs. M. J. Koniger, Cor. Sec., 497 Westminster rd.

UNIVERSALIST.

Women's League (All Souls Univ. Ch.)—1894. 163 mem. Mrs. G. Hervey, Pres.; Mrs. H. K. Davenport, Cor. Sec., 10 Stephens ct.

OTHER RELIGIOUS SOCIETIES.

Alpha Kappa Club—1881. 24 mem. Rev. F. F. Shannon, Sec., 194 Columbia Hgts.

American Bible Society—Eastern Agency, 137 Montague. Advisory Committee, Dr. L. D. Mason, W. W. Kouwenhoven, Rev. J. G. Snyder, G. M. Blauvelt; Rev. S. C. Benson, Sec.

Bkln. Bible Soc.—1840. 137 Montague. Auxiliary to Am. Bible Soc.—Rev. J. G. Snyder, Sec.

Bkln. Christian Endeavor Union—1890. E. F. Garwood, Pres., 625 E. 14th; Miss M. Jahn, Sec., 1854 E. 12th. There are 60 societies in the Union, divided as follows: Presby., 29; Cong., 11; Bapt., 3; Christian, 1; Ref., 4; Christ-Disc., 2; Prim. Meth., 2; A. M. E., 1; M P., 1; U. P., 3; Moravian, 1; Evan., 1; Und., 1. 1,900 mem. A Junior Dept. for Boys and Girls, 6-12 yrs. of age, org. 1892. 35 socs., 2,000 mem. and Intermediate Dept. for older boys and girls, org. 1908. 23 socs., 602 mem. Own and maintain fresh air camp for poor children at Huntington Sta., L. I.

Bkln. City Mission and Tract Soc.—(See Missions.)

Bkln. Clerical Union—Montauk Club. 25 mem. Robert W. Anthony, Pres.; John M. Moore, Sec., 156 Nostrand av.

Bkln. Soc. for Ethical Culture—1906. 176 S. Oxford. 300 mem. Dr. Henry Neumann, Leader; Miss F. Shettle, Sec., 720 Halsey.

Bkln. Soc. of the New Church—1868. 108 Clark. R. A. Shaw, Pres.

Bkln. S. S. Union—1816. 23 Flatbush av. Bd. of Mgrs. meets 2d M. Jan., Mar., May, Sept. and Nov. E. B. Van Buskirk, Sec., 132 Herkimer.

Council of Men's Church Clubs of Flatbush—(See Men's Church Clubs.)

Epworth League—Bkln. and L. I. Divided into North and South Dists. North Dist. has 62 Senior, 25 Junior Chapters and 5,715 mem. D. J. Cameron, Pres.; Marie Herfort, Sec., Hicksville. South Dist. has 52 Senior, 35 Junior Chapters and 4,650 mem. H. A. Merlin, Pres.; Ethel M. Selover, Sec., 1616 Beverly rd.

Federation of Churches—1920. Temp. officers. Rev. S. E. Young, Bedford Presby. Ch., Chairman; Rev. F. M. Gordon, Sec., 400 Rugby rd.

Federation of Men's Church organizations of Bkln.—5,000 mem. Org. 1910. W. M. Briggs, Pres.; J. G. Stevenson, Sec., 27 Cedar, Mhtn.

German Y. M. C. A. Assn.—1878. 30 mem. F. H. Hagmann, Pres.; G. Heitman, Sec., 9126 110th, Richmond Hill.

Kings Co. S. S. A. Assn.—Consolidated with Bkln. Sunday Schl. Union.

Sunday Observance Assn. of Kings Co.—1882. H. N. Niles, Pres., 373 Tompkins av.; Rev. T. B. Griswold, Treas.

Theosophical Soc.—1904. 95 Lafayette av. Mrs. Annie Besant, Pres.; Miss Edith Schofield, Sec., 55 Prospect pl.

Tillary St. Rescue Mission and Gardner Memorial—1891. 14 Tillary. Rev. E. D. Bailey, Pres.; Rev. T. C. Roberts-Honsfield, Supt.

Union Missionary Training Inst.—1885. 525 Clinton av. D. O. Shelton, Pres.; H. R. Monro, Treas.

Women's Guild of Plymouth Ch.—1913. Mrs. E. Meyer, Act. Pres., 275 Clinton; Miss A. L. Henken, Rec. Sec., Hotel Mohawk.

Women's Missionary Soc. of Christ Ch.—H. H. Foster, Pres.; Miss J. Morris, Sec., 502 Beach 44th, Edgemere.

Women's Natl. Sabbath Alliance (Bkln. Br.)—Mrs. H. E. Drake, Pres., 200 Schermerhorn; Mrs. A. L. Dutcher, Sec., 36 Clark.

Young Men's Christian Assn., Bkln.—Founded 1853. Gen. office, 55 Hanson pl. 16,906 mem. Average attendance of 7,137 daily. Reference libraries in 13 branches with 14,291 vols.; 13 reading rooms, with 454 magazines and newspapers; 9 gymnasiums, 1,073 dormitory rooms in 8 branches. Educational dept. in 5 branches, in 50 studies, with enrollment of 5,783. Literary societies; chess, checkers and camera clubs. Members' entertainments and weekly religious meetings. Lunch rooms in 6 branches. 4 Summer Camps. F. C. Munson, Pres.; J. W. Cook, Gen. Sec.; J. C. Armstrong, Assoc. Gen. Sec.; H. W. Northcott, Army Sec., R. P. Walker, City Industrial Sec.; G. C. Brooke, City Phy. Dir. for Industry; A. R. Klemer, City Boys Work Sec.; J. H. Field, Acct. Branches: Central, 55 Hanson pl.; C. W. Dietrich, Sec. Eastern District, Marcy av. and S. 9th; F. J. Slater, Sec. Bedford, Bedford av. and Monroe; H. Hammond, Sec. Prospect Park, 369 9th; L. H. Brown, Sec. Bush Terminal, 40th and 2d av.; A. E. Chamberlain, Sec. Highland Pk., 125 Logan; W. H. Waechter, Sec. L. I. Railroad, 45 Borden av., L. I. City; A. K. Hicks, Sec. Ft. Totten, Army, Ft. Totten, N. Y.; L. W. Draper, Sec. Ft. Hamilton, Army, Ft. Hamilton; J. H. Berry, Sec. Fort Tilden, Army, Fort Tilden, L. I.; C. E. Schuyler, Sec. Carlton av., 405 Carlton av.; R. M. Meroney, Sec. Greenpoint, Meserole av. and Lorimer; W. D. Miller, Sec. Bethelship Seaman's, Sullivan and Richards; C. Brandt, Mgr. L. I. City-Industrial, 426 Jackson av.; A. W. Walch, Sec. New Utrecht, 1841 84th; E. H. Burritt, Sec. Jamaica Community Branch, J. O. Arrol, Sec. Chapels at Rockaway Pt. and Broad Channel, Jamaica Bay. Naval Branch (affiliated), 167 Sands; W. L. Tisdale, Sec.

Young Women's Christian Assn. of Bkln.—1888. Schermerhorn, at Flatbush av. Mrs. H. M. Halsted, Pres.; Miss G. Ingraham, Treas. Central Branch, Schermerhorn, at Flatbush av.; Mrs. R. Reimer, Jr., Ch.; Miss M. A.

SOCIETIES AND ASSOCIATIONS—RELIGIOUS—BROOKLYN—MISCELLANEOUS—*Continued.*

Billington, Sec. 18 classrooms; library of 13,034 vols.; hall seating 650; assembly room seating 300; gymnasium, running track, needle baths; classes in commercial courses, domestic economy, attendant nursing, etc.; girls' work dept.; self-governing clubs. Has a general employment agency, including a nurse's registry; cafeteria and room registry. Boarding dept. 50 Nevins.; Mrs. E. Adams, Ch.; Miss E. Alexander, Sec. Eastern District Branch, Bedford av. and Keap. Org. 1903. Mrs. J. A. Mollenhauer, Ch.; Miss Alice Ward, Sec. Ashland Pl. Branch, 45 Ashland pl. Org. 1902. Mrs. R. W. Westbrook, Ch.; Miss Josephine Pinyon, Sec. Bush Terminal Branch-Industrial Centre, 35th and 3d av.; cafeteria, 40th and 2d av.; Mrs. Ralph I. Lloyd, Ch.; Miss L. B. Smith, Sec. Home for Business Women, 245 Carlton av.; Mrs. Melville H. Bearns, Ch.; Mrs. J. R. Odenwalder, Sec. International Institute, 106 Montague; Mrs. Oliver W. Ingersoll, Ch.; Miss Annie B. Kerr, Sec.

Manhattan and Bronx.

BAPTIST.

Amer. Bapt. Home Miss. Soc.—1832. 23 E. 26th. Rev. C. L. White, Exec. Sec.

Bapt. Ministers' Conference—Madison av. and 31st. 180 mem. Rev. C. W. Petty, Pres.; Rev. W. A. Spinney, Sec., 371 72d, Bkln.

Bapt. Social Union of N. Y.—1869. 145 mem. L. W. Hill, Pres.; D. H. Knott, V.-Pres., 35 Washington sq.

N. Y. City Bapt. Mission Soc. 276 5th av. Inc. 1893. Composed of delegates from all Bapt. churches in Mhtn. and Bronx. Builds churches, sustains downtown churches among foreign people in N. Y. E. L. Ballard, Pres.; C. H. Sears, D.D., Sec., 276 5th av.

CATHOLIC.

Archdiocesan Union Holy Name Soc.—1882. 457 W. 51st. 236 branches. 52,350 mem. F. J. Briggs, Pres.; E. D. Dowling, Sec., 280 B'way.

Holy Cross Lyceum—1879. 321 W. 43d. 400 mem. Rev. J. F. Flannelly, Pres.; J. A. Dowd, Sec.

Institute of Our Lady of Christian Doctrine—173 Cherry. The sisters of the institute conduct a day nursery and classes for the religious instruction of children and adults, also visit sick poor.

Soc. of St. Vincent de Paul—(See Relief Socs., Special Relief, Mhtn.)

CHRISTIAN SCIENCE.

(See Churches and Libraries.)

CONGREGATIONAL.

Cong. Church Bldg. Soc.—1853. 287 4th av. Dr. R. H. Potter, Pres.; Dr. C. E. Burton, Dr. J. R. Smith and Dr. C. H. Richards, Secs.; C. H. Baker, Treas.

Cong. Club of N. Y. and Vicinity—1879. Hotel McAlpin. 200 mem. Rev. C. H. Wilson, Pres.; C. L. Beckwith, Sec., 346 B'way.

Cong. Home Miss. Soc. (The)—1826. 287 4th av. C. E. Burton, D.D., Gen. Sec.; C. H. Baker, Treas.

Woman's Dept., Miss M. L. Woodberry, Sec.

Congregational S. S. Exten. Soc. (The)—1917. 287 4th av. C. E. Burton, D.D., Gen. Sec.; C. H. Baker, Treas.

N. Y. City Assn. of Cong. Churches—1889. 27,410 mem. Rev. G. D. Egbert, Pres.; Rev. C. J. Allen, Sec.-Treas., 1776 45th, Bkln.

LUTHERAN.

Inner Mission Soc. Evang. Luth. Ch., Inc.—600 mem. Rev. M. L. Canup, Pres.; J. S. Runyon, Sec., 502 W. 136th.

Luth. Bureau of the Natl. Luth. Council—437 5th av. Rev. L. Larson, D.D., Ch.; O. H. Pannkoke, Exec. Sec.

Luth. Ch. Extension Soc.—1890. J. A. Prigge, Pres.; Rev. F. H. Bosch, Sec., 142 W. 123d.

Luth. Emigrant's House Assn. (The)—1871. 147 W. 23d. 21 mem. M. Wulff, Pres.; Rev. D. W. Peterson, Sec., 147 W. 23d.

Luth. League of N. Y. City—1888. W. Weilage, Pres., 678 St. Nicholas av.; Miss E. Wirsing, Cor. Sec., 236 W. 65th.

N. Y. Luth. Ministers' Assn.—250 mem. 23d st. Y. M. C. A. Rev. A. S. Hardy, Pres.; Rev. R. C. Deitz, Sec., 264 78th, Bkln.

METHODIST EPISCOPAL.

Board of Education of the M. E. Ch.—1864. 150 5th av., Mhtn. 36 mem. Dr. A. W. Harris, Cor. Sec., 150 5th av.

Home and Foreign Missionary Dept. (African M. E. Ch.—1844. 62-4 Bible House. Bishop W. W. Beckett, Pres.; Rev. J. W. Rankin, Sec.

Meth. Book Concern—1789. 150 5th av. E. R. Graham, Pub. Agt.

Meth. Historical Soc. in the City of N. Y.—1892. 150 5th av. H. K. Carroll, Pres.; Rev. H. E. Woolever, Sec.

Meth. Social Union—1887. 500 mem. C. W. Erskine, Pres.; B. A. Matthews, Sec., 150 B'way.

Missions (Board of Foreign of the M. E. Ch.)—1819. 150 5th av. Bishop L. B. Wilson, Pres.; G. M. Fowles, Treas.; S. E. Taylor, LL.D., Rev. F. M. North, D.D., Cor. Secs.

N. Y. City Soc. of the M. E. Church—1866. 150 5th av. 175 managers. 25 churches and missions. Rev. M. L. Robinson, Exec. Sec.

N. Y. Preachers' Meeting of the M. E. Ch.—1817. 150 5th av. 700 mem. J. A. Cole, Pres.; W. C. Kinsey, Sec.

Woman's Foreign Mission Soc. of M. E. Ch. (N. Y. Branch)—1869. 150 5th av. 64,791 mem. Mrs. W. I. Haven, Pres.; Mrs. G. A. Wilson, Cor. Sec., 820 Livingston av., Syracuse, N. Y.

Woman's Home Miss. Soc. of N. Y. Conference of the M. E. Ch.—1882. 150 5th av. 2,459 mem. Mrs. E. J. Palmer, Pres., 103 W. 86th; Mrs. W. B. Oliver, Cor. Sec., 611 W. 111th, Mhtn.

PRESBYTERIAN.

Board of Foreign Missions of the Presb. Ch. in the U. S. A.—1837. 156 5th av. 23 mem. Rev. Geo. Alexander, D.D., Pres.; Rev. Stanley White, D.D., Rec. Sec.

Board of Home Missions of the Presb. Ch. in the U. S. A.—1872. 156 5th av. 30 mem. Rev. W. Merle-Smith, Pres.; Rev. J. A. Marquis, Gen. Sec.; Varian Banks, Asst. Treas.

Board of the Church Erection Fund of the General Assembly of Presb. Ch. in U. S. A.—1844. 156 5th av. 27 trustees. Rev. F. C. Ottman, D.D., Pres.; Rev. D. G. Wylie, D.D., Gen. Sec.; Rev. J. C. Bruce, Field Sec.; Rev. G. R. Brauer, Treas.

College Board (The)—Merged with General Bd. of Education of Presb. Ch. in U. S. A.—(See National Socs.)

Men's Assn. of the First Presby. Ch.—Thos. P. Kilgore, Sec., 65 W. B'way.

Presby. of N. Y.—1738. 189 ministers, 62 churches. Rev. H. G. Mendenhall, D.D., Mod.; J. F. Forbes, D.D., Stated Clerk, 156 5th av.

Presby. Ministers Assn. of N. Y. City and Vicinity—1861. 156 5th av. 200 mem. Rev. R. Watson, D.D., Pres.; Rev. L. W. Barney, Sec., Sound Beach, Conn.

Presby. Union of N. Y.—1886. 200 mem. Rev. A. E. Keigwin, Pres.; Rev. H. G. Mendenhall, Sec., 156 5th av.

Women's Board of Foreign Missions of the Presb. Ch.—1870. 156 5th av. 49 managers. Miss A. M. Davison, Pres.; Mrs. G. C. Aymar, Sec.

Woman's Board of Home Missions—156 5th av. Mrs. F. S. Bennett, Pres.; Miss L. H. Dawson, Gen.-Sec.

PROTESTANT EPISCOPAL.

Am. Church Missionary Soc.—1860. 281 4th av. Rev. F. J. Clark, Gen. Sec.

Archdeaconry of N. Y.—1887. R. M. Pott, Treas.; 214 E. 23d.

Church Periodical Club (P. E.)—1888. 2 W. 47th. Mrs. Otto Heinigke, Pres.; Miss M. E. Thomas, Exec. Sec.

Daughters of the King—1885. 84 Bible House. 6,000 mem. Mrs. A. Denmead, Pres.; Miss M. E. Atwood, Natl. Sec.

Girls' Friendly Soc. in Diocese of N. Y.—Diocesan office, 147 E. 34th. 8,269 mem. Mrs. J. W. Pfan, Pres.; Mrs. E. M. Hadley, Sec.

N. Y. Bible and Prayer Book Soc.—1809. E. S. Gorham, Sec., 11 W. 45th.

N. Y. P. E. City Mission Soc.—1831. 38 Bleecker. H. P. Robbins, Sec.; L. E. Sunderland, Supt., 38 Bleecker.

Presiding Bishop and Council (Domestic and Foreign Miss. Soc. of the P. E. Ch. in the U. S. of A., 1821)—281 4th av. Rt. Rev. T. F. Gailor, D.D., Pres.; Rev. F. J. Clark, Sec.; L. B. Franklin, Treas.; C. A. Tompkins, Asst. Treas. Dept. of Missions and Church Extension, J. W. Wood, D.C.L., Exec. Sec. and Act. Foreign Sec.; Rev. A. R. Gray, D.D., Sec. for Latin America; Wm. C. Sturgis, Ph.D., Educational Sec.; Rev. Thos. Burgess, Sec. for Work among Foreign Born Americans. Dept. of Religious Education, Rev. W. E. Gardner, D.D., Exec. Sec.; Rev. L. Bradner, Ph.D.,

Rev. P. Micou, M.A., Miss F. H. Withers, Secs. Dept. of Christian Social Service, Rev. C. N. Lathrop, Exec. Sec. Dept. of Publicity, Rev. R. F. Gibson, Exec. Sec.; Rev. C. E. Betticher, Editorial Sec. Dept. of Finance, L. B. Franklin, Exec. Sec. Dept. of Nation Wide Campaign, Rev. W. H. Milton, D.D., Exec. Sec.; Rev. R. W. Patton, D.D., Campaign Dir.; Rev. L. G. Wood, Field Sec.; Rev. R. Bland Mitchell, Cor. Sec. The Woman's Anxiliary, Miss M. G. Lindley, Gen. Sec.; Miss E. C. Tillotson, Educ. Sec.; Mrs. G. Biller, Field Sec.; Miss G. Hutchins, Recruiting Sec.; Miss E. I. Flanders, Office Sec.

P. E. Soc. for Promotion of Evangelical Knowledge—1848. Rev. R. H. McKim, Pres.; Alex. G. Cummins, Sec., Poughkeepsie, N. Y.

Sisterhood of the Holy Communion—1852. Parish work and visiting, nursing care of altar service, clergy, choir vestments, home for aged women, etc., 328 6th av.

Soc. for Promoting Religion and Learning—1839. Pres. (vacant). Cathedral Hgts.

Trinity Ch. Assn. (The)—1880. 211 Fulton. Rev. W. T. Manning, S. T. D., Pres.; R. M. Colt, Sec., 59 Maiden lane.

Woman's Aux. to the Presiding Bishop and Council—1871. Church Missions House, 281 4th av. Miss M. G. Lindley, Gen. Sec., 281 4th av.

REFORMED.

Board of Direction of Gen. Synod of R. Ch. in Am.—1771. 25 E. 22d. Com. L. Brower, Pres.; F. R. Van Nest, Sec.

Board of Education of the R. Ch. in Am.—1828. 25 E. 22d. 24 mem. A. T. Broek, Pres.; W. D. Brown, Cor. Sec., 25 E. 22d.

Board of Foreign Missions, R. C. A.—1832. 25 E. 22d. 27 mem. Rev. H. E. Cobb, D.D., Pres.; Rev. W. I. Chamberlain, Ph.D., Sec., 25 E. 22d. F. M. Potter, Treas.

Board of Publication and Bible School Work of the Ref. Ch. in Amer.—1856. 25 E. 22d. 30 mem. Rev I. W Gowen, Cor. Sec.

Fulton St. Noon Prayer Meeting—1857. 113 Fulton, or 58 Ann. Rev. G. H. Dowkontt, Supt.

Pastors' Assn. of the R. Ch. in N. Y. and Vicinity—1877. 25 E. 22d. Rev. Eugene Hill, Pres.; Rev. E. W. Thompson, D.D., Sec., Hastings-on-Hudson, N. Y.

Reformed Church Union—1901. 300 mem. Wm. I. Chamberlain, Pres.; W. T. Demarest, Sec., 25 E. 22d.

Woman's Board of Foreign Missions of the R. Ch. in Am.—1875. 25 E. 22d. 55 mem. Mrs. F. A. Baldwin, Pres.; Miss E. P. Cobb, Cor. Sec.

Women's Board of Domestic Missions, R. Ch. in Am.—1882. 25 E. 22d. 60 mem. Mrs. J. S. Bussing, Pres.; Mrs. J. S. Allen, Sec., 25 E. 22d.

REFCRMED EPISCOPAL.

N. Y. and Phila. Synod of Ref. Epis. Ch.—1881. 12,230 mem. Rt. Rev. R. L. Rudolph, D.D., Pres.; Rev. J. H. Clemmency, Sec., 732 N. E. Boulevard, Phila., Pa.

UNIVERSALIST.

N. Y. Univ. Club—1885. 85 mem. Object: Social and denominational. E. L. Faris, Pres.; G. O. Revere, Sec., 150 Nassau.

The Trustees of the N. Y. Univ. Relief Fund— Consolidated with the N. Y. State Convention of Universalists. See State Socs.

Univ. Women's Alliance of the Metropolitan Dist.—1895. 300 mem. Mrs. W. F. Peters, Pres.; Mrs. H. C. Greanelle, Sec., 44 W. 75th.

OTHER RELIGIOUS SOCIETIES.

Am. Bible Soc.—1816. **Bible House, 4th av. and** Astor pl. C. H. Cutting, Pres.; Rev. W. I. Haven, F. H. Mann, Gen. Secs.; Rev. L. B. Chamberlain, Rec. Sec.; G. Darlington, Asst. Treas. Eastern Agency, covering all N. Y. and New England, not cared for by local Bible socs., Rev. H. J. Scudder, Agency Sec., 137 Montague, Bkln.

Am. Church Building Fund Commission—1880. 281 4th av. Rev. C. L. Pardee, D.D., Cor. Sec., 281 4th av.

Am. Inst. of Christian Philosophy—1882. Rm. 3109, Grand Central Term. J. H. MacCracken, Pres.; A. S. Lyman, Treas.

Am. Missionary Assn.—1846. 287 4th av. N. Boynton, Pres.; G. L. Cady, Sec., 287 4th av.

Am. Swedenborg Printing and Publishing Soc., 3 W. 29th. H. W. Guernsey, Pres.; W. B. Safford, Sec.

Am. Tract Soc.—1825. Park av. and 40th. W. P. Hall, Pres.; Judson Swifth, D.D., Gen. Sec.; Louis Tag, Treas.

Bible Teachers' Training Schl.—1901. 541 Lexington av. W. W. White, Pres.; L. J. Tompkins, Sec.

Board of Domestic Missions—1832. 25 E. 22d. 27 mem. Rev. J. M. Farrar, D.D., Pres.; W. T. Demarest, Sec.

Bureau of Missions—Merged with Missionary Education Movement.

Church Assn. for Advancement of Interests of Labor—1887. 416 Lafayette. Miss H. A. Keyser, 2d V.-Pres. and Ex. Sec.

Church Mission to Deaf Mutes (The)—1872. 511 W. 148th.

Clergymen's Mutual Insurance League, Inc—1869. Rev. W. N. Dunnell, Pres.; Rev. E. B. Rice, Sec.-Treas., 212 N. Fulton av., Mt. Vernon, N. Y.

Clergymen's Retiring Fund Soc.—1874. Provides annuities for old clergymen. 650 mem. Invested Fund, $431,654. Rt. Rev. Frederick Burgess, D.D., Pres.; Rev. H. Anstice, Fin. Sec.-Treas., 281 4th av.

Intercollegiate Branch of Y. M. C. A. (Students' Club)—1889. 2240 mem. Office, 2929 B'way. Centers of Work, Violet Hut, N. Y. Univ.; Earl Hall, Columbia Univ.; Club Houses, 129 Lex. av., 346 W. 57th. E. P. Wheeler, Pres.; H. E. Edmonds, Sec., 527 Riverside drive.

Interdenominational Committee on Weekday Religious Instruction—Mrs. H. W. Farrington, Sec., 625 W. 138th.

Internatl. Christian Police Assn.—N. Y. Branch. 226 E. 58th. S. R. Kendall, Pres.; Mrs. J. L. Spicer, V.-Pres.; Rev. J. L. Spicer, Sec.-Chaplain.

Metropolitan Federation of Daily Vacation Bible Schools—1919. 90 Bible House. Rev. R. W. Anthony, Pres.; Rev. W. M. Howlett, Sec.

Natl. Bible Institute (Inc.)—1906. 214 W. 35th. D. O. Shelton, Pres.; H. R. Monro, Treas.

Needlework Guild of Amer.—(See Special Relief.)

New Church Bd. of Publication (The)—1882. 3 W. 29th. 50 mem. R. A. Shaw, Pres.; Rev. P. A. Sherer, Sec.

New Church Press, Inc. (The)—3 W. 29th. R. A. Shaw, Pres.; P. A. Sherer, Sec.

N. Y. Assn. of the New Church—1883. 1,200 mem. Rev. J. K. Smyth, Pres.; F. W. Freeman, Sec., Paterson, N. J.

N. Y. Bible and Common Prayer Book Soc.— 1809. 11 W. 45th. E. S. Gorham, Sec.

N. Y. Bible Soc.—1809. 5 E. 48th. Object: To distribute Bibles. Total distribution during past year, 550,000 volumes in 53 languages and in raised type for the blind. Has instituted third Sunday before Christmas as Universal Bible Sunday. J. C. West, Pres.; Rev. G. W. Carter, Sec.; J. H. Schmelzel, Treas.

N. Y. Churchman's Assn.—1882. 175 mem. Rev. C. L. Slattery, Pres.; Rev. John Acworth, Sec., 67 E. 89th.

N. Y. City Mission Soc.—(See Missions.)

N. Y. City S. S. Assn.—1816. 257 Metropolitan Tower. W. J. Thompson, Pres.; H. W. Hicks, Gen. Sec.

N. Y. Federation of Churches—1896. 200 5th av. A. F. Atterbury, D.D., Pres.; W. Laidlaw, Exec. Sec.

N. Y. Female Bible Soc.—1848. Bible House. 50 managers. Mrs. Theodore Weston, Pres.; Miss E. M. Olcott, Cor. Sec.; Miss E. R. Greenwood, Treas.

N. Y. Port Soc.—(See Soc. for Promoting Gospel Among Seamen in Port of N. Y.)

N. Y. Sabbath Com.—1857. Inc. 1884. 31 Bible House. T. Gilman, Ch.; Dr. D. J. McMillan, Gen. Sec.; E. F. Hyde, Treas.

Northeastern Field Comm. of the Y. W. C. A. for New England, N. Y. and N. J.—1907. 600 Lexington av. 80 committee mem., 26 secs.

Police Christian Assns.—See Internalt. Christian Police Assns.

Rescue Soc., Inc. (The)—1901. 5 and 7 Doyers. 399 mem. Dr. Thos. H. Spencer, Pres.; T. J. Noonan, Sec., 126 Bible House.

Salvation Army—(See Special Relief.)

Silver Bay Assn. for Christian Conferences and Training (The)—1904. 27 trustees. 347 Madison av. W. D. Murry, Ch.; C. C. Michener, Pres.

Silver Bay School Boys—1919. 347 Madison av. H. F. Marten, Ph.D., Prin.

SOCIETIES AND ASSOCIATIONS—RELIGIOUS—MHTN. AND BRONX—MISCELLANEOUS—*Continued.*

Soc. for Ethical Culture—1876. 64th and Central Park W. Sun. mornings, Oct.-May, at 11; Sun. evenings, Jan.-Mar., at 8. 1,100 mem. Ethical Culture Schl., 63d and Central Park W. 1879. 700 pupils. Felix Adler, Sr. Leader; 3 Leaders. R. D. Kohn, Sec., 56 W. 45th. Women's Conference—1891. 2 W. 64th. 450 mem. Mrs. H. Ollesheimer, Pres., 550 Park av.

Soc. for Promoting Gospel Among Seamen in Port of N. Y. (N. Y. Port Soc.)—1818. 166 11th av. 20 dirs. J. Yereance, Pres., 128 B'way; Rev. K. Palmer Miller, M.A., Sec., 166-168 11th av.

Theosophical Soc. (Independent)—1899. 124 W. 58th. H. W. Percival, Pres.; B. B. Gattell, Sec.

Theosophical Soc., N. Y. Lodge (Besant Branch)—1897. 2228 B'way. Mrs. E. B. Welton, Pres.; Mrs. L. Eggleston, Sec.

Vedanta—1898. 117 W. 72d. E. Shaughnessy, Pres.; A. L. Stuart, Sec. Branches in Los Angeles, San Francisco, Boston and Washington, D. C.

Volunteers of Amer.—(See Special Relief.)

Young Men's Christian Assn.—1852. 2 W. 45th. 14 branches and 23 buildings. 31,311 mem. Has libraries with 102,359 vols., reading rooms with 1,206 newspapers and magazines; 12 gymnasiums and 8 swimming pools. Facilities for outdoor athletics. 10 halls for entertainments. Educational dept. embraces 607 classes in 75 different subjects, with 10,635 students; literary societies, lectures, health talks and socials. Special work for 3,000 boy members in 8 branches. Special branches are maintained for French students, soldiers and sailors, colored men and railroad men. Six summer camps for boys. Special service rendered foreign born at Ellis Is. and on the docks. Classes in citizenship and English conducted in industries, foreign clubs and in principal branches. W. M. Kingsley, Pres.; W. T. Diack, Gen. Sec., 2 W. 45th.

Branches:

Army—Fort Jay, Fort Wood, Fort Wadsworth, Fort Slocum and Fort Schuyler. G. A. Sanford, Sec.

Bowery—8 E. 3d. R. F. Woodhull, Sec., 334 mem. Work among destitute men.

Bronx Union Branch—470 E. 161st. E. L. Moralier, Sec., 2,494 mem.

East Side—153 E. 86th. R. W. Brown, Sec. 1,616 mem.

French—109 W. 54th. Louis Bichsel, Sec., 509 mem.

Harlem—5 W. 125th. F. G. Banister, Sec. 1,007 mem.

Institute—222 Bowery. C. M. Knight, Sec. 552 mem.

Intercollegiate—129 Lexington av. and 346 W. 57th. H. E. Edmonds, Sec., 2929 B'way. 991 mem.

Mott Haven Dept. Railroad Branch—E. 150th and Spencer pl. 117 mem. F. E. Lawrence, Sec.

R. R. Branch—R. R. Men's Bldg., 309 Park av. W. W. Adair, Sec. 3,702 mem.

R. R. Branch—Penn. Sta. J. M. Rice, Sec. 961 mem.

Twenty-third St.—215 W. 23d. B. B. Farnsworth, Sec. 3,700 mem.

Washington Heights—531 W. 155th. S. Peterson, Sec. 561 mem.

West 135th (for colored men)—179 W. 135th. T. E. Taylor, Sec. 542 mem.

West Side—318 W. 57th. E. G. Wilson, Sec. 8,422 mem.

West 72d St. Dept. R. R. Branch—72d and 11th av. 271 mem. F. E. Lawrence, Sec.

West Shore Dept. R. R.—New Durham, N. J. 281 mem. W. A. Berry, Sec., New Durham.

Young Women's Christian Assn., City of N. Y. (Central Branch)—610 Lexington av. Day and evening classes in household arts, bus. and secretarial tr., gym. and swimming. Bible and world friendship program, study. Employment bureau, room registry and social clubs. Library of 23,000 vols., reference and reading rooms, open daily. Hall seating 700. Miss E. B. Wilson, Ch.; Mrs. W. A. Ransom, Treas.; Mrs. F. B. Fay, Sec.; Sarah C. Wells, Gen. Sec.

Young Women's Christian Assn. (Harlem)—1891. 124th and Lenox av. Social rooms, reading room, educational classes, gymnasium, religious meetings, boarding dept., library, industrial dept. and junior dept. Mrs. E. E. Cooley, Pres.; Miss J. W. Button, Gen. Sec.

Girls' Residence—13 Mt. Morris Pk. W. Mrs. A. J. Briggs, Supt.

Queens.

Archdeaconry of Queens and Nassau—1891. 125 mem. R. F. Duffield, Archdeacon, Garden City. Rev. G. E. Talmage, Sec., Oyster Bay, L. I.

Ft. Totten Y. M. C. A.—H. T. Rodman, Ch.; L. W. Draper, Sec.

Queens-Nassau S. S. Assn.—C. E. Barker, Pres.; J. Eckert, Sec., Ozone Park.

Young Women's Christian Assn.—1920. 30 Union Hall, Jamaica. 400 mem. Mrs. Wm. N. Griffith, Pres.; Miss Florence R. Dunham, Gen. Sec.

SCANDINAVIAN AND FINNISH SOCIETIES.

National and International.

Amer. Scandinavian Foundation—1911. 25 W. 45th, Mhtn. Object: To cultivate closer relations bet. Denmark, Norway and Sweden and the U. S. H. G. Leach, Sec.

Brooklyn.

BENEFIT.

Dagmar Soc. of Danish Women—Prospect Hall. Mrs. Johanna Olsen, Pres.; Mrs. B. Hay, Sec., 466 62d.

Dania Selskabelig Forening—Prospect Hall. Otta Sorensen, Pres.; Lorentz Pehrson, Sec., 617 5th av.

Danish Veteran Soc.—Anderson's Assembly Rooms, 16th and 3d av. 226 mem. J. Ohlman, Pres.; A. Henriksen, Sec., 503 3d, Bkln.

Danmark Velgorenheds Selskabet—Prospect Hall. J. Rasmussen, Pres., 1329 74th; V. Bancke, Sec., 1105 Halsey.

Dansk Kvindeforening Stella—Prospect Hall. Mrs. E. Thomson, Pres.; Mrs. C. Hansen, Sec., 935 Lafayette av.

Finnish Aid Soc. Imatra—740 40th. J. A. Koski, Treas., 421 54th.

Fremad, Danish Sick Benefit, Columbia Hall, Court and State, S. W. Jensen, Sec., 935 Lafayette av.

Ladies Soc., Hjordis—Fraternity Hall, 53d and 5th av. 200 mem. Mrs. J. M. Olsen, Pres.; Mrs. Sara Bemtsen, Sec., 131 57th.

Logen Nordstjernan, 89, V. O. of A.—180 mem. A. Westberg, Pres.; Hjalmar Peterson, Sec., 331 Franklin av.

Men's Aid Soc. of Norwegian Hosp.—46th and 4th av. 90 mem. E. E. Choland, 666 47th, Pres.; J. Anderson, Sec., 421 56th.

Norwegian Children's Home Assn.—43 Gubner. A. N. Rygg, Pres., 4423 3d av.; O. N. Hertzwig, Sec., 10 B'way, Mhtn.

Nytta och Noje—329 Atlantic av. 60 mem. A. Edlund, Pres.; A. Amelung, Sec., 404 DeKalb av.

Pride of Leif Erikson Circle, 979—Vasa Hall, 52d, near 3d av. 2, 4 Wed. 230 mem. Anna O. Larsen, Pres.; Mrs. O. Halvorsen, Sec., 459 42d.

Scandinavian 100 Men's Soc.—329 Atlantic av. G. Grandin, Pres.; Alfred Liljequist, Sec., 592 Vanderbilt av.

Scandinavian Soc. No. 1—329 Atlantic av. 300 mem. W. Johnson, Pres.; C. E. Nelson, Sec., 272 6th av.

South Bkln. Norwegian Sick Ben. Assn.—Trinity Norwegian Ch., 4th av. and 46th. 262 mem. T. Aanansen, Pres.; Geo. W. Eriksen, Fin. Sec., 467 85th.

Swedish Women's Soc., Freja—267 52d. Mrs. H. Molander, Pres.; Mrs. Gerda Lefren, Sec., 19 E. 5th.

SOCIAL, MUSICAL, POLITICAL, ETC.

Norwegian Natl. League—Composed of 92 delegates from 30 Norweg. Socs. O. C. Christopher, Pres., 946 42d; G. T. Ueland, Sec., 129 7th av.

Norwegian Singing Soc.—Saengerbund Hall. 60 mem. A. Wetlesen, Pres.; C. Tausan, Cor. Sec., 66 4th pl.

Sampo Craftsmen's Guild (Inc.)—740 40th. T. H. Nektan, Pres., 421 54th.

Swedish Glee Club—Saengerbund Hall. 100 mem. A. Holmgren, Pres.; A. Wilson, Sec., 330 Rutland rd.

SOCIETIES AND ASSOCIATIONS—SCANDINAVIAN AND FINNISH—*Continued.*

Manhattan and Bronx.

BENEFIT.

Cimbria Lodge, No. 257, Danish Brotherhood of A. 742 St. Anns av. V. C. Eberlin, Sec., 305 E. 206th.

Du Nord—203-7 E. 56th. 176 mem. A. Rothoff, Pres.; C. J. Swanson, Sec., 795 Courtlandt av., Bronx.

Scandinavian Sisters' Alliance—82 mem. Mrs. C. Olson, Pres.; Mrs. A. Swanberg, Sec., 33 Van Cortlandt Park av., Yonkers.

Swedish Bartholomei Kyrkans Sick Benefit Soc.—127th and Lexington av. 50 mem. Rev. E. G. Ericson, Pres.; R. Qvarnstrom, Sec., 2617 3d av.

Swedish Norwegian Soc. of N. Y.—Anderson's Assembly Rooms, 400 mem. A. Stolpe, Pres.; Emil Blomquist, Sec., 114 E. 83d.

United Swedish Societies of N. Y.—Anderson's Assembly Rooms, 16th and 3d av. Ed. E. Molin, Pres.; Mrs. A. Anderson, Cor. Sec., 280 Dean, Bkln.

SOCIAL, MUSICAL, POLITICAL, ETC.

Swedish Ladies Soc. of N. Y.—Teutonia Assembly Rooms. Mrs. H. Lind, Sec., 850 E. 164th.

Swedish Singing Soc. Lyran—International Geneva Assn. 228 mem. J. E. Hellberg, Pres.; J. H. Johnson, Sec., 1091 Park av.

SCOTTISH SOCIETIES.

Brooklyn.

Caledonia Hosp. Soc.—(See Hosp. and Disp.)

Clan Chisholm, No. 217, Order of Scottish Clans—51st and 4th av. Chief, J. W. Stirling, 467 42d; Sec., David W. Chisholm, 1742 45th.

Clan MacDonald No. 33, Order of Scottish Clans—Masonic Temple. Chief, John McCall, 1136 50th; Sec., R. K. Young, 369 Nostrand av.

Flora MacDonald Soc.—8 Nevins. 1896. 90 mem. Mrs. J. R. Spence, Pres., 623 Park pl.; Mrs. H. H. Macdonald, Sec., 9439 85th rd., Woodhaven.

Manhattan and Bronx.

Burns Soc. of the City of N. Y.—See Literary Socs., Mhtn.

Clan Graham No. 142, Order of Scottish Clans—Masonic Temple. Chief, John McPherson, 442 E. 169th; Sec., Jas. Brunton, 712 Oakland pl.

Clan MacDuff No. 81, Order of Scottish Clans—Pythian Bldg. Chief, Geo. W. Horne, 1240 Franklin av.; Sec., A. T. Kirke, 410 E. 156th.

Clan MacKenzie No. 29, Order of Scottish Clans—Grand Opera House. Chief, Wm. L. Loudon, 31 Pratt pl., Woodhaven; Sec., John Galbraith, 507 W. 1"1st.

Highland Guard—1885. 846 7th av. Wm. G. Reid, Capt.; Archd. Gray, 1st Sergt.

N. Y. Caledonian Club—846 7th av. 1856. 358 mem. Object: Preservation of Scottish literature, costumes and games. James R. Donaldson, Chief; John H. Whiteford, 4th Chieftain (Sec.).

N. Y. Scottish Soc.—309 W. 23d. 1887. 110 mem. M. McNeil, Pres.; Thos. M. Lennox, Sec., 87 B'way, Elmhurst, L. I.

St. Andrew's Soc.—105 E. 22d. Org. 1756. 650 mem. A. C. Humphreys, Pres.; Hy. Moir, Sec., 256 B way.

Queens.

Clan Scott No. 205, Order of Scottish Clans—Woodhaven. Chief, David Jamieson, 4392 Jerome av., Rich. Hill; Sec., Robt. Woodburn, 416 89th.

Richmond.

Clan Campbell No 228, Order of Scottish Clans—Port Richmond. Sec., W. H. Brown, 1238 Boulevard, Bayonne, N. J.

ORDER OF SCOTTISH CLANS.

Royal Chief, A. G. Findlay, Seattle, Wash.; Royal Tanist, Walter Scott, Mhtn., N. Y.; Royal Counsellor, T. Forsyth, San Francisco, Cal.; Royal Treas., Duncan MacInnes, Bkln., N. Y.· Royal Sec., T. R. P. Gibb, 248 Boylston, Boston, Mass.

DAUGHTERS OF SCOTIA.

Grand Chief Daughter, Mrs. M. Spence; Mrs. H. Scott, Sec., 7 Edisonia Ter., W. Orange, N. J.; Miss Annie E. Leslie, Treas., 34 Slocum, Phila., Pa.

SECRET AND BENEFIT ASSOCIATIONS.

AMERICAN ORDER OF CLANSMEN.

Brotherhood of American Citizens, patriotic, social and benevolent. The Grand Clan, San Francisco, Cal. Dr. H. Waterhouse, Grand Dir. Gen., Mrs. F. R. Apter, Grand Sec., 278 Page, San Francisco, Cal.

ANCIENT ORDER OF FORESTERS.

Org. 1745. A beneficial order. Hdqtrs., Hackensack, N. J. Meets triennially on Labor Day. D. McKellar, High Ch. Ranger, Waterbury, Conn.; R. A. Sibbald, Perm. Sec., Hackensack, N. J., and 15 Park row, Mhtn. Mem. U. S., 43,666; N. Y. State, 2,321; Mhtn. and Bronx, 498; Bkln., 539.

Brooklyn Courts: Ivy 8052, 479 Gates av.; Excelsior 8186, 9th and 6th av. Manhattan Courts: Colonial 8501, 59th and Columbus av.: Phoenix 7894, Grand Opera House; Robt. A. Sibbald 8065, 136 W. 131st.

ANCIENT ORDER OF GLEANERS.

Fraternal Benefit—Org. 1894. Detroit, Mich. G. H. Slocum, Pres., Detroit, Mich.; R. L. Holloway, Sec., Detroit, Mich.

ANCIENT ORDER OF GOOD FELLOWS.

Geo. Moeller, Gr. Master, 533 E. 88th, Mhtn.; H. F. Raabe, Hon. Gr. Sec., 80 Vanderveer, Bkln. Mem., N. Y. State, 300; Mhtn., 600; Bkln., 200; U. S., 4,400.

ANCIENT ORDER OF HIBERNIANS IN AMERICA.

Natl. officers: J. E. Deery, Natl. Pres., Indianapolis, Ind.; J. O'Dea, Natl. Sec., 1344 Colwyn, Phila., Pa. N. Y. State officers: J. T. Buckley, Pres., Utica; Denis English, Sec., Schenectady.

Brooklyn.

Jno. O'Hagan, Co. Pres., 255 49th; J. P. Kelly, Sec., 41 E. 4th.

Manhattan and Bronx.

T. R. Keane, Pres., 51 Chambers.

Queens.

P. J. Connolly, Co. Pres.; P. J. Henry, Co. Sec., 50 Van Pelt, L. I. City.

Richmond.

B. T. McKay, Co. Pres.; Dennis Keogh, Co. Sec., 56 7th av., New Brighton.

ANCIENT ORDER UNITED WORKMEN.

W. M. Narvis, Muscatine, Ia., Sup. Master Workman; E. J. Moore, Fargo, N. Dak., Sup. Recorder; E. F. Danforth, Skowhegan, Me., Sup. Treas. Mem. in U. S., 80,000. N. Y. C. Lodges under jurisdiction of the Connecticut Grand Lodge. E. S. Merrill, Grand Master, 26 W. 44th, Mhtn.

ARMENIAN GENERAL BENEVOLENT UNION

Hdqts., Cairo, Egypt. Dist. Comm. of Amer. Dr. C. H. Calusdian, Pres.; D. Dar Bedrosian, Gen. Sec., 530 Old South Bldg., Boston, Mass. Over 8,000 mem. in U. S.

ARMY AND NAVY UNION OF U. S. OF A.

Hdqtrs., 240 Longwood av., Boston, Mass.; J. J. Cosgrove, Natl. Com., 41 High, Charlestown, Mass.; D. F. Kent, Natl. Adj.

Dept. State of New York—Ed. Stubel, Dept. Com., Albany, N. Y.; H. C. Edgerton, Albany, N. Y.

BANKERS INSURANCE CORPORATION.

W. Burton, Pres.; W. E. Bell, Sec., 1st Natl. Bank Bldg., Chicago, Ill. 4,552 mem.

BENEVOLENT AND PROTECTIVE ORDER OF ELKS.

Wm. M. Abbott, Gr. Exalted Ruler, San Francisco, Cal.; F. C. Robinson, Gr. Sec., Dubuque, Ia. Mem.: U. S., 703,850; N. Y. State, 51,854; Bkln., 6,682; Mhtn., 4,926; Bronx, 1,780; Queens, 1,603; Richmond, 388. Bkln. Lodge No. 22, 144 S. Oxford; Mhtn. Lodge No. 1, 116 W. 43d; Bronx Lodge No. 871, 2050 Grand Concourse; Staten Is. Lodge No. 841, 346 Van Duzee, Stapleton.

BROTHERHOOD OF AMERICA.

Supreme Circle officers: A. Wrensch, Sup., Montclair, N. J.; J. Ruhl, Sup. Scroll Keeper, 2208 Frankford av., Philadelphia, Pa.; 12,590 mem.

SOCIETIES AND ASSOCIATIONS—*Secret and Benefit—Continued.*

BROTHERHOOD OF AMERICAN YEOMEN.

A national fraternal benefit insurance, 5th and Park, Des Moines, Ia. G. N. Frink, Gr. Foreman; W. E. Davy, Chief Correspondent. Mem. in U. S. A., 285,897. Also 3,464 juveniles.

BROTHERHOOD OF THE COMMONWEALTH.

An internatl. fraternal pension order. Supreme Council. A. J. Boultoy, Pres.; W. B. Danforth. Exec. Sec. and Treas., 1316 Av. S, Bkln. Prospect Council No. 1, 261 Prospect av., Bkln.; Concordia Council No. 2, Palm Garden, Bkln.; Flatbush Council No. 3, 854 Flatbush av., Bkln.; Arion Council No. 4, 1082 Bushwick av., Bkln.

CATHOLIC BENEVOLENT LEGION.

A denominational fraternal insurance order. Religious, Social and Benevolent. R. B. Tippett, Pres.; J. E. Dunn, Sec., 186 Remsen. N. Y. State Council: F. Fanning, Pres.; D. J. Sharkey, Sec., 168 6th av., Bkln. Total mem. in U. S., 15,748; N. Y. State, 8,630; in Bkln., 2,966; Mhtn. and The Bronx, 2,496; Queens, 316; Richmond, 116.

CATHOLIC FRATERNAL LEAGUE.

Fraternal Benefit Organization. Org. 1893. John Merrill, Pres., 185 Sumner, Boston, Mass.; J. F. Reynolds, Sec.

CATHOLIC KNIGHTS OF AMERICA.

Most Rev. W. T. McGuirl, Spiritual Dir., Bkln., N. Y.; Dr. F. Gaudin, Sup. Pres., New Orleans, La.; M. Quin, State Pres., 4610 Ft. Hamilton P'kway, Bkln., N. Y.; J. Quigley, State Sec. and Treas., 332 E. 123d, Mhtn. Mem. U. S., 25,000; State, 1,500; N. Y. City, 1,000.

CATHOLIC WOMEN'S BENEVOLENT LEGION.

Inc. Aug. 23, 1895. Hdqtrs., 165 W. 31st, Mhtn. Mrs. E. L. Loughlin, Sup. Pres.; Mrs. S. E. Skelly, Sup. Sec.; Miss R. M. Calhoun, Sup. Treas.

COURT OF HONOR.

Fraternal Beneficiary Soc.—Org. 1895. Springfield, Ill. A. L. Hereford, Pres.; W. E. Robinson, Sec., Springfield, Ill. Mem. in U. S., 77,515.

DAUGHTERS OF AMERICA.

A patriotic American fraternity. 1891. Auxiliary to the Junior Order United American Mechanics. Natl. Councilor, Mrs. I. Edwards, 626 W. 4th, Cincinnati, O.; Natl. Sec., Mrs. M. C. Roth, 1526 Florencedale av, Youngstown, Ohio. 100,000 in U. S.; 7,000 in N. Y. State. St. Councilor, Mrs. Mary E. Lee, 829 E. 216th, Bronx; St. Sec., Mrs. H. E. Van Buren, 10 Tompkins av., Ossining.

FORESTERS OF AMERICA.

Supreme Court: 275 Grove, Jersey City, N. J. P. J. O'Keeffe, S. C. R.; Thos. M. Donnelly, S. Sec.

Grand Court: 346 Fulton, Bkln. M. Roache, G. C. R.; T. F. McNulty, Gr. Sec., 346 Fulton.

Companions of the Forest of America.

Mrs. A. E. Poth, Sup. Fin. Sec., 271 W. 125th, Mhtn. Membership, 92,000.

Knights of Sherwood Forest.

Sup. Com., Geo. Wallace, Waltham, Mass.; Sup. Adj.-Gen., W. H. Moriarty, 138 Centre, Brockton, Mass.; Sup. Paymaster, H. D. Houdashall, 37 Eliot, So. Natick, Mass.

Shepherds of America.

Sup. Pastor, Ed. H. Spratt, 115 Lynhurst av., Syracuse, N. Y.; Sup. Scribe, Ed. L. Eckert, 50 Abbotsford pl., Buffalo, N. Y.; Sup. Treas., G. R. Brown, 222 Frost av., Rochester, N. Y.

Associations.

Foresters of America Home Assn. of N. Y. Home at Springfield, L. I. Robt. W. Brant, Pres.; A. J. Schoenfelder, Sec., 1048 Fox, Bronx.

FRATERNAL MYSTIC CIRCLE.

Office of the Sup. Ruling, 1913 Arch, Phila. Org. 1884. Inc. 1895. Sup. Mystic Ruler, W. C. Paul, Phila., Pa.; Sup. Recorder, J. D. Myers, 1913 Arch, Phila., Pa.; Sup. Treas., John Smiley, Phila., Pa.

F. B. Brown, Gr. Ruler, Glens Falls, N. Y.; A. W. Freeman, Gr. Recorder, 134 Clinton, Saratoga Springs, N. Y.; F. P. Leffingwell, Gr. Treas., Fonda, N. Y. Bkln., L. I., Ruling No. 212, 210 Norwood av., Bkln.; H. H. Kafe, Gr. Rec., 43 Myrtle av., Bkln.

FRATERNAL ORDER OF EAGLES.

Fraternal and beneficial, Kansas City, Mo. Org. 1898. 400,000 mem. E. D. Weed, G. W. P., Oshkosh, Wis.; J. S. Parry, Gd. Sec., Kansas City, Mo.

State: T. G. Welsh, Pres.; W. A. Neafie, Sec., Ossining, N. Y.

Brooklyn: Aerie No. 393, T. D. McArdle, Sec., 1954 Coney Is. av.; Aerie No. 583, J. W. Hill, Sec., 217 E. 69th, Mhtn.; Aerie No. 1924, W. F. Dyer, Sec., 249 54th.

Manhattan and Bronx: Aerie No. 40, F. A. Barnhard, Sec., 275 W. 23d; Aerie No. 491, W. J. Godfrey, Sec., 436 E. 138th; Aerie No. 1117, H. J. Mallon, Sec., 301 W. 113th.

Queens: Aerie No. 748, O. W. Schiffers, Sec., Howard Beach; Aerie No. 1509, J. H. Greatfield, Sec., 683 9th av., L. I. C.; Aerie No. 1544, W. T. Hushion, Sec., Jamaica.

Richmond: Aerie No. 543, C. M. Schwalbe, Sec., 7 Cottage pl., Pt. Richmond.

FRATERNAL AID UNION.

Supreme Lodge officers: V. A. Young, Sup. Pres., S. Baty, Sup. Sec., Lawrence, Kan.; T. J. Sweeney, Sup. Treas., Lawrence, Kan. Org. 1890. Natl. membership, 100,000. Columbia Council No. 2025, L. E. Doring, Pres.; J. J. F. Doyle, Sec., 246 Sackett, Bkln.

GENERAL SOCIETY OF THE WAR OF 1812.

Office, Phila., Pa., John Cadwalader, Pres.-Gen.; H. M. Leland, Sec.-Gen., 10 P. O. Sq., Boston, Mass.

Soc. of the Second War With Great Britain in State of N. Y.—1896. N. Y. State Br. of Gen.-Soc. of the War of 1812. C. Boucher, Pres., 272 W. 90th; H. H. Noble, Sec., Essex, N. Y.

GRAND ARMY OF THE REPUBLIC.

Natl. officers: Com.-in-Chf., Wm. A. Ketcham, Indianapolis, Ind.; S. V.-Com.-in-Chf., G. A. Hosley, Boston, Mass.; Surg.-Gen., C. W. Burrill, Kansas City, Mo.; Chaplain-in-Chf., W. A. Bosworth, Wichita, Kan.; Adjt.-Gen., M. D. Butler, Indianapolis, Ind.; Q. M.-Gen., C. D. R. Stowits, Buffalo, N. Y.

N. Y. State officers: Dept. Com., A. E. Stacey, Elbridge; S. V. Dept. Com., H. L. Keene, Elmira; J. V. Dept. Com., Thos. J. McConekey, Bkln.; Asst. Adjt.-Gen. and Asst. Q. M. Gen., B. F. Raze, Camillus; Medical Dir., R. P. Bush, Horseheads; Chaplain, Wm. E. Kimball, Sanquoit; Judge Adv., C. W. Stanton, Cohocton.

Memorial and Exec. Com., Kings Co. Hdqtrs., R. 12, Borough Hall, Bkln. Ch., Thos. J. McConekey; Sec. and Almoner, Hy. C. Draper; Treas., L. Finkelmeier.

Ladies of the G. A. R.

Mrs. Laura B. Prisk, Dept. Pres.; Mrs. Rosetta Drummond, Dept. Sec., 133 W. 127th, Mhtn.; Mrs. Grace H. Boles, Dept. Treas., Cato, N. Y.

GRAND UNITED ORDER OF ODD FELLOWS IN AMERICA.

Natl. officers: E. H. Morris, Gd. Master; J. F. Needham, Gd. Sec., 12th and Spruce, Phila., Pa. 641,536 mem. in America. Org. 1843.

N. Y. State officers: W. D. Brown, Dist. Gd. Master; J. F. Adair, Dist. Gd. Sec., 1201 St. Marks av., Bkln., N. Y. 11,125 mem. in State.

GUARDIANS OF LIBERTY.

Non-sectarian, non-partisan. To promote and extend benevolence. To promote and foster a spirit of patriotism. To protect free institutions, especially the public educational system. National Court—Masonic Temple, Chicago, Ill. Chas. R. Young, Chief Guardian; Rev. W. R. Collins, Chief Recorder; H. W. Korsgren, Sec. and Treas., Exec. Comm.

IMPROVED ORDER OF HEPTASOPHS.

Supreme Conclave officers: J. C. Tolson, Sup. Archon; F. E. Pleitner, Sup. Sec., Cathedral and Preston, Baltimore, Md.; J. O. Miller, Sup. Treas., 215 Montague, Bkln., N. Y. Mem.: Bkln., 1,800; Mhtn. and Bronx, 1,037; total mem., 39,000.

IMPROVED ORDER OF RED MEN

Great Sachem, A. J. Ruland, 405 Kilmer Bldg., Binghamton, N. Y.; Great Chief of Records, Edw. J. Boyd, 409 W. 47th, Mhtn.

SOCIETIES AND ASSOCIATIONS—SECRET AND BENEFIT—I. O. R. M.—*Continued.*

Degree of Pocahontas.

Great Prophetess, Frances E. Churchill, Penn Yan, N. Y.; Great Pocahontas, Jennie Harrison, 8 St. Lukes pl., Mhtn; Great Keeper of Records, Anna A. Van Alstine, Amsterdam, N. Y.

INDEPENDENT ORDER OF FORESTERS.

Org. 1874. W. H. Hunter, Sup. Ch. Ranger; G. E. Bailey, Asst. Sup. Sec., Toronto, Canada; H. J. Carpenter, City Mgr., 732 97th, Woodhaven, L. I.

INDEPENDENT ORDER OF ODD FELLOWS.

Grand Officers, Grand Lodge of N. Y. State: Harry Walker, Grand Sec., 31 Union sq. W., Mhtn. Grand Encampment of State of N. Y.—Harry Walker, Grand Scribe. Mem. State, 131,620; Mhtn. and Bronx, 12,651; Bkln., 7,124; Queens, 1,475; Richmond, 336. Total of Order in the world, 2,226,562. State officers of Rebekah Assembly: Mrs. Ida Y. Smith, Pres., L. Box 4, McGraw, N. Y.; Miss A. E. Rogers, Sec., 731 Amsterdam av., Mhtn. Kings Co. Assemblies: United Sisters No. 59; Mrs. Alvina Abert, 8801 5th av., Bkln.; Mt. Olive No. 117, Mrs. Carrie Gurnett, 383 E. 143d, Mhtn.; Williamsburg No. 525, Mrs. H. Marks, 14 Middletown, Jamaica, L. I.

Associations.

L. I. Odd Fellows Home Assn.—C. F. Crawford, Pres., 206 B'way, Mhtn.; V. C. Steuerwald, Sec., 1177A Putnam av., Bkln. Located at Hollis.

Veteran Odd Fellows Assn. of State of N. Y.—Quarterly, 2 Sat., Jan., April, July, Oct. 31 Union sq. W. Org. 1888. 300 mem. F. P. Trautmann, Pres.; Geo. W. Stuyvesant, Sec., 228 Clermont av., Bkln.

MANCHESTER UNITY.

Orig. in England 1800, America 1806. 1,500,000 mem. 450 Dists.; 6,000 lodges.

Officers of N. Y. Dist.: Prov. G. M., Adam Cockburn, 3905 B'way, Mhtn.; Prov. Cor. Sec., W. J. O'Brien, 556 W. 160th, Mhtn.

Brooklyn Lodges: Perseverance Lodge, Lorimer and Ten Eyck; Verrazzano Lodge, Spatz Hall, Lorimer and B'way.

INDEPENDENT ORDER OF TRUE FRIENDS.

Inc. 1886. Co-operative Sick Benefit Life Assurance Order. R. E. Jones, 401 B'way, Mhtn., Sup. Pres.; M. R. Clark, 468 Irving av., Bkln., Sup. Sec., A. E. Vanderheyde, 542 5th av, Mhtn., Sup. Treas. Mem.: Bkln., 700; Mhtn. and Bronx, 1,200; Queens, 100.

JUNIOR ORDER UNITED AMERICAN MECHANICS.

Natl. Council officers: Org. 1853. H. F. Lochner, N. Councilor, 318 E. B'way, Louisville, Ky.; M. M. Woods, N. Sec., Box 874, Phila., Pa. 338,000 mem. in U. S.

N. Y. State officers: Fred. H. Smith, 241 Vernon av., Bkln., S. C.; C. W. Lisle, S. Sec., 98 Moffat, Bkln. A. L. McCallum, S. Treas., West Brighton, S. I. Mem., 12,622.

JUNIOR ORDER UNITED AMERICAN MECHANICS.

(Operated under N. Y. State incorporation.)

N. Y. State officers: L. L. Bishop, Councilor; F. S. Faye, Sec., 1180 Fulton, Bkln. Mem.: Bkln., 5,132; Mhtn., 2,397; Queens, 1,295; Richmond, 1,506.

KNIGHTS OF COLUMBUS.

Supreme officers: J. A. Flaherty, Sup. Knight; M. H. Carmody, Dep. Sup. Knight; Wm. J. McGinley, Sup. Sec., Drawer 1670, New Haven, Conn. Total mem., 700,000; Greater N. Y., 80,000.

State Officers: Dr. J. J. Coyle, 220 E. 31st, Mhtn., State Deputy; F. J. Keaveney, Johnstown, State Sec.

Dist. Deps. (Bkln. and L. I.)—1st, J. M. Collins, 524 10th; 2d, D. A. Tobin, 200 Linden av.; 3d, J. A. McNamara, 165 B'way, Mhtn.; 4th, J. A. Boucher, 817 N. Y. av.; 5th, M. J. Moore, 239 76th; 6th, Dr. I. P. Byrne, 1071 Lorimer; 7th, B. J. McGinn, 8818 Boyd, Woodhaven; 8th, J. A. Giblin, 135 Bay 28th; 9th, T. A. Roesch, 36 Middleton, Jamaica; 10th, T. J. Cullen, 194 Meserole av.; 11th, O. W. Muehlenbrink, College Pt.; 12th, J. A. Hennessey, 817 Crescent av., L. I. City; 13th, D. J. Fogarty, Glen Cove; 14th, A. J. Melton, Bay Shore; 15th, J. H. Brown, Riverhead.

Dist. Deps. (Mhtn., Bronx and Richmond)—16th, J. W. King, 210 E. 53d; 17th, J. J. Sheehan, 27 Dominick; 18th, N. P. Duffy, 3494 Morris av.; 19th, J. N. Bailey, 518 E. 88th; 20th, W. J. Shells, 416 W. 149th; 21st, J. J. Cunneen, 325 W. 93d; 22d, F. J. Jones, 2082 Valentine av.; 23d, A. N. Lilly, 1 St. Nicholas ter.; 24th, J. B. Lynch, 439 E. 136th; 25th, J. A. Cougan, 2428 Frisby av.; 26th, H. Kelly, W. New Brighton.

KNIGHTS OF PYTHIAS.

Founded 1864; 55 grand lodges; 6,866 subordinate lodges; mem., 746,520. Mem. N. Y. State, 24,763; Bkln., 1,484; Mhtn. and Bronx, 8,132; Queens, 719; Richmond, 209; Nassau and Suffolk Counties, 847. There are 3 ranks—Page, Esquire and Knight—and 2 branches, the Uniform Rank (military), mem. 14,273, and Insurance Dept. (life insurance), mem. 74,651.

Supreme Lodge officers: Wm. Ladew, Sup. Chancellor, N. Y. City; G. C. Cabell, S. V. C., Norfolk, Va.; F. E. Wheaton, Sup. Keeper of Records and Seal, Minneapolis, Minn.; W. H. Loomis, Maj.-Gen. of Uniform Rank, Grand Rapids, Mich.; H. Wade, Pres. Insurance Dept., Indianapolis, Ind.

N. Y. State Grand Lodge officers: P. Canfield, Gd. Chancellor, Kingston, N. Y.; Alonzo Bedell, Gd. Keeper of Records and Seal, Haverstraw; Trustees of Pythian Home, C. W. Endel, Pres., N. Y. City; J. W. Van Demark, Sec., 130 E. 127th, Mhtn.; G. H. Stalker, Treas., Rochester, N. Y.; W. D. Bush, P.C., Ch. Publicity Comm., Domain of N. Y., 254 W. 25th, Mhtn. Ogdensburg selected as the site for the State Home and dedicated July 4, 1913.

Military Department K. of P.

N. Y. Brigade—S. Shepard, Brig. Gen., 67 Central av., Albany, N. Y.; D. S. Radcliffe, Col. and Chief of Staff, Oswego, N. Y.; Geo. W. Heath, Col. and Asst. Adj.-Gen., Albany, N. Y.; C. H. Gardiner, Col. and Asst. Insp. Gen., Amsterdam, N. Y.; Wm. Ladew, Col. and Asst. Q. M.-Gen., N. Y. City; Judge Advocate, Brig.-Gen., Wm. Grossman, 115 B'way, Mhtn.

First Regiment, U. R.

Col. Ed. W. Cox, Comm., Mechanicville, N. Y.; Lieut.-Col. J. A. Kehlbeck, 61 William, Mhtn.; Maj. J. L. Dohme, 973 Whitlock av., Bronx.

PYTHIAN SISTERS.

Minnie E. Bunting, Sup. Chief, Oklahoma City, Okla.; M. Josie Nelson, Sup. Mistress of Records and Correspondence, Union City, Ind.; Alice M. H. Boylan, Eldora, Iowa, Sup. Mistress of Finance.

State officers: I. R. Miller, Grand Ch., Fort Plain, N. Y.; Anna Du Bois, Gd. Mistress of Finance, Tottenville; Lizzie P. Frerichs, Gd. Mistress of Cor., Tottenville, S. I.

KNIGHTS OF ST. JOHN AND MALTA.

A chivalric, military and benevolent order. Founded at Jerusalem, A. D., 1048. Chartered to conduct an endowment department under the laws of the State of N. Y. in 1883. Reorg. in 1911.

Supreme Commandery—W. Buckett, M. E. Grand Master; A. F. Lamson, R. E. Grand Lieut.-Commander; F. A. Gates, R. E. Grand Chancellor, 154 Lefferts pl., Bkln.; S. P. Hartman, R. E. Grand Almoner, 42 Hart, Bkln.

Bkln. Commandery No. 1—Meets 1, 3 and 5 Thur. at Johnson Bldg. J. W. Wendell, Emt. Com.; A. F. Lamson, Fin. Chancellor, 395A Lafayette av., Bkln.

KNIGHTS OF THE GOLDEN EAGLE.

Supreme Castle: T. R. Lenich, Sup. Chief, Union City, Ind.; J. B. Treibler, Sup. Master of Records, 814 N. Broad, Phila., Pa. Bkln., 36; State, 196; U. S., 84,119.

LADIES' CATHOLIC BENEVOLENT ASSN.

Inc. 1890. Miss Kate Mahoney, 1987 15th, Troy, N. Y., Sup. Pres.; Mrs. J. A. Royer, 443 W. 11th, Erie, Pa., Sup. Rec.; Mrs. M. E. Costello, 20 N. 124th, Rockaway Park, L. I., N. Y. Sup. Treas. Mem., 155,000; N. Y. C., 6,000.

SOCIETIES AND ASSOCIATIONS—SECRET AND BENEFIT—*Continued.*

LEAGUE OF ELECT SURDS.

Grand Lodge.

A Secret Society of the Deaf of N. Y. City. Org. 1884. C. C. McMann, Grand Ruler; E. A. Hodgson, Gr. Treas., 3800 B'way, Mhtn. M. Miller, Gr. Sec. Meetings monthly. 35 mem.

LOYAL AMERICAN LIFE ASSN.

E. J. Dunn, Pres.; H. D. Cowan, Sec., Chicago, Ill. Mem. U. S., 16,362.

LOYAL ASSOCIATION.

Inc. 1894. W. A. McGarrett, Gd. Coun., P. O. Box 1, Station X, Mhtn.; Fred Wanderer, Gd. Recorder, 324 Valley Brook av., Lyndhurst, N. J.

LOYAL ORANGE INSTITUTION, U. S. A.

Sup. Grand Lodge: A. E. Armstrong, Gd. Master, Ayer, Mass.; W. J. Kirkland, Sup. Gd. Sec., 229 Rhode Island av., N. W., Washington, D. C.

N. Y. State Grand Lodge: Geo. Weirs, Gd. Master, 176 B'way, Mhtn.; R. P. Dodds, 2125 7th av., Troy, Gd. Sec. Mem., N. Y. C., 2,000.

Ladies Loyal Orange Assn.—Sup. Grand Lodge, Sup. Gr. Mistress, Mrs. M. MacGovern, 367 Carlton av., Bkln.; Sup. Gr. Sec., Mrs. S. E. Hanna, 23 N. Gilmor, Baltimore, Md.

LOYAL ORDER OF MOOSE.

Founded 1888; Lodges, 1,650. Members: Loyal Order of Moose, 546,849; Women of Mooseheart Legion, 20,018; Junior Order of Moose, 2,712. Total, 569,579.

Supreme officers: Geo. N. Warde, Gen. Dictator, Mooseheart, Ill.; J. J. Davis, Dir.-Gen., Pittsburgh, Pa.; R. H. Brandon, Sup. Sec., Mooseheart, Ill.

Brooklyn Lodge No. 14, 87 Dean; N. Y. Lodge No. 15, 1704 Municipal Bldg.; Coney Is. Lodge No. 138, 553 Neptune av., Bkln.; Staten Is. Lodge No. 422, 204 Gordon, Stapleton, S. I.; L. I. City Lodge No. 485, 740½ 11th av.; Bronx Lodge No. 1002, 455 E. 163d; Ridgewood Lodge No. 1642, 842 Fresh Pond rd., Bkln.

THE MACCABEES.

N. Y. State officers: J. J. Volk, Gt. Com., Buffalo; Gt. Camp office, 916 Delaware av., Buffalo, N. Y.; Deputies, A. Popp, 466 W. 151st, Mhtn. Mem. State, 60,000; total mem., 350,000.

Bkln. Maccabee Council, composed of representatives from tents in Bkln., meet on the 3d Wed. of each month at Atlantic av. and Court. Nathan Manasse, Sec., 414 Macon, Bkln.

WOMEN'S BENEFIT ASSN. OF THE MACCABEES.

Great Officers: Mrs. C. L. McDannell, Gt. Com., 916 Delaware av., Buffalo, N. Y.; Mrs. M. Fay, Dist. Dep., 63 Charlton, Mhtn.; Mrs. M. A. Tully, Dist. Dep., 403 1st, Bkln.

MASONIC.

STATE.

Grand Master, Robt. H. Robinson, N. Y. City; Gd. Sec., R. J. Kenworthy, 23d and 6th av., Mhtn. Number lodges, 888.

Mem.: Bkln., 27,264; Mhtn. and Bronx, 58,767; Queens, 4,458; Richmond, 2,227; N. Y. State, 234,894.

District Deputy Grand Masters in New York City.

T. J. Towers, Queens, 365 Fulton, Jamaica.
C. A. Tonsor, 1st Kings, 226 St. James pl., Bkln.
J. L. Fleming, 2d Kings, 315 Lincoln pl., Bkln.
R. D. M. Brown, 3d Kings, Corn Ex. Bank, 13 William, Mhtn.
H. W. Stimpson, 1st Mhtn., 220 W. 57th, Mhtn.
E. M. Stimpson, 2d Mhtn., 2 Rector, Mhtn.
C. Felix, 3d Mhtn., 770 St. Nicholas av., Mhtn.
J. H. Reed, 4th Mhtn., 1 Liberty, Mhtn.
G. B. Roane, 5th Mhtn., 126 10th av., Mhtn.
M. B. Bernstein, 6th Mhtn., 1 Wall, Mhtn.
A. A. Wiener, 7th Mhtn., 601 W. 168th, Mhtn.
H. Moerchen, 8th, Mhtn., 484 Warburton av., Yonkers.
G. Kotzenberg, 9th Mhtn., 1319 Teller av., Mhtn.
J. A. Caras, 10th Mhtn., 30 Broad, Mhtn.
G. Mord, Richmond, 1026 Bay, Rosebank.
J. Bell, Bronx, 240 Echo pl., Mhtn.

Ancient and Accepted Scottish Rite. Northern Masonic Jurisdiction.

Officers of Sup. Council, Barton Smith, M. P. Sov. Grand Com., Toledo, O.; R. A. Shirrefs, 299 B'way, Mhtn., Sec. Gen.; J. L. Thomas, **Dep. for N. Y. State.**

Cerneau Rite.

Supreme Council: Max Scheur, Sov. Gr. Comr.; A. C. Dupont, Lt.-Gr. Comr., Mhtn.; L. Loeb, Gr. Orator and Minister of State, Mhtn.; R. F. Downing, Gr. Sec.-Gen., 201 Dean, Bkln.; R. A. Guinsburg, Gr. Treas.-Gen., Mhtn., Sup. Council Rooms, 806 Temple Court, Mhtn.

Consistories.

Grand Consistory, State of N. Y.: E. B. Guild, M.D., Gd. Com.-in-Chief, Mhtn.; F. E. Francisco, Gd. Sec., 29 B'way, Mhtn.; R. A. Guinsburg, Gd. Treas., Mhtn.

Royal Arch Masons.

State officers: J. L. Cheney, G. H. P., Syracuse, N. Y.; C. C. Hunt, Gr. Sec., 46 W. 24th, Mhtn.; J. A. Crane, Gr. Treas., Rochester. Mem.: Bkln., 4,076; Mhtn. and Bronx, 7,049; Queens, 1,145; Richmond, 596; in State, 48,494.

Royal and Select Masters.

Grand Council meets in N. Y. City, Aug. 22 and 23, 1921.
Grand Master, H. H. Kendall, Corning, N. Y.
Grand Recorder, G. E. Hatch, Rochester, N. Y.
Mem. in Mhtn., 736; Bkln., 470; Bronx, 290; State, 9,381.

Grand Encampment Knights Templar, U. S. A.

Grand Master, J. K. Orr, Atlanta, Ga.; Deputy Gr. M., J. W. Chamberlin, St. Paul, Minn.; Gd. Rec., F. H. Johnson, Masonic Temple, Louisville, Ky. No. Gd. Commanderies, 48; subordinate Commanderies, 7; total mem., 315,426. Next triennial conclave meets April 25, 1922, New Orleans, La. DeWitt Clinton Commandery No. 27, Knights Templar, Masonic Temple, Clermont and Lafayette avs., Bkln. I. S. Waters, Recorder, 197 Waverly av.

Nobles of the Mystic Shrine.

BROOKLYN.

Kismet Temple meets monthly on call. J. W. Downing, Potentate; J. A. Morison, Recorder, 92 Herkimer.

MANHATTAN.

Mecca Temple, on call. T. G. Price, Potentate; L. N. Donnatin, Recorder, 107 W. 45th.

Masonic Aid Associations.

BROOKLYN.

Masonic Free Employment Bureau, Masonic Temple. To assist the brethren and their dependents to secure positions. J. H. Erb, Mgr.

Williamsburg Board of Relief. 1025 Lafayette av. R. Morris, Pres.; John Milford, Sec., 827 Bedford av.

MANHATTAN.

German Masonic Temple Assn.—220 E. 15th. Louis G. Burger, Pres.; L. Kleinbohl, Sec.

Masonic Board of Relief, 71 W. 23d, Tu. and Sa. evgs. R. S. Wardle, Sec., 71 W. 23d.

RICHMOND.

Staten Isl. Masonic Mut. Benefit Assn.—Port Richmond. 300 mem. W. M. Braman, Sec., P. O. Box 303.

Veteran Associations.

Bkln. Masonic Veterans—Aurora Grata Cathedral, Bedford av. and Madison. Isaac S. Waters, Rec. Sec., 41 Ormond pl.

Masonic Veterans of N. Y.—1872. Masonic Hall, W. 24th, Mhtn. S. D. Hubbard, Pres.; R. S. Wardle, Sec., 589 Carlton av., Bkln.

Eastern Star.

Mrs. Clara S. Ellithorp, Gd. Matron, 140 Bleecker, Gloversville, N. Y. Col. T. H. Roberts, Gd. Patron, Bkln., N. Y.; Mrs. A. M. Pond, Gd. Sec., Masonic Hall, 46 W. 24th.

Order of the Amaranth.

Supreme Council meets in Minneapolis, Minn., 3d M. in June. H. F. Lewis, Supt. Royal Matron. Grand Court of N. Y. meets 1st W. and Th. in June in Watertown, N. Y. Isabel Sidway, Grand Royal Matron; Mrs. Annie Vass, Grand Sec., 494 Jefferson av., Bkln. 60 courts in N. Y. State.

Prince Hall Masons State of N. Y.

G. Master, David W. Parker; Dep. G. Master, Harry A. Williamson; S. G. Warden, D. T. Teagle; J. G. Warden, J. E. Mason, Ithaca; G. Treas., Harvey E. Williams, N. Y. C.; G. Sec., A. A. Schomburg, 105 Kosciusko, Bkln. Lodges in N. Y. State, 33. Mem. N. Y. State, 2,820; Mhtn. and Bronx, 1,400; Bkln. and **Queens, 550.**

SOCIETIES AND ASSOCIATIONS—SECRET AND BENEFIT—MASONIC—*Continued.*

Rite of Memphis.

M. I. Ellis B. Guild, 96 deg., Sovereign G. Master Gen.

MODERN BROTHERHOOD OF AMERICA.

Org. 1897. Mason City, Ia. A. Hass, Sup. Pres.; E. L. Balz. Sup. Sec., Mason City, Ia. Mem. U. S., 81,000.

MODERN WOODMEN OF AMERICA.

93 Nassau, Mhtn.

A fraternal beneficiary society. Natl. officers: A. R. Talbot, Head Consul, Lincoln, Neb.; A. N. Bort, Head Clerk, Rock Island, Ill.; State Dep. Head Consul, M. J. Cahill, 93 Nassau, Mhtn.

Monitor Assn. Naval Veterans—1861-1865—Meets 165 Waverly av., Bkln., 3d Wed., Jan., April, July and Oct. Henry W. Speight, Capt.; Fred E. Haskins, Sec. and Paymaster, 767 Washington av., Bkln.

NATL. ASSN. NAVAL VETERANS, 1861-1865.

Org. 1887. Com. Comdg., Loomis Scofield, New Canaan, Conn.; Fleet Sec. and Paymaster, H. F. McCollum, 40 Shelter, New Haven, Conn.; Judge Advocate, F. E. Haskins, 767 Washington av., Bkln.

NATL. ASSN. OF LETTER CARRIERS.

Kenois Bldg., 11th and G, N. W., Washington, D. C. Edw. J. Gainor, Natl. Pres., Muncie, Ind.; E. J. Cantwell, Natl. Sec., Washington, D. C.; M. T. Finnan, Asst. Natl. Sec., Washington, D. C. Mem., 35,000. Jos. Tinnelly, State Pres., Albany, N. Y.; LeRoy B. Van Duzer, State Sec., Rochester, N. Y. Mem. in Mhtn. and Bronx, 2,543; Bkln., 1,145; Queens, 200; Richmond, 58.

NATL. ORDER DAUGHTERS OF ISABELLA.

Supreme Regent, Mrs. G. H. Walsh, 4241 B'way, Mhtn.; Natl. Sec., M. F. Kelly, 309 Genesee, Utica, N. Y.

State Regent, Mrs. M. K. McInerney, 145 So. 3d av., Mechanicsville, N. Y. Mem. U. S., 60,000; State, 15,000; Mhtn. and Bronx, 2,200; Bkln., 1,000; Queens, 1,400; Richmond, 725.

NATL. ORG. MASTERS, MATES AND PILOTS OF AMERICA.

J. H. Pruett, Natl. Pres., 423 49th, Bkln.; M. D. Tenniswood, Natl. Sec., 308 Vine, Camden, N. J. Total mem. U. S., 15,000; State, 3,700; N. Y. C., 3,000.

United Assn. No. 1, Masters, Mates and Pilots of America—1886. 2,300 mem. A. C. Howell, Pres.; Wm. A. Maher, Sec., 5 Front, Mhtn.

NATIONAL PROTECTIVE LEGION.

Org. 1890. Geo. A. Scott, Pres.; H. C. Lockwood, Sec., Waverly, N. Y.

NATIONAL UNION ASSURANCE SOCIETY.

Org. 1881. 53,246 mem. N. Y. State, 1,946; Mhtn. jurisdiction, 1,231. Senate officers: D. A. Helpman, Pres., Toledo, O.; E. A. Myers, Sec., Toledo, O.; C. G. Bentley, Treas., Cleveland, O.

NORTH AMERICAN UNION.

(Consolidated in 1917 with Fraternal Aid Union.)

ORDER OF HERMAN'S SONS.

Org. 1840. 57,000 mem. Hdqts., 253 Atlantic av., Bkln. H. Havecker, Pres.; A. Schwarz, Sec., 338 E. 98th, Mhtn.

ORDER OF MUTUAL PROTECTION.

S. J. Mueller, Jr., Sup. Pres., 1523 Masonic Temple, Chicago, Ill.; G. Del Vecchio, Sup. Sec., Masonic Temple, Chicago, Ill.

ORDER OF OWLS.

Sup. Pres., John W. Talbot, South Bend, Ind.; Dep. Sup. Pres., C. J. Kelly, 1377 B'way, Bkln.; Sup. Sec., W. Baley, South Bend, Ind. Mem. in Mhtn., 1,175; Bkln., 5 317; Queens, 510.

ORDER OF SCOTTISH CLANS.

See Scottish Societies.

ORDER OF THE GOLDEN SEAL.

Fraternal Benefit Ins. Inc. 1902. Pres., Hill Montague, Richmond, Va.; Vice Pres., M. B. Ferguson, Richmond, Va.; Sup Sec., A. F. Souton, Roxbury, N. Y.; Treas., J. F. Bouton, Roxbury, N. Y. Total mem., 10,000; Mhtn., Bronx and Bkln., 1,500.

ORDER OF THE IROQUOIS.

A Fraternal Beneficiary Order. Hdtrs., 811 Iroquois Bldg., Buffalo, N. Y. J. E. Smith, Sup. Pres., 834 Michigan av., Buffalo, N. Y.; C. F. Jekel, Sup. Sec., Buffalo, N. Y.; Dr. E. S. Streng, Sup. Treas., Buffalo, N. Y.; Dr. E. L. Frost, Sup. Med. Dir., 212 Mass. av., Buffalo, N. Y.; Sup. Marshal, F. E. Currier, 189 Halsey st., Bkln. Org. under laws of N. Y. and doing business in N. Y., Penn., N. J., Conn., Ohio, Mich., Ky.

Brooklyn Lodge, Washington No. 106, meets in Johnston Bldg. 1st and 3d Wed. J. M. Freileweh, Sec., 25 Fuller pl.

ORDER SONS OF ST. GEORGE.

Sup. Pres., J. Orrell, 169 A, Lowell, Mass.; Sup. Sec., W. Willis, 3029 E. 92d, Chicago, Ill. Mem.: U. S., 28,416; N. Y. State, 4,216.

Grand Lodge.

Grand Pres., W. Fowler, 3 Melrose, Utica, N. Y.; Gr. Sec., J. A. Pinchbeck, 1 Madison av., Mhtn. Order of the Daughters of St. George. Cleveland, O.—1885. Sup. Pres., Mrs. M. A. Sandiford, 70 Liberty, N. Adams, Mass.; Sup. Sec., Eliza Connell, 100 Whittier, Providence, R. I.; Mem. 8,500.

Brooklyn Lodges: Anglo Saxon No. 48, W. Swannell, 268 Prospect av.; Magna Charta No. 49, T. Winsper, Sec., 866 Bushwick av.; Longfellow No. 94, S. Albinson, Sec., 265 Putnam av.; Shaftesbury No. 135, A. E. Graham, Sec., 133 Kent.

L. I. City Lodge: White Rose No. 315, W. T. Blunt, Sec., 554 9th av.

ORDER UNITED AMERICAN MEN.

D. J. Read, State Councilor, 1019 Emery, Fulton, N. Y.; E. Billings, Sec., 1868 9th av., Watervliet, N. Y. Mem.: Bkln., 100; N. Y. State, 2,100.

Brooklyn Council: America Council No. 13, 1028 Gates av., J. L. Springstead, Rec. Sec., 85 Myrtle av.

ORDER UNITED COMMERCIAL TRAVELERS OF AMERICA.

A Secret Beneficial Order. Inc. 1888. Hdqtrs., Park and Russell, Columbus, O. Sup. officers: W. B. Emerson, Sup. Counselor; W. D. Murphy, Sup. Sec., Columbus, O. N. Y. State: A. Shafer, Albany, N. Y. W. M. Winn, Gd. Sec., Utica, N. Y. Mem.: Bkln., 136; Mhtn. and Bronx, 678; N. Y. State, 6,860; in U. S. and Canada, 93,475. Meets June 9, 10, 11, 1921, in Schenectady, N. Y.

2 Brooklyn Councils: B. A. G. Reuter, 1560 E. 14th, and R. V. Kinney, 811 Halsey, Secs.

2 Manhattan Councils: C. H. Kohrs, 203 W. 78th, and J. M. Wile, 630 W. 172d, Secs.

RAILWAY MAIL ASSOCIATION.

Org. 1891. Inc. 1898. Branches in each of the 14 divisions of the country. Pres., E. J. Ryan, 604 Colorado Bldg., Washington, D. C.; V.-Pres., C. M. Harvey, 390 N. Exchange, St. Paul, Minn.; W. M. Collins, Industrial Sec., 604 Colorado Bldg., Washington, D. C.; Sec., O. J. Williams, Orchard Park, N. Y. Second Div. has branches in: N. Y. City, R. D. Hoover, Pres., Weehawken, N. J.; J. F. Bennett, Pres., 2d Div., Alleghany, N. Y.; Phila., Pa. C. H. Jolls, Pres., Wyoming, Del.; Utica, A. L. Frank, Pres.; Utica, N. Y.; Albany, F. T. Sorrell, Pres., Morrisonville, N. Y.; Buffalo, F. G. Hehr, Pres., Buffalo, N. Y.; Binghamton, C. E. Whitaker, Pres., Binghamton, N. Y.; Harrisburg, H. H. Wert, Pres., Harrisburg, Pa.; Williamsport, T. D. S. Bordner, Pres., Williamsport, Pa.; Baltimore, E. M. Boone, Pres., Baltimore, Md.

ROYAL ARCANUM.

Founded Boston, June 23, 1877, with 9 members. L. R. Geisenberger, Lancaster, Pa., Sup. Regent; S. N. Hoag, 407 Shawmut av., Boston, Mass., Sup. Sec.

State: L. C. Roake, Peekskill, Gd. Regent; D. A. Brown, Gd. Sec., 215 Montague, Bkln. Membership: Total in N. Y. State, 35,250; U. S. and Canada, 135,495.

ROYAL LEAGUE.

Fraternal Benefit. Org. 1883. W. E. Hyde, Sup. Archon; Chas. E. Piper, Sup. Scribe, 1601 Masonic Temple, Chicago, Ill. Mem. U. S., 23,192.

ROYAL NEIGHBORS OF AMERICA.

A Fraternal Beneficiary Society, auxiliary to the Modern Woodmen of America. Mem. 438,721. N. Y. State, 8,330. National officers: Sup. Oracle, Mrs. E. Child, Janesville, Wis.; H. M. Carlson, Sup. Recorder, Rock Island, Ill.; Sup. Receiver, Mrs. E. Foster, Chandler, Okla.

State officer: Supervising Dep., N. Y. State, Mrs. P. Kirkpatrick, 234 Georgia, Buffalo.

SOCIETIES AND ASSOCIATIONS—SECRET AND BENEFIT—*Continued.*

SONS OF VETERANS.

Natl. officers: Com.-in-Chief, H. D. Sisson, Pittsfield, Mass.; Sec., H. H. Hammer, Reading, Pa. Mem. 60,000.

N. Y. Div. officers: Div. Com., A. J. Clark, Utica; Div. Sec., W. S. Beilby, 164 Woodbine av., Rochester. Total mem. in N. Y. State, 5,058.

Sons of Veterans Auxiliary (N. Y. Div.), Mrs. M. E. Stapleton, Pres., Albany.

Sons of Veterans Auxiliary, Miss M. Tredo, Natl. Pres.; Miss M. Arold, Sec., Paterson, N. J.

National Alliance Daughters of Veterans: Miss Anna B. Dunham, Lockport, N. Y., Pres.

N. Y. Dept. Daughters of Veterans: Mrs. K. Hoeheiller, Pres., Buffalo, N. Y.; Miss R. Kirsch, Sec., 288 Hickery, Buffalo, N. Y.

Brooklyn Camps: 20, F. Obst, Com., 342 Tompkins av.; 23, F. Oliver, Com., 5407 3d av.; 28, R. McGowan, Com., 551 E. 16th, Mhtn.; 79, G. J. Whalen, Com.; 106, 96th, Woodhaven; 92, A. Goebel, Com.; 1034, Atlantic av.; 135, G. Sattler, Com., 403 Himrod; 168, F. Kellerman, Com., 351 42d.

SONS AND DAUGHTERS OF LIBERTY.

Natl. officers: Councilor, W. J. Smith. Natl. Sec., W. V. Edkins, 1604 E. Passyunk av., Phila, Pa.

State Sec., Lottie A. McClure, 171 Hillside av., Jamaica, N. Y. 100,000 mem. in U. S., 12,000 in N. Y.; Bkln., 4,000; Mhtn., 1,480; Richmond, 108; L. I., 2,000.

TELEGRAPH AND TELEPHONE LIFE INSURANCE ASSOCIATION.

Org. 1867. 5,000 mem. James Robb, Pres.; L. Dresdner, Treas.; N. M. Giffen, Sec., 195 B'way, Mhtn.

THEATRICAL MUTUAL ASSOCIATIONS.

Fraternal and Benevolent. Mem. 22,000. Grand Lodge org. 1889. D. F. Pierce, Gd. Pres.; E. Hollenkamp, Gr. Sec.-Treas., 50 E. Court, Cincinnati, O.

Brooklyn Lodge, 30. Org. 1891. 250 mem. C. J. McFadden, Pres, 90 Dean.

New York Lodge 1. Org. 1866. 450 mem. J. A. Casey Pres.; G. C. Krant, Sec.-Treas., 132 W. 90th.

TRAVELERS' PROTECTIVE ASSN. OF AMER.

Natl. Hdqtrs., St. Louis, Mo. Natl. Pres., R. J. White; Sec.-Treas., T. S. Logan, 915 Olive, St. Louis, Mo.

State Hdqtrs., Commodore Hotel, Mhtn. State Pres., P. F. Schmitt; State Sec. and Treas., L. C. Gosselin, 327 E. 63d, Mhtn. Mem., 95,000.

TRIBE OF BEN HUR.

R. H. Gerard, Sup. Chief, Crawfordsville, Ind.; John C. Snyder, Sup. Scribe, Crawfordsville, Ind.; W. W. Goltra, Sup. Keeper of Tribute, Crawfordsville, Ind.; J. F. Davidson, Sup. Med. Exam., Crawfordsville, Ind. Mem.: Bkln., 31; Mhtn., 707; N. Y. State, 4,121; U. S., 78,156.

UNION VETERAN LEGION OF THE U. S.

Natl. Council, J. S. Du Shane, New Castle, Pa.; Adj-Gen., J. M. Martin, New Castle, Pa.

Natl. Ladies' Union Veteran Legion. Natl. Pres., Anna L. Kicker, St. Louis, Mo.

UNITED ANCIENT ORDER OF DRUIDS.

A. M. Beasley, Sup. Arch., Linton, Ind.; C. G. N. Geider, Sup. Sec., 14 W. Ohio, Indianapolis, Ind.

N. Y. State officers: J. Bosch, N. G. A.; H. Freudenthal, Gr. Sec., 426 Clinton av., Albany. Mem.: Bkln., 175; Mhtn., 350; State, 1,953; U. S., 22,375.

UNITED NATIONAL ASSOCIATION POST OFFICE CLERKS.

Natl. officers: C. P. Franciscus, Pres., Sta. T, N. Y. P. O.; John J. Grogan, Sec., Wheeling, W. Va. State officers: P. J. Nolan, Pres., Albany; G. A. Murphy, Sec., College Point. Mem., 3,000.

Bkln. Branch—J. Z. Adams, Pres.; G. E. Van Nostrand, Rec. Sec.

New York Branch—N. Y. P. O., Mhtn. T. F. Slevin Pres. Auditor office, N. Y. P. O.; A. O. Murphy, Sec., Sta. N. N. Y. P. O.

UNITED ORDER OF THE GOLDEN CROSS.

Sup. Comr., J. P. Burlingame, Providence, R. I.; Sup. Keeper of Records, W. R. Cooper, Knoxville, Tenn.; Sup. Treas., F. W. Rauskolb, 16 Franklin, Medford, Mass.

N. Y. State officers: Grand Comr., Chas. Knapp, 1737 Sedgwick av., Bronx; Gr. Keeper of Records, J. F. Dorsheimer, 331 W. 24th, Mhtn.; Gr. Treas., W. A. Crouse. Mem.: State, 893; Bkln. and Queens, 384; Mhtn. and Bronx, 226; Richmond, 9.

UNITED SPANISH WAR VETERANS.

Reorg. April, 1904. An amalgamation of the Natl. Army and Navy Spanish War Veterans, Natl. Assn. Spanish-American War Veterans and the Natl. Encampment Service Men of the Spanish War.

National Encampment.

Com.-in-Chief, Wm. Jones, Farwell Bldg., Detroit, Mich.; Adj.-Gen., P. S. Rigney, Farwell Bldg., Detroit, Mich.

New York State Department.

Headquarters, Rm. 7, City Hall, N. Y. City. Dept. Comdr., T. F. Gannon; Dept. Adj., W. S. Goodwin; Dept. Q. M., Bernard J. Pierce.

U. S. VETERAN NAVY.

Commodore Fred'k Abel, 1636 71st, Bkln.; Fleet Sec., J. S. Drew, 745 Columbus av., Mhtn.; Fleet Paymaster, J. J. Butler, West Haven, Conn. Org. 1889. 4,682 mem. Qualification, service in the U. S. Navy, Rev. Cutter Service or Marine Corps during any war or in any wars that may come.

WOODMEN OF THE WORLD.

Fraternal Beneficiary Soc. Org. Omaha, Neb. 1890. Hdqtrs., Omaha, Neb. Sov. Camp officers: Sov. Com., W. A. Fraser, Omaha, Neb.; Sov. Adv., B. W. Jewell; Sov. Clk., J. T. Yates, Omaha, Neb. Head Camp, Jurisdiction of N. Y. Head Consul, E. T. Lowery, Buffalo, N. Y.; Head Advr., J. O'Donnell, N. Y. C.; Head Banker, A. H. Noeller, Niagara Falls, N. Y.; Head Clerk, E. O. Rose, Binghamton, N. Y.; Dist. Mgr., O. L. Forrester, 930 Madison, Bkln., N. Y.; Dist. Mgr., A. A. Hall, 441 106th, Richmond Hill. Juvenile and Industrial Dept., Gen. Mgr., O. L. Forrester, Shubert Bldg., Bkln. Mem., 9,991,151. No. of camps, 23,750. Mem. N. Y. State, 24,238. No. of camps, N. Y. State, 282.

WOODMEN CIRCLE.

A Fraternal Beneficiary Soc., auxiliary to the Woodmen of the World. Mem., 204,120; N. Y. C., 3,316. No. of Groves, 4,849. Sup. officers: Sup. Guardian, Emma B. Manchester, Omaha, Neb.; Sup. Banker, Nora M. DeBolt, Oklahoma City, Okla.; Sup. Clk., Dora Alexander, Omaha, Neb.; State Supervisor, Mrs. M. E. Long, Supreme Mgr., N. Y. City.

State officers: Grand Guardian, Emma La Tour, Buffalo; Grand Clk., Katherine B. Holland, Niagara Falls; Grand Banker, Tessie M. Rose, Bingham, N. Y.

MISCELLANEOUS BENEFIT SOCIETIES.

National.

Benev. Soc. of the U. S. for Propagation of Cremation—Inc. 1910. 949 Willoughby av., Bkln. 5,100 mem. F. Loechel, Pres.; Geo. Vermaeten, Sec., 1328 Barnes av., Bronx.

Clergymen's Mutual Ins. League of the P. E. Ch.—1869. Object, mutual insurance of relief to families of deceased members. Treas., Rev. E. B. Rice, 212 N. Fulton av., Mt. Vernon, N. Y.

Fraternal Aid Union—Lawrence, Kan. Org. 1890. 93,642 mem. V. A. Young, Pres.; Saml. S. Baty, Sec., Lawrence, Kan.

Hotel Men's Mutual Benefit Assn. of U. S. and Canada—Chicago, Ill. Org. 1879. 1,400 mem. Tyrrell, Pres.; J. K. Blatchford, Sec., Auditorium Tower, Chicago.

Natl. Fraternal Congress of America—1886. 5,538,000 mem. G. P. Kirby, Pres., 923 Ohio Bldg., Toledo, O. W. E. Futch, Sec., 1136 B. of L. E. Bldg., Cleveland, O.

Navy Mutual Aid Assn.—Room 1641, Navy Dept., Washington, D. C. Org. 1879. 1,310 mem. Adm. W. S. Benson, Pres.; Paymaster, H. W. Balthes, Sec.

Security Benefit Assn.—Topeka, Kan. Org. 1892. 250,000 mem. J. M. Kirkpatrick, Pres.; J. V. Abrahams, Sec.

Workmen's Sick and Death Benefit Fund—9 7th, Mhtn. Org. 1884. 53,000 mem. Paul Flaeschel, Pres.; Paul Sturm, Fin. Sec.

SOCIETIES AND ASSOCIATIONS—SECRET AND BENEFIT—MISCELLANEOUS—*Continued.*

Brooklyn.

Ackerman Benev. Assn.—A. Margolin, Pres.; A. Streicher, Fin. Sec.

Associated Employes of Bureau of Bldgs of Boro. of Bkln.—1907. 94 mem. John Conlon, Pres., E. F. McEnerney, Sec., 267 9th.

Beacon Light Ladies' Sick Benefit Assn.—1560 B'way. Org. 1880. 56 mem. Mrs. L. Goodbread, Pres.; Mrs. Minnie Kircher, Sec., 135 Cornelia.

Bkln. Mutual Aid Assn.—50 mem. Howard av. and Madison. J. W. Sudlow, Pres.; R. B. Gilmore, Sec., 120 Woodbine. Sect. 1—Howard av. and Madison; J. W. Sudlow, Pres.; R. B. Gilmore, Sec., 120 Woodbine.

Bkln. Mutual Aid Sick Benefit Assn.—No. 4, 92 mem. A. H. Graham, Pres.; F. H. Clement, Sec., Meets every Th. No. 7, 69 mem. F. T. Collier, Pres.; Wm. Bergemann, Sec., 126 Marcy av. Meets every M.

Bkln. Post Office Clerks' Mutual Benefit Assn.—Federal Bldg. Org. 1901. 375 mem. G. E. Van Nostrand, Pres.; Thos. J. Donnelly, Sec.; William Plath, V.-Pres.; Val Korn, Treas.

Bkln. Rapid Transit Employes' Benefit Assn.—1 Jamaica av. Org. 1902. 10,500 mem. G. W. Edwards, Pres.; H. E. Tiffany, Sec.

Bkln. Teachers' Life Assurance Assn.—1,610 mem. E. G. Colgan, Pres.; Mary B. Hart, Sec., 1242 Pacific.

Bkln. Teachers' Relief Assn.—1907. 4,750 mem. Miss E. L. Johnston, Pres.; Emily C. Powers, Sec., 56 Macon.

Daniel Bahr Relief Circle—211 Montrose av. 1894. Hy. Fisher, Pres.; Thos. Withers, Sec., 2027 Bleecker.

F. W. Foley Mutual Aid Club—335 Union. J. Dolan, Pres.; W. Stewart, Sec.

Kings Co. Civil Employees Benev. Assn.—1902. Hall of Records, Bkln. 300 mem. Louis Miller, Pres.; Frank L. Van Cleef, Sec., Hall of Records.

Knickerbocker Hgts. Assn.—716 Knickerbocker av. 114 mem. P. Butterworth, Pres.; Wm. Seliger, Sec., 182 Maujer.

Lawrence Mutual Aid Assn.—Inc. 1906. Bridge and Willoughby. 150 mem. T. Brizell, Pres., 94 Myrtle av; T. Summers, Rec. Sec., 131 Johnson.

Letter Carrier's Mutual Benefit Assn.—317 Washington. Chas. Keller, Pres., P. O. Sta. V.; G. J. Teagle, Sec.

Long Is. R. R. Employees Mutual Relief Assn.—L. I. R. R. office. P. H. Woodward, Ch., Gen. Pass. Agt.

Mhtn. Relief Circle—Org. 1879. 144 Wyckoff av. 80 mem. H. Scheick, Pres.; W. A. Lagatutta, Rec. Sec., 349 Cornelia.

Martha Washington Sick Benefit—100 mem. 554 Glenmore av. Elsor Torsk, Pres.; Mrs. Ida Ruefner, Sec., 869 Barbey.

Mutual Benefit Assn.—23d Infantry. 1877. 200 mem. R. P. S. Webster, Pres.; R. D. Crane, Sec., 1317 E. 17th.

Natl. Fraternal Soc. of Deaf (Div. 23)—1908. 185 mem. T. J. Cosgrove.

Natl. Institute of Inventors—Executive offices, 118 Fulton, Mhtn. L. J. Wing, Pres.; W. H. Kennedy, Sec., 338 W. 86th, Mhtn.; Paul R. Fay, Ex. Sec., 56 E. 122d, Mhtn. (For mutual aid, betterment and protection of inventors of North America.)

O. K. Club—State and Court. M. G. Rywelski, Pres.; C. H. Chambers, Rec. Sec., 2242 Church.

Post Office Station S. Mutual Aid Soc.—C. S. Lawrence, Pres.; H. O'Neill, Sec., Sta. S.

St. Agnes' Total Abstinence Benev. Soc.—Hoyt and Sackett. Org. 1879. 100 mem. Edw. McErney, Pres.; P. McGuire, Sec., 393 President; J. Brown, Treas., 388 12th. Su., 11 a.m.

Schweizer Verein of Bkln.—689 Seneca av. Swiss sick and death benefit. E. Baenninger, Pres.; H. Wuersch, Sec., 42 Rector, Woodhaven, L. I.

Spinner Club No. 16, Inc.—297 Irving av. 50 mem. J. Schauder, Big Chief; G. Scherer, Sec., 264 Irving av.

Trustees of Widows' and Orphans' Fund Vol. Fire Dept., Former City of Bkln.—Boro. Hall. J. H. Ruggles, Pres.; A. D. Bennett, Sec.; F. E. Pouch, Treas., 305 Adams.

United Retail Grocers' Assn. of Bkln. Mutual Benefit Horse Fund—P. Becker, Pres.; Fred Luppens, Sec., 1344 Flatbush av.

Wallabout Market Benev. Assn.—1888 Labor Lyceum. Chas. Gigrich, Pres.; Conrad Botsch, Sec., 211 Windsor pl., Bkln.

West Indian Benevolent and Social League—1892. C. Rollock, Pres.; W. E. Martin, Sec., 85 Rochester av.

Manhattan and Bronx.

Amceha: Soc.—1904. 780 mem. Sick and death benefit. Saml. Simms, Pres.; S. N. Higbie, Sec., 135 W. 42d.

Bremer Verein (Sick and Death Ben. Soc.)—A. Becker, Pres.; E. Beusmann, Sec., 2520 Gates av.

Circulation Club of N. Y.—1904. 2 Duane. F. P. O'Raw, Pres.; W. M. Henry, Sec.

Corkmen's Pat. Benev. Prot. Assn.—1888. 201 E. 67th. 750 mem. J. D. Fitzgerald, Pres.; T. M Hayes, Sec., 359 Jay, Bkln.

Geneva Soc. of Hotel and Restaurant Employes of America—1887. 800 mem. D. Block, Pres., 236 W. 43d; R. Liebel, Sec.

Insurance Clerks' Mutual Benefit Assn.—Org. 1872. 1,960 mem. A. M. Thorburn, Pres., 62-64 William.

Mutual Benefit Assn.—1905. Custom House, Mhtn Employes of the classified customs service, N. Y. District. 1,200 mem. J. A. Bangs, Pres.; J. S. Long, Sec.

Netherlands Soc.—Thiessen's Hall, 130 3d av., Mhtn. D. G. Verschuur, Pres., 65 Nassau, Mhtn.; J. van Folker, Sec., 626 75th, Bkln.

N. Y. Fire Dept. Benev. Assn., 220 E. 59th; J. J. Donohue, Pres., 817 Webster av., Bkln.; M. V. Stokes, Sec., 3226 Hull av., Bronx.

N. Y. Physicians' Mutual Aid Assn.—17 W. 43d. Org. 1868. 2,666 mem. G. R. Pisek, Pres.; Jas. Pedersen, Treas., 40 E. 41st.

N. Y. Railways' Assn.—769 7th av. Frank Hedley, Pres.; J. J. Shea, Sec.

N. Y. Telegraphers' Aid Soc.—1880. 1,000 mem. 195 B'way. C. J. Lemaire, Pres.; Miss M. E. Saunders, Rec. Sec.

N. Y. Veteran Police Assn.—Police Hdqtrs., Grand and Centre. 2,000 mem. B. Keleher, Pres., 115 B'way, Mhtn.; J. J. Churchill, Sec., 1381 Bergen, Bkln. Meets 2d Th.

Patrolmen's Ben. Assn.—63 Park row. J. P. Moran, Pres., 5803 6th av., Bkln.

Patrolmen's Endowment Org.—205 E. 56th. Jas. Coughlin, Ch., 45 Maurice av., Elmhurst.

Police Lieutenants' Benevolent Assn.—145 Riverside dr. John H. Ayres, Pres.

Postal Employees' Mutual Aid Assn.—General P. O., N. Y. C. Org 1895. 860 mem. Lewis J. Gallagher, Pres.; J. T. McCarthy, Sec.

Stewards' Assn. of N. Y. C.—1890. 200 mem. U. De Lisle, Pres.; A. Hauser, Sec., 107 W. 38th.

Traffic Squad Benev. Assn. P. D. N. Y.—1908. Police Club, 145 Riverside dr. P. F. Crane, Pres., 138 W. 30th; Michael Tierney, Sec, Tr. C., 138 W. 30th; D. J. O'Sullivan, Treas.

Uniformed Firemen's Assn.—1917. Room 402, World Bldg. 4,115 mem. A. E. Guinness, Pres.; A. Rosenberg, Sec.

Young Men's Benev. Assn.—1889. 500 mem. Benevolence and education, sick, death benefits and own cemetery. Meyer Sindel, Pres., 299 B'way; Hy. Bier, Sec.

Queens.

College Point, St. Joseph's Soc.—Org. 1872. 80 mem. C. F. Bux, Jr., Pres.; J. Koegel, Sec., 128 10th, College Point.

Richmond.

Natl. Assn. of Letter Carriers, Br. No. 99—1904. Tompkinsville. 48 mem. C. Rutz, Pres., New Brighton, S. I.; W. Brinley, Sec., Tompkinsville.

Richmond Light and Railroad Employes' Beneficial Assn.—1901. New Brighton. R. L. Rand, Pres.; Miss A. M. Stillwell, Treas.; F. Spall, Sec., Richmond Light and R. R. Co., New Brighton.

27,996 GRADUATED FROM PUBLIC SCHOOLS

Public schools in the greater city graduated 27,996 students, June, 1920. This represented 94.4 per cent. of the entire class up for graduation. Of the total number graduated there were 14,623 girls and 13,373 boys. Brooklyn schools exceeded the others, having a total of 11,587 graduations. Manhattan was next with 10,244, and figures for the other boroughs were: Bronx, 4,621; Queens, 2,651, and Richmond, 544.

U. S. CASUALTIES IN WORLD WAR.

Final figures on Army casualties in the World War are contained in the annual report of Surgeon General Ireland, made public Dec. 1, 1920, showing 34,249 killed and 224,089 wounded.

SOCIETIES AND ASSOCIATIONS—*Continued.*

SOCIAL CLUBS.

Note—Organizations listed under other classifications of this chapter have more or less of a social character, but to avoid repetition are not included in following list:

International and National.

American Club—1919. 95 Piccadilly, London, W., Eng. 700 mem. Social intercourse for Americans in London. Francis E. Powell, Pres.; Edw. F. Edwards, Sec.

Am. Club of Paris (The)—1904. 32 rue Taitbout, Paris. 1,450 mem. Lewis Niles Roberts, Pres.; J. L. Gimel, Sec.

Anglo-Am. Hospitality Club—1920. London, Eng. Undertakes entertainment of Amer. visitors in English homes. Lady Denman, Pres.

Ends of the Earth—1903. 300 mem. Rudyard Kipling, Ch. Honorary Council; C. B. Vaux, Sec., Wistar Inst., Phila., Pa.

English Speaking Union—1918. Trafalgar Bldgs., Trafalgar sq., London, W. C. 4,000 mem. A. J. Balfour and W. H. Taft, Pres.; Earl of Reading, Ch.; John E. Wrench, Sec.

Internatl. League of Press Clubs—1892. 25,000 mem. T. J. Keenan, Pres., Pittsburgh, Pa.; L. G. Early, Sec., Reading, Pa. P. O. Box 95.

Internatl. Optimist Club—1919. 2,000 mem. W. H. Harrison, Pres.; H. G. Hill, Sec., Pennsylvania av., Indianapolis, Ind.

Natl. Assn. of the Friars—1904. Geo. M. Cohan, Abbot, 110 W. 48th.

Professional Chauffeurs' Club of Am.—1903. 10 W. 60th. 1,000 mem. F. W. Hopler, Pres.; H. Holzmann, Treas.; D. Lawrence, Sec.

Brooklyn.

Anawanda—191 Monroe.. 1895. 75 mem. Sidney H. Weinberg, Pres.; P. Cohen, Sec., 190 Hart.

Anvil Chorus—1908. Jas. Dunne, Pres.; W. R. Redmond, Sec., 44 Court.

Arcady Club—314 Wythe av. F. T. Dixson, Pres.

Arthur J. Boyle Assn.—1909. 150 mem. Mostly Government employees. J. T. O'Grady, Pres.; J. E. Whistance, Sec.

Associated Brewery Clerks of N. Y. C. and Vicinity—Palm Garden, Wilson and Greene avs.; F. A. Clemenz, Pres.; J. Vogt, Sec.

Bankers' Club of Bkln.—1914. Chamber of Commerce Bldg. 135 mem. C. J. Obermayer, Pres.; W. A. Fischer, Sec., People's Trust Co.

Bkln. Club (The)—131 Remsen. 370 mem. 1865. C. J. Edwards, Pres.; F. H. Timpson, Sec.

Bkln. College Club—1919. 400 mem., J. A. Reilly, Pres., 44 Court; L. J. Mannion, Sec., 908 Greene Av.

Bkln. College Junior Auxiliary—1920. 1125 Carroll. 225 mem. Miss Marie V. Hillmann, Pres.; Miss Mary E. McCaffrey, Sec., 2739 Bedford av.

Bkln. Heights Seminary Club—1885. 18 Pierrepont. 350 mem. Miss Ellen Y. Stevens, Pres.; Miss A. Piper, Sec., 7522 Ridge blvd.

Bkln. Press Club—1912. 5 Willoughby. 200 mem. G. Bloch, Pres.; C. M. Armstrong, Sec.; J. F. Lane, Fin. Sec.-Treas.

Bkln. 60 Club—1919. 373 9th. 800 mem. H. A. Spaulding, Pres.; Miss M. Flaherty, Sec.

Cambridge Club—1890. 50 mem. Mrs. D. C. Seitz, Pres.; Mrs. S. Frost, Sec., 751 Westminster rd.

Cathedral Club—85 6th av. 1900. 425 mem. Leo J. Hickey, Pres.; B. B. Gillespie, Treas.; J. W. Lowell, Sec.

Catholic—(See Religious Socs., Catholic.)

Catholic Young Women's League—1919. 48 St. Paul's pl. 135 mem. Mrs. Eliz. Cunn'ngham, Dir.; Miss M. D. Buckley, Sec., 58 Rutland rd.

Central League of Central Cong. Church—R. M. Gray, Pres.; Miss G. R. Hoffman, Sec., 161 Putnam av.

Chiropean Soc.—1896. 346 Clinton av. Miss Julia F. Ring, Pres.; Mrs. Chas. H. Gillespie, Cor. Sec., 1141 Bergen.

Church Club of the Diocese of L. I.—1894. 170 Remsen. 100 mem. J. C. Klinck, Pres.; G. M. Allen, Sec., 1430 46th.

Columbian Club of L. I.—231 Jamaica av. J. W. Schopp, Pres.; Thos. Hammill, Sec.

Commerce—1912. 750 Mhtn. av. 250 mem. W. S. Miller, Pres.; J. E. MacDermott, Sec.

Congress Club of Kings Co.—1900. (Republican.) 586 Bedford av. 650 mem. Geo. Stark, Pres.; T. W. Christy, Sec.

Cortelyou—1896. Bedford av. and Av. D. 300 mem. Wm. Von Elm, Pres.; E. D. Gerber, Fin. Sec.

Dyker Heights Club—1907. 86th and 13th av. E. Frank Colyer, Pres.; J. O. Collyer, Sec., 8201 13th av.; Harry K. Mehrer, Treas.

East End Club, Inc.—1907. 1121 Liberty av. W. Wrage, Pres.; D. Walsh, Jr., Cor. Sec., 1122 Liberty av., Bkln.

Eastern District Club—1913. 725 Driggs av. 45 mem. L. Zahler, Pres.; D. Small, Sec., 183 Rochester av.

Eckford—1865. 95 B'way. 215 mem. A. W. Welch, Pres.; P. J. Maher, Sec., 1424 Sterling pl.

Edison—1906. 8 Nevins. W. T. Fairbairn, Ch.

Entre Nous—1914. 106 Wilson. 200 mem. J. J. Crawford, Pres.; J. A. Driscoll, Sec.

Excelsior—1854. 45 mem. D. Chauncey, Pres.; A. E. Smylie, Sec., 106 John.

Farmers—1883. 603 Grand. 100 mem. S. Allen, Pres.; Chas. Dahlbender, Sec.

Fawcett—1913. 1765 79th. 150 mem. J. J. Pollaci, Pres., 1427 75th; E. Craig, Sec.

Flatbush Boys' Club—(See Relief of Children, Bkln.)

Flatbush Gas Co. Employees' Assn.—300 mem. 273 Clarkson. L. S. Troell, Pres.; G. H. Evans, Sec.; J. P. Mulvihill, Ch. of Entertainment Com.

Hamilton—1882. 146 Remsen. 610 mem. E. P. Maynard, Pres.; H. A. Ingraham, Sec.

Hanover—1890. 563 Bedford av. 220 mem. C. C. Mollenhauer, Pres.; Chas. B. Andrews, Sec.

Heights Casino—75 Montague. 300 mem. Ed. Cornell, Pres.

Huron—1908. 48 Thatford av. 225 mem. Wm. J. H. Birken, Pres.; D. Goldmintz, Sec.

Illuminati Club—(See Literary Socs.)

Kilowatt—1909. 8 Nevins. 500 mem. H. G. Disque, Pres.; H. Trottner, Sec., 360 Pearl.

Kings Co. Grand Jurors Assn.—(See Boards of Trade and Civic Improvement Assns.)

Knickerbocker Field Club—1889. E. 18th and Tennis Court. 400 mem. F. M. Brooks, Pres.; F. A. Cottrell, Sec., 396 McDonough.

Knickerbocker Heights Assn.—718 Knickerbocker av. 100 mem. P. Butterworth, Pres.; John Smith, Sec., 1379 Jefferson av.

Liberty Hose Assn.—1866. 10 mem. H. H. Brennan, Pres.; H. A. Mandeville, Sec., 108 Van Siclen av.

Lincoln—Inc. 1879. 65-67 Putnam av. 200 mem. C. H. Luscomb, Pres.; Jay Stone, Sec.

Long Is. Harvard Club—B. M. Langstaff, Pres.; Warren J. Kibby, Sec.-Treas., St. Albans, L. I.

Masonic Club of Bkln. (The)—1908. 1160 Bedford av. 350 mem. B. V. W. Owens, Pres.; S. A. Coombs, Sec.

Midwood—(Re-named Union League Club.)

Montauk—25 8th av. Inc. 1889. 650 mem. W. H. English, Pres.; B. A. Greene, Sec., 265 Berkeley pl.

Neighborhood Club—1920. 104 Clark. Saml. N. Jones, Pres.; Harriet Fitts, Sec., 104 Clark.

Old 13th Reg. Hut, Inc.—1919. 150 mem. 1320 Myrtle av., E. A. DeYoung, Com., Alex Pisciotta, Sec., 1440 DeKalb av.

Pilgrim Club of Ch. of Pilgrims—1917. 109 Remsen. E. S. Green, Pres.; R. M. Montgomery, Jr., Sec.

Pratt Inst. Women's Club—1914. 166 Willoughby av. Mrs. Nellie G. Taylor, Soc. Sec.

Prospect Club—(See Literary Socs.)

Ryder—1909. 165 Carroll. 125 mem. Chas. Esposito, Pres.; S. De Nicola, Sec.

Service Club of Greater N. Y., Inc.—1916. 149 Adams. 212 mem. T. J. Gillane, Pres., 219 Concord; G. A. Michaud, Sec.-Treas., 150 Adams.

Spinner Club No. 16 (Inc.)—1904. 50 mem. 297 Irving av. J. Schauder, Big Chief; Geo. Scherer, Sec., 264 Irving av.

Stuyvesant Assn.—1907. 957 Lafayette av. 92 mem. John McGovan, Pres.; F. A. Linden, Sec.; E. Jones, Treas.

Tavern Club—1902. 4 Court sq. Geo. E. Brower, Pres.; W. F. Atkinson, Sec., 44 Court.

Terrace Club of Flatbush—(See Country Clubs.)

Union League Club (formerly Midwood Club)—1917. E. 21st. 350 mem. F. J. H. Kracke, Pres.

United Victory Club—1919. 375 Union. 350 mem. T. F. Flynn, Pres; D. Dugan, Sec., 684 Warren.

Unity Club of Bkln.—1897. Grant sq. 600 mem. H. E. Lewis, Pres.; Ira Skutch, Sec.

University—1901. 109 Lafayette av. 446 mem. W. A. Mosscrop, Pres.; T. W. Hanigan, Sec.

Who-R-We?—1919. Jackson pl. and Prospect av. 75 mem. E. Hollan, Pres.; I. Murphy, Sec.; J. McIntyre, 344 17th.

Williamsburgh Luncheon Club—1918. 84 Broadway. 320 mem. R. C. Irish, Pres.; Hy. Mollenhauer, Jr., Sec.

SOCIETIES AND ASSOCIATIONS—SOCIAL CLUBS—*Continued.*

Manhattan and Bronx.

Aldine Club—1889. 200 5th av. 900 mem. Dr. O. S. Marden, Pres.

Amen Corner—1902. Waldorf-Astoria. 35 mem. T. F. Smith, Pres.; J. J. Montague, V.-Pres.; W. Leary Treas.; J. V. Gwin, Sec.

Arkwright—1893. 320 B'way. 1,000 **residents, 200 non-residents.** J. H. Snook, Pres.; Wm. Widnall, Jr., **Sec.**

Army and Navy—1889. 18 Gramercy Park. 2,750 mem. Rear Admiral B. A. Fiske, U. S. N., Retired, Pres.; Brig. Gen. W. J. Nicholson, U. S. A., Retired, V.-Pres.; Capt. W. B. Franklin, U. S. N., Treas.; Theo. S. Farrelly, Late Capt., U. S. A., Sec.

Associates of the Engineer Corps and Co. K, 7th Regt., N. G., N. Y.—1868. 400 mem. R. G. Mead, Pres.

Authors—1882. Carnegie Bldg., 7th av. and 56th. 254 mem. E. Ingersoll, Sec.

Bankers Club of **Amer.**—1915. 120 B'way. 2,900 mem. A Barton Hepburn, Pres; Ralph Lane, Sec.

Barnard Club of the City of N. Y.—1894. Carnegie Hall. 550 mem. **Walter Bogert, Pres.; Miss** Louise Tibbetts, Sec.; Ed. J. Gillies, Treas.; Mrs. G. R. Boynton, Ch. House Comm., 58 W. 57th.

British Schools and Universities Club—1895. 115 Franklin. 475 mem. Rev. John Williams, Pres.; V. F. Clarendon, Sec., 115 Franklin; H. W. Souter, Treas., Rm. 620. 1472 B'way.

Brown Univ.—44 W. 44th. 250 mem. A. B. Meacham, Pres.; C. B. Fernald, Sec.

Brownson Catholic—1894. 348 E. 146th. 180 mem. Dr. J. F. Buckley, Pres.; J. B. Lynch, Sec.

Calumet—1879. 12 W. 56th. S. O. Edmonds, Pres.; S. F. Barry, Sec.

Camera—1896. 121 W. 68th. 200 mem. J. N. McKinley, Pres; M. W. Tingley, Sec.

Camp Fire Club of America—Marshall McLean, Pres.; Arthur F. Rice, Sec., 15 E. 40th.

Carroll—1919. 120 Madison av. 6,000 mem. Miss May Jenkins, Sec.

Cathedral Club—1887. 144 E. 50th. C. A. Dempsey, Pres.; F. X. Dempsey, Treas.; J. J. Conlin, Cor. Sec.

Catholic—1871. 120 Central Park S. 1,450 mem. T. F. Farrell, Pres.; E. A. Arnold, Sec.

Catholic Writers' Guild—1920. Suite 1606, 220 W. 42d. 500 mem. T. Meehan, Pres.; T. C. Quinn, Sec., 434 W. 20th.

Chelsea—1895. 500 mem. W. B. Mack, Pres.; J. J. Mack, Sec.

Cherokee Club—(See Political Clubs, Dem.)

Church Club of N. Y. (The)—1887. 53 E. 56th. 500 mem. H. L. Hobart, Pres.; F. S. Marden, Sec.

City Bank Club—1904. 55 Wall. 3,200 mem. Percy West, Pres.; J. K. Hayden, Sec.

City Club—1892. 55 W. 44th. 2,100 mem. N. S. Spencer, Pres.; R. P. Ingersoll, Sec.

City College Club—1890. 371 Grand av. 300 mem. B. M. Briggs, M.D., Pres.; J. Holman, Sec.

Clergy Club of N. Y. and Neighborhood (Inc.)—1915. 200 5th av. 698 mem. A P Atterbury, DD., Pres.; Dr. W. Laidlaw, Registrar.

Collectors'—1896 120 W. 49th. 125 mem. Dr. J. B. Chittenden, Pres.; H. M. Lewy, Sec.

Colony Club (The)—1903. 1,844 mem. 564 Park av. **Miss R. Morgan, Pres.;** Mrs. M. Ellsworth, Sec.

Columbia—325 W. 108th. Inc. 1890. 300 mem. O. Rothschild, Pres.; L. Phillips, Sec.

Columbia Univ. Club—1901. 4 W. 43d. 2,190 mem. Chas. H. Mapes, Pres.; H. K. Masters, Sec., 233 B'way.

Commerce Club—1915. 31 Nassau. 815 mem. L. Szymanski, Pres.; Wm. A. Brockwell, Exec. Sec.; Beatrice Smith, Sec.

Cornell—1889. 30 W. 44th. 1,100 mem. E. N. Sanderson, Pres.; F. M. Coffin, Sec.

Cosmopolitan—1909. 133 E. 40th. W. S. Morse.

Criterion Club of the Metropolis—1894. 683 5th av. 300 mem. H. Rawitser, Pres., 285 W. B'way; W. J. Wittenberg, Sec., 11 B'way.

Cygnet—1883. 84th and E. River. 50 mem. S. A. **Magarigal, Pres.;** H. Gennerich, Sec., 1626 Av. A.

Diomedians of N. Y.—1919. 51 W. 48th. 100 mem. Wm. Lilly, Pres.; Don R. Almy, Sec., 46 Cedar.

Dixie—1904. Hotel Astor. 200 mem. Mrs. E. W. Inslee, Pres.; Mrs. J. D. Richards, Sec., 56 W. 58th.

Dotards of 1848 (The)—1915. 12 mem. W. E. Iselin, **Pres.; A. W. Evarts, Treas.;** L. K. Wilmerding, **Sec., E. Islip, L. I.**

Down Town Assn.—1860. 60 Pine. 1,178 mem. A. P. Whitehead, Pres.; O. S. Seymour, Sec., 60 Pine.

Engineers—1888. 32 W. 40th. 2,300 mem. Lansing C. Holden, **Pres.; Jos. Struthers, Sec.**

Friars—See National Socs.

Gamut Club—Hotel Wellington. 300 mem. Miss Mary Shaw, Pres.; Miss Mary Rehan, Sec., 252 W. 92d.

Green Room—1902. 664 mem. 139 W. 47th. H. Corthell, Prompter; F. Burt, Call Boy; J. F. Stephens, Angel; R. Stuart, Copyist.

Guaranty—140 B'way. 3,000 mem. J. J. Gaul, Pres.; H. P. Engle, Sec.

Hardware—1892. 253 B'way. 250 mem. R. G. Thompson, Pres.; J. Ed. Ogden, Sec.

Harmonie—1852. 4-6 E. 60th. 900 mem. A. B. Spingarn, Pres.; W. R. Rose, Sec., 4 E. 60th.

Harvard—1865. 27 W. 44th. 5,445 mem. R. P. Perkins, Pres.; F. Rogers, Sec., 27 W. 44th.

Hungry Club—1906. 35 mem. **James Freixas,** Sec.-Treas., 250 W. 85th.

India House—1914. 1 Hanover sq. J. A. Farrell, Pres.; M. Egan, Sec.

Jekyl Island—1885. 126 Le Roy. 77 mem. W. B. James, Pres.; J. A. Falk, Sec.

John Rackey Saturday Night Club—21 Frankfort. John Rackey, Pres.; A. Kronmueller.

Lambs (The)—1875. 130 W. 44th. 1,500 mem. R. H. Burnside, Shepherd; I. S. Cobb, Boy; C. A. Stevenson, Sec.

Lawyers' (The)—1887. 115 B'way. 1,200 mem. W. A. Butler, Pres.; R. G. Babbage, Sec.; L. F. Goldrick, Mgr.

Lehigh Club of N. Y.—1902. 35 W. 39th. 700 mem.

Le Salon—180 Madison av. Countess de Castlevecchio, Pres., Islip, L. I.; Miss Alberta Gallatin, Cor. Sec.

Lotos—1870. 110 W. 57th. 1,254 mem. **Chester S. Lord, Pres.;** Chas. M. Schwab, Vice-Pres.

Machinery Club of the City of N. Y.—1907. 1,300 mem. J. R. Vandyck, Pres.; Fred Stadelman, Sec., 50 Church.

Manhattan Matinee Club—1916. Waldorf-Astoria. 200 mem. Jessie Emerson Moffat, Pres.; Mrs. P. G. Sawyer, Sec., 26 St. Nicholas pl.

Marine Insurance Club—1898. 600 mem. 27 William. E. W. Morren, Pres.

Masonic Club of N. Y. (The)—Masonic Hall, 24th, nr. 6th av. 1,600 mem. Wm. H. Miller, **Pres.;** Geo. W. Gale, Sec.

Merchants (The)—1871. 108 Leonard. 400 mem. J. C. Wilmerding, **Pres.;** E. M. Townsend, Sec.

Merry Five Assn.—1865. 2164 Crotona av. 100 mem. T. J. Byrne, Pres.; W. J. McLaughlin, Sec.

Metropolis Club—105 W. 57th. 600 mem. Irving L. Ernst, Pres.; Z. D. Bernstein, Sec.

Metropolitan—1891. 1 E. 60th. 1,400 mem. F. K. Sturgis, Pres.; P. R. Pyne, Sec.

Minerva—1898. 509 W. 121st. 325 mem. Mrs. H. MacNutt, Pres.; Mrs. R. F. Cartwright, Rec. Sec., 541 W. 113th.

New Club for Men and Women—1920. 17 W. 44th (temp.), 113-123 W. 43d (perm.). S. McC. Lindsay, Pres.; Miss Charlotte S. Baker, Sec.; L. P. B. Gould, Treas.

New York—1845. 20 W. 40th. 700 mem. A. W. Morse, Pres.; J. J. Crawford, Sec.

New York Alumni Club (Univ. of Chicago)—L. J. MacGregor, Sec., care Halsey Stuart & Co., 49 Wall.

New York Press—1870. 21 Spruce. 1,000 mem. E. P. Howard, Pres.; C. H. Redfern, Sec.

N. Y. Swiss Club—1882. P. O. Box 982. 350 mem. R. F. Schwarsenbach, Pres.; J. Huber, Sec.

N. Y. Times Assn.—1911. 217 W. 43d. **150 mem. Dr. Van B. Thorne, Pres.**

Nippon—161 W. 93d. 450 mem. R. Arai, Pres.; S. Shinozaki, Sec.

Our Own Club (9th Ward)—1883. 275 Bleecker. 75 mem. John Molter, Pres.; G. E. Macoy, Sec.

Over Seas Club—N. Y. Branch—1910. Majestic Hotel. H. J. Riley, V.-Pres.; A. F Inverarity, Hon. Sec., P. O. Box 614, Scarsdale, N. Y.

Owl—1883. 448 W. 50th. 250 mem. H. W. Beyer, Pres.; B. J. Foss, Sec., 495 9th av.

Park Bank Club—1915 214 B'way. 450 mem. T. B. Carlton, Pres.; Miss Anna Bentel, Sec.

Pleiades Club—Geo. F. Curtis, Pres.; William H. Ross, Sec., 109 Fair [illegible] City, N. J.

Police Club of the City of N. Y.—1919. 145 Riverside dr. 300 mem. J. C. Harriss, Pres.; J. A. Faurot, Sec.

Princeton Club of N. Y. (The)—1899. **Vanderbilt** av., cor. 44th. 2,200 mem. R. E. Dwight, Pres.; S. G. Etherington, Sec., 50 E. 42d.

SOCIETIES AND ASSOCIATIONS—SOCIAL CLUBS—MANHATTAN AND BRONX—*Continued.*

Pro Club—1911. 65 W. 119th. 100 mem. J. E. Golding, Pres.; H. Rubin, Sec.

Progress—Central Park West and 88th. Inc. 1865. 600 mem. M. Eisner, Pres.; Louis Gans, Sec.

Quarter Century—1915 J. C. Bangs, Pres.; J. F. Carroll, Sec., Collectors Dept., Custom House.

Railroad Club of N. Y. (The)—1907. 30 Church. 1,200 mem. E. H. Gary, Pres.; R. B. Kay, Sec.

Railway Mail Club of N. Y. (Inc.)—1895. 14 Vesey. 800 mem. B. L. Brand, Pres.; T. H. Russell, Mgr.

Rocky Mountain Club of N. Y.—1907. 1,200 mem. 65 W. 44th. John Hays Hammond, Pres.; H. Wall, Sec.

Rutgers Club—1891. 216 Lenox av. 260 mem. Benjamin Cohen, Pres.; L. Abrams, Sec.

St. Laurent Assn.—1910. 135 mem. 5 E. 35th. Miss Helen C. McGee, Pres.; Miss E. Levins, Sec.

St. Lawrence Univ. Club—(See Alumni Assn.)

St. Nicholas Soc.—1835. 43 Cedar. 650 mem. Alfred Wagstaff, Pres.; F. I. Lockman, Sec.

Schnorer Club of Morrisania—1881. Eagle av. and E. 163d. 350 mem. W. S. Sullivan, Pres.; John J. Beisiegel, Sec., 105 E. 192d.

Southland Club—Waldorf-Astoria. Mrs. Simon Baruch, Pres., 51 W. 70th.

Sterling Cob Web Club—1908. 823 Mhtn. av. 70 mem. J. J. Skivington, Pres.; Jas. C. Conboy, Sec.

Stewards' Assn. of N. Y. C.—Inc. 1890. 30 E. 42d. 200 mem. Jas. Ringgold, Pres.; A. Hauser, Sec.

Stock Exchange Luncheon Club (The)—1904. 18 Wall. 510 mem. Wm. A. Greer, Pres.; G. M. Sidenberg, Sec.

Sunrise—1893. 500 mem. E. C. Walker, Sec., 211 W. 138th.

Technology Club—1903. 17 Gramercy Pk. 1,000 mem. L. D. Gardner, Pres.; F. Mathesius, Jr., Sec.

Thirteen Club—1882. 226 mem. Col. J. F. Hobbs, Chief Ruler; Lonnie Hobbs, Scribe, Rm. 221, 1495 B'way.

Three Arts Club of N. Y. C.—1903. 340 W. 85th. 683 mem. Mrs. J. H. Hammond, Pres.; Mrs. R. H. Hoadley, Jr., Sec.

Tough—1865. 243 W. 14th. 400 mem. Wm. Lawrence, Pres.; Ed. Johnson, Rec. Sec.

Union—1836. 5th av. and 51st. 1,600 mem. L. K. Wilmerding, Vice-Pres.; C. K. Beekman, Sec.

Universal Netherlands Federation; Div. New Netherlands—Con. J. A. Schrikker, Pres., 44 Beaver; J. Van Folker, Sec., 626 75th, Bkln.

Union League—1863. 1 E. 39th. 1,800 mem. Henry P. Davison, Pres.; G. W. McGarrah, Treas.; H. A. Cushing, Sec.

U. S. Diamond Club of N. Y.—1915. 95 Nassau. 114 mem.

University—1865. 1 W. 54th. 4,800 mem. A. B. Hepburn, Pres.; S. H. Ordway, Sec.

Univ. of Pa.—1,250 mem. Wm. L. Saunders, Pres.; L. Martin, Sec., 135 William.

Vacation Assn.—1910. 2?8 Madison av. Miss G. R. Smith, Pres.; Mrs. N. Carlton, V.-Pres.; Miss G. E. Lachlan, Sec.

Vatel Club—216 W. 60th. 1,200 mem. E. Panchard, Pres.; T. W. Stucky, Sec.

Vigor Club—1913. 84 W. 119th. 100 mem. Ellis Goldberg, Pres.; B. Goldman, Sec.

West Side Club—1888. 270 W. 84th. 300 mem. E. W. Palmer, Pres.; C. H. Doud, Sec.

Whitehall Club—1910. 17 Battery pl. 800 res. mem. 209 non-res. mem. M. C. Keith, Pres.; E. J. Beinecke, Sec.

Workers Amusement Club—1915. 142 W. 118th. 400 mem. Mrs. A. Simmons.

Yale—1897. 50 Vanderbilt av. 4,756 mem. M. M. Buckner, Pres.; L. Platt, Sec.

Queens.

Adelphi Social—1889. 225 mem. J. Hoenig, Pres.; H. E. Simon, Sec., 33 S. 14th, College Point.

College Point Club—1906. 60 mem. Alfred Scheckell, Pres.; A. E. Miller, Sec., 616 13th, College Point.

Columbia—1897. 21st, bet. 7th and 8th avs., Whitestone. 250 mem. G. Kefer, Pres.; C. S. Colden, Sec., Whitestone.

Jamaica—1891. Herriman av. and Grove, Jamaica. 150 mem. W. H. Shannon, Pres.; E. P. Ramsey, Sec.

Jamaica Women's Club—1888. Herriman av., Jamaica. 130 mem. Mrs. S. Palmer, Pres.; Mrs. C. B. Jameson, Sec., 4 Park View av.

Laurelton Club—1910. Laurelton. 102 mem. H. S. Terbell, Pres.; Geo. A. Nelson, Sec., Laurelton, L. I.

Progress Club—1912. Woodhaven. C. W. Wolfe, Pres.; H. J. Ahlheim, Sec., 380 Ferry.

Men's Club of Forest Hills Gardens—L. Abbott, Pres.; L. Beecher Stowe, Sec., Greenway South. Forest Hills Garden.

Mettco Club—Nolins and Mettco avs. Howard Beach. 1915. 162 mem. E. C. Kraus, Pres.; Mildred M. Correll, Sec.

Niantic—1863. Sanford av., Flushing. 98 mem. L. Littlejohn, Sr., Pres.; W. T. Wilcox, Sec., Flushing.

Queens Borough Club—1901. Ozone Pk. H. Voizard, Pres.; J. B. McCook, Jr., Sec., 4220 Rockaway rd., Ozone Pk.

Rockaway Beach Pioneers—1910. Rockaway Beach. John Jamieson, Pres.; George Bennett, Sec., 26 N. 121st, Rockaway Pk.

Winter Colony Club—1919. Miss Gertrude Conolly, Pres., 73 N. 118th, Rockaway Park. Miss May O'Connor, Sec., 73 N. 7th av., Rockaway Park.

Richmond.

Amicita Assn.—1886. Pleasant Plains. 100 mem. Jos. C. Seguine, Pres.; W. M. Lebert, Sec., Prince Bay; W. A. Swade, Treas.

S. I. Ladies Club—1880. Livingston. 220 mem. Mrs. Hy. T. Boody, Pres.; Mrs. J. E. Ridgway, Sec., 324 Bard av., W. New Brighton.

Woman's Club of S. I. (The)—New Brighton, 1893. 175 mem. Mrs. W. A. Boyd, Pres.; Mrs. F. A. Franklin, Cor. Sec., 461 Oakland av., West New Brighton.

SPANISH SOCIETIES.

Brooklyn.

BENEVOLENT.

"La Nacional" Mutual Aid Society—27 Fort Greene pl. Gerardo Moscosco, Pres.

TOBACCO TRADE.

"Los Escogedores"—102 Pineapple. *M. Alvarez.

"Union de Rezagadores"—*Escolastico Uriona.

*President. †Secretary.

Manhattan.

SOCIAL.

Club Ibero Americano—200 W. 72d. *M. Ayala; J. A. Thomen, Treas.

BENEVOLENT.

"Centro Hispano Americano"—29 E. 20th. *J. Gomez. †C. Claros.

SPORTING CLUBS.

AERO CLUBS.

International Federation Aeronautique Internationale—Paris.

National.

Aerial League of America—1917. 280 Madison av., Mhtn. Major R. G. Landis, Sec.

Aero Club of Amer.—297 Madison av. 1905. 2,500 mem. A. R. Hawley, Pres.; A. Post, Sec.

Amer. Flying Club—1919. 11 E. 38th. 1,500 mem. Lawrence La T. Driggs, Pres., A. H. Johns, Sec.

ARCHERY CLUBS.

National.

Natl. Archery Assn. of U. S.—R. P. Elmer, M.D., Pres.; W. H. Palmer, Jr., Wayne, Pa., Sec.-Treas.

Beechview-Bon Air Archery Club—O. L. Hertig, Pres.; W. D. Douthitt, Sec., 68 Pasadena, Pittsburgh, Pa.

Keystone Archers—Dr. O. L. Hertig, Pres., Pittsburgh, Pa.; Dr. R. P. Elmer, Sec., Wayne, Pa.

Wayne Archers—W. H. Palmer, Pres.; Mrs. John Dunlap, Sec.-Treas., Wayne, Pa.

ATHLETIC CLUBS.

National.

Amateur Ath. Union—R. Weaver, Pres.; F. W. Rubien, Sec., 290 B'way, Mhtn.

Military Ath. League—F. H. Norton, Pres.; Capt. C. J. Dieges, Sec., 15 John, Mhtn.

Natl. Collegiate Ath. Assn.—1905. Dean F. W. Nicolson, Sec., Wesleyan Univ., Middletown, Conn.

State.

Flower City A. S.—1915. 2,000 mem. J. T. O'Grady, V.-Pres.; J. R. Powers, Sec., 118 Berkly Bldg., Rochester, N. Y.

Mercury—Yonkers and Central av., Yonkers, N. Y. 1905. 100 mem. C. J. Schlobohm, Pres.; J. D. Hickerson, Sec.

Newburgh Wheelmen—49 Grand, Newburgh, N. Y. 1890. 250 mem. Geo. Mason, Pres.; R. E. Diebold, Sec., 245 Wisner av., Newburgh.

SOCIETIES AND ASSOCIATIONS—SPORTING CLUBS—*Continued.*

Brooklyn.

Bkln.-Queens Police Ath. Club—240 Centre, Mhtn. 1915. 2,300 mem. M. A. Noonan, Pres.; F. C. Kruse, Sec.

Bkln. Park Playgrounds Ath. Assn.—Litchfield Mansion. 1915. 2,000 mem. J. N. Harman, Pres.; J. J. Downing, Sec.

Central Congregational Ath. Assn.—Hancock, nr. Franklin av. J. W. Atherton, Pres.; W. L. Thompson, Mgr., 231 Lenox rd.

Crescent Ath. Club—129 Pierrepont. 1884. Country house and grounds, Shore rd. and 85th, Bay Ridge. 2,610 mem. A. S. Hart, Sec.

Danish Ath. Club—Prospect Hall. R. Hansen, Pres.; M. Andreasen, Sec., 209 11th, Bkln.

Elite—358 Vernon av. Inc. 1910. 150 mem. M. J. Solomon, Pres.; Max Abrams, Sec.

Emmanuel Ath. Assn.—1895. 131 Steuben. 100 mem. A. E. Parkhouse, House Sec.

14th Regt. A. A.—8th av. and 14th. Capt. Le Roy Bellows, Pres., 2110 82nd.

47th Regt. Ath. Assn.—355 Marcy av. 900 mem. Col. W. J. Jeffreys, Pres.; Capt. T. S. Mahoney.

Holy Trinity Ath. Club of St. Luke's—53 mem. 230 Hall. J. F. Heinbockel, Pres.; J. W. Ogilvie, Sec.

Millrose—Bay 11th and 784 B'way. Mhtn. 1910. V. Dysert, Pres.; Fred Schmertz, Sec., 318 E. 19th.

Monitor—Wm. Wassmuth, Jr., Pres.; C. F. Kirchner, Sec., 165 McDougal.

Natl. A. C.—11 Cedar. J. G. Sullers, Pres.; F. W. Werner, Sec.

Smart Set Ath. Club—1904. 511 McDonough. 125 mem. G. W. Lattimore, Pres.; W. E. D. Robinson, Sec., 1656 Dean.

13th C. D. C., A. A.—Sumner and Jefferson avs. Capt. J. C. Hardmeyer, Pres., 395 St. Johns Pl.

Twenty-third Regt. Ath. Assn.—Bedford and Atlantic avs. 1905. Frank I. Loomis, Pres.; F. H. Smith, Sec., 115 Broadway, Mhtn.

Visitation Parish Club—77 Verona. 1911. 200 mem. W. E. Hughes, Pres.; J. S. Farrell, Sec., 324 Van Brunt.

Women's Ath. Club—1918. 25 Clinton. 200 mem. Mrs. J. P. Cowley, Pres.; Loretta L. Delaney, Sec., 129 Berkeley pl.

Manhattan and Bronx.

Alpha Physical Culture Club, Inc.—126 W. 131st. 1904. 125 mem. Oscar H. Williams, Pres.; R. L. Hutchins, Jr., Sec., 262 St. James pl., Bkln.

Bohemian Gymnastic Assn. ("Sokol")—420-424 E. 71st. 1867. 1,165 mem. J. Modr, Pres.; M. A. Klein, Sec.

Catholic Ath. League—321 W. 43d. 11,000 mem. 35 clubs. Rev. J. F. Ferris, Pres.; M. B. Mulligan, Sec.-Treas., 694 Union av., Bronx.

Church Ath. League of N. Y.—535 W. 135th. 1902. 22 clubs. F. J. Delaney, Pres.; Maj. E. S. Bettelheim, Jr., Sec.-Treas.

City Ath. Club—1908. 50 W. 54th. 1,000 mem. S. R. Guggenheim, Pres.; S. T. Stern, Sec., 41 Park Row.

Continental A. C.—1919. 5 Columbus Circle, N. Y. C.

East Side House Ath. Assn.—540 E. 76th. 150 mem. J. F. Reilly, Pres.; H. Kuntz, Sec.

Fencers—109 W. 54th, N. Y. C. 1883. 225 mem. G. H. Breed, Sec.-Treas.

First Bohemian Ath. Club—413 E. 71st. 1910. 50 men. O. Havranek, Pres.; J. Havranek, Sec.

Fresh Air Club—1890. 80 mem. H. E. Buermeyer, Pres.; Mortimer Bishop, Sec., care of N. Y. A. C., Central Park South.

Glencoe—154th and 7th av. 1907. 320 mem. J. J. Hewes, Pres.; Max J. Tea, Sec.

Grace Ath. Club—415 E. 13th. 225 mem. Rev. B. Washburn, Pres.; T. Drain, Sec.

Harlem Sporting Club—14 E. 135th. 1916. B. Gibson, Mgr.; M. Wittenberg, Sec.

Inter. Settlement Ath. Assn.—1904. 15 Settlements. Chas. H. Warner, Pres., 283 Rivington.

Irish-Amer.—159 E. 60th. 2,276 mem. P. J. Conway, Pres.; H. G. Bannon, Sec.

Martinique A. and S. Club—156th and Beck. 1913. 102 mem. C. Gabriel, Pres.; M. H. Friedman, Cor. Sec.

Metropolitan Assn. (of Amateur Ath. Union of the U. S.), 290 B'way—1891. 200 clubs. F. W. Rubien, Pres.

Metropolitan Life Ins. Ath. Assn.—12 E. 24th. J. L. Sherin, Pres.; T. Lynch, Sec.

Morningside—1348 St. Nicholas av. 1908. 150 mem. I. Lehmann, Pres.; Al. King, Treas., 359 Lenox av.

N. Y. Ath. Club—Central Park So. and 6th av.; Country House, Travers Island, Pelham Manor. 1868. 6,400 mem. Geo. J. Corbett, Pres.; F. R. Fortmeyer, Sec.

Huckleberry Indians—Huckleberry Island, L. I. Sound. 200 mem. R. J. Schaefer, Big Chief; R. O. Haubold, Scribe, 95 William.

Pastime—114 E. 159th. 1877. 250 mem. K. F. Hearns, Pres.; S. Krause, Sec.

Public Schools Ath. League—157 E. 67th. 1903. All P. S. of N. Y. City. G. W. Wingate, Pres.; A. K. Aldinger, Act. Sec.

Girls' Branch—Miss C. S. Leverich, Pres.; Miss E. A. O'Keefe, Exec. Sec., 157 E. 67th.

League of Neighborhood Centers—500 Park av. 1904. W. J. McAuliffe, Pres.; Samuel Berkowitz, Sec.

St. Anselm's—673 Tinton av. 1909. 250 mem. J. McInerney, Pres.; Ed. McCormick, Sec., 3276 Decatur.

St. Anselm's (Ladies) A. C.—1917. 57 mem. Miss U. R. Corley, Pres.; Miss J. Wolski, Sec., 751 Hewitt pl., Bronx.

St. Bartholomew's Boys' Club—209 E. 42d. 1889. 490 mem. J. Barnes, Pres.; Rev. J. F. Talcott, Sec.; Geo. McVicker, Supt.

St. George's—207 E. 16th. 1887. 500 mem. F. H. Walsh, Ch.; F. W. Meyer, Sec.

Union Settlement—231 E. 104th. 1896. 200 mem. J. Kelleher, Pres.; J. F. Cooke, Sec., 166 E. 105th.

Queens.

Steinway Civic & Ath. Assn.—1915. 500 mem. F. J. Speyres, Pres.; W. Karstedt, Sec., Shore rd., Astoria.

Warlow—Whitestone. 1894. 275 mem. J. Bechamp, Pres.; I. Pearsall, Sec.

Woodhaven (Inc.)—50 Benedict av., Woodhaven. 1895. 109 mem. W. H. Betz, Pres.; W. J. Lerner, Sec.

Richmond.

Aquehonga—Brighton and Academy pl., Tottenville. 1920. 165 mem. J. G. Morrill, Pres.; Chas. L. Bennett, Sec., Tottenville.

Bon Ton—Mariners Harbor. 1900. 15 mem. J. R. Jones, Pres.; Wm. Bailey, Sec.

AUTOMOBILE CLUBS.

National.

Amer. Automobile Assn.—1902. 501 5th av., Mhtn. and Albee Bldg., Washington, D. C. 44 State Assns., 600 clubs. 250,000 aggregate mem. D. Jameson, Pres.; J. N Brooks, Sec.

State.

N. Y. State Automobile Assn.—1903. 128 clubs. 22,700 mem. H. W. Robbins, Pres.; H. W. Baker, Sec., 108-110 State, Albany.

Brooklyn.

L. I. Automobile Club—1255 Bedford av. 1900. 1,000 mem. T. F. Condon, Pres.; R. H. Breninger, Sec.

Manhattan and Bronx.

Automobile Club of Amer. (The)—54th, west of B'way. Inc. 1899. 2,556 mem. To promote development of motor carriages, secure improved highways. Honorary members, President of U. S., Governor of N. Y., Mayor of N. Y. City. Alex. J. Hemphill, Pres.; E. Thompson, Sec.

Touring Club of Amer.—243 W. 39th. E. R. Mixer, Pres.; G. Gouge, Sec

BOAT CLUBS.

National.

Amer. Power Boat Assn.—1903. 30,000 mem. A. L. Judson, Pres.; G. C. Krusen, Sec., 329 N. 15th, Phila., Pa.

Middle States Regatta Assn.—R. Sturcke, Pres.; C. F. Muller, Sec.-Treas., Rm. 5418, Grand Cent. Terml., Mhtn.

Natl. Assn. of Amateur Oarsmen—Composed of rowing clubs of U. S., representing a membership of 50,000 Jas D Denegre, Pres; J J. Nolan, Sec., P. O. Box 1640, Washington, D. C.

Brooklyn.

Ariel Rowing—Ft. Bay 21st. 100 mem. A. C. Weiss, Pres.; Herbert Kisse, Sec.

Ben Ma Chree—Bay 32d. 1892. 100 mem. W. O. Dudley, Com.; J. G. Moran Sec., 2229 85th, Bensonhurst.

Brooklyn Rowing—Ft. 16th av. 175 mem. R. G. Clark, Pres.; J. L. Cassidy, Sec., 556 74th.

Ivy—1905. Old Mill. P. Harty, Pres.; J. Hunt, Sec., 125 Meeker av.

L. I. Rowing Assn.—1885. 3,500 mem. Comprises Bkln. Rowing, Flatbush Boat, Nautilus Boat, Seawanhaka Boat, Ravenswood Boat, Crescent A. C., Sheepshead Bay Rowing, Ariel Rowing, Varuna Boat Clubs. R. H. Pelton, Pres.; T. J. Brennan, Sec., 143 Liberty, Mhtn.

SOCIETIES AND ASSOCIATIONS—SPORTING CLUBS—BOAT—*Continued.*

Nautilus—Ft. of 22d av. 1883. 175 mem. C. W. Ruprecht, Pres.; H. A. Osborn, Treas.; E. F. Lanchantin, Sec.; T. J. Lanheady, Jr., Capt.; G. W. Byrne, 1st Lieut.; F. Kavanagh, 2d Lieut.

Sheepshead Bay Boat Owners' Assn.—Capt. F. Plage, Pres., 79 Elton; Capt. D. Martin, Jr., Sec., Sheepshead Bay.

Sheepshead Bay Rowing Club—Sheepshead Bay, N. Y. C.

Tamaqua—1912. Emmons av. and 19th, Sheepshead Bay.

Varuna—Sheepshead Bay. 1875. 125 mem. A. W. Hudson, Pres.; F. A. Furey, Capt., 3035 Ocean av.

Manhattan and Bronx.

Atalanta—152d and Harlem R. 1848. 100 mem. J. J. F. Mulcahy, Pres.; J. F. Innes, Sec.

First Bohemian—156th and Harlem R. 1881. 140 mem. Anton Jursik, Pres.; J. Havelka, Fin. Sec., 338 E. 71st; F. Sticha, Capt.; A. Kalbac, Cor. Sec., 702 8th av., Astoria, L. I.

Harlem Regatta Assn.—Composed of 15 clubs. 1872. H. Lauer, Sec. 342 W. 47th.

Metropolitan Rowing—Harlem R., nr. Jerome av. 1880. 150 mem. W. Burns, Pres.; A. Kinerim, Sec., 3147 Decatur av., Bronx.

Nassau—Macomb's Dam Park and 161st. 1867. 85 mem. O. J. Stephens, Pres.; T. F. Russell.

N. Y. Motor Boat Club—147th and Hudson R. Inc. 1908. Chas. D. Farriss, Com.; F. J. Minkel, Sec.

Nonpareil Rowing—Speedway Course and Harlem R. 1874. 150 mem. H. H. Michaels, Pres.; Jas. T. Coughlin, Jr., Sec., 585 6th, Bkln.

Union—Speedway and Dyckman 1872. 110 mem. J. A. Hughes, Pres.; W. Falb, Sec.

Waverley—167th and Hudson R. 1859. 130 mem. R. E. Kirchner, Pres.; A. E. Redpath, Sec., 501 W. 173d.

Wells, Inc.—Hudson R. and 166th. Clubhouse, 415 E. 13th. 40 mem. J. W. Stumpf, Pres.; J. Gugenhan, Sec.; G. W. Burke, Treas.

Queens.

Flushing—Point Ruth, Flushing. 45 mem. J. F. Rogen, Pres.; Geo. Scholze, Sec., 131 Main.

Oriental Boat and Fishing Club—Rockaway Beach. 1900. 18 mem. H. C. Mandel, Sec., 548 3d av., Mhtn.

Ravenswood—Ft. 9th av. and Bowery Bay. P. O. Box 28, L. I. City. 1882. 125 mem. J. D. Hampton, Pres.; Eug. Quinn, Sec., 79 Corona av., Elmhurst, L. I.

Seawanhaka—Corona. 1868. 125 mem. J. Effler, Pres.; Carl Searing, Sec., 98 Beech, Flushing.

Richmond.

Clifton—Edgewater st. 1880. 100 mem. A. G. Thompson, Pres.; H. J. Dahl, Sec.; L. Rachmiel, Capt., Rosebank, S. I.

Long Island.

Bay Shore Motor Boat—Inc. 1910. Bay Shore. 85 mem. H. M. Brewster, Com.; Frank Coombs, Sec., Bay Shore.

Maidstone—1916. Easthampton. J. C. Lawrence, Pres.; A. H. Culver, Sec.

BOXING.

Internatl. Sporting Club—1919. A. J. D. Biddle, Pres.; Adam Emple, Sec., 340 Madison av.

CANOE CLUBS.

Amer. Canoe Assn.—1880. 1,500 mem. H. M. Schwartz, Com.; S. B. Burnham, Sec., Box 23, Providence, R. I.

Amer. Canoe Assn. (Atlantic Div.)—O. Tyson, V.-Com.; J. B. Clarke, Purser, 56 Seaman av., Mhtn.

Brooklyn Canoe Club—Gravesend Bay. W. S. Hallett, Com.; W. M. Davis, Purser, 1724 74th.

Knickerbocker—167th and Hudson River, Mhtn. H. Brooks, Com.; W. J. Ebbels, 80 Maiden lane.

N. Y.—Ft. Totten, L. I.—1871. 120 mem. H. G. Pimm, Com.; C. L. Pultz, Sec., 408 E. 18th. Bkln.

Sheepshead Bay Canoe Club—1710 Emmons av., N. Y. C.

Yonkers Canoe, Glenwood—Yonkers, N. Y. 1886. 48 mem. Alden D. Tompkins, Com.; R. O. Phillips, Jr., Sec., 257 Warburton av., Yonkers.

CHECKER CLUBS.

Brooklyn.

Grattan—535 Myrtle av. Meets Fri. evgs. John McCaffrey, Pres.; J. T. Keveney, Sec., 601 Grand av.

CHESS CLUBS.

State.

N. Y. State Chess Assn.—D. F. Searle, Pres., Rome, N. Y.

Brooklyn.

Bkln.—4 and 5 Court sq. 150 mem. W. Underhill, Pres.; C. A. Neff, Sec.

Bkln. Inst.—100 mem.

Eastern District—22 mem. H. S. V. Cortelyou, Pres.; E. O. Dewing, Sec., 234 Linden av., Bkln.

Labor Lyceum—1907. 949 Willoughby av. 20 mem. C. Schneider, Pres.; H. Walter, Sec.

Manhattan.

Manhattan—Sherman Sq. Hotel. 1877. 170 mem. A. Martinez, Pres.; J. F. Rice, Sec.

Isaac L. Rice Progressive—219 2d av. 1915. 260 mem. S. Shore, Pres.; O. Chajes, Sec.

Richmond.

S. I.—Savings Bank Bldg., Stapleton. 50 mem. G. A. Barth, Pres.; C. Broughton, Sec., 55 Beach, Stapleton.

COUNTRY CLUBS.

(*Maintains golf course.)

Adirondack League Club—29 B'way, Mhtn. 1890. 323 mem. W. P. Hall, Pres.; N. P. Lewis, Sec. Owns preserve of 70,000 acres and has 3 clubhouses.

Amityville—Amityville, L. I. R. J. Ireland, Pres.; E. J. Heartt, Sec.

*Arion—Greenwood Lake, N. J. E. H. Hupe, Pres.; M. Werner, Sec.

*Ardsley—Ardsley-on-Hudson, N. Y. 1895. 700 mem. F. Q. Brown, Pres.; Geo. E. Dickinson, Sec., 1 B'way, Mhtn.

Baldwin, Inc.—J. F. Cotte, Pres.; R. F. Smith, Sec., Baldwin, L. I.

*Belleclaire—Bayside. 1919. 300 mem. R. D. Blackman, Pres.; L. Lee, Sec. and Treas., 2173 B'way, N. Y. C.

*Broadway—1916. Flushing. 450 mem. H. C. Monroe, Pres.; Jas. F. Conroy, Cor. Sec., 149 Amity, Flushing.

*Canoe Brook—Summit, N. J. 1902. Golf and tennis. 140 acres. W. G. Libby, Sec., Summit, N. J.

*Century—White Plains, N. Y. 1898. 300 Mem. G. M. Sidenberg, Pres.; W. E. Beer, Sec., 52 B'way, Mhtn.

*Cherry Valley—Garden City, L. I. Arthur E. Whitney, Pres.; E. D. Gerard, Sec., Garden City, L. I.

Country Club of Flushing—1887. W. C. Calk'ns. Jr., Pres.; P. B. Brewster, Sec.

*Country Club of Westchester—Westchester, N. Y. 1877. 250 mem. G. T. Adee, Pres.; H. H. Boyesen, Sec., Westchester, N. Y.

*Crescent Athletic—Country house, Shore Road and 85th. (See Athletic Clubs, Bkln.)

Douglaston—Douglaston, L. I. Inc. 1917. 125 mem. C. B. Knight, Pres.; Chas. M. Burtis, Sec., Douglaston, L. I.

*Dunwoodie—Yonkers. 1905. J. E. Freeman, Pres.; H. C. Smith, Sec.

Edgemere—Edgemere, L. I. 1904. F. N Lancaster, owner; B. S. Lyndeman, Mgr.

Elmira—Elmira, N. Y. 1897. 600 mem. J. R. Clarke, Pres.; F. F. Jewett, Sec.

*Engineers Country Club—Roslyn, L. I. 1917. 450 mem. C. G. M. Thomas, Pres.; A. S. Pratt, Sec.

Fairview—Elmsford, N. Y. 1910. 270 mem. G. A. Harris, Pres.; N. M. Cohen, Sec., 694 B'way, Mhtn.

*Flushing—Whitestone av., Flushing. 1887. 200 mem. W. E. Calkins, Jr., Pres.; P. B. Brewster, Sec.

Garden City—W. H. Amerman, Pres.; R. Ballantine, Sec.

*Glen Ridge—1920. 425 mem. W. D. Lyon, Pres.; P. L. Thomson, Sec., 87 Oxford, Glen Ridge.

*Great Neck—Great Neck, L. I. A. B. Olsen, Sec.-Treas., 31 Nassau, Mhtn.

*Hempstead—Hempstead, L. I. 1920. J. Richards, Pres.; F. B. Hawkins, Treas.; W. F. McCulloch, Sec., Hempstead, L. I.

*Hudson River—1915. 255 mem. Col. W. B. Thompson, Pres.; Edwin C. Brenn, Sec., 212 5th av., Mhtn.

*Huntington—Huntington, L. I. 1915. 200 mem. Ray Morris, Pres.; S. A. Everitt, Sec.

*Huntington Bay—1920. Huntington, L. I. Geo. B. Cortelyou, Pres.

*Inwood—Inwood, L. I. 350 mem. A. T. Steiner, Pres.; Morton Wild, Sec.

SOCIETIES AND ASSOCIATIONS—SPORTING CLUBS—COUNTRY—*Continued.*

*Jamaica—Jamaica, L. I. 1916. 200 mem. H. J. Mullen, Pres.; R. B. Duyckinck, Sec., 4 Chapin av., Jamaica, L. I.

Kew Gardens—Kew Gardens, L. I. 1915. 250 mem. E. W. Shipman, Pres.; C. R. Smith, Sec., Kew Gardens.

*Knollwood—White Plains. W. C. Breed, Pres.; D. S. Edmonds, Sec., 35 Nassau, Mhtn.

L. I.—Eastport, L. I. 1886. C. S. Lord, Pres.; C. P. Easton, Treas.; H. L. Finch, V.-Pres., 120 B'way, Mhtn.; Chas. McDermott, Sec.

*Maidstone—Easthampton, L. I. Dr. G. E. Munroe, Pres.; D. W. McCord, Sec., Easthampton, L. I.

*Malba Field Club—Whitestone, L. I. 1914. I. J. Merritt, Pres.; E. O. Champ, Sec.

Maplewood Field—Maplewood, N. J. 1903. 350 mem. A. Owen, Pres.; Harry Clark, Sec., Maplewood av., Maplewood, N. J.

Marine and Field—Bath Beach, Bkln. 1885. 400 mem. E. J. Grant, Pres.; F. C. Wilsox, Sec.

Meadow—Southampton, L. I. G. Livingston, Pres.; A. E. Schermerhorn, Treas.; H. P. Robbins, Sec., Southampton, L. I.

*Meadow Brook—Westbury, L. I. 1881. 185 mem. E. L. Winthrop, Jr., Pres.; F. R. Appleton, Jr., Sec.-Treas., 59 Wall, Mhtn.

Milburn—Baldwin, L. I. 1915. 125 mem. J. S. Blume, Pres., 80 Maiden lane; Chas. Lipshitz, Sec.

*Nassau—Glen Cove, L. I. 1896. 350 mem. H. F. Whitney, Pres.; H. C. Martin, Sec., 25 Madison av., Mhtn.

*North Fork—1911. Cutchogue, L. I. 150 mem. A. S. Moore, Pres.; F. C. Barker, Sec., Mattituck, L. I.

*North Hempstead—Port Washington, L. I. 1916. 235 mem. John H. Love, Pres.; L. W. Armstrong, Sec., Plandome, N. Y.

*North Shore—Glen Head, L. I. 440 mem. Auxiliary to Harmonie Club, N. Y. C. Simon J. Klee, Pres.; T. A. Peyser, V.-Pres., 1 Madison av., N. Y. C.; E. S. Lorsch, Sec.; J. F. Loeb, Treas.

*Ocean—Far Rockaway, L. I. 1900. 110 mem. Wm. Goldman, Pres.; J. Marcus, Sec., Far Rockaway, L. I.

*Pelham—1920. Pelham Manor. M. D. Rogers, Ch., 266 Mad'son av., Mhtn.

*Piping Rock—Locust Valley, L. I. 1911. H. R. Winthrop, Pres.; F. L. Crocker, Sec., 5 Nassau, Mhtn.

Quogue Field Club—Quogue, L. I. Inc. 1887. G. C. Stevens, Pres.; O. H. Smith, Sec., Quogue, L. I.

*Richmond Co.—Dongan Hills, N. Y. 1888. 385 mem. H. J. Fuller, Pres.; R. Monell, Sec., 14 Wall, Mhtn.

Rockville Centre Club—R. H. D. Malin, Pres.; T. M. Donaldson, Sec.

Rumson—Rumson, N. J. 1908. 470 mem. T. N. McCarter, Pres.; J. W. Brown, Sec., 65 B'way, N. Y. C.

Schroon Lake—Schroon Lake, N. Y. 1913. 52 mem. M. L. Cushman, Pres.; B. F. Saxon, Sec., 233 E. 61st.

Shelter Island—Shelter Isl. Heights, N. Y. 1901. C. L. Morse, Pres.; M. Edson, Sec., 65 Dey, Mhtn.

*Siwanoy—Mt. Vernon, N. Y. 1901. 400 mem. S. A. Scribner, Pres.; A. H. Appel, Sec.

*South Shore Field—Bay Shore, L. I. 1903. 200 mem. Golf, tennis, trap shooting, bathing. G. A. Ellis, Jr., Pres.; J. R. Hyde, Sec., 33 W. 42d, Mhtn.

*Suffolk Country Club (formerly Bellport Golf Club)—Bellport, L. I. 225 mem. 18h; 6,270 yds. Course to open in spring. 1918. F. Edey,

Terrace Club of Flatbush—1576 Ocean av., Bkln. 1907. 250 mem. E. M. Backus, Jr., Pres.; N. MacCallum, Sec.

Turf and Field—18 E. 41st and Belmont Park, Queens. 1895. F. K. Sturgis, Pres.; J. G. Livingston, Sec.; H. A. Buck, Asst. Sec.

*Tuxedo—Tuxedo Park, N. Y. 1885. 400 mem. P. Lorillard, Hon. Pres.; P. Tuckerman, Sec.

*Westhampton—Westhampton Beach, L. I. 1891. 18-hole Golf Course. 500 mem. R. H. MacDonald, Pres.; B. Herbert Smith, Treas.; F. Crampton, Sec.

*Woodmere—Woodmere, L. I. 1915. L. J. Robertson, Pres.; I. H. Lehman, Sec., 111 B'way, Mhtn.

*Wykagyl—New Rochelle, N. Y. 1905. 450 mem. H. V. Gaines, Pres.; C. P. Odell, Sec., 311 W. 43d, Mhtn.

CRICKET CLUBS.

Bensonhurst Cricket and Field Club (Inc.)—1905. Bay 43 and Bath av. 35 mem. A. B. Bailey, Pres.; N. Evelyn, Sec., 497 Prospect pl.

Brooklyn—Grounds, Prospect Park. J. Rodgers, Pres.; Harry Rushton, Sec., 1932 Arthur av., Mhtn.

Kings Co.—Dr. E. C. Huskinson, Pres.; H. D. Hoyle, Sec., 344 Lafayette av., Bkln.

METROPOLITAN CLUBS.

Columbia Oval—Geo. S. Shaw, Pres.; A. Jeffrey, Sec., 1034 5th av., Mhtn.

Manhattan—A. J. White, Pres.; F. C. Maher, Sec., 1205 Carroll, Bkln.

Metropolitan District Cricket League—J. H. Eckersley, Pres.; H. Rushton, Sec., 1932 Arthur av., Mhtn.

N. Y. Veteran Cricketers' Assn.—Dr. E. V Brendon, Pres.; J. S. Bretz, Capt., 250 W. 54th, Mhtn.; J. L. Evans, Sec.-Treas., 3219 3d av., Mhtn.

N. Y. and N. J. Cricket Assn.—Edgar O. Challenger, Pres.; F. F. Kelly, Sec., 243 W. 99th, Mhtn.

CYCLING CLUBS.

National.

Century Road Club Assn. (Natl. Board)—J. Mitchell, Pres., Greenwich, Conn.; L. Seehof, Natl. Sec., 1126 Park av., Mhtn.

Century Road Club of Amer.—1891. 500 mem. Harry B. Hall, Pres., 76 6th av., Whitestone, N. Y.; C. E. Nylander, Sec., 118 Haven av., Mhtn.

League of Amer. Wheelmen—Wm. M. Frisbie, Pres.; A. Bassett, Sec., 105 Central av., Newtonville, Mass.

Natl. Cycling Assn.—1893. To control and direct cycle racing in U. S. D. M. Adee, Pres.; P. Thomas, Sec., North Tarrytown, N. Y.

Brooklyn.

Whirling Dervishes—1893. 100 mem. Frank La Manna, Crank Pres.; H. B. Fullerton, Cyclometer Sec., Medford, L. I.

Manhattan and Bronx.

Calumet Cyclers—83 W. 134th. 1892. 160 mem. J. H. Murray, Pres.; W. J. Ames, Sec.

Century Road Club Assn. (N. Y. Div.)—M. Halpern, Sec., 307 W. 54th.

Firemen's—1895. 125 mem. J. Crawley, Pres.; G. F. Ricketts, Sec., 142 W. 63d.

GOLF CLUBS.

Apawamis—Rye, N. Y. 1890. 800 mem. 18h; 6,170 yds. W. H. Conroy, Pres.; H. E. White, Sec., 31 Nassau, Mhtn.

Baltusrol—Baltusrol, N. J. 1895. 750 mem. 18h; 6,210 yds. R. S. Sinclair, Pres.; Lou s Keller, Sec., 29 B'way, Mhtn.

Bedford Golf and Tennis Club (Inc.)—Bedford, N. Y. 1905. 90 mem. 9h; 3,100 yds. A. D. Partridge, Pres.; H. D. Kountze, Sec., 257 B'way, Mhtn.

Belle Terre (Community Club)—Port Jefferson, L. I. (Controlled by Belle Terre Bondholders' Protective Comm.)

Bellport—Bellport, L. I. (Now Suffolk Country Club.)

Blind Brook—Port Chester, N. Y. 1916. 150 mem. 18h; 6,162 yds. Wm. H. Childs, Pres.; A. W. Erickson, Sec., 381 4th av., Mhtn.

Brentwood—Brentwood, L. I. 1916. 70 mem. 9h; 1,800 yds.

Bridgehampton—1900. 95 mem. 9h; 2,250 yds. Wm. Crawford, Pres.; W. E. Quimby, Sec., Bridgehampton, L. I.

Brooklyn-Forest Park—At entrance to Forest Park. 260 mem. 18h; 5,496 yds. J. W. Kent, Pres.; W. J. Myers, Sec., 70 Beekman, Mhtn.

Buffalo Golf Club—Buffalo. 1914. 308 mem. 18h; 5,500 yds. E. G. Oliver, Pres.; W. H. Turner, Sec., 77 Pearl.

Cherry Valley Club—Garden City, L. I. 18h; 6,336 yds. W. M. Cruikshank, Pres.; E. D. Gerard, Sec., Garden City, L. I.

Cobble Hill—Elizabethtown, N. Y. 1896. 150 mem. 9h; 2,862 yds. A. N. Hand, Pres.; Rev. H. H. Pittman, Sec., Elizabethtown, N. Y.

Crescent Club, Bay Ridge—9h. (See Athletic Clubs.)

Dutchess Golf and Country Club—Poughkeepsie, N. Y. 9h; 2,740 yds. W. A. Wetterau, Pres.; Wm. M. Cumming, Sec., 16 Washington, Poughkeepsie, N. Y.

Fox Hills—Clifton, S. I. 1900. 400 mem. 18h; 6,200 yds. J. J. O'Donohue, Jr., Pres.; G. G. Worthley, Sec., 68 William, Mhtn.

Garden City Golf Club—1899. 350 mem. 18h; 6,400 yds. F. M. Bacon, Jr., Pres.; G. L. Hubbell, Sec., Garden City, L. I.

SOCIETIES AND ASSOCIATIONS—SPORTING CLUBS—GOLF—*Continued.*

Gedney Farm—White Plains, N. Y. 1913. 250 mem. 18h; 6,280 yds. Thos. E. Conklin, Pres.; Wm. T. Hart, Sec., 12 E. 44th, Mhtn.

Glenburnie—Glenburnie, N. Y. 1911. 130 mem. 9h; 2,195 yds. H. D. Whittlesey, Pres.; E. B. Walton, Sec.

Governor's Island—Governor's Island, N. Y. C. 1902. 43 mem. 9h; 2,910 yds.

Guggenheim Private Golf Course—Port Washington.

Hollywood—Course at Deal, N. J. 400 mem. 18h; 6,950 yds. H. Content, Pres.; M. S. Guiberman, Sec., 32 Liberty, Mhtn.

Gun Hill Golf Club—Van Cortlandt Park. 1918. 3650 Jerome av. 18h; 5,286 yds. W. M. Covill, Pres.; B. R. Abbott, Sec.

Hudson River Golf Assn.—R. F. Tompkins, Pres.; J. E. Barringer, Sec., Poughkeepsie, N. Y.

Knickerbocker Field Club—(See Social Clubs.)

Lake George Club—Diamond Point, N. Y. 1908. 130 mem. H. W. Guernsey, Pres.; S. Homer, Sec., Diamond Point-on-Lake George, N. Y.

Lake Placid Club—Lake Placid, N. Y. 1898. 18h; 6,301 yds. 9h; 3,100 yds. 9h; 1,377 yds. 9h; 1,010 yds. M. Dewey, Pres.

Lake Ronkonkoma—Lake Ronkonkoma.

Lido—1916. Long Beach, L. I. 18h; 6,424 yds. (Controlled by The Lido Corpn.)

Links—Roslyn, L. I. City. Office, 38 E. 62d, Mhtn. C. B. McDonald, Pres.; F. L. Crocker, Sec.

Mahopac—Lake Mahopac, N. Y. 1898. 197 mem. 18h; 5,800 yds. E. C. Dusenbury, Pres.; Wm. C. Hynard, Sec., 39 W. 29th, Mhtn.

Maidstone—Easthampton, L. I. 1892. 100 mem. 18h; 6,004 yds. Dr. G. E. Munroe, Pres.; D. W. McCord, Sec., Easthampton, L. I.

Malba Field Club—1914. Whitestone, L. I. 9h; 2,500 yds. I. J. Merritt, Pres.; E. O. Champ, Sec.

Manhattan—Pelham Bay Park, N. Y. 1908. 53 mem. 18h; 6,316 yds. J. S. Hamilton, Pres.; R. H. Sarver, Sec., 510 W. 140th.

Metropolitan Golf Assn.—102 clubs within 55 miles of N. Y. City, Inc. L. I. C. J. Sullivan, Pres.; A. H. Pogson, Sec., 45 Nassau, Mhtn.

Midland—Hempstead, L. I. 75 mem. J. L. Van Vranken, Pres.; W. F. McCulloch, Sec., Hempstead, L. I.

Mohawk—Schenectady, N. Y. 1898. 1,158 mem. 18h; 6,384 yds. M. R. Rice, Pres.; T. A. McLoughlin, Sec., Gen. Electric Co., Schenectady, N. Y.

Mosholu Golf Links—Van Cortlandt. 1914 18h; 5,284 yds. (Public.) Dept. of Parks issues yearly and daily permits.

Mt. Kisco—1916. Mt. Kisco, N. Y. 100 mem. R. S. Brewster, Pres.; M. Taylor, Sec., 5 Nassau, Mhtn.

Nassau—Glen Cove, L. I. 1896. 300 mem. 18h; 6,300 yds. H. W. Maxwell, Pres.; H. C. Martin, Sec., 25 Madison av., Mhtn.

Natl. Golf Links of Amer.—Shinnecock Hills, L. I. 1909. 450 mem. 18h; 6,300 yds. C. B. Macdonald, Pres.; Dan'l Chauncey, Sec., 61 B'way, Mhtn.

N. Y. Golf Club—Van Cortlandt. 1902. 18h; 5,359 yds. E. S. Dreux, Pres.; H. E. Back, Sec.

N. Y. Newspaper Golf Club—18h; 5,359 yds. F. T. Pope, Pres.; C. A. Dailey, Sec.-Treas., 600 W. 192d, Mhtn.

North Hempstead—Port Washington, L. I. 1916. 225 mem. 18h. 6,200 yds. J. H. Love, Pres.; E. M. Strong, Sec., 1 W. 34th, Mhtn.

North Shore—Glen Head, L. I. 1914. 450 mem. 18h; 6,365 yds. S. J. Klee, Pres.; E. S. Lorsch, Sec.

Oakland—Bayside, L. I. 1896. 375 mem. 18h; 6,000 yds. S. Brinckerhoff Thorne, Pres.; Graig Colgate, Sec., 49 Wall, Mhtn.

Onondaga Golf and Country Club—Fayetteville, N. Y. 1900. 500 mem. 18h; 6,319 yds. E. I. White, Pres.; A. C. Stevens, Sec., Syracuse, N. Y.

Pelham Bay Park Course—18h; 6,315 yds. Public annual and daily permits.

Quaker Ridge—1916. Mamaroneck, N. Y. 275 mem. W. R. Hochster, Pres.; D. F. Sicher, Sec., 15 William, Mhtn.

Rockaway Hunting Club—Cedarhurst, L. I. 1878. 408 mem. 9h; 3,000 yds. Wm. A. Hazard, Pres.; O. S. Seymour, Sec.

Sag Harbor—Sag Harbor. 25 mem. Dr. C. H. Tillinghast, Pres.; B. D. Corwin, Sec.

Salisbury Links—Westbury. Semi-public. Two courses 18 h. each, about 6,425 yds. each. Apply J. J. Lannin, Garden City Hotel.

St. Albans—1916. St. Albans, L. I. 18h; 6,290 yds. W. M. Tomlins, Jr., Pres.; Dr. W. V. Pascual, Sec., 690 St. Marks av., Bkln.

St. Andrews—Mt. Hope, N. Y. 1887. 18th; 6,003 yds. 369 mem. Walter Douglas, Pres.; Wm. T. Manypenny, Sec., 257 4th av., N. Y. C.

St. George's—Stony Brook.

Sands Point—Port Washington.

Sargowana—Sheepshead Bay.

M. Schiff Private Golf Course—Oyster Bay.

Sayville—Sayville. Inc. 130 mem. 9h; 1,909 yds. Arthur Murphy, Pres.; E. B. Clark, Sec., Sayville, L. I.

Shinnecock Hills—Southampton, L. I. 1892. 125 mem. 18h; 6,140 yds. M. J. O'Brien, Pres.; Fred'k A. Snow, Sec., 52 B'way, N. Y. C.

Sleepy Hollow—Scarborough on Hudson, N. Y. 1912. 900 mem. Finley J. Shepard, Pres.; G. B. Francis, Sec., 74 B'way, Mhtn.

Sound Beach Golf and Country Club—Sound Beach, Conn. 9h; 3,100 yds. M. B. Foster, Pres.; P. D. Adams, Sec., Sound Beach, Conn.

South Shore Field—Bay Shore, L. I. 1903. 18h; 5,750 yds. G. A. Ellis, Jr., Pres.; J. R. Hyde, Sec., 33 W. 42d.

Twaalfskill—Kingston, N. Y. 1902. 175 mem. 9h; 2,930 yds. J. D. Schoonmaker, Pres.; C. H. De La Vergne, Sec.

U. S. Golf Assn.—766 Broad, Newark, N. J. Governing body of all golf clubs in U. S. 1894. G. H. Walker, Pres.; W. D. Vanderpool, Sec.

Van Schaick Island Country Club—Troy, N. Y. 1900. 411 mem. 9h; 3,250 yds. A. Gillespie, Pres.; J. Heatly, Sec., 58 Hudson av., Green Island, N. Y.

Westbrook—1895. East Islip, L. I. 9h; 3,120 yds. J. B. Stanchfield, Pres.; E. S. Knapp, Sec.-Treas.

Wee Burn—1897. Noroton, Conn. 200 mem. 9h; 3,080 yds. E. H. Delafield, Pres.; Marion G. Weed, Sec., Noroton, Conn.

Wheatley Hills—East Williston, L. I. 18h; 6,160 yds. Ed. E. B. Adams, Pres.; H. W. Chatfield, Sec., 15 Dey, N. Y. C.

Whiteface Inn Golf Club—Whiteface, N. Y. 1916. 9h. Address J. J. Sweeney, Mgr., Whiteface Inn, Whiteface, N. Y.

Whitney's Private Golf Course—Manhasset.

Woodmere Club—Inc. 1912. Woodmere, L. I. 349 mem. L. J. Robertson, Pres.; A. W. Weil, Sec., 170 B'way, Mhtn.

Woodhaven Golf Club—Forest Park, Woodhaven. 18th; 5,320 yds. Woodhaven.

Yahnundasis—New Hartford, N. Y. 1897. 300 mem. 18h; 6,000 yds. Sherrill Sherman, Pres.; F. W. Owen, Sec., 116 Liberty, Mhtn.

HUNTING AND FISHING CLUBS.

Adirondack League Club—29 B'way, Mhtn. 1890. 323 mem. W. P. Hall, Pres.; N. P. Lewis, Sec.

Amer. Rifle Team of S. I.—Inc. 1892. 75 mem. 203 Canal, Stapleton, S. I. J. V. Adamo, Capt., Stapleton; W. A. Dausch, Rec. Sec.

Barnegat—35 Warren, Mhtn. 1912. 200 mem. C. L. Wright, Pres.; M. S. Squires, Sec.

Bay Shore Boatmen's Assn.—Bay Shore, L. I. 65 mem. W. Bishop, Pres.; G. C. Smith, Sec.

Boone and Crockett—1887. 100 mem. Geo. B. Grinnell, Pres.; Kermit Roosevelt, Sec., 151 E. 74th, Mhtn.

Carman's River—Brookhaven, L. I. F. J. Horne, Pres.; Geo. C. Pennell, Sec., 70 Beekman, Mhtn.

Chelsea Plantation—South Carolina. O. M. Eidlitz, Pres.; F. K. Gaston, Sec., 30 E. 42d. Mhtn.

Columbia Fishing—Eltingville, S. I. N. Y. office, Beekman, Mhtn. 1887. 30 mem. J. W. Runpf, Pres.; Chas. Eppleur, Sec., 19 Church, Mhtn.

Coram Gun—Coram, L. I. 1897. 10 mem. T. J. Smith, Pres.; F. W. Shaw, Sec.-Treas., Patchogue, L. I.

Gilbert Rod and Gun—Amityville, L. I. 1884. 35 mem. A. E. Hendrickson, Pres.; G. W. Barnard, Sec., Amityville, L. I.

Glenwood Fishing—Glenwood, L. I. 1882. 16 mem. F. Youngs, Capt.; J. Gaylord, Sec., 161 India, Bkln.

Great Meadow Gun—Jamesport, L. I. 1909. 105 mem. J. E. Weir, Pres.; Howard H. Downs, Sec., South Jamesport, L. I.

Guaranty Rod and Gun—311 W. 41st, Mhtn.

Great Kills and Giffords, S. I. 1898. 35 mem. J. J. Webb, Pres.-Sec.

SOCIETIES AND ASSOCIATIONS—SPORTING CLUBS—HUNTING AND FISHING—*Continued.*

Liberty Island Rod and Gun—The Raunt, Jamaica Bay. 1897. 20 mem. Capt. T. Price, Pres.; J. Rausch, Sec. and Treas, 67 Atlantic av., Bkln.

Meadow Brook—(See Country Clubs.)

Melrose Rod, Gun and Boat—Clubhouse, Plum Beach. E. W. Smith, Pres.; C. H. Smith, Sec., 246 South, Mhtn.

Narrow Bay Gun—Center Moriches. O. C. Grinnell, Jr., Pres.; W. B. Growtage, Sec.-Treas.

Nassau Rod and Gun—Nassau-by-the-Sea. 1906. J. C. Stevens, Pres.; Philip Hauser, Sec., 1064 Union, Bkln.

Natl. Beagle Club of Amer.—J. W. Appleton, Pres.; R. Turnbull, Sec., 49 Broad, Mhtn.

N. Y. Assn. for Protection of Game—1844. 61 mem. Alfred Wagstaff, Pres.; R. B. Lawrence, Sec., 43 Cedar, Mhtn.

N. Y. Fishing—Richmond Valley, S. I. 1883. 50 mem. Jos. A. Hassmer, Pres.; C. H. Graham, Treas., 71 B'way, Mhtn.; R. A. Bogart, Sec.

Orient Gun—D. T. Latham, Pres.; F. H. Terry, Sec., Orient, L. I.

Prospect Gun—Meadow Island, Jones' Inlet, Freeport, L. I. 1882. 31 mem. H. B. Wesselman, Pres.; F. J. MacRae, Sec., 55 William, Mhtn.

Rockaway Hunting—Cedarhurst, L. I. Has 18 hole course. 300 mem. W. A. Hazard, Pres.; O. S. Seymour, Sec., 54 William, Mhtn.

Southside Sportsmen's—Oakdale, L. I. 1866. 100 mem. John Mulligan, Pres.; B. Hollister, Sec., 20 Exchange pl., Mhtn.

State Fish, Game and Forest League—1865. Membership of 125 clubs. Frank D. Sargent, Pres.; L. C. Andrews, Sec., Elmira, N. Y.

Stereo Fishing—Canarsie, Bkln. 1883. 26 mem. A. B. Winter, Pres.

Suffolk Hunt—Southampton, L. I. 1911. 120 mem. R. Newton, Jr., M. F. H.

Undine Fishing—Undine Island, Jamaica Bay, N. Y. 1881. 50 mem. H. F. Simons, Pres.; C. Hauptner, Sec., 32 W. 33d, Mhtn.

Union Sportsmen's—Valhalla, N. Y. W. E. Tufts, Pres.; J. C. Dalton, Sec, 782 Lincoln pl, Bkln.

United Angler's League—63 Park row. 1903. 1,000 mem. Dr. B. M. Briggs, Pres.; Jas. W. Studley, Fin. Sec., World Bldg., Mhtn.

Wyandanch—1872. Smithtown, L. I. 50 mem. S. Aldrich, Sec., 29 B'way, Mhtn.

KENNEL CLUBS.

Airedale Terrier Club of L. I.—1910. 100 mem. R. Tileston, Pres.; J. Reid, Sec.-Treas., 606 Fulton, Bkln.

Amer. Fox Terrier Club—W. Rutherfurd, Pres.; H. H. Hunnewell, Sec.-Treas., 87 Milk, Boston, Mass.

Amer. Kennel—221 Fourth Av., Mhtn. 1884. H. H. Hunnewell, Pres.; Newton H. Day, Sec.

Am. Spaniel—G. Greer, Pres.; R. P. Keasbey, Sec.; 175 5th av., Mhtn.

Boston Terrier Club of N. Y.—W. H. Purcell, Mgr., 29 B'way, Mhtn.

Bronx Co. Kennel Club—Bronx. W. H. Purcell, Mgr., 29 B'way, Mhtn.

Bull Dog Club of Amer.—100 mem. J. F. Trown, Pres.; J. Harry Rushton, Sec., Asbury Park, N. J.

Bull Terrier Club of Amer.—1897. 65 mem. S. L. Libby, Sec., East Williston, N. Y.

Collie Club of N. Y.—W. H. Purcell, Mgr., 29 B'way, Mhtn.

Great Dane Club of Amer.—1891. 41 mem. J. B. Miller, Pres.; C. H. Mantler, Sec, 51 Front, Mhtn.

Irish Setter Club of America—J. S. Wall, V.-Pres.; Mrs. H. M. Talbot, Sec., Atlantic, Mass.

Japanese Spaniel Club of Amer.—Mrs. R. T. Harrison, Pres.; Mrs. E. H. Berendsohn, Sec., 204 Berkeley pl., Bkln.

Ladies Kennel Assn. of Am.—1900. Miss L. Alger, Pres.; Miss J. M. Sheffield, Sec., 6 E. 37th.

L. I. Kennel Club—Johnson Bldg., Bkln. 250 mem. John Collins, Pres.; W. H. Purcell, Mgr., 29 B'way, Mhtn.

Nassau County Kennel Club—Belmont Park, L. I. Theo. Offerman, Pres.; Dr. E. H. Berendsohn, Sec., 204 Berkeley Pl., Bkln.

Newark Kennel Club—Newark, N. J. W. H. Purcell, Mgr., 29 B'way, N. Y. C.

North Jersey Shore Kennel Club—W. H. Purcell, Mgr., 29 B'way, Mhtn.

Plainfield Kennel Club—Plainfield, N. J. W. H. Purcell, Supt., 29 B'way, Mhtn.

Pointer Club of Amer.—70 mem. H. D. Kirkover, Buffalo, Pres.; J. C. Weller, Sec.-Treas., 792 E. 169th, Bronx.

Queensboro Kennel Club—Astoria, L. I. W. H. Purcell, Mgr., 29 B'way, Mhtn.

Richmond Co. Kennel Club—Staten Island. W. H. Purcell, Mgr., 29 B'way, Mhtn.

Rumson Kennel Club—Red Bank, N. J. W. H. Purcell, Supt., 29 B'way, Mhtn.

St. Bernard Club of Amer.—Grand Rapids, Mich. 1888. 50 mem. Col. J. Ruppert, N. Y. Pres.; D. E. Waters, Sec., Grand Rapids, Mich.

Scottish Terrier Club of Amer.—1900. 90 mem. F. G. Lloyd, Pres.; Miss M. Brigham, Sec., North Grafton, Mass.

Toy Spaniel Club of Amer.—Mrs. G. E. Tobey, Pres.; Mrs. G. O. Kolb, Sec., West Hartford, Conn.

Welsh Terrier Club of Amer.—1900. 45 mem. F. G. Lloyd, Pres.; Miss G. de Copper, Sec., 754 Park av., Mhtn.

Westchester Kennel Club—Gedney Farm, White Plains, N. Y. W. H. Purcell, Mgr., 29 B'way, Mhtn.

Westminster Kennel—61 B'way, Mhtn. 1878. R. H. Williams, Pres.; L. A. Eldridge, Sec.

Yorkshire Terrier Assn., N. Y. C.—W. H. Purcell, Mgr., 29 Bway., N. Y. C.

LAWN TENNIS CLUBS.

National.

In addition to following clubs many of the Country, Golf and Yacht Clubs maintain courts.

U. S. Lawn Tennis Assn.—The governing body of all recognized lawn tennis clubs in America. Annual meeting held in N. Y. in Feb. J. S. Myrick, Pres., 38 Nassau, Mhtn.; G. W. Wightman, Sec., 60 State, Boston, Mass.; P. B. Williams, Field Sec., 20 Broad, Mhtn.

Brooklyn.

Albemarle—1909 Church av. and Story. 13 mem. J. C. Coe, 508 E. 5th, Pres.; B. Moffat, Sec.

Bay Ridge Field Club (Inc.)—1890. 60 mem. G. A. Boyce, Pres.; A. Sawyer, Sec., 423 75th.

Crescent Athletic—Grounds at Bay Ridge. E. Ditmars, Ch., 38 8th av.

Heights Casino—1904. 350 mem. Edw. Cornell, Pres.; G. H. Thirkield, Sec., 75 Montague.

Kingsboro. Inc. 1917. (formerly Parkside)—Courts at Lefferts and Bedford avs. 60 mem. A. H. Dodge, Pres.; P. F. W. Ruther, Sec., 55 Wall, Mhtn.

Kings County—Grounds at Kingston av. and Montgomery. 110 mem. F. B. Ogilvie, Pres.; J. W. Anderson, Sec., 173 Amity.

Knickerbocker Field Club—(See Social Clubs.)

Parkway Tennis Club—1902. Ditmas av. and E. 5th. 40 mem. T. N. Sissosway, Pres.; J. W. Maclee, Sec., 296 E. 8th.

Terrace Club of Flatbush—1576 Ocean av. Inc. 1904. 250 mem. E. M. Backus, Jr., Pres.; Le R. Norand, Sec., 1040 E. 19th.

Manhattan and Bronx.

Bedford Golf and Tennis—(See Golf Clubs.)

Columbus Univ. Tennis—East Hall, 116th and B'way. Jose A. Sosa, Mgr.

Hamilton Grange—Convent av. and 149th. F. C. Hayden, Pres.; W. A. Tice, Sec., 450 W. 147th.

Harlem—135th and 8th av. 1895. 65 mem. P. J. Goold, Pres.; E. Bry, Sec., 7 W. 22d.

N. Y. Athletic—Grounds, Travers Island, Pelham Manor, N. Y. G. J. Corbett, Pres.; F. R. Fortmeyer, Sec.; H. W. Wilson, Chairman Tennis Comm.

N. Y. Tennis Club—B'way and 238th. C. B. Winne, Pres.; S. L. Butler, Sec., 418 Central Pk. W.

Seventh Regt. Tennis—7th Regt. Armory. 200 mem. A. C. Postley, Pres., 449 Greenwich. W. D. Cunningham, Sec., 253 W. 99th.

University Heights Tennis Club—1905. Harlem River Terrace, Bronx. 105 mem. H. R. Howard, Pres.; Sherman Hall, Sec., 2287 Loring pl.

Queens.

Elmhurst—1902. 9th, Elmhurst. 150 mem. F. Hartel, Pres.; Chas. E. Richart, Sec., Denman, Elmhurst, N. Y.

Murray Hill Park—Myrtle av. and 13th, Flushing, L. I. F. L. Greiffenberg, Pres.; C. W. Seymour, Sec. and Treas, 43 W. 6th, Flushing.

Prospect Hill—Alsop, Jamaica. 1915. 40 mem. Martha Haeberle, Pres., 58 Victoria.

West Side Tennis Club—Clubhouse and grounds, Forest Hills, L. I. Mhtn. Grounds, 93d and Amsterdam av. 960 mem. Wm. A. Campbell, Sec., 2 Rector, Mhtn.

SOCIETIES AND ASSOCIATIONS—SPORTING CLUBS—LAWN TENNIS—*Continued.*

Richmond.

Clifton Tennis Club—Arrochar, S. I. C. Knight, Sec.-Treas., 1062 Woolworth Bldg., N. Y. C.

New Dorp Field Club—New Dorp, S. I. 1909. 50 mem. A. W. Roberts, Pres.; C. Henderson, Sec.

S. I. Cricket and Tennis—1905. 200 mem. H. G. Van Vechten, Sec., 425 Richmond Terrace, N. Brighton.

S. I. Ladies' Club—1877. Livingston, W. N. Brighton. Mrs. H. T. Boody, Pres.; Mrs. T. M. Logan, Sec., Davis av., West New Brighton.

Long Island.

Baldwin Tennis Club—1911. Merrick rd., Baldwin, L. I. R. F. Smith, Pres.; Rennie Smith, Sec., Harrison av., Baldwin.

Garden City Club—1895. 206 mem. N. Floyd, Jr., Pres.; L. V. Morris, Sec., Garden City, L. I.

Hay Harbor Club—Fisher's Isl. 1909. 575 mem. D. S. Willard, Pres.; Wm. M. Austin, Sec.

Nassau Country Club—Glen Cove, L. I. 1896. 350 mem. H. F. Whitney, Pres.; H. C. Martin, Sec., 25 Madison av., Mhtn.

Rockville Centre—G. A. Powers, Pres.; H. B. Wright, Sec., Rockville Centre, L. I.

POLO CLUBS.

Islip Polo Club—Bay Shore, L. I. 1912. H. T. Peters, Pres.; A. Pinkerton, Sec., 92 Liberty, Mhtn.

Polo Assn.—30 Church. 1890. 1,500 mem. H. L. Herbert, Ch.; W. A. Hazard, Sec.-Treas., 29 B'way, Mhtn.

RACING CLUBS.

Amer. Trotting Assn.—127 So. Ashland Blvd., Chicago, Ill. W. P. Ijams, Pres.; W. H. Smollinger, Sec.

Brooklyn Jockey Club—374 Adams, Bkln. Race Course, Gravesend, L. I. J. Shevlin, Pres.; F. Rehberger, Racing Sec.

Cuba-Amer. Jockey and Auto Club—Oriental Park, Marianao, Havana, Cuba. M. Nathanson, Racing Sec., 4232 Grand blvd., Chicago, Ill.

Jockey Club—18 E. 41st, Mhtn. August Belmont, Ch.; H. K. Knapp, Sec.-Treas.

Kentucky Jockey Club—Louisville, Ky. J. N. Camden, Pres.; M. J. Winn, V.-Pres. and Gen. Mgr.; S. Goodpaster, Sec. and Treas.

Metropolitan Jockey Club—Jamaica, L. I. M. Corbett, Pres.; W. C. Edwards, Gen. Mgr., 50 Court, Bkln.

Natl. Steeplechase and Hunt Assn.—18 E. 41st, Mhtn. Amalgamated 1899. A. Belmont, Pres.; H. W. Bull, Hon. Sec.

Natl. Trotting Assn.—Hartford, Conn. J. C. Welty, Pres.; W. H. Gocher, Sec., Hartford, Conn.

New Louisville Jockey Club—Louisville, Ky. C. F. Grainger, Pres.; H. C. Applegate, Sec.

Piping Rock Racing Assn.—Locust Valley, L. I. J. E. Davis, Pres.; F. J. Bryan, Racing Sec., 18 E. 41st, Mhtn.

Queens Co. Jockey Club—Race course at Aqueduct, L. I. J. Shevlin, Pres.; F. Rehberger, Racing Sec., 374 Adams, Bkln.

Saratoga Assn.—18 E. 41st, Mhtn. R. T. Wilson, Pres.; George H. Bull, Sec.-Treas.; A. McL. Earlocker, Racing Sec.

Turf and Field Club—(See Country Clubs.)

United Hunts Racing Assn.—H. A. Buck, Sec., 18 E. 41st, Mhtn.

Westchester Racing Assn.—Belmont Pk., Queens, L. I. August Belmont, Pres., 43 Exchange pl., Mhtn.; H. I. Pelz, Sec.

RACQUET AND TENNIS CLUBS.

Racquet and Tennis Club—370 Park av., Mhtn. 1,950 mem. H. K. Knapp, Pres.; Sherman Day, Sec., 370 Park av.

Tuxedo Park Tennis and Racquet—Tuxedo Park, N. Y. 1899. R. Moore, Supt.

RIDING AND DRIVING CLUBS.

National.

Natl. Horse Show Assn.—16 E. 23d, Mhtn. 1883. 500 mem. R. A. Fairbairn, Pres.; Chas. W. Smith, Sec.

Brooklyn.

Flatbush Riding School—507-511 Flatbush av. G. H. Willers, Prop.

Riding and Driving Club of Bkln.—Vanderbilt av. and Prospect Park Plaza. T. L. Leeming, Pres.; E. A. Ames, Sec., 390 Park pl.

Manhattan and Bronx.

Coaching Club—G. G. Haven, Sec., 30 Broad.

N. Y. Riding—Central Park W. and 66th. 1873. 52 mem. J. Delahunty, Pres.; O. Seidenberg, c., Central Park W. and 66th.

Riding Club—7 E. 58th. 1881. 700 mem. Saml. T. Peters, Pres.; D. B. Pratt, Sec.

Road Drivers' Assn. of N. Y.—1889. 25 Dyckman. 217 mem. E. Carpenter, Sec.

Long Island.

Nassau Driving Club—Mineola Fair Grounds. 1909. 125 mem. Edw. Shoemaker, Pres.; W. Gartrell, Sec., New Hyde Park.

Piping Rock Horse Show Assn.—Locust Valley. P. D. Cravath, Pres.; G. W. Gall, Sec., 18 E. 41st, Mhtn.

SKATING CLUBS.

Amer. Amateur Hockey League—R. J. Bell, Pres.; R. L. von Bernuth, Sec., 2 Wall, Mhtn.

Crescent Ath. Club—Skating interests in charge of a committee. G. G. Hallock, Jr., Ch., 896 Lincoln pl.; Wm. Dobby, Mgr., 384A 5th, Bkln.

Internat. Skating Club of Am.—1912. Iceland, 52d and B'way, Mhtn. Irving Brokaw, Pres., 985 5th av., Mhtn.

Internatl. Skating and Hockey Union of Amer.—1907. C. Fellowes, Pres., 1966 B'way, Mhtn.; J. Harding, Sec.-Treas., Hotel Vermont, Burlington, Vt.

St. Nicholas Hockey—K. B. Gordon, Pres.; R. L. von Bernuth, Sec., 2 Wall, Mhtn.

TRAP, RIFLE AND REVOLVER SHOOTING CLUBS.

National.

Amer. Trapshooting Assn.—460 4th av., Mhtn. E. R. Galvin, Pres.; Stoney McLinn, Sec.-Mgr.

Natl. Rifle Assn. of Amer.—Brig. Gen. F. H. Phillips, Jr., Sec., Woodward Bldg., Washington, D. C.

U. S. Revolver Assn.—1900. A. M. Poindexter, Pres.; A. C. Hulburt, V.-Pres.; Capt. W. A. Morrall, Sec., Hotel Virginia, Columbus, O.

State.

N. Y. State Rifle Assn.—Maj.-Gen. C. F. Roe, Pres.; Capt. W. H. Palmer, Sec., 141 B'way, Mhtn.

Brooklyn.

Bkln. Rifle Club—32 mem. R. Rutherford, Pres.; L. Miller, Sec., 102 South Oxford.

Fountain Gun (Inc.)—1877. J. A. Carney, Sec., 93 Nassau, Mhtn.

Parsonage Island—Shoots at Hook Creek, L. I., monthly. Dr. Fulda, Pres.; S. Short, Sec., 1148 Lafayette av.

Manhattan and Bronx.

Old Guard Rifle Club—1912. Capt. P. J. Rocchiette Pres.; Capt. W. I. Joyce, Sec.-Treas., 307 W. 91st.

Seventh Regiment Rifle—66th and Park av. 1880. 450 mem. Col. Wade H. Hayes, Pres.; D. S. Steele, Sec.

Zettler Rifle—69 W. 23d. 1874. 57 mem. Outdoor ranges, Union Hill, N. J. A. Begerow, Pres.; F. Hecking, Sec.

Queens.

Empire State Gun—L. I. City. 1902. R. H. Gosman, Pres., 75 Hill, L. I. City.

Long Island.

Fahys Rifle—Sag Harbor. 186 mem. A. Kiernan, Pres.; Theo. Biechele, Sec., Sag Harbor.

Islip Town Rifle—1916. 72 mem. R. Bachia, Jr., Pres.; J. V. Jerome, Sec., East Islip.

Neguntatogue Club—Bruno Gnilka, Pres.; Jos. Warta, Sec., Lindenhurst, L. I.

Wilhelm Tell Rifle—Lindenhurst. 1909. 40 mem. W. F. Wild, Pres.; O. Hillhardt, Sec.

WHIST CLUBS.

Amer. Whist League—1891. 10,000 mem. One week each year a congress is held, in which players from all parts of the country participate in matches and tournaments. Officers: E. S. Brown, Pres., Cleveland, O.; W. E. Byrnes, Sec., Cleveland, O.

Knickerbocker Whist Club, N. Y.—6 W. 40th, Mhtn. C. L. Patton, Pres.; S. S. Lenz, Treas.

Metropolitan Whist Assn.—Mrs. H. E. Wallace, Pres.; Miss M. H. Campbell, Sec., 121 E. 30th, Mhtn.

Whist Club—13 W. 36th. 1894. 165 mem. Henry de F. Weekes, Pres.; W. M. K. Olcott, Sec.

Women's Whist League—Meets annually in different cities. Meets in N. Y. City, 1921. Mrs. Francis Winslow, Pres., Yonkers, N. Y.; Mrs. G. H. Reed, Treas., 65 Crescent av., Jersey City, N. J.

YACHT AND POWER BOAT CLUBS.

National.

U. S. Power Squadrons, Inc.—1912. 600 mem. H. M. Williams, Chief Com.; F. C. Scofield, Sec., 78 Montgomery, Newburgh, N. Y.

SOCIETIES AND ASSOCIATONS—SPORTING CLUBS—YACHT AND POWER BOAT—*Continued.*

Brooklyn.

Ambrose Channel—2270 Cropsey av. 80 mem. A. H. Selling, Com.; P. Darby, Sec.

Amer. Model—Sailing sta., Riches Pt., Jamaica Bay. 1896. R. Ferguson, Com.; P. H. Bell, Sec., 92 16th, Bkln.

Atlantic—Sea Gate, Inc. 1866. 500 mem. E. L. Doheny, Com.; E. I. Graff, Sec., 60 B'way, Mhtn.

Bay Ridge—1910. Bay 47th and Harnay av. 130 mem. A. McMonigle, Pres.; L. P. Ernst, Sec., 267 55th.

Bensonhurst—Ft. 20th av. A. Kissel, Jr., Com.; Ed. M. La Roche, Sec.

Bergen Beach—Bergen Beach. 1901. 105 mem. F. Doebeli, Com.; F. Schmitt, Treas.; T. H. Morley, Rec. Sec.

Brooklyn Motor Boat Club—Gravesend Bay Clubhouse, 2270 Cropsey av. 1897. 125 mem. C. Guden, Com.; J. H. Petersen, Sec., 291 Pearl, Bkln.

Brooklyn Yacht Club—C. V. Dyckman, Com.; A. MacDougall, Sec., 233 B'way, Mhtn.

Canarsie Yacht Club—Canarsie. A. F. Roth, Com.; E. C. Wolf, Sec., 597 5th av., N. Y. C.

Crescent Ath. Club Yacht Dept., Bay Ridge— A. F. Aldridge, Ch.

Diamond Pt.—1911. Canarsie. 150 mem. W. H. Ebner, Com.; W. Perkins, Sec., Conklin av., Canarsie.

Excelsior—Ft. 60th, Bkln. Inc. 1889. W. D. Martin, Com.; J. L. Fredlund, Sec.

Flatlands—1905. J. W. A. Butler, Com.; R. Sheafer, Sec., 1526 Flatbush av.

Gravesend Bay—1905. 115 mem. Geo. W. Raff, Com.; J. J. Grace, Sec., Clubhouse, ft. 25th av.

Old Mill Y. C. of Pleasant Point—Jamaica Bay. Inc. 1910. 200 mem. G. L. Sillence, Com.; Wm. J. Lewis, Sec., 653 2d av., N. Y. C.

Prospect Pk. Model Yacht Club—Prospect Pk. H. P. Taylor, Com.; G. F. Hoyt, Sec., 635 Grand av.

Sea Gull—Sand Bay, Canarsie. 60 mem. Philip Peters, Com.; J. Ostheimer, Sec., 338 E. 58d.

Sheepshead Bay—1902. 3070 Emmons av., L. W. Seeligsberg, Com.; Chas. Huethwohl, Sec., 3070 Emmons av.

Tamaqua—Sheepshead Bay. F. A. Filsner, Com., T. V. Gould, Sec.

Williamsburgh—College Pt., L. I. 1868. 63 mem. J. C. Fisher, Com.; H. Rohs, Jr., Sec., 139 Russell.

Yacht Masters and Engineers Assn.—Tebo's Yacht Basin, Ft. of 23d, Bkln. 1894. 260 mem. P. P. Langdahl, Pres.; T. Meyer, Sec.

Yacht Racing Assn. of Gravesend Bay—A. Aldrich, Pres.; J. N. Birch, Sec., Gravesend Bay, N. Y. C.

Manhattan. Bronx and Vicinity.

Atalanta Boat Club—152d and Harlem River, at 7th av. 1848. 250 mem. J. P. Levins, Com.; V. H. Zagat, Sec., 973 Summit av., Highbridge.

Bronx County Yacht Club—Clason Pt. Geo. Bing, Jr., Com.; C. F. Gilfrich, Cor. Sec.

Colonial—Hudson River, north of 138th. A. M. Garretson, Com.; M. G. Vautsinas, Rec. Sec.

Columbia—86th and N. R. J. A. Harriss, Com.; J. McKinlay Wight, Sec., 80 Maiden la.

Federal Motor Boat (Inc.)—142d and Hudson River. 1913. 76 mem. J. R. Gannon, Com.; L. E. Glocker, Sec., 576 W 131st

Handicap Yacht Racing Class—30 mem. 1906. G. P. Granbery, Pres., 5 Nassau; H. L. Stone, Sec., 239 4th av.

Hudson River—92d and H. R. 1875. 150 mem. G. Fisher, Com.; W. E. Church, Sec., 340 B'way.

Hudson River Yachting Assn.—1905. 17 clubs. W. A. Ranney, Pres.; J. H. Acker, Sec., 641 Washington, Mhtn.

Huguenot—New Rochelle, N. Y. 1894. 127 mem. H. H. Van Renssalaer, Com.; H. E. McCormick, Sec., 346 Main, New Rochelle, N. Y.

Morrisania—Old Ferry Point, Bronx. 1896. 150 mem. Harry Hansen, Com.; Jos. Desser, Sec., Old Ferry Pt., Bronx.

New York—37-41 W. 44th. 1844. 2,300 mem. J. P. Morgan, Jr., Com.; G. A. Cormack, Sec.

N. Y. Motor Boat—147th and Hudson River. Inc. 1908. 235 mem. A. M. Coyle, Jr., Com.; L. R. Browne, Sec.

Waterway League of Conn.—Bridgeport, Conn. 1915. 2,700 mem. F. Elliott, Pres.; J. R. Gebhart, Sec., 335 John, Bridgeport.

Westchester Motor Boat Club—1911. Clason Point, N. Y. 52 mem. Chas. Heppler, Com.; W. Effinger, Sec., 764 Forest av., Bronx.

Queens.

Bayside—Bayside. 1902. 350 mem. Wm. Teller, Com., Waldo av., Bayside.

Jamaica Bay—Hollands Sta., Rockaway Beach. J. Michel, Com.; H. Wood, Sec.

Jefferson—Holland's Sta., Rockaway Beach. 1897. 25 mem. Jacob Rech, Com.; G. Einsel, Sec., 78 Bedford, Mhtn.

Rockaway Park—Rockaway Park. 1915. 96 mem. **J. Friedenberg, Com.; J. Opkenheim, Sec.. 132 W. 88th, Mhtn.**

Rockaway Point—Rockaway Point. 1911. 125 mem. F. S. Lockwood, Com.; B. A. H. Smith, Sec., 195 B'way, Mhtn.

Richmond.

Mariners Harbor (Inc.)—Mariners Harbor 1910. 125 mem. G. Schwedfeiger, Com.; D. E. Davis, Sec., Elizabeth, N. J.

Ocean—Ft. Water, Stapleton. 1905. 70 mem. E. Wanty, Com.; J. P. Mannewitz, Sec.

Stapleton, S. I.—1896. 200 mem. Geo. Cramer, Com.; G. H. Winters, Sec., 81 Highview av., New Brighton.

Long Island.

Babylon—Babylon. 1903. T. D. Downing, Com.; H. C. Hepburn, Sec., P. O. Box 858, Babylon.

Bay Shore Motor Boat—Bay Shore. Inc. 1910. 85 mem. H. M. Brewster, Com.; F. T. Hulse, Sec., Bay Shore.

Belle Harbor—Belle Harbor. 1905. 500 mem. Chas. J. O'Brien, Com.; J. Halstead Patterson, Sec., 371 E. 31st, Bkln.

Bellport Bay—Bellport. 1905 120 mem. Dr. R. B. Stanley, Com.; J. R. Watkins, Sec. and Treas., Bellport.

Cedarhurst—Lawrence. 1909. 150 mem. D. H. Cox, Com., 15 William, Mhtn.; J. A. Barnard, Sec.

Centreport—Centreport. 1906. L. D. Andrews, Com.; L. L. Lockwood, Sec., Centreport.

Glenwood—Glenwood. 1910. 47 mem. Geo. M. Diamond, Com.; J. G. Attwood, Sec., 765 Westminster rd.

Great Peconic Bay—So. Jamesport. S. L. Jacques, Com.

Handicap Yacht Racing Class of L. I. Sound —1906. 125 mem. Geo. P. Granbery, Pres., 15 Nassau, Mhtn.; T. L. Grace, Sec., 2 Wall, Mhtn.

Hempstead Harbor—Glen Cove. 1891. 107 mem. J. S. Appleby, Com.; E. Valentine, Purser, Glen Cove.

Huntington—Huntington. 1890. 100 mem. W. N. Brown, Com.; R. E. Bayles, Sec., Huntington.

Independent Y. and B. C.—Northport. C. S. Mott, Com.; E. G. Emans, Sec.

Ketewomoke—Halesite. 100 mem. D. H. Ketcham, Com.; H. A. Roselle, Sec., Halesite.

Keystone—Woodmere. 1892. 75 mem. F. M. Jensen, Com.; H. T. de Rivira, Sec.

Knickerbocker—Port Washington. 1874. 200 mem. P. C. Gallagher, Com.; J. O. Sinkinson, Sec., P. O. Box 68, Sta. D, Mhtn.

Manhasset Bay—Port Washington. 1891. 300 mem. Edgar A. Sierck, Com.; Waldo Grose, Sec., Port Washington.

Mattituck—1910. 150 mem. LeRoy S. Reeve, Com.; H. R. Reeve, Sec., Mattituck.

Northport—Northport. 1907. 50 mem. J. B. Morrell, Com.; H. F. Burns, Sec., Northport.

Point o' Woods—Point o' Woods. 1899. 100 mem. Dr. E. M. Alger, Com.; W. M. Parke, Sec., 120 B'way, N. Y. C.

Port Washington—Port Washington. Wm. Miller, Sec., 80 Bay View av., Port Washington.

Quantuck—Westhampton Beach. 1896. 150 mem. B. Brower, Com.; T. Kimball, Sec.-Treas.

Robinson—East Patchogue. 1894. 60 mem. S. N. Robinson, Com.; J. J. Robinson, Sec., E. Patchogue.

Sag Harbor—Sag Harbor. 1897. 100 mem. Wm. S. Eaton, Com.; E. P. Eaton, Sec.; C. E. Fritts, Treas.

Sea Cliff—Sea Cliff. 1892. 85 mem. E. J. Hogan, Com.; J. Mattemore, Sec., Sea Cliff, L. I.

Seawanhaka-Corinthian—Oyster Bay. 1871. 500 mem. Ralph Ellis, Com.; Henry R. Hayes, Sec., 120 B'way.

Shelter Island—Chequit Point, Shelter Island Heights. 1886. 90 mem. G. N. Webster, Com.; O. A. Keep, Sec., 59 Dey, N. Y. C.

Shinnecock Bay—Quogue. 1895. 25 mem. W. A. Keys, Jr., Com., **33 E. 17th, Mhtn.; G. W. Betts, Jr., Sec.**

SOCIETIES AND ASSOCIATONS—SPORTING CLUBS—YACHT AND POWER BOAT—*Continued.*

South Bay—Patchogue. L. C. Hafner, Com.; Chas. Sommers, Sec.

South Shore—Freeport. 300 mem. F. C. S. Knowles, Com.; Frank Alcorn, Rec. Sec., 19 Miller av., Freeport.

Unqua Corinthian—Amityville. 1900. 178 mem. L. Smyth, Com.; W. F. Ploch, Sec.

Westhampton Country Club—Yacht Squadron. 1891. Westhampton Beach.

Yacht Racing Assn. of L. I. Sound—1895. 23 clubs. J. W. Alker, Pres.; C. A. Marsland, Sec., 200 5th av., N. Y. C.

Yacht Racing Assn. of Southeastern L. I.—Quantuck Yacht Club, Westhampton Country Club Yacht Squadron, Moriches Yacht Club.

MISCELLANEOUS CLUBS.

National.

Assn. of College Track Coaches of America—1919. J. F. Moakley, Pres., Cornell Univ.; H. Hillman, Sec., Dartmouth Coll.

League of Amer. Sportsmen—1898. Composed of organizations in 48 States. G. O. Shields, Pres., 1110 Simpson, Bronx, N. Y.; H. M. Beach, Sec.

Brooklyn.

Bkln. Bowling Green Club—Parade Ground, Prospect Park. 1903. 75 mem. A. M. Clonney, Pres.; C. W. Gallaer, Sec., 485 E. 49th, Bkln.

Manhattan.

Woman's Swimming Assn.—1917. 308 W. 59th. 250 mem. (limited). Mrs. Winifred Pym, Pres.; Miss Rae Lehman, Sec., 3 E. 17th.

TEMPERANCE SOCIETIES.

WOMAN'S CHRISTIAN TEMPERANCE UNION

World's Convention of the W. C. T. U. meets triennially. Rosalind, Countess of Carlisle, Pres., Castle Howard, York, Eng.; V.-Pres., Miss A. A. Gordon, Evanston, Ill.; Hon. Secs.; Miss A. E. Slack Ripley, Derbyshire, Eng.; Mrs. Blanch Johnston, Barrie, Ont., Can.; Hon. Act. Treas., Mrs. Ella A. Boole, 525 5th, Bkln.

Natl. W. C. T. U.—Miss A. A. Gordon, Pres.; Mrs. F. P. Parks, Cor. Sec., Evanston, Ill.

N. Y. State Officers: Mrs. E. A. Boole, Pres., 156 5th av., Mhtn.; Mrs. L. M. De Silva, Cor. Sec.

Kings County.

County Officers—Mrs. W. W. Wickes, Pres.; Mrs. W. A. Bell, Cor. Sec., 1617 Beverly rd.

New York County.

County Officers: Mrs. D. L. Colvin, Pres.; Mrs. J. D. Minnick, Cor. Sec., 418 W. 118th.

Queens and Nassau Counties.

County Officers—Mrs. John Dayton, Pres.; Mrs. J. McCall, Cor. Sec., Elmhurst.

Richmond County.

County Officers: Mrs. S. A. Hall, Pres.; Mrs. Hendrickson, Cor. Sec., Springfield av., W. New Brighton, S. I.

Suffolk County.

County Officers—Mrs. E. A. Tyler, Pres., Smithtown Branch; Mrs. E. H. Bennett, Cor. Sec., Southampton.

(For N. Y. City and Long Island Auxiliary Unions see pages 334-335, 1917 Eagle Almanac.)

ANTI-SALOON LEAGUE OF AMERICA.

Org. 1895. Bishop L. B. Wilson, Pres., Mhtn.; F. Copeland, Treas., Columbus, O.; S. E. Nicholson, Sec., Richmond, Ind.; Rev. E. J. Moore, Asst. Gen. Supt., Westerville O.; Rev. P. A. Baker, Gen. Supt., Westerville, O.; Wayne B. Wheeler, Gen. Counsel and Legislative Dir., 30 Bliss Bldg., Washington, D. C.; E. H. Cherrington, Supt. Publishing Interest and Ed., Westerville, O.; Rev. H. H. Russell, Supt. Lincoln-Lee Legion, Westerville, O.; Natl. Hdqtrs., 30 Bliss Bldg., Washington, D. C., and Westerville, O.

Anti-Saloon League of N. Y., 156 5th av. W. H. Anderson, State Supt.; M. M. O'Dell, Asst. State Supt.; Anne B. Tubbs, Information Sec.

The American Issue (Weekly), official organ of the Anti-Saloon League of N. Y., R. O. Everhart, Editor.

CATHOLIC TOTAL ABSTINENCE UNION OF AMERICA.

Org. 1872. Mem. 100,000. Rev. J. G. Beane, Pres.; Rev. M. J. O'Connor, Treas.; T. E. McCloskey, Sec., Danbury, Conn.

INDEPENDENT ORDER OF RECHABITES.

Org. Eng., 1835; America, 1842. Total mem., 1,100,000. Officers of the High Tent: T. W. Newman, High C. R.; J. R. Mahoney, High Sec., 324 Pa. av., S. E., Washington, D. C.

Intercollegiate Prohibition Assn.—Hdqtrs., 14 W. Washington, Chicago, Ill. Inc. 1901. 125,000 active and alumni mem. D. A. Poling, Pres.; H. S. Warner, Sec. and Treas.

INTERNATIONAL ORDER OF GOOD TEMPLARS.

International Supreme Lodge—675,000 mem.; 70 grand lodges; 13,000 lodges; ritual in 18 different languages. Lars O. Jensen, Int. Chief Templar, Bergen, Norway. Tom Honeyman, Int. Sec., 160 Hill, Glasgow, Scotland.

Natl. Grand Lodge—Dr. C. A. Carlson, N. C. T., Youngstown, O.; N. Sec., W. O. Wylie, Beverly, Mass.

Grand Lodge of N. Y.—Geo. H. Higbie, G. C. T.; A. M. Leffingwell, G. Sec., Watertown, N. Y.

Brooklyn.

Kings County Officers: D. G. Simpson, D. C. T., **201 Amity, Mrs. Margaret Darrock, Sec., 1924 8th av.**

Manhattan and Bronx.

Dist. Officers: T. Gilmore, D.C.T., 1924 8th av., Bkln., O. A. Shipstead, D., Sec., 44 W. 115th Mhtn.; D. S. Gillies, 539 W. 144th, D. Dep.; Mrs. C. Lockwood, D. S. J. W., 555 W. 149th, Mhtn.

Queens—Nassau County.

Dist. Officers: T. A. Druce, Jr., Dist. C. T., Woodhaven; F. E. Farmer, Sec., Pt. Washington, L. I.

Suffolk County.

Dist. Officers: E. M. Osborne, Easthampton, Dist. Chief Templar; Mrs. C. H. G. Vail, Dist. Sec., Quogue.

NATIONAL TEMPERANCE SOCIETY AND COMMISSION ON TEMPERANCE.

Hdqts., 105 E. 22d, Mhtn. Rev. D. S. Dodge, D.D., Pres.; Gov. C. E. Milliken, Ch.

SONS OF TEMPERANCE.

Natl. Division—E. L. Hohenthal, So. Manchester, Conn., M. W. P.; **Ross Slack, 4539 N. 20th,** Phila., Pa., M. W. S.

TEMPLARS OF HONOR AND TEMPERANCE.

D. I. Robinson, Supreme Templar, Gloucester, Mass.; C. S. Woodruff, Supreme Recorder; Allendale, N. J.; Wm. D. Putnam, Grand Templar, Fredonia, N. Y.; A. Y. Freeman, Grand Recorder, Fredonia, N. Y.

MISCELLANEOUS.

Church Temperance Soc.—1881. 88 St. Nicholas av. Rev. James V. Chalmers, Pres.; Rev. J. Empringham, D.D., Natl. Supt.

Prohibition Trust Fund Assn.—1890. C. E. Manierre, Counsel, 7 E. 42d, N. Y. C. E. L. G. Hohenthal, So. Manchester Ct., Pres.; J. C. Crawford, Sec., 152 Prospect av., Mt. Vernon, N. Y.

VETERAN FIREMEN'S ASSOCIATIONS.

State.

Volunteer Firemen's Assn. of the State of N. Y. —1872. 1,200 mem. Walter S. Gedney, Pres.; Thomas Honohan, Sec., Frankfort.

Southern N. Y. Vol. Firemen's Assn.—1896. 90 Livingston. 600 mem. G. H. Schiffmacher, Pres.; J. H. Downing, Sec., 488A Chauncey.

Brooklyn.

Aryowius Exempt Vol. Firemen's Assn.—1893. 103 Pineapple. T. F. Fallon, Pres.; J. J. Campbell, Sec., 57 Middagh.

Bkln. Vol. Firemen's Assn.—1885. Room 10, Borough Hall. 293 mem. J. B. Byrne, Pres.; D. J. McGonigle, Sec., 20 Warren pl.

Exempt Firemen's Assn.—1882. Bedford and Metropolitan avs. 110 mem. G. E. Tilt, Pres.; Wm. Young, Sec., 1222 B'way.

Exempt Firemen's Assn. of Town of New Lots —1886. 450 Liberty av. 100 mem. P. J. Kelly, Pres.; G. W. Rhodebeck, Sec., 177 Richmond.

Exempt Firemen's Benevolent Fund of Co. of Kings—2267 Church av. Wm. H. Swartwout, Pres.; Wm. P. Goebel, Sec., 575 76th.

SOCIETIES AND ASSOCIATIONS—VETERAN FIREMEN'S—*Continued.*

Flatbush Vol. Firemen's Assn.—1890. 2267 Church av. 260 mem. W. H. Swartwout, Pres.; J. J. Bollinger, Sec., 232 Rogers av.

Flatlands Vol. Firemen's Assn.—200 mem. J. H. Conk, Pres.; H. M. Butecke, **Sec.,** 9501 **Av. L.**

Gravesend **Exempt** Vol. Firemen's Assn.—1888. W. 8th, Coney **Island.** 290 mem. Wm. E. Johnson, Pres.; F. G. Walther, Sec., 2700 Ocean av.

Kings Co. Vol. Firemen's Assn.—1891. Boro Hall, Rm. 8. F. P. Gallagher, Pres.; W. P. Goebel, Sec., 575 76th. Composed of delegates from all veteran and exempt assns. in county.

New Utrecht Exempt Firemen's Assn.—1895. 257 Bay Ridge av. 195 mem. T. J. O'Connell, **Pres.; T. F. Hogan, Sec., 1075 60th.**

Vet. Firemen's Assn. of 20 Years' Active Service in Fire Dept. of the City and Boros. of Bkln. and Queens—1897. Boro Hall. 540 mem. **T. F. Nevins, Pres.; C. E. Field, Sec., 365 Jay.**

Vet. Vol. Firemen—1887. 305 Adams. R. Lott, Pres.; F. E. Pouch, Sec., 305 Adams.

Vol. **Firemen's Exempt** Assn. of Bkln. (The) —Borough Hall. 80 mem. T. A. Welwood, **Pres.;** D. J. McGonigle, Sec., 20 Warren pl.

Manhattan.

Assn. of Exempt Firemen, City of N. Y.—1842. 200 mem. 10 Greenwich av. George W. Collier, Pres.; Wm. O'Hearn, Fin. Sec., 10 Greenwich av.

Exempt Firemen's **Benev.** Assn. of 23d Ward, **Bronx** Co.—1875. 2801 3d av. 53 mem. C. H **Kirk, Pres.**, 1109 **Washington** av.; H. Paine, Sec.

Exempt Firemen's Benev. Fund of City of N. Y. (The Trustees)—1798. 10 Greenwich av. Jno. Mulligan, Pres.; A. Collier, Sec.

Vol. Firemen's Assn. of the City of N. Y.—1884. 220 E. 59th. 50 mem. Wm. H. Thomas, Pres.; C. P. Ling, Sec., 402 E. 83d; John Mulligan, Treas.

Queens.

Exempt Firemen's **Benev.** Assn., College Pt.—1897. 509 14th. 285 mem. J. Konzet, Sec., 516 10th, C. Pt.

Exempt Firemen's Assn.—1885 170 Lockwood, L. I. City. 165 mem. J. W. Bishop, Pres.; H. Daniel Mulligan, Sec., 301 1st av., L. I. C.

Exempt Firemen's Assn. of Flushing—144 Amity. 1897. 360 mem. J. F. Ryan, Pres.; J. J. McConnell, Sec., 144 Amity, Flushing.

Exempt Firemen's Assn. of the 5th Ward, Far Rockaway. 1898. 348 mem. Frank Baldwin, Pres.; F. D. Doolittle, Sec., Far Rockaway.

Exempt Firemen's Assn. of the Town of Newtown, L. I.—1897. 642 mem. H. Ringe, Pres.; Jas. McCron, Sec., 16 Toledo, Elmhurst.

Vet. Firemen's Assn.—1890. 156-158 Grand av., L. I. City. 190 mem. Jas. J. Rider, Pres.; J. M. Smyth, Sec., 409 B'way, L. I. City.

Vet. Vol. Firemen's Assn., Jamaica—1897. No. Washington. 325 mem. G. Oswald, Pres.; F. Zimmer, Sec.

Woodhaven Exempt Vol. Firemen's Assn.—Woodhaven. 1897. 492 mem. F. Clapp, Pres.; C. E. Singer, Rec. Sec.

Richmond.

Vet. Firemen's Assn. of the North Shore Fire Dept. of S. I.—1896. W. New Brighton. 500 mem. H. W. O'Reilly, Pres., 236 Taylor; Wm. Snedeker, Sec., W. New Brighton.

WAR VETERANS' ASSOCIATIONS.

AMERICAN LEGION.

Composed of veterans of the war with Germany —those who served honorably in uniform in the army, navy or marine corps (male or female) of the U. S. between April 6, 1917, and Nov. 11, 1918.

It is non-military, non-sectarian, non-racial, non-political. It exacts only that all of its members shall be 100 per cent. American. Natl. Hdqtrs., **Indianapolis, Ind.**

National.

Commander-in-Chief, F. W. Galbraith, Jr., Cincinnati, O.; Adj., L. L. Bolles, Wash.

State.

N. Y. State Dept.—Hall of Records, Mhtn. C. G. Blakeslee, Comdr., Binghamton; G. S. Kelly, Adj., Tarrytown.

District Chairmen—J. M. Blackwell, 1st Judicial Dist., 63 Wall, Mhtn.; L. Sullivan, 2d Judicial Dist., Woodmere; A. S. Callan, 3d Judicial Dist., Chatham; R. C. Booth, 4th Judicial Dist., Plattsburgh; J. B. Tuck, 5th Judicial Dist., Syracuse; C. W. Kress, 6th Judicial Dist., Watkins; J. F. Gallivan, 7th Judicial Dist., Rochester; W. R. Pooley, 8th Judicial Dist., Buffalo; H. Zulauf, 9th Judicial Dist., Yonkers.

MISCELLANEOUS.

National and State.

American Flying Club.—1919. 1,500 mem. 11 E. 38th, N. Y. C. World's War Veterans. L. LaT. Driggs, Pres.; H. Johns, Sec.

Army and Navy Legion of Valor of U. S. of A.—1907-8. 300 mem. Dr. Geo. W. Brush, Com., 633 E. 16th, Bkln. A. A. Forman, Q.M., 44 Court, Bkln.

Military Order of the World War—(See Patriotic and Commemorative Socs.)

Overseas Service League—1919. 119 W. 40th, Mhtn. Mrs. Lucy W. Pheater, Pres., 344 W. 88th, Mhtn.; Miss Eliz. A. Cullen, Sec.

Soc. of Amer. Wars. Commandery of the State of N. Y.—1910. G. M. Hammond, M.D., Major U. S. A., Pres.; Clarence A. Manning, Sec., 144 E. 74th, Mhtn.

Spanish-American War Veterans of N. Y. State —(See Secret and Benefit.)

Veteran Assn. of Dept. of the South and Atlantic Blockading Squadrons—1890. 50 mem. C. B. Newkirk, 489 Washington, Bkln., Pres.

Veterans of Foreign Wars—1899. 32 Union sq., Mhtn. R. G. Woodside, Comm.-in-Chief; Walter I. Joyce, Qrmr.-Gen.; R. C. Johnson, Judge Advocate Gen., Aberdeen, S. D.

Brooklyn.

Associated Veterans of the 14th Regt.—1920. 14th Regt. Armory. Edw. Riker, Comm.; Jos. A. Henahan, Adj.; C. Hader, Treas.

Civil War Veterans' Assn.—1908. 45 mem. 1013A Gates av. T. F. Boyle, Pres.; C. G. Hall, Sec., 943 Gates av.

Forty-seventh Regt., N. Y. State, Vet. Vol. Inf., "Washington Greys"—1861-1865. 40 mem. W. Scott, Pres.; C. W. Waagle, Sec.-Treas., 1306 Myrtle av. Reunion, Sept., 1921.

Forty-eighth Regt., N. Y. Vols., Vet. Assn.—1880. J. H. Rayner, Sec., 106 Hall.

Fourteenth Regt. N. Y. S. M. Civil War Vet. Assn. 1920. 14th Regt. Armory. 100 mem. Ed. Ricker, Pres., 115 Woodruff av.; W. H. H. Pinckney, Sec., 439A Monroe.

Ironsides Vet. Assn. of 176th Regt., N. Y. V.— 1909. 25 mem. C. T. Schondelmeier, Pres.; O. W. Marvin, Sec., 458 Macon.

One Hundred and Seventy-third N. Y. Vol. Vet. Assn.—1892. R. 2, Boro. Hall. P. Bender, Sec., 2708 Av. G.

Soc. of the Third Division—1920. 81 Hanson pl. Ed. M. Allen, Pres.; H. R. Koop, Sec.-Treas., 232 Logan.

United **Spanish War Veterans. (See Secret and Benefit.)**

Vet. Assn. of the Thirteenth Regt.—1874. 700 mem. Major T. Fleming, Pres.; J. J. F. Doyle, Sec., 246 Sackett.

Vet. Assn. of the 23d Regt.—1870. 800 mem. J. H. Shearman, Pres.; H. J. Barringer, Sec., 934 Sterling pl.

Veterans of the 127th Regt., N. Y. Vols.—1880. 112 mem. John Carr, Pres.; **R. F. Gurney, Sec., Greenlawn, N. Y.**

War Vet. and Sons Assn. of the U. S. of A.—1888. Room 13, Boro. Hall. 175 mem. W. A. Stubner, Pres.; Wm. Lycett, Sec.-Treas., 399 Lincoln rd.

Manhattan and Bronx.

Military Order of Foreign Wars of the U. S., N. Y. Commandery—1895. 149 B'way. 450 mem. Col. W. G. Bates, U. S. A., Pres.; Major R. A. de Russy, Sec., 52 B'way.

Military Order of the World War, Manhattan Chapter—60 E. 34th. S. H. Wolfe, Comdr.

Old Guard of City of N. Y.—1826. 307 W. 91st. 225 mem. Maj. E. H. Snyder, Com.; Capt. W. A. Damer, Adj.

United Spanish War Veterans. (See Secret and Benefit.)

Vet. Assn.—1884. 73d N. Y. V. 128 W. 17th. 35 mem. J. McCloskey, Pres.; **J. H. Campbell,** Sec., 304 Graham av., Bk'n.

Vet. Assn. 71st Regt., N. G., N. Y.—Armory. 1868. 600 mem. Louis F. Stein, Pres.; W. I. Joyce, Sec., 32 Union sq.

Veteran Corps of the Artillery (constituting the Military Soc. of the War of 1812—(See Patriotic and Commemorative Socs.)

SOCIETIES AND ASSOCIATIONS—WAR VETERANS'—MISCELLANEOUS—*Continued.*

Veterans of Foreign Wars, George Washington Post—1919. 309 W. 23d. 150 mem. M. D. Lund, Comdr.; Alvin Nashley, Adj., 46 Ft. Washington av.

Veterans of the 7th Regt.—1859. 7th Regt. Armory. 1,900 mem. A. V. Pancoast, Sec., 65 W. 68th.

War Veterans of the 9th Regt., N. G., N. Y. 1871—9th N. G. Inf., 1907, C. A. C., 125 W. 14th, Mhtn. 1871. 650 mem. G. M. Pollard, Com.; J. A. Thatcher, Adj., Bkln.

Queens.

Seventh Regt. Assn. of L. I.—1911. Capt. W. C. Roe, Pres.; Capt. H. L. Dayton, Sec., Bayside, L. I.

WORKING GIRLS' CLUBS.

(In addition to following, the Y. W. C. A. maintains girls' clubs.)

Brooklyn.

Good Will Club—41 Tompkins pl. 1887. 84 mem. Miss M. Dowd, Pres., 602 11th; Mrs. M. H. Brock, Sec.

Manhattan and Bronx.

Abbot E. Kittredge Club for Girls—1889. 440 E. 57th. 300 mem. Wm. H. Hamilton, Pres.; Ida S. Hutchison, Supt.

Co-operative Girls' Club—1891. 342 W. 23d. Julia E. Van Emburg, Supt.

Dolly Madison Club—184 Eldridge. 12 mem. Miss Flora Fein, Pres.; Miss Bee Galerstein, Sec., 620 W. 138th.

Enterprise Club—1888. 266 W. 40th. 20 mem. Miss M. U. Hoffman, Pres.; Miss Eva Huxel, Sec., 750 Melrose av., Bronx.

N. Y. League of Women Workers—6 E. 45th. 21 clubs affiliated with this org. Mrs. Kenneth J. Muir, Pres., 58 W. 68th; Mrs. R. Helmer, Sec., 37 Madison av.; Miss Helen D. McGlade, Org. Sec.

Clubs affiliated with—Acorn Club, 209 Concord, Bkln.; Domestic Circle, 501 W. 50th, N. Y. C.; Fern Club, 243 24th, Guttenberg, N. J.; Friendly Club, 318 E. 82nd, N. Y. C.; Good Will Club, 24 Grove, Amsterdam, N. Y.; Good Will Club of Bkln., 41 Tompkins pl., Bkln.; Holly Club, 394 Clinton av., West Hoboken, N. J.; Industrial Society, 220 Willow av., Hoboken, N. J.; Irene Club, 501 W. 50th, N. Y. C.; Jersey City Circle, 110 Hutton, Jersey City, N. J.; Kappa Phi, 2 W. 64th, N. Y. C.; Kittredge Club, 440 E. 57th, N. Y. C.; Myrtle Club, 993 Bergenline av., Woodcliff, N. J.; Prospect Hill Club, 411 E. 5[illegible] N. Y. C.; United Club, 243 E. 34th, N. Y. C.; Unity Club, 52 Orawaupum, White Plains, N. Y.; Wahco, 241 B'way, N. Y. C.; Woman's Institute Club, 38 Palisade av., Yonkers, N. Y.; Bronx Girls' Community Club, 434 E. 154th, N. Y. C.; Girls' Community Club of College Point, College Point, L. I.

Prospect Hill Working Girls' Club—1884. 411 E. 50th. 30 mem. Mrs. Eagan, Pres.; Miss M. Hennesey, Sec., 311 E. 51st.

United Club—1917. 243 E. 34th. 540 mem. Miss A. Besuzzi, Pres.; Miss E. L. Young, Sec.

SOCIETIES AND ASSOCIATIONS UNCLASSIFIED.

International.

Intl. Assn. Chiefs of Police—1893. J. M. Quigley, Pres.; J. L. Beavers, Sec., Atlanta, Ga.

Intl. Assn. of Fire Engineers—1873. Denver, Col. 670 mem. J. F. Healy, Pres., Chief, Fire Dept., Denver, Col.

Intl. Reform Bureau—1895. 206 Pennsylvania av., Washington, D. C. 12,000 mem. Rev. Robt. Watson, Pres., N. Y. City; Rev. Wilbur T. Crafts, Sec.

Intl. Soc. for Personal Identification—Hotel McAlpin, Mhtn. H. P. de Forest, Pres.; Frank A. Byrne, Sec.-Treas., 1428 E. 10th, Bkln.

Lake Mohonk Conference on Internatl. Arbitration—1895. H. C. Phillips, Sec., Mohonk Lake, N. Y.

Parliament of Peace and Universal Brotherhood—1913. Katherine Tingley, Pres.; Joseph H. Fussell, Cor. Sec., Pt. Loma, Cal.

Travel Club of America—1912. Grand Centl. Palace, Mhtn. H. C. Walsh Pres.

Universal Negro Improvement Assn.—Marcus Garvey, Pres., 56 E. 135th, Mhtn.

World's Court League (Inc.)—2 W. 13th, Mhtn. T. E. Burton, Pres.; C. H. Levermore, Sec.

National.

Amer. Anti-Wage Slavery Soc.—1910. Rudolf Modest, Pres.; A. Schlesinger, Sec., 1199 Boston rd., Bronx, N. Y. City.

Amer. Arbitration League—Inc. 1909. Object: Peace through arbitration and national security through preparedness for defense. Woodrow Wilson, W. H. Taft, Hon. Prests.; Henry Clews, Pres.; A. B. Humphrey, Ex. Dir., 54 W. 40th, Mhtn.

Amer. Asiatic Assn.—1898. 627 Lexington av., Mhtn. 300 active mem. To promote good relations with Asiatic nations. L. C. Griscom, Pres.; J. Foord, Sec.; J. R. Patterson, Treas.

Amer. Assn. for Intl. Conciliation—407 W. 117th, Mhtn. N. M. Butler, Ch.; H. S. Haskell, Sec.

Amer. Assn. for Labor Legislation—1906. 131 E. 23d, Mhtn.; T. L. Chadbourne, Pres.; John B. Andrews, Sec.

Amer. Assn. for Organizing Family Social Work—1911. 130 E. 22d, Mhtn. Mrs. W. H. Lothrop, Pres; Francis H. McLean, Field Sec.

Amer. Bison Soc.—1907. 700 mem. E. Seymour, Pres., 45 Wall; M. S. Garretson, Sec.

Amer. Chemical Soc.—W. A. Noyes, Pres.; C. L. Parsons, 1709 G, Washington, D. C.

Amer. Colonization Soc.—1817. 515 Colorado Bldg., Washington, D. C. Hy. L. West, Pres., Paul Seeman, Sec.

Amer. Folk-Lore Soc.—1888. C. M. Barbean, Pres.; Chas. Peabody, Sec., Peabody Museum, Cambrige, Mass.

Amer. Forestry Assn.—1882. 1410 H st., N. W., Washington, D. C. 18,000 mem. C. L. Pack, Pres.; P. S. Ridsdale, Ex. Sec.

Amer. Frugality Assn.—1917. Natl. Hdqtrs., [illegible] Lee av., Bkln., N. Y. Miss L. M. Riegelman, M.D., Pres.; Mrs. Wm. E. Coles, Gen. Sec.

Amer. Home Econom'cs Assn.—Miss Mary E. Sweeney, Pres.; Miss S. F. Cooper, Sec., Battle Creek Sanitarium, Battle Creek, Mich.

Am. Institute of City of N. Y.—1828. 322 W. 23d, Mhtn. 1,200 mem. J. W. Bartlett, Pres.; E. F. Murdock, Sec.

Am. Inst. of Criminal Law and Criminology—Chicago, Ill. 500 mem. Edwin M. Abbott, Sec., Philadelphia, Pa.

Amer. Inst. of Electrical Engineers—1884. 11,838 mem. 33 W. 39th, Mhtn. A. W. Berresford, Pres.; F. L. Hutchinson, Sec., 33 W. 39th.

Amer. Metric Assn.—1916. 156 5th av., Mhtn. Dr. G. F. Kung, Pres.; H. Richards, Jr., Sec.

Amer. Numismatic Assn.—1891. 650 mem. W. C. Moore, Pres.; H. H. Yawger, Gen. Sec., 73 Linden, Rochester, N. Y.

Amer. Numismatic Soc.—1858. B'way at 156th, Mhtn. 658 mem. E. T. Newell, Pres.; H. Wood, Curator; S. P. Noe, Sec.

Amer. Ornithologists' Union—Fd. 1883. Inc. 1888. 1,150 mem. J. H. Sage, Pres.; T. S. Palmer, Sec., 1939 Biltmore, Washington, D. C.

Amer. Peace Soc.—Washington (publishers of magazine "Advocate of Peace"). Hon. A. J. Montague, Pres.; A. D. Call, Sec., Washington, D. C.

Amer. Philatelic Soc.—1886. 1,850 mem. Promotion of stamp collecting. H. H. Wilson, Pres., Bkln.; Dr. H. A. Davis, Sec., 3421 Colfax av., Denver, Col.

Amer. Public Health Assn.—169 Massachusetts av., Boston, Mass. Dr. M. P. Ravenel, Pres., Univ. of Missouri; A. W. Hedrich, Sec.

Amer. Scenic and Historical Preservation Soc.—1895. 154 Nassau, Mhtn. G. F. Kunz, Pres.; E. H. Hall, Sec.

Amer. School Citizenship League—1908. 405 Marlborough, Boston, Mass. 44 State branches. R. J. Condon, Pres.; Mrs. Fannie Fern Andrews, Sec.

Amer. Soc. for Psychical Research—1905. 44 E. 23d. 1,010 mem. Miss G. O. Tubby, Act. Sec.; Walter F. Prince, Ph.D., Act. Dir. of Research.

Am. Soc. of Equity—1899. Madison, Wis. Arthur Sampson, Sec.-Treas.

Amer. Social Hygiene Assn., 105 W. 40th, Mhtn. Dr. W. F. Snow, Gen. Dir.; J. H. Foster, Exec. Sec.

Amer. Union Against Militarism—203 Westory Bldg., Wash., D. C. O. G. Villard, Chair.

Anti-Cigarette League—Eastern Division. 12 Beechwood rd., Verona, N. J. Dr. A. Ed. Keigwin, Pres.; Miss S. Carlew, Sec.-Treas.; Mrs. G. F. Burnett, State Supt.

Anti-Profanity League—1902. Object: To discourage profanity. 27,000 mem. R. D. Sawyer, Gen. Sec., Ware, Mass.

Assn. of Urban Universities—1915. Chancellor. F. A. Hall, Pres., Washington Univ., St. Louis, Mo.; F. B. Robinson, Sec.-Treas., Col. of City of N. Y.

SOCIETIES AND ASSOCIATIONS—UNCLASSIFIED—NATIONAL—*Continued.*

Atlantic Deeper Waterways Assn.—1907. 818 Crozer Bldg., Phila., Pa. J. H. Moore, Pres.; W. H. Schoff, Sec.-Treas.; D. Shuster, Asst. Sec.

Bald Head Club of America—1912. Lakeville, Ct. 1,000 mem. W. A. Warner, Pres., New Haven, Ct.; W. W. Norton, Sec., Lakeville, Ct.

Boy Scouts of Amer.—1910. 379,121 scouts organized in 503 local councils. Natl. Council, 200 5th av., Mhtn. C. H. Livingstone, Pres.; Jas. E. West, Chf. Scout Exec. Object, character development and citizenship training of adolescent boys through program of outdoor activities. Bkln. office, 201 Montague. Registered scouts in Bkln. jurisdiction, 4,691.

Camp Directors' Assn. of America—1910. F. L. Bryant, Pres.; Eugene H. Lehman, Sec., 216 W. 100th, Mhtn.

Carnegie Hero Fund Commission—Oliver Building, Pittsburgh, Pa. 1904. C. L. Taylor, Pres.; F. M. Wilmot, Sec. and Mgr. Endowment fund of $5,000,000. For scope and object of fund see Eagle Almanac, 1907, p. 341.

China Soc. of Amer.—1912. 300 mem. L. L. Seaman, Pres.; A. B. Humphrey, Ch., 31 Nassau, N. Y. City.

Citizens' Alliance for Good Government—1920. Carl Gerke, Pres., Flushing, L. I.; John Hering, Sec., 532 B'way, Astoria, L. I.

English Folk-Dance Soc. (U. S. Branch)—1915. Mrs. J. J. Storrow, Pres.; Chas. Peabody, Sec.-Treas., Cambridge, Mass.

Genl. Fed. Women's Clubs—1888. 9,000 clubs. 2,500,000 mem. Mrs. Thos. G. Winter, Pres., 415 Maryland Bldg., Washington, D. C.

Indian Rights Assn—1882. 995 Drexel Bldg., Phila., Pa. 800 mem. H. Welsh, Pres.; M. K. Sniffen, Sec.

Inter-Racial Council—120 B'way, C. Du Pont, Pres.; F. A. Kellor, Sec.

League to Enforce Peace—1915. 22 W. 19th, Mhtn. 400,000 mem. W. H. Taft, Pres.; W. H. Short, Sec.

Natl. Anti-Horse Thief Assn.—1854. 40 000 mem. T. J. Sargent, Pres., Newkirk, Okla.; J. M. Pence, Sec.-Treas., Morrisonville, Ill.

Natl. Assn. for the Advancement of Colored People—1909. 70 5th av., Mhtn. 90,000 mem. M. Storey, Pres.; J. W. Johnson, Act. Sec.

Natl. Assn. of Audubon Socs.—Inc. 1905. 4,000 mem. Wm. Dutcher, Pres.; T. G. Pearson, Sec., 1974 B'way, Mhtn.

Natl. Assn. of Directors of Girls Camps—1914. Meets in N. Y. and Boston. 75 mem. E. H. Lehman, Pres., Highland Manor, Tarrytown, N. Y.; R. W. Currier, Sec., N. J. Law Schl., Newark, N. J.

Natl. Assn. of Travelers' Aid Soc.—25 W. 43d, Mhtn. G. Colgate, Pres.; R. Taggart, Treas.; V. V. Johnson, Sec. Non-sec. Composed of non-commercial agencies interested in the protection of travelers, especially women and children.

Natl. Civil Service Reform League—1881. 8 W. 40th, Mhtn. 20 local assns. R. H. Dana, Pres.; N. W. Marsh, Sec.

Natl. Congress of Mothers and Parent Teacher Assns.—1897. 1201 16th, N. W., Washington, D. C. 218,000 mem. Mrs. M. P. Higgins, Pres.; Mrs. Geo. P. Chandler, Sec.

Natl. Consumers' League—1899. 44 E. 23d, Mhtn. 89 branches in 16 States. N. D. Baker, Pres.; Mrs. Florence Kelly, Sec.

Natl. First Aid Assn. of Am. (The)—Inc. Federal Charter. 1905. (See page 338, 1916 Eagle Almanac, for scope of work). R. G. Wells, Act. Pres., hdqtrs., Cooper Tavern Bldg., Arlington, Mass.; Mary Kensel Wells, Sec.; F. H. Morse, M.D., Medical Dir.

Natl. Founders' Assn.—1898. 650 mem. W. H. Barr, Pres.; J. M. Taylor, Sec., 29 S. LaSalle, Chicago, Ill. Investigation and adjustment of labor disputes. Member of Natl. Indusl. Conf. Board, representing 75% of factories, to make scientific study of industrial economic problems.

Natl. Haymakers' Assn. of U. S. (Beneficial)—1878. A. W. Finch, Natl. C. H.; Mahlon Trumbauer, Natl. C. of S., 8110 Frankford av., Phila., Pa.

Natl. Housewives League—1911. 327 W. 101st, Mhtn. Mrs. J. D. Heath, Pres.; Mrs. Sara O. West, Sec.

Natl. Industrial Council—1907. 30 Church, Mhtn. J. Kirby, Jr., Ch.; J. P. Bird, Sec.

Natl. Information Bureau—1918. 1 Madison av. A co-operative effort for the standardization of national, social, civic and philanthropic work. G. D. Pope, Pres.; A. T. Burns, Sec.

Natl. One-Cent Letter Postage Assn.—1910. 50,000 mem. To secure an equalization of postage rates to cost of service on each class of mail. C. W. Burrows, Pres., 1881 E. 23d, Cleveland, O.; G. T. McIntosh, Sec.-Treas., 1240 Huron rd., Cleveland, O.

Natl Optimists' Club—W. H. Harrison, Pres., Louisville, Ky.; H. G. Hill, Sec., Indianapolis, Ind.

Natl. Prohibition Assn.—1907. H. C. Parsons, Pres.; Chas. L. Chute, Sec. and Treas., 132 State, Albany, N. Y. To study and invest'gate the work of probation officers, juvenile and other social courts and promote their work in the U. S.

Natl. Research Council—1918. By exec. order Pres. of the U. S. 1201 16th, Washington, D. C. J. R. Angell, Ch.; Vernon Kellogg, Sec.

Natl. Social Unit Orgn.—1916. 117 W. 46th, N. Y. C. Wilbur C. Phillips, Sec., N. Y. C.

Natl. Spiritualists' Assn.—1893. Auxiliary organizations for membership. G. B. Warne, Pres.; G. W. Kates, Sec., 600 Penna. av., Washington, D. C.

Natl. Tax Assn.—1906. 1,000 mem. Zenas W. Bliss, Pres.; A. E. Holcomb, Sec., 195 B'way, Mhtn.

Natl. Women's Life Saving League—1911. 25 Clinton, Bkln. 2,000 mem. Miss M. F. Mehrtens, Pres.; Bessie Simons, Sec. Object: To teach women and children swimming.

Naval History Soc.—1909. 35 W. 42d, Mhtn. 600 mem. To discover and procure data relating to naval history and American seamen. Col. James Barnes, Pres.; Rear Adm. Bradley A. Fiske, Sec.; R. S. Sloane, Treas.

Pilgrims of the U. S.—1902. 800 mem. A. E. Gallatin, Sec., 217 B'way.

Playground and Recreation Assn. of Amer.—1906. 1 Madison av., Mhtn. Jos. Lee, Pres.; H. S. Braucher, Sec., 1 Madison av.

Soc. for Amer. and British Friendship—1919. 516 Madison av., Mhtn. Dr. N. Dwight Hillis, Pres.; D. D. Irvine, Sec.

Soc. for Upholding the Sanctity of Marriage—1920. Summit, N. J. Rev. M. H. Gates, Pres.; Rev. Walker Gwynne, Sec., Summit, N. J.

Sponsor's Soc. of U. S. Navy—210 mem. Mrs. R. T. Hall Pres.; Miss N. D. Barney, Sec., Washington, D. C.

U. S. Council of Natl. Defence—1916. For the co-ordination of industries and resources for natl. security and welfare. Sec. of War, N. D. Baker, Ch.; E. K. Ellsworth, Ch. Clk., Washington, D. C.

U. S. Hay Fever Assn.—1873. Mrs. Geo. K. Camp, Pres., Irvington, N. J.; Miss L. B. Gachus, Treas. and Sec., Bethlehem, N. H.

United Writers of Amer.—1917. 1199 Boston rd. Alexander Schlesinger, Pres.; W. I. Slawson, Sec.-Treas.

Universal Bro. and Theosophical Soc.—1875. International Hdqts. at Point Loma. Reorg. 1898 by Katherine Tingley, Leader; J. H. Fussell, Sec., Point Loma, Cal.

World Purity Federation—1900. La Crosse, Wis. 30,000 mem. B. S. Steadwell, Pres.

World War Objectors—1920. Rand School, 7 E. 15th, Mhtn. Jos. Brandon, Pres.; A. H. Smith, Sec.

State.

Committee of Ninety-six, N. Y. State Com.—1920. L. F. Franklin, Ch.; G. S. Viereck, Sec., 202 E. 42d, Mhtn.

Law and Order Union of N. Y. State—1903. 15 William, Mhtn. 500,000 mem. Dwight Braman, Pres.; Miss E. Wagle, Sec.

North Country Garden Club—1914. 35 mem. Mrs. J. P. Morgan, Pres.; Miss A. D. Weeks, Sec., Cold Spring Harbor, L. I.

N. Y. Civic League—1910. 452 B'way, Albany. W. Sheafe Chase, Pres., 481 Bedford av., Bkln.; Rev. O. R. Miller, State Supt.; H. P. Freece, Treas.

N. Y. State Colonization Soc.—1885. Object: To colonize Africans in the U. S. to the coast of Africa. Eben C. Sage, Pres.; L. G. Myers, Treas., 61 B'way, Mhtn.

N. Y. State Federation of Women's Clubs—Mrs. Walter S. Comley, Pres., Portchester; Mrs. Wm. H. Purdy, Sec., 136 Park av., Mt. Vernon.

N. Y. Tax Reform Assn.—1891. 29 B'way, N. Y. C. 600 mem. W. G. Low, Pres.; A. C. Pleydell, Sec.

Prison Assn. of N. Y.—135 E. 15th, Mhtn. O. F. Lewis, Gen. Sec.

Vet. Assn. 1st Battalion, N. M. N. Y.—Hon. H. L. Satterlee, Pres.; W. S. Newhouse, Sec., 87 Liberty, Mhtn.

SOCIETIES AND ASSOCIATIONS—Unclassified—*Continued.*

Brooklyn.

Adelphi College Associates—1913. 200 mem. Object: To foster higher education in Bkln., in particular through financial support of Adelphi College as a college for women. Wm. McCarroll, Pres.; A. G. Fradenburgh, Sec., Adelphi College.

Adelphi College Aux.—1913. 575 mem. Object: To foster higher education of women in Bkln. Mrs. S. Wilson, Pres.; Miss E. W. Draudt, Cor. Sec., Adelphi College.

Alliance of Women's Clubs of Bkln.—1902. Composed of Presidents and delegates from women's clubs of borough. Mrs. R. C. Talbot-Perkins, Pres.; Mrs. C. E. Donnellon, Sec., 849 Carroll.

Bkln. City Girls' Club—1920. 169 Livingston. Frances Froelich, Pres.; Barbara Matthees, Sec.; Mrs. Emma Mooney, Treas.

Brooklyn Girl Scouts—200 Montague. Mrs. Maude Canfield, Commissioner; Miss Anna Harvey, Dep. Commr., Adelphi College; Jos. T. Stevens, Treas., Nassau National Bank.

Bkln. Protective Tenants' Union—1919. 219 Sackman. 8,000 mem. H. Rich, Pres.; L. Orlinger, Sec.

Bkln. Signal Corps—801 Dean. Maj. E. Bigelow, Pres.; Capt. E. B. Esbach, Sec.

Bkln. Stamp Club—1919. Howard av. and Hancock. 40 mem. R. M. Osborne, Pres.; Wm. Lycett, Sec., 399 Lincoln rd.

Bkln. Woman's Single Tax Club—1890. 40 mem. Mrs. W. A. Cornell, Pres.; Miss J. A. Rogers, Sec., 485 Hancock.

Brotherhood of the Commonwealth—(See Soc. and Ben., Miscel.)

Colored Big Sister Club—1918. 583 Franklin av. 50 mem. Miss M. B. Trotman, Pres.; Mrs. Jerome Peterson, Sec., 380 Monroe.

Ellsworth Relief Circle—1861. Labor Lyceum, Willoughby and Myrtle av. 83 mem. C. Laut, Pres.; H. Bauer, Sec., 51 Nostrand av.

Gates-Franklin Residents League—Mrs. R. C. Talbot-Perkins, Pres.; Miss F. Williams, Sec., 284 Gates av.

Historic Boys' Club—1891. 40 mem. Dr. C. J. Harbordt, Pres.; J. A. Kellett, Sec., 346 B'way, Mhtn.

Kings Co. Anti-Mosquito Assn.—Wm. T. Donnelly, Pres.; H. B. Maurer, Sec., 299 B'way, Mhtn.

L. I. Council of Women's Clubs—1895. 103 clubs. Mrs. C. B. Smith, Pres., Flushing; Mrs. M. Barrett, Sec., 69 Pilling.

Motor Corps of Amer. (Bkln. Corps)—92 Herkimer. Capt. M. M. Ogilvie, 1st Lt. J. M. Cantwell, 1st Lt. C. H. Miller.

Natl. League for Women's Service—Kings Co. Branch, 54 Lafayette av. Mrs. W. Gibb, Ch.; Miss M. B. Geary, Sec., 64 Lafayette av.

Navy Employes' Welfare Assn.—90 Park av. R. T. Broaddhus, Pres.; E. H. Markolf, Sec.-Treas.

Navy War Workers' League of U. S. Navy Yards and Naval Stations—Wm. Barr, Pres.; E. H. Markolf, Sec., 149 Waverly av.

Syrian Centre—Clinton and Pacific. R. C. Agne, Director.

Unity Child Welfare Assn.—1911. Unity House, Gates av. and Irving pl. 200 mem. Mrs. A. J. Boulton, Pres.; Mrs. G. W. Leach, Sec., 48 McDonough.

Upanin Club—1911. Affords temporary home and Shelter for young men without home and friends. Acc. 16. 1 Middagh. R. J. Wilkin, Pres.; E. Byk, Sec.

Manhattan and Bronx.

Amer. Chemical Soc. (N. Y. Sect.)—2,400 mem. R. H. McKee, Ch.; H. G. Sidebottom, Sec.-Treas., 17 Battery pl.

Am. Embassy Assn.—1909. 505 5th av. B. C. Jones, Pres.; F. D. Pavey, Sec.

Assn. for the Protection of the Adirondacks—154 Nassau. 1901. 750 mem. J. G. Agar, Pres.; E. H. Hall, Sec., 154 Nassau.

Betterment League of N. Y.—Hotel Astor. 500 mem. Mrs. N. B. Van Slingerland, Pres.; Miss Alice E. Ives, Sec., 11 W. 64th.

Camp Fire Girls—1912. 31 E. 17th, Mhtn. 150,000 mem. R. Garrett, Act. Pres.; L. F. Scott, Sec.; J. A. Potter, Treas.

Central Park Shakespeare Garden Comm.—1916. Mrs. C. C. Cowl, Pres.; Mrs. G. G. Gould, V.-Pres. and Sec., 106 W. 78th.

Chemists' Club of N. Y.—1898. 52 E. 41st. 1,712 mem. E. Hendrick, Pres.; J. R. M. Klotz, Sec., 120 B'way.

City Midday Club—25 Broad. 1901. 575 mem. H. W. Taft, Pres.; R. Talbot, Sec.

Civil Service Reform Assn.—1877. 8 W. 40th. 890 mem. S. H. Ordway, Pres.; G. T. Keyes, Sec.

Collector's Club—1896. 100 mem. Dr. G. B. Chittenden, Pres.; Harry M. Levy, Sec., 120 W. 49th.

Community Service—1919. 1 Madison av. Jos. Lee, Pres.; H. S. Brancher, Sec.

Congress of State Socs.—Mrs. T. J. Vivian, Pres. and Founder, 312 Manhattan av.; Mrs. C. D. Hirst, Cor. Sec., 137 W. 75th.

Consumers' League—289 4th av. Miss Amey Aldrich, Pres.; Mrs. Clara M. Tead, Sec.

Far Western Travelers' Assn.—1510 B'way. J. B. Patten, Pres.

Friends of Russian Freedom—1907. 500 mem. Herbert Parsons, Pres.; J. B. Reynolds, Ch. of Ex. Com., North Haven, Conn.

General Soc. of Mechanics and Tradesmen of City of N. Y.—1789. 20 W. 44th. Jas. Hopkins, Pres.; R. T. Davies, Sec.

Girls Scouts—1912. 189 Lexington av. Mrs. Juliette Low, Founder; Mrs. A. O. Choate, Pres.; Mrs. Jane D. Rippin, Dir.

Gridiron Club—100 mem. Hotel Astor, Hdqts. Mrs. A. A. A. Brooks, Pres., Manhattan Ct. Hotel Apartments.

Harmony Fellowship Club—Mrs. W. B. Smith, Pres., 452 Riverside dr.

Honest Ballot Assn.—1912. 843 mem. To insure honest elections. J. Byrne, Pres.; S. K. Rapp, Sec., 18 W. 34th.

Humanitarian League—1914. Misha Appelbaum, Founder and Pres., 228 W. 75th.

Inkowa Club—12 W. 40th. Miss G. Parker, Chn.; Miss E. Harner, Dir.

Japan Soc.—1907. 25 W. 43d. 1,500 mem. 1,300 of whom are Amer. Object: To diffuse among Amer. a more accurate knowledge of people of Japan. F. A. Vanderlip, Pres.; E. C. Worden, Sec., 25 W. 43d.

Kiwanis Club—Hotel McAlpin. R. A. M. Hobbs, Pres.

League for Industrial Rights—1902. 135 B'way. 2,000 mem. W. Wood, Ch.; L. F. Sherman, Sec.

League of Foreign Born Citizens—1913. 303 5th av., 95 2d av., 407 E. 73d. 5,000 mem. N. Phillips, Pres.; S. W. Levine, Sec.

League of Free Nations Assn.—1918. 3 W. 29th. James G. McDonald, Pres.; Miss C. Merriman, Sec.

Life Saving Benev. Assn. of N. Y.—Inc. 1849. 51 Wall. Makes awards in recognition of highly meritorious service. C. Eldert, Pres.; F. D. Denton, Treas.

Mhtn. Single Tax Club—1888. Union sq. 1,000 mem. J. R. Brown, Pres.; E. H. Underhill, Sec.

Metropolitan League of Savings and Loan Assn.—1890. 47 assns. affiliated. W. D. Carter, Pres.; A. W. McEwan, Sec., 2161 Bathgate av.

N. Y. Anti-Vivisection Soc.—1908. 456 4th av. Mrs. D. Belais, Pres.; Mrs. J. L. Boynton, Sec.

N. Y. City Federation of Women's Clubs—Mrs. H. Lilly, Pres.; Miss Andrews, Sec., 138 E. 40th.

N. Y. Community Trust—1920. Alvin W. Krech, Pres.; F. J. Parsons, Act. Dir., 55 Cedar.

N. Y. Numismatic Club—1908. 216 W. 102d, Mhtn. 80 mem. A. R. Frey, Pres.; F. C. C. Boyd, Sec.

N. Y. Peace Soc.—1906. For International Justice and Friendship. O. S. Straus, Pres.; C. H. Levermore, Sec., 70 5th av., Mhtn.

N. Y. Soc. for the Suppression of Vice—215 W. 22d. 250 mem. J. S. Sumner, Sec.

No Strike Assn.—1918. Rm. 1100, 154 Nassau. 360 mem. A. I. du Pont, Ch.; B. Woods, Sec.

Non-Smokers' Prot. League—1910. 101 W. 72d. 2,000 mem. Opposed to smoking in public places. Dr. C. G. Pease, Pres.; E. di Pirani, Sec.

Parole Officers' Assn.—Rm. 2500, Municipal Bldg. 38 mem. Jas. J. Doherty, Pres.; H. Stein, Sec.

Philatelic Soc. of N. Y.—1891. 120 W. 49th. 100 mem. Hy. Clotz, Pres.; J. W. Scott, Sec.

Probation Officers' Assn. of City Magistrates' Courts, City of N. Y.—J. J. Fitzgerald, Pres.; D. J. O'Shea, Sec., 44 Court, Bkln.

Professional Woman's League—144 W. 55th. Inc. 1893. 500 mem. Helen W. Ritchie, Pres.

Rainy Day Club—1896. 450 mem. Hotel Astor. Mrs. A. M. Palmer, Pres.; Mrs. O. Kahn, Cor. Sec.

Riverside Castle Club—Mrs. W. B. Smith, Pres.; Mrs. D. S. Pike, Sec.-Treas., 843 West End av.

Shipmasters' Club of N. Y.—1913. 600 mem. Promotion of safety at sea. A. B. Conner, Pres., 51 Wall; James Moorhead, Treas.

Soc. for Instruction in First Aid to the Injured—105 E. 22d. Org. 1883. J. A. Wade, Pres.; L. F. Bishop, Sec.

SOCIETIES AND ASSOCIATIONS—UNCLASSIFIED—MANHATTAN AND BRONX—*Continued.*

Soc. for Prevention of Crime—1878. 50 Union sq. C. E. Bruce, Pres.; T. D. Kenneson, Sec.; Samuel Marcus, Counsel; H. C. Barber, Supt.

Soc. for Suppression of Unnecessary Noise—1907. Mrs. I. L. Rice, Pres.; Miss Muriel Rice, Sec., 12 E. 87th.

Soc. of Chemical Industry—1895. Amer. Sect., 52 E. 41st. 1,500 mem. S. R. Church, Ch.; A. Rogers, Hon. Sec.

Surveyors' Customs Welfare Assn.—J. S. Long, Pres.; T. M. Hyatt, Sec.; U. S. Barge Office, Battery Park

Travelers' Aid Soc. of N. Y.—1905. 465 Lexington av. Wm. F. Morgan, Pres.; V. M. Murray, Gen. Sec.. Agents of society meet all boats and trains, to assist, without charge, all travelers, especially women and girls.

U. S. Junior Naval Reserve—1915. 12,000 mem. 2:80 B'way. Wm. A. Blair, Ch.; Ed. A. Oldham, Ex. Sec. For the training of boys for sea service and better citizenship. American crews for American ships.

Vacation Assn.—1915. 38 W. 39th. 200 admin. mem. 800 taxpayers. 10,000 associate mem. Miss G. Robinson Smith, Pres.; Miss G. E. Lachlan, Sec.

Victory Club—Hotel Pennsylvania. N. Drew, Pres.; D. S. Pike, Sec., 843 West End av.

Women's City Club—1915. 22 Park av. Miss M. G. Hay, Pres.

Wool Club—1895. 260 B'way. 500 mem. F. E. Kaley, Pres.; R. McBratney, Sec.

IMMIGRATION AND EMIGRATION.

Increase or decrease of population by arrival and departure of aliens during fiscal year ended June 30, 1920, by races.

RACES.	Admitted—Immigrant.	Admitted—Non-Immigrant.	Total.	Departed—Emigrant.	Departed—Non-Emigrant.	Total.	Inc. (+) or dec. (—).
African (black)	8,174	5,425	13,599	1,275	2,118	3,393	+10,206
Armenian	2,762	198	2,960	584	91	675	+ 2,285
Bohemian and Moravian	415	135	550	259	59	318	+ 232
Bulgarian, Serbian and Montenegrin	1,064	1,770	2,834	23,844	1,893	25,737	—22,903
Chinese	2,148	11,698	13,843	2,961	11,248	14,209	— 363
Croatian and Slovenian	493	727	1,220	7,481	268	7,749	— 6,529
Cuban	1,510	7,477	8,987	1,598	7,567	9,165	— 178
Dalmatian, Bosnian and Herzegovinian	63	22	85	1,533	85	1,618	— 1,533
Dutch and Flemish	12,730	4,423	17,153	3,016	4,341	7,357	+ 9,796
East Indian	160	121	281	162	42	204	+ 77
English	58,366	35,260	93,626	11,659	33,588	45,247	+48,379
Finnish	1,510	320	1,830	1,447	557	2,004	— 174
French	27,390	10,892	38,282	7,026	8,008	15,034	+23,248
German	7,338	1,830	9,168	4,178	1,305	5,483	+ 3,685
Greek	13,998	1,426	15,424	20,319	1,948	22,267	— 6,843
Hebrew	14,292	3,231	17,523	358	1,025	1,383	+16,140
Irish	20,784	4,330	25,114	4,635	3,838	8,473	+16,641
Italian (north)	12,918	3,046	15,964	8,159	2,213	10,372	+ 5,592
Italian (south)	84,882	28,885	113,767	80,955	8,727	89,682	+24,085
Japanese	9,279	6,895	16,174	4,238	11,415	15,653	+ 521
Korean	72	9	81	14	22	36	+ 45
Lithuanian	422	43	465	719	25	744	— 279
Magyar	252	54	306	14,619	208	14,827	—14,521
Mexican	51,042	17,350	68,392	6,412	4,742	11,154	+57,238
Pacific Islander	17	33	50	3	5	8	+ 42
Polish	2,519	8,931	11,450	18,392	1,223	19,615	— 8,165
Portuguese	15,174	964	16,138	4,859	1,086	5,945	+10,193
Roumanian	898	956	1,854	21,490	1,023	22,513	—20,659
Russian	2,378	683	3,061	1,151	391	1,542	+ 1,519
Ruthenian (Russniak)	258	136	394	693	32	725	— 331
Scandinavian (Norwegians, Danes and Swedes)	16,621	8,529	25,150	8,246	12,174	20,420	+ 4,730
Scotch	21,180	7,655	28,835	2,577	4,888	7,465	+21,370
Slovak	3,824	1,372	5,196	11,568	478	12,046	— 6,850
Spanish	23,594	7,442	31,036	5,144	5,159	10,303	+20,733
Spanish-American	3,934	5,102	9,036	1,126	4,413	5,539	+ 3,497
Syrian	3,047	991	4,038	1,652	730	2,382	+ 1,656
Turkish	140	55	195	1,340	173	1,513	— 1,318
Welsh	1,462	735	2,197	195	303	498	+ 1,699
West Indian (except Cuban)	1,546	1,989	3,535	626	1,948	2,574	+ 961
Other peoples	1,345	435	1,780	1,802	388	2,190	— 410
Totals	430,001	191,575	621,576	288,315	139,747	428,062	+193,514

MOTOR TRAFFIC OVER CITY BRIDGES.

The growth of motor traffic since 1917 and the relative importance of the various bridges as automobile highways is shown in the following daily average traffic table of the Department of Plant and Structures, City of New York:

DAILY AVERAGE TRAFFIC.

Name of Bridge.	1917 Motor.	1917 Horse.	1917 Total.	1917 Trucks & Autos. Per Ct.	1919 Motor.	1919 Horse.	1919 Total.	1919 Trucks & Autos. Per Ct.
Brooklyn	3,150	1,910	5,060	62	3,295	3,310	6,605	50
Manhattan	11,266	3,093	14,359	78	*20,214	1,010	21,304	95
Williamsburg	6,248	4,029	10,277	61	12,422	3,997	16,419	76
Queensboro	12,206	1,226	13,431	91	17,594	1,207	18,801	94
Willis Avenue	5,308	3,858	9,166	58	9,136	2,745	11,881	77
Third Avenue	2,165	2,460	4,625	47	2,974	1,654	4,628	64
Madison Avenue	5,893	1,686	7,579	78	12,921	1,193	14,114	92
145th Street	5,359	704	6,063	88	4,213	440	4,653	91
Hamilton Avenue	5,603	6,361	11,964	47	2,703	1,509	4,212	"
Vernon Avenue	3,754	2,387	6,141	61	4,566	1,209	5,775	79
Ship Canal	4,170	218	4,388	95	3,776	156	3,932	96
Eastchester	1,142	47	1,189	96	3,648	62	3,710	98
Other Bridges	31,364	26,732	58,096	54	42,391	19,844	62,235	68
Grand totals	97,627	54,711	152,338	64	139,933	38,336	178,269	78

*Includes busses.

LABOR UNIONS AND OFFICIALS

New York State Industrial Commission.

By an act of the Legislature of 1915, the N. Y. Dept. of Labor was reorganized and placed under the administration of 5 commrs. at an annual salary of $8,000 each, the official designation of the dept. becoming "State Industrial Commission—Dept. of Labor." Thus the new Commission has taken over the State Dept. of Labor the Workmen's Compensation Commission, the State Insurance Fund, the State Bureau of Mediation and Arbitration, the State Bureau of Inspection, the State Bureau of Industrial Hygiene, the State Bureau of Labor Statistics and information, the State Employment Bureau, the Bur. of Industries and Immigration, the Bur. of Boilers and Explosives of the former Fire Marshal's Dept. and the State Bureau to Formulate an Industrial Code, all of which have branch offices in Bkln., Mhtn., Buffalo, Rochester and Syracuse. Employment Bureau branches are also located in Yonkers, Schenectady, Utica, Syracuse, Elmira, Binghamton, Rochester, Buffalo, Watertown, Jamestown, Dunkirk, Niagara Falls, Albany, Bronx, Mhtn., Bkln., L. I. City.

Personnel of State Industrial Commission. Dept. of Labor, Including Heads of Depts.

Commissioners—E. F. Boyle, Ch., Mhtn.; F. Perkins, N. Y. C.; J. M. Lynch, Syracuse; H. D. Sayer, Richmond Hill; C. W. Phillips, Rochester; salary, $8,000 each per annum. Sec., E. W. Buckley, Mhtn., $6,000; First Deputy Commissioner, J. L. Gernon, Bkln., $6,000; 2d Dep. Comnr., W. C. Archer, Mt. Vernon, $6,000; 3d Dep. Commr., E. D. Jackson, Buffalo, $6,000; Counsel, B. L. Shientag, Mhtn., $7,000; 1st Asst. Counsel, F. H. Cunningham, Mhtn., $5,000; Assts. to Counsel, P. M. Daly, $4,000; F. Wilmot, $3,000; A. A. Fansky, $3,000; C. Whelan, Bkln., $2,750; Mgr. State Insurance Fund, L. W. Hatch, Albany, $8,000; Asst. Mgr. State Ins. Fund, N. W. Muller, Mhtn., $5,000; Actuary, vacant, $7,000; Inspector of Risks, W. Newell, Neponsit, L. I., $4,250; Chf. Div. of Claims, W. S. Pendleton, Bkln., $4,000; Chf. Medical Exam., Dr. Raphael Lewi, Mhtn., $6,000; Medical Exam., Dr. H. B. Boyle, $3,250; Dr. Chas. Steinhauser, $2,500; Dr. F. J. O'Brien, $2,500; Medical Advisor to State Ins. Fund, Dr. H. T. Radin, Bkln., $3,500; Dep. Commrs., Compensation Bur., T. J. Curtis, Mhtn., $4,000; J. C. Brown, Mhtn., $4,000; W. A. Abbott, Bkln., J. P. Boyle, N. Y. (Albany office), $4,000 each; D. M. Stone, Bkln., $4,000; W. C. Richards, Parish, and J. P. Richardson (Syracuse office), $4,000 each; C. K. Blatchley, N. Y. (Rochester office), $4,000; J. McLusky, Syracuse, and O. Lang (Buffalo office), $4,000 each; Dep. Commrs., Industrial Code—R. J. Cullen, Mhtn., $4,000; T. C. Eipper, Bkln., $4,000; Asst. Secs. of Com.—M. J. Wallace, Mhtn., $3,750; N. J. Rosenberg, Mhtn., $3,750; V. T. Holland, Albany, $3,750; Cashier, A. F. Pentz, Bkln., $3,750; Chf. Acct., P. J. McDermott, Spring Valley, N. Y., $3,250; Editor, Official Bulletin, W. A. Marakle, Rochester, $3,000; Chf. of Div. of Homework Inspection, D. O'Leary, Glens Falls, $3,250; Chf. Mercantile Insp., C. B. Ash, Yonkers, $4,000; Chf. Statistician, E. B. Patton, Albany, $4,500; Asst. Chf. Statistician, G. A. Stevens, Bronx, $3,500; Chf. of Div. of General Statistics, S. B. Dicker, Ithaca, $2,800; Chf. of Div. of Industrial Accidents and Diseases, T. K. Lewis, Albany, $2,800; Chf. of Div. of Special Investigations, vacant, $2,800; Mediator of Industrial Disputes, M. J. Reagan, Bronx, $3,250; Chf. Investigator, M. K. Clark, Mhtn., $3,500; Chf. Eng., Bureau of Boilers and Explosives, G. A. O'Rourke, Albany, $3,750.

Industrial Council (Advisory).
Serving without salary.

H. D. Sayer, Ch.; J. C. Clark, Buffalo; C. A. Chase, Syracuse; R. H. Curran, Rochester; G. E. Emmons, Schenectady; J. P. Holland, N. Y. C.; R. C. Stofer, Norwich; T. M. Gafney, Syracuse; M. Scott, N. Y. C.; M. H. Christopherson, Yonkers, E. W. Buckley, Sec.

International Federation of Trade Unions.

W. A. Appleton, England, Pres.; J. Ondegeest, Holland, Sec.

American Federation of Labor.

Headquarters, A. F. of L. Bldg., Washington, D. C.

(Composed of 110 natl. and internatl. unions, 5 depts., 46 State branches, 950 city central unions and 1,264 local trade and Federal unions.)

President, Samuel Gompers, Washington, D. C.; 1st Vice-Pres., James Duncan, Quincy, Mass.; 2d Vice-Pres., J. F. Valentine, Cinn., O.; 3d Vice-Pres., F. Duffy, Indianapolis, Ind.; 4th Vice-Pres., Wm. Green, Indianapolis, Ind.; 5th Vice-Pres., W. D. Mahon, Detroit, Mich.; 6th Vice-Pres., T. A. Rickert, Chicago, Ill.; 7th Vice-Pres., J. Fischer, Indianapolis, Ind.; 8th Vice-Pres., M. Woll Chicago, Ill.; Sec., Frank Morrison, Wash., D. C.; Treas., D. J. Tobin, Indianapolis, Ind. (The above officers also comprise the Executive Council.)

Departments of American Federation of Labor.

Building—†W. J. Spencer, Washington, D. C.

Metal Trades—†A. J. Berres, Washington, D. C.

Mining—*J. Lord, Washington, D. C.

Railroad Employes—*B. M. Jewell, Washington, D. C.

Union Label Trades—†J. J. Manning, Washington, D. C.

A. F. of L. Fraternal Organizations.

Women's Trade Union League, The National—*Mrs. Raymond Robins, 64 W. Randolph, Chicago, Ill.

Women's Interl. Union Label League—Mrs. A. B. Field, Harting Block, Elwood, Ind.

Farmers' Educational and Co-operative Union of America—*C. S. Barrett, Union City, Ga.

American Society of Equity—*J. H. Carnshan, Madison, Wis.

International Unions Affiliated With American Federation of Labor.

Actors and Artists of America, Associated—H. Montford, 207 E. 54th, N. Y. C.

Asbestos Workers, Interl. Assn. of Heat and Frost Insulators—†T. J. McNamara, 803 Holland Bldg., St. Louis, Mo.

Bakery and Confectionery Workers Interl. Union of America—C. Iffland, 212 Bush Temple of Music, Chicago, Ill.

Barbers' Interl. Union, Journeymen—†J. Fischer, 222 E. Michigan, Indianpolis, Ind.

Bill Posters and Billers of America, Interl. Alliance—W. McCarthy, 1482-90 B'way, Fitzgerald Bldg., N. Y. C.

Blacksmiths, Interl. Brotherhood—†Wm. F. Kramer, Transportation Bldg., 608 So. Dearborn, Chicago, Ill.

Boiler Makers, Iron Ship Builders and Helpers of America, Interl. Brotherhood—†F. P. Reinmeyer, 309 Wyandotte Bldg., Kansas City, Kan.

Bookbinders, Interl. Brotherhood—D. T. Davies, 222 East Michigan, Indianapolis, Ind.

Boot and Shoe Workers Union—†C. L. Baine, 246 Sumner, Boston, Mass.

Brewery Flour, Cereal and Soft Drink Workers of America, Interl. Union of the United—J. Rader, 2347-49-51 Vine, Cincinnati, O.

Bricklayers, Masons and Plasterers, Interl. Union of America—†W. Dobson, Univ. Park Bldg., Indianapolis, Ind.

Brick and Clay Workers of America, The United—†W. Tracy, 166 West Washington, Chicago, Ill.

Bridge and Structural Iron Workers, Interl. Assn.—†H. Jones, 304 American Central Life Bldg., Indianapolis, Ind.

Broom and Whisk Makers' Union, Interl.—†W. R. Boyer, 851 King pl., Chicago, Ill.

Carmen of America, Brotherhood Railway—†E. W. Weeks, 507 Hall Bldg., Kansas City, Mo.

Carpenters and Joiners of America, United Brotherhood—F. Duffy, Carpenters' Bldg., Indianapolis, Ind.

Carvers' Assn. of North America, Interl. Wood—F. Detlef, 230 Woodbine, Bkln., N. Y.

Cigarmakers' Interl. Union of America—*G. W. Perkins, Monon Bldg., Chicago, Ill.

Clerks, Brotherhood of Railway—†C. M. Owens, 407 Second National Bank Bldg., Cincinnati, O.

Clerks' International Protective Assn., Retail—†H. J. Conway, Lock Drawer 248, Lafayette, Ind.

Clerks' Natl. Federation of Postal—†T. F. Flaherty, A. F. of L. Bldg., Washington, D. C.

Conductors' Order of Sleeping Car—†W. O. Murphy, 360-361 Union Station, Kansas City, Mo.

Coopers' Interl. Union of North America—†W. R. Deal, Bishop Bldg., Kansas City, Kan.

Cutting Die and Cutter Makers, Interl. Union—†L. S. Rantz, 156 Short, Brockton, Mass.

Diamond Workers' Protective Union of America—*A. Meyer, 323 Washington, Bkln., N. Y.

Draftsmen's Unions, Interl. Federation of Technical Engineers, Architects—*C. L. Rosemund, 201 A. F. of L. Bldg., Washington, D. C.

---

*President. †Sec.-Treas.

LABOR UNIONS AND OFFICIALS—*Continued.*

Electrical Workers of America, Interl. Brotherhood—C. P. Ford, I. A. of M. Bldg., 9th and Mt. Vernon pl., Washington, D. C.

Elevator Constructors, Interl. Union—†F. J. Schneider, Perry Bldg., 16th and Chestnut, Philadelphia, Pa.

Engineers' Beneficial Assn. of U. S. of America, Natl. Marine—G. A. Grubb, 311-315 I. A. of M. Bldg., 9th and Mt. Vernon pl., Washington, D. C.

Engineers, Interl. Union of Steam and Operating—†H. M. Comerford, 6334 Yale av., Chicago, Ill.

Engravers' Union of No. America, Interl. Photo.—†H. F. Schmal, Nicholas Bldg., 1504 South Grand av., St. Louis, Mo.

Engravers' League, Interl. Steel and Copper Plate—†A. J. Marsh, Y. M. C. A., Orange, N. J.

Federal Employees Natl. Federation—†E. J. Newmyer, 1423 New York av., N. W., Washington, D. C.

Fire Fighters, Interl. Assn.—W. A. Smith, Washington, D. C.

Firemen, Interl. Brotherhood of Stationary—†C. L. Shamp, 3615 North 24th, Omaha, Neb.

Foundry Employees, Interl. Brotherhood—†G. Bechtold, Hill Bldg., 2604 Gravois av., St. Louis, Mo.

Fur Workers' Union of U. S. and Canada, Interl.—†A. Wennels, 9 Jackson av., L. I. City, N. Y.

Garment Workers of America, United—†B. A. Larger, Bible House, N. Y. C.

Garment Workers' Union, Interl. Ladies—†A. Baroff, 32 Union sq., N. Y. C.

Glass Bottle Blowers' Assn. of U. S. and Canada—H. Jenkins, Colonial Trust Co. Bldg., 13th and Walnut, Philadelphia, Pa.

Glass Workers' Union, American Flint—†C. J. Shipman, Ohio Bldg., Toledo, O.

Glass Workers, Window, Natl.—T. Reynolds, 419 Electric Bldg., Cleveland, O.

Glove Workers, Union of America, Interl.—†Elizabeth Christman, 64 W. Randolph, Chicago, Ill.

Granite Cutters' Interl. Assn. of America—*J. Duncan, 25 School, Quincy, Mass.

Hatters of North America, United—†M. Lawlor, 73 Bible House, N. Y. C.

Hod Carriers, Bldg. and Common Laborers' Union of America, Interl.—†A. Persion, 25 School, Quincy, Mass.

Horseshoers of U. S. and Canada, Interl. Union of Journeymen—†H. S. Marshall, 605 Second Natl. Bank Bldg., Cincinnati, O.

Hotel and Restaurant Employees' Interl. Alliance and Bartenders' Intl. League of America—†J. L. Sullivan, Commercial Tribune Bldg., Cincinnati, O.

Iron, Steel and Tin Workers, Amalgamated Assn.—†F. Keightly, House Bldg., Smithfield and Water, Pittsburg, Pa.

Jewelry Workers' Union, Interl.—†Abraham Greenstein, 63 Park Row, N. Y. C.

Lathers, Interl. Union of Wood, Wire and Metal J. B. Bowen, 401 Superior Bldg., Cleveland, O.

Laundry Workers' Interl. Union—†H. L. Morrison, Box 11, Station 1, Troy, N. Y.

Leather Workers, United, Interl. Union—†J. J. Pfeiffer, Postal Bldg., Kansas City, Mo.

Letter Carriers, Natl. Assn.—†E. J. Cantwell, Kenois Bldg., 11th and G Washington, D. C.

Letter Carriers' Natl. Federation of Rural—*J. R. Smith, Marshall, Mich.

Lithographers' Interl. Protective and Beneficial Assn. of U. S. and Canada—†J. M. O'Connor, Langdon Bldg., 309 B'way, N. Y. C.

Longshoremen's Assn., Interl.—†J. J. Joyce, Brisbane Bldg., Buffalo, N. Y.

Machinists, Interl. Assn.—†E. C. Davison, Washington, D. C.

Marble, Slate and Stone Polishers, Rubbers and Sawyers, Interl. Assn.—*S. C. Hogan, 446 E. 149th, N. Y. C.

Masters, Mates and Pilots, American Assn.—M. D. Tenniswood, 308 Vine, Camden, N. J.

Meat Cutters and Butcher Workmen of North America, Amalgamated—†D. Lane, 166 W. Washington, Chicago, Ill.

Metal Workers' Interl. Alliance, Amalgamated Sheet—†W. L. Sullivan, 122 South Ashland blvd., Chicago, Ill.

Mine, Mill and Smelter Workers, Interl. Union—†E. Mills, Denham Bldg., Denver, Col.

Mine Workers of America, United—†W. Green, Merchants Bank Bldg., Indianapolis, Ind.

Molders' Union of North America, Interl.—V. Kleiber, 530 Walnut, Cincinnati, O.

Musicians, American Federation—W. Kerngood, 3535 Pine, St. Louis, Mo.

Oil Field, Gas Well and Refinery Workers of America—†H. L. Hope, 208½ W. 112th, Ft. Worth, Tex.

Painters, Decorators and Paperhangers of America, Brotherhood—†J. C. Skemp, Drawer 99, Lafayette, Ind.

Paper Makers' Interl. Brotherhood—*J. T. Carey, 25 S. Hawk, Albany, N. Y.

Patrolmen Brotherhood of Railroad—†C. B. Thayer, 822 Ohio, Chicago, Ill.

Pattern Makers' League of North America—*J. Wilson, Rooms Second Natl. Bank Bldg., 9th and Main, Cincinnati, O.

Pavers, Rammermen, Flag Layers, Bridge and Stone Curb Setters, Interl. Union—E. I. Hannah, 240 E. 57th, N. Y. C.

Paving Cutters, Union of U. S. of America and Canada—C. Bergstrom, Lock Box 130, Rockport, Mass.

Piano and Organ Workers' Union of America, Interl.—*C. Dold, 166 W. Washington, Chicago, Ill.

Plasterers' Interl. Assn. of U. S. and Canada, Operative—†T. A. Scully, Castell Bldg., Middletown, O.

Plumbers and Steam Fitters of U. S. and Canada, United Assn.—†T. E. Burke, Bush Temple of Music, Chicago, Ill.

Polishers, Metal, Interl. Union—†C. R. Atherton, Neave Bldg., Cincinnati, O.

Potters, Natl. Brotherhood of Operative—†J. T. Wood, Box 6, East Liverpool, O.

Powder and High Explosive Workers of America, United—†H. A. Ellis, 503 S. Minnesota av., Columbus, Kan.

Print Cutters' Assn. of America, Natl.—R. Heinl, 124 North, Jersey City, N. J.

Printers and Color Mixers of U. S., Machine, Natl. Assn.—E. Gentzler, 1107 West Princess, York, Pa.

Printers' Union of North America, Inter'l. Steel and Copper Plate—J. E. Goodyear, 1630 W. Louden, Philadelphia, Pa.

Printing Pressmen's and Assistants' Union of North America, Internatl.—J. C. Orr, Sec., Pressmen's Home, Tenn.

Pulp, Sulphite and Paper Mill Workers of U. S. and Canada, Interl. Brotherhood—*J. P. Burke, P. O. Drawer K, Fort Edward, N. Y.

Quarryworkers, Interl. Union of North America—†F. W. Suitor, Scampini Bldg., Barre, Vt.

Railway Employees of America, Amalgamated Assn. of Street and Electric—*W. D. Mahon, 104 E. High, Detroit, Mich.

Railway Mail Assn.—*E. J. Ryan, 604 Colorado Bldg., Washington, D. C.

Roofers' Damp and Waterproof Workers' Assn. United Slate and Tile—†J. M. Gavlak, 3643 W. 47th, Cleveland, O.

Sawsmiths' Natl. Union—†H. Milan, 1234 Oxford, Indianapolis, Ind.

Seamen Union of America, Interl.—†T. A. Hanson, 355-359 North Clark, Chicago, Ill.

Signalmen of America, Brotherhood Railroad—†T. A. Austin, I. A. of M. Bldg., 9th and Mt. Vernon pl., Washington, D. C.

Stage Employees of America, Interl. Alliance of Theatrical—†F. G. Lemaster, 107 W. 46th, N. Y. C.

Stereotypers' and Electrotypers' Union of North America, Interl.—†C. A. Sumner, 3110 Olive, Kansas City, Mo.

Stonecutters' Assn. of North America, Journeymen—†J. Blasey, 528 American Central Life Bldg., Indianapolis, Ind.

Stove Mounters' Interl. Union—†F. Grimshaw, 1210 Jefferson av., East, Detroit, Mich.

Switchmen's Union of North America—†M. R. Welch, 39 North, Buffalo, N. Y.

Tailors' Union of America, Journeymen—T. Sweeney, cor. E. 67th and Stony Island av., Chicago, Ill.

Teachers, American Federation—*C. B. Stillman, 1620 Lake av., Wilmette, Ill.

Teamsters, Chauffeurs, Stablemen and Helpers of America, Interl. Brotherhood—†T. L. Hughes, 222 E. Michigan, Indianapolis, Ind.

Telegraphers, Order of Railroad—C. B. Rawlins, Star Bldg., St. Louis, Mo.

Telegraphers' Union of America, The Commercial—*R. H. Johnson, 113 S. Ashland blvd., Chicago, Ill.

Textile Workers of America, United—†S. A. Conboy, Bible House, N. Y. C.

Timber Workers, Interl. Union—†J. M. Norland, 202 Maynard Bldg., Seattle, Wash.

Tobacco Workers' Interl. Union—†E. Lewis Evans, 50-51 Iroquois Life Bldg., Louisville, Ky.

Transferrers' Assn of America, The Steel Plate—J. A. McCaskie, 65 North 11th, Newark, N. J.

*President. †Sec.-Treas.

LABOR UNIONS AND OFFICIALS—*Continued.*

Tunnel and Subway Constructors' Interl. Union —T. Pacelli, 162 E. 118th, N. Y. C.

Typographical Union, Interl.—†J. W. Hays, Newton Claypool Bldg., Indianapolis, Ind.

Upholsterers' Interl. Union of North America—*J. H. Hatch, 142 E 80th, N. Y. C.

Weavers' Amalgamated Assn., Elastic Goring—J. Hurley, 19 W. Ashland av., Brockton, Mass.

Weavers' Protective Assn., American Wire—†C. C. Bradley, 987 Halsey, Bkln., N. Y.

State Branches of the American Federation of Labor.

Alabama—L. Bowen, 910 Farley Bldg., Birmingham.

Arizona—T. A. French, 238 E. Washington, Phoenix.

Arkansas—L. H. Moore, 216 New Hollenberg Bldg., 5th and Scott, Little Rock.

California—P. Scharrenberg, Underwood Bldg., 525 Market, San Francisco.

Colorado—Ed. Anderson, Box 1108, Denver.

Connecticut—I. M. Ornburn, 215 Meadow, New Haven.

Florida—L. R. Campbell, Box 490, Miami.

Georgia—J. A. McCann, Box 890, Savannah.

Idaho—Al. Reynolds, Labor Temple, Boise.

Illinois—V. A. Olander, 164-166 W. Washington, Chicago.

Indiana—A. J. Fritz, 31-32 United Bldg., Indianapolis.

Iowa—E. C. Willey, StarPrinting Co., Sioux City.

Kansas—C. Hamlin, Labor Temple, Pittsburgh.

Kentucky—P. J. Campbell, Box 305, Louisville.

Louisiana—E. H. Swally, Box 291, Shreveport.

Maine—H. B. Brawn, Box 22, Augusta.

Maryland-District of Columbia—N. A. James, 606 5th, N. W., Washington, D. C.

Massachusetts—Martin T. Joyce, Rooms 12-13, Pemberton Bldg., Boston.

Michigan—J. J. Scannell, 766 Dickerson av., Detroit.

Minnesota—G. W. Lawson, 75 W. 7th, St. Paul.

Mississippi—J. W. Jones, Box 158, Meridian.

Missouri—F. W. Brand, Roth Bldg., St. Joseph.

Montana—J. T. Taylor, Gold Block, Helena.

Nebraska—F. M. Coffey, Box 886, Lincoln.

New Hampshire—C. H. Bean, Jr., 31 Chestnut, Franklin.

New Jersey—H. F. Hilfers, 16-18 Clinton, Newark.

New Mexico—J. J. Votew, 113 West Lead av., Albuquerque.

New York—E. A. Bates, 14 Jones Bldg., Utica.

North Carolina—C. G. Worley, Box 652, Asheville.

North Dakota—N. M. Aune, Box 299, Grand Forks.

Ohio—T. J. Donnelly, Columbus Savings and Trust Bldg., Columbus.

Oklahoma—G. B. Johnson, Baltimore Bldg., Oklahoma City.

Oregon—W. E. Kinsey, 412 Stock Exchange Bldg., Portland.

Pennsylvania—C. F. Quinn, M 1-3 Commonwealth Trust Co. Bldg., Harrisburg.

Porto Rico—Free Federation of Workingmen—R. Alonso, Box 807, San Juan.

Rhode Island—L. A. Grace, 37 Weybossett, Providence.

South Carolina—J. L. Davis, Room 500, Loan and Exchange Bank Bldg., Columbia.

Tennessee—W. C. Birthwright, 307½ 2d, N., Nashville.

Texas—R. McKinley, Box 417, Temple.

Utah—A. E. Harvey, Labor Temple, Salt Lake City.

Vermont—A. Ironside, 33 Ayers, Barre.

Virginia—J. Gribben, Labor Temple, Newport News.

Washington—L. W. Buck, Maynard Bldg., Seattle.

West Virginia—J. L. Pauley, Arcade, Charleston.

Wisconsin—J. J. Handley, 37 Metropolitan Block, Milwaukee.

Wyoming—W. A. James, Mine Workers Bldg., Cheyenne.

Federal Unions Chartered Direct by A. F. of L.

The following subordinate Federal unions in N. Y. have no parent internatl. union and hence are chartered direct by the A. F. of L.:

Artificial Limb Workers (N. Y.), W. Wagensell, 473 Harman, Bkln.

Awning and Tent Workers, F. Nold, 8 Orange, Buffalo.

Awning and Tent Workers, Max Opotheker, 53 Broome, N. Y. C.

*President. †Sec.-Treas.

Basket Makers Protective (N. Y.), J. Sekulski, 143 N. 8th, Bkln.

Bath Workers and Masseurs, D. J. Cole, 534 W. 178th, N. Y. C.

Bed Spring Makers, (Gr. N. Y.), B. Weinstein, 276 Marcy av., Bkln.

†Boilermakers' Helpers, G. W. Ford, 426 Liberty, Newburgh.

Bookkeepers, Stenographers and Accountants (N. Y. and vicinity), Miss Ann Hogan, 32 Union sq., N. Y. C.

Bkln. Navy Yard Laborers (Bkln.), W. B. Wyatt, 127 W. 141st, N. Y. C.

Brushmakers, G. A. Betz, 227 Manhattan av., Bkln.

Brushmakers, M. Schneicle, 81 Willet, N. Y. C.

Building Insp. Protective (Gr. N. Y.), J. Hopkins, 507 W. 186th, N. Y. C.

Button Workers, Ivory, Seth Clum, 181 N. Hamilton, Poughkeepsie.

Button Workers, Pearl, J. Kazatko, 512 E. 17th, N. Y. C.

Button Workers, Pearl, J. Cerny, 116 Grove, Winfield, L. I.

Button Workers, Ivory—A. Stanchi, 206 Skillman av., Bkln.

Cement Mill Workers, E. Smith, 48 Missouri, Glens Falls.

Chasers' Protective (N. Y.), A. Whalen, 1352 St. Marks av., Bkln.

City and County Public Service, S. Reilly, 101 W. 63d, N. Y. C.

Civil Service Inspectors (Gr. N. Y.), W. H. Scheer, 132 E. 127th, N. Y. C.

Cloth Examiners and Shrinkers (Gr. N. Y.), W. H. Roberts, 80 Edgecomb av., N. Y. C.

Coach and Car Cleaners, Minnie Johnson, 247 W. 137th, N. Y. C.

Cotton and Burlap Bag Makers, F. F. Kellerman, 351 42d, Bkln.

Crane Followers and Platform Workers, G. W. Briskie, 1020 Eastern av., Schenectady.

Cutters, United Neckwear, M. A. Ullmann, 123 E. 23d, N. Y. C.

Drivers and Tenders, Marine, E. Tuck, 456 E. 49th, N. Y. C.

Drug and Chemical Workers (Gr. N. Y.), J. Tucker, 47 Atlantic, Maspeth, L. I.

Egg Inspectors, M. Klinger, 326 Greenwich, N. Y. C.

Elevator Operators and Starters, D. N. Moore, 130 W. 132d, N. Y. C.

Elevator Starters and Operators (N. Y.), J. R. Elliott, 136 3d av., N. Y. C.

Fancy Feather and Flower Workers (Gr. N. Y.), Miss Clara Bodian, 328 S. 1st, Bkln.

Federal Labor, L. C. Gaiser, 1341 Michigan av., Niagara Falls.

Federal Labor, W. J. Davies, 1559 Steuben, Utica.

Federal Labor, F. Gildea, 397 Vliet, Cohoes.

Federal Labor, J. D. Harrington, Box 38, Hudson Falls.

Federal Labor, L. Barrone, 45 W. 3d, Dunkirk.

Federal Labor, M. Hall, 595 South Division, Buffalo.

Federal Labor, T. J. Thomas, 734 Armstrong av., Rome.

Federal Labor, I. J. Velzy, 8 Prospect, Silver Creek.

Federal Labor (N. Y.), C. Hoffman, 246 Grand, Maspeth, L. I.

Federal Labor (Beacon), F. Banks, Glenham.

‡Federal Labor (N. Y.), T. M. Rollins, Jr., 15 Wood pl., Yonkers.

Federal Labor, W. A. Costello, 65 North Lansing, Albany.

Federal Labor, E. Glassford, 125 Port Watson, Cortland.

Federal Labor, C. L. Sawyer, 1353 Lake, Elmira.

Felt, Panama and Straw Hat Trimmers and Operators, United; Minnie Teitlebaum, 7 E. 15th, N. Y. C.

Garage Workers, J. Walsh, 319 W. 58th, N. Y. C.

General Merchandise Packers and Porters, O. Haeuser, 228 E. 22d, N. Y. C.

Gold Beaters (Gr. N. Y. and vicinity), W. Quandt, 33 Wilton av., Glendale.

Hard Rubber Turners (N. Y.), P. Salley, 85 Sands, Bkln.

Hospital Attendants, Wm. Moritz, 414 E. 85th, N. Y. C.

Hospital Attendants, J. Power, Box 116, Central Islip, L. I.

Janitors, Schoolhouse, C. Hamcox, 22 Dow, Troy.

Janitors, Superintendents and Assistants, E. G. Klotsch, 302 W. 87th, N. Y. C.

Japanners and Sheet Metal Truckers, A. V. Gould, 521 Chrisler av., Schenectady.

LABOR UNIONS AND OFFICIALS—*Continued.*

Keepers and Matrons Assn., Dept. of Correction, J. F. Ryan, 82 W. 105th, N. Y. C.

Kodak and Film Workers, Irene Hoctor, 16 Holmes, Rochester.

Last Makers (N. Y.), R. Roche, 252 Midwood, Bkln.

Library Employees, Miss E. Wheclock, 540 W. 124th, N. Y. C.

Lumber Handlers (Gr. N. Y.), W. Roche, 123 Eckford, Bkln.

Metal Bed Workers, N. Verazub, care of Pritsky, 1420 Madison av., N. Y. C.

Moving Picture Theater Attendants, L. Simon, 77 Eldridge, N. Y. C.

Moving Picture Employes, L. Simon, 77 Eldridge, N. Y. C.

Neckwear Makers, United; Miss May Oberst, 7 E. 15th, N. Y. C.

Newspaper Carriers (Gr. N. Y.), M. Kellerman, 8525 B'way, N. Y. C.

Optical Workers, M. J. Murtha, 360 Hudson av., Rochester.

Ordnancemen's, G. Storch, 463 Shepherd, Bkln.

Packers and Shippers, F. E. McGann, 5 Eldredge, Hoosick Falls.

Paoor Plate and Bag Makers, M. Gordon, 71 E. 115th, N. Y. C.

Picture Frame Workers, United; R. Porter, 570 Teasdale pl., Bronx.

Pipe Caulkers and Repairers, W. Hanrahan, 51 Marvin, Buffalo.

Plate and Window Glass Handlers (N. Y.), J. Mininsohn, 732 Rockaway av., Bkln.

Potash Workers, J. A. Borey, 92 Broad, Albany.

Public School and Bldg. Cleaners (Gr. N. Y.), H. S. Pickenpack, 102 Douglas, Jamaica.

Public Service Employees, State; G. E. Suffern, Box 500, Elmira.

Rag and Paper Sorters, S. Culotto, 13 Monroe, N. Y. C.

Railway Station (N. Y.) **Porters and Cleaners**, G. J. Franklin, 45 North, White Plains.

Rubber Specialty Workers, Eva Dame, 33 1st, Hoosick Falls.

Rubber Workers, P. Anderson, 222 Skillman av., Bkln.

Sail Makers (Port of N. Y.), E. J. Rooney, 615 Gates av., Bkln.

Salt Workers, *A. L. Hovey, 310 8th, Watkins.

Sea Food Workers, United: F. Wilson, 231 E. 34th, N. Y. C.

Slate Workers, O. W. Jones, 23 Williams av., Granville.

Station Attendants, N. E. Snead, 25 15th, Corona, L. I.

Stenographers, Typewriters, Bookkeepers and Assistants, W. M. Mahoney, 322 Deer, Dunkirk.

Stenographers, Typewriters, Bookkeepers and Assistants, H. W. Stickney, 526 Page, Schenectady.

Stenographers, Typewriters, Bookkeepers and Assistants, G. E. Greenwood, 796 River, Troy.

Suspender Makers, M. Kenigsberg, 175 E. B'way, N. Y. C.

Tenement House Insp. (Gr. N. Y.), J. Bolger, 618 12th, Bkln.

Theater Employees, W. B. James, 1100 State, Schenectady.

Theatrical Doormen's (N. Y.), F. Rothenstein, 97 S. 8th, Bkln.

Theatrical Tailors and Dressers, A. Lippman, 226 Pennsylvania av., Bkln.

Theatrical Wardrobe Attendants, Mrs. M. Angle, 630 Eagle av., N. Y. C.

Trained Nurses, Rose Maxwell, 948 Bergen, Bkln.

Tuck Pointers' Protective (Buffalo), E. Faust, R. F. D. No. 4, Lockport.

Umbrella Handle and Stick Makers, United; S. Rearman, 175 E. B'way, N. Y. C.

Umbrella Workers, United; M. B. Fabian, 683 E. 23d, N. Y. C.

Ushers, Theater (Gr. N. Y. and vicinity), B. Weinstein, 276 Marcy av., Bkln.

Warehouse Employees, J. Scanlon, 333 E. 30th, N. Y. C.

Watchmen's (Schenectady), E. H. Garling, 47 Center, Ballston.

Watchmen's Protective, Port, J. J. Shea, 81 Horatio, N. Y. C.

Water Works Employees, D. J. Larkey, 185 3d av., Albany.

Window Cleaners' Protective, I. Demchuk, 217-19 E. 6th, N. Y. C.

Wire Sewers' Protective Assn. (N. Y.), Miss Sadie Fanning, 987 Halsey, Bkln.

Woolen and Cotton Clip Sorters, A. Silverman, 151 Clinton, N. Y. C.

---

*President.

New York State Federation of Labor.

Affiliated with the A. F. of L. 1864. Pres., James P. Holland, 229 E. 47th, Mhtn.; Vice-Prests., Theo. M. Guerin, Troy; Thos. J. Curtis, N. Y. C.; Geo. C. King, Buffalo; Emanuel Koveleski, Rochester; Jos. A. Mullaney, Elmhurst, L. I.; J. Dehan, N. Y. C.; H. A. Engle, Schenectady; J. Sullivan, N. Y. C.; J. C. Imhof, N. Y. C.; Wm. F. Kehoe, N. Y. C.; Miss Nellie Kelly, Syracuse; Sec.-Treas., E. A. Bates, 14 Jones Bldg., Utica; Legislative Committee—Thos. D. Fitzgerald, Albany, Ch.; William R. Ferguson, Oneida; M. Schiebeling, Schenectady; J. M. O'Hanlon, Troy, Wm. E. Brown, Utica. Legal Adviser, F. X. Sullivan, 46 Cedar, Mhtn. Legislative Committee Hdqtrs., Rm. 223, Arkay Bldg., Albany. Education Committee—P. J. Brady, Ch., 812 Municipal Bldg., Mhtn. Prison Committee—J. J. Mulholland, Ch., 190 Bowery, Mhtn. Health Committee—J. M. Lynch, Ch., 223 Arkay Bldg., Albany.

Allied Printing Trades Council of N. Y. State.

P. J. Brady, Pres., Photo Engr. Union, 924 Pulitzer Bldg.; D. Ahearn, V.-Pres., Paper Cutters' Union, 502 Pulitzer Bldg.; F. Tague, Typographical Union, Syracuse; J. McArdle, V.-Pres., Mailers' Union, 924 Pulitzer Bldg., N. Y.; F. W. Wells, V.-Pres., Pressmen's Union, Rochester; L. DeVeze, V.-Pres., Stereotypers' Union, N. Y.; J. C. Boyer, V.-Pres., Electrotypers' Union, N. Y.; M. J. Nicholson, V.-Pres., Photo Engr. Union, N. Y.; Wm. J. Walsh, V.-Pres., Electrical Workers, N. Y.; J. P. Burke, V.-Pres., Int. Bro. P. S. & P. M. W., Fort Edward, N. Y.; J. T. Carey, V.-Pres., Int. Bro. of Paper Makers, Albany, N. Y.; J. L. Hartnett, Sec.-Treas., Typographical Union, 2649 6th av., Troy; E. W. Edwards, Organizer, Int. Printing Pressmen and Assts. Union, 924 Pulitzer Bldg.

Allied Printing Trades Council of N. Y. City.

Meets 4th Thurs. at 6 P.M. at Rm. 923, World Bldg. L. DeVeze, Pres.; D. Ahearn, Vice-Pres.; S. G. Kelly, Sec.; J. McArdle, Treas.; F. Katsch, Sergt.-at-Arms; Wm. Doerr, J. Brosnan, M. Apy, J. P. Mines, C. Daly, Trustees. Affiliated unions and secretaries—Photo Engr. Union No. 1, R. Lee, 502 Pulitzer Bldg.; Typographical Union No. 6, J. O'Connell, 616 Pulitzer Bldg.; Typographical Union No. 7 (German), W. Osterman, 16 No. William; Typographical Union No. 83 (Jewish), A. Feigin, 211 E. B'way; Typographical Union No. 131 (Bohemian), C. Jerabek, 304 E. 70th; Typographical Union No. 261 (Italian), U. Penza, 295 Lafayette; Typographical Union No. 440 (Hungarian), A. Szego, 937 E. 181st; Mailers No. 6, C. Gallagher, 924 Pulitzer Bldg.; Stereotypers No. 1, Wm. Walsh, 924, Pulitzer Bldg.; Pressmen (Web) No. 25, I. Rosenthal, 527, Pulitzer Bldg.; Pressmen (Cylinder) No. 51, J. E. Donnelly, 150 Nassau; Job Press and Platen No. 1, F. Cafferty, 150 Nassau; Press Feeders No. 23, 150 Nassau; Bookbinders Nos. 1-3, F. Langdon, Bible House, N. Y. C.; Bookbinders No. 6 (blank book workers), J. Nevins, 504 Pulitzer Bldg.; Bookbinders No. 9 (Paper Rulers), E. Brereton, 504 Pulitzer Bldg.; Bindery Women's Union No. 43, Miss Margaret Reynolds, 403 World Bldg.; Paper Cutters No. 119, Wm. E. Platt, 504 Pulitzer Bldg.; Paper Handlers No. 1, A. G. Hayes, 510 Pulitzer Bldg.; Stampers and Goldlayers No. 22, J. Wortman, 41 E. 29th; N. Y. Ink Workers No. 2, 150 Nassau, J. B. Ritchey; Polish Typographical Union No. 816, W. J. Mackiewicy, Grand, nr. Elm Grove Park, Maspeth, N. Y.; Hellenic Typographical Union No. 8[illegible] D. Lalos, 423 E. 52d.

Central Union Label Council.

Composed of unions having labels, stamps, buttons, shop or store cards to designate their products. Meets Bldg. Trades Hall, 12th, 1st Monday in each month, at 8 P.M. Geo. Behrerd, Pres.; C. E. Sinnigen, Sec., Rm. 512A, 367-73 Fulton, Bkln. Dist. Council No. 1. S. Schwartz, Sec., 902-4 B'way, Bkln.; meets at Bkln. Labor Lyceum, 949 Willoughby av., 2d and 4th M., 8 P.M.

Unaffiliated Organizations.

Brotherhood Locomotive Engineers—W. S. Stone, Pres., B. of L. E. Bldg., Cleveland, Ohio.

Brotherhood of Locomotive Firemen and Enginemen—*Timothy Shea, 901 Guardian Bldg., Cleveland, O.

Brotherhood of Railroad Trainmen—A. E. King, American Trust Bldg., Cleveland, Ohio.

Order of Railway Conductors of America—C. E. Whitney, The Masonic Temple, Cedar Rapids, Iowa.

LABOR UNIONS AND OFFICIALS—*Continued.*

Knights of Labor.

General Master Workman, J. W. Hayes, 615 F, N. W., Washington, D. C. General Worthy Foreman, W. A. Denison, 615 F, N. W., Washington, D. C. General Sec.-Treas., F. W. Borhill, 615 F. N. W., Washington, D. C.

National Women's Trade Union League.

Hdqtrs., 64 W. Randolph, Chicago, Ill. Pres., Mrs. Raymond Robins, Chicago; Vice-Pres., Rose Schneidermann, Mhtn.; Sec.-Treas., Emma Steghagen, Chicago.

Central Board of Allied Bookbinding Leagues of New York City.

Meets at Rm. 504, World Bldg., 3d Monday, 6 P.M. Pres., Jeremiah Ryan, Rm. 504, World Bldg.; Sec., D. J. Ahearn, Rm. 504, World Bldg.

City Central Unions of the State.

Albany—Central Federation of Labor, J. J. Dillon, Sec., 45 2d.
Amsterdam—Central Labor Union, Mrs. F. J. Goller, 59 Arnold av.
Auburn—Central Labor Union, T. H. Mohan, Sec., 61 Steele.
Batavia—Central Labor Union, E. J. Deffner, 135 Bank.
Binghamton—Central Labor Union, J. Ryan, 77 State.
Buffalo—Central Labor Council, G. W. Bork, Sec., 385 Ellicott.
Cohoes—Cent. F. of L., E. J. Allen, 36 Hoosick, Troy.
Corinth—Central Trades and Labor Assembly, C. E. Salisbury, Box 150.
Corning—Central Labor Union, E. H. Painter, 323 E. Tioga av.
Cortland—Central Trades and Labor Assembly, M. F. Bolt, 61 Owego.
Dunkirk and Vicinity—United Trades and Labor Council, Emil Hagberg, Sec., 329 Deer.
Elmira—Central Trades and Labor Assembly, G. E. Reedy, 503 Wells.
Fort Edward—Trades Assembly, Henry Hussard, Sec., Box 100.
Fulton—Trades and Labor Assembly.
Geneva—F. of L., M. F. Tracy, Box 162.
Glens Falls—Central Trades and Labor Assembly, M. D. Foley, 18 Stewart av.
Gloversville—Central Labor Union, N. Van Valkenburgh, Sec., 16½ Elm.
Hoosick Falls—Central Labor Union, T. J. Davock, 9 White.
Hornell—Central Labor Union, E. E. Knapp.
Ithaca—Central Labor Union, W. D. Hammond, Sec., Box 186.
Jamestown—Central Labor Council, H. A. Hartman, Sec., Box 462.
Kingston—Central Trades and Labor Council, F. Richardson, Sec., 233 Smith av.
Lackawanna—Central Labor Union, A. Kiefer, 108 Cherry.
Lancaster—Central Labor Union, J. H. Wright, Sec., 39 School.
Little Falls—Trades Assembly, J. McCarthy.
Lockport—Central Labor Union, J. L. Smith, 222 South.
Middletown—Central Labor Union, J. F. Walsh, 78 Wisner av.
Mt. Kisco—Central Labor Union, J. L. Fishbaugh.
Mt. Vernon—Central Labor Union, H. Wildberger, Jr., 119 S. High.
Newburgh—Central Labor Union, Miss Emma McCauley, Sec., 150 B'way.
New Rochelle—Central Labor Union, J. Chambers, 617 S. 7th av., Mt. Vernon.
New York—Central Trades and Labor Council, John Sullivan, Pres.; W. F. Kehoe, Sec., 107 W. 47th.
Niagara Falls—Trades and Labor Council, W. J. Boeldt, 1629 10th.
Norwich Trades Assembly, W. J. McGrugan, 33 Canassawata.
Ogdensburg—Trades and Labor Council, G. E. Farley, Sec., 56 Albany av.
Olean—Trades and Labor Council, D. Burleigh, Box 401.
Oneida—Trades Assembly, L. C. Woodcock, 46 Seneca.
Oneonta—Trades and Labor Council, J. Meader, Box 302.
Oswego—United Trades and Labor Assembly, E. M. Benzing, 114 E. 1st.
Peekskill—Trades and Labor Council, Robert Cross, 660 Main.
Plattsburg—Trades and Labor Assembly, A. A. Commo, 4 Margarette.
Port Jervis—Central Labor Union, C. E. Dailey, 56 Hudson.
Poughkeepsie—Trades and Labor Council, Miss E. M. Berrigan, 11 Morrison.
Rochester—Central Trades and Labor Council, W. L. Burke, 28½ Jefferson av.
Rome—Central Labor Union, N. McCraig, Sec., 500 Robert.
Salamanca—Central Labor Union, P. J. Meyers, 640 Broad.
Saranac Lake—Central Labor Union, J. J. Murphy, 105 B'way.
Saratoga Springs—Central Labor Union, J. H. Brainard, 9 Pavilion pl.
Schenectady—Trades Assembly, F. A. Soellner, Sec., 9 Howard.
Syracuse—Central Trades and Labor Assembly, H. M. Woodard, Sec., 476 S. Salina.
Tonawanda—Central Labor Union, R. Cramer, 271 Oliver, N. Tonawanda.
Troy—Central Federation of Labor, T. J. Purcell, Sec., Federation Hall.
Utica—Trades and Labor Assembly, J. Brown, Sec., 1120 Downer av.
Walden—Central Labor Union, *Nathaniel Nutt, Walden P. O.
Watertown—Central Trades and Labor Assembly, O. A. Badcock.
White Plains—Central Labor Union, E. W. Berges, Sec., 35 Grove.
Yonkers—Federation of Labor, J. B. Towers, 173 Stanley av.

Central Organizations of Labor in Metropolitan District.

BROOKLYN.

Board of Delegates of the Building Trades of Bkln. and L. I.—196 State. 2d and 4th Fr., 10 A.M. Sec., Charles Burns, Rm. 500, Arbuckle Bldg.

Cigarmakers Int. Label League of Bkln.—926 B'way, Tu. Sec., Wm. Strauss, 926 B'way.

Combined Assn. of Engineers—W. F. Brundage, Sec., 316 8th.

District Assembly No. 220, K. of L.—3 Ralph av., 3d Th., 8 P.M. Master Workman, John McCarthy, 3249 Fulton; Sec., C. Hill, 240 9th av.

Painters and Decorators Dist. Council No. 29—10 DeKalb av. Sec., Thomas McCall, 98 King.

Shoe Workers Joint Council No. 7—Waverly Hall, Th. Sec., David Joseph, 80 Reid av.

Steam and Operating Engineers Exec. Board—Temple Bar. Sec., W. M. Gavan, 644 Bushwick av.

BRONX.

Board of Representatives of Building Trades—Tremont and 3d avs., Th., 10 A.M. Sec., J. P. McGrane, Arthur Bldg.

MANHATTAN.

Bakery and Confectionery Workers Joint Bd.—210 5th. Sec., J. H. Hesse, 231 E. 26th.

Boilermakers Dist. Council No. 2—G. A. Daly, 37 Cortlandt, Mhtn.

Brewery Workmen's Joint Council—243 E. 84th, Mhtn., and 945 Willoughby av., Bkln., alt. Th., 8 P.M. Sec., C. Weyell, 243 E. 84th.

Bricklayers, Masons and Plasterers Exec. Committee—36th and 9th av., F., 8 P.M. Sec., Thomas Murray, 1217 Bryant av., Bronx.

Butchers' Dist. Council No. 2 (Brotherhood)—200 E. 45th. J. Pfeiffer, Sec.

Cigarmakers Label Committee—953 3d av. Sec., D. Levy.

Coopers' Internatl. Union Joint Executive Bd.—243 E. 84th. Sec., Albert Streicher, 1476 St. Lawrence av.

Dis. Council No. 1 of Pavers, Rammermen, Wood Block, Brick and Iron Slag Pavers, Flag-Layers, Bridge and Stone Curb Setters of Gr. N. Y. and Vic.—249 E. 57th, N. Y. C.; J. E. Pritchard, Pres.; Chas. Martin, Sec.

Executive Council United Board Business Agents of Bldg Trades of Gr. N. Y., 953 3d av., Mhtn., 4th M., 2 P.M.

Internatl. Brotherhood of Teamsters and Chauffeurs Dist. Council No. 16—107 W. 47th. 2d Tu., 8 P.M. T. J. Lyons, Sec., 572 16th, Bkln.

Internatl. Cigarmakers Joint Advisory Bd.—Sec., J. C. Hilsdorf, 509 E. 88th.

Internatl. Molders Union Conference Board—67 St. Marks pl., 1st and 3d Sa., 8 P.M. Sec., Bernard Kelly, 19 Park Row.

Internatl. Union of Steam Engineers Joint Executive Bd., 166 E. 60th, 1st M., 8 P.M. Sec., Robert Ross, 2078 Walton av.

LABOR UNIONS AND OFFICIALS—*Continued.*

Joint Board United Brotherhood of Tailors—142 2d av., Mhtn.. F., at 8 P.M. Sec.-Treas., Joseph Schlossberg, 89 Delancey.

Joint Executive Bd. of Hotel Employees—121 2d av., M. Sec., A. Toby, 121 2d av.

Laborers Union Protective Soc. General Council—229 E. 47th, 1st and 3d M., 8 P.M. Sec., M. Sullivan, 229 E. 47th.

Longshoremen's Union Protective Assn. Executive Board—164 10th av., 2d and 4th Su., 2 P.M. Sec., D. Sullivan, 259 9th av.

Metal Polishers, Buffers, etc., Internatl. Union Dist. Council No. 1—25 3d av., 1st and 3d Th. Sec., J. T. Cortello.

National Labor Council, Inc.—Subdiv. No. 1, Labor Council of Gr. N. Y. and Vic.—7 E. 15th, N. Y. 2d and 4th Su. at 10 A.M.

N. Y. Building Trades Council, A. F. of L.—12 St. Marks pl. Sec., R. D. Tompkins.

Piano and Organ Workers Joint Bd.—1551 2d av., 3d M. Sec., John Walz, 488 14th av., L. I. City.

Sheet Metal Workers Dist. Council—Sec., G. Park, 33 Tichenor pl., Montclair, N. J. Meets 24 Union sq., Mhtn.

United Assn. of Plumbers and Gasfitters Dist. Council—305 8th av. Sec., H. McGowan, 422 E. 77th.

United Bd. of Business Agents—12 St. Marks pl. Tu. and F., 10 A.M. Sec., R. D. Tompkins, 154 E. 54th.

United Brotherhood of Carpenters and Joiners Joint Dist. Council of Gr. N. Y.—142 E. 59th, 1st and 3d W., 8 P.M. Sec.-Treas., E. H. Neal, 142 E. 53d.

United Hebrew Trades—175 E. B'way, M., 8 P.M. Sec., M. Finestone.

Women's Trade Union League—7 E. 15th. 1st M. Pres., Rose Schneidermann.

QUEENS.

Board of Representatives of the Bldg. Trades of Queens, Nassau and Suffolk, 374 Jackson av., L. I. City, W., 8 P.M. Sec., Charles Burns, 374 Jackson av., L. I. City.

Brotherhood of Painters, Decorators and Paperhangers, Dist. Council No. 28—274 Fulton, Jamaica, W. Sec., Jacob Ziegler, 151½ 5th av., L. I. City.

RICHMOND.

Central Trades and Labor Council—Sec., T. H. Fischer, 16 Clinton, Tompkinsville.

NORTH HEMPSTEAD.

United Brotherhood of Carpenters and Joiners, Dist. Council—Odd Fellows Hall, Fort Washington, 2d and 4th F. Sec., Charles L'Hommedieu, Jr., Manhasset, L. I.

National Association of Manufacturers.

Pres., S. C. Mason; Sec., G. S. Boudinot; Treas., Henry Abbott; Gen. Mgr., J. P. Bird. Hdqrs., 50 Church, N. Y. "The Natl. Assn. of Mfrs. disapproves absolutely of strikes and lockouts and favors an equitable adjustment of all differences between employers and employees by any amicable method that will preserve rights of both parties. Employees have the right to contract for their services in a collective capacity, but any contract that contains a stipulation that employment should be denied to men not parties to the contract is an invasion of the constitutional rights of Amer. workmen, is against public policy, and is in violation of conspiracy laws. This assn. declares its unalterable antagonism to the closed shop and insists that the doors of no industry be closed against American workmen because of their membership or non-membership in any labor organization."

Building Trades Employers' Association of the City of New York.

Pres., Ronald Taylor; 1st Vice-Pres., F. B. Tuttle; 2d Vice-Pres., A. N. Chambers; Treas., M. F. Westergren; Chairman Bd. of Governors, C. J. Kelly; Sec., S. B. Donnelly, 34 W. 33d.

MERCHANT MARINE OF THE UNITED STATES.

(From the reports of the Bureau of Navigation.)

Year.	In Foreign Trade.		In Coastwise Trade.		Whale Fisheries.		Cod and Mackerel Fisheries.	Total.	Annual inc. (+) or dec. (—).
	Steam.	Total.	Steam.	Total.	Steam.	Total.			
	Tons	Tons.	Tons.	Tons.	Tons.	Tons.	Tons.	Tons.	Per cent.
1860	97,296	2,379,000	770,641	2,644,867	.....	166,841	162,764	5,353,868	+ 4.06
1870	192,544	1,448,840	882,551	2,638,247	.....	67,954	91,460	4,246,507	+ 2.41
1880	146,604	1,314,402	1,064,954	2,637,686	.....	38,408	77,538	4,068,034	— 2.43
1890	192,705	928,062	1,661,458	3,409,435	4,925	18,638	68,367	4,424,497	+ 2.71
1900	337,356	816,795	2,289,825	4,286,516	3,986	9,899	51,629	5,164,839	+ 6.18
1910	533,468	782,517	4,330,896	6,668,966	3,509	9,308	47,291	7,508,082	+ 1.61
1911	582,186	863,495	4,505,567	6,720,313	3,544	9,176	45,806	7,638,790	+ 1.74
1912	616,053	923,225	4,543,276	6,737,046	3,653	8,876	45,036	7,714,183	+ 0.99
1913	667,896	1,019,165	4,646,741	6,817,013	3,252	8,611	15,573	7,886,551	+ 2.23
1914	720,609	1,066,288	4,688,240	6,818,363	4,265	9,864	26,700	7,928,688	+ 2.23
1915	1,346,164	1,862,714	4,578,567	6,486,384	3,682	8,829	15,397	8,389,429	+ 5.49
1916	1,573,705	2,185,008	4,315,579	6,244,550	1,789	6,707	33,384	8,469,649	+ 0.95
1917	1,855,484	2,440,776	4,559,008	6,392,583	2,250	5,623	32,055	8,871,037	+ 4.74
1918	3,013,603	3,599,213	4,433,337	6,282,474	2,178	4,493	38,338	9,924,518	+11.87
1919	5,992,028	6,065,376	4,395,701	6,201,426	2,177	4,350	36,148	12,907,300	+30.05
1920	9,193,001	9,924,694	4,596,470	6,357,706	1,921	3,901	37,723	16,324,024	+26.47

VESSELS BUILT IN THE UNITED STATES.

Year.	New England coast.		On entire seaboard.		*Miss. and tributaries.		On Great Lakes.		Total*		Sail.		Steam and gas.	
	No.	Tons.	No.	Tons.	No.	Tons.	No.	Tons.	No.	Tons.	No.	Tons.	No.	Tons.
1890	208	78,577	756	169,091	104	16,506	191	108,526	1,051	294,123	505	102,873	418	159,045
1900	199	72,179	1,107	249,006	215	14,173	125	130,611	1,447	393,790	504	116,460	422	202,528
1910	111	23,442	887	167,829	193	5,488	281	168,751	1,361	342,068	127	19,358	936	257,993
1911	94	23,653	1,004	190,612	202	6,398	216	94,157	1,422	291,162	82	10,092	969	227,231
1912	95	23,052	1,076	136,485	206	5,286	224	90,898	1,505	232,669	95	21,221	1,051	153,493
1913	95	27,131	1,022	247,318	234	7,930	219	90,907	1,475	346,155	72	28,610	1,004	243,408
1914	79	21,934	887	251,683	133	8,018	131	56,549	1,151	316,250	51	13,749	778	224,225
1915	89	18,551	.777	184,605	144	5,499	147	16,467	1,157	225,122	51	8,021	751	154,990
1916	62	37,568	609	238,181	140	4,973	126	44,691	937	325,413	34	14,765	624	250,125
1917	84	52,526	993	518,958	157	6,185	147	139,336	1,297	664,479	64	43,185	801	513,243
1918	105	88,302	1,225	1080,437	135	5,409	168	215,022	1,528	1300,868	115	83,629	929	1090,996
1919	146	177,758	1,529	2875,733	107	3,716	317	507,172	1,953	3326,621	84	79,234	1,524	3157,091
1920	131	208,023	1,615	3475,872	185	10,300	267	394,467	2,067	3880,639	115	132,184	1,678	3660,023

*Including canal boats and barges.

Of the world's shipping, 16.3 per cent. are oil-burners, coal-burners 76 per cent., internal combustion engines 1.7 per cent. and 6 per cent. sail, according to Lloyd's Register of Shipping.

The Panama Canal is now self-sustaining. During the last fiscal year the total operating expenses were $6,548,272, and receipts were $8,935,871.

RELIGIOUS DENOMINATIONS.

Baptist.

Northern Baptist Convention, organized 1907. Members, 1,285,416; churches, 9,101; value of church property, $32,990,600. D. C. Shull, Pres., Sioux City, Iowa; Rev. M. A. Levy, Sec., Pittsfield, Mass.

Baptist Missionary Convention of State of N. Y. (State Missions)—276 5th av., Mhtn. Rev. Wm. A. Granger, Pres.; Rev. E. B. Richmond, Sec.; O. R. Judd, Treas. 186,769 mem.; 987 churches.

Christian Science.

Discoverer and founder, Mary Baker Eddy. The Mother Church of the denomination, The First Church of Christ, Scientist, is in Boston, Mass. Churches throughout the world are branches of this church. There are 1,800 churches and societies in this and foreign lands.

Congregational.

Natl. Council of Cong. Churches of U. S.—Org. 1871 at Oberlin, O.; Hdqtrs., 287 Fourth av., N. Y. C.; Rev. H. Churchill King, D.D., Oberlin, O., Mod.; Rev. R. A. Hume, D.D., India, Asst. Mod.; Rev. W. N. De Berry, D.D., Springfield, Mass., Asst. Mod.; F. F. Moore, N. Y. C., Treas. 808,122 mem. in the U. S.; 728,619 Sunday School scholars; 808,266 ministers; 5,959 churches; $3,756,986, benevolent contributions: $12,195,872, home expenditures; aggregate salaries of pastors, $5,891,280; average, $1,431; aggregate value of property, 5,495 churches, $104,661,812; invested funds of 1,780 churches, $13,638,285; debts of 1,023 churches, $3,442,256; number of churches having parsonages, 2,961; number of churches receiving missionary aid, 1,161.

New York Cong. Conference—Org. 1834. Hon. Clark H. Hammond, Buffalo; Rev. Willard P. Harmon, Sec., Ticonderoga; Rev. Chas. W. Shelton, Treas., 287 4th av., Mhtn. Meeting in 1921, Plymouth Ch., Syracuse, May 17, 18, 19.

Evangelical.

German Evangelical Synod of North America—Rev. J. Baltzer, Pres., 6328 Emma av., St. Louis, Mo.; Rev. A. H. Becker, V.-Pres., New Orleans, La.; Rev. G. Fischer, Sec., 671 Madison, Milwaukee, Wis.; Rev. H. Bode, Treas., 1714 N. Euclid av., St. Louis, Mo.; 1,390 congregations in 19 districts; 1,131 ministers; 47 teachers in parochial schools; 269,842 communicants; 132,669 Sunday School scholars; value of church property, $20,258,847; new church buildings, $658,900; paid debts on churches, $384,591.

Latter Day Saints.

Church of Jesus Christ of Latter Day Saints—Org. April 6, 1830. Hdqtrs., Salt Lake City, Utah. Heber J. Grant, Pres. Total number of members in world, upward of 600,000. Sunday School members, 250,000. Missionaries (exclusive of those working in home churches), about 1,600. Eastern State Hdqtrs., 273 Gates av., Bkln.; Geo. W. McCune, Pres.; Jos. G. Jensen, Sec., 273 Gates av.

Lutheran.

United Lutheran Church in America. Organized in N. Y. City, Nov., 1918. Office, 437 5th av., Mhtn. Rev. F. H. Knubel, D.D., LL.D., Pres., N. Y. City; Rev. M. G. G. Scherer, D.D., Sec., N. Y. C.; E. Clarence Miller, Treas., Philadelphia, Pa., 42 synods, 2,755 ministers, 3,750 congregations, 782,807 communicants, 1,058,398 baptized members, 457,357 S. S. scholars. Value of church property, $57,519,334. 11 theological seminaries, 6 academies, 14 colleges, 11 orphans' homes, 10 homes for the aged, 1 home for defectives, 8 deaconess' motherhouses and 4 hospitals. Evangelical Lutheran Synod of New York and New England—Saml. G. Trexler, D.D., Pres., 16 E. 48th, Mhtn.; Hy. C. Erbes, Sec., 69 Grape, Rochester, N. Y. New York Ministerium, United Luth. Ch. in Amer.—Rev. O. Krauch, Pres., Buffalo, N. Y.; Rev. T. Posselt, Sec., 1343 Fulton av., Bronx; Rev. J. F. Holstein, Treas., 77 Midwood, Bkln. New York Conference of the New York Ministerium—Rev. J. G. F. Blaesi, Pres., 1077 Dean, Bkln.; Rev. F. Noeldeke, Sec., 762 E. 219th, Bronx.

Methodist Episcopal.

Bishops of the Methodist Episcopal Church—W. F. Anderson, Cincinnati, O.; Anton Bast, Copenhagen, Denmark; J. F. Berry, Philadelphia, Pa.; G. H. Bickley, Singapore, S. S.; L. J. Birney, Shanghai, China; Edgar Blake, Paris, France; F. M. Bristol, Chattanooga, Tenn.; C. W. Burns, Helena, Mont.; William Burt, Buffalo, N. Y.; M. W. Clair, Monrovia, Liberia; R. J. Cooke, Athens, Tenn.; Earl Cranston, New Portsmouth, O.; F. B. Fisher, Calcutta, India; J. W. Hamilton, Washington, D. C.; M. C. Harris, Tokyo, Japan; J. C. Hartzell, Blue Ash, O.; T. S. Henderson, Detroit, Mich.; E. H. Hughes, Boston, Mass.; E. S. Johnson, Cape Town, Africa; R. E. Jones, New Orleans, La.; F. T. Keeney, Foochow, China; F. D. Leete, Indianapolis, Ind.; A. W. Leonard, San Francisco, Cal.; E. C. Locke, Manila, P. I.; W. S. Lewis, Peking, China; F. J. McConnell, Pittsburgh, Pa.; W. F. McDowell, Washington, D. C.; C. L. Mead, Denver, Col.; O. B. Mitchell, St. Paul, Minn.; Thomas Nicholson, Chicago, Ill.; Thomas Neely, Philadelphia, Pa.; J. L. Nuelsen, Zurich, Switzerland; W. F. Oldham, Buenos Ayres, Argentina, S. A.; Mr. Quayle, St. Louis, Mo.; E. G. Richardson, Atlanta, Ga.; J. E. Robinson, India; J. W. Robinson, Bombay, India; W. O. Shepard, Portland, Ore.; Isaiah B. Scott, Nashville, Tenn.; H. Lester Smith, Bangalore, India; Homer C. Stuntz, Omaha, Neb.; W. P. Thirkield, Mexico City, Mexico; J. M. Thoburn, Meadville, Pa.; F. W. Warne, Lucknow, India; E. L. Waldorf, Wichita, Kan.; Herbert Welch, Seoul, Korea; L. B. Wilson, New York City.

District Superintendents of the Methodist Episcopal Church, New York area—New York Conference—G. W. Grinton, Kingston, N. Y.; H. E. Wright, Newburgh, N. Y.; Wallace MacMullen, 150 5th av., New York City; G. A. MacDonald, Poughkeepsie, N. Y. New York East Conference—W. L. Davison, 20 7th av., Bkln., N. Y.; J. H. Bell, 504 Whitney av., New Haven, Conn.; W. H. Kidd, West Park, Stamford, Conn.; A. S. Kavanagh, 352 Clinton av., Bkln., N. Y. Newark Conference—T. G. Spencer, 224 Prospect, Westfield, N. J.; J. R. Wright, 161 Harrison av., Jersey City, N. J.; F. C. Baldwin, 500 Park av., East Orange, N. J.; C. C. Woodruff, 390 Park av., Paterson, N. J. East German Conference—John Lutz, 3714 Av. D, Bkln., N. Y.; Henry Vollberg, 713 Garden, Hoboken, N. J. Eastern Swedish Conference—Herman Young, 47 E. 31st, Bkln., N. Y.; Albert Hallen, 30 Glen, Malden, Mass.; H. E. Wyman, 9 Webster, Malden, Mass. Oliver S. Baketel, 150 5th av., New York City., Editor, Methodist Year Book and General Minutes. Total membership, Methodist Episcopal Church, 4,179,522; total ministers, 20,151; church buildings, 29,834; Sunday School scholars, 4,324,458; value of church and parsonage property (exclusive of schools), $278,119,493.

Methodist Protestant.

Officers of the Gen. Conference of the Methodist Protestant Church (natl. body)—Rev. T. H. Lewis, D.D., LL.D., 2844 Wisconsin av., Washington, D. C., Pres.; Rev. C. H. Beck, D.D., 219 6th, Pittsburgh, Pa., Sec. There are two annual conference dists. with churches in N. Y. State: Eastern Conference, Rev. F. W. Varney, D.D., White Plains, N. Y., Pres.; Rev. B. F. Day, D.D., Inwood, L. I., Sec. The Onondaga Conference, Rev. E. D. Ridgeway, Richfield Springs, N. Y., Pres.; Rev. J. H. Richards, Arkport, N. Y., Sec.

Presbyterian.

Officers of the General Assembly of the Presbyterian Church in the United States of America—Office, 515 Witherspoon Bldg., Phila., Pa. Rev. S. S. Palmer, D.D., Mod., Columbus, O. Office of Stated Clerk, vacant. 40 synods, 288 Presbyteries, 9,924 ministers, 9,769 churches, 1,637,105 communicants, 1,351,260 Sunday School members, $43,071,072 total contributions.

• Protestant Episcopal.

Domestic and Foreign Missionary Soc. of the Prot. Epis. Church in the U. S. of Amer. Hdqtrs., Church Mission House, 281 4th av., N. Y. C.

Diocesan House of L. I., 170 Remsen, Bkln.

The Protestant Episcopal Church consists of 69 dioceses and, including Panama, of 21 Missionary Dists. within the U. S. and their possessions, under the care of 119 Bishops, as follows (Title, Rt. Rev.). Alabama, C. M. Beckwith, Montgomery; Albany, R. H. Nelson, Albany, N. Y.; Arkansas, J. R. Winchester, Little Rock; E. T. Demby, Bishop Suff.; E. W. Saphore, Suffragan, Little Rock; Atlanta (Georgia), H. J. Mikell, Atlanta; Bethlehem (Penn.), E. Talbot, So. Bethlehem; California, W. F. Nichols, San Francisco; E. L. Parsons, Bishop Coad.; Central New York, C. T. Olmsted, Utica; Coad., C. Fiske, Syracuse; Chicago, C. P. Anderson; S. M. Griswold, Suff., Chicago; Colorado, Den., I. P. Johnson; Connecticut, C. B. Brewster, Hartford; Suffragan, E. C. Acheson, Middletown, Conn.; Dallas (Texas), A. C. Garrett, Dallas; H. T. Moore, Coad., Dallas; Delaware, vacant; Duluth (Minn.),

RELIGIOUS DENOMINATIONS—PROTESTANT EPISCOPAL—*Continued.*

J. D. Morrison, Duluth: East Carolina, T. C. Darst, Wilmington, N. C.; Easton (Md.), vacant; Erie (Pa.), R. Israel, Erie; Florida, E. G. Weed, Jacksonville; Fond du Lac (Wis.), R. H. Weller, Fond du Lac; Georgia, F. F. Reese, Savannah; Harrisburg (Pa.), J. H. Darlington, Harrisburg; Indianapolis (Ind.), J. M. Francis, Indianapolis; Iowa, T. N. Morrison, Davenport; H. S. Longley, Coad., Des Moines, Iowa; Kansas, J. Wise, Topeka; Kentucky, C. E. Woodcock, Louisville; Lexington (Ky.), L. W. Burton, Lexington; Long Island (N. Y.), Frederick Burgess, Garden City; Los Angeles (Cal.), J. H. Johnson, Pasadena; Louisiana, Davis Sessums, New Orleans; Maine, B. Brewster, Portland; Marquette (Mich.), G. M. Williams (retired), Annapolis, Md.; R. L. Harris, Marquette; Maryland, J. G. Murray, Baltimore; Massachusetts, William Lawrence, Boston; S. G. Babcock, Suffragan, Boston; Michigan, C. D. Williams, Detroit; Milwaukee (Wis.), W. W. Webb, Milwaukee; Minnesota, F. A. McElwain, Minneapolis, Minn.; Mississippi, Theo Du Bose Bratton, Battle Hill, Jackson; W. H. Green, Bishop Coad.; Missouri, D. S. Tuttle, Coad., F. F. Johnston, St. Louis; Montana, W. F. Faber, Helena; Nebraska, E. V. Shayler, Omaha; Newark (N. J.), E. S. Lines, Newark; W. R. Stearly, Coad., Newark, N. J.; New Hampshire, E. M. Parker, Concord; New Jersey, Paul Matthews, Trenton; New York (vacant); North Carolina, J. B. Cheshire, Raleigh; M. B. Delany, Bishop Suff.; Northern Indiana (Ind.), John H. White, South Bend; Ohio, W. A. Leonard, Cleveland; F. DuMoulin, Coad., Cleveland, O.; Olympia (Wash.), F. W. Keator, Tacoma; Oregon, W. T. Sumner, Portland; Pennsylvania, Philip M. Rhinelander; T. J. Garland, Suffragan, Phila.; Pittsburg (Pa.), Cortlandt Whitehead, Pittsburg; Quincy (Ill.), Edward Fawcett, Quincy; Rhode Island, J. de W. Perry, Jr., Providence; Sacramento (Cal.), Wm. H. Moreland, Sacramento; South Carolina, W. A. Guerry, Charleston; Southern Ohio, Boyd Vincent, Cincinnati; T. I. Reese, Coad., Columbus, Ohio; Southern Virginia, B. D. Tucker, Norfolk; A. C. Thomson, Suff., Portsmouth; Southwestern Virginia, R. C. Jett, Roanoke, Va.; Springfield (Ill.), G. H. Sherwood, Springfield; Tennessee, T. F. Gailor, Memphis, Coad., T. Meatty, Chattanooga; Texas, G. H. Kinsloving, Austin; Coadj., C. S. Quin, Houston; Vermont, A. C. A. Hall, Burlington; G. Y. Bliss, Coadj., Burlington, Vt.; Virginia, W. C. Brown, Richmond, Va.; Washington (D. C.), Alfred Harding, Washington; West Texas, J. S. Johnston (retired), Kerrville, Texas; W. T. Capers, San Antonio; West Va., W. L. Gravatt, Charleston; West Missouri, S. C. Partridge, Kansas City, Mo.; West Mich., J. N. McCormick, Grand Rapids; Western Mass., T. F. Davies, Springfield; Western N. Y., Chas. H. Brent, Buffalo; Suff., D. L. Ferris.

MISSIONARY DISTRICTS—U. S.

Alaska, P. T. Rowe, Seattle, Wash.; Arizona, J. W. Atwood, Phoenix; Asheville (N. C), J. M. Horner, Asheville; Idaho, F. H. Touret, Boise; Eastern Oregon, R. L. Paddock, Hood River; Honolulu (H. I.), H. B. Restarick; Nevada, G. C. Hunting, Reno; New Mexico, F. B. Howden, Albuquerque, N. M.; North Dakota, J. P. Tyler, Fargo; North Texas, E. A. Temple, Amarillo, Tex.; Oklahoma, T. B. Thurston, Oklahoma City; Philippines, G. Mosher, Manila; Porto Rico, C. B. Colmore, San Juan, P. R.; Virgin Islands, C. B. Colmore (in charge); Salina (Kan.), G. A. Beecher, in charge; San Joaquin (Cal.), L. C. Sanford, Fresno; Spokane, Herman Page, Spokane; Utah, A. W. Moulton; South Dakota, H. L. Burleson, Sioux Falls; W. P. Remington, Suff.; Southern Florida, Cameron Mann, Orlando; Western Nebraska, G A. Beecher, Hastings; Wyoming, N. S. Thomas, Cheyenne. Total, 5,960 clergy; 8,586 churches; contributions, $21,451,346; 1,085,068 communicants; 47,979 Sunday School teachers; 412,450 Sunday School scholars.

MISSIONARY DISTRICTS—FOREIGN.

Liberia, W. H. Overs; Shanghai (China), F. R. Graves, Shanghai; Hankow (China), L. H. Roots, Hankow, Anking (China), D. T. Huntington, Anking; Tokyo (Japan), John McKim, Tokyo; Kyoto (Japan), H. St. G. Tucker, Kyoto; Brazil, L. L. Kinsolving, Rio de Janeiro; Cuba, H. R. Hulse, Havana; Mexico, H. D. Aves, Guadalajara, Mexico; Haiti, C. B. Colmore (in charge); Canal Zone, J. C. Morris, D.D.; Santo Domingo, C. B. Colmore (in charge).

Reformed Church in America.

General Synod of the Reformed Church in Amer.—Rev. J. Fred. Berg, D.D., Pres., 900 Flatbush av., Bkln.; Rev. Jasper S. Hogan, D.D., V.-Pres., New Brunswick, N. J.; Rev. Henry Lockwood, D.D., Stated Clerk, East Millstone, N. J.; Rev. C. P. Case, D.D., Permanent Clerk, Poughkeepsie, N. Y. Offices of the Board of the Church, 25 E. 22d, Mhtn. Total number of churches, 727; ministers, 803; communicants, 133,783; Sunday School enrollment, 128,393; contributions for benevolent purposes, $876,920; congregational purposes, $1,827,422.

Reformed Episcopal.

Officers of the General Council of the Reformed Episcopal Church.

Bishop S. Fallows, Pres. and Presiding Bishop, 1618 W. Adams, Chicago, Ill.; Rev. W. T. Way, D.D., Sec., 1611 N. Carolina, Baltimore, Md.; Geo. Wagner, Treas., 4418 Pine, Phila.

Presiding Bishop and Bishop of the Missionary Jurisdiction of the Northwest and West and Coadj. Bishop of the Synod of Chicago, Samuel Fallows; Bishop of the New York and Philadelphia Synod, R. L. Rudolph, 103 S. 36th, Phila. Special Missionary Jurisdiction of the South, Bishop A. L. Pengelley, 75 Charlotte st., Charleston, S. C.; Bishop in charge of Synod of Canada and of missionary jurisdiction of the Pacific, Willard Brewing, 491 Euclid av., Toronto, Can. 100 ministers, 12,000 communicants, 10,849 Sunday School members, 90 parishes and churches; total offerings, $500,680; value of church property, less incumbrance, $2,198,720.

Roman Catholic Church.

The Apostolic Delegation — Most Rev. John Bonzano, D.D., Apostolic Delegate, 1811 Biltmore, Washington, D. C. Vy. Rev. Mons. Aluigi Cossio, Auditor; Rev. J. A. Floersh, Sec. Archbishops: Baltimore, His Eminence James Cardinal Gibbons; Boston, His Eminence William Cardinal O'Connell; Chicago, Most Rev. G. W. Mundelein; Cincinnati, Most Rev. Henry Moeller; Dubuque, Ia., James J. Keane; Milwaukee, Wis., S. G. Messmer; New Orleans, Most Rev. J. W. Shaw; New York, Most Rev. Patrick J. Hayes, D.D.; Oregon (Portland), Alexander Christie; Philadelphia, Most Rev. Dennis J. Dougherty, D.D.; St. Louis, Most Rev. J. J. Glennon; St. Paul, Minn., M. R. Austin Dowling, D.D.; San Francisco, Most Rev. E. J. Hanna; Most Rev. Albert T. Daeger, O.F.M.; Santa Fe, N. Mex., Archbishop of Heliopolis, Robert Seton, Pau, France; Titular Archbishop, Joseph Weber, Chicago, Ill. Number of Catholics in U. S., 17,735,553; 16,181 churches, 110 seminaries, 8,944 students, 2 cardinals, 16 archbishops, 91 bishops, 21,019 priests.

Diocese of Brooklyn—Est. 1853. Comprises Kings, Queens, Nassau, Suffolk counties, 1,007 sq. miles. Bishop, Rt. Rev. Charles Edward McDonnell, D.D., 367 Clermont av.; Vicars-Gen., Rt. Rev. T. E. Malloy, D.D., S.T.D., Auxiliary Bishop 367 Clermont av.; Rt. Rev. Mgr. Joseph McNamee and George Kaupert; Chancellor, Rev. F. X. Driscoll, S.T.L., 101 Greene av.; Asst. Chancellor, Rev. J. J. Oppel; Sec., Rev. James T. Kelty, S.T.L. Diocesan Consultors: Rt. Rev. Mgrs. G. W. Kaupert, V. G.; Jos. McNamee, V. G.; J. T. Woods, V. F.; Edward W. McCarty, M. G. Flannery, LL.D. Examiners of the Clergy: Vy. Rev. Mgr. J. F. Hoffman, Rt. Rev. Mgr. M. G. Flannery, Vy. Rev. H. F. Farrell, V. F.; Vy. Rev. Mgr. J. J. Corrigan, Revs. Peter Donohue, M. A. Fitzgerald, J. L. Belford, T. J. O'Brien.

Recapitulation—Bishops, 2; priests, 584; churches, 227; seminaries, 1; academies, 14; orphan asylums, 11; hospitals, 9; colleges for boys, 3; industrial schools, 4; young people under Catholic care, 78,993; homes for aged poor, 4; parishes with parochial schools, 115; pupils, 69,995; Catholic population, 819,217.

Archdiocese of N. Y.—Est. 1808; created an archbishopric in 1850. Comprising the Boroughs of Mhtn., The Bronx and Richmond, Counties of Westchester, Putnam, Rockland, Dutchess, Ulster, Sullivan, Orange, also Bahama Islands. 9,138 sq. miles.

Most Rev. P. J. Hayes, D.D.; Rev. J. P. Dineen, Sec., 452 Madison av., N. Y. C.; archbishop, Rt. Rev. Mgr. J. F. Mooney, V.G.; Chancellor, Vy. Rev. Mgr. J. J. Dunn, D.D., Chancery Office, 23 E. 51st, Sec.; Diocesan Consultors, Rt. Rev. Mgr. M. J. Lavelle, Rt. Rev. Mgr. John Edwards, Rt. Rev. Mgr. Jas. H. McGean, Rt. Rev. Mgr. Jas. J. Flood, Supt. of S. S., Rev. M. A. Delaney.

RELIGIOUS DENOMINATIONS—ROMAN CATHOLIC—*Continued.*

Recapitulation—Bishop, 1; priests, 1,110; churches, 391; chapels, 199; stations, 35; seminaries, 10; orphan asylums, 8; hospitals, 30; industrial and reform schools, 39; homes for aged, 5; emigrant homes, 7; day nurseries, 25; school for deaf mutes, 3; parish schools in city and out, 188; pupils, 93,692; Catholic population, 1,325,000.

Unitarian.

Amer. Unitarian Assn.—Org. 1825. Rev. S. A. Eliot, D.D., Pres., Boston; H. C. McDougall, Franklin, N. H.; Chas. A. Lory, Fort Collins, Col.; F. H. Hiscock, Syracuse, N. Y.; Wm. H. Taft, New Haven, Conn.; J. L. Mauran, St. Louis, Mo.; Geo. Soule, New Orleans, La.; W. H. Alexander, Edmonton, Can.; W. H. Carruth, Palo Alto, Cal., V.-Pres.; Rev. L. C. Cornish, Sec., Boston, Mass.; W. Forbes Robertson, Asst. Sec., 28 Beacon, Boston, Mass.; Henry M. Williams, Treas., Boston, Mass. 461 churches, 521 ministers.

Universalist.

Officers of the General Convention—R. S. Galer, Pres., Mt. Pleasant, Iowa; H. R. Childs, V.-Pres., N. Y. C.; Rev. R. F. Etz, Sec., 359 Boylston, Boston, Mass.; J. B. Horton, Treas., Boston, Mass. Trustees—Rev. V. E. Tomlinson, Worcester, Mass.; R. S. Galer, Iowa; Rev. L. S. McCollester, Tufts College, Mass.; Rev. R. E. Sykes, Canton, N. Y.; L. A. Ames, New York; Rev. J. F. Albion, Portland, Me.; W. A. Presbrey, Providence, R. I.; Mrs. C. E. Rice, Springfield, Mass.; J. M. Tilden, Galesburg, Ill.; C. L. Hutchinson, Chicago, Ill. 675 parishes, 58,566 members, 45,000 Sunday School members, 640 churches; value church property, $18,641,200.

MISSIONS.

Brooklyn.

(See also Church Tables and Relief Societies.)

BKLN. CITY MISSION AND TRACT SOC.

44 Court, C. H. Fuller, Pres.; F. H. Parsons, Treas., 60 Wall, Mhtn.; Dr. U. G. Warren, Supt.

Services and classes conducted, 2,644; total attendance, 114,275; interviews about personal religion, 1,809; Bibles, Testaments and Portions distributed, 855; visits made and received, 12,350; found employment, 175; garments distributed, 1,318; meals, 8,595; lodgings furnished free, 3,352.

CITY MISSION CENTERS AND STATIONS.

Atlantic Av. Goodwill Center, Atlantic and Grand avs.; Hamilton Av. Mission (Scandinavian), 92 Hamilton av. Rev. Chas. Cedarholm; Meeker Memorial Mission (Sailors), 92 Hamilton av., Rev. Chas. Cedarholm, Bernard Carlson; York St. Goodwill Center, Rev. S. C. Hearn, Rev. Giovanni Tron; House of Goodwill, 80 Willoughby, Rev. C. Park, Mrs. C. Park.

GOODWILL INDUSTRIES OF BKLN., INC.

Hdqtrs., 269 State. Branch Stores, 216 Fulton, 2106 Fulton, 156 Bedford av. Rev. C. Park, Supt.

WOMAN'S BRANCH, HDQTRS., 44 COURT.

Lincoln's Mission, 1699 Atlantic av.; York St. Ital. Center, York and Gold. King's Daughters' House, 18 Sidney pl.

Manhattan.

N. Y. CITY MISSION SOC.

105 E. 22d, Mhtn. Wm. S. Coffin, Pres.; S. Baker, Treas.; A. H. McKinney, D.D., Supt.

Objects of the society are to promote morality and religion among the poor and destitute of N. Y. C. by employment of missionaries, diffusion of evangelical truth and establishment of Mission Churches, Chapels, Sunday Schools, etc. Aims at the evangelization of the city in its most destitute parts. Has services in English, German, Italian, Spanish, Yiddish. Holds property in churches valued at over $600,000, all free of incumbrance. Has Sunday Schools, Libraries, Reading Rooms, Open-Air Services, Lecture Courses, 4 large Gymnasiums. Roof Playgrounds and various other instrumentalities for extending influence.

CHURCHES.

Olivet Church, 59 2d; DeWitt Memorial Church, 280 Rivington; Broome St. Tabernacle, 395 Broome; Charlton St. Memorial Church, 34 Charlton; Spanish Church, 109 E. 22d.

NUMBER OF CHURCHES IN NEW YORK CITY.

Denominations.	Bkln.	Mhtn. & Bronx.	Queens.	Rich-mond.	Total.
Baptist	52	41	10	5	108
Calvinistic Methodist	..	1	..	..	1
Christian	2	..	1	..	3
Christian Science	5	13	5	1	24
Congregational	30	10	9	..	49
Catholic Apostolic	..	2	..	..	2
Disciples of Christ	4	3	1	1	9
Evangelical Assn.	7	2	4	1	14
Evan. Synod of N. A.	1	..	..	..	1
Friends	2	2	..	..	4
Ger. Ev. Syn. of N. A.	..	2	..	..	2
Jewish	56	89	5	..	150
Lutheran	69	50	31	7	157
Methodist Episcopal	45	50	21	13	129
Meth. Epis. African.	3	5	4	2	14
Meth. Epis. Af. Zion	4	2	..	..	6
Methodist Free	2	..	..	..	2
Methodist Primitive	2	..	..	..	2
Methodist Protestant.	2	..	1	..	3
Moravian	..	2	..	4	6
Pentecostal	3	..	..	..	3
Presbyterian	43	64	19	2	128
Presbyterian Ref.	..	2	..	..	2
Presbyterian United.	4	3	..	..	7
Protestant Episcopal.	58	89	29	13	189
Reformed in America	23	24	17	4	68
Reformed in the U. S.	4	2	..	..	6
Reformed Catholic	..	1	..	..	1
Reformed Episcopal	2	1	1	..	4
7th Day Adventists	4	4	..	..	8
Swedenborgian	2	..	..	..	2
Unitarian	5	3	..	1	9
Universalist	3	1	..	..	4
Miscellaneous	21	22	6	1	50
Roman Catholic	120	150	44	19	333
Total	579	644	206	75	1,500

Foreign Government loans floated in the United States and outstanding on July 1, 1920, amounted to $11,820,866,078.

NUMBER OF CHURCHES IN NASSAU AND SUFFOLK COUNTIES.

Denominations.	Suffolk County.	Nassau County.	Total.
Baptist	11	7	18
Christian Science	..	4	4
Congregational	12	2	14
Jewish	2	1	3
Lutheran	7	12	19
Methodist Episcopal	47	29	76
Meth. Episcopal African	7	6	13
Meth. Epis. Af. Zion	5	3	8
Methodist Episcopal Ger.	..	2	2
Methodist Protestant	3	3	6
Pentecostal	1	..	1
Presbyterian	35	13	48
Protestant Episcopal	35	27	62
Reformed	1	..	1
Reformed in America	..	5	5
Universalist	1	..	1
Miscellaneous	..	1	1
Roman Catholic	41	31	72
Total	208	146	354

NEW YORK STATE REVENUES.

The total State General Revenue receipts during the fiscal year ending June 30, 1920, were $115,591,606.99, against $79,833,633 for 1919. A marked increase was shown in the revenues from corporations, aggregating $33,729,407 in 1920, against $27,101,387 in 1919.

The inheritance tax totals reached $21,259,640 in 1920, against $13,339,582 in 1919, while the stock transfer stamp tax netted $10,048,998 in 1920, against $6,989,317 in 1919. Miscellaneous receipts, which include those collected from conservation, insurance, hospitals, education, farms and markets, and industrial commissions, amounted to $7,515,257, against $6,705,552 the previous year.

The direct State tax required for retiring bond issues incurred for the building of highways and canals and the acquiring of the forest preserve totaled $15,058,317, against $15,067,918 in 1919.

NEW YORK CITY CHURCHES.

BROOKLYN.

Name of Church and Location.	Name of Pastor and Address.	Organized	Contrib'g Mem.	S. S. Members.	Total Amt. Raised	Value Church Prop'ty.
Baptist.						
Baptist Temple, 3d av., c. Schermerhorn	J. C. Massee, 211 Lafayette av....	1823	1,000	1,500	$46,000	$308,000
Bay Ridge (Swedish), 257 Bay Ridge av.	A. J. Hulbert, 370 74th............	1910	95	140	6,000	10,000
Bedford Heights, Bergen, c. Rogers av.	C. L. Laws, 1273 Carroll	1888	175	333	12,000	40,000
Berean (col'd), Bergen, nr. Rochester av.	A. C. Mathews, 189A Chauncey....	1851	545	275	6,218	75,000
Bergen St., 697 Bergen..................	Vacant	1901	45	75	1,050	....
Bethany (col'd), Clermont av., c. Atlantic	K. L. Warren, 286 Herkimer......	1887	800	350	12,000	75,000
Bethel (colored), 265 Bergen..............	Timothy White, 405 Dean.........	1907	400	200	6,000	30,000
Borough Park, 48th st. and 13th av......	Vacant	1898	100	87	5,200	25,000
Bushwick Av., Bushwick, cor. Weirfield.	J. L. Hynes..........................	1889	325	400	7,767	85,000
Calvary, 14th st., near Fourth av........	Geo. Rittenhouse, 311 12th.........	1899	501	331	13,187	100,000
Central, Adelphi St., 170 Adelphi, united	with Hanson Place.					
Concord (col'd), 165 Adelphi.............	Vacant	1847	1,100	600	20,000	110,000
East End, 263 Van Sicklen av............	Vacant	1887	150	250	4,000	10,000
Ebenezer Swedish, 607 Herkimer	W. Kohler, 297 Park pl.............	1897	112	72	3,652	16,000
Emmanuel, Lafayette av., c. St. James pl.	A. A. Shaw, 376 Ryerson...........	1881	937	750	53,400	310,000
Euclid Avenue, Euclid av., n. Liberty av.	J. W. Hakes, 12 Hill	1899	97	273	3,597	12,000
§First in Pierrepont st....................	(See Baptist Temple).					
First (col'd), E. 15th, Sheepshead Bay.	J. H. Dennis, 144 Fulton.....	1899	98	60	2,265	15,000
First, Canarsie, Remsen av., Canarsie..	S. Thompson, 909 95th, Woodh'en.	1901	35	44	534	5,500
First in Wmsbgh., Lee av. and Keap..	R. D. Lord, 379 Washington av...	1839	854	327	18,250	110,000
First E.N.Y., Hendrix, nr. Arlington av.	Vacant	1863	221	111	3,534	30,000
First Free, united with First in Williamsburgh.						
First German, E.D., Montrose, nr. Union	P. Wengel, 97 Halleck av..........	1834	350	250	6,500	000
First Italian, 16 Jackson..................	V. Coletta, 171 Monitor............	1911	180	250	3,000	000
First Norwegian, 4th av. nr. 32d........	Otto E. C. Hansen, 361 4th av.....	1903	109	130	5,200	60,000
First Swedish, 513-517 Dean	O. J. Engstrand, 126 Underhill av	1884	417	250	5,200	80,000
Friendship, (colored) 447 Elton...........	R. E. Edwards, 376 Ashford	1910	30	75	1,283	000
Grace, 6th av. & 53d.......................	Wm. A. Spinney, 553 54th.........	1885	450	500	5,000	000
Greene Avenue, Greene av., nr. Lewis..	Chas. F. McKoy, 816 Greene av....	1854	1,109	551	18,788	000
Greenwood, 7th av. and 6th st...........	F. W. O'Brien, 183 Pros. Pk. W..	1858	350	325	27,000	000
Hanson Pl., Hanson pl. & S. Portland av..	S. M. Lindsay, 476 Clinton av......	1854	600	500	15,000	000
Holy Trinity (col.), DeKalb av., n. F'k'n.	C. D. Patterson, 443 Franklin av..	1898	500	300	6,500	5,000
Kenilworth, Bedford av. & Ave. G......	E. W. Van Aken, 2409 Ave. G...	1913	160	150	3,000	100,000
Lefferts Park, 76th st. and 14th av......	E. H. Lovett, 146 S. Portland av.	1896	125	285	7,500	40,000
Lenox Road, Lenox rd. & Nostrand av..	Harvey W. Chollar, 366 Lenox rd.	1872	400	550	8,000	50,000
McDonough St., Patchen av. cor. McD'gh	W. F. Allton, 401 Decatur.........	1889	119	214	5,437	33,000
Marcy Avenue, Marcy and Putnam avs.	John M. Moore, 516 Nostrand av...	1872	987	1,402	47,335	200,000
Memorial, 8th av. and 16th st............	M. A. Slade, 61 Sherman..........	1891	150	328	4,500	35,000
Mount Calvary, (colored) Greene and Tompkins.	S. W. Timms............					
Mt. Lebanon (col'd), Howard, nr. Herkimer.	J. Wm. Hamlin, 91 Sackman......	1891	700	325	7,500	12,000
Prospect Park, Av. C and E. 4th st......	C. E. Morris, 446 E. 4th............	1899	130	175	4,500	22,000
Redeemer, Cortelyou rd. and Ocean av..	H. F. Perry, 2304 Newkirk av.....	1900	312	472	16,200	35,000
St. Nich. Av. Gr. Bap. Mis., 89 St. Nich. av.	P. Wengel, 97 Halleck av..........	1890	....	110	......	5,000
Salem, Snyder av. & Prospect...........	S. L. Arrington, 90 Prospect.......	1910	160	55	1,440	8,000
Second German, 455 Evergreen av.......	W. J. Zirbes, 455 Evergreen av....	1881	210	250	10,000	55,000
Sixth Avenue, 6th av., cor. Lincoln pl..	David Miller, 433 3d...............	1872	300	350	12,800	60,000
Strong Place, Strong pl., cor. Degraw..	F. H. Adams, 54 Strong pl........	1849	479	265	24,500	80,000
Sumner Av., Sumner av., cor. Decatur...	Vacant	1865	100	75	3,600	88,000
Tabernacle, Clinton st. and 3d pl........	Vacant	1862	78	175	5,726	....
Union, Noble, near Manhattan av.......	G. M. MacDonald, 106 Noble......	1900	250	225	4,000	5 000
Washington Av., Wash'n, cor. Gates av.	Robert McCaul, 25 Clinton........	1861	700	300	26,396	2 5,000
Wmsbg. Jewish Msn., Throop av. & Walton	L. Cohn, 27 Throop av..............	1894	125	100	67,000	90,000
Christian.						
Church of the Evangel, 678 Leonard.....	H. A. Barton, 810 E. 35th..........	1838	110	100	1,400	15,000
Vanderveer Park, N. Y. av., n. Av. D..	L. F. Johnson, 270 E. 32d.........	1910	100	185	3,000	13,000
Christian Scientist.						
First Church of Christ, Dean & N.Y. av..	F. S. Bartlett, First Reader.......	1892	....	....	......	... ...
Second Ch. of Christ, 67th, 3d & 4th avs	C. A. Johnston, First Reader.....	1909	....	....	......	... ...
Third Ch. of Christ, 261 E. 21st........	J. F. Phillips, First Reader.......	1915	....	....	......	... ...
Fourth Ch. of Christ, 181 Lincoln pl....	Miss I. D. Carter, First Reader...	1919	....	....	......	... ...
Society 4521 Ft. Hamilton P'kway.....	J. K. MacHaffie, First Reader....	1919	....	....	......	....
Congregational.						
Bethesda, now St. Mark's.						
Borough Pk, 49th, nr. Ft. Ham. Pkway.	H. S. Baker	1901	160	277	2,500	24,000
Bushwick Av., Bushwick, cor. Cornelia..	J. L. Clark, 47 Linden..............	1885	1,500	1,000	10,000	100,000
Central, Hancock, near Franklin av.....	S. Parkes Cadman, 2 Spencer pl....	1854	2,912	560	125,530	225,000
Ch. of the Evangel, Bedford & Hawthorne	A. E. Roraback, 215 Fenimore....	1907	420	325	7,300	75,000
Ch. of the Pilgrims, Henry, cor. Remsen	Richard Roberts, 266 Hicks	1844	350	80	27,057	200,000
Clinton Av., Clinton, cor. Lafayette av..	Nehemiah Boynton, 379 Wash'n av	1847	690	150	33,000	200,000
Finnish Golgotha, 733 44th...............	J. E. Lillback, 1071 48th...........	1912	203	30	5,500	27,500
Flatbush, E. 18th and Dorchester road..	L. T. Reed, 455 E. 18th............	1899	1,575	950	50,000	150,000
Italian Ch. of Redeemer, 440 Clinton..	....	1903	125	110	......	48,000
Kings Highway, Av. P, cor. 18th........	C. A. Lincoln, 1400 E. 21st........	1911	230	260	6,700	15,000
Lewis Av., Lewis av., cor. Madison......	Vacant	1877	987	363	22,553	23,450
Mapleton Park, 65th, near 18th av........	Edward W. Robinson, 6416 22d av..	1910	125	250	2,500	12,000
*Mayflower, Lawrence and Johnson	I. W. Henderson, 105 Col'b'a hts..	1843	....	350	......	30,000
Nazarene (colored), Troy av. & Herkimer.	H. H. Proctor, 1597 Pacific....	1869	400	175	7,000	20,000
Ocean Av., Ocean av. and Ave. I.......	E. M. Halliday, 1058 E. 21st.......	1903	250	275	17,700	100,000
Park Slope, 8th av. and 2d..............	R. W. McLaughlin, 253 Garfield pl.	1868	415	325	27,000	125,000
Parkville, 18th av. and E. 5th	Chas. J. Allen, 1776 45th st......	1866	434	600	8,000	50,000
Pilgrim Swedish Ev'ngel, 413 Atlantic...	H. A. Bentson, Y.M.C.A., Hanson pl.	1883	475	300	16,250	42,845
Plymouth, Orange, near Henry..........	Newell Dwight Hillis, Ply'h Inst.	1847	2,460	600	41,000	564,830
Puritan Chapel, Lafayette av., cor. Marcy (branch of Tompkins Av. Cong.)..	Ernest E. Youtz, 40 McDonough..	....	800	1,012	......	70,000
Rockaway Av., Rockaway, near Blake..	Vacant	1868	23	60	900	4,000
Rugby, E. 49th, nr. Linden av...........	J. A. Hansen, 216 E. 43d...........	1913	68	130	2,200	6,500
St. Mark's, 461 Decatur..................	Chas. W. Dane, 536 McDonough...	1859	350	475	5,550	40,000
St. Paul's New York av. & Sterling pl..	Geo. R. Andrews, 960 Sterling pl..	1912	750	505	10,000	83,500

*Missions. §Corporate name, First in Pierrepont Street.

BROOKLYN CHURCHES—*Continued.*

Name of Church and Location.	Name of Pastor and Address.	Or-gan-ized	Con-trib'g Mem.	S. S. Mem-bers.	Total Amt. Raised	Value Church Prop'ty.
Congregational—Continued.						
South, Court, cor. President	R. A. McConnell, 553 8th	1851	1,189	356	$14,828	$150,006
South Sunday School, 118 4th pl	R. A. McConnell, 533 8th	....	....	400	......	....
Tompkins Av., Tompkins, cor. McDonough	J. Percival Huget, 244 Decatur	1875	1,794	1,986	70,197	350,000
Tabernacle (Swedish), 326-330 56th st	Roy Lundgren, 1029 73d	1901	80	360	11,500	22,800
Willoughby Av., Wil'ghby av., nr. Grand.	O. James, 337 Adelphi	1909	125	200	1,800	....
Disciples of Christ.						
Borough Park Christian, 12th av. & 45th.	E. B. Kemm, 1158 50th	1906	79	100	2,344	20,000
First Ch. of Christ, P'k pl. & V'db't	M. W. Williams, 241 Park pl	1876	150	140	10,000	50,000
Flatbush Christian, Dorchester & Marl'b	Vacant	1904	439	610	11,000	65,000
Second Ch. of Christ, Humboldt	F. R. Nichols, 46 Oakland	1887	106	100	2,000	10,000
Evangelical Association.						
Church of Peace, Ridg'w & Nichols av.	E. M. Glasow, 195 Nichols av	1910	175	300	5,000	27,000
Emanuel, 400 Melrose	G. A. Linder, 400 Melrose	1887	250	500	6,000	18,000
Friedenskirche—See Church of Peace.						
St. John's, 1737 Linden	C. Philipbar, 1735 Linden	1904	240	500	6,000	50,000
St. Paul's, 541-543 Leonard	C. H. Benseler, 570½ Leonard	1883	115	120	4,239	20,000
Salem, 1200 Jefferson av	A. D. Pfost, 1198 Jefferson av	1890	225	250	4,000	19,500
Zion's, 446 Liberty av	H. G. Hazelstein, 444 Liberty av.	1889	125	150	4,550	18,000
Evangelical Synod of N. A.						
Bethlehem, Ger., Cortelyou rd. and O.	P'kway. W. E. Bourquin, 595 E. 7th	1906	200	300	4,500	30,000
Friends.						
Friends (Hicksite), 110 Schermerhorn	Anna L. Curtis, Sec., 110 Scherm'n.	1835	425	70	......	....
Religious Soc. of Friends (Orth'x), Lafayette, c. Washington	C. E. Tebbetts, 56 S. Oxford	1837	210	100	7,500	30,000
Jewish.						
Ahawath Israel, 108 Noble	Max Brody, Sec., 108 Noble	1903	160	....	......	30,008
Ahawath Achim, 710-712 Quincy	J. H. Paymer, 776 Lafayette av.	1868	90	130	20,000	15,000
Ahavas Chesed, 742 Jefferson av	Rabbi Doobin, 229 Keap	1892	120	120	......	30,000
Ahawath Sholom Beth Aron, 98 Scholes.	K. Solomon, Cantor, 126 Vernon av	1895	14	....	1,500	20,000
Anshe Emes, 136 Stanhope	Vacant	1904	200	125	......	25,000
Aqudath Achim Anshei, 49 Malta	Morris Hessel, Sec., New Lots rd. and Williams av.	1907	...	....	......	56,000
Aguadas Achim Bnei Jacob 238 Wyona	I. Altman, Sec., 1666 Union	1903	120	....	......	10,000
Asifas Israel, 420 Wallabout st	Jeal Magulensky, 420 Wallabout st.	1885	40	52	5,000	9,000
Baith Israel Anshei Emes, Har. & Court	I. Goldfarb, 360 Clinton	1856	200	425	15,000	105,000
Beth El of Bor. Park, 12th av. & 41st	L. H. Spero, Sec., 1246 40th	1902	125	....	2,000	20,000
Beth El, 110 Noble, Greenpoint	S. J. Rome, 1031 Lorimer	1886	60	150	4,000	8,000
Beth Elohim, 274 Keap	S. R. Cohen, 1421 Ditmas av	1851	1,500	150	16,000	116,000
Beth Elohim. (See 8th Av. Temple.)						
Beth Emeth, Church av. & Marlboro rd.	S. J. Levinson, 522 E. 8th	1911	450	350	16,000	75,000
Beth Hamidrash, Hagadol, Sackman &	Belmont. B. Fleischer, 345 Sackman	1897	130	....	6,979	25,000
Beth Israel of Brownsville, 349 Christop	her av. J. Spatt, 424 Sackman	....	....	....	......	....
Beth Hifah, Hopkinson, c. Sumner av.	S. Buchler, 788 Park pl	1895	300	....	......	60,000
Beth Jacob Ansche Scholom, 274 S. 3d	S. T. Galubowski, 260 Hewes	1872	200	175	10,000	75,000
Beth Jehuda, 904-908 Bedford av	S. Buchler, 788 Park pl	1890	200	40	......	55,000
Beth Sholom, People's Temple, 20th and Benson av.	H. K. Jacobs, 8422 19th	1905	200	200	7,500	40,000
B'nai Israel of Bay Ridge	J. Katz, 478 41st	1900	250	100	15,000	90,000
B'nai Israel, 4th av. & 54th	Jacob Katz	1904	350	250	5,500	10,000
B'nai Jacob, 136 Prospect av	B. Rosenson	1887	115	...	5,800	15,000
B'nai Jacob, 525 Marcy av	L. J. Risikoff, 48 Moore	1914	500	150	3,000	25,000
B'nai Sholaum, 399 9th. Dr. M. Fried	lander, 10 Pr'p't pk., S. W	1890	560	300	9,000	65,000
B'nai Yits'k Nusach Hoari, 445 Georgia	av. H. S. Warshavsky, 554 Vermont	1915	55	55	4,000	13,000
Bkln. Jewish Center, E. Parkway, bet. Bkln. and N. Y. aves	I. H. Levinthal, 1233 E. P'kway.	1919	180	150	250,000	500,000
Chevra Beth Yakov Zvie, 50 Moore	E. Lehrer, Pres., 168 Boerum	1916	....	175	......	....
Chevra Kadisho, 93 Moore	L. Berman, 76 McKibbin	....	100	....	......	....
Chevrah Kad'a Anche Emeth, W. 5th, C. I.	J. Aginskee, 3040 W. 1st	1899	53	....	......	....
Cong. Cr'n'g Glory of Is'l of E.N.Y., 479A	Ashf'd. A. Karlin, Sec. 505 Ashf'd	....	350	....	......	30,000
Cong. Men of Justice (Anshe Zedek), 1674 Park pl.	J. Rosenblum, Sec., 1660 Prospect pl	1919	59	....	2,000	40,000
Eighth Av. Temple, 8th av., Garfield pl.	Alex. Lyons, 526 8th	1861	175	275	......	150,000
Emanuel Temple, 14th av. and 49th	B. Rubern Weilerstein	....	150	....	......	75,000
Etz Chaim, 467 Stone av	M. H. Rabinowitz, 198 Thatford av.	1894	145	175	......	15,000
First Bklyn. Roumanian American, 224	Hopkins, Morris Schachtar, 72 Van Buren	1895	250	....	5,000	33,000
First Cong. Ansho Sfard of Boro. Park.	14th av., cor. 45th.	1915	130	....	......	45,000
House of Aaron, 11 Beaver	J. Gerstein, 79 Cook	1897	....	....	......	4,500
House of Abraham, 73 Debevoise	L. J. Risikoff, 48 Moore	1915	300	60	900	4,000
Machzike Talmud Torah, 1319 43d	S. J. Borowsky, 1530 55th	1911	900	....	......	65,009
Mount Sinai, State and Hoyt	M. Silverman, 209 Underhill ave.	1882	500	200	7,000	40,000
Oheb Zedek, Howard av., nr. Herkimer.	C. Smolin, 1515 St. Johns pl	1897	60	....	......	20,000
People's Temple of Bensonhurst, Bay Parkway and 85th st.	H. K. Jacobs	1910	100	150	......	....
Rabbi Eliuhu Gaove	A. H. Canter, 1806 Bergen	1915	75	100	1,000	6,500
Shaare Tefilla, 51-53 Watkins	J. Adler, Pres., 138 Watkins	1893	110	....	......	25,000
Shaari Zedek, Putnam av., nr. Reid av.	M. Silber, 611 Jefferson av	1902	308	300	14,000	100,000
Sons of Israel, 21st & Benson avs	Samuel Sacks, 216 Bay 23d	1896	140	180	20,000	35,000
Talmudical Schl. of Bkln., 655 Wil. av.	J. Gerstein, 28 Porter av	1909	700	....	12,000	26,000
Temple Ahavath Sholom, Av. R & E. 17th	S. Peiper, 1786 E. 19th	1912	100	150	......	60,000
Temple Israel, Bedford & Lafayette avs.	L. D. Gross, 570 Pacific	1869	200	200	......	150,000
Temple Petach Tikvah, Lincoln pl., cor. Rochester av.	R. H. Melamed, 1423 Lincoln pl	1914	325	300	24,000	100,000
Temple Sinai, Arlington av., c. Bradford	Dr. Sachs	....	100	....	......	....
Tiferes Israel, 23 Siegel	F. Weinlass, 103 Hopkins	....	....	....	......	....
Tifareth Israel, 397 14th	M. Port, 395 14th	....	....	....	......	....
Tifereth Zion Talmud Torah, E. Pky. &	Prospect pl. Jos. Koplowitz	1905	400	....	5,000	12,000
Zemach Zedek, 125 Moore	H. Lewis, Pres., 244 Boerum	188[illegible]	200	....	......	70,000
Lutheran.						
Advent, E. 12th and Av. P	A. F. Walz, 1617 E. 14th	1909	240	200	3,100	2,200
Ascension, 13th av. and 81st	M. J. Kluttz, 1316 48th	1908	44	75	1,200	15,000
Bethany (Norw.), 73d & 10th av	J. C. Herre, 1044 73d	181[illegible]	85	220	2,200	23,000

BROOKLYN CHURCHES—*Continued.*

Name of Church and Location.	Name of Pastor and Address.	Organized	Con-trib's Mem.	S. S. Members.	Total Amt. Raised	Value Church Prop'ty.
Lutheran—Continued.						
Bethesda (Norw.) Woodhull, nr. Columbia.	J. C. Herre, 1044 73d	....	....	112	......	$40,000
Bethlehem (Swedish), 3d av. & Pacific	F. Jacobson, 490 Pacific st	1874	880	621	$11,169	147,900
Bethlehem, Marion, near Reid av	F. W. Behnke, 481 Decatur	1888	600	275	5,490	28,000
Bethlehem, 51st, nr. 6th av	A. W. Herbert, 654 54th	1903	160	138	3,500	10,000
Bethlehem (Nor.), Russell, nr. Nassau av.	(United with 1st Scandinavian).					
Calvary, Rochester av. and Herkimer	Vacant	1888	125	300	4,500	25,000
Christ, 1084 Lafayette av	C. B. Schuchard, 793 Quincy	1895	500	430	13,000	150,000
Emanuel, 415-21 7th	Emil Roth, 421 7th	1884	450	350	5,000	65,000
Epiphany, 831-835 Sterling pl	Wm. H. Stutts, 837 Sterling pl	1908	423	225	4,700	35,000
Finnish, 752 44th	S. Ilmonen, 715 43d	1890	155	135	2,150	25,000
Finnish Seamen's Mission, 529 Clinton	K. Makinen, 2 W. 117th, Mhtn	1887	100	40	16,000	25,000
First Scandinavian, 152 Russell	E. Risty, 163 Monitor	1894	100	75	1,500	10,000
German Evang., Schermerhorn, nr. Court	Jacob W. Loch, 183 Stratford rd	1841	500	300	34,000	250,000
Good Shepherd, 315 Fenimore	W. G. Brunn, 315 Fenimore	1909	85	100	1,200	110,000
Good Shepherd, 75th and 4th av	C. D. Trexler, Pastor, 148 74th	1906	752	800	62,000	80,000
Grace, Bushwick av. and Weirfield	C. F. Intemann, 1251 Bushwick av.	1902	525	400	8,303	100,000
Holy Trinity, Jefferson & Knickerbocker avs.	C. H. Dort, 477 Irving av	1915	190	300	10,000	....
Immanuel, S. 9th, near Driggs av	John Holthusen, 177 S. 9th st	1875	500	250	14,000	90,000
Immanuel (Swedish), 521 Leonard	Eric Bowman	1894	200	100	3,821	21,000
Incarnation, 4th av., bet. 53d and 54th	H. S. Miller, 5323 4th av	1902	500	350	9,000	65,000
Mediator, 68th and Bay Pkway	F. D. Haffner, 129 Sheridan av	1912	53	75	800	8,000
Messiah, Russell, nr. Nassau av	R. C. Deitz, 141 Russell	1899	438	565	12,045	65,000
Norwegian Seaman's, 111 Pioneer	Christen Bruun, 134 Senator	1879	1,500	30	12,000	25,000
Our Saviour (Danish), 193-195 9th	R. Andersen, 193-195 9th st	1878	....	....	......	18,000
Our Saviour, 21 Covert	A. R. G. Hanser, 37 Covert	1901	560	360	15,000	55,000
Our Saviour (Norwegian), 632-636 Henry	S. Turmo, 630 Henry	1866	310	225	4,000	35,000
Redeemer, Lenox rd., nr. Flatbush av	S. G. Weiskotten, 200 Fenimore	1894	400	200	......	....
Redeemer, 991 E. P'kway	E. J. Flanders, 1345 Sterling pl	1912	164	150	4,348	40,000
Reformation, Barbey, nr. Arlington av	H. C. Kline, 227 Arlington av	1898	600	400	10,000	48,000
St. Andrew's, St. Nicholas av. & Harmon	C. H. Hirzel, 196 St. Nicholas av.	1906	500	900	7,000	40,000
St. Jacobi, 4th av., bet. 54th and 55th	H. C. A. Meyer, 5406 4th av	1889	191	400	5,894	85,000
St. John's (Swedish-Finnish), 44th and 8th av.	J. Gullans, 672 46th	1913	125	82	2,600	6,000
St. John's, 268 Hamilton av	V. A. M. Mortensen, 564 2d	1917	43	62	......	....
St. John's, Maujer, nr. Humboldt	A. J. Beyer, 197 Maujer st	1844	500	350	6,638	80,000
St. John's, 283 Prospect av	Rev. F. B. Clausen, 281 Prospect av	1861	900	600	11,540	50,000
St. John's, 223 New Jersey av	C. J. Lucas, 223 New Jersey av	1847	458	825	3,461	50,000
St. John's, Greenpoint, Milton, n. Mhtn. av	H. C. Offerman	1857	210	600	4,210	75,000
St. John's (Lithuanian), 145 Skillman av.	Geo. Matzat, 106 Creek, Maspeth	1905	45	15	1,130	5,000
St. John's, 84th and 16th av	Lewis Happ, 8619 19th av	1891	400	375	......	50,000
St. Luke's, Washington, nr. DeKalb avs.	W. A. Snyder, 127 Willoughby av	1869	750	300	11,000	125,000
St. Mark's, Bushwick & Jefferson avs.	Paul Woy, 907 Willoughby av., and S. J. E. Frey, 30 Jefferson.	1868	2,000	500	......	200,000
St. Mark's, 42 E. 5th st	W. H. Steup, 337 E. 5th st	1908	125	110	2,643	10,000
St. Matthew's, E. 92d, nr. Flatlands av.	T. A. Petersen, E. 93d st, Canarsie	1880	200	80	4,000	20,000
St. Matthew's, 6th av. and 2d	G. B. Young, 543 3d	1859	400	250	7,000	125,000
St. Matthew's, 197-203 N. 5th	G. Sommer, 197 N. 5th st	1864	100	300	......	25,000
St. Paul's, West 5th, Coney Island	J.F.W. Kitzmeyer, 497 Neptune av.	1907	224	283	2,130	24,000
St. Paul's, Palmetto, c. Knickerbocker av	J. P. Riedel, 267 Palmetto st	1887	500	400	......	....
St. Paul's, Henry, near 3d pl	J. Huppenbauer, 11 3d pl	1872	263	200	2,973	30,000
St. Paul's, S. 5th, cor. Rodney	H. C. Wasmund	1853	780	500	11,921	150,000
St. Paul's (Swedish), 392 McDonough	John Eastlund, 392 McDonough	1889	336	175	2,753	31,780
St. Paul's, E. 40th and Av. J	F. Holter, 1011 E. 38th	1919	75	50	2,300	6,000
St. Peter's, 94 Hale av	Arthur Brunn, 45 Hale av	1898	602	341	5,861	24,000
St. Peter's, Bedford av., near DeKalb	J. J. Heischmann, 457 Greene av.; J. G. F. Blaesi, Jr., past., 1077 Dean	1867	2,200	1,084	47,624	238,529
St. Philip's, 287 McKinley av	A. Wuerstlin, 9423 Av. L	1914	90	147	......	12,000
St. Stephen's, E. 28th and Newkirk av	Luther D. Gable, 448 E. 28th	1898	572	915	7,200	45,000
Salem (Swedish), 414-18 46th	J. A. Anderson, 418 46th	1904	400	550	7,900	30,000
Salem (Danish), 128 Prospect av	J. Knudsen, 213 13th	1895	92	60	4,000	23,000
Tabor (Swedish), Ashford, nr. Glenmore av	Student	1888	85	70	750	6,000
*Trinity, 249 Degraw	Hugo H. Burgdorf, 204 Baltic st	1886	300	200	6,500	30,000
Trinity Ch. of Flat'b., Coney Isld ave. & Av G.	Geo. C. Koenig, 336 Parkville av	1915	100	75	3,000	12,500
Trinity (Norwegian), 4th av. & 46th st.	S. O. Sigmond, 411 46th	1890	300	500	20,000	90,000
Wartburg Chapel, Georgia av., nr. Fulton	O. Hanser, 46 Sheffield av	1875	....	5	......	....
Zion, Henry, near Clark	E. C. J. Kraeling and E. G. Kraeling, Jr., Pastors, 132 Henry	1855	1,000	200	7,000	100,000
Zion, Bedford av., nr. Church	P. F. Jubelt, 2251 Bedford av	1888	260	290	4,200	35,000
Zion (Norwegian), 63d and 4th av	H. Halvorson, 414 63d st	1908	450	700	25,000	85,000
Zion (Swedish), 59th and 11th av	Jos. D. Danielson, 1070 59th	1897	175	125	4,750	14,000
Methodist Episcopal.						
Bkln. No. & So. N. Y. E. Conf. Dist. Supts.	Wm. H. Davison, 62 Montague; A. S. Kavanagh	....	....	....	......	....
Andrews, Richmond, nr. Fulton	Wm. D. Tuckey, 95 Richmond	1854	250	350	4,300	49,000
Buffalo Avenue, Bergen and Buffalo av	Wm. W. Gillies, 17 Revere pl	1894	70	150	1,800	15,000
Bushwick Av. Central, Bushwick, cor. Madison	G. E. Bishop, 1018 Madison	1886	2,111	2,912	26,000	182,000
Corner-Stone Temple, Mhtn. av. & Noble	D. O. Osterheld, 1005 Lorimer	1911	563	420	9,000	120,000
Cropsey Av., Cropsey av. and Bay 35th	Chas. D. Norman, 226 Bay 35th	1844	128	230	2,800	28,500
Eighteenth St., near 5th av	W. I. Bowman, 215 17th	1840	399	500	8,000	46,000
Embury Memorial, Decatur & Lewis av.	Geo. E. Pickard, 230 Decatur	1866	900	400	15,000	100,000
Fenimore St., Fenimore and Rogers av	Claude C. Coile, 266 Fenimore	1889	400	375	6,000	35,000
First Place, 1st pl., corner Henry	Harry S. Crossett, 158 Summit	1849	300	175	4,000	50,000
First (Sands St.) Henry, cor. Clark	W. M. Nesbit, Hotel St. George	1794	215	145	6,000	120,000
Flatlands, E. 40th and Flatlands av	E. E. Wright, 435 51st st	1850	85	133	1,000	8,000
Fourth Avenue, 4th av., corner 47th	W. A. Richard, 4614 4th av	1872	900	1,300	16,500	65,000
Goodsell Memorial, Sheridan and McKinley avs.	Wm. C. Craig, 79 Sheridan av	1888	200	400	6,700	45,000
Grace, Bay Ridge, 4th & Ovington avs.	H. H. DuBois, 368 Ovington av	1830	250	600	7,000	8,700
Grace, 7th av., corner St. Johns pl	Roy E. Manne, 29 7th av	1878	407	267	8,000	115,000
Greene Av. (German), 1171 Greene av	Henry Mueller, 1169 Greene av	1887	284	374	7,700	24,000
Hanson Place, Hanson pl., cor. St. Felix	Harry K. Miller, 159 Lafayette av.	1858	800	600	30,000	300,000

*Chapels at 186 Conover and 691 Coney Island av.

BROOKLYN CHURCHES—*Continued.*

Name of Church and Location.	Name of Pastor and Address.	Organised	Contrib'g Mem.	S. S. Members.	Total Amt. Raised	Value Church Prop'ty.
Methodist Episcopal—Continued.						
Immanuel (Swedish), 426 Dean	C. G. Westerdahl	1845	400	300	$5,000	$75,000
Janes, Monroe, corner Reid av	Paul E. Edwards	18[illegible]	1,943	1,275	27,000	135,000
Knickerbocker Av. M. E., Knkbr., c. Menehan	Carl E. Bash, 249 Woodbine st	189[illegible]	350	650	4,250	22,000
Marcy Av., Marcy av., cor. Penn	Chas. Stephan, 318 Marcy av	1846	150	284	8,556	58,000
New York Av., 121 New York av	J. W. Langdale, 962 Sterling pl	1856	989	756	32,050	215,000
Norwegian, Bethelship, 297-299 Carroll	A. M. Treistad, 391 Clinton	1874	312	150	5,000	50,000
Norwegian, St. Paul, Bethelship Mis'n.	Rich'd & Sull'an. A. M. Treistad.	....	....	....	......	....
Nostrand-DeKalb, Nostrand av., cor. Quincy	H. B. Munson, 378 Nostrand av	1861	500	600	10,000	150,000
Ocean P'kway, Ocean pky. & Foster av.	W. B. West	1865	400	350	9,217	100,000
Prospect Av., Greenwood & Prospect avs	W. M. Hughes, 530 Greenwood av	1886	231	400	4,400	30,000
Prospect Pl., (German), between 5th and 6th avs.	J. H. F. Boese, 44 Pros. pl.	1856	100	100	4,000	....
St. John's, Bedford av. and Wilson	H. S. Scarborough, 530 Bedford av.	1870	650	600	25,000	162,000
St. Mark's, Ocean av., cor. Beverly rd.	Robt. M. Moore, 1695 Albemarle rd.	1903	900	800	47,470	16,000
Salem (German), Vanderveer Pk., E. 38th and Av. D	John Lange, 3714 Ave. D	1884	75	60	2,000	12,000
Sheepshead Bay, Ocean & Voorhees avs.	C. W. Severance, 3087 Ocean av	1895	120	159	......	31,000
Simpson, Clermont and Willoughby avs.	Albert E. Beebe	1834	575	425	32,000	150,000
Sixth—See 18th St. M. E.						
Sixth Avenue, 6th av. and 8th	H. C. Whitney, 453 7th	1884	400	420	9,000	85,000
South Third St., Hewes and S. 3d	Jas. H. Lockwood, 411 S. 3d	1832	263	228	3,500	80,000
Summerfield, Washington & Greene avs.	F. D. Torrey, 117 St. James pl.	1851	317	150	11,000	70,000
Sunset Park M. E., 7th av. & 45th	J. M. Beckstrom, 654 47th	1909	250	535	9,000	38,000
Swedish Bethany, St. Johns pl., nr. Albany av.	C. F. Edwards	1891	115	80	2,575	15,000
Swedish Elim, 48th and 7th av	Edw. Stromberg, 719 52d	1898	172	170	3,500	40,000
Union, Leonard, cor. Conselyea	E. M. Johnson, 352 Adelphi	1896	75	100	2,050	20,000
Vanderveer Pk., E. 31st & Glenwood rd.	Geo. M. Brown, 658 E. 32d	1900	500	524	12,000	33,000
Warren Street, 307 Warren	E. L. Fox, 307 Warren	1852	192	409	1,800	31,500
Wesley, Glenmore and Atkins avs	P. St. J. Cohman, 831 Glenmore av	1883	242	381	2,730	17,250
Williams Avenue, 50 Williams av	....	1865	342	374	7,500	41,000
Methodist Episcopal—African.						
Bethel A.M.E., Schenectady av., cor. Dean	C. E. Wilson, 671 Herkimer	1848	190	103	4,500	25,000
Bridge Street A. M. E., 313 Bridge	W. S. Carpenter, 182 Duffield	1818	1,200	800	15,000	70,000
St. John's A.M.E., Howard & Atlan. av.	A. L. Bouldin, 11 Dewey pl	1890	40	36	800	....
Methodist Epis.—Afric'n, Zion						
Boyle A.M.E. Zion, 837 Bergen	J. W. Buddin	1901	115	80	2,575	15,000
First A.M.E. Zion, W. 3d, Coney Island	A. L. Lightfard, 2770 W. 15th	1890	28	36	600	3,000
Fleet St. Ml. A.M.E.Zion, B'dge, n. Myrtle.	P. A. Wallace, 347 Bridge	1885	986	428	16,154	58,500
Ralph A.M.E.Z., 416 Ralph av	J. H. Mason, 16 Dewey rd	1832	250	200	4,900	25,000
Methodist Free.						
Brooklyn Free Meth., 122 16th	F. F. Shoup, 124 16th st	1878	80	173	10,000	30,000
Hooper Street, 76 Hooper	H. W. Hodge	1873	40	50	3,500	18,000
Methodist Primitive.						
First, Park pl., near Nostrand av	J. Proude, M.A., 378 New York av.	1841	125	80	3,200	30,000
Orchard, 47-49 Oakland	Lee Ashton, 47 Oakland	1874	81	108	1,680	12,500
Methodist Protestant.						
Christ, Coney Island av. & Ave. I	T. T. Martin, 1104 E. 3d	1914	56	80	2,500	10,000
Grace (Canarsie), E. 92d & Church lane.	C. S. Kidd, 755 E. 89th	1830	300	250	5,000	25,000
Pentecostal.						
Bedford Ch. of the Nazarene, Weirfield and Evergreen av.	Wm. E. Riley, 63 Orient av	1895	35	106	1,217	....
John Wesley, Saratoga av. & Sumpter	W. H. Hoople, 277 Brooklyn av	1896	108	249	7,600	35,000
Nazarene, Utica av., bet. Bergen & Dean	E. T. French, 258 Albany av	1894	106	209	4,296	9,000
Presbyterian.						
Ainslie St., Ainslie, nr. Manhattan av	Vacant	1854	133	337	3,600	50,000
Arlington Av., Arlington av., cor. Elton.	John H. Kerr, 268 Arlington av	1890	569	655	10,247	60,000
Italian Br., Elton & Arlington avs	S. L. Testa, 962 Bedford av	1912	36	75	150	....
Linwood Br., 336 Ashford	Dr. J. H. Kerr, 268 Arlington av	1898	61	142	1,000	....
Bedford, Dean, cor. Nostrand av	S. Edward Young, 1273 Pacific	1894	690	756	27,980	175,000
Bensonhurst, First, 23d av. and 83d	E. B. MacDonald, 1780 W. 9th	1901	171	170	3,000	25,000
Bethany, McDonough and Howard av	L. O. Rotenbach, 203 Macon	1888	591	450	12,340	50,000
Beverly Rd., Beverly rd. & E. 8th	L. P. Armstrong, 508 5th	1900	235	190	5,000	27,500
B'hw'k Av., B'hw'k av. & Menehan	H. E. Schnatz, 975 Bushwick av	1868	450	440	6,000	81,000
Central, Marcy and Jefferson avs	J. F. Carson, 258 Jefferson av	1894	3,212	1,000	50,469	125,000
Franklin Av. Br. Italian, 165 Franklin av.	S. L. Testa, 962 Bedford av	1907	320	175	2,160	15,000
Classon Av., Classon av. and Monroe	R. M. Huston, 33 Monroe	1867	699	249	27,814	200,000
Cuyler, 358 Pacific st	J. R. Campbell, 360 Pacific	1907	275	450	4,200	30,000
Duryea, Sterling pl. and Underhill av	W. G. Clark-Duff, 362 Sterling pl	1887	204	475	17,923	100,000
Ebenezer, Stockholm, nr. St. Nicholas av.	C. C. Jaeger, 369 Stockholm st	1894	220	285	2 800	20,000
First, Henry, near Clark	L. Mason Clarke, 128 Henry st	1822	1,575	487	53,183	200,000
‡City Park Branch, 209 Concord	V. G. Burns, 209 Concord	1866	—	—	—	40,000
Flatbush, E. 23d and Foster av	H. H. Field, 657 E. 23d	1904	375	280	10,000	40,000
Glenmore Av., Glenmore av. & Doscher.	A. J. Penney, 298 Crescent	1899	137	325	2,640	10,000
Grace, Stuyvesant av., cor Jefferson	Robt. H. Carson, 744 Putnam av	1889	710	285	32,000	113,500
Greene Av., Greene av., b. Reid & Patchen avs.	W. L. Gallup, 1121 Bedford	1871	300	125	8,242	60,000
Halsey St., 1155-1157 Halsey	C. H. Schwarzbach, 1159 Halsey st	1886	60	85	1,300	20,000
Homecrest, Av. T and E. 15th	Edward L. Tibbals, 2198 Ocean av.	1900	275	300	8,000	25,000
Irving Sq., Weirfield and Wilson	Arthur F. Kurtz, 84 Weirfield	1902	347	509	7,416	29,000
Lafayette Av., Lafayette av. cor. S. Oxford	C. C. Albertson, 180 Wash'gton Pk	1857	2,391	550	141,643	400,000
*Gregg Chapel, 190 4th av	L. B. Verdoja, 645 Degraw	1908	170	150	3,000	500
†Cumberland St., 103 Cumberland	....	1864	....	....	......	....
Lefferts Park, 15th av. and 72d	T. B. Griswold, 1622 69th	1900	205	225	3,600	20,000
Memorial, 7th av. and St. Johns pl	John Barlow, 50 7th av	1867	465	125	26,870	170,000
Mount Olivet, Evergreen av., c. Troutman.	T. W. Malcolm, 823 Greene av	1887	390	375	5,220	18,000
Noble St., Noble, cor. Lorimer	R. R. Greenwood, 140 Noble	1869	361	360	22,000	65,000
Olivet, Bergen, nr. 6th av	J. G. Snyder, 9 8th av	1901	231	315	4,480	18,000

*Missions. †Statistics included in Lafayette Avenue Church. ‡Statistics included in First Church, Henry and Clark.

BROOKLYN CHURCHES—*Continued.*

Name of Church and Location.	Name of Pastor and Address.	Organized	Contrib'g Mem.	S. S. Members.	Total Amt. Raised	Value Church Prop'ty.
Presbyterian—Continued.						
Prospect Heights, 8th av. and 10th	E. D. Bailey, 1014 8th av	1888	1,000	400	$16,000	$50,000
S. Third St., S. 3d, cor. Driggs av	N. W. Wells, 155 South 3d st	1844	417	210	18,750	50,000
Siloam (colored), 404-8 Lafayette av	G. S. Stark, 286 Clifton pl	1848	300	130	5,254	33,000
Spencer Memorial, Clinton and Remsen	Vacant	1858	155	152	8,000	160,000
Syrian Protestant	R. A. Bishara, 201 Clinton	....	....	....	......	....
Throop Av., Throop av. and Macon	Wm. Carter, 362 Jefferson av	1862	[illegible]	442	24,300	125,000
Union Ch. of Bay Ridge, Ridge Blvd & 80th	H. H. Leavitt, 179 82d	1895	827	438	34,020	88,622
Wells Memorial, Glenwood & Argyle rds.	D. E. McCurry, M.A., 1117 Glen'd rd.	1906	250	175	8,500	75,000
Westminster, Clinton, corner 1st pl	Frank E. Simmons, 356 Henry	1856	400	250	8,000	50,000
Willoughby Av. (Ger.), 860 Willoughby av.	L. Wolferz, 497 Hart	1884	130	100	3,500	25,000
Wyckoff Hts., Harmon, nr. St. Nicholas av	L. L. Daniel, 8566 112 st., Richmond Hill	1904	384	549	4,475	20,000
Presbyterian—United.						
E. Brooklyn, Eldert Lane and Etna. Jos	L. Hervey, 627 Ferry, Woodh'n, L.I.	1902	300	875	......	40,000
Second, Bond and Atlantic av	Wm. M. Nichol, 463 Pacific	1858	60	60	2,652	30,000
South, 75th, nr. 6th av	Vacant	1913	80	150	1,850	20,000
Westminster, Bainbridge & Hopkinson av	A. H. Crosbie, 702 Decatur st	1894	181	360	2,178	20,000
Protestant Episcopal.						
Bishop, Dio. of L. I., Rt. Rev. Frederick Burgess, D.D., LL.D., Gar. C.						
*Advent, 75th and 17th av	R. R. Upjohn, 1676 69th av	1910	300	100	8,000	20,000
All Saints, 7th, cor. 7th av	E. S. Harper, 792 Carroll	1869	750	350	16,000	100,000
*Annunsiazione (Ital.), 1412 67th	J. Castelli, 1366 66th	1906	200	93	311	14,100
Ascension, Kent and Manhattan av	W. L. Greenwood, 129 Kent	1860	400	200	5,000	50,000
Atonement, 17th, near 5th av	Chas. C. Kelsey	1864	275	250	4,588	50,000
Calvary, E. D., 966 Bushwick av	John Williams, 1114 Bushwick av	1849	300	350	14,249	95,000
Christ, cor. Clinton and Harrison	W. De Forest Johnson, 326 Clinton	1834	250	120	20,000	225,000
*Christ Chapel, Wolcott and Van Brunt	H. L. Rice, 383 Clinton	1867	200	230	4,800	1,000,000
Christ, E. D., Bedford, nr. Division av	W. S. Chase, 481 Bedford av	1846	300	125	8,000	225,000
Christ, Ridge blvd. and 73d	J. H. Fitzgerald, 7301 Ridge Blvd	1853	400	450	10,191	101,000
*Emmanuel, 2635 E. 22d	A. R. Cummings, 193 Berkeley pl	1915	101	168	3,274	28,500
*Epiphany, E. 17th, cor. av. R	H. E. Payne, 1722 Av. R	1906	150	129	3,851	28,000
Good Shepherd, McDonough, nr. Lewis av.	Robert Rogers, 306 McDonough	1879	750	250	23,000	100,000
Grace Church, 46 Grace Court	C. F. J. Wrigley, 53 Remsen	1847	600	310	35,514	....
Grace, E.D., Conselyea, near Lorimer	Wm. G. Ivie, 65 Conselyea	1853	110	60	2,327	40,000
Holy Apostles, Greenwood, nr. Prospect av	G. F. Banbach, 623 Greenwood av	1890	350	411	8,000	35,000
*Holy Cross, 176 St. Nicholas av	James Williams, 176 St. Nicholas av	1896	300	350	5,784	20,000
Holy Spirit, Bay Parkway and 82d	T. C. Johnson, 2211 82d	1887	200	100	5,500	60,000
Holy Trinity, Montague, cor. Clinton	J. Howard Melish, 157 Montague	1840	630	150	42,588	200,000
Incarnation, Gates, bet. Classon & Fr'klin	A. W. E. Carrington, 239 Gates av.	1867	600	157	10,429	....
Messiah, Greene & Clermont avs	St. Clair Hester, 207 Washing'n pk	1850	1,204	125	21,500	350,000
Nativity, Ocean av. and Av. F	Andrew Fleming, 450 E. 26th	1899	362	245	9,911	80,000
Redeemer, 4th av., cor. Pacific	T. J. Lacey, 4th av. and Pacific	1853	343	103	7,371	154,000
*St. Agnes, 2005 60th	Vacant	1914	80	50	400	6,200
*St. Albans, Farragut rd., cor. E. 94th	F. C. Stevens, 9406 Av. F	1890	350	305	3,000	10,000
St. Andrew's, 50th and 4th av	J. W. Gill	1889	600	200	7,000	45,000
St. Ann's, Clinton and Livingston	G. A. Oldham, 131 Clinton	1784	600	250	30,000	500,000
St. Augustine's, St. Edwards, n. Myrtle av.	G. F. Miller, 121 N. Oxford	1875	390	100	4,434	16,500
*St. Barnabas' (col.), 726 Belmont av	C. G. Howell, 725 Belmont av	1907	118	86	2,726	12,200
St. Bartholomew's, Pacific, nr. Bedford av	Frank M. Townley, 1227 Pacific	1881	800	260	21,965	170,000
St. Clement's, Penn'vania, c. Liberty av.	H. W. R. Stafford, Queens, L. I	1888	92	....	2,400	40,100
*St. Gabriel's, Nostrand av. nr. Hawthorne	G. T. Baker, 345 Martense	1906	320	140	4,150	20,000
St. George's, Marcy av. and Gates	Chas. G. Clark, 264 Monroe	1869	732	250	11,000	75,000
St. James', St. James pl. & Lafayette av.	E. M. Thompson, 305 Lafayette av	1868	300	45	17,476	125,000
St. John's, St. Johns pl., nr. 7th av	T. B. Holland, 139 St. Johns pl	1827	795	200	22,164	100,000
†St. John's Hos., Atlantic av., c. Albany	Geo. D. Graeff, 1521 Atlantic av	1852	120	....	......	....
*St. John's, 99th, cor. Ft. Hamilton av.	W. A. Swan, 9818 Ft. Hamilton av	1834	170	80	2,791	27,500
St. John the Baptist, Webster av. and Ocean Parkway	J. W. Crowell, 725 E. 5th	1859	175	150	5,158	25,000
St. Jude, 55th, cor. 14th av	J. C. Stephenson, 1376 55th	1899	309	125	4,406	41,000
St. Luke's, Clinton av., nr. Fulton	H. C. Swentzel, 528 Clinton av	1842	750	125	15,834	....
*St. Lydia, Glenmore av. and Crystal	H. S. Frazer, 528 Bainbridge	[illegible]	100	100	1,500	10,000
*St. Margaret's Chapel, 1061 42d	J. C. Stephenson, 1376 55th	1902	....	65	......	5,500
St. Mark's, Brooklyn av. & E. P'kway.	A. L. Charles, 309 Brooklyn av	1837	500	257	9,000	68,000
St. Mark's, 230 Adelphi, nr. DeKalb av.	W. J. Ehrhard, 263 Clermont av	1850	305	110	5,702	65,000
St. Martin's, 293 President	F. W. Davis, 293 President	1854	323	26	4,577	35,000
St. Mary's, Classon av., c. Willoughby.	J. Clarence Jones, 230 Classon av	1834	901	327	19,365	125,000
St. Matthew, McDonough and Tompkins	F. W. Norris, 180 Macon st	1859	675	135	10,024	100,000
St. Michael's, 217 High	J. E. Gerstenberg, 219 High	1847	200	125	5,100	50,000
St. Paul's, Church av. & St. Pauls pl	W. J. Gardner, 68 St. Pauls pl	1836	1,635	530	32,608	250,000
St. Paul's, Clinton, cor. Carroll	A. C. Wilson, 199 Carroll	1849	200	87	12,152	250,000
St. Philips, 11th av., cor. 80th	John H. Sattig, 1063 81st	1899	450	250	11,000	70,000
*St. Philip's (colored), 1606 Dean	N. P. Boyd, 1610 Dean	1899	300	225	2,657	....
*St. Simon's, Av. K, cor. E. 12th	R. W. Kenyon, 1241 Dean	1911	130	160	2,600	8,000
St. Stephen's, Patchen av., c. Jefferson.	H. J. Glover, 547 Madison	1867	350	156	9,210	42,500
St. Thomas', Bushwick av., cor. Cooper.	Duncan M. Genns, 67 Moffat	1872	1,346	792	17,702	150,000
St. Timothy's, Howard av. nr. Atlantic	Chas. E. Taylor, 51 Irving pl	1889	100	125	2,200	11,800
*Transfiguration, Ridgewood & Autumn avs.	A. J. Lovelee, 193 Autumn av.	1894	350	225	3,400	35,000
Trinity, Arlington, cor. Schenck av	Jacob Probst, 70 Barbey	1854	480	196	9,119	63,000
Reformed Church in America.						
Church of Jesus, 64-66 Menehan	Christian Oswald, 79 Harman	1891	125	200	2,029	25,000
Church-on-the-Hhts., Pierrepont, n. Henry	T. W. Davidson, 47 Pierrepont	1851	....	....	......	....
Dutch Evangelical, Conklin av., Canarsie	J. Meier, 1155 E. 93d	1876	220	300	......	....
Edgewood, 53d and 14th av	Alex. Wouters, 1118 54th st	[illegible]	300	225	6,000	45,000
First Ch. of W'msb'g, Bedford av. & Clymer.	S. C. Hearn, Act. Pastor, 191 York	[illegible]	129	90	3,500	100,000
Flatbush (First), Flatbush & Church avs	J. Frederic Berg, 2103 Ken. Ter.	1654	520	600	......	220,000
F'tb'h Second, Church & Bed. avs	H. J. Wahl, 2170 Bedford av	1874	180	135	4,000	60,000
Flatlands, Kouwenhoven pl. and E. 40th.	C. W. Roeder, 1260 E. 40th	1654	390	787	9,240	35,000
Grace, Lincoln rd. and Bedford av	G. Wm. Carter, 155 Lincoln rd	1903	160	280	11,000	140,000
Gravesend, 145 Neck rd	O. M. Fletcher, 145 Neck rd	1655	315	350	8,468	150,000

*Missions. †Chapel.

BROOKLYN CHURCHES—*Continued.*

Name of Church and Location.	Name of Pastor and Address.	Organized	Contrib'g Mem.	S. S. Members.	Total Amt. Raised	Value Church Prop'ty.
Reformed Church in America—Continued.						
Greenwood Heights, 7th av. and 45th st.	Vacant	1891	190	350	$4,000	$30,000
Kent St., 149 Kent	H. B. Kerschner	1849	360	208	7,000	150,000
New Brooklyn, Herkimer, cor. Dewey pl.	F. C. Erhardt, 1062 Herkimer	1852	330	354	3,935	40,000
New Lots, New Lots rd. & Schenck av.	H. C. Hasbrouck, 653 Schenck av.	1824	103	107	1,605	37,000
New Utrecht, 18th av., bet. 83d and 84th	A. Roosenraad, 1828 83d	1677	340	350	9,000	....
Ocean Hill, Herkimer, cor. Hopkinson	Andrew Hageman, 1239 Herkimer	1885	100	262	2,574	25,000
Old First, 7th av. and Carroll	John W. Van Zanten	1654	750	200	......	250,000
S. Bushwick, Bushwick av. and Himrod	A. J. Meyer, 15 Himrod	1851	519	897	8,800	65,000
South, 4th av. and 55th	R. A. Watson, 425 56th	1838	874	1,001	13,422	75,000
Trinity, Union av. and Scholes	G. G. Wacker, 144 Penn	1853	300	400	5,000	60,000
Chapel, 267 St. Nicholas av	G. G. Wacker, 144 Penn	1853	....	300	......	10,000
Twelfth St., 12th, near 5th av	J. C. Rauscher, 136 Prospect Pk. W.	1858	1,000	900	12,500	125,000
Woodlawn, Av. M and E. 9th	J. G. Addy, 1460 E. 10th	1906	238	221	3,382	25,000
Reformed Church in the U. S.						
Christ Evangelical, 54 Wyona	Paul Wienand, 54 Wyona	1864	385	320	6,373	30,000
St. Mark's Ev. Ref., 601 Onderdonk av., R'	g'w'd. M. J. H. Walenta, 1739 Grove	1906	275	450	4,656	22,000
Ger. Emanuel, 410 Graham av	W. Walenta, 396 Graham av	1877	455	350	5,000	35,000
St. Luke's Evang. Ref., 55 Sutton	H Bran, 60 Hausman	1903	167	98	3,058	15,000
Reformed Episcopal.						
Grace, Herkimer and Saratoga av	T. R. Lawler, 225 Chauncey	1896	135	120	1,500	10,000
Redemption, 602 Leonard	Vacant	1877	90	75	1,400	8,000
Seventh Day Adventists.						
English Bkln., Patchen & Greene avs.	W. R. Andrews, 122 Jefferson av.	1877	425	225	30,000	25,000
First Bkln. Dan.-Nor., 675 Hicks	L. M. Halsvick, 275 86th	1894	130	126	6,000	12,000
First German, 1831 Gates av	B. E. Miller, 1703 Gates av	1901	325	400	30,000	80,000
Second Brooklyn, 1661 Dean	J. K. Humphrey, 141 W. 131st, Mhtn.	1906	70	60	76	700
Swedenborgian.						
Ch. of New Jerusalem, Monroe pl. & Clark	Vacant	1868	135	50	4,000	100,000
First Ger. New Ch. of Bkln., Jef'n & Kn	ick'er av. Paul Harth, 217 Weirfield	1883	40	26	......	30,000
Unitarian.						
Ch. of the Saviour, Pierrepont-Monroe pl.	J. H. Lathrop, 38 Pierrepont	1833	500	70	15,000	125,000
Willow Place Chapel, 26 Willow pl	W. J. Greene, 50 Monroe pl	1865	200	125	......	50,000
Fourth, E. 19th and Beverly rd	N. J. Springer, 613 E. 14th	1900	150	70	4,300	37,000
Second, Clinton, cor. Congress	C. H. Lyttle, 76 Columbia Hts	1851	200	40	10,000	20,000
Unity (Third), Gates av., c. Irving pl.	F. J. Gauld	1867	50	25	4,000	55,000
Universalist.						
All Souls, Ocean, cor. Ditmas av	A. Eugene Bartlett, 725 Ken. pl	1845	375	230	15,000	115,000
Ch. of Good Tidings, Stuyvesant av. and	Madison. C. H. Vail, 548 Monroe	1886	175	100	3,000	60,000
Ch. of Our Father, Grand av., c. Leffert	s pl. T. E. Potterton, 57 Lefferts pl.	1842	....	100	7,000	85,000
Miscellaneous.						
Brethren Church, 354 60th	J. S. Noffsinger, 358 60th	1889	100	250	......	20,000
Bkln. Ethical Culture Soc., Acad. of M	us. Hy. Neumann, 24 Willow	1906	300	50	7,500	....
Christian & Miss'y All'ce, 1560 Nostrand	A. Winn, Act., 1560 Nostrand av.	1901	50	....	2,000	....
Ch. of Divine Light (Spir.), Quincy, nr. Re	id av. E. C. Resch, 752 Jefferson av	1904	....	....	......	30,000
Ch. of Jesus Christ of L.D.Sts. (Mormon)	Gates & F'n. Geo. W. McCune, 265 Gates	1830	200	75	......	45,000
Ch. of the Second Advent, 1174 Bedford	av. Supply	1886	45	....	3,000	20,000
First Moravian, Jay, nr. Myrtle av	F. E. Grunert, 347 Jay	1854	100	125	4,000	50,000
Gospel Lighthouse, 1244 Myrtle av	William Coxe, 1244 Myrtle av	1905	100	80	600	....
Grace Gospel, Bainbridge, n. Saratoga av	Henri F. Gondret, 707 Halsey	1893	410	475	8,000	25,000
Independent Ch. of the Covenant	S. G. Tnydall, 416 30th	1920	....	....	......	20,000
Internat. Bible Students' Assn., Mas. T	emple. J. F. Rutherford, 124 Col. hts.	1909	....	....	......	....
Latter Day Saints Reorg. Ch., Park pl. and Schenectady av	J. F. Sheehy, 1361 St. Johns pl	1870	250	180	3,500	16,000
Meserole Av., 128 Meserole av	J. E. Jaderquist, 20 Banta, Elmhurst, L. I.	1899	56	75	2,200	10,000
Norw. Evan. Free (Indpt.) 15th & 4th av	N. W. Nelson, 578 Prospect av	1897	250	150	22,134	50,000
Young Girls' Home, 225 9th	....	....	....	....	......	....
People's Church (Ind.), 77 Sutton	W. Fred Silleck, 2123 Av. G	1899	25	50	500	7,500
Pillar of Fire, 123 Sterling pl	L. S. Wolfgang	....	....	....	......	....
Reformed Presbyt., 452 Monroe	R. C. Montgomery, 271 Madison st	1857	34	10	1,748	10,000
St. Nicholas, Syrian, G'k Ortho., Cath., Cath. 345 State	Rt. Rev. Aftimios, Bishop. B. M. Kerbawy, Dean, 124 Pacific.	1902	650	150	3,600	100,000
So. Bkln. Gospel Ch., 4th av., cor. 56th.	Geo. H. Dowkontt, 421 56th st	1898	150	160	4,500	40,000

Roman Catholic Churches of Brooklyn.

Bishop, Rt. Rev. Charles Edward McDonnell, D.D., 367 Clermont av Auxiliary Bishop, Rt. Rev. Thomas E. Molloy, D.D., 367 Clermont av.

Name of Church and Location.	Name of Pastor.	Organized	No. of P'r'hioners	S. S. Members	Value Ch'ch Prop.
*All Saints', Throop av., cor. Thornton st	Geo. Kaupert, 2 assistants	1867	4,000	400	$325,000
*Annunciation, N. 5th st., cor. Havemeyer	Nicodemus Petkus, 2 assistants	1863	3,000	...	200,000
*Assumption, Cranberry st	Wm. B. Farrell, 2 assistants	1842	2,500	488	300,000
*Blessed Sacrament, Euclid av. and Fulton st.	J. M. Kiely, 2 assistants	1891	2,000	260	45,000
Sts. Cyryl and Methodius, 123 Eagle st	Emil F. Strenski, 2 assistants	1918	.....	...	....
*Epiphany, 100-104 South 9th st	Edward A. Duffy, 2 assistants	1904	3,000	450	200,000
*Fourteen Holy Martyrs, Central av. & Covert.	Bernard Kurz, 1 assistant	1878	325	500	25,000
Guardian Angel, Ocean Pkway, nr. Neptune av.	Joseph F. Conway	1880	300	110	75,000
*Holy Cross, Church av., near Rogers av	J. T. Woods, 4 assistants	1852	4,000	1,200	300,000
Holy Family, 98th st. and Rockaway av	John Reynolds	1895	450	100	25,000
Holy Family (Slovak) Nassau av., nr. 15th st.	John J. Jurosko	1905	1,500	350	30,000
*Holy Family, 13th st., near 4th av	John S. Gresser, 2 assistants	1880	2,000	450	175,000
*Holy Innocents, 17th st. and Beverly rd	Francis McMurray, 2 assistants	1909	1,500	300	60,000
*Holy Name of Jesus, Pros. Pk. W. & Pros. av.	Charles Vitta, 2 assistants	1887	5,500	700	150,000
Holy Rosary, Chauncey st. and Reid av	John McEnroe, 2 assistants	1889	3,525	510	100,000
*Immaculate Conception, Leonard & Maujer sts.	Thomas Horan, 2 assistants	1853	5,065	1,000	125,000
*Immac. Heart of Mary, Ft. Ham. av., E. 4th.	M. J. Tierney, 2 assistants	1841	6,200	450	300,000

*Has a parochial school.

BROOKLYN CHURCHES—*Continued.*

Name of Church and Location.	Name of Pastor.	Organized	No. of P'r'h ioners	S.S. Members.	Value Church Prop'ty
Roman Catholic Churches—Continued.					
*Most Holy Trinity (German), 132-136 Montrose av	G. A. Metzger, 3 assistants	1893	2,500	600	$100,000
*Nativity, Church of The, Classon, cor. Madison	John L. Belford, 2 assistants	1871	5,000	600	250,000
Our Lady of Angels, 74th st. and 4th av	M. J. Flynn, 2 assistants	1892	1,121	470	80,000
Our Lady of Charity, Dean, nr. Schenectady	Louis Caporaso, 1 assistant	1904	3,021	140	25,000
*Our Lady of Consolation, Metropolitan & Berry	A. Jarka, 1 assistant	1908	2,000	350	75,000
*Our Lady of Czenstochova, 25th, nr. 4th av	B. Puchalski, 1 assistant	1896	2,010	200	100,000
*Our Lady of Good Counsel, Putnam, nr. Ralph av	Peter Donohue, 3 assistants	1886	4,600	1,100	250,000
Our Lady of Guadaloupe, 73d st., nr. 15th av	Thos. Cloke, 2 assistants	1906	900	175	75,000
Our Lady of Lebanon (Maronite), Hicks, nr. State	Khairullah Stephen	1903	200	100	25,000
Our Lady of Loretto (Ital.), Pacific & Sackman	V. Sorrentino, 2 assistants	1894	7,000	800	120,000
*Our Lady of Lourdes, B'way & De Sales pl	John McMahon, 5 assistants	1857	6,200	6.5	250,000
*Our Lady of Mercy, Schermerhorn, nr. Bond	J. J. McAteer, 2 assistants	1872	4,100	820	250,000
Our Lady of Miraculous Medal, 2453 Ralph st	J. J. Oppel	—	.....	...	....
*Our Lady of Mt. Carmel (Ital.), N. 8th & Union av.	P. Saponara, 1 assistant	1887	8,250	560	26,000
*Our Lady of Peace (Italian), 526 Carroll st	Franciscan Fathers	1901	8,000	610	100,000
*Our Lady of Perpetual Help, 59th st. & 5th av.	Redemptorist Fathers	189[illegible]	8,000	1,500	500,000
Our Lady of Pilar (Spanish)	A. Canas, 1 assistant	1916	.....	...	....
Our Lady of Refuge, Ocean and Foster avs	Robt. O'Donovan, 1 assistant	1912	800	90	50,000
Our Lady of the Presentation, Rock'y & St. M'ks.	John I. Whelan, 1 assistant	1887	1,200	250	100,000
*Our Lady of the Rosary of Pompeii, Seigel st.	O. Silvestri, 2 assistants	1895	12,046	400	150,000
*Our Lady of Solace, W. 17th st. & Mermaid av.	Walter Kerwin, 1 assistant	1900	1,000	500	40,000
*Our Lady of Sorrows, Morgan av. & Harrison pl	F. X. Wunsch	1891	2,000	3,000	80,000
Our Lady of Victory, Throop av., nr. McDon'gh.	Jas. J. Woods, 3 assistants	1868	5,000	800	500,000
*Queen of All Saints, Lafayette & Vanderbilt	James J. Coan, 2 assistants	1913	2,518	412	397,000
Sacred Heart, Barren Island	Attended from St. John's Cantius	1907	1,500	350	10,000
*Sacred Heart, Clermont av, near Park av	Thomas Leonard, 2 assistants	1873	6,000	1,500	300,000
*Sacred Hearts of Jesus and Mary, Deg'w & Hicks	John Vogel, 5 assistants	1879	2,000	2,000	200,000
St. Agatha, 50th nr. 7th av	Martin Fitzpatrick, 1 assistant	1912	2,500	600	100,000
*St. Agnes, Hoyt st., cor. Sackett st	Jas. F. Flynn, 2 assistants	1878	7,500	1,670	750,000
*St. Aloysius, Onderdonk av. and Stanhope st	John W. Hauptman, 2 assistants	1892	2,815	654	350,000
*St. Alphonsus, 177-183 Kent av	Geo. Metzger, 1 assistant	1873	750	150	40,000
*St. Ambrose, Tompkins av., cor. DeKalb av	Louis M. O. Blaber, 3 assistants	1883	4,000	400	200,000
*St. Anne's, Front st., cor. Gold st	John Patterson, 1 assistant	1860	4,500	500	125,000
*St. Antony of Padua, Manhattan av. & Milton.	P. F. O'Hare, 4 assistants	1856	12,500	2,000	500,000
St. Athanasius, 62d st. and 22d av	E. J. Donnelly	1913	900	200	60,000
*St. Augustine, 6th av., cor. Sterling pl	E. W. McCarty, 3 assistants	1870	6,000	850	600,000
*St. Barbara, Bleecker st. and Central av	James J. Kuntz, 3 assistants	1893	3,000	400	250,000
*St. Benedict, Fulton st., near Ralph av	Joseph Traenkle, 2 assistants	1852	1,600	300	185,000
*St. Bernard, Hicks st., cor. Rapelye st	Charles W. Hamma	1872	600	120	80,000
St. Blaise, Kingston av. and Maple st	Vincent De Giovanni	1907	4,000	500	10,000
*St. Boniface, Duffield st., nr. Willoughby st	M. Lang, 1 assistant	1854	1,240	300	75,000
*St. Brendan's, Av. O and E. 12th st	T. A. Hickey, 2 assistants	1907	800	1,000	105,000
*St. Brigid's, Linden st. and St. Nicholas av	John C. York, 3 assistants	1883	7,000	1,300	200,000
St. Casimir's (Polish), 40 Greene av	G. W. Kubec	1874	700	35	45,000
*St. Catharine of Alexandria, 41st & Ft. Ham'n pky.	John J. O'Neill, 2 assistants	1902	5,000	900	250,000
St. Catherine of Genoa, Albany, nr. Linden av.	Fredk. Hentz, 1 assistant	1910	1,150	75	10,000
*St. Cecilia, Herbert st., nr. N. Henry st	E. J. McGoldrick, 3 assistants	1869	13,000	2,500	650,000
*St. Charles Borromeo's, Sidney pl. & Livingston	Thos. J. O'Brien, 2 assistants	1850	5,333	600	200,000
St. Columbkille, 140-146 Dupont st	Theodore King, 1 assistant	1908	2,000	400	60,000
St. Edward, St. Edward st. and Leo pl	James F. Mealia, 2 assistants	1891	3,500	500	150,000
St. Elias (Greek Rite), Leonard, nr. Gr'np't av	P. Keshelak	1891	1,200	50	25,000
St. Finbar, Bay 20th st. and Bath av	W. A. Gardiner, 1 assistant	1881	510	160	75,000
*St. Francis Assisi, Lincoln rd. & Nostrand av.	F. X. Ludeke, 2 assistants	1897	1,200	275	125,000
St. Francis of Paola, Old Bhk Rd, nr. Skillman	L. Russo	....	.....	...	....
*St. Francis de Chantal, 57th st. and 13th av	John O'Loughlin, 2 assistants	1892	1,500	400	43,000
*St. Francis Xavier, Carroll st. and 6th av	D. J. Hickey, 3 assistants	1886	4,500	100	500,000
St. Gabriel, New Lots rd. and Linwood st	Thomas Fitzgerald, 2 assistants	1900	2,500	600	50,000
St. George (Lithuanian), 207 York st	Anthony P. Kodis	1910	1,150	150	11,500
*St. Gregory, Brooklyn av. & St. Johns pl	M. Fitzgerald, 2 assistants	1906	2,000	250	75,000
St. Ignatius, Nostrand av. and Carroll st	Jesuit Fathers	1909	2,000	300	....
*St. James Pro-Cathedral, Jay st., cor. Chapel.	F. J. O'Hara, 2 assistants	1822	5,000	1,000	500,000
St. Jerome, Newkirk and Nostrand avs	Thomas F. Lynch, 2 assistants	1901	3,000	250	300,000
*St. John the Baptist, Willoughby & Lewis avs.	Vincentian Fathers	1868	8,000	500	500,000
*St. John the Evangelist, 21st, near 5th av	Thomas S. Duhigg, 2 assistants	1849	10,000	500	220,000
*St. John's Cantius, Blake and New Jersey avs.	Theodore Regulski, 1 assistant	1902	2,000	120	60,000
*St. John's Chapel, Clermont av., nr. Greene av.	(Affiliated with Queen of All Saints.)	1878	2,518	412	....
*St. Joseph, Pacific st., near Vanderbilt av	Wm. T. McGuirl, 3 assistants	1853	10,000	1,200	500,000
*St. Leonard of Port Maurice, 70 Hamburg av	Geo. D. Sander, 2 assistants	1872	8,000	1,425	400,000
*St. Louis (French), Ellery st., nr. Nostrand av	Wm. T. Conklin, 1 assistant	1869	600	300	100,000
St. Lucy's (Italian), Kent av., near Park av	Alfonso Arcese, 1 assistant	1894	3,000	450	30,000
*St. Malachy, Van Sicklen av., nr. Atlantic av.	D. J. Cherry, 2 assistants	1854	2,000	550	60,000
St. Mark, E. 14th st. and Shore rd	D. J. McCarthy, 1 assistant	1868	1,400	200	25,000
*St. Martin of Tours, Knickerb'k'r av. & Hancock	James H. Lynch, 2 assistants	1906	2,000	500	60,000
*St. Mary, Mother of Jesus, 85th st., c. 23d av.	H. F. Murray, 2 assistants	1889	1,000	300	30,000
St. Mary, Queen of Angels, S. 4th & Roebling	Sylvester Remeika	1892	4,900	550	45,000
*St. Mary, Star of the Sea, Court, cor. Luqueer.	James Corrigan, D.D., 2 assistants	1855	12,628	1,450	250,000
*St. Matthew, Utica av. and Lincoln pl	William Costello, 3 assistants	1885	3,100	200	175,000
*St. Matthias, Catalpa, nr. Woodward	Nicholas M. Wagner, 2 assistants	1908	4,000	200	75,000
*St. Michael, 4th av. and 42d st	Patrick Cherry, 3 assistants	1870	10,500	1,600	400,000
*St. Michael (German), 225 Jerome st	Capuchin Fathers	1900	400	100	150,000
†St. Michael Archangel (Ital.), 230 Concord st	Joseph R. Agrella, 1 assistant	1881	4,235	500	12,000
*St. Nicholas, Devoe and Olive sts	J. P. Hoffmann, 2 assistants	1866	3,500	550	150,000
*St. Patrick, Kent av., cor. Willoughby av	John E. Cherry, 2 assistants	1843	12,021	1,714	324,000
*St. Patrick, 95th st. and 4th av	Jeremiah J. Kent, 2 assistants	1852	1,300	300	65,000
*St. Paul, Court st., cor. Congress	Michael G. Flannery, 3 assistants	1836	2,000	700	350,000
*Sts. Peter and Paul, Wythe av., nr. S. 2d st	John Lyle, 2 assistants	1837	9,000	1,000	360,000
*St. Peter, Hicks st., cor Warren st	M. A. Fitzgerald, 2 assistants	1859	7,500	165	175,000
St. Rita, 279 Essex st	Leopold Arcese, 1 assistant	1912	5,000	600	52,000
St. Rocco (Italian), 27th st., near 4th av	A. de Donatis	1900	5,000	200	7,000
St. Rosalia's (Italian), 62d st. and 14th av	Locksley A. Appo, 2 assistants	1907	5,000	200	10,000

*Has a parochial school. †Kindergarten.

BROOKLYN CHURCHES—*Continued.*

Name of Church and Location.	Name of Pastor.	Organized	No. of P'r'h-ioners	S. S. Mem-bers.	Value Ch'ch Prop.
Roman Catholic Churches—Continued.					
*St. Rose of Lima, Parkville av., Parkville	J. McAleese, 2 assistants	1870	725	310	$150,000
*St. Saviour's, 6th st. and 8th av	Jas. J. Flood, 2 assistants	1905	2,556	700	300,000
Sts. Simon and Jude, Av. T and Van Sicklen st.	John J. McCarron, 1 assistant	1898	600	100	35,000
St. Stanislaus' Martyr, 14th st., near 6th av	Fred. M. Lund, 1 assistant	1890	1,200	425	000
*St. Stanislaus' Kostka (Polish), 164 Driggs av.	Leo Wysiecki, 1 assistant	1896	2,000	600	,000
*St. Stephen, Summit st., cor. Hicks st	John G. FitzGerald, 2 assistants	1859	6,000	800	000
*St. Teresa, Classon av. and Sterling pl	Jos. McNamee, 4 assistants	1874	6,100	950	000
*St. Thomas Aquinas, 9th st. and 4th av	James Smyth, 2 assistants	1874	7,600	660	78,000
St. Thomas Aquinas, Flatbush & Flatlands avs.	E. W. Dullea, 1 assistant	1883	700	80	[illegible],000
*St. Vincent de Paul, N.6th, bt.Bedford&Driggs	John Geary, 2 assistants	1860	8,000	1,950	500,000
Spanish Mission, 38 Front	Vincentian Fathers	1911	300	200	......
*Transfiguration, Hooper st., cor. Marcy av	W. J. Maguire, 2 assistants	1874	5,500	650	210,000
*Visitation, Verona st., cor. Richards	William L. Long, 2 assistants	1854	7,500	700	300,000

*Has a parochial school.

Recapitulation, Brooklyn Churches.

Denominations.	Con-trib'g Mem.	S.S. Mem-bers.	Total Amount Raised.	Value Church Property
Baptist	17,768	14,421	$524,292	$2,765,200
Christian	162	255	4,460	28,000
Christian Science	......	......	....	....
Congregat onal	21,181	12,307	525,625	2,835,125
Disciples of Christ.	688	850	23,344	135,000
Evangelical Assn.	1,130	1,820	29,789	152,500
Evang. Sy. of N. A.	200	300	4,500	30,000
Friends	635	170	7,300	30,000
Jewish	*	3,122	480,179	2,586,000
Lutheran	25,491	20,584	500,091	3,441,909
Meth. Episcopal	19,010	19,764	453,913	3,191,950
M. E. African	1,430	939	20,300	95,000
M. E. Afric. Zion	1,379	744	24,229	101,500
Meth. Free	195	368	16,500	73,000
Meth. Primitive	206	188	4,881	42,500
Meth. Protestant	356	370	7,500	35,000
Pentacostal	249	564	13,113	44,000
Presbyterian	20,564	13,689	636,076	2,799,122
Pres. United	621	585	6,080	110,000
Prot. Episcopal	24,451	11,583	$563,008	$5,137,414
Ref. Ch. in Amer.	7,743	8,517	115,455	1,617,000
Ref. Ch. in U. S.	1,282	1,218	19,117	102,000
Ref. Episcopal	225	195	2,900	18,000
Roman Catholic	†	60,502	....	20,555,500
7th Day Adventist.	950	811	66,076	117,700
Swedenborgian	175	76	4,000	130,000
Unitarian	1,100	330	33,300	287,000
Universalist	530	430	25,000	260,000
Miscellaneous	2,720	1,830	130,782	430,500
Totals	666,822	178,692	$4,243,209	$52,050,920

*Number of families, 11,909. There are numerous "Holiday Churches" in N. Y. C., of which there is no official record and are not listed above.
†Number of parishioners, 444,462.

MANHATTAN AND BRONX.

Name of Church and Location.	Name of Pastor and Address.	Organized	Con-trib'g Mem.	S. S. Mem-bers.	Total Amt. Raised	Value Church Prop'ty.
Baptist.						
Abyssinian (colored), 242 W. 40th	A. C. Powell, 227 W. 136th	1808	1,600	500	$50,000	$350,000
Alexander Av., Alex. av., cor. E. 141st	G. B. Kierstead, 338 E. 141st	1872	350	650	8,000	120,000
Ascension, 291 E. 160th	F. W. Hagar, 386 E. 161st	1864	170	200	6,600	15,000
Baptist Temple, 159 W. 132d	M. B. Hucless, 159 W. 132d	1899	804	244	10,000	75,000
Calvary, 123 W. 57th	John R. Straton, 123 W. 57th	1847	828	150	30,000	1,000,000
Central, 92d and Amsterdam av	F. M. Goodchild, 144 W. 93d	1842	626	225	28,376	625,000
Central Park, 235 E. 83d	M. W. Pullen, 235 E. 83d	1855	160	200	4,000	60,000
Creston Av., c. Creston av. and E. 188t	h. A. C. Thomas, 146 E. 188th	1905	450	175	8,000	100,000
Day Star, 512-514 W. 157th	R. J. Brown, 503 W. 161st	1888	500	95	4,500	75,000
Ebenezer (Primitive), 1218 Intervale av.	J. McConnell, 206 E. 163d	1806	51	....	......	......
Emmanuel, White Plains av., n. E. 216th.	Vacant	1888	...	....	......	55,000
Fifth Avenue, 2-8 W. 46th	C. Woelfkin, 8 W. 46th	1841	659	250	298,267	500,000
First, Broadway, cor. W. 79th	I. M. Haldeman, D.D., 389 W. End av.	1762	765	200	31,000	750,000
First Czecho Slovak, 429 E. 77th	A. Hok, 124 E. 85th	1907	50	100	800	15,000
First German, 336 E. 14th	J. R. Miller, 2352 2d av	1846	120	75	1,850	100,000
First German of Harlem, 220 E. 118th	F. Busch, 220 E. 118th	1874	180	100	3,000	50,000
First Hungarian, 227 E. 80th	N. Dulitz	....	....	....	......	......
First Italian, 1 Henry st	Carmine Pagano, 300 Gates av., Bln.	1894	40	45	2,000	12,500
First Russian, 2d av. and 10th	G. A. Podlesney	1916	....	....	......	......
First Swedish, 141 E. 55th	Arvid Gordh, 141 E. 55th	1867	430	150	20,595	165,000
First Swedish Finnish	Isak Roy, 673 E. 137th	....	....	....	......	......
First Union of Bronx, 595 Courtland av.	P. H. Lee, 597 Courtland av	1915	360	175	7,000	25,000
Harlem, 219 E. 123d st	A. Chambers, 213 E. 123d	1901	90	1,600	6,000	60,000
Immanuel, 411 E. 75th	K. Roth, 218 E. 70th	1894	95	50	3,000	30,000
Judson Mem., Wash. Sq. S., c Thomp'n	A. R. Petty, 39 Gleane, Elmh., L. I.	1838	100	250	9,600	550,000
Madison Av., 30 E. 31st	G. C. Moor, 30 E. 31st	1848	523	374	39,000	680,000
Mariner's Temple, Oliver, cor. Henry	W. N. Hubbell, 3 Henry	1843	106	150	3,100	125,000
Metropolitan, 128th & 7th av	W. W. Brown, 143 W. 131st	1912	2,498	960	41,748	200,000
Mount Morris, 5th av., nr. 127th	C. W. Petty, 28 W. 127th	1844	600	1,200	23,000	150,000
Mount Olivet, 161 W. 53d	W. P. Hayes, 316 W. 52d	1878	2,000	200	11,000	190,000
North, 232 W. 11th	R. F. Y. Pierce, acting	1827	100	76	5,550	100,000
St. John the Baptist	P. L. Buffa, 2411 Lorillard pl	....	....	....	......	......
Second Avenue, 164 Second av	R. P. Sanford, 164 2d av	1898	100	200	6,000	120,000
Second German, 407 W. 43d	Wm. A. Lipphard, 409 W. 43d	1855	168	175	4,156	80,000
Sixteenth, 255 W. 16th	C. C. Prentice, 401 W. 152d	1833	187	250	8,000	75,000
Third German	R. Hoefflin, 1127 Fulton av	....	....	....	......	......
Tremont, Tremont and Webster avs	L. G. Simon, 270 E. 176th	1885	250	300	8,500	120,000
Trinity, 800 E. 224th, nr. Barnes av	B. T. Harvey, Lakewood, N. J.	1899	120	125	1,831	7,500
Union, 204 W. 63d	G. H. Sims, 131 W. 131st	1898	3,160	612	15,565	106,000
Wadsworth Avenue, 124 Wadsworth av.	E. S. Holloway, 461 Ft. Wash. av.	....	440	....	......	......
Washington Heights, 420 W. 145th	H. Pattison, 849 St. Nicholas av	1906	700	250	19,000	250,000
Calvinistic Methodist.						
Ebenezer (Welsh), 505 W. 155th	D. M. Richards, 393 Edgecombe av	1846	350	65	7,966	83,000
Christian Scientist.						
First, 1 W. 96th st	W. R. Best, 1st R., 204 W. 81st	1887	....	....	......	......
Second, Central Park W. and 68th st	C. E. Heitman, 1st R., 344 W. 72d.	1891	....	....	......	......
Third, 58th, e. of Park av	G. Falkenstein, 1st R., 628 W. 114th	1895	....	....	......	......

MANHATTAN AND BRONX CHURCHES—*Continued.*

Name of Church and Location.	Name of Pastor and Address.	Organized	Contrib'g Mem.	S. S. Members.	Total Amt. Raised	Value Church Prop'ty.
Christian Scientist—Continued.						
Fourth, Fort Washington av. and 178th.	J. H. Frames, 1st R.	1896	....	....	......	......
Fifth, 34 W. 43d	H. C. Burr, 1st R.	1913	....	....	......	......
Sixth, 1301 Boston rd.	S. S. Bettman, 1st R.	1907	....	....	......	......
Seventh, 112th, e. of B'way	J. Jaburg, 1st R.	1918	....	....	......	......
Eighth, 103 E. 77th	R. S. Ross, 1st R.	1919	....	....	......	......
Ninth, Park Av. Hotel	G. Alexander, 1st R.	1919	....	....	......	......
Tenth, 163 W. 57th	E. B. Sanford, 1st R.	19[illegible]	....	....	......	......
Eleventh, 2562 Briggs av.	F. Reeder, 1st R.	1919	....	....	......	......
Twelfth, Anderson Galleries	W. V. Cole, 1st R.	1920	....	....	......	......
Society, 547 W. 146th	M. Fabricant, 1st R.	1920	....	....	......	......
Congregational.						
Armenian, Evang., 207-215 E. 30th	A. A. Bedikian, 207 E. 30th	1897	273	....	$7,748	......
Bedford Park, Bainbridge av. and 201st	R. L. Peterson, 309 E. 201st	1890	304	201	5,737	$52,500
Broadway Tabernacle, 56th and B'way	Chas. E. Jefferson, 121 W. 85th	1840	1,377	400	72,000	1,000,000
Bethany, 455 10th av.	James A. McCague, 5 Hamilton ter	1867	315	225	2,177	75,000
Camp Memorial, 141 Chrystie	D. B. Minor, 33 E. 22d	1859	30	75	1,000	40,000
Forest Avenue, 166th and Forest av.	A. M. Reoch, 761 E. 166th	1851	234	195	3,600	35,000
Immanuel, 308 W. 139th (Swedish)	Carl Hanson, 308 W. 139th	1900	180	230	30,000	45,000
Manhattan, 76th and B'way......Chas.	H. Parkhurst, act., Hotel Ansonia	1896	245	41	......	500,000
North New York, E. 143d, nr. Willis av.	Wm. H. Kephart, 415 E. 143d	1890	800	650	10,000	100,000
Pilgrim, 175th, cor. Concourse, Bronx	H. M. Brown, 1808 Concourse	1892	150	120	6,000	90,000
Catholic Apostolic.						
Central, 417 W. 57th st.	H. O. DuBois, 417 W. 57th	....	....	....	......	......
Harlem German, 202 W. 114th st.	A. Hermann, 1224 Union av.	....	500	....	......	30,000
Disciples of Christ.						
Central, 142 W. 81st	F. S. Idleman, 107 W. 82d	1809	500	200	14,000	125,000
Russian Christian Ch., 147 2d av.	John Johnson, 147 2d av.	1910	50	34	476	......
Second, 595 E. 169th	L. H. Couch, 1342 Franklin av.	1863	130	250	5,000	80,000
Evangelical Association.						
Dingeldein Mem'l (German), 429 E. 77th.	C.F.Zimmerer,1228 Napier, Rich.H.	1883	53	60	1,450	12,000
First Ch. of Ev. Assn., 424 W. 55th	Daniel Bast	1844	75	90	3,000	60,000
German Evangelical Synod of N. A.						
St. Paul's, 2136 Newbold av.	J. P. Schwab, 2134 Newbold av.	1801	172	353	3,417	20,000
St. Paul's (German), 159 E. 112th	H. Rexroth, 107 E. 112th	1888	145	150	1,900	20,000
Friends.						
Friends' Meeting House, 221 E. 15th	No pastor. Anna L. Curtis, Sec.	1681	500	40	......	500,000
Twentieth St. (Orthodox), 144 E. 20th	No pastor	1704	....	....	5,748	180,000
Jewish.						
Adath Jeshurun, 112 E. 110th	M. Slomka, Pres.	1896	25	....	....	10,000
Adath Jashurun Anshe Kamenitz, 50-52 Attorney.	I. Goldenberg, 460 Grand	1886	250	46	....	42,000
Adath Jeshurun of Jassy, 58-60 Rivington	Morris Graubart, Sec.	1904	200	....	3,500	95,000
Adath Israel of N. Y., 203 E. B'way	G. W. Margolies	1901	9,000	....	......	......
Adath Wolkowisk, 203 Henry	M. Levy, Pres.	1887	120	....	....	....
Ahawath Abraham B'nai Kolo, 48 Av. D	....	1875	118	....	....	....
Ahawath Achim Anshe Hungaria, 70 Columbia.	P. Friedman, 56 Lewis	1883	150	....	....	20,000
Ahawath Sholom Anshe Winetza, 92 Hester.	Joel Limon, 1571 Fulton av.	1888	75	....	2,100	5,000
Ahawath Zedek Anshe Tinkowitz, 89 Henry.	*M. Greenberg	....	150	....	....	....
Anschel Cheutschover Chasam Sophor, 10 Clinton.	B. B. Guth, 103 Av. A.	1840	500	....	2,000	80,000
Anshe Achim, Anshe Kurland, 175 Eldridge.	*M. Bluestone	....	150	....	....	50,000
Anshe Chesed, 114th and 7th av.	Jacob Kohn, 235 W. 110th	1895	600	275	150,000	275,000
Anshe Lebedowe and Rodsilower, 245 D'n.	S. Epstein, 245 Division	1886	120	....	10,000	20,000
Anshe Sineer and Wilna, 290-292 Madison	S. Goldberg, 327 Madison	1871	100	350	6,000	100,000
Anshe Sholom Koldonov, 33 Jefferson	*S. Rakowitz, 26 Jefferson	1885	150	....	....	45,000
Anshey Bobruisk, 203 Henry	A. Rivkin, 66 Rutgers	1890	200	286	....	....
Ateres Zvie, Madison av. and 121st	F. Light, 178 E. 108th	1890	70	100	2,000	35,000
Atereth Israel, 323 E. 82d	M. Fried, 329 E. 79th	1882	65	96	5,000	45,000
Beth El, 5th av. and 76th	Samuel Schulman, 55 E. 92d	1874	225	350	60,000	1,500,000
Beth Hachneses Anshe Bialostok	J. Eskolsky, 256 E. B'way	1903	250	50	35,000	75,000
Beth Hakeneseth Anshe Alshan V'Ivie, 63 M'tgom'y.	Hyman Lipnitzky	1889	125	800	25,000	....
Beth Hakeneseth Anshe Slutzk, 34 Pike.	....	1906	375	....	20,000	45,000
Beth Hamidrash Hagadol Adasz Jeshurun, 463 E. 145th.	B. Rosenfeld	....	65	....	6,000	....
Beth Hamidrash Hagadol of Harlem, 110 E. 105th.	M. Levine, 34 W. 116th	1905	200	....	75,000	135,000
Beth Hamidrash Hagadol, 60 Norfolk	*R. Granowitz	1852	200	100	10,000	150,000
Beth Hamedrash Hagadol (Bronx), 827 Forest av.	Rabbi Olishefsky	1905	80	80	20,000	50,000
Beth Hamidrash Hagadol Anshe Ungard, 277 7th.	Moses Wemberger	1882	300	....	3,500	45,000
Beth Israel Bikur Cholim, 72d & Lex. av	....	1845	400	450	12,000	150,000
Beth Israel, 252 W. 35th	L. Shmulewitz, 460 W. 34th	1890	100	200	5,000	50,000
Beth Joseph Anshe Rachwoluwka, 88 Monroe.	M. Fridland, 145 Henry	....	100	....	....	....
Brith Sholom—Benei Jitzchok, 6 Av. D.	Chaim A. Friedman, 53 Av. D	1882	92	....	7,500	30,000
Central Synagogue, 55th & Lex. av.	Nathan Krass	1846	1,500	300	....	750,000
Cong. of People of City of Bobruisk, 203	Henry A. Rivkin, 66 Rutgers	....	299	....	....	......
Darech Amuno, 2 Van Nest pl.	*M. Morrison, 252 Bleecker	....	250	....	3,000	60,000
Dukler, Mugain Abraham, 87-89 Attorney	Rabbi David Frankel, 349 E. 4th	....	....	....	....	....
Emanuel, 521 5th av..H.G.Enelow,521 5th av.,	& Jos. Silverman, 45 E. 75th	1845	1,007	250	50,000	3,000,000
Emunath Israel, 301 W. 29th	A. Sachs, Sec.	1885	130	....	1,000	45,000
Ez Chaim of Yorkville, 107 E. 92d	D. Davidson, 71 E. 92d	1902	225	125	9,500	26,000
First Galician, 87 Attorney	*S. Schnee, 67 E. 7th	1881	219	600	1,800	65,000
First Rouman'n Amer. Cong., 89 Riv'n.	*N. Rosenzweig	1885	350	....	3,000	110,000
Free Synagogue, Carnegie Hall	S. S. Wise, 23 W. 90th	1907	1,000	1,000	100,000	200,000
Hand-in-Hand, Consolidated with Sinai	Cong. of the Bronx.					
Harlem Home of Daughters of Israel, 32-34 E. 119th.	P. Jaches, 1391 Mad. av	....	....	....	....	....
Hebrew Tabernacle, 218 W. 130th	E. Lissman, 417 Riverside Drive.	1905	150	300	135,000	70,000
Israel of Harlem, 120th and Lenox av.	Maurice H. Harris, 254 W. 103d	1873	600	300	40,000	340,000
Kahal Adath Jeshurun, 12-16 Eldridge	*L. Bloom	1886	200	....	....	120,000
Kehal Adath Jeshurun of Jassay, 97 Forsyth.	*L. H. Braunstein	....	375	....	....	....
Kehilath Israel, 1162 Jackson av.	L. Finkelstein, 631 E. 168th	1905	100	175	....	50,000
Kehilath Jeshurun, 119 E. 85th	M. S. Margolies, 1225 Madison av.	1882	1,000	135	....	125,000
Khol Adath Kurland, 25 W. 115th	P. Jaches, 1391 Madison av.	....	....	....	....	....
Kol Israel of Harlem, 24-28 W. 114th	S. Buchler, 1800 7th av.	1903	375	200	16,000	75,000
Kol Israel Anshe Poland, 20-22 Forsyth	M. S. Buchler	1870	200	....	......	150,000

*Presidents, others Rabbis.

MANHATTAN AND BRONX CHURCHES—*Continued.*

Name of Church and Location.	Name of Pastor and Address.	Organized	Contrib'g Mem.	S. S. Members.	Total Amt. Raised	Value Church Prop'ty.
Jewish—Continued.						
Kolbuszower Teitelbaum Chevra Banai Chajim Machne Rubin, 622 E. 5th	L. Leiman, 111 E. 7th	1893	380	....	$2,000	$25,000
Lubowitz and Homle, 169 Henry	....	1903	150	....	1,750	23,000
Montefiore Congregation, Hewett pl., nr. Macy pl.	Alex. Basle, 830 E. 163d.	1897	500	255	12,000	65,000
Mount Neboh, 150th, nr. B'way	A. Eiseman, 610 W. 156th	1911	295	500	75,000	125,000
Mount Zion, 37-41 W. 119th	Benj. A. Tintner, 3 W. 122d	1889	100	250	....	100,000
M'wasereth Zion, 188 Stanton	*J. Feller	....	125	....	....	....
Nachlath Zevi, 65-67 E. 109th	M. N. Kaplan, 22 E. 108th	1881	1,000	....	1,200	75,000
New People's Synagogue, 151 Clinton	S. Buchler, 1800 7th av	1913	300	100	3,500	....
New Synagogue, B'way, bet. 76th and 77th.	E. Frisch, 140 Claremont av.	1915	400	100	....	....
Oheb Zedek, 116th, west of 5th av	Philip Klein, 137 W. 119th	1873	400	....	....	150,000
Ohel Torah, 804 E. 6th	S. Schwartz, 956 Kelly	1902	500	300	2,000	6,000
Orach Chaim, 1463 Lexington av	M. Hyamson, 115 E. 95th	1879	125	150	....	50,000
Oshmaner and Trab Assn., 68 E. B'way	A. Shreero, 115 Madison	....	100	....	....	....
People's Synagogue, 197 E. B'way	J. Tarlau, 530 W. 153d	1895	650	600	....	....
Pincus Elijah, 118 W. 95th	....	....	115	155	....	40,000
Peni-El, 525 W. 147th	J. Blau, 600 Riverside dr	1907	150	200	20,000	90,000
Poel Zedek Anshe Ella, 126-128 Forsyth.	A. A. Klein, 202 E. B'way	1886	125	....	12,000	150,000
Rodeph Sholom, Lexington av. and 63d	R. Grossman, 1347 Lexington av	1842	750	300	....	300,000
Rzeszower-Karcziner, 70 Willett	S. Burnstein, 122 Goerck	1886	220	75	....	25,000
Shaaray Tefila, 156-162 W. 82d	F. de Sola Mendes, 154 W. 82d	1846	600	350	30,000	200,000
Shaare Berocho, 80-82 W. 126th. Consolidated with Israel of Harlem.						
Shaari Zedek, 23 W. 118th	Vacant	1838	600	....	....	75,000
Sharith B'nai Israel, 22 E. 113th	J. A. Dolgenos, 1771 Madison av	1881	70	500	3,000	26,000
Shearith Israel (Span.-Portuguese), 99 Central Park West	H. P. Mendes, 99 Central Park W.	1855	500	200	....	1,000,000
Sheerith Judah, 543 W. 145th	H. Cohen, 202 W. 119h	1913	55	....	11,000	....
Sinai Cong. of Bronx, Stebbins av. and E. 163d.	M. Reichler, 860 E. 161st.	1911	550	600	12,000	60,000
Talmud Torah Yagistover, 32 Rutgers	*E. Rosenblum, 396 Grand	1872	60	....	2,000	35,000
Talmud Torah Yagustaver, 122 W. 129th	C. Jaches, 200 W. 111th	...	....	....	....	....
Talmud Torah Beth Abraham, 532 E. 146th.	A. Gallant, 494 E. 140th	1898	150	....	20,000	35,000
Tifereth Israel, 1038-42 Prospect av	B. Kallenberg, 1042 Prospect av	1916	76	....	....	65,000
Tiffereth Israel, 2481 Valentine av	M. Kopfstein, 1393 Franklin av	[illegible]	126	....	....	45,000
Tiffereth Israel, 126 Allen	J. Lotz, 90 Orchard	1872	200	....	8,500	80,000
Tifferth Jerusholoim, 240 Madison	M. Sobel	1887	120	....	12,000	30,000
West End Synagogue, 156 W. 82d	N. Stern, 201 W. 79th	1846	600	350	30,000	200,000
Zemach Zedek Nusach Hoari, 184 Henry	B. Sosensky, 216 Clinton	1893	200	....	....	....
Zera Jacob, Washington, cor. 175th	S. Gelich, 1818 Bathgate av	1900	150	35	2,000	19,[illegible]
Zichron Ephraim, 67th, near 3d av	Rev. Dr. B. Drachman, 128 W. 121st	1889	1,400	1,000	20,000	250,000
Lutheran.						
Advent, B'way and 93d	A. Steimle, 174 W. 93d	1897	365	202	16,978	275,000
Atonement, Edgecombe av. & W. 140th.	C. E. Frontz, 39 Hamilton Terrace	1899	550	457	17,517	120,000
Bethany, 582 Teasdale pl. G. V.	B. Schumann, 903 Caudwell av	1893	200	249	3,600	13,850
Christ, 406 E. 19th	G. U. Wenner, 319 E. 19th	1868	297	122	4,890	65,000
Concordia, Brook av. and 142d	H. Pottberg, 505 E. 142d	1906	270	230	......	35,000
Emmanuel, Brown pl. and 137th	P. M. Young, Brown pl. and 137th.	1901	228	310	5,200	50,000
Epiphany, 70-74 E. 128th	M. L. Canup, 70 E. 128th	1880	400	150	8,517	40,000
Ev. Luth. Hebrew Mission, 250 E. 101st.	N. Friedmann, 1427 Longfellow av	1883	....	....	2,200	500
Fordham, 2430 Walton av	F. H. Meyer, 2431 Morris av	1915	263	201	6,300	30,000
Grace, 123 W. 71st	J. A. Weyl, 107 W. 68th	1886	420	225	5,000	85,000
Grace, Valentine av., cor. 199th	Aug. Koerber, 2924 Valentine av	1905	260	310	6,500	35,000
Gustavus Adolphus (Swedish), 151 E. 22d	Mauritz Stolpe, 217 E. 49th	1865	1,000	300	11,653	176,202
Harlem (Finnish), 171 E. 121st	K. Makinen, 2002 5th av	1903	120	50	2,400	....
Harlem Swedish, 74 W. 126th	A. F. Borgendahl, 72 W. 126th	1894	630	225	1,287	6,900
Holy Comforter, Woodycrest av. & W. 165th	A. P. Schwab, 1070 Woodycrest av	1911	200	170	10,000	12,500
Holy Trinity, 65th and Central Park W.	Paul E. Scherer, 3 W. 65th	1868	410	182	30,000	350,000
Holy Trinity, 881 E. 167th	F. H. Lindemann, 881 E. 167th	1899	200	110	7,000	17,000
Holy Trinity (Slovak), 334 E. 20th	L. A. Engler, 230 E. 19th	1904	500	....	1,500	....
Immanuel, 88th, cor. Lexington av	Geo. F. Schmidt, 1376 Lex. av	1863	1,390	610	42,850	350,000
Immanuel (Nor. & Scan.), 1410 Vyse av.	I. Thoraldsen, 1790 Clinton av	1895	50	50	1,500	6,000
Luth. Emigrant Mission, 147 W. 23d	G. G. F. Haas, Grymes Hill, S. I.	1869	....	....	....	110,000
Messiah (Swedish), Brook av. and 144th.	John Johnson, 424 E. 141st	1907	225	200	3,000	17,000
Our Saviour, Audubon av. and 179th	A. S. Hardy, 523 W. 179th	1898	127	156	4,780	45,000
Our Saviour (Norwegian), 237 E. 123d	J. C. Gram, 241 E. 123d	1896	240	60	4,000	50,000
Redeemer, 422 W. 44th	F. C. G. Schumm, 422 W. 44th	1895	275	140	3,195	60,000
St. James, Madison av., cor. E. 73d	J. B. Remensnyder, 900 Madison av	1827	225	101	8,024	400,000
St. John's, 79-83 Christopher	F. E. Oberlander, 79 Christopher	1855	319	320	11,455	85,000
St. John's, 217 E. 119th	H. C. Steup, 229 E. 124th	1864	500	400	15,060	45,000
St. John's, 1343 Fulton av	T. O. Posselt, 1343 Fulton av	1860	720	400	6,800	85,000
St. Luke's, 233-239 W. 42d	Wm. Koepchen, 431 W. 43d	1850	....	....	......	......
St. Luke's, 1724 Adams	W. Rohde, 1722 Adams	1898	154	135	......	7,000
St. Mark's, 323-327 6th	Vacant	1848	100	40	3,600	70,000
St. Mark's, 242d and Martha av	O. H. Trinklein, Yonkers, N. Y.	1913	126	120	......	22,500
St. Matthew's, Convent av. and 145th	A. Wismar, 419 W. 145th	1664	450	300	......	......
St. Matthew's, 376 E. 156th	Wm. T. Junge, 385 E. 155th	1862	...	350	3,000	46,500
St. Paul's Evang., 313 W. 22d	H. A. Kropp, 317 W. 22d	1841	73	100	3,534	140,000
St. Paul's, 147 W. 123d	Fred H. Bosch, 142 W. 123d	1864	940	400	10,060	150,000
St. Paul's, Lafontaine av. and 178th	Karl Kretzmann, 585 E. 178th	1898	410	300	7,920	30,000
St. Paul's, 796 E. 156th	G. H. Tappert, 796 E. 156th	1882	400	420	6,294	40,000
St. Peter's, 437 E. 140th	O. C. Mees	1893	617	400	11,400	60,000
St. Peter's, Lexington av. and 54th	A. R. Moldenke, 132 E. 54th	1862	700	700	17,000	125,000
St. Peter's, 219th st., Williamsbridge	F. Noeldeke, 757 E. 218th	1894	119	160	2,955	15,000
St. Stephen's, 1001 Union av	Paul Roesener, 999 Union av	1893	275	300	12,000	42,000
St. Thomas, E. 175th & Topping av	A. J. Traver, 1770 Gr. Concourse	1908	325	300	15,000	45,000
Trinity, cor. Westchester & Glebe avs.	Paul Sander, 2260 Ellis av	1913	110	115	2,500	3,000
Trinity (German), 139 Av. B	Otto Graesser, 602 E. 9th	1843	400	45	4,360	75,000
Trinity, 164 W. 100th	E. Brennecke, 168 W. 100th	1889	900	300	11,000	135,000
Trinity (Danish), 1179 Hoe av	A. C. Kildegaard, 1179 Hoe av	1903	85	35	2,800	20,000
Washington Heights, W. 153d & B'way.	C. B. Rabbow, 546 W. 153d	1895	360	250	6,860	80,000
Zion, 341 E. 84th	Wm. Popcke, 338 E. 84th	1892	1,800	1,028	6,000	125,000

*Presidents, others Rabbis.

MANHATTAN AND BRONX CHURCHES—*Continued.*

Name of Church and Location.	Name of Pastor and Address.	Organized	Contrib'g Mem.	S. S. Members.	Total Amt. Raised	Value Church Prop'ty.
Methodist Episcopal.						
Battery Swedish, 127 W. 89th	O. K. Sundberg, 2407 B'way	1887	130	55	$6,700	$100,000
Bedford Street, Bedford and Morton	United with Metropolitan Temp.					
Beekman Hill, 319 E. 50th	Geo. Adams, 321 E. 50th	186[illegible]	215	76	3,895	125,000
Bethel, Grand Concourse & 177th	C. O. Forsgren	1901	60	120	4,000	50,000
Blinn Memorial, Lexington av. & E.103d	H. J. Schuckai, 140 E. 103d	1890	160	200	5,300	61,000
Boston Road, Boston rd. & E. 172d	H. J. Hartman, 870 E. 175th	1831	150	100	2,675	85,000
Calvary, 7th av., cor. W. 129th	W. P. Odell, 2290 7th av	1886	600	450	20,000	200,000
Centenary, Washington av. and 166th	F. B. Crispell, 1074 Washington av.	1850	300	410	5,400	100,000
Chelsea, Fort Washington av. & 178th	G. B. Smith, 701 W. 177th	1848	240	228	6,000	100,000
Church of All Nations, 9 2d av	J. R. Henry, 9 2d av	1906	250	400	6,500	350,000
Ch. of the Saviour, 111th, cor. Lex'tn av	A. H. Wilson, 111th, cor. Lex. av.	1869	298	235	1,160	100,000
Cornell Memorial, 231 E. 76th	W. C. Phelps, 231 E. 76th	1869	115	500	1,400	100,000
Crawford Mem'l, White Plains av. and 218th	L. H. Caswell, 54 Glen av., Mt.V.	1895	290	264	......	255,000
Duane, 294 Hudson	A. Jamieson, 292 Hudson	1794	40	20	7,500	50,000
Elton Avenue (German), Elton av. & E. 158th.	F. Hagner, 456 E. 158th	1850	166	200	3,000	30,000
First German, 48 St. Marks pl	E. W. Piglow, 48 St. Marks pl	1841	60	50	13,500	25,000
Five Points Mission, 69 Madison	F. J. Belcher, 69 Madison	1856	45	600	36,286	300,000
Fordham, 2543 Marion av	A. Thompson, 2543 Marion av	1872	135	313	7,000	110,000
Grace, 131 W. 104th	F. B. Harris, 131 W. 104th	1867	1,000	450	30,000	250,000
Hadley Rescue Mission, 293 Bowery	J. Callahan, 293 Bowery	1904	....	....	8.000	......
Jefferson (Italian), 407 E. 114th	A. M. D. Riggio, 407 E. 114th	1895	300	400	3,000	200,000
John St., 44 John	L. R. Streeter, 73 Willow, B'kln	1766	175	100	5,000	300,000
Madison Av., Madison av. and 60th	R. W. Sockman, 480 Park av	1881	600	240	70,000	400,000
M. E. Church, Mott av., cor. E. 150th	A. H. Nesbitt, 157 E. 150th	1886	[illegible]	3,800	......	90,000
Metropolitan Temple, 7th av. and 14th	J. W. Chasey, 60 7th av	1834	250	300	15,000	250,000
Morris Heights, 1788 Sedgwick av	W. H. Westerfield, 1801 Popham av	1890	70	120	......	35,000
Park Avenue, Park av., cor. 86th	S. W. Grafflin, 106 E. 86th	1837	400	300	8,000	850,000
People's, 225-233 E. 61st	B. F. Saxon, 223 E. 61st	1866	250	225	7,000	140,000
People's Home, 545 E. 11th	L. G. Davis, 543 E. 11th	1868	85	165	2,000	40,000
St. Andrew's, 122 W. 76th	Allan MacRossie, 37 Madison av	1889	250	170	14,000	200,000
St. James', Madison av. and E. 126th	G. L. Nuckolls, 1981 Madison av.	1833	426	349	15,000	115,000
St. Mark's (colored), 231 W. 53d	W. H. Brooks, 237 W. 53d	1871	1,500	300	45,600	200,000
St. Paul's, West End av. and W. 86th	R. L. Forman, 550 West End av	1835	627	220	32,044	390,000
St. Paul's (German), 308 E. 55th	H. Houst, 320 E. 55th	1874	40	55	1,250	48,000
St. Stephen's, 228th and Marble Hill av	Chas. L. Mackey, 144 W. 228th	1826	84	65	3,000	54,000
Salem, 102 W. 133d	F. A. Cullen, 234 W. 131st	1885	900	600	10,000	120,000
Second (German), 346 W. 40th	A. Sleitz, 350 W. 40th	1840	100	80	2,300	65,000
Swedish, Lexington av., cor. 52d	C. A. Seaberg, 323 E. 50th	1882	225	160	7,000	250,000
Tremont German, 1841 Bathgate av	Wm. Hesskamp, 1841 Bathgate av.	1904	75	70	1,800	25,000
Tremont, E. 178th and Washington av	W. H. Moser, 454 E. 178th	1850	450	600	8,000	80,000
Trinity, City Island av. & Bay, City Is	C. A. Whitemarsh, 113 Bay, City Is.	1878	225	283	3,500	25,000
Trinity, 318 E. 124th	W. P. Lord, 36 Clark, Bkln	1859	125	50	2,000	100,000
Union, 48th, west of B'way	J. G. Benson, 233 W. 48th	1894	200	190	25,000	250,000
Wakefield Grace, Wh. Plains av., n.241st	D. F. Crawford, Treas., 4746 White Plains av	1888	100	125	2,000	40,000
Wash'gton Hts., Amster'm av., c.W.153d.	J. E. Price, 1868 Amsterdam av	1868	800	250	15,000	110,000
Washington Square, 139 W. 4th	J. S. Stone, 133 W. 4th	1820	100	150	16,000	130,000
West Side, 461 W. 44th	A. M. Morgan, 463 W. 44th	1862	230	140	4,700	35,000
Westchester, 2547 E. Tremont av	A. L. Faust, 2547 E. Tremont av	1808	247	248	5,700	60,000
Willis Avenue, Willis av. and E. 141st	J. E. Zeiter, 401 E. 141st	1850	625	500	16,000	150,000
Woodlawn, 241st and Katonah av	W. R. Blackie, 239 E. 237th	1875	142	162	4,400	41,000
Methodist Episcopal—African.						
Bethel A. M. E., 52-60 W. 132d	M. W. Thonston, 58 W. 132d	1819	1,000	550	28,000	110,000
Emmanuel A. M. E., 148 W. 62d	A.A. Amos, 430 Vanderbilt av., Bk	1902	75	65	4,000	15,000
*Metropolitan A. M. E., 132 W. 134th	A. L. Wilson, 185 W. 134th	1901	120	115	3,000	......
Mission of Simon of Cyrene, 331 W. 37th	P. E. Paul, 202 W. 143d	1913	70	45	1,600	300
Union A. M. E., 109 W. 131st	J. G. Ryder, 109 W. 131st	1818	153	101	5,678	15,000
Methodist Epis.—African, Zion						
Mother A. M. E. Zion, 151 W. 136th	J. W. Brown, 110 W. 139th	1796	1,400	525	35,000	135,000
Rush Memorial, A. M. E. Zion, 58 W. 138th.	G. M. Oliver, 2470 7th av.	1843	600	150	12,000	80,000
Moravian.						
Second, Wilkins av. and Jennings	E. S. Wolle, 859 Jennings	1852	150	160	2,000	55,000
Third (Moravian), 224 W. 63d	F. T. Trafford, 218 W. 63d	1901	250	209	13,000	......
Presbyterian (Presbytery of N. Y., 156 5th av.).						
Adams Memorial, 207 E. 30th	H. L. Rambo, 207 E. 30th	1886	350	202	6,300	75,000
Ascension (Ital.), 340 E. 106th	A. Stasio, 152 E. 116th	1906	415	350	800	75,000
Beck Memorial, 980 E. 180th	M. Bartlett, 980 E. 180th	1814	525	440	8,640	100,000
Bedford Park, Bainbridge av. & 200th	Geo. Mair, 213 E. 201st	1900	350	217	5,824	30,000
Bethany, 420 E. 137th	D. R. Wylie, 50 Morningside Drive	1875	210	326	3,600	100,000
Bethlehem Chapel, 196 Bleecker	E. L. Walz, 133 E. 73d	1847	252	224	1,870	100,000
Bohemian Brethren, 589 W. 165th	V. Ziegler	1906	44	....	......	......
Brick, 5th av. and 37th	Wm. P. Merrill, 112 E. 36th	1767	....	184	2725,905	......
Broadway (formerly Fourth av.), B'way & 114th.	W.D.Buchanan, 305 W. 106th	1825	961	481	......	......
Central, Madison av. and 57th	D. W. Wylie	1821	1,150	517	8,800	600,000
Chelsea, 212 W. 23d	Wm. N. Ross, 214 W. 23d	1908	350	125	18,000	350,000
Chinese Church, 225 E. 31st	Huie Kin, 225 E. 31st	1910	102	126	1,984	40,000
Christ, 344 W. 36th	T. F. Savage, 1 W. 64th	1888	700	700	5,000	250,000
Church of the Covenant, 310 E. 42d	G. C. Hunter, 150 E. 40th	1893	515	455	4,000	50,000
Ch. of the Gospel, 196 Bleecker	T. Barbieri, 196 Bleecker	1918	112	....	250	......
Church of the Puritans, W. 130th & 5th av.	R. B. Clark, 15 W. 130th	1871	525	200	10,000	200,000
Ch. of the Sea and Land, 61 Henry	W. D. Hall, 61 Henry	1864	451	687	15,327	160,000
East Harlem, 233 E. 116th	H. V Yergin, 200 E. 116th	1887	397	185	885	50,000
Emmanuel Ch., 737 6th	G. E. Schibrede, 737 6th	1858	880	780	4,300	200,000
Faith, 359 W. 48th	R. F. Jenney, 510 W. 112th	1888	400	225	9,000	80,000
Fifth Avenue, 5th av. and 55th	J. Kelman, 7 W. 55th	1808	2,000	275	340,833	2,000,000
First Pres., 5th av., 11th and 12th	G. Alexander, 47 University pl	1716	1,894	292	185,755	1,000,000
First of Morrisania, Wash. av., n.E.168th.	M. F. Johnston, 1205 Washington av.	1849	576	352	7,489	100,000
First of Throggs Neck, Westchester	Vacant	1854	123	205	1,650	40,000
First of Williamsbridge, 734 E. 225th	A. D. Gantz, 730 E. 225th	1900	200	350	3,000	45,000

*Missions.

MANHATTAN AND BRONX CHURCHES—*Continued.*

Name of Church and Location.	Name of Pastor and Address.	Organized	Contrib'g Mem.	S. S. Members.	Total Amt. Raised	Value Church Prop'ty.
Presbyterian—Continued.						
Ft. George, W. 186th & St. Nicholas av.	L. R. Hartley, 1545 St. Nicholas av	1917	300	450	......	$120,000
Ft. Washington, W. 174th & B'way	J. McNeill, 461 Ft. Washington av	1913	600	550	$15,000	650,000
Fourth, West End av., cor. W. 91st	E. W. Work, 631 West End av	1787	700	300	31,500	350,000
Fourth Av. (now Broadway).						
French Evangelical, 126 W. 16th	Paul D. Elsesser, 126 W. 16th	1849	665	118	6,500	65,000
Good Shepherd, 152 W. 66th	D. E. Lorenz, 134 W. 80th	1888	450	200	9,500	125,000
Gospel, 196 Bleecker	T. Barbieri, 7 King	....	....	....	......	......
Greenwich, 145 W. 13th	W. H. Matthews	1846	359	140	16,110	125,000
Harlem, N. Y., Mt. Morris Pk. W. and	122d. F. W. Evans	1915	836	280	17,000	200,000
Holy Trinity (Ital.), 153d, nr. Morris av.	J. W. Vavolo, 253 E. 153d	1911	135	155	500	70,000
Home St., Home and West Farms rd.	Robt. M. Russell, Jr., 40 E. 39th.	1910	225	250	4,580	50,000
Hunts Point, Coster and Spofford av	B. D. Hall, 710 Coster	1911	207	291	2,305	40,000
Italian Ch. of the Covenant	R. Valenti, 424 Mott av	....	....	....	......	......
John Hall Memorial, 342 E. 63d	P. F. Landis	1908	....	500	2,500	200,000
John Huss, Church and Neighb'd Hse.	V. Pisek, 347 E. 74th	1874	317	926	5,994	110,000
Labor Temple, 2d av. and 14th	J. C. Day, Dir.	1910	1,000	700	34,000	300,000
Madison Avenue, Madison av. and 73d	H. S. Coffin, 129 E. 71st	1899	1,697	1,952	94,000	750,000
Church House, 432 3d av	Lee W. Beattie, 432 3d av	1886	74	300	2,000	200,000
Morningside, Morningside av. & W. 122d.	P. E. Baker, 600 W. 122d	1894	180	225	5,261	110,000
Mount Washington, Dyckman & B'way.	W. D. Knight, 616 W. 207th	1846	193	275	6,647	80,000
North, 525 W. 155th	J. R. Mackay, 3750 B'way	1905	1,488	615	25,000	250,000
Northminster, 141 W. 115th	S. C. Craig, 238 W. 113th	1905	300	150	2,000	70,000
Olmstead Av., Newbold av. & Olmstead.	M. F. Clarke, 1417 Overing	1910	173	140	1,955	72,000
Park Av., Park av. and 85th	Tertius van Dyke, 1010 Park av	1846	250	195	6,500	500,000
Rendall Memorial, 258 W. 133d	W. R. Lawton, 173 Wil'by, Bkln.	1899	....	....	......	......
Riverdale, Riverdale av., Bronx	R. Mackenzie, Riverdale av. & 248th	1863	200	100	17,747	30,000
Rutgers, B'way, cor. W. 73d	D. Russell	1797	400	177	40,000	800,000
St. James' (colored), 59 W. 137th	F. M. Hyder, 206 W. 137th	1895	1,200	309	10,000	75,000
St. Nicholas Av., 141st & St. Nicholas av	E. W. Brown, 58 Hamilton Terrace	1891	520	400	17,500	250,000
Second, W. 96th and Central Park West	R. Watson	1756	824	275	23,042	400,000
Seventh Ch. of Jesus Christ, 138 Broome	J. T. Wilds, 134 Broome	1818	347	96	10,000	300,000
Spring Street, 246 Spring	J. W. Darr, 45 Dominick	1811	250	200	3,500	250,000
Tremont, Grand Concourse and 178th	J. H. Hartman, 240 E. Tremont av.	1854	450	300	7,500	75,000
University Hts., Fame pl. and Univ. av.	P. B. Wightman, 2200 Loring pl.	1900	402	412	10,006	125,000
Van Nest, Morris Park & Barnes avs.	G. M. Elsbree, 1822 Hunt av	1905	502	400	10,500	75,000
West End, W. 105th, cor. Amsterdam av	A. E. Keigwin, 324 W. 103d	1888	2,207	800	64,836	400,000
West Park, W. 86th, cr. Amsterdam av.	A. H. Evans	1829	547	281	47,620	900,000
Woodlawn Hgts., 240th & Martha av	C. B. Swartz, 206 E. 200th	1912	200	190	3,000	40,000
Woodstock, Prospect av. and 165th	James Cromie, 1068 Tinton av	1890	300	400	4,000	200,000
Presbyterian Reformed.						
Second, 308 W. 122d	W. McCarroll, 1182 Woodycrest av		210	200	6,000	55,000
Third, 327 W. 33d	F. M. Foster, 305 W. 29th	1848	111	150	5,200	......
Presbyterian—United.						
East 187th St., E. 187th and Tiebout av.	A. Heughs, E. 187th and Tiebout av	1902	80	160	6,950	50,000
Second, Audubon av., cor. W. 172d	J. P. Lytle, 512 W. 172d	1831	173	150	8,000	85,000
West Forty-fourth Street, 434 W. 44th	H. H. Wallace, 426 W. 44th	1856	150	122	4,712	60,000
Protestant Episcopal. Bishopric	of New York, vacant.					
All Angels, W. 81st and West End av	S. DeL. Townsend, 251 W. 80th	1859	1,530	250	53,967	....
All Saints, Henry and Scammel	K. S. Guthrie, 292 Henry	1824	20	34	160	150,000
All Souls, St. Nicholas av. and 114th	C. Macon, 88 St. Nicholas av	1850	400	150	12,000	200,000
Ascension, 5th av. and 10th	P. S. Grant, 7 West 10th	1827	497	109	73,909	833,046
Ascension Memorial, 251 W. 43d	J. F. Steen, 257 W. 44th	1863	198	100	6,565	175,000
Beloved Disciple, 59 E. 89th	Geo. R. Van DeWater, 65 E. 89th.	1870	250	150	21,000	200,000
Calvary, 4th av. and 21st	Theodore Sedgwick, 103 E. 21st	1836	1,200	300	45,000	......
Chapel of the Comforter, 10 Horatio	C. C. Clark, 10 Horatio	1914	200	160	......	....
Chapel Good Shepherd, Blackwell's Isl'd	S. N. Ussher, 44 E. 76th	1889	....	....	......	75,000
Christ, W. 71st, cor. Broadway	John R. Atkinson, 213 W. 71st	1793	400	150	......	900,000
Christ, Riverdale av. and 252d	G. W. White	1866	....	....	......	90,000
Christ the Consoler, ft. of E. 27th	E. V. Collins, Bellevue Hospital	1830	....	....	......	City
Ch. of the Advocate, Wash'n av. & 181st	Geo. N. Deyo, 2119 Washington av.	1899	405	390	4,290	31,000
Ch. of Holy Comforter, 341 W. Houston	A. R. Mansfield, 25 South	1847	....	....	......	50,000
Ch. of Holy Faith, E. 166th & Trinity av	C. S. Gregg, 698 E. 166th	1880	1,000	250	6,391	100,000
Ch. of San Salvatore (Ital.), 359 Broome	Sisto J. Noce, 359 Broome	1870	500	350	......	200,000
Ch. of the Mediator, Kingsbridge av. &	W. 231st. J. Campbell, 260 W. 231st	1855	250	240	12,853	250,000
Ch. of the Resurrection, 115 E. 74th	E. Russell Bourne, 63 E. 75th	1866	75	60	3,000	250,000
Du St. Esprit (French), 45-47 E. 27th	A. V. Wittmeyer, 606 W. 137th	1687	250	100	7,500	....
Epiphany, Lexington av. and 35th	W. T. Crocker, 143 E. 35th	1835	....	....	......	....
Grace (West Farms), Vyse av., nr. 177th	A. E. Bentley, 1907 Vyse av	1843	490	200	4,500	30,000
Grace, 800 Broadway	C. L. Slattery, 804 Broadway	1809	....	585	338,218	......
Grace Chapel, 414 E. 14th	Eliot White, 92 4th av	1896	Included in Grace Ch.			
Grace, City Island av. & Pilot, City Is.	J. McVickar Haight, Rec., 44 C. Is. av.	1880	30	41	627	13,000
Grace-Emmanuel, 216 E. 116th	W. K. McGown, 1925 7th av	1894	500	150	6,500	85,000
Heavenly Rest, 551 5th av	Herbert Shipman, 3 E. 45th	1870	1,000	250	60,000	1,000,000
Holy Apostles, 28th and 9th av	L. A. Dix Edelblute, 360 W. 28th.	1844	620	250	13,000	250 000
Holy Communion, 6th av. and 20th	Henry Mottet, 47 W. 20th	1846	500	190	......	....
Holy Cross, 300 E. 4th	W. K. Damuth, 35 Washington sq.	1875	....	....	......	....
Holy Nativity, 204th and Bainbridge av	C. F. Kennedy, 3061 Bainbridge av	1907	250	200	5,980	33,700
Holy Rood, 179th & Ft. Wash. av. Gustav	A. Carstensen, D.D., 715 W. 179th.	1893	....	....	......	225,000
Holy Trinity Ch., W. 122d cor. Lenox av.	H. P. Nichols, 18 W. 122d	1868	450	200	32,000	400,000
Incarnation, Mad. av., c. 35th. H. P. Silver,	209 Madison av.; Rev. G. F. Taylor and H. Glaser, Asst	1852	652	80	137,408	....
Incarnation Chapel, 240 E. 31st	G. F. Taylor, 236 E. 31st	1858	600	350	26,000	....
Little Church Around the Corner. (See	Transfiguration)					
Messiah Chapel, 206 E. 95th	M. N. Wilson, 206 E. 95th	1891	400	120	861	45,000
St. Albans', Ogden av. and 163d	M. K. Crawford, 979 Ogden av	1899	175	80	3,500	50,000
St. Andrew's, 4th av., cor. 50th	R. Harold	....	....	....	......	......
St. Andrew's, 5th av., cor. 127th	A. E. Ribourg	1829	600	250	......	200,000
St. Ann's, St. Anns av., nr. 140th	H. G. Willis, St. Anns av. & 140th.	1841	754	450	7,606	254,125
St. Barnabas' Chapel, 306 Mulberry	L. E. Sunderland, 38 Bleecker	1878	....	....	......	......
St. Bartholomew's, Park av. & 54th	Leighton Parks, 107 E. 50th	1835	2,920	1,200	293,547	1,000,000
St. Bartholomew's Chapel, 211 E. 42d	P. G. Favour, 209 E. 42d	1896	400	400	3,000	......

MANHATTAN AND BRONX CHURCHES—*Continued.*

Name of Church and Location.	Name of Pastor and Address.	Organized	Contrib'g Mem.	S. S. Members.	Total Amt. Raised	Value Church Prop'ty.
Protestant Episcopal—Continued.						
Swedish Chapel, 123 E. 127th	E. G. Ericson, 125 E. 127th	1891	300	125	......	......
St. Clement's, 423 W. 46th	Thomas A. Sparks, 423 W. 46th	1830	500	250	......	......
St. Cyprian's Chapel (col'd), 171 W. 63d	J. W. Johnson, 173 W. 63d	1905	700	500	$5,000	$200,000
St. David's, 384 E. 160th	E. G. Clifton, 313 E. 157th	1896	597	305	371,474	60,000
St. Edmund's, Morris av., cor. E. 177th.	J. C. Smiley, 206 E. Tremont av.	1884	360	132	4,432	48,000
St. Edward the Martyr, 12 E. 109th	P. C. Pyle, 14 E. 109th	1883	106	65	6,000	75,000
St. George's, Stuyvesant sq	Karl Reiland, 209 E. 16th	1811	2,000	1,102	118,005	620,000
St. George's Chapel, 661 E. 219th	D. S. Agnew, 661 E. 219th	1894	125	188	3,000	25,000
St. Ignatius', West End av. and 87th	Wm. P. McCune, 552 West End av.	1872	294	87	19,510	370,000
St. James', 71st, cor. Madison av	F. W. Crowder, 829 Park av	1810	600	512	150,000	1,433,886
Ch. of the Holy Trinity, 312-32 E. 88th.	Jas. V. Chalmers, Vicar, 332 E. 88th	1897	390	964	......	....
St. James' (Fordham). Jerome av., cor.	190th. DeW. L. Pelton, 3 E. 190th.	1853	600	350	8,000	300,000
St. John the Divine (Cathedral), 112th,	nr. Amst'm. H. C. Robbins	1872	....	....	......	....
St. John the Evang., 224 Waverley pl	J. A. Wade, 224 Waverley pl	1856	350	225	12,000	150,000
St. Luke's, Convent av., cor. W. 141st	W. T. Walsh	1820	600	500	21,500	375,000
St. Margaret's, 940 E. 156th	H. H. Gifford	1899	300	180	3,500	65,000
St. Mark's in the Bouwerie, E. 10th &	2d av.. W. N. Guthrie, 232 E. 11th.	1795	....	....	......	....
St. Mark's Hall, 234 E. 11th		....	....	....	......	....
St. Mark's Mem'l Chapel, 288 E. 10th	P. C. Valence, 288 E. 10th	1879	....	....	......	....
St. Mark's Parish House, 288 E. 10th	Wm. N. Guthrie, 288 E. 10th	1879	....	201	......	....
St. Mary the Virgin, 139 W. 46th	J. G. H. Barry, D.D., 144 W. 47th.	1868	420	211	54,548	879,393
St. Mary's, Alexander av., nr. E. 142d	J. A. MacNulty, 338 Alexander av.	1854	600	250	6,000	40,000
St. Mary's, 101 Lawrence	C. B. Ackley, 101 Lawrence	1823	500	300	6,092	103,720
St. Matthew's, 28 W. 84th	Arthur H. Judge, 82 W. 84th	1854	585	182	26,000	261,662
St. Ann's, Deaf Mutes, 511 W. 148th	John Chamberlain, 460 W. 149th	1852	325	40	1,753	50,000
St. Michael's, Amsterdam av. and 99th.	T. McCandless, 225 W. 99th	1807	400	250	......	....
St. Paul's, Wash'n av. & St. Pauls pl.	H. F. Taylor, 1446 Washington av.	1849	550	220	......	100,000
St. Peter's, Westchester av., Westches'r	Joseph A. Foster, Westchester av.	1693	830	350	26,000	300,000
St. Peter's, W. 20th, near 9th av	O. S. Roche, 346 W. 20th	1831	425	200	8,000	175,000
St. Philip's, 212 W. 134th	H. C. Bishop, 217 W. 133d	1819	1,000	1,085	44,217	531,500
St. Simeon's, 165th and Sheridan av	R. J. Walker, Sheridan av. & 165th	1905	250	150	6,000	100,000
St. Stephen's, 122-128 W. 69th	Nathan A. Seagle, 120 W. 69th	1805	325	68	18,218	530,000
St. Stephen's Chapel, 4355 Vireo av	R. W. Cochrane, 4308 Martha av.	1896	145	67	1,400	20,000
St. Thomas', 5th av. and W. 53d	E. M. Stires, 3 W. 53d	1823	2,929	141	307,305	1,730,000
St. Thomas' Chapel, 230 E. 60th	J. S. Haight, 229 E. 59th	1894	1,275	690	7,000	400,000
Transfiguration, 1 E. 29th	G. C. Houghton, 1 E. 29th	1848	1,200	307	49,781	1,500,000
Trinity, Broadway, opp. Wall	W. T. Manning, 4 Washington sq.	1697	1,238	175	27,789	17,500,000
Chapel of the Intercession, B'way & 1	55th. M. H. Gates, 540 W. 155th	1846	1,451	8,160	......	......
St. Agnes', W. 92d, nr. Columbus av.	W. W. Bellinger, 115 W. 91st	1892	2,700	761	......	......
St. Augustine's Chapel, 105 E. Houst'n	L. D. Rhodes, 105 E. Houston	1870	454	273	......	....
St. Chrysostom's Ch'l, 7th av. & W. 39th	C. Nelson Moller, 550 7th av	1866	748	268	22,000	650,000
St. Cornelius Ch'l, Governor's Island	E. B. Smith, Governor's Island	1845	....	....	......	82,000
St. Luke's Chapel, 483 Hudson	E. H. Schlueter, 477 Hudson	1821	755	300	......	....
St. Paul's Chapel, Fulton & Vesey	Joseph P. McComas, 29 Vesey	1766	175	50	......	5,000,000
Trinity Chapel, 15 W. 25th	J. W. Sutton, 18 W. 25th	1855	200	....	10,000	......
Trinity, E. 164th, nr. Boston rd., Bronx	A. S. Hull, 591 E. 164th	1889	186	....	......	....
Zion and St. Timothy, 234 W. 57th	Fred. Burgess, Jr., 334 W. 57th	1890	500	100	22,671	250,000
Reformed Church in America.						
Anderson Memorial, 675 E. 183d	J. A. De Boer, 675 E. 183d	1892	107	201	2,500	25,000
Bethany Memorial, 1st av., cor. 67th	A. B. Churchman, 400 E. 67th	1898	250	275	1,800	200,000
Church of the Comforter, 279 E. 162d	R. H. MacCready, 279 E. 162d	1894	160	250	28,000	62,000
Elmendorf Chapel, 171 E. 121st	A. A. Pfanstiehl, 171 E. 121st	1660	400	325	......	60,000
Evangelical, 351 E. 68th	Julius Jaeger, 355 E. 68th	1758	100	120	4,998	100,000
Fordham Manor, Kin'sbdge rd. & Claflin ter	J. M. Hodson, Davidson av. c. 190th	1696	190	142	4,601	60,000
Fourth (German), 410 W. 45th	A. E. Wirth	1856	114	112	4,026	......
Grace, 7th av. and 54th	J. R. Duryee, 139 E. 36th	1879	270	150	7,100	150,000
Hamilton Grange, W. 149th c. Convent av	A. F. Mabon, 459 W. 149th	1874	226	193	9,965	175,000
Mott Haven, E. 146th, nr. 3d av	O. M. Voorhees, 350 E. 146th	1851	200	275	4,000	200,000
New York Collegiate:						
Collegiate (St. Nicholas), 5th av. & 48th	M. J. MacLeod, Cedar Knolls, B'xv'e.	1628	....	....	......	....
Collegiate (Marble), 5th av. & W. 29th	D. J. Burrell, 1 W. 29th	1628	725	108	32,000	......
Collegiate (W. End), W. End av. & W. 77th	H. E. Cobb, 370 West End av	1892	600	200	......	....
Collegiate (Mid. Ch.), 112 2d av	E. F. Romig, 50 7th	1628	600	300	......	....
Faith Mission, 241 W. 60th	Thos. H. Johnson	1913	109	104	......	....
Fort Washington, Ft. W'h'n av. & 181st	I. H. Berg, 415 Ft. Washington av	1909	....	....	......	100,000
Fulton St. Noon Prayer Meet., 113 Fulton.	Geo. H. Dowkontt, Supt.	1857	....	....	......	....
Knox Memorial, 405 W. 41st	E. G. W. Meury, 405 W. 41st	1858	910	1,408	......	......
Vermilye Chapel, 416 W. 54th	W. R. Ackert, 416 W. 54th	1891	350	389	2,000	200,000
Ref. Ch. of Harlem, 267 Lenox av	Edgar Tilton, Jr., 269 Lenox av	1660	600	250	9,500	300,000
Manor Church, 350 W. 26th	F. E. Bolster, 350 W. 26th	1855	....	....	......	115,000
Union (High Bridge), Ogden av. & 169th.	D. G. Verwey, 1176 Woodycrest av.	1874	303	300	6,162	75,000
West Farms, Prospect av. & Fairmount pl	W. N. MacNeill, 783 Fairm't pl.	1839	165	150	2,000	......
Zion, Stebbins av. and Chisholm	A. F. Hahn, 1288 Stebbins av	1836	240	270	3,000	125,000
Reformed Church in the U. S.						
Martha Memorial, 419 W. 52d	E. F. Burger, 438 W. 47th	1880	225	170	4,500	50,000
St. Paul's, 606-612 E. 141st	J. Schmitt, 612 E. 141st	1852	428	413	4,621	75,000
Reformed Catholic.						
Christ Mission, 331 W. 57th	H. P. Morgan, 331 W. 59th	1883	....	....	......	65,000
Reformed Episcopal.						
First Y.W.C.A., 53d & Lexington av	P. T. Edrop, 194 Clinton, Bkln	1874	100	100	3,000	......
Seventh Day Adventists.						
German New York, Eagle av. and 163d.	D. N. Wall, 499 E. 176th	....	130	90	7,974	5,000
Harlem (Col.), 144 W. 131st	J. K. Humphrey, 141 W. 131st	1910	600	450	25,000	50,000
Seventh Day Adv. Temple, 120th & Len	ox av. C. B. Haynes, 322 Convent av	1898	500	411	42,000	500 000
Swedish Manhattan, 137th, nr. Willis av.	S. F. Svensson, 436 E. 138th	....	83	62	3,434	......
Unitarian.						
All Souls, 4th av. and 20th	Wm. L. Sullivan	1819	400	40	25,000	700,000
Lenox Av., Lenox av., cor. W. 121st	M. St. C. Wright, 490 Riverside dr.	1887	150	....	10,000	100,000
West Side, B'way and 117th	C. F. Potter, Pelham, N. Y.	....	....	....	......	......
Universalist.						
Ch. Divine Paternity, Cent. Pk. W. & 76th.	Rev. J. F. Newton, 4 W. 76th	1838	450	75	......	800,000

MANHATTAN AND BRONX CHURCHES—*Continued.*

Name of Church and Location.	Name of Pastor and Address.	Organized	Contrib'g Mem.	S. S. Members.	Total Amt. Raised	Value Church Prop'ty.
Miscellaneous.						
Amer. Greek Orthodox, 233 E. 17th.....	I. N. W. Irvine, 18 E. 90th.......	1920	....	....	......	......
Broome St. Tabernacle(Ital.), 395 Broome	Joseph Brunn, 395 Broome	1884	325	500	$3,000	$300,000
Church of God, 2134 Grand av., Bronx..	C. J. Blewitt, 2134 Grand av......	1907	....	....	1,000	70,000
Church of God, 334-6 E. 14th...........	C. J. Blewitt	1898	....	....	7,500	....
Church of God, 774 E. 223d............	A. A. Bolitho, 2132 Grand av......	1898	....	....	......	......
Ch. of the Strangers (Deem's Mem'l)	309 W. 57th. P. M. Spencer.........	1868	360	200	10,000	250,000
Ch. of Jesus Christ of Latter Day Saints (Mormon), 151 W. 125 & 273 Gates av., Bn.	G. W. McCune, 265 Gates av., Bkln.	1830	450	60	......	4,500
Community Ch. of N.Y., Park av. & 34th...	John Haynes Holmes, 61 E. 34th..	1825	465	200	20,000	1,000,000
DeWitt Memorial, 280 Rivington.........	W. T. Elsing, 280 Rivington.......	1881	480	450	1,700	90,000
First (7th Day Bap.), Judson Memorial,	Washington Sq. So................	1845	....	....	......	......
First Ch. of Divine Science, Waldorf-A	stor.a. W. J.2Murray, 113 W. 87th.	....	64	37	2,700	......
Hungarian Reformed 346-348 E. 69th....	Zoltan Kuthy, 344 E. 69th..........	1895	1,250	125	7,814	75,000
Mariners', 166 11th av..................	K. P. Miller, 542 W. 124th.........	1856	....	....	......	......
Metropolitan Tabernacle, 104th & B'way.	Wm. Allan	1917	214	180	22,000	......
New Jerusalem, 114 E. 35th.............	Julian K. Smyth, 230 W. 59th......	1816	234	40	12,000	225,000
Olivet Memorial, 59 2d	H. L. Oldfield, 63 2d	1867	375	309	2,196	40,000
People's Tabernacle, 52 E. 102d.........	Henry M. Tyndall, 56 E. 102d......	1894	200	200	......	250,000
Sears Philosophy, Princess Theatre....	F. W. Sears, 110 W. 34th..........	1906	3,000	....	19,600	......
St. Nicholas Russian Orth. Cathedral, 15	E. 97th. L. Turkevich, 15 E. 97th..	1893	5,000	....	......	275,000
Soc. for Ethical Culture, Central Pk. W.	& 64th. Dr. Felix Adler	1876	1,200	....	......	......
Waldensian (Italian and French services), 405 W. 41st..........................	Rev. B. Tron, 366 W. 25th.........	1910	160	25	2,500	......
West Side Mission, 269-271 W. 47th......	C. E. White, 309 W. 46th...........	1897	40	90	1,200	1,000

Roman Catholic Churches of Manhattan and Bronx.

Archbishop of New York, Most Reverend Patrick J. Hayes, D.D., Archbishop, Res. 452 Madison av.

Name of Church and Location.	Name of Pastor.	Organized	No. of P'r'hioners	S. S. Members.	Value Ch'ch Prop.
*All Saints, Madison av. and E. 129th st........	J. W. Power, 3 assistants...........	1880	10,000	800	$250,000
*Annunciation, W. 131st st. and Convent av..	W. L. Penny, 4 assistants...........	1852	7,000	1,187	450,000
*Ascension, 215 W. 107th st..................	E. M. Sweeney, 4 assistants.........	1896	7,300	500	500,000
*Assumption, 427 W. 49th st..................	James Veit, 1 assistant............	1858	5,000	538	250,000
*Blessed Sacrament, S. E. cor. B'way and 71st.	Wm. J. Guinan, 4 assistants........	1887	6,500	315	450,000
*Corpus Christi, S. E. cor. B'way and 121st st..	John H. Dooley, 3 assistants........	1906	2,500	300	225,000
*Epiphany, 373-375 2d av.....................	P. J. Harold, 3 assistants..........	1868	9,000	425	300,000
Good Shepherd, 207th & B'way, (Bldg.).........	T. J. McNichol, 3 assistants........	1911	2,000	325	100,000
*Guardian Angel, 511-513 W. 23d st............	J. F. Raywood, 2 assistants.........	1888	3,000	600	150,000
*Holy Cross, 333 W. 42d st....................	Vacant, 3 assistants	1852	8,000	1,547	400,000
*Holy Family, Castle Hill & Watson av., U'port	U. C. Nageleisen, 1 assistant.......	1895	1,500	105	75,000
*Holy Innocents, 124-128 W. 37th st...........	Thos. J. Lynch, 2 assistants........	1866	2,000	50	1,000,000
*Holy Name, N. W. cor. Amsterdam av, W. 96th	J. B. Curry, 4 assistants...........	1868	12,000	418	775,000
Holy Rosary, 438-442 E. 119th st.	Thos. F. Kane, 4 assistants.........	1884	7,000	1,060	250,000
*Holy Spirit, Burnside and Aqueduct avs......	J. D. Roach, 2 assistants...........	1901	1,500	135	125,000
*Holy Trinity, 205-211 W. 82d st..............	J. G. McCormick, 4 assistants.......	1898	6,000	390	500,000
*Immaculate Conception, 503-511 E. 14th st.....	T. W. Tierney, 3 assistants.........	1855	80,000	1,636	250,000
*Immaculate C'ception (Ital.mis.), E. Gun Hill	rd. & Holl. av. R. Tonini, 2 assts.	1903	1,200	300	25,000
*Immaculate Conception (Ger.), 389 E. 150th....	Wm. Tewes, 7 assistants............	1853	5,000	620	400,000
*Incarnation, St. Nicholas av. and 175th st....	J. F. Delany, 3 assistants..........	1908	4,500	300	175,000
Mary, Help of Christians, 431 E. 12th st........	P. Beccaria, 3 assistants..........	1908	18,000	800	85,000
*Most Holy Redeemer, 173 E. 3d st., nr. Av. A.	Joseph Schmidt, 6 assistants	1842	1,000	150	300,000
Most Precious Blood, 113 Baxter st.............	P. Savastano, 3 assistants..........	1890	18,000	800	200,000
Nativity, 46-50 2d av..........................	Daniel J. Quinn, 2 assistants.......	1842	1,850	400	125,000
Notre Dame, 40 Morningside Drive...............	A. N. Arcibal, Adm., 1 assistant..	1910	3,500	700	300,000
*Our Lady Queen of Angels, 228 E. 113th st....	Fulgentius Brem, 4 assistants.......	1886	4,000	400	100,000
Our Lady of Esperanza, 156th & Riverside dr.	A. Buisson, 2 assistants............	1911	5,000	375	225,000
*Our Lady of Good Counsel, 232 E. 90th st....	J. N. Connolly, 4 assistants........	1886	9,000	804	700,000
Our Lady of Grace (Gr'k Albanese), 14 Stanton	C. Pinnola	1907	2,500	325	35,000
Our Lady of Guadaloupe (Span.), 229 W. 14th..	O. Caron, 7 assistants..............	1902	25,000	210	100,000
*Our Lady of Loretto (Ital. mission), 303-305	Elizabeth. Jos. Sillipigni, 3 assts.	1891	15,000	1,200	92,000
*Our Lady of Lourdes, 463-467 142d st..........	J. H. McMahon, 4 assistants........	1901	2,000	300	425,000
*Our Lady of Mercy, 2502 Marion av............	P. N. Breslin, 3 assistants..	1882	5,000	146	150,000
*Our Lady of Mt. Carmel (Ital.), 447 E. 115th st.	Gaspare Dalla, 6 assistants.......	1887	10,000	1,300	175,000
Our Lady of Mt. Carmel (Ital.), 187th st & Belm	ont av. Jos. Caffuzzi, 2 assistants.	1907	3,000	245	47,000
Our Lady of Peace, 62d, nr. Lexington av.......	Philip Leone, 1 assistant..........	1918	1,100	125	70,000
*Our Lady of Perpetual Help, 321 E. 61st st.....	James Hayes, 9 assistants....	1887	6,000	900	200,000
*Our Lady of Pity (Ital.), E. 151st, nr. Morris a	v. F. Oppici, 2 assistants....... ...	1908	11,000	400	50,000
Our Lady of Pompeii (Ital.), 210-214 Bleecker st	Anthony Demo, 3 assistants........	1892	20,000	1,500	100,000
Our Lady of Rosary, 7 State st.................	M. J. Henry, 2 assistants..........	1883	700	80	125,000
*Our Lady of Scapular of Mt.Carmel, 28th,1st av	Denis O'Connor, 5 assistants.......	1888	7,200	850	300,000
Our Lady of Solace, White Plains rd&Van N't av	D. J. Curley, 1 assistant...........	1903	2,000	400	100,000
*Our Lady of Sorrows, 107 Pitt st..............	V. Buessing, 4 assistants...........	1867	5,000	110	100,000
*Our Lady of Victory, 171st st. and Webster av.	B. F. Galligan, 2 assistants........	1909	1,500	200	40,000
Our Lady of Vilna (Lithuanian), 568-570 Broome	st. J. Shestokas..................	1909	2,500	225	42,500
Our Saviour, 183d & Washington av., (Bldg.)..	Francis P. Duffy, 2 assistants.....	1912	4,000	175	90,000
*Resurrection, 282 W. 151st	T. F. Murphy, 3 assistants.........	1908	4,500	800	150,000
*Sacred Heart, Shakespeare av., High Bridge.	J. J. Lennon, 2 assistants..........	1875	1,500	150	125,000
*Sacred Heart of Jesus, 449-456 W. 51st.......	J. F. Mooney, 5 assistants.........	1876	12,000	840	625,000
*Sacred Heart of Jesus and Mary (Ital.), E. 33d	Jos. Congedo, 2 assistants.........	1915	7,000	800	75,000
*St. Adalbert, 420 E. 156th, bet. Elton & Melrose	J. Zaniewicz	1898	2,000	175	95,000
*St. Agnes, 143-149 E. 43d.....................	H. A. Brann, 4 assistants..........	1873	6,500	250	400,000
St. Albert's (Belgian), 431 W. 47th st...........	Jos. Stillemans, 1 assistant........	1916	4,000	200	75,000
St. Aloysius, 209-217 W. 132d st................	Patrick J. Minogue, 3 assistants....	1899	6,000	520	195,000
*St. Alphonsus, 312 West B'way.................	John J. Frawley, 7 assistants......	1847	8,000	300	502,000
*St. Ambrose, 513 W. 54th st...................	P. F. Guinevan, 2 assistants.......	1897	3,500	850	150,000
St. Andrew, Duane st. and City Hall pl.......	L. J. Evers, 3 assistants...........	1842	1,100	225	450,000
*St. Angela Merici, Morris av. and 163d st.....	John J. Harrington, 2 assistants...	1889	2,500	200	100,000
*St. Ann, 112-116 E. 12th st....................	W. J. Sinnott, 2 assistants.........	1852	2,000	500	300,000
St. Ann (Ital.), 306-310 E. 110th st............	Eucherio Perini, 2 assistants......	1911	10,000	490	125,000

*Has a parochial school.

MANHATTAN AND BRONX CHURCHES—*Continued.*

Name of Church and Location.	Name of Pastor.	Organized	No. of P'r'h-ioners	S. S. Members.	Value Ch'ch Prop.
Roman Catholic—Continued.					
*St. Anselm, 152d st. and Tinton av	B. Kevenhoerster, 4 assistants	1891	1,500	390	$225,000
*St. Anthony of Padua, 826-830 E. 166th st	J. F. Rummel, 2 assistants	1903	3,000	300	100,000
*St. Anthony of Padua (Ital.), 153 Sullivan st.	A. Silvioni, 6 assistants	1866	23,400	1,500	420,000
St. Anthony (Ital.), Commonwealth av. and Mansion	P. Maltese, 1 assistant	1908	2,000	300	40,000
*St. Athanasius, 880-884 Tiffany	W. F. Dougherty, 1 assistant	1906	1,800	190	150,000
*St. Augustine, 167th, bet. Franklin & Fulton.	John J. McCabe, 3 assistants	1849	4,300	600	400,000
*St. Barnabas, 241st & Martha av	M. A. Reilly, 1 assistant	1910	600	230	105,000
St. Benedict the Moor (colored), 342-344 W. 53d.	T. M. O'Keefe, 1 assistant	1883	2,500	110	67,000
St. Bernard, 330-336 W. 14th	J. F. Smith, 4 assistants	1868	8,000	1,000	340,000
*St. Boniface, 2d av., cor 47th st	F. X. E. Albert, 2 assistants	1858	3,000	150	125,000
*St. Brendan, 207th st. and Perry av	W. A. Courtney, 1 assistant	1908	1,200	125	70,000
*St. Brigid, 121-123 Avenue B	P. J. Magrath, ? assistant	1848	1,200	300	250,000
*St. Catherine of Genoa, 502-504 W. 153d st	P. E. McCorry, 3 assistants	1887	3,000	230	250,000
*St. Catherine of Sienna, 420 E. 69th	Ignatius Smith, 3 assistants	1897	6,000	800	325,000
*St. Cecilia, 118-124 E. 106th st	M. J. Phelan, 4 assistants	1874	5,000	1,200	300,000
*St. Charles Borromeo, 213-219 W. 141st st	F. H. Wall, 3 assistants	1888	7,000	670	500,000
*St. Clare's (Ital.), 434-436 W. 36th st	M. Sergenti, 1 assistant	1903	10,000	350	175,000
*St. Clement (Polish), 406 W. 40th	J. Letanche, 1 assistant	1909	3,000	225	60,000
*St. Columba, 337-341 W. 25th st	T. A. Thornton, 3 assistants	1845	6,000	695	200,000
St. Cyril (Croatian), 62 St. Marks pl	B. Snoj, 1 assistant	1916	1,150	190	50,000
Sts. Cyril and Methodius (Croatian), 552 W. 50th st.	I. Petricak	1914	3,000	600	60,000
St. Elizabeth, 187th st. and Broadway	W. J. Stewart, 3 assistants	1869	2,500	200	125,000
St. Elizabeth of Hungary, 217 E. 83d st	M. A. Tamassy	1891	4,100	110	65,000
St. Frances of Rome, Richardson av., Wakefield	F. P. Moore	1897	800	165	50,000
*St. Francis of Assisi, 141 W. 31st st	Anselm J. Kennedy, 3 assistants	1840	1,000	200	1,000,000
St. Francis de Sales, E. 96th, bet. Lex. & Park.	John F. Brady, 3 assistants	1894	7,000	900	250,000
*St. Francis Xavier, 42-48 W. 16th st	Patrick J. Casey, 8 assistants	1847	5,000	1,000	700,000
*St. Gabriel, 310-312 E. 37th st	W. Livingston, 5 assistants	1858	14,000	200	300,000
St. George (Syrians), 98 Washington st	A. Bachewate, 2 assistants	1916	3,000	100	30,000
*St George (Greek-Ruthenian), 23 E. 7th st	N. Pidhorecki, 1 assistant	1906	2,000	160	35,000
*St. Gregory, 119-121 W. 89th st	W. F. Hughes, 4 assistants	1908	5,000	200	275,000
*St. Ignatius Loyola, Park av. and 84th st	Jas. M. Kilroy, 8 assistants	1851	14,000	1,000	1,000,000
*St. James, 32 James st	V P. McGean, 4 assistants	1827	6,000	250	350,000
*St. Jean Baptiste (Fr.), 76th & Lex. av.	A. Letellier, 8 assistants	1882	7,500	700	800,000
*St. Jerome, Alexander av. and 138th st	G. T. Donlin, 4 assistants	1869	4,500	200	600,000
St. Joachim (Ital.), 22-28 Roosevelt st	V. Jannuzzi, 4 assistants	1888	17,000	800	170,000
*St. John, 230th st. & Kingsbridge av	F. X. Kelly, 1 assistant	1886	1,500	185	125,000
*St. John the Baptist (German), 211 W. 30th st.	Ludger Werth, 4 assistants	1841	1,500	180	400,000
*St. John Chrysostom, 167th st. and Hoe av	B. F. Brady, 2 assistants	1899	2,500	206	200,000
*St. John the Evangelist, 55th st. and 1st av	J. J. Flood, 5 assistants	1881	7,500	1,200	425,000
St. John Nepomucene (Slav), 350-354 E. 57th st.	Stephen Krasula, 1 assistant	1895	1,800	67	75,000
St. John the Martyr (Bohemian), 252-254 E. 72d	J. A. Lane, 2 assistants	1903	2,000	300	100,000
*St. Joseph, 61-65 6th av	J. Edwards, 4 assistants	1833	16,000	260	1,000,000
*St. Joseph (German), 404-418 E. 87th	G. Bruder, 2 assistants	1873	7,500	900	383,000
*St. Joseph, W. 125th, cor. Morningside av	G. H. Huntmann, 3 assistants	1860	6,500	360	425,000
*St. Joseph, Bathgate av. and 176th st	Patrick Morris, 1 assistant	1873	2,500	230	450,000
*St. Joseph (Maronite), 46 Washington	F. Wakim	1891	1,000	125	60,250
St. Leo, 9-11 E. 28th	Francis P. J. Cummings	1880	1,125	....	250,000
St. Lucy (Ital.), 336-342 E. 104th st	P. J. Lennon, 3 assistants	1900	8,000	800	95,000
*St. Luke's, 138th st., near St. Anns av	D. J. McMackin, 3 assistants	1897	3,500	700	150,000
St. Malachy, 241-245 W. 49th st	Vacant, 2 assistants	1902	3,000	325	250,000
St. Margaret, Riverdale av. and 260th st	J. N. Aylward, 1 assistant	1887	750	150	50,000
*St. Mark the Evangelist (colored), 61-63 W. 138th.	C. J. Plunkett, 3 assistants	1906	3,500	350	150,000
St. Martin of Tours, E. 182d & Grote	E. J. O'Gorman, 2 assistants	1899	1,500	400	200,000
*St. Mary, 215th st. and White Plains road	Henry P. Tracy, 1 assistant	1866	1,200	346	100,000
*St. Mary, Grand, cor. Ridge st	J. M. Byrnes, 2 assistants	1826	1,200	65	600,000
*St. Mary Magdalen (Ger.), 581 E. 17th st	A. L. Strube	1873	800	175	120,000
St. Mary Star of the Sea, City Island	A. C. Mearns	1887	500	86	50,000
St. Matthew, 215-217 W. 67th st	W F. Meehan, 3 assistants	1902	5,000	644	175,000
*St. Michael, 424 W. 34th st	Wm. F. Dougherty, 4 assistants	1857	7,000	1,800	1,000,000
*St. Monica, 406-411 E. 79th st	A. J. Kenny, 3 assistants	1879	7,500	404	550,000
*St. Nicholas of Tolentine, Andrews & Fordham	B. J. Zeiser, 3 assistants	1906	2,300	325	125,000
*St. Nicholas (German), 125-133 2d st	J. A. Nageleisen, 1 assistant	1833	1,200	200	450,000
*St. Patrick, Mott, Mulberry and Prince	J. F. Kearney, 4 assistants	1809	28,000	600	800,000
*St. Patrick's Cathedral, 50th st. and 5th av	M. J. Lavelle, 8 assistants	1879	15,000	1,700	6,000,000
*St. Paul's, 115 and 123 E. 117th st	J. McQuirk, 3 assistants	1835	7,500	1,000	550,000
*St. Paul the Apostle, Columbus av. and 60th st.	Thos. F. Burke, 28 assistants	1858	12,000	1,800	900,000
*St. Peter, 18-22 Barclay st	J. H. McGean, 4 assistants	1785	5,000	790	1,000,000
*Sts. Peter and Paul, St. Anns av. and 159th st.	Thomas F. Duffy, 3 assistants	1897	3,500	450	225,000
*St. Philip Neri, 3025 Concourse	D. Burke, 2 assistants	1898	5,000	400	150,000
*St. Pius, 416-418 E. 145th st	F. M. Fagan, 1 assistant	1906	1,500	270	125,000
St. Raphael, 504-510 W. 41st st	M. J. Duffy, 3 assistants	1886	11,000	700	350,000
*St. Raymond, Walker and Castle Hills av	E. McKenna, 4 assistants	1842	3,000	360	225,000
*St. Rita of Cascia, 145th and College av	J. P. O'Brien, 3 assistants	1900	8,000	340	100,000
St. Roch, 732 E. 150th st	C. Cassaneti, 1 assistant	1899	1,500	90	30,000
St. Rose, 34-36 Cannon st	P. McNamee, 2 assistants	1868	1,200	435	300,000
St. Rose of Lima, 502-508 W. 165th st	John R. Mahoney, 3 assistants	1901	4,000	400	250,000
St. Sebastian (Ital.), 312 E. 24th st	Romamus Simoni	1916	4,100	320	50,000
St. Simon Stock, Valentine av. and 183d st	W. G. O'Farrell, 1 assistant	1920	2,200	300	70,000
*St. Stanislaus, 103-107 7th st	Ig. J. Bialdyga, 2 assistants	1872	5,600	165	250,000
*St. Stephen, 147-149 E. 28th st	Francis P. J. Cummings, 6 assts	1848	6,000	1,200	850,000
St. Stephen of Hungary (Magyar), 420 E. 14th st	J. Froehlich	1902	3,000	290	50,000
*St. Teresa, 16-18 Rutgers st	J. T. McIntyre, 2 assistants	1863	1,000	250	600,000
*St. Thomas Aquinas, 1905-1913 Daly av	D. F. Coyle, 2 assistants	1890	3,000	900	100,000
*St. Thomas the Apostle, 118th, w. St. Nicholas av.	J. B. McGrath, 4 assistants	1889	7,000	550	600,000
*St. Valentine (Polish), E. 221st, Williamsbridge.	C. Czarkowski	1900	1,200	97	25,000
*St. Veronica, 149-155 Christopher	P. H. Drain, 4 assistants	1889	4,000	450	600,000
*St. Vincent de Paul (French), W. 23d, bet. 6th & 7th.	T. Wucher, 7 assistants	1840	10,000	300	500,000
*St. Vincent Ferrer, 873 Lexington av	J. R Heffernan, 15 assistants	1867	8,500	890	750,000
*Transfiguration (Ital.), 23-27 Mott st	John Voghera, 4 assistants	1827	5,000	1,000	175,000

*Has a parochial school.

MANHATTAN AND BRONX CHURCHES—*Continued.*

Recapitulation, Manhattan and Bronx Churches.

Denominations.	Con-trib'g Mem.	S.S. Mem-bers.	Total Amount Raised.	Value Church Property.
Baptist	19,350	10,196	$717,238	$7,221,000
Calvinistic Meth.	350	65	7,966	88,000
Catholic Apostolic	500	......	....	30,000
Christian Science	......	......	....	....
Congregational	3,889	2,127	138,262	1,937,500
Disciples of Christ	730	484	19,476	205,000
Evangelical Assn.	128	150	4,450	72,000
Friends	500	40	5,748	680,000
Ger. Ev. Sy., N. A.	317	503	5,317	40,000
Jewish	*	12,167	1,121,850	11,261,000
Lutheran	18,181	11,465	363,602	3,773,552
Meth. Episcopal	14,705	11,310	252,210	6,630,000
Meth. Epis. Af.	1,418	936	41,883	14,300
M. E. Afric. Zion	2,000	675	47,000	215,000
Moravian	400	369	15,000	55,000
Presbyterian	32,314	20,528	3,926,315	15,267,000
Pres. Reformed	321	350	11,200	155,000
Pres. United	403	432	19,662	195,000
Prot. Episcopal	43,982	19,963	$2,534,777	$40,930,032
Ref. Ch. in Am.	6,286	5,390	115,552	1,797,000
Ref. Ch. in U. S.	653	583	9,121	125,000
Reformed Catholic	......	......	....	65,000
Ref. Episcopal	100	100	3,000	......
Roman Catholic	†	73,634	....	47,875,770
7th Day Adventist	1,393	1,013	78,458	550,000
Unitarian	1,115	240	55,000	7,800,000
Universalist	450	75	....	800,000
Miscellaneous	13,352	2,216	92,960	1,580,500
Totals	1106916	174,921	$9,589,047	149,262,034

*Number of families, 31,303. There are numerous "Holiday Churches" in N. Y. C., of which there is no official record and are not listed above.
†Number of parishioners, 912,775.

QUEENS.

Name of Church and Location.	Name of Pastor and Address.	Organized	Contrib'g Mem.	S. S. Members.	Total Amt. Raised	Value Church Prop'ty.
Baptist.						
Ebenezer (colored), S. Prince, Flushing	B. S. Ryland, 117 Washington	1876	200	75	$9,000	$25,000
Elmhurst, Whitney av., cor. Judge	E. C. Platner, 52 Baxter av	1900	179	146	3,964	25,000
First, Flushing, Sanford av. and Union	George Douglas, 178 Union	1856	125	200	7,200	50,000
First, Flushing av., nr. Grove, Jamaica	W. H. Sobey, 143 Grove, Jamaica	1869	224	196	5,545	31,000
First, L. I. City, 11th, nr. Ely av	C. E. Sumpp	1869	46	56	......	......
First Woodside, 5th and Woodside av	John A. Courtright, 20 First st., Woodside	1880	70	200	3,270	20,000
Forest Parkview Chapel, Glendale	J. L. Hynes	1912	100	150	200	1,500
Richmond Hill, 114th & 91st av	R. E. Hunt, 114 91st av., R. H.	1898	335	383	6,529	130,000
Union C'se, 1st & Shaw av., Union C'se	J. Donaldson, 4015 Ferris, W'dh'vn	1891	330	580	8,820	20,000
Wyckoff, Summerfield & Forest av., Ev'g'n	G. C. McKiernan, 576 Leonard	1886	155	300	......	25,000
Christian.						
Springfield Docks	A. T. Langley, Springfield Docks	1917	30	60	......	4,000
Christian Science.						
Far Rockaway (First)	H. H. Weinstock, 1st R	....	....	....	......	......
Flushing (First)	A. Plishke, 1st R	1912	....	....	......	......
Forest Hills Soc.	Mrs. A. C. Boyd, 1st R	....	....	....	......	......
Jamaica (First)	G. J. Bagley, 1st R	....	....	....	......	......
Richmond Hill (First)	H. A. Stenson, 1st R	1913	....	....	......	......
Congregational.						
Broadway, 22d st., Flushing	Vacant	1905	20	60	600	4,000
Cedar Manor Chapel	O. W. Orell, 53 Hanson pl., Bkln.	1909	37	85	......	5,000
Christ, Columbia av. & 85th rd., Wood'n	R. L. Minich, 8518 85th, Woodhaven, L. I.	1911	310	300	6,000	30,000
Church in the Gardens, Forest Hills	D. D. Latshaw	1913	140	175	7,200	80,000
First, Bowne av. & Lincoln, Flushing	Geo. D. Egbert, 77 Bowne av	1851	350	275	11,000	80,000
First Rockaway Beach, Blvd. & 94th	J. C. Green, 305 Boulevard	1885	400	333	6,000	40,000
First, Walker & Grafton avs., W'dhaven	W. J. Buchanan, 1111 Walker av	1863	250	175	4,500	40,000
Pilgrim, Ridgewood & Oxford, R'd Hill	T. Williams, 10422 89th, Rich. Hill	1903	301	450	7,362	41,500
Union, 86th av. & 115th, R'd Hill	A. M. Ellis	1886	600	500	8,000	50,000
Disciples of Christ.						
Ridgewood Hgts. Christian Ch., Forest av. and Linden, Queens	K. Page, 611 Forest av., Bkln	1910	169	180	2,850	65,000
Evangelical.						
Bethany, 109th, nr. Jamaica av., R. H.	F. G. Fischer, 8765 109th	1919	32	20	500	8,000
Collegiate Union, 45 Grand av., Corona	Vacant	1868	440	630	3,400	31,000
Emmanuel, Bigelow and Jerome avs., Woodhaven	O. H. Penten, 2146 93d, Woodhaven	1879	97	59	2,600	16,000
Leverich Memorial, 46th & Burnside, Cor	J. E. Carlin, 14 Hanover, Elmh'st	1916	360	350	1,800	13,000
Jewish.						
Derech Emunah, Vernon & Ocean avs.	J. Glovitch, Arverne	1905	400	150	10,000	100,000
Rockaway Beach, Blvd. and Dodges	J. Kohn, Boulevard and Dodges	1894	60	40	6,000	25,000
Temple Israel, Roanoke st., Far R'kaway	I. Landman	1908	230	311	20,000	60,000
Temple Israel, 10 S. Fairview av., R'kaw	ay Beach. H. Germansky	1895	78	78	2,500	20,000
Temple Israel, Jamaica	G. Lipkind, Hollis	1918	175	....	......	45,000
Lutheran.						
Bethany, Elmhurst	H. W. Petersen, 25 Horton	....	....	....	......	......
Christ, 5th, nr. Jackson av., Woodside	H. F. Bunke, 144 5th, Woodside	1896	100	90	3,500	7,000
Christ, Rosedale	G. L. Kieffer, Rosedale	1913	57	50	2,500	3,000
Christ, Jerome av., cor. Ferry, Woodh'vn	H. E. Meyer, 3910 Jerome av	1880	350	450	6,000	60,000
Covenant, Elm and Buchanan avs	Rgwd. G. U. Preuss, 2402 Catalpa	1910	600	7,000	10,000	50,000
Emanuel, Darvall, cor. Alburtis av., Corona	E. G. Holls, 116 Alburtis av., Cor.	1887	125	200	3,000	......
Emmaus, Cornelia & Anthon av., Ridge	wood. T. S. Frey, 842 Anthon av	1904	600	300	......	......
Eng. Luth., 20 Bell av., Bayside	F. J. Muehlhaeuser, 22 Bell av		....	....	......	......
Eng. Luth., 182 Main, Port Washington	F. J. Muehlhaeuser, 22 Bell av., Bayside, L. I.	....	....	....	......	......
Good Shepherd, Ashby & Horan avs., So.	Ozone Park. C. H. Thomsen	1911	213	200	2,400	15,000
Grace, Creed av., Queens	L. S. Wagner, Queens	1916	70	60	......	15,000
Holy Trinity, Hollis ......A. L.	Dillenbeck, Palatina av., Hollis	1908	125	140	4,800	20,000
Immanuel, 21st nr. 8th av. Whitestone	H. C. Wolk, 57 N. 8th av	1894	380	100	4,000	18,000
Redeemer, Copeland & Fosdick avs., Gl	endale. Theo. Kuehn, Glendale	1909	190	250	3,000	17,000
St. Andrew's, Glen Morris	C. D. Zinssmeister, 401 Eldert lane	1915	45	65	2,000	18,500
St. Jacobus, Winfield, Middagh and Sinclair av	F. E. Tilly, Sinclair av., Woodside P. O.	1867	350	310	6,000	35,000

QUEENS CHURCHES—*Continued.*

Name of Church and Location.	Name of Pastor and Address.	Organized	Contrib'g Mem.	S. S. Members.	Total Amt. Raised	Value Church Prop'ty.
Lutheran—Continued.						
St. John's, 6th av. & 14th, College Point	**Arthur H. Halfman, College Point**	1857	250	3,000	$4,000	$56,000
St. John's, 186 Percy, Flushing	C. Geo. Kaestner, 184 Percy	1893	79	65	......	15,000
St. John's Evang., 114th no. of Jamaica av., Richmond Hill	A. L. Benner, 8626 114th, R. Hill	1903	675	700	11,790	43,000
St. John's, 7 Martin, Maspeth	O. Graeser, Jr., 454 Woodward av., Bkln.	....	....	....	......	......
St. Luke's, Yarmouth & Downing, W'dh'n	E. R. Jaxheimer, 8068 87th rd., W'd'n.	1908	375	550	6,000	40,000
St. Mark's, N. Y. av., Jamaica	K. Riebesell, New York av., Jam.	1909	135	215	3,000	2,500
St. Paul's, Richmond Hill	P. B. Frey, 719 Stoothoff av	1902	297	256	3,500	15,200
St. Paul's, Dunton	C. G. Toebke, 12503 103d av., R. H.	1915	110	200	4,500	5,000
Salem (Swedish), 8th av., L. I. C.	H. Luther Wilson	1897	109	80	1,200	6,000
Trinity, Corona	H. Luther Wilson	1906	55	45	834	7,000
Trinity, Middle Village	D. W. Peterson, 12 Juniper av., Mid. Vil'ge.	1863	170	700	3,500	80,000
Trinity, 8th av., nr. Jamaica av., L. I. City	C. Merkel, 345 8th av., L. I. C.	1890	450	450	6,500	35,000
Trinity, cor. Andrew & Pacific, Masp'th.	Wm. H. Pretzsch, 35 Andrew	1899	325	375	2,000	10,000
Methodist Episcopal.						
Bayside, Palace av. & West, Bayside	P. E. Shoemaker, Bayside	1891	229	206	4,970	28,500
Corona Italian Mission, 52 Moore	A. Sartorio, 52 Moore, Corona	1910	30	100	1,000	5,000
Corona, Kingsland & Alburtis avs., Cor.	Geo. W. Servis, 30 Alburtis av., Cor.	1880	60	100	2,000	16,500
Elmhurst, Medina pl. and Gerry av	W. D. Beach, 8 Medina pl	1839	600	685	11,000	22,000
Epworth, 8th av. and 20th, Whitestone	A. Y. Holter, 5 E. 20th	1850	144	182	2,590	14,000
First, Amity st., Flushing	W. W. W. Wilson, 188 Amity, Flushing, L. I.	1811	585	450	17,402	70,000
First, Springfield Gardens	S. E. Lawson, Springfield G'dens.	1867	300	400	4,000	35,000
First, Temple & Crescent, Astoria	A. J. Smith, 238 Temple	1841	500	482	7,900	65,500
First, Kimball, c. Hatch avs., Oz. P'k.	Wm. MacNicholl	1891	170	290	5,000	23,000
First, Minnetonka av., Hollis	A. C. Flandreau, Hollis	1894	156	246	7,423	26,500
First, Church & Beaufort, Rich. Hill	D. D. Irvine, 1017 Church, R. H.	1890	600	1,293	12,500	48,000
First German, 80 Academy, L. I. City	H. R. Houst, 78 Academy, L. I. C.	1887	65	50	1,200	25,000
First Italian, Van Alst av. & Lincoln, Ast'a.	A. Sartorio, 52 Lincoln, Astoria	1905	200	200	1,836	25,000
Glendale, Tesla pl.	F. Gunton, 3 Simpson, Forest Park	1896	25	95	1,500	7,000
Jamaica, 430 Fulton st., Jamaica	Geo. C. Fort, 428 Fulton, Jamaica.	1807	725	710	20,134	172,000
Maspeth, Columbia pl., Maspeth	J. W. Eggleston	1854	200	300	5,000	30,000
Middle Vil'ge, Metropolitan av., Mid. Vil.	Chas. Bell, 297 Hewes, Bkln.	1768	64	244	1,160	14,000
Ridgewood Hts. (Ger.), Woodward av. & Grove.	G. Bobilin, 606 W'dw'd av. Bn.	1895	300	250	6,500	50,000
Shaw Avenue, Union Course	F. Steihler, 78 Shaw av., W'h'n	18[illegible]2	350	450	4,000	30,000
Trinity, 86th av. & 108 st., Rich. H.	J. J. Foust, 8644 106th, Rich. Hill.	1907	413	596	4,973	23,000
Van Alst Av., 190 Van Alst av., L. I. C.	D. C. Winship, 190 Van Alst av	1864	148	250	2,500	42,500
Methodist Episcopal—African.						
Allen Ch'p'l, Washington & South, Jam.	T. G. Clark, 17 Hackett	1843	250	140	2,224	10,500
Macedonia A.M.E., 159 Lincoln, Flush'g	G. R. Coverdale, 50 Monroe	1810	200	150	3,000	9,000
St. Mark's A. M. E., Elmhurst	W. H. Jones, 54 Corona av., E'h't	1828	40	34	900	75,000
St. Peter's, Douglaston	C. J. Lawton, 15 W. 135th, Mhtn.	1870	20	22	450	3,000
Methodist Protestant.						
Centreville Avenue, Aqueduct, L. I.	G. H. Jackson, Lynbrook	1857	22	110	1,000	3,000
Presbyterian. (Presbytery of Brooklyn-Nassau.)						
Astoria, 954 Boulevard, Astoria	D. Wills, 557 Academy	1846	300	225	4,700	25,000
Bohemian Brothers Friendly Chapel, 149 Potter av., Astoria	V. Ziegler, 149 Potter av	1906	68	....	710	10,000
Calvary, Maspeth	S. F. Muir, 690 8th av., Mhtn.	1916	100	150	......	12,000
First Ger. E. W'msb'g, 28-40 Prospect av.	John Dietz, 34 Prospect av, R'gw'd	1863	518	706	9,034	150,000
First, Barclay & Murray, Flushing	C. H. Hodges, 15 Botanic pl	1905	100	145	5,212	16,000
First, Greenw'd av., nr. Atlantic, Rich. H.	J. J. MacDonald, D.D., 802 111th av., R'd. Hill	1905	230	200	6,000	15,000
First, Fulton & Clinton av., Jamaica	A. Magill, 25 Clinton av	1662	671	498	12,530	150,000
First of Newtown, Queens blvd., Elmh's	H. A. Northacker, 10 Queens Blvd.	1652	356	293	5,383	150,000
French Evang., 4176 Chich'r av., W'dh'n	G. Baechler, Chichester av., W'dh'n	1887	80	56	1,175	15,000
Glen Morris, Woodhaven	J. A. Harrer, St. Albans	1920	50	75	......	......
Jamaica, Hillside	J. MacInnes, Jamaica	....	151	179	......	......
Ravenswood, L. I. City	W. S. Wallace, 42 Wardell, L. I. C.	1891	43	86	1,020	7,000
Ridgewood, Forest & Halleck avs., R'd'w'd.	A. B. Rhinow, 983 Forest av	1853	700	1,000	......	80,000
Rosedale, Rosedale	C. M. Rutherford, Sp'ld Gardens.	1905	75	160	2,000	10,000
Russell Sage Memorial, Far Rock'w'y	J. M. Thompson, Far Rockaway	1888	261	177	12,490	400,000
St. Albans	J. A. Harrer, St. Albans	....	76	....	......	......
Springfield, Springfield av. & Broadway	W. J. Macdonald, Sp'gf'd Gardens	1867	200	310	7,238	50,000
Whitestone	W. S. Wallace, 42 Wardell, L. I. C.	1871	46	53	646	6,000
Woodhaven First, Jeromo at 94th	Woodhaven. J. Allison MacRury	1866	330	285	3,000	25,000
Protestant Episcopal.						
All Saints', Bayside	Chas. A. Brown, Bayside	1892	200	230	8,394	79,600
All Saints', Lefferts Blvd, R'd. Hill	H. W. Armstrong, Richmond Hill	1901	214	115	1,800	9,000
Annunciation, Cooper, nr. Webster av., Glendale.	W. P. S. Lander, Box 109 Freeport	1895	135	150	1,512	15,000
Epiphany, McCormick & Kimball avs., Ozone Park.	Wm. Wilkinson	1888	200	150	2,500	28,000
Grace, 41st, Corona	A. G. Roberts, 37 41st, Corona	1906	135	130	2,875	15,000
Grace, 315 Fulton, Jamaica	R. T. Homans, 62 Clinton av	1702	1,000	637	25,574	200,000
Grace Chapel, 89 Merrick road	R. T. Homans, S. W. Day	....	50	150	......	......
Grace, 11th av. and 18th, Whitestone	Wm. Jenkins, Whitestone, L. I.	1859	96	117	4,356	60,000
Redeemer, Crescent & Temple, Astoria	W. C. Charlton, 765 Crescent, Ast'a	1866	600	781	8,580	78,000
St. Andrew's Mission, 204 17th av., Astoria.	Vacant	1902	60	200	3,500	4,000
Resurrection, Church st., Richmond Hill	W. P. Evans, 401 Church, R. H.	1874	160	150	6,249	40,000
St. Andrew's-by-the-Sea, Belle Harbor	G. R. Wood, Chelsea sq., Mhtn.	1905	50	40	559	10,000
St. Gabriel's, Fulton st., Hollis	C. W. French, Hollis	1888	150	115	2,700	40,000
St. George's, Franklin st., Astoria	H. L. Lonsdale, 212 Franklin	1827	....	....	......	......
St. George's, Main st., Flushing	H. D. Waller, 45 Locust	1761	....	225	25,000	150,000
St. James', B'way & Corona av., Elmh'st	E. M. McGuffey, Elmhurst	1704	400	250	10,312	250,000
St. John's, Mott av., Far Rockaway	W. A. Sparks, Far Rockaway	1882	400	150	10,998	60,000
St. John's, Van Alst av. & 10th, L. I. City	E. Helm, 590 Rogers av., Bkln.	1866	190	120	1,631	30,000
St. John's, Sanford av. & Wilson, Flush'g	G. W. Eccles, 5 Bullard pl	1911	140	200	6,600	39,000
St. Joseph's, Franklin av., Queens	Vacant	1880	80	80	3,000	48,000
St. Luke's, Forest Hills	Archdeacon Duffield, Gar. City, L. I.	1913	75	50	5,000	14,000
St. Mary's Chapel, Laurel Hill	F. S. Griffin, Maspeth	1888	37	22	612	10,000
St. Matthew's, Woodhaven	F. V. Baer, 475 Willard av	1913	240	302	10,000	40,000

QUEENS CHURCHES—*Continued.*

Name of Church and Location.	Name of Pastor and Address.	Organized	Contrib'g Mem.	S. S. Members.	Total Amt. Raised	Value Church Prop'ty.
Protestant Episcopal—Continued.						
St. Paul's Chapel, 13th & 1st av., College Pt.	B. Mottram, 611 13th, College Pt.	1864	270	225	$5,318	$30,000
St. Paul's, Striker av. & 8th, W'dside.	A. G. Roberts, 37 41st, Corona....	1873	89	135	16,000	25,000
St. Peter's, Rosedale. H. W. Stafford	Sedgwick, Queens	1909	60	48	650	9,000
St. Saviour's, Maspeth	F. S. Griffin, Maspeth..............	1847	155	100	2,401	8,000
St. Stephen's, Grand & N. 1st, Jamaica	W. S. McKinney, 41 Grand........	1902	110	100	......	5,000
St. Thomas', Vernon av., Ravenswood...	A.G.Roberts, 104 W.Hayes av.,Cor.	1839	75	85	550	15,000
Zion, Douglaston	R. M. W. Black, Douglaston......	1830	200	75	4,200	75,000
Reformed (North Classis of L. I.)						
Evang. of Woodhaven, Woodhaven and Ridgewood avs., Woodhaven...........	P. H. Land, 107 E. 34th, Mhtn....	1913	111	100	3,000	10,000
First, 1st av. & 10th, College Point.......	H. Sluyter, 611 10th	1876	280	329	5,540	30,000
First German, Far Rockaway............	A. Q. Wettstein, Far Rockaway..	1909	80	65	2,500	30,000
First, 100 Academy st., L. I. City........	F. A. Scofield, 102 Academy, L.I.C.	1875	240	300	2,975	27,000
First Newtown, B'way & Union av., Elmh'st.	C. K. Clearwater, 23 Vietor pl	1731	250	200	4,500	75,000
Flushing, Bowne av. & Amity, Flush'g	T. H. MacKenzie, 37 S.Parsons av.	1846	497	300	16,600	75,000
Forest Park, Hillside av.&Ferry, Wdhvn	F. L. Cornish, Woodhaven..........	1839	401	410	7,500	45,000
German Second, 526 2d av., Astoria.....	Dr. C. D. F. Steinfuhrer, 520 2d av..	1854	138	65	1,966	30,000
Jamaica Dutch, Fulton & Ray, Jam'ca.	R. K. Wick, 221 Fulton st..........	1702	560	595	15,000	250,000
Queens, Jericho rd.&Creed av., Queens..	D. E. Lyon	1858	107	300	4,905	50,000
Ref. Ch. of Astoria, Remsen st., Astoria	Geo. S. Bolsterle, 73 Remsen.......	1836	215	125	4,000	70,000
Ridgewood (Dutch), Evergreen	G. R. Israel, 1839 Decatur, Everg'n.	1890	140	175	2,711	15,000
St. Paul's G.E., Herrim'n & Hillside av, J'ca.	F. Stoebener, 120 Herriman av.	1872	340	180	2,285	60,000
Steinway, Ditmas av. & 11th av..........	P. F. Strauss, 770 11th av., L. I. C...	1891	210	340	4,075	25,000
Sunnyside, 310 Buckley st., L. I. City...	C. M. Severance, 310 Buckley st. L. I. City	1895	50	75	1,000	15,000
Winfield, Woodside and Lee avs........	Wm. T. Adams, 19 Lenox av.....	1907	100	175	1 500	10,000
Zion (German), Horton, Elmhurst......	J. G. Bosshart, Ivy, Elmhurst....	1862	300	200	2,000	16,000
Reformed Episcopal						
Christ, South Ozone Park	Wm. P. Mackay, 103 Presberger av.	1909	50	80	600	10,000
Miscellaneous.						
Bethel Union S. S., Hawtree Creek rd., Wdhvn.	J. M. Bergen, Supt....	1805	50	60	1,200	4,000
Ch. of the Nazarene, Springfield Gardens.	G. H. Rowe, N. Y. av. and Foster pt., Jamaica	....	35	108	1,200	3,600
Church of Forest Hills, Forest Hills....	G. Sheppard, 160 Harvest	1911	120	130	5,000	38,000
Friends Meeting, B'way, Flushing......	T. C. Bell, Correspondent, Bayside	1636	70	40	1,000	20,000
United Ch. Ch. of Am., 41 Prospect, L.I.C.	C. Nelson, 1938 Grove, Bkln.........	1870	200	100	......	......
Union Evang. Ch. (Ind), 4th av. & 14th, College Pt.	Vacant		40	80	2,500	20,000

Roman Catholic Churches of Queens.

Name of Church and Location.	Name of Pastor.	Organized	No. of P'r'h-ioners	S. S. Members.	Value Ch'ch Prop.
*B. V. M. Help of Christians, Winfield Junction	J. F. Naab, 1 assistant...........	1854	800	340	$130,000
*B. V. M. Mt. Carmel, Newton av., Astoria.....	Chas. Gibney, 2 assistants...........	1841	4,000	1,000	150,000
*Church of the Presentation of the Blessed Virgin Mary, Flushing & Shelton, Jamaica..	J. M. Scheffel, 1 assistant...........	1886	2,500	400	90,000
*Gate of Heaven, Ozone Park....................	Fathers of Mary	1904	1,200	200	50,000
*Holy Child Jesus, Richmond Hill...............	Thomas A. Nummey, 1 assistant....	1910	600	200	50,000
*Holy Cross (Polish), Maspeth.....................	Adalbert Nawrocki	1912	300	350	10,000
*Nativity (Italian), Woodhaven....................	J. B. Garbottini	1909	705	205	8,000
Our Lady of Mt. Carmel, Astoria................	Chas. F. Gibney, 2 assistants......	....	....	...	.....
*Our Lady of Sorrows, Shell rd., Corona.........	Wm. Dwyer, 2 assistants..............	1870	3,237	380	150,000
Queen of Martyrs, Forest Hills....................	Joseph R. McLaughlin..................				
Sacred Heart, Bayside	Philip Brady, 1 assistant............	1895	700	180	18,000
*St. Adelbert's (Polish), Elmhurst..................	Anthony Witkowski, O.M.C., 1 asst.	1892	2,700	165	20,000
St. Bartholomew, 4th, Elmhurst.....................	F. X. Uleau, 2 assistants............	1906	750	180	65,000
*St. Benedict Joseph, Morris Park...............	Wm. Kerwin, 1 assistant..............	1893	2,000	350	40,000
St. Camillus, Seaside	Joseph Brady	1912	150	20	50,000
St. Clements, So. Ozone Park....................	Anthony E. Bourke......................	1913	200	200	12,000
*St. Elizabeth, Atlantic av. & 3d, Woodhaven..	Gustav Baer	1873	2,000	162	25,000
*St. Fidelis, High and 15th, College Point.......	Ambrose Schumack, 2 assistants.....	1856	2,000	400	120,000
*St. Francis de Sales, Belle Harbor..............	James W. Foran	1906	500	300	85,000
St. Gerard Magella, Hollis	Edward Harley	1906	7,000	500	15,000
St. Gertrude's, Edgemere, Summer Church.....	Herbert Farrell, 2 assistants	1912	1,000	200	18,000
Sts. Joachim and Anne, Hollis av., Queens......	F. W. Dotzauer.........................	1896	700	100	30,000
St. Joan of Arc, Elmhurst.........................	Ward Meehan, ...	1920			
St. Josaphat (Polish), Bayside	B. Malinowski	1910	1,200	180	20,000
*St. Joseph's, Long Island City..................	Peter Henn, 2 assistants	1879	4,010	140	125,000
*St. Joseph's (Polish), Rockaway rd., Jamaica.	Stanislaus Rysiekiewicz, 1 assistant	1904	1,800	400	85,000
St. Leo (Ital.), Sycamore av. & Elm, Corona..	C. Caruana, 1 assistant	1903	2,100	200	33,000
*St. Luke, 11th av., Whitestone...................	F. J. Dillon	1870	1,200	300	150,000
*St. Margaret, Middle Village	John P. Gopp	1860	525	160	90,000
*St. Mary's, Hunter's Point, Long Island City..	Wm. J. Dunne, 2 assistants	1868	5,000	700	150,000
*St. Mary Magdalen, Springfield Gardens.......	John Tinney, 1 assistant	1907	800	60	40,000
*St. Mary's Star of the Sea, Far Rockaway.....	Herbert Farrell, 2 assistants	1854	2,500	400	150,000
*St. Michael's, Union and Madison, Flushing..	Eugene J. Donnelly, 2 assistants...	1841	2,500	600	200,000
*St. Monica, Washington st., Jamaica..........	Richard Schenck, 1 assistant.......	1838	3,000	700	75,000
St. Pancras, Glendale	Francis O. Siegelack, 1 assistant...	1898	225	115	30,000
*St. Patrick's, Dutch Kills, L. I. C............	Joseph P. McGinley, 2 assistants....	1862	2,000	600	180,000
St. Pius the V, Jamaica	M. Legnani	1909	1,000	150	15,000
St. Raphael, Blissville, Long Island City........	Edward A. Holley, 1 assistant......	1865	1,800	600	160,000
St. Rita, Boulevard, near Webster av............	Michael Heffernan, 1 assistant	1894	900	300	40,000
*St. Rose of Lima, So. R'kw'y Bh., F'v'w av & Cedar pl.	Jas. J. Bennett	1886	1,500	100	150,000
St. Sebastian, Woodside............................	Michael Walsh, 1 assistant.	1894	1,800	300	75,000
St. Stanislaus, Maspeth	Joseph A. Bennett	1871	1,500	450	20,000
St. Thomas, Benedict av., Woodhaven	Andrew Klarmann, 2 assistants....	1908	1,000	150	100,000
St. Virgilius, Broad Channel	Attended from Rockaway Beach..	1914			
Transfiguration, Hull av., Maspeth	A. N. Malukas	1908	1,400	30	25,000

*Has a parochial school.

QUEENS CHURCHES—*Continued.*

Recapitulation, Queens Churches.

Denominations.	Con-trib'g Mem.	S.S. Mem-bers.	Total Amount Raised.	Value Church Property	Denominations.	Con-trib'g Mem.	S.S. Mem-bers.	Total Amount Raised.	Value Church Property
Baptist	1,663	1,987	$44,058	$347,500	Prot. Episcopal	5,171	5,106	$170,872	$1,359,100
Christian Science	......	......	....	....	Reformed	4,019	3,934	82,057	833,000
Christian	30	60	....	4,000	Ref. Episcopal	55	80	600	10,000
Congregational	2,371	2,268	47,800	364,000	Roman Catholic	†	12,347	....	3,049,000
Disciples of Christ.	169	180	2,850	65,000	Miscellaneous	350	506	12,800	91,000
Evangelical	927	1,059	8,300	68,000					
Jewish	*	579	28,500	205,000	Totals	103,444	50,185	$708,257	$8,998,300
Lutheran	6,420	9,756	95,490	617,200					
Meth. Episcopal	5,864	7,456	125,218	772,500					
M. E. African	510	346	5,350	97,000					
Meth. Prot.	22	110	1,000	3,000					
Presbyterian	4,066	4,365	73,462	1,113,000					

*Number of families, 943. There are numerous "Holiday Churches" in N. Y. C., of which there is no official record and are not listed above.
†Number of parishioners, 70,822.

RICHMOND.

Name of Church and Location.	Name of Pastor and Address.	Organized	Con-trib'g Mem.	S. S. Mem-bers.	Total Amt. Raised	Value Church Prop'ty.
Baptist.						
First, Hamilton av., New Brighton....	W. A. Pugsley, 236 Hamilton av.	1884	112	102	$3,359	$30,000
Mariners Harbor	A. M. Winsor	....	....	....	......	......
Park, Park av. & Vreeland, Pt. Rich	mond. H. Winton, Pt. Richmond.	1840	400	275	7,771	25,000
St. Philip's (col'd), Elm st., Pt. Rich'd	E.W.Lipscomb, 31 Trantor pl., Pt.R.	1887	200	100	15,000	3,000
South, Main st., Tottenville............	Rev. Harrison Johnson, Tottenville	1869	60	160	1,800	12,000
Christian Science.						
First Church of Christ, N. Brighton....	J. D. Manton, Tompkinsville.......	1900	....	....	......	......
Disciples of Christ.						
Church of Christ, Wash. av.............	J. A. Deojay, 301 Wash. av........	1914	50	45	2,000	1,500
Evangelical (Union).						
Community Ch., Shore rd., Charleston..	E. P. McLean, New Brunswick, N.J.	1893	60	120	400	3,500
Lutheran.						
Bethlehem, Ft. Wadsworth	M. T. Holls	....	....	....	......	......
Immanuel, New Springville	H. A. Meyer, 2024 Richmond av...	1911	74	63	1,718	6,185
Lutheran Evan., 191 Beach, Stapleton..	Fred'k Sutter, 171 Beach, Tpksvle.	1856	625	450	15,174	130,000
Scandinavian Zion, Av.B,P.R'd. R. O. Sig	mond, 1621 Castleton av., Pt. R'd.	1893	200	200	20,000	30,000
Scandinavian, N. Brighton..............	J. C. Hougum, 2:6 Benziger av., N.B.	1892	70	85	1,000	3,000
St. John's, Port Richmond.........J. C.	Borth, 212 Jewett av., Pt. Richm'd.	1852	400	160	5,550	45,000
St. Paul's Ger. Eng., W.N.Brighton....	R. I. Eichler, 90 Caroline.........	1899	85	56	1,200	17,000
Methodist Episcopal.	(Newark Conference.)					
Asbury, Richmond av., New Springville	Supply	1802	96	80	1,000	6,000
Dickinson, Linoleumville	L. G. Gunn, 3980 Richmond T'ke..	1840	75	130	3,400	9,000
Bethel, Amboy rd. & Bethel av., Tot'v'e.	O. L. Joseph, 7260 Amboy rd., T'le	1840	252	339	10,010	35,000
Grace, c. Heb'ton & Castleton avs., Pt. Ri	ch'd. W. J. Hampton, 213 Heb'n av.	1867	430	464	7,722	50,000
Graniteville	G. H. Cooley, Pt. Richmond.......	1909	....	195	......	3,800
Italian Mission	....	....	....	113	......	......
Kingsley	H. B. Leech, 134 Cebra av., T'le..	....	....	225	......	23,000
St. Mark's, Princes Bay. D. H. Gridl	ey, 6144 Amboy rd., P. Bay........	1871	260	250	4,000	20,000
St. Paul's, Amboy av., Tottenville.....	J. F. Bindenberger, 7559 Amboy rd.	1859	255	250	4,907	40,000
Summerfield, Mariners' Harbor..........	D. O. Cowles, Mariners Harbor..	1839	350	320	6,500	25,000
Trinity, Delafield & Elizabeth, W. B'ton	H. E. Curts, 578 Delafield av.....	1839	415	452	6,100	70,000
*Wandell Memorial, Concord............	Supply	1902	48	90	1,073	12,000
Woodrow, Prince Bay	S. O. Rusly, Prince Bay...........	1787	42	62	1,356	16,000
Methodist Episcopal—African.						
Bethel Tabernacle, 51 Vandeezer st., Tompkinsville	P. E. Paul, Tompkinsville.........	1918	30	40	2,200	4,000
Mt. Zion, Bloomingdale rd, Rossville...	L. A. Roach, Rossville, S. I.......	1875	25	30	200	3,000
Moravian.						
United Brethren's Church on S. I.						
†Castleton Corners, Richm'd t'np'e, Ca	stleton Corners. F. R. Nitzschke, 1646 Richmond tnpke., W.N.Bghtn	1873	83	197	5,399	......
†Great Kills, 74 Hillside Terrace........	P. M. Greider, Great Kills.........	1895	300	500	10,000	......
†New Dorp, Richmond rd., New Dorp..	E. S. Hagen, New Dorp............	1763	....	....	......	......
Stapleton Moravian, Osgood av., Staple	ton, S. I. P.T.Shultz, 90 Osgood av	1889	100	200	2,000	12,000
Presbyterian.						
Calvary, Bement av., W. New B'ton...	M. Ramsay, 280 Bement av......	1872	426	276	6,900	50,000
First of Edgewater, Stapleton...........	J. A. Fraser, 32 Brownell, St'p'ton	1856	235	245	8,635	90,000
Protestant Episcopal.						
All Saints, Mariners' Harbor...........	A. H. Ohse, Chelsea Square.......	188	60	60	2,100	16,000
Ascension, West New Brighton..........	Pascal Harrower, W. N. Brighton	1869	495	350	8,500	80,000
Christ, Franklin av. & 2d, New Brighton	D. H. Browne, New Brighton....	1846	761	221	18,020	172,700
Holy Comforter, Eltingville	K. R. Buchanan	1865	100	30	......	9,000
Most Holy Redeemer, 45 Jewett av., Pt.	Richmond. Carmelo Di Sano	....	....	....	......	......
St. Andrew's, Richmond rd..............	O. F. Moore, Dongan Hills........	1708	450	150	6,500	225,000
St. John's, New York av., Clifton......	J. R. Harding, 550 W. 157th, Mhtn.	1708	654	312	13,075	......
St. Luke's, Shore rd. & St. Luke's av.,	Rossville. T. Burgess	1847	175	100	3,500	40,000
St. Mary's, Davis av., W. New Brighton	Francis L. Frost, W.NewBrighton	1853	300	152	8,500	80,000
St. Paul's Memorial, 93 St. Pauls av., T	'nk'le. G.L.Wallis, 225 St.Pauls av.	1833	136	50	2,500	75,000
St. Simon's, Stapleton	W. W. Mix, Stapleton	1853	75	125	1,850	29,000
St. Stephen's, Tottenville	English Crooks	1880	150	60	2,814	12,500
Trinity, 3d st., New Dorp	Rev. K. R. Buchanan, New Dorp.	1896	60	78	2,500	15,000
Reformed.						
Brighton Heights, Tompkins av. and F	ort pl. J. H. Brinckerhoff, 17 Lenox pl., New Brighton......	1823	605	315	12,000	75,000
Mariner's Har., Rich'd ter.&Lockman av	Vacant	1905	100	150	2,000	15,000
St. Peter's, Charleston	Jacob Ganss, Kreischerville........	1882	36	48	250	8,000
Staten Island, Richmond av., Port Rich	m'd. O.L.F.Mohn, 278 Heberton av.	1665	340	288	8,800	60,000
Unitarian.						
Ch. of the Redeemer, Clinton av., N.Brig	hton. G. C. Cressey, 68 Clinton av..	1852	100	40	2,500	50,000
Miscellaneous.						
Immanuel (Union), Westerleigh..........	C. R. Kingsley	1894	200	284	......	35,000

***Mission.** †**These churches compose one church organized under incorp. title "United Brethren."**

RICHMOND CHURCHES—*Continued.*

Roman Catholic Churches of Richmond.

Name of Church and Location.	Name of Pastor.	Organized	No. of P'r'h-ioners	S. S. Members.	Value Ch'ch Prop.
Blessed Sacrament, West New Brighton	F. J. Heaney, 1 assistant	1910	800	140	$40,000
*Immaculate Conception, Targee st, Stapleton	Daniel A. Quinn, 1 assistant	1887	1,500	300	160,000
Our Lady of Good Counsel, Tompkinsville	M. A. Ryan, 4 assistants	1899	800	250	100,000
*Our Lady Help of Christians, Tottenville	J. F. Malloy, 1 assistant	1890	1,000	80	30,000
Our Lady Star of Sea, Huguenot Park	J. F. Malloy	1916	400	125	18,000
Our Lady Mt. Carmel (Ital.), West New Brighton	Louis Riccio, 2 assistants	1916	4,000	550	40,000
St. Adalbert, John st, Port Richmond	J. Brzozlewski	1901	505	230	40,000
St. Ann, Dongan Hills, S. I.	Jos. A. Farrell	1915	1,000	600	38,000
St. Anthony's (Polish), Decker av., Linoleumvil	Anthony Gryguc	1910	1,000	125	25,000
St. Clement's, Mariner's Harbor	Jas. E. Goggin, 1 assistant	1910	700	400	35,000
St. Joachim and St. Ann Chapel, Mount Loretto	M. J. Fitzpatrick, 2 assistants	1883	1,900	300	200,000
*St. John Baptist de la Salle, Stapleton	Jos. Kirschoffer	1900	1,000	166	50,000
St. Joseph, Washington av, Rossville	J. T. Kelly	1867	700	100	20,000
St. Joseph (Ital.), 94 St. Marys av., Rosebank	A. Catoggio, 1 assistant	1902	1,500	300	16,000
*St. Mary's, N. Y. av, Rosebank	C. J. Cronan, 1 assistant	1852	1,500	301	110,000
*St. Mary of the Assumption, Port Richmond	J. C. Campbell, 2 assistants	1877	1,600	240	100,000
St. Patrick, 45 Garretson av, Richmond	C. J. Parks, 1 assistant	1862	500	50	27,500
*St. Peter, St. Marks pl, New Brighton	C. A. Cassidly, 2 assistants	1839	2,500	500	150,000
*The Sacred Heart, West New Brighton	T. J. Heafy, 1 assistant	1875	2,500	300	125,000

*Has a parochial school.

Recapitulation, Richmond Churches.

Denominations	Con-trib'g Mem.	S.S. Mem-bers.	Total Amount Raised.	Value Church Property.
Baptist	772	637	$27,930	$76,000
Christian Science	......	......	....	....
Disciples of Christ	50	45	2,000	1,500
Evangelical	60	120	400	3,500
Lutheran	1,454	1,014	44,642	236,185
Meth. Episcopal	2,222	2,437	45,302	290,000
Meth. Epis. Af.	105	70	21,000	7,000
Moravian	483	897	17,349	12,000
Presbyterian	661	534	15,535	140,000

Denominations.	Con-trib'g Mem.	S.S. Mem-bers.	Total Amount Raised.	Value Church Property.
Prot. Episcopal	3,265	1,638	$68,541	$749,200
Reformed	1,081	801	23,050	148,000
Roman Catholic	†	4,997	....	1,264,500
Unitarian	100	40	2,500	30,000
Miscellaneous	200	297	....	35,000
Totals	35,858	13,527	$268,249	$2,992,805

†Number of parishioners, 26,405.

MUSEUMS IN NEW YORK CITY.

Brooklyn.

BKLN. BOTANIC GARDEN—See index.

CENTRAL MUSEUM OF THE BROOKLYN INSTITUTE OF ARTS AND SCIENCES, Eastern parkway and Washington av. Open week days, 9 A.M. to 6 P.M.; Sun., 2 to 6 P.M. Pay days, Mon. and Tues. (See also index.)

CHILDREN'S MUSEUM—Branch museum of The Brooklyn Institute of Arts and Sciences, in Bedford Park, Brooklyn av. and Park pl. Free. Open 10 A.M. to 5 P.M. wk. days; 2-5 P.M. Sun. Curator, Anna B. Gallup.

Manhattan.

AMERICAN MUSEUM OF NATURAL HISTORY—W. 77th and Central Park West. Open 9 A.M. to 5 P.M.; Sun., 1 P.M. to 5 P.M. Always free. Reached by 6th or 9th av L to 81st, subway to 79th; 8th av. or Columbus av. surface cars. (See also index.)

AMERICAN NUMISMATIC SOC.—B'way and 156th, Mhtn. Has collection of coins, medals and decorations and Numismatic Library. Open 10 A.M. to 5 P.M. week days except Mon, 1 to 5 P.M. Sun. (See also index.)

AQUARIUM—(See index.)

BOTANIC GARDEN—(See index.)

DYCKMAN HOUSE—204th and B'way. Built in 1873. Historical relics. Open 9 A.M. to 4 P.M.

HISPANIC SOC. OF AM. MUSEUM AND LIBRARY—156th, west of B'way. Open 9 A.M. to 5 P.M., except the month of Aug., New Year's Day, Lincoln's and Washington's Birthdays, Decoration Day, 4th of July, Thanksgiving and Christmas. Library is closed Sun. and Mon. (See also index.)

WASHINGTON HDQTS. (Jumel Mansion)—160th and 162d, bet. Edgecomb av. and Jumel Terrace. Open daily and Sun., 9 A.M. to 5 P.M. Free every day. Reached by B'way subway to 157th st. sta., 6th av. "L" to 155th, as well as by surface cars and 5th av. bus No. 3, which passes the house. Used as a museum of Revolutionary relics.

METROPOLITAN MUSEUM OF ART—Central Park E. and 82d. Open 10 A.M. to 6 P.M. in summer, 10 A.M. to 5 P.M. in winter; Sun., 1 P.M. to 6 P.M. Pay days, Mon. and Fri., 25c. Reached by 5th av. stage, Madison av. cars to 82d, 3d av. L to 84th, Lexington av. subway to 86th. Paintings, sculpture, architectural models, arms, armor, Egyptian and classical antiquities, European and American decorative arts, Chinese and Japanese, Indian, Persian and other near Eastern art. (See also index.)

POE COTTAGE—Poe Park, Kingsbridge rd. and Grand Blvd. Concourse.

ROGER MORRIS MANSION—See Washington Hdqts. this page.

SAFETY INST. OF AMERICA (maintains the Amer. Museum of Safety)—261 Madison av. Open daily, except Sun., 9 A.M. to 5 P.M., and in the evening to classes and societies by special arrangement. Closed on Thanksgiving, Christmas, New Year's and July 4th days, and also Sat. afternoons during July and Aug.

VAN CORTLANDT HOUSE—Van Cortlandt Park, B'way and 242d, Bronx. Open daily 10 A.M. to 5 P.M.; Sun., 2 P.M. to 5 P.M. Free every day except Thur., when fee of 25c. is charged. Reached by subway to 242d. Used as museum of Colonial relics and maintained by Soc. of Colonial Dames of N. Y. State.

ZOOLOGICAL PARK—(See idex.)

RAILROAD FATALITIES AND INJURIES.

According to figures of the Interstate Commerce Commission, fewer persons were killed on railroads during 1919 than in any year since 1898, and fewer were injured than in any year since 1910. The figures are summed up as follows by *Bradstreet's:* During 1919 a total of 6,978 persons were killed and 149,053 injured, compared with 6,859 killed in 1898 and 119,507 injured in 1910. Of the killed, 273 were passengers, as were 7,456 of the injured. Railroad employees killed during the year numbered 2,138, and 131,018 were injured. Fewer trespassers on railroads were killed in 1919 than during any year of the commission's records, which go back to 1890. Last year 2,553 trespassers were killed and 2,658 injured.

GARRITSEN PARK GIFT.

Brooklyn is again indebted to two of its most generous citizens, Frederic B. Pratt and Alfred T. White, for their splendid gift of 143 acres of land and water in and about the historic Garritsen's Basin for park purposes. This gift is only one of the many which they have made toward the improvement of living conditions in Brooklyn.

PUBLIC SCHOOLS OF THE CITY OF NEW YORK.

HEADQUARTERS, Park av. and 59th st., Mhtn. Bkln. Office, 131 Livingston st.

THE BOARD OF EDUCATION.

Bd. of Education consists of 7 members appointed by the Mayor for a term of 7 yrs. (1918 appointees excepted). It consists of 2 members from Mhtn., 2 from Bklyn. and 1 each from Bronx, Queens and Richmond, who serve without pay. The members and year when term expires are:

Anning S. Prall, Pres., 160 College av., West New Brighton, S. I., 1926; George J. Ryan, V. Pres., 236 Lincoln, Flushing, L. I., 1922; Arthur S. Somers, 988 Sterling pl., Bkln., 1925;; Frank D. Wilsey, V. Pres., Spuyten Duyvil, Bronx, 1921; Mrs. Emma L. Murray, 71 E. 96th, Mhtn., 1923; Dr. John A. Ferguson, 962 Bushwick av., Bkln., 1924; Morris S. Stern, 2013 5th av., Mhtn., 1927.

SALARIES are fixed by the Bd. of Education in compliance with the State law. (See schedules.)

POWERS AND DUTIES.

To perform duties imposed upon boards of education by statute; to create or abolish positions and bureaus; to appoint all employees; to have care and control of school properties; to purchase and furnish apparatus, books and supplies; to establish and maintain all free schools, school libraries, lecture courses, playgrounds, recreation and social centers and reading rooms; to authorize courses of study and contents; to authorize and determine text books from lists recommended; and to prescribe regulations and by-laws for the conduct of its proceedings and business affairs.

Committees of Board of Education: Committee on Finance, Salaries and Supplies: Mr. Prall, chairman; Mr. Ryan, Mr. Stern, Dr. Ferguson.

Committee on Buildings and Sites: Mr. Stern, chairman; Mr. Somers, Dr. Ferguson.

Committee on By-Laws: Mr. Ryan, chairman; Mr. Somers, Mrs. Murray.

Committee on Day Schools: Dr. Ferguson, chairman; Mr. Wilsey, Mr. Stern.

Committee on Special Schools: Mr. Stern, chairman; Mr. Ryan, Dr. Ferguson.

Committee on Care of Buildings: Mr. Ryan, chairman; Mr. Wilsey, Dr. Ferguson.

Committee on Local School Boards: Dr. Ferguson, chairman; Mrs. Murray, Mr. Ryan.

APPOINTMENTS OF THE BOARD OF EDUCATION.

Office of Superintendent of Schools.

The Supt. of Schools is appointed by the Bd. of Education for a 6-yr. term. Powers and duties: Supervision and direction over all employees except members of Board of Examiners; transfer of teachers on recommendation of Bd. of Supts., such transfers to be submitted to Bd. of Education for consideration and action; reporting of violations of regulations and suspension of employees pending action of Bd. of Education; licensing of teachers on recommendation of Bd. of Examiners; as chief executive officer, supervision over all educational activities under the direction and control of the Bd. of Education.

Supt. of Schools, William L. Ettinger....$12,000
790 Riverside drive, Mhtn. Term expires Mar. 14, 1922.

Head Clerk, J. H. Pitts, $4,800; Sec. to Bd. of Supts., T. E. Bussey, $4,800; Clerks, F. L. Mills, $5,500; C. C. Sherrick, $3,096. Clerks and Stenographers, etc., $624 to $2,820.

Board of Superintendents.

The Bd. of Superintendents consists of Supt. of Schools and 8 Associate Supts., whose terms of office are 6 yrs. All members of teaching staff are appointed by Bd. of Education on recommendation of Bd. of Supts.

Assoc. City Supts.—Salaries, $8,250 each; E. D. Shimer, 104 Union av., Jamaica; E. B. Shallow, 1090 Dean, Bkln.; A. W. Edson, 680 St. Nicholas av., Mhtn; G. Straubenmuller, 169 W. 88th, Mhtn.; C. E. Meleney, 509 E. 16th, Bkln.; Wm. J. O'Shea, 145 W. 88th; J. H. Walsh, 8502 Fort Hamilton av., Bkln.; Wm. McAndrew, 2758 Kingsbridge Ter., Kingsbridge, Mhtn.

OFFICE HOURS.

Ettinger: Ch.; *Th., 3 to 5 P.M. Edson: *Th., 3 to 5 P.M.; at P. S. 10, Eagle av. and 163d, The Bronx; *Sat., 9 A.M. to 12 M. McAndrew: *Tu., 3 to 5 P.M. Shimer: M., 3 to 5 P.M. at P. S. 82, Kaplan av., Hammond and Horton, Jamaica, L. I.; Tu., 3 to 5 P.M., Sat., 9 A.M. to 12 M. at 131 Livingston, Bkln. O'Shea: M., 3 to 5 P.M. at P.S. 17, 327 W. 47th, Mhtn.; *Wed., 3 to 5 P.M.; *Sat., 9 A.M. to 12 M. Shallow; M., 4 to 5 P.M. at 131 Livingston, Bkln.; *Sat., 9 A.M. to 12 M. Straubenmuller: *Tu., 3 to 5 P.M.; *Sat., 9 A.M. to 12 M. Meleney, *Th., 3 to 5 P.M.; *Sat., 9 A.M. to 12 M. Walsh: Fri., 3 to 5 P.M. at P. S. 50, Driggs av. and S. 3d, Bkln.; Sat., 9 A.M. to 12 M. at 131 Livingston, Bkln.

Assignments of Associate Superintendents.

Meleney—Div. I, comprising Local School Bd. Dists. 1, 2, 3, 4, 5, 6, 7, 9. Div. VII, high schools. Special assignment, supervision of Dir. of Art in High Schools.

O'Shea—Div. II, comprising L. S. Bd. Dists. 8, 10, 11, 12, 13, 14, 15, 16. Special assignment, nomination, transfer, appt. of teachers in all branches of the service; absences, leaves of absence; resignations and retirements; experience certification; service approval; rules of service; war activities (temporary).

*Offices at 500 Park av., Mhtn.

Edson—Div. III, comprising L. S. Bd. Dists. 17, 18, 19, 20, 21, 22, 23, 24. Div. IX, Probationary Sch., Truant Sch. and Parental Sch.; Attendance Bur. Special assignment: Classes for exceptional children—anemic, blind, crippled, deaf, speech defects tuberculosis and ungraded. Visiting teachers. Supervision of Director of Speech Improvement, Inspector of Ungraded Classes, Inspector for the Blind.

Shallow—Div. IV, comprising L. S. Bd. Dists. 26, 27, 28, 29, 30, 37, 47, 48. Special assignment; Sites, buildings, leases and structural modifications of existing buildings.

Walsh—Div. V, comprising L. S. Bd. Dists. 31, 32 33, 34, 35, 36, 38, 39. Special assignment: Organization of classes in elementary schools.

Shimer—Div. VI, comprising L. S. Bd. Dists. 25, 40, 41, 42, 43, 44, 45, 46. Special assignment: Studies and text books for all schools, supervision of following named directors and assistant directors: Music, Physical Trg. and Educational Hygiene and Kindergartens.

McAndrew—Div. VIII, extension activities, comprising evening schools of all types; non-industrial continuation classes; community centers; after school athletic centers; lecture service; visual instruction; vacation schools and summer activities. Special assignment: Supervision of following: Director of Ev. Sch. and Continuation Classes, Director of Community Centers, Vacation Schools and Playgrounds and Director of Lectures.

Straubenmuller—Div. X, vocational day schools, industrial co-operative and continuation classes and training schools for teachers. Div. XI, intermediate schools, intermediate depts. (7th, 8th and 9th grades in elementary schools) and 7th, 8th and 9th grades in all prevocational schools. Special assignment: School gardens. Supervision of Director of Vocational Activities and Cooking, the former being responsible for supervision of Directors and Assistant Directors of Drawing, Manual Training and Sewing. The Director of Vocational Activities also acts as technical adviser to Associate Superintendents Meleney and McAndrew.

27 District Superintendents.

Appointed on recommendation of Board of Supts.; salary, $6,600 each.

Name and residence.	Assigned to	Dists.
Jas. Lee, 456 W. 141st, Mhtn..........	10	11
Cecil A. Kidd, Park Av. Hotel, Mhtn..	2	3
C. W. Lyon, 2410 Clarendon rd., Bkln..	25	40
E. W. Stitt, 1543 St. Nicholas av., Mhtn.	4	5
R. G. McGray, Mrs., 119 W. 71st, Mhtn.	6	9
Henry W. Jameson, 1925 7th av., Mhtn.	23	24
Jos. H. Wade, 454 W. 153d, Mhtn....	21	22
Wm. O'Flaherty, 163 Bush, Bronx.....	17	18
J. P. Conroy, 167 W. 94th, Mhtn.....	15	16
C. E. Franklin, 463 3d av., Astoria.....	41	42
John Dwyer, 456 W. 153d, Mhtn......	19	20
J. S. Taylor, 2275 Loring pl., Bronx....	1	7
Henry E. Jenkins, 250 W. 11th, Mhtn..	27	29
J. M. Edsall, 177 8th av., Bkln.......	28	30
J. J. McCabe, 614 St. Marks av., Bkin.	31	34
B. Veit, Healy av., Far Rockaway, L. I.	32	36
Grace S. Forsythe, 20 W. 72d, Mhtn...	33	35

PUBLIC SCHOOLS OF THE CITY OF NEW YORK—APPOINTMENTS OF BD. OF ED.—*Continued.*

Name and Residence.	Assigned to Dists.
Lizzie E. Rector, 210 Madison av., Mhtn.26	37
J. T. Nicholson, 534 W. 150th, Mhtn...12	14
Arthur C. Perry, Jr., 163 Macon, Bkln.43	44
Wm. A. Boylan, 770 St. Nich. av., Mhtn.45	46
J. J. Reynolds, 732A Jefferson av., Bkn.38	39
Thomas O. Baker, 453 Bement av., W. N. Brighton, S. I....................47	48
John S. Wade, 2267 Andrews av., Bronx. 8	13

For offices of above see Local School Boards.

Special Assignments.

J. L. Tildsley, Spuyten Duyvil, High Schools; J. S. Roberts, 596 Riverside drive, Junior High Schools; Wm. E. Grady, 1476 Ocean P'kway, Bkln., Office of Supt. of Schools, $7,500.

Directors and Inspectors of Special Branches.

Kindergarten—Dir., Fanniebelle Curtis; Asst. Dir., Luella A. Palmer, Jane H. Nicholson.

Sewing—Annie L. Jessup, Mrs., Mhtn.; Bronx, Richmond; Minnie L. Hutchinson, Bkln., Queens.

Cooking—Dir., Grace Schermerhorn; Asst. Dir., Martha Westfall.

Music—Dir., G. H. Gartlan; Asst. Dir., J. P. Donnelly.

Art—High Schools, J. P. Haney.

Drawing—Elementary Schools, F. H. Collins.

Manual Training and Drawing—Elementary Schools, Asst. Dir., A. W. Garritt.

Lectures—Dir., Ernest L. Crandall; Asst. Dir., Wendel M. Thomas.

High School Organization—Dir., Herman H. Wright.

Modern Languages in High Schools—Dir., Lawrence A. Wilkins.

Vocational Activities—George J. Loewy, Dir.

Evening Schools and Continuation Classes—Morris E. Siegel, Dir.

Physical Training—Dir., A. K. Aldinger, M. D.; Asst. Dirs., Jessie H. Bancroft, Josephine Beiderhase, Abner P. Way, Adela J. Smith.

Community Centers, Vacation Schools and Vacation Playgrounds—Eugene C. Gibney, Dir.

Inspector of Classes for the Blind—Frances E. Moscrip.

Inspector of Playgrounds and Recreation Centers—Mae H Beattys.

Inspectors of Public School Athletics—J. J. McHugh, R. A. Patterson, M. A. Jones, Emily A. O'Keefe, Christine Dobbins.

Inspector of Ungraded Classes—Elizabeth E. Farrell; Asst. Insps., Elizabeth A. Walsh, Mrs. Elizabeth Teas Wood.

Speech Improvement—Dir., Frederick W. Martin.

Supervisors of Continuation Classes—Mrs. Anna H. Wilcox, Sarah Elkus.

Asst. Dirs. of Educational Hygiene—Dirs. Frances Cohen, I. H. Goldberger.

Board of Examiners.

Geo. J. Smith, Ch., 1920-21.

Consists of 4 examiners, appointed by the Bd. of Education. They examine all applicants for licenses to teach. Eligible lists are prepared in order of standing. Salaries, $7,700 each.

J. C. Byrnes, 86 Franklin pl., Flushing, L. I.; W. L. Hervey, 351 W. 114th; J. A. O'Connell, 57 W. 126th; G. J. Smith, 260 W. 57th, Mhtn.

Secretary, F. V. Daly, $3,600. Clerks and Stenographers, $702 to $2,640.

Bureau of Supplies.

The Supt. of School Supplies is executive officer of the Board respecting purchase, storing and distribution of supplies, printing for the Board, transportation of school children, etc. Term, 6 yrs. Expires Mar. 6, 1922.

Supt., Patrick Jones, $9,000; Dept. Supt., A. L. Brasefield, $4,000; Fuel Engineer, J. R. Cave, $4,500; Clerks, Geo. G. Brown, $2,700; Ed. St. Leger, $4,000; W. F. McCabe, Rufus J. Suits, Anthony Wahle, Henry F. McGuckin, $3,096; other Clerks, Fuel Insprs., Engnrs., etc., $858 to $2,640.

Superintendent of School Buildings.

The Supt. of School Bldgs. is the executive officer of the Board in all matters relating to school buildings. Term, 6 yrs. Expires Feb. 20, 1922.

Superintendent, C. B. J. Snyder, $11,000; Dept. Supts. Sch. Bldgs., A. W. Ross, F. A. Collins, H. M. Devoe, C. M. Morgan, C. E. Dobbin, each $6,500; S. R. Brick, $5,500.

Sanitary Asst., J. J. Sheridan, $5,500; Asst. Chief Sanitary Div., C. Nixon, $4,000; Chief Heating and Ventilating Div., F. G. McCann, $5,500; Asst. Chf. Heating and Vent. Div., J. H. Lindsay, $4,200; Chf. Elec. Div., S. A. Thomas, $5,500; Chief Furniture Div., Trimble Foster, $4,500; Asst. Chief Furniture Div., James J. McCue, $4,000; Asst. Eng., Charles Tilgner, $4,000; Asst. Chief Elec. Div., C. A. Kassenbrock, $4,200; Ch. Clk., J. E. Douglass, $5,500; Clerks, H. S. Grinleese, $3,312; Jacob C. Jung, $2,820; Sten., Ellen C. Ives, $2,640; Stenographers, Clerks, etc., $702 to $2,470.

INSPECTORS, DRAUGHTSMEN, ETC.

Gen. Insps., M. F. Long, P. E. Mellon, A. Haywood, J. Mallon, J. W. Morgan, T. H. Mackey, $3,312; Engineer, E. J. Lance, $3,528; Asst. Engineers, Eugene Schon, $4,320; G. Kong, $3,600; S. S. Rathbun, $3,312; Insp. of Iron and Steel, T. H. Graham, $3,312; Gen. Insp. Repairs, W. H. McCord, W. B. Tocher, J. J. McKinney, $3,312; Insp. of Heat and Vent., D. Donalds, $3,096, and 12 at $2,820; Mechanical Draughtsman, C. F. Wolfsfeld, $3,312; Mechanical Engineer, T. J. A. Rahilly, $3,312; Architectural Draughtsmen, A. H. Hallock, P. B. Ruggles, $3,528; L. M. Thorn, S. E. Kingman, J. Frees, M. Bause, E. G. Hopped, R. H. F. Halsey, L. P. Pitt, $3,312, and others from $2,470 to $3,096; Electrical Insps., Insp. of Painting, Insp. of Electrical Conductors, Insps. of Masonry and Carpentry, Structural Steel Draughtsmen, Mechanical Draughtsmen and other employees, $3,096 to $1,482.

Other Employees of the Board.

SECRETARY'S OFFICE.

Sec. A. E. Palmer, $6,500; Chief Clerk, T. A. Dillon, $4,000; Clerks, C. Herr, $3,960; Mary Anglin, Elizabeth V. Bennett, Morris Warschauer, $3,096; Trial Stenographer, J. M. Connolly, $3,096; Stenos. and other employees, $868 to $2,820.

Confidential Secretaries, Laura P. O'Meara, $3,096; Mary Selonik, $2,470; Henry Eisenhauer, $1,700.

BUREAU OF AUDIT AND ACCOUNTS.

Auditor, H. R. M. Cook, $7,500; Dep. Aud., F. D. Chambers, $6,000; Ch. Clerk, F. Gerst, $4,000; Bookkeeper, J. B. Payne, $4,200; Clerks, J. L. Higgins, G. L. Graef, $4,200; E. J. Whitlock, Chas. J. Gilman, $3,096; Examiners of Claims, W. Hagan, R. C. Nicholson, J. H. Rooney, R. M. Bingham, $3,096; Clerks, Stenographers and other employees, $702 to $2,820.

DIVISION OF REFERENCE AND RESEARCH.

Director, Eugene A. Nifenecker, $7,000; Chief Clerk, W. S. West, $4,200; Clerk, Wm. C. McGregor, $3,528; Statistician, Lawrence F. Hogan, $3,096; other employees, $624 to $2,640.

DIRECTOR OF LECTURES.
(Office, 157 E. 67th, Mhtn.)

Director, Ernest C. Crandall, $6,600; Asst. Director, W. M. Thomas, $4,500; Stenos. and Typrs. and other employees, $702 to $2,262.

BUREAU OF LIBRARIES.

C. G. Leland, Supt., $5,000; Clerk, Clarence Dow, $2,640.

BUREAU OF PLANT OPERATION.

Supt., R. W. Rodman, $7,500; Chief Clerk, Jos. Miller, $4,500; Supervisor of Janitors, A. J. Maguire, $3,600; Assts., John S. Bannon, Frank Bergan, Thos. Dibbins, each $3,312; other employees, $1,170 to $2,470.

Offices of District Supts., Clerks and Stenographers, $1,014 to $1,950.

SCHOOL LUNCHES.

Manager, Maude J. Bleier, $2,470; Assts., Cooks and Helpers, $1,014 to $1,638.

PHYSICIANS TO EXAMINE APPLICANTS FOR TEACHERS' LICENSES.

Jas. P. Hunt, 44 E. 48th, Mhtn.; E. Helen Knight, 15 Ft. Washington av., Mhtn., $2,600.

MEDICAL INSPECTORS OF UNGRADED CLASSES.

Dr. Harriet F. Coffin, 426 E. 26th st.; Dr. Elizabeth I. Adamson, 240 Waverly pl., $3,600.

EMPLOYEES OTHER THAN PRINCIPALS AND TEACHERS IN TRUANT AND PARENTAL SCHOOLS.

Mhtn.—Mary K. Leonard, Matron Supt., $2,470, and 8 other employees from $624 to $1,170.

Bkln.—(Annex to Parental)—12 employees from $624 to $1,326.

Parental (Queens)—29 employees from $195 to $1,638.

PUBLIC SCHOOLS OF THE CITY OF NEW YORK—APPOINTMENTS OF BD. OF ED.—*Continued.*

BUREAU OF ATTENDANCE.

154 E. 68th, Mhtn.

Statutory Title—Bureau of Compulsory Education, Schl. Census and Child Welfare. Dir., J. W. Davis, $7,700; Asst. Dir., G. H. Chatfield, $5,500. Est. by act of the Legislature effective May 1, 1914 (Chap. 470-471, Laws of 1914). Chief Clerk, J. H. Smyth, $2,470; Stenographer, Mary H. O'Connell, $2,640; other Clks., Stenos., etc., $702 to $1,950; Attendance Officers (salaries, see Salary Schedules); Div. Supervising Attendance Officers, J. L. Coppinger, C. T. Gartlan, Dist. Supv. Attendance Officers. Felicia Cafferata, E. Loewing, O. T. Martin, J. S. McCloskey, W. J. Black, Jennie F. Walsh, P. E. Rausch, T. M. Purcell, V. M. Collins, E. M. Michelbacher, C. T. Graham, H. Kelly, W. T. Byrnes, J. A. Carlin, Jessie Frank, T. A. Tydinge, A. B. Ripley, J. J. Ludeke, T. F. Donovan, J. J. Farrell, W. E. O'Leary, J. F. Rorke, F. A. Craig, A. F. Carruthers, H. M. Donnolly, J. E. McGuire, 279 other Attendance Officers.

LOCAL SCHOOL BOARDS..

Each consists of 6 members, 5 appointed by Borough Pres. for a period of 5 years, and 1 member of the Board of Education. A Dist. Supt. is assigned to advise with board. Districts are numbered from 1 to 48. Following are the schools in each district, and the names and addresses of the members of each board. The duties of a Local Board are: To visit schools once each quarter; to make recommendations with respect to matters affecting the interests of the schools; subject to the by-laws, to transfer teachers from school to school, excuse absences of teachers, hear charges against principals and teachers and make recommendations thereon, and perform such other duties as may be required under said by-laws; to provide by-laws regulating the exercise of the powers and duties vested in it; to elect a Sec. and determine his duties. The Sec. is authorized to administer oaths and take affidavits in matters pertaining to the schools of the district, and possesses powers of Commissioner of Deeds, but is not entitled to fees or emoluments.

Assignments of Board Members to Local School Board Districts.

MANHATTAN.

Mr. Stern—Dists. 1, 2, 3, 4, 5, 6, 7 and 9.

Mrs. Murray—Dists. 8, 10, 11, 12, 13, 14, 15 and 16.

THE BRONX.

Mr. Wilsey—Dists. 17, 18, 19, 20, 21, 22, 23 and 24.

BROOKLYN.

Dr. Ferguson—Dists. 26, 27, 28, 29, 30, 37, 38 and 39.

Mr. Somers—Dists. 25, 31, 32, 33, 34, 35, 36 and 40.

QUEENS.

Mr. Ryan—Dists. 41, 42, 43, 44, 45 and 46.

RICHMOND.

Mr. Prall—Dists. 47 and 48.

Manhattan.

No. 1—Schools 1, 21, 23, 29, 38, 44, 106, 108, 112, 114, 130, 134, 162 and 177. Board: M. A. Rofrano, Ch., 11 Oliver; Mrs. A. Pisani, Sec., 2 Oliver; J. J. Goldstein, 72 Madison; Miss M. I. Hannon, 82 Greenwich; J. B. Golden, 21 Spruce; J. S. Taylor, Dist. Supt., Office, P. S. 44.

2—Schools 2, 7, 42, 62, 65, 75, 92, 120, 137. Board: Max Herbst, Ch., 460 Grand; L. J. Frank, Sec., 70 Jefferson; Ella G. Mark, 27 Rutgers; Dr. C. Goldman, 128 Henry; Mrs. Clara Maret, 146 Henry; Cecil A. Kidd, Dist. Supt., Office, P. S. 65.

3—Schools 12, 22, 31, 34, 88, 97, 110, 147. Board: Max Bresler, Ch., 278 E. B'way; I. B. Scheiber, Sec., 263 Henry; Dr. Bernard Zaglin, 273 Rivington; Mrs. I. O. Goldman, 425 Grand; Mrs. Mary A. Brewer, 283 Rivington; Cecil Kidd, Dist. Supt., Cffice, P. S. 65.

4—Schools 4, 13, 20, 35, 79, 91, 140, 160, 161, 174. Board: Mrs. H. Brodman, Ch., 186 Suffolk; A. D. Lindemann, 153 Rivington; Mrs. Esther Koppelman, Sec., 144 Rivington; John Graubard, 40 Stanton; Dr. H. Theaman, 142 Rivington; E. W. Stitt, Dist. Supt., Office, P. S. 25.

5—Schools 15, 36, 61, 64, 71, 105, 126, 131, 188. Board: Mrs. Louis Glicksman, Ch., 89 Av. B; D. M. Schoenfeld, 366 E. 8th; Mrs. Thos. Bowe, 263 7th; Dr. W. I. Sirovitch, 539 E. 6th; Wm. Weiss, 619 E. 5th; E. W. Stitt, Dist. Supt., Office, P. S. 25.

6—Schools 14, 19, 25, 40, 47 (Deaf), 50, 63, 104, 122, Stuyvesant High, Wash. Irving High, Man. Trade S. Board: Dr. Louis Haupt, Ch., 232 E. 19th; Tobias Roth, Sec., 309 E. 6th; Dr. Meyer Wolff, 61 2d av.; M. J. Bergin, 224 E. 5th; Mrs. E. Van Zile, 103 E. 17th; Mrs. Ruth McGray, Dist. Supt., Office, P. S. 27.

7—Schools 3, 8, 11, 16, 26, Textile, 28, 32, 33, 41, 45, 48, 56, 95, 107, Julia Richman High. Board: J. Mulligan, Ch., 493 8th av.; Mrs. C. N. Shepard, Sec., 9 Chelsea sq.; Chas. A. Bohlen, 46 Perry; J. J. Morris, 265 W. 25th; Vincent Pepe, 40 Washington sq. S.; Mrs. John Zimmerman, 534 9th av.; J. S. Taylor, Dist. Supt., Office, P. S. 44.

8—Schools 9, 17, 51, 58, 67, 69, 84, 87, 93, 94, 127, 141, 166, DeWitt Clinton High, High School of Commerce. Board: Mrs. Cora L. Magnus, Ch., 28 W. 96th; Mrs. Dora T. Rosett, Sec., 302 Central Pk. W.; Morton Stein, 251 W. 89th; Dr. H. E. Hale, 64 W. 50th; Bernard Naumberg, 53 W. 73d; John E. Wade, Dist. Supt., Office, P. S. 93.

9—Schools 18, 27, 59, 70, 73, 74, 76, 82, 116, 135, 183, Murray Hill Voc. S. Board: Jas. J. McLarney, Ch., 874 Lex. av.; Miss Minna Boehm, Sec., 210 E. 68th; Elwood Hendrick, 139 E. 40th; Rev. Graham C. Hunter, 150 E. 40th; Mrs. H. M. Kennaday, 780 Park av.; Mrs. Ruth G. McGray, Dist. Supt., Office, P. S. 27.

10—Schools 6, 30, 37 (Probationary), 53, 66, 77, 96, 151, 158, 190. Board: Maurice Bloch, Ch., 62 E. 90th; Mrs. Adele C. Epstein, Sec., 20 E. 88th; Benj. Blumenthal, 981 Park av.; Mrs. Harry Hastings, 7 E. 87th; Mrs. J. Loeb, 5 E. 84th; Dr. Jas. Lee, Dist. Supt., Office, P. S. 6.

11—Schools 72, 86, 109, 121, 150, 171. Board: Benj. Ulman, Ch., 1874 3d av.; Ed. J. Fay, Sec., 129 E. 94th; J. S. Donohue, 121 E. 94th; Mrs. Marg. Heineman, 168 E. 94th; Mrs. Jas. H. Marsh, 176 E. 95th; Dr. Jas. Lee, Dist. Supt., Office, P. S. 6.

12—Schools 57, 83, 101, 102, 168, 172, Ward's Island. Board: Benj. Ulman, Ch., 2004 2d av.; Dr. J. J. Tierney, Sec., 182 E. 111th; Thos. V. Stack, M.D., 169 E. 111th; Mrs. America Mannarino, 109 E. 111th; Miss Frances Greenberg, 23 E. 111th; J. T. Nicholson, Dist. Supt., Office, P. S. 101.

13—Schools 10, 54, 81 (Model), 165, 170, 179, 184, Wadleigh High, N. Y. Training S. Board: Wm. Chorosh, Ch., 1851 7th av.; Jos. V. Mitchell, Sec., 494 Central Pk. W.; Mrs. Chas. P. Dietz, 217 W. 105th; G. W. Enright, 90 Morningside dr.; Mrs. W. E. Wilkinson, 609 W. 115th; John E. Wade, Dist. Supt., Office, P. S. 93.

14—Schools 24, 39, 68, 85, 103, 159. Board: Wm. M. Silber, Ch., 2111 5th av.; Dr. John Beuermann, Sec., 1891 Lexington av.; Miss Bertha Gage, 405 E. 116th; Mrs. Katherine A. Kerr, 390 Pleasant av.; J. T. Nicholson Dist. Supt., Office, P. S. 101.

15—Schools 5, 43, 68, 119, 157, 186, 192. Board: Mrs. J. J. Rooney, Ch., 619 W. 145th; Mrs. Elizabeth G. Alexander, Sec., 547 W. 123d; Chas. F. Bishop, 601 W. 148th; David E. Goldfarb, 62 Hamilton Terrace; John P. Leo, Jr., 611 W. 146th; J. P. Conroy, Dist. Supt., Office, P. S. 157.

16—Schools 46, 52, 89, 90, 115, 132, 169, Geo. Washington High, Vocational S. for Boys. Board: Frank E. Karelsen, Ch., 540 W. 165th; W. J. Geraty, Sec., 409 Edgecomb av.; Dr. Johanna B. Leo, 520 W. 182d; David C. Lewis, 550 W. 180th; Mrs. Teresa G. Lindheim, 523 W. 187th; J. P. Conroy, Dist. Supt., Office, P. S. 157.

Bronx.

17—Schools 1, 9, 18, 22, 29, 30, 31, 43, Theo. Roosevelt High. Board: Dr. W. E. Howley, Ch., 191 Alexander av.; Dr. Francis L. Donlon, Sec., 470 E. 138th; Mrs. John Johnson, 424 E. 141st; Geo. Price, 461 E. 140th; Michael J. Sullivan, 343 E. 141st; Wm. O'Flaherty, Dist. Supt., Office, P. S. 27.

18—Schools 3, 25, 27, 37, 38, 52. Board: F. S. Frankfurter, Ch., 807 Courtlandt av.; Jacques Mautinband, Sec., 486 E. 141st; Arthur A. Barr, 424 E. 157th; Mrs. Catherine Goodwin, 479 E. 141st; Frank Grady, 406 E. 152d; Wm. O'Flaherty, Dist. Supt., Office, P. S. 27.

19—Schools 10, 23, 35, 39, 48, 51, Morris High. Board: Jos. L. Levine, Ch., 832 Manida; Louis G. Friess, Sec., 972 Woodycrest av.; Mrs. Mary Fitzpatrick, 919 Ogden av.; Dr. J. W. Maller, 303 E. 161st; Mrs. Jacob L. Markel, 1119 Forest av.; John Dwyer, Dist. Supt., Office, P. S. 10.

PUBLIC SCHOOLS OF THE CITY OF NEW YORK—LOCAL SCHOOL BOARDS—*Continued.*

20—Schools 11, 20, 40, 53, 54. Board: Louis Castagnetta, Ch., 1105 Hoe av.; Mrs. Sadie Brown, Sec., 1118 Forest av.; Ambrose G. Christ, 1189 Franklin av.; Dr. Otto J. Scheina, 1143 Hoe av.; Aubrey J. Parody, 272 E. 169th; John Dwyer, Dist. Supt., Office, P. S. 10.

21—Schools 2, 4, 42, 50, 55. Board: Theo. E. Thompson, Ch., 1779 Washington av.; W. F. Olpp, Sec., 1384 Clinton av.; Andrew I. Albert, 728 Crotona Pk. E.; Harold C. Knoepel, 1815 Morris av.; Jos. H. Wade, Dist. Supt., Office, P. S. 44.

22—Schools 6, 7, 24, 26, 28, 33, 44, 49, 58, Evander Childs High. Board: Paul T. Davis, Ch., 3121 Sedgwick av.; Nathan Loewus, Sec., 1895 Grand Concourse; Albert E. Wheeler, 702 W. 121st; Harry B. Chambers, 205 E. 176th; Mrs. Philip J. Kearns, 2311 Grand Concourse; Jos. H. Wade, Dist. Supt., Office, P. S. 44.

23—Schools 5, 8, 19, 32, 45, 46, 56. Board: Herbert A. Knox, Ch., 2759 Bainbridge av.; Geo. W. M. Clark, Sec., 88 E. 236th; Mrs. Thos. A. Hand, 3323 Decatur av.; Mrs. Ellsworth J. Healy, LeRoy Hall, Fordham; Mrs. Katherine W. O'Brien, 2126 Mapes av.; Henry W. Jameson, Dist. Supt., Office, P. S. 21.

24—Schools 12, 13, 14, 15, 16, 17, 21, 34, 36, 41, 47. Board: Dominic A. Trotter, Ch., 2079 Benedict av.; Mrs. May G. Goggin, Sec., 1541 St. Lawrence av.; Dr. Cornelius O'Grady, 1477 Commonwealth av.; Clarence W. Beach, 427 Beach av.; Ed. R. Koch, 3642 Olinville av.; Henry W. Jameson, Dist. Supt., Office, P. S. 21.

Brooklyn.

25—Schools 61, 63, 109, 149, 173, 174. Board: Dr. Milton Schreiber, Ch., 105 Penn av.; Mrs. Sadie Lessall, Sec., 301 Penn av.; Dr. L. Simmons, 642 Sutter av.; Sigmund Trapani, 138 New Jersey av.; Chas. W. Lyon, Dist. Supt., Office, P. S. 63.

26—Schools 48, 80, 81, 95, 97, 100, 128, 163, 164, 177, 180, New Utrecht High. Board: Allison L. Adams, Ch., 8634 20th av.; Mrs. Arthur Stern, Sec., 116 Bay 26th; Wm. Burke, 62 Av. Q; Samuel W. Gumpertz, Dreamland, C. I.; Mark Nave, 2825 W. 24th; Miss Lizzie E. Rector, Dist. Supt., Office, P. S. 140.

27—Schools 1, 4, 5, 7, 8, 9, 11, 12, 14, 15, 42, 45, 67, 77, 111, 133, Girls' Commercial High, Bkln. Vocational School for Boys. Board: Mrs. John Guilfoyle, Ch., 179 Nassau; Mrs. Jennie E. Tomes, Sec., 502 Classon av.; Harriet L. Bedell, 81 Nassau; Mrs. Mary A. Strack, 194 Washington av.; Mrs. Lydia M. Salmon, 166 Sands; Henry E. Jenkins, Dist. Supt., Office, 131 Livingston.

28—Schools 6, 13, 27, 29, 30, 32, 40, 46, 47, 58, 60, 78, 124, 142. Board: Dr. J. A. O'Reilly, Ch., 405 Union; Wm. S. Butler, 49 2d pl.; Rose Brenner, 252 Carroll; Susan G. Harkins, 302 Hicks; Jas. M. Edsall, Dist. Supt., Office, 131 Livingston.

29—Schools 3, 41, 44, 54, 55, 83, 93, 138, 148, 167, Boys' High, Girls' High, Commercial High, Training School for Teachers. Board: Jas. F. Hurley, Ch., 97 Decatur; Martin E. Moriarity, Sec., 431 Jefferson av.; Mrs. Allan M. Gordon, 1675 Union; Michael D. Michaels, 441 Jefferson av.; Mrs. Catherine W. Stengle, 138 Halsey; Henry E. Jenkins, Dist. Supt., Office, 131 Livingston.

30—Schools 2, 10, 39, 82, 94, 107, 130, 131, 136, 146, 154, 169, 172, Manual Training High. Board: Gustav Hartung, Ch., 548 2d; Mrs. Sadie Steinbrink, Sec., 18 Fuller pl.; Jas. J. Daly, 318 9th av.; Dr. Ralph I. Lloyd, 450 9th; Geo. A. Viemeister, 1013 12th; James M. Edsall, Dist. Supt., Office, 131 Livingston.

31—Schools 16, 19, 33, 37, 50, 69, 71, 122, 157, 166, Eastern Dist. High. Board: Mrs. Wm. S. Troy, Ch., 130 Hewes; Mrs. Martha Nugent, Sec., 628 Wythe av.; Mrs. Augustus C. Newman, 500 Bedford av.; Robt. J. Dickie, 272 Hewes; Jas. J. McGinty, 72 S. 2d; Jas. J. McCabe, Dist. Supt., Office, P. S. 50.

32—Schools 25, 26, 28, 35, 57, 70, 79, 129, 144, 156. Board: Saml. H. Cragg, Ch., 612 Willoughby av.; Jennie E. Rodell, Sec., 605 Putnam av.; Geo. N. Hanna, 609 Macon; Mrs. Clotilde Hollman, 488 Monroe; Geo. W. Martin, 367 McDonough; Benj. Veit, Dist. Supt., Office, P. S. 26.

33—Schools 18, 21, 36, 43, 49, 52, 88, 117, 141, 147, 168. Board: David H. Moore, Ch., 105 Powers; Mrs. Elizabeth Grismer, Sec., 194 Powers; Mrs. Meyer Weill, 683 Grand; Robt. S. Du Bois, 263 Manhattan av.; John J. McCusker, 109 Powers; Mrs. Grace Forsythe, Dist. Supt., Office, P. S. 145.

34—Schools 17, 20, 22, 23, 31, 34, 38, 59, 110, 126, 132, 143. Board: Wm. J. Cosby, Ch., 88 N. Henry; Geo. J. Brigham, 887 Manhattan av.; Dr. Ignatius Byrne, 1071 Lorimer; Mrs. Margaret Raynor, 11 Apollo; Jas. J. McCabe, Dist. Supt., Office, P. S. 50.

35—Schools 24, 53, 68, 74, 75, 86, 106, 116, 123, 145, 151, 162, Bushwick High. Board: Ferdinand Fraas, Ch., 376 Himrod; Mrs. Catherine Ohle, 1111 Lafayette av.; Francis A. F. Frisse, 18 Harmon; Mrs. Katherine A. Haggerty, 32 Linden; Gasper Liota, 31 Starr; Mrs. Grace Forsythe, Dist. Supt., Office, P. S. 145.

36—Schools 56, 73, 84, 85, 87, 113, 137, 155, 178. Board: Harrison C. Glore, Ch., 1035 Madison; Mrs. Helen A. Braun, 105 Woodbine; Sydney Masone, 28 Pleasant pl.; Daniel J. Morrison, 40 Cornelia; Dr. Walter J. O'Connell, 990 Decatur; Benj. Veit, Dist. Supt., Office, P. S. 26.

37—Schools 102, 103, 104, 105, 112, 118, 127, 140, 160, 170, 176, Bay Ridge High. Board: John R. Pinover, Ch., 7320 14th av.; Mrs. Mary E. Dwyer, Sec., 311 54th; Vincent Tanzola, 6823 Ridge Boulevard; Michael T. Fay, 369 72d; Lizzie E. Rector, Dist. Supt., Office, P. S. 140.

38—Schools 89, 90, 92, 96, 98, 99, 119, 120, 134, 139, 152, 153, 179, Erasmus Hall High. Board: Arthur C. Dore, Ch., 599 E. 5th; Mrs. Herman Gottlieb, 1523 E. 14th; Mrs. Matilda O'Connor, 1315 E. 35th; Rev. J. Fredric Berg, 900 Flatbush av.; Francis J. Sullivan, 38 Rutland rd.; Jas. J. Reynolds, Dist. Supt., Office, Erasmus Hall H. S.

39—Schools 66, 91, 114, 115, 121, 125, 135, 150, 165, 175. Board: Fredk. H. Campbell, Ch., 1221 Remsen av.; Mary M. Dammann, 412 Stone av.; Jos. Goldstein, 138 Chester; Miss Helen L. Chester, 1599 E. 96th; Baruch Miller, 461 Rockaway av.; Jas. J. Reynolds, Dist. Supt., Office, Erasmus Hall High.

40—Schools 62, 64, 65, 72, 76, 108, 158, 159, 171. Board: Chas. E. Smith, Ch., 110 Arlington av.; Geo. Keiser, Sec., 150 Autumn av.; Mrs. Petronella Leese, 5 Sunnyside av.; John C. Creveling, 235 Arlington av.; Mrs. Wm. J. Flannery, 238 Arlington av.; Chas. W. Lyon, Dist. Supt., Office, P. S. 63.

Queens.

41—Schools 1, 4, 5, 6, 7, 8, 9, 83, 84, 85, Bryant High. Board: Francis J. Schleicher, Ch., Nott and Ely avs., L. I. City; John Andrews, Sec., 134 8th, L. I. City; Jos. Brown, 427 Hopkins av., L. I. City; Mrs. Mary Matthews, 516 Graham av., L. I. City; Cornelius E. Franklin, Dist. Supt., Office, Bryant High.

42—Schools 2, 10, 11, 12, 13, 15, 16, 19, 72, 73, 76, 78, 80, 86, 89, 92, Newtown High. Board: Francis B. Carland, Ch., 24 Astoria av., Corona; Geo. S. Ethier, Sec., 93 Lamont av., Elmhurst; Otto Loibl, 62 Greenpoint av., Woodside; Jos. F. McDonell, Washington av., Laurel Hill; John A. Rapelye, Morris and Chicago avs., Elmhurst; Cornelius E. Franklin, Dist. Supt., Office, Bryant High.

43—Schools 33, 34, 35, 36, 37, 38, 39, 40, 42, 43, 44, 45, 48, 49, 50, 82, 95, 96, Far Rockaway High, Jamaica High, Jamaica Training. Board: Fred. Bradley, Ch., 23 Cannonbury rd., Jamaica; Jos. P. Rudden, 48 Washington, Jamaica; Mrs. Leon DuBois, 5 Amherst av., Jamaica; Mrs. Jas. J. Halpin, Washington av., Rosedale; Cecil B. Ruskay, 37 Neilson av., Far Rockaway; Arthur C. Perry, Jr., Dist. Supt., Office, P. S. 82.

44—Schools 46, 51, 53, 54, 55, 56, 57, 58, 59, 60, 61, 62, 63, 64, 65, 66, 90, 97, 100, Richmond Hill High. Board: David M. Wolff, Ch., 138 Vanderveer pl., Richmond Hill; Mrs. Lillian M. Radford, Sec., Ridge av., Glen Morris; Dr. Henry Stoesser, 171 Shaw av., Union Course; Mrs. Bertha Schaeffler, 1217 Woodhaven av., Woodhaven; Rev. Allen L. Benner, 528 114th, Richmond Hill; Arthur C. Perry, Jr., Dist. Supt., Office, P. S. 82.

45—Schools 67, 68, 71, 74, 75, 77, 81, 88, 91, 93. Board: Edward N. Kassel, Ch., 338 Thompkins pl., Glendale; Louis A. Richter, Sec., Webster av., Glendale; Mrs. Maude A. Davis, 8 Brown pl., Maspeth; Christian A. Smith, 140 Hallock av., Ridgewood; Wm. A. Boylan, Dist. Supt., Office, Morris Bldg., Flushing.

PUBLIC SCHOOLS OF THE CITY OF NEW YORK—LOCAL SCHOOL BOARDS—*Continued.*

46—Schools 3, 14, 17, 18, 20, 21, 22, 23, 24, 25, 26, 27, 28, 29, 30, 31, 41, 79, 87, 94, 98, 99, 101, Flushing High. Board: Mrs. Anna M. Sinclair, Ch., 14th and Myrtle av., Flushing; Frank H. Sincerblaut, Newton pl., Kew Gardens; Mrs. M. E. L. Dayton, Sec., Bay View Terrace, Bayside; Jacob Eifert, 25th, Flushing; Fred S. Rauber, Manhattan ct. and Prince, College Pt.; Wm. A. Boylan, Dist. Supt., Office, Morris Bldg., Flushing.

Richmond.

47—Schools 16, 17, 18, 19, 20, 21, 22, 23, 24, 25, 26, 27, 29, 39, Curtis High. Board: Geo. L. Egbert, Ch., 48 Arietta, Tompkinsville; Mrs. Ralph McKee, Sec., 18 Central av., Tompkinsville; Mrs. Jas. Adamson, Westerleigh, West N. Brighton; Miss Laura Botsford, Prospect av., New Brighton; Mrs. Geo. Wm. Curtis, 192 Bard av., West N. Brighton; Thos. O. Baker, Dist. Supt., Office, Borough Hall, New Brighton.

48—Schools 1, 2, 3, 4, 5, 6, 7, 8, 9, 10, 11, 12, 13, 14, 15, 28, 31, 32, 33, 34. Board: Jas. M. Talbot, Ch., 126 8th, New Dorp; Mrs. Norman S. Walker, Sec., Hillbrook Cottage, Dongan Hills; Chas. A. Bruns, 13 Thempkins, Stapleton; Miss M. Elise Johnson, 58 Central av., Tompkinsville; Miss Laura Getman, 5336 Arthur Kill rd.; Thos. O. Baker, Dist. Supt., Office, Borough Hall, New Brighton.

SALARY SCHEDULES, ENTIRE CITY.

The last general salary legislation took effect Aug. 1, 1920, when the Lockwood-Donohue Law became effective. A teacher appointed to a supervisory or teaching position, who has previously taught in a lower position, is placed in the schedule for the higher position at the salary next above that to which such teacher would be entitled in the lower position. A member of the supervising and the teaching staff receives salary and increment provided in said schedule for the year which corresponds to his or her year of service in such schedules, unless her services for the year immediately preceding have been declared by a majority vote of Bd. of Supts. to be unsatisfactory, after opportunity to be heard.

Elementary and Intermediate Schools—Salary Schedules Ia, Ib and Ic.

Years of service.	*Schedule Ia.	†Schedule IaI. See note a.	Years of service as such.	‡Schedule Ib. See note b.	§Schedule IbI. See notes a b	¶Schedule Ic. See note b.
1st......	$1,500	$1,600	1st......	$1,900	$2,000	$1,900
2d......	1,625	1,725	2d......	2,050	2,150	2,050
3d......	1,750	1,850	3d......	2,200	2,300	2,200
4th......	1,875	1,975	4th......	2,350	2,450	2,350
5th......	2,000	2,100	5th......	2,500	2,600	2,500
6th......	2,125	2,225	6th......	2,650	2,750	2,650
7th......	2,250	2,350	7th......	2,800	2,900	2,800
8th......	2,375	2,475	8th......	2,950	3,050	2,950
9th......	2,500	2,600	9th......	3,100	3,200	3,100
10th.....	2,625	2,725	10th.....	3,250	3,350	3,250
11th.....	2,750	2,850				
12th.....	2,875	2,975				
Subseq't years...	2,160	2,260				

(a) This schedule shall apply in all cases only during the continuance of assignment by Bd. of Supts. (b) In this schedule credited gross teaching service over and above 3 yrs. shall be counted.

*Teachers of kindergarten to 6B classes, incl. †Teachers of 1A to 6B classes, assigned as senior teachers. ‡Teachers of 7A and higher classes. §Teachers of 7A and higher classes assigned as senior teachers. ¶Teachers of music, drawing, phys. train., shopwork, sewing, cooking, French, German, Spanish, Italian, vocational or trade subjects, ungraded classes, teachers in parental schls., truant scls., probationary schls. and schls. for the deaf. Teachers of open air, tubercular, blind, crippled, cardiopathic classes and teachers of speech improvement.

A teacher in an elem. sch., with 3 years' experience in teaching, one of which years shall have been in the P. S. of N. Y. C., may be temporarily assigned to a school for the deaf without diminution of salary.

Teachers in the parental school, serving as teachers in evenings, receive maintenance.

Teacher-clerks and clerical and visiting assistants in schools for the deaf:

Year of service as such.	Schedules Id. Teacher-Clerks.	Ie. Teacher-Clks. Assigned to Parental School.	If. Clerical & Visiting Assts. in Schls. for the Deaf.
1	$1,200	$1,560	$1,560
2	1,300	1,690	1,690
3	1,400	1,820	1,820
4	1,500	1,950	1,950
5	1,600	2,080	2,080
6	1,700	2,210	2,210
7	1,800	.....	2,340
8	.....	.....	2,470
9	.....	.....	2,600

ASSISTANT PRINCIPAL IN PARENTAL SCHOOL.

Schedule Ig.

	(1) With lodging and maintenance.	(2) Without lodging and maintenance.
1st year	$2,800	$3,400
2d year	2,900	3,500
3d year	3,000	3,600

SCHEDULE Ih—TEACHERS OF CONTINUATION CLASSES.

(a) Teachers of common branches in continuation classes, not forming part of a P. S. organization under a principal or teacher in charge, in one establishment, 1st hr., $1.95; for each addl. hr., $1.30; maximum compensation in same estbl., $5.85.

(b) Teachers of subjects of high schl. grades and teachers of commercial and other vocat'l subjects in continuation classes not forming part of a P. S. organization under a principal or teacher in charge, per hr., $1.95; maximum compensation, $7.80.

(c) Teachers of elem. and vocat'l subjects in compulsory continuation classes in elem. schls. shall receive compensation provided for same grade of work in other classes in elem. schls.

ASSTS. TO PRINCIPALS AND TEACHERS IN CHARGE OF TRUANT AND PROBATIONARY SCHOOLS.

Year of service as such.	Schedule Ij. Assistants to principals in day elem. schls.	Schedule Ik. Teachers in charge of truant and probat'y schls.
1st	$3,400	$3,700
2d	3,500	3,800
3d	3,600	3,900

Principals of Day Elem. Schls. and Heads of Model Schls., having 25 or more classes, incl. junior high scls., elem. schls. having junior high schl. depts., and schls. having high schl. depts., principals of Schls. for Deaf, principals of Continuation, Prevocat'l, Parental and Probationary Schls.

Year of service as such—Schedule Il: 1st, $3,750; 2d, $4,000; 3d, $4,250; 4th, $4,500; 5th and subsequent years, $4,750.

High Schools and Training Schools for Teachers.

TEACHERS.

SCHEDULES IIa, IIaI, IIb AND IIc.

Year of service as teacher in high or tr. schls.	*Schedule IIa.	†Schedule IIaI. See note a.	Year of service as such.	‡Schedule IIb. See note b.	§Schedule IIc.
1st.......	$1,900	$2,405	1st.......	$3,200	$1,400
2d.......	2,050	2,600	2d.......	3,400	1,500
3d.......	2,200	2,680	3d.......	3,600	1,600
4th.......	2,350	2,760	4th.......	3,800	1,700
5th.......	2,500	2,940	5th.......	4,000	1,800
6th.......	2,650	3,120	6th.......	4,200	1,900
7th.......	2,800	3,300	7th.......	.....	2,000
8th.......	2,950	3,480	8th.......	.....	2,100
9th.......	3,100	3,660	9th.......	.....	2,200
10th......	3,250	3,840	10th......	.....	2,300
11th......	3,400	4,020	11th......	.....	2,400
12th......	3,550	4,200			
13th......	3,700	4,380			
subseq't years...	3,150	3,650			

(a) This schedule shall apply in all cases only during the continuance of the assignment by the Bd. of Education on the recommendation of the Bd. of Supts. (b) In this schedule credited gross

PUBLIC SCHOOLS OF THE CITY OF NEW YORK—SALARY SCHEDULES—*Continued.*

teaching service in high or training schls. over and above 5 yrs. shall be counted.

*Asst. teachers, model teachers and critic teachers. †Teachers assigned in charge of annexes or assigned as administrative assts. ‡First assts. §Clerical, laboratory, library, placement and investigation assts.

PRINCIPALS.

Year of service as such.	Schedule IId. Schools having 25 or more teachers.	Schedule IIdl. Schools with less than 25 teachers.
1st	$5,500	$5,000
2d	6,000	.....
3d	6,500	.....

Vocational and Trade Schools.

Year of service as such.	Schedule IIIa. Principals of vocational or trade schools.	*Schedule IIIb. Teachers assigned in charge of vocational or trade schools.
1st	$4,800	$4,200
2d	5,000	4,320
3d and subsequent years	5,200	4,440

*This schedule shall apply in all cases only during the continuance of assignment by the Bd. of Education on the recommendation of the Bd. of Supts.

TEACHERS IN VOCATIONAL SCHOOLS FOR BOYS.

	Schedule			
Year of service.	IIIc	†IIId.	‡IIIe.	§IIIf.
1st	$2,145	$2,535	$2,145	$1,560
2d	2,340	2,615	2,340	1,690
3d	2,535	2,700	2,535	1,820
4th	2,615	2,880	2,615	1,950
5th	2,700	3,060	2,700	2,080
6th	2,880	3,240	2,880	2,210
7th	3,060	3,420	3,060	.....
8th	3,240	3,600	3,240	.....
9th	3,420	3,780	3,420	.....
10th & sub. yrs...	3,600	.....	3,600	.....

(a) In this schedule credited gross teaching service over and above 3 yrs. shall be counted. (b) This schedule shall apply in all cases only during the continuance of assignment by the Bd. of Supts. (c) The non-vocat'l subjects in a vocat'l or tr. schl. for boys shall be English, history and civics and geography.

*Teachers of vocat'l or trade subjects. †Teachers of trade mathematics and science. ‡Teachers of phys. tr. and teachers of non-vocat'l subjects assigned to vocat'l or trade schls. (see notes a, b, c). §Teacher clerks assigned to vocat'l or trade schls. (see note b).

TEACHERS ET AL. IN TRADE SCHOOLS FOR GIRLS.

Yrs. of service as such.	Schedule					
	*IIIg.	†IIIh.	‡IIIj.	§IIIk.	¶IIIl.	‡IIIm
1st	$2,640	$2,100	$2,000	$2,145	$1,820	$1,560
2d	2,840	2,280	2,150	2,340	1,950	1,690
3d	3,040	2,460	2,300	2,535	2,080	1,820
4th	3,240	2,640	2,450	2,615	2,210	1,950
5th	3,440	2,820	2,600	2,700	2,340	2,080
6th	3,640	3,000	2,750	2,880	.....	2,210
7th	3,840	3,180	2,900	3,060	.....	.....
8th	.....	3,360	3,050	3,240	.....	.....
9th	.....	3,540	3,200	3,420	.....	.....
10th and subsequent yrs.	.....	.....	3,350	3,600	.....	.....

(a) In this schedule credited gross teaching service over and above 3 yrs. shall be counted. (b) This schedule shall apply in all cases only during the continuance of the assignment by the Bd. of Supts. (c) The non-vocat'l subjects in a vocat'l or trade schl. for girls shall be English, history and civics and geography and any other of the common branches.

DIRECTORS, ASSISTANT DIRECTORS ET AL. SCHEDULE IV a-IV m.

Dirs. of music, art, drawing, phys. tr.—IVa, 1st yr., $4,800; 2d, $4,940; 3d, $5,080; 4th, $5,220; 5th, $5,360; 6th, $5,500.

Dirs. of speech improvement, high schl. organization and modern languages in high sch's.—IVb, 1st yr., $4,440; 2d, $4,680; 3d, $4,730; 4th, $5,000.

Asst. dirs. of music, manual tr., phys. tr. and educational hygiene—IVc, 1st yr., $3,600; 2d, $3,825; 3d, $4,050; 4th, $4,275; 5th, $4,500.

Asst. dirs. of kindergarten and cooking—IVe, 1st yr., $2,880; 2d, $3,060; 3d, $3,240; 4th, $3,420; 5th, $3,600; 6th, $3,780.

Insps. of P. S. athletics—IVj, 1st yr., $2,600; 2d, $2,760; 3d, $2,940; 4th, $3,120; 5th, $3,300.

Sups. of continuation classes—IVk, 1st yr., $2,640; 2d, $2,880; 3d, $3,120; 4th, $3,360.

Insps. of playgrounds and recreation centers—IVl, 1st yr., $2,340; 2d, $2,470; 3d, $2,600; 4th, $2,640; 5th, $2,760.

Visiting teachers—IVm, 1st yr., $1,430; 2d, $1,560; 3d, $1,90; 4th, $1,820; 5th, $1,950; 6th, $2,080; 7th, $2,210; 8th, $2,340; 9th, $2,470.

A teacher of modern foreign languages assigned to the supervision of such languages is paid add. compensation at rate of $400 per annum.

Teachers assigned to control and management of after-school athletics are paid at rate of $3.25 for service in an afternoon, in an eve., or on a Sat. or holiday.

District Supt., assigned to assist Supt. of Schools, $7,500.

SUPERINTENDENT OF SCHOOLS ET AL. SCHEDULE V.

Supt. of Schools, $12,000; Associate Supt., $8,250; Member of Bd. of Examiners, $7,700; Dist. Supt., $6,600; Dir. Attendance, $7,700; Asst. Dir. of Attendance, $5,500; Dir. of Reference, Research and Statistics, $7,000; Asst. Dir. of Reference, Research and Statistics, $5,000; Dir. of Lectures, $6,600; Asst. Dir. of Lectures, $4,500; Dirs. of Community Centers, Vacation Schls. and Vac. Playgrounds and of Ev. Schls. and Continuation Classes, $7,000; Supt. of Libraries, $5,000; Dir. of Vocational Activities, $7,500; Medical Inspectors of Ungraded Classes, $3,600; Physician to Examine Candidates for Licenses, $2,600.

SUBSTITUTE TEACHERS.

Substitutes in Elementary Schools, Schedule VIa. Per day of actual service.

Common branches, $5.20; modern languages, $5.20; music, drawing, sewing, cooking and physical training, $5.20; ungraded classes, visiting teachers, $5.20; tubercular and anaemic classes, without lodging and maintenance, $5.20; tubercular and anaemic classes, with lodging and maintenance, $3.90; vocational or trade subjects in girls' classes, $5.20; vocational or trade subjects in boys' classes, $6.50; shopwork, $6.50; kindergarten, morning session, $3.25; afternoon session, $2.60; both sessions in one school, $5.20; schools for the deaf, $5.20.

Clerical and visiting assts. in schools for deaf, $5.85; teacher clerk, $5.20; parental, truant and probationary, $5.20; pupil teacher, $2; teacher clerk in parental school, $5.85.

Teachers of common branches in continuation classes, not forming part of a P. S. organization, under a principal or teacher in charge, in one estbl., for 1st hr., $1.95; for each addl. hr., $1.30; maximum compensation in same estbl., $5.85.

Teachers of subjects of high school grades and teachers of commercial and other vocational subjects in continuation classes, not forming part of a P. S. organization, under a principal or teacher in charge, per hr., $1.95; maximum compensation, $7.80.

Teachers of elementary and vocational subjects in compulsory continuation classes in elementary schools shall receive the compensation provided for same grade of work in other classes in elementary schools.

SUBSTITUTES IN HIGH SCHOOLS—SCHEDULE VIb.

Teachers of mechanic arts (metal and woodworking and kindred branches), $7.80; teachers of vocational agriculture, $9.10; other substitute teachers, $6.50; machine shop assts., $7.80; teacher in training (78c. per hr.), $3.90 per day of actual service.

*Heads of trade depts. †Dept. vocat'l teachers. ‡Teachers of vocat'l or trade subjects. §Teachers of phys. training and cooking and teachers of non-vocat'l subjects assigned to vocat'l or trade schls. (see notes a, b and c). ¶Placement and investigation assignments. ‡Clerical and financial assts.

SUBSTITUTES IN VOCATIONAL OR TRADE SCHOOLS—SCHEDULE VIc IN SCHOOLS FOR GIRLS.

Placement and investigation teacher, $6.50; Dept. vocat'l teacher, $7.80; vocat'l or trade subjects, $6.50; 1st asst. teacher of vocat'l or trade subjects, $5.85; 2d asst. teacher of vocat'l or trade subjects, $4.55; jun. asst. teacher of vocat'l or trade subjects, $3.25; teacher-clk., $5.85; asst. teacher-clk., $4.55; vocat'l or trade helper, $1.95 per day of actual service.

PUBLIC SCHOOLS OF THE CITY OF NEW YORK—SALARY SCHEDULES—*Continued.*

Sub. teachers of non-vocat'l subjects and sub. teachers of phys. training and cook'ng employed for 6 hrs. of instruction per day shall receive the rate of compensation provided for sub. teachers of their respective licenses, with add. compensation at the rate of $1 per day.

IN SCHOOLS FOR BOYS.

Vocat'l or trade subjects, $7.80. Teacher-Clk., $5. Sub. teachers of non-vocat'l subjects and sub. teachers of phys. training employed for 6 hrs. of instruction per day shall receive rate of compensation provided for sub. teachers of their respective licenses, with add. compensation at rate of $1 per day.

EVENING SCHOOLS—SCHEDULE VII.

Principals of eve. high and eve. tr. schls., $9.10; gen. assts. in eve. high and eve. tr. schls., $6.50; teachers in eve. high and eve. tr. schls., $6.50; laboratory assts. in eve. high and eve. tr. schls., $3.90; principals of eve. elem. schls., $7.80; teachers in charge of eve. elem. schls., having no principals, but having 12 classes or more, $6.50 per evening. Teachers in charge of eve. elem. schls., having no principals, but having less than 12 classes, $5.20; gen. assts. in eve. elem. schls., $3.90; teachers in eve. elem. schls., $3.90; supvs. of special subjects, $7.80; sub. teachers in trade subjects, in eve. high and eve. tr. schls., $6.50; sub. teachers of other subjects in eve. high and eve. tr. schls., $3.90; sub. teachers of trade subjects in eve. elem. schls., $3.90; sub. teachers of other subjects in eve. elem. schls., $2.60; tool boys, $1.95 per evening.

VACATION SCHOOLS—SCHEDULE VIII.

Supervisors, $7.80 per day; Princ'pals, $5.85; Teachers in Charge, $5.20; Teachers, $3.90; Kindergartners, $3.90; Kindergarten Helpers, $1.95; Substitutes, $1.95 per session.

VACATION PLAYGROUNDS AND RECREATION CENTERS—SCHEDULE IX.

Supervisors, $7.80; principals, $5.20; teachers in charge, $3.90; teachers, $3.25; asst. teachers, $2.28; jr. asst. teachers, $1.30; teachers of swimming or teachers in charge of baths, $3.90; librarians (playgrounds), $2.28; librarians (community centers), $3.25; pianists, $2.60; substitutes, $1.95; attendants (eve. playgrounds), $1.96 per session.

ATTENDANCE OFFICERS—SCHEDULE X.

	Schedule Xa.	Xb.	Xc.	Xd.
Year of service as such.	Attendance officers.	Dist. supv. attendance officers. (See Note a)	Div. supv. attendance officers. (See Note a)	Chief attendance officer. (See Note a.)
1st	$1,560	$2,554	$3,240	$4,176
2d	1,690	2,680	3,456	4,464
3d	1,820	2,808	3,672	4,752
4th	1,950	.....	.....	.....
5th	2 080	.....	.....	.....
6th	2,210	.....	.....	.....
7th	2,340	.....	.....	.....

(a) Schedule applies in all cases only dur'ng continuance of assignment by Bd. of Education.

SPECIAL AND EVENING SCHOOLS.

Hunter College.

Park av. and 68th, Mhtn.—Estab. Feb. 1, 1870. A liberal college education, with the specific purpose of training teachers for the city schools, is given free to girls resident of N. Y. City. Graduates receive A.B. degree, which qualifies them for temporary teaching license.

George S. Davis, Pres. of College. Trustees: Wm. G. Wilcox, Ch.; W. H. Gilpatrick, Mrs. S. J. Kramer, Mrs. J. M. Price, Mrs. Michael J. Mulqueen, Edward C. McParland, Jas. H. Robinson, Lincoln Cromwell, Elizabeth S. Williams. Ex-officio, A. S. Prall and G. S. Davis; E. C. Hunt, Sec.

College of the City of New York.

St. Nicholas Terrace and 139th, Mhtn.—Sidney E. Mezes Pres. Trustees: Geo. McAneny, Ch.; Albert Weiss, F. P. Bellamy, Chas. H. Tuttle, J. W. Hyde, Sec.; Lee Kohns, W. F. McCombs, B. M. Baruch. M. J. Strook. Ex-officio, A. S. Prall.

Truant and Parental Schools.

Manhattan Truant—215 E. 21st. Mary K. Leonard, Matron-Supt.

Bkln. Truant—Jamaica av., opp. Enfield. Annex of N. Y. Parental.

N. Y. Parental—Jamaica rd., Flushing. Borough of Queens. J. S. Fitzpatrick, Principal.

TRAINING SCHOOLS—Manhattan.

Location.	Principals.	Janitors.	Cl'r'ms	Tchrs.	Reg't'r
N. Y. Training Sch., 119th, nr. 7th av. (P. S. 81)	Theory Department, Hugo Newman (B.-G.)	Alex. McGill ...	..	37	581
	*†Model Dept., Emma L. Johnston (B.-G.)	....	21	*27	*863
Brooklyn.					
Maxwell Tr'ng Sch., Park pl, nr. Nostrand.	Theory Dept., Emma L. Johnston (B.-G.).	Jas. Gallagher...	..	51	607
Prospect pl., nr. Nostrand av. (P.S.138)..	*†Model Dept., Emma L. Johnston B.-G.).	....	38	*39	*1637
Queens.					
Jamaica Training Sch.	Theory Dept., A. C. McLachlin (B.-G.)...	S. F. Bowen.....	..	14	238
Flush'g&H'ghl'd avs...	*†Model Dept., A. C. McLachlin (B.-G.)...	....	17	*17	*794

*Included in Elementary School recapitulation. †Kindergarten.

Recapitulation of Training Schools.

Theory Dept.

Teachers, including principals	105
Register	1.376

Vocational and Trade Schools.

Detailed statistics under list of Public Schools.

Vocational Schl. for Boys (The Cyrus H. McCormick)—138th and 139th, west of 5th av. (P. S. 100). C. J. Pickett, Prin. Mhtn. Trade Schl. for Girls—22d and Lexington av. Florence M. Marshall, Prin. Murray Hill Vocational Schl. —37th and 38th, west of 2d av. (P. S. 49), Chas. Harper. Brooklyn Vocational Schl.—Cary Bldg., Jay and Nassau, Jas. H. Allen.

Recapitulation of Vocational and Trade Schools.

Mhtn.—Register, 2,342; teaching positions, 179. Bkln. register, 539; teaching, 26. Totals, register, 2,881; teaching positions, 205.

Continuation Schools.

East Side, Chrystie and Hester sts. (P. S. 7), Franklin J. Keller, Prin.; register, 2,338. West Side, Greenwich av., west of 6th av. (P. S. 41). Chas. W. Laffiin, Teacher in Charge; register, 1,672. Brooklyn, Ryerson st., nr. Myrtle (P. S. 69), Teacher in Charge, I. David Cohen; register, 1,970. Queens, Borden and Van Alst avs., L. I. City; register, 600; John E. Kiffen, Teacher in Charge. Staten Island, Heterton av., Port Richmond, Jas. A. Harrigan, Teacher in Charge; register, 352. Total register, 6,932.

Recapitulation of Elementary, Truant and Parental Schools.

Detailed statistics under list of Public Schools.

Borough.	Register.	Cl'ses.	Kind'rgart'ns. Register.	Kind'rgart'ns. Cl'ses.
Manhattan	278,727	13,174	6,856	310
Bronx	112,830	4,657	2,746	104
Brooklyn	303,948	14,694	7,266	328
Queens	70,003	4,120	1,752	90
Richmond	18,000	1,097	447	23
Totals	$783,508	$37,742	†19,066	†855

†Included in $. Note—In addition to the teaching positions there are 946 principals and assistants not teaching.

PUBLIC SCHOOLS, PRINCIPALS, REGISTER, ETC.

HIGH SCHOOLS—Manhattan.

Name and Location.	Principals.	Janitors.	Teachers	Register
*DeWitt Clinton, 10th av., 58th-59th.	F. H. J. Paul (B.)	John B. McCauley	201	5155
*George Washington, B'way and Academy, (P. S. 52)	Arthur A. Boylan (B.-G.)		43	1091
*High Schl. of Com., 65th and 66th, nr. B'way	Harold B. Buttrick (B.)	John Reilly	147	3607
Stuyvesant, 15th-16th, nr. 1st av.	E. R. Von Nardroff (B.)	H. J. Lowe	224	5313
Wadleigh, 114th and 115th, nr. 7th av	S. H. Rowe (G.)	Gilman Dedrick	121	3069
Wash'g't'n Irv'ng, Irv'ng pl., 16 & 17th.	E. C. Zabriskie (G.)	Patrick Dowd	230	5402
*Julia Richman, 60 W. 13th	Michael H. Lucey (G.)	J. A. Lindsay	156	3622
Haaren Co-operative, Hubert and Collister, (P. S. 44)	R. Wesley Burnham (B.-G.)		22	307
Bronx.				
Morris, 166th, nr. Boston rd	E. E. Bogart (B.-G.)	Edward Cassin	145	3789
*Evander Childs, E. 184th, Field pl., Creston and Morris avs	Gilbert S. Blakely (B.-G.)	J. B. Babcock	129	3276
*Theodore Roosevelt, Mott and Walton avs., 144th and 146th (P. S. 31)	W. R. Hayward (B.-G.)	Ernest Easty	63	1528
Brooklyn.				
*Bay Ridge, 4th av., 67th, Senator.	Kate E. Turner (G.)	Gustaf Gustafson	92	2209
*Boys', Marcy, Putnam avs. and Madison	Arthur L. Janes (B.)	Francis X. Polser	150	3688
*Bushwick, Irving av., Madison and Woodbine	Milo F. McDonald (B.-G.)	Chas. Brundage	117	2896
*Com'c'l, Albany av., Bergen, Dean	Gilbert J. Raynor (B.)	Patrick Freeman	139	3570
*E'n Dist., Marcy av., Rodney&Keap.	W. T. Vlymen (B.-G.)	Jos. F. O'Day	98	2510
Erasmus Hall, Flat.av., n.Church av.	J. H. Low (B.-G.)	Edw. P. Mullin	162	4179
Girls', Nostrand av., Macon and Halsey	W. L. Felter (G.)	John Dowling	83	2027
*Girls' Commercial, St. Marks and Classon avs. (P. S. 42)	Evelyn W. Allen (G.)		51	1593
*Manual Training, 7th av., 4th and 5th	H. M. Snyder (B.-G.)	Chas. T. Mellen	156	3804
*New Utrecht, 86th, nr. 18th av. (P. S. 101)	Harry A. Potter (B.)	W. H. Miller	38	846
Queens.				
Bryant, Wilbur av., Academy and Radde, L. I. C.	P. E. Demarest (B.-G.)	James Barnes	60	1333
Far Rockaway, Dinsmore and Roanoke avs.	A. G. Belding, Acting	Wm. Scarlet	28	610
Northern blvd. and Union	Harold G. Campbell	Eph. Hoag	53	1309
Newtown, Chicago and Gerry avs., Elmhurst	J. D. Dillingham (B.-G.)	D. R. Miller	68	1507
Jamaica, Hillside and Union avs.	C. H. Vosburgh (B.-G.)	Wm. Fairbairn	61	1443
*Richmond Hill, 114th av. and 91st	Irving A. Hazen (B.-G.)	John J. Luddin	66	1648
Richmond.				
*Curtis, Hamilton av. and St. Marks pl., N. Brighton	D. D. Feldman (B.-G.)	W. H. Brundage	57	1459

*Have annexes.

Recapitulation of High Schools.

Boroughs, total register and number of instructors, incl. principals: Manhattan, 27,566, 952; Bronx, 72,789, 340; Brooklyn, 27,321, 996; Queens 7,850, 342; Richmond, 1,459, 58. Totals, 72,789 registered; 2,688 instructors, incl. principals.

PUBLIC SCHOOLS—Manhattan.

School Number.	Location. (Schools marked * have no kindergartens.)	School Name.	Principals.	District.	Cl'sr'ms	Teachers	Register.
1.	Henry, Catharine and Oliver		Mary R. Davis (B.-G.)	1	66	57	2472
2.	116 Henry	Henry Rutgers	Ellen A. G. Phillips (B.-G.)	2	55	59	2238
3.	Hudson and Grove	B. D. L. Southerland	Loretta M. Rochester (B.-G.)	7	48	51	2049
4.	Rivington, Ridge and Pitt	William Pitt	Mary C. Donohue (B.-G.)	4	51	58	2182
5.	Edgecomb av., 140th-141st	Alexander S. Webb	Stephen F. Bayne (B.-G.)	15	63	79	3222
6.	Madison av. and 85th	Lillie Devereux Blake	Kath. D. Blake (B.-G.)	10	42	38	1483
7.	Chrystie and Hester	George T. Trimble	Franklyn J. Keller (B.-G.)	3	32	32	1290
8.	29 King	Richard Varick	Margaret N. Wheaton (B.-G.)	7	29	32	1421
9.	82d and West End av	John Jasper	Teresa E. Bernholz (B.-G.)	8	31	32	1182
*10B	St. Nicholas av. and 117th	St. Nicholas	E. R. Birkins (B.)	13	35	35	1477
10P			Hester A. Roberts (B.-G.)	13	33	39	1483
11.	314 W. 17th	William T. Harris	Benjamin B. Greenberg (B.)	7	32	32	1062
12.	Madison and Jackson sts	The Corlears	Elizabeth Walker (B.-G.)	3	62	61	2444
13.	E. Houston and Essex	James Watt	May Jackson (B.-G.)	4	52	53	2340
14.	225 E. 27th	Lafayette B. Olney	G. L. Hentz (B.-G.)	6	65	68	2717
15.	4th and 5th, near Av. D		Margaret Knox (B.-G.)	5	64	71	2819
16.	208 W. 13th	Josiah H. Zabriskie	Chas. M. Landesman (B.-G.)	7	27	27	[illegible]
17.	348 W. 28th	La Salle	Kath. A. McCann (B.-G.)	8	49	51	1188
18.	121 E. 51st	John Winthrop	Hy. H. Goldberger (B.-G.)	9	35	34	1187
19.	344 E. 14th	William M. Evarts	R. G. Powers (B.-G.)	6	59	67	2380
20.	Rivington, Forsyth & Eldridge	Forsyth	Wm. Krampner (B.-G.)	4	63	64	2480
21.	Mott and Elizabeth	John Doty	A. J. Pugliese (B.-G.)	1	48	55	2786
22.	Stanton and Sheriff	Hamilton Fish	Carrie E. Krowl (B.-G.)	3	61	61	2480
*23.	Mulberry and Bayard	Columbus	J. D. Reardon (B.-G.)	1	39	45	2188
*24.	128th, west of Madison av	Mt. Morris	John J. O'Reilly (B.)	14	28	28	1182
25.	4th and 5th, near 1st av	Schiller	C. C. Roberts (B.-G.)	6	65	70	2482
27.	41st and 42d, east of 3d av	Thomas A. Edison	Sol E. Du Bois (B.-G.)	9	54	58	2145
28.	257 W. 40th	John Newton	Anna A. Short (B.-G.)	7	36	37	1529

PUBLIC SCHOOLS OF THE CITY OF NEW YORK—MANHATTAN—*Continued.*

School Number.	Location. (Schools marked * have no kindergartens.	School Name.	Principals.	District.	Cl'sr'ms	Teacher	Register
29.	Washington, Albany & Carlisle.	....	Magnus Gross (B.-G.)........	1	17	17	699
30.	220 E. 88th..........................	Yorkville..................	Albert Loewenthan (B.-G.).	10	46	45	1741
31.	Monroe and Gouverneur	Patrick F. McGowan..	Sarah H. Conant (B.-G.)...	3	48	55	2452
32.	357 W. 35th..........................	William Wood............	J. H. Grotecloss (B.-G.).....	7	41	42	1691
33.	418 W. 28th..........................	Chelsea......................	Alida S. Williams (B.-G.)..	7	46	46	1960
34.	Broome and Sheriff...............	Herman Ridder............	Geo. E. Vogel (B.-G.)......	3	46	31	1098
35.	160 Chrystie	Wendell Phillips.........	Louise E. Tucker (B.-G.)..	4	30	31	1159
36.	710 E. 9th..........................	Tompkins Square	Ellen T. O'Brien (B.-G.)...	5	31	32	1253
*37.	113 E. 87th (Probationary Sch.)	John Barry...............	Hazen Chatfield (B.)........	10	15	16	169
38.	Dominick, Clark & Broome.....	Vittoria Colonna.......	Margaret Aitken (B.-G.)..	1	52	58	2480
*39B	125th and 126th, nr. 2d av......	Harlem......................	Henry Levy (B.)............	14	31	31	1450
39P	....	....	Helen M. Hynes (B.-G.)...	14	39	46	2069
*40.	320 E. 20th..........................	George W. Wingate....	W. K. Franklin (B.)........	6	33	33	1315
41.	36 Greenwich av.....................	Greenwich.................	Jennie G. Bowtell (B.-G.)..	7	26	20	791
42.	Hester, Ludlow and Orchard...	Benjamin Altman.......	Rufina A. Carls (B.-G.)....	2	51	53	2299
43.	129th and Amsterdam av........	Manhattanville...........	J. K. Van Denberg (B.-G.).	15	63	85	3044
44.	Hubert and Collister..............	St. Johns Park..........	John E. Brown (B.-G.).....	1	19	19	650
45.	225 W. 24th..........................	Peabody....................	Maude I. Price (B.-G.).....	7	22	20	768
46.	156th and St. Nicholas av.......	Stinson McIver...........	H. S. Platt (B.-G.)..........	16	60	67	2761
*47.	225 E. 23d (School for Deaf)....	Gallaudet..................	Carrie W. Kearns (B.-G.)..	6	35	35	300
48.	124 W. 28th..........................	Abram S. Hewitt.......	Mary L. Gordon (B.-G.)....	7	22	15	548
50.	211 E. 20th..........................	Gramercy..................	Katherine Bauer (B.-G.)...	6	31	34	1355
51.	519 W. 44th	Elias Howe................	Jos. Chankin (B.-G.)........	8	52	50	1860
52.	Vermilyea av. Academy & Bway	Inwood......................	B. Louis Snyder (B.-G.)....	16	31	43	1789
*53.	79th and 80th and 3d av.........	Salome Purroy...........	Kate Van Wagenen (B.-G.)	10	50	52	2106
54.	104th and Amsterdam av........	....	Margaretta Uihlein (B.-G.).	13	44	44	1787
56.	351 W. 18th..........................	Gansevoort................	Alice V. Parle (G.)..........	7	30	27	1009
57.	176 E. 115th	George Bancroft.........	E. A. Duggan (B.-G.).......	12	62	86	3496
58.	317 W. 52d..........................	William L. Marcy......	Martha Adler (B.-G.).......	8	27	25	955
59.	228 E. 57th..........................	Louisa Lee Schuyler....	Mary C. Bergen (B.-G.).....	9	61	57	2141
61.	12th, East of Av. B...............	John Eaton................	Jessie B. Colburn (B.-G.)..	5	48	65	2710
*62.	Hester, Essex and Norfolk......	Seward Park	Robert B. Brodie (B.-G.)...	2	115	114	4492
63.	3d and 4th, east of 1st av........	William McKinley.....	Lena Kemp (B.-G.).........	6	49	57	2638
64.	9th and 10th, east of Av. B.....	Henry P. O'Neil........	Louis Marks (B.-G.)........	5	61	84	2994
65.	Eldridge and Forsyth.............	Charles Sumner ...	Elizabeth S. Harris (B.-G.).	2	59	58	2233
66.	88th st., near 1st av..............	Chester A. Arthur......	C. Augusta Sanger (B.-G.).	10	28	30	1253
67.	120 W. 46th..........................	Astor........................	Annie E. Cunningham(B-G)	8	9	9	353
68.	116 W. 128th........................	....	Ida Ikelheimer (B.-G.)......	15	43	47	1752
69.	125 W. 54th..........................	Matthew J. Elgas......	Thos. J. Boyle (B.-G.)......	8	50	50	1861
70.	75th and 76th, nr. 3d av.........	Richard Riker............	Abraham Smith (B.-G.)....	9	39	46	1771
*71.	188 7th	Van Rensselaer.........	Sarah A. Robinson (G.).....	5	40	36	1337
72.	Lexington av., 105th-106th......	....	Mary M. Cummings (G.)....	11	37	63	2842
73.	209 E. 46th..........................	Josephine Shaw Lowell..	Kath. F. McCarthy (B.-G.).	9	30	31	1332
74.	220 E. 62d..........................	William Blackstone....	Fred M. Scheider (B.-G.)...	9	48	48	1983
75.	157 Henry	Jacob T. Boyle.........	Henrietta R. Scheider. B.-G.)	2	16	19	866
76.	Lexington av. and 68th...........	....	Mary A. Magovern (B.-G.).	9	41	41	1685
*77.	1st av., 85th and 86th............	Carl Shurz...............	Matilda B. Lemlein (B.-G.)	10	55	52	2026
78.	Pleasant av. and 119th...........	Henry Clay...............	Mary H. Donohue (B.-G.)..	14	68	84	3943
79.	38 1st	Joseph J. Little.........	W. L. Bulkley (B.-G.)......	4	34	35	1342
82.	1st av. and 70th....................	Agassiz.....................	H. J. Heidenis (B.-G.)......	9	33	36	1513
*83.	109th and 110th, near 3d av.....	Galvani.....................	David Goldwasser (B.).....	12	57	83	3414
84.	430 W. 50th..........................	Henry A. Rogers.......	Isabel W. Smith (B.-G.)...	8	33	32	1265
85.	1st av. and 117th..................	William Marconi.......	Felix Arnold (B.-G.)........	14	49	49	2136
86.	Lexington av. and 96th...........	Nathan Hale..............	Margaret P. Duggan(B.-G.)	11	43	67	3021
87.	77th and Amsterdam av..........	William T. Sherman....	Geo. G. Weinberger (B.-G.)	8	31	27	1016
88.	Rivington and Lewis..............	Rivington..................	Bella Strauss (B.-G.).......	8	38	39	1725
89.	Lenox av., 134th and 135th......	Lenox.......................	Jacob M. Ross (B.-G.)......	16	47	61	2368
90.	147th-148th, nr. 7th av..........	Riverside..................	Jennie Birmingham (B.-G.)	16	66	82	3303
91.	Stanton and Forsyth	Wheelock..................	Emma Sylvester (B.-G.)....	4	53	66	2798
92.	Broome and Ridge.................	Grace H. Dodge.........	Mary B. Kinkeldey (B.-G.)	2	46	52	2068
93.	Amsterdam av. and 93d..........	....	Laura Charlton (B.-G.)....	8	42	41	1769
94.	Amsterdam av. and 68th.........	Henry Kiddle............	Pauline Goerlich (B.-G.)..	8	39	39	1617
95.	W. Houston and Clarkson	Hudson Park	Harold Peyser (B.-G.)......	7	62	78	2992
96.	Av. A, 81st and 82d..............	Richard Kelly	Eliza S. Pell (Mrs.) (B.-G.)	10	71	65	2822
97.	Mangin, n. of Stanton...........	Mangin.....................	Edward Mandel (B.-G.)....	3	47	50	1976
101.	111th, near Lexington av........	Andrew S. Draper......	Millicent Baum (B.-G.)	12	59	75	3280
102.	113th, east of 2d av..............	Cartier......................	Emma V. Haggerty (B.-G.)	12	34	55	2488
103.	119th and Madison av............	Elbridge T. Gerry......	Kate A. Condon (B.-G.)...	14	54	77	3135
104.	16th and 17th, near 1st av......	Rutherford................	Ottilia M. Beha (B.-G.)....	6	45	55	2231
105.	269 E. 4th..........................	George G. Meade.......	Hannah Wehle (B.-G.).....	5	18	22	961
106.	Lafayette, near Spring..........	Francis Marion..........	Susan McCormick (B.-G.)..	1	24	24	871
107.	272 W. 10th	....	Clare Kleiser (B.-G.).......	7	20	20	734
108.	60 Mott	Verdi........................	Margaret P. Rae (B.-G.)..	1	16	22	893
*109.	99th-100th, bet. 2d and 3d avs..	Century....................	Ed. J. McNally (B.)........	11	52	56	2585
110.	Broome and Cannon	Florence Nightingale ..	Adeline E. Simpson (B.-G.)	3	39	44	1791
112.	83 Roosevelt	Roosevelt..................	Irene M. Dunphy (B.-G.)...	1	10	12	529
114.	James, Oliver and Oak sts......	Vandewater...............	Jos. T. Griffin (B.-G.)......	1	59	63	2689
115.	176th & 177th, nr. St. Nicholas.	Humboldt..................	Chas. F. Thellusson (B.-G.)	16	42	55	2174
116.	32d and 33d, near 2d av.........	Mary Lindley Murray...	Catherine I. Tillman(B.-G.)	9	21	26	1167
119.	133d and 134th, near 8th av.....	James Russell Lowell..	Harriet A. Tupper (B.-G.).	15	62	65	2656
*120.	187 Broome (Probationary Sch.).	Thomas Hughes.........	Olive M. Jones (B.).........	2	12	12	174
121.	227 E. 102d........................	Galileo......................	Emma C. Haviland (B.-G.).	11	46	53	2443
122.	9th and 1st av.....................	Silas Wright	Eliz. I. Dowling (B.-G.)....	6	35	53	2596
*126.	536 E. 12th	Rosa Bonheur............	Rose Davidson (B.).........	5	17	24	1012
127.	515 W. 37th	Dearborn..................	Margaret M. Wilson (B.-G.)	8	19	20	906
130.	143 Baxter	De Soto	Anna I. Mathews (B.-G.)..	1	16	19	766
131.	272 E. 2d...........................	Hannibal Hamlin.......	Anna M. Foley (B.-G.).....	5	15	16	617
132.	182d and Wadsworth av.........	Fort Washington........	Thomas C. Halligan (B.-G.)	16	49	63	2570
134.	63 Pearl.............................	Peter Minuit..............	M. Martha Steelman (B.-G.)	1	4	4	124
135.	1st av. and 51st..................	Beekman Hill............	Kate M. Stephens (B.-G.)..	9	34	37	1581
137.	Grand, Ludlow and Essex......	Cyrus W. Field.........	Harriet V. R. Field (B.-G.).	3	31	32	1330

PUBLIC SCHOOLS OF THE CITY OF NEW YORK—MANHATTAN—*Continued.*

School Number.	Location. (Schools marked * have no kindergartens.)	School Name.	Principals.	District.	Cl'sr'ms	Teachers	Register.
*140.	116 Norfolk	Henry George	Annie M. Atkinson (B.-G.)	4	22	34	1009
141.	462 W. 58th	Amsterdam	Kate A. Walsh (B.-G.)	8	32	33	1481
147.	Henry and Gouverneur	Gouverneur	W. A. Kottman (B.-G.)	3	53	57	2430
150.	95th-96th, near 1st av	Martha Washington	Alice Jackson (B.-G.)	11	50	62	2900
151.	1st av. and 91st	Miles M. O'Brien	Agnes O'Brien (B.-G.)	10	36	37	1531
157.	St. Nicholas av., 126th-127th	John Hancock	Elise W. Kornmann (B.-G.)	15	52	57	2208
158.	Av. A., 77th and 78th	Bayard Taylor	B. W. Purcell (B.-G.)	10	72	76	2983
159.	119th-120th, near 2d av	Elmer Ellsworth	Helen A. Stein (B.-G.)	14	62	73	3260
160.	Rivington and Suffolk	James E. Sullivan	C. D. Fleming (B.-G.)	4	47	47	1879
161.	Ludlow and Delancey	Delancey	Amelia F. Patterson(B.-G.)	4	25	16	722
*162.	36 City Hall pl		Branch of No. 23	1	4	..	...
165.	108th-109th, near Amsterdam av		Jacob Theobald (B.-G.)	13	44	44	1697
166.	89th, near Columbus av		John F. Reigart (B.-G.)	8	27	26	968
168.	104th-105th, near 2d av	Richard Montgomery	Ella C. McNair (B.-G.)	12	57	76	3244
169.	Audubon av., 168th and 169th	Audubon	Frank A. Schmidt (B.-G.)	16	44	54	2106
*170G	111th and 112th, nr. Lenox av.	Julia Ward Howe	Margaret F. O'Connell (G.)	13	36	38	1566
*170P			Eloise K. Fisher (B.-G.)	13	28	36	1611
171.	103d and 104th, near 5th av	Patrick Henry	M. J. Willson (B.-G.)	11	59	80	3481
172.	108th and 109th, east of 2d av	James Otis	Margt. F. Brangan (B.-G.)	12	50	51	2516
*174.	Attorney, near Rivington	Oliver Goldsmith	Elizabeth J. Hofer (B.-G.)	4	31	31	1393
177.	Market and Monroe	Roger Bacon	Mary L. Brady (B.-G.)	1	46	53	2231
179.	101st & 102d, nr. Amsterdam av.	Daniel Webster	Fred. A. Berghane (B.-G.)	13	41	39	1649
183.	66th and 67th, east of 1st av	Robert Louis Stevenson	Anne J. Farley (B.-G.)	9	33	34	1490
184.	116th and 117th, e. of Lenox av.	J. Fenimore Cooper	Jas. B. T. Demarest (B.-G.)	13	62	80	3558
186.	145th & 146th, nr. Amsterdam av	Alexander Hamilton	T. Adrian Curtis (B.-G.)	15	64	77	3061
*188B	Mhtn., e. Houst'n, Lewis & E. 3	Lewis	Edward F. O'Connor (B.)	5	50	42	1806
188G	Mhtn., e. Houst'n, Lewis & E. 3		Ellen M. Phillips (B.-G.)	5	47	50	1973
190.	82d, near 2d av	Paul Revere	Sarah Goldie (B.-G.)	10	32	34	1503
192.	Amsterdam av. and 136th	Henry Rice	Maurice B. Lewis (B.-G.)	15	41	42	1179
	Vocational Sch. for Boys, 138th, west of 5th av., P. S. 100	Cyrus McCormick	Chas. J. Pickett	..	74	44	256
*	Murray Hill Voc. Sch., 37th, west of 2d av., P. S. 49		Chas. Harper (B.)	..	..	28	475
*	Man. Tr. Sch., 22d & Lex. av.		Florence M. Marshall (G.)	..	..	93	894
	Textile Sch., 124 W. 30th, P.S. 28	Carlisle	W. H. Dooley	..	..	14	256
*	School for Deaf (see P. S. 47).						
*	Truant School, 215 E. 21st		Mary K. Leonard, Mn. Spt. (B)	6	1	2	23

PUBLIC SCHOOLS—Bronx.

School Number.	Location.	School Name.	Principals.	District.	Cl'sr'ms	Teachers	Register.
*1.	College av. and 145th	College Avenue	Abby P. Leland (B.)	17	22	25	917
2.	3d av., near 169th	Morrisania	Elizabeth D. Haas (B.-G.)	21	43	63	2379
3.	157th, east of Courtlandt av	Melrose	Burt P. Seelye (B.-G.)	18	60	68	2748
4.	Fulton and 3d avs. and 173d	Crotona	Simon Hirsdansky (B.-G.)	21	63	69	2758
5.	Webster av. and 189th	Fordham	Elizabeth C. Rottger (B.-G.)	23	22	33	1471
6.	Bryant, Tremont and Vyse avs.	West Farms	G. K. Martin (B.-G.)	22	36	59	2709
7.	Kingsbridge av. and 232d	Kingsbridge	Frederic Ernst (B.-G.)	22	25	38	1318
8.	Mosholu P'kway & Briggs av.	Isaac Varian	Robt. S. Stantial (B.-G.)	23	28	31	1178
9.	491 E. 138th, near Brook av	Jonathan D. Hyatt	Elias Silberstein (B.-G.)	17	48	61	2474
10.	Eagle av. and 163d	Eagle Avenue	Samuel Viertel (B.-G.)	19	63	80	3053
11.	169th and Ogden av	Highbridge	C. W. Hawkins (B.-G.)	20	32	38	1525
12.	Overing, Benson & Frisby avs	Westchester	John F. Condon (B.-G.)	24	33	35	1495
13.	216th and Willett av.	Williamsbridge	F. D. Sherman (B.-G.)	24	31	35	1316
*14.	Eastern bvd., Throgg's Neck	Throgg's Neck	Chas. W. Moore (B.-G.)	24	13	15	539
*15.	Dyre av., Eastchester		Branch of No. 16	24	4	..	...
16.	Carpenter av., nr. 240th, Wakef'd	Wakefield	Elijah Jenks, Jr. (B.-G.)	24	42	36	1331
*17.	Fordham av., City Island	City Island	Edwin F. Wilson (B.-G.)	24	9	8	346
18.	Courtlandt av., near 148th		Elizabeth M. Ball (B.-G.)	17	22	22	882
19.	234th & 235th, near Kepler av. Woodlawn	Edward Eggleston	Caroline E. Hoefling (B.-G.)	23	13	12	323
20.	Fox, Simpson and 167th	Charles James Fox	Mary A. Curtis (B.-G.)	20	43	75	3312
21.	225th-226th, nr. White Plains av	Phillip H. Sheridan	Eliza A. Caterson (B.-G.)	24	21	26	1029
*22.	599 E. 140th		Branch of No. 30	17	6	..	...
23.	165th, Tinton and Union avs	Woodstock	John King Clark (B.-G.)	19	40	64	2954
24.	Kappock st., Spuyten Duyvil		Branch of No. 7	22	6	..	...
25.	Union av. and 149th	Phil Kearny	Mary A. Carr (B.-G.)	18	38	58	2436
26.	Andrews and Burnside avs	Burnside Avenue	H. T. McLaughlin (B.-G.)	22	19	27	1016
27.	St. Anns av., 147th and 148th	St. Mary's Park	Arthur T. Gorton (B.-G.)	18	61	70	7802
28.	Tremont av. & Mt. Hope pl	Mount Hope	L. A. Beardsley (B.-G.)	22	52	74	3139
29.	Cypress av., 135th and 136th	Port Morris	Jacob J. Shufro (B.-G.)	17	44	58	2416
30.	141st, near Brook av	Walton	Mary A. Conlon (B.-G.)	17	53	76	3061
31.	Mott & Walton avs., 144th-146th	William Lloyd Garrison	Mary A. Regan (B.-G.)	17	20	30	1198
32.	183d, Beaum't & Cambrell's avs.	Belmont	Hugh C. Laughlin (B.-G.)	23	62	113	4655
33.	Jerome & Walton avs, n of 184th	Timothy Dwight	Frederick J. Reilly (B.-G.)	22	28	34	1403
34.	Amethyst av., nr. Morris Pk. av	Van Nest	Wm. H. Story (B.-G.)	24	37	40	1634
35.	163d, Grant and Morris avs	Franz Sigel	Ellen C. Gilbert (B.-G.)	19	28	32	1367
36.	E. 177th & Castle Hill av. Unionport	Unionport	Morgan Washburn (B.-G.)	24	27	24	894
37.	145th and 146th, c. of Wils av.		Gabriel R. Mason (B.-G.)	18	49	55	2279
38.	157th and 158th, 3d & Brook avs		Mary M. Fitzsimons (B.-G.)	18	28	32	1339
39.	Longwood av., Kelly and Beck	Longwood	Anna V. McCarthy (B.-G.)	19	50	75	3104
40.	Prospect av., Jennings st. and Ritter pl.	Prospect Avenue	Henry E. Hein (B.-G.)	20	61	92	3861
41.	Olinville av. and Magenta, Olinville		Catherine D. Frey (B.-G.)	24	16	19	745
42.	Wash'n av. & Claremont Pkway	Claremont	Eugene B. Gartlan (B.-G.)	21	46	75	3316
43.	Brown pl., 135th and 136th	Jonas Bronck	W. A. Hannig (B.-G.)	17	59	82	3498
44.	Prospect av. and 176th	David G. Farragut	Plowden Stevens, Jr. (B.-G.)	22	45	72	3325
45.	189th and Hoffman	Paul Hoffman	Angelo Patri (B.-G.)	23	73	96	3944
46.	196th, Bainbridge & Briggs av	Edgar Allan Poe	John D. Haney (B.-G.)	23	38	38	1430
47.	Rand'ph and St. Lawrence av.	John Randolph	E. F. McSorley (B.-G.)	24	33	34	1414
48.	Spofford av., Coster and Faile.	Joseph Rodman Drake	Julius Bluhm (B.-G.)	19	46	58	2235

PUBLIC SCHOOLS OF THE CITY OF NEW YORK—Bronx—*Continued.*

School Number.	Location. (Schools marked * have no kindergartens.)	School Name.	Principals.	District.	Cl'sr'ms	Teachers	Register.
*49.	281st and Riverside av..........	Riverdale..................	Alice F. Halpin (B.-G.).....	22	9	9	239
50.	Bryant and Vyse avs., nr. 172d.	Clara Barton..............	Thos. J. Donohue (B.-G.)..	21	49	75	3323
51.	158th, Jackson and Trinity avs.	James K. Paulding.....	Hugh J. Smallen (B.-G.)...	19	47	54	2294
52.	Kelly, nr. Av. St. John.........	Thomas Knowlton.......	W. P. McCarthy (B.-G.)...	18	57	78	3147
53.	168th, Findlay and Teller avs..	....	W. J. Henwood (B.-G.)....	20	50	69	2859
54.	Intervale av., Freeman and Chisholm	Intervale..................	E. R. Maguire (B.-G.).....	20	40	100	3838
55.	St. Paul's pl., Wash'ngton and Park avs.	....	Wm. Rabenort (B.-G.).....	21	47	77	3391
56.	207th, Hull and Decatur avs....	....	Branch of No. 8............	23	16	..	...
*57.	Washington av., c. 176th........	....	Anna C. Johnston	22	19	26	1109

PUBLIC SCHOOLS—Brooklyn.

School Number.	Location.	School Name.	Principals.	District.	Cl'sr'ms	Teachers	Register.
1.	Adams, cor. Concord............	John Adams	Anna E. Darrow (B.-G.)...	27	22	19	687
2.	47th, near 3d av...................	Bergen.....................	F. W. Memmott (B.-G.).....	30	34	40	1626
3.	Hancock, near Bedford av......	Bedford....................	LaSalle H. White (B.-G.)...	29	29	49	2058
4.	Berkeley pl., near 5th av........	Charles A. Schieren......	Eva C. Wood (B.-G.)......	27	26	31	1202
5.	Tillary, Bridge and Lawrence...	McLaughlin Park.........	W. J. O'Leary (B.-G.).....	27	48	70	2635
6.	Baltic & Warren, near Smith..	....	Clara C. Calkins (B.-G.)...	28	34	48	1899
7.	York, near Bridge...............	John Jay..................	Edith Horton (B.-G.).......	27	28	33	1441
8.	Hicks, Middagh and Poplar.....	Robert Fulton............	Mary Walsemann (B.-G)...	27	26	31	1178
9.	Vanderbilt av. & Sterling pl...	Prospect Hill............	Wm. M. Rainey (B.-G.)....	27	57	60	2190
10.	7th av., 17th and Prospect av..	Peter Rouget.............	Edwin B. Uline (B.-G.)....	30	44	40	1500
11.	Washington av., nr. Greene av	....	F. F. Harding (B.-G.)......	27	31	30	1153
12.	Adelphi, near Myrtle av........	Fort Greene	Frederick Schoedel (B.-G.)..	27	30	34	1372
13.	Degraw, near H'cks.............	Calvin Patterson	M. Margot Elmer (B.-G.)..	28	30	42	1645
14.	Navy, cor. Concord..............	City Park	Ellen F. Quinn (B.-G.)......	27	19	22	874
15.	3d av., cor. State & Schermerh'n.	Schermerhorn............	Andrew I. Sherman (B.-G.)	27	28	28	997
16.	Wilson, near Bedford av.........	Leonard Dunkley........	Lewis H. Tuthill (B.-G.)...	31	59	71	2844
17.	Driggs av., cor. N. 5th..........	Henry D. Woodworth...	Thos. P. Smith (B.-G.)......	34	34	53	1975
*18.	Maujer, near Leonard...........	Edward Bush	Earl P. Haynes (B.-G.).....	33	44	43	1662
19.	S. 3d, cor. Keap	John W. Bulkley........	John W. Rafferty (B.-G.)..	31	61	76	3175
20.	Union av. and Keap.............	DeVoe......................	Matilda C. S. Brooks (B.)..	34	14	21	834
21.	McKibbin, near Manhattan av.	McKibbin..................	Beatrice P. King (B.-G.)...	33	18	25	1135
22.	Java, near Manhattan av........	Greenpoint................	Laura Black (B.-G.).........	34	22	22	846
23.	C'nselyea, Humboldt & Skillm'n	Old Bushwick............	Everett Barnes (B.).........	34	47	53	2318
24.	Arion pl., c Beaver & Belvidere	Belvidere..................	Augusta D. Moore (B.-G.)..	35	49	50	2100
25.	Lafayette av., near Sumner av.	Lafayette..................	Isidore Springer (B.-G.)....	32	37	66	2971
26.	Quincy st., near Ralph av....	Quincy.....................	F. K. Perkins (B.-G.)......	32	50	47	1756
27.	Nelson and Hicks................	Agnes Y. Humphrey....	P. J. Behan (B.-G.).........	28	37	47	2072
28.	Herkimer, near Ralph av.......	....	Sara L. Rhodes (B.-G.).....	32	28	38	1696
29.	Columbia and Amity............	Columbia..................	Amelia Schaller (B.-G.)....	28	18	28	1031
30.	Conover, Sullivan & Wolcott....	Wolcott....................	R. F. McCormack (B.-G.)..	28	48	40	1653
31.	Dupont, near Manhattan av.....	Samuel F. Dupont......	Julia L. Kelly (B.-G.)......	34	41	43	1645
32.	Hoyt and President..............	Hoyt........................	Frances A. Weiss (B.-G.)..	28	30	45	1751
33.	Heyward, near Broadway.......	Thomas Heyward, Jr...	Caroline R. Gipner (B.-G.).	31	27	26	948
*34.	Norman av., Eckford & Oakland	Oliver H. Perry..........	Martha A. Youngs (B.-G.).	34	49	[illegible]	[illegible]
35.	Decatur and Lewis av...........	Decatur....................	F. B. Graham (B.-G.)......	32	47	47	1887
*36.	Stagg, near Bushwick av........	John McNamee..........	Abraham London (B.-G.)..	33	40	41	1704
37.	S. 4th, near Berry...............	Sylvester Malone	Fannie H. Decker (B.-G.)..	31	29	31	1251
38.	N. 7th, near Bedford av........	Robert Emmet...........	Dora M. Coughlan (B.-G.)..	34	16	22	894
39.	6th av., cor. 8th..................	Henry Bristow	Mary McSwyny (B.-G.).....	30	27	27	1057
*40.	15th, near 4th av................	James Weir...............	W. S. S. Newton (B.-G.)...	28	35	38	1596
41.	Dean and New York av..........	Franklin W. Hooper...	Martha A. Kane (B.-G.)...	29	17	16	581
42.	St. Marks, near Classon av....	Concord....................	Eliz. F. Doherty (B.-G.)...	27	28	34	1486
*43.	Boerum, near Manhattan av...	Walt Whitman............	Jas. A. O'Donnell (B.)......	33	51	59	2349
44.	Throop av., cor. Putnam av....	Israel Putnam............	John F. Harris (B.-G.).....	29	45	51	2369
45.	Lafayette av., nr. Classon av..	DeKalb.....................	W. L. Huntley (B.-G.)......	27	39	39	1556
46.	Union, near Henry	Frances Parkman.......	Anna L. McDevitt (B.-G.)..	28	26	39	1680
47.	Pacific and Dean, near 3d av...	Pacific.....................	Margt. J. McCooey (B.-G.).	28	33	36	1377
48.	60th and 18th av.................	Mapleton..................	F. B. Spaulding (B.-G.)....	26	31	47	1938
49.	Maujer, near Graham av........	Daniel Maujer...........	Katharine C. Knobbe (B-G)	33	20	23	962
50.	Driggs av. and S. 3d............	John D. Wells...........	Oswald Schlockow (B.-G.).	31	52	75	3154
52.	Ellery, near Broadway..........	William Ellery..........	Freda Freifeld (B.-G.)......	33	14	15	575
53.	Troutman, near Central av.....	Paolo Toscanelli.........	Margaret Wilson (B.-G.)...	35	38	45	2028
54.	Walworth, near Myrtle av......	Samuel C. Barnes......	Erna L. Behnken (B.-G.)..	29	27	41	1758
55.	Floyd, near Tompkins av......	Stockton...................	Mary A. Mason (B.-G.).....	29	41	52	2280
*56.	Bushwick av. and Madison......	Thos. W. Field..........	Winifred T. C. Davies(B-G)	36	20	22	914
57.	Reid av., cor. Van Buren.......	Whitelaw Reid..........	Eliz. M. Braine (B.-G.)....	32	17	19	834
*58.	Degraw, near Smith	Degraw.....................	Sidney M. Fuerst (B.-G.)..	28	17	20	747
59.	Leonard, near Nassau av.......	Horace Greeley..........	Branch of No. 34...........	34	14	..	...
60.	4th av., cor. 20th................	Greenwood................	Sarah B. Van Brunt(B.-G.)	28	18	18	810
*61.	Fulton & N. J. av. (Prob. Sch.)	Ditmas Jewell...........	Lucille Nichol (B.)...........	25	7	9	152
62.	Bradford, near Liberty av......	Bradford..................	Mabel F. Dodge (B.-G.)....	40	12	15	668
63.	Hinsdale, near Glenmore av....	Hinsdale...................	Anne Griffin (B.-G.)........	25	18	32	1276
64.	Berrim'n, Belmont & Atkins avs	Berriman..................	W. F. Kurz (B.-G.).........	40	75	71	3065
65.	Richmond, near Ridgewood av.	....	Mary E. Duncan (B.-G.)....	40	20	19	697
66.	Osborn & Watkins, nr Sutter av	Lew Wallace	Kathleen M. Kennedy(B.-G.)	39	43	61	2634
67.	N. Elliott pl., near Park av....	Elliott.....................	Marietta Riley (B.-G.).....	27	10	17	699
68.	Bushwick av., cor. Kosciusko..	Kosciusko.................	Fannie A. Irvine (B.-G.)....	35	24	25	1029
69.	Ryerson, near Myrtle av........	Ryerson....................	Zillah A. Powers (B.-G.)..	31	16	17	633
70.	Patchen av. Macon & McDon'gh	Thomas McDonough.....	Samuel Katz (B.-G.).......	32	31	37	1461
71.	Heyward, near Lee av..........	Edward Rutledge........	Martha S. McL'ghlin (B-G)	31	20	25	1154
72.	New Lots rd. and Schenck av.	New Lots	Thos. D. Murphy (B.-G.)..	40	27	50	2325
73.	McDougal, cor. Rockaway av...	William J. Morrison....	Ambrose Cort (B.-G.).......	36	39	48	2109
*74.	Kosciusko, near B'way..........	Almon G. Merwin.......	John Lieberman (B.-G.)....	35	28	28	1113
75.	Evergreen av., cor. Ralph......	Evergreen-Grove.........	Wm. S. Mills (B.-G.).......	35	50	50	1913
76.	Wyona, near Jamaica av.......	Independence............	Rosamond L. Goertner(B.G)	40	24	31	1292
77.	2d, near 6th av..................	William Penn............	G. B. Germann (B.-G.)....	27	42	43	1701
78.	Pacific, near Court..............	Seth Thayer Stewart.....	John K. Bolen (B.-G.)......	28	26	29	1111
79.	Kosciusko, near Sumner av....	Evangeline E. Whitney..	Branch of No. 25	32	16	..	...

PUBLIC SCHOOLS OF THE CITY OF NEW YORK—BROOKLYN—*Continued.*

School Number.	Location. (Schools marked * have no kindergartens.)	School Name.	Principals.	District.	Cl'sr'ms	Teachers	Register.
*80.	W. 17th & 19th, nr. Neptune av	Neptune	John J. Loftus (B.-G.)	26	32	92	2748
*81.	Harway av. and Stryker	Unionville	Helena E. Horan (B.-G.)	26	4	4	168
82.	4th av., cor. 36th	J. Edward Swanstrom	Temperance Gray (B.-G.)	30	26	28	1150
83.	Bergen & Dean, c. Schenectady	Isaac Newton	Albert E. King (B.-G.)	29	48	54	2259
*84B	Glenmore and Stone avs	Glenmore	Saul Badanes (B.)	36	47	54	2350
84G	....	....	Susie A. Griffin (B.-G.)	36	47	58	2555
85.	Evergreen av., Eldert & Covert	....	C. E. Springmeyer (B.-G.)	36	55	58	2308
86.	Irving av., cor. Harman	Irvington	Harriet A. Kerby (B.-G.)	35	30	31	1291
*87.	Herkimer, cor. Radde pl	Grover Cleveland	Ella Kelly (B.-G.)	36	27	36	1577
88.	Vandervoort pl., cor. Thames	Vandervoort	Annie J. O'Neil (B.-G.)	33	26	32	1340
89.	Newkirk av., E. 31st & E. 32d.	Vanderveer Park	Alice E. B. Ritter (B.-G.)	38	32	44	1824
90.	Bedford and Church avs	Flatbush	Lucy E. Stone (B.-G.)	38	12	18	786
91.	E. N. Y. & Albany avs. & Maple	Albany Avenue	Georgiana E. Brown (B-G.)	39	27	30	1264
92.	Rogers av. and Robinson	....	Louise Castle (B.-G.)	38	38	50	2238
93.	N. Y. av. and Herkimer	William H. Prescott	Wm. C. Allen (B.-G.)	29	37	40	1426
94.	6th av., 50th and 51st	Longfellow	Frank B. Stevens (B.-G.)	30	46	56	2352
95.	Van Sicklen, near Neck rd	Gravesend	Katherine M. Keyes (B.-G.)	26	27	39	1727
*96.	Ocean av. and Ave. U	....	Branch of No. 153	38	4	..	...
97.	Benson and 25th avs	James D. Lynch	A. E. Eichman (B.-G.)	26	11	20	720
98.	Av. Z, E. 26th and E. 27th	Sheepshead Bay	John J. Winter (B.-G.)	38	17	17	899
99.	Ave. K., bet. E. 9th and 10th	Midwood	Jas. C. Rogers (B.-G.)	38	30	39	1746
100.	W. 3d, near Park pl	Coney Island	Jas. F. Smith (B.-G.)	26	16	31	1383
102.	71st, cor. 2d av	Bay View	J. J. Malarkey (B.-G.)	37	34	42	1777
103.	14th av., 53d and 54th	Borough Park	Francis W. Powers (B.-G.)	37	32	45	2133
104.	92d, 5th and Gelston avs	Fort Hamilton	Frank Pickelsky (B.-G.)	37	24	27	1109
105.	10th av. & 59th	Blythebourne	Gertrude M. Paulsen (B.-G.)	37	14	26	1167
106.	Putnam, Hamb'g avs. & Cornelia	Edward Everett Hale	Jos. V. Witherbee (B.-G.)	35	50	50	2016
107.	8th av., cor. 13th	John W. Kimball	Marg. E. Bacon (B.-G.)	30	26	28	1147
108.	Linwood, cor. Arlington av	Arlington	Fred. W. Mar (B.-G.)	40	44	50	1951
109.	Dumont av., Powell & Sackman	Isidor Straus	Jos. F. Wingebach (B.-G.)	25	82	116	5213
110.	Monitor, cor. Driggs av	Monitor	James T. Carey (B.-G.)	34	41	57	2347
111.	Sterling pl., cor. Vanderbilt av.	Algernon S. Higgins	Branch of No. 9	27	28	..	...
112.	15th av., 71st and 72d	Lefferts Park	Thos. H. Hughes (B.-G.)	37	24	50	2112
113.	Evergr'n av, Moffat & Chauncey	Isaac Chauncey	Mary C. V. Connolly (B.-G.)	36	26	31	1303
114.	Remsen av., nr. Av.F, Canarsie	Ryder	Maurice B. Brandt (B.-G.)	39	25	26	1190
115.	E. 92d., bet. Avs. L & M, Canarsie	Canarsie	Kath R. Callahan (B.-G.)	39	8	9	351
116.	Knickerb'k'r av, Grove & Ralph	Plymouth	Agnes E. DeMonde (B.-G.)	35	28	29	1297
117.	B'shwick av, Stagg & Ten Eyck	Ten Eyck	Julia Byrne (B.-G.)	33	23	26	1045
*118.	4th av., 59th and 60th	Charles Dudley Warner	F. J. Arnold (B.)	37	28	34	1311
119.	Av. K, E. 38th and E. 39th	Amersfoort	Helen E. Warner (B.-G.)	38	22	28	1206
120.	Barren Island	Barren Island	Jane F. Shaw (B.-G.)	38	7	6	162
*121.	E. 55th and Ave. C	Livingston	Kate B. Fyfe (B.-G.)	39	1	1	37
122.	Harris'n av, Heyw'd & Rutl'dge	William H. Harrison	W. M. Simmons (B.-G.)	31	38	43	1769
123.	Irving and Willoughby avs	Suydam	Jos. G. Furey (B.-G.)	35	53	53	2187
124.	4th av. and 13th and 14th	Silas B. Dutcher	Margaret Davidson (B.-G.)	28	24	23	915
125.	Blake, Rockaway & Thatf'd avs	Richard H. Dana	Mary E. Quinn (B.-G.)	39	24	36	1675
126.	Meserole av., Lorimer & G'rnsey	John Ericsson	Jos. A. Haniphy (B.-G.)	34	45	60	2253
127.	7th av., 78th and 79th	McKinley Park	Josephine M. Burnett (B-G)	37	25	32	1187
128.	21st av., 83d and 84th	Bensonhurst	Fred. F. Crooker (B.-G.)	26	37	63	2701
129.	Quincy, near Stuyvesant av	Gates	E. P. Crowell (B.-G.)	32	37	41	1701
130.	Ocean Parkway & E. 5th	Parkside	Bernard Colton (B.-G.)	30	31	29	1204
131.	Ft. Hamilton av., 43d and 44th.	....	Grace Bowtell (B.-G.)	30	32	34	1472
132.	Manhattan & Metropolitan avs.	Conselyea	Emily C. Powers (B.-G.)	34	31	57	2521
*133.	Butler, bet. 4th and 5th avs	William A. Butler	Anna G. Bauer (B.-G.)	27	26	32	1323
134.	18th av., near Ocean Parkway.	Parkville	Jas. S. Morey (B.-G.)	38	24	32	1443
135.	Church av. and E. 48th	Rugby	Isabel M. McElhinney (B.-G.)	39	8	13	529
136.	4th av., 40th and 41st	Charles O. Dewey	Warren M. Van Name (B.-G.)	30	30	40	1577
137.	Saratoga av. & Chauncey	Bainbridge	Mary A. Ward (B.-G.)	36	31	33	1315
139.	Cortelyou, Rugby & Argyle rds.	Cortelyou	Gerald W. Griffin (B.-G.)	38	31	34	1447
140.	60th, west of 4th av	Winfield Scott	Minnie C. Ledwith (B.-G.)	37	42	43	1766
141.	Leonard, McKibbin and Boerum	Lucy Larcom	Anna M. Olsson (G.)	33	44	58	2298
142.	Henry and Rapelye	Stranahan	Annie A. L. Egan (B.-G.)	28	31	49	2063
143.	Havemeyer, N. 6th & N. 7th	Havemeyer	Mary R. Fitzpatrick (G.)	34	41	59	2432
144.	Howard av. & Prospect pl	Lincoln Park	Giles J. Swan (B.-G.)	32	48	85	3673
145.	Central av. and Noll	Andrew Jackson	G. M. Davison (B.-G.)	35	47	52	2273
146.	18th & 19th, bet. 6th & 7th avs.	Louisa M. Alcott	Jennie M. Mackay (B.-G.)	30	49	51	2159
147B	Bush'k av., Siegel & McKib'n.	Isaac S. Remsen	Olive Mordorf (B.-G.)	33	38	52	3064
147G	....	....	Marie B. Campbell (B.-G.)	33	36	51	2022
148.	Ellery, Hopkins & Delmonico pl	Hopkins	Rufus A. Vance (B.-G.)	29	46	62	2796
149.	Sutter av., Vermont & Wyona.	East New York	Robert Comin (B.-G.)	25	55	86	3984
150.	Christopher av. and Sackman	Christopher	Lydia A. Miller (B.-G.)	39	51	72	3045
151.	Knick'bkr av. Halsey & Weirf'd	Irving Park	Katharine R. Brady (B.-G.)	35	35	35	1430
152.	Av. G, E. 23d and E. 24th	Glenwood	Frederic L. Luqueer (B.-G.)	38	33	44	1909
153.	Homecrest av., Av. T & E. 12th	Homecrest	Jos. M. Sheehan (B.-G.)	38	38	45	1796
154.	11th av., Windsor pl. & Sherman	Windsor Terrace	Margaret Laing (B.-G.)	30	26	30	1209
155.	Eastern Parkway & Herkimer	Nicholas Herkimer	Emily N. Goodwin (B.-G.)	36	44	58	2417
156.	Sutter av. and Grafton	Waverly	Byron W. Baker (B.-G.)	32	69	106	4629
157.	Kent av., near Myrtle	Franklin	Bryan J. Reilly (B.-G.)	31	60	67	2946
158.	Warwick and Belmont avs	Warwick	Nathan Peyser (B.-G.)	40	50	74	3132
159.	Pitkin av., Hemlock & Crescent.	Pitkin	Addie D. Williams (B.-G.)	40	34	38	1780
160.	Ft. Hamilton av., 51st and 52d.	William T. Sampson	Helena M. Curran (B.-G.)	37	31	42	1851
162.	St. Nicholas av. & Suydam st	Willoughby	Annie B. Moriarty (B.-G.)	35	47	46	1639
163.	Benson & 17th avs. & Bay 14th.	Bath Beach	Mary E. Lynch (B.-G.)	26	37	50	2363
164.	14th av., 42d and 43d sts	Rodney	Augustus Ludwig (B.-G.)	26	47	65	2807
165.	Lott & Hopkinson avs. & Amboy	John Lott	Alex. Fichandler (B.-G.)	39	35	53	2511
*166.	S. 4th, nr. Havemeyer	George L. A. Martin	Margaret M. Shaw (B.-G.)	31	11	15	422
167.	Schenectady av. & E'st'n Pkwy.	Parkway	Floyd R. Smith (B.-G.)	29	47	77	3329
168.	Throop av., Bartlett & Whipple	Bartlett	Robt. J. Frost (B.-G.)	32	45	51	2143
169.	7th av., 43d and 44th	Sunset Park	Anna E. Clemency (B.-G.)	30	33	41	1723
170.	6th and Stewart av., 71st & 72d.	Lefferts	Francis R. Kelley (B.-G.)	37	31	34	1536

PUBLIC SCHOOLS OF THE CITY OF NEW YORK—BROOKLYN—*Continued.*

School Number.	Location. (Schools marked * have no kindergartens.)	School Name.	Principals.	District.	Cl'ar'ms	Teachers	Register.
171.	Ridgew'd, Lincoln & Nichols avs.	Abraham Lincoln	Lyman A. Best (B.-G.)	40	51	58	2442
172.	4th av., 29th and 30th	Gowanus	Mary E. Elmore (B.-G.)	30	26	32	1406
173.	Penna. av., bet. Liberty and Glenmore avs.	Liberty	Honor E. Quinn (B.-G.)	25	49	60	2507
174.	Dumont, Alabama & W'ms avs	Dumont	Ida L. Morrison (B.-G.)	25	50	81	3728
175.	Blake and Hopkinson avs. and Bristol	Hopkinson	Kate McKee (B.-G.)	39	45	75	3482
176.	68th, 12th and Bay Ridge avs.	Ovington	Jesse C. Bell (B.-G.)	37	31	52	2194
177.	Av. P. & West av.	Marlboro	Harriet R. Dailey (B.-G.)	28	5	7	267
178.	Dean, nr. Saratoga av.	St. Clair McKelway	Chas. E. O'Neill (B.-G)	36	49	65	2601
179.	Av. C, E. 2d and 3d	Kensington	Henry Ludwig (B.-G.)	38	47	54	2328
180.	18th av. and 67th	Homewood	Rose V. Marshall (B.-G.)	26	11	16	483
*	Bkln. Voc. Sch., Carey Bldg., Jay and Nassau		Jas. H. Allen (B.)	..	..	28	539
*	Truant Sch'l—Jamaica av., opp. Enfield		J. S. Fitzpatrick (B.)	..	6	6	102

PUBLIC SCHOOLS—Queens.

School Number.	Location.	School Name.	Principals.	District.	Cl'ar'ms	Teachers	Register.
1.	9th and Van Alst av., L.I.C.	Hunter's Point	W. L. Cremin (B.-G.)	41	40	39	1697
*2.	Hulst and Nelson avs., L. I. C.	Sunnyside	Branch of No. 80	42	8	..	...
3.	Colonial av & Liv'gston, F. Hills	Forest Hills	Mary A. Hoppe (B.-G.)	46	10	15	573
4.	Prospect nr. Beebe av., L.I.C.	Darwin	Robert L. Conant (B.-G.)	41	42	46	1852
5.	Academy, nr. Grand av., L.I.C.	Van Dyke	Matthew D. Quinn (B.-G.)	41	27	32	1306
6.	Steinway, nr. Pat'son av., L.I.C.	John H. Thiry	Thomas H. Sweeney (B.-G.)	41	36	50	2074
7.	Van Alst, nr. Flush'g av., L.I.C	Astoria	Mamie Fay (B.-G.)	41	41	42	1804
*8.	St'n'y av., n. Ditmars av., L.I.C.	John A. Dix	Branch of No. 84	41	8	..	...
9.	Munson, nr. Astoria av., L.I.C.	Hallett's Cove	Branch of No. 7	41	6	..	...
*10.	Astoria av., nr. Frye, Woodside	Phoebe Cary	Branch of No. 92	42	1	..	...
11.	Woodside av., Woodside	Woodside	Theophilus Johnson (B.-G.)	42	23	23	884
12.	Sinclair av., near Fisk av., Winfield	James B. Colgate	Branch of No. 78	42	10	..	...
13.	Parcell st., nr Chicago, Elmh'st	Cement C. Moore	Branch of No. 89	42	6	..	...
14.	Van Dusen, Orentes & 51st, Corona Hts.	Fairview	Josephine M. Nordman (B-G)	46	39	50	1960
*15.	Junction & Hayes avs., Corona	Luona	Emily C. Curry (B.-G.)	42	14	15	580
16.	Alburtes av. nr Gunther, Corona	Corona	J. J. Jenkins (B.-G.)	42	40	43	1715
17.	Tremann av. & Strong, Corona.	Martense	Branch of No. 14	46	12	..	...
*18.	Corona & Alburtis avs., Corona	Francis A. Walker	Branch of No. 14	46	4	..	...
19.	41st & Roosevelt av., Corona	Lake	Branch of No. 16	42	6	..	...
20.	Sanford av. & Union, Flushing.		A. S. Taylor (B.-G.)	46	27	27	1024
*21.	37th av. & Union, Flushing		Branch of No. 23	46	4	..	...
22.	Sanford av. Murray, Flushing		Frances J. Cronan (B.-G.)	46	25	29	1174
23.	35th and Union, Flushing		Edna H. Ash (B.-G.)	46	17	17	666
24.	Holley av. & Robinson, Flush'g		Isabel Lincoln (B.-G.)	46	5	5	214
25.	Kissena rd. & Melbourne av., Flushing	Richard A. Proctor	George H. Dildine (B.-G.)	46	4	5	184
26.	67th av. & Fresh Meadow rd., Flushing		Carrie H. Yarrow (B.-G.)	46	4	4	197
.	122d & 14th av., College Point	College Point	George W. Dorland (B.-G.)	46	32	35	1330
.	115th, College Point	Tallman	Branch of No. 27	46	6	..	...
27.	22d av. & 125th, College Point	Poppenhusen	Branch of No. 27	46	8	..	...
*29.	12th av., nr. Cross Island rd., Whitestone	John D. Locke	Branch of No. 79	46	8	..	...
31.	Boulevard & 46th av., Bayside.	Bayside	Branch of No. 41	46	12	..	...
33.	222d & Bellwood av., Creedmoor	Creedmoor	Branch of No. 34	43	4	..	...
34.	Springfield rd. & Hollis av., Q's	John Harvard	Geo. R. Dutton (B.-G.)	43	14	17	682
35.	191st & Canonbury rd., Hollis	Woodhull	Clara E. Bell (B.-G.)	43	12	18	510
*36.	Everett & Westchester av., St. Albans	St. Albans	Phoebe A. Combes (B.-G.)	43	4	5	185
*37.	140th av., nr. Coomb, Springfield	Springfield	W. E. Hendrie (B.-G.)	43	11	15	645
*38.	Brookville Boulevard, nr. 137th, Rosedale	Rosedale	John H. Miller (B.-G.)	43	5	6	216
39.	Dinsmore & Nameoke av., Far Rockaway	Far Rockaway	Sanford J. Ellsworth (B-G.)	43	18	31	1232
40.	Lambertville av. & Union Hall, Jamaica	Samuel Huntington	Frank K. Montfort (B.-G.)	43	39	49	2128
41.	35th av. & 214th pl., Bayside	Crocheron	Jennie L. Potter (B.-G.)	46	20	23	950
*42.	Blvd. & Beach 67th, Arverne	R. Vernam	Branch of No. 44	43	8	..	...
*43.	Blvd. & Beach 110th, Rkwy Pk.	Rockaway Park	Branch of No. 44	43	8	..	...
44.	Blvd. & Beach 94th, Rkwy B'h.	P. Sarsfield Gilmour	William M. Gilmore (B.-G.)	43	35	65	2671
45.	Garfield, nr. Rockaway blvd., Jamaica South	Baisley Park	Branch of No. 96	44	16	..	...
*46.	Old South rd., Woodhaven	Daniel Boone	Isabella A. Boulton (B.-G.)	44	12	12	471
48.	South and Carlisle, Jamaica	William Wordsworth	Branch of No. 40	43	4	..	...
49.	Brenton av., Jamaica	Brenton	Branch of No. 95	43	12	..	...
-50.	Liverpool & Humboldt av., Jamaica	Talfourd Lawn	Margaret Scott (B.-G.)	43	17	27	1165
51.	Church av., near Jamaica av., Richmond Hill	Arthur Middleton	Branch of No. 56	44	5	..	...
53.	114th, n. Atlantic av., Morris Pk	Charles Carroll	Branch of No. 62	44	8	..	...
54.	Hillside av. & 126th, R. H.	Hillside Avenue	Helen T. Daily (B.-G.)	44	13	18	673
*55.	130th & 97th av., R. H.	John Morton	Branch of No. 57	44	4	..	...
56.	86th av. & 114th, R. H.	Jacob A. Riis	Catherine Sheehan (B.-G.)	44	26	25	912
57.	124th & 101st av., Morris Park	Morris Park	Mary A. Cooley (B.-G.)	44	19	26	1078
58.	Walker & Beaufort avs., Woodhaven	Woodhaven	C. B. Jameson (B.-G.)	44	45	48	1923
*59.	83d & Rockaway blvd., Woodhaven	University Place	A. D. Stetson (B.-G.)	44	11	11	435
*60.	87th rd. & 90th, Bklyn Hills	Snedeker	Branch of No. 97	44	4	..	...
61.	89th av. & 102d, Bklyn Hills	Alonzo B. Cornell	Branch of No. 66	44	4	..	...
62.	107th, nr. 101st av., Ozone Park	Chester Park	Mary E. McQuirk (B.-G.)	44	18	23	881

PUBLIC SCHOOLS OF THE CITY OF NEW YORK—QUEENS—*Continued.*

School Number.	Location. (Schools marked * have no kindergartens.)	School Name.	Principals.	District.	Cl'sr'ms	Teachers	Register.
63.	Pitkin av., n. Woodhaven blvd. South Woodhaven	Old South	Branch of No. 46	44	4	..	...
64.	101st av. & 83d. Union Course	Andre Ampere	Mabel Sondheim (B.-G.)	44	8	10	306
65.	78th, nr. Jamaica av., Union Course	Pascal	Branch of No. 97	44	8	..	...
66.	102d & 85th av., Bkln. Manor	Oxford	Frances H. Seeley (B.-G.)	44	22	22	764
*67.	Central av. and Olmstead pl., Glendale		Branch of No. 91	45	12	..	...
68.	St. Felix av. and Seneca, Evergreen	Cambridge	Kate R. Hickey (B.-G.)	45	24	23	834
71.	Forest av., near Metropolitan av., E. Williamsburg	East Williamsburgh	Maurice I. Jewell (B.-G.)	45	53	46	1753
72.	Maspeth av., nr. Clermont, Maspeth	George Clinton	Robert Eadie (B.-G.)	42	20	27	1258
73.	La Forge, nr. Grand, Maspeth	William Cowper	Branch of No. 3	42	4	..	...
74.	Star & Woodw'd av., E. Wmsbg.	Woodward Avenue	Winifred L. Northey (B.-G.)	45	8	5	159
*75.	Bl'cker & Seneca av., Ridgew'd	Max Muller	Branch of No. 81	44	8	..	...
76.	Montgomery & Congress avs., Laurel Hill	Rapelye	Josephine McC. Klohr (B.-G.)	42	13	11	415
77.	Seneca av. and George, Ridgewood Park		Jas. J. O'Regan (B.-G.)	45	51	51	1809
78.	Maurice av. and Carroll place, Winfield	James A. Garfield	Fred H. Mead (B.-G.)	42	29	31	1209
79.	7th av. and 14th, Whitestone	Frances Lewis	William H. Carr (B.-G.)	46	26	21	803
80.	Greenp't av., nr. Bradley av., L. I. C.	Blissville	Melvin Hix (B.-G.)	42	22	15	619
81.	Cypress av., Ralph & Bleecker Evergreen	Jean Paul Richter	William H. Dumond (B.-G.)	45	55	58	2117
82.	Kaplan av. & Le Roy pl., Jamaica	Hammond	Imogene G. Bradford (B-G)	43	15	17	682
83.	Vernon av., bet. Pierce and Graham avs., L. I. C.	Ravenswood	W. J. McGrath (B.-G.)	41	28	32	1356
84.	11th av., nr. Ditmars av., Steinway	Steinway	Jos. T. P. Callahan (B.-G.)	41	39	40	1580
85.	2d av., nr. Woolsey, L. I. C.	Humphrey Davy	John J. Dempsey (B.-G.)	41	34	29	1092
86.	Creek st., nr. Grand, Maspeth		Jas. A. Dugan (B.-G.)	42	25	27	924
87.	Weiss av. & Pulaski, Middle Village	Middle Village	Matthew A. Devlin (B.-G.)	46	32	29	1168
88.	Fresh Pond rd. & Catalpa av., Ridgewood Heights	Seneca	J. H. Rohrbach (B.-G.)	45	31	32	1285
89.	Gleane & Britton av., Elmh'st.	Elmhurst	Almeron W. Smith (B.-G.)	42	49	53	2291
90.	109th, nr. Jamaica av., R. H.	Horace Mann	J. A. Loope (B.-G.)	44	37	35	1295
91.	Central, Folsom and Fosdick avs., Glendale	Richard Arkwright	J. W. Drumm (B.-G.)	45	43	37	1467
92.	Hays av., 42d & 43d, N. Corona	Charles P. Leverich	Agnes A. Cording (B.-G.)	42	25	29	1193
93.	Forest & Madison avs., Ridgewood Hts.	Euclid	T. M. Donohue (B.-G.)	45	45	45	1839
94.	Cutter av. & Old House Landing rd., Little Neck	David D. Porter	Anna Brett (B.-G.)	46	9	10	311
95.	Harvard av. & Canonbury rd., Jamaica	Eastwood	Mary A. Flynn (B.-G.)	43	29	35	1374
96.	Rockaway bldv. and 131st, So. Ozone Park		Bridget C. Peixotto (B.-G.)	43	31	26	1104
97.	85th & Shipley, Woodhaven	Forest Park	Martin Joyce (B.-G.)	44	35	42	1710
98.	Main st., Douglaston	Douglaston	Jos. Gill	46	6	6	197
*99.	Cuthbert pl., nr. Lefferts blvd., Kew Gardens		Elizabeth Cadzow	46	2	2	100
*100.	Lefferts, Glen Morris		Ellen M. Kenny (B.-G.)	44	4	5	145
*101.	Children's Lane & Russell pl., Forest Hills Gardens		Branch of No. 3	46	4	..	...
*	Kissena rd., Reeves and Melbourne avs., Flushing	N. Y. Parental	J. S. Fitzpatrick (B.)	46	6	5	177

PUBLIC SCHOOLS—Richmond.

School Number.	Location.	School Name.	Principals.	District.	Cl'sr'ms	Teachers	Register.
1.	Academy pl., Tottenville	Tottenville	Nathan J. Lowe (B.-G.)	48	29	23	844
*2.	Weiner, Richmond Valley	Richmond Valley	Ava A. Butler (B.-G.)	48	2	1	33
3.	Latourette, Pleasant Plains	Pleasant Plains	K. Eloise Kinne (B.-G.)	48	13	10	369
4.	Arthur Kill rd., Kreischerville	Kreischer	H. F. Albro (B.-G.)	48	9	6	211
*5.	Amboy rd., Huguenot	Huguenot	Annie E. Cole (B.-G.)	48	6	6	260
*6.	Rossville av., Rossville	Betsey Ross	Benj. B. Chappell (B.-G.)	48	4	4	128
*7.	Arthur Kill rd., Greenridge	Greenridge	Laura K. Cropsey (B.-G.)	48	2	2	57
8.	Lindenwood av., Great Kills		Frank G. Ingalls (B.-G.)	48	22	17	724
*9.	Knight av., New Dorp	De Vries	Branch of No. 8	48	6	..	...
*10.	Richmond rd., New Dorp	Egbert	Anna T. Dermody (B.-G.)	48	2	2	68
11.	Jefferson av., Dongan Hills	Thomas Dongan	Alfred D. B. Mason (B.-G.)	48	11	15	681
12.	Steuben, Stapleton	Ralph Waldo Emerson	Thos. C. Harty (B.-G.)	48	20	20	759
13.	Pennsylvania av. & Anderson pl., Rosebank	Rosebank	Esle F. Randolph (B.-G.)	48	33	29	1152
14.	Broad and Wright, Stapleton	Vanderbilt	Frank Hankinson (B.-G.)	48	34	35	1401
15.	Grant & Park av., Tompk'v'le.	Daniel D. Tompkins	Mary M. Conway (B.-G.)	48	21	21	808
16.	Monroe av., Tompkinsville	Henry W. Slocum	John J. Driscoll (B.-G.)	47	24	27	973
17.	Prospect av. & Linden, New Brighton	New Brighton	Samuel McK. Smith (B.-G.)	47	33	40	1599
18.	Broadway, West New Brighton	John Greenleaf Whittier	T. F. Donovan (B.-G.)	47	33	34	1240
19.	Greenleaf av, W. New Bright'n		G. Alvin Grover (B.-G.)	47	15	16	591
20.	Heberton av., Port Richmond	Port Richmond	Lewis H. Denton (B.-G.)	47	33	34	1431
21.	Hooker pl., Port Richmond	Elm Park	G. J. Jennings (B.-G.)	47	30	30	1214
*22.	Washington & Columbus avs., Graniteville	Graniteville	Branch of No. 21	47	12	..	...
23.	Cedar, nr. Andros av., Mariners Harbor	Mariner Harbor	David J. Keator (B.-G.)	47	24	24	1007

PUBLIC SCHOOLS OF THE CITY OF NEW YORK—RICHMOND—*Continued.*

School Number	Location. (Schools marked * have no kindergartens.)	School Name.	Principals.	District.	Cl'sr'ms.	Teachers.	Register.
*24.	Washington av., Summerville..	Summerville...	Margaret McDonough(B.-G.)	47	3	2	73
*25.	Chelsea rd., Bloomfield	Bloomfield...............	Branch of No. 26...........	47	2	..	...
26.	Richmond turnpike & Wild av., Linoleumville	Carteret..................	Elsie Gardner (B.-G.).......	47	15	14	539
*27.	Richmond av., New Springville	Springville...............	Lillian Boeddinghaus(B.-G.)	47	2	1	27
*28.	Centre, Richmond	Richmond..................	Anna M. Martin (B.-G.)...	48	4	4	120
29.	Manor rd., W. New Brighton..	Castleton Corners.......	Branch of No. 30...........	47	5	..	...
30.	Fisk av., W. New Brighton....	Westerleigh...............	Wm. B. Rafferty (B.-G.)...	47	20	24	910
*31.	Pleasant av., Bogardus C'ners.	Guyon......................	Julia Hurd (B.-G.).........	48	2	1	30
32.	Osgood av., Stapleton............	Grymes.....................	Branch of No. 15...........	48	8	..	...
*33.	Midland av., Grant City........	Grantland.................	Branch of No. 11...........	48	3	..	...
34.	Fingerboard rd., Rosebank......	Fort Wadsworth........	C. W. Sutherland (B.-G.)..	48	9	9	479

NEW PUBLIC SCHOOL BUILDINGS UNDER CONSTRUCTION.

Manhattan: P. S. 83 (addition); P. S. 130 (new), Baxter and Hester.

BRONX—P. S. 6 (addition); P. S. 38 (new), St. Anns av., Rae and Carr and Hagney pl.; P. S. 43 (addition); P. S. 37 (new), Crotona and Belmont avs., E. 180th and 181st; P. S. 59, Bathgate av. and E. 182d, P. S. 61, Crotona Park East and Charlotte; P. S. 62, Leggett av., bet. So. blvd. and Fox.

BROOKLYN: P. S. 20 (new), Driggs av., N. 4th, N. 5th and Roebling; P. S. 29 (new), Henry, bet. Baltic and Harrison; P. S. 73 (addition); P. S. 80 (addition); P. S. 97 (new), Stillwell av. and Av. S; P. S. 100 (new), W. 1st and Sheepshead Bay rd.; P. S. 144 (addition); P. S. 181, N. Y. av. and E. 34th, bet. Tilden and Snyder avs.; P. S. 182, Dumont, Vermont and Livonia avs. and Wyona; P. S. 185, 2d av. and 86th.

QUEENS: P. S. 3 (new), Colonial av., Livingston and Meteor, Forest Hills; P. S. 39 (addition); P. S. 50 (new), Liberty, Bryant and Jerome avs., South Jamaica; Bryant H. S. (addition); Newtown H. S. (addition).

RICHMOND: P. S. 11 (new), Cromwell av., Dongan Hills.

TEACHERS' COUNCIL TO ADVISE BOARD OF EDUCATION.

The Teachers' Council is composed of 45 representatives from voluntary teachers' organisations, the representation being distributed among the various elements of the teaching staff. It has a twofold function: (a) The furnishing of information and the opinions of principals and teachers upon questions submitted by the Bd. of Education or by the Bd. of Superintendents; and (b) the introduction of recommendations concerning any of the problems affecting the welfare of the schools and the teaching staff. Pres., Wm. J. McAuliffe, 372 E. 194th, Bronx; V.-Pres., Agnes M. Marshall, P. S. 9, Bkln.; Rec. Sec., S. McKee Smith, P. S. 17, Richmond; Cor. Sec., Louise A. Schreiker, 522 W. 145th, Mhtn. Meets at Bd. of Ed. Bldg., 3d Friday in Sept. and 2d Friday each month, except July and Aug. Advisory Bd. on Industrial Education: Mrs. Sara A. Conboy, Ch.; Frederick Alfred, E. J. Deering, Samuel B. Donnelly and John J. Mulholland.

SCHOOL TEACHERS' RETIREMENT FUND.

N. Y. City and the school teachers share in equal amount the cost of pension benefits to be provided (law enacted 1917). The cost represents for future entrants into the teaching force approximately 10% of their average salaries. One-half of this, or 5%, is contributed by the teachers and the other half, or 5%, by the city. These contributions develop a fund, out of which the pensions are paid on the expiration of the required period of service. For present employees the city not only provides ½ of their ultimate retirement allowance, but in addition makes up the arrearages due to accrued liability. This is done for each teacher in proportion to the length of his service.

The retirement plan involves two factors: (1) An annuity of 25% of the final salary, paid out of the contributions of the teacher, and (2) a service pension of 25% of the average final salary, paid for out of the contributions of the city. In addition to this benefit, each teacher is insured against disability occurring at any time after 10 years of service to an amount of 20% of the final salary, which is provided by the contributions of the city with such additional sum as may be purchased in the form of an annuity out of the teachers' contributions made up to the time of his retirement on disability.

The Dept. of Insurance has supervision over the conduct of the business of the fund.

The Retirement Board consists of the Pres. of the Board of Education, the Comptroller of N. Y. C., 2 members appointed by the Mayor, one of whom shall be a member of the Board of Education, and 3 members elected by representatives of the supervising and teaching force. The Board: Annig S. Prall, Ch.; Chas. L. Craig, John A. Ferguson, T. W. Churchill, Clara C. Calkins, Fredk. Z. Lewis, Agnes M. Craig.

ROCKEFELLER GIFTS FOR PUBLIC WELFARE.

A statement, issued Nov. 24, 1920, announced a new gift by John D. Rockefeller of $63,763,357.37 in securities to the Laura Spelman Rockefeller Memorial, an institution founded after Mrs. Rockefeller's death in 1915 to give support to the many religious and charitable institutions in which she was interested. Mr. Rockefeller's gifts for public welfare now total close to $500,000,000. Up to 1915 his gifts had amounted to $250,000,000. Since that time, among other donations, he has given $82,000,000 to the Rockefeller Foundation, $70,000,000 to the General Education Board, $10,000,000 to the Rockefeller Institute and the above mentioned gift of $63,000,000 to the Laura Spelman Rockefeller Memorial.

BROOKLYN SUBWAY TRAFFIC INCREASE.

The report of the Interborough Rapid Transit Co. shows that Brooklyn business on the Interborough Subway has increased 16 per cent. in one year. In July, 1919, there were 3,621,830 fares paid at the Brooklyn stations of the subway and in July, 1920, there were 4,197,470 fares paid.

EXPENDITURES ON NON-ESSENTIALS.

Experts in the Department of the Treasury, figuring from the tax returns, estimate that the country spends the following sums annually in non-essentials:

Chewing gum	$50,000,000
Candy	1,000,000,000
Cigarettes	800,000,000
Soft drinks, including ice cream and soda	350,000,000
Perfumery and cosmetics........	750,000,000
Cigars	510,000,000
Tobacco and snuff	800,000,000
Furs	300,000,000
Carpets and luxurious clothing....	1,500,000,000
Automobile and parts............	2,000,000,000
Toilet soaps	400,000,000

CEMETERY IN ENGLAND FOR AMERICAN SOLDIERS.

The War Department has decided that the 550 American soldiers who died on British soil are to be buried permanently in Great Britain. The bodies will be concentrated in a cemetery near London, under the perpetual care of the United States Government.

POSTAL REGULATIONS

CLASSES OF MAIL.

Domestic matter is divided into four classes:

1st—Embraces letters, postal cards, post cards, all matter wholly or partly in writing or sealed against inspection, postage 2c. (postal and post cards, 1c.). Limit of weight, same as for 4th class.

2d—Newspapers and periodicals in their entirety which have been entered as "Second Class Matter." Parts of publications are third-class matter. Postage 1c. for each 4 ozs. or fraction thereof when mailed by other than publisher; postage to be fully prepaid or will be disposed of as waste. No limit of weight.

3d—Sections of periodicals, newspaper clippings, not embraced in the term "book"; circulars and matter wholly in print on paper, blue prints, proof sheets, corrected proof sheets and manuscript copy accompanying the same, engravings, lithographs. Also facsimile copies made by a mechanical process, provided they are mailed at the post office window in the minimum number of 20 identical copies. Postage 1c. each 2 ozs. or fraction thereof. Limit of weight, 4 lbs. Books and miscellaneous printed matter over 4 lbs. can be sent by parcel post.

4th—Fourth class matter embraces that known as domestic parcel post mail, and includes merchandise, farm and factory products, seeds, cuttings, bulbs, roots, scions and plants, books (including catalogues), miscellaneous printed matter weighing more than 4 lbs., and all other mailable matter not embraced in the first, second and third classes, not exceeding 70 lbs. in first, second and third zones, 50 lbs. in other zones, not greater in size than 84 in. in length and girth combined.

Rates of Postage, to be fully prepaid, unsealed, are as follows:

(a) Parcels weighing 4 ounces or less, except books, seeds, plants, etc., 1 cent for each ounce or fraction thereof, any distance.

(b) Parcels weighing 8 ounces or less, containing books, seeds, cuttings, bulbs, roots, scions and plants, 1 cent for each 2 ounces or fraction thereof, regardless of distance.

(c) Parcels weighing more than 8 ounces, containing books, seeds, plants, etc., parcels of miscellaneous printed matter weighing more than 4 pounds, and all other parcels of fourth-class matter weighing more than 4 ounces, are chargeable, according to distance or zone, at the pound rates shown in the following table, a fraction of a pound being considered a full pound.

Forwarding Mail Matter.

Matter of the first class, including post and postal cards, can be forwarded until it reaches the addressee.

What Cannot Be Mailed.

All transient second-class matter and all matter of the third or fourth class not wholly prepaid; and letters and other first-class matter not prepaid one full rate—2c.

Parcels post matter limit 1st, 2d and 3d zones, 70 lbs.; 50 lbs. other zones. See fourth-class above. Poisons and obscene literature.

Unmailable.

Every letter, writing, circular, postal card, picture, print, engraving, photograph, newspaper, pamphlet, book or other publication, matter or thing of any kind in violation of the provisions of the Espionage Law.

All matter containing advertisements of intoxicating liquors or solicitations of orders therefor when addressed to any place or point in any State or Territory where it is unlawful either to advertise such liquors or to solicit orders therefor.

PARCELS POST SYSTEM.

The domestic parcels post delivery went into effect Jan. 1, 1913. On Feb. 26, 1913, the limit of weight of parcels of fourth-class mail for delivery within the first, second and third zones was increased to 70 lbs. and for other zones to 50 lbs. Each parcel must bear the return name and address of the sender or it will not be accepted for mailing.

Insured Parcels Post.

4th class or domestic parcel post mail may be insured against loss, rifling or damage in amt. equivalent to its value up to $5 for a fee of 3c., $25 for 5c., $50 for 10c., or $100 for 25c., in addition to postage. Both postage and fee must be paid by postage stamps affixed to parcel. Such mail may be insured at any post office or sta. thereof, or by rural carriers, but must not be deposited in st. mail boxes or in mail drops at post offices.

Meat and Meat Products.

Salted, dried, smoked or cured meats and other meat products may be admitted to the mails and may be transported, regardless of distance, from one State or Territory or the Dist. of Columbia to another State or Territory or the Dist. of Columbia, when they comply with the regulations as promulgated by the Dept. of Agriculture, which requires that a certificate be furnished showing that such meat or meat-food product has been either inspected and passed or exempted from inspection according to Act of Congress of June 30, 1906.

Parcels Post Rates.

Weight, in lbs.	1st Zone, 50 mi. Local rate.	1st Zone, 50 mi. Zone rate.	2d Zone, 150 mi.	3d Zone, 150-300 mi.	4th Zone, 300-600 mi.	5th Zone, 600-1,000 mi.	6th Zone, 1,000-1,400 mi.	7th Zone, 1,400-1,800 mi.	8th Zone, all over 1,800 mi.
1...	$.05	$.05	$.05	$.06	$.07	$.08	$.09	$.11	$.12
2...	.06	.06	.06	.08	.11	.14	.17	.21	.24
3...	.06	.07	.07	.10	.15	.20	.25	.31	.36
4...	.07	.08	.08	.12	.19	.26	.33	.41	.48
5...	.07	.09	.09	.14	.23	.32	.41	.51	.60
6...	.08	.10	.10	.16	.27	.38	.49	.61	.72
7...	.08	.11	.11	.18	.31	.44	.57	.71	.84
8...	.09	.12	.12	.20	.35	.50	.65	.81	.96
9...	.09	.13	.13	.22	.39	.56	.73	.91	1.08
10...	.10	.14	.14	.24	.43	.62	.81	1.01	1.20
11...	.10	.15	.15	.26	.47	.68	.89	1.11	1.32
12...	.11	.16	.16	.28	.51	.74	.97	1.21	1.44
13...	.11	.17	.17	.30	.55	.80	1.05	1.31	1.56
14...	.12	.18	.18	.32	.59	.86	1.13	1.41	1.68
15...	.12	.19	.19	.34	.63	.92	1.21	1.51	1.80
16...	.13	.20	.20	.36	.67	.98	1.29	1.61	1.92
17...	.13	.21	.21	.38	.71	1.04	1.37	1.71	2.04
18...	.14	.22	.22	.40	.75	1.10	1.45	1.81	2.16
19...	.14	.23	.23	.42	.79	1.16	1.53	1.91	2.28
20...	.15	.24	.24	.44	.83	1.22	1.61	2.01	2.40
21...	.15	.25	.25	.46	.87	1.28	1.69	2.11	2.52
22...	.16	.26	.26	.48	.91	1.34	1.77	2.21	2.64
23...	.16	.27	.27	.50	.95	1.40	1.85	2.31	2.76
24...	.17	.28	.28	.52	.99	1.46	1.93	2.41	2.88
25...	.17	.29	.29	.54	1.03	1.52	2.01	2.51	3.00
26...	.18	.30	.30	.56	1.07	1.58	2.09	2.61	3.12
27...	.18	.31	.31	.58	1.11	1.64	2.17	2.71	3.24
28...	.19	.32	.32	.60	1.15	1.70	2.25	2.81	3.36
29...	.19	.33	.33	.62	1.19	1.76	2.33	2.91	3.48
30...	.20	.34	.34	.64	1.23	1.82	2.41	3.01	3.60
31...	.20	.35	.35	.66	1.27	1.88	2.49	3.11	3.72
32...	.21	.36	.36	.68	1.31	1.94	2.57	3.21	3.84
33...	.21	.37	.37	.70	1.35	2.00	2.65	3.31	3.96
34...	.22	.38	.38	.72	1.39	2.06	2.73	3.41	4.08
35...	.22	.39	.39	.74	1.43	2.12	2.81	3.51	4.20
36...	.23	.40	.40	.76	1.47	2.18	2.89	3.61	4.32
37...	.23	.41	.41	.78	1.51	2.24	2.97	3.71	4.44
38...	.24	.42	.42	.80	1.55	2.30	3.05	3.81	4.56
39...	.24	.43	.43	.82	1.59	2.36	3.13	3.91	4.68
40...	.25	.44	.44	.84	1.63	2.42	3.21	4.01	4.80
41...	.25	.45	.45	.86	1.67	2.48	3.29	4.11	4.92
42...	.26	.46	.46	.88	1.71	2.54	3.37	4.21	5.04
43...	.26	.47	.47	.90	1.75	2.60	3.45	4.31	5.16
44...	.27	.48	.48	.92	1.79	2.66	3.53	4.41	5.28
45...	.27	.49	.49	.94	1.83	2.72	3.61	4.51	5.40
46...	.28	.50	.50	.96	1.87	2.78	3.69	4.61	5.52
47...	.28	.51	.51	.98	1.91	2.84	3.77	4.71	5.64
48...	.29	.52	.52	1.00	1.95	2.90	3.85	4.81	5.76
49...	.29	.53	.53	1.02	1.99	2.96	3.93	4.91	5.88
50...	.30	.54	.54	1.04	2.03	3.02	4.01	5.01	6.00
51...	.30	.55	.55	1.06	....	....	....	....	....
52...	.31	.56	.56	1.08	....	....	....	....	....
53...	.31	.57	.57	1.10	....	....	....	....	....
54...	.32	.58	.58	1.12	....	....	....	....	....
55...	.32	.59	.59	1.14	....	....	....	....	....
56...	.33	.60	.60	1.16	....	....	....	....	....
57...	.33	.61	.61	1.18	....	....	....	....	....
58...	.34	.62	.62	1.20	....	....	....	....	....
59...	.34	.63	.63	1.22	....	....	....	....	....
60...	.35	.64	.64	1.24	....	....	....	....	....
61...	.35	.65	.65	1.26	....	....	....	....	....
62...	.36	.66	.66	1.28	....	....	....	....	....
63...	.36	.67	.67	1.30	....	....	....	....	....
64...	.37	.68	.68	1.32	....	....	....	....	....
65...	.37	.69	.69	1.34	....	....	....	....	....
66...	.38	.70	.70	1.36	....	....	....	....	....
67...	.38	.71	.71	1.38	....	....	....	....	....
68...	.39	.72	.72	1.40	....	....	....	....	....
69...	.39	.73	.73	1.42	....	....	....	....	....
70...	.40	.74	.74	1.44	....	....	....	....	....

POSTAL REGULATIONS—PARCELS POST SYSTEM—*Continued.*

Note—The local rate applies to parcels mailed under the following conditions:

(1) At any post office for local delivery at such office.

(2) At any city letter carrier office, or at any point within its delivery limits, for delivery by carriers from that office.

(3) At any post office from which a rural route starts, for delivery on such route, or when mailed at any point on a rural route for delivery at any other point thereon.

Collect on Delivery.

The sender of a mailable parcel on which the postage is fully prepaid may have the price of the article and the charges thereon collected from the addressee on payment of a fee of 10c. in stamps affixed, provided the amount to be collected does not exceed $50, and for a fee of 25c. in stamps, provided the amount to be remitted does not exceed $100. Such a parcel will be insured against loss, rifling or damage without additional charge, in an amount equivalent to its actual value, but not to exceed $50 or $100, according to whether a 10c. or 25c. fee was paid.

A C. O. D. parcel will be accepted only at a money order office and when addressed to a money order office. Money order offices are designated in the Parcels Post Guides by an asterisk (*) or a dagger (†). The C. O. D. tag must show the amount due the sender and the money order fee necessary to make the remittance. The addressee will not be permitted to examine contents of a C. O. D. parcel until it has been receipted for and all charges paid. A parcel may be refused when it is tendered for delivery, but after delivery has been effected it cannot be returned on account of dissatisfaction with contents or amount collected.

A C. O. D. parcel may be sent "Special Delivery" by affixing stamps for the special delivery fee, in addition to the regular postage.

Parcels Post Firm Books.

Individuals and firms mailing 3 or more Insured or C. O. D. parcels at one time are recommended to use a firm book which renders it unnecessary to fill out the mailing office and senders receipt, and which greatly facilitates the handling of these parcels. These books will be furnished by the P. O. upon request.

DOMESTIC RATES.

The domestic rates apply to the United States, Porto Rico, Guam, Philippine Islands, Shanghai (China), Cuba, *Canada, *Mexico, Hawaii, Republic of Panama, the Panama Canal Zone, Tutuila (U. S. Samoa), Midway Island, Virgin Islands of the U. S. Parcels for Shanghai, China, must have customs declaration.

Parcels cannot be insured or sent C. O. D. if addressed to members of military units in the U. S., unless such parcels are clearly and definitely addressed, showing the rank of the addressee, his company and regiment, the camp, cantonment, etc., at which the addressee is stationed, and the State in which it is located.

War-Stamp Tax.

A war-stamp tax of 1c. for each postage charge of 25c. or fractional part of 25c. must be paid on parcels on which the postage amounts to not less than 25c. each. The tax is not applicable to parcels on which the postage amounts to less than 25c. Special delivery insurance or C. O. D. fees are not included in computing the postage for war-stamp tax.

War-stamp tax does not apply to parcels sent to Am. Forces abroad, Porto Rico, Philippine Islands, Canal Zone, Virgin Islands of the U. S., Guam, Tutuila and Manua and other islands of the Samoan group belonging to the U. S., U. S. Naval vessels, parcels addressed to foreign countries, parcels mailed by the Am. Red Cross, to be exclusively in connection with their work for the benefit of U. S., and parcels sent by officers or employes of the U. S., or of any State, Territory, or the District of Columbia in the discharge of Govermental functions.

U. S. Forces in Europe.

Domestic rates and conditions apply, except that the limit of weight on parcels post packages is 25 lbs. Rate of postage, 12c. a lb. or fraction.

FOREIGN RATES.

Mail matter addressed to countries in the Universal Postal Union is subject to the following rates: Letters and sealed packages, 5c. for 1 oz. or fraction thereof and 3c. for each additional oz. or fraction thereof, if prepaid, and double that rate if not prepaid, except England, Ireland, Scotland, Wales, Bahamas, Barbados, British Guiana, British Honduras, Canada, Cuba, Dominican Republic, Dutch West Indies, Leeward Islands (Antigua with Barbuda and Redonda, St. Kitts or St. Christopher, Nevis, with Anguilla, Dominica, Montserrat, and the Virgin Islands, British), Mexico, Newfoundland, New Zealand, Republic of Panama, Trinidad, including Tobago, and the Windward Islands (Grenada, St. Vincent, The Grenadines and St. Lucia), which is 2c. per oz.

Postal and private mail cards, 2c. each.

Printed matter of every kind, commercial papers, samples of merchandise, 1c. each 2 ozs. or fraction thereof, but at least 5c. must be paid on each packet of commercial papers and 2c. on each packet of samples of merchandise.

Exceptions for Cuba, Mexico, Canada and Republic of Panama.

Matter mailed in the United States addressed to Cuba, Mexico, Canada and Republic of Panama is subject to the following rates and conditions:

Letters, 2c. for each oz. or fraction of an oz. Postal cards and post cards, 1c. Double postal cards (with paid reply), 2c. Second-class matter (newspapers and periodicals), 1c. for each 4 ozs. or fraction thereof. No limit of weight. Printed matter (except second class): 1c. for each 2 ozs. or fraction thereof. Limit of weight 4 lbs. 6 ozs., except for single volumes of printed books, and except single volumes of printed books not exceeding 10 lbs. in weight for Canada. Packages of miscellaneous printed matter and packages of books weighing over 4 lbs., but not over 4 lbs. 6 ozs., may also be sent as fourth-class matter at the rate of 12c. a lb. Canada and Cuba, 4 lbs. 6 oz. Mdse. for Mexico and to Panama up to 50 lbs. may also be sent in Int'n'l Parcel Post mail up to 20 lbs.

Articles of every kind that are admitted to the domestic mails of the U. S. may be sent by mail for delivery in the City of Shanghai, China, at the postage rates and under the conditions which apply to similar articles addressed for delivery in the U. S.

Articles mailed in the U. S. addressed to the officers and men of the U. S. Navy in the U. S. Naval Hospital at Yokohama, Japan, will be subject to the same conditions and rates of postage as articles mailed in the U. S. addressed to officers and men on U. S. Naval vessels.

Fourth-class matter (domestic parcel post; see also Circular 111) not exceeding 4 ozs. in weight (except seeds, plants, etc.), is subject to the rate of 1c. for each oz. or fraction of an oz., and when exceeding 4 ozs. in weight is subject to the rate of 12c. a lb. or fraction thereof. Packages of seeds, plants, etc., not exceeding 8 ozs. in weight are subject to the rate of 1c. for each 2 ozs. or fraction of 2 ozs., and when exceeding 8 ozs. are subject to the rate of 12c. a lb. or fraction thereof. Limit of weight 4 lbs. 6 ozs., except for a single book.

Commercial papers, samples, printed books and miscellaneous printed matter may be mailed at the Postal Union postage rates and under the conditions applicable to such articles in foreign mails. Any foreign mailable matter, except parcel post mail for certain foreign countries, may be registered, but cannot be sent as insured mail. Sealed articles, other than letters in their usual and ordinary form, are unmailable. But unsealed packages may contain sealed articles which cannot be safely transmitted.

The following articles are absolutely excluded from the mails to the above countries: All packages closed against inspection and not in usual form of a letter; publications which violate any copyright law of Canada, Cuba, Mexico or Republic of Panama. Liquids and fatty substances (except samples) are unmailable to Cuba and Republic of Panama.

Customs declarations must be attached to all parcels of fourth-class matter and all packages sent by foreign parcel post to Cuba, Mexico and Republic of Panama. The customs regulations of Cuba also require a consular invoice with each parcel of merchandise representing a value of $5 or more. Parcels up to 50 lbs. in weight may be

POSTAL REGULATIONS—*Foreign Rates—Continued.*

sent by foreign parcel post under the conditions of the parcel post convention with Panama. Parcels may also be sent by foreign parcel post under the conditions of the parcel post convention with Mexico. The limit of weight is 20 lbs. Matter addressed to Mexico must, in all cases, bear as part of the address the name of the State in which the city or town is located. For example, Acapulco, Guerrero, Mexico; not Acapulco, Mexico.

Rates and conditions in regard to mails to foreign countries not in the Universal Postal Union are the same as to those in it, with the following exceptions. Domestic rates and conditions apply to mail matter addressed to officers or members of the crews of vessels of war of the United States and the U. S. Naval Hospital, Yokohama, to matter sent to the United States Postal Agency at Shanghai, China, and, in the main (see exceptions) to that sent to Canada, Cuba, Mexico and the Republic of Panama. The domestic rate applies also to letters, but not to other articles, addressed to England, Ireland, Scotland, Wales, Bahamas, Barbados, British Guiana, British Honduras, Canada, Cuba, Dominican Republic, Dutch West Indies, Leeward Islands (Antigua with Barbuda and Redonda, St. Kitts or St. Christopher, Nevis with Anguilla, Dominica, Montserrat and the Virgin Islands, British), Mexico, Newfoundland, New Zealand, Republic of Panama, Trinidad, including Tobago, and the Windward Islands (Grenada, St. Vincent, The Grenadines and St. Lucia).

Foreign Parcels Post.

Dimensions—Greatest length, 3½ ft. greatest length and girth combined, 6 ft.; greatest weight, 11 lbs.; except to Colombia, to which the greatest length is limited to 2 ft., with the greatest girth at 4 ft., and except Argentina, to which round (spherical) packages must not exceed 19 inches in diameter. Long (cylindrical) packages must not exceed 8 inches in diameter and 4 ft. 11 inches in length.

Parcels Post Countries.

The foreign parcels post service has been extended to practically every country of the world. Parcels may be sent direct to some countries, while to others they are sent through either England or France and are subject to a transit charge. For list of countries requiring a transit charge see pages 158 and 159 of the annual Postal Guide for 1920, which may be examined at any U. S. P. O.

Parcels may be addressed to the following countries in excess of the regular 11-pound weight limit: Ecuador, Mexico and Salvador, 20 pounds; Argentina, Brazil, Bulgaria, Colombia, Costa Rica, Curacao, Dominican Republic, Guatemala, Haiti, British Honduras, Republic of Honduras, Lithuania, Nicaragua, Paraguay, Peru and Roumania, 22 pounds, and to Panama, 50 pounds.

Money Order Fees.

Fees for money orders payable in the United States (which includes Hawaii, Porto Rico and Virgin Islands, U. S.) and its possessions comprising the Canal Zone (Isthmus of Panama), Guam, the Philippines, and Tutuila, Samoa; also for orders payable in Bahamas, Bermuda, British Guiana, British Honduras, Canada, Cuba, Martinique, Newfoundland, at the United States postal agency at Shanghai, China, and in certain islands in the West Indies: Not exceeding $2.50, 3c.; over $2.50 to $5, 5c.; over $5 to $10, 8c.; over $10 to $20, 10c.; over $20 to $30, 12c.; over $30 to $40, 15c.; over $40 to $50, 18c.; over $50 to $60, 20c.; over $60 to $75, 25c.; over $75 to $100, 30c.

Fees for International Money Orders.

The following rates to all foreign countries are in effect:

For orders from 1c. to $10, 10c.; $10.01 to $20, 20c.; $20.01 to $30, 30c.; $30.01 to $40, 40c.; $40.01 to $50, 50c.; $50.01 to $60, 60c.; $60.01 to $70, 70c.; $70.01, to $80, 80c.; $80.01 to $90, 90c.; $90.01 to $100, $1.

Registered Mail.

Domestic—Any mailable article, except unsealed 4th class matter (parcel post), may be registered at any post office in the United States. Parcels containing 4th class matter may also be registered if sealed and the usual fee and postage at the 1st class rate are paid. The fee on registered matter domestic or foreign, is 10c. for each letter or parcel, to be affixed in stamps, in addition to the postage. Limit of weight, 1st class, is same as 4th class. Parcel post, 50 and 70 lbs. Limit of weight, 2d class, none. Limit of weight, 3d class, 4 lbs.

The postal authorities give an indemnity for lost or rifled domestic first-class registered matter up to $50, and for lost 3d class domestic registered matter to the extent of $25, or the actual value of the lost article, when it is less than $25.

Foreign—Any article of mail matter, except parcels post packages for certain foreign countries may be registered, provided that when presented for registration the postage thereon is fully prepaid by postage stamps affixed, also the registration fee, which is uniformly 10c. Indemnity on account of loss of foreign registered mail, except parcel post, not to exceed 50 francs, provided the loss is not due to circumstances beyond control, such as acts of war, earthquakes and tempest.

Special Delivery System.

A special 10c. stamp, when attached to a letter or package, or ordinary stamps, in addition to the lawful postage, with "special delivery" marked on wrapper, will entitle such to immediate delivery within carrier limit of a free delivery office bet. hours of 7 A.M. and 11 P.M. daily, by messengers.

When ordinary stamps are used, the words "special delivery" must be placed on the envelope or wrapper, directly below but never on the stamps.

Airplane Mail Service.

Airplane mail service to Phila., Pa., and Wash., D. C., was established May 15, 1918. Later postal air service was opened to Chicago and N. Y., and between Chicago, Ill., and Cleveland Ohio. Mail carried by airplane is charged with postage at the rate of 2c. an oz. or fraction thereof. Such mail shall consist of matter of the 1st class, including sealed parcels not exceeding 30 in. in length and girth combined. Postage must be fully prepaid.

POSTAL SAVINGS BANK SYSTEM.

Information for Depositors.

The Postal Savings System is established for the purpose of providing facilities for depositing savings at interest with the security of the U. S. Government for repayment. Accounts may be opened and deposits made by any person of ten years of age or over in his or her own name, and by a married woman in her own name and free from any interference or control by her husband.

How to Open an Account.

To open an account a person must fill out and sign an application. Deposits will be received in the form of either Postal Savings Cards properly completed to the amount of $1, or cash not to exceed $2,500 for any one account. Deposits are evidenced by postal savings certificates issued in fixed denominations of $1, $2, $5, $10, $20, $50, $100, $200 and $500, each bearing the name of the depositor, the number of his account, the date of issue, the name of the depository office and the date on which interest begins. No account may be opened for less than $1.

Savings Cards and Stamps.

Postal Savings Cards and Postal Savings Stamps, valued at 10c. each, are sold at the retail stamp windows of the General Post Office and at all stations.

Amounts less than $1 may be saved for deposit by the purchase of 10c. postal savings cards and 10c. postal savings stamps. Each card contains blank spaces to which savings stamps may be affixed. A postal savings card with nine 10c. savings stamps thus affixed will be accepted as a deposit of $1. Savings cards and stamps will be redeemed without the issue of savings certificates. Deposits may be made by mail.

Two Per Cent. Interest Paid.

Interest on any deposit is payable annually at the rate of 2% per annum, computed on each savings certificate separately. No interest will be paid on money which remains on deposit for a fraction of a year only. Deposits will bear interest from the first of the month next following that in which deposited. In-

POSTAL REGULATIONS—POSTAL SAVINGS BANK SYSTEM—*Continued.*

terest will continue to accrue on a savings certificate as long as it remains outstanding, certificates being valid until paid, without limitation as to time. Compound interest is not allowed on an outstanding certificate, but a depositor may withdraw interest payable and include it in a new deposit, which will bear interest at the regular rate. A depositor may at any time withdraw the whole or any part of his deposits to his or her credit with interest payable, by surrendering savings certificates, properly indorsed, for the amount desired. Deposits to, or withdrawals from, an account may be made by depositor's representative upon properly filling out forms provided for that purpose, or by mail.

BROOKLYN POST OFFICE.

Federal Bldg., Washington and Johnson.

W. C. Burton, P. M., $6,000; P. J. Cleary, Asst. P. M.; W. H. Keane, Sec.; J. F. Hallahan, Postal Cashier; J. A. T. Carrougher, Supt. of Mails; John A. Brennan, Asst. Supt. of Mails in charge of Registry Division; J. E. Collins, Cashier Money Order Division; J. F. Roarty, Examiner of Stations; Chas. D. Romeyn, Foreman; F. T. Norris, Chief Bookkeeper; J. Harry Conlin, Asst. Supt. of Mails, Inquiry Dept.; M. A. Cunningham, Asst. Supt. of Mails, in charge of Delivery.

Collections and Deliveries.

Time of collections will be found in printed form on all mail boxes.

Deliveries—3 to 4 in residential dist. bet. 7 a.m. and 5:25 p.m. 5 to 7 in business dist. bet. 7:15 a.m. and 5:30 p.m.; market dist., 6:30 a.m. to 3:45 p.m.

Carrier Stations and Superintendents.

A—661 B'way. J. C. Vielbig.
B—1266 Fulton. E. J. Rorke.
C—5009 6th av. G. L. C. Jacobson.
D—1915 Fulton. W. F. Costello.
E—2581 Atlantic av. J. L. Keresey.
Flatbush—961 Flatbush av. W. F. Morris.
G—746 Manhattan av. J. E. Bennet.
Bath Beach—1884 86th. S. V. Fonner.
Ridgewood—1600 Myrtle av. T. B. Lavens.
Blythebourne—13th av. and 55th. R. W. King.
Times Plaza—Flatbush av., L. I. R. R. Depot. G. W. Barrell.
Coney Island—Surf av., opp. W. 17th. J. J. Noonan.
Fort Hamilton—9110 5th av. T. Barrett.
Sheepshead Bay—Av. U. & E. 16th. P. F. Ralph.
P—76 Thatford av. H. Hassler.
Vanderveer—Nostrand av. and Av. H. S. P. Fisher.
S—1075 Lafayette av. J. F. Halloran.
T—155 Hamilton av. J. M. McArdle.
V—383 8th. J. A. Hamilton.
W—B'way and S. 8th. E. Thompson.
Y—Southwest cor. 47th & Gravesend av. H. Kraft.
Kensington—305 Church av. J. F. Plunkett.
New Lots—946 Glenmore av. F. W. Schuttler.
Pratt—Willoughby av. & Steuben. D. F. Carroll.
St. Johns Place—1234 St. Johns pl. J. J. Barry.
Bush Terminal—34th, bet. 2d and 3d avs. W. J. Morrison.
Upton Branch—Camp Upton, N. Y. J. J. Dowd, Clerk in Charge.
Post Office Garage—3d av. and Union. J. A. Doherty.

Money Order Business.

	Transactions.	Amount.
Domestic orders issued	$1,443,307	$16,877,262.41
Internatl. orders issued	31,171	468,817.39
Combined fees	......	114,887.08
Domestic orders paid	1,210,373	13,963,409.29
Internatl. orders paid	4,756	170,405.02
Totals for 1919	$2,692,607	$31,594,781.19

Business of Brooklyn Post Office, Fiscal Years Ending June 30.

	1919.	1920.
Total receipts	$5,224,728.04	$5,647,044.98
Total expenditures	3,689,867.74	4,212,642.70
Net revenues	$1,534,860.30	$1,254,402.28

Registry Statistics.

	1919.	1920.
Domestic letters and parcels registered	666,812	715,655
Foreign letters and parcels registered	130,629	448,227
Total paid registrations	797,441	1 163,882
Official fee	135,192	132,957

Increase in paid registrations, 366,441.

	1919.	1920.
Ins. parcels mailed	1,318,122	1,732,175
C. O. D. parcels mailed	71,662	126,891

Inquiry Department.

	June 30, 1919.	June 30, 1920.
No. letters held for postage	180,271	189,818
No. supplied with stamps by sender or addressee	125,211	150,903
No. not supplied with stamps and sent to D. L. O.	55,060	38,915
Misdirected letters forwarded	79,720	83,101
Misdirected letters, D. L. O.	19,514	21,912
Misdirected letters returned	18,887	20,222
Illegible and unaddressed, D L. O.	10,328	9,313
Unmailable, sent to D. L. O.	160,016	161,716
Unclaimed letters, D. L. O.	716,201	759,161
Valuable dead, from D. L. O.	204,222	231,219
Valuable dead letters delivered	189,991	219,828
Valuable dead letters returned	14,231	11,391
Packages received misdirected	35,044	36,112
Packages held for postage	7,530	8,104
Packages sent to D. L. O.	421	512
Packages returned to sender	12,820	14,435
Packages (contrary to reg. of Postal Union) sent to D. L. O.	1,121	1,817
Packages forwarded	4,127	4,982
Unclaimed packages, D. L. O.	1,916	2,121

Brooklyn Postal Savings Bank Transactions.

July 1, 1919, to July 1, 1920.

	New accounts.	No. deposits.	Gross amount.
1919.			
July	2,812	18,485	$1,214,560
August	2,719	20,272	1,250,608
September	2,585	18,876	1,178,087
October	2,319	16,822	1,035,011
November	2,225	17,413	1,091,955
December	2,279	18,547	1,211,065
1920.			
January	2,882	20,575	1,245,872
February	2,105	17,865	1,081,099
March	2,335	19,517	1,298,281
April	2,275	18,592	1,276,204
May	2,369	18,914	1,306,315
June	2,347	18,331	1,298,033
Totals	29,252	223,709	$14,482,035

NEW YORK POST OFFICE.

Office of the Postmaster, General Post Office, 8th av., 31st to 33d.

T. G. Patten, Postmaster; T. F. Murphy, Asst. P. M.; E. M. Norris, Supt. of Mails; Charles Lubin, Supt. of Delivery; E. S. Post, Supt. of Registry; W. S. Mayer, Auditor. Postal receipts for the calendar year, 1920, $46,387,483.03.

Collections and Deliveries.

Time of collections indicated on all boxes.

Deliveries at Gen. P. O.—7:45, 9:30, 10:45 A.M., 12:00 M., 2:00, 3:50 P.M. Market section, 6:30 A.M.

Carrier Stations and Superintendents.

Postal Savings Bank at General P. O. and all stations except Pelham, Pelham Manor, Morris Heights and City Island.

A—N. E. cor. Prince and Greene; J. A. McNamee. B—45 Suffolk; C. E. Callan. C—13th and 9th av.; W. F. Taylor. CITY HALL—B'way and Park Row; J. J. McCrum. CITY ISLAND—S. W. cor. City Island av. and Bay; J. W. Miller. COLLEGE STATION—305-307 W. 140th, nr. 8th av.; D. F. McAnanly. D—4th av., S. W. cor. 13th; F. Rothmann. F—149-155 E. 34th; R. P. Geoghegan. FORDHAM STATION—2519 Webster av.; J. J. McCann. FOREIGN STATION—Morton, cor. West; T. C. Walter. FOX ST. STATION—West side Fox, bet. 167th and 169th; J. Cronin. G—217-225 W. 51st; T. A. Gallagher. GRAND CENTRAL—110 E. 45th; J. J. Kiely. H—178-180 W. 102d; J. P. Daly, Jr. HAMILTON GRANGE—W. 146th, bet. B'way and Amsterdam av.; W. Harris. HIGH BRIDGE—W. 165th, bet. Lind and Summit avs.; W. F. Delanoy. HUDSON TERMINAL STATION—Cortlandt St. Bldg.; T. P. Owens. I—232-234 W. 116th, bet. 7th and 8th avs.; J. P. Quigley. J—309-311 W. 125th, bet. 8th and St. Nicholas avs.; J. J. McKelvey. K—202-204 E. 88th; P. G. Ottendorfer. KINGSBRIDGE—5233 B'way, bet. 226th and 227th; P. J. Herrlich. L—147 E. 125th; J. H. Welch. M—2088

POSTAL REGULATIONS—New York Post Office—*Continued.*

Amsterdam av. MADISON SQ.—310 4th av., bet. 23d and 24th; R. Morrisey. MORRIS HEIGHTS—W. 177th, nr. Cedar av.; F. A. Textor. N—B'way, cor. 69th; Jos. Grainsky. O—112-116 W. 18th; J. P. Morr's. P—Custom House; E. V. Smith. PELHAM BRANCH—Pelham, N. Y., 5th av., bet. 2d and 3d; Seth T. Lyman. PELHAM MANOR BRANCH—Pelham Manor, N. Y.; F. Bergman. R—436 Westchester av.; J. M. Moran. S—Lafayette, cor. Howard; J. Cordell. T—507-509 E. 165th; L. J. Mulvihill. TIMES SQ. STATION—231 W. 39th; J. Willon. TOMPKINS SQ. STATION—12th and Av. B; W. L. Baldwin. TREMONT—1931 Washington av., bet. 177th and 178th; A. Frank. U—3d av. and 103d; J. F. Emmerich. V—N. W. cor. W. B'way and Beach; J. S. Conmy. W—160-162 W. 83d; F. Miller. WALL ST. STATION—165-169 Pearl, cor. Pine and Pearl; E. E. Doherty. WASHINGTON BRIDGE—Amsterdam av., nr. 186th; W. J. Donovan. WESTCHESTER—1471 Winsbrige rd.; P. M. Cassidy. WEST FARMS—1054 Tremont av.; F. J. Buhrendorf. WILLIAMSBRIDGE—White Plains av., nr. Gun Hill rd.; John Knewitz. X—373-375 E. 138th. Y—1160-1162 3d av.; J. C. Tobin.

Mails Between P. O. Stations.

Mail matter deposited at a P. O. station, for delivery in district of another station, is dispatched direct to the latter. Dispatches from 6 to 49 times week days, 1 to 35 times Su. There are 184 numbered sta. in Mhtn. and Bronx.

QUEENS COUNTY POST OFFICES.

Long Island City Post Office.
51 Jackson Av.

Postmaster, J. W. Kelly, Oct. 8, '14 $3,600; Asst. Postmaster, J. B. Keegan, $2,000; Supt. Mails, M. Reidy; Supt. Postal Savings Banks, F. X. Hussey; Supt. Astoria Station, D. J. McInerny.

Collections and Deliveries.

Collections begin at 5, 7, 10:30, 11:30 A.M., 2, 3:40, 6, 8:30 P.M. Due at Post Office one hour after time of beginning. Sun., 2 p.m.

Deliveries begin at 7, 10, 11 A.M., 2, 2:30, 3:30 P.M.

STATIONS—Steinway Av.—F. Wagenstein, Supt.; 307 Steinway av. Clerks are in charge of following: 1, 3d av. and B'way; S. Boockstaber. 2, 212 3d av.; E. Steinicke. 3, 911 Steinway av.; H. G. Sims. 4, cor. Webster and Vernon avs.; F. Schluer. 5, Bridge Plaza; G. Hines. 6, 101 Greenpoint av.; A. Kulis. 7, 133 Fulton av.; C. A. Riehl. 8, 813 2d av.; J. Kopejzna. 9, 338 Flushing av.; N. Oxman. 10, 215 Crescent; W. Gardin. 11, 252 Grand av.; J. M. Bensen.

Jamaica Post Office.
Union Hall, nr. Fulton.

Postmaster, D. F. Shea, Feb. 1, '15, $3,800; Asst. Postmaster, Skidmore Pettit, Jr., $2,600.

BRANCHES—Richmond Hill—Supt., E. L. Kabus. Woodhaven—Supt., S. H. Hitchcock. Queens—Supt., J. A. Simon. Springfield Garden—Supt., N. B. Ashmead.

SUB-STATIONS—1, Ozone Park—F. E. Niblette, 4192 Jerome av. 2, Morris Park—Thos. Gilmartin, Atlantic and Church. 3, Brooklyn Hills—M. M. Loewenthal, Liberty av., Jamaica. 4, Union Course—S. H. Hill, 39 Snedeker av. 5, Hollis—C. Cerat, Fulton, nr. Palatine av. 7, Woodhaven—A. S. Chamberlain, 1240 Jamaica av. 8, Woodhaven—J. J. Hill, 1191 Jamaica av. 9, Jamaica—F. Himmelfarb, Washington and South. 10, D. S. Sher, Fulton and Homer Lee, Jamaica. 11, South Woodhaven—F. Guarino, 3955 B'way. 12, Richmond Hill—J. J. Huether, 2398 Jamaica av. 13, J. J. Schafton, Woodhaven. 14, Jamaica—B. Gertz, 376 Fulton. 15, Jamaica South—O. Winzerling, New York and Meyer avs. 16, Jamaica—Alex. Kramer, Rockaway rd. and South. 17, William Mindlin, Hillside and Flushing avs., Jamaica. 18, Queens—R. C. Schmadel, Fulton and Lynn av. 19, Kew Gardens—A. Nieman, 153 Lefferts av. 20, Richmond Hill Circle—Thos. G. Prytherch, Bergen Landing rd. 21, Woodhaven—M. L. Dayton, Jamaica av. and Forest P'kway. 22, Rosedale—I. F. Hoechle, Gildersleeve av., nr. Clifton av. 24, M. Guarino, B'way and Wicks. 25, Jamaica—A. E. King, Fulton and Queens blvd. 26, So. Morris Pk.—S. Schachter, Church and Liberty. 27, Jamaica—S. Kemp, 292 N. Y. av. Hook Creek—Chas. Humbert, H. C. Station.

Flushing Post Office.
103 Amity St.

Postmaster, A. J. Kennedy, May 6, '13 $3,600; Asst. Postmaster, Herman Notbohm, $2,000; Supt. Mails, W. H. Stevenson, $1,800; Asst., F. Boyle $1,600.

INDEPENDENT STATIONS—Bay Side, College Point, Fort Totten, Corona, Douglaston, Elmhurst, Forest Hills, Maspeth, Whitestone, Woodside.

SUB-STATIONS—1, Murray Hill. 2, Winfield Junction. 3, Corona—A. Martinez. 4, Laurel Hill—E. H. Inglis. 5, Middle Village—Mrs. H. Ballay. 6, Corona—J. Portugaloff. 7, Elmhurst—J. Linhart. 8, Maspeth. 9, B'way—Theo. Klatt. 10, Little Neck—A. B. Richert. 11, Corona—H. Weingarten. 12, Winfield—C. A. Buchbinder. 13, Middle Village—J. A. Brandle. 14, Elmhurst—N. B. Michel. 15, Elmhurst—H. Burmeister. 16, Flushing—P. Wechler.

Other Queens Post Offices.

Broad Channel, Etta Shaw, April 1, '13 Comm. †Far Rockaway, Mar. 30, '14 $3,200. Ft. Totten, G. H. Martens, May 18, '14 $1,100.

†Comprising postal stations at Hammels and Arverne.

RICHMOND COUNTY POST OFFICES.

Staten Island, Tompkinsville, F. O. Driscoll, Postmaster, Jan. 8, '17........................$3.500

Stations at Great Kills, Mariners Harbor, New Brighton, New Dorp, Port Richmond, Prince Bay, Rosebank, Stapleton, Tottenville, West New Brighton.

Richmond (vacant) $1,000

BOY SCOUTS OF AMERICA.

The organization of boys in the U. S., known as the Boy Scouts of America, was incorporated Feb. 10, 1910.

It has as its Hon. Pres., Woodrow Wilson, Pres. of the U. S. There is a Natl. Council, comprising eminent citizens from all walks of public life, and also local councils.

Early in 1911, the Bkln. Local Council was organized. Present local officers are: J. C. Cropsey, Pres.; L. D. Stapleton and F. E. Franzen, Vice-Pres.; E. C. Granberry, Treas.; Frederick Bruckbauer, Commr.; A. D. Murphy, Field Executive; A. W. Beeny, Dep. Field Executive. Borough Hdqtrs., 201 Montague.

Any boy, of any nationality, of any creed, twelve years of age or older, may become a Boy Scout if he promises to keep the Scout oath and law and prepares himself for simple tests on the composition and history of the American flag and the significance of the Scout badge and can make several cordage knots.

The number of registered Scouts under the jurisdiction of the Bkln. Council is about 7,000.

The borough is divided into districts, a Dist. Council co-ordinating the work in each dist. These districts and officers are: Bedford—Wm. Van Kleeck, Jr., Pres.; Benj. Anchell, Commr.. Bay Ridge—G. E. Hix, Pres.; Wm. Beyer, Commr. Bushwick—John Bladen, Pres.; F. O. Nowaczek, Commr. Columbia Heights—H. M. Howard, Pres.; A. T. Shorey, Commr. East N. Y.—C. B. Law, Pres.; A. F. A. Witte, Commr. Flatbush—T. I. Chatfield, Pres.; R. C. Hynds, Commr. Fort Greene—Nathan Lane, Jr., Pres.; E. H. Marsh, Commr. Prospect Heights—Herbert McCreary, Pres. Stuyvesant—L. E. Meeker, Pres.; F. J. Davis, Commr. Williamsburg—D. T. Wilson, Pres.; DeForest Jones, Commr. Sheepshead Bay—J. G. Needham, Pres.; C. E. Bingham, Commr.

WHERE TO OBTAIN PASSPORTS.

Any American citizen, or native or resident of the insular possessions who is entitled to the protection of the United States, may make application for passport in the Passport Agency, Custom House, New York City, which is the only office officially designated for this purpose in Greater New York. Outside of Greater New York applications may be made before the clerk of any United States District Court or State Court authorized by law to naturalize aliens.

STATISTICS OF THE PRINCIPAL COUNTRIES OF THE WORLD.

See also notes at end of table.

Countries.	Population.	Square Miles.	Capitals.	Gov't.	Present Head.	Acceded.
Abyssinia (Africa)	8,000,000	350,000	Adis Ababa	Desp. Mon.	Waizeru Zauditu	Feb.11,'17
Afghanistan (Asia)	6,380,500	245,000	Kabul	Abs. Mon.	Amanullah Khan	Feb.20,'19
Albania (Europe)	825,000	11,000	Durazzo	Prov. Gov	...	...
Andorra (Europe)	5,231	191	And'ra la-Vieille	Republic	Syndic	...
Argentine Republic	8,284,266	1,153,119	Buenos Ayres	Republic	Hipolito Irigoyen	Oct.12'16
Armenia (Asia)	2,159,000	26,130	Erivan	Republic	Chamber	...
Austria (Europe)	6,412,430	32,076	Vienna	Republic	Michael Mayr, Chan.	Nov. '20
Azerbaijan (Asia)	4,616,000	40,000	Baku	Republic	Natl. Council	...
Baluchistan (Asia)	834,703	134,638	Kalat	Khanate	Mir Mahmud Khan II.	Nov., '93
Belgium (Europe)	7,571,387	11,373	Brussels	Lim. Mon.	Albert I	Dec.17,'09
Congo (Africa)	15,000,000	909,654	Boma	Colony	M. Henry, Gov. Gen.	Jan.4,'16
Bhutan (Asia)	250,000	20,000	Punakha	Protect'ate	Sir Ugyen Wangchuk	——, '07
Bolivia (So. America)	2,889,970	514,155	Sucre	Republic	Prov. Govt	...
Brazil (So. America)	30,492,250	3,275,510	Rio de Janeiro	Republic	Dr. Epitacio Pessoa	Apr.13,'19
British Empire	428,165,364	13,153,712	London	Lim. Mon.	George V	May 6, '10
U. K. (Br. Isles)	46,516,250	121,633	London	Lim. Mon.	George V	May 6, '10
England	34,045,290	50,874	London	Lim. Mon.	George V	May 6, '10
Wales	2,025,202	7,466	Carnarvon	Lim. Mon.	George V	May 6, '10
Scotland	4,700,904	30,405	Edinburgh	Lim. Mon.	George V	May 6, '10
Ireland	4,390,219	32,586	Dublin	Lim. Mon.	George V	May 6, '10
Malta (Europe)	228,534	118	Valetta	Colony	Lord Plumer	——, '19
Gibraltar (Europe)	25,367	2	Gibraltar	Colony	Sir H. L. Smith-Dorrien	June 22,'19
Indian Emp. (Asia)	315,156,396	1,802,386	Delhi	Imp'r'lism	Lord Chelmsford, V'y	Mar., '16
Aden (Asia)	46,165	220	Aden	Colony	Sir W. S. Delamain	...
Bahrein Isls. (Asia)	110,000	35	Manama	Protect'ate	Sheikh Isa	——, 1869
Brunei (Asia)	30,000	4,000	Brunei	Protect'ate	Moh'ed Jemaeulalam	May 11,'06
Ceylon (Asia)	4,110,367	25,332	Colombo	Colony	Sir Wm. H. Manning	Apr.30,'18
Cyprus (Asia)	274,108	3,584	Nicosia	Colony	M. Stevenson, Sec	...
Hong Kong (Asia)	529,000	391	Victoria	Cr'n Colony	Sir R E Stubbs	——, '19
Malay States (Asia)	800,000	43,106	Kuala Lumpur	Federation	Sir L. N. Guillemard	——, '19
North Borneo (Asia)	208,183	31,106	Sandakan	Territory	A. C. Pearson	——, '15
Sarawak (Asia)	600,000	42,000	Kuching	Sover'gnty	Raja Brooke	May,'17
Sikkim (Asia)	87,920	2,818	Gangtok	Protect'ate	H. H. Tashi Namgyal	Dec.5,'14
Straits Settlements	795,214	1,600	Singapore	Colony	Sir L. N. Guillemard	——, 19
Weihaiwei (Asia)	147,177	285	Weihaiwei	Territory	Sir J. H. S. Lockhart, C'r	——, '02
Union of S. Africa	5,973,394	473,100	CapeTn., Pretoria	Self-Gov. Col	Pr. Arthur of Con'ght.	June,'20
Ascension (Africa)	196	34	Georgetown	Colony	Maj. H. G. Grant	——, 19
Basutoland (Africa)	404,507	11,716	Maseru	Territory	E. C. F. Garraway, Com'	...
Bechuanaland (Afr.)	125,350	275,000	Mafeking	Protect'ate	J. C. MacGregor, Com'r.	...
East Africa or Kenya	4,038,000	246,822	Nairobi	Protect'ate	Sir E. Northey	——, '14
Egypt (Africa)	11,287,359	363,181	Cairo	Protect'ate	Ahmed Fuad Pasha, Sul	Oct.9,'17
Gambia (Africa)	138,401	4,500	Bathurst	Protect'ate	Sir E. J. Cameron	Feb.,'14
Gold Coast (Africa)	1,503,386	80,000	Accra	Colony	Gen. F. G. Guggisberg	——, '19
Mauritius (Africa)	377,083	720	Port Louis	Colony	Sir H. H. Bell	——, '16
Nigeria (Africa)	16,500,000	336,000	Lagos	Colony & Prot	Sir Hugh Clifford	——, '14
Nyassaland (Africa)	1,138,736	39,573	Blantyre	Protect'ate	Sir Geo. Smith	...
Rhodesia (Africa)	1,750,000	450,000	Salisbury	Territory	Br. S. Africa Company	Oct.29,'89
St. Helena (Africa)	3,604	47	Jamestown	Colony	Maj. H. E. S. Cordeaux	——, '12
Seychelles (Africa)	24,691	156	Victoria	Colony	Sir E. Fiennes, Bart.	——, '03
Sierra Leone (Afr.)	1,403,132	31,000	Freetown	Protect'ate	R. J. Wilkinson	——, '16
Somaliland (Africa)	310,000	68,000	Berbera	Protect'ate	G. F. Archer	May,'14
Sudan (Africa)	3,380,531	984,520	Khartoum	Protect'ate	Gen. L. O. F. Stack	...
Swaziland (Africa)	99,959	6,536	Mbabane	Protect'ate	D. Honey (Res. Com'r)	...
Uganda (Africa)	2,887,800	109,119	Kampala	Protect'ate	Sir R. T. Corydon	——, '11
Zanzibar (Africa)	197,199	1,020	Zanzibar	Protect'ate	Sir E. Northey	...
Canada (N. Amer.)	8,361,000	3,729,665	Ottawa	Dominion	Duke of Devonshire	Aug.19,'16
Labrador (N. Am.)	4,016	120,000	St. Johns	Depend'cy	Sir C. A. Harris	Oct.,'17
Newfoundland (N.A.)	250,707	42,734	St. Johns	Colony	Sir C. A. Harris	Oct.,'17
Br. Honduras (Am.)	42,333	8,598	Belize	Cr'n Colony	E. Hutson	...
West Indies (Am.)	1,733,900	12,550	...	Colonies	...	...
Br. Guiana (S. Am.)	313,859	89,480	Georgetown	Colony	Sir W. Collet	...
Falkland Is. (S. A.)	3,275	6,500	Port Stanley	Colony	Sir W. D. Young	——, '15
Australia (Oceania)	4,455,005	2,974,581	Canberra	Com'w'lth	Lord Foster	June16,'20
New Zealand (Oc'ia)	1,099,295	103,861	Wellington	Dominion	Viscount Jellicoe	Apr.,'20
Fiji (Oceania)	139,541	7,083	Suva	Colony	Sir C. H. Rodwell	Oct.,'15
Papua (Oceania)	234,768	272,000	Port Moresby	Territory	J. H. P. Murray	...
Pacific Is. (Oceania)	203,068	15,459	...	Colonies	...	...
Bulgaria (Europe)	5,517,700	47,750	Sofia	Cont. Mon.	Boris III	Oct.,'18
Chile (S. America)	4,500,000	289,829	Santiago	Republic	A. Alessandri	Dec.,'20
China (Asia)	342,639,000	4,278,352	Peking	Republic	Hsu Shi Chang	Oct.10,'13
China Proper	316,271,000	1,532,800	Peking	Provinces	Hsu Shi Chang	Oct.10,'13
Manchuria (Asia)	14,917,000	363,700	Mukden	Territory	Hsu Shi Chang	Oct.10,'13
Mongolia (Asia)	2,600,000	1,367,953	Urga	Territory	Jeb'tsun D'a Hutuktu	...
Tibet (Asia)	6,500,000	463,200	Lhasa	Territory	Dalai Lama	...
E. Turkestan (Asia)	2,491,000	550,579	Urmchi	Province	...	...
Colombia (S. America)	6,000,000	440,846	Bogota	Republic	Marco Fidel Suarez	Aug.7,'18
Costa Rica (C. Am.)	441,342	23,000	San Jose	Republic	Frederico T. Grandos	Apr.11,'17
Cuba (West Indies)	2,888,095	45,881	Havana	Republic	M. G. Menocal	May 20,'13
Czechoslovakia	13,811,655	58,048	Prague	Republic	T. G. Masaryk	May 27,'20
Danzig (Europe)	200,000	579	Danzig	Free City	High Commr	...
Denmark (Europe)	3,107,582	17,922	Copenhagen	Lim. Mon.	Christian X	May 14,'12
Iceland (N. Atlantic)	85,188	39,756	Reykjavik	Dependency	Christian X	May 14,'12
Greenland (N. Amer.)	13,517	46,740	Sydproven	Lim. Mon.	Christian X	May 14,'12
Ecuador (S. America)	2,000,000	116,000	Quito	Republic	Dr. J. L. Tamayo	Sept.1,'20
Esthonia (Europe)	1,750,000	23,160	Reval	Republic	Constituent Assembly	...
Finland	3,000,650	125,689	Helsingfors	Rep.	Prof. Stahlberg	Aug.,'19
France (Europe)	39,601,509	207,054	Paris	Republic	Alexandre Millerand	Sept.23,'20
Alsace-Lorraine	1,874,014	5,605	Strassburg	Territory	...	...
Fr. India (Asia)	268,499	196	Pondicherry	Colony	M. A. Duprat	...
Indo China (Asia)	16,990,229	256,000	Saigon	Protect'ate	A. Sarrault	...
Algeria (Africa)	5,563,828	343,500	Algiers	Colony	M. Jonnart	Jan.29,'13
Morocco (Africa)	6,000,000	231,500	Fez	Protect'ate	Mulai Yussef	Aug.18,'12

STATISTICS OF THE PRINCIPAL COUNTRIES OF THE WORLD—*Continued.*

Countries.	Population.	Square Miles.	Capitals.	Gov't.	Present Head.	Acceded.
France—Continued.						
Tunis (Africa)	1,780,527	50,000	Tunis	Protect'ate	E. Flandin	Oct.,'18
Sahara (Africa)	800,000	1,544,000	Timbuktu	Territory	M. Van Vollenhoven	
W. Africa (Africa)	12,061,315	1,745,000	Dakar	Colonies	M. Angoulvant	Jan.22,'13
Equat. Africa	9,000,000	669,000	Brazzeville	Colonies		
Madagascar (Africa)	3,545,264	228,000	Antananarivo	Colony	M. Schramek	Jan.'13
Reunion (Africa)	173,822	970	St. Denis	Colonies	M. J. T. Piat, B.C.	
African Isls. (Afr.)	......	2,191		Colony	M. Schramek	Jan.,'18
Fr. Somaliland	206,000	5,790	Djibonti	Colony		
St. Pierre (W.Indies)	4,652	93	St. Pierre	Colonies	P.J.F.Staniforth,B.C.	
Martinique (W. Ind.)	194,000	385	Fort de France	Colony	H. J. Meagher, B.C.	
Guadaloupe (W.In.)	212,430	722	Pointe-a-Pitre	Colony	J. E. Devaux, B.C.	
Fr. Guiana (S. Am.)	49,009	32,000	Cayenne	Colony		
New Caled'a (Oc'a)	50,608	7,650	Noumea	Colony	H. C. Venables, B.C.	
Society Isls. (Oc'a)	31,477	1,520	Papeete	Colonies	A. Richards, B.C.	
Georgia (Asia)	3,176,000	80,706	Tiflis	Republic	Cabinet	
Germany	55,086,000	171,910	Berlin	Republic	F. Ebert	Feb.11,'19
Prussia	40,165,219	134,650	Berlin			
Bavaria	6,887,291	30,346	Munich			
Saxony	4,806,661	5,787	Dresden			
Wurtemburg	2,437,574	7,534	Stuttgart			
Baden	2,142,833	5,823	Karlsruhe			
Hesse	1,282,051	2,968	Darmstadt			
Meck'b'g Schwerin	639,958	5,068	Schwerin			
Meck'b'g Strelitz	106,442	1,131	Neu Strelitz			
Oldenburg	483,042	2,482	Oldenburg			
Saxony	......	5,787	Dresden			
Anhalt	331,128	888	Dessau			
Brunswick	494,339	1,424	Brunswick			
Saxe-Altenburg	216,128	511	Altenburg			
Saxe-Cob'g-Gotha	257,177	762	Coburg, Gotha			
Saxe-Meiningen	278,762	953	Meiningen			
Lippe	150,937	469	Detmold			
Reuss (Elder B'h)	72,769	122	Greiz			
Reuss (Y'ger B'h)	152,752	319	Gera			
Schaumb'g-Lippe	46,652	131	Buckeburg			
Schw'zb'rg-Rud't	100,702	363	Rudolstadt			
Schw'zb'rg-Sond'n	89,917	333	Sonderhausen			
Waldeck	61,707	433	Arolsen			
Bremen	295,715	99	Bremen			
Hamburg	1,014,664	160	Hamburg			
Lubeck	116,599	115	Lubeck			
Greece (Europe)	8,000,000	60,000	Athens	Lim. Mon	Constantine	Dec.,'20
Crete (Europe)	353,000	3,365	Canea	Occupation	Constantine	Dec.,'20
Islands (Europe)	229,000	1,160		Occupation	Constantine	Dec.,'20
Guatemala (C. Amer.)	2,200,000	48,290	Guatemala	Republic	Carlos Herrera	Sept.15,'20
Haiti (West Indies)	2,500,000	10,204	Port-au-Prince	Republic	Sudre Dartiguenave	Aug.12,'15
Hedjaz (Asia)	750,000	100,000	Jidda	Kingdom	Husein Ibor Ali	Nov.,'16
Honduras (C. Amer.)	926,000	44,275	Tegucigalpa	Republic	Rafael L. Gutierrez	Feb.1,'20
Hungary (Europe)			Budapest	Republic	Adm. von Horthy	Mar.1,'20
Italy (Europe)	36,740,000	110,632	Rome	Con. Mon	V. Emanuele III	July 29,'00
Eritrea (Africa)	450,000	45,800	Asmara	Colony	N. G. de Martino	—, '16
Somaliland (Africa)	400,000	139,430	Mogadicho	Colony	Cerrina Ferroni	—, '18
Tripoli (Africa)	529,176	406,000	Tripoli	Colony	Gen. V. Garioni	—, '18
Tientsin Conc. (Asia)	17,000	20		Concession		
Japan (Asia)	78,261,856	260,738	Tokio	Con. Mon	Emperor Yoshihito	July 30,'12
Korea (Chosen)	17,412,871	84,738	Seoul	Dependency	Adm. Saito, Gov. Gen.	Aug.12,'19
Formosa (Taiwan)	3,698,918	13,991	Taihoku	Depend'cy	Baron K. Den, Gov. G.	Oct.29,'19
Sakhalin (Karaguto)	36,100	13,253	Toyohara	Territory	K. Nagai, Gov	—, '19
Kwantung (Asia)	515,147	1,256	Ryojun	Concession	Governor Gen.	
Jugo-Slavia (See Serbs, Croats and Slovenes, Kingdom of)						
Latvia (Europe)	2,500,000	24,400	Riga	Republic	Constituent Assembly	
Liberia (Africa)	2,100,000	40,000	Monrovia	Republic	Hon. C. D. B. King	Jan.1,'20
Liechtenstein (Eur.)	10,716	65	Vadus	Con. Mon	John II	Nov.12,'58
Lithuania (Europe)	4,651,000	36,532	Vilna	Republic	A. Sonetona	Apr.4,'19
Luxemburg (Europe)	259,891	998	Luxemburg	Con. Mon	G'd Duchess Charlotte	Jan.9,'19
Mesopotamia (Asia)	2,849,000	143,250	Baghdad	Br. Mand'y		
Mexico (N. America)	15,501,684	767,190	Mexico	Republic	Alvaro Obregon	Dec.1,'20
Monaco (Europe)	22,956	8	Monaco	Princip'ty	Albert I	Sept.10,'89
Montenegro (Europe)	436,789	5,880	Cettinje	Lim. Mon	Nicholas I	Aug.14,'60
Morocco (Africa)	6,000,000	2,315,000	Fez	Abs. Desp	Mulai Yusef	Aug.18,'12
Nepal (Asia)	5,600,000	54,000	Katmandu	Mil. Olig'hy	Trib'bana Bir Bikram	Dec.11,'11
Netherlands (Europe)	6,778,699	13,196	Amsterdam	Lim. Mon	Wilhelmina Queen	Nov.23,'90
Java and Madura	34,157,383	50,557	Batavia	Colony	D. Fock	Feb.21,'21
Sumatra (Malaysia)	5,027,073	159,739	Padang	Colony	D. Fock	Feb.21,'21
Borneo (Malaysia)	1,544,503	212,737	Pontianak	Colony	D. Fock	Feb.21,'21
Other E. Indies	6,271,041	312,096		Colony		
Surinam (W. Indies)	107,827	46,060	Paramaribo	Colony	G. J. Staal	
Curacao (W. Indies)	57,195	403	Willemstad	Colony		
Nicaragua (C. Am.)	746,000	49,200	Managua	Republic	Diego M. Chamorro	Jan.1,'21
Norway (Europe)	2,632,010	125,001	Christiania	Lim. Mon	Haakon VII	Nov.18,'05
Oman (Asia)	500,000	82,000	Muskat	Abs. Mon	Seyyid T'mar bin Feysil	Oct.5,'13
Palestine (Asia)	675,000	13,724	Jerusalem	Br. Mand'y	Sir H. Samuel	June,'20
Panama (C. Amer.)	450,000	32,380	Panama	Republic	Dr. Belisario Porra	Oct.1,'20
Paraguay (S. Amer.)	1,050,000	196,000	Asuncion	Republic	Dr. Manuel Gondra	Aug.15,'20
Persia (Asia)	9,500,000	628,000	Teheran	Lim. Mon	Ahmad Shah	July 16,'09
Peru (S. America)	4,620,201	722,461	Lima	Republic	A. B. Lequia	Sept.24,'19
Poland (Europe)	27,906,340	146,506	Warsaw	Republic	Jos. Pilsudski	Nov.3,'20
Portugal (Europe)	5,957,985	35,490	Lisbon	Republic	Antonio Almeida	Aug.6,'19
Port India (Asia)	548,472	1,638	Panjin	Colony		
Macao (Asia)	74,866	4	Macao	Colony	Col. Miranda	
Timer (Malaysia)	377,815	7,330	Dilly	Colony	F. da Camara	
Cape Verde Is. (Af.)	149,793	1,480	Praia	Colony		
Port. Guinea (Afr.)	289,000	13,940	Bolama	Colony	Dr. Sequeira	
S. Thome & Prin'pe	58,907	360	Sao Thome	Colony	Dr. Machada	

STATISTICS OF THE PRINCIPAL COUNTRIES OF THE WORLD—*Continued.*

Countries.	Population.	Square Miles.	Capitals.	Gov't.	Present Head.	Acceded.
Portugal (Cont.).						
Angola (Africa)	2,124,361	484,800	S. Paulo de L'da	Colony	Maj. do Mallos	...
Mozambique (Afr.)	3,000,000	428,132	LourencoMarq'es	Colony	Governor Gen.	...
Rumania (Europe)	16,500,000	120,000	Bucharest	Con. Mon	Ferdinand I	Oct.11,'14
Russia	...	...	Moscow	Soviet	...	...
European Russia	...	...	Moscow	Soviet	...	...
Caucasia (Europe)	...	...	Tiflis	Province	...	...
Cent. Asia	...	...	Tashkend	Province	...	...
Siberia (Asia)	...	...	Irkutsk	Province	...	...
Khiva (Asia)	646,000	24,000	Khiva	Vassalage	Sayid-Asfendiar-Khan	——,'10
Bokhara (Asia)	1,250,000	83,000	Bokhara	Depend'cy	Sayid-Mir-Alim Khan	Jan.6,'11
Salvador (C. Amer.)	1,336,000	13,176	San Salvador	Republic	Jorge Melendez	Mar.1,'19
San Marino (Europe)	11,648	38	San Marino	Republic	Captains Regent	...
Santo Dom'go(W.Ind.)	955,159	19,332	Santo Domingo	Republic	F. Henriquez Carvajal	July 25,'16
Serbs, Croats, Slovenes	14,000,000	100,000	Belgrade	Con. Mon	Peter I	June 2,'03
Siam (Asia)	10,000,000	195,000	Bangkok	Abs. Mon	Rama VI	Oct.23,'10
Spain (Europe)	19,950,817	190,050	Madrid	Lim. Mon	Alphonso XIII	May 17,'86
Canary Isls. (Africa)	506,414	3,342	Las Palmas	Province	Alphonso XIII	May 17,'86
Cadiz and Centa	476,047	2,834	Cadiz	Province	Alphonso XIII	May 17,'86
Fernando Po (Afr.)	23,844	814	Santa Isabel	Colony	Governor General	...
Rio de Oro (Afr.)	...	109,200	...	Colony	Governor General	...
Sp. Guinea (Afr.)	200,000	9,470	...	Colony	Governor General	...
Presidios, etc.	60,000	100	Melilla	Colonies	Governor	...
Sweden (Europe)	5,813,850	173,035	Stockholm	Lim. Mon	Gustav V	Dec.8,'07
Switzerland (Europe)	3,937,000	15,976	Berne	Republic	Edmond Schulthess	Jan.1,'21
Syria (Asia)	3,133,500	106,740	Damascus	Fr. Mand'y	...	...
Turkey(OttomanEmp.)	12,077,900	210,154	Constantinople	Con. Mon	Mohammed VI	July 3,'18
European	1,891,000	10,882	Constantinople	...	Mohammed VI	July 3,'18
Asia Minor	10,186,000	199,272	...	Con. Mon	Mohammed VI	July 3,'18
Ukraine (Europe)	46,000,000	498,100	Odessa	Directory	...	...
United States (Am.)	105,708,771	2,973,774	Washington	Republic	Woodrow Wilson	Mar.4,'13
Alaska (N. Am.)	54,889	590,884	Juneau	Territory	Thomas Riggs	Ap.26,'18
Canal Zone (C.Am.)	22,858	333	Balboa	Special	Gen. C. Harding, Gov.	Jan.11,'17
Porto Rico (W.Ind.)	1,299,809	3,435	San Juan	Territory	A. Yager, Gov	Nov.20,'13
Virgin Isls. (W.In.)	26,051	132	...	Territory	Adm. J. W. Oman	Ap.18,'19
Hawaii (Oceanic)	255,912	6,449	Honolulu	Territory	C. J. McCarthy, Gov.	May 4,'18
Philippine Isls.	10,350,640	114,400	Manila & Baguio	Territory	F. B. Harrison, Gov.	Sept.2,'13
Guam (Oceania)	13,275	210	Agana	Territory	Capt. I. C. Wettengel	June 3,'20
Samoan Isls. (Oc'a)	8,056	77	Pago Pago	Naval Sta.	Capt. Waldo Evans	Nov.11,'20
Uruguay (S. Amer.)	1,429,585	72,153	Montevideo	Republic	Dr. Baltasar Brum	Mar.1,'19
Venezuela (S. Amer.)	2,844,618	398,594	Caracas	Republic	J. Vincente Gomez	May 3,'15

AUSTRIA was proclaimed a Republic on Nov. 12, 1918, and the Govt. taken over by a Natl. Assembly. According to the boundaries fixed by the Treaty of St. Germain, Sept. 10, 1919, the new Republic consists of the former Austrian provinces of Upper Austria, Lower Austria, Salzburg, North Tyrol, Styria, Carinthia, Vorarlberg and German Western Hungary.

BRITISH EMPIRE—India. As a result of administrative changes in 1912 India is now divided into 15 provinces: Madras, 14,500,000 pop.; Bombay, 19,500,000; Bengal, 45,500,000; Agra and Oudh, 47,000,000; Burma, 12,000,000; Bihar and Orissa, 34,500,000; Central Provinces and Berar, 14,000,000; Assam, 6,750,000; N. W. Frontier Province, 2,250,000; Ajmer-Merwara, 500,000; Coorg, 175,000; Baluchistan, 400,000; Delhi, 390,000; Andaman and Nicobar Islands, 26,000.

The Union of S. Africa is divided into the following provinces: Cape of Good Hope, Natal, Transvaal and Orange Free State. Pretoria is the seat of government and Cape Town is the seat of legislature.

Egypt. Negotiations relating to independence proceeding.

Canada includes nine provinces, Prince Edward Island, Nova Scotia, New Brunswick, Quebec, Ontario, Manitoba, British Columbia, Alberta and Saskatchewan, with the Northwestern Territory and Yukon Territory.

British West Indies consist of six groups, Bahamas, Barbados, Jamaica with Turks Island, Leeward Islands, Trinidad with Tobago and Windward Islands.

CZECHOSLOVAKIA came into existence Oct. 28, 1918, and includes Bohemia, Moravia, Silesia and Slovakia, hitherto belonging to the Austro-Hungarian Monarchy. The population is made up of 8,054,036 Czechoslovaks, 3,828,974 Germans, 1,071,578 Magyars, 432,929 Karpatho-Russians and 424,130 other races.

DENMARK—Parts of Northern Schleswig have been returned to Denmark in accordance with plebiscite.

FRENCH POSSESSIONS. French India is divided into five provinces: Pondicherry, Karikal, Chandernagar, Mahe, Yanaon. Indo-China consists of six States and protectorates: Cochin China, Annam, Cambodia, Tonking, Laos, Kwang Chang Wan.

The greater portion of the former German Colony of Cameroon has been placed under French administration.

GERMANY. On Nov. 9, 1918, the abdication of the German Emperor was announced and from that date Germany became a Republic. The Council of People's Commissioners in Berlin took over the Government and the reigning Kings and Princes of the Federal States were either deposed or abdicated. By the Treaty of Versailles, June 28, 1919, Germany agreed to the following territorial rearrangement: Alsace-Lorraine was ceded to France; the greater part of West Prussia and a part of Eastern Silesia were ceded to Poland; a part of Upper Silesia to Czechoslovakia; Memel to the Allies; Danzig to the Allies; Eupen and Malmedy to Belgium. Provision was made in the Treaty to settle the ultimate fate of certain areas by plebiscite via The Saar Basin after 15 years; Schleswig in two zones, one zone of which has since elected to return to Danish rule; and districts in West Prussia, Southern East Prussia and in Upper Silesia.

The former colonial possessions of Germany were placed under the administration of the Allied Nations as follows: German East Africa, British; Southwest Africa, British; Togoland, British and French; Cameroon, British and French; German New Guinea, which consists of all territories held in Germany in the Western Pacific, is under Australian, New Zealand and Japanese administrations.

GREECE. After the death of King Alexander, on Oct. 25, 1920, a plebiscite was held, which resulted in a large majority in favor of the return of King Constantine.

HUNGARY. The new State is roughly about half the size of the old kingdom. Statistical returns not available.

POLAND. The area and population of the Polish State cannot be exactly stated until its boundaries are definitely decided.

TURKEY. According to the Treaty between the Allies and Turkey the Empire ceded Thrace to Greece; Smyrna to be administered by Greece under Turkish sovereignty for five years, when a plebiscite is to be held; Mesopotamia, Palestine, Syria, Armenia and the Hedjaz became independent, the first three under mandatories; Kurdestan granted autonomy; Castellorizo and the Dodecanese ceded to Italy.

STATISTICS OF LEADING AMERICAN CITIES.

Cities.	Standing.†	Population U. S. Census, 1920.	Dept. of Health: Area Sq. Miles.	Dept. of Health: Annual Death Rate per 1,000.	Dept. of Health: Annual Birth Rate per 1,000.	Department of Finance: Assessed Property Value: Real.	Department of Finance: Assessed Property Value: Personal.	Department of Finance: Tax Rate per $1,000 of Assessed Value.	Department of Finance: Per Cent. of Real Val. to Ass'd Val.	Department of Finance: Net Public Debt.	Department of Finance: Annual Cost of Maintaining City Government.	Department of Finance: Per Capita Cost of Maintaining City Government.	Dept. of Education: Number of Pupils in Public Schools.	Dept. of Education: Number of Principals and Teachers.	Dept. of Education: Annual Cost of Maintaining Public Schools.	Fire Dept.: Regular.	Fire Dept.: Volunteer.	Fire Dept.: Average Annual Cost of Force.	Police Department: Number of Force.	Police Department: Average Annual Number of Arrests.	Police Department: Average Annual Cost of Force.
Akron, O.	**32**	**208,435**	**23.8**	**11.5**	**24.5**	***$375,000,000**	....	$20.60	75	$7,654,388	$1,400,560	$6.71	28,941	780	$1,586,208	149	...	$237,937	130	11,582	$227,807
Albany, N. Y.	60	113,344	19.10	17.01	17.63	101,116,620	$1,491,000	26.60	100	10,243,217	2,850,736	25.32	10,100	420	860,685	196	...	332,916	196	3,882	309,781
Atlanta, Ga.	33	200,616	26	15.52	17.40	160,150,429	73,000,000	16.25	70	3,709,000	5,148,772	25.66	29,000	756	915,000	235	...	534,521	282	16,481	462,680
Baltimore, Md.	8	733,826	91.3	17.06	26.32	433,621,158	402,065,020	21.30	100	41,403,523	18,809,476	32.43	96,598	2,505	4,748,455	858	...	1,312,252	1,095	50,027	1,670,981
Birmingham, Ala.	36	178,270	52.00	17.84	15.53	*125,000,000	....	15.00	60	8,350,571	2,534,444	14.21	28,250	725	526,750	220	...	363,309	128	15,715	133,549
Boston, Mass.	7	748,060	47.34	15.63	12.00	1,256,072,300	176,523,335	19.04	100	48,329,646	32,833,918	43.89	123,392	3,423	9,088,181	1,194	...	2,864,040	1,568	67,947	2,832,675
Bridgeport, Conn.	44	143,538	14.6	13.1	29.9	121,009,492	46,480,537	20.70	100	5,703,836	4,288,291	28.21	25,235	690	1,517,011	260	...	711,141	266	2,521	523,003
Buffalo, N. Y.	12	506,775	42.16	14.30	28.70	597,634,615	10,540,500	29.24	90	36,875,219	22,382,204	44.03	62,000	2,473	....	922	...	2,038,946	1,045	31,236	1,963,141
Cambridge, Mass.	63	109,694	6.5	13.14	.....	124,300,000	17,216,000	31.30	100	5,546,018	4,549,329	41.46	15,731	528	938,877	160	...	271,469	197	3,822	289,519
Camden, N. J.	58	116,309	7.25	16.40	22.37	98,558,055	15,153,085	24.50	100	4,215,802	2,414,036	20.84	19,260	562	732,746	120	...	283,500	200	4,341	260,000
Chicago, Ill.	2	2,701,705	200.00	12.52	24.4	1,174,665,872	375,696,133	53.60	33⅓	45,875,100	52,545,128	19.44	393,918	9,116	23,076,278	2,336	...	5,017,098	5,120	91,457	9,454,331
Cincinnati, O.	16	401,247	72.00	15.87	17.31	468,150,130	244,668,890	15.72	100	32,027,442	9,208,478	22.94	54,472	1,678	4,209,756	675	...	1,371,241	767	17,235	1,094,750
Cleveland, O.	5	796,836	56.64	13.4	2.4	794,461,320	594,596,970	17.75	75	70,046,122	8,702,466	12.90	122,634	3,496	9,386,267	941	...	1,451,440	1,171	23,761	1,713,762
Columbus, O.	28	237,031	22.79	14.13	18.1	*313,000,000	....	14.00	100	10,174,234	3,596,523	15.98	33,039	1,240	2,173,330	386	...	610,000	285	8,034	363,055
Dallas, Tex.	42	158,976	23.00	12.00	18.8	105,283,650	50,396,700	21.00	50	8,011,566	4,498,951	28.19	28,185	829	1,261,496	249	...	487,710	200	26,058	227,832
Dayton, O.	43	152,559	29.00	11.56	20.9	*216,164,740	....	21.00	100	6,540,000	1,700,000	11.14	22,750	631	1,075,751	173	...	315,120	175	5,062	281,000
Denver, Col.	25	256,369	59.00	13.93	13.77	225,341,200	126,727,835	23.50	100	18,011,400	3,591,206	40.00	51,314	1,414	2,231,450	235	...	380,000	273	9,642	348,000
Des Moines, Ia.	52	126,468	54.00	20.9	.....	*178,264,455	....	13.87	25	7,689,686	2,014,042	15.92	25,348	848	1,954,542	199	...	395,500	136	6,380	225,000
Detroit, Mich.	4	993,739	84.5	13.7	27.4	1,241,406,100	457,744,450	20.66	100	26,901,334	37,925,052	38.00	139,604	3,937	7,063,224	1,182	...	3,500,000	1,667	39,602	3,369,893
Duluth, Minn.	70	98,917	64.00	9.82	23.24	51,687,407	20,791,576	53.00	38	3,071,400	1,220,771	12.34	16,284	519	640,000	123	...	252,423	94	5,245	182,429
Elizabeth, N. J.	72	95,682	9.7	12.05	27.62	73,804,400	14,028,144	27.40	100	2,476,948	2,213,387	24.17	13,296	388	725,081	133	...	263,000	118	3,048	210,000
Erie, Pa.	75	93,372	8.00	12.09	27.76	*90,502,254	....	.....	100	2,859,409	1,193,206	12.77	13,140	409	1,033,926	129	...	209,320	118	3,048	210,000
Fall River, Mass.	54	120,485	41.00	13.12	28.71	69,921,600	60,823,950	26.00	100	5,361,191	7,528,427	62.48	15,897	585	823,789	174	...	240,000	184	2,962	307,320
Fort Worth, Tex.	65	106,482	24.94	16.73	12.53	58,489,675	23,746,635	18.50	75	6,190,768	1,017,603	9.78	18,349	459	636,000	154	...	204,282	...	......	....
Grand Rapids, Mich.	48	137,634	18.00	11.5	20.7	133,083,705	64,731,263	20.01	...	3,283,200	2,523,270	18.83	20,707	783	1,399,387	270	...	510,515	108	2,231	183,006
Hartford, Conn.	46	138,036	18.00	12.21	29.46	140,410,031	136,969,175	28.75	80	6,366,893	5,006,047	36.27	23,429	699	1,069,740	260	...	583,700	230	6,570	324,436
Houston, Tex.	45	138,076	25.00	11.05	12.42	113,582,560	17,563,130	18.00	50	11,862,585	2,492,498	22.19	25,000	626	629,000	156	...	186,291	155	12,231	208,261
Indianapolis, Ind.	21	314,194	41.00	13.9	19.4	*602,000,000	....	26.80	100	4,000,000	4,000,000	12.72	42,890	1,364	3,001,640	335	...	411,863	404	13,426	638,243
Jersey City, N. J.	23	297,864	13.2	13.5	20.7	319,075,028	50,772,250	30.97	100	8,526,781	9,636,094	32.66	37,211	1,167	2,540,621	440	...	980,450	546	9,944	775,183
Kansas City, Kan.	67	101,177	12.00	16.1	22.8	*105,795,872	....	9.35	...	7,428,718	3,580,090	35.38	17,350	453	814,283	114	...	170,393	95	4,700	98,000
Kansas City, Mo.	19	324,410	63.00	15.00	18.1	187,584,900	108,259,210	14.50	70	9,242,000	3,780,309	11.05	53,933	1,617	3,133,945	402	...	648,286	554	51,821	630,000
Lawrence, Mass.	73	94,270	7.25	13.35	27.0	74,640,975	30,018,355	31.20	100	3,281,480	3,593,403	38.00	12,124	366	550,509	86	50	158,418	121	3,310	243,243
Los Angeles, Cal.	10	576,673	35.2	12.98	17.39	576,628,220	59,519,745	16.00	40	33,875,887	8,734,000	15.16	105,110	3,537	7,398,150	785	...	1,486,275	550	67,481	1,304,234
Louisville, Ky.	29	234,891	27.00	16.9	17.2	151,500,000	80,000,000	19.80	74	1,126,900	5,684,835	24.2	32,645	972	1,393,851	330	...	627,254	429	7,981	667,959
Lowell, Mass.	61	112,759	14.00	15.82	29.73	69,322,300	25,181,123	21.90	100	3,178,199	3,800,867	35.18	13,109	355	694,984	152	12	268,271	5	4,629	255,498
Lynn, Mass.	69	99,148	11.33	11.95	22.47	81,169,340	17,109,767	21.80	82	3,954,453	2,330,340	22.84	13,297	402	742,968	176	...	330,000	109	2,898	169,960
Memphis, Tenn.	40	162,351	16.00	22.26	12.60	96,921,550	13,195,297	17.50	60	7,523,000	4,211,617	28.96	22,261	661	738,960	262	...	403,565	190	8,646	245,000
Milwaukee, Wis.	13	457,147	25.85	11.0	23.5	419,074,285	102,164,840	20.74	100	14,730,750	13,712,623	31.16	63,523	1,638	3,060,745	586	...	1,044,569	628	10,000	911,520
Minneapolis, Minn.	18	380,582	53.39	11.56	21.37	175,696,283	51,337,412	39.43	40	28,665,358	9,000,000	23.65	63,623	1,958	4,300,000	544	...	997,739	380	12,227	689,527
Nashville, Tenn.	56	118,342	18.2	27.73	18.29	*92,028,728	....	15.00	75	8,318,000	1,900,000	15.96	20,375	403	89,406	168	...	276,210	150	14,000	181,000
Newark, N. J.	15	414,216	23.40	12.57	25.7	407,562,097	91,589,750	37.00	100	28,615,808	17,421,873	42.00	76,149	2,101	4,817,514	758	...	1,450,841	842	15,357	1,389,202
New Bedford, Mass.	53	121,217	19.39	13.25	27.09	67,237,350	40,791,882	23.20	...	7,062,975	2,735,944	24.59	16,207	472	903,202	146	...	254,292	237	2,354	331,904
New Haven, Conn.	39	162,519	18.00	12.63	26.47	*188,865,393	....	19.75	100	6,129,945	4,575,115	28.17	30,197	850	1,236,849	230	105	478,067	280	12,000	446,000

*Real and Personal. †Subject to correction.

STATISTICS OF LEADING AMERICAN CITIES—*Continued.*

Cities.	Miles from New York.	Time from New York.	Department of Streets and Public Works: Total Miles of Streets.	Total Miles of Paved Streets.	Annual Cost of Cleaning Streets.	Annual Cost of Removing Garbage and Ashes.	Total Miles of Sewers.	[illegible]al Cost of Street Lighting: Gas.	Electricity.	Lighting Plant Owned by City?	Water Works Department: Daily Capacity of Water Works. Gallons.	Average Daily Consumption. Gallons.	Miles of Mains.	Total Cost of Works.	Water Plant Owned by City?	Mayor: Name of Mayor and Political Party.	Salary.	Term Expires.
Akron, O.	625	19	375	125	$100,000	$88,000	225	......	$113,000	No	30,000,000	2000,000	.	$11,505,000	Yes	Carl F. Beck ... Rep.		[illegible]n. '22
Albany, N. Y.	142	3	197	111	118,154	*	132	......	103,555	No	25,000,000	20,200,000	164	3,099,000	Yes	Jas. R. Watt ... Rep.	4,000	Dec. '21
Atlanta, Ga.	882	24	350	244	135,000	$265,000	333	......	150,000	No	85,000,000	25,000,000	400	6,000,000	Yes	J. L. Key ... Dem.	4,000	Dec. '22
Baltimore, Md.	188	5	440	422	45169	343,836	823	233,565	390,325	No	128,000,000	85,000,000	845	19,226,037	Yes	W. F. Broening ... Rep.	6,000	May '23
Birmingham, Ala.	1043	23	400	36	....	....	250	......	......	No	‡	‡	‡	‡	‡	N. A. Barrett ... Com.	5,000	Nov. '21
Boston, Mass.	217	7	601	176	556,830	1,106,933	961	196,866	489,021	No	173,000,000	89625,400	576	17,055,000	Yes	A. J. Pe[illegible]rs ... N. P.	10,000	Feb. '22
Bridgeport, Conn.	55	1½	193	113	118,000	135,000	146	......	121,539	No	45,000,000	31,000,000	295	....	No	Clifford B. Wilson ... Rep.	6,000	Nov. '21
Buffalo, N. Y.	410	9	638	461	401,485	813,223	578	252,755	290,942	No	275,000,000	135,577,694	620	18,722,006	Yes	G. S. Buck ... Rep.	8,000	Dec. '21
Cambridge, Mass.	220	7	125	31	60,000	160,000	162	7,165	71,966	No	30,000,000	10,908,011	133	6,745,894	Yes	E. W. Quinn ... Dem.	5,000	Jan. '22
Camden, N. J.	91	3	250	90	26,040	56,682	97	105,000	......	No	40,000,000	13,750,000	25¼	2,000,000	Yes	Charles H. Ellis ... Rep.	5,000	Jan. '22
Chicago, Ill.	900	20	3251	2112	1,373,038	1,609,805	2526	158,565	909,661	[a]Yes	1050000,000	890,000,000	3015	82,000,000	Yes	Wm. Hale Thompson. Rep.	18,000	Apr. '23
Cincinnati, O.	744	20	970	622	313,423	82,796	542	56,313	340,357	No	110,000,000	50,000,000	759	25,000,000	Yes	J. Galvin ... Rep.	10,000	Dec. '21
Cleveland, O.	568	18	886	577	†529,683	....	771	††424,584	......	[a]Yes	360,000,000	135,000,000	1200	33,000,000	Yes	W. S. Fitz Gerald ... N. P.	10,000	Jan. '22
[illegible]bus, O.	624	19	400	231	189,343	179,000	397	......	194,700	Yes	75,000,000	18,872,000	346	4,318,501	Yes	J. J. [illegible]mpson ... Rep.	6,000	Jan. '24
Dallas, Tex.	1815	52	411	169	170,000	145,000	307	......	99,862	No	33,500,000	9,000,000	241	8,565,176	Yes	F. W. Wozencraft ... Dem.	4,000	May '21
[illegible]ton, O.	813	19	250	110	49,970	49,928	225	30,000	100,000	No	16,200,000	22,000,000	244	3,750,000	Yes	J. M. Switzer ... Com.	1,800	Dec. '21
Denver, Col.	1930	70	889	60	130,000	....	640	......	[b]200,000	No	80,000,000	53,803,655	617	15,000,000	Yes	Dewey C. Bailey ... Rep.	3,000	June '23
Des Moines, Ia.	1200	37	530	139	83,807	69,000	214	34,528	107,761	No	30,000,000	8,622,548	205	3,500,000	Yes	H. H. Barton ... Rep.	3,500	Apr. '22
Detroit, Mich.	743	21	1290	697	255,400	316,883	977	......	904,000		[illegible]31,997,985	151,543,036	1328	17,486,000	Yes	J. Couzens ... Rep.	8,000	Jan. '22
Duluth, Minn.	1538	47	241	61	15,000	*	120	......	34,340	Yes	18,902,000	8,464,288	170	3,541,552	Yes	C. R. [illegible]ley ... N. P.	4,000	Apr. '21
Elizabeth, N. J.	11	½	...	...	....	....	...	......	......	...	....	....	...	....	...	V. Mravlag ... Rep.	4,000	Dec. '22
Erie, Pa.	525	12	...	...	....	....	...	......	......	...	40,000,000	22,609,885	169	36,759,539	Yes	M. B. Kitts ... Dem.	3,500	Jan. '24
Fall River, Mass.	177	5	156	43	[illegible]	63,685	87	15,184	104,027	No	33,000,000	5,906,955	129	2,642,579	Yes	[illegible]es H. Kay ... Rep.	[illegible]	Jan. '23
Forth Worth, Tex.	2296	96	345	250	20,000	....	193	......	35,300	No	25,000,000	8,000,000	175	2,000,000	Yes	W. D. Davis ... Dem.	3,600	Apr. '21
Grand Rapids, Mich.	860	17	317	70	40,000	†145,935	234	......	68,000	Yes	25,000,000	14,000,000	242	2,566,778	Yes	J. McNabb ... N. P.	1,500	May '21
Hartford, Conn.	112	3	175	20	177,529	165,124	152	......	92,537	No	212,300,000	12,0[illegible]800	207	8,778,898	Yes	N. C. Brainard ... Rep.	6,000	May '22
Houston, Tex.	1739	48	600	245	75,009	48,000	224	......	80,000	No	22,000,000	9,[illegible]000	174	1,300,000	Yes	A. E. Amerman ... Dem.	7,500	Apr. '21
Indianapolis, Ind.	806	23	693	364	158,118	196,337	500	6,000	160,000	No	120,000,000	30,000,000	440	11,000,000	No	C. W. Jewett ... Rep.	7,500	Jan. '22
Jersey City, N. J.	1	..	203	144	403,623	141,873	135	......	177,967	No	560,000,000	50,500,000	241	[c]7,100,000	Yes	Frank Hague ... Dem.	8,000	May '21
[illegible]sas City, Kan.	.312	39	274	158	26,246	....	131	29,972	47,917	Yes	20,000,000	17,233,000	155	2,769,049	Yes	H. A. Mendenhall ... Rep.	4,500	Apr. '21
Kansas City, Mo.	1312	39	1200	584	274,929	60,000	660	70,000	180,000	No	105,000,000	47,000,000	645	10,500,000	Yes	J. Cowgill ... Dem.	7,500	Apr. '22
Lawrence, Mass.	259	6	106	51	27,066	84,862	82	......	60,973	No	6,000,000	4,430,000	105	2,160,950	Yes	Wm. P. White ... N. P.	3,500	Jan. '22
Los Angeles, Cal.	310	114	2782	516	406,532	243,467	1258	......	302,000	Yes	335,000,000	135,000,000	1490	38,000,000	Yes	M. P. Snyder ... N. P.	4,500	July '21
Louisville, Ky.	854	30	340	110	43,652	121,890	288	......	192,000	No	72,000,000	32,490,000	408	10,975,000	Yes	Geo. W. Smith ... Rep.	5,000	Nov. '21
[illegible]ell, Mass.	253	6	200	23	19,911	31,854	107	34,334	68,238	No	12,000,000	6,711,721	162	7,945,432	Yes	P. D. Thompson ... N. P.	3,000	Jan. '22
Lynn, Mass.	228	6	150	35	38075	89,483	93	......	64,977	No	20,000,000	8,500,000	135	6,000,000	Yes	W. H. Creamer ... Dem.	5[illegible]	[illegible]n. '22
Memphis, Tenn.	1163	40	308	196	40,000	75,000	315	......	125,000	No	30,000,000	16,000,000	282	3,857,700	Yes	J. R. Paine ... Dem.	6,000	[illegible]. '24
Milwaukee, Wis.	985	29	494	414	[illegible]	543,634	556	89,266	167,274	No	106,000,000	61,891,603	564	9,396,172	Yes	Daniel W. Hoan ... Soc.	800	Apr. '24
Minneapolis, Minn.	1317	48	881	152	220,000	‡‡54,000	445	92,000	233,000	No	56,000,000	29,500,000	595	9,737,553	Yes	J. E. Meyers ... Rep.	6,000	July '21
Nashville, Tenn.	1004	33	342	50	37,000	8000	164	......	100,000	Yes	30,000,000	13,360,000	215	4,500,000	Yes	Wm. [illegible]n ... Dem.	6,000	Oct. '21
Newark, N. J.	9	¼	334	275	341,706	520,086	314	77,436	218,594	No	50,000,000	45,000,000	440	22,534,588	Yes	C. P. Gillen ... Dem.	8,500	May '21
New Bedford, Mass.	2[illegible]0	6	192	139	111,258	114,622	143	......	120,000	No	26,000,000	9,650,567	174	4,496,704	Yes	Chas. S. Ashley ... Dem.	7,500	Jan. '22
New Haven, Conn.	76	2	205	110	97,000	40,000	130	29,376	61,415	No	65,000,000	34,500,000	328	....	No	David E. Fitzgerald ... Dem.	7,500	Jan. '22

*Not removed by city. †Incl. removal of garbage and ashes. [a]City owns electric but not gas plant. [b]Gas and electricity. [c]Does not incl. cost of Boonton Reservoir and [illegible]uit lines. ‡ [illegible] [illegible]rought from Birmingham [illegible] Works and resold. ††Includes [illegible]ost of gas and electricity. ‡‡Removal of garbage only.

STATISTICS OF LEADING AMERICAN CITIES—*Continued.*

Cities.	Standing.†	Population U. S. Census 1920.	Dept. of Health: Area Sq. Miles.	Annual Death Rate per 1,000.	Annutl Birth Rate per 1,000.	Department of Finance: Assessed Property Value: Real.	Personal.	Tax Rate per $1,000 of Assessed Value.	Per Cent. of Real Val. to Ass'd Val.	Net Public Debt.	Annual Cost of Maintaining City Government.	Per Capita Cost of Maintaining City Government.	Dept. of Education: Number of Pupils in Public Schools.	Number of Principals and Teachers.	Annual Cost of Maintaining Public Schools	Fire Dept.: Regular.	Volunteer.	Average Annual Cost of Force.	Police Department: Number of Force.	Average Annual Number of Arrests.	Average Annual Cost of Force.
New Orleans, La.	17	387,219	196	12.39	21.71	$173,468,682	$70,609,333	$22.00	75	$ 3601,145	$3,213,943	$8.89	51,595	1,369	$1,886,722	455	....	$494 400	464	23,239	$483,916
New York, N. Y.	1	5,620,048	317	12.28	24.00	8,626,121,707	296,508 187	.....	100	‡624365937	246,916,622	43.93	931 468	23,010	45,765,043	6,067	675	11,161,437	10,887	199,099	20,534,695
Manhattan	..	2,284,103	21.3	12.39	21.71	5,186,771,887	227,063,250	24.90	100	....	....	.....	339,755	8,416	......	....	....	......	....	.....	....
Bronx	..	732,016	41.4	13.78	28.07	753,308,264	17,211,200	25.30	100	....	....	.....	131,212	3,226	......	....	....	......	....	.....	....
Brooklyn	..	2,018,356	60.9	12.28	24.00	1,937,811,205	41,192,900	25.40	100	....	....	.....	356,295	8,680	......	....	....	......	....	.	....
Queens	..	469,042	112	12.93	22.07	636,409,159	8,792,100	25.40	100	....	....	.....	83,535	2,165	......	....	....	......	....	.....	....
Richmond	..	116,531	57.19	20.40	24.61	111,821,192	2,246,635	25.30	100	....	....	.....	20,671	523	......	....	....	......	....	.....	....
Norfolk, Va.	59	115,777	10	12.00	[illegible]	68. [illegible]	22,205,120	19.00	75	10,229,000	3,078,353	3435	18,300	560	834,000	174	....	336,607	267	7,360	461,456
Oakland, Cal.	31	[illegible]	56	12.5	18.00	138,427 950	26,537,146	24.00	60	7,222,860	3,674,697	16.98	49,186	1,381	2,932,267	344	....	629,112	225	11,589	350,243
Omaha, Neb.	34	191,601	38	10.5	22.5	*64,104,388	....	49.00	20	9,861,438	2,068,000	10.78	35,067	1,111	2,533,331	331	....	571,135	275	25,553	348,918
Paterson, N. J.	49	135,866	8.36	15.65	21.51	92,778,565	19,711,179	20.40	100	6,566,409	2,270,158	18.15	22,985	675	1,253,857	213	....	[illegible]	167	4,371	272,015
Philadelphia, Pa.	3	1,823,158	129.59	14.52	[illegible]	1,941,467,934	693,630,026	21.50	100	144,109,150	48,520,872	26.62	237,514	6,060	12,274,788	1,666	....	2,746,194	4,475	75,618	6,726,248
Pittsburgh, Pa.	9	588,193	42	16.3	24.3	802,571,410	....	21.00	85	29,026,296	12,521,165	21.58	86,823	2,610	5,156,921	906	....	1,729,712	892	46,404	1,139,411
Portland, Ore.	24	258,288	66.3	11.00	14.9	226,679,806	58,661,245	10.80	75	14,541,950	5,234,873	21.04	45,279	1,300	3,741,022	440	150	[illegible]	373	17,000	603,477
Providence, R. I.	27	237,595	18.29	13.22	21.68	287,064,360	195,499,040	21.50	100	14, [illegible]	12,651,069	53.60	38,619	1,064	1,881,686	294	....	672,000	434	8,439	928,284
Reading, Pa.	64	[illegible]	6	11.43	20.54	*68,695,788	....	22.00	75	1,836,439	1,157,499	10.73	16,000	440	731,843	....	5,855	82,726	110	1,615	160,865
Richmond, Va.	38	171,667	24.3	23.79	23.94	139,397,978	102,624,769	19.50	75	12 569,097	5,051,069	29.40	30,219	984	1,271,453	267	....	[illegible]	213	12,124	377,755
Rochester, N. Y.	23	295,750	21.09	12.45	22.97	273,843,471	1,025,250	23.24	80	[illegible]	9,408,878	31.00	60,088	1,465	2,257,563	470	100	12,297	360	4,998	669,014
St. Louis, Mo.	6	772,897	62	14.3	13.2	667,857,200	150,000,000	23.50	80	19,964,000	16,935,243	21.91	106 991	2,625	6,324,345	842	....	1,311,362	1,176	49,630	2,411,386
St. Paul, Minn.	30	284,595	55.44	9.56	16.66	106,309,261	41,207,499	53.00	40	8,300,941	10,374,337	44.22	33,000	1,144	2,415,000	484	....	[illegible]	325	8,070	398,780
Salt Lake City, Utah	57	[illegible]	51.54	12.02	23.84	135,053,346	70,928,066	11.00	100	6,850,046	2,996,953	25.37	24,000	860	1,858,956	102	....	149,237	115	4,605	202,391
San Antonio, Tex.	41	161,379	36	15	21.04	96,833,690	36,451,157	22.50	75	7,563,000	1,790,590	11.1	25,504	695	[illegible]	200	....	267,519	231	17,068	267,559
San Francisco, Cal.	11	[illegible]	46.50	14.75	17.34	585,105,569	234,322,429	31.80	50	34,322,600	21,185,666	4169	70,626	1,856	3,468,418	898	....	2,004,186	962	26,673	1,792,118
Scranton, Pa.	47	137,783	20	18.4	22.00	60,386,545	47,610,090	13.10	80	1,335,376	1,332,368	9.67	24,113	688	1,177,993	196	....	329,530	146	5,384	165,000
Seattle, Wash.	20	[illegible]	94.47	11.05	19.90	199,635,368	46,187,678	30.55	50	16,279,400	8,958,804	26.21	42 615	1,536	[illegible]	606	....	1,118,492	517	21,876	901,831
Spokane, Wash.	66	104,437	39.25	7.57	13.82	58,824,950	20,667,367	57.75	50	5,415,925	2,483,210	23.77	21,311	630	1,200,760	157	....	268,175	106	3,416	167,136
Springfield, Mass.	51	[illegible]	39.9	13.69	26.73	202,524,420	29,173,315	24.50	100	8,588,355	4,707,173	36.31	22 648	787	1,694,634	274	....	[illegible]	182	3,393	342,128
Syracuse, N. Y.	37	171,717	18	13.9	24.8	171,249,479	493,919	23.17	90	8,330,986	4,212,872	24.50	22,300	690	1,339,962	290	....	537,215	239	5,012	415,995
Tacoma, Wash.	71	96,965	43.6	9 46	15.31	43,263,530	16,240,050	23.00	46.5	4,794,619	1,321,263	13.62	18,203	508	1,022,237	144	30	283,356	93	9,576	152,665
Toledo, O.	26	[illegible]	33	[illegible]	19.59	291,109,110	141,336,410	27.4	100	8,859,854	5,170,269	21.26	39,877	1,058	2,168,980	235	....	373,563	332	6,990	367,029
Trenton, N. J.	55	119,289	9	24.8	32.1	76,177,195	16,030,800	24.20	100	6,110,437	1,665,169	16.13	17,764	533	1,098,709	89	....	240 522	151	5,231	282,978
Utica, N. Y.	74	94,156	....	....	....	87,795,495	628,600	23.67	100	2,930,065	2,705,156	.....	16,000	480	914,612	135	....	239,721	114	3,814	163,218
Washington, D. C.	14	437,571	62.24	13.99	18.07	426,623,630	415,013,651	15.00	67	2,152,626	21,393,007	48.88	65 298	2,096	4,155,790	650	....	1,271,060	993	48,930	1,381,520
Wilmington, Del.	62	110,168	11.29	17.12	28.27	108,958,675	....	17.55	100	6. [illegible]	1,584,114	14.94	13,707	391	604,873	28	800	[illegible]	165	3,620	280,000
Worcester, Mass.	35	179,754	38.49	26.25	46.72	191,368,550	40,636,230	26.60	100	8,448,538	7,837,700	43.6	29,147	883	1,971,672	267	12	388,789	300	8,733	494,500
Yonkers, N. Y.	68	0 [illegible]	21	106	22.3	160,869,445	1,896,250	22.25	100	15,243,711	4,181,551	41.72	18,000	600	1,500,000	129	400	[illegible]	198	3,084	343,392
Youngstown, O.	50	132,358	25	14.3	29.66	*243,000,000	....	16.40	33⅓	6,158,733	1,200,000	9.06	22,157	592	1,401,124	92	....	169,128	156	10,340	400,000

†Subject to correction. *Real and Personal. ‡Net Funded Debt, Sept. 1, 1920.

STATISTICS OF LEADING AMERICAN CITIES—*Continued.*

Cities.	Miles from New York.	Time from New York.	Department of Streets and Public Works. Total Miles of Streets.	Total Miles of Paved Streets.	Annual Cost of Cleaning Streets.	Annual Cost of Removing Garbage and Ashes.	Total Miles of Sewers.	Annual Cost of Street Lighting. Gas.	Annual Cost of Street Lighting. Electricity.	Lighting Plant Owned by City?	Water Works Department. Daily Capacity of Water Works. Gallons.	Average Daily Consumption. Gallons.	Miles of Mains.	Total Cost of Works.	Water Plant Owned by City?	Mayor. Name of Mayor and Political Party.	Salary.	Term Expires.
New Orleans, La.	1364	32	525	352	$593,903	$197,000	508	....	$256,750	No	50,000,000	39,000,000	[illegible]06	$10,500,000	[illegible]	A. J. McShane ... Dem.	10,000	Dec. '24
New York, N. Y.	....	..	3543	2226	3,443,362	3,259,353	2290	$825,020	2,331,535	No	955,000,000	660,200,000	[e]3014	[f]2020993[illegible]2	Yes	Jno. F. Hylan ... Dem.	15,000	Dec. '21
Manhattan	....	..	484	472	....	....	534	....	....	No	585,000,000	417,400,000	1348	139,372,000	Yes	[e]H. H. Curran ... Rep.	7,500	Dec. '21
Bronx	....	..	487	203	....	....	379	....	....	..	‡.......	‡.......	....	‡.......	‡...	[e]H. R. Bruckner ... Dem.	7,500	Dec. '21
Brooklyn	....	..	1258	885	....	....	853	....	....	No	320,000,000	181,600,000	1125	46,500,000	Yes	[e]Edw. Riegelmann ... Dem.	7,500	Dec. '21
[illegible]ns	....	..	1078	478	....	....	360	....	....	No	20,000,000	44,200,000	262	4,187,000	Prt	M. E. Connelly ... Dem.	5,000	Dec. '21
Richmond	....	..	320	257	....	....	93	....	....	No	27,000,000	17,000,000	273	4,333,000	Yes	[e]C. D. Van Name ... Dem.	5,000	Dec. '21
Norfolk, Va.	346	12	180	95	†360,000	....	115	....	56,500	No	10,000,000	7,250,000	25	2,000,000	Yes	A. L. Roper ... Pres.	1,800	Sep. '23
Oakland, [illegible]	3250	[illegible]06	568	430	171,680	††19,426	432	37,255	125,823	No	26,000,000	19,714,000	962	22,000,000	No	[illegible] L. D[illegible]e ... Rep.	4,200	June '23
[illegible]a, Neb.	1383	40	675	250	70,000	45,000	390	25,000	140,000	Yes	68,000,000	20,866,754	360	6 [illegible]33	Yes	E. P. Smith ... Dem.	5,000	May '21
Paterson, N. J.	17	½	207	127	50,000	100,000	141	8,000	80,102	No	62,000,000	9,600,000	154	....	No	F. J. Van N[illegible] ... Dem.	3,500	Dec. '21
Philadelphia, Pa.	90	2	250	200	2, [illegible]000	2,300,000	1420	....	1,305,289	[d]No	320,000,000	320,000,000	1894	65,000,000	Yes	J. H. Moore ... Rep.	12,000	Jan. '24
Pittsburgh, Pa.	431	13	1036	542	[c]402,024	....	634	....	429,826	Yes	190,000,000	115,000,000	706	28,000,000	Yes	E. V. [illegible] ... N. P.	10,000	Jan. '22
Portland, Ore.	3181	115	844	400	[illegible]	†......	528	....	194,148	No	67,500,000	29,767,000	762	12,807,529	Yes	G. L. Baker ... Rep.	6,000	June '21
Providence, R. I.	189	5	268	74	7 [illegible]26	39,000	252	....	245,954	No	68 000,000	21,560,396	437	7,802,647	Yes	Jos. H. [illegible] ... Dem.	[illegible]	Jan. '23
Reading, Pa.	148	4	125	27	55,000	32,000	121	15,000	75,000	No	[illegible],000	15,400,000	125	4,750,000	Yes	J. K. Stauffer ... Rep.	3,500	Jan. '24
Richmond, Va.	344	11	374	82	88,724	131,765	230	7,372	74,904	Yes	32,000,000	31,314,877	251	4,500,000	Yes	George Ainslie ... Dem.	6,500	Sep. '24
Rochester, N. Y.	371	7	401	276	202,420	323,433	361	....	¶362,995	No	37,000,000	23,000,000	458	13,000,000	Yes	Hiram H. Edgerton ... Rep.	7,500	Dec. '2[illegible]
St. Louis, Mo.	1048	29	955	703	93,7[illegible]4	140,730	878	595,728	127,336	No	160,000,000	104,110,744	1013	32,756,769	Yes	Henry W. Kiel ... Rep.	10,000	Apr. '21
St. [illegible], Minn.	300	27	290	55	184,500	52,664	433	161,116	161,116	No	40,000,000	17,025,230	439	7,127,615	Yes	L. C. Hodgson ... N. P.	5,000	June '22
Salt Lake [illegible], Utah	2452	72	500	71	[illegible]293	43,165	286	....	70,017	No	47,000,000	26,000,000	319	4,075,000		[illegible]. C. Neslen ... Dem.	4,200	Jan. '25
San Antonio, Tex.	2222	63	650	104	174,660	96,000	247	....	53,500	No	65,000,000	16,000,000	205	4,500,000	No	S. C. Bell ... N. P.	5,000	May '21
San Francisco, Cal.	3250	106	860	485	530,010	[b].....	510	....	[illegible]000	No	44,000,000	37,000,000	627	35,900,000	No	Jas. Rolph, Jr. ... N. P.	6,000	Jan. '24
[illegible]n, Pa.	146	4	153	61	44,373	99,287	125	....	62,424	No	30,000,000	25,000,000	...	... .	....	A. T. Connell ... Rep.	5,000	Jan. '22
Seattle, Wash.	3232	102	130	293	174,182	20[illegible]000	514	....	202,113	Yes	67,000,000	33 [illegible]000	718	13,947,107	Yes	Hugh M. Caldwell ... Rep.	7,500	Mch. '22
Spokane, Wash.	2840	192	395	71	57,740	55,000	150	....	64,288	No	84,500,000	20,182,100	357	4,850,000	Yes	Chas. A. Fleming ...	3,600	Jan. '22
Springfield, Mass.	142	4	156	101	225,000	198,000	153	....	151,000	No	17,000,000	11,920,000	227	5,758,921	Yes	E. F. Leonard ... Rep.	6,000	Jan. '23
Syracuse, N. Y.	291	6	275	115	193,331	190,116	230	....	181,077	No	121,000,000	26, 6 [illegible]	225	5,860,756	Yes	H. H. Fa[illegible] ... Rep.	6,500	Dec. '21
Tacoma, Wash.	3225	102	306	[illegible]09	52,052	[b].....	301	....	54,373	Yes	54,000,000	23,330,000	285	5,657,270	Yes	C. M. Riddell ... N. P.	4,000	May '22
Toledo, O.	733	19	610	244	81,902	68,819	280	....	129,331	No	101,000,000	28,000,000	415	7,500,000	Yes	C. Schrieber ... N. P.	7,500	Jan. '22
Trenton, N. J.	57	1½	150	66	60,000	43,500	105	15,000	6300	No	30,000,000	16,000000	176	2,866,700	Yes	Fredk. W. Donnelly ... Dem.		M[illegible]y '22
Utica, N. Y.	238	5	...	...	.	....	...	....	....	....	....	....	...	....	....	J. K. O'Conner ... Rep.	6,500	Dec. '21
Washington, D. C.	226	6	522	374	375,000	750,000	746	186,270	212,960	No	65,000,000	62,553,490	639	20,712,705	Yes	L. Brownlow[a], Pres., Com.	5,000	Feb. '21
Wilmington, Del.	118	4	167	82	41,070	67,523	135	15,987	41,457	No	24,000,000	14,835,446	138	3,636,356	Yes	W. G. Taylor ... Rep.	2,000	June '21
Worcester, Mass.	127	4	223	28	93,157	31,629	248	15,279	[illegible]	No	32,000,000	14,628,000	314	8,069,119	Yes	P. F. Sullivan ... Dem.	5,000	Jan. '22
Yonkers, N. Y.	19	½	153	130	121,442	180,165	75	87,009	87,668	No	31 000,000	9,420 485	166	4,241,328	Yes	W. J. Wallin ... Rep.	6 500	Dec. '21
[illegible]n, O.	632	18	275	150	31,543	26,000	150	....	¶75,000	No	315,000,000	11,300,000	211	2,613 012	Yes	F. J. Warnock ... Rep.		[illegible]c. '21

* I[illegible]des removal of garbage and a[illegible]s. †Does not [illegible]e garbage and a[illegible]s, [illegible]t operates incinerator. ††Disposal only. ‡Included in figures for Mhtn. ¶Gas and electricity. [a]Apptd. by Pres. of U. S. [b]Private co[illegible]ct. [d]Gas pl[illegible]nt owned by city and leased. [c]Excl. of high pressure. [e]Borough President. [f]Total d[illegible]isbursements for Catskill [illegible]s (in addition to figures in [illegible]umn), $128,154,089.

PRESIDENTS OF THE UNITED STATES.

	Name.	Born.	Resided at election and burial place.	Politics.	Inaugural.	Died.
1	George Washington......	Feb. 22, 1732	Mount Vernon, Va..	Federalist...	1789	Dec. 14, 1799
2	John Adams..............	Oct. 30, 1735	Quincy, Mass........	Federalist...	1797	July 4, 1826
3	Thomas Jefferson.........	Apr. 13, 1743	Monticello, Va......	Democrat*...	1801	July 4, 1826
4	James Madison...........	Mar. 16, 1751	Montpelier, Va......	"	1809	June 28, 1836
5	James Monroe............	April 28, 1758	Oak Hill, Va.†......	"	1817	July 4, 1831
6	John Quincy Adams......	July 11, 1767	Quincy, Mass........	Federalist...	1825	Feb. 23, 1848
7	Andrew Jackson..........	Mar. 15, 1767	Hermitage, Tenn...	Democrat....	1829	June 8, 1845
8	Martin Van Buren.......	Dec. 5, 1782	Kinderhook, N. Y...	"	1837	July 24, 1862
9	William Henry Harrison.	Feb. 9, 1773	North Bend, O......	Whig.........	1841	April 4, 1841
10	John Tyler.................	Mar. 29, 1790	Williamsburg, Va.†.	Democrat....	1841	Jan. 18, 1862
11	James Knox Polk........	Nov. 2, 1795	Nashville, Tenn.....	"	1845	June 15, 1849
12	Zachary Taylor...........	Nov. 24, 1784	Baton Rouge, La.†..	Whig.........	1849	July 9, 1850
13	Millard Fillmore..........	Jan. 7, 1800	Buffalo, N. Y........	"	1850	Mar. 9, 1874
14	Franklin Pierce...........	Nov. 23, 1804	Concord, N. H......	Democrat....	1853	Oct. 8, 1869
15	James Buchanan..........	April 23, 1791	Wheatland, Pa.†....	" ...	1857	June 1, 1868
16	Abraham Lincoln.........	Feb. 12, 1809	Springfield, Ill.......	Republican..	1861	April 15, 1865
17	Andrew Johnson..........	Dec. 29, 1808	Greenville, Tenn....	" ..	1865	July 31, 1875
18	Ulysses S. Grant..........	April 27, 1822	Washington, D. C.†	" ..	1869	July 23, 1885
19	Rutherford B. Hayes....	Oct. 4, 1822	Fremont, O..........	" ..	1877	Jan. 17, 1893
20	James A. Garfield........	Nov. 19, 1831	Mentor, O.†	" ..	1881	Sept. 19, 1881
21	Chester A. Arthur........	Oct. 5, 1830	New York City†....	" ..	1881	Nov. 18, 1886
22	Grover Cleveland.........	Mar. 18, 1837	Buffalo, N. Y.†......	Democrat....	1885	June 24, 1908
23	Benjamin Harrison.......	Aug. 20, 1833	Indianapolis, Ind...	Republican..	1889	Mar. 13, 1901
24	Grover Cleveland..........	Mar. 18, 1837	New York City†....	Democrat....	1893	June 24, 1908
25	William McKinley........	Jan. 29, 1843	Canton, O...........	Republican..	1897	Sept. 24, 1901
26	Theodore Roosevelt.......	Oct. 27, 1858	Oyster Bay, N. Y...	" ..	1901	Jan. 6, 1919
27	Wm. H. Taft..............	Sept. 15, 1857	Cincinnati, O.......	" ..	1909	Living.
28	Woodrow Wilson	Dec. 28, 1856	Princeton, N. J....	Democrat...	1913	Living.
29	Warren G. Harding§......	Nov. 2, 1865	Marion, O...........	Republican.	....	Living.

*Jefferson, Madison and Monroe belonged to the first Republican party. †The tomb of Monroe is in Richmond, Va.; of Tyler, in Richmond, Va.; of Taylor, in Springfield, Ky.; of Buchanan, in Lancaster, Pa.; of Grant, in Mhtn., N. Y. City; of Garfield, in Cleveland, O.; of Arthur, in Albany, N. Y.; of Cleveland, in Princeton, N. J. §Elected Nov. 2, 1920; to be inaugurated March 4, 1921.

VICE PRESIDENTS OF THE UNITED STATES.

	Name.	Born.	Resided at election and burial place.	Politics.	Qualified.	Died.
1.	John Adams	Oct. 30, 1735	Quincy, Mass.	Federalist.....	1789	July 4, 1826
2.	Thos. Jefferson	April 13, 1743	Monticello, Va.	Republican....	1797	July 4, 1826
3.	Aaron Burr	Feb. 6, 1756	New York City*........	Republican....	1801	Sept. 14, 1836
4.	Geo. Clinton	July 26, 1739	Orange Co., N. Y.*....	Republican....	1805	April 20, 1812
5.	Elbridge Gerry	July 17, 1744	Marblehead, Mass.*	Republican....	1813	Nov. 23, 1814
6.	Daniel D. Tompkins	June 21, 1774	Westchester Co., N. Y.†	Republican....	1817	June 11, 1825
7.	John C. Calhoun	Mar. 18, 1782	Abbeville Dist., S. C.*..	Republican....	1825	Mar. 31, 1850
8.	Martin Van Buren	Dec. 5, 1782	Kinderhook, N. Y.......	Democrat......	1833	July 24, 1862
9.	Richard M. Johnson	Oct. 17, 1781	Bryant's Station, Ky.*	Democrat......	1837	Nov. 19, 1850
10.	John Tyler	Mar. 29, 1790	Williamsburg, Va.......	Democrat......	1841	Jan. 18, 1862
11.	George M. Dallas	July 10, 1792	Philadelphia, Pa.......	Democrat......	1845	Dec. 31, 1864
12.	Millard Fillmore	Jan. 7, 1800	Buffalo, N. Y...........	Whig...........	1849	Mar. 7, 1874
13.	William R. King	April 6, 1786	Dallas Co., Ala........	Democrat......	1853	April 18, 1853
14.	John C. Breckenridge	Jan. 21, 1821	Lexington, Ky.	Democrat......	1857	May 17, 1875
15.	Hannibal Hamlin	Aug. 27, 1809	Hampden, Me.*	Republican....	1861	July 4, 1891
16.	Andrew Johnson	Dec. 29, 1808	Greenville, Tenn.	Republican....	1865	July 31, 1875
17.	Schuyler Colfax	Mar. 23, 1823	South Bend, Ind........	Republican....	1869	Jan. 13, 1885
18.	Henry Wilson	Feb. 12, 1812	Natick, Mass.	Republican....	1873	Nov. 22, 1875
19.	William A. Wheeler	June 30, 1819	Malone, N. Y...........	Republican....	1877	June 4, 1887
20.	Chester A. Arthur	Oct. 5, 1830	New York City*	Republican....	1881	Nov. 18, 1886
21.	Thos. A. Hendricks	Sept. 7, 1819	Indianapolis, Ind.	Democrat......	1885	Nov. 25, 1885
22.	Levi P. Morton	May 16, 1824	New York City	Republican....	1889	May 16, 1920
23.	Adlai E. Stevenson	Oct. 23, 1835	Bloomington, Ill.	Democrat......	1893	June 1, 1914
24.	Garret A. Hobart	June 3, 1844	Paterson, N. J.	Republican....	1897	Nov. 21, 1899
25.	Theo. Roosevelt	Oct. 27, 1858	Oyster Bay, N. Y.......	Republican....	1901	Jan. 6, 1919
26.	Chas. W. Fairbanks........	May 11, 1852	Indianapolis, Ind.	Republican....	1905	June 4, 1918
27.	Jas. S. Sherman............	Oct. 24, 1855	Utica, N. Y.............	Republican....	1909	Oct. 30, 1912
28.	Thomas R. Marshall......	Mar. 14, 1854	Columbia City, Ind......	Democrat.......	1913	Living.
29.	Calvin Coolidge§............	July 4, 1872	Northampton, Mass.....	Republican.....	....	Living.

*The tomb of Burr, who died in Port Richmond, S. I., is in Princeton, N. J.; of Clinton, in Washington, D. C.; of Gerry, in Washington, D. C.; of Calhoun, in Washington, D. C.; of R. M. Johnson, in Frankfort, Ky.; of Hamlin, in Bangor, Me.; of Arthur, in Albany, N. Y. †Tompkins died on Staten Island, N. Y. §Elected Nov. 2, 1920; to take oath of office March 4, 1921.

PRESIDENTIAL SUCCESSION.

Upon the death of the Pres., the Vice-Pres. succeeds to office. (Constn., Art. II, Sec. 5.)

Record of succession. Harrison, by John Tyler, April 4, 1841; Taylor, by Millard Fillmore, July 9, 1850; Lincoln, by Andrew Johnson, April 15, 1865; Garfield, by Chester A. Arthur, Sept. 19, 1881; McKinley, by Theodore Roosevelt, Sept. 14, 1901.

Succession: In case of removal, death, resignation, or inability both of Pres. and Vice-Pres.: Sec. of State, Sec. of Treas., Sec. of War, Atty. Gen., Postm. Gen., Sec. of Navy, Sec. of Interior. (Act of Jan. 19, 1886, 24 Stat., 1.)

Dept. of Agriculture and Dept. of Commerce and Labor were organized after passage of presidential succession act.

PRODUCTION OF COAL, 1913 TO 1920.

In millions of gross tons

Year.	U. S.	United Kingdom.	Germany.	France.	Grand total.
1913	509	287	188	40	1,024
1914	458	266	159	29	912
1915	475	253	144	20	892
1916	527	256	156	21	960
1917	582	248	165	28	1,023
1918	605	228	158	29	1,020
1919	486	230	115	22	853
1920 (est.).....	548	237	122	32	939

THE BROTHERHOOD BANK.

The Brotherhood of Locomotive Engineers' Co-operative National Bank opened its temporary headquarters at St. Clair av. and Ontario st., Cleveland, O., on Nov. 1. So far as known, this is the first co-operative commercial bank in the United States, although there are many such banks in Europe. It is the first labor bank. The institution has a capital of $1,000,000, and Grand Chief Warren S. Stone, of the Brotherhood, is its first president.

UNITED STATES GOVERNMENT

EXECUTIVE.

	Salary.
President of the United States—Woodrow Wilson, N. J.	*$75,000
Vice President—Thos. R. Marshall, Ind	12,000
Sec. to Pres.—Jos. P. Tumulty, N. J.	7,500
Executive Clerk—Rudolph Forster, Va.	5,000
Chief Clerk—Joseph M. Sharkey, N. J.	4,000

The Cabinet.

In order of succession to the Presidency:
Secretary of State—Bainbridge Colby, N. Y.
Secretary of Treasury—David F. Houston, Mo.
Secretary of War—Newton D. Baker, Ohio.
Attorney General—A. Mitchell Palmer, Pa.
Postmaster General—Albert S. Burleson, Tex.
Secretary of Navy—Josephus Daniels, N. C.
Secretary of Interior—John Barton Payne, Ill.
Sec. of Agriculture—Edwin T. Meredith, Ia.
Sec. of Commerce—Joshua W. Alexander, Mo.
Secretary of Labor—Wm. B. Wilson, Pa.

Department of State.

The Secretary of State is charged, under direction of the President, with the duties appertaining to correspondence with the public ministers and consuls of the U. S., and with the representatives of foreign powers accredited to the U. S.; and to negotiations of whatever character relating to the foreign affairs of the U. S. He is regarded as the first in rank among members of the Cabinet.

	Salary.
Sec. of State—Bainbridge Colby, N. Y.	$12,000
Counselor—Norman H. Davis, N. Y.	7,500
Asst. Sec.—Vacant	5,000
2d Asst. Sec., A. A. Adee, D. C.	4,500
3d Asst. Sec.—Van S. Merle-Smith, N. Y.	4,500
Director of the Consular Service—W. J. Carr, N. Y.	4,500
Chief Clerk—Ben. G. Davis, Neb.	3,000
Solicitor—Fred. K. Neilsen, Neb.	5,000
Chief War Trade Board—F. T. St. John Perret, La.	4,000
Chief Latin Amer. Division—Sumner Welles, N. Y.	4,500
Chief Div. of Far Eastern Affairs—John VanA. MacMurray, D. C.	4,500
Chief Div. Near Eastern Affairs—Warren D. Robbins, Mass.	4,000
Chief Div. Mexican Affairs—Chas. M. Johnston, N. Y.	4,500
Chief Div. Russian Affairs—Arthur Bullard, D. C.	4,000
Chief Div. Western European Affairs—R. W. Bliss, N. Y.	4,500
Chief Diplomatic Bur.—W. E. Stewart, Ohio (Acting)	2,100
Chief Consular Bur.—Herbert C. Hengstler, Ohio	3,000
Chief Bur. of Appointments—Miles M. Shand, N. J.	2,250
Chief Div. Passport Control—Philip Adams, Mass.	2,500
Chief Bur. of Indexes and Archives—David A. Salmon, Conn.	2,500
Chief Bur. Accts.—Wm. McNair, Mich.	2,450
Chief Bur. Rolls and Lib.—John A. Tonner, Ohio	2,100
Foreign Trade Adviser—Wesley Frost, Ky. (Acting)	4,000

Department of the Treasury.

The Secretary of the Treasury is charged by law with the management of the national finances.

	Salary.
Secretary of the Treasury—David F. Houston, Mo.	$12,000
Assistants—S. P. Gilbert, Jr., N. Y.; A. W. McLean, N. C.; Ewing Laporte, Mo.; Jas. H. Moyle, Utah; Nicholas Kelly, N. Y.	5,000
Chief Clerk—W. G. Platt, Mo.	4,300
Supervising Architect—Vacant	6,000
Director of Mint—R. T. Baker, Nevada.	5,000
Chief of the Bureau of Engraving and Printing—Jas. L. Wilmeth, Ark.	6,000
Chief App't Division—Jas. E. Harper, S. C.	3,000
Chief Customs Div.—G. W. Ashworth, Md.	4,500
Chief Loans and Currency—Chas. N. McGroarty, Ala.	3,500
Chief Stationery and Printing—Frederick F. Weston, Iowa	2,500
Commissioner Public Debt.—Wm. S. Broughton, Ill.	6,000
Supt. of Mails—S. M. Gaines, Ky.	2,500
Govt. Actuary—Jos. S. McCoy, N. J.	4,000
Register—W. S. Elliott, Ga.	4,000
Compt. Treas.—W. W. Warwick, Ohio	6,000
Treasurer U. S.—John Burke, No. Dak.	8,000
Comp. of Currency—J. S. Williams, Va.	12,000
Com. of Internal Rev.—Wm. W. Williams, Ala.	10,000
Federal Prohibition Com.—John F. Kramer, Ohio	7,500
Solicitor of Int. Rev.—Carl A. Mapes, Mich.	6,000
Solicitor of Treas.—Lawrence Becker, Ind.	4,500
Com. of Accounts and Deposits—R. G. Hand	.....
Auditor of Treas.—Samuel Patterson, Neb.	4,000
Auditor of War Dept.—J. L. Baity, Mo.	4,000
Auditor of Interior—J. E. R. Ray, Neb.	4,000
Auditor of Navy—Edward Luckow, Wis.	4,000
Auditor of State—E. D. Hearne, Del.	4,000
Auditor of Post Office—C. A. Kram, Pa.	5,000
Chief Secret Service—W. H. Moran, D.C.	4,500
Supervising Surg.-Gen. Public Health and Marine Hosp.—Hugh S. Cummings, Va.	5,000

*Allowance of $25,000 additional for traveling expenses.

GENERAL CUSTOMS APPRAISERS OF MERCHANDISE.

Salary $9,000 each.

B. S. Waite, Mich.; W. B. Howell, N. J.; G. S. Brown, Md.; J. B. Sullivan, Ia.; I. F. Fischer, N. Y.; E. G. Hay, Minn.; C. P. McClelland, N. Y., W. C. Adamson, Ga., and Geo. E. Weller, N. Y.

Department of War.

	Salary.
Secretary of War—N. D. Baker, Ohio	$12,000
Asst. Sec.—Wm. R. Williams, Ohio	5,000
Asst. and Ch. Clk.—J. C. Scofield, Ga.	4,000
Private Sec. to Sec.—B. F. Fiery, Ohio.	2,500
Chief of Staff—Gen. Peyton C. March	10,000
Chief Cavalry—Maj. Gen. W. A. Holbrook	8,000
Chief Field Artillery—Maj. Gen. Wm. J. Snow	8,000
Chief of Infantry—Maj. Gen. Chas. S. Farnsworth	8,000
Chief of Chaplains—Col. John T. Axton.	6,500
Chief, Coast Artillery—Maj.-Gen. F. W. Coe	8,000
Adjt.-Gen.—Maj.-Gen. P. C. Harris	8,000
Insp.-Gen.—Maj.-Gen. J. L. Chamberlain.	8,000
Judge Advocate-Gen.—Maj.-Gen. E. H. Crowder	8,000
Qrmr.-Gen.—Maj.-Gen. Harry L. Rogers	8,000
Chief of Finance—Brig. Gen. H. M. Lord	6,000
Surg.-Gen.—Maj.-Gen. M. W. Ireland	8,000
Chief of Engnrs.—Maj. Gen. Lansing H Beach	8,000
Chief of Ord.—Maj.-Gen. Clarence C. Williams	8,000
Chief Signal Officer—Maj.-Gen. G. O. Squier	8,000
Bur. of Insular Affairs—Maj. Gen. Frank McIntyre	8,000
Chf. Mil. Div.—Maj. Gen. Jesse McI. Carter	8,000
Chf. Motor Transport Corps—Brig.-Gen. Chas. B. Drake	6,000
Dir. Military Aeronautics—Maj. Gen. C. T. Menoher	8,000
Dir. Chemical Warfare Service—Brig. Gen. A. A. Fries	6,000

Department of Justice.

	Salary.
Atty. Gen.—A. Mitchell Palmer, Pa.	$12,000
Solicitor Gen.—Wm. L. Frierson, Tenn.	10,000
Private Sec.—Robt. T. Scott, Va.	3,600
Asst. to Atty. Gen.—Frank K. Nebeker, Utah	9,000
Asst. Atty. Generals—Frank Davis, Jr., Ohio; Robt. P. Stewart, S. D.; Thos. J. Spellacy, Conn.; Annette A. Adams, Cal.; Leslie C. Garnett, Pa., each	7,500
Asst. Atty. Gen., Customs Div.—Bert Hanson, N. Y.	
Dir. Div. Investigation—Wm. J. Flynn, N. Y.	7,500
Solicitor for P. O. Dept.—W. H. Lamar, Md.	5,000
Solicitor for Int. Dept.—C. D. Mehaffie, Ore.	5,000

UNITED STATES GOVERNMENT—EXECUTIVE—*Continued.*

	Salary.
Solicitor of Treas.—Lawrence Becker, Ind.	5,000
Chief Clerk—C. E. Stewart, Ala.	4,000
Attorney in Charge of Titles—Charles S. Lawrence, Tenn.	3,500
Attorney in Charge of Pardons—Jas. A. Finch, N. Y.	3,600
Supt. of Prisons and Prisoners—D. S. Dickerson, Nev.	4,000
Appt. Clerk—C. B. Sornborger, Vt.	2,000

Post Office Department.

	Salary.
Postmaster Gen.—A. S. Burleson, Tex.	$12,000
First Asst. P. M. G.—J. C. Koons, Ind.	5,000
Second Asst.—Otto Praeger, Tex.	5,000
Third Asst.—Alex. M. Dockery, Mo.	5,000
Fourth Asst.—James I. Blakslee, Pa.	5,000
Dir. Postal Savings System—Malcolm Kerlin, D. C.	4,800
Purchasing Agt.—Robt. L. Maddox, Ky.	4,000
Chief Clerk—Ruskin McArdle, Tex.	4,000
Chief P. O. Inspr.—G. M. Sutton, Mo.	4,000
Gen. Supt. Div. Rural Mails—Geo. L. Wood, Md.	3,000
Supt. Post Office Service Division—Goodwin D. Ellsworth, N. C.	4,000
Gen. Supt. Ry. Mail Service—Wm. I. Denning, Ga.	4,000
Supt. Foreign Mails—S M. Weber, Md.	3,000
Supt. M. O.—Chas. E. Matthews, Okla.	2,750
Supt. Dead Letters—M. M. McLean, Tex.	2,500

Department of the Navy.

The Secretary of the Navy performs such duties as the President, who is Commander-in-Chief, may assign him, and has superintendence of construction, manning, armament, equipment and employment of vessels of war.

	Salary.
Sec. of the Navy—Josephus Daniels, N. C.	$12,000
Asst. Sec.—Gordon Woodbury, N. H.	5,000
Private Sec. to the Secretary—E. E. Britton, N. C.	2,500
Chief Clerk—F. S. Curtis, Ohio	3,000
Chief of Naval Operations—Admiral Robt. E. Coontz	10,000
Chief of Bur. of Navigation—Rear Admiral Thos. Washington	8,000
President Board of Inspection and Survey for Ships—Rear Adm. G. W. Kline	8,000
Chief of Steam Engineering—Engineer-in-Chief—*Robt. S. Griffin, Va.	8,000
Chief of Medicine and Surgery—Surgeon-General E R. Stitt, S. C.	8,000
Chief of Construction and Repair—Chief Constructor D. W. Taylor, Va.	8,000
Chief of Yards and Docks—Rear Admiral Chas. W. Parks	8,000
Chief of Supplies and Accounts—Vacant.	
Chief of Ordnance—Rear Admiral Chas. B. McVay, Col.	8,000
Dir. Naval Communications—Rear Adm. W. H. G. Bullard	8,000
Dir. of Naval Intelligence—U. T. Long, N. C.	8,000
Judge Adv. Gen.—Rear Admiral Geo. R. Clark	8,000
Major-General, Commandant of Marine Corps—Maj.-Gen. John A. Lejeune	8,000

Department of Interior.

The Secretary of the Interior is charged with supervision of public business relating to patents for inventions, pensions and bounty lands, public lands and surveys, the Indians, education, railroads, geological survey, reclamation of arid lands, investigation of methods of mining, appliances to prevent accidents to miners, and treatment of ores and other mineral substances, Hot Springs Reservation, Ark.; Yellowstone National Park, Wyo.; Casa Grande Ruin, Ariz.; the Yosemite, Sequoia, Gen. Grant and Lassen Volcanic Parks, Cal.; Mt. Rainier, Wash.; Crater Lake, Ore.; Wind Cave, S. D.; Platt, Okla.; Sullys Hill, N. D.; Mesa Verde, Colo.; Rocky Mountain, Colo.; Glacier, Mont.; Hawaii National Park and Mt. McKinley Natl. Park in Territory of Alaska; certain hospitals and eleemosynary institutions in the Dist. of Columbia, distribution of appropriations for agricultural and mechanical colleges in the States and Territories, the custody and distribution of certain public documents; the work of constructing Gov. railroads in Alaska; also exercises certain other powers in relation to territories of U. S.

	Salary.
Secretary—John Barton Payne, Ill.	$12,000
Asst. Sec.—Selden G. Hopkins, Wyo.	4,500
Chief Clerk—Ezekiel J. Ayers, N. J.	4,000
Com.-Gen. Land Office—Clay Tallman, Nevada	5,000
Com. of Patents—R. F. Whitehead, Va.	5,000
Com. of Pensions—F. D. Byington, Md.	5,000
Com. Indian Affairs—Cato Sells, Texas	5,000
Com. of Education—P. P. Claxton, Tenn.	5,000
Dir. Geological Survey—G. O. Smith, Me.	6,000
Dir. and Chief Engineer Reclamation Service—Arthur P. Davis, Kans.	7,500
Dir. Bur. of Mines—Fred. G. Cottrell, Cal.	6,000
Dir. of Natl. Park Service—S. T. Mather, Ill.	4,500

Department of Agriculture.

The Secretary of Agriculture is charged with the supervision of public business relating to the agricultural industry, with the duty of issuing rules and regulations for the protection, maintenance and care of the National Forest Reserves. He also is charged with carrying into effect laws prohibiting transporation by interstate commerce of game killed in violation of local laws and excluding from importation certain noxious animals. Has authority to control importation of other animals.

	Salary.
Sec. of Agriculture—E. T. Meredith, Ia.	$12,000
Asst. Sec.—E. D. Ball, Md.	5,000
Solicitor—R. W. Williams, D. C.	5,000
Private Sec. to Sec.—W. J. O'Leary, N. Y.	2,500
Chief Clerk—R. M. Reese, D. C.	3,500
Chief Weather Bur.—C. F. Marvin, O.	5,000
Chief, Office of Farm Management—H. C. Taylor, Va.	4,000
Chief of Bureau of Animal Industry—John R. Mohler, Ohio	5,000
Statistician and Chief of Bureau of Crop Est.—L. M. Estabrook, Tex.	4,000
Chemist and Chief of Bureau of Chemistry—C. L. Alsberg, Mass.	5,000
Dir. States Relations—A. C. True, Conn.	4,500
Entomologist and Chief of Bureau of Entomology—L. O. Howard, N. Y.	4,500
Biologist and Chief of Bureau of Biological Survey—E. W. Nelson, Ariz.	3,500
Forester and Chief of Forest Service—W. B. Greeley, Col.	5,000
Ch. Insecticide and Fungicide Board—J. K. Haywood, N. Y.	3,300
Chief of Bureau of Plant Industry—Wm. A. Taylor, Mich	5,000
Physiologist and Asst. Chief of Bur. of Plant Industry—K. F. Kellerman, O.	4,000
Chief of Div. of Accounts and Disbursements—A. Zappone, D. C.	4,000
Chf. Publication Div.—John L. Cobbs, Jr., Ind.	3,500
Chief Bureau of Soils—M. Whitney, Md.	4,000
Dir. Office of Public Roads and Rural Engineering—T. H. MacDonald, Iowa.	4,500
Chief, Office of Markets and Rural Organizations—Geo. Livingston	4,500
Ch. Fed. Horticultural Bd.—C. L. Marlatt, Kan.	4,000

Department of Commerce.

The Secretary of Commerce is charged with the work of promoting the commerce of the United States and its mining, manufacturing, shipping, fishery and transportation interests. His duties also comprise the investigation of the organization and management of corporations (excepting railroads) engaged in interstate commerce; the administration of the Lighthouse Service and the aid and protection of shipping thereby; the taking of the census, and the collection and publication of statistical information connected therewith, the making of coast and geodetic surveys; the collecting of statistics relating to foreign and domestic commerce; the inspection of steamboats, and the enforcement of laws relating thereto for the protection of life and property.

	Salary.
Sec. of Commerce—Joshua W. Alexander, Mo.	$12,000
Asst. Sec.—Edwin F. Sweet, Mich.	5,000
Private Sec. to Sec.—Wm. B. Yancey, Mich.	2,500

*With the rank of Rear-Admiral.

UNITED STATES GOVERNMENT—Executive—*Continued.*

	Salary.
Solicitor—F. G. Wixson, D. C.	5,000
Ch. Clk. and Supt.—E. W. Libbey, D. C.	3,000
Disbursing Clerk—C. E. Molster, D. C.	3,000
Chief of Appt. Div.—Clifford Hastings, Wash.	2,500
Chief, Bureau of Foreign and Domestic Commerce—R. S. MacElwee, N. Y.	6,000
Director of Census—S. L. Rogers, N. C.	6,000
Supt. Coast and Geodetic Survey—E. Lester Jones, Va.	6,000
Supervising Inspector General, Steamboat Inspection Service—G. Uhler, Pa.	4,000
Comr. of Fish and Fisheries—H. M. Smith, D. C.	6,000
Comr. of Navigation—E. T. Chamberlain, N. Y.	4,000
Comr. of Lighthouses—G. R. Putnam, Ia.	5,000
Dir., Bur. Standards—S. W. Stratton, Ill.	6,000

Department of Labor.

The Secretary of Labor is charged with the duty of fostering, promoting, and developing the welfare of the wage earners of the United States, improving their working conditions, and advancing their opportunities for profitable-employment. He has power under the law to act as mediator and to appoint commissioners of conciliation in labor disputes whenever in his judgment the interests of industrial peace may require it to be done.

	Salary.
Secretary of Labor—Wm. B. Wilson, Pa.	$12,000
Asst. Secretary—Louis F. Post, Ill.	5,000
Solicitor—R. B. Mahany, Ala.	5,000
Chief Clerk—Sam. J. Gompers, D. C.	3,000
Disbursing Clerk—Geo. W. Love, Ohio.	3,000
Priv. Sec. to Sec.—E. S. McGraw, Pa.	2,500
Chief Div. of Publications and Supplies—Henry A. Works, D. C.	2,500
Appointment Clerk—R. C. Starr, S. C.	1,800
Dir. Gen., Employment Service—John B. Densmore, Mont.	5,000
Com., Div. of Conciliation—Hugh L. Kerwin, Pa.	4,250
Comr.-Gen. of Immigration—Anthony Caminetti, Cal	5,000
Comr. of Naturalization—R. K. Campbell, Va.	4,000
Dir. of Citizenship—R. F. Crist, D. C.	4,000
Comr. of La or Stats.—Ethelbert Stewart, D. C. b	5,000
Chief Clerk and Statistician Bureau of Labor Statistics—Chas. E. Baldwin, Ill.	3,000
Chf. Children's Bur.—J. C. Lathrop, Ill.	5,000
Dir. Bureau Industrial Housing and Transportation—Robt. Watson, D. C.	7,000
Dir. Women in Industry Service—Mary Anderson, Ill.	5,000

Independent Departments.

SMITHSONIAN INSTITUTION.

Chancellor, Edward D. White, La.
Secretary, Charles D. Walcott.

UNITED STATES BUREAU OF EFFICIENCY.

Chief, H. D. Brown; sr. acct., H. N. Graves; labor-saving devices, W. E. Wilmot; efficiency ratings, W. H. McReynolds; chief clerk and disbursing officer, Miss D. F. Fridley; librarian, Florence C. Bell.

FEDERAL RESERVE BOARD.

Ch., David F. Houston, Sec. of the Treas.; J. S. Williams, Compt. of Currency. Gov., W. P. G. Harding, term expires Aug. 9, 1922. Vice-Gov., Edmund Platt, term expires Oct. 26, 1928. A. C. Miller, term expires Aug. 9, 1924. C. S. Hamlin, term expires Aug 9, 1926. D. C. Wills, term expires Dec. 7, 1930.

FEDERAL TRADE COMMISSION.

Commsnrs.—Ch., Huston Thompson, N. B. Gaskill, John G. Pollard, Victor Murdock and John F. Nugent; sec., J. P. Yoder.
Administrative Div.—Asst. sec., W. R. Choate; custodian and chief clerk's office, C. H. Becker; chief Div. of Personnel, Luther H. Waring; auditor and disbursing clerk's office, C. G. Duganne.
Economic Div.—Chief Economist, Francis Walker.
Legal Div.—Chief Counsel, A. F. Busick; Act. Chf. Exam., M. F. Hudson.

UNITED STATES SHIPPING BOARD.

Ch., Admiral Wm. S. Benson, term of 6 years from Nov. 10, 1920; Frederick I. Thompson, of Alabama, term of 5 years from Nov. 10, 1920; Joseph N. Teal, of Oregon, term of 4 years from Nov. 10, 1920; John A. Donald, of N. Y. City, term of 3 years from Nov. 10, 1920; Chester E. Rowell, of California, term of 2 years from Nov. 10, 1920; Guy D. Goff, of Wisconsin, term of 1 year from Nov. 10, 1920. Salary of each, $12,000.

PAN-AMERICAN UNION.

Dir.-Gen., L. S. Rowe, Washington, D. C., $7,500; Asst. Dir., F. J. Yanes, Venezuela, $4,000; Counselor, Franklin Adams, Cal., $3,600.

INTERSTATE COMMERCE COMMISSION.
Salary, $10,000.

Edgar E. Clark, Ia., Ch.; B. H. Meyer, Wis.; W. M. Daniels, N. J.; C. B. Aitcheson, Ore.; C. C. McChord, Ky.; Henry C. Hall, Col.; Robt. W. Woolley, Va.; John B. Eastman, Mass.; H. J. Ford, N. J.; Mark W. Potter, N. Y.; Jas. Duncan, Mass.; Sec., George B. McGinty, $5,000.

CIVIL SERVICE COMMISSION.

Pres., M. A. Morrison, Ind., $4,500; Geo. R. Wales, Vt., $4,000; Mrs. Helen H. Gardner, D. C., $4,000; Chf. Exam., H. A. Filer, Md., $3,000; Sec., J. T. Doyle, N. Y., $2,500.

U. S. COUNCIL OF NATIONAL DEFENSE.

The Council—Ch., Sec. of War; Sec. of Navy, Sec. of Interior, Sec. of Agriculture, Sec. of Commerce, Sec. of Labor.
Advisory Commsn.—Ch., Daniel Willard; B. M. Baruch, H. E. Coffin, Hollis Godfrey, Samuel Gompers, Dr. F. H. Martin, Julius Rosenwald; dir. of council and of advisory commsn., H. N. Shenton; Asst. to Dir., E. K. Ellsworth.

ALIEN PROPERTY CUSTODIAN.

Alien Property Custodian, F. P. Garvan; Managing Dir., H. E. Ahern; Dir. Bur. of Administration, A. G. Belt; Dir. Bur. of Trusts, H. B. Caton; Gen. Counsel, Wm. Sabine.

U. S. TARIFF COMMISSION.

Ch., Thos. Walker Page; Vice-Ch., Samuel McCall, Mass.; Commsrs., D. J. Lewis, of Md.; W. S. Culbertson, of Kan.; E. P. Costigan, of Col.; Sec., J. F. Bethune.

U. S. EMPLOYEES' COMPENSATION COMMISSION.

Ch., J. J. Keegan; C. H. Verrill, Mrs. F. C. Axtell; Sec., S. R. Goilbart, Jr.; Med. Dir., John W. Trask; Chf. Statistician, R. T. Hoage; Atty., S. D. Slentz; chief claim examr., John W. Edwards; disbursing agt., A. H. Gardes.

FEDERAL BOARD FOR VOCATIONAL EDUCATION.

Ch., Sec. of Labor, Wm. B. Wilson; Sec. of Commerce, J. W. Alexander; Sec. of Agriculture, E. T. Meredith; Commsnr. of Education, P. P. Claxton; Vice-Ch., J. P. Munroe, representative of manufacturing and commercial interests; C. F. McIntosh, representative of agricultural interests; A. E. Holder, representative of labor, 110 F st., sec., E. J. Aronoff; chief clerk, C. E. Alden.

THE PANAMA CANAL.

Gen. purchasing officer and chief of office, A. L. Flint; chief clerk, purchasing dept., E. D. Anderson; asst. to chief of office, R. L. Smith; appt. clerk, E. E. Weise.
On the Isthmus—Gov. of Canal, Brig.-Gen. Chester Harding, Corps of Engrs., U. S. Army, Balboa Heights; engr. of maintenance, Lieut. Col. J. J. Morrow, U. S. Army, Balboa Heights, C. Z.

COMMISSION ON NAVY YARDS AND NAVAL STATIONS.

Commnrs., Rear Adm., G. W. McElroy, Rear Adm. W. L. Capps (CC.), Rear Adm. H. H. Rousseau (CEC.), Capt. F. T. Chambers (CEC.).

NATIONAL ADVISORY COMMITTEE FOR AERONAUTICS.

Ch., Dr. C. D. Walcott; Prof. J. S. Ames (ch. exec. comm.), Col. T. H. Bane (U. S. A.), Capt. T. T. Craven (U. S. N.), Dr. W. F. Durand, Prof. J. F. Hayford, Prof. C. F. Marvin, Maj. Gen. C. T. Menoher (U. S. A.), Prof. M. I. Pupin, Rear Adm. D. W. Taylor (U. S. N.), Orville Wright; Sec., Dr. S. W. Stratton; Asst. Sec. and Special Disbursing Agent, J. F. Victory.

AMERICAN NATIONAL RED CROSS.

Natl. Officers—Pres., Woodrow Wilson; Vice Pres., W. H. Taft, New Haven, Conn.; R. W. de Forrest, 30 Broad, N. Y. C.; Treas., J. S. Williams; Counselor, Wm. L. Frierson; Sec., Miss M. T. Boardman.
Central Comm.—Ch., Dr. Livingston Farrand; Gen. Mgr., F. C. Munroe.

UNITED STATES GOVERNMENT—EXECUTIVE—*Continued.*

U. S. BOARD OF MEDIATION AND CONCILIATION.

Commsnr., W. L. Chambers: Asst. Commsnr., Whitehead Kluttz. Board of Mediation and Conciliation, Ch., M. A. Knapp; W. L. Chambers, Whitehead Kluttz. Sec., Wm. J. Hoover.

THE INTERNATIONAL JOINT COMMISSION.

U. S. Section—Ch., Obadiah Gardner; C. D. Clark; Sec., Wm. H. Smith.

Canadian Section—Ch., C. A. Magrath; H. A. Powell, K. C.; Wm. Hearst, K. C. M. G.; Sec., L. P. Burpee.

INT'N'L BOUNDARY COMM'S'N, U. S. AND C.

For defining and marking boundary between U. S. and Canada, except on Great Lakes and St. Lawrence River. For marking and surveying boundary between Alaska and Canada.

Comm'r.—E. C. Barnard; Eng. to comms.—J. H. Van Wagenen; Chief clerk and disbursing officer—Burton Fuller.

Canadian Section—Commr., J. J. McArthur, Dep. of Interior, Ottawa, Canada.

INT'N'L BOUNDARY COMM'S'N, U. S. AND MEXICO.

American Section—Commsr., Lucius D. Hill; Sec., W. F. Tinsley; Consulting engn., H. P. Corbin.

Mexican Section—Commsr., Antonio Prieto, Mexico City, Mexico; Sec., F. A. Pesqueria, El Paso, Tex.; Consulting engn., Manuel Bancalari, Juarez, Mexico.

U. S. SECTION OF INT'N'L HIGH COMM'S'N.

Ch., David F. Houston, Sec. of Treas.; Vice-Ch., J. B. Moore, N. Y. C.; J. H. Fahey, Boston, Mass.; Herbert Fleishhacker, San Fran., Calif.; D. U. Fletcher, U. S. Senator from Fla.; A. J. Peters, mayor of Boston, Mass.; Samuel Untermeyer, N. Y. C.; P. M. Warburg, N. Y. C.; J. H. Wigmore, dean of law school, Northwestern Univ., Chi., Ill.; Sec., L. S. Rowe, Pan American Union.

U. S. GEOGRAPHIC BOARD.

Ch., Dr. C. H. Merriam, Dep. of Agriculture.; Sec., C. S. Sloane, geographer, Census Bur., Dep. of Commerce. Ch. exec. comm., Frank Bond, chief clerk, Genl. Land Office, Dep. of Interior.; G. D. Ellsworth, sup., Div. of P. O. Service, P. O. Dep.; Wm. C. Barnes, asst. forester, Forest Service, Dep. of Agriculture; J. N. B. Hewitt, ethnologist, Bur. of American Ethnology, Smithsonian Institution; D. M. Hildreth, topographer, P. O. Dep.; J. W. McGuire, U. S. Coast and Geodetic Survey; W. McNeir, Chief Bur. of Acc., Dep. of State; J. S. Mills, editor and asst. chief of div., Dep. of Treas.; J. E. Payne, chief of proof sec., Gov. Print. Office; G. R. Putnam, Commnr. Bur. of Lighthouses, Dep. of Commerce; Rear Adml. L. H. Chandler, hydrographer, Dept. of Navy.

COMMISSION OF FINE ARTS

Ch., Chas. Moore, Detroit, Mich.; Vice-Ch., C. A. Platt, W. M. Kendall, J. R. Pope, J. L. Greenleaf, Wm. S. Kendall, Jas. E. Fraser; Sec. and Exec. Officer, Maj. C. S. Ridley, U. S. A.; Clerk to Comsn., H. P. Caemmerer.

PECUNIARY CLAIMS ARBITRATION COM'S'N.

Arbitrator, C. P. Anderson, N. Y.; Counsel and joint sec., Marshall Morgan, Tenn.

NATIONAL HOME FOR DISABLED VOLUNTEER SOLDIERS.

(National Military Home, Ohio.)

Branches.—Central, Dayton, Ohio; Northwestern, Milwaukee, Wis.; Eastern, Togus, Me.; Western, Leavenworth, Kansas.; Marion, Marion, Ind.; Pacific, Santa Monica, Cal.; Danville, Danville, Ill.; Mountain, Johnston City, Tenn.; Battle Mountain Sanitarium, Hot Springs, S. Dak.

Managers.—Pres. of U. S., Chief Justice, Sec. of War (ex officio), Washington, D. C.; Gen. G. H. Wood, pres. National Military Home, Dayton, Ohio.; Capt. J. C. Nelson, 1st vice pres., Logansport, Ind.; Maj. J. W. Wadsworth, 2d vice pres., Genesee N. Y.; S. Catherwood, sec., Hoopeston, Ill.; Col. H. H. Markham, Pasadena, Cal.; Menander Dennett, Lewiston, Me.

Gen. treas., Col. C. W. Wadsworth. Insp. gen. and chief surgeon, Col. Jas. A. Mattison.

JUDICIAL.

United States Supreme Court.

Chief Justice Edward D. White of Louisiana; born 1845; appointed 1910....... $15,000

Associate Justices at a salary of $14,500 each:

	Born.	App.
Joseph McKenna, Cal.............	1843	1898
Oliver W. Holmes, Mass...........	1841	1902
William R. Day, Ohio.............	1849	1903
Jas. C. McReynolds, Tenn.........	1862	1914
Willis Van Devanter, Wyo.........	1859	1910
Mahlon Pitney, N. J..............	1858	1912
Louis D. Brandeis, Mass..........	1856	1916
Jno. H. Clarke, Ohio	1857	1916

Term of office—For life.

Clerk, Jas. D. Maher, D. C.	$6,000
Marshal, Frank K. Green, D. C.	4,500
Reporter, Ernst Knaebel, Col...........	4,500

United States Circuit Court.

The salary of the Circuit Judges of the United States Courts is $7,000 each.

The Circuit and District Judges within circuit and the Justice of the Supreme Court for the circuit constitute a Circuit Court of Appeals.

1st—Justice Holmes of Mass. Districts of Me., N. H., Mass. and R. I.

Circuit Judges—Geo. H. Bingham, Concord, N. H.; Chas. F. Johnson, Portland, Me., and Geo. N. Anderson, Boston, Mass.

2d—Justice Louis D. Brandeis, Mass. Districts of Vt., Conn., Northern N. Y., Eastern N. Y., Southern N. Y. and Western N. Y.

Circuit Judges—H. G. Ward, N. Y.; Chas. M. Hough, N. Y.; H. W. Rogers, New Haven, and Martin T. Manton, N. Y.

3d—Justice Mahlon Pitney of N. J. Districts of N. J., Eastern Pa., Western Pa., Middle Pa. and Delaware.

Circuit Judges—J. W. Davis, Trenton, N. J.; Victor B. Woolley, Wilmington, Del.; Jos. Buffington, Pittsburgh, Pa.

4th—Chief Justice Edward D. White of La. Districts of Md., Northern and Southern W. Va., Eastern and Western Va., Eastern N. C., Western N. C. and S. C.

Circuit Judges—Chas. A. Woods, Florence, S. C.; J. C. Pritchard, Asheville, N. C., and Martin A. Knapp, D. C.

5th—Justice James C. McReynolds of W. Va. Districts of Northern Ga., Southern Ga., Northern Fla., Southern Fla., Northern Ala., Middle Ala., Southern Ala., Northern Miss., Southern Miss., Eastern La., Western La., Northern, Eastern, Western and Southern Texas and Canal Zone.

Circuit Judges—R. W. Walker, Huntsville, Ala., N. P. Bryan, Jacksonville, Fla.; A. C. King, Atlanta, Ga.

6th—Justice Wm. R. Day of O. Dists. of Northern O., Southern O., Eastern Mich., Western Mich., Eastern Tenn., Middle Tenn., Western Tenn., Eastern and Western Ky.

Circuit Judges—Arthur C. Denison, Grand Rapids, Mich.; M. H. Donahue, Columbus, O., and L. E. Knappen, Grand Rapids, Mich.

7th—Justice John H. Clarke, of Ohio. Districts of Ind., Northern Ill., Eastern Ill., Southern Ill., Eastern Wis., Western Wis.

Circuit Judges—Francis E. Baker. Hammond, Ind.; Samuel Alschuler, Chicago, Ill.; Julian W. Mack, Chicago, Ill.; Evan A. Evans, Madison, Wis., and Geo. T. Page, Peoria, Ill.

8th—Justice Willis Van Devanter of Wyo. Districts of Minn., Northern Ia., Southern Ia., Eastern Mo., Western Mo., Eastern Ark., Western Ark., Neb., Colo., Kan., N. Dakota, S. Dakota, Oklahoma, Utah, Wyoming and New Mexico.

Circuit Judges—Walter H. Sanborn, St. Paul, Minn.; William C. Hook, Leavenworth, Kan.; Walter I. Smith, Council Bluff, Iowa; J. E. Carland, Wash., D. C., and Kimbrough Stone, Kansas City, Mo.

9th—Justice Joseph McKenna, San Francisco, Cal. Districts of Arizona, Northern and Southern Cal., Ore., Nev., Eastern and Western Wash., Idaho, Montana, Territories of Alaska and Hawaii.

Circuit Judges—William W. Morrow, San Francisco, Cal.; William B. Gilbert, Portland, Ore.; Erskine M. Ross, Los Angeles, Cal.; Wm. H. Hunt, Wash., D. C.; Chas. S. Lobingier, Nebr., to hear appeals from U. S. Consuls in China and Corea.

District Judges.

Alabama (M.)—H. D. Clayton, Montgomery.
Alabama (N.)—Wm. I. Grubb, Birmingham.
Alabama (S.)—R. T. Ervin, Mobile.
Arizona—Wm. H. Sawtelle, Tucson.
Arkansas (E. D.)—Jacob Trieber, Little Rock.
Arkansas (W. D.)—F. A. Youmans, Fort Smith.

UNITED STATES GOVERNMENT—JUDICIAL—*Continued.*

California (N.)—Wm. C. Van Fleet, San Francisco; Maurice T. Dooling, San Francisco.
California (S)—B. F. Bledsoe and O. A. Trippet, Los Angeles.
Colorado—Robert E. Lewis, Denver.
Connecticut—E S. Thomas, New Haven.
Delaware—H. M. Morris, Wilmington.
Florida (N. D.)—Wm. B. Sheppard, Pensacola.
Florida (S. D.)—R. M. Call, Jacksonville.
Georgia (N. D.)—S. H. Sibley, Athens.
Georgia (S. D.)—B. D. Evans, Savannah.
Idaho—F. S. Dietrich, Boise.
Illinois (N. D.)—G. A. Carpenter and Kenesaw M. Landis, Chicago.
Illinois (E. D.)—Geo. W. English, Danville.
Illinois (S. D.)—Louis FitzHenry, Peoria.
Indiana—A. B. Anderson, Indianapolis.
Iowa (N. D.)—Henry T. Reed, Cresco.
Iowa (S. D.)—Martin J. Wade, Davenport.
Kansas—John C. Pollock, Kansas City.
Kentucky (W. D.)—Walter Evans, Louisville.
Kentucky (E. D.)—A. M. J. Cochran, Maysville.
Louisiana (E. D.)—R. E. Foster, New Orleans.
Louisiana (W. D.)—Geo. W. Jack, Shreveport.
Maine—Clarence Hale, Portland.
Maryland—John C. Rose, Baltimore.
Massachusetts—James M. Morton, Jr., Boston.
Michigan (E. D.)—Arthur J. Tuttle, Detroit.
Michigan (W.D.)—C. W. Sessions, Grand Rapids.
Minnesota—Wilbur F. Booth, Minneapolis, and Page Morris, Duluth.
Mississippi (N. & S. D.)—E. R. Holmes, Jackson.
Missouri (E. D.)—C. B. Faris, St. Louis.
Missouri (W. D.)—A. S. Van Valkenburgh, Kansas City.
Montana—Geo. M. Bourquin, Butte.
Nebraska—Thomas C. Munger, Lincoln, and J. W. Woodrough, Omaha.
Nevada—E. S. Farrington, Carson City.
New Hampshire—Edgar Aldrich, Littleton.
New Jersey—John Rellstab, Trenton; C. F. Lynch, Newark, and Jos. L. Bodine, Trenton.
New Mexico—Colin Neblett, Santa Fe.
New York (N. D.)—Geo. W. Ray, Norwich, and Frank Cooper, Albany.
New York (S. D.)—John C. Knox, Learned Hand, Julius M. Mayer and A. N. Hand, N. Y. City.
New York (E. D.)—Thos. I. Chatfield and Edwin L. Garvin, Bkln.
New York (W. D.)—John R. Hazel, Buffalo.
North Carolina (E. D.)—H. G. Connor, Wilson.
North Carolina (W. D.)—J. E. Boyd, Greensboro. and E. Y. Webb, Shelby.
North Dakota—Charles F. Amidon, Fargo.
Ohio (N. D.)—John M. Killits, Toledo, and D. C. Westernhaver, Cleveland.
Ohio (S. D.)—John W. Peck, Columbus, and John E. Sater, Columbus.
Oklahoma (E. D.)—R. L. Williams, Muskogee.
Oklahoma (W. D.)—J. H. Cotteral, Guthrie.
Oregon—C. E. Wolverton and R. S. Bean, Portland.
Pennsylvania (E. D.)—J. W. Thompson and Oliver B. Dickinson, Philadelphia.
Pennsylvania (M. D.)—C. B. Witmer, Sunbury.
Pennsylvania (W. D.)—W. H. S. Thomson and Chas. P. Orr, Pittsburgh.
Rhode Island—Arthur L. Brown, Providence.
South Carolina (E. D.)—H. A. M. Smith, Charleston.
South Carolina (E. D.)—H. H. Watkins, Anderson.
South Dakota—James D. Elliott, Sioux Falls.
Tennessee (E. and M. D.)—Edward T. Sanford, Knoxville.
Tennessee (W. D.)—J. E. McCall, Memphis.
Texas (E. D.)—W. Lee Estes, Texarkan.
Texas (W. D.) Duval West, San Antonio, and W. R. Smith, El Paso.
Texas (N. D.)—Edward R. Meek, Dallas, and J. C. Wilson, Fort Worth.
Texas (S. D.)—Jos. C. Hutcheson, Jr., Houston.
Utah—T. D. Johnson, Salt Lake City.
Vermont—H. B. Howe, Windsor.
Virginia (E. D.)—E. Waddill, Jr., Richmond.
Virginia (W. D.)—H. C. McDowell, Lynchburg.
Washington (W. D.)—Edward E. Cushman, Tacoma, and Jeremiah Neterer, Tacoma.
Washington (E. D.)—F. H. Rudkin, Spokane.
West Virginia (N. D.)—Vacant.
West Virginia (S. D.)—B. F. Keller, Charleston.
Wisconsin (E. D.)—Ferdinand A. Geiger, Milwaukee.
Wisconsin (W. D.)—Vacant.
Wyoming—John A. Riner, Cheyenne.

U. S. Courts in the Territories.

Alaska—(1st Div.), Robt. W. Jennings, Juneau; (2d Div.), W. A. Holzheimer, Nome; (3d Div.), F. M. Brown, Valdez; (4th Div.), C. E. Bunnell, Fairbanks.
Canal Zone—District Judge—J. W. Hanan, Ancon.

District of Columbia—Court of Appeals—C. J. Smyth, Chief Justice; J. A. Van Orsdel, Chas. H. Robb, Associate Justices.

District of Columbia—Supreme Court—Walter I. McCoy, N. J., Chief Justice; Wm. Hitz, Ashley M. Gould, Thos. J. Bailey, Wendell P. Stafford, Frederick L. Siddons, Associate Justices.

Hawaii—Supreme Court—Chief Justice, Jas. L. Coke, Honolulu; Asso. Justices, Samuel B. Kemp and Wm. S. Edings, Honolulu. Judges Circuit Courts—First Circuit, C. S. Franklin, John T. De Bolt and J. J. Banks, Honolulu; Second Circuit, L. L. Burr, Wailuku, Maui; Third Circuit, J. W. Thompson, Kailua; Fourth Circuit, C. K. Quinn, Hilo; Fifth Circuit, Wm. C. Achi, Jr., Lihue; U. S. District Judges, H. W. Vaughan and J. B. Poindexter, Honolulu.

Porto Rico—Supreme Court—Chief Justice, Jose C. Hernandez, San Juan; Associate Justices, Emilio del Toro, San Juan; Pedro De Aldrey, San Juan; H. M. Hutchison, Adolf Grant Wolf, San Juan. District Judge, Peter J. Hamilton, San Juan.

United States Court of Claims.

Chief Justice, Edward Campbell, Ala....$6,500
Judges—James Hay, Vt.; Geo. E. Downey, Ind.; F. W. Booth, Ill.; S. J. Graham, Pa., $6,000 each.

Court of Customs Appeals.

Presiding Judge, vacant; Associate Judges, James F. Smith, Cal.; Orion M. Barber, Vt.; Marion De Vries, Cal.; George E. Martin, Ohio, $7,000 each. Marshal, Frank H. Briggs, Me., $3,000. Clerk, Arthur B. Shelton, D. of C., $3,500.

UNITED STATES DISTRICT ATTORNEYS.

Alabama—No. Dist., Erle Pettus, Birmingham; Middle Dist., T. D. Samford, Montgomery; So. Dist., A. D. Pitts, Mobile.
Alaska—1st Div., J. A. Smiser, Juneau; 2d Div., J. M. Clements, Nome; 3d Div., W. A. Munly, Valdez; 4th Div., R. F. Roth, Fairbanks.
Arizona—T. A. Flynn, Phoenix.
Arkansas—Etn. Dist., June P. Wooten, Little Rock; Wtn. Dist., Jas. S. Holt, Ft. Smith.
California—No. Dist., F. M. Silva, San Francisco; So. Dist., John R. O'Connor, Los Angeles.
Canal Zone—A. C. Hindman, Ancon.
Colorado—H. B. Tedrow, Denver.
Conn.—Ed. L. Smith, Hartford.
Delaware—Jas. H. Hughes, Jr., Wilmington.
Dist. of Columbia—J. E. Laskey, Washington.
Florida—No. Dist., J. L. Neeley, Pensacola; So. Dist., H. S. Phillips, Tampa.
Georgia—No. Dist., Hooper Alexander, Atlanta; So. Dist., J. W. Bennett, Savannah.
Hawaii—S. C. Huber, Honolulu.
Idaho—J. L. McClear, Boise.
Illinois—No. Dist., C. F. Clyne, Chicago; Etn. Dist., J. G. Burnside, Danville; So. Dist., E. C. Knotts, Springfield.
Indiana—F. Van Nuys, Indianapolis.
Iowa—No. Dist., F. A. O'Connor, Dubuque; So. Dist., E. G. Mon, Ottumwa.
Kansas—Fred Robertson, Kansas City.
Kentucky—Wtn. Dist., W. V. Gregory, Louisville; Etn. Dist., T. D. Slattery, Covington.
Louisiana—Etn., Dist., Henry Mooney, New Orleans; Wtn. Dist., Joseph Moore, Shreveport.
Maine—J. F. A. Merrill, Portland.
Maryland—R. R. Carman, Baltimore.
Mass.—D. J. Gallagher, Boston.
Michigan—Etn. Dist., J. E. Kinnane, Detroit; Wtn. Dist., M. H. Walker, Grand Rapids.
Minnesota—Alfred Jaques, St. Paul.
Mississippi—No. Dist., W. S. Hill, Clarksdale; So. Dist., J. P. Alexander, Jackson.
Missouri—Etn. Dist., Jas. E. Carroll, St. Louis; Wtn. Dist., S. O. Hargres, Kansas City.
Montana—Geo. F. Shelton, Helena.
Nebraska—T. S. Allen, Lincoln.
Nevada—Wm. Woodburn, Jr., Reno.
New Hampshire—F. H. Brown, Concord.

UNITED STATES GOVERNMENT—JUDICIAL—*Continued.*

New Jersey—E. H. Geran, Trenton.
New Mexico—Summers Burkhart, Albuquerque.
N. Y.—No. Dist., D. B. Lucey, Utica; So. Dist., F. G. Caffey, N. Y. C.; Etn. Dist., Le Roy W. Ross, Bkln.; Wtn. Dist., S. T. Lockwood, Buffalo.
North Carolina—Etn. Dist., E. F. Aydlett, Elizabett City; Wtn. Dist., S. J. Durham, Charlotte.
No. Dakota—M. A. Hildreth, Fargo.
Ohio—No. Dist., E. S. Wertz, Cleveland; So. Dist., Jas. R. Clark, Cincinnati.
Oklahoma—Etn. Dist., C. W. Miller, Muskogee; Wtn. Dist., H. M. Peck, Oklahoma City.
Oregon—L. W. Humphreys, Portland.
Penn.—Etn. Dist., Chas. D. McAvoy, Phila.; Middle Dist., R. L. Burnett, Scranton; Wtn. Dist., D. J. Driscoll, Pittsburgh.
Porto Rico—M. M. Martin, San Juan.
Rhode Island—P. C. Cannon, Providence.
South Carolina—Etn. Dist., F. H. Weston, Charleston; Wtn. Dist., J. W. Thurmond, Greenville.
So. Dakota—E. W. Fiske, Sioux Falls.
Tennessee—Etn. Dist., W. T. Kennerly, Chattanooga; Middle Dist., Lee Douglas, Nashville; Wtn. Dist., W. D. Kyser, Memphis.
Texas—Etn. Dist., E. J. Smith, Sherman; No. Dist., R. E. Taylor, F. N. North; Wtn. Dist., Hugh R. Robertson, San Antonio; So. Dist., D. E. Simmons, Houston.
Utah—I. B. Evans, Salt Lake City.
Vermont—V. A. Bullard, Burlington.
Virginia—Etn. Dist., Julian Gunn, Richmond; Wtn. Dist., Jos. H. Chitwood, Roanoke.
Washington—Wtn. Dist., Robt. C. Saunders, Seattle; Etn. Dist., F. A. Garrecht, Spokane.
W. Virginia—No. Dist., S. W. Walker, Martinsburg; So. Dist., L. H. Kelly, Charleston.
Wisconsin—Etn. Dist., H. A. Sawyer, Milwaukee; Wtn. Dist., A. C. Wolfe, Madison.
Wyoming—C. L. Rigdon, Cheyenne.

WORK OF THE 66TH CONGRESS.

(1st Session (Extraordinary) of 66th Congress, and part of 2d session.)

The first or extraordinary session of the 66th Congress, which convened on May 19, 1919, at the call of the President, passed but few bills of importance. Pres. Wilson, in a speech to Congress at the opening of the session, laid down a program of the legislation he desired. The principal request was action by the Senate on the Treaty of Peace. The Senate devoted practically its entire time to the consideration of the Treaty. Meanwhile the House passed a number of bills, some of which were acted upon by the Senate, others were acted upon during the 2d session of the 66th Congress, which convened on Dec. 2, 1919.

Laws Passed.

The following legislation has been passed by both the House and Senate and is now upon the statute books:

Return of the telephone, telegraph and cable lines of the country to their owners.

Adoption of woman suffrage constitution amendment.

Enactment of prohibition enforcement bill.

Enactment of provisions for vocational training and rehabilitation of wounded soldiers and sailors and appropriation for the same.

Extension and enlargement of the food control act, as urged by the President, with a view of preventing hoarding and profiteering, and with additional penalties for the violation of the statute.

Provision for additional travel pay for enlisted men discharged from the Regular Army.

Authorizing enlisted men who served in the world war to retain their uniforms and personal equipment.

Incorporation of the American Legion.

Amendment of the War Risk Insurance Act, increasing the allowance in certain classes of serious injury.

Repeal of the daylight saving law.

Provision for additional compensation for employees of the Postal Service.

Legislation to facilitate the marketing of agricultural products, including livestock, by increasing amount which banks may loan on paper secured by such commodities.

Amendment to the Federal Reserve Act to enable national banks to assist in the facilitation of export trade.

Legislation making more stringent the restrictions and prohibitions surrounding the entry of aliens.

Provision for the completion of the railroad in Alaska.

Provision for the punishment for the transportation of stolen vehicles.

Provision for completion and payment of necessary construction work in Army camps and cantonments.

Provision in aid of relief for the stricken peoples of the Near East by providing for an organization for that purpose.

Provision for the further regulation of vessels operated by the Shipping Board.

Creation of office of general of the Armies of the U. S. in terms providing for the appointment of J. J. Pershing to that office.

Provision for an ambassador to Belgium.

Edge bill for the organization of private corporations, under the Federal Reserve Board, for the financing of foreign trade.

Work of the Second Session, 66th Congress.

Congress convened at noon on Dec. 1, 1919, for the second, or first regular session, of the 66th Congress. This session ran until June 5, 1920, when final adjournment was taken so that the members could attend the national conventions.

On Dec. 2 President Wilson transmitted, in writing, his annual message to Congress. Since his inauguration as President, this was only the second time in which Mr. Wilson had not appeared in person to address Congress. The President made no specific reference in this message to the Treaty of Versailles, except to make it clear that in his opinion the establishment of peace must be the first step toward a restoration of normal conditions. His principal recommendations for legislation were as follows:

Establishment of a national budget system; reorganization of the taxation system with simplifications of the income and excess profits taxes; readjustment of the tariff system to protect new American industries; recognition and relief for the veteran soldiers of the World War, particularly in the way of Government farms as proposed by Secretary of the Interior Lane; an enlarged program for rural development in recognition of the farmers' part in the war, and measures which will remove the causes of political restlessness in our body politic.

Congress immediately, after convening, resumed consideration of the bill for the return of the railroads to private ownership. This bill was passed early in 1920 and received the approval of the President.

Other important pieces of legislation enacted were:

A bill providing for the operation of the American merchant marine and creating a new Shipping Board.

Water power bill for the development of water power under Federal regulation.

Oil, Gas and Coal Land Leasing bill for the leasing of the remaining public lands containing coal, oil and gas.

Congress enacted a budget bill, but because of a provision taking away from the President the authority to remove the Comptroller of the Treasury, it was vetoed. This bill has been since introduced with the objectionable feature eliminated. It is expected to be passed at the present session.

The House also passed a bill providing a bonus for soldiers of the World War. This bill is now pending in the Senate.

The present session of Congress, the third one of the 66th, has witnessed the introduction and passage of a resolution recreating the War Finance Committee, with authority to loan money to the farmers, that they may sell their crops to foreign countries. This resolution is awaiting the approval of the President.

There has also been introduced a bill placing higher duties on the importation from foreign countries of agricultural commodities. This is designed to help maintain higher prices in the United States, so that the farmers may sell their crops at a profit.

The present session has also undertaken the formation of a new general tariff revision bill. This bill will not be taken up at this session.

UNITED STATES DEPARTMENTS IN NEW YORK CITY.

U. S. Circuit Court of Appeals.

MANHATTAN—Post Office Building.

The Circuit Court of Appeals, 2d circuit, is composed of Judges H. G. Ward, H. W. Rogers, C. M. Hough, M. T. Manton, $8,500 each, and the Supreme Court Justice assigned to that circuit, Justice L. D. Brandeis.

Clerk—Wm. Parkin; salary, $4,500.

United States District Court.

Southern District of New York.

MANHATTAN—Post Office Building.

Judges of District Court—L. Hand, J. M. Mayer, A. N. Hand, J. C. Knox, $7,500.

Clerk—Alex. Gilchrist, Jr. Dep. Clerk, Wm. Tallman.

U. S. Atty.—F. G. Caffey, $10,000; Asst. Attys. —E. B. Barnes, B. A. Matthews, J. Hunter, Jr.; K. Lorenz, M. S. Mattuck, J. S. Johnson, J. M. Ryan, E. H. Reynolds, E. F. Unger, G. Cotter, G. W. Taylor, D. V. Cahill, John E. Joyce, H. E. Kelley, J. Fine, A. C. Rothwell, L. D. Schwartz, Jerome Simmons; salaries, $5,000 to $1,600.

Special Assts. to U. S. Atty.—H. A. Guiler, D. Nicoll, Jr., J. E. Walker, J. W. Osborne, 2d; L. B. Duerr, P. B. Olney, Jr., G. F. Goldthwait, R. S. Holmes, J. J. Lilly, T. Megorden, F. L. McGurk, R. A. Peattie.

Chief Clerks—W. J. Etgen, J. V. B. Merritt and Jerry Bonner.

Marshal—T. D. McCarthy, $5,000.

U. S. Comm'rs—S. R. Betts, H. W. Goodrich, E. L. Owen, Herbert Green and S. M. Hitchcock, New York; E. J. Collins, Newburgh; D. B. Deyo, Kingston.

Eastern Dist. of New York.

BROOKLYN—Post Office Building.

Dist. Judges—Thos. I. Chatfield, E. L. Garvin, $7,500.

Clerk—P. G. B. Gilkes.

Dep. Clerks—Joseph G. Cochran, J. H. Proctor.

Marshal—J. M. Power, $4,000; Chief Dep. Marshal, Wm. H. Parry.

U. S. Attorney—Leroy W. Ross, $4,500.

Regular Asst. U. S. Attorneys—J. T. Eno, H. Harvey Harwood, C. J. Buchner, R. N. Gilmore, J. J. Licari, W. E. J. Collins, C. J. McWilliams, R. J. Barry.

U. S. Commissioners—J. J. Allen, M. F. McGoldrick, J. Gray, J. H. McCabe, F. P. Nohowel, E. D. Hennessy, H. D. Barmore and H. S. Rasquin.

Collector of Customs Office.

Custom House, Bowling Green, Manhattan.

"A" Div. (Administration), B. R. Newton, Collector, $12,000; H. C. Stuart, Spl. Dep. Coll., $6,500; F. Kaley, Supt. of Supplies, $4,500; M. Fluhrer, Pvt. Sec., $3,800; J. C. Williams, Dep. Col., $3,500; F. N. Dodge, Appointment Clk., $2.800; 1st Div. (Marine), S. W. Hamilton, Clk. and A. D. C., $4,000; E. J. Donohue, Chf. Clk., $3,200; 2d Div. (Entry). W. P. Zwinge, Clk. and A. D. C., $4,000; R. V. Friedrichs, Chf. Clk., $3,500; J. J. Viele, Chf. Entry Clk., $3,200; 3d Div. (Moneys and Accounts), E. S. Hawkins, Chief, $4,500; W. T. Black, in charge Cashier s Bur., $4,200; F. T. Leahy, in charge Warehouse Bur., $4,200; G. W. Brinck, in charge Disbursement Bur., $3,000; S. C. Duryea, Supt. of Warehouses, $3.100; 4th Div. (Records). H. L. Swords, Dep. Coll., $3,000; 5th Div. (Liquidating), E. J. Allendorf, Clk. and A. D. C., $4,500; C. B. Winne, Chf. Clk., $3,200; 7th Div. (Law), M. P. Andrews, Solicitor to the Coll., $5,500; E. Barnees, Asst. Solicitor, $3,800; W. R. Eaton, Chf. Clk., $3 200.

Naval Office of Customs.

Custom House, Bowling Green, Mhtn.

The Naval Office directly represents the Treasury Dept. at N. Y., in the final accounting for all customs revenues collected in this district. (For duties of Naval Officer see page 391, 1916 Eagle Almanac.)

Naval Officer, H. Otto Wittpenn; Controller, T. J. Skuse; Dep. Naval Officer, G. N. See. Chiefs of Divisions and Bureaus, J. A. Bangs, A. Eaton, N. J. Mullins, C. B. Sweeney, H. E. Jones. Mem. of Board of U. S. Civil Service Examiners, T. J. Skuse.

Surveyor's Dept.

Custom House, Bowling Green, Mhtn.

Surveyor, T. E. Rush, $8,000; Spec. Dep., W. F. Buechler, $4,500; Act. Dep. Sur. and Sec. to Surveyor, B. S. Ashby, $3,200; Chief, Inspection, Wm. Tierney, $4,000; Chief, Baggage Bureau, Alex. McKeon, $3,500; Bureau of Customs Guards, W. W. Trumble, $3,000; Dep. Surveyors in charge of Districts, $3,000 each: W. T. Brophy, Dist. 1; M. M. Comeys, Dist. 2; J. T. McNally, Dist. 3; J. L. Whalen, Dist. 4; W. R. Sanders, Dist. 5; M. P. Jackson, Dist. 6; J. Hennessey, Jr., Dist. 7; J. F. Curran, Dist. 8.

U. S. Bureau of Foreign & Domestic Commerce.

R. 734, Custom House, Bowling Green, Mhtn.

The Government's bureau to develop the various manufacturing industries of the U. S. and markets for their products at home and abroad, to stimulate export trade. Is a clearing house for commercial information of all kinds, and has a well organized and efficient system for its collection and distribution, furnishes Amer. mfgrs. and exporters definite information as to specific opportunities to sell their goods in foreign countries.

Appraiser's Office.

641 Washington, Mhtn.

Appraiser Port of N. Y., J. K. Sague, $8,000; Spec. Dep. Appr. and Asst. Appr., 1st and 10th Divs., G. W. Wolf, $4,000; Dep. Appr. and Asst. Appr., 3d Div., C. W. Bunn, $4,000; Dep. Appr. and Asst. Appr., 8th Div., C. C. Keenan, $4,000; Asst. Appr., 2d Div., M. F. Tanahey; 4th Div., N. G. Schlamm; 5th Div., C E. Victory; 6th Div., F. S. Terry; 7th Div., T. J. Burns; each $3,500; Chf. Clk., E. M. Barber, $3,500.

Sub-Treasury.

Wall and Nassau, Mhtn.

Asst. Treas., M. Vogel, $8,000; Cashier, U. S. Grant, $4,200; Asst. Cash., F. P. Chapman, $3,600; Chief Clerk, C. L. Blair, $3,000; Paying Tellers, E. R. Lynch and Jas. P. Espie, $3,000 each; Receiving Teller, Chas. M. Le Furge, $2,800; Bond Clerk, H. D. Sherer, $2,800.

United States Assay Office.

32 Pine, Mhtn.

Supt. V. M. Bovie, $5,000; Assayer, G. R. Comings, $3,000; Supt. of Melting and Refining, Elry J. Wagor, $3,500.

Steamboat Inspection Service Bureau.

(Under Dept. of Commerce.)

Custom House, Mhtn.

Super. Insp. of Steam Vessels, 2d Dist., H. M. Seeley, $3,450; Local Insps., G. T. Charloton and J. L. Crone, each $2,950; Clks. to Superv. Insp., J. Specter, $1,500; G. Reich, $1,000; Chief Clk. to Local Insps., T. B. Martin, $1,500; Clks. to Local Insps., W. C. Osborne, $1,500; F. J. Dunlea, $1,400; J. J. Daly, $1,400; B. Kohn, B. A. Jones, S. A. Noyes, J. A. Luhrs, each $1,200; J. A. Kehl, $1,000; Asst. Inspectors of Hulls, F. J. Smith, C. M. Bunce, H. R. Campbell, T. H. Foster, H. Jones, J. Watkinson, H. Wellman, C. H. Smith, E. J. Millikin, E. Keane, J. H. Mathews, W. A. Harvey, G. N. Francisco, W. E. Disley, J. H. Bethel, W. J. Barry, A. S. Johnstone, T. F. Dalton, W. Mason, T. E. Norton, each $2,500; Asst. Insps. of Boilers, J. J. McCarthy, W. G. Fenwick, W. H. Powers, P. J. O'Reilly, J. L. Moran, J. W. Waters, J. Egan, F. L. Dennis, J. W. Wilson, F. Kelly, J. Smith, P. J. Hunt, J. Mason, A. D. Fitzgerald, J. B. Riley, R. K. Griswold, W. J. Johnston, each $2,500.

United States Internal Revenue.

BROOKLYN.

1ST DISTRICT, N. Y.—Federal Bldg. Comprising all of Long Island and Richmond.

Bertram Gardner, Collector, $6,000; Wm. Berker, Chf. Office Dep., $3,600; E. M. Muller, Chf. Field Dep., $3.300; F. E. O'Leary, Chf. Income Tax Div., $3,300; F. D. Roach, Cash., $2,500; Wm. M. Farmer, Bkpr., $2,500; P. S. Davis, Chf. Estate Div., $2,400; Ellen M. Jameson, Chf. Sales Tax Div., $2,000.

Division Deputies—J. A. McNally, $2,000; P. P. McGuirk, $2,000; F. Scheide, $2,000; G. M. Goodale, $2,000; J. J. Ruppell, $1,800; J. W. McHenry, $1,800; O. Fitzpatrick, $1,800; S. Kapper, $2,000; 5 at $1,700, 4 at $1,600, 15 at $1,500.

Narcotic Deputy—Belle M. McMahon, $1,500.

STATISTICS OF LEADING AMERICAN CITIES—*Continued.*

Cities.	Standing.†	Population U. S. Census 1920.	Dept. of Health: Area Sq. Miles.	Dept. of Health: Annual Death Rate per 1,000.	Dept. of Health: Annual Birth Rate per 1,000.	Department of Finance: Assessed Property Value: Real.	Department of Finance: Assessed Property Value: Personal.	Department of Finance: Tax Rate per $1,000 of Assessed Value.	Department of Finance: Per Cent. of Real Val. to Ass'd Val.
New Orleans, La.	17	387,219	196	12.39	21.71	$173,468,682	$70,609,333	$22.00	75
New York, N. Y.	1	5,620,048	317	12.28	24.00	8,626,121,707	396,506,155	.....	100
Manhattan	..	2,284,103	21.3	12.39	21.71	5,186,771,887	227,033,350	24.80	100
Bronx	..	732,016	41.4	13.78	28.07	753,308,264	17,211,200	25.30	100
Brooklyn	..	2,018,356	60.3	12.28	24.00	1,937,811,205	41,192,900	25.40	100
Queens	..	469,042	112	12.93	22.07	636,409,159	8,792,100	25.40	100
Richmond	..	116,531	57.19	20.40	24.61	111,521,192	2,246,635	25.30	100
Norfolk, Va.	59	115,777	10	12.00	26.00	68,218,724	22,205,120	19.00	75
Oakland, Cal	31	216,361	56	12.5	18.00	138,427 950	26,537,145	24.00	60
Omaha, Neb	34	191,601	38	10.5	22.5	*64,104,388	....	49.00	20
Paterson, N. J.	49	135,866	8.36	15.65	21.51	92,778,565	19,711,170	20.40	100
Philadelphia, Pa	3	1,823,158	129.59	14.52	23.53	1,941,467,934	693,630,026	21.50	100
Pittsburgh, Pa	9	588,193	42	16.3	24.3	802,571,410	....	21.00	85
Portland, Ore	24	258,288	66.3	11.00	14.9	226,679,805	58,561,245	10.80	75
Providence, R. I.	27	237,595	18.29	13.22	21.68	287,064,360	195,499,040	23.50	100
Reading, Pa	64	107,784	6	11.43	20.54	*68,695,788	....	22.00	75
Richmond, Va	38	171,667	24.3	23.79	23.94	139,397,978	102,624,769	19.50	75
Rochester, N. Y.	23	295,750	21.09	12.45	22.97	275,843,471	1,025,250	23.24	80
St. Louis, Mo	6	772,897	62	14.3	23.3	667,887,200	150,000,000	23.50	80
St. Paul, Minn	30	284,595	55.44	9.56	16.66	106,309,261	41,207,490	53.00	40
Salt Lake City, Utah	57	118,110	51.54	12.02	23.84	135,053,346	70,928,066	11.00	100
San Antonio, Tex	41	161,379	36	15	21.04	95,833,690	36,451,157	22.50	75
San Francisco, Cal	11	508,410	46.50	14.75	17.34	585,105,569	234,332,429	31.30	50
Scranton, Pa	47	137,783	20	18.4	22.00	60,386,545	47,610,090	13.10	80
Seattle, Wash	20	315,652	94.47	11.05	19.90	199,635,368	46,187,678	30.55	50
Spokane, Wash	66	104,437	39.25	7.57	13.82	58,824,950	20,667,367	57.75	50
Springfield, Mass	51	129,563	39.9	13.69	26.73	202,524,420	29,172,315	24.30	100
Syracuse, N. Y.	37	171,717	18	13.9	24.8	171,249,479	493,919	23.17	90
Tacoma, Wash	71	96,965	43.6	9 46	15.31	43,363,580	16,240,060	23.00	46.5
Toledo, O	26	243,109	33	13.38	19.59	291,109,110	141,336,410	27.4	100
Trenton, N. J.	55	119,289	9	24.8	32.1	76,177,195	16,030,800	24.20	100
Utica, N. Y.	74	94,156	....	....	....	87,795,495	628,600	23.67	100
Washington, D. C.	14	437,571	62.24	13.99	18.07	426,623,630	415,013,651	15.00	67
Wilmington, Del	62	110,168	11.29	17.12	28.27	108,958,675	....	17.50	100
Worcester, Mass	35	179,754	38.49	26.25	46.72	191,368,550	40,636,270	26.60	100
Yonkers, N. Y.	68	100,176	21	10.6	22.3	160,869,445	1,396,250	22.35	100
Youngstown, O.	50	132,358	25	14.3	29.66	*243,000,000	....	16.40	33⅓

Cities.	Department of Finance: Net Public Debt.	Department of Finance: Annual Cost of Maintaining City Government.	Department of Finance: Per Capita Cost of Maintaining City Government.	Dept. of Education: Number of Pupils in Public Schools.	Dept. of Education: Number of Princi-pals and Teachers.	Dept. of Education: Annual Cost of Maintaining Public Schools	Fire Dept.: Regular.	Fire Dept.: Volunteer.	Fire Dept.: Average Annual Cost of Force.	Police Department: Number of Force.	Police Department: Average Annual Number of Arrests.	Police Department: Average Annual Cost of Force.
New Orleans, La.	$36,601,145	$3,213,943	$8.89	$51,595	1,369	$1,886,722	455	....	$494,400	464	23,239	$483,916
New York, N. Y.	‡624365937	246,916,622	43.93	931 468	23,010	45,765,043	6,067	675	11,161,437	10,887	199,099	20,534,695
Manhattan	....	....	.....	339,755	8,416	....	....	....	....	....	....	....
Bronx	....	....	.....	131,212	3,226	....	....	....	....	....	....	....
Brooklyn	....	....	.....	356,295	8,680	....	....	....	....	....	....	....
Queens	....	....	.....	83,535	2,165	....	....	....	....	....	....	....
Richmond	....	....	.....	20,671	523	....	....	....	....	....	....	....
Norfolk, Va.	10,229,000	3,078,353	34.35	18,300	560	834,000	174	....	336,607	267	17,360	461,456
Oakland, Cal	7,222,860	3,674,697	16.98	49,186	1,381	2,932,267	344	....	629,113	225	11,589	350,243
Omaha, Neb	9,861,438	2,068,000	10.78	35,067	1,111	2,533,331	331	....	571,135	275	25,553	348,918
Paterson, N. J.	6,566,409	2,270,158	18.15	22,985	675	1,253,857	213	....	333,900	167	4,371	272,015
Philadelphia, Pa	144,109,150	48,520,872	26.62	237,514	6,060	12,274,788	1,666	....	2,746,194	4,475	75,618	6,726,248
Pittsburgh, Pa	29,026,296	12,521,165	21.58	86,823	2,610	5,156,921	906	....	1,729,712	892	46,404	1,139,411
Portland, Ore	14,541,950	5,234,873	21.04	45,279	1,300	3,741,022	440	150	800,000	373	17,000	603,477
Providence, R. I.	14,001,043	12,651,069	53.60	38,519	1,064	1,881,686	294	....	672,000	434	8,439	928,284
Reading, Pa	1,836,439	1,157,499	10.73	16,000	440	731,843	....	5,855	82,725	110	1,615	160,865
Richmond, Va	13,569,097	5,051,069	29.40	30,219	984	1,271,453	267	....	310,234	213	12,124	377,755
Rochester, N. Y.	19,888,779	9,408,878	31.00	50,088	1,465	2,257,563	470	100	912,197	380	4,998	669,014
St. Louis, Mo	19,964,000	16,935,243	21.91	106 991	2,625	6,324,345	842	....	1,311,362	1,176	49,630	2,411,386
St. Paul, Minn	8,300,941	10,374,337	44.22	33,000	1,144	2,415,000	484	....	749,194	325	8,070	398,780
Salt Lake City, Utah	6,850,046	2,996,953	25.37	24,000	860	1,858,956	102	....	149,237	115	4,605	202,391
San Antonio, Tex	7,563,000	1,790,590	11.1	25,504	695	918,059	200	....	267,519	231	17,068	267,559
San Francisco, Cal	34,322,600	21,185,666	41.69	70,626	1,856	3,468,418	898	....	2,004,186	962	26,673	1,792,118
Scranton, Pa	1,335,376	1,332,368	9.67	24,113	688	1,177,993	195	....	329,530	146	5,384	165,000
Seattle, Wash	16,279,400	8,958,804	26.21	42 615	1,536	4,213,402	606	....	1,118,492	517	21,876	901,831
Spokane, Wash	5,415,925	2,483,210	23.77	21,311	630	1,200,760	157	....	268,175	106	3,416	157,136
Springfield, Mass	8,588,355	4,707,173	36.31	22 648	787	1,694,634	274	....	488,241	182	3,393	342,128
Syracuse, N. Y.	8,330,986	4,212,872	24.50	22,300	690	1,339,962	290	....	537,215	238	5,012	415,995
Tacoma, Wash	4,794,619	1,321,263	13.62	18,203	508	1,022,237	144	30	283,356	93	9,576	152,665
Toledo, O	8,859,854	5,170,269	21.26	39 877	1,058	2,168,980	235	....	373,563	332	16,090	357,029
Trenton, N. J.	6,110,437	1,665,169	16.13	17,764	533	1,098,709	139	....	240 622	151	5,231	282,978
Utica, N. Y.	2,930,055	2,706,156	.....	16,000	480	914,612	135	....	239,721	114	3,814	163,218
Washington, D. C.	2,152,626	21,393,007	48.88	65 298	2,096	4,155,790	650	....	1,271,060	993	48,930	1,381,520
Wilmington, Del	6,385,100	1,584,114	14.94	13,707	391	604,873	28	800	105,000	165	3,620	280,000
Worcester, Mass	8,448,538	7,837,700	43.6	29,147	883	1,971,672	267	12	388,789	300	8,738	494,500
Yonkers, N. Y.	15,243,711	4,181,551	41.72	18,000	600	1,500,000	129	400	259,339	193	3,084	342,392
Youngstown, O.	6,158,733	1,200,000	9.06	22,157	592	1,401,124	92	....	169,128	156	10,340	400,000

†Subject to correction. *Real and Personal. ‡Net Funded Debt, Sept. 1, 1920.

STATISTICS OF LEADING AMERICAN CITIES—*Continued.*

Cities.	Miles from New York.	Time from New York.	Department of Streets and Public Works.								Water Works Department.					Mayor.		
			Total Miles of Streets.	Total Miles of Paved Streets.	Annual Cost of Cleaning Streets.	Annual Cost of Removing Garbage and Ashes.	Total Miles of Sewers.	Annual Cost of Street Lighting. Gas.	Annual Cost of Street Lighting. Electricity.	Lighting Plant Owned by City?	Daily Capacity of Water Works. Gallons.	Average Daily Consumption. Gallons.	Miles of Mains.	Total Cost of Works.	Water Plant Owned by City?	Name of Mayor and Political Party.	Salary.	Term Expires.
New Orleans, La.	1364	32	525	352	$593,[illegible]93	$197,000	508	....	$256,750	No	50,[illegible]00[illegible]	39[illegible]00[illegible]		$[illegible]80,[illegible]0,[illegible]00	Yes	A. J. McShane........Dem.	10,000	Dec. '24
New York, N. Y.	....	..	3543	2226	3,443[illegible]82	3,259,353	2290	$825,020	2,331,535	No	[95,000,000	660,200,000	*3014	^{f}2020993[illegible]2	Yes	Jno. F. [illegible]h........Dem.	15,000	Dec. '21
Manhattan	....	..	484	472	....	....	534	....	....	No	85[illegible]0,000	417[illegible]0,00	1348	19,372,[illegible]00	Yes	^{e}H. H. [illegible]h........Rep.	7,500	Dec. '21
Bronx	....	..	487	203	....	....	379	....	....	..	‡........	‡........	....	‡........	‡...	^{e}H. R. Bruckner......Dem.	7,500	[illegible] '21
Brooklyn	....	..	1258	885	....	....	[illegible]53	....	....	No	,[illegible]90,000	181,[illegible],[illegible]00	1125	46,500,000	Yes	^{e}[illegible]w. Riegelmann....Dem.	7,500	Dec. '21
Queens	....	..	108	478	....	....	60	....	....	No	20,000,000	44,200,000	62	4,187,000	Prt	M. E. Connelly......[illegible]em.	[illegible]00	Dec. '21
Richmond	....	..	320	257	....	....	93	....	....	No	27,000,000	17,000,000	273	4,333,000	Yes	^{e}C. D. Van Name.....Dem.	5,000	Dec. '21
Norfolk, Va.	346	12	180	95	†360,000	....	115	....	56,500	No	10,000,000	7,250,000	25	2,000,000	Yes	A. L. Roper............Pres.	[illegible]00	S[illegible]. '23
Oakland, Cal.	3250	[illegible]6	58	130	[illegible]0	††19,426	432	37,255	125,823	No	26,000,000	19,71[illegible] 00	82	22,000,000	No	[illegible]ohn L. Davie..........Rep.	4,200	[illegible]uhe '23
Omaha, Neb.	183	40	675	[illegible]0	70,000	45,000	390	25,000	140,[illegible]00	Yes	68,000,000	20,866,754	80	7,169,633	Yes	E. P. Smith...........Dem.	6,000	May '21
Paterson, N. J.	17	½	207	127	50,000	[illegible]0 00	141	8,000	80,[illegible]02	No	62,000,000	9,600,000	154	....	No	F. J. Van Noort......Dem.	3,500	Dec. '21
Philadelphia, Pa.	90	2	1350	1200	2,800,[illegible]00	2[illegible]0,00	140	....	1,305,289	^{d}No	320,000,000	320,000,000	1894	65,000,000	Yes	J. H. Moore............Rep.	12,000	Jan. '24
[illegible]h, Pa.	431	13	[illegible]36	542	*402,024	....	634	....	429,826	Yes	190,000,000	115,000,000	[illegible]6	28,000,000	Yes	E. V. Babcock........N. P.	10,000	Jan. '22
Portland, Ore.	3181	115	844	400	249,67[illegible]	†......	528	....	194,148	No	67,500,000	29,767,000	762	12,807,529	Yes	G. L. [illegible]r............Rep.		[illegible]he '21
[illegible]e, R. I.	189	5	[illegible]8	74	173,826	39,000	252	....	245,954	No	68,000,000	21,560,396	437	7,802,647	Yes	Jos. H. Gainer........Dem.	6,600	Jan. '23
Reading, Pa.	148	4	125	27	55,000	32,000	121	15,000	75[illegible]00	No	19,000,000	15,[illegible]0,[illegible]00	125	4,750,000	Yes	J. K. Stauffer.........Rep.	3,500	Jan. '24
Richmond, Va.	344	11	374	82	88,724	131,765	230	7,372	74,904	Yes	32,000,[illegible]00	31,314,877	251	4,500,000		[illegible]e [illegible]lie ....Dem.	6,500	Sep. '24
Rochester, N. Y.	371	7	401	276	202,420	323,433	361	....	¶[illegible]8,[illegible]95	No	37,000,000	23,000,000	458	13,000,000	Yes	Hiram H. Edgerton...Rep.	7,500	[illegible] '21
St. [illegible]is, Mo.	1048	29	95	[illegible]3	93,7[illegible]4	140,730	878	595,728	127,336	No	160,000,000	104,110,744	1013	32,756,769	Yes	Henry W. Kiel.........Rep.	10,000	[illegible] '21
St. Paul, Minn.	100	27	290	55	184,500	52,664	433	161,116	161,116	No	40,000,000	17,025,230	139	7,127,615	Yes	L. C. Hodgson.........N. P.	5,000	June '22
Salt Lake City, Utah	2452	72	[illegible]0	71	92,193	43,165	286	....	70,017	No	47,[illegible]00,[illegible]00	26,[illegible]00,[illegible]00	319	4,075,000	Yes	C. C. Neslen..........Dem.	4,200	Jan. '25
San Antonio, Tex.	2222	63	60	[illegible]4	174,660	96,000	247	....	53,500	No	65,000,000	16,000,000	85	4,500,000	No	S. C. Bell..............N. P.	5,000	May '21
San Francisco, Cal.	[illegible]	106	860	485	530,010	^{b}......	510	....	¶500,000	No	44,000,000	37,000,000	627	35,900,000	No	Jas. Rolph, Jr.........N. P.	6,000	Jan. '24
Scranton, Pa.	146	4	153	61	44,373	[illegible]987	125	....	62,424	No	30,000,000	35,000,[illegible]00	...	... .	....	A. T. Connell..........Rep.	5,000	Jan. '22
Seattle, Wash.	3232	102	1[illegible]0	[illegible]3	174,182	420,000	514	....	202,113	Yes	[illegible]00	33,000,000	718	13,947,107	Yes	Hugh M. Caldwell....Rep.		[illegible]h. '22
Spokane, Wash.	2840	192	395	71	57,740	55,000	16	....	64,288	No	84,500,[illegible]0	20,[illegible]2,100	357	4,850,[illegible]00	Yes	Chas. A. Fleming...........	3,600	Jan. '22
Springfield, Mass.	142	4	[illegible]6	101	225,000	198[illegible]00	153	....	151,000	No	17,000,000	11,920,000	227	5,758,921	Yes	E. F. Leonard..........Rep.	6,000	Jan. '23
Syracuse, N. Y.	291	6	275	115	193,331	[illegible],116	30	....	181,077	No	121,000,000	26,660,[illegible]00	225	5,860,736	Yes	H. H. Farmer..........Rep.		[illegible]c. '21
Tacoma, [illegible]	3225	102	[illegible]6	[illegible]9	52,052	^{b}......	301	....	54,373	Yes	54,000,000	23,330,000	285	5,657,270	Yes	C. M. Riddell..........N. P.	[illegible]00	May '22
Toledo, O.	733	19	610	244	81,902	68,819	280	....	129,331	No	101,000,000	28,000,[illegible]00	415	7,500,000	Yes	C. Schrieber ....N. P.	7,500	Jan. '22
Trenton, N. J.	57	1⅙	150	66	60,000	43,500	[illegible]5	15,000	63,[illegible]20	No	30,000,000	16[illegible]0,[illegible]00	176	2,[illegible]86,[illegible]00	Yes	Fredk. W. Donnelly...Dem.	5,250	May '22
Utica, N. Y.	238	5	...	...	....	....	...	....	....	....	....	....	...	....	....	J. K. O'Conner.......Rep.	6,500	Dec '21
[illegible]h. D. C.	26	6	522	374	375,[illegible]00	750,000	746	186,270	212,960	No	65[illegible]00[illegible]0	62,553,490	[illegible]	20,712,[illegible]65	Yes	L. Brownlow^e, Pres., Com.	5,000	Feb. '21
Wilmington, Del.	118	4	167	82	41,070	67,523	135	15,987	41,457	No	24[illegible]00[illegible]	14,835[illegible]46	138	3,536,[illegible]36	[illegible]	W. G. Taylor..........Rep.	2,000	June '21
Worcester, [illegible]s.	1[illegible]7	4	223	28	93,157	31,629	248	15,279	185[illegible]	No	32[illegible]00[illegible]00	14,628[illegible]00	314	[illegible]9,119	Yes	P. F. Sullivan........Dem.	5[illegible]00	Jan. '22
Yonkers, N. Y.	10	⅙	153	130	121,442	180,165	75	87,009	87[illegible]68	No	31,000,000	9,420,485	166	[illegible]41,328	Yes	W. J. Wallin..........Rep.	6,500	Dec. '21
Youngstown, O.	632	18	275	150	31,543	26,[illegible]00	150	....	¶75[illegible]0	No	13[illegible]00[illegible]0	11,300[illegible]00	211	2,613,012	Yes	F. J. Warnock..........Rep.	6,000	Dec. '21

I[illegible]es removal of garbage and ashes. †Does [illegible]nt remove garbage and ashes, but operates incinerator. ††Disposal only. ‡Included in figures for [illegible]. ¶ G[illegible]s and electricity. [illegible]ptd. by [illegible]s. of U. S. ^{b}Private contract. ^{d}Gas plant owned by city and leased. ^{e}Excl. of high pressure. ^{e}Borough President. ^{f}Total disbursements for Catskill [illegible]ks (in addition to figures in column), $128,154 [illegible].

UNITED STATES DIPLOMATIC AND CONSULAR SERVICE—*Continued.*

Nanking—John K. Davis, C., Ohio.
Shanghai—Edwin S. Cunningham, C. G., Tenn.
Swatow—Myrl S. Myers, C., Pa.
Tientsin—S. J. Fuller, C. G., Wis.
Tsinanfu—C. E. Gauss, C., Conn.

COLOMBIA.

Barranguilla—Arthur C. Frost, C., Mass.
Cartagena—Edgar C. Soule, C., Tex.
Santa Marta—Leroy R. Sawyer, C., Mass.

COSTA RICA.

Port Limon—Stewart E. McMillin, C., Kans.
San Jose—Claude E. Guyant, C., Ill.

CUBA.

Cienfuegos—Frank Bohr, C., Kan.
Habana—Carlton Bailey Hurst, C. G., D. C.
Nueva Gerona, Isle of Pines—Chas. Forman, C., La.
Neuvitas—Geo. G. Duffee, C., Ala.
Santiago de Cuba—H. D. Clum, C., N. Y.

CZECHO-SLOVAKIA.

Prague, Bohemia—Chas. S. Winans, C., Mich.
Free City of Danzig—Wm. Dawson, C., Minn.

DENMARK AND DOMINIONS.

Copenhagen—Marion Letcher, C. G., Ga.

DOMINICAN REPUBLIC.

Puerto Plata—Wm. A. Bickers, C., Va.
Santo Domingo—Geo. A. Makinson, V. C., Cal.

ECUADOR.

Guayaquil—F. W. Goding, C. G., Ill.

FINLAND.

Helsingfors—L. A. Davis, C., N. Y.
Viborg—H. B. Quarton, C., Iowa.

FRANCE AND DOMINIONS.

Algiers, Algeria—E. A. Dowd, C., Neb.
Bordeaux—Theo. Jaeckel, C., N. Y.
Brest—Sample B. Forbus, C., Miss.
Calais—Thos. D. Davis, C., Okla.
Cette—A. J. Lespinosse, C., N. Y.
Dakar, Senegal—W. J. Yerby, C., Ark.
Dunkirk—Paul C. Squire, C., Mass.
Guadeloupe, W. I.—John S. Calvert, C., N. C.
Havre—A. E. Ingram, C., Cal.
La Rochelle—Wm. W. Brunswick, C., Kan.
Lille—A. L. Burnell, C., Me.
Limoges—Eugene L. Belisle, C., Mass.
Lyon—Clarence Carrigan, C., Cal.
Marseilles—Alphonse Gaulin, C. G., R. I.
Martinique, W. I.—Thos. R. Wallace, C., Iowa.
Nancy—P. H. Cram, C., Me.
Nantes—Maxwell K. Moorhead, C., Pa.
Nice—Wm. D. Hunter, C., Minn.
Paris—Alexander M. Thackara, C. G., Pa.
Rouen—M. B. Kirk, C., Ill.
Saigon, French-Indo China—Karl de G. MacVitty, C., Ill.
St. Etienne—Wm. H. Hunt, C., N. Y.
Strassburg—Wm. J. Pike, C., Pa.
Tahiti, Society Islands—H. F. Withey, C., Mich.
Tananario, Madagascar—J. G. Carter, C., Ga.
Tunis—H. N. Cookingham, C., N. Y.

GERMANY.

(No Consuls.)

GREAT BRITAIN AND DOMINIONS.

Adelaide, Australia—Henry P. Starrett, C., Fla.
Aden, Arabia—A. E. Southard, C., Ky.
Auckland, N. Z.—A. A. Winslow, C. G., Ind.
Barbados, W. I.—John J. C. Watson, C., Ky.
Belfast, Ireland—Wm. P. Kent, C., Va.
Belize, Honduras—W. W. Early, C., N. C.
Birmingham, Eng.—W. T. Gracey, C., Cal.
Bombay, India—John C. Moomaw, V. C., Va.
Bradford, Eng.—W. J. Young, C., Ill.
Bristol, Eng.—Robertson Honey, C., N. Y.
Calcutta, India—A. W. Weddell, C. G., Va.
Calgary, Alberta—Samuel C. Reat, C., N. Y.
Campellton, N. B.—G. Carlton Woodward, C., Pa.
Cape Town, Cape of Good Hope—C. J. Pisar, V. C., Wis.
Cardiff, Wales—Chas. E. Asbury, C., Ind.
Charlottetown, P. E. I.—C. Ludlow Livingston, C., Pa.
Colombo, Ceylon—Robt. L. Keiser, C., Ind.
Cornwall, Ont.—Thos. D. Edwards, C., S. D.
Dublin, Ire.—F. T. F. Dumont, C., Pa.
Dundee, Scot.—H. A. Johnson, C., D. C.
Dunfermline, Scot.—H. D. Van Sant, C., N. J.
Durban, Natal—W. W. Masterson, C., Ky.
Edinburgh, Scot.—Hunter Sharp, C., N. C.
Fernie, B. C.—Norton F. Brand, C., N. D.
Fort William and Port Arthur, Ont.—John O. Sanders, C., Tex.
Georgetown, Guiana—C. W. Davis, C., N. Y.
Gibraltar, Spain—R. L. Sprague, C., Mass.
Glasgow, Scot.—Geo. E. Chamberlin, C., N. Y.
Halifax, N. S.—E. N. Gunsaulus, C. G., Ohio.
Hamilton, Bermuda—A. W. Swalm, C., Iowa.
Hamilton, Ont.—Jose De Olivares, C., Mo.
Hong Kong, China—Wm. H. Gale, C. G., Va.
Hull, Eng.—John H. Grout, C., Mass.
Johannesburg, Transvaal—Fred. D. Fisher, C., Ore.
Karachi, India—E. V. Richardson, C., N. Y.
Kingston, Jamaica—C. L. Latham, C., N. C.
Kingston, Ont.—Felix S. S. Johnson, C., N. J.
Leeds, Eng.—Percival Gassett, C., D. C.
Liverpool, Eng.—Horace L. Washington, C., D. C.
London, Eng.—Robt. P. Skinner, C. G., Ohio.
London, Ont.—G. Russell Taggart, C., N. J.
Madras, India—L. G. Dawson, C., Va.
Malta, Maltese Isls.—Carl R. Loop, C., Ind.
Manchester, Eng.—Ross E. Holaday, C., Ohio.
Melbourne, Australia—Thos. Sammons, C. G., Wash.
Moncton, N. B.—B. M. Rasmusen, C., Iowa.
Montreal, Quebec—Jas. L. Rogers, C. G., Ohio.
Nairoli, British East Africa—Stillman W. Eells, C., N. Y.
Nassau, N. P.—L. A. Lathrop, C., Cal.
Newcastle, N. S. W.—L. N. Sullivan, C., Pa.
Newcastle-on-Tyne, Eng.—F. C. Slater, C., Kans.
Niagara Falls, Ont.—Jas. B. Milner, C., Ind.
Nottingham, Eng.—Calvin M. Hitch, C., Ga.
Ottawa, Ont.—John G. Foster, C. G., Vt.
Penang, Straits Settlements—R. S. McNiece, C., Utah.
Plymouth, Eng.—John D. Wise, C., Va.
Port Elizabeth, Cape of Good Hope—John W. Dye, C., Minn.
Prescott, Ont.—F. C. Denison, C., Vt.
Prince Rupert, B. C.—E. A. Wakefield, C., Me.
Quebec, Quebec—E. H. Dennison, C., Ohio.
Queenstown, Ireland—Mason Mitchell, C., N. Y.
Rangoon, India—Chas. H. Thorling, V. C., N. Y.
Regina, Saskatchewan—J. H. Johnson, C., Tex.
Riviere du Loup, Quebec—L. P. Briggs, C., Mich.
St. John, N. B.—Henry S. Culver, C., Ohio.
St. John's, N. F.—Jas. S. Benedict, C., N. Y.
St. Stephens, N. B.—A. B. Garrett, C., W. Va.
Sarnia, Ont.—H. W. Diederich, C., D. C.
Sault Ste. Marie, Ont.—G. W. Shotts, C., Mich.
Sheffield, Eng.—Wm. J. Grace, C., N. Y.
Sherbrooke, Quebec—E. L. Adams, C., N. Y.
Singapore Straits Settlements—A. G. Snyder, C. G., W. Va.
Southampton, Eng.—J. M. Savage, C., N. J.
Stoke-on-Trent, Eng.—Wm. F. Doty, C., N. Y.
Swansea, Wales—A. B. Cooke, C., S. C.
Sydney, N. S.—Chas. M. Freeman, C., N. H.
Sydney, Australia—E. J. Norton, C., Tenn.
Toronto, Ont.—C. W. Martin, C., Mich.
Trinidad, W. I.—H. D. Baker, C., Ill.
Vancouver, B. C.—F. M. Ryder, P. G., Conn.
Victoria, B. C.—R. B. Mosher, C., D. C.
Windsor, Ont.—M. J. Hendrick, C., N. Y.
Winnipeg, Man.—Jos. I. Brittain, C. G., O.
Yarmouth, N. S.—John N. McCunn, C., Wis.

GREECE.

Athens—Will L. Lowrie, C. G., Ill.
Patras—Geo. K. Stiles, C., Md.
Saloniki—L. B. Morris, C., Pa.

GUATEMALA.

Guatemala—Frederick Simpich, C., Wash.

HAITI.

Cape Haitien—A. M. Warren, C., Ind.
Port au Prince—J. B. Terres, C., N. Y.

HONDURAS.

Ceiba—Parker W. Buhrman, C., Va.
Puerta Cortes—A. H. Gerberich, V. C., Pa.
Tegucigalpa—Geo. K. Donald, C., Ala.

ITALY.

Catania—Robt. R. Bradford, C., Nebr.
Florence—W. R. Dorsey, C., Md.
Genoa—David F. Wilbur, C. G., N. Y.
Leghorn—Lucien Memminger, C., S. C.
Milan—North Winship, C., Ga.
Naples—Homer M. Byington, C., Conn.
Palermo—Louis G. Dreyfus, Jr., C., Cal.
Rome—F. B. Keene, C. G., Wis.
Turin—J. E. Haven, C., Ill.
Venice—Jas. B. Young, C., Pa.

JAPAN.

Dairen, Manchuria—M. D. Kirjassoff, C., Conn.
Kobe—John K. Caldwell, C., Ky.
Nagasaki—R. S. Curtice, C., Pa.
Nagoya—H. F. Hawley, C., N. Y.
Seoul, Chosen—R. S. Miller, C. G., N. Y.
Taihoku, Taiwan—H. B. Hitchcock, C., N. Y.
Yokohama—Geo. H. Scidmore, C. G., Wis.

UNITED STATES DIPLOMATIC AND CONSULAR SERVICE—*Continued.*

LIBERIA.

Monrovia—Jos. L. Johnson, C. G.

MEXICO.

Acapulco—John A. Gamon, C., Ill.
Aguascalientes—L. K. Zabriskie, C., Conn.
Chihuahua—Jas. B. Stewart, C., N. Mex.
Ciudad Juarez—E. A. Dow, C., Neb.
Ensenada, Lower California—W. C. Burdett, C., Tenn.
Frontera—L. B. Blohm, C., Ariz.
Guadalajara—A. J. McConnico, C., Miss.
Guaymas—B. F. Yost, C., Kan.
Manzanillo, Colima—H. L. Walsh, C., Ind.
Matamoras—Gilbert R. Willson, C., Tex.
Mazatlan—Wm. E. Chapman, C., Okla.
Mexicali, Lower California—Walter F. Boyle, C., Ga.
Mexico—Nathaniel B. Stewart, C. G., Ga.
Monterey—Thos. D. Bowman.
Nogales—F. J. Dyer, C., Cal.
Nuevo Laredo—Randolph Robertson, C., Tex.
Piedras Negras—Wm. P. Blocker, C., Tex.
Progresso—O. G. Marsh, C., Wash.
Salina Cruz—Lloyd Burlingham, C., N. Y.
Saltillo—Harold Playter, C., Cal.
San Luis Potosi—Knox Alexander, V. C., Mo.
Tampico—C. I. Dawson, C., S. C.
Torreon, Coahuila—Chester Donaldson, C., N. Y.
Vera Cruz—P. H. Foster, C., Tex.

MOROCCO.

Casa Blanca—T. B. L. Layton, C., La.
Tangier—Maxwell Blake, C. G., Mo.

NETHERLANDS AND DOMINIONS.

Amsterdam—Frank W. Mahin, C., Iowa.
Batavia, Java—John F. Jewell, C., Ill.
Curacao, W. I.—B. S. Rairden, C., Me.
Medan, Sumatra—Carl O. Spamer, C., Ind.
Rotterdam—Geo. E. Anderson, C. G., Ill.
Soerabaya, Java—Harry Campbell, C., Kans.

NICARAGUA.

Bluefields—John R. Bradley, C., Okla.
Corinto—Henry S. Waterman, C., Wash.

NORWAY.

Bergen—Geo. N. Ifft, C., Idaho.
Christiana—John B. Osborne, C. G., Pa.
Stavanger—R. S. S. Bergh, C., N. D.
Trondhjem—M. A. Jewett, C., Mass.

PANAMA.

Colon—Julius D. Dreher, C., S. C.
Panama—Soren Listoe, C. G., Minn.

PARAGUAY.

Asuncion—H. H. Balch, C., Pa.

PERSIA.

Tabriz—Gordon Paddock, C., N. Y.
Teheran—Ralph H. Bader, C., Va.

PERU.

Callao—Jas. H. Roth, V. C., Cal.

POLAND.

Lemberg, Galicia—J. Preston Doughten, C., Del.
Warsaw—Leo J. Keena, C. G., Mich.

PORTUGAL AND DOMINIONS.

Funchal, Madeira—Wm. L. Jenkins, C., Pa.
Lisbon—W. S. Hollis, C. G., Mass.
Loanda, Angola—R. P. Clark, C., N. H.
Lourenco Marquez, E. Africa—John A. Ray, C., Tex.
Oporto—Samuel H. Wiley, C., N. C.
St. Michaels, Azores—Drew Linnard, C., Ala.

ROUMANIA.

Bucharest—E. C. Kemp, C., Fla.

RUSSIA.

Reval—C. H. Albrecht, C., Pa.
Riga—John P. Hurley, C., N. Y.
Tiflis—C. K. Moser, C., Va.
Vladivostok, Siberia—David B. Macgowan, C., Tenn.

SALVADOR.

San Salvador—L. W. Franklin, V. C., Md.

KINGDOM OF SERBS, CROATS AND SLOVENES

Belgrade—K. S. Patton, C., Va.
Zagreb—A. R. Thomson, C., Ind.

SIAM.

Bankok—J. P. Davis, C., Ga.

SPAIN AND DOMINIONS.

Barcelona—V. W. O'Hara, V. C., Kan.
Bilboa—H. M. Wolcott, C., N. Y.
Cadiz—B. Harvey Carroll, C., Tex.
Huelva—Horace Remillard, C., Mass.
Madrid—E. E. Palmer, C., R. I.
Malaga—Gaston Smith, C., La.
Palma de Mallorca—Jas. H. Goodier, C., N. Y.
Santander—M. L. Stafford, C., Cal.
Seville—R. W. Harnden, C., Cal.
Teneriffe, Canary Islands—F. A. Henry, C., Del.
Valencia—J. R. Putnam, C., Ore.
Vigo—Edward I. Nathan, C., Pa.

SWEDEN.

Goteborg—Walter H. Sholes, C., Okla.
Malmo—Maurice C. Pierce, C., Wis.
Stockholm—Dominic I. Murphy, C. G., D. C.

SWITZERLAND.

Basel—Philip Holland, C., Tenn.
Berne—Thornwell Haynes, C., Ala.
Geneva—L. W. Haskell, C., S. C.
St. Gall—Gebhard Willrich, C., Wis.
Zurich—Geo. H. Murphy, C. G., N. C.

TURKEY AND DOMINIONS.
(No Consuls.)

URUGUAY.

Montevideo—David J. D. Myers, C., Ga.

VENEZUELA.

La Guaira—H. C. von Struve, C., Tex.
Maracaibo—D. G. Dwyer, C., Col.
Puerto Cabello—Wm. P. Garrety, C., N. Y.

Officers Not Elsewhere Listed.

Apia, Samoa—Quincy F. Roberts, V. C., Tex.; Aleppo—J. B. Jackson, C., Ohio; Tsingtau, China—W. R. Peck (C), Cal.; Alexandria, Egypt—Lester Maynard, C., Cal.; Bagdad—Thos. R. Owens C., Ala.; Constantinople—G. B. Ravndal, C. G., S. D.; Damascus—Geo. W. Young, C., Md.; Jerusalem—O. A. Glazebrook, C., N. J.; Smyrna—Geo. Horton, C. G., Ill.; Beirut—Paul Knabenshue, C., Ohio; Trieste—Jos. E. Haven, C., Ill.; Samsoun—S. Pinkney Tuck, C., N. Y.

Consular Officers Temporarily Unassigned or Temporarily Assigned to the Dept. of State.

Name, where assigned, whence appointed.
W. L. Avery, unassigned, Mont.; Felix Cole, Dept., D. C.; Hernando de Soto, Dept., Cal.; H. H. Dick, Dept., S. C.; Wesley Frost, Dept., Ky.; E. L. Harris, unassigned, Ill.; Lewis Heck, on leave without pay, Pa.; J. Paul, Jameson, Dept., Pa.; N. T. Johnson, Dept., Okla.; Tracy Lay, Dept., Ala.; H. D. Learned, unassigned, Pa.; P. C. Lee, Dept., Col.; W. A. Leonard, Dept., Ill.; G. L. Logan, unassigned, Ark.; E. L. Neville, Dept., Ohio; L. C. Pinkerton, Dept., Mo.; DeWitt C. Poole, Dept., Ill.; D. D. Shepard, Dept., D. C.; R. C. Tredwell, Dept., Ind.

FOREIGN EMBASSIES AND LEGATIONS IN THE UNITED STATES.

Unless otherwise indicated, names given are those of Envoys Extraordinary and Ministers Plenipotentiary. (*) Indicates Ambassador Extraordinary and Plenipotentiary.

Argentina—Dr. T. A. Le Breton.*
Austria-Hungary—No representative.
Belgium—E. de Cartier de Marchienne.*
Bolivia—Vacant.
Brazil—Mr. Augusto Cochrane de Alencar.*
Bulgaria—Mr. Stephen Panaretoff.
Chile—Senor Don Beltran Mathieu.*
China—Yung Kwai, Chg. D'Affrs.
Cuba—Dr. Carlos Manuel de Cespedes.
Colombia—Dr. Carlos Adolfo Urueta.
Costa Rica—Senor Don Odarro Beeche.
Czechoslovakia—Mr. Karel Halla, Chg. D'Affrs.
Denmark—Constantin Brun.
Dominican Republic—Licdo Emilio C. Joubert.
Ecuador—Dr. Don Rafael H. Elizalde.
Finland—Armas H. Saastamoinen.
France—J. J. Jusserand.*
Germany—No representative.
Great Britain—Sir Auckland Geddes.*
Greece—Vacant.
Guatemala—Dr. Julio Bianchi.
Haiti—Vacant.
Honduras—Senor J. Antonio Lopez Gutierrez.
Italy—Signor Giuseppe Brambilla, Chg. D'Affrs.
Japan—Kijuro Shidehara.*
Luxemburg—Baron Raymond de Waha, Chg. D'Affrs.
Mexico—Salvado Diego-Fernandez, Chg. D'Affrs.
Montenegro—Gen. A. Gvosdenovitch.
Netherlands—J. T. Cremer.
Nicaragua—Senor Don Diego Manuel Chamorro.
Norway—Mr. H. H. Bryn.
Panama—Vacant.

FOREIGN EMBASSIES AND LEGATIONS IN THE UNITED STATES—*Continued.*

Paraguay—Vacant.
Persia—Mirza Abdul Ali Khan Sadigh-es-Saltaneh.
Peru—Federico Alfonso Pezet.*
Poland—Prince Casimar Lubomirski.
Portugal—Viscount de Alte.
Roumania—Mr. N. H. Lahovary, chg. d'affrs.
Russia—Mr. Boris Bakhmeteff.*
Salvador—Don Salvador Sol M.
Serbs, Croats and Slovenes—Dr. Slavko Y. Grouitch.
Siam—Phya Prabha Karavongse.
Spain—Senor Don Juan Riano y Gayangos.*
Sweden—Vacant.
Switzerland—Marc Peter.
Uruguay—Dr. Jacobo Varela.
Venezuela—Dr. Don Santos A. Dominici

CONSULS IN NEW YORK CITY.

Accredited representatives of foreign countries having offices in New York, where residents of the country represented may apply for advice and protection. Unless otherwise indicated, names are those of Consul-Gen.

Argentine Republic—Ernesto C. Perez, 17 Battery pl.
Austria-Hungary—(In charge of Swedish Consulate).
Belgium—Pierre Mali, 25 Madison av.
Bolivia—Jose M. Gutierrez, 233 B'way.
Brazil—Helio Lobo, 17 State.
Bulgaria—(Vacant) 140 Liberty.
Chile—Emilio Edwards Bello, 165 B'way.
China—Juming C. Suez, 291 B'way.
Colombia—Jose M. Arango, 17 Battery pl.
Costa Rica—J. Rafael Oreamuno, 2 Rector.
Cuba—Felipe T. y Cruz, 44 Whitehall.
Czecho-Slovak—Francois Kopecky, 31 E. 17th.
Denmark—George Bech, C., 8 Bridge.
Dominican Republic—M. de J. Camacho, 17 Battery pl.
Ecuador—Gustave R. de Ycaza, 17 Battery pl.
Finland—Axel Solitander, 443 Broome.
France—Gaston Liebert, 9 E. 40th.
German Empire—(In charge of Swiss Consulate).
Great Britain and Ireland—H. G. Armstrong, 44 Whitehall,; Office for Shipping Seaman, 25 South.
Greece—Theodore Papagannopoulo, 11 St. Lukes pl.
Guatemala—(Vacant).
Haiti—Andre Faubert, 33 B'way.
Honduras—Armando Lopez Ulloa, 31 B'way.
Italy—Chev. Romolo Tritonj, 20 E. 22d.
Japan—Kyo Kumasaki, 165 B'way.
Korea—(See Japan).
Liberia—Edw. G. Merrill, C., 326 W. 19th.
Mexico—Bernardino Mena Brito in charge, 120 B'way.
Monaco—Paul Fuller, 10 Bridge.
Montenegro—Wm. F. Dix.
Netherlands—P. Staal, 90 West.
Nicaragua—Fernando Elizondo, 80 Wall.
Norway—Hans H. Th. Fay, 17 State.
Panama—Belisario Porras, Jr., 11 B'way.
Paraguay—W. W. White, 233 B'way.
Persia—H. H. Topakyan, 40 W. 57th.
Peru—Eduardo Higginson, 42 B'way.
Poland—Stefan Grotowski, 40 W. 40th.
Portugal—G. de S. Duarte, 140 Nassau.
Roumania—Tilestan Wells C., 43 Cedar.
Russia—M. Oustinoff, 55 B'way.
Salvador—Trinidad Romero, 42 B'way.
Serbia—Vladislav Savitch, 443 W. 22d.
Siam—F. Warren Sumner, 81 New.
Spain—Alejandro Berea, C., 8 State.
Sweden—Olaf H. Lamm, 119 Nassau.
Switzerland—Louis H. Junod, 100 5th av.
Turkey—Represented by Consul of Spain.
Uruguay—Mario L. Gil, 17 Battery pl.
Venezuela—Pedro R. Rincones, 80 Wall.

UNITED STATES TERRITORIES AND DEPENDENCIES.

DISTRICT OF COLUMBIA.

The Dist. of Columbia is the seat of the Federal Gov. and is situated on east bank of the Potomac River, bet. Maryland and Virginia.

ALASKA.

Alaska, one of the non-contiguous possessions of the U. S., is in the extreme northwest of North America, bordering on the Pacific and Arctic oceans and Bering Sea. The Aleutian Islands, 150 in number, which form a portion of it, stretch nearly to Asia. It was formerly known as Russian America and was purchased by the U. S. under the treaty of 1867 for $7,200,000. The area is 590,884 sq. miles. Alaskan Engineering Commsn., Wm. C. Edes, Ch., was created under act of Mar. 12, 1914, which empowered, authorized and directed the President to locate, construct, operate, or lease a railroad, or railroads, to connect the interior of Alaska with one or more of the open navigable ports. Thos. Riggs, Jr., is Govr. of Alaska.

HAWAII.

The Hawaiian Islands, annexed to the United States by the signature of the President, July 7, 1898, lie in the North Pacific, little more than 2,000 miles west of the U. S., 3,400 miles from Yokohama and 4,800 miles from Hong Kong. The Legislature of the Territory of Hawaii consists of 2 houses, Senate (15 members) and House of Representatives (30 members). Hawaii is represented in the Congress of the U. S. by a delegate. Present delegate, J. K. Kalanianaole, Rep. Chas. J. McCarthy is the Governor of Hawaii at a salary of $7,000.

PANAMA CANAL DIRECTORY.

Executive Department.

Hdqtrs., Balboa Heights.

Brig.-Gen. Chester Harding, U. S. A., Gov., Ala., *$10,000.

Washington (D. C.) Office.

A. L. Flint, Ohio, Gen. Purchasing Officer and Chf. of Office, $4,620; E. D. Anderson, Chf. Clk., Purchasing Dept., $3,600; E. E. Weise, Appointment Clk., Wis., $2,250.

THE PHILIPPINE ISLANDS.

The Philippine Archipelago is made up of Luzon, Visayas, Mindanao, Mindoro, Palawan and Sulu.

By act of Congress approved Aug. 29, '16, the legislative authority is vested in the Philippine Legislature, composed of 2 houses, 1 the Senate (24 members) and the other House of Representatives (90 members). The Philippine Legislature opened its 1st session under this law on Oct. 16, '16, and on being organized the Philippine Commission ceased to exist, and the members thereof vacated their offices.

Administrative Officers.

Hdqtrs., Manila.

Gov.-Gen., Francis Burton Harrison; Vice-Gov. and Sec. of Public Instruction, Charles E. Yeater; Sec. of the Interior, Teodoro M. Kalaw; Sec. of Commerce and Communications, Dionisio Jakosalem; Sec. of Justice, Quintin Paredes; Sec. of Finance, Alberto Barretto; Sec. of Agriculture and Natural Resources, Galicano Apacible.

PORTO RICO.

Porto Rico is 108 miles east to west, and 37 to 43 miles across; total area, 3,606 square miles. It is 1,050 miles from Key West, Fla.

Under the Organic Act of March 2, 1917, the legislative powers in Porto Rico are vested in a Legislature consisting of 2 houses, the Senate and House of Representatives. The Senate consists of 19 members elected for terms of 4 yrs. by the qualified electors of Porto Rico. House of Representatives consists of 39 members elected for 4 yrs. by the qualified electors. The members of the Senate and House of Representatives receive compensation at the rate of $7 per day for 90 days of each session and $1 per day for each additional day of such session while in session. Regular sessions of the Legislature are held biennially, convening on the 2d Monday in Feb.

Porto Rico Government.

Hdqtrs., San Juan.

Gov., Arthur Yager; Atty. Gen., Salvador Mestre; Treas., Jose E. Benedicto; Comr. of the Interior, Guillermo Esteves; Comr. of Education, Paul G. Miller; Comr. of Agriculture and Labor, Manuel Camunas; Comr. of Health, Alejandro Ruiz Soler; Exec. Sec., Ramon Siaca Pacheco.

VIRGIN ISLANDS.

(Danish West Indies.)

The Danish West Indies, comprising Islands of St. Thomas, St. John and St. Croix, were acquired by purchase from Denmark for sum of

UNITED STATES TERRITORIES AND DEPENDENCIES—*Continued.*

$25,000,000, in accordance with treaty ratified Jan. 17, 1917. They were formally taken over by the U. S. on March 31, 1917, and renamed "The Virgin Islands of the U. S." Their government is under direction of Navy Dept.

The President, in accordance with authority conferred upon him by act of Congress, March 3, 1917, to provide a temporary government for the islands, appointed Rear Admiral Joseph W. Oman, Gov., and early in April Oman assumed the duties of the office.

Half a century ago negotiations were begun looking to the acquisition of the islands, which were desired by the U. S. on account of their strategic position. But it was not until Aug. 4, 1916, that the convention arranging for the transfer was signed, this being ratified by the U. S. Senate on Sept. 7, 1916, and the final ratifications exchanged in Washington on Jan. 17, 1917. Congress, in addition to the $25,000,000 to be paid for the purchase of the islands, appropriated $100,000 for the expenses of the government.

GUAM.

The Island of Guam was ceded to the United States by Spain by the treaty of Paris, signed Dec. 10, 1898. It is 5,200 miles from San Francisco and 900 miles from Manila.

Administrative Officer.

Governor, Capt. I. C. Wettengel, U. S. N.

MILITARY EDUCATIONAL SYSTEM OF THE UNITED STATES.

(Prepared by the Adjutant General's Office, U. S. A.)

The Military Educational System of the United States is under the supervision and co-ordination of the General Staff of the Army. The system provides for the military education of the officers and enlisted men of the Army. It contemplates that all officers upon being newly commissioned from West Point, from the ranks, from civil life, or from any other source, shall pursue a year's basic course at the special service schools of their respective arms. Upon completion of this, they are assigned to duty with troops of their arm of the service for a minimum period of two years.

I. The War Plans Division of the General Staff is charged with the supervision of all military, educational and vocational training throughout the army. It is in charge of a director, who is an assistant to the Chief of Staff.

II. Special Service Schools are maintained for each arm of the service as follows: The Infantry School, Camp Benning, Georgia; the Cavalry School, Fort Riley, Kansas; the Field Artillery Schools, Fort Sill, Oklahoma, and Camp Knox, Kentucky; the Coast Artillery School, Fort Monroe, Virginia; the Engineer School, Camp Humphreys, Virginia; the Signal Corps School, Fort Leavenworth, Kansas; the Signal Corps School, Camp Alfred Vail, New Jersey; the Air Service Schools at the various flying fields; the Tank Corps School, Camp Meade, Maryland; the Ordnance School of Application, Aberdeen Proving Ground, Maryland; the Ordnance School of Technology, Watertown, Mass.; the Ordnance School of Operation, Maintenance, and Repair, Raritan Arsenal, New Jersey; the Army Medical School, Washington, D. C.; the Motor Transport School, Camp Holabird, Maryland, and the Chemical Warfare School, Lakehurst, New Jersey; the Finance School, Ft. Washington, Maryland.

These schools are under the direct supervision and control of the chiefs of the respective arms or services. The object of the courses for officers is to develop and standardize the instruction and training of officers in the technique and tactics of their respective arm or service.

Basic courses, where officers are sent upon their initial entry into the Regular Army, are maintained at the five special service schools of the following combatant arms of the service, viz.: infantry, cavalry, field artillery, coast artillery, and engineers. These basic courses have for their object: So to qualify all officers upon their initial entry into the service that they may function intelligently on being assigned to duty with their arm of the service.

Advanced courses for the training of officers are maintained. They are of such scope as will completely fit the graduates for the performance of all duties that devolve upon officers of their grade in their respective arm of service.

III. General Service Schools, including (a) the School of the Line and (b) the General Staff School located at Fort Leavenworth, Kansas, and (c) the General Staff College, Washington, D. C., are under the direct supervision and control of the Chief of Staff of the army. It is contemplated that the officer will spend his first school year at the School of the Line. On the recommendation of the school faculty, which is based on his competitive class standing, he is eligible for the course at the General Staff School the succeeding year. The third year of his military education is to be spent, if practicable, on duty with troops of arms of the service other than that with which he has previously served. Having received the recommendation of the General Staff School faculty at the end of his second year, the officer is eligible to enter the General Staff College at the beginning of his fourth year. This course continues for one year, at the end of which period the officer's school education is complete and he is eligible for detail on the War Department Staff after having complied with the law as to eligibility for detached duty from his own arm of the service.

The School of the Line, Fort Leavenworth, Kansas. The object of this school is to train officers (a) in the combined use of all arms and services functioning with a division, including the functioning of corps and army troops and services in their relation to the division, in accordance with a uniform doctrine approved by the War Department; (b) in the duties and responsibilities of field officers with regard to education and training in the army.

The General Staff School, Fort Leavenworth, Kansas. The object of this school is to train selected officers, who have completed the course in the School of the Line, for higher tactical command and for duty as General Staff officers with tactical units. In addition, special courses are conducted for General officers and selected officers of the technical and administrative services.

The General Staff College, Washington, D. C. The object of this institution is to train selected officers who have completed the course in the General Staff School for high command and for duty in the War Department, General Staff. In addition, special courses are conducted for General Officers, and for selected officers of the technical and administrative services.

IV. Unit Schools for Officers. These schools include those for officers which are under the direct control of territorial or tactical commanders. Their primary object is the training and instruction of officers of all grades with a view to securing uniform and efficient training of the troops or personnel under their respective commands. The courses are conducted concurrently with and closely co-ordinated with the training schedules or work of the troops or personnel under the student officers.

V. Unit Schools for Enlisted Men. These schools include schools for the military training and instruction of enlisted men. They have for their object (a) to prepare non-commissioned officers, selected privates, and enlisted specialists to carry out efficiently the schedule of training or work in progress; (b) to insure proper uniformity and co-ordination in the training of work of different elements of the same command; (c) to provide such additional technical and tactical instruction as may be practica le and suited to the needs of the students. b

VI. Special Service Schools for Enlisted Men. Courses are established at the special service schools enumerated in paragraph II above, for the special training and instruction of enlisted men. The objects of the schools are (a) to train selected non-commissioned officers in the duties of junior officers of their respective arm or service; (b) to give special training to selected enlisted men in the duties of non-commissioned officers and enlisted specialists of their respective arm or service.

VII. The Reserve Officers' Training Corps consists of units established under the provisions of Section 40-53 of the National Defense Act (act of June 3, 1916) in civil educational institutions under a system of regulations and

MILITARY EDUCATIONAL SYSTEM OF THE UNITED STATES—*Continued.*

instructions prescribed by the Secretary of War. These units are composed of students and represent the various branches of the military service. The military instruction is conducted by army officers detailed for the purpose who are designated as professors of military science and tactics. The Reserve Officers' Training Corps consists of a senior division organized in general in colleges and universities which require four years of collegiate study for a degree and a junior division established at other approved institutions. Military training in the Reserve Officers' Training Corps is carried on from three to five hours each week throughout the four academic years, and also includes attendance at a summer camp of six weeks' duration. Upon the satisfactory completion of the four-year course, including the camp training, the students are eligible for appointment as second lieutenants in the Officers' Reserve Corps of the army.

VIII. General and Vocational Education of Soldiers. The Army school system provides for the enlisted personnel, elementary and advanced education, and vocational training. Education is voluntary, except for illiterates and non-English speaking recruits. Recruit Educational Centers have been established within the several territorial departments where intensive specialized training is given this class of student. In the advanced general education, an opportunity is given the soldier to pursue work preparatory to college and to West Point.

Vocational training is offered with the dual purpose of providing the Army with the technicians needed, and to qualify the soldier for a place in the industrial world on his return to civil life. The courses now offered are: Automotive, electrical, building, textile, food, animal transportation, metals, printing, medicine, highway construction and topography, steam, gas and electrical power, music, leather, machine, business, agriculture and miscellaneous. The "applicatory" or "learning by doing" method of instruction is followed in both the general education and vocational courses.

Funds are provided by Congressional appropriation. The instructors are qualified civilians and officers and soldiers within the service. A Special Educational School has been established for the purpose of developing courses along vocational and general educational lines, and for the instruction of teachers to insure uniform standards of achievement throughout the Army. Any Army recruiting officer will furnish detailed information concerning courses, and posts, camps and stations at which such courses are taught.

THE SPECIAL SERVICE SCHOOLS.

IX. The Infantry School, Camp Benning, Georgia; the Cavalry School, Fort Riley, Kansas; the Field Artillery Schools, Fort Sill, Oklahoma; Camp Knox, Kentucky, and Camp Bragg, North Carolina; the Coast Artillery School, Fort Monroe, Virginia, and the Engineer School, Camp Humphrey, Virginia, are established for the purpose of (a) training officers for their specific duties in command of troops; (b) the tactical and technical training of their arms and services; (c) training selected non-commissioned aand enlsted specialists for their respective arms and services.

X. The Signal Corps School, Fort Leavenworth, Kansas, for the training of officers and selected enlisted men for the tactical duties of the Signal Corps.

XI. The Signal Corps School, Camp Alfred Vail, New Jersey, for the training of officers and enlisted men in the technical duties of the Signal Corps.

XII. The Air Service Schools are maintained at the several flying fields for the practical training of officers and enlisted men as aviators, and the duties incident thereto.

XIII. The Tank Corps School, Camp Meade, Maryland, for the training of officers and enlisted men of the Tank Corps in the technique, tactics, and practical mechanical operation of military tanks.

XIV. The Ordnance School of Application, Aberdeen Proving Ground, Maryland, for the instruction of officers of the Ordnance Department in mechanical and chemical engineering.

XV. The Ordnance School of Technology, Watertown, Mass., for the instruction of officers in shop practice, shop administration, and the general administration of the Ordnance Department, except that of the field service thereof.

XVI. The Ordnance Operation, Maintenance and Repair School, Raritan Arsenal, New Jersey, for the training of officers and enlisted men in the specialized branches of ordnance work.

XVII. The Army Medical School, Washington, D. C., for the training of officers and selected enlisted men in the administrative work and medical procedure pertaining to the Medical Corps. The Army Medical School at Washington provides a course of training and instruction for prospective officers of the Medical Corps covering a period of one year.

XVIII. The Motor Transport School, Camp Holabird, Maryland, provides practical courses of training for officers and enlisted men in the technical and mechanical operation of motor transport. They also have excellent vocational training schools in which enlisted men may pursue a sixteen weeks' course to qualify in the several trades pertaining to motor industry.

XIX. The Chemical Warfare School, Lakehurst, N. J., for the training of officers and enlisted men in the technical and tactical duties of the Chemical Warfare Service.

XX. The Army Bandleaders' School, Fort Jay, Governor's Island, N. Y., for the training of bandmasters and selected enlisted men for service with army bands. Graduates of the Bandleaders' School are eligible for appointment as bandleaders in the service. The Institute of Musical Art of New York gives a number of scholarships to students at the school.

XXI. School for Bakers and Cooks, at many of the large cantonments a specially prepared course of training for enlisted men to qualify them for duty as bakers and cooks in the service These schools operate under the direction of the Quartermaster Corps.

AIR MAIL.

The Air Mail was inaugurated May 15, 1918, and has been in continuous operation ever since. The first route was between New York and Washington, a distance of 218 miles. The routes between Cleveland and Chicago, and New York and Cleveland, were established in 1919, the route between Chicago and Omaha on May 15, 1920; the route between Chicago and St. Louis on Aug. 16, 1920, and the route between Chicago and Minneapolis on Sept. 1, 1920.

Between its inauguration and Sept. 1, 1920, the Air Mail operations covered 957,108 miles of flying. In that time it carried 38,027,440 letters. The cost of operation, including interest on investment, total or partial wrecking of planes, replacements of damage to planes, death and injury compensation, etc., amounted to $1,147,926.26 for 2¼ years, or $1.18 per mile. More than one-third of this cost of operation was not cash expenditure, but represents the original cost to the Army and Navy of surplus war material, which the Post Office Dept. put to use in carrying the mails. First-class mail has been advanced in delivery to the public 18 to 24 hours.

With the inauguration of the through Transcontinental Air Mail on Sept. 8, 1920, Postmaster General Burleson has extended the American Air Mail Service over 1,463 miles of new territory, reducing the transit time of mails between New York and San Francisco from 91 hours to 57 hours in the winter months and to 54 hours in the summer. Preparations have been made for night flying over the plains in the spring of 1921 between Chicago and Cheyenne, and this will reduce the time of transit of the Air Mail to 45 hours, against 91 hours by rail.

More than 49,000 farmers of the United States now use motor trucks on their farms, so the Bureau of Agriculture reports, and, whether because of the motors or otherwise, horses are becoming fewer. The 21,109,000 horses on farms and ranches at the opening of the year 1920 represented a decrease of 373,900 from the number of a year previous.

UNITED STATES ARMY.

The Army of the United States underwent a general reorganization in accordance with an executive order of the President on Sept. 1, 1920. On that date, in accordance to the Army Act of June 4, 1920, an order was issued establishing the Army into corps for the purposes of administration, training and tactical control. The corps areas fixed were as follows:

First Corps Area to embrace the States of Maine, New Hampshire, Vermont, Massachusetts, Rhode Island and Connecticut. Hdqtrs. at Boston, Mass.

Second Corps Area to embrace the States of New York, New Jersey and Delaware. Hdtrs. at Governor's Island, New York.

Third Corps Area to embrace the States of Pennsylvania, Maryland, Virginia and the District of Columbia. Hdqtrs. at Fort McHenry, Md. (temporarily at Baltimore, Md., until space is vailable at Fort McHenry, Md.).

Fourth Corps Area to embrace the States of North Carolina, South Carolina, Georgia, Florida, Alabama, Tennessee, Mississippi and Louisiana. Hdqtrs. at Fort McPherson, Georgia (temporarily at Charleston, S. C., until space is available at Fort McPherson, Ga.).

Fifth Corps Area to embrace the States of Ohio, West Virginia, Indiana and Kentucky. Hdqtrs. at Fort Benjamin Harrison, Ind.

Sixth Corps Area to embrace the States of Illinois, Michigan and Wisconsin. Hdqtrs. at Fort Sheridan, Ill. (temporarily at Chicago, Ill., until space is available at Fort Sheridan, Ill.).

Seventh Corps Area to embrace the States of Missouri, Kansas, Iowa, Nebraska, Minnesota, North Dakota, South Dakota and Arkansas. Hdqtrs. at Fort Crook, Neb.

Eighth Corps Area to embrace the States of Texas, Oklahoma, Colorado, New Mexico and Arizona. Hdqtrs. at Fort Sam Houston, San Antonio, Tex.

Ninth Corps Area to embrace the States of Washington, Oregon, Idaho, Montana, Wyoming, Utah, Nevada and California. Hdqtrs. at Presidio of San Francisco, Cal. (temporarily at San Francisco, Cal., until space is available at Presidio of San Francisco, Cal.)

Upon the establishment of these Corps Areas the six Territorial Departments, now embracing the continental area of the United States, shall be discontinued and the following will obtain:

The Island of Porto Rico, with the islands and keys adjacent thereto, will, for administrative purposes, be attached to the Second Corps Area. The Territory of Alaska will be attached to the Ninth Corps Area for the same purposes.

For purposes of administrative and tactical control, in connection with the border patrol and field operations incident thereto, such part of the State of Arizona as lies west of the 114° meridian and south of the 33° parallel is attached to the Ninth Corps Area.

For the purposes of inspection or maneuvers of plans for mobilization, war, demobilization, etc., the nine Corps Areas will, upon their establishment, be grouped into three Army Areas as indicated:

FIRST ARMY AREA—First, Second and Third Corps Areas.

SECOND ARMY AREA—Fourth, Fifth and Sixth Corps Areas.

THIRD ARMY AREA—Seventh, Eighth and Ninth Corps Areas.

The following assignments of General Officers are made:

Assts. to the Chief of Staff and members of the War Dept. General Staff. Maj. Gen. William G. Haan, U. S. Army; Brig. Gen. Henry Jervey, U. S. Army; Brig. Gen. Dennis E. Nolan, U. S. Army.

Commanders of Corps Areas—First Corps Area, Maj. Gen. David C. Shanks, U. S. Army; Second Corps Area, Maj. Gen. Robert L. Bullard, U. S. Army; Third Corps Area, Maj. Gen. Adelbert Cronkhite, U. S. Army; Fourth Corps Area, Maj. Gen. John F. Morrison, U. S. Army; Fifth Corps Area, Maj. Gen. George F. Read, U. S. Army; Sixth Corps Area, Maj. Gen. Leonard Wood, U. S. Army; Seventh Corps Area, Maj. Gen. Omar Bundy, U. S. Army; Eighth Corps Area, Maj. Gen. Joseph T. Dickman, U. S. Army; Ninth Corps Area, Maj. Gen. Hunter Liggett, U. S. Army.

Division Commanders—Fourth Div., Maj. Gen. Charles H. Muir, U. S. Army. Fifth Div., Maj. Gen. John L. Hines, U. S. Army.

Brigade and District Commanders—First Div., Brig. Gen. Clarence Edwards, U. S. Army; Brig. Gen. William S. Graves, U. S. Army; Brig. Gen. Dwight E. Aultman, U. S. Army. Second Div., Brig. Gen. James H. McRae, U. S. Army; Brig. Gen. Hanson E. Ely, U. S. Army; Brig. Gen. (to be appointed), George Van Horn Moseley, U. S. Army. Third Div., Brig. Gen. Robert C. Davis, U. S. Army. Fourth Div., Brig. Gen. George S. Duncan, U. S. Army; Brig. Gen. Richard M. Blatchford, U. S. Army. Fifth Div., Brig. Gen. Andre W. Brewster, U. S. Army; Brig. Gen. U. G. McAlexander, U. S. Army. Sixth Div., Brig. Gen. Mark L. Hersey, U. S. Army. Seventh Div., Brig. Gen. Harry H. Bandholtz, U. S. Army. Philippine Dept., Brig. Gen. Charles G. Treat, U. S. Army. Hawaiian Dept., Brig. Gen. Joseph E. Kuhn, U. S. Army. Panama Dept., Brig. Gen. Edwin P. Babbitt, U. S. Army. South Atlantic Coast Artillery District, Brig. Gen. Johnson Hagood, U. S. Army.

CAMPS AND SERVICE SCHOOLS.

General Service Schools, Fort Leavenworth, Kan.; Brig. Gen. Hugh A. Drum, U. S. Army. Infantry School, Camp Benning, Ga.; Brig. Gen. Walter H. Gordon, U. S. Army. Field Artillery School, Fort Sill, Okla.; Brig. Gen. Earnest Hinds, U. S. Army. Camp Knox, Ky.; Brig. Gen. William Lassiter, U. S. A.

The following named General Officers report for duty to districts along the Mexican Border: Brig. Gen. Grote Hutcheson, U. S. Army; Brig. Gen. Robert L. Howze, U. S. Army; Brig. Gen. Malin Craig, U. S. Army.

AUTHORIZED STRENGTH OF THE REGULAR ARMY.

Under the provisions of the Act of Congress, approved June 4, 1920, the total authorized peace strength of the Regular Army, including the Philippine Scouts, has been increased to 17,726 officers and 280,000 enlisted men, classified according to branch of service, as follows:

Branch of Service.	Off'crs.	Enlisted Men.	Total.
General officers of the line	68	......	68
Gen. Staff Corps (War Dept.)	[1]88	......	88
Adjt. General's Dept.	117	......	117
Insp. General's Dept.	62	......	62
Judge Adv. General's Dept.	115	......	115
Quartermaster Corps	1,054	20,000	21,054
Finance Dept.	142	900	1,042
Medical Dept.:			
Surg. General and 2 assts.	3	[2]14,000	[2]16,437
Medical Corps	1,820		
Med. Administrative Corps	140		
Dental Corps	299		
Veter'nary Corps	175		
Ordnance Dept.	353	4,500	4,853
Chemical Warfare Service	101	1,200	1,301
Bureau of Insular Affairs	3	......	3
Chaplains	[4]242	......	242
Professors, U. S. Mil. Academy	7	......	7
Military storekeeper	1	......	1
Infantry[5]	4,201	110,000	114,201
Cavalry	951	20,000	20,951
Field Artillery	1,901	37,000	38,901
Coast Artillery Corps	1,201	30,000	31,201
Air Service	1,516	[6]16,000	17,516
Corps of Engineers	602	12,000	12,602
Signal Corps	301	5,000	5,301
Miscellaneous[7]	2,263	9,400	11,663
Total Regular Army[8]	17,726	280,000	297,726

[1]Does not include the Chief of Staff and his 4 assistants, who are included among the general officers of the line. [2]Maximum authorized until June 30, 1921. Thereafter not to exceed 5 per cent. of the actual strength, commissioned and enlisted, of the Regular Army. [3]Does not include the authorized strength (approximately 1,500) of the Army Nurse Corps or the authorized number (approximately 35) of contract surgeons. [4]The authorized number of chaplains will vary slightly with changes in the number of unassigned recruits. [5]Includes all tank units and the Porto Rico Regiment of Infantry. [6]Includes flying cadets, not to exceed 2,500. [7]Includes General Staff with troops, detached officers' list, detached enlisted men's list, military attache and unassigned recruits. [8]Includes officers and enlisted men of the Philippine Scouts, but does not include warrant officers, the Corps of Cadets at the U. S. Military Academy (with an authorized strength of 1,334) or the officers and enlisted men on the retired list.

UNITED STATES ARMY—*Continued.*

ACTUAL STRENGTH OF THE ARMY.

The actual strength of the entire Military Establishment on June 30, 1919, and June 30, 1920, by branches of service, is shown in the following table:

Branch of Service.	June 30, 1919 Officers.	June 30, 1919 Enlisted Men.	June 30, 1919 Total.	June 30, 1920 Officers.	June 30, 1920 Enlisted Men.	June 30, 1920 Total.
General officers and aides	215	......	215	193	......	196
Staff Corps and departments	27,632	192,932	220,564	5,390	48,775	47,165
Infantry[1]	10,621	182,752	193,373	3,453	49,107	62,560
Cavalry	957	19,682	20,639	965	15,812	16,777
Field Artillery	2,672	35,584	38,156	1,034	14,723	15,757
Coast Artillery Corps	1,207	14,328	15,535	1,019	15,126	16,145
Air Service	2,928	21,187	24,115	1,069	8,289	9,358
Corps of Engineers	[2]3,694	[2]83,007	86,701	303	4,574	4,877
Signal Corps	710	9,498	10,208	253	4,695	4,948
Miscellaneous	27,152	192,190	219,342	1,561	16,817	25,368
Totals	[3]77,688	751,160	[5]828,848	[4]16,232	177,918	[6]193,150
Philippine Scouts	278	7,719	7,997	219	6,930	7,149
Aggregate	77,966	758,879	836,845	15,451	184,848	200,299

[1]Including tank units. [2]Including Transportation Corps. [3]Including 67,656 emergency officers. [4]Including 7,232 emergency officers. [5]To this total 37 warrant officers should be added. [6]To this total 56 warrant officers should be added.

RATES OF PAY TO OFFICERS, ACTIVE AND RETIRED.

Grade.	Pay of Officers in Active Service. Pay of Grade. Year	M'nth	Monthly Pay.[a] After 5 y's 10%	After 10 yrs 20%	After 15 y's 30%	After 20 y's 40%	Pay of Retired Officers.[c] Pay of Grade. Year	M'nth	Monthly Pay. After 5 y's	After 10 yrs	After 15 y's	After 20 y's
General of the Armies of U. S.	$13,500	......	......	......	......	......	......	......	......	......	......	......
General	10,000	$833.34	......	......	......	......	$7,500	$625.00	......	......	......	......
Lieutenant-General	9,000	750.00	......	......	......	......	6,750	562.50	......	......	......	......
Major-General	8,000	666.67	......	......	......	......	6,000	500.00	......	......	......	......
Brigadier-General	6,000	500.00	......	......	......	......	4,500	375.00	......	......	......	......
Colonel	4,000	333.33	$366.67	$400.00	[b]$416.67	$416.67	3,000	250.00	$275.00	$300.00	$312.50	$312.50
Lieutenant-Colonel	3,500	291.67	320.83	350.00	[b]375.00	375.00	2,624	218.75	240.62	262.50	281.25	281.25
Major	3,000	250.00	275.00	300.00	325.00	[b]333.33	2,250	187.50	206.25	225.00	243.75	250.00
Captain	2,400	200.00	220.00	240.00	260.00	280.00	1,800	150.00	165.00	180.00	195.00	210.00
First lieutenant	2,000	166.67	183.33	200.00	216.67	233.33	1,500	125.00	137.50	150.00	162.50	175.00
Second lieutenant	1,700	141.67	155.83	170.00	184.17	198.33	1,275	106.25	116.87	127.50	138.12	148.75

[a]Officers below rank of brig.-gen. receive 10% on yearly pay of grade for each term of 5 years' service, not to exceed 40% in all. (Except colonel, lieut.-col. and major.) [b]Maximum pay of a colonel is $5,000, that of lieut.-col. $4,500, and that of major, $4,000. [c]Retired officers receive 75% of pay of their grade (salary and increase). No increase of longevity after retirement unless retired for wounds received in battle.

Forts in Vicinity of New York City.

FORT HAMILTON, N. Y.—On southwest shore of L. I., commanding "Narrows." Reservation, 155 acres. P. O., Ft. Hamilton Sta.

FORT HANCOCK, N. J.—At Sandy Hook, N. J. Reservation, 1,366 acres. P. O., Ft. Hancock, N. J.; Teleg. Sta., Sandy Hook, N. J. R. R. Sta., Highlands, N. J.

FORT JAY, N. Y.—On Governors Island, N. Y. Harbor Reservation, 172 acres.

FORT SCHUYLER, N. Y.—On Throg's Neck, L. I. Sound, 4½ miles from Westchester, N. Y. City. P. O. Teleg. and R. R. Sta. Reservation, 52 acres. Sub post, Ft. Totten.

FORT SLOCUM, N. Y.—David's Island, southwest extremity of L. I. Sound, 2 miles from New Rochelle. Reservation, 86 acres. P. O., New Rochelle, N. Y.; Teleg. Sta., Ft. Slocum.

FORT TILDEN, N. Y.—Rockaway Point, L. I. Comdg. entrance to N. Y. Harbor. 290 acres. P. O., Rockaway Beach.

FORT TOTTEN, N. Y.—On East River, 2¼ miles from Whitestone, L. I. Reservation, 136 acres. P. O. and Teleg. Sta., Ft. Totten, N. Y.; R. R. Sta., Whitestone and Bayside.

FORT WADSWORTH, N. Y.—On Staten Island, commanding "Narrows." Reservation, 230 acres, P. O. and Teleg. Sta., Rosebank, S. I.

FORT WOOD—On Bedloe's Island, N. Y. Harbor, 1⅝ miles southwest of the Battery, N. Y. City; 1⅛ miles from Jersey shore. Reservation, 13 acres. P. O. and R. R. Sta., N. Y.

Strength and Casualties of U. S. Army in World War.

The size of the American Army increased from April 6, 1917, to Nov. 11, 1918, from 190,000 to 3,665,000 men, of whom more than 2,000,000 were in France. The appropriations for the War Dept., on the executive side alone, were increased in that period from $2,000,000 a year to $20,000,000; and the civilian employees had increased from about 2,000 to about 25,000.

CASUALTIES.

The most reliable data available in Dec., 1920, showed that a total of 33,483 members of the American Expeditionary Forces (incl. 382 who lost their lives at sea through act of the enemy) were killed in action during the entire period of hostilities; that 12,883 died from wounds received in action; 22,359 died from diseases; 3,890 died from accident and other causes; and 183,876 were wounded in action. Total, 256,491. These figures include all reported casualties among members of the American Expeditionary Forces, whether serving in Europe or Siberia.

U. S. ARMY LOSSES IN OTHER WARS.

WAR OF 1812.

Less than 1,600 killed, 3,500 wounded.

CIVIL WAR.

The number of casualties in the Volunteer and Regular armies of the U. S. during the war of 1861-65, according to a statement prepared by the Adj.-General's Office, was as follows: Killed in battle, 67,058; died of wounds, 43,012; died of disease, 199,720; other causes, such as accidents, murder, Confederate prisons, etc., 40,154; total died, 349,944; total deserted, 199,105. Number of soldiers in Confederate service who died of wounds or disease (partial statement), 133,821; deserted (partial statement), 104,428. Number of U. S. troops captured during the war, 212,608; Confederate troops captured, 476,169. Number of U. S. troops paroled on the field, 16,431; Confederate, 248,599. Number of U. S. troops who died while prisoners, 30,156; Confederate, 30,152.

SPANISH AND PHILIPPINE WARS.

From wounds or disease. Officers, enlisted men: May 1, 1898, to June 30, 1899, 224; 6,395. June 30, 1899, to July 1, 1900, 74; 1,930. July 1, 1900, to June 30, 1901, 57; 1,932.

1916 MEXICAN CRISIS.

From wounds and disease: March 15, 1916, to Jan. 28, 1917, 3 officers, 40 enlisted men.

NATIONAL GUARD.

The aggregate strength of the National Guard drafted into Federal service was 12,100 officers and 367,223 enlisted men.

UNITED STATES NAVY.

During the 12 months ending Oct. 1, 1920, the United States Navy was strengthened by the addition of 125 new vessels. Of this number 1 was a battleship, the Tennessee; 84 were destroyers, 12 submarines, 8 Eagle boats, 1 fuel ship, 1 ammunition ship, 1 gunboat, 6 minesweepers and 11 fleet tugs. This left under construction Oct. 1 11 battleships, 6 battle cruisers, 10 scout cruisers, 1 gunboat, 8 auxiliary vessels, including 2 ordered during the year; 52 destroyers, 49 submarines, including the 3 fleet submarines ordered March, 1920, and 3 fleet tugs. With the exception of the Battleship California, launched Nov. 20, 1919, and due for completion in 1921, the destroyers, 20 of the submarines and the 3 fleet tugs, the vessels now under construction for the Navy all belong to the three-year naval program adopted by Congress.

The following summary shows the strength of the United States Navy, including ships building, of July 1, 1920:

Summary of Vessels in the United States Navy, July 1, 1920.

Class and Type.	Fit for service, including those under repair.		Under construction.		Authorized but not yet placed.		Totals.	
	Number.	Displacement.	Number.	Displacement.	Number.	Disp'ment.	Number.	Displacement.
Battleships.								
Battleships, first line	16	435,750	11	421,900	..	..	27	857,650
Battleships, second line	21	296,704	..	..	..	..	21	296,704
Monitors, second line	6	20,974	..	..	..	..	6	20,974
Sub-total	43	753,428	11	421,900	..	..	54	1,175,328
Cruisers.								
Battle cruisers, first line	..	......	6	261,000	..	..	6	261,000
Cruisers, second line	16	173,730	..	..	..	..	16	173,730
Light cruisers, first line	..	......	10	71,000	..	..	10	71,000
Light cruisers, second line	3	11,250	..	..	..	..	3	11,250
Aircraft carrier, second line	..	......	1	19,360	..	..	1	19,360
Mine layers, second line	4	16,096	..	..	..	..	4	16,096
Sub-total	23	201,076	17	351,360	..	..	40	552,436
Destroyers.								
Destroyers, first line	214	252,578	70	85,009	12	..	296	337,587
Destroyers, second line	21	15,582	..	..	..	..	21	15,582
Light mine layers	14	16,674	..	..	..	..	14	16,674
Sub-total	249	284,834	70	85,009	12	..	331	369,843
Submarines.								
Submarines, first line	49	22,961	45	..	..	..	94	22,961
Submarines, second line	48	17,202	..	..	..	..	48	17,202
Fleet submarines, first line	1	([2])	5	..	6	..	12	([3])
Sub-total	98	40,163	50	..	6	..	154	40,163
Patrol Vessels.								
Eagles	55	27,500	..	..	..	..	55	27,500
Submarine chasers	112	8,624	..	..	..	..	112	8,624
Gunboats	28	44,183	2	3,150	..	..	30	47,333
Yachts	10	10,072	..	..	..	..	10	10,072
Sub-total	205	90,379	2	3,150	..	..	207	93,529
Totals, fighting ships	618	1,369,880	150	861,419	18	..	786	2,231,299
Auxiliaries.								
Special types	46	304,445	8	87,040	1	10,000	55	401,485
Fuel ships	22	288,306	3	46,400	..	..	25	334,706
Tugs	40	33,580	4	4,000	..	..	44	37,580
Mine sweepers	46	43,700	..	..	..	..	46	43,700
Sub-total	154	670,031	15	137,440	1	10,000	170	817,471
Unclassified	23	71,546	..	..	..	..	23	71,546
Grand total	795	2,111,457	165	998,859	19	10,000	979	3,120,316

The following table shows a comparison of the strength of the enlisted and enrolled personnel of the Navy on June 30, 1919 and 1920:

Comparative Strength of the Enlisted and Enrolled Personnel on June 30, 1919 and 1920.

	1919.	1920.	Decrease.
United States Navy	169,279	107,601	61,678
United States Naval Reserve Force	81,258	1,349	79,909
Total	250,537	108,950	141,587

Navy Yards and Stations.

Boston, Mass.; Charleston, S. C.; Great Lakes Naval Training Station, Ill.; Guam, M. I.; Guantanamo, Cuba; Hawaii; Indian Head Proving Ground; Key West, Fla.; Mare Island, Cal.; Narragansett Bay, R. I.; New Orleans, La.; New York, N. Y. Norfolk, Va.; Pensacola, Fla.; Philadelphia, Pa.; Philippine Islands, Olongopo; Portsmouth, N. H.; Puget Sound, Wash.; San Francisco, Cal.; Tutuila, Samoa; Washington, D. C.

Brooklyn Navy Yard.

The Brooklyn Navy Yard was established Feb. 23, 1801, when the first land, 23 acres, was bought from John Jackson for $40,000. It now comprises 197 acres (land 126, water 71), situated on Wallabout Channel of the East River, and has a water front of nearly 3 miles, protected by a sea wall of granite and concrete.

The frigate Fulton, first steam war vessel, was constructed at this yard in 1815.

Naval Academy, Annapolis, Md.

The students of the Naval Academy are styled midshipmen. 4 are allowed for each Senator, Representative and Delegate in Congress, 2 for District of Columbia and 15 each year from United States at large. 100 appointments may be made annually from the enlisted men of the Navy. The appointments from District of Columbia and at large are made by the President. 1 is allowed from Porto Rico. The appointment from Porto Rico is made on recommendation of the Gov. of Porto Rico. Appointees from the Philippines are not to be appointed as commissioned officers upon graduation.

The course for midshipmen is 4 years, at the expiration of which time examination for graduation takes place.

Certificates from colleges and high schools will not be accepted in lieu of the entrance examinations at the Naval Academy; all candidates must take the prescribed mental and physical examination before being admitted.

Midshipmen who pass the examination for graduation are appointed to fill vacancies in the lower grades of the line of the Navy and of the Marine Corps in order of merit.

Candidates allowed for Congressional Districts, for Territories and for the District of Columbia must be actual residents of the Districts or Territories, respectively, from which they are nominated. All candidates must, at the time of their examination for admission,

UNITED STATES NAVY—*Continued.*

be between the ages of 16 and 20 years. A candidate is eligible for examination on the day he becomes 16 and is ineligible on the day he becomes 20 yrs. of age. The pay of a midshipman is $600 a year while at the Academy, pay commencing at admission. Supt., Capt. E. W. Eberle, Naval Academy, Annapolis, Md.

ENLISTMENT IN THE U. S. NAVY.

The term of enlistment of enlisted men of the Navy is four years, except machinists in Aviation Schools, who must enlist for **three years. Minors over the age of 18 may be enlisted without consent of parents or guardians. Only such persons shall be enlisted as can reasonably be expected to remain in the service. Every person, before being enlisted must pass the physical examination prescribed in the medical instructions. Applicants for enlistment must be American citizens, able to read and write English, and when enlisted must take the oath of allegiance. No person under the age of 17 can be enlisted.**

PAY OF COMMISSIONED OFFICERS OF THE NAVY.

(Acts of May 13, 1908; March 3, 1915; May 22, 1917; Oct. 6, 1917; July 1, 1918.)

Rank.	Pay.
Admiral (in command of fleet)	$10,000
Vice-Admiral (second in command of fleet)	9,000
Rear-Admiral (upper half*); Chief of Bureaus and Judge Advocate General	$8,000
Rear-Admiral (lower half*) (and commodore)	6,000
Captain	4,000
Commander	3,500
Lieut-Commander	3,000
Lieutenant	2,400
Lieutenant (junior grade)	2,000
Ensign	1,700

*By act of Aug. 29, 1916, rear admirals, for pay and allowance purposes, are designated as either upper or lower half.

PAY OF WARRANT OFFICERS.

(As provided by Acts of May 13, 1908; March 3, 1915, and March 4, 1917.)

	At sea.	On shore or other duty.	On leave or waiting orders
First 3 yrs.' service	$1,500	$1,125	$875
Second 3 yrs.' service	1,625	1,250	1,000
Third 3 yrs.' service	1,750	1,625	1,125
Fourth 3 yrs.' service	2,000	1,750	1,250
After 12 yrs.' service	2,250	2,000	1,500
Mates.			
In service, Aug. 1, 1894	1,500	1,125	875
Ap'd since Aug. 1, 1894	1,125	875	625

U. S. MARINE CORPS.

Two battalions of United States Marines were authorized by a resolution of the Continental Congress on Nov. 10, 1775. After the conclusion of the American Revolution very few Marines were enlisted, but there were always a few to maintain continuity until July 11, 1798, when an Act of Congress established the Marine Corps as it exists today, with a strength of 37 officers, including a Major-Commandant and 848 enlisted men. The statutory strength of the Marine Corps today is 1,235 officers and 27,400 enlisted men, or a total of 28,635 Marines.

TONNAGES OF THE NAVIES OF THE WORLD.

Ships Built.

Type.	Great Britain. No.	Great Britain. Tonnage.	United States. No.	United States. Tonnage.	France. No.	France. Tonnage.	Japan. No.	Japan. Tonnage.	Italy. No.	Italy. Tonnage.
Battleships	46	962,750	32	675,690	17	327,950	12	277,822	9	158,060
Battle cruisers	10	247,500	..	....	..	....	4	110,000	..	....
Cruisers	21	248,900	19	161,750	9	107,252	5	58,206	4	38,462
Light cruisers	81	346,720	..	....	..	....	7	29,290	6	19,638
Flotilla Leaders	26	44,842	.	....	..	....	..	....	8	10,832
Destroyers	375	385,547	265	305,696	63	36,860	59	35,912	35	22,766
Torpedo boats	31	8,685	..	......	50	4,917	..	....	90	16,852
Submarines	165	116,150	105	50,673	55	26,292	23	6,352	77	21,511

Ships Building.

Country.	No.	Ton'ge.
Great Britain	39	77,823
Japan	109	690,735
France	20	164,168
Italy	32	146,921
United States.	52	840,707

Capital Ships Building and Projected.

Type.	Italy.		Great Britain	Un'd States.		Japan.		France.	
Battleships	4	123,600	......	11	421,900	7	261,400	4	123,600
Battle cruisers	0	....	......	6	211,800	8	320,000		......

Note—There is no reliable data in regard to Russia.

THE WORLD'S SHIPPING IN GROSS TONS.

	June, 1914.	June, 1920.
United Kingdom	18,892,000	18,111,000
British Dominions	1,632,000	2,032,000
United States	4,287,000	14,525,000
Germany	5,135,000	419,000
Norway	1,957,000	1,980,000
France	1,922,000	2,963,000
Japan	1,708,000	2,996,000
Holland	1,472,000	1,773,000
Italy	1,430,000	2,118,000
Austria-Hungary	1,052,000	....
Sweden	1,015,000	996,000
Greece	821,000	497,000
Spain	884,000	937,000
Denmark	770,000	719,000
World's total	45,404,000	53,905,000

Difference between 1914 and 1920, 8,501,000.

World's Tonnage Being Built.

World's tonnage under way July 1, 1919	8,017,000
World's tonnage under way July 1, 1920	7,720,000
U. S. tonnage under way July 1, 1919	3,874,000
U. S. tonnage under way July 1, 1920	2,106,000
United Kingdom tonnage under way July 1 1919	2,524,000
United Kingdom tonnage under wry July 1, 1920	3,578,000

The British railways employ 10,000 female clerks.

VALUE OF BRITAIN'S TRADE.

The annual statement of the trade of the United Kingdom with foreign countries and British possessions during the year 1919 was issued in Nov., 1920, as a blue book. Abstracts from the summary tables show that under imports from foreign countries the total value in the last fiscal year was £1,043,585,573 compared with £893,115,932 in 1918. From the British possessions, including the protectorates, the total reached £582,570,639, compared with £423,034,971 in 1918; thus showing a gross total of imports in 1919 of £1,626,156,212, compared with £1,316,150,903 in the previous year. Under exports, it is shown that the total value of the produce and manufactures of the United Kingdom sent to foreign countries in 1919 was £593,015,062, compared with £323,056,875 in the previous year. The value of exports to the British possessions, including the protectorates, in 1919 was £205,620,314 as compared with £178,362,122 in 1918. Together, a gross amount was reached of £798,635,376 as against £501,418,997 in 1918. A summary of the total value of the exports of foreign and colonial merchandise to foreign countries and the British possessions, including the protectorates, gives an amount of £164,749,301, as compared with £30,945,081 in 1918.

Twenty-four Russian Communists were deported from New York City Dec. 23, 1920, sailing on the Imperator for Soviet Russia.

UNITED STATES GOVERNMENT PENSIONS.

PENSIONERS AND AMOUNTS PAID DURING THE FISCAL YEAR ENDED JUNE 30, 1920.

States and Territories.	No.	Amount.
Alabama	2,045	$736,445.45
Alaska	44	15,845.29
Arizona	653	235,158.36
Arkansas	5,995	2,158,919.41
California	20,892	7,523,627.04
Colorado	6,002	2,160,440.23
Connecticut	7,130	2,567,655.60
Delaware	1,427	513,891.24
District of Columbia	6,470	2,239,976.39
Florida	3,654	1,315,878.47
Georgia	2,079	748,689.48
Idaho	1,383	498,045.96
Illinois	41,981	15,119,998.31
Indiana	35,905	12,930,108.60
Iowa	20,080	7,230,209.61
Kansas	23,632	8,510,355.83
Kentucky	15,545	5,598,065.40
Louisiana	3,203	1,153,464.36
Maine	10,297	3,708,155.65
Maryland	8,566	3,084,787.92
Massachusetts	24,695	8,893,163.40
Michigan	24,695	8,954,023.69
Minnesota	9,481	3,414,297.72
Mississippi	2,130	767,05 .60
Missouri	29,078	10,470,569.35
Montana	1,625	585 195.
Nebraska	10,415	3,75 649.
Nevada	246	8 589.
New Hampshire	4,770	1,71[illegible],772.
New Jersey	14,966	5,389,555.00
New Mexico	1,369	493,004.[illegible]
New York	50,963	18 352,795.56
North Carolina	2,379	856,725.49
North Dakota	1,892	681,347.04
Ohio	58,160	20,944,579.20
Oklahoma	7,963	2,867,635.57
Oregon	5,718	2,059,166.16
Pennsylvania	55,924	20,139,350.87
Rhode Island	3,061	1,102,327.32
South Carolina	1,132	407, 3.84
South Dakota	3,781	1,361, 3.71
Tennessee	12,369	4,454,654.28
Texas	5,600	2,016,622.00
Utah	741	266,848.92
Vermont	4,673	1,682,840.77
Virginia	4,002	1,441,200 25
Washington	7,280	2,621,673.60
West Virginia	7,478	2,692,977.35
Wisconsin	14,251	5,132,034.38
Wyoming	549	197,705.89
Totals	583,538	$211,943,069.42
Canal Zone	12	4,321.44
Insular Possessions:		
Guam	3	1,080.36
Hawaii	65	23,407.80
Philippines	105	37,812.60
Porto Rico	13	4,681.56
Virgin Islands	1	360.12
Totals	187	$67,342.44

Total number in Foreign Countries, 3,453; total amount, $1,280,581.35. Grand total number, 592,190; grand total amount, $213,295,314 65.

UNITED STATES PENSIONERS.

Fiscal Year.	Total.	Number of Pensioners.	Fiscal Year.	Total.	Number of Pensioners.
1866	$15,857,714.88	126,722	1895	144,150,814.51	970,524
1867	21,275,767.04	155,474	1896	142,212,080.07	970,678
1868	23,654,529.70	169,643	1897	143,937,500.42	976,014
1869	29,077,774.08	187,963	1898	148,765,971.26	993,714
1870	29,952,486.64	198,686	1899	142,502,570.68	991,519
1871	29,381,871.62	207,495	1900	142,303,887.39	993,592
1872	30,703,999.81	232,229	1901	142,400,279.28	997,735
1873	27,985,264.53	238,411	1902	141,335,646.95	999,446
1874	31,173,573.12	236,241	1903	141,752,870.50	996,545
1875	30,253,100.11	234,821	1904	144,942,987.74	994,762
1876	28,951,288.34	232,137	1905	144,864,694.15	998,441
1877	29,217,281.05	232,104	1906	142,523,557.76	985,971
1878	27,818,509.53	223,998	1907	141,464,522.90	967,371
1879	34,502,163.06	242,755	1908	155,894,049.63	951,687
1880	57,624,256.36	250,802	1909	164,826,287.50	946,194
1881	51,655,464.99	268,830	1910	162,631,729.94	921,083
1882	55,779,408.06	285,697	1911	159,842,287.41	892,098
1883	63,019,222.10	303,658	1912	155,435,291.03	860,294
1884	60,747,568.47	322,756	1913	176,714,907.39	820,200
1885	68,564,513.46	345,125	1914	174,484,053.41	785,239
1886	67,336,159.51	365,783	1915	167,298,126.44	748,147
1887	77,506,397.99	406,007	1916	160,811,812.25	709,572
1888	82,465,558.94	452,557	1917	162,457,908.90	673,111
1889	92,309,688.98	489,725	1918	181,862,944.36	646,895
1890	109,620,232.52	537,944	1919	223,592,484.37	624,427
1891	122,013,326.94	676,160	1920	214,690,328.74	592,190
1892	144,292,812.91	876,068			
1893	161,774,372.36	966,012	Total,	$5,871,664,004.56	....
1894	143,950,702.48	969,544			

PENSIONERS ON THE ROLL JUNE 30, 1920, AND JUNE 30, 1919.

	1920.	1919.	Gain.	Loss.
Regular Establishments:				
Invalids	14,477	14,655	....	178
Widows	2,899	2,922	....	23
Minor children	259	251	8	.....
Mothers	1,211	1,217	....	6
Fathers	169	161	8	.....
Brothers, sisters, sons and daughters	9	8	1	.....
Helpless children	7	4	3	.....
Civil War:				
Act Feb. 6, 1907—Survivors	410	579	....	169
Act of May 11, 1912—Survivors	234,756	260,127	....	25,371
General law—				
Invalids	8,152	10,418	....	2,266
Widows	39,346	42,773	....	3,427
Minor children	62	86	....	24
Mothers	129	189	....	60
Fathers	11	17	....	6
Brothers, sisters, sons and daughters	635	683	....	48
Helpless children	388	399	....	11
Act June 27, 1890—				
Invalids	202	267	....	65
Minor children	1,519	1,698	....	179
Helpless children	512	507	5	.....
Act Apr. 19, 1908—				
Widows without children	245,170	247,940	....	2,770
Act Aug. 5, 1892—				
Nurses	109	129	....	20
War with Spain:				
Invalids	23,144	23,382	....	238
Widows	1,233	1,262	....	29
Minor children	123	131	....	8
Mothers	1,965	2,100	....	135
Fathers	283	303	....	20
Brothers, sisters, sons and daughters	1	2	....	1
Helpless children	5	6	....	1
Act July 16, 1918—				
Widows	3,371	992	2,379	.....
Minors	306	72	234	.....
Helpless children	1	1	....	.....
War of 1812:				
Widows	71	81	....	10
War with Mexico:				
Survivors	148	215	....	67
Widows	2,421	2,738	....	318
Brothers, sisters, sons and daughters	2	2	....	.....
Indian Wars:				
Survivors	3,745	3,436	309	.....
Widows	2,483	2,027	456	.....
World War:				
Invalids	76	61	15	.....
Widows	41	44	....	3
Minor children	4	3	1	.....
Mothers	6	6	....	.....
Fathers	1	1	....	.....
Totals	592,190	624,427	3,419	35,656
Net loss to the roll	.....	......	.....	32,237

PRINCIPAL PORTS OF U. S.

Total tonnage entering at and clearing from Custom Districts:

		Total Vessels.	Total Tonnage.
New York City,	entered	4,628	13,610,098
	Cleared	4,558	14,030,827
Ohio (Cleveland),	entered	3,504	3,104,446
	Cleared	4,138	4,607,966
New Orleans,	entered	1,556	3,101,010
	Cleared	1,636	3,414,010
Philadelphia,	entered	1,083	2,773,108
	Cleared	1,222	3,270,196
Washington,	entered	4,395	2,618,070
	Cleared	4,358	2,776,023

The statistics of passports issued by the Department of State show that as an average 34,000 passports a year have been issued during the last eight years. The peak year during this period was 1919, following the armistice, during which year more than 98,000 passports were issued.

U. S. TREASURY CONDITION, DECEMBER 2, 1920.

CASH ASSETS AND LIABILITIES.

General Fund.

ASSETS.	
Available gold	$291,779,294.85
Available silver dollars	16,048,807.00
United States Notes	6,391,348.00
Federal Reserve Notes	16,574,508.00
Federal Reserve Bank Notes	4,335,932.55
National Bank Notes	13,824,084.13
Certified checks on banks	82,041.49
Subsidiary silver coin	3,634,344.75
Minor coin	1,027,192.66
Silver bullion	36,224,791.76
Unclassified (unsorted currency, etc.)	15,284,911.43
Deposits in Federal Land Banks	800,000.00
Deposits in Fed. Reserve Banks	46,113,727.33
Deposits in Spec. Depositaries account of sales of certifs. of indebtedness	48,553,000.00
Deposits in Foreign Depositaries:	
To credit of Treas., U. S.	7,553,211.28
To credit of other Govt. Officers	41,234,975.25
Deposits in National Banks:	
To credit of Treas., U. S.	11,313,065.36
To credit of other Govt. Officers	12,444,469.09
Deposits in Philippine Treasury:	
To credit of Treas., U. S.	2,781,238.92
Total	$576,000,943.85

LIABILITIES.	
Treasurer's checks outstanding	$493,684.26
Deposits of Gov. Officers:	
Post Office Department	17,561,681.53
Bd. of Trustees, Postal Savings System (5% reserve)	7,548,611.08
Other deposits	52,014.31
Comptroller of Currency, agent for creditors of insolvent banks	1,313,464.97
Postmasters, clerks of courts, etc.	63,531,869.13
Deposits for:	
Redemption of Federal Reserve Notes (5% fund, gold)	278,380,921.11
Redemption of Federal Reserve Bank Notes (5% fund)	11,825,011.55
Redemption of National Bank Notes (5% fund)	23,558,752.44
Retirement of addl. circulating notes, Act May 30, 1908	105,110.00
Exchanges of currency, coin, etc.	18,402,263.40
	$420,773,383.72
Net balance	155,227,560.13
Total	$576,000,943.85

Note—The amount to the credit of disbursing officers and agencies Dec. 2 was $950,520,744.48. Book credits, for which obligations of foreign Govts. are heli by the U. S., amount to $35,736,629.06.

Under the acts of July 14, 1890, and Dec. 23, 1913, deposits of lawful money for the retirement of outstanding natl. bank and Federal Reserve Bank notes are paid into the Treasury as miscellaneous receipts, and these obligations are made under the acts mentioned a part of the public debt. The amount of such obligations Dec. 2 was $27,143,001.

$1,197,497 in Federal Reserve notes, $3,433,109 in Federal Reserve Bank notes and $11,927,946 in national bank notes are in the Treasury in process of redemption and are charges against the deposits for the respective 5 per cent. redemption funds.

RECEIPTS AND DISBURSEMENTS.

Total receipts of the U. S. Government from all sources, excl. of postal receipts, for the year ended June 30, 1920, were $22,556,760,387.42. The total disbursements fcr the same period were $23,178,189,511.33, showing deficit of $621,429,123.91.

U. S. Treasury Balance Sheet, Receipts and Disbursements, 1916 to 1920.

For Fiscal Year.	1920.	1919	1918	1917	1916
I. Ordinary receipts	$6,704,414,437.63	$4,647,603,852.46	$4,174,010,585	$1,118,174,126	$779,664,552.49
Ordinary disbursements	6,141,745,240.08	15,365,362,741.76	8,966,532,266	1,147,898,991	724,492,998.90
Excess of receipts over disbursements	562,669,197.55	*10,717,758,889.30	*4,792,521,680	*29,724,865	55,171,553.59
II. Panama Canal receipts	9,039,670.95	6,777,046.55	6,414,570	6,150,669	2,869,995.28
Panama Canal disbursements	9,465,056.54	12,265,775.08	20,787,624	19,262,798	17,503,728.07
Excess of receipts over disbursements	*425,385.59	*5,488,728.53	*14,373,054	*13,112,129	*14,633,732.79
III. Public-debt receipts	15,852,345,949.79	29,075,976,515.75	16,974,889,209	2,428,017,799	58,452,402.50
Public-debt disbursements	17,036,444,271.25	15,837,566,009.13	7,706,879,075	677,544,782	24,668,913.50
Excess of receipts over disbursements	*1,184,098,321.46	13,238,410,506.62	9,268,010,134	1,750,473,017	33,783,489.00
Excess of all receipts over all disbursements	*621,429,123.91	*1,059,349,775.36	*343,472,604	788,755,707	74,321,309.80
Balance in General Fund at close of year	1,226,164,935.26	1,002,732,042.00	$967,247,123	$1,066,983,861	$178,491,415.58

*Excess of disbursements over receipts.

BROOKLYN DAILY EAGLE GRAND CANYON DEDICATION TOUR.

The Eagle organized and conducted a Grand Canyon National Park Dedication Tour in April-May, 1920. The tourists, numbering 119, left New York on April 8; they returned on May 8, having passed through 21 States, with three side trips into Mexico. The tour included practically all the beauties and wonders and historic points of interest in the Southwest and California, the distance covered by train being 7,835 miles, and 1,154 miles covered by automobile. The tour, which was organized with the co-operation of the National Park Service and on the invitation of the Secretary of the Interior, had as its central feature the dedication of the Grand Canyon as a national park. The dedication exercises were held on April 30 at the Powell Monument in the Grand Canyon, Governor Thomas E. Campbell of Arizona, Director Mather of the National Park Service, as well as Edward M. Bassett and Meier Steinbrink of The Eagle party, assisting in the ceremonies.

At the Grand Canyon The Eagle tourists raised a fund of $1,835.50 for a permanent memorial to mark the dedication of the canyon as a national park by The Eagle party. At a meeting of the tourists at the Brooklyn Club in June it was unanimously approved that the memorial should take the form of an information booth located at a convenient location in the canyon.

BROOKLYN EAGLE TOURS SINCE THE CHICAGO EXPOSITION.

Destination and date; World's Fair at Chicago—two special trains, 1893; Duluth, by way Great Lakes, 1895; Cotton State Exposition, Atlanta, 1895; St. Lawrence River and Saguenay, 1896; Tennessee Centennial, Nashville, 1897; Nova Scotia, 1898; Great Lakes to Duluth, 1898; Porto Rico, 1899; California and Yellowstone, 1899; Europe, 1900; Pan-American Exposition, Buffalo, 1901; Louisiana Purchase Exposition, St. Louis, 1904; California Exposition, 1905; Jamestown Exposition, 1907; Seattle Exposition, 1909; Canada, 1910; Europe, 1910; Panama-Pacific Exposition, 1915; National Park Tour, 1919.

One hundred and fifty-four thousand seven hundred cars and trucks enter and leave Manhattan daily, according to three recent traffic surveys. The motor vehicles crossing the bridges total 139,900, those reaching New York by ferry number 14,846.

SENATE OF THE SIXTY-SEVENTH CONGRESS.

The 67th Congress will come into existence March 4, 1921. For Senate of the 66th Congress see 1920 Eagle Almanac, p. 293.

Senators are chosen by direct vote of the people for a term of 6 yrs. Salary, $7,500 per yr. and mileage. Salary of V.-Pres., $12,000.

President......V.-Pres., Calvin Coolidge, Mass.

Term expires.	Senator	Home address.
	ALABAMA.	
1927	Oscar W. Underwood, D.	Birmingham
1925	J. Thomas Heflin, D.	Lafayette
	ARIZONA.	
1927	Ralph H. Cameron, R.	Phoenix
1923	Henry F. Ashurst, D.	Prescott
	ARKANSAS.	
1927	Thaddeus H. Caraway, D.	Jonesboro
1925	Joseph T. Robinson, D.	Lonoke
	CALIFORNIA.	
1927	Samuel M. Shortridge, R.	Menlo Park
1923	Hiram W. Johnson, R.	Sacramento
	COLORADO.	
1927	Samuel D. Nicholson, R.	Leadville
1925	Lawrence C. Phipps, R.	Denver
	CONNECTICUT.	
1927	Frank B. Brandegee, R.	New London
1923	George P. McLean, R.	Simsbury
	DELAWARE.	
1923	J. O. Wolcott, D.	Dover
1925	L. Heisler Ball, R.	Marshalton
	FLORIDA.	
1927	Duncan U. Fletcher, D.	Jacksonville
1923	Park Trammell, D.	Tallahassee
	GEORGIA.	
1927	Thomas E. Watson, D.	Thomson
1925	William J. Harris, D.	Cedartown
	IDAHO.	
1927	Frank R. Gooding, R.	Gooding
1925	William E. Borah, R.	Boise
	ILLINOIS.	
1927	William B. McKinley, R.	Champaign
1925	Medill McCormick, R.	Chicago
	INDIANA.	
1927	James E. Watson, R.	Rushville
1923	Harry S. New, R.	Indianapolis
	IOWA.	
1927	Albert B. Cummins, R.	Des Moines
1925	William S. Kenyon, R.	Fort Dodge
	KANSAS.	
1927	Charles Curtis, R.	Topeka
1925	Arthur Capper, R.	Topeka
	KENTUCKY.	
1927	Richard P. Ernst, R.	Covington
1925	Augustus O. Stanley, D.	Henderson
	LOUISIANA.	
1927	Edwin S. Broussard, D.	New Iberia
1925	Joseph E. Ransdell, D.	Lake Providence
	MAINE.	
1923	Frederick Hale, R.	Portland
1925	Bert M. Fernald, R.	West Poland
	MARYLAND.	
1927	Ovington E. Weller, R.	Baltimore
1923	J. I. France, R.	Port Deposit
	MASSACHUSETTS.	
1923	Henry Cabot Lodge, R.	Nahant
1925	David I. Walsh, D.	Fitchburg
	MICHIGAN.	
1923	Charles E. Townsend, R.	Jackson
1925	T. H. Newberry, R.	Grosse Point Farms
	MINNESOTA.	
1923	Frank B. Kellogg, R.	St. Paul
1925	Knute Nelson, R.	Alexandria
	MISSISSIPPI.	
1923	John Sharp Williams, D.	Benton
1925	Byron P. Harrison, D.	Gulfport
	MISSOURI.	
1927	Selden P. Spencer, R.	St. Louis
1923*	James A. Reed, D.	Kansas City
	MONTANA.	
1923	Henry L. Myers, D.	Hamilton
1925	Thomas J. Walsh, D.	Helena
	NEBRASKA.	
1923	Gilbert M. Hitchcock, D.	Omaha
1925	George W. Norris, R.	McCook
	NEVADA.	
1927	Tasker L. Oddie, R.	Reno
1923	Key Pittman, D.	Tonopah
	NEW HAMPSHIRE.	
1927	George H. Moses, R.	Concord
1925	Henry W. Keyes, R.	Haverhill
	NEW JERSEY.	
1923	J. S. Frelinghuysen, R.	Raritan
1925	Walter E. Edge, R.	Atlantic City
	NEW MEXICO.	
1923	A. A. Jones, D.	East Las Vegas
1925	A. B. Fall, R.	Three Rivers
	NEW YORK.	
1927	James W. Wadsworth, R.	Groveland
1923	William M. Calder, R.	Brooklyn
	NORTH CAROLINA.	
1927	L. S. Overman, D.	Salisbury
1925	F. M. Simmons, D.	Newbern
	NORTH DAKOTA.	
1927	Edwin F. Ladd, R.	Fargo
1923	Porter J. McCumber, R.	Wahpeton
	OHIO.	
1927	Frank B. Willis, R.	Ada
1923	Atlee Pomerene, D.	Canton
	OKLAHOMA.	
1927	J. W. Harreld, R.	Oklahoma City
1925	Robert L. Owen, D.	Muskogee
	OREGON.	
1927	Robert N. Stanfield, R.	Portland
1925	Charles L. McNary, R.	Salem
	PENNSYLVANIA.	
1927	Boies Penrose, R.	Philadelphia
1923	Philander C. Knox, R.	Pittsburgh
	RHODE ISLAND.	
1923	Peter Goelet Gerry, D.	Providence
1925	LeBaron B. Colt, R.	Bristol
	SOUTH CAROLINA.	
1927	Ellison D. Smith, D.	Florence
1925	N. B. Dial, D.	Laurens
	SOUTH DAKOTA.	
1927	Peter Norbeck, R.	Redfield
1925	Thomas Sterling, R.	Vermilion
	TENNESSEE.	
1923	Kenneth McKellar, D.	Memphis
1925	John K. Shields, D.	Knoxville
	TEXAS.	
1923	C. A. Culberson, D.	Dallas
1925	Morris Sheppard, D.	Texarkana
	UTAH.	
1927	Reed Smoot, R.	Provo
1923	William H. King, D.	Salt Lake City
	VERMONT.	
1927	William P. Dillingham, R.	Montpelier
1923	Carroll S. Page, R.	Hyde Park
	VIRGINIA.	
1923	Claude A. Swanson, D.	Chatham
1925	Carter Glass, D.	Lynchburg
	WASHINGTON.	
1927	Wesley L. Jones, R.	North Yakima
1923	Miles Poindexter, R.	Spokane
	WEST VIRGINIA.	
1923	Howard Sutherland, R.	Elkins
1925	Davis Elkins, R.	Morgantown
	WISCONSIN.	
1927	Irvine L. Lenroot, R.	Superior
1923	Robert M. LaFollette, R.	Madison
	WYOMING.	
1923	John B. Kendrick, D.	Sheridan
1925	Francis E. Warren, R.	Cheyenne

Republicans	59
Democrats	37
Total	96

NEW YORK CITY CONGRESSMEN, SIXTY-SEVENTH CONGRESS.

Dist.	
1.	F. C. Hicks, Pt. Washington, L. I.
2.	J. J. Kindred, Wolcott av., L. I. C.
3.	J. Kissel, 12 Thornton, Bkln.
4	Thomas H. Cullen, 265 President, Bkln.
5.	A. L. Kline, 238A Carlton av., Bkln.
6.	W. I. Lee, 214 Parkside av., Bkln.
7.	M. J. Hogan, 171 Warren, Bkln.
8.	Chas. G. Bond, 1701 E. 22d, Bkln.
9.	A. N Petersen, 319 Highland blvd., Bkln.
10.	L. D Volk, 140A Floyd, Bkln.
11.	D. J. Riordan, 29 Oliver, Mhtn.
12.	Meyer London, 275 E. B'way, Mhtn.
13.	C. D. Sullivan, 185½ Forsyth, Mhtn.
14.	N. D. Perlman, 440 5th, Mhtn.
15.	Thos. J. Ryan, 407 W. 44th, Mhtn.
16.	W. Bourke Cochran, 130 E. 67th, Mhtn.
17.	O. L. Mills, 4 E. 69th, Mhtn.
18.	J. F. Carew, 333 E. 68th, Mhtn.
19.	W. M. Chandler, 238 W. 103d, Mhtn.
20.	Isaac Siegel, 104 E. 116th, Mhtn.
21.	M. C. Ansorge, 575 Riverside dr., Mhtn.
22.	A. J. Griffin, 371 E. 140th, Mhtn.
23.	A. E. Rossdale, 412 E. Tremont av., Bronx.
24.	B. L. Fairchild, Pelham.

HOUSE OF REPRESENTATIVES, SIXTY-SEVENTH CONGRESS.

The 67th Congress will come into existence on March 4, 1921. For House of Representatives, 66th Congress, see 1920 Eagle Almanac, p. 294.

Congressmen are elected for a term of 2 years by direct vote of the people. Salary, $7,500 per year and mileage. Salary of Speaker, $12,000. Those marked * served in 66th Congress. Where names have no district number, they were elected at large.

Dist.

ALABAMA.

1 J. McDuffie, D*......Monroeville
2 J. R. Tyson, D.....Montgomery
3 H. B. Steagall, D*.........Ozark
4 F. L. Blackmon, D*....Anniston
5 W. B. Bowling, D....Lafayette
6 W. B. Oliver, D*.....Tuscaloosa
7 Lilius B. Rainey, D*...Gadsden
8 E. B. Almon, D*.....Tuscumbia
9 G. Huddleston, D*..Birmingham
10 W. B. Bankhead, D*.....Jasper

ARIZONA.

Carl Hayden, D*...........Phoenix

ARKANSAS.

1 W. J. Driver, D.........Osceola
2 W. A. Oldfield, D*....Batesville
3 J. . Tillman, D*...Fayetteville
4 Otis Wingo, D*.........De Queen
5 H. M. Jacoway, D*..Dardanelle
6 S. M. Taylor, D*......Pine Bluff
7 T. B. Parks, D.............Hope

CALIFORNIA.

1 C. F. Lea, D*.......Santa Rosa
2 J. E. Raker, D*.........Alturas
3 C. F. Curry, R*.....Sacramento
4 Julius Kahn, R*..San Francisco
5 J. I. Nolan, R*...San Francisco
6 J. A. Elston, R*.........Berkeley
7 H. E. Barbour, R*.......Fresno
8 A. M. Free, R..........San Jose
9 Vacant ....
10 H. Z. Osborn, R*...Los Angeles
11 P. D. Swing, R........El Centro

COLORADO.

1 W. N. Vaile, R*.........Denver
2 C. B. Timberlake, R*....Sterling
3 G. U. Hardy, R*...Canyon City
4 E. T. Taylor, D*.Glenwood Spng

CONNECTICUT.

1 E. H. Fenn, R.....Withersfield
2 R. P. Freeman, R*.New London
3 J. Q. Tilson, R*.....New Haven
4 Schuyler Merritt, R*..Stamford
5 J. P. Glynn, R*..........Winsted

DELAWARE.

C. R. Layton, R*..Georgetown

FLORIDA.

1 H. J. Drane, D*.......Lakeland
2 Frank Clark, D*.....Gainesville
3 J. H. Smithwick, D*..Pensacola
4 W. J. Sears, D*.......Kissimmee

GEORGIA.

1 J. W. Overstreet, D*...Sylvania
2 Frank Park, D*........Sylvester
3 C. R. Crisp, D*........Americus
4 W. C. Wright, D*......Newnan
5 W. D. Upshaw, D*......Atlanta
6 J. W. Wise, D*....Fayetteville
7 Gordon Lee, D*....Chickamauga
8 C. H. Brand, D*.........Athens
9 Thomas M. Bell, D*.Gainesville
10 Carl Vinson, D*....Milledgeville
11 W. C. Lankford, D*....Douglas
12 W. W. Larsen, D*........Dublin

IDAHO.

Burton L. French, R*...Moscow
Addison T. Smith, R*.Twin Falls

ILLINOIS.

1 M. B. Madden, R*......Chicago
2 J. R. Mann, R*.........Chicago
3 E. W. Sproul, R.........Chicago
4 J. W. Rainey, D*.......Chicago
5 A. J. Sabath, D*.......Chicago
6 J. J. Gorman, R........Chicago
7 M. A. Michaelson, R...Chicago
8 S. H. Kunz, D..........Chicago
9 F. A. Britten, R*.......Chicago
10 C. R. Chindblom, R*...Chicago
11 I. C. Copley, R*..........Aurora
12 C. E. Fuller, R*........Belvidere
13 J. C. McKenzie, R*...Elizabeth
14 W. J. Graham, R*.........Aledo
15 E. J. King, R*........Galesberg
16 Clifford Ireland, R*.......Peoria
17 F. H. Funk, R.....Bloomington
18 J. G. Cannon, R*......Danville
19 A. F. Moore, R.......Monticello

Dist.

20 G. L. Shaw, R......Beardstown
21 L. E. Wheeler, R*...Springfield
22 W. A. Rodenberg, R*.E.St.Louis
23 E. B. Brooks, R*........Newton
24 T. S. Williams, R*....Louisville
25 Ed. E. Denison, R*......Marion
R. Yates, R*..........Springfield
Wm. E. Mason, R*......Chicago

INDIANA.

1 O. R. Luhring, R*...Evansville
2 Oscar E. Bland, R* ....Linton
3 J. W. Dunbar, R*..New Albany
4 J. S. Benham, R*......Benham
5 Everett Sanders, R*.TerreHaute
6 R. N. Elliott, R*...Connersville
7 Merrill Moores, R*..Indianapolis
8 A. H. Vestal, R*......Anderson
9 F. S. Purnell, R*..........Attica
10 W. R. Wood, R*.......Lafayette
11 Milton Kraus, R*............Peru
12 L. W. Fairfield, R*......Angola
13 A. J. Hickey, R*.......Laporte

IOWA.

1 W. F. Kopp, R....Mt. Pleasant
2 H. E. Hull, R*...Williamsburg
3 B. E. Sweet, R*.........Waverly
4 G. N. Haugen, R*....Northwood
5 J. W. Good, R*...Cedar Rapids
6 C. W. Ramseyer, R*..Bloomfield
7 C. C. Dowell, R*....Des Moines
8 H. M. Towner, R*.......Corning
9 W. R. Green, R*.......Audubon
10 J. L. Dickinson, R*......Algona
11 W. D. Boies, R*........Sheldon

KANSAS.

1 D. R. Anthony, R*.Leavenworth
2 E. C. Little, R*....Kansas City
3 P. P. Campbell, R*....Pittsburg
4 H. Hoch, R*..............Marion
5 J. C. Strong, R*....Blue Rapids
6 H. B. White, R*.......Mankato
7 J. N. Tincher, R*..Medicine Lodge
8 R. E. Bird, R..........Wichita

KENTUCKY.

1 A. W. Barkley, D*.....Paducah
2 D. H. Kincheloe, D*.Madisonville
3 R. Y. Thomas, Jr., D*.Cen. City
4 Ben Johnson, D*......Bardstown
5 C. F. Ogden, R*......Bardstown
6 A. B. Rouse, D*.....Burlington
7 J. C. Cantrill, D*....Georgetown
8 R. Gilbert D..........Shelbyville
9 W. J. Fields, D*......Olive Hill
10 J. M. Robsion, R*..Barbourville

LOUISIANA.

1 James O'Connor, D*..N. Orleans
2 H. G. Dupre, D*..New Orleans
3 W. P. Martin, D*....Thibodaux
4 J. N. Sandlin, D.........Minden
5 R. J. Wilson, D*...Harrisonburg
6 G. K. Favrot, D...Baton Rouge
7 L. Lazaro, D*........Washington
8 J. B. Aswell, D*...Natchitoches

MAINE.

1 C. L. Beedy, R.........Portland
2 W. H. White, Jr., R*..Lewiston
3 J. A. Peters, R*........Ellsworth
4 I. G. Hersey, R*........Houlton

MARYLAND.

1 T. A. Goldsborough, D...Denton
2 A. A. Blakeney, ...Catonsville
3 J. P. Hill, R...........Baltimore
4 J. C. Linthicum, D*..Baltimore
5 S. E. Mudd, R*.........La Plata
6 F. N. Zihlman, R*..Cumberland

MASSACHUSETTS.

1 A. T. Treadway, R*.Stockbridge
2 F. H. Gillett, R*.....Springfield
3 C. D. Paige, R*......Southbridge
4 S. E. Winslow, R*...Worcester
5 J. J. Rogers, R*.........Lowell
6 W. W. Lufkin, R*........Essex
7 R. S. Maloney, R.....Lawrence
8 F. W. Dallinger, R*..Cambridge
9 C. L. Underhill, R..Somerville
10 Peter F. Tague, D*.......Boston
11 G. H. Tinkham, R*......Boston

Dist.

12 J. A. Gallivan, D*.........Boston
13 R. Luce, R*...............Easton
14 L. A. Frothingham, R.N.Easton
15 W. S. Greene, R*....Fall River
16 Joseph Walsh, R*.New Bedford

MICHIGAN.

1 G. P. Codd, R............Detroit
2 E. C. Michener, R*.......Adrian
3 W. H. Frankhauser, R.Hillsdale
4 J. C. Ketcham, R......Hastings
5 C. E. Mapes, R*..Grand Rapids
6 P. H. Kelley, R*.......Lansing
7 L. C. Cramton, R*........Lapeer
8 J. W. Fordney, R*......Saginaw
9 J. C. McLaughlin, R*.Muskegon
10 R. O. Woodruff, R.....Bay City
11 F. Douglas Scott, R*....Alpena
12 W. Frank James, R*...Hancock
13 V. M. Brennan, R........Detroit

MINNESOTA.

1 Sydney Anderson, R*.Lanesboro
2 F. Clague, R.....Redwood Falls
3 C. R. Davis, R*........St. Peter
4 Oscar E. Keller, R*....St. Paul
5 W. H. Newton, R*..Minneapolis
6 H. Knutson, R*........St. Cloud
7 A. J. Volstead, R*.Granite Falls
8 O. J. Larson, R...........Duluth
9 Halvor Steenerson, R*.Crookston
10 T. D. Schall, R*....Minneapolis

MISSISSIPPI.

1 J. E. Rankin, D..........Tupelo
2 B. G. Lowrey, D.Blue Mountain
3 B. G. Humphreys, D*.Greenville
4 T. U. Sisson, D*..........Winona
5 R. A. Collins, D........Meridian
6 P. B. Johnson, D*..Hattiesburg
7 P. E. Quin, D*....McComb City
8 J. W. Collier, D*......Vicksburg

MISSOURI.

1 F. C. Millspaugh, R......Canton
2 W. W. Rucker, D*..Keytesville
3 H. F. Lawrence, R.....Cameron
4 C. L. Faust, R........St. Joseph
5 E. C. Ellis, R.......Kansas City
6 W. O. Atkeson, R.........Butler
7 R. C. Patterson, R...Springfield
8 S. C. Roach, R.......Linn Creek
9 T. W. Hukriede, R...Warrenton
10 C. A. Newton, R*......St. Louis
11 H. B. Hawes, D........St. Louis
12 L. C. Dyer, R*..........St. Louis
13 M. E. Rhodes, R*..........Potosi
14 E. D. Hays, R*.Cape Girardeau
15 I. V. McPherson, R*.....Aurora
16 S. A. Shelton, R......Marshfield

MONTANA.

1 W. J. McCormick, R..Missoula
2 C. W. Riddick, R*..Lewistown

NEBRASKA.

1 C. F. Reavis, R*......Falls City
2 A. W. Jefferis, R*.........Omaha
3 R. E. Evans, R*....Dakota City
4 M. O. McLaughlin, R*.....York
5 W. E. Andrews, R*....Hastings
6 M. P. Kinkaid, R*.......O'Neill

NEVADA.

S. S. Arentz, R.........Simpson

NEW HAMPSHIRE.

1 S. E. Burroughs, R*.Manchester
2 E. H. Wason, R*........Nashua

NEW JERSEY.

1 F. F. Patterson, Jr., R*.Camden
2 I. Bacharach, R*..Atlantic City
3 T. F. Appleby, R....Asbury Pk.
4 E. C. Hutchinson, R*..Trenton
5 E. R. Ackerman, R*..Plainfield
6 R. Perkins, R...Woodcliff Lake
7 A. H. Radcliffe, R*....Paterson
8 H. W. Taylor, R........Newark
9 R. W. Parker, R........Newark
10 F. R. Lehlbach, R*......Newark
11 A. E. Olpp, R......W. Hoboken
12 C. F. X. O'Brien, D.Jersey City

NEW MEXICO.

N. Montoya, R......Albuquerque

HOUSE OF REPRESENTATIVES, SIXTY-SEVENTH CONGRESS—*Continued.*

NEW YORK.

Dist.
1 F. C. Hicks, R*..Pt. Washington
2 J. J. Kindred, D.........Astoria
3 John Kissel, R..........Brooklyn
4 T. H. Cullen, D*......Brooklyn
5 A. L. Kline, R..........Brooklyn
6 W. I. Lee, R............Brooklyn
7 M. J. Hogan, R.........Brooklyn
8 C. G. Bond, R...........Brooklyn
9 A. N. Peterson, R......Brooklyn
10 L. D. Volk, R*.........Brooklyn
11 D. J. Riordan, D*....New York
12 Meyer London, Soc..New York
13 C. D. Sullivan, D*....New York
14 N. D. Perlman, R*....New York
15 T. J. Ryan, R.........New York
16 W. Bourke Cockran, D. New York
17 Ogden L. Mills, R....New York
18 J. F. Carew, D*.......New York
19 W. M. Chandler, R..New York
20 Isaac Siegel, R*.......New York
21 M. C. Ansorge, R.....New York
22 A. J. Griffin, D*.......New York
23 A. B. Rossdale, R...........Bronx
24 B. L. Fairchild, R........Pelham
25 J. W. Husted, R*......Peekskill
26 Hamilton Fish, Jr., R..Garrison
27 C. B. Ward, R*..........Debruce
28 P. G. Ten Eyck, D.......Albany
29 J. S. Parker, R*............Salem
30 F. Crowther, R*....Schenectady
31 B. H. Snell, R*.........Potsdam
32 L. W. Mott, R*..........Oswego
33 Homer P. Snyder, R*. Little Falls
34 J. D. Clarke, R..............Delhi
35 Walter W. Magee, R*..Syracuse
36 Norman J. Gould, R*. Seneca Falls
37 A. B. Houghton, R*.....Corning
38 T. B. Dunn, R*.......Rochester
39 A. D. Sanders, R........Stafford
40 S. W. Dempsey, R*....Lockport
41 C. MacGregor, R*........Buffalo
42 J. M. Mead, D*.....Lackawanna
43 D. A. Reed, R*..........Dunkirk

NORTH CAROLINA.

1 H. S. Ward, D......Washington
2 Claude Kitchin, D*. Scotland N'k
3 S. M. Brinson, D*......Newbern
4 E. W. Pou, D*........Smithfield
5 C. M. Stedman, D*..Greensboro
6 H. L. Lyon, D.........Whiteville
7 W. C. Hammer, D.....Asheboro
8 R. L. Doughton, D*. Laurel Sp'gs
9 A. L. Bulwinkle, D....Gastonia
10 Zeb Weaver, D*.........Asheville

NORTH DAKOTA.

1 O. B. Burtness, R..Grand Forks
2 G. M. Young, R*.....Valley City
3 J. H. Sinclair, R*......Kenmare

OHIO.

1 Nicholas Longworth, R* Cin'nati
2 A. E. B. Stephens, R*..No. Bend
3 R. G. Fitzgerald, R......Dayton
4 J. L. Cable, R*..............Lima
5 C. J. Thompson, R*.....Defiance
6 C. C. Kearns, R*........Batavia
7 S. D. Fess, R*...Yellow Springs
8 R. C. Cole, R*............Findlay
9 W. W. Chalmers, R.......Toledo
10 I. M. Foster, R*..........Athens
11 E. D. Ricketts, R*........Logan
12 J. C. Speaks, R........Columbus
13 J. T. Begg, R*.........Sandusky
14 C. L. Knight, R............Akron
15 C. E. Moore, R*......Cambridge
16 J. H. Himes, R............Canton
17 W. M. Morgan, R........Newark
18 Frank Murphy, R*..Steubenville
19 J. G. Cooper, R*....Youngstown
20 M. C. Norton, R.......Cleveland
21 H. C. Gahn, R.........Cleveland
22 T. E. Burton, R........Cleveland

OKLAHOMA.

Dist.
1 T. A. Chandler, R.........Vinita
2 Alice M. Robertson, R. Muskogee
3 C. D. Carter, D*........Ardmore
4 J. C. Pringey, R........Chandler
5 F. B. Swank, D..........Norman
6 L. M. Gensman, R......Lawton
7 J. V. McClintic, D*.......Snyder
8 M. Herrick, R..............Perry

OREGON.

1 W. C. Hawley, R*........Salem
2 N. J. Sinnott, R*....The Dalles
3 C. N. McArthur, R*...Portland

PENNSYLVANIA.

1 W. S. Vare, R*............Phila.
2 G. S. Graham, R*........Phila.
3 H. C. Ransley, R*.........Phila.
4 G. W. Edmonds, R*......Phila.
5 J. J. Connolly, R.........Phila.
6 G. P. Darrow, R*..........Phila.
7 T. S. Butler, R*..West Chester
8 H. W. Watson, R*...Langhorne
9 W. W. Griest, R*.....Lancaster
10 C. R. Connell, R........Scranton
11 C. D. Coughlin, R..Wilkes-Barre
12 J. Reber, R*.............Pottsville
13 F. B. Gernerd, R......Allentown
14 L. T. McFadden, R*....Canton
15 E. R. Kiess, R*....Williamsport
16 I. C. Kline, R............Sunbury
17 B. K. Focht, R*......Lewisburg
18 A. S. Kreider, R*......Annville
19 J. M. Rose, R*.......Johnstown
20 E. S. Brooks, R*..........York
21 E. J. Jones, R*.........Bradford
22 A. M. Wyant, R....Greensburg
23 S. A. Kendall, R*....Meyersdale
24 H. W. Temple, R*..Washington
25 M. W. Shreve, R*............Erie
26 W. H. Kirkpatrick, R....Easton
27 N. L. Strong, R*......Brookville
28 H. J. Bixler, R......Johnsonburg
29 S. G. Porter, R*......Pittsburgh
30 M. Clyde Kelly, R*....Braddock
31 J. M. Morin, R*.......Pittsburgh
32 G. E. Campbell, D*..Pittsburgh
Vacant ....
J. McLaughlin R..........Phila.
W. J. Burke, R* .....Pittsburgh
A. H. Walters, R*....Johnstown

RHODE ISLAND.

1 C. Burdick, R*..........Newport
2 W. R. Stiness, R*.......Cowesett
3 Ambrose Kennedy, R*. Woons'et

SOUTH CAROLINA.

1 W. T. Logan, D......Charleston
2 J. F. Byrnes, D*............Aiken
3 F. H. Dominick, D*..Newberry
4 J. J. McSwain, D......Greenville
5 W. F. Stevenson, D*....Cheraw
6 P. H. Stoll, D*.........Kingstree
7 H. P. Fulmer, D...........North

SOUTH DAKOTA.

1 C. A. Christopherson, R* Sioux Falls
2 R. C. Johnson, R......Aberdeen
3 W. Williamson, R.......Oacoma

TENNESSEE.

1 C. Reese, R........Elizabethtown
2 J. W. Taylor, R*.....La Follette
3 Joe Brown, R........Chattanooga
4 W. S. Clouse, R........Cookeville
5 E. L. Davis, D*.......Tullahoma
6 J. W. Byrns, D*.......Nashville
7 L. P. Padgett, D*......Columbia
8 L. A. Scott, R..........Savannah
9 F. J. Garrett, D*........Dresden
10 Hubert F. Fisher D*. Memphis

TEXAS.

1 Eugene Black, D* ...Clarksville
2 J. C. Box, D*........Jacksonville
3 M. G. Sanders, D.........Canton
4 Samuel Rayburn, D*....Bonham
5 H. W. Sumners, D*. ....Dallas
6 Rufus Hardy, D*.......Corsicana
7 C. S. Briggs, D*.......Galveston
8 D. E. Garrett, D.........Houston
9 J. J. Mansfield, D*....Columbus
10 J. P. Buchanan, D*...Brenham
11 Thos. Connally, D*.......Marlin
12 F. C. Lanham, D*.....Ft. Worth
13 L. W. Parrish, D*....Henrietta
14 H. M. Wurzbach, R......Seguin
15 J. N. Garner, D*..........Uvalde
16 C. B. Hudspeth, D*......El Paso
17 T. L. Blanton, D*.......Abilene
18. M. Jones, D*...........Amarillo

UTAH.

1 D. B. Colton, R...........Vernal
2 E. O. Leatherwood, R. Salt Lake C.

VERMONT.

1 F. L. Greene, R*.....St. Albans
2 P. H. Dale, R*......Island Pond

VIRGINIA.

1 S. O. Bland, D*..Newport News
2 J. T. Deal, D..............Norfolk
3 A. J. Montague, D*...Richmond
4 P. H. Drewry, D......Petersburg
5 R. A. James, D*........Danville
6 J. P. Woods, D*.........Roanoke
7 T. W. Harrison, D*. Winchester
8 R. W. Moore, D*..........Fairfax
9 C. B. Slemp, R*. Big Stone Gap
10 H. D. Flood, D*....Appomattox

WASHINGTON.

1 J. F. Miller, R*..........Seattle
2 L. H. Hadley, R*....Bellingham
3 A. Johnson, R*..........Hoquiam
4 J. W. Summers, R*. Walla Walla
5 J. S. Webster, R*........Spokane

WEST VIRGINIA.

1 B. L. Rosenbloom, R..Wheeling
2 G. M. Bowers, R*..Martinsburg
3 S. F. Reed, R*.......Clarksburg
4 H. C. Woodyard, R*....Spencer
5 W. Goodykoontz, R*. Williamson
6 L. S. Echols, R*......Charleston

WISCONSIN.

1 H. A. Cooper, R...........Racine
2 Edward Voigt, R*....Sheboygan
3 J. M. Nelson, R...........Madison
4 J. C. Kleczka, R*.....Milwaukee
5 W. H. Stafford, R....Milwaukee
6 F. Lampert, R*..........Oshkosh
7 J. D. Beck, R..............Viroqua
8 E. E. Browne, R*......Waupaca
9 D. G. Classon, R*........Oconto
10 J. A. Frear, R*............Hudson
11 A. P. Nelson, R*.....Grantsburg

WYOMING.

F. W. Mondell, R*....Newcastle

Territories.

HAWAII.

Del., J. K. Kalanianaole, R*. Waikiki

ALASKA.

D. A. Sutherland, R..............

PORTO RICO.

Res. Comr., F. C. Davila*. San Juan

PHILIPPINES.

Res. Comr., J. C. DeVeyra*....Leyte
Res. Comr., I. Gabaldon. San Isidro

Recapitulation.

Democrats	132
Republicans	300
Socialist	1
Vacancies	2
Total	435

RATIO OF REPRESENTATION IN HOUSE OF REPRESENTATIVES.

Constitution, 1789, ratio 30,000	65
First Census, 1790, ratio 33,000	106
Second Census, 1800, ratio 33,000	142
Third Census, 1810, ratio 35,000	186
Fourth Census, 1820, ratio 40,000	213
Fifth Census, 1830, ratio 47,700	242
Sixth Census, 1840, ratio 70,680	232
Seventh Census, 1850, ratio 93,423	237
Eighth Census, 1860, ratio 127,381	243
Ninth Census, 1870, ratio 131,425	293
Tenth Census, 1880, ratio 151,911	332
Eleventh Census, 1890, ratio 173,900	357
Twelfth Census, 1900, ratio 194,182	391
Thirteenth Census, 1910, ratio 211,877	435

The Government collected $51,000,000 in taxes on soft drinks during 11 months of the year 1920.

Of the inhabitants of Mexico less than one in three on an average is able to read or write.

IMPORTANT COMMITTEES OF THE SIXTY-SIXTH CONGRESS

THE SENATE.

Chairman of each committee is named first.

Agriculture and Forestry—Messrs. Gronna, Page, Norris, Kenyon, Wadsworth, France, McNary, Capper, Keyes, Gore, Smith of S. C., Smith of Ga., Ransdell, Johnson of S. Dak., Kendrick and Harrison.

Appropriations—Messrs. Warren, Smoot, Jones of Wash., Curtis, Kenyon, Sherman, Gronna, Hale, Spencer, Phipps, Newberry, Overman, Owen, Smith of Md., Culberson, Smith of Ariz., Gay, Harris, Glass and Jones of N. Mex.

Banking and Currency—Messrs. McLean, Page, Gronna, Norris, Frelinghuysen, Penrose, Calder, Newberry, Keyes, Owen, Hitchcock, Pomerene, Fletcher, Kendrick, Henderson and Walsh of Mass.

Canadian Relations—Messrs. Hale, Sherman, Wadsworth, Spencer, Newberry, Kendrick, Myers, Walsh of Mass. and Harris.

Census—Messrs. Sutherland, La Follette, McLean, Townsend, New, Calder, Moses, Sheppard, Ashurst, King, McKellar and Walsh of Mass.

Civil Service and Retrenchment—Messrs. Sterling, Cummins, La Follette, Smoot, Colt, Ball, Capper, McKellar, Ransdell, Kirby, Wolcott and Heflin.

Claims—Messrs. Spencer, Gronna, Wadsworth, Fernald, Frelinghuysen, New, Keyes, Capper, Robinson, Johnson of S. Dak., Beckham, Trammell, Wolcott and Henderson.

Coast Defenses—Messrs. Frelinghuysen, Fernald, Nelson, Calder, Lenroot, Ball, Smith of Md., Gerry, Wolcott, Chamberlain and Swanson.

Commerce—Messrs. Jones of Wash., Nelson, Sherman, Harding, Fernald, Calder, Lenroot, Colt, McNary, Ball, Edge, Fletcher, Chamberlain, Ransdell, Sheppard, Simmons, Reed, Kirby, Dial and Hefl'n.

Cuban Relations—Messrs. Johnson of Cal., Knox, McCormick, Underwood and Dial.

Education and Labor—Messrs. Kenyon, Borah, Page, McLean, Sterling, Phipps, Smith of Ga., Jones of N. Mex., McKellar, Wolcott and Walsh of Mass.

Finance—Messrs. Penrose, McCumber, Smoot, La Follette, Dillingham, McLean, Curtis, Watson, Calder, Sutherland, Simmons, Williams, Thomas, Gore, Jones of N. Mex., Gerry and Nugent.

Foreign Relations—Messrs. Lodge, McCumber, Borah, Brandegee, Fall, Knox, Harding, Johnson of Cal., New, Moses, Hitchcock, Williams, Swanson, Pomerene, Smith of Ariz., Pittman and Shields.

Forest Reservations and Protection of Game—Messrs. Hitchcock, Overman, Meyers, Thomas, McLean, Sherman, New, Warren and Edge.

Geological Survey—Messrs. Smith of Ariz., Smith of S. C., Trammell, Norris, Sutherland, Penrose and Dillingham.

Immigration—Messrs. Colt, Dillingham, Penrose, Sterling, Johnson of Cal., Keyes, Edge, Gore, Nugent, King, Harris, Harrison and Phelan.

Indian Affairs—Messrs. Curtis, La Follette, Gronna, Fall, Fernald, McNary, Spencer, Nelson, McCormick, Ashurst, Owen, Johnson of S. Dak., Walsh of Mont., Kendrick, Jones of N. Mex. and Nugent.

Interoceanic Canals—Messrs. Borah, Page, Cummins, Colt, Calder, Knox, Johnson of Cal., Edge, Walsh of Mont., Simmons, Phelan, Kirby, Trammell and Ransdell.

Interstate Commerce—Messrs. Cummins, Townsend, La Follette, Poindexter, McLean, Watson, Kellogg, Fernald, Frelinghuysen, Elkins, Smith of S. C., Pomerene, Meyers, Robinson, Underwood, Wolcott and Stanley.

Judiciary—Messrs. Nelson, Dillingham, Brandegee, Borah, Cummins, Colt, Sterling, Fall, Norris, Kellogg, Culberson, Overman, Reed, Ashurst, Shields, Walsh of Mont., Smith of Ga. and King.

Manufactures—Messrs. La Follette, Lodge, Kenyon, Fernald, McNary, Gronna, Smith of S. C., Pomerene, Jones of N. Mex., Reed and Walsh of Mass.

Military Affairs—Messrs. Wadsworth, Jr., Warren, Sutherland, New, Frelinghuysen, Johnson of Cal., Knox, Lenroot, Spencer, Capper, Chamberlain, Hitchcock, Fletcher, Myers, Thomas, Sheppard, Beckham, Kirby and McKellar.

Mines and Mining—Messrs. Poindexter, Sterling, Sutherland, McCormick, Phipps, Newberry, Henderson, Walsh of Mont., Ashurst and Phelan.

National Banks—Messrs. Kellogg, Lenroot, Elkins, Gerry and Dial.

Naval Affairs—Messrs. Page, Penrose, Lodge, Poindexter, Hale, Ball, McCormick, Newberry, Keyes, Swanson, Smith of Md., Phelan, Pittman, Walsh of Mont., Gerry, Trammell and King.

Patents—Messrs. Norris, Brandegee, Knox, Kellogg, Kirby, Smith of S. C. and Gore.

Pensions—Messrs. McCumber, Smoot, Poindexter, Sherman, New, Elkins, Ball, Walsh of Mont., Johnson of S. Dak., King, Gay, Walsh of Mass. and Gerry.

Philippines—Messrs. Harding, Kenyon, Knox, Johnson of Cal., McNary, Curtis, Frelinghuysen, Hale, Fletcher, Beckham, Phelan, Hitchcock, Robinson, Chamberlain and Shields.

Railroads—Messrs. Lenroot, Lodge, Warren, Dillingham, Phipps, Newberry, Gerry, Reed, Smith of Ariz., Williams and Smith of S. C.

Territories—Messrs. New, McLean, Jones of Wash., Harding, Hale, Borah, Smoot, Pittman, Owen, Phelan, Nugent and Chamberlain.

Woman Suffrage—Messrs. Watson, Jones of Wash., Nelson, Cummins, Johnson of Cal., Jones of N. Mex., Owens, Ransdell and Johnson of S. Dak.

HOUSE OF REPRESENTATIVES.

COMMITTEES OF THE HOUSE.

Chairman of each committee is named first.

Ways and Means—Messrs. Fordney, Green of Iowa, Longworth, Hawley, Treadway, Copley, Mott, Young of N. Dak., Frear, Tilson, Bacharach, Hadley, Timberlake, Bowers, Kitchin, Henry T. Rainey, Hull of Tenn., Garner, Collier, Dickinson of Mo., Oldfield, Crisp, Carew and Martin.

Appropriations—Messrs. Good, Davis of Minn., Madden, Anthony, Vare, Cannon, Slemp, Wood of Ind., Cramton, Wason, Magee, Tinkham, French, Elston, Dempsey, Shreve, Ogden, Byrns of Tenn., Sisson, McAndrews, Evans of Mont., Eagan, Buchanan, Gallivan, Byrnes of S. C., Small, Dent, Rubey, Holland, Hastings, Ayres and Smith of N. Y.

Judiciary—Messrs. Volstead, Graham of Penn., Dyer, Walsh, Reavis, Husted, Currie of Mich., Classon, Boies, Christopherson, Yates, Goodykoontz, Thomas, Igoe, Gard, Whaley, Caraway, Neely, Steele and Sumners of Tex.

Banking and Currency—Messrs. McFadden, Dale, McCullough, King, Scott, Nelson of Wis., Strong of Kan., Echols, Brooks of Penn., Hill, Luce, Burdick, Phelan, Eagle, Wingo, Steagall, Hamill, Lonergan, Brand and Stevenson.

Interstate and Foreign Commerce—Messrs. Esch, Hamilton, Winslow, Parker, Sweet, Stiness, Cooper, Ellsworth, Denison, Sanders of Ind., Merritt, Webster, Jones of Penn., Sims, Doremus, Barkley, Rayburn, Montague, Coady, Dewalt and Sanders of La.

Rivers and Harbors—Messrs. Kennedy of Iowa, Costello, Dempsey, Emerson, Osborne, Freeman, Strong of Penn., Juul, Radcliffe, Hickey, Layton, Foster, Michener, Small, Booher, Gallagher, Scully, Taylor of Ark., Dupre, Lea of Cal. and Cleary.

Merchant Marine and Fisheries—Messrs. Greene of Mass., Edmonds, Rowe, Scott, White of Me., Lehlbach, Burroughs, Curry of Cal., Ricketts, Chindblom, Crowther, Randall of Wis., Andrews of Md., Hardy of Tex., Dooling, Lazaro, Kincheloe, Bankhead, Wright, Davis of Tenn. and Cullen.

Agriculture—Messrs. Haugen, McLaughlin of Mich., Wilson of Ill., Ward, McKinley, Hutchinson, Purnell, Voight, McLaughlin of Neb., Riddick, Tinches, Hulings, Lee of Ga., Candler, Rubey, Young of Tex., Jacoway, Lesher, J. W. Rainey and Kalanianaole.

Foreign Affairs—Messrs. Porter, Rogers, Temple, Kennedy of R. I., Browne, Moores of Ind., Mason, Newton of Minn., Dickinson of Iowa, Ackerman, Smith of Ill., Begg, Houghton, Flood, Linthicum, Goodwin of Ark., Stedman, Sabath, Huddleston, Connally and Smith of N. Y.

Military Affairs—Messrs. Kahn, McKenzie, Greene of Vt., Morin, Crago, Hull of Iowa, Sanford, James, Kearns, Fuller of Mass., Miller, Dent, Fields, Quin, Caldwell, Wise, Olney, Harrison, Fisher and Kalanianaole.

Naval Affairs—Messrs. Butler, Britten, Mudd, Peters, Hicks, McArthur, Darrow, Kraus, Lufkin, Stephens of Ohio, McPherson, Padgett, Riordan, Oliver, Venable, Vinson, Kettner, Ayres and Nicholls.

Indian Affairs—Messrs. Snyder, Campbell of Kan., Johnson of S. Dak., Dallinger, Hernandez, Rhodes, Sinclair, Randall of Wis., Jefferis, Cole, Reber, Kelly of Penn., Carter, Hayden, Sears, Tillman, Gandy, Hastings, Weaver and McKiniry.

IMPORTANT COMMITTEES OF SIXTY-SIXTH CONGRESS—HOUSE OF REP.—*Continued.*

Territories—Messrs. Curry of Cal., Johnson of Wash., Dowell, Sinnott, McFadden, Baer, Ramsey, Brooks of Penn., Strong of Kan., Monahan, Watkins, Ferris, Weaver, Lankford, Davey, Humphreys, Almon, Grigsby and Kalanianaole.

Insular Affairs—Messrs. Towner, Fuller of Ill., Glynn, Focht, Nolan, Hersey, Zihlman, Knutson, Fairfield, MacGregor, Kleczka, Garrett, Brumbaugh, Sullivan, McKeown, Robinson of N. C., Jones of Tex., Dominick and Bland of Va.

Railways and Canals—Messrs. Wheeler, Goodall, Lehlbach, Benham, Monahan of Wis., Brooks of Penn., Thompson of Ohio, Keller, Welty, Drane, Godwin of N. C., Cullen, McLane and Mead.

Mines and Mining—Messrs. Rhodes, Kinkaid, Monahan of Wis., Echols, Robsion of Ky., Brooks of Ill., Burke, Luhring, Wingo, Welling, Dooling, Parrish and Howard.

Education—Messrs. Fess, Towner, Dallinger, Vestal, Burroughs, King, Reed of N. Y., Robsion of Ky., Sears, Bankhead, Brand, Blanton, Donovan and Nelson of Mo.

Labor—Messrs. Smith of Mich., Nolan, Hersey, Zihlman, Gould, Bland of Ind., MacCrate, Murphy, Evans of Neb., Maher, Casey, Carss, Major and Hoey.

Patents—Messrs. Nolan, Lampert, Wheeler, Vestal, Burke, Jefferis, MacCrate, Swope, Campbell of Penn., Johnston of N. Y., Babka, Davis of Tenn. and McDuffie.

Pensions—Messrs. Sells, Kiess, Knutson, Walters, White of Me., Robsion of Ky., Cole, Kleczka, Mead, McGlennon, Wilson of Penn., Smithwick, Upshaw and Carss.

War Claims—Messrs. Focht, Snell, Zihlman, Reed of W. Va., Ramsey, Strong of Kan., Evans of Neb., Reed of N. Y., Kleczka, Clark of Fla., John W. Rainey, Mooney, Wilson of Penn., O'Connell and Stoll.

Election of President, Vice President and Representatives in Congress—Messrs. Lampert, Mapes, Fess, Andrews of Neb., Brooks of Ill., White of Kan., Reed of N. Y., Rucker, Dominick, Wright, Pell and Briggs.

Alcoholic Liquor Traffic—Messrs. Smith of Idaho, Smith of Mich., Schall, Sinclair, Strong of Kan., Upshaw and Box.

Irrigation of Arid Lands—Messrs. Kinkaid, Sinnott, Little, Smith of Idaho, Baer, Hernandez Summers of Wash., Barbour, Thompson of Ohic Taylor of Col., Hayden, Welling, Evans of Nev and Hudspeth.

Immigration and Naturalization—Messrs. Johnson of Wash., Siegel, Knutson, McCulloch, Taylor of Tenn., Kleczka, Vaile, White of Kan., Swope, Sabath, Raker, Wilson of La., Welty, Box and Rainey of Ala.

Census—Messrs. Siefele, Fairfield, Hersey, Langley, Towner, Wheeler, Glynn, Barbour, Aswell, Larsen, Stephens of Miss., Bee, Brinson and Milligan.

Roads—Messrs. Dunn, Sells, Williams, Ramsey, Dowell, Rose, Ricketts, Benham, Robsion of Ky., Evans of Neb., Summers of Wash., Andrews of Md., Monahan of Wis., Stephens of Miss., Doughton, Aswell, Almon, Jones of Tex., Larsen, McKeown and Moore of Va.

Woman Suffrage—Messrs. Mann of Ill., Little, Elliott, Nolan, Edmonds, Burroughs, Nelson of Wis., MacCrate, Raker, Clark of Fla., Mays, Sullivan and Blanton.

SELECT COMMITTEES.

Water Power—Messrs. Esch, Sinnott, Haugen, Hamilton, Smith of Idaho, McLaughlin of Mich., Winslow, Elston, Anderson of Minn., Sims, Ferris, Doremus, Taylor of Col., Lee of Ga., Barkley, Raken and Candler.

To Investigate War Expenditures—Messrs. Graham of Ill., McKenzie, Frear, Johnson of S. Dak., Reavis, Magee, McCulloch, Bland of Ind., Jefferis, MacGregor, Flood, Garrett, Doremus, Donovan and Lea of Cal.

To Investigate the Shipping Board—Messrs. Walsh, Kelley of Mich., Hadley, Foster, Steele and Connally.

Budget—Messrs. Good, Campbell of Kan., Madden, Hawley, Temple, Tinkham, Purnell, Byrns of Tenn., Kitchin, Garner, Taylor of Col. and Howard.

POLITICAL DIVISIONS OF THE U. S. SENATE AND HOUSE OF REPRESENTATIVES

Congress.	Senate.					House of Representatives.				
	Senators.	Republicans.	Democrats.	Third Party.	Vacant	Representatives.	Republicans.	Democrats.	Third Party.	Vacant
Forty-fourth	66	46	29	...	1	293	107	181	3	2
Forty-fifth	76	39	36	1	...	293	137	156	...	...
Forty-sixth	76	33	43	...	...	293	128	150	14	1
Forty-seventh	76	37	37	2	...	293	152	130	11	...
Forty-eighth	76	40	36	...	...	325	119	200	6	...
Forty-ninth	76	41	34	...	1	325	140	182	2	1
Fiftieth	76	39	37	...	...	325	151	170	4	...
Fifty-first	84	47	37	...	...	330	173	156	1	...
Fifty-second	88	47	39	2	...	333	88	231	14	...
Fifty-third	88	38	44	3	1	357	126	220	8	3
Fifty-fourth	88	42	39	5	...	357	246	104	7	...
Fifty-fifth	90	46	34	10	...	357	206	134	16	1
Fifty-sixth	90	53	26	11	...	357	185	163	9	...
Fifty-seventh	90	56	29	3	2	357	198	153	5	1
Fifty-eighth	90	58	32	...	...	386	207	178	...	1
Fifty-ninth	90	58	32	...	...	386	250	136	...	...
Sixtieth	92	61	29	...	2	386	222	164	...	...
Sixty-first	92	59	32	...	1	391	219	172	...	...
Sixty-second	92	49	42	...	1	391	162	228	1	...
Sixty-third	96	44	51	1	...	435	127	290	18	...
Sixty-fourth	96	39	56	1	...	435	193	231	8	3
Sixty-fifth	96	42	53	1	...	435	216	210	9	...
Sixty-sixth	96	48	47	1	...	435	237	191	7	...
Sixty-seventh	96	59	37	...	...	435	300	132	1	2

RECENT SESSIONS OF CONGRESS.

Congress.	Session	Begun.	Adjourned.	Length in days	President Pro Tempore of the Senate.	Speaker of the House of Representatives.
Sixtieth	1	Dec. 2, 1907	May 30, 1908	181	Wm. P. Frye, Maine	Joseph G. Cannon, Ill.
	2	Dec. 7, 1908	Mch. 3, 1909	87	do.	do.
Sixty-first	1	Mch. 15, 1909	Aug. 5, 1909	144	Wm. P. Frye, Maine	do.
	2	Dec. 6, 1909	June 21, 1910	202	do.	do.
	3	Dec. 5, 1910	Mch. 3, 1911	89	do	do.
Sixty-second	1	Apr. 4, 1911	Aug. 22, 1911	141	Vacant	Champ Clark, Mo.
	2	Dec. 4, 1911	Aug. 26, 1912	267	do.	do.
	3	Dec. 2, 1912	Mch. 3, 1913	92	do.	do.
Sixty-third	1	Apr. 7, 1913	Dec. 1, 1913	239	Jas. P. Clarke, Ark.	do.
	2	Dec. 1, 1913	Oct. 24, 1914	328	do.	do.
	3	Dec. 7, 1914	Mch. 3, 1915	87	do.	do.
Sixty-fourth	1	Dec. 6, 1915	Sept. 8, 1916	278	do.	do.
	2	Dec. 4, 1916	Mch. 3, 1917	90	Willard Saulsbury, Del.	do.
Sixty-fifth	1	Apr. 2, 1917	Oct. 6, 1917	188	do.	do.
	2	Dec. 3, 1917	Nov. 21, 1918	354	do.	do.
	3	Dec. 2, 1918	Mar. 3, 1919	92	do.	do.
Sixty-sixth	1	May 19, 1919	Nov. 19, 1919	185	Albert B. Cummins, Ia.	Fred. H. Gillett, Mass.
	2	Dec. 1, 1919	June 5, 1920	188	do.	do.

GOVERNORS OF NEW YORK STATE.

COLONIAL.

Governors.	Terms.	Governors.	Terms.	Governors.	Terms.
Adrian Joris	1623-1624	Col. William Smith		James DeLancey, Lt.-Gov	1755
Cornelius Jacobzen Mey.	1624-1625	Col. Abraham De Peyster	1701	Sir Charles Hardy	1755-1757
William Verhulst	1625-1626	Col. Peter Schuyler		James DeLancey, Lt.-Gov	1757-1760
Peter Minuit	1626-1633	John Nanfan, Lt.-Gov	1701-1702	Cadwallader Colden, Pres.	1760-1761
Wouter Van Twiller	1633-1638	Lord Cornbury	1702-1708	Cadwallader Colden, Lt.-Gov.	1761-1762
William Kieft	1638-1647	Lord Lovelace	1708-1709	Robert Monckton	1762-1763
Petrus Stuyvesant	1647-1664	Peter Schuyler, Pres.	1709	Cadwallader Colden, Lt.-Gov.	1763-1765
Richard Nicolls	1664-1668	Richard Ingoldsby, Lt.-Gov.	1709	Sir Henry Moore	1765-1769
Francis Lovelace	1668-1673	Gerardus Beekman, Pres.	1710	Cadwallader Colden, Lt. Gov.	1769-1770
Anthony Colve	1673-1674	Robert Hunter	1710-1719	Earl of Dunmore	1770-1771
Edmond Andros	1674-1683	Peter Schuyler, Pres.	1719-1720	William Tryon	1771-1774
Thomas Dongan	1683-1688	William Burnet	1720-1728	Cadwallader Colden, Lt.-Gov.	1774-1775
Francis Nicholson	1688-1689	John Montgomerie	1728-1731	Peter Livingston	1775
Jacob Leisler	1689-1691	Rip Van Dam, Pres.	1731-1732	William Tryon	1775-1777
Henry Sloughter	1691	William Cosby	1732-1736		
Benjamin Fletcher	1692-1698	George Clarke, Lt.-Gov.	1736-1743		
Earl of Bellomont	1698-1699	George Clinton	1743-1753		
John Nanfan, Lt.-Gov.	1699-1700	Sir Danvers Osborne	1753-1755		
Earl of Bellomont	1700-1701				

STATE.

Governors.	Residence.	Elected.	Term.
George Clinton[a] (1739-1812)	Ulster County	July 9, 1777	1777-1795
John Jay (1745-1829)	New York City	April 1795	1795-1801
George Clinton (1739-1812)	Ulster County	April 1801	1801-1804
Morgan Lewis (1758-1832)	Dutchess County	April 1804	1804-1807
Daniel D. Tompkins (1774-1825)	Richmond County	April 1807	1807-1816
John Tayler[b] (1742-1829)	Albany, Albany County	March 1817	1817
De Witt Clinton (1769-1828)	New York City	Nov. 1817	1817-1822
Joseph C. Yates[b] (1768-1837)	Schenectady, Schenectady County	Nov. 6, 1822	1822-1824
De Witt Clinton (1769-1828)	New York City	Nov. 2, 1824	1825-1828
Nathaniel Pitcher[b] (1777-1836)	Sandy Hill, Washington County	Feb. 11, 1828	1828
Martin Van Buren (P.) (1782-1862)	Kinderhook, Columbia County	Nov. 5, 1828	1829
Enos T. Throop[c] (1784-1874)	Auburn, Cayuga County	Mar. 12, 1829	1829-1832
William L. Marcy (1786-1857)	Troy, Rensselaer County	Nov. 7, 1832	1833-1839
William H. Seward (1801-1872)	Auburn, Cayuga County	Nov. 7, 1838	1839-1842
William C. Bouck (1786-1859)	Fultonham, Schoharie County	Nov. 8, 1842	1843-1844
Silas Wright (1795-1847)	Canton, St. Lawrence County	Nov. 5, 1844	1845-1846
John Young (1802-1852)	Geneseo, Livingston County	Nov. 3, 1846	1847-1848
Hamilton Fish (1808-1893)	New York City	Nov. 7, 1848	1849-1851
Washington Hunt (1811-1867)	Lockport, Niagara County	Nov. 5, 1850	1851-1852
Horatio Seymour (1810-1886)	Deerfield, Oneida County	Nov. 2, 1852	1853-1854
Myron H. Clark (1806-1892)	Canandaigua, Ontario County	Nov. 7, 1854	1855-1856
John A. King (1788-1867)	Queens County	Nov. 4, 1856	1857-1858
Edwin D. Morgan (1811-1883)	New York City	Nov. 2, 1858	1859-1862
Horatio Seymour (1810-1886)	Deerfield, Oneida County	Nov. 4, 1862	1863-1864
Reuben E. Fenton (1819-1885)	Frewsburgh, Chautauqua County	Nov. 8, 1864	1865-1868
John T. Hoffman (1828-1888)	New York City	Nov. 3, 1868	1869-1872
John A. Dix (1798-1879)	New York City	Nov. 5, 1872	1873-1874
Samuel J. Tilden (1814-1886)	New York City	Nov. 3, 1874	1875-1876
Lucius Robinson (1810-1891)	Elmira, Chemung County	Nov. 7, 1876	1877-1880
Alonzo B. Cornell (1832-1904)	New York City	Nov. 4, 1879	1880-1882
Grover Cleveland[d] (P.) (1837-1908)	Buffalo, Erie County	Nov. 7, 1882	1883-1884
David B. Hill[e] (1843-1910)	Elmira, Chemung County	Jan. 6, 1885	1885-1891
Roswell P. Flower (1835-1899)	New York City	Nov. 3, 1891	1892-1894
Levi P. Morton (1824-1920)	Rhinecliff, Dutchess County	Nov. 6, 1894	1895-1896
Frank S. Black (1853-1913)	Troy, Rensselaer County	Nov. 3, 1896	1897-1898
Theodore Roosevelt (P.) (1858-1919)	Oyster Bay, Nassau County	Nov. 8, 1898	1899-1900
Benjamin B. Odell, Jr.[f] (1854—	Newburgh, Orange County	Nov. 6, 1900	1901-1904
Frank W. Higgins (1856-1906)	Olean, Cattaraugus County	Nov. 8, 1904	1905-1906
Charles E. Hughes[h] (1862—	New York City	Nov. 6, 1906	1907-1910
Horace White[k] (1865—	Syracuse, Onondaga County	Oct. 6, 1910	1910
John A. Dix (1860—	Thomson, Washington County	Nov. 8, 1910	1911-1912
William Sulzer[o] (1863—	New York City	Nov. 5, 1912	1913-1914
Martin H. Glynn[p] (1870—	Albany, Albany County	Oct. 17, 1913	1913-1914
Charles S. Whitman[q] (1868—	New York City	Nov. 3, 1914	1915-1919
Alfred E. Smith (1873—	New York City	Nov. 5, 1918	1919-1921
Nathan L. Miller (1868—	Syracuse, Onondaga County	Nov. 2, 1920	1921-1923

[a]The Constitution of 1777 did not specify the time when the Governor should enter on the duties of his office. Governor Clinton was declared elected July 9, and qualified the same day. On the 13th of February, 1787, an act was passed for regulating elections, which provided that the Governor and Lieutenant-Governor should enter on the duties of their respective offices on the 1st of July after their election. The Constitution of 1821 provided that the Governor and Lieutenant Governor shall, on and after the year 1823, enter on the duties of their respective offices on the 1st of January. [b]Lieutenant-Governor, Acting Governor. [c]Lieutenant-Governor, became Governor upon resignation of Martin Van Buren, March 12, 1829. Elected November, 1830, for a full term. [d]Elected President of the United States in 1884, and resigned the office of Governor January 6, 1885. [e]Lieutenant-Governor, became Governor upon resignation of Grover Cleveland, January 6, 1885. Elected November 6, 1885, for a full term, and re-elected November 6, 1888. [f]Re-elected November 4, 1902. [h]Re-elected November 3, 1908. [k]Lieut. Gov.; upon resignation of Gov. Hughes, Oct. 6, 1910 (P.) President of United States. [o]Removed by impeachment Oct. 18, 1913. [p]Lieut.-Gov.; succeeded upon removal of Gov. Sulzer. [q]Re-elected Nov. 7. 1916.

WALL ST. BOMB EXPLOSION.

The banking house of J. P. Morgan & Co. was damaged and the Wall Street district severely shaken at noon on Sept. 16, 1920, by the explosion of a bomb, which caused 36 fatalities and injured more than 200 persons. Fifteen of the dead were residents of Brooklyn and Queens. More than $1,000,000 damage was done. The New York Stock Exchange closed for the day immediately after the explosion.

NEW YORK CITY FACTORIES.

Figures issued by the State Industrial Commissioners show that on June 30, 1919, there were 46 887 factories in New York City, located by boroughs as follows: Manhattan, 32,323; Brooklyn, 10,496; Bronx, 1,801; Queens, 1,962; Richmond, 305.

It is estimated that prohibition has increased the demand for confectionery 30 per cent.

NEW YORK STATE GOVERNMENT.

EXECUTIVE.

Governor.

The State Constitution provides that "The executive power shall be vested in a Governor."

The Governor is elected for 2 years. He must be a citizen of the United States, 30 years of age and for 5 years previous to his election a resident of this State. Lieutenant Governor, Secretary of State, Comptroller, Treasurer, Attorney General, State Engineer and Surveyor, known as State Officers, are elected by the people at the same time as Governor, and serve for 2 years. Terms expire Dec. 31, 1922.

Gov., Nathan L. Miller, $10,000; Sec., W. W. Smith, $7,000; Exec. Auditor, J. S. Parsons, $5,000; Counsel, Prof. Charles T. Stagg, Ithaca, $5,000; Executive Legal Asst., O. L. Potter, $5,000; Mil. Sec., Maj. Ranulf Compton, $3,000; Asst. Sec., G. B. Graves, $4,500; Requisition Clk., J. A. Waldron, $1,800.

Lieutenant Governor.

Presides over the Senate; has vote in case of tie. Jeremiah Wood, $5,000. (Term exp. Dec. 31, 1922.)

Secretary of State.

Keeper of State archives, in connection with which he has numerous specific duties. See Executive Law, Chap. 23, Laws 1909, secs. 20-34.

Sec. State, John J. Lyons, $8,000 (elected 2 yrs. term exp. Dec. 31, 1922); 1st Dep., A. B. Parker, $5,000; Asst. Dep., B. F. Fox, $2,200; 2d Dep. and Chf. Clk., C. W. Taft, $4,500; Priv. Sec., Wm. Bonner, $2,500· Confid. Clk., Gabriel Tischler, $2,500; Land Clk., C. V. Hooper, $3,000; Exam. Corp., F. S. Sharp, $4,500; Asst. Corp. Exam., L. I. Luther, $2,750; Corp Clk., W. T. Fletcher, $2,200; Confid. File and Index Clk., Mark Stern, $2,200; Bkpr., F. J. Laraway, $1,320; Clk. and Statis., Charles McKallor, $1,800; 45 Stenos, 26 Clks., Messgrs., etc.

N. Y. AUTOMOBILE OFFICE—B'way and 65th. Ch. of Bureau, F. P. Redmond, $4,500; Cashrs., A. Loeffel, $1,800; Herbert Conklin, $1,900; Albert Katz, $1,500, and Belle Natkiel, $900.

State Treasurer.

Custodian of all State moneys. Has special powers in regard to sale and conversion of securities held by Supt. of Insurance in trust for insurance co's. Custodian of State Teachers Retirement Fund and Insurance Fund of State Industrial Commsn. Treas., N. Monroe Marshall, $6,000 (elected 2 yrs.; term expires Dec. 31, 1922); Dep. Treas., Jas. J. Hamilton, $5,000; Acct. and Trans. Clk., Ellsworth Crum, $2,300; Cash., * F. J. Seaver, $4,000; Asst. Cash., J. J. Caldwell, $2,750; Auditor and Paying Teller, Isaac Blauvelt, $4,000; Clk., B. L. Taber, $1,980; Clk., R. L. McMahon, $1,800; 3 Clks., 2 Stenos., 1 Mess.

State Engineer and Surveyor.

Must be practical engnr. Has charge of all engrng. in connection with State work except that pertaining to highways. He is a Commsnr. of Land Office, member of Canal Board, and State Bd. of Equalization of Assessments, Hospital Developing Commsn. and Board of Canvassers. Engineer and Surveyor, Frank M. Williams, $8,000 (elected 2 years; term exp. Dec. 31, 1922). Dep. R. G. Finch, $6,000; Spec. Dept., Friend P. Williams, $7,000; Chf. Clk., Charles R. Waters, $3,600.

Div. Engrs.—Eastern Div., E. D. Hendricks; Middle Div., Guy Moulton; Western Div., L. C. Hubburd, $5,000 each.

State Comptroller.

Superintends fiscal affairs, audits all accounts against State, designates banks for State funds, collects taxes, etc. (See also chap. 23, Laws 1909, secs. 40-44.)

Compt., Jas. A. Wendell, $8,000. Elected 2 yrs., term exp. Dec. 31, 1922; Dep. Comptrs., Wm. J. Maier, F. M. Farwell, E. P. Kearney, each $6,000; Sec. to Compt., C. H. Dorn, $4,000; Asst. Dep. Compt., C. H. Mullens, $3,850; Stenos. (Albany) to Compt., $1,900 to Dept., $1,500; (N. Y.), to Compt., $2,000, to Dep., $2,000, 1 Steno., $3,000; Clks., Detectives, Special Agts., etc., $1,500 to $3,600; Tel. Oper., $1,500.

FINANCE BUR.—Voucher Clk. and Auditor, J. B. Wood, $5,500; Supervising Accountant, W. P. Boone, $5,500; Auditor Prison Accts., N. I. Martin, $4,000; Document Clk., E. D. Thompson, $3,600; Chf. Acct., S. G. Jeffrey, $3,400; Entry Clk., H. C. Price, $3,100.

AUDIT BUREAU—Auditor, J. J. Magilton, $5,500; Auditor of Revenues, J. S. Nichols, $3,500; Confidential Exam., F. J. Meagher, 3,000.

LAND TAX BUREAU—Chf. Clk., G. R. Kehoe, $5,000.

TRANSFER TAX BUR.—Chief, W. E. Stephens, $5,000.

Bkln. office, 215 Montague—Apprs., D. H. Ralston, P. H. Seligman, W. G. Price, J. D. Moore, $5,000 each; Atty., L. A. Wray, fees.

Mhtn. office, 233 B'way—Apprs., C. B. Largy, C. Schwenzel, G. B. Compton, A. P. Ludden, A. J. Berwin, Chas. Sweeney, H. Copp, Wm. J. Campbell, $5,000 each; Atty., L. B. Gleason, $10,000; and office equipment and disbursements.

Bronx office, 2808 3d av.—Apprs., F. Wynne, A. B. Simonds, E. W. Bradbury; Atty., John Boyle Jr., $5,000 each.

Queens office, L. I. City—Appr., W. B. Ashmead, $4,000.

Richmond office, 85 Water, Stapleton—Appr., C. E. Smith, $1,000; Atty., C. A. Marshall, fees.

Nassau Co.—Appr., J. N. Gehrig, $2,800; Atty., (vacant), fees.

Suffolk Co.—Appr., A. M. Tasker, $2,000.

CORPORATION TAX BUR.—Chf. Clk., H. G. Savage, $4,250.

MUNICIPAL ACCTS. BUR—Director, C. R. Hall, $5,000; Exam., Wm. Arnstein, $4,000.

STOCK TRANSFER TAX BUR.—Chf. Clk., F. S. McCaffrey, $3,500.

CORPORATION TAX BUR.—Chf. Clk., N. Y. office, A. Dateasandro, $3,500; Chf. Clk. Albany office, F. A. Codding, $3,200; examr., W. H. Ludden, $4,250.

HIGHWAY BUR.—Highway Audit Clk., W. N. Sherritt, $4,500.

CANAL BUR.—Chf. Clk., G. M. Spawn, $4,000.

STATE PRINTING BOARD—Expt. Printer—F. C. Foster, $4,250.

INCOME TAX BUR.—Main office, Albany, Dir., Mark Graves, $6,000; Asst. Dirs., J. P. Somers, 1 vacant, each $4,500; E. A. Foley, A. C. Calhoun, F. G. Zimmer, each $4,000; Chf. Fld. and Audit Sec., J. J. Donovan, $4,000; Chf. Resident Sec., B. J. Rice, $4,000; Chf. Office Information Sec., J. J. Malone, $4,000; Chf. Cor. Sec., J. T. Taaffe, $3,200; Chf. File Sec., H. L. Butler, $3,000; Statis., M. S. Howard, $3,000.

Albany Dist., Office—Dist. Dir., R. H. Palmer, $3,500.

Manhattan Office—Asst. Dir., J. H. Elliott, $4,500; Dist. Dir., M. H. Becker, $4,000; Asst. Cash., L. J. Le Rolle, $3,800; Exec. Clk., E. L. Johnson, $3,500.

Brooklyn Office—Dist. Dir., H. B. Cocheu, $4,000; Asst. and Cash., J. M. Walters, $3,800.

Bronx Office—Dist. Dir., T. W. Whittle, $4,000; Asst. Dir. and Cash., J. P. Conway, $3,000.

Jamaica Office—Dist. Dir., G. U. Harvey, $3,500; Asst. Dir. and Cash., E. L. Ryon, $3,300.

White Plains Office—Dist. Dir., C. D. Whittemore, $3,500.

Buffalo Office—Dist. Dir., Henry Sollheimer, $4,000; Asst. Cash., G. W. Crane, $3,800.

Rochester Office—Dist. Dir., J. M. Mangan, $3,250.

Syracuse Office—Dist. Dir., A. A. Kocher, $3,250.

Utica Office—Dist. Dir., F. J. Graff, $3,250.

Elmira Office—Dist. Dir., L. C. Andrews, $3,000.

Binghamton Office—Dist. Dir., H. B. Mulford, $3,000.

Kingston Office—Dist. Dir., J. De Puy Hasbrouck, $3,000.

Attorney General.

Prosecutor and defender of all actions in which State is interested. Has charge of all legal business. Atty. Gen., C. E. Newton, $10,000, elected 2 years; term exp. Dec. 31, 1922; 1st Dep.,* T. F. Fennell, $8,000; 2d Dep.,* G. L. Fisher, $6,000; 3d Dep.,* A. E. Rose, $5,000; Deps.,* E. J. Mone, $6,000; W. W. Chambers, $6,000; C. T. Dawes, $6,000; E. A. Gifford, $5,000; H. C. Henderson, $5,000; B. Coe Turner, $5,000; J. S. Y. Ivins, $5,000; M. V. Ryan, $5,000; E. G. Griffin, $4,200; T. Paul McGannon, $4,200; G. A. Frank, $4,200; A. T. Selkirk, $4,200; I. Belanger, $2,500; J. A. Burnham Jr., $3,000.

---

*Exempt civil service class.

NEW YORK STATE GOVERNMENT—EXECUTIVE—ATTORNEY GENERAL—*Continued.*

COURT OF CLAIMS—Dep. (in charge), C. D. Davie, $6,000; F. K. Cook, $5,000; J. H. Clogston, $5,000; M. H. Quirk, $5,000; W. E. Thorpe, $6,000; H. P. Nevins, $5,000; James Gibsons, Jr., $5,000; A. C. Ryder, $5,000; E. M. Brown, $4,200; H. W. Eble, $4,200; C. A. Clark, $4,000; P. J. Finn, $5,000, and A. A. Armitage, $4,500; 3 Stenos., Land and Opinion Clk., W. J. Conway, $3,500; Private Sec., L. W. Gett, $3,500; Chf. of Land Bur., E. H. Leggett, $4,250; Hearing Steno., W. M. Thomas, $3,000; Steno. and Rec. Clk., A. L. O'Connell, $2,500; Audit Clk., E. J. Grogan, $3,500; Steno. to Atty. Gen.,* Hilda A. Krein, $1,800; Fin. Clk.,* A. C. Quenan, $1,500; Conf. Clk.,* M. E. Templeton, $1,500; 12 Stenos., 1 Law Librarian, 1 Mess., 4 Laborers, 1 Tel. Oper., 1 Relief Oper.

CONSERVATION BUREAU—Dep.* (in charge), A. F. Jenks, $6,000; Asst. Deps.,* W. T. Moore, $4,500; B. F. Sturgis, $4,000; E. W. Howe, $4,000; Atty., J. O. Bates, $2,750; 3 Stenos.

N. Y. CITY BUR.—49 Chambers, Mhtn. Dept.,* R. S. Conklin, $6,000; S. E. Berger, $5,000; W. J. Smith, $4,000; Chas. P. Robinson, $4,000; R. P. Beyer, $4,000; C. S. Amsel, $4,000; 1 Law Clk., 1 Spec. Investigator, 3 Process Servers, 6 Stenos., 1 Mess., 1 Laborer, 1 Tel. Oper.

ADMINISTRATIVE DEPARTMENTS.

BOARDS AND COMMISSIONS IN NEW YORK STATE.

Public Service Commission.*

FIRST DISTRICT.

49 Lafayette St., N. Y. City.

The Public Service Comm'n for the 1st Dist. has supervision over all transportation, lighting and steam co's. in N. Y. C. (1 Com'r apptd. by Gov. for 5 yrs; salary $15,000. Three deputies appointed by Comm'r, salary $7,500 each.) Comr., residence and expiration of term—Alfred M. Barrett, Commr., Queens, May 5, 1924; C. V. Halley Jr., Dep. Commr., the Bronx, no stated term of office; vacant; Dep. Commr., no stated term of office; M. T. Donnelly, Kings, no stated term of office; Sec., James Blaine Walker, $6,000; Asst. Sec., F. N. Robinson, $4,000; Counsel, Terrence Farley, $10,000; Asst. Counsel, T. H. Ward, $6,000; Ely Neuman, $8,000; H. M. Chamberlain, $5,500; G. H. Stover, $5,400; John A. Mullan, $4,000; Miles W. O'Brien, Jr., $4,000; Chf. of Transit Bur., A. Bassett, $6,000; Elec. Engr., R. H. Nexsen, $5,000; Chf. Statisn., A. F. Weber, $7,500; Chf. Gas Engr., William Merrifield, $5,000; Grade Crossing Engr., W. L. Selmer, $3,250.

The Commission also employs approximately 275 other employees, such as elec. engrs., inspts., acctnts., statisns., clks., etc.

The former duties of the Commission in respect to construction of rapid transit lines have been transferred to the office of the Transit Construction Commr., and its employees engaged in rapid transit construction activities, have been transferred to that office.

SECOND DISTRICT.

Albany.

Second District has supervision over all transportation co.'s incl. stock yard co.'s., gas and illuminating co.'s furnishing steam for heat or power in State outside N. Y. City; also all teleg. and telephone co.'s in the State. (Ap. by Gov. Term 5 yrs. Salary, $15,000.) Albany office, 91 State st.

Comr., Residence and expiration of term—C. B. Hill, Buffalo, Ch., Feb. 1, 1923; G. R. Van Namee, Watertown, Feb. 1, 1925; Frank Irvine, Ithaca, Feb. 1, 1921; J. A. Barhite, Rochester, Feb. 1, 1922; J. A. Kellogg, Glens Falls, Feb. 1, 1924; Counsel,* L. P. Hale, $10,000; Sec., F. X. Disney, $6,000; Exec. Clk., E. C. McEntee, $5,000; Chf. Clk. Records, A. H. Moore, $2,500; Supt. of Pub. and Compilation, T. Z. Root, $2,500; Chf. Div. Statis. and Accts.,* H. C. Hasbrouck, $5,000; Ch. Engr.,* Div. of Light, Heat and Power, C. A. Volz, $5,000; Ch. Div. of Tel and Tel.,* E. B. Rogers, $4,500; Asst. Ch. Div. of Tel. and Tel.,* W. I. Sweet, $3,250; Ch. Div. Tariffs,* W. E. Griggs, $4,500; Maint. and Operation Insps.,* J. B. Stouder, W. G. Himes, $3,200 each; Equip., G. Bradley, W. J. Corliss, J. J. Gill, $2,700 each; Ch. Div. Steam Railroads and Elec., C. R. Vanneman, $5,000; Ch. Div. Capitalization, J. J. Hubbard, $4,500.

5 Sec. to Comm.,* and approx. 100 insp., testers, stens., bookkeepers, etc.

N. Y. C. OFFICE, ROOM 403, HALL OF RECORDS—Asst. Ch. Div. Tel. and Tel.,* W. I. Sweet, in charge.

Buffalo office, Underhill Bldg., Buffalo, N. Y.—F. V. Leonard in charge.

Office Transit Construction Commr.

49 Lafayette St., N. Y. City.

Has supervision of construction and equipment of new rapid transit facilities; supervises carrying out of provisions of contracts with operating companies. (Apptd. by Gov. for 5 yrs.; salary $15,000.)

J. H. Delaney, 317 Washington av., Bklyn, N. Y., Commr. Apptd, by Gov. with consent of Senate; term 5 yrs.; term expires Feb. 1, '24; salary $15,000 per annum, paid by the city.

D. L. Ryan, Dep. Commr.; L. C. White, Counsel; F. J. Sinnott, Sec.; J. B. Trainer, Sec. to Commr.; Arthur McKinney, J. W. Horan Asst. Secs.; P. B. Gaynor, Ch. of Accts.; H. A. D. Hollman, Audtr.; C. F. Smollin, Chf. Clk.; D. L. Turner, Chf. Engr.; Robert Ridgway, Engr. Subway Constn.; Sverre Dahm, Dep. Engr. Subway Constn.; H. N. Latey, Elec. Engr.; A. I. Raisman, Designing Engr., Div. of Designs; J. O. Shipman, Div. Engr., 1st Div.; J. H. Myers, Div. Engr., 2d Div., 70 E. 45th st.; Tel. Murray Hill 6597; C. V. V. Powers, Div. Engr., Bur. Contract Adjustment; J. T. Kane, Designing Engr., Sta. Finish Div.; R. H. Jacobs, Div. Engr., Track Div.; G. L. Lucas, Gen. Inspt., Div. Material Insptn.

Superintendent of Insurance.

Has control of insurance companies transacting business in this State. Companies outside of State must obtain yearly renewals to transact business. All companies are examined by this office. Supt. Insurance, Jesse S. Phillips, $10,000. (Appointed by Gov.; term 3 yrs.; exp. July 1, 1921.) 1st Dep., H. D. Appleton, $7,000; Actuary, C. G. Smith, $6,000; Asst. Actuary, G. H. Hipp, $4,000; Ch. Bur. of Frat. Assns., T. F. Behan, $5,500; Ch. Bur. of Co-op. Assns., G. E. Merrigold, $5,500; Acct., T. W. Meany, $4,250; Tax Clk. and Cashr., J. T. Wilkins, $3,500; Statis., C. S. Crippen, $3,600; Ch. Clk., E. M. Cadman, $3,200; Asst. Statis., F. C. Willis, $2,400; Registrar, J. S. Andrews, $3,000; Confid. Sten., Margaret T. Hart, $2,400; Gen. Clk., G. B. Fowler, $2,100; Bkpr., J. A. Meany, $2,600; Counsel, H. J. Drake, $5,000; Examr., G. H Jamison, $3,250; 39 Clks., 21 Stenos., Proofreaders, etc.

N. Y. City Office—165 B'way. 2d Dep. Supt., F. R. Stoddard, Jr., $6,500; Ch. Exam. Life Cos., N. B. Hadley, $6,000; Ch. Exam. Fire Cos., S. Deutschberger, $6,000; Ch. Exam. Casualty Cos., A. F. Saxton, $6,000; Ch. Exam. Fraternal Cos., J. E. Diefendorf, $5,500; Aud. and Actuary, Charles Hughes, $6,000; 46 Exam. Ch. Liq. Bur., C. C. Fowler, $5,000; Rating Exp., E. J. O'Dea, $2,000; R. A. Elmer, $3,500; I. Fuld, $3,500; C. H. Gardner, $3,250; 50 other Examrs., 21 Clks., 14 Stenos., Mess., etc.

Superintendent of Public Works.

Supv. over navigation and maintenance of State canals. Supt., C. L. Cadle, Rochester, $10,000 (apptd. by Gov.; term, 2 yrs.; exp. Dec. 31, 1922); Dep. Supt., J. E. Doyle, $6,500; Asst. Dep., A. M. O'Neill, $5,000; Priv. Sec. to Supt., F. P. Keenan, $2,800; Asst. Supts. (each $3,500). Estn. Div., T. R. Crane, Schenectady; Middle Div., P. J. Cawley, Syracuse; Westn. Div., Charles McDonough, Rochester; Fin. Clk., H. M. Hulsapple, $4,800; Audr., E. L. Walsh, $4,800; Clk. Statistics, J. E. Winne, $2,700; Canal Traffic Agent, J. W. Grady, $4,750.

Superintendent of Banks.

Supervision of banks and trust co.'s operated under State laws; also savings banks and other financial institutions. All such institutions are examined by his officers and must make reports. The expenses of Dept. are paid by pro rata of direct assessments on these institutions. Supt., George V. McLoughlin, $10,000. (Ap. by Gov. for 3 yrs.; exp. July 1, 1923). 1st Dep., N. J. Macdonald, $6,000; 2d Dep., Geo. Overocker, $5,500; 3d Dep., George Coleman, $5,000; 4th Dep., F. H. Warder, $4,500; Priv. Sec.,* E. F. Glynn, $3,500; Exam. in Charge of Reports and Tabulation of Accts., P. N. Shippe, $16 a day;

*Exempt civil service class.

NEW YORK STATE GOVERNMENT—ADMINISTRATIVE—SUPT. OF BANKS—*Continued.*

Ch. Liquidation Bureau, (vacant) (salary paid by liquidating banks); Exams. *Met. Dist., A. T. Campbell, $22 a day; Eastern Dist., Albany, (vacant); Central Dist., Syracuse, H. J. Young, $19 a day; Western Dist., Buffalo, Claude Hutchins, $19 a day; Savings Bank Exams., *Met. Dist., J. S. Love, $14 a day; outside of Met. Dist., B. D. Haight, $18 a day.

Commissioner of Excise.

Issues liquor tax certificates, collects liquor taxes and penalties, investigates and prosecutes violations of excise law.

Comr., H. S. Sisson, Buffalo, $7,000 (apptd. by Gov. for 5 yrs.; exp. April 1, 1921); Dep. Jay Farrier, $5,000; 2d Dep., C. V. Platt, $4,000; Chf. Counsel, H. D. Sanders, $5,500.

STATE BOARDS OF EXAMINERS.

(With yrs. when term expires.)

MEDICAL EXAMINERS—1921, Matthias Nicoll, Jr., Albany, Pres.; 1921, A. W. Booth, Elmira; 1921, A. B. Miller, Syracuse; 1923, H. B. Minton, Bklyn.; 1923, R. H. Williams, Rochester; 1923, M J. Stearns, Ogdensburg; 1922, Wm. H. Park, Mhtn.; 1922, L. S. Pilcher, Bkln.; 1922, E. H. King, Saratoga Springs; sec., W. D. Cutter, Education Bldg., Albany.

DENTAL EXAMINERS—1922, J. B. West, Elmira; 1922, Stephen Palmer, Poughkeepsie; 1922, J. G. Roberts, Buffalo; 1923, H. J. Burkhart, Rochester; 1923, O. J. Gross, Schenectady; 1924, E. A. Holbrook, Bkln.; 1924, A. R. Cooke, Syracuse; 1921, George Evans, Mhtn.; 1921, A. M. Wright, pres., Troy; sec., M. J. Perry, Education Bldg., Albany; 1922, D. W. McLean, Mt. Vernon; 1922, J. G. Roberts, Buffalo.

NURSE EXAMINERS—1924, Carolyn E. Gray, N. Y. C.; 1925, Lydia Anderson, Bkln.; 1921, Grace Comeron, Ft. Covington; 1922, Sara J. Ford, Lakewood, N. J.; 1923, Edith Atkin, Troy; 1925, Lillian Reed, Rochester; 1925, Sister Immaculata, Albany.

CERTIFIED PUBLIC ACCT. EXAMINERS—1921, C. S. McCulloh, Sec., N. Y. C.; 1923, J. W. Mason, Mt. Vernon; 1922, F. W. Lafrentz, N. Y. C.

CERTIFIED SHORTHAND REPORTERS EXAMINERS—1922, L. F. Cragin, Buffalo; 1921, Samuel Bruckheimer, Albany; 1920, Wm. C. Booth, Mhtn.

EXAMINERS IN OPTOMETRY—1922, F. A. Woll, N. Y. C.; 1925; W. W. Bissell, Sec., Rochester; 1921, H. C. Watts, Syracuse; 1922, G. R. Fox, Buffalo; 1921, Thos. McBurnie, Bkln.

VETERINARY EXAMINERS—1925, Ralph Knight, Olean; 1923, H. S. Beebe, pres., Albion; 1921, R. W. Gannett, Sec., Bkln.; 1924, Otto Faust, Poughkeepsie; 1922, G. A. Knapp, Millbrook.

PHARMACY EXAMINERS—This Board was reorganized by Chap. 422, the Laws of 1910. It is composed of 9 mem., selected by the State Regents, to hold office for 3 yrs. Terms expire on Aug. 1 each yr.; 4 are selected from N. Y. City.

University of State of New York.

DEPT. OF EDUCATION.

Conducted by the Bd. of Regents of the Univ. of the State of New York. The Regents (12) are elected by the Legislature, 1 each yr., to serve 12 yrs. The Commissioner of Education is appointed by the Regents to serve during their pleasure. The Pres. of Univ. and Commr. acts as the executive officer of the Regents. He has power to suggest necessary depts. of educational work and is responsible for administration and discipline of the minor officers. The Bd. of Regents has sole power of appointments and removals within the jurisdiction of the Univ. of the State of N. Y.

BOARD OF REGENTS.

Name, residence and expiration of term—Pliny T. Sexton, Chan., Palmyra, 1926; Al ert Vander Veer, Vice-Chan., Albany, 1927; W. G. Kellogg, Ogdensburg, 1928; Wm. Nottingham, Syracuse, 1930; Chester S. Lord, Bkln., 1922; T. J. Mangan, Binghamton, 1931; Adelbert Moot, Buffalo, 1924; C. B. Alexander, Tuxedo, 1925; H. L. Bridgman, Bkln., 1929; James Byrnes, Mhtn., 1932; Comr. Educ. (Act.), Frank B. Gilbert; Wm. J. Wallin, Yonkers, 1921; Wm. Bondy, Mhtn., 1923; Dep. Comr. and Counsel, F. B. Gilbert, $7,000; Asst. Comrs., Geo. M. Wiley, $5,500; A. S. Downing, $6,000; C. F. Wheelock, $5,500.

*Exempt civil service class.

CHIEFS AND DIRECTORS OF DIVISIONS—Science, J. M. Clarke, $5,500; State Lib., J. I. Wyer, $5,500; Admin., H. C. Case, $4,500; Attend., J. D. Sullivan, $4,000; Ed. Exten., W. R. Watson $3,500; Exams. and Insp., A. W. Skinner, $4,250; State Historian and Dir. of Archives and History, Jas. Sullivan, $5,500; Sch. Bldgs. and Grounds, F. H. Wood, $3,750; Asst. to Dep. Comr. in charge of Law Div., Irwin Esmond, $3,500; Schl. Lib., S. Williams, $3,500; Agricultural and Industrial Education, L. A. Wilson, $5,500; Visual Instn., A. W. Abrams, $3,750.

STATE COLLEGE FOR TEACHERS.

Pres., A. R. Brubacher, Albany, N. Y.

STATE NORMAL SCHOOLS.

School, principal and when opened—Oswego, J. G. Riggs, 1862; Brockport, A. C. Thompson, 1867; Fredonia, M. T. Dana, 1868; Cortland, H. DeW. De Groat, 1869; Potsdam, R. T. Congdon, 1869; Buffalo, H. W. Rockwell, 1871; Geneseo, J. V. Sturges, 1871; New Paltz, J. C. Bliss, 1886; Oneonta, P. I. Bugbee, 1889; Plattsburg, G. K. Hawkins, 1890.

G. C. Dickman, Mhtn., 1923; J. H. Rehfuss, Bkln., 1922; B. M. Hyde, Rochester, 1922; Jacob Diner, N. Y. City, 1923; John Hurley, Little Falls, 1923; J. L. Lascoff, Mhtn., 1920; Wm. Mansfield, Albany, 1921; W. G. Gregory, Buffalo, 1921; C. B. Sears, pres., Auburn, 1921; W. L. Bradt, Sec., Albany, Education Bldg.

ARCHITECTURAL EXAMINERS — D. E. Waid, 1922, Pres., N. Y. C.; W. P. Bannister, 1921, Sec., N. Y. C.; A. L. Brockway, 1924, Syracuse; E. B. Green, 1925, Buffalo; Frederick L. Ackerman, 1923, Mhtn.

ENGINEERING EXAMINERS—W. J. Wilgus, Mhtn.; Percy A. Barbour, Mhtn.; H. G. Reist, Schenectady; A. H. Hooker, Niagara Falls; Victor M. Palmer, Rochester.

Council of Farms and Markets.

Empowered to direct and supervise administration of Depts. of Agriculture, Foods and Markets, and Weights and Measures, and the cold storage bureau of State Health Dept. The Council, which is apptd. by Legislature, consists of 1 member from the State at large and 1 from each of the judicial dists. of the State. Wm. E. Dana, Pres. of Council, whose other members are: May B. Van Arsdale, N. Y. C.; E. L. Rockefeller, Bkln.; J. Y. Gerow, Washingtonville; F. W. Howe, Syracuse; Datus Clark, Peru; J. G. Pembleton, Owego; L. L. Morrell, Kinderhook; Wm. F. Pratt, Batavia. E. R. O'Malley, Commr. Public Markets of N. Y., is ex-officio member of Council. Sec., H. W. Leversee, Cohoes.

Commission of Foods and Markets.

Comr., Dr. E. H. Porter, apptd. by Council, $6,000; Dep., A. E. Brown, $5,000; Sec., Dr. F. E. Foster, $3,500. The dept. is to assist in the distribution of farm produce and to aid in the organization of co-operative societies among producers and consumers for the purpose of securing more direct business relations between them. The comr. is empowered to establish local markets wherever he deems them necessary.

Commissioner of Agriculture.

Protects against domestic animal and plant diseases; aids agricultural development, etc.

Com., Geo. E. Hogue, $8,000; Dep. Commrs.,* H. B. Winters, $4,000; S. C. Shaver, Cobleskill, $5,000; Sec., W. S. Green, Rochester, $3,000; Counsel, G. L. Flanders, Albany, $4,000. Agricultural Exp. Sta. located at Geneva. Dir. of Staff, W. H. Jordan. A Bd. of Control, composed of 9 trustees, including Gov. and Comm. of Agriculture, is the governing body.

STATE AGRICULTURAL SCHOOLS.

Morrisville, estab., Laws 1908. Schoharie, Cobleskill; estab., Laws 1911. Long Island, Farmingdale; estab., Laws 1912; St. Lawrence Univ., Canton; estab., Laws 1906. Alfred; estab., Laws 1908. Delhi; estab., Laws 1913.

Advisory Board for Promotion of Agriculture.

Geological Hall, Albany.

Created to consider plans for promotion and direction of agricultural education and advancement of interest in country life.

Board consists of 12 mem., 3 of whom are appointed by the Gov., others being as follows: Commr. of Education, Commr. of Agriculture, Dir. of N. Y. State College of Agriculture, Dir. of N. Y. Agricultural Experiment Sta., Dir. of N. Y. State Veterinary College, Dir. of Dean of State Schls. of Agriculture at Alfred Univ., Alfred, N. Y.; St. Lawrence Univ., Canton, N. Y., and Morrisville, N. Y., and a member of State Fair Commsn., to be designated by Commsn.

The board reports annually to Gov. its views and recommendations upon above matters and serves without compensation.

Names, residences and when appointed:

B. C. Davis, Ch., Alfred, ex-officio; C. S. Wilson, Sec., Ithaca, ex-officio; John H. Finley, Albany, ex-officio; B. T. Galloway, Ithaca, ex-officio; W. H. Jordan, Geneva, ex-officio; V. A. Moore, Ithaca, ex-officio; H. E. Cook, Canton, ex-officio; F. G. Helyar, Morrisville, ex-officio; C. A. Wieting, Cobleskill, Aug. 4, 1911; J. A. D. S. Findlay, Salisbury Mills, Nov. 22, 1911; J. R. Day, Syracuse, Mar. 28, 1913; vacancy.

Department of Health.

Commissioner of Health investigates causes of epidemics and disease, and methods for their prevention, has general supervision over public water supplies, sewage disposal, etc.; supervision over local health officials (except New York City); keeps records of births, marriages, deaths, enforcement of Public Health Law and Sanitary Code, investigation of sources of mortality.

Comm., H. M. Biggs, M.D., $8,000 (ap. by Gov. Jan. 29, 1920, term 6 yrs.); Dep. Comm., Matthias Nicoll Jr., $6,000; Sec., J. A. Smith, M.D., $5,000; Asst. to Dep. Comm., B. R. Rickards, S.B., $3,750; Exec. Clk. F. D. Beagle, $4,500; Dir. of Laboratories, A. B. Wadsworth, $7,000; Chemist, L. W. Wachter $3,400; Dir. Bureau, Communicable Diseases, E. S. Godfrey, Jr., M.D., $4,250; Chf. Engr., Theo. Horton, $5,500; Prin. Asst. Engr., C. A. Holmquist, $3,500; Dirs. Div. Vital Statis. O. R. Eichel, M.D., $4,250; Child Hygiene, M. E. Rose, M.D., $4,500; Dir. Div. of Tuberculosis M. F. Lent, M.D., $3,500; Dir. Div. of Veneral Diseases, J. S. Lawrence, M.D., $4,000; Dir. Div. Public Health Nursing, Mathilde S. Kuhlman, R.N., $3,500.

Public Health Council.

Authorized to establish and from time to time amend sanitary code and deal with any matter affecting preservation and improvement of public health in the State. Composed of the Commr. of Health and 6 mem. appointed by Gov., at least 3 of whom shall be physicians. Term, 6 yrs.; salary of appointive mem., $1,000 and expenses. H. M. Biggs, M.D., ex-officio, Ch.; Simon Flexner, M.D., Jacob Goldberg, M.D., T. M. Prudden, M.D., Homer Folks, Mrs. Elmer Blair, H. N. Ogden.

Civil Service Commission.

General supervision over examinations and appointments to the classified Service of State and of the 18 counties with 100,000 population or more. Ap. by Gov.

Pres., W. G. Rice, term 6 yrs. from Feb. 1, 1919, $5,000; Comrs., J. C. Clark, 6 yrs. from Feb. 1, 1915, $5,000; Mrs. C. B. Smith, 6 yrs. from Feb. 1, 1917, $5,000; Sec., J. C. Birdseye, $4,500; Asst. Sec., G. R. Hitchcock, $3,300; Chf. Examr., J. W. Steven, $4,000; Asst. Chf. Examr., A. B. Zerus, $3,000; 36 employees, $720 to $3,000.

Superintendent State Prisons.

General supervision over all State Prisons; appoints wardens, physicians and chaplains. The Comptroller appoints the clerks of the prison.

Supt., Charles F. Rattigan, $8,000 (ap. by Gov., term 5 yrs.); Dep. Supt., J. E. Long, $4,500; Industrial Agent, J. L. Schneider, $2,000; Industry Clk., F. H. Duel, $4,000; Supt. Matteawan Hosp., R. F. C. Kelb, $4,500; Supt. Dannemora Hosp., Dr. J. R. Ross, $4,000.

AUBURN PRISON, Auburn, N. Y.—Warden, E. S. Jennings, $5,000; Clk., G. A. Teller, $2,000.

CLINTON PRISON, Dannemora, N. Y.—Warden, H. M. Kaiser, $5,000; Clk., F. A. Justin, $2,200.

SING SING PRISON, Ossining, N. Y.—Warden, L. E. Lawes, $5,000; Clk., D. M. Vail, $2,320.

GREAT MEADOW PRISON, Comstock, N. Y.—Warden, Wm. Hunt, $5,000; Clk., R. A. Hall, $2,100.

Board of Parole.

Composed of Supt. of State Prisons and 2 mem. ap. by Gov. for 5 yrs., who get $3,600 each, as follows:

E. E. Larkin, Plattsburg, to Sept. 14, 1922; G. W. Benham, Auburn, to July 3, 1922.

Superintendent Public Buildings.

Supt., Otto Jantz, $5,000 (ap. by Gov., Lieut.-Gov. and Speaker, as trustees of public bldgs., term 2 yrs.); Dep. Supt., W. J. Wendell, $3,500; Chf. Engr., J. F. Miller, $3,200; Chf. Clk., S. A. Smith, Jr., $2,580.

State Industrial Commission.

State Industrial Commn. (est. 1915, succeeding former offices of Commr. of Labor and Workmen's Compensation Commn.), Capitol, Albany. Mhtn. office, 124 E. 28th st. To enforce labor law and the workmen's compensation law. Comrs., E. F. Boyle, Ch.; J. M. Lynch, H. D. Sayer, C. W. Phillips, Frances Perkins; salary, $8,000 each. (Apptd. by Gov., term 6 yrs.); Sec., E. W. Buckley, $6,000; Dep. Comrs., 1st, J. L. Gernon, $6,000; 2d, Wm. C. Archer, $6,000; 3d, E. D. Jackson, $6,000.

INDUSTRIAL COUNCIL (ADVISORY)—H. D. Sayer, Ch.; E. W. Buckley, Sec.; R. A. Day, N. Y. C.; J. C. Clark, Buffalo; M. M. Davidson, Firthcliffe; R. H. Curran, Rochester; C. M. Winchester, Albany; J. P. Holland, Mhtn.; Samuel Rothschild, Gloversville; T. M. Gafney, Syracuse; Melinda Scott, Mhtn.; A. E. Parsons, Syracuse.

BUR. OF INSPECTION—J. M. Lynch, Supv. Commr. Under immediate charge of 1st Dep. Commr. To inspect and enforce provisions of labor law in factories and shops (including bakeries and laundries), mercantile establishments, tenement bldgs. in which home work is done; mines, quarries and tunnels under construction; also to enforce provisions of labor law concerning public work and bldg. work. J. L. Gernon, 1st Dep. Commr., salary $6,000. Office, 124 E. 28th st.

BUR. OF STATISTICS AND INFORMATION—Frances Perkins, Supvr. Comr. Under immediate charge of a chief statistician. To collect, prepare and publish information, statistical or otherwise, in relation to labor and industries in State. E. B. Patton, Chf. Stat., salary, $5,000. Office, Capitol, Albany.

BUR. OF EMPLOYMENT—H. D. Sayer, Supv. Commr. Under immediate charge of a dir. To establish and maintain throughout State a system of public employment offices. Dr. D. S. Flynn, Dir.; salary, $4,000. Office 124 E. 28th st., Mhtn.; registration branches, 310 Jay st., Bkln.; 112 W. 46th st., 58 Cooper sq., 184 W. 135th st., Mhtn.; 2733 3d ave., Bronx.

BUR. OF MEDIATION AND ARBITRATION—Frances Perkins, Supv. Commr. Under immediate charge of 3d Dep. Commr. To endeavor by mediation or arbitration to effect amicable settlement of labor disputes; may also make public investigation of causes of disputes. 3d Dep. Comr. (chf. mediator), E. D. Jackson, salary, $6,000. Office, Capitol, Albany.

BUR. OF INDUSTRIES AND IMMIGRATION—H. D. Sayer, Supv. Commr. Under immediate charge of a chf. invest. To investigate condition of aliens in State and to administer law relating to registration of employment agencies with Industrial Commission, and licensing of immigrant lodging places by that officer. Marian K. Clark, Chf. Investigator; salary, $3,000. Office, 124 E. 28th st., Mhtn.

BUR. OF WORKMEN'S COMPENSATION—E. F. Boyle, Supv. Comr. Under immediate charge of 2d Dep. Commr. To administer Workmen's Compensation Law. W. C. Archer, 2d Dep. Commr.; salary, $6,000. Office 124 E. 28th st., Mhtn.

LEGAL BUREAU—C. W. Phillips, Supv. Commr. Under immediate charge of B. L. Schlentag, Chf. Counsel; salary, $7,000.

BUR. OF WOMEN IN INDUSTRY—Frances Perkins, Supvr. Comr.; Nelle Schwartz, Chf. of Bur., $2,500 per annum. To make special investigations with respect to industries in which women are employed.

BUR. OF BOILERS AND EXPLOSIVES—J. M. Lynch, Supvr. Comr.; G. A. O'Rourke, Chf. Engr., $3,500. Has jurisdiction over boilers and storage and handling of explosives.

Hospital Development Commission.

Organized to adopt a general plan of hospital development. Comprises the Ch. of the State Hospital Commsn., State Engnr., State Architect, Ch. of Senate Finance Comm., Ch. of Assembly Ways and Means Comm., a member of one of the Legislative financial comms., representing the minority, and 2 members apptd. by Gov.—W. B. James, N. Y. C., and B. W. Arnold, Albany.

NEW YORK STATE GOVERNMENT—ADMINISTRATIVE—*Continued.*

State Hospital Commission.

Exclusive jurisdiction over the insane. All private insane institutions must get license from Comm. 1st 2 comms., doctor and lawyer, respectively.

Comm., C. W. Pilgrim, M.D., $7,500 (ap. by Gov., term indefinite); Comm. A. D. Morgan, F. A. Higgins (ap. by Gov., term 6 yrs.); Sec., E. S. Elwood; Med. Insp., J. L. Van De Mark, $5,000 each; Aud., F. W. Kyte, $5,000; Asst. Aud., J. H. Flinn, $3,350; State Hosp. Treas., L. M. Farrington, $3,500; Statn., H. M. Pollock, $3,500; Spec. Agents, Clks., etc.

SUPTS. STATE HOSPITALS FOR INSANE—Binghamton, Dr. C. G. Wagner, $5,500; Bkln., Dr. I. G. Harris, $4,600; Buffalo, Dr. F. W. Parsons, $4,000; Central Islip, Dr. G. A. Smith, $6,000; Gowanda, Dr. C. A. Potter, $4,200; Hudson River, Dr. W. G. Ryon, $4,300; Kings Park, Dr. W. C. Garvin, $4,000; Mhtn., Dr. M. B. Heyman, $4,200; Middletown, Dr. M. C. Ashley, $5,400; Rochester, Dr. E. H. Howard, $5,500; St. Lawrence, Dr. P. G. Taddiken, $4,000; Utica, Dr. R. H. Hutchings, $5,300; Willard, Dr. R. M. Elliott, $5,500.

State Tax Commissioners.

They are appointed by the Gov. for a term of 3 yrs. They must officially visit every county in State, at least once in 2 yrs.; inquire into methods of assessment and taxation; furnish local assessors with information and forms; hear and determine appeals from local equalizations within the several counties; annually fix and determine valuation of each special franchise subject to assessment in each city, town or tax district, and prepare an annual report to the Legislature.

Pres., M. J. Walsh, Dec. 31, 1921, $8,500; J. J. Merrill, Dec. 31, 1920, $8,000; J. D. Smith, Dec. 31, 1922, $8,000; Geo. M. Haight, Sec., $4,000; W. E. Sill, Counsel, $4,200. Dep. Tax Commrs., Special Franchises, P. B. Wittmer, $4,750; Corpns., N. W. Canfield, $4,750. Mortgage Tax, R. E. Thompson, $4,750; Local Assessments, Statistics and Equalization, L. K. Rockefeller, $4,750; Administration, M. M. France, $4,750.

Department of Architecture.

Prepares plans and specifications and supervises construction of all hospitals, prisons, armories, educational, charitable and other bldgs. erected by State.

L. F. Pilcher, State Arch. (ap. Exp. Dec. 31, 1922), $10,000; C. A. Sussdorff Exec. Dep., $6,000; T. M. Newton, Asst. Dep., $5,000; J. T. McNally, Ex. Sec., $4,000; H. J. Hichman, Asst. Dep., $3,500; R. C. Taggart, Chf. Engr., $4,250; D. M. Collier, Chf. Insp., $3,750; A. A. Wiedenbeck, Ex. Clk., $2,500.

Department of Highways.

F. S. Greene, Comr., Sands Points (ap. Apr. 8, '19; term 5 yrs.), $10,000; Paul Schultze, 1st Dep. Comr., Troy, $6,000; A. W. Brant, N. Y. C., 2d Dep Comr., $5,000; Chas. Van Amburgh, Binghamton, 3d Dep. Comr., $5,000; I. V. A. Huie, N. Y. C., Sec., $5,000; F. R. Pennock, Asst. Sec., Chittenango, $3,000; vacancy, Auditor, $6,000; 9 Div. Engrs., $5,000; each; J. H. Sturdevant, 1st Div., Columbus Inst., 11 Washington, Poughkeepsie; H. O. Schermerhorn, 2d Div., 1 Daniel, Albany; R. F. Hall, 3d Div., Cleveland Bldg., Watertown; L. F. Brownell, 4th Div., Chamber of Commerce Bldg., Utica; H. E. Smith, 5th Div., 901 Press Bldg., Binghamton; W. M. Acheson, 6th Div., 433 So. Salina, Syracuse; C. M. Edwards, 7th Div., 423 Cutler Bldg., Rochester; Perry Filkin, 8th Div., St. Ann Federation Bldg., Hornell; C. J. McDonough, 9th Div., 703 Main, Buffalo.

State Probation Commission.

Seven members; 4 are appointed by the Gov. for terms of 4 yrs. each; 1 by the State Bd. of charities from among its members; 1 by the State Comm. of Prisons from among its members, and the Comm. of Education is a member ex-officio. The duties are to collect and publish information and secure the enforcement of the Probation Law, to keep informed as to the work of all probation officers in the State and from time to time to inquire into their conduct and efficiency. No compensation, but traveling expenses. (Date is expiration of term.) E J. Butler, Pres., Mhtn., July 1, 1922; E. C. Blum, Mhtn, July 1, 1924; A. T. Clearwater, Kingston, July 1, 1921; Henry Marquand, Bedford Hills, April 4, 1921; Mary E. Paddon, Mhtn., July 1, 1923; Henry Solomon, Mhtn., Jan. 6, 1922. State Education Commissioner, ex-officio; Sec., C. L. Chute, $3,750.

Court of Claims.

The Court of Claims, which superseded Bd. of Claims on Mar. 9, 1897, was, by chap. 856 of laws of '11, in turn superseded by a Bd. of Claims with powers and jurisdiction of said court. Chap. 1 of laws of '15 restores the Court of Claims.

The Court of Claims has jurisdiction to hear and determine private claims against the State. It may also hear and determine any claim on part of State against claimant or against his assignor at time of assignment and must render judgment for such sum as should be paid by or to State. But the court has no jurisdiction of a claim submitted by law to any other tribunal or officer for audit or determination except where the claim is founded upon express contract and such claim or some part thereof has been rejected by such tribunal or officer. In no case shall any liability be implied against the State and no award shall be made in any claim against the State except upon such legal evidence as would establish liability against an individual or corp. in a court of law or equity.

The court is regularly composed of 3 judges who are apptd. by Gov. by and with advice and consent of Senate. The 1st appts. under chap. 1 of the laws of '15 restoring Court of Claims were for terms of 3, 6 and 9 yrs. respectively. Hereafter the term of office of each judge will be 9 yrs.

By chap. 1 of the laws of '15 the Gov., in order to relieve congested condition of calendar, was given authority to appoint, by and with advice and consent of Senate, not more than 2 additional judges whose term of office would expire on Jan. 1, '18. By Chap. 255, Laws of 1917, the terms of the additional judges in office, when the act went into effect, were extended to Feb. 1, 1918, and the authority of the Gov. to appt. additional judges, under the restrictions therein named, was continued indefinitely.

Each judge of Court of Claims receives an annual salary of $8,000 and all actual and necessary expenses in discharge of their official duties. Judges, residence and when terms expire: F. M. Ackerson, presiding, Niagara Falls, Dec. 31, '29; W. W. Webb, Rochester, Dec. 31, '23; S. W. Smith, Chatham, Dec. 31, 1926.

Additional judges, appointed under chap. 1 of Laws of '15, and by Chap. 255, Laws 1917. Charles Morschauser, Poughkeepsie, Feb. 1, '21; W. D. Cunningham, Ellenville, Feb. 1, '21; F. D. Colson, Clk., $4,200.

State Commission of Prisons.

7 Commissioners (compensation, $10 per diem, not to exceed $1,000 per year), term exp. June 21 each year.

J. S. Kennedy, Pres., N. Y. C., '21; L. C. Weinstock, V.-Pres., N. Y. C., '23; Mrs. S. L. Davenport, Bath, '24; M. H. Pierce, Gouverneur, '21; Chas. S. Rogers, Hudson, '22; Mrs. C. D. Patten, Saratoga Springs, '24; H. Solomon, N. Y. C., '22; Sec., J. F. Tremain, $4,000; Chf. Clk., P. G. Roosa, $3,500.

Adjutant General's Office.
(See Index, "N. Y. State Militia.")
Albany office, 158 State St.

N. Y. office (N. Y. State Arsenal), 35th and 7th av., N. Y. C.

Adj.-Gen., Brig.-Gen. J. Leslie Kincaid, $7,500 (ap. by the Gov., term exp. with Gov.); Assts. to Adj.-Gen., Col. E. J. Westcott, $4,500; Col. J. Weston Myers, $3,750; Dir. of Bur., Maj. C. W. Abrams, $3,000; Capt. B. H. Mull, $3,000.

Military Training Commission.

Composed of the Maj. Gen. commanding Natl. Guard, ex-officio, who shall be ch., and 2 other members, 1 to be appointed by the Board of Regents of the State Univ. and 1 by the Governor. Terms of appointed members, 4 yrs. No compensation but necessary travel expenses. The Commn. shall advise and confer with the Bd. of Regents as to courses of instruction in physical training to be prescribed for all children over 8 yrs. of age, in elementary and secondary schools; shall recommend to the Regents a programme of physical training for the schools; shall prepare a course of military training for all boys in the State over 16 and not over 19 yrs. of age; shall have power to provide for observation and inspection of the work in physical and military training, prescribe rules and regulations for compulsory attendance during periods of military training, regulate individual exemptions from the prescribed military training, maintain and co-operate with the colleges in the State or with the Federal authorities in maintaining courses of instruction for male teachers and physical instructors, and others who volunteer and are accepted by the commsn.

Commsn.: Maj.-Gen. J. F. O'Ryan, N. Y. C.; (Act.) F. H. Gilbert, Com. of Education, Albany; G. J. Fisher, M.D., N. Y. C.; Insp. of Physical Training, T. A. Storey, M.D., $5,000; Chief Supervising Officer, Military Training, Brig.-Gen. W. H. Chapin, $5,000; Supervising Officer, Vocational Training, H. G. Burdge, $5,000; Sec., T. C. Stowell, $2,500.

Department of State Police.
(New York State Troopers.)

Duty is to prevent and detect crime and apprehend criminals. Must not exercise powers within limits of any city to suppress rioting and disorder, except by direction of the Gov. or upon request of the mayor of the city with approval of the Gov., who appoints Supt.

Supt., Maj. G. F Chandler, $5,000; Dep. Supt., Capt. G. P. Dutton, $3,500; Capt. Troop K, W. W. Robinson; Capt. Troop D, Stephen McGrath; Capt. Troop G, E. F. Tobey; Capt. Troop K, J. A. Warner, $1,800 each; Ex. Clk, S. C. Beagle, $2,500; Insp., A. B. Moore, $1,800.

Barracks located at Batavia, tel. No., Batavia 156. Oneida, tel. Oneida 8. Albany, tel. West 1684. White Plains, tel. White Plains 44.

Conservation Commission.
(Chap. 318, Laws of 1915.)

The Conservation Comm. succeeded to powers and duties of Forest Purchasing Bd., Forest Fish and Game Comn., Comn. of Water Power on Black River and State Water Supply Comn. The Gov. apps. 1 Conservation Comnr. for term of 6 yrs., at an annual salary of $8,000 and necessary expenses. The Comn. apps. a Sec. and other officials. Through the div. of lands and forests are administered all laws relating to tree culture, reforestation, care and management of State parks, reservations, etc., now or hereafter under jurisdiction of Conservation Comn.; through the div. of fish and game all laws relating to State jurisdiction over fish and game, and protection and propagation thereof, including shellfish; through div. of waters all laws relating to State jurisdiction over water storage, hydraulic development, water supply, river improvement, drainage, irrigation and navigation of waters outside canals. The Commn. also has complete supervision and jurisdiction over State Reservation at Saratoga Springs. (Ap. Jan. 1, '15. Term 6 yrs.).

Comnr., G. D. Pratt, $8,000; Dep. Comnr., Alex. Macdonald, $6,000; Sec., W. S. Carpenter, $4,000; Counsel, Marshall McLean, $6,000.

DIV. OF LANDS AND FORESTS—Supt. of Forests, C. R. Pettis, $5,000; Asst. Supt. of Forests, W. G. Howard, $3,250; 1 Chf. Land Surveyor. 5 Foresters, 6 Dist. Forest Rangers, force of 65 Forest Rangers, 55 Mountain Observers, etc.

DIV. OF FISH AND GAME—Chf. Game Protector, L. Legge, $5,000; Fish Culturist, John W. Titcomb, $4,000; Supvr. of Marine Fisheries, E. B. Hawkins, $3,000; 12 Div. Insps., 131 Game Protrs.

DIV. OF WATERS—Div. Engr.; A. H. Perkins, $5,000; Insp. of Docks and Dams, A. R. McKim, $4,000; Asst. Engrs., E. H. Sargent and Russell Suter, $3,500 each; Engrs., Levellers, Rodmen, etc.

DIV. OF SARATOGA SPRINGS—J. G. Jones, Supt., $5,000; C. B. Elmore, Act. Sec., $2,400; Herbert Ant, Chemist, $2,400.

State Board of Charities.

Visit all incorporated or unincorporated charitable institutions, city, county or State, in receipt of public funds for the care of inmates, except those for insane. There are 12 mem. of board, 1 from each judicial dist., and 3 from N. Y. City. Ap. for 8 yrs. N. Y. C. office, 287 4th av., Mhtn.

W. R. Stewart, Pres., N. Y. C.; term expires Mar. 23, 1921; L. K. Frankel, N. Y. C., May 28, 1921; V. F. Ridder, N. Y. C., May 28, 1921; D. W. Burdick, Ithaca; M. J. Mulqueen, Mhtn., 1921; C. H. Lewis, Syracuse, 1923; Mrs. Lillie B. Werner, Rochester, 1924; W. H. Gratwick, V.-Pres., Buffalo, 1925; Mrs. B. G. Higley, Hudson Falls, 1926; Mrs. M. H. Glynn, 1927; J. R. Kevin, Bkln., 1927; H. Marquand, Bedford Hills, 1923; Sec., C. H. Johnson, $6,000; Chf. Clk., W. D. Ives, $3,200; Supt. of State Alien Poor, R. W. Hill, $3,650; Supt. of Insp., R. W. Wallace, $3,750; Supt. Div. Children, J. H. Foster, $3,650; Supt. Div. Medical Charities, C. E. Ford, $3,500. N. Y. C. office, 287 4th av.; Supt., J. B. Prest, $3,700. 5 Transfer Agents, 24 Insprs., 30 Clks., and Stenos.

CHARITABLE INSTS. & REFORMATORIES.

Salaries on sliding scale, based on length of service.

Craig Colony for Epileptics, Sonyea—Dr. W. T. Shanahan, Supt., $4,000 to $4,750.

House of Refuge, Mhtn.—Col. E. C. Barber, Supt., $4,000 to $4,500.

Letchworth Village, Thiells, Rockland Co.—C. S. Little, M.D., Supt., $4,500 to $5,000.

N. Y. State Hospital for Crippled and Deformed Children, West Haverstraw—Dr. J. J. Nutt, Supt., $2,500 to $3,500.

N. Y. State Hospital for the Treatment of Incipient Pulmonary Tuberculosis, Raybrook—Dr. H. A. Bray, Supt., $3,500 to $3,750.

N. Y. State Reformatory, Elmira and Eastern, N. Y. Reformatory, Napanoch—F. L. Christian, M.D., Supt., $5,000.

N. Y. State Reformatory for Women, Bedford—Mrs. Anna H. Talbot, Supt., $3,000 to $3,500.

N. Y. State Soldiers and Sailors' Home, Bath—J. C. F. Tillson, Comt., $3,500.

N. Y. State Training Schl. for Girls, Hudson—Dr. Hortense V. Bruce, Supt., $3,000 to $3,500.

N. Y. State Woman's Relief Corps Home, Oxford—Col. J. S. Graham, Supt., $2,500.

Rome State Schl. for Mental Defectives, Rome—Dr. C. Bernstein, Supt., $4,500.

State Agricultural and Industrial Schl., Industry, N. Y.—H. H. Todd, Supt., $4,000.

N. Y. State Schl. for Mental Defectives, Newark—Supt., E. A. Nevin, M.D., $4,000 to $4,500.

Syracuse State Schl. for Mental Defectives—Dr. O. H. Cobb, Supt., $4,000.

Thomas Indian Schl., Iroquois—Mrs. Emily P. Lincoln, Supt., $2,500 to $2,750.

Western House of Refuge for Women, Albion—Mrs. F. P. Daniels, Supt., $2,000 to $2,500.

N. Y. State Schl. for the Blind, Batavia—C. A. Hamilton, Supt., $3,000 to $3,250.

ASSOCIATIONS.

State Charities Aid Assn.—Homer Folks, Sec., 105 E. 22d, N. Y. C.

State Conference of Charities and Correction—O. F. Lewis, Mhtn., Pres.; R. W. Wallace, Sec., Albany.

SUPPORTED SCHLS. FOR BLIND AND DEAF.

Albany Home Schl. for the Oral Instruction of the Deaf, Albany—Quincy McGuire, Prin.

Central N. Y. Institution for Deaf-Mutes, Rome—O. A. Betts, Prin.

Institution for the Improved Instruction of Deaf-Mutes, Lexington av., N. Y. C.—Harris Taylor, Prin.

Le Couteulx St. Mary's Institution for the Improved Instruction of Deaf-Mutes, Buffalo—Sister Mary Anne Burke, Prin.

N. Y. Institute for the Education of the Blind, 9th av. and 34th, N. Y. C.—E. M. Van Cleve, Prin.

N. Y. Institution for the Instruction of the Deaf and Dumb, 163d, N. Y. C.; I. B. Gardner, Prin.

Northern N. Y. Institution for Deaf-Mutes, Malone—E. C. Rider, Prin.

St. Joseph's Institute for Improved Instruction of Deaf-Mutes. Girls' Dept., Westchester, Miss J. F. O'Hara; Boys' Dept., Bkln., Miss A. M. Larkin, branch Westchester—Miss Rose A. Fagan, Prin.

Rochester School for the Deaf, Rochester, T. C. Forrester, Prin.

Fiscal Supervisor.

Empowered to examine into all matters connected with financial management of, and to revise all estimates for supplies for State charitable insts., incl. reformatories. Fiscal Supv., F. R. Utter, $6,000 (ap. by Gov.; term, 5 yrs.; exp. June 10, 1922); 1st Dep., Henry O'Brien, $5,000; 2d Dep., T. H. Lee, $4,250; Chf. Clk., W. J. Baier, $2,750; Est. Clk., J. B. Kelly, $2,800; Chf. Insp., D. C. Kaye, $2,700.

NEW YORK STATE GOVERNMENT—ADMINISTRATIVE—*Continued.*

Legislative Bill-Drafting Department.

Estab. 1913 by Legislative act. Two comm. ap. by Temp. Pres. of Senate and Speaker of Assembly; R. C. Cummings, $6,500; Wm. J. McCormick, $5,000; Dep., B. S. Rude, $4,500; Clks., Stenos., etc.

New York City Health Officer.

Port of New York. Must be doctor of medicine. General superintendence of Quarantine Est. Health officer, L. E. Cofer, M.D., $12,500. (Ap. by Gov.; term 4 years; exp. Feb. 1, 1922.)

New York City Port Wardens.

Port of New York. Exclusive cognizance relating to surveys of vessels and their cargoes arriving at Port of N. Y. in distress or damaged in port. They specify amount of damage and judge repairs necessary to render vessel again seaworthy. Paid by fees.
(Ap. by Gov.; term 3 years.)

PORT WARDENS AND RESIDENCE—E. M. Price, Bellport, term exp. Jan. 27, 1920; D. Albert Marinelli, Mhtn., term exp. Mar. 16, 1922; S. Rendt, N. Y. C.; term exp. Apr. 28, 1923; J. A. Farley, Grassy Point, erm. exp. Mar. 30, 1922; John Guilfoyle, Bkln., term exp. May 18, 1922; S. A. Judge, Northport, term exp. July 14, 1922; J. V. Lyons, Mhtn., term exp. Dec. 5, 1923; Chas. W. Ferry, N. Y. C., term exp. May 13, 1921; Jeremiah O'Connor, N. Y. C., term exp., Mar. 16, 1922.

Retirement Pensions Commission.

Commn. to inquire into subject of retirement pensions, allowances and annuities for State and municipal employees, apptd. by the Gov.: C. F. Horton, Buffalo; J. J. Merrill. Josephine W. Wickser, Buffalo; Joseph Hoag, Mhtn.; W. M. Thomas, Albany. The commsn. also includes the Supt. of Insurance, as provided by law, and 1 Senator and 1 Assemblyman.

Superintendent of Elections.

Supt., Henry S. Renaud, N. Y. C. (term 4 yrs.; exp. Dec. 31, 1922); $5,000.

Inst. for Study of Malignant Diseases.

E. J. Meyer, M.D., Buffalo; Wm. H. Gratwick, Buffalo; J. G. Milburn, Mhtn.; J. W. Wadsworth, Jr., Groveland; Chas. Cary, M. D., Buffalo; James Erving, M.D., Ithaca; Hermann M. Biggs, M.D., ex-officio.

Commission to Appraise Value of Lands in Albany for New State Building.

Property in question situated west of Capitol, comprising 2 blocks. App. by Trustees of Public Bldgs. Compensation, $25 per diem. Commrs., F. C. Herrick, J. P. Failing, W. M. Douglas, Albany.

West Side Improvement Commission.

Created by Chap. 720, Laws 1917, to investigate practical effect and progress made in carrying out law under which opportunity was given N. Y. C. and the N. Y. Central R. R. to discontinue the use, by the railroad, of sts. at grade, abolish the use of steam as motive power, expand freight facilities and bring about various improvements in connection therewith. The 1st Dist. Public Service Commsn. is given a part in solution of the problem. Commrs., Wm. H. Van Benschoten, Ch., N. Y. C.; R. S. Rounds, N. Y. C.; C. A. Beard, N. Y. C.; H. L. Stoddard, N. Y. C.; C. C. Miller, N. Y. C.; H. C. Todd, Saratoga Springs; D. W. Ainsworth, Albany; J. C. Clark, N. Y. C., Counsel.

Dir. Weights and Measures.

W. T. White, Albany, $3,500 and expenses; term subject to Foods and Markets Dept.'s discretion; Asst. Dir., C. J. Reynolds, $2,000; 3 Insps., $1,400 each.

Board of Law Examiners.

Pres., Edward H. Letchworth, Buffalo; term exp. Dec. 31, 1920. No salary. Sec.-Treas., F. M. Danaher, term exp. Dec. 31, 1921; fees not to exceed $2,000 and such addtl. allowance as Court may direct.

Examination of all persons applying to be admitted to practice as attorneys and counselors in Courts of Record of N. Y. State are appointed to be held for the 1st and 2d depts. of the State for 1921 as follows:

Mhtn., at Examination Room of Mncpl Civil Service Com., Room 1417 Mncpl Bldg., except in June, when it will be held in Gym. Annex, Columbia Univ. Tu. and Wed., Jan. 11, 12; Tu. and Wed., Apr. 12, 13; Tu. and Wed., June 29, 30; Th. and Fr., Oct. 13, 14, at 8:45 a.m.

Board of Embalming Examiners.

(Ap. by Gov.; term 3 yrs.) Exams., †J. J. McLarney, Mhtn., term exp. Dec. 5, 1922; †W. J. Phillips, Sec., Albany; term expires Dec. 5, 1922; H. Sauerwein, Buffalo; term exp. Dec. 5, 1923; W. A. Drinkwine, Syracuse; term exp. Dec. 5, 1921; C. F. Moadinger, Bkln.; term exp. Dec. 5, 1921; salary, $200; Sec., $1,000 additional.

Commissioners of Land Office.

Lieut. Gov., State Comp., Speaker of Assembly, State Treas., Secy. of State, Attorney Gen., State Engineer.

Commissioners of Canal Fund.

Lieut. Gov., Secy. of State, State Comptroller, State Treasurer, Attorney General.

Board of Canvassers.

Secy. of State, State Comptroller, Attorney Gen., State Treasurer, State Engineer.

Board of Equalization.

State Tax Commissioners and Commissioners of the Land Office.

State Printing Board.

Entrusted with control of all printing done for the State. Its mem. are Sec. of State, State Compt. and the Atty. Gen.

State Boxing Commission.

J. L. Johnson, Mhtn., 1924; E. W. Ditmars, Bkln., 1922; W. G. Hooke, Yonkers, 1923.

License Committee.

Lawrence McGuire, Mhtn.; Capt. D. W. Wear, Binghamton; Col. C. E. Walsh, Albany.

Board of Classification.

Fiscal Supervisor, Supt. of Prisons, State Commission of Prisons, Lunacy Commission. The Board fixes and determines prices on all labor performed and all articles manufactured and furnished to the State, its political departments, or its public institutions. It also determines styles, patterns, designs and qualities of articles to be manufactured in public offices and public institutions of State.

Canal Board.

Lieut. Gov., Secy. of State, State Comptroller, State Treasurer, Attorney Gen., State Engineer, Supt. of Public Works. John A. O'Connor, Engineer in charge of construction of Barge Canal terminals.

Narcotic Drug Control Commission.

W. R. Herrick, Comm., N. Y. C., $6,000; term 6 yrs. (ap. by Gov., term exp. Dec. 2, 1925); 1st Dep., Sara Graham-Mulhall, Mhtn., $3,500; 2d Dep., F. C. Marrill, Sherrill, $3,500; 3d Dep., Dr. John Seeley, Woodhull, $3,500; To control the sale of narcotic drugs. The commsn. is charged with the duty of registering by certificate all sales throughout the State, beginning Feb. 1, 1919.

Racing Commissioners.

Three appts. by Gov. for 5 yrs. No compensation: James W. Wadsworth, Sr., Geneseo; John Sanford, Amsterdam; Harry K. Knapp, 34 E. 35th st., Mhtn.

Bronx Parkway Commissioners.

Three appts. by Gov. for 5 yrs.; salary, $2,500; Madison Grant, Mhtn., 1922; F. H. Bethell, Scarsdale, 1921; W. W. Niles, N. Y. C., 1923.

Fire Island State Park Commissioners.

Five appts. by Gov. and Senate; tm. 5 yrs: J. E. King, Islip; G. Fishel, Babylon; J. P. Balter, Babylon; T. A. Clark, Bkln; exp. Mar. 25, 1924; Edw. Thompson, Huntington; exp. Feb. 4, 1925.

Commissioners for Promotion of Uniformity of Legislation in United States.

Three appts. by Governor and Senate; no term. Expenses. Charles T. Terry, Mhtn.; G. G. Bogert, Cornell University, Ithaca; C. C. Alden, Buffalo.

State Fair Commission.

5 Appointments with Lt.-Gov. and Com. of Agriculture, ex-officio; salary, $2,000 and expenses; F. B. Parker, Elba, 1921; Pierre Lorillard, Jr., Tuxedo, 1922; H. K. Williams, Dunkirk, 1923; G. R. Fitts, McLean, Mar. 1, 1925; J. H. Cahill, Syracuse, Mar. 1, 1924.

NEW YORK STATE GOVERNMENT—ADMINISTRATIVE—*Continued.*

Inter-State Taxation Commission.

Apptd. by Gov. to meet representatives of Cal. and other States as may be in attendance thereat in a congress or convention to consider relation of State and Fed. govts. in respect of taxation. Comnrs., Martin Saxe, Mhtn; W. H. Knapp, Canandaigua; Lawson Purdy, N. Y. C.; J. A. Blair, Mhtn.; Allyn Young, Ithaca; E. R. A. Seligman, Mhtn.; J. M. Gray, Bkln.

Palisades Interstate Park Commission.

Five appointed by Gov. of N. Y. and 5 by Gov. of N. J.; tm. 5 yrs.; exp. Feb. 12 in year indicated. Office, 346 B'way, Mhtn. The N. Y. members are: E. L. Partridge, 1925, Cornwall; G. W. Perkins, 1921, Riverdale; J. Du Pratt White, 1924, Nyack; Wm. H. Porter, 1923, Mhtn., and W. A. Harriman, 1922, Arden.

The Watkins Glen Reservation.

Five Comrs., ap. by Gov.; terms 5 yrs. J. D. Macreery, Watkins, 1926; L. H. Durland, Watkins, July 21, 1927; J. E. Frost, Watkins, 1923; F. L. Miller, Watkins, 1922; C. W. Fletcher, Montour Falls, 1921; O. H. Waltz, Ithaca, 1924; O. A. Leonard, Elmira, 1925.

State Board of Geographic Names.

Empowered to determine and establish correct historical and etymological form of place names in the State, as well as to determine form and propriety of new place names proposed for general use, and to recommend adoption of correct forms. 5 mem., Comn. of Education and State Geologist being ex-officio mem., together with 3 mem. apptd. by Gov., serving without compensation; term, 6 yrs. J. H. Finley, Ch.; J. M. Clarke, Sec. and Exec. Officer; H. P. Baker, 1923; Arnold J. F. Van Laer, H. L. Fairchild; terms exp. 1925.

New York State Nautical School.

Maintained at N. Y. City, aboard a proper vessel, to give instruction in science and practice of navigation, seamanship, steam and electrical engnrg., to teach pupils from several counties of the State, who have qualifications of good moral character, elementary education and physical fitness. Board of Governors comprises J. H. Finley, Comr. of Education; E. W. Brown, N. Y. C., 1922; W. R. Evans, Buffalo, 1923; A. B. Conner, Mhtn., 1923; Reginald Fay, N. Y. C., 1921; Capt. N. L. Cullen, Mhtn., 1922; C. H. Bissikumer, Albany, 1921; M. H. Tracy, Mhtn., 1921; Rafael Rios, Mhtn, 1922.

State Commission for the Blind.

Apptd. by Gov., trm., 5 yrs.; no compensation, save expenses. Duty is to maintain a complete registration of blind in N. Y. State and also one or more bureaus of information and industrial aid.

Comrs., C. S. Davis, Rochester, 1922; Miss Mary V. Hun, Albany, 1924; C. J. Himmelsbach, Buffalo, 1923; M. C. Migel, N. Y. C., 1921; W. M. Mehl, M.D., Buffalo, 1925.

Legislative Library.

Located in State Capitol; open throughout year. C. R. Skinner, Librarian, $2,500.

State Aviation Commission.

Apptd. by Gov. to make study of subject of regulation and promotion of aeronautics by the State and to report to Gov. their suggestions for legislation, together with bills prepared for purpose of carrying out such suggestions for introduction in Legislature during the session. Col. J. De Mont Thompson, N. Y. C.; Robert Graves, N. Y. C.; A. R. Hawley, N. Y. C.; F. S. Voss, N. Y. C.; C. D. Hakes, Albany; F. H. Allen, N. Y. C., and H. B. Herts, N. Y. C.

CATSKILL WATER SUPPLY

New York City's Catskill Mountain water-supply system is being developed by the Board of Water Supply, which was created by Act of Legislature, chapter 724, laws of 1905. This legislation followed an eight years' campaign for an additional water-supply for N. Y. C. which began with a report presented on March 15, 1897, to the Manufacturers' Asso. of Bkln., by a special comm. of which Charles N. Chadwick was Chairman.

The Catskill water-supply system is the greatest which has ever been undertaken and ranks among the most notable enterprises ever carried out by any city, state or nation. For magnitude and cost and for the variety, complexity and difficulty of the physical problems involved it stands with the great canals, transcontinental railroad lines and New York's own rapid-transit railway system.

Catskill water has its origin in the Esopus and Schoharie watersheds, with an area of 257 and 314 sq. miles, respectively; these watersheds are situated in the sparsely-populated central and eastern portions of the Catskill mountains, and each of them will be called upon to yield upward of 250 million gallons of water daily in order to supply the 500 million gallons daily which the Catskill aqueduct was constructed to carry.

The first instalment of the Catskill system, covering the development of the Esopus watershed, was substantially completed and put into service in 1917, and since that time Catskill water has been delivered continuously into the five boroughs of the city at the rate of about 400 million gallons daily, which is approximately two-thirds the average daily water consumption of Gr. N. Y.

The portions of the system completed for the Esopus development include the Ashokan impounding reservoir in Ulster county, an artificial lake 12 miles long; the Catskill aqueduct, extending 92 miles from the Ashokan reservoir to the northern boundary of N. Y. C.; the Kensico storage reservoir near White Plains; the Hill View equalizing reservoir in the City of Yonkers; the Silver Lake terminal reservoir on Staten Island, and 35 miles of tunnel and pipe-lines within the city limits for delivering the water to the distribution system. The area of the surface of the Ashokan reservoir is equivalent to that of Manhattan Island below 110th st. and the water which all the Catskill reservoirs together hold would fill the North river from the Battery to Hastings.

Water from the Catskill sources is delivered within the city by gravity, the water flowing from the Ashokan reservoir to the city and into the distribution pipes under such pressure that it need not be pumped before it reaches the people who use it.

Of the 92 miles of the Catskill aqueduct between the Ashokan reservoir and the city line, 61 miles were constructed in open cut, nearly all of which is the standard cut-and-cover type 17 ft. high by 17 ft. 6 in. wide. The remaining 31 miles consist of tunnels driven through hills and mountains and in solid rock under wide, deep valleys. The most important of these valleys to be crossed was that of the Hudson river, where a circular tunnel 14 ft. in diameter was constructed at a depth of 1,100 ft. beneath the river surface. The cut-and-cover aqueduct and the tunnels are more than big enough for railroad trains to pass through them with ample clearances.

The city tunnel, which is 18 miles long and located at depths varying from 200 to 750 ft. below the street surface, carries the water from the Hill View reservoir to the distribution system in the Bronx and Manhattan and to two terminal shafts in Bkln.; from the latter shafts steel and cast-iron pipe-lines extend into Queens and Richmond, respectively.

Operations on the second stage of the Catskill water system, covering the development of the Schoharie watershed, are being actively carried on. This work comprises the construction of the Gilboa dam, forming the Schoharie reservoir, from which the water will be carried by the Shandaken tunnel, also now under construction, a distance of 18 miles to the Esopus creek, where it will flow through the present channel into the Ashokan reservoir.

For surveys, real estate, construction, engineering and general supervision, and all other items except interest on the bonds, the total cost of the completed Catskill system will be about $177,000,000 of which $22,000,000 is for the Schoharie works. To Sept. 30, 1920, $144,618,190.91 had been expended.

N. Y. STATE BUDGETS.

For year	Budget appropriations.	Per capita.
1912	$43,074,192.58	4.61
1913	52,866,582.35	5.53
1914	59,465,690.97	6.21
1915	47,899,527.74	4.94
1916	63,997,271.86	6.51
1917	59,103,450.08	5.93
1918	79,742,834.21	7.89
1919	81,525,271.31	7.95
1920	95,840,983.77	9.22
1921	145,219,906.60	13.79

The British Museum contains more than 16,000 copies of the Bible.

NEW YORK STATE JUDICIARY.

COURT OF APPEALS.

Court consists of a Chief Judge and 6 Asso. Judges, elected by entire State for 14 yrs.; salary Chf. Judge, $14,200; Asso. Judges, $13,700 each.

Chf. Judge—Frank H. Hiscock, Syracuse, term exp. Dec. 31, 1926.

Asso. Judges—Emory A. Chase, Catskill, Dec. 31, 1924; John W. Hogan, Syracuse, Dec. 31, 1923; Cuthbert W. Pound, Lockport, term exp. Dec. 31, 1930; Benj. N. Cardoso, N. Y. C., term exp. Dec. 31, 1931; Chester B. McLaughlin, Pt. Henry, term exp. Dec. 31, 1926; Frederick E. Crane, Bkln., Dec. 31, 1934.

Asso. Judge (Sup. Court Justice temporarily designated by Gov.)—William S. Andrews.

Clk., R. M. Barber, Albany, $6,000; Dep. Clk., Wm. J. Armstrong, Albany, $4,500; Remitting Clk., John Ludden, Troy, $3,300; Certificate Clk., Rufus Kimball, Albany, $2,500; Chancery Clerk, Harry B. Caso, Albany, $2,400; Consultation Clk., A. S. Brolley, Albany, $4,500.

SUPREME COURT.

Composed of 107 justices. The State is divided into 9 judicial dists. and into 4 judicial depts. 22 of the Sup. Court Justices are assigned by the Gov. to Appellate Div.

1st Dist.—City and County of New York. (For Justices see N. Y. Co. Govt.)

2d Dist.—Richmond, Nassau, Suffolk, Kings and Queens Counties. (For Justices see Kings Co. Govt.)

3d Dist.—Columbia, Rensselaer, Sullivan, Ulster, Albany, Greene and Schoharie Cos. Justices and expiration of terms—A. V. S. Cochrane, Hudson, Dec. 31, 1928; W. O. Howard, Troy, Dec. 31, 1930; E. A. Chase, Catskill, Dec. 31, 1924; Wm. P. Rudd, Albany, Dec. 31, 1921; G. D. B. Hasbrouck, Kingston, Dec. 31, 1926; Chas. E. Nichols, Jefferson, Dec. 31, 1930; Harold J. Hinman, Albany, Dec. 31, 1932.

4th Dist.—Warren, Saratoga, St. Lawrence, Washington, Essex, Franklin, Clinton, Montgomery, Hamilton, Fulton and Schenectady Cos. Justices and expiration of terms—H. V. Borst, Amsterdam, Dec. 31, 1927; J. M. Kellogg, Ogdensburg, Dec. 31, 1921; H. T. Kellogg, Plattsburg, Dec. 31, 1931; C. C. Van Kirk, Greenwich, Dec. 31, 1932; James McPhillips, Glens Falls, Dec. 31, 1921; E. C. Whitmyer, Schenectady, Dec. 31, 1925.

5th Dist.—Onondaga, Jefferson, Oneida, Oswego, Herkimer and Lewis Cos. Justices and expiration of terms—W. M. Ross, Syracuse, Dec. 31, 1920; I. R. Devendorf, Herkimer, Dec. 31, 1926; E. S. K. Merrell, Lowville, Dec. 31, 1923; I. G. Hubbs, Pulaski, Dec. 31, 1925; L. C. Crouch, Syracuse, Dec. 31, 1927; Wm. S. Andrews, Syracuse, Dec. 31, 1927; F. M. Calder, Utica, Dec. 31, 1931; J. L. Cherrey, Syracuse, Dec. 31, 1931; E. B. Alverson, Dexter, Dec. 31, 1931

6th Dist.—Otsego, Delaware, Madison, Chenango, Tompkins, Broome, Chemung, Schuyler, Tioga and Cortland Cos. Justices and expiration of terms—W. L. Smith, Elmira, Dec. 31, 1926; R. C. Davis, Cortland, Dec. 31, 1929; Geo. McCann, Elmira, Dec. 31, 1927; Theodore R. Tuthill, Binghamton, Dec. 31, 1933; M. H. Kiley, Cazenovia, Dec. 31, 1926; A. L. Kellogg, Oneonta, Dec. 31, 1930.

7th Dist.—Livingston, Ontario, Wayne, Yates, Steuben, Seneca, Cayuga, Monroe Cos. Justices and expiration of terms—A. P. Rich, Auburn, Dec. 31, 1928; J. B. M. Stephens, Rochester, Dec. 31, 1927; Benjamin B. Cunningham, Rochester, Dec. 31, 1933; W. W. Clark, Wayland, Dec. 31, 1928; S. N. Sawyer, Palmyra, Dec. 31, 1921; R. J. Thompson, Canandaigua, Dec. 31, 1930; A. J. Rodenbeck, Rochester, Dec. 31, 1930.

8th Dist.—Erie, Chautauqua, Cattaraugus, Orleans, Niagara, Genesee, Allegany and Wyoming Cos. Justices and expiration of terms—H. L. Taylor, Dec. 31, 1927; F. W. Kruse, Olean, Dec. 31, 1922; J. S. Lambert, Fredonia, Dec. 31, 1921; L. H. Marcus, Buffalo, Dec. 31, 1933; Alonzo G. Hinkley, Buffalo, Dec. 31, 1933; C. H. Brown, Belmont, Dec. 31, 1928; C. B. Wheeler, Buffalo, Dec. 31, 1921; F. C. Laughlin, Buffalo, Dec. 31, 1923; C. A. Pooley; Buffalo, Dec. 31, 1924; John Woodward, Buffalo, Dec. 31, 1924; W. C. Dudley, Buffalo, Dec. 31, 1930; G. W. Cole, Salamanca, Dec. 31, 1928; Chas. B. Sears, Buffalo, Dec. 31, 1931; G. E. Pierce, Buffalo, Dec. 31, 1933.

9th Dist.—Westchester, Putnam, Dutchess, Orange and Rockland Cos. Justices and expiration of terms—I. N. Mills, Mt. Vernon, Dec. 31, 1921; A. S. Tompkins, Nyack, Dec. 31, 1934; Joseph Morschauser, Poughkeepsie, Dec. 31, 1933; M. J. Keogh, New Rochelle, Dec. 31, 1922; Wm. P. Platt, White Plains, Dec. 31, 1928; J. A. Young, New Rochelle, Dec. 31, 1929; A. H. F. Seeger, Newburgh, Dec. 31, 1929.

APPELLATE DIVISION.

1st Dept.—County of New York. Justices and expiration of designation—J. P. Clarke, Pres. (1st Dist.), Dec. 31, 1926; V. J. Dowling (1st Dist.), Dec. 31, 1924; E. S. K. Merrell (5th Dist.), Dec. 31, 1923; F. C. Laughlin (8th Dist.), Dec. 31, 1923; A. R. Page (1st Dist.), Feb. 3, 1921; W. L. Smith (6th Dist.), Dec. 31, 1922; Eugene A. Philbin (1st Dist.), May 5, 1924; Samuel Greenbaum (1st Dist.), Dec. 31, 1924.

2d Dept.—Kings, Queens, Richmond, Nassau, Suffolk, Rockland, Westchester, Orange, Dutchess and Putnam Cos. Justices and expiration of designations—A. F. Jenks, Pres. (2d Dist.), Dec. 31, 1923; A. E. Blackmar (2d Dist.), Dec. 31, 1922; A. P. Rich (7th Dist.), Aug. 10, 1922; Harrington Putnam (2d Dist.), Dec. 31, 1921; I. N. Mills (9th Dist.), Dec. 31, 1920; Wm. J. Kelly (2d Dist.), W. H. Jaycox (2d Dist.), temp. designations.

3d Dept.—Columbia, Rensselaer, Sullivan, Ulster, Albany, Greene, Schoharie, Warren, Saratoga, St. Lawrence, Washington, Essex, Franklin, Clinton, Montgomery, Hamilton, Fulton, Schenectady, Otsego, Delaware, Madison, Chenango, Tompkins, Broome, Chemung, Schuyler, Tioga and Cortland Cos. Justices and expiration of designations—J. M. Kellogg, Pres. (4th Dist.), Dec. 31, 1921; Jno. Woodward (8th Dist.), March 1, 1923; A. V. S. Cochrane (3d Dist.), Jan. 1, 1926; H. T. Kellogg (4th Dist.), Jan. 1, 1923; M. H. Kiley (6th Dist.), Jan. 1, 1926.

4th Dept.—Onondaga, Jefferson, Oneida, Oswego, Herkimer, Lewis, Livingston, Ontario, Wayne, Yates, Steuben, Seneca, Cayuga, Monroe, Erie, Chautauqua, Cattaraugus, Orleans, Niagara, Genesee, Allegany and Wyoming Cos. Justices and expiration of designations—F. W. Kruse, Pres. (8th Dist.), Dec. 31, 1922; Wm. W. Clark (7th Dist.), Dec. 31, 1926; J. S. Lambert (8th Dist.), Dec. 31, 1923; R. L. Davis (6th Dist.), Jan. 1, 1926; I. G. Hubbs (5th Dist.), May 20, 1923.

COURT REPORTERS.

Sup. Court, Austin B. Griffin; State, J. N. Fiero, each, $5,000; Miscellaneous, Wm. V. R. Irving, $4,500, and $500 for publishing Dept. reports.

IRISH HOME RULE BILL.

The Irish Home Rule Bill, as slightly modified by the House of Lords, was adopted by the House of Commons on Dec. 21, 1920. Under the bill two self-governing parliaments are established, one for Northeast Ulster at Belfast and the other for the rest of Ireland at Dublin. A Federal Council elected in equal parts by the two legislatures forms a connecting link.

The demand for a separate parliament for Ireland was first advanced at Westminster by an Irish party under the leadership of Isaac Butt (born 1813, died 1879), who was succeeded by Charles Stewart Parnell (born 1846, died 1891). After many failures to pass a bill through both Houses of Parliament, a Home Rule Bill was eventually placed on the Statute Book in 1914, with a suspensory clause for the duration of the war. In the later stages of the war, however, the extreme party of the Irish politicians developed their organization under the name of Sinn Fein ("Ourselves Alone") and demanded complete severance from Great Britain and the recognition of an Irish Republic. Various efforts have been made by the Cabinet to arrive at a solution of the Irish problem and the Home Rule Bill now on the Statute Book is in lieu of the 1914 bill.

According to statistics prepared by the Collector of Internal Revenue, patrons of the theaters in Manhattan alone paid a tax amounting to $783,891.42 during the month of January, 1920, representing a sum of nearly $8,000,000 spent in theater tickets.

NEW YORK STATE LEGISLATURE.

SENATE.

Senators are elected every 2 years (even years); salary, $1,500, and mileage.

Jeremiah Wood, Lieut.-Gov. and Pres. of Senate, Albany. Home P. O., Lynbrook.

Clayton R. Lusk, Cortland, Pres. Pro Tem. E. A. Fay, Potsdam, Clerk, $3,000.

QUEENS.

1. *G. L. Thompson, R., Kings Park.
2. *J. L. Karle, R., Glendale.
3. *P. J. McGarry, D., 71 Greenpoint av., L. I. C.

KINGS.

4. M. S. Harris, R., 1179 51st.
5. *D. F. Farrell, D., 378 17th.
6. W. T. Simpson, R., 523 6th.
7. *C. C. Lockwood, R., 954 Greene av.
8. *A. W. Burlingame, Jr., R., 391 Fulton.
9. G. M. Reischmann, R., 250 Eldert.
10. *J. F. Twomey, D., 151 Java.
11. A. L. Katlin, R., 175 Hewes.

MANHATTAN.

12. *J. J. Walker, D., 6 St. Lukes pl.
13. *J. J. Boylan, D., 418 W. 51st.
14. *Bernard Downing, D., 195 Monroe.
15. Nathan Straus, Jr., D., 33 W. 42d.
16. M. G. McCue, D., 734 3d av.
17. S. M. Meyer, R., 20 Exchange pl.
18. *S. A. Cotillo, D., 235 E. 116th.
19. William Duggan, R., 61 E. 21st.
20. W. V. Tolbert, R., 90 Pinehurst av.

BRONX.

21. *H. G. Schackno, D., 360 E. 166th.
22. Edmund Seidel, Soc., 2066 Mohegan av., Bronx.
23. G. H. Taylor, R., 95 Brandt pl., Bronx.

RICHMOND.

24. C. E. Smith, R., Stapleton.

STATE.

25. *G. T. Burling, R., White Plains.
26. H. S. Duell, R., Yonkers.
27. *C. H. Baumes, R., Newburgh.
28. *J. E. Towner, R., Towners.
29. *C. W. Walton, R., Kingston.
30. F. L. Wiswall, R., Watervliet.
31. F. E. Draper, R., Troy.
32. F. W. Kavanaugh, R., Waterford.
33. *M. Y. Ferris, R., Ticonderoga.
34. W. T. Thayer, R., Chateaugay.
35. T. D. Robinson, R., Mohawk.
36. *F. M. Davenport, R., Clinton.
37. *F. B. Pitcher, R., Watertown.
38. G. R. Fearon, R., Syracuse.
39. A. J. Bloomfield, R., Richfield Springs.
40. *C. R. Lusk, R., Cortland.
41. *Seymour Lowman, R., Elmira.
42. *C. J. Hewitt, R., Locke.
43. *W. A. Carson, R., Rushville.
44. *John Knight, R., Arcade.
45. *J. L. Whitley, R., Rochester.
46. J. B. Mullan, R., Rochester.
47. W. W. Campbell, R., Lockport.
48. *Parton Swift, R., Buffalo.
49. W. E. Martin, R., Buffalo.
50. *L. W. H. Gibbs, R., Buffalo.
51. D. H. Ames, R., Franklinville.

RECAPITULATION.

Republicans	40
Democrats	10
Socialist	1

*Re-elected.

ASSEMBLY.

Assemblymen are elected every year; salary, $1,500 per year and mileage.

H. E. Machold, Ellisburg, Speaker; F. W. Hammond, Syracuse, Clerk, $3,000.

ALBANY—1, *E. C. Campbell, R., Albany; 2, J. T. Merrigan, D., Albany; 3, J. M. Gaffers, R., Cohoes, R. F. D.

ALLEGANY—*W. Duke, Jr., R., Wellsville.

BRONX—1, *A. H. Henderson, D., 304 E. 162d; 2, *E. J. Flynn, D., 529 Courtlandt av.; 3, *Benjamin Antin, D., 920 Ave. St. John; 4, *Samuel Orr, Soc., 833 E. 167th; 5, William Lyman, D., 926 Southern blvd.; 6, *T. J. McDonald, D., 876 E. 224th; 7, *J. V. McKee, D., 870 E. 175th; 8, E. J. Walsh, D., 2384 Tiebout av.

BROOME—1, *E. B. Jenks, R., Whitney Point; 2, *F. E. Whitcomb, R., Union.

CATTARAUGUS—L. G. Kirkland, R., Randolph.

CAYUGA—*L. F. Hager, R., Victory, R. F. D., Red Creek.

CHAUTAUQUA—1, J. S. Wright, R., Falconer; 2, *J. A. McGinnies, R., Ripley.

CHEMUNG—*J. J. Richford, R., Elmira.

CHENANGO—*Bert Lord, R., Afton.

CLINTON—*C. M. Harrington, R., Plattsburg.

COLUMBIA—G. H. Finch, R., Claverack.

CORTLAND—*Irving F. Rice, R., Cortland.

DELAWARE—*L. R. Long, R., New Kingston.

DUTCHESS—1, *Griswold Webb, R., Clinton Corners; 2, *F. L. Gardner, R., Poughkeepsie.

ERIE—1, *G. E. D. Brady, R., Buffalo; 2, *J. W. Slacer, R., Buffalo; 3, *August Seelbach, R., Buffalo; 4, *A. T. Beasley, D., Buffalo; 5, *A. B. Borkowski, R., Buffalo; 6, *G. H. Rowe, R., Buffalo; 7, *H. A. Zimmerman, R., Buffalo; 8, *N. W. Cheney, R., Eden.

ESSEX—F. L. Porter, R., Crown Point.

FRANKLIN—A. H. Ellsworth, R., Fort Covington.

FULTON-HAMILTON—*E. Hutchinson, R., Green Lake.

GENESEE—*C. P. Miller, R., South Byron.

GREENE—F. G. Jacobs, R., South Cairo.

HERKIMER—J. A. Evans, R., Little Falls.

JEFFERSON—*H. E. Machold, R., Ellisburg.

KINGS—1, J. A. Warren, R., 173 Joralemon; 2, *J. J. Mullen, R., 1197 E. 19th; 3, *F. J. Taylor, D., 47 Wolcott; 4, P. A. McArdle, D., 559 Bedford av.; 5, *J. H. Caulfield, Jr., R., 872 Madison; 6, J. R. Crews, R., 256 Hart; 7, J. J. Kelly, D., 5516 4th av.; 8, *M. J. Reilly, D., 452 Baltic; 9, *J. T. Carroll, R., 735 50th; 10, *L. V. Doherty, R., 161 Remsen; 11, *J. F. Bly, R., 627 Prospect pl.; 12, J. G. Moore, R., 532 5th; 13, J. J. Wackerman, D., 294 Maujer; 14, Henry Jager, Soc., 153 S. 2d; 15, *J. J. McLaughlin, D., 319 Eckford; 16, L. G. Moses, R., 1958 67th; 17, *F. A. Wells, R., 215 Montague; 18, *Theodore Stitt, R., 966 St. Marks av.; 19, F. X. Giaccone, R., 149 Wilson av.; 21, W. J. O. Gempler, R., 711 Knickerbocker av.; 21, W. F. Clayton, R., 224 E. 16th; 22, L. J. Druss, R., 282 Jerome; 23, *C. Solomon, Soc., 601 Howard av.

LEWIS—M. B. Moran, R., Lowville.

LIVINGSTON—*G. F. Wheelock, R., Leicester.

MADISON—J. A. Brooks, R., Cazenovia.

MONROE—1, *J. A. Harris, R., East Rochester, R. F. D. No. 2; 2, *S. L. Adler, R., Rochester; 3, *H. B. Crowley, R., Rochester; 4, G. L. Lewis, R., Barnard; 5, *F. W. Judson, R., Coldwater.

MONTGOMERY—S. W. McCleary, R., Amsterdam.

NASSAU—1, *T. A. McWhinney, R., Lawrence; 2, *T. Roosevelt, R., Oyster Bay.

NEW YORK—1, *P. J. Hamill, D., 585 Broome; 2, F. R. Galgano, D., 42 Kenmare; 3, *T. F. Burchill, D., 347 W. 21st; 4, *Samuel Dickstein, D., 304 E. B'way; 5, *C. D. Donohue, D., 140 Nassau; 6, *S. Ullman, R., 268 E. 7th; 7, *N. B. Fox, R., 150 Nassau; 8, M. D. Reiss, R., 23 7th; 9, E. R. Rayher, R., 150 W. 95th; 10, Bernard Aronson, R., 128 W. 11th; 11, F. H. Nichols, R., 550 W. 113th; 12, J. J. O'Connor, D., 55 Liberty; 13, *R. B. Wallace, R., 351 St. Nicholas av.; 14, F. L. Hackenburg, D., 261 B'way; 15, *Joseph Steinberg, R., 320 B'way; 16, *Maurice Bloch, D., 407 E. 88th; 17, N. Lieberman, R., 51 Chambers; 18, *O. M. Kiernan, D., 163 E. 89th; 19, *Marguerite L. Smith, R., 21 W. 122d; 20, M. G. Di Pirro, R., 311 E. 121st; 21, *J. C. Hawkins, R., 228 W. 137th; 22, M. E. Reiburn, D., 665 W. 160th; 23, *G. N. Jesse, R., 621 W. 179th.

NIAGARA—1, *D. E. Jeffery, R., Lockport; 2, *N. V. V. Franchot, 2d, R., Niagara Falls.

ONEIDA—1, *H. W. Booth, R., Utica; 2, *L. M. Martin, R., Clinton; 3, *C. J. Williams, R., Remsen.

ONONDAGA—1, *M. J. Soule, R., Euclid; 2, *G. J. Chamberlin, R., Syracuse; 3, T. K. Smith, R., Syracuse.

ONTARIO—C. C. Sackett, R., Canandaigua.

ORANGE—1, *A E. Brundage, R., Newburgh; 2, *C. L. Mead, R., Middletown.

ORLEANS—*F. H. Lattin, R., Albion.

OSWEGO—E. A. Barnes, R., Oswego.

OTSEGO—J. C. Smith, R., Oneonta.

PUTNAM—J. R. Yale, R., Brewster.

QUEENS—1, *P. A. Leininger, D., 640 Academy, L. I. City; 2, *Bernhard Schwab, D., Ridgewood; 3, *E. J. Neary, R., East Elmhurst; 4, *N. M. Pette, R., Jamaica; 5, *R. Halpern, R., Richmond Hill; 6, *Henry Baum, R., Woodhaven.

RENSSELAER—1, *H. C. Morrissey, R., Troy; 2, *A. Cowee, R., Berlin.

RICHMOND—1, *T. F. Cosgrove, D., New Brighton; 2, E. V. Frerichs, R., Tottenville, S. I.

ROCKLAND—*G. H. Peck, R., West Haverstraw.

*Re-elected.

NEW YORK STATE LEGISLATURE—ASSEMBLY—*Continued.*

ST. LAWRENCE—1, *F. L. Seaker, R., Gouverneur; 2, *E. A. Everett, R., Potsdam.
SARATOGA—*C. C. Smith, R., Saratoga Springs.
SCHENECTADY—1, *H. E. Blodgett, R., Schenectady; 2, W. W. Campbell, R., Schenectady.
SCHOHARIE—H. M. Greenwald, R., Cobleskill.
SCHUYLER—*C. W. Hausner, R., Montour Falls.
SENECA—*G. A. Dobson, R., Seneca Falls.
STEUBEN—1, *E. E. Cole, R., Bath; 2, D. C. Hunter, R., Canisteo.
SUFFOLK—1, *J. G. Downs, R., Cutchogue; 2, Paul Bailey, R., Amityville.
SULLIVAN—J. G. Gray, R., Liberty.
TIOGA—*D. P. Witter, R., Berkshire.
TOMPKINS—*Casper Fenner, R., Lake Ridge via Ludlowville.
ULSTER—*S. B. Van Wagenen, R., Station R, Kingston.

*Re-elected.

WARREN—*Stewart MacFarland, R., Glens Falls.
WASHINGTON—H. A. Bartholomew, R., Whitehall, R. F. D. No. 1.
WAYNE—*C. H. Betts, R., Lyons.
WESTCHESTER—1, *T. Channing Moore, R., Bronxville; 2, *W. W. Westall, R., White Plains; 3, S. C. Mastick, R., Pleasantville; 4, *Mitchell Trahan, R., Yonkers; 5, *George Blakely, R., Yonkers.
WYOMING—*B. P. Gage, R., Warsaw.
YATES—*J. M. Lown, R., Penn Yan.

RECAPITULATION.

Republicans	119
Democrats	28
Socialists	3
Total	150

POLITICAL CALENDAR, 1921.

(Subject to changes by the Legislature of 1921.)

Primary Petitions.

To designate candidates, petitions must contain 3% of the enrolled voters of party in political subdivision, but need not exceed the number mentioned below, namely:

2,000 signatures for candidates to be voted by all voters of State.

1,500 signatures for Justice of Supreme Court, Judge of Court of General Sessions, Judge of City Court, N. Y. C., or any other office voted for by all the voters in a city of over 1,000,000 inhabitants.

1,000 signatures for any office to be filled by all the voters of any other city of the first class or of any county or borough containing more than 250,000 inhabitants.

500 signatures for any office in a county or borough containing more than 25,000 and not more than 250,000 inhabitants, or city of second class or any Congressional or Senatorial district.

250 signatures for any office to be filled by all the voters of any other county or any city of the third class or of any Assembly district.

JULY 5—First day for signing petition.

AUG. 16 to AUG. 23—Dates for filing designating petitions.

SEPT. 2—Last day to decline designation.

SEPT. 6—Last day to fill vacancy after declination.

SEPT. 8—Certification by Secretary of State to Custodian of Primary Records of designations filed in his office.

SEPT. 20—Fall primary. Hours for voting in New York City, 3 P.M. to 9 P.M. Hours for voting outside New York City, 7 A.M. to 9 P.M.

SEPT. 26—Last day for Custodian of Primary Records to certify result of election to Secretary of State. Custodian must also furnish to Secretary of State, on same date, names and addresses of nominees of various parties for Justice of Supreme Court, Representative in Congress, State Senator and Member of Assembly, where original designations were not filed with said Secretary of State.

Town Nominations.

OCT. 4 to 11—Dates for filing party nominations.

OCT. 15—Last day to decline party nominations.

OCT. 18—Last day to fill vacancy in party nominations.

OCT. 4 to 18—Dates for filing independent nominations.

OCT. 22—Last day to decline independent nominations.

OCT. 25—Last day to fill vacancy in independent nominations.

Independent Nominations.

To nominate independently signatures must be obtained to the number of:

12,000 for State-wide offices, with at least 50 from each county (Fulton and Hamilton considered as one).

5% of total vote for Governor in any political subdivision, except that

3,000 may nominate a candidate for any political subdivision.

1,500 may nominate a candidate for a borough or county office.

SEPT. 27 to OCT. 4—Dates for filing independent nominations.

OCT. 10—Last day to decline independent nomination.

OCT. 14—Last day to fill vacancy of independent nominations.

Board of Elections or County Clerk should immediately certify list of nominations together with address of nominees of all parties to Secretary of State.

Registration.

New York City—Personal Registration.

OCT. 10, 11, 12, 13, 14—5 P.M. to 10:30 P.M.
OCT. 15—7 A.M. to 10.30 P.M.

Cities and Villages of 5,000 or More Inhabitants (except N. Y. C.)

Personal Registration.

OCT. 14, 15—7 A.M. to 10 P.M.
OCT. 21, 22—7 A.M. to 10 P.M.

Outside of Cities and Villages of 5,000 or More Inhabitants.

Non-Personal Registration.

OCT. 15, 22—7 A.M. to 10 P.M.

Nov. 8, General Election.

Polls open 6 A.M. and close 6 P.M.

Statements under Corrupt Practices Act and Penal Law.

NOV. 18—Last day to file candidates' expense statements. (Penal Law, §776.)

NOV. 28—Last day to file committee statements of expense.

Note—Candidates should file statements in accordance with the provisions of Sec. 776 of Penal Law as follows: Where district is greater than a county, except districts in New York City, with Secretary of State. In New York City candidates should file with Commissioner of Elections. Candidates for town, village or city offices should file with town, village and city clerks, respectively, unless there is no city clerk, then it should be filed with the Clerk of the Common Council.

All committee statements of expense should be filed with the Secretary of State.

Officers to be Voted for at the General Election, Nov. 8, 1921.

THROUGHOUT THE STATE, MEMBERS OF ASSEMBLY.

CITY OF NEW YORK—Mayor, Comptroller, Pres. Board of Aldermen, Pres. of the Boroughs.

MANHATTAN—Sheriff, District Attorney, County Clerk, Register, Judge City Court, 2 Judges Court of Sessions.

BRONX—District Attorney, Register, Sheriff.

BROOKLYN—Two County Judges, Sheriff, Register.

RICHMOND—Sheriff.

QUEENS—County Judge.

ONE JUDGE, SUPREME COURT, 2d Judicial Dist. (Kings, Queens, Richmond, Nassau and Suffolk Counties).

BATTLE OF L. I. MONUMENT.

A monument was unveiled at Greenwood Cemetery on Aug. 27, 1920, as a memorial to the heroes who took part in the Battle of Long Island. The monument, known as the Altar of Liberty, is the gift of Charles H. Higgins and is a heroic bronze figure of Minerva standing beside an altar of granite, the four sides of which are decorated with bronze plates carrying historical and commemorative inscriptions. The statue is the work of a Brooklyn sculptor, F. Wellington Ruckstull.

MILITIA OF NEW YORK STATE

NEW YORK GUARD.

The N. Y. Guard is commanded, under the orders of the Governor, by Maj. Gen. John F. O'Ryan, with hdqtrs. at Room 829, Mncpl. Bldg., N. Y. C., and consists of 1 Signal Batl., 1 Regt. Engrs., 1 Batl. Engrs., 3 Regts. F. A., 3 Regts. Coast Defense Command, 12 Regts. Inf., 1 Sanitary Train, 4 Field Hospitals, 3 Ambulance Cos., 1 Motor Machine Gun Batl., 1 Regt. Cav., 1 Squadron Cav.

Commander-in-Chief, Nathan L. Miller, Albany, N. Y. Staff of the Governor—Brig. Gen. J. Leslie Kincaid, The Adj. Gen. of the State; Chief of Staff, Major Ranulf Compton, Military Sec. to the Governor.

Aides, Detailed—Commodore Louis M. Josepthal, N. Y. Naval Militia; Col. Rodman Wanamaker, Inf., N. Y. G.; Col. H. K. Bird, Inf., N. Y. N. G.; Lt. Col. J. T. Loree, Q M. C., N. Y. G.; Lt. Col. H. J. Cookingham, Reserve List; Lt. Col. G. G. Shepard, Reserve List; Lt. Col. H. C. Wilder, Reserve List; Maj. R. Guggenheim, Reserve List; Major B. A. Flood, Reserve List; Capt. R. J. Ryan, 3d Inf., N. Y. N. G.; Capt. C. J. Mangan, 1st Field Art., N. Y. N. G.; 2d Lt. Cornelius Vanderbilt, Jr., Reserve List.

Office of the Adjutant General of the State—158 State, Albany; telephone Main 5456 and 5457. Brig. Gen. J. Leslie Kincaid, the Adjt. Gen. of the State; Lt. Col. Edward J. Westcott, Asst. Adjt. Gen.; Comm. L. M. Josephthal, Asst. to the Adjt. Gen.; Maj. B. H. Mull, Dir. Finance Bureau; C. W. Abrams, Dir. Personnel Bureau.

State Arsenal, N. Y. C.—463 7th av.; tel., Greely 354. Col. J. W. Myers, Quartermaster Corps, N. G. N. Y., Asst. Adj., Gen. officer in charge; U. S. Property and Disbursing Officer.

Militia Council—The Comd. Gen., Div., ex-officio, The Adj. Gen. of the State, ex-officio; The Comd. Officer, Naval Militia, ex-officio; Ch. of the Military Comm. of the Senate and Assembly, ex-officio.

Armory Commission—Col. F. W. Ward, Sec.; Capt. J. A. Coffey, Asst. Sec., 158 State, Albany. tel. Main 663.

New York Guard—Hdqtrs., Div., N. Y. G. 829 Mncpl. Bldg., N. Y. C.; tel. Worth 8673; Maj. Gen. J. F. O'Ryan, Comdg.

Staff—Col. F. W. Ward, Chief of Staff; Lt. Col. Edward Olmstead, Asst. Chf. of Staff; Lt. Col. W. T. Starr, Asst. Chf. of Staff; Major W. R. Wright, Asst. Chf. of Staff; Lt. Col. Ed. McLeer, Jr., Div. Adjt.; Maj. A. L. Reagan, Asst. Div. Adjt.; Capt. J. A. Walsh, Asst. Div. Adjt.; Col. J. F. Daniell, A. G. Dept.; Col. T. F. Donovan, A. G. Dept.; Lt. Col. G. G. Hollander, A. G. Dept.; Capt. L. F. Knust, A. G. Dept.; Lt. Col. H. T. Kingsbury, Judge Adv., Gen. Dept.; Col. W. I. Taylor, Coast Defense Officer; Lt. Col. S. Whitney, Machine Gun Office Div.; Lt. Col. R. W. Maloney, Signal Officer; Lt. Col. J. M. Wainwright, Insp. Gen. Dept.; Lt. Col. J. T. Loree, Q. M. C., Qmr.; Lt. Col. H. S. Sternberger, Q. M. C.; Lt. Col. L. Collis, Q. M. C., Asst. Qmr.; Lt. Col. P. E. Nagle, Q. M. C.; Maj. R. T. Moniz, Asst. Div. Qmr.; Maj. H. W. Tayler, Q. M. C.; Capt. J. I. McWilliams, Q. M. R., Div.; Capt. G. W. Peppard, Qmr. Corps, Div.; First Lt. C. L. Bubbs, Asst. to Qmr., Div.; Capt. J. H. Florsheimer, Qmr. Corps, Div.; Lt. Col. J. J. Daly, Div. Ord. Officer; 1st Lt. J. W. Heasly, Jr., Q. M. C.; Capt. J. M. Sabater, Q. M. C.; Maj. T. H. Lewis, Ord. Dept., Div.; Maj. J. A. S. Mundy, Ord. Dept.; Col. W. C. Montgomery, M. C., Surgeon; Lt. Col. L. A. Salisbury, Div. Surgeon; Lt. Col. J. F. Dunseith, M. C. (S. C. and D.); Capt. R. M. Ballantyne, Medical Corps; Lt. Col. M. F. Carney, Dental Corps, Div.; Maj. A. N. Towner, Vet. Corps, Div.; Capt. G. B. Gibbons, Aide, F. A., N. Y. G.; Capt. Theodore Crane, Aide, Cavalry, N. Y. G. Strength, 4,448 officers and enlisted men.

Organizations attached—1st Batl. Sig. Corps, 104 E. 34th, N. Y. C.; Maj. J. C. Fox, Comdg.

22d Regt. Engrs., 216 Ft. Washington av., N. Y. C.; Lt. Col. F. E. Humphreys, Comdg.

47th Batl. Engrs., 355 Marcy av., Bkln.; Maj. W. E. Corwin, Comdg.

1st M. G. Batl., 216 Ft. Washington av., N. Y. C.; Maj. J. C. Mansfield, Comdg.

1st Cav., 1579 Bedford av., Bkln., N. Y.; Col. M. D. Bryant, Comdg.

8th Coast Defense Command, 29 West Kingsbridge rd., N. Y. C.; Col. E. F. Austin, Comdg.

9th Coast Defense Command, 125 W. 14th, N. Y. C.; Col. J. J. Byrne, Comdg.

13th Coast Defence Command, 357 Sumner av., Bkln., N. Y.; Col. Sydney Grant, Comdg.

Sanitary Train, 56 W. 66th, N. Y. C.; Lt. Col. R. P. Wadhams, Comdg.

1st Field Hosp., 56 W. 66th, N. Y. C.; Maj. H. C. Russell, Comdg.

2d Field Hosp., Armory, Elk and Lark, Albany, N. Y.; Maj. J. F. Rooney, Comdg.

3d Field Hosp., 355 Marcy av., Bkln., N. Y.; Maj. W. C. Griswold, Comdg.

4th Field Hosp., Syracuse, N. Y.; Maj. H. B. Pritchard, Comdg.

2d Ambulance Co., 900 Main, East Rochester, N. Y.; Capt. W. D. Edwards, Comdg.

3d Ambulance Co., 56 W. 66th, N. Y. C.; Capt. M. W. Barnum, Comdg.

4th Ambulance Co., State Armory, Syracuse, N. Y.; Capt. W. N. Street, Comdg.

Squadron A., Cav., 1339-1349 Madison av., N. Y. C.; Maj. N. H. Egleston, Comdg.

52D FIELD ARTILLERY BRIGADE—171 Clermont av., Bkln.; Brig. Gen. D. C. Wild, Jr.; Maj. F. de Figaniere, Adjt.; 1st Lt. F. A. Willis, Aide; 2d Lt. H. Rathbone, Aide. Strength, 1,713 officers and men.

Organizations attached—1st F. A., 1988 B'way, N. Y. C.; Col. J. T. Delaney.

2d F. A., 171 Clermont av., Bkln.; Col. R. W. Marshall.

65th F. A., 29 Masten, Buffalo; Col. L. P. Hubbell.

FIRST BRIGADE—Hdqtrs., 104 E. 34th, N. Y. C.; tel. Murray Hill 8488; Brig. Gen. G. R. Dyer; Maj. G. A. Daly, Adj.; Maj. J. P. Askin, Insp.; Maj. M. F. Loughman, Eng. Officer; Maj. T. C. McDonald, O. O.; Maj. B. H. Mull, Asst. Qmr., Capt. W. W. Barbour, Aide; Capt. L. P. Sauger, Aide. Strength, 4,266 officers and men.

Organizations attached—7th Inf.; Col. W. H. Hayes; Hdqtrs., 643 Park av., N. Y. C.

12th Inf.; Col. N. R. Burr; Hdqrs., 120 W. 62d, N. Y. C.

15th Inf.; Col. W. J. Schieffelin; 2217 7th av., N. Y. C.

69th Inf.; Col. J. Phelan; Hdqrs., 68 Lexington av., N. Y. C.

71st Inf.; Col. J. H. Wells; Hdqrs., 106 E. 34th, N. Y. C.

SECOND BRIGADE—Hdqrs., 1322 Bedford av., Bkln.; tel. Prospect 22; Brig. Gen. James Robb; Maj. C. H. Newman, Adj.; Maj. A. C. Vandiver, Judge Advocate; Maj. C. E. Potts, Ordn. Officer; Maj. L. C. Donovan, Qmr. Strength, 1,877 officers and men.

Organizations attached; 14th Inf.; Hdqrs. at Bkln, N. Y.; Col. Frederick Baldwin, Comdg.

23d Inf.; Hdqtrs. at Bkln., N. Y.; Col. T. Fairservis, Comdg.

THIRD BRIGADE—Hdqrs., 176 State, Albany; tel, Main 1913; Brig. Gen. J. W. Lester, Maj. D. F. Nial, Adj.; Maj. E. J. Wilson, Qtmr.; Maj. G. J. Winslow, Insp.; Maj. Fred. M. Beckwith, Judge Adv.; Maj. Ed. J. Parish, Ordn. Officer. Strength, 3,021 officers and men.

Organizations attached, 1st Inf.; Col. R. A. Egan; Hdqtrs. at Newburgh; Cos. A. C. at White Plains, N. Y., D., Mt. Vernon, N. Y., Cos. E. L. at Newburgh, N. Y., F., Warwick, N. Y., G., Yonkers, N. Y., H., Mount Vernon, N. Y., I., Middletown, N. Y., K., Poughkeepsie, N. Y., M., Kingston, N. Y. Machine Gun Co., Pine Plains.

2d Inf.; Col. R. H. Gillet, Hdqrs. at Troy, N. Y., Cos. A. C. at Troy, B., Cohoes, D., Saranac, Platoon at Plattsburg, E. F., Schenectady, G., Gloversville, H., Amsterdam, I., Whitehall, K., Glens Falls, L., Saratoga Springs, M., Hoosick Falls.

10th Inf.; Col. C. E. Walsh; Hdqrs. at Albany.; Cos. A. B. C. D. at Albany, Catskill, Hudson Oneonta, Oneida, Walton, Utica; (2) Cos. Mohawk, Rome (N. G. Co.).

FOURTH BRIGADE—Hdqtrs., 451 Main, Buffalo; tel., Seneca 1362; Brig. Gen. E. S. Jennings; 1st Lt. F. H. Bloomer, Aide; 1st Lt. C. D. Osborne, Aide; Maj. E. G. Ziegler, Adjt.; Maj. D. J. Cadotte, Judge Adv.; Maj. C. S. Martin, Ordn. Officer; Capt. H. B. Parry, Insp. Strength, 2,868 officers and men.

Organizations attached: 3d Inf.; Col. J. S. Thompson; Hdqtrs. at Syracuse (1) Co.; Rochester (3) Cos.; Geneva, Oswego, Canandaigua, Platoon at Newark, Medina, Ogdensburg: Platoon at Massena, Malone; Platoon at Chateauguay, Watertown; Platoon at Pulaski, Auburn.

4th Batl.; Maj. W. K. Whitley; Hdqtrs. at Elmira, Binghamton (2) Cos.; Corning, Ithaca, Deposit, Owego, Hornell, Elmira.

74th Inf. Col. W. R. Pooley; Hdqtrs. at Buffalo; Buffalo (9) Cos.; Jamestown, Niagara Falls (2) Cos., Olean, Tonawanda.

MILITIA OF NEW YORK STATE—NEW YORK GUARD—*Continued.*

NAVAL MILITIA OF NEW YORK STATE.

The Naval Militia of the State comprises Hdqrs., 1st, 2d, 3d and 4th Battalions and the 1st, 2d, 3d, and 4th Separate Divisions.

The Hdqtrs., Naval Militia, N. Y., is located on board the U. S. S. Granite State, ft. of W. 97th, N. Y. C., and consists of the following officers: Commodore, R. P. Forshew, Commanding; Capt. A. B. Fry, Chief of Staff; Capt. R. L., J. C. MacEvitt, Surgeon; Lieut. Comdr. H. W. York, Ordnance Officer; Lt. Comdr. R. C. Lee, Nav. and Sig. Officer; Lt. Comdr. W. L. Sawyer, Aide; Lt. Comdr. R. R. Riggs; Lt. Comdr. L. W. Hesselman.

The office of Hdqtrs., Naval Militia, N. Y., is located at Room 2203, Mncpl. Bldg., N. Y. C.

The 1st Battalion consists of Hdqtrs., 1 Aeronautic Div., 1 Marine Co. and 10 Divs., one of the latter being a Separate Division. All of the units of the 1st Battalion are located on board the U. S. S. Granite State with the exception of the 7th Separate Div., which is located at New Rochelle. The 1st Battalion is commanded by Comdr. W. B. Wait. Strength, officers and men, 860.

The 2d Battalion consists of Hdqtrs., 9 Divisions, 1 Aeronautic Division and 1 Marine Co., which are located at Armory, ft. of 52d st., Bkln., N. Y., and is commanded by Capt. E. T. Fitzgerald. Strength, officers and men, 1,134.

The 3d Battalion consists of Hdqtrs., 13 Separate Divisions, 1 Aeronautic Section and 2 Marine Companies, and they are located as follows: Hdqtrs., 2d, 6th and 7th Divisions, Rochester, N. Y.; 3d, 5th and 11th, Buffalo, N. Y.; 1st, Dunkirk, N. Y.; 4th, Watertown, N. Y.; 8th, Niagara Falls, N. Y.; 9th, Oswego, N. Y.; 10th, Fulton, N. Y.; 12th, Syracuse, N. Y.; 13th, Ogdensburg, N. Y.; 1st Marine Co., Tonawanda, N. Y.; 2d Marine Co., Rochester, N. Y.

The 3d Batt. is commanded by Comdr. W. J. Graham, Rochester State Ar'y, Rochester, N. Y. Strength, officers and men, 963.

The 4th Batt., commanded by Capt. E. C. DeKay, Room 1234, Mncpl. Bldg., N. Y. C., consists of Hdqtrs., 11 Separate Divisions and 1 Aeronautic Section located as follows: 2d, 5th, 7th and 11th Divs., Staten Island, N. Y.; 9th and 10th, Yonkers, N. Y.; 1st, Peekskill, N. Y.; 3d, Poughkeepsie, N. Y.; 4th, Albany, N. Y.; 6th, Flushing, N. Y.; 8th, Ossining, N Y.; Aeronautic Section, Beacon, N. Y. Strength, officers and men, 1,007.

In addition there are 4 Separate Divisions, which are attached to Hdqtrs., Naval Militia, N. Y. They are located as follows: 1st Separate Div., Port Chester, N. Y.; 2d and 3d Separate Divs., Mount Vernon, N. Y.; 4th Separate Div., Eastchester, N. Y. Strength of the Naval Militia, Officers and men, 4,272.

UNITED STATES MILITARY ACADEMY AT WEST POINT.

Each Senator, Congressional district and Territory, including Porto Rico, Alaska and Hawaii, is entitled to have two cadets at the academy; the District of Columbia, four cadets. There are also eighty-two appointments at large, two of whom are appointed upon the recommendation of the Vice-President, specially conferred by the President of the United States. The law (act of May 4, 1916) authorizes the President to appoint cadets to the United States Military Academy from among enlisted men in the Regular Army and National Guard, the total number not to exceed one hundred and eighty at any one time.

Appointments are usually made one year in advance of date of admission, by the Secretary of War, upon the nomination of the Senator or Representative. These nominations may either be made after competitive examination or given direct, at the option of the Representative. The Representative may nominate two legally qualified second candidates, to be designated first and second alternates. The alternates will receive from the War Department a letter of appointment, and will be examined with the regular appointee, and the better qualified will be admitted to the academy in the event of the failure of the principal to pass the prescribed preliminary examinations. Appointees to the Military Academy must be between seventeen and twenty-two years of age, except in the following case: That during the calendar years 1919, 1920 and 1921 any appointee who has served honorably and faithfully not less than one year in the armed forces of the United States or allied armies in the late war with Germany, and who possesses the other qualifications required by law, may be admitted between the ages of seventeen and twenty-four years; Provided, That whenever any member of the graduating class shall fail to complete the course with his class by reason of sickness, or deficiency in his studies or other cause, such failure shall not operate to delay the admission of his successor. Appointees must be free from any infirmity which may render them unfit for military service, and able to pass, unless a satisfactory certificate is submitted, a careful examination in English grammar, English composition, English literature, algebra through quadratic equations, plane geometry, United States history, and the outlines of general history. The Secretary of War is authorized to permit not exceeding four Filipinos to be designated, one for each class, by the Governor-General of the Philippine Islands, to receive instruction at the United States Military Academy at West Point; Provided, That the Filipinos undergoing instruction shall receive the same pay, allowances and emoluments as are authorized by law for cadets at the Military Academy appointed from the United States, to be paid out of the same appropriations; And provided further, That said Filipinos undergoing instruction, on graduation shall be eligible only to commissions in the Philippine Scouts; serve for eight years, unless sooner discharged.

The course of instruction, which is quite thorough, requires four years; Provided, That any person heretofore nominated in accordance with regulations for appointment to fill a vacancy which would have resulted from the graduation of a cadet during the present year, may be so appointed notwithstanding the retention of such cadet at the academy; Provided further, That any cadet now at the academy may at his option, exercised prior to June 11, 1920, continue at the academy one additional year and postpone thereby his prospective graduation, and cadets not electing so to prolong their course shall be graduated in the years assigned to their respective classes prior to the passage of this Act. The course is largely mathematical and professional. The principal subjects taught are mathematics, English, French, drawing, drill regulations of all arms of the service, natural and experimental philosophy, chemistry, chemical physics, mineralogy, geology, electricity, history, international, constitutional and military law, Spanish, civil and military engineering, art and science of war, and ordnance and gunnery.

From about the middle of June to the end of August cadets live in camp, engaged only in military duties and receiving practical military instruction. Cadets are allowed but one leave of absence during the four years' course, and this is granted at the expiration of the first two years. The pay of a cadet is $1,174.20 per year and with proper economy is sufficient for his support.

Upon graduating, cadets are commissioned as Second Lieutenants in the United States Army. The whole number of cadets graduated from 1802 to 1920, inclusive, has been 6,809. It is virtually absolutely necessary for a person seeking an appointment to apply to his Senator or Member of Congress. The Superintendent is Brig.-Gen. Douglas MacArthur, U. S. A., and the military and academic staff consists of 15 persons. Number of cadets June 15, 1920, was 701.

METROPOLITAN DISTRICT OF NEW YORK.

The population of the Metropolitan District, as given by the Census Bureau, Dept. of Commerce, for 1920, is 8,311,451.

New York City	5,620,048
Nassau County, N. Y.	83,930
Westchester County, N. Y.	344,086
Rockland County, N. Y.	45,548
Bergen County, N. J.	210,688
Essex County, N. J.	651,807
Hudson County, N. J.	629,124
Middlesex County, N. J.	162,334
Passaic County, N. J.	259,148
Union County, N. J.	199,832
Monmouth County, N. J.	104,906
Total population	8,311,451

COURT OF INTERNATIONAL JUSTICE

Following is the text of the draft scheme for the institution of a permanent Court of International Justice adopted by an advisory committee of international jurists at the Hague, June 16-July 24, 1920, and presented to the Council of the League of Nations. On Dec. 13, 1920, the Assembly of the League of Nations adopted the statute for an International Court of Justice, with an amendment eliminating compulsory jurisdiction. The Assembly meets next in Sept., 1921, and if the statute is ratified by a majority of the members of the League the judges will then be elected and the court constituted.

Chapter I.

ORGANIZATION OF THE COURT.

Article 1—A Permanent Court of International Justice, to which parties shall have direct access, is hereby established, in accordance with Article 14 of the Covenant of the League of Nations. This court shall be in addition to the Court of Arbitration organized by the Hague Convention of 1899 and 1907, and to the special tribunals of arbitration to which States are always at liberty to submit their disputes for settlement.

Article 2—The Permanent Court of International Justice shall be composed of a body of independent judges, elected regardless of their nationality, from among persons of high moral character, who possess the qualifications required, in their respective countries, for appointment to the highest judicial offices, or are jurisconsults of recognized competence in international law.

Article 3—The Court shall consist of 15 members: 11 judges and 4 deputy judges. The number of judges and deputy judges may be hereafter increased by the Assembly, upon the proposal of the Council of the League of Nations, to a total of 15 judges and 6 deputy judges.

Article 4—The members of the Court shall be elected by the Assembly and the Council from a list of persons nominated by the national groups in the Court of Arbitration, in accordance with the following provisions:

Article 5—At least three months before the date of the election the Secretary-General of the League of Nations shall address a written request to the members of the Court of Arbitration, belonging to the States mentioned in the Annex to the Covenant or to the States which shall have joined the League subsequently, inviting them to undertake, by national groups, the nomination of persons in a position to accept the duties of a member of the court.

Article 6—Before making these nominations, each national group is hereby recommended to consult its highest court of justice, its legal faculties and schools of law and its national academies and national sections of international academies devoted to the study of law.

Article 7—The Secretary-General of the League of Nations shall prepare a list, in alphabetical order, of all the persons thus nominated. These persons only shall be eligible for appointment, except as provided in Article 12, paragraph 2.

The Secretary-General shall submit this list to the Assembly and to the Council.

Article 8—The Assembly and the Council shall proceed to elect by independent voting first the judges and then the deputy judges.

Article 9—At every election the electors shall bear in mind that not only should all the persons appointed as members of the Court possess the qualifications required, but the whole body also should represent the main forms of civilization and the principal legal systems of the world.

Article 10—Those candidates who obtain an absolute majority of votes in the Assembly and the Council shall be considered as elected.

In the event of more than one candidate of the same nationality being elected by the votes of both the Assembly and the Council, the eldest of these only shall be considered as elected.

Article 11—If, after the first sitting held for the purpose of the election, one or more seats remain to be filled, a second and, if necessary, a third sitting shall take place.

Article 12—If, after the third sitting, one or more seats still remain unfilled, a joint conference, consisting of six members, three appointed by the Assembly and three by the Council, may be formed at any time at the request of either the Assembly or the Council, for the purpose of choosing one name for each seat still vacant, to submit to the Assembly and the Council for their respective acceptance.

If the committee is unanimously agreed upon any person, who fulfills the required conditions, he may be included in its list, even though he was not included in the list of nominations made by the Court of Arbitration.

If the Joint Conference is not successful in procuring an election, those members of the Court, who have already been appointed, shall within a time limit, to be arranged by the Council, proceed to fill the vacant seats by selection from amongst those candidates who have obtained votes either in the Assembly or in the Council.

In the event of an equality of votes amongst the judges, the eldest judge shall have a casting vote.

Article 13—The members of the Court shall be elected for nine years. They may be re-elected. They shall continue to discharge their duties until their places have been filled.

Though replaced, they shall complete any cases which they may have begun.

Article 14—Vacancies which may occur shall be filled by the same method as that laid down for the first election.

A member of the Court elected to replace a member, the period of whose appointment has not expired, will hold the appointment for the remainder of his predecessor's term.

Article 15—Deputy judges shall be called upon to sit in the order laid down in a list.

This list shall be prepared by the Court, having regard first to the order in time of each election and secondly to age.

Article 16—The exercise of any function which belongs to the political direction, national or international, of States, by the members of the Court, during their terms of office, is declared incompatible with their judicial duties.

Any doubt upon this point is settled by the decision of the Court.

Article 17—No member of the Court can act as agent, counsel or advocate in any case of an international nature.

No member may participate in the decision of any case in which he has previously taken an active part, as agent, counsel or advocate for one of the contesting parties, or as a member of a national or international Court, or of a Commission of Inquiry, or in any other capacity.

Any doubt upon this point is settled by the decision of the Court.

Article 18—A member of the Court cannot be dismissed unless, in the unanimous opinion of the other members, he has ceased to fulfill the required conditions.

When this happens a formal notification shall be given to the Secretary-General.

This notification makes the place vacant.

Article 19—The members of the Court, when outside their own country, shall enjoy the privileges and immunities of diplomatic representatives.

Article 20—Every member of the Court shall, before taking up his duties, make a solemn declaration in open Court that he will exercise his powers impartially and conscientiously.

Article 21—The Court shall elect its President and Vice-President for three years; they may be re-elected.

It shall appoint its Registrar.

The duties of Registrar of the Court shall not be considered incompatible with those of Secretary-General of the Permanent Court of Arbitration.

Article 22—The seat of the Court shall be established at The Hague. The President and Registrar shall reside at the seat of the Court.

Article 23—A session shall be held every year. Unless otherwise provided by rules of Court this session shall begin on the 15th of June and shall continue for so long as may be necessary to complete the cases on the list. The President may summon an extraordinary meeting of the Court whenever necessary.

COURT OF INTERNATIONAL JUSTICE—*Continued.*

Article 24—If, for some special reason, a member of the Court considers that he cannot take part in the decision of a particular case, he shall so inform the President.

If, for some special reason, the President considers that one of the members of the Court should not sit on a particular case, he shall give notice to the member concerned.

In the event of the President and the member not agreeing as to the course to be adopted in any such case, the matter shall be settled by the decision of the Court.

Article 25—The full Court shall sit, except when it is expressly provided otherwise. If 11 judges cannot be present, deputy judges shall be called upon to sit, in order to make up this number. If, however, 11 judges are not available, a quorum of 9 judges shall suffice to constitute the Court.

Article 26—The expenses of the Court shall be borne by the League of Nations, in such a manner as shall be decided by the Assembly upon the proposal of the Council.

Article 27—The Court shall frame rules for regulating its procedure. In particular, it shall lay down rules for summary procedure.

Article 28—Judges of the nationality of each contesting party shall retain their right to sit in the case before the Court.

If the Court includes upon the Bench a judge of the nationality of one of the parties only, the other party may select from among the deputy judges a judge of its nationality, if there be one. If there should not be one, the party may choose a judge, preferably from among those persons who have been nominated as candidates by some national group in the Court of Arbitration.

If the Court includes upon the Bench no judges of the nationality of the contesting parties, each of these may proceed to select or choose a judge, as provided in the preceding paragraph.

Should there be several parties in the same interest, they shall, for the purpose of the preceding provisions, be reckoned as one party only.

Judges selected or chosen as laid down in paragraphs 2 and 3 of this article shall fulfill the conditions required by Articles 2, 16, 17, 20, 24 of this statute. They shall take part in the decision on an equal footing with their colleagues.

Article 29—The judge shall receive an annual salary to be determined by the Assembly of the League of Nations upon the proposal of the Council. This salary must not be decreased during the period of a judge's appointment.

The President shall receive a special grant for his period of office, to be fixed in the same way.

Deputy judges shall receive a grant, for the actual performance of their duties, to be fixed in the same way.

Traveling expenses incurred in the performance of their duties shall be refunded to judges and deputy judges who do not reside at the seat of the Court.

Grants due to judges selected or chosen as provided in Article 28 shall be determined in the same way.

The salary of the Registrar shall be decided by the Council upon the proposal of the Court.

A special regulation shall provide for the pensions to which the judges and Registrar shall be entitled.

Article 30—The expenses of the Court shall be borne by the League of Nations in such a manner as shall be decided by the Assembly upon the proposal of the Council.

Chapter II.

COMPETENCE OF THE COURT.

Article 31—The Court shall have jurisdiction to hear and determine suits between States.

Article 32—The Court shall be open of right to the States mentioned in the Annex to the Covenant, and to such others as shall subsequently enter the League of Nations. Other States may have access to it. The conditions under which the Court shall be open of right or accessible to States which are not members of the League of Nations shall be determined by the Council, in accordance with Article 17 of the Covenant.

Article 33—When a dispute has arisen between States, and it has been found impossible to settle it by diplomatic means, and no agreement has been made to choose another jurisdiction, the party complaining may bring the case before the Court. The Court shall, first of all, decide whether the preceding conditions have been complied with; if so, it shall hear and determine the dispute, according to the terms and within the limits of the next article.

Article 34—Between States which are members of the League of Nations, the Court shall have jurisdiction (and this without any special convention giving it jurisdiction) to hear and determine cases of a legal nature, concerning: (a) The interpretation of a treaty; (b) any question of international law; (c) the existence of any fact which, if established, would constitute a breach of an international obligation; (d) the nature or extent of reparation to be made for the breach of an international obligation; (e) the interpretation of a sentence passed by the Court.

The Court shall also take cognizance of all disputes of any kind which may be submitted to it by a general or particular convention between the parties. In the event of a dispute as to whether a certain case comes within any of the categories above mentioned, the matter shall be settled by the decision of the Court.

Article 35—The Court shall, within the limits of its jurisdiction as defined in Article 34, apply in the order as follows:

1. International conventions, whether general or particular, establishing rules expressly recognized by the contesting States
2. International custom, as evidence of a general practice, which is accepted as law.
3. The general principles of law recognized by civilized nations.
4. Judicial decisions and the teachings of the most highly qualified publicists of the various nations, as subsidiary means for the determination of rules of law.

Article 36—The Court shall give an advisory opinion upon any question or dispute of an international nature referred to it by the Council or Assembly. When the Court shall give an opinion on a question of an international nature, which does not refer to any dispute that may have arisen, it shall appoint a special commission of from three to five members. When it shall give an opinion upon a question which forms the subject of an existing dispute, it shall do so under the same conditions as if the case had been actually submitted to it for decision.

Chapter III.

PROCEDURE.

Article 37—The official language of the Court shall be French. The Court may, at the request of the contesting parties, authorize another language to be used before it.

Article 38—A State desiring to have recourse to the Court shall lodge a written application, addressed to the Registrar. The application shall indicate the subject of the dispute and name the contesting parties. The Registrar shall forthwith communicate the application to all concerned. He shall also notify the members of the League of Nations through the Secretary-General.

Article 39—If the dispute arises out of an act which has already taken place or which is imminent, the Court shall have the power to suggest, if it considers that circumstances so require, the provisional measures that should be taken to preserve the respective rights of either party.

Pending the final decision, notice of the measures suggested shall forthwith be given to the parties and the Council.

Article 40—The parties shall be represented by agents.

They may have counsel or advocates to plead before the Court.

Article 41—The procedure shall consist of two parts, written and oral.

Article 42—The written proceedings shall consist of the communication to the judges and to the parties of statements of cases, counter-cases and, if necessary, replies; also all papers and documents in support.

These communications shall be made through the Registrar, in the order and within the time fixed by the Court.

COURT OF INTERNATIONAL JUSTICE—*Continued.*

A certified copy of every document produced by one party shall be communicated to the other party.

Article 43—The oral proceedings shall consist of the hearing by the Court of witnesses, experts, agents, counsel and advocates.

For the service of all notices upon persons other than the agents, counsel and advocates, the Court shall apply direct to the Government of the State upon whose territory the notice has to be served.

The same provision shall apply whenever steps are to be taken to procure evidence on the spot.

Article 44—The proceedings shall be under the direction of the President, or, in his absence, of the Vice-President: if both are absent, the senior judge shall preside.

Article 45—The hearing in Court shall be public, unless the Court, at the written request of one of the parties, accompanied by a statement of his reasons, shall otherwise decide.

Article 46—Minutes shall be made at each hearing and signed by the Registrar and the President.

These minutes shall be the only authentic record.

Article 47—The Court shall make orders for the conduct of the case, shall decide the form and time in which each party must conclude its arguments, and make all arrangements connected with the taking of evidence.

Article 48—The Court may, even before the hearing begins, call upon the agents to procure any document, or to supply to the Court any explanations. Any refusal shall be recorded.

Article 49—The Court may at any time entrust any individual, bureau, commission or other body that it may select with the task of carrying out an inquiry or giving an expert opinion.

Article 50—During the hearing in Court the judges may put any questions considered by them to be necessary, to the witnesses, agents, experts, advocates or counsel. The agents, advocates and counsel shall have the right to ask, through the President, any questions that the Court considers useful.

Article 51—After the Court has received the proofs and evidence within the time specified for the purpose, it may refuse to accept any further oral or written evidence that one party may desire to present, unless the other side consents.

Article 52—Whenever one of the parties shall not appear before the Court, or shall fail to defend his case, the other party may call upon the Court to decide in favor of his claim. The Court must, before doing so, satisfy itself, not only that it has jurisdiction in accordance with Articles 33 and 34, but also that the claim is supported by substantial evidence and well founded in fact and law.

Article 53—When the agents, advocates and counsel, subject to the control of the Court, have presented all the evidence, and taken all other steps that they consider advisable, the President shall declare the case closed.

The Court shall withdraw to consider the judgment.

The deliberations of the Court shall take place in private and remain secret.

Article 54—All questions shall be decided by a majority of the judges present at the hearing. In the event of an equality of votes, the President or his deputy shall have a casting vote.

Article 55—The judgment shall state the reasons on which it is based.

It shall contain the names of the judges who have taken part in the decision.

Article 56—If the judgment given does not represent, wholly or in part, the unanimous opinion of the judges, the dissenting judges shall be entitled to have the fact of their dissent or reservations mentioned in it. But the reasons for their dissent or reservations shall not be expressed in the judgment.

Article 57—The judgment shall be signed by the President and by the Registrar. It shall be read in open court, due notice having been given to the agents.

Article 58—The judgment is final and without appeal. In the event of uncertainty as to the meaning or scope of the judgment, the Court shall construe it upon the request of any party.

Article 59—An application for revision of a judgment can be made only when it is based upon the discovery of some new fact, of such a nature as to be a decisive factor, which fact was, when the judgment was given, unknown to the Court and also to the party claiming revision, always provided that such ignorance was not due to negligence.

The proceedings for revision will be opened by a judgment of the Court expressly recording the existence of the new fact, recognizing that it has such a character as to lay the case open to revision, and declaring the application admissible on this ground. The court may require previous compliance with the terms of the judgment before it admits proceedings in revision. No application for revision may be made after the lapse of five years from the date of the sentence.

Article 60—Should a State consider that it has an interest of a legal nature which may be affected by the decision in the case, it may submit a request to the Court to be permitted to intervene as a third party. It will be for the Court to decide upon this request.

Article 61—Whenever the construction of a convention in which States, other than those concerned in the case, are parties, is in question, the Registrar shall notify all such States forthwith. Every State so notified has the right to intervene in the proceedings; but if it uses this right, the construction given by the judgment will be as binding upon it as upon the original parties to the dispute.

Article 62—Unless otherwise decided by the Court, each party shall bear its own costs.

THE NOBEL PRIZES.

The Nobel Peace Prize for 1920 was conferred on President Wilson of the United States. The only two Americans who have in the past received the Peace Prize were Theodore Roosevelt in 1906 and Elihu Root in 1912. The Nobel Peace Prize carries with it a grant of about $40,000 from the fund left for that purpose by Alfred B. Nobel, the Swedish scientist, and the inventor of dynamite, who died in 1896. The Peace awards have been: 1901, Henri Dunant, Swiss, and Fr. Passy, French; 1902, E. Ducommun and A. Gobat, both Swiss; 1903, W. R. Cremer, English; 1904, The Institution of Internatl. Law, the 1st award, to an institution; 1905, Baroness von Suttner, Austrian; 1906, Pres. Theodore Roosevelt, American; 1907, Ernesto Theodoro Moneta, Italian, and Louis Renault, French; 1908, K. P. Arnoldson, Swede, and M. F. Bajer, Dane; 1909, Baron d'Estournelles de Constant, French, and M. Beernaert, Belgian; 1910, Internatl. Permanent Peace Bureau, Berne; 1911, Prof. T. M. C. Asser, founder of the Inst. de Droit Internatl., Dutch, and Alfred Fried, editor of the Journal Freidens-Warte of Vienna, Austrian; 1912, U. S. Senator Elihu Root, of N. Y., American; 1913, Senator Henri La Fontaine, formerly Pres. of the Permanent Internatl. Peace Bureau at Berne; 1916 and 1917, Internatl. Red Cross Comm. of Geneva. Other Nobel Prizes awarded in 1920 were: For distinction in chemical research, Herr Haber, Germany; in medical science, for the years 1919 and 1920, Dr. Jules Bordet, Belgium, and Prof. August Krogh, Denmark; for physics, Dr. Charles Edouard Guillaume Breteuil, head of the Internatl. Bureau of Weights and Measures; for literature, Knut Hamsum, Norway. Also during the year 1920 Carl Spitteler, Switzerland, was awarded the 1919 prize for literature.

The total expenditures of the United States Peace Commission, from Dec. 1, 1918, to Dec. 4, 1920, amounted to $1,651,191, according to a special message transmitted by President Wilson to the Senate on Dec 8, 1920.

The amount of taxes collected by the Internal Revenue Bureau during the fiscal year 1919-1920 was $5,407,580,251. This is the largest amount of taxes ever collected in the history of the nation.

CITY OF NEW YORK MUNICIPAL GOVERNMENT.

The Govt. of the City of New York has 3 officials elected by the whole city, the Mayor, the Comptroller and the Pres. of the Bd. of Aldermen. The last is Vice-Mayor. There is a Borough Pres. for each of the 5 boroughs, elected simultaneously with the Mayor, and deputies of borough depts. apptd. with the presidents as executives. The general city depts. are filled by appointees of the Mayor, who also names members of the Bd. of City Magistrates. The legislative branch is the Bd. of Aldermen, elected by districts. Certain constitutional officers of counties are still elected, though they are paid out of the city budget, and the counties are otherwise not considered. The charter of 1901, which went into effect Jan. 1, 1902, defines the functions of all depts.

CHARTER OF THE CITY OF NEW YORK.
(Complete text, with 1920 Amendments, Eagle Library No. 216.)

The charter of the City of New York is a development of the charters of the former cities, New York, Brooklyn and Long Island City, differing from all of them, however, by the introduction of the principle of local control over local affairs. In this feature the charter provides a system of govt. more nearly like that of London and continental cities. For a history of charter making see Introduction to Eagle Library No. 216.

SEAL AND FLAG.

The City of New York adopted on June 24, 1915, as its official emblem, a new flag, combining the colors of the United Netherlands—orange, white and blue (blue next to flagstaff)—under which the city was settled, with the design of the municipal seal, under which English authority replaced the Dutch. Founded by the Dutch in 1626, as "New Amsterdam," it was named "New York" in 1664, and a year later, on June 24, 1665, the municipal govt. was formally transferred to the Mayor and Bd. of Aldermen of the City of New York, as successors in office of the burgomasters and schepens of the City of New Amsterdam.

Seal of The City of New York.
Adopted June 24, 1915.

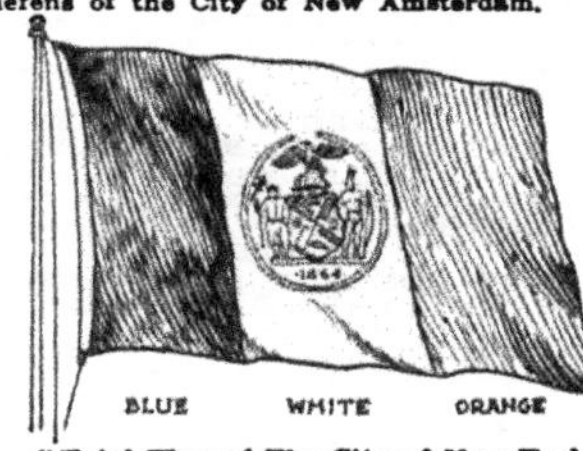

Official Flag of The City of New York.
Adopted June 24, 1915.

EXECUTIVE DEPARTMENT.

THE MAYOR'S OFFICE.

Room 5, City Hall, 9 A.M. to 5 P.M.; Sat. to 12 M.

The executive power of the city is vested in the Mayor, the Presidents of the Boroughs and the officers of the depts. The Mayor is the chief executive officer. His term begins on the 1st day of Jan. after his election and continues for 4 yrs. He is eligible for re-election. The Mayor appoints the heads of depts. and commissioners, except those over which the Presidents of the Boroughs have jurisdiction, and except, also, the head of the Dept. of Finance. He can remove at any time any official appointed by him, except the members of the Bd. of Education, trustees of the Coll. of the City of N. Y., and trustees of some hospitals, and certain judicial officers. He himself can be removed from office by the Governor, after a hearing, upon charges.

The Mayor has the power of veto over all ordinances and resolutions of the Bd. of Aldermen, but if he does not disapprove they become laws after a lapse of 10 days, or the next meeting after 10 days. (For duties of Mayor see N. Y. City Charter, Eagle Library No. 119.)

Mayor, J. F. Hylan, $15,000; elected 4 yrs.; term expires Dec. 31, 1921. Sec., J. F. Sinnott,* $6,500; Asst. Sec., F. W. Rokus, $5,800; Exec. Sec., A. Kelly,* $4,800; Chf. Clk., J. J. Glennon, $4,000; Exec. Clk., A. H. Allen, $2,340; Clk., J. H. Marron, $2,700; Exec. Steno., S. R. Kelf, $2,300; Conf. Steno., L. McNamara, $2,000; Estelle E. Frankfort, $2,100; Clks., J. G. Conlon, $3,060; J. T. Curtin, $2,700; J. F. Fitzsimmons, $2,574; F. J. Finnegan, $2,000; Acct., E. J. McLoughlin, $2,180; Stenos., Katherine H. Newman, $1,980; Jennie A. McGuigan, $1,760; Tel. Oper., Jos. A. Caulfield, $1,495; Chauffeur Attendant, J. W. Eppse, $1,880.

Mayor's Bureau of Weights and Measures.

372 Mncpl. Bldg., Hall of Records, Rm. 6. Also offices in Bkln., 23 DeKalb av., and Queens, 48 Jackson av.

Com., Jos. J. Holwell, $5,500; Chf. Insp., A. Lutz, $2,160; Conf. Insp., Mrs. K. Haenlain, $1,620; 8 Sealers, $1,600 to $2,580; 18 Insps., $1,495 to $1,920; 4 Clks., $660 to $1,440; 3 Stenos. and Tpes., $840 to $1,140; 3 Laborers at $912.

*Exempt from Civil Service.

Dept. of Public Markets.

Municipal Bldg., Mhtn.

Comr., E. J. O'Malley, $7,500; Dep. Comrs., vacant, $6,500; S. Buchler, G. A. Colgan, Mrs. B. W. Wezzmiller, $5,500 each; Sec., W. D. J. McCarthy, $4,000; Sec. to Comm., T. F. McGrath, $3,000; Gen. Insp., Chas. Winter, $3,500.

City Marshals.

City Marshals are appointed by the Mayor for terms of 6 yrs. They are paid by fees. Following is list, with year of appointment:

MANHATTAN.

C. Jacobs, 48 Charlton, '06; S. H. Krisky, 166 Suffolk, '13; A. Levine, 158 W. 141st, '15; H. H. Lazarus, 220 E. 115th; J. McCann, 421 W. 57th, M. Cohen, 260 Madison, '04; J. T. Pangburn, 36 Perry, '03; H. F. Tiernan, 168 W. 141st, '13; L. L. Vanderhoven, 344 E. 124th, '03; A. L. Blau, 10 W. 93d, '03; G. Boden, 637 2d av., '03; F. Boylan, 459 W. 23d, '15; A. Freeman, 76 Madison, '06; S. Cohen, 124 W. 112th, '09; E. J. Healey, 42 Barrow, '03; R. J. Hoffmeister, 202 E. 96th, '12; W. J. Kelly, 446 W. 51st, '06; J. J. Larkin, 217 E. 35th, '09; B. Horn, 269 Madison, '09; J. Ether, 33 7th, '04; M. Florea, 103 E. 123d, '15; A. Bauer, 116 E. 117th, '15; C. Kemp, 167 E. 121st, '15; W. Leishman, 280 St. Nicholas av., '15; A. Adisky, 386 Grand, '15; P. J. Gaffney, 50 E. 89th, '15; D. Greenblatt, 37 Attorney, '15; N. Gluck, 396 8th av., '15; J. Cash, 269 W. 118th, '15; M. J. Dobson, 360 W. 45th, '15; S. J. Peyser, 300 W. 68th, '17; F. W. Geraty, 403 W. 127th, '17; Frank Martoccia, 1:3 6th av.; D. Leef, 214 Rivington; B. Greenberg, 9 W. 111th.

BRONX.

E. L. Van Orden, 2557 3d av., '13; J. J. Haggerty, 1220 Gilbert pl.; S. Barnett, 1046 Hoe av., '15; C. J. Moshier, 457 E. 168d, '16; F. Donnelly, 785 Forest av.

CITY OF NEW YORK MUNICIPAL GOVERNMENT—EXECUTIVE DEPARTMENT—*Continued.*

BROOKLYN.

D. Goldberg, 402 Sackman, '06; H. McBride, 87 Rutledge, '12; R. J. Brown, 770 Metropolitan av., '12; P. N. Carroll, 138 Norwood av.; F. C. Metzger, 126 Kenilworth pl., '04; J. Casey, 581½ 18th; J. C. Ryan, 121 Washington av., '15; D. L. Hicks, 476 12th, '10; D. E. McBride, 535 45th, '10; W. H. Lyons, 620 Park pl.; M. J. Gaynor, 362 S. 1st; G. R. Henry, 638 DeKalb av.; L. Heyman, 401 Bushwick av.; N. J. Zielinski, 229 Nassau; J. Powers, 726 Halsey; D. L. Thomas, 344 Quincy; W. B. Winschel, 74 Henry; H. Wolkof, 788 Eastern P'kway.

QUEENS.

C. Diestal, 226 Nott av., L. I. City, '04; J. C. Cole, Wittier, Queens, '04; T. F. Maguire, 102 Amity, Flushing, '10; Wm. E. Cassidy, 706 Bleecker, Ridgewood, '16; James F. Sullivan, 45 Hardenbrook av., Jamaica, '16; C. F. Connelly, 1026 Dickens av., Far Rockaway, '11.

RICHMOND.

Ed. Kane, Linoleumville, S. I., '11; Geo. W. Perry, 91 Broad, Stapleton, S. I., '11.

LEGISLATIVE DEPARTMENT.

The legislative power of the city is vested in the Bd. of Aldermen, consisting of 67 members elected for 2 yrs., in the Pres. of the Bd. and the Presidents of the Boroughs. The salary of the Aldermen is $3,000 per yr. The Pres. of the Bd. receives $7,500 a yr. He is elected by the city for 4 yrs. (See City Charter.)

THE LOCAL IMPROVEMENT BOARDS.

The Aldermanic districts are divided into 25 local improvement districts. (See index.) The Pres. of the Borough as chairman and the Aldermen residing in each local improvement district constitute the local board. The local boards are empowered to initiate such improvements as grading and paving streets and constructing sewers, subject to the approval of the Bd. of Estimate, if they involve an assessment. (See City Charter.)

BOARD OF ALDERMEN.

Room 12, City Hall, Mhtn., 9 A.M. to 5 P.M.

Fiorello H. L. La Guardia, Pres. of Bd.; W. P. Kenneally, Vice-Ch.; Ch. Finance Com., F. A. Cunningham, Clk., P. J. Scully.

Manhattan.

GREENWICH—1, B. E. Donnelly, D., 44 Charlton; 2, M. Stapleton, D., 22 City Hall pl.; 3, S. F. Roberts, D., 167 8th av.

CORLEARS HOOK—4, L. Zeltner, D. and R., 408 Madison; 6, A. Beckerman, S., 705 E. 5th.; 8, M. Graubard, D., 201 Forsyth.

CHELSEA—5, J. F. McCourt, D., 415 W. 35th; 7, C. A. McManus, D., 345 W. 48th; 9, T. H. O'Kane, D., 858 10th av.

KIPS BAY—10, Wm. P. Kenneally, D., 223 E. 17th; 12, W. T. Collins, D., 201 E. 30th; 14, Thos. M. Farley, D., 321 E. 65th.

BROADWAY—11, Wm. F. Quinn, R., 237 W. 74th; 21, L. F. Cardini, R., 937 6th av.; 23, B. M. Falconer, R., 701 Madison av.

ST. NICHOLAS—13, J. J. Sullivan, R., 207 W. 106th; 25, S. R. Morris, D. and R., 151 W. 117th; 27, C. H. Roberts, R., 233 W. 139th.

WASHINGTON HEIGHTS—15, M. A. Burke, R., 127 Manhattan; 17, C. S. Bostwick, R., 3750 B'way; 19, J. W. Friedman, R., 630 W. 172d.

HELL GATE—16, Edw. Cassidy, D., 333 E. 79th; 18, J. N. Knoesel, D., 309 E. 89th; 20, T. J. Sullivan, D., 114 E. 101st.

HARLEM—22, C. Novello, R., 220 E. 116th; 24, C. J. McGillick, D., 2033 Madison av.; 26, G. W. Harris, R., 75 W. 141st.

Bronx.

MORRISANIA—28, E. W. Curley, D., 260 Brook av.

CHESTER—29, A. G. Halberstadt, D., 780 N Oak Drive; 30, J. M. Fitzpatrick, D., 1828 Hunt av

CROTONA—31, J. R. Ferguson, D., 369 E. 169th; 32, A. Braunstein, S., 667 Trasdale pl.

VAN CORTLANDT—33, Chas. A. Buckley, D., 2333 Creston av.; 34, R. Hannoch, D., 1064 Grant av.; 35, T. W. Martin, D., 3072 Bailey av.

Brooklyn.

HEIGHTS—36, A. V. Gorman, R., 237 Bergen; 37, P. H. Larney, D., 252 High; 38, F. A. Cunningham, D., 237 Baltic.

BEDFORD—39, F. D. McGarey, D., 175 Marcy av.; 40, J. Wirth, R., 729 Putnam av.; 41, S. Schmalheiser, R., 827 Park av.

BAY RIDGE—42, J. J. Molen, D., 150 23d; 43, G. J. Joyce, D., 29 3d; 44, C. W. Dunn, D., 651 53d.

PROSPECT HEIGHTS—45, A. Ferrand, R., 218 DeKalb av.; 46, D. J. Stewart, R.; 47, T. F. Layden, R., 728A Carroll.

WILLIAMSBURG—48, J. Gabriel, R., 310 Maujer, 49, J. W. Sullivan, D., 148 N. 8th; 50, P. J. McGuinness, D., 134 Franklin.

FLATBUSH—51, H. F. X. Savarese, R., 1352 69th; 52, F. Smith, R., 105 McDonough; 53, J. J. Keller, R., 44 Woodruff av.

BUSHWICK—54, J. T. Moehringer, R., 325 Stockholm; 55, C. Mueller, R., 290 Menahan; 56, B. C. Vladeck, S., 233 Keap.

NEW LOTS—57, C. H. Haubert, D., 1335 Jefferson av.; 58, C. J. Moore, R., 119 Crystal; 59, A. I. Shiplacoff, S., 612 Saratoga av.

Queens.

NEWTOWN DISTRICT—60, S. J. Burden, D., 144 11th, L. I. C.; 61, H. A. Alwell, D., 26 William, Glendale; 62, F. J. Schmitz, D., 404 11th, College Point.

JAMAICA DIST.—63, C. A. Post, R., 254 Lincoln, Flushing,; 64, W. B. Hazelwood, R., 8553 106th, Rich. Hill.

Richmond.

STATEN ISLAND DIST.—65, W. T. Warren, D., 29 Van Buren, N. Brighton; 66, John J. O'Rourke, D., 52 Gordon, Stapleton; 67, Edw. J. Atwell, D., 12 Vreeland, Port Richmond.

Recapitulation—Members of Board: Dem., 37; Rep., 27; Soc., 4. Boro. Presidents: Dem., 4; Rep., 1; Pres. of Bd., Rep., 1.

Attaches, Board of Aldermen.

Municipal Bldg., Mhtn.

Clk. Bd., P. J. Scully, $7,500; 1st Dep. City Clk., M. J. Cruise, $5,500; Asst. Chf. Clk., D. W. McCoy, $2,772; Steno., R. J. White, $2,520; Com. Clk., J. J. Flaherty, $3,500; Clk. to Bd. Comm., Mrs. A. C. Donner, $2,160; Ordinance Clk., F. J. Martin, $4,000; Clk. Records, C. A. Glaser, $3,330; Commr. Deeds Clk., T. J. Millett, $2,180; Clks., T. C. Waterman, $2,620; C. R. Shopland and G. McFarlane, $2,160 each; R. J. Maloney, $1,823; Librarian, P. Baer, $2,772; Journal Clk., J. F. Sullivan, $2,160; Sertg.-at-Arms, M. J. McGowan, $2,088; 8 Assts. to Sergt.-at-Arms, $1,823 each.

Office President Board of Aldermen.

City Hall, Mhtn., Room 11.

Pres. Bd., Fiorello H. LaGuardia, $7,500 (elected 4 yrs., term expires Dec. 31, '21; Asst. to Pres., F. Oppikofer, $5,500; Exam., F. K. Bowers,* $4,000; Leg. Clk., Wm. O'Connor,* $2,700; Sec., Miss Charlotte Delafield,* $2,640; Steno., Miss Marie M. Fisher,* $2,100; Law Clk., M. J. Diserio,* $1,800; Process Server, vacant,* $1,495.

City Clerk's Office.

Municipal Bldg., 2d floor.

The Bd. of Aldermen shall appoint a city clerk for a term of 6 yrs., to act as clerk of the Bd. of Aldermen. He has charge of all papers and documents of the city not otherwise provided for. It is his duty to keep the records of the Bd. of Aldermen open for public inspection at reasonable times. His signature is necessary to all leases by the city of its property, and to all grants as well as all bonds of city. Marriage licenses, auctioneer's licenses, shooting licenses and electric sign permits are also given in this office. He may appoint a deputy in each of the boroughs.

MANHATTAN.

City Clk., P. J. Scully, $7,500 (term exp. Dec. 31, 1921); 1st Dep., M. J. Cruise,* $5,500; Cash., T. B. Jones, $3,140; Custodian, J. F. Nash, $2,160; Electric Sign Clk., G. H. Ott, $2,520; Clk., J. H. Cross, $2,616; Steno. and Typist, G. O'Brien, $1,823.

BRONX.

Borough Hall, 177th and 3d av.

Dep. City Clk., Thos. J. McCabe,* $2,280.

BROOKLYN.

Borough Hall.

Dep. City Clk., J. F. Quayle, $3,800; Electric Sign Clk., J. Litt, $2,160; Chief Clk., T. F. Maher, $2,280.

---

*Exempt from Civil Service.

CITY OF NEW YORK MUNICIPAL GOVERNMENT—LEGISLATIVE DEPARTMENT—*Continued.*

QUEENS.

Court House, Jackson av., L. I. C.
Dep. City Clk., Wm. R. Zimmerman,* $2,616.

RICHMOND.

Borough Hall, St. George.
Dep. City Clk., J. R. Dalton, $1,800.

Marriage License Bureau.

Fee $1. License good until used.

MANHATTAN.
Municipal Bldg.

Chf. C'k., E. W. Hart, $3,140; 8 Clks. and 3 Interpreters, $1,823 each.

BRONX.
Borough Hall, 177th and 3d av.

Clk., Stuart Harris, $2,616; Dep. City Clk., T. J. McCabe, $2,280.

(See City Clerk's office for Brooklyn, Queens and Richmond.)

ADMINISTRATIVE DEPARTMENTS.

FINANCE DEPARTMENT.

Municipal Bldg., Mhtn., 9 A.M. to 5 P.M. (July, Aug., 9 A.M. to 4 P.M.) and 12 M. on Sat.

The Comptroller of N. Y. City is head of the Dept. of Finance, which has control of the fiscal affairs of the corporation.

There are 8 bureaus in this dept., including the Bureau of the City Chamberlain.

Following is a list of the bureaus and divisions of the Dept. of Finance, together with names of principal officers and employees:

EXECUTIVE DIVISION.

Comp., C. L. Craig, $15,000; elec. 4 yrs.; exp. Dec. 31, 1921; Dep. Coms., vacant, $8,500; A. J. Philbin,* F. J. Prial,* each $7,500; Asst. Dep., P. A. Whitney, $6,500; Sec. of Dept., C. F. Kerrigan, $7,000; Clks., John Korb, Jr., $4,100; M. E. Brennan, $3,150; 3 Clks., etc., 2 Stenos. and 3 Messgs., 1. Sp. Exam., 1 Typ. Acct., 1 Laborer.

CHIEF CLERK'S OFFICE.

Ch. Clk., Valentine F. Keller, $3,560; 28 Clks., etc.

REAL ESTATE DIVISION.

Aps. Real Est. (vacant), $6,500; 1 Appraiser Real Est., A. J. Rinn, $4,500; Clks., John J. McDermott, $2,520; Nicholas Deevy, $2,544; 7 Clks., 1 Steno., 1 Top Draftsman.

STOCK AND BOND DIVISION.

Ch. Clk., A. C. Baur, $4,640; Clk., J. J. Koehler, $3,500; 25 Clks., etc.

ENGINEERING DIVISION.

Ch. Engr., Chandler Withington, $7,000; 28 Asst. Engs., Insps., etc.

Auditing Bureau.

DIVISION OF ADMINISTRATION.

Ch. Aud., D. E. Kemlo, $6,500; Ch. Exam. of Accts. of Inst., T. W. Hynes, $5,500; C'ks., T. G. Morgan, $2,772; E. J. Smith, $2,832; 24 C'ks., etc.

DIVISION OF AUDITORS AND EXAMINERS.

Ch. Clk., P. L. Kenney, $5,000; Aud. of Accts., C. A. Hart, J. G. Benning, M. A. Fitzgerald, J. J. Flanagan, M. Levy, Patr'ck F. O'Connell, Robt. O. O'Connor, E. W. Ivins, John A. Hamilton, Jas. P. McInerney, $3,500 each; W. A. Griffith, $3,000; Jas. W. Wells, $2,520; 32 Clks., etc.

INSPECTION DIVISION.

Ch. Insp., M. F. Hayes, $4,500; 42 Clks., Insps., Exams., etc.

DIVISION OF REFUNDS.

Bkpr., D. Rotschild, $4,000; 18 Clks., etc.

CENTRAL PAYROLL DIVISION.

Fin. Clk., A. M. Steinert, $3,900; Exam., Geo. J. Gibbons, $3,070; 50 Clks., etc.

PAY DIVISION.

Cashs., William N. McNamara, $2,892; W. J. Popper, $2,844; J. J. Plunkett, $2,892; A. P. Lincoln, R. C. Whiting, $2 844 each; Fin. Clk., Wm. P. McClunn, $3,000; Cash., 37 Clks., etc.

BUREAU OF ACCOUNTANCY.

Ch. Acct., D. MacInnes, $8,000; 21 Accts., Bkprs., Clks., etc.

DIVISION OF RECEIPTS.

Aud. Receipts, H. H. Rathyen, $4,500; 26 Clks., etc.

DIVISION OF DISBURSEMENTS.

Aud. Disbursements, J. J. Kelly, $4,500; 42 Clks., etc.

LAW AND ADJUSTMENT BUREAU.

Chief, Maurice Breen, $5,500; Med. Exam., J. H. Byrne, $4,333; Exams., Robt. B. Jordan, $4,000; P. J. McEvoy, $2,820; 62 Clks., etc.

Bureau of Municipal Investigation and Statistics.
Municipal Bldg., Mhtn.

Supv., Stat. and Exam., R. B. McIntyre, $6,500; 36 Accts., etc.

*Exempt civil service class.

Bur. for Collection City Revenue.

Municipal Bldg., Mhtn.

Col. City Rev., T. J. Moynahan, $4,500; Dep. Col of City Rev., M. S. Raunheim, $2,772; 8 Cashs., C'ks., etc.

Bureau for the Collection of Taxes.

Rec. Taxes, Wm. C. Hecht, $5,000; 3 Clks., etc.

MANHATTAN.
Municipal Bldg.

Dep. Rec. Taxes, J. J. McDonough, $4,500; Cashs., E. F. McLaughlin, $3,250; T. T. Kuester, $2,160; 27 Clks., etc.

BRONX.

Arthur and Tremont avs.

Dep. Rec. Taxes, E. H. Healy, $3,000; 16 Clk., etc.

BROOKLYN.

248 Duffield.

Dep. Rec. Taxes, F. H. Norton, $4,500; 33 Clks., etc.

QUEENS.

5 Court Square, L. I. C.

Dep. Rec. Taxes, Anthony Moors, $3,000; 23 Clks., etc.

RICHMOND.

Borough Hall, St. George.

Dep. Rec. Taxes, J. DeMorgan, $3,200; 7 Clks., etc.

Bur. Collection Assessments and Arrears.

MANHATTAN.

Municipal Bldg., Mhtn.

Col. Assts. and Arrs., T. F. McAndrews, $5,300. 18 Clks., etc.

BRONX.

Tremont and Arthur avs.

Dep. Col. Assts. and Arrs., S. T. Shay, $2,700; 19 Clks., etc.

BROOKLYN.

248 Duffield.

Dep. Col. Assts. and Arrs., M. E. Dooley, $4,000; 24 Clks., etc.

QUEENS.

5 Court Square, L. I. City.

Dep. Col. Assts. and Arrs., F. M. Becker, $2,700; 17 Clks., etc.

RICHMOND.

Borough Hall, St. George.

Dep. Col. Assts. and Arrs., T. A. Braniff, $2,700; 9 Clks., etc.

Bureau of City Chamberlain.

Municipal Bldg., Mhtn.

Chamberlain appointed by Mayor pursuant to City Charter. Chamberlain, P. Berolzheimer,* $12,000; Dep. Cham., C. Sweeney,* $5,500; Sec. to Cham., Miss A. A. Robinson,* $3,000.

Commissioners of Sinking Fund.

The Mayor, Comptroller, Chamberlain, Pres. of Bd. of Aldermen and Ch. of Finance Com. of Bd. of Aldermen. John Korb, Sec., Municipal Bldg. (no salary).

Clk., Bertha Schmitt, $2,640; Steno., Anna Conroy, $1,860.

DEPARTMENT OF PLANT AND STRUCTURES

Main Office, Municipal Bldg., Mhtn.

The Commissioner is appointed by the Mayor. His jurisdiction includes the construction, repair, management and maintenance of all bridges of the City of New York, which extend across waters of a navigable stream or have a terminus in two or more boroughs.

Beginning July 1, 1918, the Commr. assumed jurisdiction over the Mncpl. ferries, and subject to the approval of the Commrs. of the Sinking Fund, he has power to establish new ferries and lease franchises for ferries.

The Commr. has charge of 42 bridges and the Staten Island, 39th St. (Bkn.) and 92d St.-Astoria

CITY OF NEW YORK MUNICIPAL GOVERNMENT—ADMINISTRATIVE DEPARTMENTS—*Continued.*

Ferries and the City Bus Service. The cost of the bridges, including property, amounts to $120,800,000. The cost of the ferries, including terminals and ferryboats, amounts to $12,492,914.

ADMINISTRATIVE—Com., Grover A. Whalen, $7,500; 2 Dep. Coms., W. W. Mills, John Mara, $5,500 each; Sec. to Com., F. C. Riegelman, $3,400; Exam., F. Richter, $4,640; Asst. Sec., F. J. Ryan, $4,500.

CLERICAL STAFF—Bkpr., E. Joyce, $2,970; Clks., H. E. Cunningham, $2,970; D. M. Simpson, $2,970; H. B. Baldwin, $2,772; 3 Bkprs., 45 Clks., 15 Stenos., 8 Mess., 2 Telephone Opers.

ENGINEERING STAFF—Chf. Engr., Edward A. Byrne, $7,500; Asst. Engr., F. W. Perry, $5,500; C. I. Crocker, $5,360; J. A. Knighton, A. McLean, $5,060 each; O. M. Kelly, J. R. Geoghan, $4,100; S. Hamburger, $4,000; J O. Eckersley, $4,000; 29 Asst. Engrs., $1,872 to $4,000; Transitmen, $1,920 to $2,772; 11 Draughtsmen (Steel), $2,184 to $3,000; 1 Leveler, $2,088; Insps. of Masonry and of Steel, etc.

MAINTENANCE OF BRIDGES.

Force composed of Riveters, Bridge Mechanics, Carpenters, Wiremen, Painters, Bridge Tenders, Laborers, etc.

OPERATION OF FERRIES.

30 Captains, $3,000 each; 34 Chf. Marine Engrs., $2,700 each; 24 Marine Engrs., $2,400 each; 32 Oilers, $1,720 each; 42 Water Tenders, $1,720 each; 155 Marine Stokers, $1,720 each; 17 Quartermasters, $2,280 each; 24 Mates, $1,800 each; Ticket Agents, Ticket Choppers, Deckhands, Boilermakers, Carpenters, Machinists, Laborers, Cleaners, Painters, etc.

CITY BUS SERVICE.

Established to meet emergencies of discontinued trolley lines, 46 routes—75,000,000 passengers in one year. Fare, 5c.

TENEMENT HOUSE DEPARTMENT.

Municipal Bldg., Mhtn.

Commissioner appointed by Mayor. This dept. is charged with enforcement of the Tenement House Law and certain provisions of the Charter, and with collecting and recording of information in regard to tenement houses. (See City Charter.)

Manhattan and Richmond.

Com., Frank Mann, $7,500; 1st Dep. Com., J. P Finnerty,* $4,700; Supt., C. A. Saffer,* $3,080; Sec. to Com., E. J. Byrne,* $2,851; Sec. to 1st Dep., M. Sinnott,* $2,376; Steno. to Com., E. L. Dowling,* $2,088; Ch. Insps., W. A. Robertson, $3,440; S. H. Lavelle, $3,500; Ch. Clk., F. A. Smith, $3,200; Plan Exam., E. J. Carroll, $2,544; 133 Clks., $660 to $2,616; 4 Plan Exams., $1,732 to $2,376; 118 Insps. of Tenmts., $1,464 to $2,534; 40 Stenos. and Copyists, $860 to $1,968.

Bronx.

559-61 E. Tremont av.

Supt., W. C. Martin, $3,500; Chf. Insp., J. White, $2,772; 50 Insps., Clks., etc.

Brooklyn and Queens.

503 Fulton, Bkln.

Executive Bureau.

2d Dep. Com., T. R. Farrell,* $4,500; Supt., P. J. Walsh, $2,880; Ch. Insp., S. H. Lavelle, $3,500; J. D. Caird, $2,772; 130 Insps., Clks., etc.

BOARD OF REVISION OF ASSESSMENTS.

Consists of the Comptroller, Corporation Counsel and President of the Dept. of Taxes and Assessments, without salary as members of said Board. The Board has and performs all powers and duties relative to the revision, correction and confirmation of assessments for any public improvement within the city other than assessments made by commissioners appointed by Court of Record, and those confirmed by Board of Assessors, without objections from property owners.

John Korb, Sec., Finance Dept. (no salary), Municipal Bldg., Chambers and Centre, Mhtn.

COMMON LANDS FUND COMMISSION OF LATE TOWN OF GRAVESEND.

Municipal Bldg.

Commissioners: The Mayor and Comptroller. No salary.

LAW DEPARTMENT.

Municipal Bldg., 9 A.M. to 5 P.M.; Saturdays, 9 A.M. to 12 M.

CORPORATION COUNSEL.

The Corporation Counsel is the attorney and counsel for the City of New York, the Mayor, the Board of Aldermen and each and every officer, board and department of the city, and conducts all the law business of the city. The Corporation Counsel may appoint 75 assistants to conduct the business of the department. The main office of the department is in Mhtn. and a branch office is maintained in Bkln., at 153 Pierrepont. Other branches may be maintained at his discretion in the other boroughs. (See City Charter.) The Corporation Counsel is appointed by the Mayor for a term of four years.

MAIN OFFICE.

Corp. Counsel, John P. O'Brien, $15,000; Sec., J. H. Johnston, $5,000; Steno. to Corp. Counsel, Miss M. I. Neary, $1 800; 1st Asst., G. P. Nicholson, $8,500; Assts., C. D. Olendorf, $10,000; W. H. King, J. A. Donnelly, A. Sweeny, $7,500 each; C. J. Druhan, J. F. O'Brien, $7,000 each; R. L. Tarbox, R. J. Culhane, E. G. Nelson, J. A. Stover, J. J. Fitzgerald, $6,500 each; C. J. Nehrbas, J. Lehman, E. J. Kohler, M. M. Fertig, $6,000 each; W. E. C. Mayer, J. P. Morrissey, W. A. Walling, $5 500 each; H. H. Torborg, W. B. Caughlan, I. F. Cohen, C. C. Marrin, J. J. Haggerty, M. L. Strauss, $5,000 each; G. H. Cowie, J. P. O'Connor, G. E. Draper, E. Fay, H. W. Mayo, J. Beihilf, D. C. Broderick, C. J. Carroll, $4,500 each; R. M. De Acosta, E. S. Benedict, I. Phillips, L. W. Eisenberg, $4,000 each; H. S. Worthley, J. Moroney, $3,780 each; M. Salomon, W. S. Allen, E. J. Talley, S. Plumer, V. Victory, W. H. Kehoe, C. A. O'Neil, T. F. Curley, J. J. Sheehan, J. F. Caponigri, E. F. Bennett, A. D. Hahn, W. Russell, $3,500 each; J. B. Miller, $3,280; A. Stern, C. E. La Lanne, M. Strasbourger, H. S. Lucia, S. Frontera, C. Horowitz, H. B. Woods, M. M. Dolphin, $3,000 each; Dep. Assts., W. H. Doherty, $3,250; F. E. Smith, $3,100; C. W. Miller, J. A. Devery, E. J. Kenney, J. L. Pascal, $2 940 each; A. J. Hyatt, $2,850; H. J. Shields, $2,640; J. J. Mead, C. Bradshaw, $2,508 each; J. H. Miles, R. H. Reid, $2,310 each; Junior Assts., H. Taylor, W. Augenmeyer, $2 100 each; W. Flatto, $2,040; A. S. Allenikoff, $2,000; C. B. Kelly, $1,980; E. Guilfoyle, $1,950; H. Hertzhoff, $1,800; J. T. Condon, S. J. Resnick, $1,780 each; E. F. Barrett, $1,650.

BUREAU FOR THE RECOVERY OF PENALTIES

Municipal Bldg., Mhtn.

Asst. in Ch., J. I. Berry,* $5,500; Assts., W. T. Kennedy, $4,500; A. M. Kross, $3,500; Dep. Assts., M. J. Kelly, $3,440; M. Flanagan, $3,300; F. E. V. Dunn, $3,008; J. D. O'Sullivan, $3,270; M. H. Murphy, $3,140; Jun. Assts., J. P. Morris, $2,772; W. J. Leonard, $2,970; S. Lippman, $2,232; M. Rosenthal, $2,040; Law Clk., T. J. Murphy, $2,616; Chf. Clk., G. G. P. Jackson, $3,700; Asst. Chf. Clk., W. E. Fay, $3,330; 8 Clks., 7 Stenos., 5 Process Servers, 2 Law Clks.

BUREAU FOR THE COLLECTION OF ARREARS FOR PERSONAL TAXES.

Municipal Bldg., 17th floor, Mhtn.

Asst., E. J. Murphy,* $5,500; Asst., S. Hoffman,* $4,200; Dep. Asst., J. F. Sullivan $2,818; Jr. Asst., Thos. J. Kinsella, $2,074; 11 Clks., 6 Stenos., 1 Typewriting Copyist, 12 Special Process Servers at $1.35 for each process actually served.

BUREAU STREET OPENINGS.

Municipal Bldg.

Asst. in Ch., J. J. Squier,* $7,500; Assts., L. H. La Motte,* $5,100; E. F. Reynolds,* $4,000; Dep. Assts., C. A. Molloy, $2,940; S. J. Benson, $2,520; Chf. Clk., F. J. Flynn, $3,000; Bkpr., J. Hahn, $1,680; 17 Clks., 8 Stenos., 6 Computers of Assessments, 2 Topographical Draughtsmen.

Brooklyn Branch,

153 Pierrepont.

Asst. in Ch., J. A. Solovei,* $5,500; Assts., P. J. MacDwyer,* $4,000; A. G. Tonkonogy,* $3,500; Dep. Asst. H. S. Campion, $3,750; Ch. Clk., E. A. Reilly, $3,500; 4 Jr. Assts., 1 Title Exam., 2 Clks., 2 Stenos., 1 Mess.

Queens Branch.

Municipal Bldg., L. I. City.

Asst. in Ch., J. G. Matthews,* $5,000; Asst., F. S. Higgins,* $3,500; Dept. Assts., Nathan Goldstein, $3,440; W. F. Kuh, J. G. McCarthy, $3,270 each; Chf. Clk., J. J. McConnell, $1,823; 2 Clks., 3 Stenos., 1 Mess.

TITLE DIVISION.

Municipal Bldg., Mhtn.

Asst. in Ch., P. Tiernan, $3500; Ch. Clk., J. A. Kane, $3,008; Asst., J. D. Lyons, $2,924; 12 Title Exams., 1 Law Clk., 1 Steno.

---

*Exempt civil service class.

CITY OF NEW YORK MUNICIPAL GOVERNMENT—LAW DEPARTMENT—*Continued.*

Brooklyn.

LAW DEPT.

153 Pierrepont, 9 A.M. to 5 P.M.; Saturdays, 9 A.M. to 12 M.

Asst. Corp. Counsel, in Ch., W. B. Carswell,* $10,000; Asst., W. R. Wilson,* $7,500; J. P. Reilly,* $4,750; J. B. Shanahan,* $4,100; D. P. Goldstein,* $3,500; Law Clk., C. R. Hartman, $2,830; Ch. Clk., S. K. Probasco, $4,500; Clks., Stenos., Exams., Process Servers, etc.

DEPT. OF TAXES AND ASSESSMENTS.

Municipal Bldg., Mhtn.

Commissioners appointed by the Mayor, one designated as Pres. Deputies appointed by the Com. (See City Charter.)

Pres., J. A. Cantor, $8,000; Sec. to Pres., W. A. Boeckel, $3,000; Coms., L. M. Swasey, G. H. Payne, J. P. Sinnott, A. Murphy, Jos. O'Grady, R. Williams, $7,000 each; Sec., C. R. Tyng,* $5,000; Exam. and Aud., W. J. King, $5,000; Assts. to Com., J. M. Grunert,* F. F. Straul, J. P. Hicks,* F. P. Coakley,* B. A. Ruoff,* E. H. Kaufman,* E. Duffy,* $3,000 each; C. Dep. Real Estate, F. J. Bell, $5,500; Surveyor, H. W. Vogel, $7,500.

Manhattan.

Hall of Records.

Dep. in Ch., R. E. of Corp., J. J. Hart, $4,700; Dep. in Ch., P. Est., R. E. L. Howe, $4,700; Dep. in Ch., P. J. Kelly, $5,000; Dep. T. Comms., R. J. Delehanty, $4,200; F. T. Cahill, $3,350; J. O'Connell, $3,950; Geo. E. McKenna, $3,420; H. Schumacher, $3,900; H. Bayer, W. B. Hogan, $3,600 each; J. Quinn, $3,540; T. W. Cullen, $3,350; R. F. Hendrickson, Chas. Strobel, $3,420 each; W. A. Munger, $3,350; G. T. Watterson, $3,350; P. F. McDonald, $2,520; 45 Clks., $600 to $2,100; 3 Searchers, $1,650 to $2,100; 4 Stenos., $1,495 to $2,060; 3 Book Type. at $1,380; 3 Messgrs., $1,540 to $2,100.

Bronx.

Arthur and Tremont avs.

Dep. in Ch., M. H. Kinsley, $4 200; Dep. T. Coms., O. C. Naumann, $3,700; W. L. Cunningham, J. R. Peterson, $3,450; M. P. Mulhall, $3,280; N. B. Levenson, $3,100; R. Miller, $3,100; W. J. Gilon, James Ryan, $2,930; D. J. McDonald, A. M. Field, J. J. T. Judge, E. T. Brennan, $2,920 each; 15 Clks., $1,060 to $1,800.

Brooklyn.

503 Fulton st.

Dep. in Ch., W. P. Burke, $4,700; Dep. T. Coms., G. W. Adee, $4,200; J. J. Sullivan, $2,880; P. A. Kinkel, C. J. Dunne, J. M. McNamara, F. E. Johnson, T. A. Moorehead, H. J. Levy, $3,950 each; C. DeWitt, D. B. Hutton, T. F. J. Brennan, E. A. Goetting, $3,900 each; D. Van Vleck, G. M. Brown, $3,780 each; Geo. M. Roe, A. Masset, R. W. Walden, A. C. Bernstein, I. N. Natkins, T. J. Hanlon, N. Knox, $3,420 each; J. 'ONeill, H. Milhard, J. Waldman, $3,350 each; 31 Clks., $1,293 to $2,340; 1 Searcher, $2,232; 1 Steno., $2,232; Mess., $1,376; 2 Book Typewriters, $1,683 each.

Queens.

Tax Bldg., Court House sq., L. I. City.

Dep. in Ch., M. Mulcahey,* $4,700; Dep. T. Coms., C. M. Lawless, $3,400; M. F. Dugan, A. J. Caplis, $3,780 each; J. J. Tracey, $3,950; T. Walsh, J. H. Storey, $3,600 each; J. A. Murray, G. W. Hilley, W. L. Nagle, $3,540 each; F. A. Dede, R. F. Tighe, $3,450 each; G. P. Frahm, C. Corkey, J. J. Fagan, D. M. Donegan, $3,420 each; H. G. Wilson, $2,100; E. J. Tracey, P. J. Cronin, $3,350 each; P. Mason, J. J. Heaphy, $2,880;; F. A. Uihlein, $1,146 to $2,232; 24 Clks., $1,146 to $2,232; Mess., $1,980; 1 Book Type., $1,683; Steno. and Type., $1,823.

Richmond.

Borough Hall, New Brighton.

Dep. in Ch., J. J. A. Hasson, $3,950; Dep. T. Coms., G. C. Demsey, $2,050; C. A. Mulligan, $3,600; W McMullen, $3,540; F. W. Pfaff, $3,450; Hy. Kathmann, $3,300; F. G. Stuart, $2,900; 8 Clks., $1,680 to $2,500; 1 Steno., $2,230; Asst. Surveyor, $2,760.

DEPARTMENT OF HEALTH.

S. W. cor. Centre and Walker, Mhtn.

The Board of Health consists of the Commissioner of Health, at a salary of $7,500 per year, appointed by the Mayor; the Police Commissioner and the Health Officer of the Port. Their duty is to enforce, so far as practicable, all the laws of the State and the provisions of the Sanitary Code within the city limits and the waters adjacent thereto for the preservation of human life and the care, promotion and protection of health.

BOARD OF HEALTH—Pres., R. S. Copeland, M.D., Health Comr.; R. E. Enright, Police Comr.; L. E. Cofer, M.D., Health Officer, Port of New York.

Acting with no salary are doctors composing the following boards: Medical Advisory Bd., 11 mem.; Medical Examining Bd., 5 mem.; Attdg. Phys. to Hosp., 35 mem.; Asst. Attdg. Phys., 30 mem.; Vis. Phys. to Hosp., 23 mem.; Hon. Consultants, 12 mem.; Advisory Council of about 150 mem.

OFFICE OF COMMISSIONER—Comr., Royal S. Copeland, M.D., $7,500; Sec. to Comr., J. S. Bestar, $4,100; Steno. and Type., $2,376; 7 Clks., $760 to $2,772.

OFFICE OF THE DEPUTY COMR. AND SANITARY SUPT.—Dep. Comr. and Sanitary Supt., F. J. Monaghan, M.D., $6,500; Sec. to Dep. Comr., T. J. Clougher, $3,500; 4 Asst. Sanitary Supts., A. J. O'Leary, M.D., $4,250; H. T. Peck, M.D., $4,250; J. H. Barry, M.D., $4,250; B. S. Harwood, M.D., $4,250; 4 Med Insps., $1,767 to $3,500; 1 Sanitary Insp., J. Lonergan, $3,600; 1 Sanitary Engr., E. Winship, $3,206; 1 Sanitary Insp., J. Oberwager, $2,448; 2 Clks., $900 to $2,520; 2 Stenos. and Typewriters, $1,376 to $1,610; 1 Typewriting Copyist, $1,288.

LAW DIVISION—Law Clk., W. T. Fetherson, $4,000; 4 Clks., $920 to $2,232; 1 Insp. of Foods, $2,304; 2 Stenos. and Typewriters, $1,020 to $1,610; 1 Typewriting Copyist, $1,288.

OFFICE OF THE SECRETARY—Sec. of Dept. and to Board of Health, C. L. Kohler, $5,500; Ch. Clk. of Dept., W. J. O'Connor, $3,500; Asst. Engr., J. C. Wolfe, $3,350; 105 Clks., $660 to $3,050; 26 Stenos. and Typewriters, $1,020 to $1,739; 4 Typewriting Copyists, $1,288 to $1,376; 14 Telephone Opers., $1,112 to $1,610; 3 Messgrs., $1,217 to $1,683; 3 Sanitary Insps., $2,016 to $2,520; 1 Attendant, $1,464; 1 Storekeeper, $2,616; 3 Drivers, $1,445 to $1,478; Insp. of Repairs and Supplies, $2,304; Insp. of Foods, $2,304; 18 Laborers, $1,185 to $1,445; 7 Auto Truck Drivers, $1,537 to $1,610; Architectural Draftsman, $1,944; Foreman of Laborers, $2,304; Janitor, $1,610; 63 Cleaners, $800; 2 Elevator Attendants, $1,522; 2 Watchmen, $920; 8 Auto Enginemen, $1,445 to $2,016.

DIVISION OF AUDIT AND ACCOUNTS—Clk. in Ch., H. A. Schickling, $3,920; 21 Clks., $760 to $2,772; 2 Accountants, $2,520 to $2,616; 3 Bookkeepers, $1,708 to $2,088; 1 Laboratory Asst., $1 537; 1 Steno. and Typewriter, $1,020; 1 Typewriting Copyist, $1,464.

DIVISION OF INSTITUTIONAL INSPECTION—Chief of Division, H. G. MacAdam, M.D., $3,500; 24 Med. Insps., $1,464 to $3,300; 2 Clks., $760 to $2,040; 1 Steno. and Typewriter, $1,020.

PUBLIC HEALTH EDUCATION—Dir., S. D. Hubbard, M.D., $4,280; 2 Med. Insps., $2,760 to $3,980; 3 Clks., $760 to $2,851; 2 Stenos. and Typewriters, $1,200 to $1,823; 1 Laborer, $1,445.

BUREAU OF RECORDS—Registrar of Records, W. H. Guilfoy, $5,500; 5 Asst. Registrars of Records, $3,500 to $4,280; Tabulator, $3,074;; 6 Med. Clks., $1,464 to $2,016; 26 Clks., $760 to $2,520; 4 Hollerith Opers., $1,200; Bookbinder's Seamstress, $1,288; 2 Photographers, $1,464 to $1,823; Driver, $1,478; 3 Laborers, $1,445; 6 Stenos. and Typewriters, $1,020 to $1,823; 6 Typewriting Copyists, $1,288 to $1,464.

SANITARY BUREAU—Asst. Sanitary Supt., A. Blauvelt, M.D., $4,580; 2 Med. Insps., $1,560 to $1,872; 67 Sanitary Insps., $1,686 to $3,250; 6 Clks., $660 to $2,304; 2 Stenos. and Typewriters, $864 to $1,200; 3 Foremen of Laborers, $1,495 to $1,823; 15 Laborers, $1,185 to $1,445; 60 Patrolmen, $2,280; 2 Sergeants, $2,700; 1 Lieutenant, $3,300.

CHILD HYGIENE—Dir., S. Josephine Baker, M.D., $5,600; 140 Med. Insps., $1,406 to $4,280; 328 Nurses, $1,405 to $2,376; 59 Nurses' Assts., $800 to $1,050; 10 Dentists, $1,244 to $2,184; 1 Chief, Division of Employment Certificates, $2,376; 15 Clks., $760 to $2,232; 6 Stenos. and Typewriters, $1,020 to $1,823.

PREVENTABLE DISEASES—Dir., L. I. Harris, M.D., $5,600; 44 Med. Insps., $1,464 to $3,500; 193 Nurses, $1,405 to $3,500; 1 Dentist, $1,767; 10 Veterinarians, $2,160 to $3,330; 9 Physicians (Sup. Clinic), $1,708 to $2,160; 86 Asst. Physicians, Clinic, $488 to $966; 33 Clks., $760 to $2,232; 8 Hospital Clks., $1,200 to $1,708; 6 Stenos. and Typewriters, $1,020 to $1,610; 3 Typewriting Copyists, $1,040 to $1,200; 4 Domestics, $780 to $924; Watchman, $1,445; 4 Disinfectors, $1,212 to $1,478; Cook, $982.

*Exempt civil service class.

CITY OF NEW YORK MUNICIPAL GOVERNMENT—DEPARTMENT OF HEALTH—*Continued.*

FOOD AND DRUGS—Dir., L. P. Brown, $5,500; 100 Insps. of Foods, $1,586 to $3,500; Chief Division of Milk Inspection, $2,772; 15 Sanitary Insps., $1,823 to $2,304; 9 Chemists, $1,448 to $3,008; 3 Laboratory Assts., $1,020 to $1,683; 10 Clks., $760 to $2,376; 3 Stenos. and Typewriters, $1,288 to $1,610; 1 Typewriting Copyist, $1,040; 1 Laborer, $1,445; 2 Laboratory Helpers, $824 to $953; 9 Veterinarians, $2,160 to $2,616.

BUREAU OF LABORATORIES—Dir., W. H. Park, M.D., $6,500; 5 Asst. Dirs., $3,008 to $3 920; 1 Med. Insp., $3,260; 2 Chemists, $1,823 to $2,160; 21 Bacteriologists, $1,464 to $3,350; 6 Bacteriologist Diagnosticians, $1,464 to $2,160; 1 Insp. of Foods, $1,944; Librarian, $1,683; 13 Clks., $763 to $2,376; 2 Stenos. and Typewriters, $1,020 to $1,376; 3 Typewriting Copyists, $920 to $1,537; 61 Laboratory Assts., $1,020 to $1,823; 14 Laborers, $1,092 to $1,445; 46 Laboratory Helpers, $760 to $1,288; 1 Mess., $1,445.

BUREAU OF HOSPITALS—Dir., R. J. Wilson, M.D., $5,350; 4 Dietitians, $940 to $2,616; 14 Hospital Clks., $1,040 to $2,851; 1 Steno. and Typewriter, $1,537; 147 Laborers, $590 to $1,823; 10 Drivers, $1,420 to $1,610; 34 Physicians, $1,443 to $3,250; 5 Internes, $440; 167 Nurses, $400 to $1,782; 3 Matrons, $1,332 to $1,398; 2 Storekeepers, $1,288 to $1,944; 11 Asst. Institutional Clks., $540 to $1,040; 1 Typewriting Copyist, $1,288; 11 Elevatormen, $1,299 to $1,445; 3 Butchers, $1,244 to $1,288; 8 General Mechanics, $1,445 to $1,944; 2 Watchmen, $906 to $1,445; 8 Orderlies, $1,132 to $1,299; 95 Hospital Attendants, $220 to $1,100; 218 Domestics, $340 to $1,078;; 13 Ambulance Enginemen, $1,610; 3 Med. Insps., $2,328 to $2,772; 3 Chaplains, $300 to $1,040; 2 Gardeners, $1,376; 6 Telephone Switchboard Opers., $964 to $1,288; 2 Laboratory Assts., $964 to $1,064; Dentist, $1,443; Architectural Draftsman, $2,758; Insp of Foods, $1,980; Baker, $1,214; Electrician, $1,823; Foreman of Mechanics, $1,944; 12 Helpers, $340 to $480; Fireman, $1,376; Stationary Engr., $1,610; Tinsmith, $1,478; Plumber, $1,465; Blacksmith, $1,478; 3 Carpenters, $1,507; Dairyman, $1,187.

Manhattan.

Asst. Sanitary Supt., Alonza Blauvelt, M.D., $4,580; Chief, Div. of Sanitary Insp., Richard Walsh, $3,000; Chief, Div. of Child Hygiene, R. H. Willis, M.D., $3,780; Chief, Div. of Preventable Diseases, Victor Neesen, M.D., $3,600; Chief, Div. of Food and Drug Insp., H. W. Taylor, $2,618; Willard Parker and Reception Hospital, Hosp. Phys., A. Dickson, M.D., $2,310.

Bronx.

3731 3d av.

Asst. Sanitary Supt., A. J. O'Leary, M.D., $4 250; Chief, Div. of Child Hygiene, M. L. Ogan, M.D., $2,328; Chief, Div. of Preventable Diseases, Charles Bartels, M.D., $2,400; Chief, Div. of Sanitary Insp., Thomas McCarthy, $3 250; Chief, Div. of Food and Drug Insp., Thomas M. McMeekan, $2 772; Asst. Chf. Clk., W. A. Flynn, $2,160; Riverside Hospital, Hospital Phys., F. S. Westmoreland, M.D., $2,772.

Brooklyn.

Willoughby and Flatbush av.

Asst. San. Supt., H. T. Peck, M.D., $4,250.

BUREAU OF GENERAL ADMINISTRATION—Asst. Ch. Clk., J. J. Kearney, $2,232; 26 Clks., $720 to $2 232; 6 Stenos., $1,200 to $1,739; 1 Type. Copyist, $1,288; 3 Tele. Opers., $1,464 to $1,537; H. Aumack, Engr. in Ch., $8 per diem; 2 Firemen, $5.50 per diem; 3 Laborers, $1,445; 24 Cleaners, $800; 2 Elevator Opers., $1,522; Janitor, $1 610.

SANITARY BUREAU—Med. Insp. in Ch., H. A. Newman, M.D., $2,550; 21 Sanitary Insps., $1,586 to $2,304.

BUREAU OF RECORDS—Asst. Registrar of Records, S. J. Byrne, M.D., $3,500;; 2 Med. Clks., $1,739 to $2,016; 6 Clks., $920 to $2,088; 2 Stenos., $1,200 to $1,640; 1 Type. Copyist, $1,288.

BUREAU OF PREVENTABLE DISEASES—Borough Chief., J. H. Plath, M.D., $3,500; 10 Med. Insps., $1,634 to $2,040; 3 Sup. Clinic Phys., $1,767; 25 Clinic Phys., $488 to $966; 59 Nurses $1,466 to $1,739; 3 Veterinarians, $2,160.

BUREAU OF FOOD AND DRUGS—Borough Chief, Walter Drennan, $2,820; 22 Insps., $1,659 to $2,304; 2 Veterinarians, $2,520; 5 Clks., $760 to $1,823; 1 Type. Copyist, $1,464.

BUREAU OF CHILD HYGIENE—Borough Chief, Laura Reigelman, M.D., $3,500; 42 Med. Insps., $1,464 to $2,184; 4 Dentists, $1,244 to $1,488; 123 Nurses, $1,405 to $1,739; 24 Nurses' Assts., $800 to $1,040.

FLOATING DAY CAMP RUTHERFORD, ft. of B'way—Phys. in Ch., E. W. Lawrence, M.D., $488; 4 Nurses, $1,537 to $1,683; 3 Helpers, $982 to $1,445; 3 Domestics, $780 to $804.

KINGSTON AV. HOSPITAL, Fenimore and Kingston av.—Rec. Phys., W. T. Cannon, M.D., $2,760; 6 Hosp. Phys., $1,659 to $2,541; 1 Med. Insp., $2,544; 3 Internes, $440; Supt. of Nurses, $1,798; 56 Nurses, $700 to $1,332; 5 Clks., $920 to $1,683; 1 Matron, $1,398; 6 Auto Enginemen, $1,610; 5 Drivers, $1,478; 38 Laborers, $916 to $1,823; 1 Butcher, $1,288; 3 Tele. Opers., $1,012 to $1,288; 1 Gardener, $1,537; 1 Elevator Oper., $1,445; 1 Laboratory Asst., $1,064; 81 Domestics, $300 to $976; 2 Mechanics, $1,478 to $1,683; 1 Orderly, $1,132; 2 Hosp. Atts., $1,076 to $1,940; 4 Engrs., $8 per diem; 6 Firemen, $5.50 per diem.

Queens.

374 Fulton, Jamaica.

Asst. Sanitary Supt., J. H. Barry, M.D., $4,250; Borough Chf., Bureau of Child Hygiene, R. W. Fowler, M.D., $3,500; Borough Chf., Bureau of Preventable Diseases, V. Mildenberg, $3,500; Chf., Div. of Sanitary Insps., M. Green, $2,400; Chf., Div. of Food and Drugs Inspection, C. A. Matthews, $2,304; Asst. Chf. Clk., G. R. Crowley, $3,000; Asst. Registrar of Records, C. H. Lynn, M.D., $3,500; Physician in Charge of Queens oro Hospital, F. Westmorland, M.D., $2,520. b

Richmond.

514 Bay, Stapleton.

Asst. Sanitary Supt., B. S. Harwood, M.D., $4,250; Chief Div. of Child Hygiene, W. C. Buntin, M.D., $1,830; Baby Health Sta., Miss Grace Haven, $1,537; 4 Nurses, $1,587 each; 3 Nurses, $1,683 each; 3 Phys., $1,708 each; Chief, Div. of Sanitary Insp., B. R. Williams, $2,376; 5 Insps., $1,708 to $1,944; Chief, Div. of Food and Drugs Insp., Walter Schaibly, $1,948; 2 Insps., $1,659 to $1,823; Asst. Ch. Clk., C. E. Hoyer, $3,050; Asst. Registrar of Records, J. F. Walsh, M.D., $3,500; Bur. of Preventable Diseases, J. D. Dickson, M.D., $1,708; 3 Patrolmen, $2,280 each; 5 Clks., $720 to $1,823; 2 Stenos., $1,064 to $1,290.

BELLEVUE AND ALLIED HOSPITALS.

Office, Bellevue Hosp., 26th and 1st av., Mhtn.

The Charter placed Bellevue, Harlem, Gouverneur and Fordham Hospitals under the jurisdiction of a Board of Trustees, to be appointed by the Mayor, and took them from control of Charities Dept. The Neponsit Beach Hospital for Children was subsequently added to the department.

BOARD OF TRUSTEES—(No salary.) Pres., Dr. J. W. Brannan; Sec., J. G. O'Keeffe. Members, Mrs. B. W. Lissburger, J. A. Farley, M. Weinberg, H. C. Wright, Dr. J. W. Pereilli, B. S. Coler, Com. of Public Welfare, ex-officio.

GENERAL ADMINISTRATION — Gen. Med. Supt., Geo. O'Hanlon, M.D., $6,000; Gen. Supt., Training Schools, Carrie J. Brink, $2,574; Dir. Laboratories, D. Symmers, M.D., $5,000; Sec. to Pres., E. J. Halligan,* $3,060; Aud. and Ch. Clk., G. A. White, $3,240; Purchasing Agent, P. J. Hart, $2,460; Sup. Eng., F. Lemke, $2,770; Clks. and Stenos.

BELLEVUE HOSPITAL—1st Asst. Med. Supt., M. L. Fleming, M.D., $4,000; 2d Asst. Med. Supt., J. J. Hill, M.D., $3,000; Asst. Supt., J. F. McHale, $2,500; Dir. of Alcoholic and Psychopathic Services, M. S. Gregory, $4,000; Roentgenologist, I. S. Hirsch, M.D., $2,100; Supt. Nurses, vacant, $2,180. Helpers, Nurses, etc.

TRAINING SCHOOL—Women pupils.

TRAINING SCHOOL FOR ATTENDANTS—Men pupils.

SCHOOL FOR MIDWIVES — Women pupils. Nurse in charge, A. E. Aikman.

DAY CAMP "BOAT SOUTHFIELD"—Ft. E. 27th. Nurses and Helpers.

GOUVERNEUR HOSPITAL—Gouverneur Slip, cor. Front. Asst. Supt., Jessie Stowers, $2,100. Nurses, Helpers and Assistants.

DAY CAMP "JOHN H. HUDDLESTON"—Ft. of Jackson, Mhtn. Nurses and Helpers.

HARLEM HOSPITAL—Lenox av., cor. 136th. Asst. Supt., C. D. O'Neil, $2,750. Nurses and Helpers.

FORDHAM HOSPITAL—Crotona av. and Southern blvd. Sup. Nurse, H. Malmgren, $2,000. Helpers and Assistants.

NEPONSIT BEACH HOSP. FOR CHILDREN—R'way Park. Asst. Supt., J. T. W. Brass, $2,100. Nurses, Helpers, etc.

*Exempt civil service class.

CITY OF NEW YORK MUNICIPAL GOVERNMENT—*Continued.*

BOARD OF WATER SUPPLY.

Municipal Bldg., Mhtn.

Created under Chap. 724, Law of 1905; consists of 3 commissioners appointed by Mayor. Charged with the development of Catskill Mtns. sources as an additional water supply for N. Y. City.

Coms., George J. Gillespie, Pres.; J. P. Sinnott, L. J. O'Reilly, $12,000 each.

ADMINISTRATION—Sec., B. F. Einbigler, $6,000; Asst. Sec., R. T. Stanton, $3,000; Aud., H. C. Buncke, $7,000; Ch. Bureau of Claims, J. H. McManus, $5,500; 3 Conf. Secs., $2,200 to $2,600; Bkpr., J. M. Carroll, $4,400; 10 Clks., $1,500 to $3,200; 6 Stenos., $1,500 to $1,800; 3 Investigators of Claims, $1,620 to $1,800; 1 Asst. Eng. at $2,520.

POLICE BUREAU—13 Sergts., $1,920; 36 Patrolmen, $1,500 to $1,700; 4 Caretakers, $1,080; 4 Hostlers, $1,080; 1 Clk. at $3,200.

ENGINEERING BUR.—(Hdqtrs. Dept.) Ch. Engr., J. W. Smith, $16,000; Dep. Ch. Engr., T. Merriman, $10,000; Cons. Engrs., J. R. Freeman, W. H. Burr, $3,000 each; Des. Engr., F. F. Moore, $6,500; 1 Mech. Engr., $4,500; 1 Architect, $4,500; 1 Asst. Engr., $4,500; 3 Asst. Engrs., $4,320; 8 Asst. Engrs., $3,960; 4 Asst. Engrs., $3,600; 1 Asst. Engr., $3,240; 3 Asst. Engrs., $3,060; 1 Asst. Engr., $2,880; 4 Topo. Dftsmen., $2,520 to $2,880; 1 Arch. Dftsman., $2,700; 1 Mech. Dftsman., $2,700; 1 Chemist, $3,696; 1 Insp., $2,520; 1 Insp., $2,160; 1 Photographer, $2,880; 1 Rodman, $1,680; 1 Axeman, $1,440; 1 Ch. Clk., $4,500; 1 Priv. Sec., $2,200; 7 Clks., $900 to $2,520; 6 Stenos., $1,800 to $1,950; 1 Tel. Oper., $1,750; 1 Cataloger, $1,620; 1 Auto Eng., $1,850; 1 Laborer, $1,440.

RESERVOIR DEPT.—Grand Gorge, N. Y. Dept. Engr., G. G. Honness, $8,500; Div. Engrs., C. M. Clark, W. B. Hunter, $5,400 each; J. A. Guttridge, $4,800; 1 Asst. Engr., $4,320; 4 Asst. Engrs., $3 700; 1 Asst. Engr., $3,600; 5 Asst. Engrs., $3,240; 1 Asst. Engr., $2,880; 1 Asst. Engr., $2,700; 6 Asst. Engrs., $2,600; 1 Asst. Engr., $2,520; 1 Asst. Engr., $2,400; 1 Asst. Engr., $2,200; 3 Asst. Engrs., $2,160; 1 Asst. Engr., $2,000; 15 Insps., $2,160 to $2,280; 7 Transitmen, $1,980 to $2,160; 6 Rodmen, $1,680; 3 Axemen, $1,440; 10 Clks., $680 to $2,200; 3 Stenos., $1,200; 1 Stenotypist, $1,200; 1 Storekeeper, $2,000; 5 Auto Eng., $1,850 to $2,000; 1 Auto Truck Driver, $1,520; 1 Foreman, $1,620; 1 Janitress, $1,100; 20 Laborers, $4.20 to $4.80 per day; 14 Gagekeepers, $72 to $144 per annum.

DEPARTMENT OF WATER SUPPLY, GAS AND ELECTRICITY.

The Commr. of Water Supply, Gas and Electricity, aptd. by Mayor, has charge of all property connected with supply and distribution of water for public use; use and transmission of gas, electricity, steam, etc.

Manhattan.

Municipal Bldg.

ADMINISTRATION—Com., N. J. Hayes; J. J. Dietz,* $6,500; Sec. to Dep., N. F. Donahue, $3,500; Ch. Clk., T. M. Murphy, $4,500; Sec. to Com., C. A. White, $3,500; Clk., L. F. McCann, $3,500.

DIV. OF SUPPLIES—Act. Chf., E. J. Beardsley, $4,000; Clk., J. T. Brodly, $2,424; Insps. of Supplies, Storekprs., Clks. and Stenos., $720 to $1,500.

BUR. OF WATER SUPPLY—Chf. Engr., M. H. Smith, $9,000; Dep. Chf. Engr., W. W. Brush $7,500; Assts., $2,100 to $2 500; Assts., Draftsmen, etc., $900 to $1,740; Clks., $600 to $1,800; Stenos., etc.

INVESTIGATION AND DESIGN—Asst. Engr. in Ch., J. Goodman, $3,750; Asst. Engrs., Draftsmen, $900 to $2,700.

MECHANICAL INSPECTION—Mech. Engr., Wm. Flannery, $2,524; 1 Draftsman, $900; Inspectors, $1,200 to $1,800.

LABORATORY—Chf. Chem., F. E. Hale, $4,000; Asst. Chem., Clks., Laborers, etc.

WATERSHED (Croton)—4 Asst. Engrs., $1,800 to $2,280; Assts., Transitmen, San. Insps., Foremen, Auto Engmn., Laborers, etc.

PUMPING (Mhtn. and Bronx)—Mech. Engr., Draftsman, $1,800; Enginemen, Coal Sampler, Tel. Opers., Clks., Oilers, Stokers, Laborers, etc.

DISTRIBUTION—Asst. Engr., Wm. Hauck, $3,300; Supt. of Repairs, John Mead, $3,000.

BUR. GAS AND ELECTRICITY—Chf. Engr., P. J. Keegan, $7,100; Clk., J. J. McHugh, $2,520.

STREET AND PARK LIGHTING—Supt., Gen. Insp., W. G. Quirk, $3,360; Insps., Draftsmen, Clks., Stenos., etc.

*Exempt civil service class.

LIGHTING PUBLIC BLDGS.—Insps., Clks., Stenos., Pub. Exams., etc.

ELECTRICAL INSPECTION—Elec. Eng., H. S. Wynkoop, $5,000; Act. Chf. Insp., J. Honey, $2,448; Insps., Clks., Stenos., etc.

GAS EXAMINATION—Act. Chf. Gas Insp., W. R. Birdsley, $2,448; 8 Insps., $1,500 to $2,400.

BUR. WATER REGISTER—Water Reg., D. F. Finon, $5,500; Chf. Clk., T. F. Bannon, $3,320; Bkpr., Cashs., Clks., Stenos., Insps. of Meters and Water Consumption, Messgs., Foremen, Asst. Foremen and Laborers.

Bronx.

Tremont and Arthur avs.

Dep. Com., A. H. Liebenau, $5,000; Clks., Stenos., etc.

ELECTRICAL INSPECTION—Chf. Insp., F. J. Fitzpatrick, $2,750; Clks., Stenos., etc.

BUR. WATER REGISTER—Chf. Clk., Cashs., Clks., Stenos., Insps. Meters, etc.

BUR. OF LAMPS AND LIGHTING—Chf. Insp., Clks., Stenos., Insps., etc.

ENGINEERING BUREAU—Asst. Engr., Insps., Labs., Clks.

Brooklyn.

50 Court.

Dep. Com., C. M. Sheeban,* $6,000; Steno., Tel. Oper., Clks., etc.

BUR. WATER SUPPLY—Boro. Engr., C. B Bull, $5,000; Clks., Stenos., etc.

PUMPING—Supv. Engr., Wm. A. Drew, $8 per day; Clk., Engmn., Oilers, Stokers, Laborers, etc.

DISTRIBUTION—Asst. Eng., J. S. Vertefeinlle, $3,008; Foreman of Maintenance, J. S. Lynch, $3,200; Transitman, Draftsmen, Rodmen, Axeman, Clks., Foremen, Assts., Insps., Laborers, etc., per diem.

WATERSHED—Auto Engineman, Foreman, Laborers, etc.

BUR. OF GAS AND ELECTRICITY—Street and Park Lighting—Gen. Insp., J. F. Bussing, $3,008; Clks., Steno., Insp., etc. Public Bldgs. and Lighting—Gen. Insp., A. J. Moran, $3,008; Steno., Insp., Clks., etc.

ELECTRICAL INSPECTION—Chf. Insp., N. A. Cassidy, $2,280; Insps., Steno., Clk., etc.

BUR. WATER REGISTER—Water Register, M J. Trudden, $4,000; Chf. Clk., C. O. Davis, $2,970; Cash., Clks., Stenos., Insps., Mess., etc.

Queens.

Mncpl. Bldg., L. I. City—Dep. Com., Jas. Butler,* $5,000; A. F. Hitzel, $1,924; Stenos., etc.

BUR. OF WATER SUPPLY—Bor. Engr., Wm. F. Laase, $4,460; Steno. and Type., Clks., Foremen, Draftsmen, Transitman, Rodmen, etc.

PUMPING—Pumping stations at Bayside and Flushing. Engmn., Oilers, Stokers, Labs., etc.

DISTRIBUTION—Asst. Engr., B. J. Bleistein, $2,865.

CONSTRN.—Traisitman, R. Ankener, $2,544; Rodmen, Insps.

BUR. OF GAS AND ELECTRICITY—Street and Park Lighting—Gen. Insp., C. Krauss, $2,448; Gen. Insp. of Pub. Bldgs., R. J. Keogh, $1,944; Clks., Insps., etc.

BUR. ELECTRICAL INSPECTION—Chf. Insp., J. H. Burke, $3,008; Insps., Clks., etc.

BUR. OF WATER REGISTER—Chf. Clk., R. H. Clausen, $2,520; Cash., Insps., Clks., Steno., Foreman and Labs.

Richmond.

Municipal Bldg., St. George—Dep. Com., J. L. Vail, *$4,000; Clk., Steno., etc.

BUR. WATER SUPPLY—Boro. Engr., W. V. Barnes, $3,200; Asst. Engrs., Draftsman, Rodmen, Axman, Stenos., etc.

PUMPING—Supv. Engr., J. J. Taylor, $8 per diem; Engrs., Laborers and Helpers.

DISTRIBUTION—Transitman, F. S. Sims, $1,944.

BUR. OF GAS AND ELECTRICITY (Electrical Inspection)—Csf. Insp., G. Sheridan, $3,206; Insps., etc.

BUR. WATER REGISTER—Chf. Clk., James Cullen, $2,520; Cash., Clks., Insps., Labs., etc.

DEPARTMENT OF CORRECTION.

Central Office, Municipal Bldg., Mhtn.

The Comm. of Correction, appointed by the Mayor, has charge of all penal institutions of the City for care and custody of criminals and misdemeanants, except police sta. houses and

CITY OF NEW YORK MUNICIPAL GOVERNMENT—DEPT. OF CORRECTION—*Continued.*

civil prisons in charge of Sheriff. He is to classify persons in his charge. As far as possible employment is to be given to all persons under his charge for not more than 8 hrs. a day.

Comm., Jas. A. Hamilton,* $7,500; Dep. Com., Wm. Dalton,* $6,000; Sec., R. L. Tudor,* $4,000; Priv. Sec., Mrs. M. C. Murtha, $3,250; Warden (Super.), H. O. Schleth, $4,000; Dept. Steward, A. Goldner, $3,500; 1 Asst. Steward, $1,800; 10 Clks., $560 to $2,000; 4 Stenos. and Type., $1,229 to $1,944; 2 Tel. Opers., $1,229 to $1,500.

BUR. OF AUDIT AND ACCOUNTS—Aud., W. J. Donovan, $4,500; 12 Clks, $920 to $2,772.

PURCHASING BUREAU—Sr. Storekeeper, C. D. Almstead, $2,772; Purch. Agt., W. A. Lamb, $2,880; Asst. Purch. Agt., $1,932; 5 Clks., $968 to $1,683; 3 Asst. Storekeepers, $1,000 each; Insp. of Supplies, $1,800.

BUREAU OF REGISTRATION AND PASSES Room 2532, Municipal Bldg. Information furnished regarding prisoners and passes issued for all departmental insts. Prison Reg., J. E. Elliott, $1,860; Clks., $560 to $2,000.

CENTRAL OFFICE STABLES—R. L. Robinson, in Ch., $2,000; Drivers, Hostlers, Motor Truck Drivers and Auto Enginemen.

BUR. OF REPAIRS AND CONSTRUCTION—Gen. Insp., J. J. Lewis, $2,500; Arch. Draftsman and Designer, S. S. McGrath, $2,508; Ch. Enginemen, W. Denton, $2,508; Sr. Insp. of Light and Power, J. H. Schroeder, $2,120; Industrial Instructor (trades) $1,560.

STEAMBOATS AND PIERS—Pilots, F. W. Parkinson, P. Bedson, T. Berry, O. Williams, $2,280 each; Engrs., Stokers, Deckhands and Mates.

CITY PRISON—Centre and Franklin (The Tombs)—Warden, J. J. Hanley, $3,240; Dep. Warden, T. McManus, $2,310; Hd. Kpr., J. B. Donovan, $1,440; Kprs. and Assts.

N. Y. PENITENTIARY—Blackwell's Isl.—Act. Warden, J. A. McCann, $2,520; Dep. Warden, M. J. Feeley, $2,310; Kprs. and Assts.

MUNICIPAL FARM, RIKER'S ISL.—Warden, H. C. Honeck, $2,770; Kprs. and Assts.

CITY PRISON, BKLN.—149 Raymond. Warden, R. Barr, $2,770; Dep. Warden, J. Bremel, $2,310; Kprs. and Assts.

CITY PRISON, QUEENS—Court House, L. I. City. Warden, F. W. Fox, $2,770.

NEW HAMPTON FARMS—New Hampton, Orange Co., N. Y. (N. Y. C. Reformatory) Supt., L. E. Lawes, $3,480; Asst. Supt., S. W. Brewster, $2,100; Hd. Kpr., Kprs. and Instrs.

DISTRICT PRISONS—Warden, P. A. Mallon, $3,240; 7 Dist. Prisons in Mhtn.; 6 Hd. Prison Kprs., $1,740 to $1,860; Phy., $1,496; Clk., $1,128; 2 Cooks, $820 to $1,056.

REFORMATORY PRISON—Harts Island. Dep. Warden, M. Breen, $2,310; Supt. of Industries, J. E. King, $3,000.

RECEPTION HOSPITAL AND CLEARING HOUSE (Women)—Sup. of Women, Mary M. Lilly, $2,100.

BD. OF ESTIMATE AND APPORTIONMENT.

The Bd. of Estimate and Apportionment is constituted according to Sec. 226, City Charter. Bet. 1st day of Oct. and 1st day of Nov., the Bd. of Estimate and Apportionment prepares a budget of amounts required to pay expenses of city during coming yr. When such budget is prepared it is submitted to Bd. of Aldermen, which may decrease any appropriations, but may not increase any. Such decrease may be vetoed by Mayor and can be overridden only by a three-fourths vote of Bd. of Aldermen. In important instances the Bd. of Estimate and Apportionment may issue bonds for public improvements without concurrence of Bd. of Aldermen. The Bd. of Estimate and Apportionment also has charge of granting of franchises, which was formerly vested in Bd. of Aldermen. Regular meetings of Bd. are held on Fris., at 10:30 A.M., at City Hall, Mhtn.

The Board and votes—Mayor, J. F. Hylan, 3; Compt., C. L. Craig, 3; Pres. Bd. Alderman, Fiorello H. La Guardia 3; Pres. Boro. Mhtn., Henry H. Curran, 2; Pres. Boro. Bkln., Edw. Riegelmann, 2; Pres. Boro. Bronx, Henry Bruckner, 1; Pres. Boro. Queens, M. E. Connolly, 1; Pres. Boro. Richmond, C. D. Van Name, 1.

COMMITTEES OF THE BOARD—Franchises—The Mayor, Ch.; The Comptroller, Pres. Bor. Mhtn., Pres. Bor. Bronx, Pres. Bor. Queens. City Plan and Public Improvements—Pres. Bor. Bronx, Ch.; the Comptroller, Pres. Bor. Mhtn., Pres. Bor. Bkln, Pres. Bor. Queens, Pres. Bor. Richmond, the Mayor, ex-officio. Assessments—Pres. Boro. Bkln., Ch.; the Mayor, the Comptroller, Pres. Bd. of Aldermen, Pres. Bor. Mhtn., Pres. Bor. The Bronx, Pres. Bor. Queens, Pres. Bor. Rich. Finance and Budget—The Comptroller, Ch: the Mayor, Pres. Bd. Aldermen, Pres. Bor. Mhtn., Pres. Bor. Bkln., Pres. Bor. The Bronx, Pres. Bor. Queens, Pres. Bor. Rich. Salaries and Grades—Pres. Bor. Queens, Ch.; Pres. Bor. Mhtn., Pres. Bor. Bkln., the Mayor, ex-officio.

SECRETARY'S OFFICE (including Division of Investigation)—Municipal Bldg. Sec., Jos. Haag,* $7,500; Asst. Sec., J. Matthews,* $5,500; Dir., F. P. Bent,* $6,500; Asst. Engrs., J. W. Reed, $5,500; W. H. Roberts, $5,000; A. G. Culver, $3,920; E. Riordan, W. D. Murray, T. M. Kelly, $3,500 each; R. C. Strahan, $3,350; W. King, $3,300; W. J. Larkin, $3,000; Mech. Engr., A. T. Smith, $3,500; Chf. Clk., F. J. O'Connor,* $4,000; Clks., J. C. Deering, $4,000; E. P. O'Connor, $3,700; F. H. Sigerson and J. J. O'Brien, $3,000 each; M. V. Murphy, $2,970; B. M. Ross, $2,580; W. C. Fitzpatrick, S. Wiener, $2,520 each; H. E. Taylor, $2,400; 23 Clks., $900 to $2,200; Exams., P. J. McGowan, $5,240; E. Feeney, $4,350; W. F. O'Connell, $4,100; T. J. Patterson, T. P. Eustace, H. V. Brockway, $3,560 each; John A. Cahill, $3,500; J. F. Hazrick, T. V. Tully, W. J. Loughran, $2,951 each; J. V. Dixon, $2,880; Municipal Exam., C. Baumgarten, $2,520; Accountant, W. J. Cobb, $3,250; Expert Accountants, G. W. J. Angell, $3,800; J. W. McDonald, $3,500; Stenos., J. H. Schwarting, $3,500; L. T. H. Albers, N. I. Stich, $2,880 each; 12 Stenos. and Typewriters, $1,464 to $1,980; 3 Typewriting Copyists, $1,376 to $1,464; Photographer, $2,040; 2 Tel. Opers., $1,200 and $1,317.

DIVISION OF PUBLIC IMPROVEMENTS—Municipal Bldg. Chf. Engr., N. P. Lewis, $12,000; Dep. Chf. Engr., A. S. Tuttle, $8,000; Sanitary Engr., K. Allen, $4,900; Asst. Engrs., F. F. Fuess, $4,300; F. W. Koop, $4,250; V. S. Moon, $3,900; B. Scheiman, A. W. Tidd, $3,600; L. Durham, $3,300; C. T. Nafey, $3,100; Chemist, W. T. Carpenter, $2,640; 5 Draftsmen, $2,340 to $2,700; Clk., J. W. Meade, $3,074; 4 Clks., $720 to $1,944; 4 Stenos. and Typewriters, $1,500 to $1,980.

DIVISION OF FRANCHISES—Municipal Bldg. Asst. Engr., J. A. McCollum, $6,500; E. W. Libaire, $4,100; C. H. Vanderbilt, $3,800; F. P. Pierce, $3,250; Topographical Draftsman, $2,400; Clks., V. McLaughlin, $4,070; J. D. McGann, $3,650; 3 Clks., $800 to $1,800; 2 Stenos. and Typewriters, $1,683 and $1,960.

DEPARTMENT OF DOCKS.

Pier A, North River.

The Commissioner of the Dept. of Docks is appointed by the Mayor and is also Dir. of the Port. Two deputies are appointed by the Com. The Com. has general charge of all waterfront and wharf property and, subject to approval of Commissioners of the Sinking Fund, he also has the following power: To establish bulkhead lines. Subject to approval by Sec. of War. Lease all wharf property belonging to the city. Subject to approval of Comm. of Sinking Fund. (See City Charter.)

Com., Murray Hulbert, $7,500; 1st Dep. Com.,* M. Cosgrove, $6,500; 2d Dep. Com.* H. A. Meyer, $5,500; Sec. to Dept., $4,000; Sec. to Com., J. T. Eagan, $3,500; Chf. Clk., J. McKenzie, $4,000; Aud., J. M. Phelan, $5,500; Chf. Engr., T. F. Keller, $6,500; 16 Asst. Engrs., $1,739 to $2,040; 23 Clks., $1,659 to $3,300; 13 Stenos., $900 to $2,376; 5 Messgrs., $1,659 to $1,823; 9 Chainmen and Rodmen, $2,520 to $5,500; 13 Draftsmen, $1,900 to $2,520; 4 Hydrographers, $1,600 to $2,520; 1 Leveler, $2,088; 2 Transitmen and Computer, $2,520 and $2,952; 2 Transitmen, $2,100 and $2,520; 1 Gen. Foreman, $2,400; 15 Insps. of Dredging, $1,815 to $2,178; 3 Marine Engrs., $1,980; 3 Pilots, $2,280; 19 Dock Masters, $2,772; 1 Dockmaster, $3,140; 1 Foreman Carpenter, $1,920; 1 Auto Truck Driver, $1,637; Oiler, $5.60 per day; 1 Eng. Locomobile, $1,968; 1 Foreman of Yard, $2,520; 1 Conf. Insp., $3,740; 1 Conf. Insp., $2,970; 2 Storekeeper's Helpers, $1,445 each; 1 Telephone Oper., $1,610. For Dockmaster's offices see index. 1 Expert Blue Printer, $1,830; 16 Insps., Pier Bldg., $2,000 to $2,178; 6 Rodmen, $1,560; 1 Mate, $1,380.

*Exempt civil service class.

CITY OF NEW YORK MUNICIPAL GOVERNMENT—*Continued.*

MUNICIPAL CIVIL SERVICE COMMISSION.

Municipal Bldg., Mhtn.

Three commissioners are appointed by the Mayor pursuant to Sec. 123 of City Charter.

Pres., M. Cukor, $6,000; Coms., T. R. Killilea, Wm. Drennan, $5,000 each; Sec., C. I. Stengle, $5,500; Sec. to Pres., M. Healy, $2,772; Asst. Sec., M. L. Sigerson, $3,500; Ch. Clk., Geo. H. Eberle, $3,680; Appli. Clk., J. F. McDonald, $3,140; Certif. Clk., W. M. Tighe, $3,140; Inform. and Complaint Clk., T. Casey, $2,200; Act. C. Ex., T. C. Murray, $5,500; Exams., M. B. Upshaw, $4,760; Jas. A. Rafferty, $4,180; L. A. Merrill, $3,440; M. C. Ihlseng, $3,800; C. S. Shaughnessy, $3,680; Wm. B. Clarke, $3,440; F. S. Thorpe, B. Gillam, F. E. Kavanagh, J. A. Higgins, $3,206 each; E. C. Evans, L. B. Widder, $2,772 each; L. L. Whitney, $3,008; B. Steinberg, $3,140; E. J. Ellison, $3,008; Med. Ex., J. A. Kene, $3,140; Phys. Ex., J. A. Ruddy, $3,300; Finger Print Clk., P. Ryan, $2,088; 37 Clks., $660 to $2,448; 15 Stenos., $992 to $2,400; 194 Monitors at $6 per day. Other Exams. at $10 per day; 8 Investigators at $2,304; 6 Investigators at $2,232; 4 Investigators at $2,160; 1 Tab., $1,610; 3 Attendants, $1,268 to $1,944; 1 Tel. Oper., $1,112; 1 Super. Monitor, $1,800.

COMMISSIONER OF ACCOUNTS.

Municipal Bldg., Mhtn.

Commissioner appointed by Mayor and removed at pleasure, pursuant to Sec. 119 of City Charter.

Com., D. Hirshfield,* $7,500; Dep. Coms., H. H. Klein* and W. D. Loudoun, $5,500 each; Chief of Staff, J. McGinley, $5,240; Sec. to Comm., A. Regozin, $2,640; Exam. Accts., P. F. Atlee,* $4,100; W. G. Domidion,* $4,000; B. M. Cole,* $3,920; L. B. Hubbard,* $3,560; G. Morrell, J. H. Quinn, J. P. Divver,* $3,500 each; T. C. Quinn,* J. Strouse,* R. Holde,* $3,200 each; F. P. Treanor,* $3,074; J. J. McKenna,* $2,832; P. J. Maloney, J. Goodstein, $2,616 each; C. J. O'Leary, $2,400; Stenos. to Com., M. F. Hook,* $2,160; M. C. Brady,* $2,088; 50 Accts., $1,756 to $3,680; 24 Clks., $660 to $2,280; 4 Stenos. and Typrs., $1,366 to $2,040; 2 Typr. Copyists, $980 and $992; 9 Ex. Insps., $1,824 to $2,760; 1 Eng. Insp., $2,256; 1 Exam. Eng., $3,200; 1 Asst. Eng., $2,664; Tel. Oper., $1,100; 1 Law Exam., $3,700; 1 Exam., $3,000; 1 Computer, $2,184.

BOARD OF CITY RECORD.

Municipal Bldg., Mhtn.

For duties of Board of City Record see City Charter, Sec. 1526. The Supervisor is elected by majority vote of Mayor, Comptroller and Corporation Counsel, who comprise the Board, serving without salary. The City Record is the official journal of the City of New York. It is published daily at 9 A.M. (except holidays). The subscription price is $20 a year; 10 cents a copy. Distribution Office, 125 Worth.

Sup., P. J. Brady, $6,000; Dep. Sup., H. McMillen, $3,500; Ch. Clk., Rose McShane, $2,200; Editor, William Viertel, $3,300; Stationer, E. J. Plunkett; Bkbdr., J. W. McAvoy; Insp. of Printing, J. J. McCue, $2,850 each; Acct., B. B. Gillespie, $4,006.

CHIEF MEDICAL EXAMINER.

Municipal Bldg., Mhtn.

Chf. Med. Exam., Chas. Norris, M.D., $7,500; G. P. LeBrun, Sec., $3,500; Asst. Med. Exams., Drs. B. Schwartz, T. H. Gonzales, C. S. Cassasa, Geo. Hohmann, $4,100 each; Steno., J. Casey, $2,376; Thos. Prendeville, $2,580; J. M. Shea, $2,232; Clks., J. M. Tobin, $2,376; Edw. Doonan, $2,520; J. G. Woodlock, $2,376; F. A. Perry, $1,823; A. M. Simpson, $968; J. Aneckstein, $1,980; Miss L. Bausch, Tel. Oper., $1,708; Laboratory Asst., I. Silverman, $1,288.

Bronx.

1918 Arthur av.

Asst. Med. Exams., K. S. Kennard, J. Riegelman, $4,100 each; Chf. Clk., Wm. T. Austin, $3,330; Asst. Clks., Wm. H. Brown, W. Rausch, $2,376.

Brooklyn.

Dept. Health Bldg., Willoughby and Flatbush av.

Asst. Med. Exams., Chas. Wuest, M. E. Marten, C. Boettiger, $4,100 each; Chf. Clk., P. J. Coffey, $3,330; Clks., Thos. Gamble, Wm. Kearney, $2,376 each; M. Dannhauser, $1,824; Steno., J. M. Shea, $2,232.

*Exempt civil service class.

Queens.

Town Hall, Jamaica.

Asst. Med. Exams., W. H. Mammack, H. W. Neail, $3,600 each; Chf. Clk., A. Humm, $2,880; Clk., Wm. Bartel, $1,495.

Richmond.

2d, New Brighton.

Asst. Med. Exam., Geo. Mord, $4,100; Chf. Clk., A. Fulton, $2,520; Clk., Chas. Hoefle, $2,376.

DEPARTMENT OF PARKS.

The Park Board consists of five commissioners, one having administrative jurisdiction in Mhtn., one in The Bronx, one in Bkln., one in Queens and one in Richmond. They are appointed by the Mayor. The Board adopts regulations for administration of the department and ordinances for government of parks. (See City Charter.)

PARK BOARD, Mncpl. Bldg.—Pres., F. D. Gallatin; Comrs., J. N. Harman, J. P. Hennessy, A. C. Benninger, Thos. R. McGinley, $7,500 each; Sec., Willis Holly, $4,500; Landscape Arch., J. V. Borgevin, $4,500; Asst. Landscape Arch., J. F. Gatringer, $3,200; Photographer H. V. Letkemann, $1,823.

Manhattan.

Municipal Bldg.

Com., F. D. Gallatin, Sec. to Com., J. J. Ryan, $3,350; Bkpr., M. Mayer, $2,520; Ch. Eng., E. A. Miller,* $5,500; Dir. of Recreation, William J. Lee, $4,220; Purchasing Clk., J. J. McCarthy, $2,616; Prin. Asst. Eng., W. F. Richards, $3,200; 16 Clks., $720 to $2,520; 4 Stenos., $1,823 to $2,160.

Brooklyn.

Litchfield Mansion, Prospect Park.

Com., John N. Harman; Sec., H. J. Kempf, $3,250; Supt., B. Rothberg, $4,800; Eng., E. J. Mullane*, $4,000; Conf. Sec. to Com., Mrs. W. A. Combes, $2,068; Sup. of Recreation, J. J. Downing, $2,856; Ch. Clk., E. S. Ryan, $2,760; Gen. Foreman, J. A. McKinney, $2,448; Foreman of Repairs, J. I. Crozier, $2,400; 2 Stenos., $1,823; 8 Clks., $840 to $2,232; 5 Arboriculturists, $2,520 each; Prop. Clk., R. J. Flynn, $2,520; 5 Insps. of Tree Complaints, $1,610 each; 800 Employees, $4.50 to $10 per diem.

MUSEUM OF ARTS AND SCIENCES—Eastern P'kway and Washington av. Dir. of Museums, Wm. H. Fox, $6,500; 3 Curators, $3,500 each; Bus. Mgr., L. T. Hart, $3,200; Librarian, $2,904.

Queens.

"The Overlook," Forest Park, Richmond Hill, near Union Turnpike.

Com., A. C. Benninger, $5,500; Sec., B. M. Patten, $3,660; Chf. Clk., J. Pasta, $2,616; Asst. Eng., J. J. Kelly, $3,000; Asst. Landscape Arch., A. V. Grande, $2,544; Forester, J. F. Burns, $3,200; about 200 Employees, paid by day or month.

Bronx.

Zbrowski Mansion, Claremont Park.

Com., J. P. Hennessey, $5,500; Priv. Sec., H. Geiger,* $3,500; Bkpr., J. H. Bergen, $3,200; 5 Clks., $1,175 to $2,232; 3 Stenos., $1,390 to $1,823; 1 Tel. Oper., $1,342; 1 Mess., $1,586.

ENGR'S OFFICE—Chief Engr., E. J. Fanelly, $4,500; Asst. Engr., F. A. L. Seymour, $3,000; Asst. Arch. Landscape, A. G. Waldreason, $2,976; Insps., Rodmen, etc.

SUPT'S OFFICES—Supt., W. T. Wager,* $4,500; Asst. Supts., W. Kelly, $2,256; C. Trede, $2,376; Head Gardener, J. F. Walsh, Jr., $3,008; 16 Foremen, $1,744 to $2,616; about 500 Employees, paid by day or month.

ART COMMISSION.

Office, City Hall, Mhtn.

Member ex-officio: Pres. Art Com., R. W. de Forest, Pres. Met. Museum; V. Pres. Art Com., F. L. Babbott, Pres. Bkln. Inst.; J. F. Hylan, Mayor; W. Barclay Parsons, Trustee, N. Y. Public Library. Members: Welles Bosworth, Architect; H. W. Watrous, Painter; R. Aitken, Sculptor; L. V. Lockwood, Sec.; L. Ouidin, R. T. H. Halsey, Asst. Secs.; H. Rutgers, Marshal, $3,600; Alice S. Clark, Clk., $1,800.

DEPARTMENT OF LICENSES.

57 Center, Mhtn.

Com., J. F. Gilchrist,* $7,500; Dep. Coms., J. J. Sexton,* J. F. Geraghty,* $5,000 each; Sec. to Com., J. J. Caldwell, $2,650; Chf. Insp., J. O. McShane, $3,500; Chf., Bkln. Office, 381 Fulton, J. J. Brackman, $3,500; Chf. Div. of Licensed Vehicles, J. Brennen, $3,500.

CITY OF NEW YORK MUNICIPAL GOVERNMENT—*Continued.*

BOARD OF ELECTIONS.

Gen. Office, Municipal Bldg., Mhtn.

Coms., J. R. Voorhis, Pres., C. E. Heydt, Sec., James Kane, J. A. Livingston, $6,000 each; Chf. Clk.,* S. H. Cohen, $4,700; Dep. Chf. Clk.,* T. J. Kenny, $3,950.

Manhattan.

Municipal Bldg.

Chf. Clk., W. C. Baxter, $4,550; Dep. Clk.,* Patrick Cooke, $3,500.

Bronx.

442 E. 149th.

Chf. Clk.,* J. L. Burgoyne, $2,950; Dep. Clk.,* T. F. Stapleton, $2,500.

Brooklyn.

26 Court.

Chf. Clk.,* Geo. Russell, $3,700; Dep. Clk.,* Adam H. Leich, $3,350.

Queens.

64 Jackson av., L. I. City.

Chf. Clk.,* H. W. Sharkey, $3,250; Dep. Clk.,* H. Homer Moore, $2,760.

Richmond.

Borough Hall, New Brighton.

Chf. Clk.,* A. M. Ross, $2,700; Dep. Clk.,* A. M. Donaldson, $2,460.

DEPARTMENT OF STREET CLEANING.

Municipal Bldg., Mhtn.

The Com. of Street Cleaning (appointed by Mayor, pursuant to Sec. 533 of City Charter) has control of sweeping and cleaning of streets, removal of ashes, garbage, snow, etc., and framing ordinances regulating use of sidewalks for disposition of refuse, except in Queens and Richmond, where authority is vested in the Bor. Presidents. Contracts for disposition of street sweepings, ashes and garbage are made by the Comr.

Manhattan.

GENERAL ADMINISTRATION—Comr., J. P. Leo,* $7,500; Dep. Comr., Mhtn., J. J. Nugent,* $5,500; Office Dep. Comr., F. A. Eschmann, $5,500; Gen. Sup., A. A. Taylor, $4,600; Asst. Sup., J. W. Asip, $3,600; Sup. Final Dis., E. P. Greene, $3,700; Asst. Sup. Final Dis., A. Pierce, $3,000; Pri. Sec. to Comr., E. J. Meehan, $3,500; Chf. Clk., J. J. O'Brien, $4,600; Chf. Bkpr., J. S. McCann, $4,000; Clk. Pensions, C. Murphy, $2,340; Law Clk., H. N. Steinert, $4,240; Master Mech., $3,000; 7 Med. Exams., $3,400 each; 1 Chf. Vetern., $3,000; 6 Veterns., $2,304; 83 Clks., Stenos., Mess., etc.

UNIFORMED FORCE—Dist. Supts., P. Hynes, R. H. Hicks, J. S. Malcolm, J. F. Reilly, T. Flynn, Jr., P. Flaherty, J. M. Hayden, W. F. Ward, J. Murray, J. J. Condon, W. J. Powell, J. J. Kiernan, T. J. Reilly, J. Pope, C. Schierbaum, A. E. L. Newiger, $3,000 to $3,330; 52 Sec. Foremen, $2,064 each; 25 Stable Foremen, $2,400 each; 181 Assts., $1,848 each; 34 Dump Insps., $2,064 each; 44 Assts., 149 Mechanics, paid by day.

Bronx.

2804 3d av.

Dep. Comr., J. W. Brown,* $5,500; Bor. Supt., M. N. O'Donnell, $3,330; Dist. Supts., J. J. Byrne, Jas Minchin $3,200 each; W Ward, $3,000; Clk., J. B. Rooney, $2,520; 12 Sec. Foremen, $2,064 each; 3 Stable Foremen, $2,400 each; 3 Dump Insps., $2,064 each.

Brooklyn.

50 Court.

Dep. Comr., M. Laura,* $5,000; Executive Clk., J. A. Maguire, $2,100; Clks. and Stenos.

UNIFORMED FORCE — Boro. Insp., M. J. O'Brien, $3.330; Dist. Supts., P. J. Cunningham, M. J. Ward, F. C. Gannon, Wm. Reil, J. J. Byrne, Chas. Summers, $3,200 each; R. J. Dolan, J. P. Josephs, $3,000 each; 40 Sec. Foremen, $2,064 each; 15 Dump Insps., 40 Asst. Foremen, 9 Stable Managers, $2,400 each; 9 Assts., 47 Mechanics, employed by day.

Queens.

63 Jackson av., L. I. C.

Appointed by Boro. Pres.

Supt., D. Ehntholt,* $4,000; Dist. Supts., A. Williams, D. E. Whitney, R. J. Munson, Wm. J. Walters, Jos. J. Carlin, $2,700 each; Chf. Clk., P. F. Guidera, $2,100; 4 Clks., 1 Steno., Foremen, Laborers, etc.

*Exempt civil service class.

Richmond.

Borough Hall, New Brighton, S. I.

Supt., J. E. Minnahan, $4,000; Asst. Supt., R. D. Rice, $3,000; Clks., J. C. Schnibbe, $2,340; J. W. Johnston, $2,400; L. Baumann, $1,944; Steno., R. F. Rice, $1,512; 5 Insps., 12 Foremen, 1 Auto Engmn.

DEPARTMENT OF PUBLIC WELFARE.

Municipal Bldg. (See index Hosp., Homes and Rel. Socs.)

The head of Dept. of Public Welfare is the Com. of Public Welfare appointed by Mayor. He can appoint three deputies. He has general charge of hospitals, asylums and almshouses of city. The main office shall be in Mhtn.

Manhattan and Bronx.

Main Office, Municipal Bldg.

Com., B. F. Coler, $7,500; 1st Dep. Com., S. A. Nugent, $6,500; 2d Dep. Com., P. J. Carlin, $5,500; 3d Dep. Com., Matthew Hawkins, $5,000; Dr. J. F. Fitzgerald, $6,000, Gen. Med. Supt.; Conf. Steno., E. Schmitt, $2,736; Sec., J. McKee Borden,* $4,000; Ch. Eng., J. J. Herrick, $5,000; Aud., G. T. Broad, $3,100; Gen. Insp., Miss M. C. Tinney,* $4,250; Priv. Sec., $3,320.

CITY MORTUARY—29th and 1st av. Supt. of Mortuary, M. J. Rickard, $2,616; Helpers.

BUR. INVESTNS.—Dir., V. Dodworth, $4,500; Clks., Soc. Investgrs., etc. Main office, Mncpl. Bldg., Mhtn. Dist. offices, 124 E. 59th Mhtn.; Tremont and Arthur avs., Bronx; 327 Schermerhorn, Bkln.; Flushing, L. I.; New Brighton, S. I.

GENERAL DRUG DEPT.—Chemist, vacant; Clks., Assts., etc.

MUNICIPAL LODGING HOUSE—432 E. 25th. Supt., E. E. McMahon, $2.541; Helpers.

EMERGENCY HOSP.—Ft. E. 70th. Under jurisdiction Metropolitan Hosp. Dir. in Ch., W. H. Conley, $5,050.*

CITY HOSP.—Blackwell's Island. Supt., C. B. Bacon, M.D., $4,756. Helpers, Cooks, etc.

CITY HOSP. TRAINING SCHL.—Blackwell's Island. Supt., Miss T. H. Le Febore, $2,310.

N. Y. C. HOME FOR THE AGED AND INFIRM—Blackwell's Island. Supt., C. J. Cosgrove, $2541; Nurses Orderlies Helpers etc.

STOREHOUSE—Blackwell's Island. Gen. Storekeeper, H. Scheitlin, $3,500; Clks. and Helpers.

METROPOLITAN HOSP.—Blackwell's Island. Med. Supt., W. H. Conley, $5,050; Dep. Med. Supt., N. W. Thompson, $3,270.

MET. TRAINING SCHL.—Blackwell's Island. Supt., Agnes S. Ward, $2,574; Nurses and Helpers.

N. Y. C. CHILDREN'S HOSP. AND SCHL.—Randall's Island. Med. Dir., Dr. J. S. Rickards, $4,250; Clks., Helpers and Nurses.

STEAMBOATS—Helpers, Pilots, Engineers, etc.

Brooklyn and Queens.

Office, 327 Schermerhorn.

Dep. Com., P. J. Carlin, $5,500.

KINGS COUNTY HOSP.—Clarkson and Albany av. Gen. Med. Supt., Dr. M. D. Jones, $3,750; Dep. Med. Supt., Dr. F. M. Bauer, $3,430; Helpers, Clks., Nurses, etc.

N. Y. C. HOME FOR AGED AND INFIRM. Bkln. Div.—Clarkson and Albany av. Dr. T. I. Price, Dep. Med. Supt., $3,430; Helpers, etc.

GREENPOINT HOSP.—Kingsland av. and Bullion, Supt., R. G. Laub, $3,430; Supt. of Training Schl., N. McCarthy, $2,310; Helpers, Clks., Nurses, etc.

CUMBERLAND ST. HOSP.—109 Cumberland. Act. Supt., Dr. W. F. Jacobs, $3,400; Helpers, Nurses, etc.

BRADFORD ST. HOSP.—113 Bradford. Chf. Nurse in Ch., $1,389; Nurses and Helpers.

CONEY ISLAND HOSP.—Coney Island. Supt., A. Eberle, $2,770; Nurses and Helpers.

Richmond.

Boro. Hall, St. George.

BUREAU OF INVESTIGATIONS—Supt., Mrs. E. McGowan, $2,016.

SEA VIEW HOSP.—Castleton Corners. Farm Colony and Mortuary. Dir., Dr. G. Kremer, $4,500; Helpers, etc.

PAROLE COMMISSION.

Municipal Bldg., Mhtn.

Created by Chap. 579, Laws of 1915. Jurisdiction over inmates committed to N. Y. City Reformatory, N. Y. C. Penitentiary and Workhouse, on indeterminate sentences.

CITY OF NEW YORK MUNICIPAL GOVERNMENT—PAROLE COMMISSION—*Continued.*

Members—B. de N. Cruger, Ch., $7,500; M. Fogarty, $5,500; F. A. Lord (Dec. 28, 1927), $5,500. Ex-officio, J. A. Hamilton, Commr. of Correction; R. E. Enright, Police Commr., no salary. T. R. Minnick, Sec., $3,500; Ch. Parole Officer, Jas. J. Flynn, $2,820.

ARMORY BOARD.

Municipal Bldg., Mhtn.

The Mayor, Comptroller, Pres. of Bd. of Aldermen, Brig.-Gen. 1st Brig., Brig.-Gen. 2d Brig., Com. Officer Naval Mil., Pres. Dept. of Taxes and Assets; Sec., C. D. Rhinehart,* $4,500; Supt. Con. Rep. and Sup., L. V. Meehan, $3,800; Steno., L. M. Sweet, $3,200; Insp. of Rep. and Sup., Robert Telfer, $2,700; Insp. of Rep. and Sup., T. J. York, $2,520; Insp. Masonry, W. F. Stone, $1,980; Bkpr., C. J. Barry, $2,520; Clks., J. F. X. McCarty, $2,232; C. F. Finnerty, $2,172; M. M. Walker, $1,220.

BOARD OF ASSESSORS.

809 Municipal Bldg., Mhtn.

3 Assessors appointed by Mayor; duties defined Sec. 943, City Charter.

Assessors, Wm. C. Ormond, Pres., $5,500; A. T. Sullivan, M. Simmons, $5,000 each; 7 Clks., $1,944 to $3,000; 2 Stenos., $1,683 to $2,892; 1 Mess., $1,610; 1 Draftsman, $2,676.

BOARD OF STANDARDS AND APPEALS.

Room 914, Municipal Bldg., Mhtn.

Ch., W. E. Walsh. Mems.: J. J. Beatty, John De Hart, A. J. Boulton, J. P. Holland, Jas. Kearney, John Kenlon, Fire Ch.; Thos. J. Drennan, Fire Com.; R. P. Miller, Supt. of Bldgs., Mhtn.; P. J. Reville, Supt. of Bldgs., Bronx; A. E. Kleinert, Supt. of Bldgs., Bkln.; J. W. Moore, Supt. of Bldgs., Queens; W. J. McDermott, Supt. of Bldgs., Richmond; Sec., J. A. McMahon, $4,500. Meets Tuesdays, 10 A.M.

EXAMINING BOARD OF PLUMBERS.

Municipal Bldg., 9th floor, Mhtn.

Mems. of Bd.: M. J. McGrath, T. J. Gorman, J. J. Hassett, ex-officio mems., A. J Griffin. Exams. are held monthly.

BOARD OF PURCHASE.

Municipal Bldg., Mhtn.

Com., G. A. Whalen, Ch.; Com. J. F. Gilchrist, Com. J. A. Hamilton; A. E. Hull, Sec., $5,500; A. L. Meehan, Asst. Sec., $4,500; P. B. Mitchell, Gen. Insp., $4,300; Exam., D. V. Daff, $4,640; Eng., F. L. Belknap, $4,000; 32 Clks., $560 to $4,000; 13 Stenos. and Typr. Copyists, $926 to $2,520.

BOARD OF AMBULANCE SERVICE.

Municipal Bldg., Mhtn.

Composed of Commr. of Police, Commr. of Public Welfare, Pres. Bd. of Trustees Bellevue and Allied Hospitals and 2 citizens app. by Mayor. (See City Charter.) No salary.

COMN. OF ESTIMATE AND APPRAISAL.

Municipal Bldg., 17th floor, Mhtn.

Clk., W. H. Jasper, $4,500.

PUBLIC SERVICE COMMISSION.

(See index.)

BANK COMMISSION.

Charter Section 196.

The Mayor, Chamberlain and Comptroller shall by a majority vote, by written notice to Compt., designate the banks or trust cos. in which all moneys of City of N. Y. shall be deposited, and may, by like notice in writing, from time to time, change the banks and trust cos. thus designated.

BOARD OF HAZARDOUS TRADES.

Municipal Bldg., Mhtn.

To formulate recommendations of rules and regulations for diminishing fire dangers in the conduct of hazardous trades. Members, designated by Fire Com., are: J. M. Hannon, Dep. Fire Comr. and Ch.; W. F. Thompson, Dep. Fire Comr. B. & Q.; J. Kenlon, Ch. of Dept.; J. B. Martin, Asst. Ch. of Dept.; P. J. Gillespie, Sup. Insp. Bureau of Fire Prev.; J. F. Dixon, Asst. Insp. of Combustibles; D. D. Gallagher, Sec.

BOROUGH GOVERNMENTS.

PRESIDENTS AND COMMRS. OF PUBLIC WORKS.

The Presidents of five boroughs are elected at the same time as Mayor, for period of 4 yrs.; their present terms expiring Dec. 31, '21. Borough Presidents, within their respective boroughs, have charge of highway, sewer and topographical work; of care of public bldgs. and offices, and of enforcement of bldg. code; Presidents of Boroughs of Queens and Richmond also have charge of street cleaning.

Among the miscellaneous powers of Borough Pres are following: Licensing of sub-surface vault spaces; removal of encumbrances upon the sidewalks and highways; control over projecting signs; granting permission to use and open streets for any purpose; construction and maintenance of all bridges and tunnels, except those crossing navigable streams; care of public baths, comfort stations and placing of street signs. (See City Charter.)

Manhattan.

Municipal Bldg.

Pres., Henry H. Curran, $7,500; Boro. Sec., C. H. Woodward,* $6,000; Sec. to Pres., A. L. Smith, Jr.,* $5,000; Conf. Insp., W. J. Lyons, $3,500; Steno. to Pres., Miss Harriet Mullen, $2,736; Clk., $2,520; Steno. and Mess.

COM. OF PUBLIC WORKS—Municipal Bldg. Com., C. H. Fay,* $7,500; Asst. Com., J. S. Shea, $6,500; Sec. to Com., Miss Harriet E. Porritt,* $4,040; Aud., H. H. Lloyd, $4,500; Steno. to Com., H. J. Stanton, $2,160; Cons. Eng., A. Schaeffer,* $7,500; Asst. Engs., $2,160 to $5,000; Bkpr., $2,232; Stenos., $1,512 to $2,400; Clks., $720 to $5,000.

Bronx.

177th and 3d av.

Pres., H. Bruckner, $7,500; Sec. of Boro., A. W. Glatzmayer, $4,700; Sec. to Pres., Thos. J. Dolen,* $5,000; Cons. Eng., L. Haffen,* $7,500; Eng. in Ch., J. H. Fitch, $6,500.

COM. OF PUBLIC WORKS—Com., Wm. J. Flynn, $7,500; Asst. Com., Jos. Hawatsch,* $4,700; Sec. to Com., Geo. B. Hefter,* $3,700.

Brooklyn.

Borough Hall

Pres., Edw. Riegelmann, $7,500; Sec., F. Fogarty,* $5,500; Boro. Sec., Miss Sarah Stephenson, $4,250; Con. Eng., P. P. Farley, $7,500; Clk. in Ch., W. J. Cantwell, $3,800; Conf. Insp., J. E. Corrigan, $3,000; 1 Chf. Clk., $3,500; 1 Asst. Eng., $3,500; 1 Sp. Exam., $4,000; 14 Stenos., $1,464 to $2,400; 13 Clks., $720 to $1,220; 9 Clks., $1,586 to $2,160; 7 Clks., $2,340 to $3,500; 1 Mess., $1,708; 5 Tel. Opers., $1,100 to $1,610; 1 Att., $1,525.

COM. OF PUBLIC WORKS—Com., Jos. Guider,* $7,500; Asst. Com., Jos. Fennelly,* $6,000; Sec. to Com., Chas. Minsterer,* $4,000.

Queens.

Borough Hall, L. I. City.

Pres., Maurice E. Connolly, $5,000; Sec. to Pres., H. Hall, $4,300; Steno. to Pres., E. Sonderocker, $2,400; Sec. of Bor., Jos. Flanagan,* $5,000; Conf. Insp., A. Twombley,* $2,520.

COM. OF PUBLIC WORKS—Com., F. X. Sullivan,* $6,500; Asst. Com., W. A. Shipley, $4,500; Sec. to Com., J. Gerold, $3,000; Cons. Eng., C. B. Moore,* $7,500.

Richmond.

Borough Hall, New Brighton, S. I.

Pres., C. D. Van Name, $5,000; Sec., G. T. Egbert,* $3,750; Sec. to Pres., H. J. Jamison, $4,000; Steno. to Pres., J. J. Doran,* $2,520; 6 Clks., $800 to $2,772; 2 Messgrs., $1,830 to $1,944.

COM. OF PUBLIC WORKS—Com., J. E. Bowe,* $5,500; Asst. Com., R. R. McKee, $4,100; Sec. to Com., W. H. Durkin, $3,200; Chf. Clk., W. B. Kenney, $3,640; 8 Clks., $1,040 to $2,772; 2 Stenos., $2,400 and $2,928.

BUREAU OF ENGINEERING.

The Chf. Engineer of this bureau is appointed by the Bor. Pres. to carry out Sec. 388 of the City Charter, which says that the Pres. of the Bor. has jurisdiction in his borough over regulating, grading, curbing, flagging and guttering of streets; constructing and repairing public roads, viaducts, tunnels and sewers, paving and repaving streets, laying of all surface railroad tracks; filling in sunken and fencing vacant lots; the issue of permits to construct vaults under sidewalks, and to builders and others to use the streets.

Manhattan.

Municipal Bldg., 21st floor.

BUR. OF ENGINEERING—Chf. Eng., C. M. Pinckney, $6,620; Prin. Asst. Eng., E. N. Raleigh, $5,500; Asst. Engrs., W. E. Dey, $4,500; R. Lewis, $4,160; R. A. MacGregor, $3,640; and J. J. Mur-

*Exempt civil service class.

CITY OF NEW YORK MUNICIPAL GOVERNMENT—BUREAU OF ENGINEERING—*Continued.*

phy, $3,580; Asst. Engrs., $2,100 to $4,000; Supt. Asphalt Plant, C. H. Doherty, $3,440; Transitmen, $2,300 to $2,600; Levelers, Rodmen, $1,500 to $2,500; Axemen, $1,500 to $1,700; Draftsmen, $2,000 to $2,600; Insps., $1,600 to $2,550; Clks., $1,000 to $3,500; Gen. Insps., $1,800 to $3,500; Foremen paid by annual salary; Masons, Bricklayers, Laborers paid by day; Mess. and Attds., $1,495 to $1,945.

Bronx.

Sewers and Highways.

Tremont and 3d avs.

MAINTENANCE—Supt. Hghys., A. J. Largy,* $4,700; Eng. of Maint., J. P. Binzen, $4,700; Chf. Clk., E. Schweitzer, $3,350; Permit Clk., C. H. Buntinx, $2,520; 11 Clks., 1 Cashier, 1 Transitman, 1 Rodman, 1 Steno. and Typewriter, 2 Typewriter Copyists, 1 Attendant, 1 Mess., 1 Supt. of Asphalt Plant, 1 Gen. Insp., 1 Gen. Insp. and Foreman, 1 Gen. Foreman of Stable and Yards, 2 Gen. Foremen, 19 Insps., 41 Foremen, 1 Storekeeper's Helper, 1 Asst. Foreman, 8 Rammers, 20 Pavers, 392 Labs., 4 Flaggers, 19 Carts, 3 Hostlers, 3 Stablemen, 5 Drivers, 6 Steam Roller Engrs., 6 Firemen, 1 Bricklayer, 2 Asphalt Foremen, 37 Asphalt Workers, 3 Carpenters, 3 Painters, 2 Machinists, 1 Helper, 1 Wheelwright, 2 Blacksmiths, 2 Helpers, 57 Teams.

ENGINEERING BUREAU—Eng.-in-Charge, J. H. Fitch, $6,500; 1 Asst. Engr., 3 Clks., 1 Typr. Copy., 1 Steno. and Typr.

SEWER DIVISION—Asst. Engr., E. F. Austin, $4,700; 9 Asst. Engrs., 5 Transitmen, 3 Draftsmen, 3 Levelers, 8 Rodmen, 2 Axemen, 1 Clk., 1 Steno. and Type.

TOPOGRAPHICAL DIVISION—Asst. Engr., J. C. Hume, $4,700; 5 Asst. Engrs., 3 Transitmen, 6 Draftsmen, 2 Levelers, 4 Rodmen, 3 Clks., 1 Steno. and Type., 1 Searcher.

HIGHWAYS DIVISION—Asst. Eng., F. F. McDowell, $4,700; 10 Asst. Engrs., 7 Transitmen, 3 Draftsmen, 3 Levelers, 12 Rodmen, 5 Axemen, 1 Clk., 1 Copy. Type.

DIV. OF SUBSURFACE STRUCTURES—Asst. Eng., N. B. K. Hoffman, $3,880; 1 Asst. Eng., 1 Transitman, 5 Rodmen.

Brooklyn.

50 Court.

Supt., Hy. Hesterberg,* $6,000; Chf. Eng., H. H. Smith, $5,500; Asst. Engrs., J. Schmitt, $4,900; A. E. Allen, W. R. Tenney, $4,500 each; G. Berry, E. D. Rhame, J. Strachan, $3,920 each; H. J. Barker, $3,500; L. Burt, $3,140; O. Claussner, $3,350; Wm. J. Shea, $3,008; Chem., W. H. Broadhurst, $3,440; Chf. Clk., W. F. McGowan, $3,600; 1 Asst. Engrs., at $2,544; 8 at $2,520; Supt. Asphalt Plant, J. H. Garahan, $3,500; 2 Eng. Insps., $2,500; 4 Transitmen, $2,304 to $2,520; 2 Topo. Draftsmen, $2,232 to $2,376; 1 Leveler, 3 Rodmen, 3 Axemen, $1,610 to $2,232; 1 Asst. Chem., $2,448; Junior Chem., $2,016; 25 Clks., $896 to $2,952; Stenos. and Typrs., $1,525 to $2,100; 1 Copyist, 1 Mess., 6 Auto Engns., 1 Driver, 51 Insps., 3 Gen. Foremen, 944 Insps., Foremen, Pavers, Rammers, Flaggers, Laborers, Asphalt Workers, etc. Per diem vehioular force; 175 Trucks, Wagons, Carts, etc.

DIVISION OF INCUMBRANCES AND PERMITS—Supt., C. J. Cassidy, $3,200; 5 Insps., $1,872 to $2,040; 1 Foreman, 10 Laborers.

TOPOGRAPHICAL BUR.—209 Montague. Chf. Eng., C. R. Ward, $6,000; Asst. Engs., A. C. Forbes, $4,500; E. C. Ranson, $3,680; G. W. Hebert, $3,500; N. W. Stanley, $3,350; 8 Asst. Engrs. at $2,772; 2 at $2,970; 6 Transitmen, $2,376 to $2,520; 2 Topo. Draftsmen, $2,520 each; 2 Rodmen, $1,823 to $1,944; 1 Searcher, $2,520; 3 Axemen, $1,610; Mess., $1,647; 1 Clk., $1,823; 1 Steno., $1,683.

Queens.

Subway Bldg., Hunters Pt. and Van Nest avs., L. I. City.

Supt., Dr. J. J. Kindred, $4,500; Eng. in Ch., J. Rice, $6,620; 10 Transitmen, $1,800 to $2,520; 22 Asst. Engs., $2,304 to $4,500; 30 Draftsmen, $1,769 to $3,008; 12 Rodmen, $1,464 to $1,944; 12 Axemen, $1,537 to $1,610; 3 Chainmen, $1,823; 4 Eng. Insps., $2,160 to $2,520; 21 Insps. (Highways), $1,823 to $2,088; 35 Insps., Sewer Const., $1,586 to $2,136; 54 Clks. and Stenos., $840 to $2,952; Foremen, Pavers, Carpenters, Blacksmiths, Striper, Painters, Bricklayers, Drivers and Laborers, paid mostly by day.

TOPOGRAPHICAL BUR.—Municipal Bldg., L. I. City. Eng. in Ch., C. U. Powell, $6,500; Asst. Eng., L. Schoonmaker, $4,500; 24 Asst. Engs., $2,520 to $3,800; 19 Transitmen, $1,830 to $2,520; 35 Topo. Draftsmen, $1,872 to $2,952; 2 Computers, $2,520; 5 Rodmen, $1,512 to $1,823; 18 Axemen, $1,405 to $1,683; 4 Stenos. and Typrs., $1,376 to $1,739; 1 Clk., $2,772; 2 Clks., $1,376; 4 Messgrs., $1,525 to $1,872; 1 Auto Engn., $1,823.

Richmond.

Borough Hall, St. George, S. I.

Supt. Highways,* R. Bailey, $4,000; Chf. Clk., E. B. Sheeran, $3,330; Clks., A. Greenwald, $2,280; J. J. Gunning, $1,739; F. W. Musgrove, $1,823; Stenos., J. M. Owens, $1,800; F. H. Birmelin, $2,160; Cash., F. M. Ohliger, Jr.,* $2,304; Asst. Engrs., A. G. Bouton, W. J. Noonan, $3,000 each; 3 Insps., $2,448 each; Auto Engn., G. H. Kress, Jr., $1,830; 1 Insp., $1,920; 3 Auto Truck Drivers, $1,537 each; Ch. Insp., $2,772.

BUR. OF ENGINEERING—Engr., T. S. Oxholm, $5,500; Asst. Engrs., L. W. Freeman, $4,100; V. H. Reichelt, $3,350; Ellarson Stout, $3,600; H. Mouronval, W. B. Grubbe, $3,200 each; T. B. Oakley, W. R. Borst, $3,000 each; T. P. Edwards, $2,772; F. Muller, H. I. Lurye, $2,880 each; W. Selmer, $2,772; F. E. Engelman, $2,520; R. J. Millner, $2,448. In addition 49 employees that include Transitmen, Computers, Rodmen, Axemen, Topo. Draftsmen, Clks., Steno. and Typr., Typr. Copys., Insps., Foremen, Laborers, Drivers, Auto Enginemen, etc.

BUREAU OF SEWERS.

The Pres. of the Bor. has charge in his borough of all matters relating to public sewers and drainage of city; and prepares plans for and supervises construction of all sewers. He can contract for materials to be used in the maintenance. He appoints officials in charge. The city is authorized to acquire title to all lands required for such purposes.

Manhattan.

(See Bur. of Engineering.)

Bronx.

(See Bur. of Engineering.)

Brooklyn.

Mechanics Bank Bldg., 10th floor.

Supt., J. J. Browne,* $5,500; Asst. Supt. of Maint. and Rep., T. J. McGee, $3,300; Chf. Eng., A. J. Griffin, $5,500; Asst. Engrs., G. T. Hammond, $4,500; F. R. Bartlett, $5,000; J. C. Riedel, $4,500; G. E. Winslow, Wm. A. Markey, F. C. Bates, $3,500 each; L. A. Walsh, $3,920; W. S. Moore, I. H. Kirby, $3,500 each; J. H. Vogt, $3,500; H. J. Lynch, D. T. Pithethly, F. O. Schellenberg, W. G. Closson, Asst. Engrs., $3,008 each; J. L. Pittaluga, G. H. Knight, Chas. Harper, $2,970 each; Peter Farley, $3,008; Jos. C. Zengerle, $2,280; W. P Hennessy, $2,970; Foremen Rep. Yd., G. E. Higgins, $2,520; F. Lingsweller, $2,424; Chas. T. McPauley, Foreman, $2,520; 10 Clks., $824 to $3,080; 9 Stenos. and Typists and Copyist, $1,464 to $2,280; 46 Rodmen, Transitmen, Axemen, Draftsmen and Asst. Engr., $1,464 to $2,544; Foremen, Insps., Laborers, Stokers, Drivers, etc., mostly paid by day.

Queens.

Queens Subway Bldg., L. I. City.

Supt., J. R. Higgins, $4,500; Chf. Clk., H. A. Bornscheuer, $2,520; Act. Chf. Eng., H. Tait, $4,500; Eng. of Const., J. F. Perrine, $4,300; Eng. of Design, F. Seeley, $4,400; Eng. of Maint., E. W. Firth, $3,350; 9 Asst. Engs., $2,100 to $3,300; 36 Draftsmen, Clks., etc., $1,317 to $3,008; 35 Insps., $1,560 to $2,160; 5 Ward Foremen, $2,136 each; Laborers, Engs., Stokers, etc., paid by day.

Richmond.

Boro. Hall, St. George, S. I.

Supt. of Sewers, C. P. Cole,* $4,000; Clk., E. A. Taylor, $1,830; Transitman, F. A. Dillon, $2,448; 2 Insps., $1,800 to $3,000; Foremen, Drivers, Laborers, etc. Supts. apptd. by Boro. President.

BUREAU OF BUILDINGS.

Manhattan.

Municipal Bldg., 20th floor.

Supt., R. P. Miller,* $7,500; Chf. Insps., R. C. Bastress,* F. C. Kuehnle,* Asst. Supt., W. D. Brush, $4,500 each; Sec. to Supt., W. Goldstecker,* $3,500; Clks., $660 to $2,520; Stenos., $1,200 to $2,112; Messgrs., $1,376 to $1,823; Insps., $1,512 to $3,140; Asst. Engs., $2,208 to $3,200; Eng. Insps., $2,016 to $2,160.

*Exempt civil service class.

CITY OF NEW YORK MUNICIPAL GOVERNMENT—BUREAU OF BUILDINGS—*Continued.*

Bronx.

3d av. and 177th.

Supt., P. J. Reville,* $6,000; Asst. Supt., C. L. Halberstadt,* $4,200; Sec. to Supt., R. J. Connolly, $3,250; Chf. Insp., E. Odell, $3,700; Chf. Clk., C. T. Ulman, $3,330; Gen. Insp., Thos. T. Petersen, $3,140; 3 Asst. Engs., $1,800 to $2,544; Chf. Plan Exam., $3,000; Plan Exam., $2,328; Insp. Arch. Eng., $2,970; 45 Insps., $1,683 to $2,544; 9 Clks., $760 to $2,520; 3 Messgrs., $1,823; 2 Stenos., $1,739; 1 Copyist, $1,405.

Brooklyn.

Boro. Hall.

Supt., A. E. Kleinert,* $6,500; Asst. Supt., Wm. Stone,* $4,500; Sec. to Supt., Valentine Theisen,* $2,640; Chf. Clk., W. W. Richards, $4,000; Chf. Insp., T. P. Flanagan,* $4,000; Chf. Insp., J. J. Kilcourse, $3,250; Chf. of Public Safety Div., J. C. Snackenberg, $3,250; Chf. Plan Exam., J. J. Koen, $3,420; Chf. Insp. of Plumbing, Wm. J. Allen, $2,400; 18 Clks., $660 to $2,520; 69 Insps. Carp. and Masonry, $1,586 to $2,760; 21 Insps. Plumbing, $1,872 to $2,760; 12 Insps. Elevators, $1,683 to $2,160; 2 Insps. Plastering, $1,944 each; 2 Messgrs., $1,366 to $1,390; 4 Stenos. and Type., $1,525 to $1,836; 4 Insps. Iron and Steel, $1,683 to $2,160; 6 Asst. Eng., $2,160 to $3,200; 8 Plan Exams., $1,830 to $1,944; 2 Process Servers, $1,537 to $1,586.

Queens.

Hackett Bldg., L. I. City.

Supt., J. W. Moore,* $4,500; Asst., E. F. Cunningham,* $3,500; Sec., C. Fredericks,* $2,620; Chf. Clk., G. A. Brown, $2,500; Chf. Insp., C. F. Bales,* $3,008.

Richmond.

Boro. Hall, St. George, S. I.

Supt., W. J. McDermott, $4,500; Asst., J. E. Murphy, $3,000; Sec. to Supt., L. A. Quinlan,* $1,830; Chf. Clk., J. Nolan, $3,800; Clks., J. A. Simonson, $2,520; H. M. Speight, $2,232; Steno., W. P. Reilly, $1,920; Eng. Insp., A. B. Comins, $2,160; Plan Exam., John Davies, $1,944; Chf. Insp., R. Langere, $3,500; 11 Insps., $1,683 to $2,280; Auto Engineman, $1,944.

BUR. OF PUBLIC BLDGS. AND OFFICES.

Manhattan.

Municipal Bldg., 20th floor.

Supt., F. H. Hines,* $5,500; Supv. Insp., B. J. Corcoran, $3,320; Asst. Eng., J. H. Stewart, $4,350; Asst. Eng., W. J. Gillen, $3,500; Mech. Engs., G. S. Eble, $3,300; A. T. Brice, $3,000; S. P. DeLemos, $3,000; Arch. Draftsman, H. H. Rice, $2,592; Clks., $620 to $2,088; Janitors, $1,440 to $2,376; Attds., $1,575; Tele. Opers., $1,200 to $1,823; Elev. Attds., $1,586; Stat. Engs., Firemen, Mechs., Foremen, Elevatormen, Laborers, etc., paid by the day.

Bronx.

Tremont and 3d avs.

Supt., P. J. Kane, $4,700; Clk., J. J. Naughton, $2,580; Tel. Oper., Alice T. Tierney, $1,550; Attds., Foremen, Cleaners, Elevatormen, Watchmen, etc.

Brooklyn.

50 Court.

Supt., Jas. J. Byrne,* $6,000; Chf. Clk. (vacant), $3,800; Asst. Eng., W. R. Griffith, $3,500; 6 Clks., $656 to $2,200; 5 Insps., $1,800 to $2,300; 10 Janitors, 350 Attds., Elevatormen, Laborers, Cleaners, Watchmen, etc.

Queens.

Borough Hall, L. I. C.

Supt., Jos. Sullivan,* $4,000; Chf. Clk., W. E. Everitt, $2,520; Assts. mostly paid by day.

Richmond.

Boro. Hall, St. George, S. I.

Supt., J. Timlin, Jr.,* $4,000; Clk., C. Kuttruff, $2,520; Clk. (vacant); Foremen and Laborers, Janitors, Driver, Cleaners, Engs., Stokers, Elevatormen.

COUNTY OFFICIALS IN GREATER NEW YORK.

NEW YORK COUNTY.

Surrogate's Court.

Hall of Records.

Sur., J. P. Cohalan,‡ $15,000; elect. trm., 14 yrs., exp. Dec. 31, 1922; Sur., J. A. Foley,* $15,000, elect. trm., 14 yrs., exp. Dec. 31, 1933; Chf. Clk., W. R. DeLano,* $11,000; Comr. of Rec., J. T. Curry,* $5,500; Dep. Chf. Clk. (vacant), $6,500; Asst. Dep. Chf. Clk., W. H. Down, $4,500; Law Assts., A. T. O'Leary,* $7,200; A. J. Barrett,* $7,000; R. Cummins,* $7,000; H. E. Nagle,* $6,000; W. B. Farrell,* $6,000 Clk. of Ct., D. J. Dowdney,* $6,000; Dep. Clk. of Ct., J. H. Nagle, $3,600; Clk. Add'l Pt. of Ct., James O'Hara, $3,600; Clk. to Sur., J. F. Brosnan,* John J. Cray,* $4,200 each; Stenos., P. Jones, J. F. Pruden, $4,500 each; Sup. of Sup., T. F. Doherty, $3,180; Cal. Clk. and Supt. of Copyists, E. G. McGinnis, $2,220; Prob. Clk., J. Washburn, $6,000; Asst. Prob. Clks., B. A. Jackson, $3,180; J. A. Killoran, J. E. Quinn, $2,220 each; Admn. Clk., H. C. Moore, $4,500; 1st Asst. Admn. Clk., J. A. Lynch, $3,180; Acct. Clk., C. J. Donovan, $3,600; Sup. Rec. Clks., T. C. Glennon, $2,700; 27 Clks., $1,708 to $2,401; 8 Ct. Attds., $2,500 each; 3 Messgrs., $2,820 each; 6 Stenos.

TRANSFER TAX DEPT.—Trans. Tax Asst., J. J. Kearney,* $6,500; Trans. Tax Clk., J. Keenan, $2,400; Asst., M. J. Ford, $1,800; Rec. Clk. (vacant), $1,300; Steno., M. V. Fitzgerald, $1,200.

Sheriff's Office.

31 Chambers.

Shff., D. H. Knott, $12,000; elect. trm., 4 yrs., exp. Dec. 31, 1921; Un. Sheriff, J. V. Coggey, $6,500; Counsel, G. W. Olvany, $6,500; Asst. Counsel, Geo. H. Engel, $4,000; Chf. Clk., J. A. Bell, $4,500. Dep. Sheriffs at $3,500: J. J. Coakley, Wm. A. Glennon, C. Kramer, J. C. Hackett, C. Plunkett, P. J. Halloran, J. P. Murphy, J. F. Neilson, L. Ressler, B. Gorman, T. F. Burke, W. Cuff, W. T. Fitzsimmons, P. J. Conlin, N. P. Sinnott. Asst. Dep. Sheriffs at $2,280: Wm. J. Gallagher, N. Marinelli, M. Eisenstein, L. W. Rooney, F. Donnelly, J. A. Lanman, L. D. Curtin, H. Smullen, T. J. Cunningham, S. Juskovitz, T. Kane, C. P. Coyle, J. D. Sullivan, Wm. Lee, P. O'Keefe. Ent. Clk., T. J. McMahon, $2,880; Asst. Ent. Clk., L. Marconnier, $1,944; Bond Clk., T. A. Ellis, $2,160; Cash., F. P. Young, $2,760; Asst. Cash., A. F. Caridi, $2,280; Aud., E. H. Warker, $3,200; Asst. Aud., G. M. Gruber, $2,232; Asst. Clk., T. P. McElvoy, $2,040; Jy. Clk., D. McCarthy, $1,823; Warden, Eugene Johnson, $3,250; Dep. Warden, E. Redeke, $2,088; 4 Clks., $1,647 to $1,823; 9 Guards, $1,920 each; 11 Kprs., $1,622 each; Steno., Copyists, Mess., etc.

District Attorney's Office.

Criminal Courts Bldg.

PROFESSIONAL STAFF—Dist. Atty., Edw. Swan, $15,000; elect. term, 4 yrs., exp. Dec. 31, 1921. Asst. Dist. Atty., Joab H. Banton,* $12,000; Asst. Dist. Attys., $10,000: G. N. Brothers,* J. T. Dooling,* R. S. Johnstone,* W. A. McQuaid,* A. I. Rorke,* R. C. Taylor.* Asst. Dist. Attys., $7,500: T. L. Waugh,* O. W. Bohan,* J. M. Donohue,* E. P. Kilroe,* S. Markewich,* M. R. Ryttenberg,* J. E. Smith.*

DEP. ASST. DIST. ATTYS.—J. G. Wallace,* A. Blogg Unger,* $5,500 each; G. A. Lavelle,* $5,000; J. D. Edelson,* H. W. Hastings,* J. F. Joyce,* T. A. McGrath,* J. E. McDonald,* F. Q. Morton,* F. J. Sullivan,* S. Tekulsky,* J. Forrester,* J. C. Myers,* J. F. O'Neil,* $4,500 each; J. Cardone,* T. J. Whalen,* $4,000 each; L. Lazarus,* E. Weil,* H. M. R. Goodman,* M. H. Panger,* $3,500 each; M. J. Driscoll,* P. F. Marro,* $4,000 each; J. T. Hogan,* W. O'Shaughnessy,* $2,880 each; D. Direnzo,* H. Kastenbaum,* A. Lehman,* M. A. Lynch,* R. Rothenberg,* J. F. Wheaton,* $2,800 each; L. C. Carlino,* J. R. Hennis,* E. B. McGuire,* J. B. Stanchfield, Jr., P. L. F. Sabbatine,* S. Untermyer,* $2,400 each; Med. Asst., O. H. Schultze, M.D.,* $5,500; Priv. Sec., $4,680.

ADMINISTRATIVE STAFF—Chf. Clk., J. T. Neary,* $6,000; Dep. Chf. Clk., A. Fay, $4,350; Dep. Chf. Clk. and Aud., J. J. Buckley, $4,350; Clk., J. Kennaly, $3,250; Grand Jury Clk., E. J. Kelly, $3,250; 18 Clks. at $2,880; 4 Clks. at $2,400; 23 Stenos., $2,220 to $3,250; Chf. Process Server, J. P. Donnellan, $2,904; 49 Process Servers, $1,830 to $2,220; Messgrs., etc.

BUR. OF SPECIAL SESSIONS INFORMATION—Dep. Asst. Dist. Attys., R. D. Petty,* $5,500; B. D. Dineen,* $3,250; 3 Clks., $2,880; 1 Clk., $3,250; 1 Law Steno., $1,830; 12 Process Servers, $1,830 to $2,200.

Register's Office.

Hall of Records.

Reg., J. A. Donegan,* $12,000; elect. trm., 4 yrs., exp. Dec. 31, 1921; Dep., E. P. Holahan,* $5,500; Asst. Dep., M. Holzman,* $3,500; Chf. Clk., Chas. W Schluter, $3,900; Chf. Statis. Clk., J. A. O'Reilly, $3,900; Chf. Block Index Clk., W. F. Hull,* $3,500; Cashs., M. B. Hoffman,* $2,520; T. Murray.

*Exempt civil service class.

$2,160; Chat. Mort. Clk., P. F. Glennen, $3,330; Sup. of Index, A. Weigand, $3,250; Search. and Exam., M. Werden, $2,640; Chf. Rec. Clk., A. Spies, $3,074; Sup. of Index, E. J. Reilly, $2,520; Sec., Grace M. Mahoney,* $3,300; 50 Clks., $1,823 to $2,232; 1 Steno., $1,823; 14 Custodians, $1,146 to $1,823; 15 Folio Writers, per folio 5c.

PRESERVATION OF PUBLIC RECORDS—Chf. Clk., S. S. Lipschutz, $3,074; 8 Clks., $1,683 to $1,944; 3 Bkbdrs., $2,150 each.

MORTGAGE TAX BUR.—Spe. Dep. Reg., L. J. Donegan,* $4,400; Cash., B. F. Plunkett, $3,300; Exam., J. B. Doland, $3,300; Steno., $500.

REINDEXING DEPT.—Spe. Dep. Reg., M. J. McCarthy $5,600; Asst. Spe. Dep. Reg., J. P. Davenport, $3,800; Ch. Sur., J. B. Gill, $2,772; Exam. in Ch., $3,232; 25 Abstractors, $1,420 to $1,940; 6 Laborers, $1,445; Steno., $700.

City Court.

32 Chambers, Mhtn.

Elected for 10 yrs.; salary $12,000, jurisdiction only over N. Y. City, as it was constituted before consolidation, and extends to common law action, involving property to $2,000 value.

JUSTICES, EXPIRATION OF TERMS AND CLERKS—Chf., E. F. O'Dwyer, Dec. 31, 1927; L. Wendel, J. M. Callahan, G. Hartman, Dec. 31, 1929; L. A. Valente, Edw. B. La Fetra, Dec. 31, 1921; A. G. Meyer, A. Finelite, J. L. Walsh, P. Schmuck, Dec. 31, 1927; Stenos., C. T. Tinkham, C. J. Barnes, J. R. Potts, J. R. Stevenson, G. C. Kiesel, Wm. J. Norton, C. H. Redfern, T. F. Falvey, C. J. Doran, G. H. Gordon, $3,300 each; Conf. Steno., J. J. Murphy, $2,340; Intprs., P. F. Schmitt, J. Rollins, A. A. Wimmer, $2,200 each; Clk., F. J. Goodwin, $6,000; Dep. Clks., F. J. Smith, $3,450; T. J. Sullivan, $3,060; Wm. C. Blaney, $4,000; L. Heft, $2,575 each; Lib., Louis Schaefer, $3,000; Asst. Clks., 12 at $2,574 each; 7 at $2,100 each; Tele. Oper., $1,140; Attds., 1 at $1,920; 24 at $1,800 each; 2 at $1,350 each.

County Clerk.

County Court House.

Co. Clk., William F. Schneider, $15,000; 1st Dep. Co. Clk., W. B. Selden,* $6,500; 2d Dep. Co. Clk., G. E. Best,* $4,500; 3d Dep. Co Clk., F. H. Warder, $3,500;; Counsel, J. A. Allen, $5,500; Supv. Clk., W. F. Schneider, Jr., $3,500; Aud., J. A. Wrede, $3,350; Equity Clk., D. J. Begley, $4,000; Law Clk., E. J. Horn, $3,500; Gen. Clk., E. B. Schwartz, $3,000; 75 Gen. Clks., $1,040 to $3,330; 6 Laborers, $1,445 each.

Commissioner of Jurors.

Stewart Bldg., Room 127.

Com., F. O'Byrne,* $6,000; Asst. Com., F. P. Simpson,* Sec., J. T. Carmody,* $3,800 each; Clk., C. H. Lindroth, $2,640; Clk., F. H. Cahoon, $2,400; 17 Clks., $1,920 to $2,220; 9 Messgrs. and Notice Servers, $1,823 to $1,920; 2 Messgrs., $1,920.

Commissioner of Records.

Hall of Records.

Com., C. K. Lexow,* $7,500; Dep., E. J. Driscoll,* $5,500; Supt., D. McEvoy,*, $4,000; Asst. Supt., F. J. Dotzler,* $3,600; Sec., W. G. Rose,* $2,160; Chf. Clk., J. Weintraub, $2,580; 49 Exam. Rec. Clks., Asst. to Rec. Clks., Stenos., Type. Copyists, Supv. Repair, etc., Bkbdrs., 11 Labs.

Public Administrator.

Hall of Records.

Adm., W. M. Hoes,* $10,000; Asst., F. W. Arnold,* $5,500; Chf. Clk., J. J. Connell, $3,700.

BRONX COUNTY.

County Court.

Tremont and Arthur avs.

Co. Judge, L. D. Gibbs, $12,500; elect. trm., 6 yrs., exp. Dec. 31, 1925. Sec., D. R. Kaplan, $3,100; Ct. Steno., Robt. Hamburger, $4,200; 14 Clks., Steno., Attendants, Detectives, etc.

Surrogate's Court.

Bergen Bldg., Tremont and Arthur avs.

Sur., G. M. S. Schulz,* $10,000; elect. trm., 6 yrs., exp. Dec. 31, 1925; Law Asst. and Clk. to Sur, F. Sigel,* $4,200; Chf. Clk. and Clk. of Court, H. H. Reilly,* $5,000; Adm. Clk., A. C. Otto, $4,000; Pro. Clk., G. F. Stiebeling, $4,500; Guardian Clk., Chas. Stein, $3,074; Cash., E. N. Patterson,* $3,500; Conf. Steno., B. V. Duffy, $2,520; Attend., T. Fitzgerald,* $2,160; Ct. Steno., H. M. A. Meyer, $2,851; Rec. Clks., P. F. Callahan, $1,830; R. Unger, $1,823.90; E. I. Havel, $1,823.90; Guardian Acct. Clk., H. W. Cook, $2,760; Index Clk., C. Mulvey, $2,160; Senior Clk., P. Sattler, $2,088; Acct. Clk., S. Boneparth, $3,140; Sten., G. W. Orthey, $2,400; Attend. and Mess., C. Cerussi, $1,944; Tr. Tax Clk., I. Silver, $2,500; Clk., F. J. Donnelly, $968.

Public Administrator.

2808 3d av.

Adm., E. E. L. Hammer, $4,500; Chf. Clk., Jno. Collins; Clk and Steno., C. M. Streubert. (City does not pay clerks' salaries.)

Sheriff's Office.

1932 Arthur av.

Shff., T. H. O'Neil, $10,000; elec. for unexp. term, exp. Dec. 31, 1921; Un. Shff., E. H. Miller,* $5,500; Counsel, Wm. A. Keating,* $5,000; Sec., D. J. Byrne, $3,000; Cash., J. M. Barrett, $3,000; Chf. Clk., W. S. O'Neill,* $3,000; Clks., J. O'Connor,* H. G. McCord, $1,823 each; T. Gleason, $1,683; H. P. Mulvany, $1,376; Steno., Miss M. F. Kennedy,* $1,823; Tel. Oper., Miss S. C. McLaughlin, $1,464; Mess., J. Donar, $1,823; Warden, Bronx Co. Jail, E. K. Butler, $2,640; Auc., J. J. Donovan, fees; Dep. Shffs., J. J. Hanraty,* J. J. Dooley, J. McCarthy,* J. L. Devine,* J. A. Bergen,* F. Conlon,* L. J. Fagan, J. H. Gebe, T. E. Fox, C. Broschart, $3,500 each; Asst. Dep. Shffs., P. Vormbaum,* J. E. Fitzpatrick,* M. J. Lyons,* J. Wegman,* C. Thoman, $1,800 each.

District Attorney.

Bergen Bldg.

Dist. Attorney, E. J. Glennon, $10,000; Asst. Dist. Attys., F. V. Oliver,* A. Cohn,* P. A. Hatting,* W. F. Quigley,* $5,000 each; Miss Julia A. Gainey, E. Chapman,* F. A. Dixon,* $4,500; J. P. Adlerman,* P. J. Tracy, G. De Leuta, $3,500 each; Aud., T. G. Emes, $2,750; Stenos. to Asst. Dist. Attys., D. M. Mahoney, J. Daly, $2,000 each; Miss Theresa A. Quilty, $1,495; T. A. Cryan,* $1,500; Interp., Jos. Pistone,* $1,500; Co. Dects., J. O'Hara,* T. H. Cobb, F. J. Clark, E. J. Skennion, W. P. Corbett, P. Fleischer, A. Burger, J. P. Luke, $1,700 each; Clk. to Gr. Jury, J. E. Moran, $1,700; Warden to Gr. Jury, Jas. Clark, $1 700; Process Servers, P. McDermott, E. McIntosh, $1,700; Indictment Clk., Thomas F. Quinn; Inform. Clk., D. T. O'Keefe, $1,800 each; Bail and Recognizance Clk., E. M. O'Gorman, $2,300; Clk., H. J. Fliederblum, $2,640; Tel. Oper., Margaret M. Feehan, $1,000; Mess., B. Hirsch, $1,700; Police Dept., Thomas Gleason.

Register's Office.

Tremont and Arthur avs.

Reg., Edward Polak, $10,000; elect. trm., 4 yrs., exp. Dec. 31, 1921; Dep. Reg., T. A. Maher,* $4,500; Asst. Dep. Reg., J. F. Healy, $3,500; Chf. Clk., J. P. Rice,* Cash., Jas. J. O'Donnell, $3,250 each; Sec., T. F. Driscoll,* Exam., A. E. Crowley; Sat. Clk., J. B. Corcoran, Chf. Index Clk., A. Liberi, $3,074 each; Steno., Edna Polak, $1,823; Bkpr., Emil L. Newman, $2,232; Chf. Record Clk., H. D. Frisbie, $2,520; Land Title Exams., W. Ascher, $4,000; 4 Clks., $2,376; 4 Clks., $2,088; 1 Clk., $2,160; 17 Clks., $1,944; 1 Clk., $1,592; 2 Clks., $1,439; 1 Clk., $1,406; 1 Bkbdr., $2,150; 1 Tel. Oper., $1,200; 1 Custodian, $1,980; 2 Custodians, $1,823; 2 Draftsmen, $1,464; 5 Laborers, $1,445; 10 Recording Clks., 5c. per folio.

MORTGAGE TAX DEPT.—Special Dep. Reg., T. F. Quinn, $3,000; Cash., B. Lipshay,* $2,250; Exam., W. D. Austin, $2,800.

County Clerk.

161st and 3d av.

Co. Clk., Robert L. Moran, $10,000; Dep. Co. Clk., C. F. Griffin,* $4,500; Asst. Dep. Co. Clk., J. J. Daly,* $3,500; Sec., F. X. Conlon,* $2,640; Counsel, J. Kadel,* $3,500; Ch. Clk., C. F. Carroll,* $3,250; Cash., E. F. Gilson,* $3,250; Notarial Clk., H. M. Schiffer, $3,250; Equity Clk., J. Cunnion, $3,500; Docket Clks., M. W. Jonas, S. H. Hecker, D. Rieback, $2,088 each; Lis Pendens and Lien Clk., F. Knezek, $2,232; Executive Clk., N. J. Eberhard, $3,320; Filing and Registration Clk., H. Linn, $2,040; Index Clk., L. Myerson, $1,830; Asst. Equity Clk., F. J. Quinn, $2,160; Comparing Clk., N. Metzger, $2,376; General Clks., J. H. Leddy, $3,000; I. L. Hirscher, $2,160; J. S. Readdy, $1,944; F. B. Egan, $1,920; J. H. Malone, $1,823; Clks., E. L. Geary, $1,830; J. Cahill, $1,739; J. Reisman, $1,683; A. Wolf, $1,610; D. Deutsch, $1,610; Recording Clk., F. F. Stahl, $1,439; Searcher, T. F. Haggblom, $2,520; 3 Messgrs., $1,464 each; 1 Mess., $1,376; 1 Bkdr., $1,800; 1 Lab., $1,317.

*Exempt from Civil Service.

CITY OF NEW YORK MUNICIPAL GOVERNMENT—COUNTY OFFICIALS—BRONX CO.—*Con.*

Commissioner of Jurors.

Arthur and Tremont avs.

Com., J. A. Mason,* $6,000; Asst. Com., J. A. Pachler,* Sec., J. E. Barkley,* $3,000 each; Chf. Clk., J. J. McMullin, $2,200; Clk., F. B. Bower, $1,800; Clk., Sten. and Typ., S. Goldschmidt, $1,980; July Notice Servers, C. F. Newman, D. W. Burke, C. D. McGuire, $1,540 each; Mess., J. A. Theis, $720.

KINGS COUNTY.

County Court.

120 Schermerhorn, nr. Smith.

Judge Wm. R. Bayes, trm. exp. Dec. 31, 1921; Judge, Reuben L. Haskell, elect. trm. exp. Dec. 31, 1925; Judge, J. Grattan MacMahon, elect. trm. exp. Dec. 31, 1924; Judge, Geo. W. Martin, elect. trm. exp. Dec. 31, 1921; Judge Mitchell May, trm. exp. Dec. 31, 1921, $12,500 each; Chf. Clk., John L. Gray,* $7,500; Dep. Chf. Clk., T. E. Griffin,* $5,000; Conf. Clks., P. Kraemer,* J. P. Carroll,* A. Werther,* C. E. Lemken, E. J. Allen,* $2,750 each; Stenos., L. A. Zimmerman, J. F. Kirkland, T. F. Darcy, R. E. Roberts, Geo. Rea, $4,500 each; G. R. Leonard, $2,100; Chf. Ct. Att., T. F. Buttling, $3,800; Asst. Chf. Ct. Att., S. B. Crane, $3,300; Clks., C. H. Foley, G. H. Murphy, B. F. Childs, $3,800 each; J. J. Gartland, $4,000; J. G. Fitzgerald, $3,200; J. H. Meehan, $3,800; G. W. McCluskey, $4,000; A. Levy, W. M. Cahill, $3,300 each; J. F. M. Anderson, F. F. Schulz, R. W. Gross, J. C. Rogers, T. O'Shea, Edward Rowland, $3,000 each; J. G. Giambalvo, $3,500; W. A. O'Connell, $3,100; D. W. Corrigan, $1,800; J. Bochner, $3,500; Detecs. J. Bagnarillo, J. F. Davis, N. Klaboe, $3,300 each; Co. Detecs., J. F. Tevlin, J. Astarita, $3,200 each: J. Shanahan, $2,000; Warden, Gr. Jy., M. J. Wheeler,* $3,500. 24 Attendants, $1,500 to $2,200; Steno., Wm. R. Foley, $4,000; Mess., $2,000; Tel. Oper., $1,200; 3 Prob. Officers, $1,800; Tel. Oper., $700; Laborers, etc.

Surrogate's Court.

Hall of Records.

Sur., Geo. A. Wingate, $15,000, elect. trm. 6 yrs., exp. Dec. 31, 1925; Chf. Clk. and Clk. of Ct., J. H. McCooey,* $9,000; Prob. Clk., J. V. Cain, $4,500; Acct. Clk., J. F. Regan, $5,000; Adm. Clk., J. J. Meagher, $4,000; Steno., F. Driscole, $3,000; Gdn. Acct. Cl., J. F. Belford, $4,000; Chf. of Rec. and Intpr., P. Bellman, $3,500; Law Asst., J. H. Schmid, $6,000; Index Clk., H. J. Wall, $2,750; Asst. Adm. Cl., M. R. Kays, $3,640; Cal. Clk., E. F. Bannigan, $3,000; Asst. Prob. Clk., G. B. Keenan, $2,640; Cert. and Fin. Clk., J. R. McDonald, $3,500; Asst. Acct. Clk., D. S. Brower, $3,000; Asst. Chf. of Rec., E. F. Duffy, $1,700; L. W. Faubel, $2,000; J. B. Scholl, $2,000; L. People, $2,000; Chf. Custd., Jas. E. Lennon, $1,800; 25 Ct. Officers, Clks., Mess.

Sheriff's Office.

50 Court.

Shff., John Drescher, $15,000, elect. trm. 2 yrs., exp. Dec. 31, 1921; Un. Shff., W. Schnitzspan, $6,500; Counsel, C. F. Murphy, $5,500; Chf. Clk., H. W. Whalen,* $3,300; Asst. Clk., E. A. Carbona,* $2,760; Eqty. Clk., J. H. Van Deusen,* $2,760; Asst. Eqty. Clk., C. F. Eckman,* $2,520; Sec., Miss Marie Frugone,* $2,040; Dep. Shffs. at $2,904—Geo. Owens, J. J. D'Amato,* A. De Martini,* M. Green,* H. Meyer,* J. E. McAvoy,* J. J. Brennan,* G. W. Meine,* Asst. Deps., $2,040 each—C. F. Williams,* W. Gerber,* J. McKeon,* G. Gunther,* J. Lennon,* A. C. Cowan,* S. Frank,* Wdn., R. Wright,* $3,500; Dep. Wdn., C. S. Francisco,* $2,640; Acct., M. Persico,* $2,160; Bkpr., H. Jacobs,* $2,040; Conf. Steno., D. Bregnan, $1,823; 8 Keepers, $1,708 each. etc.

District Attorney.

Livingston and Court.

Dist. Atty., H. E. Lewis, $15,000; elect. trm., 4 yrs., exp. Dec. 31, 1923; Assts., E. Caldwell,* H. N. Warbasse,* G. A. Voss,* $7,500 each; H. G. Anderson,* R. E. Hemstreet,* H. H. Kellogg,* A. E. Richardson,* $6,500 each; L. Goldstein,* J. E. Ruston, E. W. Cooper,* $6,000 each; B. T. Hock,* T. P. Peters,* $5,500 each; N. Selvagge,* $5,000; J. V. Gallagher,* $4,500; Dep. Assts., J. R. Hurley,* H. P. McCormick, $4,000 each; R. Wilson,* $3,500; H. Wandmaker,* $3,140; Med. Asst., E. M. Vaughan, $3,500; Chf. Clk., L. E. Birdseye,* $5,500; 7 Clks., $2,160 to $2,640; 9 Stenos., $2,160 to $2,520; 2 Stenos to Gd. Jy., $2,160 to $2,640; 12 Co. Detects., $2,040 to $2,160; 6 Process Servers, $1,823 each; 1 Mess., $1,708; 1 Dkpr., $1,708; 1 Tel. Oper., $1,464.

*Exempt from Civil Service.

Public Administrator.

44 Court.

Appointed by Surrogate; term, 5 yrs.

Adm., Frank V. Kelly'* $5,500; Chf. Clk., W. A. Manning, $2,640; Atty., P. B. Hanson, $3,500.

Register.

Hall of Records.

Reg., Ed. H. Maddox, $12,000; elect. trm., 2 yrs., exp. Dec. 31, 1921. Dep. Reg., J. Bartscherer,* $5,500; Asst. Dep. Reg., J. J. V. Dunn,* $3,850; Counsel, R. M. Johnston, $3,850; Sec., T. F. Livingston,* $2,400; Expert Clk., J. C. McDermott, $4,070; Land Title Exam., J. T. McGill, $3,850; Chf. Block Index Clk., L. L. Sanford, $3,300; Chf. Search and Exam., A. M. Milligan, $3,600; Tick. Clk., J. Swan, $3,480; Chf. Clk. of Copyists, P. V. Hickoy, $3,410; 1st Asst. Tick. Clk., E. H. Hand, $2,616; Chf. Current Index Clk., J. F. Carney, $2,616; Chf. Clk. of Rec., E. Hammond, $2,616; Bkpr., Wm. B. Vernan, $2,880; Exec. Clk., F. G. Kernan, $2,340; Chattel Mtg. Clk., C. E. Hauser, $2,616; Satisfaction Clk., A. D. Ecke, $2,520; Abstract Clks., 3 at $2,280 to $2,376; Asst. Cash., J. A. Gamble, $2,616; Steno., J. E. O'Connor, $2,376; Asst. Index Clks., 1 at $2,376; Asst. Index Clks., 6 at $2,160; Comparers, 4 at $2,376; Asst. Comparers, 3 at $2,376; Asst. Exams., 2 at $2,880; Entry Clk. at $2,376; Mailing Clk. at $2,160; Asst. Tick. Clks., 2 at $1,944 and $1,980; Chattel Mtg. Clk., $1,980; Clks., 3 at $2,088; Clks., 6 at $1,980; Clks., 5 at $1,800; Clks., 8 at $1,794; Clk., 1 at $1,944; Clk., 1 at $1,560; Custodians, 5 at $1,711 to $1,440; Tel. Oper., $1,680; Messgrs., 7 at $1,440, 1 at $1,296; Keeper of Coat Room, $1,422; Copyists, 35 at $1,440 to $1,872.

MORTGAGE TAX DEPT.—Dep., L. Miller, $4,200; Exam. Mort., W. J. A. Rooney, $3,000; Cash., G. W. Criss,* $3,400; Clk., J. O'Donnell, $2,000.

County Clerk.

Hall of Records.

Co. Clk., W. E. Kelly, $12,000; elect. trm., 4 yrs., exp. Dec. 31, 1923; Dep. Co. Clk., W. J. Heffernan, $6,000; Counsel, A. G. McLaughlin, $4,000; Asst. Dep. Co. Clk., Jos. V. Lemaire, $3,820; Bkpr., Geo. Loader, $2,851; Sec., J. M. Tully, $2,400; Notarial Clk., T. M. Burke, $3,330; Cash., J. R. Coblens, $2,640; Clk., Law Dept., F. J. Asip, $3,320; 30 Clks., $1,500 to $3,000.

Commissioner of Jurors.

387 Fulton.

Com., J. Brenner,* $6,000; Dep., E. L. Welker,* $4,000; Sec., L. M. Swasey, Jr., $3,250; Clk., D. F. M. Ferguson, $2,772; Fine and Exempt Clk., J. R. Carroll, $2,520; 7 Clks. at $2,160; 9 Jury Notice Servers at $1,823 each; 1 Steno., $1,464.

Commissioner of Records.

Hall of Records.

Com., E. O'Connor,* $5,000; Dep., C. H. Wilson,* $4,000; Supt., F. S. Schackne;* Asst. Supt., M. Hyman,* $3,000 each; Sec., D. Hunter,* $2,000; Chf. Clk., D. McQueen, $3,162; Chf. of Map Div., Fred W. Beers, $2,530; Chf. of Locating Div., S. O. Mosscrop, $2,300; Chf. of Index Div., J. H. Johnson $2,300; Chf. of Town Records Div. and Translator, F. L. Van Cleef, $2,300; Chf. of Comparing Div., C. W. Maynard, $2,300; Sup. of Copying, W. E. Soper, $2,530; 1 Asst. Chf. of Divs., $2,185, and 1 Asst. Chf. of Div., $1,840; 2 Stenos., 45 Clks., Laborers, etc., from $1,300 to $2,070.

QUEENS COUNTY.

Surrogate's Court.

364 Fulton, Jamaica.

Sur., Daniel Noble, $10,000; elec. trm. 6 yrs., exp. Dec. 31, 1922; Clk. of Ct., W. F. Hendrickson,* $5,000; Ct. Steno., W. F. Rockstroh, $2,640; Clk. to Sur., P. M. Pelletreau,* $4,000; Prob. Clk., Wm. A. Brooks, $3,500; Acc. Clk., R. McC. Robinson, Jr., $3,500; Index Clk., G. R. Creed, $2,520; Gdship. Clk., J. F. Fiesel, $3,500; 3 Copyists, etc.

County Court.

Court House, Jackson av., opposite 12th, L. I. City.

Judge, B. J. Humphrey, $12,500; elect. trm., 6 yrs., exp. Dec. 31, 1921; Sp. Dep. Clk., E. J. Smith, $5,000; Asst. Sp. Dep. Clks., E. J. Juster, $3,500; E. J. Clarke, B. J. Funke, $3,500; Conf. Clk. to Co. Judge, H. A. O'Brien,* $3,250 Ct. Crier, T. F. McDermott, $3,000; Intpr., F. Granieri, $2,700; Steno. Co. Ct., J. J. Sullivan, $4,200; Chf. Att. Co. Ct., S. Nostrand, $2 700; 3 Co. Detectives, each $3,000; 3 Atts., Co. Ct., $2,500 each.

CITY OF NEW YORK MUNICIPAL GOVERNMENT—COUNTY OFFICIALS—QUEENS CO.—*Con.*

Sheriff.

Court House, L. I. City.

Shff., John Wagner, term exp. Dec. 31, 1923, $10,000; Un. Shff., Hy. Vogt,* term exp. Dec. 31, 1923, $3,250; Counsel to Shff.,* R. L. Smith, $3,250; Chf. Clk., H. B. Jones,* $2,616; Cash., P. S. Heuss.

District Attorney.

Court House, L. I. City.

Dist. Atty., Dana Wallace, $8,000; elect. trm. 3 yrs., exp. Dec. 31, 1923; Assts., H. Vollmer, Jr.,* $4,500; Frank E. Phillips,* R. P. Bell,* W. B. Hazelwood,* $3,500; Dept. Asst., J. Lonardo,* $2,772; Chf. Clk., G. Mann,* $3,140; Legal Ex., A. J. Chambers, $3,074; Clk., T. A. Lynch, $2,088; Clks., Stenos., etc.

County Clerk.

364 Fulton, Jamaica.

Co. Clk., Edw. W. Cox,* $8,000; elec. trm. 3 yrs., exp. Dec. 31, 1921; Dep. Co. Clk., J. Theofel, $5,500; Asst. Dep. Clk., P. F. Albrecht, $3,900; Fin. Clk., Chas. Lauer, $3,250; Priv. Sec., E. F. Keenan, $2,700; E. J. Kiely, Counsel, $3,500; 120 other Clks., $1,000 to $3,000.

Public Administrator.

364 Fulton, Jamaica.

Adm., R. White,* $3,500.

Commissioner of Jurors.

Court House, L. I. City.

Com., T. C. McKennee,* $5,000; Asst., J. Wagner,* $3,250; Chf. Clk., J. King, $2,160; Clk., M. J. Mullen, $1,823; O. J. Schumacher, $1,823; Jury Notice Server, Richard A. Homeyer, $1,610; Steno., Alta M. Luckings, $1,376.

RICHMOND COUNTY.

County Judge and Surrogate.

Court House, Richmond.

Co. Judge and Sur., J. H. Tiernan, $7,600; elec. trm. 6 yrs., exp. Dec. 31, 1923; Clk. of Sur. Ct., W. Finley,* $4,000; Sten., T. Kenny, $3 800; F. W. Owens, Sec., $3,000 (Class Service); Conf. Clk., L. Feil,* $2,376; Clk., A. Wells, $2,574; Clk., W. Fabiszewski, $1,280; Prob. Officer, W. J. Ruggles, $1,560; Clk., A. F. Deegan, $1,128.

Sheriff.

Court House, St. George.

Shff., W. K. Walsh, $6,000; elect. trm., 3 yrs., exp. Dec. 31, 1921.

Un. Shff., P. J. Finn,* $3,250; Dep. Shff., E. Peterson,* $2,160; Counsel to Shff., W. C. Casey, $1,920; 4 Guards, $1,823 each; 1 Jailer, $2,088; 1 Fingerprint Clk., $1,944; Motor Driver, $1,610; 1 Clk., $1,944; 1 Steno., $1,610; 1 Matron, $1,288; 1 Phys., $1,244; 1 Guard, $1,537; 1 Farm Hand, $940; 1 Cook, $904.

District Attorney.

Court House, St. George.

Dist. Atty., J. Maloy, $5,000; elec. trm. 3 yrs., exp. Dec. 31, 1922; Assts., A. V. Norton,* $3,500; C. B. Dullea,* $3,500; J. M. Braisted,* $2,500; Chf. Clk., F. C. Vitt,* $2,500; Grand Jury Stenos., T. J. Walsh, $1,500; Elsa M. Becker, $2,000; Mess., W. J. Corey, Sr., $1,500; Pro. Serv. and Clk., J. H. Brennan, $1,800; Intpr., B. Scalano, $1,805.

County Clerk.

Court House, New Brighton.

Co. Clk., C. L. Bostwick, $5,000; elec. trm. 3 yrs., exp. Dec. 31, 1923; Dep., J. P. Kelly,* $3,250; Chf. Clk., W. Hurst, $2,880; 12 Clks.

Commissioner of Jurors.

Court House, New Brighton.

Com., E. I. Miller, $2,500; Asst. J. J. McCaughey * Clk., W. J. Kane, $2,160 each.

Public Administrator.

Office, Port Richmond (Mhtn. office, 31 Nassau). Adm., W. T. Holt,* fees.

NEW YORK CITY JUDICIARY.

SUPREME COURT.

The Supreme Court is the highest court of original jurisdiction in all actions in law and equity and in criminal cases. Members are elected by the people of the State for 14 yrs. The State is divided into 9 judicial districts. The Counties of New York and Bronx form the **1st Dist. The Counties of Kings, Queens, Richmond,** Nassau and Suffolk form the 2d Dist. The salary of each Justice is $17,500. **See also index for State Judiciary for Judges of other districts.**

1st District.

Manhattan.

JUSTICES AND EXPIRATION OF TERMS—Appellate Div.—John P. Clarke, Dec. 31, 1929; V. J. Dowling, Dec. 31, '32; S. Greenbaum, Dec. 31, 1923; F. C. Laughlin, Dec. 31, '32; Edgar S. K. Merrell, Dec. 31, '32; A. R. Page, Dec. 31, '23; Walter L. Smith, Dec. 31, '32.

OFFICIAL REFEREES—John J. Freedman, Henry A. Gildersleeve and J. W. Goff, $11,500 each; L. Zeller, $7,500; Librarian and Consult. Clk., G. T. Campbell, $5,000; Confed. Clk., B. H. Doane, $5,000; Crier, E. J. Hinch, $4,000; Dep. Clk., P. A. Halpin, $3,500; Asst. Clk., E. E. Ford, $3,500.

JUSTICES' CLERKS—F. J. Clarke to Clarke; B. L. Schwartz to S. Greenbaum $3,000; E. E. Ford to Dowling; C. W. Roberts to Laughlin; G. S. Reed to Merrell; C. L. Bristol, Jr., to Page; G. L. Lewis to Smith; $4,000 each.

TRIAL AND SPECIAL TERMS—Justices—Nathan Bijur, Dec. 31, 1923; D. F. Cohalan, Dec. 31, '25; V. M. Davis, Dec. 31, '30; F. B. Delehanty, Dec. 31, '29; T. F. Donnelly, Dec. 31, '26; M. L. Erlanger, Dec. 31, '34; E. R. Finch, Dec. 31, '29; John Ford, Dec. 31, '34; E. J. Gavegan, Dec. 31, '23; L. A. Giegerich, Dec. 31, '34; W. P. Burr, Dec. 31, '34; C. L. Guy, Dec. 31, '34; H. D. Hotchkiss, Dec. 31, '25; I. Lehman, Dec. 31, '22; R. Lydon, Dec. 31, '32; J. V. McAvoy, Dec. 31, '31; R. H. Mitchell, Dec. 31, '30; G. V. Mullan, Dec. 31, '30; J. E. Newburger, Dec. 31, '33; M. W. Platzek, Dec. 31, '34; J. A. Tierney, Dec. 31, '29; R. F. Wagner, Dec. 31, '32; B. S. Weeks, Dec. 31, '28; E. G. Whitaker, Dec. 31, '26; P. J. McCook, Dec. 31, '33; I. Wasservogel, Dec. 31, '34; F. J. O'Malley, Dec. 31, '34; F. Martin, Dec. 31, '34.

JUSTICES' CLERKS—H. B. Alexander, to Lehman; R. H. Arnold, to Tierney; H. S. Flynn, to Mullan; W. E. Keleher, to Whitaker; T. F. Keogh, to Guy; R. R. Murphy, to Mitchell; J. G. McTigue, to Cohalan; J. C. Madigan, to Gavegan; J. J. Murphy, to Weeks; A. O'Connell, to Delehanty; G. W. Pawson, to Davis; T. J. Walsh, to McAvoy; F. de L. Cunningham, to Hotchkiss; D. R. Daly, to Giegerich; P. H. Gregory, to Platzek; W. A. Maguire, to Newburger; J. O. Wingrave, to Finch; J. F. Crater, to Wagner; A. F. Burke, to Lydon; R. Field, to Bijur; M. A. Ford, to Ford; L. A. Higgins, to Donnelly; W. Hecht, Jr., to Wasservogel; P. McQuillan, to O'Malley; J. A. Pateracki, to Martin; $5,000 each.

SPECIAL DEP. CLERKS—C. E. Bensel, Jr., $4,500; C. Boese, E. M. Coe, G. F. Lyon, $4,000 each; J. McNierney, J. B. F. Smith, J. R. Cherry, $5,000 each; E. Bodine, W. A. Brady, M. H. Brown, W. G. Clark, J. F. Dalton, J. A. Delehey, P. H. Dunn, S. Ford, T. M. Gibbons, T. F. O'Connor, C. A. Grant, E. J. Hughes, J. W. Jones, C. H. Smith, T. F. McDevitt, F. W. Maguire, W. P. Miner, M. M. O'Brien, Jas. Owens, E. R. Carroll, $4,000 each.

ASST. SPEC. DEP. CLERKS—E. A. Bernholz, J. F. Berrigan, R. Blum, H. J. Callahan, J. M. Cannon, W. J. Butler, J. A. Dooley, J. P. Doyle, J. J. Duffy, H. W. Ellperin, A. Elterich, M. J. Flannelly, C. Freedman, B. Friedman, J. Gilliland, J. E. Gleason, J. B. Kavanagh, T. E. Keenan, S. H. Keating, Geo. Kelly, J. Kelly, J. H. Loos, J. F. McCabe, J. McLoughlin, W. H. O'Brien, J. Levine, J. L. Maher, E. C. Quigg, T. J. Quinn, H. Richter, E. F. Roche, W. E. Rooney, W. T. Shannon, M. Streicher, G. W. Sweeney, W. L. Taylor, J. A. Tierney, W. Turk, C. L. Wendel, H. W. Boyce, E. F. Horan, J. R. McLaughlin, R. E. Nicholls, J. Spielberg, C. J. Irving, J. F. Flynn, E. R. Gibbons, D. J. O'Sullivan, $2,500 each; W. H. Penney, $3,500.

STENOGRAPHERS—H. E. Anstie, W. C. Booth, B. S. Bottome, W. B. Bottome, C. B. Bull, J. D. Carson, E. J. Curtis, F. T. Harris, R. J. July, J. E. Keese, B. F. Keinard, G. Kemp, J. F. Martin, C. A. Morrison, B. Moynahan, C. J. O'Callaghan, A. G. Previn, R. L. Randall, J. A. Russell, R. W. Ryan, P. B. Sheridan, J. Standfast, H. S. Van Demark, H. W. Wood, J. A. Kikmund, H. L. Davis, N. Behrin, G. M. Laubshire, E. J. A. Murphy, $4,200 each.

Telephone Operators—C. Lynch, $2,000; F. J. Manley, $1,800; E. K. Williams, $1,800. 140 Attendants in all departments.

---

*Exempt from Civil Service.

CITY OF NEW YORK MUNICIPAL GOVT.—JUDICIARY—SUPREME COURT—*Continued.*

Second District.

Borough Hall, Bkln.

JUSTICES AND EXPIRATION OF TERMS—Appellate Div.—A. J. Jenks, P. J., Dec. 31, '26; H. Putnam, Dec. 31, '24; A. E. Blackmar, Dec. 31, '23; W. J. Kelly, Dec. 31, '31; W. H. Jaycox, Dec. 31, '34; I. M. Mills, Dec. 31, '34; A. P. Rich, Dec. 31, '28.

OFFICIAL REFEREES—Josiah T. Marean, Bkln.; Wm. T. Dickey, Bkln.; E. B. Thomas, Bkln.; M. H. Hirschberg, Newburgh; H. T. Ketcham, Bkln.; Lester W. Clark, Staten Is., $11,500 each.

Court House, Bkln.

TRIAL AND SPECIAL TERMS—Justices—I. M. Kapper, Dec. 31, '23; J. Aspinall, Dec. 31, '24; C. H. Kelby, R. Benedict, J. C. Van Siclen, Dec. 31, '25; D. F. Manning, Dec. 31, '26; S. Callaghan, Dec. 31, '29; J. C. Cropsey, Dec. 31, '30; L. L. Fawcett, Edw. Lazansky, Dec. 31, '31; L. B. Faber, Dec. 31, '32; A. L. Squiers, Dec. 31, '33; N. S. Dike, J. MacCrate, S. B. Strong, Dec. 31, '34.

CLERKS.

(Within jurisdiction of Kings.)

Gen. Clk., C. S. Devoy, $5,000; Asst. Gen. Clk., J. J. McQuade, $4,500; Clks., W. P. Leggatt, L. A. Cohn, H. M. Burtis, G. C. Manning, $4,250 each; F. L. Chadwick, F. H. Barre, R. E. Jackson, A. J. Buttling, L. J. Farrell, J. McMullan, G. McHenry, $3,750 each; Jos. Gilbert, W. S. Gibbs, L. H. Washburn, J. J. Rush, D. S. Murphy, $3,250 each; T. E. Holt, A. J. Higgins, G. M. Conrady, J. Brosnan, S. J. Tormey, T. J. White, $2,750 each; Stenos., W. P. Cherry, F. E. Meakin, Frank Rawlings, J. Happel, C. H. Marshall, Chas. F. H. Pagan, Clarence J. Tobin, Chas. J. Joyce, J. H. Ruehmling, F. N. Applegate, Louis Granat, W. R. Duryea, $4,200 each; Con. Attndt., C. J. Dalton,* $3,500; 6 Intprs., $3,300; 1 Typewriter Oper., $2,500; 1 Con. Telephone Oper., $1,100.

CLERKS TO JUSTICES.

Clerks to each Justice (exempt), salaries, $4,000; Clerk to Justice Kelly, A. O. Sherwood; Aspinall, M. Mott; Blackmar, J. B. Stevens; Kapper, C. D. Cords; Kelby, E. F. Harding; Benedict, G. I. Woolley; Putnam, H. S. Sullivan; Fawcett, H. W. Smith; Lazansky, J. J. Fox; Jenks, T. M. Jenks; Mills, H. D. Brown; Jaycox, R. P. Lee; Van Siclen, H. C. Frey; Manning, T. J. Sefton; Rich, L. A. Pierce; Callaghan, Geo. Serenbetz; Cropsey, G. J. Whalen; Squires, Miss Henriette Fuchs; Strong, Miss Cecilia McKenzie; Dike, T. Scott; MacCrate, F. Meyer.

COURT OF GENERAL SESSIONS.

Bldg. for Criminal Courts, Centre, Lafayette and Franklin, Mhtn.

Held by the Judges of the Court of General Sessions; salaries, $17,500; elected for 14 yrs.

JUSTICES, EXPIRATION OF TERMS AND CLERKS—O. A. Rosalsky, T. C. T. Crain, Dec. 31, '34; J. F. Mulqueen, A. J. Talley, Dec. 31, '21; C. C. Nott, Jr., J. F. McIntyre, Dec. 31, '31; Clk., E. R. Carroll, $5,500; Dep. Clks., G. F. Spinney, W. N. Penney, E. K. Cowing, W. Hannah, W. R. Boenke, E. Chambers, J. F. Court, J. J. Smith, T. W. Goggin, S. F. Spellman, $4,500 each; J. J. Ryan, Alex. Rosalsky, G. W. Hamilton, S. Steinberg, $4,500 each; Asst. Clk., S. Wolf, $4,500; Stenos., T. W. Osborne, F. S. Beard, P. P. McLaughlin, J. E. Lynch, A. G. Russell, L. Lutz, $5,040 each; Intprs., D. Villamena, M. Moustaki, E. J. Rosenthal, F. Fischer, Wm. Landau, $3,500 each; War. of Gr. Jury, H. McLaughlin; War. Add. Gr. Jury, J. A. Mossel, $2,400 each; 9 Rec. Clks., $3,500 each; 7 Clks. to Judges at $4,500; 6 Chf. Attds. and 56 Attds. at $2,500 each; Court Crier at $3,600.

COURT OF SPECIAL SESSIONS.

Salary of Chf. Justice, $10,000; 1 Asso. Justice at $9,000. Appointed by Mayor for term of 10 yrs. See Sec. 1406-1409 City Charter; also Inf. Courts, Law, Chap. 659, Laws 1910. Court is held by 8 Justices in districts as follows:

Part I, Criminal Courts Bldg., Mhtn. Part II, Athenaeum Bldg., Atlantic av. and Clinton, Bkln.; held on every day except Sat. and Sunday. Part III, Town Hall, Jamaica, Queens, held on Tues. Part IV, County Court House, St. George, Richmond; held on Wed. Part V, Bergen Bldg., Tremont and Arthur avs.; held on Thur. Part VI, Circuit Court.

JUSTICES, EXPIRATION OF TERMS AND CLERKS—F. Kernochan, Chf., July 1, '26; Arthur C. Salmon, July 1, '28; A. E. Voorhees, Dec. 31, '29; Joseph F. Moss, July 1, '29; Moses Herman, July 1, '21; J. J. McInerney, Dec. 31, '21; J. J. Freschi, July 1, '25; H. W. Herbert, July 9, '25; C. Edwards, Dec. 31, '25; D. F. Murphy, Nov. 26, '27; G. J. O'Keefe, Dec. 31, '28; E. J. Healey, May 2, '22; John I. Cotter, Sec. to Ch. Justice, $2,790; Chf. Clk., Frank Smith, $6,000; Clk., J. P. Hilley, $4,500; Dep. Clks., W. M. Fuller, $4,000; W. L. Trafford, $2,376; Chf. Prob. Officer, J. J. Ryan, $3,600; Intpr., C. H. LeMon, $2,000; Dep. Clk., J. J. Dorman, $4,000; Clks., Bronx, W. E. Cullen, $2,000; Kings, J. L. Kerrigan, $4,000; Queens, H. S. Moran, $2,376; Richmond R. Brown, $2,200.

Children's Court.

Franklin Chase Hoyt, Presiding Justice; Cornelius F. Collins, S. D. Levy, M. M. L. Ryan, R. J. Wilkin, JJ., $10,000 each; Ch. Clk., A. Ragan, $6,080; B. J. Fagan, Chf. Prob. Officer, $4,100.

MHTN. (Parts I and II)—137 E. 22d. Clk., D. A. Lambert, $5,000.

BKLN. (Part III)—102 Court. Clk., Wm. C. McKee, $3,700.

BRONX (Part IV)—355 E. 137th. Clk., B. J. Schneider, $3,070.

QUEENS (Part V)—30 Union Hall st., Jamaica. Clk., J. J. Ryan, $3,070.

RICHMOND (Part VI)—Borough Hall, St. George. Clk., E. E. Kenny, $2,640.

Court held daily in Parts I, II and III; Mon., Th. and Sat. of each week in Part IV; Tu. and Fri. of each week in Part V; Wed. of each week in Part VI.

MUNICIPAL COURTS.

Manhattan.

Elected by the electors of each municipal dist.; term, 10 yrs. See Sec. 1350, N. Y. City Charter; salary $9,000 a yr., except in Queens and Richmond, where it is $7,000; salary of Steno. in each court, $2,160; Intprs., $1,500; attdts., $1,500.

1ST DIST., 145 Grand, Justices and expiration of terms—Wm. J. A. Caffrey, John Hoyer, Wm. F. Moore, Dec. 31, 1929; Clk., T. O'Connell, $3,500; Dep. Clk., P. Wheelan, $3,500; Asst. Clks. at $3,500, J. J. Finn, J. Muldoon, T. F. Campbell, R. Duffy, M. Haggerty.

2D DIST., 264 Madison, Justices and expiration of terms—M. Eder, W. Blau, Benj. Hoffman, Dec. 31, 1929; A. J. Levy, Dec. 31, 1923; J. Panken, Dec. 31, 1927; Clk., H. C. Perry, Dep. Clk., W. H. Burns, $3,500 each; Asst. Clks., T. Fitzpatrick, Andrew Lang, C. F. Regan, Peter Hughes, P. J. Paul, J. T. Koenig, N. J. White, E. A. Ahearn, $3,500 each.

3D DIST., 314 W. 54th, Justices and expiration of terms—T. E. Murray, T. F. Noonan, Dec. 31, 1929; Clk., P. H. Bird, Dep. Clk., J. J. Dalton, Asst. Clk., George Sexton, Asst. Clk., J. T. Nevins, $3,000 each.

4TH DIST., 207 E. 32d, Justices and expiration of terms—M. F. Blake, Dec. 31, 1927; J. G. McTigue, Dec. 31, 1930; Clk., W. J. Murphy; Dep. Clk., T. F. Winters; Asst. Clk., Elizabeth M. Barry, $3,000 each.

5TH DIST., 2565 B'way, Justices and expiration of terms—F. Spiegelberg, Wm. Young, Dec. 31, 1927; A. Ellenbogen, Dec. 31, 1924; Clk., J. H. Servis, $3,500; Dep. Clk., H. W. Baldwin, $3,500; Asst. Clks., J. Schloss, S. Harris, G. Snedden, F. A. Stahl, $3,500 each.

6TH DIST., 155 E. 88th, Justices and expiration of terms—Jacob Marks, Dec. 31, 1927; T. A. Leary, Dec. 31, 1929; Clk., C. J. Dunn, $3,500; Dep. Clk., S. J. Meagher, $3,500; Asst. Clks., T. F. Bezley, P. Sullivan, $3,500 each.

7TH DIST., 360 W. 125th, Justices and expiration of terms—J. R. Davies, S. C. Crane, S. Friedlander, Dec. 31, 1928; Clk., J. P. Burns, $2,500; Dep. Clk., V. J. Hahn, $3,500; Asst. Clks., Chas. Cogut, M. J. Fay, J. A. H. Sealy, $3,500 each.

8TH DIST., Sylvan pl. and 121st, Justices and expiration of terms—Leopold Prince, Dec. 31, 1927; Carroll Hayes, Dec. 31, 1929; Clk., Hugh H. Moore, $3,000; Dep. Clk., D. J. Sullivan, $3,000.

9TH DIST., 624 Madison av., Justices and expiration of terms—Edgar J. Lauer, Dec. 31, 1925; William C. Wilson, George L. Genung, Frank J. Coleman, Jr., Dec. 31, 1927; Clk., Martin H. Early; Dep. Clk., Elijah T. Keehn, $3,000 each; Asst. Clks., Chas. Healy, W. S. Cross, I. Elliott, D. H. Sanford, N. H. Knox, Mary Pursell, $3,000 each.

CITY OF NEW YORK MUNICIPAL GOVT.—JUDICIARY—MUNICIPAL COURTS—*Continued.*

Bronx.

1ST DIST., 1400 Williamsbridge rd., Justice and expiration of term. Part I—Peter A. Sheil, Dec. 31, 1927; Part II—Harry Robitzek, Dec. 31, 1927; Clk., Stephen Collins, $3,000; Dep. Clk., P. A. Ryan, $3,000; Asst. Clks., J. N. Murphy, T. J. Kiernan.

2D DIST., 162d and Washington av., Justice and expiration of term. Part I—M J. Scanlan, Dec. 31, 1927; Clk., M. J. Burke, $3,000; Dep. Clk., J. Monaghan, $3,000. Part II—Wm. E. Morris, Dec. 31, 1921; Asst. Clks., J. M. Dennerlein, Wm. Klapp. $3,000 each.

Brooklyn.

1ST DIST., 106 Court, Justice and expiration of term—J. A. Dunne, Dec. 31, 1929; Clk., C. M. Byrne, $3,000; Dep. Clk., D. McGonigle, $3,000; Asst. Clks., W. Mutell, M. J. Wofer, $3,000 each; Steno., N. F. O'Callahan, $2,340.

2D DIST., 495 Gates av., Justices and expiration of term—J. R. Farrar, Dec. 31, 1929; O. G. Esterbrook, Dec. 31, 1927; Clk., J. J. McManus, $3,000; Dep. Clk., C. W. Jannicky, $3,000; Asst. Clks., J. Herries, Fred Marsland, $3,000 each.

3D DIST., 6 Lee av., Justices and expiration of terms—W. J. Bogenshutz, Dec. 31, 1928; Chas. J. Carroll, Dec. 31, 1929; Chf. Clk., J. M. Carpenter, $3,500; Dep. Clk., (vacant).

4TH DIST., 14 Howard av., Justice and expiration of term—J. S. Strahl, Dec. 31, 1929; Clk., Wm. A. Nelson, Jr., $3,000; Dep. Clk., P. J. Eiseman, $3,000.

5TH DIST., 53d and 3d av., Justice and expiration of term—C. Furgueson, Dec. 31, 1929; Clk., J. J. O'Leary, $3,500; Dep. Clk., S. Licari, $2,500.

6TH DIST., 236 Duffield, Justices and expiration of terms—W. D. Niper, Dec. 31, 1925; E. M. Doughty, Dec. 31, 1927; Clk., W. R. Fagan. $3,500; Dep. Clk., W. H. Burgess, $3,500; Asst. Clks., G. Holske, J. S. Cohen, $3,500 each.

7TH DIST., 31 Penn av., Justices and expiration of terms—C. B. Law, Dec. 31, 1925; H. C. Glore, Dec. 31, 1930; Clk., J. W. Toumey, $3,500; Dep. Clk., J. F. Ward, $3,500; Asst. Clks., L. Messenger, W. R. Harris, $3,500 each.

Queens.

1ST DIST., 115 5th, L. I. City, Justice and expiration of term—J. Hetherington, Dec. 31, 1929; Clk., J. F. Cassidy, $2,500; Dep. Clk., E. J. Dennen, $2,500.

2D DIST., B'way and Justice, Elmhurst, Justice and expiration of term—John M. Cragen, Dec. 31, 1929; Clk., W. Repper; Dep. Clk., L. Lang, $2,500 each.

3D DIST., 1908 Myrtle av., Glendale, Justice and expiration of term—A. Christman, Jr., Dec. 31, 1929; Clk., J. H. Nuhn; Dep. Clk., T. Kohlweiss, $2,500 each.

4TH DIST., Fulton and Flushing av., Jamaica, Justice and expiration of term—E. F. Hazleton, Dec. 31, 1929; Clk., Jos. Kestler, $3,000; Dep. Clk., J. F. Ryan, $3,000.

Richmond.

1ST DIST., Lafayette and Fillmore, New Brighton. Justice and expiration of term—T. C. Brown, Dec. 31, 1929; Clk., T. E. Cremins, $3,000.

2D DIST., Stapleton, Justice and expiration of term—A. J. B. Wedemeyer, Dec. 31, 1929; Clk., Wm. Wedemeyer, $3,000.

CITY MAGISTRATES COURTS.

Manhattan and Bronx.

Office, 300 Mulberry.

Term, 10 yrs.; appointed by the Mayor; salary, Chf. Magis., $11,000; City Magis., $8,000.

Magistrates and expiration of terms—Wm. McAdoo, Chf., June 30, 1925; J. S. Schwab, July 1, 1921; W. A. Sweetser, June 30, 1929; F. H. Mancuso, June 30, 1930; Thos. J. Nolan, June 30, 1929; Geo. W. Simpson, June 27, 1929; J. H. Norris, Apr. 30, 1927; Max Levine, Aug. 15, 1929; R. C. Ten Eyck, July 1, 1921; C. N. Harris, M. P. Breen, F. X. McQuade, June 30, 1922; P. T. Barlow, B. J. Douras, Apr. 30, 1923; Chas. S. Simms, July 1, 1923; J. E. McGeehan, Aug. 15, 1923; E. V. Frothingham, M. Koenig, Apr. 30, 1925; W. B. Cobb, July 8, 1925; A. Brough, F. B. House, Apr. 30, 1927; Jos E. Corrigan, N. J. Marsh, July 14, 1927; Chf. Clk., F. Oliver,* $6,080; Sec. to City Mag., R. E. Broderick, $3,500 Asst. Ch. Clk., J. Bernhard, $3,030; Chf. Prob. Officer, E. J. Cooley, $4,100; Dep. Chf. Prob. Offr., Geo. J. Lavender, $3,250; Supv. Finger Prints, A. A. Hart, $2,851.

DISTS. AND CLERKS—Clk. salary, $3,250; exempt Civil Service. 1st Dist.—Criminal Courts Bldg., T. A. Geary; 2d—Jefferson Market, E. Demarest; 3d—1st and 2d av., I. Rice; 4th—151 E. 57th, E. T. Tyrrell; 5th—121st and Sylvan pl., Thos. A. Clark; 6th—161st and Brook av., A. Creelman; 7th—314 W. 54th, Jay Finn; 8th—1014 E. 181st (vacant); 9th—Night Court for Females, 125 6th av., C. Anthes; 10th—Night Court for Males, 151 E. 57th, A. Volgenan; 11th—Domestic Relations Court, 151 E. 57th, G. P. Richter; 12th—1130 St. Nicholas av., J. H. Hanan; 13th—Domestic Relations Court, 1014 E. 181st, A. Wilson; Mun. Term., Part I, Mun. Bldg., J. Lynch (Act.); Traffic Court, 301 Mott, R. J. Sheridan.

Brooklyn, Queens and Richmond. Office, 44 Court, Bkln.

City Magistrates, $8,000 each.

MAGISTRATES AND EXPIRATION OF TERMS—H. H. Dale, Dec 31, '29; F. S. Mullin,‡ Dec. 31, '25; M. S. Brown, June 30, '29; J. T. O'Neill, June 30, '30; E. J. Dooley, L. H. Reynolds, J. V. Short, J. J. Walsh, Chas. J. Dodd, J. C. McGuire, May 1, '21; G. H. Folwell, A. H. Geismar, Dec. 31, '27; J. Kochendorfer, Dec. 31, '25; A. E. Steers, July 2, '23; F. A. McCloskey, Sept. 23, '25; Thomas F. Doyle,† July 30, '27; H. Milled,† J. J. Conway,† Wm. T. Croak, Dec. 31, '27; Dep. Chf. Clk., W. F. Delaney, $5,000; Dep. Chf. Prob. Offr., J. T. Coffey, $2,750.

TRAFFIC COURT—Mag., L. C. Fish, Jan. 1, 1930, $7,000.

DISTS. AND CLERKS—(Court Clk. salary $2,750; Queens $2,574, except 3d Dist., and Richmond, where it is $2,200; exempt civil service.)—1st Dist., 318 Adams, J. H. Esquirol; 5th, Williamsburg Bridge Plaza, John McKeon; 6th, 495 Gates av.; Chas. Nitze; 7th, 31 Snyder av., W. J. Hunter; 8th, West 8th, C. I., H. Hasenflug; 9th, 5th av. and 23d, D. F. King; 10th, 133 New Jersey av., H. Rayfiel.

DOMESTIC RELATIONS COURT—Myrtle and Vanderbilt avs.—P. J. Donnelly.

Mun. Term, Part 2—2 Butler. J. E. Dowdell.

Women's Night Court—318 Adams, S. H. Finkel, Act. Clk.

QUEENS—1st Dist., 115 5th, L. I. City, W. E. McGee; 2d, Town Hall, Flushing, B. H. Hewlett; 3d, Central av., Far Rockaway; 4th Town Hall, Jamaica, W. N. George.

RICHMOND—1st Dist., Village Hall., N. B. W. C. Casey; 2d, Village Hall, Stapleton, M. Brennan, Clerk.

†Serve in Queens. ‡Serve in Richmond.

THE RHODES SCHOLARSHIPS.

Statement for the Academic Year 1919-1920.

Ninety-eight Rhodes Scholars came into residence for the first time during the year. The number of Scholars actually in residence for either the whole or some part of the academic year 1919-1920 was 183—viz., 105 from the British Empire and 78 from the United States of America. There were also in residence four ex-Scholars, of whom three were from the British Empire and one from the United States of America. In the course of the year thirty-two Scholars either went out of residence or, although remaining in residence, completed the term of their Scholarship.

The academic year, 1920-1921 started with 220 Rhodes Scholars in residence. A further 60 come into residence in January, 1921.

The results of the 1920 annual election of Rhodes Scholars to represent the United States at the University of Oxford were announced on Sept. 26, 1920, by Prof. Frank Aydelotte, Mass Inst. of Technology, the American secretary of the Rhodes trustees. The quota for the United States was, as in 1919, sixty-four, instead of the normal thirty-two, thus making up for the postponement of elections during the war. In 1921 the quota for the United States will be thirty-two, and two-thirds of the States will elect one man each, while those which in 1920 made two appointments, will have no election. Alexander B. Trowbridge (Cornell Univ.), of Flushing, L. I., received the New York State 1920 appointment.

The offices of the Rhodes Trust are at Seymour House, Waterloo place, London, S. W. In the United States application may be made to Prof. Frank Aydelotte, Mass. Inst. of Technology, Cambridge, Mass.

FIRE DEPARTMENT, CITY OF NEW YORK.

Headquarters, Municipal Bldg., Manhattan, Brooklyn Office, 367 Jay st.

The Fire Commr. is the head of the Fire Dept. He is required to appoint 2 deps. The Commr. is treasurer of the dept. and has to give a bond of $20,000. He is also trustee of the Fire Dept. Relief Fund, for which he has to give a bond of $100,000. The Commr. has power to select the heads of bureaus and assts. and as many officers and firemen as may be necessary. A pension bureau is connected with the dept. A tax of 2% is laid on the business of foreign insurance companies, which shall go to this pension fund.

The Bureau of Fire Prevention has charge of all matters relating to the prevention of fires, including those relating to the storage, sale, transportation or use of combustibles or explosives; to the installation and maintenance of automatic or other fire alarm systems and fire extinguishing equipment; to the means and adequacy of exits from all buildings, structures, vessels, places and premises in which numbers of persons work, live or congregate from time to time for any purpose, except tenement houses and except factories as defined by the Labor Law.

MANHATTAN, BRONX AND RICHMOND.

Commr., T. J. Drennan, $7,500; Dept. Commr. (E), J. M. Hannon, $5,500; Sec. of Dept. (E), J. A. Mackey, $4,000; Sec. to Com. (E), A. J. Keogh, $4,000; Clk. in Charge of Relief and Life Insurance Funds, P. J. Quigley, $4,100; Asst. Sec. of Dept., G. A. Perley, $3,500; Clk., M. P. Corrigan, $3,000; R. P. Colligan, $3,100; other Clks., Messgrs. and Stenos., $1,040 to $2,616.

(See Municipal Chap. for Bd. of Hazardous Trades.)

(See 1918 Eagle Almanac for list of Engine, Hook and Ladder and Hose Companies and Addresses.)

Bureau of Fire.

Chief of Dept., John Kenlon, $10,000; Asst. Chief of Dept., J. B. Martin, $6,500; Dep. Chiefs, W. T. Beggin, H. B. Helm, J. Binns, E. J. Worth, J. Crawley, T. F. Dougherty, J. J. Burns, T. J. Hayes, J. F. King, G. L. Ross, each $5,500. Chiefs of Battalion, Patk. Walsh, W. Jones, J. J. Mooney, J. J. Walsh, G. J. McKenna, J. F. Sherlock, E. L. Cooke, Wm. Clark, C. R. Griffiths, Gerhardt Webber, W. F. Williams, Luke Flanagan, George Bauer, D. J. Curtin, Michael Ruddy, B. F. Carlock, J. F. Hennessy, S. S. Poling, T. F. Barrett, F. J. Gray, J. C. Brogan, J. Spencer, J. J. Henry, T. F. Larkin, each $4,490; Chief Med. Officer, J. E. Smith, $5,200; Med. Officers, E. B. Ramsdell, John J. White, F. M. Banta, W. J. Tierney, H. L. Reis, each $4,250; Chaplains (E), J. H. Ivie, Patrick O'Connor, each $1,830; Clks. and Stenos.

DIVISION OF PLACES OF PUBLIC ASSEMBLY.

Chf. of Batl., J. J. T. Waldron, in Ch.; 2 Captains, $3,600 each; 1 Lieutenant, $3,200; 8 Firemen, 1st grade, $2,280 each; 1 Steno. and Type., $1,680.

Bureau of Fire Prevention.

Municipal Bldg., Mhtn.

EXECUTIVE DIVISION

Chief (E), W. F. Doyle, $6,500; 1 Spec. Investgr. (E), $3,280; 1 Sup. Insp., $3,000; Clk., T. F. Lantry, $1,823.

DIVISION OF VIOLATIONS AND AUXILIARY FIRE APPLIANCES.

Chf. Exam., M. J. Reidy, $2,976; 43 Insps. of Fire Prev., $1,512 to $2,520; 2 Process Servers, $1,376 each; 1 Eng. Insp., $1,872; 1 Insp. Masonry, $1,739; 3 Asst. Engrs., $2,160 to $2,448; 1 Exam., $2,448; 4 Clks., $1,040 to $1,944.

ELECTRICAL DIVISION.

Asst. Elec. Engr., E. Hohn, $2,976; 1 Insp. of Fire Prev., $2,016; 6 Elec. Insps., $1,823 to $1,872; 1 Fireman, $2,280.

PLAN ROOM.

Chf. Exam., Max Cohen, $2,760; 2 Eng. Insps., $2,304 each; 1 Lieut., $3,200; 2 Fire Prev. Insps., $1,872; 1 Fireman, 1st grade, $2,280.

STENOGRAPHIC DIVISION.

3 Stenos. and Types., $1,200 to $1,944; 13 Type. Copyists, $800 to $1,376.

DIVISION OF RECORDING.

19 Clks., $800 to $2,520; 3 Insps. of Fire Prev., $1,739 to $1,823; 3 Firemen, $2,280 each.

(E) Exempt from Civil Service.

DIVISION OF COMBUSTIBLES.

Act. Insp. of Combustibles, J. F. Dixon, $3,400; Cash., J. Mahoney, $2,520; 11 Asst. Insps. of Combustibles, $1,464 to $2,304; 6 Insps. of Blasting, $1,823 to $2,232; 3 Eng. Insps., $1,732 to $2,448; 5 Insps. of Fire Prev., $1,739 to $1,944; 4 Clks., $900 to $2,160.

BUREAU OF FIRE INVESTIGATION.

Chief Fire Marshal, T. P. Brophy, $5,500; Dep. Chf. Fire Marshal, J. P. Prial, $4,100; Assts., H. W. de Malignon, $2,976; J. McGough, $2,760; R. J. Sheehan, $2,448; S. B. Willis, $2,448; W. A. Finn, $2,304; P. R. Kilgallen, $2,304; John J. Cashman, Wm. J. Cassidy, Wm. G. Copeland, Wm. F. Emerson, Jas. Tierney, each $2,232; J. Winkler, $1,830; Intpr., A. Niflot, $2,160; Steno. and Type., J. L. McKeon, $2,352; Clk., J. J. Dwyer, $2,160.

BROOKLYN OFFICE—Asst. Fire Marshals Wm. R. Ferris, $2,760; R. F. Walsh, $2,544; E. J. Shields, $2,544; A. N. Flamm, $2,304; W. B. Anderson, $2,160; Steno. and Type., Hannah K. Fagan, $1,944.

Bureau of Fire Alarm Telegraph.

Ch. of Bureau, V. Fendrich, $4,000.

DIVISION OF ENGINEERING.

Asst. Elec. Engrs., Jerome F. Langer, $3,500; William F. Hennessy, $3,080; D. A. Kane, $2,520; A. J. Neuman, $2,520; Fire Telegraph Expert, E. A. Faller, $3,000; 5 Draftsmen, $1,806 to $2,376; Insps., 3 at $1,823 to $2,040; Cable Testers, 5 at $1,706 to $1,872; Stenos. and Types., $1,146; 1 at $1,944.

EXECUTIVE DIVISION.

Clks., 1 at $2,232, 1 at $2,088, 1 at $1,944, 1 at $1,040. Steno. and Type., 1 at $1,944.

DIVISION OF OPERATION.

Dispatchers in charge of Boroughs: Mhtn., W. G. Linson, $2,544. Bkln., J. J. Welsh, $2,760. Bronx, J. G. Stephens, $2,544. Queens, T. S. Mahoney, $2,088. Richmond, T. J. Cusack, $2,736. Fire Telegraph Dispatchers, 1 at $2,736, 1 at $2,640, 6 at $2,544, 1 at $2,304, 11 at $2,160, 8 at $2,088, 1 at $1,944, 1 at $1,872, 4 at $1,823, 5 at $1,708, 2 at $2,328; Tel. Opers., 1 at $1,610, 4 at $1,537, 4 at $1,464, 6 at $1,317, 1 at $1,200.

DIVISION OF MAINTENANCE.

Supt., W. H. Snyder, $2,976; Chf. Insp., A. P. Martin, $2,520; Foreman Cable Splicer, Joseph Strauss, $2,550; Cable Splicers, 15 at $2,400; Foreman Lineman, Martin J. Moroney, $2,550; Linemen, 33 at $2,400; Insps. Fire Alarm Boxes, 1 at $1,944, 1 at $1,739, 1 at $1,708; Batterymen, 2 at $1,823, 7 at $1,683, 2 at $1,610, 3 at $1,488; Batteryman's Asst., 1 at $1,488; Instrument Makers, 2 at $1,944; Laborer, 1 at $1,317; Auto Enginemen, 3 at $1,823, 1 at $1,464; Wiremen, 1 at $1,560, 4 at $1,495; Drivers, 4 at $1,445; Bricklayer, 1 at $8.50; Painters, 3 at $9; Electricians, 2 at $9; Laborers, 5 at $5.

Bureau of Repairs and Supplies.

Chief of Bureau, H. J. Treacy, $4,480; Clk., W. J. Collins, $2,520.

PURCHASING DIVISION.

Clerks, J. Liberman, $2,976; J. S. Julian, $2,160; other Clks. and Stenos., $1,317 to $2,040.

DIVISION OF HORSES.

Foreman of Laborers, J. J. Canavan, in charge, $2,160; 4 Hostlers, 2 Drivers, 2 Stablemen, $1,437 to $1,708; 4 Horseshoers, $2,000 each.

DIVISION OF APPARATUS.

Chief of Battalion, R. J. Marshall in charge, $4,490; Clks., J. L. Glenmore, $2,232; J. Deaken, $2,088; 1 Mech. Draftsman, $1,740; 9 Clks., $1,100 to $2,040; 163 Mechanics and other employees.

DIVISION OF STORES.

F. McCaffrey, in Charge, $2,520; Bookkeeper, E. Winter, $2,088; Clk., J. A. Kavanagh, $1,823.

DIVISION OF BUILDINGS.

Insps. of Bldgs., C. S. McCarthy and J. R. Sliney, each $2,520; Arch. Draftsmen, A. R. Weismuller and G. Stirratt, $2,304 each; Insp. Masonry Construction, A. J. Fleming, $2,160; Clk., E. Kinney, $2,340; 50 Mechanics, Drivers and Labs.

BROOKLYN AND QUEENS.

365-367 Jay st., Brooklyn.

Dept. Com's (E), W. F. Thompson, $5,500; Steno., Elvie K. Macoy, $2,340; Mess., T. P. Donovan, $2,160; 3 Laborers, 5 Cleaners, 1 Elevator Attend.

FIRE DEPARTMENT, CITY OF NEW YORK—BROOKLYN AND QUEENS—*Continued.*

Bureau of Fire.

Dep. Chief in Charge, John O'Hara, $7,500; Dep. Chiefs: F. W. Goderson, 10th Div.; Patrick Maher, 11th Div.; T. R. Langford, 12th Div.; John Davin, 13th Div., each $5,500; 21 Battalion Chiefs, each $4,490. Chaplains: (E) H. A. Handel, R. J. Hamilton, $1,830 each. Clerk, J. E. Ray, $2,520.

DIVISION OF PLACES.

Public Assembly Capt. E. A. Soden, in charge, $3,700; 4 Firemen, 1st grade, $2,283 each.

Bureau of Fire Prevention.

Dep. Chief, W. H. Swartwout, $4,500; 1 Steno. and Type., $1,610; 1 Insp. Bur. Fire Prev., $2,160.

DIV. VIOLATIONS & AUX. FIRE APPLIANCES.

Insp. of Fire Prevention, D. A. Mahoney in Charge, $2,160; 1 Insp., $2,448; 14 Insps., $1,739 to $2,304.

DIVISION OF RECORDS.

1 Clk., $1,944; 2 Clks., $1,464; 4 Types., $1,040 to $1,317; 8 Clks., $800 to $1,112; 5 Firemen, 1st grade, $2,280 each.

ELECTRICAL DIVISION.

C. A. Hanson, $1,944; 1 Eng. Insp., $2,760; 1 Elec. Insp., $1823.

DIVISION OF COMBUSTIBLES.

Asst. Insp. of Combustibles J. A. McCabe, $2,304; Cash., J. C. Harris, $2,520; 7 Asst. Insps. of Combustibles, $1,830 to $2,304; 3 Fire Prev. Insp., $1,739 to $2,060; 1 Bookkeeper, $1,823; 1 Blasting Insp., $2,160.

Salaries of Uniformed Force Members.

Dep. Chief in Charge, $7,500; Dep. Chiefs, $5,500; Chief of Battalions, $4,490; Capts., $3,700; Lieuts., $2,200; Engineers of Steamers, $2,520; Marine Engineers, $1,980; Pilots, $2,280; Firemen, 1st grade, $2,280; 2d grade, $1,980; 3d grade, $1,769; 4th grade, $1,769.

Volunteer Fire Companies in Queens Borough

Bayside Eng. Co., 17; Rosedale Chemical Fire Eng. Co., 20; Springfield Chemical Eng. Co., 35; Rosedale H. & L. Co., 15; Queens H. & L. Co., 51; Hollis H. & L. Co., 20; St. Albans H. & L. Co., 22; Bayside Enterprise H. & L. Co., 26; Black Stump H. & L. and Bucket Co., 25; Active H. & L. and Hose Co. 1, 27; Forest Hills Hose Co., 75; Creedmoor Hose Co., 20; Queens Hose Co. 2, 24; Springfield Hose Co., 1, 20; Columbia Hose Co. 1, 50; Douglaston Hose Co., 25; 17 companies; 472 men.

FIRE DEPARTMENT STATISTICS.

MANHATTAN, BRONX AND RICHMOND.

1920.	Fires.	Loss on build.	Loss on contents.	Total.
Jan.	979	$464,240	$1,274,245	$1,738,485
Feb.	701	347,795	968,940	1,316,735
Mar.	835	266,390	824,550	1,090,940
Apr.	775	221,025	530,170	751,195
May	689	188,965	1,028,858	1,217,823
June	674	105,690	581,015	686,706
July	675	75,320	529,320	604,640
Aug.	537	136,430	861,145	997,575
Sept.	686	169,160	473,730	642,890

BROOKLYN AND QUEENS.

	Fires.	Loss on build.	Loss on contents.	Total.
Jan.	609	$182,840	$309,955	$492,795
Feb.	439	174,230	340,215	514,445
Mar.	508	123,215	149,880	273,095
Apr.	506	141,655	744,475	886,130
May	436	103,745	118,705	222,450
June	418	105,900	209,730	315,630
July	406	188,305	249,280	437,585
Aug.	293	78,170	114,000	192,170
Sept.	443	106,900	333,545	440,445

COST OF FORCE.

	1920. allowance.
Mhtn., The Bronx, Richmond, Bkln. and Queens	$12,385,353.19

COST OF APPARATUS, SUPPLIES, ETC.

Mhtn., Bronx, Richmond, Bkln. and Queens, $775,200.

Maintenance, Vol. system, Queens	$15,400
Maintenance, Vol. system, Richmond	10,800
Total	$26,200

MEMBERSHIP OF FIRE DEPARTMENT.

Regular—Mhtn. and Bronx	3,054
Regular—Bkln. and Queens	2,687
Regular—Richmond	257
Volunteer system—Queens	472
Volunteer system—Richmond	203
Total	6,673

IMPORTS AND EXPORTS.

According to returns of the Department of Commerce, the value of the leading items of the import and export trade of the United States is as follows:

Imports.	1919-20.	1918-19.
Animals, live	$49,136,672	$40,924,766
Articles returned	69,150,382	32,634,281
Art works	30,479,428	6,947,363
Breadstuffs	59,977,601	47,850,655
Chemicals, drugs and dyes	177,969,526	150,225,186
Cocoa, crude	72,946,064	35,953,990
Coffee	310,701,872	143,089,619
Copper, crude	24,902,792	29,642,979
Copper, manufactured	65,106,842	84,931,967
Cotton, raw	156,918,719	37,633,612
Cotton, manufactured	111,874,821	34,762,723
Fertilizers	38,578,063	5,883,376
Fibers, cured	86,630,841	103,874,757
Fibers, manufactured	141,389,218	98,824,770
Fish	38,773,551	28,058,506
Fruits and nuts	124,773,197	68,234,657
Furs, undressed	103,772,044	37,965,713
Hides and skins	376,892,462	149,288,544
Rubber, crude	280,358,788	161,837,031
Iron and steel	37,423,289	24,306,839
Leather and manufactures	40,327,091	15,423,184
Meats and dairy products	42,424,105	60,445,083
Oils	195,141,567	144,621,251
Paper	63,407,279	46,551,731
Precious stones	114,019,472	52,367,057
Seeds	113,032,112	35,212,664
Silk, raw	454,573,638	217,517,484
Silk manufactures	87,728,181	29,349,198
Sugar	688,127,380	309,403,314
Tea	25,800,742	24,390,722
Tin, ore and pig	92,799,236	73,559,534
Tobacco, unmanufactured	78,164,290	66,329,689
Tobacco manufactures	13,274,307	9,983,622
Vegetables	46,569,851	33,687,306
Wood and manufactures	157,367,368	92,289,532
Wool, raw	212,848,568	224,414,983
Wool, manufactured	43,537,552	13,279,481
All imports	$5,238,621,668	$3,095,720,068

Exports.	1919-20.	1918-19.
Agricultural implements	$36,724,902	$42,662,724
Breadstuffs	808,471,226	954,647,337
Automobiles	233,252,376	116,304,973
Cars	53,111,368	30,419,889
Chemicals and dyes	159,009,927	148,063,531
Coal, anthracite	40,667,538	30,927,815
Coal, bituminous	132,299,978	75,826,696
Coal, bunker	58,245,950	38,282,697
Cotton, raw	1,381,707,502	873,579,669
Cotton, manufactures of	364,036,786	232,206,566
Electric machinery	87,208,413	80,714,124
Explosives	28,215,657	122,730,877
Fertilizers	32,925,408	9,405,242
Fish	42,178,071	37,219,828
Fruits and nuts	118,326,019	71,292,813
Furs and skins	38,883,097	14,612,015
Glass and glassware	25,906,621	21,898,185
Rubber manufactures	69,226,716	43,856,782
Iron and steel and manuf'es	932,675,866	1,065,021,193
Leather	199,772,357	126,525,495
Shoes	78,064,947	50,506,986
Meats and dairy products	771,006,760	1,166,110,958
Naval stores	36,504,797	17,777,497
Oil cake	30,611,141	16,668,763
Oil, mineral	426,497,967	344,233,216
Oil, vegetable	96,225,582	59,067,320
Paper and manufactures	73,717,425	84,080,312
Paraffin	31,403,933	24,557,386
Silk, manufactures of	26,945,293	22,354,896
Spirits and wines	30,224,313	12,911,178
Sugar, refined	131,771,308	81,569,680
Tobacco, leaf	271,940,888	189,894,417
Tobacco, manufactured	51,551,794	35,297,692
Vegetables	36,517,381	53,143,012
Wood and manufactures of	168,574,578	104,557,896
Wool manufactures	56,223,360	31,191,387
Zinc manufactures	26,984,162	24,526,166
All exports	$7,950,429,180	$7,081,461,938

More than 200 restaurants in Greater New York are owned and run by Chinese

Babylon is believed to have been the first city to attain a population of a million.

POLICE DEPARTMENT, CITY OF NEW YORK.

Headquarters, Centre and Broome Sts., Mhtn.

Commissioner and Deputies.

Commissioner (e), Richard Enright.......$7,500
1st Dep. Comr. (e), J. A. Leach.......... 6,500
2d Dep. Comr. (e), J. Daly.............. 6,500
3d Dep. Comr. (e), J. A. Faurot.......... 6,500
4th Dep. Comr. (e), J. J. Cray............ 6,500

5th Dep. Comr. (e), vacant; Special Dep. Comr., J. A. Harriss, Spl. Dep. Comr., A. A. Ryan, Spl. Dep. Comr., J. M. Shaw, Spl. Dep. Comr., R. Wanamaker, Spl. Dep. Comr., T. Coleman Du Pont, Spl. Dep. Comr., Ed. A. Guggenheim, Spl. Dep. Comr., Dr. Carleton Simon, Hon. Dep. Chief of Police, K. S. Williams. (Without compensation.)

Sec. to Comr. (e), W. Gillespie..........$4,500
Sec. to 1st Dep. Comr. (e), G. O. Woodelton 2,880
Sec. to 2d Dep. Comr. (e), S. A. Rudd.... 2,880
Sec. to 3d Dep. Comr. (e), Florence Dooling 2,880
Sec. to 4th Dep. Comr. (e), G. McNulty.... 2,880
Sec. to Dept. (e), F. P. Nicklas........ 3,800

Inspection Districts.

Chief Insp., W. J. Lahey, $7,500.

BOROUGH INSPECTOR.

Bkln. and Queens, Thos. H. Murphy, $5,300.

DIST. INSPECTORS.

(Salary, $4,900.)

1—Wm. A. Coleman, 118 Clinton, Mhtn.
2—J. S. Bolan, 16 Beach, Mhtn.
3—Wm. F. Boettler, 150 W. 68th, Mhtn.
4—Thos. V. Underhill, 153 E. 67th, Mhtn.
5—C. F. Cahalane, 229 W. 123d, Mhtn.
6—J. F. Sweeney, 1925 Bathgate av., Bronx.
7—Geo. C. Liebers, Webster av., Bronx Park.
8—Thos. F. Walsh (Act.), St. George, S. I.
10—B. R. Sackett, Av. U and E. 15th, Bkln.
11—Thos. McDonald, 2 Liberty av., Bkln.
12—B. J. Hayes, 154 Lawrence av., Bkln.
14—Wm. T. Davis (Act.), 72 Poplar, Bkln.
15—C. A. Formoso, 627 Gates av., Bkln.
16—Jos. A. Conboy, 194 Clymer, Bkln.
17—Thos. T. Ryan, 85 4th, L. I. City.
18—Thos. J. Kelly, Flushing av. & Fulton, Jamaica.

Above Dists. comprise following precincts:

1—5th, 7th, 13th, 15th, 17th and 21st.
2—1st, 4th, 6th, 14th, 16th and 18th.
3—22d, 23d, 26th, 28th and 32d.
4—25th, 29th, 31st, 35th, 39th and 43d.
5—36th, 37th, 38th, 40th and 42d.
6—45th, 46th, 47th, 49th and 50th.
7—51st, 53d, 54th, 56th and 57th.
8—60th, 63d, 65th and 66th.
10—67th, 68th, 70th, 72d and 73d.
11—80th, 82d, 83d, 85th, 87th and 88th.
12—74th, 76th, 78th and 79th.
14—89th, 91st, 92d and 93d.
15—94th, 95th, 96th, 97th, 98th.
16—101st, 102d, 103d, 104th and 105th.
17—109th, 111th, 112th and 113th.
18—116th, 118th, 120th, 123d and 125th.

Division National Defense.

Insp., Alfred W. Thor, 240 Centre, Mhtn.

Marine Division.

Marine Insp., J. W. Hallock, Pier A, N. R.

Traffic Division.

Insp., J. O'Brien, 138 W. 30th, Mhtn.

Subdiv. A, City Hall, Capt. P. J. Cray; Subdiv. B, 138 W. 30th, Capt. J. W. O'Connor; Subdiv. C, 229 W. 123d, Capt. J. D. Ormsby; Subdiv. D, 308 Classon av., Bkln., Capt. J. L. Falconer; Subdiv. E, 275 Church, Richmond Hill, Capt. J. J. Butler; 3d Pct., 179 Washington, Bkln., Capt. E. J. Toole; 27th Pct., E. 59th, Mhtn., Capt. P. Corcoran; 33d Pct., Central Pk., Capt. J. Brown; 77th Pct., Prospect Pk., Capt. E. J. Burns.

Detective Division.

240 Centre, Mhtn.

Act. Insp., commanding Detective Division, John D. Coughlin; Capt., commanding Homicide Squad, Arthur A. Carey.

Bureau of Criminal Identification, Lt. John J. Allen.

Commanding Bkln. and Queens—Act. Capt., Lt. John J. McCloskey.

1st Dist., Capt. Wm. H. Kinsler; 2d, Capt. T. Fay; 3d, Capt. H. McQueeney; 4th, Capt. T. F. Walsh; 5th, Capt. J. Duane; 6th, Capt. L. M. Haupt; 7th, Act. Capt., Lt. A. Wines; 8th, Capt. G. Busby; 9th, Act. Capt., Lt. E. L. Van Wagener; 10th, A.D.S. 1, Sgt. J. J. Ryan; 11th, Act. Capt., Lt. H. Duane; 12th, Act. Capt., Lt. J. J. Sullivan; 14th, Act. Capt., Lt. J. J. Gallagher; 15th, Act. Capt., Lt. D. Moriarty; 16th, Act. Capt., Lt. D. J. Carey; 17th, Capt. P. Randles; 18th, Capt. T. Mullarky.

Borough Headquarters and Other Officials.

MHTN. AND BRONX, 240 CENTRE.

Chf. Clk., R. K. Walsh, $4,100; 1st Dep. Clk., Grant Crabtree, $4,000; 2d Dep. Clk., A. H. G. Evans, $3,500; Prop. Clk. (e), J. A. Murray, $3,140; Supt. of Telegraph, M. R. Brennan, $4,000; Steno., J. H. Saunders, $3,400; Bkpr., E. J. Healey, Jr., $4,000; Bkpr., G. B. Hawthorne, $3,500; Steno., W. J. Rafferty, $2,232; Steno. to Comm., S. L. Grant, $2,340; Steno. to 1st Dep. Comr., P. H. Enright, $2,280; Steno. to 2d Dep. Comr., Rose Delaney, $1,860; Steno. to 3d Dep. Comr., M. Treister, $1,860; Steno. to 4th Dep. Comr., C. Underhill, $1,850; Steno. to Spec. Dep. Comr., F. Donahue, $2,520; Asst. Prop. Clks., J. C. Farley and Cornelius J Cronin, $2,280 each; Investigator, H. W. Dearborn, $2,304; Foreman Printer, J. J. Connelly, $2,707; Arch. Draftsman, B. P. Wilson, $2,772; Exec. Clk., A. E. O'Hara, $2,880; Veterinary Surg., $2,448; Foreman of Mechanics, $2,806; 2 Boiler Insps., $2,280 each; Janitor Eng., $2,700; Pilot, $2,280; 2 Marine Engs., $2,280 each; Launch Eng., $1,823; 4 Marine Stokers, $1,720 each; 2 Marine Oilers, $1,720 each; Cook and Steward, $1,632; 4 Job Compositors, $45 per week each; 2 Pressmen at $46 per week; 4 Electricians, $9 per day; Wireman, $9 per day; 4 Linemen, $8 per day; 42 Clks., $1,403 to $3,330; 10 Stenos., $1,464 to $2,040.

Chf. Surg., P. J. Murray, $6,500; 17 other Surgs., $4,400 each. Surgical Dists. 1 to 17; C. E. Nammack, D. J. Donovan, J. D. Gorman, M. Williams, C. J. Dillon, W. B. Brouner, E. T. Higgins, T. D. Lehane, F. R. Oastler, E. V. Hubbard, D. D. Jennings, T. A. McGoldrick, P. F. O'Hanlon, F. J. Murray, D. H. Morris, J. J. McGowan, P. J. Yorke; Hon. Neurologist, G. F. Boehme; Hon. Optometrist, H. A. Cohen; Hon. Consultant Surg., E. H. Fiske; Hon. Pediatrist, A. H. Hansen; Hon. Consultant Surg., C. G. Heyd; Hon. Dental Surgs., L. F. Gieberick, E. Appel, C. Hansen.

Patrolmen in Mhtn., 2,882; Bronx, 813.

BROOKLYN, 70-76 POPLAR.

In Charge, Thos. H. Murphy, Boro. Insp.

Prop. Clk., C. J. Cronin, $1,900; Asst. Supt of Telegraph, Wm. Allan, $3,800.

Patrolmen in Bkln., 2,932.

QUEENS, TOWN HALL, JAMAICA, AND 85 4TH, L. I. C.

Insp., T. J. Kelly, $4,900. Insp., T. T. Ryan, $4,900.

Patrolmen in Queens, 744.

RICHMOND, ST. GEORGE.

Insp., G. C. Lilbers, $4,900.

Patrolmen in Richmond, 128.

The Uniformed Force.

Composed of the following in order of rank:

Chief Inspector.... / Bor. Inspectors..... / Inspectors	24	Sergeants	769
Surgeons	18	Patrolmen	9,887
Captains	103	Matrons	56
Lieutenants	524	Supt. Telegraph	1
		Asst. Supt. Tel......	1

Police Women.

56 Police Women at $2,280 for 1st grade; $1,920 for 4th grade and $1,769 for 5th, 6th and 7th grades. 29 Patrol Women at $1,290 for 4th grade and $1,769 for 5th, 6th and 7th grades.

Special work of various kinds is done by details from the Uniformed Force, as follows:

Detective Bureau.

Captain	7	1st Grade Detecs.....	149
Lieutenants	43	Detectives	566

Marine Division.

Inspector, 1; Lieutenants, 3; Sergeants, 7; Patrolmen, 61.

(e) Exempt from Civil Service.

POLICE DEPARTMENT, CITY OF NEW YORK—*Continued.*

Traffic Regulation.

Inspectors	1	Mounted Patrolmen	87
Captains	9	Motorcycle Patrol	107
Lieutenants	31	Foot Patrolmen	1,080
Sergeants	56	Bicycle Patrol	9

Public Offices.

Lieutenants, 4; Patrolmen, 15.

Total Mounted.

Lieutenants, 2; Sergeants, 25; Patrolmen, 279.

Total Bicycle.

Sergeants, 92; Patrolmen, 976.

Total Motorcycle.

Lieutenants, 2; Sergeants, 15; Patrolmen, 122.

MAGISTRATES' COURTS TO WHICH PRECINCTS REPORT.

CITY MAGISTRATES' COURTS.

Manhattan.

1st Dist. Court, 110 White St.—1st Precinct (Mhtn. end of Bkln. & Mhtn. Bridges), 4th, 5th, 6th and 7th Precincts.

2d Dist. Court, Jefferson Mkt.—14th, 16th, 18th and 23d Precincts and Health Squad.

3d Dist. Court, 2d av. and 2d—13th, 15th, 17th. Wmsbrg. Bridge arrests (Mhtn. end).

4th Dist. Court, 151 E. 57th—21st, 25th, 29th, 31st and Queensboro Bridge arrests (Mhtn. end).

5th Dist. Court, 121st and Sylvan pl.—35th, 39th and 43d Precincts, Harbor Precinct B.

7th Dist. Court, 314 W. 54th—22d, 26th, 28th, 32d and 33d Precincts.

Separate Court for Women, 125 6th av.—Where any females will be arraigned charged with prostitution of any character, intemperance and shoplifting.

10th Dist. Court, 151 E. 57th—Night Court for males.

11th Dist. Court, 151 E. 57th—Domestic Relations.

12th Dist. Court—1130 St. Nicholas av.—36th, 37th, 38th, 40th and 42d Precincts.

Children's Court, 137 E. 22d.

Traffic Court, 301 Mott.

Municipal Term.—Mncpl. Bldg., Room 500.

Special Sessions—Center and White sts.

Bronx.

6th Dist. Court, 161st and Brook av.—45th, 46th, 47th, 50th and 57th Precincts.

8th Dist. Court, 1014 E. 181st—49th, 51st, 53d, 54th and 56th Precincts.

13th Dist. Court, 1014 E. 181st—Domestic Relations.

Children's Court, 355 E. 137th.

Special Sessions—Bergen Bldg., Tremont and Arthur avs.

Brooklyn.

1st Dist. Court, 318 Adams—91st, 92d, 93d and 99th Precincts, Sub-Division D and Bridge Precinct (Bkln. end of Bkln. and Mhtn. Bridges).

Traffic Court, 182 Clermont av.—Entire Borough of Bkln.

Domestic Relations Court, Myrtle and Vanderbilt avs.—Entire Borough of Bkln.

5th Dist. Court, Williamsburg Bridge Plaza—101st, 103d, 105th, 104th and 102d Precincts and Wmsbg. Bridge arrests (Bkln. end).

6th Dist. Court, 495 Gates av.—87th, 97th, 95th, 94th, 96th and 98th Precincts.

7th Dist. Court, 31 Snyder av.—73d, 74th, 77th, 79th, 82d and 88th Precincts and Harbor C.

8th Dist. Court, W. 8th, Coney Isl.—67th, 70th and 72d Precincts.

9th Dist. Court, 5th av. and 23d—68th, 76th, 78th, 89th and 90th Precincts and Harbor A.

10th Dist. Court, 133 New Jersey av.—80th, 83d and 85th Precincts.

Woman's Night Court, 318 Adams—Entire Borough of Bkln.

Municipal Term, Part 2, 2 Butler—Entire Borough of Bkln.

Queens.

1st Court, 115 5th, L. I. City—111th and 109th Precincts and Queensboro Bridge arrests (Queens end).

2d Court, Town Hall, Flushing—113th and 112th Precincts., B'way and Linden av.

3d Court, Central av., Far Rockaway—125th and 123d Precincts, Central and Mott avs.

4th Court, Town Hall, Jamaica—116th, 118th, 120th, 123d and 125th Precincts.

Richmond.

1st Court, Village Hall, N. Brighton—65th Precinct.

2d Court, Village Hall, Stapleton—66th, 63d and 60th Precincts, Washington Park Stapleton; Children's Court, Borough Hall, St. George; Spl. Sessions, New County Court House, St. George.

POLICE HONOR MEDAL MEN.

One Act. Det. Sergeant and 6 Patrolmen were selected in 1920 to receive medals in recognition of special acts of bravery in 1919. The medal men so chosen were:

A. D. S. Joseph A. Walsh, Dept. Medal.
Patl. Harry Cohen, Rhinelander Medal for Valor.
Patl. John J. Walsh, Isaac Bell Medal for Bravery.
Patl. J. J. Deveny, Peter F. Meyer Medal.
Patl. Geo. S. Lane, Auto Club of America Medal.
Patl. John F. Monahan, Bkln. Citizen Medal.
Patl. John J. Wimmer, Walter Scott Medal.

The medals were formally presented by the Mayor at the reviewing stand for the 1920 parade.

COMPARATIVE TABLE OF ARRESTS IN NEW YORK CITY FOR 11 YEARS.

	Entire City										
Offense.	1909	1910	1911	1912	1913	1914	1915	1916	1917	1918	1919
Grand larceny	5,001	4,839	5,150	4,520	4,022	4,556	4,651	4,546	4,933	4,869	5,193
Burglary	2,680	1,898	2,196	2,135	2,364	2,151	2,217	2,476	2,973	2,244	3,100
Robbery	839	826	615	502	556	669	637	1,106	1,275	1,143	1,744
Arson	49	48	50	61	66	44	43	156	45		24
Homicide	755	567	366	417	351	433	453	491	579	615	649
Felonious assault	4,312	4,481	4,309	4,099	4,444	4,605	4,912	5,210	4,567	3,485	3,771
Intoxication	30,233	28,733	31,994	30,640	31,727	30,269	30,194	17,099	13,844	7,090	5,562
Drunk, disorderly	7,026	7,046	4,773	4,965	4,480	2,772	2,183	2,206	2,292	1,553	1,293
All offenses: (Inc. Sum'nses)											
Males	135,962	141,928	130,917	148,358	146,766	166,175	186,196	174,684	163 992	152,296	199,099
Females	31,989	26,373	21,264	21,907	25,254	23,456	25,633	26,217	23,921	17,863	21,050

NEW YORK SUBWAY AND "L" TRAFFIC.

Year.	Elevated. (In round figures)	Subway. (In round figures)	Total. Exact fig's.
1905	266,000,000	72,000,000	339,104,820
1906	257,000,000	137,000,000	395,716,386
1907	282,000,000	166,000,000	449,287,884
1908	282,000,000	200,000,000	483,285,640
1909	276,000,000	238,000,000	514,680,342
1910	293,000,000	268,000,000	562,788,395
1911	301,000,000	276,000,000	578,154,088
1912	304,000,000	302,000,000	607,244,697
1913	306,000,000	327,000,000	634,316,516
1914	311,000,000	340,000,000	651,886,671
1915	301,000,000	345,000,000	647,378,266
1916	312,000,000	371,000,000	683,752,114
1917	349,000,000	414,000,000	763,574,065
1918	352,000,000	418,000,000	770,998,335
1919	348,000,000	461,000,000	809,355,658
1920	369,000,000	586,000,000	955,133,110

METROPOLITAN NEW YORK MOTOR REGISTRATION.

1914.		1920.	
Passenger cars	65,084	Passenger cars	208,000
Commercial	11,143	Commercial	64,500
Dealers	604	Dealers	1,618
Chauffeurs	47,875	Chauffeurs	155,000

This shows an increase in business in 1920 over 1914 of about 410 per cent.

BILLS INTRODUCED IN N. Y. STATE LEGISLATURE.

Yr.	Sen. bills.	As'bly bills.	Total.	Yr.	Sen. bills.	As'bly bills.	Total.
1911	1,713	1,955	3,668	1917	1,647	1,734	3,381
1912	1,254	1,605	2,859	1918	1,041	1,535	2,576
1913	1,858	2,223	4,081	1919	1,512	1,507	3,019
1914	1,326	1,502	2,828	1920	1,732	1,710	3,442
1916	1,477	1,596	3,073				

BUDGET OF THE CITY OF NEW YORK.

According to Section 226 of the Charter of the City of New York, the Bd. of Estimate and Apportionment (composed of the Mayor, Comptroller, Pres. of Bd. of Ald., and Presidents of Boros. of Mhtn., Bronx, Bkln., Queens and Richmond), from figures furnished by the heads of all departments not later than Sept. 10, annually between Oct. 1 and Nov. 1, prepares a budget of amounts estimated as requisite for the conduct of the city's business during the ensuing year. Public hearings thereon are mandatory, and within 5 days after budget is made and amounts therein authorized, it must be submitted to the Bd. of Ald. and adopted by said Board within 20 days after being convened by the Mayor in special session. Should the latter Board fail to act within such time, the budget as originally submitted stands. Board of Ald. may reduce, but cannot increase the budget, said reductions, if any, being final. Budget must then be signed by Mayor and Comptroller within 10 days, the former also having power to reduce, but not increase same. Thereafter budget is filed with the City Clerk as a public document.

COMPARISON OF 1919 AND 1920 BUDGETS.

Department.	1920.	1921.
Bd. of Ald., City Clerk..	$302,840.00	$408,542.30
Bd. of Est. and Appt....	368,999.00	384,286.67
Employees Retire't Sys..	......	585,295.00
Comrs. of Sinking Fund.	3,890.00	4,700.00
The Mayoralty	71,247.00	80,281.00
Dept. of Finance	1,547,248.00	1,970,691.33
City Chamberlain	1,617,243.00	2,055,684.33
Law Dept.	1,030,493.00	1,324,114.00
Dept. of Taxes and Assts	640,281.00	756,621.00
Board of Elections.......	2,129,915.00	2,046,521.00
Mncpl. Civil Serv. Comsn	211,772.00	255,248.00
Commissioner of Accts..	252,530.00	298,634.00
Bur. Weights & Meas'es	67,169.00	79,560.00
Dept. of Licenses........	196,703.40	221,520.00
Dept. of Public Markets.	209,785.20	196,776.15
Board of Assessors.......	38,333.00	42,734.75
Art Commission	7,526.60	8,411.60
Exam. Bd. of Plumbers.	7,210.00	7,984.00
Pres., Borough of Mhtn.	4,061,207.79	5,278,873.75
Pres., Bor. of The Bronx	1,820,293.93	2,543,327.95
Pres., Borough of Bkln..	3,914,568.59	5,475,829.20
Pres., Borough of Queens	3,805,424.58	5,092,033.80
Pres., Bor. of Richmond	1,252,386.11	1,572,838.97
Dept. of Education—		
General School Fund..	39,316,531.80	61,941,051.08
Special School Fund....	49,408,582.12	77,946,038.77
College of City of N. Y.	820,468.65	1,059,422.70
Hunter Col., C. of N. Y.	640,516.98	785,379.66
Teachers' Ret'mt System	2,611,033.00	2,920,672.00
N. Y. Public Library....	993,585.00	1,120,037.60
Bkln. Public Library....	632,119.32	709,679.32
Queens Bor. Pub. Lib..	223,731.50	252,806.58
Dept. of Parks, Park Bd.	32,895.00	41,723.00
Dept. of Parks, Mhtn....	1,300,853.85	1,574,590.75
Dept. of Parks, Bronx..	654,416.58	802,601.25
Dept. of Parks. Bklyn..	1,019,465.13	1,220,579.50
Dept. of Parks, Queens.	314,465.00	396,382.75
Dept. of Parks, Richm'd	......	56,448.00
Jumel Mansion	5,964,100	7,293.00
Grant's Tomb	5,000.00	7,000.00
N. Y. Pub. Library Bldg.	55,000.00	55,000.00
Metln. Museum of Art..	300,000.00	623,509.96
N. Y. Aquarium..........	54,891.00	65,653.00
Amer. Mus. Nat. History	295,140.00	457,176.00
N. Y. Botanical Garden.	160,000.00	200,442.80
N. Y. Zoological Garden.	237,930.97	282,400.00
Bkln. Inst. Arts & Sci'ces	130,000.00	163,407.00
Children's Museum, Bkln.	18,500.00	23,350.00
Bkln. Bot. Gar. & Arb'm	87,500.00	90,050.80
Bronx Parkway Comn...	81,000.00	169,200.00
Staten I. Assn. Arts&Sci.	6,800.00	8,201.00
Police Dept.	24,595,186.71	28,349,407.64
Fire Dept.	13,186,753.19	17,033,082.28
Armory Board	392,025.73	438,559.00
Bd. of Stand. & Appeals	38,810.00	42,687.00
U. S. Vol. Life Sav. Crps	6,887.00	7,795.00
Dept. of Health..........	4,729,832.92	5,733,076.17
Dept. of Pub. Welfare..	7,497,561.43	8,201,147.67
Board of Child Welfare..	2,084,492.00	3,081,635.00
Bellevue & Allied Hosps.	2,835,623.96	3,313,291.42
Bd. of Ambulance Service	116,960.00	121,844.00
Tenement House Dept...	671,383.00	804,079.00
Dept. of Water Supply, Gas and Electricity....	7,513,150.34	10,775,149.80
Dept. of St. Cleaning...	13,163,523.54	16,790,036.33
Payments to Charitable Insts.	8,149,387.50	8,146,850.00
Com'ment Insane Persons	4,000.00	4,800.00
Dept. of Correction......	2,331,214.20	2,447,336.00
Parole Commission	101,292.00	113,896.00
Dept. Plant & Structures	3,432,416.95	5,722,850.40
Municipal Garage Service	115,065.00	217,998.63
Dept. of Docks..........	1,123,274.30	1,754,530.55
City Court	283,470.00	339,689.00
Court of Spec. Sessions—		
Adult Court	285,929.00	326,008.00
Children's Court	279,786.00	330,672.00
City Magistrates' Courts.	1,191,877.00	1,396,281.00
Municipal Courts	1,069,435.00	1,245,147.00
Office of Chief Medical Examiner	112,499.00	127,303.00
Bd. of City Record, N.Y.C.	1,093,730.00	1,394,841.00
Board of Purchase.......	151,679.00	170,206.00
Advertising	95,000.00	115,000.00
Debt. Service	74,811,538.66	106,528,527.30
Tax Deficiency	$1,675,000.00	$1,680,000.00
Rent	655,122.57	742,616.51
Miscellaneous, N. Y. C..	495,323.00	444,323.00
Total, City of New York	$256,441,440.16	$313,459,633.54

County Government

NEW YORK COUNTY.

Department.	1920.	1921.
County Clerk	$170,218.00	$205,782.
District Attorney	548,821.00	640,268.
Register	259,649.00	307,205.
Comr. of Records	100,000.00	100,000.
Comr. Records, Su. Court	90,970.00	77,198.
Commissioner of Jurors..	67,870.00	78,942.
Public Administrator	31,833.00	.367.
Sheriff	186,028.00	37,867.00
State Gd. & Naval Mil..	332,642.00	339,055.00
Payments to Charitable Insts.	90,560.00	93,150.00
Supreme Court, 1st Dept.	1,048,078.80	1,211,395.88
Supreme Court, 1st Dept., Maintenance of App. Div. Court House......	32,905.92	46,279.34
Court of General Sessions	422,200.00	479,785.00
Surrogate's Court	255,510.00	310,594.00
Fees and Expenses of Jurors	600,000.00	600,000.00
Disbursements and Fees	15,000.00	53,000.00
Stenographers' Fees	30,000.00	33,000.00
Witnesses' Fees	11,000.00	11,000.00
Board of City Record....	39,000.00	39,000.00
Miscellaneous	62,869.40	121,771.00
Totals, New York Co....	$4,365,155.12	$5,010,659.22

BRONX COUNTY.

Department.	1920.	1921.
County Clerk	$81,617.00	$97,727.00
District Attorney	116,045.00	139,987.00
Register	115,612.00	150,776.00
Commissioner of Jurors..	24,641.00	29,316.00
Public Administrator	4,497.00	4,940.00
Commissioner of Records.	24,785.00	44,314.00
Sheriff	153,851.00	183,188.00
State Gd. & Naval Mil..	94,428.00	97,820.00
Payments to Charitable Inst.	27,320.00	29,500.00
Supreme Court, 1st Dept.	147,541.26	170,997.00
Supreme Court, 1st Dept., Maintenance of App. Div., Court House......	4,615.08	6,631.06
Law Library	2,585.50	3,263.00
Surrogate's Court	54,608.00	65,856.00
County Court	48,710.00	67,801.00
Fees and Expenses of Jurors	70,000.00	85,000.00
Stenographers' Fees	750.00	1,400.00
Witnesses' Fees	1,000.00	1,700.00
Board of City Record....	15,000.00	15,000.00
Miscellaneous	50,784.50	57,143.50
Totals, Bronx County..	$1,038,390.34	$1,247,990.44

KINGS COUNTY.

Department.	1920.	1921.
County Clerk	$121,766.00	$142,690.00
District Attorney	184,385.00	273,682.16
Register	328,906.00	354,048.20
Comr. of Records	100,000.00	114,016.25
Comr. of Jurors..........	45,590.00	53,240.00
Public Administrator	14,693.00	17,051.00
Sheriff	107,655.00	123,765.00
State Gd. & Naval Mil.	244,014.00	260,865.00
Payments to Charitable Inst	61,250.00	63,050.00
Supreme Court, 2d Dept.	407,650.00	474,800.00
Supreme Court, 2d Dept., App. Div.	92,381.33	110,818.00
Supreme Court, 2d Dept., App. Term	18,500.00	23,550.00
Surrogate's Court	125,600.00	161,111.00
County Court	287,906.00	319,773.00
Supreme Court Library..	10,800.00	12,450.00
Fees and Expenses of Jurors	180,000.00	182,000.00

BUDGET OF THE CITY OF NEW YORK—KINGS COUNTY—*Continued.*

Department.	1920.	1921.
Disbursements and Fees.	$4,000.00	$5,700.00
Witnesses' Fees	3,000.00	3,300.00
Board of City Record	23,900.00	31,900.00
Miscellaneous	51,832.00	59,815.58
Totals, Kings County	$2,413,908.33	$2,786,530.19

QUEENS COUNTY.

Department.	1920.	1921.
County Clerk	$228,066.00	$271,147.00
District Attorney	53,557.00	65,397.00
Commissioner of Jurors	14,873.00	19,227.45
Public Administrator	1,280.00	3,668.50
Sheriff	54,212.00	63,025.00
State Gd. & Naval Mil.	13,542.00	14,235.00
Payments to Charitable Inst.	9,300.00	13,400.00
Supreme Court	90,150.42	99,080.39
Supreme Court, 2d Dept., App. Div.	25,052.23	31,243.83
Surrogate's Court	41,750.00	46,893.00
County Court	49,860.00	56,207.00
Supreme Court Library	3,270.00	4,081.00
Fees and Expenses of Jurors	60,000.00	60,000.00
Disbursements and Fees.	300.00	700.00
Witnesses' Fees	1,500.00	1,200.00
Board of City Record	8,000.00	13,000.00
Miscellaneous	6,962.00	4,672.00
Totals, Queens County.	$661,664.65	$767,177.17

RICHMOND COUNTY.

Department.	1920.	1921.
County Clerk	$32,090.00	$41,
District Attorney	22,905.00	28,
Commissioner of Jurors	6,900.00	7,
Sheriff	51,625.00	58,852.00
State Gd. & Naval Mil.	15,372.00	16,[illegible].00
Payments to Charitable Inst.	3,775.00	5,300.00
Supreme Court	24,361.08	27,461.21
Supreme Court, 2d Dept., App. Div.	4,612.08	5,523.73
Supreme Court Library	16,851.00	11,864.00
County Ct. and Sur. Ct.	31,589.00	37,644.00
Fees and Expenses of Jurors	13,800.00	14,500.00
Witnesses' Fees	700.00	700.00
Board of City Record	3,700.00	3,700.00
Miscellaneous	1,490.00	1,928.00
Totals, Richmond Co.	$229,770.16	$258,225.94
Totals, All Counties	$8,708,888.60	$10,070,582.96
Totals, City of N. Y. and Counties	$265,150,328.76	$323,530,216.50
Direct State Tax	$8,539,156.37	$22,041,183.27
Grand total	$273,689,485.13	$345,571,399.77

BUDGET APPROPRIATIONS FROM 1898 TO 1920, INCLUSIVE.

Year.	Interest on City Debt.	Redemption of City Debt.	Per Cent. of Budget for Interest on City Debt.	Total Budget Appropriations.	Per Capita.	To Provide for Deficiencies in Collection of Taxes.	Grand Total Budget.
1898	$9,629,382.39	$4,536,828.99	12.429	$76,518,964.80	$23.80	$954,119.97	$77,473,084.77
1899	11,430,778.74	12,046,061.34	12.223	91,830,204.22	27.86	1,689,877.81	93,520,082.03
1900	11,707,544.95	7,939,073.35	12.897	89,160,499.40	26.34	1,618,473.08	90,778,972.48
1901	12,100,206.05	10,332,173.18	12.335	96,374,244.19	27.60	1,726,169.24	98,100,413.43
1902	12,937,776.26	10,194,494.75	13.119	96,889,582.46	26.90	1,730,018.42	98,619,600.88
1903	13,276,709.68	10,417,359.17	13.671	95,596,822.03	25.68	1,522,209.07	97,119,031.10
1904	15,188,951.64	14,552,338.40	14.239	104,987,289.89	27.35	1,687,667.20	106,674,955.09
1905	17,101,850.89	12,164,843.84	15.573	108,072,776.47	27.29	1,744,816.56	109,817,593.03
1906	18,459,015.38	12,657,191.83	15.803	114,960,428.66	28.13	1,845,061.71	116,805,490.37
1907	20,799,880.82	14,458,564.55	16.324	127,421,505.65	29.73	3,000,000.00	130,412,505.66
1908	24,576,622.57	15,878,250.29	17.483	140,572,266.17	31.78	3,000,000.00	143,572,266.17
1909	29,671,070.13	17,552,008.20	19.314	153,622,701.06	33.65	2,922,447.08	156,545,148.14
1910	32,178,760.49	14,264,935.23	20.222	159,128,270.37	33.39	4,000,000.00	163,128,270.37
1911	34,214,137.09	16,447,684.90	20.866	163,967,835.16	32.90	10,000,000.00	173,967,835.16
1912	35,473,685.93	15,780,842.24	19.951	177,802,889.77	34.37	3,287,366.74	181,090,256.51
1913	38,453,876.67	16,523,504.67	20.195	190,411,441.16	35.44	2,300,000.00	192,711,441.16
1914	37,745,836.58	14,865,681.07	19.801	190,495,551.62	34.11	2,500,000.00	192,995,551.62
1915	42,411,903.85	17,403,477.19 *17,000.00	21.10	192,877,694.08	34.22	6,112,092.44	198,989,786.52
1916	42,020,934.84	21,192,275.27	20.11	208,956,177.54	35.98	4,000,000.00	212,956,177.54
1917	43,284,252.12	26,460,316.83	21.00	206,115,016.82	40.83	5,000,000.00	211,115,016.82
1918	47,663,019.54	17,927,440.48	20.28	235,023,759.20	40.96	3,100,000.00	238,662,514.18
1919	48,949,997.62	17,656,940.48	20.43	239,502,905.27	41.74	1,835,000.00	248,025,434.88
1920	49,751,993.42	7,834,545.24	18.18	265,150,328.76	†44.14	1,675,000.00	273,689,485.13
1921	53,501,482.0?	11,802,045.24	15.48	323,530,216.50	‡57.56	1,680,000.00	345,571,399.77

*Amount required to reimburse City's Agent for its expenses incurred in payment of coupons on the City of N. Y. †Per capita cost is based on N. Y. C. Health Dept. 1919 est., pop., 6,006,794. ‡Per capita cost is based on U. S. Census 1920 pop., 5,620,048.

SUMMARY OF TOTAL APPROPRIATIONS FOR CITY AND COUNTIES

	Approp. 1920.
The City of New York	$256,441,440.16
County of New York	4,365,155.12
County of The Bronx	1,038,390.34
County of Kings	2,413,908.33
County of Queens	661,664.65
County of Richmond	229,770.16
N. Y. State Tax	8,539,156.37
Total	$273,689,485.13

	Approp. 1921.
The City of New York	$313,459,633.54
County of New York	5,010,659.22
County of The Bronx	1,247,990.44
County of Kings	2,786,530.19
County of Queens	767,177.17
County of Richmond	258,225.94
N. Y. State Tax	22,041,183.27
Total	$345,571,399.77

TAX RATES—CITY AND COUNTY PURPOSES—1913-1920.

	New York Co.	Bronx Co.	Kings Co.	Queens Co.	Richmond Co.
1920	2.39	2.44	2.43	2.41	2.52
1919	2.32	2.37	2.33	2.37	2.41
1918	2.36	2.40	2.40	2.41	2.46
1917	2.02	2.08	2.07	2.09	2.12
1916	2.04	2.09	2.08	2.06	2.13
1915	1.87	1.94	1.92	1.95	2.24
1914	1.78	1.77	1.84	1.80	1.90
1913	1.81	....	1.85	1.85	1.92

All peace-time records in recruiting for the Regular Army were broken in Oct., 1920, when 17,625 enlistments were accepted.

Statisticians figure that the populations of the world average 110 women to every 100 men.

Oxford University for the first time in its history of 900 years has recently conferred degrees upon its women students.

More than a million patients pass through the New York hospitals every year.

BRIDGES OVER THE EAST RIVER.

The management of the Bridges is under control of the Commissioner of Plant and Structures, appointed by the Mayor. (See Municipal Government Chapter, Dept. of Plant and Structures.)

BROOKLYN BRIDGE.

Year ending December 1, 1920.

TROLLEY CAR STATEMENT.

Total number of cars crossing Bridge.... 1,013,003
Daily average 2,768

ELEVATED TRAIN STATEMENT.

Total number of cars crossing Bridge..... 822,888
Daily average 2,248

Total Receipts.

Fiscal years ending December 1.

1884,* $682,775.42; 1885, $622,680.31; 1886, $870,307.43; 1887, $938,281.21; 1888, $1,012,254.82; 1889, $1,120,024.16; 1890, $1,239,493.90; 1891, $1,176,447.95; 1892, $1,801,661.48; 1893, $1,590,140.03; 1894, $1,476,598.85; 1895, $1,628,378.04; 1896, $1,404,318.47; 1897, $1,363,731.03; 1898, $802,717.46; 1899, $422,666.37; 1900, $381,612.57; 1901, $434,105.12; 1902, $375,581.77; 1903, $351,292.96; 1904, $425,165.06; 1905, $369,838.56; 1906, $385,413.16; 1907, $393,498.43; 1908, $449,860.11; 1909, $432,075.73; 1910, $452,448.43; 1911, $411,868.63; 1912, $313,380.50; 1913, $296,778.63; 1914, $289,801.29; 1915, $298,701.92; 1916, $278,366.34; 1917, $254,091.70; 1918, $248,544.23; 1919, $253,531.23; 1920, $271,636.26.

Roadway tolls abolished July 18, 1911, by the Board of Aldermen.

*From May to December.

Total Expenditures.

Fiscal years ending December 1.

1884, $552,647.78; 1885, $560,928.23; 1886, $951,944.68; 1887, $989,461.22; 1888, $831,497.22; 1889, $1,267,115.19; 1890, $1,075,436.71; 1891, $1,732,280.88; 1892, $1,716,530.82; 1893, $1,655,908.23; 1894, $1,521,660.94; 1895, $1,647,316.56; 1896, $1,640,490.24; 1897, $1,228,143.24; 1898, $779,949.30; 1899, $286,076.98; 1900, $251,261.56; 1901, $322,311.33; 1902, $328,731.90; 1903, $303,046.62; 1904, $394,812.36; 1905, $387,489.38; 1906, $368,596.04; 1907, $406,881.97; 1908, $401,182.47; 1909, $438,355.10; 1910, $442,018.95; 1911, $374,662.05; 1912, $305,375.84; 1913, $344,114.04; 1914, $323,066.46; 1915, $308,193.18; 1916, $244,860.02; 1917, $210,330.72; 1918, $216,064.51; 1919 and 1920 (figures not available from Dept.).

Statistics of the Structure.

Construction commenced Jan. 3, 1870. Opened May 24, 1883. Elevated railroad opened Sept. 24, 1883. Surface railway began operation Jan. 23, 1898. Size of Mhtn. caisson, 172x102 ft., of Bkln. caisson, 168x102 ft. Mhtn. tower contains 46,945 cubic yds. masonry, Bkln. tower contains 38,214 cubic yds. masonry. Depth of tower foundation below high water, Bkln., 45 ft.; Mhtn., 78 ft. Size of Mhtn. tower, high water line, 140x59 ft. Size of Mhtn. tower at roof course, 136x53 ft. Height of towers above high water, 272 ft. Heights of roadway at center of bridge, 139 ft. above mean high water. Clear height of bridge for channel width of 400 ft., 133 ft. above mean high water. Height of roadway at towers above high water, 119 ft. 3 in. Grade of roadway, 3¼ ft. in 100 ft. Height of towers above roadway, 152 ft. 9 in. Weight of each anchor plate, 23 tons. Diameter of each cable, 15¾ in. First wire was run out May 29, 1877. Length of each single wire, 3,578 ft. 6 in. Ultimate strength of each cable, 14,600 tons. Weight of wire, 11 ft. per pound. Each cable contains 5,296 parallel (not twisted) galvanized steel, oil coated wires, closely wrapped to a solid cylinder, 15¾ in. in diameter. Permanent weight suspended from cables, 13,820 tons. Width of bridge, 86 ft. Length of river span, 1,595 ft. 6 in. Length of each land span, 930 ft. Length of Bkln. approach, 998 ft.; of Mhtn. approach, 1,562 ft. 6 in. Total length of carriageway, 6,016 ft. Total cost of constr. to Dec. 31, 1915, $17,909,412.

WILLIAMSBURG BRIDGE.

Year ending December 1, 1920.

TROLLEY CAR STATEMENT.

Brooklyn Lines.

Total number of cars crossing Bridge...... 873,236
Daily average 2,386

New York Lines.

Total number trolley cars crossing Bridge.. 191,299
Daily average 522

New York and Brooklyn Lines Combined.

Total number trolley cars crossing Bridge.1,064,535
Daily average 2,902

ELEVATED TRAIN STATEMENT.

Total number of cars crossing Bridge....... 599,361
Daily average 1,638

Total Receipts.

Fiscal years ending December 1.

1904, $50,084.88; 1905, $102,014.87; 1906, $141,864.96; 1907, $153,167.82; 1908, $169,803.50; 1909, $255,568.01; 1910, $275,432.20; 1911, $214,564.30; 1912, $132,301.10; 1913, $121,401.50; 1914, $96,793.07; 1915, $93,963.76; 1916, $94,971.84; 1917, $103,765.38; 1918, $77,348.87; 1919, $88,458.94; 1920, $41,645.84.

Roadway tolls abolished July 18, 1911, by the Board of Aldermen.

No collection of tolls from Elevated R. R. Cos. since August, 1913—in litigation.

Total Expenditures.

Fiscal years ending December 1.

1904, $37,098.00; 1905, $71,646.72; 1906, $131,789.34; 1907, $127,762.12; 1908, $163,769.36; 1909, $252,737.06; 1910, $298,599.25; 1911, $303,571.02; 1912, $272,237.31; 1913, $244,115.37; 1914, $207,615.33; 1915, $226,979.10; 1916, $182,480.07; 1917, $162,330.69; 1918, $167,404.44; 1919 and 1920 (figures not available from Dept.).

Statistics of the Structure.

Construction commenced Nov. 7, 1896; formal opening, Dec. 19, 1903. Surface railway for Bkln. lines began operation Nov. 3, 1904. Surface railway for Mhtn. lines began operation Feb. 9, 1905. Elevated railway began operation Sept. 16, 1908. Length of main span, center to center of towers, 1,600 ft. Length of entire bridge, 7,308 ft. Width of bridge, main span over all, 118 ft. Height of bridge above mean high water, 135 ft. for channel width of 400 ft. Height of masonry towers above mean high water, 23 ft. Height of cables at towers above mean high water, 333 ft. Width of each two carriageways, 20 ft. Number of trolley tracks, 4. Number of elevated railway tracks, 2. Weight of steel in cables and suspenders, 4,900 tons; in other parts main bridge, 26,300 tons; in approaches, 16,600 tons. Diameter of cables, outside of wires, 18¾ inches. Number of wires in each cable, 7,696. Size of each wire in cables (No. 6), about 3-16 inch. Length of each of the cable wires, about 2,985 ft. Quantities of material used in the bridge: Timber, about 8,000,000 ft. B. M.; excavation, about 125,000 cubic yards; concrete masonry, about 60,000 cubic yards; stone masonry, about 130,000 cubic yards; steel, 47,800 tons. Total cost of constr. to Dec. 31, 1915, $15,091,497.

QUEENSBORO BRIDGE.

Year ending December 1, 1920.

TROLLEY CAR STATEMENT.

Total number of cars crossing Bridge...... 233,886
Daily average 639

Total Receipts.

Fiscal years ending December 1.

1909, $59,091.34; 1910, $84,892.50; 1911, $71,069.20; 1912, $38,585.04; 1913, $38,511.33 (*$37,203.83); 1914, $40,588.50 (*$38,834.44); 1915, $42,832.66 (*$39,128.48); 1916, $39,541.46 (*$36,244.67); 1917, $38,729.41; (*$29,823.54); 1918, $26,639.38 (*24,393.60); 1919, $28,024.09 (*$23,519.12); 1920, $23,219.10 (*$18,733.73).

Roadway tolls abolished July 18, 1911, by the Board of Aldermen.

*Portion of total amt. certified to Compt. for collection.

Total Expenditures.

Fiscal years ending December 1.

1909, $62,824.19; 1910, $105,464.97; 1911, $94,145.59; 1912, $89,134.34; 1913, $88,354.71; 1914, $86,171.82; 1915, $85,694.56; 1916, $100,645.46; 1917, $124,735.94; 1918, $94,705.64; 1919 and 1920 (figures not available from Dept.).

Statistics of the Structure.

The general plan for a cantilever bridge, from 2d av., bet. 59th and 60th, Mhtn., across Blackwell's Island to an intersection with Jane st., L. I. City, was submitted to the Sec. of War, Dec. 2, 1899. Nov. 15, 1900, the ordinance authorizing construction was approved by the Mayor, and on Feb. 21, 1901, the plans were approved by the War Dept. On June 27, 1901, the contract for the construction of the 6 masonry piers was let to Ryan & Parker, for $745,547.

Construction of the piers was commenced July 19, 1901, and was completed June 10, 1904, at a total cost of $858,565.01. The contract for the steel superstructure was let to the Pennsylvania Steel Co., Nov. 20, 1903, and was completed June 15, 1908. Total cost of constr. to Dec. 31, 1915, was $12,873,364.

BRIDGES OVER THE EAST RIVER—*Continued.*

The total length of this bridge, from the east side of 2d av., Mhtn., to Jackson av., L. I. City, including the Queens Plaza, is 8,601 ft., or from 2d av., Mhtn., to Crescent, L. I. City, 7,449 ft.

The length of the spans are: Manhattan anchor span, 469.5 ft. West Channel span, 1,182 ft. Island span, 630 ft. East Channel span, 984 ft. Queens anchor span, 459 ft. The clear height over river channels is 135 ft. Plans were approved by the Art Commission Feb. 10, 1903. The bridge was opened for pedestrians and vehicles on March 30, 1909. The celebration of the completion of the bridge was commenced June 12, 1909. The operation of surface cars on the bridge began Sept. 19, 1909. Elevated railroad trains first used the bridge, July 23, 1917.

MANHATTAN BRIDGE.

TROLLEY CAR STATEMENT.

Year ending December 1, 1920.

Total number of cars crossing Bridge..... 132,409
Daily average 362

Total Receipts.

Fiscal years ending December 1.

1910, $69,901.83; 1911, $59,308.59; 1912, $1.506.95; 1913, $12,509.57 (*$6,281.68); 1914, $12,266.23 (*$11,535.48); 1915, $13,582.88 (*$12,757.63); 1916, $23,067.70 (*$13,373.23); 1917, $39,797.36 (*$13,537.16); 1918, $44,351.84 (*$14,443.32); 1919, $43.673.60 (*$13,686.02); 1920, $44,387.97 (*$9 539.41).

Roadway tolls abolished July 18, 1911, by the Board of Aldermen.

*Portion of total amt. certified to Compt. for collection.

Total Expenditures.

Fiscal years ending December 1.

1910, $47,348.14; 1911, $60,918.15; 1912, $60,705.04; 1913, $62,913.27; 1914, $64,506.66; 1915, $58,872.20; 1916, $65,-313.01 1917, $56,301.36; 1918, $59,070.64; 1919 and 1920 (figures not available from Dept).

Statistics of the Structure.

The Manhattan Bridge is the greatest suspension bridge in the world. It extends from Bowery and Canal, Mhtn., to Nassau and Bridge, Bkln. The ordinance authorizing construction was approved by the Mayor Jan. 8, 1900, and Jan. 29, 1900, the Sec. of War approved the plans. Construction commenced on Oct. 1, 1901. The Bkln. tower foundation contract was let to J. C. Rodgers, May 1, 1901, for $471,757, and the foundation was completed in Dec., 1902. The Mhtn. tower foundation contract was let to J. C. Rodgers Dec. 22, 1902, for $482,726.56, and the foundation was completed in April, 1904. On July 9, 1903, the contract for masonry pedestals on top of the tower foundations was let to J. C. Rodgers for $150,000. The Bkln. anchorage contract was let to Kosmos Engineering Co., Jan. 24, 1905, for $1,312,554, and the Mhtn. anchorage contract was let to Williams Engineering and Contracting Co., Feb. 9, 1905, for $1,197,000. Each anchorage is 237 ft. long by 183 ft. wide. The contract for furnishing the metal work for the anchorages and constructing the towers, cables, suspenders and suspended superstructure was let to the Ryan-Parker Construction Co. on June 15, 1906, at a price of $6,493,223. The steel towers over which the cables are swung are 336 ft. high. They are constructed on masonry piers which extend 92 ft. below and 32 ft. above mean high water level. The largest steel plates in these towers are 362 in. long, 88½ in. wide, and 2½ in. thick, weighing each 16,460 pounds. The first wire rope for the temporary cables supporting footwalks was strung on June 15, 1908. The first cable wire was strung August 10, 1908; the last one on Dec. 10, 1908. These four cables contain 37,888 galvanized acid steel wires. Diameter of cables, 21¼ in. Length of each wire about 3,224 ft.

The contract for the construction of the masonry piers, surface and sub-surface changes and steel superstructure of the Mhtn. and Bkln. approaches was entered into with J. C. Rodgers on Dec. 20, 1907, for $2,168,304.

On June 18, 1909, a contract was entered into with the Lord Electric Co. for the construction of railings, roadway and footwalk pavements and tracks and electrical equipments, the total cost of which was $394,162. Contract for improvement of Mhtn. plaza with Wm. P. Seaver for $317,380, dated Jan. 18, 1912. Contract for improvement of Bkln. plaza with North-Eastern Construction Co. for $596,400, dated June 23, 1913. The total length of the bridge is 6,855 ft. and the extreme width 122 ft. 6 in. The elevation above mean high water at center is 135 ft. Provision is made for 4 trolley and 4 subway tracks, one 35-ft. roadway and two promenades. each 13 ft. 7 in. wide.

On Dec. 31, 1909, the roadway was opened to the public. On July 18, 1910, the east footwalk was opened to pedestrians. On May 11, 1911, the west footwalk was opened to pedestrians. Local surface car traffic commenced Sept. 4, 1912. Subway trains first used the bridge, June 22, 1915. Total cost of constr. to Dec. 31, 1915, was $16,698,189.

NEW YORK CONNECTING RAILROAD BRIDGE.

The N. Y. Connecting Railroad cantilever bridge over Hell Gate from the Astoria section of Queens, crossing Ward's and Randall's Islands to the Port Morris region of the Bronx is an important railway connection with Bkln. The Pennsylvania and New Haven Systems share interests. Starting from the yards of the N. Y., N. H. & H. R. R. Co. at 142d in the Bronx, the line passes over numerous streets and is carried on a steel viaduct with concrete piers some 4,064 ft. to the Bronx Kills, which it crosses on a two-span Bascule Bridge of the Strauss type, each span 175 ft. long; thence on steel viaduct 1,900 ft. long to Little Hell Gate, which it crosses by three deck truss spans 296 ft. long and one span 260 ft. long; thence on steel viaduct 2,570 ft. long to Hell Gate Arch 977 ft. 6 in.; thence on steel viaduct 2,828 ft. long; thence partly on viaduct and embankment. At Hell Gate there has been built the most massive bridge structure of its kind in this country. It has huge granite piers 250 ft. high and a span of 1,107 ft. The clear height above mean high water is 135 ft. The great steel structure, rising in a parabolic arch, has four tracks, two for passenger trains and two for freight. The train floor level is below the crown of the arch and suspended from it. The estimated weight of steel in the viaducts and bridges together, about 3 miles long, is 75,000 tons. From the Long Island end of the bridge the pass. tracks continue partly on a viaduct and partly on embankment to the Sunnyside yards of the Penn. R. R. in L. I. City. The freight tracks continue through Queens to Fresh Pond and the East New York part of Brooklyn; whence they follow the route of the Manhattan Beach Railroad to Flatbush and then the Bay Ridge branch of that road to the waterfront at 65th st. The passenger connection between the Pennsylvania System and the New Haven is via the tunnels of the former from New Jersey to Long Island, and thence by the Connecting Railroad to Port Morris, where the New Haven road practically begins.

NEWTOWN CREEK.

Although less than four miles from its source, among the oil refineries of Blissville and Greenpoint, L. I., to its mouth at the East River, Newtown Creek is known as one of the "world's busiest waterways." The Mississippi River, from New Orleans to St. Paul, is 1,[illegible] miles in length and flows through a great industrial and agricultural district. Recent figures show that 5,220,000 tons of cargo are carried annually on the upper and lower reaches of the longest river in the world, while the annual average of tonnage carried on the little four-mile Newtown Creek was 5,620,060.

257 MILES OF B. R. T.

Since the opening of the Montague Street and 60th Street Queens tunnels under the East River, the Brooklyn Rapid Transit Company has had in operation 257½ miles of rapid transit road.

PETROLEUM IN MEXICO.

Mexico's 1920 production of petroleum amounted to 140,000,000 barrels, or one-fifth of the world's total, according to official estimates given out by the Mexican Embassy. This compares with a production of 88,000,000 barrels in 1919 and more than twice as much as 1918 and 1917.

VITAL STATISTICS, OCT., 1919, TO SEPT., 1920, OF NEW YORK CITY.

	Total Deaths.	Death Rate Thousand	Deaths Under 1 Year Old.	Deaths at 65 Yrs. and Over.	Total Births.	Birth Rate Per Thousand
Manhattan.						
October, 1919	2,103	8.9:	369	407	5,129	21.74
November ..	2,187	9.58	297	497	4,230	18.52
December ...	2,616	11.09	352	584	5,240	22.21
January, 1920	3,811	15.87	479	713	4,782	19.92
February ...	5,033	22.40	676	830	4,809	21.40
March	3,178	13.23	567	585	5,183	21.37
April	2,901	12.48	453	580	4,745	20.42
May	2,551	10.62	417	508	4,403	18.34
June	2,106	9.06	349	409	5,148	22.15
July	2,031	8.43	410	358	5,050	21.08
August	2,152	9.26	510	349	4,776	20.55
September ..	2,078	8.94	352	426	4,675	20.12
Bronx.						
October, 1919	459	8.87	80	100	1,232	22.48
November ..	483	9.22	66	104	1,032	19.46
December ..	656	11.97	97	165	1,318	24.04
January, 1920	938	16.51	131	183	1,204	2[illegible].19
February ...	1,305	24.56	166	238	1,317	24.78
March	735	12.94	108	176	1,317	23.18
April	622	11.21	88	134	1,277	23.23
May	618	10.88	81	133	1,179	20.76
June	570	10.37	81	123	1,325	24.10
July	491	8.64	62	107	1,282	22.57
August	509	9.26	93	82	1,195	21.74
September ..	492	8.95	86	136	1,127	20.50
Brooklyn.						
October, 1919	1,585	9.02	241	396	4,127	23.49
November ..	1,718	10.10	213	457	3,819	22.46
December ..	1,908	10.86	275	472	4,199	23.90
January, 1920	2,791	15.53	352	646	4,249	23.64
February ...	4,121	24.50	572	806	4,151	24.68
March	2,577	14.34	405	570	4,586	25.52
April	2,170	12.47	329	403	4,[illegible]66	23.96
May	2,081	11.58	311	504	3,773	20.99
June	1,684	9.68	263	346	4,316	24.81
July	1,549	8.62	282	301	4,147	23.07
August	1,653	9.50	338	360	4,143	23.82
September ..	1,593	9.16	307	336	4,010	23.05

	Total Deaths.	Death Rate Thousand	Deaths Under 1 Year Old	Deaths at 65 Yrs. and Over.	Total Births.	Birth Rate Per Thousand
Queens.						
October, 1919	338	9.80	57	65	825	23.93
November ..	346	10.37	37	103	745	22.33
December ..	406	11.74	60	97	817	23.70
January, 1920	610	17.13	62	142	827	23.23
February ...	824	24.73	100	159	762	22.87
March	478	13.42	69	125	852	23.93
April	477	13.84	75	128	805	23.36
May	451	12.66	70	114	779	21.88
June	378	10.97	45	85	774	22.46
July	368	10.34	52	65	880	24.72
August	384	11.14	60	77	829	24.06
September ..	343	9.95	58	76	784	22.75
Richmond.						
October, 1919	129	14.67	25	34	232	26.38
November ..	117	14.92	10	38	201	23.61
December ..	120	13.64	16	25	249	28.31
January, 1920	181	20.20	24	65	218	24.33
February ..	240	28.64	26	66	216	25.77
March	160	17.83	25	55	259	28.91
April	151	17.42	27	41	213	24.57
May	97	10.82	13	27	230	25.67
June	125	14.42	28	35	247	28.49
July	127	14.18	15	41	257	28.69
August	134	15.46	24	33	207	23.88
September ..	134	15.45	28	43	273	31.49
Total New York City.						
October, 1919	4,614	9.05	752	1,002	11,545	22.65
November ..	4,857	9.84	623	1,199	10,027	20.32
December ..	5,705	11.19	800	1,343	11,823	23.20
January, 1920	8 331	15.98	1,048	1,749	11,280	21.64
February ...	11,523	23.64	1,540	2,099	11,255	23.06
March	7,128	13.67	1,174	1,511	12,147	23.30
April	6,321	12.52	972	1,286	11,206	22.20
May	5,798	11.02	892	1,286	10,364	19.89
June	4,833	9.64	764	998	11,810	23.42
July	4,566	8.76	821	872	11,616	22.29
August	4,831	9.58	1,025	901	11,150	22.10
September ..	4,640	9.20	831	1,017	10,869	21.55

Mortality and Births in New York City, 1919.

	Total Deaths.	Annual Death Rate.	Deaths Under 1 Year Old	Deaths at 65 Years and Over.	Typhoid Fever.	Measles.	Pulmonary Tuberculosis	Cancer.	Pneumonia.	*Bright's Disease.	Infantile Paralysis.	Influenza.	Births. Total.	Births. Annual Birth Rate.	Births. Still Births.
City of N. Y.	74,433	12.39	10,639	14,418	121	318	7,395	5,147	6,194	5,007	15	4,834	130,377	21.71	5,984
Manhattan	33,937	12.20	4,928	6,874	51	143	3,597	2,293	2,654	1,802	7	1,974	56,546	20.34	2,613
Bronx	8,616	13.34	1,093	1,609	11	9	920	670	711	375	..	619	14,788	22.90	654
Brooklyn	24,512	11.84	3,679	5,441	43	51	2,252	1,715	2 225	2,256	7	1,727	47,526	22.95	2,246
Queens	5,253	12.93	715	1,088	10	8	474	367	432	443	1	394	8,966	22.07	372
Richmond	2,115	20.40	224	406	6	7	152	102	172	131	..	120	2,551	24.61	99

*And acute nephritis. †Department of Health estimate.

Mortality and Births in Suburban Towns, 1919.

	Total Deaths	Annual Death Rate.	Deaths Under 1 Year	Deaths at 60 Years and Over.	Typhoid Fever	Measles	Pul. Tub.	Cancer	Pneumonia All Forms	Brights Disease	Infantile Paralysis	Influenza	Total Births	Annual Birth Rate.	Stillbirths
Hempstead, Nassau Co...	768	9.3	80	283	1	1	51	58	94	*	..	52	1123	14.3	21
North Hempstead, "	349	12.3	63	115	..	1	21	20	82	*	..	29	700	24.7	28
Oyster Bay§ "	227	6.3	28	90	..	..	21	16	27	*	..	8	349	9.6	12
Brookhaven, Suffolk Co...	392	17.9	16	146	2	1	66	14	45	*	..	38	318	14.5	13
Huntington, "	181	10.1	26	90	2	..	7	22	27	*	..	4	300	16.8	10
Southold, "	117	11.7	9	66	..	2	4	11	8	*	..	5	202	20.2	11
Mamaroneck, W'ch'er Co.	88	9.2	9	38	..	..	4	10	12	*	..	4	143	14.9	3
Mount Vernon, "	467	10.9	51	192	..	..	19	24	39	57	..	45	838	19.6	36
New Rochelle, "	367	10.9	51	135	..	1	16	33	42	27	..	28	649	19.2	24
Ossining, "	150	14.5	9	76	..	..	9	13	13	15	..	12	211	20.4	9
Peekskill, "	202	12.9	18	84	..	..	14	17	14	17	..	10	263	16.8	19
Port Chester, "	204	12.0	40	66	1	1	12	11	120	14	..	16	508	30.0	14
White Plains, "	258	12.3	23	89	1	..	18	21	41	18	..	7	372	17.8	18
Yonkers, "	1,077	10.9	181	294	1	..	107	80	160	86	2	40	2224	22.4	62
Totals for N. Y. State....	143,401	13.2	18,976	49.465	374	355	12 814	10166	17,096	10,540	35	8,047	226269	20.8	9,568

*Data for these districts not available for 1919. §Does not include Glen Cove, now a city, formerly part of Oyster Bay.

GREAT EARTHQUAKES.

In last 52 years Italy leads the list with 200,000 killed in disaster of 1908. 1868, Ecuador and Peru, 25,000 killed. 1885, Cashmere, 70,000 homes destroyed. 1902, Martinique, 32,500 killed. 1908, Sicily and Italy, 200,000 killed.

CANADIAN PROSPERITY.

Canadian exports for the year ended Sept. 30, 1920, amounted to $1,219,523,896, almost half of the Canadian national debt. Official estimates place the wealth of the Canadian people at $16,000,000,000, and their aggregate income, $2,500,000,000.

REAL ESTATE SITUATION.

The real estate market in New York City during the year 1919 was marked by a series of spectacular deals which caused real estate values to advance by leaps and bounds. The activity was caused principally by the shortage of housing facilities and the stoppage of building construction. The latter condition was brought about by the high cost of building material and labor. These unsettled conditions, students of real estate contend, were the natural consequences of the war. However, a halt was called to the wild speculation in apartment buildings, when landlords boosted rents to such a degree that "rent strikes" frequently occurred. The final effect of the traffic was the enactment of rent legislation, which dealt a disastrous blow to the real estate boom.

The market recovered somewhat from this restrictive legislation in the early part of the spring of 1920, but the attitude of the courts in their interpretation of the rent laws, real estate brokers said, discouraged investors from doing business in real estate, particularly in property affected by the rent laws. The auction market during the year 1920 was exceedingly interesting from the standpoint of the student of real estate. The demand for vacant land began to be felt when improved property found new buyers. This demand became apparent in all sections of the city, particularly in the subway zones.

Following is a classified list of new buildings and other structures for the five boroughs for the year 1920:

Brooklyn.

DWELLINGS—BRICK.

	Number buildings.	Number families.	Estimated cost.
One-family	485	485	$4,334,500
Two-family	450	900	5,063,850
Store and two-family	132	264	1,478,500
Tenements	53	645	3,077,900
Totals	1,119	2,294	$13,954,750

DWELLINGS—FRAME.

	Number buildings.	Number families.	Estimated cost.
One-family	1,682	1,682	$8,798,848
Two-family	356	712	3,243,875
Totals	2,038	2,394	$12,042,723
Total brick and frame dwellings	3,157	4,688	25,997,473
Miscellaneous	1,239	.....	707,443
Totals	4,396	.....	$26,704,916

OTHER THAN DWELLINGS.

	No. buildings.	Est. cost
Factories and storage	248	$8,690,487
Garages and stables	3,617	14,491,436
Stores	122	2,545,900
Theaters	25	4,007,000
Churches	10	424,000
Office buildings	8	98,300
Banks	2	160,000
Hotels	1	10,000
Schools	5	7,570,000
Bath houses	2	500,000
Miscellaneous	162	4,346,910
Total other than dwellings	4,202	$36,844,032
Grand total new buildings	8,598	63,549,048
Illuminated signs	851	234,863
Ground signs	50	6,685
Elevators	149	837,878
Amendments inc. cost of plan	3,090	1,332,312
Plumbing for buildings	2,505	341,118
Total new operations	15,243	$66,301,904

ALTERATIONS.

	No. buildings.	Est. cost
One-family dwellings	1,451	$2,099,190
Two-family dwellings	1,316	1,914,665
Store and two-family	542	788,425
Tenements	924	1,306,265
Factories and storage	569	2,616,640
Garages and stables	302	849,390
Stores	300	914,712
Theaters	37	182,375
Hotels	16	42,730
Schools	6	69,900
Churches	18	150,240
Office buildings	31	1,483,015
Clubs	8	34,200
Hospitals	18	$180,300
Miscellaneous	626	1,793,815
Total alteration	6,164	$14,425,862
New buildings and other structures	15,243	66,301,804
Grand totals, building operations	21,407	$80,727,666

Manhattan.

NEW BUILDINGS.

	No. buildings.	Est. cost
Dwellings, over $50,000	8	$1,170,000
Dwellings, $20,000 to $50,000	10	205,000
Dwellings under $20,000	4	38,500
Tenements	22	13,565,000
Hotels	3	1,915,000
Stores, lofts, etc., over $30,000	27	6,591,000
Office buildings	81	44,668,400
Manufactories and workshops	23	8,232,700
School houses	3	500,000
Churches	1	60,000
Public buildings, municipal	11	1,676,800
Public buildings, places of amusement, etc.	25	5,140,000
Hospitals	8	5,350,000
Stables and garages	482	6,348,318
Other securities	51	403,802
Totals	783	$96,199,860

ALTERATIONS.

	No. buildings.	Est. cost
Dwellings	1,171	$11,050,000
Tenements	678	4,142,825
Hotels	100	1,937,500
Stores, lofts, etc.	667	4,630,160
Office buildings	414	13,498,840
Manufactories and workshops	366	2,746,050
Schoolhouses	39	601,180
Churches	34	494,500
Public buildings, municipal	21	299,100
Public buildings, places of amusement, etc.	125	2,123,330
Stables and garages	184	1,468,200
Totals	4,008	$42,999,703
Grand totals for Manhattan	4,791	$139,199,564

Queens.

NEW BUILDINGS.

Classification.	No.	Est. val.
Frame dwellings	2,985	$15,907,963
Brick dwellings	536	5,085,800
Frame stores and dwellings	75	348,550
Brick stores and dwellings	69	802,900
Brick tenements	23	1,750,000
Public buildings, amusements	44	496,815
Public buildings, municipal	2	255,000
Manufactories and workshops	112	8,038,100
Churches	10	254,000
Schools	2	600,000
Storage, warehouses, etc	78	821,325
Office buildings	32	564,950
Garages	2,570	2,966,748
Stables	19	30,650
Other frame structures	337	169,747
Totals	6,914	$38,092,548

ALTERATIONS.

	Number.	Cost.
Frame dwellings	2,144	$1,125,028
Brick dwellings	52	56,460
Frame stores and dwellings	280	306,960
Brick stores and dwellings	115	117,975
Frame tenements	21	13,210
Brick tenements	5	3,500
Frame stores and tenements	7	22,325
Brick stores and tenements	14	36,200
Public buildings, amusements	48	113,635
Public building, municipal	1	2,000
Manufactories and workshops	223	1,200,785
Churches	11	37,715
Schools	10	455,400
Hotels, boarding houses, etc	15	33,380
Hospitals	1	15,000
Storage warehouses, etc.	47	167,705
Office buildings	41	289,442
Garages	100	392,827
Stables	47	132,930
Other frame structures	146	45,447
Totals	3,328	$4,567,924
New structures	6,914	38,092,548
Grand total building operations	10,242	$42,660,572

REAL ESTATE SITUATION—*Continued.*

Bronx.

NEW BUILDINGS.

	Number.	Cost.
Brick dwellings, over $50,000 and $50,000	1	$100,000
	11	285,500
Brick dwellings less than $20,000	221	2,058,400
Brick tenements over $15,000	24	3,610,000
Stores over $3,000	9	615,000
Stores between $15,000 and $3,000	7	125,000
Stores less than $15,000	15	86,750
Office buildings	5	219,000
Manufactories and workshops	83	1,491,600
Schoolhouses	5	1,750,000
Churches	6	683,000
Public buildings, municipal	2	230,000
Public buildings, places of amusement	12	1,698,600
Stables and garages	394	4,061,425
Frame dwellings	312	1,619,075
Other structures	8	2,300
Total new buildings	1,115	$18,585,600

ALTERATIONS.

	Number.	Cost.
Brick dwellings	76	$168,250
Frame dwellings	360	742,480
Brick tenements	61	150,250
Frame tenements	30	37,650
Stores	37	101,000
Office buildings	10	60,400
Manufactories and workshops	47	332,150
Schools	5	821,500
Churches	13	88,400
Public buildings	17	255,400
Stables and garages	39	149,450
Miscellaneous	2,619	32,211
Total alterations	3,314	3,739,141
Total new buildings	1,115	$18,585,600
Total alterations	3,314	3,739,141
Grand totals	4,429	$22,324,741

Richmond.

NEW BUILDINGS.

	Number.	Cost.
Frame dwellings	1,271	$3,420,293
Brick dwellings	26	247,021
Factories and workshops	104	234,848
Garages and stables	396	269,068
Office buildings	11	185,662
Stores	28	50,260
Churches	2	78,250
Public buildings, places of amusement	21	344,100
Other securities	157	454,404
Total new buildings	2,015	$5,283,926

ALTERATIONS.

	Number.	Cost.
Frame dwellings	496	$296,635
Brick dwellings	6	24,600
Manufactories and workshops	15	$41,500
Garages and stables	48	26,627
Tenements	5	2,390
Stores	29	9,585
Churches	4	2,740
Office buildings	9	74,790
Public buildings, places of amusement	15	826,618
Theaters	1	450
Other structures	44	21,860
Total alterations	672	$1,331,795
Total new buildings	2,015	5,283,926
Total building operations	2,687	$6,615,721

RECAPITULATION, N. Y. CITY.

Brooklyn	21,407	$80,727,660
Manhattan	4,791	139,199,564
Queens	10,242	42,660,572
Bronx	4,429	22,324,741
Richmond	2,687	6,615,721
Grand total City of New York	43,556	$291,528,264

APARTMENT HOUSES.

Plans were filed in Bkln. last year for 68 apartment houses with 1,084 apartments, to cost $3,684,550, as compared with 154 in 1919, with 1,680 apartments, costing $4,540,000; plans were filed in Mhtn. last year for 27 tenements, with 1,342 apartments, and to cost $16,8330,000, as compared with 32 in 1919, with 1,210 apartments, which cost $7,035,000; in the Bronx 21, with 800 apartments, to cost $3,684,550, as compared with 67 in 1919, with 2,599 apartments, to cost $8,086,000; in Queens, 20, with 286 apartments, to cost $1,516,000, as compared with 17 in 1919, with 206 apartments, to cost $872,500, the only boro showing a gain.

CONVEYANCES AND MORTGAGES.

Brooklyn.

1919.	Conveyances.	Misc'l Papers.	No. Mortgages.	Amount.
November	6,704	92	7,329	$19,080,700
December	6,888	109	8,244	23,329,300
1920.				
January	6,000	85	7,103	21,995,500
February	4,486	67	5,648	15,110,800
March	6,465	112	7,265	26,418,600
April	7,325	127	8,303	25,842,750
May	6,324	122	7,166	21,092,800
June	5 299	82	6,234	17,509,000
July	4,423	51	5,879	15,974,900
August	3,158	55	4,336	10,367,600
September	4,064	61	4,725	13,772,400
October	4,229	70	5,299	13,174,200
November	3,385	63	4,892	12,103,200

MAYFLOWER TERCENTENARY.

Three hundred years ago the Pilgrim Fathers left Plymouth, England, on their voyage for liberty, and landed in New England. The efforts of the Pilgrims, at first in vain, to escape from England to Holland, their reunion and sufferings in that country, the departure from Delfthaven in July, 1620; the sailing from Southampton on Aug. 5, 1620, of the ships Mayflower and Speedwell, and the subsequent dismissal from the enterprise of the latter ill-fated vessel, the final departure of the Mayflower from Plymouth on Sept. 6, 1620; the arrival two months later at New Plymouth, the subsequent hardships of the Pilgrims and the eventual triumphant events and achievements arising as direct results from the expedition, form a chain of events constituting one of the most moving episodes of history. During the year 1920 a large number of commemorative functions were organized in the United States, the United Kingdom and Holland, and pageants, plays and processions have been popular features in a number of towns where homage has been paid to the Pilgrim Fathers.

N. Y. SUB-TREASURY TO BE PRESERVED.

David F. Houston, Secretary of the Treasury, announced that, although the New York City Sub-Treasury would be discontinued at the close of business, Dec. 6, 1920, and its functions taken over by the Federal Reserve Banks and other organizations, the building itself would be retained by the Treasury Department because of its historic significance.

LOCAL OPTION IN SCOTLAND.

The "Act to Promote Temperance in Scotland," passed by the Parliament of Great Britain and Ireland in 1913, came into force on June 1, 1920. For the purpose of the act the country is divided into areas, and it is provided that if ten per cent. of the electors in any area sign a requisition demanding a poll, then a poll shall be taken on the question of adopting. 1. A no-change resolution. 2. A limiting resolution. 3. A no-license resolution. The last-named resolution means that during the period in which a no-license resolution remains in force, no license shall be granted, except in the case of an inn or hotel or premises bona fide used as a restaurant. To carry a no-license resolution requires at least 55 per cent. of the votes recorded, and not less than 35 per cent. of the total electorate. Elections were held for a number of areas in Nov. and Dec., 1920, when no-license resolutions were adopted in some areas, but the majority of areas favored a no-change or limiting plan.

MARRIAGE LICENSES, NEW YORK CITY.

Number of marriage licenses issued in the different Boroughs of New York City, 1920: Manhattan, 43,024; Bronx, 7,449; Brooklyn, 23,155; Queens, 4,224; Richmond, 1,086. Total, 78,938.

The first Labor college in the United States opened in 1920 at Springfield, Mass. It is to be conducted under the joint direction of Amherst College and the Labor Unions of Springfield and Holyoke.

STATISTICS OF THE FIVE BOROUGHS OF NEW YORK CITY.

Greater New York City. (All Boroughs.)

Population (U. S. Census, 1920)	5,620,048
Assessed property value (real)	$8,626,121,707
Assessed property value (personal)	296,506,185
Average daily consumption of water (gallons)	660,200,000
Total Police Force	10,887
Annual cost of Police Dept.	$20,534,695
Membership Fire Dept. (regular)	6,067
Membership Fire Dept. (voluntoer)	675
Annual cost of Fire Dept.	$11,161,437
Register in Public Schools	931,468
Register in High & Training Schls.	72,789
Total teachers and principals	23,010

For further statistics consult index.

Brooklyn.

Population (U. S. Census, 1920)	2,018,356
Total area (80.95 sq. miles)	51,807 acres
Area excl. marsh lands)	45,158 acres
Park area	1,158 acres
Per cent. of total area covered by parks	2.49
Cemetery area (estimated)	1,638 acres
Average daily consumption of water (gallons)	181,600,000
Length of streets	1,258 miles
Length of paved streets	885 miles
Register Public schools	356,295
Register High Schools	27,321
Wards	32
Congressional Districts	8
Senate Districts	8
Assembly Districts	23
Election Districts	977
Aldermanic Districts	23
Tax rate (per $1,000)	$25.40

Manhattan.

Population (U. S. Census, 1920)	2,284,103
Total area (21.9 sq. miles)	14,056 acres
Park area	1,487 acres
Per cent. total area covered by parks.	10.57
Cemetery area (estimated)	51 acres
Average daily consumption of water including Bronx (gallons)	471,000,000
Length of streets	484 miles
Length of paved	472 miles
Register in Public Schools	339,775
Register in High Schools	27,566
Wards	22
Congressional Districts	9
Senate Districts	9
Assembly Districts	23
Election Districts	997
Aldermanic Districts	27
Tax rate (per $1,000)	$24.80

Bronx.

Population (U. S. Census, 1920)	732,016
Total area (33.87 sq. miles)	21,680 acres
Park area	3,929.19 acres
Per cent. total area covered by parks.	18.12
Cemetery area (estimated)	403 acres
Length of streets	487 miles
Length of paved streets	203 miles
Register in Public Schools	131,212
Register in High Schools	8,593
Wards	2
Congressional Districts	3
Senate Districts	3
Assembly Districts	8
Election Districts	381
Aldermanic Districts	8
Tax rate (per $1,000)	$25.30

Queens.

Population (U. S. Census, 1920)	469,042
Area (121.11 sq. miles)	77,516 acres
Area (excl. marsh lands)	67,141 acres
Park area	1,186.47 acres
Per cent. total area covered by parks	1.583
Cemetery area (estimated)	1,960 acres
Average daily consumption of water (gallons)	44,200,000
Length of streets	1,078 miles
Length of paved streets	478 miles
Register in Public Schools	83,535
Register in High Schools	7,850
Wards	5
Congressional Districts (incl. Long Island)	2
Senate Districts	2
Assembly Districts	6
Election Districts	291
Aldermanic Districts	5
Tax rate (per $1,000)	$25.40

Richmond

Population (U. S. Census, 1920)	116,531
Area (57.18 sq. miles)	36,600 acres
Park area	63 acres
Cemetery area (estimated)	408 acres
Length of streets	320 miles
Length of paved streets	257 miles
Average daily consumption of water (gallons)	17,000,000
Register in Public Schools	20,671
Register in High Schools	1,459
Wards	5
Senate Districts (incl. Rockland Co.)	1
Congressional District	1
Assembly Districts	2
Election Districts	76
Aldermanic Districts	3
Tax rate (per $1,000)	$25.30

STATE NICKNAMES AND STATE FLOWERS.

Alabama—Cotton State, goldenrod; Arizona———, sequoia cactus; Arkansas—Bear State, apple blossom; California—Golden State, poppy; Colorado—Centennial State, columbine; Delaware—Blue Hen State, peach blossom; Florida—Peninsula State; Georgia—Cracker State, Cherokee rose; Idaho— ——, syringa; Illinois, Sucker State, violet; Indiana—Hoosier State, carnation; Iowa—Hawkeye State, wild rose; Kansas—Sunflower State, sunflower; Kentucky—Blue Grass State, blue grass; Louisiana—Pelican State, magnolia; Maine—Pine Tree State, pine cone; Maryland—Old Line State; Massachusetts—Bay State; Michigan—Wolverine State, apple blossom; Minnesota—Gopher State, moccasin; Mississippi—Bayou State, magnolia; Montana—Stub Toe State, bitter root; Missouri— ——, goldenrod; Nebraska— ——, goldenrod; Nevada—Silver State; New Hampshire—Granite State; New Jersey—Jersey Blue State, sugar maple (tree); New York—Empire State, rose; North Carolina—Old North State; North Dakota—Flickertail State, goldenrod; Ohio—Buckeye State; Oklahoma— ——, mistleto; Oregon—Beaver State, Oregon grape; Pennsylvania—Keystone State; Rhode Island—Little Rhody, violet; South Carolina—Palmetto State; South Dakota—Sunshine State, pasqueflower (anemone patens), with motto, "I Lead"; Tennessee—Big Bend State; Texas—Lone Star State, bluebonnet; Utah— ——, Sego lily; Vermont—Green Mountain State, red clover; Virginia—The Old Dominion; Washington—Evergreen State, rhododendron; West Virginia—The Panhandle; Wisconsin—Badger State.

INCOME TAX PAYERS.

More than 5,600,000 firms and individuals were income tax payers in 1920, according to figures made public in Sept., 1920, by the Bureau of Internal Revenue. These figures also reveal that about 3,000,000 taxpayers had already paid their income taxes in full. The Bureau's statement shows that 4,000,000 persons were paying income taxes on incomes of $5,000 or less and that fewer than 600,000 of this number had not paid their taxes in full, choosing the alternative method of payment by installments. Individual returns for incomes in excess of $5,000, including those individuals and firms, numbered 700,000. Approximately half of this number paid all income taxes to the Government in the first two tax installments. Nearly 350,000 corporations filed income tax returns.

BRITISH COAL STRIKE.

The strike of British coal miners began on Oct. 16, 1920, with a walkout of 1,000,000 men. To meet the situation orders were at once issued directing darkening all electric signs and store windows and limiting the use of gas and electricity for power and household consumption. The strike spread to other industries. In North Yorkshire iron works, coke ovens, furnaces and mills closed and in other parts of the country iron works were idle. On Oct. 28 a settlement was arrived at on the basis of an immediate advance of 2 shillings in wages, with a sliding scale to determine future rise or fall according to output.

INFORMATION FOR MUNICIPAL TAXPAYERS.

Calendar for Taxpayers.

April 1—Commence to assess.

Oct. 1—Annual record of assessed valuation of real and personal estate open for inspection.

Nov. 15—Real estate books close.

Nov. 30—Personal books close.

Feb. 1—Make up assessment rolls.

Mar. 1—Deliver to Bd. of Aldermen.

Mar. 3—Bd. of Aldermen fix tax rate.

Mar. 28—Deliver to Receiver of Taxes.

May 1—All personal taxes and half real estate taxes payable in May. If second half paid, rebate at rate of 4% per annum to Nov. 1.

June 1—Interest at 7% runs from May 1 on unpaid taxes due in May.

Aug., Third Tues.—Hearing on assessments on shareholders of banks.

Nov. 1—2d half of real estate taxes payable.

Dec. 1—Interest at 7% from Nov. 1 on unpaid taxes due in Nov.

Dec. 15 to 31—Bank taxes payable.

(See pages 524-525, 1916 Eagle Almanac, for list of taxable and exempt personal property, deductions, etc.)

Taxable Real Estate.

The total assessed value of real estate for 1919 was $8,428,322,753. For 1920 it was $8,626,122,557. The increase over 1919 is $197,799,804.

Following tabulated statement shows assessed valuation of real estate by sections and wards in the boroughs constituting N. Y. City for year 1920, as compared with assessed valuation for year 1919:

MANHATTAN.

	Assessment Roll, 1919.	Assessment Roll, 1920.	Increase.
Section 1	$769,944,780	$780,064,180	$10,119,400
Section 2	431,918,830	435,385,730	3,466,900
Section 3	982,691,750	999,503,800	16,814,050
Section 4	707,951,450	728,325,100	20,373,650
Section 5	1,008,903,750	1,015,557,400	6,653,650
Section 6	225,261,026	226,235,626	967,600
Section 7	433,847,670	436,266,420	2,418,750
Section 8	181,555,790	183,743,890	2,188,100
Totals	$4,742,082,046	$4,805,048,146	$63,002,100
Real Est., Corps.	111,559,000	113,739,925	2,180,925
Spec. Franch...	262,170,575	267,947,816	5,777,241
Totals	$5,115,811,621	$5,186,771,887	$70,960,266

THE BRONX.

	Assessment Roll, 1919.	Assessment Roll, 1920.	Increase.
Section 9	$140,326,156	$141,684,576	$1,358,420
Section 10	147,072,370	150,475,920	3,403,550
Section 11	203,746,120	217,377,915	13,631,795
Section 12	40,812,261	41,958,261	1,146,000
Section 13	19,564,005	19,585,445	21,440
Section 14	18,204,265	18,563,505	359,240
Section 15	29,363,891	29,494,466	130,575
Section 16	17,865,763	18,324,803	459,040
Section 17	16,991,945	17,089,595	97,650
Section 18	17,702,235	18,172,235	470,000
Totals	$51,649,011	$672,726,721	$21,077,710
Real Est.,Corps.	51,283,250	51,408,650	125,400
Spec. Franch...	28,876,711	29,172,893	296,182
Totals	$731,808,972	$753,308,264	$21,499,292

BROOKLYN.

	Assessment Roll, 1919.	Assessment Roll, 1920.	Increase.
Section 1	$156,346,000	$165,755,600	$9,409,600
Section 2	86,609,316	88,874,200	2,264,884
Section 3	118,311,435	118,282,790	*28,645
Section 4	135,725,250	137,784,910	2,059,660
Section 5	101,140,465	107,268,965	6,128,490
Section 6	164,429,965	169,672,540	5,242,575
Section 7	105,456,475	106,860,350	1,403,875
Section 8	110,963,440	112,461,790	1,498,350
Section 9	69,110,575	69,563,050	452,475
Section 10	46,221,510	47,034,010	812,500
Section 11	95,086,100	96,694,095	1,607,995
Section 12	61,496,340	67,538,785	6,042,445
Section 13	50,887,505	52,512,515	1,625,010
Section 14	6,811,880	7,117,485	305,605
Section 15	23,076,885	24,479,035	1,402,150
Section 16	117,211,840	124,555,115	7,343,275
Section 17	47,083,425	50,173,690	3,090,265
Section 18	61,595,245	61,899,320	304,075
Section 19	38,614,385	40,347,515	1,733,130
Section 20	43,463,965	46,621,270	3,157,305
Section 21	43,748,045	56,926,610	13,178,565
Section 22	19,903,945	20,009,445	105,500
Section 23	21,631,670	22,577,220	945,550
Section 24	10,557,180	10,861,400	304,270
Section 25	5,780,511	5,755,111	25,400
Totals	$1,741,263,302	$1,811,626,806	$70,363,504
Real est., Corps.	38,220,650	39,164,350	943,700
Spec. Franch...	85,640,000	87,020,049	1,380,049
Totals	$1,865,123,952	$1,937,811,205	$72,687,253

QUEENS.

	Assessment Roll, 1919.	Assessment Roll, 1920.	Increase.
Ward 1	$134,027,710	$139,570,550	$5,542,840
Ward 2	145,219,965	156,170,525	10,950,560
Ward 3	76,307,505	78,637,570	2,330,065
Ward 4	135,205,925	141,768,020	6,562,095
Ward 5	50,041,385	53,547,910	3,506,525
Totals	$539,802,490	$569,694,575	$29,892,085
Real Est., Corps.	36,586,400	37,577,450	991,050
Spec. Franch...	28,438,586	29,137,134	698,548
Totals	$604,827,476	$636,409,159	$31,581,683

RICHMOND.

	Assessment Roll, 1919.	Assessment Roll, 1920.	Increase.
Ward 1	$27,670,450	$29,358,225	$1,687,775
Ward 2	20,008,540	16,602,905	*3,405,635
Ward 3	25,449,525	27,038,275	1,588,750
Ward 4	17,581,690	19,193,125	1,611,435
Ward 5	10,301,945	10,574,020	272,075
Totals	$101,012,150	$102,766,550	$1,754,400
Real Est., Corps.	5,182,850	4,620,800	*562,050
Spec. Franch...	4,555,732	4,434,692	*121,040
Totals	$110,750,732	$111,822,042	$1,071,310

*Decrease.

RECAPITULATION.

Borough.	Assessment Roll, 1919.	Assessment Roll, 1920.	Increase.
Manhattan.....	$5,115,811,621	$5,186,771,887	$70,960,266
The Bronx ...	731,808,972	753,308,264	21,499,292
Brooklyn.......	1,865,123,952	1,937,811,205	72,687,253
Queens..........	604,827,476	636,400,159	31,581,683
Richmond......	110,750,732	111,822,042	1,071,310
Totals	$8,428,322,753	$8,626,122,557	$197,799,804

CORPORATION REAL ESTATE.

Corporation real estate, exclusive of value of property, assessed as real estate, under Chap. 712 of Laws of 1889, known as Franchise Law:

Borough.	Assessment Roll, 1919.	Assessment Roll, 1920.	Increase.
Manhattan......	$111,559,000	$113,739,925	$2,180,925
The Bronx......	51,283,250	51,408,650	125,400
Brooklyn........	38,220,650	39,164,350	943,700
Queens..........	36,586,400	37,577,450	991,050
Richmond......	5,182,850	4,620,800	....
Totals	$242,832,150	$246,511,175	$4,241,075
	....	242,832,150	562,050
Net increase	....	$3,679,025	$3,679,025

Total Number of Parcels Assessed by Boroughs.

Borough.	1916.	1917.	1918.	1919.	1920.
Manhattan.....	94,209	93,383	92,352	91,805	91,109
The Bronx.....	67,748	68,183	68,551	68,689	69,214
Brooklyn........	219,146	220,460	222,850	224,040	226,503
Queens..........	143,548	145,989	147,521	148,927	151,674
Richmond......	36,645	38,112	39,226	40,103	41,480
Totals..........	561,294	566,127	570,500	573,564	579,980

Assessed Valuations of Corporations.

Borough.	1919.	1920.	Increase.
Manhattan.......	$53,076,350	$65,562,100	$12,485,750
The Bronx.......	1,583,450	1,123,600	*459,850
Brooklyn.........	3,722,900	6,163,550	2,440,650
Queens............	802,000	960,650	158,650
Richmond........	411,250	373,600	*37,650
Totals............	$59,595,950	$74,183,500	$14,587,550

*Decrease.

Comparative statement showing assessed valuation of personal property on final assessment rolls for 1919 and 1920 in N. Y. City:

INFORMATION FOR TAXPAYERS—*Continued.*

Personal Property.

Borough.	Valuation 1919.	Valuation 1920.	Decrease.
Manhattan.....	$291,286,700	$227,063,350	$64,223,150
The Bronx	12,674,400	17,211,200	*4,536,800
Brooklyn.........	44,907,205	41,192,900	3,714,305
Queens...........	10,934,300	8,792,100	2,142,200
Richmond.......	2,610,175	2,246,635	363,540
Totals...........	$362,412,780	$296,506,185	$65,906,595

*Increase.

Summary of assessed valuations of personal property shown on annual record, values cancelled and amount held on final assessment rolls:

	Annual Record.	Additions.	Cancelled.	Assessment Roll.
Manhattan	$556,432,500	$1,324,150	$330,693,300	$227,063,350
The Bronx	49,181 000	160,100	32,129,900	17,211,200
Brooklyn..	145,569,250	275,700	104,652,050	41,192,900
Queens....	27,954,550	149,800	19,312,250	8,792,100
Richmond.	6,810,100	33,340	4,596,805	2,246,635
Totals	$785,947,400	$1,943,190	$491,384,305	$296,506,185

Tax Rates.

MANHATTAN AND BRONX.

The yearly rate in New York (Manhattan) for the period since 1876 is as follows:

1876....	2.00	1886....	2.29	1896....	2.14	1905...	1.490
1877....	2.65	1887....	2.16	1897....	2.10	1906...	1.478
1878....	2.55	1888....	2.22	1898....	2.01	1907...	1.484
1879....	2.58	1889....	1.95	N.Y. County		1908....	1.61407
1880....	2.53	1890....	1.97	1899....	2.44	1909...	1.67804
1881....	2.62	1891....	1.90	1900....	2.24	1910...	1.75790
1882....	2.25	1892....	1.85	1901....	2.317	1911...	1.72248
1883....	2.25	1893....	1.82	1902....	2.273	1912...	1.83
1884....	2.29	1894....	1.79	1903....	1.413	1913...	1.81
1885....	2.40	1895....	1.91	1904....	1.513		

1914..........................	Manhattan, 1.78;	Bronx, 1.77.
1915..........................	Manhattan, 1.87;	Bronx, 1.94.
1916..........................	Manhattan, 2.04;	Bronx, 2.09.
1917..........................	Manhattan, 2.02;	Bronx, 2.08.
1918 Real.................	Manhattan, 2.36;	Bronx, 2.40.
1918 Personal...........	Manhattan, 2.33;	Bronx, 2.37.
1919 Real	Manhattan, 2.32;	Bronx, 2.37.
1919 Personal...........	Manhattan, 2.32;	Bronx, 2.37.
1920 Real.................	Manhattan, 2.48;	Bronx, 2.53.
1920 Personal...........	Manhattan, 2.39;	Bronx, 2.44.

BROOKLYN.

The following table shows the rate of taxation in Kings County (Brooklyn) since 1881:

1881....	2.38	1892....	2.77	1903.....	1.489	1914.....	1.84
1882....	2.33	1893....	2.85	1904.....	1.572	1915.....	1.92
1883....	2.60	1894....	2.62	1905.....	1.562	1916.....	2.08
1884....	2.63	1895....	2.74	1906.....	1.537	1917.....	2.07
1885....	2.90	1896....	2.90	1907.....	1.554	1918 Real..	2.40
1886....	2.65	1897....	2.83	1908...	1.67021	1918 Per'l .	2.37
1887....	2.76	1898...	None	1909....	1.7378	1919 Real..	2.36
1888....	2.74	1899....	2.36	1910...	1.81499	1919 Per'l..	2.36
1889....	2.94	1900....	2.32	1911...	1.75502	1920 Real..	2.54
1890....	2.58	1901.....	2.388	1912......	1.87	1920 Per'l.	2.43
1891....	2.56	1902.....	2.358	1913......	1.95		

QUEENS AND RICHMOND.

	1920 Real.	1920 Per.	1919 Real.	1919 Per.	1918 Real.	1918 Per.	1917.	1916.
Queens...	2.54	2.41	2.37	2.33	2.41	2.34	2.09	2.06
Rich'd....	2.53	2.52	2.41	2.41	2.46	2.43	2.12	2.13

(See page 526, 1916 Eagle Almanac, for explanation of tax rates.)

Total names on annual record, Oct. 1, 1919, by Boroughs, number cancelled and number held on final assessment rolls for 1920:

	Annual Record.	Cancelled.	As'm't Roll.
Manhattan	41,952	13,512	28,440
The Bronx	8,614	2,962	5,652
Brooklyn	18,395	8,702	9,693
Queens	4,812	2,688	2,124
Richmond	1,262	617	645
Totals	75,085	28,481	46,554

Water Tax.

Payment of bills—Frontage bills are due and payable annually in advance on Jan. 1. Bills for metered water are payable when rendered. Where premises are not metered, $5 a season is charged for hose. Where metered, no special charge is made. When frontage bills are not paid by April 1, 5% penalty is added. On July 1 an additional 10% (making 15% in all) is added on all unpaid rates. (See page 527, 1916 Eagle Almanac, for addl. details.)

The annual frontage rates on premises wholly or partly unmetered are based on following schedule:

Front, width.	1 Story.	2 Story.	3 Story.	4 Story.	5 Story.
16 ft. and under.	$4.00	$5.00	$6.00	$7.00	$8.00
16 to 18 ft........	5.00	6.00	7.00	8.00	9.00
18 to 20 ft........	6.00	7.00	8.00	9.00	10.00
20 to 22½ ft......	7.00	8.00	9.00	10.00	11.00
22½ to 25 ft......	8.00	9.00	10.00	11.00	12.00
25 to 30 ft........	10.00	11.00	12.00	13.00	14.00
30 to 37½ ft......	12.00	13.00	14.00	15.00	16.00
37½ to 50 ft......	14.00	15.00	16.00	17.00	18.00

For each additional story $1 per annum is added, and for each additional 10 ft. or part thereof, above 50 ft. in front width of building, $2 shall be added.

METER RATES.

Where water is furnished for business consumption 10c. per 100 cu. ft. (For extra and miscellaneous rates see page 471, 1917 Eagle Almanac.)

Assessed Valuations, 1897 to 1920.

Year.	Real.	Personal.	Totals.
1897	*$2,463,125,687	$419,679,395	$2,882,815,082
1898	*2,532,516,819	548,987,900	3,081,504,719
1899	2,932,445,464	545,906,565	3,478,352,029
1900	3,168,547,700	485,574,493	3,654,122,193
1901	3,237,778,261	550,192,612	3,787,970,873
1902	3,330,647,579	526,400,139	3,857,047,718
1903	*4,751,532,826	680,866,092	5,432,398,918
1904	5,015,463,779	625,078,878	5,640,542,657
1905	5,221,584,301	690,561,926	5,912,146,227
1906	5,738,487,245	567,306,940	6,305,794,185
1907	6,240,480,602	554,861,313	6,795,341,915
1908	6,722,415,789	435,774,611	7,158,190,400
1909	6,807,179,704	443,320,855	7,250,500,559
1910	7,044,192,674	372,644,825	7,416,837,499
1911	7,858,840,164	357,922,123	8,216,762,287
1912	7,861,898,890	342,963,540	8,204,862,430
1913	8,006,647,861	325,421,340	8,332,069,201
1914	8,049,859,912	340,295,560	8,390,155,472
1915	8,108,760,787	352,051,755	8,460,812,542
1916	8,207,822,361	376,530,150	8,584,352,511
1917	8,254,549,000	419,156,315	8,673,705,315
1918	8,339,638,851	251,414,875	8,591,053,726
1919	8,428,322,753	362,412,780	8,790,735,533
1920	8,626,122,557	296,506,185	8,922,628,742

*See page 526, 1916 Eagle Almanac, showing how valuations for these years were ascertained.

Bank Shares.

Tax on Bank Shares by Boroughs, from 1902 to 1918

Year.	Mhtn.	Bronx.	Bkln.	Q'ns.	Ric'd.	Tax.
1902..	$1,929,640	$4,189	$78,627	$3,701	$3,490	$2,019,650
1903..	2,574,871	2.997	76,875	6,707	5,148	2,666,600
1904..	2,596,261	3,206	81,184	6,607	4,275	2,691,535
1905..	2,670,676	3,667	79,477	6,924	3,425	2,764,171
1906..	2,781,894	4,281	103,978	7,374	4,037	2,901,566
1907..	3,035,153	5,677	87,478	10,642	4,810	3,142,761
1908..	2,985,490	9,106	78,996	12,795	5,017	3,091,406
1909..	3,126,013	10,198	107,233	14,707	5,106	3,263,259
1910..	3,308,254	10,688	100,184	21,080	5,329	3,445,538
1911..	3,439,613	12,064	86,411	21,974	5,430	3,565,494
1912..	3,357,464	12,162	91,551	22,519	5,615	3,489,312
1913..	3,474,716	12,472	86,080	24,725	5,768	3,603,763
1914..	3,499,359	12,795	84,049	24,952	5,954	3,627,111
1915..	3,485,128	12,808	80,409	22,204	6,025	3,606,575
1916..	3,551,363	13,221	81,871	23,035	6,256	3,675,748
1917..	3,898,965	13,551	83,966	25,265	6,601	4,028,351
1918..	4,142,136	12,853	83,061	26,262	6,840	4,271,154
1919..	4,637,429	12,912	86,301	33,715	7,236	4,777,595

Assessment is made as of June 1 and tax is payable Dec. 31.

Bank share assessments are not incl. in aggregate assessments of real and personal property submitted in this report.

Receipts by City of New York Under Income Tax Laws, January to July 1, 1920.

New York State Income Tax—Article 16 of Tax Law

New York Co., Bor. of Manhattan......	$6,573,235.84
Bronx Co., Bor. of The Bronx............	954,673.28
Kings Co., Bor. of Brooklyn..............	2,455,803.04
Queens Co., Bor. of Queens...............	806,526.24
Richmond Co., Bor. of Richmond.......	141,711.84
Totals	$10,931,950.24
Corporation Income Tax—Article 9A of Tax Law:	
Amount received to July 1, 1920..........	5,255,782.41
Total receipts in 1920	$16,187,732.65

Note—The total receipts from the tax on incomes under Article 16 are divided as follows: One-half to the State and one-half to the several counties in the proportion that the assessed valuation of the real property in each county bears to the aggregate assessed valuation of the real property of the State.

The total receipts from the tax under Article 9A are divided as follows: Two-thirds to the State and one-third to the several counties in which the principal offices of the corporation are located.

INFORMATION FOR TAXPAYERS—*Continued.*

Assessed Value Real Estate, All Boroughs.

As corrected by Board of Taxes and Assessments on applications and exemptions under various laws.

Borough.	Manhattan.	The Bronx.	Brooklyn.	Queens.	Richmond.
Assessed value, Oct. 1, 1919	$4,924,806,521	$727,700,921	$1,897,760,621	$608,466,970	$112,422,575
Increase on notice	45,000	....	58,475	460,900	1,000
Reductions by Commissioners	2,487,750	1,489,400	7,342,650	925,655	869,090
Exemptions	3,216,700	1,852,900	38,945,250	356,225	4,028,800
Parsonage	282,500	188,000	489,200	253,000	102,200
Clergy	40,500	34,600	214,150	89,025	31,275
Pensions	....	650	36,690	21,940	4,860
Total reductions	$6,027,450	$3,565,550	$47,029,940	$1,645,845	$5,036,225
Corrected valuations	$4,918,824,071	$734,135,371	$1,850,791,156	$607,272,025	$107,387,350
Special Franchise	267,947,816	29,172,893	87,020,049	29,137,134	4,434,692
Assessed valuation, Feb. 1, 1920	$5,186,771,887	$753,308,264	$1,937,811,205	$636,409,159	$111,822,042

Classification of Buildings.

Class 1, one-family dwellings, designed as such, however used. Class 2, two-family dwellings. Class 3, tenements without elevators. Class 4, hotels and elevator apartment houses. Class 5, warehouses, loft dwellings and department stores. Class 6, office buildings. Class 7, factories. Class 8, stables and garages. Class 9, theaters. Class 10, special structures:

Class.	1.	2.	3.	4.	5.	6.	7.	8.	9.	10.	Total.
Manhattan	23,592	2,602	40,423	2,299	7,842	796	1,351	2,141	182	3,476	84,694
The Bronx	13,412	8,669	10,924	75	123	79	422	2,256	19	3,721	39,700
Brooklyn	67,948	53,879	48,750	285	1,734	174	3,167	9,957	108	7,398	198,400
Queens	44,869	17,853	6,527	209	68	107	1,107	8,214	30	4,081	83,065
Richmond	17,538	2,464	554	65	91	32	501	1,686	4	1,010	23,945
Totals	167,359	85,467	107,178	2,933	9,858	1,188	6,548	24,244	343	19,686	424,804

Assessed Value of Real and Personal Estate, by Boroughs.

MANHATTAN.

Year.	Real Estate.	Personal.
1905....	$3,820,754,181	$563,390,790
1906....	4,105,352,281	447,184,550
1907....	4,391,970,951	432,654,158
1908....	4,534,536,431	327,810,632
1909....	4,614,446,256	332,202,634
1910....	4,743,916,785	293,030,453
1911....	5,037,872,685	289,797,952
1912....	5,035,485,413	251,467,122
1913....	5,126,942,595	265,512,335
1914....	5,149,250,760	287,768,270
1915....	5,145,802,495	292,349,590
1916....	5,129,830,629	317,187,300
1917....	5,088,344,403	339,106,700
1918....	5,094,601,238	194,775,200
1919....	5,115,811,621	291,286,700
1920....	5,186,771,887	227,063,350

BRONX.

Year.	Real Estate.	Personal.
1905....	$274,859,593	$16,673,625
1906....	355,779,602	18,028,857
1907....	396,687,730	14,115,699
1908....	441,228,718	11,539,680
1909....	462,704,008	13,959,671
1910....	493,757,919	7,716,550
1911....	605,222,933	4,986,895
1912....	616,521,378	4,595,198
1913....	640,340,593	5,094,060
1914....	658,632,013	5,761,200
1915....	$677,126,664	$6,804,800
1916....	698,869,196	6,265,500
1917....	714,226,994	9,524,400
1918....	726,129,198	7,257,100
1919....	731,808,972	12,674,400
1920....	753,308,264	17,211,200

BROOKLYN.

Year.	Real Estate.	Personal.
1905....	$940,982,302	$90,911,363
1906....	1,072,007,172	87,722,310
1907....	1,181,221,910	92,866,547
1908....	1,334,864,335	83,448,072
1909....	1,354,809,840	84,332,190
1910....	1,404,036,521	59,331,825
1911....	1,659,171,283	55,855,616
1912....	1,674,742,409	48,753,985
1913....	1,680,013,591	46,296,870
1914....	1,671,175,330	39,296,065
1915....	1,691,912,426	43,606,010
1916....	1,752,360,970	43,789,090
1917....	1,790,901,437	57,502,715
1918....	1,826,813,885	39,683,575
1919....	1,865,123,952	44,907,205
1920....	1,937,811,205	41,192,300

QUEENS.

Year.	Real Estate.	Personal.
1905....	$140,404,990	$9,094,738
1906....	159,446,205	9,694,428
1907....	217,668,775	11,191,262
1908....	296,458,980	9,908,830
1909....	$308,112,605	$9,673,200
1910....	334,563,960	5,258,480
1911....	446,569,352	5,339,875
1912....	456,750,539	6,396,750
1913....	477,792,836	6,740,350
1914....	488,696,756	5,915,150
1915....	509,515,978	7,635,650
1916....	539,394,614	6,711,060
1917....	569,865,007	10,266,200
1918....	591,599,075	7,909,400
1919....	604,827,476	10,934,300
1920....	636,409,159	8,792,100

RICHMOND.

Year.	Real Estate.	Personal.
1905....	$44,581,235	$5,490,810
1906....	45,901,965	4,676,296
1907....	52,931,286	4,062,205
1908....	65,326,826	3,067,397
1909....	67,106,965	3,153,160
1910....	67,917,489	2,207,487
1911....	80,003,911	1,942,785
1912....	78,309,151	1,750,485
1913....	81,558,246	1,777,225
1914....	82,114,453	1,554,875
1915....	84,403,224	1,655,705
1916....	87,866,952	2,577,200
1917....	91,211,159	2,756,300
1918....	100,495,455	1,689,600
1919....	110,750,782	2,610,175
1920....	111,822,042	2,246,635

Special Franchises, From 1900 to 1920.

(ASSESSED VALUATIONS FIXED BY THE STATE BOARD OF TAX COMMISSIONERS, UNDER TAX LAW, SECTION 43.)

Year.	Manhattan.	The Bronx.	Brooklyn.	Queens.	Richmond.	Total.
1900	$166,763,669	$7,272,249	$39,250,552	$4,036,817	$2,356,064	$219,679,351
1901	160,954,887	7,466,283	35,084,220	5,768,494	2,060,810	211,334,194
1902	167,169,240	9,071,700	37,522,490	5,264,900	1,591,825	220,620,155
1903	177,447,700	9,573,100	41,124,700	5,528,000	1,510,825	235,184,325
1904	189,944,100	10,791,600	43,790,950	5,496,600	1,498,200	251,521,450
1905	228,054,000	14,117,000	52,206,950	6,232,600	1,583,000	303,193,550
1906	268,565,750	13,992,000	68,787,750	8,333,300	1,800,500	361,479,300
1907	336,346,500	21,521,000	95,311,300	11,688,700	1,997,500	466,855,000
1908	346,569,200	23,610,300	103,900,150	15,902,070	2,508,750	492,490,470
1909	334,299,800	23,209,400	98,976,500	14,876,700	2,639,500	474,001,900
1910	328,012,100	20,076,100	100,218,200	14,917,800	2,185,400	465,409,600
1911	324,651,100	27,443,600	109,940,300	16,400,400	2,582,700	481,018,100
1912	277,836,600	23,305,400	94,615,990	15,031,989	2,358,780	413,148,799
1913	297,674,923	24,741,625	98,440,849	15,428,524	2,575,660	438,861,581
1914	282,194,094	26,147,758	78,261,638	15,446,039	2,370,782	404,420,311
1915	265,840,985	25,010,258	73,017,854	14,288,994	2,314,979	379,973,070
1916	280,248,618	32,053,720	91,107,508	18,786,164	3,156,652	425,352,662
1917	302,494,867	35,939,013	94,532,547	24,436,374	4,164,844	461,567,645
1918	282,825,592	32,097,927	92,659,654	27,479,105	4,411,730	439,474,008
1919	262,170,575	28,876,711	85,640,000	28,438,586	4,555,732	409,681,604
1920	267,947,816	29,172,893	87,020,049	29,137,134	4,434,692	417,712,584

COST OF WORLD WAR TO U. S.

The net cost of the war to the American Government was fixed by Secretary Houston on Dec. 8, 1920, at $24,010,000,000. This represents the adjusted expenditure of the Treasury, excluding all other outlay which had no relation to the actual prosecution of the war during the period from April 6, 1917, to June 30, 1920. Total expenditures by the Govt. during the period covered, excepting only postal disbursements from postal revenues, were $38,830,312,895.

THEATRES IN NEW YORK CITY.

Brooklyn.

Academy of Music, Lafayette av. and St. Felix. Seats 2,200. H. T. Swin, Mgr. Supt.

Bay Ridge, 72d and 3d av. Seats 1,868. Wm. Fox, Mgr.

Bedford Theatre, Bedford av. and Bergen. Seats 2,024. H. W. Moore, Mgr.

Brevoort, 1274 Bedford av. Seats 2,030. E. Hoffman, Mgr.

Brighton Beach Music Hall, Brighton Beach.

Casino, Flatbush av., nr. State. Seats 1,572. J. C. Sutherland, Mgr.

Comedy, 194 Grand. Seats 1,138. Wm. Fox, Mgr.

Crescent, Flatbush av. and Fulton. Seats 1,550. J. M. Howard, Gen. Mgr.

DeKalb, 1155 DeKalb av. Seats 2,500. G. W. Powell, Mgr.

Empire, Ralph av. and Quincy. Seats 2,000. J. H. Curtin, Mgr.

Farragut, Flatbush and Rogers avs. Seats 2,500. J. D. Fink, Mgr.

Fifth Av., 5th av. and 4th. Seats 1,100. D. Schaefer, Mgr.

Flatbush Theatre, Church and Flatbush avs. Seats 1,600. B. S. Moss, Mgr.

Folly, Graham av. and Debevoise. Seats 1,975. H. H. Lipkowitz, Mgr.

Fulton, 1283 Fulton. Seats 1,525. A. Sichel, Mgr.

Gayety, Throop av. and B'way. Seats 1,610. Louis Kreig, Mgr.

Halsey, Halsey, nr. B'way. Seats 2,500. Geo. W. Powell, Mgr.

Keeney's, 300 Livingston.

Keith's Theatres: Orpheum, Fulton, nr. Flatbush av.; seats 1,872. Bushwick, B'way and Howard av.; seats 2,240. Prospect, 9th, nr. 5th av.; seats 2,433. Greenpoint, Manhattan av. and Calyer; seats 1,822. Monroe, B'way and Monroe; seats 600. Madison, B'way and Madison; seats 600.

Loew's Theatres: Bijou, Smith and Livingston; seats 1,700. Brevoort, see above. Broadway, B'way, nr. Myrtle av.; seats 2,125. Fulton, see above. Metropolitan, 392 Fulton; seats 3,700. Palace, E. N. Y. av. and Douglas; seats 1,650. Warwick, Fulton and Jerome; seats 1,500.

Majestic, Fulton, nr. Rockwell pl. Seats 1,800. H. F. Kinsey, Mgr.

Montauk, Livingston and Hanover pl. Seats 1,550. L. S. Werba, Lessee and Mgr.

New Brighton, Br. Beach. Geo. Robinson, Mgr.

Olympic, 342 Adams.

Oxford, State, nr. Flatbush av. Seats 774. O. Muller, Mgr.

Rialto, Flatbush av. and Cortelyou Rd.

Ridgewood, Myrtle and Cypress avs. Seats 2,154. Wm. Fox, Mgr.

Star, Jay, nr. Fulton. Seats 1,500. Columbia Amusement Co., Props.

Strand, Fulton, nr. Rockwell Pl. Seats 3,500. E. L. Hyman, Managing Dir.

Teller's Shubert, B'way and Howard av. Seats 1,800. Management of L. C. Teller and H. S. Ascher.

Manhattan and Bronx.

Academy of Music, 14th and Irving pl. Seats 2,478. W. David, Mgr. Dir.

American, 260 W. 42d. Seats 3,000. M. Loew, Mgr.

Apollo, W. 42d. Selwyn & Co., Mgrs.

Astor, B'way and 45th. Seats 1,125.

Audubon, Wm. Fox, 165th and B'way. Seats 2,638.

Belasco, 44th, nr. B'way. Seats 1,000. David Belasco, Mgr.

Belmont, 48th, e. of B'way. R. G. Herndon, Mgr.

Bijou, 45th, w. of B'way. Seats 600. Management of Messrs. Shubert. D. M. Cauffman, Mgr.

Bim's Standard, B'way, cor. 90th. Seats 1,476. B. K. Bimberg, Mgr.

Booth, 45th, w. of B'way. Seats 700. Winthrop Ames, Dir.

Bramhall, 138 E. 27th. Seats 250. B. Davenport, Mgr.

Broadhurst, 44th, w. of B'way. Seats 1,120. George Broadhurst, Dir.

Broadway, B'way and 41st. Seats 1,550. Leon D. Langsfeld, Mgr.

Bronx Opera House, 149th, e. of 3d av. Seats 1,920. M. Silverstein, Mgr.

Capitol, B'way, at 51st. Seats 5,300. E. Bowes, Mgr.

Casino, B'way and 39th. Seats 1,455. Sam and Lee Shubert, Inc., Mgrs.

Central, B'way and 47th. Lee and J. J. Shubert, Mgrs.

Century, Central Pk. W. and 62d. Seats 3,000. Lee and J. J. Shubert, Dirs.

City, 114 E. 14th. Seats 1,998. Wm. Fox, Mgr.

Cohan & Harris, 226 W. 42d. Seats 1,055. Budd Robb, Mgr.

Cohan's, see George M. Cohan's.

Coliseum, B'way and 181st. Seats 3,500. B. S. Moss, Mgr.

Columbia, 7th av. and 47th. Seats 1,350. J. Herbert Mack, Mgr.

Comedy, W. 41st, e. of B'way. Seats 688. Lee and J. J. Shubert, Dirs.

Cort, 48th, e. of B'way. Seats 1,029. B. Klawans, Mgr.

Criterion, B'wav and 44th. Seats 891. H. Riesenfeld, Dir.

Crotona, 177th and Park av. Seats 2,400. Wm. Fox, Mgr.

Dyckman, 207th and Sherman av. Seats 1,400. B. S. Moss, Mgr.

Eltinge, 236 W' 42d. Seats 893. A. C. Barney, Mgr.

Empire, B'way and 40th. Seats 1,099. Chas. Frohman, Mgr.

Forty-fourth St., 216 W. 44th. Seats 1,500. W. W. Rowland, Mgr.

Forty-eighth St., 157 W. 48th. Seats 969. Wm. A. Brady, Dir.

Frazee, 42d, bet. 7th and 8th avs. Seats 780. Lee and J. J. Shubert, Dirs.

Fulton, 46th, w. of B'way. Seats 924. Oliver D. Bailey.

Gaiety, B'way and 46th. Seats 806.

Garrick, 35th, nr. 6th av. Seats 537. The Theatre Guild, Inc., Mgrs.

George M. Cohan's, B'way and 43d. Seats 1,104. Harry Davis, Mgr.

Globe, B'wav and 46th. Seats 1,192. Chas. Dillingham, Mgr.

Grand Opera House, 8th av. and 23d. Seats 2,155. Charles Meyerson, Mgr.

Greenwich Village, 7th av. and 4th. Seats 374. F. Conroy and H. Meltzer, Mgrs.

Harris, 42d, bet. 7th and 8th avs. See Frazee Theatre.

Henry Miller's, 124 W. 43d. Seats 950. H. Miller, Mgr.

Hippodrome, 6th av., 43d to 44th. Seats 5,300. Chas. Dillingham, Mgr.

Hudson, 44th, nr. B'way. Seats 1,075. Mrs. H. B. Harris, Mgr.

Hurtig & Seamon's New Theater, 125th, nr. 8th av. Seats 1,853. Lou Hurtig, Mgr.

Irving Place, Irving pl. and 15th. Seats 1,100. Maurice Schwartz, Dir.

Japanese Garden, 97th and B'way. Seats 1,636. Wm. Fox, Mgr.

Jewish Art Theatre, Madison Sq. Garden. Seats 1,084. S. Shore, Mgr.

Keith's Theatres: Palace, B'way and 47th: seats 1,751. Colonial, B'way and 62d; seats 1,494. 81st St., B'way and 81st; seats 2,125. Riverside, B'way and 96th; seats 1,863. Hamilton, B'way and 146th; seats 1,851. Alhambra, 7th av. and 126th; seats 1,435. Royal, Westchester and Bergen avs.; seats 2,201. Fordham, Fordham rd. and Valentine av.; seats 2,460. Jefferson, 14th, nr. 3d av.; seats 1,971. Harlem Opera House, 125th, nr. 7th av.; seats 1,748.

Knickerbocker, B'way, cor. 38th. Seats 1,420. H. G. Sommers, Mgr.

Lexington, Lexington av. and 51st.

Liberty, 234 W. 42d. Seats 1,350. Klaw & Erlanger, Mgrs.

Loew's Theatres: American, see above. Av. B, Av. B and 5th; seats 1,800. Boulevard, So. Blvd. and Westchester av.; seats 2,100. Burland, 985 Prospect av.; seats 1,500. Circle, B'way and 60th; seats 1,650. Delancey St., Delancey and Suffolk; seats 1,800. 86th St., 162 E. 86th; seats 1,450. Elsmere, Crotona P'kway and Elsmere pl.; seats 1,575. 42d St., Lexington av. and 42d; seats 1,250. Greeley Sq., 30th and 6th av.; seats 1,850. Lincoln Sq., 1947 B'way; seats 1,600. National, 149th and Bergen av.; seats 2,400. New York, see below. 116th St., 132 W. 116th; seats 1,850. Orpheum, 86th and 3d av.; seats 3,000. Rio, 160th and B'way; seats 2,100. Seventh Av., 124th and 7th av.; seats 1,600. Spooner, 963 So. Blvd.; seats 1,800. Victoria, 233 W. 125th; seats 2,400. Victory, 156th and 3d av.; seats 1,800.

Longacre, 48th, nr. B'way, Seats 1,005. Frand Theatre Co., Props.

Little Theatre, 44th, w. of B'way. Seats 518. Oliver, Morosco, Lessee.

THEATRES IN NEW YORK CITY—*Continued.*

Lyceum, 149 W. 45th. Seats 957. W. W. Walter, Mgr.
Lyric, 213 W. 42d. Sam. S. & Lee Shubert, Mgrs.
Madison, Madison, nr. B'way. Seats 600.
Manhattan Opera House, 34th, nr. 8th av. Seats 3,800.
Maxine Elliott's, 39th, nr. 6th av. Seats 938. G. J. Appleton, Mgr.
McKinley Square, 169th and Boston rd. Seats 1,800. Inwood Theatres Corp.
Metropolitan Opera House, B'way, 39th and 40th. Seats 3,372. G. Gatti-Casazza, Mgr.
Morosco, 45th, w. of B'way. Seats 925. Oliver Morosco, Mgr.
Nemo, 110th and B'way. Seats 950. Wm. Fox, Mgr.
New Amsterdam, 214 W. 42d. Seats 1,702. Erlanger, Dillingham & Ziegfeld, Lessees.
New York, 1520 B'way. Seats 2,800. M. Loew, Mgr.
Nora Bayes, W. 44th, nr. B'way. Lee and J. J. Shubert, Dirs.
Olympic, E. 14th, nr. 3d av. Seats 758. S. Kraus, Mgr.
Park, B'way and 59th. Seats 1,541. L. J. Anhalt, Mgr.
People's, 201 Bowery. Seats 1,612. Mazda Amusement Corp., Lessees and Mgrs.
Playhouse, 141 W. 48th. Seats 879. A. O. Brown, Mgr.
Plymouth, 45th, w. of B'way. Seats 1,042. A. Hopkins, Mgr.
Princess, 39th, nr. B'way. Seats 299. F. R. Comstock, Mgr.
Proctor's Fifth Av., B'way and 28th. Seats 1,400. Wm. H. Quaid, Mgr.
Proctor's Fifty-eighth St., 58th, nr. 3d av. Seats 1,942. J. Buck, Mgr.
Proctor's, 125th, nr. Park av. Seats 1,600. F. F. Proctor, Mgr.
Proctor's, 23d, nr. 6th av. Seats 1,331. M. J. Duffy, Mgr.
Prospect, Prospect and Westchester av. Seats 1,600. B. S. Moss, Mgr.
Provincetown Players, 133 Macdougal. Seats 190. G. C. Cook and J. Light, Dirs.
Punch and Judy, 155 W. 49th. Seats 299. Chas. Hopkins, Mgr. and Producer.
Regent, 116th and 7th av. Seats 1,900. B. S. Moss, Mgr.
Republic, 42d, w. of B'way. Seats 914. A. H. Woods, Mgr.
Rialto, Times sq. Motion pictures. Seats 2,000. Hugo Riesenfeld, Dir.
Riviera, 97th and B'way. Seats 1,900. A. M. Lighton, Mgr.
Rivoli, B'way and 49th. Seats 2,125. Hugo Riesenfeld, Dir.
Second Av. Theatre, 35 2d av. Seats 1,896. J. Edelstein, Mgr.
Selwyn, 42d, w. of B'way. Seats 1,051. Selwyn & Co., Mgrs.
Shubert, 44th, nr. B'way. Seats 1,395. L. L. Gallagher, Mgr.
Standard, B'way, cor. 90th. Seats 1,476. B. K. Bimberg, Mgr.
Stanley, 7th av. at 41st. Seats 650. Leon D. Langsfeld, Mgr.
Star, 107th and Lexington av. Seats 2,253. Wm. Fox, Mgr.
Strand, B'way and 47th. Seats 3,500. R. A. Jones, Mgr.
Symphony, B'way and 95th. Seats 1,600. J. W. Springer, Mgr.
Theater Francais, 35th, nr. 6th av. Seats 452. L. L. Bonheur, Mgr.
Thirty-ninth Street, 39th, nr. B'way. Seats 673. R. F. Ronchetti, Mgr.
Times Sq., W. 42d. Selwyn & Co., Mgrs.
Vanderbilt, W. 48th. Seats 780. L. D. Andrews, Mgr.
Washington, 149th and Amsterdam av. Seats 1,541. Wm. Fox, Mgr.
Winter Garden, 50th and B'way. Seats 1,573. Jas. E. Early, Mgr.

UNITED STATES RECLAMATION SERVICE.

Arthur P. Davis, Dir., New Interior Bldg., 18th and F, N. W., Washington, D. C. Western Office, Tramway Bldg., Denver, Col. Employees: Washington Office, 100; Western, 5,000 (varies). Expenditures per year about $8,000,000.

The Reclamation Service was organized as a bureau of the Interior Dept., under the Reclamation Act of June 17, 1902. It is engaged in the investigation, construction and operation of irrigation works in the arid and semi-arid States of the West. Thirty projects have been authorized for construction or operation for irrigation of lands in Arizona, California, Colorado, Idaho, Montana, Nebraska, Nevada, New Mexico, North Dakota, Oregon, South Dakota, Texas, Utah, Washington and Wyoming. These projects aggregate 3,200,000 acres and the major works aid in serving an additional 1,000,000 acres under private canals that generally get stored water from the Government reservoirs. The funds for this work have come chiefly from the sale of public lands; and the money expended is returned to the fund by easy payments of settlers, usually in twenty annual instalments, without interest, in accordance with the Reclamation Extension Act of Aug. 13, 1914.

The Service has built on the 30 projects over 12,000 miles of canals, ditches and drains, including 100,000 canal structures and involving the excavation of 174,000,000 cubics yards of materials. In connection with this work there have been constructed 100 storage and diversion dams, with an aggregate volume of 13,700,000 cubic yards, including the Arrowrock Dam, highest in the world (349 ft.), the Elephant Butte Dam on the Rio Grande, forming the largest artificial irrigation reservoir in the United States, and the longest roller crest dam in the world, located on the Grand River in Colorado. The Service has built 95 tunnels, 983 miles of road, 83 miles of railroad, 3,141 miles of telephone line, a dozen power plants and 651 miles of transmission lines; and is also mining coal and has manufactured 1,676,0[illegible] barrels of cement and sand cement. The net construction cost to June 30, 1919, was $123,853,000.

Over 150,000 persons are living on the 40,000 farms irrigated by the Service. Of the 3,200,000 acres above referred to, water is now available for 1,800,000 acres, and of this 1,100,000 were harvested in 1919, producing crops worth over $88,000,000, or an average of over $80 per acre. The additional lands using stored water yielded crops worth $50,000,000 more.

Public land farm units on the several projects are opened for settlement from time to time as canals are extended to make irrigation water available. Under present law, soldiers of the World War have a preference right to enter these farms and at recent openings have taken all units.

Information in regard to farms available for settlement may be obtained by addressing Statistician, U. S. Reclamation Service, Dept. of the Interior, Washington, D. C.

THE NEW YORK COMMUNITY TRUST.

The New York Community Trust offers a plan for the utilization of wealth, and for its wise and efficient application to charitable, benevolent or educational purposes. The trustees consist of nineteen New York City Trust Companies and Banks, with Alvin W. Krech, President of the Equitable Trust Company, as Chairman of the Trustees Committee.

Individuals desiring to give during their lifetime or under their will any sum, large or small, to be devoted to charitable, benevolent or educational objects, either definitely specified or without any stated object, may place it in trust with a trust company or bank of their own choosing, provided only it is a member of The New York Communty Trust. It will be possible under the Community Trust plan for a donor to leave funds so that the principal of his gift, invested in securities carefully restricted for trust funds, will be kept intact for all time by the responsible agents provided and acting under the State laws as to investments. Furthermore, that so long as his special charity or philanthropy shall exist, it will receive the income from his gift, and if through unforeseen circumstances or by reason of changes in the social viewpoint or the needs of the community, his charity ceases to exist or no longer serves any large public good, the income will continue to be used for the benefit of other approved purposes, as nearly in line with his desires as possible. The Acting Director is Frank J. Parsons, 55 Cedar st., Mhtn.

NEW YORK CITY WATERFRONT DEVELOPMENT

By Murray Hulbert, Commissioner of Docks.

In order to provide wharfage accommodations to meet the constant demands and take advantage of the remarkable opportunities that have fallen to the lot of this nation, the Dock Department of the City of New York is laying down what is probably the most comprehensive plan that has ever been formulated at one time for waterfront development anywhere in the world.

From the Administration of Washington to that of Wilson, less than 3 per cent. of the total appropriation made by Congress for river and harbor improvements was spent in the Port of New York—an aggregate of $20,0000,000.

By successive acts of Congress, enacted annually since 1914, the Federal Government stands committed to an appropriation of more than $100,000,000 for modernizing the channels in New York Harbor and its tributaries, and the city will, within the period of the expenditure of this sum, invest two or three times that amount in the construction of wharves and docks and terminal facilities.

Pier Construction.

The 12 large piers planned for the easterly shore of Staten Island, one of which will be maintained as an open pier for transient and miscellaneous wharfage, are rapidly becoming a reality. The last pile in one of these piers has been driven and the other eleven are rapidly approaching completion, and it is expected will be shedded and ready for occupancy before the end of 1921.

A great deal has been said about the lack of cargo handling appliances in the Port of New York.

Three distinct types of piers are being constructed at Staten Island.

Two of the piers are 209 ft. in width, with two-story sheds and aprons on each side, and will be equipped with elevators and all modern cargo handling devices, including a large fleet of industrial trucks, tractors and trailers.

Two piers are 130 ft. in width, with two-story sheds thereon, and will be fitted with cargo masts and cargo and electric winches, operated in connection with the ship's tackle.

The remaining eight piers, built according to the particular wishes of each lessee, are 125 ft. in width, and will also be equipped with cargo masts and electric winches. The completion and operation of these piers will, therefore, be a great test in the solution of the freight handling problem in New York Harbor, through an ideal comparison of the various methods employed as above outlined.

A system of warehouses, with railroad terminal and classification yard, on the upland in the rear of these structures, has been laid out by the Department during 1920 and is now before the Board of Estimate and Apportionment for a public hearing and approval.

Reconstruction of Piers for Steamship Wharfage.

With the letting of a contract by the Federal Government for the removal of Shell Reef, extending along the Manhattan side of the East River, from Corlears Hook to Bellevue Hospital, the Department of Docks undertook the reconstruction of piers inaccessible, except for boats of very light draft.

Piers at E. 18th and E. 25th are now completed and shedded and ready for service, while the piers at Stanton, E. 5th and E. 20th have been reconstructed, and the steel sheds are being erected and they will be ready for occupancy on or soon after the first of the year, and work is about to be begun on the pier at the foot of E. 4th and E. 26th.

On the North River, pier at the foot of W. 35th has been reconstructed and before the end of the present year will be ready for use as a steamship pier.

After 40 years of unsuccessful effort, the Department of Docks finally persuaded the Federal Government to grant an extension of the pierhead line between Piers Old No. 1 and No. 7, North River, thereby enabling the Department to erect 3 modern piers in this locality of sufficient length to be commercially economical, and proceedings have been instituted to condemn the property, and it is expected that work of construction will be begun early in 1921.

Consideration is, meanwhile, being given to the building of two additional stories on this shed, to be used for office purposes.

Modernization of the North River.

A lay-out for the modernization of the North River, between Vesey and Perry, was prepared and adopted by the Commissioners of the Sinking Fund on July 29, 1920.

18 modern steamship piers of adequate length and width and sufficient slip room between them are proposed in substitution for the 32 narrow and out-of-date existing piers. For many years various plans have been considered for relieving congestion on the marginal street, but the erection of any improvement of a permanent character was prohibited under the provisions of the Charter. The present Dock Commissioner brought about the passage of the Lynch Bill, removing this obstacle, and a plan has been devised for the construction of an elevated roadway along the bulkhead from Riverside Drive to Battery Park, connecting with the piers and with warehouses to be erected over the marginal street, thus affording ample relief not only for the present, but for the future.

Occupation by the Street Cleaning Department of a valuable pier site at Canal has been recognized as an economic waste and a most modern disposal station, erected entirely of steel and concrete, is being constructed under the old Brooklyn Bridge, on the Manhattan side, for the disposal of ashes and other waste material, collected south of Canal.

As soon as this improvement can be completed and put in service, the ramshackle pier at the foot of Canal, North River, will be demolished and a modern pier, 1025 ft. long and 150 ft. wide, the first under the new plan adopted July 29, 1920, will be erected, thus affording a protection to and means of ventilating the vehicular tube.

There is now pending before the Secretary of War an application by the Commissioner of Docks for the extension of the pierhead line from Perry north to 72d, North River, and should it be approved, a comprehensive plan will be prepared and submitted to the Commissioners of the Sinking Fund for approval, embracing the remaining commercial waterfront area on the North River side of Manhattan, for constructive improvement.

Bay Ridge Improvement.

Designs for a modern dock terminal in the Bay Ridge district have been completed. The necessary privately owned property has been acquired and the Department of Docks are now waiting the authority and authorization of the necessary funds by the Board of Estimate and Apportionment to advertise and let contracts and proceed with the work.

The designs include four steamship piers, with sheds fitted with modern freight handling devices, at least two stories in height, and a connecting warehouse system on the upland.

Particular attention has been given to the architectural features of this terminal because of its proximity to park property. It is hoped that it will be well under way before the end of 1921.

Jamaica Bay.

Construction of a pier, to be utilized for the disposal of street cleaning and other material, has been begun and is expected to be completed on or shortly after the 1st of January, 1921. Congress is expected to authorize the enlargement of the existing project for a 30-ft. channel. The Department of Docks submitted to the Sinking Fund (which approved) and the Board of Estimate and Apportionment plans, estimates and application for authority to advertise and let contract for the construction of a modern terminal, a typical plan for which has been worked out by the Commissioner of Docks and his engineering force, as a result of his visit during the summer of 1920 to Antwerp, Rotterdam, Amsterdam, Hamburg, Marseilles, Bordeaux, Southampton, London, Liverpool and Manchester.

GLEN COVE OFFICIALS.

J. E. Burns, Mayor and Supr.; C. P. Valentine, Commr. Finance; Bryan Murray, Jr., Commr. Public Safety; L. T. Simonson, Commr. Public Works; H. F. Weber, Commr. Accounts; Wm. Weldon, Jr., City Clerk.

PLAN OF FUTURE RAPID TRANSIT SYSTEM

Plans for extending the rapid transit system of New York City, so that it will accommodate the growth of population for the next twenty-five years, were completed in Sept., 1920, by Daniel L. Turner, chief engineer in the office of John H. Delaney, Transit Construction Commissioner.

The plan provides for 830 miles of single track to be added to the present 616 miles of subway and elevated lines. At pre-war prices the estimated cost of the completed plan is $175,000,000, and at present prices, $350,000,000 exclusive of equipment.

For the twenty-five-year program, based on present-day utilization of tracks and present type of equipment, the proposed additional trunk lines would be able to develop a capacity of approximately 5,000,000,000 passengers per year.

Summary of the Plan.

New Manhattan-All City Lines: An eight-track, double deck trunk line under 8th and Amsterdam avs., only four tracks to be constructed at one time, and so located under the roadway as not to interfere with future construction of another four-line unit; and a trunk line under Madison av., to relieve the Lexington Av. Line.

The Eighth-Amsterdam Av. Trunk Line would be connected with distributing and collecting branches, both at its northern and southern extremities. The northern extremity will be at 155th st., where it is suggested a branch be built to cross the Harlem River and traverse the Bronx through 161st st., Longwood and Randall avs., to the Throggs Neck section. This branch would be connected with a projected Manhattan-Bronx-to-the-Ocean Crosstown Line. Another branch would traverse upper Manhattan via Fort Washington to Spuyten Duyvil, thence via Netherland av., through the Riverdale section.

Below 155th st. the line would be under Amsterdam av., approximately to 103d st., where the existing Lenox Av.-West Farms connection might be taken in. From this point to 86th st. a six-track line is projected. At 86th st. two tracks might come in from Queens via an under-river tunnel. At 57th st. two tracks, possibly those devoted to the Lenox Av.-West Farms connection, might go down 10th av.

Steinway Tunnel Connection.

At 41st st. the Steinway Tunnel Line from Queens would connect with the Eighth Av.-Amsterdam Av. Trunk Line. At 23d st. a line from Bkln. would connect with the trunk service. Below 23d st. the line would be six-track, through 8th av. and Hudson st. At Bedford st., the southern extremity of the trunk line, two tracks would turn to the east, to be later extended into and through B'way, Bkln. At Grand st. two more tracks would continue southward under Hudson and Washington sts. to the Battery, and cross to Bkln. via Governor's Island and Hamilton av. to 3d av., Bkln. This would permit all of the collecting and distributing branches of the southern extremity of the trunk line to enter and traverse Bkln. Borough.

It is explained that this new trunk line would offer the closest possible connection with the Pennsylvania and the New York Central stations and the tubes to New Jersey from all parts of the city.

The principal new line to be provided on the east side of Mhtn. is a proposed Madison Av. Line. This line would begin at the Harlem River as a four-track trunk line, with a possible two-track connection to the Bronx, and extend down Madison av. to 86th st., where two tracks would branch to the east into and through Queens, which, together with the two-track branch from the Eighth Av.-Amsterdam Av. Line on the west side, would constitute a four-track trunk line to Queens.

Six-Track Line Provided For.

From 86th st., south to 23d st., the Madison Av. Line would be a six-track line. At 23d st. one two-track branch would extend down 5th av., Greene and Church sts. to about Chambers st., where eventually the line would turn west under the Hudson River to New Jersey and to Richmond. At Madison av. and 23d st. two tracks would terminate.

The other tracks would extend down 3d av. to about 3d st., where they would turn east and cross the East River to Bkln., connecting with a four-track trunk line in B'way, this trunk line in Bkln. thus being served by an east side two-track connection via Madison av., and a west side two-track connection via the projected Eighth Av. Line.

Another facility tentatively laid down provides for the upper west side of Mhtn. a two-track line from the end of the Interborough Rapid Transit Broadway-Seventh Av. route, up Central Park West, through 8th or 7th av. to the Harlem River. It was said that the effect of such a line would be to immediately relieve the existing west side elevated road by providing superior facilities for the territory east of Morningside Park and north of Central Park. Such a line would pierce territory in part inadequately served from 59th to 155th st.

Brooklyn.

Many petitions have been received by the Transit Construction Commissioner asking for the extension of the Brooklyn Rapid Transit Broadway Line from 59th st. to Washington Heights via 8th av. to 116th st. and thence via St. Nicholas av. and B'way to the city's northern limits.

Bkln. is not as prominent as Mhtn. in the scheme of rapid transit extension. But this Borough, like all of the others, received close study with the result that the plan provides for the building of a subway-tunnel connection via Livingston and Washington sts. into Mhtn. to a connection with the two tracks of the B. R. T. Subway which now terminates at City Hall, Mhtn. This two-track subway could temporarily, it is explained, connect with the Fulton St. Elevated Line at or near Ashland pl. Other parts of the proposals to aid Bkln. are:

Another two-track subway and tunnel crossing to Mhtn., starting at Fulton st., Bkln., in the neighborhood of Ashland pl. and routing through State st. and via a tunnel to a connection with the spur provided at the lower end of the Whitehall St. Subway of the New York Municipal Railway. With this new crossing constructed, it probably would be desirable to extend a four-track subway through Fulton st., Bkln., to East New York. This done, the Montague St. Tunnel could be given over to the exclusive use of the Centre St. Loop and Nassau St. Line.

Relief for the Fourth Av. Subway could be provided by a new and direct subway and river tunnel connection into and through Mhtn. for the Culver Line, and a crosstown line through Bkln., connecting the Brighton Beach Line at Franklin av. with the Astoria branch in Queens. Such a line would provide convenient crosstown facilities within a convenient distance of the waterfront in Bkln. and would interest practically all other rapid transit lines in Bkln. and afford a convenient medium of interchange.

The Bronx.

For the central section of lower Bronx a three-track line along Morris av., from the Harlem River to lower Tremont, thence easterly through the congested section adjacent to Crotona Park by way of Tremont av. to Long Island Sound. This line would be in addition to the projected 161st St. Crosstown Line, which will tap the Hunts Point section, with one branch extending through Unionport to Throggs Neck and another by way of Riker's Island to Steinway and through Queens to the Forest Park section of that borough and to East New York.

Extensions of the existing rapid transit lines from the junction of Gun Hill and White Plains rds., along the former highway to Boston rd., and thence northeasterly, and of the Westchester-Pelham Bay Park Line through Williamsbridge rd. to Rodman's Neck, are also laid down.

Queens.

In addition to the connecting and distributing sections of the Eighth Av.-Amsterdam Av. and Madison Av. Trunk Lines to and through Queens, that borough will be brought into direct connection with Bkln. by means of the proposed crosstown line connecting the Brighton Beach Line at Franklin av. and by giving Queens direct access to Coney Island. Flushing and the North Shore will be connected up with the dual system by means of the extension of the Corona Line, jointly operated by the Interborough and B. R. T. Railways.

PLAN OF FUTURE RAPID TRANSIT SYSTEM—*Continued.*

Richmond.

Richmond will be provided with its first rapid transit facilities by means of tunnels under the Narrows, which will connect with the southern extremity of the existing Fourth Av. Rapid Transit Line. The matter of extending the lines from the tubes under the Narrows, through Staten Island, will be determined by the development of the general city plan for the Island.

Many Extensions Contemplated.

Concerning extensions, the proposed improvements suggest for the near future the lengthening of the Corona Branch of the Steinway Tunnel from its present terminal to Main st., Flushing; the extension of the tunnel line from its proposed terminus at 7th av. and 41st st., west through 41st st. to a connection with the proposed Amsterdam-Eighth Av. Trunk Line and a two-track extension of the B. R. T. Subway from 59th st. and 7th av. up Central Park West and 8th or 7th av. to the Harlem River. Other proposed extensions are:

Extension of the New York Municipal Railway Broadway-Fourth Av. Line from a connection at B'way and City Hall Park, via Ann st. and the East River to Bkln., and via Brooklyn Bridge terminal property, Washington st., Livingston st., DeKalb av. and Fort Greene pl. to a connection with the Fulton St. Elevated Line at or near Ashland pl.

Extension of the B. R. T. Fourth Av. Subway, Bkln., by way of a two-track tunnel under the Narrows to the Borough of Richmond.

Extension of the Nostrand Av. Subway of the Interborough Company south into and through Coney Island.

Extension of the Astoria Branch of the Steinway Tunnel Line south through Queens and Bkln. to a connection with the Brighton Beach Line in Bkln., thereby providing a Bkln. crosstown line.

Extension of the two tracks of the Interborough-Seventh Av.-Broadway Line, now terminating at the Battery, from a point at Greenwich and Liberty sts., via Liberty st., Maiden lane and the East River to Brooklyn, and thence via Hicks st., Union st., 7th av. and Gravesend av. to a connection with the Culver Line.

MAYORS OF NEW YORK CITY PRIOR TO CONSOLIDATION.

Up to 1774 the Mayor was appointed by the Governor of the Province, and from 1784 to 1820 by the Appointing Board of the State of New York, of which the Governor was the head. From 1821 to the amendment of the Charter in 1829, the Mayor was appointed by the Common Council. In 1898 the term of the first Mayor of Greater New York began.

Mayors.	Terms.	Mayors.	Terms.	Mayors.	Terms.
Thomas Willett	1665	Jacobus van Cortlandt	1719-1720	Isaac L. Varian	1839-1841
Thomas Delavall	1666	Robert Walters	1720-1725	Robert H. Morris	1841-1844
Thomas Willett	1667	Johannes Jansen	1725-1726	James Harper	1844-1845
Cornelius Steenwyck	1668-1670	Robert Lurting	1726-1735	Wm. F. Havemeyer	1845-1846
Thomas Delavall	1671	Paul Richard	1735-1739	Andrew H. Mickle	1846-1847
Matthias Nicolls	1672	John Cruger, Sr.	1739-1744	William V. Brady	1847-1848
John Lawrence	1673	Stephen Bayard	1744-1747	Wm. F. Havemeyer	1848-1849
William Dervall	1675	Edward Holland	1747-1757	Caleb S. Woodhull	1849-1851
Nicholas de Meyer	1676	John Cruger, Jr.	1757-1766	Ambrose C. Kingsland	1851-1853
S. van Cortlandt	1677	Whitehead Hicks	1766-1776	Jacob A. Westervelt	1853-1855
Thomas Delavall	1678	David Matthews	1776-1784	Fernando Wood	1855-1858
Francis Rombouts	1679	James Duane	1784-1789	Daniel F. Tiemann	1858-1860
William Dyre	1680-1681	Richard Varick	1789-1801	Fernando Wood	1860-1862
Cornelius Steenwyck	1682-1683	Edward Livingston	1801-1803	George Opdyke	1862-1864
Gabriel Minville	1684	De Witt Clinton	1803-1807	C. Godfrey Gunther	1864-1866
Nicholas Bayard	1685	Marinus Willett	1807-1808	John T. Hoffman	1866-1868
S. van Cortlandt	1686-1687	De Witt Clinton	1808-1810	T. Coman (act'g mayor)	1868
Peter Delanoy	1689-1690	Jacob Radcliff	1810-1811	A. Oakey Hall	1869-1872
John Lawrence	1691	De Witt Clinton	1811-1815	Wm. F. Havemeyer	1873-1874
Abraham De Peyster	1692-1695	John Ferguson	1815	S. B. H. Vance (acting)	1874
William Merritt	1695-1698	Jacob Radcliff	1815-1818	William H. Wickham	1875-1876
Johannes De Peyster	1698-1699	Cadwallader D. Colden	1818-1821	Smith Ely	1877-1878
David Provost	1699-1700	Stephen Allen	1821-1824	Edward Cooper	1879-1880
Isaac de Riemer	1700-1701	William Paulding	1825-1826	William R. Grace	1881-1882
Thomas Noell	1701-1702	Philip Hone	1826-1827	Franklin Edson	1883-1884
Philip French	1702-1703	William Paulding	1827-1829	William R. Grace	1885-1886
William Peartree	1703-1707	Walter Bowne	1829-1833	Abraham S. Hewitt	1887-1888
Ebenezer Wilson	1707-1710	Gideon Lee	1833-1834	Hugh J. Grant	1889-1892
Jacobus van Cortlandt	1710-1711	Cornelius W. Lawrence	1834-1837	Thomas F. Gilroy	1893-1894
Caleb Heathcote	1711-1714	Aaron Clark	1837-1839	William L. Strong	1895-1897
John Johnson	1714-1719				

MAYORS OF GREATER NEW YORK.

Name.	Residence.	Term.	
Robert A. Van Wyck (1849—1918)‡	135 E. 46th st., Mhtn	1898-1901	Four years.
Seth Low (1850—1916)		1902-1903	Two years.
George B. McClellan (1865—	37 Madison av., Mhtn	1904-1909	*Six years.
William J. Gaynor (1851—1913)§		1910-1913	Four years.
Ardolph L. Kline† (1858—	238 Carlton av., Bkln	1913—unexpired Gaynor term.	
John P. Mitchel (1879-1918)**		1914-1917	Four years.
John F. Hylan (1868—	959 Bushwick av., Bkln	1918—	Four years.

*Two terms, first, 2 yrs; second, 4 yrs. §Died at sea, Sept. 10, 1913, on S. S. Baltic, while on voyage to Europe for recuperation. †Pres. Bd. of Ald., succeeded to mayoralty. **Killed in fall from airplane, July 6, 1918. ‡Died in Paris, Nov. 15, 1918.

MAYORS OF BROOKLYN PRIOR TO CONSOLIDATION.

Name.	Term.	Name.	Term.	Name.	Term.	Name.	Term.
George Hall	1834	F. B. Stryker	1846-8	M. Kalbfleisch	1861-3	James Howell	1878-81
Jonathan Trotter	1835-6	Edward Copeland	1849	Alfred M. Wood	1864-5	Seth Low	1882-5
Jere'h Johnson	1837-8	Samuel Smith	1850	Samuel Booth	1866-7	D. D. Whitney	1886-7
Cyr. P. Smith	1839-41	Conklin Brush	1851-2	M. Kalbfleisch	1868-71	Alfred C. Chapin	1888-91
Henry C. Murphy	1842	Ed. A. Lambert	1853-4	Sam'l S. Powell	1872-3	David A. Boody	1892-3
Joseph Sprague	1843-4	George Hall	1855-6	John W. Hunter	1874-5	C. A. Schieren	1894-5
Thos G. Talmage	1845	S. S. Powell	1857-60	F. A. Schroeder	1876-7	F. W. Wurster	1896-7

A direct all-American line of cable from Brazil to the United States will be established soon by the laying of a cable from Rio de Janeiro to Cuba, with North American connection at Barbados.

Australians are by far the most prolific letter writers in the world. They average 150 letters per head each year, as against an average of 80 for the people of the United States and Canada.

OLD U. S. COINS AND PREMIUM VALUES THEREON.

(Premium, Subject to Condition, Estimated by J. Lehrenkrauss & Sons.)

Copper.

HALF CENTS—1793, .50—$3; 1796, $5—$25; 1797, lettered edge .25—$2.50; 1802, .10—$2; 1831, $3—$20; 1836, $5—$20; 1840-49, $4—$20; 1852, $6—$15.

Any ½ cent commands premium of 5c. to 15c.

CENTS (LARGE)—1793, Liberty cap, pole, $2.50—$8; 1793, chain, Liberty, period and no period, $3—$15; 1793, strawberry sprig, wreath, $3—$8; 1793, olive sprig over date, $1.50—$2; 1793, chain, Ameri (instead of America), $3—$8; 1793, chain, America, $3—$8; 1793, Liberty cap, $3.50—$10; 1796, Fillet head (hair tied), .50—$2.50; 1799, over 1798, $10—$50; 1804, $3.50—$20; 1809-11, head to left, .50—$2; 1811 over 1810, .50—$2.50.

All other dates, if in perfect condition, command a premium, more or less.

SMALL CENTS—1856 (nickel), flying eagle, $2—$5; 1877 (bronze), Indian head, .05—.25; 1909 V. D. B. Lincoln head (proof), .10—.25.

TWO CENT (BRONZE)—1873, $1—$2.

THREE-CENT (NICKEL)—1877, $1—$2.

FIVE-CENT (NICKEL)—1877, $1—$2.

Silver.

THREE-CENT PIECES—1863, .25—.75; 1864, $1—$2; 1865-1872, .20—.75.

HALF DIMES—1794, flowing hair, $1.50—$3.50; 1796, $2—$5; 1797, $2—$5; 1801, $1—$2; 1802, $30—$50; 1803, .50—$1.50; 1805, $2—$3.50; 1846, .50—$1.

1795, 1800, 1860 and 1864 also command a fair premium.

DIMES—1804, $6—$25.

1796, 1797, 1798, 1800, 1801, 1802, 1803, command a large premium, and 1809, 1811, 1822 and 1846 command a fair premium; 1859, Obverse, Reverse 1860, $3—$5.

TWENTY-CENT PIECES—1876, C. C. mint mark only, .50—$1; 1877, 1878, $1.50—$2 (proofs only).

QUARTERS—1796, $2—$5; 1804, $1.50—$3; 1823, $20—$40; 1827, $30—$50; 1853, Liberty seated, without arrow heads at sides of date, $2—$4; 1866 (without "In God We Trust"), $2.50—$5; 1893, Columbian or Isabel, .30—.40.

HALF DOLLARS—1796, Fillet head, 15 stars, $30—$45; 1796, Fillet head, 16 stars, $20—$35; 1797, Fillet head, 15 stars, $20—$35; 1838, O between date and bust, $5—$30; 1838 Liberty cap seated, $10—$30; 1853, without arrow heads at sides of date; no rays around eagle, $20—$35; 1892-3, Columbian, no premium; 1794, 1801, 1802, 1807, 1815 and 1866 (without "In God We Trust") command a fair premium.

DOLLARS—1794, head flowing hair, $30—$70; 1804, large eagle, $800—$1,500; 1836, flying eagle, C. Gobrecht on base, $10—$30; 1838, flying eagle, Gobrecht on base, plain edge, $70—$100; milled edge, $20—$30; 1839, flying eagle, Gobrecht on base, plain edge, $70—$100; milled edge, $20—$25; 1851-52, Liberty seated, $15—$50; 1858, Liberty seated, $10—$25; 1866 (without "In God We Trust"), $3—$6. Slight premium on many other dates if coins are in good condition.

Gold.

DOLLARS—1863, $3—$5; 1864, $3—$5; 1865, $6—$9; 1875, $20—$25. Other dates, $1.90—$6; common, $1.75—$2.10; 1803-1903, Jefferson-McKinley, $1.75—$2; 1904, Lewis & Clark, $1.80—$2.80; 1905, Lewis & Clark, $1.80—$2.80.

QUARTER EAGLES ($2.50)—1796, without stars, $10—$25; 1796, 13 stars, $10—$30; 1797, $25—$50; 1798, 1806, 1827, $10—$25; 1821, 1824, 1825, $10—$20; 1834, with "E Pluribus Unum," $15—$50.

1802, 1804, 1805, 1807, 1808, 1829, 1830, 1831, 1832, 1833, 1875 command premium of $3—$9.

THREE DOLLAR—1854 D mint, $4—$10; 1870, S mint, $100—$300; 1873, $12—$20; 1875, $25—$35; 1876, $20—$50. Some other dates as high as $6.

Common dates, $3.50—$4.75.

FOUR-DOLLAR—"STELLA"—1879, $30—$40; 1880, $60—$75.

HALF EAGLES ($5)—1795 Large Eagle, 1797, $15—$35; 1795 Small Eagle, 1796, 1798 Large Eagle, 1799, 1818, 1820, 1823, 1826, 1830, $10—$25; 1824, 1825, 1827, 1831, 1832, 1833, 1834, with "E Pluribus," $20—$75; 1815, $500—$750; 1822, $750—$1,250; 1828, 1829, $50—$125; and many other dates of smaller premium.

EAGLES ($10)—1795 Small Eagle, 1796-97, 1804, $15—$25; 1798, $25—$45; 1797 Large Eagle, 1799, 1800, 1801, 1803, $12—$15.

DOUBLE EAGLES ($20)—1849, only one specimen is known. It is in the U. S. Mint at Phila. and valued at $5,000; 1881-87, without any mint mark, $21—$30; 1907, flying eagle, date in Roman letters, $21—$22.50.

FIFTY DOLLAR GOLD PIECES—Round or octagon, any date, $75—$140.

PRINCIPAL INDUSTRIES OF METROPOLITAN DISTRICT OF NEW YORK.

	Value of products.	No. of estabs.
1. Clothing	$546,682,000	6,229
2. Printing and publishing	230,961,000	3,647
3. Smelting and refining copper	207,752,000	5
4. Textiles	179,209,000	1,003
5. Slaughtering and meat packing	148,621,000	263
6. Foundry and machine shop products	128,194,000	2,612
7. Petroleum refining	113,770,000	10
8. Tobacco manufactures	103,564,000	2,006
9. Bread and other bakery products	97,632,000	3,391
10. Millinery and lace goods, not elsewhere specified	78,032,000	1,488
11. Electrical machinery, apparatus and supplies	54,904,000	226
12. Gas, illuminating and heating	54,166,000	35
13. Paint and varnish	42,076,000	159
14. Chemicals	39,989,000	81
15. Copper, tin and sheet iron products	38,004,000	636
16. Patent medicines, compounds and druggists' preparations	37,820,000	597
17. Coffee and spice, roasting and grinding	32,742,000	107
18. Confectionery	32,110,000	244
19. Jewelry	31,800,000	685
20. Boots and shoes, including cut stock and findings	31,559,000	227
21. Men's furnishing goods	31,376,000	319
22. Lumber and timber products	29,949,000	418
23. Fur goods	29,251,000	838
24. Musical instruments, pianos, organs and materials	27,747,000	142
25. Furniture and refrigerators	27,719,000	648
26. Leather, tanned, curried and finished	26,051,000	92
27. Food preparations, not elsewhere specified	22,421,000	236
28. Leather goods, not elsewhere specified	22,308,000	260
29. Boxes, fancy and paper	18,233,000	260
30. Artificial flowers and feathers and plumes	16,467,000	372
31. Shipbuilding, including boat building	16,237,000	106
32. Brass, bronze and copper products	14,243,000	302
33. Paper goods, not elsewhere specified	13,657,000	100
34. Automobile, including bodies and parts	13,442,000	183
35. Hats, fur, felt	13,016,000	70
36. Rubber goods, not elsewhere specified	11,727,000	56
37. Gas, electric fixtures, lamps and reflectors	11,682,000	176
38. Marble and stone work	11,803,000	346
39. Hats and caps, other than felt, straw and wool	10,999,000	289
40. Belting and hose, woven and rubber	10,907,000	10
41. Cars and general shop-construction and repairs by steam railroad companies	10,594,000	27
42. Fancy articles, not elsewhere specified	10,281,000	300
All other industries	729,997,000	...

Air-mail service between the United States and Cuba was inaugurated on Nov. 1, 1920, with the departure of two seaplanes from Key West to Havana.

In the year ending June 30, 1920, the average immigrant family brought two and a half times as much money as in the year ending June 30, 1914.

CATHOLIC EDUCATIONAL SYSTEM—DIOCESE OF BROOKLYN

PERSONNEL OF THE SCHOOL BOARD.

Pres., Rt. Rev. Charles E. McDonnell, D.D.; 1st V. P., Rt. Rev. Mgr. George Kaupert, V.G.; 2d V. P., Rt. Rev. Mgr. Joseph McNamee, V.G.; Supt., Rev. Joseph V. S. McClancy, 749 Linwood st., Brooklyn, N. Y.

Kings County.

Rt. Rev. Mgr. A. Arcese, Very Rev. Mgr. D. J. Hickey, Very Rev. Mgr. F. Strenski, Very Rev. Mgr. F. X. Ludeke, Very Rev. Mgr. B. Puchalski, Rev. J. F. Mealia, J. J. Flood, J. J. McAteer, E. A. Duffy, J. W. Hauptmann, M. P. Fitzgerald, D. F. Cherry, J. H. Lynch, T. J. O'Brien, J. M. Kiely, M. Lang, P. J. Cherry, J. J. O'Neil, D. McCarthy, J. R. Agrella.

Queens County.

Rev. J. P. McGinley, P. Henn, A. Nawrocki, D.D.

Nassau County.

Very Rev. I. Zeller, V.F.; Very Rev. L. Fuchs, V.F.; B. O'Reilly, W. F. McGinnis, D.D.

Suffolk County.

Rev. P. Schwartz, T. W. Connolly, A. Cizmowski.

DIOCESAN BOARD OF COMMUNITY SUPERVISORS.

Franciscan Brothers—Bro. Jarlath, O.S.F., 41 Butler. Christian Brothers—Bro. Anselm, 22 No. Henry. Brothers of Mary—Bro. John Banzer, 306 Warwick. Brothers of the Sacred Heart—Bro. Matthias, 270 Newkirk av. Xavier Brothers—Bro. Urban, 2540 Church av. Sisters of St. Joseph—Sr. M. Angelita, 241 Prospect Park West and Sr. M. Camilla, 834 Pacific. Sisters of St. Dominic—Sr. M. Chrysostom, O.S.D., 23 Thornton. Sisters of Charity—Sr. Gertrude Aloysia, 202 Congress. Sch. Sisters of Notre Dame—Sr. M. Betra, Glen Cove, N. Y. Sisters of Mercy—Mother Mary Bernard, 273 Willoughby av. Sisters of the Holy Family of Nazareth—Sr. Mary Theobalda, Conshohocken, Pa. Sisters of the Sacred Heart of the Virgin Mary—Mother M. Gerard, Marymount, Tarrytown, N. Y. Felician Sisters—Sr. Mary Angelica, Lodi, N. J. Daughters of Wisdom—Sr. Marie, 1219 McCormick av., Ozone Park, N. Y. Sisters of Christian Charity—Sr. M. Wigberta, 1918 Fulton. Missionary Sisters of the Sacred Heart—Sr. M. Stanislaus, 138 Van Brunt. Missionary Franciscan Sisters—Sr. M. Philomena, 670 Carroll. Sisters of the Holy Names of Jesus and Mary—Sr. Mary Irene, W. 17th, Coney Island, Brooklyn.

Brooklyn—Grade Schools.

(School, rector's name, address, principal and address. Sr. is abbreviation for Sister.)

1—St. Agnes, J. Flynn, 417 Sackett; Sr. Seraphine, 419 Degraw.

2—All Saints, Rt. Rev. Mgr. Geo. Kaupert, 115 Throop av.; Sr. M. Chrysostom, O.S.D., 23 Thornton.

3—St. Aloysius, J. Hauptmann, Onderdonk av. and Stanhope; Sr. M. Cesla, O.S.D., 1817 Stanhope.

4—St. Alphonsus, H. J. Pfeifer, 177 Kent; Sr. M. Martinella, 174 Java.

5—St. Ambrose—L. M. O. Blaber, 222 Tompkins av.; Sr. John Francis, 756 DeKalb av.

6—St. Anne, J. J. Patterson, 251 Front; Sr. M. Peter, 237 Front.

7—Annunciation—N. J. Petkus, 259 No. 5th; Sr. M. Emerentiana, O.S.D., 64 Havemeyer.

8—St. Antony, Rt. Rev. Mgr. P. O'Hare, 862 Manhattan av.; (Boys' Dept.), Bro. Athanasius, 714 Leonard; (Girls' Dept.), Sr. M. Francisca, 878 Manhattan av.

9—Assumption, W. B. Farrell, 64 Middagh; Sr. Angelita Marie, 202 Congress.

10—St. Augustine, Rt. Rev. Mgr. E. W. McCarthy, 116 6th av.; (Boys' Dept.), Bro. Alban, 58 Park pl.: (Girls' Dept.), Sr. M. Evangelista, 45 Sterling pl.

11—St. Barbara, J. J. Kuntz, 311 Central av.; (Boys' Dept.), Bro. Michael, 137 Menahan; (Girls' Dept.), Sr. M. Catherine, O.S.D., 144 Bleecker.

12—St. Benedict, Jos. Traenkle, 927 Herkimer; Sr. Wigberta, 1918 Fulton.

13—St. Bernard, Chas. Hamma, Hicks, near Woodhull; Sr. M. Avellina, O.S.D., 103 Rapelye.

14—Blessed Sacrament, J. M. Kiely, 200 Euclid av.; Sr. M. Raymondina, 189 Chestnut.

15—St. Boniface, Martin Lang, 109 Willoughby; Sr. M. Felicitas, O.S.D., 107 Willoughby.

16—St. Brendan's, T. A. Hickey, 1225 E. 12th; Sr. Joseph, Av. O and E. 13th.

17—St. Brigid, J. C. York, 409 Linden; Sr. Mary Imelda, 419 Linden.

18—St. Catherine of Alexandria, J. J. O'Neill, 1119 41st; Sr. M. Sacred Heart, 41st and Ft. Hamilton av.

19—St. Cecelia, Rt. Rev. Mgr. Edw. McGolrick, 84 Herbert: (Boys' Dept.), Bro. Anselm, 22 No. Henry; (Girls' Dept.), Sr. St. Luke, 21 Monitor.

20—St. Charles, J. Vogel, P.S.M., 550 Hicks; Sr. M. Stanislaus, 138 Van Brunt.

21—St. Charles Borromeo, T. J. O'Brien, 21 Sidney pl.; (Boys' Dept.), Bro. Adrian, 23 Sidney pl.; (Girls' Dept.), Sr. Marguerite Marie, 202 Congress.

22—Sts. Cyril and Methodius, Very Rev. Mgr. E. Strenski, 123 Eagle; Sr. M. Charitas, 90 Dupont.

23—Epiphany, E. A. Duffy, 96 So. 9th; Sr. M. Michaela, 98 So. 9th.

24—Fourteen Holy Martyrs, B. Kurtz, Central av. and Covert; Sr. M. Morgia, O.S.D., 142 Covert.

25—St. Francis of Assisi, Very Rev. Mgr. F. X. Ludeke, 319 Maple; Sr. Mary Edward, 396 Lincoln rd.

26—St. Francis de Chantal, P. J. O'Laughlin, S.P.M., 1273 68th; Sr. M. Adelgundis, O.S.D., 1274 57th.

27—St. Francis Xavier, Very Rev. Mgr. D. J. Hickey, 225 6th av.; (Boys' Dept.), Bro. Eugene, 41 Butler; (Girls' Dept.), Sr. Agnes Regina, 697 Carroll.

28—St. Gregory, M. P. Fitzgerald, 1006 Sterling pl.; Sr. M. Dominic, 987 St. Johns pl.

29—Holy Cross, Rt. Rev. Mgr. J. Woods, 2530 Church av.; (Boys' Dept.), Bro. Urban, 2540 Church av.; (Girls' Dept.), Sr. Mary John, 12 Prospect.

30—Holy Family, J. Gresser, 206 14th; Sr. M. Maud, O.S.D., 222 13th.

31—Holy Family (Slovak), J. J. Jurasko, 21 Nassau av.; Sr. Mary Alix, 21 Nassau av.

32—Holy Innocents, F. J. McMurray, 1718 Beverly rd.; Sr. M. Cecilia, 1722 Beverly rd.

33—Holy Name, Chas. Vitta, 245 Prospect Park West; Sr. M. Adrian, 241 Prospect Park West.

34—Holy Trinity, Geo. Metzger, 138 Montrose av.; (Boys' Dept.), Bro. George Ley, 153 Johnson av.; (Girls' Dept.), Sr. M. Narcissa, O.S.D., 157 Graham av.

35—Immaculate Conception, T. F. Horan, 72 Maujer; Sr. M. Eugene, 189 Leonard.

36—Immaculate Heart of Mary, M. J. Tierney, 119 East 4th; Sr. St. Stanislaus, 155 East 2nd.

37—St. James, Very Rev. Mgr. F. J. O'Hara, Cathedral pl., 155 East 2d; (Boys' Dept.), Bro. Austin, 264 Jay; (Girls' Dept.), Sr. M. Chrysostom, 223 Jay.

38—St. Jerome, T. F. Lynch, 2900 Newkirk av.; Sr. Mary Ambrose, 455 East 29th.

39—St. John Baptist, Very Rev. John W. Moore, C.M., 75 Lewis av.; Sr. M. Vincentella, 80 Lewis av.

40—St. John Cantius, Theo. Regulski, 477 New Jersey av.; Sr. M. Felicia, 480 Vermont.

41—St. John Evangelist, T. S. Duhigg, 21st, near 5th av.; (Boys' Dept.), Rev. Edmund A. Kean, 250 21st; (Girls' Dept.), Sr. Rose Geraldine, 250 22d.

42—St. Joseph, Very Rev. Mgr. W. T. McGuirl, 856 Pacific; (Boys' Dept.) Bro. Domnus, 41 Butler; (Girls' Dept.), Sr. Marie Louise, 834 Pacific.

43—St. Leonard, Geo. D. Sander, 199 Jefferson; Sr. M. Vincent, O.S.D., 274 Melrose.

44—St. Malachy, D. Cherry, 129 VanSicklen av.; Sr. St. Ephrem, 2791 Atlantic av.

45—St. Mary, Mother of Jesus, H. F. Murray, 2305 85th; Sr. M. Julia, 2311 84th.

46—St. Mary, Star of the Sea, Very Rev. Mgr. Jas. J. Corrigan, 467 Court; (Boys' Dept., Bro. Ambrose, 41 Butler; (Girls' Dept.), Sr. Mary Pauline, 193 Luqueer.

47—St. Matthew, Wm. J. Costello, 1123 Eastern Parkway; Sr. Teresa Augusta, 250 Utica av.

48—St. Matthias, N. M. Wagner, 1861 Catalpa av.; Sr. M. Alcantara, 1871 Catalpa av.

49—St. Michael, R. J. Cherry, 352 42nd; Sr. M. Irenaeus, 369 43d.

50—St. Michael, Fr. Martin, O.M.Cap., 225 Jerome; (Boys' Dept.), Bro. John, 306 Warwick; (Girls' Dept.), Sr. M. Philomene, O.S.D., 235 Jerome.

51—Nativity, J. L. Belford, 20 Madison; Sr. M. Raymond, 30 Madison.

52—St. Nicholas, Very Rev. Mgr. J. P. Hoffman, 26 Olive; Sr. M. Prudentia, O.S.D., 287 Powers.

53—Our Lady of Consolation, A. A. Jarka, 183 Metropolitan av.; Sr. Mary Baptista, 175 Metropolitan av.

CATHOLIC EDUCATIONAL SYSTEM—BROOKLYN GRADE SCHOOLS—*Continued.*

54—Our Lady of Czestochova, Very Rev. Mgr. B. Puchalski, 183 25th; Sr. M. Eudoxia, 170 25th.

55—Our Lady of Good Counsel, P. J. Donohue, 915 Putnam av.; (Boys' Dept.), Bro. Pacificus, 921 Putnam av.; (Girls' Dept.), Sr. Mary James, 895 Putnam av.

56—Our Lady of Lourdes, M. McMahon, S.P.M., 11 DeSales pl.; Sr. Rose Madeline, 34 Aberdeen.

57—Our Lady of Mercy, J. McAteer, 234 Schermerhorn; Sr. M. Bauline, 385 State.

58—Our Lady of Peace, V. Pianigiani, O.F.M., 522 Carroll; Sr. M. Philomene, 670 Carroll.

59—Our Lady of Perpetual Help, J. Barron, C.SS.R., 526 59th; Sr. M. Martine, 560 59th.

60—Our Lady of Pompeii, O. Silvestri, 225 Seigel; Sr. M. Hedwig, O.S.D., 167 Graham av.

61—Our Lady of Solace, W. A. Kerwin, Mermaid av. and West 19th; Sr. Mary Irene, 2876 West 17th.

62—Our Lady of Sorrows, F. X. Wunsch, 83 Morgan av.; Sr. M. Placida, O.S.D., 27 Harrison pl.

63—St. Patrick, John F. Cherry, 285 Willoughby av.; (Boys' Dept.), Bro. Mark, 918 Kent av.; (Girls' Dept.), Sr. M. Mercedes, 273 Willoughby av.

64—St. Patrick, J. J. Kent, 4th av. and 95th; Sr. M. Pulcheria, O.S.D., 420 95th.

65—St. Paul, Rt. Rev. Mgr. M. G. Flannery, 223 Congress; Boys' Dept., Bro. David, 41 Butler; (Girls' Dept.), Sr. Gertrude Aloysia, 202 Congress.

66—St. Peter, M. A. Fitzgerald, 117 Warren, (Boys' Dept.), Bro. Albert, 41 Butler; (Girls' Dept.), Sr. Eleanor Mary, 202 Congress.

67—Sts. Peter and Paul, J. B. Lyle, 71 South 3d; Sr. St. Joseph, 61 South 3d.

68—Queen of All Saints, Rt. Rev. Mgr. J. J. Coan, 300 Vanderbilt av.; (Boys' Dept.), Bro. Aubert, 73 Greene av.; (Girls' Dept.), Sr. Irmina, 292 Washington av.

69—St. Rose of Lima, Jas. McAleese, 269 Parkville av.; (Boys' Dept.), Bro. Matthias, 270 Newkirk av.; (Girls' Dept.), Sr. St. William, 259 Parkville av.

70—Sacred Heart, Thos. Leonard, 41 Adelphi; (Boys' Dept.), Bro. Hilary, 41 Butler; (Girls' Dept.), Sr. M. Michael, 273 Willoughby av.

71—Sacred Hearts of Jesus and Mary, J. Vogel, 503 Hicks; Sr. M. Pauline, 490 Hicks.

72—St. Saviour, Jas. J. Flood, 611 8th av.; Sr. M. Benitia, 590 6th.

73—St. Stanislaus, L. Wysiecki, Humboldt and Driggs av.; Sr. M. Dyonisia, 185 Driggs av.

74—St. Stephen, Very Rev. Mgr. J. Fitzgerald, 108 Carroll; (Boys' Dept.), Bro. Brendan; (Girls' Dept.), Sr. Maria Magdalena, 202 Congress.

75—St. Teresa, Rt. Rev. Mgr. McNamee, V.G., 563 Sterling pl.; Sr. M. Adele, 560 Sterling pl.

76—St. Thomas Aquinas, J. Smyth, 249 9th; Sr. M. Berchmans, 262 9th.

77—Transfiguration, Very Rev. Mgr. M. Maguire, 263 Marcy av.; Sr. M. Stella, 267 Hewes.

78—St. Vincent de Paul, J. F. Geary, 167 North 6th; (Boys' Dept.), Bro. Aidan, 41 Butler; (Girls' Dept.), Sr. St. Neri, 165 North 5th.

79—Visitation, Wm. L. Long, 98 Richard; Sr. Mary Thomas, 96 Visitation pl.

Queens—Grade Schools.

1—St. Adalbert, A. Witkowski, Carter, Elmhurst, L. I.; Sr. M. Erazma, Carter, Elmhurst, L. I.

2—St. Benedict Joseph, Wm. Kerwin, 932 Church; Sr. Francis Joseph, 924 Church, Morris Park, L.I.

3—St. Elizabeth, G. E. Baer, Digby; Sr. M. Damian, O.S.D., Digby, Woodhaven.

4—St. Fidelis, A. Schumack, High; Sr. M. Concordia, High, College Point.

5—St. Francis de Sales, J. M. Foran, Washington av.; Sr. St. George, 216 Beach 130th, Belle Harbor.

6—Holy Child Jesus, T. A. Nummey, 8578 112th; Sr. M. Carmelite, Brandon av., Richmond Hill.

7—Holy Cross, A. Nawrocki, Clinton av.; Sr. M. Rose, 124 Clinton av., Maspeth.

8—St. Joseph, S. Rysiakiewicz, 313 Rockaway rd.; Sr. M. Ildephonse, 331 Rockaway rd., Jamaica.

9—St. Joseph, Peter Henn, 515 Grand av.; Sr. M. Seraphine, O.S.D., 607 Grand av., Long Island City.

10—St. Luke, F. J. Dillon, 138 South 11th av.; Sr. M. Antoinette, O.S.D., 128 South 11th, Whitestone.

11—St. Margaret, John P. Gopp, 74 Pullis av.; Sr. M. Christine, O.S.D., 70 Pullis av., Middle Village.

12—St. Mary, Wm. J. Dunne, 118 5th; Rev. Mother St. Joseph, 120 3rd, Long Island City.

13—St. Mary, Gate of Heaven, P. Vaque, Oxford and Jerome avs.; Sr. Agnes of the Sacred Heart, 1219 McCormick av., Ozone Park.

14—St. Mary, Help of Christians, J. F. Naab, 25 Ramsey; Mother Cajetan, O.S.D., Monroe, Winfield.

15—St. Mary, Star of the Sea, H. F. Farrell, Clark av.; (Boys' Dept.), Bro. Timothy; (Girls' Dept.), Sr. M. Damian, Central av., Far Rockaway.

16—St. Mary Magdalene, John Tinney, Willow pl.; Sr. Florian Marie, O.S.D., Willow pl., Springfield Gardens, L. I.

17—St. Michael, Rt. Rev. Mgr. E. J. Donnelly, 63 Madison av.; Sr. M. Sidonia, Sanford av., Flushing.

18—St. Monica, Rich. Schenck, 42 Washington av.; Sr. Andree Marie, 36 Prospect, Jamaica.

19—Nativity, J. B. Garbottini, Shoe and Leather and Canal, Jamaica; Sr. M. Helen, Canal, Woodhaven.

20—Our Lady of Mt. Carmel, Chas. Gibney, 31 Newtown av.; Sr. M. Maud, 58 Flushing av., Astoria.

21—Our Lady of Sorrows, W. K. Dwyer, Polk av.; Sr. M. Dolorita, 152 Alburtis av., Corona.

22—St. Pancras, Fr. Siegelack, Myrtle av.; Sr. M. Mechtildis, O.S.D., DeBoe pl., Glendale.

23—St. Patrick, J. P. McGinley, 123 Academy; Sr. M. Cornelia, 196 Crescent, L. I. City.

24—Presentation—J. M. Scheffel, 78 Flushing av.; Sr. M. Gabriel, O.S.D., 215 Shelton av., Jamaica.

25—St. Thomas Apostle, A. Klarmann, Syosset and Boyd av.; Sr. M. Rose Gertrude, 460 Benedict av., Woodhaven.

Nassau County—Grade Schools.

1—St. Agnes, P. Quealy, College pl.; Sr M. Petra, O.S.D., College pl., Rockville Centre.

2—St. Boniface, Very Rev. Ignatius Zeller, V.F.; Sr. M. Euphrasia, O.S.D., Elmont, L. I.

3—St Brigid, Wm. F. McGinnis, D.D.; Sr. M. Christina, Westbury.

4—St. Hedwig, F. Wilamowski; Sr. Mary Bridget, Linden, Floral Park, L. I.

5—Holy Ghost, F. Videnz; Sr. M. Martina, O.S.D., New Hyde Park, L. I.

6—St. Ignatius, Lawrence Fuchs, V.F.; Sr. M. Rosarita, O.S.D., Hicksville.

7—St. Joachim, H. C. Jordan, Central av.; Sr. F. Borgia, Central av., Cedarhurst, L. I.

8—St. Patrick, B. J. O'Reilly; Sr. M. Petra, Glen Cove, L. I.

Suffolk County—Grade Schools.

1—St. Andrew, P. L. Rickard; Sr. Marie Dolores, Sag Harbor, L. I.

2—St. Joseph, Jas. H. Casey; Sr. M. Genevieve, Babylon.

3—St. Francis Xavier Academy; Sr. M. Immacuine, East Islip.

4—Our Lady of Perpetual Help, T. E. Farrenkopf; Sr. M. Teresa, O.S.D., Lindenhurst.

Elementary Academy Schools.

1—St. Agnes Seminary; Sr. M. Flavia, 287 Union, Bkln.

2—St. Angela's Hall; Sr. M. Celestine, 292 Washington av., Bkln.

3—St. Francis Xavier Academy; Sr. M. Immaculata, 697 Carroll st., Bkln.

4—St. Joseph's Academy; Sr. Marie Louise, 834 Pacific, Bkln.

5—Our Lady of Victory Academy; Sr. M. Dominic, 149 McDonough, Bkln.

6—Our Lady of Wisdom Academy; Sr. Agnes, 1219 McCormick av., Ozone Park, L. I.

7—Sacred Heart Boarding School; Sr. St. Hilary, Hempstead, L. I.

8—Academy of the Sacred Heart; Mother Basil, Sag Harbor, L. I.

9—Star of the Sea Academy; Sr. St. Germaine, 601 Central av., Far Rockaway.

10—Visitation Academy; Sr. Francis Agnes, Ridge blvd. and 89th, Bkln.

11—Academy of St. Joseph; Sr. M. Loretto, Brentwood, L. I.

Institutional Schools.

1—Angel Guardian Home; Sr. M. Basil, 12th av. and 64th, Bkln.

2—St. Charles Hospital; Sr. Joseph, Port Jefferson, L. I

3—Convent of Mercy; Sr. M. Stanislaus, 273 Willoughby av., Bkln.

4—St. John's Home; Sr. St. Mark, 992 St. Marks av., Bkln.

CATHOLIC EDUCATIONAL SYSTEM—INSTITUTIONAL SCHOOLS—*Continued.*

5—St. John's Protectory; Sr. M. Adelaide, Hicksville, L. I.
6—St. Joseph's Institute for Deaf Mutes; Miss Margaret Moran, 113 Buffalo av., Bkln.
7—St. Joseph's Orphan Asylum; Sr. Miriam Regina, 735 Willoughby av., Bkln.
8—St. Joseph's Home; Sr. Agnes Marie, Flushing, L. I.
9—St. Malachy's Ocean Home; Sr. St. Liguori, Rockaway Park, L. I.
10—St. Mary of the Angels; Sr. Mary Gregory, Syosset, L. I.
11—Nazareth Trade School; Mother M. Cajetana, O.S.D., Farmingdale, L. I.
12—St. Rose Industrial School; Sr. M. Rufina, O.S.D., Melville, L. I.
13—St. Vincent's Home; Sr. M. Honora, O.S.D., Boerum pl., Bkln.

Settlement Schools.

1—Italian Mission; Miss M. C. Maginness, 38 Front, Bkln.

Brooklyn High Schools.

1—St. Agnes; Sr. M. Flavia, 287 Union.
2—St. Aloysius; Sr. M. Cesla, O.S.D., 1817 Stanhope.
3—All Saints; Sr. M. Chrysostom, 23 Thornton.
4—St. Angela's Hall; Sr. M. Celestine, 286 Washington av.
5—St. Augustine (Boys); Bro. Alban, 58 Park pl; (Girls) Sr. M. Evangelista, Sterling pl. and 6th av.
6—St. Barbara (Boys); Bro. Michael, 137 Menahan; (Girls) Sr. M. Catherine, O.S.D., 144 Bleecker.
7—St. Francis Xavier; Sr. M. Immaculata, 697 Carroll.
8—Holy Trinity; Bro. George, 153 Johnson av.
9—St. James (Boys); Bro. Austin, 254 Jay; (Girls) Sr. M. Chrysostom, 250 Jay.
10—St. Joseph's Commercial; Sr. Mary, 342 Bridge.
11—St. Leonard; Bro. Gerard, 138 S. 4th.
12—Mercy Commercial School; Sr. Mary Helena, 176 Taaffe pl.
13—St. Michael (Boys); Bro. John, 306 Warwick; (Girls) Sr. M. Philomena, O.S.D., 625 Liberty av.
14—St. Nicholas; Sr. M. Prudentia, O.S.D., 287 Powers.
15—St. Saviour; Sr. M. Benitia, 590 6th.
16—St. Teresa; Sr. M. Adele, 560 Sterling pl.
17—Visitation; Sr. Francis Agnes, Ridge blvd. and 89th.

High Schools—Queens County.

1—St. Agnes; Sr. M. Concordia, College Pt., L. I.
2—Our Lady of Wisdom; Sr. Agnes, 1219 McCormick av., Ozone Park, L. I.

High Schools—Suffolk County.

1—St. Joseph; Sr. M. Loretto, Brentwood, L. I.

Colleges.

MEN.

1—Brooklyn College; Pres., Rev. Jos. A. Farrell, S.J., 1125 Carroll, Bkln.
2—Cathedral College; Pres., Rev. A. J. Reichert, D.D., Washington and Atlantic avs.
3—St. Francis College; Pres., Rev. Bro. Jarlath, O.S.F., 41 Butler.
4—St. John's College; Pres., Rev. Edw. L. Carey, C.M., 75 Lewis av.

WOMEN.

1—St. Joseph's; Registrar, Sr. Mary Sacred Heart, 245 Clinton av., Bkln.

B. R. T. STRIKE.

On July 16, 1920, Lindley M. Garrison, as receiver of the Brooklyn Rapid Transit System, offered an increase in wages of 10% over the wage scale on Aug. 1, 1919. On July 28 the Committee of Employees, with whom the receiver had made an agreement under date of Dec. 16, 1919, presented demands for the recognition of the Amalgamated Assn. of Street and Electric Railway Employees of America; for the establishment of a closed shop, and wage increases of more than 50% in some cases. The receiver refused to consider any demands tending towards a closed shop on the property and his position was approved by Judge Julius M. Mayer of the U. S. District Court, who appointed the receiver. The Union Committee thereupon appealed to Mayor Hylan, who designated Transit Construction Comr. John H. Delaney to act as mediator. Comr. Delaney held several conferences with the receiver and with the committee, and on Aug. 23 the committee withdrew from discussion the demands for a closed shop. Negotiations between the receiver and the committee were then started, but came to an end when the committee demanded that the receiver and Judge Mayer agree to unlimited arbitration of all financial questions involved in their demands. Judge Mayer declined to abdicate his duty as a judge, although indicating that he would ratify any arbitration award if it were in the financial ability of the receiver to pay it. The committee again appealed to Mayor Hylan and Comr. Delaney and these officials upheld the Court and the receiver. Comr. Delaney in a public statement on Aug. 27, said:

"If a strike ensues, the responsibility will be on the Union leaders and not on the receiver. There is no justification for a strike now. A strike would be for the purpose of establishing a closed shop and complete Union control and not for wages and hours, which could be settled without a strike. Even should a strike be called, no settlement could prevail beyond the financial ability of the receiver to pay."

The Union held a mass meeting on Saturday night, Aug. 28, at which Mayor Hylan spoke and asked the members to defer the strike for one or two weeks to enable him to effect an amicable adjustment of the matter. Early Sunday morning, after the Mayor had left the meeting, a strike was called and immediately put into effect.

The operation of surface lines was completely suspended as a result of the strike for three days. During that period the company organized and trained a force of strike breakers and surface line operation was resumed on Wednesday, Sept. 1, on a small scale. As the men gradually returned to work, the service on the surface lines was extended and within a month was practically normal again.

The operation of the subway and elevated lines was maintained without interruption throughout the entire strike period, although during the first few days it was materially curtailed. During the early days of the strike the public authorities held various meetings and conferences to endeavor to bring it to an end, but without result.

The police handled the strike situation most effectively and promptly suppressed any and all attempts of violence on the part of the strikers. There was little or no disorder incidental to the strike, the most serious incident being the stoning of a Sea Beach train by strikers, causing the death of a passenger, for which act five of the strikers later admitted their guilt and were sentenced to terms in prison. Another incident of the strike was a collision between two surface cars on the Flatbush Av. Line at the Willink Entrance of Prospect Park, resulting in the death of one passenger.

OLD LONG ISLAND MAP.

What is probably the oldest map of the North Shore section of Long Island, including the Flushing and Hempstead sections, in existence, was recently found by George F. Swenson of Flushing while searching among some Colonial records. The title of the map is "A platt of ye sitication of the turns and places on ye westerly end of Long Island to Hempstead." The map was drawn by Col. Hubbard on July 3, 1666, more than two centuries and a half ago. The shore is marked out into much the same divisions as at present. Flushing Bay is found as "Ffushing Bay," while Little Neck Bay was known as "Math Gar Bay." One of the most interesting features of the map is the drawing of a tiny house on the "rever" (now Flushing Creek), which is marked as "Mr. Coes mill house." The building is still standing on the same location, which is now part of Corona.

Rocky Hill road is designated as "Roodwale to Hempstead," while Jamaica ave., which is the artery connecting Flushing with Jamaica, is simply marked "Roode." "Whitestone roode," on the map, has now disappeared, but it is thought that it was the road which formerly ran from Flushing to Whitestone, and from there to College Point along the shore of Powell's Cove.

POLITICAL ORGANIZATIONS.

DEMOCRATIC.

National.

Natl. Dem. Club—617 5th av., Mhtn. 900 mem. J. M. Riehle, Pres.; Wm. H. Jasper, Sec., 617 5th av.

Natl. Dem. League of Clubs—1919. Hdqtrs., Castle Hall Bldg., Indianapolis, Ind. 750,000 mem. J. E. Raker, Pres.; C. R. Cameron, Sec.; F. S. Clark, Treas.

State.

Dem. Editorial Assn. of N. Y. State—F. C. Parsons, Pres., Cortland; A. R. Kessinger, Ch. Ex. Com., Rome.

Brooklyn.

ASSEMBLY DISTRICT CLUBS, HEADQUARTERS AND LEADERS.

1—Seawanhaka—106 Concord. 1,000 mem. John J. Delaney, Pres.; J. J. Quinn, Sec.; J. J. Browne, L.

First A. D. Dem. Assn.—350 Atlantic av. 600 mem. Joseph F. Dooley, Pres.; J. C. McDermott, Sec.; John F. Quayle, L.

2—Kings Highway Dem. Club—1120 Kings Hwy. Jas. Blanchfield, Pres.; G. Morrell, Sec.; Jos. Fennelly, L.

3—Third A. D. Dem. Club—314 Clinton. 1,400 mem. J. E. Dowdell, Pres.; A. J. Farrell, Sec.; James Kane, L.

4—Seneca Club, 130 Taylor. F. V. Kelly, Pres.; A. C. Hall, Sec.; T. J. Drennan, L.

5—Jefferson Club—735 Hancock. 700 mem. H. S. Sullivan, Pres.; A. C. Moran, Sec.; Jas. J. Sexton, L.

6—Sixth A. D. Reg. Dem. Assn.—116 Tompkins av. J. J. Dorman, Pres.; C. W. Jannicky, L.

7—Seventh A. D. Dem. Assn.—589 4th av. J. Howard, Pres.; B. Nolan, Sec.; W. J. Heffernan, L.

8—Eighth A. D. Club—170 Bergen. C. M. Byrne, Pres. and L.

9—Ninth A. D. Reg. Dem. Org.—259 Ovington av. T. F. Wogan, Pres. and L.; T. M. Bradshaw, Sec.

10—Washington Club—241 Prospect pl. J. J. Kney, Pres.; B. F. Underhill, Sec.; J. J. McQuade, L.

11—Andrew Jackson Club—271 Adelphi. T. A. Dempsey, Pres.; W. R. Foley, Sec.; Jos. A. Guider, L.

12—Twelfth A. D. Dem. Club—435 9th. A. Harting, Pres.; H. T. Rogers, Sec.; T. E. Griffin, L.

13—Thirteenth A. D. Reg. Dem. Club—1911. Geo. Lindsay, Pres., 40 Bushwick pl.; Chas. A. Sherlein, Sec., 529 Grand.

14—Fourteenth A. D. Dem. Club—267 Bedford av. 2,500 mem. J. T. Hagan, Sec., 64 Grand; D. J. Carroll, L.

15—Reg. Dem. Org. of 15th A. D.—776 Manhattan av. J. Bulger, Pres.; C. Conlon, Fin. Sec.; J. A. McQuade, L.

15—Ladies' Reg. Dem.—Miss M. McQuade, Pres.; Mrs. P. Knoot, Sec.; Miss M. O'Connor, L.

United Dem. Club—60 mem. 1918. D. C. Ruth, Pres.; J. F. Duhamel, Sec., 203 Bay 28th.

16—White House Dem. Club—11 Church av. Chas. R. Ward, L.

17—Wigwam—590 Gates av. J. L. Shea, Pres.; J. J. Leonard, Rec. Sec.; P. B. Hanson, L.

18—Madison Club—922 St. Marks av. A. S. Somers, Pres.; T. O'Shea, Sec.; J. H. McCooey, L.

19—Nineteenth A. D. Dem. Assn.—24 Jefferson. August Hasenflug, Pres.; H. Kranz, Sec.; R. Hasenflug, L.

20—Twentieth A. D. Reg. Dem. Org.—1155 Bushwick av. 1,500 mem. J. W. Tuomey, Sec.; W. F. Delaney, L.

21—Flatbush Dem. Club—830 Flatbush av. Chas. H. Fuller, Pres.; J. Abel, Cor. Sec.; H. Hesterberg, L.

22—Twenty-second A. D. Dem. Club—179 Hendrix. Chas. E. Russell, Pres.; R. W. Jones, Sec.; J. P. Sinnott, L.

23—A. D. Co. Reg. Dem. Club—1120 Herkimer. 2,200 mem. H. Shorenstein, L. N. J. Hickey, Pres.; A. J. Man, Sec.

OTHER DEMOCRATIC ORGANIZATIONS.

Andrew Jackson Club of 20th A. D.—429 Central av. F. A. Miller, Pres.; L. Kroner, Sec.

Bkln. Dem. Club—1888. Johnston Bldg. 800 mem. H. B. Hammond, Pres.; Emil J. Pettinato, Sec. and Treas., 5711 17th av.

Brownsville Dem. Star Club—357 Rockaway av. Dr. L. Greenebaum, Pres.; S. L. Silverstein, Sec.

Colonial Dem. Club 13th A. D.—Grand and Graham av. J. J. Lennon, Pres.; T. W. A. Crowe, Sec.

Downtown Dem. Club—1918. 26 Court. Miss Sarah Stephenson, Pres.; Mrs. M. F. Merchant, Sec.

E. D. Dem. Club—38 Throop av. Wm. Hawley, Pres.; P. M. Koorse, Fin. Sec.; H. Heyman, Treas.

Eighth Ward Dem. Club—294 28th. P. H. Malone, Pres.; John Nichols, Sec., 414 33d.

Hannibal Dem. Club—1910. 1,400 mem. R. L. Perry, Pres., 875 Fulton.

Jefferson (11th A. D.)—1914. 398 Franklin av. Geo. T. Nichols, Pres.; J. A. Potts, Sec.

Jefferson—1876. 136 Greenpoint av. 1,500 mem. T. A. O'Connor, Pres.; Wm. Craig, Sec.

Juanita Dem. Club—271 Adelphi. 400 mem. Chas. J. Healy, Pres.; Geo. D. Wilson, Sec.

Kings Co. Dem. Women's Forum—1919. 5 Court sq. Mrs. S. McC. Minsterer, Pres.; Mrs. Laura Mulcaire, Sec.

Kings Highway Dem. Club—1634 E. 15th. Jas. A. Blanchfield, Pres.; Jno. Savarese, Sec.; John E. Stoddard, Treas., 1654 E. 15th.

Langan Club (22d A. D.)—84 Williams av. S. Silsbiger, Pres.; G. F. Young, Sec.

Lawrence F. Carroll Assn.—1878. 220 Grand. 1,500 mem. Daniel J. Donovan, Pres.; Wm. Dermody, Sec.

Metropolitan Dem. Club—1910. 1516 Metropolitan av. H. Ringe, Pres.; J. Doster, Sec.

Michael F. Luby Dem. Club—1416 Gates av. R. Werbeck, Pres.; H. Doyle, Sec.

Pontiac Club—1915. 252 President. 850 mem. E. R. Judge, Pres.; J. J. Mullady, Sec., 95 Luquer.

P. H. McCarren Dem. Club—1919. 263 So. 1st. 350 mem. Phil Casidy, Ch., Sim. Barene, Sec.

Reg. Dem. League 23d A. D.—1905. 1,630 mem. 403 Sutter av. J. I. Gottlieb, Pres.; A. Stein, Sec.

Reg. United Colored Democracy of Kings Co. (Inc.)—1908. 36 St. Felix. 350 mem. O. W. Fulcher, Pres.; Emory Jones, Sec.

Seymour Club—163 Bedford av. 1,150 mem. J. H. Tully, Pres.; J. J. Collins, Sec.

Sheepshead Bay Reg. Dem. Assn., Inc., Union Club House, E. 16th and Av. Z. C. Boyle, Pres.; Miss Grace McKeon, Sec.

Sixteenth A. D. Coney Island Dem. Reg. Org.—120 Bay 25th. C. Furgueson, Pres.; J. Avitable, Sec., 2868 W. 14th, Coney Island.

Third Ward Young Men's Dem. Club—1890. 350 Atlantic av. 100 mem. M. J. O'Brien, Pres.; J. P. Carroll, Sec., 189 Montague.

Tiger Head Assn.—427 Wilson av. 125 mem. J. J. Campbell, Pres.; A. Baum, Sec.

Twenty-first A. D. Dem. Club—1510 Flatbush av. P. J. Sullivan, Pres.; P. P. Damm, Sec.

Twenty-second Ward Dem. Assn.—341 9th. 300 mem. J. E. Collins, Pres.; W. J. Conklin, Sec.

Twenty-third A. D. Women's Dem. Org. 1231 Herkimer. Mrs. Laura Mulcaire, Pres.

Woodrow Wilson Dem. Club, 6th A. D.—162 Vernon av. S. J. Lagusker, Pres.; Jacob Levy, Sec.

Women's Reg. Dem. Assn. of 2d A. D.—1917. 1634 E. 15th. Mary A. Corbett, Pres.; Mrs. Bridget Bryan, Sec.

Wyandance Dem. Club (15th A. D.)—157 Nassau av. H. Johnson, Pres.; J. J. O'Neill, Fin. Sec., 53 Diamond.

Young Men's Dem. League of Kings Co.—J. J. F. Doyle, Pres., 246 Sackett, Dr. J. J. Wagner, Sec., 28 7th av.

Young Women's Dem. League of Kings Co.—182-188 Flatbush av. Mrs. Wm. P. Mulry, Sec., 283 Parkside av.

Manhattan.

ASSEMBLY DISTRICT CLUBS, HEADQUARTERS AND LEADERS.

1—Huron Club, 590 Broome. D. E. Finn, L.

Downtown Tammany Club, 59 Madison. T. F Foley, L.

2—Tammany Club, 263 Grand. M. S. Levine, L.

T. D. Sullivan Assn., 161 Bowery. H. C. Perry, L.

3—Tammany Club, 303 W. 12th. C. W. Culkin, L.; H. P. Dausch, Sec.

Horatio Seymour Tammany Club, 267 W. 25th. F. J. Goodwin, L.; Wm. L. Kavanagh, Sec.

Tammany Club, 271 W. 33d. Wm. Dalton, L.

4—J. F. Ahearn Assn., 290 E. B'way. J. Carroll, Pres.; O. McGinty, Sec.; J. F. Ahearn, L.

Tammany Club, 290 E. B'way. P. J. Scully, L.

5—Tammany Club, 315 W. 42d. P. J. Dooling, L.; J. J. Burke, Sec.

POLITICAL ORGANIZATIONS—DEMOCRATIC—MANHATTAN—*Continued.*

The McManus Assn., 728 9th av. T. J. McManus, L.; T. F. McGrath, Sec.; Mrs. B. McCarthy, L.
J. F. Curry Assn., 413 W. 57th. J. F. Curry, L.
6—Jefferson Club, 247 7th. David Lazarus, L.
7—Amsterdam Dem. Club, 131 W. 64th. J. J. Hagan L.; M. Ingram, Sec.
8—Tammany Club, 67 St. Marks pl. S. Goldenkrans and F. Bauman, Lds.; S. Salinger, Sec.
9—Tamarora Club, 133 W. 97th. Mrs. P. Lau, L.; Wm. Farrell, Pres.; W. H. Rocholl, Sec.
10—Tammany Club, 129 W. 14th. Geo. W. Olvany, L.
Tammany Club (Tonkawa Club), 109 W. 47th. G. L. Donnellan, L.
Iroquois Club, 139 W. 14th. G. W. Olvany, Pres.
11—Monongahela Dem. Club, 293 Manhattan av. J. J. Hines, L.
12—Anawanda Club, 345 2d av. C. F. Murphy, L.; Jerome Craig, Sec.
Tammany Central Assn., 226 E. 32d. M. J. Cruise, L., and Anna Montgomery, L.
Tammany Club, 790 3d av. J. C. McTigue, Pres.; J. J. McQuade, Sec.; E. F. Boyle, L.
13—Shenandoah Club, 327 W. 126th. J. H. O'Connell, L.
14—Wyandot Club, 232 E. 58th. J. V. Coggey, L.
Tammany Club, 222 E. 71st. Wm. C. Blaney, L.
15—Osceola Club—1036 Park av. J. T. Mahoney, L.
16—Tammany Club, 326 E. 86th. M. Cosgrove, L.
17—Wichita Club, 1523 Madison av. N. Burkan, L.
Tammany Club, 46 W. 115th. S. Marx, L.
18—Tammany Club, 1600 Lexington av. J. J. Dietz, L.; E. T. Tyrrell, Sec.
Pocasset Club, 208 E. 116th. H. W. Hubbard, L.; E. J. Kelly, Sec.
19—Cayuga Club, 2043 7th av. Wm. Allen, Miss A. Mathews, Lds.
20-Tammany Club, 2310 3d av. P. E. Nagle, L.
Mohawk Club, 2310 3d av. F. J. Hendrick, K. Keely, Lds.
21—Tammany Club, 728 St. Nicholas av. E. P. Holahan, L.
22—Wm. L. Marcy Tammany Assn.—533 W. 148th. J. J. F. Mulcahy, Pres.; J. P. Burns, Sec.
23—Minqua Club, 1389 St. Nicholas av. J. Mara, L.; A. Codding, Sec.

Bronx.

1—Reg. Dem. Org., 312 St. Anns av. J. F. Geragnty, L.
2—Samoset Dem. Club, 2d Elec. Dist., 384 E. 155th. H. Bruckner, Pres.; E. A. Miller, L.
3—P. J. Kane Dem. Club, 750 Prospect av. P. J. Kane, L., Exec. Mem.
4—Jackson Dem. Club, 1175 Boston rd. S. A. Nugent, L.
5—Star Dem. Club—957 Whitlock av., John J. Daly, L.
6—Cheppewa Club, 1447 Ferris pl., T. H. O'Neil, L.
7—A. H. Murphy Assn., 862 Tremont av. A. H. Murphy, L.
8—North End Dem. Club, 195th and Webster av. C. A. Buckley, L.; J. F. Condon, Pres.
9—Tackamuk Club, 447 E. 167th. A. H. L'ebenau, L.

OTHER DEMOCRATIC ORGANIZATIONS.

Cherokee Club (Tammany Hall)—1879. 334 E. 79th. 1,600 mem. S. J. Meagher, Pres.; T. O'Sullivan, Sec.; S. Ruddy, L.
City Democracy—1917. 30 E. 42d. M. W. Littleton, Ch.
Delaware Club—1894. 222 E. 71st. 650 mem. M. J. Delehanty, Pres.; R. J. Maloney, Cor. Sec.
Miami Club of 18th A. D. (South)—1901. 1451 Lexington av. 500 mem. John J. McCarthy, Jr., Pres.; E. T. Tyrell, Sec.
N. Y. Dem. League of Clubs—P. Belmont, Pres.; E. O. Towne, Sec., 1402 B'way, Mhtn.
Tammany Hall Dem.—145 E. 14th. David H. Knott, Ch.; T. F. Smith, Sec.
Tammany Soc.—1789. 145 E. 14th. 2,000 mem. J. R. Voorhis, Gd. Sachem; T. F. Smith, Sec.
Waupanoag Dem. Club—2538 3d av., Bronx. F. C. Humphrys, L.

Queens.

Amerind Dem. Club of Elmhurst—1912. 800 mem. M. O. Smedley, Pres.; Chas. M. McWilliams, Sec., Elmhurst.
Andrew Jackson Dem. Club of 4th Ward of Queens, Union and Kimball avs., Richmond Hill. Thos. Doherty, Pres.; G. Van Tussenbrock, Jr., Sec., Woodhaven.
Fourth A. D. Dem. Club—412 Fulton, Jamaica. J. R. Higgins, Pres.; A. Lopard, Sec.
Hebrew Ind. Dem. Club—1899. L. I. City. 172 mem. F. A. Simons, Pres.; M. Hirshthal, Sec., 191 Main, Astoria.
Hillcrest Dem. Club of Jamaica—L. T. Gresser, Pres.; H. J. Stemmann, Sec., 69 Gilbert, Jamaica.
Jefferson Dem. Club—1913. M. J. Lally, Sec., 8 Beach 91st, Rockaway Beach.
North Side Dem. Assn.—1,000 mem. Cor. Kingsland and Way avs.
Corona. James Butler, Pres.; Ed. Jester, 69 Alburtes av., Corona, Sec.
Powhatan Dem. Club—1906. 332 11th av., L. I. City. 250 mem. Chas. Fredericks, Pres.; A. G. Fries, Sec., 140 15th av., L. I. City.
Young Men's Dem. Club of Flushing—1909. 200 mem. J. H. Nix, Pres.; J. McGrath, Sec.

REPUBLICAN.

National.

League of Rep. State Clubs—Washington, D. C. E. F. Colladay, Pres.; Wm. H. Estey, Cor. Sec.
Natl. Rep. League—John Hays Hammond, Pres.; W. B. Brewster, Sec.; D. B. Atherton, Treas., 2 Rector, Mhtn.
Natl. Rep. College League—89 State, Boston, Mass. 314 clubs, 15 depts. 100,000 mem. A. E. Lunt, Harvard Uni., Pres.
Natl. Women's Rep. Assn.—105 W. 40th Mhtn. Miss H. V. Boswell, Pres.; Miss Mary Wood, Sec., 400 Riverside Drive, Mhtn.

State.

Rep. Editorial Assn., State of N. Y.—1894. 150 mem.
Rep. League of Clubs—1902. Woolworth Bldg., Mhtn. 93,000 mem. 277 clubs, assns., minor leagues, etc. J. A. Stewart, Pres.; C. M. Turner, Sec., Bkln.

Brooklyn.

ASSEMBLY DISTRICT CLUBS, HEADQUARTERS AND LEADERS.

1—First A. D. Rep. Club, 127 Remsen. D. H. Ralston, L.; H. O. Barmore, Pres.; O. A. Eberle, Jr., Sec.
2—Second A. D. Rep. League, Inc. M. B. Campbell, L.
3—Sixth Ward Rep. Club, 105 Rapelyea. 1899. 200 mem. A. De Martini, Pres.; F. Kretsch, Sec.; R. H. Laimbeer, Jr., L.
4—Fourth A. D. Rep. Club, 590 Bedford av. S. Engel, Pres.; W. H. Bradford, Sec.; J. S. Gaynor, L.
5—Kings Co. Rep. Club, 202 Patchen av. T. McCann, Pres.; P. M. Dow, Sec.; C. G. C. Lockwood, L.
6—Sixth A. D. Rep. Club, 44 Sumner av. J. Diemer, L.; C. S. Amsel, Sec.
7—Seventh A. D. Rep. Club, 425 50th. C. S. Devoy, L.; J. H. Osborn, Sec., 459 63d.
8—Federal Rep. Club, 318 Union. E. O. Brandes, Pres.; J. Brenner, L.; A. D. Stiles, Sec.
9—Ninth A. D. Rep. Club, 7604 4th av. W. H. Eagleson, Pres.; J. F. Fanning, Sec.; C. S. Warbasse, L., 131 76th.
10—Tenth A. D. Rep. Club, 175 S. Oxford. C. F. Murphy, Pres and L.; A. Sebring, Sec.
11—Eleventh A. D. Rep. Hdqtrs., 352 Greene av. A. E. Vass, L.; John Drescher, Pres.; F. V. S. Hallenbeck, Sec.
12—Twelfth A. D. Rep. Club, 409 9th. J. E. Brady, Pres.; J. W. Mackay, Sec.; J. T. Rafferty, L.
13—Thirteenth A. D. Rep. Club, 247 Mhtn. av., J. D. Moore, L.; J. Skelton, Pres.; W. Haits, Sec.
14—Fourteenth A. D. Rep. Club, 356 Bedford av., G. A. Owens, L.; A. J. Joa, Pres.; W. H. Knapp, Sec.
15—Alpha Rep. Club, 138 Nassau av. R. Wright, Exec. Committeeman, L.; J. M. Manee, Pres.; A. B. Gilmor, Sec.
16—Sixteenth A. D. Rep. Club, 8739 20th av. P. S. Seery, Pres.; D. Manezon, Sec.; F. Oppikofer, L.
17—Invincible Club, 73 Herkimer. L. M. Swasey, Pres. & L.; E. C. Chapman, Sec.
18—Eighteenth A. D. Rep. Club, 2431 Church av. F. J. H. Kracke, L.; J. A. Hilton, Pres.; Walter F. Clayton, Sec.
19—Nineteenth A. D. Rep. Club, 608 Hart. 800 mem. J. Bartscherer, L.; J. T. Moehringer, Pres.; B. T. Westervelt, Sec., 105 Troutman.
20—Unity Rep. Club, cor. Bushwick and Gates avs. 350 mem. H. C. Glore, Pres.; C. Winklehaus, 1041 Bushwick av., Sec.; W. Schnitzspan, L.

POLITICAL ORGANIZATIONS—REPUBLICAN—BROOKLYN—*Continued.*

21—21st A. D. Rep. Club, 2431 Church av. F. J. H. Kraesle, L.

22—Twenty-second A. D. Rep. Club, 236 Barbey. J. A. Livingston, L.; C. J. Bode, Pres.; W. S. Tuley, Sec.

23—Republican Club of the 23d A. D., 1108 Herkimer, E. J. Brown, Pres.; W. D. Ludden, L.; A. Bilewicz, Sec.

OTHER REPUBLICAN ORGANIZATIONS.

Bkln. Young Rep. Club—Johnston Bldg. 500 mem. E. H. Wilson, Pres.; F. A. Cottrell, Sec.

Bushwick Rep. Club—1920. 425 Wilson av. 460 mem. G. T. Smith, Pres.; J. E. McGovern, Sec., 1364 Gates av.

Columbus Rep. Club—1920. 210 Carroll. H. Naciarone, Pres.

Congress Club of Kings Co.—1900. 600 mem. 586 Bedford av. Geo. Stark, Pres.; Thos. W. Christy, Sec., 167 Taylor.

Cypress Hills Rep. Club—71 Lincoln av. Wm. Perry, Pres.; Frank Weber, 143 Nicholas av.

Eagle Rep. Club (23d A. D.)—1905. 353 Rockaway av. 750 mem. M. Snyder, Pres.; Alex. Bilewicz, 1545 St. Marks av., Sec.

E. N. Y. Rep. Club—800 Sutter av. I. M. Lerner, Pres.; J. Levinson, Sec.

Flatbush Rep. League of the 16th and 2d A. D.—W. K. Van Meter, Pres., 1830 E. 2d.; A. Firman, Sec., 1403 Av. P.

Italian-American Rep. Club of 19th A. D.—312 Melrose. 200 mem. J. Vidone, Pres.; J. Bertolino, Sec.

John J. Scully, Rep. Club (Inc.)—1907. 910 Bergen. Wm. Macauley, Pres., 809 Classon av.; Alex. H. White, Sec., 685 Sterling pl.

20th A. D. Reg. Rep. Club, Inc.—1903. 62 Woodbine. 600 mem. R. E. Weber, Pres.; J. Konz, Sec.

Original Woman's Rep. Club—1893. 50 mem. Mrs. K. M. Bostwick, Pres.; Mrs. W. W. Court, Sec., 405 Park pl.

Logan Club—1893. 292 Flatbush av. W. H. Tappey, Pres., 422 1st; J. Dawson, Sec.

Prospect Hill Rep. Club (12th A. D.)—1902. 150 mem. T. O. Grills, Pres.; Chas. Herter, Sec., 422 54th.

Thirteenth A. D. Rep. Club—1896. 247 Manhattan av. 400 mem. J. Skelton, Pres.; Wm. F. Haitg, Sec., 156 Leonard; J. D. Moore, Ex. Me n.

Twelfth A. D. Women's Rep. Club—1919. 7th av. and 9th. Miss Bertha Irish, Pres.; A. L. Kinudsen.

Twentieth A. D. Women's Rep. Club. Mrs. Lillian Finch, Pres.

Twenty-eighth Ward Rep. Club, Inc.—1897. 637 Knickerbocker av. 360 mem. Henry Werner, Pres.; Theo. Hilderbrandt, Sec., 1520 Putnam av.

Woman's Rep. Union League—1896. 60 mem. Mrs. C. W. Fisk, Pres., 67 Pros., E. Orange, N. J.; Mrs. Herbert Taylor, Sec., 8544 101st, Richmond Hill.

Young Men's Rep. League—2431 Church av. L. Silk, Pres.; D. L. Nogel, Sec.-Treas., 373 Lincoln rd.

Manhattan.

ASSEMBLY DISTRICT CLUBS, HEADQUARTERS AND LEADERS.

1—(W. Dist.) Reg. Rep. Club, 32 Macdougal. W. G. Rose, L.; R. Petrocelli, Sec.

2—(W. Dist.) Reg. Rep. Club, 32 Macdougal. A. Dalessandro, L.

(Middle Dist.) Reg. Rep. Club, 233 Lafayette. J. E. March, Pres.; Thos. J. Barrymore, Sec.

Lincoln League Reg. Rep. Club, 274 Grand. Jacob Meyer, Sec., 242 Grand.

3—(Middle Dist.) Rep. Club, 269 8th av. B. F. Fox, L.; H. H. Brownlee, Pres.; C. Conlin, Sec.

(N. Dist.) Rep. Club, 265 W. 34th. M. H. Blake, L.; D. Morton, Pres.; F. J. Kennon, Sec.

Rep. Club, 318 W. 14th. R. M. Greenbank, Pres.; Chas. E. Prescott, Sec.

4—Fourth A. D. Rep. Club, 436 Grand. Alex. Wolf, L., 299 B'way.

5—(S. Dist.) Active Rep. Club, 670 8th av. H. W. Beyer, L.; R. Dailey, Sec.

(N. Dist.) Rep. Club, 467 W. 57th. 500 mem. A. P. Ludden, L.; W. Hahn, Pres.; Jennie C. Wilson, Sec.

6—Federal Club, 44 Av. C. S. S. Koenig, L.; G. Tischler, Sec.

7—Rep. Org. Club, 2228 B'way. A. J. Berwin, L. N. R. Becker, Pres.; J. J. Griffin, Sec.

8—Progress Rep. Club, 310 E. 14th. J. Samuel, L.; J. Kostman, Sec.

9—Riverside Rep. Club. 157 W. 97th. Chas. E. Heydt, L.; S. Marks, Pres.; Wm. G. Bragg, Sec.

10—Reg. Rep. Club, 8 W. 28th. A. P. Nevin, Pres.; A. M. Mauder, Sec.

11—Hamilton Rep. Club, 550 W. 113th. R. P. Levis, L.; Chas. Griffiths, Pres.; L. W. Bond, Fin. Sec.

12—(S. Dist.) Wm. Henkel Rep Club, 383 3d av. Dennis J. Hanlon, Pres.; John T. Guy, Sec.; Wm. Henkel, L.

(Middle) East Side Rep. Club, 230 E. 36th. J. S. Shea, L.; O. A. Witte, Sec.

(N. Dist.) Rep. Club, 409 E. 51st. C. K. Lexow, L.; Edw. Wilson, Sec.

13—Reg. Rep. Club, 824 St. Nicholas av. V. J. Hahn, L.

14—(S. Dist.) Ivy Club, 324 E. 72d. J. Pabian, L.; T. Mallee, Sec.

(N. Dist.) Reg. Rep. Club, 324 E. 72d. H. Hoffman, L.

15—Rep. Club, 1041 Madison av. W. Chilvers, L.; S. Berger, Pres.; A. Mandelbaum, Sec., 78 E. 94th.

16—(S. Dist.) Rep. Union, 308 E. 79th. C. W. Ferry, Pres.; C. A. Schenck, Sec.; Wm. C. Hecht, Jr., Ex. Mem.

17—(S. Dist.) Rep. Club, 1664 Madison av. S. Krulewitch, L.

(N. Dist.) Liberty Rep. Club, 69 W. 113th. R. Oppenheim, L.

18—(N. Dist.) Rep. Club, 158 E. 116th. Chas. B. Largy, L.

(Middle West) South Union Rep. Club, 1536 Madison av. B. Schwartz, Pres. and L.; J. W. Mathias, Sec.

(S. Dist.) Reg. Rep. Club, 1707 3d av. E. S. Berce, L.

19—Central Rep. Club, 23 W. 124th. J. J. Lyons, L.

20—Rep. Club, 107 E. 125th. F. K. Bowers, L.; C. H. Wheelock, Pres.; Mario Di Pierra, Sec.

21—Mhtn. Rep. Club, 474 W. 141st. R. S. Conklin, L.; Wm. V. Goldie, Pres.; J. F. Heim, Sec.

22—Reg. Rep. Club, 1723 Amsterdam av. and 135 Hamilton pl. J. A. Bolles, L. and Pres.; S. Kirschner, Sec.

23—Reg. Rep. Org., 573 W. 181st. C. H. Woodward, L.

Bronx.

(Executive Districts).

1—North Side Rep. Club, 2661 3d av. Wm. H. Ten Eyck, L.; B. Hahn, Pres.; G. Tarrant, Sec.

2—(2d Dist.) John Hay Rep. Club, 412 E. Tremont av. P. Wynne, L.

4—Pioneer Rep. Club, 1324 Franklin av. E. W. Bradbury, L.; Chas. E. Singer, Pres.; H. Isaacs, Sec.

5—Prospect Rep. Club, 892 Prospect av. H. B. Harris, L.

6—Bronx Rep. Club, 3549 Willett av. J. J. Knewitz, L.

7—Tremont Rep. Club, 800 E. Tremont av. M. J. Reagan, L. C. E. Buchner, Pres.; M. Rosenblum, Sec.

8—Park Rep. Club, 4778 3d av. T. W. Whittle, L..; H. K. Davis, Pres.; T. J. Casey, Sec.

9—Hunt's Point Rep. Club, 1029 E. 163d. Samuel J. Joseph, L.

10—Bronx County Rep. Club, 152d and Melrose av. Chas. Rathfelder, L.

OTHER REPUBLICAN ORGANIZATIONS.

Central Rep. Club—23 W. 124th. 890 mem. A. B. Murtha, Pres.; L. Simon, Sec., 209 W. 118th.

East Side Rep. Club—1899. 230 E. 36th. 300 mem. D. Thompson, Pres.; O. A. Witte, Sec.; J. S. Shea, L.

Harlem Rep. Club—1887. 23 W. 124th. 100 mem. R. H. Hardy, Pres.; A. Bauer, Sec.

Hell Gate Rep. Club—1891. 344 E. 86th. 400 mem. A. O. Neal, Pres.; W. Nadolny, Sec.

Hungarian Rep. Club of the City of N. Y.—1896. 138 W. 119th. 615 mem. Marcus Helfand, Pres.; Dr. Jos. Brumiller, Sec.

Loyal Rep. Club—233 Lafayette, 52 mem. Jas. E. March, Pres.; Jesse S. C. Spota, Sec.

North Side Rep. Club—1888. 3661-63 3d av. 540 mem. B. Hahn, Pres.; T. J. Miley, Jr., Sec., 349 E. 142d.

POLITICAL ORGANIZATIONS—REPUBLICAN—*Continued.*

Patriotic Rep. Club of N. Y.—1894. 185 E. 79th. 300 mem. J. Oppenheimer, Pres., 173 E. 79th; A. Berger, Sec.

Progress Rep. Club—1889. 310 E. 14th. 700 mem. J. Kostman, Pres.; N. Friedman, Sec.

Natl. Rep. Club, Inc.—1879. 54 W. 40th. 1,962 mem. Chas. D. Hilles, Pres.; Oscar W. Shrhom, Sec.

U. S. Grant Rep. Club—1895. 133 Bowery. 386 mem. John Cassidy, Pres.; J. Moran, Sec., 133 Bowery.

West Side Club—1888. 270 W. 84th. 300 mem. F. A. Baggs, Pres.; C. H. Doud, Sec.

Woman's Rep. Club—Delmonico's. 1899. 227 mem. Mrs. J. G. Wentz, Pres.; Mrs. H. S. Schley, Sec., 24 W. 54th.

Queens.

Jamaica Rep. Club—19 Union Hall. J. A. Green, Pres.; A. S. Westervelt, Sec.

Rep. Club of Queens Co.—1908. 400 mem. F. Walter, Pres.; H. Van Alst, Sec., 522 Jamaica av., L. I. C.

Richmond Hill Rep. Club—1901. 350 mem. H. Vollmen, Jr., Pres.; W. T. Edgerton, Sec., 528 Birch, Richmond Hill.

Roosevelt Rep. Club of Queens—5th A. D. C. N. Neppell, Pres.; R. M. Murdock, Sec.

Third E. D. Rep. Club (4th A. D.)—B'way and Ocean av. G. Livett, Pres.; J. T. Case, Sec., 1145 Hatch av., Ozone Park.

Third Ward Rep. Club—1898. Flushing. 250 mem. E. C. Hunt, Pres.; Mrs. L. Sorenson, Sec.

Wyckoff Rep. Club—586 Woodward av., Ridgewood Hgts. H. Vogt, Pres.; O. J. Schumacher, Sec.

Richmond.

Reg. Rep. Org.—Tompkinsville. J. P. Thompson, Ch.; T. A. Braniff, Sec., Tompkinsville, S. I.

MISCELLANEOUS.

National and State.

Amer. Prot. Tariff League—1888. 339 B'way, Mhtn. 775 mem. A. H. Heisey, Pres.; W. F. Wakeman, Sec. and Treas., 339 B'way, Mhtn.

Anti-Imperialist League—1898. M. Storey, Pres.; D. G. Harkins, Jr., Treas., 10 Tremont, Boston, Mass.; E. Winslow, Sec., 202 Prospect, New Haven, Conn.

Women's Natl. Single Tax League—(See Miscell. Soc., Natl.)

The Committee of Forty-eight—15 E. 40th, Mhtn. For a conference of Liberal.; J. A. H. Hopkins, Ch., Morristown, N. J.; J. W. McConaghy, V.-Ch., Greenwich, Conn.; Allen McCurdy, Sec.; Chas. H. Ingersoll, Treas., 315 4th av.

Brooklyn.

Citizens' Union—(See Mhtn.)

Corridor Club—348 Fulton. 150 mem. T. J. Dody, Pres., 303 Clermont av.; Ed F. Black, Sec.

Citizens' Union (20th A. D.)—G. W. Ernest, Ch., 450 Evergreen av.

Citizens' League of 22d Assem. Dist.—1891. 996 Blake av. 1,200 mem. J. Hessel, Ex. mem.; J. Jena, Sec., 198 Hendrix.

Flatbush Women's Club—Mrs. Eliz. Osborne, Pres., 235 Ocean P'kway.

Independent Citizens' League of Nations Assn. of Bkln—1920. 8 Nevins. H. B. Hammond, Pres.; Mary E. Bittner, Sec.; H. Healy, Treas.

Manhattan and Bronx.

Bronx County Club—1912. 1223 Tinton av. E. A. Martin, Pres.; C. T. Rudershausen, Sec.

Citizens' Union—1897. 41 Park Row. Wm. Jay Schieffelin, Ch.; Walter T. Arndt, Sec.; Sam. A. Lewisohn, Treas.; Leonard M. Wallstein, Counsel.

Four by Four Club—1920. 120 W. 23d. 1,000 mem. Capt. Rainsford, Pres.; Alice McK. Kelly, Sec.

Huron Club—590 Broome. 800 mem. L. H. Harison, Pres.; James O'Hara, Sec. 45 King.

Ind. Citizens' League—1901. 5,500 mem. Dr. Cherurg, Pres.; R. L. Cherurg, Sec., 39 St. Marks pl., Mhtn.

Ind. Club of the West Side—114 mem. A. P. W. Seaman, Pres.; H. L. Stein, Sec., 176 W. 81st.

Queens.

Good Citizenship League—117 Sanford av., Flushing. 268 mem. Mrs. R. Phillips, Pres.; Mrs. W. J. Hamilton, Sec., 215 So. Parsons av.

HISTORY OF THE STRUGGLE FOR WOMAN SUFFRAGE.

Colonial Period—Under several Colonial governments women voted.

At the time of American Revolution—Women demanded to be included in Government. Abigail Adams wrote to her husband, John Adams: "If women are not represented in this new republic, there will be another revolution."

In 1848—Woman's Rights Convention at Seneca Falls, N. Y., arranged by Lucretia Mott and Elizabeth Cady Stanton, the first big suffrage demonstration in this country.

From 1848 to Civil War—Efforts made to have State laws altered to include women. Susan B. Anthony became a leader in the movement for political freedom during this period.

At the close of Civil War—Suffragists attempted to secure an interpretation of the 14th and 15th Amendments that would permit women to vote.

In 1872—Miss Anthony made the test of voting at the polls. She was arrested, refused to pay her fine, but was never jailed.

In 1875—Miss Anthony drafted the Woman Suffrage Amendment, which reads: "The right of citizens of the United States to vote shall not be denied or abridged by the United States or by any State on account of sex."

In 1878—The amendment introduced in Senate by Senator Sargent of California.

State campaigns—Side by side with the effort to secure Federal action, the State campaigns begun in 1848 were continued. Miss Anthony always advocated securing suffrage by Federal action and protested against the necessity of laborious State campaigns. By the end of 1912 women had won the right to vote in 9 States: Wyoming (1869); Colorado, Utah and Idaho (1894); Washington (1910); California (1911), and Kansas, Arizona and Oregon (1912). In 1913 the women of Illinois won State and Presidential suffrage. In 1914 the women of Montana and Nevada were enfranchised. In 1917 the women of New York, in 1918 the women of Oklahoma, South Dakota and Michigan obtained full suffrage, and in 1919 Iowa, Tenn., Wis., Ind., Maine, Minn. and Mo. granted Presidential suffrage.

When the National Woman's Party, then called the Congressional Union, was organized in 1913 to concentrate on a campaign for Federal amendment, no action or even debate on the Federal Amendment had taken place in Congress since 1887. Politicians were opposed and political party platforms silent about the amendment. Within seven years every political party had included in its platform an equal suffrage plank. President Wilson had publicly appealed for the passage of the amendment as "a vitally necessary war measure," and the amendment had been passed by both houses of Congress and ratified by 36 States.

SUGAR EXPORTATION.

In 1914 the United States exported 195,205 tons of granulated sugar; in 1915, 481,787 tons; in 1916, 788,326 tons; in 1917, 505,397 tons; in 1918, 203,615 tons, and in 1919, 737,849 tons. During the years 1915, 1916, 1917, 1918 and 1919 a great portion of the sugar listed as exportation was sugar bought by the British Government from the planters and shipped to the United States to be refined on a toll basis. This sugar, therefore, cannot be classed as American owned or traded sugar. This sugar was owned and bought by England and France.

NEW REAL ESTATE VALUES FOR ALL BOROS.

Borough.	1921.	1920.
Brooklyn	$2,348,200,561	$1,397,760,621
Manhattan	5,620,873,155	4,024,806,521
Bronx	825,777,396	727,700,921
Queens	683,630,885	608,466,970
Richmond	123,535,470	107,387,350
Totals	$9,608,017,467	$8,266,122,383

The first State Federation of women's clubs was organized in Maine, in 1892.

LOCAL, STATE AND NATIONAL POLITICAL COMMITTEES.

DEMOCRATIC.

Democratic County Committee of Kings County.

Composed of 1,721 members. Elected by Election Districts. Each Dist. is entitled to representation at ratio of 1 member to every 100 votes cast at last Gubernatorial election and 1 other member.

Hdqtrs., 4-5 Court sq.

Officers: C. W. Berry, Ch.; J. J. Dorman, 1st Vice-Ch.; F. V. Kelly, Mrs. J. Kane, Sec.; T. H. Cullen, Cor. Sec., 256 President; J. D. Fairchild, Treas.; G. N. Young, Ex. Cl., 180 Sterling pl.

EXECUTIVE COMMITTEE.

1, J. J. Browne, Mrs. M. Guilfoyle, J. J. Quayle, Mrs. M. V. Walters; 2, J. Fennelly, Miss L. Murphy; 3, J. Kane, Mrs. A. L. Patterson Jones; 4, T. J. Drennan, Mary T. Harrington; 5, J. J. Sexton, Mrs. M. Greehy; 6, C. W. Jannicky, Mrs. C. D'Oench; 7, W. J. Heffernan, Mrs. A. L. Ward; 8, P. J. Diamond, Mrs. E. Parks; 9, T. F. Wogan, Mrs. E. J. Meagher; 10, J. J. McQuade, Mrs. M. J. Harris; 11, J. A. Guider, Honour B. Gelson; 12, T. E. Griffin, Mrs. E. M. Joyce; 13, G. W. Lindsay, Miss E. Skeahan; 14, D. J. Carrol, Mrs. C. I. Carroll; 15, J. A. McQuade, Estelle Corcoran; 16, K. F. Sutherland, Jennie McMahon; 17, P. B. Hanson, Mrs. M. Abel; 18, J. H. McCooey, Mrs. S. McRae Minsterer; 19, H. Hasenflug, Mrs. P. Katkse; 20, W. F. Delaney, Mrs. H. A. Braun; 21, H. Hesterberg, Mrs. M. F. O'Malley; 22, J. P. Sinnott, Miss G. Vaughan; 23, Hyman Shorenstein, Agnes Riley.

Democratic General Committee of N. Y. County.

Tammany Hall, E. 14th.

J. H. Knott, Ch. Gen. Com.; P. F. Donohue, Treas.; T. F. Smith, Sec.

EXECUTIVE COMMITTEE.

Composed of representatives from each Assembly Dist. Ed. F. Boyle, Ch.; T. F. Smith, Sec., as follows:

1—D. E. Finn, T. F. Foley. 2—M. S. Levine, H. C. Perry. 3—C. W. Culkin, F. J. Goodwin, Wm. Dalton. 4—J. F. Ahearn, P. J. Scully. 5—T. J. McManus, P. J. Dooling, J. F. Curry. 6—David Lazarus. 7—J. J. Hagan. 8—S. Goldenkranz. 9—T. Williams. 10—G. W. Olvany, G. L. Donnellan. 11—J. J. Hines. 12—M. J. Cruise, C. F. Murphy. 13—J. H. O'Connell. 14—T. M. Farley. 15—J. Mahoney. 16—S. J. Ruddy, M. Cosgrove. 17—S. Marx, N. Burkan. 18—J. J. Dietz, H. W. Hubbard. 19—Wm. Allen. 20—P. E. Nagle. 21—E. P. Holahan. 22—J J. McCormack. 23—J. Mara. County Comm. is composed of 10,315 members.

Democratic County Committee of Bronx County.

862 Tremont av.

A. H. Murphy, Ch. Ex. Comm.; J. M. Callahan, Pres.; D. J. Carr, Treas.; K. S. Kennard, M.D., Sec.

EXECUTIVE COMMITTEE AND DISTRICTS.

1—Jas. W. Brown, May Skeffington, J. F. Geraghty, Catherine Goodwin. 2—E. Miller, Mary Clark. 3—P. J. Kane, Marie Arthur. 4—S. A. Nugent, Helen McRedmond. 5—J. J. Daly, Sara Friedman. 6—T. H. O'Neil, Margaret Behan. 7—A. H. Murphy, C. F. Griffin, Mary E. Shea. 8—Chas. Buckley, Rosina M. Ryan. 9—A. H. Liebnau, May F. Kennedy.

Democratic General Committee of Queens County.

Headquarters, 9 Jackson av., L. I. City.

Officers—M. O. Smedley, Ch., Elmhurst; W. N. George, Sec., Richmond Hill; J. Theofel, Treas., Flushing.

Executive Committee—M. O. Smedley, Ch.; W. N. George, Sec., 88 Maple, Rich. Hill; Chas. Fredericks, M. J. Reidy, Mrs. Mary Mathews; Mrs. Julia A. McLaughlin, Mrs. Irene Vandenhoff, T. F. Creem, Mrs. Frances Stenger, Mrs. Lucy R. Krug, Mrs. Ellen Robinson, E. W. Cox, J. T. Kelly, F. Meyer, R. H. Williams, Mrs. Katherine Crogan, Mrs. Martha Patterson, Mrs. Mary E. Mullen, J. Theofel, J. R. Higgins, Mrs. Elizabeth Doyle, Mrs. Anna M. Sinclair, Mrs. Irene G. Lane, R. Richardson, P. F. Albrecht, J. Michels, Mrs. Dorothea Courten, Dr. Maria M. Vinton, Mrs. Ethel L. Adrian, Mrs. Lillian Brunjes, V. A. Klebauer, P. Duggan, A. C. Benninger, W. E. Blake, W. N. George, Elizabeth McKenna, Bertha Gerold.

Democratic General Committee of Richmond

EXECUTIVE COMMITTEE.

Headquarters, cor. Church and Richmond Terrace, New Brighton, S. I.

Officers—(Vacant), Ch.; A. V. Norton, Sec.; Thos. Cremins, Treas.

Democratic County Committee, Nassau.

Members of Democratic County Committee, elected at the spring primary election held on the 6th April, 1920:

FIRST ASSEMBLY DISTRICT.

Town of Hempstead.

G. P. Rohr, Seaford; J. N. Seaman, Wantagh; N. Meyer, Bellmore; D. Smith, East Meadow; H. Leich, Merrick; C. Johnson, B. J. Loonan, R. Malone, F. Duffy, E. A. Rice, J. J. Shea, Freeport; C. D. De Lap, Roosevelt; L. H. McMahon, A. C. Vandewater, T. J. Hartnett, Hempstead; S. D. Ward, Garden City; L. E. Kirwin, W. H. Agnew, G. B. Keene, Hempstead; F. B. Cotte, T. J. Reardon, C. Miller, Baldwin; J. M. Adell, Long Beach; M. B. Pettit, F. W. Shaw, S. Pettit, Oceanside; T. J. Buckman, H. B. Adams, S. L. Smith, R. D. Woodcock, Rockville Centre; C. Sielaff, Hempstead; L. J. Moran, A. R. Lent, Lynbrook; G. H. Schiffmacher, East Rockaway; J. J. Derrick, H. T. Ackley, Lynbrook; W. Sherrer, Floral Park; J. F. Schroeter, Hempstead; J. M. Herman, D. J. Bergen, Valley Stream; L. J. Lincoln, Woodmere; J. G. Divver, W. D. Reilly, Cedarhurst; J. Loucheim, J. Lynch, Lawrence; R. H. Abrams, W. F. Bates, Inwood; F. N. Box, Wantagh; L. J. Weed, Garden City; J. Brendel, Bellerose; J. Daub, Hewlett; M. Sackman, Lynbrook; T. P. Brennan, Meadowmere; J. A. Dougherty, Roosevelt.

SECOND ASSEMBLY DISTRICT.

Town of Oyster Bay.

H. C. Weiden, Farmingdale; M. Romacho, Central Park; J. Puvogel, Hicksville; T. J. O'Neil, Jericho; J. M. French, F. McQuade, Oyster Bay; D. T. Horton, East Norwich; E. J. Fisher, W. O'Keefe, Oyster Bay; C. Weeks, Locust Valley; A. R. Ketcham, Farmingdale; H. T. Dollard, Oyster Bay; T. A. Olsen, Glenwood Landing; W. F. Britt, F. Schmitz, W. J. Burns, J. W. Branigan, Sea Cliff; O. J. West, Bayville; W. J. Hofmann, Massapequa; J. Schlick, Hicksville; J. S. Burke, Syosset.

Town of North Hempstead.

T. O'Connell, D. B. Allen, Manhasset; W. W. Wood, Roslyn; H. F. Burdick, J. B. Corley, Pt. Washington; P. N. Krug, F. W. Van Wagner, Mineola; E. O'Connor, G. Hesse, Jr., Westbury; M. Smith, Pt. Washington; J. J. Hughes, Great Neck Station; J. B. Blome, New Hyde Park; J. Stapleton, A. Hamilton, Roslyn Heights; H. Colbert, Pt. Washington; W. J. McKenna, J. Milk, Westbury; F. P. Krug, Jr., Mineola.

City of Glen Cove.

G. M. Rehill, H. Curran, M. H. Stapleton, B. J. Hill, T. J. Ryan, H. Hults, K. E. Savage, J. Wansor, D. J. Fogarty, Glen Cove.

Democratic County Committee of Suffolk.

F. P. Nohowel, Ch., Bay Shore; B. J. Boyle, Sec.; C. P. Edwards, Treas..

Town of Huntington—R. Cronin, Cold Spring Harbor; J. McBrien, T. Connell, C. Sammis, R. H. La Clair, Huntington; F. G. Gubler, Huntington Station; J. T. Leiper, Melvile; G. W. Smith, Greenlawn; H. Henschel, L. A. Judge, Northport; V. Schneider, E. Northport; F. Goldsmith, Jr., Commack; J. J. Robinson, Huntington; L. Hahn, Huntington Station.

Town of Smithtown—J. S. Huntting, Smithtown Branch; J. Amey, St. James; C. Lyons, J. Lynam, Kings Park.

Town of Babylon—R. H. Pearsall, J. Stanton, I. E. Smith, Babylon; L. Wilson, Deer Park; E. Gleste, F. Sheide, Lindenhurst; E. I. Ketcham, R. D. Melick, S. T. Haff, Amityville; G. A. Bedell, Farmingdale; W. Ricketts, Babylon; H. R. Bunce, Amityville.

Town of Islip—H. Horan, Babylon; F. P. Nohowel, Bay Shore; M. J. Ward, Islip; G. Hall, East Islip; A. C. Edwards, Sayvile; J. R. Woods, Bayport; M. McKearny, Central Islip; A. Bartik, Bohemia; W. Van Popering, Sr., West Sayvile; G. Walter, Brentwood; G. Doyle, F. Creedon, Bay Shore; C. Bollinger, Islip; W. T. Edds, Sayville; M. P. Mannix, Central Islip.

Town of Brookhaven—J. A. Shipman, Stony Brook; A. Hawkins, Setauket; C. B. Tooker, R. Patterson, Port Jefferson; M. S. Warner, Millers Place; J. D. Terry, Lake Ronkonkoma; L. H. Davis, Coram; C. J. Bauer, Manorvile; A. Chapman, East Moriches; C. D. Hawkins, Center Moriches; G. Kraemer, Bellport; J. S. Bishop, C. W. Coleman, C. J. Mapes, G. Jones, Patchogue; R. Werner, Blue Point; J. E. Hayes, Medford; J. Stephani, North Bellport; W. F. Butler, S. Mc-

Cann, Patchogue; M. Schroeder, Port Jefferson Station; W. O. Lyons, Setauket; J. S. Dreyer, Port Jefferson; G. C. Raynor, Lake Ronkonkoma; H. G. Seaman, Eastport; G. D. Hulse, Center Moriches; W. M. Hodges, Bellport; J. Foster, J. Hallock, W. C. Rittenhouse, I. Coleman, J. H. O'Connor, Patchogue.

Town of Riverhead—J. A. Rowland, Wading River; J. Q. Adams, F. D. O'Keefe, F. G. Downs, F. Blasl, Riverhead; G. C. Young, R. A. Young, Aquebogue.

Town of Southold—R. C. Shanklin, Fisher's Island; P. Douglas, Orient; S. Nowel, East Marion; E. A. Rackett, S. Thomas, J. P. Grady, J. P. Cantlin, M. Cassidy, Greenport; L. W. Korn, C. H. Bechtold, Southold; A. David, Peconic; C. Garvey, Cutchogue; W. M. Boutcher, E. L. Tuthil, Mattituck.

Town of Shelter Island—H. E. Jennings, Shelter Island.

Town of Easthampton—S. M. Bennett, Easthampton; M. J. Morouney, Sag Harbor; W. D. Kelsey, Amagansett; G. S. Miller, Springs; S. Kline, Easthampton.

Town of Southampton—G. Cunningham, B. J. Boyle, Sag Harbor; T. Maran, Bridgehampton; F. R. Foster, Water Mill; C. P. Edwards, B. D. Sab'n, G. H. White, Southampton; J. W. Clark, Good Ground; J. F. Terrel, East Quogue; S. S. Stevens, Westhampton; E. F. Raynor, Eastport; G. A. Vail, Riverhead.

Democratic New York State Committee.

Headquarters, 448 B'way, Albany, N. Y. Ch., W. W. Farley; Treas., E. E. Perkins; Acting Sec., R. J. Powers, Albany, N. Y.; N. E. Mack, Buffalo, Natl. Committeeman; Sergt.-at-Arms, Chas. Weisz, N. Y. C.; Clk., A. E. Hoyt, Albany, N. Y.

(First, county; 2d, district; 3d, name; 4th, address.)

Albany—1, H. W. Blanchard, Albany; 2, W. V. Cooke, Albany; 3, W. F. Bryne, Loudonvile.

Allegany—1, W. M. Sweet, Cuba.

Bronx—1, L. J. Haffen, 308 E. 162d; 2, G. F. Lynch, 250 Willis av.; 3, P. J. Kane, 513 Concord av.; 4, S. A. Nugent, 115 Boston rd.; 5, J. J. Daly, 945 E. 163d; 6, T. H. O'Neil, 2577 Poplar; 7, A. H. Murphy, 1800 Arthur av.; 8, J. H. Murphy, 1882 Grand Con.

Broome—1, C. S. Darling, Binghamton; 2, Wm. W. Farley, Binghamton.

Cattaraugus—1, Clare Willard, Allegany.

Cayuga—1, C. F. Ratigan, Auburn.

Chautauqua—1, P. S. Guinnane, Jamestown; 2, L. A. Kilburn, Dunkirk.

Chemung—1, D. Sheehan, Elmira.

Chenango—1, J. H. Curtis, Rockdale.

Clinton—1, M. J. Callahan, Keeseville.

Columbia—1, J. Conror, Philmont.

Cortland—1, F. C. Parsons, Cortland.

Delaware—1, J. J. Farrell, Walton.

Dutchess—1, H. Morganthau, Jr., Hopewell Jct., R. F. D.; 2, J. E. Mack, Poughkeepsie.

Erie—1, J. Oppenheimer, Buffalo; 2, G. Klein, Buffalo; 3, J. Schueler, Buffalo; 4, T. P. Coughlin, Buffalo; 5, F. Roskwitalski, Buffalo; 6, W. C. Culliton, Buffalo; 7, F. M. Stage, Akron; 8, W. W. Parker, East Aurora.

Essex—1, R. Lockwood, Ticonderoga.

Franklin—1, Dr. J. C. Russell, Saranac Lake.

Fulton-Hamilton—1, J. H. Danforth, Gloversville.

Genesee—1, S. W. Brown, Batavia.

Greene—1, T. J. O'Hara, Prattsvile.

Herkimer—1, F. C. Harter, Herkimer.

Jefferson—1, C. E. Norris, Carthage.

Kings—1, J. J. Browne, 97 Johnson; 2, Jos. Fennelly, 1404 Av. C; 3, J. Kane, 195 Congress; 4, T. J. Drennan, 87 S. 9th; 5, J. Sexton, 681 Monroe; 6, Chas. W. Jannicky, 57A Vernon av.; 7, W. J. Heffernan, 598 4th av.; 8, P. J. Diamond, 119 3d pl.; 9, T. F. Wogan, 461 Ovington av.; 10, J. J. McQuade, 291 Park pl.; 11, J. A. Guider, 678 Park pl.; 12, T. E. Griffin, 496 6th av.; 13, G. W. Lindsay, 40 Bushwick pl.; 14, D. J. Carroll, 135 N. 3d; 15, J. A. McQuade, 124 Milton; 16, K. F. Sutherland, 2834 W. 1st; 17, P. B. Hanson, 525 Herkimer; 18, J. H. McCooey, 908 St. Marks av.; 19, H. Hasenflug Sr., 93 Jefferson; 20, W. F. Delaney, 1110 Bushwick av.; 21, H. Hesterberg, 9 Lenox rd.; 22, J. P. Sinnott, 118 Arlington av.; 23, Hyman Shorenstein, 449 Saratoga av.

Lewis—1, H. G. Gould, Lyons Falls.

Livingston—1, M. L. Gamble, Groveland.

Madison—1, H. T. Lewis, Morrisville Station.

Monroe—1, N. J. Streb, Rochester; 2, N. M. Bowie, Rochester; 3, L. K. Mezger, Rochester; 4, Jas. F. Leary, Rochester; 5, G. E. Warner, Rochester.

Montgomery—1, vacant.

Nassau—1, LeRoy Weed, Garden City; 2, E. J. Deasy, Glen Cove.

New York—1, T. F. Foley, 15 Oliver; 2, H. C. Perry, 339 Broome; 3, Wm. Dalton, 486 7th av.; 4, J. F. Ahearn, 296 E. B'way; 5, P. J. Dooling, 460 W. 43d; 6, D. Lazarus, 271 7th; T. T. Hagan, 172 W. 82d; 8, S. Goldenkrantz, 68 St. Marks pl.; 9, T. A. Williams, 166 W. 99th; 10, G. L. Donnellan, 135 W. 47th; 11, J. J. Hines, 373 W. 116th; 12, C. F. Murphy, 305 E. 17th; 13, J. H. O'Connell, 484 St. Nicholas av.; 14, F. M. Farley, 321 E. 65th; 15, J. T. Mahoney, 1211 Madison av.; 16, S. Ruddy, 142 E. 83d; 17, S. Marx, 1846 7th av.; 18, N. J. Hayes, 164 E. 111th; 19, Wm. Allen, 92 Morningside av.; 20, P. E. Nagle, 51 E. 129th; 21, E. P. Holohan, 770 St. Nicholas av.; 22, J. J. McCormick, 575 E. 155th; 23, J. Mara, 215th and Park Terrace.

Niagara—1, N. D. Fish, N. Tonowanda; 2, M. J. Gormley, Niagara Falls.

Oneida—1, J. D. Smith, Utica; 2, F. J. Henkle, Paris; 3, J. W. McMahon, Rome.

Onondaga—1, W. G. Stuart, Skaneateles; 2, W. H. Kelly, Syracuse; 3, R. P. Byrnes, Syracuse.

Ontario—1, J. Colmey, Canandaigua.

Orange—1, H. W. Chadeayne, Newburgh; 2, C. C. Bogart, Middletown.

Orleans—1, D. A. White, Medina.

Oswego—1, J. Gray, Parish.

Otsego—1, C. G. Tennant, Cooperstown.

Putnam—1, W. C. Osborn, Garrison.

Queens—1, T. F. Greem, L. I. City; 2, J. T. Quinn, Ridgewood; 3, M. O. Smedley, Elmhurst; 4, J. R. Higgins, Jamaica; P. F. Albrecht, Ozone Park; C. Berger, 2420 Putnam av., Ridgewood.

Rensselaer—1, G. B. Fitzgerald, Troy; 2, J. C. Riley, Hoosick Falls.

Richmond—1, M. J. Cahill, New Brighton; 2, J. L. Vail, Rosebank.

Rockland—1, J. Osborn, Nyack.

St. Lawrence—1, D. H. Corcoran, Ogdensburg; 2, J. M. Sullivan, Potsdam.

Saratoga—1, B. J. Gaffney, Saratoga Springs.

Schenectady—1, G. W. Cooper, Schenectady; 2, P. F. McGowan, Schenectady.

Schoharie—1, George M. Palmer, Cobleskill.

Schuyler—1, J. M. Quick, Watkins.

Seneca—1, A. H. Traphagen, Waterloo.

Steuben—1, G. W. Lane, Corning; 2, J. A. Killeen, Hornell.

Suffolk—1, G. C. Young, Aquebogue; 2, F. Sheide, Lindenhurst.

Sullivan—1, G. N. Hembdt, Monticello.

Tioga—1, G. A. Scott, Waverly.

Tompkins—1, L. C. Rumsey, Ithaca.

Ulster—1, J. J. McGrath, Phoenicia.

Warren—1, J. J. McCabe, Glens Falls.

Washington—1, W. A. Huppuch, Hudson Falls.

Wayne—1, J. J. O'Brien, Wolcott.

Westchester—1, F. H. Waldorf, New Rochelle; 2, P. A. Murphy, White Plains; 3, J. J. Sinnott, No. Tarrytown; 4, T. A. Brogan, Yonkers; 5, M. J. Walsh, Yonkers.

Wyoming—1, J. E. Murphy, Pearl Creek.

Yates—1, E. R. Bordwell, Penn Yan.

Women's Dem. State Committee—Mrs. J. S. Crosby, Ch., 27 W. 82d, Mhtn.

Democratic National Committee.

Hdqts., Woodward Bldg., Washington, D. C. Homer S. Cummings, Ch., Stamford, Conn.; J. Bruce Kremer, Vice-Ch., Butte, Mont.; S. B. Amidon, Vice-Ch., Wichita, Kan.; E. G. Hoffman, Sec., Ft. Wayne, Ind.; W. R. Hollister, Exec. Sec., Washington, D. C.; W. W. Marsh, Treas., Waterloo, Iowa; W. D. Jamieson, Dir. of Finance, Washington, D. C.; W. J. Cochran, Dir. of Publicity, Washington, D. C.

Alabama—W. T. Sanders, Athens; Mrs. J. D. McNeel, Birmingham.

Arizona—W. L. Barnum, Phoenix; Mrs. B. J. McKinney, Tucson.

Arkansas—V. M. Miles, Fort Smith; Mrs. J. D. Head, Texarkana.

California—I. B. Dockweiler, Los Angeles; Mrs. C. F. Donohoe, Oakland.

Colorado—M. G. Saunders, Pueblo; Mrs. Gertrude A. Lee, Denver.

Connecticut—Homer S. Cummings, Stamford; Miss Caroline Ruutz-Rees, Greenwich.

Delaware—J. O. Wolcott, Dover; Miss Lena Evans, Newark.

Florida—J. T. G. Crawford, Jacksonville; Mrs. Lois K. Mayes, Pensacola.

Georgia—C. Howell, Atlanta; Mrs. F. I. McIntire, Savannah.

Idaho—R. H. Elder, Coeur d'Alene; Theresa M. Graham, Coeur d'Alene.

LOCAL, STATE AND NATIONAL POLITICAL COMMITTEES—DEMOCRATIC—NATL. COM.—*Con.*

Illinois—C. Boeschenstein, Edwardsville; Mrs. A. L. Smith, Chicago.
Indiana—E. G. Hoffman, Fort Wayne; Miss J. E. Landers, Indianapolis.
Iowa—W. W. Marsh, Waterloo; Miss A. B. Lawther, Dubuque.
Kansas—S. B. Amidon, Wichita; Mrs. W. A. Cochel, Kansas City, Mo.
Kentucky—J. N. Camden, Versailles; Mrs. C. Cantrill, N. Y. City.
Louisiana—S. B. Hicks, Shreveport; Mrs. J. E. Friend, New Orleans.
Maine—D. J. McGillicuddy, Lewiston; Mrs. Wm. R. Pattangall, Augusta.
Maryland—J. W. Smith, Snow Hill; Mrs. J. G. Briscoe, Hagerstown.
Massachusetts—E. W. Quinn, Cambridge; Mrs. M. F. Sullivan, Fall River.
Michigan—W. F. Connolly, Detroit; Mrs. L C. Boltwood, Grand Rapids.
Minnesota—F. E. Wheaton, Minneapolis; Mrs. P. Olesen, Cloquet.
Mississippi—O. G. Johnson, Clarksdale; Miss H. Mitchel, Jackson.
Missouri—E. F. Goltra, St. Louis; Mrs. B. A. Jenkins, Kansas City.
Montana—J. B. Kremer, Butte; Mrs. R. R. Purcell, Helena.
Nebraska—W. H. Thompson, Grand Island; Dr. Jennie Callfas, Omaha.
Nevada—S. Pickett, Reno; Mrs. J. D. Finch, Reno.
New Hampshire—R. C. Murchie, Concord; Dorothy B. Jackson, Concord.
New Jersey—R. S. Hudspeth, Jersey City; Mrs. J. J. Billington, Jersey City.
New Mexico—A. A. Jones, Sante Fe; Mrs. W. F. Kirby, Tucumcari.
New York—Norman E. Mack, Buffalo; Miss E. Marbury, N. Y. C.
North Carolina—A. W. McLean, Lumberton; Miss M. O. Graham, Raleigh.
North Dakota—H. H. Perry, Ellendale; Mrs. S. Johnson, Grand Forks.
Ohio—G. White, Marietta; Mrs. B. B. Pyke, Cleveland.
Oklahoma—G. L. Bowman, Kingfisher; Mrs. D. A. McDougal, Sapulpa.
Oregon—Dr. J. W. Morrow, Portland; Mrs. Rose Shieffelin, Medford.
Pennsylvania—J. F Guffey, Pittsburgh.
Rhode Island—P. H. Quinn, Providence; Mrs. R. E. Newton, Providence.
South Carolina—J. G. Evans, Spartanburg; Mrs. H. I. Manning, Sumpter.
South Dakota—J. Mee, Centerville; Mrs. W. Hickey, Sioux Falls.
Tennessee—C. Hull, Carthage; Miss C. Williams, Memphis.
Texas—T. B. Love, Dallas; Mrs. C. Johnson, Tyler.
Utah—J. H. Moyle, Salt Lake City; Mrs. Maude D. Porter, Ogden.
Vermont—F. H. Puffey, Rutland; Mrs. C. M. Brislin, Rutland.
Virginia—Carter Glass, Lynchburg; Mrs. B. B. Munford, Richmond.
Washington—A. R. Titlow, Tacoma; Mrs. E. D. Christian, Spokane.
West Virginia—C W. Ossenton (acting), Fayetteville; Mrs. R. McG. de Berric, Grafton.
Wisconsin—J. Martin, Green Bay; Mrs. G. E. Bowler, Sheboygan.
Wyoming—P. J. Quealy, Kemmerer; Mrs. R. D. Hawley, Douglas.
Alaska—L. J. Donohoe, Cordova; Mrs. J. W. Troy, Juneau.
District of Columbia—J. F. Costello, Mrs. T. F. Walsh.
Hawaii—J. H. Wilson, Honolulu; Mrs. L. L. McCandless, Honolulu.
Philippines—R. E. Manly, Naga Camarines; Mrs. K. Williams, Manila.
Porto Rico—H. W. Dooley, San Juan; Miss E. Martin, San Juan.
Canal Zone—M. A. Otero, Ancon; Mrs. D. F. Reeder, Ancon.

REPUBLICAN.

Republican General Committee of Kings County.

Rep. Genl. Committee of Kings Co. Composed of 2,855 mem. Elected by Election Dists. Each dist. entitled to representation at ratio of 1 mem. to every 100 votes cast at last Gubernatorial election. Hdqtrs., 26 Court.

Officers County Com.: A. E. Vass, Ch.; F. H. Stevenson, Sec.; W. P. Rae, Treas.; J. D. Moore, Sergt-at-Arms.

Officers Exec. Com.: Jacob Livingston, Ch.; A. D.—1, D. H. Ralston; 2, M. B. Campbell; 3, R. E. Laimbeer; 4, J. S. Gaynor; 5, C. C. Lockwood; 6, R. L. Gledhill; 7, J. Feltner; 8, Jacob Brenner; 9, C. S. Warbasse; 10, C. F. Murphy; 11, A. E. Vass; 12, J. T. Rafferty; 13, J. D. Moore; 14, G. A. Owens; 15, Richard Wright; 16, F. Oppikofer; 17, L. M. Swasey; 18, W. G. Price; 19, J. Bartscherer; 20, Wm. Schnitzspan; 21, F. J. Kracke; 22, Jacob A. Livingston; 23, W. D. Ludden.

Republican General Committee of New York Co. 105 W. 40th.

S. S. Koenig, Pres.; C. E. Heydt, 1st V.-Pres.; Helen V. Boswell, 2d V.-Pres.; O. L. Mills, Treas.; J. N. Boyle, Sec.; J. L. Higgins, Asst. Sec.

EXECUTIVE COMMITTEE.

S. S. Koenig, Ch., 105 W. 40th. J. N. Boyle, **Sec.; O. L. Mills, Treas. (For hdqtrs. of members of Exec. Com., see Republican Dist. Clubs.)**
A. D.—1, Jos. Levenson, W. G. Rose; 2, A. Dalessandro, J. Rosenberg; 3, B. F. Fox, M. H. Blake, R. M. Greenbank; 4, Alex. Wolf; 5, H. W. Beyer, A. P. Ludden; 6, S. S. Koenig; 7, A. J. Berwin; 8, G. C. Nordinger; 9, Chas. E. Heydt; 10, F. R. Stoddard, Jr.; 11, R. P. Levis; 12, Wm. Henkel, J. S. Shea, C. K. Lexow; 13, V. J. Hahn; 14, J. Pabian, C. W. Ferry; 15, W. Chilvers; 16, Wm. C. Hecht, A. O. Neal; 17, R. Oppenheim; 18, C. B. Largy, B. Swartz; 19, D. B. Costuma; 20, F. K. Bowers; 21, R. S. Conklin; 22, J. A. Bolles; 23, C. H. Woodward.

Republican General Committee, Bronx County.

Headquarters, 412 E. Tremont av. R. W. Lawrence, Pres.; Chas. Rathfelder, Treas.; P. Wynne, Sec.

EXECUTIVE COMMITTEE AND DISTRICTS.

R. W. Lawrence, Ch., 3549 Willett av. A. D. 1, A. D. Brunner; 2, P. Wynne; 3, A. B. Simonds; **4, E. W. Bradbury; 5, H. B. Harris; 6, J. J. Knewitz; 7, M. J. Reagan; 8, T. W. Whittle; 9, S. J. Joseph; 10, Chas. Rathfelder.**

Republican General Committee of Queens Co.

Hdqtrs., 246 Jackson av., L. I. City. Officers—J. H. DeBragga, Ch., 2309 Decatur, Ridgewood; P. Campbell, Sec., 105 Woolsey av.; F. H. Woodruff, Treas.

EXECUTIVE COMMITTEE.

J. H. DeBragga, Ch.; J. Wagner, H. Vogt, R. L. Smith, F. Hulbert, G. Vreeland, F. E. Knauss.

CHAIRMEN ASSEMBLY COMMITTEE.

1st, J. Gordon, Mrs. E. Van Alst; 2d, Chas Hahn, Mrs. E. Schumacer; 3d, G. Alexander, Miss B. L. Babcock; 4th, E. C. Hunt, Mrs. E. M. Winslow; 5th, W. B. Hazelwood, Mrs. H. Vander Clute; 6th, F. L. Plass, Madeline Jacoby.

Republican General Committee of Richmond Co.

Hdqtrs., S. I. Bldg., Tompkinsville. J. P. Thompson, Ch.; C. J. Sharrett, V.-Ch.; T. A. Braniff, Sec., Tompkinsville; A. E. Johnson, Treas., Tottenville.

EXECUTIVE COMMITTEE.

Wards: 1st, G. L. Nichol; 2d, H. E. Buel; 3d, James C. Smith; 4th, John Timlin, Jr.; 5th, James Lring; member at large, Mrs. Leonie Vosburgh.

Republican County Committee, Nassau County.

Jeremiah Wood, Ch., Lynbrook; Byron C. Gould, Treas., Port Washington; Wm. Cornell, Sec., Lynbrook; T. Roberts, Seaford; F. A. Nolan, Central Park; W. F. Southard, Wantagh; J. J. Molloy, Bellmore; F. Mangels, Smithville South; W. W. Louden, East Hempstead; B. S. Carman, Merrick; S. P. Pettitt, C. B. Williams, H. R. Smith, R. G. Anderson, C. Lewis, J. J. Dunbar, Freeport; W. Pearsall, J. J. Boston, J. McCaffrey, Roosevelt; H. Harms, Hempstead; G. B. Van Sicklen, Garden City; G. S. Smith, C. U. Stowe, W. R. Jones, C. Gittens, J. E. Patterson, A. G. Patterson, Hempstead; W. H. Raynor, C. Smith, R. S. Homan, Baldwin; B. Molitor, Long Beach; E. Ramsden, R. H. Smith, Oceanside; E. J. Bennett, O. H. Tuthill, C. C. Van Deusen, P. F. Weidersum, Rockville Centre; P. G. Ohrtman, Woodfield; G. F. Hubbell, Garden City; C. W. Randell, Garden City Estates; Jeremiah Wood, Malverne; W. Cornell, S. Pearsall, H. E. Lister, Lynbrook; D. L. Van Wicklen, East Rockaway; C. Plant, T. Christianson, Lynbrook; Wm. Hendrickson, Valley Stream; P. J. Herman, Franklin Square; H. Baer, New Hyde Park; A. H. Goldsmith, Floral Park; N. D. Sturgess, Bellerose; E. R. Frasco, Elmont; A. J. Hendrickson, F. Hammill, Valley Stream; W. H. Latham, Hewlett; T. Brower,

LOCAL, STATE AND NATIONAL POLITICAL COMMITTEES—REPUBLICAN—NASSAU CO.—*Con.*

Woodmere; J. G. Ehlen, Meadowmere; J. H. Foster, Inwood; C. F. Craft, E. F. McGinn, Cedarhurst; W. D. Burtis, Woodmere; A. Weston, T. A. McWhinney, C. W. Smith, Lawrence; A. Gunther, G. W. Doughty, Inwood.

Town of North Hempstead—C. Snedeker, C. E. Remsen, G. C. Hyde, E. Schmidt, E. MacFerran, A. Kohler, B. C. Gould, R. E. Allen, M. Rhodes, A. Westervelt, W. V. Pearsall, F. Powers, W. E. Sexton, M. R. Schenck, C. W. Smith, C. D. Stryker, J. L. Dowsey, C. F. Lawrence, Wm. McCarty, L. D. Chase, P. L. Snedeker, C. F. Bertanzel, E. W. Weeks, J. F. Buhler, R. L. Bacon, T. LeBouttlier.

Town of Oyster Bay—C. Beierling, J. Robinson, J. Baunsbach, F. Tappan, R. E. Ebbets, C. J. Remsen, Mrs. C. Loeb, F. Davis, J. Merritt, Mrs. W. I. Clarke, C. Luyster, C. I. Wood, C. S. Chellborg, E. Tilford, J. W. Anderson, L. J. Monico, S. J. Titus, E. Conlin, H. Lee, G. Muller, J. T. Mills, J. Bryce.

Glen Cove City—W. E. Luyster, W. H. Seaman, A. W. Howell, T. Miller, H. F. Weber, W. T. Welden, Jr., S. W. Mudge.

Republican County Committee of Suffolk.

F. S. Pulver, Ch.; Mrs. I. B. Sammis, Treas.; Harry Lee, Sec., Riverhead.

Town of Huntington—C. H. Newman, M. Bunce, Cold Spring Harbor; H. A. Murphy, A. V. Sammis, H. A. Rosell, W. Sammis, W. B. Gibson, Ruth H. Palmer, Ida B. Sammis, Allison E. Lowndes, Huntington; C. J. Fox, C. Devoe, Huntington Station; R. Schmidt, F. E. Baylis, Melville; Mary F. Lockwood, J. Deans, Greenlawn; S. M. Scudder, Anna Clerke, R. W. Hawkins, Grace A. Green, Northport; J. Enderling, Jr., Lillian Stiles, E. Northport; C. S. Burr, Commack; H. S. Brush, Kate E. Jackman, Huntington; C. Cornehlsen, G. Holzapfel, Huntington Station.

Town of Smithtown—J. Evans Crane, Sarah B. Peterson, Smithtown Branch; C. M. Smith, Isabell Lefferts, St. James; G. L. Thompson, W. H. Clayton, J. F. Kelly, D. L. Reynold, Kings Park.

Town of Babylon—J. C. Robbins, Josephine McLachlin, B. B. Wood, Louise Sammis, E. A. Taylor, Ethel A. Snedecor, Babylon; R. F. Soper, Florence V. Donner, Deer Park; A. A. Arnold, J. G. Wiebel, Anna Keller, Lindenhurst; P. Bailey, F. E. Wychoff, C. O. Ireland, W. T. Louden, Anna L. Evans, Amityville; Kathleen Franke, Farmingdale; J. Philip Denton, Farmingdale; B. F. Mott, Ida J. Van Brunt, Babylon; J. C. Howell, Amityville.

Town of Islip—R. Baylis, Babylon; F. T. Hulse, Lucy D. Dietrich, Bay Shore; E. Smith, Maude Schlemmer, Islip; Mary E. Smith, F. Markvart, East Islip; E. Fellerath, Charlotte Sawyer, Sayville; F. Rogers, Edna Brown, Bayport; Lucy J. Rhodes, G. Dow, Central Islip; A. Thuma, W. Stochl, Bohemia; T. Lokker, Louise E. Ockers, West Sayville; C. B. Cooper, Brentwood; W. H. Robbins, Etta L. Whitman, J. M. Dodson, Mabel Carll, Bay Shore; C. M. Grover, Emma Hubbs, Islip; L. Hiddink, Jane Hoag, Sayville; Margaret R. Mulligan, J. Donlon, Central Islip.

Town of Brookhaven—J. A. Squire, W. H. Bennett, Stony Brook; May W. Strong, H. R. Jayne, Julia O. Bonelli, Q. A. Learch, G. Tobiason, Cornelia Moger, Port Jefferson; C. Barrand, N. Tuthill, Millers Place; W. Court, Arabelle Dare, Lake Ronkonkoma; J. M. Ashton, Yaphank; E. F. Howell, Matilda Pille, Manorville; H. H. Benjamin, L. B. Reeve, East Moriches; Luella Howell, W. Rogers, Center Moriches; E. J. Weidner, E. Hulse, Bellport; W. B. Smith, Blanche M. Belmont, R. T. Baker, Augusta Pape, H. Paine, C. N. Butler, Jr., Ruth Underwood, Patchogue; Arline P. Moffit, J. R. Snedecor, Blue Point; S. E. Terry, Holtsville; R. MacIntosh, Angeline Perry, East Patchogue; R. A. Newton, B. M. Sherwood, R. B. Ackerly, O. F. Karlein, Patchogue; H. Smith, Inez Squires, Port Jefferson Station; Esther Tyler, C. J. Aldrich, Sarah G. Downs, R. Wheeler, Port Jefferson; F. G. Hallock, Marjorie Witte, Lake Ronkonkoma; H. Mott, Eva D. Raynor, Eastport; H. A. T. Hedges, Laura A. Penny, Center Moriches; J. H. Morton, Freida Esperson, Bellport; E. J. King, Ella M. Robinson, W. DeMullen, Annie Glover, W. C. Miller, Carrie F. Griffing, Grace Homan, A. Still, E. Chuichiolo, Georgiana Schulze, Patchogue.

Town of Riverhead—C. Rowley, Wading River; J. W. Kratoville, Margaret Lucas, W. A. Nugent, Clara J. Lane, A. H. Prudent, R. W. Wiey, V. L. Case, Harry Lee, Theresa Morell, Riverhead; J. J. Cole, H. L. Tyler, Jamesport.

Town of Southold—F. Hine, Fisher's Island; E. Latham, Mary D. Young, Orient; I. M. Rogers, Susan Bennett, East Marion; W. J. Mills, W. F. Conklin, F. Corwin, Blanche Adams, A. Tasker, Florence Rackett, F. B. Thornhill, R. B. Conklin, E. S. Tillinghast, Greenport; N. Davis, F. E. Booth, G. C. Terry, F. T. Jennings, Southold; F. D. Richmond, Peconic; H. Jacobs, New Suffolk; C. P. Tuthill, Cutchogue; P. B. Ruland, Ida M. Torrey, G. L. Penny, Florence Morton, Mattituck.

Town of Shelter Island—I. Clark, Belle Dickerson, Shelter Island.

Town of Easthampton—N. C. Osborne, Amy J. Newton, Easthampton; Rose Bates, E. Jones, Sag Harbor; S. J. Kelsey, Retta Vail, Amagansett; F. D. Schellinger, Bertha Finch, Springs; J. M. Strong, S. Jennie Baker, Easthampton.

Town of Southampton—F. S. Pulver, Mary Morris, G. Farley, Minnie Dalzell, Sag Harbor; H. M. Hallock, F. C. Schenck, Bridgehampton; C. B. Foster, Edna M. Dimon, Water Mill; Pauline Sabin, C. A. Payne, F. Phillips, H. Robinson, R. R. Kendrick, DeLancey Kountze, Southampton; A. F. Squires, C. L. Jackson, Good Ground; C. W. Brown, Harriet V. Carman, East Quogue; A. P. Rogers, Ida Atwater, B. G. Halsey, Ida J. Tuthill, Westhampton; F. C. Havens, Flanders; A. J. Fisher, Riverhead.

Republican N. Y. State Committee.

Headquarters—43 W. 39th, Mhtn.
Chairman—Geo. A. Glynn.
Secretary—L. B. Gleason, Delaware Co.
Treasurer—H. K. Bird.
B. H. Snell, Ch. Ex. Com.

Women's Republican State Exec. Comm.—Mrs. Arthur L. Liverman, Ch., Yonkers, N. Y.

Order of following is: 1st, County; 2d, Assembly District; 3d, name; 4th, address.

Albany—1, W. A. Glenn, Albany. 2, J. H. Rea, Albany; 3, H. M. Sage, Menands.
Allegany—F. R. Utter, Friendship.
Bronx—1, Chas. Rathfelder, 440 E. 156th. 2, P. Wynne, 124 Featherbed lane. 3, A. B. Simonds, 656 E. 160th. 4, E. W. Bradbury, 631 E. 168th. 5, H. B. Harris, 960 Prospect av. 6, F. W. Newbold, 2411 Butler pl. 7, M. J. Reagan, 2046 Prospect av. 8, T. W. Whittle, 2332 University av.
Broome—1, H. D. Ballard, Binghamton. 2, N. A. Boyd, Binghamton.
Cattaraugus—A. T. Fancher, Salamanca.
Cayuga—Chas. J. Hewitt.
Chautauqua—1, Glenn A. Frank, Jamestown. 2, H. B. Lyon, Dunkirk.
Chemung—H. C. Mandeville, Elmira.
Chenango—J. J. Ray, Norwich.
Clinton—J. H. Moffitt, Plattsburg.
Columbia—O. Drumm, Hudson.
Cortland—F. J. Bentley, Cortland.
Delaware—E. H. Axtell, Deposit.
Dutchess—1, M. Smith, Millbrook. 2, G. Schlude, Poughkeepsie.
Erie—1, W. A. Cowan, 68 Court, Buffalo. 2, W. G. Humphrey, 1858 Niagara, Buffalo. 3, L. J. Schmidt, 221 Cherry, Buffalo. 4, J. T. Claris, 629 Clinton, Buffalo. 5, W. C. Tenjost, 87 Krettner, Buffalo. 6, E. R. Miller, 496 Northampton, Buffalo. 7, A. R. Atkinson, Kenmore. 8, F. F. Holmwood, Orchard Park, Erie Co.
Essex—P. J. Finn, Ticonderoga.
Franklin—A. MacDonald, St. Regis Falls.
Fulton and Hamilton—C. Durey, Green Lake.
Genesee—F. B. Parker, Batavia.
Greene—W. E. Thorpe, Catskill.
Herkimer—E. Small, Herkimer.
Jefferson—A. B. Parker, Watertown.
Kings—1, D. H. Ralston, 121 Henry. 2, M. B. Campbell, 4654 Bedford av. 3, R. H. Laimbeer Jr., 309 B'way, Mhtn. 4, J. S. Gaynor, 136 Keap. 5, G. Marshall, 271 Lewis av. 6, R. L. Gledhill, 324 Hart. 7, J. Feltner, 156 23d. 8, J. Brenner, 252 Carroll. 9, C. S. Warbasse, 131 76th. 10, Chas. F. Murphy, 292 Clinton av. 11, A. E. Vass, 131 Quincy. 12, J. T. Rafferty, 242 Garfield pl. 13, J. D. Moore, 155 Ainslie. 14, G. A. Owens, 117 South 1st. 15, R. Wright, 55 Jewell. 16, F. Oppikofer, 2760 Ocean P'kway. 17, L. M. Swasey, 42 Herkimer. 18, W. G. Price, 1366 Park. 19, J. Bartscherer, 178 Evergreen av. 20, W. Schnitzpan, 53 Woodbine. 21, F. J. H. Kracke, 11 Kenmore pl. 22, J. A. Livingston, 448 Ridgewood av. 23, W. D. Ludden.
Lewis—Chas. S. Mereness, Jr., Lowville.
Livingston—J. F. Connor, Mt. Morris.
Madison—M. E. Tallett, De Ruyter.
Monroe—1, J. W. Hopkins, Pittsford. 2, J. L. Hotchkiss, Rochester. 3, W. H. Craig, Rochester. 4, G. W. Aldridge, So. Rochester. 5, E. W. Arnold, Adams Basin.

LOCAL, STATE AND NATIONAL POLITICAL COMMITTEES—REPUBLICAN—N. Y. STATE—*Con.*

Montgomery—Geo. K. Morris, Amsterdam.
Nassau—1, G. W. Doughty, Inwood. 2, K. L. Bacon, Westbury.
New York—1, Jos. Levenson, 243 Canal. 2, A. Dalessandro, 30 Macdougal. 3, B. F. Fox, 402 W. 29th. 4, A. W. Wolf, 299 B'way. 5, A. P. Ludden, 341 W. 56th. 6, S. S. Koenig, 27 Cedar. 7, S. Selig, 2039 B'way. 8, Wm. Berkowitz, 229 E. 5th. 9, C. E. Heydt, 2 Rector. 10, C. Schmelzel, 54 W. 40th. 11, R. P. Levis, 42 B'way. 12, J. S. Shea, 157 E. 31st. 13, V. J. Hahn, 360 W. 125th. 14, J. Pabian, 525 E. 72d. 15, W. Chilvers, 35 Nassau. 16, W. C. Hecht, Jr., 169 E. 83d. 17, R. Oppenheim, 1867 7th av. 18, C. B. Largy, 101 E. 116th. 19, J. J. Lyons, 2040 7th av. 20, F. K. Bowers, 2071 5th av. 21, R. S. Conklin, 34 Pine. 22, J. A. Bolles, 154 Nassau. 23, C. H. Woodward, 61 B'way.
Niagara—1, J. P. Mackenzie, No. Tonawanda. 2, G. M. Tuttle, Niagara Falls.
Oneida—1, T. O. Cole, Utica. 2, M. B. Hall, Vernon. 3, W. P. Binks, Rome.
Onondaga—1, J. F. Mathews, Solvay. 2, C. E. Dorr, 108 W. Pleasant av. 3, L. A. Saxer, Syracuse.
Ontario—L. G. Hoskins, Geneva.
Orange—1, J. B. Corwin, Newburgh. 2, G. F. Gregg, Goshen.
Orleans—T. A. Kirby, Albion.
Oswego—Francis D. Culkin, Oswego.
Otsego—F. M. Smith, Springfield Center.
Putnam—E. S. Agor, Mahopac Falls.
Queens—1, J. Wagner, L. I. C. 2, H. Vogt, 657 Woodward av. 3, R. L. Smith, Woodside. 4, W. B. Ashmead, Jamaica. 5, G. F. Vreeland, Rockaway Beach. 6, R. H. Wickert, 818 Cypress av., Ridgewood.
Rensselaer—1, F. H. Meter, Troy. 2, C. V. Collins, Troy.
Richmond—1, G. Cromwell, Dongan Hills, S. I., N. Y. 2, A. E. Johnson, Tottenville.
Rockland—W. G. Hamilton, Stony Point.
St. Lawrence—1, J. C. Tullock, Ogdensburgh. 2, B. H. Snell, Potsdam.
Saratoga—W. J. Dodge, Ballston Spa.
Schenectady—1, T. C. Brown, Schenectady. 2, W. S. Hamlin, Amsterdam.
Schoharie—E. J. Eckerson, Cobleskill
Schuyler—S. F. Northrup, Watkins.
Seneca—N. J. Gould, Seneca Falls.
Steuben—1, H. O. Elkins, Bath. 2, B. C. DeWitt, Hornell.
Suffolk—1, H. Lee, Riverhead. 2, Wm. H. Robbins, Bay Shore.
Sullivan—M. J. McGibbon, Liberty.
Tioga—(Vacant).
Tompkins—E. C. Stewart, Ithaca.
Ulster—P. Elting, Kingston.
Warren—L. W. Emerson, Warrensburg.
Washington—E. C. Rogers, Hudson Falls.
Wayne—C. H. Betts, Lyons.
Westchester—1, J. A. Mahlstedt, New Rochelle. 2, W. L. Ward, Port Chester. 3, F. Montross, Peekskill. 4, Chas. D. Millard, Tarrytown. 5, D. J. Cashin, Yonkers.
Wyoming—J. E. Nash, Silver Springs.
Yates—A. T. Halstead, Rushville.
Women's Div.—Mrs. J. F. Yawger, Ch., 808 West End av., Mhtn.

REP. WOMEN'S STATE EXEC. COMM.—1919. 43 W. 39th, Mhtn. Mrs. A. L. Livermore, Pres.; Mrs. W. H. Ives, Sec.

Republican National Committee.

Hdqtrs., Woodward Bldg., Washington, D. C.

W. H. Hays, Ch.; J. T. Adams, V.-Ch.; J. B. Reynolds, Sec.; F. W. Upham, Treas.; E. P. Thayer, Sgt -at-Arms.

Alabama—O. D. Street, Guntersville.
Arizona—A. B. Jaynes, Tucson.
Arkansas—H. L. Remmel, Little Rock.
California—Wm. H. Crocker, San Francisco.
Colorado—J. F. Vivian, Denver.
Connecticut—J. H. Roraback, Hartford.
Delaware—T. C. du Pont, New York City.
Florida—G. W. Bean, New York City.
Georgia—H. L. Johnson, Atlanta.
Idaho—J. W. Hart, Rigby.
Illinois—L. Y. Sherman, Springfield.
Indiana—J. B. Kealing, Indianapolis.
Iowa—J. T. Adams, Dubuque.
Kansas—D. W. Mulvane, Topeka.
Kentucky—A. T. Hert, Louisville.
Louisiana—E. Kuntz, New Orleans.
Maine—G. P. Gannett, Augusta.
Maryland—W. P. Jackson, Salisbury.
Massachusetts—J. W. Weeks, West Newton.
Michigan—F. M. Warner, Farmington.
Minnesota—I. A. Caswell, St. Paul.
Mississippi—M. J. Mulvihill, Vicksburg.
Missouri—J. L. Babler, St. Louis.
Montana—O. H. P. Shelley, Helena.
Nebraska—R. P. Howell, Omaha.
Nevada—G. Wingfield, Reno.
New Hampshire—F. W. Estabrook, Nashua.
New Jersey—H. F. Kean, New York City.
New Mexico—H. O. Bursum, Socorro.
New York—C. D. Hilles, New York City.
North Carolina—J. M. Morehead, Charlotte.
North Dakota—G. Olson, Grafton.
Ohio—R. K. Hynicka, New York City.
Oklahoma—J. L. Hamon, Ardmore.
Oregon—R. E. Williams, Portland.
Pennsylvania—Boies Penrose, Philadelphia.
Rhode Island—F. S. Peck, Providence.
South Carolina—J. W. Tolbert, Greenwood.
South Dakota—W. C. Cook, Sioux Falls.
Tennessee—J. W. Overhall, Nashville.
Texas—H. F. MacGregor, Houston.
Utah—E. Bamburger, Salt Lake City.
Vermont—E. S. Kinsley, Rutland.
Virginia—C. B. Slemp, Big Stone Gap.
Washington—G. E. Kelly, Tacoma.
West Virginia—V. L. Highland, Clarksburg.
Wisconsin—A. T. Rogers, Madison.
Wyoming—P. Sullivan, Casper.
Dist. of Columbia—E. F. Colladay, Washington.
Alaska—J. C. McBride, Juneau.
Philippine Islands—H. B. McCoy, Manila.
Porto Rico—R. H. Todd, San Juan.
Hawaii—R. W. Shingle, Honolulu.

PROHIBITION PARTY.

KINGS CO. COMMITTEE—Hdqtrs., 306 Schermerhorn. John McKee, 113 Columbia Heights, Ch. Ex. Com.; Wm. E. Moore, V.-Ch., 508 Lexington av.; John D. Snyder, Treas., 295 Midwood; J. W. Quail, Sec., 293 Stuyvesant av.; Miss Susie E. Hughes, Cor. Sec., 453 15th.

NEW YORK CO. COMMITTEE—Geo. K. Hinds, Ch., 92 Riverside dr.; R. J. McAusland, Cor. Sec., 945 Columbus av.; A. T. Hule, Rec. Sec.; A. R. Lewis, Fin. Sec.; W. F. Rawlins, Treas.; A. H. Saunders, Ch. Ex. Com.

BRONX CO. COMMITTEE—A. H. Stillman, Ch., 2096 Boston rd.; A. W. Pfluger, Sec., 4038 Barnes av.

QUEENS CO. COMMITTEE—L. W. Farr, Ch., 8 Clayton pl., Jamaica; Hy. Schauss, Sec.; S. E. Pratt, Treas.

RICHMOND CO. COMMITTEE—Harlow McMillen, 1647 Richmond turnpike, W. New Brighton, Ch.; Mary E. Rudman, 1st V.-Ch.; Anna S. Wort, 2d V.-Ch.; H. C. Horton, Sec., W. New Brighton; J. B. Dorman, Treas.; 76 mem. of committee.

NASSAU CO. EXEC. COMMITTEE—Wm. Varney, Ch., Rockville Centre; Secs., Geo. H. Jackson, Lynbrook; W. A. Simons, E. Rockaway; C. Dickson, Woodmere; Treas., G. Gregory, Great Neck.

SUFFOLK CO. COMMITTEE—J. A. Duryea, Ch., Huntington; W. E. Bryant, Treas., Huntington; H. W. Livingston, Sec., Islip; E. M. Osborne, Easthampton; H. B. Bishop, Southampton.

N. Y. STATE EXECUTIVE COMMITTEE.

Hdqtrs., 40 State, Rochester, N. Y. W. H. Burr, Ch., Rochester; Mrs. D. Leigh Colvin, N. Y., Supt. Women's Dept.; N. D. Cramer, Sec., Elmira; L. Hoag, Treas., Binghamton; O. S. Bishop, J. F. Gillespie, A. W. Pierson, Mary H. Bishop, F. L. Lockwood, C. Z. Spriggs, W. E. Moore.

NATIONAL EXECUTIVE COMMITTEE.

Hdqtrs., 729 Manhattan Bldg., Chicago, Ill. V. G. Hinshaw, Ch., Chicago, Ill.; Mrs. Ida B. Wise Smith, V.-Ch., Cedar Rapids, Ia.; Mrs. F. E. Beauchamp, Sec., Lexington, Ky.; H. P. Faris, Treas., Clinton, Mo.; R. H. Patton, Springfield, Ill.; E. L. G. Hohenthal, So. Manchester, Conn.; F. E. Baldwin, Elmira, N. Y.; W. G. Calderwood, Minneapolis, Minn.; B. E. P. Prugh, Harrisburg, Pa.

SOCIALIST PARTY.

NATIONAL EXECUTIVE COMMITTEE.

Morris Hillquit, 19 W. 44th, N. Y. C., N. Y.; James Oneal, 112 4th av., N. Y. C., N. Y.; Wm. M. Brandt, St. Louis, Mo.; J. I. Hagel, Okla.; Wm. M. Henry, Ind.; E. I. Melms, Milwaukee, Wis.; G. E. Roewer, Boston, Mass.; Bertha H. Mailly, 7 E. 15th, Mhtn.

EXECUTIVE SECRETARY.

Otto Branstetler, 220 S. Ashland bld., Chicago, Ill.

INTERNATIONAL SECRETARY.

Morris Hillquit, 30 Church, N. Y. C.

LOCAL, STATE AND NATIONAL POLITICAL COMMITTEES—SOCIALIST—*Continued.*

N. Y. STATE EXECUTIVE COMMITTEE.

Hdqtrs., 467 B'way, Albany. Chas. W. Nooman, Sec.

KINGS COUNTY EXECUTIVE COMMITTEE.

Hdqtrs., 61 Graham av. A. Pauly, Ch.; I. M. Chatcuff, Sec.; Comm., H. Chait, Frances Mabel, A. N. Shulman, W. B. Robinson, B. Shainblura, N. Wainess, G. W. Klein, A. H. Carlin, B. Brandes, W. Shapiro.

N. Y. COUNTY EXECUTIVE COMMITTEE.

Hdqtrs., 7 E. 15th, Mhtn. S. J. Block, Ch.; H. Volk, Sec.; Julius Gerber, Exec. Sec.; A. Lee, Treas.; S. E. Beardsly, Ed. F. Cassidy, Olga Long, F. Crossmith, H. Rück, I. Alexander, J. Axelrad, I. Silverman.

BRONX COUNTY EXECUTIVE COMMITTEE.

Hdqtrs., 1167 Boston rd. E. Seidel, Ex. Sec.; A. Vidoms, Treas.

RICHMOND CO. EXECUTIVE COMMITTEE.

Hdqtrs., 22 Roff, Stapleton. R. Rochow, Ch.; M. Newman, Sec.

SUFFOLK COUNTY EXECUTIVE COMMITTEE.

Wm. Drensiki, Ch., Huntington; C. Schneider, Treas., Huntington Sta.; O. Grausalke, Sec., Patchogue.

SOCIALIST LABOR PARTY.

A. Petersen, Natl. Sec., 45 Rose, N. Y. C., N. Y.

Representative on Internatl. Socialist Bureau, B. Reinstein.

NATIONAL EXECUTIVE COMMITTEE.

California, Max J. Michel; Connecticut, H. Ogens; Illinois, S. J. French; Massachusetts, H. M. Lichtenstein; Minnesota, W. E. McCue; Missouri, H. J. Poelling; New Jersey, J. C. Butterworth; New York, P. E. DeLee; Ohio, J. D. Goerke; Virginia, D. L. Munro; Washington, J. C. Schaefer; Pennsylvania, W. H. Thomas.

Language Federation—Bulgarian: A. Nasteff, Baltimore, Md. Hungarian: F. C. Zermann, N. Y. C. So. Slavonian: S. Theofanov, Dayton, O.

N. Y. STATE EXECUTIVE COMMITTEE.

Hdqtrs., 45 Rose, Mhtn. A. Orange, State Sec.; J. J. Donohue, E. A. Archer, Lazarus Abelson, Jos. Manblatt, Henry Kuhn, J. P. Quinn, B. Greenbaum, F. Dormagen.

FARMER-LABOR PARTY.

N. Y. STATE EXECUTIVE COMMITTEE.

W. Kohn, Ch.; E. H. Markolf, Sec.; N. Fine, Exec. Sec.; Dr. Alcan Hirsch, Treas.; Maud Schwartz, C. H. Larsen, New York County; W. Reichle, L. S. McDermott, Bronx; A. Lefkowitz, H. DeFrem, Queens County; P. Umstader, A. Hirsch, Westchester County; E. H. Markolf, J. McGuire, Kings County.

NEW YORK COUNTY OFFICERS.

T. Jones, Ch.; N. Fin, Sec.; A. McVitty, Fin. Sec.; P. F. Byrne, Treas.; Ben Howe, Organizer.

BRONX COUNTY OFFICERS.

L. S. McDermott, Ch.; P. Donahue, V.-Ch.; M. Whalen, Rec. Sec.; E. Cross, Cor. Sec.; T. Keane, Campaign Mgr.

KINGS CO. OFFICERS AND EXEC. COMMITTEE

Hdqtrs., Saengerbund Hall, Bkln. J. McGuire, Pres.; E. H. Markolf, 1st V.-Pres.; Johanna Lindlof, 2d V.-Pres.; M. Gorrin, Sec.; Mrs. J. Geise, Fin. Sec.; M. Naddler, Treas.; Dr. M. William, Ch. Campaign Committee; O. Lamberger, E. Schneelock, L. Schneider, F. Schmidt, L. I. Rines, J. Gordon, L. Lombardo, B. D. Gross, R. H. Haskell.

NEW YORK CITY CENTRAL COMMITTEE.

W. Kohn, Ch.; A. Lefkowitz, V.-Ch.; E. Bohm, Sec.; Florence Blackstone, Treas.

CITIZENS UNION.

Hdqtrs., 41 Park Row, Mhtn. Wm. Jay Schieffelin, Ch.; J. H. Cohen, W. G. Wilcox, H. Pushae Williams, V.-Chs.; W. Talmadge Arndt, Sec.; S. A. Lewisohn, Treas.; L. M. Wallstein, Counsel.

WOMAN SUFFRAGE ASSOCIATIONS.

International.

Internatl. Woman Suffrage Alliance—1904. Org. in Berlin, Ger. Mrs. C. C. Catt, Pres., 404 Riverside drive, Mhtn., N. Y.; Miss C. Macmillan, Sec., hdqtrs., 11 Adams, Adelphi, London. 30 nations affiliated.

National.

Natl. Am. Woman's Suffrage Assn.—1869. 171 Madison av., Mhtn. 2,000,000 mem. Mrs. C. C. Catt, Pres.; Mrs. F. J. Shuler, Sec., 171 Madison av.

Natl. Woman's Party—Mrs. O. H. P. Belmont, Member of Exec. Comm., 13 E. 41st, Mhtn.

LEAGUE OF WOMEN VOTERS.

National.

Hdqtrs., Munsey Bldg., Washington, D. C. Maud Wood Park, Ch.; Mrs. P. R. Jacobs, Sec.

State.

New York State League of Women Voters (formerly N. Y. State Woman Suffrage Party)—1896. 303 5th av., N. Y. C. 6,000 volunteer officers, 1,012,000 enrolled. Mrs. F. A. Vanderlip, Ch.; Mrs. Vanderbilt Webb, Sec.

Brooklyn.

League of Women Voters—Mrs. G. Notman, Ch.; Mrs. E. L. C. Goddard, Cor. Sec. Consists of 23 Assembly Districts, with district leaders as follows:

1, Mrs. H. E. Dreier; 2, Mrs. A. M. Johnson; 3, Mrs. J. F. Doyle; 4, Mrs. A. Mackintosh; 5, Mrs. M. Semonite; 6, Mrs. M. Enright; 7, Mrs. Mae Read; 8, vacant; 9, Mrs. E. Boyce; 10, Miss M. A. Horn; 11, Mrs. S. C. Vause; 12, Miss C. Behrisch; 13, vacant; 14, Mrs. N. W. Wells; 15, Mrs. N. Raddatz; 16, Mrs. M. Ochsenreiter; 17, Mrs. E. D. Bush; 18, Mrs. M. J. McCurrach; 19, Mrs. J. Blank; 20, Mrs. C. O. Blaisdell; 21, Dr. I. Scott; 22, Mrs. F. C. Zimmerh; 23, Mrs. J. B. Kantcr.

Women's League of Voters—3d Assembly Dist., Kings Co. Hdqtrs., Public Library, Clinton and Union. Mrs. J. J. F. Doyle, Leader; Miss Irva McNevin, Sec., 33 Tompkins pl.; Mrs. Wm. Ferguson, Treas., 430 Clinton.

Manhattan and Bronx.

League of Women Voters—Hdqtrs., 37 W. 39th. City officers: Miss M. G. Hay, Ch.; Miss A. W. Sterling, Cor. Sec.; Mrs. H. L. Pratt, Treas.

Directors: Bkln., Mrs. A. P. Hutchins; Mhtn., Dr. K. B. Davis; Bronx, Miss E. Bayreuther; Queens, Miss E. Macdonald; Richmond, Mrs. C. E. Simonson.

Mhtn. Branch—Mrs. Chas. L. Tiffany, Ch.; Miss R. Glogau, Cor. Sec.; Mrs. B. Hanson, Treas. Consists of 23 Assembly Districts, with district leaders as follows:

1, Miss M. Fay; 2, Miss J. Schain; 3, vacant; 4, Miss I. Oppenheimer; 5, vacant; 6, vacant; 7, Mrs. R. Craft; 8, vacant; 9, Miss S. Peters; 10, Miss E. Stebbins; 11, Miss R. T. Oliver; 12, Miss H. Hill; 13, Miss E. D. Prendergast; 14, Mrs. J. Wademan; 15, Mrs. E. Parsons; 16, vacant; 17, Mrs. E. R. Weisberg; 18, Mrs. F. Woolston; 19, Mrs. F. A. Halsey; 20, vacant; 21, vacant; 22, Mrs. A. Kamholz; 23, Mrs. D. A. Kilborn.

Bronx Branch—Hdqtrs., 442 W. 238th. Mrs. H. Wilson, Ch. Consists of 8 Assembly Districts, with leaders as follows. 1, vacant; 2, Miss M. Lonergan; 3 and 4, vacant; 5, Mrs. M. Bowen; 6, Miss Gregory; 7, Mrs. O. Pierce; 8, Mrs. J. K. Small.

Queens.

League of Women Voters, Queens Borough—Mrs. A. Trowbridge, Ch.; Mrs. D. R. Rodger, Sec.

Richmond.

S. I. League of Women Voters—Mrs. W. G. Willcox, Ch., W. New Brighton; Mrs. J. L. Robertson, Cor. Sec., Bement av., W. New Brighton.

OTHER SUFFRAGE ORGANIZATIONS.

Anna Howard Shaw Civic League—Dr. Sophie Klenk, Pres., 1806 Caton av.

People's Political League of Kings Co.—Mrs. R. C. Talbot-Perkins, Pres., 1161 Fulton.

Bkln. Woman's Republican Union League—1896. Mrs. C. W. Fisk, Pres., 482 Greene av.; Mrs. Herbert Taylor, Sec., Richmond Hill.

Elizabeth Cady Stanton Political Equality League—Mrs. Orion White, Pres., 172 Madison.

Trade Union Woman's Suffrage League of Greater N. Y.—1914. A. J. Boulton, Pres.; F. A. Byrne, Sec.-Treas., 1428 E. 10th.

Rising Sun Woman Suffrage League—Mrs. M L. Rimes, Pres., 246 Lake dr., Mt. Lakes, N. J.; Dr. A. J. Sherman, Sec.; Mrs. N. B. Van Slingerland, Founder.

ANTI-SUFFRAGE ORGANIZATIONS.

National.

Natl. Assn. Opposed to Woman Suffrage—1911. 213 Oxford Bldg., Washington, D. C. Miss Mary G. Kilbreth, Pres.; Miss Margaret R. Grundy, Sec.

State.

Women Voters' Anti-Suffrage Party (formerly N. Y. State Assn. Opposed to Woman Suffrage)—218 St. James pl., Bkln. Mrs. D. H. Morton, Ch.; Mrs. B. Aymar Sands, Sec.

ASSEMBLY DISTRICT BOUNDARIES OF NEW YORK CITY.

(Population figures, 1920 U. S. Census.)

BROOKLYN.

1st—E. River and Congress, to Columbia, Warren, Clinton, Amity, Court, Dean, Boerum, Bergen, Nevins, Atlantic av., Bond, Fulton, Hudson av., DeKalb av., Navy, Lafayette, Raymond, Willoughby, St. Edwards, Bolivar, Raymond, Myrtle av., Prince, Johnson, Navy, Flushing av., Clinton av., Wallabout Channel. Pop., 86,912. 38 E. D.

2d—Sutter and Williams av., to Blake av., Pennsylvania av., Hegeman av., New Jersey av., Vienna av., Pennsylvania av., Jamaica Bay, boundary of Kings and Queens Co. south of Barren Island to Atlantic Ocean, west, and north, through Atlantic Ocean to Ocean P'kway, Av. J, E. 5th, Av. I, E. 4th, Elmwood av., E. 3d, Foster av., E. 17th, Av. I, Flatbush av., E. 34th, Av. J, Schenectady av., Glenwood rd., E. 46th, Farragut rd., Schenectady av., Clarendon rd., Ralph av., Church av., E. 91st, Linden av., Rockaway P'kway, Church av., E. 98th, Lott av., Thatford av., Livonia av., Osborn, Dumont av., Thatford av., Sutter av., to Williams av. Pop., 109,104. 49 E. D.

3d—E. River, Buttermilk Channel and Congress, Columbia, Warren, Clinton, Amity, Court, 1st pl., Summit, Hicks, Rapelyea, Hamilton av., 3d av., 24th, 4th av., 54th, 3d av., 59th, 4th av., 61st, 3d av., 63d, N. Y. Bay, to Buttermilk Channel, and E. River to Congress. Pop., 90,760. 27 E. D.

4th—E. River and B'way, to Berry, So. 6th, B'way, Havemeyer, So. 4th, Rodney, B'way, Division av., Harrison av., Rutledge, Marcy av., Walton, Wallabout, Harrison av., Flushing av., Nostrand av., Willoughby av., Spencer, Myrtle av., Washington Pk. or Cumberland, DeKalb av., Navy, Lafayette, Raymond, Willoughby, St. Edwards, Bolivar, Raymond, Myrtle av., Prince, Johnson, Navy, Flushing av., Clinton av., Wallabout Channel. Pop., 82,336. 38 E. D.

5th—Lewis av. and Van Buren, to Stuyvesant av., Quincy, Reid av., Greene av., B'way, Hopkinson av., McDonough, B'way, Eastern P'kway, Truxton, Stone av., McDougal, Saratoga av., Fulton, Ralph av., Herkimer, Rochester av., Atlantic av., Utica av., Pacific, Schenectady av., Fulton, Sumner av., McDonough, Lewis av., Van Buren. Pop., 67,808. 45 E. D.

6th—Nostrand and Flushing avs., to B'way, Greene av., Reid av., Quincy, Stuyvesant av., Van Buren, Lewis av., Greene av., Nostrand av., Flushing av. Pop., 85,895. 39 E. D.

7th—3d av. and 65th, to 6th av., 49th, 7th av., 40th, Ft. Hamilton av., Gravesend av., Terrace pl., 11th av., 17th, Terrace pl., Prospect av., Hamilton av., 3d av., 24th, 4th av., 54th, 3d av, 59th, 4th av., 61st, 3d av., 61st, Pop., 77,455. 36 E. D.

8th—Hamilton av. and Prospect av., to 4th av., Garfield pl., 5th av., St. Marks av. or pl., 4th av., Bergen, Boerum pl., Dean, Court, 1st pl., Summit, Hicks, Rapelyea, Hamilton av., Prospect av. Pop., 79,658. 29 E. D.

9th—40th and 13th av., 41st, 14th av., 46th, 13th av., 70th, 14th av., 75th, 15th av., Bath av., Bay 8th, Sharp av., 15th av., Gravesend Bay, south and west through Gravesend Bay to Narrows, thence N. Y. Bay to 63d, 3d av., 65th, 6th av., 49th, 7th av., 40th, Ft. Hamilton P'kway, 39th, 12th av., 40th, 13th av. Pop., 92,754. 48 E. D.

10th—Prospect Park W. and Union, to Carroll, 8th av., Garfield pl., 7th av., Carroll, 6th av., 5th, 5th av., 6th, 4th av., Garfield pl., 5th av., St. Marks av. or pl., 4th av., Bergen, Nevins, Atlantic av., Bond, Fulton, Hudson av., DeKalb av., St. Felix, Fulton, Ft. Greene pl., Hanson pl., So. Oxford, Fulton, Greene av., Vanderbilt av., DeKalb av., Franklin av., Lafayette av., Franklin av., Greene av., Waverly av., Atlantic av., Classon av., St. Marks av., Grand av., Washington av., Sterling pl., Classon av., St. Johns pl., Washington av., Malbone, Flatbush av., Prospect Pk. Plaza, Prospect Park W. and Union. Pop., 75,835. 51 E. D.

11th—DeKalb av. and St. Felix, to Washington Park or Cumberland, Myrtle av., Spencer, Willoughby av., Nostrand av., Lafayette av., Bedford av., Dean, N. Y. av., Park pl., Nostrand av., Eastern P'kway, N. Y. av., Sterling pl., Washington av., St. Johns pl., Classon av., Sterling pl., Washington av., Grand av., St. Marks av., Classon av., Atlantic av., Waverly av., Greene av., Franklin av., Lafayette av., Franklin av., DeKalb av., Vanderbilt av., Greene av., So. Oxford, Fulton, Hanson pl., Ft. Greene pl., Fulton, St. Felix, DeKalb av. Pop., 78,062. 56 E. D.

12th—Prospect av. and 4th av., to Terrace pl., 17th, 11th av., Terrace pl., Gravesend av., Fort Hamilton P'kway, 39th, 12th av., 40th, 13th av., 41st, 14th av., 37th, 15th av., West, Av. C, E. 9th, Beverly rd., Coney Island av., Caton av, Parade pl., Parkside av., Ocean av., Flatbush av., Prospect Pk. Plaza, Prospect Park W., Carroll, 8th av., Garfield pl., 7th av., Carroll, 6th av., 5th, 5th av., 6th, 4th av., Prospect av. Pop., 77,872. 52 E. D.

13th—Lorimer and Jackson, to Leonard, Skillman av., Graham av., Jackson, Manhattan av., Bayard, Graham av., Driggs av., Humboldt, Richardson, Kingsland av., Meeker av., Newtown Creek, Kings and Queens Cos., to Flushing av., Morgan av., Johnson av., White, Boerum, Bushwick av., Moore, Humboldt, McKibbin, Graham av., Siegel, Leonard, B'way, Bartlett, Throop av., Flushing av., Harrison av., Lorimer, Throop av., Walton, B'way, Lorimer, Jackson. Pop., 83,437. 28 E. D.

14th—E. River and B'way, Berry, So. 6th, B'way, Havemeyer, So. 4th, Rodney, B'way, Division av., Harrison av., Rutledge, Marcy av., Walton, Wallabout, Harrison av., Lorimer, Throop av., Walton, B'way, Lorimer, Frost, Union av., No. 12th, Berry, No. 11th, E. River, B'way. Pop., 97,344. 30 E. D.

15th—No. 11th and E. River, to Newtown Creek, Meeker av., Kingsland av., Richardson, Humboldt, Driggs av., Graham av., Bayard, Manhattan av., Jackson, Graham av., Skillman av., Leonard, Jackson, Lorimer, Frost, Union av., No. 12th, Berry, No. 11th, E. River. Pop. 73,027. 33 E. D.

16th—Foster av. and E. 3d, to Elmwood av., E. 4th, Av. I, E. 5th, Av. J, Ocean P'kway, Atlantic Ocean, Gravesend Bay, 15th av., Sharp av., Bay 8th, Bath av., 15th av., 75th, 14th av., 70th, 13th av., 46th, 14th av., 44th, 15th av., 50th, 16th av., 49th, 19th av., 47th, Parkville av., Gravesend av., Foster av., E. 3d. Pop., 97,110. 44 E. D.

17th—N. Y. av. and Park pl., to Bkln. av., Atlantic av., Albany av., Prospect pl., Rochester av., St. Marks av., Ralph av., Prospect pl., Howard av., Pacific, Ralph av., Atlantic av., Utica av., Pacific, Schenectady av., Fulton, Sumner av., McDonough, Lewis av., Greene av., Nostrand av., Lafayette av., Bedford av., Dean, N. Y. av. Pop., 75,487. 46 E. D.

18th—Sterling and N. Y. av., to Eastern P'kway, Nostrand av., Park pl., Bkln. av., Atlantic av., Albany av., Prospect pl., Rochester av., St. Marks av., Ralph av., Prospect pl., Howard av., Sutter av., Thatford av., Dumont av., Osborn, Livonia av., Thatford av., Lott av., E. 98th, Church av., Rockaway P'kway, Linden av., E. 91st, Church av., Ralph av., Clarendon rd., Schenectady av., Farragut rd., E. 46th, Glenwood rd., Schenectady av., Av. J, E. 34th, Flatbush av., Av. I, E. 29th, Germania pl., Flatbush av., E. 29th, Foster av., E. 28th, Newkirk av., E. 29th av., Nostrand av., Church av., N. Y. av., Sterling. Pop., 95,245. 57 E. D.

19th—Boundary line of Kings and Queens Cos. and Stanhope, to Hamburg av., DeKalb av., B'way, Flushing av., Throop av., Bartlett, B'way, Leonard, Siegel, Graham av., McKibbin, Humboldt, Moore, Bushwick av., Boerum, White, Johnson av., Morgan av., Flushing av., to boundary line of Kings and Queens Cos. Pop., 86,719. 28 E. D.

20th—Stanhope and boundary line of Kings and Queens Cos., Wilson av., DeKalb av., B'way, Hopkinson av., McDonough, B'way, Eastern P'kway, Bushwick av., Highland blvd., boundary bet. Kings and Queens Cos., to Stanhope. Pop., 99,357. 64 E. D.

21st—Sterling and N. Y. av., to Church av., Nostrand av., Av. D, E. 29th, Newkirk av., E. 28th, Foster av., E. 29th, Flatbush av., Germania pl., E. 29th, Av. I, E. 17th, Foster av., Gravesend av., Parkville av., 47th, 19th av., 49th, 16th av., 50th, 15th av., 44th, 14th av., 37th, 15th av., West, Av. C, E. 9th, Beverly rd., Coney Island av., Caton av., Parade Pk., Parkside av., Ocean av., Malbone, Flatbush av., Sterling, N. Y. av. Pop., 84,484. 59 E. D.

22d—B'way and Eastern P'kway to Jamaica av., Alabama av., Atlantic av., Williams av., Blake av., Pennsylvania av., Hegeman av., New Jersey av., Vienna av., Pennsylvania av., Jamaica Bay, E. of Duck Pt. Marsh, to boundary line of Kings and Queens Cos., Highland blvd., Bushwick av., Eastern P'way. Pop., 122,637. 58 E. D.

23d—Fulton and Alabama av., B'way, Eastern P'kway, Truxton, Stone, McDougal, Saratoga av., Fulton, Ralph av., Herkimer, Rochester av., Atlantic av., Ralph av., Pacific, Howard av., Sutter av., Williams av., Atlantic av., Alabama av., Fulton. Pop., 99,058. 28 E. D.

ASSEMBLY DISTRICT BOUNDARIES OF NEW YORK CITY—*Continued.*

MANHATTAN

1st—E. River and Gouverneur Slip, to Water, Scammel, Cherry, Gouverneur, Grand, Clinton, Henry, Catharine, Division, Chrystie, Canal, B'way, Broome, Sullivan, Spring, McDougal, W. Houston, Bedford, 7th av., Christopher, Bleecker, Charles, Greenwich, W. 10th, Hudson River and Bedloe's, Ellis and Oyster Islands. Pop., 137,532. 40 E. D.

2d—Clinton, Grand, to Essex, Broome, Ludlow, E. Houston, 2d av., E. 4th, B'way, W. 3d, 6th av., W. Washington pl., 7th av., Bedford, W. Houston, McDougal, Spring, Sullivan, Broome, B'way, Canal, Chrystie, Division, Catharine, Henry, Clinton, Grand. Pop., 147,115. 31 E. D.

3d—W. 10th, Hudson River, Greenwich, Charles, Bleecker, W. 11th, W. 4th, Bank, Bleecker, 8th av., W. 14th, 7th av., W. 37th, 8th av., W. 40th, Hudson River, W. 10th. Pop., 113,098. 49 E. D.

4th—E. River, Gouverneur Slip, Gouverneur, Water, Scammel, Cherry, Gouverneur, Grand, Essex, Broome, Ludlow, Stanton, Suffolk, E. Houston, Sheriff, Stanton, Gouverneur Slip. Pop., 94,980. 23 E. D.

5th—W. 40th and Hudson River, W. 40th, 8th av., W. 43d, 7th av., W. 44th, 8th av., W. 57th, 9th av., Columbus av., W. 63d, Hudson River, W. 40th. Pop., 103,166. 52 E. D.

6th—E. River and Stanton, Sheriff, E. Houston, Av. B, E. 10th, Av. C, E. 12th, Av. A, E. 14th, 1st av., E. 15th, 2d av., E. 16th, 1st av., E. 17th, Av. B, E. 8th, E. River, Stanton. Pop., 99,165. 26 E. D.

7th—W. 63d and Hudson River, Columbus av., 9th av., W. 58th, 8th av., B'way, W. 62d, Central Park W., W. 81st, Columbus av., W. 94th, Amsterdam av., W. 86th, B'way, W. 83d, Hudson River, W. 63d. Pop., 85,486. 53 E. D.

8th—Av. B and E. Houston, Suffolk, Stanton, Ludlow, E. Houston, 2d av., E. 4th, B'way, Astor pl., 4th av., E. 14th, Irving pl., E. 15th, 3d av., E. 16th, 2d av., E. 15th, 1st av., E. 14th, Av. A, E. 12th, Av. C, E. 10th, Av. B, E. Houston. Pop., 109,522. 28 E. D.

9th—W. 83d and Hudson River, B'way, W. 86th, Amsterdam av., W. 94th, Columbus av., W. 81st, Central Park W., W. 104th, Columbus av., W. 103d, Amsterdam av., W. 101st, Hudson River, W. 83d. Pop., 82,994. 53 E. D.

10th—B'way and W. 3d, 6th av., W. Washington pl., Christopher, Bleecker, W. 11th, W. 4th, Bank, Bleecker, 8th av., W. 14th, 7th av., W. 37th, 8th av., W. 43d, 7th av., W. 44th, 8th av., W. 55th, 7th av., W. 52d, 6th av., W. 53d, 5th av., E. 47th, Madison av., E. 49th, Lexington av., E. 40th, 3d av., E. 34th, Lexington av., E. 22d, 3d av., E. 15th, Irving pl., E. 14th, 4th av., Astor pl., B'way, W. 3d. Pop., 79,801. 48 E. D.

11th—Hudson River and W. 101st, to Amsterdam av., W 103d, Columbus av., W. 104th, Central Park W., W. 110th, 7th av., W. 118th, St. Nicholas av., W. 119th, Morningside Park E., W. 116th, Amsterdam av., W. 114th, B'way, W. 116th, Hudson River, W. 101st. Pop., 79,314. 47 E. D.

12th—E. 18th and E. River, to Av. B, E. 17th, 1st av., E. 16th, 3d av., E. 22d, Lexington av., E. 34th, 3d av., E. 40th, Lexington av., E. 52d, 1st av., E. 54th, to E. River, to E. 18th, including Blackwell's Island. Pop., 121,539. 53 E. D.

13th—W. 116th and Hudson River, to B'way, W. 114th, Amsterdam av., W. 116th, Morningside av., E., W. 124th and Hancock pl., Mhtn. av., W. 123d, 8th av., W. 128th, 7th av., W. 136th, Hudson River, to W. 116th. Pop., 76,008. 43 E. D.

14th—E. 54th and E. River to 1st av., E. 52d, 3d av., E. 74th, Lexington av., E. 76th, 3d av., E. 77th, to Av. A, E. 84th, E. End av., E. 81st, E. River, to E. 54th. Pop., 120,879. 44 E. D.

15th—E. 49th and Lexington av., to Madison av., E. 47th, 5th av., W. 53d, 6th av., W. 52d, 7th av., W. 55th, 8th av., W. 57th, 9th av., W. 58th, 8th av., B'way, W. 62d, Central Park W., transverse rd. at W. 97th, across Central Park, through and along transverse rd., at 97th, 5th av., E. 104th, Madison av., E. 101st, Park av., E. 96th, Lexington av., E. 79th, 3d av., E. 76th, Lexington av., E. 74th, 3d av., E. 52d, Lexington av., E. 49th. Pop., 96,072. 55 E. D.

16th—E. 81st and E. River, to East End av. E. 84th, Av. A, E. 77th, 3d av., E. 79th, Lexington av., E. 89th, 3d av., E. 100th, 2d av., E. 98th, E. River, to E. 81st. Pop., 108,117. 54 E. D.

17th—E. 101st and Park av., to Madison av., E. 104th, 5th av., transverse rd. at E. 97th, extending across said transverse rd. in Central Park to Central Park W. at 97th, W. 110th, 7th av., W. 118th, E. and W. 118th, Park av., E. 101st. Pop., 85,668. 36 E. D.

18th—E. 98th to 2d av., E. 100th, 3d av., E. 89th, Lexington av., E. 96th, Park av., E. 117th, 3d av., E. 118th, 2d av., E. 115th, E. River, E. 98th. Incl. Ward's Island. Pop., 141,790. 37 E. D.

19th—Park av. and E. 118th, to St. Nicholas av., W. 119th, Morningside av. E., W. 12th and Hancock pl., Mhtn. av., W. 123d, 8th av., W. 128th, 7th av., W. 136th, Lenox av., W. 137th, Madison av., E. 128th, 5th av., E. 124th, Madison av., E. 120th, Park av., E. 118th. Pop., 78,052. 44 E. D.

20th—E. River and 115th, to 2d av., E. 118th, 3d av., E. 117th, Park av., E. 120th, Madison av., E. 124th, 5th av., E. 128th, Madison av, E. 134th, Harlem River, E. River, E. 115th, incl. Randall's Island and the Sunken Meadows. Pop., 83,156. 26 E. D.

21st—W. 136th and Hudson River, to Lenox av., W. 137th, Madison av., E. 134th, Harlem River, E. 144th, 8th av., W. 145th, Edgecombe av. or Colonial P'kway, W. 155th, St. Nicholas av., Convent av., W. 142d, Hamilton pl., W. 144th, Hudson River, W. 136th. Pop., 76,982. 46 E. D.

22d—W. 144th and Hudson River, to Amsterdam av., Hamilton pl., W. 142d, Convent av., St. Nicholas av., W. 155th, Edgecome av. or Colonial P'kway, W. 145th, 8th av., W. 144th, Harlem River, W. 162d, Fort Washington av., W. 161st, Riverside Drive, W. 165th, Hudson River, W. 144th. Pop., 74,895. 51 E. D.

23d—W. 165th and Hudson River, to Riverside Drive, W. 161st, Fort Washington av., W. 162d, Harlem River, Spuyten Duyvil Creek, Ship Canal, to Hudson River, to W. 165th. Pop., 88,787. 60 E. D.

BRONX.

1st—E. 140th and E. River, to Locust av., E. 141st, Jackson av., E. 145th, Trinity av., E. 149th, St. Anns av., E. 156th, Cauldwell av., E. 164th, Boston rd., 3d av., Weiher court, Washington av., E. 165th, Park av., E. 162d, Grant av., E. 161st, Morris av., E. 150th, Melrose av., E. 149th, Bergen av., Willis av., E. 143d, 3d av., E. 142d, Alexander av., E. 140th, Brook av., E. 132d, Lincoln av., Harlem River, Bronx Kills, E. River. Pop., 110,315. 52 E. D.

2d—Lincoln av. and Harlem River, to E. 132d, Brook av., E. 140th, Alexander av., E. 142d, 3d av., E. 143d, Willis av., Bergen av., E. 149th, Melrose av., E. 150th, Morris av., E. 161st, Grant av., E. 162d, Park av., E. 165th, Washington av., Weiher court, 3d av., E. 166th, Washington av., E. 175th, Park av., E. 177th, E. 176th, Anthony av., E. Tremont av., Mount Hope av., E. 176th, Morris av., Mount Hope pl., Walton av., E. 177th, W. 177th, W. Tremont av., Macombs rd., Featherbed lane, Aqueduct av., W. 172d, Harlem River, to boundary line bet. N. Y. and Bronx Cos., then south along boundary, through Harlem River, to Lincoln av. Pop., 117,611. 67 E. D.

3d—E. 140th and E. River, to Locust av., E. 141st, Jackson av., E. 145th, Trinity av., E. 149th, St. Anns av., E. 156th, Cauldwell av., E. 163d, Union av., E. 160th, Westchester av., E. 163d, Tiffany, Southern blvd., Barretto, Garrison av., Hunts Pt. av., Lafayette av., Bronx River, E. River, to W. 140th. Including Riker's, So. Brothers and No. Brothers Island. Pop., 83,042. 38 E. D.

4th—E. 163d and Cauldwell av., to Union av., E. 160th, Prospect av., Freeman, Bristow, Jennings, Charlotte, E. 170th, Wilkins av., Boston rd., E. 172d, Seabury pl., Boston rd., Southern blvd., E. 175th, Crotona Park North, Arthur av., E. 175th, Washington av., E. 166th, 3d av., Boston rd., E. 164th, Cauldwell av. Pop., 84,195. 35 E. D.

5th—Prospect av. and Westchester av., Freeman Bristow, Jennings, Charlotte, E. 170th, Wilkins av., Boston rd., E. 172d, Seabury pl., Boston rd., Southern blvd., E. 175th, Boston rd., Hoe av., E. 174th, Bronx River, So to Lafayette av., Hunts Pt. av., Garrison av., Barretto, Southern blvd., Tiffany, E. 163d, Westchester av. Pop., 88,428. 44 E. D.

6th—Hoe av. and E. 174th, Boston rd., Vyse av., E. Tremont av., Boston rd., E. 178th, Bryant av., E. 180th, Boston rd., Bronx Park South, Southern blvd., Pelham av., Bronx River, E. 233d, Mt. Vernon av., northerly boundary line of City of N. Y., E. River, Bronx River, E. 174th. Pop., 70,482. 36 E. D.

7th—E. 175th and Park av., Arthur av., Crotona Pk. North, E. 175th, Boston rd., Vyse av., E. Tremont av., Boston rd., E. 178th, Bryant av., E. 180th, Boston rd., Bronx Park South, Southern blvd., Pelham av., Cambreling av., E. 189th, Hoffman, E. 187th, Lorillard pl., E. 184th, Park av. Pop., 89,123. 43 E. D.

ASSEMBLY DISTRICT BOUNDARIES OF NEW YORK CITY—BRONX—*Continued.*

8th—E. 177th and Park av., to E. 176th, Anthony av., E. Tremont av., Mount Hope av., E. 176th. Morris av., Mount Hope pl., Walton av., E. 177th, W. 177th, W. Tremont av., Macomb's rd., Featherbed lane, Aqueduct av., W. 172d, Harlem River, to boundary line bet. N. Y. and Bronx Cos., Hudson River, to northerly boundary line of City of N. Y., easterly along boundary line to Mt. Vernon av., E. 233d, Bronx River, south through Bronx River, Pelham av., Cambreling av., E. 189th, Hoffman, E. 187th, Lorillard pl., E. 184th, Park av. Pop., 88,820. 66 E. D.

QUEENS.

1st—Boundary bet. Kings and Queens Cos. in Newtown Creek, bulkhead line of E. River, prolonged; thence to center line of Dutchkills Creek, to prolongation thereof until intersected by prolongation of Rapelje av. or 4th av.; thence Jackson av., Old Bowery Bay rd., Astoria av. or Flushing av., Woolsey av., Steinway av. or 10th av., Potter av., Kouwenhoven or 9th av., Bowery Bay and E. River; thence to beginning, incl. Berrians Island. Citizen pop., 78,805. 46 E. D.

2d—On line dividing Brooklyn and Queens Cos. in Newtown Creek, center line of Dutchkills Creek, prolonged; thence to Woodbine, Woodward av., Palmetto. Grand View av., Linden. Forest av., Gates av., Fresh Pond rd., Hancock, Hughes or Woodbine, L. I. R.R., Woodhaven av., Yellowstone av., to intersection of Lawn av. with Mill Creek; thence to point opposite intersection of Junction and Newtown avs.; to Justice, Laconia or Broad, Queens blvd., Grand, Calamus rd., Fisk av., Woodside av., Skillman av., Greenpoint av., Celtic av., Dickinson av., Middleburg av., Woodside av., Jackson av., 4th av., Rapelje av., intersection of center line to Dutchkills Creek, to boundary line bet. Brooklyn and Queens. Pop., 73,273. 44 E. D.

3d—Jackson av. and Woodside av., Middleburg av., Dickinson av., Celtic av., Greenpoint av., Skillman av., Woodside av., Fisk av., Calamus rd., Grand, Queens blvd., Laconia or Broad, Justice, intersection of Junction av., to point on Mill Creek, opposite intersection of Junction and Justice or Newtown rd., thence following Mill Creek to intersection of Yellowstone av. and Lawn av. at Mill Creek, to Flushing Creek, Strong's Causeway, Ireland Mill rd., Lawrence, to Bradford av., Main, Lincoln av., Union av., Whitestone av., Bayside av., Little Bayside rd., Poppenhusen av., Bell av., Mulford av., Little Neck Bay, following boundary line bet. Queens Co. and The Bronx and Queens Cos. and Mhtn. to intersection of Kouwenhouven or 9th av., Potter av., Steinway or 10th av., Woolsey av., Astoria av., Old Bowery Bay rd., Jackson av. or Woodside av. Pop., 76,593. 49 E. D.

4th—Little Neck Bay, where same is intersected by Mulford, prolonged, thence to Bell av., Poppenhusen av., Saxe, Bayside av., Whitestone av., Union av., Lincoln av., to Main, Bradford av., Lawrence, Ireland Mill rd., Flushing Creek and Strong's Causeway, along Flushing Creek to intersection of line bet. 2d and 4th Wards, Newtown rd., Lefferts av., Atlantic av., So. Cochran av., Garden, Van Wyck av., Old Lincoln av., Rockaway blvd. or Rockaway rd., to line bet. Bkln. and Nassau at Hook Creek, to prolongation of Mulford av. and Little Neck Bay. Pop., 83,175. 52 E. D.

5th—Line bet. Bkln. and Queens and Atlantic av., to Ferry, Jamaica av., Gherardi or Woodland av., Syosset or 3d, Thrall, Syosset or Russell, Woodhaven av., Jamaica av., Waterbury, prolongation thereof to Myrtle av., along boundary line bet. 2d and 4th Wards, to Newtown rd., Lefferts av., Atlantic av., So. Cochran av., Garden, Van Wyck av., Old Lincoln av., to Rockaway rd. or Rockaway blvd., to boundary line bet. Queens and Nassau at Hook Creek, thence through Far Rockaway to Atlantic Ocean, to intersection of boundary line bet. Bkln. and Queens, thence to Atlantic av. Pop., 83,228. 52 E. D.

6th—At intersection of line bet. Bkln. and Queens, to Woodbine, Woodward av., Palmetto av., Grand View av., Linden, Forest av., Gates av., Fresh Pond rd., Hancock, Hughes or Woodbine, L. I. R.R., Woodhaven av., Woodhaven or Yellowstone av., Mill Creek and Lawn av., Flushing Creek, the line bet. 2d and 4th Wards, to prolongation of Waterbury, Jamaica av., Woodhaven av., Syosset or Russell, Thrall, Syosset or 3d, Gherardi av., Jamaica av., Ferry, Atlantic av., to the line bet. Bkln. and Queens, thence to intersection of Woodbine, to point or place of beginning. Pop., 73,968. 54 E. D.

RICHMOND.

1st—Beginning at Upper N. Y. Bay at ft. of Vanderbilt av., to Richmond rd., Rockland av. (formerly Egbert av.), Bradley av. (formerly Manor rd.), Willow Brook rd., Watchogue rd., to a brook known as Palmer's Run, Forest av. (formerly Cherry lane), to intersection of Post and Jewett avs., to Kill van Kull, to Upper N. Y. Bay. Pop., 55,681. 43 E. D.

2d—Beginning at Upper N. Y. Bay at ft. of Vanderbilt av., Richmond rd., Rockland av., Bradley av., to Willow Brook rd., Patchogue rd., to Palmer's Run, Forest av., to intersection of Post and Jewett avs., to Kill van Kull, following State boundary line along Kill van Kull and Newark Bay to Staten Island Sound, or Arthur Kill, thence Raritan Bay and Lower N. Y. Bay to Narrows.

In addition to above territory following: All of Shooters Island, so much of Buckwheat Island as is within State of N. Y., Prall's Island, Meadow Island, Hoffman Island, Swinburne Island and Great Kills Point. Pop., 60,850, 33 E. D.

ELECTION AND ASSEMBLY DISTRICTS TOTALS IN N. Y. C.

Mhtn., 997 election dists.; The Bronx, 381; Bkln., 977; Queens, 291; Richmond, 76. Grand total; 2,712.

MANHATTAN.

1st A. D., 40 E. D.; 2d, 31; 3d, 49; 4th, 23; 5th, 52; 6th, 26; 7th, 53; 8th, 28; 9th, 58; 10th, 48; 11th, 47; 12th, 58; 13th, 48; 14th, 44; 15th, 55; 16th, 54; 17th, 36; 18th, 37; 19th, 44; 20th, 26; 21st, 46; 22d, 51; 23d, 60. Total, 997.

BRONX.

1st A. D., 52 E. D.; 2d, 67; 3d, 38; 4th, 35; 5th, 44; 6th, 36; 7th, 43; 8th, 66. Total, 381.

BROOKLYN.

1st A. D., 38 E. D.; 2d, 49; 3d, 27; 4th, 38; 5th, 45; 6th, 39; 7th, 36; 8th, 29; 9th, 48; 10th, 51; 11th, 56; 12th, 52; 13th, 28; 14th, 30; 15th, 33; 16th, 44; 17th, 46; 18th, 51; 19th, 28; 20th, 64; 21st, 59; 22d, 58; 23d, 28. Total, 977.

QUEENS.

1st A. D., 46 E. D.; 2d, 44; 3d, 49; 4th, 52; 5th, 46; 6th, 54. Total, 291.

RICHMOND.

1st A. D., 43 E. D.; 2d, 33 Total, 76.

POLITICAL DISTRICTS.

The following table shows at a glance Assembly districts in each Congressional and Senatorial districts:

Assembly Dist.	Congressional. Dist.	N.Y. Senatorial Dist.
	BROOKLYN.	
13, 15, 19	3	10
3, 7, 8	4	5
11, 12, 10	5	6
17, 18, 21	6	8
1, 4, 14	7	11
2, 9, 16	8	4
20, 22	9	9
5, 6, 23	10	7
Parts of	MANHATTAN.	
1, 2	11	12
3, 5	15	13
4, 6, 8	13	14
7, 9, 12	19	15
12, 14	16	16
10, 15, 17	17	17
16, 18	18	18
13, 19, 20	21-22	19
21, 22, 23	21-22	20
	BRONX.	
1, 2, 3	22	21
Parts of 1, 2, 3, 4, 5, 6, 7, 8	23	22
3, 5, 6, 7	24	23
	QUEENS.	
1, 2, 3	2	2
4, 5, 6	2	3
Parts of 4, 5, 6	9	..
Parts of 3, 4	1	..
	RICHMOND.	
1, 2	11	24

BROOKLYN VOTE, 1920—For President and Governor.

1st Assembly District.

Elec. Dist.	Reg'trat'n. Male.	Reg'trat'n. Female.	Cox, Dem.	Harding, Rep.	Smith, Dem.	Miller, Rep.
1	302	62	148	169	213	98
2	329	152	224	187	340	78
3	342	93	143	240	288	85
4	327	130	218	185	300	92
5	432	110	118	269	259	209
6	364	152	208	240	351	97
7	307	168	220	179	329	87
8	347	136	170	234	309	82
9	304	77	189	144	284	56
10	334	199	212	245	338	108
11	363	175	234	229	346	102
12	368	129	175	271	280	144
13	337	136	174	270	237	156
14	277	135	163	262	191	147
15	317	157	79	319	181	204
16	325	162	127	294	201	238
17	318	189	150	306	298	140
18	315	132	127	276	221	163
19	295	162	134	290	258	145
20	330	261	209	334	328	204
21	317	184	163	254	334	85
22	366	113	94	232	229	93
23	358	181	166	312	336	137
24	278	249	189	288	299	165
25	309	170	193	237	257	123
26	349	343	188	428	290	333
27	346	220	145	370	295	272
†28	439	363	82	382	157	292
29	352	296	132	454	226	368
30	377	324	132	459	262	347
31	342	152	167	275	251	169
†32	392	347	109	287	163	232
†33	451	417	63	258	114	301
34	347	182	231	241	335	117
35	335	136	201	224	357	67
*36	...	...	65	223	127	161
*37	...	...	112	168	193	81
*38	...	...	102	387	170	315
	11910	6582	5891	10491	9909	6132

Total registration, 18,492.

2d Assembly District.

Elec. Dist.	Reg'trat'n. Male.	Reg'trat'n. Female.	Cox, Dem.	Harding, Rep.	Smith, Dem.	Miller, Rep.
1	148	102	59	167	155	103
2	365	307	143	464	300	295
†3	377	331	73	278	177	371
4	401	263	139	477	325	262
5	400	252	130	429	336	213
6	357	247	130	407	333	196
7	400	277	211	379	407	170
8	353	198	193	306	336	173
9	371	276	178	401	350	206
10	403	261	224	359	364	200
11	377	258	245	354	394	178
12	336	207	147	329	269	188
13	404	230	144	336	317	157
14	373	239	208	325	365	162
†15	459	291	214	217	320	109
16	409	176	167	362	285	217
17	324	229	221	283	338	159
18	123	82	54	125	125	59
†19	423	319	111	275	216	171
†20	463	337	105	238	159	180
†21	407	346	73	224	155	133
22	397	291	192	427	317	250
23	404	266	159	447	318	267
24	311	144	106	304	232	150
25	12	14	13	11	11	11
26	225	111	41	201	95	177
27	204	83	27	139	74	77
28	292	159	92	316	220	159
29	215	108	80	217	170	100
30	326	153	97	312	285	183
31	391	181	17	171	128	68
32	384	128	32	126	100	61
33	285	110	18	115	90	49
34	306	126	24	140	117	52
35	377	170	31	159	120	71
36	394	189	26	127	99	61
37	452	202	17	146	146	45
38	364	225	11	95	108	40
39	454	179	22	144	116	58
40	415	194	17	139	148	50
41	415	185	22	178	164	67
42	341	160	28	220	166	94
43	271	121	82	258	166	139
44	24	14	11	21	20	5
*45	...	...	38	254	112	174
*46	...	...	62	154	144	77
*47	...	...	71	197	156	119
*48	...	...	110	284	202	173
*49	...	...	73	349	181	229
	14931	8731	4688	12400	10077	6687

Total registration, 23,662.

*New Elec. Dist. created after last day of registration.

†Election Districts divided for Election Day on account of heavy registration.

3d Assembly District.

Elec. Dist.	Reg'trat'n. Male.	Reg'trat'n. Female.	Cox, Dem.	Harding, Rep.	Smith, Dem.	Miller, Rep.
1	378	255	328	246	445	122
2	163	119	159	96	218	38
3	307	121	189	194	295	79
4	342	43	116	221	228	83
5	301	124	130	236	242	120
6	296	178	210	211	311	115
7	317	182	197	247	290	143
8	272	211	170	268	292	122
9	324	63	145	187	253	81
10	340	76	199	165	298	59
11	229	84	150	122	210	34
12	301	98	203	139	265	55
13	260	111	138	202	230	80
14	319	120	196	195	305	66
15	311	118	232	154	312	51
16	319	113	223	157	315	54
17	310	46	93	198	180	85
18	394	93	104	304	221	137
19	310	62	123	204	209	90
20	332	147	171	244	290	90
21	355	159	172	283	280	130
22	344	167	128	325	275	135
23	336	124	108	273	209	128
24	378	190	150	244	283	189
25	367	145	140	305	282	131
26	297	113	126	207	231	99
27	383	198	169	335	344	129
	8585	3450	4469	6062	7313	2637

Total registration, 12,035.

4th Assembly District.

Elec. Dist.	Reg'trat'n. Male.	Reg'trat'n. Female.	Cox, Dem.	Harding, Rep.	Smith, Dem.	Miller, Rep.
1	285	144	168	195	284	74
2	329	140	75	237	228	94
3	330	186	165	239	310	92
4	329	206	170	265	319	112
5	350	211	128	316	316	119
6	357	154	76	266	269	98
7	339	134	100	236	255	72
8	342	112	91	217	225	89
9	382	179	87	302	248	135
10	294	143	77	249	197	122
11	367	218	116	295	274	119
12	415	266	157	380	369	175
13	370	235	115	386	284	228
14	289	141	200	187	307	69
15	350	183	70	264	271	108
16	336	217	125	314	298	125
17	372	241	169	326	345	141
18	348	251	109	382	318	178
19	360	211	143	302	301	146
20	286	164	114	259	227	141
21	340	234	108	329	303	139
22	335	176	90	318	261	125
23	294	87	73	200	156	100
24	367	102	114	278	223	162
25	324	88	138	215	251	93
26	339	96	117	283	204	170
27	379	82	140	270	245	147
28	406	148	207	290	352	123
29	137	72	84	109	145	42
30	336	144	240	203	360	73
31	286	157	183	219	277	108
32	225	147	170	169	255	71
33	173	136	104	175	186	94
34	342	206	232	255	342	132
35	337	233	288	243	427	91
36	351	151	282	234	345	115
37	394	128	183	275	318	136
38	460	127	187	353	325	174
	12657	6249	5396	10005	10510	4527

Total registration, 18,906.

5th Assembly District.

Elec. Dist.	Reg'trat'n. Male.	Reg'trat'n. Female.	Cox, Dem.	Harding, Rep.	Smith, Dem.	Miller, Rep.
1	361	215	137	355	309	167
2	337	242	130	328	231	270
3	301	320	124	465	218	358
4	351	315	191	412	316	272
5	309	286	140	416	277	243
6	267	216	121	322	248	182
7	396	212	87	412	203	264
8	408	246	125	449	280	286
9	342	299	151	438	270	294
†10	358	354	121	300	218	186
11	358	313	154	468	281	215
12	377	243	137	395	290	225
13	374	301	140	445	327	233
14	321	221	120	346	262	174
15	358	201	146	347	290	188
16	380	267	148	432	307	236
17	364	266	152	400	358	152
18	382	238	149	383	320	178
19	350	246	153	395	314	179
20	335	295	164	434	306	257
21	269	263	131	284	223	163
†22	393	320	82	336	198	208
23	316	271	154	379	299	210
24	335	308	145	448	288	294
25	348	291	166	430	307	256
26	371	300	162	467	329	265
27	221	165	98	262	196	151
28	410	266	176	450	362	241
29	376	248	144	430	272	277
30	329	218	123	379	223	252
31	359	296	170	443	357	241
32	281	208	77	387	240	192
33	323	227	127	364	254	211
34	317	180	77	387	225	222
35	367	210	104	418	285	230
36	373	211	116	404	282	181
37	296	160	89	329	242	144
38	279	167	127	275	249	128
39	337	230	147	374	328	166
40	360	181	108	302	208	173
41	395	150	125	285	248	131
42	335	229	167	346	346	144
43	310	193	135	319	307	127
*44	...	...	63	159	124	97
*45	...	...	57	156	119	90
	14527	10588	5846	16690	12167	9471

Total registration, 25,115.

6th Assembly District.

Elec. Dist.	Reg'trat'n. Male.	Reg'trat'n. Female.	Cox, Dem.	Harding, Rep.	Smith, Dem.	Miller, Rep.
1	258	106	81	203	166	107
2	365	154	34	181	122	100
3	358	122	39	237	155	101
4	278	116	22	205	113	104
5	285	141	44	227	158	110
6	311	133	36	211	145	99
7	335	132	21	183	111	84
8	327	115	91	222	210	86
9	326	147	73	256	189	118
10	344	138	84	230	210	107
11	362	228	105	295	252	150
12	302	208	96	290	236	155
13	288	142	41	206	161	78
14	314	133	75	189	174	80
15	362	170	41	262	193	99
16	307	150	48	251	229	90
17	341	150	27	280	208	126
18	327	128	43	174	121	84
19	331	170	62	243	182	104
20	325	199	93	293	268	108
21	311	132	87	244	242	89
22	375	172	134	299	274	142
23	362	180	59	142	261	153
24	315	197	107	291	261	141
25	347	179	99	285	269	117
26	272	160	78	246	211	113
27	310	160	71	290	204	196
28	274	189	33	231	162	118
29	355	220	97	317	268	134
30	374	185	86	291	241	131
31	326	168	44	241	190	108
32	276	131	93	249	193	137
33	133	90	69	143	102	84
34	346	212	129	330	303	147
35	267	212	94	289	220	109
36	235	183	52	266	176	136
37	315	209	101	307	252	144
38	366	278	134	426	298	235
39	338	246	157	341	284	193
	12342	6489	2921	9943	8019	4676

Total registration, 18,8[illegible]1.

BROOKLYN VOTE, 1920—FOR PRESIDENT AND GOVERNOR—*Continued.*

7th Assembly District.

Elec. Dist.	Reg'trat'n. Male.	Reg'trat'n. Female.	Cox, Dem.	Harding, Rep.	Smith, Dem.	Miller, Rep.
1	312	263	176	355	336	171
2	356	232	203	320	364	135
3	370	232	233	295	366	134
4	332	315	220	267	383	84
5	390	220	235	310	425	102
6	289	153	115	274	236	136
7	362	232	215	302	363	150
8	330	170	160	304	322	113
9	363	207	198	312	314	158
10	384	232	196	340	343	145
11	310	155	123	267	246	132
12	358	186	128	335	265	162
13	298	173	120	300	246	140
14	286	155	122	272	223	146
15	340	216	162	345	300	173
16	310	170	92	323	222	174
17	312	186	142	301	288	124
18	372	217	156	360	291	195
19	330	234	167	319	309	158
20	413	177	179	335	352	136
21	350	164	139	292	281	115
22	243	106	94	209	271	139
23	84	43	43	60	79	19
24	324	143	150	293	246	122
25	289	111	150	204	229	89
26	378	85	157	261	264	122
27	375	72	119	267	251	105
28	332	172	197	236	300	129
29	367	130	140	310	286	149
30	295	112	139	221	241	93
31	349	153	164	276	280	138
32	359	149	164	273	271	139
33	352	160	194	251	312	113
34	322	122	163	225	258	102
35	344	175	208	259	276	102
36	2	1	...	3	...	...
	11562	5913	5562	9891	10012	4534

Total registration, 17,475.

8th Assembly District.

Elec. Dist.	Reg'trat'n. Male.	Reg'trat'n. Female.	Cox, Dem.	Harding, Rep.	Smith, Dem.	Miller, Rep.
1	395	202	200	313	369	124
2	337	142	200	215	331	97
3	366	236	288	250	424	107
4	334	136	220	81	312	84
5	352	131	224	193	314	103
6	345	161	225	229	337	107
7	279	137	163	205	273	68
8	308	170	235	189	340	82
9	347	157	154	282	271	149
10	418	199	196	346	376	158
11	375	175	201	88	335	128
12	360	170	157	291	313	138
13	395	81	82	339	331	141
14	379	57	93	292	200	163
15	364	160	270	204	370	77
16	335	162	251	206	364	64
17	372	201	232	288	356	145
18	308	257	237	286	340	155
19	375	210	237	273	396	102
20	336	166	204	227	312	101
21	245	85	132	166	230	61
22	294	137	185	205	283	81
23	318	135	205	210	228	74
24	278	89	162	161	261	46
25	359	113	168	245	305	76
26	318	136	291	136	371	41
27	406	213	218	342	351	105
28	352	103	175	316	300	129
29	352	133	177	247	281	112
	9982	4454	5788	6726	9278	3098

Total registration, 14,436.

9th Assembly District.

Elec. Dist.	Reg'trat'n. Male.	Reg'trat'n. Female.	Cox, Dem.	Harding, Rep.	Smith, Dem.	Miller, Rep.
1	330	137	22	214	152	92
2	356	177	61	325	254	136
3	318	160	87	373	223	124
4	339	165	89	294	285	99
5	445	203	133	405	293	209
6	399	202	109	392	269	181
7	314	213	173	305	302	153
8	371	269	154	410	361	208
9	361	157	60	355	276	137

*New Elec. Dist. created after last day of registration.

†Election Districts divided for Election Day on account of heavy registration.

9th A. D.—Continued.

Elec. Dist.	Reg'trat'n. Male.	Reg'trat'n. Female.	Cox, Dem.	Harding, Rep.	Smith, Dem.	Miller, Rep.
10	429	285	152	435	349	217
11	68	35	23	69	47	35
12	325	100	61	314	172	178
13	458	215	151	430	352	188
14	406	260	142	464	323	228
15	353	193	138	330	287	161
16	413	270	151	467	376	222
17	378	266	232	364	407	144
18	400	269	219	379	443	138
19	394	203	148	351	321	181
20	395	236	142	416	338	199
†21	438	302	89	275	198	167
22	402	243	152	428	302	238
23	371	191	118	367	284	183
24	207	146	91	217	185	106
25	357	186	142	338	291	164
26	333	150	155	278	281	116
†27	419	300	71	162	125	93
†28	459	323	79	251	172	152
29	390	287	190	437	344	256
30	356	295	191	408	369	210
31	329	287	176	382	336	[illegible]
32	326	261	229	319	374	155
33	347	235	171	354	313	189
34	327	223	146	355	296	176
35	366	217	131	383	287	213
36	390	277	165	438	325	249
37	203	157	98	220	172	131
38	292	224	128	300	247	222
†39	430	328	96	227	174	132
40	375	266	161	435	325	254
†41	442	413	88	256	183	152
42	369	245	200	352	344	180
43	413	224	208	378	361	186
*44	...	...	47	232	121	144
*45	...	...	135	300	257	169
*46	...	...	111	368	197	174
*47	...	...	134	226	208	122
*48	...	...	124	340	221	226
	15592	9735	6276	16010	13111	8199

Total registration, 25,347.

10th Assembly District.

Elec. Dist.	Reg'trat'n. Male.	Reg'trat'n. Female.	Cox, Dem.	Harding, Rep.	Smith, Dem.	Miller, Rep.
1	379	235	187	379	332	[illegible]
2	290	217	204	275	328	131
3	264	275	167	326	272	196
4	259	233	161	281	235	195
5	232	323	95	420	175	321
6	72	99	34	123	62	94
7	287	296	124	412	223	299
8	198	137	76	226	143	157
9	390	262	147	446	254	309
10	330	278	87	467	147	376
11	321	152	124	331	228	211
12	383	231	152	401	266	268
13	355	155	138	304	258	163
14	290	233	132	336	211	243
15	426	244	180	422	346	200
16	274	149	128	251	295	148
17	184	93	74	163	146	82
18	337	226	163	334	310	171
19	367	240	258	293	411	147
†20	379	342	90	237	161	152
21	313	241	169	337	256	216
22	353	241	220	313	335	179
23	375	239	241	316	378	119
24	336	336	251	378	349	276
25	335	218	219	317	352	173
26	377	162	233	254	375	107
27	232	108	147	154	224	79
28	85	40	35	79	60	53
29	309	167	208	224	289	125
30	265	106	104	229	189	136
31	131	53	39	118	103	52
32	295	253	180	321	292	199
33	339	349	174	471	318	307
34	332	316	160	438	295	295
35	123	58	90	76	129	36
36	149	158	93	195	174	102
37	138	122	44	203	124	123
38	314	307	155	389	245	289
39	336	334	140	475	276	323
40	218	231	186	236	301	115
41	276	271	196	304	304	178
42	250	272	156	326	234	238
43	226	268	164	297	258	187

10th A. D.—Continued.

Elec. Dist.	Reg'trat'n. Male.	Reg'trat'n. Female.	Cox, Dem.	Harding, Rep.	Smith, Dem.	Miller, Rep.
44	333	215	208	287	327	137
45	350	190	184	307	334	151
46	205	150	143	178	245	75
47	264	202	177	259	297	133
48	323	230	165	343	326	158
49	329	250	211	317	326	187
50	400	108	136	300	294	134
*51	...	...	128	198	194	180
	11328	10691	7658	15066	12782	9336

Total registration, 22,019.

11th Assembly District.

Elec. Dist.	Reg'trat'n. Male.	Reg'trat'n. Female.	Cox, Dem.	Harding, Rep.	Smith, Dem.	Miller, Rep.
1	420	98	165	346	192	242
2	362	198	145	360	235	259
3	384	311	160	478	284	341
4	285	266	152	355	221	275
5	284	374	116	392	214	283
6	299	251	179	314	294	194
7	333	332	207	406	338	264
8	319	306	170	305	287	174
9	316	267	198	331	332	209
10	83	75	42	111	74	76
11	95	94	62	118	90	86
12	344	224	193	335	322	[illegible]
13	311	224	190	291	303	171
14	329	182	183	285	307	129
15	296	136	178	214	264	111
16	346	174	192	291	329	143
17	376	198	160	334	304	175
18	300	171	159	271	266	144
19	388	285	220	410	354	239
20	381	323	152	475	278	381
21	347	314	100	495	223	353
22	316	325	149	440	260	328
23	326	366	117	510	250	360
24	83	66	30	113	61	81
†25	344	275	88	334	181	225
26	215	228	104	301	172	226
27	311	266	166	364	272	235
28	317	266	165	371	314	203
29	347	344	185	448	295	315
30	353	343	172	443	296	303
31	301	306	148	404	262	290
32	385	150	178	288	338	180
33	266	222	147	299	256	181
34	309	263	135	383	256	266
35	295	268	121	420	223	302
36	337	277	162	396	294	252
37	292	252	140	372	94	191
38	311	208	163	307	301	161
39	347	301	198	406	354	235
40	164	125	73	205	166	105
41	293	227	143	332	290	173
42	386	297	170	427	404	196
43	393	271	154	440	323	256
44	451	218	241	398	417	196
45	253	195	192	206	307	82
46	329	255	144	407	323	202
47	191	165	117	213	206	114
48	191	161	89	236	190	132
49	262	177	169	152	258	57
50	148	157	88	189	178	102
51	383	280	201	417	370	233
52	298	303	182	369	319	121
53	358	239	225	323	378	151
54	318	241	230	279	371	140
55	273	170	133	245	258	109
*56	...	...	37	183	86	130
	15503	12010	8477	18435	14907	11193

Total registration, 27,513.

12th Assembly District.

Elec. Dist.	Reg'trat'n. Male.	Reg'trat'n. Female.	Cox, Dem.	Harding, Rep.	Smith, Dem.	Miller, Rep.
1	276	130	131	240	228	134
2	279	193	152	257	272	149
3	335	179	172	313	297	158
4	325	175	175	281	304	137
5	298	247	175	328	309	176
6	286	194	165	263	284	125
7	273	165	126	271	234	161
8	373	189	182	321	302	163
9	290	148	154	234	256	91
10	294	154	176	224	283	102
11	326	221	151	339	290	213
12	299	184	145	292	280	150
13	261	237	178	278	273	191
14	136	128	65	180	145	102

BROOKLYN VOTE, 1920—FOR PRESIDENT AND GOVERNOR—*Continued.*

12th A. D.—Continued.

Elec. Dist.	Reg'trat'n. Male.	Reg'trat'n. Female.	Cox, Dem.	Harding, Rep.	Smith, Dem.	Miller, Rep.
15	258	319	155	291	365	167
16	341	326	229	403	359	265
17	309	311	216	349	330	211
18	220	209	147	259	251	142
19	214	177	152	218	243	106
20	277	294	154	376	280	270
21	230	301	102	281	205	175
22	304	258	170	362	286	245
†23	365	362	220	355	222	253
24	359	346	214	436	417	244
25	266	268	210	272	308	162
26	242	216	162	273	273	152
27	266	214	138	319	256	183
28	335	314	222	374	331	237
29	332	203	149	312	290	182
30	354	313	228	397	389	228
31	352	276	196	385	346	223
32	347	196	166	294	312	133
33	369	222	178	343	364	154
34	352	180	199	288	331	141
35	338	199	137	312	278	170
36	245	178	107	295	219	165
37	369	241	174	376	325	203
38	315	211	158	323	313	157
39	353	235	179	353	336	193
40	367	227	180	362	330	198
41	329	188	134	314	191	225
42	295	161	126	304	228	159
43	360	219	195	321	355	145
44	327	227	193	312	325	178
45	265	186	133	270	226	172
46	309	239	130	384	242	256
47	330	259	119	388	282	202
48	387	199	110	347	293	148
49	408	249	146	396	341	187
50	292	121	36	218	161	67
51	349	142	78	304	247	114
*52	...	...	51	159	93	115
	15793	11133	8140	16047	14560	8982

Total registration, 26,926.

13th Assembly District.

Elec. Dist.	Male.	Female.	Cox, Dem.	Harding, Rep.	Smith, Dem.	Miller, Rep.
1	345	149	281	141	251	141
2	202	48	50	148	111	89
3	357	112	116	306	250	145
4	349	130	170	251	287	114
5	350	136	121	301	280	116
6	344	159	152	311	319	118
7	293	129	93	290	197	167
8	405	127	119	303	241	158
9	272	142	101	254	205	152
10	280	121	101	266	257	111
11	336	125	148	273	297	97
12	327	116	111	289	259	128
13	322	169	100	287	266	112
14	242	93	94	205	205	73
15	347	121	64	281	201	121
16	330	126	54	267	192	107
17	359	170	132	283	273	123
18	265	131	83	264	324	96
19	414	133	157	338	339	114
20	425	138	76	328	248	153
21	293	122	62	282	234	87
22	302	94	35	260	181	107
23	350	122	61	184	150	91
24	330	99	22	174	105	94
25	342	115	52	243	210	82
26	336	118	45	163	157	58
27	318	89	28	185	127	80
28	369	128	38	197	163	66
	9204	3462	2666	7077	6209	3107

Total registration, 12,666.

14th Assembly District.

Elec. Dist.	Male.	Female.	Cox, Dem.	Harding, Rep.	Smith, Dem.	Miller, Rep.
1	303	79	167	178	254	67
2	305	91	172	170	269	67
3	334	132	151	234	265	99
4	337	146	77	203	189	79
5	291	115	75	152	182	61
6	320	138	144	203	262	72
7	372	178	75	184	244	52

*New Elec. Dist. created after last day of registration.

†Election Districts divided for Election Day on account of heavy registration.

14th A. D.—Continued.

Elec. Dist.	Male.	Female.	Cox, Dem.	Harding, Rep.	Smith, Dem.	Miller, Rep.
8	314	133	29	165	143	54
9	411	129	45	208	195	77
10	370	135	38	173	167	52
11	328	112	55	182	155	39
12	272	98	98	178	211	62
13	365	141	94	239	307	102
14	239	208	228	159	352	44
15	244	89	136	164	312	66
16	384	142	116	337	272	161
17	284	52	47	245	156	136
18	211	84	96	167	185	67
19	330	114	104	114	228	92
20	324	91	106	194	235	60
21	382	164	78	152	201	42
22	340	138	44	181	173	66
23	289	112	61	164	176	50
24	263	107	30	125	121	45
25	333	126	62	164	163	56
26	342	165	39	189	177	75
27	237	102	60	164	147	83
28	215	68	31	150	120	56
29	370	153	79	251	212	111
30	413	188	74	353	264	141
	9510	3729	2711	5775	6237	2216

Total registration, 13,239.

15th Assembly District.

Elec. Dist.	Male.	Female.	Cox, Dem.	Harding, Rep.	Smith, Dem.	Miller, Rep.
1	282	124	168	202	280	84
2	342	158	170	280	335	100
3	327	185	160	257	307	88
4	343	190	186	292	314	136
5	350	172	186	287	348	106
6	280	139	140	245	251	129
7	298	214	170	308	303	156
8	391	162	210	301	364	128
9	354	222	157	360	308	171
10	303	109	179	179	271	59
11	380	175	176	315	331	140
12	301	133	152	239	252	101
13	288	138	120	263	247	112
14	298	150	130	296	236	152
15	264	179	138	271	264	122
16	321	163	162	280	300	119
17	306	200	150	294	289	126
18	337	137	152	258	327	77
19	288	196	184	250	306	113
20	396	206	230	292	390	119
21	301	154	148	247	291	75
22	301	147	168	206	303	68
23	334	104	165	206	274	73
24	283	83	120	210	230	79
25	303	111	143	233	275	79
26	339	187	182	296	311	150
27	393	171	236	280	388	99
28	336	225	220	298	356	147
29	407	217	158	399	349	194
30	367	198	233	289	375	119
31	331	155	165	268	308	104
32	366	178	167	319	307	146
33	473	75	65	410	174	250
	10989	6306	5483	9113	9953	3922

Total registration, 16,295.

16th Assembly District.

Elec. Dist.	Male.	Female.	Cox, Dem.	Harding, Rep.	Smith, Dem.	Miller, Rep.
1	381	175	62	365	268	156
2	404	216	70	440	329	169
3	341	178	106	323	256	148
†4	481	231	53	175	161	61
5	391	273	181	422	316	253
6	389	243	139	388	298	206
7	293	165	116	293	234	151
8	382	201	88	401	315	175
9	355	185	104	353	282	165
10	384	191	140	346	329	143
11	328	164	128	276	271	131
12	453	85	45	420	319	209
13	349	211	156	367	335	178
14	338	170	109	359	264	196
15	378	242	159	387	337	168
16	428	218	145	392	361	168
†17	388	327	130	320	248	185
†18	460	307	92	339	244	143
19	416	232	127	413	326	210
20	334	165	102	348	261	164
21	295	130	81	255	202	136
22	354	172	119	304	283	132
23	325	224	90	312	250	145
24	347	207	115	314	274	154
25	323	168	114	244	267	96

16th A. D.—Continued.

Elec. Dist.	Male.	Female.	Cox, Dem.	Harding, Rep.	Smith, Dem.	Miller, Rep.
26	440	237	90	396	343	157
27	400	263	130	404	335	197
28	391	218	103	404	298	195
29	360	164	154	296	297	135
30	331	168	128	292	286	125
31	348	158	140	303	274	150
32	347	169	149	272	290	116
33	341	156	100	255	244	102
34	289	110	146	195	272	67
35	407	120	104	289	211	88
36	366	160	90	235	252	75
37	306	159	99	176	230	53
38	441	177	63	201	222	42
39	404	195	69	195	246	57
†40	466	267	81	261	213	109
*41	...	...	49	334	333	139
*42	...	...	54	150	103	94
*43	...	...	34	190	127	86
*44	...	...	33	96	105	30
	14954	7791	4585	13500	11621	6069

Total registration, 22,745.

17th Assembly District.

Elec. Dist.	Male.	Female.	Cox, Dem.	Harding, Rep.	Smith, Dem.	Miller, Rep.
1	366	287	134	449	278	272
2	329	297	196	381	329	234
3	424	229	158	381	340	182
4	341	310	171	404	271	281
5	313	227	123	360	280	199
6	420	230	120	389	320	184
7	380	239	152	369	286	236
8	322	205	136	288	258	151
9	274	159	72	274	184	142
10	285	187	109	264	227	139
11	262	276	102	387	213	253
12	299	259	112	406	270	229
13	262	287	135	372	247	239
14	172	180	100	224	208	117
15	338	352	189	443	290	336
16	337	256	148	376	283	214
17	333	358	137	490	286	321
18	314	286	102	453	199	338
19	379	314	140	453	303	285
†20	391	412	161	428	297	274
21	319	234	135	373	242	238
22	306	274	172	379	297	238
†23	387	390	94	356	165	279
24	301	329	124	455	214	356
25	276	281	101	413	244	260
26	374	296	138	475	278	326
27	267	322	117	440	230	309
28	182	248	82	320	156	230
29	285	302	129	419	247	297
30	152	171	76	234	160	146
31	418	220	159	410	324	218
32	337	368	160	488	291	340
33	334	360	202	457	341	286
34	195	211	114	259	207	161
35	244	290	175	314	289	306
36	368	242	110	430	247	267
37	268	143	125	336	304	140
38	244	143	42	299	107	201
39	284	131	114	254	230	122
40	187	128	98	196	149	100
41	357	190	190	316	312	163
42	437	207	156	434	376	252
43	464	240	134	378	322	154
44	352	170	50	249	177	108
*45	...	...	32	127	70	90
*46	...	...	81	207	138	131
	13879	11239	5807	16288	11271	10234

Total registration, 25,118.

18th Assembly District.

Elec. Dist.	Male.	Female.	Cox, Dem.	Harding, Rep.	Smith, Dem.	Miller, Rep.
1	343	280	195	375	343	214
†2	351	394	101	377	308	269
3	335	268	179	333	336	219
4	278	318	153	330	300	253
5	345	302	162	411	317	345
6	306	339	162	397	297	362
7	348	350	190	475	329	310
8	326	328	189	384	327	260
9	274	377	85	368	238	224
10	283	350	144	312	287	161
11	359	234	182	301	335	156
12	258	306	171	353	254	148
13	359	335	654	352	314	171
14	323	167	105	351	275	80
15	254	159	131	330	261	97
16	200	165	66	[illegible]	[illegible]	79

BROOKLYN VOTE, 1920—For President and Governor—*Continued.*

18th A. D.—Continued.

Elec. Dist.	Reg'trat'n. Male.	Reg'trat'n. Female.	Cox, Dem.	Harding, Rep.	Smith, Dem.	Miller, Rep.
17	334	180	65	329	298	117
18	418	240	101	434	363	161
19	317	217	110	337	294	150
20	325	294	120	451	289	296
†21	423	289	37	318	182	176
22	389	124	165	296	257	174
23	275	175	147	250	232	118
24	274	197	140	286	259	153
25	399	220	234	340	357	170
26	364	241	200	344	328	208
†27	392	324	102	222	182	130
28	264	169	88	334	189	207
29	364	259	116	442	266	277
30	215	143	117	215	196	111
31	234	186	107	280	174	189
32	369	321	153	498	285	331
33	360	230	134	387	265	230
34	346	217	112	360	253	206
35	341	170	158	277	290	115
36	387	181	62	331	324	68
37	314	165	33	283	204	104
38	447	218	76	313	258	125
39	324	161	82	239	202	109
40	400	167	24	170	123	66
41	349	158	35	193	180	61
42	278	132	72	229	202	91
43	295	145	107	134	200	45
44	466	236	34	327	227	130
45	425	201	42	242	189	100
46	368	162	34	158	121	73
47	370	143	24	141	105	68
48	404	156	25	192	118	86
*49	...	...	88	144	145	92
*50	...	...	39	247	146	128
*51	...	...	85	255	159	170
	16292	10701	5516	15484	12496	8169

Total registration, 26,993.

19th Assembly District.

Elec. Dist.	Reg'trat'n. Male.	Reg'trat'n. Female.	Cox, Dem.	Harding, Rep.	Smith, Dem.	Miller, Rep.
1	380	143	69	372	243	199
2	423	159	69	397	233	207
3	346	137	64	335	227	131
4	345	158	54	382	240	185
5	310	168	24	332	152	171
6	359	184	59	390	227	198
7	328	131	42	313	188	144
8	407	168	76	415	293	158
9	414	166	54	442	271	165
10	348	180	75	361	246	151
11	323	178	68	348	225	167
12	322	156	63	355	210	164
13	196	96	43	199	148	75
14	378	178	56	391	217	204
15	344	175	133	298	284	141
16	320	184	145	303	295	132
17	391	182	108	386	275	138
18	295	167	96	296	251	121
19	382	166	93	278	248	113
20	357	143	53	296	171	158
21	373	124	76	313	247	107
22	319	158	23	147	103	68
23	263	115	24	126	84	76
24	347	136	34	244	151	103
25	332	138	47	191	147	78
26	307	100	23	162	93	91
27	342	141	53	190	185	71
28	299	113	24	156	99	72
	9562	4234	1743	8417	5743	3828

Total registration, 13,796.

20th Assembly District.

Elec. Dist.	Reg'trat'n. Male.	Reg'trat'n. Female.	Cox, Dem.	Harding, Rep.	Smith, Dem.	Miller, Rep.
1	313	168	65	363	221	156
2	308	114	67	389	207	108
3	277	175	69	339	239	145
4	338	151	66	378	266	123
5	319	122	56	324	202	143
6	427	154	78	413	285	157
7	301	138	83	311	235	126
8	365	131	50	296	213	114
9	299	167	97	295	252	135
10	324	228	101	402	248	220
11	346	221	95	395	300	170
12	310	200	96	375	307	141

*New Elec. Dist. created after last day of registration.

†Election Districts divided for Election Day on account of heavy registration.

20th A. D.—Continued.

Elec. Dist.	Reg'trat'n. Male.	Reg'trat'n. Female.	Cox, Dem.	Harding, Rep.	Smith, Dem.	Miller, Rep.
13	324	210	116	371	294	171
14	303	176	73	356	223	167
15	329	185	66	406	236	209
16	307	151	61	338	226	134
17	265	114	60	208	216	103
18	213	119	68	258	168	115
19	298	133	63	326	231	110
20	246	106	72	244	206	91
21	353	194	118	350	321	118
22	277	174	64	328	228	128
23	311	139	81	296	242	116
24	339	158	96	346	243	171
25	348	242	111	422	277	223
26	327	186	96	378	241	213
27	276	198	84	347	209	200
28	250	207	109	310	228	165
29	352	232	116	424	290	225
30	270	139	71	306	214	149
31	300	183	98	31	241	163
32	347	168	104	332	274	145
33	335	131	106	297	238	124
34	248	122	73	258	204	100
35	286	190	88	362	253	165
36	292	176	100	336	255	141
37	261	173	81	313	220	149
38	283	199	104	338	214	191
39	374	249	102	471	262	276
40	310	232	130	364	253	212
41	324	214	91	407	242	234
42	364	243	118	448	290	261
43	288	222	103	373	246	183
44	344	234	135	405	316	205
45	267	158	116	284	237	138
46	298	207	106	375	291	156
47	306	220	87	403	242	219
48	345	203	122	392	294	176
49	365	225	119	412	307	175
50	327	186	122	353	294	135
51	336	204	127	355	275	162
52	309	204	121	334	243	196
53	380	251	136	439	300	228
54	358	259	157	412	342	194
55	279	179	115	315	250	166
56	337	203	114	386	264	214
57	340	196	125	377	273	187
58	333	207	104	378	301	149
59	319	164	78	346	200	190
60	341	165	108	353	257	174
61	290	202	133	318	274	161
62	297	235	115	379	240	232
63	238	140	78	268	183	134
64	324	154	176	244	308	92
	20099	11728	6211	22069	16075	10562

Total registration, 31,827.

21st Assembly District.

Elec. Dist.	Reg'trat'n. Male.	Reg'trat'n. Female.	Cox, Dem.	Harding, Rep.	Smith, Dem.	Miller, Rep.
1	366	281	154	444	311	285
†2	420	404	76	339	183	229
3	334	311	127	470	262	330
†4	401	363	119	214	177	155
5	339	324	159	463	279	327
6	331	282	152	425	279	281
7	309	243	138	384	280	230
8	336	276	165	403	320	240
9	316	227	125	360	261	211
10	385	222	230	315	351	181
11	372	254	165	396	294	244
12	361	315	178	444	323	271
13	293	209	154	303	248	200
14	266	236	115	350	199	257
15	340	218	179	328	328	164
16	374	294	185	421	316	271
17	367	197	193	311	340	144
18	327	189	178	295	298	139
19	321	193	117	349	256	184
20	306	210	131	335	252	194
21	365	307	174	457	340	270
22	276	202	115	312	235	181
23	343	243	121	413	261	255
24	357	287	102	475	237	332
25	215	212	64	338	138	251
26	231	214	61	363	140	277
27	349	326	118	513	242	391
28	182	149	72	245	150	163
29	239	196	88	324	177	220
30	362	309	107	516	227	379
31	296	282	124	391	254	242
32	317	249	113	397	232	262
33	300	242	158	336	363	213
34	393	307	154	482	304	316

21st A. D.—Continued.

Elec. Dist.	Reg'trat'n. Male.	Reg'trat'n. Female.	Cox, Dem.	Harding, Rep.	Smith, Dem.	Miller, Rep.
†35	409	314	104	327	195	232
†36	385	319	145	526	279	384
37	334	273	138	436	282	279
38	278	309	96	467	198	359
39	160	158	34	239	82	182
40	183	222	71	299	136	224
41	349	293	113	489	252	344
42	356	309	144	477	325	278
43	372	290	153	414	312	288
44	308	240	103	406	215	272
45	342	201	137	348	264	198
46	341	256	127	409	300	226
47	341	246	187	334	319	174
48	309	171	111	326	254	161
49	307	163	95	346	221	183
50	365	260	139	403	314	216
51	432	272	178	411	332	229
52	211	132	36	190	161	70
53	263	142	25	148	116	64
54	315	158	66	301	229	135
55	237	154	51	344	221	141
56	313	211	137	322	295	163
*57	...	...	50	314	114	242
*58	...	...	96	297	172	215
*59	...	...	62	187	112	131
	18087	13860	7206	21711	14458	13670

Total registration, 31,947.

22d Assembly District.

Elec. Dist.	Reg'trat'n. Male.	Reg'trat'n. Female.	Cox, Dem.	Harding, Rep.	Smith, Dem.	Miller, Rep.
1	40	40	25	66	62	28
2	269	91	76	232	191	97
3	233	211	79	409	248	196
4	262	233	91	376	329	217
5	299	189	145	299	267	166
6	305	257	122	281	259	233
7	333	243	135	392	254	257
8	307	255	128	371	258	227
9	337	246	103	428	271	232
10	347	256	101	469	252	292
11	354	264	118	475	287	278
12	258	196	80	352	319	193
13	287	205	57	399	191	217
14	276	175	73	339	185	199
15	345	215	90	421	228	246
16	353	248	70	492	226	309
17	305	204	86	383	231	217
18	412	275	126	494	354	350
19	365	238	101	444	362	248
20	422	257	119	480	332	236
21	350	239	117	408	285	217
22	391	220	134	425	289	251
23	355	159	91	343	235	170
24	384	172	132	350	264	188
25	417	198	114	422	332	189
26	410	217	112	396	305	182
27	355	144	77	285	229	125
28	329	140	57	253	190	110
29	335	130	61	183	176	67
30	380	158	61	302	202	149
31	349	145	67	280	206	134
32	359	151	71	300	225	138
33	289	134	53	212	167	104
34	348	168	112	299	207	113
35	340	149	89	364	231	195
36	348	182	331	54	257	150
37	340	152	80	318	205	160
38	420	262	145	464	322	133
39	281	178	74	339	212	172
40	392	197	102	407	297	172
41	299	154	90	397	193	163
42	375	193	111	388	254	184
43	379	231	99	414	261	216
44	341	177	71	341	262	147
45	363	160	85	294	231	118
46	366	177	45	244	196	118
47	329	159	28	204	147	81
48	279	123	40	202	164	69
49	332	151	47	249	201	87
50	379	153	28	195	122	101
51	307	148	77	196	111	57
†52	506	218	36	184	141	64
53	273	124	35	158	118	79
54	385	153	32	256	154	133
55	341	138	31	231	136	106
56	349	134	50	287	186	127
57	252	119	59	246	145	132
*58	...	...	10	92	56	33
	19373	10511	4927	18498	12785	9679

Total registration, 29,884.

BROOKLYN VOTE, 1920—FOR PRESIDENT AND GOVERNOR—*Continued.*

23d Assembly District.

Elec. Dist.	Reg'trat'n. Male.	Reg'trat'n. Female.	Cox, Dem.	Harding, Rep.	Smith, Dem.	Miller, Rep.
1	368	191	119	380	264	203
2	351	196	89	366	241	187
3	296	179	126	288	237	156
4	398	214	174	374	370	145
5	382	183	163	314	327	146
6	372	202	117	366	241	224
7	381	163	114	361	275	167
8	238	62	57	196	141	94
9	382	145	50	290	206	134
10	387	136	27	248	107	173

23d A. D.—Continued.

Elec. Dist.	Reg'trat'n. Male.	Reg'trat'n. Female.	Cox, Dem.	Harding, Rep.	Smith, Dem.	Miller, Rep.
11	308	185	43	222	157	134
12	340	180	29	253	220	88
13	426	212	59	253	204	122
14	361	156	23	208	152	90
15	311	157	24	202	132	90
16	402	189	28	189	164	61
17	366	191	22	230	173	83
18	353	144	35	202	167	74
19	410	230	25	150	124	78
20	374	180	25	143	111	59

23d A. D.—Continued.

Elec. Dist.	Reg'trat'n. Male.	Reg'trat'n. Female.	Cox, Dem.	Harding, Rep.	Smith, Dem.	Miller, Rep.
21	378	168	25	134	97	66
22	332	232	33	223	160	96
23	283	168	34	163	117	80
24	337	156	40	184	130	102
25	381	142	21	214	146	97
26	349	163	24	193	124	84
27	322	152	18	189	137	76
28	377	165	34	170	138	66
	9965	4839	1588	6704	5065	3195

Total registration, 14,304.

STATE SENATORS—Kings County.

S.D.	Democratic.		Republican.		Socialist.		Prohibition.	
4	K. Sutherland	24633	M. S. Harris	29279	Jos. Stein	9092	R. E. Neidig	276
5	D. F. Farrell	20222	J. F. McLaughlin	15353	M. Lewis	1461	E. R. Keeler	342
6	L. M. Black Jr	27253	W. T. Simpson	41973	B. Jackson	2274	F. F. Schoap	429
7	M. Ross	10217	C. C. Lockwood	29229	D. P. Berenberg	11518	Charles Osgood	171
8	F. Conklin	22369	A.W. Burlingame Jr.	44363	G. Giefer	7079	E. M. Waring	668
9	J. J. Morris	17938	G. M. Reischman	30524	M. Schechter	6351	G. H. Warwick	340
10	J. Twomey	16407	E. Clifton	14824	H. S. Berlin	5422	J. B. Davis	122
11	D. J. Carroll	18216	A. J. Katlin	18554	H. Rogoff	6465	L. C. Brown	327

FOR MEMBERS OF THE HOUSE OF REPRESENTATIVES—Kings County.

C.D.	Democratic.		Republican.		Socialist.		Prohibition.	
3	C. J. McWilliams	15219	J. Kissel	16568	H. W. Laidler	5257	F. Koakley	146
4	T. H. Cullen	21069	J. J. Astarita	14684	A. Fagin,	1408	M. Schimpf	319
5	Edw. Cassin	27645	A. L. Kline	42118	J. M. Chatcuff	2047	W. Nichol	574
6	W. F. H. Geoghan	22471	W. T. Lee	44516	W. W. Passage	6867	L. Johnson	1095
7	J. P. Maher	16551	M. J. Hogan	20482	J. J. Caronel	6561	C. E. Gildersleeve	446
8	W. E. Cleary	22586	C. G. Bond	30908	V. H. Lawn	9124	A. J Copeland	386
9	D. J. O'Connell	20868	A. N. Peterson	27886	W. B. Rob'nson	6600	F. E. Merchon	278
10	G. H. Rhodes	14067	L. D. Volk	25801	J. O'Neal	11529	B. Cook	181

Congress, 10th Dist., Short Term.

G. H. Rhodes, Dem., 13943; L. D. Volk, 25608; J. O'Neill, Soc., 11512.

Associate Judges of the Court of Appeals.

Frederick E. Crane, Dem.-Rep., 284,868; Abram I. Elkus, Dem., 150,048; Emory A. Chase, Rep., 206,502; Leon A. Malkiel, Soc., 43,973; Jacob Axelrad, Soc., 41,678; Coleridge A. Hart, Proh., 2,602; Francis E. Baldwin, Proh., 1,845; Swinburne Hale, Farmer-Labor, 6,062; Thomas F. Dwyer, Farmer-Labor, 8,787.

Justices of the Supreme Court for the Second Judicial District.

Edwin L. Garvin, Dem., 147,635; Burt Jay Humphrey, Dem., 132,863; Edward Ward McMahon, Dem., 133,253; Townsend Scudder, Dem.-Citz., 155,286; Charles J. Druhan, Dem., 105,421; Joseph Aspinall, Rep.-Citz., 216,740; Selah B. Strong, Rep., 200,509; Norman S. Dike, Rep., 244,230; John MacCrate, Rep., 202,221; Walter H. Jaycox, Rep.-Citz., 190,784; Morris Wolfman, Soc., 43,653; Hyman Rivkin, Soc., 41,783; Isidore Kayfetz, Soc., 40,193; Philip Satra, Soc., 38,798; Francis M. Testa, Soc., 34,269; Charles A. Wilson, Proh., 2,108; Asa F. Smith, Proh., 1,961; Harold D. Watson, Proh., 1,614; Walter G. Howell, Proh., 1,529; David A. Howell, Proh., 1,681; Robert H. Haskell, Farmer-Labor, 14,811; James P. Kohler, Farmer-Labor, 6,570; Joseph Goldstein, Farmer-Labor, 8,630; Jacob S. Strahl, Farmer-Labor, Am. Constl., Non-Partisan, 96,311; Edmond Congar Brown, Single Tax, 2,028.

Municipal Court, 7th District.

H. C. Glore, Rep., 32434; G. H. Boyce, Dem., 25098; L. P. Goldberg, Soc., 14453.

For Members of the Board of Aldermen to Fill Vacancies.

46th Ald. Dist.—J. L. Dempsey, Dem., 6884; D. J. Stewart, Rep., 11888; W. Shapiro, Soc., 431; A. F. Smith, Proh., 150.

51st Ald. Dist.—J. J. Dunn, Dem., 16304; H. H. F. Savarese, Rep., 23732; J. Tunin, Soc., 5021.

Assembly.

1st A. D.—J. J. Griffith, Dem., 7,076; F. Morton, Rep., 8,110; F. C. Hazleth, Soc., 507; C. A. Montgomery, Proh., 95.

2d A. D.—W. Brown, Dem., 5,918; J. J. Mullen, Rep., 9,496; A. L. Carlin, Soc., 5,394; L. S. Zicler, Jr., Proh., 71.

3d A. D.—F. J. Taylor, Dem., 5,473; G. W. Harris, Rep., 4,067; L. Mendelson, Soc., 459; W. G. Blythe, Proh., 56.

4th A. D.—P. A. McArdle, Dem., 7,453; S. L. Krooks, Rep., 6,437; H. Nemsen, Soc., 2,301; F. B. Newman, Proh., 118.

5th A. D.—H. P. Fearon, Dem., 6,173; J. Caulfield, Jr., Rep., 14,935; M. Lorentz, Soc., 1,009; C. Vantin, Proh., 174.

6th A. D.—M. G. Soloman, Dem., 3,913; J. E. Crews, Rep., 7,262; H. Fruchter, Soc., 5,388; G. C. Munn, Proh., 48.

7th A. D.—J. J. Kelly, Dem., 7,489; T. F. Monahan, Rep., 6,664; W. Radilin, Soc., 738; E. E. Hand, Jr., Proh., 243.

8th A. D.—M. J. Reilly, Dem., 7,244; F. J. Sheridan, Rep., 4,466; F. Sharblum, Soc., 329; E. H. Brown, Jr., Proh., 82.

9th A. D.—J. W. Conklin, Dem., 8,431; J. T. Carroll, Rep., 12,299; M. G. Kramer, Soc., 1,526; W. B. Hantsch, Proh., 179.

10th A. D—B. F. Grey, Dem., 8,279; L. V. Doherty, Rep., 12,739; S. Camen, Soc., 584; R. M. Low, Proh., 353.

11th A. D.—W. E. Warland, Dem., 8,659; J. F. Bly, Rep., 16,518; S. Spindel, Soc., 681; W. A. Fergerson, Proh., 185.

12th A. D.—J. F. Rice, Dem., 9,824; G. J. Moore, Rep., 12,899; F. Smith, Soc., 1,121; T. Thompson, Proh., 137.

13th A. D.—J. G. Wackerman, Dem., 4,482; J. L. Zito, Rep., 4,191; S. Parloff, Soc., 2,278; J. Broeder, Proh., 50.

14th A. D.—A. B. Yacunda, Dem., 4,054; A. R. Finkelstein, Rep., 2,739; H. Jaeger, Soc., 4,856; B. T. R. Balch, Proh., 69.

15th A. D.—J. J. McLaughlin, Dem., 7,856; H. Sprigade, Rep., 5,955; P. Mueller, Soc., 495; W. W. Locke, Proh., 93.

16th A. D.—P. M. Kleinfeld, Dem., 8,212; L. G. Moses, Rep., 8,619; L. Tomash, Soc., 2,685; T. C. R. Horsfield, Proh., 130.

17th A. D.—Jose Pidgeon, Dem., 6,727; F. A. Wells, Rep., 13,658; S. Rubin, Soc., 1,379; G. B. Hillard, Proh., 177.

18th A. D.—V. Curren, Dem., 7,211; T. Stith, Rep., 11,634; B. S. Riley, Soc., 4,734; O. Christason, Proh., 209.

19th A. D.—B. C. Klingman, Dem., 4,348; F. X. Giaconne, Rep., 4,708; M. Rubin, Soc., 2,909; G. Liotta, Proh., 26.

20th A. D.—G. J. Braun, Dem., 10,086; J. O. Gempler, Rep., 16,502; L. Weil, Soc., 1,747; W. T. Pfast, Proh., 208.

21st A. D.—J. D. White, Dem., 8,688; W. F. Clayton, Rep., 18,281; B. C. Hammond, Soc., 1,438; J. D. Snyder, Proh., 236.

22d A. D.—L. Emmett, Dem., 8,552; L. J. Druss, Rep., 12,807; J. Kooperman, Soc., 4,995; L. Y. Becker, Proh., 189.

23d A. D.—J. Schneider, Dem., 1,867; J. Ricca, Rep., 4,316; C. Solomon, Soc., 6,785; J. Metz, Proh., 30.

BROOKLYN VOTE, 1920—*Continued.*

KINGS COUNTY ENROLLMENT FIGURES.

A. D.	Democrat. Male.	Democrat. Female.	Democrat. Total.	Republican. Male.	Republican. Female.	Republican. Total.	Socialist. Male.	Socialist. Female.
First	4,909	2,360	7,269	6,314	3,677	9,991	130	74
Second	5,005	2,282	7,287	7,027	4,468	11,496	1,417	1,040
Third	4,668	1,773	6,441	3,427	1,429	4,856	157	60
Fourth	5,197	2,396	7,593	5,965	2,888	8,843	399	339
Fifth	4,872	2,950	7,822	8,717	6,763	15,480	194	126
Sixth	3,848	1,726	5,574	6,307	3,239	9,546	987	706
Seventh	5,483	2,512	7,995	5,167	2,909	8,076	194	98
Eighth	5,741	2,451	8,192	3,844	1,714	5,558	103	31
Ninth	5,633	3,150	8,783	8,495	5,481	13,976	318	231
Tenth	5,403	3,528	8,931	7,893	6,467	14,360	142	80
Eleventh	6,191	3,785	9,976	9,527	8,042	17,569	137	96
Twelfth	6,057	3,813	9,870	8,414	6,365	14,779	206	150
Thirteenth	4,534	1,484	6,018	3,590	1,472	5,062	580	312
Fourteenth	4,419	1,312	5,731	3,238	1,104	4,342	890	591
Fifteenth	6,644	2,887	9,531	3,940	2,143	6,083	140	40
Sixteenth	6,046	2,754	8,800	6,965	3,666	10,631	530	436
Seventeenth	4,523	2,974	7,497	8,277	7,396	15,673	278	204
Eighteenth	5,639	3,139	8,778	8,311	5,742	14,053	921	851
Nineteenth	3,322	1,189	4,511	4,754	2,144	6,898	797	499
Twentieth	7,269	3,190	10,459	11,195	7,387	18,582	399	161
Twenty-first	5,540	3,406	8,946	11,212	9,232	20,444	249	221
Twenty-second	6,030	2,535	8,565	10,604	6,093	16,697	1,086	803
Twenty-third	2,992	1,067	4,059	4,607	1,799	6,406	1,448	1,164
Totals	119,965	58,663	178,628	157,780	101,622	259,402	11,702	8,313

BROOKLYN VOTE.

Treasurer, H. F. Kreuger, Soc., 45,115; J. McKee, Proh., 1,761; J. A. Withers, Soc.-L., 971; J. E. Cronk, Far.-L., 6,698.

Atty. Genl., D. J. Meserole, Soc., 45,632; W. H. Burr, Proh., 2,932; J. Donohue, Soc.-L., 1,711; F. R. Serri, Far.-L., 6,805.

State Eng. and Surveyor, V. Karapetoff, Soc., 46,509; A. S. Light, Proh., 1,729; C. C. Crawford, Soc.-L., 2,863.

U. S. Senator, J. Panken, Soc., 49,102; E. A. Boole, Proh., 9,121; H. Carlson, Soc.-L., 1,192; R. Schneiderman, Far.-L., 6,622.

CALIFORNIA IRRIGATION PROJECT.

One of the greatest engineering projects ever attempted in this country was launched when the California Realtors were in annual session at Los Angeles recently. The plan involves an expenditure of $500,000,000. More than 12,000,000 acres of land in California will be supplied with needed water, and lands that today are lying idle will soon be brought into production. This water will be supplied by two giant canals approximately 700 miles long, running the length of the State, connecting ten rivers and including a series of sub-canals that will give the State a complete irrigation system.

STATE ELECTIONS.

(As reported to Eagle Almanac by the Secretaries of States.) (For Governors of States see index.)

State.	Yr.	Office.	Dem.	Rep.	Soc.	Proh	F.-L
Ala.	1920	Pres.	163,254	74,690	2,369	757	....
	1913	Gov.	54,746	14,497	1,186	....	....
Ariz.	1920	Pres.	29,546	37,016	125	4	1
	1920	Gov.	31,385	37,060	....	....	....
Ark.	1920	Pres.	107,409	71,117	6,111	....	....
	1920	Gov.	126,477	65,381	4,542	....	....
Cal.	1920	Pres.	229,191	624,992	64,076	25,085	....
	1918	Gov.	251,189	387,547	29,003	....	....
Col.	1920	Pres.	104,936	173,248	8,046	2,807	3,016
	1918	Gov.	105,000	107,726	....	....	....
Conn.	1920	Pres.	120,721	229,238	10,350	1,771	1,947
	1920	Gov.	119,912	230,792	10,154	1,817	1,896
Del.	1920	Pres.	39,911	52,858	988	986	....
	1920	Gov.	41,038	51,895	148	....	....
Fla.	1920	Pres.	90,515	47,527	5,189	5,124	....
	1920	Gov.	103,407	23,788	2,823	....	....
Ga.	1920	Pres.	107,162	41,089	465	8	....
	1918	Gov.	59,000	.....	....	....	....
Idaho	1920	Pres	46,579	88,975	38	32	....
	1920	Gov.	33,509	75,748	....	....	....
Ill.	1920	Pres.	534,395	1420480	74,747	11,216	49,630
	1920	Gov.	731,551	1243148	58,998	9,876	56,480
Ind.	1920	Pres.	511,364	696,370	23,228	13,235	16,626
	1916	Gov.	325,060	337,831	22,156	15,454	....
Iowa	1920	Pres.	227,921	634,674	16,981	4,197	10,321
	1918	Gov.	175,568	161,451	....	....	....
Kan.	1920	Pres.	185,447	369,195	15,510	....	....
	1920	Gov.	214,927	319,826	15,407	....	....
Ken.	1920	Pres.	456,497	452,480	6,409	3,250	....
	1919	Gov.	214,114	254,290	4,221	10,717	....
La.	1920	Pres.	86,994	30,090	....	....	....
	1920	Gov.	52,792	1,206	....	....	....
Me.	1920	Pres.	58,961	136,355	2,214	....	....
	1920	Gov.	70,047	135,393	....	....	....
Md.	1920	Pres.	180,626	236,117	8,876	....	1,645
	1919	Gov.	112,240	112,075	2,799	1,663	....
Mass.	1920	Pres.	276,691	681,153	32,267	....	....
	1920	Gov.	290,350	643,869	20,079	....	....
Mich.	1920	Pres.	233,450	762,865	28,947	9,646	....
	1920	Gov.	310,566	703,180	23,542	6,990	11,817
Minn.	1920	Pres.	142,994	519,421	56,106	11,489	....
	1920	Gov.	91,293	415,805	5,124	....	....
Miss.	1920	Pres.	69,277	11,576	1,639	....	....
	1920	Gov.	63,313	10,962	1,615	....	....
Mo.	1920	Pres.	574,799	727,162	20,242	5,142	3,291
	1920	Gov.	580,626	722,024	19,489	3,974	3,003
Mont.	1920	Pres.	57,370	109,430	....	....	12,204
	1920	Gov.	74,875	111,113	....	....	12,204
Neb.	1920	Pres.	119,608	251,093	9,600	6,041	....
	1920	Gov.	130,433	152,863	9,600	6,041	....
Nev.	1920	Pres.	9,803	15,479	1,864	....	....
	1920	Gov.	10,402	11,550	494	....	....
N. H.	1920	Pres.	62,662	95,196	1,235	....	....
	1920	Gov.	62,080	93,021	1,235	....	....
N. J.	1920	Pres.	256,887	611,541	27,141	4,734	2,200
	1919	Gov.	217,486	202,976	11,014	6,098	....
N. M.	1920	Pres.	46,668	57,634	....	....	1,097
	1920	Gov.	46,668	57,634	....	....	1,097
N. Y.	1920	Pres.	781,238	1871167	203201	19,653	18,413
	1920	Gov.	1261812	1335878	159804	35,509	69,908
No. C.	1920	Pres.	305,447	242,848	446	....	....
	1920	Gov.	308,151	230,175	336	....	....
No. D.	1920	Pres.	37,422	160,072	8,283	....	....
	1920	Gov.	112,292	116,934	....	....	....
Ohio	1920	Pres.	780,037	1182022	57,147	294	....
	1920	Gov.	918,962	1039835	42,889	294	....
Okla.	1920	Pres.	216,390	244,320	25,685	....	....
	1920	Gov.	217,677	247,824	25,685	....	....
Ore.	1920	Pres.	80,009	143,592	9,801	3,595	1,515
	1918	Gov.	65,440	81,077	6,480	....	....
Pa.	1920	Pres.	503,202	1218215	70,021	42,612	....
	1918	Gov.	297,567	547,833	18,706	27,360	....
R. I.	1920	Pres.	55,062	107,463	4,351	320	....
	1920	Gov.	55,963	109,138	3,292	....	....
So. C.	1920	Pres.	64,170	2,610	26	....	....
	1920	Gov.	62,233	2,244	26	....	....
So. D.	1920	Pres.	35,657	110,692	....	906	....
	1920	Gov.	31,583	102,834	....	....	....
Tenn.	1920	Pres.	206,558	219,829	2,239	....	....
	1920	Gov.	185,890	229,143	2,113	....	....
Tex.	1920	Pres.	289,688	143,155	8,194	....	....
	1918	Gov.	177,371	12,520	21,106	....	....
Utah	1920	Pres.	56,639	81,555	3,159	....	4,475
	1920	Gov.	54,913	83,518	2,843	....	2,300
Vt.	1920	Pres.	20,919	68,212	....	774	....
	1920	Gov.	18,917	66,494	....	1,180	....
Va.	1920	Pres.	141,670	87,456	807	856	240
	1917	Gov.	.....	.....	....	....	....
Wash.	1920	Pres.	84,298	223,137	8,913	3,800	7,246
	1920	Gov.	66,079	210,662	....	....	....
W. Va.	1920	Pres.	220,789	282,007	5,618	1,528	....
	1916	Gov.	143,324	140,569	....	....	....
Wis.	1920	Pres.	113,422	498,576	80,635	8,647	....
	1920	Gov.	247,746	366,247	71,126	6,047	....
Wyo.	1920	Pres.	17,429	35,691	1,288	265	....
	1918	Gov.	13,640	23,825	10	....	....

MANHATTAN VOTE, 1920—For President and Governor.

1st Assembly District.

Elec. Dist.	Reg'trat'n. Male.	Reg'trat'n. Female.	Cox, Dem.	Harding, Rep.	Smith, Dem.	Miller, Rep.
1	399	149	74	231	255	65
2	415	207	93	211	309	67
3	249	99	46	99	198	13
4	393	187	119	167	286	37
5	397	169	256	117	362	27
†6	516	201	109	94	178	33
7	449	186	105	201	331	44
8	297	150	147	113	260	32
9	473	169	101	246	333	73
10	286	130	193	139	277	74
11	363	169	201	220	374	71
12	346	121	222	188	347	78
13	303	85	193	168	298	37
14	323	121	247	167	348	65
15	430	148	260	278	464	72
16	473	117	326	196	440	70
17	...	...	...	...	...	...
18	187	13	124	44	157	9
19	511	121	156	396	437	104
20	626	112	237	320	430	118
21	385	136	253	231	376	95
22	364	111	247	183	374	59
23	362	165	384	116	465	28
24	227	90	197	77	248	26
25	283	77	174	144	262	52
26	330	102	230	184	301	92
27	373	133	227	208	328	96
28	302	103	141	225	243	103
29	363	194	285	235	418	92
30	352	166	304	178	424	58
31	166	130	140	122	187	67
32	376	180	224	276	360	136
33	272	138	236	148	315	62
34	386	155	196	276	326	147
35	373	147	207	205	415	63
36	376	178	243	259	384	97
37	348	162	184	256	326	108
38	393	153	219	240	355	97
39	65	28	21	49	47	22
*40	...	...	87	137	208	48
	13461	5201	7372	7236	12435	2632

Total registration, 18,662.

2d Assembly District.

Elec. Dist.	Reg'trat'n. Male.	Reg'trat'n. Female.	Cox, Dem.	Harding, Rep.	Smith, Dem.	Miller, Rep.
1	159	47	66	88	143	24
2	321	58	99	242	275	70
3	229	80	53	153	162	45
4	602	158	70	258	290	80
5	435	136	43	234	203	70
6	219	100	68	153	150	58
†7	585	158	62	176	169	69
8	464	149	73	315	278	160
9	430	153	66	320	228	160
10	476	155	117	238	269	98
11	478	145	93	299	246	80
12	388	135	168	232	236	144
13	306	106	61	184	201	69
14	366	99	88	228	188	130
15	450	46	170	218	264	112
16	417	61	193	188	288	67
17	536	64	224	290	571	5
18	61	4	31	32	61	0
19	474	103	80	439	288	188
†20	648	73	159	203	303	58
21	632	72	266	269	378	123
22	506	80	150	287	312	109
23	233	65	69	123	166	36
24	410	85	146	326	302	130
†25	645	79	54	226	165	106
26	520	122	76	468	310	206
27	632	123	85	490	299	268
28	308	155	101	280	278	128
*29	...	...	64	166	156	61
*30	...	...	257	61	249	81
*31	...	...	132	208	224	101
	11720	2830	3374	7382	7631	2968

Total registration, 14,550.

3d Assembly District.

Elec. Dist.	Reg'trat'n. Male.	Reg'trat'n. Female.	Cox, Dem.	Harding, Rep.	Smith, Dem.	Miller, Rep.
1	354	163	314	158	389	58
2	375	178	266	218	404	66
3	163	105	96	148	163	70

*New Elec. Dist. created after last day of registration.

†Election Districts divided for Election Day on account of heavy registration.

3d A. D.—Continued.

Elec. Dist.	Reg'trat'n. Male.	Reg'trat'n. Female.	Cox, Dem.	Harding, Rep.	Smith, Dem.	Miller, Rep.
4	255	133	233	125	299	49
5	334	160	299	156	372	63
6	388	173	319	196	418	74
7	354	171	302	158	400	46
8	309	124	230	153	312	59
9	360	196	218	286	328	167
10	238	210	212	181	302	84
11	220	137	151	161	240	66
12	318	151	227	191	325	77
13	396	166	274	207	385	87
14	279	127	251	107	304	44
15	303	142	237	162	324	61
16	363	138	210	234	344	84
17	303	217	292	187	376	92
18	409	164	207	274	359	100
19	346	169	180	267	313	128
20	362	200	206	278	321	149
21	303	141	207	187	286	97
22	399	228	215	228	337	197
23	299	164	153	229	244	130
24	352	162	217	237	323	123
25	406	246	272	295	366	182
26	417	146	259	228	380	75
27	367	301	244	359	374	219
28	359	248	247	292	317	209
29	407	149	183	284	298	161
30	400	273	309	264	450	129
31	488	175	326	241	461	86
32	386	157	222	231	335	90
33	336	113	160	224	271	100
34	407	176	239	273	365	132
35	287	159	221	180	306	78
36	307	108	179	167	259	76
37	395	114	238	206	343	87
38	357	166	263	204	368	91
39	403	191	265	277	395	122
40	324	162	168	247	267	182
41	270	66	123	168	213	71
42	622	187	135	419	277	256
43	423	210	226	331	388	156
44	412	157	214	284	358	119
45	309	112	152	206	246	99
46	267	102	137	176	254	45
47	397	139	119	339	276	152
48	243	108	126	179	219	67
49	327	99	76	281	218	109
	16988	7980	11619	11068	15586	5104

Total registration, 24,968.

4th Assembly District.

Elec. Dist.	Reg'trat'n. Male.	Reg'trat'n. Female.	Cox, Dem.	Harding, Rep.	Smith, Dem.	Miller, Rep.
1	211	106	222	62	260	17
2	338	141	191	114	201	26
3	396	147	130	119	244	27
4	473	199	271	184	448	111
5	414	185	197	258	343	123
6	373	139	194	171	276	77
7	387	208	170	219	309	97
8	427	218	82	197	245	76
9	396	157	98	195	302	90
10	381	190	145	185	315	77
11	315	118	107	118	213	49
12	426	140	101	201	295	87
13	355	230	118	215	256	71
14	449	191	124	257	292	108
15	375	162	95	242	224	113
16	409	144	76	228	230	63
17	380	154	126	176	267	52
18	238	87	51	123	117	53
19	446	178	107	239	267	75
20	373	145	66	180	216	65
21	417	143	106	232	294	54
22	433	149	49	208	188	91
28	319	106	147	118	252	29
	8761	3637	2977	4231	6146	1600

Total registration, 12,398.

5th Assembly District.

Elec. Dist.	Reg'trat'n. Male.	Reg'trat'n. Female.	Cox, Dem.	Harding, Rep.	Smith, Dem.	Miller, Rep.
1	408	149	136	328	280	175
2	282	168	195	194	314	66
3	436	139	262	234	377	88
4	271	104	115	212	230	77
5	433	159	279	230	388	115
6	341	155	241	200	376	63
7	339	122	196	209	296	85
8	318	179	161	268	300	131
9	301	193	171	255	299	119
10	436	146	205	271	344	123
11	102	46	39	88	70	56

5th A. D.—Continued.

Elec. Dist.	Reg'trat'n. Male.	Reg'trat'n. Female.	Cox, Dem.	Harding, Rep.	Smith, Dem.	Miller, Rep.
12	287	245	175	294	296	159
13	263	121	159	189	259	74
14	252	118	161	167	247	59
15	338	119	169	206	291	83
16	265	168	174	205	277	86
17	287	166	168	226	280	102
18	370	164	249	227	331	114
19	402	201	243	290	389	113
20	313	172	148	266	279	128
21	302	119	146	214	232	111
22	321	141	221	172	313	61
23	214	92	133	129	199	45
24	278	154	238	147	327	41
25	291	160	189	206	314	88
26	461	214	274	312	500	94
27	317	180	206	242	336	90
28	373	169	227	241	358	103
29	223	101	140	148	215	67
30	329	127	190	194	311	72
31	277	158	162	235	265	109
32	143	115	154	83	203	32
33	239	115	143	183	231	71
34	317	193	206	232	315	103
35	309	153	131	257	246	133
36	464	240	134	411	288	335
37	461	154	242	271	383	107
38	412	197	212	292	370	123
39	362	144	231	206	388	36
40	308	102	179	170	287	43
41	280	181	134	279	238	154
42	471	232	202	381	341	225
43	460	173	310	229	439	77
44	229	146	192	132	261	67
45	202	137	174	123	253	43
46	201	203	259	179	359	63
47	297	154	125	256	208	134
48	210	112	61	288	106	223
49	462	244	298	288	464	107
50	402	258	296	280	434	117
51	205	125	175	126	248	39
52	258	135	45	286	121	177
	16654	8147	9655	11750	15475	5204

Total registration, 24,801.

6th Assembly District.

Elec. Dist.	Reg'trat'n. Male.	Reg'trat'n. Female.	Cox, Dem.	Harding, Rep.	Smith, Dem.	Miller, Rep.
1	424	233	68	260	284	131
2	391	217	81	259	263	109
3	306	107	35	235	149	136
4	299	164	49	251	180	122
5	341	183	38	272	157	178
6	361	177	61	255	238	96
7	343	160	81	222	202	126
8	379	199	60	255	190	146
9	358	166	48	225	178	123
10	380	187	31	308	174	166
11	334	181	56	262	109	136
12	412	189	32	254	182	131
13	441	205	49	315	219	181
14	275	175	42	201	152	111
15	362	182	46	257	160	169
16	264	158	28	173	130	82
17	422	225	29	276	167	145
18	426	220	40	366	188	128
19	321	159	65	188	155	111
20	321	156	63	281	190	146
21	465	126	97	352	274	152
22	329	182	184	281	302	157
23	325	177	252	190	346	83
24	272	192	244	172	334	68
25	368	186	215	267	356	103
26	341	211	242	244	359	116
	9263	4783	2336	6521	5728	3358

Total registration, 14,046.

7th Assembly District.

Elec. Dist.	Reg'trat'n. Male.	Reg'trat'n. Female.	Cox, Dem.	Harding, Rep.	Smith, Dem.	Miller, Rep.
1	266	186	76	323	144	228
2	397	198	148	361	284	207
3	321	112	131	237	256	99
4	373	194	88	404	194	254
5	203	55	100	119	170	45
6	311	207	157	283	270	164
7	268	155	133	234	250	111
8	329	227	190	305	309	161
9	375	139	209	228	352	84
10	316	190	165	227	283	98
11	346	188	216	278	318	151

MANHATTAN VOTE, 1920—FOR PRESIDENT AND GOVERNOR—*Continued.*

7th A. D.—Continued.

Elec. Dist.	Reg'trat'n. Male.	Reg'trat'n. Female.	Cox, Dem.	Harding, Rep.	Smith, Dem.	Miller, Rep.
12	311	248	108	393	194	304
13	349	310	149	430	269	260
14	373	330	174	431	334	269
15	190	161	97	212	183	111
16	376	169	152	320	256	152
17	318	253	149	364	286	226
18	354	332	126	494	276	338
†19	386	345	74	302	171	190
†20	432	374	50	251	121	177
†21	338	384	81	230	128	177
†22	403	331	61	167	118	102
23	402	296	126	500	270	356
24	285	306	96	453	201	342
25	336	373	130	502	267	363
26	308	297	129	421	267	278
†27	423	312	95	210	156	144
28	329	326	146	470	261	331
†29	461	366	63	313	165	204
†30	344	380	37	285	105	211
†31	418	417	91	331	225	326
32	362	297	157	447	291	291
33	303	236	142	250	217	163
34	300	219	133	339	259	200
35	308	213	176	366	278	147
36	363	266	218	346	372	172
37	261	190	129	271	264	127
38	316	229	189	293	316	146
39	366	283	150	444	257	326
40	385	299	135	477	328	263
41	258	225	203	317	316	188
42	334	250	253	275	408	121
43	249	189	164	245	277	116
44	276	287	161	352	289	224
45	315	355	158	424	283	284
*46	...	...	68	237	118	177
*47	...	...	102	340	198	233
*48	...	...	72	261	160	173
*49	...	...	74	374	171	269
*50	...	...	105	350	189	161
*51	...	...	94	284	194	175
*52	...	...	63	281	147	196
*53	...	...	68	270	146	190
	15037	11639	6761	17110	12591	10304

Total registration, 26,676.

8th Assembly District.

Elec. Dist.	Male.	Female.	Cox, Dem.	Harding, Rep.	Smith, Dem.	Miller, Rep.
1	321	126	32	170	151	60
2	375	164	45	196	218	60
3	278	155	34	201	170	73
4	373	107	43	231	179	88
5	434	150	65	275	234	106
6	402	154	76	236	236	92
7	265	100	40	193	172	64
8	391	137	70	204	239	58
9	420	179	66	303	237	138
10	472	160	82	344	266	140
11	325	130	52	205	206	58
12	353	165	69	283	240	107
13	353	161	120	227	267	87
14	231	78	80	126	154	45
15	5	7	1	10	5	4
16	396	154	86	263	264	84
17	313	104	67	199	227	47
18	483	163	76	314	265	129
19	305	123	40	208	167	71
20	317	152	77	288	233	125
21	433	181	40	259	188	171
22	441	194	74	348	244	164
23	545	159	103	336	314	184
24	238	136	93	229	322	95
25	266	122	103	190	236	57
26	435	149	74	282	260	96
27	387	135	105	264	248	118
28	466	207	177	320	343	149
	10108	3952	1990	6704	6185	2620

Total registration, 14,060.

9th Assembly District.

Elec. Dist.	Male.	Female.	Cox, Dem.	Harding, Rep.	Smith, Dem.	Miller, Rep.
1	198	190	80	288	158	207
2	224	249	116	315	206	217
3	295	315	163	278	287	250

*New Elec. Dist. created after last day of registration.

†Election Districts divided for Election Day on account of heavy registration.

9th A. D.—Continued.

Elec. Dist.	Reg'trat'n. Male.	Reg'trat'n. Female.	Cox, Dem.	Harding, Rep.	Smith, Dem.	Miller, Rep.
4	269	261	99	385	251	236
5	308	319	132	426	307	253
6	331	294	138	413	300	247
7	291	200	132	316	255	174
8	270	262	133	329	267	193
9	314	254	208	397	360	227
10	255	230	124	319	254	116
†11	367	345	182	444	332	288
12	281	231	137	222	287	174
13	332	262	230	330	361	168
14	312	203	146	307	274	151
15	394	280	191	406	390	218
16	346	265	228	313	387	155
†17	428	291	107	246	186	154
18	322	212	201	262	336	113
19	336	241	140	359	332	147
20	410	213	220	311	407	116
21	384	240	144	390	287	244
22	338	196	105	345	237	191
23	238	181	123	250	214	160
24	241	228	135	290	266	151
25	180	206	108	238	192	143
26	266	222	176	252	279	145
27	351	230	178	330	343	153
28	265	147	173	195	282	76
29	373	208	223	274	382	109
30	283	180	158	235	266	116
31	351	159	169	251	310	104
32	266	135	130	221	247	90
33	344	264	124	419	304	241
34	300	268	85	450	293	237
†35	415	264	64	269	183	151
36	289	224	72	398	220	252
37	339	272	117	418	279	349
38	320	336	162	428	298	285
39	299	286	132	393	281	242
40	303	267	121	410	267	261
41	294	248	124	375	269	225
42	334	290	145	420	289	271
43	458	349	65	299	193	111
†44	446	307	75	244	182	134
†45	403	341	62	302	164	208
46	351	292	110	461	250	307
47	290	331	130	422	268	278
48	314	312	91	468	207	352
*49	...	...	92	166	200	50
*50	...	...	74	301	198	166
*51	...	...	69	303	147	219
*52	...	...	67	251	180	176
*53	...	...	49	261	141	161
	15318	12298	6959	17526	14053	10061

Total registration, 27,616.

10th Assembly District.

Elec. Dist.	Male.	Female.	Cox, Dem.	Harding, Rep.	Smith, Dem.	Miller, Rep.
1	221	188	124	233	181	170
2	327	201	193	281	333	126
3	350	242	162	353	285	219
4	308	217	180	283	302	145
5	272	190	134	273	245	160
6	277	202	220	216	318	108
7	243	202	142	245	233	143
8	239	183	166	207	230	144
9	290	163	202	208	271	124
10	287	194	205	239	309	115
11	173	116	115	135	173	82
12	342	311	196	366	304	265
13	315	396	176	402	296	280
14	238	364	140	386	242	280
15	320	266	148	359	260	244
16	298	256	148	337	263	227
17	272	253	128	319	215	243
18	300	262	143	349	249	230
19	212	118	95	190	180	99
20	284	297	169	341	271	287
21	343	315	178	411	289	286
22	333	216	121	361	220	265
23	336	198	201	254	303	146
24	266	262	148	331	267	199
25	249	126	117	209	201	127
26	305	143	117	283	218	181
27	356	238	154	361	295	211
28	257	365	140	412	220	323
29	322	324	178	389	290	275
30	247	242	136	310	228	212
31	343	255	173	361	284	244
†32	374	385	138	207	142	197
33	358	297	141	440	214	354

10th A. D.—Continued.

Elec. Dist.	Reg'trat'n. Male.	Reg'trat'n. Female.	Cox, Dem.	Harding, Rep.	Smith, Dem.	Miller, Rep.
34	206	180	114	290	184	208
35	521	44	171	285	273	179
36	110	32	34	75	66	41
37	191	83	67	166	126	96
38	293	147	65	332	134	247
39	450	89	108	342	239	202
†40	647	310	80	369	167	284
41	253	309	144	405	239	304
42	361	283	165	407	259	304
43	417	165	156	352	302	189
44	377	177	124	327	260	190
45	500	208	192	425	364	232
46	105	67	47	110	76	77
*47	...	...	103	239	150	187
*48	...	...	43	376	120	296
	14178	10001	6729	14551	11279	9692

Total registration, 24,179.

11th Assembly District.

Elec. Dist.	Male.	Female.	Cox, Dem.	Harding, Rep.	Smith, Dem.	Miller, Rep.
1	299	279	130	384	258	261
2	358	334	123	510	293	329
3	386	298	174	428	328	259
4	341	317	185	419	326	268
5	341	301	188	374	315	240
6	315	288	185	360	318	209
7	325	244	167	341	311	170
8	329	330	213	367	354	219
9	369	225	182	332	358	135
10	376	217	195	329	328	165
11	331	255	171	271	306	218
12	234	221	146	276	273	140
13	366	269	167	336	344	194
†14	386	354	73	260	171	166
15	351	268	189	381	391	184
16	328	257	115	415	298	234
17	341	244	173	340	312	180
18	252	146	112	225	233	86
19	307	254	161	333	324	166
20	414	239	89	413	361	151
21	358	283	208	364	392	167
22	359	178	120	307	346	102
23	421	204	125	386	353	150
24	402	216	156	354	366	131
25	269	196	130	286	290	115
26	342	206	188	295	343	141
27	304	253	217	309	377	132
28	391	237	193	346	396	137
29	447	207	197	321	385	112
30	301	156	145	245	297	90
31	331	154	174	278	329	112
32	342	222	191	289	325	128
33	257	241	171	277	306	135
34	280	310	201	318	334	186
35	332	280	207	350	349	192
36	184	233	121	259	185	187
37	181	278	135	263	206	186
38	368	296	130	471	342	252
39	307	322	157	424	310	269
†40	385	386	105	234	180	152
41	353	315	169	410	335	249
42	287	318	180	389	297	251
43	342	318	127	474	320	271
44	316	331	128	465	300	284
45	167	158	56	269	143	176
*46	...	...	70	255	161	168
*47	...	...	111	265	218	153
	14854	11697	7210	16146	14376	8698

Total registration, 26,551.

12th Assembly District.

Elec. Dist.	Male.	Female.	Cox, Dem.	Harding, Rep.	Smith, Dem.	Miller, Rep.
1	366	197	169	288	314	135
2	251	188	133	206	254	88
3	236	177	157	195	272	80
4	295	135	211	174	303	76
5	322	132	246	139	342	38
6	309	224	198	207	333	78
7	270	173	194	186	304	68
8	355	203	279	163	407	67
9	425	117	263	217	408	75
10	226	160	185	195	316	76
11	53	31	41	30	54	16
12	515	185	137	171	225	66
†13	504	296	308	302	480	103
14	284	274	254	229	364	110
15	436	161	257	247	412	82
16	321	186	243	208	371	75
17	410	158	199	284	348	123
18	323	192	233	230	366	93
19	336	162	226	219	314	106

MANHATTAN VOTE, 1920—FOR PRESIDENT AND GOVERNOR—*Continued.*

12th A. D.—Continued.

Elec. Dist.	Reg'trat'n. Male.	Reg'trat'n. Female.	Cox, Dem.	Harding, Rep.	Smith, Dem.	Miller, Rep.
20	234	205	153	219	349	102
21	230	161	163	194	365	82
22	281	162	292	306	424	50
23	323	180	188	341	326	111
24	306	174	261	163	345	71
25	370	188	178	278	341	122
26	282	106	158	184	245	84
27	351	143	177	245	313	86
28	285	186	206	208	324	77
29	290	160	244	168	351	49
30	345	164	260	177	391	51
31	466	179	272	286	433	105
32	460	139	354	258	398	40
33	414	182	227	282	397	98
34	293	168	221	194	332	77
35	375	141	190	248	341	84
36	296	151	239	216	385	63
37	291	287	181	328	314	172
38	318	169	201	215	322	90
39	384	166	224	253	369	91
40	333	168	219	228	362	83
41	229	166	180	169	269	80
42	347	192	254	215	366	90
†43	546	174	152	212	239	98
44	280	168	195	187	281	84
45	281	234	221	227	305	127
46	360	216	244	251	384	93
47	334	175	221	214	349	85
48	247	175	93	247	224	100
49	294	157	140	246	257	114
50	234	140	128	196	264	57
51	365	117	311	115	364	45
*52	...	...	121	190	216	94
*53	...	...	86	161	191	48
	17012	8741	10776	11302	17141	4477

Total registration, 25,753.

13th Assembly District.

Elec. Dist.	Reg'trat'n. Male.	Reg'trat'n. Female.	Cox, Dem.	Harding, Rep.	Smith, Dem.	Miller, Rep.
1	307	295	123	405	233	294
2	338	305	181	360	262	264
3	154	320	143	275	194	232
4	224	468	163	414	226	349
5	210	338	166	322	282	202
6	243	405	203	367	283	246
7	232	452	230	343	328	260
8	329	319	224	332	391	147
9	331	323	216	332	361	197
10	202	228	112	262	233	139
11	242	283	129	330	247	212
12	216	118	83	184	191	69
13	233	216	136	260	229	143
14	329	151	169	276	287	139
15	146	70	96	95	155	80
16	375	210	170	321	326	138
17	416	200	158	376	362	137
18	423	222	153	373	377	137
19	313	258	163	350	306	159
20	314	305	145	401	297	245
21	456	188	230	320	413	119
22	414	178	183	286	398	67
23	315	184	193	245	302	104
24	399	267	173	392	384	197
25	361	311	173	412	390	190
26	307	224	94	386	291	195
27	250	219	194	231	306	100
28	284	181	188	280	331	126
29	337	128	100	311	234	174
30	262	186	146	262	238	166
31	333	255	80	402	194	273
32	401	229	143	395	292	234
33	406	215	112	416	291	216
34	280	153	85	285	180	174
35	296	160	86	297	213	153
36	117	97	63	133	127	68
37	321	205	131	304	326	95
†38	535	230	120	307	277	51
39	364	224	108	321	373	126
40	376	317	166	440	362	239
41	408	282	184	411	422	173
42	301	237	121	350	273	182
*43	...	...	96	168	213	56
	13190	10176	6358	13612	12380	7274

Total registration, 23,366.

*New Elec. Dist. created after last day of registration.

†Election Districts divided for Election Day on account of heavy registration.

14th Assembly District.

Elec. Dist.	Reg'trat'n. Male.	Reg'trat'n. Female.	Cox, Dem.	Harding, Rep.	Smith, Dem.	Miller, Rep.
1	331	169	127	262	312	104
2	214	116	113	171	315	86
3	407	184	197	290	324	91
4	273	182	156	321	367	96
5	221	90	90	163	307	47
6	256	191	151	218	298	79
7	436	170	194	257	341	89
8	347	162	129	224	270	98
9	346	223	196	311	387	112
10	254	160	155	184	344	69
11	352	173	176	265	314	106
12	346	160	170	346	278	113
13	419	190	227	296	354	153
14	509	153	223	294	417	101
15	334	195	171	238	296	93
16	247	157	142	167	247	51
17	326	186	163	234	310	84
18	341	226	184	262	348	90
19	318	174	116	236	266	80
20	364	259	206	307	379	111
21	412	176	141	275	314	88
22	246	201	184	225	301	102
23	182	134	136	141	235	42
24	261	174	199	177	312	64
25	409	167	137	290	296	120
26	502	189	173	344	381	114
27	472	180	208	301	386	113
28	370	190	195	250	365	66
29	343	216	213	247	363	92
30	353	141	104	291	264	117
31	444	200	88	378	262	166
32	323	140	126	282	268	123
33	331	143	104	256	231	106
34	293	139	139	211	246	81
35	385	170	165	267	338	82
36	523	178	159	336	369	127
†37	587	168	45	196	143	101
38	379	163	147	276	324	105
39	288	176	95	237	199	113
40	336	327	127	305	273	148
41	373	190	126	264	302	81
42	358	216	144	306	308	123
43	401	173	119	343	303	106
*44	...	...	68	204	156	104
	15298	7640	6692	11256	13071	4301

Total registration, 22,938.

15th Assembly District.

Elec. Dist.	Reg'trat'n. Male.	Reg'trat'n. Female.	Cox, Dem.	Harding, Rep.	Smith, Dem.	Miller, Rep.
1	20	33	15	33	25	21
2	202	136	106	188	170	116
3	345	251	150	372	254	257
4	342	316	158	440	262	333
†5	402	354	49	332	119	265
6	291	330	109	450	315	334
7	310	309	104	451	201	341
8	409	256	145	430	300	131
9	329	297	82	385	299	119
10	350	331	121	491	224	386
11	472	142	142	412	232	316
12	362	270	201	348	348	173
13	105	86	95	117	157	55
14	186	204	95	252	156	192
15	217	202	83	305	169	195
†16	413	380	80	318	149	243
17	281	293	121	408	215	303
18	301	206	164	267	275	159
19	275	274	177	277	203	291
20	220	209	154	224	219	153
21	225	271	102	350	164	290
22	265	196	147	260	252	143
†23	343	427	74	272	129	220
†24	362	354	81	299	177	195
25	350	239	206	297	356	166
26	368	337	145	499	252	383
27	207	259	133	285	219	214
28	281	296	86	412	213	285
29	332	297	169	398	315	254
30	322	235	174	389	245	240
31	250	284	145	326	318	160
32	217	255	143	274	244	176
33	269	202	146	248	296	96
34	328	242	204	293	353	141
35	293	206	174	245	273	147
36	414	243	217	334	423	133
37	268	240	147	307	299	152
38	267	326	130	310	265	189
39	263	217	116	304	238	176
40	279	275	195	293	345	148
41	280	238	157	296	318	136
42	262	171	120	242	264	97

15th A. D.—Continued.

Elec. Dist.	Reg'trat'n. Male.	Reg'trat'n. Female.	Cox, Dem.	Harding, Rep.	Smith, Dem.	Miller, Rep.
43	271	206	214	295	275	[illegible]
44	230	157	78	336	317	[illegible]
45	265	157	69	259	333	109
46	324	173	64	214	221	71
47	350	193	53	331	335	64
48	406	162	39	192	158	81
49	261	165	55	216	206	82
50	136	64	23	79	65	85
51	70	48	22	60	82	30
52	87	63	57	65	97	37
*53	...	...	67	253	115	134
*54	...	...	48	275	105	215
*55	...	...	60	281	108	224
*56	...	...	51	322	106	169
	14768	11946	6361	16378	12339	10680

Total registration, 26,709.

16th Assembly District.

Elec. Dist.	Reg'trat'n. Male.	Reg'trat'n. Female.	Cox, Dem.	Harding, Rep.	Smith, Dem.	Miller, Rep.
1	85	63	48	66	82	16
2	270	160	86	250	221	85
3	153	100	56	145	154	30
4	558	151	69	258	330	91
5	279	144	93	218	215	41
6	301	165	130	260	276	92
7	274	149	92	289	208	97
8	211	125	106	173	308	61
9	410	178	169	272	332	80
10	296	190	149	280	305	186
11	259	146	132	306	360	76
12	284	155	141	301	248	78
13	378	93	121	219	239	77
14	346	116	114	304	340	73
15	377	162	159	252	311	76
16	327	172	177	242	396	75
17	364	223	160	312	341	134
18	360	163	160	203	282	53
19	436	185	169	332	366	96
20	294	222	178	271	329	107
21	334	181	208	249	345	90
22	355	180	140	270	284	89
23	304	169	130	248	273	81
24	336	145	108	288	347	74
25	361	200	134	279	385	108
26	414	193	148	345	317	136
27	302	191	161	260	308	83
28	339	183	116	285	380	161
29	249	203	114	263	346	95
30	317	195	128	316	300	106
31	217	141	69	221	182	85
32	226	169	111	248	236	80
33	281	179	90	211	358	108
34	403	219	197	324	331	105
35	331	199	188	253	219	106
36	318	190	171	246	297	99
37	238	178	135	308	261	66
38	354	202	167	309	313	141
39	379	150	180	222	307	59
40	381	203	173	315	350	104
41	211	121	83	167	197	38
42	241	162	114	207	353	61
43	326	155	144	237	287	66
44	215	133	148	163	254	87
45	308	181	128	259	277	91
46	170	117	68	167	159	69
47	316	196	175	358	302	107
48	330	143	115	209	239	71
49	275	114	121	194	250	53
50	402	144	126	365	332	58
51	492	175	159	254	332	89
52	430	147	111	215	259	71
53	413	145	83	210	188	91
54	170	64	21	95	61	46
	16300	8709	6938	12813	14247	4947

Total registration, 25,509.

17th Assembly District.

Elec. Dist.	Reg'trat'n. Male.	Reg'trat'n. Female.	Cox, Dem.	Harding, Rep.	Smith, Dem.	Miller, Rep.
1	161	111	14	96	53	53
2	387	192	27	133	138	48
3	400	204	80	300	277	90
4	293	132	33	184	136	78
5	435	166	47	236	208	79
6	302	144	80	198	195	75
7	467	185	39	312	197	100
8	328	131	36	164	161	53
9	335	144	39	170	147	66
10	432	161	175	[illegible]	266	86
11	399	173	60	226	289	97
12	457	174	46	[illegible]	[illegible]	36

MANHATTAN VOTE, 1920—For President and Governor—*Continued.*

17th A. D.—Continued.

Elec. Dist.	Reg'trat'n Male.	Reg'trat'n Female.	Cox, Dem.	Harding, Rep.	Smith, Dem.	Miller, Rep.
13	301	132	48	207	200	66
14	304	138	58	233	205	74
15	378	165	138	321	327	125
16	280	177	70	217	253	141
17	316	145	66	281	254	89
18	359	123	47	210	199	70
19	230	130	52	159	167	57
20	339	156	60	225	247	61
21	426	146	68	293	296	63
22	428	178	66	359	329	113
23	331	114	58	209	243	23
24	416	223	95	407	337	172
25	363	159	90	318	333	79
26	331	165	83	236	306	125
27	381	155	42	359	267	154
28	309	130	59	252	241	72
29	340	153	51	240	229	78
30	409	163	80	178	233	83
31	353	144	49	181	194	64
32	309	119	59	270	283	69
33	300	117	36	238	221	68
34	377	188	104	366	360	110
35	409	229	108	355	376	123
36	322	168	46	326	286	98
37	...	...	...	...	...	...
38	...	...	...	...	...	...
	12597	5644	2284	8988	8667	3072

Total registration, 18,241.

18th Assembly District.

Elec. Dist.	Reg'trat'n Male.	Reg'trat'n Female.	Cox, Dem.	Harding, Rep.	Smith, Dem.	Miller, Rep.
1	385	225	204	330	410	109
†2	433	306	101	215	228	29
3	282	166	134	237	293	78
4	263	159	146	200	283	62
†5	499	221	88	142	168	53
6	214	120	74	150	160	65
7	282	158	173	162	278	59
8	326	170	108	232	237	103
9	393	176	122	215	286	63
10	529	165	67	220	192	95
11	504	167	69	304	221	127
12	469	165	147	374	317	86
12	427	213	213	226	379	55
14	464	224	109	233	254	99
†15	587	202	18	196	109	98
16	410	161	149	251	324	80
17	368	215	117	259	292	91
18	237	186	200	234	372	57
19	549	140	77	442	283	237
20	546	117	53	497	238	272
21	469	219	156	309	321	102
22	381	185	67	200	213	64
23	295	155	143	220	287	77
24	437	176	107	318	275	130
25	423	216	150	279	315	100
26	384	139	56	366	220	195
27	405	168	118	372	312	170
28	187	51	164	51	129	76
29	543	132	57	498	290	241
30	485	196	239	344	443	126
31	329	166	78	162	201	62
32	380	193	108	278	273	115
33	484	217	140	402	346	178
34	147	71	57	101	122	31
*35	...	...	108	198	224	68
*36	...	...	128	142	224	36
*37	...	...	105	211	243	74
	13516	6086	4350	9472	9762	3773

Total registration, 19,552.

19th Assembly District.

Elec. Dist.	Reg'trat'n Male.	Reg'trat'n Female.	Cox, Dem.	Harding, Rep.	Smith, Dem.	Miller, Rep.
1	404	170	54	259	216	82
2	199	104	45	148	141	49
3	339	123	57	255	243	72
4	320	228	91	375	222	222
5	326	174	91	315	282	125
6	435	174	87	361	313	123
7	308	199	79	319	270	137
8	326	231	126	340	354	129
9	336	216	149	333	308	168
10	232	131	141	163	241	62
11	261	253	133	324	253	194
12	274	254	193	276	307	166

*New Elec. Dist. created after last day of registration.

†Election Districts divided for Election Day on account of heavy registration.

19th A. D.—Continued.

Elec. Dist.	Reg'trat'n Male.	Reg'trat'n Female.	Cox, Dem.	Harding, Rep.	Smith, Dem.	Miller, Rep.
13	212	173	123	225	227	112
14	311	186	158	368	197	129
15	286	186	83	308	233	148
16	332	289	171	368	356	193
17	289	222	108	343	234	317
18	315	223	205	276	331	138
19	352	209	132	324	264	180
20	260	158	74	277	203	139
21	373	246	121	418	277	243
22	409	213	151	369	273	340
23	327	202	133	311	268	174
24	356	200	185	283	306	138
25	338	260	167	346	326	178
26	303	229	137	319	281	161
27	243	192	165	193	268	91
28	218	212	[illegible]	245	223	124
29	180	131	79	203	164	115
30	265	199	81	316	198	117
31	251	210	118	254	237	136
32	242	193	75	303	158	198
33	315	247	179	306	315	163
34	240	127	46	253	128	157
35	316	192	7	450	162	269
36	419	281	39	530	207	333
37	356	209	12	457	147	292
38	412	248	7	522	187	312
39	434	249	24	518	123	396
40	370	198	8	450	132	293
41	333	148	6	425	161	240
42	356	192	28	426	174	257
43	184	78	20	203	94	117
44	246	104	57	242	151	119
	13594	8650	4260	14199	10154	7648

Total registration, 22,250.

20th Assembly District.

Elec. Dist.	Reg'trat'n Male.	Reg'trat'n Female.	Cox, Dem.	Harding, Rep.	Smith, Dem.	Miller, Rep.
1	278	82	93	155	195	55
2	297	140	84	216	202	85
3	478	187	149	290	317	117
4	426	240	232	302	403	116
5	340	190	197	257	322	118
†6	527	224	116	205	259	58
7	381	150	161	258	395	102
8	383	229	178	330	362	145
9	150	118	71	166	147	88
10	372	209	219	258	349	125
11	376	228	233	307	393	133
12	379	196	87	392	210	251
13	452	171	242	287	406	103
14	453	221	186	376	309	206
15	496	196	186	386	404	141
16	387	176	185	285	337	110
17	375	170	175	278	301	123
18	453	154	149	271	302	108
19	472	147	125	315	303	133
20	449	201	167	376	338	166
21	399	133	160	349	268	150
22	435	135	82	330	243	131
23	489	128	82	443	295	205
24	432	81	50	371	236	164
25	318	81	94	232	200	109
*36	...	...	145	156	214	71
	9997	4195	3788	7591	7619	3316

Total registration, 14,192.

21st Assembly District.

Elec. Dist.	Reg'trat'n Male.	Reg'trat'n Female.	Cox, Dem.	Harding, Rep.	Smith, Dem.	Miller, Rep.
1	299	240	149	322	290	181
2	247	200	121	277	254	150
3	282	228	131	322	264	189
4	290	260	110	392	313	178
5	278	210	94	333	236	193
6	298	272	131	361	287	217
7	217	135	78	259	209	108
8	242	156	100	263	251	109
9	280	229	174	280	316	140
10	262	242	155	284	292	142
†11	396	335	98	211	174	124
12	281	228	138	340	267	208
†13	406	335	75	196	174	99
14	236	152	103	238	208	125
15	196	121	41	224	127	135
16	203	127	3	282	116	155
17	182	108	12	242	105	135
18	368	237	26	451	190	276

21st A. D.—Continued.

Elec. Dist.	Reg'trat'n Male.	Reg'trat'n Female.	Cox, Dem.	Harding, Rep.	Smith, Dem.	Miller, Rep.
19	274	169	109	272	229	137
20	304	208	92	357	232	200
†21	442	279	6	337	121	314
22	425	256	6	546	223	300
23	389	224	9	524	237	273
24	328	204	2	452	177	258
25	35	32	2	52	17	34
†26	473	252	6	292	146	132
27	414	210	5	525	262	229
28	297	145	52	295	165	157
29	329	183	47	379	186	231
30	445	211	13	505	253	257
†31	494	258	39	160	98	89
32	376	210	195	308	372	103
33	213	106	99	151	205	46
34	347	211	154	331	306	158
35	208	213	115	277	235	145
36	279	269	156	337	313	172
37	247	260	110	359	229	239
38	251	227	113	330	229	210
39	401	342	146	423	356	261
40	272	256	152	318	269	195
41	300	262	138	364	251	233
*42	...	...	123	237	222	128
*43	...	...	123	246	231	128
*44	...	...	3	258	86	156
*45	...	...	19	324	150	158
*46	...	...	11	428	178	256
	12506	8751	3776	14664	10064	7979

Total registration, 21,263.

22d Assembly District.

Elec. Dist.	Reg'trat'n Male.	Reg'trat'n Female.	Cox, Dem.	Harding, Rep.	Smith, Dem.	Miller, Rep.
1	270	284	172	341	305	208
2	418	246	189	368	408	139
†3	458	306	114	224	224	109
4	327	250	197	332	340	179
5	289	206	136	282	285	125
6	204	134	120	174	221	71
7	296	234	127	351	281	201
8	162	136	106	166	167	109
9	244	214	105	312	254	160
†10	446	299	64	232	175	121
11	236	276	146	302	272	163
12	379	249	191	352	315	173
13	329	260	134	389	356	157
14	322	214	116	345	304	140
15	200	159	88	224	220	89
16	253	262	153	325	290	189
17	231	216	146	260	261	128
18	237	182	91	289	216	159
19	287	247	179	329	284	205
20	273	276	132	383	247	260
21	352	269	187	376	380	168
22	277	229	141	327	299	160
23	272	239	147	320	302	172
24	292	218	121	325	284	166
25	326	239	112	385	265	227
26	341	249	94	438	206	229
27	241	152	87	279	221	141
28	327	201	159	312	318	141
29	368	299	185	413	344	238
30	384	200	153	361	354	136
31	347	273	162	396	384	163
32	294	202	84	359	286	163
33	368	228	73	470	353	189
34	6	4	6	1	9	1
35	270	223	152	287	291	147
36	380	193	168	286	330	102
37	428	207	202	313	377	117
38	332	185	181	269	338	102
39	238	156	139	196	267	68
40	...	...	...	...	...	...
41	351	195	165	292	355	120
42	259	134	132	194	246	68
43	266	149	141	188	262	80
44	332	181	166	274	307	121
45	408	169	162	313	307	111
46	251	129	117	193	229	66
47	351	180	125	294	279	135
48	223	102	92	188	193	74
49	198	112	23	242	114	133
*50	...	...	76	250	164	157
*51	...	...	64	325	223	160
	14313	9966	6613	14845	13814	7140

Total registration, 24,279.

MANHATTAN VOTE, 1920—FOR PRESIDENT AND GOVERNOR—*Continued.*

23d Assembly District.

Elec. Dist.	Reg'trat'n. Male.	Reg'trat'n. Female.	Cox, Dem.	Harding, Rep.	Smith, Dem.	Miller, Rep.
1	427	222	95	500	372	213
2	339	204	117	342	325	187
3	165	122	72	171	128	115
4	244	140	148	204	243	98
5	342	198	107	361	331	145
6	376	211	239	295	422	92
7	274	184	159	249	290	111
8	378	274	188	293	399	194
9	405	225	219	329	396	152
10	352	269	185	419	301	243
11	375	293	110	511	355	253
12	328	222	157	320	341	130
13	314	229	134	341	299	168
14	314	219	88	388	328	143
15	270	222	174	323	277	158
16	296	249	157	322	286	176
17	304	212	134	301	309	126

*New Elec. Dist. created after last day of registration.

†Election Districts divided for Election Day on account of heavy registration.

23d A. D.—Continued.

Elec. Dist.	Reg'trat'n. Male.	Reg'trat'n. Female.	Cox, Dem.	Harding, Rep.	Smith, Dem.	Miller, Rep.
18	337	232	139	371	300	198
19	294	223	128	333	278	162
20	447	251	158	394	407	157
21	283	166	83	273	241	111
22	420	237	168	389	388	169
23	296	192	120	310	303	112
24	297	222	150	321	316	151
25	263	228	85	352	201	228
26	260	242	89	359	239	203
27	440	193	112	444	312	243
28	286	211	90	318	262	149
29	335	250	113	379	317	180
30	224	230	95	319	216	204
31	239	200	78	316	225	163
32	317	279	141	397	284	258
33	207	167	96	258	191	151
34	273	214	108	320	253	171
35	289	231	135	335	279	173
36	283	212	150	274	286	143
37	292	227	124	331	262	184
38	315	238	133	358	289	192
39	325	239	116	345	309	178
40	297	199	123	317	265	171

23d A. D.—Continued.

Elec. Dist.	Reg'trat'n. Male.	Reg'trat'n. Female.	Cox, Dem.	Harding, Rep.	Smith, Dem.	Miller, Rep.
†41	416	326	91	222	195	117
42	297	236	126	251	252	225
43	343	258	178	346	350	183
44	309	239	156	340	309	180
45	288	214	91	363	250	198
46	335	243	105	408	253	248
47	298	262	144	356	261	237
48	320	216	127	331	299	155
49	330	232	127	350	319	159
†50	517	330	99	240	234	106
51	342	219	150	338	323	274
†52	404	311	89	246	219	117
53	307	234	183	289	318	150
54	276	198	142	264	296	114
55	353	262	146	396	330	207
56	321	213	159	313	326	144
57	267	211	137	298	237	186
*58	...	...	103	231	209	118
*59	...	...	110	281	287	101
*60	...	...	82	208	173	113
	18259	13002	7700	19753	17275	9925

Total registration, 31,261.

Members of the State Senate.

12th Dist.—J. J. Walker, Dem., 14,027; J. Shapiro, Rep., 8,507; M. Loeb, Soc., 5,724.

13th Dist.—J. J. Boylan, Dem., 23,205; W. H. Brady, Rep., 16,491; F. Witherspoon, Soc., 1,723.

14th Dist.—B. Downing, Dem., Fus., 20,255; S. E. Beardsley, Soc., 14,654.

15th Dist.—N. Strauss, Jr., Dem., 36,549; A. Ottinger, Rep., 31,920; A. D. L. Montanye, Soc., 1,906; G. B. Youngs, Far.-L., 315.

16th Dist.—M. G. McCue, Dem., 28,245; T. Mallee, Rep., 13,131; H. W. Berger, Soc., 4,885.

17th Dist.—J. Miller, Dem., 2,707; S. M. Meyer, Rep., 30,098; S. Silverman, Soc., 8,460.

18th Dist.—S. A. Cotillo, Dem., 16,612; W. P. Hartman, Rep., 12,727; M. S. Calman, Soc., 8,085.

19th Dist.—E. J. Downing, Dem., 18,627; W. Duggan, Rep., 26,474; E. F. Dutton, Soc., 4,426.

20th Dist.—B. E. Burston, Dem., 24,153; W. V. Tolbert, Rep., 37,775; F. Poree, Soc., 3,640.

Justice, Municipal Court, 4th District.

J. G. McTigue, Dem., 18,564; J. Goode, Rep., 16,402; E. A. Lynn, Soc., 2,634.

Associate Judges of the Court of Appeals.

	Mhtn.	Bronx.
Frederick E. Crane, Dem., Rep.	295,597	109,467
Abram I. Elkus, Dem.	176,744	67,869
Emory A. Chase, Rep.	172,086	61,828
Leon A. Malkiel, Soc.	46,442	34,801
Jacob Axelrad, Soc.	43,316	33,072
Coleridge A. Hart, Proh.	1,838	633
Francis E. Baldwin, Proh.	1,184	397
Swinburne Hale, Far.-L.	8,269	2,631
Thomas F. Dwyer, Far.-L.	11,784	3,928

Justice of the City Court.

	Mhtn.	Bronx.
Thomas T. Reilley, Dem.	168,310	64,061
Gustave Hartman, Rep.	206,137	77,018
Jacob Hillquit, Soc.	49,542	36,306

Judges of the Court of General Sessions.

Thomas C. T. Crain, Dem., Rep., Proh., 340,189; Otto A. Rosalsky, Dem., Rep., Proh., 337,893; Isaac Sackin, Soc., 50,929; William Karlin, Soc., 51,849.

Justices of the Supreme Court for the 1st Judicial District.

	Mhtn.	Bronx.
Francis Martin, Dem.	188,871	82,117
William P. Burr, Dem.	194,385	79,531
Edward J. McGoldrick, Dem.	188,770	72,924
Edward Swann, Dem.	183,930	75,150
Leonard A. Giegerich, Dem., Rep.	323,985	118,332
John Ford, Dem., Rep.	319,378	118,606
Charles L. Guy, Dem., Rep.	321,518	117,189
M. Warley Platzek, Dem., Rep.	310,440	110,450
Mitchell L. Erlanger, Dem., Rep.	315,085	113,411
James O'Malley, Rep.	202,977	69,091
Isidor Wasservogel, Rep.	196,929	67,000
Henry K. Davis, Rep.	186,690	69,688
Robert McC. Marsh, Rep.	179,562	59,681
Alexander Kahn, Soc.	50,614	36,662
Morris Gisnet, Soc.	46,936	34,817
Adolph Warshow, Soc.	46,712	34,305
Jacob Hennefeld, Soc.	46,131	34,090
S. John Block, Soc.	47,713	34,621
Jacob Bernstein, Soc.	45,790	34,185
Henry Gilbert, Soc.	44,666	32,957
Benjamin Marcus, Soc.	44,197	33,047
Samuel Fried, Soc.	42,493	31,498
Benjamin W. Burger, Sing. Tax	4,423	1,367

RECAPITULATION—PRESIDENT AND GOVERNOR, CITY OF NEW YORK.

Boroughs.	Registration.	President. Cox, Dem.	Harding, Rep.	Debs, Soc.	Watkins, Proh.	Cox, Soc.-L.	Christensen, Far.-L.	Governor. Smith, Dem.	Miller, Rep.	Cannon, Soc.	Thompson, Proh.	Quinn, Soc.-L.	Malone, Far.-L.
Manhattan	503,811	134,308	275,194	45,046	463	567	7,077	268,418	135,434	34,220	1,115	582	19,848
The Bronx	199,423	45,611	106,012	32,823	211	452	1,949	105,558	43,388	25,583	540	405	10,093
Brooklyn	495,161	119,545	292,452	45,098	733	638	3,473	244,362	153,923	34,534	3,029	795	21,445
Queens	135,252	35,296	94,268	6,143	142	262	1,204	75,938	45,140	4,361	741	262	8,649
Richmond	30,355	9,371	17,857	712	111	48	170	15,337	10,542	426	282	51	908
Totals	1,364,112	344,131	785,783	129,822	1,660	1,967	13,873	709,823	392,927	99,124	5,707	2,095	60,943

ENROLLMENT NEW YORK CITY, 1921.

Counties.	Democrats. Male.	Democrats. Female.	Republican. Male.	Republican. Female.	Socialist. Male.	Socialist. Female.	Prohibition. Male.	Prohibition. Female.
New York	127,570	61,585	138,009	91,179	12,570	7,493	853	872
Bronx	53,214	26,247	47,325	29,504	8,446	6,509	328	291
Kings	119,965	58,663	157,780	101,622	11,702	8,313	875	1,182
Queens	46,271	21,754	38,633	27,321	1,738	803	239	336
Richmond	11,352	4,546	7,257	5,000	220	94	120	212
Totals	358,372	172,795	389,004	254,626	34,676	23,212	2,415	2,893

BRONX VOTE, 1920—For President and Governor.

1st Assembly District.

Elec. Dist.	Reg'trat'n. Male.	Reg'trat'n. Female.	Cox, Dem.	Harding, Rep.	Smith, Dem.	Miller, Rep.
1	453	198	183	376	370	160
2	366	163	136	254	285	82
3	365	206	145	238	314	63
4	345	181	119	232	266	72
5	344	187	120	198	236	72
6	425	252	178	307	371	101
7	382	181	88	225	232	75
8	394	221	136	267	308	74
9	439	234	118	263	275	95
10	248	152	64	205	168	80
11	316	224	164	294	336	107
12	271	200	153	271	292	113
13	406	264	238	361	435	152
14	416	219	220	321	367	160
15	333	161	73	169	207	38
16	380	229	112	239	266	78
17	299	165	152	267	284	103
18	235	146	136	205	235	94
19	343	190	129	279	290	112
20	373	185	157	267	307	83
21	300	116	109	218	239	69
†22	485	231	95	228	239	84
23	492	166	157	393	385	130
24	431	258	135	387	341	186
25	405	187	161	343	378	88
26	299	155	74	332	272	110
27	387	126	87	330	254	128
28	448	249	171	419	451	147
29	427	175	148	376	350	131
30	413	217	160	384	397	109
31	345	164	138	305	326	84
32	413	189	138	373	324	147
33	401	221	120	415	338	153
34	335	181	131	309	312	114
35	325	159	95	306	271	95
†36	464	247	90	330	276	119
37	394	218	157	361	345	125
38	452	220	124	418	371	136
39	352	167	86	288	297	67
40	135	88	67	128	129	55
41	400	213	174	345	306	122
42	394	216	167	373	361	148
43	414	213	166	363	375	126
44	303	186	146	267	287	97
45	39	29	25	38	39	23
46	333	216	179	314	336	140
47	456	200	189	362	407	134
48	463	262	99	184	209	61
49	450	181	106	422	361	195
*50	...	...	77	151	166	57
*51	...	...	54	145	127	63
*52	...	...	105	247	236	90
	18093	9418	6741	15092	15349	5417

Total registration, 27,511.

2d Assembly District.

Elec. Dist.	Reg'trat'n. Male.	Reg'trat'n. Female.	Cox, Dem.	Harding, Rep.	Smith, Dem.	Miller, Rep.
1	426	232	183	368	347	210
†2	524	230	107	206	205	81
†3	496	269	195	193	314	61
4	378	216	259	261	407	99
5	235	224	180	280	311	139
6	234	124	163	137	261	37
†7	464	378	159	165	260	56
8	384	222	134	268	261	37
9	414	227	181	361	340	171
10	397	242	259	316	418	129
11	229	155	107	204	220	66
12	284	164	144	205	275	73
13	326	180	207	218	333	84
14	285	205	180	257	317	106
15	391	211	248	277	371	143
16	373	197	188	314	337	146
17	279	191	208	224	315	91
†18	571	151	77	251	198	113
19	587	104	72	461	260	237
20	243	147	122	233	230	114
21	426	278	224	468	354	241
22	305	253	212	299	328	179
23	354	307	144	443	334	261
24	360	267	179	300	374	114
25	299	229	181	300	341	131
†26	336	325	89	139	157	40
27	396	233	164	367	382	127
†28	380	215	126	323	358	104
†29	465	331	88	216	212	83
30	150	105	59	146	142	62
31	283	196	120	296	305	97
32	420	254	182	358	359	157
33	278	202	126	306	283	118
34	314	234	114	369	299	159
†35	451	288	148	324	324	139
36	324	220	106	312	323	107
37	281	210	116	286	244	130
†38	473	242	28	99	111	38
39	251	218	148	324	298	135
40	392	208	121	261	296	94
41	404	196	71	210	220	59
42	271	187	60	202	198	81
43	482	217	77	211	221	66
†44	468	244	66	143	169	53
45	163	109	29	109	111	38
46	373	226	151	320	316	132
†47	395	338	131	338	281	183
48	316	230	95	290	243	149
†49	462	300	75	255	182	140
50	309	246	176	339	319	167
51	302	196	180	249	300	105
42	333	236	218	279	345	141
53	412	273	193	405	349	239
54	370	281	254	364	403	207
†55	465	334	156	285	284	159
*56	...	...	164	178	250	78
*57	...	...	128	162	198	67
*58	...	...	153	164	243	56
*59	...	...	46	247	160	125
*60	...	...	281	146	281	136
*61	...	...	86	302	234	146
*62	...	...	47	141	128	53
*63	...	...	53	174	168	64
*64	...	...	31	82	89	27
*65	...	...	72	133	121	81
*66	...	...	67	158	169	69
*67	...	...	59	170	165	98
	20322	12419	9303	17417	18235	7796

Total registration, 32,751.

3d Assembly District.

Elec. Dist.	Reg'trat'n. Male.	Reg'trat'n. Female.	Cox, Dem.	Harding, Rep.	Smith, Dem.	Miller, Rep.
1	309	153	129	246	292	70
2	391	238	142	350	349	117
†3	475	250	58	177	180	57
4	431	235	126	344	340	119
5	428	238	171	359	398	102
6	352	173	131	272	276	114
7	288	149	68	232	204	89
8	354	217	81	297	260	113
9	433	224	97	380	321	119
10	427	203	65	257	250	85
11	452	232	86	308	289	105
12	324	198	117	306	294	115
13	437	227	108	375	330	142
14	406	185	79	276	266	85
15	21	6	2	21	16	5
16	291	170	98	261	269	73
17	391	196	170	276	347	94
18	392	248	112	221	266	62
19	274	185	86	213	247	67
20	348	164	26	180	197	37
21	326	152	42	159	166	45
22	328	180	35	249	218	64
23	408	203	83	278	313	65
24	311	170	85	267	293	69
25	443	241	114	387	336	161
26	356	153	69	321	310	86
27	394	166	78	270	287	80
28	452	225	67	386	361	109
29	470	220	49	331	300	101
30	352	212	72	325	312	87
31	392	189	64	310	274	93
32	438	206	72	325	335	84
33	267	195	46	331	284	104
34	384	186	140	246	297	76
35	377	207	96	312	366	70
36	430	221	96	362	329	138
37	[illegible]	[illegible]	45	21	57	8
*38	...	...	23	111	127	26
	12304	7685	3218	10341	10456	3236

Total registration, 20,589.

4th Assembly District.

Elec. Dist.	Reg'trat'n. Male.	Reg'trat'n. Female.	Cox, Dem.	Harding, Rep.	Smith, Dem.	Miller, Rep.
1	370	166	61	226	219	71
2	433	240	103	320	334	97
3	359	202	48	246	232	71
4	380	225	107	255	297	83
5	406	233	145	283	357	75
6	383	225	111	273	298	107
7	375	238	112	334	336	112
8	301	194	97	308	242	135
9	210	251	186	288	355	114
10	379	265	153	340	347	139
11	272	183	159	236	301	86
12	339	201	99	287	310	81
13	380	227	201	259	395	74
14	285	231	195	256	365	79
15	353	235	91	353	324	123
16	323	224	127	301	304	109
17	304	182	83	253	271	76
18	384	228	123	317	323	108
19	367	190	92	236	349	80
20	344	198	39	176	187	129
21	374	256	80	356	296	123
22	426	271	124	317	310	140
23	417	256	141	279	317	112
24	282	172	96	225	236	78
25	378	205	75	237	277	63
26	355	209	74	319	265	106
27	443	202	61	228	233	72
28	392	202	44	175	215	43
29	372	231	73	264	295	81
30	474	215	39	206	120	94
31	471	232	89	287	275	115
32	361	155	65	184	192	61
33	414	188	41	144	131	52
34	376	185	63	147	208	45
35	485	217	51	207	226	66
	13049	7534	3548	9121	9742	3202

Total registration, 20,583.

5th Assembly District.

Elec. Dist.	Reg'trat'n. Male.	Reg'trat'n. Female.	Cox, Dem.	Harding, Rep.	Smith, Dem.	Miller, Rep.
1	262	143	44	249	200	101
2	410	219	114	329	335	102
3	224	167	80	281	253	119
4	408	239	88	329	322	101
5	440	216	65	311	298	86
†6	499	215	48	183	190	50
7	346	192	76	326	296	96
†8	523	247	26	150	148	37
†9	486	235	41	197	189	67
10	406	182	73	290	302	88
11	443	220	84	407	383	102
12	456	234	96	379	387	86
13	347	154	78	322	385	116
14	294	178	102	269	262	101
15	407	217	105	331	342	110
16	401	186	64	347	359	69
†17	497	249	28	148	135	60
18	399	260	139	353	364	130
19	406	258	157	344	364	137
20	457	221	82	296	308	86
21	372	184	79	264	264	68
22	394	197	81	289	292	86
23	438	233	88	360	338	108
†24	472	249	45	173	187	66
25	332	167	59	247	231	73
26	379	203	113	286	312	80
27	399	237	78	329	334	89
28	440	232	106	335	333	113
29	340	208	86	281	275	96
30	412	326	91	300	330	89
31	328	192	59	209	245	57
32	441	200	55	268	243	78
33	331	198	59	222	224	68
†34	490	246	7	102	105	17
35	417	223	60	244	258	65
36	450	207	88	277	269	88
37	322	165	62	135	238	38
38	434	232	59	276	273	79
*39	...	...	63	221	220	69
*40	...	...	51	288	292	72
*41	...	...	46	199	209	63
*42	...	...	107	270	325	63
*43	...	...	59	140	165	52
*44	...	...	36	151	163	40
	15309	9039	3307	11786	11847	3540

Total registration, 23,348.

6th Assembly District.

Elec. Dist.	Reg'trat'n. Male.	Reg'trat'n. Female.	Cox, Dem.	Harding, Rep.	Smith, Dem.	Miller, Rep.
1	397	213	166	378	337	170
2	336	229	168	328	351	131
3	398	208	137	401	329	181

*New Elec. Dist. created after last day of registration.

†Election Districts divided for Election Day on account of heavy registration.

BRONX VOTE, 1920—FOR PRESIDENT AND GOVERNOR—*Continued.*

6th A. D.—Continued.

Elec. Dist.	Reg'trat'n. Male.	Reg'trat'n. Female.	Cox, Dem.	Harding, Rep.	Smith, Dem.	Miller, Rep.
4	352	209	167	328	332	131
5	335	212	238	258	350	121
6	467	238	208	416	408	179
7	398	203	166	380	320	184
8	385	209	173	370	306	196
9	321	226	204	299	316	159
10	409	230	251	340	401	151
11	407	215	198	356	344	173
12	275	156	132	253	245	116
13	420	261	204	407	404	153
†14	447	272	137	324	302	144
†15	468	260	96	249	244	110
16	396	206	97	400	298	182
17	459	201	155	379	329	163
18	321	217	162	308	292	135
19	391	231	120	406	219	173
20	372	219	150	357	318	172
21	415	278	198	426	360	215
22	415	187	123	398	264	231
23	445	143	110	411	282	226
24	414	191	155	368	318	189
25	390	216	175	349	342	177
26	401	222	177	362	360	149
27	345	238	137	401	276	238
28	290	244	153	342	299	181
29	343	196	134	343	269	186
30	375	216	134	399	226	189
31	338	147	77	365	222	203
32	458	217	128	405	321	157
†33	529	272	80	297	167	188
*34	...	...	40	83	84	37
*35	...	...	53	163	142	57
*36	...	...	124	225	192	141
	12902	7182	5326	12274	10774	5888

Total registration, 20,084.

7th Assembly District.

Elec. Dist.	Reg'trat'n. Male.	Reg'trat'n. Female.	Cox, Dem.	Harding, Rep.	Smith, Dem.	Miller, Rep.
1	304	211	145	232	268	104
2	276	170	124	250	272	125
3	416	229	129	222	310	76
4	390	212	122	240	278	95
5	341	238	124	309	311	109
6	273	196	128	216	263	93
7	321	215	136	269	205	97
†8	412	235	120	293	279	136
9	192	148	70	205	167	96
10	389	232	82	337	306	111

*New Elec. Dist created after last day of registration.

†Election Districts divided for Election Day on account of heavy registration.

7th A. D.—Continued.

Elec. Dist.	Reg'trat'n. Male.	Reg'trat'n. Female.	Cox, Dem.	Harding, Rep.	Smith, Dem.	Miller, Rep.
11	308	198	126	241	288	92
12	361	220	102	266	256	96
13	413	264	112	339	333	122
†14	486	239	77	176	187	62
15	402	235	63	341	291	133
16	354	244	79	299	272	109
17	389	257	121	259	220	158
18	356	175	68	274	220	97
19	428	246	125	291	344	92
20	368	209	118	273	290	95
21	348	192	115	221	252	87
22	332	197	154	247	286	119
23	394	247	230	312	406	106
24	383	216	95	257	249	102
25	376	208	195	282	344	117
26	312	215	110	232	246	95
27	253	193	142	221	251	100
28	239	190	136	239	261	104
29	373	262	205	345	404	133
30	111	34	9	100	58	48
31	414	264	229	324	398	143
32	312	183	101	284	243	126
33	326	187	92	278	241	116
34	302	203	80	254	202	108
35	428	254	114	269	282	93
36	344	235	104	241	271	82
37	327	162	70	251	222	89
38	280	75	33	227	168	89
39	337	177	126	275	284	121
40	383	69	56	287	208	115
41	490	104	55	356	245	141
*42	...	...	68	93	132	30
*43	...	...	38	184	149	73
	14238	7328	4728	11230	11143	4435

Total registration, 22,566.

8th Assembly District.

Elec. Dist.	Reg'trat'n. Male.	Reg'trat'n. Female.	Cox, Dem.	Harding, Rep.	Smith, Dem.	Miller, Rep.
1	486	348	160	347	300	207
2	376	314	192	429	330	270
†3	411	332	161	279	251	182
4	345	298	164	411	303	256
5	328	248	144	380	296	218
6	364	231	150	376	312	194
7	396	258	198	385	371	191
8	361	255	228	328	404	147
†9	477	349	69	169	139	91
†10	500	391	118	346	221	235
11	306	250	158	355	298	212
12	339	331	258	372	386	236
†13	404	336	106	249	206	149
†14	398	333	77	220	166	122
15	313	194	170	300	323	130

8th A. D.—Continued.

Elec. Dist.	Reg'trat'n. Male.	Reg'trat'n. Female.	Cox, Dem.	Harding, Rep.	Smith, Dem.	Miller, Rep.
16	373	223	166	365	339	187
†17	454	316	109	237	242	190
18	373	240	171	363	371	161
19	327	131	133	231	275	82
20	253	169	132	239	364	102
21	383	216	187	288	365	104
22	171	51	33	143	104	65
23	486	191	126	428	370	162
24	358	186	122	247	295	68
†25	397	330	213	246	340	106
26	248	225	195	249	297	137
27	281	322	163	279	300	135
28	316	258	209	305	368	145
†29	481	257	110	297	235	163
†30	453	342	125	330	270	185
31	379	282	171	438	339	269
32	338	278	173	375	316	222
33	412	284	249	387	416	191
†34	433	269	146	215	244	113
35	329	217	223	271	336	159
36	292	173	97	330	195	116
37	348	344	217	405	404	219
†38	430	283	117	201	209	105
39	273	252	208	282	322	158
40	320	276	341	205	385	148
41	285	241	175	303	331	145
†42	417	306	114	238	228	115
†43	379	345	96	212	184	122
†44	443	397	113	213	218	103
45	384	291	216	406	382	216
46	310	242	157	341	299	218
47	357	281	202	394	361	193
48	376	312	226	400	409	216
49	364	255	217	353	337	159
†50	448	306	202	218	290	116
*51	...	...	55	134	220	109
*52	...	...	27	186	131	99
*53	...	...	122	357	328	156
*54	...	...	120	208	226	110
*55	...	...	116	218	206	129
*56	...	...	129	249	250	125
*57	...	...	123	207	387	159
*58	...	...	88	116	133	60
*59	...	...	119	232	227	124
*60	...	...	94	166	156	104
*61	...	...	91	189	137	139
*62	...	...	89	238	205	112
*63	...	...	113	181	197	90
*64	...	...	128	214	235	112
*65	...	...	154	298	266	185
*66	...	...	102	178	149	121
	18431	13560	9871	18751	18062	9707

Total registration, 31,991.

BOROUGH OF THE BRONX.

Lieut. Gov., J. W. Hughan, Soc., 31,241; B. G. Dietrich, Proh., 433; J. D. Crowley, Soc.-L., 812; R. E. Haffey, Far.-L., 6 126.

Sec. of State, C. W. Noonan, Soc., 34,500; I. B. Taylor, Proh., 602; M. Phalor, Soc.-L., 632; W. H. Auver, Far.-L., 3,556.

Comptroller, A. P. Randolph, Soc., 35 471; W. C. Gray, Proh., 471; J. L. Lee, Soc.-L., 669; H. H. Fincke, Far.-L., 3,334.

Treasurer, H. F. Kreuger, Soc., 35,275; J. McKee, Proh., 472; J. A. Withers, Soc.-L., 598; J. E. Crank, Far.-L., 3,225.

Atty. Gen., D. J. Meserole, Soc., 34,964; W. H. Burr, Proh., 1,202; J. Donohue, Soc.-L., 927; F. R. Serri, Far.-L., 2,988.

State Eng. and Surveyor, V. Karapetoff, Soc., 35 657; A. S. Light, Proh., 401; C. C. Crawford, Soc.-L., 1,374.

U S Senator, J. Paulin, Soc, 38,641; E. A. Bolle, Proh., 1,224; H. Carlson, Soc.-L., 560; R. Schneiderman, Far.-L., 3,194.

Justices of the Supreme Court, 1st Jud. Dist.

F. Martin, Dem., 82,117; W. P. Burr, Dem., 79,531; E. J. McGoldrick, Dem., 72,924; E. Swann, Dem., 75,150; L. A. Giegerich, Dem. and Rep., 118,332; J. Ford, Dem. and Rep., 118,606; C. L. Guy, Dem. and Rep., 117,189; M. W. Platzek, Dem. and Rep., 110,450; M. L. Erlanger, Dem. and Rep., 113,411; J. O'Malley, Rep., 69,091; F. Wasservogel, Rep., 67,000; H. K. Davis, Rep., 69,688; R. McC. Marsh, Rep., 59,681; A. Kahn, Soc., 36,662; M. Gismet, Soc., 34,817; A. Warshow, Soc., 34,305; J. Hennefeld, Soc., 34,090; S. J. Bloch, Soc., 34,621; J. Bernstein, Soc., 34,185; H. Gilbert, Soc., 32,957; B. Marcus, Soc, 33,047; S. Fried, Soc., 31,498; B. W. Burger, Single Tax, 1,367.

Congress.

22d Dist.—A. J. Griffin, Dem., 14,316; W. J. Murphy, Rep., 10,711; P. J. Murphy, Soc., 4,740.

23d Dist.—R. F. McKinny, Dem., 36,833; A. B. Rossdale, Rep., 38,907; A. Josephson, Soc., 22,947.

24th Dist.—J. V. Gauley, Dem., 13,808; B. L. Fairchild, Rep., 20,230; G. Orr, Soc., 12,892.

State Senate.

21st Dist.—H. G. Schackno, Dem., 21,999; J. Yule, Rep., 20,949; J. Loeb, Soc., 9,472.

22d Dist.—A. Cohn, Dem., 16,209; P. A. Abeles, Rep., 18,141; E. Seidel, Soc., 22,126.

23d Dist.—J. J. Dunnigan, Dem., 28,760; G. H. Taylor, Rep., 28,785; L. Weitz, Soc., 9,152.

County Clerk.

R. L. Moran, Dem., 76,199; P. Wynne, Rep., 62,846; M. Leffert, Soc., 37,319.

Justice of the City Court.

T. T. Reilley, Dem., 64,061; G. Hartman, Rep., 77,019; J. Hillquit, Soc., 36,306.

Member of Board of Aldermen.

(To fill vacancy.)

Bronx, 29th Ald. Dist.—A. G. Halberstadt, Dem., 2,823; W. J. Brennan, Rep., 2,196; E. Deutsch, Soc., 321.

QUEENS VOTE, 1920—For President and Governor.

1st Assembly District.

Elec. Dist.	Reg'trat'n. Male.	Reg'trat'n. Female.	Cox, Dem.	Harding, Rep.	Smith, Dem.	Miller, Rep.
1	298	85	159	186	256	64
2	301	123	240	151	331	47
3	290	134	238	145	320	41
4	304	170	217	216	342	66
5	220	177	213	147	292	53
6	291	114	206	165	312	50
7	299	209	244	229	376	91
8	315	158	193	223	292	84
9	343	132	160	255	305	104
10	391	172	173	328	364	116
11	330	165	147	275	301	86
12	315	119	112	261	231	130
13	354	155	136	333	252	182
14	317	184	137	323	280	144
15	337	215	165	367	329	171
16	290	105	129	227	237	81
17	319	189	110	339	269	149
18	327	175	131	300	291	92
19	294	168	111	307	283	93
20	267	150	105	267	245	86
21	326	181	116	319	283	128
22	350	175	105	261	273	150
23	276	124	74	285	200	114
24	355	203	133	342	329	116
25	270	160	118	260	252	105
26	300	184	135	316	285	128
27	341	193	154	318	305	126
28	175	155	109	198	202	91
29	355	252	176	366	348	171
30	281	198	151	287	266	154
31	270	147	92	281	221	126
32	328	149	109	306	238	143
33	311	161	144	284	275	125
34	278	141	130	257	245	107
35	288	177	144	292	238	148
36	413	208	226	329	407	117
37	351	178	168	303	302	139
38	199	126	96	189	188	80
39	343	205	173	307	350	89
40	304	165	156	274	315	83
41	344	123	101	261	223	104
42	366	172	147	300	312	107
43	347	140	110	314	255	130
44	343	173	116	332	282	146
45	293	170	105	292	240	124
46	381	189	118	348	288	138
	14440	7558	6721	12743	13039	6115

Total registration, 21,998.

2d Assembly District.

Elec. Dist.	Reg'trat'n. Male.	Reg'trat'n. Female.	Cox, Dem.	Harding, Rep.	Smith, Dem.	Miller, Rep.
1	371	139	320	170	407	60
2	311	182	270	172	384	51
3	328	189	130	316	299	114
4	293	189	161	275	320	103
5	225	104	60	219	154	81
6	322	108	130	241	263	80
7	352	142	309	169	392	56
8	365	131	113	317	231	174
9	260	82	73	227	178	81
10	302	137	58	331	245	98
11	300	135	55	347	271	94
12	345	144	44	380	292	102
13	317	153	81	356	260	135
14	262	148	83	297	210	183
15	249	162	77	278	214	112
16	310	122	66	320	231	117
17	369	192	112	384	311	142
18	332	173	116	343	303	125
19	277	135	69	287	228	92
20	276	127	70	273	234	76
21	357	158	79	374	300	124
22	289	149	65	336	260	93
23	291	111	53	308	231	94
24	302	164	75	313	238	119
25	210	103	48	218	173	74
26	268	144	45	294	203	115
27	254	118	60	282	183	109
28	350	167	101	378	312	125
29	352	126	105	308	271	102
30	328	125	84	300	247	94
31	292	145	98	270	248	96

*New Elec. Dist. created after last day of registration.

†Election Districts divided for Election Day on account of heavy registration.

2d A. D.—Continued.

Elec. Dist.	Reg'trat'n. Male.	Reg'trat'n. Female.	Cox, Dem.	Harding, Rep.	Smith, Dem.	Miller, Rep.
32	307	176	83	341	256	136
33	322	196	111	335	279	139
34	356	187	116	372	292	153
35	232	106	40	187	146	51
36	274	116	87	240	231	65
37	359	142	88	355	257	117
38	379	166	136	334	274	153
39	409	167	125	371	294	176
40	395	96	130	290	290	89
41	272	126	90	274	238	110
42	306	168	112	314	261	127
43	290	196	141	303	282	188
44	314	225	119	383	256	215
	13680	6488	4581	13182	11443	4740

Total registration, 20,168.

3d Assembly District.

Elec. Dist.	Reg'trat'n. Male.	Reg'trat'n. Female.	Cox, Dem.	Harding, Rep.	Smith, Dem.	Miller, Rep.
1	285	73	61	243	171	98
2	304	144	104	282	245	104
3	304	100	76	259	186	121
4	306	121	119	231	237	79
5	281	141	113	260	230	104
6	409	218	209	342	364	152
7	388	195	137	360	217	142
8	285	94	132	214	248	75
9	287	158	116	271	250	111
10	248	240	140	311	242	199
†11	408	308	107	186	161	124
12	325	248	200	313	316	186
13	331	201	254	331	386	138
14	318	209	168	300	293	152
15	206	142	120	197	192	120
16	299	266	179	336	290	212
17	386	195	144	371	300	175
18	327	169	149	283	273	123
19	307	211	162	299	331	102
20	285	233	152	314	323	119
21	329	157	95	328	245	144
22	244	145	108	237	217	87
23	307	136	73	315	233	133
24	318	160	96	313	264	122
25	213	144	120	204	226	78
26	285	134	146	229	251	98
27	264	152	115	218	228	87
28	279	148	127	222	250	92
29	316	180	151	290	282	118
30	418	158	126	335	285	142
31	346	140	100	272	267	97
32	320	102	107	228	237	88
33	368	119	162	181	221	87
34	249	150	160	197	226	114
35	303	181	168	239	255	134
36	263	166	142	264	240	135
37	250	163	133	239	215	134
38	403	248	219	383	336	241
†39	456	274	142	245	249	129
40	334	217	144	360	246	240
41	279	157	90	281	242	103
42	314	129	96	296	233	186
43	310	166	99	328	265	138
44	351	171	122	345	237	159
45	265	160	108	373	270	165
46	289	141	119	270	258	112
47	285	174	125	294	224	173
*48	...	...	142	218	238	106
*49	...	...	116	183	185	103
	14677	8138	6500	13590	12480	6370

Total registration, 22,815.

4th Assembly District.

Elec. Dist.	Reg'trat'n. Male.	Reg'trat'n. Female.	Cox, Dem.	Harding, Rep.	Smith, Dem.	Miller, Rep.
1	323	251	121	423	216	296
2	390	193	106	402	218	238
3	287	188	91	351	194	226
4	274	180	96	319	202	195
5	376	165	123	341	231	251
6	331	188	102	359	236	190
7	316	129	166	230	254	91
8	378	191	153	362	271	197
9	393	188	78	406	239	199
10	327	169	105	308	240	145
11	312	154	123	276	248	120
12	342	184	124	335	243	188
13	390	117	85	302	183	177
14	284	235	119	353	219	239
15	283	222	113	363	240	216

4th A. D.—Continued.

Elec. Dist.	Reg'trat'n. Male.	Reg'trat'n. Female.	Cox, Dem.	Harding, Rep.	Smith, Dem.	Miller, Rep.
16	267	162	100	288	207	163
17	398	248	125	456	328	202
18	343	346	109	522	267	328
19	336	234	143	350	252	248
20	220	208	81	313	150	247
21	422	213	154	396	282	309
22	243	174	107	275	192	170
23	312	230	138	372	275	214
24	299	273	127	390	255	236
25	319	267	128	429	216	319
26	256	166	85	296	179	186
27	240	123	71	250	145	134
28	336	213	104	407	250	220
29	326	219	107	377	189	244
30	415	253	150	434	262	291
31	353	254	137	415	266	274
32	316	244	112	325	230	278
33	525	356	120	303	219	204
34	448	373	87	232	150	152
35	298	162	97	321	185	207
36	363	271	137	442	248	312
37	386	299	169	452	285	303
38	243	192	121	274	202	188
39	332	239	154	373	273	199
40	235	207	125	296	185	231
41	231	220	99	328	157	256
42	310	245	142	382	228	267
43	324	269	158	384	229	299
44	275	250	167	322	229	235
45	214	259	144	307	187	242
46	313	225	163	326	249	218
47	155	190	115	201	141	166
48	276	255	141	344	217	246
49	350	203	136	336	258	194
50	284	176	124	282	215	155
*51	...	...	71	223	153	209
*52	...	...	106	349	196	237
	13373	13608	6249	17901	11595	11452

Total registration, 26,981.

5th Assembly District.

Elec. Dist.	Reg'trat'n. Male.	Reg'trat'n. Female.	Cox, Dem.	Harding, Rep.	Smith, Dem.	Miller, Rep.
1	324	240	91	444	235	277
2	298	211	92	384	243	198
3	334	254	123	411	282	234
4	349	267	126	448	276	251
5	286	262	109	383	302	134
6	345	294	188	444	288	278
7	346	274	140	427	284	259
8	327	237	136	381	280	207
9	359	260	185	439	308	228
10	233	164	61	310	165	183
11	350	269	115	425	291	226
12	231	161	93	265	189	147
13	278	198	76	368	230	198
14	406	277	138	487	304	292
15	357	264	111	455	280	250
16	265	196	88	324	235	134
17	254	190	91	321	214	178
18	265	185	91	327	225	180
19	234	173	84	293	207	141
20	370	128	138	311	283	180
21	375	222	133	384	298	177
22	441	204	113	428	292	223
23	406	163	142	363	304	172
24	290	159	99	277	205	157
25	278	127	108	252	241	98
26	273	163	93	295	222	145
27	362	211	128	373	285	192
†28	508	294	108	347	230	185
†29	466	335	77	259	163	161
30	265	164	109	271	234	129
31	308	247	143	364	278	206
32	285	250	166	327	281	169
33	345	225	151	360	275	199
34	310	257	135	393	260	250
35	348	224	139	385	266	233
36	263	203	107	310	228	161
37	248	165	95	281	210	147
38	382	233	137	422	295	231
39	279	142	115	251	212	87
40	260	104	76	223	175	89
†41	439	278	135	305	216	110
42	350	195	184	305	358	137
43	351	167	207	258	351	98
44	300	183	135	290	276	131
45	342	117	115	198	215	92

QUEENS VOTE, 1920—FOR PRESIDENT AND GOVERNOR—*Continued.*

5th A. D.—Continued.

Elec. Dist.	Reg'trat'n. Male.	Reg'trat'n. Female.	Cox, Dem.	Harding, Rep.	Smith, Dem.	Miller, Rep.
46	485	148	160	376	349	168
47	274	112	71	233	187	91
48	428	185	100	376	320	144
49	340	210	152	347	327	162
†50	491	254	162	176	247	81
51	267	194	130	287	263	141
52	359	169	164	301	295	152
*53	...	...	89	186	212	56
*54	...	...	100	280	211	144
*55	...	...	124	179	226	77
*56	...	...	116	207	330	96
	15735	12272	6259	18515	13479	9028

Total registration, 28,007.

6th Assembly District.

Elec. Dist.	Reg'trat'n. Male.	Reg'trat'n. Female.	Cox, Dem.	Harding, Rep.	Smith, Dem.	Miller, Rep.
1	368	181	92	392	278	177
2	260	123	59	280	215	100
3	227	101	65	228	193	80
4	332	126	95	307	238	110
5	252	129	53	293	131	125
6	365	185	96	399	296	168
7	288	196	77	356	271	126
8	280	139	53	302	208	116
9	276	160	87	283	216	118
10	303	151	65	322	250	111
11	280	183	98	317	262	124
12	292	183	78	349	257	126
13	263	139	68	272	248	79
14	297	183	88	333	283	104
15	227	170	72	298	189	147
16	342	170	67	373	362	136
17	313	160	91	329	263	124
18	236	124	49	276	179	116
19	280	151	84	301	234	121
20	239	101	63	253	158	128
21	328	225	119	377	316	131
22	254	133	74	272	224	99
23	306	219	112	364	305	144
24	310	192	116	349	277	156
25	267	159	52	331	201	153
26	290	155	60	337	234	129
27	286	198	54	384	264	143
28	256	125	52	252	169	108
29	331	209	102	383	276	167
30	264	157	107	284	263	107
31	321	203	133	337	284	128
32	306	181	71	303	235	145
33	306	156	108	322	268	130
34	389	182	64	443	277	171
35	348	205	119	395	295	159
36	289	125	84	261	211	181
37	328	142	85	311	225	116
38	334	166	93	298	257	100
39	308	156	49	369	214	155
40	300	230	79	415	243	213
41	282	201	102	349	216	307
42	366	234	138	419	305	209
43	301	202	85	363	235	181
44	289	232	120	447	294	243
46	300	197	79	368	228	179
46	335	260	117	432	258	250
47	328	250	81	448	270	233
48	236	179	97	292	195	179
49	256	189	87	329	183	209
50	293	173	117	318	234	167
51	365	125	65	276	208	102
†52	418	394	66	295	140	219
53	334	247	121	431	360	219
*54	...	...	90	290	150	227
	15944	9439	4588	18166	12891	8006

Total registration, 25,383.

*New Elec. Dist. created after last day of registration.

†Election Districts divided for Election Day on account of heavy registration.

Gov., J. D. Cannon, Soc., 4,361; G. F Thompson, Proh., 741; J. P. Quinn, Soc.-L., 262; D. F. Malone, Far.-L., 8,649.

Lieut. Gov., J. W. Hughan, Soc., 5,500; E. G. Dietrich, Proh., 572; J. D. Crowley, Soc.-L., 428; R. E. Haffey, Far.-L., 5,025.

Sec. of State, C. W. Noonan, Soc., 6,049; S. B. Taylor, Proh., 559; W. H. Auyer, Far.-L., 3,395; M. Phalor, Soc. L., 379.

Comptroller, A. P. Randolph, Soc., 6,235; W. C. Gray, Proh., 645; H. H. Fincke, Far.-L., 3,165; J. D. Lee, Soc. L., 338.

Treasurer, H. F. Kreuger, Soc., 6,159; J. McKee, Proh., 444; J. A. Withers, Soc. L., 291; J. E. Cronk, Far.-L., 2,960.

Atty.Gen., D. J. Meserole, Soc., 6,280; W. H. Burr, Proh., 886; J. Donohue, Soc. L., 571; F. R. Serri, Far.-L., 2,641.

State Engr. and Surveyor, V. Karapetoff, Soc., 6,269; A. S. Light, Proh., 457; C. C. Crawford, Far.-L., 1,070.

U. S. Senator, J. Pankin, Soc., 6,214; E. A. Bode, Proh., 2,424; H. Carlson, Soc. L., 356; R. Schneiderman, Far.-L., 2,792.

Members of Congress.

1st Dist.—A. J. Kennedy, Dem., 5,234; F. C. Hicks, Rep. and Proh., 8,082; D. T. Hinckley, Soc., 274.

2d Dist.—J. J. Kindred, Dem., 42,530; R. Hantusch, Rep., 40,201; W. Burkle, Sr., Soc., 5,872; W. E. Keys, Proh., 608.

9th Dist.—D. J. O'Connell, Dem., 9,333; A. N. Petersen, Rep., 13,550; W. B. Robinson, Soc., 821; F. E. Mershon, Proh., 100.

Sheriff.

J. Flanagan, Dem., 58,198; J. Wagner, Rep., 64,322; B. Wolf, Soc., 5,229; J. A. Nebgen, Far.-L., 2,223.

District Attorney.

L. T. Gresser, Jr., Dem., 33,662; D. Wallace, Rep., 49,120; L. Roper, Soc., 5,174; D. O'Leary, Far.-L. and Peo., 38,052.

State Senate.

2d Dist.—C. Berger, Dem., 25,945; J. L. Karle, Rep., 42,162; M. H. Mainland, Soc., 3,235.

3d Dist.—P. J. McGarry, Dem., 28,662; A. C. Kinzl, Rep., 23,838; C. Ress, Soc., 3,831.

Assembly.

1st A. D.—P. A. Leninger, Dem., 10,006; F. M. Kenna, Rep., 7,961; A. Prouspiel, Soc., 1,218.

2d A. D.—B. Schwab, Dem., 8,740; R. F. Murphy, Rep., 7,673; M. Palm, Soc., 1,386.

3d A. D.—G. W. Byrnes, Dem., 7,835; E. J. Neary, Rep., 10,833; H. Straus, Soc., 1,263.

4th A. D.—E. A. Homer, Dem., 7,415; N. M. Pette, Rep., 15,214; S. C. Smith, Soc., 848; M. C. Beardsley, Proh., 208.

5th A. D.—J. C. Donovan, Dem., 9,742; R. Halpern, Rep., 18,912; L. H. Strohman, Soc., 1,156.

6th A. D.—F. A. Locke, Dem., 9,792; H. Baum, Rep., 11,551; A. M. Weunis, Soc., 1,522.

Justices of the Supreme Court for the Second Judicial District.

Edwin L. Garvin, Dem., 52,085; Burt Jay Humphrey, Dem., 75,408; Edward W. McMahon, Dem., 47,943; Townsend Scudder, Dem., Cit., 59,119; Charles J. Druhan, Dem., 41,275; Joseph Aspinall, Rep., Cit., 57,302; Selah B. Strong, Rep., 55,033; Norman S. Dike, Rep., 61,121; John MacCrate, Rep., 55,393; Walter H. Jaycox, Rep., Cit., 50,907; Morris Wolfman, Soc., 5,736; Hyman Rivkin, Soc., 5,223; Isidore Kayfetz, Soc., 5,039; Philip Satra, Soc., 5,083; Francis M. Testa, Soc., 4,972; Charles A. Wilson, Proh., 647; Asa F. Smith, Proh., 574; Harold D. Watson, Proh., 444; Walter G. Howell, Proh., 400; David A. Howell, Proh., 323; Robert H. Haskell, Far.-L., 3,996; James P. Kohler, Far.-L., 2,327; Joseph Goldstein, Far.-L., 1,869; Jacob S. Strahl, Far. L., Amer. Const., non-partisan, 16,582; Edmond C. Brown, S. T., 639.

Associate Judges of Court of Appeals.

Frederick E. Crane, Dem., Rep., 91,227; Abram I. Elkus, Dem., 46,135; Emory A. Chase, Rep., 60,208; Leon A. Malkiel, Soc., 6,178; Jacob Axelrad, Soc., 5,427; Coleridge A. Hart, Proh., 742; Francis E. Baldwin, Proh., 538; Swinburne Hale, Far.-L., 2,808; Thomas F. Dwyer, Far.-L., 4,984.

N. Y. STATE VOTE ON AMENDMENT AND PROPOSITION, 1920.

Total vote on Constitutional Amendment relative to State indebtedness:
For, 1,117,546. Against, 630,265.
Total vote on Soldiers' Bonus Proposition:
For, 1,454,940. Against, 673,292.

THE TOWN HALL.

113-123 West 43d St., Manhattan.

Formal opening Jan. 12, to 18, inclusive, 1921. Exercises afternoons and evenings. Committee of arrangement: Henry W. Taft, Chairman; Frank A. Vanderlip, Henry Morgenthau, A. Barton Hepburn, Mrs. Henry A. Alexander, Otto H. Kahn, Morgan J. O'Brien, Robert Erskine Ely, Mary B. Cleveland. The Town Hall contains a large auditorium for the assembly of gatherings interested in civic and educational movements. There are club rooms, a library and committee rooms. The plan is a revival of the New England town meeting idea.

STATE-OWNED MOTOR VEHICLES.

Thirty thousand cars and trucks are serving the various departments of the governments of the 48 States. Twenty-three thousand of this total are trucks and automobiles used by the States for the improvement of highways. About 4,500 of the remainder are passenger cars, which the authorities have purchased for the needs of official business.

RICHMOND VOTE, 1920—For President and Governor.

1st Assembly District.

Elec. Dist.	Reg'trat'n. Male.	Reg'trat'n. Female.	Cox, Dem.	Harding, Rep.	Smith, Dem.	Miller, Rep.
1	216	148	118	208	177	138
2	202	211	125	246	184	177
3	209	128	122	175	191	96
4	258	147	144	224	217	132
5	288	154	144	234	260	110
6	222	89	119	172	193	81
7	200	88	117	141	191	71
8	258	171	141	245	213	153
9	337	166	175	272	276	157
10	123	60	62	110	110	62
11	349	149	194	220	296	107
12	212	146	114	222	191	136
13	244	176	230	173	284	89
14	255	159	195	177	264	101
15	240	174	139	243	211	164
16	278	217	194	257	267	179
17	328	180	237	230	323	126
18	495	165	223	333	360	190
19	211	109	112	180	175	113
20	275	212	149	290	237	182
21	243	152	152	220	215	133
22	205	112	72	217	122	134
23	259	175	103	280	183	192
24	205	153	93	235	154	160
25	263	163	100	287	177	276
26	253	246	107	350	175	271
27	215	94	84	192	165	88
28	163	84	111	103	141	63
29	223	119	85	229	148	186
30	175	151	64	242	126	163
31	245	140	116	226	216	98
32	269	115	114	236	210	117
33	236	98	139	150	214	65
34	183	76	94	122	155	60
35	230	72	106	162	151	98
36	257	156	217	171	324	60
37	181	109	87	183	144	107
38	198	144	109	204	180	124
39	279	133	135	226	236	119
40	199	108	80	202	147	118
41	246	148	150	228	244	109
42	200	93	92	172	190	74
43	265	188	137	287	224	181
	10383	6078	6590	9283	8871	5453

Total registration, 16,460.

2d Assembly District.

Elec. Dist.	Reg'trat'n. Male.	Reg'trat'n. Female.	Cox, Dem.	Harding, Rep.	Smith, Dem.	Miller, Rep.
1	251	128	129	217	208	129
2	252	70	126	163	199	75
3	218	91	141	156	194	83
4	193	93	101	168	140	117
5	301	158	167	262	266	149
6	224	149	105	215	190	116
7	207	96	73	201	152	101
8	292	128	130	240	222	131
9	344	149	149	310	308	129
10	393	176	173	309	287	182
11	257	141	97	258	200	143
12	387	245	156	395	233	277
13	248	72	44	236	89	149
14	286	93	71	234	153	122
15	310	163	92	326	189	212
16	250	158	63	305	121	226
17	348	144	118	312	212	191
18	372	168	154	304	266	184
19	418	145	195	304	310	169
20	271	82	106	205	184	95
21	412	139	227	274	348	124
22	387	147	117	335	214	192
23	340	119	101	306	167	202
24	266	82	95	215	187	94
25	262	117	91	235	166	137
26	304	118	111	250	195	136
27	189	70	68	163	108	91
28	185	96	62	192	92	141
29	299	212	112	362	192	258
30	320	112	126	257	204	148
31	379	194	105	403	211	267
32	211	139	87	235	126	164
33	198	127	81	227	133	156
	9574	4321	3773	8574	6466	5089

Total registration, 13,895.

BOROUGH OF RICHMOND.

Other Candidates—Pres., E. V. Debs, Soc., 712; A. S. Watkins, Proh., 111; W. W. Cox, Soc.-L., 48; P. P. Christensen, Far.-L., 170.

Governor, J. D. Cannon, Soc., 426; G. F. Thompson, Proh., 282; J. P. Quinn, Soc.-L., 51; D. F. Malone, Far.-L., 906.

Lieut. Gov.—J. W. Hughan, Soc., 575; E. G. Dietrich, Proh., 228; J. D. Crowley, S. L., 72; R. E. Haffey, F. L., 545.

Sec'ty of State—C. W. Noonan, Soc., 622; F. B. Taylor, Proh., 248; M. Phalor, S. L., 69; W. H. Auyer, F. L., 343.

Comptroller—A. P. Randolph, Soc., 1,049; W. C. Gray, Proh., 220; J. D. Lee, S. L., 56; H. H. Fincke, F. L., 325.

Treasurer—H. F. Kreuger, Soc., 663; J. McKee, Proh., 206; J. A. Withers, S. L., 46; J. E. Cronk, F. L., 294.

Atty. Genl.—D. P. Meserole, Soc., 641; W. H. Burr, Proh., 271; J. Donohue, S. L., 75; F. R. Serri, F. L., 229.

State Eng. & Suvy.—V. Karapetoff, Soc., 647; A. S. Light, Proh., 199; C. C. Crawford, S. L., 150.

U. S. Senator—J. Panken, Soc., 648; E. A. Boole, Proh., 1,416; H. Carlson, S. L., 60; R. Schneiderman, F. L., 126.

Associate Judges of the Court of Appeals.

Frederick E. Crane, Dem., Rep., 18,242; Abram I. Elkus, Dem., 10,034; Emory A. Chase, Rep., 11,683; Leon A. Malkiel, Soc., 665; Jacob Axelrad, Soc., 556; Coleridge A. Hart, Proh., 283; Francis E. Baldwin, Proh., 205; Swinburne Hale, Far.-L., 278; Thomas F. Dwyer, Far.-L., 372.

Justices of the Supreme Court for the 2d Judicial District.

Edwin L. Garvin, Dem., 12,185; Burt Jay Humphrey, Dem., 11,206; Edward Ward McMahon, Dem., 10,788; Townsend Scudder, Dem. and Citz., 12,738; Charles J. Druhan, Dem., 5,994; Joseph Aspinall, Rep. and Citz., 11,974; Selah B. Strong, Rep., 11,469; Norman S. Dike, Rep., 11,511; John MacCrate, Rep., 11,227; Walter H. Jaycox, Rep. and Citz., 11,210; Morris Wolfman, Soc., 683; Hyman Rivkin, Soc., 602; Isidore Kayfetz, Soc., 577; Philip Satra, Soc., 592; Francis M. Testa, Soc., 574; Charles A. Wilson, Proh., 268; Asa F. Smith, Proh., 250; Harold D. Watson, Proh., 220; Walter G. Howell, Proh., 207; David A. Howell, Proh., 181; Robert H. Haskell, F. L., 356; James P. Kohler, F. L., 282; Joseph Goldstein, F. L., 304; Jacob S. Strahl, F. L., A. C. and Non-P., 1,468; Edmond Congar Brown, S. T., 117.

Congress, 11th Congr. District.

D. F. Riordan, Dem., 11,454; W. F. Wakeman, Rep., 13,608; R. Rochow, Soc., 710.

Senator, 24th Sen. Dist.

J. A. Lynch, Dem., 12,508; C. E. Smith, Rep., 12,820; E. Veeck, Soc., 681.

Members of Assembly.

1st A. D.—T. Cosgrove, Dem., 8,251; L. J. Kipper, Rep. and Proh., 5,562; W. H. Dearing, Soc., 430.

2d A. D.—G. P. Reynaud, Dem., 5,095; E. B. Frerichs, Rep., 5,993; O. Eichele, Soc., 391; W. E. Sharroth, Proh., 161.

County Clerk.

C. L. Bostwick, Dem., 14,791; J. Laing, Rep., 10,986.

BRONX COUNTY VOTE.

Members of Assembly (Bronx).

1st A. D.—A. H. Henderson, Dem., 10,583; T. F. Faillace, Rep., 8,264; L. Bright, Soc., 4,768.

2d A. D.—E. J. Flynn, Dem., 13,200; F. F. Latham, Rep., 10,936; K. Reely, Soc., 5,041.

3d A. D.—B. Antin, Fus., 9,032; S. A. DeWitt, Soc., 8,765.

4th A. D.—H. F. McRedmond, Fus., 8,158; S. Orr, Soc., 9,902.

5th A. D.—W. Lyman, Fus., 11,211; M. H. Laing, Soc., 9,006.

6th A. D.—T. J. McDonald, Dem., 8,409; H. V. Becher, Rep., 8,062; M. Scheler, Soc., 1,504.

7th A. D.—J. V. McKee, Dem., 8,116; C. Tremonti, Rep., 5,772; A. Rosen, Soc., 6,403.

8th A. D.—E. J. Walsh, Dem., 13,629; C. A. Conners, Rep., 13,498; F. E. Nadelman, Soc., 1,816.

Prohibition—No candidates.

According to the Bureau of Industries and Immigration, 345,672 industrial accidents were reported in New York State in the fiscal year 1919-1920, an increase over the previous year of 57,228, and involving a direct loss to the State under the Workmen's Compensation Law of more than $40,000 a day.

The first Olympic games were held in 1453 B.C.

New York City has more than 100,000 clubwomen.

The first English Bible was printed in 1535.

RECAPITULATION—PRESIDENT AND STATE OFFICERS, BOROUGH OF BROOKLYN.

Assembly District.	Registration.	President. Cox, Dem.	President. Harding, Rep.	Governor. Smith, Dem.	Governor. Miller, Rep.	Lieut. Gov. Fitts, Dem.	Lieut. Gov. Wood, Rep.	Secty. of State. Mills, Dem.	Secty. of State. Lyons, Rep.	Comptroller. Berry, Dem.	Comptroller. Wendell, Rep.	Treasurer. Healy, Dem.	Treasurer. Marshall, Rep.	Atty. Genl. Mott, Dem.	Atty. Genl. Newton, Rep.	State Eng. and Surveyor. McLoud, Dem.	State Eng. and Surveyor. Williams, Rep.	U. S. Senator. Walker, Dem.	U. S. Senator. Wadsworth, Rep.
1 ..	18492	5891	10491	9908	6132	7557	7679	6431	8706	7440	7689	6802	8326	6509	8419	6471	8444	6657	8149
2 ..	23662	4688	12400	10077	6687	7479	8507	5899	9958	7024	8659	6379	9407	5968	9841	6096	9768	5975	9310
3 ..	12035	4459	6052	7312	2637	6881	3653	5232	4362	6015	3609	5640	3915	6403	4036	5351	4092	5346	4086
4 ..	18906	5396	10005	10610	4527	7953	6164	6366	7792	7482	6641	7015	7111	6729	7169	6742	7203	6626	6949
5 ..	25116	6846	16680	12167	9471	8856	12225	6919	14152	8601	12529	7628	13569	7339	13732	7190	13569	7461	13025
6 ..	18831	2921	9943	8019	4676	6537	6284	4063	7691	4810	6684	4259	7376	4026	7538	3988	7503	3999	7091
7 ..	17475	5562	9891	10012	4534	7876	6200	6785	7277	8495	5908	7386	6886	7078	6983	7111	7023	7023	6969
8 ..	14436	5788	6726	9278	3008	7496	4054	6469	5189	7358	4314	7096	4521	6778	4714	6866	4672	6724	4793
9 ..	25347	6276	16010	13111	8189	9762	10885	7941	12918	10098	10991	8547	12208	8173	12172	8106	12622	8155	11908
10 ..	25019	7658	16066	12782	9336	10019	11454	8238	13291	9898	11423	9017	12451	8648	12707	8679	12543	8975	11657
11 ..	29613	8477	18425	14907	11193	11547	13996	9203	16381	11508	13907	10125	15408	9536	15843	9610	15702	10203	14549
12 ..	26926	8140	16047	14560	8982	11151	11617	9002	13931	11111	11766	9837	13094	9433	13278	9353	13416	9678	12531
13 ..	12666	2666	7077	6209	3107	4659	4130	3805	4862	4258	4345	3989	4618	3846	4734	3662	4835	3504	4768
14 ..	13229	2711	5775	6237	2316	4609	3043	3754	3738	4104	3291	3933	3494	3777	3565	3729	3536	3671	3436
15 ..	16295	5483	9113	9953	3922	8081	5242	7005	6377	7967	5477	7671	5783	7262	5956	7227	6053	7346	5720
16 ..	22745	4585	13590	11621	6069	8474	8272	6779	10018	7921	8770	7112	9629	6866	9658	6721	9759	6619	9646
17 ..	25118	5807	16288	11277	10234	8280	12569	6591	14265	8168	12501	6993	13558	6714	13913	6698	13794	7102	12668
18 ..	26993	6516	15484	12495	8169	9137	14671	7075	12607	8628	10890	7474	12103	7212	13297	7049	12273	7356	11223
19 ..	13786	1743	8417	5743	3828	3935	6222	3929	6061	3438	5641	3184	6898	3069	15954	3010	6060	2975	6915
20 ..	31827	6211	22069	16075	10662	11562	14728	8903	17760	10963	15376	9564	16995	9176	17227	9125	17302	9425	16889
21 ..	31947	7295	21711	14458	13670	10694	16682	8497	19091	10699	16663	8925	18539	8607	18819	8702	18564	9116	17393
22 ..	29884	4927	18498	12785	9579	9064	12610	7018	14742	8457	13297	7415	14344	7078	14608	7077	14619	7187	13986
23 ..	14804	1588	6704	5065	3195	3320	4176	2437	4872	2723	4450	2508	4659	2384	4743	2284	4715	2164	4528
Ttls.	495161	119545	292452	244562	152923	182648	199952	147432	236131	177157	204824	158499	222892	151581	237906	150748	227967	153387	217089

Other Candidates—Pres., E. V. Debs, Soc., 45098; A. S. Watkins, Proh., 733; W. W. Cox, Soc. L., 638; P. P. Christensen, Far.-L., 3473.

Governor, J. D. Cannon, Soc., 34534; G. F. Thompson, Pro., 3029; J. P. Quinn, Soc.-L., 795; D. F. Malone, Far.-L., 21445.

Lt. Gov., J. W. Hughan, Soc., —; E. J. Deitrich, Proh., —; J. D. Crowley, Soc.-L., —; R. E. Haffey, Far.-L., —.

Sec. of State, C. W. Noonan, Soc., 44976; Z. B. Taylor, Proh., 2036; M. Phalor, Soc.-L., 1018; W. H. Auyer, Far.-L., 7672.

Comptroller — A. P. Randolph, Soc., 45684; W. C. Gray, Proh., 2450; J. De Lee, Soc.-L., 1127; H. H. Fincke, Far.-L., 6935.

(See also p. 383.)

MANHATTAN.

Assembly District.	Registration.	President. Cox, Dem.	President. Harding, Rep.	Governor. Smith, Dem.	Governor. Miller, Rep.	Lieut. Gov. Fitts, Dem.	Lieut. Gov. Wood, Rep.	Secty. of State. Mills, Dem.	Secty. of State. Lyons, Rep.	Comptroller. Berry, Dem.	Comptroller. Wendell, Rep.	Treasurer. Healy, Dem.	Treasurer. Marshall, Rep.	Atty. Genl. Mott, Dem.	Atty. Genl. Newton, Rep.	State Eng. and Surveyor. McLoud, Dem.	State Eng. and Surveyor. Williams, Rep.	U. S. Senator. Walker, Dem.	U. S. Senator. Wadsworth, Rep.
1 ..	18662	7572	7325	12435	2632	10063	5661	8789	4982	9496	4064	8479	4131	9394	4186	9245	4289	9179	4198
2 ..	14550	3374	7393	7631	2963	5307	4043	4464	4753	4778	4383	4702	4367	4590	4470	4614	4495	4605	4388
3 ..	24968	11619	11068	15886	5104	13116	6728	10573	9351	12774	7087	12536	7369	12237	7418	12220	7517	12300	7544
4 ..	12398	2977	4231	6146	1600	5381	1749	4527	2446	4794	2059	4729	2169	4715	2186	4727	2244	4348	2023
5 ..	24801	9655	11750	15475	5204	12514	6829	9861	9744	12078	7365	11967	7489	11616	7625	11552	7650	11548	7896
6 ..	14046	2236	6521	5728	3358	4030	4301	3057	5079	3338	4731	3188	4807	3232	4801	3062	4919	3060	4591
7 ..	26676	6761	17110	2591	10804	9322	12911	7189	15225	8770	13257	8273	13755	7915	14114	7923	14013	8185	13784
8 ..	14060	1990	6704	6185	2620	4365	3516	2213	4471	3417	4074	3232	4174	3226	4215	3104	4219	2896	4066
9 ..	27616	6959	17526	14053	10061	10198	12782	7658	15446	9378	13476	8781	14162	8296	14498	8241	14358	8563	14156
10 ..	24179	6729	14551	11279	9692	8572	11638	7176	13135	8042	11895	7563	12521	7438	12632	7326	12565	7923	11892
11 ..	26551	7219	16146	14376	8598	10762	11038	7693	1436	9669	12013	9196	12636	8734	12841	8759	12709	8868	12620
12 ..	25753	10776	11302	17141	4477	14224	6120	12126	8469	13785	6602	13636	6807	13279	6939	13226	7016	12989	6871
13 ..	23366	6339	13612	12380	7274	9132	9244	6561	11949	8417	10043	8023	10536	7492	10583	7651	10584	8255	9716
14 ..	22938	6692	11256	13071	4301	10191	6008	7947	8245	9672	6440	9864	6482	9281	6737	9312	6840	8902	6916
15 ..	26709	6361	16378	12339	10080	9040	12399	6832	14681	8307	12918	7687	12630	7643	13658	7649	13506	7592	13447
16 ..	25509	6938	12813	14347	4367	11192	6136	8630	8953	10545	6900	10490	7050	10086	7154	10173	7418	9575	7763
17 ..	18241	2284	8988	8667	3072	5908	4450	2364	6778	4283	5591	4034	5829	3865	5874	3713	5890	3590	5540
18 ..	19552	4350	9472	9762	3773	6885	5388	5209	7117	6289	5808	6210	5904	5986	5937	6032	6047	5764	6027
19 ..	22250	4260	14199	10154	7648	7144	9542	4226	12848	6074	10347	6220	10480	5651	10815	5560	10723	5457	10875
20 ..	14192	3778	7591	7619	3316	5557	4632	3741	6519	4980	5035	4964	5099	4750	5186	4682	5250	4669	5191
21 ..	21263	3776	14664	10064	7979	6467	10246	4661	12339	5494	10914	5213	11456	4941	11573	4958	11415	4780	11659
22 ..	24279	6613	14845	13814	7140	10352	9436	7301	12775	9407	10561	8926	11061	8455	11266	8457	11230	8390	11248
23 ..	31261	7700	19749	17275	9925	12653	13284	8783	17197	11107	14648	10875	15482	9875	15786	9940	15501	9928	16354
Ttls.	503820	134308	275294	268418	135434	202370	176054	153720	226865	184888	190201	179368	197386	172697	200394	172130	200397	171266	197783

Other Candidates — Pres., E. V. Debs, Soc., 45046; A. S. Watkins, Proh., 463; W. W. Cox, Soc.-L., 567; P. P. Christensen, Far.-L., 7077.

Gov., J. D. Cannon, Soc., 34220; G. F. Thompson, Proh., 1115; J. P. Quinn, Soc.-L. 582; D. F. Malone, Far.-L., 19848.

Lieut. Gov., J. W. Hughan, Soc., 42233; E. G. Dietrich, Proh., 1206; J. D. Crowley, Soc.-L., 1428; R. E. Haffey, Far.-L., 13928.

Sec. of State, C. W. Noonan, Soc., 45714; I. B. Taylor, Proh., 1232; M. Phalor, Soc.-L., 935; W. H. Auyer, Far.-L., 9360.

RECAPITULATION—PRESIDENT AND STATE OFFICERS, BOROUGH OF THE BRONX.

Assembly District.	Registration.	President. Cox, Dem.	President. Harding, Rep.	Governor. Smith, Dem.	Governor. Miller, Rep.	Lieut. Gov. Flitts, Dem.	Lieut. Gov. Wood, Rep.	Secty. of State Mills, Dem.	Secty. of State Lyons, Rep.	Comptroller. Berry, Dem.	Comptroller. Wendell, Rep.	Treasurer. Healy, Dem.	Treasurer. Marshall, Rep.	Atty. Genl. Mott, Dem.	Atty. Genl. Newton, Rep.	State Eng. and Surveyor. McLoud, Dem.	State Eng. and Surveyor. Williams, Rep.	U. S. Senator. Walker, Dem.	U. S. Senator. Wadsworth, Rep.
1 ..	27511	6741	15092	15349	5417	11571	7907	9149	10463	10785	8779	10444	9082	10191	9167	10075	9396	9715	9820
2 ..	32751	9072	17417	17954	7796	14083	10336	10873	13623	13126	11145	12764	11564	12348	11824	12205	11825	12023	11857
3 ..	20589	3218	10341	10156	3236	7373	4846	5143	6889	6101	5739	5705	6132	5227	6313	5420	6326	4958	6192
4 ..	20682	3448	9121	9742	3202	7018	4482	5066	6142	5901	5198	5395	5548	5447	5629	5378	5594	4945	5512
5 ..	23248	3207	11786	11847	3540	8368	5433	5575	7744	6466	6616	6033	6935	5735	7281	5677	7192	5127	7111
6 ..	29081	5326	12274	10774	5888	8548	7544	6924	9282	8222	7956	7877	8320	7648	8435	7575	8578	7452	9663
7 ..	25566	4728	11230	10669	4443	8714	6170	6228	8259	7590	6903	7229	7248	6921	7450	6921	7439	6686	7317
8 ..	31991	9871	18751	18447	9866	14550	12712	11102	16295	14037	13243	13389	13960	12767	14341	12716	14374	12676	14249
Ttl.	199427	45611	106012	105568	43388	80061	59130	60004	78727	72228	65609	69036	68790	66594	70340	65977	70624	63582	70210
QUEENS.																			
1 ..	21598	6721	12548	13045	5116	11866	6708	9296	8458	10632	7002	10838	7381	10092	7482	10013	7593	9938	7603
2 ..	20168	4351	13182	11438	4846	9107	6771	7672	8410	9655	7390	8148	7924	7993	7966	7955	8219	7688	8255
3 ..	22815	6500	13590	12504	6380	10400	7829	9060	9371	10157	8119	9761	8629	9437	8797	9432	8776	9373	9636
4 ..	26087	9249	17934	11730	11283	9314	13229	8940	14667	9123	13431	8210	14404	7865	14645	8607	14492	8153	13535
5 ..	28087	0657	18547	14313	9441	8552	14975	8540	14978	10878	12644	9814	13776	9153	13956	9425	13949	9264	13771
6 ..	25863	4588	18160	12896	8074	9619	11102	7617	13242	8987	11958	8042	12945	7766	13133	7752	13308	7709	13122
Ttls.	155552	32296	94268	75938	45140	57825	60064	50187	69124	58432	60544	54313	65053	52536	65977	52578	66237	52135	64923
RICHMOND.																			
1 ..	16460	5598	9283	8871	5453	7635	6171	6981	6876	7546	6520	7229	6603	7128	6655	7019	6679	7018	6305
2 ..	13895	3773	8574	6466	5089	5190	5785	4794	6227	5105	5617	4794	6160	4806	6101	4730	6115	4724	5602
Ttls..	30355	9371	17857	15337	10542	12825	11956	11775	13103	12651	12137	12023	12763	11934	12756	11749	12794	11742	11907

Other Candidates (Bronx) — Pres., E. V. Debs, Soc., 32921; A. S. Watkins, Proh., 214; W. W. Cox, Soc.-L., 452; P. P. Christensen, Far.-L., 1948.

Gov., J. D. Cannon, Soc., 25583; G. F. Thompson, Proh., 540; J. P. Quinn, Soc.-L., 406; D. F. Malone, Far.-L., 10993.

For other Bronx County candidates see p. 390.

Other Candidates (Queens) — Pres., E. V. Debs, Soc., 6143; A. S. Watkins, Proh., 142; W. W. Cox, Soc.-L., 262; P. P. Christensen, Far.-L., 1204.

For other candidates, Borough of Richmond, see p. 393.

OTHER CANDIDATES—MHTN.—*Con.*

Comptroller, A P. Randolph, Soc., 47,437; W. C. Gray, Proh., 1,374; J. D. Lee, Soc.-L., 1,074; H. H. Fincke, Far.-L., 9,673.

Treasurer, H. F. Kreuger, Soc., 46,635; J. McKee, Proh., 1,081; J. A. Withers, Soc.-L., 805; J. E. Cronk, Far.-L., 9,371.

Atty. Gen., D. J. Meserole, Soc., 46,255; W. H. Burr, Proh., 2,576; J. Donahue, Soc.-L., 1,998; F. R. Serri, Far.-L., 9,328.

State Eng. and Surveyor, V. Karapetoff, Soc., 47,280; A. S. Light, Proh., 1,176; C. C. Crawford, Soc.-L., 3,472.

U. S. Senator, J. Pankin, Soc., 50,884; E. A. Boole, Proh., 4,436; H. Carlson, Soc.-L., 804; R. Schneiderman, Far.-L., 10,001.

Members of Assembly.

1st A. D.—P. J. Hamill, Dem., 9,532; H. C. Parke, Rep., 4,102; H. Leventhal, Soc., 2,692.

2d A. D.—F. R. Galgano, Dem., 5,931; M. Weiner, Rep., 3,937; H. Havidon, Soc., 2,813.

3d A. D.—T. F. Burchill, Dem., 12,002; W. A. Restle, Rep., 6,990; J. Mullen, Soc., 878; R. J. Ryan, Far.-L., 1,148.

4th A. D.—S. Dickstein, Dem., Fus., 6,774; T. S. Malkiel, Soc., 4,228.

5th A. D.—C. D. Donahue, Dem., 11,529; J. McCann, Rep., 8,073; W. B. Williams, Soc., 838.

6th A. D.—S. Ullman, Dem., Fus., 7,045; E. Rosenberg, Soc., 5,446.

7th A. D.—R. E. O'Boyle, Dem., 8,113; N. B. Fox, Rep., 13,798; H. Karp, Soc., 800; G. H. Macy, Sing. Tax, 101.

8th A. D.—M. D. Reiss, Dem., Fus., 6,267; L. Waldman, Soc., 6,053.

9th A. D.—P. P. Costello, Dem., 8,958; E. R. Rayher, Rep., 13,727; J. Strobel, Soc., 930.

10th A. D.—W. A. Morgan, Dem., 7,973; B. Aronson, Rep., 11,737; T. D. Mygatt, Soc., 1,035.

11th A. D.—C. Stuart, Dem., 9,448; F. H. Nichols, Rep., 12,124; S. Berlin, Soc., 1,214; R. J. Ausland, Proh., 72.

12th A. D.—J. J. O'Connor, Dem., 13,103; J. A. Jerome, Jr., Rep., 6,815; A. L. Trachtenberg, Soc., 1,722; W. H. Aldman, Proh., 120.

13th A. D.—J. J. Wilson, Dem., 7,983; R. B. Wallace, Rep., 10,370; R. Meade, Soc., 1,228.

14th A. D.—F. L. Hackenburg, Dem., 7,197; C. J. Bartunek, Rep., 6,344; G. McMullen, Soc., 2,317; A. McVitty, Far.-L., 966; E. F. Healy, Yorkville Party, 3,092.

15th A. D.—J. L. MacDonnell, Dem., 7,464; J. Steinberg, Rep., 13,757; E. Steinberger, Soc., 1,891.

16th A. D.—M. Bloch, Dem., 11,823; A. Ober, Rep., 6,160; H. Voly, Soc., 3,900.

17th A. D.—N. Lieberman, Dem., Fus., 8,062; A. Claessens, Soc., 7,325.

18th A. D.—O. M. Kiernan, Dem., 6,156; D. J. Naughton, Rep., 6,012; I. Phillips, Soc., 4,477.

19th A. D.—M. J. Healy, Dem., 6,947; M. L. Smith, Rep., 9,303; G. Campbell, Soc., 1,888; A. T. Hill, Proh., 84.

20th A. D.—L. A. Cuvillier, Dem., 4,513; M. G. Di Pirre, Rep., 5,771; A. Tuvin, Soc., 1,744; P. Brady, Proh., 97.

21st A. D.—J. T. Pathe, Dem., 4,859; J. C. Hawkins, Rep., 11,299; C. Owen, Soc., 1,032.

22d A. D.—M. E. Reiburn, Dem., 10,527; O. J. Smith, Rep., 9,433; J. Dombroff, Soc., 1,074.

23d A. D.—I. Coon, Dem., 9,055; G. N. Jesse, Rep., 16,521; J. Lyons, Soc., 2,018.

Representatives in Congress.

11th Dist., D. J. Riordan, Dem., 7,642; W. F. Wakeman, Rep., 3,753; R. Rochow, Soc., 525.

12th Dist.—H. M. Goldfogel, Dem., Fus., 8,646; M. London, Soc., 10,212.

13th Dist.—C. D. Sullivan, Dem., Fus., 8,978; C. W. Ervin, Soc., 4,925.

14th Dist.—N. D. Pearlman, Dem., Fus., 18,037; A. Lee, Soc., 8,515.

15th Dist.—P. J. Dooling, Dem., 14,970; T. J. Ryan, Rep., 18,935; C. Richter, Soc., 1,219; J. J. Reilly, Far.-L., 1,570.

16th Dist.—W. B. Cockran, Dem., 19,273; W. S. Fisher, Rep., 14,333; B. H. Mailly, Soc., 2,748.

17th Dist.—H. C. Pell, Jr., Dem., 18,340; O. L. Mills, Rep., 33,644; J. Halpern, Soc., 2,322.

18th Dist.—J. F. Carew, Dem., 12,160; H. J. O Connor, Rep., 11,145; M. McDonald, Soc., 5,668; J. A. O'Leary, Far.-L., 9,998.

19th Dist.—W. Kennelly, Dem., 23,121; W. M. Chandler, Rep., 41,821; E. Friedman, Soc., 5,667.

20th Dist.—I. Siegel, Dem., Fus., 12,602; M. Hillquit, Soc., 9,441.

21st Dist.—J. F. Donovan, Dem., 28,528; M. C. Ansorge, Rep., 48,954; R. Press, Soc., 3,873; T. F. Ryan, Far.-L., 1,824; M. Van Veen, Sing. Tax, 251.

22d Dist.—A. J. Griffin, Dem., 6,070; W. J. Murphy, Rep., 6,941; P. J. Murphy, Soc., 1,840.

VOTE OF NASSAU COUNTY, 1920

Towns.	Dist. No.	President. Cox, Dem.	President. Harding, Rep.	Governor Smith, Dem.	Governor Miller, Rep.	Lieut. Governor Fitts, Dem.	Lieut. Governor Wood, Rep.	Secretary of State. Mills, Dem.	Secretary of State. Lyons, Rep.	Compt'ler Berry, Dem.	Compt'ler Wendell, Rep.	State Treasurer Healy, Dem.	State Treasurer Marshall, Rep.	Attorney General. Mott, Dem.	Attorney General. Newton, Rep.	State Engineer McLoud, Dem.	State Engineer Williams, Rep.	Assoc. J. Ct. of Ap. Crane, Rep. & Dem.	Assoc. J. Ct. of Ap. Chase, Rep.	U. S. Senator. Walker, Dem.	U. S. Senator. Wadsworth, Rep.
Hempstead.	1	30	245	87	183	50	207	29	236	54	204	33	222	34	223	32	224	142	216	42	215
	2	8	136	18	111	10	123	8	127	11	121	11	126	9	124	8	124	87	121	8	127
	3	50	223	91	173	55	206	54	207	61	196	49	210	50	210	47	209	260	209	60	196
	4	66	334	165	198	96	266	84	289	101	262	81	285	82	283	78	290	221	277	82	273
	5	32	152	71	95	46	115	34	132	39	120	27	135	30	134	33	134	92	126	37	121
	6	32	189	70	125	50	150	44	160	49	153	37	163	39	154	40	157	121	151	42	152
	7	56	323	144	210	78	273	69	291	97	247	71	276	66	280	68	280	212	258	77	265
	8	58	401	144	276	64	362	59	359	79	318	63	351	62	345	65	352	266	336	72	331
	9	90	359	200	228	113	322	97	336	130	299	102	326	100	327	97	328	425	320	108	308
	10	141	507	222	414	167	458	154	472	185	430	154	468	150	470	152	466	614	458	163	420
	11	139	486	223	367	154	443	140	434	174	406	142	455	139	447	146	444	441	416	157	406
	12	113	418	209	287	161	344	127	363	149	337	134	361	137	360	130	367	346	343	123	365
	13	81	329	165	213	95	289	90	292	119	254	95	281	87	279	82	292	228	266	88	290
	14	41	306	126	200	57	264	54	269	62	263	52	275	46	277	45	282	326	275	55	267
	15	44	269	102	182	54	221	55	223	63	214	49	230	50	212	48	230	147	220	54	216
	16	63	206	92	179	63	204	63	200	73	186	67	198	64	202	67	198	260	193	37	128
	17	32	157	67	100	38	125	33	129	33	126	35	124	36	134	37	130	94	124	87	148
	18	70	186	106	142	96	151	89	155	92	148	85	158	76	165	75	165	192	147	143	483
	19	126	543	202	463	135	52	132	513	148	500	126	527	128	519	125	596	641	508	100	296
	20	79	342	131	282	85	322	90	314	99	304	84	322	86	322	81	324	410	315	127	315
	21	124	353	130	291	135	330	129	337	139	329	123	34	125	341	127	338	465	334	78	191
	22	89	233	122	190	81	212	84	216	85	253	80	212	82	210	80	208	301	206	118	361
	23	105	412	155	344	122	372	124	373	125	369	114	386	108	385	109	384	492	380	18	106
	24	16	127	42	90	24	107	19	111	25	109	21	111	17	113	19	112	76	110	94	198
	25	85	250	144	162	100	196	91	205	106	196	95	204	92	205	95	205	165	191	135	279
	26	124	322	192	253	131	297	125	301	140	286	126	299	123	301	125	296	435	295	64	231
	27	62	298	168	193	79	229	66	240	94	209	72	232	69	232	62	238	174	210	112	226
	28	85	251	196	140	122	204	111	208	120	199	111	211	106	206	108	205	220	189	99	254
	29	90	218	141	132	109	137	91	177	108	148	101	165	100	162	98	162	180	139	114	267
	30	112	314	160	252	114	346	110	295	121	279	112	289	113	286	114	288	402	277	110	319
	31	98	362	153	305	88	386	100	352	117	332	102	349	98	349	92	354	443	248	84	360
	32	68	421	145	329	164	596	79	392	97	374	83	185	76	292	76	390	465	383	176	537
	33	155	620	265	495	107	396	149	606	200	548	165	591	154	599	156	596	753	576	103	383
	34	89	423	177	321	50	188	165	399	112	390	110	391	100	400	102	398	499	393	53	181
	35	43	219	85	150	95	230	44	195	52	181	43	197	42	195	40	201	151	183	71	240
	36	68	238	101	250	59	259	65	256	76	241	59	259	57	262	60	255	322	246	61	247
	37	57	265	100	225	30	207	61	257	80	229	58	259	57	257	57	256	313	250	47	179
	38	36	277	72	162	96	299	33	190	39	190	36	196	35	194	33	193	150	193	123	515
	39	126	574	211	458	49	409	116	561	145	522	118	557	112	561	114	560	647	542	79	353
	40	64	350	133	319	72	331	67	380	89	349	73	374	68	371	85	375	443	361	95	282
	41	78	339	154	243	80	256	81	315	107	27	91	300	87	209	87	307	252	285	95	213
	42	78	276	113	217	85	619	85	255	94	243	83	256	85	250	85	251	194	240	113	540
	43	92	617	202	496	74	285	106	583	116	571	95	587	94	584	97	584	686	570	96	245
	44	88	300	154	197	67	263	85	262	99	238	91	250	94	246	91	259	209	226	68	249
	45	59	303	132	193	53	144	72	249	91	234	77	253	71	253	68	255	210	240	45	149
	46	31	194	97	111	63	114	47	144	54	140	47	145	50	146	48	145	96	142	58	113
	47	42	161	90	98	110	396	60	115	63	112	60	116	55	116	56	120	105	108	105	366
	48	79	429	187	320	32	163	106	394	106	390	96	404	99	407	98	403	495	396	32	145
	49	23	176	55	141	69	80	24	173	44	152	26	171	21	175	25	174	155	467	62	89
	50	49	134	105	62	79	195	67	96	69	85	67	89	59	95	62	90	99	93	59	199
	51	47	243	112	157	95	252	59	207	67	192	57	207	57	203	55	208	163	197	98	244
	52	67	314	165	188	85	246	83	265	102	245	90	262	81	263	80	272	271	255	79	243
	53	71	273	140	202	92	203	67	261	83	236	73	257	71	254	72	263	330	238	118	260
	54	91	322	160	242	31	43	81	309	101	289	85	306	78	309	82	303	384	248	24	50
	55	17	61	39	34	29	184	27	47	25	46	23	51	23	51	23	51	57	46	21	185
	56	28	199	46	177	157	320	28	158	26	185	25	188	24	190	26	188	212	184	131	334
	57	127	400	266	236	111	281	126	350	143	317	134	334	126	344	117	342	290	301	95	287
	58	85	333	169	236	65	307	82	307	90	296	92	299	89	297	88	290	382	269	79	288
	59	71	330	129	263	76	193	65	313	82	294	63	310	60	316	63	311	372	275	75	183
	60	57	224	114	159	79	226	67	206	77	191	70	194	64	199	62	200	244	173	63	238
	61	61	263	115	199	73	228	53	253	62	220	65	239	62	243	53	244	213	176	65	259
	62	58	242	112	195	46	235	60	242	65	232	65	235	61	237	64	233	298	233	46	219
	63	48	240	69	216	84	446	68	217	54	228	44	233	48	229	44	233	283	234	61	457
	64	50	616	141	379	..	..	78	458	80	441	67	463	66	469	59	462	285	441	..	..
North Hempstead.	1	93	290	141	240	97	271	100	274	93	266	93	274	86	279	92	275	366	278	105	258
	2	80	262	125	211	74	256	70	261	82	241	74	259	74	254	77	253	329	251	84	226
	3	134	264	171	226	138	249	115	272	137	252	127	261	129	268	126	257	384	255	129	251
	4	100	319	188	244	119	284	111	292	134	271	114	282	111	287	112	288	400	285	110	278
	5	85	242	124	192	92	227	92	230	99	219	91	230	90	229	100	222	318	225	94	212
	6	66	158	97	126	75	143	74	141	74	140	67	147	67	149	69	146	215	146	70	134
	7	76	322	99	288	64	319	71	313	71	309	60	319	67	313	66	315	383	309	68	301
	8	90	351	140	301	102	329	94	335	94	333	91	334	88	340	93	334	428	335	99	311
	9	37	205	80	158	48	191	46	189	52	183	44	187	47	188	43	191	232	184	46	178
	10	100	167	124	140	101	161	97	176	104	146	97	155	97	155	98	153	250	149	102	144
	11	87	192	106	167	83	188	79	190	91	184	82	195	85	192	79	194	276	190	108	168
	12	79	267	156	194	99	234	90	250	99	231	95	240	88	246	86	249	333	238	90	236
	13	92	236	159	170	101	207	102	203	103	203	102	208	101	204	100	201	303	198	104	196
	14	197	383	266	316	200	361	203	360	207	356	199	360	199	363	213	360	560	357	208	356
	15	69	256	115	207	78	240	76	246	81	235	73	244	70	244	71	247	312	241	81	227
	16	52	160	99	105	68	128	63	137	69	127	57	137	59	138	55	140	193	129	68	123
	17	65	241	97	195	62	227	60	230	64	223	63	226	57	229	61	221	284	224	63	227
	18	69	302	98	263	74	283	69	290	75	280	71	287	70	286	70	287	363	280	73	264
	19	57	281	74	254	58	270	59	274	59	268	54	272	56	274	56	272	328	272	64	268
	20	74	174	116	125	80	150	72	161	84	150	78	154	76	152	72	157	229	164	83	145
	21	32	196	70	158	37	188	33	192	43	175	32	188	35	186	35	185	319	180	45	167
	22	22	137	58	103	24	121	23	124	23	121	24	122	24	121	24	118	142	118	22	124
	23	42	131	65	104	47	118	45	122	50	120	44	124	45	122	47	122	168	119	48	117
	24	60	238	109	171	64	207	61	211	70	196	64	208	65	209	61	211	270	204	70	198
	25	53	244	82	215	53	235	53	242	58	230	53	240	53	233	50	237	295	235	67	229
	26	41	212	71	180	47	197	44	196	48	196	47	200	44	196	46	197	241	..	48	194

VOTE OF NASSAU COUNTY, 1920—*Continued.*

Towns.	Dist. No.	President.		Governor.		Lieut. Governor		Secretary of State.		Compt'ler		State Treasurer		Attorney General		State Engineer		Assoc. J. Ct. of Ap.		U. S. Senator.	
		Cox, Dem.	Harding, Rep.	Smith, Dem.	Miller, Rep.	Fitts, Dem.	Wood, Rep.	Mills, Dem.	Lyons, Rep.	Berry, Dem.	Wendell, Rep.	Healy, Dem.	Marshall, Rep.	Mott, Dem.	Newton, Rep.	McLoud, Dem.	Williams, Rep.	Crane, Rep. & Dem.	Chase, Rep.	Walker, Dem.	Wadsworth, Rep.
Oyster Bay.	1	52	254	114	191	65	230	62	236	67	229	61	234	57	236	59	237	290	223	62	219
	2	64	348	139	241	95	289	84	299	89	276	77	300	78	294	78	297	241	274	77	278
	3	37	192	94	125	49	156	48	159	49	154	39	166	41	163	39	165	120	153	40	160
	4	39	242	100	170	57	199	56	198	66	196	59	198	56	198	53	198	172	188	62	178
	5	74	275	164	175	110	229	80	259	93	242	72	247	82	248	81	252	231	238	91	209
	6	42	273	96	204	69	229	63	225	59	221	55	231	57	229	60	238	203	221	64	198
	7	57	211	117	145	68	199	51	208	54	196	53	202	52	199	55	200	251	199	66	196
	8	90	421	171	319	112	366	108	369	122	354	116	366	102	374	113	362	302	335	105	369
	9	73	222	105	169	86	183	83	183	99	167	84	184	88	180	83	187	177	176	91	159
	10	64	213	112	190	75	191	75	194	87	180	66	201	68	197	65	202	205	176	79	181
	11	64	256	77	125	75	222	61	235	86	214	68	235	64	222	68	233	219	225	71	216
	12	59	162	114	194	54	150	57	148	63	137	51	157	52	154	52	155	146	117	61	136
	13	132	314	128	134	137	292	133	293	139	282	133	295	130	293	129	292	417	281	131	278
	14	50	274	109	140	58	240	56	242	64	224	51	244	54	243	49	245	217	228	63	227
	15	73	209	86	147	84	179	81	179	92	166	82	177	82	177	79	185	172	168	78	178
	16	38	222	125	180	59	181	48	195	64	177	52	190	51	190	52	192	184	181	53	185
	17	57	198	120	148	59	169	60	169	66	155	55	168	57	170	50	176	171	163	68	146
	18	•75	252	76	95	84	225	78	229	85	221	84	224	81	220	75	228	209	202	83	215
	19	42	245	112	213	64	190	58	209	74	188	59	205	62	197	61	199	183	191	60	206
	20	26	156	91	172	42	131	34	135	42	130	37	135	34	136	34	139	167	128	40	131
	21	73	261	174	255	87	234	72	242	83	233	75	242	70	246	74	243	193	228	80	229
	22	51	271	66	234	66	234	59	246	69	245	59	247	63	239	51	252	169	198	69	225
Glen Cove.	1	142	327	213	243	177	281	167	291	173	277	168	295	160	297	163	292	323	264	173	276
	2	58	285	102	236	73	261	80	252	91	243	65	264	65	265	71	261	191	256	75	236
	3	108	318	176	228	143	248	124	265	144	241	140	251	134	251	187	249	242	242	124	262
	4	175	143	230	74	214	90	198	99	213	88	217	93	208	91	209	92	243	85	197	100
	5	120	279	167	211	112	254	128	248	139	237	125	257	129	253	125	248	278	238	137	232
	6	81	183	106	142	84	164	84	163	85	155	82	166	69	168	80	166	185	152	86	175
	7	105	271	178	192	130	231	129	234	137	220	128	233	126	225	134	222	236	206	124	235
Totals		8589	33064	15274	24795	9963	29498	9350	30050	10654	28394	9396	29603	9188	29878	9154	29933	33053	28304	9817	28001

Other Votes—Pres., Soc., Debs, 1,253; Proh., Watkins, 155; Soc.-Labor, Cox, 46; Farmer-Labor, Christensen, 182. Gov., Soc., Cannon, 925; Proh., Thompson, 495; Soc.-Labor, Quinn, 47; Farmer-Labor, Malone, 1,044; blanks, 732; void, 297. Lt. Gov., Soc., Hughan, 1,099; Proh., Deitrich, 286; Soc.-Labor, Crowley, 56; Farmer-Labor, Haffey, 475; blanks, 1,349; void, 243. Sec. of State, Soc., Noonan, 1,094; Proh., Taylor, 300; Soc.-Labor, Phalor, 48; Farmer-Labor, Auyer, 361; blanks, 1,482; void, 224. Comptroller, Soc., Randolph, 1,122; Proh., Gray, 398; Soc.-Labor, De Lee, 58; Farmer-Labor, Fincke, 367; blanks, 1,633; void, 215. State Treas., Soc., Kreuger, 1,107; Proh., McKee, 267; Soc.-Labor, Withers, 45; Farmer-Labor, Cronk, 318; blanks, 1,550; void, 208. Atty. Gen., Soc., Meserole, 1,084; Proh., Burr, 349; Soc.-Labor, Donohue, 68; Farmer-Labor, Serri, 299; blank, 1,653; void, 223. State Eng., Soc., Karapetoff, 1,100; Proh., A. S. Light, 278; Soc.-Labor, Crawford, 139; blanks, 1,772; void, 237. Asso. J. Ct. of Appeals, Dem., Elkus, 8,922; Soc., Malkiel, 1,095, Axelrod, 1,005; Proh., Hart, 329, Baldwin, 283; Farmer-Labor, Hale, 341, Dwyer, 410; blanks, 10,660; void, 350. U. S. Senator, Soc., Panken, 1,041; Proh., Boole, 1,337; Soc.-Labor, Carlson, 67; Farmer-Labor, Schneiderman, 357; blanks, 1,503; void, 213.

Justices of the Supreme Court.

Aspinall, Rep., 28,891; Strong, Rep., 25,715; Dike, Rep., 28,374; McCrate, Rep., 25,327; Jaycox, Rep., 28,644; Garvin, Dem., 8,978; Humphrey, Dem., 10,163; McMahon, Dem., 7,980; Scudder, Dem., 18,155; Druhan, Dem., 7,126; Wolfman, Soc., 1,064; Rivkin, Soc., 1,025; Kayfetz, Soc., 998; Satra, Soc., 969; Testa, Soc., 996; Wilson, Proh., 321; Smith, Proh., 290; Watson, Proh., 247; W. Howell, Proh., 239; Howell, Proh., 225; Haskell, Farmer-Labor, 430; Kohler, Far.-Lab., 306; Goldstein, Far.-Lab., 277; Strahl, Far.-Lab., 1,704; Brown, Single Tax, 87; blanks, 13,910; void, 1,134.

Other Candidates—Rep. in Cong., Kennedy, Dem., 9,809; Hicks, Rep., 29,461; Hinckley, Soc., 1,161; blanks, 2,096; void, 205.

State Senator—Carroll, Dem., 10,280; Thompson, Rep., 28,452; Bache, Soc., 1,147; blanks, 2,288; void, 180.

Amendment No. 1—For, 13,906; against, 8,978; blanks, 6,811; void, 70.

Proposition No. 1—For, 17,202; against, 11,620; blanks, 3,500; void, 171.

Members of Ass. 1st Dist.—Malone, Dem., 7,573; McWhinney, Rep., 13,778; Jackson, Soc., 949; blanks, 1,429; void, 126.

Members of Ass. 2d Dist.—Weaver, Dem., 4,370; Roosevelt, Rep., 12,420; Freidman, Soc., 1; blanks, 880; void, 68.

TAX RATES, SUFFOLK AND NASSAU COUNTIES.

SUFFOLK.

Individual tax warrants are as follows: Easthampton, $185,492; Southampton, $566,309; Shelter Is., $35,470; Southold, $256,874; Riverhead, $179,367; Islip, $631,828; Brookhaven, $634,985; Huntington, $473,077; Babylon, $283,898; Smithtown, $158,162.

Aggregate of the 10 warrants is $3,405,463, or $559,064 greater than in 1919.

The tax rates in towns and incorporated villages are as follows:

Southampton, $2.75; incorporated villages, $1.55; Huntington, 98c.; incorporated villages, 65c.; Shelter Is., $1.06; incorporated villages, 90c.; Smithtown, $1.88; Riverhead, $2.03; Brookhaven, $1.95; incorporated villages, $1.28; Easthampton, $2.22; incorporated villages, $1.23; Islip, $1.57; incorporated villages, $1.18; Southold, $1.75; incorporated villages, $1.15; Babylon, $1.68; incorporated, $1.42.

NASSAU.

Town of Hempstead—State tax, $0.38; county tax, $1.08; town, $0.29; highway, $0.24; health, $0.04.

Town of North Hempstead—State, $0.36; county, $1.03; town, $0.50; highway, $0.38; health, $0.02.

Town of Oyster Bay—State, $0.42; county, $1.20; town, $0.18; highway, $0.25; health, $0.01.

Glen Cove City—State, $0.42; county, $1.17.

Assessed valuations of real, personal and special franchise:

Town of Hempstead, $94,222,539; Town of Oyster Bay, $32,643,968; Town of North Hempstead, $48,506,529; Glen Cove City, $9,570,369.

Villages in the Tepeleni district, Southern Albania, were destroyed by an earthquake on Dec. 11, 1920, 200 persons being reported killed and 15,000 homeless.

Operation of the United States Postal Service for the fiscal year 1920 resulted in a deficit of $17,270,482, the second largest in the history of the service.

VOTE OF SUFFOLK COUNTY, 1920.

Towns.	Dist. No.	President		Governor		Lieut.-Governor		Sec. of State.		Comptroller.		State Treas.		Att'y General.		State Engineer		Asso. J. Ct. App's		U. S. Senator.	
		Cox, Dem.	Harding, Rep.	Smith, Dem.	Miller, Rep.	Fitts, Dem.	Wood, Rep.	Mills, Dem.	Lyons, Rep.	Berry, Dem.	Wendell, Rep.	Healy, Dem.	Marshall, Rep.	Mott, Dem.	Newton, Rep.	McLoud, Dem.	Williams, Rep.	Crane, (Rep.-Dem.	Chase, Rep.	Walker, Dem.	Wadsworth, Rep.
Brookhaven.	1	53	178	80	153	62	162	48	178	72	145	51	269	53	168	50	168	185	156	66	163
	2	71	235	85	188	67	198	65	204	74	192	68	201	71	202	68	206	206	178	73	180
	3	44	212	68	188	54	195	43	202	47	192	44	199	42	201	41	208	189	178	42	151
	4	82	174	99	149	78	164	74	171	84	158	80	163	85	151	72	165	188	150	68	141
	5	95	178	117	129	101	146	87	157	100	146	78	164	83	161	80	161	167	128	80	128
	6	38	130	59	119	45	129	41	130	44	129	43	131	39	132	38	132	151	119	41	115
	7	51	146	52	121	45	127	46	128	54	124	46	129	46	129	46	131	137	117	49	96
	8	27	78	38	60	29	62	29	65	30	58	28	60	28	62	26	62	78	69	35	58
	9	75	181	72	153	57	163	60	163	71	146	61	162	66	155	65	164	178	140	66	135
	10	115	236	136	197	116	214	108	219	116	211	110	218	105	215	108	216	269	183	131	197
	11	85	206	141	152	103	175	85	190	100	174	88	188	87	178	81	186	247	173	87	184
	12	49	206	65	160	41	182	37	184	44	171	34	182	25	182	34	178	191	176	39	163
	13	55	231	90	190	72	200	54	214	73	197	63	208	62	206	61	202	239	191	59	176
	14	54	137	88	99	63	117	52	124	55	117	50	121	49	128	50	122	186	113	45	87
	15	48	196	97	130	66	157	62	168	67	155	46	170	45	169	50	168	193	153	56	136
	16	47	203	88	138	58	164	61	169	63	164	50	176	52	176	53	177	195	160	68	167
	17	46	126	85	74	67	87	60	95	67	83	64	88	64	90	65	91	113	81	66	83
	18	51	163	105	106	78	119	72	122	66	125	66	130	68	136	64	126	148	117	60	134
	19	43	204	95	131	68	161	53	178	61	161	53	171	49	176	52	179	208	152	64	149
	20	57	148	89	111	64	128	55	137	69	114	58	132	52	138	53	138	140	118	49	110
	21	42	129	65	107	39	110	42	109	51	97	38	111	37	113	39	109	121	97	34	91
	22	71	165	98	120	73	144	62	147	73	131	68	137	64	142	65	140	154	128	65	120
	23	83	189	105	157	87	168	74	171	80	163	76	170	76	169	78	167	179	152	84	129
	24	74	136	106	95	83	109	79	109	85	100	69	113	69	117	72	116	150	106	65	101
	25	17	70	24	50	20	48	17	60	20	48	22	50	19	60	20	48	67	43	17	38
	26	56	86	64	79	56	77	51	82	52	75	50	81	53	80	60	80	110	72	64	72
	27	45	129	60	122	46	129	43	129	42	125	40	128	41	127	40	128	139	122	43	108
	28	41	140	69	95	56	107	47	113	56	102	51	109	51	106	54	108	137	96	47	102
	29	26	136	48	114	32	121	29	126	38	111	29	120	29	120	27	123	132	114	33	97
	30	44	196	92	143	57	177	51	180	65	114	49	170	47	167	48	172	190	149	59	146
	31	36	174	63	128	47	147	33	157	40	147	34	176	34	155	32	156	173	141	42	122
	32	16	112	43	71	25	91	18	94	21	94	21	93	16	96	18	96	87	100	35	87
Riverhead.	1	20	72	34	56	26	55	26	56	27	54	27	53	28	54	28	55	66	50	26	54
	2	75	136	121	81	92	96	79	109	80	105	56	102	83	102	82	103	136	87	78	80
	3	96	170	115	137	92	147	80	161	97	140	54	159	83	156	81	154	197	147	97	117
	4	54	180	86	137	67	158	56	162	67	146	64	164	62	161	61	158	177	136	63	115
	5	78	290	92	261	75	289	76	269	93	236	71	263	71	266	76	259	288	244	68	216
	6	67	272	99	232	80	249	72	254	84	229	69	251	71	252	67	256	290	229	69	184
	7	59	224	57	182	87	189	97	179	96	177	97	187	89	179	86	178	221	164	78	107
Southold.	1	24	54	83	45	30	45	29	46	29	44	27	37	24	49	25	48	56	44	28	49
	2	23	247	27	233	22	237	21	236	20	235	20	226	20	235	19	237	287	218	28	164
	3	47	113	37	113	85	102	33	100	43	91	38	95	31	95	34	95	110	88	42	82
	4	67	219	115	157	99	186	77	208	79	200	75	196	72	216	74	196	215	162	72	151
	5	58	188	78	158	70	163	62	171	55	172	62	169	62	168	68	165	195	140	65	144
	6	82	249	128	189	104	203	93	215	92	212	85	216	83	216	83	217	233	184	82	195
	7	82	149	115	101	87	119	77	124	73	126	78	124	76	126	73	127	184	65	60	105
	8	25	32	25	30	25	30	26	29	25	30	25	29	25	30	25	30	41	29	24	30
	9	130	157	145	140	131	148	122	155	121	149	120	166	117	157	117	164	212	136	129	127
	10	56	212	64	196	55	203	51	205	53	200	55	200	55	201	58	201	205	196	55	177
	11	72	190	83	179	68	186	64	185	66	180	62	185	62	185	59	188	212	172	65	153
	12	84	175	130	137	87	141	83	143	81	145	81	144	86	142	83	144	180	123	83	92
	13	42	183	53	169	38	178	37	172	46	156	35	173	40	166	31	173	184	159	36	157
	14	87	240	109	213	93	225	84	230	94	210	85	226	86	225	82	227	255	213	89	188
Shelter Island.	1	88	295	98	278	73	283	66	286	73	282	68	290	68	285	64	289	292	258	81	280
East-hampton.	1	122	372	145	339	124	322	103	345	115	327	101	347	101	343	95	341	375	311	134	294
	2	112	289	176	210	124	239	107	257	120	225	121	238	112	248	118	238	276	228	119	182
	3	111	217	138	183	105	206	100	204	96	197	93	202	98	198	93	201	238	183	94	188
	4	65	90	51	93	49	87	56	80	51	77	47	91	46	81	47	79	103	72	61	75
	5	144	276	166	226	132	234	135	233	132	226	126	240	123	244	128	241	295	212	131	199
Southampton.	1	160	248	217	266	172	295	148	213	171	285	156	204	156	298	165	301	332	373	147	289
	2	178	281	275	180	224	219	184	247	199	229	194	242	188	233	189	244	292	219	173	218
	3	56	215	73	189	58	202	54	204	51	204	50	205	49	210	47	211	226	198	68	188
	4	47	189	68	157	47	172	53	163	54	139	44	168	41	169	42	168	166	147	44	122
	5	69	289	153	197	95	239	75	263	91	232	83	249	73	257	67	251	296	236	67	201
	6	76	413	143	315	85	358	78	371	85	344	61	377	66	375	66	369	370	345	60	361
	7	64	293	130	273	86	236	69	253	80	233	67	250	62	247	66	248	359	216	63	235
	8	99	190	160	128	111	154	99	163	102	137	99	158	95	163	95	157	208	147	98	140
	9	94	331	121	287	93	301	94	299	86	305	82	310	96	306	86	312	352	280	90	276
	10	108	393	152	338	117	350	98	375	116	353	106	366	106	364	101	371	412	330	105	329
	11	54	243	76	202	60	209	60	209	59	208	56	215	54	214	53	215	220	199	68	174
	12	37	164	54	144	40	144	34	149	38	145	36	148	34	150	34	150	147	144	30	135
	13	37	233	54	210	42	212	37	217	37	215	33	218	33	217	84	200	117	205	33	182
Huntington.	1	70	209	97	162	79	178	79	183	87	172	77	184	71	187	77	184	229	178	78	176
	2	83	256	132	174	104	191	93	205	99	197	97	202	94	206	97	213	245	208	86	174
	3	51	281	118	206	71	243	64	248	94	215	60	253	65	251	55	262	289	233	58	225
	4	80	235	113	190	81	213	82	207	76	207	69	216	77	211	69	222	241	196	72	191
	5	92	431	151	361	100	392	108	390	110	377	90	402	90	393	92	399	491	294	109	385
	6	81	324	148	247	109	287	99	301	96	293	90	290	94	303	89	303	301	289	84	272
	7	44	197	90	143	70	160	53	179	67	154	58	163	57	168	64	160	183	146	46	162
	8	69	251	106	219	81	250	67	257	76	237	68	251	72	247	68	254	286	221	68	219
	9	202	380	234	334	209	348	202	354	220	327	204	350	210	344	195	349	547	340	196	287
	10	120	389	176	329	141	355	130	356	150	322	130	360	131	355	127	357	394	320	136	296
	11	41	218	81	156	62	176	49	186	61	174	45	191	51	182	48	187	187	170	51	172
	12	40	189	74	128	47	147	44	156	48	144	43	150	44	149	43	152	[illegible]	[illegible]	44	142
	13	126	332	171	248	122	285	106	303	126	276	106	296	101	303	100	304	343	176	120	244
	14	49	347	135	226	76	276	62	295	79	276	66	289	60	282	63	294	[illegible]	[illegible]	76	[illegible]

VOTE OF SUFFOLK COUNTY, 1920—*Continued.*

Towns	Dist. No.	President		Governor		Lieut.-Governor		Sec. of State.		Comptroller.		State Treas.		Att'y General.		State Engineer		Asso. J. Ct. App's		U. S. Senator.	
		Cox, Dem.	Harding, Rep.	Smith, Dem.	Miller, Rep.	Fitts, Dem.	Wood, Rep.	Mills, Dem.	Lyons, Rep.	Berry, Dem.	Wendell, Rep.	Healy, Dem.	Marshall, Rep.	Mott, Dem.	Newton, Rep.	McLoud, Dem.	Williams, Rep.	Crane, Rep. Dem.	Chase, Rep.	Walker, Dem.	Wadsworth, Rep.
Smithtown.	1	123	330	149	290	127	308	122	313	133	297	121	312	123	307	122	313	429	307	117	292
	2	118	250	149	217	126	231	118	236	120	232	121	235	119	232	120	234	355	226	122	227
	3	135	135	212	66	173	96	156	111	155	113	155	119	157	114	153	115	175	103	145	110
	4	140	232	206	172	145	208	128	228	146	208	132	223	132	220	132	223	353	212	135	213
	5	149	67	68	41	64	44	50	46	51	44	54	43	51	46	53	51	72	41	43	43
Babylon.	1	91	358	153	282	102	313	84	336	109	297	89	328	92	325	95	322	357	277	92	301
	2	121	306	173	248	123	279	122	279	132	269	125	279	126	278	125	278	398	271	123	256
	3	115	301	170	217	136	228	119	257	134	241	139	262	116	253	113	254	307	224	114	231
	4	40	178	79	123	52	148	37	159	52	146	42	155	43	157	43	158	167	140	40	154
	5	56	269	206	111	133	168	99	200	115	178	103	192	99	198	94	199	228	169	98	187
	6	40	275	135	146	86	186	67	217	79	206	72	216	68	221	76	219	233	196	79	196
	7	100	337	185	238	126	290	104	302	141	263	116	293	115	289	114	285	317	262	106	275
	8	83	335	153	255	98	301	80	217	110	281	80	306	79	311	82	310	337	294	78	298
	9	74	340	146	245	90	289	82	287	101	265	82	292	81	290	76	291	316	271	74	287
	10	27	97	67	55	33	84	30	86	37	70	28	84	27	86	26	87	81	69	32	69
	11	72	192	122	114	88	135	70	150	84	129	78	153	72	159	70	156	164	130	69	150
	12	28	117	67	70	38	97	32	106	43	93	32	103	44	92	29	108	150	58	32	98
Islip.	1	60	128	96	86	71	99	53	119	63	110	63	108	63	105	61	109	131	90	59	108
	2	66	335	128	267	80	304	71	311	86	296	66	316	67	311	67	311	377	306	74	296
	3	75	163	132	106	94	131	79	145	80	138	75	149	77	147	74	145	183	128	86	124
	4	87	273	181	162	115	227	94	240	104	223	82	220	82	223	82	223	265	208	93	217
	5	63	182	106	133	82	145	65	160	77	149	76	157	69	159	72	160	191	146	75	128
	6	88	278	127	214	98	235	80	253	92	241	88	248	91	248	83	241	288	228	100	221
	7	105	224	200	125	140	170	116	193	147	167	135	176	120	182	126	181	235	167	128	147
	8	80	123	110	87	77	98	66	105	72	99	71	104	66	106	65	167	124	94	71	100
	9	27	354	43	318	27	321	59	281	32	328	30	331	30	332	31	329	357	330	36	282
	10	43	75	72	39	51	53	52	51	53	47	46	56	45	57	42	55	76	49	45	51
	11	89	248	130	197	104	215	93	223	100	206	92	227	85	222	88	227	252	198	98	176
	12	72	271	147	169	88	222	83	219	94	218	78	235	77	228	76	220	228	211	97	197
	13	79	226	170	133	111	182	98	189	108	171	95	193	93	190	92	190	216	180	94	161
	14	87	332	130	259	96	295	82	295	102	298	97	300	90	303	91	300	347	285	99	264
	15	125	129	226	46	170	80	123	117	164	88	156	89	140	98	142	94	171	81	157	79
	16	41	193	92	137	58	161	40	176	57	157	41	175	38	177	41	176	179	154	39	162
	17	80	210	138	123	102	152	79	175	101	144	88	160	86	169	88	166	198	136	90	137
	18	74	223	136	164	77	202	75	204	88	198	76	205	77	206	74	206	279	204	83	185
	19	84	190	157	106	103	142	87	157	93	152	87	157	88	154	86	158	183	139	84	143
	20	46	232	115	138	62	181	38	204	52	189	43	205	43	200	41	201	198	177	39	179
Totals		8851	26729	13658	20368	10141	22652	8984	23725	10024	22230	9029	23627	8886	23638	8762	23663	27128	21290	9062	20642

Towns	Dist. No.	Justice of the Supreme Court.					Rep. in Congr's		State Senator.		Mem. Assembly. 1st Dist		2d Dist.		County Treas.		District Attorney.		Amend. No. 1.		Prop'tion No. 1.	
		Aspinall, Rep.-Cit.	Strong, Rep.	Dike, Rep.	MacCrate, Rep.	Jaycox, Rep.-Cit.	Kennedy, Dem.	Hicks, Rep.-Proh.	Carroll, Dem.	Thompson, Rep.	Garvey, Dem.	Downs, Rep.	Reylek, Dem.	Bailey, Rep.	Rayner, Dem.	Scudder, Rep.	Collins, Dem.	Young, Rep.	For.	Against.	For.	Against.
Brookhaven.	1	150	138	153	150	159	74	145	130	93	85	131	...	...	68	165	70	150	78	88	97	101
	2	140	237	142	125	141	89	188	93	174	74	185	...	...	74	188	82	178	102	100	114	136
	3	158	174	167	169	191	60	188	52	192	45	192	...	...	42	194	58	188	102	63	119	93
	4	154	167	156	151	186	78	168	83	155	74	165	...	...	70	165	81	158	98	65	37	108
	5	164	138	147	132	183	98	155	100	141	101	149	...	...	86	155	96	144	79	88	93	134
	6	126	121	124	128	136	38	144	49	130	40	126	...	...	87	91	45	132	65	57	91	63
	7	119	118	118	113	137	40	131	47	126	42	129	...	...	44	127	43	130	48	66	20	91
	8	57	58	56	58	70	25	67	32	58	31	56	...	...	27	59	33	58	22	24	37	33
	9	145	125	150	141	184	51	179	73	149	64	161	...	...	68	155	67	157	55	179	74	129
	10	207	182	197	190	222	116	211	145	181	129	133	...	...	108	217	122	197	111	85	170	107
	11	161	143	185	139	212	87	196	115	164	101	173	...	...	82	187	99	150	83	155	90	106
	12	168	134	167	156	194	47	181	48	179	43	183	...	...	33	189	46	184	96	78	100	112
	13	186	106	187	183	236	78	199	99	178	67	201	...	...	57	206	65	201	112	59	142	104
	14	180	75	115	107	156	60	119	78	101	52	120	...	...	62	125	56	121	156	39	101	57
	15	144	129	152	139	186	90	134	90	132	62	155	...	...	46	168	79	141	121	81	82	56
	16	163	141	165	159	206	59	177	79	154	64	165	...	...	50	108	63	169	108	76	124	91
	17	84	72	84	91	96	68	93	76	81	72	85	...	...	67	93	69	88	69	59	92	68
	18	84	124	125	122	123	72	125	80	118	74	118	...	...	70	123	68	129	79	68	95	64
	19	149	129	158	147	205	64	166	87	138	61	166	...	...	53	174	58	166	92	66	134	81
	20	110	84	122	115	156	73	123	87	109	72	122	...	...	61	123	61	128	78	45	109	82
	21	90	118	85	79	103	39	113	48	101	48	98	...	...	39	105	46	98	81	44	97	57
	22	92	186	85	90	100	73	137	77	127	72	131	...	...	62	138	65	130	80	63	113	87
	23	140	164	150	147	181	90	161	79	162	78	164	...	...	77	162	83	157	90	72	129	83
	24	99	107	102	99	117	79	108	87	105	76	100	...	...	159	51	71	118	67	76	102	82
	25	45	44	46	46	59	22	62	21	56	21	57	...	...	19	51	20	61	37	24	20	23
	26	76	70	81	73	80	51	83	53	81	52	80	...	...	53	77	63	75	30	60	54	63
	27	121	108	119	109	136	46	129	52	117	42	127	...	...	42	124	43	124	54	61	45	104
	28	102	93	103	101	139	53	121	62	102	65	103	...	...	53	112	59	102	63	62	77	77
	29	108	87	122	103	133	39	120	43	116	33	123	...	...	36	130	32	126	61	46	55	91
	30	160	120	167	164	194	60	156	81	175	51	155	...	...	51	158	53	159	94	66	94	120
	31	128	115	158	124	173	40	154	46	142	37	143	...	...	33	153	36	148	63	74	77	95
	32	81	81	86	86	90	34	69	31	77	31	77	...	...	24	90	28	78	29	68	71	35
Riverhead.	1	38	68	50	37	56	31	56	33	65	49	46	...	...	28	56	39	54	30	85	33	44
	2	108	93	86	87	122	96	103	94	98	96	96	...	...	83	104	82	104	111	58	85	59
	3	142	80	148	140	194	95	153	92	148	100	142	...	...	88	156	85	162	94	75	104	101
	4	145	112	156	141	180	63	166	66	154	76	145	...	...	52	171	59	167	68	94	72	91
	5	223	193	216	218	260	72	265	70	269	85	254	...	...	66	275	63	285	110	138	121	148
	6	227	171	232	233	256	63	264	69	261	89	233	...	...	82	252	63	265	84	120	89	157
	7	175	161	184	164	199	81	215	90	200	88	203	...	...	98	193	79	205	72	136	94	158

VOTE OF SUFFOLK COUNTY, 1920—*Continued.*

Towns	Dist. No.	Justice of the Supreme Court.					Rep. in Congr's.		State Senator.		Mem. Assembly. 1st Dist.		Mem. Assembly. 2d Dist.		County Treas.		District Attorney.		Amend. No. 1.		Prop'tion No. 1.	
		Aspinall, Rep.-Cit.	Strong, Rep.	Dike, Rep.	MacCrate, Rep.	Jaycox, Rep.-Cit.	Kennedy, Dem.	Hicks, Rep.-Proh.	Carroll, Dem.	Thompson, Rep.	Garvey, Dem.	Downs, Rep.	Reylek, Dem.	Bailey, Rep.	Raynor, Dem.	Scudder, Rep.	Collins, Dem.	Young, Rep.	For.	Against.	For.	Against.
Southold.	1	48	43	48	43	45	16	56	29	41	27	42	...	...	21	51	25	43	51	14	37	35
	2	226	202	225	215	234	11	262	17	247	24	240	...	...	17	242	20	247	87	55	97	106
	3	85	72	85	84	97	24	128	30	111	30	111	...	...	37	95	27	114	41	24	89	33
	4	180	131	175	173	214	81	193	88	182	92	178	...	...	71	199	73	204	116	54	126	80
	5	146	138	149	145	168	55	187	61	168	61	163	...	...	56	165	61	173	99	60	109	73
	6	191	219	197	194	224	88	230	86	214	95	205	...	...	81	223	87	226	114	51	144	70
	7	106	114	113	115	127	77	132	77	125	81	122	...	...	70	128	67	138	87	51	104	50
	8	29	29	29	30	31	24	31	26	29	27	29	...	...	24	30	22	32	26	10	29	12
	9	148	107	150	138	171	112	170	118	159	127	149	...	...	117	151	112	167	86	85	92	123
	10	184	151	187	179	206	54	208	57	200	62	196	...	...	52	201	59	197	64	76	71	111
	11	180	124	169	169	193	59	192	58	184	67	179	...	...	69	187	57	188	88	70	106	86
	12	132	112	125	133	159	80	159	83	150	97	143	...	...	83	142	90	141	81	81	105	96
	13	169	145	165	153	177	35	180	36	176	41	179	...	...	39	174	36	176	71	60	94	76
	14	224	192	224	212	231	75	238	86	216	91	221	...	...	82	224	84	225	106	91	119	96
Shelter Island.	1	253	219	246	252	277	67	308	76	284	78	275	...	...	94	264	71	286	154	112	172	137
East-hampton.	1	301	286	239	283	326	114	349	104	345	107	345	...	...	100	332	101	352	169	156	150	258
	2	216	224	221	226	238	149	219	148	207	133	[illegible]	...	...	102	253	158	218	234	67	180	71
	3	174	193	185	182	198	110	189	103	186	94	189	...	...	91	203	98	195	133	56	182	73
	4	67	83	67	66	80	45	96	46	87	45	83	...	...	44	79	43	86	49	36	48	58
	5	209	219	253	199	241	148	224	133	232	129	252	...	...	120	234	135	222	174	94	196	121
Southampton.	1	266	248	269	277	298	169	293	176	278	165	276	...	...	156	292	172	275	195	107	243	88
	2	209	225	228	233	252	204	239	245	196	213	220	...	...	187	234	211	239	218	89	283	96
	3	200	173	210	199	213	48	219	57	204	62	209	...	...	48	210	50	210	42	43	50	62
	4	144	140	150	141	164	42	172	46	166	46	168	...	...	44	170	45	166	51	61	83	93
	5	227	212	228	219	260	71	267	91	240	82	248	...	...	59	259	86	242	124	75	142	187
	6	338	312	364	339	387	65	411	70	382	75	378	...	...	63	383	74	378	190	127	188	196
	7	202	183	212	203	232	74	243	89	211	86	221	...	...	59	258	89	214	146	95	149	160
	8	151	132	152	149	177	88	175	96	160	96	159	...	...	91	164	88	166	124	80	135	110
	9	277	227	293	283	305	98	317	98	301	94	301	...	...	87	308	95	303	120	157	145	184
	10	333	312	347	330	367	121	360	117	354	112	363	...	...	103	370	103	373	188	122	207	191
	11	198	198	199	198	220	68	224	64	219	58	223	...	...	59	212	58	229	87	66	110	91
	12	136	135	139	133	152	36	157	36	154	37	149	...	..	33	148	35	149	73	41	93	51
	13	198	175	203	201	218	41	214	37	207	39	212	...	...	35	215	35	215	42	50	33	77
Huntington.	1	179	168	179	157	190	72	196	89	173	...	...	67	191	59	202	99	165	141	53	106	127
	2	194	207	193	178	217	85	236	93	224	...	...	79	211	71	234	124	201	129	105	134	139
	3	253	223	229	206	246	59	271	76	241	...	...	57	251	42	270	121	203	150	117	129	171
	4	198	211	200	185	234	75	227	93	207	...	...	61	220	59	235	135	176	134	79	134	119
	5	383	390	376	343	413	82	433	95	421	...	...	80	398	79	418	159	361	144	97	104	182
	6	238	280	260	250	270	106	290	122	269	...	...	77	298	83	316	166	237	198	136	234	156
	7	147	146	154	161	158	72	161	83	144	...	...	49	169	52	168	91	140	80	86	88	92
	8	226	239	220	215	242	64	283	75	253	...	...	63	256	55	276	90	245	125	95	137	143
	9	338	316	346	352	394	173	390	199	365	...	...	183	350	138	421	202	351	152	128	171	169
	10	308	282	317	317	347	132	369	159	39	...	..	112	362	93	401	151	337	189	123	224	176
	11	161	183	172	169	176	63	179	88	152	...	...	46	186	37	204	82	156	98	112	107	119
	12	131	141	134	124	140	53	159	76	133	...	...	45	154	35	168	83	129	76	72	92	99
	13	227	289	272	240	295	103	321	115	302	...	...	105	287	89	310	184	250	170	152	173	220
	14	269	292	277	273	280	93	274	104	260	...	...	72	269	66	293	133	241	93	129	135	126
Smith-town.	1	312	260	310	289	313	110	326	137	311	...	...	113	313	121	309	121	315	60	120	70	134
	2	233	230	234	225	251	127	235	129	230	...	...	117	232	118	234	120	238	42	85	65	95
	3	103	100	109	105	115	175	105	168	102	...	...	149	118	160	111	169	109	146	54	188	54
	4	218	209	221	227	230	144	218	167	207	...	...	127	212	126	225	151	210	93	39	94	51
	5	46	47	44	53	52	55	50	60	44	...	...	50	55	59	48	66	41	57	46	74	37
Babylon.	1	286	290	295	263	336	117	312	143	279	...	...	69	341	68	315	98	332	118	166	139	221
	2	266	266	266	247	295	136	270	147	269	...	...	109	286	120	291	119	298	84	97	89	122
	3	222	251	228	212	259	187	263	159	232	...	...	90	236	107	264	137	269	128	118	171	146
	4	97	164	100	89	106	74	129	68	130	...	...	34	167	44	160	58	147	70	43	106	57
	5	168	179	174	171	188	179	140	185	134	...	...	97	206	102	199	180	132	147	74	222	69
	6	187	201	190	190	220	146	153	160	143	...	...	72	214	69	226	141	156	173	71	283	62
	7	272	268	260	259	298	111	311	136	275	...	...	66	374	104	301	112	301	154	100	183	147
	8	290	256	292	255	298	78	321	94	302	...	...	70	324	72	315	85	310	125	153	107	224
	9	268	276	270	249	274	88	297	109	264	...	...	57	321	81	293	88	290	162	113	197	115
	10	63	71	72	63	73	36	76	34	74	...	...	24	89	31	80	31	76	53	29	64	40
	11	119	148	129	118	146	96	148	101	130	...	...	94	135	69	132	90	141	10	2	128	52
	12	92	96	92	81	103	31	105	40	94	...	...	29	109	29	110	26	102	67	35	79	37
Islip.	1	87	99	96	83	106	70	102	87	82	...	...	50	116	61	107	65	99	76	52	71	64
	2	309	273	310	280	315	72	316	81	307	...	...	67	309	64	320	74	318	100	119	94	145
	3	139	119	143	127	156	74	154	96	129	...	...	72	152	72	148	78	146	111	49	130	64
	4	211	206	212	200	231	103	232	140	189	...	...	92	238	87	241	105	216	160	87	192	104
	5	133	120	144	143	182	81	154	97	135	...	...	106	131	80	148	71	160	97	71	129	73
	6	232	177	239	219	273	103	242	172	178	...	...	104	227	94	245	108	235	139	115	169	143
	7	152	159	163	105	199	128	190	148	178	...	...	122	181	133	137	139	173	202	132	168	91
	8	90	105	95	94	101	92	81	120	67	...	...	126	68	74	100	98	78	90	66	123	61
	9	320	328	317	305	322	27	349	44	332	...	...	57	304	28	325	46	326	27	65	97	75
	10	50	45	51	43	53	49	61	57	47	...	...	44	58	44	56	52	52	55	31	54	49
	11	217	183	210	187	242	84	232	105	207	...	...	80	222	89	219	84	227	168	116	128	90
	12	193	194	204	191	221	88	258	102	197	...	...	63	235	73	230	95	227	122	75	176	71
	13	174	157	179	169	218	92	204	107	179	...	...	82	190	89	195	92	181	116	94	134	124
	14	275	215	277	243	326	98	305	126	275	...	...	140	253	101	279	90	306	145	115	165	158
	15	89	60	75	88	122	169	85	195	66	...	...	136	101	141	82	158	84	139	43	171	54
	16	169	128	173	144	164	47	164	52	156	...	...	39	166	41	171	45	161	104	79	93	119
	17	150	150	159	148	180	88	164	105	150	...	...	78	162	78	170	92	155	118	72	164	80
	18	202	171	198	196	217	82	201	102	180	...	...	79	192	82	202	72	211	79	82	96	90
	19	141	142	142	126	146	99	144	108	124	...	...	89	147	81	154	94	139	124	75	167	70
	20	178	183	173	176	184	69	188	107	147	...	...	86	169	55	190	52	193	121	72	154	67
Totals		21225	20370	21743	20567	24148	9819	23940	11164	21879	5196	12092	4176	10970	8734	23689	10313	22762	12563	9659	14468	12283

VOTE IN NEW YORK STATE, 1920—For President and Governor.

Counties.	President.						Governor.					
	Cox, Dem.	Harding, Rep.	Debs, Soc.	Watkins, Proh.	W. W. Cox, Soc.-L.	Christensen, Far.-L.	Smith, Dem.	Miller, Rep.	Cannon, Soc.	Thompson, Proh.	Quinn, Soc.-L.	Malone, Far.-L.
Albany	28,376	48,750	1,438	244	63	118	37,572	39,067	967	751	57	121
Allegany	2,799	10,898	513	441	24	22	2,886	10,428	495	588	20	30
Bronx	45,741	106,050	32,923	214	432	1,949	105,301	43,390	25,585	540	405	10,100
Broome	9,251	24,759	1,1[illegible]0	623	60	98	9,950	22,481	1,031	779	73	107
Cattaraugus	6,693	16,083	[illegible]	481	39	75	7,043	14,957	568	740	37	98
Cayuga	6,343	15,234	639	191	70	33	6,990	14,538	566	343	60	46
Chautauqua	6,781	27,618	3,143	860	114	62	8,380	25,254	2,705	1,176	111	108
Chemung	7,060	17,864	431	633	34	46	9,062	15,143	325	839	30	70
Chenango	3,735	10,116	68	282	9	14	3,197	9,866	53	293	12	36
Clinton	4,110	9,062	29	166	7	11	4,800	7,536	36	223	3	11
Columbia	5,203	9,284	211	95	15	15	5,613	8,763	188	268	12	48
Cortland	2,541	9,606	136	218	9	6	2,929	8,883	99	256	8	6
Delaware	4,528	11,719	150	269	8	27	4,171	10,893	112	392	20	104
Dutchess	9,938	21,152	882	167	36	71	12,022	18,212	758	310	36	129
Erie	40,436	99,762	15,1[illegible]1	1,430	536	521	62,315	82,730	12,222	1,947	479	544
Essex	2,218	8,042	47	61	2	9	2,822	7,660	33	139	23	37
Franklin	3,825	9,786	62	178	2	12	4,543	8,413	102	166	5	26
Fulton	3,192	10,946	888	436	42	35	4,035	9,863	800	588	33	36
Genesee	2,570	9,628	539	152	21	13	2,831	9,081	499	298	21	25
Greene	3,498	6,323	264	160	17	20	3,546	6,062	236	246	15	42
Hamilton	516	881	3	4	0	2	614	674	2	6	0	5
Herkimer	6,507	14,310	793	264	25	25	7,786	12,629	683	344	29	39
Jefferson	7,925	22,072	252	406	36	510	8,753	20,223	153	463	44	530
Kings	119,612	292,692	45,100	733	638	3,473	244,697	154,078	34,535	3,030	795	21,452
Lewis	2,673	5,906	24	76	3	10	2,731	5,444	22	93	1	11
Livingston	3,571	9,488	497	192	18	17	3,913	9,094	446	290	11	19
Madison	3,797	11,094	230	182	23	22	3,963	10,374	186	299	15	21
Monroe	28,523	73,809	11,089	1,324	298	678	38,280	64,871	8,883	2,383	340	824
Montgomery	5,911	12,835	476	134	43	26	7,252	11,390	394	225	39	46
Nassau	8,595	33,089	1,254	155	46	182	15,282	24,804	925	495	47	1,044
New York	135,249	275,013	46,049	463	567	7,079	268,316	136,580	34,223	1,117	582	19,852
Niagara	7,415	21,193	1,872	380	67	104	9,966	18,202	1,629	1,678	104	94
Oneida	15,560	36,311	2,297	412	133	78	19,744	32,181	2,038	638	133	89
Onondaga	23,308	57,008	4,707	640	221	163	29,493	51,406	4,043	1,173	213	132
Ontario	5,678	13,361	914	196	21	24	5,849	13,164	902	357	21	49
Orange	10,567	24,558	1,573	292	52	93	12,598	21,618	1,457	616	50	285
Orleans	2,266	8,305	620	176	13	30	2,487	7,793	598	319	18	41
Oswego	8,045	17,905	491	474	28	36	8,965	16,360	443	665	14	47
Otsego	6,275	12,112	134	391	13	36	5,751	11,646	83	537	10	82
Putnam	1,406	3,447	23	20	8	8	1,669	2,858	17	71	6	51
Queens	35,296	94,360	6,143	142	179	1,204	75,938	45,140	4,361	741	262	8,651
Rensselaer	20,224	28,810	1,849	278	94	116	23,774	25,451	1,526	434	88	89
Richmond	9,373	17,844	712	111	48	170	15,352	10,541	426	282	51	908
Rockland	5,057	11,169	498	80	26	67	6,817	8,874	388	219	16	281
St. Lawrence	7,213	24,651	372	282	32	56	8,023	22,644	325	325	16	58
Saratoga	6,905	16,222	351	290	17	73	9,038	13,239	216	575	21	129
Schenectady	8,741	19,208	4,941	509	117	68	12,177	16,255	4,068	877	128	120
Schoharie	3,697	5,572	30	215	11	12	3,107	5,669	26	312	7	48
Schuyler	1,231	3,827	151	138	12	9	1,157	3,727	134	118	12	17
Seneca	3,023	6,260	250	135	16	12	3,268	6,094	233	265	10	12
Steuben	7,401	18,335	1,217	784	79	52	8,015	17,020	1,113	1,167	76	59
Suffolk	8,852	26,737	596	223	38	118	13,667	2[illegible],383	435	790	43	601
Sullivan	3,623	8,029	671	98	11	26	4,419	6,777	499	236	13	143
Tioga	2,406	6,772	83	223	11	16	2,152	6,551	64	295	9	39
Tompkins	3,487	9,508	288	250	19	21	4,056	8,812	249	300	14	19
Ulster	8,759	19,001	301	455	20	76	10,174	16,129	189	774	24	198
Warren	3,227	9,009	189	101	9	20	4,704	6,815	117	232	15	40
Washington	4,124	13,647	162	123	13	24	5,486	11,522	81	227	3	58
Wayne	4,289	13,333	304	241	20	18	3,982	13,026	295	406	18	32
Westchester	28,060	76,020	6,097	435	238	485	44,367	58,796	4,691	702	237	1,938
Wyoming	2,442	9,134	294	194	16	21	2,635	8,554	292	247	18	19
Yates	1,571	5,638	52	122	2	6	1,496	5,229	34	304	2	12
Totals	781,238	1,871,167	203,201	19,653	4,841	18,413	1,261,812	1,335,878	159,804	35,509	5,015	69,908

(See page 385, 1920 Eagle Almanac, for 1916 and 1912 vote for President and 1918 vote for Governor.)

VOTE FOR AMENDMENT NO. 1 AND PROPOSITION NO. 1, ALL BOROUGHS, N. Y. CITY.

		Mhtn.	Bronx.	Bkln.	Queens.	Rich'd.	Totals.
AMENDMENT NO. 1. "Shall the proposed amendment to sections two, four, five, eleven and twelve of article seven of the Constitution, in relation to debts contracted by the State." be approved?	Yes.	234,358	89,056	216,461	66,800	12,935	619,610
	No.	99,239	47,253	1[illegible]6,290	32,594	5,976	301,352
PROPOSITION NO. 1. "Shall chapter eight hundred seventy-two of the laws of nineteen hundred and wenty, entitled 'An act making provision for issuing bonds to the amount of not to exceed forty-five million dollars for the payment of a bonus to persons who served in the military or naval service of the United States at any time between the sixth day of April, nineteen hundred and seventeen, and the eleventh day of November, nineteen hundred and eighteen, and providing for a submission of the same to the people to be voted upon at the general election to be held in the year nineteen hundred and twenty'" be approved?	Yes.	260,475	113,292	266,157	81,355	16,468	737,747
	No.	119,601	46,760	127,171	22,706	7,020	323,258

GOVERNORS OF STATES AND TERRITORIES.

States.	Governors.	Secretary of State.	Official Term of Governor. Yrs.	Official Term of Governor. Expires.	Gov. Salary.	Legislature Meets.	Legislature Time	Legislature Limit	Next Gov. St. Elec.
Alabama	T. E. Kilby, D.	W. P. Cobb	4	Jan., 1923	$7,500	Jan. 1923	Quad	54 dys	Nov. 1922
Arizona	T. E. Campbell, R.	E. R. Hall	2	Jan., 1923	6,500	Jan. 1921	Bien.	60 dys	Nov. 1922
Arkansas	T. C. McRae, D.	R. C. Hopper	2	Jan., 1923	5,000	Jan. 1921	Bien.	60 dys	Nov. 1922
California	Wm. D. Stephens, R.	F. C. Jordan	4	Jan., 1923	10,000	Jan. 1921	Bien.	90 dys	Nov. 1922
Colorado	O. H. Shoup, R.	J. R. Noland	2	Jan., 1923	5,000	Jan. 1921	Bien.	None	Nov. 1922
Connecticut	E. J. Lake, R.	D. J. Warren	2	Jan., 1923	5,000	Jan. 1921	Bien.	5 mos.	Nov. 1922
Delaware	W. D. Denney, R.	E. C. Johnson.	4	Jan., 1925	4,000	Jan. 1921	Bien.	60 dys	Nov. 1924
Florida	C. A. Hardee, D.	H. C. Crawford	4	Jan., 1925	6,000	Apr. 1921	Bien.	60 dys	Nov. 1924
Georgia	T. W. Hardwick, D.	S. G. McLendon	2	July, 1923	7,500	Jun. 1923	Bien.	50 dys	Nov. 1922
Idaho	D. W. Davis, R.	R. O. Jones	2	Jan., 1923	5,000	Jan. 1921	Bien.	60 dys	Nov. 1922
Illinois	L. Small, R.	L. L. Emmerson	4	Jan., 1925	12,000	Jan. 1921	Bien.	None	Nov. 1924
Indiana	W. T. McCray, R.	E. I. Jackson	4	Jan., 1925	8,000	Jan. 1921	Bien.	60 dys	Nov. 1924
Iowa	N. E. Kendall, R.	W. C. Ramsay	2	Jan., 1923	5,000	Jan. 1921	Bien.	None	Nov. 1922
Kansas	H. J. Allen, R.	L. J. Pettijohn.	2	Jan., 1923	5,000	Jan. 1921	Bien.	50 dys	Nov. 1922
Kentucky	Ed. P. Morrow, R.	F. A. Vaughan	4	Dec., 1923	6,500	Jan. 1922	Bien.	60 dys	Nov. 1923
Louisiana	J. M. Parker, D.	J. J. Bailey	4	May, 1920	7,500	May 1924	Bien.	60 dys	Apr. 1924
Maine	F. H. Parkhurst, R.	F. W. Ball	2	Jan., 1923	5,000	Jan. 1921	Bien.	None	Sept. 1922
Maryland	A. C. Ritchie, D.	T. W. Simmons	4	Jan., 1924	4,500	Jan. 1920	Bien.	90 dys	Nov. 1923
Massachusetts	C. H. Cox, R.	F. W. Cook	2	Jan., 1922	10,000	Jan. 1921	Ann.	None	Nov. 1922
Michigan	A. J. Groesbeck, R.	C. J. DeLand	2	Dec., 1922	5,000	Jan. 1921	Bien.	None	Nov. 1922
Minnesota	J. A. O. Preus, R.	M. Holm	2	Jan., 1923	7,000	Jan. 1921	Bien.	100dys	Nov. 1922
Mississippi	Lee M. Russell, D.	Jos. W. Power	4	Jan., 1924	7,500	Jan. 1922	Bien.	None	Nov. 1923
Missouri	A. M. Hyde, R.	C. U. Becker	4	Jan., 1925	7,500	Jan. 1921	Bien.	70 dys	Nov. 1924
Montana	J. M. Dixon, R.	C. T. Stewart.	4	Jan., 1925	7,500	Jan. 1921	Bien.	60 dys	Nov. 1924
Nebraska	S. R. McKelvie, R.	D. M. Amsberry	2	Jan., 1923	7 500	Jan. 1921	Bien.	60 dys	Nov. 1922
Nevada	E. D. Boyle, D.	Geo. Brodigan	4	Jan., 1923	7,000	Jan. 1921	Bien.	60 dys	Nov. 1922
N. Hampshire	A. O. Brown, R.	E. C. Bean	2	Jan., 1923	3,000	Jan. 1921	Bien.	None	Nov. 1922
New Jersey	Ed. I. Edwards, D.	T. F. Martin	3	Jan., 1923	10,000	Jan. 1921	Ann.	None	Nov. 1922
New Mexico	M. C. Mechem, R.	M. Martinez	2	Jan., 1923	5,000	Jan. 1921	Bien.	60 dys	Nov. 1922
New York	N. L. Miller R.	J. J. Lyons	2	Jan., 1923	10,000	Jan. 1921	Ann.	None	Nov. 1922
No. Carolina	C. Morrison, D.	J. B. Grimes	4	Jan., 1925	7,000	Jan. 1921	Bien.	60 dys	Nov. 1924
No. Dakota	L. J. Frazier, R.	Thos. Hall	2	Jan., 1923	5,000	Jan. 1921	Bien.	60 dys	Nov. 1922
Ohio	H. L. Davis, R.	H. C. Smith	2	Jan., 1923	10,000	Jan. 1921	Bien.	None	Nov. 1922
Oklahoma	J. B. A. Robertson, D.	J. S. Morris	4	Jan., 1923	4,500	Jan. 1921	Bien.	60 dys	Nov. 1922
Oregon	B. W. Olcott, R.	S. A. Kozer	4	Jan., 1923	5,000	Jan. 1921	Bien.	40 dys	Nov. 1922
Pennsylvania	W. C. Sproul, R.	C. E. Woods	4	Jan., 1923	18,000	Jan. 1921	Bien.	None	Nov. 1922
Rhode Island	E. J. San Souci, R.	J. F. Parker	2	Jan., 1923	8,000	Jan. 1921	Ann.	60 dys	Nov. 1922
So. Carolina	R. A. Cooper, D.	W. B. Dove	2	Jan., 1923	3,000	Jan. 1921	Ann.	None	Nov. 1922
So. Dakota	W. H. McMaster, R.	C. A. Burkhart	2	Jan., 1923	3,000	Jan. 1921	Bien.	60 dys	Nov. 1922
Tennessee	A. A. Taylor, R.	I. B. Stevens	2	Jan., 1923	7,500	Jan. 1921	Bien.	75 dys	Nov. 1922
Texas	P. M. Neff, D.	C. D. Mims	2	Jan., 1923	4,000	Jan. 1921	Bien.	60 dys	Nov. 1922
Utah	C. R. Mabey, R.	H. E. Crockett	4	Jan., 1925	6,000	Jan. 1921	Bien.	60 dys	Nov. 1924
Vermont	J. Hartness, R.	H. A. Black	2	Jan., 1923	3,000	Jan. 1921	Bien.	None	Nov. 1922
Virginia	Westmoreland Davis, D.	B. O. James	4	Feb., 1922	5,000	Jan. 1922	Bien.	60 dys	Nov. 1921
Washington	L. F. Hart, R.	J. G. Hinkle	4	Jan., 1925	6,000	Jan. 1921	Bien.	60 dys	Nov. 1924
West Virginia	E. F. Morgan, R.	H. G. Young	4	Mar., 1925	10,000	Jan. 1921	Bien.	60 dys	Nov. 1924
Wisconsin	J. J. Blaine, R.	E. Hall	2	Jan., 1923	5,000	Jan. 1921	Bien.	None	Nov. 1922
Wyoming	R. D. Carey, R.	W. E. Chaplin	4	Jan., 1923	4,000	Jan. 1922	Bien.	40 dys	Nov. 1922

Territories and Insular Possessions.

Territories.	*Governors.	Secretary.
Alaska	Thos. Riggs, Jr.	C. E. Davidson.
Hawaii	Chas. J. McCarthy	C. P. Iaukea.
Porto Rico	Arthur Yager	R. S. Pacheco.

Territories.	*Governors.	V.-Gov. & Treas.
Philippine Is.	F. B. Harrison	C. E. Yeater, V. G.
Guam	I. C. Wettengel	J. T. Martinez, Tr.
Canal Zone	Gen. C. Harding	A. L. Flint
Samoa (Am.)	W. Evans	....
Virgin Isls.	Adm. J. W. Oman	....

*Territorial Governors are appointed by the President.

SUFFOLK COUNTY VOTE.

Vote for Other Candidates—Pres., Debs, Soc., 598; Watkins, Proh., 235; W. W. Cox, Soc.-L., 40; Christensen, Farmer-Lab., 121. Gov., Cannon, Soc., 435; Thompson, Proh., 790; Quinn, Soc.-Lab., 43; Malone, Farmer-Lab., 601; blank, 1,577; void, 408. Lieut.-Gov., Hughan, Soc., 541; Dietrich, Proh., 513; Crowley, Soc.-Lab., 54; Haffey, Farmer-Lab., 417; blank, 3,216; void, 336. Sec. of State, Noonan, Soc., 608; Taylor, Proh., 481; Phalor, Soc.-Lab., 46; Auyer, Farmer-Lab., 328; blank, 3,396; void, 306. Comptroller, Randolph, Soc., 603; Gray, Proh., 572; De Lee, Soc.-Lab., 49; Fincke, Farmer-Lab., 335; blank, 3,766; void, 286. State Treas., Kreuger, Soc., 586; McKee, Proh., 439; Withers, Soc.-Lab., 50; Cronk, Farmer-Lab., 263; blank, 3,625; void, 270. Atty. Gen., Meserole, Soc., 608; Burr, Proh., 495; Donohue, Soc.-Lab., 63; Serri, Farmer-Lab., 239; blank, 3,729; void, 286. State Engineer, Karapetoff, Soc., 588; Light, Proh., 442; Crawford, Soc.-Lab., 130; blank, 4,022; void, 272. Assoc. Judge Ct. of Appeals, Elkus, Dem., 8,846; Malkiel, Soc., 610; Axelrad, Soc., 540; Hart, Proh., 644; Baldwin, Proh., 467; Hale, Farmer-Lab., 338; Dwyer, Farmer-Lab., 389; blank, 15,054; void, 553. U. S. Senator, Panken, Soc., 579; Boole, Proh., 2,763; Carlson, Soc.-Lab., 61; Schneiderman, Farmer-Lab., 250; blank, 4,320; void, 313.

Justice of the Supreme Court—Garvin, Dem., 9,058; Humphreys, Dem., 8,423; McMahon, Dem., 7,228; Scudder, Dem., 14,055; Druhan, Dem., 5,900; Wolfman, Soc., 584; Rivkin, Soc., 535; Kayfetz, Soc., 488; Satra, Soc., 491; Testa, Soc., 489; Wilson, Proh., 501; Smith, Proh., 470; Watson, Proh., 393; W. Howell, Proh., 403; D. Howell, Proh., 306; Haskell, Farmer-Lab., 346; Kohler, Farmer-Lab., 262; Goldstein, Farmer-Lab., 225; Strahl, Farmer-Lab., 1,041; Brown, Single Tax, 82. Rep. in Congress.—Hinckley, Soc., 737. State Senator—Bache, Soc., 714. Mem. Assembly.—1st Dist., O. Grausalka, Soc., 291; 2d Dist., Burchard, Soc., 468; Duryea, Proh., 336. Dist. Attorney.—Dreusike, Soc., 664. Co. Treasurer.—Hinckley, Soc., 677; Bryant, Proh., 423. Co. Auditor.—Hulse, Dem., 9,207; Corwin, Rep., 23,215; A. Grausalke, Soc., 628; York, Proh., 417. Supt. of Poor.—Baker, Dem.-Rep., 30,158; Schneider, Soc., 1,055; Bishop, Proh., 883. Coroner.—Luce, Dem., 9,010; Hodges Dem. 7,426; Miles, Rep., 22,868; Moore, Rep., 21,659; Palma, Soc., 675; Nauman, Soc., 613; Sammis, Proh., 664.

NEW YORK PORT TRAFFIC, 1920.

(Exclusive of Domestic.)

Month.	Entrances. No. Ships.	Entrances. Net Tonnage.	Clearances. No. Ships.	Clearances. Net Tonnage.
January	372	1,143,126	410	1,450,777
February	377	1,174,913	329	1,054,269
March	440	1,322,013	410	1,369,829
April	431	1,302,177	386	1,243,000
May	444	1,343,052	390	1,258,996
June	508	1,545,144	436	1,364,297
July	510	1,627,721	462	1,518,406
August	537	1,634,719	499	1,649,416
September	506	1,747,266	493	1,669,392

CHANGES IN COST OF LIVING IN THE UNITED STATES, 1913 TO JUNE, 1920.

(Compiled by the Bureau of Labor Statistics, U. S. Dept. of Agriculture.)

The following table shows the increase in the cost of living in the United States from 1913 to June, 1920. These figures are averages based on the prices secured in 18 cities up to Dec., 1917, and in 31 cities from Dec., 1917, to June, 1920. The first column in the table shows the per cent. that the average expenditure for each group of items is of the average total expenditure per family, and each column that follows shows the per cent. of increase, at the date given, over the average cost of each item in 1913:

Item of Expenditure.	Per cent. of total expenditure.	Per cent. of increase from 1913 (average) to:							
		Dec., 1914.	Dec., 1915.	Dec., 1916.	Dec., 1917.	Dec., 1918.	June, 1919.	Dec., 1919.	June, 1920.
Food	38.2	5.0	5.0	26.0	57.0	87.0	84.0	97.0	119.0
Clothing	16.6	1.0	4.7	20.0	49.1	105.3	114.5	168.7	187.5
Housing	13.4	...	1.5	2.3	0.1	9.2	14.2	25.3	34.9
Fuel and light	5.3	1.0	1.0	8.4	24.1	47.9	45.6	56.8	71.9
Furniture and furnishings	5.1	4.0	10.6	27.8	50.6	113.6	125.1	163.5	192.7
Miscellaneous	21.3	3.0	7.4	13.3	40.5	65.8	73.2	90.2	101.4
Totals	100.0	3.0	3.6	18.3	42.4	74.4	77.3	99.3	116.5

In Dec., 1920, the Natl. Industrial Conference Board issued a statement containing the following percentages of change in the cost of living between July, 1920, and Dec., 1920: Food, 11.9 decrease; housing, 5.1 increase; clothing, 22.9 decrease; fuel and light, 20.5 increase; sundries, 3.8 increase.

AVERAGE RETAIL FOOD PRICES ON AUG. 15, 1913, TO 1920.

(Compiled by the Bureau of Labor Statistics, U. S. Dept. of Agriculture.)

Article.	Unit.	Cents							
		1913	1914	1915	1916	1917	1918	1919	1920
Bacon	lb.	28.3	28.8	27.1	29.2	43.1	54.0	57.7	54.8
Bread	lb.	5.6	6.3	7.1	7.1	10.2	9.9	10.1	11.9
Butter	lb.	35.4	36.1	31.4	36.5	47.6	53.9	64.1	67.0
Cheese	lb.	22.0	22.8	22.8	24.4	32.8	34.6	43.5	40.5
Chuck roast	lb.	16.5	17.5	16.4	17.6	21.7	28.3	36.6	27.5
Eggs, strictly fresh	doz.	33.0	33.2	30.5	36.3	46.1	53.6	60.2	63.6
Flour	lb.	3.3	3.5	4.1	4.4	7.6	6.8	7.4	8.4
Ham	lb.	28.4	29.1	26.3	30.0	39.4	48.5	56.9	60.2
Lamb	lb.	18.9	20.6	20.5	23.1	29.7	36.9	36.4	39.7
Lard	lb.	16.1	15.6	14.1	17.6	27.7	33.1	42.0	27.9
Milk	qt.	8.8	8.9	8.8	9.0	11.4	13.6	15.5	17.0
Onions	lb.	....	....	3.1	5.0	4.6	5.5	7.8	5.6
Pork chops	lb.	21.9	25.1	21.6	24.4	34.5	42.2	46.9	45.9
Potatoes	lb.	1.9	1.9	1.4	2.4	3.5	3.9	5.6	6.0
Rib roast	lb.	20.2	21.4	20.5	21.9	25.6	32.6	32.4	34.9
Rice	lb.	8.7	8.8	9.1	9.1	10.6	13.4	15.5	18.8
Steak, round	lb.	23.2	25.1	23.8	25.7	30.8	39.6	39.5	43.7
Steak, sirloin	lb.	26.4	27.9	26.5	28.4	32.9	41.5	42.1	47.3
Sugar	lb.	5.6	7.9	6.7	8.6	10.0	9.3	11.1	22.9

CHANGES IN UNION SCALE OF WAGES, 1913 TO 1920.

(Compiled by the Bureau of Labor Statistics, U. S. Dept. of Agriculture.)

The union wage scale figures represent the minimum wage of union members employed in the trades stated in New York as of May 15, 1920, brought into comparison with like figures for preceding years back to 1913:

Trade.	Rate per hour (cents).							
	1913	1914	1915	1916	1917	1918	1919	1920
Blacksmiths	44.4	44.4	44.4	53.1	53.1	72.5	80.0	80.0
Boilermakers	41.7	41.7	41.7	46.9	49.4	70.0	80.0	80.0
Bricklayers	70.0	75.0	75.0	75.0	75.0	81.0	87.5	125.0
Building laborers	22.5	22.5	25.0	25.0	30.0	40.5	40.5	75.0
Carpenters	62.5	62.5	62.5	62.5	68.8	68.8	75.0	112.0
Cement finishers	62.5	62.5	62.5	62.5	70.0	70.0	75.0	112.5
Compositors, book and job	50.0	50.0	50.0	52.1	52.1	58.3	75.0	93.8
Compositors, newspaper	66.7	66.7	66.7	66.7	66.7	71.1	96.7	122.2
Electrotypers	62.5	62.5	65.6	68.8	68.8	68.8	75.0	109.1
Granite cutters	50.0	50.0	50.0	50.0	50.0	68.8	79.0	100.0
Hod carriers	37.5	37.5	37.4	37.5	42.5	47.0	50.0	87.5
Inside wiremen	56.3	60.0	60.0	60.0	65.0	65.0	75.0	112.5
Linotype operators, book and job	54.2	54.2	54.2	54.2	54.2	58.3	75.0	93.8
Linotype operators, newspapers	66.7	66.7	66.7	66.7	66.7	71.1	96.7	122.2
Machinists	40.6	40.6	40.6	46.9	56.3	82.0	90.0	90.0
Molders, iron	38.9	41.7	41.7	41.7	47.2	52.8	75.0	88.0
Painters	50.0	50.0	50.0	62.5	62.5	62.5	75.0	112.5
Plasterers	68.8	68.8	68.8	75.0	75.0	75.0	93.8	118.8
Plasters' laborers	40.6	40.6	40.6	43.8	46.9	56.3	62.5	87.5
Plumbers	68.8	68.8	68.8	68.8	68.8	75.0	75.0	112.5
Sheet metal workers	59.4	62.5	62.5	62.5	62.5	70.0	75.0	112.5
Stonecutters	68.8	68.8	68.8	68.8	68.8	68.8	84.4	112.5
Structural iron workers	62.5	62.5	62.5	66.3	68.8	80.0	87.5	112.5

QUEENS BRIDGES.

Name.	Water Crossing.	Type of Bridge.	Feet: Clear Height. above M. H. W.	Greatest Span.	Length of— Bridge.	Length of— App'ch.	Tot. Width of Bridge.
Vernon Avenue	Newtown Creek	Bascule	24	172	1698.6	1500	60
Greenpoint Avenue	Newtown Creek	Swing	15	206.7	282	75	32
Meeker Avenue	Newtown Creek	Swing	8	200	284	84	31
Grand Street	Newtown Creek	Swing	10	229.6	550	320	36
Borden Avenue	Dutch Kills Creek	Retractile	3.5	169	265	90	50.5
Flushing	Flushing Creek	Bascule	12	68	351	262	52
Strong's Causeway	Flushing Creek	Swing	2	135	135.2	44	33.2
Little Neck	Alley Creek	Swing	2	90	157.2	65	18

THE LEAGUE OF NATIONS.

COVENANT.

The high contracting parties, in order to promote international co-operation and to achieve international peace and security—by the acceptance of obligations not to resort to war; by the prescription of open, just and honorable relations between nations; by the firm establishment of the understandings of international law as the actual rule of conduct among governments, and by the maintenance of justice and a scrupulous respect for all treaty obligations in the dealings of organized peoples with one another—agree to this Covenant of the League of Nations.

ARTICLE 1.
(Membership.)

The original members of the League of Nations shall be those of the signatories which are named in the Annex to this Covenant and also such of those other States named in the Annex as shall accede without reservation to this Covenant. Such accession shall be effected by a declaration deposited with the Secretariat within two months of the coming into force of the Covenant. Notice thereof shall be sent to all other members of the League.

Any fully self-governing State, Dominion or Colony not named in the Annex may become a member of the League if its admission is agreed to by two-thirds of the Assembly, provided that it shall give effective guarantees of its sincere intention to observe its international obligations, and shall accept such regulations as may be prescribed by the League in regard to its military, naval and air forces and armaments.

Any member of the League may, after two years' notice of its intention so to do, withdraw from the League, provided that all its international obligations and all its obligations under this Covenant shall have been fulfilled at the time of its withdrawal.

ARTICLE 2.
(Executive and Administration Machinery.)

The action of the League under this Covenant shall be effected through the instrumentality of an Assembly and of a Council, with a permanent Secretariat.

ARTICLE 3.
(The Assembly.)

The Assembly shall consist of representatives of the members of the League.

The Assembly shall meet at stated intervals and from time to time as occasion may require at the seat of the League or at such other place as may be decided upon.

The Assembly may deal at its meetings with any matter within the sphere of action of the League or affecting the peace of the world.

At meetings of the Assembly each member of the League shall have one vote, and may have not more than three representatives.

ARTICLE 4.
(The Council.)

The Council shall consist of representatives of the principal Allied and Associated Powers, together with the representatives of four other members of the League. These four members of the League shall be selected by the Assembly from time to time in its discretion. Until the appointment of the representatives of the four members of the League first selected by the Assembly, representatives of Belgium, Brazil, Spain and Greece shall be members of the Council.

With the approval of the majority of the Assembly, the Council may name additional members of the League whose representatives shall always be members of the Council; the Council with like approval may increase the number of members of the League to be selected by the Assembly for representation on the Council.

The Council shall meet from time to time as occasion may require, and at least once a year, at the seat of the League, or at such other place as may be decided upon.

The Council may deal at its meetings with any matter within the sphere of action of the League or affecting the peace of the world.

Any member of the League not represented on the Council shall be invited to send a representative to sit as a member at any meeting of the Council during the consideration of matters specifically affecting the interests of that member of the League.

At meetings of the Council, each member of the League represented on the Council shall have one vote, and may have not more than one representative.

ARTICLE 5.
(Decision by Unanimity or Majority; Initial Meetings.)

Except where otherwise expressly provided in this Covenant or by the terms of the present Treaty, decisions at any meeting of the Assembly or of the Council shall require the agreement of all the members of the League represented at the meeting.

All matters of procedure at meetings of the Assembly or of the Council, including the appointment of committees to investigate particular matters, shall be regulated by the Assembly or by the Council and may be decided by a majority of the members of the League represented at the meeting.

The first meeting of the Assembly and the first meeting of the Council shall be summoned by the President of the United States of America.

ARTICLE 6.
(The Secretariat.)

The permanent Secretariat shall be established at the seat of the League. The Secretariat shall comprise a Secretary General and such secretaries and staff as may be required.

The first Secretary General shall be the person named in the Annex; thereafter the Secretary General shall be appointed by the Council with the approval of the majority of the Assembly.

The secretaries and staff of the Secretariat shall be appointed by the Secretary General with the approval of the Council.

The Secretary General shall act in that capacity at all meetings of the Assembly and of the Council.

The expenses of the Secretariat shall be borne by the members of the League in accordance with the apportionment of the expenses of the International Bureau of the Universal Postal Union.

ARTICLE 7.
(League Capital; Status of Officials and Property; Sex Equality.)

The seat of the League is established at Geneva.

The Council may at any time decide that the seat of the League shall be established elsewhere.

All positions under or in connection with the League, including the Secretariat, shall be open equally to men and women.

Representatives of the members of the League and officials of the League when engaged on the business of the League shall enjoy diplomatic privileges and immunities.

The buildings and other property occupied by the League or its officials or by representatives attending its meetings shall be inviolable.

ARTICLE 8.
(Disarmament.)

The members of the League recognize that the maintenance of peace requires the reduction of national armaments to the lowest point consistent with national safety and the enforcement by common action of international obligations.

The Council, taking account of the geographical situation and circumstances of each State, shall formulate plans for such reduction for the consideration and action of the several governments.

Such plans shall be subject to reconsideration and revision at least every ten years.

After these plans shall have been adopted by the several governments, the limits of armaments therein fixed shall not be exceeded without the concurrence of the Council.

The members of the League agree that the manufacture by private enterprise of munitions and implements of war is open to grave objections. The Council shall advise how the evil effects attendant upon such manufacture can be prevented, due regard being had to the necessities of those members of the League which are not able to manufacture the munitions and implements of war necessary for their safety.

The members of the League undertake to interchange full and frank information as to

THE LEAGUE OF NATIONS—*Continued.*

the scale of their armaments, their military, naval and air programs and the condition of such of their industries as are adaptable to warlike purposes.

ARTICLE 9.

(Disarmament Commission.)

A permanent commission shall be constituted to advise the Council on the execution of the provisions of Articles 1 and 8 and on military, naval and air questions generally.

ARTICLE 10.

(Territorial and Political Guarantees.)

The members of the League undertake to respect and preserve as against external aggression the territorial integrity and existing political independence of all members of the League. In case of any such aggression or in case of any threat or danger of such aggression the Council shall advise upon the means by which this obligation shall be fulfilled.

ARTICLE 11.

(Joint Action to Prevent War.)

Any war or threat of war, whether immediately affecting any of the members of the League or not, is hereby declared a matter of concern to the whole League, and the League shall take any action that may be deemed wise and effectual to safeguard the peace of the nations. In case any such emergency should arise the Secretary General shall on the request of any member of the League forthwith summon a meeting of the Council.

It is also declared to be the friendly right of each member of the League to bring to the attention of the Assembly or of the Council any circumstances whatever affecting international relations which threaten to disturb international peace or the good understanding between nations upon which peace depends.

ARTICLE 12.

(Postponement of War.)

The members of the League agree that if there should arise between them any dispute likely to lead to a rupture, they will submit the matter either to arbitration or to inquiry by the Council, and they agree in no case to resort to war until three months after the award by the arbitrators or the report of the Council.

In any case under this article the award of the arbitrators shall be made within a reasonable time, and the report of the Council shall be made within six months after the submission of the dispute.

ARTICLE 13.

(Arbitration of Justifiable Matters.)

The members of the League agree that whenever any dispute shall arise between them which they recognize to be suitable for submission to arbitration and which cannot be satisfactorily settled by diplomacy, they will submit the whole subject-matter to arbitration.

Disputes as to the interpretation of a treaty, as to any question of international law, as to the existence of any fact which if established would constitute a breach of any international obligation, or as to the extent and nature of the reparation to be made for any such breach, are declared to be among those which are generally suitable for submission to arbitration.

For the consideration of any such dispute the court or arbitration to which the case is referred shall be the court agreed on by the parties to the dispute or stipulated in any convention existing between them.

The members of the League agree that they will carry out in full good faith any award that may be rendered, and that they will not resort to war against a member of the League which complies therewith. In the event of any failure to carry out such an award, the Council shall propose what steps should be taken to give effect thereto.

ARTICLE 14.

(Permanent Court of International Justice.)

The Council shall formulate and submit to the members of the League for adoption plans for the establishment of a Permanent Court of International Justice. The court shall be competent to hear and determine any dispute of an international character which the parties thereto submit to it. The court may also give an advisory opinion upon and dispute or question referred to it by the Council or by the Assembly.

ARTICLE 15.

(Settlement of Disputes by Council or Assembly; Exclusion of Domestic Questions.)

If there should arise between members of the League any dispute likely to lead to a rupture, which is not submitted to arbitration in accordance with Article 13, the members of the League agree that they will submit the matter to the Council. Any party to the dispute may effect such submission by giving notice of the existence of the dispute to the Secretary General, who will make all necessary arrangements for a full investigation and consideration thereof.

For this purpose the parties to the dispute will communicate to the Secretary General, as promptly as possible, statements of their case with all the relevant facts and papers, and the Council may forthwith direct the publication thereof.

The Council shall endeavor to effect a settlement of the dispute, and if such efforts are successful, a statement shall be made public giving such facts and explanations regarding the dispute and the terms of settlement thereof as the Council may deem appropriate.

If the dispute is not thus settled, the Council either unanimously or by a majority vote shall make and publish a report containing a statement of the facts of the dispute and the recommendations which are deemed just and proper in regard thereto.

Any member of the League represented on the Council may make public a statement of the facts of the dispute and of its conclusions regarding the same.

If a report by the Council is unanimously agreed to by the members thereof other than the representatives of one or more of the parties to the dispute, the members of the League agree that they will not go to war with any party to the dispute which complies with the recommendations of the report.

If the Council fails to reach a report which is unanimously agreed to by the members thereof, other than the representatives of one or more of the parties to the dispute, the members of the League reserve to themselves the right to take such action as they shall consider necessary for the maintenance of right and justice.

If the dispute between the parties is claimed by one of them, and is found by the Council, to arise out of a matter which by international law is solely within the domestic jurisdiction of that party, the Council shall so report, and shall make no recommendation as to its settlement.

The Council may in any case under this article refer the dispute to the Assembly. The dispute shall be so conferred at the request of either party to the dispute, provided that such request be made within fourteen days after the submission of the dispute to the Council.

In any case referred to the Assembly, all provisions of this article and of Article 12 relating to the action and powers of the Council shall apply to the action and powers of the Assembly, provided that a report made by the Assembly, if concurred in by the representatives of those members of the League represented on the Council and a majority of the other members of the League, exclusive in each case of the representatives of the parties to the dispute, shall have the same force as a report by the Council concurred in by all the members thereof other than the representatives of one or more of the parties to the dispute.

ARTICLE 16.

(Sanctions.)

Should any members of the League resort to war in disregard of its covenants under Articles 12, 13 or 15, it shall ipso facto be deemed to have committed an act of war against all other members of the League, which hereby undertake immediately to subject it to the severance of all trade or financial relations, the prohibition of all intercourse between their nationals and the nationals of the covenant-breaking State, and the prevention of all financial, commercial or personal intercourse between the nationals of the covenant-breaking State and the nationals of any other State, whether a member of the League or not.

It shall be the duty of the Council in such case to recommend to the several governments

THE LEAGUE OF NATIONS—*Continued.*

concerned what effective military, naval or air force the members of the League shall severally contribute to the armed forces to be used to protect the covenants of the League.

The members of the League agree, further, that they will mutually support one another in the financial and economical measures which are taken under this article, in order to minimize the loss and inconvenience resulting from the above measures, and that they will mutually support one another in resisting any special measures aimed at one of their number by the covenant-breaking State, and that they will take the necessary steps to afford passage through their territory to the forces of any of the members of the League which are co-operating to protect the covenants of the League.

Any member of the League which has violated any covenant of the League may be declared to be no longer a member of the League by a vote of the Council concurred in by the representatives of all the other members of the League represented thereon.

ARTICLE 17.

(Disputes of Non-Members.)

In the event of a dispute between a member of the League and a State which is not a member of the League, or between States not members of the League, the State or States not members of the League shall be invited to accept the obligations of membership in the League for the purposes of such dispute, upon such conditions as the Council may deem just. If such invitation is accepted, the provisions of Articles 12 to 16 inclusive shall be applied with such modifications as may be deemed necessary by the Council.

Upon such invitation being given the Council shall immediately institute an inquiry into the circumstances of the dispute and recommend such action as may seem best and most effectual in the circumstances.

If a State so invited shall refuse to accept the obligations of membership in the League for the purposes of such dispute and shall resort to war against a member of the League, the provisions of Article 16 shall be applicable as against the State taking such action.

If both parties to the dispute when so invited refuse to accept the obligations of membership in the League for the purposes of such dispute, the Council may take such measures and make such recommendations as will prevent hostilities and will result in the settlement of disputes.

ARTICLE 18.

(Registration of International Engagements.)

Every treaty or international engagement entered into hereafter by any member of the League shall be forthwith registered with the Secretariat and shall as soon as possible be published by it. No such treaty or international engagement shall be binding until so registered.

ARTICLE 19.

(Revision of Former Treaties.)

The Assembly may from time to time advise the reconsideration by members of the League of treaties which have become inapplicable and the consideration of international conditions whose continuance might endanger the peace of the world.

ARTICLE 20.

(Abrogation of Understandings Not Consistent With the Covenant.

The members of the League severally agree that this Covenant is accepted as abrogating all obligations or understandings inter se which are inconsistent with the terms thereof, and solemnly undertake that they will not hereafter enter into any engagement inconsistent with the terms thereof.

In case any member of the League shall, before becoming a member of the League, have undertaken any obligations inconsistent with the terms of this Covenant, it shall be the duty of such members to take immediate steps to procure its release from such obligations.

ARTICLE 21.

(The Monroe Doctrine.)

Nothing in this Covenant shall be deemed to affect the validity of international engagements, such as treaties of arbitration or regional understandings like the Monroe Doctrine, for securing the maintenance of peace.

ARTICLE 22.

(Mandatory Tutelage of Colonies and Backward Races.)

To those colonies and territories which as a consequence of the late war have ceased to be under the sovereignty of the States which formerly governed them and which are inhabited by peoples not yet able to stand by themselves under the strenuous conditions of the modern world, there should be applied the principle that the well being and development of such peoples form a sacred trust of civilization and that securities for the performance of this trust should be embodied in this Covenant.

The best method of giving practical effect to this principle is that the tutelage of such peoples should be entrusted to advanced nations who by reason of their resources, their experience or their geographical position can best undertake this responsibility, and who are willing to accept it, and that this tutelage should be exercised by them as Mandatories on behalf of the League.

The character of the mandate must differ according to the stage of the development of the people, the geographical situation of the territory, its economic conditions and other similar circumstances.

Certain communities formerly belonging to the Turkish Empire have reached a stage of development where their existence as independent nations can be provisionally recognized subject to the rendering of administrative advice and assistance by a Mandatory until such time as they are able to stand alone. The wishes of these communities must be a principal consideration in the selection of the Mandatory.

Other peoples, especially those of Central Africa, are at such a stage that the Mandatory must be responsible for the administration of the territory under conditions which will guarantee freedom of conscience and religion, subject only to the maintenance of public order and morals, the prohibition of abuses such as the slave trade, the arms traffic and the liquor traffic, and the prevention of the establishment of fortifications or military and naval bases and of military training of the natives for other than police purposes and the defence of territory, and will also secure equal opportunities for the trade and commerce of other members of the League.

There are territories, such as Southwest Africa and certain of the South Pacific Islands, which, owing to the sparseness of their population, or their small size, or their remoteness from the centers of civilization, or their geographical contiguity to the territory of the Mandatory, and other circumstances, can be best administered under the laws of the Mandatory as integral portions of its territory, subject to the safeguards above mentioned in the interests of the indigenous population.

In every case of mandate the Mandatory shall render to the Council an annual report in reference to the territory committed to its charge.

The degree of authority, control or administration to be exercised by the Mandatory shall, if not previously agreed upon by the members of the League, be explicity defined in each case by the Council.

A permanent commission shall be constituted to receive and examine the annual reports of the Mandatories and to advise the Council on all matters relating to the observance of the mandates.

ARTICLE 23.

(Humanitarian Provisions; Freedom of Transit.)

Subject to and in accordance with the provisions of international conventions existing or hereafter to be agreed upon, the members of the League:

(a) will endeavor to secure and maintain fair and human conditions of labor for men, women and children, both in their own countries and in all countries to which their commercial and industrial relations extend, and for that purpose will establish and maintain the necessary international organizations.

(b) undertake to secure just treatment of the native inhabitants of territories under their control;

(c) will entrust the League with the general supervision over the execution of agree-

THE LEAGUE OF NATIONS—*Continued.*

ments with regard to the traffic in women and children, and the traffic in opium and other dangerous drugs;

(d) will entrust the League with the general supervision of the trade in arms and ammunition with the countries in which the control of this traffic is necessary in the common interest;

(e) will make provision to secure and maintain freedom of communications and of transit and equitable treatment for the commerce of all members of the League. In this connection, the special necessities of the regions devastated during the war of 1914-1918 shall be borne in mind;

(f) will endeavor to take steps in matters of international concern for the prevention and control of disease.

ARTICLE 24.

(Control of International Bureaus and Commissions.)

There shall be placed under the direction of the League all international bureaus already established by general treaties if the parties to such treaties consent. All such international bureaus and all commissions for the regulation of matters of international interest hereafter constituted shall be placed under the direction of the League.

In all matters of international interest which are regulated by general conventions but which are not placed under the control of international bureaus or commissions, the Secretariat of the League shall, subject to the consent of the Council and if desired by the parties, collect and distribute all relevant information and shall render any other assistance which may be necessary or desirable.

The Council may include as part of the expenses of the Secretariat the expenses of any bureau or commission which is placed under the direction of the League.

ARTICLE 25.

(The Red Cross and International Sanitation.)

The members of the League agree to encourage and promote the establishment and co-operation of duly authorized voluntary national Red Cross organizations having as purposes the improvement of health, the prevention of disease and the mitigation of suffering throughout the world.

ARTICLE 26.

(Amendments of the Covenant; Right of Dissent.)

Amendments to this Covenant will take effect when ratified by members of the League whose representatives compose the Council and by a majority of the members of the League whose representatives compose the Assembly.

No such amendment shall bind any member of the League which signifies its dissent therefrom, but in that case it shall cease to be a member of the League.

First Secretary General of the League of Nations.

The Hon. Sir James Eric Drummond, K. C. M. G., C. B.

LEAGUE OF NATIONS' MEMBERSHIP.

Original Members.

	Date of Accession.
Great Britain	Jan. 10, 1920
Canada	Jan. 10, 1920
Australia	Jan. 10, 1920
South Africa	Jan. 10, 1920
New Zealand	Jan. 10, 1920
India	Jan. 10, 1920
France	Jan. 10, 1920
Italy	Jan. 10, 1920
Japan	Jan. 10, 1920
Belgium	Jan. 10, 1920
Bolivia	Jan. 10, 1920
Brazil	Jan. 10, 1920
China*	July 16, 1920
Cuba	Mar. 8, 1920
Greece	Mar. 30, 1920
Guatemala	Jan. 10, 1920
Haiti	June 30, 1920
Hedjaz (regarded as a member of the League, according to the League Secretariat.)	
Liberia	June 30, 1920
Panama	Jan. 10, 1920
Peru	Jan. 10, 1920
Poland	Jan. 10, 1920
Portugal	Apr. 8, 1920
Roumania	Sept. 14, 1920
Serbs, Croats, Slovenes (Jugo-Slavia)	Feb. 10, 1920
Siam	Jan. 10, 1920
Czecho-Slovakia	Jan. 10, 1920
Uruguay	Jan. 10, 1920

The United States, Ecuador, Honduras and Nicaragua are signatories to the Treaty of Versailles. The United States and Ecuador have not deposited ratifications of the League of Nations. Honduras and Nicaragua became members of the League at the 1920 Assembly of the League at Geneva.

Invited Members.

	Date of Accession.
Argentine Republic	July 18, 1920
Chile	Nov. 4, 1919
Colombia	Feb. 16, 1920
Denmark	Mar. 8, 1920
Netherlands	Mar. 9, 1920
Norway	Mar. 5, 1920
Paraguay	Dec. 26, 1919
Persia	Nov. 21, 1919
Salvador	Mar. 10, 1920
Spain	Jan. 20, 1920
Sweden	Mar. 9, 1920
Switzerland	Mar. 8, 1920
Venezuela	Mar. 3, 1920

Admitted Members.

Albania	Dec. 17, 1920
Austria	Dec. 15, 1920
Bulgaria	Dec. 16, 1920
Costa Rica	Dec. 16, 1920
Finland	Dec. 16, 1920
Luxemburg	Dec. 16, 1920

Applicants for Admission to the League.

	Date of Request.
Azerbaidjan (applied to L. of N. Assembly at Geneva, Nov., 1920).	
Armenia	May 13, 1920
Esthonia	Apr. 10, 1920
Georgia	May 21, 1920
Iceland	July 2, 1919
Latvia	May 14, 1920
Liechtenstein	July 15, 1920
Lithuania	Nov. 15, 1920
Monaco	May 3, 1920
San Marino	Apr. 23, 1920
Ukraine	Feb. 25, 1920

*By ratification of Austrian Treaty.

THE LEAGUE.

The first action of the League of Nations was the International Labor Commission called by President Wilson, which met at Washington, Oct. 29, to Nov. 29, 1919. The Conference created an International Labor Organization and recommended a code of international labor laws. The second Conference of the Labor Organization was held at Genoa, June 15 to July 10, 1920, to consider the working day for sailors.

On Jan. 16, 1920, the Council of the League held its first meeting in Paris. The following countries were represented: British Empire, France, Italy, Japan, Belgium, Brazil, Spain and Greece. Ten other Council meetings have since been held; the 2d, at London, Feb. 11th to 13th; 3d, at Paris, March 13th; 4th, at Paris, April 9th to 11th; 5th, at Rome, May 14th to 19th; 6th, at London, June 14th to 16th; 7th, at London, July 9th to 12th; 8th, at San Sebastian, July 29th to Aug. 5th; 9th, at Paris, Sept. 16th to 20th; 10th, at Brussels, Oct. 20th to 28th, and the 11th, at Geneva, on and after Nov. 14th, coincident with the meeting of the Assembly. Among the work undertaken by the Council has been the calling together of the Jurists Advisory Committee at the Hague; the International Communications and Transport Commission; the Armaments Commission at San Sebastian; and the Financial Conference at Brussels. The Council has assumed jurisdiction in the Aaland Islands dispute between Sweden and Finland, with the result that those nations accepted the League as a mediator. Poland and Lithuania also agreed to accept the mediation of the League with regard to Vilna. The Coun-

THE LEAGUE OF NATIONS—*Continued.*

cil was required to make an important decision as to Switzerland. This country wished to have her military neutrality and the inviolability of her territory recognized as consistent with her membership in the League. The Council decided that the perpetual neutrality of Switzerland was in the interests of general peace, and therefore compatible with the Covenant. Under the supervision of the Council, the work of Dr. Nansen in the repatriation of prisoners of war had resulted, up to Oct. 31, 1920, in enabling 166,000 prisoners to return to their homes.

The first meeting of the Assembly of the League of Nations convened at Geneva, Switzerland, the permanent headquarters of the League, on Nov. 15, 1920. M. Paul Hymans of Belgium was chosen as President of the Assembly. There were 241 delegates in all, representing forty-one nations, including twenty-eight original members and thirteen invited members of the League. The original members attending were: Australia, Belgium, Bolivia, Brazil, Canada, China, Cuba, Czechoslovakia, France, Great Britain, Greece, Guatamala, Haiti, India, Italy, Japan, Jugo-Slavia, Liberia, New Zealand, Nicaragua, Panama, Peru, Poland, Portugal, Roumania, Siam, South Africa, Uruguay. The invited members: Argentina, Chile, Colombia, Denmark, Netherlands, Norway, Paraguay, Persia, Salvador, Spain, Sweden, Switzerland, Venezuela. China refused to sign the Treaty of Versailles, but became an original member of the League by signing the treaty with Austria at St. Germain July 16, 1920. The United States, Ecuador and Honduras were not represented at the opening of the Assembly, not having filed ratifications. The Secretary General announced, Dec. 2, 1920, that Nicaragua and Honduras had ratified the treaty and were therefore members of the League.

The following are among the general or specific acts of the Assembly:

Six new States were admitted to membership, Austria on Dec. 15; Bulgaria, Costa Rica, Finland and Luxembourg on Dec. 16, and Albania on Dec. 17. China was elected to the Council in place of Greece.

The applications of some of the smaller Baltic States were denied, because the Assembly did not wish to commit itself to a guaranty of the existing boundaries of those States, under Article X of the Covenant.

A statute was adopted for the establishment of an International Court of Justice in accordance with the plan drawn by the Jurists Advisory Committee, with an amendment eliminating compulsory jurisdiction, and subject to ratification by a majority of the members of the League. For text of draft scheme for Court of International Justice see page 320.

An International Blockade Commission was created to study the use of the League's economic weapon, but each nation must be free to decide for itself whether there has been a breach of the Covenant.

The Assembly requested the Council to ask member States to consider an agreement that armament expenditures for two years, 1922 and 1923, should not exceed similar expenditures for 1921.

Bureaus were established to deal with economic questions and international credits.

Principles were set forth and formally adopted on the mandate question.

An international conference to plan measures against the traffic in women and children was called; and a special committee was appointed to take charge of the fight against typhus and other epidemics in Eastern Europe.

The Assembly divided itself into six commissions for the study of its principal subjects, as follows:

On General Organization: Chairman, Arthur J. Balfour, Great Britain; Vice Chairman, Dr. Wellington Koo, China.

On Admission of New States: Chairman, Antonio Huneus, Chile; Vice Chairman, Dr. Juan Callos Blanco, Uruguay.

On Technical Organization: Chairman, Tomasso Tittoni, Italy; Vice Chairman, Take Jonescu, Rumania.

On the Court of International Justice: Chairman, Leon Bourgeois, France; Vice Chairman, Dr. Alfonso da Costa, Portugal.

On Finances: Chairman, Count Quinones de Leon, Spain; Vice Chairman, Senor Restrepo, Colombia.

On Disarmament, Mandates and the Economic Blockade: Chairman, Hjalmar Branting, Sweden; Vice Chairman, Senor Aguer, Cuba.

Six Vice Presidents of the Assembly were elected: H. A. van Karnabeck, Holland; Dr. Eduard Benes, Czechoslovakia; Viscount Kikujiro Ishii, Japan; Honorio Pueyrredon, Argentina; Sir George E. Foster, Canada, and Rodrigo Octavio of Brazil.

The Assembly held its final session on Dec. 18, when it adjourned until the first Monday in September, 1921.

NATIONAL DEBTS OF PRINCIPAL NATIONS.

	Pre-war.	Armistice.	Latest available.
Argentina	1913.. $732,398,000	1918.. $866,380,000	1918.. $866,380,000
Australia	1913.. 80,753,000	1918.. 975,738,000	1919.. 1,583,000,000
Australia States	1913.. 1,348,624,000	1916.. 1,741,301,000	1917.. 1,813,000,000
Austria	1913.. 2,152,490,000	1918..16,475,000,000	1919..17,668,000,000
Belgium	1914.. 825,269,000	1918.. 3,500,000,000	1920.. 4,000,000,000
Brazil	1912.. 663,667,000	1917.. 1,073,826,000	1918.. 1,118,546,000
Bulgaria	1912.. 135,300,000	1918.. 800,000,000	1919.. 2,158,000,000
Canada	1913.. 544,391,000	1918.. 1,300,000,000	1920.. 1,935,946,000
Chile	1913.. 207,704,000	1918.. 228,377,000	1918.. 228,377,000
China	1913.. 969,189,000	1916.. 1,066,649,000	1920.. 1,534,575,000
Denmark	1913.. 95,579,000	1918.. 161,700,000	1918.. 161,700,000
Ecuador	1913.. 19,780,000	1918.. 25,756,000	1918.. 25,756,000
Egypt	1913.. 459,153,000	1918.. 455,338,000	1918.. 455,338,000
Finland	1913.. 33,706,000	1916.. 34,618,000	1916.. 34,618,000
France	1913.. 6,346,129,000	1918..30,000,000,000	1920..46,025,000,000
Germany	1913.. 1,194,052,000	1919..40,000,000,000	1920..48,552,000,000
German States	1913.. 3,854,795,000	1917.. 4,341,611,000	1920.. 4,500,000,000
Greece	1913.. 206,640,000	1917.. 259,725,000	1919.. 469,367,000
Hungary	1913.. 1,731,350,000	1918.. 8,513,848,000	1920.. 9,412,000,000
India, British	1912.. 1,475,272,000	1917.. 1,546,237,000	1917 . 1,546,237,000
Italy	1913.. 2,921,153,000	1918..12,000,000,000	1920..18,102,000,000
Japan	1913.. 1,241,997,000	1918.. 1,244,375,000	1920.. 1,300,000,000
Mexico	1912.. 226,404,000	1918.. 377,333,000	1919.. 500,000,000
Netherlands	1914.. 461,649,000	1917.. 762,527,000	1919.. 961,349,000
New Zealand	1913.. 438,271,000	1918.. 734,000,000	1919.. 856,875,000
Norway	1913.. 97,215,000	1918.. 197,409,000	1920.. 250,000,000
Peru	1913.. 34,268,000	1916.. 34,015,000	1916.. 34,015,000
Poland	....	....	1919.. 1,356,600,000
Portugal	1913.. 947,603,000	1918.. 1,289,646,000	1918.. 1,289,646,000
Rumania	1913.. 316,623,000	1915.. 355,194,000	1918.. 1,022,000,000
Russia	1914.. 4,537,861,000	1917..25,000,000,000	1917..25,000,000,000
Serbia	1913.. 126,232,000	1913.. 126,232,000	1913.. 126,232,000
Spain	1914.. 1,814,270,000	1917.. 1,964,206,000	1919.. 1,985,774,000
Sweden	1913.. 161,590,000	1917.. 249,298,000	1920.. 336,420,000
Switzerland	1912.. 23,614,000	1918.. 205,489,000	1918.. 205,439,000
Turkey	1913.. 675,654,000	1917.. 1,459,000,000	1918.. 2,000,000,000
Union South Africa	1913.. 573,415,000	1918.. 780,766,000	1918.. 780,768,000
United Kingdom	1913.. 3,485,818,000	1918..36,391,000,000	1920..39,214,000,000
United States	1913.. 1,028,564,000	1918..17,005,431,000	1920..24,974,336,000

THE WORLD WAR—IMPORTANT DATES AND EVENTS

War began—Aug. 1, 1914.
Armistice signed—Nov. 11, 1918.
Duration of war—4 years, 3 months, 11 days.
United States entered—April 6, 1917.
Paris peace conference began—Jan. 18, 1919.
German peace treaty signed—June 28, 1919.
Austrian peace treaty signed—Sept. 10, 1919.

Nations Directly Involved.

United States, Great Britain, Canada, India, Australia, New Zealand, South Africa, France, Russia, Belgium, Serbia, Montenegro, Japan, Italy, Rumania, Portugal, Cuba, Panama, Greece, Liberia, China, San Marino, Siam, Brazil, Guatemala, Costa Rica, Nicaragua, Haiti.

Germany, Austria-Hungary, Turkey, Bulgaria.

Declarations of War.

Austria against Belgium, Aug. 28, 1914.
Austria against Japan, Aug. 27, 1914.
Austria against Montenegro, Aug. 9, 1914.
Austria against Russia, Aug. 6, 1914.
Austria against Serbia, July 28, 1914.
Brazil against Germany, Oct. 26, 1917.
Bulgaria against Rumania, Sept. 1, 1916.
Bulgaria against Serbia, Oct. 14, 1915.
China against Austria, Aug. 14, 1917.
China against Germany, Aug. 14, 1917.
Costa Rica against Germany and Austria-Hungary, May 24, 1918.
Cuba against Germany, April 7, 1917.
Cuba against Austria, Dec. 16, 1917.
France against Austria, Aug. 12, 1914.
France against Bulgaria, Oct. 16, 1915.
France against Germany, Aug. 3, 1914.
France against Turkey, Nov. 5, 1914.
Germany against Belgium, Aug. 4, 1914.
Germany against France, Aug. 3, 1914.
Germany against Portugal, March 9, 1916.
Germany against Rumania, Aug. 28, 1916.
Germany against Russia, Aug. 1, 1914.
Great Britain against Austria, Aug. 13, 1914.
Great Britain against Bulgaria, Oct. 15, 1915.
Great Britain against Germany, Aug. 4, 1914.
Great Britain against Turkey, Nov. 5, 1914.
Greece against Bulgaria, Nov. 23, 1916.
Greece against Germany, Nov. 28, 1916.
Guatemala against Germany, April 21, 1918.
Haiti against Germany, July 12, 1918.
Honduras against Germany, July 19, 1918.
Italy against Austria, May 24, 1915.
Italy against Bulgaria, Oct. 19, 1915.
Italy against Germany, Aug. 28, 1916.
Italy against Turkey, Aug. 21, 1915.
Japan against Germany, Aug. 23, 1914.
Liberia against Germany, Aug. 4, 1917.
Montenegro against Austria, Aug. 8, 1914.
Montenegro against Germany, Aug. 9, 1914.
Nicaragua against Austria, May 6, 1918.
Nicaragua against Germany, May 7, 1918.
Panama against Germany, April 7, 1917.
Panama against Austria, Dec. 10, 1917.
Portugal against Germany, Nov. 23, 1914.
Rumania against Austria, Aug. 27, 1916.
Russia against Bulgaria, Oct. 19, 1915.
Russia against Turkey, Nov. 3, 1914.
San Marino against Austria, May 24, 1915.
Serbia against Bulgaria, Oct. 16, 1915.
Serbia against Germany, Aug. 6, 1914.
Serbia against Turkey, Dec. 2, 1914.
Siam against Austria, July 22, 1917.
Siam against Germany, July 22, 1917.
Turkey against Allies, Nov. 11, 1914.
Turkey against Rumania, Aug. 29, 1916.
United States against Germany, April 6, 1917.
United States against Austria-Hungary, Dec. 7, 1917.

Surrender Dates.

Russia to Germany and her allies, Dec. 16, 1917.
Rumania to Germany (treaty signed), May 6, 1918.
Bulgaria to France and allies, Sept. 29, 1918.
Turkey to Britain and allies, Oct. 30, 1918.
Austria-Hungary to Allies and United States, Nov. 3, 1918.
Germany to Allies and United States, Nov. 11, 1918.

Other Important Dates.

1914.

June 28—Archduke Francis Ferdinand and wife assassinated in Sarajevo, Bosnia.
Aug. 8—Germans capture Liege.
Aug. 20—German troops enter Brussels.
Sept. 6—Allies win battle of Marne.
Sept. 14—Battle of Aisne begins.
Sept. 15—First battle of Soissons fought.
Oct. 9-10—Germans capture Antwerp.
Nov. 7—Tsingtao captured by Japanese.

1915.

Jan. 24—British win naval battle in North Sea, sinking the German cruiser Bluecher.
Feb. 19—British and French fleets bombard Dardanelles forts.
Apr. 23—Germans cross Ypres Canal.
May 7—Liner Lusitania torpedoed and sunk.
Aug. 4—Germans occupy Warsaw.
Sept. 25-30—Battle of the Champagne.
Oct. 12—Edith Cavell executed by Germans.
Dec. 15—Sir John Douglas Haig succeeds Sir John French as British Commander on Western front.

1916.

Jan. 9—British evacuate Gallipoli peninsula.
Apr. 24—Insurrection in Dublin.
June 5—Lord Kitchener lost with British cruiser Hampshire.
July 1—Battle of Somme begins.
Nov. 13—British win battle of Ancre.

1917.

Feb. 1—Germany begins unrestricted submarine warfare.
Feb. 3—President Wilson orders that Ambassador von Bernstorff be handed his passports.
Feb. 25—"Hindenburg retreat" from Somme.
Mar. 11—Successful revolution in Russia.
Mar. 15—Czar Nicholas II of Russia abdicates.
Mar. 18—British and French take Peronne, Chaulnes, Nesle and Noyon.
Apr. 4—Senate passes war resolution.
Apr. 6—House passes war resolution.
Apr. 9—Canadians take Vimy Ridge.
Apr. 15—Great French offensive between Soissons and Rheims begins.
Apr. 21—Turkey breaks off relations with U. S.
Apr. 28—Senate and House pass army draft bill.
June 13—Gen. Pershing lands in France.
June 27—American troops arrive in France.
July 20—Draft day in the United States.
Oct. 17—United States transport Antilles sunk.
Dec. 9—Jerusalem captured by Gen. Allenby.

1918.

Jan. 31—Americans take over sector on French front.
Mar. 11—American troops make successful raid on German trenches in Lorraine.
Mar. 21—Germans begin heavy offensive.
Mar. 28—Gen. Foch made commander-in-chief of Allied armies.
Mar. 29—Gen. Pershing places American forces at the disposal of Gen. Foch; offer accepted.
Apr. 20—German shock troops attack Americans near Renners Forest and take village of Seicheprey; all lost ground recovered by counter-attack.
Apr. 23—British and French attack Zeebrugge and Ostend and sink five old cruisers in harbor channels to bottle up "U" boat bases.
May 27—Germans begin second great offensive.
May 28—American troops northwest of Montdidier attack German line, take Cantigny.
May 31—Germans reach Chateau-Thierry, halted by Americans and French.
June 6—American marines gain two miles on a 2½-mile front, northwest of Chateau-Thierry.
June 7—Americans in second battle of Chateau-Thierry.
June 11—Americans complete capture of Belleau Wood.
July 18—Gen. Foch delivers heavy counter-attack.
July 21—Germans driven out of Chateau-Thierry.
July 27—Germans retreat all along the line north of the Marne.
Aug. 4—Americans take whole of Fismes; British troops advance in Picardy.
Aug. 8—British and French begin great offensive in Picardy, east of Amiens.
Aug. 22—British capture Albert.
Aug. 24—Americans advance to the Soissons-Rheims road; British capture Bray.
Aug. 28—Chaulnes taken by the French.
Sept. 1—Americans in Belgium capture Voormezeele; Australian troops capture Peronne.
Sept. 14—Americans take 150 square miles of territory in St. Mihiel offensive.
Sept. 18—British and French pierce Hindenburg line on a 22-mile front.
Sept. 26—Gen. Pershing's 1st army smashes its way seven miles deep into the German lines.
Oct. 2—St Quentin taken by the French.
Oct. 7—Americans win hot battle for possession of north end of Argonne Forest.
Oct. 8—British, French and American troops deliver assault on 20-mile front
Nov. 11—Fighting ceases at 11 a.m.

THE FINANCIAL YEAR, 1920.

The year 1920 will be remembered as the year of deflation—attempted deflation of credit, deflation of securities and deflation of commodities.

The great declines in prices of securities and commodities were the aftermath of the war-period inflation. Time and again the Governor of the Federal Reserve Board during the industrial boom of 1919, built as it was on scarcity of goods and high prices, referred to conditions as a "fool's paradise."

The year 1920 witnessed the readjustment. It began with the Federal Reserve Board's restrictions on borrowings for speculative purposes. It went forward with the word from the Federal Reserve Board that bank loans must be for essential purposes.

Stock market loans, being, so far as they were made on securities held for speculative purposes, non-essential loans, were under restriction as long ago as November, 1919. From that time on stocks declined with more or less frequent interruption clear into December of the following year.

The war, with its enormous demands for production and its enormous profits to industry, had been attended by great speculation in industrial shares, while bonds and railroad shares declined. The year 1920, with its readjustment from the war conditions to peace conditions, saw many industrial stocks fall to pre-war levels as business fell off. Following are a few samples of the declines in industrial shares on the New York stock market during the year from January to December:

	Year's High.	Dec. Low.	Decline.
Am. Hide and Leather Pf....	122	35	87
Amer. International	120½	30¼	90¼
Amer. Sugar Refining..........	142⅝	82⅛	60½
Amer. Sumatra Tobacco......	106¾	65	41¾
Amer. Woolen	165	55½	109½
Atlantic Gulf and W. I........	176½	71½	105
Baldwin Locomotive	148½	78	70½
Bethlehem Steel ...B..........	102½	48⅞	53⅝
Central Leather	104¾	30½	74¼
Endicott Johnson	147	47	100
General Electric	182	116½	65½
International Paper	91¾	38½	53¼
Maxwell Motor 1st Pf.........	63½	3¼	60¼
Republic Steel	124¾	55¼	59½
Punta Alegre Sugar...........	120	40	80
Vanadium	97	28½	68½
Worthington Pump	95½	35⅞	59⅝
United Retail Stores...........	96½	43¼	53¼
U. S. Rubber...................	140	54¼	85¾
Willys Overland Pf.......	93	26	67

Incidental to the great economic readjustment, events that will long be remembered in and out of financial circles crowded the year. Here are some of the things that stood out as of more than ordinary consequence:

January:
- Call money rates up to 20 percent.
- Severe declines in stocks.

February:
- Call money up to 25 percent.
- Federal Reserve Bank at New York reports first deficit in reserves since enactment of Federal Reserve Law.
- Esch-Cummins Bill for return of railroads to private operation on March 1 passed by Congress.
- Federal Reserve rediscount rates raised.
- Sterling exchange (demand) at low record of $3.18 for the pound. Gold at 125s. 9d. in London.
- Violent declines in stocks.

March:
- U. S. Supreme Court Decision holding U. S. Steel Corporation not a "trust."
- U. S. Supreme Court Decision holding stock dividends not income for taxation purposes.
- "Corner" in Stutz Motor stock.
- Extensive rise in stock market prices.

April:
- Outlaw railroad strike.
- Financial crisis in Japan. Japanese exchanges closed.
- U. S. Supreme Court declares Reading Company a trust and orders it dissolved.
- Many corporations declare stock dividends.
- Public protest against high prices develops "overalls" movement.
- Stock market decline resumed.

May:
- Cutting of prices by retail merchants.
- Carranza regime overthrown in Mexico.
- Heavy liquidation in stocks.

June:
- Advances in textile wages in New England followed by curtailment at woolen mills.
- Silk and shoe industries suffer from trade reaction.
- Sharp decline in price of silver.
- Federal Reserve Bank rediscount rates advanced.

July:
- Trading in wheat futures resumed. December contracts $2.72 to $2.75 a bushel.
- Railway Labor Board announces advances of 21 percent in railroad men's wages, retroactive to May 1.
- Interstate Commerce Commission grants increased freight and passenger rates to railroads.

August:
- Declines in cotton and wheat and other commodities get under way.

September:
- Price cutting by manufacturers and wholesalers as commodity prices continue to decline.
- Industrial contraction becomes pronounced.

October:
- Declines in commodity prices continue.

November:
- Stocks, cotton and wheat decline to low levels of year.
- Southern Pacific announces segregation of oil properties.

December:
- New low levels reached in stock market.

* * *

The year 1919 ended with forewarning of financial stress in the year 1920. Call money at the end of 1919 was up to 25 percent and the New York Federal Reserve Bank's ratio of reserves at the beginning of 1920 was down to 38.5 percent, compared with 46.5 percent a year previous. Things had got to the point where the banking system of the country had over-expanded its credit, the banks being passively encouraged in this by the ability to rediscount their loans at the Federal Reserve Banks at less cost than they were charging borrowers. One of the first things the Federal Reserve Board proceeded to do, therefore, was to take the profit out of rediscounting by member banks.

Wall Street was first called upon to do its part in the way of liquidation of loans. Wall Street loans on stock market collateral in July, 1919, had stood at an estimated $1,750,000,000. Throughout the year these loans were gradually and continually reduced until in December, 1920, they were estimated to stand at but $700,000,000.

This reduction in the loan account, of course, meant selling of securities, and this in turn meant falling prices. The months in which stock market declines were most pronounced were January and February, April and May and November and December.

But the process of deflation was not confined to stocks. It was applied to commodities. The Federal Reserve policy of "essential loans" only made it necessary for speculation in commodities to cease, and there were witnessed heavy declines in silk, rubber, hides and leather, sugar and finally cotton, wheat, corn and other grains.

The commodities that were in greater supply and less demand sustained the most severe declines. Silk, for instance, was one of the first commodities to feel the effects of reduced demand on the part of the consumer; at the same time the silk industry had expanded to the point of almost unlimited production. Raw silk (Sinshui No. 1) fell from $17.40 a pound in January to approximately $5 by summer. There had been heavy speculation in hides and some grades of this commodity fell during the year about to pre-war levels. Wool was similarly affected by large supplies, and at the end of the year the world's stocks of wool on hand, estimated to be two years' supply, was a world-wide problem.

In the grain markets, wheat had a spectacular fall during the latter part of the year, with surplus production in the United States, Canada, the Argentine and Australia. The world short-

THE FINANCIAL YEAR, 1920—*Continued.*

age of goods that was exploited at the beginning of the year as a reason and an excuse for high prices was met, in many lines, and, as it turned out, there was a limit to demand, since there was a limit to purchasing power the world over.

The declines in prices of leading commodities is shown in the following figures:

	High 1920	Low 1920
Wheat, per bu	$2.25	$1.79
Corn, per bu	2.31⅝	.94½
Coffee, per lb	.16¼	.06⅝
Sugar, per lb., gran.	.23	.08
Iron, ton	53.51	36.50
Lead, lb	.09½	.04⅞
Copper, lb	.19½	.13⅝
Cotton, lb.	.43¾	.15½
Print cloths	.16	.05½
Silk (Sinshui No. 1)	17.40	5.40
Rubber	.53½	.17

Bradstreet's index number of commodity prices showed a drop from the peak on Feb. 1, 1920, of 35 percent to December, 1920. The index number of the Federal Reserve Bank, figured on twelve important basic commodities, showed a drop of about 36 percent from the middle of May to the middle of November, 1920.

The rise in the price of refined sugar to 26 cents wholesale and its subsequent decline to 8 cents was an example of extreme change during the equilibrium of supply and demand. The year started with a so-called world shortage of sugar put at about 3,000,000 tons. Fear of absolute scarcity led to buying beyond immediate necessity on the part of refiners, manufacturers of goods of sugar content, wholesalers, retailers and consumers. Sugar at retail at 30 cents a pound was not uncommon. The whole world sent its sugar here to get advantage of the high prices, the Far East gave up its supply to the United States and shipments to Europe were turned back to this country. The result was that there came to be an oversupply at the high prices. Sugar that had been stored away against possible famine came out from its hiding places and the decline in price continued over the entire latter half of the year.

In nearly all lines it was a case of supply overtaking demand at high prices. Expansion of credit had given purchasing power to raise the price; uneven distribution of wealth restricted purchasing power of large numbers of consumers, restricted buying began to be felt in the markets and the necessity of payment of loans at the banks gave impetus to the price reaction. And in the meantime production of goods to meet the "world shortage" increased.

The decline in prices of agricultural products —of cotton, wheat, corn and other grains—was so drastic as to bring appeals for relief from the West and South. Cotton, wheat and corn, said the farmers, were bringing in the fall far less than cost of production. The Federal Reserve Board was appealed to without avail for credit to permit the farmers to hold back their goods. The West essayed a "strike," in refusing to market their wheat and corn at the low prices. Wheat came flowing over the border from Canada and the American farmer turned to Congress in December for tariff protection.

Estimates put of the shrinkage in the value of farm products from 1919 to 1920 at $5,000,000,000—the figure of the Department of Agriculture. Following are the leading crops and the department's estimates of quantity and value in December, 1919 and 1920. Our corn, tobacco and rice crops were the greatest in the history of the country:

	1919	1920
Corn, bu	2,917,450,000	3,232,367,000
	$3,934,234,000	$2,189,721,000
Winter wheat, bu.	731,636,000	580,513,000
	$1,543,452,000	$866,741,000
Spring wheat, bu.	209,351,000	209,365,000
	$485,020,000	$273,465,000
Oats, bu	1,248,310,000	1,524,055,000
	$895,603,000	$719,782,000
Barley, bu	165,719,000	202,024,000
	$200,419,000	$142,931,000
Potatoes, bbls	357,901,000	430,458,000
	$577,581,000	$500,974,000
Hay, tons	108,666,000	108,233,000
	$2,129,087,000	$1,809,162,000
Cotton, bales	11,030,000	12,987,000
	$1,977,073,000	$914,590,000
Tobacco, lbs	1,389,458,000	1,508,064,000
	$542,547,000	$298,001,000
Apples, bbls	147,457,000	240,640,000
	$275,463,000	$271,984,000

Restricted buying on the part of Europe was unquestionably an important factor in reducing purchases of manufactured goods here. In some lines the recovery of European industry made far lessened demand for American goods. In other cases inability to buy what with depreciated currency and adverse exchange operated to restrict our exports. The tendency has been for loss of exports of manufactured goods to be made up in part by exports of raw materials and foodstuffs, and accordingly the total export figures have not shown a sensational fall during the year. Following are the exports and imports of the United States during the twelve months ended November, 1920:

	Exports	Imports
Dec., 1919	$681,415,999	$380,710,323
Jan., 1920	722,063,790	473,823,869
Feb., 1920	645,145,225	467,402,320
Mar., 1920	819,556,037	523,923,236
April, 1920	684,319,392	495,738,571
May, 1920	745,523,223	431,004,944
June, 1920	629,376,757	552,605,534
July, 1920	651,136,478	537,118,971
Aug., 1920	578,182,691	513,111,488
Sept., 1920	605,291,257	363,290,301
Oct., 1920	751,728,570	334,098,698
Nov., 1920	675,000,000	321,000,000

The problem of financing our export trade was one of the great problems of the year 1920, although definite action to organize machinery for financing our foreign trade was not taken until near the end of the year. In December, under the direction of the American Bankers Association, a meeting of bankers and business men was held at Chicago at which a Foreign Trade Finance Corporation was formed under the Edge Act for the purpose of extending credit to foreign purchasers of American goods. The corporation is to have a capital of $100,000,000 and will be empowered to issue its debentures to American investors, at the same time taking foreign securities in return for goods shipped abroad. It will be possible to finance foreign trade thus to the extent of $1,000,000,000. Since the armistice there accumulated on the hands of the banks, of manufacturers and of business men generally unfunded foreign loans for goods purchased in America amounting to a sum estimated from $2,000,000,000 to $4,000,000,000.

1920 POPULAR VOTE FOR PRESIDENT.

The following official compilation of the popular vote for President was announced by the Associated Press on Jan. 9, 1921. They show a total popular vote of 26,759,708 for the candidates of seven parties, as compared with a total popular vote of 18,515,340 for the candidates of five parties in 1916. The returns from Tennessee alone were unofficial:

Harding, Rep.	16,141,629
Cox, Dem	9,139,866
Debs, Soc.	914,869
Watkins, Proh.	187,470
Christensen, Farm.-Lab.	252,435
Cox (W. W.), Soc.-Lab.	42,950
Macauley, Single Tax	5,747

Harding's plurality over Cox was 7,001,763. Texas returns also show: Amer. Party, 47,495; Black and Tan, 27,247.

BETELGEUSE A GIANT STAR.

The result of the measurement of Alpha Orionis or Betelgeuse, the northernmost star of the constellation Orion, by Professor Michelson's device for measuring the diameter of stars, shows that its diameter is 260,000,000 miles, or three hundred times that of the Sun. Compared with the sun in volume, it is 27,000,000 times as great. The distance of Betelgeuse from the earth is 150 "light years." That is, the light that strikes the eye started on its journey from the star 150 years ago, traveling at the rate of 186,000 miles a second.

More than 2,000 women are enrolled as students in the University of Pennsylvania.

SPORTING RECORDS.

CHAMPIONS OF 1920.

Athletics (all around)—Brutus Hamilton, Univ. of Missouri.

Automobiling—Leading driver, Gaston Chevrolet (deceased).

Baseball—World's champions, Cleveland (A. L.); Natl. League, Bkln.; Amer. League, Cleve. Champion batters—Natl. League, Rogers Hornsby, St. Louis; Amer. League, George Sisler, St. Louis.

Basketball—Natl. A. A. U., N. Y. Univ.; Intercollegiate, Pa.

Bicycling—Natl. amateur, Fred Taylor, N. Y. A. C.; Natl. professional, Arthur Spencer, Toronto, Can.

Billiards—18.1, 18.2, 14.1 balkline, Willie Hoppe, N. Y.; 3-cushion caroms, John Dayton, Sedalia, Mo.; pocket billiards, Ralph Greenleaf, Wilmington, Del. Amateur—Class A, Percy Collins, Chicago; Class B, Julian Rice, N. Y.; Closs C, Sidney Brussel, Bkln; pocket billiards, Howard Shoemaker, N. Y.

Boxing—Heavyweight, Jack Dempsey; light heavyweight, Georges Carpentier, France; middleweight, Johnny Wilson, Boston; welterweight, Jack Britton, N. Y.; lightweight, Benny Leonard, N. Y.; featherweight, Johnny Kilbane, Cleveland; bantamweight, Joe Lynch, N. Y.; flyweight, Jimmy Wilde, Wales. Amateur—108-lb. class, A. J. Devito, N. Y.; 115-lb., James Hutchinson, Phila.; 125-lb., Sol Seaman, Bkln.; 135-lb., Tommy Murphy, Kansas City; 145-lbs., Jack Schoendorf, Milwaukee; 158-lbs., Sam Lagonta, N. Y.; 175-lbs., John Burke, Pitts.; heavyweight, Carl Wicks, Boston.

Canoeing—Leo Friede, N. Y.

Chess—Jose R. Capablanca, N. Y.

Cross Country—Natl. A. A. U. senior indiv., Fred Faller, Boston; junior, W. Ritola, N. Y.; team, senior, Dorchester Club, Boston; junior, Mohawk A. C., N. Y.; intercollegiate indiv., John L. Romig, Penn State; team, Cornell.

Fencing—Sherman S. Hall, N. Y., intercollegiate, U. S. Naval Acad.

Golf—Natl. amateur, Charles Evans Jr., Chicago; open, Edward Ray, England; women's, Miss Alexa Stirling, Atlanta; Pro Golfers' Assn., Jack Hutchison, Chicago; intercollegiate indiv., Jess Sweetser, Yale; team, Princeton.

Gymnastics—Natl. all around, Joseph Oszy, N. Y.

Lawn Tennis—World's, William T. Tilden 2d; natl. singles, W. T. Tilden 2nd; Natl. doubles, William Johnston and Clarence J. Griffin; mixed doubles, Wallace F. Johnson and Mrs. H. H. Wightman; Natl. clay court singles, Roland Roberts; doubles, Roland Roberts and Vincent Richards; junior singles, Vincent Richards; doubles, Harold Godshall and Richard Hinchley; intercollegiate singles, L. M. Banks, Yale; doubles, A. Wilder and L. Wiley, Yale; women's singles, Mrs. Molla Bjurstedt Mallory; doubles, Miss Eleanor Goss and Miss Marion Zinderstein; Natl. indoor singles, W. T. Tilden 2nd; doubles, W. T. Tilden 2nd and Vincent Richards; indoor junior singles, V. Richards; doubles, V. Richards and Frank T. Anderson. Natl. indoor women's singles, Miss Helene Pollak; doubles, Miss H. Pollak and Mrs. L. G. Morris.

Court Tennis—Natl. open, Jay Gould; natl. amateur, Jay Gould; professional, Walter Kinsella.

Squash Tennis—Natl. amateur, A. V. Cordier, N. Y.; world's professional, Walter Kinsella, N. Y.

Racquets—Natl. amateur, Clarence C. Pell, Tuxedo; doubles, Jay Gould and J. W. Wear, Phila.; world's professional, Jock Soutar, N. Y.

Football—Princeton.

Motor Boating—Miss America.

Polo—Natl. open, Meadow Brook; senior, Meadow Brook; junior, Bryn Mawr.

Racing—Single G, 1:59; leading money winner, John Henry, $10,354.

Racing—Man o'War; leading money winner, Man o'War, $166,104; leading jockey, Jimmy Butwell.

Rowing—Natl. amateur, John B. Kelly, Phila.; doubles, Vasper B. C., Phila.; fours, Pennsylvania Barge Club; senior eights, U. S. Naval Academy; intercollegiate, Syracuse; New London regatta, Harvard; world's professional, Ernest Barry, England.

Shooting—Natl. singles, F. S. Wright, Buffalo; doubles, P. H. O'Brien, Butte, Mont; Grand Amer. Handicap, A. L. Ivins, Red Bank, N. J.

Socker—Ben Millers, St. Louis.

Swimming—Norman Ross; women's, Ethelda Bleibtrey, Bkln.

Trotting—Peter Manning, 2:02½; leading money winner, Peter Manning, $26,550; leading driver, Tommy Murphy, Glen Cove, L. I.; won 30 races and $59,498.

Wrestling—Ed (Strangler) Lewis, Ky. Natl. A. A. U., 108-lb. Class, Carl Benson, Bkln; 115-lb., Sam Pommow, Chicago.; 125-lb., A. Gallas, Chicago; 135-lb., George Metropoulis, Gary, Ind.; 145-lb., W. Tikka, N. Y.; 158-lb. E. Leino, N. Y.; 175-lb., Carl Kunert, Gary, Ind.; heavyweight, Nat Pendleton, N. Y.

Yachting—International race, Resolute, Amer.

ATHLETICS.

World's Amateur Records.

RUNNING.

[Event, time, holder, nation and date.]

100 yds.—9 3-5 s., D. J. Kelly, U. S. A., June 23, '06. H. P. Drew, U. S. A., Mar. 18, '14.

220 yds.—21 1-5 s., B. J. Wefers, U. S. A., May 30, 1896; R. C. Craig, U. S. A., May 28, '10; D. F. Lippincott, U. S. A., May 31, '13.

300 yds.—30 3-5 s., B. J. Wefers, U. S. A., Sept. 26, 1896.

300 yds. (indoor)— 31 2-5 s., A. D. Kelly, U. S. A., Mar. 17, '17.

440 yds. (straight away)—47 s., M. W. Long, U. S. A., Oct. 4, 1900.

440 yds. (around turn)—47 2-5 s., J. E. Meredith, U. S. A., May 27, '16.

600 yds.—1 m. 10 4-5 s., M. W. Sheppard, U. S. A., Aug. 14, '10.

880 yds.—1 m. 52 2-5 s., J. E. Meredith, U. S. A., May 13, '16.

1,000 yds.—2 m. 12 2-5 s., M. W. Sheppard, U. S. A., July 17, '10.

1,320 yds.—3 m. 2 4-5 s., T. P. Conneff, U. S. A., Aug. 21, 1895.

1 mile—4 m. 12 3-5 s., N. S. Taber, U. S. A., July 16, '15.

1-mile (indoor)—2 m. 16 s., J. W. Overton, U. S. A., Mar. 17, '17.

1⅓ mile (indoor)—6 m. 46 3-5 s., J. W. Ray, U. S. A., Jan. 24, '17.

2 miles—9 m. 9 3-5 s., A. Shrubb, England, June 11, '04

2 miles (indoor)—9 m. 11 2-5 s., J. W. Ray, U. S. A., Mar. 13, '17.

3 miles—14 m. 17 3-5 s., A. Shrubb, England, May 21, '03.

4 miles—19 m. 23 2-5 s., A. Shrubb, England, June 13, '04.

5 miles—24 m. 33 2-5 s., A. Shrubb, England, May 12, '04.

6 miles—29 m. 59 2-5 s., A. Shrubb, England, Nov. 5, '04.

7 miles—35 m. 4 3-5 s., A. Shrubb, England, Nov. 5, '04.

8 miles—40 m. 1⅗ s., A. Shrubb, England, Nov. 5, '04.

9 miles—45 m. 27 3-5 s., A. Shrubb, England, Nov. 5, '04.

10 miles—50 m. 40 3-5 s., A. Shrubb, England, Nov. 5, '04.

15 miles—1 h. 20 m. 4 2-5 s., F. Appleby, England, July 21, '02.

20 miles—1 h. 51 m. 54 s., G. Grossland, England, Sept. 22, 1894.

25 miles—2 h. 29 m. 29 2-5 s., H. Green, England, May 12, '13.

1 hour—11 mls., 1,442 yds., J. Bouin, France, July 6, '13.

2 hours—20 mls., 952 yds., H. Green, England, May 12, '13.

Metric Distances.

100 meters—10.6 s., D. F. Lippincott, U. S. A., 1912.

200 meters—21.6 s., A. Hahn, U. S. A., '04.

300 meters—36.4 s., F. Mezei, Hungary, '13.

300 meters—36.4 s., Faillot, France, '08.

400 meters—48.2 s., C. Reidpath, U. S. A., '12.

500 meters—1 m. 7.6 s., F. Rajz, Hungary, '13.

800 meters—1 m. 51.9 s., J. E. Meredith, U. S. A., '12.

1,000 meters—2 m. 32.3 s., Mickler, Germany, '13.

1,500 meters—3 m. 55.8 s., A. R. Kiviat, U. S. A., '12.

3,000 meters—8 m. 36.8 s., H. Kolehmainen, Finland, '12.

5,000 meters—14 m. 36.6 s., H. Kolehmainen, Finland, '12.

10,000 meters—30 m. 58.8 s., J. Bouin, France, '13.

10,000 meters—31 m. 20.8 s., H. Kolehmainen, Finland, '12.

SPORTING RECORDS—ATHLETICS—WORLD'S AMATEUR RECORDS—RUNNING—*Continued.*

15 kilometers—47 m. 18.6 s., J. Bouin, France, '13.

20 kilometers—1 h. 7 m. 57 s., A. Ahlgren, Sweden, '13.

1 hour—19,021 m., 90cm., J. Bouin, France, '13.

WALKING.

1 mile—6 m. 25 4-5 s., G. H. Goulding, Canada, June 4, '01.

2 miles—13 m., 11 2-5 s., G. E. Larner, England, July 13, '04.

3 miles—20 m. 25 4-5 s., G. E. Larner, England, Aug. 19, '05.

4 miles—27 m. 14 s., G. E. Larner, England, Aug. 19, '05.

5 miles—36 m. 1-5 s., G. E. Larner, England, Sept. 30, '05.

6 miles—43 m. 26 1-5 s., G. E. Larner, England, Sept. 30, '05.

7 miles—50 m. 50 4-5 s., G. E. Larner, England, Sept. 30, '05.

8 miles—58 m. 18 2-5 s., G. E. Larner, England, Sept. 30, '05.

9 miles—1 h. 7 m. 37 4-5 s., G. E. Larner. England, July 17, '08.

10 miles—1 h. 15 m. 57 2-5 s., G. E. Larner, England, July 17, '08.

15 miles—1 h. 59 m. 12 3-5 s., H. V. L. Ross, England, May 20, '11.

20 miles—2 h. 47 m. 52 s., T. Griffith, England, Dec. 30, 1870.

25 miles—3 h. 37 m. 6 4-5 s., S. C. A. Schofield, England, May 20, '11.

1 hour—8 mls. 438 yds., G. E. Larner, England, Sept. 30, '05.

2 hours—15 mls. 128 yds., H. V. L. Ross, England, May 20, '11.

Metric distances—5,000 meters—24 m. 35.8 s., T. Bildt, Sweden, '11.

10 kilometers—46 m. 28.4 s., G. Goulding, Canada, '12.

JUMPING.

[Event, height or distance, holder, nation, date.]

Standing high, 5 ft. 5 3-4 in., L. Goehring, U. S. A., June 14, '13.

Running high—6 ft. 7 5-16 in., E. Beeson, U. S. A., May 2. 14

Standing broad—11 ft. 4 7-8 in., R. C. Ewry, U. S. A., Aug. 29, '04.

Running broad—24 ft. 11 3-4 in., P. O'Connor, England, Aug. 5, '01.

Hop step and jump—50 ft. 11 in., D. F. Ahearne, U. S. A., July 31, '09.

Pole Vault—13 ft. 5½ in., F. Foss, U. S. A., Aug. 20, '20.

WEIGHT EVENTS.

[Event, distance, holder, nation, date.]

Putting 16-lb. wght.—51 ft., R. Rose, U. S. A., Aug 21, '09.

Throwing 16-lb. hammer—189 ft. 6 1-2 in., P. Ryan, U. S. A., Aug. 17, '13.

Throwing 56-lb. wght.—43 ft. 1½ in. (with unlimited run and follow), M. J. McGrath, U. S. A., Oct. 2, '17.

Throwing javelin, 65.78 meters, J. Myrra, Finland, Aug. 15, '20.

HURDLES (10 HURDLES).

[Event, time, holder, nation, date.]

120 yds. (hurdles 3 ft. 6 in. high)— 14 3-5 s., R. Simpson, U. S. A., June 3, '16.

220 yds. (hurdles 2 ft. 6 in. high)—23 3-5 s., A. Kraenzlein, U. S. A., May 28, 1898; J. I. Wendell, U. S. A., May 31, '13; Robt. Simpson, U. S. A., May 27, '16.

440 yds. (hurdles 3 ft. high)—54 3-5 s., W. H. Meanix, U. S. A., July 16, '15.

10 hurdles, metric distances—110 meters—14 4-5 s., E. Thompson, Canada, Aug. 18, '20.

200 meters—24.6 s, H. Hillman, U. S. A., '04.

400 meters—54 s., F. F. Loomis, U. S. A., Aug. 16, '20.

RELAY RACES.

[Event, time, country, holder, date.]

4 men to run equal distances—1 mile, 3 m. 18 s., Univ. of Penn., Kaufmann, Lockwood, Lippincott and Meredith, U. S. A., April 24, '15.

2 miles—7 m. 53 s., Riley Bromilow, Sheppard; Kiviat, U. S. A., Sept. 5, '10.

4 miles—17 m. 51 1-5 s., Mahoney, Marceau, Powers, Hedlund, U. S. A., June 17, '13.

Metric distances—400 meters—42 1-5 s., team of U. S. A. (C. Paddock, J. Scholz, L. Murchison, M. Kirksey), Aug. 22, '20.

800 meters—1 m. 36 s., A. F. K., Stockholm (Ljung, Petterson, Almqist, Hakansson), '08.

1,600 meters—3 m. 16.6 s., team of U. S. A. (Shepperd, Reidpath, Meredith, Lindberg), '12.

Note.—For Olympic Records made by Amer. athletes see section, 1920 Olympic games.

World's Best Records—Amateur and Prof.

[Event, record, amateur, record, professional.]

Running 100 yds.—9 3-5 s., D. J. Kelly, Spokane, Wash., June 23, '06; H. P. Drew, Berkeley, Cal., Mar. 28, '14. 9 1-2 s., A. B. Postle (downhill), Kalgoorlie, Aus., Dec. 28, '06. 9 3-5 s., E. Donovan, Boston, Mass., Sept. 2, 1895; R. Walker, Johannesburg, So. Africa, Dec. 17, '13. 9 3-5 s., A. F. Duffey, N. Y., May 31, '02.

130 yds.—12 4-5 s., Robt. Cloughen, Bkln., N. Y., Feb. 11, '09; H. P. Drew, Bkln., N. Y., Nov. 22, '13. 12 s., J. Donaldson, Sydney, N. S. W., Sept. 23, '11.

220-yds.—21 1-5 s., B. J. Wefers (straightaway), N. Y., May 30, 1896; R. C. Craig, Phila., Pa., May 28, '10; R. C. Craig, Cambridge, Mass., May 27, '11; D. J. Kelly (slight curve), Spokane, Wash., June 23, '06; D. F. Lippincott, Cambridge, Mass., May 31, '13; H. P. Drew, Claremont, Cal., Feb. 28, '14; G. Parker, Fresno, Cal., Oct. 2, '14; 21 1-4 s., J. Donaldson, Shawfield Park, Scotland, July 26, '13.

300 yds.—30 3-5 s., B. J. Wefers, N. Y., Sept. 26, 1896. 30 s., H. Hutchins, Scotland, Jan. 2, 1884.

440 yds.—47 s., M. W. Long, Guttenberg, N. J (straight), Oct. 4, 1900; 47 2-5 s., J. E. Meredith, Cambridge, Mass., May 27, '16. 47 4-5 s., B. R. Day, Perth, W. Australia, April 1, '07.

600 yds.—1 m. 10 4-5 s., M. W. Sheppard, Celtic Park, N. Y., Aug. 14, '10. 1 m. 12 s., E. C. Bredin, England, July 31, 1897; J. Nuttall, Eng., Feb. 20, 1864.

880 yds.—1 m. 52 2-5 s., J. E. Meredith, Phila., Pa., May 13, '16. 1 m. 53½ s., F. S. Hewitt, Lyttleton, N. Z., Sept. 21, '71.

¾-mile—3 m. 2 4-5 s., T. P. Conneff, Travers Isl., N. Y., Aug. 21, 1895. 3 m. 7 s., W. Richards, Eng., June 30, 1866.

1 mile—4 m. 12 3-5 s., N. S. Taber, Cambridge, Mass., July 16, '15. 4 m. 12¾ s., W. G. George, Lilliebridge, Eng., Aug. 23, '86.

2 miles—9 m. 9 3-5 s., A. Shrubb, Glasgow, Scotland, June 11, '04. 9 m. 11 1-2 s., W. Lang, Manchester. Eng., Aug. 1, 1863.

3 miles—14 m. 17 3-5 s., A. Shrubb, Stamford Bridge, England, May 21, '03. 14 m. 19 1-2 s., P. Cannon, Govan, Scotland, May 14, 1888.

4 miles—19 m. 23 3-5 s., A. Shrubb, Glasgow, Scotland, June 13, '04. 19 m. 25 3-5 s., P. Cannon, Glasgow, Scotland, Nov. 8, 1888.

5 miles—24 m. 33 2-5 s., A. Shrubb, Stamford Bridge, England, May 12, '04. 24 m. 40 s., J. White, Hackney, Wicks, May 11, 1863.

10 miles—50 m. 40 3-5 s., A. Shrubb, Glasgow, Scotland, Nov. 5, '04. 51 m. 5 1-2 s., H. Watkins, Rochdale, Sept. 16, 1899.

120 yds., high hurdles—14 3-5 s., R. Simpson, Evanston, Ill., June 3, '16.

220 yds., low hurdles—23 3-5 s., A. C. Kraenzlein, N. Y., May 28, 1898; J. I. Wendell, Cambridge, Mass., May 31, '13; R. Simpson, Columbia, Mo., May 27, '16.

Running high jump—6 ft. 7 5-16 in., E. Beeson, Berkeley, Cal., May 2, '14. 6 ft. 1-2 in., E. W. Johnston, Boston, Mass., Oct. 1, 1881.

Running broad jump—24 ft. 11 3-4 in., P. O'Connor, Dublin, Ireland, Aug. 5, '01. 23 ft. 1 in., L. A. Carpenter, Boston, Oct. 16, '96.

Run, hop, step and jump—50 ft. 11 in., D. F. Ahearne, Celtic Park, N. Y., May 30, '11. 48 ft. 8 in., T. Burrows, Worcester, Mass., Oct. 18, 1884.

Putting 16-lb. shot—51 ft., Ralph Rose, San Francisco, Cal., Aug. 21, '09.

Throwing 16-lb. hammer—189 ft. 6 1-2 in., P. Ryan, Celtic Park, N. Y., Aug. 17, '13.

Pole vault—13 ft. 5½ in., F. Foss, U. S. A., Antwerp, Belgium, Aug. 20, '20. 11 ft. 4 in. R. B. Dickerson, Ireland, July 11, 1892.

Standing broad jump—11 ft. 4 7-8 in., R. C. Ewry, St. Louis, Mo., Aug. 24, '04. 12 ft. 1 1-2 in., J. Darby, England, May 28, 1890.

Standing high jump—5 ft. 5 3-4 in., L. Goehring. Travers Isl., N. Y., June 14, '13. 4 ft. 11 in., H. Andrews, Scotland, 1875.

3 standing jumps—35 ft. 8 3-4 in., R. C. Ewry, Celtic Park, N. Y., Sept. 7, '03. 36 ft. 3 in., T. Colquitt, England, May, '07.

American Amateur Records.

RUNNING.

60-Yd.—6⅗s., L. E. Myers, N. Y. C., Dec. 12, 1882; J. W. Tewksbury, N. Y. C., Jan. 13, 1899; W. D. Eaton, Buffalo, N. Y., Sept. 6, '01; Wash-

SPORTING RECORDS—ATHLETICS—A. A. U. RECORDS—RUNNING—*Continued.*

ington Delgado, N. Y. C., Feb. 4, '01; R. Cloughen, Irish-Amer. A. C., and R. Reed, Gordon A. A., Madison Sq. Garden, N. Y. C., Dec. 1, '08; W. J. Keating, Albany, N. Y., Feb. 3, '10; R. Cloughen, N. Y. C., Jan. 28, '10; J. Wasson, Notre Dame, Chicago, Ill., Mar. 11 '11; A. T. Meyer, Irish-Amer. A. C., Paterson, N. J., Jan. 31, '14; S. Butler, Hutchinson, Kansas, H. S. Evanston, Ill., Mar. 28, '14; R. A. Carroll, Indiana Normal Schl., at Pittsburgh, Pa., July 13, '15; Jo. Loomis, N. Y., Mar. 18, '16; N. Y., Mar. 17, '17; T. G. Griffin, Pittsburgh, Pa., Dec. 4, '15.

60-Yd. Dash—6 2-5 s. (indoor), H. B. Lever, Univ. of Pa., at A. A. U.; indoor junior championships, Buffalo, N. Y., Feb. 21, '20.

70-Yd. (indoor)—7 1-5 s., J. G. Loomis, Chic. A. C., at N. Y. C., Feb. 13, '17.

75-Yd.—7⅗s., L. H. Cary, Princeton, N. J., May 9, 1891; B. J. Wefers, Boston, Mass., Jan. 25, 1896; Archie Hahn, Milwaukee, Wis., Mar. 11, '05; H. P. Drew, N. Y. C., Mar. 6, '13; A. T. Meyer, Irish-Amer. A. C., at N. Y., Mar. 2, '14.

100-Yd.—9⅗s., D. J. Kelly, Spokane, Wash., June 23, '06; H. P. Drew, Univ. of So. Cal., Berkeley, Cal., Mar. 28, '14.

100 Meters—10⅗s., R. C. Craig, Detroit Y. M. C. A.; H. P. Drew, Springfield H. S., at Eastern Tryouts, held at Cambridge, Mass., June 8, '12.

220-Yd.—21 95-100s. (electrical timing), H. Jewett, Montreal, Can., Sept. 24, 1892 (slight curve). Straightaway, 21⅕s., B. J. Wefers, N. Y. C., May 30, 1896; R. C. Craig, Phila., Pa., May 28, '10; R. C. Craig, Cambridge, Mass., May 27, '11; D. F. Lippincott, Cambridge, Mass., May 31, '13. Around half of ¼-mile path, 21⅗s., J. H. Maybury, Madison, Wis., May 9, 1896. Around part of ⅓-mile path, 21⅗s., B. J. Wefers, Travers Isl., N. Y., June 13, 1896. Around a turn ⅓-mile track, 21⅗s., P. J. Walsh, Montreal, Can., Sept. 21, '02. Slight curve, 21⅕s., Dan J. Kelly, Spokane, Wash., June 23, '06; H. P. Drew, Univ. So. Cal., Claremont, Cal., Feb. 28, '14; Geo. Parker, Fresno, Cal., Oct. 2, '14.

220-Yd.—22 ⅘s., L. Murchison, St. Louis, Mo., at Bkln., N. Y., Apr. 28, '19.

300-Yd.—30⅗s., B. J. Wefers, Travers Isl., N. Y., Sept. 26, 1896.

300-Yd. (indoor)—31 2-5 s., A. B. Kelly, Holy Cross Coll., 22d Regt. Armory, N. Y., Mar. 17, '17.

440-Yd., straightaway—47s., M. W. Long, Guttenburg Race Track, Oct. 4, 1900. Round path, 47 2-5 s., J. E. Meredith, Cambridge, Mass., May 27, '16.

440-Yd. (indoor)—49⅗s., T. J. Halpin, Buffalo, N. Y., Mar. 15, '13.

600-Yd.—1m. 10⅘s., M. W. Sheppard, Celtic Park, N. Y., Aug. 14, '10.

600-Yd. (indoor)—1m. 13⅗s., T. J. Halpin, Boston A. A., N. Y., Mar. 2, '14.

880-Yd. (indoor, board)—1m. 54⅘s., E. B. Parson, Buffalo, N. Y., Mar. 19, '04.

880-Yd.—1m. 52 2-5s., J. E. Meredith, Phila., Pa., May 13, '16. (World's record.)

1,000-Yd.—2m. 12⅗s., M. W. Sheppard, Celtic Park, N. Y., July 17, '19; 2m. 13⅗s., J. Ray, Bkln., N. Y., Apr. 28, '19.

1,000-Yd. (indoor)—2m. 14s., J. W. Overton, Yale Univ., 22d Regt. Armory, N. Y., Mar. 17, '17 J. W. Lay, Ill. A. A., March 16, '18.

1,320-Yd.—3m. 2⅘s., T. P. Conneff, Travers Isl., N. Y., Aug. 21, 1895.

1,320-Yd. (indoor)—3m. 7s., J. P. Driscoll, Buffalo, N. Y., Mar. 15, '13.

1,500 Meters—3m. 55⅘s., A. R. Kiviat, Cambridge, Mass., June 8, '12.

1-Mile (outdoor)—4 m. 16 s., J. W. Overton, Phila., Pa., Mar. 10, '17; 4m. 12⅗s., N. S. Taber, Boston A. A., Cambridge, Mass., July 16, '15.

1-Mile (indoor)—4m. 14⅗s., J. Ray, Coliseum, Chicago, Ill., Apr. 12, '19.

3,000 Meters (indoor)—8m. 35s., G. V. Bonhag, Bkln., N. Y., Dec. 16, '11.

2-Mile (outdoor)—9m. 17⅘s., T. S. Berna, Ithaca, N. Y., May 4, '12.

2-Mile (indoor)—9m. 11 2-5s., J. W. Ray, Ill. A. C., Phila., Pa., Mar. 10, '17.

3-Mile (indoor)—14m. 18⅕s., H. Kolehmainen, Bkln., N. Y., Feb. 12, '13.

3-Mile (outdoor)—14m. 32⅗s., H. Kolehmainen, Celtic Park, N. Y., Aug. 17, '13.

4-Mile (indoor, board)—19m. 39⅗s., G. V. Bonhag, N. Y. C., Feb. 5, '10.

4-Mile (outdoor)—20m. 2s., H. Kolehmainen, N. Y. C., Nov. 1, '13.

5,000 Meters (indoor)—15m. 5⅗s., G. V. Bonhag, Madison Sq. Garden, Jan 25, '12.

5,000 Meters (outdoor)—14 m. 45 s., C. F. Hunter, unattached, at Western Olympic Tryouts, Pasadena, Cal., June 26, '20.

5-Mile (indoor)—24m. 29⅗s., H. Kolehmainen, N. Y. C., Feb. 12, '13.

5-Mile (outdoor)—24m. 36 4-5s., C. Pores, Pelham Bay Naval Sta., Apr. 6, '18.

6-Mile (outdoor)—30m. 20⅗s., H. Kolehmainen, N. Y. C., Nov. 1, '13.

6-Mile (indoor)—30m. 24s., H. Kolehmainen, Buffalo, N. Y., Feb. 1, '13.

7-Mile (outdoor)—35m. 35⅘s., H. Kolehmainen, Buffalo, N. Y. C., Nov. 1, '13.

7-Mile (indoor)—35m. 36⅗s., H. Kolehmainen, Buffalo, N. Y., Feb. 1, '13.

8-Mile (indoor)—40m. 47⅘s., H. Kolehmainen, N. Y., Feb. 1, '13.

8,000-Meter (outdoor)—25m. 44s., W. J. Kramer, Celtic Park, L. I., June 2, '12.

8-Mile (indoor)—46m. ⅘s., H. Kolehmainen, Buffalo, N. Y., Feb. 1, '13.

9-Mile (indoor)—46m. ⅘s., H. Kolehmainen, N. Y. C., Nov. 1, '13.

10,000-Meter (outdoor)—31m. 43⅗s., W. J. Kramer, Cambridge, Mass., June 8, '12.

9-Mile (outdoor)—46m., H. Kolehmainen, N. Y. C., Nov. 1, '13.

10-Mile (outdoor)—51m. 3⅗s., H. Kolehmainen, N. Y. C., Nov. 1, '13.

10-Mile (indoor)—51m. 6⅘s., H. Kolehmainen, Buffalo, N. Y., Feb. 1, '13.

Hour—10 miles, 1,182½ yds., S. Thomas, N. Y. C., Nov. 30, 1889.

15-Mile—1h. 25m. 15s., J. F. Crowley, Celtic Park, N. Y., Nov. 14, '09; 1h. 22m. 24⅕s., C. Pores, Millrose A. A., N. Y. C., June 1, '19.

20-Mile—1h. 58m. 37⅗s., James Clark, Celtic Park, N. Y., Nov. 14, '09.

25-Mile—2h. 44m. 50s., M. Maloney, N. Y. C., Jan. 8, '09.

WALKING.

1-Mile (outdoor)—6m. 29⅗s., F. P. Murray, N. Y. C., Oct. 27, 1883.

1-Mile (indoor)—6m. 28s., G. H. Goulding, Buffalo, N. Y., Dec. 16, '11.

3,000 Meters (outdoor)—12 m. 56 2-5 s., W. Plant, Morningside A. C., N. Y., at Eastern Olympic Tryouts, Franklin Field., Phila., Pa., June 26, '20.

2-Mile (indoor)—13 m. 37 s., G. H. Goulding, N. Y., Mar. 18, '16.

2-Mile (outdoor)—13m. 48⅗s., F. P. Murray, Wmsbg., N. Y. C., May 30, 1884.

3-Mile (indoor)—20m. 49⅗s., G. H. Goulding, Bkln., N. Y., Mar. 30, '12.

3-Mile (outdoor)—21m. 9⅕s., F. P. Murray, N. Y. C., Nov. 6, 1883.

4-Mile (indoor)—28m. 6⅕s., G. H. Goulding, Bkln., N. Y., Mar. 30, '12.

5-Mile (outdoor)—36m. 10s., G. H. Goulding, Toronto, Central Walkers' Club, New Brunswick, N. J., Oct. 23, '15.

6-Mile (outdoor)—43m. 28⅗s., G. H. Goulding, New Brunswick, N. J., Oct. 23, '15.

7-Mile (outdoor)—50m. 40⅗s., G. H. Goulding, New Brunswick, N. J., Oct. 23, '15.

8-Mile—1h. 2m. 8⅕s., J. B. Clark, N. Y. C., Sept. 8, '80; 1h. 1m. 34s., R. F. Remer, N. Y. A. C., handicap walk, Nov. 24, '19.

9-Mile—1 h. 10 m. 8 s. 10-Mile—1 h. 17 m. 40¾ s., E. E. Merrill, Boston, Mass., Oct. 5, '80.

2 hrs. (outdoor)—14 miles, 420 yds., W. Plant, N. Y., June 17, '17; 14 miles, 430 yds. 6 in., W. Plant, N. Y. C., Nov. 9, '19.

15-Mile—2 h. 7 m. 17 3-5 s., Ed Rens, N. Y. A. C., N. Y., June 17, '17; 2h. 6m. 13⅕s., W. Plant, Morningside A. C., N. Y. C., Nov. 9, '19.

20-Mile—3 h. 3 m. 10 s. 25-Mile—4 h. 3 m. 35 s., J. B. Clark, N. Y. C., Dec. 5, '79.

1 Hour Record (outdoor)—10 miles, 1,492 yds., C. Pores, Millrose A. A., N. Y., June 1, '19.

RELAY RACING.

440-Yds. (4-man team, each man running 110 yds.)—42⅘s., Univ. of Penn., Phila, Pa., June 7, '19.

880-Yd. Relay (indoor, Olympic style, with baton, 4 men)—1m. 35⅘s., Xavier A. A. team (C. B. Clark, H. Heiland, E. Lohse, W. J. Keating), N. Y. C., Feb. 21, '12.

880-Yd. Relay (outdoor, 4 men each to run 220 yds.)—1m. 29⅘s., Univ. of Chicago team (F. T. Ward, B. Desmond, M. Baranak, D. Knight), Chicago, Ill., June 12, '15; 1m. 27⅘s., Univ. of Penn., Phila, Pa., June 7, '19.

1,760-Yd. (outdoor, 4 men, each man to run 440 yds.)—3m. 18s., Univ. of Penn., team (F. Kaufmann, J. Lockwood, D. Lippincott, J. E. Meredith), Phila., Pa., Apr. 24, '15.

SPORTING RECORDS—ATHLETICS—A. A. U. RECORDS—RELAY RACING—*Continued.*

1,760-Yd.—3 m. 21 s., All-Buffalo team (J. W. Habberfield, W. F. Koppish, M. J. Sutton and C. H. Brandt), at 74th Regt. A. A. games at Buffalo, N. Y., April 17, '20.

1,760-Yd. (outdoor, teams of 5 men, each man to run ⅕ of distance)—3m. 11⅗s., N. Y. A. C. team (W. G. Packard, E. Frick, L. C. Carey, R. T. Edwards, LeRoy Wood), Travers Isl., N. Y., June 1, '12

2-Mile—7m. 53s., Irish-Amer. A. C. team (F. Riley, J. Bromilow, M. W. Sheppard, A. R. Kiviat), Celtic Park, N. Y., Sept. 5, '10; Yale Univ. (H. Rolfe, A. Barker, H. Cooper, J. W. Overton), Phila., Pa., April 29, '16.

4-Mile (outdoor, teams of 4 men, each man to run 1 mile)—17m. 51⅘s., Boston A. A. team (Mahoney, Marceau, Powers, Hedlund), Easton, Pa., June 17, '13; Cornell Univ. (G. Taylor, J. Hoffmire, L. Windnagle, D. Potter), Phila., Pa., April 29, '16.

4-Mile (indoor)—17m. 43⅗s., Cornell Univ. team (H. N. Putnam, L. Finch, T. S. Berna, J. P. Jones), Buffalo, N. Y., Mar. 1, '12.

HURDLE RACING.

50-Yds.—4 hurdles, low (indoor), 15 yds. to 1st hurdle, hurdles 10 yds. apart, 5 yds. to finish, 6 1-5 s., J. G. Loomis, Phila., Pa., Mar. 10, '17.

60-Yds.—5 hurdles, 2 ft. 6 in. high, 7 2-5 s. (indoor); J. J. Eller, N. Y. C., Jan. 25, '13. 5 hurdles, 3 ft. 6 in. high, 8 s., F. Smithson, San Francisco, Cal., Feb. 19, '09 (indoor); F. W. Kelly, Univ. Sou. Cal., Bkln., April 27, '14. 15 yds. to 1st hurdle, 10 yds. apart, 5 yds. to finish, 8 s., J. R. Case, Olympic Club, San Francisco, Cal., Feb. 20, '14. 15 yds. to 1st hurdle, hurdles 10 yds. apart and 5 yds. to finish; 3 hurdles, 3 ft. 6 in. high, 15 yds. apart, 15 yds. start and finish, 7 2-5 s., R. G. Haskins, C. A. A., Chicago, Ill., Mar. 11, '11; 3 hurdles, 2 ft. 6 in. high, 15 yds. apart, 15 yards to finish, 6 4-5s., F. Fletcher, Notre Dame, Chicago, Ill., Mar. 11, '11.

70-Yds.—5 hurdles, 3 ft. 6 in. high, 8 4-5 s., Forrest Smithson, Madison Sq. Garden, N. Y., Mar. 10, '08.

70-Yd. High Hurdles (indoor)—9 1-5 s (Six 3 ft. 6 in. hurdles, 10 yds. apart, 10 yds. to first hurdle and 10 yds. to finish), W Smith, Cornell Univ., at Natl. A. A. U.; indoor championship at 22nd Regt. Armory, N. Y., March 13, '20.

70-Yd. High Hurdles (indoor), 9 1-5 s. (Six 3 ft. 6 in. hurdles, 10 yds. apart, 10 yds. to first hurdle, 10 yds. to finish), E F Smalley, Univ. of Pa., at Natl. A. A. U.; junior indoor track and field championships, Buffalo, N. Y., Feb. 21, '20.

70-Yds. (outdoor)—5 hurdles, 2 ft. 6 in. high, 8 2-5 s., J. J. Eller, N. Y. C., Feb. 5, '10; (indoor) 8 2-5 s., R. Eller and J. J. Eller, Madison Sq. Garden, N. Y. C., Feb. 4, '11

75-Yds. High (indoor)—9 3-5 s., Waldo Ames, Champaign, Ill., Mar. 3, '17.

75-Yds. Low (indoors)—3 hurdles, 2 ft. 6 in., 8 2-5 s., Waldo Ames, Champaign, Ill., Mar. 3, '17.

120-Yds.—5 hurdles, 3 ft. high, 17 s., W. M. Townsend, Gambier, O., May 24, '82; 6 hurdles, 3 ft. high, 17s., H. G. Otis, Nahant Beach, Mass., Sept. 28, '78; 6 hurdles, 3 ft. 6 in. high, 17⅗s., W. H. Young, Toronto, Ont., June 10, '76; 8 hurdles, 3 ft. 6 in. high, 17¼s., R. B. Jones, San Francisco, Cal., Sept. 9, '84; 10 hurdles, 2 ft. 6 in. high, 14 2-5 s., J. J. Eller, Celtic Park, Sept. 6, 1909; (indoor) 2 ft. 6 in. high, 14 2-5 s., J. J. Eller, Irish-Amer. A. C., Bkln., Feb. 23, '14; 10 hurdles, 3 ft. high, 18 1-5 s., G. H. Taylor, Rutland, Vt., Aug. 24, '83; 10 hurdles, 3 ft. 6 in. high, 14 3-5 s., Robt. Simpson, Evanston, Ill., June 3, '16.

220-Yds.—5 hurdles, 3 ft. high, 29⅗ s., F. W. Janssen, N. Y. C., July 26, '80; 6 hurdles, 2 ft. 6 in. high, 26 2-5 s., C. T. Wiegand, N. Y. C., May 4, '89; 7 hurdles, 2 ft. 6 in. high, 29 s., J. McClelland, N. Y. C., Oct. 4, '79; 8 hurdles, 2 ft. 6 in. high, 28⅗s., J. E. Haigh, N. Y. C., Sept. 6, '79; 9 hurdles, 2 ft. 3 in. high, 28⅘ s., J. S. Voorhees, Jersey City, N. J., Oct. 26, '80; 9 hurdles, 3 ft. 6 in. high, 29 3-5 s., J. B. Hanna, N. Y. C., Mar. 14, '80; 10 hurdles, 2 ft. 6 in. high, 23 3-5 s., A. C. Kraenzlein, N. Y. C., May 28, '98; 10 hurdles, 2 ft. 6 in high, 23 3-5s., J. I. Wendell, Cambridge, Mass., May 31, '13; 10 hurdles, 3 ft. high, 28 4-5 s., C. T. Wiegand, Bkln., July 10, '86; 10 hurdles, 3 ft. 6 in. high, 27 3-5 s., J. J. Eller, Celtic Park, L. I., Oct. 11, '08; 10 hurdles, 2 ft. 6 in. high, 24 4-5s. (⅙ mile track, around turn), J. J. Eller, I.-A. A. C., Travers Isl., Sept. 19, '08; J. J. Eller, Pittsburg, Pa., July 1, '11; J. J. Eller, Celtic Park, L. I., Sept. 16, '11; Robt. Simpson, Columbia, Mo. May 27, '16; 2 ft. 6 in. hurdles (outdoor, around turn), 24 4-5 s., F. W. Kelly, Univ. Sou. Cal., Los Angeles, Cal., May 21, '15.

¼-Mile—8 hurdles, 3 ft. 6 in. high, 1 m. 4 s., W. L. Allen, St. Hyacinthe, P. Q., Oct. 10, '78; 10 hurdles, 2 ft. 6 in. high, 56 2-5 s., J. Buck, Williamsbridge, N. Y., Sept. 19, '96; 10 hurdles, 3 ft. 6 in. high, 1 m. 8¼ s., R. S. Summerhayes, Montreal, P. Q., Oct. 7, '77; 15 hurdles, 2 ft. 6 in. high., 1 m. 9⅗ s., G. G. Neidlinger, Bkln., N. Y., Dec. 31, '79. 16 hurdles, 2 ft. 6 in. high, 1 m. 4 s., H. H. Moritz, N. Y. C., July 4, '79; 18 hurdles, 2 ft. 6 in. high, 1 m. 12¼ s., H. H. Moritz, N. Y. C., May 17, '79; 20 hurdles, 2 ft. 6 in. high, 1 m. 9 4-5 s., A. F. Coplan, N. Y. C., Jan. 28, '88; 10 hurdles, 2 ft. 6 in. high, 54 3-5 s., H. L. Hillman, Travers Isl., N. Y., Oct. 1, '04.

440-Yd. (outdoor)—54 1-5 s.—J. K. Norton, Olympic Club, San Francisco, at Western Olympic Tryouts, Pasadena, Cal., June 26, '20. (10 hurdles, 3 ft. high, 40 yds. to first hurdle, 40 yds. between hurdles and 40 yds. to finish.)

JUMPING.

Standing high, without weights (outdoor)—5 ft. 5⅝ in., Leo Goehring, Travers Isl., N Y., June 14, '13; (indoor), 5 ft. 4½ in., Platt Adams, N. Y. C., Jan. 25, '13.

Running high, without weights—6 ft. 7 5-16 in. (outdoor), E. Beeson, Olympic Club, Berkeley, Cal., May 2, '14.

Running high (indoor), without weights—6 ft. 4½ in., S. C. Lawrence, Boston, Feb. 9, '12.

Standing broad jump, without weights—11 ft. 4⅞ in., Ray C. Ewry, St. Louis, Aug. 29, '04.

3 standing—35 ft. 8⅞ in., Ray C. Ewry, Celtic Park, N. Y., Sept. 7, '08.

Running broad jump, without weights—24 ft. 7¼ in., M. Prinstein, Phila., Pa., April 28, '00.

Running hop, step and jump, without weights—50 ft. 11 in., D. F. Ahearne, Celtic Park, L. I., May 30, '11.

VAULTING.

Pole vault for height—13 ft. 2¼ in., M. S. Wright, Cambridge, Mass., June 8, '12; 13 ft. 3 9-16 in., F. K. Foss, Chicago A. A., Aug. 23, '19.

Pole vault for distance (indoor)—28 ft. 2 in., Platt Adams, N. Y. C., Oct. 31, '10.

THROWING HAMMER.

Regulation hammer, A. A. U. rules, weight (including handle) 16 lbs., entire lgth. 4 ft., thrown from 7-ft. circle.

16-Lb. hammer—189 ft. 6½ in., P. Ryan, Celtic Park, L. I., Aug. 17, '13.

SHOT PUTTING.

8-Lb. shot—67 ft. 7 in., Ralph Rose, Travers Isl., N. Y., Sept. 14, '07.

12-Lb. shot—57 ft. 3 in., Ralph Rose, Celtic Park, L. I., Aug. 29, '08.

16-Lb. shot—51 ft., Ralph Rose, San Francisco, Aug. 21, '09.

24-Lb. shot (outdoor)—38 ft. 10 11-16 in., P. J. McDonald, Celtic Park, L. I., Oct. 22, '11.

24-Lb. shot (indoor, from board to dirt pit)—39 ft. 3¼ in., P. J. McDonald, N. Y. C., Mar. 6, '13.

16-Lb. shot, r. and l. hand, with toe board—91 ft. 10½ in. (r. h., 50 ft. 6 in.; l. h., 41 ft. 4½ in.), Ralph Rose, Oakland, Cal., June 2, '12; r. and l. h. without toe board—91 ft. 10 in. (r. h. 49 ft. 10 in.; l. h., 42 ft.), Ralph Rose, Amer. League Park, N. Y. C., June 13, '12.

THROWING WEIGHTS.

56-Lb. weight, thrown with both hands from 7-ft. circle, without follow—40 ft. 6⅝ in., M. J. McGrath, Montreal, Can., Sept. 23, '11. With unlimited run and follow, 43 ft. 1½ in., M. J. McGrath, N. Y. A. A., Travers Isl., Oct. 2, '17.

56-Lb. weight for height—16 ft. 11¼ in., P. Donovan, Pastime A. C., San Francisco, Cal., Feb. 20, '14.

JAVELIN RECORD.

Javelin Throw—197 ft. 5¼ in., J. C. Lincoln Jr., N. Y. A. C., at the N. Y. A. C. games at Travers Isl., N. Y., Sept. 25, '20.

THROWING DISCUS

Throwing discus, Olympic style, weight 4 lbs. 6½ oz. (8 ft. 2½ in. circle)—156 ft. 1⅝ in., J. Duncan, Celtic Park, L. I., May 27, '12.

Throwing discus from 7 ft. circle—145 ft. 9½ in., J. Duncan, Celtic Park, L. I., June 2, '12.

Throwing discus (8 ft. 2½ in. circle, r. and l. hand)—252 ft. 8⅞ in., J. Duncan, Celtic Park, L. I., May 27, '12. R. h., 156 ft. 1⅝ in.; l. h., 96 ft. 7½ in.

SPORTING RECORDS—ATHLETICS—A. A. U. RECORDS—*Continued.*

ALL-AROUND TRACK AND FIELD RECORD.

All-around record—7,499 points, F. C. Thomson, Princeton U., Princeton, N. J., June 5, '13.

ROPE CLIMBING.

38 Ft. Up—16 3-5 s., L. Weissman, 92d St. Y. M. C. A., N. Y., at 12 Regt. Armory, N. Y., April 17, '20.

WORLD'S SWIMMING RECORDS.
AMATEUR AND PROFESSIONAL.

50 yds., bath, D. P. Kahanamoku (A), 23 2-5s.; open water, D. P. Kahanamoku (A), 23s.

100 yds., bath, Perry McGillivray (A), 54s.; open water, D. P. Kahanamoku (A), 53s. Professional, A. Wickham (Aus.), 1:00 4-5.

100 meters, bath, Norman Ross (A), 1:01; open water, Duke P. Kahanamoku (A), 1:00 4-5.

120 yds., bath, P. McGillivray (A), 1:08 2-5. Professional, G. R. Dungan (A), 1:13.

150 yds., bath, H. E. Vollmer (A), 1:29 4-5; open water, C. Healy (Aus.), 1:34. Professional, G. R. Dungan (A), 1:34 3-5.

200 yds., bath, Norman Ross (A), 2:06 2-5; no open water. Professional, D. Billington (E), 2:13 1-5.

200 meters, bath, Norman Ross (A), 2:21 3-5.

220 yds., bath, Norman Ross (A), 2:20 1-5; open water, P. McGillivray (A), 2:21 1-5. Professional, D. Billington (E), 2:34 4-5.

300 yds., bath, Norman Ross (A), 3:16 3-5; open water, B. Kieran (Aus.), 3:31 4-5. Professional, D. Billington (E), 3:32.

400 meters, bath, Norman Ross (A), 5.16 2-5; open water, L. Langer (A), 5:17.

440 yds., bath, Norman Ross (A), 5:05 3-5; open water, L. Langer (A), 5:17. Professional, D. Billington (E), 5:26.

500 meters, bath, H. E. Vollmer (A), 6:51 3-5.

500 yds., bath, Norman Ross (A), 5:53 2-5; open water, L. Langer (A), 6:11 2-5. Professional, D. Billington (E), 6:18.

880 yds., bath, B. Kieeran (Aus.) 11:11 3-5; open water, H. Taylor (E), 11:25 2-5. Professional, D. Billington, 11:37.

1,000 yds., bath, Norman Ross (A), 12:44 3-5; open water, L. Langer (A), 13:07 2-5. Professional, D. Billington, 13:26.

1,320 yds., bath, C. M. Daniels (A), 17:45 4-5; open water, W. Longworth (Aus.), 17:42. Professional, D. Billington (E), 17:36 2-5.

1-mile, bath, B. Kieran (Aus.), 23.16 4-5; open water, G. R. Hodgson (C), 23:34½. Professional, D. Billington (E), 24:11 1-5.

2 miles, bath, George Read (Aus.), 54:54; open water, W. Longworth (Aus.), 51:32.

SWIMMING.

Figures in parentheses indicate length of course in yards, unless stated otherwise. t—turns.

50 yds., bath (100 ft.) 1 turn—23 ⅗s., D. P. Kahanamoku, San Francisco, Cal., Aug. 6, '13; 50 yds. open tidal salt water, straightaway—23⅗s., B. R. Small, San Francisco, Honolulu, H. T., Feb. 21, '14 (swimmer not aided by tide).

100 yds., bath (75 yds., salt water), 1 turn—54⅗s., D. P. Kahanamoku, San Francisco, Cal., July 5, '13; open tidal salt water, straightaway—53s., D. P. Kahanamoku, Honolulu Bay, H. T., Sept. 5, '17; bath (20), 4 t.—54 s., Perry McGillivray, Ill. A. C., Chicago, Ill., Feb. 3, '16.

120 yds., bath (25), 4 turns—1m. 10s., C. M. Daniels, N. Y. C., Dec. 9, '08; bath (20), 5 turns—1m. 8⅗s., Perry McGillivray, Illinois A. C., bath, Chicago, Ill., Jan. 8, '14.

150 yds. free style, bath (25) 5 turns—1 m. 29 3-5 s., Tedford Cann, Detroit A. C., Detroit, Mich., at Cleveland Y. M. C. A. Bath, April 17, '20; bath (20), 7 turns—1m. 31⅕s., H. J. Hebner, Illinois A. C., bath, Chicago, Ill., Feb. 5, '14; bath (25), 5 t.—1 m. 29 4-5 s., H. E. Vollmer, N. Y. A. C., N. Y. C., Jan. 10, '16.

150 yds., backstroke, bath (25), 5 turns—1m. 53 1-5s, S. C. B. Pavlicek, Ill. A. C., Detroit, Mich., Feb. 24, '17.

200 yds., bath (20), 9 turns—2 m. 6 2-5 s., Norman Ross, Illinois A. C., Chicago, in Honolulu Y. M. C. A. Bath, Dec. 3, '19.

220 yds., bath (25), 7 turns—2 m. 19 4-5 s. Tedford H. Cann, Detroit A. C. pool, Detroit, Mich., April 10, '20; bath (30), 8 turns—2 m. 25 2-5 s., C. M. Daniels, Pittsburgh, Pa., Mar. 26, '09; bath (20), 10 turns—2m. 21s., H. J. Hebner, Illinois A. C., bath, Chicago, Ill., Jan. 8, '14; bath (75, salt water), 2 turns—2m. 26⅗s., D. P. Kahanamoku, Honolulu, H. T., Sutro bath, San Francisco, Cal., July 4, '14; open, still water (110), 1 turn—2m. 33⅗s., Perry McGillivray, Illinois A. C., Broad Ripple Pool, Indianapolis, Ind., July 31, '14; bath (25), 8 t.—2 m. 28 3-5 s., H. E. Vollmer, N. Y. A. C., N. Y., Apr. 10, '16.

250 yds., bath (25), 9 turns—2m. 48 4-5s., T. H. Cann, N. Y., Mar. 14, '17.

300 yds., bath (25), 11 turns—3m. 35⅗s., C. M. Daniels, N. Y., Mar. 4, '10; bath (20), 14 turns—3m 29⅕s., Perry McGillivray, Illinois A. C., bath, Chicago, Ill., Feb. 5, '14; bath (25), 11 t.—3 m. 34 2-5 s., H. E. Vollmer, N. Y. A. C., N. Y. C., July 18, '16.

300 meters, bath (25), 13 t.—3 m. 55⅗ s., H. E. Vollmer, N. Y. A. C., N. Y. C., July 13, '16.

440 yds., bath (75, salt water), 5 turns—5m. 22⅕s., Ludy Langer, Los Angeles A. C., Sutro bath, San Francisco, Cal., July 5, '14; open tidal salt water (110), 3 turns—5m. 37⅗s., D. P. Kahanamoku, Honolulu, H. T., June 11, '13 (swimmer not aided by tide); bath (25), 17 turns—5m. 16 2-5s., Norman Ross, Olympic Club, Detroit, Mich., Mar. 31, '17; bath (20), 21 turns—5 m 5 3-5 s., N Ross, Illinois A. C., Chicago, in Honolulu Y. M. C. A. Bath, Honolulu, T. H., Dec. 4, '10.

500 yds., bath (20), 24 turns—5m. 53 2-5s., Norman Ross, Chicago, Ill., Apr. 10, '18.

880 yds., bath (75, salt water), 11 turns—11m. 46⅗s., Ludy Langer, Los Angeles A. C., Sutro bath, San Francisco, Cal., July 3, '14; still open water (110), 7 turns—12m. 18⅗s., C. M. Daniels, Seneca Park Lake, Rochester, N. Y., Aug. 28, 09; open salt water (100) 8 turns, 11m. 13 3-5 s., N. Ross, Illinois A. C., Chicago, in Honolulu Harbor, Honolulu, T. H., Nov. 1, '19.

1,000 yds. open, still salt water (80), 12 turns—14m. 19⅗s., H. E. Vollmer, N. Y. A. C. bath, Coney Isl., N. Y., Sept. 1, '14; (150), 1 m. 53 3-5 s., H. J. Hebner, Ill. A. C., Sutre baths, San Francisco, Cal., July 16, '15.

1 mile, bath open tidal salt water, 15 turns—25m. 40⅗s., J. H. Reilly, Rye, N. Y., Sept. 16, '11; open still salt water (80), 21 turns—25m. 18⅗ s., L. J. Goodwin, Coney Isl., Sept. 4, '13.

100 meters, bath (25), 4 turns—1m. 2⅗s., C. M. Daniels, N. Y., Apr. 15, '10.

100-meter free style, straightway, (60), 1 m. 5 s., D. P. Kahanamoko, Honolulu, H. T., at Neptune Beach, Alameda, Cal., June 26, '20.

200 meters, bath (30), 7 turns—2m. 26s., C. M. Daniels, Pittsburgh, Pa., Mar. 28, '11; bath (25), 8 t.—2 m. 23⅗ s., H. E. Vollmer, N. Y. A. C., N. Y. C., April 10, '16; (100) 6 turns—2m. 21 3-5s., Norman Ross, San Francisco, Cal., Nov. 24, '16.

300 meters, bath (25), 13 turns—3m. 57⅗s., C. M. Daniels, N. Y., Mar. 4, '10.

500 meters, bath (25), 21 turns—7m. ⅗s., J. C. Wheatley, N. Y. A. C., N. Y. A. C. bath, New York City, Apr. 25, '14.

50 yds. open tidal salt water, straightaway—23 sec., D. P. Kahanamoku, Hui Nalu, Honolulu, Honolulu Harbor, H. T., June 11, '15.*

100 yds. open tidal salt water, straightaway—53 sec., D. P. Kahanamoku, Hui Nalu, Honolulu, Honolulu Harbor, H. T., Sept. 5, '17.*

100 yds., bath (75), 1 turn—54⅗s., D. P. Kahanamoku, Hui Nalu, Honolulu, Sutro baths, San Francisco, Cal., July 17, '15.

220 yds., open tidal salt water (100), 2 turns—2m. 29s., D. P. Kahanamoku, Hui Nalu, Honolulu, and George Cunha, Hui Nalu (swimming dead heat), Honolulu Harbor, H. T., June 11, '15.*

220 yds., bath (75), 2 turns—2m. 26⅗s., D. P. Kahanamoku, Hui Nalu, Honolulu, Sutro baths, San Francisco, July 16, '15.

220 yds., bath (100), 6 turns—2m. 21 3-5s., Norman Ross, Stanford, Univ., San Francisco, Cal., Nov. 24, '16.

300 yds., bath (20), 14 turns—3m. 28⅗s., Perry McGillivray, Ill. A. C., Ill. A. C. bath, Chicago, Ill., Feb. 4, '15.

440 yds., open salt water (110), 3 turns—5m. 32⅕s., Ludy Langer, Los Angeles A. C., San Francisco, Cal., July 19, '15.

500 yds., bath (75), 6 turns—6m. 13⅗s., Ludy Langer, Los Angeles A. C., Sutro baths, San Francisco, Cal., July 17, '15.

1,000 yds., open, still, salt water (84), 11 turns—13m. 59⅗s., H. E. Vollmer, N. Y. A. C., Steeplechase Park baths, N. Y., Aug. 18, '15.

1 mile, open salt water (110), 15 turns—24m. 59⅗s., Ludy Langer, Los Angeles A. C., San Francisco, Cal., July 23, '15.

---

*Not aided by tide.

SPORTING RECORDS—ATHLETICS—A. A. U. RECORDS—SWIMMING—*Continued.*

100 yds., breaststroke, bath (20), 4 t.—1 m. 10⅘ s., M. McDermott, Ill. A. C., bath, Chicago, Ill., Mar. 2, '16.

200 yds., breaststroke, bath (20), 9 turns—2m. 38⅗s., Michael McDermott, Ill. A. C., Ill. A. C. bath, Chicago, Ill., Feb. 4. '15.

200 yds. breaststroke, open water (50), 2 t.—2 m. 45⅘ s., M. McDermott, Ill. A. C., Put-in-Bay, Ohio, July 18, '16.

SWIMMING ON BACK.

880 yds., open salt water (110), 7 turns—12m. 6s., Ludy Langer, Los Angeles A. C., San Francisco, Cal., July 22, '15.

100-yds., open tidal salt water straightaway—1 m. 8 s., W. Kealoha, Hui Makani, Honolulu, in Honolulu Harbor, Honolulu, T. H., Apr. 19, '20.

100 yds., bath (20), 4 turns—1 m. 8 1-5 s., H. Kruger, St. Mary's Col., San Francisco, Cal., in Honolulu Y. M. C. A. Bath, Honolulu, T. H., Apr. 29. '20.

100-meter, bath (20), 5 turns—1 m. 16 4-5 s., H Kruger, St. Mary's Col., San Francisco, Ca., in Honolulu Y. M. C. A. Bath, Honolulu, T. H., Apr. 29, '20.

100 yds., bath (25), 3 turns—1m. 8⅗s., H. J. Hebner, Crystal bath, St. Louis, Mo., Apr. 1, '11; 100 yds., open still water, straightaway—1m. 16 4-5s., Walter Brack, Berlin, Germany, at St. Louis, Mo., Sept. 6, '04.

150 yds., bath (75, salt water), 1 turn—1m. 55⅗s., H. J. Hebner, Illinois A. C., Sutro bath, San Francisco, Cal., July 4, '14; bath (20), 7 turns—1m. 49⅗s., H. J. Hebner, Illinois A. C., Ill. A. C. bath, Chicago, Ill., Apr. 30, '14.

1,000-yd. free style, open salt water (100), 9 turns—12 m. 44 3-5 s., N. Ross. Illinois A. C., Chicago, in Honolulu Harbor, Honolulu, T. H., Nov. 1, '19.

RELAY RACING.

200-Yd. Relay. 4 men, 50 yds. each (25) bath—1 m. 39 4-5 s., Yale Univ. team (R. F. Solley, J. M. Hincks, L. P. Thurston and E. Binney, Jr.), Yale Univ. Bath, New Haven, Conn., March 17, '20.

Relay racing—250 yds., 5 men, each 50 yds. bath (25)—2 m. 10⅗s., N. Y. A. C. team (H. E. Vollmer, Walter Ramme, N. T. Nerich, H. O'Sullivan and W. R. Bennett), Rutgers College bath, New Brunswick, N. J., Mar. 10, '15.

Relay racing—400 yds., 4 men, each 100 yds., 3 m. 47 4-5 s., Illinois A. C. team at Olympic Club, San Francisco, Cal., Apr. 28, '20.

Relay racing—500 yds., 5 men, each 100 yds., bath (20)—4 m. 40⅗ s., Ill. A. C. team (A. C. Raithel, 55s.; Wm. Vosburgh, 57⅗s.; H. J. Hebner, 55s.; Perry McGillivray, 55⅕s.; D. L. Jones, 58s.), Ill. A. C. bath, Chic., Ill., April 27, '16.

Relay racing—500 yds., 5 men each, 100 yds., Illinois A. C. team at Olympic Club, San Francisco, Apr. 28, '20.

Relay racing—200 yds., 4 men, each 50 yds., bath (25)—1m. 46s., N. Y. A. C. (Geo. South, 26⅗s.; C. D. Trubenbach, 27s.; N. Nerich, 26⅗s., and C. M. Daniels, 25⅕s.), N. Y. C., Apr. 15, '10.

Relay racing—400 yds., 4 men, each 100 yds., bath (20)—3m. 46s., Illinois A. C. team (A. C. Raithel, 55s.; H. J. Hebner, 57s.; Perry McGillivray, 55⅘s.; Wm Vosburgh, 58⅕s.), Chicago, Ill., May 1, '13; 4 men, each 100 yds., bath (25)—3m. 52⅘s., Illinois A. C. (A. C. Raithel, 58⅗s.; Wm. Vosburgh, 59⅕s.; Perry McGillivray, 57s.; H. J. Hebner, 58s.), N. Y. A. C. bath, N. Y. C., May 4, 1914; 4 men, open, still water, 100 yds. course—3m. 57⅕s., Illinois A. C. (H. J. Hebner, 1m.; M. R. Mott, 1m. 2s.; A. C. Raithel, 57⅕s.; Perry McGillivray, 58s.), Broad Ripple Pool, Indianapolis, Ind., July 31, '14.

Relay racing—500 yds., 5 men, each 100 yds., bath (20)—4m. 45⅕s., Illinois A. C. team (A. C. Raithel, 55s.; H. J. Hebner, 57s.; Perry McGillivray, 55s.; Wm. Vosburgh, 58⅕s.; E. W. McGillivray, 59⅕s.), Chicago, Ill., May 1, '13; 5 men, each 100 yds., bath (25)—4m. 57s., N. Y. A. C. team (H. O'Sullivan, 1m.; N. T. Nerich, 58⅘s.; C. M. Daniels, 56⅕s.; J. H. Reilly, 1m. ⅕s.; Geo. South, 1m. 1⅘s.), N. Y. C., Mar. 18, '11.

Plunging—1 m. time limit, bath—82 ft. 9 in., F Schwedt, Detroit Y. M. C. A., Detroit, Mich., in natl. championship, Pittsburgh Natatorium, Pittsburg, Pa., Mar. 1, '20.

Women.

50 yds., free style, open tidal salt water, straightaway—29 1-5 s., F C Schroth, San Francisco, Cal., in Honolulu Harbor, Honolulu, T. H., Nov. 3, '19.

100 yds. free style, open tidal salt water, straightaway—1 m. 3 1-5 s., E. Bleibtrey, Women's Swimming Assn. of N. Y., in Honolulu Harbor, Honolulu, T. H., Apr. 17, '20.

100 yds. free style, bath (20), 4 turns—1 m. 6 1-5 s., E. Bleibtrey, Women's Swimming Assn. of N. Y., in W. 60th St. Bath, N. Y. C., Mar. 17, '20.

100-meter free style, open tidal salt water, straightaway—1 m. 12 4-5 s., E. Bleibtrey, Women's Swimming Assn. of N. Y., at Manhattan Bh., N. Y., July 10, '20.

220 yds. free style, open tidal salt water (100), 2 turns—2 m. 55 2-5 s., E. Bleibtrey, Women's Swimming Assn. of N. Y., at Manhattan Bh., N. Y., July 24, '20.

220 yds. free style, bath (20), 10 turns—2 m. 53 4-5 s., C. Boyle. Women's Swimming Assn. of N. Y., in W. 60th St. Bath, N. Y. C., Mar. 17, '20.

300-meter free style, open tidal salt water (100), 3 turns—4 m. 34 1-5 s., E. Bleibtrey, Women's Swimming Assn. of N. Y., at Manhattan Bh., N. Y., July 14, '20.

440 yds. free style, open tidal salt water (100), 4 turns—6 m. 21 3-5 s., E. Bleibtrey, Women's Swimming Assn. of N. Y., in Honolulu Harbor, Honolulu, T. H., Apr. 17, '20.

Plunging—1 m. time limit, bath—65 ft. 10 in., H Nolan of Northern High School, Detroit, in Detroit Y. M. C. A. Bath.

Swimming on the Back.

100 yds., bath (20), 4 turns—1 m. 17 3-5 s., E. Bleibtrey, Women's Swimming Assn. of N. Y., in Y. W. H. A. Bath, N. Y. C., Mar. 13, '20.

150 yds., bath (25), 5 turns—2 m. 10 1-5 s., E. Bleibtrey, Women's Swimming Assn. of N. Y., at People's Palace Bath, Jersey City, N. J., Feb. 28, '20.

100 yds., bath (20), 4 turns—1 m. 20 3-5 s., E. Bleibtrey, Women's Swimming Assn. of N. Y., at Greensburg Y. M. C. A. Bath, Greensburg, Pa., Feb. 18, '20.

100 yds., bath (25), 3 turns—1 m. 22 s., S. Bauer, Illinois A. C., Chicago, at the Detroit A. C. Bath, Detroit, Mich., Feb. 28, '20.

100 yds., bath (75), 1 turn—1 m. 24 3-5 s., S. Bauer, Illinois A. C., Chicago, at Great Lakes Naval Training Sta. Bath., Feb. 18, '20.

Best Interscholastic Records of U. S.

50 yds.—5 3-5s., E. C. Jessup, St. Louis, Mo., July 4, '04.

60 yds.—6 2-5s., S. Butler, Hutchinson, (Kan.) High School, Evanston, Ill., Mar. 28, '14.

100 yds.—9 4-5s., Ernest E. Nelson, Volkmann School, Cambridge, May 2, '08; Charles Hoyt, Greenfield High School, Chic., Ill., June 7, '13; W. J. Carten, Chic. Univ. High, Ann Arbor, Mich., Mar. 23, '14; Evan Pearson, North Central H. S., Spokane, Wash., May 20, '16.

220 yds.—21 2-5s., W. J. Carter, Jr., Chic. Univ. High, Ann Arbor, Mich., May 23, '14.

400 yds.—42 3-5s., Flank Sloman, Polytechnic H. S., San Francsico, Cal., Oct. 16, '15.

440 yds. (around turn)—48 4-5s., J. E. Meredith, Mercersburg Academy, Phila., Pa., May 18, '12; 48 1-5s. (straightaway), Frank Sloman, Polytechnic H. S., San Francisco, Cal., Oct. 16 '15.

880 yds.—1m. 55s., James E. Meredith, Mercersburg Academy, Princeton, N. J., May 4, '12.

1 mile—4m. 23 3-5s., Ed Shields, Mercersburg Acad., Port Deposit, Md., May 20, '16.

2 mile—9m. 51 3-5s., C. Boughton, Newark Central H. S., Princeton, N. J., May 23, '14.

HURDLES.

120 yds.—15 2-5s., H. Whitted, Citrus Union School, Chic., Ill., June 8, '12; H. Whitted, Citrus Union School, Stanford, Cal., Apr. 13, '12.

220 yds.—24 2-5s., C. Cory, Chic. Univ. H. S., Ann Arbor, Mich., May 23 and 24, '13; Frank Loomis, Oregon H. S., Minneapolis, Minn., May 27 '16; D. Kimball, Deerfield, Shields H. S. at Univ. of Ill., interscholastic meet champion, Illinois, May 22, '20.

JUMPING.

Running high—6 ft. 3⅝ in., W. M. Oler, Jr., Pawling School, Cambridge, Mass., May 25, '12.

Running broad—23 ft. 7 1-5 in., P. G. Stiles, Culver Military Acad., Chic., Ill., May 12, '13.

POLE VAULTING.

12 ft., 8 in., S. Landers, Oregon H. S., Minneapolis, Minn., May 27, '16.

Indoor—12 ft. 1 in., Eugene Schobinger, Harvard School, Chic., Ill., Feb. 18, '11.

PUTTING SHOT.

8-lb. (indoor)—59 ft. ⅝ in., George Bronder, Poly Prep, Bkln., N. Y., Jan. 16, '15.

SPORTING RECORDS—ATHLETICS—INTERSCHOLASTIC RECORDS—PUTTING SHOT—*Continued.*

12-lb.—55 ft. 9 in., A. M. Mucks, Oshkosh H. S., Oshkosh, Wis., Jan. 19, '12.

16-lb.—45 ft. 6¼ in., Ralph Rose, San Francisco, May 2, '02.

MISCELLANEOUS.

Throwing 12-lb. hammer—197 ft. ½ in., L. J. Talbot, Washington, Pa., May 25, '07.

Throwing discus—139 ft. 5½ in., B. L. Byrd, Champaign, Ill., May 21, '10.

Throwing jr. discus (7 ft. circle)—155 ft. 4 in., R. G. Walker, Passaic H. S., Ohio Field, N. Y. C., Apr. 18, '14.

Throwing jr. discus (8 ft. 2½ in. circle)—158 ft. 2¾ in., R. G. Walker, Passaic H. S., Castle Point, Hoboken, N. J., May 1, '15.

¼ mile relay—46 4-5s., Univ. H. S., Chic., Ill., June 11, '10.

½ mile relay—1m. 32 2-5s., Lewis Inst., at Northwestern Univ., May 23, '03.

1 mile relay—3m. 27 1-5s., Los Angeles H. S. relay team, Los Angeles, Cal., '10.

Pole vault record for boys under 10 yrs.—5 ft. 10½ in., R. E. Graves, 8 yrs 4 mo. old, Marshfield, Oregon, July 3, '12.

Throwing javelin—184 ft. 9½ in., H. B. Liversedge, Stanford, Cal., Apr. 11, '14.

National A. A. U. Championships, 1920.

JUNIOR INDOOR TRACK AND FIELD.

Held under the auspices of the 74th Inf. A. A., Buffalo, N. Y., Feb. 21, '20.

300-Yd. Dash—Won by D Caprio, Knights of St. Antony, N. Y.; E. Farrell, Todd Shipyard A. A., N. Y., 2d; L. R. Souder, Syracuse Univ., 3d; S. Hruitford, Syracuse Univ., 4th. Time, 32 4-5 s.

Running High Jump—Won by J. F. Feeney, Georgetown Univ., 5 ft. 10 in.; E. Windhovel, Meadowbrook Club, 5 ft. 9 in., 2d; A. A. Bromet, Morningside A. C., 5 ft. 9 in., 3d.

16-lb. Shot Put—Won by J Lichtman, Clark House, N. Y.; F. F. Foster, Syracuse Univ., 2d; E. Ellis, Syracuse Univ., 3d; E. Windhovel, Meadowbrook Club, Phila., 4th. Distance, 40 ft. 6½ in.

70-Yd. High Hurdle—Won by E. F. Smalley, Univ. of Pa.; A. P. Roberts, N. Y. A. C., 2d; J. W. Reynolds, Lafayette Col., 3d.

1,000-Yd. Run—Won by R. Crawford, Lafayette Coll.; L. A. Brown, Univ. of Pa., 2d; W. F. Morton, Hobart Col., 3d; H. Wigger, Paulist A. C., 4th. Time, 2 m. 19 s.

Standing Broad Jump—Won by W. Stulman, Baltimore, 10 ft. 1¼ in.; E. Busby, Meadowbrook Club, 9 ft. 11 in., 2d; L. Rudnick, Mohawk A. C., 9 ft. 9 in., 3d; M. J. Suttner, Masten Park H. S., 9 ft. 7 in., 4th.

60-Yd. Dash—Won by H. B. Lever, Univ. of Pa.; F. Conway, Morningside A. C., 2d; J. F. Dwyer, Hobart Col., 3d; W. H. Hill Jr., H. C. H. S., 4th. Time, 6 2-5 s.

2-Mile Run—Won by H. G. Helme, Lafayette H. S.; A. Craw, Bkln. A. A., 2d; A. Hisler, Meadowbrook Club, 3d; A. J. Hulsebosch, Paulist A. C., 4th. Time, 9 m. 35 2-5 s.

Standing High Jump—Won by E. Haub, Pittsburg A. A.; E. Bergquist, Bronx Church House, 2d; E. Windhovel, Meadowbrook Club, 3d; L. Rudnick, Mohawk A. C., 4th. Hgt. 4 ft. 11 in.

600-Yd. Run—Won by T. W. Habberfield, C. A. Weed's; W. D. Braunstein, N. Y. Univ., 2d; E. Balestier, Knights of St. Anthony, 3d. Time, 1 m. 16 s.

One Mile Walk—Won by H. L. Schultz, C. A. Weed's; S. W. Cobb, C. A. Weed's, 2d; M. Greenberg, Pastime A. C., 3d; J. A. Graham Jr., unattached, 4th. Time, 7 m. 5 4-5 s.

Medley Relay Race—Won by Pa. State Col.; Syracuse Univ., 2d; Paulist A. C., 3d; C. A. Weed's, 4th. Time, 8 m. 1 s.

JUNIOR OUTDOOR TRACK AND FIELD.

Held at Harvard Stadium, Cambridge, Mass., July 16, '20.

100-Yd. Run—E. O. Gourdin, unattached, Boston, won; E. B. Farrell, unattached, N. Y., 2d; R. M. Williams, U. S. Army, 3d; R. Moore, U. S. Army, 4th. Time, 10 1-5 s.

220-Yd. Run—E. B. Farrell, unattached, N. Y., won; R. Moore, U. S. Army, 2d; B. F. Machia, Boston A. A., 3d; J. J. Kehal, Enterprise Club, Phila., 4th. Time, 22 3-5 s.

440-Yd. Run—W. F. Morton, Jersey Harriers A. A., Bayonne, N. J., won; R. A. Robertson, Boston A. A., 2d; G. J. Melville, Boston A. A., 3d; E. M. Murphy, Boston A. A., 4th. Time, 50 4-5 s.

880-Yd. Run—J. A. Caffey, Boston A. A., won; W. W. Shoemaker, U. S. Army, 2d; W. Powe, Alpha P. C. C., N. Y., 3d; C. E. Snow Jr., M. I. T., Boston, 4th. Time, 2 m. 2 2-5 s.

One Mile Run—Garland Courage, N. Y. A. C., won; C. J. O'Leary, Boston A. A., 2d; Ed. Rank, Paulist A. C., N. Y., 3d; J. L. Doherty, Dorchester (Mass.) Club, 4th. Time, 4 m. 33 s.

120 Yds. High Hurdles—W. E. Massey, N. Y. A. C., won; J. Morse, Univ. of Texas, 2d; C. E. Davis, U. S. Army, 3d; E. Ellis, Syracuse Univ., 4th. Time, 16 1-5 s.

440 Yds. Hurdles—J. J. Sullivan, Boston A. A., won; L. Lloyd, Paulist A. C., N. Y., 2d; C. Brundage, Paulist A. C., N. Y., 3d; no fourth. Time, 59 sec.

Running Broad Jump—P. Coutois, Mohawk A. C., N. Y., 22 ft. 9 in., won; H. Politzer, Mohawk A. C., N. Y., 22 ft. 3½ in., 2d; B. L. Russell, U. S. Army, 22 ft. 2½ in., 3d; E. L. Bradley, Univ. of Kansas, 21 ft. 11½ in., 4th.

Running High Jump—L. A. Watson, Alpha P. C. C., N. Y., 6 ft. 2 in., won; A. Abromet, Morningside A. C., N. Y., 6 ft., 2d; H. A. Bigelow, unattached, 5 ft. 8 in., 3d; C. S. Maulsby, U. S. Army, 5 ft. 8 in., 4th.

Running Hop, Step and Jump—K. Geist, 92d St. Y. M. H. A., N. Y., 46 ft. 7½ in., won; W. Rosenberg, Glencoe A. C., N. Y., 46 ft. 3¾ in., 2d; S. Lehrer, Pastime A. C., 45 ft. 9 in., 3d; H. C. Pierce, unattached, West Newton, Mass., 42 ft. 5 in., 4th.

Pole Vault—R. W. Harwood, Boston A. A., 11 ft. 6 in., won; E. Shrader, U. S. Army, 11 ft., 2d; A. F. Fletcher, M. I. T., Boston, 11 ft. 3d; S. E. Huntley, U. S. Navy, 10 ft. 6 in., 4th.

Putting 16-lb. Shot—R. G. Hill, The Hill School, 44 ft. 10 in., won; T. Cooke Jr., Paulist A. C., N. Y., 2d; C. Vrettos, unattached, N. Y., 42 ft. ⅝ in., 3d; W. F. Wilkie, Boston A. A., 41 ft. 5⅝ in., 4th.

Throwing the 16-lb. Hammer—C. G. Dandrow, Boston A. A., 161 ft. 3 in., won; J. Conway, Pastime A. A., N. Y., 140 ft. 10¼ in., 2d; E. R. Roberts, U. S. Army, 136 ft. 10½ in., 3d; B. F. Sherman, unattached, N. Y., 122 ft. 5½ in., 4th.

Throwing 56-lb. Weight—J. Conway, Pastime A. C., N. Y., 29 ft. 4½ in., won; E. R. Roberts, U. S. Army, 28 ft. 6 in., 2d; F. L. Skidmore, Univ. of South, Sewanee, Tenn., 26 ft. 9 in., 3d; R. G. Lehman, U. S. Army, 26 ft., 4th.

Throwing the Discus—W. K. Bartlett, Univ. of Oregon, 136 ft. ½ in., won; R. G. Walker, N. Y. A. C., 133 ft. 7½ in., 2d; J. G. Boyle, Los Angeles A. C., 130 ft. 4 in., 3d; Chris Vrettos, unattached, N. Y., 126 ft. 7¾ in., 4th.

Throwing the Javelin—J. Mahon, Texas A. & M. Col., 175 ft. 7½ in., won; L. Perrine, Univ. of Idaho, 163 ft. 10¼ in., 2d; M. A. Phillips, St. Stanislaus Coll., St. Louis, Mo., 166 ft., 3d; E. L. Bradley, Univ of Kansas, 155 ft. 6½ in., 4th.

The following events were not held this year: 220 yds. low hurdles, 5-mile run, 3-mile walk.

POINTS SCORED.

Boston A. A., 32; U. S. Army, 23; unattached, 18; N. Y. A. C., 13; Pastime A. C., N. Y., 12; Paulist A. C., N. Y., 10; Mohawk A. C., N. Y., 8; Alpha P. C. C., N. Y., 7; Jersey Harriers, Bayonne, N. J., 5; Univ. of Oregon, 5; 92d St. Y. M. H. A., N. Y., 5; Hill School, 5; Texas A. & M. Col., 5; Univ. of Texas, 3; M. I. T., Boston, 3; Morningside A. C., N. Y., 3; Glencoe A. C., N. Y., 3; Univ. of Idaho, 3; Univ. of Kansas, 2; Univ. of South, Sewanee, Tenn., 2; St. Stanislaus Col., St. Louis, Mo., 2; Los Angeles A. C., 2; Enterprise Club, Phila., 1; U. S. Navy, 1; Syracuse Univ., 1; Dorchester (Mass.) Club, 1.

SENIOR INDOOR TRACK AND FIELD.

Held under the auspices of the Amateur Athletic Union of the U. S. at the 22d Regt. Armory, N. Y. City, March 12, '20.

Running High Jump—Won by W. L. Whalen, Boston A. A.; E. Erickson, Bronx Church House, 2d; R. W. Landon, Yale Univ., 3d; H. Troup, Rutgers Col., 4th. Hgt. 6 ft. 3½ in.

Putting 16-lb. Shot—Won by P. J. McDonald, N. Y. A. C., 45 ft. 3¼ in.; J. Lawlor, Boston A. A., 42 ft. 11¼ in., 2d; H. S. Elsey, Mohawk A. C., 42 ft. 10 in., 3d; W. F. Wilkie, unattached, 41 ft. 6½ in., 4th.

Standing Broad Jump—Won by W. I. Reid, M. Brown School, Providence, 10 ft. 4⅛ in.; J. C. Hoskins, Chicago A. A., 10 ft. 1⅞ in., 2d; P. Courtis, N. Y. Univ., 10 ft. 1⅛ in., 3d; S. Kronman, Clark House A. A., 10 ft. ⅛ in., 4th.

60-Yd. Run—Won by L. Murchison, N. Y. A. C.; H. Lever, Univ. of Pa., 2d; P. White, unattached, 3d; F. Conway, Morningside A. C., 4th. Time 6 2-5 s.

SPORTING RECORDS—ATHLETICS—TRACK AND FIELD—A. A. U. RECORDS—*Continued.*

1,000-Yd. Run—Won by J. Ray, Illinois A. C.; L. C. Cutbill, Boston A. A., 2d; H. Baker, Glencoe A. C., 3d; T. J. O'Brien, Yale Univ., 4th. Time, 2 m. 15 1-5 s.

300-Yd. Run—Won by L. Murchison, N. Y. A. C.; F. Conway, Morningside A. C., 2d; R. S. Maxam, Univ. of Pa., 3d; J. J. O'Brien, 4th. Time, 32 s.

70-Yd. High Hurdle—Won by W. Smith, Cornell Univ.; E. F. Smalley, Univ. of Pa., 2d; M. Burke, Illinois A. C., 3d; W. Meanix, Boston A. A., 4th. Time, 9 1-5 s.

600-Yd. Run—Won by E. W. Eby, Univ. of Pa.; F. L. Murrey, Princeton Univ., 2d; C. Shaw, Columbia Univ., 3d; M. R. Gustafson, Univ. of Pa., 4th. Time, 1 m. 16 4-5 s.

2-Mile Run—Won by H. Helm, Lafayette H. S., Buffalo; M. Bohland, Paulist A. C., 2d; R. McMahon, Mass. Inst of Technology, 3d; A. Hisler Jr., Meadowbrook Club, 4th. Time, 9 m. 34 3-5 s.

One Mile Walk—Won by J. B. Pearman, N. Y. A. C.; W. Plant, Morningside A. C., 2d; R. F. Remer, Amer. Walkers' Ass., 3d; W. J. Rolker, N. Y. A. C., 4th. Time, 6m. 39 4-5 s.

1⅜ Medley Relay—Won by Illinois A. C.; Millrose A. A., 2d; Lafayette Coll., 3d; Pa. State Coll., 4th. Time, 7 m. 42 2-5 s.

Standing High Jump—Won by B. W. Adams, N. Y. A. C., hgt. 5 ft. 1 in.; T. S. Clark, N. Y. A. C., 5 ft. 1 in., 2d; E. Berquist, Bronx Church House, 4 ft. 11 in., 3d; S. Kronman, Clark House A. A., 4 ft. 11 in., 4th. Adams won the jump-off, breaking the tie for the first place, and Berquist won the jump-off, breaking tie for third place.

POINTS SCORED.

N. Y. A. C., 29 points; Univ. of Pa., 15; Boston A. A., 12; Morningside A. C., 8; Illinois A. C., 7; Cornell, 5; Moses Brown Sch., Providence, R. I., 5; Lafayette H. S., Buffalo, 5; Bronx Church House, 5; Millrose A. A., 5; Yale, 3; Chicago A. A., 3; Paulist A. C., 3; Princeton, 3; Lafayette Col., 3; Mohawk A. C., 2; Glencoe A. C., 2; N. Y. Univ., 2; Clark House, 2; Mass. Inst. of Tech., 2; Columbia Univ., 2; Amer. Walkers' Ass., 2.

SENIOR OUTDOOR TRACK AND FIELD.
FINAL OLYMPIC TRYOUTS.

Held at Harvard Stadium, Cambridge, Mass., July 17, '20.

100 Yd. Run—L. Murchison, N. Y. A. C., won; C. W. Scholz, Univ. of Mo., 2d; C. W. Paddock, Los Angeles A. C., 3d; M. M. Kirksey, Olympic Club, San Francisco, 4th. Time, 10 s.

220-Yd. Run—C. W. Paddock, Los Angeles A. C., won; M. M. Kirksey, Olympic Club, San Francisco, 2d; L. Murchison, N. Y. A. C., 3d; G. B. Messengale Univ. of Mo., 4th. Time, 21 2-5 s.

440-Yd. Run—F. J. Shea, U. S. Navy, won; J. E. Meredith, N. Y. A. C., 2d; R. S. Emory, Chicago A. A., 3d; C. G. Bretnall, Cornell Col., Iowa, 4th. Time, 49 s.

880-Yd. Run—E. Eby, Chicago A. A., won; D. N. Scott, U. S. Army, 2d; T. Campbell, Yale Univ., 3d; A. B. Sprott, Los Angeles A. C., 4th. Time, 1 m. 54 1-5 s.

One-Mile Run—J. W. Ray, Illinois A. C., won; E. B. Curtis, 2d; L. M. Shields, Meadowbrook Club, Philadelphia, 3d; J. J. Connolly, Boston A. A., 4th. Time, 4 m. 16 1-5 s.

120-Yd. High Hurdles—H. E. Barron, Meadowbrook Club, Philadelphia, won; W. Yount, Los Angeles A. C., 2d; W. Smith, Chicago A. A., 3d; F. S. Murray, N. Y. A. C., 4th. Time, 15 1-5 s.

440-Yd. Hurdles—F. F. Loomis, Chicago A. A., won; J. K. Norton, Olympic Club, San Francisco, 2d; A. G. Desch, Unattached, N. Y., 3d; C. D. Daggs, Los Angeles A. C., 4th. Time, 55 s.

Running Broad Jump—S. Butler, Dubuque Coll., Iowa, 24 ft. 3 in., won; S. Landers, Chicago A. A., 23 ft. 5 in., 2d; R. L. Templeton, Leland Stanford Univ., 22 ft. 8 in., 3d; J. W. Merchant, Olympic Club, San Francisco, 22 ft. 4⅞ in., 4th.

Running High Jump—J. Murphy, Multnomah A. A. C., Portland, Ore., 6 ft. 4¼ in., won; R. W. Landon, N. Y. A. C., and H. B. Muller, Olympic Club, San Francisco, tied for 2d at 6 ft. 3⅛ in., Landon won jump off; W. L. Whalen, Boston A. A., R. L. Templeton, Olympic Club, San Francisco, O. Cory, Los Angeles A. C., A. Richards, Ogden A. A., Utah, Egon Erickson, Unattached, N. Y., C. G. Krogness, Chicago A. A., all tied for 4th, 6 ft. 2⅛ in. Whalen won jump off.

Running Hop, Step and Jump—S. Landers, Chicago A. A., 48 ft. 7 9-10 in., won; D. F. Ahearn, Illinois A. C., 47 ft. 9 in., 2d; K. Geist, 92d St. Y. M. H. A., 46 ft. ⅛ in., 3d; C. E. Jacquith, Chicago A. A., 45 ft. 9¼ in., 4th.

Pole Vault—F. K. Foss, Chicago A. A., and E. E. Meyers, Chicago A. A., 13 ft. 1 in., tied for 1st; Foss won jump off; E. E. Knourek, Illinois A. C., and E. E. Jenne., Wash. State Coll., 12 ft. 10 in., tied for 3d; Knourek won jump off.

Putting 16-Lb. Shot—P. J. McDonald, N. Y. A. C., 47 ft. ¼ in., won; H. B. Liversedge, U. S. Navy, 46 ft. 1¼ in., 2d; G. H. Bihlman, Olympic Club, San Francisco, 45 ft. 2⅛ in., 3d; H. G. Cann, N. Y. A. C., 44 ft. 6 in., 4th.

Throwing 16-Lb. Hammer—P. Ryan, Loughlin Lyceum, Brooklyn, N. Y., 169 ft. 4 in., won; M. J. McGrath, N. Y. A. C., 166 ft. 3½ in., 2d; J. M. McEacheron, Olympic Club, San Francisco, 156 ft. 8½ in., 3d; B. Bennett, Chicago A. A., 153 ft. 4¼ in., 4th.

Throwing 56-lb. Weight—P. J. McDonald, N. Y. A. C., 37 ft. 11¼ in., won; M. J. McGrath, N. Y. A. C., 36 ft. 10½ in., 2d; P. Ryan, Loughlin Lyceum, Brooklyn, N. Y., 36 ft. 6 in., 3d; T. Anderson, St. Christopher Club, 32 ft. 8⅛ in., 4th.

Throwing the Discus—A. R. Pope, Univ. of Wash., 146 ft. 5 in., won; K. G. Bartlett, Univ. of Oregon, 141 ft. 9⅝ in., 2d; R. M. Evans, Los Angeles A. C., 134 ft. 11⅛ in., 3d; M. R. Husted, Chicago A. A., 134 ft. 7½ in., 4th.

Throwing the Javelin—M. S. Angier, Illinois A. C., 192 ft. 10 in., won; J. C. Lincoln, N. Y. A. C., 187 ft. 3 in., 2d; K. L. Wilson, Chicago A. A., 172 ft. 5⅛ in., 3d; J. F. Hanner, Leland Stanford Univ., 172 ft. 5 in., 4th.

SPECIAL OLYMPIC TRYOUT EVENTS.

5,000-Meter Run—H. H. Brown, Boston A. A., won; C. Furnes, Purdue Univ., 2d; J. T. Simmons, N. Y. A. C., 3d; I. C. Dresser, N. Y. A. C., 4th. Time, 15 m. 26 s.

10,000 Meter Run—F. W. Faller, Dorchester (Mass.) Club, won; R. E. Johnson, Morgan Community, Pittsburg, 2d; G. Cornetta, N. Y. A. C., 3d; M. Bohland, Paulist A. C., N. Y., 4th. Time, 32 m. 15 s.

3,000-Meter Walk—W. Plant, Morningside A. C., N. Y., won; W. J. Rolker, N. Y. A. C., 2d; J. B. Pearman, N. Y. A. C., 3d; T. A Moroney, St Anselms A. C., N. Y., 4th. Time, 13 m. 8 s.

The following A. A. U. Championship Events were not held this year: 220-Yard Low Hurdles, Five-Mile Run, Three-Mile Walk.

POINTS SCORED.

Chicago A. A., 35; N. Y. A. C., 34; Illinois A. C. 15; Los Angeles A. C., 14; Olympic Club, San Francisco, 14; U. S. Navy, 11; Loughlin Lyceum, Brooklyn, N. Y., 7; Meadowbrook Club, Philadelphia, 7; Dubuque Coll., Iowa, 5; Multnomah A. A. C., Portland, Ore., 5; Univ. of Wash., 5; Univ. of Mo., 4; Univ. of Ore., 3; U. S. Army, 3; Boston A. A., 2; Yale Univ., New Haven, Conn., 2; Unattached, 2; 92d St. Y. M. H. A., 2; Wash. State Coll., 1; St. Christopher Club, N. Y., 1; Cornell Coll., Iowa, 1.

ALL-AROUND AND FIVE RELAYS

Were not held.

WRESTLING.

Held under the auspices of the Birmingham A. C., Birmingham, Ala., Apr. 5th and 6th, '20.

108-lb. Class—Won by K. Benson, Swed.-Amer. A. C.; S. Berry, Birmingham A. C., 2d. Time, 1 m. 26 s.

115-lb. Class—Won by S. Pammow, Chic. Hebrew Inst.; K. Benson, Swed-Amer. A. C., 2d. Time, 2 m. 7 s.

125-lb. Class—Won by A. Gallas, Greek Olympic Club; T. Jaffe, Birmingham A. C., 2d. (Forfeit.)

135-lb. Class—Won by G. Metropoulis, Gary Y. M. C. A., Gary, Ind.; B. Johnson, Birmingham A. C., 2d. (Decision.)

145-lb. Class—Won by W. Tikka, Fin.-Amer. A. C., N. Y.; P. Metropoulis, Gary Y. M. C. A., Gary, Ind., 2d. (Decision.)

158-lb. Class—Won by E. Leino, N. Y. A. C.; W. Maurer, Chic. Hebrew Inst, 2d. Time, 5 m. 52 s.

175-lb. Class—Won by K. Kunert, Gary Y. M. C. A., Gary, Ind.; F. Meyer, Chic. Hebrew Inst, 2d. (Decision.)

Heavy Class—Won by N. Pendleton, N. Y. A. C.; Babe Taylor, Birmingham A. C., 2d. Time, 7 m. 54 s.

BOXING.

Held under the auspices of the Boston A. A., Boston, Mass., Apr. 5th and 6th, '20.

108-lb. Class—Semi-final bouts—A. J. De Vito, N. Y., beat J. Manning, So. Boston, 3 rounds.

SPORTING RECORDS—ATHLETICS—A. A. U. RECORDS—BOXING—*Continued.*

2d Bout—W. Cohen, N. Y., beat B. Bass, Phila., 3 rounds.

Final Bout—A. J. De Vito beat W. Cohen, 3 rounds.

115-lb. Class—Semi-final bouts—J. Hutchinson, Phila., beat F. Heuke, Milwaukee, 3 rounds.

2d Bout—N. Brock, Cleveland, beat A. Donza, New Orleans, 3 rounds.

Final Bout—Hutchinson beat Brock, 3 rounds.

125-lb. Class—Semi-final bouts—T. Murphy, Kansas City, Mo., beat M. Kleinman, Cleveland, 3 rounds.

2d Bout—B. Ponteau, N. Y., beat R. Dinsmore, Huntington Sch., 3 rounds.

Final Bout—T. Murphy, Kansas City, Mo., beat B. Ponteau, N. Y., 3 rounds.

145-lb. Class—Semi-final bouts—J. Schoendoerf, Milwaukee, beat L. Aldrin, N. Y., 3 rounds.

2d Bout—R. Helton, Kansas City, beat H. C. Boblin, Brockton, 4 rounds.

Final Bout—J. Schoendoerf beat R. Helton, 4 rounds.

158-lb. Class—Semi-final bouts—S. Lagonia, N. Y., beat J. J. Hares, N. Y., 2 rounds.

2d Bout—F. Grayber, Pittsburg, beat G. Farquhar, Los Angeles, Cal., 3 rounds.

Final Bout—S. Lagonia, N. Y., beat F. Grayber, Pittsburg, 3 rounds.

175-lb. Class—Semi-final bout—J. Burke, Pittsburg, beat E. Eagan, New Haven, 3 rounds.

Final Bout—J. Burke, Pittsburg, beat R. Patterson, San Francisco, Cal., 3 rounds.

Heavyweight Class—Semi-final bouts—K. Wicks, Dorchester, beat E. Eagan, New Haven, 3 rounds.

Second Bout—J. Burke, Pittsburg, defaulted to J. Geroux, Boston (injured hand).

Final Bout—Wicks beat Geroux, Boston, 1 round.

GYMNASTICS.

FINAL OLYMPIC TRYOUTS.

Report on natl. gymnastic championships of the A. A. U. held at 23d St. Y. M. C. A., N. Y. City, July 22, '20.

Long Horse—Won by V. Winsjansen, Norwegian Turn Verein, 839 points; 2d, J. Oszy, N. Y. A. C., Gym. Assn., 837 points; 3d, M. Wanderer, Phila. Turngemeinde, 834 points; 4th, F. Berg, Norwegian T. and A. C., 827 points.

Horizontal Bar—Won by C. Rottmann, N. Y. Turn Verein, 839 points; 2d, J. Oszy, N. Y. A. C., 831 points; 3d, G. Rathgeb, Detroit Y. M. C. A., 788 points; 4th, P. Krempel, Los Angeles A. C., 714 points.

Parallel Bars—Won by J. Oszy, N. Y. A. C., 838 points; 2d, C. Rottmann, N. Y. T. V., 804 points; 3d, F. Kris, Bohemian Gym. Ass., 796 points; 4th, P. Krempel, Los Angeles A. C., 766 points.

Side Horse—Won by C. M. Cremer, N. Y. A. C., 850 points; 2d, J. B. Richter, D. A. Sokol Gym. Assn., 790 points; 3d, C. Rottmann, N. Y. T. V., 760 points; 4th, J. Oszy, N. Y. A. C., 755 points.

Flying Rings—Won by J. D. Gleason, Los Angeles A. C., 862 points; 2d, P. Krempel, Los Angeles A. C., 802 points; 3d, A. Pfeiffer, Newark, N. J., Natl. T. V., 785 points; 4th, J. Oszy, N. Y. A. C., 769 points.

Rope Climb—Won by L. Weissman, 92d St. Y. M. H. A., 8 s.; 2d, E. C. Iglesias, Bronx U. Br. Y. M. C. A.; 3d, P. Kluge, N. Y. T. V.; 4th, H. Kowista, Detroit Y. M. C. A.

Indian Club Swinging—Won by R. W. Dutcher, N. Y. A. C., 274 points; 2d, I Yanousky, Newark, N. J., N. T. V., 259 points; 3d, J. L. McCloud, N. Y. A. C., 258 points; 4th, A. Wilsen, Anchor A. C., 244 points.

Tumbling—Won by A. W. Nugent, Newark, N. J., N. T. V., 833 points; 2d, J. F. Lunn, U. S. N. R. F. & N. Y. A. C., 820 points; 3d, A. Kimball, Newark, N. J., Y. M. C. A., 753 points; 4th, O. Deamsey, Newark, N. J., N. T. V., 723 points.

All Around Championships—Won by J. Oszy, N. Y. A. C., 2,752 points; 2d, C. Rottmann, N. Y. T. V., 2,680 points; 3d, F. Kriz, Bohemian Gym. Ass., 2,625 points; 4th, P. Krempel, Los Angeles A. C., 2,582 points.

SENIOR OUTDOOR SWIMMING CHAMPIONSHIPS—MEN.

100 Yds.—Held under the auspices of the Chicago A. A. at the Lincoln Park Lagoon, Chicago, Ill., July 10, '20.

Won by Duke Kahanomoku, Honolulu; Pau Kealoha, Honolulu, 2d; N. Ross, Illinois A. C., 3d; J. K. Gilman, U. S. Navy, 4th. Time, 55 2-5 s.

440 Yds.—Held under the auspices of the Chicago A. A. at Lincoln Park Lagoon, Chicago, Ill., July 11, '20.

Won by N. Ross, Illinois A. C., Chicago; W. H. Harris, Honolulu, 2d; P. Kealoha, Honolulu, 3d; F. K. Kahele, U. S. Navy, 4th. Time, 5 m. 40 2-5 s.

One Mile—Held under the auspices of the Chicago A. A. at the Lincoln Park Lagoon, Chicago, Ill., July 10, '20.

Won by E. Bolden, Illinois A. C.; L. Langer, Honolulu, 2d; F. K. Kahele, U. S. Navy, 3d; Leo Giebel, N. Y. A. C., 4th. Time, 25 m. 26 2-5 s.

Long Distance Swim—Held under the auspices of the Riverton Yacht Club, Riverton, N. J., July 17, '20.

Won by E. J. Bolden, Illinois A. C., Chicago; V. H. Kiffee, Brooklyn, 2d; Ralston, Meadowbrook Club, 3d; McCurdy, Phila. Swimming Club, 4th; Levand, Phila. Swimming Club, 5th; J. Showell, Riverton, 6th; G. Corner, Riverton, 7th; Elverson, Camden Y. M. C. A., 8th; Brown, Flushing High, N. Y., 9th; Gunther, Charleston, W. Va., 10th; Rosborough, Phila. Swimming Club, 11th; Titus, Phila. Swimming Club, 12th; Bell, Riverton, 13th; Davisson, Riverton, 14th; Pagel, Philadelphia, 15th; Einhorn, Philadelphia, 16th; Ferry, E. Rutherford, N. J., 17th; Nicholas, Pitman, N. J., 18th; Longaker, Philadelphia, 19th; Brennan, Riverton, 20th. Time, 2 h. 9 m. 17 s.

JUNIOR OUTDOOR SWIMMING—MEN.

100 Yds.—Held under the auspices of the Hawaiian Association, Honolulu, T. H., April 17, '20.

Won by Pua Kealoha, Honolulu; Warren Kealoha, Honolulu, 2d; Clarence Lane, Honolulu, 3d. Time, 55 3-5 s.

880 Yds.—Held under the auspices of the United Labor League of Pittsburg at West View Park, Sept. 6, '20.

Won by Adam Smith, Erie Y. M. C. A.; G. F. Pawling Jr., unattached, Philadelphia, Pa., 2d; C. Crownover, Philadelphia, 3d; R. Spangle, 4th. Time, 12 m. 55 2-5 s.

One Mile—Held under the joint auspices of Detroit A. C. and Detroit Boat Club, at Detroit, Mich., Sept. 6, '20.

Won by M. Coolly, Duluth Boat Club; Ehrlich, Detroit, 2d; J. Gilbreath, Detroit, 3d. Time, 19 m. 4 4-5 s.

SENIOR INDOOR SWIMMING—MEN.

100-Yd. Swim—Held under the auspices of the Brookline Swimming Club, Brookline, Mass., March 11, 1920.

Won by T. Cann, Detroit A. C., C. Brown, Chicago A. C., 2d; H. J. Hebner, Illinois A. C., 3d; L. Handy, Detroit A. C., 4th. Time, 53 3-5 s.

220-Yd. Free Style Swim—Held under the auspices of the Detroit A. C., Detroit, Mich., on April 10, '20.

Won by A. Cann, Detroit A. C.; C. Brown, Chicago A. C., 2d; P. McGillivray, Illinois A. C., 3d; W. L. Wallen, Illinois A. C., 4th. Time, 19 4-5 s.

500-Yd. Swim—Held under the auspices of the Great Lakes A. C., U. S. Naval Training Sta., Great Lakes, Ill., on March 24, '20.

Won by W. L. Wallen, Illinois A. C., Chicago; C. Brown, Chicago A. A., 2d; F. R. Pickel, Chicago A. A., 3d.; E. T. Bolden, Great Lakes A. A., 4th. 6 m. 14 3-5 s.

150-Yd. Back Stroke—Held under the auspices of Marion Club, Indianapolis, Ind., May 15, '20.

Owing to size of pool it was necessary to swim the race in two heats, the time of each competitor to decide his position in the race.

First Heat—Won by P. McGillivray, Illinois A. C.; H. Fergus, Chicago A. A., 2d. Time, 1 m. 48 4-5 s.

Second Heat—Won by L. Handy, Detroit A. C.; A. Siegel, Illinois A. C., 2d. Time, 1 m. 50 3-5 s.

Order of placing in race:

Won by P. McGillivray, Illinois A. C.; Leo Handy, Detroit A. C., 2d; A. Siegel, Illionois A. C., 3d.; H. Fergus, Chicago A. A., 4th. Time, 1 m. 48 4-5 s.

Fancy Diving Championship—Held under the auspices of Los Angeles A. C., Los Angeles, Cal., April 22, '20.

Won by C. Swendsen, Los Angeles A. C.; E. Field, unattached, 2d; L. Kuehn, Multnomah, Portland, 3d; Clarence Pinkston, Stanford University, 4th.

Plunge for Distance—Held under the auspices of the Pittsburg Aquatic Club, at the Pittsburg Natatorium, Pittsburg, Pa., on March 11, '20.

SPORTING RECORDS—ATHLETICS—SWIMMING—*Continued.*

Won by F. Schwedt, Detroit A. C., 82 ft. 8 in.; R. H. Meagher, Yale Univ., 80 ft., 2d; F. R. Jorn, Detroit Y. M. C. A., 78 ft., 3d; R. Boyle, Pittsburg A. A., 74 ft. 8 in., 4th.

JUNIOR INDOOR SWIMMING—MEN.

500-Yd. Swim—Held under the auspices of Philadelphia Turngemeinde, Philadelphia, Pa., on March 4, '20·

Won by G. Cunha, Meadowbrook Club, Philadelphia; M. Armstrong, unattached, Philadelphia, 2d; M. Raphael, U. S. S. Conn., 3d; Elmer Schill, Philadelphia Turngemeinde, 4th. Time, 25 1-5 s.

100-Yd. Swim—Held under the auspices of Pittsburg A. A., Pittsburg, Pa., on March 19, '20·

Won by Jack Love, Pittsburg A. A.; H. Q. Taylor, Univ. of Pittsburg, 2d; A. Straub, Pittsburg A. A., 3d; J. McGuire, Pittsburg A. A., 4th. Time, 60 4-5 s.

220-Yd. Swim—Held under the auspices of the Cleveland Y. M. C. A., Cleveland, Ohio., April 17, '20·

Won by L. Handy. Detroit A. C.; D. Nixon, Detroit A. C., 2d. Time, 2 m. 3¾ s.

500-Yd. Swim—Held under the auspices of the Minneapolis A. C., Minneapolis, Minn., on March 10, '20·

Won by A. Thompson. Milwaukee A. C.; M. Lampher, St. Paul A. C., 2d; B. Curry, Univ. of Minnesota, 3d. Time, 6 m. 42 2-5 s.

100-Yd. Breast Stroke Swim—Held under the auspices of the Los Angeles A. C., at the Venice Pool, Los Angeles, on April 17, '20·

Won by S. I. Messenger, Los Angeles A. C.; Dr R. Vint, Los Angeles A. C., 2d; C. Fletcher, San Diego Rowing Club, 3d; R. Triest, Los Angeles A. C., 4th. Time, 1 m. 19 s.

Fancy Diving—Men (1919 Championship).—Held under the auspices of Multnomah A. C., Portland, Ore., Nov. 22, '19·

Won by L. Kuehn, Multnomah A. C., Portland, Ore.; E. Field, Spokane A. C., Spokane, Wash., 2d; P. Patterson, Olympic Club, San Francisco, Cal., 3d.

Water Polo—Men—Held under the auspices of the Detroit A. C., Detroit, Mich., on April 10, '20.

Won by N. Y. A. C.; Detroit A. C., 2d.

SENIOR OUTDOOR SWIMMING—WOMEN.

100 Yds. Straightway—Held under the auspices of the Hawaiian Association, Honolulu, T. H., April 19, '20·

Won by Miss Ethelda Bleibtrey, Women's Swimming Assn., N. Y.; Miss Charlotte Boyle, Women's Swimming Assn., 2d; Miss Helen Moses, Honolulu, 3d. Time, 1:05 1-5 s.

National Long Distance Swim—Held under the joint auspices of the Detroit A. C. and Detroit Boat Club, at Detroit, Mich., Sept. 6, '20·

Won by Marie Curtis, Detroit A. C.; Miss Kulman, Duluth, 2d; Miss McBean, Detroit, 3d. Time, 49 m. 37 s.

JUNIOR OUTDOOR SWIMMING—WOMEN.

440 yds., held under the auspices of the Birmingham A. C., Birmingham, Ala., Aug. 7, '20· Won by Miss Mary Launey, Birmingham; Miss Garnett Launey, Birmingham, 2d; Miss Christine Tobie, Birmingham, 3d. Time, 9m. 48s.

SENIOR INDOOR SWIMMING—WOMEN.

50 yds., held under the auspices of the Los Angeles A. C., Los Angeles, Cal., May 12, '20· Won by Miss Ethelda Bleibtrey, N. Y. Women's Swimming Assn.; Miss Thelma Finn, Los Angeles A. C., 2d; Mrs. F. C. Schroth, Oakland A. C., San Francisco, 3d; Miss Charlotte Boyle, N. Y. Women's Swimming Assn., 4th. Time, 29 1-5s.

100 yds., held under the auspices of the Women's Swimming Association at W. 60th St. Pool, N. Y. City, March 16, '20· Won by Miss Ethelda Bleibtrey, Women's Swimming Assn.; Miss Charlotte Boyle, Women's Swimming Assn., 2d; Miss Ruth Smith, Morningside A. C., 3d. Time, 1m. 6 1-5s.

500 yds., held under the auspices of Marion Club, Indianapolis, Ind., May 15, '20· Owing to size of pool it was necessarly to swim the race in two heats of two each, the time of each competitor to decide her position in the race. First heat, won by Miss Woodbridge, Detroit A. C.; Miss T. Darby, Indianapolis, 2d. Time, 7m. 46 2-5s. Second heat, won by Miss Regina Reis, Indianapolis, unattached; Miss E. Donnelly, Independent A. C., Indianapolis, 2d. Time, 8m. 23s. Order of placing in the race, won by Miss M. Woodbridge, Detroit A. C.; Miss Regina Reis, Indianapolis, unattached, 2d; Miss T. Darby, Indianapolis, 3d. Time, 7m. 46 2-5s.

100 yds., breast stroke, held under the auspices of Philadelphia Turngemeinde, Philadelphia, Pa., on April 24, '20· Won by Miss Eleanor Smith, Morningside A. C.; Miss Ruth Smith, Morningside A. C., 2d; Miss Marie Hillegass, Philadelphia Turngemeinde, 3d; Miss Elizabeth Becker, Philadelphia Turngemeinde, 4th. Time, 1m. 25 1-5s.

Fancy dive, held under the auspices of the Detroit A. C., Detroit, Mich., on April 10, '20· Won by Miss Thelma Payne, Multnomah A. A. C., Portland, Ore. (128.14 points); Mrs. V. Malcomson, Detroit A. C. (124.13 points), 2d; Miss Helen Wainwright, Women's Swimming Assn. of N. Y. (114.89 points), 3d; Betty Grimes, unattached, Minneapolis (112.20 points), 4th.

JUNIOR INDOOR SWIMMING—WOMEN.

50 yds., held under the auspices of the Philadelphia Turngemeinde, Philadelphia, Pa., March 27 '20· Won by Miss Irene Guest, unattached; Miss Elizabeth Becker, Philadelphia Turners, 2d; Miss Mabel Arklie, Philadelphia Turners, 3d. Time, 31s.

100 yds., held under the auspices of the Cleveland A. C., at Cleveland, Ohio, Feb. 20, '20· Won by Miss Ruth Smith, Morningside A. C.; Miss Eleanor Smith, Morningside A. C., 2d; Miss Margaret Woodbridge, Detroit A. C., 3d. Time, 1m. 10s.

100 yds., back stroke, held under the auspices of the Greensburg (Pa.) Y. M. C. A., on Feb. 18, '20. Won by Miss Ethelda Bleibtrey, Women's Swimming Assn. of N. Y.; Miss Eleanor Smith, Morningside A. C., N. Y., 2d; Miss Alice Lord, Women's Swimming Assn. of N. Y., 3d. Time, 1m. 20 3-5s.

Plunge for distance, held under the auspices of Pittsburg A. A., Pittsburg, Pa., on March 19, '20· Won by Miss Mela Freeman, Civic A. C., Pittsburg; Miss Alma Gilespie, Schenley High School, Pittsburg, 2d; Miss E. Mahoney, Civic A. C., Pittsburg, 3d. Distance, 45 ft. 3 in.

400 yds., relay, held under the auspices of the Detroit A. C., Detroit, Mich., April 10, '20· Won by the Women's Swimming Assn. of N. Y. (Gertrude Ederle, Helen Meany, Eileen Riggin, Helen Wainwright); Detroit A. C., first team, 2d; Detroit A. C., 2d team, 3d. Time, 5m. 3 2-5s.

NOTEWORTHY SWIMMING PERFORMANCES

WOMEN.

50 yds., back stroke, bath (20), 2 turns—35s., Ethelda Bleibtrey, Women's Swimming Assn. of N. Y., at W. 60th St. Bath, N. Y. City, March 17, '20·

50 yds., back stroke, open tidal salt water, straightaway—36s., Ethelda Bleibtrey, Women's Swimming Assn. of N. Y., in Honolulu Harbor, Honolulu, T. H. April 17, '20·

50 yds., back stroke, bath (75)—35s., Sybil Bauer, Illinois A. C., Chicago, Ill., in Great Lakes Naval Training Sta. Bath, Great Lakes, Ill., Feb. 18, '20·

50 yds., back stroke, open tidal salt water, straightaway—39s., Ruth Scudder, Honolulu, in Hilo Harbor, Honolulu, T. H., Nov. 12, '19·

50 yds., breast stroke, open tidal salt water, straightaway—45 4-5s., Ruth Scudder, Honolulu, in Hilo Harbor, Honolulu, T. H., Nov. 11, '19·

MEN.

50 yds., back stroke, bath (20), 2 turns—29 3-5s., Warren Kealoha, Hui Makani, Honolulu Y. M. C. Bath, Honolulu, T. H., April 30, '20·

Plunging—75 ft. in 40s., R. H. Meagher, Yale Univ., in Yale Bath, New Haven, Conn., Feb. 20, '20·

JUNIOR CROSS COUNTRY.

Held over the Van Cortlandt Park Course, N. Y. City, Nov. 8, '19·

1, J. Simmons, Syracuse Univ., 33:00 3-5; 2, L. Watson, Syracuse Univ., 33:05; 3, Wm. Ritola, Finnish-Amer., 33:20; 4, J. O'Connor, St. Anselm's, 33:32; 5, J. McGuinnis, Mohawk, 33:39; 6, B. Prim, Finnish-Amer., 33:59; 7 J. Losgar, St. Anselm's, 34:10; *8, A. J. Hulsebosch, Paulist, 34:11; *9, G. Cornetta, N. Y. A. C., 34:22; 10, H. C. Johnson, Syracuse Univ., 34:26; *11, T. Halpine, unattached, 34:30; 12, R. Spear, Paulist, 34:37; 13, M. Fellman, Syracuse Univ., 34:33; *14, V. Voteretsas, Millrose, 34:35; 15, J. Fleck, Syracuse Univ., 34:55; *16,

---

*Individual entries; not counted in team scores.

SPORTING RECORDS—ATHLETICS—JUNIOR CROSS COUNTRY—*Continued.*

F. Titterton, unattached, 34:56; 17, J. Goff, St. Christopher, 35:04; 18, S. Jackson, St. Christopher, 35:10; *19, C. de Stefano, Millrose, 35:11; 20, V. Segretto, Morningside, 35:12; 21, C. Mitchell, St. Christopher, 35:13; 22, W. Campbell, Syracuse Univ., 35:14; 23, H. Wigger, Paulist, 35:19; 24, J. Losero, Paulist, 35:25; 25, W. Nouppa, Finnish-Amer., 35:26; 26, C. A. Hall, Mohawk, 35:34; 27, G. Williams, St. Christopher, 35:39; 28, C. Beagan, St. Anselm's, 35:40; 29, J. Brooks, Mohawk, 35:55; 30 W. Rose, Syracuse Univ., 35:57; 31 W. Hillman, Finnish-Amer., 35:58; 32, W. Stokeley, St. Christopher, 35:59; 33, J. Lehmann, Morningside, 36:03; 34, T. O'Connor, St. Anselm's, 36:05; *35, W. Johanning, unattached, 36:06; 36, E. Wilson, Mohawk, 36:13.

Team Scores—Syracuse Univ., 32; Finnish-Amer. A. C., 81; St. Christopher Club, 84; St. Anselm's A. A., 87; Mohawk A. C., 101; Paulist A. C., 110; St. Anselm's A. A., 135; Morningside A. C., 135.

SENIOR CROSS COUNTRY.

Held over the Van Cortlandt Park Course, N. Y. City, Nov. 29, '19.

1, F. Faller, Dorchester Club, 32:26 1-5; 2, C. Pores, Millrose, 32:40 4-5; *3, W. Ritalo, Finnish-Amer. A. C., 33:04; 4, J. Henigan, Dorchester Club, 32:26; *5, J. C. Geiger, Baltimore, 33:53; 6, A. J. Hulsebosch, Paulist, 34:04; 7, W. Giannakopulos, Millrose, 34:11; 8, M. Devaney, Millrose, 34:24; 9, J. Losgar, St. Anselm's, 34:26; 10, P. Flynn, Paulist A. C., 34:23; *11, T. Halpine, unattached, 34:25; 12, V. Voteretsas, Millrose, 34:36; 13, J. Losero, Paulist A. C., 34:55; 14, R. Spear, Paulist A. C., 34:58; 15, H. Wigger, Paulist A. C., 35:04; 16, C. Horne, Dorchester Club, 35:09; *17, P. Trivoulidas, unattached, 35:14; 18, C. de Staffano, Millrose, 35:32; 19, L. Davis, Dorchester Club, 35:36; 20, T. Henigan, Dorchester Club, 36:06; 21, J. E. O'Connor, St. Anselm's, 36:09; *22, R. Ohman, unattached, 36:11; 23, T. O'Connor, St. Anselm's, 36:13; 24, J. Soukop, St. Anselm's, 36:31; 25, C. Beagon, St. Anselm's, 36:35; 26, J. Giorgio, Paulist A. C., 39:19; 27, J. Warose, St. Anselm's, 39:24.

Team Scores—Millrose A. A., 36; Paulist A. C., 45; Dorchester Club, 48; St. Anselm's A. A., 81.

Miscellaneous.

BASKETBALL.

Held under the auspices of Atlanta A. C., Atlanta, Ga., March 10, 11, 12 and 13, '20. Won by N. Y. Univ. (49), Rutgers College, New Brunswick, N. J. (24). Members N. Y. Univ. team; Holman, Goeller, Delaney, Cann, Storey (captain), Mooney and Baker.

HANDBALL.

Junior, Doubles—Held under the auspices of the Detroit A. C., Detroit, Mich., March 2 to 6, '20. Won by A. L. Henry and E. J. Smith, Detroit A. C.

Championship, Singles—Held under the auspices of the Los Angeles A. C., Los Angeles, Cal., May 22 to 29, '20. Won by M. Gold, Los Angeles A. C.; G. Klawiter, unattached, 2d; Bill Ranft, Los Angeles A. C., 3d.

Championship, Doubles—Held under the auspices of the Los Angeles A. C., Los Angeles, Cal., May 22 to 29, '20. Won by K. Klawiter, unattached, and R. Retzer, Los Angeles A. C.; Bill Ranft, Los Angeles A. C., and M. Gold, Los Angeles A. C., 2d; M. Laswell, Los Angeles A. C., and G. Haskell, Los Angeles A. C., 3d.

TUG-OF-WAR.

Won by Aland A. C.; Atlas A. C., 2d; Finnish-Amer. Club, 3d.

10-MILE RUN.

Held under auspices of Metropolitan A. A. U. at Glenn Pk., Yonkers, N. Y., Dec. 5, '20.

F. Faller, Dorchester A. A., Boston, 55m. 20s., won; Frank Zuna, Paulist A. C., 57m. 31s., 2d; Peter Trivoulides, Millrose A. A., 57m. 36s., 3d. Sol Silverstein, Glencoe A. C., 58m. 19s., 4th; Fred Travalene, Mohawk A. C., 5th; A. Michelson, unattached, Stamford, 6th; John Wiberg, Mohawk A. C., 7th; Edwin White, Holy Cross Lyceum, 8th; Harry Rosen, Morningside A. C., 9th; Harry Parkinson, Morningside A. C., 10th.

7-MILE WALK.

Held under auspices of Metropolitan A. A. U. at Glenn Pk., Yonkers, N. Y., Dec. 5, '20.

J. Pearson, N. Y. A. C., 55m. 1-5s., won; R. Remmer, Amer. W. A., 55m. 32 3-5s., 2d; W. Roiker, N. Y. A. C., 58m. 1 2-5s., 3d; E. Zulch, Amer. W. A., 58m. 48 4-5s., 4th; J. Farrell, St. Anselm's A. C., 59m. 2 3-5s. 5th; M. Greenberg, Pastime A. C., 59m. 17 4-5s., 6th.

3,000-METER STEEPLECHASE.

(Final Olympic tryouts.)

Held under the auspices of N. Y. A. C., at Travers Isl., N. Y., July 10, '20.

Won by P. J. Flynn, Paulist A. C.; M. A. Devaney, Millrose A. A., 2d; A. J. Hulsebosch, Paulist A. C., 3d; R. B. Watson, Kansas State Agricl. Coll., 4th. Time, 9m. 58 1-5s.

PENTATHLON.

(Final Olympic tryouts.)

Held under the auspices of the Loughlin Lyceum, Bkln., N. Y., July 5, '20.

Won by Brutus Hamilton, Univ. of Missouri, 17 points; R. Le Gendre, Georgetown Univ., 19 points, 2d; E. L. Bradley, Univ. of Kansas, 22 points, 3d; L. Perrine, Univ. of Idaho, 26 points, 4th; R. N. Irving, Univ. of Idaho, 30 points, and Joseph L. Baker, Univ. of Michigan, 30 points, tied.

Running Broad Jump—Won by Bradley with 23 ft.; LeGendre, 22 ft. 8 in., 2d; Hamilton, 21 ft. 10 in., 3d; Helbig, 21 ft. 1 in., 4th; Perrine, 20 ft. 11½ in., 5th; Baker, 20 ft. 5½ in., 6th; Shea, 20 ft. 5 in., 7th; Irving, 20 ft. 4¾ in., 8th; Bartels, 20 ft. 3¾ in., 9th; Clapp, 20 ft. 2 in., 10th; Misbach, 20 ft., 11th; Bray, 19 ft. 11½ in., 12th; Harmer, 19 ft. 10½ in., 13th; Dunne, 19 ft. 8 in., 14th; Lichtman, 19 ft. 5 in., 15th; Masuda, 19 ft. 4 in., 16th; O'Connor, 19 ft. 3 in., 17th; Liversedge, 18 ft. 3 in., 18th; Huntley, 18 ft. 8 in., 19th; Hutchinson, 18 ft., 20th; Guthner, 17 ft. 10½ in., 21st; Fahrney, 17 ft. 8 in., 22d; McLoughlin, 16 ft. 6½ in., 23d.

Throwing the Javelin—Won by Liversedge, with 169 ft. 8 in.; Perrine, 162 ft. 6½ in., 2d; Irving, 162 ft. 6 in., 3d; Hamilton, 161 ft. 9½ in., 4th; Dunne, 154 ft. 7½ in., 5th; Helbig and LeGendre, tied for 6th, each with 145 ft. 4½ in.; Clapp, 142 ft. 9 in., 8th; Bray, 141 ft. 2¾ in., 9th; Bartels, 139 ft. 4½ in., 10th; Huntley, 138 ft., 11 in., 11th; Bradley, 137 ft. 11 in., 12th; Masuda, 136 ft. 10 in., 13th; Lichtman, 135 ft. 4½ in., 14th; Guthner, 133 ft. 8 in., 15th; Fahrney, 132 ft. 11 in., 16th; Harmer, 127 ft. 9 in., 17th; Baker, 117 ft. 9 in., 18th; Shea, 113 ft. 9 in., 19th; Misbach, 106 ft., 20th; Hutchinson, 104 ft. 7½ in., 21st; O'Connor, 103 ft. 11 in., 22d; McLoughlin fouled on three trials.

200-Meter Run—Hamilton and Bradley, 23 3-5s. tied for first; LeGendre and Guthner, 23¾s., tied for third; Harmer, 24 2-5s., 5th; Shea, Baker, Bray and Bartels, 24 3-5s., tied for 6th; Perrine, Clapp, Helbig and Dunne, 24 4-5s., tied for 10th; Lichtman, 25s., 14th; Irving and Liversedge, 25 1-5s., tied for 15th; Misbach, 25 2-5s., 17th; Masuda, 25 3-5s., 18th; Huntley, 24 4-5s., 19th; Fahrney, 27 2-5s., 20th; Hutchinson, 27 3-5s., 21st; McLoughlin and O'Connor did not run.

Throwing the Discus—Won by Clapp, with 129 ft. 1¼ in.; Irving, 123 ft. ½ in., 2d; Dunne, 121 ft. 7½ in., 3d; Baker, 120 ft. 9 in., 4th; Bartels, 118 ft. 2½ in., 5th; Hamilton, 117 ft. 7½ in., 6th; Bradley, 111 ft., 7th; LeGendre, 105 ft. 1½ in., 8th; Bray, 100 ft. 8½ in., 9th; Perrine, 99 ft. 1 in., 10th; Shea, 92 ft. 5 in., 11th; Helbig, 77 ft., 12th.

1,500-Meter Run—Won by LeGendre, 5 min. 8s.; Perrine, 5m. 14s., 2d; Bradley, 5m. 14 4-5s., 3d; Hamilton, 5m. 15 2-5s., 4th; Baker, 5m. 15 3-5s., 5th; Irving, 5m. 15 4-5s., 6th.

DECATHLON.

(Final Olympic tryouts.)

Held under the auspices of the N. Y. A. Club at Travers Isl., N. Y., July 15, '20.

Won by Brutus Hamilton, Univ. of Missouri, 7022.9815; Everett L. Bradley, Univ. of Kansas, 6965.118, 2d; R. L. LeGendre, Georgetown Univ., 6587.7885, 3d; H. G. Goelitz, Illinois A. C., 6461.531, 4th; E. L. Vidal, U. S. A., 6430.969, 5th; E. Ellis, Syracuse Univ., 6217.9985, 6th; L. Perrine, Univ. of Idaho, 6122.700, 7th; W. Yount, Los Angeles A. C., 6064.812, 8th; H. A. Jewett, Cornell Univ., 6028.9525, 9th; W. F. Bartels, Univ. of Pennsylvania, 5893.458, 10th; T. A. Farrell, N. Y. A. C., 5774.2485, 11th; C. E. Huntley, U. S. N., 5830.301, 12th; A. S. Roberts, Boston A. A., 5047.535, 13th.

*Individual entries; not counted in team scores.

SPORTING RECORDS—Athletics—*Continued.*

U. S. Navy Atlantic Fleet Boxing and Wrestling Championships.

Held at Madison Square Garden, N. Y. City, Dec. 1, 1920.

WRESTLING.

Middleweight Class—Seaman A. L. Berkowitz, Jacksonville, Fla., U. S. S. Bridge, defeated Seaman Janaak, U. S. S. Arizona, half Nelson, 2m. 5s.

Lightweight Class—Seaman F. Ames, Beacon Falls, Conn., U. S. S. North Dakota, defeated Seaman W. Howard, N. Y. City, U. S. S. Nevada, on points, 15m.

Welterweight Class—Seaman E. C. Simon, Shelby, O., defeated Coxswain H. L. Rogers, N. Y. City, U. S. S. Arizona, on points, 15m.

Heavyweight Class—Fireman O. Finney, Alma, Ark., U. S. S. Bridge, defeated Fireman L. Bartels, North Bend, O., U. S. S. Florida, on points, 15m.

Light Heavyweight Class—Chief Yeoman E. C. Bibeault, Brooklyn, N. Y., defeated Fireman W. Paradis, New Bedford, Mass., U. S. S. Pennsylvania, half Nelson and body lock, 54s.

BOXING.

Bantamweight Class—Fireman L. M. Gordon, North Bend, O., U. S. S. North Dakota, defeated Mess Attendant M. Soriano, Orton Bataan, P. I., 6 rounds, judges' decision.

Featherweight Class—Seaman H. O. Sutton, Syracuse, N. Y., U. S. S. Pennsylvania, defeated Seaman F. C. Kelly, Philadelphia, U. S. S. Nevada, 6 rounds, judges' decision.

Lightweight Class—Seaman M. Castelucci, Bayonne, N. J., U. S. S. Nevada, defeated Fireman B. H. Hilliard, Buffalo, N. Y., U. S. S. Utah, 7 rounds, judges' decision.

Welterweight Class—Fireman A. Urquidez, Los Angeles, Cal., defeated Seaman S. S. Markowitz, Brooklyn, N. Y., U. S. S. Utah, 7 rounds, referee's decision.

Heavyweight Class—Fireman J. L. Duman, Malone, N. Y., U. S. S. Columbia, defeated Fireman H. H. Anderson, Chicago, U. S. S. Florida, 5 rounds, stopped by referee.

Light Heavyweight Class—Coxswain M. F. Fenton, Washington, D. C., U. S. S. Nevada, defeated Fireman T. H. Van Billiard, South Bethlehem, Pa., U. S. S. Oklahoma, 7 rounds, judges' decision.

Middleweight Class—Seaman DeW. R. Bell, Newburgh, N. Y., U. S. S. Arizona, defeated W. Wellenmann, Philadelphia, U. S. S. Nevada, 6 rounds, judges' decision.

Public Schools Athletic League.

ELEMENTARY SCHOOLS INDOOR RECORDS.

(Weight Classifications Only.)

40-yd. dash (75-lb. class)—6s.; M. Unger, P. S. 184, Mhtn.; J. McArevey, P. S. 37, Bronx; I. Goldshein, P. S. 10, Bronx; Novick, P. S. 26, Bronx (record made in trial heats), Dec. 14, '18; J. Unger, P. S. 184, Mhtn., Dec. 20, '19.

50-yd. dash (80-lb. class)—6 4-5s.; H. Linicus, P. S. 9, Bronx; J. McMahon, P. S. 6, Mhtn., Dec. 15, '06.

50-yd. dash (85-lb. class)—6 2-5s.; Frankfort, P. S. 54, Bronx, Dec. 15, '17.

60-yd. dash (95-lb. class)—7 3-5s.; C. Atwood, P. S. 186, Mhtn (in heat), Feb. 22, '08; I. Hamberger, P. S. 10, Mhtn (in heat); E. DeRivera, P. S. 44, Bronx, Dec. 28, '12.

60-yd. dash (100-lb. class)—7 2-5s.; Schlossberg, P. S. 62, Mhtn., Dec. 11, '09; M. White, P. S. 43, Mhtn., Dec. 16, '11; P. Rabinowitz, P. S. 164, Bkln (in heat); V. Olivieri, P. S. 19, Mhtn., Dec. 28, '12; P. Baida, P. S. 9, Bkln (in heat), Dec. 19, '14; A. Davis, P. S. 164, Bkln. (in heat), Dec. 19, '14; Meyer, P. S. 10, Mhtn. (semi-final heat), Dec. 19, '14; Donashefsky, P. S. 62, Mhtn. (in heat), Dec. 18, '15; Borison, P. S. 62, Mhtn., (in heat), Dec. 18, '15; G. Adachi, P. S. 160, Bkln., Dec. 15, '17.

70-yd. dash (115-lb. class)—8 1-5s.; Harry Schultz, P. S. 6, Mhtn., Dec. 17, '19; F. Zittel, P. S. 23, Queens, Dec. 16, '11; M. Wilkoff, P. S. 143, Bkln., Dec. 19, '14.

100-yd. dash (unlimited weight class)—11s.; W. Strahan, P. S. 10, Bronx, Dec. 11, '09; F. Goodwin, P. S. 5, Mhtn., Dec. 17, '10.

220-yd. dash (unlimited weight class)—26 1-5s.; F. Suarez, Jr., P. S. 3, Bkln., Dec. 15, '06.

220-yd. relay (70-lb. class)—30 2-5s.; P. S. 40, Mhtn (Esposito, Karp, Gentile, Dubner), Dec. 20, '19.

360-yd. relay (80-lb. class)—47 2-5s.; P. S. 77, Mhtn. (E. Hauser, T. Garten, W. Moore, J. Kreiger); P. S. 40, Mhtn. (G. Ottinger, C. Walters, D. Adelman, D. Farley); P. S. 3, Bronx (W. Brouse, T. O'Rourke, A. Albrecht, I. Grenbaum), Nov. 28, '07.

360-yd. relay (85-lb. class)—46s.; P. S. 40, Mhtn. (Perillo, Merklin, Hand, Riccobono), Dec. 20, '19.

440-yd. relay (95-lb. class)—55s.; P. S. 40, Mhtn. (H. Marshall, E. Denroche, W. Craig, J. Moss), Dec. 15, '06.

440-yd. relay (100-lb. class)—55s.; P. S. 37, Mhtn. (W. Finnigan, L. Arminini, R. Cheappe, J. Fitzpatrick), Dec. 19, '14.

440-yd. relay (115-lb. class)—52 4-5s.; P. S. 43, Mhtn. (E. Healey, J. Glick, A. Suglia, H. Friedman), Dec. 16, '16.

880-yd. relay (unlimited weight class)—1m. 47 3-5s.; P. S. 6, Mhtn. (Gorham, G. Holder, Szilage, Jones), Dec. 11, '09; P. S. 43, Mhtn. (A. DeWitt, J. Riordan, E. Elliott, H. Reilly), Dec. 27, '12.

Running high jump (80-lb. class)—4 ft. 4 in.; Simpson, P. S. 77, Mhtn., Feb. 22, '08.

Running high jump (85-lb. class)—4 ft. 9½ in.; E. Benzinger, P. S. 42, Bronx, Dec. 18, '15.

Standing broad jump (80-lb. class)—8 ft. 1½ in.; J. Hinrichsen, P. S. 32, Bronx, Dec. 12, '08.

Standing broad jump (85-lb. class)—8 ft. 5⅝ in.; C. Schening, P. S. 90, Queens, Dec. 19, '14.

Running high jump (95-lb. class)—4 ft. 7 in.; Kesler, P. S. 77, Mhtn., Feb. 22, '08; H. Baker, P. S. 9, Bkln., Dec. 12, '08.

Standing broad jump (95-lb. class)—8 ft. 8 in.; Katz, P. S. 43, Bkln., Dec. 12, '08.

Running high jump (100-lb. class)—5 ft. ⅝ in.; M. Silberstein, P. S. 46, Mhtn., Dec. 18, '15.

Standing broad jump (100-lb. class)—8 ft. 10⅜ in.; I. Shambaum, P. S. 62, Mhtn., Dec. 16, '11; M. Stelzer, P. S. 22, Mhtn., Dec. 19, '14.

Putting 8-lb. shot (115-lb. class)—40 ft. 7 in.; M. Cohen, P. S. 62, Mhtn., Dec. 16, '16.

Standing broad jump (115-lb. class)—9 ft. 3 in.; Brod, P. S. 62, Mhtn., Dec. 18, '15.

Running high jump (unlimited weight class)—5 ft. 3½ in.; G. Corcoran, P. S. 184, Mhtn., Dec. 19, '14.

Putting 8-lb. shot (unlimited weight class)—40 ft. 5 in.; A. Berken, P. S. 164, Bkln., Dec. 15, '17.

Putting 12-lb. shot (unlimited weight class)—40 ft. 4½ in.; A. Kurzman, P. S. 186, Mhtn., Dec. 18, '15.

SPECIAL INDOOR NOVICE RELAY—D. T'K.

352-yd. relay (80-lb. class)—49 3-5s.; P. S. 24, Mhtn. (M. Myles, J. Schmidt, B. DeLara, J. Greenberg), Mar. 17, '06.

352-yd. relay (95-lb. class)—48s.; P. S. 24, Mhtn. (A. Block, W. Board, A. Guider, J. McMahon), March 17, '06.

704-yd. relay (110-lb. class)—1m. 23 2-5s.; P. S. 62, Mhtn. (I. Kupperman, M. Gordon, N. Smith, I. Goldstein), March 17, '06.

704-yd. relay (unlimited weight class)—1m. 21s.; P. S. 24, Mhtn. (L. Tohnach, E. Earlie, C. Grubb, M. Newmark), March 17, '06.

SWIMMING.

20 yds. (80-lb. class)—13 4-5s.; J. Fulton, P. S. 67, Mhtn., April 17, '09.

20 yds. (85-lb. class)—11s.; A. Santiago, P. S. 141, Mhtn., April 20, '18.

40 yds. (95-lb. class)—29 4-5s.; S. Lothian, P. S. 58, Mhtn., April 17, '09.

40 yds. (100-lb. class)—24s.; J. Watt, Jr., P. S. 9, Bkln., April 17, '15.

50 yds. (100-lb. class)—33s.; A. Brown, P. S. 27, Queens, May 3, '19.

60 yds. (115-lb. class)—35s.; H. Florence, P. S. 40, Mhtn., April 20, '18.

80 yds. (unlimited weight class)—48s.; H. Giebel P. S. 14, Mhtn., April 20, '18.

160-yd. relay (unlimited weight class)—1m. 46 4-5s.; P. S. 9, Bkln. (Coghe, McGary, Schriver, Underhill), April 21, '17.

400-ft. relay (unlimited weight class)—1m. 29 1-5s.; P. S. 40, Mhtn. (Bondy, Pastorino, Petruso, Zimmerman), May 3, '19.

HIGH SCHOOL INDOOR RECORDS.

Events for Juniors.

100-yd. dash—10 4-5s.; L. Perkins, H. S. of Commerce, Jan. 6, '06; Ottman, DeWitt Clinton H. S., Jan. 6, '06; B. Levinson, E. D. H. S., Jan. 28, 1911.

220-yd. dash—24 3-5s.; A. Engels, Commercial H. S., Jan. 28, '11.

SPORTING RECORDS—ATHLETICS—PUBLIC SCHOOLS ATHLETIC LEAGUE—*Continued.*

Events for Seniors.

50-yd. dash—6s.; E. C. Jessup, Boys H. S., Dec. 26, '03.

70-yd. dash—8 s.; H. Turchin, Townsend Harris Hall, Jan. 26, '12.

100-yd. dash—10 2-5s.; J. Ravenell, H. S. of Commerce, Jan. 29, '10; Peter White, Stuyvesant H. S., Jan. 30, '15.

220-yd. dash—24 1-5s.; A. Van Winkle, Boys H. S., Jan. 28, '11.

440-yd. dash—53 3-5s.; F. Brady, DeWitt Clinton H. S., Jan. 28, '11.

880-yd. run—2m. 5s.; A. Lent, Stuyvesant H. S., Jan. 26, '12; E. Ballister, Morris H. S., Jan. 30, '15.

1-mile run—4m. 43 2-5s.; J. Fleck, Morris H. S., Jan. 29, '16.

400-yd. high hurdles—14s.; George Hughes, Flushing H. S., Jan. 30, '15; duplicated performance Jan. 29, '16.

440-yd. relay (100-lb class)—52 2-5s.; Manual Training H. S. (R. Palmer, A. Reed, J. Blecher, H. Obst), Jan. 29, '10.

880-yd. relay (120-lb. class)—1m. 41 1-5s.; Manual Training H. S. (E. Shannon, I. Bruns, E. Feuerstein, C. Luce), March 8, '13.

850-yd. midget relay—1m. 49 4-5s.; Morris H. S. (Wilson, Flood, Hands, Blum), Jan. 6, '06.

880-yd. freshman relay—1m. 43 2-5s.; H. S. of Commerce (G. Young, K. Lozier, J. Adler, C. Burgess), Jan. 29, '10.

704-yd. freshman relay—1m. 24 3-5s.; Boys H. S. (C. S. Bryce, L. E. Fackner, E. B. Jones, A. G. Salmon), Dec. 26, '03.

1 mile relay championship—3m. 35s.; Manual Training H. S. (A. Clunan, A. Cozzens, F. Youngs, Danielson), March 7, '08.

Running high jump—5 ft. 8¾ in.; W. M. Oler, DeWitt Clinton H. S., Jan. 23, '09; Courtois, Stuyvesant H. S., Jan. 25, '19.

Putting 12-lb. shot—48 ft. 4⅛ in.; J. Sinclair, Stuyvesant H. S., Jan. 29, '16.

EVENING HIGH SCHOOLS.

70-yd. dash (120-lb. class)—8s.; A. Pendleton, Morris Eve. H. S., March 26, '15.

70-yd. dash (unlimited weight class)—7 4-5s.; J. Behnken, N. Y. Eve. H. S., April 11, '13; W. Elliott, Bkln. Eve. H. S., March 25, '15.

100-yd. dash—11s.; C. Beckman, Manual Training Eve. H. S., Jan. 29, '10; C. Mundt, N. Y. Eve. H. S., Jan. 28, '11.

220-yd. dash—24s.; R. Schulze, N. Y. Eve. H. S., March 26, '15.

880-yd. relay (120-lb. class)—1m. 44 2-5s.; Harlem Eve. H. S. (H. Foster, H. Richardson, E. Herberg, N. Hoffman), March 21, '14.

1-mile relay—3m. 47 3-5s.; N. Y. Eve. H. S. (H. Weinberg, G. Ralston, J. Foley, F. Safarowic), March 21, '14.

Running high jump—5 ft. 9⅛ in.; G. Trefry, Bkln. Eve. H. S., March 26, '15.

Putting 12-lb. shot—46 ft.; T. Cook, N. Y. Eve. H. S., April 11, '13.

SPECIAL INDOOR NOVICE RELAYS—D. T'K.

704-yd. relay (100-lb. class)—1m. 31 1-5s.; Stuyvesant H. S. (Sucker, Farrington, Brennan, Reinhardt), March 17, '06.

1,408-yd. relay (120-lb. class)—3m. 9 1-5s.; Morris H. S. (H. Gaffney, W. Bennett, V. Murray, H. Zoller), March 17, '06.

1408-yd. relay (heavyweight class)—3m. 7s.; Commercial H. S. (L. Andrews, W. Calvin, H. Gray, L. Stevenson), March 17, '06.

SWIMMING.

Tub race (20 yds.)—17 2-5s.; Guiteras, H. S. of Commerce, Feb. 26, '07.

50 yds.—27 2-5s.; H. Vollmer, Stuyvesant H. S., March 13, '13.

75 yds.—57 3-5s.; M. Thompson, H. S. of Commerce, Feb. 26, '08.

100 yds.—1m. 2 1-5s.; T. Cann, H. S. of Commerce, March 12, '15.

200 yds.—2m. 49 1-5s.; H. W. Roger, Townsend Harris Hall, March 11, '10.

220 yds.—2m. 39s.; C. Ross, Erasmus Hall H. S. (in trial heat two days prior to date of championship meet), Jan. 14, '19.

Relay race (160 yds.)—1 m. 47 4-5s.; H. S. of Commerce (O'Neil, H. Greenwald, J. Boyle, M. Thompson), Feb. 26, '07.

Relay race (200 yds.)—2m. 13 2-5s.; H. S. of Commerce (Rohes, Purcell, Kernel, M. Thompson), Feb. 27, '09.

Relay race (266 yds.)—3m. 2s.; DeWitt Clinton H. S. (Richards, McAuliffe, Moore, Hanratti), March 11, '10.

Relay race (800 ft.)—2m. 42s.; Erasmus Hall H. S. (J. Burrill, R. Franken, H. McMullen, C. Ross), Jan. 16, '19.

Plunge for distance—69 ft. 6 in.; L. Glebel, Stuyvesant H. S., March 12, '15.

Junior (or First Year Students) High School.

50 yds.—32s.; J. Arnold, Manual Training H. S., April 25, '19.

100 yds—1m. 17 2-5s.; Kennedy, Stuyvesant H. S., April 25, '19.

200 feet breast stroke—1m. 2-5s.; Morgan, Stuyvesant H. S., April 25, '19.

220-yd. swim—3m. 22s.; Walcutt, Townsend Harris Hall, May 14, '20.

400-ft. relay—1m. 28s.; H. S. of Commerce (Roses, Slotsky, Mare, Friedman), May 14, '20.

800-ft. relay—3m. 9 4-5s.; Stuyvesant H. S. (Laskas, Treull, Scheibler, Kennedy), April 25, '19.

EVENT CLOSED TO NAUTICAL SCHOOL.

66 yds. 18 in.—55 2-5s.; S. Williams, U.S.S. Newport, March 11, '10.

SKATING.

440 yds.—54 1-5s.; L. Cremin, DeWitt Clinton H. S., March 15, '07.

880 yds.—1m. 56 4-5s.; L. Barnett, DeWitt Clinton H. S., March 15, '07.

1 mile—3m. 59 2-5s.; L. Cremin, DeWitt Clinton H. S., March 15, '07.

ELEMENTARY SCHOOLS—OUTDOOR RECORDS.

40-yd. dash (75-lb. class)—5 4-5s.; J. Shapiro, P. S. 16, Bkln., June 16, '17; Daichman, P. S. 64, Mhtn., June 16, '17; Lawrence, P. S. 168, Bkln., June 8, '18; H. Sokel, P. S. 184, Mhtn., June 14, '19.

50-yd. dash (80-lb. class)—6 2-5s.; C. Schneider, P. S. 77, Mhtn., June 15, '07; H. Beebe, P. S. 144, Bkln., June 6, '08.

50-yd. dash (85-lb. class)—6 2-5s.; V. Valle, P. S. 83, Mhtn., June 14, '13.

60-yd. dash (95-lb. class)—7s.; L. Jackson, P. S. 89, Mhtn., June 12, '09.

60-yd. dash (100-lb. class)—6 4-5s.; Borison, P. S. 62, Mhtn., June 17, '16.

70-yd. dash (115-lb. class)—8s.; N. Patto, P. S. 77, Mhtn., June 15, '07; E. Murphy, P. S. 28, Bronx, June 12, '09; C. Schneider, P. S. 77, Mhtn., June 10, '11.

100-yd. dash (unlimited weight)—10 2-5s.; F. Zittel, P. S. 20, Queens, June 14, '13.

220-yd. dash—25s.; J. Weaver, P. S. 166, Mhtn., June 16, '06.

20-yd. relay (70-lb. class)—28 4-5s.; P. S. 167, Bkln. (J. Kiely, A. Taub, F. Barnet, Noren), June 16, '17.

260-yd. relay (80-lb. class)—44 4-5s.; P. S. 77, Mhtn. (L. Posnelsky, F. Sharpell, H. Kurth, B. Schenck), June 15, '07.

360-yd. relay (85-lb. class)—43 4-5s.; P. S. 40, Bronx (Finkelbrand, Joseph, Meller, Sladen), June 17, '16.

440-yd. relay (95-lb. class)—53 3-5s.; P. S. 40, Mhtn. (G. Lamm, C. Waters, E. Denroche, C. Foverschner), June 15, '07.

440-yd. relay (100-lb. class)—52 2-5s.; P. S. 10, Mhtn. (H. Dubia, W. Giesen, S. Rose, W. Porter). June 14, '13.

440-yd. relay (115-lb. class)—50 2-5s.; P. S. 24, Mhtn. (King, Fleck, Harker, McKernan), June 15, '07.

880-yd. relay (115-lb. class)—1m. 48s.; P. S. 15, Bkln (A. Whitlock, F. Lampe, T. Shotten, W. McGonigal), June 15, 1906.

880-yd. relay (heavyweight)—1m. 41s.; P. S. 24, Mhtn. (Friedman, Kelley, Heller, DeLuna), June 15, '07.

Running broad jump (80-lb. class)—17 ft.; J. Keller, P. S. 77, Mhtn., June 15, '07.

Running broad jump (85-lb. class)—16 ft. 7 in.; C. Silverstone, P. S. 40, Bronx, June 14, '13.

Running high jump (80-lb. class)—4 ft. 6 in.; A. Willetts, P. S. 9, Bkln., June 12, '09.

Running high jump (85-lb. class)—4 ft. 11 in.; Kantrowitz, P. S. 62, Mhtn., June 12, '15.

Running broad jump (95-lb. class)—16 ft. 11¼ in.; C. Thompson, P. S. 144, Bkln., June 15, '07.

Running high jump (95-lb. class)—4 ft. 11⅛ in.; R. Crowe, P. S. 32, Bronx, June 6, '08.

Running broad jump (100-lb. class)—16 ft. 11 in.; D. Shutkind, P. S. 30, Mhtn., June 25, '10.

Running high jump (100-lb. class)—5 ft.; M. Zerchner, P. S. 42, Bronx; C. Levine, P. S. 64,

SPORTING RECORDS—ATHLETICS—PUBLIC SCHOOLS ATHLETIC LEAGUE—*Continued.*

Mhtn., June 1, '12; Johnson, P. S. 10, Mhtn., June 12, '15.

Putting 8-lb. shot (115-lb. class)—40 ft. 4 in.; C. Walsh, P. S. 100, Bkln., June 12, '09.

Running broad jump (115-lb. class)—18 ft. 8¾ in.; N. Sloane, P. S. 12, Bronx, June 15, '07.

Running high jump (115-lb. class)—4 ft. 9 in.; F. Hanek, P. S. 23, Bronx, June 16, '06.

Putting 8-lb. shot (unlimited weight class)—43 ft. 5½ in.; F. Gollik, P. S. 51, Bronx, June 14, '19.

Putting 12-lb. shot (heavyweight)—39 ft. 7½ in.; H. A. Clinton, P. S. 12, Bronx, June 6, '08.

Running high jump (unlimited weight class)—5 ft. 4 in.; Levy, P. S. 10, Mhtn., June 17, '16.

SWIMMING.

20 yds.—17 3-5s.; H. Slifka, P. S. 10, Mhtn., July 1, '11.

40 yds.—35 2-5s.; A. Moor, P. S. 40, Mhtn., July 1, '11.

60 yds.—52 1-5s.; D. McCann, P. S. 168, Bkln., July 1, '11.

80 yds.—1m. 4-5s.; J. Agid, P. S. 160, Mhtn., July 1, '11.

Relay (160 yds.)—3m. 16 4-5s.; P. S. 128, Bkln. (H. Lawson, F. Fay, F. LaDolce, L. Lake), July 1, '11.

HIGH SCHOOL OUTDOOR RECORDS.

Junior Events.

100-yd. dash—10 3-5s.; George McNulty, Erasmus Hall H. S., May 27, '05; D. Friend, Manual Training H. S., May 29, '09.

220-yd. run—23 3-5s.; George McNulty, Erasmus Hall H. S., May 27, '05; B. Taylor, Boys H. S., May 23, '08.

Senior Events.

100-yd. dash—10 1-5s.; B. Wefers, DeWitt Clinton H. S., May 27, '16.

220-yd. dash—22 1-5s.; Bonaparte, Morris H. S., May 31, '13.

440-yd. dash—52 1-5s.; W. Albrecht, Stuyvesant H. S., May 29, '15.

880-yd. run—2m. 3 1-5s.; F. Jenkins, Far Rockaway H. S., June 10, '14.

1 mile run—4m. 34 1-5s.; R. Crawford, Flushing H. S., May 25, '18.

120-yd. high hurdles—16 3-5s.; V. B. Havens, Boys H. S., May 23, '08.

120-yd. low hurdles—26 2-5s.; H. Starr, Boys H. S., May 27, '05.

440-yd. relay (100-lb. class)—50s.; H. S. of Commerce (Meyer, Gettelson, Usher, Alpert), May 31, '15.

880-yd. relay (120-lb. class)—1m. 38 3-5s.; Townsend Harris Hall (C. Weg, L. Levine, A. Von Bonin, O. Tabor), June 3, '10.

1 mile relay (unlimited weight class)—3m. 31 4-5s.; Morris H. S. (H. Schulman, J. Bonaporte, E. Ballister, J. Taub), May 31, '15.

Running high jump—5 ft. 9⅞ in.; Clark, DeWitt Clinton H. S., June 7, '19.

Running broad jump—21 ft. 6 in.; D. Brown, Jamaica H. S., June 10, '14.

Pole vault—10 ft. 9 in.; A. Belcher, Jamaica H. S., and B. Goggins, Boys H. S., May 28, '10.

Putting 12-lb. shot—49 ft. 4⅜ in.; P. Coffey, Bryant H. S., May 28, '10.

Throwing the discus (Greek style)—130 ft. 3 in.; F. Finegan, Manual Training H. S., May 28, '10.

ROWING.

1 mile (8-oared)—5m. 35s.; H. S. of Commerce, May 30, '07.

EVENING HIGH SCHOOLS OUTDOOR RECORDS.

100-yd. dash—10 3-5s.; J. Behnken, N. Y. Eve. H. S., May 17, '13; P. K. Walters, N. Y. Eve. H. S., May 16, '14; A. Pendleton, Morris Eve. H. S., May 31, '15.

220-yd. dash—23 4-5s.; R. Schulze, N. Y. Eve. H. S., May 31, '15.

440-yd. run—53s.; R. Schulze, N. Y. Eve. H. S., May 31, '15.

880-yd. run—2m. 7 3-5s.; A. Rolly, East Side Eve. H. S., May 31, '15.

1 mile run—4m. 48 1-5s.; M. Taub, Harlem Eve. H. S., May 17, '13.

1 mile relay—3m. 42 4-5s.; Harlem Eve. H. S. (V. Block, F. Plank, W. Garrettson, C. Grandgerard), May 28, '10.

Putting 12-lb. shot—45 ft. ⅛ in.; T. Cooke, Jr., N. Y. Eve. H. S., May 17, '13.

Running broad jump—19 ft. 8 in.; G. Trefry, Bkln Eve. H. S., May 31, '15.

NAUTICAL SCHOOL RECORDS—U.S.S NEWPORT.

70-yd. dash—8 3-5s.; J. A. Bain, U.S.S. Newport, March 11, '11; B. Hope, U.S.S. Newport, March 9, '12; P. Gerardi, U.S.S. Newport, March 29, '13.

220-yd. dash—30 2-5s.; P. Gerardi, U.S.S. Newport, March 29, '13.

440-yd. dash—1m. 4s.; W. Riker, U.S.S. Newport, March 9, '12.

880-yd. run—2m. 54 3-5s.; C. Duhme, U.S.S. Newport, March 11, 11.

1 mile run—5m. 34s.; T. Barry, U.S.S. Newport, March 29, '13.

Flag relay (600 yds.)—1m. 24s.; U.S.S. Newport (E. Brann, J. Bain, L. Wehle, C. Flynn, J. Pell, F. Farrier, W. Dietrich, A. Piaron, F. Gorsch, W. Malloy), March 11, '11.

Relay 880 yds.—2m. 39 4-5s.; Class A, U.S.S. Newport (E. O'Brien, R. Peterson, C. Dorgue, H. Wagner), March 9, '12.

Potota race (6 potatoes)—23 4-5s.; S. Willesen, U.S.S. Newport, March 11, '11.

Putting 12-lb. shot—36 ft. 3 in.; F. W. Gorsch, U.S.S. Newport, March 11, '11.

Running high jump—5 ft.; W. Greenhalgh, U.S.S. Newport, March 9, '12.

Rope climbing—10 1-5s.; A. I. Flynn, U.S.S. Newport, March 11, '11.

The best class records to date are as follows:

City Records.

STANDING BROAD JUMP.

5th yr., 6 ft. 6.3126 in., P. S. 32, Bronx; 6th yr., 7 ft. 0.275 in., P. S. 32, Bronx; 7th yr., 7 ft. 2.328 in., P. S. 32, Bronx; 8th yr., 7 ft. 7.417 in., P. S. 9, Bkln.

CHINNING.

5th yr., 13.1438 times, P. S. 17, Queens; 6th yr., 14.8518 times, P. S. 3, Bronx; 7th yr., 17.88 times, P. S. 12, Bronx; 8th yr., 20.592 times, P. S. 12, Bronx.

RUNNING.

5th yr., 40 yds., 5.3534s., P. S. 32, Bronx; 6th yr., 50 yds., 6.04s., P. S. 32, Bronx; 7th yr., 60 yds., 7.0937s., P. S. 10, Bkln.; 8th yr., 80 yds., 9.0845s., P. S. 10, Bkln.

AUTOMOBILE RECORDS, 1920.

April 18—J. Murphy, in Duesenberg, set world's record at Daytona, Fla., of rate of mile in 23:38s. for 153.9 miles.

April 24—T. Milton, in Duesenberg, at Daytona, Fla., set world's records—1 mile in 0:23:60 and 2 miles in 0:47:16.

April 25—T. Milton set world speed records at Daytona, Fla.—1 kilometer in 14:65, 3 miles in 1:12:18, 4 miles in 1:36:14, 5 miles in 2:00:14, ½ mile in 0:11:86 and 1 mile in 0:2356.

April 27—T. Milton, at Daytona, Fla., set world's speed 2-mile record to 0:46:24.

May 31—500-mile speedway race at Indianapolis won by G. Chevrolet in a Monroe in 5:46:16:14, average of 87.45 miles; R. Thomas, Balliot, 2d; T. Milton, Duesenberg, 3d; J. Murphy, Duesenberg, 4th; R. De Palma, Balliot, 5th.

June 19—T. Milton, Duesenberg, won 225-mile Universal trophy race at Uniontown, Pa., in 2:22:44:37, average of 94.9 miles; J. Murphy, Duesenberg, 2d; E. O'Donnell, Duesenberg, 3d; I. P. Fetterman, Monroe, 4th.

July 5—T. Milton won 225-mile speedway race at Tacoma, Wash., in 2:28:28, average of 95 miles; R. Mulford, 2d; Hearne, 3d; Klein, 4th; Sarles, 5th.

Aug. 1—G. Chevrolet set world's record for 100 miles over dirt track at Columbus, O., when he covered distance without a stop in 89m. 23s.

Aug. 28—R. De Palma, Balliot, won Elgin road race, 250 miles, in 3:09:54, average of 79.5 miles, track record. He also set record lap of 7:11; T. Milton, Duesenberg, 2d; Murphy, Duesenberg, 3d; R. Mulford, Monroe, 4th; O'Donnell, Duesenberg, 5th; Ford, Frontenac, 6th.

Sept. 6—T. Milton, Duesenberg, won 225-mile race at Uniontown, Pa., in 2:20:24, average of 96 miles an hour; J. Murphy, Duesenberg, 2d; E. Hearne, Revere, 3d.

Sept. 6—O. Loesche, Lexington, won free-for-all hill climb to Pikes Peak summit in 22:25 2-5; A. M. Cline, Lexington, 2d.

Sept. 18—R. De Palma, Balliot special, broke two world's records for circular track at Syracuse, N. Y., 10 miles in 7:47¼ and 20 miles in 16:25.

Oct. 10—T. Milton, at Phoenix, Ariz., broke world's record on dirt track, making 100 miles in 1:24:00 2-5.

SPORTING RECORDS—*Continued.*

BASEBALL.

Brooklyn won the National League baseball pennant in 1920, as it did in 1916, and it again lost the World Series when it was beaten in five out seven games by the Cleveland Americans champions. Cleveland won the first of three games scheduled in Brooklyn, and Brooklyn won the next two. Moving to Cleveland, the American League champions won four straight games and the championship of the world. In 1916 Brooklyn lost four out of five games to the Boston American League champions of that year.

Baseball conditions were much upset in the last two months of the 1920 season by the exposure of the alleged fact that when the Chicago White Sox, champions of the American League, lost five out of eight games to the Cincinnati National League champions in the World Series of 1919, eight of the White Sox had been bribed by a coterie of gamblers to "throw" the series. The eight accused players have since been indicted by the Cook County (Chicago), Ill., Grand Jury, but there is considerable doubt whether they technically violated the criminal laws.

As a consequence of the serious dissentions in the American League, in which the New York, Chicago and Boston clubs were lined up against the other five in a fight upon Pres. Ban B. Johnson, there was a movement to consolidate the three American League "insurgents" with the eight National League clubs, and one other, in a revival of the old 12-club circuit, with two clubs in many cities. The matter was finally compromised by the appointment of Judge Kenesaw Mountain Landis, of the United States District Court for the Northern District of Ill., since 1905, as a one-man arbiter of professional baseball, to take the place of the three-man National Commission. Judge Landis will retain his position on the U. S. Bench, at a salary of $7,500, and Organized Baseball will pay him $42,500 per year, bringing his total salary to $50,000 per year.

National League.

Final Standing.

Clubs.	Brooklyn.	New York.	Cincinnati.	Pittsburg.	Chicago.	St. Louis.	Boston.	Philadelphia.	Games won.	Games lost.	Per cent.
Brooklyn		15	10	12	13	15	14	14	93	61	.604
New York	7		16	13	15	11	12	12	86	68	.558
Cincinnati	12	6		12	13	13	12	14	82	71	.536
Pittsburg	10	9	10		11	11	15	13	79	75	.513
Chicago	9	7	9	11		10	15	14	75	79	.487
St. Louis	7	11	9	11	12		11	14	75	79	.487
Boston	8	10	9	7	7	11		10	62	90	.408
Philadelphia	8	10	8	9	8	8	11		62	91	.405
Games lost.......	61	68	71	75	79	79	90	91			

CLUB BATTING.

Club.	G.	AB.	R.	H.	2B.	3B.	HR.	PC.
St. Louis......	155	5,495	675	1,589	238	96	32	.289
Brooklyn	155	5,399	660	1,493	205	99	28	.277
Cincinnati ...	154	5,176	639	1,432	169	76	18	.277
New York....	155	5,309	682	1,427	210	76	46	.269
Chicago	154	5,117	619	1,350	223	67	34	.264
Philadelphia .	153	5,264	565	1,385	229	54	64	.263
Boston	153	5,218	523	1,358	168	86	23	.260
Pittsburg	155	5,219	530	1,342	162	90	16	.257

INDIVIDUAL BATTING.

Player and Club.	G.	AB.	R.	H.	HR.	PC.
Hornsby, St. L...........	149	589	96	218	9	.370
Nicholson, Pitts..........	99	247	33	89	4	.360
Young, N. Y.............	153	581	92	204	6	.351
Roush, Cin...............	149	579	81	196	4	.339
Smith, St. L.............	91	313	53	104	1	.332
Wheat, Bkn..............	148	583	89	191	9	.328
Eayrs, Bos..............	87	244	31	80	1	.328
Williams, Phila..........	148	590	88	192	15	.325
Stock, St. L.............	155	639	85	204	..	.319
Hollocher, Chi..........	80	301	53	96	..	.319
Daly, Chi................	44	90	12	28	..	.311
Meusel, Phila............	138	518	75	160	14	.309
Konetchy, Bkn...........	131	497	62	153	5	.308
Fournier, St. L..........	141	530	77	162	3	.306
Grimes, Bkn.............	43	111	9	34	..	.306
See, Cin.................	47	82	9	25	..	.305
Myers, Bkn..............	154	582	83	177	4	.304
Daubert, Cin.............	142	553	97	168	4	.304
Flack, Chi...............	135	520	85	157	4	.302
Robertson, Chi...........	134	500	68	150	10	.300
Bancroft, Phila., N. Y..	150	613	102	183	..	.299
Groh, Cin................	145	550	86	164	..	.298
Sullivan, Bos............	81	250	36	74	1	.296
Duncan, Cin..............	154	576	75	170	2	.295
Holke, Bos...............	144	551	53	162	3	.294
Smith, N. Y..............	91	262	20	77	1	.294
Stengel, Phila...........	129	445	53	130	9	.292
Johnston, Bkn...........	155	635	87	185	1	.291
Lavan, St. L.............	142	516	52	149	1	.289
Carey, Pitts.............	130	485	74	140	1	.289
Miller, Bkn..............	90	301	16	87	..	.289
Cravath, Phila...........	46	45	2	13	1	.289
Paulette, Phila..........	143	562	59	162	1	.288
Krueger, Bkn............	52	146	21	42	1	.288
Burns, N. Y..............	154	631	115	181	6	.287
Doyle, N. Y..............	137	471	48	134	4	.285
Merkle, Chi..............	92	330	33	94	3	.285
Fletcher, N. Y., Phila...	143	550	57	156	4	.284
Southworth, Pitts.......	146	546	64	155	2	.284
Heathcote, St. L.........	133	489	55	139	3	.284
O'Neil, Bos..............	112	304	19	86	..	.283
McHenry, St. L..........	137	504	66	142	10	.282
Clemons, St. L...........	112	338	17	95	1	.281
Bigbee, Pitts............	137	550	78	154	4	.280
Terry, Chi...............	133	496	56	139	..	.280
Frisch, N. Y.............	110	440	57	123	4	.280
Paskert, Chi.............	139	487	57	136	5	.279
Cruise, Bos..............	91	288	40	80	1	.278
Schmidt, Pitts...........	94	310	22	86	..	.277
Mann, Bos................	115	424	48	117	3	.276
King, N. Y...............	93	261	32	72	7	.276
Pick, Bos................	95	383	34	105	2	.274
Janvrin, St. L...........	87	270	33	74	1	.274
Barbare, Pitts...........	57	186	9	51	..	.274
Kauff, N. Y..............	55	157	31	43	3	.274
Lamar, Bkn..............	24	44	5	12	..	.273
Kilduff, Bkn.............	141	478	62	130	..	.272
Allen, Cin...............	43	85	10	23	..	.271
Carlson, Pitts...........	39	85	3	23	..	.271
Boeckel, Bos.............	153	582	70	156	3	.268
Nehf, N. Y...............	40	97	11	26	..	.268
Rath, Cin................	129	506	61	135	2	.267
Bressler, Cin............	21	30	4	8	..	.267
Kelly, N. Y..............	155	590	69	157	11	.266
Maranville, Bos..........	134	493	48	131	1	.266
Luque, Cin...............	37	64	6	17	..	.266
Barber, Chi..............	94	340	27	90	..	.265
Wingo, Cin..............	108	364	32	96	2	.264
Schultz, St. L...........	99	320	38	84	..	.263
Dillhoefer, St. L........	76	224	26	59	..	.263
Wrightstone, Phila......	76	206	23	54	3	.262
Tyler, Chi...............	29	65	6	17	..	.262
Whitted, Pitts...........	134	494	53	129	1	.261
Griffith, Bkn............	93	334	41	87	2	.260
LeBourveau, Phila......	84	261	29	67	3	.257
McQuillan, Bos..........	38	74	8	19	1	.257
Schupp, St. L...........	39	86	11	22	..	.256
Neale, Cin...............	150	530	55	135	3	.255
Olson, Bkn...............	143	637	71	162	1	.254
Miller, Phila............	98	343	41	87	1	.254
Neis, Bkn................	95	249	38	63	2	.253
Lear, N. Y...............	31	87	12	22	1	.253
Eller, Cin................	38	87	7	22	..	.253
Cutshaw, Pitts...........	131	488	56	123	..	.252
Snyder, N. Y............	87	264	26	66	3	.250
O'Farrell, Chi...........	94	270	29	67	3	.248
Rixey, Phila.............	43	101	6	25	1	.248
Rariden, Cin.............	39	101	9	25	..	.248
Kopf, Cin................	126	458	56	112	..	.245
Pfeffer, Bkn.............	30	74	5	18	..	.243
Gowdy, Bos...............	80	214	14	52	..	.243
Elliott, Bkn..............	41	112	13	27	1	.241
Toney, N. Y..............	42	96	6	23	..	.240
Schmandt, Bkn..........	28	63	7	15	..	.238
Caton, Pitts..............	98	352	29	83	..	.236
Mitchell, Bkn............	55	107	9	25	..	.234
Smith, Bkn...............	33	43	6	10	..	.233
Gonzales, N. Y..........	11	13	1	3	..	.231
Cadore, Bkn..............	35	91	4	20	2	.220
Barnes, N. Y............	45	108	10	22	..	.204
Spencer, N. Y...........	45	140	15	28	..	.200
Sallee, Cin., N. Y.......	26	38	1	7	..	.184
Marquard, Bkn..........	28	59	2	10	..	.169
Mamaux, Bkn............	41	60	5	10	..	.167
Grimes, N. Y............	26	57	5	9	..	.158
McCabe, Chi., Bkn......	44	70	11	11	..	.157
McCarty, N. Y., St. L...	41	45	2	7	..	.156
Ward, Bkn...............	19	71	7	11	..	.155
Douglas, N. Y...........	46	73	6	11	..	.151
Lefevre, N. Y............	17	27	5	4	..	.148
Statz, N. Y..............	16	30	..	4	..	.133
Benton, N. Y............	38	65	3	6	..	.092
Winters, N. Y...........	21	7	..	..	..	.000

SPORTING RECORDS—Baseball—National League—Continued.

PITCHING RECORDS.

(5 games and over.)

Pitcher, club.	W.	L.	P.C.	Pitcher, club.	W.	L.	P.C.
Mitchell, Bk..	5	2	.714	Carlson, Pit...	14	13	.519
Grimes, Bk...	23	11	.676	Cadore, Bk....	15	14	.517
Napier, Cin...	4	2	.667	Ring, Cin......	17	17	.500
Alexander, Ch.	27	11	.659	Sallee, N. Y...	6	6	.500
Toney, N. Y..	21	11	.656	Tyler, Ch......	11	12	.478
Pfeffer, Bk...	16	9	.640	Fisher, Cin....	11	11	.476
Nehf, N. Y...	21	12	.636	Hubbell, Pa...	9	11	.450
Doak, St. L..	20	12	.625	Hamilton, Pit.	10	13	.435
Cooper, Pit...	24	15	.615	Hendrix, Ch...	9	12	.429
Mamaux, Bk.	12	8	.600	McQuillan, Bos.	11	15	.423
North, St. L..	3	2	.600	Smith, Pa.....	13	18	.419
Luque, Cin...	13	9	.591	Ponder, Pit....	10	15	.400
Marquard, Bk	10	7	.588	Haines, St. L..	13	20	.394
Douglas, N.Y.	14	10	.583	Fillingim, Bos.	12	21	.364
J. Barnes, N.Y.	20	15	.571	Benton, N. Y..	9	16	.360
Ruether, Cin.	16	12	.571	Rixey, Pa......	11	22	.333
Adams, Pit..	17	13	.567	Causey, Pa.....	7	14	.333
Watson, Bos.	5	4	.556	Rudolph, Bos...	4	8	.333
Schupp, St. L.	26	13	.552	Jacobs, St. L.	4	8	.333
Smith, Bk....	11	9	.550	Carter, Ch.....	3	6	.333
Vaughn, Ch..	19	16	.543	Scott, Bos......	10	21	.323
Oeschger, Bos.	15	13	.536	Goodwin, St.L.	3	8	.273
Meadows, Pa.	16	14	.533	Martin, Ch.. ...	4	15	.211
Sherdel, St.L.	11	10	.524	May, St. L....	1	4	.200
Eller, Cin.....	13	12	.520				

American League.

Final Standing.

Clubs.	Cleveland.	Chicago.	New York	St. Louis.	Boston.	Washington.	Detroit.	Philadelphia	Games won.	Games lost.	Per cent.
Cleveland		12	9	15	16	15	15	16	98	56	.636
Chicago	10		10	14	10	17	19	16	96	58	.623
New York....	13	12		12	13	11	15	19	95	59	.612
St. Louis.....	7	8	10		13	12	12	14	76	77	.497
Boston	6	12	9	9		10	13	13	72	81	.471
Washington ..	7	5	11	9	11		9	16	68	84	.447
Detroit	7	3	7	10	9	13		12	61	93	.396
Philadelphia .	6	6	3	8	9	6	10		48	106	.312
Games lost....	56	58	59	77	81	84	93	106			

CLUB BATTING.

Clubs.	G.	AB.	R.	H.	2B.	3B.	HR.	PC.
St. Louis.....	154	5,358	797	1,651	279	83	50	.308
Cleveland ...	154	5,196	857	1,574	300	95	35	.303
Chicago	154	5,330	794	1,569	267	92	36	.295
Washington .	153	5,251	723	1,526	233	81	36	.291
New York...	154	5,176	838	1,448	268	71	115	.280
Detroit	155	5,215	651	1,408	228	72	30	.270
Boston	154	5,199	650	1,397	216	71	22	.269
Philadelphia.	156	5,258	570	1,326	219	49	46	.252

INDIVIDUAL BATTING.

Player and Club.	G.	AB.	R.	H.	HR.	PC.
Niehaus, Clev	19	9	0	4	0	.444
Sisler, St. L	154	631	137	257	19	.407
Speaker, Clev	150	552	137	214	8	.388
Jackson, Chi	146	570	105	218	12	.382
Ruth, N. Y	142	458	158	172	54	.376
Collins, Chi	153	601	115	222	3	.369
Jacobson, St. L	154	609	97	216	9	.355
Evans, Clev	56	172	32	60	0	.349
Uhle, Clev	27	32	4	11	0	.344
Tobin, St. L	147	593	94	202	4	.340
J. E. Murphy, Chi	58	118	22	40	0	.339
Rice, Wash	153	624	83	211	3	.338
Felsch, Chi	142	556	88	188	14	.338
Cobb, Det	112	428	86	143	2	.334
Weaver, Chi	151	630	104	210	2	.333
Judge, Wash	126	493	103	164	5	.333
Nunamaker, Clev	34	54	10	18	0	.333
Torres, Wash	16	30	8	10	0	.333
Sewell, Clev	22	70	14	23	0	.329
Meusel, N. Y	119	460	75	151	11	.328
Hendryx, Bos	99	363	54	119	0	.328
Milan, Wash	126	506	70	163	3	.322
Dugan, Phila	123	491	65	158	3	.322
S. O'Neill, Clev	149	489	63	157	3	.321
Witt, Phila	65	218	29	70	1	.321
Lynn, Chi	16	25	0	8	0	.320
Jamieson, Clev	108	370	69	118	1	.319
E. Smith, Clev	129	456	82	144	12	.316
Snyder, Wash	16	19	1	6	0	.316
Pratt, N. Y	154	574	84	180	4	.314
Hooper, Bos	139	536	91	167	7	.312
Brower, Wash	36	119	21	37	1	.311
Gardner, Clev	154	597	72	185	3	.310
Heilman, Det	145	543	66	168	9	.309
High, Phila	17	65	7	20	1	.308
Veach, Det	154	612	92	188	11	.307
Williams, St. L	141	521	90	160	10	.307
Earl Smith, St. L	103	353	45	108	3	.306
Schang, Bos	122	387	58	118	4	.305
J. Collins, Chi	133	495	70	150	1	.303
Chapman, Clev	111	435	97	132	3	.303
Harris, Wash	137	506	76	152	1	.300
McInnis, Bos	148	559	50	166	2	.297
Menosky, Bos	141	532	80	158	3	.297
Graney, Clev	62	152	31	45	0	.296
Bodie, N. Y	129	471	63	139	7	.295
Hale, Det	76	116	13	34	1	.293
Gedeon, St. L	153	606	95	177	0	.292
W. R. Johnston, Clev	147	535	68	156	2	.292
Ellerbe, Wash	101	336	38	98	0	.292
Hoffmann, N. Y	15	24	3	7	0	.292
Young, Det	150	594	84	173	0	.291
Roth, Wash	138	468	80	136	9	.290
J. O'Neill, Wash	86	294	27	85	1	.289
Shorten, Det	116	364	35	105	1	.288
E. Myers, Clev., Bos	28	63	10	18	0	.286
Fewster, N. Y	21	21	8	6	0	.286
Pipp, N. Y	153	610	109	171	11	.280
Karr, Bos	57	75	8	21	1	.280
Gerber, St. L	154	584	70	163	2	.279
Billings, St. L	66	155	19	43	0	.278
Severeid, St. L	123	422	46	117	2	.277
Erickson, Wash	39	83	7	23	1	.277
Manion, Det	32	80	4	22	0	.275
Lewis, N. Y	107	365	34	99	4	.271
Austin, St. L	88	280	38	76	1	.271
Schalk, Chi	151	485	64	131	1	.270
Peckinpaugh, N. Y	139	534	109	144	8	.270
J. Wood, Clev	61	137	25	37	1	.270
Scott, Bos	154	569	41	153	4	.269
C. Walker, Phila	149	585	79	157	17	.268
Shanks, Wash	128	444	56	119	4	.268
Ruel, N. Y	82	261	30	70	1	.268
Risberg, Chi	126	458	53	122	2	.266
Davis, St. L	38	94	8	25	0	.266
Strunk, Phila., Chi	109	385	55	102	1	.265
Bush, Det	141	506	85	133	1	.263
Zachary, Wash	51	111	7	29	0	.261
W. P. Johnson, Wash	35	69	7	18	1	.261
Perkins, Phila	148	492	40	128	5	.260
Pennock, Bos	38	77	7	20	0	.260
Styles, Phila	24	50	5	13	0	.260
Foster, Bos	117	386	48	100	0	.259
Welsh, Phila	100	360	43	93	4	.258
Dykes, Phila	142	546	81	140	8	.256
Ward, N. Y	127	496	62	127	11	.256
McNally, Bos	93	312	42	80	0	.256
Shannon, Wash., Phila	87	310	34	79	0	.255
Bagby, Clev	49	131	17	33	1	.252
Myatt, Phila	70	196	14	49	0	.250
G. Burns, Phila., Clev	66	116	8	29	1	.250
Keefe, Phila	32	40	3	10	0	.250
Hasty, Phila	19	24	2	6	0	.250
Jones, Det	81	265	35	66	1	.249
Hannah, N. Y	79	259	24	64	2	.247
Gharrity, Wash	131	428	51	105	3	.245
Bush, Bos	45	102	14	25	0	.245
Woodall, Det	18	49	4	12	0	.245
Wambsgans, Clev	153	565	83	138	1	.244
Jourdan, Chi	48	150	16	36	0	.240
Acosta, Wash	17	25	2	6	0	.240
Mays, N. Y	45	109	10	26	0	.239
Griffin, Phila	129	467	46	111	0	.238
Ehmke, Det	38	105	4	25	0	.238
Flagstead, Det	110	311	40	73	3	.235
Courtney, Wash	37	69	11	16	1	.232
Stanage, Det	78	238	12	55	0	.231
Ainsmith, Det	69	186	19	43	1	.231
F. Walker, Phila	24	91	10	21	0	.231
Bailey, Bos	46	135	14	31	0	.230
Shawkey, N. Y	38	100	13	23	0	.230
Pinelli, Det		284	33	65	0	.229
Thomas, Phila., Wash	108	262	27	60	1	.229
Brady, Bos	53	180	16	41	0	.228
Coveleskie, Clev	41	111	13	25	0	.225
Shocker, St. L	38	80	8	18	0	.225
Sothoron, St. L	36	72	4	16	0	.222
Thormahlen, N. Y	29	45	3	10	0	.222
Leibold, Chi	108	413	61	91	1	.220
Vitt, Bos	87	296	50	65	1	.220
Vick, N. Y	51	118	21	26	0	.220
Ellison, Det	61	155	11	34	0	.219
C. Williams, Chi	39	101	5	22	0	.218
S. P. Jones, Bos	44	92	12	20	0	.217
Morton, Clev	29	46	1	10	0	.217
Rommel, Phila	34	51	8	11	0	.216
P. Collins, St. L	23	28	5	6	0	.214
Caldwell, Clev	41	89	17	19	0	.213
Leonard, Det	28	57	2	12	0	.212
C. Johnson, Phila	18	72	6	15	0	.208

SPORTING RECORDS—BASEBALL—AMERICAN LEAGUE—*Continued.*

Player and Club.	G.	AB.	R.	H.	HR.	PC.
Picinich, Wash	48	133	14	27	3	.203
Galloway, Phila	98	298	28	60	0	.202
Moore, Phila	27	50	2	10	1	.200
Okrie, Det	21	5	1	1	0	.200
Walters, Bos	88	258	25	51	0	.198
McMullin, Chi	46	127	14	25	0	.197
Lunte, Clev	23	71	6	14	0	.197
Cicotte, Chi	37	112	10	22	0	.196
Schacht, Wash	22	26	4	5	0	.192
Shaw, Wash	38	74	6	14	0	.189
Bigbee, Phila	37	70	4	13	1	.186
Eibel, Bos	29	43	4	8	0	.186
Burrus, Phila	71	135	11	25	0	.185
Wellman, St. L	30	63	6	11	0	.175
Oldham, Det	39	69	7	12	0	.174
Hiller, Bos	17	29	4	5	0	.172
Bayne, St. L	18	35	2	6	0	.171
Thompson, St. L	22	53	7	9	0	.170
Dauss, Det	38	83	7	14	0	.169
Burwell, St. L	35	42	4	7	0	.167
Mogridge, N. Y	26	42	5	7	0	.167
Naylor, Phila	42	86	4	14	0	.163
Perry, Phila	42	83	4	13	1	.157
Kerr, Chi	46	90	12	14	0	.155
Ayres, Det	46	59	2	9	0	.153
Wilkinson, Chi	34	48	5	7	0	.146
Vangilder, St. L	24	30	3	4	0	.133
W. Collins, N. Y	36	62	8	8	0	.129
Gleich, N. Y	24	41	6	5	0	.122
Russell, Bos	17	41	2	5	0	.122
Harper, Bos	27	50	3	6	0	.120
Hoyt, Bos	22	43	3	5	0	.116
Faber, Chi	40	104	10	11	0	.106
Harris, Phila	31	55	0	7	0	.106
Quinn, N. Y	41	88	6	8	2	.091
Calvo, Wash	17	23	5	1	0	.043
McGraw, N. Y	15	7	0	0	0	.000

PITCHING RECORDS.
(Percentage of .200 or over.)

	W.	L.	P.C.
Walter Mails, Cleveland	7	0	1.000
Ray Richmond, St. Louis	2	0	1.000
Adrian Lynch, St. Louis	2	0	1.000
G. H. Ruth, New York	1	0	1.000
Roy Crumper, Detroit	1	0	1.000
H. L. Biemiller, Washington	1	0	1.000
Jas. C. Bagby, Cleveland	31	12	.721
C. W. Mays, New York	26	11	.703
Richard Kerr, Chicago	21	9	.700
Elmer Myers, Cleveland, Boston	11	5	.688
E. V. Cicotte, Chicago	21	10	.677
R. B. Caldwell, Cleveland	20	10	.667
Urban Shocker, St. Louis	20	10	.667
John Bogart, Detroit	2	1	.667
Allen Conkwright, Detroit	2	1	.667
W. N. Snyder, Washington	2	1	.667
J. J. Quinn, New York	18	10	.643
Urban C. Faber, Chicago	23	13	.639
W. Collins, New York	14	8	.636
Stanley Coveleskie, Cleveland	24	14	.632
Claude Williams, Chicago	23	14	.611
J. Robert Shawkey, New York	20	13	.606
Frank Davis, St. Louis	18	12	.600
Albert Schacht, Washington	6	4	.600
H. E. Thormahlen, New York	9	6	.600
Wm. Burreil, St. Louis	6	4	.600
Guy Morton, Cleveland	8	6	.571
J. Acosta, Washington	5	4	.556
Herbert Pennock, Boston	16	13	.552
L. J. Bush, Boston	15	15	.500
Edwin Rommel, Philadelphia	7	7	.500
Waite Hoyt, Boston	6	6	.500
Ernest G. Shore, New York	2	2	.500
George Payne, Chicago	1	1	.500
Wm. Morrisette, Detroit	1	1	.500
C. C. Hodge, Chicago	1	1	.500
Roy Sanders, St. Louis	1	1	.500
W. C. Wilson, Detroit	1	1	.500
J. T. Zachary, Washington	15	16	.484
D. E. Keefe, Philadelphia	6	7	.462
H. J. Ehmke, Detroit	15	18	.455
Allan Russell, Boston	5	6	.455
Wm. Bayne, St. Louis	5	6	.455
S. P. Jones, Boston	13	16	.448
Walter P. Johnson, Washington	8	10	.444
Geo. E. Uhle, Cleveland	4	5	.444
Roy Wilkinson, Chicago	7	9	.437
E. G. Erickson, Washington	12	16	.428
H. S. Courtney, Washington	8	11	.421
Carl Wellman, St. Louis	9	13	.409
B. Harris, Philadelphia	9	14	.391
Geo. Dauss, Detroit	13	21	.382
John C. Oldham, Detroit	8	13	.381
Jas. A. Shaw, Washington	11	18	.378
H. B. Leonard, Detroit	10	17	.370
Geo. Mogridge, New York	5	9	.357
Allan Sothoron, St. Louis	8	15	.348
Y. W. Ayres, Detroit	7	14	.333
Walter Kinney, Philadelphia	3	4	.333
Joseph DeBerry, St. Louis	2	4	.333
Robert W. Clark, Cleveland	1	2	.333
R. J. Niehaus, Cleveland	1	2	.333
Frank Okrie, Detroit	1	2	.333
Scott Perry, Philadelphia	11	25	.306
R. C. Naylor, Philadelphia	10	23	.303
Elam Vangilder, St. Louis	3	8	.273
Benj. J. Karr, Boston	3	8	.273
Harry Harper, Boston	5	14	.263
Robert Hasty, Philadelphia	1	3	.250
Patrick Martin, Philadelphia	1	4	.200

Eagle's All-Scholastic Teams of 1920.

First Team. Name.	School.	Pos.	Second Team. Name.	School.
Voigt	Commercial	P.	Clarke	Erasmus
O'Brien	Bkln. Prep	P.	Wiebe	Manual
Bell	Poly Prep.	P.	Gillespie	St. F. Pp.
Lott	Poly Prep	C.	Taylor.	Bkn. Pp.
Kennedy	St. John's Pp.	C.	Greve	Com'cial
McRae	Poly Prep	1B.	Lenkowsky	Boys' H.
Rowan	Commercial	2B.	Ruckstall	Poly Pp.
Boohecker	Erasmus	S.S.	Hawkins	Bkn. Pp.
Friedman	Erasmus	3B.	Breden	Com'cial
Petrilli	Bkln. Prep	L.F.	Schmidt	Manual
Sullivan	St. Fran. p.	C.F.	Greenbaum	Com'cial
Stevenson	Boys' High	R.F.	Sproul.	St. J. Pp.

THE WORLD SERIES, 1920.

Brooklyn was beaten in the World Series of 1920 by Cleveland, 5 games to 2. In 1916 Brooklyn also engaged in the series, losing to the Boston Red Sox, 4 games to 1. The statistics and scores follow:

FINAL STANDING.

Club.	W.	L.	PC.
Cleveland	5	2	.714
Brooklyn	2	5	.286

ATTENDANCE AND RECEIPTS.

Paid attendance	178,357
Total receipts	$564,800.00
National Commission	56,480.00
Each club's share	146,718.63
Players' share (five games)	214,882.74

WHAT PLAYERS RECEIVED.

Players' pool	$214,882.74
Winner's share	96,692.20
Loser's share	64,464.80
White Sox and Giants	32,235.44
Yankees and Reds	21,490.39

First Game.

(At Brooklyn, Tuesday, Oct. 5.)

CLEVELAND (A. L.).

	AB.	R.	H.	BB.	SO.	SH.	SB.	PO.	A.	E.
Evans, lf	2	0	0	1	0	0	0	1	0	0
Jamieson, lf	1	0	0	0	0	0	0	0	0	0
Wambsgans, 2b	3	0	0	0	1	1	0	0	2	0
Speaker, cf	4	0	0	0	1	0	0	4	0	0
Burns, 1b	3	1	1	0	1	0	0	9	1	0
Smith, rf	1	0	0	0	0	0	0	0	0	0
Gardner, 3b	4	0	0	0	0	0	0	1	3	0
Wood, rf	2	2	1	1	1	0	0	4	0	0
W. Johnston, 1b	1	0	0	0	0	0	0	0	1	0
Sewell, ss	3	0	1	0	1	0	0	3	4	0
O'Neill, c	3	0	2	0	1	0	0	3	0	0
Coveleskie, p	3	0	0	0	1	0	0	2	2	0
Totals	30	3	5	2	7	1	0	27	13	0

BROOKLYN (N. L.).

	AB.	R.	H.	BB.	SO.	SH.	SB.	PO.	A.	E.
Olson, ss	3	0	2	1	0	0	0	0	3	0
J. Johnston, 3b	3	0	0	0	1	1	0	1	3	0
Griffith, rf	4	0	1	0	0	0	0	1	0	0
Wheat, lf	4	1	1	0	0	0	0	4	0	0
Myers, cf	4	0	0	0	0	0	0	1	0	0
Konetchy, 1b	4	0	0	0	1	0	0	12	1	1
Kilduff, 2b	3	0	0	0	1	0	0	1	3	0
Krueger, c	3	0	0	0	0	0	0	7	1	0
Marquard, p	1	0	0	0	0	0	0	0	0	0
aLamar	1	0	0	0	0	0	0	0	0	0
Mamaux, p	0	0	0	0	0	0	0	0	1	0
bMitchell	1	0	1	0	0	0	0	0	0	0
cNeis	0	0	0	0	0	0	0	0	0	0
Cadore, p	0	0	0	0	0	0	0	0	1	0
Totals	31	1	5	1	3	1	0	27	13	1

a—Batted for Marquard in 6th. b—Batted for Mamaux in 8th. c—Ran for Mitchell in 9th.

SCORE BY INNINGS.

Cleveland	0	2	0	1	0	0	0	0	0	—3
Brooklyn	0	0	0	0	0	0	1	0	0	—1

2-base hits—Wood, O'Neill, 2, Wheat. Double play—Konetchy, Krueger and Johnston. Left on bases—Bkn., 5; Cleveland, 3. Hits and runs—

SPORTING RECORDS—BASEBALL—WORLD'S SERIES—*Continued.*

Off Marquard, 5 and 3 in 6 innings; Mamaux, 0 and 0 in 2; Cadore, 0 and 0 in 1. Struck out—By Marquard, 4; Mamaux, 3; Coveleskie, 3. Bases on balls—Off Marquard, 2; Coveleskie, 1. Winning pitcher, Coveleskie; losing pitcher, Marquard. Umpires—Klem (N. L.), at plate; Connolly (A. L.), 1st base; O'Day (N. L.), 2d base; Dinneen (A. L.), 3d base. Time of game—1 hour and 41 min.

Second Game.

(At Brooklyn, Wednesday, Oct. 6.)

BROOKLYN (N. L.).

	AB.	R.	H.	BB.	SO.	SH.	SB.	PO.	A.	E.
Olson, ss	4	1	1	0	1	0	0	3	2	0
J. Johnston, 3b	4	1	1	0	0	0	1	0	1	0
Griffith, rf	4	0	2	0	1	0	0	3	0	0
Wheat, lf	3	0	1	1	0	0	0	3	0	0
Myers, cf	3	0	1	0	0	0	0	2	0	0
Konetchy, 1b	3	0	0	0	0	0	0	10	1	0
Kilduff, 2b	3	0	0	0	0	0	0	2	3	0
Miller, c	3	0	0	0	1	0	0	3	1	0
Grimes, p	3	1	1	0	0	0	0	1	4	0
Totals	30	3	7	1	3	0	1	27	12	0

CLEVELAND (A. L.).

	AB.	R.	H.	BB.	SO.	SH.	SB.	PO.	A.	E.
Jamieson, lf	4	0	1	1	0	0	0	2	0	0
Wambsgans, 2b	3	0	0	0	0	0	0	3	0	0
aBurns	0	0	0	1	0	0	0	0	0	0
Lunte, 2b	0	0	0	0	0	0	0	0	0	0
Speaker, cf	3	0	2	1	0	0	0	2	0	0
E. Smith, rf	4	0	0	0	1	0	0	3	0	0
Gardner, 3b	3	0	2	1	0	0	0	1	2	0
W. Johnston, 1b	4	0	0	0	0	0	0	3	3	0
Sewell, ss	4	0	0	0	0	0	0	1	1	0
O'Neill, c	4	0	1	0	0	0	0	7	2	0
Bagby, p	2	0	0	0	0	0	0	2	1	1
bGraney	1	0	0	0	1	0	0	0	0	0
Uhle, p	0	0	0	0	0	0	0	0	0	0
cNunamaker	1	0	1	0	0	0	0	0	0	0
Totals	33	0	7	4	2	0	0	24	9	1

a—Batted for Wambsgans in 8th. b—Batted for Bagby in 7th. c—Batted for Uhle in 9th.

SCORE BY INNINGS.

Brooklyn	1	0	1	0	1	0	0	0	..—3
Cleveland	0	0	0	0	0	0	0	0	0—0

2-base hits—Griffith, Wheat, Speaker, Gardner. Double play—Gardner, O'Neill and W. Johnston. Left on bases—Cleveland, 10; Brooklyn, 4. Struck out—By Grimes, 2; Uhle, 3. Bases on balls—Off Grimes, 4; Bagby, 1. Hits—Off Bagby, 7 in 6 innings; Uhle, none in 2. Losing pitcher—Bagby. Umpires—Connolly (A. L.), at plate; O'Day (N. L.), 1st base; Dinneen (A. L.), 2d base; Klem (N. L.), 3d base. Time of game—1 hour and 55 min.

Third Game.

(At Brooklyn, Thursday, Oct. 7.)

BROOKLYN (N. L.)

	AB.	R.	H.	BB.	SO.	SH.	SB.	PO.	A.	E.
Olson, ss	2	1	1	2	0	0	0	0	6	0
J. Johnston, 3b	3	0	0	0	1	1	0	0	4	0
Griffith, rf	1	1	0	0	0	0	0	2	0	0
Neis, rf	3	0	0	0	0	0	0	0	0	0
Wheat, lf	4	0	3	0	0	0	0	1	0	1
Myers, cf	4	0	2	0	0	0	0	1	0	0
Konetchy, 1b	3	0	0	1	0	0	0	17	2	0
Kilduff, 2b	1	0	0	1	0	1	0	2	6	0
Miller, c	1	0	0	1	0	1	0	2	0	0
S. Smith, p	3	0	0	0	1	0	0	2	2	0
Totals	25	2	6	5	2	3	0	27	20	1

CLEVELAND (A. L.).

	AB.	R.	H.	BB.	SO.	SH.	SB.	PO.	A.	E.
Evans, lf	4	0	0	0	0	0	0	2	0	0
Wambsgans, 2b	3	0	0	1	0	0	0	2	2	0
Speaker, cf	4	1	1	0	0	0	0	2	0	0
Burns, 1b	3	0	0	0	1	0	0	12	0	0
Gardner, 3b	3	0	0	0	0	0	0	0	0	0
Wood, rf	3	0	0	0	1	0	0	1	0	0
Sewell, ss	2	0	0	1	0	0	0	2	3	1
O'Neill, c	3	0	2	0	0	0	0	2	2	0
aJamieson	0	0	0	0	0	0	0	0	0	0
Caldwell, p	0	0	0	0	0	0	0	0	0	0
Mails, p	2	0	0	0	0	0	0	1	3	0
Nunamaker, c	1	0	0	0	0	0	0	0	0	0
Uhle, p	0	0	0	0	0	0	0	0	1	0
Totals	28	1	3	2	2	0	0	24	11	1

a—Ran for O'Neill in 8th.

SCORE BY INNINGS.

Brooklyn	2	0	0	0	0	0	0	0	0—2
Cleveland	0	0	0	1	0	0	0	0	0—1

2-base hit—Speaker. Double plays—Mails and Burns; Olson, Kilduff and Konetchy; Wambsgans, Sewell and Burns; Johnston, Kilduff and Konetchy. Left on bases—Brooklyn, 7; Cleveland, 2. Bases on balls—Off Caldwell, 1; Mails, 4; Smith, 2. Struck out—By Mails, 2; Smith, 2. Hits—Off Caldwell, 2 in 1-3 inning; Mails, 3 in 6 2-3; Uhle, 1 in 1. Losing pitcher—Caldwell. Umpires—O'Day (N. L.), at plate; Dinneen (A. L.), 1st base; Klem (N. L.), 2d base; Connolly (A. L.), 3d base. Time of game—1 hour and 47 min.

Fourth Game.

(At Cleveland, Saturday, Oct. 9.)

BROOKLYN (N. L.).

	AB.	R.	H.	BB.	SO.	SH.	SB.	PO.	A.	E.
Olson, ss	4	0	1	0	0	0	0	1	3	0
J. Johnston, 3b	4	1	2	0	0	0	0	1	0	0
Griffith, rf	4	0	1	0	0	0	0	1	0	0
Wheat, lf	4	0	0	0	0	0	0	0	0	1
Myers, cf	3	0	0	0	1	0	0	6	1	0
Konetchy, 1b	2	0	0	1	0	0	0	5	0	0
Kilduff, 2b	3	0	1	0	2	0	0	2	3	0
Miller, c	3	0	0	0	0	0	0	7	0	0
Cadore, p	0	0	0	0	0	0	0	1	0	0
Mamaux, p	1	0	0	0	1	0	0	0	0	0
Marquard, p	0	0	0	0	0	0	0	0	1	0
Pfeffer, p	1	0	0	0	0	0	0	0	0	0
xLamar	1	0	0	0	0	0	0	0	0	0
zNeis	0	0	0	0	0	0	0	0	0	0
Totals	30	1	5	1	4	0	0	24	8	1

CLEVELAND (A. L.).

	AB.	R.	H.	BB.	SO.	SH.	SB.	PO.	A.	E.
Jamieson, lf	2	0	0	0	0	0	0	1	0	0
Evans, lf	3	0	1	0	0	0	0	0	0	0
Wambsgans, 2b	4	2	2	1	0	0	0	4	6	0
Speaker, cf	5	2	2	0	0	0	0	3	0	0
Smith, rf	1	0	1	0	0	0	0	1	0	0
Burns, 1b	2	0	1	1	1	0	0	7	0	1
Gardner, 3b	3	0	1	0	1	1	0	2	3	0
W. Johnston, 1b	1	0	0	0	1	0	0	4	0	0
Wood, rf	2	0	0	0	0	0	0	0	0	0
Graney, rf	1	0	0	0	0	0	0	0	0	0
Sewell, ss	4	0	2	0	0	0	0	1	7	1
O'Neill, c	2	0	1	2	1	0	0	4	0	0
Covaleskie, p	4	1	1	0	1	0	0	0	2	0
Totals	34	5	12	4	5	1	0	27	18	2

x—Batted for Marquard in 6th. z—Ran for J. Johnston in 9th.

SCORE BY INNINGS.

Brooklyn	0	0	0	1	0	0	0	0	0—1
Cleveland	2	0	2	0	0	1	0	0	..—5

2-base hit—Griffith. Double plays—Myers to Olson to Kilduff; Sewell to Wamby to Burns; Gardner to Wamby to Burns. Runs batted in—By E. Smith, 1; by Gardner, 1; by Burns, 2; by Griffith, 1; by Wamby, 1. Earned runs—Cleveland, 3; Brooklyn, 1. Basehits—Off Cadore, 2 in first inning; 2 in second inning, when removed; off Mamaux, 2; off Marquard, 2 in four innings; off Pfeffer, 4 in two innings. Struck out—By Cadore (W. Johnston), by Mamaux (Coveleskie); by Coveleskie (Kilduff, 2), Mamaux (Myers), by Marquard (Gardner, Burns), by Pfeffer (O'Neill). Bases on balls—Off Cadore (Wamby); off Marquard (O'Neill); off Coveleskie (Konetchy); off Pfeffer (Burns, O'Neill). Left on bases—Cleveland, 10; Brooklyn, 3. Wild pitch—Pfeffer. Passed ball—Miller. Time of game—1 hour and 56 min. Umpires—Dinneen (A. L.), behind the plate; Klem (N. L.), 1st base; Connolly (A. L.), at 2d base; O'Day (N. L.), at 3d base.

Fifth Game.

(At Cleveland, Sunday, Oct. 10.)

CLEVELAND (A. L.).

	AB.	R.	H.	BB.	SO.	SH.	SB.	PO.	A.	E.
Jamieson, lf	4	1	2	0	0	0	0	2	1	0
Graney, lf	1	0	0	0	1	0	0	0	0	0
Wambsgans, 2b	5	1	1	0	0	0	0	7	2	0
Speaker, cf	3	2	1	1	0	0	0	1	0	0
E. Smith, rf	4	1	3	0	0	0	0	0	0	0
Gardner, 3b	4	0	1	0	0	0	0	2	2	1
W. Johnston, 1b	3	1	2	0	0	1	0	9	1	0
Sewell, ss	3	0	0	1	0	0	0	2	4	0
O'Neill, c	2	1	0	2	0	0	0	3	1	1
Thomas, c	0	0	0	0	0	0	0	1	0	0
Bagby, p	4	1	2	0	0	0	0	0	2	0
Totals	33	8	12	4	1	1	0	27	13	2

SPORTING RECORDS—Baseball—World's Series—*Continued.*

BROOKLYN (N. L.).

	AB.	R.	H.	BB.	SO.	SH.	SB.	PO.	A.	E.
Olson, ss	4	0	2	0	0	0	0	3	5	0
Sheehan, 3b	3	0	1	0	0	1	0	1	1	1
Griffith, rf	4	0	0	0	1	0	0	0	0	0
Wheat, lf	4	1	2	0	1	0	0	3	0	0
Myers, cf	4	0	2	0	0	0	0	0	0	0
Konetchy, 1b	4	0	2	0	1	0	0	9	2	0
Kilduff, 2b	4	0	1	0	0	0	0	5	6	0
Miller, c	2	0	2	0	0	0	0	0	1	0
Krueger, c	2	0	1	0	0	0	0	2	1	0
Grimes, p	1	0	0	0	0	0	0	0	1	0
Mitchell, p	2	0	0	0	0	0	0	1	0	0
Totals	34	1	13	0	3	1	0	24	17	1

SCORE BY INNINGS.

Cleveland	4	0	0	3	1	0	0	0	..	—8
Brooklyn	0	0	0	0	0	0	0	0	1	—1

3-base hits—E. Smith, Konetchy. Home runs—E. Smith, Bagby. Triple play—Wambsgans, unassisted. Double plays—Olson, Kilduff and Konetchy; Jamieson and O'Neill; Gardner, Wambsgans and W. Johnston; W. Johnston, Sewell and W. Johnston. Left on bases—Brooklyn, 7; Cleveland, 6. Bases on balls—Off Grimes, 1; Mitchell, 3. Struck out—By Bagby, 3; Mitchell, 1. Hits—Off Grimes, 9 in 2 1-3 innings; Mitchell, 3 in 4 2-3. Wild pitch—Bagby. Passed ball—Miller. Losing pitcher—Grimes. Umpires—Klem (N. L.), at plate; Connolly (A. L.), 1st base; O'Day (N. L.), 2d base; Dinneen (A. L.), 3d base. Time of game—1 hour and 49 min.

Sixth Game.

(At Cleveland, Monday, Oct. 11.)

CLEVELAND (A. L.).

	AB.	R.	H.	BB.	SO.	SH.	SB.	PO.	A.	E.
Evans, lf	4	0	3	0	0	0	0	4	0	0
Wambsgans, 2b	4	0	0	0	0	0	0	1	2	0
Speaker, cf	3	1	1	0	0	0	0	3	0	0
Burns, 1b	2	0	1	1	0	0	0	10	0	0
Gardner, 3b	3	0	0	0	0	0	0	2	2	1
Wood, rf	3	0	1	0	0	0	0	2	0	0
Sewell, ss	3	0	1	0	0	0	0	2	3	2
O'Neill, c	3	0	0	0	0	0	0	3	2	0
Mails, p	3	0	0	0	1	0	0	0	1	0
Totals	28	1	7	1	1	0	0	27	10	3

BROOKLYN (N. L.).

	AB.	R.	H.	BB.	SO.	SH.	SB.	PO.	A.	E.
Olson, ss	4	0	1	0	0	0	0	4	1	0
Sheehan, 3b	4	0	0	0	1	0	0	0	3	0
Neis, rf	2	0	0	1	0	0	0	3	0	0
aKrueger	1	0	0	0	0	0	0	0	0	0
Griffith, rf	0	0	0	0	0	0	0	0	0	0
Wheat, lf	4	0	0	0	1	0	0	2	0	0
Myers, cf	4	0	1	0	0	0	0	1	0	0
Konetchy, 1b	3	0	1	1	0	0	0	9	0	0
Kilduff, 2b	4	0	0	0	1	0	0	2	2	0
Miller, c	3	0	0	0	0	0	0	3	3	0
S. Smith, p	3	0	0	0	1	0	0	0	3	0
bMcCabe	0	0	0	0	0	0	0	0	0	0
Totals	32	0	3	2	4	0	0	24	12	0

a—Batted for Neis in 8th. b—Ran for Konetchy in 9th.

SCORE BY INNINGS.

Cleveland	0	0	0	0	0	1	0	0	..	—1
Brooklyn	0	0	0	0	0	0	0	0	0	—0

2-base hits—Burns, Olson. Left on bases—Brooklyn, 7; Cleveland, 4. Bases on balls—Off Mails, 2; Smith, 1. Struck out—By Mails, 4; Smith, 1. Umpires—Connolly (A. L.), at plate; O'Day (N. L.), 1st base; Dineen (A. L.), 2d base; Klem (N. L.), 3d base. Time of game—1 hour and 34 min.

Seventh Game.

(At Cleveland, Tuesday, Oct. 13.)

CLEVELAND (A. L.).

	AB.	R.	H.	BB.	SO.	SH.	SB.	PO.	A.	E.
Jamieson, lf	4	1	2	0	0	0	1	3	0	0
Wambsgans, 2b	4	0	1	0	0	0	0	4	3	0
Speaker, cf	3	0	1	1	0	0	0	3	0	0
E. Smith, rf	3	0	0	1	0	0	0	3	1	0
Gardner, 3b	4	1	1	0	0	0	0	1	3	0
W. Johnston, 1b	2	0	1	2	0	0	1	11	1	0
Sewell, ss	4	0	0	0	0	0	0	0	6	2
O'Neill, c	4	0	1	0	1	0	0	1	0	0
Coveleskie, p	3	1	0	0	2	0	0	0	1	1
Totals	31	3	7	4	3	0	2	*26	15	3

BROOKLYN (N. L.).

	AB.	R.	H.	BB.	SO.	SH.	SB.	PO.	A.	E.
Olson, ss	4	0	0	0	0	0	0	1	1	0
Sheehan, 3b	4	0	1	0	0	0	0	2	1	1
Griffith, rf	4	0	0	0	0	0	0	3	0	0
Wheat, lf	4	0	2	0	0	0	0	3	0	0
Myers, cf	4	0	0	0	0	0	0	3	0	0
Konetchy, 1b	4	0	1	0	0	0	0	8	4	0
Kilduff, 2b	3	0	0	0	0	0	0	1	4	0
Miller, c	2	0	0	0	1	0	0	2	1	0
aLamar	1	0	0	0	0	0	0	0	0	0
Krueger, c	0	0	0	0	0	0	0	1	0	0
Grimes, p	2	0	1	0	0	0	0	0	2	1
bSchmandt	1	0	0	0	0	0	0	0	0	0
Mamaux, p	0	0	0	0	0	0	0	0	0	0
Totals	33	0	5	0	1	0	0	24	9	2

*—Olson out, hit by batted ball. a—Batted for Miller in 7th. b—Batted for Grimes in 8th.

SCORE BY INNINGS.

Cleveland	0	0	0	1	1	0	1	0	..	—3
Brooklyn	0	0	0	0	0	0	0	0	0	—0

2-base hits—Jamieson, O'Neill. 3-base hit—Speaker. Left on bases—Cleveland, 8; Brooklyn, 6 Bases on balls—Off Grimes, 4. Struck out—By Coveleskie, 1; Grimes, 2; Mamaux, 1. Losing pitcher—Grimes. Umpires—O'Day (N. L.), at plate; Dinneen (A. L.), 1st base; Klem (N. L.), 2d base; Connolly (A. L.), 3d base.

Composite Score of the Seven Games.

G., games; AB., at bat; R., runs; H., hits; Bat. Ave., batting averages; PO., put outs; A., assists; E., errors; Fldg. Ave., fielding averages.

CLEVELAND (A. L.).

	G.	AB.	R.	H.	Bat. Ave.	PO.	A.	E.	Fldg. Ave.
Evans, lf	4	13	0	4	.308	7	0	0	1000
Jamieson, lf	6	15	2	5	.333	8	1	0	1000
Wambsgans, 2b	7	26	3	4	.154	21	17	0	1000
Lunte, 2b	1	0	0	0	.000	0	0	0	.000
Speaker, cf	7	25	6	8	.320	18	0	0	1000
Burns, 1b	5	10	1	3	.300	38	1	1	.975
W. Johnston, 1b	5	11	1	3	.273	27	6	0	1000
E Smith, rf	5	13	1	4	.308	7	1	0	1000
Wood, rf	4	10	2	2	.200	7	0	0	1000
Graney, rf., lf	3	3	0	0	.000	0	0	0	.000
Gardner, 3b	7	24	1	5	.208	9	15	2	.923
Sewell, ss	7	23	0	4	.174	11	28	6	.867
O'Neill, c	7	21	1	7	.333	22	7	1	.967
Nunamaker, c	2	2	0	1	.500	0	0	0	.000
Thomas, c	1	0	0	0	.000	1	0	0	1000
Coveleskie, p	3	10	2	1	.100	2	5	1	.875
Bagby, p	2	6	1	2	.333	2	3	1	.833
Uhle, p	2	0	0	0	.000	0	1	0	1000
Caldwell, p	1	0	0	0	.000	0	0	0	.000
Mails, p	2	5	0	0	.000	1	4	0	1000
Totals		217	21	53	.244	182	89	12	.958

BROOKLYN (N. L.).

	G.	AB.	R.	H.	Bat. Ave.	PO.	A.	E.	Fldg. Ave.
Olson, ss	7	25	2	8	.320	12	21	0	1000
J. Johnston, 3b	4	14	2	3	.214	2	8	0	1000
Sheehan, 3b	3	11	0	2	.182	3	5	2	.800
Griffith, rf	6	21	1	4	.190	11	0	0	1000
Neis, rf	4	5	0	0	.000	3	0	0	1000
Wheat, lf	7	27	2	9	.333	16	0	2	.889
Myers, cf	7	26	0	6	.231	14	1	0	1000
Konetchy, 1b	7	23	0	4	.174	70	6	1	.983
Kilduff, 2b	7	21	0	2	.095	15	27	0	1000
Krueger, c	4	6	0	1	.167	10	2	0	1000
Miller, c	6	14	0	2	.143	17	6	0	1000
Marquard, p	2	1	0	0	.000	0	1	0	1000
Mamaux, p	2	1	0	0	.000	0	1	0	1000
Cadore, p	2	0	0	0	.000	1	1	0	1000
Grimes, p	3	6	1	2	.333	1	7	1	.889
S. Smith, p	2	6	0	0	.000	2	5	0	1000
Pfeffer, p	1	1	0	0	.000	0	0	0	.000
Mitchell, p	2	3	0	1	.333	1	0	0	1000
*Lamar	3	3	0	0	.000	0	0	0	.000
*Schmandt	1	1	0	0	.000	0	0	0	.000
†McCabe	1	0	0	0	.000	0	0	0	.000
Totals		215	8	44	.205	177	91	6	.967

Games won—Cleveland, 5; Brooklyn, 2. Pitchers' records—Games won: Coveleskie, 3; Bagby, 1; Mails, 1; Grimes, 1; S. Smith, 1; games lost: Marquard, 1; Grimes, 2; Cadore, 1; S. Smith, 1; Bagby, 1; Caldwell, 1. Hits—Off Marquard, 7 in 9 innings; Mamaux, 2 in 3; Cadore, 4 in 2; Coveleskie, 15 in 27; Bagby, 20 in 15; Uhle, 1 in 3; Grimes, 23 in 19 1-3; S. Smith, 10 in 17; Caldwell, 2 in ⅓; Mails, 6 in 15 2-3; Pfeffer, 4

*Pinch batter. †Pinch runner.

in 3; Mitchell, 3 in 4 2-3. Struck out—By Coveleskie, 8; Marquard, 6; Mails, 6; Mamaux, 4; Smith, 3; Uhle, 3; Bagby, 3; Grimes, 5; Pfeffer, 1; Cadore, 1; Mitchell, 1. Bases on balls—Off Mails, 6; Grimes, 9; Marquard, 3; Mitchell, 3; S. Smith, 4; Coveleskie, 2; Pfeffer, 2; Bagby, 1; Caldwell, 1; Cadore, 1. Sacrifice hits—J. Johnston, 2; Wambsgans, Kilduff, Miller, W. Johnston, Sheehan. Sacrifice fly—Gardner. Left on bases—Cleveland, 43; Brooklyn, 39. Triple play—Wambsgans, unassisted. Double plays—Konetchy, Krueger and J. Johnston; Gardner, O'Neill, W. Johnston and O'Neill; Mails and Burns; Olson, Kilduff and Konetchy; Myers, Olson and Kilduff; Gardner, Wambsgans and Burns; Jamieson and O'Neill; Wambsgans and W. Johnston; W. Johnston, Sewell and W. Johnston.

BICYCLING.

Maurice Brocco and William Coburn won the 1920 6-day bicycle race at Madison Sq. Garden, New York, Dec. 5-11.

	Mi.	L.		Mi.	L.
Brocco—Coburn....	2290	0	Egg—McNamara..	2289	8
Debaets—Persyn...	2289	9	Verri—Belloni......	2289	8
Van Hevel—Vandenburgh	2289	9	Nan Nek—Miquel..	2289	8
			Bedell—Thomas....	2289	8
Taylor—Smith.....	2289	9	Egg—McNamara...	2289	8

BOXING.

The Walker Law, permitting 15-round decision bouts, re-established boxing in New York State. The Boxing Commission consists of J. Johnson, W. G. Hooke and E. W. Ditmas. with C. A. White as secretary. License Committee—L. McGuire, D. W. Wear and C. E. Walsh, with J F. Hoey, secretary.

The visit of Georges Carpentier to America stirred up interest in the sport. His only fight in this country was with Battling Levinsky, whom he knocked out in the 4th round, at Jersey City. Carpentier is matched to fight Jack Dempsey for the world's championship next summer.

Jimmy Wilde, the English flyweight, who was outpointed by Young Jack Sharkey in his first bout in America, on Dec. 4, 1919, fought a number of battles in America during 1920 and was unbeaten.

Two titles changed hands. Johnny Wilson of Boston won the middleweight championship from Mike O'Dowd by a referee's decision in 12 rounds at Boston. Joe Lynch of New York wrested the bantamweight title from Pete Herman by referee's decision in a 15-round bout at Madison Sq. Garden.

N. Y. STATE BOXING CHAMPIONS. (Amateur.)

108 pounds—James J. Fanning.
115 pounds—Murray Schwartz.
125 pounds—Harold N. Evans.
135 pounds—Archie Walker.
145 pounds—Milton Weiss.
Middleweight—Mortimer Seligman.
Light heavyweight—Frank Adams.
Heavyweight—Frank Adams.

Jack Dempsey retained the heavyweight title by knocking out Bill Brennan at Madison Sq. Garden, Dec. 14.

Benny Leonard retained the lightweight title by knocking out Joe Welling in the 14th round at Madison Sq. Garden, Nov. 26.

Heavyweight champions—J. L. Sullivan, 1882-1892; J. J. Corbett, 1892-1894; R. Fitzsimmons, 1894-1899; J. J. Jeffries, 1899-1905; M. Hart, 1905; T. Burns, 1906-1908; J. Johnson, 1908-1915; J. Willard, 1915-1919; J. Dempsey, 1919—.

CHESS.

Like all other pastimes, chess has felt the effect of the unprecedented post-war tendency of all manner of entertainments, sport activities and the like to grip the fancy of the public at large. This state of affairs has been accentuated to a considerable extent by the presence in this country of Samuel Rzeschewski, the child prodigy from Poland, who, at the time this article was prepared, had given three public exhibitions of his skill, playing a total of 60 games, of which he won 51, drew 7 and lost 2. The past year was also noteworthy because of the negotiations for a world's championship match between Dr. E. Lasker of Berlin and J. R. Capablanca of Havana, which, it is hoped, may take place in Havana during the early part of 1921. For the first time since the outbreak of the war an international tournament, participated in by a representative field of continental players, was held in Gotenburg, Sweden, and a comparative newcomer, R. Reti, a native Czecho-Slovakia, carried off chief honors. A masters' tournament at Atlantic City, N. J., won by Marshall, the U. S. champion, and the Western championship at Memphis, Tenn., won by Edward Lasker of Chicago, were the outstanding features of American chess activities for the past year.

Chess Records for Year 1920.

27TH INTER-COLLEGIATE TOURNEY—N. Y., Jan. 1, 2 and 3, 1920—Won by Columbia, total of 10½—1½. Other scores: Harvard, 7—5; Princeton, 6½—5½; Yale, 0—12. The winning team was: Columbia, M. A. Schapiro, '23; C. B. Isaacson. '21; E. P. Wolfson, '22; W. R. Thompson, '23. The record: Columbia, 14 wins; Harvard, 9; Yale, 2; Princeton, 1. In addition, Harvard and Yale tied, the play-off also being a tie.

21ST TRIANGULAR COLLEGE LEAGUE TOURNEY—N. Y., Dec. 26, 27 and 29, 1919—Won by Cornell, total of 8½—3½. Other scores: City College, 6½—5½; N. Y. University, 6—6; Pennsylvania, 3—9. The winning team was: Cornell, H. Adelsberg, '21; H. Garfinkel, '22; A. Kevitz, '23; G. G. Neidich. '23. The record: Pennsylvania, 11 wins; Cornell, 7; City College, 1. In addition, Pennsylvania tied once with Cornell and once with Brown.

RICE PROGRESSIVE C. C. CHAMPIONSHIP—Won by O. Chajes, 8—1; Kupchik, 7½—1½; C. Jaffe, 6½—2½; H. Liebenstein, 5—4.

MATCHES BY TELEGRAPH—Feb. 21, Manhattan C. C., 6½; Boston City Club, 2½; Feb. 22, Manhattan C. C., 8; Capital City C. C. (Washington), 2; May 19 and 28, West. Electric Co. of N. Y., 7; Hawthorne Station, Chicago, 3; May 31, Bkln. C. C., 4; Kenwood C. C. (Chicago), 6.

NEW JERSEY STATE CHAMPIONSHIP—Newark Rice C. C., Feb. 22, championship won by C. E. Armstrong of East Orange, 3½—½; E. E. Cobb, South Orange, S. A. Clapp, East Orange, and H. E. Holbrook, Newark, each 3—1. Class A tourney, S. T. Smith and M. Besmer, each 2½—1½. Class B tourney, won by F. Petzold, 4—0. Class C tourney, won by M. Eichfeld, 3—0. Novice tourney, P. N. Snelling, E. Driscoll and J. Krueger, each 2—1.

CORRESPONDENCE CHAMPIONSHIP—5th American Championship Tournament of the Correspondence Chess League of America—Finals won by J. E. Narraway, Ottawa, 4—1; J. H. Norris, Hoopeston, Ill., 3—3; E. Lasker, Chicago, and J. McClure, Nashville, Tenn., each 2—3.

INTERCOLLEGIATE INDIVIDUAL TOURNAMENT—Marshall C. C., N. Y., Feb. 23 and 28—Won by M. A. Schapiro, Columbia, 4—0; P. Wolfson, Columbia, 3½—½; L. Dennon. N. Y. Univ., 3—1; B. Buss, City College, 2½—1½.

METROPOLITAN LEAGUE—N. Y. club championship won by I. L. Rice, Progressive C. C., 9—0. Other scores: Bklyn. C. C., 8—1; Columbia Univ., 7—2; Staten Island C. C.. 5½—3½; Marshall C. C., 5—4.

MANHATTAN C. C. CHAMPIONSHIP—O. Chajes and A. Kupchik (tie), each 7½—2½; R. T. Black, 6½—3½.

HIGH SCHOOL INDIVIDUAL TOURNAMENT—Bkln. C. C., Feb. 23—Won by M. K. Coleman, Erasmus, 5—0; P. Prosswimmer, Richmond Hill, 4—1; R. Bornholz, Commercial H. S., and G. Wheeler, Richmond Hill, each 3—1.

ATLANTIC CITY CHESS CONGRESS—Atlantic City, N. J., July 7-20—Masters tournament won by F. J. Marshall, N. Y., 7½—2½; C. Jaffe, N. Y., 6½—3½; E. S. Jackson, Philadelphia, and S. Mlotkowski, Los Angeles, each 5—5.

WORLD'S CHAMPIONSHIP—Dr. E. Lasker, Berlin, title-holder for 26 years, announced his abdication in favor of J. R. Capablanca of Havana, his challenger. Later, an agreement was reached to play a match of 24 games for a purse of $20,000, in Havana, during Jan. and Feb. next.

SPORTING RECORDS—*Chess—Continued.*

NEW YORK STATE CHAMPIONSHIP—Albany, Aug. 2-6—Championship tournament won by J. Bernstein, N. Y., 5—1; B. Forsberg, 4—2.

CLASS A TOURNEY—Won by G. N. Cheney, Syracuse, 6½—1½; F. R. Stevens, Schenectady, 5½—2½; M. I. Lockwood, Stapleton, and D. F. Searle, Rome, each 5—3. Class B Tourney, won by H. Nielsen, New Brighton, and J. S. Brubacher, Albany, each 7½—1½; L. P. Guckemus, Schenectady, 5—4; O. Fraser, Albany, 4½—4½. Class C Tourney, won by J. H. Morier, Rensselaer, 6—2; D. Whittle, Albany, 5½—2½.

GOTHENBURG MASTERS TOURNAMENT—Gothenburg, Sweden, Aug.—Won by R. Reti, Slovakia, 9½—3½; A. Rubinstein, Russia, 9—4; J. Bogoljuboff, Russia, 8—5; B. Kostich, Serbia; J. Mieses, Germany; Dr. S. Tarrasch, Germany, and Dr. Tartakower, Austria, each 7½—5½. Minor Tournament—Won by P. Johner, Switzerland, 10 points; W. Euwe, Holland, 9½; M. Marchand, Holland, and W. John, Berlin, each 9.

BRITISH CHAMPIONSHIP — Edinburgh, Aug.—Won by Lieut. R. H. V. Scott, London, 9—2; Sir G. Thomas, London, 8—3; E. G. Sergeant, London, 7½—3½; R. P. Michell, Kingston, 7—4.

WESTERN CHAMPIONSHIP — Memphis, Tenn., Sept. 19-26—Won by E. Lasker, Chicago, 5½—1½; J. T. Beckner, Winchester, Ky., and B. B. Jefferson, Memphis, each 4½—2½.

Samuel Rzeschewski—Poland's chess prodigy, arrived in N. Y. on Nov. 3—Simultaneous exhibitions:

Date.	Place.	Won.	Lost.	Drawn.
Nov. 2	S. S. Olympic	11	0	0
Nov. 10	West Point	19	0	1
Nov. 25	New York	15	1	4
Nov. 27	New York	17	1	2

CRICKET.

METROPOLITAN LEAGUE.

	Played.	Won.	Lost.	Drawn.	Pts
Manhattan	15	14	0	1	29
Brooklyn	15	9	2	4	22
Paterson	15	9	4	2	20
Longfellows	15	4	10	1	9
Cameron	15	4	11	0	3
Kings County	15	1	14	0	2

NEW YORK AND NEW JERSEY CRICKET ASSOCIATION.

	Won.	Lost.	Drawn.	Pts.
Manor Field	13	1	1	27
Staten Island	10	4	1	21
Brooklyn	7	4	4	18
Columbia Oval	5	9	1	11
Columbia Oval Rovers	4	11	0	8
Bensonhurst	2	12	1	5

The Halifax Cup was won by the Germantown Cricket Club.

The 1920 County Championship in England was won by Middlesex.

The tour of the Incogniti Cricket Club team in the United States and Canada resulted in the following record: Won, 6; Lost, 0; Drawn, 2.

CROSS COUNTRY.

Eagle's All-Scholastic Cross-Country Team for 1920.

Kerr, Manual.	Pierce, Poly Prep.
Peak, Commercial.	Somers, Boys' High.
Marr, Erasmus.	Weeks, Manual.
Rosenblum, Commercial.	Clark, Brooklyn Prep.

CROSS-COUNTRY RUNNING.

Intercollegiate champion—John L. Romig, Penn State.

Intercollegiate team champion—Cornell.

National senior A. A. U. champion—Fred Faller, Dorchester Club, Boston, Mass.

National senior A. A. U. team champion—Dorchester Club, Boston, Mass.

National junior A. A. U. champion—W. Ritola, Finnish-American A. C., N. Y.

National junior A. A. U. team champion—Mohawk A. C., N. Y.

FOOTBALL.

College Records.

WILLIAMS.

63	Rensselaer	6
35	Union	0
0	Harvard	38
62	Trinity	0
14	Columbia	20
31	Hamilton	7
50	Wesleyan	14
7	Amherst	14
312		99

ARMY.

36	Union	0
38	Marshall	0
27	Middlebury	0
26	Springfield	7
28	Tufts	6
17	Notre Dame	27
53	Lebanon Val.	0
90	Bowdoin	0
0	Navy	7
315		47

PENN STATE.

27	Muhlenberg	7
13	Gettysburg	0
14	Dartmouth	7
41	No. Carolina	0
100	Lebanon Val.	7
28	Penn	7
20	Nebraska	0
7	Lehigh	7
0	Pittsburg	0
259		35

CORNELL.

13	Rochester	6
55	St. Bonaventure	7
60	Union	0
42	Colgate	6
24	Rutgers	0
3	Dartmouth	14
34	Columbia	7
0	Pennsylvania	28
231		68

GEORGETOWN.

79	St. John's	0
27	N. C. State	0
28	W. Va. Wes.	7
40	Fordham	16
28	Hopkins	7
6	Navy	21
6	Georgia Tech.	35
7	W. and L.	16
0	Centre	103
0	Boston	30
221		235

HARVARD.

3	Holy Cross	0
41	Maine	0
21	Valparaiso	0
38	Williams	0
31	Centre	14
24	Virginia	0
14	Princeton	14
27	Brown	0
9	Yale	0
208		28

SYRACUSE.

55	Hobart	7
49	Vermont	0
45	Johns Hopkins	0
7	Pittsburg	7
10	Dartmouth	0
0	Holy Cross	3
14	W. and J.	0
7	Maryland	10
14	Colgate	0
201		27

LAFAYETTE.

20	Muhlenberg	0
7	Navy	12
0	Pennsylvania	7
84	Catholic U.	0
0	Pittsburg	14
10	Bucknell	7
34	Villanova	0
27	Lehigh	7
182		47

LEHIGH.

28	Lebanon Val.	0
7	West Virginia	7
9	Rutgers	0
41	Rochester	0
0	W. and J.	14
17	Carnegie Tech.	6
56	Muhlenberg	0
7	Penn State	7
7	Lafayette	27
172		61

W. AND J.

28	Bethany	0
67	Kalamazoo	0
13	Geneva	0
7	W. Va. Wes.	7
14	Lehigh	0
49	Westminster	0
0	Syracuse	14
0	Pittsburg	7
0	Carnegie Tech.	6
28	West Virginia	0
206		34

DARTMOUTH.

31	Norwich	0
7	Penn State	14
27	Holy Cross	14
0	Syracuse	10
34	Tufts	7
14	Cornell	3
44	Penn	7
14	Brown	6
28	Washington	7
199		68

NAVY.

7	N. C. State	14
12	Lafayette	7
7	Bucknell	2
0	Princeton	14
47	West. Reserve	0
21	Georgetown	6
63	So. Carolina	0
7	Army	0
164		43

WEST VIRGINIA.

14	W. Va. Wes.	0
7	Lehigh	7
13	Pittsburg	34
81	Geo. Wash.	0
0	Yale	24
3	Princeton	10
14	Wash. & Lee	10
17	Rutgers	0
20	Bethany	0
0	W. and J.	28
169		113

BROWN.

23	R. I. State	0
13	Amherst	0
32	Maine	7
14	Colgate	0
14	Springfield	0
35	Vermont	0
10	Yale	14
0	Harvard	27
6	Dartmouth	14
149		62

FORDHAM.

71	N. Y. Aggies	0
0	Boston College	20
12	Villanova	6
16	Georgetown	40
0	Detroit	39
40	Geo. Wash.	0
13	Muhlenburg	0
152		105

PITTSBURG.

47	Geneva	0
34	West Virginia	13
7	Syracuse	7
10	Ga. Tech.	3
14	Lafayette	0
27	Pennsylvania	21
7	W. and J.	0
0	Penn State	0
146		44

SPORTING RECORDS—FOOTBALL—*Continued.*

PRINCETON.
17—Swarthmore .. 6
35 Maryland State 0
34—W. and Lee.. 0
14—Navy 0
10—West Virginia. 3
14—Harvard 14
20—Yale 0
144 23

HOLY CROSS.
0—Harvard 3
14—Dartmouth ...27
3—Syracuse 0
17—Springfield ... 0
36—Colby 0
32—Hampshire S.. 0
0—Boston Col....14
102 44

WESLEYAN.
20—R. I. State.... 0
20—Trinity 0
13—N. Y. U.......13
10—Columbia 0
20—Rochester 0
—Amherst 0
17—Williams 50
104 63

N. Y. U.
7—Columbia 14
13—Wesleyan 13
13—Hamilton 14
7—Union 9
31—Trinity 20
18—Bates 21
14—Stevens 21
103 112

YALE.
44—Carnegie Tech. 0
21—U. of N. C... 0
13—Boston College.21
24—West Virginia. 0
21—Colgate 7
14—Brown 10
0—Princeton 20
0—Harvard 9
137 67

ST. LAWRENCE.
10—Vermont 7
35—St. Stephen's.. 0
24—Rochester 17
20—Buffalo 0
35—Hobart 0
0—Canisus 7
10—Middleburg ... 0
34—Clarkson Tech. 0
168 31

BOSTON COLLEGE.
20—Fordham 0
21—Yale 13
12—Springfield ... 0
34—Boston Univ.. 0
37—Tufts 0
13—Marietta 3
30—Georgetown .. 0
14—Holy Cross.... 0
181 16

COLGATE.
0—Susquehanna.. 0
7—Allegheny..... 7
0—Brown 14
6—Cornell 42
7—Yale 21
14—Rochester 21
80—St. Bon'venture 0
0—Syracuse 14
114 119

STEVENS.
12—Penn. M. C...10
10—Haverford 3
14—Swarthmore .. 7
0—Middlebury ... 0
14—Rensselaer ... 0
48—Delaware 0
30—U.S.S. Arizona.13
21—N. Y. U.......14
149 47

PENNSYLVANIA.
35—Delaware 0
7—Bucknell 0
21—Swarthmore .. 0
7—Lafayette 0
7—Virginia M. I. 27
7—Penn State....28
21—Pittsburg 27
7—Dartmouth ...44
27—Columbia 7
28—Cornell 0
167 133

AMHERST.
0—Brown 13
13—Bowdoin 0
7—Columbia 20
35—Union 0
30—Hamilton 7
0—Wesleyan 7
14—Trinity 0
14—Williams 7
113 54

COLUMBIA.
21—Trinity 0
14—N. Y. U....... 7
20—Amherst 7
0—Wesleyan 10
20—Williams 14
7—Swarthmore ..21
7—Cornell 34
7—Penn 27
96 120

RUTGERS.
7—Ursinus 14
6—Maryland Univ. 0
0—Lehigh 9
19—Virginia Poly.. 6
0—Virginia 7
0—Cornell 24
0—Nebraska 28
0—W. Virginia...17
0—Detroit 27
32 132

SCHOLASTIC TEAMS.

ADELPHI.
0—St. Francis Pr.21
0—Glen Cove.....46
2—Freeport 7
7—Barnard 0
13—Marquand 0
22 74

BOYS' HIGH.
0—Rutgers Prep..12
14—Commerce 9
0—New Utrecht.. 0
0—Poly Prep.....13
0—Commercial.... 3
0—Erasmus 3
0—Flushing 13
0—Manual 14
14 67

BROOKLYN PREP.
13—St. Jos. Prep...19
10—Princeton Prep.27
7—Hamilton Inst. 6
7—Fordham Prep.12
7—Flushing 37
10—St. John's Pr'p. 7
6—St.Peter's Prep.16
60 124

COMMERCIAL.
7—Stuyvesant..... 7
14—Manual 0
7—Poly Prep..... 0
10—Erasmus 7
3—Boys High.... 0
6—Commerce 9
37—Marquand 0
7—New Utrecht... 0
91 23

ERASMUS.
3—St. Jno.'s Prep. 0
13—New Utrecht... 6
6—Harrisb'g T'ch.40
7—Commercial ..10
7—Flushing 7
0—Manual 13
0—Boston Com... 3
3—Boys' High.... 0
0—Poly Prep.....14
39 93

MANUAL.
0—Commercial ..14
12—St. Paul's..... 0
16—Flushing 0
13—Erasmus 0
21—St. John's Prep. 6
7—Poly Prep..... 7
20—New Utrecht.. 0
14—Boys' High.... 0
103 27

FLUSHING.
0—New Utrecht..13
7—Morris 0
28—St. Johns Prep. 3
0—Manual 16
7—Erasmus 7
28—Hamilton Inst. 0
37—Bklyn. Prep... 7
13—Boys' High.... 0
0—Bingh'mt'nCen.19
120 65

MARQUAND.
6—DeWitt Clint'n 47
0—Glen Cove 21
19—Hempstead ... 0
0—Adelphi 13
0—Commercial ..37
0—McBurney 21
25 139

NEW UTRECHT.
13—Flushing 0
6—Erasmus 13
0—Boys High..... 0
0—DeWitt Clin... 7
14—Poly Prep..... 7
9—Evander Childs 0
6—White Plains..28
0—Manual 20
0—Commercial... 7
48 82

POLY PREP.
0—East Orange..13
0—Commercial... 7
13—Boys' High.... 0
7—New Utrecht..14
40—Glen Cove..... 6
7—Manual 7
14—Erasmus 0
81 47

ST. FRANCIS' PREP.
21—Adelphi 0
7—South Side....13
7—St. Peter's Pr.60
0—Stamford 76
0—Jamaica 0
0—All Hollows...12
0—Glen Cove.....52
35 213

ST. JOHN'S PREP.
0—Erasmus 3
26—South Side.... 7
3—Flushing 28
6—Manual 21
20—Canterbury.... 7
7—Bklyn. Prep...10
62 76

BKLYN. EYE. HIGH.
0—Concordia Prep.27
26—Nyack 0
0—Kingston 0
26 27

GLEN COVE.
37—Oyster Bay... 0
44—Adelphi 0
32—Lynbrook 0
34—Port Wash.... 0
21—Marquand 0
6—Poly Prep.....40
46—Freeport 0
52—St. Fran. Prep. 0
13—Corning Acad. 6
285 46

SOUTH SIDE.
7—St. Johns Prep.26
13—St. Fran. Prep. 7
20 33

FREEPORT.
0—St. Paul's..... 7
7—Adelphi 2
19—Lynbrook 0
13—Southampton.. 0
0—Southampton.. 6
18—Hempstead ... 0
7—Glen Cove.....46
64 61

ST. PAUL'S.
7—Freeport....... 0
0—Manual 12
6—Morristown ... 0
0—Hackley 21
66—Hempstead ... 0
79 33

HEMPSTEAD.
14—Alumni 0
0—Marquand 19
0—St. Paul's.....66
0—Freeport 18
14 103

LYNBROOK.
0—Glen Cove.....32
0—Freeport 19
0 51

Eagle's All-Scholastic Football Teams for 1920.

1ST TEAM. Name and School.	Pos.	2D TEAM. Name and School.
Meyers, New Utrecht.	L. E.	Starobin, Comm'l
Bronder, Poly Prep.	L. T.	Van Tronk, Erasmus
Kubat, St. Johns Pr.	L.G.	Tierney, New Utr'cht
Schaap, Boys High.	Center.	Malhame, Comm'l
Weiner, Commerc'l.	R. G.	Fanning, Manual
Ruch, Erasmus.	R. T.	Wardle, Poly Prep
E. Harrison, Bk.Pr'p.	R. E.	Miller Manual
Mattimore, Bkn. Prp.	Q. B.	Parks, Polp Prep
Bunn, Boys High.	L. H.	Schissel, Commerc'l
Greve, Com. (Capt.).	R. H.	Longua, St. Jno's P.
Beattie, Manual.	F.B.	Bell, Poly P. (Capt.)

SPORTING RECORDS—FOOTBALL—*Continued.*

1920 ROLL OF HONOR.

Adelphi — Maisel, fullback; Mason, right tackle; Dangler, quarterback; Darcy, right guard, and Aldridge, right end.

Boys High—Bunn, left halfback; Schaap, center; Conroy, left halfback; Rampell, right halfback; Peper, right end.

Brooklyn Prep.—Harrison, right end; White; fullback; Furey, left halfback; Bill, left tackle; Mattimore, quarterback.

Commercial—Creve, right halfback; Starobin, left end; Shuter, left end; Abrams, fullback; Breden, quarterback; Bloomgarten, right tackle; Kovner, left tackle; Stubbs, left guard; Sowden, right end; Weiner, right guard; Malhame, center; Schissel, left halfback.

Erasmus—Ruch, right tackle; Washington, quarterback; Chandler, left halfback; Van Tronk, left tackle; Moore, right halfback; Morris, right guard.

Manual—Beattie, fullback; Studwell, left guard; Bease, quarterback; Fanning, right guard; Miller, right end; Hart, right tackle; Kilby, left halfback.

Marquand—Yeo, fullback; Simmons, left end; Bucher, right tackle; Schiaffino, left guard.

New Utrecht—Meyers, left end; Tierney, left guard; Glass, center; Wirtz, fullback; Schaeffer, quarterback; Salemi, left halfback; Holle, right halfback; D'Auria, right halfback.

Poly Prep—Bronder, left tackle; Wardle, right tackle; Parks, quarterback; Bell, fullback; Dube, left halfback; Cook, right halfback; Lawson, center.

St. John's Prep—Kubat, left guard; Pollock, center; Longue, right halfback; Kennedy, fullback; Gaffney, left halfback.

St. Francis Prep—Sullivan, left halfback; Bartley, quarterback; Gallagher, left tackle.

GOLF.

The season of 1920 proved to be the most important in the history of American golf. Not only did Americans compete in the British and French championships, but Britishers took part in the American championships, both open and amateur. While an American, Robert A. Gardner, was runner-up in the British amateur, the British champion, Tolley, failed to qualify in the American amateur, his two traveling companions, Lord Charles Hope and Roger H. Wethered, meeting the same fate. But a Scotch amateur, T. D. Armour, qualified and lasted till the third round. In the U. S. open Ed Ray, the English pro, proved the winner.

In the British open Walter Hagen, the American open champion, made a poor showing, but redeemed himself by capturing the French open, defeating the British champion, Duncan, and Abe Mitchell, the British pro-champion.

No British women competed in America, but a delegation of fair Americans "invaded" Great Britain and France, but met with no success. However, Miss Alexa Stirling, the American champion, was successful in her invasion of Canada, as she captured the Dominion championship.

One of the outstanding features of the season was the American visit of Harry Vardon and Ed Ray, the British pros, who played a number of exhibition matches. In addition to Ray's winning the U. S. title, Vardon, though 50 years old, finished in a tie for second place. The results of their trip appear in totals below.

In the three national championships of the U. S. Golf Association only one new figure is found, that of Ray, Evans repeating his victory of 1916 in the amateur and Miss Stirling retaining her laurels. However, the national professional champion, Jack Hutchison, is new, as is the intercollegiate title-holder, Jess Sweetser.

Apart from the actual play the season was made memorable also by the visit of the American rules committee to Great Britain to confer over changes in the code and the standardization of the ball. A significant phase of the closing weeks of the season was the coming to the front of the great Lido seaside course at Long Beach, L. I., which Open Champion Ray called altogether the finest course in this country and which he thought should be the scene of the 1921 open championship. The record of the more important 1920 competitions follows.

NATIONAL CHAMPIONSHIPS.

OPEN—Won at Inverness, Toledo, by Ed Ray, of England. Leading scores: Ed Ray, 295; Harry Vardon, England, 296; Jack Hutchison, Glen View, 296; Jack Burke, Town and Country, 296; Leo Deigel, Lake Shore, 296; Chick Evans (amateur), Edgewater, 298; J. M. Barnes, Sunset Hill, 298; Bobby Jones, Atlanta (amateur), 299; W. MacFarlane, Port Washington, 299; Robert MacDonald, Bob O' Link, 300; Walter Hagen, N. Y., 301; C. W. Hackney, Atlantic City, 302; Fred McLeod, Columbia, 304; C. H. Rowe, Oakmont, 305; Frank McNamara, Cherry Valley, 305; M. J. Brady, Oakland Hills, 306. Ray's winning rounds were 74, 73, 73, 75—295, an average of 73.75.

AMATEUR—Won at Engineers, Roslyn, L. I., by Chick Evans, of Edgewater, Ill., who defeated Francis Ouimet, of Woodland, Mass., by 7 and 6; medalist, Bobby Jones, Atlanta, in play-off of tie at 154 with Fred J. Wright Jr., Albemarle, Mass. In semi-finals, Evans defeated Ned Allis, Milwaukee, 10 and 8, and Ouimet disposed of Jones by 6 and 5. In final Evans was 2 up at end of morning round.

WOMEN'S—Won at Mayfield, Cleveland, by Miss Alexa Stirling, of Atlanta, who defeated Mrs. J. V. Hurd, of Pittsburg, by 4 and 3; medalist, Miss Marion Hollins, Westbrook, L. I., 82. This was Miss Stirling's third consecutive national triumph.

PROFESSIONAL—Won at Flossmoor, Ill., by Jack Hutchison, of Glen View, who defeated J. Douglas Edgar, of Atlanta, by 1 up, in competition for Rodman Wanamaker prizes. In semi-finals Hutchison defeated Harry Hampton, Richmond, Va., by 4 and 3, and Edgar beat George McLean, Great Neck, by 8 and 7.

INTERCOLLEGIATE.—Won at Nassau by Jess Sweetser, of Yale, who defeated James C. Ward, of Williams, by 4 and 3; medalist, J. Simpson Dean, Princeton, 149. At end of morning round, Sweetser was 4 up on Ward.

The intercollegiate team championship was won at the same course by Princeton with a total of 1,269. Yale being second with 1,303. Other scores: Dartmouth, 1,338; Harvard, 1,339; Williams, 1,376; Cornell, 1,407; Penn, 1,417; Columbia, 1,421.

WESTERN CHAMPIONSHIPS.

OPEN.—Won at Olympia Fields by Jack Hutchison with 296. J. M. Barnes, of Sunset Hill, the title-holder, was tied with Harry Hampton, of Richmond, and C. W. Hackney, of Atlantic City, with the second low score of 297. Hutchison's winning rounds: 72, 73, 71 and 80—296. Other scores: William Creavy, Kansas City, 298; Eddie Loos, Ravisloe, 302; George Carney, Chicago, 304; J. J. O'Brien, Pittsburg, 306; E. Loeffler, Pittsburg, 306; L. Ayton, Chicago, 307; W. Ogg, Atlanta, 308.

AMATEUR.—Won at Memphis Country Club by Chick Evans, of Edgewater, Ill., who defeated Clarence Wolff, of St. Louis, by 5 and 4. Medalist, Bobby Jones, Atlanta, 139, made up of 69 and 70. At end of morning round, Evans was 3 up on Wolff. In semi-finals Evans beat Bobby Jones 1 up and Wolff defeated Harry Wenzler, Memphis, by 2 and 1.

SECTIONAL CHAMPIONSHIPS.

AMATEUR.—Metropolitan—Won at Apawamis by Ned Sawyer, Siwanoy, by 1 up, 37 holes; runner-up, Gardiner W. White, Nassau.

New Jersey—Won at Arcola by W. M. Reekie, Upper Montclair, by 7 and 5; runner-up, Frank W. Dyer, Upper Montclair.

Trans-Mississippi—Won at Rock Island, Ill., by Robert McKee, Des Moines, by 3 and 1; runner-up, Clarence Wolff, St. Louis.

Westchester—Won at Dunwoodie by J. S. Worthington, Siwanoy, by 5 and 4; runner-up, Walter F. Purcell, Dunwoodie.

Southern—Won at Chattanooga by Bobby Jones, Atlanta, by 11 and 10; runner-up, Ewing Watkins, Chattanooga.

Massachusetts—Won at Brookline by Fred J. Wright Jr., Albemarle, by 2 and 1; runner-up, Parker Schofield, Albemarle.

Staten Island, N. Y.—Won at Fox Hills by W. H. Follett, Fox Hills, by 8 and 6; runner-up, S. D. Bowers, Richmond County.

Eastern Interscholastic—Won at Nassau by H. G. Davis, 3d, Hill School, by 2 up; runner-up, Willis G. Jones, Tome.

Greater New York—Won at Van Cortlandt Park by Richard Walsh, Scottish-American, by 2 up; runner-up, W. T. Gotelli, unattached.

SPORTING RECORDS—GOLF—*Continued.*

Connecticut—Won at Brooklawn by Roger H. Hovey, Shuttle Meadow, by 5 and 4; runner-up, Reginald M. Lewis, Greenwich.

Middle Atlantic—Won at Country Club of Va. by Allan L. Hawse, home club, by 1 up, 20 holes; runner-up, Robert L. Finkenstaedt, Columbia.

Chicago District—Won by Dewey Webber with 78—74—152; runner-up, Chick Evans, 76—80—156.

Detroit District—Won at Bloomfield Hills by J. B. Schlotman by 10 and 9; runner-up, C. G. Waldo, Jr.

White Mountain—Won at Jefferson, N. H., by A. R. Corwin, Tedesco, with 73; runner-up, W. L. Richard, Engineers, 75.

Western Pa.—Won at Allegheny by J. I. Crawford by 3 and 1; runner-up, Frank Nash, Sewickley Y. M. C. A.

Philadelphia—Won at Huntingdon Valley by J. Wood Platt by 8 and 6, runner-up, H. H. Francine.

Pennsylvania—Won at Oakmont by S. Davidson Herron, home club, by 5 and 3; runner-up, Max R. Marston, Merion.

OPEN.—Metropolitan—Won at Greenwich by Walter Hagen, with 70 in playoff of tie at 292 with Jim Barnes, the latter scoring 74.

Mass.—Won at Commonwealth by George Bowden, Commonwealth, with 289; runner-up, Tom McNamara, Siwanoy, 297.

Philadelphia—Won at Atlantic City C. C. by Frank McNamara, Cherry Valley, with 294; runner-up, George Fotheringham, Richmond County, 299.

Penna.—Won at Oakmont by E. Loeffler, Oakmont, with 150; runner-up, S. D. Herron, amateur, of Oakmont; Fred Brand, Allegheny, and Charles Rowe, Oakmont, 160.

Southern—Won at Eastlake by J. Douglas Edgar, Druid Hills, with 302; runner-up, Bobby Jones, amateur, Atlanta, 304.

New England—Won at Wannamoisett by Louis Tellier, Brae Burn, with 145; runner-up, George Bowden, Commonwealth, 147.

Western Penna.—Won at Allegheny by E. Loeffler, Oakmont, with 150; runner-up, Charles Rowe, Oakmont, 151.

Westchester County, N. Y.—Won at Gedney Farms by Tom Kerrigan, Siwanoy, with 143; runner-up, Arthur E. Reid, Ardsley, 149.

WOMEN'S CHAMPIONSHIPS.

National—See National Championships.

Eastern—Won at Philadelphia Cricket Club by Mrs. R. H. Barlow, Merion, with 170; runner-up, Mrs. W. A. Gavin, Belleclaire, 173.

Western—Won at Oak Park, Ill., by Mrs. Fred C. Letts Jr., Onwentsia, by 2 up; runner-up, Miss Edith Cummings, Onwentsia.

Southern—Won at New Orleans by Mrs. D. Gaut, Memphis, by 3 and 1; runner-up, Mrs. D. Lowndes, Atlanta.

Metropolitan—Won at Greenwich by Mrs. Q. F. Feitner, South Shore, by 2 and 1; runner-up, Miss G. Bishop, Brooklawn.

Philadelphia—Won at Merion by Miss M. Bell, Phila. Cricket Club, by 4 and 3; runner-up, Mrs. C. F. Fox, Huntingdon Valley.

Conn.—Won at Shuttle Meadow by Miss G. Bishop, Brooklawn, with 94; runner-up, Mrs. H. C. House, Farmington C. C., 98.

Boston—Won at Belmont Spring C. C., by Miss H. S. Curtis, Essex County; runner-up, Miss E. Gordon, Wannamoisett.

Missouri—Won at Bellevue by Miss Carolyn Lee, Hillcrest, by 7 and 6; runner-up, Mrs. Lyon Wasson, St. Louis.

Griscom Cup, tri-city team championship—Won at Philadelphia Cricket Club by Philadelphia team by 9 to 6 over N. Y. in final; in first round Phila. beat Boston, 10 to 5, and N. Y. beat Boston, 10 to 5.

TEAM MATCHES.

Lesley Cup, Tri-State—Won at Merion by Penna. with 8 points to New York's 7; N. Y. beat Mass. 8 to 7.

N. J. vs. Westchester Co.—Won at Englewood by N. J., 16 to 9.

Long Island pro-amateur series—Won by F. McNamara, pro, and G. Peacock, amateur, of Cherry Valley, by 11 and 9 over G. McLean and D. Rockwell, of Great Neck, 18 holes at each course.

Inter-city—Won at Cleveland by Ravisloe C. C.; Oakwoods, Cleveland, second.

Inter-Club Trophy—Won at Forest Park, L. I., by Woodhaven, 23, vs. Brooklyn-Forest Park, 10.

Quebec vs. Brae Burn—Won at Brae Burn by latter, 14 points to 1.

MISCELLANEOUS.

American Golf Assn. Advertising Interests—Won at Shawnee by Lee Maxwell, Sleepy Hollow; runner-up, R. S. Worthington, Shawnee.

Jaques Memorial—Won at Brookline by Francis Ouimet with 300, 72-hole course record; second, P. W. Whittemore, 317.

Lynnewood Hall—Won at Huntingdon Valley by G. V. Rotan, Texas, by 4 and 3; runner-up, J. S. Dean, Princeton.

Father and Son—Won at Sleepy Hollow by W. Rossiter Betts Sr. and Jr., with 86—12—74.

Victory Cup—Won at Wykagyl by Jess Sweetser, Siwanoy, by 3 and 2; runner-up, J. G. Anderson, Siwanoy.

JUNIOR CHAMPIONSHIPS.

Metropolitan—Won at Sleepy Hollow by J. G. McMahon, Sleepy Hollow, by 3 and 2; runner-up, J. J. Leonard, Shackamaxon. Westchester County—Won at Oak Ridge by J. G. McMahon, Sleepy Hollow, by 1 up (37 holes); runner-up, Willis Jones, Mt. Kisco. Mass.—Won at Oakley by Eddie Lowery by 2 and 1; runner-up, George Aulbach. N. J.—Won at Hackensack by J. J. Leonard, Shackamaxon; runner-up, C. F. Pierson, Montclair.

SENIORS' COMPETITIONS.

U. S. Seniors' G. A. Championship—Won at Apawamis by Hugh Halsell, of Dallas, Tex., with 80—82—162. U. S. Seniors vs. Canadian Seniors—Won at Ottawa by Americans, 20 to 15.

SOUTHERN WINTER CHAMPIONSHIPS.

PINEHURST—North and South championships: Amateur, won by Francis Ouimet, Woodland, by 5 and 4; runner-up, Sam J. Graham, Greenwich. Open, won by Fred McLeod, Columbia, D. C., with 293; runner-up, Walter Hagen, N. Y., 294. Women's, won by Mrs. J. V. Hurd, Pittsburg, by 5 and 4; runner-up, Mrs. J. Raymond Price, Oakmont.

Florida—Amateur, won at St. Augustine by H. J. Willoughby, Jr., Philadelphia, by 6 and 5; runner-up, George W. Morse, Rutland. Women's, won at Palm Beach by Mrs. Quentin F. Feitner, South Shore, by 5 and 4; runner-up, Miss Elaine Rosenthal, Ravisloe. South Florida amateur, won at Palm Beach by Stewart Stickney, St. Louis, by 7 and 6; runner-up, H. J. Willoughby Jr., Philadelphia. West Coast pro, won at Belleair by Walter Hagen, N. Y., with 292; runner-up, Leo Deigel, Chicago, 304. East Coast open, won at St. Augustine by M. J. Brady, Detroit, with 292; runner-up, Leo Deigel, Chicago, 300.

CANADIAN.

Canada vs. U. S.—Won at Engineers by U. S. 10 to 4. Amateur championship—Won at Beaconsfield by C. B. Grier by 5 and 4; runner-up, T. S. Gillespie, Calgary. Open Championship—Won at Rivermead by J. Douglas Edgar, Atlanta, with 73 in play-off with T. D. Armour, amateur, Scotland, 74, and Charles Murray, pro, Montreal, 75, after tie at 298. Women's championship—Won at Hamilton by Miss Alexa Stirling, Atlanta, by 5 and 3; runner-up, Miss Kate Robertson, Montreal. Inter-provincial team match—Won at Beaconsfield by Ontario.

BRITISH CHAMPIONSHIPS.

AMATEUR.—British—Won at Muirfield by Cyril Tolley, Oxford Univ., by 1 up (37 holes); runner-up Robert A. Gardner, Chicago. Scottish—Won at Gleneagles by Gordon Lockhart. Irish—Won at Portmarnock by G. N. C. Martin, Royal Portrush, by 6 and 5; runner-up, C. W. Robertson, Delgany.

OPEN.—British—Won at Deal by George Duncan with 80, 80, 71, 72—303. Other scores: Alex Herd, second, 72, 81, 77, 75—305; Ed Ray, third, 72, 83, 78, 73—306; Abe Mitchell, fourth, 74, 73, 84, 76—307; James M. Barnes (U. S.), fifth, 79, 74, 77, 78—308. Walter Hagen, American open champion, was in 52d place with 329.

PROFESSIONAL.—British (News of the World Tournament)—Won at Mid-Surrey by Abe Mitchell by 3 and 2; runner-up, Josh Taylor. Scottish—Won at Gleneagles by Tom Fernie for fourth time with 330 (72 holes).

WOMEN'S.—British—Won at Newcastle, Ireland, by Miss Cecil Leitch by 7 and 6 (36 holes); runner-up, Miss Molly Griffiths. Eng-

SPORTING RECORDS—Golf—*Continued.*

lish—Won at Sheringham by Miss Joyce Wethered by 2 and 1; runner-up, Miss Cecil Leitch. Scotch—Won at Cruden Bay by Mrs. Watson by 5 and 3; runner-up, Miss L. Scroggie. Irish—Won at Portrush by Miss Janet Jackson for fourth time, by 5 and 4; runner-up, Mrs. R. A. Cramsie. Girls'—Won at Stoke Poges by Miss Christina Clarke by 1 up in 21 holes; runner-up, Miss Audrey Croft, title-holder.

FOREIGN CHAMPIONSHIPS OUTSIDE BRITISH ISLES.

French Open Championship—Won at La Boulie by Walter Hagen, U. S. open champion, in play-off of tie with Pierre Lafitte, of France, at 298, Hagen scoring 75—75—150 to Lafitte's 76—78—154. Abe Mitchell, British pro champion, had 299 and George Duncan, British open champion, was far away with 314. French amateur championship—Won at La Boulie by T. D. Armour, of Scotland, by 3 and 2; runner-up, Cyril Tolley, British amateur champion. French women's championship—Won at Le Touquet by Miss Cecil Leitch, British champion, by 6 and 5; runner-up, Miss Molly Griffiths, England.

Australia amateur championship—Won by Eric L. Appleby; runner-up, E. E. Howard.

South Africa open championship—Won by L. B. Waters at Johannesburg with 304, and the amateur championship by H. Gordon Stewart with 315, medal play governing in the latter as in the open.

NECROLOGY.

The first great player to be taken by death from the ranks of American-bred golfers passed away in the year in the person of Frederick Herreshoff, the amateur, who died in New York City on March 23. In 1910 Herreshoff won the Metropolitan championship, defeating J. D. Travers in the final, and in 1909 and 1916 he was the runner-up. His fame, however, was based on the fact that in the final of the 1911 National Amateur championship at Apawamis he carried Herold H. Hilton, the former British open and amateur champion, to the 37th hole, after being 6 down, going to the 24th hole.

Another great golfer to succumb was George Simpson of Chicago, former amateur champion of Scotland, but later a professional. Other pros. to die in the year were Jack Blair of Nashua, N. H., and George J. Bouse of Richmond, Va. Edward J. Rowe, former president of the Wykagyl Country Club, also passed away.

HORSE RACING.

The racing season of 1920 was the greatest, in many respects, in the history of the turf. Man o' War was the champion of the year and won 11 races. He was not defeated. He won $166,140. He not only was the best 3-year-old of the season, but beat Sir Barton, the champion 4-year-old. He was hailed as the "super-horse," the champion of champions. He beat Sir Barton in a special race for $75,000 in gold and a gold cup worth $5,000—the most valuable prize ever offered for a race in America or Europe.

Metropolitan Handicap, 1 Mile, Records.

(Year, name of winner, value and time.)

1897, Voter, $3,850, 1:40½; 1898, Bowling Brook, $4,280, 1:44; 1899, Filigrane, $6,750, 1:39¾; 1900, Ethelbert, $6,290, 1:41¼; 1901, Banastar, $6,310, 1:42; 1902, Arsenal, $9,020, 1:42; 1903, Gunfire, $11,130, 1:38½; 1904, Irish Lad, $10,880, 1:40; 1905 (dead heat), Sysonby and Race King, *$11,310, 1:41 3-5; 1906, Grapple, $10,850, 1:39; 1907, Glorifier, $10,570, 1:40 4-5; 1908, Jack Atkin, $9,620, 1:38 2-5; 1909, King James, $3,875, 1:40; 1910, Fashion Plate, $3,800, 1:37 4-5; 1911, no race; 1912, no race; 1913, Whisk Broom II, $3,475, 1:39; 1914, Buskin, $4,200, 1:37 4-5; 1915, Stromboli, $2,325, 1:39 4-5; 1916, The Finn, $3,350, 1.38; 1917, Ormesdale, $3,850, 1:39 1-5; 1918, Trompe La Mort, $3,865, 1:38 3-5; 1919, Lanius, $3,865, 1:45 2-5; 1920, Wildair, $3,865, 1:38 4-5.

Brooklyn Handicap, 1¼ Miles, Records.

(Year, name of winner, value and time.)

1896, Sir Walter, $3,000, 2:08½; 1897, Howard Mann, $7,750, 2:09¾; 1898, Ornament, $8,000, 2:10; 1899, Banastar, $8,000, 2:06¾; 1900, Kinley Mack, $8,000, 2:10; 1901, Conroy, $8,000, 2:09; 1902, Reina, $7,800, 2:07; 1903, Irish Lad, $15,150, 2:05 2-5; 1904, The Picket, $15,800, 2:06 3-5; 1905, Delhi, $15,800, 2:06 2-5; 1906, Tokalon, $15,800, 2:05 3-5; 1907, Superman, $15,800, 2:09; 1908, Celt, $3,850, 2:04 1-5; 1909, King James, $3,850, 2:04; 1910, Fitz Herbert, $4,800, 2:05 3-5; 1911, no race; 1912, no race; 1913, Whisk Broom II, $3,025, 2:03 2-5; 1914, Buckhorn, $3,250, 2:08; †1915, Tartar, $3,950, 1:50 3-5; 1916, Friar Rock, $3,850, 1:50;

---

*Purse divided.

†Distance reduced to 1⅛ miles.

1917, Borrow, $4,850, 1:49 2-5; 1918, Cudgel, $4,850, 1:50 1-5; 1919, Eternal, $4,850, 1:49 4-5; 1920, Cirrus, $5,850, 1:50.

Suburban Handicap, 1¼ Miles, Records.

(Year, name of winner, value and time.)

1894, Ramapo, $12,070, 2:06 1-5; 1895, Lazzarone, $4,730, 2:07 4-5; 1896, Henry of Navarre, $6,000, 2:07; 1897, Ben Brush, $5,850, 2:07 1-5; 1898, Tillo, $7,000, 2:08 1-5; 1899, Imp, $7,000, 2:05 4-5; 1900, Kinley Mack, $10,000, 2:06 4-5; 1901, Alcedo, $10,000, 2:05 3-5; 1902, Gold Heels, $6,800, 2:05 1-5; 1903, Africander, $16,650, 2:10 2-5; 1904, Hermis, $16,800, 2:05; 1905, Beldame, $16,800, 2:05 3-5; 1906, Go Between, $20,000, 2:05 1-5; 1907, Nealon, $16,800, 2:06 2-5; 1908, Ballot, $19,750, 2:03; 1909, Fitz Herbert, $3,850, 2:03 2-5; 1910, Olambala, $4,800, 2:04 2-5; 1911, no race; 1912, no race; 1913, Whisk Broom II, $2,900, 2:00; 1914, no race; 1915, Stromboli, $3,025, 2:05 2-5; 1916, Friar Rock, $3,450, 2:05; 1917, Boots, $4,900, 2:05 1-5; 1918, Johaen, $5,850, 2:06; 1919, Corn Tassel, $5,200, 2:02 1-5; 1920, Paul Jones, $6,350, 2:09 3-5.

The Futurity, About ¾ Mile, Records.

(Year, name of winner, value and time.)

1894, The Butterflies, $48,710, 1:11; 1895, Requital, $53,190, 1:11 2-5; 1896, Ogden, $44,290, 1:10; 1897, L'Alouette, $34,290, 1:11; 1898, Martimas, $37,130, 1:12 2-5; 1899, Chacornac, $30,990, 1:10 2-5; 1900, Ballyhoo Bey, $33,830, 1:10; 1901, Yankee, $38,685, 1:09 1-5; 1902, Savable $45,400, 1:14; 1903, Hamburg Belle, $35,940, 1:13; 1904, Artful, $43,540, 1:11 4-5; 1905, Ormondale, $42,080, 1:11 4-5; 1906, Electioneer, $37,270, 1:13 3-5; 1907, Colin, $27,075, 1:11 1-5; 1908, Maskette, $25,100, 1:11 1-5; 1909, Sweep, $24,270, 1:11 4-5; 1910, Novelty, $25,360, 1:12 1-5; 1911, no race; 1912, no race; 1913, Pennant, $15,060, 1:15; 1914, Trojan, $15,160, 1:16 4-5; 1915, Thunderer, $16,590, 1:11 4-5; 1916, Campfire, $17,340, 1:13 4-5; 1917, Papp, $15,450, 1:12; 1918, Dunboyne, $23,360, 1:12 4-5; 1919, Man o' War, $27,010, 1:11 1-5; 1920, Step Lightly, $35,870, 1:12 1-5.

Mad Hatter won the Latonia Championship Stakes at a mile and 6 furlongs on Oct. 11, '19, worth $44,090 net—the richest individual prize of the turf for 1919. Thunderclap established a world's record of 2:29 3-5 for mile and a half at Laurel, winning the Annapolis Handicap.

NATIONAL HORSE SHOW CHAMPIONS, 1920.

Pony stallions—Irvington Autocrat; Cassilis Farms.

Harness pony pairs—Hamilton Flame, Hamilton Dianthus; Mrs. F. P. Garvan.

Pony—Hamilton Flame; Mrs. F. P. Garvan.

Ponies under saddle—Never Bounce; Miss Corinne Poth.

Heavyweight harness horses — Animation; Loula Long Combs.

Horses exceeding 15.2, single harness—The Whip; John L. Bushnell.

Ladies' saddle horses—Driftwood Blaze; Mrs. Walter H. Hanley.

Ladies' saddle horses exceeding 15.2—Jean; Herbert L. Camp.

Pairs heavy harness horses, over 14.2 and not exceeding 15.2—Eva, Netherhall's Pride; Miss Isabella Wanamaker.

Pairs exceeding 15.2—Revelation, Reputation; Loula Long Combs.

Horses suitable to become hunters—Bobolink; Mrs. R. H. Halsted.

Roadster, single harness—Col. Stroller; Robert E. Moreland.

Heavyweight hunters—King Daly; Isaac H. Clothier, Jr.

Middleweight hunters—Sir Linsen; Isaac H. Clothier, Jr.

Lightweight hunters—Silver Crest; Frederic McElhone.

Hackneys, mares—Medea; William H. Moore.

SPORTING RECORDS—*Continued.*

LAWN TENNIS.

MEN'S SINGLES RANKING—1920.

1. W. T. Tilden 2d, Phila. 2. Wm. M. Johnston, San Francisco. 3. R. N. Williams 2d, Boston. 4. I. Kumagae, N. Y. 5. W. E. Davis, San Francisco. 6. C. J. Griffin, San Francisco. 7. W. Washburn, N. Y. 8. C. S. Garland, Pittsburg. 9. N. W. Niles, Boston. 10. W. F. Johnson, Phila.

MEN'S DOUBLES RANKING—1920.

1. C. J. Griffin—W. M. Johnston, San Francisco. 2. W. E. Davis—R. Roberts, San Francisco. 3. R. Harte—R. N. Williams, Boston. 4. H. Kinsey—R. Kinsey, San Francisco. 5. W. F. Johnson—S. Pearson, Phila. 6. L. Beekman—W. M. Hall, N. Y. 7. D. Mathey—W. M. Washburn, N. Y. 8. A. S. Dabney—N. W. Niles, Boston. 9. J. Weber—L. E. Williams, Chicago. 10. R. Burdick—W. T. Hayes, Chicago.

WOMEN'S SINGLES RANKING—1920.

1. Mrs. F. I. Mallory, N. Y. 2. Miss M. Zinderstein, West Newton. 3. Miss E. Tennant, Los Angeles. 4. Miss H. Baker, San Francisco. 5. Miss E. Goss, N. Y. 6. Mrs. E. Raymond, Hartsdale. 7. Miss M. Wagner, Yonkers. 8. Miss H. Pollak, N. Y. 9. Miss E. Sigourney, Boston. 10. Miss M. Grove, N. Y.

OTHER RECORDS.

National singles championship—At the West Side Tennis Club, Forest Hills, N. Y., Aug. 30, 1920. W. T. Tilden 2d of Phila., Pa., defeated W. M. Johnston of San Francisco, Cal., 6—1, 1—6, 7—5, 5—7, 6—3.

National doubles championship—At the Longwood Cricket Club, Boston, Mass., Aug. 16, 1920. W. M. Johnston and C. J. Griffin defeated W. E. Davis and R. Roberts, 6—2, 6—2, 6—3.

National clay court championship—At the Western Lawn Tennis Assn., Chicago, Ill., July 10, 1920. R. Roberts of San Francisco, Cal., defeated V. Richards of Yonkers, N. Y., 6—3, 6—1, 6—3.

Natl. clay court doubles championship—At Western Lawn Tennis Assn., Chicago, Ill., July 10, 1920. R. Roberts and V. Richards defeated W. J. Hayes and R. Burdick, 6—2, 6—2, 7—5.

Natl. clay court women's championship—At Detroit Tennis Club, Detroit, Mich., June 21, 1920. M. Zinderstein of West Newton, Mass., defeated F. Ballin of N. Y., 6—2, 7—5.

Natl. indoor singles championship—At 7th Regt. Armory, N. Y., March 27, 1920. W. T. Tilden 2d defeated V. Richards, 10—8, 6—3, 6—1.

Natl. indoor doubles championship—At 7th Regt. Armory, N. Y., March 27, 1920. W. T. Tilden 2d and V. Richards defeated S. Hardy and S. H. Voshell, 6—3, 3—6, 6—4, 12—10.

Natl. indoor women's championship—At 7th Regt. Armory, N. Y., March 15, 1920. H. Pollak defeated E. Sigourney, 8—6, 6—2.

Natl. indoor doubles championship—At 7th Regt. Armory, N. Y., March 15, 1920. H. Pollak and Mrs. L. G. Morris defeated C. Winn and G. Della Torre, 6—2, 6—4.

Natl. indoor junior championship—At 7th Regt. Armory, N. Y., Dec. 31, 1920. V. Richards defeated J. Lang, N. Y., 6—3, 6—3, 8—6.

Natl. indoor doubles championship—At 7th Regt. Armory, N. Y., Dec. 31, 1920. V. Richards and P. F. McHugh defeated A. K. Glore and E. Kuhn, 6—0, 6—4, 6—3.

Natl. indoor boys' singles championship—At 7th Regt. Armory, N. Y., Dec. 30, 1920, W. Einsmann defeated H. D. Bearmann.

Natl. veterans' championship—At West Side Tennis Club, Forest Hills, N. Y., Aug. 30, 1920. W. A. Campbell defeated R. N. Dana, 6—1, 1—6, 6—2.

Natl. father and sons' championship—At West Side Tennis Club, Forest Hills, N. Y., Aug. 30, 1920. F. G. and F. C. Anderson defeated J. D. E. and A. W. Jones, 3—6, 7—5, 6—4.

Natl. junior championship—At West Side Tennis Club, Forest Hills, N. Y., Aug. 30, 1920. V. Richards, Yonkers, N. Y., defeated W. W. Ingraham, Oakland, R. I., 6—2, 6—4, 6—1.

Natl. junior doubles championship—At West Side Tennis Club, Forest Hills, N. Y., Aug. 30, 1920. H. Godshall and R. Hinckley, Los Angeles, Cal., defeated W. W. Ingraham and A. W. Jones of Providence, R. I., 4—6, 6—3, 4—6, 7—5, 6—4.

Natl. boys' singles championship—At West Side Tennis Club, Forest Hills, N. Y., Aug. 30, 1920. J. L. Farquhar, Rutherford, N. J., defeated W. Einsmann, Bellerose, L. I., 7—5, 6—1.

Natl. boys' doubles championship—At West Side Tennis Club, Forest Hills, N. Y., Aug. 30, 1920. C. V. de Blasco and J. L. Farquhar of Rutherford, N. J., defeated W. Einsmann and G. Acker, Bellerose, N. Y., 6—3, 6—2.

Natl. girls' singles championship—At Phila. Cricket Club, Phila., Pa., Sept. 13, 1920. Miss L. Dixon of Phila. defeated Miss H. Sewell of Phila., 3—6, 6—3, 6—2.

Natl. girls' doubles championship—At Phila. Cricket Club, Phila., Pa., Sept. 13, 1920. Miss H. Sewell and Miss V. L. Carpenter of Phila. defeated Miss C. Baker of N. Y. and Miss M. Bayard of Short Hills, N. J., 6—4, 6—3.

Natl. women's singles championship—At Phila. Cricket Club, Phila., Pa., Sept. 13, 1920. Mrs. M. B. Mallory of N. Y. defeated Miss M. Zinderstein of West Newton, Mass., 6—3, 6—1.

Natl. women's doubles championship—At Phila. Cricket Club, Phila., Pa., Sept. 13, 1920. Miss E. Goss and Miss M. Zinderstein defeated Miss H. Baker and Miss E. Tennant, 13—11, 4—6, 6—3.

Natl. mixed doubles championship—At Phila. Cricket Club, Phila., Pa., Sept. 13, 1920. Mrs. G. W. Wightman and W. F. Johnson defeated Mrs. F. I. Mallory and C. Biddle, 6—4, 6—2.

N. Y. State championship for women—At N. Y. Tennis Club, Sept. 27, 1920. Miss M. Wagner of Yonkers, N. Y., defeated Miss E. V. Lynch of N. Y., 6—2, 6—0.

N. Y. State championship for men—At Orange Lawn Tennis Club, South Orange, N. J., June 14, 1920. Dean Mathey, N. Y., defeated R. S. Stoddart, Yonkers, N. Y., 6—0, 6—2, 6—2.

New England championship for men—At Hartford Golf Club, Hartford, Conn., May 31, 1920. L. M. Banks, New Haven, Conn., defeated G. W. Pike of Springfield, Mass., 6—4, 6—1, 6—2.

Middle States championship for Men—At Germantown Cricket Club, Phila., Pa., July 12, 1920. W. J. Johnson, Phila., Pa., defeated S. W. Pearson, Phila., Pa., 3—6, 6—1, 7—5, 6—1.

New England sectional doubles championship—At Agawam Hunt Club, Providence, R. I., July 12, 1920. J. W. Foster and J. Wheelwright of Boston, Mass., defeated L. B. Rice and J. S. Nicholl of Mass., 9—7, 6—4, 6—1.

Middle States championship, women—At Germantown Cricket Club, Phila., Pa., July 12, 1920. Mrs. M. B. Huff, Phila., Pa., defeated Mrs. W. P. Newhall, Phila., Pa., 6—2, 6—3.

Middle States championship doubles, men—At Germantown Cricket Club, Phila., Pa., July 12, 1920. W. J. Johnson and S. W. Pearson of Phila., Pa., defeated A. D. Thayer and R. Evans, Jr., of Phila., 6—2, 4—6, 6—2, 15—13.

Middle Atlantic championship—At Columbia Country Club, Chevy Chase, Md. (men), May 29, 1920. C. B. Doyle, Wash., D. C., defeated J. B. Moore, Sioux City, Ia., 6—3, 6—2, 6—0.

Middle Atlantic championship for women—At Columbia Country Club, Chevy Chase, Md., May 29, 1920. Miss M. Wakeford defeated Miss L. Kelley, 6—1, 2—6, 6—1.

Middle Atlantic championship, men's doubles—At Columbia Country Club, Chevy Chase, Md., May 29, 1920. C. H. Charest and W. Sweeney defeated Maj. A. Yencken and A. P. Graves, 6—2, 6—4, 3—6, 9—7.

Southern championship—At New Orleans Lawn Tennis Club, New Orleans, La., June 21, 1920. C. Y. Smith, Atlanta, Ga., defeated F. T. Payne, 6—3, 6—2.

Southern championship—At New Orleans Lawn Tennis Club, New Orleans, La. Men's doubles, June 21, 1920. E. Phelps and J. H. Bruns, New Orleans, defeated C. Y. Smith and E. Mansfield, Atlanta, 6—3, 6—2, 6—4.

Southern championship for women—At New Orleans Lawn Tennis Club, New Orleans, La., June 21, 1920. Miss E. Legendre defeated Miss M. Morgan, 6—3, 6—2.

Western championship for men—At Cincinnati Tennis Club, Cincinnati, O., June 28, 1920. W. T. Hayes, Chicago, Ill., defeated R. A. Holden, 6—0, 9—7, 5—7, 7—5.

Western championship for women—At Cincinnati Tennis Club, Cincinnati O., June 28, 1920. Miss R. Esch, Cleveland, O., defeated Miss M. Rask, Cleveland, O., 8—6, 4—6, 6—3.

Western championship for men's doubles—At Cincinnati Tennis Club, Cincinnati, O., June 28, 1920. W. T. Hayes and R. Burdick defeated L. Williams and J. Weber, 6—4, 3—6, 6—2, 6—4.

Northwestern championship—At Minneapolis Tennis Club, Minneapolis, Minn., July 17, 1920.

SPORTING RECORDS—LAWN TENNIS—*Continued.*

J. J. Armstrong defeated P. Bennett, 8—6, 6—4, 4—6, 6—4.

Northwestern championship for women—At Minneapolis Tennis Club, Minneapolis, Minn., July 17, 1920. Miss M. Davis, St. Paul, Minn., defeated Miss H. McCarthy, 6—0, 6—0.

Northwestern championship for men's doubles—At Minneapolis Tennis Club, Minneapolis, Minn., July 17, 1920. P. S. Brain and T. N. Jayne of Minneapolis defeated J. W. Adams and W. C. Burton of Minneapolis, 6—3, 7—5, 6—4.

Pacific Northwest championship for men—At Tacoma Tennis Club, Tacoma, Wash., Aug. 2, 1920. H. Kinsey, San Francisco, Cal., defeated I. Weinstein, San Francisco, 8—6, 6—1, 6—2.

Pacific Northwest championship for women—At Tacoma Tennis Club, Tacoma, Wash., Aug. 2, 1920. Miss S. Livingstone, Seattle, Wash., defeated Miss M. McDonald, Seattle, Wash., 13—11, 6—4.

Pacific Northwest championship for men's doubles—At Tacoma Tennis Club, Tacoma, Wash., Aug. 2, 1920. H. Kinsey and Mr. Scott defeated P. Neer and I. Weinstein, 6—2, 6—4, 6—3.

Mo. Valley championship for men—At Kansas City A. C., Kansas City, Mo., July 17, 1920. W. Bates, San Francisco, Cal., defeated E. Levy, San Francisco, 7—5, 8—6, 8—6.

Mo. Valley championship for women—At Kansas City A. C., Kansas City, Mo., July 19, 1920. Marjorie Hires, Kansas City, defeated Miss E. Seavey, Kansas City, 6—2, 5—7, 6—3.

Mo. Valley championship, men's doubles—At Kansas City A. C., Kansas City, Mo., July 19, 1920. C. Speice and B. Parks of Oklahoma defeated P. Smith, Amis, Ia., and M. Dubach, Kansas City, Mo., 6—0, 4—6, 10—8, 6—4.

Calif. championship for men—At Berkeley Tennis Club, Berkeley, Cal., Sept. 4, 1920. W. J. Bates defeated M. Griffin, 6—1, 3—6, 7—5, 6—4.

Calif. championship for men's doubles—At Berkeley Tennis Club, Berkeley, Cal., Sept. 4, 1920. R. Kinsey and H. Kinsey defeated W. J. Bates and W. Parker, 6—0, 6—3, 6—3.

Calif. championship for women—At Berkeley Tennis Club, Berkeley, Cal., Sept. 4, 1920. Mrs. C. G. Clute defeated Miss J. Gunsberger, 6—1, 6—1.

Davis Cup matches (preliminary)—U. S. vs. France, at Eastbourne, Eng., July, 1920. Men's singles: W. M. Johnston (U. S.), defeated A. H. Gobert (France), 6—3, 8—6, 6—3. W. T. Tilden 2d defeated W. H. Laurentz (France), 4—6, 6—2, 6—1, 6—3.

Men's doubles, U. S. vs. France—W. M. Johnston and W. T. Tilden 2d (U. S.), defeated A. H. Gobert and W. H. Laurentz, 6—2, 6—3, 6—2.

Davis Cup matches, U. S. vs. England—At Eastbourne, Eng., July, 1920. Men's singles: W. M. Johnston (U. S.), defeated J. C. Parke (Eng.), 6—4, 6—4, 2—6, 3—6, 2—6. W. T. Tilden 2d defeated A. R. F. Kingscot (Eng.), 4—6, 6—1, 6—3, 6—1.

Men's doubles, U. S. vs. England—W. M. Johnston and W. T. Tilden 2d defeated J. C. Parke and A. R. F. Kingscot, 8—6, 4—6, 4—6, 6—3, 6—2.

W. M. Johnston defeated A. R. F. Kingscot, 6—3, 4—6, 3—6, 6—4, 7—5.

W. T. Tilden 2d defeated J. C. Parke, 6—2, 6—3, 7—5, 6—3, 7—5.

Southwestern championship for men—At Dallas Club, Dallas, Tex., July 24, 1920. B. B. Hogue defeated L. Thalheimer, 6—3, 6—3, 6—0.

Southwestern championship for men's doubles—At Dallas Club, Dallas, Tex., July 24, 1920. B. B. Hogue and Mr. Wright defeated J. B. Adoue and E. Rees, 6—4, 1—6, 6—0, 6—4.

Davis Cup Matches, Finals.

Played at Auckland, New Zealand, Dec. 30 and 31, 1920, and Jan. 1, 1921.

Singles.

William T. Tilden 2d (America) defeated Norman E. Brookes (Australasia), 10—8, 6—4, 1—6 and 6—4.

William M. Johnston (America) defeated Gerald L. Patterson (Australasia), 6—4, 6—1 and 6—1.

William T. Tilden 2d (America) defeated Gerald L. Patterson (Australasia), 5—7, 6—2, 6—3 and 6—3.

William M. Johnston (America) defeated Norman E. Brookes (Australasia), 5—7, 7—5, 6—3 and 6—3.

Doubles.

William T. Tilden 2d and William M. Johnston (America) defeated Norman E. Brookes and Gerald L. Patterson (Australasia), 4—6, 6—4, 6—0 and 6—4.

ROWING.

March 27—Cambridge beat Oxford at London in 4-mile race by 4 lengths.

April 3—Yale varsity eight-oar beat Penn. at Phila. in 1 mile and 550-yard race by two-thirds length in 6:44. Yale beat Penn. in junior varsity by one-fourth length in 7:00 3-5.

April 24—Yale varsity eight beat Columbia at Derby, Conn., by 2¼ lengths in 2-mile race in 0:97 2-5. Yale won junior race by half a length in 11:21 4-5.

April 26—Navy varsity eight beat Harvard in 2-mile race at Annapolis by 4 lengths in 11:48. Navy second crew beat Harvard by 5½ lengths in 12:15. Navy plebs beat Harvard freshmen by 4 lengths in 12:24.

May 1—Princeton varsity eight won triangular races at Cambridge, Mass., over 1⅞-miles course by three-quarters of a length from Harvard. Penn. third, 9:47. Princeton freshmen beat Harvard by half a length.

May 8—Navy varsity beat Columbia at Annapolis by 5 lengths in 7:19. Navy seconds beat Columbia by 7 lengths in 7:24 4-5. Plebs beat Columbia freshmen by 10 lengths in 7:49⅕.

May 15—Cornell varsity eight won triangular race at Princeton by one-third length from Princeton; Yale third in 9:16. Cornell won freshman race by 5 lengths from Princeton in 9:18. Yale third. Princeton junior eight beat Yale in 9:30.

May 15—In 2-mile race at Annapolis, Syracuse varsity eight beat Navy by 7 ft. in 10:20 1-5. Navy won second varsity by 7 ft. in 10:21.

May 23—Cornell varsity eight beat Harvard at Ithaca in 2-mile race by 2 lengths in 10:47. Cornell freshmen beat Harvard by 4 lengths in 10:50.

May 24—Washington varsity eight beat California at Seattle, Wash., in 6:35. Washington won freshman race, 2 miles, in 10:54.

May 28—Navy varsity eight won Childs Cup in opening of Amer. Rowing Assn. regatta at Phila. in 1 mile 550-yard race by three-quarters length from Princeton. Penn. third and Columbia fourth. Time, 7:03 2-5.

May 20—Navy varsity eight won Steward's Cup at Phila. in 1 mile 550-yard race in 6:40 1-5. Syracuse 2d, Princeton 3d; Union B. C., Boston, 4th. Navy plebs won junior collegiate race in 6:31 2-5; Syracuse 2d, Princeton 3d, Harvard 4th. Vesper won from Undine in 7:19 3-5 (record). Vesper 4-scull beat N. Y. A. C. in 6:55 (record).

June 19—Syracuse won intercollegiate 2-mile varsity eight-oared race at Ithaca, N. Y., by 1⅓ lengths from Cornell in 11:02 3-5. Columbia 3d, Penn. 4th. Cornell won freshman eight-oared race in 10:45 3-5 by 4 lengths from Syracuse. Penn. 3d and Columbia 4th. Cornell junior eight won in 10:45 3-5. Syracuse 2d, Penn. 3d and Columbia 4th.

June 25—Harvard varsity eight at New London, Conn., beat Yale in 4-mile race by 6 lengths in 23:11.

July 3—Magdalen College, Oxford, won Grand Challenge Cup at Henley-on-Thames, England, beating Leander eight-oared crew by 2 lengths in 7:24. J. Beresford, Jr., won diamond sculls, beating D. H. L. Gollan in 8:57. Magdalen College won Steward's Challenge Cup, beating Thomas Rowing Club by 5 lengths in 8:08.

July 9—Lincoln Park Boat Club won Central State Rowing Assn. regatta at Chicago, with 23½ points. Grand Rapids, Mich., 15½; Western Rowing, 8; Detroit, 6.

July 10—Lincoln Park Boat Club won canoe event of regatta with 31 points. Columbia Canoe Club, 15; Grand Rapids Boat Club, 14.

July 19—Syracuse varsity eight beat Duluth Boat Club eight at Duluth, Minn., in 1¼-mile race by 2 ft. in 6:17.

July 23—Navy won intermediate eight-oared title of U. S. in national amateur regatta at Worcester, Mass. Duluth Boat Club won intermediate four-oared title. Pennsylvania Barge Club won senior international four-oared event, with Duluth 2d and Century Boat Club, St. Louis, 3d.

July 24—Results in national regatta at Worcester, Mass.: Championship singles won by J. B. Kelly, Vesper B. C., in 7:51. Senior eight championship won by Navy in 6:20, Syracuse 2d

SPORTING RECORDS—ROWING—*Continued.*

and Duluth 3d. Senior doubles won by Costello and Kelly, Vesper B. C., in 7:44. Senior quadruple title won by Undine Barge Club, Phila., in 6:54. Senior four title won by Penn Barge Club, Phila., in 7:14.

July 31—Toronto varsity eight won Harlan memorial trophy in senior eight-oared race at Royal Canadian Henley regatta at St. Catherines, Ont. Argonaut Rowing Club No. 1, 2d and Lincoln Park Rowing Club, Chicago, 3d.

SOCCER.

Soccer football more than held its own during the year 1920, which was especially noteworthy for the trip undertaken by the St. Louis All-American team to Sweden, where a record of seven victories, five draws and only two losses, was made. The National Challenge Trophy competition, under the auspices of the United States Football Association, went to the West for the first time and was won by the Ben Miller A. C. of St. Louis, which defeated the Fore River F. C. of Quincy, Mass., by 2 goals to 1 in the final round at St. Louis. In the Western semi-final the Ben Millers defeated the Packard F. C. of Detroit by 4 to 2, and in the Eastern semi-final the Fore Rivers defeated Robins Dry Dock of Brooklyn by 2 to 1. The Bethlehem Steel Corporation eleven, so long the national champions, were eliminated by Robins Dry Dock in the fifth round. The cup of the American Football Association was won by Robins Dry Dock of Brooklyn, which defeated Bethlehem by 1—0 in the final round at Harrison, N. J. Robins Dry Dock also captured the cup of the Southern New York State Football Association. Clan MacDuff of New York was first in the N. Y. State Football League, and Tebo Yacht Basin of Brooklyn first in the Metropolitan Football League.

TRAP SHOOTING.

Amer. amateur championship at single targets—F. S. Wright, Buffalo, N. Y., 197x200 and 25 straight in shoot off.

Professional championship at single targets—C. G. Spencer, St. Louis, 195x200 from 18 yds.

Amer. amateur championship at double targets—P. H. O'Brien, Butte, Mont., 92x100.

Amer. amateur 18-yd. championship—Mark Arie, Champaign, Ill., 198x200.

Women's amateur trapshooting championship—Mrs. J. H. Bruff, Pittsburgh, Pa., 85x100.

Grand Amer. handicap of clay targets—A. L. Ivins, Red Bank, N. J., 99x100 from 19 yds.

N. Y. A. C.'s amateur championship of America at clay birds—J. Clark, Jr., Worcester, Mass., 197x200.

Boston A. A.'s patriot day championship—G. H. Hunt, Boston, 143x150.

TROTTING.

Peter Manning, the leading money winner of the year, stood out among the trotters with three titles to his credit. He stepped the fastest heat of the year, a mile in 2:02½, the best time for either a gelding or a 4-year-old, and also won the fastest 3-heat race, the times being 2:03, 2:02¾ and 2:02½.

Miss Bertha Dillon carried off the honors among the 3-year-old fillies, with a mark of 2:02¾.

Among the 3-year-old pacers Frisco Jane stood at the top of the list with a mark of 2:01¼, and Rifle Grenade was the fastest 3-year-old gelding with a mark of 2:01¾.

YACHTING.

THE AMERICA'S CUP—RECORD OF RACES.

1851—Aug. 22. Royal Y. C. of England offered cup to winner of yacht race around Isle of Wight. The course was 60 miles. The race was won by the schooner yacht America, designed by George Steers for J. C. Stevens of the N. Y. Yacht Club. The America was 94 ft. over all, 88 ft. on the water line, 22½ ft. beam and 11½ ft. draft. There was no time allowance and the competing yachts ranged in size from a three-masted 392-ton schooner, the Brilliant, to the 47-ton cutter the Aurora, which came in second. The time of the America was 10 hrs. and 34 min.; that of the Aurora was 24 min. slower. The cup after that became known as the America's cup and has been successfully defended for 68 years.

1870—Aug. 8. N. Y. Y. C. course; Magic, 3.58:21; Cambria, 4:37:38.

1871—Oct. 16. N. Y. Y. C. course: Columbia, 6:19.41; Livonia, 6:46:45. Oct. 18, 20 miles to windward off Sandy Hook and return: Columbia, 3:07:41¾; Livonia, 3:18:15½. Columbia disabled in third race Oct. 19. Oct. 21, 20 miles to windward off Sandy Hook and return: Sappho, 5:39:02; Livonia, 6.09:23. Oct. 23, N. Y. Y. C. course: Sappho, 4:16:17; Livonia, 5:11:55:

1876—Aug. 11. N. Y. Y. C. course: Madeleine, 5.23:54; Countess of Dufferin, 5:34:53. Aug. 12, 20 miles to windward off Sandy Hook and return: Madeleine, 7:18:46; Countess of Dufferin, 7:46:00.

1881—Nov. 9. N. Y. Y. C. course: Mischief, 4:17:00; Atalanta, 4:45.39¼. Nov. 10, 16 miles to leeward off Sandy Hook and return: Mischief, 4:54:53; Atalanta, 5:33:47.

1885—Sept. 14. N. Y. Y. C. course: Puritan, 6:06:05; Genesta, 6:22:24. Sept. 16, 20 miles to leeward off Sandy Hook Light and return: Puritan, 5:03:14; Genesta, 5:04:52.

1886—Sept. 9. N. Y. Y. C. course: Mayflower, 5:26:41; Galatea, 5:38.43. Sept. 11, 20 miles to leeward off Sandy Hook Light and return: Mayflower, 6:49:10; Galatea, 7:18:09.

1887—Sept. 27. N. Y. Y. C. course: Volunteer, 4.53:18; Thistle, 5:12:41¾. Sept. 30, 20 miles to windward off Scotland Light and return: Volunteer, 5:42:56¼; Thistle, 5:54:45.

1893—Oct. 7. 15 miles to windward off Sandy Hook Light and return: Vigilant, 4:05:47; Valkyrie, 4:11.35. Oct. 9, triangular 30-mile course, first leg to windward: Vigilant, 3:25:01; Valkyrie, 3:35:36. Oct. 13, 15 miles to windward off Sandy Hook Light and return: Vigilant, 3:24:39; Valkyrie, 3.25:19.

1895—Sept. 7. 15 miles to windward and return, east by south, off Point Seabright, N. J.: Defender, 4:57:55; Valkyrie III., 5:08:44. Sept. 11, triangular course, 10 miles to each leg: Valkyrie III., 3:55.09; Defender, 3:55:56; won by Defender on a foul. Sept. 13 Defender sailed over the course and claimed cup and race; claim allowed.

1899—Oct. 16 15 miles to windward and return, off Sandy Hook: Columbia, 4:53:53, Shamrock, 5:04:07. Oct. 17, triangular course, 10 miles to a leg: Columbia, 3:37:00; Shamrock snapped its topmast. Oct. 20, 15 miles to leeward and return. Columbia, 3:38:09; Shamrock, 3:43:26.

1901—Sept. 28. 15 miles to windward and return, off Sandy Hook: Columbia, 4:30:24; Shamrock II., 4:31:44. Oct. 3, triangular course: Columbia, 3:12.35; Shamrock II., 3:16:10. Oct. 4, 15 miles to leeward and return: Columbia, 4:32:57; Shamrock II., 4:33:38.

1903—Aug. 22. 15 miles to leeward and return, off Sandy Hook: Reliance, 3:31:17; Shamrock III., 3.41:17. Aug. 25, triangular course, 10 miles to leg: Reliance, 3:14:54; Shamrock III., 3:18:10. Sept. 3, 15 miles to windward and return: Reliance, 4:28:04; Shamrock III. did not finish.

Summary of the America Cup Races, 1920.

Off Sandy Hook.

	Start.	Finish.	Elapsed Time.	Corrected Time.
July 15—1st race—Shamrock wins:				
Shamrock..	12:01:38	4:26:26	———	4:24:48
Resolute...	12:00:04	(Withdrew—accident.)		
July 20—2d race—Shamrock wins:				
Shamrock..	12:15:48	5:38:06	5:22:18	5:22:18
Resolute...	12:16:26	5:48:11	5:31:45	5:24:44
(Shamrock won by 2m. 29s. corrected time.)				
July 21—3d race—Resolute wins:				
Resolute...	1:00:41	5:03:47	4:03:06	3:57:05
Shamrock..	1:00:22	5:03:28	4:03:06	4:03:06
(Resolute won by 7m. 1s. corrected time.)				
July 23—4th race—Resolute wins:				
Resolute...	1:01:33	4:39:25	3:37:52	3:31:12
Shamrock..	1:01:56	4:34:06	3:41:10	3:41:10
(Resolute won by 9m. 35s. corrected time.)				
July 27—5th race—Resolute wins:				
Resolute...	2:17:00	7:52:15	5:35:15	5:28:35
Shamrock..	2:17:00	8:05:20	5:48:20	5:48:20
(Resolute won by 19m. 45s. corrected time.)				

SPORTING RECORDS—*Continued.*

MISCELLANEOUS SPORTS.

Jan. 4—Spencer and Osterleter, United States, won 6-day bike race at Melbourne, Australia.

Feb. 12—Nel Nelson, Revelstoke, won Canadian amateur ski title at Revelstoke, B. C., with jump of 185 ft. standing. Anders Haugen won pro event with standing jump of 200 ft.

Feb. 29—Anders Haugen, at Dillon, Col., set world's ski record of 213 ft.

Feb. 29—George May, Akron, Ohio, won national horseshoe pitching title at St. Petersburg, Fla.

March 13—Goulet and Magin won 6-day bike race at New York.

May 14—William Kerber, Chicago, won 1-mile world's amateur championship roller skating race at Chicago in 2:57 2-5, world's record.

May 16—William Skrivan, Chicago, defended world's amateur roller skating title at Chicago, winning 43 points. Kerber, Chicago, 28.

June 27—Arthur Nieminsky, Unione Sportiva Italiana, at New York, set cycling unpaced road race record of 5:26:40 for 108.74 miles.

July 11—In Olympic bike eliminations at Floral Park, N. Y., J. B. Freeman, St. Louis, set record of 5:24:50 for 108.74 miles.

July 11—Fred Taylor, New York A. C., won national amateur bike sprint title at Newark, N. J., with 20 points. A. Young, Newark, 18.

July 23—Joseph Oszy, New York A. C., won all-around gym title of United States in National A. A. U. events at New York. He got one first, one second and two fourths.

July 24—Herbert Sime, Chicago, won national roque title at Chicago with 344 points in twelve games. Sime is 17 years old. H. Lyman, Topeka, 318 in twelve games.

Aug. 17—J. F. Horr, Boston, at Sandusky, Ohio, won American checker title, beating J. F. Bradford, Cleveland, in finals.

Aug. 18—Lee Friede, New York, won national canoe sailing title at Clayton, N. Y., making 6 miles in 1:05:03.

Sept. 25—G. G. Chapp, Chicago, at Chicago, set world's record of 195 ft. average for quarter ounce distance bait event. His longest cast was 204 ft.

Oct. 17—Dr. H. J. Morlan, Chicago, at Chicago, set world's record in light tackle dry fly accuracy with 100 per cent.

Nov. 3—Sgt. Maj. Crittenden at Fulham Drill Hall, London, Eng., set world's amateur record for continuous club swinging of 70 hours.

Nov. 27—Ray Eaton and Harry Kaiser won 6-day bike race at 22d Regt. Armory, New York, with 836 points.

1920 OLYMPIC GAMES.

The complete summaries of the seventh Olympic games, held last summer in Antwerp, show that United States participants were victorious in the track and field events, shooting, rowing and swimming. Several world records were registered by wearers of the American shield. There were also new Olympic records accredited to the U. S. representatives. Frank Foss, the former Cornell pole vaulter, competing for the United States team, vaulted for a height of 13 ft. 5 1-3 inches, which doubtless was the greatest performance of the games. Frank Loomis, one of the Chicago A. A.'s colorbearers, covered the 400 meters hurdles event in the fast time of 54 seconds, thereby creating a world record. Among other great performances was that of R. W. Landon, winning the high jump with a mark of 1:94 meters, a new Olympic record.

Earl Thompson, although a student of Dartmouth, but representing his place of nativity, Canada, hung up a world record for the 110 hurdles by covering these timbers in 14 4-5 seconds. Harold E. Barron, a product of West Philadelphia High School and wearing the insignia of the Meadowbrook Club of that city, was upon Thompson's heels when the record was smashed.

C. T. Osborne, wearing the United States colors, won the individual shooting honors with army rifle at 300 meters standing. His score was 56 out of 60. United States won the team shoot in the combined 300 and 600-meter event with 572.

In the boxing bouts there was more or less dissatisfaction in the results. Uncle Sam's experts, however, took their defeats gracefully and finished in the matter of points only one behind Great Britain. The catch-as-catch-can wrestling bouts went to the United States with 9½ points.

John B. Kelly not only beat the world's best single scullers, but, with Paul Costello in his boat, won the double sculls, Kelly's achievement being recorded as one of the greatest of all in the entire Olympic history.

The following records have been compiled in the various events:

Chronological Record.

Apr. 24—U. S. beat Switzerland in hockey prelim., 29 to 0.

Apr. 25—Canada beat U. S. in hockey semifinal, 2 to 0.

Apr. 26—Canada won hockey title, beating Sweden, 12 to 1. Finland won figure skating title, with Norway second, England third and U. S. fourth.

Apr. 27—Grafstrom, Sweden, won first place in men's figure skating; Krogh, Norway, second; Strixrud, Norway, third; Salelow, Sweden, fourth; N. W. Niles, U. S., fifth. U. S. beat Sweden in hockey elimination, 7 to 0.

Apr. 28—U. S. won second place in hockey, beating Czechoslovaks, 10 to 0.

Apr. 29—Czechoslovaks won third place in hockey, beating Sweden, 1 to 0.

July 23—U. S. won final in trapshooting team event, with 547 out of 600. Belgium, 503; Sweden, 500; Great Britain, 488; Canada, 474. Individual U. S. score—F. M. Troeh, 94; M. Arie, 94; H. Bonser, 93; F. W. McNier, 93; F. S. Wright, 89; J. Clark Jr., 84.

July 24—U. S. got all first five places in individual trapshooting event. Mark Arie first with 95 out of 100; F. M. Troeh, 93; F. Bonner, F. S. Wright and F. Plum, 87 each; Montgomery, Canada, 85; Hamilton, Canada, 82.

July 25—Spain beat U. S. in pony polo, 13 to 3.

July 26—Norway won running-shooting event with 178; Finland, 159; U. S., 158; Sweden, 153.

July 27—England beat Belgium in pony polo, 8 to 3.

July 29—U. S. awarded third place in pony polo event.

July 29—U. S. won rifle-shooting team match at 200 meters, lying down, with 289 out of 300; France, 288; Switzerland, 281; Norway and Finland, 279 each. Denmark won team shoot at 300 meters, standing, with 265; Sweden, 255; U. S., 253; Italy, 251; France, 249.

July 30—C. T. Osborne, U. S., won individual target shoot with army rifle at 300 meters, standing, with 56 out of 60; Madison, Denmark, 55. U. S. won team shoot in combined 300 and 600-meter event with 572; Norway, 565; France, 563. U. S., South Africa and Sweden tied for first in 600-meter team shoot with 287. Johnson and Paroche, France; Kuehen, Switzerland, and Oelson, Norway, tied for first in 200-meter individual event, lying down, with perfect scores of 60. In 300-meter individual shootoff for third place Musselein, U. S., won from Loarsen, Denmark; Jamsen, Belgium, and Tiechi, Italy. In 600-meter individual shoot L. S. Spooner, U. S.; Theofilakis, Greece; Johansen, Sweden, and Erickson, Sweden, tied with 59. U. S. won shootoff for second place from Sweden in 300-meter, standing position, team event.

July 31—Great Britain won final in pony polo event, beating Spain, 13 to 11.

Aug. 2—In second shootoff tie in 600-meter rifle shooting team event U. S. won with 284; South Africa, 279. U. S. won pistol shooting team event with 2,372; Brazil second. K. T. Frederick, U. S., won individual title with 494. Afranio Costa, Brazil, 489. U. S. won small-bore rifle team match with 1,889. N. A. Muesselein, U. S., won individual title with 391. Capt. A. D. Rothrock, U. S., 386; Sergeant Fenton, U. S., 385.

Aug. 3—Guilheim Papaeuse, Brazil, won revolver target event at 30 meters with 274; R. C. Bracken, U. S., 272; Zuranap, Switzerland, 269; Frederick, U. S., 266; Harant, U. S., 264; Lane, U. S., 258; A. H. Bayles, U. S., 244. U. S. won target shoot—rifle, pistol and revolver events—won 43 points; Sweden, 11; Norway, 9; Denmark, 7; Switzerland, 5½; Brazil, 5; France, 4; South Africa, 2; Finland, 1½. U. S. won revolver match with 1,300. Greece, 1,275; Switzerland, 1,270.

SPORTING RECORDS—OLYMPIC GAMES—*Continued.*

Aug. 6—Belgium won archery match with 2,698; France, 2,491.

Aug. 10—Georges, Belgium, won 50-kilometer bicycle race in 1:16:42. Alden, England, second; Kelaar, Holland, third.

Aug. 13—France won 170-kilometer bicycle race; Sweden, second; Belgium, third. Standing to date in Olympic games—U. S., 57 points; Norway, 56; Sweden, 39; England, 20; Holland, 18; Belgium, 13; France, 10; Finland, 7; Denmark, 7; Brazil, 6; South Africa, 6; Switzerland, 5; Canada, 3; Italy, 3; Spain, 2; Greece, 2; Czechoslovakia, 1.

Aug. 15—Javelin throw, won by J. Myrra, Finland, with 65.78 meters; H. Peltonen, Finland, second; P. Johansson, Finland, third; J. J. Saaristo, Finland, fourth; Kolumberg, Esthonia, fifth (world's record). In first round of fencing, foils, U. S. beat Holland, 10 bouts to 6. Capt. H. M. Rayner, U. S., won all his bouts.

Aug. 16—100-meter dash won by C. W. Paddock, U. S., in 10 4-5s.; M. Kirksey, U. S., second; Harry Edwards, Great Britain, third; J. Scholz, U. S., fourth; Ali Khan, France, fifth; L. Murchison, U. S., sixth. 400-meter hurdles won by F. F. Loomis, U. S., in 54s. (world record). J. K. Martin, U. S., second; A. Desch, U. S., third; G. Andre, France, fourth; C. Daggs, U. S., fifth; C. Christiernssen, Sweden, sixth. Pentathlon won by E. Lethonen, Finland, 14 points; E. Bradley, U. S., 25 points; B. Hamilton, U. S., R. Legendre, U. S., and Lortinen, Finland, tied for third with 26 each; H. Lovland, Norway, 27; Ohlsson, Sweden, 30. In fencing foils France beat U. S., 14 bouts to 2. U. S. beat Denmark, 9 to 7. Italy won first place in foils by beating France, 9 to 7. U. S. won third place, beating Great Britain, 32 touches to 31.

Aug. 17—High jump won by R. W. Landon, U. S., at 1.94 meters (Olympic record). Ekelund, Sweden, and H. P. Muller, U. S., tied for second; J. Murphy, U. S.; W. Whalen, U. S., and R. H. Baker, Great Britain, tied for fourth. 5,000-meter run won by Guillemot, France, in 14:55; Nurmi, Finland, second; Backman, Sweden, third; Koskeniemie, Finland, fourth; C. E. Blewitt, Great Britain, fifth; Seagrove, Great Britain, sixth. Graeco-Roman wrestling preliminaries—Swigart, U. S., beat Rangleers, Italy, in 3 minutes with double-bar arm. 800-meter run won by A. G. Hill, Great Britain, in 1:53 2-5; E. Eby, U. S., second; B. G. D. Rudd, Great Britain, third; E. D. Mountain, Great Britain, fourth; D. M. Scott, U. S., fifth; A. L. Sprott, U. S., sixth. Tug-of-war, Great Britain beat U. S. in first round in two pulls, 13 2-5s. and 1:24. Holland beat Italy in second round.

Aug. 18—110-meter hurdles won by E. Thompson, Canada, in 14 4-5s. (world record). R. E. Brown, U. S., second; F. S. Murray, U. S., third; Wilson, New Zealand, fourth; W. Smith, U. S., fifth; C. Christiensen, Sweden, sixth. Broad jump, won by Petersen, Sweden, with 7.15 meters; C. E. Johnson, U. S., second; Abrahamsson, Sweden, third; R. Templeton, U. S., fourth; Aastad, Norway, fifth; Franksson, Sweden, sixth. Tug-of-war—Great Britain beat Belgium in 30 3-5s. Graeco-Roman wrestling prelims—In heavyweight class Hansen, Denmark, beat A. M. Weyand, U. S., in 7:00; Linford, Finland, beat E. E. Wilkie, U. S., in 30:00. In light heavyweight class, Eriksen, Denmark, beat N. Pendleton, U. S., in 22:00, when latter was disqualified for using a barred arm hold. F. W. Marchle, U. S., beat Leonardsen, Sweden. 10,000-meter walk, won by Frigerio, Italy, in 48:06 1-5; J. B. Pearman, U. S., second; C. E. J. Gunn, Great Britain, third; McMaster, South Africa, fourth; W. Behir, Great Britain, fifth; T. A. Maroney, U. S., sixth. Shotput, won by Porkola, Finland, with 14.155; Nicklander, Finland, second; H. B. Liversedge, U. S., third; P. J. McDonald, U. S., fourth; B. Nisson, Sweden, fifth; Jammer, Esthonia, sixth. Graeco-Roman wrestling prelims—In welterweight class, G. Metroupoulas, U. S., outpointed Vonyoukas, Greece; Janssens, Belgium, pinned A. R. Swigart, U. S., in 4:00. In featherweight class, Kolkonen, Denmark, beat J. Vorres, U. S., in 7:00. Friman, Finland, beat J. Gallery, U. S., in 4:00.

Aug. 19—Great Britain beat Holland in tug-of-war and won first place; Holland, second; Belgium, third; U. S. fourth; Italy, fifth. 1,500-meter run, won by A. G. Hill, Great Britain, in 4:01 4-5; P. J. Baker, Great Britain, second; M. L. Shields, U. S., third; Vohralitz, Czechoslovakia, fourth; Lundgren, Sweden, fifth; Andre, France, sixth. Hammer throw, won by P. J. Ryan, U. S., with throw of 52,875 meters; C. Lind, Sweden, second; B. Bennett, U. S., third; Svensson, Sweden, fourth; McGrath, U. S., fifth; T. L. Nicholson, Great Britain, sixth. Graeco-Roman prelims—Featherweight class, Eriman, Finland, beat Kahukouken, Finland, in 4:00. Lightweight class, Tamminen, Finland, outpointed Vare, Finland. Middleweight class, Westergren, Sweden, beat Lindfort, Finland, in 32:00. Lightweight class, Johnson, Sweden, beat Sint, Holland, in 16:00. Heavyweight class, Lindfors, Finland, beat Ahlgreen, Sweden, in 75:00.

Aug. 20—Pole vault, won by Frank Foss, U. S., with height of 4.9 meters, about 13 ft. 5½ in. (world's record); H. Petersen, Denmark, second. In jumpoff of tie for third, Myers, U. S., won; Knourek, U. S., fourth; Rydberg, Sweden, fifth; Jorgensen, Sweden, sixth. 10,000-meter run, won by Nurmi, Finland, in 31:45 2-5; Guillemot, France, second; J. Wilson, Great Britain, third; Maccario, Italy, fourth; Manhes, France, fifth; Lumatainen, Finland, sixth. 200-meter run, won by A. Woodring, U. S., in 22s.; C. W. Paddock, U. S., second; H. F. Edwards, Great Britain, third; L. Murchison, U. S., fourth; G. Davidson, New Zealand, fifth; Oostelak, South Africa, sixth. 400-meter run, won by B. G. Rudd, South Africa, in 49 3-5s.; G. Butler, Great Britain, second; Engdahl, Sweden, third; F. J. Shea, U. S., fourth; C. C. Davis, Great Britain, fifth; Dafel, South Africa, sixth. 3,000-meter steeplechase, won by P. Hodge, Great Britain, in 10:02 2-5; P. Fynn, U. S., second; Ambrosini, Italy, third; Matson, Sweden, fourth; M. Devanney, U. S., fifth; A. Hulsenbosen, U. S., sixth. Sword duelling, Switzerland beat U. S., 7 to 6; U. S. beat Czechoslovakia, 11 to 5.

Aug. 21—3,000-meter walk won by Frigiro, Italy, in 13:14 1-5; Parker, Australia, second; R. Remer, U. S., third; McMaster, South Africa, fourth; T. Maroney, U. S., fifth; C. S. Dowson, Great Britain, sixth. Hop, step and jump, won by Timios, Finland, with 14.5 meters; Jannsson, Sweden, second; Almof, Sweden, third; Shaling, Sweden, fourth; S. G. Landers, U. S., fifth; D. Ahearn, U. S., sixth. 56-pound weight put, won by P. J. McDonald, U. S., with 11,265 meters; P. J. Ryan, U. S., second; Lind, Sweden, third; A. McDiarmid, Canada, fourth; Svensson, Sweden, fifth; Peterson, Finland, sixth. Duelling sword, U. S. beat Great Britain, 8 to 7; France beat U. S., 12 to 2. Boxing, bantamweight class, S. Vogel, U. S., beat Cochon, France; E. Hartman, U. S., beat Bowling, Great Britain. Light heavyweight class, Schell, U. S., won from MacGregor, South Africa, on a foul. Lightweight class, S. Mosberg, U. S., beat Solvin, France; F. Cassidy, U. S., beat Jensen, Holland. Flyweight class, P. Zivic, U. S., beat Andreir, Belgium; F. De Genero, U. S., beat Nilsen, Norway. Graeco-Roman wrestling, finals, Finland won with 19 points; Sweden, 7; Denmark, 3; Norway, 1. Decathlon, won by H. Lovland, Norway, with 677,355 points; B. Hamilton, U. S., second; Ohlison, Sweden, third; Hjalman, Sweden, fourth; Nilsson, Sweden, fifth; Wickholm, Finland, sixth.

Aug. 22—Marathon, won by H. Kolehmainen, Finland, in 2:32:35 4-5 (Olympic record); Lossman, Esthonia, second; Biasti, Italy, third; Broos, Belgium, fourth; Tomoskoki, Finland, fifth; Roose, Denmark, sixth; J. Organ, U. S., seventh; Hansen, Denmark, eighth; Fallgren, Finland, ninth; T. Kolehmainen, Finland, tenth; C. Linder, U. S., eleventh; C. Meller, U. S., twelfth. 400-meter relay race, won by U. S. (C. Paddock, J. Scholz, L. Murchison and M. Kirksey) in 42 15s., world's record; France, second; Sweden, third; Great Britain, fourth; Denmark, fifth; Luxembourg, sixth. 3,000-meter team race, won by U. S. Order of finish: H. H. Brown, U. S., first, in 8:51 1-5; E. Bachman, Sweden, second; A. A. Schardt, U. S., third; Burtin, Great Britain, fourth; C. Bleuette, Great Britain, fifth; I. Dresser, U. S., sixth. Discus throw, won by Nicklander, Finland, with 44,685 meters; A. Taipale, Finland, second; A. R. Pope, U. S., third; O. Zallhagen, Sweden, fourth; U. K. Bartlett, U. S., fifth; Ericksson, Sweden, sixth. Swimming in 100-meter back stroke prelim.—W. Kealoha, U. S., set world record of 1:14.

SPORTING RECORDS—OLYMPIC GAMES—*Continued.*

Aug. 22—1,000-meter relay race, won by Great Britain in 3:22 1-5; South Africa, second; France, third; U. S., fourth; Sweden, fifth. Cross-country run, about 10 kilometers, won by Nurmi, Finland, in 27:15; Bachman, Sweden, second; Liimatainen, Finland, third; Wilson, Great Britain, fourth; Hegarty, Great Britain, fifth; Conquienir, Italy, sixth; (team summary: Finland, 10 points; Great Britain, 21; Sweden, 23; U. S., 36; France, 40; Belgium, 50). Boxing, heavyweight class, Rawson, Great Britain, knocked out S. Stewart, U. S., in third round; W. T. Spengler, U. S., beat Cruesen, Belgium. Light heavyweight class, E. Eagan, U. S., beat Folstock, South Africa; Soriday, Norway, beat Schell, U. S. Middleweight class, Mallin, Great Britain, beat S. Lagonia, U. S.; Prudhomme, Canada, beat Gouillet, France. Welterweight class, Wistatcher, U. S., beat Stocktaug, Norway; E. Colberg, U. S., beat Gillett, France; Schneider, Canada, beat Steen, Norway. Lightweight class, S. Mosberg, U. S., beat Grace, Great Britain; Johansen, Denmark, beat F. Cassidy, U. S.; Newton, Canada, beat Saterhang, Norway. Featherweight class, J. Zivas, U. S., beat Clausen, Denmark. Swimming, 100-meter backstroke, won by W. Kealoha, U. S., in 1:15 1-5, Olympic record; R. Gegeris, U. S., second; Blitz, Belgium, third; P. McGillivray, U. S., fourth; H. Kruger, U. S., fifth; Duke Kahanamoku, U. S., beat own record in 100-meter free-style swim, making 1:01 1-5, but it was called "no race." Water polo, U. S. beat Greece, 7 to 0; Great Britain beat Spain, 9 to 0. Tennis, in singles finals, Raymond, South Africa, beat Kumagae, Japan, 5—7, 6—4, 7—5, 6—4. In doubles Turnbull and Woodman, Great Britain, beat Kumagae and Kashio, Japan, 6—2, 5—7, 7—5, 7—5. In woman's singles Suzanne Lenglen, France, beat Miss Holman, Great Britain, 6—3, 6—0. In doubles, Mrs. McNair and Miss McKane, Great Britain, beat Mrs. Beamish and Miss Holman, Great Britain, 8—6, 6—4. In mixed doubles, Mlle. Lengler and Max Decugis, France, beat Miss McKane and Woodman, Great Britain, 6—4, 6—2. Boxing, bantamweight class, DeGenero, U. S., beat Peterson, Denmark. In light heavyweight class, Eagan, U. S., beat Sorsdal, Norway. In lightweight class, Mosberg, U. S., beat Johansen, Denmark. In heavyweight class, Rawson, Great Britain, knocked out Peterson, Denmark.

Aug. 25—Final points in boxing: Great Britain, 11; U. S., 10; Canada, 9; Denmark, 6; France, 6. Swimming: 100-meter, free stroke (women), won by Ethelda Bleibtrey, U. S.; Irene Guest, U. S., second; Frances C. Schroth, U. S., third—1:13 3-5 (Olympic record). 1,500 meter, free stroke, won by N. Ross, U. S., in 22:23 1-5; Vernot, Canada, second; Beaurepaire, Australia, third; F. K. Kahele, U. S., fourth. 400-meter breaststroke, won by Malmroth, Sweden, in 6:31 4-5; Henning, Sweden, second; Aaltoonen, Finland, third; J. Howell, U. S., fourth.

Aug. 26—Finals in gymnastic team competition. European method—Italy won with 359.855 out of 404 points; Belgium, second; France, third. In individual competition, Zomposi, Italy, won with 88.33 out of 97; Marcos, France, second; Garnier, France, third; F. J. Kriz, U. S., tenth. Catch-as-catch-can wrestling, lightweights. Svensson, Sweden, beat G. M. Metropoules, U. S., in third round; Arntella, Finland, beat J. Shimmon, U. S., in quarter finals. Featherweights, C. D. Eckerly, U. S., beat Dialetes, Greece; S. N. Gerson, U. S., beat Mackinson, Great Britain. Middleweights, MacDonald, U. S. beat Lopponen, Canada. Light heavies, W. S. Maurer, U. S., beat Sanrau, France; J. K. Redmon, U. S., beat Wilson, Great Britain. Heavyweights, N. Pendleton, U. S., beat Salida, Finland; F. J. Meyer, U. S., beat Mason, Great Britain. Water polo, Great Britain beat U. S., 7 to 2.

Aug. 27—L. E. Kuehn, U. S., won springboard diving competition; C. Pinkston, U. S., second; L. J. Ballach, U. S., third. Rowing, prelims.—J. Kelly, U. S., beat J. Jonglof, Sweden, in single sculls; Kelly and P. Costello, U. S., beat Haas and Veth, Holland, in double sculls; U. S. beat Belgium in eight-oared event; Great Britain beat Switzerland.

Aug. 28—Catch as can wrestling finals: U. S. won with 9½ points; Finland, 8; Sweden, 5½; Switzerland, 5; Great Britain, 2. Light heavyweights, Larson, Sweden, beat Courant, Switzerland, by default; C. F. Johnson, U. S., won second place in middleweights by beating A. M. Frantz, U. S., by default; W. S. Maurer, U. S., beat J. R. Redmond, U. S., for second place in light heavyweights. F. J. Meyers, U. S., and Milhoin, Sweden, tied for third in heavyweights. Rowing, prelims.—J. Kelly, U. S., beat Hatfield, New Zealand, in single sculls. U. S. eight-oared crew beat France, and Great Britain beat Norway. Swimming—Ethelda Bleibtrey, U. S., won 300-meter, free style, in 4:34 (world record); Margaret Woodbridge, U. S., second; Mrs. F. C. Schroth, U. S., third; Eleanor Uhl, U. S., fifth. 400-meter, free style, won by N. Ross, U. S., in 5:26 4-5; L. Langer, U. S., second; G. Vernot, Canada, third. Plain diving for women, won by Miss Fryland, Denmark; Miss Armstrong, Great Britain, second; Miss Oliver, Sweden, third; Aileen Riggin, U. S., fifth; Betty Grimes, U. S., sixth. In water polo U. S. beat Spain, 5 to 0.

Aug. 20—Swimming. 800-meter relay, won by U. S. (Kahanamoku, Ross, McGillivray and P. Kealoha) in 10:04 2-5 (Olympic record); Australia, second; Great Britain, third. 400-meter relay (women), won by U. S. (E. Bleibtrey, Irene Guest, Mrs. F. Schroth and Margaret Woodbridge) in 5:11 4-5. 200-meter breast stroke, won by Malcóth, Sweden, in 3:04 2-5; Henning, Sweden, second; Atlomen, Finland, third; J. Howell, U. S., fourth. 100-meter, free-style, won by Duke Kahanamoku, U. S., in 1:01 2-5 (record); P. Kealoha, U. S., second; W. W. Harris, U. S., third; Herald, Australia, fourth. Springboard diving for women, won by Aileen Riggin, U. S.; Helen Wainwright, U. S., second; Thelma Payne, U. S., third. Rowing, finals—U. S. eight-oared crew with coxswain, beat Great Britain in 2,000-meter race (about 1¼ miles) in 6:25 (world record). Jack Kelly won single sculls title, beating J. Beresford, Jr., Great Britain, in 7:35. Kelly and Costello, U. S., beat Italy by five lengths in double sculls; France, third. Switzerland won four-oared race in 6:54; U. S., second, and Norway, third. Italy won double sculls with coxswain in 7:56; France, second; Switzerland, third. Fancy diving, won by C. Pinkstone, U. S.; Aileer, Sweden, second; H. Prieste, U. S., third; L. J. Bahlback, U. S., sixth; Welliech, Brazil, seventh.

EAGLE FUND FOR DECORATING GRAVES IN FRANCE.

A fund was raised by The Eagle for the decoration of the graves of the Brooklyn dead in France on Memorial Day, under the supervision of the Paris Bureau. The people of Brooklyn welcomed the opportunity to assure themselves that the graves would be decorated and contributions reached the total of more than $600. The extensive plans of the American Legion along this same line caused the Bureau to include the photography as well as decorating the graves, the photographs being sent to the relatives of the soldiers through the Index Dept. of The Eagle. Cemeteries in France from Calais to Verdun, and in Flanders, were visited during a period from May 29 to August 30, 1920.

The United States produces more than one-half of the world's supply of cotton.

BROOKLYN DAILY EAGLE TRAIL.

When Glacier National Park opened for the season in June, 1920, The Brooklyn Daily Eagle Trail was turned over to the public. This 15-mile stretch of road, the last link in the series of motor highways uniting Banff, Canada, with Glacier Park, U. S. A., was made possible through the generosity of the members of The Brooklyn Daily Eagle National Parks Tour of 1919.

RECORD LENGTH OF SERVICE IN CONGRESS.

On Dec. 29, 1920, Representative Joseph G. Cannon of Illinois celebrated the completion of 44 years' membership of the House, having served longer in Congress than any other man in the history of the republic. Mr. Cannon first came to the House in 1872, and in Nov., 1920, was elected for the 23d time.

GENERAL CHRONOLOGY OF 1920.

January.

1. Government Sugar Control Bill for 1920 becomes law.
2. 4,500 Reds seized in raids.
3. France grants permission for removal of bodies of 20,000 American soldiers.
4. Violent earthquakes in Mexico, particularly fatal at Vera Cruz.
5. U. S. Supreme Ct. sustains constitutionality of Volstead Prohibition Enforcement Act.
7. New York Assembly suspends five Socialists.
8. W. J. Bryan, at Jackson Day banquet, urges compromise on ratification.
10. Treaty of Versailles ratified in Paris; peace becomes effective between Germany and Powers, excepting U. S.
11. Election of French Senators, first since beginning of war.
13. Pres. Wilson calls first meeting of Council of the League of Nations for Jan. 16, at Paris.
15. Senator Carter Glass leaves Treasury for Senate.
16. Prohibition Amendment goes into effect.—League of Nations formally launched in Paris, where Council meets.
17. Admiral Sims attacks Sec. Daniels in letter.—Paul Deschanel elected President of France.—Premier Clemenceau resigns; Millerand requested to form Cabinet.
20. Italian railway unions start strike for eight hour day.
21. Communist labor leaders indicted in Chicago.
22. Japanese Premier says Japan will keep her word in regard to Shantung.
23. Holland refuses surrender of former Kaiser.
24. Sec. Wilson of Labor Dept. holds American Communist Party to be revolutionary.
26. Henry P. Fletcher, U. S. Ambassador to Mexico, resigns; Matthias Erzberger, German Minister of Finance, shot and wounded at Berlin.
27. Goldman, Berkman and other deported aliens arrive at Petrograd; coal strike in Kansas ended.
28. Trial of Senator Newberry and others, charged with election offenses, begun at Grand Rapids.
29. U. S. Steel Corporation announces increase in wages.
31. British Government arrests 100 Sinn Feiners at Dublin.

February.

1. Viscount Grey writes letter to London Times favorable to Treaty reservations.
2. E. T. Meredith becomes Secretary of Agriculture, succeeding D. F. Houston, appointed Secretary of the Treasury.
7. F. K. Lane, Secretary of Dept. of Interior, resigns.
8. President Wilson accepts reservations proposed by Senator Hitchcock.
11. Council of League of Nations meets in London.—Robert U. Johnson appointed U. S. Ambassador to Rome.—Admiral Kolchak executed.
12. John Barton Payne appointed Sec. of the Interior.
13. Robert Lansing, Secretary of State, resigns at President's request.
17. Caillaux trial begins in Paris.
18. Paul Deschanel inaugurated President of the French Republic.
20. Bolsheviki take Archangel.
24. Sale by U. S. of German liners stayed by Court order.—Charles R. Crane appointed U. S. Minister to China.
25. President appoints Bainbridge Colby Secretary of State.—Asquith elected to Parliament.
28. Railroad Bill signed by President Wilson.

March.

1. Railroads returned to owners.—Supreme Court refuses to dissolve Steel Trust.
2. Governor Edwards of N. J. signs 3½ per cent. Liquor Bill.
5. Holland again refuses to deliver Kaiser.
6. Allies dispatch drastic letter to Turk leaders
7. Hotel Chamberlin, Old Point Comfort, destroyed by fire.
8. Supreme Court of U. S. declares unconstitutional the provisions of the Revenue Act imposing income tax on stock dividends.
10. Ward liner Esperanza runs ashore off Mexican coast.—House of Representatives approves peace time army of 299,000 men and 17,820 officers.
11. British Trades Unions vote against general strike.—U. S. Senate orders investigation of U. S. Grain Corporation.
12. Great Britain announces will pay all debts to U. S. with least possible delay.—New Hungarian Peace Treaty agreed upon by Peace Conference.
13. Revolt in Germany; Ebert Government overthrown by military coup d'etat; Dr. Wolfgang Kapp takes office as Chancellor.
15. U. S. Senate, by vote of 56 to 26, adopts Lodge reservation to Article X.—Emir Feisal declared King of Syria.
16. Kiel bombarded by a German cruiser and 400 persons reported killed.
17. Allies occupy Constantinople.—German revolt fails; Kapp resigns in favor of President Ebert.
18. U. S. Senate adopts 14 Lodge reservations and a reservation approving self-determination for Ireland.
19. U. S. Senate again rejects Treaty of Versailles.
20. Senator Newberry and 16 co-defendants found guilty of criminal conspiracy by Federal Grand Jury.
22. Henry Morgenthau nominated Ambassador to Mexico.
23. President ends Government price fixing on coal; distribution committees notified that they will cease to function on April 1.
24. Heavy fighting at Wessel between German Government troops and Communists.
25. T. W. Lawson arrested at Boston in drive against stock exploiters.
26. German Cabinet, headed by Premier Bauer, resigns; Mueller heads new Cabinet.
27. French Chamber of Deputies passes vote of confidence in Millerand.—Odessa occupied by Ukrainians.
28. Tornado sweeps eight States in Middle West, with heavy death toll and property loss.
29. Brotherhood of Locomotive Engineers and Brotherhood of Firemen and Enginemen formally affiliate with Am. Federation of Labor.
30. Crisis in Denmark owing to King Christian's dismissal of Zahle Cabinet.
31. Irish Home Rule Bill passes second reading in House of Commons.—France refuses Germany permission to send troops to Ruhr region.

April.

1. N. Y. State Assembly expels five Socialist Assemblymen.
3. German Govt. troops force Reds' retreat in Ruhr region.
5. Japanese troops storm and occupy Vladivostok.—New Cabinet formed in Denmark.
6. French forces seize Frankfort and four other German Rhine cities.
8. Belgian Govt. informs France that it will co-operate in occupation of Ruhr region.
9. Rail strike grows; food trains held up; mines and mills close.—House of Representatives adopts Peace resolution by majority of 93.—Salvador proposes Latin-Amer. Court of Arbitration, excluding U. S.
10. A. T. Hadley, Pres. of Yale, resigns, to take effect June, 1921.—Mexican State of Sonora revolts against Carranza Govt.
11. Rail strike gains in East; embargo on food and fuel.
12. Revolution in Guatemala forms new government with Carlos Herrera as Pres.—League of Nations favors mandate for free Armenia.
13. Sultan of Turkey proclaims Holy War against Nationalists.—Pres. Wilson names Railroad Labor Board to deal with strike situation.
14. President attends first Cabinet meeting since September, 1919.—Hunger striking Sinn Fein prisoners released from Mountjoy Prison, Dublin.
15. U. S. arrests 24 leaders in the insurgent strike of railroad men.—British Miners' Federation accepts government's offer of increase.
16. U. S. Government proposes to Allies that commercial relations be opened with Soviet Russia.—Bolshevik risings occur in Northern Italy.
17. Pres. Cabrera of Guatemala surrenders to Herrera.
19. Premiers meet at San Remo; reject Wilson demand to oust Turk.—Sir Auckland Geddes, new British Ambassador, arrives in U. S.

GENERAL CHRONOLOGY—April—*Continued.*

20. Tornado in three Southern States razes towns, with great loss of life.
22. Caillaux, former Premier of France, found guilty of dealing with enemy and sentenced to three years' imprisonment and five years' banishment.
23. Amundsen reaches Behring Sea after 19 months in Arctic.—Three U. S. warships ordered to Mexican waters.
24. N. Y. Legislature passes 2.75 Beer Bill and adjourns.—Armenia recognized as independent republic by U. S.
25. Supreme Council at San Remo offers mandate for Armenia to U. S.; Great Britain given mandate for Palestine; France for Syria.
26. San Remo Conference adjourns after adopting Franco-British declaration warning Germany of invasion if treaty is evaded.—Canada, with British Govt. sanction, opens negotiations for establishment of direct diplomatic relations with U. S.
27. Great Jewish demonstration in London approves mandate for Palestine to Great Britain.
29. Dispatch reports that American mission at Aintab has been besieged by Turks since April 1.

May.

1. May Day passes quietly in U. S.—Paris riots cost three lives.—Sonora revolutionists capture Chihuahua City and menace capital.
2. Tornado in Cherokee County, Okla., causes 54 deaths.
3. U. S. destroyers sent to Mexican waters coincident with killing of two American citizens.
5. Former German warships finally allocated by Allies.—Danish troops occupy Northern Schleswig, returned to Denmark by people's vote.
6. Polish-Ukrainian forces capture Kiev.
7. Carranza flees from capital, taken by revolutionists.—Japan accepts terms of Chinese consortium.
10. U. S. dreadnaught Oklahoma dispatched for service in Mexican waters.—Senator Lodge elected temporary chairman of forthcoming Republican National Convention.
11. Allies present Peace Treaty to Turkey.—Italian Premier Nitti resigns.—French Govt. orders dissolution of General Federation of Labor.
13. Carranza makes stand and leads men in three days' battle.—Debs nominated by Socialist Convention.
14. Germans demand French withdraw from the Main region.—Mexican Congress called to name Provisional President.
15. Senate adopts Knox resolution repealing war declarations on Austria and Germany.
16. Allied Premiers in conference at Hythe, Eng., decide as to payment of reparations by Germany.—Switzerland votes to enter League of Nations.
17. French troops evacuate Frankfort and other towns in Main Province.
18. Nation's bankers, at conference with Federal Reserve Board, pledge help to reduce prices.—Pres. Wilson appoints John Barton Payne, Sec. of the Interior, as Director General of Railroad Administration.
19. London reports capture of Enzeli, on the Caspian Sea, by Bolshevik forces.
20. Nitti again forms Ministry at request of Italian King.
21. Carranza assassinated at Tlaxcalamkongo.—Wholesale food prices drop following price cutting of dry goods and clothing.
22. San Remo Conference invites Pres. Wilson to arbitrate Armenian boundary question.
23. French President escapes death in fall from train.
24. Pres. Wilson asks Congress for power to accept mandate for Armenia.—Governor Smith signs 2.75 Beer Bill.
26. Woolen companies indicted for profiteering.—President receives British and Brazilian Ambassadors.
27. Republican Peace Resolution vetoed by Pres. Wilson.—Armenian mandate rejected by Senate Foreign Relations Committee.
28. French Chamber of Deputies, by vote of 535 to 68, express confidence in Premier Millerand's foreign policy.
29. House of Representatives passes Soldier Relief Bill.—D'Annunzio seizes Albanian port of Durazzo.
30. Graves of America's war dead in France decorated.
31. Lloyd George begins parley with Russian Soviet Minister of Trade.

June.

1. Senate rejects mandate over Armenia.—U. S. Supreme Ct. rules Federal Amendment cannot be submitted to referendum.
2. Adolfo de la Huerta elected Provisional President of Mexico.—British Cabinet decides to resume trade with Russia.
4. Hungary signs Treaty of Peace at Versailles.—Pres. Wilson vetoes Budget Bill.
5. Sixty-sixth Congress ends second session.
6. British warships open fire on Turkish Nationalist positions near the Sea of Marmora.
7. U. S. Supreme Ct. upholds Prohibition Amendment and Volstead Act.—Amer. Federation of Labor opens annual convention at Montreal.
8. Republican National Convention opens at Chicago.
9. 14 killed, 21 injured in N. Y. Central train wreck at Schenectady.
11. Federal indictment of woolen companies quashed by Court.—Austrian Cabinet and Chancellor resign.
12. Warren G. Harding nominated on 10th ballot at Republican Convention; Calvin Coolidge named for Vice President.—Giovanni Giolitti becomes Italian Premier.
13. Essad Pasha, head of Albanian delegation, assassinated in Paris.—Committee of Forty-eight announces formation of new political party.
14. Prof. Edward Capps of Princeton appointed U. S. Minister to Greece.
16. Conference of Jurists meets at The Hague, Elihu Root representing the U. S.
17. Labor Convention endorses U. S. ownership of railroads.—Louisiana Senate rejects Woman Suffrage.
20. Premiers meet in England to plan resistance to Turkish Nationalists; Venizelos offers Greek troops.—5 killed, many injured in Irish riots at Londonderry.—Fahrenbach succeeds Müller as German Chancellor.
21. Allies give Greek army free hand to crush Turks.—Earthquake levels 21 houses in suburb of Los Angeles.
22. China ratifies Austrian Peace Treaty.—French bombard Turks at Messina.
23. U. S. Court at Boston rules Communist Party of America a lawful organization and releases members ordered deported.
24. Greeks rout Turk army in opening drive.—Londonderry asks for martial law.
26. British warships bombard Turks as Greeks attack.
28. Democratic National Convention opens at San Francisco.—German Reichstag holds opening session.
30. Port of Avlona, Albania, captured from the Italians by Albanian insurgents.

July.

1. Sir Robert Borden, Prime Minister of Canada, announces retirement.—Allied nations meet at Brussels to formulate program for Spa conference.
2. Allies fix sum required from Germany for reparations at $30,000,000,000.—Greeks in new offensive take Balikesri.
3. German Reichstag adopts vote of confidence in the government.
4. Japan announces intention to occupy ports in Saghalien pending settlement for massacres.
5. Allier-German Conference meets at Spa.—Treaty returning zone in Schleswig to Denmark signed in Paris.
6. James M. Cox nominated on 44th ballot at Democratic Convention; Franklin D. Roosevelt named for Vice President.—Jurists' Commission on Creation of International Court at The Hague adopts principles of Root-Phillimore plan.
7. Justice Brandeis elected president of International Zionist Conference in London.—Trade restrictions with Soviet Russia removed by U. S. Govt.
8. Arthur Meighen succeeds Sir Robert Borden, resigned, as Premier of Canada.—Allied Premiers at Spa Conference order Germans to reduce their army to 150,000 by Oct. 1 and 100,000 by Jan. 1.
9. Germany agrees to Allies' ultimatum demanding German army be reduced to 150,000 by Oct. 1 and to 100,000 by Jan. 1.—Bolshevik forces break through Polish lines south of Dvina River.
10. Committee of Forty-eight opens convention at Chicago.

GENERAL CHRONOLOGY—July—*Continued.*

12. Britain and Japan notify League of Nations alliance is prolonged for a year.
13. U. S. fleet restores order at Spalato, Dalmatia.—British Lord Chancellor announces that women may serve on juries after July.
15. Shamrock IV wins first America's Cup race after Resolute withdraws with broken halyard.—Revolution in Bolivia overthrows Pres. Guerra.—Labor-Farmer Party nominates P. P. Christensen.
16. Los Angeles shaken by sharp earthquakes.
17. With Resolute in lead second race for America's Cup called off for lack of wind.—Jurists at The Hague complete plan for world court.
18. Gov. Cox and F. D. Roosevelt have conference with Pres. Wilson.—Joachim, son of ex-Kaiser, kills himself at Pottsdam.
19. Japan appropriates over $22,000,000 for new warships during current year.
20. Shamrock IV wins second race for America's Cup by 2 min. 29 sec. over time allowance.—U. S. Wage Board grants $600,000,000 wage increase to railroad employees.—Allied Premiers at Spa recognize Japan's right to occupy northern section of Saghalien.
21. Yachts sail dead heat in third race; handicap gives Resolute victory.—Prohibition Party opens convention at Lincoln, Neb.
22. Senator Harding formally notified at Marion, O.—Wireless telephone messages sent from Chelmsford, Eng., to St. Johns, N. F.
23. Resolute wins fourth yacht race by 9 min. 35 sec.—Prohibition Party nominates A. S. Watkins.—Troops quell riot in Belfast.
24. Soviets accept Polish armistice plea.—Southampton begins series of English celebrations honoring tercentenary of the Pilgrims.—Four earthquake shocks in California.
25. Adrianople taken by Greek forces.
26. U. S. athletes sail for Olympic Games at Antwerp.—Amundsen arrives at Nome, Alaska, after trip in Arctic.
27. Resolute wins fifth yacht race by 19 min. 45 sec., retaining America's Cup.—Republican State Convention opens at Saratoga.
28. Republican State Convention nominates ex-Judge Miller for Governor.—Villa surrenders unconditionally to Mexican Govt.—St. Gauden's statue of Lincoln unveiled in London.
29. Seven U. S. warships ordered to Turkish waters to protect American lives.
31. Billion and a half dollar rate raise granted to railways by Government.

August.

1. Canada sends challenge to compete for the America's Cup.—Polish armistice delegates arrive within Bolshevist lines.
2. Rumania serves ultimatum on Soviet Russia to withdraw troops.—British Ministers agree on martial law in Ireland.
3. Bolsheviki break off truce parley and Polish defense crumbles.
5. British North Sea squadron ordered to Baltic to reimpose blockade.
6. Irish Crimes Bill passes in House of Commons.—Militia quells riots in Illinois; five killed, many injured.—Three more killed in Denver car strike.
7. Cox, in acceptance speech, champions League of Nations.
9. Allied Premiers at Hythe decide will not send army to aid Poland.—British land Mannix at Penzance.—Bulgarian Treaty formally ratified at Paris.
10. Lloyd George in speech to Parliament hopes for peace but gives hint of war.—Turkish Peace Treaty signed at Sevres.—$30,000,000 wage increase granted express workers.
11. French Government decides to recognize Gen. Wrangel as head of de facto government of South Russia.—Pres. Wilson warns Europe U. S. opposes territory grabs.
12. Franco-British entente near breaking point.—Two Greeks attempt assassination of Venizelos in Paris.
13. Rumania, Serbia and Czechoslovakia form alliance.—Russians hammer at Warsaw's gates.
14. Belgian King formally opens Olympic games.
15. Many killed in new Irish riots.—Warsaw bombarded from three sides.
16. Polish counter-attacks drive back Reds from Warsaw.—Lloyd George defies British Labor.—Cruiser and two destroyers ordered to Baltic.
18. Suffrage Amendment ratified; Tennessee House votes 50 to 46.
20. Brest-Litovsk retaken by victorious Poles.—Irish Coercion Act put in operation.
21. Dispatch from Mexico City says that Zamora has captured and holds for ransom a British subject and five Americans.
22. Great Britain is reported to have agreed to recognize the independence of Egypt.
23. Olympic athletic events close with U. S. an easy winner.—Ulster Unionists burn city of Lisburn in reprisal for shooting of Police Inspector Swanzy.
24. South Russia in revolt against Soviet rule.—Gov. Roberts attests Tennessee vote on suffrage.—Antis seek to enjoin Colby.
25. Poles shatter Red army; 80,000 taken prisoner; Warsaw rejects terms.
26. Secretary Colby proclaims suffrage ratified by Tennessee vote and puts official seal on 19th Amendment.
28. Soviet Russia offers to discuss peace on neutral ground.—France advises Poles to drive on into Russia.
29. Eleven dead and 40 hurt in Belfast riots.
30. Assassin wounds Mustapha Kemal, Turkish National leader.
31. D'Annunzio forms new State of Quarnero and makes public text of constitution.

September.

1. Gen. Wrangel launches counter-attack against Soviet forces in South Russia.—British miners vote in favor of strike.
2. Pennsylvania miners strike closing collieries.
3. Thirty men trapped in submarine off Cape Henlopen are saved after 42 hours' imprisonment.
4. Red revolt breaks out in Italy.—Mayflower tercentenary celebration begins at Plymouth, Eng.
5. Strikers in Italy seize and fortify factories.—Obregon wins decisive victory in Mexican Presidential election.
7. Earthquake destroys Italian cities.—Poles call on League of Nations to curb Lithuanians.—Mexico refuses to accept oil protest of U. S.
8. 700,000 homeless in Italy's earthquake; hundreds of lives lost.
9. Wrangel army 12 miles from Red headquarters in South Russia.—Two killed, many injured in new Trieste riots.
10. Poles fight way nearer Grodno; take six towns, 3,300 prisoners and guns.
11. Evans beats Ouimet in final round of amateur golf championship.
13. French and Italian Premiers in conference refuse to discuss with Teutons questions arising from Peace.
14. Great Britain and France agree that Fiume shall become a part of Italy.—Red officials in Petrograd murdered.—League of Nations headquarters announces permanent Court of International Justice.—Connecticut ratifies suffrage.
16. Paul Deschanel, President of the French Republic, resigns on account of ill health.
17. Mob in Genoa rushes U. S. Consulate and tries to lower flag.
19. Rome reports Italy's Labor War near truce; workers to evacuate seized plants.
20. Lithuania and Poland submit fight to League of Nations.—Finland accepts report calling for investigation of Aland Islands question.
22. Gov. Cox's train wrecked but Democratic candidate unhurt and proceeds on tour.
23. Alexander Millerand elected 11th President of the French Republic.
24. Georges Leygues named as French Premier.—Grand Jury in Chicago finds fraud in baseball in connection with 1919 series.—International Financial Congress of the League of Nations opens at Brussels.
26. U. S. elects 64 scholars for Rhodes course at the University of Oxford.—Tokio considers negotiations with U. S. on California problem at serious stage.
27. Forts of Grodno taken by Poles in heavy fighting.—Belfast riots renewed; four Sinn Feiners slain after four police are shot.
28. Eight Chicago White Sox players indicted following World Series baseball scandal.—Lecointe wins for France possession of Gordon Bennett airplane trophy.
29. Diplomatic relations between France and Germany renewed when German Ambassador presents credentials at Paris.

GENERAL CHRONOLOGY—SEPTEMBER—*Continued.*

30. Rome reports Premier Giolitti intends seizing all arms in Italy held by citizens.—More reprisals carried out in Ireland.

October.

1. Poles capture fourth Soviet army, taking 26,650 prisoners and many guns.—Britain takes Germany into trade fold and encourages commerce.
2. Russia reported shaken by anti-Soviet strikes; army clamors for peace.
3. Pres. Wilson enters election campaign with appeal for League of Nations as drawn at Versailles.
5. Rout of Bolsheviki complete; Reds accept Polish terms and truce agreed for Oct. 8.
6. Gen. Felix Diaz ordered deported from Mexico.
7. Military operations between Poles and Lithuanians end.—Japanese fear crisis in California situation.
8. Egyptian Nationalist party leaders agree to British protectorate in plan for independence.
9. Great rebellion reported begun in Moscow against Soviets; insurgents proclaim new government.
10. Britain notifies Bolsheviki of intention to sink Russian submarines on sight.—Poles seize Vilna, Lithuanian capital.
11. Father Flanagan, "Vice President of the Irish Republic," arrested by military patrol at Ballinasloe, Ireland.—Russian Soviets sue for peace with Gen. Wrangel.
12. Russo-Polish Armistice signed at Riga.—Man o' War easy winner over Sir Barton in $75,000 horse race.—Carpentier knocks out Battling Levinsky in 4th round.
13. Sec. Daniels makes public report charging Marines with practically indiscriminate killing of natives in Haiti.
15. International consortium to aid China signed in New York by British, French, Japanese and U. S. representatives.—Court-martial ordered in Haiti episode.
16. Strike of British miners begins; Lloyd George warns nation fight is to a finish.
17. First Irish hunger striker dies in Cork jail on 68th day.—President-elect of Mexico announces all debts will be paid.
18. Fifty hurt as London mob fights police during riot in Downing street.—Both sides in British coal strike await action by Parliament.
19. More British workers idle as strike truce fails; London police suppress rioting.—Gen. Wrangel sharply repulsed by Bolsheviki.
20. Seven dead in N. Y. Central crash at Erie, Pa.—Irish inquiry voted down in House of Commons by large majority.
21. British rail and port men give notice to Lloyd George to settle strike or they will walk out.
23. British rail men postpone strike pending new coal parleys.
25. King Alexander of Greece dies from effects of monkey bites.—Terence MacSwiney, Lord Mayor of Cork, dies on 75th day of hunger strike in Brixton jail.
26. Council of League of Nations adopts Hague committee plan for international court.—Negotiations continue in effort to settle British coal strike.
27. Council of the League of Nations holds public meeting at Brussels.—Pennsylvania textile mills begin war on radical labor, notifying employees they must repudiate leaders or quit jobs.
28. Greek Parliament offers throne of Greece to Prince Paul and elects Admiral Coundouriotis regent.—British coal strike ends in compromise.
29. Italian court at Bologna sentences Cocchi, slayer of Ruth Cruger, to 27 years' imprisonment.
30. 17 men lost on concrete ship sunk in collision off Newport.
31. Body of Terence MacSwiney buried in St. Finbar's Cemetery, Cork.

November.

1. Claims of success made by managers of both major parties on eve of U. S. general election.—Prince Paul seeks call from people of Greece.
2. Senator Warren G. Harding of Ohio, Republican, elected President of the U. S. and Calvin Coolidge of Massachusetts, Vice President, in unprecedented Republican victory; Tennessee swings to Republicans, breaking the Solid South; Republicans increase majority in both House and Senate.
3. Officers of British Miners Federation declare coal strike ended and advise men to resume work.
4. French destroyer sinks Red ship in Black Sea off Batum and seizes crew of 22.
5. Gen. Wrangel retires in safety to Crimea; gets 10,000 of Budenny's Soviet cavalry.—Naval Governor of Samoa ends life with shot.
6. President-elect starts on vacation trip to Southern Texas and Panama.
7. Tripartite agreement made public whereby Great Britain, France and Italy agree to maintain their respective spheres of influence in Turkey.
8. U. S. Court rules liquor lawfully acquired can be moved from storage to the home of the owner.—Armenians driven back by Turks, who capture Kars.
9. Duchess of Marlborough awarded a decree of divorce from the Duke.—U. S. acts to prevent smuggling of Red agitators into the country.—Dispatch received reports slaying of three U. S. Red Cross aids by Soviets.—Graft, corruption and waste of millions are charged in U. S. Shipping Board deals.
10. Santa Margherita conference agrees that Fiume be free city and Jugo Slavs get Istrian line.
11. Second anniversary of Armistice Day observed by nations honoring dead in World War.—An unknown warrior accorded highest military honors by British and buried in Westminster Abbey.—Bill for Irish Home Rule passed by House of Commons.
12. Austria asks to enter League of Nations, being ready to fulfill agreements.—U. S. prepares drive against home brew.—Hunger strike in Cork called off.
13. Reds break through lines and close in on beaten army of Gen. Wrangel; demand unconditional surrender.
14. Sebastopol occupied by Bolsheviki.—Wrangel's army wiped out.—Blockades of Black Sea coast ordered by Allies.—Greek elections held.
15. League of Nations' first assembly opens at Geneva; 41 nations at first meeting; no U. S. delegates.
16. Result of Greek elections shows defeat of Venizelos.—French train guns on Sebastopol and threaten reprisals in case of loot or massacre.—Congressional Committee investigating Shipping Board hears evidence of waste and inefficiency.
17. Shipping Board inquiry told of $2,000,000,000 lost by U. S. in sale of Ship Board fleet.—Lord Robert Cecil in address to League of Nations declares League is now a going concern.
18. George Rhallis, new Premier of Greece, forms Cabinet.—King of Hedjaz recalls special mission to London.—League of Nations elects officers of commissions.
20. Harvard beats Yale in big football event by 9 field goals to 0.—Paul Hymans, speaking for first time as President, states future of League of Nations is assured.
21. Twenty-seven die in Dublin day of terror; Sinn Fein murders 12 officers; auxiliary police fire on crowd at football grounds.
22. League of Nations votes an armed force to pacify Armenia.—Western Union enjoins Daniels in cable fight.
23. Lord Robert Cecil appointed head of League of Nations committee to help Armenia.—President-elect Harding receives enthusiastic welcome at Colon.
24. Rockefeller gives $63,763,357 to charity.
25. Army wins air race and sets world's record for closed circuit racing.—British Govt. arrests Griffith, the founder of Sinn Fein.
26. Russia sends ultimatum to Turks warning them to stop Armenian move.—British officers assassinated in Dublin receive final tributes at Westminster Abbey and Westminster Catholic Cathedral.
27. Allied Premiers agree on plebiscite plan for East Silesia.—Canada staunch defender of U. S. before League of Nations.
28. Fires charged to Sinn Fein destroy cotton warehouses in Liverpool.
29. Fifteen police cadets shot dead in ambush in Ireland.—Proposed blue laws arouse nation-wide interest.
30. Pres. Wilson accepts League of Nations' invitation to serve as mediator in Armenian question.

GENERAL CHRONOLOGY—*Continued.*

December.

1. Bill is drawn to bar aliens for two years. —War on Italy is declared by D'Annunzio.
2. Allies protest return of King Constantine to rule Greece.
3. Turks mass forces for drive on Greeks.—Britain will aid mediation in Armenia and is willing to co-operate with the U. S.
4. Argentina notifies Pres. Hymans of its withdrawal from League of Nations.—Canada offers to League an amendment eliminating Article X.
5. Greek plebiscite results in overwhelming victory for King Constantine.—Sinn Fein leader asks Lloyd George to state truce terms.—Japan firmly opposes demand of U. S. for control of Pacific cable.
6. President-elect Harding is given ovation in Senate at opening of final session of the 66th Congress.
7. Nobel Peace Prize awarded to Pres. Wilson.—President urges independence for the Philippines in message to Congress.
8. Britain bars Irish inquiry by Americans and refuses to visé passports.—Pres. Wilson declines invitation to send representatives to disarmament conference at Geneva.
9. Japan offers race equality in the former German islands of the Pacific awarded her.—House of Representatives votes 151 to 9 to bar aliens.
10. Lloyd George announces martial law to be applied to certain districts of Ireland.
11. Greece formally asks Constantine to resume throne.
12. Cork City Hall, many public buildings and stores are burned.
13. King Constantine leaves Switzerland to resume the throne of Greece.—League of Nations adopts statute for Permanent International Court of Justice.—House of Representatives unanimously votes repeal of most of war-time laws.
14. Borah proposes U. S., England and Japan cut navy programs.—Assembly of League of Nations considers disarmament program.
15. Austria elected member of League of Nations.—China succeeds Greece in the Council.
16. Senate orders national building investigation.—Anti-strike bill passed by Senate.—Eleven killed in Manila riot between enlisted men of constabulary and police.—U. S. orders deportation of Martens, Soviet envoy.—Bulgaria Costa Rica, Finland and Luxemburg admitted to League of Nations.
17. International Court ratified by nine League members.—French Chamber of Deputies votes confidence in government.—Albania elected member of League of Nations.
18. Violent earthquake shakes Argentina; hundreds dead.
19. Constantine arrives at Athens and is greeted by cheering crowds.—Bishop of Cork issues decree excommunicating participants in ambuscades of Crown forces.
21. Irish Home Rule Bill, as modified by Lords, adopted by House of Commons.—Tercentenary of Pilgrims' landing celebrated at Plymouth, Mass.
22. Italians shell D'Annunzio's forces and besiege Fiume.—British troops occupy Dublin City Hall and municipal buildings.
23. Pope issues decree banning Y. M. C. A. to Roman Catholics.
24. Proclamation issued containing plans for U. S. withdrawal of military aid in Santo Domingo.—Jury disagrees in Arnstein trial and Court announces mistrial.—Irish Home Rule Bill becomes law on receiving King's assent.
26. Italian troops fight way to edge of Fiume. —Martial law becomes effective in four Irish counties, Cork, Kerry, Limerick and Tipperary.
27. Berlin tells Allies it is unable to carry out disarmament of the citizen guards.—Serious fires occur in Tipperary; six killed in fighting near Limerick when military arrest 138 persons.
28. London press seconds Senator Borah's suggestion that U. S., Great Britain and Japan curtail naval expenditures.
29. D'Annunzio leaves Fiume in airplane and municipal council agrees to capitulate.
30. Foch plans drive to split Bavaria from Germany.—Britain to support France in enforcement of disarmament terms.

LOCAL CHRONOLOGY.

January.

2. Admiral Jellicoe visits Brooklyn Navy Yard.
3. Radicals captured in raids in New York taken to Ellis Is. for deportation.
7. Governor Smith urges reversal of Dry Law ratification vote.
14. Frank A. Munsey, owner of N. Y. Sun, purchases N. Y. Herald and Evening Telegram and Paris edition of the Herald.
15. Sir Oliver Lodge arrives in New York for American lecture tour.
19. Government agents seize more than $10,000,000 worth of liquor in New York City.
21. Mayor Hylan directs city probe of B. R. T. financial methods.
23. Influenza assumes epidemic proportions in New York City.
27. Sleet storm paralyzes city traffic.
28. Influenza claims 19,763 deaths from Jan. 1 in New York City.

February.

2. Clayton and Stanley Lundy drown in Jamaica Bay.
4. Hurricane sweeps away many bldgs. at Coney Is. and Rockaway.
7. 104 passengers rescued from ship stranded off Rockaway Point.
11. 1,000 policemen detailed to help clear city streets of snow.
15. Blizzard buries Northwestern New York; trains stalled.
20. New York Republicans hold unofficial State convention and adopt a platform.
24. Dr. Maxwell Silver, Rabbi of Temple Shaari Zedek, resigns.
25. $1,000,000 shipyard fire in City Is.
26. Oil explosion at Brooklyn Union Gas Co.'s yards kills firemen.
27. Ralph Peters elected president of L. I. R. R.
28. Liebermann shoe factory in Lexington av. burns.

March.

1. Non-resident State income tax ruled invalid by Supreme Court.—Brooklyn Food Show opens.
3. U. S. agents seize 1,237 bottles of liquor on ships in harbor.
5. Board of Estimate votes $850,000 to dig channel in Jamaica Bay.
6. Villages marooned by thaw and rain followed by snow and hailstorm.
8. During first week in March 36,000 school children sent home from public schools in New York owing to scarcity of teachers.
11. 1,600 boys and girls march safely from burning Public School No. 25, Brooklyn.
12. Longshoremen and stevedores in port of New York strike for higher wages.—City votes million to buy more buses.
15. City conference moves to reduce high rents.
17. Interborough warned that subways may be taken over by city.
19. Deputy Police Commissioner Porter indicted in vice graft investigation for neglect of duty.
23. Large delegations of tenants and landlords attend rent hearing at Albany.
26. Graft charge made against Assistant Dist. Attorney Smith by Inspector Henry.
28. Daylight saving commences in New York City.
30. Assembly committee votes to oust Socialists.—Grand Jury quizzes Enright on vice.
31. Bayles Shipyard at Pt. Jefferson sold to N. Y. Dry Dock Co. for $2,225,000.

April.

1. Justice Cropsey calls Brooklyn buses a menace and grants injunction.—Governor Smith signs 10 rent bills, two more going to Mayor.—Harbor men strike.
2. H. A. Jafredson, Brooklyn man, reported murdered by Mexicans.
4. Vice conditions exposed in sermon by Dr. Straton of Calvary Church.
8. Eagle Grand Canyon National Park Dedication Tour starts with 120 in party.
9. Rail strike threatens New York City's food supply.
10. Legislature passes bill to stop Nassau Judges practising.—Strike spreads to Hudson tubes.—Brooklyn Industrial Show opens.

LOCAL CHRONOLOGY—April—*Continued.*

12. Food prices leap as rail strike grows.—Train wreck on 9th av. L.
15. Market strike menaces city's food reserves.
16. Market strike settled.—Thousands walk up as elevator men in New York City strike.
18. Lunatic kills Dr. James W. Markoe in St. George's Church, Stuyvesant sq.
19. Rail strikers lose fight and commence returning.—Nitrate ship causes spectacular fire at Bush Dock.
21. Brooklyn Horse Show opens.—Mayor approves bill for Brooklyn municipal bldg.
23. Brooklyn Federal Grand Jury indicts three big packers on profiteering charge.
25. Churches in Brooklyn collect $200,000 for the Interchurch World Movement.
26. Three arrests in New York City for profiteering in sugar.
27. Receiver named for Staten Is. trolley line.—German-Amer. political organization formed in N. Y. City.
29. Rival union formed by B. R. T. men wanting open shop.
30. Eagle tourists attend dedication of Grand Canyon National Park and raise fund for Brooklyn Eagle gateway to park.

May.

1. Atlantic fleet arrives in North River for annual visit.
4. Announcement made that 47th Regt., National Guard of Brooklyn, is to be disbanded.
5. Nine Russellites freed after nine months in jail.—Staten Is. trolley strike called off.
6. Federal agents arrest two more Brooklyn packers' managers, completing round-up of Big 5.
8. Eagle Grand Canyon National Park Dedication Tourists arrive home from month's tour.
9. Socialist Party opens convention in Madison Sq. Garden.
10. Appellate Division upholds Cropsey in barring buses.
13. 1,500 sufferers at St. Ann's P. E. Church, Bkn., attend ministrations of J. M. Hickson, English spiritual healer.
14. Brooklyn-Staten Is. bridge proposed by Transit Construction Commissioner.
17. Atlantic fleet terminates visit to New York City.—Journeymen barbers strike.
19. Outlaw strike of milk drivers curtails supply.
20. Governor Smith vetoes bill repealing Daylight Saving Law.
21. Eight trans-Atlantic liners sail from port of New York with 10,000 travelers for Europe.
25. New York City merchants plan big trucking plan to break harbor tie-up.
28. B. R. T. power house crews strike.—Debate at Carnegie Hall between Gompers and Gov. Allen of Kansas.
29. Strike of B. R. T. power house employees fails; car crews vote to stay at posts.
30. Graves of Brooklyn and L. I. soldier dead decorated at memorial exercises in France.

June.

3. Giant battleship Tennessee placed in commission at Brooklyn Navy Yard.
4. Pier unions reject proposals of Governor Smith that they return to work.
7. Gunmen in daylight raid and loot Flatbush av. shop.
9. Protestants and Jews join Roman Catholics in golden jubilee tribute to Mons. McCarty at Montauk Club.
10. Motorman killed and 15 injured in subway crash in Bronx.
11. Court of Appeals upholds stay to stop buses.—Unions threaten war on American Legion in freight strike.
12. Neighbors Day observed in Brooklyn.
15. Civic and military ovation greets Pershing on visit to Brooklyn to review 23d Regt.
19. Justice Cropsey enjoins bus operation on Lafayette av. line.
22. $250,000 in drugs seized in raid on houses in Carroll st., Bkn.
24. Torrential rain floods city, stopping subway.—12 firms, 51 men indicted for oil fraud.
29. Dollar gas for city granted by Federal Court.
30. Finance Committee of Bd. of Estimate authorizes expenditure of $100,000,000 to establish terminal markets in all boroughs.

July.

1. Twenty injured in subway crash in Bronx.—Court orders last Brooklyn bus line stopped.
2. Passenger plane makes first trip from Manhattan to Southampton, L. I.
4. Great out-of-town rush for holiday jams all terminals.
6. 300 picked Boy Scouts of America sail from New York for World Scout Convention in London.
9. Mayor Hylan announces abandonment of municipally controlled buses.
10. Transit Commr. Delaney takes over work on Eastern Parkway Subway, abandoned by contractors.—$500,000 fire in South Brooklyn leaves many homeless.
12. Sir Thomas Lipton guest at Atlantic Yacht Club dinner.
14. Dr. Tildsley defeated for re-election as Associate Supt. of Schools.—Japanese warship Kasuga visits harbor.
15. B. R. T. announces 10 percent wage increase to all employees.
16. Mayor Hylan ousts reporter from meeting of the Board of Estimate.
18. Benny Lewis, mascot of Brooklyn National League baseball team, drowned in Columbus, O.
19. Archbishop Mannix of Melbourne, Australia, given freedom of New York City.
22. Union B. R. T. men decide to ignore offer of 10 percent raise.
25. 20 percent increase in city salaries vetoed by Mayor Hylan.—Farewell reception at Metropolitan Opera House to U. S. athletes prior to sailing for Olympic Games.
27. Long Is. R. R. report shows record number of 45,666 commutation tickets in month of June.
28. B. R. T. union men submit new demands for increased wages and improved working conditions.
30. Fire on Williamsburg Bridge destroys girders and rails, suspending traffic.
31. Archbishop Mannix of Australia sails on Olympic despite Lloyd George ban.

August.

1. B. R. T. subways commence operating through Montague st. and Queensboro tunnels.
2. Long Is. farmers strike against excessive retail profits and refuse to load potatoes.—Democratic State conference meets at Saratoga Springs.
3. Governor Smith designated and ticket agreed on by Democratic leaders.—Knights of Columbus convention opens in N. Y. City.
7. 9,286 aliens reach port of New York during current week.
8. Record crowd of 400,000 visits Coney Is.
9. Board of Estimate passes new plan for city pay raise.—Five former German ships of war arrive in Hudson River.
10. B. R. T. rejects employees' demand for closed shop and wage increase.
12. Salute of 13 guns honors arrival of body of Gen. Gorgas in port.
13. Wason, treasurer of Samaritan Hosp., arrested, admits took hospital funds.
14. Employees of Manhattan and Queens Traction Co. strike.
16. Smith st. houses collapse in storm, crushing woman and boy to death.
17. Longshoremen call off strike begun March 12.—Contract halts B. R. T. strike for one month.
20. Public Service Commission denies railroads right to increase fare rates within city.
23. Interborough subway commences service on Eastern Pkway. and Nostrand av. extensions.—Crown Prince Carol of Rumania arrives in New York City.
25. L. I. R. R. submits new petition to Public Service Comm. for 20 percent increase in passenger rates.
27. Altar of Liberty in memory of heroes who fell in Battle of L. I. unveiled in Greenwood Cemetery.
28. Gov. Cox arrives in city and addresses 100,000 people at Police Field Day games.
29. B. R. T. men strike and paralyze traffic; thousands marooned at beaches.
30. B. R. T. system still tied up by strike and thousands walk to work.

September.

1. Men show signs of backdown in B. R. T. strike and offer compromise; company runs street cars in addition to subway and El trains.
3. $25,000 fire sweeps Edgemere tent city.—Big increase in service on all B. R. T. lines.

LOCAL CHRONOLOGY—SEPTEMBER—*Continued.*

4. Boy Scouts arrive in New York on return from trip overseas.

6. Franklin D. Roosevelt addresses Brooklyn Labor Day paraders.—Arnold Hartman and wife of Brooklyn crushed to death in Cave of the Winds, Niagara Falls.—2,000 B. R. T. strikers in riot with police.—Tilden beats Johnson for tennis title at Forest Hills.

7. Public Service Commr. Nixon calls strike leaders in conference; more men return to work.

10. Nine strikers alleged to have stoned Sea Beach train indicted for murder of passenger.

11. One dead, 87 hurt when strikebreaker's car on Flatbush av. line crashes into another car.

13. Schools open with record registration.—Coney Is. Mardi Gras begins.

14. Primary elections held.

16. Bomb kills 34 and injures 400 in Wall st.; Morgan's office wrecked.—Five expelled Socialist Assemblymen re-elected.

17. Deaths in bomb explosion include 15 from Brooklyn and L. I.; city offers reward of $10,500 for evidence leading to conviction.

18. B. R. T. runs 91 percent of trains; 4,141 employees have returned to work.

20. State Legislature meets in extraordinary session to consider housing problem.—Powder magazine found at Plum Beach in bomb search.

21. State Assembly ousts three Socialists, two others resign; expulsion voted 90 to 45.

23. Bomb, alight, found on Fulton St. El. at Reid av. station.—B. R. T. reports no strikebreakers now working and strike practically over.

24. Drastic laws enacted at extraordinary session of the Legislature to stop rent gouging; evictions are halted.

25. Jacob H. Schiff, noted philanthropist and financier, dies in 5th av. home after a long illness.

27. Prices fall in 11 staple lines.—Fog imperils shipping in harbor and blocks traffic.

29. Kings Co. District Attorney calls members of Brooklyn baseball team in investigation of report that 1920 series has been sold.

October.

1. All borough records broken by $496,409,405 increase in Brooklyn realty values.—100,000 families take advantage of new rent laws and defy landlords by refusing to move.

2. District Attorney exonerates Brooklyn baseball team of any taint of corruption.

4. Edison Co. of Brooklyn and others indicted for profiteering and hoarding of coal.—Judge Scudder instructs jurors to purge Nassau County of vice.

5. World Series opens at Ebbets Field, Cleveland winning first game.

6. Brooklyn wins second game of World Series.—Centennial of Jenny Lind's birth celebrated at Carnegie Hall.

7. Brooklyn wins third game of World Series.—Five killed and many hurt in explosion of tanker at Shewan's shipyard.

8. Former engineer of Brooklyn Edison Co. pleads guilty in coal case.

9. Cleveland beats Brooklyn and evens series.—Marquard, Brooklyn pitcher, arrested as ticket scalper.

10. Week's registration of 1,367,835 sets new high mark for city.—Cleveland wins fifth game of World Series.

11. Tentative city budget passed amounting to $343,394,049.—Cleveland wins sixth game.

12. Cleveland beats Brooklyn in seventh game and wins series.—Ground broken for vehicular tunnel between N. Y. City and New Jersey.

14. Kings County Lighting Co. wins fight in Federal Court for higher gas rate.

16. 75,000 World War veterans parade in Manhattan as demonstration in favor of bonus for former service men.

18. Senator Lodge addresses big Republican rally in the Brooklyn Academy of Music.

19. New rent laws declared constitutional in decision of Supreme Court in the Bronx.

21. Builder tells Lockwood Legislative Com. he gave union president $25,000 bribe to call off strike on building in city.

23. Governor Cox addresses big meeting in Madison Sq. Garden predicting world panic unless U. S. joins League of Nations.

24. Firemen overcome in fire at Winter Garden, Manhattan.

26. Nassau Sheriff and five others indicted in gambling investigation.—Gov. Smith designates Atty. Gen. Newton to prosecute the alleged building material trust.

27. Gov. Smith addresses big meeting at Tammany Hall.—City hotels and restaurants cut prices.

28. Gov. Coolidge reviews great parade and addresses capacity meeting in Carnegie Hall.

29. Candidates for Governor speak to Brooklyn audiences, Gov. Smith at Academy of Music, Miller at Palm Garden.

31. 35,000 Irish sympathizers attend demonstration at Polo Grounds in memory of Terence MacSwiney.

November.

1. Supreme Ct. Justice Hotchkiss finds rent relief laws unconstitutional and void on three counts.

2. Judge Nathan L. Miller, Republican, of Syracuse, elected Governor of N. Y. State over Governor Alfred E. Smith, Democrat; rest of Republican ticket successful; Republicans make clean sweep in local Supreme Court contest, electing all five nominees.

3. Building graft inquiry opened by Grand Jury and action expected against corrupt labor leaders.

4. Lewis Nixon resigns as Public Service Commissioner for the 1st District.—70 seized in Manhattan East Side liquor raids.

6. State Controller Eugene M. Travis held for Grand Jury, charged with defrauding State.

8. Gen. Nivelle, hero of Verdun, arrives in New York en route to Boston Mayflower tercentenary.

9. Thousands in city jobless; 60,000 workers in Brooklyn idle.

11. Armistice Day observed in city.—Tablet unveiled in Brooklyn Postoffice.—Mayor Hylan on stand in building inquiry.

12. Board of Estimate kills plan for erecting $6,000,000 municipal building in Brooklyn.

13. New State rent laws upheld by U. S. District Court for Southern District of N. Y.

14. Six children crushed to death in panic at cry of fire in motion picture theater at Catherine st., Manhattan.

15. Horse Show opens at Madison Sq. Garden.

17. Brindell, president of Building Trades Council, indicted on charge of attempted extortion; Court fixes bail at $100,000.

18. Sir Auckland Geddes, British Ambassador, in speech at Chamber of Commerce offers to U. S. the friendship of the British Empire.

20. Nine perish in Harlem fire when trapped by burning stairs.

22. Police drive on dry violators in city nets only two arrests; no liquor seized.—Morgan group buys General Motors control.

23. Grover Whalen, Commr. of Plant and Structures, admits his firm used Manhattan Courthouse site as ash dump.—Comptroller Craig refuses aid to Hylan graft inquiry and challenges sincerity of the Mayor.—Armed thugs continue holdups in city.

24. Plymouth Church Sunday School and lecture room partially destroyed by fire; stained glass windows destroyed and relics injured.—Commr. of Accounts Hirshfield indicted by Grand Jury in libel charging graft to Asst. District Attorney Smith.

25. Irish storm Union Club in Manhattan in effort to rip down British flag.—Untermyer urges city to sue Commissioner Whalen.

26. New rent laws upheld in two Supreme Court decisions.—Backer trial begins for perjury following testimony before Lockwood Committee.

27. Justice Cropsey denies railroad plea to approve rate increase.

29. Five B. R. T. strikers get 8 to 20 years sentence for killing passenger.—Borough Pres. Curran of Manhattan withdraws from city hearing on building graft.

30. Sixteen builders indicted for destroying evidence required by Lockwood Committee.—Bandits get $460,000 in daylight hold-up in Brooklyn.

December.

1. Building in Broadway, Manhattan, collapses; one dead and five buried under ruins.—Lockwood Board is told that Brooklyn Bureau fixed masonry prices in borough.

2. Five die in apartment fire in W. 57th st., Manhattan.—12 robberies added to list in Brooklyn.

LOCAL CHRONOLOGY—DECEMBER—*Continued.*

3. Builders charged with falsifying their books and Grand Jury asked to act.—2,000 tenants in Bronx on rent strike.
4. Widow of late Terence MacSwiney, Lord Mayor of Cork, given remarkable reception on arrival in New York.
5. Ammunition lighter burnt at Ft. Hamilton and shells alarm neighborhood.
6. Board of Aldermen adopt city budget amounting to $345,571,899 for 1921.
7. U. S. Army captain arrested in New York confesses Berlin sent him and 300 others to betray troops.
8. Appellate Div. of Supreme Ct. upholds new rent law.—Building material drops 40 percent after probe of Lockwood Committee alarms ring. —Ashland pl. connection with B. R. T. subway set aside.
9. Five big unions of needleworkers at meeting at Hotel McAlpin combine to fight reduction in wages; 400,000 workers affected.
10. Twenty-nine stone men indicted as anti-trust violators as effect of Lockwood Committee investigation.
11. Caruso bursts blood vessel in throat while singing at Brooklyn Academy of Music.
12. Rev. Dr. Nehemiah Boynton resigns pastorate of Clinton Av. Cong. Church, to take effect Easter, 1921.
13. Mrs. Ellen O'Grady resigns as Police Deputy, saying she cannot retain position and self-respect.
14. Dempsey beats Brennan in sensational fight at Madison Sq. Garden after receiving considerable punishment.
15. Commr. Enright denies police breakdown or crime wave in city.
16. Bandits with silent gun kill 5th av. jeweler and get $69,000.—Jewelers call on Gov. Smith to police city.—One burglar killed, two officers shot in gun fight at Huntington, L. I.
17. Police Lt. Horton killed by taxi bandits.—Mayor Hylan stands by Enright as crime wave terrorizes New York.—Lockwood Committee adjourn after Kaplan-Untermyer clash.
18. B. R. T. asks Public Service Com. for 10-ct. fare under new zone system.—Dr. Rumely found guilty of buying Evening Mail with German money.
19. Police start greatest round-up of crooks in history of city; 150 seized in first few hours.
20. Rt. Rev. Charles S. Burch, Prot. Epis. Bishop of New York, stricken on street and dies. —Trial commences of Nassau County officials on charges of conspiracy to prevent prosecution of gambling houses.
21. 769 more police voted to city by Estimate Board.—B. R. T. fare increase schedule suspended two months by Public Service Commission.
23. 800 police reservists called to aid drive on crime in city.
24. Enright resigns as Lieut. of uniformed police but remains Commissioner.—L. I. and S. I. fare raises halted by Supreme Court.—Dr. W. Hendrickson, Brooklyn minister, killed by motorcar.
26. Rival gunmen kill Monk Eastman, New York's most notorious gang leader.
27. Enright calls up 750 new police and urges anti-gun law for New Jersey.
29. Over $2,000,000 pledged at tin cup dinner at the Hotel Commodore in aid of starving children of Europe.
30. Mayor blocks new appropriation for Manhattan Courthouse.—Brindell is denied change of venue.

GENERAL NECROLOGY OF 1920.

Adams, Rt. Rev. Wm. Forbes, Protestant Episcopal Bishop, Easton, Pa., Mar. 5.
Alexander, King of Greece, Athens, Oct. 25.
Alexander, Charles McC., evangelist, Birmingham, Eng., Oct. 13.
Amette, Cardinal, Archbishop of Paris, Aug. 29.
Avery, Samuel P., patron of art, Hartford, Ct., Sept. 25.
Bankhead, John Hollis, Senator, Washington, Mar. 1.
Benedict, Benjamin L., former Bkln. Court Clk., Burlington, Vt., July 11.
Benedict, Elias C., banker and yachtsman, Greenwich, Conn., Nov. 23.
Bennett, Charles, L. I. master mariner, Milford, Conn., Feb. 26.
Benson, Col. Frederick S., Civil War veteran and gas manufacturer, Atlantic Highlands, N. J., Feb. 23.
Bliss, Rev. Dr. H. S., Pres. Amer. College, Beirut, Syria, May 2.
Bonzano, Max F., railroad man, Guilford, Conn., Oct. 31.
Borthwick, John A., formerly of Sea Cliff, L. I., Brighton, Eng., July 14.
Bowerman, Gen. Richard N., Civil War veteran, Baltimore, O., Aug. 10.
Boyd, Prof. Asa S., lecturer, Philadelphia, Nov. 2.
Broughton, Rhoda, novelist, Oxford, Eng., June 5.
Brush, Brig.-Gen. Daniel N., U. S. A., retired, Baltimore, Mar. 8.
Bullen, Arthur Henry, Elizabethan scholar, Stratford-on-Avon, Eng., Mar. 17.
Burdick, Francis M., professor of law, De Ruyter, N. Y., June 3.
Carey, Stephen W., broker, Montclair, N. J., Sept. 6.
Carranza, Venustiano, Pres. of Mexico, Mexico City, May 21.
Carruthers, Thomas C., hotel man, Mt. Vernon, N. Y., June 13.
Castle, Egerton, author, London, Sept. 17.
Choate, Wm. G., ex-judge, Wallingford, Conn., Nov. 14.
Churchill, William, philologist, Washington, June 10.
Cole, Dr. Chas. K., financier, Pasadena, Cal., Mar. 1.
Collins, Jesse, statesman, England, Nov. 21.
Cooke, Marjorie Benton, author, Manila, P. I., Apr. 26.
Cornwallis-West, Mrs., Milford, Eng., July 21.
Crane, W. Murray, former U. S. Senator, Oct. 2.
Crawford, Clifton, actor, London, June 3.
Crown Princess of Sweden (nee Princess Margaret of Connaught), Stockholm, May 2.
Crozier, Most Rev. John Baptist, Primate of Ireland, Armagh, Apr. 11.
Davies, Chas. E., ("Parson"), sporting promoter, Bedford, Va., June 28.
Delano, Warren, coal pres., killed by train at Barrytown, N. Y., Sept. 9.
De La Touche, Gaston de Pellerin, pres. La Compagnie General Transatlantique, Paris, Nov. 3.
De Morony, Duke, Paris, July 15.
Deslys, Gaby, dancer, Paris, Feb. 11.
Des Planches, Baron Edmondo, former Ambassador, Rome, Dec. 27.
Dieulafoy, Marcel, explorer, Paris, France, Feb. 26.
Dodge, Horace E., motor car manfr., Palm Beach, Dec. 10.
Doolittle, Prof. Eric, astronomer, Philadelphia, Sept. 21.
Duval, Maj. Gen. William P., San Diego, Cal., Mar. 1.
Duveen, Louis, art dealer, London, Eng., Mar. 3.
Ekengren, W. A. F., Swedish Minister to U. S., Washington, Nov. 26.
Essad, Pasha, head of Albanian delegation, assassinated, Paris, June 13.
Eugenie, former Empress of the French, Madrid, July 11.
Feng Kuo-Cheng, former President of China, Peking, Jan. 2.
Fisher, Baron, of Kilverstone (John Arbuthnot Fisher), Admiral of the Fleet, former British First Lord of the Admiralty, London, July 10.
Fisher, Mary A., founder of Fisher Home for Aged, Tenafly, N. J., June 22.
Florio, Caryl, musician and composer, Asheville, N. C., Nov. 23.
Fryer, Sir Charles E., pisciculturist, Watford, Eng., Nov. 19.
Garvice, Charles, novelist, London, March 1.
Gary, James A., former Cabinet member, Baltimore, Oct. 31.
Gibbons, Mary, sister of Cardinal, New Orleans, Dec. 2.
Gleed, Charles S., pres. Kansas City Journal, Topeka, July 25.
Glover, Phoda A., oldest suffragist, Pasadena, Cal., Oct. 6, 94.
Goldie, George, former physical director, Princeton, N. J., Feb. 23.
Gompers, Mrs. S., wife of labor leader, Washington, May 7.
Gorgas, Maj. Gen. William C., former Sur. Gen. U. S. Army, London, July 4.
Grace, Michael P., financier and shipowner, London, Eng., Sept. 20.

GENERAL NECROLOGY FOR 1920—*Continued.*

Hanna, Hugh H., sound money advocate, Indianapolis, Oct. 31.
Hartzler, Rev. Dr. H. B., editor of The Evangelical, Harrisburg, Pa., Sept. 3.
Hendricks, Francis, Republican leader, Syracuse, June 9.
Hill, Gen. Benjamin, Mexican Sec. of War, Mexico City, Dec. 15.
Hodson, Frank, chief clerk Amer. Embassy, London, Dec. 8.
Hyslop, Dr. James H., psychist, Upper Montclair, N. J., June 17.
Kerr, Thomas B., patent lawyer, Englewood, N. J., Apr. 1.
Kempff, Rear Admiral Louis, Santa Barbara, Cal., July 29.
Kimball, Benjamin A., railroad pres., Lake Winnipesaukee, Me., July 20.
Leman, Gen., defender of Liege, Liege, Belgium, Oct. 17.
Lestocq, William, theatrical manager, London, Eng., Oct. 16.
Locklear, Lt. Omar, aviator, killed, Los Angeles, Aug. 2.
Lockyer, Sir Norman, scientist and author, Sidmouth, Eng., Aug. 16.
Ludden, Col. William A., Civil War veteran, Bath, N. Y., Feb. 17.
Lyons, Capt. Martin J., old Cup Race pilot, Jacksonville, Fla., July 21.
McCormick, Dr. Charles W., M. E. divine, East Orange, N. J., Oct. 19.
McCullough, Charles H., Jr., steel, Baltimore, Apr. 8.
MacDonald, Baroness, widow of Canadian Premier, London, Eng., Sept. 5.
MacSwiney, Terence, Lord Mayor of Cork and hunger striker, Brixton Jail, London, Oct. 25.
Mann, Col. William D'Alton, editor, Morristown, N. J., May 17.
Mathers, Helen, novelist, London, Eng., Mar. 16.
Matthews, Sir Charles, director of prosecutions, London, June 6.
Mills, Mrs. Ogden, Paris, Oct. 13.
Moore, Jonathan, former Bklyn resident, St. Clair, Mich., Oct. 7.
Morrison, Dr. George E., adviser to Chinese President, London, May 30.
Morton, Levi P., former Vice President of U. S., and former Governor of N. Y., Rhinebeck, May 16, 96.
Moyer, Horace, engineer, Los Angeles, Apr. 1.
Murphy, Franklin, former Governor of N. J., Newark, N. J., Feb. 24.
Nasmyth, George, sociologist, Geneva, Switzerland, Sept. 20.
Newbold, Arthur E., financier, Phila., June 10.
Olmstead, John C., landscape architect, Brookline, Mass., Feb. 24.
O'Neill, James, actor, New London, Conn., Aug. 10.
O'Shea, John J., editor Catholic Standard and Times, Philadelphia, Mar. 2.
Parsons, Col. William Lewis, Civil War veteran, Yates Centre, Kan., Feb. 11.
Partridge, Col. John N., former Police Commr. of Bkln., Westport, N. Y., Apr. 8.
Peary, Rear Admiral Robert E., Arctic explorer, Washington, D. C., Feb. 20.
Perris, George H., war correspondent, London, Dec. 23.
Perry, Capt. Frank I., former Capt. 23d Regt., Woodbridge, N. J., Dec. 10.
Queensberry, Marquis of, Johannesburg, South Africa, Aug. 1.
Rand, Rosa, actress, Baltimore, June 10.
Reed, John, Socialist author, Moscow, Russia, Oct. 17.
Reedy, William M., editor, Reedy's Mirror, St. Louis, July 28.
Rejane, Mme., actress, Paris, June 15.
Rice, George S., engineer, Montclair, N. J., Dec. 7.
Ridgely, William B., former U. S. Controller of Currency, Apr. 30.
Ripley, Edward Payson, railroad man, Santa Barbara, Cal., Feb. 4.
Ritter, John P., novelist and editor, Newark, N. J., Aug. 3.
Riviere, Briton, artist, London, Apr. 20.
Routhier, Sir Adolph B., Canadian jurist, Irenie les Pains, Can., June 28.
Roybet, Ferdinand, artist, Paris, Apr. 11.
Roques, Gen. Pierre A., French com., Feb. 26.
Russell, Henry, vice pres. Michigan Cent. R. R. Co., Detroit, Feb. 25.
Russell, Rt. Hon. Sir T. W., Dublin, May 2.
Schreiner, Olive, author, London, Dec. 12.
Searles, Edward F., philanthropist, Methuen, Mass., Aug. 6.
See, James W., engineer, Hamilton, O., Feb. 2.
See, Milton, architect, Mt. Vernon, N. Y., Oct. 27.
Seward, Gen. William H., Civil War veteran, Auburn, N. Y., Apr. 26.
Shevlin, Peter F., newspaperman, Pittsburg, Sept. 10.
Smedley, Wm. T., artist, Bronxville, N. Y., Mar. 26.
Snow, Alpheus H., international law expert, Washington, D. C., Aug. 19.
Spedon, Samuel M., Flatbush lecturer, Atlanta, Ga., Dec. 7.
Spooner, Dr. Edward H., physician and Civil War veteran, Park Ridge, N. J., May 30.
Spurgeon, William P., editor, Washington, June 4.
Stevens, George W., pres. Chesapeake and Ohio R. R., White Sulphur Springs, Nov. 3.
Stone, William A., former Governor, Philadelphia, Mar. 1.
Stockwell, Dr. John N., astronomer, Cleveland, O., May 19.
Stuart, Sir Thomas A., scientist, Sydney, Australia, Mar. 3.
Stuck, Rev. Hudson, archdeacon and explorer, Fort Ukon, Alaska, Oct. 10.
Sullivan, Roger C., Democratic leader, Chicago, Apr. 14.
Taylor, Brig.-Gen. Frank, Civil War veteran, Seattle, May 20.
Thomas, Olive, moving picture star, died from poison, Neuilly, France, Sept. 10.
Thorn, Maj. Walter, Civil War veteran and honor medal man, Hampton, Va., July 29.
Toedt, Theodore J., singer, New Rochelle, Dec. 3.
Trumbull, Frank, railroad man, Santa Barbara, Cal., July 13.
Vail, Theodore N., chairman Am. Tel. and Tel. Co., Baltimore, Apr. 16.
Vanderbilt, William K., financier, Paris, July 22.
Vincent, Bishop John Heyl, Chautauqua founder, Chicago, May 9.
Waitt, Arthur H., railroad man, Sharon, Conn., Nov. 10.
Wanamaker, Mrs. John, Atlantic City, Aug. 20.
Ward, Mrs. Humphrey, author, London, Mar. 24.
Waterbury, James M., Jr., polo player, French Lick, Ind., Aug. 29.
Watt, Capt. James B., Cunard commodore, Las Palmas, Canary Isl., June 8.
Weed, Smith M., Democratic leader, Plattsburg, N. Y., June 7.
Weld, Gen. Stephen M., Civil War veteran, Boca Grande, Fla., Mar. 16.
Williamson, Charles N., novelist, Bath, Eng., Oct. 5.
Wilson, James, former Sec. of Agriculture, Traer, Ia., Aug. 26.
Winans, Walter, sportsman and exhibitor of horses, London, Aug. 12.
Zorn, Anders L., Swedish painter, Stockholm, Aug. 22.

NAMELESS DEAD SOLDIERS HONORED BY ENGLAND AND FRANCE.

No military potentate of high rank or great achievement who died in the course of the war received such a funeral as fell to the lot of a nameless poilu who was buried under the Arc de Triomphe on Armistice Day, 1920, in token of the eternal gratitude of the whole nation to the common soldiers who sacrificed their lives for France. The unknown poilu's only rival in honor was a nameless British private, who, on the same day, was borne through the streets of London, with King George of England as his chief mourner, to be buried in Westminster Abbey.

COTTON PRODUCTION—SOUTHERN STATES.

	1919-20	1918-19	1917-18	1916-17	1915-16
Alabama	891	756	521	659	1,255
Arkansas	899	914	1,004	1,228	847
Florida	20	34	50	60	60
Georgia	2,037	2,029	1,980	2,164	2,320
Louisiana	329	541	665	496	403
Oklahoma	825	590	1,016	905	806
Mississippi	1,046	1,154	979	924	1,100
N. Carolina	1,006	907	717	827	893
S. Carolina	1,743	1,491	1,295	1,127	1,370
Tennessee	650	543	460	610	510
Texas	3,097	2,680	3,220	3,941	3,374
Total Crop Bales	12,443	11,640	11,907	12,941	12,938

LOCAL NECROLOGY OF 1920.

The arrangement followed in this list is: Name of person, position in life, date of death and age.

Brooklyn.

Adams, Allison L., civic worker, Apr. 27, 52.
Adams, Floyd Joseph, lawyer, Feb. 10, 52.
Allabach, Dr. Louise B., osteopath, July 20, 70.
Andreas, Jeremiah J., filibuster of the '50s, Sept. 23, 88.
Applegate, Joseph H., retired fish dealer, July 6, 71.
Bacon, Col. Alexander S., lawyer and author, May 29, 66.
Badger, George W., organ manfgr., Feb. 3, 65.
Bailey, John Alex., retired fruit merchant and Eagle reader from Vol. I, No. 1, Oct. 3, 91.
Baker, Frank M., real estate, May 1, 57.
Bangs, Charlotte R., author, Mar. 26, 52.
Barlow, Everett D., lawyer, May 11, 73.
Bennett, Catherine Duryea, Apr. 3, 97.
Bennett, Francis X., former Assemblyman and Alderman, Nov. 30, 56.
Blackham, Job W., retired, May 27, 87.
Blauss, John A., pioneer lithographer, May 30, 80.
Bolen, Dr. Nicholas, dermatologist, Nov. 28, 59.
Bowne, Robert R., Civil War veteran, Oct. 19, 85.
Bress, William A., cotton expert, July 22, 63.
Brown, Maj. Frank E., surgeon, June 23, 39.
Bruce, Walter, choir leader, July 31, 70.
Buckley, Rev. Dr. J. M., Feb. 9, 83.
Bullwinkle, Dr. Henry, physician, Sept. 14, 54.
Byrne, John J., Democratic leader, May 28.
Campbell, Miss Abby H., founder of Faith Home for Incurables, Oct. 4, 83.
Chadwick, Charles N., veteran Brooklynite and Commr. of Bd. of Water Supply, Oct. 23, 73.
Chase, Dr. Walter B., gynecologist, Nov. 15, 77.
Clark, Frank A., theatrical manager, Mar. 11, 56.
Clisset, John T., B. R. T. bandmaster, Aug. 16, 56.
Cloke, Rev. Thos. J., R. C. rector, Dec. 30.
Colell, Mrs. Emma K., artist and musician, July 21, 48.
Cornell, Dr. George B., physician, June 17, 87.
Cotter, Dr. John H., physician, Sept. 15, 52.
Crandall, Jesse A., toy inventor, Aug. 13, 86.
Davenport, Henry B., pres. Home Title Insurance Co., Feb. 16, 65.
Davis, Celinda T., teacher, May 14, 80.
Davis, Harrie, newspaperman, Jan. 13, 55.
Day, Augustus P., coal merchant, Dec. 13, 86.
De Vere, Mary A., writer and poet, Aug. 6, 69.
Dickinson, Col. E. B., Civil War veteran, Apr. 29, 75.
Donovan, Richard J., lawyer and forester.
Doyle, James, fire chief, Nov. 8, 74.
Doyle, Michael E., Civil War veteran, Nov. 2, 75.
Drobegg, Dr. Gustave C., chemist, Dec. 6, 59.
Field, Mrs. Charlotte E., artist, Apr. 8, 82.
Finnigan, Michael E., lawyer, Nov. 29, 81.
Fleury, George A., pres. U. S. Title Guaranty Co., June 1, 44.
Fogarty, William H., asst. supt. of mails, Aug. 6.
Forbes, David, linen importer, Mar. 15, 71.
Ford, William H., lawyer and founder of Crescent A. C., Sept. 22, 62.
Foster, Frank E., real estate, Apr. 26, 60.
Geatons, James T., fire chief, Apr. 5, 54.
Germond, Henry S., stock broker, Nov. 15, 86.
Goodrich, Alice D., sculptress, Sept. 30, 38.
Gouley, Dr. J. W. S., Civil War surgeon, Apr. 26, 88.
Grinden, Maj. William J., vice-pres. St. Vincent de Paul Soc., Nov. 25, 50.
Haight, Eburn F., contractor, Aug. 6, 75.
Haines, Virtus L., lawyer and lecturer Bkln. Law Sch., June 28, 60.
Hall, James, deacon of Plymouth Church, May 26.
Hanselman, Rev. J. J., pastor St. Barbara's R. C. Church, May 3, 69.
Harrington, William F., lawyer and dramatic coach, July 8, 39.
Harris, Clinton S., lawyer, June 27, 69.
Haslett, Samuel E., recluse, Jan. 16, 84.
Hazen, Mrs. Horace, war worker, Aug. 25.
Hegeman, Rev. Dr. Adrian R., archdeacon of the Episcopal Diocese of Central N. Y., Feb. 27, 50.
Hemstreet, Col. William, Civil War veteran, Oct. 15, 86.
Hendrickson, Rev. Wm. H., Presb. minister, Dec. 23, 61.
Hill, Dr. Helen E., physician, Mar. 20, 80.
Hilton, Mrs. Claire N., orphanage trustee and Church worker, Oct. 16, 43.
Hooton, William A. G., Civil War veteran, Nov. 7.
Hotchkiss, Chauncey C., novelist, Dec. 15, 68.
Howell, E. F., director, Jan. 6, 65.
Huberty, Peter, former clerk of Kings Co., May 5, 74.
Hull, Fanny, oldest Bkln. Librarian, May 9, 81.
Jahn, Frederick G., inventor, Dec. 22, 58.
Jensen, Capt. John C., mariner, June 24, 87.
Jewell, Maj. Herbert S., pres. Jewell Milling Co., Oct. 1, 75.
Joerg, Dr. Oswald, physician and Egyptologist, Nov. 4, 76.
Joost, Martin, banker, Feb. 24, 77.
Kelly, Rev. Patrick F., director of St. Vincent's Home for Boys, Dec. 6, 45.
Ketcham, Henry B., lawyer, Nov. 16, 55.
Ketchum, A. C., Alderman, Apr. 18.
Kinsey, Peter, retired banker, Apr. 16, 75.
Kirkland, John, retired distiller, July 25, 97.
Klein, Samuel, provision merchant, July 19, 71.
Knapp, Dr. Mark I., physician, Nov. 26, 65.
Krim, Very Rev. George J., S.J., pres. of Bkln. College, Apr. 1, 49.
Lally, Thomas, ex-fire chief, Oct. 14, 71.
Lamb, Richard, engineer, Oct. 18, 61.
Lee, Dr. John A., pres. Kings Co. Medical Soc., Apr. 4, 48.
Lenfestey, George N., veteran volunteer fireman, June 15, 69.
Lincoln, Eva A., war worker, Sept. 11, 44.
Littell, G. F., advertising, Jan. 6, 68.
Lockitt, Clement, banker, Feb. 2, 77.
Loewenthal, Dr. H. Murray, physician, Mar. 13, 47.
Lutkins, Mrs. Annie E., old Bkln. resident, Aug. 12, 95.
McAllister, Capt. Daniel, pres. McAllister Towing and Transportation Co., Oct. 25, 75.
McCarty, Thomas E., pioneer flour merchant, July 11, 82.
McCutcheon, Maj. Henry D., Spanish-Amer. War veteran, June 13, 60.
McDonald, Daniel J., Queens Co. official, Feb. 19, 57.
McGee, James F., Supreme Ct. clerk, Mar. 18, 60.
McKinny, Alexander, lawyer and civic worker, Mar. 30, 61.
McMannus, Charles G., Civil War veteran, June 16, 80.
McWilliams, Helen F. M., a founder of Bkln. Y. W. C. A., Sept. 7, 81.
Malarkey, Prof. John J., principal P. S. 102, Nov. 6, 60.
Malloy, Rev. Michael H., Mercy Father, July 14, 64.
Marling, Joseph, undertaker and Civil War veteran, Nov. 24, 81.
Matthews, Gardiner D., former drygoods merchant, June 17, 78.
Maujer, Mary Ann, church worker, Oct. 23, 86.
Mershon, Rev. Albert L., Alliance minister, July 14, 54.
Mertens, Rev. Hermann J., Feb. 3, 61.
Moore, Peter P., produce merchant, Jan. 11, 88.
Morrow, Rev. Charles E., acting rector of St. Andrews P. E. Church, Aug. 12, 67.
Morse, Dr. Charles F., educator, Oct. 9, 59.
Muldoon, William H., sec. of Bkln. Park Dept., and former city editor Brooklyn Eagle, July 2, 72.
Mullin, Francis B., banker and lawyer, Aug. 7, 44.
Murr, Laura Hulst, horsewoman, July 27.
Namm, Adolph I., merchant, Oct. 26, 64.
Nash, Capt. Thomas J., retired captain fire dept., Dec. 14, 65.
Nielsen, Capt. C. J., cigar manfr. and yachtsman, Mar. 8, 70.
Noble, Dr. Harriet I., anatomical expert, Oct. 10, 61.
Norton, Edward J., retired fire chief, Aug. 1, 66.
Noyes, Edward V., Civil War veteran, Aug. 14, 89.
Olena, Theophilus, banker and former pres. of Bkln. Bd. of Aldermen, Sept. 21, 87.
O'Donnell, Rev. Thomas J., associate rector Ch. of the Holy Name, Aug. 19, 34.
O'Reilly, Miles, former police inspector, Dec. 8, 78.
Ormsbee, Agnes Bailey, author, Dec. 8, 62.
Patterson, Thomas V., coal merchant, Nov. 2, 47.
Pearsall, George W., real estate, lawyer, Mar. 3, 79.
Peck, Alfred Martin, printing ink manufacturer, Mar. 15, 72.
Pentacost, Rev. Dr. George F., Congregational minister, Aug. 7, 77.

LOCAL NECROLOGY OF 1920—*Continued.*

Perez, Marcellus, cigar mfr., Sept. 16, 55.
Raymond, George T., Civil War veteran, June 4, 75.
Raymond, George W., Civil War veteran, Aug. 23, 74.
Reid, Edgar T., real estate, Apr. 30, 69.
Richert, Jean, pres. Union of French Socs., July 28, 70.
Robertson, Dr. Archibald K., veterinarian, June 7, 62.
Robinson, William A., lawyer, Oct. 15, 50.
Roddy, Capt. Hugh V., Civil War veteran, Aug. 29, 90.
Rollins, Dr. Frank, H. S. principal, May 11, 59.
Rowe, Dr. Anna F., infirmary founder, Sept. 18, 62.
Saumenicht, William G., lawyer, Nov. 9, 31.
Scharmann, Herman B., pioneer brewer, Aug. 3, 82.
Schenck, Dr. Peter Lawrence, physician and Civil War veteran, Mar. 6, 76.
Schlitz, Dr. Francis A., physician and civic worker, Nov. 28, 75.
Shaen, Harry B., pres. Bkln. Sunday Sch. Union, Nov. 21, 68.
Sheldon, Dr. Samuel, prof. Bkln. Polytechnic Inst., Sept. 4, 58.
Sheppard, John W., second oldest Brooklyn volunteer fireman, Dec. 16, 87.
Schiebler, George W., silverware mfr., Sept. 13, 74.
Shields, Thomas W., artist, Sept. 20, 70.
Shute, Sarah J. M., church worker, May 4, 84.
Smith, E. M., politician, Jan. 20, 79.
Smith, Mrs. Ellen M. Cyr, author of school books, July 25.
Smith, Howard Mapes, L. I. R. R. passenger agent, Feb. 24, 71.
Smith, Matthew, old supervisor, Nov. 11, 82.
Sorrentino, Rev. Vincent, rector of Ch. of Our Lady of Loretto, June 13, 51.
Spelman, William C., merchant, Nov. 10, 86.
Sperry, Charles D., manufacturer, Mar. 30.
Sprague, Wm. L., retired P. S. principal, May 5, 70.
Stilwell, Mrs. G. W., church worker, Nov. 22, 79.
Stitt, John H., lawyer, Oct. 10, 74.
Strauss, Julius, builder, Nov. 2, 58.
Suydam, Abram V., one of oldest Brooklynites, Nov. 8, 95.
Taaffe, Msgr. Thomas, rector emeritus St. Patrick's Church, Dec. 1, 87.
Tamblyn, Evan L., lawyer, March 24, 45.
Taylor, Edward H., former alderman, Nov. 2, 55.
Teeple, John J., hardware dealer, Oct. 31.
Tichenor, Eugene R., broker, engraver and duck raiser, Aug. 27, 61.
Tiebout, Ralph H., merchant, Apr. 20, 62.
Titus, Lewis T., Civil War veteran, Nov. 25, 89.
Turner, William M., church trestee, Nov. 9, 67.
Urquhart, Capt. William Wallace, packet ship commander, Feb. 26, 81.
Van Wyck, Jacob S., lawyer, Dec. 13, 84.
Viemeister, Edmund C., lawyer, Nov. 22, 53.
Vom Hofe, Edward C., noted fisherman, Nov. 27, 75.
Voorhees, Mrs. Mary A. S., Dec. 20, 84.
Wadsworth, Mrs. C. H., church worker, Sept. 25, 90.
Walker, Russell S., bank pres., Dec. 25, 65.
Weeks, J. R., physician, Jan. 12, 64.
White, Annie Jean Lyman, philanthropist, May 23, 69.
Whittaker, Mary, retired teacher, May 10, 75.
Williams, Fred C., advertising, May 14, 61.
Woodruff, Albert C., vice-pres. Bush Terminal Co., Feb. 25, 82.
Woodruff, Phebe J., church woman, May 25, 86.
Yale, Milton H., pres. Yale Land Co., Sept. 26, 75.
Youker, Wilfred E., ex-assemblyman, Dec. 17, 44.

Manhattan and Bronx.

Ahearn, John F., Democratic leader, Dec. 19, 67.
Andrews, William Loring, book collector, Mar. 19, 82.
Bogart, Col. John, engineer, Apr. 26, 84.
Briesen, Arthur von, lawyer, May 13, 76.
Burch, Rt. Rev. Charles S., Bishop of N. Y., Dec. 20, 65.
Cahn, Julius, theatrical mgr., March 15, 62.
Carhart, Henry Brigham, office merchant, Feb. 10, 64.
Chambers, Julius, newspaperman, Feb. 12, 70.
Chappelle, Emanuel S., wine agent, Aug. 20.
Childs, Wm. H., Dem. politician, Feb. 6, 69.
Clarke, Thomas S., sculptor and painter, Nov. 16, 60.
Colman, Samuel, artist, Mar. 27, 88.
Conyers, Joseph, actor, June 25, 60.
Cowing, Rufus B., retired judge, May 7, 79.
Davies, Julien T., lawyer, May 6, 74.
De Koven, Reginald, composer, Jan. 16.
Delano, Eugene, banker, Apr. 2, 76.
Douglas, C. Noel, author and song writer, Nov. 13, 57.
Du Bois, James T., former minister to Colombia, May 27, 69.
Dugro, Philip Henry, Supreme Court Justice, Mar. 1, 64.
Eagan, Owen, fire dept. bomb expert, Mar. 2, 63.
Fairchild, Helena Rutherford, author and flower gardener, May 17.
Francolini, Joseph N., pres. Italian Savings Bank, Dec. 14.
Caines, Col. Wm. P., editor, Mar. 18, 68.
Gayley, James, steel, Feb. 25, 65.
Gordon, Julian (Mrs. Julie Cruger), novelist, July 12.
Hallen, Fred, actor, Feb. 28, 62.
Hanan, John H., shoe mfr., Aug. 25, 71.
Hawkins, Gen. Rush C., Civil War veteran, Oct. 25, 89.
Hemphill, Alex. J., banker, Dec. 29, 64.
Henry, H. F., minstrel, Jan. 30, 75.
Herreshoff, Frederick, golfer, Mar. 23, 31.
Heuel, Dr. Emil, surgeon, Aug. 11, 58.
Howells, William Dean, author, May 11, 84.
Jennings, Frederic B., lawyer, May 26, 66.
Kerr, Walter, insurance, Apr. 24, 67.
Kessler, David, Jewish actor, May 13, 60.
Levy, Abraham, noted criminal lawyer, Dec. 16, 59.
Lydecker, Col. C. E., lawyer, May 6, 68.
Malone, Judge James T., of General Sessions, suddenly in Chambers, Dec. 1, 55.
Meltzer, Dr. Samuel, inventor and scientist, Nov. 7, 69.
Mosler, Henry, historical painter, Apr. 21, 78.
Moss, Frank, lawyer, June 5, 60.
O'Donnel, Richard, vice-pres. Pennsylvania R. R., Sept. 28, 60.
O'Donovan, William R., sculptor, Apr. 20, 76.
Ohl, Josiah K., editor Evening Telegram, June 27, 57.
Pelham, Dr. M. Annette, physician, July 16, 57.
Perkins, George W., financier, June 18, 58.
Phitbin, Eugene A., Supreme Court Justice, Mar. 14, 62.
Pierson, Francis H., former managing editor Evening Telegram, Dec. 3, 58.
Platt, Frank H., lawyer, Mar. 30, 64.
Procter, Hartley E., soap mfr., May 15, 73.
Reynolds, John D., pres. Amer. Equipment Co., Dec. 3, 62.
Rockefeller, Mrs. William, Jan. 17, 77.
Roosevelt, Samuel M., portrait painter, Aug. 19, 64.
Rudd, Channing, Federal Reserve Bank officer, Nov. 8, 45.
Schiff, Jacob H., philanthropist and financier, Sept. 25, 73.
Sell, Dr. Edward H., last surviving founder Am. Acad. of Medicine, June 7, 87.
Smith, Frank S., lawyer, Nov. 15, 69.
Smith, George D., book dealer, Mar. 4, 50.
Smith, George M., managing editor of N. Y. Tribune, Nov. 22, 51.
Stack, James H., hotel manager, Feb. 27, 61.
Stanton, Robert L., assistant corporation counsel, Feb. 23.
Steele, Sanford H., lawyer, Dec. 19, 74.
Stetson, Francis Lynde, lawyer, Dec. 5, 74.
Stoddard, Rev. Dr. Charles A., theologian, June 3, 87.
Stuart, R. W., banker, May 8, 74.
Thornton, Bonnie, actress, Mar. 13.
Timberlake, Mrs. Mildred Eve, Confederate nurse and philanthropist, Feb. 24.
Tonnetti, Francis M., sculptor, May 2, 58.
Turner, Rev. Charles W., former Bkln rector, Sept. 2, 75.
Ulman, J. S., special deputy police commr., May 7, 54.
Wertheim, Jacob, cigar mfr. and philanthropist, Nov. 14, 61.
White, James Terry, author, Apr. 3, 74.

Queens and Long Island.

Aichmann, Charles, singer and banker, Elmhurst, Apr. 11, 68.
Barber, James, accountant, Babylon, Sept. 28, 52.
Bicket, Robert, retired jeweler, Whitestone, July 24, 70.

LOCAL NECROLOGY OF 1920—*Continued.*

Boeram, Julius D., Civil War veteran, Greenport, Apr. 29, 81.
Bonner, Titus, Civil War veteran, Sea Cliff, May 27, 81.
Breck, George W., sculptor, Flushing, Nov. 22, 57.
Brown, Dr. Augustus A., police surgeon, Bayside, Apr. 2, 56.
Brown, John J., Civil War veteran, Huntington, Sept. 4, 81.
Carroll, Dr. Edward J., physician, Richmond Hill, Oct. 2.
Cassidy, Joseph, former pres. of Queens, Far Rockaway, Nov. 21, 54.
Connolly, Mary, mother of Queens Boro pres., Corona, June 8, 77.
Cooper, Edward, merchant and banker, Hempstead, Apr. 19, 80.
Crandall, Harlan, retired real estate broker, Roosevelt, July 16, 72.
Davis, Buell G., organizer and editor Glen Cove Echo Glen Cove, June 30, 74.
Davis, Wm. B., real estate, Hempstead, May 7, 62.
De Bevoise, George C., real estate, Flushing, Nov. 11, 64.
Dempsey, John C., singer, Flushing, Apr. 17.
Downey, John, Civil War veteran, Flushing, May 7, 86.
Duncan, Alex. B., banker, Hempstead, May 18, 63.
Dykes, Joseph, financier, Flushing, Oct. 14, 81.
Ellsworth, Stephen P., machinist, Woodhaven, Mar. 31, 69.
Fitz, Charles R., former treas. of Suffolk County, Southampton, June 11, 57.
Garrison, Harry H., insurance, Lynbrook, Mar. 6, 44.
Geschwind, Mrs. Christina, Hicksville, July 24, 94.
Grim, James Oswald, retired and Civil War veteran, Rockville Centre, Mar. 14, 81.
Hagadorn, Charles T., retired, Bellport, Oct. 7, 85.
Hodgetts, Rev. Alfred, M. E. pastor, Aug. 17, 68.
Houghton, Mrs. Louise S., author, Huntington, Aug. 22, 81.
Jackson, Mrs. Diana B., church worker, Seaford, Oct. 31, 70.
Lane, Theodore T., lawyer, Flushing, Apr. 15, 36.
Lanehart, Dr. Louis N., surgeon, Hempstead, Apr. 25, 61.
Lynn, Wauhope, ex-judge, Good Ground, Aug. 17, 64.
McCabe, Daniel F., prominent churchman, Rockville Centre, Nov. 8, 60.
McKee, Thomas, retired, Port Washington, Feb. 8, 65.
Maxwell, Dr. Wm. H., City Supt. of Schools, emeritus, Flushing, May 3, 68.
May, Robert W., lawyer, Rockville Centre, Nov. 7, 55.
May, William H., real estate, Huntington, Feb. 28, 80.
Mayhew, Reginald F., turf writer, Hempstead, Dec. 19, 59.
Merritt, John C., farmer, Farmingdale, Nov. 29, 75.
Miller, Frederick, Sea Cliff, June 22, 52.
Moore, Fred J., accountant, Richmond Hill, July 23, 57.
Murray, Mary King, Flushing, Nov. 12, 87.
Muttee, Capt. James L., pilot, Glen Cove, Feb. 7.
Overton, Rev. Dr. Daniel H., Presbyterian minister, Islip, Aug. 22, 57.
Pearsall, Smith F., publisher, Freeport, Dec. 28, 40.
Peck, Rev. William J., pastor Union Evangelical Ch., Corona, Sept. 15, 67.
Place, William H., retired, Little Neck, Sept. 19, 73.
Post, John, supt. Presbyterian Mission, Freeport, July 19, 67.
Price, Capt. Thomas F., bank president, Greenport, Oct. 11, 82.
Raynor, Horace M., naturalist and guide, East Moriches, May 17, 78.
Remsen, Cornelius W., broker, Argyle Park, July 9, 39.
Rippere, Rev. John, Methodist clergyman, Orient, Nov. 26.
Ryerson, Mrs. Maria W., Woodhaven, Aug. 27, 94.
Sandford, Henry H., Civil War veteran, Bridgehampton, L. I., Feb. 17, 78.
Sherer, Prescott E., banker, Garden City, Aug. 11, 40.
Shourds, Col. Stephen E., Civil War veteran, Dec. 15, 76.
Skidmore, Woodhull, retired, Patchogue, Feb. 27, 85.
Sprague, S. Foster, former guide, bayman and road commr., Freeport, Nov. 15, 77.
Terry, Egbert H., retired, East Moriches, Feb. 21, 79.
Thomas, Ralph W., editor, Mar. 26, 58.
Tilly, Rev. George E., hymn writer, Jamaica, June 7, 84.
Tooker, Capt. Charles E., master mariner, June 4, 77.
Tuttle, Brewster, retired, Mar. 26, 88.
Tyler, William H., druggist, College Point, Oct. 15, 65.
Valentine, Benjamin E., lawyer, Woodmere, Aug. 15, 75.
Verity, Lawrence, Great South Bay fisherman and guide, Seaford, June 26, 99.
Wade, Harry E., builder, Richmond Hill, July 22, 48.
Wasmuth, William, entomologist, Glendale, June 8, 64.
Weeks, Rev. Wm. H., former chaplain City Hosp., L. I. City, May 28, 88.
Wicks, Frank E., boat builder, Amityville, Dec. 5, 68.
Zerbe, Mrs. Wm. H., Richmond Hill, Sept. 11, 49.
Zimmer, Mons. Henry J., founder of Mary Immaculate Hospital, Jamaica, Aug. 28, 73.

ELECTORAL VOTE BY STATES. 1908-1920.

State.	1920. Harding, Rep.	1920. Cox, Dem.	1916. Wilson, Dem.	1916. Hughes, Rep.	1912. Wilson, Dem.	1912. Roosevelt, Prog.	1912. Taft, Rep.	1908. Taft, Rep.	1908. Bryan, Dem.
Alabama	..	12	12	..	12	..	..	..	11
Arizona	3	..	3	..	3	..	..	..	..
Arkansas	..	9	9	..	9	..	..	..	9
California	13	..	13	..	2	11	..	10	..
Colorado	6	..	6	..	6	..	..	..	5
Connecticut	7	..	..	7	7	..	..	7	..
Delaware	3	..	..	3	3	..	..	3	..
Florida	..	6	6	..	6	..	..	..	5
Georgia	..	14	14	..	14	..	..	..	13
Idaho	4	..	4	..	4	..	..	3	..
Illinois	29	..	..	29	29	..	..	27	..
Indiana	15	..	..	15	15	..	..	15	..
Iowa	13	..	..	13	13	..	..	13	..
Kansas	10	..	10	..	10	..	..	10	..
Kentucky	..	13	13	..	13	..	..	..	13
Louisiana	..	10	10	..	10	..	..	..	9
Maine	6	..	..	6	6	..	..	6	..
Maryland	8	..	8	..	8	..	..	2	6
Massachusetts	18	..	..	18	18	..	..	16	..
Michigan	15	..	..	15	..	15	..	14	..
Minnesota	12	..	..	12	..	12	..	11	..
Mississippi	..	10	10	..	10	..	..	..	10
Missouri	18	..	18	..	18	..	..	18	..
Montana	4	..	4	..	4	..	..	3	..
Nebraska	8	..	8	..	8	..	..	..	8
Nevada	3	..	3	..	3	..	..	..	3
N. Hampshire	4	..	4	..	4	..	..	4	..
New Jersey	14	..	..	14	14	..	..	12	..
New Mexico	3	..	3	..	3	..	..	..	..
New York	45	..	..	45	45	..	..	39	..
N. Carolina	..	12	12	..	12	..	..	..	12
N. Dakota	5	..	5	..	5	..	..	4	..
Ohio	24	..	24	..	24	..	..	23	..
Oklahoma	10	..	10	..	10	..	..	..	7
Oregon	5	..	..	5	5	..	..	4	..
Pennsylvania	38	..	..	38	..	38	..	34	..
Rhode Island	5	..	..	5	5	..	..	4	..
S. Carolina	..	9	9	..	9	..	..	..	9
S. Dakota	5	..	..	5	..	5	..	4	..
Tennessee	12	..	12	..	12	..	..	..	12
Texas	..	20	20	..	20	..	..	..	18
Utah	4	..	4	..	..	..	4	3	..
Vermont	4	..	..	4	..	..	4	4	..
Virginia	..	12	12	..	12	..	..	..	12
Washington	7	..	7	..	..	7	..	5	..
W. Virginia	8	..	1	7	8	..	..	7	..
Wisconsin	13	..	..	13	13	..	..	13	..
Wyoming	3	..	3	..	3	..	..	3	..
Totals	404	127	277	254	435	88	8	321	162

Hawaii's pineapple pack for the season of 1920 was approximately 6,000,000 cases, as against approximately 4,450,000 cases during the season of 1919.

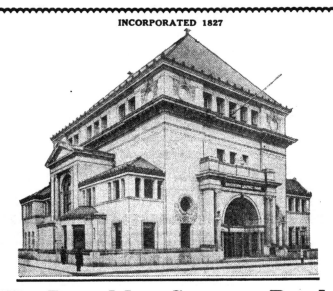

The Dime Savings Bank

OF BROOKLYN

DeKalb Avenue and Fulton Street

INCORPORATED 1859

OPEN DAILY

**From 9 A.M. to 3 P.M., except Saturdays, when the Bank closes 12 M.
Open Mondays from 5 to 7 P.M.**

OFFICERS

RUSSELL S. WALKER, President.
GEORGE W. CHAUNCEY, GEORGE T. MOON } Vice-Presidents.
FREDERICK W. JACKSON, Treasurer
PHILIP A. BENSON, Secretary
C. FRANK STREIGHTOFF, Asst. Secy.

ARTHUR S. SOMERS, President.
WALLACE L. CONNER, Secretary.
NATHAN S. JONAS, Vice President.
LOUIS C. WILLS, Vice President

Sumner Savings Bank

12 GRAHAM AVENUE, at Broadway, BROOKLYN, N. Y.

BANK BY MAIL. WE MAINTAIN A SPECIAL DEPARTMENT—IT IS AT YOUR SERVICE.
WRITE FOR PARTICULARS

ONE DOLLAR WILL OPEN AN ACCOUNT

Interest Credited in January and July Each Year on Balances from $5 to $5,000.
Open Daily 9 A. M. to 3 P. M.—Saturdays to 12 M.—Monday Nights 6-8 P. M.

FULTON SAVINGS BANK, KINGS COUNTY

OFFICERS

ADOLPH GOEPEL..................President
PETER H. REPPENHAGEN, 1st Vice-President
OTTO WISSNER............2d Vice-President
JOSEF C. M. LORENZ.........Treasurer
JOHN W. HASS................Secretary
GERARD BAETZ.................Cashier
WINGATE & CULLEN..........Counsel

TRUSTEES

P. H. Reppenhagen	Otto Wissner	T. Ellett Hodgskin	Chas. A. Schieren
John F. Hildebrand	Jacob Dangler	Herman A. Metz	Berthold Fallert
Adolph Goepel	G. Wm. Rasch	Louis Scheling	Otto E. Reimer
Richard Kny	J. Rich Mannheim	Frederick Renken	Bernard Rentrop

Henry A. Meyer

THE GREATER NEW YORK SAVINGS BANK

449-451-453 Fifth Avenue, Adjoining Corner 9th Street

Open daily (except Sundays and legal holidays) from 9 A.M. to 3 P.M. and on Monday evenings from 6 to 9 o'clock. Closes at 12 M. Saturdays. Deposits received from $1 to $5,000.00. All deposits made on or before the tenth business days of January and July, and the third business days of April and October, will draw interest from the first of these months. **One dollar will open an account.** Interest is allowed on all sums from $5 to $5,000, and is credited to the depositor's account in January and July of each year.

OFFICERS—Charles J. Obermayer, President; Alexander G. Calder, First Vice President; Wm. K. Cleverley, Second Vice President; William Obermayer, Comptroller; Thos. L. Grace Secretary; Andrew J. Lundstrom, Assistant Secretary; Charles Ruston, Counsel.

GREENPOINT SAVINGS BANK

Manhattan Avenue, corner Calyer Street

BROOKLYN, NEW YORK.

DEPOSITS, $18,300,000—INCORPORATED 1869

OFFICERS:

GEORGE W. FELTER, President.
CHARLES H. REYNOLDS, DONALD A. MANSON, Vice Presidents.
FRANK S. HARLOW, Secretary. WILLIAM J. FLEMMING, Assistant Secretary.

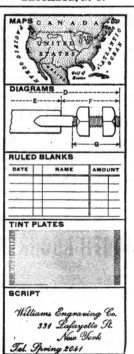

ESTABLISHED 1859

HENRY LINDENMEYR & SONS

32-34-36 BLEECKER STREET
NEW YORK CITY N.Y.

THE LINDENMEYR LINES

EVERY paper of The Lindenmeyr Lines is a good paper because it comes from a good mill, because it has passed all the tests of our experts and because it sells at a fair price.

16-18 Beekman Street
New York, N. Y.

54-56 Clinton St. ***58-60 Allyn St.***
Newark, N. J. ***Hartford, Conn.***

MAIN PAPER STOCK CO. Inc.

PAPER MAKERS' SUPPLIES

General Offices, 25 Spruce Street, corner William

Packing Houses	New York Branches	Holyoke Office
25-27-29-31 Peck Slip	321 Pearl St.	206 High St.
	423 E. 122d St.	

WILLIAM E. BROWN

FELTS FOR ALL PURPOSES

Felt and Rubber Press Blankets—Moulder and Dryer Stereo. Blankets—Tapes—Felt Wheels.

369 BROADWAY NEW YORK

NEW YORK CAMERA EXCHANGE

Do not fail to send for 1921 Bargain List

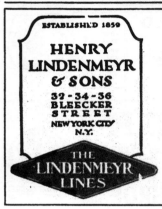

Telephone Call, 2387 Beekman **109 FULTON STREET**

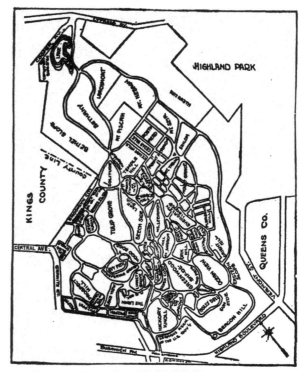

BLIND BABIES AND SMALL BLIND CHILDREN

International Sunshine Branch for the Blind. Nursery and Home at 84th St. and 13th Ave. Kindergarten at 83d St. and 13th Ave. Est. 1904. Care, maintenance and education of blind children. Daily average 30. Office phone 4315 Chelsea.

Mrs. Cynthia Westover Alden, 96 5th Ave., N. Y. City, president; Mrs. Nellie E. C Furman, secretary, 8432 107th St., Richmond Hill, N. Y.; Dr. Grace P. Macmillen, Supt. Phone 1776 Bensonhurst.

STEVENSON & MARSTERS, Inc.

STATIONERS and OFFICE OUTFITTERS

ART METAL and GLOBE WERNICKE
OFFICE FURNITURE

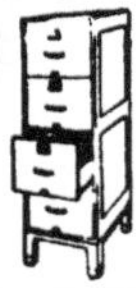

373 FULTON STREET, BROOKLYN, N. Y.

J. CONDON, Horticulturist

ARTISTIC FLORAL DECORATIONS.

The Floral Decorations of the following prominent social events were from this house: The Ihpetonga Ball, Opening Reception at the Montauk, Oxford, Riding and Driving, Marine and Field, Carleton and other Clubs; the famous dinner to Henry D. Polhemus at the Brooklyn Club, that of the "Round Table" at the Montauk, and Peary at the Hamilton; also the floral arrangement of the Beecher funeral at Plymouth Church.

Estimates Furnished and Contracts Made for Weddings and House Floral Decorations

OFFICE, 734 TO 736 FIFTH AVENUE, BROOKLYN.

GREENHOUSES (35)—291 to 313 Twenty-fourth Street, Fort Hamilton Avenue, Opposite Cemetery Entrance and Gravesend and Caton Avenues.

SAMUEL H. MOSS ✻ RUBBER STAMPS

ROBERT REED, Brooklyn Associate

Everything in the Line
Quickest Quality Service

498 Fulton St., Brooklyn
Tel. Main 0764

36 East 23d St., New York City
Tel. Gramercy 0533-4-5

MULTIGRAPHING
PUBLIC STENOGRAPHER
EMPLOYMENT EXCHANGE
YORKE MULTIGRAPHING SHOP
H. F. YORKE, PROP.
44 Court St., Temple Bar Bldg. Suite 910

Fac-simile Typewritten Letters Addressed, Filled In, Folded, Enclosed, Mailed.
Copying Done at Reasonable Rates.
Competent Office Help Furnished Without Charge.

TELEPHONE
MAIN 9516

PATRONIZE YOUR OWN HOME BOROUGH.

GENERAL CLEANING SUPPLIES

(Wholesale Only.)

Janitors' Supplies, Brushes, Brooms, Mops, Polishing Oils, Cleaning Cloths, Towel and Toilet Paper, Soaps, Disinfectants, Metal Wares, Mats, Appliances for Office Buildings, Real Estate Operators, Hospitals, Institutions, Theatres, Hotels, School Boards, Convents and kindred organizations.

Catalogues sent if requested on official stationery only.

73 Barclay St., **SAMUEL LEWIS** New York City

"I AM NOT SUPERSTITIOUS, BUT I DUBEY-LIEVE IN SIGNS."

Silk Banners
and Flags.
Pictorial
Painting
Established 1858

GUS. FRENGER

Successor to EDWARD A. DUBEY.

SIGNS

337 ADAMS STREET
Opp. the Olympic
BOROUGH OF BROOKLYN.
Telephone 3662 Main.

Manufacturer of
Wood, Wire, Glass,
Silver,
Brass Signs,
Advertising.

TELEPHONE SPRING 8170.

NEW YORK & BROOKLYN PAPER CO.

Paper Cutting of Every Description

Roll Slitting and Rewinding, Sheeting from the Roll
Roll Printing and Ruling
Flat Paper Cutting
Adding Machine Paper and Roll Paper Specialties

245-247 LAFAYETTE STREET, N. Y.

Special Sizes News or Book at Short Notice

SKINNER & COMPANY

Jones & Skinner

—DEALERS IN—

PAPER and TWINE

66 DEY STREET New York

GEORGE B. GRANGER, President ALBERT R. BORDEN, Vice-President
JOSEPH P. HANRAHAN, Sec'y-Treas.

GEORGE B. GRANGER CO., Inc.

66 BROADWAY Telephone: Rector 4574 NEW YORK CITY

ROPE, WIRE ROPE and BINDER TWINE

"Granger"	"Crescent"	"Maple Leaf"
100% Pure Manila Rope	Wire Rope	Binder Twine

New York Camera Exchange

BUY, SELL and EXCHANGE CAMERAS, LENSES, Etc.

Tel. Call, 2387 Beekman 109 FULTON STREET

Telephone Lafayette 0029

ALL-STEEL PORTABLE BUILDINGS

Garages, Boat Houses, Cabins, Bungalows, Hospitals, Etc.

Aeolipyle Combustion Damper—Saves 25% of Your Coal Bills

Ranges, Furnaces, Heaters, Roofing, Skylights, Etc.

WILLIAM BUCHANAN, 488-492 Sumner Ave., Brooklyn

Brooklyn Life

For 31 Years the Recognized and Only High Class Society, Club and Home Weekly for Brooklyn and Long Island.

HANDSOMELY ILLUSTRATED
CAREFULLY PRINTED

By Subscription $6.00 per year.
Single Numbers, 15 Cents.

BROOKLYN LIFE PUBLISHING COMPANY

307 WASHINGTON ST., BROOKLYN-NEW YORK

Brooklyn Blue Book

And Long Island Society Register for 1921

(Name Copyrighted)

The Only Directory of Its Kind Published in Brooklyn

Sent Post Paid to Any Address

for **$5.00** *by*

BROOKLYN LIFE PUBLISHING COMPANY

307 Washington Street, Brooklyn-New York

PURE **FOODS**

H-C-BOHACK CO- INC

Operating 150 Markets and Stores in Brooklyn and Long Island

GROWING EVERY DAY

1916...... 60 Stores....Sales $2,988,977.49
1920......150 Stores....Sales, approximately.....13,000,000.00

HENRY C. BOHACK, President **CHAS. G. EDEN, Vice-President**
HENRY C. BOHACK, Jr., Treasurer **ERNEST HABERLE, Secretary**

The Bohack Chain! Patronize Your Nearest Bohack Store

Brooklyn

1291 Broadway
1310 Fulton Street
1569 Fulton Street
1803 Broadway
6103 Third Avenue
5602 Fifth Avenue
220 Ralph Avenue
3005 Fulton Street
5121 Third Avenue
1080 Coney Island Avenue
1643 Broadway
1457 Broadway
1018 Flatbush Avenue
2801 Fort Hamilton Avenue
4401 Third Avenue
6924 Fort Hamilton Pkway.
1747 Flatbush Avenue
6123 Eighteenth Avenue
5102 Seventh Avenue
1421 Nostrand Avenue
377 Hancock Street
201 Ditmas Avenue
146 Jamaica Avenue
267 Brooklyn Avenue
61 Fifth Avenue
1124 Bedford Avenue
7304 Third Avenue
1412 Avenue J
302 Stuyvesant Avenue
397 Tompkins Avenue
7515 Fifth Avenue
6929 Third Avenue
2835 Fulton Street
1814 Nostrand Avenue
334 East Fourth Street
253 Troy Avenue
456 Autumn Avenue
3293 Fulton Street
7506 Third Avenue
1701 Stanhope Street
1461 Jefferson Avenue
1636 Nostrand Avenue
804 Onderdonk Avenue
664 Greene Avenue
514 Etna Street
766 Washington Avenue
666 Franklin Avenue
621 Wilson Avenue
2457 Pitkin Avenue
210 Rogers Avenue
4123 Fort Hamilton Avenue
318 Lafayette Avenue
263 Reid Avenue
1019 Hart Street
1496 Flatbush Avenue
1711 Grove Street
1114 Cortelyou Road
1212 Flatbush Avenue
4622 Seventh Avenue
3410 Fulton Street
797 Franklin Avenue
191 Howard Avenue
1701 78th St., cor. 17th Ave.
5404 Seventh Avenue
4115 Eighth Avenue
247 Sumner Avenue
9314 Third Avenue
8818 Third Avenue
511 Rogers Avenue
430 Rogers Avenue
1034 Broadway
261 Nostrand Avenue
129 Reid Avenue
319 Central Avenue
1450 Myrtle Avenue
3914 Church Avenue
171 Fifth Avenue
186 DeKalb Avenue
1625 Tenth Avenue
7910 Fifth Avenue
360 Sumner Avenue
197 Patchen Avenue
681 Sixtieth Street
273 Wyckoff Avenue
543 Evergreen Avenue
175 Saratoga Avenue
2568 Pitkin Avenue
1211 Liberty Avenue
112 Logan Street

Jamaica

399 Fulton Street
1-3 Sheldon Avenue
Bway and Remington
140 New York Avenue

Ridgewood

680 Woodward Avenue
952 Seneca Avenue
713 Forest Avenue
241 St. Nicholas Avenue
2317 Van Cortlandt Avenue
681 Fresh Pond Road
2565 Myrtle Avenue
1105 Cypress Avenue
2302 Catalpa Avenue
684 Seneca Avenue

Woodhaven

1209 Jamaica Avenue
7703 Jamaica Avenue
4134 Jamaica Avenue
10119 Jamaica Avenue
9601 Liberty Avenue

Maspeth—114 Grand Street

Winfield—12 Laurel Hill Blvd.

Richmond Hill

11320 Jamaica Avenue
4357 Jamaica Avenue
4581 Jerome near Stoothoff
12402 Metropolitan Avenue

Glendale

802 Fresh Pond Road
2433 Myrtle Avenue
3069 Myrtle Avenue

Rockaway Beach

448 Boulevard
494 Boulevard
378 Boulevard
176 Boulevard

Rockaway Park—94 Washington Avenue

Morris Park

4652 Atlantic Avenue
11813 Liberty Avenue
4827 Jerome Avenue

Corona

9 Polk Avenue
94 West Polk Avenue
53 Kingsland Avenue
86 Junction Avenue

Elmhurst

Kingsland Ave and Fifth St.
1600 Jackson Avenue
95 Corona Avenue
26 Grand Street

South Ozone Park

113 Field Avenue
4389 Jerome Avenue

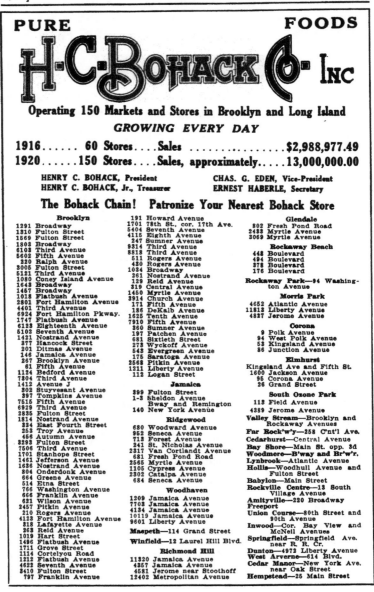

Valley Stream—Brooklyn and Rockaway Avenues
Far Rock'w'y—258 C'nt'l Ave.
Cedarhurst—Central Avenue
Bay Shore—Main St. opp. 3d
Woodmere—B'way and Br'w'r.
Lynbrook—Atlantic Avenue
Hollis—Woodhull Avenue and Fulton Street
Babylon—Main Street
Rockville Centre—13 South Village Avenue
Amityville—220 Broadway
Freeport
Union Course—80th Street and 90th Avenue
Inwood—Cor. Bay View and McNeil Avenues
Springfield—Springfield Ave. near R. R. Cr.
Dunton—4973 Liberty Avenue
West Arverne—614 Blvd.
Cedar Manor—New York Ave. near Oak Street
Hempstead—25 Main Street

STANDARD OIL COMPANY OF NEW YORK

Refiners and Dealers in All Products of Petrolenm

DEPOTS WHERE MOTOR BOATS CAN LOAD

SOCONY MOTOR GASOLINE and POLARINE OIL and GREASES.

DIRECT FROM OUR TANKS

NEW YORK BAY AND STATEN ISLAND

Bond and First Streets, Brooklyn—Gowanus Canal, S. O. Co. of N. Y.

Ulmer Park Pier—A. L. Anderson.

Ft. 69th St., So. Brooklyn—C. Poling. Barge 27A.

Port Richmond, S. I., Tottenville, S. I.—S. O. Co. of N. Y.

Stapleton, S. I.—Capt. Cattermole. Barge 30A.

EAST RIVER

Ft. N. 10th St., Brooklyn, Ft. E. 10th St., N. Y. City, Ft. E. 120th St., N. Y. City—S. O. Co. of N. Y.

Ft. E. 23rd St., N. Y. City—The Anna Service.

Ft. Walnut Ave., Bronx Kills, N. Y.—John Rehm. Barge Pt. Morris.

LONG ISLAND SOUND

Clason Point, Bronx—C. F. Quinn. Barge 59A.

Beechhurst, L. I.—Beechhurst Country Club.

City Island, N. Y.—Robert Jacobs, J. Vidal, B. F. Wood.

Mamaroneck, N. Y.—Sound Machine Shop, Inc.

Port Chester, N. Y.—J. Kapp.

College Point, L. I.—W. Needham, Frank & Walter Kraemer.

Oyster Bay, at Oyster Bay Canal Lock Co.—Ben. Seaman.

Port Washington, L. I.—H. Berg. Barge 31A.

Glenwood Landing, L. I.—James Fyfe.

Cold Spring Harbor, L. I.—E. Abrams & Son.

New Rochelle, N. Y.—A. Lion.

Huntington, L. I.—Wheeler Shipbuilding Co.

Greenport, L. I.—W. W. Griffin, G. F. Tuthill.

Fisher's Island, L. I.—A. H. Eldredge. E. M. & W. Ferguson.

Shelter Island, N. Y.—N. P. Dickerson.

CONNECTICUT

Greenwich	Bridgeport	New London
Stamford	New Haven	Groton
Rowayton	Stony Creek	Noank
S. Norwalk	Saybrook	Mystic
	Stonington	

LONG ISLAND—SOUTH SHORE

Canarsie—Wm. Moran. Barge 60A.

Flatlands Bay—Chas. G. Morse. Barges Socony, Arcade.

Sheepshead Bay—W. Lang. Barge 15A.

Rockaway Point—P. H. Reid.

East Rockaway, L. I.—S. S. Rhame.

Freeport, L. I.—J. Carcich.

Amityville, L. I.—W. J. Ketcham.

Bay Shore, L. I.—T. F. Muncey & Son.

West Sayville—F. Ockers.

Patchogue—W. R. Marran.

Montauk—E. B. Tuthill.

HUDSON RIVER

W. 140th St., N. Y. City—F. R. Welch.

Yonkers, N. Y.—S. O. Co. of N. Y., Corinthian Yacht Club, J. C. Anderson, at Germania Yacht Club.

Nyack	Saugerties
Highland Falls	Greendale
Cornwall	Catskill
Newburgh	Hudson
New Hamburg	Newton Hook
Poughkeepsie	Stuyvesant
Hyde Park	Coeymans
Kingston (Rondout)	Van Rensselaer Island
Green Island	

Van Rensselaer Island Creek—Capt. Godfrey Smith.

Rensselaer—Bailey & Parker.

Albany—Albany Yacht Club.

Lightning Source UK Ltd.
Milton Keynes UK
UKHW011113221118
332685UK00008B/1452/P

9 780428 689568